W9-BIE-190

state borders
regional borders
ROME   capital
Bari   regional capital
Pavia   provincial capital

0   100   200 km

LIECHTENSTEIN
VADUZ
AUSTRIA
BERN
SWITZERLAND
Bolzano/
Bozen
Trentino-
-Alto Adige/
Südtirol
Friuli-
-Venezia
Giulia
Belluno
Udine
Trento
Sondrio
Pordenone
Gorizia
Valle d'Aosta/
Aosta/ Aoste
Vallée d'Aoste
Varese
Como
Bergamo
Venetia
Treviso
Trieste
Novara
Lombardy
Vicenza
Vercelli
Milan
Brescia
Verona
Padua
Venice
Torino
Cremona
Piedmont
Pavia
Mantua
Rovigo
Asti
Piacenza
Alessandria
Parma
Reggio
nell'Emilia
Ferrara
Cuneo
Modena
Ravenna
Liguria
Savona
Emilia-Romagna
Genoa
Bologna
Forlì
MONACO
Imperia
La Spezia
Massa
SAN MARINO
LIGURIAN
SEA
Pisa
Lucca
Pistoia
Pesaro
Ancona
Leghorn
Tuscany
Florence
Arezzo
Marche
Siena
Macerata
YUGOSLAVIA
ELBA
Grosseto
Perugia
Ascoli
Piceno
Umbria
ADRIATIC   SEA
CORSICA
Terni
Teramo
Pescara
Viterbo
Rieti
Chieti
L'Aquila
TREMITI
Latium
Abruzzi
VATICAN
CITY
ROME
Molise
Campobasso
Frosinone
Isernia
Foggia
Latina
Caserta
Benevento
Bari
ASINARA
MADDALENA
CAPRERA
Campania
Apulia
Naples
Avellino
Brindisi
Sassari
ISCHIA
Salerno
Potenza
Matera
Taranto
CAPRI
Lecce
Nuoro
Basilicata
S.PIETRO
Sardinia
Gulf of
Taranto
Oristano
TYRRHENIAN   SEA
Cagliari
Cosenza
S.ANTIOCO
Calabria
Catanzaro
IONIAN
SEA
USTICA
LIPARI ISLANDS
Reggio di Calabria
EGADI ISLANDS
Messina
Palermo
Trapani
Canale di Sicilia
Sicily
Caltanissetta
Enna
Catania
Agrigento
Syracuse
PANTELLERIA
SICILIAN
SEA
Ragusa
TUNIS
ALGERIA
TUNISIA
MALTA
VALLETTA
PELAGIE ISLANDS

FRANCE

THE
HACHETTE
GUIDE
TO
ITALY

Acknowledgments

Special thanks to the Touring Club Italiano who produced and published this guide in Italy (1987) as Guida Turistica d'Italia, in the framework of the Hachette Guides collection.

English edition by Pantheon Books, USA, and the Automobile Association, Great Britain; French edition by Hachette-Guides Bleus.

Direction: Adélaïde Barbey.

Executive Editor: Marie-Pierre Levallois.

Editors: Isabelle Jendron and Alexandra Tufts-Simon.

Contributors: Babel Translation (London) and Thelma Clinton, Roderic Donovan, Julie Gaskill, Sheila Mooney Mall, Rosemary Perkins, Jeanette Rajadel, John Tyler Tuttle, Fabrice Ziolkowski.

Paste-up: Catherine Riand.

Cartography: T. C. I.

Illustrations: T. C. I.

Production: Gérard Piassale, Françoise Jolivot.

Photocomposition: M. C. P.-Orléans.

Manufactured in France by Maury, S. A. and Reliure Brun (Malesherbes).

First American Edition

ISBN 0-394-57045-6

ISSN 0895-3775

THE HACHETTE GUIDE TO ITALY

PANTHEON BOOKS
NEW YORK

Discover the guide

Who better than the Italians could succeed in presenting an "x-ray" of a country like Italy — a country of incomparable cultural treasures and human richness in which love of life and its pleasures plays a large part. It was this consideration which was the origin of the collaboration between Hachette Guides Bleus and the Touring Club Italiano, two publishers whose competence in creating guides is internationally recognized.

The result? The *Hachette Guide to Italy,* which, following the Hachette Guides to France and Great Britain, enlarges further the Hachette collection. This veritable data bank has been designed to enhance the traveler's stay in Italy: 4,500 hotels-restaurants, 500 camp grounds, hundreds of addresses for sports and many other free-time activities.

A thorough travel guide, this book also comprises:
● 250 high-quality maps, created by T.C.I. and adapted by Hachette Guides Bleus;
● region by region, a listing of not-to-be-missed sites and itineraries chosen either for their cultural or touristic interest;
● a selection of restaurants with commentary; red points signify *haute cuisine* and blue points good food and a rapport between quality and price;
● a Practical holiday guide, which resolves all kinds of problems faced by the traveler.

Join us in discovering the thousand and one faces of Italy — a delightful way of returning to the sources of our civilization.

The Editors

Contents

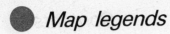

Map legends

● Itineraries

Roads

→ Itinerary (arrow indicates direction)

Alternative sightseeing route

(A3) Motorway (official number)

Main road

Other roads

Ski lifts, chair lifts

Ferry line

Borders

National border

Regional border

Cities

○ City marking beginning or end of itinerary

● City on the itinerary

Urban area

○ Other cities

Symbols

Church, church in ruins, chapel

Château, château in ruins

Villa, palace

Monument

Ruins

Prehistorical site (nurag, etc.)

Grotto

Waterfall, natural wonder

Park, garden

Hotel

Refuge

Port

Pass

Mountain peak

788 Altitude

⊕ Direction marker

● Regions

Roads

(A3) Motorway (official number)

Major road

Other major roads

Railway

Ski lifts, chair lifts

Ferry line

Borders

National border

Regional border

Provincial border

Cities

Urban area

○ Major cities

○ Other cities

Symbols

Church

Château

Monument

Ruins

Prehistorical site (nurag, etc.)

Grotto

Waterfall, natural wonder

Park, garden

Hotel

Refuge

Pass

Mountain peak

★★ Altitude

★ Highly interesting town

—3— Interesting town

● Towns and sites

⊠	postal code	≋	seaside resort
ⓘ	tourist information office	♨	spa
	bus station	⚡	ski area
	train station	★	remarkable
✈	airport	★★	exceptional
	boat line	♥	especially recommended
Λ	camp ground	→	refer to another entry

Under each locality a map reference indicates its place on the regional map.

● Hotels and restaurants

Hotels

★	simple
★★	simple but comfortable
★★★	very comfortable
★★★★	first-class establishment
L ★★★★★	luxury establishment

Restaurants

♦	pleasant
♦♦	comfortable attractive surroundings
♦♦♦	refined decor, high-quality reception and service
♦♦♦♦	exceptional surroundings, decor, reception and service
●	recommended (gourmet food)
●	recommended (good food, good value for money)

Amenities

rm	room	占	access for the handicapped
Tx	telex	⊗	no pets
ℙ	parking	⊡	pool
≶	view	⚬	tennis
〰	park or garden	⌐	golf
🔔	quiet		

Prices are given at the end of each listing.

Hotels: average price of a double room with bath. For establishments that indicate pension or half-pension, the price includes 1 or 2 meals per day for 2 people.

Restaurants: the first price given corresponds to a fixed-price item; the second to an average à la carte item.

Itineraries

Recommended tourist itineraries appear throughout the guide. As well as a map and description which can be found on the pages listed below, each itinerary is also indicated by a numbered box on the regional map.

The many faces of Italy

The country

Italy is a relatively small, densely populated country, whose rich **cultural heritage** has been crucial to the development of Western civilization. The visitor may come to Italy to enjoy the sea, the rich fragrance of the Sicilian scrub-brush, the sun of the Mediterranean, to ski in the sun on Cervino or to climb the pink Dolomite Mountains. The visitor may also enjoy landscapes embellished by man: the lakes of Lombardy, the valley of Taormina, the Tuscan hills, the Amalfi and Portofino coastlines. Italy is like a natural and cultural museum, whose masterpieces are too numerous to ever be completely catalogued. The visitor will soon discover the paradox of this enchanted country: Italy's beauty is easy to experience and almost impossible to define. Italy is proud of its famous **sites,** Rome's Sistine Chapel, Florence's Uffizi, Venice's Piazza San Marco, and of its **artists,** Raphael, Michelangelo and Leonardo da Vinci. Every city has been affected, to a greater or lesser extent, by the influence of art.

Beginnings

Italy is a country with an infinitely complex history. People first appeared on the Italian peninsula tens of thousands of years ago, but Italian history actually started 28,000 years ago. It was then that the native populations of the south, a **people of Indo-European origin,** came into contact with the more sophisticated cultures of the **Phoenicians** and the **Greeks.** From that moment, Italian history has moved forward in an unbroken, dynamic line. Much has been destroyed in Italy throughout the ages (monuments, buildings, works of art), but very little has been forgotten. This memory is crucial to the visitor's understanding of Italy.

Political fragmentation

While Italy's cultural, artistic and historical capital is Rome, until 100 years ago the country had many capitals. The existence of so many **centres of power** led to a decentralized structure that maintained stimulating interaction and diverse links with other countries. The different schools of painting (Tuscan, Umbrian, Roman, Neapolitan) are just one manifestation of Italy's political fragmentation.

This fragmentation of Italy led to strongly **individualized regions.** The individual characteristics of Tuscany, for example, differ markedly from those of Lombardy. This regional differentiation can be found throughout Italy. Italy has always been pulled in two directions. On one side, Italy is a **unified country,** a cohesive whole, and, on the other, it is still a group of individual regions, sub-regions and cities.

Italy can be seen as a collection of cities set in a garden. These cities maintained a surprising continuity from the **Middle Ages** through the **Industrial Revolution,** demonstrating an ability to reinterpret the past without fear of rebuilding. The question is often asked whether the heart of these cities developed by chance or through some grand design. How is it possible to account for Venice's Piazza San Marco, which offers such a range of contrasting styles, from Byzantine to Neoclassical? The only possible conclusion is that San Marco is the final product of generations of freewheeling imaginations for which beauty was the overriding goal.

Variety

The fragmentation of Italy politically led to a striking **variety.** Thus, in the Po Valley, towns and cities bear traces of their past as independent city-states, while, in Venetia, there are subtle indications of the long union with Venice. The layout of Ferrara, however, shows its intellectual, Renaissance origins and Vicenza is known as the city of Palladio's architecture. In central Italy, many towns stand majestically on hilltops and were strongly influenced by Romanesque and Gothic styles. Urbino is a product of the aristocratic and humanist 15C and, while Pisa belonged to the Grand Duchy, it largely consists of Romanesque elements that are unclassifiable. Southern Italy is a land of dramatic Baroque architecture — with Neapolitan, Sicilian and Lecce variants. The cities of Apulia, however, cluster around Romanesque cathedrals and Syracuse and Agrigento show strong Greek influence.

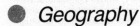

● Geography

The **geographic situation** of the peninsula is essential to an understanding of Italy. The Italian peninsula divides the Mediterranean into two basins, like a bridge between the East and the West. There are *c.* 750 miles between the northernmost and southernmost points. Sicily is only 93 miles from the coast of Africa and the Straits of Otranto (between Apulia and the Balkans) are only 45 miles wide. Because of Italy's elongated shape, no point is more than 155 miles from the sea. The peninsula has nearly 2,500 miles of coastline and Sicily and Sardinia have a further 2,175 miles. Italy covers some 120,000 square miles: 20 percent more than Great Britain or West Germany and about three-fifths the area of France. Although the landscape and climate are extremely varied, Italy is most often divided into **three regions:** the Alps, the Po Valley and the Apennine chain.

The Alps

The **Alps** enclose Italy within a gigantic barrier of peaks and glaciers that stretch from the Gulf of Genoa to Friuli. They include some of Europe's most beautiful and highest mountains, including Mont Blanc (15,780 ft, Europe's highest peak outside the Caucasus), the superb Cervino (14,692 ft), Mount Rosa, the Brenta Dolomites and Marmolada.

The Alpine mountain range is a formidable shield against weather conditions from northern Europe. It also marks the boundary of the Italian language. Yet, the Alps have never completely separated Italy from the rest of Europe: amber was carried across the Brenner Pass during prehistoric times, the Romans crossed the Alps on their marches of conquest, the Germans launched invasions through them, medieval emperors crossed them to receive tributes or sell titles of nobility, merchants and their wares passed through them as did numerous generals throughout history (Hannibal and his elephants, Napoleon and his artillery). Today it is possible to get to the top of Mont Blanc with the help of a spectacular cable-car system.

The **Dolomite Mountains** offer magnificent alpine scenery: marvelous crags of bare limestone flanked by dark fir forests. Valleys descend from the peaks to the plain, each with individual natural features, architecture and dialects.

In northwestern Italy, the three lakes of Lombardy lie where the Alps slope down into the pre-Alps. Lake Maggiore, Lake Lugano and Lake Como are splendid stretches of water ringed by picturesque shores lined with palms, cypresses and azaleas. Further east are two more lakes: Lake Iseo and Lake Garda. The gentle calm and peace of the lake region create one of the most beautiful settings in Italy.

The Po Valley

Moving south between the Alps and the Apennine Mountains, the **Po Valley** slopes gently down toward the Adriatic Sea. It covers some 15 percent of Italy, although about a third of the population lives there. It is both the agricultural heart and the first industrial centre of Italy. The valley gets its name from the Po River, the longest river in Italy (405 miles, half the length of the Rhine). Far from monotonous, the landscape has a subtle charm with rows of poplars reflected in the rice fields, rivers that meander between lush banks and fields that change colour with the seasons. To the west are the hills of Monferrato and Langhe with vineyards. To the east, the charming Berici and Euganean hills suddenly rise out of the plain and form the backdrop to some of the finest Venetian villas.

The Po delta pushes forward into the Adriatic Sea, creating lagoons in the Comacchio, as well as the more famous lagoons of Venice and Marano. The delta and lagoons form a unique environment in which the visitor may have the illusion of seeing sails of local fishing boats gliding gently over the meadows. The Alps and the Po Valley are made up of seven regions: Valle d'Aosta, Trentino, Piedmont, Lombardy, Venetia, Friuli and Emilia.

The Apennines

The **Apennine Mountains** run the entire length of the Italian peninsula, from the Gulf of Genoa to Aspromonte. These mountains are older and more weathered than the Alps. More rounded, they are often devoid of woods, sometimes wild and barren, their slopes eroded and unstable. In the spring, water from melting snow quickly swells the mountain streams. Autumn brings golden hues to the forests of chestnut trees. The rugged limestone mass of Gran Sasso d'Italia is the highest peak in the Apennine range (9,554 ft), but, for the most part, the peaks are much lower. The backbone of the range runs north-south and begins near the eastern Adriatic coast near Ancona. It gradually slopes down toward the western Tyrrhenian shore. This has created hilly areas and occasional valleys on both slopes of the range.

The region of Liguria is squeezed in between the sea, the Alps and the Apennines. It curves around a gulf and its shoreline is dotted with green headlands and rocky bays, colourful seaside villages, flowers and palms. Olive trees become a prominent feature here and remain so all the way down the coast of Italy.

On the western side of the Apennine Mountains are Tuscany, Umbria and Latium. The landscape along this route changes quickly as the roads wind, and as the latitude and altitude change. There are pine trees and the scents of the Mediterranean scrub-brush along the coast, olives and vines, hillside farms, clumps of cypresses, rounded hills and the jagged outlines of the fortified towns and the deserted remains of Etruscan dwellings.

Other geographic features

The Arno and the Tiber Rivers have flooded throughout history, sometimes with disastrous results. Extensive damage was caused to the artistic heritage of the region when the Arno last flooded in 1966; along the Tiber, an embankment was built (into the heart of Rome) following the flood of 1871.

Of particular interest are the rugged marble Apuan Alps, the metal-bearing hills of Tuscany, the Maremma (Tuscany, Latium), Lake Trasimene (the largest lake in Italy proper), the ancient volcanic landscapes and their delightful small lakes (Bolsena, Vico, Bracciano, Albano, Nemi). The beautiful island of Elba lies between Tuscany and Corsica, along with the other islets of the Tuscan archipelago. Off Mount Circeo are the Ponziane Islands.

The northernmost region along the Adriatic coast is the Marches, followed by Abruzzi and Molise. The landscape on this side of Italy is fairly uniform: a series of short parallel river valleys which come down through the hills to a sandy shoreline. In Abruzzi, where the Apennines reach their highest peaks, are extensive mountain basins. Moving south, the summer vegetation becomes yellowish, the sun climbs ever higher and prickly pears abound.

The **Tyrrhenian coast** is generally more varied and livelier than the Adriatic: It displays its most striking features in Campania: a region of clear water, volcanic rock, hills and plains. The Gulf of Naples (with Vesuvius in the background) and the fabulous islands of Capri and Ischia make up one of the most picturesque scenes in southern Italy. South of Sorento (with its citrus groves) is the green Amalfi coast, dotted with white villages. Farther south is the rugged and sun-baked region of Cilento: behind narrow fertile plains is a complex mountain landscape. Calabria is the toe of the boot of Italy, separating the Tyrrhenian and Ionian Seas. Another mountainous area, it is proud of its majestic almond trees. The virgin fir forest on the Sila plateau is one of Italy's most pleasant surprises. Farther east, the Apulia region is washed by the Adriatic and Ionian Seas and has a typical Mediterranean landscape. This area also includes the grain-producing Tavoliere, the only true plain on the Italian peninsula, and the limestone terraces of the Murge, covered with olive trees, gardens and white houses set against striking blue skies.

Leaving the peninsula, it is important to remember the Mediterranean's two largest islands: Sicily and Sardinia. The mountains along **Sicily's** northern coast are an extension of the Apennine range on the mainland. The massive volcano Etna (10,967 ft) dominates the Ionian coast from which it rises and it can be seen from almost every point on the island. Sicily's endless horizons offer some superb views: Taormina (with Etna in the background); the Conca d'Oro behind Palermo; orchards of dark green citruses. Sicily's burning sun brings summer to the island for six months out of the year.

Scattered across the sea are enchanted archipelagos: the Lipari Islands, the Aegadean Islands, distant Pantelleria and Lampedusa.

Sardinia appears as an island of broken, bare mountains without trees. A land of poor pastures, its coastline is exceptionally beautiful and an extraordinary group of islands (including la Maddelena and Caprera) fringes the wind-blown strait between Sardinia and Corsica.

● History

● The seeds of civilization

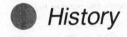

Prehistory

Italy may have been inhabited for some half a million years. Definite but rare finds extend back as far as 150,000 years and the recolonization that followed the last Ice Age began an unbroken occupation which has lasted between 20,000 to 25,000 years. The ancient history of Italy still needs to be disentangled from the Greco-Roman literary tradition, with its various names and myths. Toward the end of the prehistoric period two cultural tendencies emerged: one of migratory peoples, the other emanating from Mediterranean centres of civilization in which metal-working played a key role. Among the first inhabitants were the **Ligurians** (who occupied a much larger area than modern Liguria), the **Siculi** (who inhabited southern Italy and Latium before Sicily) and the **Sards** (who developed the agricultural and pastoral culture of Sardinia). Names that may be of Siculi and Sard origin have been found in the lists of people fought by the pharaohs of the XIX dynasty in Egypt (13C BC). Speakers of Indo-European languages entered Italy in several waves of migration. The **Veneti,** who developed the **Ateste** culture, the **Latins** and the **Oscans-Umbrians,** who spread down the backbone of the Apennines, entered by land routes; whereas the **Piceni** and the **Apulians** crossed the Adriatic from the opposite shore. It was from these that the Italic peoples descended (as opposed to the Romans).

Recent discoveries by experts increasingly stress the cultural stimulus exerted by the **Mycenaeans** via their trade routes along Italy's coasts. The **Phoenicians** developed the art of writing by means of a flexible system of alphabet, and they and the Greeks spread it through the Mediterranean world. The use of the alphabet — the first written documents in Italy date from the 8C BC — marks the dividing line beween prehistory and history. **Colonization by the Greeks** was a large-scale process, as was the Phoenician presence (which is now known to have been more extensive than once thought). These stimuli led to the emergence of the other major element in antique Italian civilization: the development of **Etruscan** culture.

The Phoenicians

The Phoenicians left their cities on the eastern shores of the Mediterranean and sailed along the shores of Africa, reaching Sicily and Sardinia. Their colony of **Carthage** established bases in Italy. The **Carthaginians** finally succeeded in controlling the whole of Sardinia and gained a toehold in western Sicily (where they fought the Greeks for control of the island). Their influence extended over the sea to the coast of Latium.

The Greeks

According to tradition, Naxos, on the Ionian coast of Sicily, was the first Greek colony in Italy (735 BC), and Syracuse was founded the following year. Expeditions from both cities spread the Greek presence along the shores of Sicily and in southern Italy, a region which became known as *Magna Graecia*. The Greek presence was the principal factor in the development of the indigenous peoples and was finally introduced into Roman culture. Besides **Naxos** and **Syracuse,** the Greek colonies in Sicily included Zancle **(Messina), Megara Hyblea, Gela, Agrigento, Selinunte, Tindari** and **Imera;** on the Ionian shores of the peninsula were **Locri, Crotone, Sybaris, Metaponte** and **Tarentum.** The Greeks founded Rhegion **(Reggio di Calabria),** passed through the Straits of Messina and into the Tyrrhenian, where they founded Elea **(Velia),** Poseidonia **(Paestum),** Neapolis **(Naples), Cuma** and **Olbia** in Sardinia. Another tradition states that the first Greek settlement was **Ischia** (Pithecussa) but Phoenicians were also present on the island and this may have marked the division of the spheres of influence in the Tyrrhenian. It did not, however, prevent the clash with Carthage to see who would control Sicily (the Greeks were victorious over Carthage at Imera in 480 BC). On the other hand, the Greek presence in Campania led to rivalry with the Etruscans. The 6C and 5C BC saw the peak of Greek power in Italy. **Tarentum** and **Syracuse** emerged as the richest and most powerful cities and they exerted full control over the surrounding regions. Rivalry between the various cities (which led to the destruction of some) did not prevent popular culture from flourishing and spreading as the magnificent ruins of Doric temples, theatres, and city walls show. This is also evident in the contents of archaeological museums: marble and bronze sculptures, rare examples of tomb paintings and an enormous number of painted ceramics. Famous Greek names are associated with Italy: Aeschylus lived and died at Gela; Plato visited Syracuse three times; Empedocles came from Agrigento; Theocritus and Archimedes were natives of Syracuse.

The Etruscans

Like Greek culture in Sicily, Etruscan culture (first of the great civilizations to develop on Italian soil) was based on cities and ocean trading. The Greeks came from the sea and essentially remained tied to the coastline, although they might have links with the peoples of the interior and establish various cultural exchanges. The Etruscans on the other hand were a people of the land who slowly moved toward the sea. Greek cities were all coastal, Etruscan cities inland and the ones nearest the Tyrrhenian had ports on the shore. Their territory took the form of a large triangle along the Tyrrhenian coast bounded by the Arno and the Tiber. They appeared in the 8C BC and reached their peak over the following two centuries. The key to their power may have been the minerals on the island of Elba and the metal-bearing hills in Tuscany. Their cities (there were twelve) were linked in a primarily religious confederation. Many of them still exist: **Volterra, Arezzo, Cortona, Perugia, Chiusi, Populonia, Vetulonia, Roselle, Vulci, Bolsena, Orvieto, Tarquinia, Cervéteri, Veio.** The Etruscans pushed to the north and south beyond the rivers Arno and Tiber. Towards the south they occupied **Campania,** extending as far as

Capua (S. Maria Capua Vetere). Here the Etruscans allied themselves with the Carthaginians and halted the maritime expansion of the Greeks. They in turn were beaten by Cuma and Syracuse in 474 BC. To the north, the Etruscans crossed the Apennines during the 6C BC and spread into the Po Valley, beyond the Po as far as the Adige, the borders of the Veneti, and the lakes of Lombardy. **Bologna** was the Etruscan city of Felsina and **Spina** in the Po delta, which has now vanished, was an unusual example of an Etruscan city which depended on trade with the Greeks who sailed up the Adriatic. However, the Etruscan presence across the Apennines was soon swept away by the Celts **(Gauls)**, who occupied the Po Valley and part of the Adriatic slopes of the Apennines at the end of the 5C. Etruscan cities were located on high ground and protected by strong walls, a combination that is still seen in central Italy. Etruscan art displays clear links with the Greeks but there is an indigenous emphasis on realism, a search for the individual in images, as opposed to the Greek stress on the ideal. The desire to peer into the future, common to all ancient cultures, manifested itself by elaborate techniques of interpreting signs in the entrails of sacrificial animals and the flight of birds. The amount of material left by the Etruscans is enormous. However, one should not be misled by the fact that the bulk of it relates to burial finds: tombs, burial objects, tomb wall paintings. The Etruscans loved life and even their cult of the dead and their concern with the after-life was expressed joyfully. Their spiritual heritage merged, almost inextricably, into Roman culture.

Sites and monuments

Materials relating to Italian **prehistory** can be found in the specialized departments of the many archaeological museums that house the finds from the nearby excavations. In Sardinia, **Santu Antine** at **Torralba** is worth visiting, as is **Barumini**. In Lombardy there are engraved rocks at the **Val Camonica Parco delle Incisioni Rupestri**. **Phoenician** sites can be found in Sardinia at **Monte Sirai** and Tharros and at **Mozia** in Sicily. The outstanding **Greek** monuments in Sicily are the **temples of Agrigento** and **Selinunte**, the **theatres at Syracuse** and **Taormina** and the **walls of Gela**. On the mainland, there is the **temple of Poseidonia-Paestum**. Besides the sites mentioned above, there are important **archaeological museums** at Palermo, Taranto and Reggio di Calabria. Greek sculptures, Roman copies and collections of Greek vases are included in numerous other Italian museums, such as the Museo Nazionale of Naples, the Museo Nazionale delle Terme in Rome and in the Vatican museums. Among the outstanding **Greek** masterpieces are the Ludovisi Throne (Museo delle Terme, Rome), the Riace bronzes (Reggio di Calabria), the Medici Venus (Uffizi, Florence), the Apollo Belvedere, the Belvedere Torso and the Laocoon (Vatican Museum, Rome). The two major **Etruscan** sites are the **necropolis of Cervétri** and the **necropolis of Tarquinia** (chamber tombs with wall paintings). Major collections are housed in the archaeological museums of Florence, Villa Giulia (Rome), Tarquinia, Volterra (Museo Guarnacci) and Ferrara. The masterpieces include the sarcophagus depicting a husband and wife and the Veio Apollo (Villa Giulia, Rome), and the winged horses and detached frescos from the tomb of the Triclinium (Tarquinia museum).

● *Italy under the Romans*

Rome once dominated the Mediterranean and Europe as far as the Rhine and the Danube. The visitor to Italy might be curious about the historical process by which Italy was Romanized and unified to a much greater extent than the rest of the Empire, thus forming the basis of modern Italy. The emergence of Rome marks a change from the world of small, fragmented, independent city-states to a stronger political organization over a large area (in the same way as the Hellenistic kingdoms developed). Indeed, Rome can be said to have found its structure in Greek culture. However, when Rome fell the small city-state re-established itself and much of subsequent Italian history can be understood as the interplay between independence for the cities and central control.

Certain scholars have explained the rise of Rome from simple village to world power by the character of its institutions (rule by consuls elected each year, the continuity of the Senate, an element of electoral democracy, the balancing of class interests by means of the right of veto by the plebs, the structure of the non-professional and unpaid army). Actually, the rise of Rome is easier to record than to explain. The first diplomatic document drawn up by the Romans was a treaty with Carthage in 510 BC.

According to tradition, Rome was founded on a precise day (21 April) in 754 BC by **Romulus,** a descendant of Aeneas of Troy, who was followed by six kings. It appears that the site may have been inhabited before that time.

Republican Rome

The establishment of republican institutions (the last king was overthrown in 509 BC) was both a national uprising of the Latins against the Etruscans and a sign of the rise of rural landowners over groups who were associated with the Etruscans. Republican Rome had to fight hard to establish its hegemony over its **Latin** cousins and neighbours. They took and destroyed **Veio,** the nearest of the Etruscan cities, in 396 BC, after a decade of struggle, and immediately afterward they were defeated at Allia (387 BC) by the **Gauls.** The latter were more intent on plunder than conquest and withdrew after having seized and sacked Rome. A much more serious threat was posed by the **Samnites,** who were expanding from the Apennines toward the more fertile plains. At the time, military campaigns were fought between harvest and sowing, yet the **three Samnite wars** lasted a total of 35 years. The last of these ended in the victory at **Sentino** in 295 BC. As a result, Rome gained control of the plain of **Campania** and of other fertile territories in **Apulia.** Rome then immediately turned against the **Senones** (Gauls) in 285 BC and established the colony of **Sena Gallica** (Senigallia) in their territory.

Roman wars

At the beginning of the third century BC the Romans were firmly established in central southern Italy, but they had only just begun to discover the wealth of the Greek cities in the far south. They began fighting **Tarentum** which turned to the Greek king **Pyrrhus of Epirus** for help. He came to Italy with an army of mercenaries and elephants and pushed back the Romans. Pyrrhus was finally beaten at the battle of **Beneventum** in 275 BC and moved on to other territories. Tarentum was conquered in 272 BC and, with it, virtually the whole of southern Italy. This had two major consequences. First, Rome began to absorb **Greek culture** despite the resistance of the conservative classes and second, control of southern Italy made Rome the natural rival of Carthage.

Rome won the **First Punic War** (264-241 BC) through its surprising ability to become a naval power practically overnight. Rome gained **Sardinia and Sicily,** its first two provinces. The fall of the wealthy Greek city of Syracuse marked the end of Greek political power in Italy after 500 years. Ten years earlier the victory over the Gauls at **Claustidium** (Casteggio, 222 BC) had opened up the **Po Valley** to the Romans, providing much land to the veterans of the long wars. Italy was now entirely under Roman control. It was at this point that **Hannibal** crossed the Alps. The Carthaginians remained in Italy for fifteen years, but were finally recalled to Africa to face other battles. Ironically, it was the **Second Punic War** (218-201 BC) fought in Italy that opened the way for Rome's conquest of the world.

Rome's foreign conquests are not relevant to this history, but two events from this period are of interest. First, availability of low cost grain from the provinces progressively did away with the small freehold farmers of Italy who were replaced by estates (Latifundia) worked by slaves. Second, Italy focused on growing crops for processing, such as vines and olives, and on animal husbandry. The **Social War** (91-89 BC) broke out with an uprising of virtually all those who had no political rights. Peace was only restored with the concession of Roman citizenship to all (89 BC), one of the most important dates in Italian history. Various generals then fought among themselves in the **civil wars** which were waged from one end of the Empire to the other, between **Marius** and **Sulla, Caesar** and **Pompey, Octavius** and **Mark Antony.** Finally the Republic became the **Empire** (through Octavius, who by a Senate decree became **Augustus** in 27 BC).

Roman Empire

While peace reigned within Italy, the Roman Empire often waged war outside its own borders. An immense city lay at the centre of the Empire and around it, numerous other cities. Some of these were actually founded by the Romans, some existed before but were rebuilt by the Romans. All were linked by an excellent network of roads. Most of the Roman architecture found in Italy dates from the Empire rather than from the Republic. In certain areas of the countryside it is still possible to see the network of roads that divided up the land

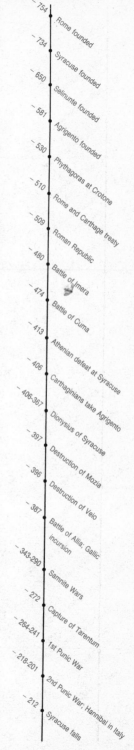

- 754   Rome founded
- 734   Syracuse founded
- 650   Selinunte founded
- 581   Agrigento founded
- 530   Phythagoras at Crotone
- 510   Rome and Carthage treaty
- 509   Roman Republic
- 480   Battle of Imera
- 474   Battle of Cuma
- 413   Athenian defeat at Syracuse
- 406   Carthaginians take Agrigento
- 406-367   Dionysius of Syracuse
- 397   Destruction of Mozia
- 396   Destruction of Veio
- 387   Battle of Allia: Gallic incursion
- 343-290   Samnite Wars
- 272   Capture of Tarentum
- 264-241   1st Punic War
- 218-201   2nd Punic War; Hannibal in Italy
- 212   Syracuse falls

Timeline (left margin):

- −91–89　Social War
- −88–79　Sulla's dictatorship
- −63　Catiline conspiracy
- −49　Caesar crosses Rubicon
- −44　Caesar assassinated
- −27　Octavius receives title of Augustus
- −13–9　Ara Pacis Augustae
- 60　Paul of Tarsus in Rome
- 64　Nero sets fire to Rome
- 72–80　Colosseum
- 79　Eruption of Vesuvius (Pompeii destroyed)
- 81　Arch of Titus
- 113　Trajan's Column
- 118–130　Hadrian's Villa at Tivoli
- 217　Opening of Baths of Caracalla
- 313　Edict of Milan
- 324–344　1st basilica of St.Peter
- c. 352　Sarcophagus of Junius Bassus
- 395　Theodosius divides Empire
- 431　Basilica of S.Maria Maggiore

among veteran centurians. In cities founded by Romans it is possible to recognize the origins of military camps in the square perimeter and in the network formed by the roads, with the two main ones crossing at right angles. **Aosta** is a fine example of this kind of design.

Each town had a certain number of public buildings which would serve practical, ideological and ornamental purposes. The **forum** (central square) was used for commerce and by the community. There were Italic **temples,** with Greco-Hellenistic decorative elements; **triumphal arches,** an exclusively Roman monument; a **theatre,** a development of the Greek structure; an **amphitheatre** and **baths,** two genuinely Roman inventions, the second of which was passed on to the Islamic world. The remains of these buildings lie scattered all over Italy.

In the countryside **villas** flourished. They acted as farming centres and, on a small scale, offered the same facilities as the towns. In spirit and in function they resemble the Renaissance villas of **Venetia.** The architecture combined walls built of squared blocks, the arches seen in Etruscan cities and Greek stylistic elements used decoratively. **Mosaic** was a basic method of decoration and the art gradually developed from geometrical motifs to more skillful *trompe-l'oeil* effects.

Architecture worked hand in hand with **sculpture:** reliefs and statues were inspired by, and often copied from, Greek works. The originality of Roman sculpture was in its emphasis on the realism and the representation of individual features, something which it owed to the Etruscans. Decorative wall **painting** seems much more original because so much of Greek painting has been lost. From the third century onward, the figurative arts leaned toward stylization, toward simplified devices for conveying meaning and toward *trompe-l'oeil*. This change was to govern the development of Byzantine and medieval art.

Roman cultural achievements are part of a universal heritage. Italy was the birthplace of many whose names have become inextricably linked with western culture: **Catullus** was born at Verona; **Virgil** at Mantua; **Cicero** at Arpino; **Horace** at Venosa; **Ovid** at Sulmona; **Sallust** near L'Aquila; **Tacitus** and **Lucretius** at Rome.

Rome, and consequently Italy, declined in importance when **Diocletian** divided the Empire in two. Its decline continued when **Constantine** founded the eastern capital of **Constantinople** (Byzantium). The Barbarians, prior to their capture of the Empire, had been invited in as 'guests'. The army, the institution that had most contributed to the longevity of the Empire, was finally almost entirely made up of them.

Christianity

Paul of Tarsus first came to Rome in 60 and **Peter** had probably arrived earlier. Both died as martyrs in Rome. As a subject of the Empire, **Jesus** saw Rome, then the undisputed centre and heart of the Empire, as the focal point of **Christianity.** By the time Constantine granted freedom of worship in the **Edict of Milan** (313), Christianity had permeated the cultural and political elite of Rome (although not the countryside: the word 'pagan' originally meant a village-dweller). Shortly afterward, the Empire adopted Christianity as its official religion. The union of the Empire with Christianity (authority in the name of God) became the key ideological issue of the Middle Ages. The connection between Christian art and that of imperial Rome — which was at a turning point — can be traced historically. The design of the Constantine basilica is a sort of statement of imperial Christian art and the basilican plan has survived for centuries.

Sites and monuments

Rome today stands as the testament to the artistic heritage of imperial Rome. **Pompeii** and **Herculaneum** are two surprisingly intact Roman provincial cities from the 1C. Works of art from these two sites form the core of the Museo Nazionale in Naples. Other sites of great interest are the excavations at **Ostia Antica** (Rome's supply port), and **Hadrian's Villa** at Tivoli. All of Italy's archaeological museums have a Roman department and there are impressive Roman ruins in hundreds of towns up and down the peninsula, from Aosta to Aquileia, from Verona (the **Arena**) to Benevento **(Trajan's Arch),** Capua (the **Amphitheatre)** and Sicily (the mosaics of **Piazza Armerina).** The main centre of **early Christian** art is also **Rome.** Many churches in Italy retain a ground plan or fragments of structure from early Christian times, which have been incorporated or have subsequently been rebuilt. Outstanding examples of mosaics can be found in the **Mausoleum of Galla Placidia** at Ravenna. Examples of the decorative arts (ivories, glass) are housed in museums and in church treasuries.

The Empire, the popes and the cities

The Empire

The Western Roman Empire (which included Italy) fell in 476. The Empire — or rather half the Empire — had been a political shell for some time, but Christian Roman culture was still very much alive. **Theodoric** and his Goths made quite a mark and his mausoleum at Ravenna, as well as the Arian mosaics in S.Appollinare Nuovo, reveal the cultural complexity of the period. The Eastern Roman Empire under Justinian soon reconquered Italy in the **Gothic War** (535-53) but the destruction was as widespread as during the Barbarian Invasions. A few years later the Lombards descended into Italy. They were much less Romanized in their culture, nor were they Christians. This led to a long-standing division in Italy, with the **Lombards** extending into the peninsula beyond Benevento, while the **Byzantines** held the coasts from Ravenna (the seat of the Byzantine Exarch) as well as Rome and a large part of southern Italy.

What is referred to as Barbarian art introduced stylistic elements from the distant homelands of the Goths and Lombards and emphasized the use of precious materials (already present in late Roman times). **Byzantine art** is, first of all, the logical development of late Roman art. It is imbued with the Christian sense of the sacred and it stresses surface and colour. Statues were no longer produced, but other kinds of sculpture flourished, as did the art of mosaic, inherited from the Romans. Another late Roman trend was simplified, idealized and ecstatic imagery. In architecture, the dominant feature became the dome, which crowns the centrally planned buildings. In Italy, the Byzantine tradition developed locally and was in intermittent contact with the East, both through the movement of small works of art and of the artists themselves. There are Byzantine masterpieces in Ravenna, Rome, Venice, southern Italy and in Sicily, and its artistic heritage forms the foundations of Italian art (especially painting) up to the Renaissance.

During centuries of Lombard and Byzantine rule, a reduced and impoverished population lived in towns clustered around (or even inside) majestic monuments which were crumbling slowly into ruin. The little they built came from stripping columns, marbles and stones from the unused Roman buildings. At the end of the 8C the **Franks** crossed the Alps and conquered the Lombard kingdom. On Christmas Day 800 Pope Leo III crowned **Charlemagne** Emperor in Rome. Direct Frank rule lasted little more than a century, but their presence and the coronation that had taken place that night had long-term consequences. The **Carolingian bequests** to the church were the basis for the formation of the papal state, which would last until the unification of Italy. The Empire (whose crown would soon become German) was to play a major role in European history, but in Italy the Emperor was mostly absent. He was soon considered a foreigner and was forced to enter Italy with his army to reach Rome. Similarly, the original common language, Latin, began to diverge into various separate national languages. Frederick II (13C) was the only emperor to be born and raised in Italy, and after him the Empire fell into decay for half a century. Finally, the Franks instituted **feudalism** in Italy.

Conflict between spiritual and temporal authority

From the coronation in 800, the pope (with universal spiritual authority and temporal authority over his states) and the emperor (with general authority) became the two protagonists of Italian history. Rarely in agreement, they fought each other by all available means, including excommunication and the creation of anti-popes. During the seven or eight centuries that make up the Middle Ages both positions changed considerably. The church, with its great cultural and moral reforms of the 10C-12C and, later, the foundation and spread of the regular orders of Franciscans and Dominicans (13C-14C), probably underwent a more profound transformation than the Empire. However, the papacy left Italy during the Avignon period (1309-77). Churches were built not only by the church authority, but also by the **city-states.** City life is a main feature of Italian history and, apart from Venice, there are virtually no cities today which did not already exist under the Romans. The city-states were independent, vigorous and highly aggressive toward each other. The **maritime cities** became involved with **overseas** trade — a very risky endeavour, but one in which profits far exceeded those of any other activity. The **maritime republics** included **Amalfi, Pisa, Genoa** and **Venice,** as well as less important cities, such as those in Apulia.

455 Vandals sack Rome
476 W. Roman Empire ends
493 Theodoric and the Goths
535-553 Gothic War
547 Consecration of S.Vitale, Ravenna
568 Lombards enter Italy
774 Franks conquer Lombard kingdom
800 Charlemagne crowned Emperor
827 Arabs occupy Sicily
1018 S.Miniato, Florence
1027 1st Norman fief in Italy
1061-1091 Normans conquer Sicily
1063-14C Pisa cathedral
1073-1086 Pope Gregory VII
1077 Henry IV at Canossa
1087-1132 S.Nicola, Bari
1094 Basilica of S.Marco, Venice
1099-1184 Modena cathedral
1120-1138 S.Zeno, Verona
1172-1185 Monreale cathedral

The comune

The cities of the Po Valley (Milan was the largest) developed a form of government known as the comune: an association of craftsmen, merchants and minor nobility. This concept spread across the Apennines to **Florence, Siena, Arezzo** and elsewhere. Goods were manufactured on a large scale, banking systems were developed and profits flowed back into agriculture. Cities grew in size not only because of the birth rate, but because of their power to attract people from outside. Some cities had to rebuild their walls several times to accommodate the expansion. Everywhere **tower houses,** magnificent **cathedrals** and **palazzi del comune** sprang up. The history of Italy depends more on the history of individual cities than on the nation as a whole.

In the 12C and 13C the cities divided their allegiances into two factions. They swore loyalty to the party of the pope (Guelph) or the emperor (Ghibelline). The cities were also often divided internally, for example the Whites and Blacks of Florence. These groupings were in part based on opposing family interests and in part on different social classes. However, this division into factions, a feature of essentially democratic life, did not prevent them from making common efforts.

In the 15C the political form of the **comune** (originally ruled by **consuls**) evolved into that of the **signoria** (government by a single powerful citizen). Such a ruler did not come from the feudal nobility, but often purchased a title from the penniless emperor. The move toward this form of government led to **territorial states,** which subjugated other cities, often by war. In the beginning the citizens themselves fought, as the Milanese and other townspeople of the **Lombard League** did in 1176, to defend their cities' freedom. However, as they grew richer, they preferred not to interrupt their business affairs and left war to professionals (the **compagnie di ventura,** and their leaders, the **condottieri**). The profession of condottiere could often become a stepping stone to the signoria.

Periods of conflict

It may seem surprising that during a period of unending wars with everyone in conflict, the country became richer. One possible explanation was offered by Machiavelli, who explained that only one person was killed in the Battle of Anghiari when the forces of the Duke of Milan met those of Florence and the pope. Mercenaries, he pointed out, fought more to take prisoners (who they could release for ransom) than to kill. Even so, for certain cities control by another meant the end of their development.

During these wars between local lords, one of the more powerful sometimes came close to forming a unified Italian monarchy. The one who came closest to this was Gian Galeazzo Visconti, Duke of Milan, who died in 1402 before he could fulfill his plans. The Signorie developed into **regional states** during the 15C.

In **Sicily,** Byzantine rule continued until the **Arabs** completed their conquest of the island, which they held for two centuries. One part of southern Italy remained Byzantine until the 11C and the **Lombard duchies** of **Benevento** and **Salerno** survived the fall of the Lombard kingdom of Pavia to the Franks (8C) and remained independent until the 12C. Another unique element in southern Italian history was the rise and fall of the **Normans.** Of Viking origin, they arrived from Normandy at the beginning of the 11C and hired themselves out as mercenaries. They soon carved out a kingdom of their own. The first countship was **Aversa** (1027); in 1071 **Robert Guiscard** took Bari, the last Byzantine stronghold, while his younger brother **Roger I** captured Sicily from the Arabs (1061-91). **Roger II** was made King of Sicily by the pope (his kingdom also included southern Italy). The mingling of Arab and Byzantine elements in Norman Sicilian art produced splendid results which can still be seen in the monuments of Palermo, Sicily, and the rest of southern Italy.

The kingdom remained largely intact, although at times Sicily was isolated from the mainland. **Constance of Altavilla's** marriage to **Henry** in 1186 united the kingdom and empire for little more than half a century. The capital, Palermo, continued to shine under Frederick II. The kingdom's origins were as a vassal of the church, and Clement IV gave its crown to the brother of St. Louis (King of France), **Charles of Anjou** (1265). The Angevin dynasty ruled the **south** for two centuries leaving its mark on the architecture. The capital was no longer Palermo but Naples. Sicily soon rose against the Angevins in the **Sicilian Vespers** of 1282 and offered the crown to **Peter III of Aragon.** From then on the island remained Spanish until the 18C. In 1442 **Alfonso V of Aragon** was named as heir of the last of the Angevins and the southern kingdom was once again reunited.

Timeline (left margin):

- 1176 — Battle of Legnano
- 1178 — The Deposition (B.Antelami)
- 1186 — Constance of Altavilla married
- 1198-1216 — Pope Innocent III
- 1208 — Abbey of Fossanova
- 1225-1235 — Cloister of S.Giovanni in Laterano
- 1226 — St.Francis of Assisi dies
- c. 1240 — Castel del Monte
- 1250 — Frederick II dies
- 1266 — Battle of Benevento: Charles of Anjou, King of S Italy
- 1271-1295 — Marco Polo in Orient
- 1282 — Sicilian Vespers
- 1288-1369 — Orvieto cathedral
- 1299-1304 — Palazzo Vecchio, Florence
- 1300 — 1st jubilee
- 1303-1305 — Giotto, Cappella degli Scrovegni, Padua
- 1309 — Pope in Avignon
- 1321 — Dante dies
- 1333 — Annunciation (S.Martini)
- 1341 — Poetic coronation of Petrarch

Cultural growth

In the 13C, the Italian language gained literary status with its three great masters: Dante Alighieri (1265-1321), Francesco Petrarca (1304-74) and Giovanni Boccaccio (1313-75). All were Tuscan and their major works, the *Divine Comedy*, the *Canzoniere* and the *Decameron*, were the basis of Italian literature.

In art, the period between the 11C and the 14C encompasses the **Romanesque** and subsequently the **Gothic** periods. In **architecture** this was the period of the great cathedrals and of the public and private palazzi. A number of regional variants of the Romanesque appeared: Lombard, Pisan, Florentine, Roman-Campanian, Apulian, Sicilian. Gothic architecture was introduced into Italy by the **Cistercians** (13C). The Italian version of this style, with the calm spaciousness and light that is a feature of churches built by Franciscans and Dominicans in almost every Italian city, worked well with the preceding Romanesque style. The cathedral in Milan is virtually the only Italian building in true northern Gothic style. The glorious secular architecture of Venice, inextricably tied to its unique lagoon setting, is quite unique.

In **sculpture** (initially meant to decorate cathedrals) the first artists, Wiligelmus and Benedetto Antelami, appeared in the Po Valley in the 12C. Major figures followed, such as Nicola and Giovanni Pisano, Tino da Camaino from Siena and the Florentines Andrea Orcagna and Arnolfo di Cambio. This period saw the reintroduction of high relief and statues. Crucifixes painted on wood are among the first examples of Italian **painting**. Much work was also done in mosaic and fresco, with the latter coming to dominate. Italy began to free itself from the Byzantine tradition in the 13C with Pietro Cavallino in Rome and Cimabue in Florence. The great innovative genius who opened the way for later Italian painting was Giotto (1266-1337). His style spread through his numerous pupils, many of whom were excellent artists in their own right. At the same time as Giotto, Duccio Boninsegna marked the beginning of the high point of Sienese painting, with other artists such as Simone Martini and Pietro and Ambrogio Lorenzetti.

Sites and monuments

The basilicas of **Ravenna**, as well as the exceptional church of S. Vitale, with their mosaics, S. Marco in **Venice** and some of its mosaics, various mosaics in Roman churches, and the mosaics in **Palermo**, **Monreale** and **Cefalù**, the Cattolica at **Stilo** and S. Marco at **Rossano** all bear witness to the survival of the Byzantine tradition. Major monuments from the Lombard period still stand at **Cividale del Friuli** and **Benevento** (S. Sofia). The Volvinius altar in S. Ambrogio in **Milan** is a superb example of **Frankish** goldsmith art.

The great number of **Romanesque** and **Gothic** monuments (11C-14C) make it impossible to give a full list. However, the visitor should always bear in mind that almost every building is the result of a long period of building or rebuilding, during which stylistic periods flow into each other. S. Ambrogio in **Milan**, S. Zeno and the Castelvecchio bridge in **Verona**, the Palazzo Ducale and the Ca' d'Oro in **Venice**, the cathedral at **Modena**, the cathedral and baptistery at **Parma**, the Prato dei Miracoli (cathedral, baptistery, leaning tower and the Camposanto) in **Pisa**, the Palazzo Vecchio, the baptistery, the campanile, S. Maria del Fiore, S. Maria Novella, S. Croce, S. Miniato, the Ponte Vecchio at **Florence**, the duomo and Palazzo Pubblico at **Siena**, the cathedral at **Orvieto**, the cloisters of S. Lorenzo and S. Paolo fuori le Mura in **Rome**, the Chiostro del Paradiso at **Amalfi**, the **Castel del Monte**, S. Nicola at **Bari** and the cathedrals of **Trani**, **Bitonto** and **Ruvo**, the duomo at **Cefalù**, the cathedral and cloister of **Monreale**, S. Gavino at **Porto Torres** and the **SS. Trinità di Saccargia** — these are just some of the many monuments.

In listing individual monuments it is important to remember that many town squares and quarters and indeed entire cities (**Lucca, Siena, San Gimignano, Perugia, Gubbio, Spoleto, Viterbo**) still bear the mark of the Middle Ages. The reliefs by Wiligelmus at **Modena** and Antelami at **Parma** are masterpieces of Romanesque sculpture, as are the bronze doors of the cathedral at Pisa and S. Zeno in **Verona**, the pulpits by Nicola and Giovanni Pisano at **Pisa** and at **Siena** and the fountain in the piazza at Perugia. For those interested in mosaics, there are S. Appollinare Nuovo in **Ravenna**, S. Marco in **Venice**, the baptistery in **Florence**, the Duomo at **Cefalù**, the Cappella Palatina and the Martorana at **Palermo**. Masterpieces of painting include Giotto's frescos (Scrovegni, **Padua, Assisi**, S.Croce, **Florence**); the *Maestà* by Duccio di Boninsegna **(Siena)**; the frescos by Simone Martini and the Lorenzetti **(Siena, Assisi)**. Museums and galleries throughout Italy contain works from this period but the most outstanding are perhaps those in **Florence** (Uffizi), **Siena** and **Pisa** (Museo Nazionale di S. Matteo).

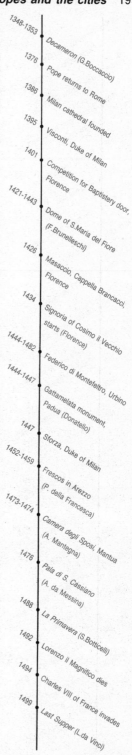

1348-1353

1376 — Decameron (G.Boccaccio)

Pope returns to Rome

1386 — Milan cathedral founded

1395 — Visconti, Duke of Milan

1401 — Competition for Baptistery door, Florence

1421-1443 — Dome of S.Maria del Fiore (F.Brunelleschi)

1426 — Masaccio, Cappella Brancacci, Florence

1434 — Signoria of Cosimo il Vecchio starts (Florence)

1444-1482 — Federico di Montefeltro, Urbino

1444-1447 — Gattamelata monument, Padua (Donatello)

1447 — Sforza, Duke of Milan

1452-1459 — Frescos in Arezzo (P. della Francesca)

1473-1474 — Camera degli Sposi, Mantua (A. Mantegna)

1476 — Pala di S. Cassiano (A. da Messina)

1488 — La Primavera (S.Botticelli)

1492 — Lorenzo il Magnifico dies

1494 — Charles VIII of France invades

1499 — Last Supper (L.da Vinci)

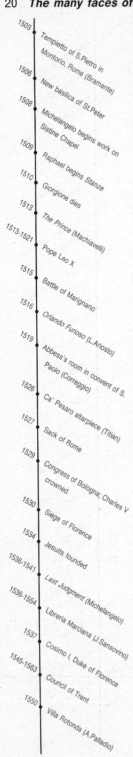

 # The Renaissance

The Renaissance was the high point of Italian civilization and is Italy's gift to the world. This is the period of greatest development for the visitor interested in art history. The multiplicity of centres of Italian art meant that there is no clear chronological break between styles and that the Renaissance's starting point is difficult to date. The Renaissance of the arts began as a Florentine phenomenon, but Rome later became its leader as the home of the major artists from the beginning of the 16C onward. The influence of these two centres spread to the rest of Italy to varying extents at different periods. This high point of creativity lasted well into the 16C (Michelangelo died in 1564) and some consider it to have continued right up to the end of the century. In Mannerism, Renaissance forms were altered, sometimes to convey a purely intellectual message and sometimes an intensely emotional and expressive one. Nevertheless, there is a coherence and progression in the dynamics of form which links the Renaissance, Mannerism and, subsequently, the Baroque.

Innovation

The Renaissance was strongly innovative. Its general trend was to shift attention from the religious spirituality of the Middle Ages, with its theocentric, otherworldly mysticism, to man on earth and to his freedom and activities. However, this art was created in large part to glorify religion, mainly by intensely religious men. Certainly there is a concern with the human condition never before attempted on this scale. In formal terms the Renaissance has its roots in Italian art (Giotto, Masaccio and Michelangelo form a direct line of descent) and in a re-evaluation of the Graeco-Roman heritage, the **rediscovery of the antique.** This heritage included sculptures that had survived or been rediscovered, buildings and written sources copied in the Middle Ages. Other distinctively Renaissance developments included **perspective,** a new technique of representing what the eye saw and a means by which the intellect gained mastery over space; the **study of anatomy** in order to portray the body accurately rather than in simplified form; **critical reflection** on the visual aspect of nature and the effectiveness of the various means of depicting it and the symbolic **significance** of iconographic material.

Period of balance

Historically, the Renaissance falls into two periods. In the second half of the 15C there was a **balance between the Italian states** which had come about from the conflicts and expansion of the preceding century. There then followed six decades during which the European powers fought for control of Italy. Freedom vanished, and foreign rule was established.

At the time of the peace of Lodi, there were five major powers: the **Duchy of Milan,** the wealthy **Republic of Venice,** which had rapidly extended its power from the lagoon through Venetia, Friuli and Lombardy as far as the Adda, the **Republic of Florence,** which under the informal overlordship of the Medici controlled the Arno Valley, the **papal states,** including Latium, the Marches, Umbria and Romagna, and, finally, the **Kingdom of Naples** (the whole of southern Italy) of Alfonso of Aragon, which also included the Spanish dominions of Sicily and Sardinia.

There were also many less powerful states. The **Duchy of Savoy** still controlled territory across the Alps. The **Republic of Genoa** controlled much but not all of Liguria; the prince-bishops of Trento, the countship of Gorizia and the city of Trieste were all Hapsburg vassals. There was the Gonzaga **Marquisate of Mantua;** the **Duchy of Ferrara** and the **Duchy of Modena** and **Reggio** were ruled by the Este family. In Tuscany there was the **Republic of Siena,** the Republic of Lucca, the Signoria of Piombino, the Fieschi at Carrara, the Malaspina in Lunigiana and at Massa. Many of these minor states were important artistic centres during the Renaissance, particularly **Mantua, Ferrara** and **Urbino.**

Foreign domination

The crisis began when **Charles VIII of France** claimed the throne of Naples on the basis of his Angevin ancestors. The kingdom was conquered easily, but his return to France proved much more difficult. In the end, Ferdinand, **King of Aragon** and then of all Spain, eventually gained the **Kingdom of Naples,** but another French king, **Louis XII,** claimed the **Duchy of Milan** as heir to Valentina Visconti and conquered it. When the Swiss beat the French at Novara in 1513, **Francis I** of France regained the Duchy of Milan in the battle of Marignano

(1515). In this way, France and Spain fought over Italy. Francis I was beaten at Pavia by the Hapsburgs and taken prisoner, but the wars continued and all the Italian states became involved on one side or another. In 1527 German troops sacked **Rome,** and **Florence** was besieged in 1530. When the heirs of the two principal adversaries, Henry II of France and Philip II of Spain, finally made peace at **Cateau-Cambrésis** in 1559, the political map of Italy had been simplified and Spain had become the dominant power.

The contrast between the political tragedy of Italy and the brilliance of its artistic and cultural achievements is striking. At the end of an essay on the cultural splendour of Italy, Fernand Braudel wrote, 'it seems to me, rightly or wrongly, that darkness may precede, and may determine every cultural leap forward'.

Cultural growth

The major figures in Italian **literature** at this time were Ludovico Ariosto (1474-1533), Niccolò Machiavelli (1469-1527), Francesco Guicciardini (1483-1540) and Torquato Tasso (1544-95). In addition, no list would be complete without Giorgio Vasari for his *Lives of the Most Excellent Painters, Sculptors and Architects,* the first and most widely read history of Italian art, and Benvenuto Cellini for his *Life* (1728), an autobiography of a major artist. Together these two books make up the best introduction to Italian art.

Cellini's autobiography shows how the arts in the Renaissance did not just include the so-called pure arts. A **master** and his **workshop** could fulfill any request by a **patron,** whether secular or religious, noble or bourgeois. It was not important whether the project was a palace or a church, a convent or a villa, furniture, tapestry, jewelry, vessels or inlay work. A town magistrate could commission paintings celebrating patriotic military feats for the council chamber from such giants as Leonardo and Michelangelo, as was the case in Florence.

Crystalline purity marks the **architecture** of the 15C. The major architects were Filippo Brunelleschi, 1377-1446 (Florence), Michelozzo, 1396-1472 (Florence), Leon Battista Alberti, 1404-72 (Florence, Mantua, Rimini) and Luciano Laurana (Urbino). In the 16C the architectural language was more directly inspired by antiquity, with a grand, open-air spaciousness. In the new genre of the villa, the emphasis lay on the interrelationship between the landscape and nature. The major figures include Donato Bramante, 1444-1514 (Milan, Rome), Michelangelo Buonarroti, 1475-1564 (Florence, Rome), Jacopo Sansovino, 1486-1570 (Venice), Giulio Romano, *c.* 1499-1546 (Mantua), Jacopo Vignola, 1507-73 (Rome, Caprarola), Andrea Palladio, 1505-80 (Vicenza, Venice, Venetia) and Galeazzo Alessi, 1512-72 (Genoa, Milan).

Gothic sculpture had already rediscovered the importance of volume, the expressiveness of line and three-dimensional statues. Renaissance **sculpture** took from this tradition and from antiquity. It knew no bounds in terms of technique or expression. Perspective was used in reliefs to convey a feeling of space; there was a freedom of modelling, a harmony of gesture, drama, dynamic balance, energy, grace, heroic force and a tragic element. The prime examples of this are mainly marbles and bronzes of the primarily Florentine Renaissance artists. They turned to the nude and to the classical vocabulary in decorative friezes, where sculpture and architecture merged. Major figures included Jacopo della Quercia (1374-1438), Lorenzo Ghiberti (1378-1455), Donatello (1387-1466), Luca della Robbia (1400-82), Andrea Verrocchio (1435-88; also a painter), Francesco Laurana, Antonio Pollaiuolo (1432-98) and, of course, Michelangelo. Vasari considers Michelangelo an expert in all the arts and cannot decide whether he was a greater architect, painter or sculptor (although it was as a sculptor that he outshone all his contemporaries and successors). Benvenuto Cellini (1500-71) produced works of great elegance. There were also a number of Mannerist sculptors, including Giambologna (1524-1608).

While **painting** today is seen as the apogee of Renaissance arts, there was a lively debate at the time between the superiority of painting and that of sculpture. The religious element, which had been predominant, was joined to a number of other genres in the painting of the 15C and the 16C: secular celebration, the portrait, mythical tales hiding a philosophical basis, paintings for private patrons, frescos, panel paintings and, of course, increasing numbers of canvases. A large number of **drawings** also survive. These were used by artists to develop ideas, as trials or as sketches, whether for their own use or for discussion with patrons. **Engraving** also came into its own as an art form. Crafts were handed down by masters who taught pupils in workshops. The pupils would then work on the master's commissions. However, every artist would strive to outdo his master and to assert his individuality, particularly in design and technique. Although there are obviously differences in quality, any attempt to rank the

1559　Treaty of Cateau-Cambrésis: Spanish domination established

1564-1587　Paintings in Scuola di S.Rocco (Tintoretto)

1571　Battle of Lepanto

1575　Gerusalemme Liberata (T. Tasso)

1585-1590　Pope Sixtus V

1607　Orfeo (C.Monteverdi)

1613-1614　Aurora in Casino Rospigliosi (G. Reni)

1623-1644　Pope Urban VIII

1624　Baldacchino of St. Peter's Basilica (G.L.Bernini)

1631-1687　S. Maria della Salute, Venice (B. Longhena)

1633　Condemnation of Galileo

1642-1660　S. Ivo della Sapienza (F. Borromini)

1656-1665　Colonnade of piazza S.Pietro (G. L.Bernini)

1680　Palazzo Carignano (G.Guarini)

1710-1717　Oratorio del Rosario, Palermo (G. Serpotta)

1713　Treaty of Utrecht: Austria supersedes Spain

immense artistic heritage found in churches, palaces and galleries must rely on matters of personal taste. Learning about the relationships between artists, the derivations, influences and the genres is more helpful in understanding the works of art than dividing them into schools, as is often done in museums. However, there is undeniably a Florentine-Tuscan style and a Venetian one, and they represent opposite poles.

Florentine genius, Masaccio (painting), Donatello (sculpture) and Brunelleschi (architecture), unleased the Renaissance. At the same time it is possible to say that the Renaissance reached its apogee and then exhausted itself with another trio: Leonardo, Raphael and Michelangelo. Such a framework fails to take Venetian painting into account. Other prominent Tuscan painters of the 15C include Fra Angelico, Paolo Uccello, Filippo Lippi, Piero della Francesca, Benozzo Gozzoli, Sandro Botticelli and Luca Signorelli. Pietro Vannucci, known as Perugino, and Pinturicchio were the Umbrian masters. In northern Italy there was Antonio Pisano, Pisanello from Verona, Cosmé Tura of Ferrara and Andrea Mantegna of Padua.

The three giants of the 16C have already been mentioned, but the inquiring Tuscan spirit of Leonardo da Vinci (1452-1519) is symbolic of the breadth of interests of the Renaissance artist. The periods he spent in Milan exerted considerable influence over the later course of Lombard painting. Raphael Santi (1483-1520) from Urbino was a pupil of Perugino and also an architect. His pupils spread his style throughout and beyond Italy. Michelangelo, another Tuscan, had enormous influence, particularly over Tuscan Mannerism. The painters of the 16C also included Andrea del Sarto of Florence, Antonio Allegri, Correggio, Francisco Mazzola, Parmigianino and Jacopo Carrucci Pontormo. Venetian painting was established by the end of the 15C and flowered during the 16C, including Giovanni Bellini, Vittore Carpaccio, Giorgione, Lorenzo Lotto, Titian, Tintoretto, Jacopo Bassano and Paolo Veronese. El Greco, who was originally from Crete, worked in Venice before becoming one of the major figures in Spanish painting.

Sites and monuments

The Renaissance flourished in **Florence, Rome** and **Venice** and they are still the cities to visit for both monuments and galleries. Other cities strongly marked by the Renaissance (major works and collections) include: **Ferrara, Urbino, Mantua, Pienza, Sabbioneta, Vicenza, Genoa** and **Milan.**

Individual works from the Renaissance are to be found in Tuscany at **Prato** (S. Maria delle Carceri), **Arezzo** (Piero della Francesca's frescos in S. Francesco), **Cortona** (Madonna del Calcinaio), **Lucca** (tomb of Ilaria del Carretto), Siena (Pinturicchio's frescos in the Libreria Piccolomini in the cathedral); in other parts of central Italy: **Orvieto** (frescos by Luca Signorelli in the Duomo), **Perugia** (S. Bernardino and the paintings by Perugino), **Todi** (S. Maria della Consolazione); in northern Italy: **Lodi** (Incoronata), **Bergamo** (Cappella Colleoni), **Padua** (the Gattamelata monument), **Verona** (Loggia del Consiglio), **Bologna** (Jacopo della Quercia's reliefs in S. Petronio), **Parma** (the Correggio frescos), **Cesena** (Biblioteca Malatestiana), **Rimini** (Tempio Malatestiana); in southern Italy: **Naples** (Porta Capuana, the triumphal arch of the Castel Nuovo), **L'Aquila** (S. Bernardino); in Sicily there are paintings by Antonello da Messina **(Palermo, Cefalù),** the fresco of the Triumph of Death **(Palermo)** and the sculptures by Antonello Gagini.

● *Regional states and foreign domination*

The political map of Italy remained the same immediately after the **peace of Cateau-Cambrésis** in 1559. However, Spain directly controlled the **Duchy of Milan, southern Italy,** the islands of **Sicily** and **Sardinia** and the small **state of the Presidi** with fortresses strategically situated along the Tuscan coastline. The only truly independent state was the **Republic of Venice** and it was constantly preoccupied with defending its overseas territories against the advance of the Turks.

The years passed and the country gradually sank into decline. Most developments were merely the consequences of events occurring in other countries.

Foreign armies criss-crossed the land, spreading the plague, fighting wars in which Italian territories were simply looted. All the major changes in Italy during this period took place due to decisions taken in the chancelleries of Europe.

War of Spanish Succession

After almost two centuries of Spanish domination the most important change occurred at the beginning of the 18C as a result of the **War of Spanish Succession.** The **treaties of Utrecht** and **Rastadt** (1713-14) gave the Spanish territories to the Austrians, with two significant exceptions: the **Duchy of Mantua** passed to Austria and was then united with Milan and the Gonzaga Marquisate of **Monferrato** went to the Duke of Savoy, Victor Amadeus II. Some years later, the partition of Italy among the various powers changed again and **Sicily** was reunited with the southern kingdom in exchange for **Sardinia.** The Spaniards were eliminated entirely. It was for this reason that when the unification was achieved, it was the king of Sardinia (rather than of Sicily) who became king of Italy.

The situation did not stabilize for several decades. Philip V, the new King of Spain who had gained his throne from the Spanish branch of the Hapsburgs as a result of the war of succession, took as his second wife **Elisabetta Farnese** of the house of Parma. She wanted her son, **Don Carlos,** to be Duke of Parma. Nonetheless, the title passed to **Francis of Lorraine,** husband of Maria Theresa. The Lorraine-Hapsburg dynasty ruled until the unification of Italy. Meanwhile, Don Carlos, a descendant of the Sun King (Louis XIV) and of a Renaissance pope, became **King of Naples.** Later, he also ascended to the throne of Spain, but the Bourbons continued to rule southern Italy until unification. Parma passed first to Austria and then to Ferdinand Bourbon (1748), another son of Philip V and Elisabetta Farnese. Some of the Italian monarchs distinguished themselves as patrons of the **Enlightenment** during the second half of the 18C.

Napoleon

It is impossible to follow in detail the whirlwind years between 1796 and 1814 when **Napoleon Bonaparte** went from general of the Army of Italy to Emperor at Fontainebleau. Dynastic Italy had been shattered, **Venice** was ceded to Austria in the treaty of Campoformio (1797), ending its thousand years of independence. Republican regimes were followed by monarchies and empires at Napoleon's whim and in accordance to the fortunes of war. Toward the end of the Empire, virtually all of Italy was French (with the exception of Sicily and Sardinia).

The **Congress of Vienna** (1815) redrew the political boundaries, but the Napoleonic era had left its mark on Italian history. It had formed groups within the population who considered themselves Italian and who hoped to express this national feeling through some form of political unity. The Risorgimento had found its roots.

Cultural growth

Italian culture made important contributions during this period. Major figures appeared, such as Galileo Galilei, the great scientist, and the Neapolitan philosopher Giambattista Vico. This period witnessed the birth of **opera,** and the theatre produced the great Venetian dramatist Carlo Goldoni, whose comedies continue to be performed in Italy and everywhere in the world. Goldoni's *Mémoires* (published in 1787) and the *Life* by Vittorio Alfieri are two books which give a clear understanding of the Italian 18C.

The **Baroque** movement in architecture invaded all of Europe. Indeed it even crossed the oceans to the colonies. It had its origins in Italy, where it grew logically out of late 16C architecture in **Rome.** As the centre of Christianity, this was where the Catholic **Counter-Reformation** developed (by orders like the **Jesuits**). It was also where talented architects such as Carlo Maderna and the Tuscan Pietro da Cortona worked. The two greatest exponents of the Roman Baroque were the Neapolitan Gian Lorenzo Bernini and Francesco Borromini from Ticino. The Baroque spread outside Rome, leaving its mark in many towns of southern Italy and Sicily, and in the north (Turin). The most innovative figures were Guarino Guarini, who came from Modena but worked mainly in Turin, and the Venetian Baldassare Longhena, who reinterpreted the style in the spirit of the lagoon. There was little **rococo** architecture in Italy. Instead, in the 18C, the dramatic and imaginative exuberance of the Baroque gave way to the noble orderliness of form of the **Neoclassical.** Interesting 18C architects include Filippo Juvarra from Messina, who worked in Turin, the Neapolitan Luigi Vanvitelli and Giuseppe Piermarini from Foligno.

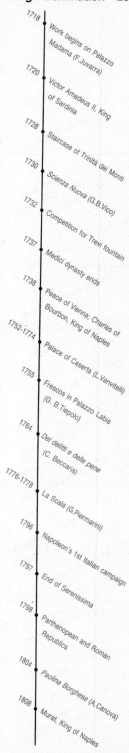

1718 — Work begins on Palazzo Madama (F.Juvarra)

1720 — Victor Amadeus II, King of Sardinia

1728 — Staircase of Trinità dei Monti

1730 — Scienza Nuova (G.B.Vico)

1732 — Competition for Trevi fountain

1737 — Medici dynasty ends

1738 — Peace of Vienna; Charles of Bourbon, King of Naples

1752-1774 — Palace of Caserta (L.Vanvitelli)

1755 — Frescos in Palazzo Labia (G. B.Tiepolo)

1764 — Dei delitti e delle pene (C. Beccaria)

1776-1778 — La Scala (G.Piermarini)

1796 — Napoleon's 1st Italian campaign

1797 — End of Serenissima

1798 — Parthenopean and Roman Republics

1804 — Paolina Borghese (A.Canova)

1808 — Murat, King of Naples

1815 Congress of Vienna

1816-1820 Piazza del Popolo (G.Valadier)

1816 Il barbiere di Sivigla (G.Rossini)

1831 Canti (G.Leopardi); Norma (V.Bellini); L'Elisir d'Amore (G.Donizetti)

1837-1842 I Promessi Sposi (A.Manzoni)

1848-1849 1st War of Independence

1853 La Traviata (G.Verdi)

c. 1855 The Macchiaioli

1859 2nd War of Independence

1860 Garibaldi and the Thousand

1861 Kingdom of Italy proclaimed

1863-1880 Mole Antonelliana (A.Antonelli)

1866 3rd War of Independence

1870 Rome captured

1882 Triple Alliance (Austria and Germany)

In **sculpture,** Bernini was the major artist of the period and was considered the only truly creative and innovative figure after Michelangelo. Other sculptors included the 17C Tuscan Francesco Mochi and, in the 18C, the virtuoso Neapolitan Giuseppe Sammartino, Giovanni Maria Morlaiter, who was active in Venetia, and Giacomo Serpotta, the master of stucco decoration.

Painting continued to flourish after the end of the Renaissance but it seemed to have been overshadowed by the great masters of the 16C and disturbed by the new religious atmosphere. Annibale Carracci was the foremost member of a family of artists from Bologna who tried to develop a new eclectic approach, drawing on the plasticity of Michelangelo, the spatial sense of Raphael, the colour of Titian and Correggio and the shading of Leonardo. The powerful personality of Michelangelo Merisi, known as Caravaggio, breathed new life into painting, although he yielded more results outside Italy than inside. Other interesting 17C artists included the Emilian Guido Reni, Domenico Zampieri, Domenichino, G. Francesco Barbieri, Guercino and the Genoese painter Bernardo Strozzi. In the 18C there was the talented but bizarre Alessandro Magnasco. However, it was in Venice that Italian painting enjoyed its final glory during the end of the Serenissima, with the splendid colour, light and space of Giambattista Tiepolo, his son Giandomenico Tiepolo with his works of consuming, foreboding melancholy, Pietro Longhi, a delightful chronicler of 18C Venetian life, and the two veduta painters, Canaletto and Francesco Guardi, who faithfully recorded the face of the city.

Sites and monuments

The major centre of **Baroque** art is **Rome.** Other cities containing a significant amount of Baroque and late Baroque architecture are **Turin, Lecce, Naples, Palermo, Catania** and the towns of southeastern Italy, which were rebuilt at the end of the 17C following a major earthquake. Key 18C buildings include the royal palace at **Caserta,** the hunting lodge of **Stupinigi,** the Villa Pisani at **Strà.** There are some fine examples of the Neoclassical in Milan.17C and 18C paintings and sculptures are scattered throughout churches, palaces, villas and museums of Italy. Caravaggio is best represented in **Rome,** Tiepolo in **Venice** and **Udine.** For a sense of the life of the period, its taste, interior decoration and the decorative arts there is the Pitti in **Florence,** the Galleria Doria-Pamphili in **Rome,** the Capodimonte, the Certosa di S.Martino and the Floridiana in **Naples** and the Museo del Settecento in the Ca' Rezzonico in **Venice.**

● *Italian unification, the Kingdom, the Republic*

The political map of Italy following the Congress of Vienna (1815), **'Restoration'** Italy, was somewhat simplified. Piedmont, Liguria and Sardinia formed the **Kingdom of Sardinia;** the **papal states** and the **Kingdom of Southern Italy** were essentially the same as they were before Napoleon; the **Grand-Duchy of Tuscany** now occupied the whole of the region. The **Austrian** Hapsburg emperors, who governed **Venetia-Lombardy** directly, dominated the rest of Italy politically. There were still two independent duchies, **Parma and Piacenza** and **Modena and Reggio.**

Risorgimento

The **Risorgimento** and unification were made possible by political developments in Europe, but they were actually triggered by an active layer of Italians who were inspired by the ideas that had come out of the French Revolution. Under Napoleon III France made a decisive intervention on the side of Piedmont leading to the defeat of the Austrians in 1859. Napoleon III was concerned for French Catholics and opposed Rome becoming the capital of Italy (and the pope losing his temporal power). Great Britain favoured the end of the Bourbon kingdom in southern Italy. Austria, obviously, was hostile to unification at its expense.

Two movements represented the forces of unity in Italy. The first was a revolutionary-republican group headed by **Giuseppe Mazzini** (1805-72), a tireless agitator, and **Giuseppe Garibaldi** (1807-82) of Nice, the inspired and brave military commander of the volunteers, who favoured a merging of the republican and royal efforts. The second movement favoured a constitutional monarchy and was led by **Camillo Benso Conte di Cavour** (1810-61), the man who could engineer the political situation from which unity might spring. Cavour died three months after the proclamation of Victor Emmanuel II as King of Italy in the parliament of Turin. Mazzini, who had been released from prison in the amnesty following the capture of Rome, died in Pisa in 1872. His final assessment of the situation: 'There is only the skeleton of Italy, not the soul'.

The revolutionary upsurge throughout Europe in 1848 swept Italy as well. **Venice** and **Milan** rebelled; the King of Sardinia, **Charles Albert,** presented a liberal constitution (the 'Statute', the institutional basis for Italian parliamentary democracy) and went to war with Austria in Lombardy (**First War of Independence,** 1848-9), fighting two unsuccessful campaigns. Mazzini declared the **Roman Republic,** which was defended by Garibaldi, but fell to the French. In Venice Daniele Manin restored the **Republic of S. Marco** but the Austrians recaptured the city after a siege. By the end of the summer of 1849, the situation was the same as before.

Ten years later, after two more campaigns, the political map of Italy was redrawn. Following Cavour's alliance with Napoleon III, the French army and **Victor Emmanuel II** (with the Sardinian-Piedmontese army) crossed the Ticino (**Second War of Independence,** 1859) and entered **Milan.** The Austrians were defeated in the bloody battles of **Solferino** and **San Martino.** Napoleon III drew up an armistice with Emperor Franz Josef, frustrating the hopes of Cavour, who resigned. However, popular movements had expelled the Grand-Duke of Tuscany and the rulers of the Po Valley duchies. The papal states had also rebelled. Having gained **Lombardy** in the war, Piedmont was able to annex **Tuscany** and **Emilia.**

A short while later, in the spring of 1860, **Garibaldi** embarked a thousand volunteers at Quarto (Genoa) to go to **Marsala** and overthrow the Boubons. He declared himself dictator of Sicily in the name of Victor Emmanuel II. He beat the Bourbon army at **Calatafimi,** took Palermo, crossed the straits and entered **Naples** triumphantly; all within the space of four months. Having obtained the agreement of Napoleon III, Cavour occupied Umbria and the papal territories in **the Marches** with the Piedmontese army. In the symbolic **Meeting of Teano** Garibaldi handed southern Italy over to Victor Emmanuel II (November 1860) and left for Caprera. The proclamation of the **Kingdom of Italy** (1861) brought the upheavals to an end and the capital was moved to Florence. **Venice** and Venetia were later united with Italy (**Third War of Independence,** 1866), as a result of an alliance with Prussia, which beat the Austrians at Sadowa. **Rome** was taken in 1870 after the withdrawal of the French garrison and the fall of Napoleon III, who was defeated by Prussia at Sedan.

Unification

The nation celebrated its first 100 years of unity only a generation ago. It has been a difficult road. Following unification, Italy was poor, generally backward, with great disparities in development. It had inherited a number of serious problems and new ones developed as the face of Europe began to change. The economy, until after the Second World War, was predominantly agricultural and industrialization was confined within the Milan-Turin-Genoa triangle. Lack of raw materials and energy sources is a fact of Italian life and the modern Italian economy is primarily based on processing. By the turn of the century, problems of an emerging proletariat had started to develop. The Piedmontese **Giovanni Giolitti** (1842-1928) was perhaps the politician with the clearest understanding of the state of affairs in Italy at the time and he strove to achieve the political integration of the socialist movement. Nevertheless, universal male suffrage was not achieved until 1919. Colonial ambitions proved more costly than profitable.

Twentieth century

Like the rest of Europe, Italy was thrown into the turmoil of the **First World War.** Italy hoped the war would lead to the completion of national unity and **Trento** and **Trieste** were indeed united with Italy at the end of the war in 1918, but the price had been high. Over 600,000 people were killed and the nation's assets fell by 26 percent. The period of **Fascist government** which followed (Benito Mussolini, 1922-43) interrupted Italy's democratic development during a generation. It was an irrational and authoritarian escape from real problems which the war had brought to light. It also led to Italy's involvement in the **Second World War** on the side of Germany. Italy was invaded by the Allies in 1943 and the fighting moved northward until 1945. The **Partisan War** (fought after the fall of Fascism) and the armistice formed the basis for a return to democratic insti-

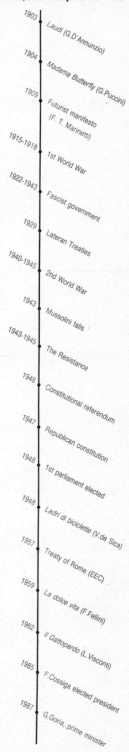

1903 Laudi (G.D'Annunzio)

1904 Madama Butterfly (G.Puccini)

1909 Futurist manifesto (F.T. Marinetti)

1915-1918 1st World War

1922-1943 Fascist government

1929 Lateran Treaties

1940-1945 2nd World War

1943 Mussolini falls

1943-1945 The Resistance

1946 Constitutional referendum

1947 Republican constitution

1948 1st parliament elected

1948 Ladri di biciclette (V.de Sica)

1957 Treaty of Rome (EEC)

1959 La dolce vita (F.Fellini)

1962 Il Gattopardo (L.Visconti)

1985 F.Cossiga elected president

1987 G.Goria, prime minister

tutions following the **Liberation** (25 April 1945). Fascism had also meant the end of the Savoyard monarchy. On 2 June 1946 the Italian people, enjoying universal male and female suffrage for the first time, voted in favour of a constitutional referendum and established the **Republic**. For the first time in their history, Italians (all Italians) held their destiny in their hands.

Despite all the internal strife, Italy had expanded during the eighty years of unity. The war had destroyed half the country, but Italy was free. Italy has never enjoyed so long a period of peace as under the Republic, nor have Italians ever been as well-off.

Cultural growth

Before and during the Risorgimento, Giacomo Leopardi wrote his *Canti* (Songs) of unparalleled intensity and purity, Alessandro Manzoni wrote *I Promessi sposi* (The Betrothed) and Ippolito Nievo wrote *Confessions of an Italian*. Following unification a number of literary figures emerged: the Tuscan Giosue Carducci, Giovanni Pascoli from the Romagna, Giovanni Verga, Gabriele D'Annunzio from Abruzzi, Luigi Pirandello from Sicily and Italo Svevo. A more recent writer, philosopher Benedetto Croce, provides a penetrating introduction to southern Italy in *History of the Kingdom of Naples*.

The 19C was the highpoint of Italian **grand opera**, with composers such as Gioachino Rossini, Gaetano Donizetti, Vicenzo Bellini and Giuseppe Verdi. 19C Italian **art**, although it did display some unusual and interesting features, lacked the relevance and vigour of previous centuries. However, major figures included the Neoclassical sculptor Antonio Canova and the **Macchiaioli** school of Tuscan painters which included Giovanni Fattori and Silvestro Lega. In the 20C **Futurism**, one of whose exponents was Umberto Boccioni, played a significant role in the avant-garde of European art.

Since the First World War Italians have been very active in the arts. Modern and contemporary art galleries (Rome, Turin, Milan and elsewhere) put on exhibitions and there are regular events such as the Venice Biennale. Works by modern Italian writers such as Carlo Levi and Italo Calvino have been translated into a number of languages. Italy has made a major contribution to the most important and popular of the modern arts: the cinema.

Practical
holiday guide

Information

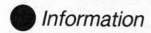

Italian National Tourist Office (ENIT)

The Italian National Tourist Office has many offices overseas, including:
- **USA:**
New York: 630 Fifth Ave, Suite 1565, New York, NY 10111 (☎ 212/2454961).
Chicago: 500 North Michigan Ave, Suite 1046, Chicago, Ill 60611 (☎ 312/6440990).
San Francisco: 360 Post St, Suite 801, San Francisco, Ca 94108 (☎ 415/3926206).
Dallas: c/o *Alitalia*, 8350 N. Central Expressway, Dallas, Tx 75206 (☎ 214/6928761).
- **Great Britain:**
London: 1 Princes St, London W1R 8AY (☎ 01/4081254).
- **Canada:**
Montreal: Store 56, Plaza 3 Place Ville Marie, Montreal, Québec (☎ 8667667).

Tourist offices can be found in regional capitals, important tourist centres and many small
towns. These offices (generally called *APT: Azienda de Promozione Turistica*) are normally
open from 8 a.m. to 12:30 p.m. and 2:00 to 6 p.m., and closed Saturday and Sunday.
However, at the height of the season the hours are often extended in large cities and tourist centres. Addresses and telephone numbers of tourist offices can be found in the *Practical Information* sections of this guide. It is also possible to obtain information by calling the
offices of *TCI (Touring Club Italiano):* at Milan, corso Italia 10, ☎ 02/852672; at Rome, v.
Ovidio 7/A, ☎ 06/388602; at Turin, p. Solferino 3 bis, ☎ 011/540177; at Bari, v. Melo 259,
☎ 080/365140. The telephone number ☎ 116 is the number for assistance for problems on
the roads; it also functions as a telephone service for foreign tourists 24 hours a day. Per-
sonnel speak several languages and furnish information and advice of all kinds.

*tourist
offices*

in Italy

Getting to Italy

There are regular Alitalia (Italian national airline) flights from *c.* 87 cities in 46 different countries: 26 in Italy, 21 elsewhere in Europe, 12 in Africa, 14 in Asia, 12 in America and 2 in
Australia. The major international airports are **Rome Fiumicino** (30 km from central Rome, 45
mn by bus to Stazione Terminini, *Alitalia* passenger information, ☎ 02/60101, other international airlines, ☎ 02/60121) and **Milan Malapensa** (46 km from central Milan, 60 mn by bus
to Stazione Centrale; passenger information, ☎ 02/74852200). Smaller international airports
are **Bologna Borgo Panigale, Cagliari Elmas, Genoa Milano-Linate, Naples Capodichino,
Olbia Costa Smeralda, Palermo Punta Raisi, Rome Ciampino, Turin Caselle, Venice Tessera.**

Alitalia has offices in many cities overseas, including:
- **USA:**
New York: 666 Fifth Ave, New York, NY 10103 (☎ 212/5828900).
Atlanta: 223 Perimeter Center Parkway, Suite 530, Atlanta, Ga 30346 (☎ 800/2235730).

air travel

information

Boston: One Exeter Plaza, 699 Boylston St, Boston, Mass 02116 (☎ 800/2235730).
Chicago: 55 East Monroe St, Suite 4635, Chicago, Ill 60603 (☎ 312/7810540).
Los Angeles: 6151 West Century Blvd, Suite 1102/1100, Los Angeles, Ca 90045 (☎ 213/5680901).
Miami: 100 North Biscayne Blvd, Suite 1707, Miami, Fla 33132 (☎ 800/2235730).
Minneapolis: 2850 Metro Drive, Suite 515, Minneapolis, Mn 55420 (☎ 800/2235730).
Newark: 1435 Morris Ave, Union, NJ 07083 (☎ 201/6434222).
Philadelphia: 2 Penn Center Plaza, Suite 1007, Philadelphia, Pa 19102 (☎ 215/5685444).
San Francisco: 421 Powell St, Suite 300, San Francisco, Ca 94102 (☎ 800/2235730).
Washington, DC: 1001 Connecticut Ave, NW, Suite 219, Washington, DC 20036 (☎ 202/3311841).
Cleveland: Lakewood Center North, 14600 Detroit Ave, Suite 710, Cleveland, Oh 44107 (☎ 800/2235730).
Dallas: 8350 North Central Expressway, Suite M2020, Dallas, Tx 75206 (☎ 800/2235730).
Houston: 1333 West Loop South, Suite 1206, Houston Tx 77027 (☎ 800/2235730).
● **Great Britain:**
London: 27/28 Piccadilly, London W1V 9PF (☎ 01/6027111).
Manchester: International House, 82/86 Deansgate, Manchester M3 2ER (☎ 061/2281653).
● **Canada:**
Montreal: 2055 Peel St, Montreal, Québec H3A 1VB (☎ 8425201).
Ottawa: PO Box 115, Station A, Ottawa, Ontario K1N 8V1 (☎ 2371460).
Toronto: 120 Adelaide St West, Suite 1202, Toronto, Ontario M5H 2E1 (☎ 3632001).
Winnipeg: 15 Greenmont Rd, Winnipeg, Manitoba R2J IT3 (☎ 800/3618050).
Hamilton: Mohawk Rd East, apt 912, Hamilton, Ontario L9A 2G6 (☎ 800/3618336).

There are many other airlines that travel to Italy from all major centres, including:

from USA   ● **Pan Am:** New York, NY (☎ 212/6872600); Washington, DC (☎ 202/8458000); toll-free number (☎ 800/2211111).
● **TWA:** New York, NY (☎ 212/2902141); Washington, DC (☎ 202/7377404); San Francisco (☎ 415/4411805); toll-free number (☎ 800/8924141).

from Great Britain   ● **British Airways:** London (☎ 01/8974000); Manchester (☎ 061/2286311); Birmingham (☎ 021/2367000).
● **British Caledonian Airways:** London (☎ 01/6684222); Manchester (☎ 061/2365118); Birmingham (☎ 021/6325504).

from Canada   ● **Air Canada:** Toronto (☎ 416/9252300); Montreal (☎ 514/3933333).

Arrival in Italy

formalities   In order to enter Italy, the visitor must have a valid national passport. For visitors from Great Britain a document satisfactorily establishing identity and nationality is sufficient. If arriving by car, the visitor must be in possession of a valid driver's license, registration papers for the car and insurance (international green card).

customs   Visitors are allowed to leave with (without payment of tax and without the intention to resell) 200 cigarettes or 100 cigarillos or 50 cigars or 250 gr of tobaccco; 1 litre of alcohol (+ 22 %) or 2 litres (− 22 %); 2 litres of wine; 50 gr of perfume; 114 litres of eau de toilette or 500 gr of coffee. For visitors from the EEC, the customs enforce these regulations lightly, making it possible to leave with rather more than is listed. For visitors from other countries, however, these regulations are enforced as listed, with the exception of cigars and cigarettes.

animals   If the visitor wishes to enter with an animal, it must be in good health and vaccinated against rabies at least 20 days and at most 11 months before arrival.

currency   The visitor is allowed to enter or leave with up to 400,000 lire per person. There is no limit to the amount of foreign currency, or other methods of payment, that a visitor may enter with. However, on leaving Italy, for any amount higher than the equivalent of 1,000,000 lire (per person), this amount will be calculated in accordance with the 'V2' form that must be filled out at customs on arrival.

exchange   Foreign currency may be changed at the frontier, in banks, international airports and major railroad stations. Exchange rates are the same throughout the country.

Money

The Italian currency is the lira. Banknotes are issued in denominations of 1,000, 2,000, 5,000, 10,000, 50,000 and 1,000,000 lire; coins of 5, 10, 20 (now little used), 50, 100, 200 and 500 lire. San Marino and Vatican City coins are also in circulation in Italy. They are the same shape and weight as their Italian equivalents (and rather rare).

Banks are open to the public from 8:30 a.m. until 1:30 p.m. and from 2:45 to 3:45 p.m. except on Saturdays, Sundays and holidays. Bank holidays are New Year's Day, Easter Monday, 25 April, 1 May, 15 August, 1 November, 8, 25 and 26 December and the patron saint's day in individual cities; half-day holidays (closing time brought forward to 11:30 a.m.) are 14 August, 24 December and 31 December. Bear in mind that in some banks exchange desks may be open shorter hours. Any amount of money may be sent from abroad to an Italian bank, but a charge will be made.

banks

Traveler's checks can be changed in banks and are accepted by many hotels, restaurants and shops. Credit cards are also widely accepted and may be used for hotels, transport, car rental, etc. Many businesses display signs indicating which methods of payment are acceptable other than cash. The most commonly recognized credit cards in Italy are *American Express* and *Visa Bank Americard;* in case of loss: *American Express,* ☎ 02/8557268, *Visa Bank Americard,* ☎ 02/40242808 or 3452260 (night and holidays).

traveler's checks

It is possible to receive money from abroad at hotels, residences or poste restante (Fermo Posta) at any post office, by means of international postal orders or telegraph. The sum sent may not exceed 100,000 lire in the case of postal orders or 200,000 lire by telegraph. Tourists may also draw against postal checks bought in their own countries on presentation of a postal credit card and valid identification (generally a passport).

money by post

Post and telephone

Italy has about 14,000 post offices. They are open from 8:25 a.m. to 2 p.m. every day except Sunday and holidays; on Saturday closing time is 12 noon. In cities and the majority of principal provincial towns the central post offices are also open until 7:30/8 p.m.; post offices at international airports are always open.

This guide indicates, locality by locality, the codes that are necessary to add before dialing a number in each area.

telephone information

Certain useful telephone numbers:
- time, ☎ 161
- wake-up calls, ☎ 114
- traffic, ☎ 194
- snow bulletin, ☎ 162
- sea forecasts, ☎ 196
- information on telephone codes and prices, Italian and European, ☎ 184; other countries, ☎ 170
- police, ☎ 112
- emergency, ☎ 113
- ACI (Automobile Club Italiano) road emergency, ☎ 116

The different regional numbers can be found in the *practical information* sections of this guide.

Calendar, events

Which season to visit?

In Italy, more than in other countries perhaps, the best season to visit depends on which region, what sites or what activities the visitor chooses. There are basically three kinds of climate on the peninsula: a continental climate in the North, a milder climate in the lake region and a Mediterranean climate on the coasts, pleasant all year round (especially in the south). The climate in Sicily is quasi African.

Summer can best be enjoyed in excursions in the mountain regions (Alps, Dolomites, Apennines), in seaside resorts on the Tyrrhenian (Bay of Naples, Amalfi) and Adriatic coasts, in Sardinia or other smaller islands, in Abruzzi, Molise or Calabria (it is better to avoid cities, which are empty of their inhabitants during school vacations and are full of tourists). Winter, tempered by the Mediterranean climate, is enjoyable on the coasts, and offers excellent skiing at Italy's many ski resorts in the Alps and the Apennines. Spring and fall, ideal seasons almost everywhere, lend perfect weather to visit Lake Garda or the other prealpine lakes, the Ligurian Riviera, Venice, Florence, Siena and other Tuscan towns, Umbria, Rome and Latium, Apulia, Naples, Sicily and Sardinia.

A large number of cultural, musical, folk and commercial events take place in Italy each year. These are listed in the regional and local *practical information* sections of this guide; tourist offices can provide more detailed information about events in each locality.

Festivals

There are many festivals, among the most famous: Palio d'Asti (Sep); Feast of the Redeemer and Historic Regatta in Venice (Sep); chess matches with living pieces in Marostica (Sep, even-numbered years); Palio delle Contrade in Siena (Jul and Aug); jousting in Arezze (Sep); Palio della Balestra in Sansepolcro (Sep); in Florence: Scoppio del Carro (Easter), Festa del Grillo (Ascension), football matches in costume in the piazza della Signoria (Jun), Festa delle Rificolone (Sep); candle race in Gubbio (May); jousting in Foligno (Sep); tournament in Ascoli Piceno (Aug); Corpus Christi floral procession in Genzano;'Macchina' di Santa Rosa procession in Viterbo (Sep); in Naples: Festa di Piedigrotta (Sep), of San Gennaro (May and Sep) and of the Madonna del Carmine (Jul), crêches in the Christmas period; feast of San Nicola in Bari (May); feast of the almond in blossom in Agrigento (Feb); Cavalcata Sarda (May) and candlestick procession (Aug) in Sassari; Feast of Sant'Efisio in Cagliari (May); parade of the Mamuthones in Mamoiada (Sant'Antonio and carnivals).

carnivals   The liveliest and most famous carnival is in Venice; major carnivals also take place in Viareggio (procession of allegorical floats), Oristano (Sartiglia equestrian competition), Ivrea (historical reconstruction and 'battle of the oranges'), as well as Acireale, Fano, Verona, Ronciglione, Bagolino, Milan.

Fairs, exhibitions and trade shows

Grande Fiera d'Aprile in Milan (80 other specialist shows: film, fashion, sport, tourism, etc.), ☎ 02/3454251; Fiera Internazionale del Levante in Bari (Sep), ☎ 080/206111; Fiera Internazionale del Mediterraneo in Palermo (May-Jun), ☎ 091/543755. International trade fairs are also held in Bolzano (Sep), Bologna (Jun), Gorizia (May), Messina (Aug), Padua (May), Pordenone (Sep) and Trieste (Jun). Specialist international events (frequently on exhibition sites where general trade fairs are taking place) include the Salone dell'Automobile in Turin (Apr-May), ☎ 011/6569; Salone Nautico Internazionale (boat show) in Genoa (autumn), ☎ 010/53911; Fiera dell'Agricoltura in Verona (Mar), ☎ 045/588111; ready-to-wear fashion show in Florence (spring and autumn; Pitti Moda, ☎ 055/219331); craft fair (Apr-May) and antiques fair (Sep-Oct) also in Florence; wine fairs in Verona (Vinitaly, Apr), Palermo (Medivini, May) and Marsala (May and Sep); goldsmiths' shows in Vicenza (Jan and Jun) and Arezzo (Sep); children's book fair in Bologna (Mar-Apr); fishing and water sports in Ancona (Jun); ceramics at Faenza (Jun-Sep) and Gualdo Tadino (Aug-Sep); marble in Carrara and in Sant'Ambrogio di Valpolicella (Verona, Sep); chairs in Torreano di Martignacco (Udine, May); stamps in Riccione (Aug). The oldest and most famous regional craft fairs are the Fiera Millenaria in Sant'Orso at Aosta (31 Jan and Aug). National art, craft and antiques fairs in Todi, Sarnano, Saluzzo, Pennabilli, Urbino (to mention only a few). The principal antiques fairs occurring on particular days are: Arezzo, Brugine, Castiglione Olona, Desenzano del Garda (1st Sun in month), Bergamo, Lucca, Nizza Monferrato, Ravenna (3rd Sun in month); Arma di Taggia and Modena (last Sun in month). There are countless gastronomic fairs; the best-known include the white truffle fair in Alba (Oct), black truffles in Norcia (Feb), wine in Asti (Sep), honey in Montalcino (Sep), chestnuts in Soriano (Oct), snails in Borgo San Dalmazzo (Dec).

Religious events

Holy Week processions are numerous, particularly in the south (*practical information* sections of guide). The most famous and the most spectacular include the Processione dell'Addolorata e dei Misteri in Taranto, the Processione dei Misteri il Venerdì Santo in Trapani, the Processione dei Misteri on Corpus Christi Day in Campobasso. The Feast of the Redeemer in Nuoro (Aug) and other festivals in that region (in Finni, Orgosolo, Mamoiada) are moving. The religious celebrations in Loreto are particularly renowned: 15 Aug and 8 Sep (Feast of the Birth of the Virgin), 10 Dec (Feast of the Translation of the Santa Casa). The most lavish religious festivals are concentrated in Rome: the great assembly of the faithful for the papal blessing in St. Peter's Square at Easter; Feast of St. Peter and St. Paul with solemn service in St. Peter's; Feast of the Immaculate Conception; Christmas services. For information on papal audiences inquire at the Ufficio Informazioni Pellegrini e Turisti in St. Peter's Square (on the left of the basilica).

● *Traveling in Italy*

Italy in two or three weeks

To aid in your choices, the following are several proposed trips:

Lombardy Lakes, Venice, Florence and Rome

Day 1 Milan★★ - Seto Calende - Stresa★ - Borromean Islands - Verbania Intra - ferry to Laveno - Varese - Como★ - Cadenabbia or Bellagio★. **Day 2** Como - Bergamo★★ - Desenzano del Garda - excursion to Sirmione★ and Gardone Riviera★. **Day 3** from Desenzano del Garda to Venice, stops at Verona★★, Vicenza★★ or Padua★★. **Days 4 and 5** Venice★★. **Day 6** Venice: excursion to Murano, Burano and Torcello★. **Day 7** from Venice to Florence stopping in Padua★★ or Bologna★★. **Days 8 and 9** Florence★★. **Day 10** from Florence to Rome stopping in Orvieto★. **Days 11 and 12** Rome★★. **Day 13** Rome: excursion to Tivoli★ and Villa Adriana★★ or the Castelli Romani. **Day 14** return to Milan.

Milan, Venice, Florence, Rome and Naples

Day 1 from Milan★★ - to Sirmione★ stopping in Bergamo★★ and Brescia★. **Day 2** from Sirmione to Venice stopping in Verona★★ and Vicenza★★. **Days 3 and 4** Venice★★. **Day 5** from Venice to Florence stopping in Padua★★ or Ferrara★. **Day 6** Florence★★. **Day 7** Florence and Siena. **Day 8** Siena★★ then from Val da Chiana to Rome. **Day 9** Rome★★. **Day 10** Rome to Naples. **Day 11** Naples★★. **Day 12** Naples, excursion to Herculaneum★★ or the archaeological site at Pompeii★★. **Day 13** Naples: excursion to Capri★★. **Day 14** return to Milan.

Turin, Florence, Rome, Naples and Venice

Day 1 from Turin★★ to Rappallo★, stop possible in Genoa★★ and Portofino★★. **Day 2** from Rapallo to Pisa★★. **Day 3** Pisa - Lucca★★ - Florence. **Day 4** Florence★★. **Day 5** Florence - Siena★★. **Day 6** from Siena to Perugia. **Day 7** Perugia★★ - Rome. **Days 8 and 9** Rome★★. **Day 10** from Rome to Naples★★. **Day 11** Naples: excursion to Pompeii★★. **Day 12** from Naples to Pescara (brief detours possible in Campania, Latium and Abruzzi). **Day 13** from Pescara to Pesaro★ stopping in Ancona★ - Urbino. **Day 14** Urbino★★. **Day 15** Urbino-Pesaro - from Pesaro to Forli stopping in Rimini★ - Ravenna. **Day 16** Ravenna★★ then from Ravenna to Venice, stops possible at the abbey of Pomposa★ and Chioggia★. **Days 17 and 18** Venice★★. **Day 19** from Venice to Vittorio Veneto★ - Cortina d'Ampezzo★★. **Day 20** from Cortina d'Ampezzo to Bolzano via the Grande Strada delle Dolomiti (→ Trentino-Alto Adige). **Day 21** from Bolzano to Turin.

Sicily and Sardinia

Day 1 Messina★ - to Catania★★ - excursion to Etna★ - Taormina★★. **Day 2** from Taormina to Syracuse★★ - excursion to Noto★. **Day 3** from Syracuse to Enna - visit the Roman villa of Casale di Piazza Armerina★ - Gela★ - Agrigento. **Day 4** Agrigento★★. **Day 5** Agrigento - Selinunte★ from Castelvetrano to Segesta★ to Palermo. **Day 6** Palermo★★ and excursion to Monreale★. **Day 7** from Palermo to Messina stopping in Cefalù★ and Tindari and possibly making a detour to Milazzo.

Day 1 Olbia - Costa Smeralda - Palau - Maddalena and Caprera★ islands - from Maddalena by ferry to Santa Teresa Gallura or to Palau again and then by road to Santa Teresa Gallura. **Day 2** Santa Teresa Gallura - Tempio Pausania - Castelsardo - Porto Torres - Alghero★. **Day 3** Alghero - Sassari - by the Carlo Felice superstrada to SS.Trinità di Saccargia★, to the Santu Antine nurag★ and finally to Macomer, Nuoro. **Day 4** Nuoro - Lago Omodeo - Ghilarza - Losa nurag★ - Oristano - excursion to the Tharros★ ruins - Oristano. **Day 5** from Oristano to Cagliari, making a detour to Sanluri for the Su Nuraxi nurag★ near Barumini. **Day 6** Cagliari - Nora★ ruins - Costa del Sud - island of Sant'Antioco - ferry from Calasetta to Carloforce - island of S.Pietro - ferry from Carloforte to Portoscuso - Monte Sirai - Iglesias - Cagliari. **Day 7** Cagliari★.

Theme vacations

It is also possible to plan a trip with a theme in mind, for example:

● Tracing the path of the Etruscans: Florence, Volterra, Cortona, Chiusi, Grosseto, Tarquinia, Cerveteri, Veio, Rome.
● Tracing the path of Greek civilization: Tarento, Metaponte, Sybaris, Crotone, Locri, Reggio di Calabria, Giardini-Naxos, Taormine, Megara, Hyblaea, Syracuse, Palazzolo Acreido, Gela, Agrigento, Selinunte, Segesto, Palermo, as well as the Greek sites in Campania (Paestum, Elea-Velia, Cumes).

● Tracing the path of Roman antiquities: Viterbo, Civita Castellana, Sutri, Ostia Antica, Tivoli, Palestrina, Ferentino, Alatri, Albano Laziale, Cori, Terracina, Santa Capua Vetere, Benevento, Cumeo, Porizzoles, Bacoli, Baia, Naples, Herculanum, Pompey, Castellammare di Stabbia, Capri.
● Tracing the path of the Renaissance: Besides the evident centres of Florence, Rome and Venice, the chief representative works can be visited on the following two itineraries:
from Olona to the Adriatic: Castiglione Olona, Milan, Vigevano, Lodi, Parma, Sabbioneta, Mantua, Ferrara, Cesena, Rimini.
from Urbino to Siena: Urbino, Arezzo, Sansepolcro, Perouse, Spello, Montefalco, Todi, Orvieto, Montepulciano, Pienza, abbey of Mount Oliveto Maggiore, Siena.

Italy by car

Italy has about 6,000 km of highways and a further network of minor roads allowing rapid movement from one part of the country to another in safety and comfort. There are special facilities for foreign motorists traveling in Italy: coupons for gasoline discounts and free use of the highway system, free help in case of emergency.

gasoline and toll coupons

Foreign citizens or Italians resident abroad driving a car with foreign license plates are entitled to buy special packages available at *ACI-ENIT* frontier stations. They contain gasoline discount coupons and coupons for free highway tolls. The package (which may be purchased abroad from *ENIT* offices and certain banks and agencies) is offered in 4 different versions:
- the 'Italia' package (which may be used throughout the country) contains 12 gasoline coupons each worth 15,000 lire, sold at a total discount of 27,000 lire, and five free highway toll coupons each worth 2,000 lire.
- the 'Italia Centro' package contains a further coupon for 120,000 lire, sold at a discount of 27,000 lire, exchangeable against 6 gasoline coupons each worth 20,000 lire in *ACI-ENIT* offices in Latium, Abruzzi, Molise, Campania, Apulia, Basilicata, Calabria, Sicily and Sardinia (addresses listed on back of booklet); 3 more free highway toll coupons.
- the 'Italia Sud' package contains a further coupon for 240,000 lire, sold at a discount of 54,000 lire, exchangeable against 12 coupons each worth 20,000 lire in *ACI-ENIT* offices in Molise, Campania, Basilicata, Calabria, Sicily and Sardinia; 5 more free highway vouchers and a free 16,000 lire highway voucher exchangeable against 8 2,000 lire coupons at the same offices.
- the 'Italia-Sud/Basilicata, Calabria, Sicily and Sardinia' package contains a further coupon for 360,000 lire, sold at a discount of 81,000 lire, exchangeable against 18 coupons each worth 20,000 lire in *ACI-ENIT* offices in the regions concerned; 5 more free highway vouchers and a free 16,000 lire highway voucher also exchangeable against 2,000 lire coupons.
Gasoline coupons for 15,000 and 20,000 lire and highway coupons for 2,000 lire are valid throughout Italy; unused gasoline coupons will be bought back up to two years after purchase. Each package (only one may be bought per year) contains the Carta Carburante Touristica which must be shown whenever reductions are claimed; before fuel is supplied the registration number of the vehicle must be written on the back of each coupon.

help on the road

The *ACI (Automobile Club Italiano)* assistance service has over 900 depots on call 24 hours per day. Assistance from *ACI* is obtained by telephoning ☎ 116 from normal roads. Any vehicle with foreign license plates has the right to unlimited free assistance on roads or highways. First aid assistance consists of roadside repairs (in the case of minor breakdowns) or towing the vehicle to the nearest *ACI* depot. A tourist with the Carta Carburante Turistica is entitled to a free 'second car' for a maximum period of 10 days if his vehicle needs repairs taking more than 12 hours (as a result of breakdown or accident).

car rental

Car rental firms have offices in almost all provincial centres, in many tourist resorts, and at airports and main railway stations (addresses are given in the *practical information* sections of the guide). The following are the major car rental firms' booking offices:
— AVIS: Turin ☎ 011/501107, Milan ☎ 02/7561020, Venice ☎ 041/964141, Genoa ☎ 010/255598, Florence ☎ 055/213629, Rome ☎ 06/47011, Naples ☎ 081/7801174, Bari ☎ 080/323357, Catania ☎ 095/347975.
— HERTZ: Rome ☎ 06/547991, Milan ☎ 02/20483, Turin ☎ 011/6508844, Florence ☎ 055/298205, Naples ☎ 081/400400.
— MAGGIORE: Rome ☎ 06/851620, Milan ☎ 02/5243846.

highways

Italian highways are the skeleton of the road system, and it is difficult to avoid using them for at least part of the journey. The principal ones are: A1 Milan-Rome (for Bologna and Florence); A4 Turin-Venice (for Milan and Verona); A22 Modena-Brenner; A12 Ventimiglia-Livorno; A7 Milan-Genoa; A15 Parma-La Spezia; A13 Padua-Bologna; A11 Florence-La Spezia; A2 Rome-Naples; A24 and A25 Rome-L'Aquila and Rome-Pescara; A14 Bologna-Taranto (for Ancona, Pescara and Bari); A3 Salerno-Reggio di Calabria; A19 Palermo-Catania.

tolls

Almost all highways are subject to toll; exceptions are Salerno-Reggio di Calabria, Palermo-Catania and Palermo-Mazara del Vallo, also some highway connections with urban areas.

Remember that free vouchers can be used for payment provided that the charge is equal to or higher than their value (difference to be paid in cash); payment can also be made in one of the major foreign currencies.

The distances given in the following tables are calculated according to the shortest or quickest routes, and are intended only as a guide; there is always more than one route to the same place (and there are always particular reasons for preferring a given route, such as places to be visited or the amount of time available for the journey). — table of distances

	Anc.	Ber.	Bol.	Bri.	Flo.	Gen.	Mil.	Nap.	Pad.	Par.	Rav.	Rom.	Tur.	Ven.
Ancona		793	495	578	263	511	426	399	297	312	161	319	545	308
Bergamo			254	1021	327	199	47	814	193	160	314	601	182	226
Bologna				892	105	295	210	592	115	96	74	379	329	152
Brindisi					834	1058	992	375	863	878	727	563	1111	874
Florence						227	298	490	217	184	136	277	395	254
Genoa							142	714	365	198	370	501	170	398
Milan								785	234	122	285	57	140	267
Naples									704	671	548	219	882	741
Padua										181	134	491	369	37
Parma											171	485	241	214
Ravenna												366	404	145
Rome													669	528
Turin														402
Venice														

SICILY

	Agrigento	Catania	Messina	Palermo	Syracuse
Agrigento		167	264	128	214
Catania			97	208	61
Messina				235	158
Palermo					255

SARDINIA

	Cagliari	Nuoro	Olbia	Oristano	Sassari
Cagliari		182	268	93	211
Nuoro			102	92	120
Olbia				178	103
Oristano					121

Italy by plane

Alitalia provides air links throughout Italy, along with *ATI, Aligiulia* and *Transavio* (for which companies *Alitalia* is agent) and *Alisarda*. There are regular flights between the principal cities and between the mainland and the islands (Sardinia, Sicily, Elba, Pantelleria, Lampedusa and the Trémiti).

Italian airports: Alghero-Fertilia; Ancona-Falconara; Bari-Palese; Bergamo-Orio al Serio; Bologna-Borgo Panigale; Brindisi; Cagliari-Elmas; Catania-Fontanarossa; Florence-Peretola; Genoa; Lamezia-Sant'Eufemia; Lampedusa; Milan-Linate; Milan-Malapensa; Naples-Capodi- — airports chino; Olbia-Costa Smeralda; Palermo-Punta Raisi; Pantelleria; Pescara; Pisa; Reggio di Calabria; Rimini-Miramare; Rome-Fiumicino; Rome Ciampino; Trapani-Birgi; Trieste-Ronchi dei Legionari; Turin-Caselle; Venezia-Tessera; Verona Villafranca (telephone numbers for airports and the relevant travel agents are listed in the practical information sections of the guide).

tickets

The following list of reduced fares applies to economy class on internal flights only:

— 90% for children up to the age of 2 (without right to a seat or baggage allowance);
— 50% discount for children between the over 2 and under 12;
— 30% discount for young people over twelve and under 22;
— 30% discount on selected flights at certain times (at the time of writing services to and from Rome involving Milan, Turin, Genoa, Venice, Bari, Palermo, Catania and the Milan-Naples service);
— discounts for families of at least 3: 50 % for one of the parents and for children over 12 and under 22; 75 % for children over 2 and under 12.

information

Alitalia Rome: Passenger Agency v. Bissolati 13 ☎ 06/46881; internal flight bookings ☎ 06/5454; international flight bookings ☎ 06/5455; information on national and international flights ☎ 06/5465; fares ☎ 06/479971; night service (booking and information, 11 p.m. -6.45 a.m.) ☎ 06/60103746/7/8. Milan: Passenger Agency v. Albricci 5 ☎ 02/62811; internal flight bookings ☎ 02/2836; international flight bookings ☎ 02/2828. *ATI* Naples Capodichino ☎ 081/7091111; Aligiulia Ronchi dei Legionari airport, Trieste ☎ 0481/779898; Transavio Milan v. Zanella 43/1 ☎ 02/7420010; Alisarda Olbia Passenger Agency corso Umberto 105 ☎ 0789/69300.

Italy by train

The Italian rail system is over 16,000 kilometres long. Information and booking offices for seats and couchettes are open from 7 a.m. to 11 p.m. in the larger stations; these stations generally also have an exchange office (near the rail information windows), telephone service, tourist offices and car rental. Telephone numbers for rail information are listed in the *practical information* sections of the guide (for all principal provincial towns and other important centres).

tickets

— tourist tickets for travel any where: individual tickets available only to foreigners and Italians resident abroad; they allow 1st or 2nd class travel throughout the network for an unlimited number of journeys (they are not subject to supplements and seat bookings are free of charge).

— *biglietti chilometrici:* tickets available for up to 5 persons and valid for 2 months; for travel individually or collectively up to 3,000 km or 20 complete journeys (practical if many trips planned).

The state railways also accept the Inter-Rail card for young people, Eurailpass, Rail Europe Senior and other tickets approved under international conventions (some also available in Italy: inquire at travel agents or rail offices).

Ferries

The state railways also provide sea links between the mainland and the major islands, Sicily and Sardinia: several ferries per day (carrying trains, cars and foot passengers) depart from Villa San Giovanni and Reggio di Calabria for Messina, and from Civitavecchia for Golfo Aranci. Voyages to Sicily last c. 35/55 minutes and to Sardinia about 8 hours and 30 minutes. Numerous shipping companies run services to the Italian islands. Major operators include: Adriatica di Navigazione (for the Trémiti Islands and the Adriatic) Venice Zattere 1411 ☎ 041/781611; Tirrenia Navigazione (for Sicily and Sardinia) Naples Rione Sirignano 2 ☎ 081/7201111; Grandi Traghetti (for Sicily and Sardinia) Genoa v. Fieschi 17 ☎ 010/589331; Navarma Lines (for Elba) Portoferraio v. Elba 4 ☎ 0565/918101; Aliscafi Snav (hydrofoils; for Ponza, Ischia, Prcida, Capri, the Aeolian Islands and Naples-Palermo) Messina v. S.Ranieri 22 ☎ 0907765; Siremar (for the Aeolian and Aegean islands) Palermo v. F.Crispi 120 ☎ 091/582688; Toremar (for Elba and the other islands of the Tuscan archipelago) Livorno Scali del Corso 5 ☎ 0586/22772; Caremar (for Ischia, Capri and the other islands of the Ponziano archipelago) Naples molo Beverello ☎ 081/313882; Sardinia Ferries (for Livorno-Olbia) Genoa p. Dante 5A ☎ 010/593301. Despite the frequency of services in high season, sailings to the more visited islands can be very full in the peak period; in particular, it is essential to make reservations on the car ferry to and from Sardinia (in July and August) if you wish to avoid long lines at departure.

● *Shopping and museum visits*

Shopping

On Saturdays and Sundays, unless in a large city or a much-frequented resort, tourist offices, banks and travel agencies are closed. Store hours vary according to the town (a municipal decision) and the season, but they are normally open from 9 a.m. to 1 p.m. and 4 to 7:30 p.m. They are closed Sunday and a half-day during the week (often Monday morning). Food stores (including supermarkets) are normally closed Monday or Wednesday afternoon. Bars normally are open from 7 a.m. to 8 or 10 p.m. In tourist areas, stores stay open every day, sometimes never closing.

Museums

In general museums and monuments are open from 9 a.m. to 2 p.m. on weekdays (some are also open in the afternoon from 5 to 7 p.m.), from 9 a.m. to 1 p.m. on holidays and Sundays, and closed Monday. If a holiday falls on a Monday, closing moves to Tuesday. Other days when museums and monuments are generally closed are: 1 Jan, Easter, 25 Apr, 1 May, first Sun in June, 15 Aug and 25 Dec (with exceptions). It is possible to buy tickets until noon. Archaeological sites are open from 8 a.m. to one hour before sunset; it is possible to buy tickets up to one hour before closing. Private museums and art galleries have their own hours. The most important churches are generally closed from 12:30 to 3:30 p.m.
For help in understanding terms used in visiting museums or other sites, there is an *Art and architectural terms guide* at the end of this *Practical holiday guide*.

Accommodation and gastronomy

Hotels

Italian hotels (more than 40,000) are classified by law into six categories carrying star markings: from 1 to 5 stars, preceded by an L for the deluxe category. This guide lists about 3,000 hotels. It is a varied selection, from luxurious to modest. Facilities are listed (for example, parking on premises, sports facilities, access for handicapped, whether animals are permitted, etc.), as well as the maximum price of a double room and of breakfast (if price is not included), and periods when the hotel is closed. The principal Italian hotel chains include (with their central booking points): *Altahotels Milan* ☎ 02/8490278, Rome ☎ 06/492772; *Best Western* Milan ☎ 02/6888651; *Ciga Hotels* Milan ☎ 02/62661, Rome ☎ 06/4757198; *Dolomiti Residence Hotels* Trento ☎ 0461/984100; *Eurotel* Bolzano ☎ 0471/42345; *Interhotel* Milan ☎ 02/8400363; *Jolly Hotels* Milan ☎ 02/77031, Rome ☎ 06/4940541, Valdagno ☎ 0445/410200; *MotelAgip* and *Hotels Semi* Rome ☎ 06/546831; *Space Hotels* Rome ☎ 06/4940346, Milan ☎ 02/801591, Turin ☎ 011/544947; *Starhotels* Milan ☎ 02/8831, Bologna ☎ 051/270924, Florence ☎ 055/352185, Rome ☎ 06/4774.

Alternative accommodation

The organization *Interhome* has about 2,000 apartments that can be booked directly (Milan, v. S.Sempliciano 2, ☎ 02/3452511). It is also possible to exchange your own home with that of a family resident in Italy. Information from *Home Exchange International,* Milan, p. Mirabello 1, ☎ 02/65173. — rentals

The 50 and more hostels (listed in this guide) are open to any one aged 8 or above who is a member of *AIG (Associazione Italiana Alberghi della Gioventù).* A card is issued by local and provincial *AIG* committees (for Lombardy and Milan, *TCI* office, corso Italia 10). Information: *AIG,* Rome, Quadrato della Concordia 9, ☎ 06/5913702. — youth hostels for children The majority of Italian *Kinderheim,* offering summer-camp style sea or mountain vacations for children, are members of *AKI (Associazione Kinderheime Italiani),* Milan, v. V.Monti 33, ☎ 02/4982588.

vacation villages Italy also has a number of hotel-like complexes providing bungalows, chalets and cabins. For information and reservations: *Club Méditerranée,* Milan, corsia dei Servi 11, ☎ 02/778663, Rome, v. Emilia 68, ☎ 06/4745951, Turin, Galleria S.Federico 10, ☎ 02/852672, Bari, v. Melo 259, ☎ 080/365140, Rome, v. Ovidio 7/a, ☎ 06/388602, Turin, p. Solferino 3 bis, ☎ 011/540177; *Vacanze,* Milan, v. Rastrelli 2, ☎ 02/85391; *Valtur,* Milan, corso Venezia 5, ☎ 02/791733, Rome, p. di Spagna 85, ☎ 06/6784588, Turin, v. Alfieri 22, ☎ 011/516016 (villages run by these organizations are listed in this guide).

farm vacations Farm tourism is increasing in Italy. As well as the beauty of the natural setting, these vacations offer sports (particularly horseback riding), study (nature, craft and cooking courses) and work. This guide lists some farm vacation centres region by region in the *practical information* sections; fuller information is provided by *Agriturist,* Rome, corso Vittorio Emanuele 101, ☎ 06/6512832, or by regional *Agriturist* associations; addresses are provided in the *practical information* sections.

Camping

There are approximately 2,300 camp sites in Italy, and a star classification is planned. Not all regions have yet completed the classification.

Individuals are not allowed to camp independently in the Valle d'Aosta, and vehicles or trailers equipped for camping are allowed to stay only during the daytime. Elsewhere, local regulations vary from region to region (information from tourist offices). *Federcampeggio* (Calenzano, Florence, ☎ 055/882391 Telex 570397) operates a camping centre for visitors *(Centro Nazionale Campeggiatori Stranieri)* which will provide information and assistance of any kind. It is generally useful to carry the Carnet Camping International, which guarantees insurance, some advantages relating to fees and individual pitches offered, and also functions as an identity card (available from touring and motoring and camping organizations in your country of origin). More than 500 camp sites are listed in this guide; *Campeggi e Villaggi Turistici in Italia,* produced by *TCI* and *Federcampeggio,* provides a fuller list.

Gastronomy

Italy has thousands of restaurants; this guide lists approximately 1,500. Each restaurant is evaluated in such a way as to provide a choice for the visitor. The evaluations are, of course, based on the standards of the cuisine, but also take into account ambiance, decor and service. Especially recommended restaurants offering haute cuisine are indicated by a red point; those offering gourmet cuisine and good ambiance are indicated by a blue point. Many people believe that Italian gastronomy is limited to spaghetti and pizza. They are wrong for two reasons: first, there exist as many different kinds of cuisine as there are regions of Italy and second, the range of dishes is enormous; Italian cuisine has no 'taboos'. It must be remembered that, as long ago as the times of the Romans, Italians appreciated the fine art of eating.

Without doubt, Italian cuisine originated from humble roots, from ingredients that were readily available and not expensive, but the art and imagination of Italian chefs took over and transformed these simple ingredients into many wonderful specialties. Fish, such as cod, originally prepared because of its inexpensive and nutritious qualities, is today served proudly at the table of the most important people.

specialties Seafood is best represented in the coastal areas, whereas the plain of the Po and Tuscany offer excellent beef and the Apennine regions specialize in lamb and kid (heritage of their pastoral tradition). Rice is often used in the cooking of the Po regions and in Naples (Italy is the biggest producer of rice in the EEC); pork, found in every region, is generally presented as sausages of many different forms and tastes, or as ham (smoked or raw). Tomatoes, imported from America (corn also, base of polenta, a specialty of northern Italy), were quickly integrated into Italian cuisine. Of course, the aromatic herbs that add flavour to everything must not be forgotten.

Pasta, which now is consumed worldwide, is generally served by the Italians at the beginning of a meal — between the hors d'oeuvres (*antipasti* means before the pasta) and the main course, never as an accompanying dish. Enriched by a sauce or chopped meat, pasta can also be eaten as the main course. For help in understanding names of dishes on restaurant menus, there is a *Menu guide* at the end of this *Practical holiday guide.*

Wine

Wines are classified according to the EEC system as *vini di tavola* (table wines), *vini di tavola a indicazione geografica* (table wines with a place name attached), *vini tipici* (wines typical of a specific area; fall between DOC and table wine); restaurants usually have red and white *vini sfusi*; these are open wines at a lower price, which is sometimes their only virtue, although some are excellent.

The most important categories are DOC and DOCG. DOC and DOCG are VQRRD wines (quality wines produced in specific regions) designated regionally according to EEC and Italian regulations. The appellations DOC and DOCG are awarded by decree; the initials stand for 'Denominazione di Origine Controllata' and 'Denominazione di Origine Controllata e Garantita', and are printed on the label. At the moment there are only 5 DOCG, two from Piedmont, 'Barbaresco' and 'Barolo', three from Tuscany, 'Chianti Classico', 'Brunellodi Montalcino' and 'Vino Nobile di Montepulciano', all red wines. White wine consumption is increasing at the moment. In cellars offering a stock of vintage wines it is possible to taste and compare wines and buy under expert guidance.

● *Menu guide*

Abbacchio milk-fed lamb.
Acciughe anchovies.
Aglio garlic.
Agnello lamb.
Agnolotti crescent-shaped, meat-filled pasta.
Agrodolce sweet and sour.
Amaretti small, crunchy macaroons.
Anatra duck.
Anguilla eel.
Animelle sweetbreads.
Aragosta spiny lobster.
Arrosto roast meat.
Baccala dried salt cod.
Bagna cauda hot anchovy-flavoured dipping sauce for raw vegetables.
Biete Swiss chard.
Bistecca (alla Fiorentina) grilled beefsteak (seasoned with pepper and olive oil).
Bollito misto mixed boiled meat.
Brodetto fish soup.
Brodo broth.
Bucatini long, thick, hollow pasta.
Budino pudding.
Burro butter.
Cacciagione game.
Cacciucco alla Livornese seafood stew typical of the Leghorn area.
Calamari squid.
Cannellini dried white beans.
Cappellacci pumpkin-stuffed pasta.
Cappelletti meat- or cheese-stuffed pasta ('little hats').
Carciofi (alla giudia) (flattened and fried young) artichokes.
Casalinga home-style.
Cassata moulded ice-cream dessert.
Cassata alla Siciliana sponge cake layered with sweetened ricotta and decorated with chocolate butter cream.
Castagna chestnut.
Cavolo cabbage.
Ceci chickpeas.
Cipolla onion.
Conchiglie seashell pasta.
Coniglio rabbit.
Contorni vegetable side dishes.
Costoletta chop.
Cotechino large, spicy pork sausage.
Cotoletta cutlet.
Cozze mussels.
Crespelle crêpes.

Crostata pie or tart.
Dolci desserts.
Fagioli beans.
Fagiolini string beans.
Farsumauru Sicilian stuffed beef.
Fedelini very thin spaghetti.
Fegatini di pollo chicken liver.
Fegato liver.
Fetta slice.
Fichi figs.
Finocchio fennel.
Formaggio cheese.
Fragole strawberries.
Frittata omelette.
Frittura fried foods.
Frutti di mare seafood (esp. shellfish).
Funghi (trifolati) mushrooms (sauteed with garlic and parsley).
Fusilli spiral-shaped spaghetti.
Gamberi shrimp.
Gamberoni prawns.
Gelato ice cream.
Gnocchi dumplings made of cheese (di ricotta), of potatoes (di patate), cheese and spinach (verdi) or semolina (alla romana).
Gramigna short, curly, tubular pasta.
Granchio crab.
Granita flavoured ice.
Grissini bread sticks.
Insalata salad.
Involtini stuffed meat rolls.
Lenticchie lentils.
Lepre hare.
Luganega fresh pork sausage.
Lumache snails.
Maiale pork.
Mandorle almonds.
Manzo beef.
Mela apple.
Melanzana eggplant.
Miele honey.
Minestra soup or pasta course.
Minestrone vegetable soup.
Mostarda fruits pickled in vinegar.
Nocciola hazelnut.
Noce walnut.
Oca goose.
Ortaggi vegetables.
Ostriche oysters.
Pane bread.
Panna heavy cream.

Pansotti triangular dumplings stuffed with cheese and greens, usually served with a walnut sauce.
Pasta asciutta pasta served plain or with a sauce.
Pasticceria pastry.
Penne quill-shaped pasta.
Peperoni green or red sweet pepper.
Pesca peach.
Pesce fish.
Pignoli pine nuts.
Piselli peas.
Pizzoccheri noodles made from buckwheat flour.
Pollame poultry.
Pollo chicken.
Polpette meatballs.
Pomodoro tomato.
Porcini boletus mushrooms.
Prezzemolo parsley.
Ragu meat sauce or stew.
Riso rice.
Risotto braised rice.
Rognoncini kidneys.
Salsa sauce.
Salsicce fresh sausage.
Saltimbocca veal scallop topped with prosciutto and a sage leaf, in a white wine sauce.
Salvia sage.
Sarde sardines.
Sedano celery.
Semifreddo mousse, chilled pudding.
Seppia cuttlefish.
Sformato vegetable mould.
Sgombro mackerel.
Sogliola sole.
Spezzatino stew.

Spiedino food served on a skewer.
Spumone light, foamy ice cream.
Strangolapreti 'priest stranglers', small, nugget-shaped eggless pasta.
Sugo sauce.
Tacchino turkey.
Tartufi truffles.
Tonnarelli square spaghetti.
Tonno tuna.
Torta cake.
Tortelli type of ravioli stuffed with greens and ricotta.
Tortellini ring-shaped dumplings stuffed with meat or cheese, served either in broth or in a cream sauce.
Totani squid.
Trenette thin noodles served with potatoes and a sauce of cheese, basil and garlic (pesto).
Triglia red mullet.
Trota trout.
Ucelletti, uccellini small, roasted birds.
Uovo egg.
Uva grapes.
Uva passa raisins.
Verdura greens.
Verza Savoy cabbage.
Vitello veal.
Vongole clams.
Zabaglione dessert of warm whipped egg yolks and Marsala wine.
Zafferano saffron.
Zampone spicy stuffed pig's trotter.
Zucchero sugar.
Zucchine zucchini.
Zuppa soup.
Zuppa inglese pound cake steeped in rum-flavoured custard.

 Art and architectural terms guide

Ambulatory: passageway surrounding a choir.
Apse: extreme eastern end of a church, beyond the choir, usually rounded in shape.
Architrave: lowest division of an entablature resting in Classical architecture immediately on the capital of a column.
Archivolt: arch surrounding an opening or doorway.
Art nouveau: decorative style that enjoyed great success just before WWI. Its characteristic curves were drawn from the supple shapes of stems and leaves.
Baroque: architectural style that began in 17C Italy. Breaking with the formal strictness of Classicism, it maintained the basic elements but used them within an original framework of curves and counter-curves. The result was a monumental and sumptuous effect enhanced by richly sculpted and painted figures and brought to life by the play of light and shade.
Barrel vault: vault formed by a semicircular arch extended perpendicular; it is a broken vault if the arch is a broken arch.
Basilica: oblong building ending in a semicircular apse.
Bastion: jutting construction at the corner of a fortification.
Battlement: parapet with open spaces that surmounts a wall.
Buttress: masonry block reinforcing a wall.

Choir: part of the nave of a church reserved for singers during services.
Classical: the basic elements of Classical architecture were those of Greek and Roman antiquity, noted for symmetry and harmony, such as in the combination of pillars and lintel, or that of pillar and arch.
Clerestory: outside wall of a building that rises above an adjoining roof and contains windows.
Console: architectural element projecting from a wall to form a bracket.
Cornice: molded and projecting horizontal element that crowns an architectural composition.
Crossing: space at the intersection of nave and transept.
Curtain wall: stretch of wall between two rows of a fortification.
Diptych: picture painted or carved on two hinged tablets.
Entablature: topmost section of a wall or storey, usually supported on columns or pilasters.
Flamboyant: last phase of the Gothic style, heavily ornamented with profuse curves and counter-curves, arcatures and stone lacework.
Flying buttress: external support abutting a structure and designed to resist the thrust of vaulting.
Frieze: part of the entablature between the architrave and the cornice; a sculptured or richly ornamented band (as on a building).

Gothic: essentially religious architectural style predominant from the end of the 12C until the Renaissance; churches in the form of the Roman cross were typified by ogival arches and vaulting, spacious, well-lighted side aisles surmounted by a gallery or triforium.

Groined vault: vault formed by the intersection of two vaults of equal size.

Lintel: horizontal piece of stone or timber surmounting a rectangular opening.

Loggia: roofed open gallery, especially at an upper storey overlooking an open court.

Machicolation: opening between corbels supporting a parapet at the top of a fortification, used for defense.

Mullion: stone upright dividing a window.

Narthex: vestibule at a church's entrance, not to be confused with the porch that opens to the outside.

Nave: central section of a church, between choir and western entrance.

Neoclassicism: late 18C architectural style inspired by Roman antiquity.

Neo-Gothic: 19C architectural movement that advocated a return to the Gothic style, opposed to the various Classically inspired movements that had predominated since the Renaissance.

Ogive: diagonal arch supporting a vault.

Order: in Classical architecture, a grouping composed of column, capital and architrave.

Orientation: placement of a church, with the choir toward the east in the direction of Jerusalem.

Pediment: section of the faade, usually triangular, placed on top of the entablature.

Pendentive: part of the groined vault that springs from a single pier or corbel.

Pilaster: flattened column, in a wall but projecting from it.

Pilgrim church: church with side aisles extended into the ambulatory around the choir to accommodate large numbers of worshippers at places of pilgrimage.

Retable: architectural ornament above an altar; a painted panel in the final Gothic period.

Rococo: 18C decorative style typified by a profusion of garlands, stucco-work and sculpture with graceful lines and delicate colouring.

Romanesque: 10C and 11C architectural style characterized by churches in the form of a Roman cross, with rounded arches and barrel vaulting.

Rood screen: sculpted screen separating choir from nave.

Side aisle: sections of a church on either side of the nave.

Stalls: seats for the clergy on either side of the choir.

Tracery: decorative openwork in the head of a Gothic window.

Transept: transverse section of a church, terminating the main nave and forming the symbolic cross-shape of the building.

Tympanum: panel above a church doorway, usually sculpted.

Abruzzi

▶ Abruzzi is a region of craftsmen, fishermen, farmers and shepherds, of olive groves, vineyards and orchards. Its character lies in the link between nature and human activity. A narrow coastal strip separates inviting beaches from gentle hills and farther inland are forests of beech, chestnut and oak. An Apennine chain divides maritime Abruzzi from the mountainous part of the region, where rivers have carved out deep gorges. Essentially, Abruzzi is a mountainous area. The countryside has few inhabitants and the villages are concentrated on the sides of slopes. The landscape offers wonderful and varied views: steep deserted places on inaccessible mountain tops, endless valleys and dark masses of forests. Nature is at its most fascinating in the Abruzzi National Park, which covers the Upper Sangro Valley on the border with Latium. Many animals live in the park, including bear, chamois, wolf and otter. The Middle Ages was Abruzzi's most original creative period and important monuments from this era have been preserved. Although Abruzzi displays an archaic picture, like the rest of Italy, it is in the process of transformation. □

● Don't miss

At L'Aquila, S. Bernardino★★ and S. Maria di Collemaggio★★; at Atri, the cathedral★; at Lanciano, S. Maria Maggiore★; at Sulmona, l'Annunziata★; at Teramo, the cathedral★; the abbey of S. Clemente at Casauria★★ near Pescara; S. Giovanni at Venere★ near Ortona. Trips to Campo Imperatore★ in the Gran Sasso d'Italia and to the Abruzzi National Park.

● Brief regional history

10C-4C BC
The Italic tribes. In the wake of the pre-Indo-European **culture of the Piceni** (to which can be attributed the statue known as the **Warrior of Capestrano,** → Chieti), **Italic tribes** moved into the region. Their lifestyle was predominantly pastoral. ● The **Piceni** and the **Pretuzi** lived along the shores from the Tronto to the Pescara, the **Peligni** inhabited the Sulmona Valley and the **Vestini** lived on the plateau between the Aterno and Tirino Valleys. The **Marsi** dwelt along the banks of the Fùcino and the **Equi** in the mountains between Marsica and Fùcino.

4C BC-5C AD
The Romans. The legions first crossed Abruzzi to aid Lucera (Apulia, 325 BC). The subsequent **conquest** of the region was achieved at the cost of a number of wars with the stubborn **Samnites.** ● The Romans' failed attempt at expansionism provoked the **Italici revolt** (90 BC), during which Italic tribes amassed an army of 100,000 and established their capital at **Corfinio,** in Peligni territory. Four years of war followed, with 300,000 victims. ● During the Augustan era, the whole of the present-day region (apart from the area around Teramo, which was in *Picenum*) formed part of the larger area of **Sabina and Samnium,** which was then subdivided into **Valeria** and **Samnium.** ● Roman settlements included: **Auxanum** (Lanciano), **Histonium** (Vasto), **Ortona,** **Teate** (Chieti), **Pinna** (Penne), **Hatria** (Atri), **Interamia Praetutiorum** (Teramo), **Sulmo** (Sulmona, the home of Ovid) and **Amiternum** (near L'Aquila, birthplace of the historian Sallust).

6C-11C
Comitatus aprutinus. The region underwent numerous changes of government because it formed a border between N and S Italy. ● During the Gothic

War (6C), the Byzantine exarch Longinus created the **Duchy of Teate** (Chieti). ● The **Lombards** divided the region between their duchies of Spoleto and Benevento. ● During the Carolingian era, the names *Aprutium* and **Comitatus Aprutinus** came into being. ● In 843 the region was called the **contado della Marsia** and it was subsequently joined to the **contea di Teate.**

12C-19C
The Southern Kingdom. The Norman King of Sicily, William I, was invested with feudal power over the region by the English Pope Adrian IV in the 12C. However, the Normans remained mainly in Molise. ● The Swabian Emperor **Frederick I** created the smaller region of **Iustitieratus Aprutii,** whose chief town was **Sulmona.** Thus, Abruzzi became part of the Kingdom of Southern Italy, an area that, despite many difficulties, maintained its own identity until 1860. ● It appears that L'Aquila was founded in 1254 to sustain the anti-imperial rebellion in W Abruzzi. ● At the **battle of Tagliacozzo** in 1268 the last of the Swabians, the Emperor **Conrad,** was defeated and captured and the **Anjou dynasty** finally

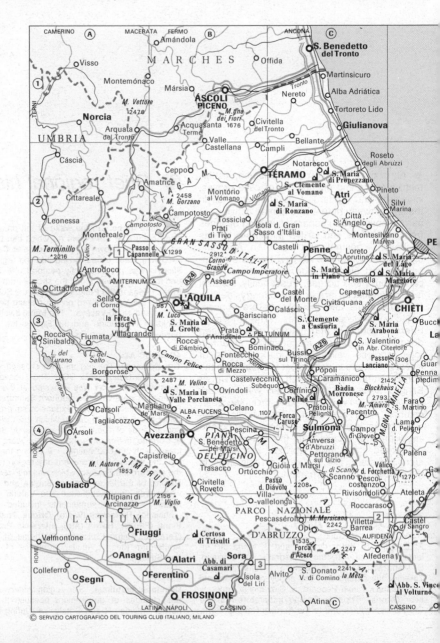

© SERVIZIO CARTOGRAFICO DEL TOURING CLUB ITALIANO, MILANO

became the rulers of southern Italy. ● In 1294, Pietro Angeleri, a hermit from Abruzzi, succeeded to the papacy as **Celestine V** only to resign after a few months. ● The region fell into combative factions. It took part in the wars that started after the assassination (1345) of Andrea of Hungary, the husband of **Queen Giovanna** of Naples, and also in the wars of succession that took place after the Queen's death in 1382. ● The mercenary leader **Braccio da Montone** made a bid for supremacy in central Italy, but was defeated and killed beneath the walls of **L'Aquila** in 1424. ● **Alfonso of Aragon,** King of Sicily, succeeded Giovanna II. He was deposed once, but finally prevailed in 1442, and the **Aragonese dynasty** reigned for a short time. ● 1441 saw the death of the popular preacher **St. Bernard of Siena,** who had spent the last part of his life wandering in the mountains of Abruzzi. ● Charles VIII of France attempted to regain Naples for the Angevins during the **Italian Wars.** The Hapsburgs' victory led to a period of **Spanish domination** of the south, as **Charles V** had set his sights on the powerful **fortress of L'Aquila** (1534). ● In 1524, Gian Pietro Carafa, bishop of **Chieti,** founded the **Order of the Teatini.** He later became Pope Paul IV. ● In 1684 the province of **Teramo** was joined to the provinces of L'Aquila and Chieti. ● After the War of Spanish Succession, which began in the 18C, the Kingdom of Southern Italy passed from Spain to **Austria** and then to the **Bourbons** in 1735. ● During the Napoleonic era, the poet **Gabriele Rossetti** (from Vasto) was Secretary of Public Education under Napoleon's brother-in-law **Joachim Murat.** He later lived in exile in London, where his son, Dante Gabriel Rossetti, became one of the founders of the pre-Raphaelite movement. ● In 1852, a French company began the work of **draining Lake Fùcino.**

cathedral in Teramo

Sheep tracks

The movement of flocks from their summer pastures in the mountains to winter pastures on the plains once meant the slow process of herding them along sheep tracks. Despite the pastoral image of Abruzzi, current statistics present a somewhat different picture. Sheep rearing is in decline and has been replaced by other factors within the local economy. Only one seventeenth of all the sheep in Italy are in Abruzzi, and the region is sixth in sheep rearing in the country. The grassy sheep tracks are now merely a reminder of the economic and social history of the region. Recent research has traced the course of the 14 major tracks, 71 minor tracks and 13 branches. The main winter destination was the Tavoliere di Puglia. During Aragon rule (15C), when a customs checkpoint was set up at Foggia, the prescribed width of the tracks was laid down as 364 ft, and all farmers who owned more than twenty sheep were obliged to pass through customs.

19C-20C
Italy. Bourbon rule in Naples came to an end in 1860, after **Garibaldi's campaign.** ● The Bourbon garrison in the fortress at **Civitella del Tronto** did not surrender until 20 May 1861, three months after Gaeta. ● **Pescara,** fourth province in Abruzzi, was established in 1927. ● **Molise** was separated from Abruzzi and established as a region in 1963.

Facts and figures

Location: On the Adriatic Sea between the Rivers Tronto and Trigno, Abruzzi is a harsh, majestic, mountainous area. The line of mountains in the E, coastal part includes the highest peaks in the Italian peninsula: Mt. Laga, 8,064 ft; the Gran Sasso d'Italia, 9,553 ft; the Maiella, 9,163 ft. Other ridges belonging to the Apennine chain are to be found on the W side.
Area: 10,794 sq km.
Climate: High altitude combined with southerly latitude (the region is level with Tuscany and Latium) produce a climate of extremes; the cooling effect of the Adriatic is less than that of the Tyrrhenian Sea. As a result winters are sometimes quite cold, whereas the summers are extremely hot on the coast.
Population: 1,236,060 inhabitants.
Administration: The regional capital is L'Aquila, situated 2,342 ft above sea level. The regional council is based in L'Aquila and Pescara, which has the highest population in the region. The other provincial capitals, apart from Pescara, are Chieti and Teramo.

 Practical information

Information: tourist offices in principal towns and main centres.
SOS: public emergency services, ☎ 113; emergency police service, ☎ 112; emergency road service, *ACI,* ☎ 116.
Weather: forecasts, ☎ 085/991991 (for districts of L'Aquila and Pescara, ☎ 191); road conditions, ☎ 085/994994 (for districts of L'Aquila, Pescara and Teramo, ☎ 194) or *ACI,* ☎ 06/4212; snow reports, ☎ 089/992992 (for district of Pescara, ☎ 162); shipping forecasts, ☎ 085/996996 (for district of Pescara, ☎ 196).
Farm vacations: *Associazone regionale Agriturist,* at Pescara, v. Catullo 39, ☎ 085/61544.

Bagpipe players

At Christmas, shepherd bagpipe players leave their flocks and come to town. The musicians wear sheepskin waistcoats and boots. The custom is a well-loved reminder of past times. The bag part of the instrument is no longer made of animal skin but from the inner tube of a tire. Nevertheless, the origin of the bagpipes is extremely ancient. The Romans called them tibia utricolaris, and it appears that Nero liked to play them as a change from the lyre. The pipe (which has a sound similar to the oboe) enjoys an equally long history. In Abruzzi, pipes are made from almond wood as well as from olive and cherry.

Events: *International Jazz festival* and summer drama season, at Pescara; *International Puppet Theatre, music and architecture show,* drama and concert season and Papal Pardon at L'Aquila; *Giugno Teramano, Good Friday procession,* at Chieti; *festival of the Madonna del Ponte, Squilla festival* and *procession of the Dead Christ,* at Lanciano; *festival of St. Antony* and *theatre in the square,* at Scanno; *wagon parade,* at Atri; *historical procession,* at Maggiolata and Ortona; *Rodeo Pentro,* at Montenero Val Cocchiara (→ Castel di Sangro); *procession of snake catchers,* at Cocullo (→ La Marsica).

The 'little devil', the guitar and the seven virtues

The 'little devil' (diavulillo in dialect) refers to the hot chili pepper. In Abruzzi, it is added to everything except desserts and fruit. Guitar in this case means a small wooden frame with strips of steel stretched across it at close intervals. A sheet of egg pasta is pressed through it with a rolling pin, forming small, neat square strips known as maccheroni alla chitarra. According to religious teaching, there are seven virtues. In traditional Abruzzi cuisine, these 'virtues' consist of a thick, rich soup prepared from the first fresh vegetables of the season. It is a joyous celebration of passing from one agricultural season to another. The key to the dish is the number seven: seven kinds of meat, seven kinds of root vegetable, seven green vegetables, seven seasonings and seven types of pasta. The cooking time is seven hours.

Nature parks: *Abruzzi National Park* (→), main office, at Rome, v. del Curato 6, ☎ 06/6543584, management, at Pescasséroli, ☎ 0863/91315, district offices (guided tours, camping authorization, assistance, use of shelters), at Pescasséroli, v. Consultore 1, ☎ 0863/91955, at Civitella Alfedena, v. Nazionale, ☎ 0864/89170; reservations for wolves at Civitella Alfedena, for deer at Villavallelonga (→ La Marsica), for chamois at Bisegna. *Riserva della Valle dell'Orfento* (→ Caramanico Terme, La Maiella).

Zoos and amusement parks: *La Rupe* park, at Civitella Casanova (→ Penne); *Davalos* park, at Pescara.

Nature conservation: *WWF Delegazione Abruzzo,* at L'Aquila, v. Svolta della Misericordia 2, ☎ 0862/28274; *Pescasséroli Ufficio Zona Parco Nazionale d'Abruzzo; LIPU,* at L'Aquila, v. Svolta della Misericordia 2, ☎ 0862/28274, at Pescara, v. Ravasco 36, ☎ 085/72590 (birdwatching courses at Abruzzi National Park, nature observatory on the Maiella).

Excursions: marked long distance routes: in Abruzzi National Park, Alta Via Est-Ovest (from Roccaraso to Sora, three stops) and Alta Via Nord-Sud (from Villavallelonga to Civitella Alfedena, four stops), recommended May-Oct; in the Gran Sasso group, *Trekking del Gran Sasso* (from Castel del Monte to Pietracamela, four stops), recommended mid-Jun-late Sep. Information from *CAI:* Avezzano, v. Marconi, ☎ 0863/20736; Chieti, v. Arniense 119, ☎ 0871/41313; Fara San Martino, v. Napoli 31; Guardiagrele, v. Modesto della Porta 3; L'Aquila, v. XX Settembre 15, ☎ 0862/24342; Pescara, p. S. Cuore 4; Sulmona, Palazzo SS. Annunziata; Teramo, v. N. Sauro 46; Ente Parco Nazionale d'Abruzzo, Pescasséroli, ☎ 0863/91955; Rome, v. del Curato 6, ☎ 06/6543584; *La Montagna,* Rome, v. Colonna 44, ☎ 06/351549; *Cooperative del Parco* (tourist services management), at Barrea, Civitella Alfedena, Opi, San

Donato Val Di Comino (Frosinone), Pescassèroli and Gioia dei Marsi.

Cycling: assistance and information from cycling groups affiliated with *UDACE* (42) throughout the region. Seaside routes at the Abruzzi National Park and at La Maiella.

Horseback riding: *Federazione italiana sport equestri,* regional committee at Rome, v. Flaminia Nuova 213, ☎ 06/3278547; riding schools at Chieti and Pescara. *ANTE* centre at L'Aquila.

Skiing: the main ski areas are in the regions of Gran Sasso d'Italia, Marsica and the mountains of the Maiella range.

Flying: *Aeroclub L'Aquila,* at Preturo Airport, ☎ 0862/609013; at Pescara Airport, v. Tiburtina, ☎ 085/2069887 (also gliding).

Hang gliding: *Federazione italiana Volo Libero,* ☎ 015/538703.

Fishing: *Federazione italiana pesca sportiva,* at Avezzano, v. XXIV Maggio 5; at Chieti, p. Umberto I 7; at Pescara, v. Rigopiano 65, ☎ 085/27740. For fishing regulations (permitted, forbidden waters, etc.) apply to relevant federal sections.

⬤ Towns and places

The ABRUZZI COAST

The Abruzzi Adriatic Coast is today an area of modern marinas and lidos, which are often coupled with older villages situated on the hilly hinterland. The *torri saracene* (Saracen towers), where inhabitants once kept watch for pirates, are a reminder of the reason why, in the past, settlers moved inland.

▶ **Alba Adriatica,** at the mouth of the River Vibrata, is the most northerly seaside resort in Abruzzi. It has a spacious beach. ▶ Behind the beach at **Tortoreto Lido** is a landscape of gentle green hills. ▶ After **Giulianova** (→) is **Roseto degli Abruzzi,** among pine groves. ▶ The beach at **Pineto** is beautifully situated. The pine grove from which it takes its name stretches for more than 2 km. ▶ Next is **Silvi Marina** which also has a wealth of vegetation. ▶ **Silvi Paese,** slightly inland *(3.5 km),* offers a splendid view of the coast. ▶ **Montesilvano Marina** has extensive beaches. 12 km inland is **Città Sant'Angelo,** with the 14C collegiate church of S. Michele. ▶ Next is **Pescara** (→). ▶ There is a lively beach at **Francavilla al Mare.** The town hall contains two paintings by the local artist F.P. Michetti *(see caretaker).* ▶ Farther on are **Ortona** (→) and **Vasto** (→). ☐

Practical information ⎯⎯⎯⎯⎯⎯⎯⎯⎯⎯

ALBA ADRIATICA, ⊠ 64011, ☎ 0861.
≋
ⓘ p. Moro 6/8, ☎ 72426.

Hotels:
★★★ *Eden,* lungomare Marconi 438, ☎ 77251, 52 rm Ⓟ ⬚ ⬚ ⬚ closed Oct-Apr, 64,000; bkf: 9,000.
★★★ *Haway,* at Villa Rosa *(2.5 km N),* lungomare Italia 62, ☎ 73923, 48 rm Ⓟ ⬚ ⬚ closed Oct-Apr, 59,000.
★★★ *Impero,* lungomare Marconi 216, ☎ 72422, 60 rm Ⓟ closed Oct-Apr, 60,000; bkf: 8,000.
★★★ *King,* lungomare Marconi 55, ☎ 77749, 70 rm Ⓟ ⬚ ⬚ closed Oct-Apr, 60,000; bkf: 9,000.
★★★ *Maxim's,* at Villla Rosa, lungomare Italia 9, ☎ 72620, 105 rm Ⓟ ⬚ ⬚ ⬚ closed 21 Sep-30 Apr, 60,000.
★★★ *Meripol,* lungomare Marconi, ☎ 77744, 44 rm Ⓟ ⬚ closed 16 Sep-19 May, 61,000.
★★★ *Riccione,* v. Vittoria 309, ☎ 72337, 65 rm Ⓟ ⬚ ⬚ closed Oct-Apr, 50,000.
★★★ *Royal,* lungomare Marconi 208, ☎ 72644, 64 rm Ⓟ closed 21 Sep-14 May, 50,000; bkf: 6,000.
★★★ *Sporting,* lungomare Marconi 414, ☎ 72510, 40 rm Ⓟ ⬚ closed 16 Sep-14 May, 60,000; bkf: 5,000.
★★ *Joli,* v. Olimpica 3, ☎ 77477, 27 rm Ⓟ ⬚ ⬚ closed Oct-Apr, 44,000; bkf: 4,000.

⚁ *Eucalyptus,* v. Abruzzi 105, 250 pl, ☎ 73356.

FRANCAVILLA AL MARE, ⊠ 66023, ☎ 085.
≋
ⓘ p. Sirena, ☎ 817169.

Hotels:
★★★ *Mare Blu,* v. Alcione 159, ☎ 816038, 27 rm Ⓟ ⓑ ⬚ closed Oct-Apr, 45,000; bkf: 6,000.
★★★ *Punta de l'Est,* v. Alcione 188, ☎ 819474, 48 rm Ⓟ closed Oct-Apr, 50,000; bkf: 5,000.

Restaurants:
♦♦♦ *Casa Mia,* v. Alcione 115/A, ☎ 817147, closed Mon and Jan. Outside service in summer. Regional seafood: cannelloni with lobster, baked sea bass, 27/38,000.
♦♦♦ *Nave,* p. Sirena 12, ☎ 817115, closed Wed, Sep and Christmas. Covered veranda overlooking beach. Creative cuisine: cartoccio mare e monti, monkfish with ham, 25/32,000.

⚁ *Paola,* v. Tosti 101, 80 pl, ☎ 817525 (all year).

Recommended
Discotheque: *Subway,* v. Alcione 159, ☎ 810032 or 816038 (open Sat and Sun in winter, daily in summer).
Events: *Michetti* national painting competition; *national writing competition for children and teenagers.*
Tennis: contrada Alento, ☎ 4910493; contrada Carletto, ☎ 818639.

MONTESILVANO MARINA, ⊠ 65016, ☎ 085.
≋
ⓘ v. Europa, ☎ 830396.

Hotels:
★★★ *City,* v. Europa 77, ☎ 838468, 45 rm Ⓟ Pens. closed Oct-Apr, 60,000.
★★★ *Promenade,* v. Moro 63, ☎ 838221, 98 rm Ⓟ ⬚ 53,500. Rest. ♦♦♦ 25/35,000.
★★★ *Sund,* v. Riviera, ☎ 73845, 126 rm Ⓟ ⬚ ⓑ ⬚ ⬚ closed Oct-May, 62,500; bkf: 5,000.

Restaurant:
♦♦ *Remo,* v. Vestina 448, ☎ 4682301, closed Mon. Regional cuisine: pastachitarra, spit-roasted quails and pigeons, 25/35,000.

PINETO, ⊠ 64025, ☎ 085.
≋
ⓘ v. D'Annunzio 123, ☎ 9491745.

Hotels:
★★★ *Astoria,* v. De Gasperi 1, ☎ 9490460, 30 rm Ⓟ ⬚ ⬚ closed Oct-May, 63,000; bkf: 7,000.
★★★ *Corfù,* v. Michetti, ☎ 9399082, 51 rm Ⓟ ⬚ closed Oct-Apr, 55,000; bkf: 8,000.
★★★ *Garden,* v. D'Annunzio 203, ☎ 939339, 51 rm ⬚ closed 21 Sep-19 May, 60,000; bkf: 8,000.
★★★ *Italia,* p. Marconi 6, ☎ 9491794, 28 rm ⬚ closed Oct-May, 60,000; bkf: 5,000.
★★★ *Residence,* v. D'Annunzio 207, ☎ 9490404, 52 rm Ⓟ ⬚ closed Oct-May, 60,000; bkf: 8,000.

⚐ *International,* contrada Torre Cerrano, 130 pl, ☎ 930639.

ROSETO DEGLI ABRUZZI, ⊠ 64026, ☎ 085.

≋
ⓘ p. della Stazione, ☎ 8991157.

Hotels:
★★★ *Albatros,* v. Nazionale 76, ☎ 8999110, 24 rm Ⓟ ▥ ♿ ⚒ 62,000; bkf: 5,000.
★★★ *Clorinda,* lungomare Roma 30, ☎ 8991270, 27 rm Ⓟ closed 21 Sep-30 Apr, 55,000; bkf: 5,000.
★★★ *Mion G.H.,* lungomare Trento 101, ☎ 8992290, 85 rm Ⓟ ▥ ⚒ ⅍ closed 21 Sep-31 May, 61,000.
★★★ *Miramare,* lungomare Roma 50, ☎ 8990230, 40 rm ⚒ closed Oct-Apr, 60,000; bkf: 3,500.
★★ *Moro,* lungomare Trento 47, ☎ 8990211, 24 rm 47,000.
★★ *Tartaruga,* v. Marcantonio 3, ☎ 8996166, 30 rm ⚒ closed Nov-Jan, 47,000.
★★ *Tonino,* v. Mazzini 15, ☎ 8993110, 20 rm Ⓟ ▥ ⚒ closed Oct-Mar, 47,000.

Restaurant:
♦ *Tonino,* v. Volturno 11, ☎ 8990274, closed Mon and 23 Dec-15 Jan. Regional seafood: rigatoni with crab, fish stew, 20/35,000.

⚐ *Eurocamping Roseto,* lungomare Trieste, 400 pl, ☎ 8993179 (all year).

Recommended
Marina: *Circolo nautico Vallonchini,* ☎ 8990258 (private).
Motocross: at *Centovie track,* run by *Moto club Roseto* (next to tourist offices), ☎ 8991157.
Sports arena: v. Ponte dell'Olmo, ☎ 8941203.

SILVI MARINA, ⊠ 64029, ☎ 085.

≋
ⓘ lungomare Garibaldi 158, ☎ 930343.

Hotels:
★★★ *Abruzzo Marina,* v. Garibaldi 196, ☎ 930397, 130 rm Ⓟ ▥ 49,000; bkf: 7,000.
★★★ *Ideal,* rampa Fiume 12, ☎ 930339, 45 rm Ⓟ ▥ ⚒ closed Oct-Mar, 56,000; bkf: 7,000.
★★★ *Mion,* v. Garibaldi 8, ☎ 930421, 70 rm Ⓟ ▥ ⊠ ⅍ closed Oct-Apr, 100,000.
★★★ *Miramare,* v. Garibaldi 90, ☎ 930235, 51 rm Ⓟ ▥ closed Oct-Feb, 50,000; bkf: 6,000.
★★★ *Orsa Maggiore,* v. Colombo 41, ☎ 930010, 40 rm ⊠ closed Oct-Apr, 57,000; bkf: 7,000.
★★★ *Parco delle Rose,* v. Garibaldi 30, ☎ 932342, 65 rm Ⓟ ▥ ⚒ ⊠ closed 16 Sep-14 May, 70,000; bkf: 10,000.
★★★ *San Paolo,* v. Romani 31, ☎ 930371; 48 rm Ⓟ ▥ ♿ ⚒ 70,000; bkf: 10,000.

⚐ *Europe Garden,* v. Arenile N, 160 pl, ☎ 932733.

SILVI PAESE, ⊠ 64028, ☎ 085.

Restaurant:
● ♦♦♦ *Vecchia Silvi,* ☎ 930141, closed Tue except summer. With fireplace and internal gardens. Regional cuisine: raviolini bella Elena, leg of lamb, 23/33,000.

Recommended
Cycling: *G.S. Abruzzo Diesel,* SS 16 at 437-km marker.

TORTORETO LIDO, ⊠ 64019, ☎ 0861.

≋
ⓘ v. Archimede 15, ☎ 787726.

Hotels:
★★★ *Costa Verde,* v. Sirena 384, ☎ 786647, 52 rm Ⓟ ▥ ⊠ closed Oct-Apr, 60,000; bkf: 8,000.
★★ *River,* v. Leonardo da Vinci 21, ☎ 786125, 27 rm Ⓟ ⚒ closed Oct-Apr, 45,000.

⚐ *Welcome Riviera d'Abruzzo,* v. Sirena 524, 406 pl, ☎ 786341.

┌─────────────────────────────────────┐
│ Looking for a locality? Consult the index at the back │
│ of the book. │
└─────────────────────────────────────┘

B-C5

The Abruzzi National Park is situated in the upper valley of the Sangro, on the borders with Latium and Molise. It consists of 400 sq km of land, plus a protected area of 200 sq km. About 60 percent of the park is pine, beech, maple and chestnut forests. The wealth of protected animal life includes 300 species of birds, 40 species of mammals and 30 species of reptiles and amphibians. The most notable animals to be found are the Abruzzi bear *(Ursus arctos marsicanus)* and the wolf. Deer, wild cats, otters, squirrels, Orsini snakes, goshawks, sea crows and yellow salamanders can also be found. Chamois live in the highest meadowlands.

▶ The administrative centre of the park is at **Pescásséroli** (3,829 ft), the birthplace of the philosopher Benedetto Croce. The visitors' centre has a natural history museum and several areas where animals can be viewed in semi-captivity. ▶ By the Monte Ceraso cableway and then on foot (1 hr) the **Rifugio Pesco di Iorio** (6,004 ft) is reached (panorama). ▶ Close to the park entrance (visitors' centre featuring the Apennine wolf, museum, enclosure with wolves in the natural state) is the picturesque town of Civitella Alfedena (3,684 ft), overlooking the artificial Lake Barrea. ▶ The visitors' centre at **Villavallelonga**, NE above the Fucino Valley, has deer (museum, enclosure with animals in the natural state). ▶ Other visitors' centres are at **Bisegna**, on the road to Cocullo (chamois, museum, animal enclosure), **San Donato Val di Comino**, toward Latium (roedeer, museum, animal enclosure) and **Pizzone**, on the way to Molise (natural history exhibition). ◻

Practical information

CIVITELLA ALFEDENA, ⊠ 67030, ☎ 0864.

Hotel:
★★★ *Valdirose,* v. Sotto ai Cerri, ☎ 89110, 59 rm Ⓟ ⚐ ▥ 40,000; bkf: 5,000.

PESCASSEROLI, 3,829 ft, ⊠ 67032, ☎ 0863.

⚵ ski lifts, cross-country skiing, instruction.
ⓘ v. Piave, ☎ 91461.
🚌 at Castel di Sangro and Avezzano, ☎ 556220.

Hotels:
★★★★ *G.H. del Parco,* v. S. Lucia 3, ☎ 91356, 118 rm Ⓟ ▥ ♿ ⊠ closed 1 Apr-14 Jun except weekends and 1 Oct-21 Dec, 90,000; bkf: 10,000.
★★★ *Pinguino,* at Collacchi, ☎ 91482, 19 rm Ⓟ ⚐ ▥ closed Jun and Oct, 40,000.
★★★ *Scoiattolo,* at Collacchi, ☎ 91340, 20 rm ⚐ ⚒ closed 5-30 Nov, 40,000.

Restaurant:
♦♦ *Caminetto,* v. Principe di Napoli 16/A, ☎ 91615, closed Mon and 1-25 Jun. Regional cuisine: pasta chitarra with mutton sauce, cannolicchi with red chicory, 14/25,000.

⚐ *Sant'Andrea,* at Sant'Andrea, 100 pl, ☎ 912173 (all year).

L'Aquila 115, Rome 207 km
Pop. 723 ⊠ 67030 ☎ 0864   C5

In the upper Sangro Valley, Alfedena is dominated by the remains of a castle with an octagonal tower.

▶ The parish church of **Ss. Pietro e Paolo** has a 13C portal. ▶ There are very old houses in the historical part of town. ▶ Findings from the **Campo Consolino necropolis** are evidence of the Samnite culture of the 9C-6C

BC. They will be housed in the Civic Museum, currently being reorganized. Items unearthed include bronzes, pieces of armour and soldiers' belts, necklaces, vases and other pottery. ▶ To the N *(15 mn walk by footpath)* are the remains of **Aufidena,** once a settlement of Caraceni Samnites. Still to be seen are traces of the walls (over 1 mile long) and of the acropolis. ▶ 3 km SE is the artificial **Lake Montagna Spaccata** (3,497 ft). ▶ 10 km SE *(scenic route)* is the tableland of **Campitelli** (4,659 ft), with meadows, beech forests, and the Meta range in the background. □

Practical information ───────────────

ⓘ p. Umberto I, ☎ 87394.

ATRI

Teramo 40, L'Aquila 76, Rome 237 km
Pop. 11,516 ⊠ 64032 ☎ 085   C2

There is a close connection between the town and the nearby sea. Coins minted here in the 4C BC bear images of fish and anchors. The town dominated much of the surrounding territory culturally, economically and politically (from the 16C-18C it was referred to as the 'State of Atri'). Traces of past grandeur are evident in the density and richness of the architectural heritage.

▶ The late 13C Romanesque-Gothic **cathedral★** with its flat-topped façade stands on the remains of some Roman baths (mosaic floor underneath the altar; reservoir in the crypt). The interior contains a 15C cycle of frescos as well as the largest church organ in Abruzzi (6,000 pipes). ▶ Around the cloister at the back is the **Museo Capitolare** (9 a.m.-12 noon and 4-8 p.m. from 15 Jun-15 Sep; reserve in advance at other times, ☎ 87241), displaying ecclesiastical items, jewelry and wooden sculpture. ▶ The churches of **S. Agostino** and **S. Domenico** both have 15C portals. ▶ The austere **Palazzo dei Duchi Acquaviva** is the town hall. ▶ From the **Villa Comunale** is a splendid view of the sea, the Maiella and the Gran Sasso. ▶ The **bolge** along the SS to Teramo are gullies formed by erosion, known locally as *scrimoni.* □

Practical information ───────────────

ⓘ v. Roma 1, ☎ 87300.
Restaurant:
♦ *Campana d'Oro,* p. Duomo 23, ☎ 870177, closed Tue. Restored trattoria. Regional cuisine: charcoal-grilled lamb, brochettes, 16/25,000.
Recommended
Events: *folk-singing and wagon procession* (mid-Aug).
Technical tourism: visits to *Camper* stained glass workshop, v. S. Domenico 5, ☎ 87363.

AVEZZANO

L'Aquila 61, Rome 105 km
Pop. 34,870 ⊠ 67051 ☎ 0863   B4

After an earthquake in 1915 and the bombings of 1944, little remained of Avezzano, which today appears as a modern town. It is the centre of the Fùcino Valley, situated at its westernmost edge.

▶ The town hall contains an interesting **archaeological collection** *(a.m. business hours).* Most of the exhibits come from **Alba Fucens** (→). ▶ A **Musem of Country Life and Sheep Farming** is currently being established at the offices of the Ente Fùcino. The collection can be seen by applying to the porter's desk. ▶ 10 km N is **Albe** and, nearby, the remains of the ancient town of **Alba Fucens★** with basilica, baths, theatre, amphitheatre and fortress walls. The Romanesque church of **S. Pietro★** *(caretaker in the town)* is built over a pre-existing

temple of Apollo. Inside is a beautiful 13C ambo★. ▶ *C.* 18 km SE is the **Satellite Ground Station** (→ La Marsica). □

Practical information ───────────────

ⓘ at Cese, ☎ 32291.
Hotel:
★★★ *Principe,* v. Corradini, ☎ 551146, 60 rm Ⓟ ⌗ No restaurant, 60,000; bkf: 3,000.
Restaurant:
♦♦ *Aquila,* corso della Libertà 62, ☎ 554152, closed Mon. Regional cuisine: roast lamb, mozzarella cooked on a spit, 20/26,000.
Recommended
Cycling: *G.S. Gentile,* v. Cavour 50.
Horseback riding: *Ippica Marsicana,* at Ponte Romano, v. Tiburtina Valeria; *Circolo ippico Punto Rosso,* at Corcumello *(19 km SW),* v. Pi La Civita, ☎ 54154 (associate of *ANTE*).

BOMINACO

L'Aquila 32, Rome 151 km
Pop. 95 ⊠ 67020 ☎ 0862   B3

The Romanesque **church of S. Maria★** (12C-13C), once part of a Benedictine abbey, is at the top of Mt. Buscito (3,842 ft). Inside is an ambo (1180), a ciborium and a Paschal candelabrum. Just below is the Gothic church of **S. Pellegrino★** (1263), decorated with 13C-14C Byzantine-style frescos. □

CAMPO DI GIOVE

L'Aquila 82, Rome 172 km
3,490 ft pop. 914 ⊠ 67030 ☎ 0864   C4

This village stands in the shadow of Tavola Rotonda (6,703 ft), one of the peaks of the Maiella. The old part of the village has 15C houses: note particularly Casa Quaranta. Via del Sacco commemorates the sacking of the town. The women's traditional costume has a short skirt, rare in Abruzzi. □

Practical information ───────────────

⌇ cable car, ski lifts, instruction.
Hotel:
★★ *Fonte Romana,* v. Caramanico 9, ☎ 40111, 22 rm Ⓟ ⌗ ⌗ closed Sep-Jun except Christmas, 27,000; bkf: 3,500.

CAMPOTOSTO

L'Aquila 47, Rome 162 km
Pop. 982 ⊠ 67013 ☎ 0862   B2

Campotosto is on the banks of the largest artificial lake in Abruzzi *(14 sq km).* A trip round the lake offers views as far as the Gran Sasso d'Italia. □

Practical information ───────────────

Hotel:
★★ *Valle,* v. Roma 57, ☎ 900119, 9 rm ⌇ ⌗ ⌗ closed Oct-Apr, 38,000; bkf: 4,000.

In preparing for your trip, consult the pages pertaining to the regions. You will find there the description of the region you wish to visit, as well as a list of sites that must be seen, a brief history and practical information.

CASTEL DI SANGRO

L'Aquila 106, Rome 197 km
Pop. 5,218 ⊠ 67031 ☎ 0864   D5

Encircled by mountains, the town, in turn, is grouped around a cliff topped by the remains of a castle. The castle was built on the remains of a Roman or Caracene fortress. The older houses seem to cling to the cliffside. The old-world charm remains intact.

▶ The town centre, partly rebuilt after the devastation of the Second World War, retains a number of **medieval and Renaissance houses:** note in particular the **Casa del Leone.** ▶ The Baroque church of the **Assunzione** (1695-1727) has a portico on either side from an earlier Renaissance building. The interior is rich in furnishings, hangings, bronzes *(Baptism of Jesus)* and wooden altar frontals (16C *Ascent to Calvary).* ▶ In the **Biblioteca Civica** is a Samnite bronze bull and other archaeological exhibits.

Environs

▶ 10 km along a scenic road is **Montenero Val Cocchiara** (2,930 ft), a village set against a background of bare mountains. ▶ A nearby hollow, **Il Pantano,** is the bed of a dried-up lake. The first Sunday after 15 August, a rodeo takes place here. ▶ Nearby, in the vicinity of **S. Lorenzo,** are the remains of **Italic walls.**   ◻

Practical information _____

Recommended
Events: *Rodeo Pentro* at Montenero Val Cocchiara, *(10 km SW,* first Sun after 15 Aug).

CASTELLI

Teramo 40, L'Aquila 96, Rome 215 km
Pop. 1,740 ⊠ 64041 ☎ 0861   B-C2

Castelli is beautifully situated on a wooded spur, with Mt. Camicia in the background. Since the 13C it has produced highly prized pottery, which was renowned from the 15C-18C. 16C-17C pieces are on display in the **Museo della Ceramica di Castelli,** in a 16C cloister *(9 a.m.-12 noon and 3:30-5 p.m.).* ▶ The parish church contains a 13C polychrome wooden statue. ◻

Practical information _____

Recommended
Craft workshops: *G. Simonetti,* Villagio Artigianato, ☎ 979493 or 979347 (majolica); *Facciolini,* Villagio Artigianato, ☎ 979182 (ceramics).

CELANO

L'Aquila 49, Rome 118 km
Pop. 10,512 ⊠ 67043 ☎ 0863   B4

Celano sits on a hill at the N edge of the Fucino Valley. ▶ **Piccolomini Castle★** is one of the most remarkable in Abruzzi. The main building, which has four corner towers, is surrounded by an irregular outer wall with towers and keeps. There is an attractive inner courtyard. ▶ Around the castle is a picturesque old village. ▶ **S. Maria Valleverde** contains an important painting of *Christ and Simon of Cyrene on the road to Calvary.* ▶ The **church of S. Giovanni Battista** contains some 15C Tuscan school frescos. ▶ The organ in the church of **S. Angelo** dates from 1737.

Environs

▶ 2 km S, then 1.5 hrs by footpath, is the **Gole di Celano★** (gorge), which is more than 5 km long with steep sides as deep as 984 ft in places. ▶ 15 km SE is **Pescina,** birthplace of Cardinal Mazarin (1602-61), prime minister of France during the regency of Anne of Austria. Viale Francia is the cardinal's birthplace (small **museum,** *by appointment,* ☎ *82156).*   ◻

Practical information _____

Environs

PESCINA, ⊠ 67057, ☎ 0863.

Restaurant:
◆ *Filippone,* v. Medaglia d'Oro Barbati 5, ☎ 81156, closed Fri. Regional cuisine: polenta with sausage, charcoal-grilled lamb, 20/25,000.

CHIETI

L'Aquila 89, Rome 200, Milan 585 km
Pop. 55,262 ⊠ 66100 ☎ 0871   D3

Chieti is known for its collections in the achaeological museum, the cathedral and the Roman remains. However, relatively modern buildings are found among the older ones. Variations in the architectural styles (Baroque, late Baroque, 19C, art nouveau) present an elegant ensemble.

▶ The **cathedral** (B1-2) dates from the 9C. It was largely rebuilt in the 14C. The campanile (1335-1498) is of interest. ▶ V. Chiarini goes from the cathedral to corso Marrucino, the main street, which is flanked by churches and palazzi. The church of **S. Francesco della Scarpa** (B2) is Baroque but of medieval origin; the Baroque church of **S. Domenico** houses the **Museo Diocesano d'Arte Sacra** containing 15C-16C paintings and frescos. ▶ In v. de Lolli is the **Pinacoteca Costantino Barbella** (B2; *9 a.m.-1 p.m.;closed hols)* displaying works from the 14C-20C. Of particular interest is a preparatory drawing for the *Massacre of the Innocents,* by Luca Giordano, a bronze self-portrait by Vincenzo Gemito, paintings and sculptures. ▶ The **Tempietti Romani** (B1) are the remains of three temples dating from the 1C. ▶ Farther on are the remains of the **Roman theatre** (B1). On the edge of town are the ruins of the **Roman baths** (B2; *apply to the Museo Archeologico),*including a remarkable reservoir. ▶ Within the attractive gardens of the **Villa Comunale** is the **Museo Archeologico Nazionale★** (C1; *9 a.m.-1 p.m.;closed Mon),* with interesting prehistoric and early historical exhibits. Note particularly findings relating to pre-Roman funerary cults in Abruzzi (fuerary artifacts from the Campovalano necropolis and from Capestrano and Alfedena) and sculptures, especially the **Warrior of Capestrano.** ▶ The **belvedere** of the Villa Comunale offers a view S to the Maiella. ▶ 1 km away, in the direction of Pescara, is the octagonal church of **S. Maria del Tricalle,** which was rebuilt in the late 15C. ▶ (→ La Maiella).   ◻

Practical information _____

ⓘ v. B. Spaventa 29 (B1), ☎ 65231.
✈ at Pescara, ☎ 085/206245; *Alitalia,* v. Asinio Herio 14 (B1), ☎ 41990.
🚂 ☎ 52211 (Chieti Scalo).
🚌 from p. Vittorio Emanuele (B2).

Hotels:
★★★ *Dangio,* at Tricalle, v. Solferino 20, ☎ 34356, 38 rm
ⓟ ⪦ 57,000.
★★★ *Sole,* v. dei Domenicani 1 (B2a), ☎ 66681, 50 rm. No restaurant, 57,000.

Restaurants:
● ◆◆◆ *Venturini,* v. de Lollis 10 (B2c), ☎ 65863, closed

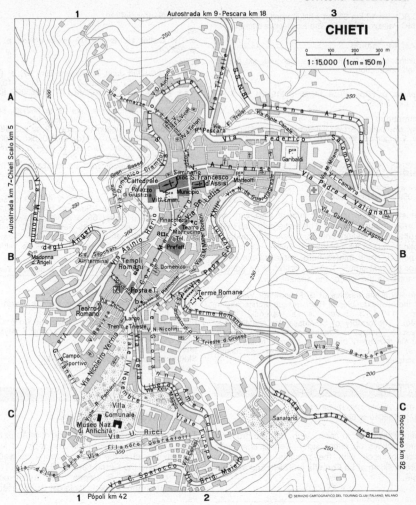

CHIETI

0   100   200   300 m

1 : 15.000   (1 cm = 150 m)

Tue and 1-20 Jul. Beautiful terrace. Regional cuisine: pappardelle montanara, ciambotta, 20/32,000.
♦ **Nino,** v. Principessa di Piemonte 7 (B1-2 b), ☎ 65396, closed Fri and Aug. Regional cuisine: pollo cacciatora, baked rabbit, 18/25,000.

Recommended
Archery: *Compagnia Arcieri Teatini,* corso Marrucino 39, ☎ 32955.
Cycling: *G.S. D'Arcangelo,* v. Pescara 133, ☎ 64241.
Events: *Good Friday procession.*
Horseback riding: *Circolo ippico Abruzzese,* v. Gizio (Chieti Scalo), ☎ 582266 (riding school).
Sports centre: Colle dell'Ara, ☎ 587260; v. dei Peligni, ☎ 65725.
Tennis: at Piana Vincolato, ☎ 63942.

> For help in understanding terms when visiting museums or other sites, see the *Art and Architectural Terms Guide* at the end of the Practical Holiday Guide.

CIVITELLA DEL TRONTO

Teramo 18, L'Aquila 91, Rome 202 km
Pop. 5,854 ⊠ 64010 ☎ 0861   B-C1

Once a place of great strategic importance, Civitella del Tronto endured many sieges; the Bourbon fortress was one of the last to surrender in 1861.

▶ The medieval, Renaissance and Baroque buildings lend a distinctive air (note the portal at v. Roma 18). ▶ The **parish church** was built in the 16C; the church of **S. Francesco** has an elaborate rose window. Inside is a 15C walnut wood chancel. ▶ The **fortress** at the top of the town offers a **view★** from the Fiori and Campli Mountains to the Adriatic.

Environs

▶ 7.5 km S is the 13C church of **S. Pietro.** Inside *(keys from the parish priest at Campovalano)* is a late Roman sarcophagus, the tomb of a marble seller. ▶ Just below is **Campovalano,** with the remains of an Italic **necropolis**

(7C-5C BC). ▶ 13 km SE, on a hill, **Campli** has old hous-ies, a 14C Palazzo Comunale and a collegiate church. ☐

Practical information _____

✗ chairlifts to Mt. Piselli at San Giacomo, ski lifts at Mt. Piselli, instruction.

Hotel:
★★ **Zunica**, p. Filippi Pepe 14, ☎ 91319, 21 rm ╡ ⌁ 35,000; bkf: 3,000.

Recommended
Archery: *Compagnia Arcieri Valvibrata*, at Sant'Egidio alla Vibrata, v. Liguria 6, ☎ 807240.

CORFINIO

L'Aquila 54, Rome 150 km
Pop. 1,000 ⊠ 67030 ☎ 0864   C4

The most important traces of ancient *Corfinium* are the *morroni* (mausoleums). The settlement was once the capital of the Peligni and, for a year, the capital of the Italic league in its war against Rome. During the latter period, coins minted here displayed the name Italia for the first time. Today, Corfinio is an agricul-tural centre on the site of the ancient town.

▶ 1 km SW is the **basilica of S. Pelino**★ (or Valvense), one of the best examples of Romanesque architecture in Abruzzi (11C-12C). Inside is a splendid pulpit (1176-80). The oratory of S. Alessandro contains two 14C frescos. Nearby is a **museum** of ancient Corfinium *(ask at the presbytery or apply in advance to the parish priest at Corfinio)* displaying weapons, bronzes, lamps and inscriptions.   ☐

GAMBERALE

Chieti 92, L'Aquila 128, Rome 211 km
Pop. 671 ⊠ 66040 ☎ 0872   D4

Gamberale lies on a crest, with the Sangro and Aventino Valleys on either side. Behind is a large expanse of rock with the remains of a **castle**. ▶ There is skiing at **La Forcella** (4,921 ft) and at **Valle del Sole**.   ☐

Practical information _____

✗ ski lifts, instruction at La Forcella and Valle del Sole.

Hotel:
★★ **Fonte**, v. S. Domenico, ☎ 946102, 34 rm ℗ ╡ ⌁ ⌁ closed 21 Apr-19 Jun and 1 Oct-4 Dec, 45,000; bkf: 5,000.

GIULIANOVA

Teramo 26, L'Aquila 100, Rome 211 km
Pop. 21,795 ⊠ 64022 ☎ 085   C1

Giulianova was founded in 1470 by Giulio Antonio Acquaviva, Duke of Atri, for the inhabitants of **Castel San Flaviano**, which had been almost completely de-stroyed in 1460. The old town is up on a hill, not far from the coast and **Giulianova Lido**.

▶ The Renaissance **Duomo** of S. Flaviano dates from the foundation of the town. A valuable silver reliquary is dis-played inside (1396). ▶ The **Pinacoteca Comunale Vin-cenzo Bindi** exhibits some 19C Neapolitan canvases and a collection of letters from the Risorgimento period *(9 a.m.-12 noon and 3-6 p.m.; 9 a.m.-12 noon Sat; closed Sun)*. ▶ 2 km away is the restored Romanesque church of **S. Maria a Mare**, with an elegant portal.   ☐

Practical information _____

≋
ℹ v. Galilei 18, ☎ 862013 (main office); p. Roma, ☎ 862226.

Hotels:
★★★★ **G.H. Don Juan**, lungomare Zara 97, ☎ 867341, 148 rm ℗ ⌁ ⅙ ⊟ ⌁ closed 21 Sep-17 May, 110,000.
★★★ **Atlantic**, lungomare Zara 117, ☎ 863029, 53 rm ℗ ⌁ closed Oct-Apr, 60,000.
★★★ **Cristallo**, lungomare Zara 73, ☎ 862780, 54 rm ℗ ⌁ ⌁ closed Christmas, 65,000; bkf: 6,000.
★★★ **Promenade**, lungomare Zara 119, ☎ 862338, 60 rm ℗ ⌁ ⊟ closed 26 Sep-14 May, 60,000; bkf: 10,000.
★★★ **Ritz**, lungomare Zara 50, ☎ 863470, 50 rm ℗ ⌁ closed Oct-Apr, 55,000; bkf: 7,000.
★★★ **Smeraldo**, lungomare Zara, ☎ 863806, 80 rm ℗ ⌁ ⊟ 61,000.

Restaurants:
● ◆◆◆ **Beccaceci**, v. Zola 28, ☎ 862550, closed Mon eve, Tue and 15-31 Dec. Seafood: fish grills, 30/42,000.
◆◆◆ **Torrione**, p. Buozzi 63, ☎ 863895, closed Mon, Sun eve in winter and 10 Jan-15 Feb. In 17C aristocratic dwelling, beautiful terrace overlooking sea. Creative cui-sine: indrucchi with fish sauce, costoletta valdostana, 30/45,000.

⚓ *Holiday*, lungomare Zara, 400 pl, ☎ 864425; *Tam Tam*, lungomare Rodi S, 300 pl, ☎ 865002.

Recommended
Farm vacations: *Fattoria Cerreto*, at Colle Cerreto *(9 km W)*, ☎ 866679.
Horseback riding: *Fattoria Cerreto*, at Colle Cerreto, ☎ 866679 (excursions across Abruzzi in 7 days; over-night accommodation).
Marina: ☎ 862224.
Skating: lungomare Spalato, ☎ 865544.
Swimming: v. Ippodromo, ☎ 862668.

Il GRAN SASSO D'ITALIA

From L'Aquila *(125 km, 1 day; map 1)*

This snow-capped massif, focal point of Abruzzi, con-sists of 35 km of bare, limestone rock. It includes the only glacier in the Apennine range, as well as its highest peak, the Corno Grande (9,554 ft). This itin-erary circles the S slopes. The usual point of approach on the N side is Isola del Gran Sasso d'Ita-lia.

▶ From **L'Aquila** (→), the route goes up through the wood-ed valletta del Raiale towards **San Vittorino** to the isolat-ed **Passo delle Capannelle** (4,262 ft). ▶ At **Assergi** (2,907 ft) is the Romanesque church of S. Maria Assunta (12C), with a crypt partly dug out of the rock. It con-tains a 15C silver urn. ▶ Nearby is **Fonte Cerreto** (3,674 ft). From there, it is a 15-minute journey by funicular to Campo Imperatore, which can also be reached by the **tra-foro del Gran Sasso** (tunnel). ▶ Once under the bed of a pre-historic lake, the plateau is almost 27 km long and more than 7 km wide, with an average height of 5,250 ft. ▶ Near the terminal of the funicular (6,975 ft) is an **alpine garden** (7,218 ft), containing more than 400 spe-cies of plants and an observatory. ▶ A 40-minute walk away is the **Rifugio Duca degli Abruzzi** (7,834 ft), which offers a beautiful view of the W side of the moun-tain. ▶ On the way down from Campo Imperatore is a crossroads with a turn-off for the **Rifugio Fonte Vetica** (5,354 ft), which stands in the shadow of Mt. Camicia (8,412 ft). ▶ From there, a winding road leads to the resort of **Castel del Monte** (4,298 ft, two interesting churches: Madonna del Suffragio and S. Marco Evange-lista). ▶ The road descends steeply across the plain of San Marco to **Calascio** (3,970 ft, 16C terra-cotta in the Convent of S. Maria delle Grazie) and **Santo Stefano di Sessànio** (4,104 ft), a medieval village. ▶ Next is a steep

1. Il Gran Sasso d'Italia

descent to **Barisciano** (2,923 ft), with beautiful views on the way, and finally to **L'Aquila**.　□

Practical information

CAMPO IMPERATORE, 6,988 ft, ✉ 67010, ☎ 0862.
☈ ski lifts and ski instruction.

Recommended
Botanical garden: visits on request; apply to the University of L'Aquila, ☎ 6446301.
Observatory: visits, ☎ 606130; information at the Osservatorio dell'Università di Roma, ☎ 06/347056 or 3452147.

FONTE CERRETO, ✉ 67010, ☎ 0862.
☈ cable car to Campo Imperatore (→), ski lifts at Mt. Cristi *(6 km E)*.

Hotel:
★★★ *Fiordigigli,* ☎ 606171, 72 rm Ⓟ ⌘ closed 1 Oct-20 Dec, 60,000; bkf: 4,000.

GUARDIAGRELE

Chieti 30, L'Aquila 127, Rome 230 km
Pop. 10,288 ✉ 66016 ☎ 0871　　　　　　　　　D3

Guardiagrele, on a spur at the foot of the E slopes of the Maiella, was the birthplace of Nicola da Guardiagrele, one of the most famous artists from Abruzzi. Active at the beginning of the 15C, he was a sculptor and goldsmith and was influenced by Tuscan artists. The traditions of goldsmithing and wrought-iron work have been preserved in the town.

▶ The church of **S. Maria Maggiore★** is an 11C Romanesque building. The campanile (1110-1202) is in the centre of the façade, which has a Gothic portal. On the r. side, beneath the portico, is a fresco of St. Christopher (1473). The sacristy contains illuminated manuscripts, and a museum is being prepared to house the most important pieces from the **treasury,** including the silver processional cross with enamel and filigree work (1431), one of Nicola da Guardiagrele's masterpieces. ▶ The 14C church of **S. Francesco** has a Romanesque-Gothic portal and a 15C cloister. A collection of sculptures and fragments from church buildings in the town and surrounding area can be found in the **Biblioteca Civica** *(3:30-7 p.m. wkdays; closed Mon).* ▶ From the garden of the

Villa Comunale is a view of the Gran Sasso, the Maiella and the sea.　□

ISOLA DEL GRAN SASSO D'ITALIA

Teramo 29, L'Aquila 89, Rome 208 km
Pop. 5,170 ✉ 64045 ☎ 0861　　　　　　　　B-C2

This town is in the Mavone Valley (also known as the Valle Siciliana, a deformation of *via Cecilia,* the name of the ancient Roman way that passed through it). In the old quarter are houses with Latin mottos engraved on the windows.

▶ The S. Sebastiano chapel contains 15C frescos. ▶ The town is the northern starting point for the **Gran Sasso** (→). Higher up, near Fano a Corno, is the beginning of the **traforo del Gran Sasso** *(motorway tunnel, 10 km).* ▶ 2.5 km along the road to Tossicia is the **santuario di S. Gabriele,** the most frequented shrine in Abruzzi. ▶ 5.5 km farther is **Tossicia,** interesting for its 15C houses and the church of S. Antonio Abate, which has a portal occupying almost all of the façade. ▶ 3 km along the Mavone Valley road is the 12C-13C Romanesque church of **S. Giovanni al Mavone** or ad Insulam, situated among the ruins of a monastery *(keys from the house nearby).* ▶ 8.5 km farther along the same road is the isolated 12C church of **S. Maria di Ronzano.** The presbytery contains 12C frescos *(keys from the parish priest at Castel Castagna).*　□

Practical information

ISOLA DEL GRAN SASSO D'ITALIA

Hotel:
★ *Insula,* borgo S. Leonardo 78, ☎ 97202, 15 rm ⌂ ⌘ closed 21 Oct-14 Mar except Christmas, 31,000; bkf: 5,000.

Environs

FANO ADRIANO, 2,444 ft, ✉ 64044, ☎ 0861, 32 km NW.
☈ ski lifts at Prato Selva *(9 km SW).*

Restaurant:
◆◆◆ *Augusto,* circonvallazione dei Merletti, ☎ 95144, closed Tue and 15-31 Oct. Regional cuisine: scrippelle 'mbusse, tegamino alla montanara, 17/25,000.

PRATI DI TIVO, 4,337 ft, ⊠ 64047, ☎ 0861, 33 km SW.
ⵊ ski lifts, cross-country skiing, instruction.

Hotels:
★★★★ *Miramonti,* ☎ 95621, 90 rm P ⌕ ⚒ 🖼 ⌁ closed
16 Apr-19 Jun and 16 Sep-19 Dec, 84,000.
★★ *Gran Sasso Tre,* ☎ 95639, 13 rm P ⌧ closed Christmas, 40,000; bkf: 5,000.

TOSSICIA, ⊠ 64049, ☎ 0861, 7.5 km N.

Recommended
Craft workshops: *I Telai del Gran Sasso,* at Azzinano,
☎ 698003 (hand-woven cloth); *I. Vignoli,* at Chiarin,
☎ 698353 (copper).
Farm vacations: information next to the *Comunità Montana del Gran Sasso* (zone O), ☎ 69322.

LANCIANO

Chieti 48, L'Aquila 145, Rome 240 km
Pop. 33, 281 ⊠ 66034 ☎ 0872   D3

Lanciano, built on three hills, is situated 12 km from
the coast. The oldest church in town is that of
S. Biagio. Until the 17C, the life of Lanciano revolved around commercial traffic and the sea. A
twice-yearly fair attracted merchants from Holland,
Germany, Turkey, Albania and Greece.

▶ In the old part of the town buildings are grouped in a
network of alleyways in the quarters of Lancianovecchia,
Borgo, Sacca (the ghetto) and Civitanova. ▶ The Cistercian Gothic church of **S. Maria Maggiore★** (1227) has
been altered and enlarged. A silver cross by Nicola da
Guardiagrele (1422) is displayed in the sacristy. ▶ The
cathedral (p. Plebiscito), rebuilt along Neoclassical lines,
is supported by four arches of a bridge dating from the
reign of the Emperor Diocletian (2C-3C). ▶ The 13C
church of **S. Francesco** contains a reliquary recording a
eucharistic miracle of the 8C. The 13C church of S.Agostino has a Baroque interior and contains a silver bust of
St. Simon by Nicola da Guardiagrele. ▶ The **Museo
Civico** *(to be opened shortly)* will exhibit neolithic and
medieval material, 15C-16C paintings and early printed
books. ▶ Traces of the 11C **walls,** with 15C additions,
can be seen surrounding the old part of the town.   ☐

Practical infomation _____

ℹ p. Plebiscito, ☎ 32245.

Hotel:
★★★ *Excelsior,* v. Rimembranze 19, ☎ 23113, 82 rm P
ᕳ 60,000; bkf: 6,000.

Restaurant:
● ♦♦♦ *Taverna Ranieri,* v. De Crecchio 42, ☎ 32102,
closed Mon. Two rooms with important paintings, indoor
garden and terrace. Excellent regional and international
cuisine: pappardelle with wild boar, kid with cheese and
egg, 25/40,000.

Recommended
Events: *Settembre Lancianese, festival of the Madonna
del Ponte* and *procession* (8 Sep), *Squilla festival* (23
Dec), *procession of the Dead Christ* and *mystery play of
the Resurrection* at Easter.
Fairs: *Fiera dell'Agricoltura e della Tecnica* (early Apr),
☎ 41747.
Instruction: *Amici della Musica,* v. Asilo 4, ☎ 23228 (Jul-
Aug; music).

L'AQUILA*

Rome 115, Milan 675 km
Pop. 64,963 ⊠ 67100 ☎ 0862   B3

On a bank above the Aterno River, this town was
founded in the 13C. A 13C fountain with ninety-
nine jets of water commemorates the ninety-nine

castles from which the town was originally formed,
each having a square, a church and a fountain. Enclosed by an irregular triangle of walls, the
town follows the plan of a checkerboard. L'Aquila
is still predominantly medieval in appearance despite
the disastrous earthquake of 1703 and offers striking
views of the encircling mountains: the Gran Sasso,

© SERVIZIO CARTOGRAFICO DEL TOURING CLUB ITALIANO, MILANO   Avezzano

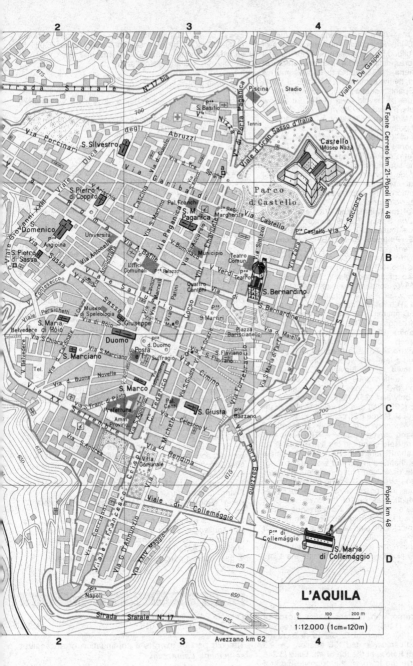

L'AQUILA

0   100   200 m

1:12.000 (1cm=120m)

Avezzano km 62

the Velino and the Sirente. The historical capital of Abruzzi, in the 14C it was the second most important town in S Italy after Naples. It has an intensely rich architectural and artistic heritage, and several of its monuments occupy an important place in the national artistic heritage.

▶ At the centre of the town, two fountains grace the p. del Duomo (C3), where there is a daily market. The **Duomo** (C3) was rebuilt in 1703 with a Neoclassical façade. Inside is the tomb of Cardinal Agnifili (1480). ▶ The main street, corso **Vittorio Emanuele** (B3), is partly flanked by arcades. The **Quattro Cantoni** intersection is a popular local meeting place. ▶ The church of **S. Bernardino★★** (B4) stands at the top of a picturesque

street.   Built from 1454-72, it has a Renaissance façade (1527-40).   The 18C interior contains numerous works of art; the carved and gilded Baroque ceiling★ of the nave; a terra-cotta★ by Andrea della Robbia; the **mausoleum of S. Bernardino of Siena★** by Silvestro dell'Aquila and his students (1505); and, by the same artist, the tomb of Maria Pereira★.   ▶ The Spanish **castle★** (1534-49) stands in a park at the NE corner of the old town (A-B4).   It is now the **Museo Nazionale d'Abruzzo** *(9 a.m.-2 p.m.; 9 a.m.-1 p.m. hols; closed Mon)* with collections of archaeology, sacred art, regional pottery and contemporary art.   There are numerous items of 12C-18C Abruzzi sacred art, including the **wooden doors★** of S. Maria in Cellis di Carsoli (1132) and of S. Pietro di Alba Fucens (12C); a group of 13C-16C polychrome **sculptures★** in wood and terra-cotta and the *Stories of S. Giovanni da Capestrano★* (15C) and a processional cross by Nicola da Guardiagrele (1434).   In the E bastion is the *elephas meridionalis* skeleton (a 1.5 million-year-old fossil).
▶ The quarters N of the Duomo and W of corso Vittorio Emanuele.   ▶ Via Sassa (B2) is flanked by medieval and 16C Baroque houses.   Of interest are the Romanesque church of **S. Pietro di Sassa** (B2), the **church of Beata Antonia** *(entrance through a small courtyard at no. 29A)* with a fresco of the *Crucifixion* (15C) and the palazzetto Fiore (no. 56) with its Renaissance courtyard.   ▶ The **Museo di Speleologia V. Rivera** (B2; *by appointment,* ☎ *26540)* contains exhibits from caves in various parts of the world.   ▶ The church of **S. Domenico** in p. Angioina (B2) retains parts of the 14C building.   ▶ The 13C-15C church of **S. Pietro di Coppito** (B2) contains 15C-16C frescos.   ▶ The I. side of the church of **S. Maria di Paganica** (B3; 1308) and the 18C **Palazzo Franchi** face each other across the same square.   ▶ **S. Silvestro** (A2-3) is a beautiful 14C church with 15C frescos and a late 15C wooden *Crucifixion*.
▶ **The S part of town.**   ▶ **S. Flaviano** (C3) is a late 13C church with a Romanesque portal and polygonal apses.   Inside are 15C frescos.   ▶ The church of **S.Giusta** (C3), built between 1257-1349, contains a lavish gilded wooden altar (16C-17C) and an inlaid Gothic chancel.   ▶ The church of **S. Marco** (C3) contains a 15C wooden sculpture of the *Madonna and Child*.   ▶ **S. Marciano** (C2) has an interesting carved portal.   ▶ The early 14C church of **S. Maria di Roio** stands in the same square as the 18C Persichetti and Revere palazzi.   ▶ The **fontana★** (B1) is unusual: first installed in 1272, it was later enlarged.   It has a double basin and ninety-nine jets of water emerging from unique structures.   ▶ The most important piece of architecture in Abruzzi is **S. Maria di Collemaggio★★** (B4), which rises out of the town walls.   It was built in the late 13C, along Romanesque-Gothic lines.   The flat-topped façade (mid-14C) is made of geometrically shaped blocks of pink and white stone.   Of note are the three portals and three rose windows.   Inside, the nave and two aisles have been restored to their original design.   A chapel contains the tomb of **St. Celestine★** (1517).

Environs

▶ 2 km away, near the cemetery, is the church of the **Madonna del Soccorso**, with its Renaissance façade of pink-and-white stone (1496).   ▶ 7 km along the road to Popoli is the early 13C church of **S. Giusta di Bazzano** with a small, vaulted campanile and 13C frescos.   ▶ 9.5 km away is **pineta di Roio★**, at the top of **Mt. Luco** (3,248 ft), which rises above the town on the opposite bank of the Aterno and provides a splendid view★.   ▶ 10 km along the SS to Teramo, at **San Vittorino**, are the Romanesque church of S. Michele and, at the foot of the hill, the ruins of the ancient Sabine (later Roman) town of *Amiternum* (destroyed in the 11C) with remains of a theatre and amphitheatre.   ▶ **Fossa** *(19 km SE, in the Aterna Valley)* is on a mountain slope with a ruined castle at the top.   The parish church contains a Gothic wooden statue of the *Madonna*.   The 13C Cistercian Gothic church of **S. Maria delle Grotte** *(just before the town, keys from caretaker at no. 16 along the same road)* contains **fres-**

cos★ of the Benedictine (13C) and Tuscan schools (14C-15C).   ▶ The ski resort of **Campo Felice** (5,085 ft, → the Sirente plateau) is reached by way of Lucoli.   ▶ → Gran Sasso d'Italia.   □

Practical information _____

⚅ p. S.Maria Paganica 5 (B3), ☎ 25149; v. XX Settembre 8 (C2), ☎ 22306.
✈ at Pescara, ☎ 085/206245; *Alitalia,* corso Vittorio Emanuele 23 (B3), ☎ 20468.
▚▚ (B1), ☎ 20497.
▄▄ from p. S. Bernardino (B3).

Hotels:
★★★ *Cannelle,* p. Le Cannelle (B1 b), ☎ 6981, 130 rm ℗ ▥ ⚭ ▭ ⏦75,000; bkf: 8,000.
★★★ *Castello,* p. Battaglione Alpini (A3 a), ☎ 29147, 44 rm ℗ ⌇ 62,000; bkf: 7,000.
★★★ *Duca degli Abruzzi,* v. Giovanni XXIII 10 (B2 c), ☎ 28341, 85 rm ℗ ⌇ 70,000; bkf: 6,000.

Restaurants:
● ♦♦♦ *Tre Marie,* v. Tre Marie 3 (B3 e), ☎ 20191, closed Mon and Christmas.   With 18C fireplace.   Regional cuisine: ciufolotti, nocchette alla pastorella, 35/45,000.
♦♦ *Salette Aquilane,* at Coppito, ☎ 639145, closed Sun eve, Mon and Jul, 25/35,000.
♦ *Aquila da Remo,* v. S. Flaviano 9 (C3 d), ☎ 22010, closed Sat and Christmas.   Regional cuisine: saltimbocca, roast meats, 20/30,000.
♦ *Scannapapera,* at Pile, v. Salaria Antica Est 2, ☎ 315052, closed Sat.   Regional cuisine: mutton stew, chicken with anchovies, 15/25,000.

⚐ *Gran Panorama,* contrada Vetoio, SS 17, ☎ 315351 (all year).

Recommended
Botanical garden: p. dell'Annunziata 1 (B2), ☎ 6446301.
Convention centre: *Le Cannelle,* v. S. Maria del Ponte, ☎ 6981.
Events: *international puppet theatre* (Jun-Jul), theatre season at the Teatro Stabile, ☎ 62946 and other theatrical events *(Associazione Teatrale Abruzzese Molisana,* ☎ 61779), *music and architecture show* (Jul-Aug), concert season in the Auditorio del Castello *(Società Aquilana Concerti,* ☎ 69761), *Papal Pardon* (historical religious event, Aug).
Fairs: antiques fair (May-Jun); arts and crafts fair (Aug).
Flying: *Preturo airport,* ☎ 609013 (gliding).
Hang gliding: *D.S. Fr. D'Arni* school, v. Sallustio 33, ☎ 22320.
Horseback riding: *Centro Agriturismo a cavallo tra i Castelli Aquilani,* v. Sassa 56, ☎ 64004 or 20117.
Instruction: *Centro internazionale della Chitarra,* v. Tre Marie 2, ☎ 62160 (music).
♥ gastronomy: nougat with chocolate and honey.

LORETO APRUTINO

Pescara 24, L'Aquila 111, Rome 227 km
Pop. 7,071 ✉ 65014 ☎ 085   C2-3

The old part of town is a continuation of an ancient settlement, *Laurentum.*

▶ At the top of the town is the parish church of **S. Pietro Apostolo** (15C), which has a Renaissance portal and a loggia with large Romanesque mullions.   ▶ Next to the **Palazzo Acerbo** is an annex that houses the **Galleria delle Ceramiche Abruzzesi★** *(private gallery, temporarily closed)* containing a large collection of regional pottery from the 15C-19C.   ▶ The library in the **Palazzo Casamarte di Campotino** contains documents and relics relating to Corsica.   ▶ 1.3 km S is the isolated abbey church of **S. Maria in Piano.**   Its frescos are considered among the most interesting in the region.   □

Practical information ———————

Recommended
Wine: visits to the *Valentini* vineyard, v. del Baio 2, ☎ 826138 (Montepulciano, Cerasuolo and Trebbiano wines; arrange in advance).

La MAIELLA

From Chieti *(203 km, 1 day; map 2)*

The landscape of La Maiella ranges from idyllic to awesome. The towns and villages are rich with reminders of an illustrious past.

▶ After leaving **Chieti** (→) the itinerary passes **Bucchianico** on the l., where there are several interesting churches. The medieval Banderesi festival is held here in May. ▶ The route continues along this winding road, which offers splendid views. ▶ After **Pretoro** detour to the r. up to **Passo Lanciano** (4,285 ft), amid woodlands, then up to **Blockhaus** (7,027 ft), where the road ends. The visitor is now in the heart of the Maielletta (6,545 ft) and surrounding mountains (Mt. Acquaviva, 8,979 ft, and Mt. Amaro, 9,163 ft). ▶ Continue through **Guardiagrele** (→) and **Bocca di Valle** (unusual caveshrine decorated with coloured tiles) and up as far as **Pennapiedimonte**, a village built on flights of steps with an 18C parish church. ▶ At the foot of Mt. Amaro is **Lama dei Peligni**; from there, take a brief detour to the cable-car station at **Grotta del Cavallone** *(reserve in advance, ☎ 910118 or 91221)*. ▶ Travel along the **tagliata degli Abruzzi**, which goes through a desolate but intriguing landscape, bare of vegetation. At **Palena** is the charming 18C church of the Rosario. ▶ At **valico della Forchetta** (4,166 ft), the landscape flattens out into extensive meadowlands. ▶ After **Pescocostanzo** (→) is **Rivisóndoli** (4,330 ft), which is on the side of Mt. Calvary and is famed for its 'living Nativity'. ▶ After **Roccaraso** (→) travel 9 km across the **Plain of Cinquemiglia**, situated at an altitude of over 4,101 ft. This area is subject to violent snowstorms. Packs of wolves roamed free here until recently, and the region was a haunt of bandits during the 19C. ▶ The road now begins to descend, coming to **Pettorano sul Gizio** (where the women wear a particularly beautiful traditional costume), then to the **Sulmona Valley** which offers a view of the Gran Sasso and the Morrone Mountains. ▶ After **Pacentro** (→ Sulmona), the road ascends to **Passo San Leonardo** (4,206 ft), but then dips to **Caramànico Terme**, a thermal resort with a distinctive, old-world appearance, situated in a sheltered spot in a valley (note the church of S. Maria Maggiore, 15C). ▶ Near **San Valentino in Abruzzo Citeriore** are caves of geological interest. The 18C parish church of Ss. Valentino e Damiano was designed by Luigi Vanvitelli. ▶ Finally, return to **Santa Maria Arabona** (→) and **Chieti.** □

Practical information ———————

BUCCHIANICO, ⊠ 66011, ☎ 0871.

Recommended
Cycling: *G.S. Santoferrara*, v. Piana 1.
Events: *Sagra dei Banderesi* (festival commemorating historic event, May), ☎ 685166.

CARAMANICO TERME, ⊠ 65023, ☎ 085.
⚓ (Apr-Nov), ☎ 92216 or 92446.
ℹ v. Fonte Grande 3, ☎ 92209 or 92348.

Hotel:
★★ *Petit Hotel Viola*, v. della Libertà 9, ☎ 92332, 28 rm ℗
⚜ ⚘ 48,000; bkf: 2,500.

Recommended
Nature park: guided excursions in the Riserva orientata Valle dell'Orfento, visitors' centre, ☎ 92284.

FARA SAN MARTINO, ⊠ 66015, ☎ 0872.

Hotel:
★★★ *Camerlengo*, v. Macchia del Fresco, ☎ 980136, 44 rm ℗ ⚙ 🖃 ⚘ 45,000; bkf: 5,000.

Recommended
♥ pasta factory: *De Cecco* visit by prior arrangement, ☎ 980421.

LAMA DEI PELIGNI, ⊠ 66010, ☎ 0872.

Recommended
Events: *Dance of the Doll* and *fireworks* for St. Barbara (26 Dec), Comune, ☎ 91221.
Spelunking: visits to the Grotta del Cavallone (via cable car, ☎ 910203), by prior arrangement, ☎ 910236 or 910118.

PASSO LANCIANO, ⊠ 66010 (Pretoro), ☎ 0871.
⚡ ski lifts at Passo Lanciano and la Maielletta, cross-country skiing, ski instruction.

Hotel:
★★★ *Mamma Rosa*, at Mirastelle-Fonte Tettoni *(4 km S)*, ☎ 896143, 43 rm ℗ ⚜ ⚘ ⚘ closed May and Oct, 40,000; bkf: 5,000.

⚓ *La Maielletta*, 220 pl, ☎ 896132 (all year).

PASSO SAN LEONARDO, ⊠ 67030, ☎ 0864.
⚡ ski lifts, cross-country skiing, ski instruction.

PRETORO, ⊠ 66010, ☎ 0871.

Hotel:
★★ *Scoiattolo*, at Calvario *(3 km)*, SS Maielletta 7, ☎ 898123, 35 rm ⚜ ⚙ ⚘ 45,000; bkf: 5,000.

Recommended
Events: *Festival of S. Domenico* with procession of snake catchers (May), Comune, ☎ 898131.

RIVISONDOLI, ⊠ 67036, ☎ 0864.
⚡ cable cars, ski lifts, instruction, skating.

2. La Maiella

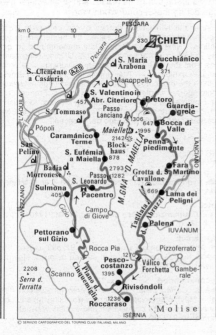

© SERVIZIO CARTOGRAFICO DEL TOURING CLUB ITALIANO, MILANO

ⓘ p. Municipio, ☎ 69351.

Hotels:
★★★ *Cinque Miglia,* SS 17 at 134-km marker, ☎ 69151, 64 rm ℙ ⚡ ▣ ⌖ 48,000.
★★★ *Como,* v. Alighieri 45, ☎ 69127, 44 rm ℙ ⚏ closed 16 Apr-14 Jun and 16 Sep-4 Dec, 44,000; bkf: 5,000.
★★★ *Impero,* v. Fonticella 40, ☎ 69112, 70 rm ℙ ⚏ ⚡ closed 21 Mar-Jun and Sep-19 Dec, 50,000; bkf: 9,000.
★★★ *Victoria,* v. Marconi 19, ☎ 69113, 40 rm ℙ ⚏ ⚡ closed Apr-Jun and Sep-27 Dec, 40,000.

Recommended
Events: *nativity play* with traditional costumes (Jan).
Horseback riding: *Centro nazionale Turismo Equestre ANTE,* strada comunale for Roccaraso, ☎ 69334.

La MARSICA

From Pòpoli to Avezzano *(168 km, 1 day; map 3)*

The wild land of the Marsi (an Italic tribe that broke away from the Sabines) has an undeniable fascination. Over the centuries, the landscape has been altered, radically in parts. Nevertheless, La Marsica still offers varied and beautiful views and places to visit. Possible departure points are the Sulmona Valley and the plain of Fùcino (the latter is the site of a lake, reclaimed just over a century ago). The route winds through a surprising landscape of harsh peaks, dark gorges, sunny lakes and quiet woods.

▶ **Popoli** is at an important road junction at the entrance to the gorge of Pescara and contains the church of S. Francesco (15C façade) and the **Taverna ducale** (14C, originally a shop). From there, take the SS 17 SE through the Sulmona Valley to reach **Corfinio** and the **basilica of S. Pelino★** (r., → Corfinio). A detour to the **Badia Morronese** and **Fonte d'Amore** (l., → Sulmona) leads to **Sulmona** (→). The route continues along a side valley of the Sagittario. ▶ After reaching **Anversa degli Abruzzi,** take the fork N to **Cocullo,** a place famous for its procession of snake catchers. It takes place on the first Thursday in May and attracts a large gathering. Snakes are captured alive and wound around a statue of St. Dominic. ▶ Next, the route goes SE and across the spectacular **gola del Sagittario** (c. 10 km long and extremely deep). ▶ The road climbs steeply to **Lake Scanno,** which lies in the shadow of the Montagna Grande, and to Scanno (→). Next it climbs, amid beautiful scenery, to **Passo Godi** (5,131 ft), the highest point in the itinerary (view★). ▶ The route continues into the Sangro basin until **Villetta Barrea** (on the shore of an artificial lake) with its beautiful 16C and 18C houses. ▶ The road to Opi leads into the Abruzzi National Park (→). The first turn on the l. leads to **Camosciara** (3,609 ft) in an enchanting mountain setting. It is a 30-minute walk to the **cascata delle Ninfe** (waterfall over 328 ft high) and the **Rifugio Belvedere della Liscia** (4,462 ft). The second turn *(access on foot only)* goes to Val Fondillo. Visit the **grotta delle Fate** *(1:30-2 p.m.)* and the **passaggio dell'Orso** (5,485 ft). ▶ After **Opi** (4,101 ft), go past a gorge, then descend towards **Pescassèroli,** then up again to the **Passo del Diavolo** (4,593 ft). ▶ Next, the route goes to **Gioia dei Marsi** and on to Pescina (→ Celano). ▶ **San Benedetto dei Marsi** stands on the E edge of the plain, on the site of the ancient Marsi settlement of *Marruvium* (remains of *morroni* or Roman tombs). ▶ On the other side of the plain is **Trasacco.** Only a tower remains from the 12C castle. The church of **Ss. Rufino and Cesidio** (13C-17C) has separate portals for men and women. It contains sculptures spanning the period from the Romanesque to the Renaissance and traces of frescos. ▶ Finally, the route arrives at **Luco dei Marsi** and Avezzano (→). □

Practical information —————————————

COCULLO, ✉ 67030, ☎ 0864.

Recommended
Events: *snake catchers' procession* (May), ☎ 49117.

GIOIA DEI MARSI, ✉ 67055, ☎ 0863.
ⓘ v. Montagnano, ☎ 88838.

Hotel:
★★★★ *Filippone,* SS 83, ☎ 88111, 40 rm ℙ ⚡ ⚏ & ▣ 50,000; bkf: 3,000.

LUCO DEI MARSI, ✉ 67056, ☎ 0863.

Recommended
Horseback riding: *Circolo ippico La Petogna,* contrada Petogna, ☎ 528382 (associate of *ANTE*).

OPI, ✉ 67030, ☎ 0863.
ⓘ v. S. Giovanni, ☎ 91622.

⚲ *Le Foci di Opi,* at Le Foci di Opi, v. Fonti dei Cementi, 130 pl, ☎ 912233 (all year).

POPOLI, ✉ 65026, ☎ 085.
ⓘ next to Taverna Ducale.

Hotel:
★★★ *Tre Monti,* v. Tiburtina, ☎ 98481, 60 rm ℙ ⚡ 40,000.

Restaurant
♦ *Giuliani,* v. Capponi 33, ☎ 98214, closed Mon. Seafood: freshwater crayfish, grilled stuffed trout, 20/35,000.

Recommended
Wine: visits to the *Pietrantoni* vineyard, at Vittorito *(6 km S),* v. S. Sebastiano 38, ☎ 0864/727102 (Montepulciano, Cerasuolo, Trebbiano wines; groups by prior arrangement).

ORTONA

Chieti 29, L'Aquila 126, Rome 227 km
Pop. 22,029 ✉ 66026 ☎ 085   D3

Ortona lost much of its artistic and architectural heritage during the Second World War.

▶ Note the two Gothic portals of the **cathedral** (1312, rebuilt) and, opposite, the ceramic tile **monument to war victims.** Next to the cathedral is a **museum and art gallery** *(telephone in advance, ☎ 912393)* displaying paintings from the 14C onward, pottery, silverware and architectural exhibits. ▶ The unfinished **Palazzo Farnese** houses the **pinacoteca** exhibiting old paintings as well as contemporary works. ▶ In the church of **S. Francesco** is the cappella del Crocifisso containing a fresco to which a miracle was attributed in the 16C. ▶ To the NW are two beaches: **Lido Riccio** and **Lido dei Saraceni.** □

Practical information —————————————

ORTONA
≋
ⓘ p. Municipio, ☎ 912841.
⛴ hydrofoil daily (summer only) to the Tremiti Islands, *Adriatica,* ☎ 912650.

Hotel:
★★★ *D'Annunzio,* v. Giro degli Ulivi 11, ☎ 914401, 27 rm ℙ ⚡ No restaurant, 41,500.

Restaurant:
♦♦ *Miramare,* largo Farnese 15, ☎ 912593, closed Sun and 15 Nov-31 Dec. Seafood: stewed octopus, steamed prawns, 20/35,000.

Recommended
Events: *Corteo delle Chiavi d'Argento* (procession, first Sat in May); *Maggiolata Abruzzese* (folk singing) and *contemporary painting competition and exhibition* (Aug).
Marina: ☎ 912290.

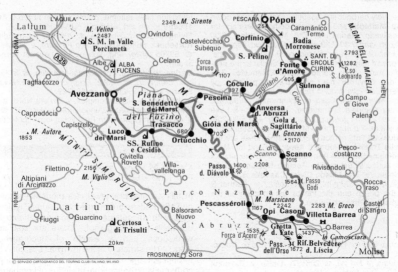

3. La Marsica

Sailing: *Lega Navale,* largo Giardini Eden; main office, v. Cervana (at Saraceni), ☎ 9061042.

Environs

LIDO RICCIO, ⊠ 66026, ☎ 085.
≋

Hotel:
★★★★ *Mara,* ☎ 9190416, 75 rm Ⓟ 🔄 ⊞ 🖪 ⁄° closed 16 Sep-14 May, 75,000.

⚓ *Torre Mucchia,* 52 pl, ☎ 9196298 (all year).

MARINA DI SAN VITO, ⊠ 66035, ☎ 0872.

Hotels:
★★★ *Garden,* contrada Portelle, ☎ 61164, 40 rm Ⓟ 🔄 ৬ ⊠ closed Nov-Mar except 1 Dec-10 Jan, 50,000.
★★ *Miramare,* v. Vespucci 1, ☎ 61072, 36 rm Ⓟ ৬ closed Christmas, 45,000.

PENNE

Pescara 31, L'Aquila 125, Rome 228 km
Pop. 11,907 ⊠ 65017 ☎ 085   C2

A town spanning two hills and characterized by a network of streets and alleyways (the *salita dell'Annunziata* is especially picturesque). It has a number of interesting buildings, mostly 16C; note the **Palazzo Friuli,** the **Palazzo del Bono** and also the medieval **Casa dei Vestini.**

▶ The **cathedral** contains a crypt that dates from the 10C, and, in the presbytery, the altar of Bishop Oderisio (1182-90). ▶ In the Palazzo Vescovile next door is the **Museo Civico-Diocesano** *(9 a.m.-12 noon and 4-7 p.m. Jul-Sep; at other times apply to parish priest).* Note the 14C wooden crucifix and the processional cross by Nicola da Guardiagrele. ▶ There is another processional cross by the same artist in the church of **S. Giovanni** (14C apse and campanile). ▶ The church of **S. Agostino** has a late 15C campanile. ▶ The church of **S. Maria in Colleromano** (14C) stands on a slope just outside the Baro-

que porta di S. Francesco. It has a 13C-14C portal and Baroque altars.

Environs

▶ **Farindola** (5,019 ft, *15 km*) and **Rigopiano** (4,101 ft, *24 km*), both resorts on the slopes of the Gran Sasso, offer splendid views. ▶ 20 km S is **Civitella Casanova** and the nearby **La Rupe** zoo and park. 9.6 km farther is **Carpineto della Nora,** with the evocative remains of the 10C Badia di S.Bartolomeo nearby. ☐

Practical information ─────────────

PENNE

Restaurant:
♦♦ *Calesse,* largo S. Francesco 2, ☎ 8279014, closed Tue. Converted 18C olive press. Regional cuisine: ravioli di ricotta, lamb with cheese and egg, 15/28,000.

Recommended
Cheese: visits to *Ilex* cheese factory at Elice *(20 km N),* v. Lungofino 141, ☎ 9609195 (by prior arrangement).

Environs

CIVITELLA CASANOVA, ⊠ 65010, ☎ 085, 20 km S.

Recommended
Animal park: *La Rupe,* ☎ 845192.

PESCARA

L'Aquila 97, Rome 208, Milan 570 km
Pop. 131,974 ⊠ 65100 ☎ 085   D2

Pescara originally consisted of two villages, Pescara and Castellammare Adriatico on either side of the mouth of a canal. They gradually merged into a single town, which now shares, with L'Aquila, the status of regional capital.

► N of the lively harbour is a beautiful seafront walk down **lungomare Matteotti** and the **viale della Riviera** as far as **Montesilvano Marina.** ► The **Museo Ittico** *(8:30 a.m.-1:30 p.m. and 2:30-7:30 p.m. mid-Jun-mid Sep, a.m. only the rest of the year; closed hols)* has collections, including one of fishing equipment. ► Parallel to the seafront is the main street, **corso Vittorio Emanuele.** The **Palazzo del Governo** has a renowned painting by F.P. Michetti, *La Figlia di Jorio (business hrs).* ► In the S part of the town is the **Casa di D'Annunzio** (birthplace of the writer Gabriele D'Annunzio, 1863-1938; → Lake Garda; *9 a.m.-2 p.m.; Jul-Aug 9 a.m.-1.p.m. and 5:30-7:30 p.m.; hols 9 a.m.-2 p.m.; closed Mon).* The museum contains antiques and mementos. In the same house are the **Museo delle Tradizioni Popolari Abruzzesi** and the **Mostra Archeologica Didattica Permanente.** ► D'Annunzio's mother is buried in the nearby **Tempio Nazionale della Conciliazione.** ► The **Museo Civico Cascella** is in viale Marconi *(8:30 a.m.-1:30 p.m.; closed hols).* ► Farther S between the beach and the Pineta Dannunziana is the garden suburb of **Pescara Pineta.**   □

Practical information ―――――――――――――

≋
ⓘ v. Nicola Fabrizi 171, ☎ 4211707; p. Sacro Cuore, ☎ 378110.
✈ v. Tiburtina *(4 km W),* ☎ 206197; *Alitalia,* v. Ravenna 3, ☎ 26632. Bus from p. Stazione.
▒▒▒ ☎ 378172.
▒▒▒▒ from p. Stazione.
▃▃▃ car ferry to Split (Yugoslavia), daily Jul-mid-Sep except Sat and Sun, Banchina Sud, ☎ 65247; *Ferry Boat,* Stazione Marittima, ☎ 63792.
Car rental: *Avis,* corso Vittorio Emanuele 16/18, ☎ 23442; *Hertz,* v.Tiburtina 289/1, ☎ 53900; *Maggiore,* v. Piave 10, ☎ 389167.

Hotels:
★★★★ *Carlton,* v. Riviera 35, ☎ 373125, 71 rm Ⓟ 93,000.
★★★★ *Esplanade,* p. I Maggio 46, ☎ 292141, 145 rm Ⓟ ⟨ ঙ ✺ 120,000; bkf: 15,000.
★★★ *Maja,* v. Riviera 201, ☎ 71545, 44 rm ✺ 65,000; bkf: 6,000.
★★★ *Plaza Moderno,* p. Sacro Cuore 55, ☎ 375148, 70 rm ✺ 63,500.
★★★ *Regent,* lungomare Colombo 64, ☎ 60641, 127 rm Ⓟ closed 16 Nov-28 Feb, 52,000; bkf: 6,000.
★★ *Ambra,* v. Forti 38, ☎ 378247, 55 rm Ⓟ 48,000; bkf: 2,000.

Restaurants:
● ♦♦♦ *Guerino,* v. Riviera 4, ☎ 23065, closed Tue except summer. Along most elegant part of beach, with beautiful terraces overlooking sea. Excellent seafood: fish with ham, mixed roast fish, homemade wines, 30/45,000.
♦♦ *Nastro Azzurro,* p. Rinascita 20/3, ☎ 22475, closed Tue, Wed and 20 Oct-20 Nov. Mixed cuisine: linguine with cuttlefish sauce, baked sea bass with potatoes, 20/35,000.
♦♦ *Terrazza Verde,* largo Madonna 6, ☎ 413239, closed Wed and Christmas. Service outside in summer. Regional cuisine: potato gnocchi, pappardelle with goose sauce, 20/25,000.
♦ *La Cantina di Jozz,* v. delle Caserme 61, ☎ 690383, closed Sun eve, Mon, May and Dec. Regional cuisine, 15/22,000.

⚓ *Internazionale,* lungomare Colombo, 100 pl, ☎ 65653.

Recommended
Ceramics: visits to the *Cerartis* workshop, at Sambuceto *(6 km SE),* v. Salara (industrial zone), ☎ 2060156.
Children's facilities: *Parco Davalos,* at the beginning of the SS to Francavilla, ☎ 28246 (8 a.m.-8 p.m., free admission).
Cycling: *G.S. Grande,* corso V. Emanuele 368, ☎ 206161; *G.S. Marano,* lungomare Emanuele 34, ☎ 21482; *G.S. Marano,* v. De Amicis 20, ☎ 23848.
Events: *international jazz festival* (Jul), the *Ennio Flaiano international competition* in drama, film, literature and

television (Jul), summer drama season at the D'Annunzio Theatre (open air), *Matteotti cycling trophy* (Jul).
Flying: airport, v. Tiburtina, ☎ 2069887 (also gliding).
Horseback riding: *Club ippico Pescara,* v. D'Avalos 204, ☎ 60766 (show ring, school; international horse show in Jul).
Marina: ☎ 694140; *Pescara* nautical club, ☎ 374230; *Circolo Canottieri,* ☎ 28382, *Gruppo vela Lega Navale.*
Sports arena: v. Elettra, ☎ 692929.
Swimming: *Le Najadi* complex, v. Riviera Nord, ☎ 71435.
Wine: *Enoteca Europa,* lungofiume Paolucci 67, ☎ 28355.
♥ gastronomy: *parrozzo* (traditional local confection).

PESCOCOSTANZO

L'Aquila 95, Rome 191 km
Pop. 1,385 ⊠ 67033 ☎ 0864   C4

In this architectural jewel in a mountain setting, 15C and 16C houses are mingled with *vignali,* typical dwellings with an outside staircase and landing and an unusually protruding roof. There are also artisans' workshops and a wealth of decorative stone work. The structure of the town has scarcely changed throughout the centuries. It boasts a tradition of craftsmanship dating from the influx of Lombard craftsmen into the area from the 15C to the 18C. There is a flourishing cottage industry in pillow-lace making; traditional filigree and wrought-iron work continue.

► The **collegiate church★** of S. Maria del Colle is one of the most interesting in Abruzzi. It contains a wealth of stucco and wood and bronze work. It has beautiful 17C coffered ceilings, a set of 18C wrought-iron railings and an 11C wooden polychrome statue of the Madonna del Colle. ► The **museum** nearby displays paintings, sculpture and silver *(telephone in advance,* ☎ *66130).* ► P. Umberto I is enclosed on all sides by 16C-17C buildings, including the former monastery of S. Scolastica. More beautiful houses are in and near the corso Roma. ► 7 km away is **Bosco di Sant'Antonio,** where a hermitage stands in a beech forest.   □

Practical information ―――――――――――――

PESCOCOSTANZO
⛷ ski lifts, cross-country skiing, ski instruction.

Recommended
Crafts: pillow lace, carved wooden articles, jewelry.
Youth hostel: *Ostello Le Torri,* v. Roma 23, ☎ 66112.

Environs
BOSCO SANT'ANTONIO, ⊠ 67033, ☎ 0864, 7 km W.

Restaurant:
♦♦ *Faggeto,* ☎ 67100, closed Fri. Regional cuisine: tacconi with broccoli, polenta with sausage, 20/25,000.

PIANELLA

Pescara 18, L'Aquila 95, Rome 206 km
Pop. 6,913 ⊠ 65019 ☎ 085   C3

On a slope just NW of Pianella is the Romanesque church of **S. Maria Maggiore** (12C, *keys from the house nearby)* containing a 12C pulpit★ and 12C-15C frescos. 7 km NE is **Moscufo.** In the 12C church of **S. Maria del Lago** *(keys from the house to the r. opposite the cemetery)* is a splendid pulpit★ by Nicodemo da Guardiagrele (1159), as well as remains of 13C-14C frescos. 27 km SW is **Civitaquana,** whose parish church of **S. Maria delle Grazie** has an interesting interior.   □

PRATA D'ANSIDONIA

L'Aquila 22, Rome 141 km
Pop. 645 ⊠ 67020 ☎ 0862   B3

The Baroque parish church of **S. Nicola** contains a magnificent ambo★ (1240; *apply to the caretaker in the house nearby*), which was originally in the church of S. Paolo di Peltuino (→). 2 km away on a hill are the ruins of the ancient town of Peltuinum. Stretches of wall and remains of the theatre can be seen; excavations are in progress. Nearby *(accessible on foot only)* is the former church of **S. Paolo di Peltuino,** which was rebuilt in the 12C-13C with Roman materials.   □

ROCCARASO

L'Aquila 97, Rome 189 km
Pop. 1,650 ⊠ 67037 ☎ 0864   C-D5

Roccaraso is a vacation and winter sports resort in a wooded setting on the **piano del Prato.**

▶ About 3 km away on the Cinquemiglia plateau (→ La Maiella) is the **Laghetto Pantaniello.** ▶ 5 km E, overlooking the Sangro Valley, is **Pietransieri.** ▶ From the **sacrario di M. Zurrone** *(c. 8 km)* are splendid views of the Cinquemiglia and Prato plateaus. ▶ 9 km away on a scenic road *(or chair lift)* is the **Aremogna plateau** (4,593-5,249 ft), frequented by skiers.   □

Practical information _____

ROCCARASO
⌇ cable-car station, ski lifts, cross-country skiing, ski instruction, skating.
ⓘ v. Roma 60, ☎ 62210.

Hotels:
★★★ *Excelsior,* v. Roma 29, ☎ 62479, 38 rm ℗ ⌇ closed 11 Apr-30 Jun and 6 Sep-19 Dec, 46,000.
★★★ *Grande Albergo,* v. Roma 21, ☎ 62124, 60 rm ℗ closed 11 Apr-30 Jun and 16 Sep-7 Dec, 50,000; bkf: 5,000.
★★★ *Iris,* v. Iris 5, ☎ 62194, 40 rm, 50,000; bkf: 10,000.
★★★ *MotelAgip,* SS 17 at 136-km marker, ☎ 62443, 57 rm ℗ ☖ ⌇ 51,000; bkf: 10,000.
★★★ *Suisse,* v. Roma 22, ☎ 62139, 48 rm ℗ ⌇ 40,000; bkf: 5,000.

Environs

AREMOGNA, ⊠ 67030, ☎ 0864, 9 km SW.

Hotel:
★★★ *Boschetto,* ☎ 62297, 48 rm ℗ ⌇ ⌇ ⌇ closed 16 Apr-30 Jun and 1 Sep-30 Nov, 36,000; bkf: 8,000.

⚓ *Del Sole,* at Piana del Leone, 100 pl, ☎ 62532.

SAN CLEMENTE A CASAURIA**

Pescara 37, L'Aquila 52 km
Pop. 180 ⊠ 65020 ☎ 085   C3

This abbey was founded in the 9C near the ancient settlement of *Interpromium;* it was restored in the 12C. It is one of the most beautiful examples in Abruzzi of the transition in style from Romanesque to Cistercian Gothic *(apply to warden).* In the centre of the splendid portico★ is a door★ with bronze wings (1192). The simplicity of the interior sets off the elaborate pulpit★, which is supported by four columns. Treasures include a 13C Paschal candelabrum and a beautiful ciborium taken from an early Christian sarcophagus. The cross-vaulted crypt survives from the older building.   □

SAN CLEMENTE AL VOMANO

Teramo 29, L'Aquila 102 km
⊠ 64024 ☎ 085   C2

This church was built in the 9C and rebuilt in 1108. It has a Romanesque portal. Inside are a magnificent ciborium★, capitals made from Roman materials, and a statue of St. Clement. A few km away is the Romanesque-Gothic church of **S. Maria di Propezzano,** which contains 15C frescos *(keys from the house nearby).* The convent next door has a spacious cloister with 17C frescos by a Polish artist, S. Maiesky.   □

Practical information _____

Restaurant:
◆◆ *Tre Archi,* at Guardia Vomano, SS 150, ☎ 898140, closed Wed and Nov. Regional cuisine, 20/30,000.

SAN GIOVANNI IN VENERE*

Chieti 49, L'Aquila 146 km
                                            D-E3

This is one of the most interesting churches in Abruzzi, dating from the 8C, but rebuilt in 1165 and renovated since. In the façade is the della luna **portal★.** Both sides are decorated with reliefs of alternating sacred and profane scenes. The interior is Cistercian in its simplicity. The conjoined monastery has a spacious, bright cloister.   □

Practical information _____

Hotel:
★★★ *Giardino,* at Fossacesia, v. della Marina 69/71, ☎ 607359, 26 rm ℗ ⌇ 48,000; bkf: 3,000.

SANTA MARIA ARABONA*

Pescara 26, L'Aquila 70 km
                                            C-D3

Situated among pine trees on a hill overlooking Manoppello Scalo, this 13C church is the earliest example of Cistercian Gothic architecture in Abruzzi *(private, visitors allowed).* The presbytery contains a Paschal candelabrum and a fine tabernacle. The walls are decorated with frescos.   □

SCANNO

L'Aquila 106, Rome 155 km
Pop. 2,644 ⊠ 67038 ☎ 0864   C4

At Scanno, the picturesque mountain landscape blends with the quaint architecture in the old part of town, where medieval, Renaissance and Baroque architecture coexist. The women's traditional costume is reminiscent of the Balkans, as is the antique jewelry worn on special occasions and the design of the pillow lace and gold- and silverware made by local craftsmen. The best time to savour the atmosphere is when a wedding is in progress. However, any Sunday women can be seen in the traditional dress: full black or dark blue skirt, puffed sleeves, a small hat worn at a slight angle and a bodice with silver buttons.

▶ The old part of town, on the hillside, has narrow streets with steps flanked by **rows of 15C-16C houses** and small palazzi. ▶ The church of **S. Eustachio** has an interesting Romanesque portal. ▶ 2 km away is **Lake Scanno** (3,254 ft), the largest natural lake in Abruzzi, in which the surrounding mountains are reflected. ▶ There is a magnificent view from **Mt. Rotondo**, which can be reached by chair lift. □

Practical information _____

Ƨ ski lifts, instruction.
ⓘ v. S. Maria della Valle 12, ☎ 74317.

Hotels:
★★★ *Mille Pini*, ☎ 74387, 19 rm Ⓟ ⚹ ⚌ ⚘ 48,000; bkf: 7,000.
★★★ *Park Hotel*, v. Riviera 6, ☎ 74624, 67 rm Ⓟ ⚹ ⚘ 45,000; bkf: 8,000.
★★★ *Seggiovia*, v. Tanturri 42, ☎ 74371, 26 rm ⚘ 40,000; bkf: 6,000.
★★★ *Vittoria*, v. Di Rienzo 46, ☎ 74398, 27 rm Ⓟ ⚹ ⚘ ⚲ 48,000; bkf: 8,000.
★★ *Belvedere*, p. S. Maria della Valle 3, ☎ 74314, 32 rm ⚹ ⚘ 40,000; bkf: 5,000.

Restaurant:
♦♦ *Archetti*, v. Silla 8, ☎ 74645, closed Tue except summer. Reconstruction of old-fashioned tavern in cellar of 16C building. Regional cuisine: beans with mountain herbs, charcoal-grilled trout, 22/30,000.

Recommended
Events: *Festival of S. Antonio* and *Travi procession* (15-16 Jun), *theatre in the square, wedding procession and folk festival* (Aug), *Sagra del coregone* and *end-of-year procession* (Dec).
Swimming: v. del Lago, ☎ 747251.

SIRENTE PLATEAU

B3-4

The Sirente plateau is divided by the plains of Ovíndoli and Rocca di Mezzo and traversed by 14 km of winding, picturesque road, which runs from Ovíndoli to Rocca di Cambio. The few scattered villages are medieval in appearance.

▶ From **Ovíndoli** (4,511 ft), the length of the plateau stretching toward the NW is visible. ▶ Farther on is **Rovere** (4,635 ft), after which the road narrows toward **Rocca di Mezzo** (4,360 ft), with its interesting old houses. The sacristy of the parish church *(apply to the parish priest, ☎ 91396; currently being reorganized)* contains church articles, wooden statues and 15C reliquaries. ▶ Finally the route arrives at **Rocca di Cambio** (4,701 ft), the highest village in Abruzzi. **Serralunga** (5,626 ft, accessible by chair lift) is above the ski stations of the **plain of Campo Felice** (5,003 ft), which can also be reached by road from **Lùcoli.** □

Practical information _____

OVÍNDOLI, ✉ 67046, ☎ 0863.
Ƨ ski lifts, instruction.

Hotels:
★★★ *Magnola Palace*, v. del Ceraso 89, ☎ 705144, 80 rm Ⓟ ⚹ ⚌ ⚘ ▭ ⚲ closed Nov, 60,000; bkf: 4,000.
★★★ *Moretti*, v. del Ceraso 30, ☎ 705174, 40 rm Ⓟ ⚹ ⚌ ⚘ 60,000.
★★★ *Park Hotel*, v. del Ceraso, ☎ 705221, 58 rm Ⓟ ⚌ 60,000.

ROCCA DI CAMBIO, ✉ 67047, ☎ 0862.
Ƨ ski lifts, cross-country skiing, instruction, sled run at Campo Felice.
ⓘ municipio, ☎ 918107; Società Campo Felice, ☎ 912003.

ROCCA DI MEZZO, ✉ 67048, ☎ 0862.
Ƨ ski lifts at Rovere.
ⓘ municipio, ☎ 91316.

Hotel:
★★★★ *Caldora*, v. Colli della Mula, ☎ 917174, 80 rm Ⓟ ⚹ ⚹ ⚲ closed Easter-14 Jun and 16 Sep-Christmas, 48,000; bkf: 5,000.

Restaurant:
♦♦ *Ruota*, largo Barberini 1/B, ☎ 91488, closed Mon, 20/30,000.

S. MARIA IN VALLE PORCLANETA*

L'Aquila 71 km

B4

It is worth negotiating the difficult 3-km route from Rosciolo de' Marsi to see this 11C Romanesque church. The interior *(caretaker at Rosciolo, at no. 45, near the crossroads)* is divided by a rare iconostasis (12C) and contains an interesting pulpit★ (1150). At **Rosciolo de' Marsi** is the picturesque church complex of **S. Maria della Grazie.** □

SULMONA

L'Aquila 68, Rome 154 km
Pop. 24,293 ✉ 67039 ☎ 0864

C4

'Sulmo mihi patria est' (Sulmo is my homeland), Ovid declared; consequently, the town's coat of arms bears the letters SMPE. There are other reminders of Ovid in the Fonte d'Amore and the so-called Villa d'Ovidio. The outstanding feature of the town, however, is the successive blending of architectural styles (medieval, Renaissance, Baroque), which is at its most harmonious in the church of the Annunziata and the adjacent palazzo. The town is surrounded by the Sulmona Valley, with the outlines of the Gran Sasso, Sirente, Genzana and Maiella in the distance.

▶ The **Annunziata★** (originally 14C) consists of a Baroque church and a Gothic-Renaissance **palazzo★** (15C-16C). ▶ The palazzo houses the **Museo Civico** *(in the process of rearrangement)*, which displays archaeological remains, medieval sculptures, 14C-17C paintings and a magnificent collection of jewelry (14C-15C). ▶ In p. del Carmine stands the church of **S. Francesco della Scarpa** with its remarkable 13C Gothic portal★. ▶ Next to it is the Renaissance **Fontana del Vecchio.** ▶ The church of **S. Maria della Tomba** has a 15C façade. Inside are remains of 15C frescos and a 17C terra-cotta *Madonna and Child*. ▶ Inside the **Duomo** (S. Panfilo) is a 13C wooden *Crucifixion.* The crypt contains a magnificent 12C Byzantine-style **relief★** *(Enthroned Madonna)*, a silver engraved and enamelled bust of St. Panfilo (15C) and a 12C bishop's chair.

Environs

▶ 5 km N is the **Badia Morronese** (or di S. Spirito), a complex of monastery buildings dating from the 12C, now used as a prison. Nearby are the remains of the **santuario di Ercole Curino** (1C BC), or the Villa d'Ovidio as it is also called (stretches of wall, traces of fresco, a mosaic floor). On the same site is what is said to have been Ovid's **Fonte d'Amore.** A little farther is the church of **S. Onofrio,** containing the 13C altar where Pope Celestine V used to celebrate mass. From here, there is a view★ of the entire Sulmona Valley. ▶ 8 km E at the foot of Mt. Morrone are **Pacentro** and the towers of Cantelmo Castle (14C). □

Practical information _____

SULMONA
ⓘ v. Roma 21, ☎ 53276.

Hotels:
★★★ *Europa Park,* SS 17, ☎ 34641, 105 rm [P] ▦ 🖕 ❄
♨ 62,000; bkf: 7,000.
★★ *Armando's,* v. Montenero 15, ☎ 31252, 18 rm [P]
❄ 34,000.

Restaurants:
◆ *Cesidio,* p. Solimo 25, ☎ 52724, closed Fri. Regional cuisine: sagne with beans, charcoal-grilled lamb, 15/25,000.
◆ *Clemente,* vico del Vecchio 11, ☎ 52284, closed Thu and Christmas. In 19C building near Fontana del Vecchio. Regional cuisine: penne verdi with mushrooms, fritto misto, homemade wines, 16/22,000.

Recommended
Events: *trade fair of craft work* from Abruzzi and Molise (Jul-Aug).
❦ gastronomy: sugared almonds, Abruzzi cassate.

Environs

PACENTRO, ⊠ 67030, ☎ 0864, 8 km E.

Recommended
Events: *Corsa degli Zingari* (horse races, Sep), Comune, ☎ 41114.

Pope Celestine V

The Morronese abbey near Sulmona is now a prison. It was founded by Pietro Angeleri (according to a chronicler, 'a hermit who led a life of harshest penitence'), who drew Benedictine anchorites to the site. His own hermitage was on higher ground, half way up Mt. Morrone near the church of S. Onofrio. After the death of Pope Nicholas IV, the cardinals, who were assembled in Perugia, could not agree on a successor and the papacy remained vacant for two years. Finally, they chose Pietro Angeleri who was crowned Pope Celestine V on 29 May 1294 in L'Aquila. He remained pope for a mere five months and nine days, after which he abdicated and fled to Mt. Sant'Angelo on the Gargano to resume his hermit's life. He was accused by Dante of cowardice, but the chronicler, more charitable, said that he resigned for the good of his soul. He was succeeded by Boniface VIII who, fearing that Celestine's controversial resignation might be used to incite a schism, imprisoned him in Monte Fumone castle near Alatri. Less than two years later, Celestine died. He was canonized by Pope Clement V in 1313.

TAGLIACOZZO

L'Aquila 76, Rome 91 km
Pop. 6,383 ⊠ 67069 ☎ 0863   A4

The **Palazzo Ducale** *(under restoration)* was built by the Orsini family in the 14C. On one side is a frescoed loggia. The chapel also contains frescos. The Gothic church of **S. Francesco** has a simple interior with cross vaulting. Piazzetta Argoli and p. dell'Obelisco are both surrounded by elegant 15C-16C houses with loggias.

Environs

▶ 2 km SE, near the **santuario di S. Maria dell'Oriente,** is a small museum of oriental exhibits. ▶ 12 km away in the valley below **Cappadocia** are the **sorgenti del Liri** (springs). Above Cappadocia is the ski resort of **Campo**

Rotondo (4,593 ft). ▶ 15 km away, on the slopes of Mt. Midia (5,702 ft), is another ski resort, **Marsia** (4,757 ft).☐

Practical information

TAGLIACOZZO
ⓘ p. Argoli, ☎ 6318.

Hotel:
★★★ *Miramonti,* variante Tiburtina Valeria 87, ☎ 6581, 22 rm [P] ▦ ♨ 42,000.

⚐ *Velino,* v. Tiburtina Valeria, 200 pl, ☎ 6253 (all year).

Recommended
Archery: *Compagnia Arcieri del Cavaliere,* at Càrsoli (25 km NW), v. Roma 10, ☎ 99254.
Cycling: *G.S. Donzelli,* v. XXIV Maggio 4, ☎ 6422.
Horseback riding: *Circolo ippico Valle Verde,* v. Secondo Castello 8 (associate of *ANTE*).

Environs

MARSIA, ☎ 67060, ☎ 0863.
⌇ ski lifts.

TERAMO

L'Aquila 74, Rome 185, Milan 550 km
Pop. 51,438 ⊠ 64100 ☎ 0861   B-C2

The Romans called the town *Interamnia Praetutiorum:* 'between the rivers of the Pretuzi'. The two rivers, the Tordino and the Vezzola, still run on either side. Only recently has proof of the existence of the Roman town been brought to light. Numerous buildings exist from the medieval and Renaissance periods. The modern town has expanded W, away from its original strategic position between the rivers. ▶ The buildings of historic and artistic interest are concentrated in the **old part** of the town, which is largely E of p. Martiri della Libertà (A-B2). The **cathedral★** (B2) was built in the 12C and extended in the 14C. In the centre of the façade is a Gothic portal (1332). The interior contains a polyptych★ and a silver **altar frontal★** by Nicola da Guardiagrele. It consists of thirty-four square panels plus a rectangular one. ▶ Along largo dell'Anfiteatro are the remains of the **Roman theatre** and **amphitheatre** (B2). ▶ In largo Melatini (B2) are the medieval **casa dei Signori di Melatino** and the 13C-14C Romanesque-Gothic church of **S. Antonio** (B2). ▶ Corso De Michetti leads to Porta Reale and the spacious p. Caduti della Libertà. At the far end of the latter is the church of the **Madonna delle Grazie** (B3), which contains a polychrome wood *Madonna and Child.* ▶ The **Villa Comunale** houses the **Museo e Pinacoteca Civica** (A1; *9 a.m.-2 p.m. and 3-7 p.m. Jun and Sep; 9:30 a.m.-2.00 p.m. Mon; 9:30 a.m.-12:30 p.m. hols*) containing 15C-18C paintings and majolica work from Castelli.   ☐

Practical information

ⓘ v. del Castello 10 (A1), ☎ 54243.
✈ at Pescara, ☎ 085/206245; *Alitalia,* p. Martiri della Libertà (A-B2), ☎ 53441.
🚌 (B3), ☎ 411732.
🚕 from p. S. Francesco (A2-3).

Hotels:
★★★ *Abruzzi,* v. Mazzini 18 (A1 a), ☎ 53043, 50 rm [P] ❄ No restaurant, 59,000; bkf: 5,000.
★★★ *Sporting,* v. De Gasperi 41 (A2-3 b), ☎ 414723, 55 rm [P] ▦ ❄ ▤ 70,000; bkf: 6,000.

Restaurants:
◆◆◆ *Duomo,* v. Stazio 9 (B2 c), ☎ 311274, closed Mon. Regional cuisine: scrippelle 'mbusse, charcoal-grilled lamb and kid, 20/30,000.
◆ *Tre Galli,* v. 558174, closed Mon. Regional cuisine: mozzarella allateramana, galantine of turkey, 20/28,000.

TERAMO

0   100   200 m

1 : 15 000 (1 cm=150 m)

© SERVIZIO CARTOGRAFICO DEL TOURING CLUB ITALIANO, MILANO

Penne km 66

Recommended

Craft workshops: *A. Perticari,* at Nepezzano, strada Nazionale, ☎ 558143 (hand-woven rugs and fabrics).
Events: *Giugno Teramano* (prose, poetry, folklore, gastronomy; May-Jul), ☎ 3241.
Sports arena: v. Ponte Vezzola, ☎ 552470.
Swimming: v. Acquaviva, ☎ 410428.
Tennis: v. De Albentiis; v. Acquaviva, ☎ 411649.
♥ gastronomy: local sweets, charcuterie, herb-based cordials.

VASTO

Chieti 71, L'Aquila 166, Rome 271 km
Pop. 31,234 ⊠ 66054 ☎ 0873   E3-4

According to tradition, Vasto was founded by Diomedes on his return from the Trojan War. It stands on the site of a Roman settlement. Still visible are remains of an amphitheatre, reservoirs and fragments of walls in an area that was once hit by a landslide (and is now an archaeological walk).

▶ In the town centre, the **Duomo** retains the portal from the original 13C building. The **Palazzo D'Avalos** (18C) will house the **Museo Civico** (*10 a.m.-12 noon and 6-10 p.m.; apply to town hall or, if closed, tourist office*), which contains archaeological exhibits, some of them from the necropolis of *Histonium,* and an art gallery with works by artists from Abruzzi. ▶ The **castle** dates from the 13C. ▶ The church of **S. Maria Maggiore** (11C, 14C campanile) contains a painting of the *Spiritual Marriage of St. Catherine* attributed to Veronese. ▶ On the coast nearby is **Marina di Vasto.**   □

Practical information

VASTO
ⓘ p. del Popolo 18, ☎ 2312.

Hotel:
★★ *Panoramic,* v. Smargiassi 1, ☎ 2700, 44 rm ℗ 46,000; bkf: 4,000.

Restaurants:
● ♦♦♦ *Corsaro,* at Porto di Vasto, ☎ 50113, closed Mon in winter. With beach area. Seafood: membretti with shrimps, mixed fried or roast fish, 35/50,000.
♦♦ *Jeannot,* loggia Amplingh, ☎ 55000, closed Tue and Christmas. View over gulf. Excellent seafood: cavatelli, roast fish, 20/45,000.

Recommended
Events: *organ music festival* (Jul-Aug).
Marina: ☎ 50340.

Environs

MARINA DI VASTO, ⊠ 66055, ☎ 0873, 2 km SE.
≈

ⓘ v. Dalmazia, ☎ 2180 (summer).

Hotels:
★★★ *Caravel,* v. Dalmazia 124, ☎ 53053, 18 rm ℗ ⩗ ⫶ No restaurant, 45,000; bkf: 5,000.
★★★ *President,* v. Dalmazia 136, ☎ 801444, 68 rm ℗ ⩗ ⫶ 50,000; bkf: 5,000.
★★★ *Royal,* v. Dalmazia 100, ☎ 801950, 28 rm ℗ ⫶ closed Dec-Mar, 50,000; bkf: 4,000.
★★★ *Sabrina,* contrada S. Tommaso, ☎ 801449, 73 rm ℗ ⫶ 50,000; bkf: 4,000.
★★★ *Sporting,* contrada S. Tommaso, ☎ 801464, 22 rm ℗ ⫶ 46,000; bkf: 6,000.

⋏ *Sea Garden,* at S. Tommaso, 175 pl, ☎ 801097; *Uliveto,* at Casarsa, 120 pl, ☎ 55952.

Apulia

▶ With miles of beaches, clear water and a sunny blue sky, Apulia resembles paradise. Around Foggia is the largest plain in Italy after that of the Po River in the N. It consists of huge grain fields, while the rest of the region, especially round Bari and Matera, abounds with olive groves, vineyards, orchards and vegetable gardens. The great mountainous peninsula of Gargano extends into the Adriatic Sea for more than thirty miles. It is covered with deep forests that hide small villages. The *gravina* in the Murgia region inland from Bari is a rocky fissure running across the land and splitting it into numerous gorges and ravines. This was a delight for medieval hermits and anchorites who dug caves into its steep cliffs and decorated them with Byzantine frescos. The artistic treasures of the region equal in importance those of most other parts of Italy: it was here that the influences of Romanesque, Byzantine, Arab, Lombard and Norman architecture converged and were absorbed, resulting in magnificent cathedrals and majestic castles that men have never ceased to admire. The *trulli* are amazing constructions that do not aspire to architectural distinction. They are cylinder-shaped houses with a cone top that stand in rows along certain village streets, often inhabited by the same family for generations. They go back to the Stone Age, although many of the existing ones are copies of older ones. Throughout Apulia the people are warm and friendly. They were kept in semi-slavery by feudal barons and invading hordes for centuries, but today, with their astounding agricultural development, they enjoy a good life. □

 ## Don't miss

At Bari★★, the Cathedral★★ and S. Nicola★★; at Bitonto★, the Cathedral★★; the Castel del Monte★★; the grottos★★ of Castellana; at Lecce★★, S. Croce★★; near Manfredonia, S. Maria di Siponto★★; Monte Sant'Angelo★, la Foresta Umbra★ and the picturesque coastal towns of the Gargano peninsula; at Taranto★, the Museo Nazionale★★; at Trani★, the Cathedral★★ and at Troia, the Cathedral★★.

Facts and figures

Location: *Apulia is at the heel of the boot. The heel, however, represents only one third of its territory because it extends inland along the Adriatic coast as far as the Gargano peninsula. The medieval division of the region — the Capitanata in the N, the Terra di Bari in the middle and the Terra di Otranto in the S — is almost the same today. The Capitanata covers the Gargano peninsula and the Tavoliere plain. The Terra di Bari covers the Murgie, a succession of plateaus, and the Terra di Otranto comprises the hilly peninsula of Salento, the easternmost part of Italy between the Gulf of Taranto and the Adriatic Sea. The archipelago of the Tremite Islands, in the Adriatic, is part of this region.*
Area: *19,348 sq km.*
Climate: *Mediterranean, with blue skies and heat in summer (Foggia is said to be the warmest town in Italy); variable in other seasons, rain limited to the autumn months; snow is rare and early spring is often very warm.*
Population: *3,946,871 inhabitants.*
Administration: *The capital of Apulia is Bari; the other four provincial capital towns are Brindisi, Foggia, Lecce and Taranto.*

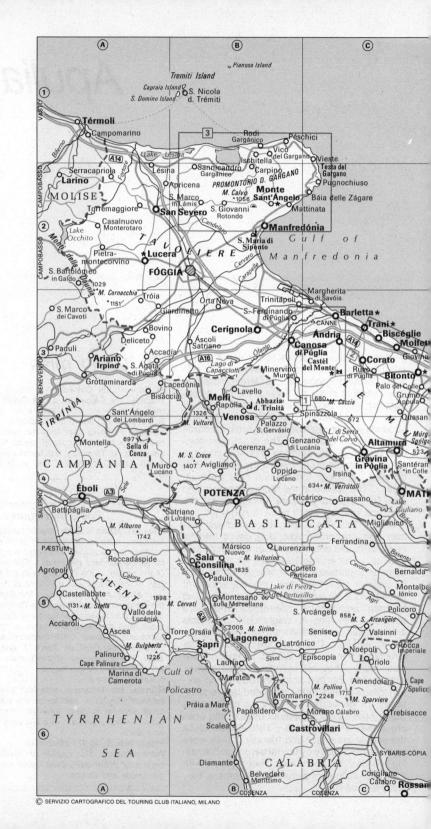

Ⓐ　　　　　Ⓑ　　　　　Ⓒ

◦ *Pianosa Island*

Tremiti Island

Capraia Island ◦ S. Nicola
S. Domino Island ◦ d. Trémiti

① ◦ Térmoli
◦ Campomarino

◦ Rodi　　◦ Péschici
Gargánico

◦ Vico
del Gargano ◦ Vieste

◦ Serracapriola　Lésina ◦ Sannicandro　Ischitella
　　　　　　　　　Gargánico　◦ Carpino　◦ Testa del
Larino　　◦ Apricena　　　　　　　　　　Gargano
　　　　　　　　　　　PROMONTÓRIO D. GARGANO ◦ Pugnochiuso
MOLISE　　◦ S. Marco　M. Calvo
　　　　　in Lámis　▲1056　Monte
◦ Torremaggiore　　◦ S. Giovanni　Sant'Angelo　◦ Báia delle Zágare
　　　　　　San Severo　Rotondo　　　　　◦ Mattinata

② ◦ Casalnuovo
Lake　　Monterotaro
Occhito
　　　　◦ Pietra-
Monti della Daunia　montecorvino
◦ S. Bartolómeo
in Galdo　1029
　　　▲ M. Cornacchia
◦ S. Marco　1151
dei Cavoti
　　◦ Bovino

◦ Lucera

FÓGGIA

TAVOLIERE

◦ S. Maria di
Siponto

Manfredónia

Gulf of

Manfredonia

◦ Tróia
◦ Giardinetto
◦ Orta Nuova　◦ Trinitápoli
　　　　　　　　　　◦ Margherita
　　　　　　　　　　di Savóia
S-Ferdinando
di Púglia　　Barletta ★
◦ Cerignola　　　CANNE　Trani ★

◦ Paduli

③ ◦ Ariano
Irpino
◦ Grottaminarda
◦ Deliceto
◦ Accadía
◦ Áscoli
Satriano
Andria　　Biscéglie
Canosa　　Molfet
di Púglia
Castèl
del Monte　Corato
◦ S. Ágata
di Púglia
A16
Lago di
Capacciotti
◦ Minervino
Murge
Ruvo
di Púglia　Bitonto
Palo del Colle

Bisáccia
◦ Lacedónia
◦ Lavello
Melfi　◦ Rapolla
Venosa
◦ Abbazia
d. Trinità
Spinazzola
680 ▲ M. Caccia
672　Grumo
Áppula

◦ Quasan

IRPÍNIA
◦ Sant'Ángelo
dei Lombardi
1326
M. Vulture
Palazzo
S. Gervásio
Genzano
di Lucánia
L. di Serra
del Corvo
Múrg
Sgóíg
523

④ CAMPÁNIA
◦ Montella
697 ▲
Sella di
Conza
◦ Muro
Lucano
M. S. Croce
1407　Avigliano
◦ Acerenza
Altamura
Gravina
in Púglia
Santéran
in Colle

◦ Éboli
A3
POTENZA
◦ Óppido
Lucano
◦ Irsina
634 ▲ M. Verrútoli
MAT
◦ Battipáglia
Sele
◦ Satriano
di Lucánia
◦ Tricárico
◦ Grassano
Lake
S. Giuliano
Bráccano
PÆSTUM
M. Alburno
1742
BASILICATA
◦ Migliónico

⑤ ◦ Roccadáspide
◦ Agrópoli
Calore
CILENTO
◦ Castellabate
1131 ▲ M. Stella
◦ Acciaroli
Sala
Consilina
1835
◦ Padula
Tanagro
◦ Márssico
Nuovo　M. Volturino
◦ Corleto
Perticara
Laurenzana
Ferrandina
Basento
Montalba
Iónico
Cavone
◦ Bernalda
Lake di Pietra
del Pertusillo
1898
M. Cervati
Vallo della
Lucánia
◦ Montesano
sulla Marcellana
Agri
S. Arcángelo
858 ▲ M. S. Arcángelo
◦ Policoro
◦ Ascea
◦ Torre Orsáia
2005 ▲ M. Sirino
Lagonegro
◦ Senise
◦ Valsinni
M. Bulgherla
◦ Palinuro　1225
Cape Palinuro
◦ Sapri
Sinni
◦ Latrónico
◦ Episcopía
◦ Noépoli
◦ Oriolo
Rocca
Imperiale

⑥ ◦ Marina di
Camerota
Gulf of
◦ Láuria
◦ Maratea
Policastro
◦ Práia a Mare
◦ Papasidero
Mormanno
M. Pollino
2248
1713
◦ Amendolara
Cape
Spulic
M. Sparviere
◦ Trebisacce

TYRRHENIAN

SEA

◦ Scalea
Morano Cálabro
Castrovillari

◦ Diamante
CALÁBRIA
SYBARIS-CÓPIA
Corigliano
Cálabro
Rossa

◦ Belvedere
Maríttimo

Ⓐ　　　　　Ⓑ COSENZA　　COSENZA　Ⓒ

0   10   20   30   40   50 km

ADRIATIC   SEA

BARI**
Torre a Mare
Modugno
Bitetto
Mola di Bari
Adélfia
Rutigliano
Polignano a Mare
Casamassima
Conversano
Monópoli
Acquaviva
d. Fonti
Castellana
Grotte
Grotte di
Castellana
EGNAZIA
Savelletri
Putignano
Torre Canne
Selva
Fasano
Gióia
del Colle
Noci
Locorotondo
Alberobello
Ostuni
Martina
Cisternino
Carovigno
Franca
Céglie
Messápico
Punta Penne
S. Andrea Island
Castellaneta
S. Vito
dei Normanni
BRÍNDISI*
Laterza
Móttola
Crispiano
Villa
Castelli
Punta d. Contessa
Ginosa
Massafra
Latiano
Mesagne
Palagiano
Grottáglie
San Pietro
Vernótico
Marina
di Ginosa
TÁRANTO
Francavilla
Fontana
Oria
San Dónaci
METAPONTUM
Chéradi
Island
S. Giórgio
Iónico
Fragagnano
Sava
Squinzano
S. Maria
di Cerrate
Lido di
Metaponto
Cape
S. Vito
Pulsano
Lizzano
Mandúria
Campi
Salentina
San Cataldo
Marina
di Pulsano
Avetrana
LECCE*
Marúggio
Leverano
Monteroni
di Lecce
Roca Vécchia
Cape
dell'Ovo
Porto
Cesáreo
Copertino
Melendugno
Martano
Nardò
Galatina
Otranto
Galátone
S. Maria
al Bagno
Aradeo
Máglie
Cape
d'Otranto
Gallípoli
Muro
Leccese
S. Cesárea
Terme
S. Andrea Island
Parábita
Poggiardo
Grotta
Zinzulusa
Casarano
Ruffano
Taviano
Taurisano
Alliste
Ugento
Tricase
AUSÉNTUM.
Alessano
Marina
di Nováglie
Gagliano
del Capo
Marina
di Léuca
Cape S. Maria
di Léuca

PENISOLA

SALENTINA

Canale   d'Otranto

Gulf

of   Taranto

IONIAN   SEA

CROTONE

● *Brief regional history*

S. Nicola in Bari

8C-4C BC

Greeks and Apulians. The Romans called the inhabitants of the E coast of S Italy Apulians and their country Apulia. This was probably a corruption of *Iapigi*, which was the Greek name for these people. ● The Apulians were Indo-Europeans of **Illyrian** background, who came, it is surmised, from across the Adriatic. ● Their tribes were called **Dauni** in the Capitanata region, **Peucezi** in the Bari region and **Messapi** in the Salento peninsula. ● In their traditions and culture they were very close to the Greeks, who themselves founded many cities in Apulia and called the whole of Italy **Magna Graecia** (Greater Greece). ● The city of **Taranto** was founded by Greeks from Sparta in 8C BC. It became one of the richest and most powerful cities in the Mediterranean and fought with the Apulian tribes over a long period.

4C BC-5C AD

Roman conquest and domination. The **Samnites,** an aggressive people from the mountains, were constantly at war with the Apulians for their pasture land. The Apulians appealed to **Rome** for help in 325 BC. ● After several difficult wars, the Romans finally subjugated the Samnites and then found themselves confronted with **Taranto,** then the greatest power in the S peninsula. ● The struggle between Rome and Taranto was long and bitter, and Taranto was forced to seek help overseas from **Pyrrhus,** King of Epirus. ● The city could not be saved and finally it was occupied by Rome in 272 BC. ● Rome next contended with the Carthaginians for control of the Mediterranean. It was in Apulia, near **Canne,** that the Romans were utterly crushed by the Carthaginian general **Hannibal** in 216 BC. ● Later, when Rome was a world power, it built the **Via Appia** across Apulia as a link with the city of Brindisi, the nearest Italian port to the Middle East.

6C-12C

Longobards, Arabs, Byzantines and Normans. Rome's long rule of Apulia was brought to an end by invading barbarians and rulers of the E part of the Empire, at Byzantium. The **Byzantines** were in the S of the peninsula over various periods, but were hampered by the **Longobards,** N barbarians who had settled near Naples, founding the **Duchy of Benevento.** Later, after forcing the Byzantines out of Apulia, occupied **Bari** and **Brindisi** (7C). ● The **Arabs** arrived next, taking Bari in 840 and Taranto in 842. The Byzantines, who had maintained a foothold in the Salento peninsula in the S of Apulia, reacted and in a counter-offensive chased the Moors from Bari in 875 and from Taranto in 883. The Byzantine occupation lasted a few hundred years, and this explains the Byzantine influence in architecture and the presence side by side in the region of the monasticism of the Benedictines, and that of the Basilians. ● With peace, the ports on the coast began to flourish (Trani, Molfetta, Barletta and Bari) and much trade was done with the Dalmatian coast, with Amalfi, then a flourishing city on the Tyrrhenian Sea and with Venice. ● It is said that the **Normans** arrived in Italy in small groups, as peaceful pilgrims intent on visiting the famous sanctuary of San Michele at Monte Sant'Angelo in Apulia. Instead of returning home, however, they offered their services as mercenaries to the local barons. Within a generation their military skill and political astuteness enabled them to set up a barony of their own under Robert Guiscard and eventually, after having wrested Sicily from the Moors, they united the whole of S Italy under their dominion. This Norman kingdom developed trade with the Middle East and prospered.

cathedral in Troia

S. Croce in Lecce

cathedral in Ruvo di Puglia

12C-19C
Apulia part of S Italy. As invaders swarmed into S Italy, Apulia changed masters, but gained little freedom. One of the best periods for the region was when it was governed by the great Norman King **Frederick II**, when the land was relatively peaceful and commerce thrived. ● In 1266 the **Angevins** (French) came, followed in 1442 by the **Aragonese** (Spanish); they ruled from the major cities as feudal overlords with the help of local barons and land-owning classes at the expense of the more independent cities of the coast. ● In the 15C the threat of the Turks was felt all over Europe, and, when in 1480 they occupied the port of **Otranto** in Apulia, the atavistic fear of Islam brought about by the terrible Moorish raiding and pillaging of centuries before returned. ● After the defeat of the Turks, Apulia was occupied by France and Spain before finally being incorporated into the **Bourbon Kingdom of Naples and Sicily** (1735). ● It was not freed until 1860 when **Garibaldi,** forming a united Italy, chased the Bourbons away, and it became part of the new Kingdom of Italy.

 Practical information

Information: tourist offices in provincial capitals and main towns; tourist information service *TCI*, at Bari, v. Melo 259, ☎ 080/365140.
SOS: emergency services, ☎ 113; police emergency, ☎ 112; road emergency *ACI,* ☎ 116.
Weather: forecasts, ☎ 080/976976 (from provincial capitals, ☎ 191); road conditions, ☎ 080/975000 (from provincial capitals, ☎ 194); sea conditions, ☎ 080/977977 (from Bari, Brindisi and Lecce, ☎ 196).

Vacation villages: *TCI Villages,* at Tremiti Islands; *Club Méditerranée,* at Otranto; *Valtur,* at Marina di Ostuni (→ Ostuni) and at Otranto.

Farm vacations: *Associazione Regionale Agriturist,* at Bari, v. Petroni 23, ☎ 080/365025.

Fairs: *Fiera Campionaria internazionale del Levante,* at Bari; *Fiera internazionale dell'agricoltura,* at Foggia; *Ascension Day Exhibition,* at Francavilla Fontana.

Events: opera, ballet and concerts at the *Petruzzelli* and *Piccini* theatres; *Castle Festival* and *Festival of S. Nicola* of Bari; *Festival of S. Oronzo; International Music Festi-*

val, *Doll Fair,* at Lecce; *Festival of S. Cataldo,* at Taranto; *Holy Week Procession,* at Bari, Brindisi, Molfetta, Ginosa (→ Marina di Ginosa), Gallipoli, Taranto; *Corpus Christi Procession of the Caparisoned Horse,* at Brindisi; *Tournament* among the various town quarters and *Historical Cortège,* at Oria; *Pageant* featuring the *Disfida a Barletta* (an incident during siege of town by French in 1503 where, in a contest between 13 chosen knights of Italy and 13 of France, the Italians were victorious), at Barletta; *Mount Gargano Study Centre cultural meeting,* at Monte Sant'Angelo; *Carnival Festivities,* at Gallipoli, Putignano (→ La Murgia dei Trulli); *Summer Open Air Meetings,* at Fasano (→ La Murgia dei Trulli); *International tennis tournaments,* at Lecce and Bari.

Nature parks: *Le Cesine Nature Reserve,* of the *WWF* (→ Lecce).

Animal reserves: *Safari Zoo,* at Fasano (→ La Murgia dei Trulli); marine exhibits, at Bari and at Trani.

Environmental protection: *WWF,* at Bari, v. Boccapianola 1, ☎ 080/5210307 (regional delegation); at Brindisi, v. Municipio 1; at Lecce, c/o Museo Missionario Cinese, v. Monti S. Michele 2; at Taranto, v. Bruno 32, ☎ 099/379559; at Barletta, v. De Nittis 15; at Manfredonia, Franciscan Convent S. Maria delle Grazie, v. Tribuna 101 (supervises *Le Cesine Reserve,* → Lecce; nature studies centre at *Torre Guaceto Reserve,* information from regional delegation or at Brindisi, ☎ 0831/884364); *Lipu Bari,* v. Boccapianola 1, ☎ 080/233900 (excursions and instruction in birdwatching).

Hiking: most interesting areas are in Gargano region where there are specially marked routes in Umbra Forest and on S coast; information from *CAI Bari,* PO BOX 530; *Gioia del Colle,* v. P. Amedeo 49; *Centro Visitatori Foresta Umbra* (near Comando Forestale), ☎ 0884/91104.

Apulian wines

In the Milanese dialect an osteria (wine bar) is often called a Trani. This refers to the port of Trani in Apulia, from where wine has been exported for centuries. The vineyards of Apulia go back to the time when man gave up hunting and settled down to farming. Their cultivation was considerably extended a century ago (1870) when considerable quantities of Apulian wine, of good colour and body, were bought by French wine merchants for the purpose of blending it with their own. The phylloxera had ravaged the vineyards of France and spared those of Apulia. In a few years, stimulated by these exports, the local vineyards trebled their surfaces. The earliest recorded exports of Apulian wines seem to have been those of the Phoenicians who some 3,000 years ago were in contact with local growers and shipping out loads of wine. Horace wrote 2,000 years ago that 'the wines of Taranto have no need to be jealous of those of Falerno'. This was praise indeed for not only was Horace a connoisseur of wines, but the Falernian wines, from vineyards under Vesuvius, were in his day the greatest of all wines, the ones drunk by the court and the Emperor. Apulian wines have continued to be acclaimed down the centuries and today Apulia is one of the leading wine-producing regions in Italy. The DOC (official control label) is only granted to certain well-known brands of wine and only covers a fraction (about 2.4 %) of total Italian wine production. There are many wines in Apulia and every one is worth trying. Begin, perhaps, with a Lucera Cacc'e mmite, a ruby red wine, dry and palatable. In the local dialect its name means 'drink up and pour yourself another glass.'

Apulian cuisine

Apulian cuisine has been called simple *because it uses simple ingredients but it consists of many succulent and tempting dishes. The appetizing displays of shellfish found in all the restaurants of the coastal towns of Apulia are a gourmet's delight. They include luscious oysters, tasty mussels, clams, cockles and sea urchins. The best dishes in Apulian cuisine are based on greens and olive oil such as 'ncapriata, a delicate purée of broad beans that are dried and boiled, seasoned with crude olive oil and topped with endives or boiled turnip tops. Ciceri e tria is tagliatelle with boiled chick peas in an oil and onion sauce. Melanzanata di Lecce is fried sliced eggplant baked with tomatoes, onion, basil and pecorino cheese. Tiella is a dish of mushrooms, onions and sliced potatoes, prepared with oil, garlic and spices. Cardoncelli are magnificent Apulian artichokes which are boiled and baked with black olives and a fricassée of beaten egg, cheese and spices. The most common Apulian dish is* orecchiette, *a form of noodles served with turnip tops seasoned with chopped anchovies or simply in a ragù sauce. The favourite meat in Apulia is lamb, roasted or cooked on a spit. The tripe of lamb makes* gnumeriddi, *a dish particularly appreciated around Bari.*

Cycling: various cycling clubs affiliated to *UDACE* can be found throughout region for assistance and information; suggested itineraries: circular 100 km tour starting at Bari to Sammichele di Bari, Alberobello, Locorotondo, Mar-

tina Franca, Torre Canne, Castellana grottos, Polignano a Mare, Mola di Bari; tour of the Gargano Mountains with excursion to Umbra Forest (5 days).

Horseback riding: *Bari Regional Committee of Italian Federation of Equestrian Sports,* v. Ferrarese 23, ☎ 080/211799; riding school, at Bitetto (→ Cathedrals in the Bari Area) and at Lecce.

Sailing: *Lega Navale,* at Bari, corso Vittorio Veneto 9, ☎ 080/237766; at Barletta, v. Cristoforo Colombo, ☎ 0883/33354; at Brindisi, v. Vespucci, ☎ 0831/418824; at Bisceglie, v. Libertà, ☎ 080/928149; at Otranto, v. del Porto, ☎ 0836/81509; at Taranto, lungomare Vittorio Emanuele III, ☎ 099/93801; at Trani, molo S. Antonio, ☎ 0883/44832.

Canoeing: at Bari, school affiliated to *Italian Federation of Canoe-Kayaks.*

Golf: *Riva dei Tessali Golf Course* (→ Marina di Ginosa).

Flying: *Aeroclub Bari Palese,* at airport, ☎ 080/373163; at Foggia, *Gino Lisa Airport,* ☎ 0881/76016; at Lecce, *San Cataldo Airport,* ☎ 0832/650042.

Caving: interesting sites include grottos of Castellana, of Putignano and of Polignano a Mare (→ La Murgia dei Trulli); the Zinzulusa grotto (→ The Salentine Peninsula); for information: *Grotte di Castellana* ☎ 080/735511; *Grotte di Putignano,* ☎ 080/731967; *Albergo Grotta Palazzese,* ☎ 080/740261; tourist offices of Castro Marina, ☎ 0836/97317.

Fishing: *Federazione Italiana Pesca Sportiva,* at Bari, molo Pizzoli, ☎ 080/210685; at Brindisi (nr Coni), v. Dalmazia 21C; at Foggia, v. Duomo 17, ☎ 0881/71872; at Lecce, v. Palma 62; for fishing regulations (permitted and prohibited waters, etc.) apply to relevant federal departments.

Archery: *Fitarco,* at Bari, p. Mater Ecclesiae 5/A; affiliated clubs at Manduria, Francavilla Fontana, Bari and Lecce.

● *Towns and places*

ACQUAVIVA DELLE FONTI

Bari 28, Rome 477 km
Pop. 18,945 ✉ 70021 ☎ 080   D4

Acquaviva delle Fonti is a picturesque name that means water of the fountains. It is a reference to the water in plentiful supply that lies in the hollow of the Murgie where the town is situated.

▶ The **cathedral** is 15C but was probably originally Romanesque. The **Palazzo del Principe** (municipio) is an interesting Baroque building. ▶ The **Museo della civiltà contadina pugliese** *(7 a.m.-1 p.m.; notify Comune,* ☎ *677203)* is in the Castello Caracciolo at **Sammichele di Bari,** 6 km E. ▶ 14 km W is the **Mercadante Forest,** which covers 258 acres.   □

Practical information _____

Restaurant:
♦♦ **Ghiottone,** v. Pepe 83, ☎ 762253, closed Mon and Aug. Regional cuisine: maccheroncini with nut sauce, fried seaweed, 25/45,000.

ALBEROBELLO*

Bari 55, Rome 502 km
Pop. 10,068 ✉ 70011 ☎ 080   D4

Alberobello seems like a magical forest from a book of fairy tales. It is a town whose architectural scheme was laid out in prehistoric times. With more

than 1,000 *trulli* — round pointed houses with white walls — it shimmers magically in the sunlight.

▶ The two sections of the town known as Monti and Aia Piccola contain most of the trulli, set along winding, hilly roads. From the open doors it is possible to see how they are built inside — a central room, communicating by an arched passage with the kitchen and the bedrooms. The people are friendly in Alberobello and it is possible to visit their homes. The finest trullo, and the tallest with two floors, stands in the small square behind the main church (→ La Murgia dei Trulli).   □

Practical information _____

 p. del Popolo, ☎ 721916.

Hotels:
★★★★★ **Trulli,** v. Cadore 28, ☎ 721130, 19 rm Ⓟ ▨ &
◪ closed Nov-Mar, 110,000; bkf: 12,000.
★★★★ **Astoria,** v. Bari 11, ☎ 721190, 47 rm Ⓟ ▨ &
66,000; bkf: 7,000.
★★★ **Lanzilotta-Cucina dei Trulli,** p. Ferdinando IV 31, ☎ 721511, 25 rm Ⓟ & 39,000; bkf: 6,000.

Restaurants:
♦♦ **Trullo d'Oro,** v. Cavallotti 29, ☎ 721820, closed Mon. Set among the trulli. Regional cuisine, 20/35,000.
♦ **Publiese,** v. Don Gigante 4, ☎ 721437, closed Tue except summer and Nov. Set among the trulli. Regional cuisine, 20/25,000.

Don't forget to consult the Practical Holiday Guide: it can help in solving many problems.

ALTAMURA

Bari 45, Rome 461 km
Pop. 52,902 ✉ 70022 ☎ 080   C4

Altamura sits on a height in the Murgie region. It
owes much to Frederick II who rebuilt it after it had
been destroyed by the Moors. He constructed a high
wall around it (hence its name) and regrouped in it
the surviving Greek, Latin and Jewish peoples of the
surroundings. The Emperor also gave the imposing
cathedral which still dominates the city today.

▶ The splendid Romanesque-Gothic **cathedral** (1232) was
rebuilt after the earthquake of 1316 and again in 1500. It
has a magnificent rosette★ and portal★. Inside the original structure has been preserved in spite of renova-
tions. ▶ The church of **S. Nicolo dei Greci** has a 15C
portal and reliefs. ▶ The **Museo Civico** (9 a.m.-2 p.m.;
closed Mon) contains prehistoric and medieval material. ▶ On v. Bari are megalithic remains. ▶ 6 km N is
pulo di Altamura, one of the largest limestone gorges in
Apulia; it was inhabited in neolithic times. ▶ 9 km SE at
the **masseria Jesce** are a series of tufa grottos and a
small Greek church with frescos.   ▢

Practical information

ⓘ p. della Repubblica 11, ☎ 843930.

Hotel:
★★★ **Autostello,** v. Matera 2/A, ☎ 8711742, 22 rm ℙ ⋙
58,000; bkf: 7,000.

Restaurant:
● ◆◆◆ **Del Corso-U Cecatidde,** corso Federico di Sve-
ria 76, ☎ 841453, closed Tue and Jul. Regional cuisine:
cavatelli with mushrooms, orecchiette and turnip tops,
30/50,000.

ANDRIA

Bari 56, Rome 399 km
Pop. 86,391 ✉ 70031 ☎ 0883   C3

Andria is a typical example of one of the big agricultural towns that are developing in S Italy. It was one
of Frederick II's favourite towns. The great Emper-
or, talked about in this part of the world as if he had
only died recently, buried two of his wives here.

▶ The **Duomo** dates from 9C-10C but has been completely rebuilt. In the crypt are the tombs of Jolanda
of Brienne, second wife of Frederick II, and Isabel of
England, his third wife. ▶ In the **Museo Diocesano**
(9:30 a.m.-12:30 p.m.; closed Mon) are many precious
works of art that were formerly kept in the
Duomo. ▶ The nearby **Palazzo Ducale** (14C) is an
impressive building. ▶ Among Andria's notable churches
are **S. Domenico**, with remains of Gothic cloister, and **S. Francesco** and **S. Agostino**, both with Gothic
portals. ▶ 2.3 km NW the church of **S. Maria di Miracoli**
(16C-17C) has been rebuilt over a Byzantine
grotto. ▶ The monument to the famous **Disfida di
Barletta** is 6 km along the road to Corato, up a short side
road.   ▢

Practical information

Restaurant:
◆◆◆ **Siepe,** v. Bonomo 97/B, ☎ 24413, closed
Fri. Regional cuisine: orecchiette with turnip tops, risotto
with seafood. 20/30,000.

> For the translation of a name of a meat, a fish or a
> vegetable, for the composition of a dish or a sauce,
> see the *Menu Guide* at the end of the Practical Holi-
> day Guide; it lists the most common culinary terms.

Recommended
♥ wines: *Rivera* vineyard, v. Alto Adige 139,
☎ 82862 or 82371 (telephone before visiting).

BARI**

Rome 449, Milan 878 km
Pop. 369,576 ✉ 70100 ☎ 080 .   D3

The changes that in recent years have been taking
place all over S Italy, and perhaps in Apulia more than
anywhere else, are evident in a city like Bari where
there is much that is very old alongside much that is
modern. Bari's division into an old town and a new
town creates two separate worlds. Old Bari is reminiscent of a city of the Middle East, a part of the world
it has traded with and exchanged ideas with from the
earliest times. It has the same narrow and winding
streets with small square houses. Most of these
streets are near the magnificent basilica of Saint
Nicola, the patron saint of the town. Away from old
Bari is la Citta Nuova (new city). This is not new by
modern standards because it dates from 1813 when
Joachim Murat, Napoleon's brother-in-law and then
King of the Two Sicilies, laid it out in a series of wide
avenues, crossed at right angles by equally broad
streets. This area has since developed and become
the modern part of town with elegant shops and pala-
tial hotels.

▶ **La Citta Vecchia** (old city). The basilica of
S. Nicola★★ (B5) is a prototype of Apulian Romanesque
architecture with a façade in three sections, high tiers of
arches, a powerful transept and a continuous wall that
surrounds the three apses and the three naves divided by
columns and pillars. The basilica was built between 1087
and 1197. The **ciborium★** (canopy) over the High Altar
is 12C; the marble **episcopal seat★** and the monument
to Bona Sforza, Queen of Poland, are 16C. The **altar
of S. Nicola★** in laminated silver (1684) is in the r. apse
while on the l. is a *Madonna and Saints★* painted in 1476
by B. Vivarini. The **treasure** in the Museo (guided visits
Mon, Fri and Sat 10 a.m.-12 noon) is very valuable
and includes a glazed copper plate showing S. Nicola
crowning Ruggero II king. ▶ In front of the basilica
is the rebuilt **portico dei Pellegrini**; to the r., beyond the
arch of S. Nicola (14C), is the small church of S. Gregorio (11C-12C). ▶ Following a revolt, the Norman king William the Bad ordered Bari destroyed. In 1156 the town
was razed, but S. Nicola miraculously was spared.
▶ The **cathedral★★** (B5) was rebuilt shortly
afterward in Romanesque style on the site of the old
Byzantine duomo; it has a superb high window in the
apse wall. The large building on the cathedral's l., known
as the *trullo,* is an old baptistery which was changed into
a sacristy in the 17C. Inside are a noteworthy High Altar
baldachin and an episcopal throne; the crypt was renovated in the 18C. Many old codexes and manuscripts
are conserved in the archives, some dated earlier than
1050. ▶ The **museum** (9 a.m.-1 p.m.) is next to the
cathedral. ▶ The huge size of the **castle★** (B4) is due, in
part, to its central part being in the form of a quadrilateral with two towers. This was how Frederick II planned
it when he had it rebuilt over the remains of an earlier
Byzantine-Norman castle. Its massive appearance is
also strengthened by the sloping bulwarks and the towers
over the entrance gate which were added in the
16C. The castle is well worth visiting (partially closed for
renovation; normally open 9 a.m.-1 p.m. and 4-7 p.m.;
closed Mon). Inside is the **Gipsoteca** with copies of
interesting Apulian sculptures. ▶ The **coast road** named
after the Roman Emperor Augustus follows the ancient
walls on the E side of the city (B5). ▶ The **Palazzo della
Provincia** (C-D5-6) on the sea front (lungomare Nazario
Sauro) contains the **Pinacoteca Provinciale**, a museum
devoted mostly to Apulian sculpture and paintings of

the medieval period. It also contains works by Venetian artists, such as polyptychs and paintings on wood by Vivarini; *Martyrdom of St. Peter*★ by Giovanni Bellini and paintings by Paris Bordone, Tintoretto and Veronese. ▶ The **Museo Archeologico** has the most complete collection of antiquities to be found in Apulia (D4-5; *9 a.m.-2 p.m.; closed Sun*), many dating from 7C-3C BC. It has a collection of bronzes with arms, helmets and belts from the tombs of Greek warriors and gold and silver antique jewelry. ▶ The **Acquario Provinciale** (B4; *9 a.m.-1 p.m. and 4:30-7 p.m.; Sun 8:30 a.m.-12:30 p.m.*) is at the beginning of the quay

Pizzoli on the Gran Porto. ▶ The **Orto Botanico** (arboretum, v. G. Amendola 175; *notify in advance*, ☎ 339549) has many interesting samples of the regional vegetation. ▶ The **Museo Etnografico Africa-Mozambico** is near the convent of S. Fara (v. gen. Bellomo 94; *10 a.m.-12 noon Wed, Fri and Sun; 5-7 p.m. Tue and Thu*).

Environs

▶ 8 km S, the **church of the Ognissanti** is situated in open country among almond trees and vineyards. It has a dome that is a perfect example of the Romanesque style of architecture. Near it are the 11C remains of a Bene-

dictine abbey. ▶→ Cathedrals in the Bari Area and La Murgia dei Trulli. □

Practical information

i p. Moro 33/A (D5), ☎ 225327 or 228855; corso Vittorio Emanuele 68 (C5), ☎ 219951; *TCI*, v. Melo 259 (D5), ☎ 365140.

✈ *Bari Palese*, ☎ 374654; *Alitalia*, v. Argiro 56, ☎ 369288, buses from v. Calefati 39 (C5), ☎ 216609.

🚂(D5), ☎ 216801.

🚌 from largo Ciaia (D6), p. Eroi del Mare (C5), corso Italia (D5), p. Moro (D5).

🚢 car ferry departures several times a week for Yugoslavia (Dubrovnik and Bar), weekly for Greece; Stazione Marittima, molo S. Vito (B4), ☎ 235205.

Car rental: *Avis*, v. L. Zuppetta 5/A, ☎ 540266, airport, ☎ 373390; *Hertz*, p. Moro 47, ☎ 225616, airport, ☎ 373666; *Maggiore*, v. Carulli 12/22, ☎ 544300, airport, ☎ 374647.

Hotels:

★★★★ *Grand Hotel Ambasciatori*, v. Omodeo 51, ☎ 410077, 177 rm 🅿 🛋 🚿 & 🖂 Very modern with heliport and swimming pool on the roof, 150,000; bkf: 14,000.

★★★★ **Grand Hotel Leon d'Oro,** p. Moro 4 (D5 a), ☎ 235040, 116 rm P ✷ 115,000; bkf: 7,000.
★★★★ **Jolly,** v. Petroni 15 (D5 b), ☎ 364366, 164 rm P 160,000.
★★★★ **Palace Hotel,** v. Lombardi 13 (C4 c), ☎ 216551, 210 rm P & 234,000; bkf: 11,000.
★★★ **Apelusion,** at Torre a Mare, v. Martiri Resistenza 23, ☎ 300352, 51 rm P ▩ ▭ ✎ 53,500; bkf: 4,500.
★★★ **Baia,** at Palese, v. Vittorio Veneto 29/A, ☎ 320288, 54 rm P & ✷ 70,000; bkf: 8,000.
★★★ **Boston,** v. Piccinni 155 (C4 d), ☎ 216633, 72 rm P No restaurant, 130,000.
★★★ **Grand Hotel & d'Oriente,** corso Cavour 32 (C5 e), ☎ 544422, 172 rm P No restaurant, 110,000.
★★★ **Majesty,** v. Gentile 87/B, ☎ 491099, 67 rm P ▩ ▭ ✎ closed Christmas, 81,000; bkf: 7,300.
★★★ **MotelAgip,** at Torre a Mare, SS 16 at 816-km marker, ☎ 300001, 95 rm P 75,000.
★★★ **Palumbo,** at Palese, v. Vittorio Veneto 31, ☎ 320779, 14 rm P ▩ & ✷ 87,000; bkf: 8,000.
★★★ **Plaza,** p. L. di Savoia 15 (D5 f), ☎ 540077, 40 rm ✷ closed Aug and Christmas, 116,000; bkf: 8,000.
★★★ **Victor,** v. Nicolai 69 (D4 g), ☎ 216600, 75 rm P & ✷ No restaurant, 115,000.
★★★ **Windsor Residence,** v. parallela Amoruso 62/7, ☎ 510011, 79 rm P ✷ 89,000.

Restaurants:
● ♦♦♦ **Pignata,** v. Melo 9 (C5 m), ☎ 232481, closed Wed and Aug. Elegant and tastefully furnished. Regional cuisine: orecchiette with turnip tops, roast kid, 35/50,000.
● ♦♦♦ **Vecchia Bari,** v. Dante 47 (C5 p), ☎ 215496, closed Fri and Aug. Originally an olive oil warehouse. Regional cuisine: tagliatelle with mushrooms, terrine Bari style, 45/50,000.
♦♦♦ **Due Ghiottoni,** v. Putignani II (C5 h), ☎ 232240, closed Sun and 5-20 Aug. Seafood and regional cuisine, 30/35,000.
♦♦♦ **Marc Aurelio,** v. Fiume I (C5 i), ☎ 212820, closed Mon. Excellent service. Regional cuisine, 24/33,000.
♦♦♦ **Panca,** P. Massari 8/10/12 (C4 l), ☎ 216096, closed Wed. Elegant with open fireplace. Regional cuisine: Bari pie, crustaceans, 20/35,000.
♦♦♦ **Taberna,** at Carbonara di Bari, v. Ospedale di Venere 8, ☎ 350557, closed Mon, Jul-Aug. Romantic setting. Regional cuisine, 20/50,000.
♦♦♦ **Sorso Preferito,** v. De Nicolo 46 (C5 n), ☎ 235747, closed Sun. Traditional Apulian osteria. Regional cuisine, 25/35,000.

⚓ San Giorgio, at San Giorgio, SS 16 at 809-km marker, 200 pl, ☎ 491175 (all year).

Recommended
Archery: *Compagnia Arcieri della Murgia,* p. Mater Ecclesiae 5/A, ☎ 510054; *Compagnia Arcieri Bari,* v. Podgora 111.
Canoeing: *Scuola CUS Bari,* lungomare Starita 1/B, ☎ 441779 (instruction).
Cycling: *G. S. De Benedictis,* v. Nitti 23, ☎ 344345; *G. S. Frenauto Bari,* v. G. Albanese 4.
Discothèque: *Boogie-Boogie,* at Capurso, v. Ognissanti, ☎ 651138.
Events: opera, ballet and concerts at *Petruzzelli Theatre,* ☎ 218295 and *Piccinni Theatre,* ☎ 218567; *Festival castello,* at Castle (theatre, cinema, music, Jul-Aug); *Festival of St. Nicholas* (pageant and procession, 7-8 May); *Procession of Mysteries* at Holy Week.
Fairs: *Fiera Campionaria Internazionale del Levante* (Fair of the East, Sep), ☎ 206111; special exhibitions all year on site of fair.
Flying: Aeroclub at *Bari Palese airport,* ☎ 373163 (instruction).
Sailing: *Lega Navale,* corso Vittorio Veneto 9, ☎ 237766 (instruction).
Swimming: v. Maratona 3, ☎ 441766 (instruction); v. Campione 17, ☎ 228247; strada provinciale per Triggiano 9, ☎ 491503.
Youth hostel: *Ostello del Levante,* v. N. Massaro 343, ☎ 320282.

♥ acquarium: *Acquario,* molo Pizzoli (B4), ☎ 211200; wines: *De Pasquale,* v. M. di Montrone 87, ☎ 213192.

BARLETTA*

Bari 55, Rome 397 km
Pop. 84,900 ⊠ 70051 ☎ 0883   C3

Barletta is famous for a huge bronze statue over 18 ft high — the *Colossus of Barletta.* The statue dates from the 4C and is said to be of the Emperor Valentinian I. It was in Constantinople until the 13C when the Venetians carried it off secretly. Gales blew the ship with the statue onto the Apulian coast where it was wrecked and the Colossus found a home at Barletta purely by chance. Barletta is also famous for the *Disfida di Barletta.* The *Disfida,* or challenge, took place in February 1503. At the time the Spaniards and French were at war in S Italy, with the Italians supporting the Spaniards. A captured French officer told a Spanish one that the Italians were useless as soldiers and that the country was destined to remain under foreign domination forever. The Spanish officer informed the Italians and a duel was arranged between thirteen Italian officers and thirteen French officers, all mounted. The Italians routed the French and captured them. Later the French were defeated by the Spaniards who took over the Kingdom of Naples and Sicily, as well as the rest of S Italy. The famous *Disfida* took place in open country near Andria and not at Barletta, although it has always been associated with Barletta.

▶ In the **medieval part** of town in the p. della Sfida (B3), the names of the Italian knights who took part in the *Disfida* appear in a **shrine** and inside the palazzo, on the l., rooms contain a reproduction of the famous challenge with period arms and uniforms *(9 a.m.-1 p.m. and 4-6 p.m.; Sun 9 a.m.-1 p.m.; closed Mon).* ▶ The church of **S. Andrea** is at the top of a flight of steps in a street going down to the port (B3); it has a splendid 12C portal and in the sacristy a *Madonna* by Alvise Vivarini (1483). ▶ The **Duomo★** (B3), built in 1150 in Romanesque-Apulian style and enlarged in the 14C-15C, is closed for repairs. The 14C painting on wood known as *The Madonna of the Challenge* because it was taken out in procession by the clergy when they went to meet the winners has been temporarily removed from the duomo to the church of Nazareth (B2). ▶ The **castle** (B3) dominates the piazza facing the port and the sea. It was built in the 13C and four corner ramparts were added in the 16C. ▶ The **Museum** and the **Pinacoteca Comunali** (B2-3; *9 a.m.-1 p.m.; closed Mon and hols)* have archaeological and medieval collections (including a bust of Frederick II), Renaissance sculpture, furniture and arms. The **De Nittis Gallery** houses 168 works of the Apulian painter De Nittis, as well as many works by 17C-19C Neapolitan artists. ▶ The *Colossus of Barletta* stands in front of the basilica of **S. Sepolcro★** (B2), in a Burgundy-Gothic style dating from the 13C. It has a remarkable **treasure** comprising Limoges porcelain, 15C ikons and many frescos. ▶ In the church of **S. Agostino** (B1), which dates from the 13C, there is a polyptych by Andrea del Salerno and his assistants (1522) and a stone frontal with the *Annunciation* in Romanesque style on the altar.   ☐

Practical information _____

≋
ℹ p. Moro (B2), ☎ 31373.

Hotels:
★★★★ **Artù,** p. Castello 67 (B3 a), ☎ 31721, 32 rm P ▩ 80,000; bkf: 8,000.
★★★ **Royal,** v. De Nittis 13 (C2 b), ☎ 31139, 34 rm P & 75,000; bkf: 6,000.

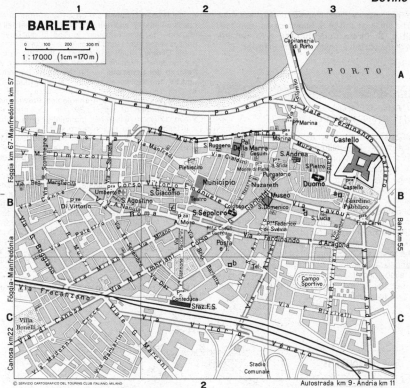

BARLETTA

0   100   200   300 m
1 : 17000 (1cm =170 m)

PORTO

Restaurants:
♦♦♦ *Bacco,* v. Sipontina 10 (B2 c), ☎ 38398, closed Mon, Jan and Aug. Intimate setting. Regional cuisine: ravioli with fish stuffing, rice with nettles and strawberries, 45/75,000.
♦♦♦ *Brigantino,* v. Litoranea di Levante, ☎ 333445. Modern with swimming pool. Regional cuisine: risotto, seafood, 25/45,000.
♦ *Casaccia,* v. Cavour 40 (B3 d), ☎ 33719, closed Mon. In historic part of town. Regional cuisine: spaghetti and shellfish sauce, lobster, 25/35,000.

Recommended
Events: re-enactment of *Disfida di Barletta* (last Sun in Aug).
Marina: ☎ 31020.
Sailing: *Lega Navale,* v. C. Colombo, ☎ 33354 (instruction, also fishing).
Sports: *Palazzetto dello sport,* v. Manzoni, ☎ 34764.

BITONTO*

Bari 17, Rome 432 km
Pop. 50,727 ✉ 70032 ☎ 080   C3

Bitonto is a town dominated by its huge 13C Romanesque cathedral. It stands in the medieval quarter, an area of narrow streets and winding lanes.

▶ The **cathedral★★** was built in a relatively short time by architects who were influenced by the basilica of S. Nicola in Bari. The church which must be considered one of the finest examples of Apulian-Romanesque architecture, is flanked by long arcades surmounted by a fine gallery. The interior is also noble. The pulpit dates from 1229. ▶ In the adjoining bishop's residence is the **Museo Diocesano e Pinacoteca A. Marena** *(Fri 10 a.m.-12 noon).* ▶ In the same ancient part of town are the 11C **S. Caterina di Alessandria** church; the **Palazzo Vulpano Sylos** (15C) with a splendid portal and courtyard and the church of **S. Francesco** (13C façade). ▶ The **Museo Civico E. Rogadeo** (v. Rogadeo 52; *Jul-Aug 8:30 a.m.-12:30 p.m.; other months Mon-Thu 2-7 p.m.; Fri and Sat 8:30 a.m.-12:30 p.m.; closed Sun)* has archaeological finds and interesting 19C-20C paintings by Apulian artists. ▶ There are several impressive **rural churches** dating from the 11C-12C in the countryside toward Terlizzi and Molfetta *(contact the honorary inspector of Soprintendenza,* ☎ *617296).*   □

Practical information

ℹ porta Baresana.

Hotels:
★★★ *Hotel SI,* v. Giovanni XXIII, ☎ 617341, 18 rm Ⓟ ♨ ✺ 63,000; bkf: 5,000.
★★★ *Nuovo,* v. E. Ferrara 21, ☎ 611178, 38 rm Ⓟ ✺ 40,000; bkf: 5,000.

BOVINO

Foggia 36, Bari 168, Rome 399 km
Pop. 5,055 ✉ 71023 ☎ 0881   A3

To the W of Bovino is a gorge, the **Vallo di Bovino,** which was once infamous for the dark deeds of the brigands that took place there. Bovino sits on a ridge and has a fine **Duomo** dating from the 10C. The small church of **S. Marco** dates from 1197 and that of **S. Pietro** from the 11C-12C. All that remains of the old ducal castle is a round **tower.**   ☐

BRINDISI

Bari 114, Rome 551, Milan 995 km
Pop. 91,118 ⊡ 72100 ☎ 0831   E4

The coat-of-arms of Brindisi has two columns and the head of a deer. The columns are said to represent the ones in the port, supposedly built by the Romans to mark the end of the Via Appia. This road ran from Rome across Italy to Brindisi, which has the only natural port on the Adriatic and is the obvious departure point for the Middle East. The word for deer in the local patois is *brunda* from whence Brindisi came, it refers to the many canals and inlets of the port which are like the antlers of a deer. The port of Brindisi is like a loch that, as it goes inland, splits into two arms; the town is built on the spit of land between the two channels. These are deep and easily navigable so that, almost inevitably, especially after the opening of the Suez Canal, Brindisi became the main Mediterranean port for the E.

▶ The **Roman columns** are on a rise in front of the port; one is intact (B3) and dates from 2C; the other fell in 1528 and only its base remains. ▶ The p. del Duomo (B3) houses many interesting buildings and monuments. There is the **Duomo,** which was rebuilt in the 18C (in the apse are pavement mosaics from the 12C). There are also the **Palazzo del Seminario** (17C), the **loggia Balsamo** (13C) and the two Gothic arcades of the **portal** known as the Knights Templar. ▶ Also on the piazza is the palazzo that houses the **Museo Archeologico Provinciale Francesco Ribezzo** *(9 a.m.-12:30 p.m.; summer also Sat 9 a.m.-12 noon),* which has many interesting archaeological finds from the region surrounding Brindisi. ▶ The round church of **S. Giovanni al Sepolcro** (B2; 11C-12C) was built by the Knights Templar on their return from a crusade. ▶ The church of **S. Benedetto** (B2), originally 11C and since rebuilt, still retains its primitive campanile. Inside are Romanesque columns; the **cloister★** was once part of a 11C monastery. ▶ The **Castello Svevo** owes its rectangular towers to Frederick II; at the end of the 15C Ferdinand I of Aragon enlarged it and built the round towers. ▶ The **Porta Mesagne,** a fine 13C arch, opens in the 15C walls built by Charles V. To the l. are some Roman basins that drained the acqueduct. The church of **S. Lucia** still retains parts of the original 11C-12C building and inside are 12C frescos and an impressive crypt. ▶ The **chiesa del Cristo** (C3), originally built in 1230, has an inspiring polychrome façade and a fine rosette; inside are wooden sculptures from the 13C. ▶ The **Monumento al Marinaio** (Monument to the Sailor; A3) dominates the central basin of the port. It was

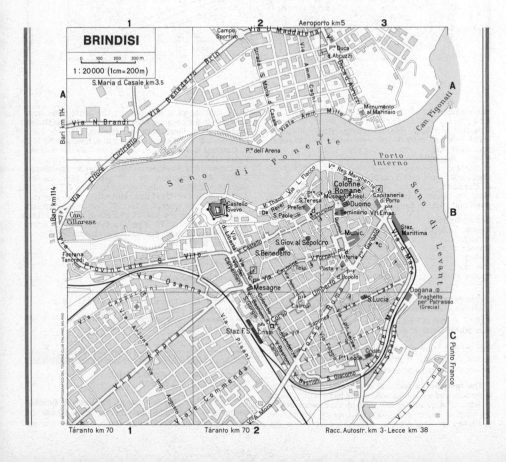

built in 1933 and is in the form of a giant rudder (174 ft high). From the top of the monument is a superb view over the surrounding region and the sea.

Environs

▶ 2 km N is the magnificent medieval church of **S. Maria del Casale**★, a 13C Romanesque-Gothic building with 14C Byzantine frescos inside. In the lunette of the inside portal there is an extraordinary *Universal Judgment* by Rinaldo da Taranto. ▶ 14 km SW is **Mesagne**, a very old town with a castle that was originally built in the 11C (since renovated). The town also contains the church of S. Lorenzo (9C-10C), the church of Carmine (14C) and the Baroque church of Matrice. In the palazzo del Comune the **Museo Civico U. Grafanei** *(9 a.m.-1 p.m.; closed wkends)* has some interesting archaeological finds. ☐

Practical information _____

ⓘ p. E. Dionisi (B3), ☎ 21944; v. C. Colombo 88 (B2), ☎ 222813; v. Rubini 19, ☎ 21091 (head office); information kiosks at p. Cairoli (C2) and in front of railway station. ✈ A. Papola, at Casale *(5 km N),* ☎ 412141; bus service from main railway station; *Alitalia,* corso Garibaldi 53 (B3), ☎ 29091.
🚃 (C2), ☎ 21975.
🚢 from v. Dalmazia and v. Colombo (C2).
🚢 car ferries for Greece (three times a week in winter, daily in summer, several times a day in Jul and Aug); information: *Adriatica di Navigazione,* ☎ 222509 or 23950; *Hellenic Mediterranean Lines,* ☎ 28531.
Car rental: *Avis,* v. del Mare 50, ☎ 26407, airport, ☎ 418826; *Hertz,* v. S. Francesco 13, ☎ 26515, airport, ☎ 412109; *Maggiore,* p. F. Crispi 13, ☎ 25838, airport, ☎ 418155.

Hotels:
★★★★ *Internazionale,* lungomare Regina Margherita 26 (B3 a), ☎ 23473, 87 rm ℗ 90,000; bkf: 7,000.
★★★★ *Majestic,* corso Umberto 151 (C2 b), ☎ 222941, 68 rm ℗ 105,000.
★★★★ *Mediterraneo,* v. Moro 70, ☎ 82811, 60 rm ℗ 90,000; bkf: 7,000.

Restaurants:
◆◆ *Botte,* corso Garibaldi 72/76 (B3 c), ☎ 28400, closed Mon and Nov. Veranda in summer. Regional cuisine: orecchiette with meatballs, Brindisi pie, 18/30,000.
◆◆ *Colonne,* v. Colonne 57 (B3 e), ☎ 28059, closed Tue. Dining in garden in summer. Regional cuisine: gnocchi with shellfish sauce, mussels au gratin, 30/40,000.
◆ *Cantinone,* v. De Leo - p. Dante ☎ 222122, (B2 d), closed Tue. Regional cuisine, 15/25,000.

Recommended
Events: *Holy Week Procession; Corpus Christi Procession* (Jun); *Bacchus week* (spring); *City of Brindisi Festival* (art, folklore, cultural events Jun-Sep).
Horseback riding: *Mitrano Sporting Club,* Tenuta Mitrano SS 379 toward Bari, ☎ 451077 (associate of *ANTE*).
Sailing: *Lega Navale,* v. Vespucci, ☎ 418824 (instruction).
Sports: *Palazzetto dello Sport,* v. Ruta, ☎ 418944.
Swimming: at Materdomini (pool).
Technical tourism: tour of port with guide Sun a.m., details from *Agenzia Gioia,* ☎ 26146.
Tennis: v. Ciciriello, ☎ 21057.
Youth hostel: *Ostello EPT,* at Casale, v. N. Brandi 4, ☎ 413100.

CANOSA DI PUGLIA

Bari 76, Rome 373 km
Pop. 30,971 ⊠ 70053 ☎ 0883   B-C4

In 1096-7 a great army under Godfrey de Bouillon and Bohemund of Otranto set out for the Holy Land on the First Crusade. They captured Antioch and Jerusalem from the Saracens and Bohemund became King of Antioch. A few years later Godfrey de Bouillon

was dead and Bohemund was captured by the Saracens. Bohemund was the son of Robert Guiscard, first Norman Duke of Apulia and Calabria, and after several years of imprisonment he was ransomed and brought home. He never left Apulia again and is buried in the cathedral grounds in Canosa.

▶ **Bohemund's tomb** is in a small courtyard reached from the r. transept of the church; it is an unusal monument of Romanesque design with Oriental influences. This is particularly noticeable in the **bronze door**★ of the mausoleum by Ruggero da Melfi (12C), which has Arab-inspired decorations. ▶ The **cathedral**★, built at the beginning of the 11C but since renovated, is an imposing building. Inside are an 11C pulpit★ and an episcopal throne★ on a base of elephants. ▶ The **Museo Civico** *(winter 8 a.m.-2 p.m.; summer also 5-7 p.m.; closed Mon)* in the Palazzo Casieri has archaeological and medieval material. ▶ In v. Cadorna there are three **Lagrasta sepulchres** *(see caretaker).* They are funeral chambers dug in the tufa from the 4C and have been used several times for burials. ▶ 1 km along the road to Cerignola is a **Roman Arch** and 2.5 km farther is a Roman bridge from the imperial period. ▶ S of the village are the remains of the basilica of **S. Leucio** *(see caretaker),* a Byzantine construction of the 5C-6C. ☐

Practical information _____

Restaurant:
◆ *Vecchia Canosa,* v. M. Pagano 5, ☎ 63074, closed Tue and Jul. In a natural grotto in old town. Italian and regional cuisine: troccoli with mushrooms, roast lamb, 25/30,000.

CASARANO

Lecce 42, Bari 193, Rome 641 km
Pop. 18,188 ⊠ 73042 ☎ 0833   F5

Casarano is an old town with a 17C church with Baroque altars. In the S part of town the church of **S. Maria della Croce** *(see caretaker or get keys in municipio)* has a cupola and choir vault covered in mosaic (5C) and 12C frescos in the vault of the nave. ☐

Practical information _____

Restaurant:
◆ *Buongustaio,* v. Ruffano 70, ☎ 331390, closed Tue and Aug. Regional cuisine: orechiette alla salentina, papardelle with salmon sauce, 20/35,000.

Recommended
Craft workshops: *E. Falcone,* at Ruffano *(9 km SE),* v. Elena 50, ☎ 692013 (terra-cotta).

CASTEL DEL MONTE

From Barletta *(91 km, 1 day; map 1)*

Castel del Monte is called the crown of Apulia. It is a massive construction, impressive from all angles standing alone on a height in the Murgia. Frederick II was a great builder and he constructed this castle as an outpost against Papal troops attacking his kingdom from the N. It is an octagonal building, flanked by eight towers which themselves are octagonal. The fountain in the courtyard (long ago vanished) was octagonal also and the castle had eight rooms on its two floors. Sixteen years after Frederick's death, Charles of Anjou with a French army routed the army of Manfred, Frederick's son, and locked his children up in the castle. This splendid edifice, which symbolized the glory of Frederick's reign, also marked the downfall of his dynasty.

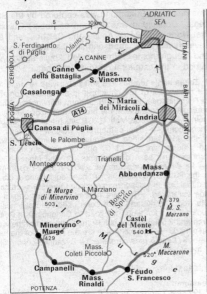

1. Castel del Monte

▶ Leaving **Barletta** (→) the route proceeds inland along the Ofanto River. ▶ At **Canne della Battaglia** a column marks the spot where the great battle between the Carthaginians, led by Hannibal, and the Roman armies took place in 216 BC. The Romans were annihilated, losing 70,000 of the 80,000 men they had in the field. Digging in the battlefield area continues although the **Museum Cannense** is closed at present for reorganization. Arms and other objects from this site can be seen in the museum at Barletta. The ancient city of Canne was situated on a nearby hill and excavations there have uncovered walls and the E gate, as well as a series of streets with shops. The remains of two Christian basilicas can also be seen. The nearby necropolis *(presently being reorganized)* is not the burial ground of the fallen in the great battle as was thought at one time; it is part of a cemetery of medieval Canne (9C-11C). Nearby are the ruins of a prehistoric Apulian village from the 6C-3C BC and a **menhir** (prehistoric monumental stone) of the Bronze Age. ▶ Beyond **Canosa di Puglia** (→) is **Minervino Murge**, which probably was named for a temple to Minerva that stood on the site of the present church of the Madonna della Croce near the grotto of S. Michele. ▶ **Castel del Monte★★** can be seen in the distance, a crown of stone on a lonely height *(9 a.m.-1 hr before sunset Apr-Oct; 9 a.m.-1 p.m. Nov-Mar)*. The castle, over the course of centuries, has been looted and has lost all its mosaics and marble decorations. It had a degree of comfort unheard of in its time, including baths with running water collected from rainwater on the terraces. The halls and rooms of the castle are still very beautiful because of the harmony of the clear stone and the red marble. ▶ The route continues to Barletta by way of Andria (→). ☐

Send us your comments and suggestions; we will use them in the next edition.

Practical information _____

CASTEL DEL MONTE, ⊠ 70031, ☎ 0883.

Restaurant:
♦♦ *Agriturist al Murgiano,* SS 170, ☎ 82849, closed Wed. Adjoins farm co-operative with overnight accommodation and fresh produce on sale. Regional cuisine: roast lamb, local cheeses, 18/28,000.

CATHEDRALS IN THE BARI AREA

From Bari *(68 km, 1 day; map 2)*

Cathedrals have always been erected for a variety of motives. As well as the obvious religious motive, they have also been erected for economic and political reasons. In medieval times it was essential that a cathedral be not only a house of God, but also the possessor of holy relics of a great saint. Equipped with such a cathedral, a town drew enormous benefits from the thousands of pilgrims it attracted annually, its rulers enjoyed great prestige as the overseers of a holy place, and the people felt secure under the protection of *their* saint and venerated him with grandiose ceremonies and processions. All towns wanted such a cathedral, knowing that whatever the initial cost it would soon be repaid. The problem for most towns was that holy relics were not easy to find. They nearly all seemed to be in the Middle East and their owners were quite unwilling to part with them. This resulted in foraging expeditions, as in 1087 when sailors of Bari returned home with the bones of St. Nicholas. This resulted in a dramatic change in the habits of pilgrims. Until then they had made a detour to the Gargano to visit the shrine of St. Michael and then embarked for the Holy Land at one of the many ports along the coast. Now they went straight to Bari where they were able to visit the shrine of St. Nicholas and take a ship to their destination. Cathedrals are named after royal figures, popes or saints, and it is forgotten that the actual work of building these edifices was done by hundreds of artisans whose names are lost forever. They formed an army of engineers, designers, labourers and architects. Sometimes the work took more than a century and many spent their whole lives on a job. Many skilled workers went abroad in pursuit of work, learning new trends and techniques that they would introduce into their designs once they returned home. This happened in Apulia perhaps more than anywhere else and its cathedrals were built with Byzantine, Norman, Sicilian, French, Spanish and Arab influences. These influences can be noted in many of the cathedrals around Bari.

▶ Starting in **Bari** (→) the route leads to **Bitetto** with a 13C cathedral. It has had its interior rebuilt following the original Romanesque design. The church of S. Maria Veterana has many late Gothic frescos *(Sun 7-8 a.m.; keys with secretary of the congregation).* ▶ At **Palo del Colle** there is a church with a font of late Gothic design; it was rebuilt in the 16C but retains its original campanile. From **Bitonto** (→) the route continues to **Terlizzi** where there is the church of S. Rosario with a 12C portal with reliefs. In the Pinacoteca De Napoli *(9 a.m.-12 noon, presently being reorganized)* there are works of the 19C painter Michele de Napoli. ▶ **Ruvo di Puglia** (→) has one of the finest cathedrals in Apulia. ▶ Three striking churches may be seen at **Corato**: S. Maria Maggiore, with a 13C portal with reliefs, the Gothic S. Domenico and S. Vito (11C-12C). ▶ The route arrives at the Adriatic at **Trani** (→) and follows the coast to the SE. ▶ The 11C-13C

2. Cathedrals in the Bari Area

cathedral of **Bisceglie** is in the medieval part of town. Also noteworthy are the 11C church of S. Adoeno and the church of S. Margherita (1197) with three 12C Gothic tombs inside. Nearby are three towers, all that remain of a Norman castle. In the Museo Civico Archeologico are reports on the well-known **dolmen of Chianca**, a megalithic monument *(c. 5 km S, nr service station on motorway)*. ▶ After **Molfetta** (→) the route leads to **Giovinazzo** with its medieval cathedral close to the sea. It was built in 1283 and much of the original structure is still preserved; it has a Baroque interior. ▶ From here return to Bari. □

Practical information _____

BISCEGLIE, ⊠ 70052, ☎ 080.
≋
ℹ v. Vittorio Veneto 10/7, ☎ 922369.

Hotel:
★★★★★ *Villa,* SS 16, ☎ 950148, 34 rm Ⓟ ⌂ ⊗ ⊠ closed Nov, 120,000; bkf: 9,000.

⚓ *La Batteria,* at Salsello, 170 pl, ☎ 950009.

Recommended
Sailing: *Lega Navale,* v. Libertà, ☎ 928149 (instruction).

BITETTO, ⊠ 70020, ☎ 080.

Recommended
Horseback riding: *Ippodromo Ulivi,* strada provinciale Modugno-Bitetto at 113-km marker, ☎ 621092 (instruction).

GIOVINAZZO, ⊠ 70054, ☎ 080.
≋

Hotel:
★★★ *Riva del Sole,* SS 16, ☎ 832166, 90 rm Ⓟ ⌂ ᕕ ⊗ ⊠ ♪ 115,000; bkf: 8,500.

⚓ *Baia Trincea,* at Trincea, 100 pl, ☎ 991165; *Campo Freddo,* SS 16, 240 pl, ☎ 931112.

CERIGNOLA

Foggia 37, Bari 95, Rome 400 km
Pop. 52,050 ⊠ 71042 ☎ 0885   B3

Cerignola stands in the middle of an immense plateau called the Tavoliere, a flat expanse of wheat fields

extending as far as the eye can see and only broken here and there by farm buildings. This region is also known as the Catapana.

▶ In the cathedral is a striking *Madonna di Ripalta,* a 12C ikon of the Virgin. ▶ 26 km W is the site of the Roman town of Herdoniae, which flourished from 1C BC-11 AD. □

Practical information _____

Restaurant:
♦ *Vincenzo,* corso Garibaldi 35, ☎ 21844, closed Sat. Regional cuisine: troccole with cuttle-fish sauce, orecchiette, 20/25,000.

Recommended
♥ wines: *Torre Quarto,* at Quarto, ☎ 23097 (telephone before visiting).

CONVERSANO

Bari 30, Rome 479 km
Pop. 21,088 ⊠ 70014 ☎ 080   D3

Conversano is a small rural town that sits on a ledge in the Murgie region surrounded by olive groves and cherry trees.

▶ The picturesque **castle** in the main square is of Norman origin. It offers a fine view of the coast and the sea below. ▶ The 14C Romanesque-Gothic **Duomo** is well worth visiting, as is the 9C church of **S. Benedetto** with three domes, a Baroque campanile and an interior renovated in the 17C. The adjoining convent has a Romanesque cloister *(see caretaker).* Also interesting is the nearby church of **S. Cosma e Damiano** with a rich Baroque interior. ▶ 10.5 km NW at **Rutigliano** is the 12C church of S. Maria della Colonna with a splendid polyptych by A. Vivarini (1450). □

Practical information _____

ℹ p. Castello 14, ☎ 751228.

Recommended
Craft workshops: *T. Garia,* at Rutigliano, v. Turi 64, ☎ 669249 (terra-cotta).

The arrow (→) is a reference to another entry.

FOGGIA

Bari 133, Rome 352, Milan 759 km
Pop. 157,371 ⊠ 71100 ☎ 0881   A-B2

Foggia's name is said to come from the Latin word the Romans used to designate the silos into which they packed the grain from the abundant harvest on the surrounding plain. During the Middle Ages feudal lords found it more profitable to turn the flat expanse to pasture and every year millions of sheep were brought down from the Abruzzi mountains to graze. In 1447 Alfonso of Aragon put a charge on the sheep entering the plain; this became known as 'the sheep tax' and was not abolished until 1806 when Joseph Bonaparte was governing the region. Today the plain is given over to wheat, with small areas of fruit orchards and vineyards, and Foggia has become a large modern city.

▶ The Norman **cathedral** (1172) was partially rebuilt in the 18C after an earthquake damaged its upper structure. It houses the **Icona Vetere**, a Byzantine ikon supposedly discovered on the day that the city was founded. ▶ An arch★ with reliefs is all that remains of the palace of Frederick II and it is now over the front of the building containing the **Museo e Pinacoteca Comunali** (p. Nigri 1; *9 a.m.-1 p.m.; Wed and Fri 5-8 p.m.; closed Sun*), which houses a collection of palaeolithic objects, archaeological material found in the region, a picture gallery with paintings by local artists from 19C to the present, a section devoted to the traditional crafts of Foggia and mementos of Foggia-born composer Umberto Giordano (1867-1948). ▶ The church **del Calvario** (1693), with five chapels, forms a picturesque Baroque complex. ▶ The beautiful public gardens **(villa Comunale)** have walks lined with ilexes, palm trees and charming statues.   □

Practical information ———————————

⬜ v. E. Perrone 17, ☎ 23650.
✈ *Gino Lisa (5 km S)*, ☎ 73959; *Alidaunia*, ☎ 71236 (daily flights to the Tremiti Islands).
🚌 ☎ 21015.
🚖 from v. Galliani, from railway station and from p. Vittorio Veneto.
Car rental: *Avis*, at railway station, ☎ 78912; *Maggiore*, v. XXIV Maggio 76/78, ☎ 73173.

Hotels:
★★★★ *Cicolella*, XXIV Maggio 60, ☎ 3890, 125 rm ℗ closed Aug and Christmas, 154,000; bkf: 10,000. Rest. ● ♦♦♦ closed Sat and Sun. Elegant and traditional with terrace for open-air dining. Regional cuisine: orecchiette, grilled fish, 30/48,500.
★★★★ *Palace Sarti*, v. XXIV Maggio 48, ☎ 23321, 78 rm, 70,000; bkf: 10,000.
★★★ *President*, v. degli Aviatori 80, ☎ 20139, 132 rm ℗ ⬜ ⬜ ⬜ 71,000; bkf: 6,000. Rest. ♦♦♦ Regional cuisine, 30/45,000.

Restaurants:
♦♦♦ *Cicolella in Fiera*, v. Fortore, ☎ 32166, closed Mon eve and Tue. Open-air service under pines of fairgrounds. Regional cuisine, 30/45,000.
♦♦ *Amerigo-Nuova Bella Napoli*, v. Azariti 26, ☎ 26188, closed Sun and Christmas. Splendid patio in old part of city. Seafood, 25/40,000.

Recommended
Craft workshops: *A. Pipoli*, v. Chiuso Belvedere, ☎ 47354 (wrought iron); *Terra e Fuoco*, v. Giardino 10, ☎ 23626 (ceramics); *E. Radogna*, rione Martucci 6/A, ☎ 27236 (wax work).
Cycling: *G.S. Cicloamatori F. Coppi*, c/o *Bicisport*, v. G. D'Orso; *G.S. Avis-Aido Foggia*, v. N. Sauro 2, ☎ 45761; *G.S. Fildaunia*, v. Bari; *Unione ciclistica Foggia*, v. Rione S. Pio X 57, ☎ 32256.
Fairs: *Fiera internazionale dell'agricoltura* (International

Agricultural Fair, Apr-May), ☎ 32111; *Apulian Craftswork Show* (Oct).
Fencing: *Palazzetto scherma*, rione Biccari, ☎ 43957.
Flying: *Aeroclub*, at *Gino Lisa Airport*, ☎ 76106 (instruction).
Sports: *Palazzetto dello Sport*, v. Ofanto, ☎ 730190.
Swimming: v. Pinto, ☎ 40519.

FRANCAVILLA FONTANA

Brindisi 33, Bari 107, Rome 557 km
Pop. 33,634 ⊠ 72021 ☎ 0831   E4

Francavilla (free city) was granted its freedom by Phillip I of Anjou, Prince of Taranto. He was greatly impressed when a Byzantine ikon of the Madonna was found in the vicinity (1310) and gave help and encouragement to the town's development. Francavilla is an agricultural community laid out with straight avenues and crossing streets and it contains many Baroque buildings.

▶ The **Imperial Palace** (municipio; 15C-18C) has been enlarged and renovated over several centuries; it has a balcony with Baroque arcades and a courtyard. ▶ The **Duomo** was built in the 17C. ▶ 8 km along the road to Ceglie Messapico is the **specchia Miano**, a circular stone construction and one of the best preserved of the Messapian monuments. (Messapii were forerunners of Apulians). ▶ 10 km E is **Latiano** with a **Museum of Traditional and Popular Arts** *(telephone before visiting, ☎ 729743)*.   □

Practical information ———————————

Recommended
Archery: *Compagnia Arcieri Rudiae*, at Villa Castelli, v. Ruthe Tarpea 9.
Fairs: *Mostre dell'Ascensione* (Ascension Day Show, local handicrafts, May), ☎ 341767.

GALATINA

Lecce 20, Bari 171, Rome 628 km
Pop. 28,695 ⊠ 73013 ☎ 0836   F5

Galatina contains a splendid Gothic church, **S. Caterina★**. It was built in 1384-91 by the Orsini family and has a splendid rosette on its façade and a central portal with carvings and reliefs. The interior is covered in frescos by 15C painters who were probably from Emilia or the Marches. The Gothic tomb of Raimondello Orsini is in the presbytery; behind the altar there is an octagonal chapel built in the 15C by G. Antonio Orsini who is buried there. Another interesting church is **SS. Pietro e Paolo** with a Baroque façade. The **Museo Civico d'Arte Pietro Cavoti** (corso Re d'Italia 51; *a.m.-2 p.m.; closed Sat*) contains works by the painter Mose Lillo.

▶ 3.8 km E is **Soleto** with a parish chruch with Gothic campanile; the nearby 14C church of S. Stefano has 14C-15C frescos (note very rare portrayal of Christ as a priest). ▶ 9 km SW, among the Baroque buildings of **Galatone**, is the church of the Sanctuary of the Crucifixion (1710) with a sumptuous interior.   □

Practical information ———————————

Hotel:
★★*Maurhotel*, v. Pavia 10, ☎ 61971, 24 rm 🍴 43,000; bkf: 9,000.

Restaurant:
♦*Capanna*, v. Turati 25, ☎ 64048, closed Sun. Regional cuisine: barley maccheroncini, swordfish, 22/28,000.

Recommended
Fairs and markets: *Mostra mercato nazionale dell'Industria, del Commercio e dell'artigianato (industry, commerce and crafts show, Jun).*

GALLIPOLI

Lecce 37, Bari 190, Rome 628 km
Pop. 20,265 ✉ 73014 ☎ 0833   E5

Surrounded by a land that is rocky and dry, with olive trees and vines in profusion, Gallipoli sits on the coast on a neck of land pushing out into the Ionian Sea. It is a beautiful city encircled by the sea. At the far end of the neck of land lies old Gallipoli, the one the Greeks founded. Farther from the sea is modern Gallipoli, a bustling commercial centre with a busy port.

▶ **Old Gallipoli** (B1) is actually an island since the time in the 16C when the Spaniards dug a canal across the isthmus, probably as an extra precaution against attacks from the land upon the castle. It has narrow winding streets and low houses with white walls. **Borgo** is the name given to modern Gallipoli (A-B2-3). ▶ The **Hellenistic Fountain** (B2), rebuilt in 1560 over an ancient one, has some very old reliefs of mythological goddesses, transformed into fountains, surrounded by Baroque decorations added in more recent times. ▶ The **castle** (B1) was built by the Angevins and renovated in the 16C. Its fortifications go as far as the fishing port of Canneto. ▶ The Baroque **cathedral** (1630) has many 17C-18C paintings by local artists. ▶ The **Museo Civico** (B1; *9 a.m.-1 p.m. and 5-7 p.m.; 4-6 p.m. in winter*) has archaeological collections and paintings relating to the city. ▶ The church of **S. Francesco** has a fine painting on wood by Giovanni Pordenone. ▶ It is possible to take a boat ride around the old city of Gallipoli and there are many fine views. ▶ At **Alezio** *(6 km E)* the **Museo Civico** *(8 a.m.-12 noon and 2-4 p.m.; 4:30-6:30 p.m. in summer)* has many archaeological finds from a 6C-2C BC burial ground being excavated nearby.   ☐

Looking for a locality? Consult the index at the back of the book.

Practical information

≋
🛈 corso Roma (B2), ☎ 476290.

Hotels:
★★★★*Grand Hotel Costa Brada,* at Baia Verder, litoranea per Leuca, ☎ 22551, 58 rm Ⓟ ⬚ ✷ ▭ ♪º 108,000; bkf: 15,000.
★★★*Cristina,* v. Ariosto 2, ☎ 22541, 33 rm ⌁ No restaurant, 55,000; bkf: 5,000.
★★★*Sirenuse,* at Baia Verder, litoranea per Leuca, ☎ 22536, 120 rm Ⓟ ⬚ 占 ✷ ▭ ♪º Pens. 89,000.
Restaurant:
◆◆ *Marechiaro,* lungomare Marconi (A2 a), ☎ 476143, closed Tue in winter. On small island with bridge to mainland; facilities for mooring boats. Seafood: risotto pescatora, lobster, roast crayfish, 20/25,000.

⚓*Vecchia Torre,* at Torre Sabea, ☎ 261083.

Recommended
Events: *Gallipoli Carnival; Good Friday procession.*
Farm vacations: *La Masseria,* at Torre Sabea, ☎ 281014.
Marina: ☎ 473165.
♥ **wines:** *Calo Vineyard,* at Alezio, v. Garibaldi 56, ☎ 281045 (Rosé of Salento wine; reserve in advance).

Il GARGANO

From Manfredonia *(183 km, 1 day; map 3)*

The Gargano promontory sits like a spur on the boot of Italy, breaking the almost straight line of the Adriatic coast. It is a hilly limestone plain with many grottos and gorges and covered in forests. The sea has sculpted its high cliffs, making caves with arches and vaults that can be visited by boat. There are also many inlets with sandy beaches. Where the coast is flat, the wind and waves have made sand dunes that, shoring up pools of water, created lakes like Lesina and Varano. The vegetation is varied and profuse and the forests have many trees including maple, sycamore, ash, oak, yew and pine. Wild mountain goats roam the hills and boars can still be found roam-

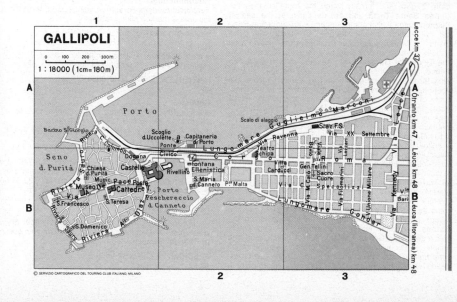

GALLIPOLI
0 100 200 300m
1 : 18000 (1cm= 180m)

© SERVIZIO CARTOGRAFICO DEL TOURING CLUB ITALIANO, MILANO

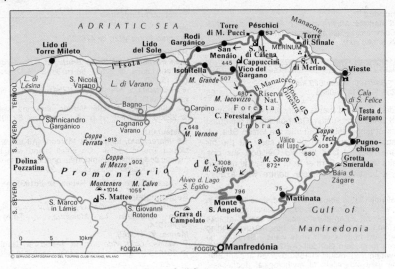

A D R I A T I C   S E A

3. Il Gargano

ing the undergrowth. In the sky fish hawks can be seen swooping down from great heights to the sea. Until recently the peninsula was isolated because of lack of communications, but now these have been improved, land has been cleared and farming has been started around the villages strewn across the plain. The forests are being worked, and tourism is being developed in a way that, it is hoped, will not destroy the natural surroundings.

▶ Leaving from **Manfredonia** (→) a scenic route goes past Rodi Garganico to reach **Mattinata** in a valley of olive groves with a fine beach. ▶ Passing above the **Baia delle Zagare** and turning inland the route crosses the **Coppa Santa Tecla** and arrives again at the sea at **Pugnochiuso**, a village surrounded by luxuriant sub-tropical vegetation on a tongue of land with two inlets. ▶ Moving past other small bays the winding road passes through an immense pine forest and goes up to the **Testa del Gargano**. ▶ The next stop is **Cala San Felice**, an inlet where caves open onto the sea. ▶ Passing through cultivated land and by sandy beaches the route arrives at **Vieste** (→). ▶ It then winds to the sanctuary of **S. Maria di Merino** near ancient *Merinum*, which dates from Roman times. ▶ The next picturesque village is **Peschici**, on a high cliff with a beach way below. ▶ The scenic route now follows the partially wooded N Gargano coast, beyond Valazzo to **San Menaio**, in a hollow among citrus farms and with a pine forest at its back, and then to **Rodi Garganico** on a rocky spur. The road next leads over a sandy rise, known locally as L'Isola, which cuts Lake Varano off from the sea. ▶ **Lido di Torre Mileto** lies on the strip of land separating Lake Varano from Lake Lésina. Out to sea from here are the Tremiti Islands (→). ▶ Returning to Valazzo the route joins the SS 528 that cuts across the Gargano. ▶ The village of **Vico del Gargano** lies on a slope facing out to sea and after leaving the village the road enters the magnificent Umbra Forest★, full of beech, pine and maple. The buildings of the Forestry Administration *(information about excursions into forest)* are at a crossroads where this route goes to Vieste. Nearby are a

small lake and a refuge where deer are raised. ▶ From Monte Sant'Angelo (→) the route descends toward the sea and Manfredonia. □

Practical information ────────────

BAIA DELLE ZAGARE, ⊠ 71030, ☎ 0884. ≋

Hotel:
★★★ *Baia delle Zagare*, ☎ 4155, 150 rm ℙ ⌇ ⛾ ⅍ ⁘ closed 16 Sep-May. Bungalows sitting in an olive grove, 110,000; bkf: 6,000.

FORESTA UMBRA, ⊠ 71030, ☎ 0884.

Recommended
Technical tourism: *Forestry Administration*, ☎ 91104 (picnic areas, marked hiking routes).

ISOLA DI VARANO, ⊠ 71010, ☎ 0884.

Hotel:
★★★★ *Bufalara*, v. Uria, ☎ 97037, 60 rm ℙ ⌇ ⛾ ⁘ closed Nov-Mar, 75,000; bkf: 4,000.

MATTINATA, ⊠ 71030, ☎ 0884. ≋

Hotels:
★★★★ *Alba del Gargano*, corso Matino 102, ☎ 4771, 45 rm ℙ ⛾ ⅍ closed 15-30 Oct, 90,000.
★★★ *Apeneste*, p. Turati 3/4, ☎ 4747, 26 rm ℙ ⛾ ▭ 70,000.

Restaurants:
● ♦♦ *Papone*, SS 89 at 144-km marker, ☎ 4749, closed Mon and Nov. In old olive oil factory. Regional cuisine: orecchiette and greens, risotto with shellfish, 20/35,000.
♦ *Portoghese*, v. Pellico 3, ☎ 4321, closed Fri. Family-run trattoria. Regional cuisine: fried small eels, crayfish, 20/25,000.

⚓ *Europa*, at Funni, v. Mare, 144 pl, ☎ 4452; *Fontana delle Rose*, at Mattinatella, 130 pl, ☎ 4028; *San Lorenzo*, at Cala dei Saraceni, 150 pl, ☎ 4152.

PESCHICI, ⊠ 71010, ☎ 0884. ≋

i v. XXIV Maggio, ☎ 94425.

⛴ several weekly sailings (Jun-Sep) to the Trémiti Islands, Rodi Gargànico and Manfredonia; hydrofoil sailings bi-weekly to the Trémiti Islands, *Adriatica,* ☎ 94074.

Hotels:
★★★★ *Valle Clavia,* at Valle Clavia, ☎ 94209, 42 rm ℗ ⨾ ⍩ closed 16 Sep-May, 80,000; bkf: 8,000.
★★★ *Solemar,* at San Nicola, ☎ 94186, 50 rm ℗ ⨾ ⨾ ⊟ closed 26 Sep-14 May, 78,000; bkf: 2,000.
★★ *Passiaturo,* v. Libetta 30, ☎ 94124, 18 rm ⨾ 55,000; bkf: 4,000.
★★ *Peschici,* v. S. Martino, ☎ 94195, 42 rm ℗ ⨾ ⅙ ⍩ 55,000; bkf: 6,000.

Restaurants:
◆◆◆ *Grotta delle Rondini,* borgo Marina, ☎ 94007, closed Oct-Mar. Dug out of rock with porthole looking onto natural grotto; sunny terrace. Seafood: risotto with shellfish, snails, 25/35,000.
◆◆ *Frà Stefano,* v. Forno 8, ☎ 94141, closed Oct-Mar. In historic building. Seafood: grilled fish and lobster, roast lamb, 25/30,000.
⚓ *San Nicola,* at San Nicola, 700 pl, ☎ 94024; *Manacore,* at Manacore, ☎ 94050; *Parco degli Ulivi,* at Padula, 500 pl, ☎ 94208.

RODI GARGANICO, ⊠ 71012, ☎ 0884.
≋
i p. Garibaldi 4, ☎ 95054.
⛴ several sailings a week (daily in summer) to the Trémiti Islands, also by hydrofoil *Adriatica (c.* 40 mns), ☎ 95031.

Hotels:
★★★ *Miramare,* v. XX Settembre 2/4, ☎ 95025, 29 rm ℗ 53,000; bkf: 4,000.
★★★ *Mizar Vacanze,* at Lido del Sole, v. Ippocampo 1, ☎ 97021, 50 rm ℗ ⨾ ⍩ closed 21 Sep-19 May, 60,000; bkf: 7,000.

Restaurant:
◆ *Gabbiano,* v. Trieste 14, ☎ 95283, closed Thu. Facing sea and beach. Seafood: orecchiette, mussels in sauce, 20/30,000.
⚓ *Lido del Mare,* at Lido del Sole, 150 pl, ☎ 97039; *Siesta,* at Lido del Sole, 500 pl, ☎ 97030.

SAN MENAIO, ⊠ 71010, ☎ 0884.
≋

Hotel:
★★★ *Nettuno,* v. Lungomare 36/38, ☎ 98131, 30 rm ℗ closed Oct-Mar, 40,000.
⚓ *Calenella,* SS 89 at 78.5-km marker, ☎ 98105; *Valle d'Oro,* SS 528 at 1.8-km marker, 150 pl, ☎ 91580 (all year).

TORRE FORTORE, ⊠ 71010, ☎ 0882.

Hotel:
★★★ *Maddalena,* v. Saturno 78, ☎ 95076, 80 rm ℗ ⨾ ⊟ ⍩ closed 21 Oct-19 Apr, 78,000; bkf: 6,000.

Restaurant:
◆ *Due Galli,* ☎ 95109, closed Tue and 15-30 Sep. Faces the sea. Seafood, 20/30,000.

GIOIA DEL COLLE

Bari 39, Rome 480 km
Pop. 27,603 ⊠ 70023 ☎ 080   D4

Gioia del Colle is a small town dominated by a Norman **castle** with massive angular towers. It was erected in 1230 on the site of an earlier Byzantine castle by Frederick II who realized that the town held a strategic position on the road from Bari to Taranto.

▶ The castle now houses the **Museo Archeologico Nazionale** *(9 a.m.-1 p.m.; closed Mon),* which contains material dating from prehistory to 3C BC recovered from the

Mount Sannace site. ▶ 5.5 km along the road to Pulignano is the **Mount Sannace prehistoric site** *(caretaker in residence)* where excavations are now taking place. An early Apulian city of some importance must have been here, and parts of houses, public buildings, an acropolis and burial grounds have been unearthed. □

Practical information _____

Restaurant:
◆◆ *Gran Gala,* v. per Acquaviva, ☎ 833432, closed Fri and Nov. Regional cuisine: cavatelli alla gioiese, orecchiette country style, 20/30,000.

Recommended
Cycling: *G.S. Gioiauto Renault,* v. V. Emanuele 129.
▼ cheese: *F. lli Capurso,* v. Dante 101, ☎ 831171 (telephone before visiting).

GRAVINA IN PUGLIA

Bari 57, Rome 450 km
Pop. 37,041 ⊠ 70024 ☎ 080   C4

Gravina means gully and the town is built on the very edge of a deep one through which torrents of water roar during the rainy season. There are numerous grottos in the steep walls of the gully where people used to seek shelter in times of trouble.

▶ **S. Michele** is a grotto-church, dug out of rock on the edge of the gully; it has 10C-14C Byzantine frescos and at one time was the cathedral of the old troglodyte city *(keys with residents or at nearby S. Agostino church).* ▶ The crypt of the old church of S. Vito Vecchio, with 13C Byzantine frescos has been reconstructed in the **Museo Pomarici Santomasi** *(9 a.m.-1 p.m. and 4-7 p.m.; closed Sat p.m. and Sun; see caretaker).* The museum also houses archaeological collections, ceramics, 17C-18C paintings and Murgia folklore material. ▶ The **Duomo** was renovated in Renaissance style in the 15C; it has a 15C giltwood ceiling and a carved wood choir. ▶ The church of **S. Sofia** contains the beautiful tomb of Angela Castriota Scanderbeg *(c.* 1518), wife of the Albanian patriot. ▶ The 16C church **del Purgatorio** has two skeletons in the spandrels of the arches of its portal and bears on its pillars referring to the Orsini family (Orso means bear), the feudal overlords of the region for 400 years; the family's chapel, with tombs, has paintings by F. Guarino and A. Solimena. ▶ There are also heraldic references in the 16C church of the **Madonna delle Grazie** *(near railway station).* In the lower part of its front are bosses with three towers with battlements, while its rosette displays the wings of a crowned eagle; these were the emblems of Monsignor Giustiniani da Chio. ▶ The **castle** of Frederick II (1231) is on the N side of town. □

Practical information _____

Restaurant:
◆◆ *Grotta,* corso Di Vittorio 22, ☎ 851776, closed Mon. Regional cuisine: orecchiette with cabbage, pork sausages with mushroom au gratin, 25/40,000.

GROTTAGLIE

Taranto 22, Bari 75, Rome 554 km
Pop. 29,090 ⊠ 74023 ☎ 099   D-E4

Grottaglie specializes in the production of handmade ceramics and copies of Greek amphoras. The **Matrice** church was renovated in Romanesque style in 1379; traces of this can still be seen in the lower part of its façade which has a fine portal with a rosette.

▶ A short distance from Grottaglie in the **gravina Foranese** (gorge) is a Byzantine church with frescos and, in a grotto above it, a Calvary carved in the 17C. The **gra-**

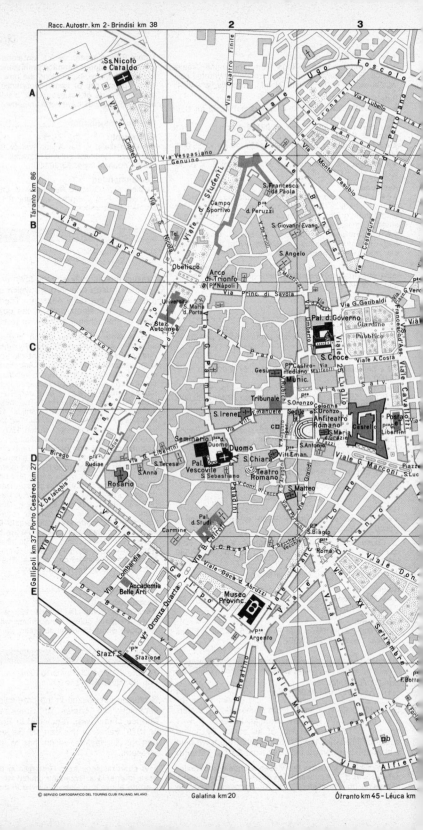

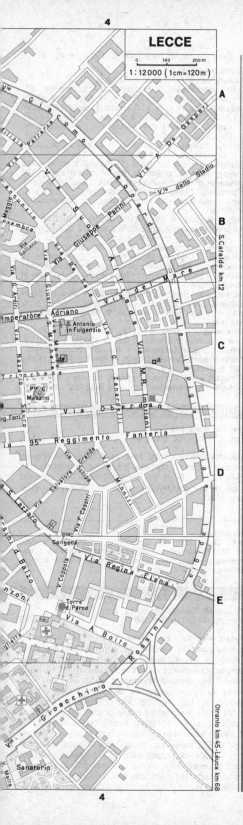

vina di **Casalpiccolo** also has a grotto-church with frescos. ☐

Practical information

Recommended
Craft workshops: *Jonio Ceramiche*, v. S. Sofia 25, ☎ 661667 (ceramics).
Events: *Christmas Eve Holy Mass* in grotto del Bucito with traditional costumes, information from Comune, ☎ 661452.

LECCE*

Bari 152, Rome 603, Milan 1,034 km
Pop. 93,883 ⊠ 73100 ☎ 0832   F5

Lecce, capital of the Salento region, is a charming city with many beautiful monuments and art treasures. This is due in part to the stone quarried in the region which is soft and honey-coloured. Lecce is known as a Baroque city because in the 17C its architects and sculptors decided to cover their city's ancient monuments — without in any way altering their structure — with a light coat of the then-new fashion called the Baroque; this resulted in the façades of the city's churches and palaces being ornamented with gargoyles, eagles, monkeys, dragons, saints, ribbons, flowers and fruit, all carved from the beautiful Lecce soft stone. These artists did not confine themselves to decorating major monuments; they also ornamented houses, balconies, courtyards, even humble dwellings in side streets. The result was that the whole city 'went Baroque' and still remains that way, but this 'Lecce Baroque', as it is called, differs from the Baroque style found elsewhere in Europe in that there is nothing massive or imposing about it; on the contrary, it is all light, airy and gay, making a walk through the streets a consummate pleasure.

▶ There are many fine buildings in the **Piazza del Duomo★** (D2): the splendid **Palazzo del Seminario★** (Giuseppe Cino, 1709) with tall pilasters has an inner courtyard with a charming Baroque stone curb surrounding a well; the **Palazzo Vescovile** (1632) with an airy loggia stands beside the **Duomo★** and its slim campanile★. The Duomo was renovated in 1659-70 by Giuseppe Zimbalo and its interior has rich altars with twisted pilasters and many excellent paintings. ▶ In piazza Castromediano (C2-3) is the church **del Gésu** (1579) with sumptuously decorated altars in the transept and apse and many fine paintings; it stands behind the **municipio** (17C). ▶ The **basilica di S. Croce★★** (C3; 1548-1646) is generally considered one of the finest of all the buildings in the Lecce Baroque style. It took almost 100 years to complete and among the major artists who worked on it were G. Riccardi (lower part of façade), A. Zimbalo (central portal) and G. Zimbalo (the upper part); Riccardi was also responsible for the pure and sober lines of the decoration in the interior. ▶ To the l. of the church stands the **Palazzo del Governo★**, formerly a convent; G. Zimbalo and G. Cino were responsible for its façade and Riccardi created the courtyard which was finally completed by G. Zimbalo. ▶ The Baroque church of **S. Chiara**, E of the Duomo, is generally attributed to Cino (1694). Nearby the **Roman theatre** (D2) is said to have been built under the reign of the Emperor Hadrian (76-138). ▶ Another church very much in the Lecce Baroque style is that of **S. Matteo.** ▶ Two other interesting churches in the same style are the church **del Rosario** (D1), the last work of G. Zimbalo, with fantastic decorations on the complex façade and extravagant altars inside, and the church **del Carmine** (D-E2), renovated by Cino in 1717. ▶ **Piazza S. Oronzo** is in the old part of the city; the column in the middle of it is Roman, similar to the one in Brindisi. The Romans, it is said, planned to put both in Brindisi marking the end there of the Via Appia. Somehow the people of

Lecce got hold of one of the columns and put it up in their city in 1666. Digging is going on in the piazza with a view to unearthing a **Roman amphitheatre**★ of the 2C. Next to this Roman site is the Palazzo del Seggio or del **Sedile** (1592), which used to be the seat of the comune; beside it is the former church of **S. Marco** (1543). ▶ The **Museo Provinciale Sigismondo Castromediano**★ (E2; *9 a.m.-1 p.m. and 3:30-7:30 p.m.; hols 9:30 a.m.-1 p.m.; closed Sat*) is divided into three sections: the Antiquarium, with an important collection of old Apulian and Greek vases, terracottas and bronzes; the topographical section, with collections of antiquities from the Lecce region (the display of sculptures found in the local Roman theatre are of particular interest); the Pinacoteca, with paintings by local artists and painters of the Venetian, Roman and Neapolitan schools. It also contains sculptures, covers for the Gospels and other holy books, 17C-18C ceramics, Venetian glassware and ivories. ▶ There is an **Arch of Triumph** at the Porta Napoli (B-C2) erected in 1548 to honour Charles V of Spain; beyond it there is an obelisk dedicated to Ferdinand I of Naples. ▶ In front of the arch the v. S. Nicola leads to the church of **S. Nicolo e Cataldo**★, of special interest because of its variety of architectural influences. It was built by the Normans in 1180 and is basically Romanesque, but it has a Byzantine dome. The whole façade was ornamented with Baroque designs by G. Cino in 1716, but he left the portal in its original form revealing the different decorative styles that had been used. Thus, of the three friezes framing the door the first is Byzantine, the second is Romanesque and the third is Islamic. Inside there are three naves and 15C-17C frescos. ▶ In v. Monte S. Michele (C4) is the Chinese museum — **Museo Missionario Cinese** *(9 a.m.-1 p.m. and 4-7 p.m. Tue, Thu and Sat)*.

Environs

▶ 3 km SW is the **site of Rudiae,** an ancient Roman town with an ancient paved Roman road, early Apulian tombs and the ruins of an amphitheatre. It was the birthplace of the poet Ennius (239-169 BC). ▶ 1205 km NE is **San Cataldo,** a Lecce seaside resort; it has a fine beach and is surrounded by a pine forest; on its S side it has a breakwater built by the Romans to make an artificial harbour. ▶ 5.7 km S is **San Cesario di Lecce,** where there is a Palazzo Ducale containing a collection of contemporary art *(8-11 a.m. and 4-7 p.m.).* ▶ → The abbey of Santa Maria di Cerrate and the Salentine Peninsula.   ☐

Practical information _____

ⓘ p. S. Oronzo (C-D2-3, in the Sedile), ☎ 24443; v. Monte S. Michele (C-4, head office), ☎ 54117; v. Zanardelli 66, ☎ 56194.

🚂 (E-F1), ☎ 21016; *Ferrovie del Sud Est* (E-F1), ☎ 41931.

🚌 from v. Adua (C1-2), ☎ 21850.
Car rental: *Maggiore,* v. Daurio 76, ☎ 20184.

Hotels:
★★★★ **President,** v. Salandra 6 (C4 a), ☎ 51881, 154 rm Ⓟ 122,000; bkf: 15,000.
★★★ **Palme,** v. Leuca 90 (F3 b), ☎ 647171, 96 rm Ⓟ 🍽 ✕ 90,000; bkf: 8,500.
★★★ **Risorgimento,** v. Augusto 19 (D2 c), ☎ 42125, 57 rm Ⓟ ♿ ✕ In 18C palace with period decoration, 86,000; bkf: 8,000.

Restaurants:
◆◆◆ **G. & G.,** v. IV Finite, ☎ 45888, closed Wed and Aug. In garden surrounded by glass. Seafood: spaghetti and scampi, lobster au gratin, 25/35,000.
◆◆◆ **Plaza,** v. 140º Reggimento Fanteria 10 (C4 d), ☎ 25093, closed Sun and Aug. Regional cuisine, 16/30,000.
◆◆◆ **Satirello,** strada provinciale Lecce-Torre Chianca, ☎ 656121, closed Tue and 1-15 Jul. 17C white-washed farmhouse with lovely garden. Regional cuisine: cannulate leccese, meat and fish, 20/36,000.

⚓ *Torre Rinalda,* at Torre Rinalda, 150 pl, ☎ 652161.

Recommended
Archery: *Società Out Line,* v. Adriatica.
Craft workshops: *A. Mazzotta,* v. Stampacchia 21, ☎ 25942 (wrought iron); *F. Palazzo,* v. Adua 48, ☎ 43072 (wrought iron); *F. Don,* v. D'Amelio 1, ☎ 22593 (papier mâché); *F. Delle Site,* v. Adua 54, ☎ 20560 (dolls); *A. Cesari,* at San Pietro in Lama, v. XX Settembre, ☎ 627800 (ceramics).
Cycling: *Velodromo degli Ulivi,* at Monteroni di Lecce, v. Provinciale, ☎ 627719 (racing).
Events: *Festival of S. Oronzo* (24-26 Aug); summer opera season; open-air theatre in Roman amphitheatre (Jul); *International Musical Festival* (Aug); *Dolls' Fair* (Dec); *International Tennis Tournament* (spring).
Farm vacations: *Azienda Scalilla,* at Melendugno, ☎ 831124.
Flying: *Aeroclub,* at San Cataldo Airport, ☎ 650042.
Horseback riding: *Associazione Salentina Sport Equestri,* v. Leuca 233, ☎ 41513 (instruction); *Financial Trust Company,* at Lizzanello, v. Castri 30, ☎ 651389; *Centro Ippico Jo Strafel,* at Copertino, v. Est Grottella 10 (associate of *ANTE*); riding grounds, v. Arnesano (trotting races, spring and summer challenges and trials), also at Mater Domini.
Nature parks: *Riserva Le Cesine* (c. 18 km NE toward San Cataldo), guided visits Thu and Sun 9:30 a.m.-2:30 p.m.; groups on Sat; book in advance, ☎ 631392, closed mid-Sep-mid-May.
Swimming: v. di Ussano 55 (F2), ☎ 44022 (instruction).
Tennis: p. Arco di Tronfo (B-C2), ☎ 45834.
Wines: *Covis,* at Squinzano, v. Brindisi 181, ☎ 745142.
Youth hostels: *Ostello Adriatico,* at San Cataldo, v. Maneli 103, ☎ 650026.
♥ display wood and papier mâché, statuettes for creche, wrought iron, permanent display, v. Rubichi 21, ☎ 46758.

LOCOROTONDO

Bari 64, Rome 518 km
Pop. 12,630 ✉ 70010 ☎ 080   D-E4

Locorotondo is a small town an a hill whose houses sit in a circle. It contains a lovely s-shaped church, della Greca. From the Serra hill there is a splendid view of the countryside of the Itria Valley, covered with trulli.   ☐

Practical information _____

Restaurant:
◆◆ **Casa Mia,** v. Cisternino at 207-km marker, ☎ 711218, closed Tue in winter and Nov. Also a discothèque. Regional cuisine: orecchiette with turnip tops, roast rabbit, 25/30,000.

LUCERA*

Foggia 18, Bari 150, Rome 381 km
Pop. 33,464 ✉ 71036 ☎ 0881   A2

Arabs, who were part of the population of Sicily when it was ruled by Frederick II, were among the most unruly of his subjects; once incorporated into his armies, however, they proved some of his best soldiers. He decided to remove some of them from Sicily to Apulia (which he also ruled), where there would be less fighting with Christians. Between 1224-46 he transferred many of them to Apulia and founded, some 10 miles from Foggia, the city of *Luceria Saracenorum,* a town with mosques, camels and 60,000 Moslems. This was a colossal undertaking. Frederick II took care of his Moslem citizens and in return they served him well and even half a century after his death this was a flourishing town, an Islamic island among the surrounding Chris-

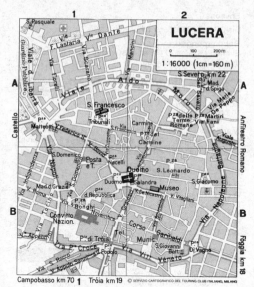

LUCERA

0 100 200m

1 : 16000 (1cm = 160m)

Campobasso km 70 **1** Tróia km 19 © SERVIZIO CARTOGRAFICO DEL TOURING CLUB ITALIANO, MILANO

and displays fossils of fauna of the Pleistocene epoch (mammoth, rhinoceros) and prehistoric stone instruments. The town also has some fine Baroque churches **(Madonna delle Grazie, Addolorata, Matrice)** with examples of Leccese altars. ◻

Practical information _____

Recommended
Craft workshops: *A. Solazzo,* at Surano *(11 km SE),* ☎ 93119 (carpets, tapestries, fabrics).
Sports: *Palazzetto dello sport,* v. Leuca ☎ 23461.

MANDURIA

Taranto 35, Bari 130, Rome 571 km
Pop. 31,418 ⊠ 74024 ☎ 099   E5

Manduria contains an ancient ghetto where Jews were confined; it has been kept unchanged and the small houses have no windows and are decorated in the manner of the 15C-16C. The **Duomo** has a 15C façade, but its campanile is 12C. The triangular piazza in the city centre is dominated by the imposing **Palazzo Imperiale.** The town library has a small archaeological collection with ceramics from a burial ground from 4C BC *(8 a.m.-2 p.m.; winter also 4-6 p.m.).* NE of town are ancient fortifications from 5C-3C BC and the Plinian Fountain *(caretaker)* in a grotto. ◻

Practical information _____

Restaurant:
♦ ***Castello,*** p. Garibaldi, ⊠ 672738, closed Mon and Aug. Regional cuisine, 23/29,000.
⚲ *Tiziana,* at Suri, 500 pl., ☎ 675891.

Recommended
Archery: *Compagnia Arcieri dei Messapi,* v. S. Lucia 8A, ☎ 672176.
Horseback riding: *Azienda Agrituristica La Staffa,* v. per San Pietro in Bevagna, ☎ 672676.

MANFREDONIA

Foggia 39, Bari 119, Rome 411 km
Pop. 55,665 ⊠ 71043 ☎ 0884   B2

Manfredi, the son of Frederick II, founded Manfredonia in 1256; his castle, surrounded by gardens, faces the quay and the port.

▶ The **Castello di Manfredi** houses the **Museo Archeologico Nazionale del Gargano** *(9 a.m.-1 p.m. and 4-7 p.m.; closed Mon)* which has 8C BC vases of the Greek Mycenean epoch and engraved 7C-6C BC steles (stone slabs). ▶ The **cathedral** has a 13C *Madonna and Child.* ▶ The church of **S. Domenico** has 13C frescos. ▶ 3 km on the road to Foggia in a deserted region near a pine forest is the church of **S. Maria di Siponto**★★. At one time this was the cathedral of the ancient city of the same name; it is an unusual building in the Byzantine style (11C), built on a square plan with a dome. 7.5 km farther is the striking church of **S. Leonardo di Siponto**★ (12C), formerly an abbey of the Teutonic Knights; on its l. side is a fine portal★ with 12C reliefs. ◻

Practical information _____

≋
ℹ corso Manfredi 26, ☎ 21998.
🚢 daily steamer sailings to Rodi Garganico and Tremiti Islands, several times a week to Pugnochiuso, Vieste and Peschici, *Adriatica,* ☎ 22888.

tians. Given the intolerance of the times this could not last and eventually Charles II of Anjou, after the Angevins had taken over the region, gave orders for the Moslem population to be liquidated and for the city to be destroyed. The remains of the town, peopled by a few Christians, was renamed Città di Santa Maria, although in time the old name of Lucera returned.

▶ The **Duomo**★ (B1-2), built by Charles II of Anjou, is one of the finest examples of Angevin Gothic architecture extant in S Italy; it remains almost the same as when it was built, having been spared renovation and reconstruction. Inside is a Crucifixion★ from the 14C. ▶ The medieval church of **S. Domenico** (B1) underwent a Baroque transformation and has an inlaid altar and a carved choir (1640). ▶ The **Museo Civico G. Fiorelli** (B2) *(9 a.m.-1 p.m. and 5-7 p.m.; winter 4-6 p.m.; 9 a.m.-1 p.m. Sat and hols; closed Mon)* has some outstanding archaeological material including a marine Venus★ which is a Roman IC copy of an original Greek statue from the school of Praxiteles, a mosaic pavement of the same period and a bust of Proserpina★; there are also many bronzes and paintings. ▶ The church of **S. Francesco** (A1) was built during the reign of Charles II and has some fine 14C, 15C and 17C frescos. ▶ The **castle** *(off map; same visiting times as Museum)* is on the hill of Monte Albano to the W of the city; Charles II of Anjou built it on what was originally a palace of Frederick II, adding powerful walls and massive towers. Inside the castle are the ruins of Frederick's palace and the remains of an Angevin church and some Roman buildings. ▶ E of the city *(off map)* is the Roman amphitheatre from 1C BC; two of its entrances have been rebuilt and its auditorium, dug out of the hill, is still visible. ◻

MAGLIE

Lecce 29, Bari 179, Rome 640 km
Pop. 15,386 ⊠ 73024 ☎ 0836   F5

Maglie is a small town that houses the interesting **Museo Paleontologico** *(8 a.m.-1 p.m.; Thu and Sat also 5-7 p.m.; winter 4-6 p.m.; Sun 10 a.m.-12 noon; closed Mon and hols).* It is in the Palazzo Capece

Hotels:
★★★★ *Cicolella,* at Lido di Siponto, ☎ 21463, 18 rm ℗ ♨ ☂ closed Nov-Easter, 61,000; bkf: 6,000.
★★★★ *Gargano,* v. Beccarini 2, ☎ 27621, 46 rm ℗ ⌧ 65,000; bkf: 4,000.

Restaurant:
♦♦ *Porto-da Michele,* p. della Libertà 3, ☎ 21800, closed Wed and Christmas. Seafood, 30/40,000.

⚓ *Gargano-Lido Romagna,* SS 159 at 3.8-km marker, 300 pl, ☎ 371063; *Ippocampo e African Beach,* SS 159 at 10.8-km marker, ☎ 371121.

Recommended
Craft workshops: *G. Olivieri,* v. Di Vittorio 117, ☎ 23986 (telephone before visiting; carved and decorated furniture).
Cycling: *G. S. Cicli Castriotta,* v. Beccarini 7, ☎ 23424.
Marina: ☎ 23871; at Gargano, ☎ 38158.
Sports: *Palazzetto dello sport,* strada Ruggiano.

MARGHERITA DI SAVOIA

Foggia 56, Bari 69, Rome 410 km
Pop. 11,804 ⌧ 71044 ☎ 0883   C3

Margherita di Savoia was named for the first Queen of Italy. Before that it was called Salina di Barletta. Its salt-works are the largest in Italy (75 % of national consumption) and one of the most important in Europe. It has been a salt-producing area since the 3C BC. The best time to visit the region is late summer because this is when the salt is gathered. The salt residues are used in a nearby spa in curative waters.　□

Practical information —————————
♨ (Jun-mid-Oct), ☎ 755402 or 755107.
≋
ℹ p. Marconi 9, ☎ 754012.

⚓ *Tritone,* at Canna Fresca, v. del Mare, 130 pl, ☎ 754445.

Recommended
Tennis: v. Rose (Regina zone), ☎ 761693.

MARINA DI GINOSA

Taranto 40, Bari 106, Rome 481 km
Pop. 3,140 ⌧ 74025 ☎ 099   D4-5

Pine trees form a background to this long beach in the Gulf of Taranto. The town of Ginosa is 21 km inland, high on the edge of a gorge with caves and cliff churches containing 10C-11C Byzantine frescos.　□

Practical information —————————
MARINA DI GINOSA

Hotels:
★★★★ *Golf Hotel,* at Riva dei Tessali, ☎ 6439007, 75 rm ℗ ♨ ♨ ⌧ ☂ ♪ (18) 1/2 Pens. closed Nov-Mar, 115,000.
★★★ *Europa Park Hotel,* v. della Chiesa 4, ☎ 627144, 45 rm ℗ ♨ ⛄ ⌧ closed Nov-Easter, 58,000; bkf: 4,000.

⚓ *Internazionale,* v. della Pineta, 100 pl, ☎ 627153.

Recommended
Golf: at Riva dei Tessali *(11 km NE),* ☎ 6439007 (18 holes).
Tennis: v. Fiume 15, ☎ 627572.

> For the translation of a name of a meat, a fish or a vegetable, for the composition of a dish or a sauce, see the *Menu Guide* at the end of the Practical Holiday Guide; it lists the most common culinary terms.

Environs
GINOSA, ⌧ 74013, ☎ 099.

Recommended
Events: *Passion of Christ,* costume pageant on Good Friday, Comune, ☎ 624255.

MARINA DI PULSANO

Taranto 20, Bari 110, Rome 548 km
⌧ 74026 ☎ 099   D5

Marina di Pulsano is one of the finest beaches in the Gulf of Taranto. Facing the blue waters of the Ionian Sea, it is surrounded by a lovely pine forest.　□

Practical information —————————
Hotels:
★★★★ *Eden Park,* at Lido Silvana, ☎ 633091, 55 rm ℗ ♨ ⛄ ⌧ ☂ closed 26 Sep-24 May, 124,000; bkf: 8,000.
★★ *Sud,* at Monte d'Arena, ☎ 633026, 48 rm ℗ ♨ 35,500; bkf: 4,200.

MARTINA FRANCA*

Taranto 31, Bari 74, Rome 524 km
Pop. 43,926 ⌧ 74015 ☎ 080   D4

Martina Franca is a showcase for the Baroque and rococo styles of architecture. This small town of winding streets contains homes and palaces whose soft blond stone is carved with marvelous convolutions and whose balconies have wrought-iron balustrades shadowing the streets. In the 10C, people from Taranto founded a village on Mount S. Martino to escape the Saracens. Four centuries later, Philip of Anjou enlarged it, built a fortified wall around it with 12 square towers and 12 round ones and gave it a number of franchises, hence the name Franca.
▶ The wall and the twenty-four towers are gone, and four **gates** are all that remain. ▶ The **Ducal Palace** has wrought-iron balustrades and 17C frescos. It is now the municipio. ▶ The church of **S. Martino** with a sumptuous Baroque façade stands beside the austere campanile of the old Gothic church. On the l. of the church are the **Palazzo della Corte** (1760) and the **Torre dell'Orologio** (1734). ▶ There are interesting **palazzetti** in v. Cavour. ▶ The church of **S. Domenico** has a rococo façade and a Baroque interior. The church of **Carmine** is on a ledge and offers a lovely view over the green Itria Valley dotted with white-washed trulli dwellings.　□

Practical information —————————
ℹ p. Roma 37, ☎ 705702.

Hotels:
★★★ *Dell'Erba,* v. dei Cedri 1, ☎ 901055, 49 rm ℗ ♨ ♿ ⛄ ⌧ 70,000; bkf: 6,000.
★★★ *Park Hotel San Michele,* v. Carella 9, ☎ 705355, 80 rm ℗ ♨ ⛄ ⌧ Villa in park, 81,000.

Restaurants:
♦♦ *Spiedo - da Antonietta,* v. Virgilio 30, ☎ 706511, closed Wed in winter. Regional cuisine, 20/25,000.

Recommended
Events: *Concorso Oppico Nazionale* (National Riding Competition, Jul); *Festival of the Itria Valley* (Jul-Aug).
Farm vacations: *Azienda Semeraro,* at Cisternino *(10 km NE),* ☎ 713668.
Horseback riding: *Okay Associazione Sport Equestri,* v. D'Annunzio 21, ☎ 705011.

> Looking for a locality? Consult the index at the back of the book.

MASSAFRA

Taranto 18, Bari 76, Rome 514 km
Pop. 28,419 ⊠ 74016 ☎ 099   D4

Massafra is just beyond the industrial fringe of Taranto. It is divided by a deep ravine with walls riddled with caves, troglodyte dwellings and Greek Orthodox Christian crypts.
▶ Massafra contains a 14C **castle** that was renovated in the 16C. ▶ From the two viaducts there is a splendid view of the **gravina di S. Marco★**. Innumerable cacti cover the walls of this ravine and countless grottos were dug in its sides by anchorites during the Middle Ages. They are decorated with religious frescos *(guided tours, 4:30-7 p.m.; telephone Comune before visit, ☎ 687903)*. ▶ Among the most interesting are the cavechurch of **S. Marco** with three naves and two apses, the cave-church of **La Candelora** and the cave-church of **S. Leonardo** (with 13C-14C frescos). ▶ 1 km along the bottom of the ravine reached by a splendid Baroque stairway is the **Sanctuary of the Madonna of the Scala,** built over an ancient Greek orthodox church; the fresco (12C-13C) on the altar is from the original church. Beside it, partly in ruins, is the crypt of the Buona Nuova with a 13C fresco on its altar. From the portico it is possible to descend to an 8C-9C crypt that is oblong with a semi-circular apse at its end. Close by the sanctuary is the **Farmacia del Mago Greguro** (pharmacy of wizard Greguro), a mysterious series of intercommunicating caves. The monks that once lived here used the recesses as deposits for their medicinal herbs.   □

Mystery of the cliff people

In narrow limestone valleys like Gravina and Massafra there are many caves dug out of the rock. They were used as dwelling places and as churches. At first they were thought to have been excavated and used by anchorites and other hermits of the Eastern Orthodox Christian church, but now archaeologists are inclined to consider them to have been the homes used by the peasantry when they were forced to escape inland up the mountains from Longobard incursions or from the cruel raids of the Moors. It is not easy to date them because the many wall paintings they contain seem to show Byzantine influences. However, they do not appear to be older than the 10C and the Byzantines had left hundreds of years before then.

Practical information _____
ℹ️ v. Garibaldi 3.

Restaurant:
♦♦ *Rocce,* v. Magna Grecia 28, ☎ 681607, closed Mon. Farmhouse redone with veranda for dining in summer. Regional cuisine: risotto and shellfish, orecchiette with ricotta, 25/30,000.

⚓ *Verde Mare,* at Marina di Ferrara, 110 pl, ☎ 685125.

MESAGNE

Brindisi 14, Bari 125, Rome 574 km
Pop. 30,734 ⊠ 72023 ☎ 0831   E4

Mesagne was destroyed by Manfred, son of Frederick II, in 1254. He later rebuilt its **castle**, which has since been restructured several times. The Palazzo del Comune contains the **Museo Civico U. Granafei** *(9 a.m.-1 p.m.; closed wkends)*. It houses archaeological finds from the surrounding region

including 7C-2C BC material from burial sites. The church of **S. Lorenzo** at the town's entrance is 9C-10C.   □

MOLFETTA

Bari 25, Rome 425 km
Pop. 65,427 ⊠ 70056 ☎ 080   C3
See map on page 88.

Today only fishing boats rest at their moorings in the port of Molfetta, an ancient town of houses with terraced roofs. In the Middle Ages, however, it was a thriving commercial centre, trading especially with Ragusa on the other side of the Adriatic Sea. It was frequented by Greeks, Dalmatians, Venetians, Slavs and people from Amalfi, many of whom built houses and made their homes here.

▶ The 12C-13C **Vecchio Duomo★** (A2) is a splendid Romanesque edifice with three naves; the central one has three domes on the outside hidden by pyramidal covers on polygonal drums. The two campanile on the sides of the apse emphasize the building's unusual structure. ▶ The 17C **cathedral** (A-B2) has a grandiose Baroque façade and in its interior there is a fine painting of the *Assumption of the Virgin Mary* by C. Giaquinto, as well as a 16C painting on wood of the *Dormition of the Virgin.* ▶ In the Episcopio (bishop's house; A-B2) is a small museum *(telephone before visiting, ☎ 911559)* with a collection of archaeological finds from the pulo pit of Molfetta as well as illuminated and painted codexes, one of which has a *Pietà* by B. Cavallino. ▶ The public gardens (**Villa Garibaldi)** and the church of **S. Bernardino** (1451), with a fine 14C tryptych by Tuccio d'Andria, are on the p. Garibaldi (B3) which is the centre of town. ▶ The **pulo pit** is 2 km SW; it is a chasm with a series of grottos, many of which were inhabited in the neolithic period.   □

Practical information _____
ℹ️ corso Dante (A2).

Hotel:
★★★ *Garden,* provinciale per Terlizzi, ☎ 911222, 63 rm
🅿️ ⌗ ✧ ✐ 60,000.

Restaurants:
♦♦♦ *Alga Marina,* SS 16 at 779-km marker, ☎ 948091, closed Mon and Nov. Regional cuisine: tagliatelle with meat sauce, grilled lobster, 35/45,000.
♦♦♦ *Astoria,* SS 16 at 779-km marker, ☎ 941141, closed Fri and Nov. Regional cuisine: risotto and shellfish sauce, lobster on the spit, 25/35,000.

Recommended
Events: *Processions of Good Friday and Easter Saturday; Arts and Crafts Show* (Jul); *Religious Festival of the Sea* (8 Sep); *National Philatelic Exhibition* (Nov).
Marina: ☎ 911076.
Sports: *Palazzetto dello sport,* p. Sturzo ☎ 948039.
Tennis: v. Gramsci, ☎ 948059.

MONTE SANT'ANGELO*

Foggia 54, Bari 135, Rome 427 km
Pop. 16,871 ⊠ 71037 ☎ 0884   B2

According to tradition, the citizens of Siponto (→ Manfredonia) were aided in resisting the barbarians by the appearance in a grotto on Monte Sant'Angelo of the Archangel Michael. In consequence, a church was consecrated here in 493. In reality the sanctuary was built over a Byzantine abbey in the second half of the following century when the Longobards, who had established themselves in the region and created the Duchy of Benevento, were organizing themselves politically and ecclesiastically. They turned Monte Sant'Angelo into a national shrine where pilgrims

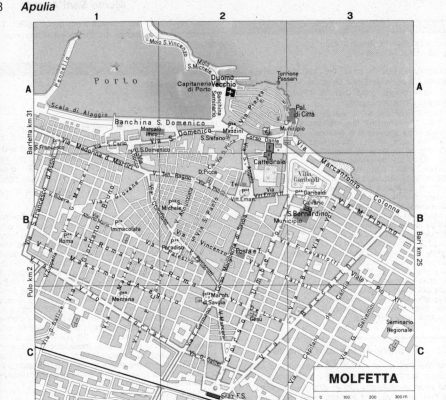

MOLFETTA

0　100　200　300 m

1 : 14000　(1cm = 140 m)

1 Autostrada km 4 - Terlizzi km 9　　2

© SERVIZIO CARTOGRAFICO DEL TOURING CLUB ITALIANO, MILANO

and Crusaders called. Today, it still draws large crowds. It sits on a spur of the Gargano promontory with a spectacular view of the surrounding mountains and the sea.

▶ The shrine of **S. Michele**★ (A1-2) is at the end of town in a small square dominated by an octagonal campanile (1273). Passing through two arches and descending to a courtyard is a **church** with a Romanesque portal and bronze **imposts**★ brought from Constantinople in 1076. Its interior has a single nave with an ogival vault. The grotto of the Archangel opens onto the church and has a 15C statue of St. Michael in alabaster, a 12C episcopal throne★ and a niche into which the Holy Water from the rock flows. Excavations under the grotto have uncovered rooms of the Carolingian period (9C) with 10C-11C frescos. ▶ Steps in front of the campanile lead to the ruins of the Romanesque church of S. Pietro where it is possible to see, on the l. of the apse *(ask caretaker)*, the **tomb of Rotari**★ (A2), King of the Longobards, which is probably an 11C baptistery. To the r. of this church is the Romanesque church of **S. Maria Maggiore** (1170) with a beautiful carved portal and 13C-16C paintings in the Byzantine style. ▶ The **Museo Tancredi di Arti e Tradizioni garganiche** (A2; *9:30 a.m.-12:30 p.m. and 3:30-7 p.m.*) has archaic material and specimens of traditional arts and crafts. The **castle** (A1) dates from the Norman period, but was enlarged by the Aragonese (1494). ▶ In the SW of the town is the **Junno district,** beside the ravine, many of the small houses date from the 17C. ▶ 9.2 km SW is the old monastery church of

S. Maria di Pulsano, a 6C building partly dug out of rock and rebuilt in the 12C.　　　□

Practical information ————————

ℹ v. Giordani 17 (A2).

Hotel:
★★★ **Rotary,** v. per Pulsano, ☎ 62146, 24 rm ℗ ⇇ ⇘ ♿ ✖ closed Nov, 45,000; bkf: 3,000.

Restaurant:
♦♦ **Poggio del Sole,** v. per Pulsano 10, ☎ 61092, closed Wed in winter, Nov and Jan. Splendid view. Regional cuisine: orecchiette, roast kid, 15/20,000.

⚠ *Monaco,* at Macchia Libera, 220 pl., ☎ 23489.

Recommended
Events: cultural and traditional events organized by Gargano Study Centre (Jul-Aug).

La MURGIA DEI TRULLI

From Bari to Monopoli *(128 km, 1 day; map 4)*

La Murgia dei Trulli is the name of the SE part of the tableland of the Murge (→ Castel del Monte and the Murgia Region). It is a hilly region that slopes down toward the Adriatic and the Gulf of Taranto. A large number of peasants remain on the land here, unlike

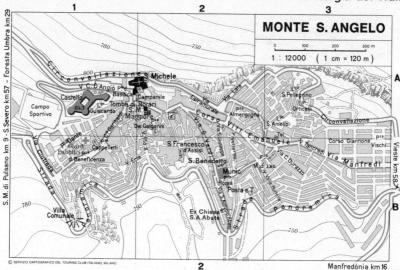

other areas of Apulia where the countryside is deserted.

▶ Leaving Bari (→), the route follows the coast in the direction of Brindisi. ▶ The Angevin Castle (1278) at **Mola di Bari** was altered in the 16C and again in following centuries. There is a 13C **cathedral** in the older section of town, which was transformed in the 16C into a Renaissance building by Dalmatian architects. ▶ The ancient part of **Polignano a Mare** is located on the edge of a high cliff facing out to sea; in the **Matrice church** there is statuary, a stone creche by Stefano da Putignano (15-16C), a 16C choir in wood and, in the sacristy, five panels of a polyptych of B. Vivarini (1472). ▶ Many nearby grottos can be visited by boat including the **grotta Palazzese** (view★ of extraordinary sea erosions) and the **grotta dei Colombi.** ▶ Turning inland, the route arrives at **Castellana Grotte★** on the edge of a hollow; its 16C church of S. Francesco has some fine Baroque altars. SE of the town near the convent of S. Maria della Vetrana is the **Specchia grande** (large mirror), an ancient sepulchral mound with a series of concentric rings; it is empty now and may have been used as a lookout. 2 km SW is the **Grotte di Castellana★★,** the largest series of caves in the Italian peninsula; they were dug out of the limestone rock by an ancient underground river and may be visited, with a guide, with a choice of two routes: one, 1,500 ft *(11 a.m., 1, 4 and 7 p.m. Apr-Sep);* the other covering *c.* two miles *(8:30 a.m.-12:15 p.m. and 2:30-6 p.m. Apr-Sep; 9 a.m.-12 noon and 2-5 p.m. Oct-Mar).* The temperature in the caves is 15° centigrade, 59° fahrenheit. ▶ Another **grotto★,** 1 km NW of **Putignano,** can also be visited *(8 a.m.-12 noon and 2 p.m.-sunset).* In the town is the church of **S. Pietro,** a 12C building that was converted to the Baroque style in the 17C. In the Palazzo Romanazzi, the **Museo Civico** *(in preparation)* will have rococo church fittings, 17C-18C paintings, silverware and arms. ▶ The itinerary leads now into the heart of the Murgia dei Trulli past **Alberobello** (→), **Martina Franca** (→) and **Locorotondo** (→), all containing many interesting sights. ▶ Returning toward the sea from **Selva di Fasano** across a region with white trulli and Mediterranean vegetation, the route goes through **Fasano,** which has a Safari-Zoo where over 600 animals, including lions, tigers, bears and wolves, roam freely in its large park *(9:30 a.m.-sunset).* ▶ Arriving at the sea at **Savelletri,** the roads follows the Adriatic coast to the N. ▶ The ruins at **Egnazia** are among the most important archaeological sites in Apulia. There is a **Museo** *(wkdays 9 a.m.-1 p.m.)* with many special displays (Mosaic of the Three Graces★ 2C-3C), a large Apulian burial room★★ (4C-3C BC) and a **burial ground** (1C). The ancient city of **Gnathia** was a village of huts (13C-12C BC), which later was a Greek town and then a Roman one; traces of its walls are still visible. In the **excavation area** remains have been found of two ancient Christian churches dating from the 4C-6C. On a hill is a 4C BC temple; the Roman port was where the inlet is, N of the hill. The last stop on the route is at nearby **Monopoli,** where there is the **castle** built by Frederick II and the Romanesque church of **S. Maria Amalfitana** with a crypt that once was an old Byzantine church. At v. S. Domenico 73 is the cliff shrine of the **Madonna del Soccorso** (11C); the cathedral has a Byzantine *Madonna* from c. 1280 and paintings by Palma il Giovane, F. de Mura and others. □

Practical information

CASTELLANA GROTTE, ⊠ 70013, ☎ 080.
ℹ p. Garibaldi 5, ☎ 735191; information office at grottos.

Hotel:
★★ *Esploratore - Matarrese,* p. Anelli 12, ☎ 735503, 17 rm ⌚ 50,000; bkf: 5,000.

Restaurants:
♦♦♦ *Chiancafredda,* v. Chiancafredda 4, ☎ 736710, closed Tue and Nov. A palazzo in a beautiful setting among olive groves. Regional cuisine: chicory and cheese, roast lamb, 25/35,000.
♦♦ *Taverna degli Artisti - da Ernesto e Rosa,* v. Matarrese 23/27, ☎ 736234, closed Thu and Nov-Mar. Near grotto, summer dining in garden. Regional cuisine: riccioli carrettiera, lamb on the spit, 18/22,000.

Recommended
Events: *Local Festival* (Sep 8), *Alternative Music Meetings* in the grottos (Jun).
Horseback riding: *Equitazione Castellanese,* v. Conversano 47, ☎ 735047.

FASANO, ⊠ 72015, ☎ 080.
ℹ p. Ciaia 10, ☎ 713086.

Recommended
Events: *Estate Silvana* (Silvan summer); opera and concerts; *Christmas Among the Trulli.*

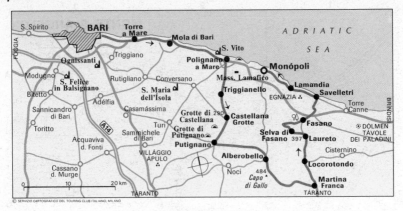

4. La Murgia dei Trulli

Trulli

Trulli *are round houses with cone tops found only in a few villages in the region of Bari. They are built of uncemented stones set out, row upon row edging inwards, until they meet at the tapering top; at this point a decorative pinnacle, with some simple religious or magical decoration, is set up over the summit. The earliest known trullo dates back to the 13C, but most are more recent and they continue to be built. At one time it was thought that they were devised during the Middle Ages to thwart Ferdinand I of Aragon. During his reign over Apulia, he gave orders that the peasants were not to be allowed to build permanent homes. In this way he could move them around from place to place as they were needed. The peasants answered with the trullo which could easily be taken down when news arrived that the King's men were coming to inspect the village. This theory has since been discounted. The method used to build the trulli is similar to that employed to erect certain houses known as 'sugar loaves' near Aleppo in Syria. It would have been possible for Apulian men on the Crusades to have seen them and brought back the idea. Archaeologists in Greece excavating the ruins of Mycenae, have found that this same principle was used there for constructing houses known as tholos. This would link the trulli of Apulia with the Aegean civilization of the third millenium BC.*

Zoo: *Zoo-Safari,* at S. Elia, ☎ 713055 or 714455.

MOLA DI BARI, ✉ 70042, ☎ 080.

⚓ *Caloria,* at Caloria, SS 16, 80 pl, ☎ 644897.

Recommended
Marina: ☎ 641573.

MONOPOLI, ✉ 70043, ☎ 080.

Hotels:
★★★ *Cala Corvino,* v. Moro 4, ☎ 802922, 156 rm P ⅏ ✄ ✉ ⌇ 86,500; bkf: 4,500.

★★★ *Gemini Due,* at Sicarico, SS 377 at 8.7-km marker, ☎ 803133, 45 rm P ⅏ ⅙ ✉ ⌇ 68,000.
★★★ *Max,* v. Vittorio Veneto 241, ☎ 802591, 31 rm P 66,000; bkf: 6,000.

Restaurant:
◆◆◆ *Villa Meo-Evoli,* ☎ 803052, closed Tue and Nov. In park of 17C villa. Regional and international cuisine: fresh local produce, olive oil from adjoining factory, 30/40,000.

⚓ *Santo Stefano,* at Santo Stefano, 300 pl, ☎ 745685 (all year).

Recommended
Sports: *Palazzetto dello sport,* v. Fiume, ☎ 802919.
POLIGNANO A MARE, ✉ 70044, ☎ 080.
≋
ℹ p. Regina Margherita.

Hotel:
★★★★ *Grotta Palazzese,* v. Narciso 59, ☎ 740261, 14 rm P ✄ 85,000; bkf: 6,000.

Recommended
Caving: visit by boat to Palazzese and dei Colombi grottos, information from *Hotel Grotta Palazzese,* ☎ 740261.

PUTIGNANO, ✉ 70017, ☎ 080.
ℹ v. Margherita di Savoia 18, ☎ 731532.

Hotel:
★★★ *Plaza,* v. Roma, ☎ 731266, 41 rm P ✄ No restaurant, 68,000; bkf: 4,800.

Recommended
Caving: Putignano or Trullo grottos (caretaker on premises), information: *Grotte di Putignano,* v. Turi 18, ☎ 731967.
Events: *Carnival,* of medieval origin.

SAVELLETRI, ✉ 72015, ☎ 080.

Restaurant:
◆◆◆ *Renzina,* p. Roma 6, ☎ 729075, closed Fri and Aug. Shaded veranda on sea. Seafood: pappardelle with lobster sauce, grilled swordfish or lobster, 30/40,000.

Recommended
Events: *Festival of Fish* (Aug).

SELVA DI FASANO, ✉ 72010, ☎ 080.
ℹ at Fasano, ☎ 713086.

Hotel:
★★★ **Sierra Silvana**, v. Castelluccio, ☎ 799322, 120 rm
Ⓟ 🐾 ♨ ♿ 🏊 ⊠ 🅿 closed Nov-Feb, 72,000; bkf: 8,000.

Restaurant:
● ♦♦♦ **Fagiano - da Vittorio**, v. Toledo 13, ☎ 799157, closed Mon in winter and Nov. Refined and tastefully furnished. Regional cuisine: roast kid, carpaccio with truffles, 35/40,000.

⚓ *Monacelle*, 400 pl, ☎ 809261 (all year).

NARDO

Lecce 24, Bari 173, Rome 622 km
Pop. 29,097 ⊠ 73048 ☎ 0833   E-F5

Nardo is a picturesque town with many Baroque buildings. The lively **piazza Salandra**, circled with galleries and balconies, has at its centre a column with the *Madonna of the Immaculate Conception* (1769). Nardo also contains a Romanesque-Gothic cathedral with 14C frescos.   □

Practical information _____

⚓ *Sant'Isidoro*, at Sant'Isidoro, ☎ 813665.

ORIA

Brindisi 32, Bari 113, Rome 663 km
Pop. 14,994 ⊠ 72024 ☎ 0831   E4

Oria is an ancient Apulian site, where Frederick II built a powerful **castle★** in the 13C. It is a triangular fortress to which the Angevins later added towers. In the castle is a collection *(9 a.m.-12 noon)* with ceramics, arms and ancient Apulian finds. In the courtyard, the 9C crypt of Ss. Chrysanthus and Daria (husband and wife, early Roman martyrs stoned to death) was probably part of an earlier cathedral on the site. Oria's **cathedral** was rebuilt in 1750 and its **museum** in the municipio has many specimens of regional finds *(office hrs)*. 5 km SE, the **shrine of S. Cosimo della Macchia** attracts many pilgrims. Not far away is a zoo with an aquarium and a small museum.   □

Practical information _____

Recommended
Events: *La Quaremma Festival* (Feb); *Pageant* with *Tournament between the town's various quarters* (Jul-Aug).

OSTUNI

Brindisi 35, Bari 80, Rome 530 km
Pop. 31,770 ⊠ 72017 ☎ 0831   E4

Each year in Ostuni the walls of houses and the church, as well as the pavements and flights of steps in the streets, are whitewashed so that the town is startlingly white. It stands on three hills, contrasting with the blue of the sky. Below it, by the sea, are rocky spurs and sandy inlets. It has a **cathedral**, at the top of the medieval part of town, which dates from the 15C and has a late Gothic façade.   □

Practical information _____

ⓘ p. Libertà 63, ☎ 971268.

Hotel:
★★★ **G. H. Rosa Marina**, at Marina di Ostuni, ☎ 970061, 197 rm Ⓟ 🐾 ⊠ 🅿 73,000.

Restaurants:
♦♦♦ **Chez Elio**, v. dei Colli, ☎ 972030, closed Mon and Sep. High on a hill with view of town, woods and sea. Mixed cuisine: crustaceans, kid on the spit, 20/35,000.
♦♦ **Vecchia Ostuni**, largo Lanza 9 ☎ 973308, closed Tue and 1-15 Nov. Regional mixed cuisine: risotto with shellfish sauce, roast kid, 25/35,000.

⚓ *Costa Merlata*, at Marina di Ostuni, 250 pl, ☎ 973064; *Pilone*, at Marina di Ostuni, 570 pl, ☎ 970075.

Recommended
Events: *La Palomma* (Apr); *Cavalcade of S. Oronzo* and *Festival of Times Gone By* (Aug).
Marina: at Villanova di Ostuni *(6 km N)*, ☎ 970210.
Swimming: at Rosa Marina, ☎ 970240.
Vacation villages: *Hotel Villaggio Valtur*, at Marina di Ostuni (May-Sep), information at Milan, ☎ 02/791733, at Rome, ☎ 06/6784588.

OTRANTO

Lecce 38, Bari 192, Rome 642 km
Pop. 4,986 ⊠ 73028 ☎ 0836   F5

Otranto is Italy's easternmost city. In 1480 it was taken by the Turks and the remains of 560 victims of that tragic event are in the **cathedral★**, in the Chapel of the Martyrs. The cathedral, the major monument of the town, dates from the 11C. It has a beautiful 14C Gothic rosette on its façade, and in its 11C **crypt★** are Byzantine frescos. Its vast mosaic pavement is especially interesting. It is black and white and depicts the Tree of Life, with scenes from the Bible, stories from Arthurian legends and animal pictures. It was done in 1166. The older part of the city is partially surrounded by its ancient walls and above it stands a massive 15C Aragonese **castle**.   □

Practical information _____

≋
ⓘ lungomare Kennedy, ☎ 81436.
🚢 daily car ferry sailings for Corfu and Igoumenitsa (Jun-Oct), *Ellade Viaggi*, ☎ 81578.

Hotel:
★★★ **Miramare**, lungomare Terra d'Otranto, ☎ 81023, 68 rm Ⓟ No restaurant, 56,000; bkf: 5,000.

⚓ *Mulino d'Acqua*, v. S. Stefano, 450 pl, ☎ 81391.

Recommended
Events: *Arts and Crafts Show* in the Castle (Aug); musical performances; *Luci sul mare* (Lights on sea; Sep).
Horseback riding: *Country Club Alimini* (associate of *ANTE*).
Marina: ☎ 81073.
Sailing: *Lega Navale*, v. del Porto, ☎ 815090.
Vacation villages: *Club Méditerranée* (Jun-Sep, information, at Milan, ☎ 02/778663, at Rome, ☎ 06/475951; *Villaggio Valtur* (Jun-Sep, information, at Milan, ☎ 02/791733 at Rome, ☎ 06/6784588.

PORTO CESAREO

Lecce 28, Bari 159, Rome 600 km
Pop. 3,623 ⊠ 73010 ☎ 0833   E5

Porto Cesareo, on the SW side of the Salerno peninsula, is a fishing village and seaside resort. It is surrounded by fortifications that were built as defenses against the Turks. It has a Marine Biology Centre and a museum of the sea, **Museo Talassografico**, on v. Russo *(if closed, see caretaker at v. Respighi 11)*. □

Practical information _____

≈ ⓘ v. Silvio Pellico 32, ☎ 846086.

Hotel:
★★★ *Scoglio,* ☎ 569079, 30 rm ⌂ ⚓ On private island linked to mainland by road, 67,000; bkf: 5,000.

Restaurant:
◆◆◆ *Veliero - da Oronzino,* v. Muratori 42, ☎ 846201, closed Tue and Nov. Regional cuisine: orecchiette cociolina, cavatelli rughetta, 25/40,000.

RUVO DI PUGLIA

Bari 36, Rome 441 km
Pop. 23,963 ⊠ 70037 ☎ 080   C3

Horace, in one of his poems, described a journey he made from Rome to Brindisi with his patron, Maecenas, and wrote, 'and tired we arrived at last at Ruvo'. Two thousand years later Ruvo is still flourishing. It is a country town that produces grapes, almonds and wine. In Horace's time it was well-known for its beautiful ceramics.

▶ Ruvo's 12C Romanesque **cathedral**★ seems almost to anticipate later Gothic architecture because of its upward sweep. The severity of its façade is lessened by the beauty of its rosette and lovely portal. ▶ The **Museo Jatta**★ (p. Bovio 35; *wkdays 9:30 a.m.-12 noon*) has a collection of more than 1,700 ancient vases, some Greek and others made locally between 5C-3C BC.   ☐

Practical information _____

Hotel:
★★★★ *Pineta,* prolungamento corso Piave, ☎ 811578, 22 rm ℗ ⌂ ⚓ closed Nov, 56,000; bkf: 6,000.

Restaurant:
◆ *Cemener,* v. Garibaldi 20, ☎ 811794, closed Sun noon and Jul. Regional cuisine, 20/25,000.

The SALENTINE PENINSULA

From Lecce to Gallipoli *(154 km, 1 day; map 5)*

The Salentine Peninsula, the heel of the Italian boot, is not only the most S part of Apulia, but also the most E part of Italy. It faces the Adriatic Sea on one side and the Gulf of Taranto on the other, and nowhere does it rise more than a few hundred feet above sea level. The coast is broken by rocky spurs which at its extreme S point near Santa Maria di Leuca become cliffs. There are coves and sandy beaches everywhere.

▶ Leaving **Lecce** (→) the route goes along the SS 16 to **Maglie** (→). Here it turns inland and heads for the E coast of the peninsula at **Otranto** (→). The route becomes scenic as it proceeds S. ▶ From the **Faro di Capo d'Otranto** (lighthouse of Cape Otranto) it is possible to see the opposite side of the Strait of Otranto, the mountains of Albania and Epirus and the island of Corfu. ▶ **Santa Cesarea Terme** is a charming seaside resort that sits on a cliff top. It has health-giving natural springs that gush from four grottos. ▶ Just before arriving at Castro, a road descends to **grotta Zinzulusa**★ *(Mar-Oct 10 a.m.-1 p.m. and 2-7 p.m.; Jul-Aug 9:30 a.m.-7 p.m.),* the most interesting grotto in Apulia. It is 500 ft long and comprises the Corridoio delle Meraviglie (hall of marvels), rich in stalactites and stalagmites, and a cavern called the Duomo that was inhabited in palaeolithic times. A little further N it is possible to reach the **grotta Romanelli** by boat *(30 mns).* This was also used by paleolithic peoples and has the oldest wall paintings and graffiti in Italy. ▶ The route then arrives at **Castro**, which is divid-

ed into **Castro Superiore,** with a 15C castle and a cathedral with 12C Romanesque remains and a small Byzantine church, and **Castro Marina** in the inlet below. ▶ On a piazza at the extreme end of **capo di Santa Maria di Leuca,** there is a 17C church dedicated to S. Maria di Finibus Terrae (of land's end). It stands on the site of an ancient temple dedicated to Minerva and it is popularly believed that a pilgrimage to this shrine ensures entry into Heaven. ▶ From nearby **Leuca** it is possible to visit by boat several caves with openings on the bay, among them **grotta Porcinara** on Ristola Point. ▶ Although it dates from prehistoric times it was originally manmade. ▶ Following the coast around the Gulf of Taranto the route arrives at **Marina San Giovanni**, which is near the old Roman port of *Usentum.* ▶ The route turns inland now and passing **Casarano** (→) arrives in **Matino,** where the 15C Marquis del Tufo had a fortified residence. ▶ Going on in the direction of the sea the route reaches the church of **San Pietro di Samaria.** This is a 13C building with Gothic elements, but it was constructed in accordance with a Byzantine plan that gave it two domes. Tradition has it that this is the spot where the Apostle Paul, en route from Palestine to Italy, disembarked. ▶ Shortly afterward the route ends at **Gallipoli** (→).   ☐

Practical information _____

CASTRO, ⊠ 73030, ☎ 0836.

Hotels:
★★★ *Orsa Maggiore,* v. Litoranea per S. Cesarea, ☎ 97029, 28 rm ℗ ⌂ ⚓ 75,000.
★★★ *Piccolo Mondo,* v. Litoranea per S. Cesarea, ☎ 97035, 50 rm ℗ ⌂ ☐ ✍ closed Oct-Apr. Series of chalets in park, 60,000.

CASTRO MARINA, ⊠ 73030, ☎ 0836.

≈ ⓘ p. Dante, ☎ 97317.

Restaurant:
◆ *Zinzulusa,* v. Zinzulusa, ☎ 97326, closed Fri. Seafood: shellfish, orecchiette alla ricotta, 18/30,000.

Recommended
Marina: ☎ 97064.

MARINA DI LEUCA, ⊠ 73030, ☎ 0833.

≈ ⓘ lungomare Colombo, ☎ 753161.

Hotels:
★★★★ *Approdo,* v. Panoramica 1, ☎ 753016, 54 rm ℗ ⌂ ☐ ✍ 95,000; bkf: 10,000.
★★★ *Terminal,* lungomare Colombo ☎ 753009, 60 rm ℗ closed Nov-Mar, 65,000; bkf: 10,000.

Restaurant:
◆◆◆ *Mamma Rosa,* at Patu, v. Alighieri 18, ☎ 752063, closed Fri. With fireplace and banquet room. Regional cuisine: tripe, rabbit with potatoes, 12/20,000.

⚠ *Santa Maria di Heuca,* SS 275 at 35.8-km marker, 400 pl, ☎ 792276 (all year).

MARINA DI SAN GIOVANNI, ⊠ 73059, ☎ 0833.

Hotels:
★★★ *Poker d'Assi,* v. Re Pirro 4, ☎ 931088, 41 rm ℗ ⌂ ☐ closed Oct-Apr, 45,000; bkf: 6,000.
★★★ *Poseidone,* v. Lungomare, ☎ 931055, 90 rm ℗ ⌂ ⌂ ☐ ✍ closed 21 Sep-31 May, 60,500; bkf: 6,000.
★★★ *Tito,* v. Lungomare, ☎ 931054, 26 rm ℗ ⌂ ⚓ closed 11 Sep-31 May, 47,000.

SANTA CESAREA TERME, ⊠ 73020, ☎ 0836.

≈ ⚕ (Jun-Nov), ☎ 944070.
ⓘ v. Roma 209, ☎ 944043.

Hotel:
★★★ *Macine,* v. Fontanelle 37, ☎ 944305, 75 rm ℗ ⌂ closed Nov-Mar except 1 Dec-15 Jan, 53,000; bkf: 6,200.

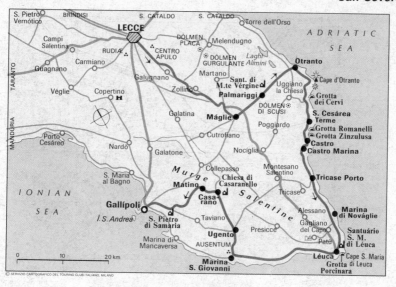

5. The Salentine Peninsula

⚓ *Scogliera*, litoranea per Castro, 300 pl, ☎ 944216 (all year); *Porto Miggiano*, litoranea per Castro, 60 pl, ☎ 944303.

UGENTO, ⊠ 73059, ☎ 0833.

⚓ *Riva di Ugento*, litoranea per Santa Maria di Leuca, 900 pl, ☎ 931040.

SAN GIOVANNI ROTONDO

Foggia 40, Bari 142, Rome 352 km
Pop. 22,247 ⊠ 71013 ☎ 0882   B2

San Giovanni Rotondo, on the S side of the Gargano promontory in an inlet with many fresh springs, is ringed by mountains. It was founded in the 11C around a small church which stood on the road pilgrims took on their way to the Shrine of Monte Sant' Angelo. Today it is still visited by pilgrims because Padre Pio da Pietrelcina (1887-1968), famed for his saintliness, lived most of his life here.

▶ The **Rotonda** from which the town takes its name is an ancient baptistery near the 13C church of **S. Onofrio.** ▶ 2 km W near the **convent of S. Maria delle Grazie** (where Padre Pio lived) are a modern **shrine** and the **Foundation for Mitigating Suffering** that Padre Pio founded with contributions from all over the world. ▶ Nearby some steps lead to the **Via Crucis** (Stations of the Cross) with bronzes by F. Messina.   ▫

Practical information _____

ℹ p. Europa, ☎ 856240.

Hotels:
★★★ *Gaggiano*, v. Cappuccini 144, ☎ 853701, 56 rm ℗ ▩ ▤ 42,000; bkf: 5,000.
★★★ *Parco delle Rose*, v. Moro 71, ☎ 856161, 50 rm ℗ ▩ ᴕ ▤ ᴪ 42,000.

★★ *Vittoria*, v. S. Vittoria 4, ☎ 856292, 24 rm ℗ closed 10-30 Jan, 35,000.

Restaurant:
♦♦ *Costanzo*, v. Santa Croce 9, ☎ 852285, closed Sun eve, Mon and Oct-Nov. Regional cuisine, 25/35,000.

SAN SEVERO

Foggia 29, Bari 153, Rome 320 km
Pop. 54,851 ⊠ 71016 ☎ 0882   A-B2

San Severo, on the edge of the Apulian plateau, contains vineyards that produce a renowned white wine. In the town's centre near the **Palazzo di Città** is the church of **S. Severino** with its original 12C Romanesque façade. The church of **S. Nicola** and the church of the **Benedettine** are Baroque. There is a small **archaeological collection** in the Biblioteca Comunale in v. Zannotti.   ▫

Practical information _____

ℹ v. S. Giuseppe 4, ☎ 21942.

Hotels:
★★★ *Cicolella*, v. 2 Giugno 20, ☎ 23977, 77 rm ℗ ᴕ 65,000; bkf: 5,000.
★★★ *Milano*, v. Teano Appulo 10, ☎ 75643, 50 rm ℗ 60,000; bkf: 3,000.

Restaurant:
● ♦♦♦ *Botte*, v. Colonna 10, ☎ 75048, closed Tue except if hol. Like a medieval tavern with massive tables, visible beams and bronze lamps. Regional cuisine: cicatelle country style, endives and beans, 24/30,000.

Recommended
Technical tourism: *Civitacquario*, at San Paolo di Civitate, v. Buon Remo 7, ☎ 51393 (aquarium makers; telephone before visiting).

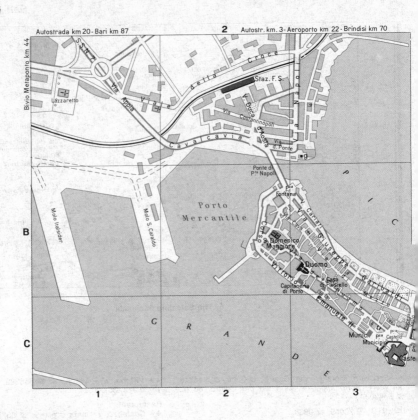

Autostrada km 20 - Bari km 87   **2**   Autostr. km. 3 - Aeroporto km 22 - Brindisi km 70

SANTA MARIA DI CERRATE*

Lecce 15, Bari 145, Rome 596 km

                              F5

The abbey of Santa Maria di Cerrate was founded in the 12C by the Norman, Tancred, Duke of Lecce. It was inhabited by Basilian monks. Next to the abbey is the **Museo delle Arti e delle Tradizioni popolari del Salento** (popular arts and traditions; *9:30 a.m.-1:30 p.m. and 3:30-7:30 p.m.; 7 p.m. Sun and hols; closed Mon*). It houses furniture and tools, as well as frescos of the church. ☐

TARANTO*

Bari 99, Rome 514, Milan 962 km
Pop. 243,120 ⊠ 74100 ☎ 099   D4-5

Taranto was founded as a Greek colony by the Spartans *c.* 700 BC and soon became one of the leading cities of Magna Grecia, as this part of the peninsula was called. Perhaps its most splendid period was in the 4C-3C BC when Archytas lived. Archytas of Taranto (430-360 BC) was one of antiquity's greatest men. A philosopher and friend of Plato, he was interested in science, music and mathematics. He governed Taranto between 361-351 BC. It was said to have had a population of 300,000, a staggering number hardly ever reached by other cities until the Industrial Revolution. Inevitably the city came up against the expanding Romans. The struggle was a

long one and in the end Taranto was captured and destroyed. Taranto was later rebuilt and Greek refugees returned there. It remained a Greek city almost until the end of the Roman Empire.

▶ At the entrance to the port of Taranto, a small island separates the Outer Sea (the Gulf of Taranto) from the Inner Sea (harbour). The old city was built, for the most part, on this island and hearly all the finds in the **Museo Nazionale★★** (C4; *9 a.m.-2 p.m.; Sun 9 a.m.-1 p.m.*) come from it. There are collections of Greek statues, material from burial grounds, a wide range of ceramics, jewelry, adornments and decorated terracotta vases illustrating everyday life in Magna Grecia. Among the most notable objects are two *kore★* (statues of young girls); a **head of a woman★★** (perhaps Artemis or Aphrodite) of the school of Praxiteles; a stele★ (stone slab) depicting a warrior; the head of a bearded man★, possibly Heracles, of the school of Lysippus; a series of **portraits★** in the popular manner found in a Roman burial ground of the 1C BC; **pavement mosaics★**; **bas-reliefs★** from tombs; **ornaments★** in terracotta from the eaves and cornices of ancient buildings and temples; a magnificent **sarcophagus★★** (500 BC) with remains of paintings on it; **gold and silver ornaments★** including broochs, rings, bracelets and necklaces; a splendid **diadem★** decorated with gold and enamel vine branches together with **gold earrings★** in the form of grapes from a burial ground at Canosa and a variety of decorated **vases, statuettes★** and **masques★★** (worn by actors). The topographical section is presently closed because it is being reorganized, but it also contains much interesting material from the grottos and burial grounds of Apulia. The prehistorical section is also closed at the moment, but it must be visited when it is opened *(shortly)* because of its magnificent collections of palaeolithic and neolithic objects and finds going back to the 15C-16C BC. ▶ The **Museo Oceanografico** (marine museum; C4; *wkdays 9 a.m.-6 p.m.*) will interest all who love the sea. It is at v. Roma 3, near the Istituto Talasso-grafico (marine studies). ▶ In the **Villa Peripato** (C4-5), the beautiful public gardens where pine and palm trees grow, there is a splendid view from a terrace over the Inner Sea. In these gardens is the **Museo del Sotto-suolo** *(9 a.m.-1 p.m. and 5-7 p.m.; closed Mon)*. This is a museum of caving. ▶ The **Lungomare Vittorio Ema-nuele III** (C-D4) is a lovely walk lined with pine, almond and palm trees along the Mar Grande. ▶ The 18C **castle** (C3), beyond the swing bridge over a navigable channel, is now used by the Italian Navy (Taranto is a naval base); it also houses a small **Museo della Marina.** ▶ The v. del Duomo (B-C3) crosses the small island on which the **Citta Vecchia** is built, which remains very much as it was during the Middle Ages. Two **pillars** stand at the start of the street; they are all that remain of an old Greek temple of 6C BC. Further on, in v. Paisiello is the house

still retains its original 13C façade and presbytery, while inside the altars are in the Lecce Baroque style. □

Practical information _____

ⓘ corso Umberto 113 (C4-5), ☎ 21233; corso Umberto 121, ☎ 24457 (head office).
🚇 (A2), ☎ 411801.
🚌 from p. Castello (C3).
Car rental: Avis, corso Umberto 61, ☎ 26071; *Hertz,* v. Pupino 19, ☎ 91943; *Maggiore,* v. T. d'Aquino 52, ☎ 24811.

Hotels:
★★★★ *Grand Hotel Delfino,* v. Virgilio 66 (E5 a), ☎ 3205, 198 rm Ⓟ 🍴 ♿ ⌧ 130,000; bkf: 10,000.
★★★★ *Palace,* v. Virgilio 10 (E5 b), ☎ 94771, 73 rm Ⓟ 🏊 134,000; bkf: 13,000.
★★★★ *Park Hotel Mar Grande,* v. Virgilio 90 (E5 c), ☎ 330861, 93 rm Ⓟ 🍴 ⌧ 124,000; bkf: 13,000.

TARANTO

0   100   200   300 m

1 : 17000 (1cm= 170m)

SERVIZIO CARTOGRAFICO DEL TOURING CLUB ITALIANO, MILANO

Marina di Pulsano km 22

where Giovanni Paisiello, the composer, was born. ▶ The **Duomo★** (B3; 10C-11C) has been renovated and altered several times and now has a Baroque façade (1713). The three arms of the end section, with a cupola, were originally a Byzantine church. At the end of the r. nave is the chapel of S. Cataldo, patron saint of Taranto (17C-18C). ▶ The church of **S. Domenico Maggiore** (B2)

★★★ *Plaza,* v. d'Aquino 46 (C4 d), ☎ 91925, 112 rm Ⓟ ♿ 🏊 85,000; bkf: 6,000.

Restaurants:
● ◆◆◆ *Gambero,* v. del Ponte 4 (A3 g), ☎ 411190, closed Mon. Terrace looking onto Inner Sea. Mixed cuisine: pappardelle and crayfish, roast meats, 25/40,000.
◆◆ *Assassino,* lungomare Vittorio Emanuele III 29 (D4 e),

Tarantella

The Tarantella is a lively dance that has been popular all over S Italy since at least the 14C. Many people think it originated in Naples — an idea certain composers like Liszt, Chopin and Mendelssohn endorsed, introducing the dance into their music and calling it Neapolitan. However, there are Sicilian, Calabrian and Apulian tarantellas as well. Taranto could rightly claim the dance because its name comes from that city. Somehow the tarantella has become associated with the tarantula, a spider whose name has also been linked with Taranto. It is claimed that the insect has a dangerous bite and that its victims are taken over by a frenzy that incites them to jump about and dance. Over the centuries, the tarantula and the tarantella became associated in the minds of the peasants of S Italy. It was considered that the dance could serve as a sort of musical therapy — the patient being encouraged to dance on, faster and faster, with the resultant sweating ridding him of the spider's poison. Actually, the tarantella is a dance for courting couples and has to be performed with a partner, accompanied by musicians playing the mandolin, the guitar or the accordieon and, above all, the tambourine; this last is also shaken and tapped by the dancers themselves.

☎ 92041, closed Sun and Aug. Regional mixed cuisine: mussels au gratin, grilled fish and meat, 25/35,000.
♦ **Barcaccia**, corso Due Mari 22 (C4 f), ☎ 26461, closed Mon. Near old city with view over inner and outer harbours. Regional cuisine, 25/35,000.

Recommended
Events: *Procession of the Madonna Addolorata and of the Mysteries* (Holy Thursday and Good Friday); *Feast of San Cataldo* (10 May); *Feast of Our Lady, Queen of the Sea* (Sep).
Hippodrome: *Paolo VI, v. per Montemesola,* ☎ 422142.
Horseback riding: *Circolo Ippico Villa S. Domenica,* at Lama, ☎ 572534; *Le Monacelle,* first crossing for Talsano on road to San Giorgio Ionico, ☎ 325809 (associate of *ANTE*).
Sailing: *Lega Navale, lungomare Vittorio Emanuele III,* ☎ 93801.
Swimming: v. F. Bruno (E5); ☎ 97182; Villa Martiri, Partigiani.

Brindisi 48, Bari 67, Rome 517 km
Pop. 224 ⊠ 72010 ☎ 080   E4

Torre Canne is located in a lovely bay with a sandy beach. Torricella and l'Antesana are the names of two springs of curative mineral waters in the **Parco delle Terme** (spa).   ☐

Practical information _____

≋
♨ (Mar-Oct), ☎ 720133.
ⓘ at Fasano, ☎ 713086.

Hotel:
★★★ **Levante**, v. Appia 14, ☎ 720026, 100 rm Ⓟ ⚲ ♨ ▣ ✍ closed Nov-Mar, 72,000; 4,000.

For help in understanding terms when visiting museums or other sites, see the *Art and Architectural Terms Guide* at the end of the Practical Holiday Guide.

Ä *Le Dune, at Bizzarro, 450 pl,* ☎ 720061.

Bari 42, Rome 414 km
Pop. 45,776 ⊠ 70059 ☎ 0883   C3

Trani is a picturesque town. The sight of its Duomo, in the piazza at the edge of the sea with waves breaking against its steps, is quite startling. The rose-coloured church is flanked by a very tall campanile.

▶ The **cathedral★★** (A2), begun in the 11C and finished in the 13C, is one of the finest examples of Apulian Romanesque architecture. The splendid **bronze door★** by Barisano da Trani (*c.* 1180) is in the centre portal. The campanile was rebuilt after the last war using original materials. The **crypt of S. Nicola★**, inside under the transept, is lined with small pillars. The adjacent church of **S. Maria** has another crypt. Below this crypt is the **tomb of S. Leucio,** which is pre-Romanesque. ▶ In the vicinity is the **Museo Diocesano** *(8 a.m.-1 p.m. and 4-6 p.m. Mon, Wed and Fri; closed Sun)* with paintings and medieval sculptures and bas-reliefs. ▶ The **castle** (A1-2), built by Frederick II (1233-49) and rebuilt in the 14C and again in the 15C, is being renovated. ▶ The 12C **Ognissanti Church** (A-B2) was part of the Hospice of the Knights Templar. ▶ The medieval part of town (A-B2) remains almost intact. It contains a synagogue and several interesting churches, among them **S. Giacomo** (A1-2); **S. Andrea** (B2) and **S. Francesco** (B2). ▶ There is a **Museo delle Carrozze** (coach museum; *telephone before visiting,* ☎ 42641) in the 17C Palazzo Antonacci (B3). ▶ In the public gardens in the **Villa Comunale** (B3) is a **Mini Aquarium** *(spring and summer 10 a.m.-12 noon and 5-8 p.m. or 6-10 p.m.).* ▶ The old Benedictine abbey of **S. Maria di Colonna** with, in its church, remains of an 11C-12C building is on a small tongue of land 2 km SE. ☐

Practical information _____

ⓘ corso Vittorio Emanuele 92, ☎ 583443 (head office); p. della Repubblica (B2-3), ☎ 43295 (information).

Hotel:
★★★★ **Trani,** corso Imbriani 137 (C1-2 a), ☎ 42340, 51 rm Ⓟ ⚲ 61,700.

Restaurant:
♦♦♦ **2 Mori,** lungomare Colombo 110, ☎ 401051, closed Wed and 5-20 Jan. View over the sea and open fireplace. International and mixed cuisine: farfalloni with salmon, orecchiette with nuts, 38/45,000.

Recommended
Aquarium: at Villa Comunale (B3).
Marina: ☎ 583763.
Sailing: Lega Navale, molo S. Antonio, ☎ 44832 (also skindiving).

A-B1

These rocky islands with pine trees and vineyards, a dozen or so miles off the N coast of the Gargano promontory, were called *Diomedeae* by the ancients, after Diomedes, the Homeric hero who was supposedly buried here. There are three large islands, San Domino, San Nicola and Capraia (also called Capperara because of its abundance of capers), and a smaller one called Cretaccio, little more than a yellow clay islet. Another island to the NE, which more rightly could be called a rock, is Pianosa, on which a lighthouse has been built. Except for Pianosa, the islands can be reached by boat from various points on the coast, but the best trip is from Manfredonia, which offers a view of the whole coast.

TRANI

0   100   200 m

1 : 13000 (1 cm = 130 m)

© SERVIZIO CARTOGRAFICO DEL TOURING CLUB ITALIANO, MILANO

2 Autostrada km 8 - Corato km 13   3   all'Ospedale

▶ **San Nicola** is a long and narrow island rising high out of the sea with a town reached by a series of steps going up between the mountain and the old defensive walls. High above, the church of **S. Maria a Mare** dominates the island. It was rebuilt in 1045 over an older church and has a double narthex, a Renaissance portal with bas-reliefs by Dalmatian sculptors, a Romanesque mosaic pavement and a Gothic wooden polyptych, carved in the second half of the 15C. It was part of a Benedictine abbey which played an important part in the history of the island. The abbey was closed down by Ferdinand IV of Naples who turned the island into a penal colony (1792). In 1843 another Bourbon banished here the more unruly elements of the Naples slums and to this day the inhabitants speak Neapolitan instead of the local patois. It was only recently realized that the island was suited for tourism. ▶ **San Domino** is the largest and most attractive of the Tremiti Islands. There is a pine forest overlooking the rocky cliffs and there are grottoes that can only be reached by boat. ▶ **Capraia**, with high cliffs, has on its shores some curious rocks in the form of bridges that the local inhabitants call *archetielli* or little arches; it also has two sandy coves. □

Practical information ⎯⎯⎯⎯⎯⎯⎯⎯⎯⎯

ℹ️ municipio, at San Nicola, ☎ 0882/663002; *TCI*, at San Domino, ☎ 0882/663018.

🚢 daily summer sailings from Ortona, Vasto and Termoli (in winter only from Termoli), from Manfredonia and Rodi Garganico (twice a week in non-summer months),

several times a week in summer from Pugnochiuso, Vieste and Peschici; hydrofoil sailings daily (May-Oct) from Ortona and Vasto, several times a day in summer from Termoli, *Agenzia Domenichelli Cafiero*, ☎ 0882/663008.

SAN DOMINO, ✉️ 71040, ☎ 0882.

Hotels:
★★★★ *Kyrie,* ☎ 663232, 64 rm Ⓟ 🛁 ♨ ⌘ 🖼 Pens. closed 26 Sep-24 May, 145,000.
★★★ *San Domino,* v. dei Cameroni, ☎ 663027, 28 rm ♨ ⌘ 70,000; bkf: 5,500.

Restaurant:
♦♦ *Cabbiano,* ☎ 663044. Mediterranean style building with lovely garden and splendid views. Seafood: cannelloni, pomegranates alla parmigiana, 30/45,000.

Recommended
Events: *National and International Underwater Races.*
Vacation villages: *Villaggio TCI* (closed Oct-May), information, at Milan, ☎ 02/85261; at Bari, ☎ 080/365140; at Rome, ☎ 06/6874432; at Turin, ☎ 011/540177.

TROIA

Foggia 23, Bari 155, Rome 386 km
Pop. 7,937 ✉️ 71029 ☎ 0881   A3

Troia sits on a hill overlooking the Apulian plateau. It is especially noted for its **cathedral★★**. Built in 1093 over a Byzantine structure, it is considered to be the masterwork of Romanesque art in the Capitanata region. It has Byzantine and Islamic influences. The **rosette**★ on its façade is highly ornamented and its **bronze door**★ is by Oderisio da Benevento (1119). Inside are three naves decorated with small bas-reliefs. The **treasure** consists of illuminated manuscripts of the 12C-13C, silver and Arab ivory and enamels. It is going to be moved to the **Museo Diocesano** in the Convent of the Benedictine Nuns in front of the cathederal *(for treasure and museum contact treasurer,* ☎ *970258).* The Baroque church of **S. Giovanni** and 11C church of **S. Basilio** are interesting, as is the 11C **Palazzo Tricarico.** The **Museo Civico** in the Palazzo Vasto *(contact commander of police)* has archaeological and modern sections.   □

VIESTE

Foggia 97, Bari 179, Rome 420 km
Pop. 13,247 ⊠ 71019 ☎ 0884   C1

Vieste, at the E end of the Gargano, is a picturesque town renowned for its medieval quarter. It has a **castle** built by Federick II (rebuilt in the 16C-17C) with a splendid view★ of the Gargano promontory and the Adriatic coast. The **cathedral,** which was rebuilt in the 18C, still retains remnants of an 11C one. It is possible to visit the **grotta Cam**-pana by boat *(1 hr, full visit to all grottos takes 3-4 hrs).*   □

Practical information ─────────────

≋
ⓘ   corso Vittorio Emanuele II 1, ☎ 78806.
🚢   several weekly sailings in summer to Tremiti Islands and to Manfredonia, Peschici and Rodi Garganico, *Gargano Viaggi,* ☎ 78501.

Hotels:
★★★★ *Pizzomunno Vieste Palace Hotel,* ☎ 78741, 183 rm Ⓟ ⟨ 🔍 📶 ☒ ⁄° closed Nov-Mar. Elegant, pine forest with long beach, 182,000; bkf: 18,000.
★★★ *Aranci,* p. Madonna delle Grazie 10, ☎ 78577, 76 rm Ⓟ ☒ Pens. closed 5 Nov-24 Mar, 98,000.
★★★ *Mediterraneo,* v. Madonna della Libera, ☎ 77025, 85 rm Ⓟ 📶 ☒ ⁄° Pens. closed Dec-Mar, 94,500.

Restaurants:
♦♦ *Kambusa,* v. XXIV Maggio 13, ☎ 77163, closed Thu except summer and Nov-Mar. Regional cuisine: troccoli with cuttle-fish sauce, mussels and stuffed cuttle-fish, 20/30,000.
♦♦ *Rugantino,* v. XXIV Maggio 14/16, ☎ 78620, closed Fri and 1-10 Oct. Regional cuisine: orecchiette ragù, fish, grills, 15/25,000.

⚓ *Crovatico,* at Crovatico, litoranea Vieste-Peschici at 9-km marker, 170 pl, ☎ 76487; *Oriente,* at Santa Maria di Merino, 500 pl, ☎ 76371; *Porticello,* at Santa Lucia, litoranea Vieste-Peschici at 4-km marker, 108 pl, ☎ 76125; *Punta Lunga,* at Defensola, litoranea Vieste-Peschici at 2-km marker, 300 pl, ☎ 76031.

Basilicata ●

Basilicata lies between the 'heel' (Apulia) and the 'toe' (Calabria) of the boot-shaped Italian peninsula, extending from the Alps southward into the Mediterranean. It is 90 percent mountainous with the Apennines crossing it from N to S. The largest part of the region is E of the watershed where the four major rivers—the Sinni, the Agri, the Basento and the Bràdano—flow into the Gulf of Taranto and the Ionian Sea. The smaller W part, on the other side of the Apennines between Calabria and Campania, faces the Gulf of Policastro and the Tyrrhenian Sea. For centuries, this was one of the poorest and most isolated parts of the south and it is only now emerging from seclusion thanks to major government renovation schemes. Basilicata was not always economically backward. Colonists from Greece, more than 2,500 years ago, founded towns and trading posts along the Gulfs of Taranto and Policastro. These were busy centres for commerce and learning, but even before the fall of the Roman Empire, the region began to decline due to pillaging of the coastal settlements by pirates and barbarians. The inhabitants gradually abandoned the coast for the mountains, building villages inland, away from the threat of raiders and the dangerous malarial marshlands along the coastlines. Most of the towns still are inland—including the two regional capitals, Matera and Potenza. Because it was so economically underdeveloped, Basilicata became one of Italy's least populated regions, with the highest rate of emigration in the whole peninsula. All this has changed over the past few decades. The coastal swamps have been drained and turned into fertile farmland and major roads have been built over the Apennines linking the region to the rest of Italy. Efforts have been made to start industries, the largest being the giant petro-chemical plant at Pisticci. The coastlines along the Ionian and the Tyrrhenian Seas are being developed for tourism and new resorts with magnificent beaches have sprung up. The tendency to avoid the flatlands and cling to hill-top villages is finally being reversed and many inhabitants are returning to the coast. Although a great deal has been achieved, there is still much to be done and government officials are the first to admit that centuries of neglect cannot be corrected overnight. At least the long period of stagnation is over—a dynamic situation has been created and changes have begun. Basilicata, a sun-drenched land of hills and mountains, olives and vineyards, now looks to an assured future. ☐

● *Don't miss*

The Duomo ★ at Matera; the scenic route to the Sassi ★ with many splendid views; the Tavole Palatine ★ at Metaponto; the Provincial Archaeological Museum ★ at Potenza; the Monticchio Lakes ★ near Rionero in Vulture, and the Abbey della Trinità ★ at Venosa.

● Brief regional history

7C-3C BC
Greeks and Lucanians. Many cities were founded on the coast of Basilicata, in the Gulf of Taranto, at a time when it was considered a 'Greek lake'. Among them are **Siris** (7C BC) whose inhabitants traded extensively with the East and adopted the practice of wearing brightly coloured Eastern clothes; **Metaponto** (7C BC), still in existence today; and **Heraclea** (built *c.* 433 BC and now called **Policoro**). ● In due course the **Lucanians,** an Italic people, swept down from the mountains and took **Posidonia,** Taranto and much of Calabria and Basilicata.

3C BC-5C AD
Romans. The **Lucanians** submitted to Rome in 298 BC, but they sided, nevertheless, with **King Pyrrhus,** when this Hellenistic monarch crossed the Adriatic, with his armies and his elephants, to help the city of Taranto ward off Rome. It was at *Heraclea* that Pyrrhus defeated the Roman army and its consul (general) Laevinus (280 BC). ● In the end Pyrrhus was defeated and Basilicata became a Roman province which later, under Caesar Augustus, was called *Lucania*.

6C-10C
Longobards and Byzantines. After the fall of the Western Roman Empire (476 AD), the **Longobards** incorporated Basilicata in their **Duchy of Benevento**

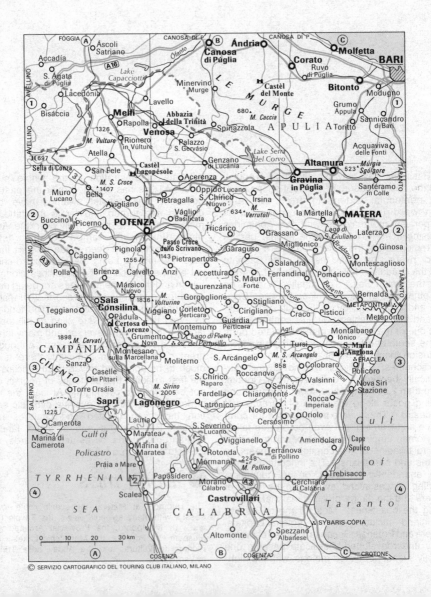

(847) and later into the **Principality of Salerno.** ● It was during this period that, due to the breakdown of the administration in the area, the lower parts of the country were allowed to revert to swamp (with **malaria** as a consequence), **raids by Moorish pirates** went unchecked and the population began to move from the coast to the uplands. ● During the 9C-10C, with the revival of the Eastern Roman Empire, the S of Italy came under **Byzantine rule.** The name, Basilicata, is derived from *basilikos*, the name of the Byzantine administration.

cathedral in Acerenza

Easter Procession at Basile nel Vulture

This is held on Good Friday afternoon in honour of the passion and death of Christ. The Stations of the Cross are commemorated in a procession that starts from the church of the Madonna delle Grazie and covers three miles. There are many participants; all, including the leading actors, local inhabitants. They include thirty-three little girls dressed in white to celebrate the years of Jesus' life; the character of Malco, the man who struck Jesus; Christ carrying the Cross, evoked by an actor bound with ropes and wearing his shoes back to front as a sign of penitence. His face is covered and he is obliged to remain doubled up throughout the ceremony. A second Christ, the 'Ecce Homo' Christ crowned in thorns, remains immobile from beginning to end. Among many personages, one of the strangest is the gypsy woman, dressed in a brightly coloured costume, whose breast glitters with gold brooches and other valuable jewelry on loan for the occasion from other local women. As a result, she is escorted throughout the procession by two police officers to safeguard the villagers' treasures.

11C-13C
Normans and Swedes. The castle at **Melfi** (1059) was one of the first fortresses which the energetic **Normans,** who had come from France, built in

the region. Pope **Nicholas II** recognized these Norman conquests at Melfi by creating **Robert Guiscard** Duke of Calabria and Apulia, as well as a vassal of the church. ● At Melfi, too, in 1129, a feudal assembly of barons paid homage to **Roger II** who was about to assume the crown and, finally, it was to Melfi that **Frederick II** of Sweden came for his coronation after inheriting the Southern Kingdom.

13C-19C
Governed from a distance. The kingdom of Southern Italy, to which Basilicata belonged, was governed at first from Palermo, in Sicily, and later from Naples, but because of difficulties in communication, Basilicata, locked away behind the Apennines, remained isolated, virtually cut off from the central administration. ● In the succeeding centuries, there was a constant power struggle between the local feudal barons and the kings at Naples.

Facts and figures

Location: *At the foot of the Italian peninsula, between the regions of Apulia (to the E), Campania (to the W) and Calabria (to the S). Mt. Pollino (7,450 ft) is the highest peak in the Apennine range that runs through the area. It has an extinct volcano, Mt. Vulture (4,350 ft). The W coast fronts the Gulf of Policastro and the Tyrrhenian Sea, while the longer S coast faces the Ionian Sea and the Gulf of Taranto.*
Area: *9,992 sq km.*
Climate: *Mediterranean but varied because of the complexity of the landscape. In winter, in the mountainous regions, it can be as cold as in N Italy, with snow in the highest parts. The climate is at its best in the highlands in spring and autumn, and summer heat is tempered on the coast by sea breezes.*
Population: *614,522 inhabitants, making the region the second lowest in population density and the third lowest in numbers of inhabitants.*
Administration: *Potenza is the regional capital; the other provincial capital is Matera.*

 Practical information

Information: tourist offices in principal towns and other centres.

SOS: emergency services, ☎ 113; police emergency, ☎ 112; road emergency *(ACI)*, ☎ 116.

Weather forecast: ☎ 191; road conditions, ☎ 194 or *(ACI)* ☎ 06/4212; sea conditions, ☎ 196.

Farmhouse accommodation: *Associazione Regionale Agriturist*, at Matera, v. XX Settembre 39, ☎ 0835/214565.

Events: *Festival of S. Bruno*, at Materano; *crèche* (with actors), at I Sassi; *Good Friday Festival* and *Festival of S. Gerard*, at Potenza; *Procession of the Holy Spirit*, at Melfi.

Nature park: at Pollino (on Calabrian side of mountain; → Lagonegro).

Nature reserve: *WWF* regional delegation, at Matera, v. Sette Dolori 10, ☎ 0835/211506; at Potenza, v. Marconi 49, ☎ 0971/72697. Guided tours to *Pantano di Pignola* *reserve* (nr Potenza), San Giuliano reserve, at Matera, ☎ 0835/210820, Policoro woods and many other places of interest for nature lovers.

Zoo: at Lagonegro.

Excursions: most interesting are Mt. Pollino (network of marked footpaths), departures from Francavilla sul Sinni, San Severino Lucano, Viggianello, Rotonda and Senise May-Nov. Information from *CAI Matera*, c/o *Circolo La Scaletta* (mountaineering club).

Skiing: ski lift to Madonna di Viggiano (→ Grumento Nova), to Lake Laudémio (→ Lagonegro), and ski at Sellata Pierfaone (→ Potenza).

Flying: *Aeroclub F. Pricolo*, at Grumento Nova, ☎ 0975/65010.

Lucanian salami

Cooking has a long tradition in Basilicata, but it is not remarkable. However, it does claim one culinary invention, the spiced sausage, a tasty morsel which in Italy is often called lucanica, *indicating its origin in Lucania. As early as the first century, the Roman writer Varro tells of Roman soldiers stationed in Lucania stuffing a pig's gut with chopped meat seasoned with spices. Local gastronomes assert that the best sausages come from Picerno, Maratea, Montemilioni and Lauria.*

Towns and places

ACERENZA

Potenza 40, Rome 403 km
Pop. 3,391 ⊠ 85011 ☎ 0971   B2

Acerenza is perched on a crag high above the Bràdano River Valley. From a distance it looks like a fortified city because of the reinforced houses on the edge of the cliff. One of the region's most important monuments is the Romanesque-Gothic **cathedral,** built in 11C and renovated after 1281. The portico with truncated columns (12C Apulian-Romanesque style) has an arch resting on columns supported by curious groups of men and monkeys; the splendid apse is full of movement. The interior has three naves; a cloister encloses the presbytery. The crypt contains frescos (renovated 16C).   □

AVIGLIANO

Potenza 20, Rome 383 km
Pop. 11,518 ⊠ 85021 ☎ 0971   A2

In Avigliano, the traditional costume worn by women was held in high esteem. It included large earrings and a headdress made of silk and supported by a wooden frame. There is a lovely church, **S. Maria** (17C), with a Baroque façade and a portico decorated with diamond shapes.   □

Practical information _____

Recommended
Craft workshops: *T. Lovallo*, v. Vallebona, ☎ 82170 (furniture, carved wooden items).

BRADANO AND BASENTO

From Matera to Potenza *(186 km, 1 day; map 1)*

See map on page 103.

This excursion starts from Matera, follows the Bràdano River down to the sea, and returns inland up the Basento River Valley to Potenza. The roads along these two rivers, the most important in Basilicata, have been traveled since ancient times. The route provides a clear understanding of the physical structure of the region. The hills are mostly rounded and bare and the earth is sunburned.

▶ From **Matera** (→) the rough, broken landscape remains unchanged for most of the journey with fields yellowed by the summer heat. ▶ **Montescaglioso** has a Benedictine abbey (11C), rebuilt during the Angevin period (1300), renovated in the 15C. The cloister is enhanced by Renaissance-style windows and a fine stone wall. The Baroque parish church of Ss. Peter and Paul contains a sculpted choir. ▶ The route continues along the Bràdano where giant aloes announce the approach of the sea. ▶ **Tavole Palatine** (Palatine Tables) is the name given to a Doric temple near the bridge over the River Bràdano, not far from **Metaponto.** Some distance from the sea, up the Basento River Valley, stands the white village of **Bernalda** which Bernardino of Barnaudo (hence its name), secretary to the Aragonese king, built to a regular plan in 1470. ▶ **Ferrandina,** the next village, lies high up the valley. It was built in 1490 by Frederick of Aragon and named after the king's father, Ferrandino. The town's coat of arms bears a Latin motto of six words all starting with F—*Fredericus Ferrantis Filius, Ferrandinam Fabricare Fecit* (Frederick, son of Ferrante, built Ferrandina). 'Ferlandine' is the name for textiles made in the district. Up the mountain road separating this valley from that of the Bràdano is **Miglionico** where there is a castle with massive round towers (15C). The church of S. Francesco contains a painting★ by Cima da Conegliano. ▶ Next are **Grottole,** located on two hills near the main road, **Grassano** and **Tricarico** (→). After **Tre Cancelli,** the route circles the slopes of Mt. Capolicchio, through one of the thickest oak forests in Basilicata, and by way of **Vaglio Basilicata** (→) reaches Potenza (→).   □

Practical information _____

BERNALDA, ⊠ 75012, ☎ 0835.

Restaurant:
♦♦ **Da Fifina,** corso Umberto 63/65, ☎ 743134, closed Sun and Sep. Next to a butcher's shop; both are run by same family. Regional cuisine, 20/25,000.

⚠ *Agriturismo Country Camping*, at San Marco, ☎ 747050.

FERRANDINA, ⊠ 75013, ☎ 0835.

Hotel:
★★★ **Ulivi,** at Borgo Macchia, SS 407 at 77-km marker, ☎ 757020, 49 rm P ⅏ ⚬ 46,000.

CHIAROMONTE

Potenza 132, Rome 440 km
Pop. 2,578 ⊠ 85032 ☎ 0973   B3

Chiaromonte lies on a hilltop between the valleys of the Sinni and Serrapótamo Rivers. It contains much of interest, including the remains of the **castle of Sanseverino** (14C). Its walls (13C) may be seen from the lower part of the town. The **Palazzo Giura** (17C)

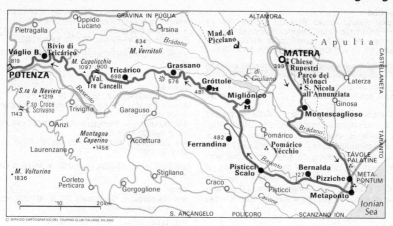

1. Bradano and Basento

has a fine portico.   There are various archaeological sites in the surrounding countryside; finds are on display in the Museo Nazionale della Siritide at Policoro (→ From Sea to Sea). □

Practical information _____

Hotel:
★★ *Ricciardi*, v. Calvario 27, ☎ 571031, 24 rm Ⓟ ⚿. 20,000; bkf: 2,000.

GRUMENTO NOVA

Potenza 66, Rome 429 km
2,529 ft pop. 2,050 ✉ 85050 ☎ 0975   A-B3

Grumento Nova is picturesque, offering an unbroken view over the whole Agri River Valley and the artificial lake of **Pietra del Pertusillo**.   5 km E, near the lake, **excavation** continues on the old Roman town of *Grumentum*, one of the chief cities of ancient Lucania, destroyed c. 1,000 by the Saracens.   The theatre (1C-2C), the amphitheatre (1C) and a Roman house with splendid mosaics have already been unearthed.   The church of S. Maria Assunta is nearby.   420 km N along the main road is the **Santuario del Monte** or Madonna di Viggiano (5,660 ft), a shrine. □

Practical information _____

⚡ cableway and skiing at Madonna di Viggiano *(24 km N)*.
ⓘ municipio, at Viggiano, ☎ 61142.

Restaurant:
♦♦♦ *Romantica*, at Lago del Pertusillo, ☎ 953125, closed Mon. Regional cuisine: ferricelli all'antica, fish, 20/25,000.

Recommended
Aeroclub: *F. Pricolo*, nr Pantanelle, ☎ 65010.

IRSINA

Matera 48, Potenza 65, Rome 428 km
Pop. 7,185 ✉ 75022 ☎ 0835   B2

Irsina lies half-way along the Bràdano River Valley.   It was formerly called Montepeloso but the name was

changed to its present one in honour of an ancient town, *Irsum,* nearby.

▶ The **cathedral** (13C) was rebuilt in the 18C but still has its original campanile.   Inside is a marble **baptismal font**.   In the crypt of the church of **S. Francesco** (originally a 12C chapel) there are 14C frescos by a Neapolitan painter *(refer to parish priest).* ▶   The **Ianora Museum** *(private, visits a.m. only)* has prehistoric objects, coins and women's traditional costumes. □

LAGONEGRO

Potenza 100, Rome 386 km
2,185 ft pop. 6,261 ✉ 85042 ☎ 0973   A-B3

In antiquity, the town's coat of arms displayed a duck called a merganser, flying over water (perhaps how the town derived its name), but it was changed in the 16C to St. Michael killing the dragon to show that the people had rid themselves of their feudal masters and demolished their castle.   The story is interesting because it recalls that, until recent times, there were no common lands in Basilicata, only feudal ones, an important factor in the region's social and economic history.

▶ The **older part** of town lies on the W side of Mt. Sirino, on the edge of a cliff with splendid views of the surrounding mountains.   The remnants of an ancient castle sit on top of a rocky peak.   ▶ There is a **zoo** *(private, visitors admitted)* 2 km away in the Noce Valley with tigers, jaguars, bears and other wild animals.   ▶ 8 km SE lies **Lake Sirino**.   ▶ **Lake Remno** or Laudemio (4,977 ft) is located on the N slopes of Mt. Sirino in wooded country some 22 km E. □

Practical information _____

⚡ cableway to Lake Laudemio (Mt. Sirino *22 km NE*).
ⓘ municipio, ☎ 21031.

Hotel:
★★★ *San Nicola*, p. della Repubblica, ☎ 21457, 48 rm Ⓟ ⚿ ⅋ closed Christmas, 33,000; bkf: 3,000.

Restaurant:
♦ *Montesirino*, v. Colombo 106, ☎ 21181. Regional and Italian cuisine, 18/26,000.

Recommended
Nature parks: *Pollino Nature Park* on Lucano side of Mt. Pollino. Information from *Commando Gruppo Forestale*, at Rotonda *(48 km SE)*, municipio, ☎ 61005.
Wildlife park: SS 19 *c.* 2 km toward Fortino, ☎ 21767.

LAVELLO

Potenza 72, Rome 359 km
Pop. 13,044 ⊠ 85024 ☎ 0972   A-B1

There are **medieval streets** and a castle in the old centre of the town on a spur facing the Ofanto Valley. The castle is used as a municipio; it has a **Museum of Antiquities** *(apply to local officials)* housing part of the archaeological finds from the surroundings (most of these are in the museum at Melfi →). The **church of St. Ann** contains a painting by A. Stabile (1594) of the *Annunciation.* The manmade Lake of Abate Alonia lies 4 km SW near a small wood.　　□

Practical information ————————————

Hotel:
★★★ *San Barbato,* SS 93 at 53.3-km marker, ☎ 83813, 38 rm P ⋘ ⁂ ⌫ ⌁ closed Christmas, 54,000; bkf: 3,500. Rest. ◆◆ closed Fri. Regional cuisine: cavatelli with chickpeas, saltimbocca San Barbato, Aglianico del Vulture wine, 20/28,000.

MARATEA

Potenza 129, Rome 423 km
Pop. 5,168 ⊠ 85046 ☎ 0973   A-B4

Maratea is situated on the slopes of Mt. S. Biagio, offering a magnificent view over the Gulf of Policastro, the only part of the peninsula where Basilicata faces the Tyrrhenian Sea.

▶ Along the rocky coast, with its seaside resorts of **Fiumicello-Santa Venere, Porto, Aquafredda** and **Marina di Maratéa,** are many **caves,** the best of which, at Marina di Maratéa, features stalagmites and stalactites. ▶ 4.5 km beyond the sanctuary of S. Biagio and the remains of ancient Maratéa is the Mt. S. Biagio lookout (2,047 ft) with a fine view★ of the surrounding mountains and sea.　　□

Practical information ————————————

MARATEA
ⓘ p. del Gesù 32, ☎ 876900.
Car rental: Maggiore, v. Sospiro 17, ☎ 876104.

Hotel:
★★★★ *Grand Hotel di Maratéa,* at Santa Caterina, ☎ 876996, 157 rm P ⋚ ⋘ ⅙ ⌫ ⌁ closed Oct-Easter, 230,000.

Restaurant:
● ◆◆◆ *Taverna Rovita,* v. Rovita 13, ☎ 876588, closed Oct-May. Regional cuisine: risotto with asparagus, involtini alla Materana, 30/35,000.

⚓ *Maratéa,* at Castrocucco, 200 pl, ☎ 879097 (all year).

Recommended
Discothèque: Le Stelle, v. della Pernia, ☎ 876996.
Marina: ☎ 376321.
Technical tourism: visit to *C. Romeo* wickerwork factory, v. Citroselli.

Environs

ACQUAFREDDA, ⊠ 85041, ☎ 0973, 12 km NW.
≋
Hotels:
★★★★ *Villa del Mare,* SS 18, ☎ 878007, 75 rm P ⋚ ⋘ ⌫

closed 16 Oct-30 Mar. On a rocky spur above beach to which it is linked by elevator, 70,000; bkf: 10,000.
★★★ *Villa Cheta Elite,* v. Timpone 24, ☎ 878134, 20 rm P ⋘ closed Oct-Easter, 55,000; bkf: 8,000.

FIUMICELLO-SANTA VENERE, ⊠ 85040, ☎ 0973, 5 km W.
≋
Hotels:
★★★★ *Santavenere,* ☎ 876910, 40 rm P ⋚ ⋚ ⋘ ⌁ closed Oct-May. On a headland in a large park running down to the sea, 135,000.
★★ *Murmann,* v. Fiumicello 1, ☎ 876931, 18 rm P ⋚ ⋘ ⁂ 6 Nov-30 May, 54,000.
★★ *Settebello,* ☎ 876277, 25 rm P ⋘ ⁂ closed Oct-May, 44,000.

MARINA DI MARATEA, ⊠ 85040, ☎ 0973, 8 km S.
≋
Hotel:
★★ *Marisdea,* v. Castrasela 10, ☎ 879003, 45 rm P ⋚ ⋘ ⌁ closed Oct-Mar, 39,500.

PORTO, ⊠ 85040, ☎ 0973, 5 km W.
≋
Restaurant:
◆◆ *Zà Mariuccia,* v. Grotte 2, ☎ 876163, closed Thu and 15 Dec-28 Feb. A seafront trattoria with fine terrace. Seafood, 28/30,000.

MATERA*

Potenza 99, Rome 460, Milan 930 km
Pop. 51,535 ⊠ 75100 ☎ 0835   C2

Matera's houses, built of brick or porous hillside stone, run down the rocky escarpment on which the Duomo is built to the edge of the cliff. Known as the *Sassi* of Matera, they form an intricate labyrinth of narrow streets and steps, one house often supported by another below it. They are mostly in a style which was prevalent in the 17C and architecturally interesting. However for the post-war government they represented little more than a maze of slums and their inhabitants were lodged elsewhere in modern apartments. The *Sassi* were not pulled down. Today they stand empty and are a tourist attraction.

▶ The interior of the church of **S. Giovanni Battista** (B2; early 13C) is Gothic-Burgundian. ▶ The church of **S. Francesco d'Assisi** (B2), renovated in 1670, has a choir with eight panels of a **painting★** by Bartolomeo Vivarini (15C). ▶ From the piazzale of the Duomo there is an interesting view over the N side of the *Sassi* (Sasso Barisano; B-C3). ▶ The Apulian Romanesque **Duomo** (B3) has a fine campanile★ and portal with a rosette; its sides have two sculptured portals and richly carved windows. Inside (renovated 17C-18C) are the **Madonna della Bruna,** a Byzantine-style 13C fresco; the 16C chapel of the Annunciation; 16C sculptures and a 15C carved choir. ▶ The **Museo Nazionale Ridola** (C2; *9 a.m.-2 p.m.; hols 9 a.m.-1 p.m.; closed Mon)* is housed in the former monastery of S. Chiara (1698); it has prehistoric artifacts, including neolithic ceramics, ceramics from the Bronze and Iron Ages and documentation on various archaeological sites in the Materano region. ▶ The **Pinacoteca d'Errico** (C3; *9 a.m.-1 p.m.; Sun 9 a.m.-12 noon)* houses an important collection of 17C and 18C paintings, mainly of the Neapolitan school. ▶ The **strada panoramica★,** the scenic route of the *Sassi* (A-C2-3), provides spectacular views over the low-lying **Sasso Caveoso** and **Sasso Barisano** and runs steeply along the side of the cliff. The v. B. Buozzi, crossing the Sasso Caveoso, reaches the piazzale of the small church of **S. Pietro Caveoso** (B-C3), then the church of **S. Maria de Idris** (C3), built almost entirely out of the rock. From here it contin-

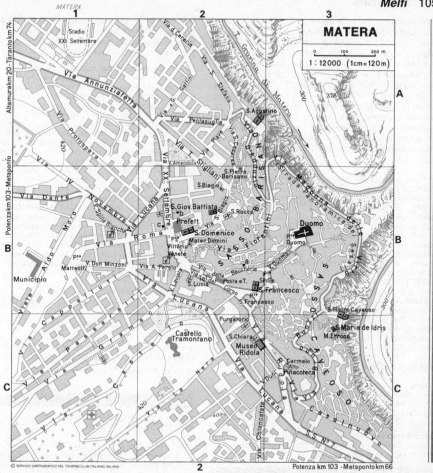

© SERVIZIO CARTOGRAFICO DEL TOURING CLUB ITALIANO, MILANO

ues to a cemetery and **small church** with 11C Byzantine frescos. A **permanent agricultural show** is held at the vico Solitario, behind the church of S. Pietro Caveoso. After circling the escarpment on which the cathedral is built, the road offers an excellent view over the lower Sasso Barisano and ends at the piazzale of the church of **S. Agostino** (A2; 17C façade) which affords another fine view of the gully and the city. ▶ Again along the scenic route on the E side of the gorge (crossing the SS 7 at 6 km in the direction of Laterza) are more **hillside churches** built out of rock and located on the edge of the cliff (*it is advisable to hire a guide*). □

Practical information

ℹ️ P. Vittorio Veneto 19 (B1), ☎ 211188; v. de Viti de Marco 9 (B1), ☎ 212488.

🚆 (B1), ☎ 211015.

🚌 from v. Nazionale (A1 off map), ☎ 213980.

Hotel:
★★★ **De Nicola**, v. Nazionale 158, ☎ 214821, 76 rm 🅿 💧 👤 ♨ 50,000; bkf: 4,000.

Restaurants:
♦♦ **Bocconcino**, vico Lombardo 52 (B2a), ☎ 221625, closed Mon. Overlooking the *Sassi Barisano* district. Regional cuisine: involtini d'agnello alla brace, spiedini misti, 25/35,000.
♦♦ **Da Mario**, v. XX Settembre 14 (B2b), closed Sun. Regional cuisine, 20/30,000.

♦♦ **Moro**, vico IV Cappelluti 2, ☎ 212181, closed Sat. Regional cuisine: orecchiette al ragù, sformato di tagliolini, 20/30,000.
♦ **Trattoria Sorangelo**, v. Lucana 48 (B2c), ☎ 216799, closed Sun and Aug. Regional cuisine, 18/20,000.

Recommended
Archery: *Compagnia arcieri Materarco*, v. Capelluti 4.
Events: *Fèstival of S. Bruna* (2 Jul); *Materano July Festival* (music, ballet, films); *Summer Theatre Festival* (Jul-Aug); *Sassi creche* (Dec).
Horseback riding: *Tenuta La Volpe*, v. Traetta 8, ☎ 210965 or 221633 (associate of *ANTE*).
Technical tourism: visit *Cooperativa abbazia S. Angelo* (graphic art) and *A. Fiore* workshop (hand embroidery) at Montescaglioso.
Tennis: v. Europa, ☎ 221797.

MELFI

Potenza 61, Rome 351 km
Pop. 15,742 ✉ 85025 ☎ 0972   A1

The Norman occupation of S Italy and Sicily began as an infiltration by foreign soldiers and ended with the establishment of a kingdom. It all started at Melfi. The eleven Altavilla (Hauteville) brothers, of Viking origin, came from Normandy, along with their vassals, soldiers and servants, offering themselves as mercenaries to the local barons. They were hired by the Longobard prince of Salerno to fight the Byzantines. In 1043 they met at Melfi and named William Altavilla a count and their leader. The existence of the new County of Melfi was later acknowledged by the Emperor Henry III. This was not the first Norman establishment in Italy (about 15 years earlier, by a similar trick, Rainulpho Drengot had himself made Count of Aversa), but it was the first settlement of the Altavilla brothers, who were to go on to create the southern kingdom. Built with the lava of a volcanic hill, at the N foot of Vulture Mountain, surrounded by thick ramparts, Melfi still lies in the shadow of its Norman castle.

▶ The square **castle**, with many-sided towers, was renovated by Frederick II, rebuilt by Charles I of Anjou, and altered again in the 14C. The chapel has a large Flemish painting of the *Crucifixion* (1589). ▶ **The Museo Nazionale Archeologico** *(9 a.m.-2 p.m.; Sun 9 a.m.-1 p.m.; closed Mon)* is in the castle and houses much prehistoric and pre-Roman material. The **Sarcophagus of Rampolla★** is a Roman (2C) sculptured stone coffin, brought from Asia Minor, now in one of the castle's towers. ▶ The **Duomo**, rebuilt several times after having been destroyed by earthquakes, still has its original campanile (1153), a fine example of Norman architecture; there is a Byzantine-style fresco of the *Madonna* in one of the chapels. ▶ A 14C crucifix may be seen in the **church of the Cappuccini**, built on a mound in front of the castle. ▶ The cliffside churches of the **Madonna delle Spinelle, S. Margherita** *(near the cemetery;* 13C Byzantine frescos) and **S. Lucia** are all of interest. ▶ Nearby is Mt. Vulture (→). ☐

Practical information ―――――――――――

Hotels:
★★★ *Due Pini,* p. Stazione, ☎ 21031, 45 rm Ⓟ ⓵ ⊗ 49,000; bkf: 4,000.
★★ *Castagneto,* SS 401 at 3-km marker, ☎ 24363, 25 rm Ⓟ ⑭ ⓵ ⊗ 29,000.

Recommended
Events: *Procession of the Holy Spirit* on Pentecost Sunday (Seventh Sun after Easter).

METAPONTO

Matera 48, Potenza 110, Rome 469 km
Pop. 541 ⊠ 75010 ☎ 0835   C3

17C and Romantic paintings show the Doric columns (remains of Greek temple) called the Palatine Tables, standing in swamps among overgrown vegetation. Since then, the central plain near the sea has been the subject of vast land reclamation schemes, becoming a flourishing agricultural zone and the Greek columns have been restored. Ancient Metaponto, which stood several hundred yards to the l. of the present town, was founded in the 7C BC. The people of Metaponto claimed that their city was really considerably older and had been established by Greeks returning from the Trojan War. They showed visitors tools which, they said, had been used to build the Wooden Horse that brought about the downfall of Troy. It does seem certain that many of the Pythagoreans, expelled from the city of Croton, came to Metaponto; and Pythagoras himself is supposed to have been among them. Cicero tells us that when he visited Metaponto he was shown the house where Pythagoras was reported to have lived centuries before. Hannibal, the Carthaginian general at war with Rome, is also said to have set up camp near Metaponto and it

was here, the story goes, that a messenger approached his tent and threw at his feet the head of his brother Hasdrubal, who had just been defeated by the Romans on the Metaurus River.

▶ The **Museum of Antiquities** along the main road to Taranto *(summer 9 a.m.-1 p.m. and 3:30-6:30 p.m.; winter 9 a.m.-12 noon and 2-5 p.m.; closed Mon)* has many archaeological finds unearthed in ancient Metaponto including silver, jewelry, statuettes and bronzes from graves. ▶ Nearby, at the Bradano River bridge are the **Tavole Palatine★**, the remains of a 6C BC Doric temple probably dedicated to the goddess Hera, of which fifteen columns are still standing. The columns acquired the name of Palatine Tables much later, during the Middle Ages, when they were imagined to be the legs of a giant table used by Charlemagne's Paladins, sworn enemies of the Moors who raided the coasts. ▶ On the road leading into town toward the railway station, there is a small archaeological site called the **Tombs of Crucinia.** A little farther, a side street leads to the **Parco Archeologico Città** where excavations currently underway have uncovered an ancient theatre, temples to Apollo Licio (with Doric columns), Hera and Athena-Aphrodite (all 6C-5C BC) as well as an Ionian temple (5C BC). In one part of the old city, an entire district was occupied by potters. Several master potters, whose work was renowned in antiquity, were among them.   ☐

Practical information ―――――――――――

LIDO DI METAPONTO, ⊠ 75010, ☎ 0835, 2.5 km SE. ≋
ⓘ v. delle Sirene, ☎ 741933.

Hotel:
★★★ *Turismo,* v. delle Ninfe 5, ☎ 741918; 61 rm ⑭ ⓵ ⊗ closed 11 Oct-31 Mar, 52,000; bkf: 4,000.

⚠ *Riva dei Greci,* Strada Turistica Archeologica, 200 pl, ☎ 741818.

PISTICCI

Matera 47, Potenza 93, Rome 352 km
Pop. 17, 713 ⊠ 75015 ☎ 0835   C3

Old Pisticci has rows of small white houses standing on a hill among olive groves between the Bavento and Cavone Rivers, and in the valley important reserves of methane gas have been found. This has resulted in major industrial development in the region.

▶ The **Chiesa Madre** in the centre of the town (rebuilt 16C) still has its original (13C) sculptured portal and campanile. ▶ In Terravecchia district are the remains of an old medieval **castle** and of a tower. ▶ 1 km E is the abbey of **S. Maria del Casale** (11C) with a fine portal and sculptured rosette. It was built by the Normans. ▶ **Marina di Pisticci,** on the Ionic seacoast, lies 24.5 km SE. It has two beaches, at San Teodoro and San Basilio.   ☐

Practical information ―――――――――――

Hotel:
★★★ *MotelAgip,* at Pisticci Scalo *(7 km N),* SS 407 at 24-km marker, ☎ 462007, 64 rm Ⓟ 64,300.

POTENZA

Rome 363, Milan 929 km
Pop. 65,234 ⊠ 85100 ☎ 0971   A2

Potenza has been the capital of Basilicata since 1806, when the ruling French decided that it was more accessible to Naples than Matera, the former provincial seat. The rivalry between the two cities continued; in 1820, the Italian Independence Movement divided the region into W Lucania and E Lucania,

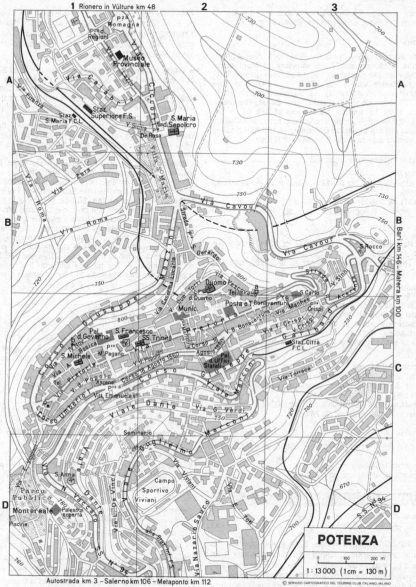

Autostrada km 3 – Salerno km 106 – Metaponto km 112

© SERVIZIO CARTOGRAFICO DEL TOURING CLUB ITALIANO, MILANO

POTENZA

0   100   200 m

1 : 13 000 (1 cm = 130 m)

with Potenza and Matera as their respective capitals. When the Bourbons returned briefly to govern, the two provinces were reunited as Basilicata and Potenza once again became the capital. In 1927, Mussolini reestablished the two Lucanias with their separate capitals. The postwar republican government brought back Basilicata with Potenza as its provincial seat and thus it has remained.

▶ **The old town,** around which the modern city has developed, lies along a hill and is crossed by the **via Pretoria** (C2), where residents stroll and shop. ▶ The Duomo (B2) is dedicated to S. Gerardo, who was bishop of the town. It was renovated in the 18C, but still has the orig-

inal structure (12C) with a rosette on the façade and an apse from the same early period. ▶ The **church of S. Francesco** (built 1274) has a 15C portal and campanile and nave with a Gothic apse, as well as a Renaissance **De Grasis tomb** (16C) and a Byzantine wooden *Madonna* (13C). ▶ **S. Michele** (CI) is a small Romanesque church (11C-12C) with a 15C predella (painted altarpiece) and paintings. ▶ The **Museo Archeologico Provinciale**★ *(closed for repairs)* houses, among many treasures, a collection of geometrical vases with red silhouettes, a Corinthian helmet (6C BC), a shield (4C BC), ex voto statuettes, pottery and terra-cotta objects from the temples of ancient Metaponto, Greek sculpture (6C BC *Kouros* or boy), the goddess Persephone on a throne and many inscriptions in Greek, Latin and the Oscan language.

Environrons

▶ 5 km along the SS 7 Appia towards Ruoti, near a group of farms, is the unusual **Rural Museum of Montocchio** *(caretaker on the premises).* ▶ 14 km along the SS 92 are the **Rifreddo woods** at 3,837 ft. ▶ 18 km along the provincial road to Abriola is the **Sellata Pass** (4,118 ft, *view*); 25 km along the road are **Sellata-Pierfaone** (skiing; 5,174 ft) and **La Maddelena** (4,370 ft). ▶ At 42 km, following the main Basentana road, are Castelmezzano and the **Lucanian Dolomites** (4,166 ft), so called because they resemble the Dolomites of N Italy. □

Practical information

POTENZA
ⓘ v. Alianelli 4 (CI), ☎ 21812; v. Cavour 15 (head office), ☎ 21839.
🚆 (A1), ☎ 54630.
🚌 from p. Bologna (B1); Ospedale Nuovo; P. Crispi (C3).

Hotels:
★★★ ***Park Hotel,*** SS 407 *(5 km SE),* ☎ 22811, 120 rm Ⓟ ♨ 🐕 🍽 64,000.
★★★ ***Tourist,*** v. Vescovado 4 (B2 a), ☎ 25955, 87 rm Ⓟ 54,000; bkf: 4,000.

Restaurants:
● ♦♦♦ ***Taverna Oraziana,*** v. Orazio Flacco 2 (CI c), ☎ 21851, closed Fri and Aug. Regional cuisine: strascinati alla potentina, homemade wine, 25/40,000.
♦♦ ***Fuori le Mura,*** v. IV Novembre 34 (C1 b), ☎ 25409, closed Mon. Regional cuisine: baccalà a ciaudedda, maiale e salsicce alla brace, Aglianico del Vulture wine, 28/30,000.

Recommended
Events: *Good Friday Procession* with tableau vivant; *Festival of S. Gerardo,* with traditional parade of Turks (29-30 May).
Swimming: parco Montereale (D1), ☎ 56344.
Tennis: v. Argilla Vecchia, ☎ 24116.

Environs

SELLATA PIERFAONE, 5175 ft, ✉ 85010, ☎ 0971, 18 km S.
⛷ ski lifts, cross-country skiir g.
ⓘ municipio, at Abriola, ☎ 923001.

RIONERO IN VULTURE

Potenza 46, Rome 366 km
Pop. 12,443 ✉ 85028 ☎ 0972 A1

This district produces wines, both still (Aglianico del Vùlture) and sparkling, spirits and mineral water from various springs in the region. The gable of the campanile and the dome of the **church of Matrice** are overlaid with green and yellow majolica tiles. Nearby is Mt. Vulture (→). □

Practical information

Restaurant:
♦♦ ***Pergola,*** v. Lavista, ☎ 721179, closed Tue, 15/23,000.

Recommended
Wines: visit to *Paternoster* wine producers, at Barile, v. Nazionale 1, ☎ 770224 (Agliatico del Vùlture wine; contact before visiting).

From SEA TO SEA

From Marina di Maratea to Nova Siri Stazione *(155 km, 1 day; map 2)*

This itinerary leads from the rocky coasts of the Gulf of Policastro to the sandy beaches of the Gulf of Taranto, from the Tyrrhenian to the Ionian Sea, Basilicata's two seacoasts, taking in many lovely sites along the Sinni River Valley.

▶ Leaving **Marina di Maratéa** and the island of San Ianni at Punta degli Infreschi and going up to **Maratéa** (→), the route crosses the first mountain ridge at **la Colla Pass** (2,270 ft). ▶ On the other side is the valley of the Noce River which flows into the Tyrrhenian and marks the boundary between Basilicata and Calabria. ▶ After passing **Lauria** at a bend in the Noce, the route crosses the watershed between the two seas and reaches the valley of the Sinni River, where the vegetation changes from Mediterranean to almost alpine. ▶ On the l. of the valley is **Latrónico** and, in turn, **Fardella, Chiaromonte** (→) and **Valsinni.** Then comes **Policoro** and the Ionian coast, reached through an area of reclaimed land and new industries on the plain between the Sinni and Agri Rivers. The **National Museum of the Siritide** *(9 a.m.-2 p.m.; summer 3:30-4 p.m.; hols 9 a.m.-1 p.m.; closed Mon)* offers archaeological collections from the ancient Greek towns of **Siris** and **Herakleia** as well as prehistoric sites. It is possible to visit Policoro castle, set on an elongated hill, where five sections of a Greek city have been excavated along with a shrine to the goddess Demeter (7C BC) and an old temple. ▶ The journey ends on the Ionian coast road at **Nova Siri Stazione** (→ Torre Bollita) on the border of Calabria. □

Practical information

LAURIA, ✉ 85044, ☎ 0973.

Hotels:
★★★ ***Isola di Lauria,*** p. Insorti d'Ungheria 6, ☎ 823905, 36 rm Ⓟ ♨ 🐕 🍽 51,000; bkf: 4,000. Rest. ♦♦♦ ***Mignon*** Regional cuisine: cavatelli Ruggero, coniglio alla cacciatora, 22/32,000.
★★★ ***Santa Rosa,*** at Lauria Superiore, v. XXV Aprile 8, ☎ 822113, 35 rm Ⓟ 🐕 35,000; bkf: 4,000.

NOVA SIRI STAZIONE, ✉ 75020, ☎ 0835.
≋

Hotel:
★★★ ***Siris,*** v. Magna Grecia 2, ☎ 877054, 70 rm Ⓟ ♨ 🐕 🍽 55,000; bkf: 4,000.

Restaurant:
♦ ***Trappola,*** v. Marittimo 6, ☎ 877021, closed Fri and Nov-Feb. Seafood, 20/40,000.

⛺ *Soleado,* 350 pl, ☎ 877019.

S. MARIA D'ANGLONA

Pisticci 35, Matera 73 km
C3

This is the cathedral of Anglona, standing alone on a hill (862 ft). The town itself no longer exists—it was destroyed in 410 by the Goths and although it was rebuilt and flourished under the Byzantines, it finally fell into disrepair and comprised only a few old houses at the time of Frederick II. The present church was originally constructed in the 11C, but has been rebuilt several times. Inside *(if custodian is absent, see parish priest at Tursi)* there are primitive 11C-12C frescos including one of the martyrdom of a female saint. The nearby Bishop's Palace is now a residence for the clergy. □

For the translation of a name of a meat, a fish or a vegetable, for the composition of a dish or a sauce, see the *Menu Guide* at the end of the Practical Holiday Guide; it lists the most common culinary terms.

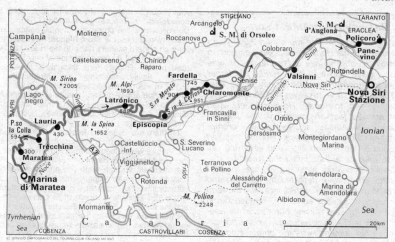

2. From Sea to Sea

TRICARICO

Potenza 46, Matera 54, Rome 409 km
Pop. 7,161 ☒ 75019 ☎ 0835   B2

Architecturally, this is a medieval town and its oldest sections (the Civita) have changed little since the Middle Ages. The *Rabatana* district remains very much as it was when besieged by the Saracens in the 11C. The Norman Baron Robert Guiscard had the **cathedral** erected in the 11C. It has been rebuilt since but still has its 13C campanile. All that remains of the castle is the massive round **tower** (15C).   ☐

Practical information _____

Recommended
Technical tourism: visit to *Salumificio Tricharese Lucania*, meat processors and manufacturers of sausages and salamis, v. della Matine 10, ☎ 723388 (reserve in advance).

VAGLIO BASILICATA

Potenza 15, Rome 378 km
Pop. 2,190 ☒ 85010 ☎ 0971   B2

The former convent of **S. Antonio** has a late 16C portal; in the annex of the **church** are early 17C carved and gilded wooden altars and a 16C altar frontal.

▶ On the outskirts of **Serra di Vàglio** (3,592 ft) archaeologists have unearthed an ancient settlement (8C-3C BC) surrounded by a wall dating from the 4C BC. Splendid Greek terra-cottas and indigenous ceramics have been found. ▶ Near **Madonna di Rossano di Vàglio** (3,015 ft) a large Oscan sanctuary consecrated to the goddess Mefite (a water divinity) has been discovered. It dates from the 4C BC.   ☐

VENOSA

Potenza 66, Rome 374 km
Pop. 12,054 ☒ 85029 ☎ 0972   B1

The **castle,** a massive square building with round towers on each corner, has in its courtyard a 16C

open gallery built by Duke Pirro del Balzo. At the other end of the v. Vittorio Emanuele (the town's main street) is the **cathedral** (1470). Nearby, in a lane running off v. F. Frusci, is the so-called house of Horace, the remains of a semicircular *tepidarium*. To the NE is the monastic **Abbey of the Trinity★** *(presently being renovated; for the caretaker inquire at the nearby church of S. Rocco),* considered a masterpiece of Norman art in S Italy. Excavation in the **chiesa vecchia** (old church; 11C) unearthed mosaic pavements belonging to the previous Early Christian cathedral; the interior has Byzantine frescos and the tomb of Alberada, first wife of Robert Guiscard. The **chiesa nuova★** (new church) was begun in 1135 in French-influenced Romanesque-Gothic style, using material from an old amphitheatre, from still older churches and from Jewish catacombs, but it was never completed. The **Palazzo Abbaziale** (Abbey Palace) has a gallery with twin arches (triple arches on the upper storey) and a small chapel with an Islamic-type dome. On the side of the abbey, archaeologists have uncovered the remains of a very early Christian baptistery and a number of buildings belonging to a Roman colony that include baths and part of a house similar to the amphitheatre located in front of the abbey *(under restoration).*   ☐

Practical information _____

ℹ Palazzo Bisceglia, p. Orazio Flacco.

Il VULTURE

From Potenza *(189 km, 1 day; map 3)*

Il Vulture is the only extinct volcano on the E side of the Apennines. When it was active, elephants and hippopotamuses, hunted by palaeolithic man, roamed around Basilicata. The volcano has two peaks, Mt. Vulture (4,350 ft) and Mt. Pizzuto di S. Michele (4,143 ft). A smaller peak, with two craters filled with water forming the lakes of Monticchio, lies between them. The surrounding countryside is very fertile, due to the volcanic ash, and the craters of the two major peaks are thickly wooded with

Basilicata's greatest son

Basilicata's greatest son lived more than 2,000 years ago. Horace (Quintus Horatius Flaccus) was born in Venosa in 64 BC and his tale is fascinating. He was the son of a slave who was later freed. His father devoted all his energy, time and money to his education. The school at Venosa was not good enough, so Horace was sent to Rome. He was twenty when his father learned that aristocratic youths finished their education in Athens, so Horace was promptly dispatched there. In Greece, Horace mingled with the sons of the Roman elite, and when the call went out to take up arms against the would-be dictator Octavian, everyone, including Horace, prepared for battle. They were defeated by Octavian and Horace's property was confiscated, including the farm his father had just bequeathed to him. He worked in Rome as a clerk to earn a living but also wrote poetry which soon won him a reputation in literary circles. Among his admirers was the greatest poet of the day, Virgil, who befriended him and introduced him to people of influence. Octavian had become Caesar Augustus, emperor of the Roman world. He, too, admired the poetry and asked to meet the writer. Horace's past was forgotten and he was given another farm, nearer Rome, in the Sabine hills. This son of Venosa was the last of the great poets of the ancient world and not until many years later would others of his calibre—men like Dante and Shakespeare—come forward.

a large variety of trees, including oak, chestnut, beech, maple, lime and ash.

▶ From Potenza (→) travel N along a winding road with many clear views over the surrounding landscape. ▶ Arrive at the **Castle of Lagopésole★** (2,719 ft); it stands high above the road and has four square towers, one on each corner of the square building. The castle

was begun in the time of Frederick II (*c.* 1242) but never completed. ▶ The village of **Atella** (1,640 ft) has a 14C Duomo with a fine portal and a squat campanile incorporating twin arches. ▶ From **Rionero in Vulture** (→) a road through superb scenery rises up the side of Mt. Vulture to a height of 4,084 ft over a distance of only 5.5 km. ▶ The road of this itinerary runs through picturesque country before finally reaching the **Monticchio Lakes★** (2,152 ft). A narrow stretch of land, with the ruins of the Benedictine abbey of **San Ippolito** (12C), separates Lago Piccolo (to the E) from Lago Grande (to the W). **San Michele,** a former Benedictine abbey, built near a grotto and rebuilt during the 18C, lies not far from Lago Piccolo; there are Byzantine frescos in the chapel (11C). A funicular operates from this point *(10 mn)* to the top of Mt. Vulture where the road from Rionero arrives. ▶ From the spa **Monticchio Bagni** proceed along the NW side of the mountain through **Melfi** (→) and **Rapolla,** delightfully located on a steep slope. This town has a 13C Gothic cathedral with an impressive portal (1,253); of interest too is the 12C Byzantine church of S. Lucia★ with its dome and the church of S. Biagio which has a carved 13C wooden Madonna (apply to the cathedral for visits). Move on to **Venosa** (→) where the return journey begins down the valleys until reaching **Meschito** (1,952 ft), which at one time was inhabited by Albanians; there are 16C frescos in the church of the Madonna del Caroseno. Arrive back at Potenza after passing **Forenza** (2,473 ft), **Acerenza** (→) and **Pietragalla** (2,752 ft). □

Practical information

MONTICCHIO LAKES, ⊠ 85020, ☎ 0972.

Hotel:
★ *Restaino,* ☎ 731052, 18 rm Ⓟ 🚗 📶 🍽 closed 21 Nov-28 Feb, 26,000; bkf: 3,000.

Restaurant:
● ♦♦ *Marziano,* ☎ 731027, closed Jan-Feb. Old tree trunks are part of decor. Regional cuisine: tagliatelle alla boscaiola, trippa alla lucana, 20/30,000.

🏕 *Belvedere,* 40 pl, ☎ 731034 (all year).

RAPOLLA, ⊠ 85027, ☎ 0972.

♨ (May-Oct), ☎ 760113.

3. Il Vulture

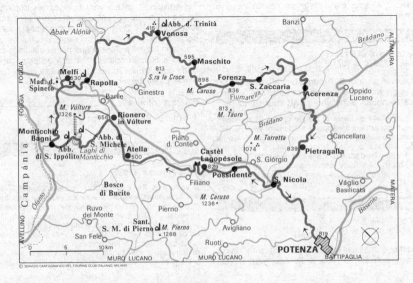

Calabria

▶ In the 17C, when travelers were taking the 'grand tour', Calabria was a sort of *terra incognita* on the other side of the Straits of Messina that they gazed at from Sicily, admiring the outlines of the Aspromonte range and the mass of Mount Pollino. Until the beginning of this century, Calabrian shepherds wore their traditional attire—a tightly buttoned waistcoat, a red scarf serving as a belt, a jacket with turned up sleeves and a cone-shaped hat—and were lampooned by the northern Italian and foreign press as typical examples of the backward Italian. All that has changed with the arrival of the *autostrada* (superhighway), the airliner and mass tourism; people swarm to the warm sandy Mediterranean beaches of Calabria. In addition to the sunny climate, the balmy sea and the hospitality and fascinating traditions of the people, there are other reasons to visit Calabria: its historical ruins that date from ancient times and its archaeological finds that make its museums among the world's most entrancing; the region of Byzantine Calabria with many fine examples of architecture in the Byzantine style; and the Sila, the wild and strange region of forests and lakes that is still completely unspoiled. □

● Don't miss

Santa Maria della Roccella★ near Catanzaro Marina; the Duomo★ at Cosenza; the cathedral at Gerace; the National Museum★ at Reggio di Calabria; the Museo Diocesano★ and San Marco★ at Rossano; the Cattolica★ at Stilo and the cathedral★ at Tropea. The Sila plateau★ is a beautiful spot to visit.

● Brief regional history

8C-3C BC
Greek colonies. *C.* 8C BC, the Phoenicians, who commanded the sea route along the coast of N Africa, brought spices, perfumes and pearls to Italy. They traded mostly with the Etruscans, who controlled the Tyrrhenian coast and parts of S Italy. Soon the **Greeks,** crossing the Ionian Sea, began to arrive on the other side of the Italian peninsula to found colonies, and Greek cities came into existence along the coastlines of S Italy. Calabria, Crotone, Caulonia, Medma, Locri Epizephyrii, Ipponio and Reggio can be traced back to this period.

3C BC-5C AD
Rome. The **Roman Republic** began expanding into S Italy and soon a power struggle developed with the Greek colonies led by Taranto. ● The Greeks were defeated and Calabria, with the rest of the south, became Roman territory. ● In 73-71 BC, **Spartacus,** who led a slave revolt against Rome and was defeated, escaped down the peninsula with his followers. In Calabria they tried to cross the Straits of Messina to Sicily but were caught by the Roman general **Crassus** by the River Silarus (where today the town of Sele stands) and were defeated. Spartacus was killed. ● The Romans, for administrative purposes, made Calabria part of the region of **Lucania** and **Bruttii.**

6C-10C
Byzantines, Longobards and Saracens. After the fall of the W Roman Empire, Italy became part of the Byzantine Empire. ● During this time, Italy was being continually invaded by barbarians. Italy was invaded by the **Saracens** (Moslems) who were eventually expelled by the Byzantines with the help of the **Longobards,** barbarians who had come down from the N.

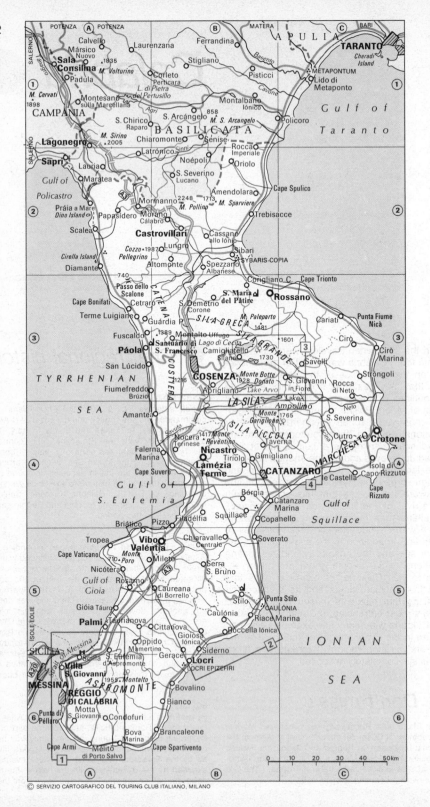

11C-18C
Kingdom of Naples. Foreign conquests continued. In the 11C the **Normans** arrived and soon Pope Nicholas II gave **Robert of Guiscard** the title of **Duke of Calabria and of Apulia.** ● A century later the **Swedes** occupied the region (1194) and still later the **Angevins** (1266) from France, who were superseded, in 1442, by the **Aragonese** from Spain. ● Finally, the Kingdom of Naples and the surrounding region, which included Calabria, became a Spanish possession and was governed by a **Spanish viceroy** (16C). ● In 1715 the **Bourbons** took over most of S Italy. ● During these centuries of foreign occupation, the mountainous inland regions of Calabria were cut off from the government on the coast, because of lack of communication, and suffered much from feudal **barons.** ● Only **Cosenza**, in the 14C, enjoyed a certain amount of autonomy and prosperity. ● It was during the Spanish occupation that **Thomas Campanella** (1568-1639) was born at Stilo. Campanella, a poet and philosopher, became a European figure with the publication of *City of the Sun,* in which he described an imaginary city equitably governed for the benefit of all its inhabitants. At once the Spanish viceroy in Naples had him prosecuted on a charge of attempting to overthrow the government. He was arrested, and after being tortured, was sentenced to perpetual imprisonment. Campanella spent twenty-seven years in jail before Pope Urban I had him freed and brought to Rome. He later went to France where he was honoured by King Louis XIII and Cardinal Richelieu and where he died.

19C-20C
The French and modern Italy. The **Bourbons,** who had taken over S Italy from the Spaniards, were ousted by **Napoleonic troops** after the French Revolution. ● Later, Napoleon's forces were defeated by the British, who put the Bourbons back on the throne of the Kingdom of Naples. ● The Bourbons were expelled for the second time after the **Battle of Aspromonte** when Calabria became part of the **United Kingdom of Italy** and, after World War II, of the **Italian Republic.**

Towers facing the sea

Around the coast of Calabria there are towers, round or square, placed strategically on heights affording a good view of the sea. Local people call them the Saracen towers, but in fact they were built to keep at bay marauding Turkish pirates, and they are found not only on the Italian coast, but throughout the Mediterranean. Philip II of Spain, a sworn enemy of the Turks, had the towers built as defenses and in 1567 there were 313 in the Kingdom of Naples and 137 in Sicily. Much later, during the Napoleonic wars, a British fleet attacked French-held Corsica at Martella point. One of the towers there put up such a resistance, keeping the British fleet at a distance with its blazing guns, that the British were much impressed. As a result the British decided to build their own towers. It is thus possible to see on the coasts of Kent, Sussex and Essex and on the coast of Ireland forts that the local people call 'Martello towers' which are direct copies of the towers of Calabria and S Italy.

Facts and figures

Location: Calabria, occupying the 'toe' of the Italian peninsula, is a long (400 km) and narrow region (maximum width 30 km), extending to the Tyrrhenian Sea on one side and the Ionian Sea on the other. It is a mountainous area with the Lucanian range (Mt. Pollino 7,341 ft) to the N, the Sila plateau (Mt. Botte Donato 6,325 ft) and the Serre Mountains in the centre and the Aspromonte range to the S. In Roman history, Calabria was the name applied to the province of Leuce (Apulia), in the 'heel' or SE extremity of Italy. The name Calabria was later transferred to the territory of the Bruttii, after its subjugation by the Longobards, and that area remains Calabria today.
Area: 15,080 sq km.
Climate: Mediterranean on the coasts and the rare plains, continental in the mountains with snow on the highest peaks all year round. Because of this range of climates, aloes, oleanders and almond trees can be found on the coasts, while firs and larches can be seen on the Sila plateau.
Population: 2,096,134 inhabitants.
Administration: Calabria has three provinces—Catanzaro, Cosenza and Reggio Emilia where the legal, taxation and education authorities are established; the Regional Council sits in Reggio di Calabria.

 Practical information

Information: tourist offices in principal towns and other centres.

SOS: emergency services, ☎ 113; police emergency, ☎ 112; road emergency *(ACI),* ☎ 116.

Weather forecast: ☎ 0961/976976 (from Catanzaro and Reggio di Calabria, ☎ 191); road conditions, ☎ 0961/975000 (from Catanzaro and Reggio di Calabria, ☎ 194), or *ACI,* ☎ 06/4212; snow information, ☎ 075/992992; sea conditions, ☎ 0961/977977 (from Catanzaro, ☎ 196).

Farmhouse accommodation: *Associazione Regionale Agriturist,* at Catanzaro, v. XX Settembre 42, ☎ 0961/45084.

Events: *Festival of Calabrian Costume,* at Cosenza; *Spring Festival,* at Reggio di Calabria with traditional procession; *San Rocco Festival,* at Palmi; *Carnival of Pollino* and *International Festival,* at Castrovillari; *Festival of the Sea,* at Pizzo (→ Le Serre); *Calabrian Gastronomic Festival,* at Crotone; *Good Friday Procession,* at San Gioanni in Fiore; *Vibo Six-Day Musical Festival; Enactment of the Holy Crucifixion,* at Tiriolo; *Easter Saturday Historical Procession,* at Caulonia; *Holy Week ancient rites,* at San Demetrio Corone and in all other Italian towns; *Sila Cup Car Race,* at Camigliatello Silano; *citrus fruits fair,* at Reggio di Calabria.

Nature parks: the Parco Nazionale of Calabria is in three sections: Sila Grande, Sila Piccola and Aspromonte. Head office, at Cosenza, v. della Repubblica 26, ☎ 0984/26544; other offices: at Catanzaro, v. Cortese, ☎ 0961/21731, and at Reggio di Calabria, v. Prolungamento Torrione, ☎ 0965/22410. Forestry protection posts in Sila Grande, at Camigliatello Silano, *Cava Melis,* ☎ 0983/71141, at Cupone, ☎ 0962/978144, at Germano, ☎ 0984/992481; in Sila Piccola, at Buturo, ☎ 0961/ 931317; in Aspromonte, at Basilico, ☎ 0965/

743020. Lake Angitola (→ Le Serre) is a protected site. A regional park on the Calabrian side of Mt. Pollino is presently being laid out.

Nature reserves: *WWF* regional office, at Lamezia Terme, v. Carducci 2, ☎ 0968/29548; branches: for Mt. Pollino, at Castrovillari, v. Raganello 6, ☎ 0981/21803; at Cosenza, *Cooperativa Avvenire,* contrada Bosco de Nicola, ☎ 0984/8515470; at Crotone, v. Ruffo 15, ☎ 0962/23546; at Catanzaro, v. Magenta 21, ☎ 0961/601166; at Palmi, v. Serre 20, ☎ 0966/45548; at Pizzo, v. M. Salomone 286, ☎ 0963/231732; at Reggio di Calabria, v. N. Furnari 72, ☎ 0965/58474 (for Lake Angitola). *LIPU* branches: at Pellaro, ☎ 0965/359404 (spring excursions to Saline Joniche swamp for bird-watching); at Crotone, ☎ 0962/28008 (excursions to mouth of Neto River); at Castrovillari, v. Alfano 36, ☎ 0981/21615.

Holiday villages: *Valtur Holiday villages,* at Simeri (→ Catanzaro), at Capo Rizzuto (→ Crotone), at Nicotera Marina, for information, ☎ 02/791733, Milan or ☎ 06/6784588 (Rome); *Triton Holiday Villages,* at Sellia Marina (→ Catanzaro); *Sabbie Bianche Holiday Villages,* at Tropea, for information, ☎ 02/85391 (Milan).

Rambling and hiking: areas of particular interest are Sila Grande in Cosenza province (from Camigliatello Silano), Sila Piccola in Catanzaro province (from Villaggio Mancuso e Tirivolo) and Aspromonte in Reggio di Calabria province (from Gambarie; best May-Oct, no indicated long-distance routes). Information from: *CAI,* at Reggio di Calabria, v. Vittorio Emanuele 99, at Gambarie, ☎ 0965/743075; *Gente in Aspromonte Excursion Association,* at Reggio di Calabria, v. Reggio Campi, ☎ 0965/23328.

Cycling: help and information may be obtained from *UDACE* cycling clubs throughout Calabria; excursions include the Tyrrhenian coast from Praia a Mare to Villa San Giovanni or the Ionian coast from Reggio di Calabria to Rocca Imperiale or from one coast to the other crossing the Sila region.

Horseback riding: *Italian Federation of Equestrian Sports,* at Reggio di Calabria, v. Aschenez 140, ☎ 0965/330105 (regional office); affiliated riding schools at Catanzaro, Cosenza, Gioia Tauro, Reggio di Calabria and Sibari.

Sailing: *Lega Navale,* at Crotone, Sanità wharf, ☎ 0962/27240.

Marinas

A recent phenomenon has radically changed the geography of the Calabrian coast: the appearance of marinas. For centuries, the Calabrians had taken refuge inland against invasions and malaria. New railroads and highways along the coast and land reclamation of marshes have brought the people of Calabria nearer the coastal regions. Some villages in the back country have been deserted and new towns have appeared which simply append 'Marina di...' to the name of the old village. Initially, these were agricultural communities which covered the coast with vegetable gardens, olive trees and vines. They have progressively turned toward tourism and leisure activities.

Skiing: locations in the Aspromonte and La Sila regions offer skiing.

Golf: at Simeri-Crichi (→ Catanzaro).

Flying: *Crotone Aeroclub,* at airport, ☎ 0962/793173; at *Lamezia Terme Airport,* ☎ 0968/53189; at *Reggio di Calabria Airport,* ☎ 0965/320035.

Fishing: *Federazione Italiana Pesca Sportiva,* at Catanzaro, v. A. Daniele 28, ☎ 0961/21630; at Cosenza, corso Mazzini 286, ☎ 0984/21892; at Palmi, p. I Maggio 7 (inquire for fishing conditions: permitted waters, prohibitions, etc.).

Archery: *Fitarco,* at Catanzaro, corso Mazzini 45, ☎ 0961/42411; affiliated centres at Lamezia Terme and Scalea (→ Praia a Mare).

Gastronomy

According to tradition, brides-to-be in Calabria must know at least a dozen ways of making spaghetti. A few of these are fusilli *or* fischietti *(lace bobbins or little whistles, cylindrical shaped pasta three in long with a hole through them);* ricci di donna *(curled like a woman's hair);* filatieddi *(of strawlike thickness);* paternostri *(pierced small cubes);* capiddi d'angilu *(angel's hair);* pizzicotti *(kneaded rounds of pasta);* cannaruozzoli *(like bent canes);* ricchie 'i prieviti *(priest's ear);* rascatelli *(like tagliatelle) and* sagne. *This last is a succulent dish of stuffed lasagne, baked in the oven and served with meatballs, sliced boiled eggs and mozzarella, covered in grated pecorino (sheep's-milk cheese) and seasoned with artichoke sauce.* Strangugliaprieviti *(literally priest stranglers) in spite of its fearsome name is nothing more than an appetizing local kind of gnocchi. Calabrian cuisine is based essentially on its two main food sources—fish from the long sea coasts and farm produce from the inland regions. Some unusual dishes are* melanzane a scapece, *eggplant pickled with aromatic herbs,* ovotarica *(caviar from tuna), served in slices with olive oil and tomatoes; swordfish served in slices and prepared a* ghiotta *(rolled in breadcrumbs, fried in oil and served with capers),* alla bagnerese *(in evaporating water) or roasted on a grate and served with* salmoriglio *(a sauce of parsley, marjoram and lemon in olive oil); and* mustica, *whitebait and similar fish, dried in the sun, covered in peppers and preserved in oil.*

Wedding presents

An old Calabrian marriage custom in use until quite recently was for shepherds to make the stiffeners for the stays of their fiancees. They would use the flexible wood of the orange tree, making stiffeners about a foot long. They would then carve them with various designs. The designs had special meanings: a bird represented purity; branches and leaves, fecundity; the sun, the male; a knot, the tie between the married partners. The young men worked at carving while away with their sheep in the high pastures. When the wedding took place, the bridegroom gave the bride a present symbolizing the union and the tasks which she would have to perform. To offer a dibble, used for planting bulbs, meant that she would work in the fields; a shuttle, that she would be a weaver; a distaff, that she would spin wool, and a mould, for shaping bread and cakes, meant that she would stay in the kitchen to look after the family.

The arrow (→) is a reference to another entry.

● Towns and places

ALTOMONTE

Cosenza 64, Catanzaro 156, Rome 488 km
Pop. 4,501 ⊠ 87042 ☎ 0981   B2

The church of **S. Maria della Consolazione**★ stands at the top of the old part of Altomonte and is reached through rising narrow streets and steps. It is French Gothic (1360) and is flanked by a massive campanile. In the interior are fine 14C-15C sculptures and three funeral monuments. Next to the church in a former Dominican convent is the **Museum** *(8:30 a.m.-1 p.m. and 2-6:30 p.m.)*. It contains paintings and wood sculpture, as well as a splendid portrait of S. Ladislaus★ possibly by Simone Martini (1283-1344), the Sienese master.   □

AMANTEA

Cosenza 43, Catanzaro 67, Rome 514 km
Pop. 11,609 ⊠ 87030 ☎ 0982   A-B4

Amantea sits perched on a hill looking out over the Tyrrhenian Sea. High above the town are ruins of an ancient **castle** and in the town, the charming church of **S. Bernardino** (15C). Inside there is a *Madonna and Child* by A. Gagini (1505).   □

Practical information _____

AMANTEA

Hotels:
★★★ *Palmar*, SS 18, ☎ 42043, 46 rm ℗ ⬭ 60,000; bkf: 4,000.
★★ *San Gabriele*, v. Lava Gaenza 87, ☎ 41704, 36 rm ℗ ⬭ & ⬥ closed 16 Sep-14 Apr, 31,000; bkf: 3,000.

Environs

CAMPORA SAN GIOVANNI, ⊠ 87032, 8 km S.

Hotel:
★★ *Confortable*, SS 18 ☎ 46048, 24 rm ℗ ⬭ closed Nov, 50,000; bkf: 4,000.
🜊 *La Principessa*, SS 18 at 379-km marker, 90 pl, ☎ 46047 (all year).

CORECA, ⊠ 87032, 5 km S.

Hotel:
★★★ *Scogliera*, SS 18, ☎ 46219, 38 rm ℗ ⬭ & 50.000; bkf : 4,000. Rest. ♦♦♦ closed Tue and Nov. - Regional cuisine : seafood, risotto alla marinara, 20/30,000.

L'ASPROMONTE

From Reggio di Calabria *(144 km, 1 day; map 1)*

L'Aspromonte sits at the W extremity of the Sila range and rises to a height of 6,420 ft. It offers a wonderful view of both the Ionian and Tyrrhenian Seas, as well as the Straits of Messina and Sicily. It is covered with dry riverbeds full of flowers in summer, which turn into roaring torrents in winter. Its upper slopes are forested, mostly with chestnuts, oaks and beeches, while citrus fruits and vines grow on the lower ones. Evergreen junipers grow plentifully in the more sheltered parts.

▶ From **Reggio di Calabria** (→) follow the coastal road S, along the Straits of Messina, passing through small seaside resorts and reach **Melito di Porto Salvo** where berga-

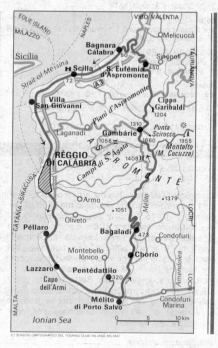

1. L'Aspromonte

mot essence, used in perfume, is produced. A short distance further, take a scenic route that rises *(after 7.5 km)* to **Pentedattilo** (1,233 ft), a partially abandoned village that is located below a rocky range with five peaks. ▶ The road now leads inland towards Aspromonte and becomes narrower and steeper; citrus trees are replaced by forests. ▶ At **Bagaladi** (1,555 ft) there is a church with a marble *Annunciation*, by A. Gagini (1504). ▶ Climbing higher, pass through **Sella Entrata** (4,620 ft) and then begin the slow descent to the coast. On the r., a road leads to the top of *Montalto* or Monte Cocuzza (6,415 ft), which is surmounted by a statue of the *Redeemer*. The view★ from here is incomparable and, since the Straits of Messina are hidden, Calabria and Sicily seem to be one unseparated land. ▶ At **Gambarie** (4,690 ft), which lies in a forest of beech and fir trees, a chair lift goes up practically to the top of **Puntone di Scirocco** (5,450 ft). ▶ Just before the road to Gambarie another road leads among the pines *(for 1.3 km)* to **Cippo Garibaldi** (4,312 ft), where a monument has been erected to Garibaldi who was severely wounded here after his attempt to take Rome from the popes (29 Aug 1862). ▶ Continuing along the main road, descend to **Sant'Eufemia d'Aspromonte** (1,575 ft) where the parish church has a beautiful statue of the *Madonna* (1568). Finally, the road leads to the coast at **Bagnara Calabra** (180 ft). ▶ Take the coast road, passing through **Scilla** and **Villa San Giovanni,** back to Reggio di Calabria.   □

Practical information _____

BAGNARA CALABRA, ⊠ 89011, ☎ 0966.
ⓘ p. Marconi 3, ☎ 371319.

Hotel:
★★ *Rose,* corso Vittorio Emanuele 37, ☎ 371088, 25 rm
⌘ 60,000; bkf: 5,000.

GAMBARIE, ⊠ 89050, ☎ 0965.
⚡ chair lifts, skating.
ⓘ municipio, ☎ 743081.

Hotel:
★★ *Excelsior,* p. Mangeruca 1, ☎ 743049, 48 rm 60,000.

MELITO DI PORTO SALVO, ⊠ 89063, ☎ 0965.
≋
⚓ *Stella Marina,* at Anna, 300 pl, ☎ 787001 (all year).

CAMIGLIATELLO SILANO

Cosenza 32, Catanzaro 128, Rome 553 km
4,555 ft pop. 728 ⊠ 87052 ☎ 0984   B3

Camigliatello Silano is the departure point for magnificent excursions into the woods in the heart of the Sila Grande (→). 15 km S is **Silvana Mànsio** (5,274 ft), isolated in the greenery of the woods. 12.5 km NE is **Lake Cecita** or Lake Mucone at a height of 4,057 ft. It is an artificial lake that was formed from the damming for hydro-electrical purposes of the Mucone River. It is a paradise for trout fishermen. An excursion to **Mt. Botte Donato** (6,905 ft) (*28 km,* passing through **Fago del Soldato** (5,192 ft) and continuing on SE through dense and majestic forests) is well worth undertaking if only for the spectacular views.   □

Practical information _____

⚡ cableway, chair lifts, cross-country skiing, instruction.

Hotels:
★★★ *Aquila & Edelweiss,* v. Stazione 11, ☎ 978044, 40 rm ℗ ⋙ ♿ ⌘ 85,000; bkf: 5,000.
★★★ *Cristallo,* v. Roma 91, ☎ 978016, 51 rm ℗ ⌘ 70,000; bkf: 5,000.
★★★ *Leonetti,* v. Roma 48, ☎ 978075, 40 rm ℗ ⌘ closed 15 Jan-15 Jul and 15 Sep-30 Nov, 50,000; bkf: 5,000.
★★★ *Sila,* v. Roma 7, ☎ 978484, 36 rm ℗ ⋙ ⌘ 76,000; bkf: 6,000.
⚓ *La Fattoria,* nr Labonia, 200 pl, ☎ 978364 (all year).

CASSANO ALLO IONIO

Cosenza 70, Catanzaro 162, Rome 468 km
Pop. 18,996 ⊠ 87011 ☎ 0981   B2

Cassano Allo Ionio is an ancient town and a spa that looks out over the plain of Crati. There is a **cathedral** in the lower part of the city that was completely rebuilt at the end of the 18C. Its campanile dates from 1608 and inside are paintings and sculptures (16C-18C). In the nearby Palazzo Vescovile work is going on in preparation for a **Museo Diocesano,** which is to house 16C-18C art by Calabrian artists.   □

Practical information _____

♨ ☎ 71376 (May-Oct).

┌───┐
│ Don't forget to consult the Practical Holiday Guide: it │
│ can help in solving many problems.   │
└───┘

Le CASTELLA

Catanzaro 49, Rome 602 km
Pop. 1,049 ⊠ 88070 ☎ 0962   C4

On a small island in the Gulf of Squillace, where the sun rises out of the sea, there sit the solitary ruins of a **castle**★ that dates from the Aragonese period.   □

Practical information _____

Hotels:
★★★ *Club Le Castella,* ☎ 795054, 253 rm ℗ ⋙ ⌘ ▤
⁄° Pens. closed Nov-Apr. In large park, central building surrounded by small cottages, 160,000.
★★ *Annibale,* v. Duomo, ☎ 795004, 20 rm ℗ ⋙ ⌘
⁄° 55,000.

⚓ *Annunziata,* 600 pl, ☎ 795052; *Conchiglie,* at Isola di Capo Rizzuto, 300 pl, ☎ 791185; *Oasi,* at Isola di Capo Rizzuto, 500 pl, ☎ 791628; *Poker,* at Isola di Capo Rizzuto, 250 pl, ☎ 791642; *Scogliera,* at Isola di Capo Rizzuto, 300 pl, ☎ 791172 (all year); *Stella del Sud,* 300 pl, ☎ 795039 (all year); *Torre,* at Isola di Capo Rizzuto, 250 pl.

CASTROVILLARI

Cosenza 72, Catanzaro 168, Rome 453 km
Pop. 21,191 ⊠ 87012 ☎ 0981   B2

Castrovillari is a farming community located in a fertile hollow. Although farming is now carried on with modern agricultural methods, this town retains many links with the past.

▶ Among Castrovillari's ancient structures are a square Aragonese **castle** (1490) and the church of **S. Giuliano.** ▶ The **Civic Museum** (*8:30 a.m.-1:30 p.m.; summer also 4-6:30 p.m.; closed hols*) houses archaeological finds and sculpture and paintings by A. Alfano. ▶ The 17C church of **S. Maria di Castello** stands isolated on a nearby hill. Inside is a Byzantine-style fresco of the *Madonna and Child* (14C). ▶ Excursions can be made from the town to the Pollino massif which towers over the N part of Calabria.   □

Practical information _____

ⓘ corso Calabria 45, ☎ 27067; v. Garibaldi 37, ☎ 21292.

Hotels:
★★★ *Motel A.S.T.J.,* corso Calabria 103, ☎ 21720, 45 rm ℗ 70,000; bkf: 6,000.
★★ *Unione,* corso Garibaldi 60, ☎ 26596, 18 rm ℗ 40,000; bkf: 3,000.

Restaurant:
● ♦♦♦ *Alia,* v. Jetticelle, ☎ 46370, closed Sun. Rebuilt farmhouse with garden. Excellent cuisine, 25/35,000.

Recommended
Events: *International Folklore Festival* and *Pollino Carnival* (Feb).

CATANZARO

Rome 609, Milan 1,175 km
Pop. 101,622 ⊠ 88100 ☎ 0961   B-C4

Catanzaro was probably founded by the Byzantines in the late 9C or early 10C when they re-occupied Calabria after ousting the Saracens with the help of the Longobards. The Graeco-Byzantine cultural imprint has remained. Catanzaro has been called the city of the three V's — for S. Vitalian, patron saint of the city; for vento (wind), which blows hard on the rocky spur on which Catanzaro is built; and for velvets, since the city has always had a flourishing trade in them. At the Silk Fabrics Fair, which was held at

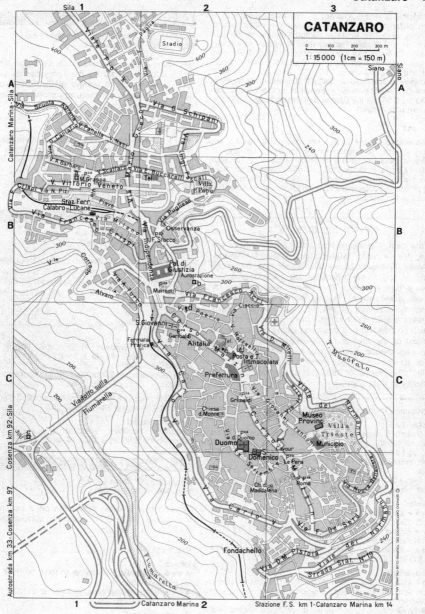

Santa Chiara (near the municipio, C3) and which lasted for a fortnight, buyers came from all over Italy and even from beyond the Alps. In 1688 the trade received a severe blow from which it never really recovered when a plague swept through the city.

▶ **Corso Mazziani** (C-D2-3), a large avenue with 19C buildings on each side, runs through the older part of the town ending at p. Matteotti (B2), where the newer areas begin. The medieval town, on both sides of the corso,

is full of narrow winding streets interspersed with ramps and steps linking the different levels of the town. There are 17C palaces, Baroque portals and open galleries among the ancient residences. ▶ The church of the **Rosary** or S. Domenico (C-D2) can be reached by steps in v. Tribunali. It has an 18C Neoclassical façade and the interior is late Baroque. Among its many works of art, the 15C statue of the *Redeemer* and the *Madonna of the Rosary*★ by the Flemish painter Dirk Hendricksz are outstanding. ▶ In the Duomo (C2), rebuilt in 1960, there is a remarkable bust of S. Vitalian. ▶ The **Villa Trieste** (C3), a short distance away looking out over the valley toward the sea, also has busts of famous people in its gardens. ▶ The **Museo Provinciale** (C3; *open Thu and Fri 10 a.m.-12 noon*) has a variety of prehistoric, Greek and Roman material; a collection of Graeco-Byzantine, medieval and 18C-19C coins; 16C-17C paintings including a *Madonna* by Antonello de Saliba (1508) and some modern paintings. ▶ There is a beautiful marble statue by A. Gagini (1504) in the **Chiesa dell'Osservanza** (B2) in the modern part of town.

Environs

▶ **Catanzaro Marina** is 13.5 km away; a further 1.5 km along a side road leads to the imposing remains of **S. Maria della Roccella**★ (or Roccelletta), a church that possibly dates from the 12C and that reveals Arab, Norman and Byzantine influences. Close by is the archaeological site of **Scolacium** with remains of a Roman theatre, amphitheatre and baths. □

City of the three V's

In the past, Catanzaro was know as the city of the three V's — vento, Vitaliano, velluto (wind, Vitaliano, velvet). The wind blows relentlessly over the rocky crag on which the village is set. Vitaliano is the town's patron saint. The village was famous for its silk velvet works. Having learned about silk from eastern merchants in the 11C, Catanzaro artisans turned the town into the center of a prosperous industry which counted up to a thousand looms and employed a third of the town's 16,000 inhabitants. During a two-week period, traders from all over Europe would flock to the village fair (near the present-day city hall). The plague of 1688 put an end to the textile industry in Catanzaro.

Practical information ——————————

CATANZARO
ⓘ Galleria Mancuso (C2), ☎ 29823 (head office); p. Rossi (C2), ☎ 45530.
✈ at Lamazia Terme *(35 km W)*, ☎ 0968/53082; *Alitalia*, corso Mazzini 74 (C2), ☎ 27435.
▓▓ (D3 off map), ☎ 71022; *Calabrian Lucanian Railways* (B1), ☎ 45521.
▓▓ from p. Matteotti (B2).

Hotels:
★★★★ *Guglielmo,* Tedeschi 1 (B1 a), ☎ 26532, 46 rm P ▓ ⓑ 120,000; bkf: 12,000.
★★★ *Grand Hotel,* p. Matteotti (B2 b), ☎ 25605, 79 rm P ⚡ No restaurant, 103,000.
★★★ *MotelAgip,* at Fiumarella crossroads (C1 c), ☎ 51791, 76 rm P 103,000.

Restaurants:
♦♦♦ *Uno Più Uno,* v. San Nicola (C2 e), ☎ 23180, closed Mon and Sun in Jun-Sep. Regional cuisine: risotto with cuttlefish sauce, rolled anchovies, 20/30,000.
♦♦ *La Griglia,* v. Poerio 26 (C2 d), ☎ 23118, closed Sun, 10-25 Aug. Regional cuisine, 25/35,000.

Recommended
Golf: *Porto d'Orra,* at Simeri-Crichi *(18 km E)*, ☎ 34045.
Horseback riding: *La Laganusa,* ☎ 31606.

Environs

CATANZARO MARINA, ⊠ 88063, ☎ 0961, 13 km S. ≋

Hotel:
★★★ *Stillhotel,* v. Melito Porto Salvo, ☎ 32851, 30 rm P ≼ ⚡ 75,000; bkf: 6,000. Rest. ♦♦♦ *Brace* ☎ 31340, closed Mon. Seafood, 22/35,000.

CETRARO

Cosenza 55, Catanzaro 147, Rome 468 km
Pop. 10,999 ⊠ 87022 ☎ 0982   A3

Cetraro is a lovely seaside resort sitting on a hill from which it looks out across the Tyrrhenian Sea. At its feet is the beach of **Marina di Cetraro.** To the N along the rocky coast there are **grottos** to visit; they are well worth a boat trip. □

Practical information ——————————

Hotel:
★★★★ *Grand Hotel San Michele,* contrada Bosco 8/9, ☎ 91012, 73 rm P ⚄ ▓ ▭ ⌐ ⌣ closed Nov. Former private villa on rocky spur with elevator to beach below, 100,000.

▲ *La Grotta,* at Cetraro Porto, 87 pl, ☎ 91257; *Lido dei Pini,* at Cetraro Marina, 80 pl, ☎ 91384.

CIRO MARINA

Catanzaro 103, Rome 561 km
Pop. 13,499 ⊠ 88072 ☎ 0962   C3

On the Ionian coast between the mouth of the Lipuda River and Punta Alice (where there are remains of a Doric **temple** of Apollo Aleus, possibly 5C BC), Ciro Marina is an important fish market and produces excellent wines. □

Practical information ——————————

Hotels:
★★★ *Costa Elisabeth,* at Ciro, SS 106 at 291-km marker, ☎ 34087, 42 rm P ▓ ▭ ⌐ closed 1-15 Nov, 60,000; bkf: 5,000.
★★★ *Gabbiano,* at Punta Alice, ☎ 31849, 40 rm P ⚄ ⌐ 65,000.

▲ *Punta Alice,* at Punta Alice, 400 pl, ☎ 31160; *Torrenova,* at Torrenova, 120 pl, ☎ 31482.

Recommended
Children's facilities: camping at *Centri Rousseau:* information, at Milan, v. Vico 10, ☎ 02/468496.

COPANELLO

Catanzaro 22, Rome 626 km
Pop. 140 ⊠ 88060 ☎ 0961   B4

Copanello is a lovely little town on a beach on the Ionian Sea not far S of Catanzaro, surrounded by the rocky Punta di Staletti. □

Practical information ——————————

Hotels:
★★★★ *Copanello,* SS 106, ☎ 911004, 30 rm P ≼ ▓ ⚡ ▭ Pens. 110,000.
★★★★ *Villagio Guglielmo,* at Lido, ☎ 911321 155 rm P ▓ ▭ ⌐ Pens. 110,000.

Recommended
Craft workshops: *Commodaro,* at Squillace *(10 km NW)*, v. F. Pepe, ☎ 912233.

COSENZA

Catanzaro 92, Rome 518, Milan 1,084 km
Pop. 106,373 ⊠ 87100 ☎ 0984   B3

Called Consentia by the Romans, Cosenza lies at the confluence of the Crati and Busento Rivers and is surrounded by hills. The ancient part of town, which has steep and narrow streets, is joined by the Mario Martire Bridge to the modern part, which is well laid

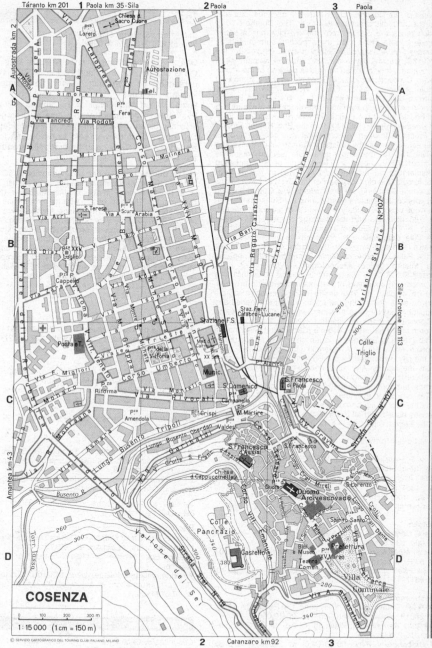

COSENZA

0   100   200   300 m

1 : 15 000 (1 cm = 150 m)

© SERVIZIO CARTOGRAFICO DEL TOURING CLUB ITALIANO, MILANO

Catanzaro km 92

out with fine buildings. Silk, leather goods, furniture and pottery are manufactured here, and there is a lively trade in cereals, fruit, olive oil and cloth.

▶ **Piazza Campanella** (C2), on the l. bank of the Busento near the bridge, lies where the two parts of the city come

together and offers a good view of the confluence of the rivers. ▶ In the piazza, the church of **S. Domenico** (originally 15C) has been rebuilt in the Baroque style and the only evidence of the previous church is a large arched portico and a fine rosette. Inside are a *Madonna della Febbre*, a 16C Neapolitan sculpture, and a 17C choir and chapel of the Rosary, rich in Baroque carvings, stuccos, frescos and gilt ornamentation. ▶ The **Duomo**★ (D3), which faces the piazza from the old city, has a sober façade in tufa stone with three portals surmounted by rosettes. It is Cistercian-Gothic in style, dates from the 12C-13C, was rebuilt in the 18C and has recently been renovated. Inside are an admirable painting of the *Immaculate Conception* by Luca Giordano and the tomb★ of Isabel of Aragon, a 13C French work. ▶ In the nearby **Palazzo dell'Arcivescovado** (D3; Archiepiscopal Palace) work is nearly completed on a **Interdiocesan Museum**. It will house part of the Duomo's treasures including a Sicilian enamel cross★ (13C), a gift of the Holy Roman Emperor Frederick II when the cathedral was consecrated, as well as ivory works by artists of the school of Benvenuto Cellini, 15C-18C paintings, gold plate, sacred vestments and old manuscripts. ▶ The church of **S. Francesco d'Assisi** (C2) can be reached by walking up the **via Seggio**, through the old (15C) part of the town *(or by car along the corso Garibaldi)*. It was originally a Gothic building but was considerably altered during the Renaissance and Baroque periods; inside are wood carvings, some interesting 18C paintings and the Baroque chapel of St. Catherine. ▶ The Prefecture (regional government building), the **Villa Comunale** with its extensive gardens and the Teatro Comunale are all on the piazza XV marzo (D3), as is the **Palazzo dell'Accademia Cosentina**, which houses the **Museo Civico Archeologico** *(8:30 a.m.-2 p.m.; closed Sun & hols)* where archaeological finds, including an important collection of Calabrian prehistoric bronzes, are on display. ▶ The **castle** (D2), a massive square fort on a hill dominating the town, was strengthened and rebuilt by the Normans and the Swedes, these last being responsible for the octagonal tower. ▶ Inside the 17C church of **S. Francesco di Paolo** (C3) are a striking marble tomb (1593), a Baroque wooden choir and a remarkable triptych (early 16C). A splendid view of the two parts of the city, separated by the Busento River, can be seen from the nearby Alarico Bridge, which is close to the confluence of the two rivers. According to tradition, the Goths temporarily changed the course of the Busento River in order to bury their king, Alaric, in its bed. Alaric was the first of the barbarians to sack Rome, in 410, and he was buried with all the treasure that he had plundered in the Eternal City. □

Practical information —————————————

ⓘ v. P. Rossi (Al off map), ☎ 390595; v. Tagliamento 15 (B2; head office), ☎ 27821.
🚂 (C2), ☎ 27080; *Ferrovie Calabro Lucane* (B2), ☎ 24961.
🚌 from bus station (A2), ☎ 35323.
Car rental: *Maggiore*, v. degli Alimena 31/H, ☎ 71249.

Hotels:
★★★ **Centrale**, v. del Tigrai (B2 a), ☎ 73681, 48 rm P 85,000; bkf: 6,000.
★★★ **MotelAgip**, SS 19 at crossroads with SS 107, ☎ 839101, 65 rm P 🛝 94,000.
★★★ **San Francesco**, nr Commenda, v. Ungaretti, ☎ 861721, 144 rm P 🖃 82,000; bkf: 5,000.

Restaurants:
● ◆◆◆ **Calavrisella**, v. Gerolamo De Rada 11A (A1 b), ☎ 28012, closed Sat and Sun eve, 20/40,000.
◆◆ **Villa Bernaudo**, v. Piave 55 (Cl-2 d), ☎ 22026, closed Sun, 15/23,000.
◆ **Giocondo**, v. Piave 53 (B-C2 c), ☎ 29810, closed Sat and Aug, 23/40,000.

Recommended

Events: musical season and plays at *Teatro Rendano*, ☎ 23971; *Festival of the Calabrian Costume* (spring every other year).
Horseback riding: *San Valentino*, v. G. Santoro 15, ☎ 33825.
Nature park: *Parco Nazionale della Calabria*, v. della Repubblica 26, ☎ 26544 (head office).

Catanzaro 69, Rome 593 km
Pop. 59,899 ⊠ 88074 ☎ 0962   C4

One of Crotone's most famous sons was Milon, the Greek athlete who flourished in 6C BC. He was unbeatable as a wrestler, winning the Olympic and Pythian games wrestling contests twelve times. Milon was a pupil of the famous philosopher Pythagoras who taught at one time in Crotone. He also captained the Crotonian army that defeated the Sybarites. Crotone was said to have been founded by Greeks in 710 BC and its acropolis stood facing the sea where the castle is today.

▶ The **Duomo** has a sober and harmonious 16C façade but the church for the most part has been rebuilt. Inside is a much revered image of the *Madonna di Capo Colonna*. ▶ The 16C castle with its large round towers dominates the port. ▶ The **Museo Archeologico Statale** *(winter 9 a.m.-2 p.m.; summer 9 a.m.-1 p.m. and 3-5 p.m.; Sun 9 a.m.-1 p.m.; closed Mon)* displays prehistoric and Graeco-Roman finds from the Crotone region. ▶ At **Capo Colonna** *(11 km SE)* all that remains of the **Sanctuary of Hera Lacinia**, which in antiquity comprised a large number of buildings surrounded by a wall, is the base of a Doric temple (5C BC) and one column. □

Practical information —————————————

≋ .
ⓘ v. Firenze 47, ☎ 23185.
✈ at Isola di Capo Rizzuto *(14 km SW)*, ☎ 791150.
Car rental: *Maggiore*, v. M. Nicoletta 149, ☎ 27725, airport, ☎ 27725.

Hotels:
★★★ **Casarossa**, toward Capo Colonna, ☎ 29825, 182 rm P 🛝 🖃 ♪ closed Oct-May, 90,000.
★★★ **Costa Tiziana**, toward Capo Colonna, ☎ 25601, 112 rm P 🛝 🖃 ♪ closed 20 Dec-20 Jan, 80,000; bkf: 8,000.
★★ **Tortorelli**, v. Gramsci, ☎ 29930, 16 rm P 🛝 42,000; bkf: 3,000.

Restaurants:
● ◆◆◆ **Bella Romagna**, v. Poggioreale 87, ☎ 21943, closed Sun and Dec-Jan. Seafood: with risotto and pasta, swordfish, 25/40,000.
◆◆◆ **Girarrosto**, traversa Tedeschi 5, ☎ 22043, closed Sun and Dec. Regional cuisine, 25/35,000.
⚓ *Alfier*, at Capo Colonna, v. Campione, 350 pl, ☎ 25050 (all year).

Recommended

Events: *Festival of Calabrian Cuisine* (Aug or Sep).
Flying: aeroclub, at airport, ☎ 793173.
Sailing: *Lega Navale*, at Moletto Sanità, ☎ 27240 (instruction).
Vacation villages: *Village Valtur*, at Capo Rizzuto (closed Oct-Apr), information: at Milan, ☎ 02/791733, at Rome, ☎ 06/6784588.

Cosenza 76, Catanzaro 137, Rome 444 km
Pop. 5,121 ⊠ 87023 ☎ 0985   A2-3

Diamante is located on a small headland on the Tyrrhenian coast. A number of unusual murals may be seen on the houses of the old part of town. To the S are the sandy beaches of **Marina di Belvedere** *(7.5 km)* and of **Sangineto Lido** *(13 km)*. The small island of **Cirella** is to the N, as is Cirella itself, on a spur and at the foot of a hill surmounted by the ruins of **Cirella Vecchia** (Old Cirella), which was destroyed by the Napoleonic fleet in 1806. The nearby mausoleum is a Roman tomb dating from imperial times. ☐

Practical information ⎯⎯⎯⎯⎯⎯

DIAMANTE

≋

ⓘ corso Vittorio Emanuele 57.

Hotels:

★★★★ *Ferretti*, v. Lungamore, ☎ 81428, 45 rm Ⓟ ₩ ▣ ⟋⁰ closed Oct-Mar, 80,000; bkf: 6,000.

★★★ *Focesi*, nr Monache, ☎ 81515, 120 rm Ⓟ ₩ ⚘ ⟋⁰ closed Nov-Mar, 50,000; bkf: 4,000.

Environs

CIRELLA, ⊠ 87020, ☎ 0985, 4 km N.

Hotel:

★★★ *Guardacosta*, v. Veneto 76, ☎ 86012, 58 rm Ⓟ ⟨ △ ₩ ▣ ⟋⁰ closed Oct-Mar, 70,000; bkf: 6,000.

⚔ *Internazionale Cirella*, at Acchio, 180 pl, ☎ 86003; *Mare Blu*, v. Riviere 60, 150 pl, ☎ 86097.

GERACE

Reggio di Calabria 96, Catanzaro 108, Rome 692 km
Pop. 2,994 ⊠ 89040 ☎ 0964   B5-6

Gerace is a picturesque medieval town, rising inland on a series of three terraces towards the top of a hill. Rebuilt after the earthquake of 1783, it is divided into three parts. The first is the *Borgo* where the ancient shops of the potters are dug out of the soft rock; the second is the *Borghetto* and the third the *Baglio*. The *Baglio* offers a wide view over the country below; it was here that the population took refuge when danger threatened. It overlooks a deep natural crevice beyond which stands the solitary castle which, at one time, could only be reached by a slender drawbridge.

▶ The **cathedral,** consecrated in 1045, restored under the Swedes and since altered and renovated, is the largest place of worship in Calabria and an edifice of the utmost importance. In the interior, which is bare and solemn, there are several old pagan pillars, which were taken from Greek temples at nearby Locri, and there are also similar columns in the crypt. A sculptured *Madonna* of the Pisan school (14C) may be seen in the 16C chapel behind the altar. A tomb of the Ruffo family, of the late Pisan school (1372), can be seen. ▶ In the church of **S. Francesco** (1252) are a 14C tomb and inlaid woodwork on the main altar (1664). ▶ Byzantine-style statues may be seen in the small church of **S. Giovanello.** ▶ The **castle** offers a magnificent view. ▶ The **Terme di Antonimina** comprise the **Acque Sante Locresi** (Holy Waters of Locri). ☐

Practical information ⎯⎯⎯⎯⎯⎯

⚑ at Bagni di Antonimina, ☎ 312040 (Apr-Nov).
ⓘ municipio, ☎ 356003.

GIOIA·TAURO

Reggio di Calabria 57, Catanzaro 110, Rome 654 km
Pop. 17,564 ⊠ 89013 ☎ 0966   A5

Gioia Tauro is on the border of the Rosarno plain. A region that produces olive oil and grows grapes, olives and citrus fruit, it is currently developing several new industries. It has many long streets and modern buildings which join up, toward the sea, with those of **Marina di Gioia Tauro.** ☐

Send us your comments and suggestions; we will use them in the next edition.

Practical information ⎯⎯⎯⎯⎯⎯

ⓘ motorway service area west of motorway, ☎ 52402.

Hotel:

★★★ *Park Hotel*, v. Nazionale 18, ☎ 51159, 44 rm Ⓟ ₩ 60,000.

Recommended

Horseback riding: *Circolo Ippico della Piana*, corso Garibaldi 120, ☎ 51443.

LAMEZIA TERME

Catanzaro 35, Rome 580 km
Pop. 65,409 ⊠ 88046 ☎ 0968   B4

On the N side of the plain of S. Eufemia, Lamezia Terme is a vast and scattered comune formed in 1968 by uniting the old centres of Nicastro and Sambise with the modern town of S. Eufemia Lamezia. **Nicastro,** where the administrative offices of the comune are located, is built against a projection of Mount Reventino. The old locality of S. Teodoro, dominated by the ruins of the Norman Swedish castle, is worth a visit. The **Terme di Caronte** are in a valley 8 km W of **Sambiase,** a well-known wine-producing centre. **Gizzeria Lido,** on the sea, is 4 km NW of S. Eufemia di Lamezia. ☐

Practical information ⎯⎯⎯⎯⎯⎯

≋
⚑ ☎ 331180 or 331980 (May-Nov)
ⓘ at Nicastro, corso Numistrano 1, ☎ 21405.
✈ at S. Eufemia Lamezia, ☎ 53082.
Car rental: *Hertz*, at airport, ☎ 51533; *Maggiore*, at airport, ☎ 51331.

Hotel:

★★★ *Grand Hotel Lamezia*, at S. Eufemia Lamezia, p. Lamezia, ☎ 53021, 104 rm Ⓟ ⚅ closed Easter and Christmas, 55,000; bkf: 3,000.

⚔ *La Vela*, at S. Eufemia Lamezia, ☎ 51576; *Ulisse*, at S. Eufemia Lamezia, SS 18 at 403-km marker, 120 pl.

Recommended

Archery: *Compagnia Arcieri Lametini*, ☎ 26334.
Craft workshops: *Cooperativa Annunziata*, at Serrastretta *(22 km NE of Nicastro)*, ☎ 81186 (wooden chairs and toys).
Flying: at airport, ☎ 53189 (instruction).
Tennis: at Nicastro, ☎ 21708.

LOCRI

Reggio di Calabria 96, Catanzaro 98, Rome 702 km
Pop. 13,261 ⊠ 89044 ☎ 0964   B6

There is a grim story told about *Locri Epizephyrii* (Locri of the West Wind), an ancient Greek colony founded *c.* 700 BC. Dionysius the Elder, tyrant of Syracuse, after capturing Rhegium and most of what today is Calabria in 356 BC, made his kingdom the greatest power in Europe. While visiting these new territories he met a certain Aristides and asked for one of his daughters in marriage. Aristides replied that he would sooner see his daughter dead than married to a despot. Outraged, Dionysius had all Aristides' children killed. 'Though I am utterly shattered by what you have done to me', Aristides is said to have replied, 'I do not regret my action.' Commenting on this anecdote some four centuries later, Plutarch was to write 'This is carrying the question of honour a bit too far.'

▶ Modern Locri is not very far from the ancient town. The site of **Locri Epizephyrii**, where digging is going on, is 3.5 km along the main road to Bovalino. The **Locri Museum** is at the entrance to the site *(winter 9 a.m.-2 p.m. and 3-5:30 p.m.; Sun 9 a.m.-1 p.m.; closed Mon)* where, among major finds, are some terracotta votive tablets belonging to the Temple of Persephone (5C BC). Some walls and part of a building, the remains of a 5C Ionic temple, are behind the museum. ▶ A Graeco-Roman **temple** *(visiting hours same as museum)* and a Doric temple are in an enclosure in the direction of the hills; the remains of the temple of Persephone are higher up near some water works and military installations. ▶ The seaside resort of **Siderno** *(5 km)* lies among the citrus trees in the direction of Punta Stilo.   □

Practical information ───────────────

≋
ℹ v. Matteotti (corner of v. Fiume), ☎ 29600.

Hotel:
★★★ *Demaco*, v. Lungomare 28, ☎ 20247, 33 rm ℗ ⦉⦊ ⌚ 65,000; bkf: 5,000.

⚑ *Caravan Sud,* at Siderno Marina, 75 pl, ☎ 342767; *Helios,* at Portigliola Marina, 400 pl, ☎ 361069.

LUNGRO

Cosenza 75, Catanzaro 167, Rome 483 km
Pop. 3,210 ⊠ 87010 ☎ 0981   B2

A number of **Albanians** arrived as refugees in the 15C in Calabria after their national hero George Castriota, known as Scanderbeg, died and the Turks reoccupied their country. Lungro, high up over the valley of the Crati River and the plain of Sibari, is their spiritual centre and the seat of an eparchia (diocese) of the Greek-Catholic rite. In the cathedral of **S. Nicola di Mira** there are a notable screen with ikons and a painting found in the ruins of the old church of 1547.   □

MORANO CALABRO

Cosenza 80, Catanzaro 172, Rome 446 km
Pop. 5,144 ⊠ 87016 ☎ 0981   A-B2

Morano Calabro is positioned on the steep side of a cone-like hill, crowned by the ruins of a castle, with Mount Pollino rising majestically in the distance. The streets are narrow and steep and the houses fall away, as if tumbling on top of each other. This unusual layout has attracted many artists.

▶ The 15C church of **S. Bernardino**, at the town's entrance, has a Gothic portal and a roof in the Venetian style *(presently being restored; caretaker on premises).* ▶ The **Museo della Civiltà Contadina** (rural objects and peasant life) is currently being set up in the monastery adjacent to the church. The material at this time may be seen only by special request *(to the Comune).* ▶ The Baroque **Collegiate church** has a *Madonna* by Antonello Gagini and other works of art. ▶ There are statues by Pietro Bernini in the church of **S. Pietro.** ▶ The church of **S. Nicola** has a Gothic portal.   □

NICOTERA

Catanzaro 96, Rome 639 km
Pop. 7,434 ⊠ 88034 ☎ 0963   A5

Nicotera, on the lower slopes of a group of hills enclosing the Gulf of Gioia Tauro, boasts a fine view over the Rosarno plain. It is laid out on a typically Nor-

man radial plan with the cathedral and the castle in the centre and streets running off like spokes of a wheel to the encircling walls. The manufacture of cloth, a very ancient industry, is still carried on in the Jewish quarter, called the Giudecca.

▶ The late Baroque, rebuilt **cathedral** has a *Crucifixion* from 1593 and, in the chapel on the r. of the presbytery, a *Madonna delle Grazie* by Antonello Gagini. ▶ The **Diocesan Museum of Sacred Art** *(8:30 a.m.-12:30 p.m. and 4:30-6:30 p.m.)* in the nearby bishop's palace has architectural remains, paintings (chiefly 16C-19C), sculpture, embroidered vestments and religious articles and old manuscripts. ▶ The **Archaeological Museum** *(8:30 a.m.-12:30 p.m. and 3-6 p.m.)* is housed in the castle (partly rebuilt in 18C) and has prehistoric, Graeco-Roman and medieval material.   □

Practical information ───────────────

Hotel:
★★★ *Miragolfo,* v. Corte 68, ☎ 81470, 100 rm ℗ 57,000; bkf: 5,000.

Restaurant:
♦ *La Pergola,* toward S. Ferdinando, ☎ 88033. Regional cuisine: pasta and chickpeas, mixed meats on the spit, 15/25,000.

⚑ *Mimosa,* at Nicotera Marina, 200 pl, ☎ 81397; *Sayonara,* at Nicotera Marina, ☎ 81944.

Recommended
Vacation villages: *Valtur Village,* at Nicotera Marina (closed Oct-Apr), information, at Milan, ☎ 02/791733, at Rome, ☎ 06/6784588.

PALMI

Reggio Calabria 49, Catanzaro 117, Rome 661 km
Pop. 18,693 ⊠ 89015 ☎ 0966   A5

Palmi is a small modern city, rebuilt after the earthquake of 1908, that sits on a height on the Tyrrhenian coast called the **Costa Viola.**

▶ Traditional and ethnographic material is presently being arranged in a museum *(8:15 a.m.-1:15 p.m. and 3:30-5:30 p.m.; closed Sun)* housed in the **Casa della Cultura Leonida Repaci.** Collections include objects used for work by peasants and fishermen, musical instruments and finds from 7C BC-9C AD recovered from sites in the ancient city of **Taureaunum.** ▶ **Marina di Palmi** is at the lower end of Palmi itself; along the coast to the N are the beaches of **Lido di Palmi** and **Taureana.** ▶ From **Mount S. Elia** there is a dazzling view, and it is possible to see the distant Mount Etna and the Lipari Islands.   □

Practical information ───────────────

PALMI
≋
ℹ v. Tripepi 72, ☎ 23294; p. I Maggio 4, ☎ 22192.

Hotels:
★★★ *Costa Viola,* at Torre, ☎ 22016, 42 rm ℗ ⦉⦊ ⊗ 59,000; bkf: 5,000. Rest. ♦♦♦ Seafood: swordfish with salmoriglio sauce, ling alla Calabrese, 15/25,000.
★★ *Garden,* p. Lo Sardo, ☎ 23645, 25 rm ℗ ⦉⦊ 50,000; bkf: 3,000.

Recommended
Craft workshops: *V. Latino,* at Seminara v. Basilica 14, ☎ 317124.
Cycling: *G.S. Palmi,* v. Trodio 30, ☎ 46115.
Events: *S. Rocco Festival* (Aug 16).

Environs
TAUREANA ⊠ 89010, ☎ 0966, 5 km N.

Hotel:
★★★ *Arcobaleno,* ☎ 46275, 51 rm ℗ ♿ ⌂ ⊗ ⁒ 88,000.

⚑ *San Fantino,* v. San Fantino, 200 pl, ☎ 46306 (all year).

Customs and superstitions

Calabria was cut off from the rest of Italy for long periods and it developed customs and superstitions different from those of other parts of the peninsula. The Casa della Cultura (museum) at Palmi houses items that attest to these customs and superstitions. Among these items are masks that at one time were hung by doors of houses; those who went in or out had to touch them each time to ward off bad luck. Other strange objects include babbaluti, bottle-shaped figures with human likenesses. By means of the babbaluti, the people showed their contempt for their rulers. They created babbaluti that looked like Spanish policemen or the Emperor Franz Joseph of Austria or a local feudal lord.

PAOLA

Cosenza 34, Catanzaro 94, Rome 487 km
Pop. 17,191 ⊠ 87027 ☎ 0982   A3

Francesco d'Alessio's simple faith was disturbed by the ostentatious luxury in 16C papal Rome and he obtained permission to open a convent in his native Paola, where he was born in 1416. This is how the order of the Minim friars — so called because they wished to be the least of all friars — came into being.

▶ The **house** where Saint Francis di Paola was born has been turned into the **Church of the Addolorate.** It is on an avenue with small chapels where majolica tablets depict his life story. The present convent was built in the 18C and the church has a Renaissance and Baroque façade. There are relics of the saint in a chapel (16C) which also has a Flemish painting (16C) and a silver cross (15C). ▶ 6.5 km N of **Marina di Paola** is the beach of **Marina di Fuscaldo.** □

Practical information ——————

≋
ⓘ p. IV Novembre, ☎ 5583.

Hotels:
★★★ **Alhambra,** SS 18, ☎ 2790, 40 rm P ⌑ ⌘ 50,000.
★★★ **Terminus,** at Marina, p. Stazione, ☎ 3454, 56 rm P ⌘ 42,500; bkf: 4,000.

⚑ *Bahja,* nr Castagnaro, 500 pl, ☎ 3144.

PRAIA A MARE

Cosenza 103, Catanzaro 198, Rome 417 km
Pop. 5,760 ⊠ 87028 ☎ 0985   A2

Praia means beach. There is a small Spanish fort on the shore which faces the **isola di Dino.** On the isola di Dino are steep rocky cliffs and several grottos *(visit by boat, 2.5 km).* The **Madonna della Grotta** sanctuary is in a cave above the town. 12 km S the old town of **Scalea** reaches down to the coast where a modern seaside resort has been built. □

Practical information ——————
PRAIA A MARE
≋
ⓘ v. Giugni, ☎ 72489.

Hotels:
★★★ **Garden,** v. Roma 8, ☎ 72829, 41 rm P ⌑ ⚅ Pens. closed Oct-Mar, 62,000.
★★★ **Major,** v. Alighieri 44, ☎ 72410, 60 rm P ⌘ closed Oct-Apr, 60,000; bkf: 7,000.

★★ **Casetta Bianca,** at Fiuzzi, v. Nazionale 25, ☎ 72335, 22 rm P ⌑ closed Oct-Apr, 40,000; bkf: 4,000.
⚑ *Internazionale sul Mare,* at Fiuzzi, 290 pl, ☎ 72211.

Recommended
Craft workshops: *G. Codella,* v. Cavalier Longo, ☎ 72807.
♥ discothèque: *Moana,* at Lido di Tortora, v. Filimarco, ☎ 72325.

Environs

SCALEA ⊠ 87029, ☎ 0985, 12 km S.
≋
ⓘ v. Nazionale 18, ☎ 21157.

Hotels:
★★★★ **De Rose,** corso Mediterraneo, ☎ 20273, 66 rm P ⌑ ⌘ ⚞ Elegant building overlooking beach, 77,000; bkf: 6,000.
★★★ **Talao,** corso Mediterraneo 66, ☎ 20444, 45 rm P ⌘ ⌑ ⚞ 60,000; bkf: 6,000.

Recommended
Archery: *Compagnia Arcieri Center sport,* v. s. Maria 9, ☎ 20500.

REGGIO DI CALABRIA

Catanzaro 159, Rome 703, Milan 1,270 km
Pop. 175,646 ⊠ 89100 ☎ 0965   A6

Reggio di Calabria was originally a prosperous Greek colony, but in 281 BC it fell into the hands of the Romans. Later it was taken at different times by the Goths, Saracens and Normans. The modern town is well laid out along the seafront having been twice rebuilt after earthquakes in 1783 and 1908. Except for the museum there is now no trace of Greece, although nature remains unchanged — the olive, the almond, the aloe and the oleander grow under the luminous sky.

▶ The celebrated **Museo Nazionale** (B2; *winter 9 a.m.-1 p.m. and Tue, Thu and Sat also 3-6 p.m.; summer 9 a.m.-1 p.m. and 3-6 p.m.; Sun 9 a.m.-1 p.m.; closed Mon)* must be visited. It has splendid collections of material from archaeological sites in both Calabria and Basilicata that shed light on the culture and civilization of ancient Magna Graecia. In addition to the recently acquired **bronzes of Riace**★★ and specimens of **votive tablets**★ found at the temple of Persephone at Locri, there is a group in terra-cotta (5C BC) and a marble group (5C BC). In the medieval and modern sections are two **paintings** by Antonello da Messina, *Saint Jerome*★ and *Abraham and the Angels*★ (1457), as well as *Return of the Prodigal Son*★ by Mattia Preti. ▶ A walk along the **lungomare**★ (C-D1-2) offers wonderful views over the Straits of Messina, Mt. Etna and the Lipari Islands. At the end of the lungomare are part of a **wall** (D1) that dates from the 4C BC and remains of **Roman baths** (E1). ▶ Inside the **Duomo** (E2) are tombs of bishops dating from the 18C and the remarkable Baroque chapel of the Holy Sacrament with marble mosaic work. ▶ All that remains of the **castle** (D2), built during the Aragonese period (16C), are two round towers and part of the wall connecting them. □
Practical information ——————

ⓘ v. D. Tripepi (C2), ☎ 98496; air terminal, ☎ 320291; v. Roma 5 (B2; head office), ☎ 21171; v. Roma 3 (B2), ☎ 92012; central railway station (E-F1), ☎ 27120.
✈ *Tito Minniti,* at Ravagnese, ☎ 320287; buses from central railway station; *Alitalia,* corso Garibaldi 521 (E1), ☎ 331444.
🚌 (E-F1), ☎ 98123.
🚃 from central railway station (E-F1).
⚓ ferries to Messina several times a day, *Ferrovie dello Stato* (A1), ☎ 97957; weekly sailings to Catania, Syracuse and Naples; three sailings a week to Malta

Bronze statues of Riace

Glory came to Calabria at last—and to Reggio in particular—when on 16 August 1972 a scuba diver found two bronze male nude statues off its shore. It was the archaeological find of the century. The statues were dubbed 'The Young Man' and 'The Old Man'; the first was 6 ft 6 in height, the second 6 ft 7 in. The statues were cleaned in Reggio and then sent to specialists in Florence to be renovated—a job that took nearly two years. The bronzes were Greek and dated from the 5C BC. They were of warriors—their left hands are shaped as if holding a shield and their right hands a sword, though these articles are unfortunately lost. Experts have decided that they are the work of Phidias, the 5C Athenian, regarded as the greatest sculptor of antiquity although until now there was no single masterpiece of his extant. How had the statues come to be in the sea off Riace? There was a simple and convincing explanation. After the Battle of Marathon (490 BC) where the Greeks routed a large invading Persian army, they commemorated the event by having twelve specially cast statues placed in their most sacred temple, the sanctuary of Delphi. Some of the twelve statues were the work of Phidias. Centuries later, when the Romans occupied Greece, they looted the museums and the temples. The two statues were on their way from Greece to Rome by sea when the ship carrying them went down off Riace. Although none of this was impossible, some people found the story a little too contrived, but all agreed on the beauty of the statues and the extraordinary luck of their remaining 2,500 years on the seabed and being found by chance. The bronzes first went on display in Florence and then in Rome and crowds queued for hours to see them. There was enthusiasm about them everywhere except in Reggio where there were near-riots. The people wanted back 'their' statues and they were afraid that the Florentines or the Romans would keep them. Finally they were returned to Reggio where they are on display. As for the theory about Phidias, they will have none of it. Pliny the Elder, a Roman writer, asserted that a contemporary sculptor did marvelous nude statues revealing the veins and the muscles of the models just as in the bronzes of 'The Young Man' and 'The Old Man'. That sculptor was Pythagoras and he was born in Reggio di Calabria. The people of Reggio decided that Pythagoras must be the sculptor of their statues.

at Tirrenia, ☎ 92032; hovercraft to Messina; summer daily sailings to Lipari Islands, *SNAV*, ☎ 29568.
Car rental: *Avis*, at airport, ☎ 320023; *Hertz*, at port, ☎ 332223, at airport, ☎ 320093; *Maggiore*, corso Garibaldi 320, ☎ 94980, at airport, ☎ 320148.

Hotels:
★★★★ *Grand Hotel Excelsior*, v. Vittorio Veneto 66 (B2 a), ☎ 25801, 92 rm Ⓟ 146,000.
★★★ *Fata Morgana*, at Gallico Marina, v. Lungomare, ☎ 370009, 32 rm Ⓟ ◪ 84,000; bkf: 4,000.
★★★ *Palace Hotel Masoanri's* (B2 b), ☎ 26433, 65 rm Ⓟ No restaurant, 98,000.
★★★ *Primavera*, v. Nazionale 177, ☎ 47081, 62 rm Ⓟ 85,000; bkf: 7,000.

Restaurants:
● ♦♦♦ *Bonaccorso*, v. Battisti 18 (E1 c), ☎ 96048,

closed Fri and Aug. Regional cuisine: maccheroni alla pastorella, swallows' nests soup, 25/40,000.
● ♦♦♦ *Conti*, v. Giulia 2 (C-D2 d), ☎ 29043, closed Mon except Aug and mid-Sep. Regional cuisine, 20/32,000.
♦♦♦ *Mimmo*, at Gallico Marina, v. Marina 16, ☎ 370013, closed Mon except summer. Regional cuisine: fettucine with mushrooms, swordfish, 16/21,000.
♦ *Baylik*, v. Leone 1/5, ☎ closed Thu and Jul. Seafood: risotto with cuttlefish, grilled stockfish and swordfish, 20/30,000.
♦ *Kalura*, at Catona, v. Bolzano, ☎ 301453, closed Mon and Nov. Regional cuisine, 18/22,000.

⋀ *Paradiso*, at Gallico Marina, v. Marina, 150 pl, ☎ 302482.

Recommended
Clay pigeon shooting: v. D'Annunzio 5, ☎ 21854.
Cycling: *G.S. Cicli Jiriti*, p. Stadio Nord, ☎ 591169.
Events: *Primavera di Reggio; Folklore Procession* (Sep).
Fairs and markets: *Oils and Essences of Citrus Fruit Fair* (Mar), ☎ 43044.
Flying club: *dello Stretto Airport*, ☎ 320035.
Horseback riding: *Club Ippico Reggino*, v. Gebbione, ☎ 51468.
Swimming: p. Stadio, ☎ 54533.
▼ wine: *Bottiglieria Pellarese*, at Pellaro, v. Sottolume 28, ☎ 359957.

Festival of the Madonna in Reggio

At the end of summer, when the last of the fruit has been picked, the people of Reggio are busy with the large cooking pots in which the tomato juice for the following year is prepared. On their balconies salted tomatoes rest in wicker baskets drying in the sun. This is also the time for the Festival of the Madonna, which lasts a week and where many events take place that date from pre-Christian times. Gypsies and hawkers sell wickerwork, wrought iron objects and embroidered tablecloths and the streets are crowded with people eating honey-flavoured cakes shaped like animals or women. Some people attend Mass, either inside the church or outside where loudspeakers relay the ceremony. In the evening, everyone dances the lively tarantella to the sounds of bagpipes and accordions. On the day of the festival a procession wends its way through the streets of Reggio to the accompaniment of music and singing, trumpet playing and fireworks.

ROSSANO

Cosenza 90, Catanzaro 160, Rome 512 km
Pop. 32,906 ✉ 87067 ☎ 0983   B-C3

Rossano, facing the Ionian Sea, lies between the last slopes of the Sila Greca and the plain of Sibari and is surrounded by terraced hills with majestic olive trees. It is one of the most important centres of early medieval Byzantine art and culture in Calabria.

▶ The **cathedral**, in the upper part of the city, although rebuilt in a Baroque style, has retained much of its medieval construction, especially in the apse. The portal is Renaissance, as is the roof. It has a precious Byzantine *Madonna* (C8-9C) called *acheropita* (not painted by human hand). ▶ The **Diocesan Museum**★ nearby (*winter 10:30 a.m.-12 noon and 4-6 p.m.; summer 10:30 a.m.-12 noon and 5-7 p.m.; Sun 9 a.m.-12 noon*), in addition to 15C-16C material and medieval precious manuscripts, houses one of the oldest and most valuable Greek gospel miniature manuscripts, the **Codex Purpureus★**, 188 leaves of purple parchment containing the

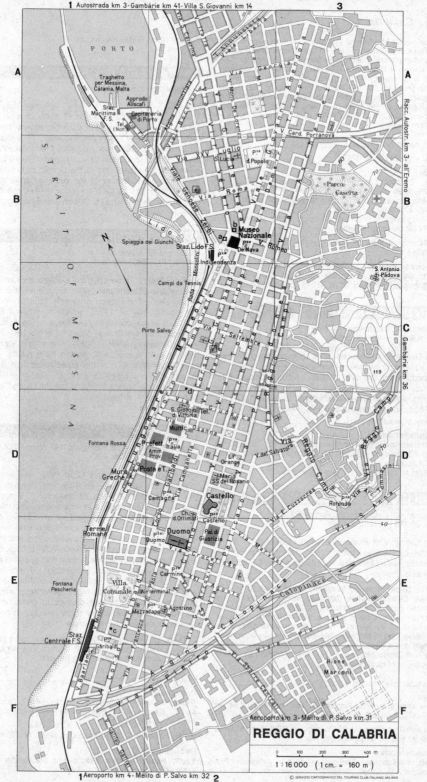

Top margin: 1 Autostrada km 3 - Gambárie km 41 - Villa S. Giovanni km 14 — 3

Page number: 125

Right margin: Racc. Autostr. km 3 - all'Éremo · Gambárie km 36

Bottom margin: 1 Aeroporto km 4 - Mélito di P. Salvo km 32 — 2 · Aeroporto km 3 - Mélito di P. Salvo km 31

REGGIO DI CALABRIA

Scale: 1 : 16 000 (1 cm. = 160 m)
0 100 200 300 400 m

© SERVIZIO CARTOGRAFICO DEL TOURING CLUB ITALIANO, MILANO

Notable labels: PORTO · STRAIT OF MESSINA · Traghetto per Messina, Cátania, Malta · Approdo Aliscafi · Staz. Marittima F.S. · Capitaneria di Porto · Museo Nazionale · Parco Caserta · S. Antonio di Pádova · Spiaggia dei Giunchi · Staz. Lido F.S. · Campi da Tennis · Porto Salvo · Munic. · Fontana Rossa · Prefett. · Amm. Prov. · Posta e T. · Mura Greche · Castello · Camagna · Terme Romane · Duomo · Fontana Pescheria · Villa Comunale · Air terminal · S. Agostino · Staz. Centrale F.S. · Rione Marconi

Gospels of St. Matthew and St. Mark. ▶ There are several fine Byzantine churches such as the **Chiesa della Panaghia** and the small church of **S. Maria del Pilerio.** ▶ The best known is **S. Marco**★ (10C-11C), outside the town on a cliff from where several grottos can be seen that were, at one time, inhabited. The church, which is laid out in a square, has three apses and five small cupolas and remains one of the most interesting Byzantine constructions in Calabria. ▶ The Church of **S. Maria del Patire**★ is 18 km away. ☐

Practical information _____

ⓘ p. Metteotti 2, ☎ 32137.

Hotels:
★★★ *Europa Lido Palace,* at Rossano Stazione, ☎ 22095, 55 rm Ⓟ ⚿ 66,000; bkf: 4,000.
★★ *Murano,* at Lido S. Angelo, ☎ 25370, 38 rm Ⓟ ⚞ ⚲ 57,000; bkf: 6,000.
★★ *Scigliano,* at Rossano Stazione, v. Margherita 257, ☎ 21846, 36 rm Ⓟ 51,000.

⚿ *Marina di Rossano,* at Rossano Stazione, 400 pl, ☎ 22069.

Recommended
Craft workshops: *Tessitura Artistica Calabrese,* at Longobucco, v. Monaci 12, ☎ 71048 (fabrics; closed Sun).

SAN DEMETRIO CORONE

Cosenza 54, Catanzaro 146, Rome 515 km
Pop. 4,503 ⊠ 87069 ☎ 0984   B3

San Demetrio Corone became an important Albanian cultural centre following their arrival here in 1468. It is located on the NW slopes of the wooded Sila Greca. The Italo-Albanian College contains the church of **S. Adriano**★ which dates from the 11C-12C and has mosaic flooring and 14C frescos. ☐

Practical information _____

Recommended
Craft workshops: *Cooperativa Anamide,* at Vaccarizzo Albanese, ☎ 0983/84142 (machine and hand weaving of fabrics).
Events: traditional *Holy Week Ceremonies.*

SAN GIOVANNI IN FIORE

Cosenza 60, Catanzaro 85, Rome 583 km
Pop. 20,318 ⊠ 87055 ☎ 0984   C3

San Giovanni in Fiore, in a scenic position on the E slopes of the Sila Grande (→), grew up around the powerful abbey founded in 1189 by Abbot Gioacchino da Fiore.

▶ The **Badia Florense** *(presently being restored)* is in a severe Cistercian style that was renovated during the Baroque period. It still retains its Gothic portal, windows and the rosette of the apse, as well as the crypt that houses the tomb of its founder. ▶ **S. Maria dèlle Grazie,** in the upper part of the town, has some Baroque sculptured portals and a sumptuous interior. ▶ The **Museo Faunistico** in v. Cappuccini *(9 a.m.-1 p.m.; closed Sun)* has many specimens of local fauna. ☐

Practical information _____

Hotel:
★★★ *Dino's,* v. della Repubblica 166, ☎ 992370, 34 rm Ⓟ ⚿ ⚲ 46,000; bkf: 6,500.

⚿ *Lago Arvo,* Passo della Cornacchia, SS 108 bis at 5-km marker, 550 pl, ☎ 997060 (all year).

Recommended
Craft workshops: *Cooperativa Nuova Artigiana Florense,* v. A.G. Lopez, ☎ 992271 (modern carpets).

Events: *Good Friday Procession.*

SANTA MARIA DEL PATIRE*

Rossano 19, Cosenza 86 km
                B3

The church of Santa Maria del Patire is built on a plateau from which there is a splendid view★ over the reclaimed plain of Sibari and the sea. Only the ruins remain of the great monastery of the order of Saint Basil (Greek Orthodox Church), built 1101-05. The portals of the church are in the Gothic style while the polychrome decoration of the external apse is Norman-Sicilian; the basilica's interior, with three naves, has fine mosaic paving (12C) with animal designs. ☐

SANTA SEVERINA

Catanzaro 69, Rome 618 km
Pop. 2,718 ⊠ 88070 ☎ 0962   C4

Santa Severina is perched on a steep rock on the N side of the Marchesato, with a distant view of the Ionian Sea. The district of **Grecia** (abandoned after the earthquake of 1783), which is entirely Byzantine, has some interesting buildings. The **cathedral,** renovated several times, dates from the 13C and the adjacent **baptistery**★ (8C-9C) is a round Byzantine building with a cupola sustained by 8 pillars. Typically Byzantine, too, is the small church of **S. Filomena** (11C) with its round cupola. The massive Norman **castle** is well-preserved, but its central interior part was rebuilt in the 15C. ☐

SCILLA

Reggio di Calabria 23, Catanzaro 138, Rome 682 km
Pop. 5,741 ⊠ 89058 ☎ 0965   A5-6

The story of Scylla and Charybdis, sea monsters living on the rock between Sicily and Italy, is one of the best known legends of antiquity. Homer, Ovid and many others wrote that Scylla, who lived in a cave on the side nearest to Italy, was a six-headed dragon with twelve feet and the bark of a dog who snatched and devoured sailors from passing ships and that, on the other side, Charybdis lurked under a huge fig tree and thrice a day swallowed down and spouted out the waters, creating a gigantic whirlpool. There is some basis for this legend, since it is here that the Ionian and the Tyrrhenian Seas meet, generating whirlpools and strong currents that change in direction every six hours, and even today ships passing through the Straits must navigate with care.

▶ There are two small beaches below the town of Scilla, which is perched high on a cliff. Citrus fruit is grown on land and swordfish are caught in the sea. ☐

Practical information _____

Restaurant:
♦*Alla Pescatora,* v. Colombo 32, ☎ 754147, closed Tue and 20 Dec-31 Mar. Seafood: all freshly caught in the sea below, 20/30,000.

⚿ *Aspromonte Club dei Pioppi,* at Melia, ☎ 755149.

Recommended
Youth hostel: *Ostello Principessa Paola del Belgio,* v. Nazionale, ☎ 754033.

SERRA SAN BRUNO

Catanzaro 63, Rome 675 km
Pop. 6,421 ⌧ 88029 ☎ 0963   B5

Serra San Bruno is a fine hilly town surrounded by forests of beech and fir trees on the slopes of Mount Pecoraro, the highest peak in the Serre (→) range.

▶ The **church of the Addolorata,** with its graceful 18C façade, houses a large shrine in marble and precious stone originally executed in 1631-50 by C. Fanzago and G.A. Gallo for the Carthusian monastery, but placed in the church after the monastery was destroyed in the 1783 earthquake. ▶ The 18C **Matrice Church** has four statues, also originally in the monastery, with pedestals and bas-reliefs by D. Muller (1611). ▶ The **Carthusian monastery** *(1 km S)* is on the edge of a forest of fir trees *(visits for men only, from Wed after Easter-Oct, 10-11:30 a.m.; Sat 4-5:30 p.m.; closed winter and Sun; ring to be accompanied by a friar).* The Carthusian Order was founded by S. Bruno. He also founded a community at La Torre. The 11C monastery was rebuilt after the earthquake inside a wall with towers and has modern buildings in a pseudo-Gothic style; in the church is a 16C silver bust of S. Bruno. ▶ In the wood, 1.5 km from the monastery, is the church of **S. Maria del Bosco** which marks the site where it was decided to found the original Carthusian monastery; the holy water, a pillar and a statue of the saint are said to be miraculous.   ☐

Practical information _____

Recommended
Craft workshops: *D. Grenci,* at Brognaturo ☎ 74077 (deluxe pipes).

Le SERRE

From Pizzo Service Station on Naples-Reggio motorway to Marina di Gioiosa Ionica *(115 km, 1 day; map 2)*

The Serre range, S of the Sila chain and N of Aspromonte, is the lowest line of peaks between the Tyrrhenian and Ionian Seas and consequently the most accessible and the first to be occupied by the population moving inland from the coasts when these were no longer secure. The land is arid and olive trees are cultivated on terraces.

▶ Starting at the **Pizzo Service Station** on the Naples-Reggio autostrada, the route passes the artificial **Lake Angitola** and the small town, of **San Nicola da Crissa,** rebuilt after the 1783 earthquake. Crossing some high passes, it then descends into the wooded valley of **Serra San Bruno** and its Carthusian monastery. ▶ The road continues, at times passing through beech forests and at times bare land, until it reaches the **Pietra Spada Pass** (4,870 ft) where there is a good view of the Ionian Sea far below. It then descends through forests until the maintenance point of Mangiatorella near where *(4 km)* a side road leads to **Ferdinandea,** an interesting building that was formerly a Bourbon armaments factory *(no visits).* Returning to the main road, the descent continues past steep, rose-coloured slopes of Mounts Consoline and Stella, arriving at **Stilo,** a town built against a hill and topped by the ruins of a 16C castle. Here also is the **Cattolica★,** an 11C Byzantine church *(contact caretaker in advance, v. Salerno 16, ☎ 71341).* The church is in the form of a cube with five cylindrical drums covering five cupolas on its roof. This last, with curved tiles, is rather like a flattened umbrella. Inside are Byzantine frescos. ▶ The **Duomo** has a Gothic-Swedish portal (14C), some medieval bas-reliefs and inside a 17C *Madonna d'Ognissanti* by G.B. Caracciolo. ▶ The road twists going down, but still allows magnificent views of the sea below. After passing the Stilaro torrent, near the spot where Emperor Otto II was defeated by the Byzantines and Saracens, the road arrives at the coast at **Monas-**

2. **Le Serre**

terace Marina** with its splendid promenade along the seafront. The archaeological sites of **Caulonia,** an old Greek city, are a little farther N, but all that remains of the ancient town are the bases of some temples and part of a wall. ▶ Following the seafront and turning S by the beach the route passes **Riace Marina** where in 1972 the famous bronze statues now in the museum in Reggio were found. The route then arrives at **Roccella Ionica.** The upper part of this town, dominated by the ruins of its castle, is no longer inhabited; in the lower part, in the church of S. Vittore is a painting by Mattia Preti and a 15C wooden crucifix. ▶ The route ends at **Marina di Gioiosa Ionica,** which has remains of an ancient Roman theatre and a large medieval tower.   ☐

Practical information _____

MARINA DI GIOIOSA IONICA, ⌧ 89046, ☎ 0964. ≋
ⓘ v. Fratelli Rosselli, ☎ 55216.

Hotels:
★★★ **Miramare,** v. Colombo 2/A, ☎ 55342, 37 rm Ⓟ ⌘ 60,000; bkf: 5,000.
★★★ **San Giorgio,** v. I Maggio 3, ☎ 55064, 88 rm Ⓟ ⌂ ⌘ ⌷ closed 1 Oct-14 May, 70,000; bkf: 5,000.

PIZZO, ⌧ 88026, ☎ 0963.
≋
ⓘ castle, ☎ 231551.

Hotels:
★★★ **Grillo,** v. Prangi, ☎ 231632, 62 rm Ⓟ ⌂ closed Oct-Jun, 76,000; bkf: 6,000.
★★ **Sonia** v. Prangi 114, ☎ 231315, 47 rm Ⓟ 55,000; bkf: 4,000.

Restaurant:
♦ *Medusa*, v. Salomone, ☎ 231203, closed Mon except summer. Seafood: scampi, risotto alla marinara, 15/25,000.

⚓ *Europa*, at Marinella, SS 522 at 2-km marker, 160 pl, ☎ 264036; *Pinetamare*, SS 18 at 420-km marker, 500 pl, ☎ 264071.

Recommended
Events: *Festival of the Sea* (Jul).
Marina: ☎ 231470.
Nature park: protected area of Lake Angitola, information from *WWF*, ☎ 221732.
Youth hostel: *Ostello Gioacchino Murat*, Castello di Pizzo, ☎ 231551.

ROCCELLA IONICA, ✉ 89047, ☎ 0694.
≈

Hotel:
★★*Villa Giovanna*, v. Cavone, ☎ 84139, 12 rm P 𝕨 Former 18C villa with original ceilings and floors, 50,000.

⚓ *Ala Bianca*, SS 106 at 111-km marker, 168 pl, ☎ 84903; *Uliveto*, nr Badessa, ☎ 84881.

Recommended
Events: *Procession on Saturday before Easter*, at Caulonia *(13 km N)*, ☎ 81002 (Comune).

SIBARI

Cosenza 71, Catanzaro 167, Rome 483 km
Pop. 1,802 ✉ 87070 ☎ 0981   B2

Sybaris was founded in 720 BC by Achaean and Trezene Greeks on the coast of Calabria. The Sybarites later established other colonies along the coast, among them Posidonia and Paestum. They derived their great wealth, which enabled them to live luxuriously, from their trade with the Etruscans. Sybaris was destroyed in 510 BC by the Crotonians. Sybaris was forgotten and even its original site was lost. It was only recently, after marshland on the plain of Crati was drained for land reclamation purposes, that archaeologists traced its location.

▶ The town that today is called Sibari has no connection with Sybaris except its name. ▶ The **Museo della Sibaritide** *(summer 9 a.m.-2 p.m. and 5-7 p.m.; winter 9 a.m.-2 p.m.; Sun 9 a.m.-1 p.m.)* has many archaeological finds from the tombs around Francavilla Marittima, as well as bronzes and ceramics from the nearby temple of Athena. ▶ On the newly built Ionic state road, before the Crati bridge, there are **sites** that have recently been excavated in which traces of houses said to have been those of ancient **Sybaris** have been found, as well as others said to be of **Thurii**. The most important **finds** are on display in the **Parco del Cavallo**.   ☐

Practical information _____
Hotels:
★★★ *Bagamayo*, at Bruscate, ☎ 74253, 50 rm P 𝕨 ✿ 🎣 ⚓ closed Nov-Mar, 71,000. Rest. ♦♦♦ Regional cuisine: seafood, roast meats, pasta, 30/40,000.
★★★ *Magna Grecia*, v. Stazione 1, ☎ 74257, 52 rm ✿ 60,000; bkf: 7,000.

⚓ *Millepini*, at Bruscate, ☎ 74056; *Pineta di Sibari*, at Fuscolara, ☎ 74135; *Sibari*, at Fuscolara, 340 pl, ☎ 74088.

Recommended
Farm vacations: *Azienda Volta del Ponte*, ☎ 71031.
Horseback riding: *Circolo ippico Salicetta*, nr Salicetta, ☎ 74137.

┌─────────────────────────────────────┐
│ Don't forget to consult the Practical Holiday Guide: it │
│ can help in solving many problems. │
└─────────────────────────────────────┘

Sybaris and the sybarites

Sibari, a short distance from the Gulf of Taranto and the Ionian Sea, is a large Calabrian town with a prosperous farming community near the site of ancient Sybaris, one of the great cities of Magna Graecia renowned in ancient times throughout the Mediterranean for the luxurious living and self-indulgence of its inhabitants. Sybaris disappeared long ago and only recently, after the draining of the marshlands around the plain of Crati, traces of it have been found. Yet how famous it was in its time! Its inhabitants, supposedly effeminate and luxury-loving, had to fight many wars with neighbouring towns—and were usually victorious. It was said that they taught their horses to dance to the sound of pipes, and on one occasion when they were attacked by the armies of the city of Croton (modern Crotone), they played the pipes, making their horses dance and causing utter confusion in the ranks of the enemy who was easily routed. In spite of their many victories, the Sybarites were ultimately defeated by the Crotonians who destroyed their city (510 BC). The Sybarites were so notorious for their dissipation and hedonism that the name sybarite still means one who loves pleasure and lives in luxury.

La SILA GRANDE

From Cosenza *(212 km, 1 day; map 3)*

Of all the southern Apennine mountain ranges, the Sila is the one that comes nearest to recalling the time when the whole Italian peninsula was covered in dense forests. Even the name, which comes from the Latin *silva* (a wood) bears this out. The mountains form the watershed between the Gulf of Squillace on the Tyrrhenian side, where they are fairly steep, and the S part of the Gulf of Taranto on the Ionian, where their declivity is much less abrupt. The flora and fauna are similar throughout, changing uniformly between 5,000 and 6,500 ft (maximum height is that of Mt. Botte Donato at 6,904 ft), and subdivisions such as Sila Greca to the N, Sila Grande in the centre and Sila Piccola to the S are solely for convenience.

▶ After leaving **Cosenza** (→) the route passes through the Crati Valley and begins ascending toward the Sila range. ▶ The villages on the route are of medieval origin, lying off the main road, and most have fine churches. The church of S. Giorgio, at **Zumpano** is austere and contains a triptych by B. Vivarini. S. Barbara at **Rovito** has filigreed portals and rosettes on its façade, while S. Michele at **Celico** has a 15C exterior and is Baroque inside. (Celico is the birthplace of Joachim da Fiore (1130-1202), a medieval monk and mystic.) The church of S. Francesco di Paola at **Spezzano della Sila** was built in 1455-8 and has a Baroque interior. ▶ At the top of the **Monte Scuro Pass** (5,794 ft) is a splendid view of the whole of the Sila Grande. There is also a memorial stone to the Calabrian novelist N. Misasi. ▶ The route then arrives at **Lorica**, a village on the banks of **Lake Arvom**, probably the most attractive of the artificial lakes in the region. It is reminiscent of a Norwegian fjord with its high mountains and dark pine forests. ▶ After passing the road repair hut at the top of the **Ascione Pass** (5,000 ft) and crossing the valley of the Savuto River, the route continues to the NE toward **Lake Ampollino**. **Trepido Soprano**, on its E shore, is a village of a few houses on a spur overlooking the lake. ▶ Still in the midst of

SALERNO   CASTROVILLARI   Fossiata   ROSSANO

Mavigliano   Rose   S I L A   Lake Cecita   1708   Serra Toppale
Crati   Arente   1431   M. Pettinascura   1454
Serra la Guàrdia   Lese

PAOLA   Valico di M. Scuro   Camigliatello   G R A N D E
Rovito   1616   Silano   Lake Ariamacina   Germano
750 Célico
Zumpano   M. Botte   Lake
COSENZA   429   744   1928 Donato   Silvana   Votturino   CROTONE
800 Spezzano   Mánsio
della Sila   1405   Ramundo

Mendicino   Pietrafitta   Lorica   S. Giovanni   1049
in Fiore
Aprigliano   L A'   1280   S I L A   Neto
Lake Arvo   1881   1371   Croce di
Paternò   Montenero   Agnara
Busento   Cálabro   lassa   1279
Dománico   Cellara   1384   Colle d'Ascione   Lake   Trepidò   Ampollino   CROTONE
1233   Ampollino   Soprano
Rogliano
Savuto   0   5   10km
CATANZARO   CATANZARO

SERVIZIO CARTOGRAFICO DEL TOURING CLUB ITALIANO, MILANO

3. La Sila Grande

pine forests, the route crosses the **Croce di Agnara Pass** (4,909 ft), then the Neto, and finally reaches **San Giovanni in Fiore** (→). ▶ The return journey is a more northerly route that passes by **Lake Cecita**, through **Camigliatello Silano** and ends in Cosenza.   □

Practical information

LORICA, 4,705 ft ⊠ 87050, ☎ 0984.
↗ cableway, ski lifts.
ⓘ v. Nazionale, ☎ 997069.

Hotel:
★★★ *Grand Hotel Lorica*, v. Libertà 57, ☎ 997039, 100 rm ℗ ≶ 52,000; bkf: 4,000.

TREPIDO SOPRANO, 4,662 ft, ⊠ 88073, ☎ 0962.
↗ ski lifts at Villaggio Palumbo.
ⓘ at Cotronei, ☎ 44202.

La SILA PICCOLA

From motorway service station at Lamezia Terme to Catanzaro *(121 km, 1 day; map 4)*
See map on page 130.

Like the Sila Grande, the Sila Piccola is lovely country, wooded and mountainous. The surroundings, however, are generally less enclosed and glimpses of the Tyrrhenian and Ionian Seas are readily available.

▶ This route starts at the **Lamezia Terme exit** on the Naples-Reggio di Calabria autostrada. ▶ **Nicastro** is a small town that was built when the Baroque style flourished in the 17C, after having been destroyed in the 1738 earthquake. The remains of a Norman-Swedish castle may be seen in the old quarter of S. Theodoro; its women occasionally wear the traditional Calabrian costume. ▶ At **Platania**, a village settled by Albanians overlooking the valley, is the first sight of the Silano landscape. ▶ The **Acquabona Pass** (3,653 ft) is a point of departure for further excursions higher up into the mountains and to the top of Mt. Reventino (5,074 ft) from where it is possible to see as far as the Etna volcano in Sicily and Mt. Pollino to the N. ▶ This itinerary, however, goes on to **Soveria Mannelli** where a stone slab commemorates the surrender (in 1860) of a body of Bourbon troops

to Garibaldi. ▶ From **Coraci** the ridge of **Bocca di Piazza** is reached after crossing a forest of chestnut trees. ▶ Next comes the high valley of the Savuto River where a picturesque route by a ledge of fir trees leads on to the plateau where the village of **Mancuso** is located. Here there are superb views over both seas far below. ▶ Reaching **Zagarise** on a rocky spur, the route has already descended to the hills where olive trees grow. At this point it is possible to take a good side road, which quickly leads back up into the mountains to the **Forestry Guards House of the Gariglione** (5,930 ft). This is the name of a wood full of imposing trees and comes from *gariglio*, a dialect word for a kind of oak. ▶ After Zagarise, continue to **Taverna**, a picturesque village on the S slopes of the Sila Piccola and the birthplace of the painter Mattia Preti. Unfortunately his paintings, which were in the village church of S. Domenico, have had to be moved. The excursion ends at Catanzaro (→).   □

Practical information

DECOLLATURA, ⊠ 88041, ☎ 0968, 5 km N of Acquabona Pass.

Hotel:
★★ **Cardel**, villaggio Cesariello, ☎ 61334, 35 rm ℗ ⚶ ⚱
☒ ⚲ closed 1-25 Nov, 40,000.

VILLAGGIO MANCUSO, 4,615 ft, ⊠ 88050, ☎ 0961.
↗ ski lift at Cicicilla.

Hotel:
★★★ *Grand Hotel Parco delle Fate*, ☎ 922057 ℗ ⚶ ⚲
⚲ closed 1 Oct-14 Jun, 66,000. Rest. ♦♦♦ Regional cuisine: striscioni with special sauce, Sila mushrooms, 30/40,000.

SOVERATO

Catanzaro 31, Rome 636 km
Pop. 10,315 ⊠ 88068 ☎ 0967   B5

Soverato, on the Gulf of Squillace, is made up of **Soverato Marina** with a 16C fort and **Soverato Superiore** with a parish church. Inside the church are a

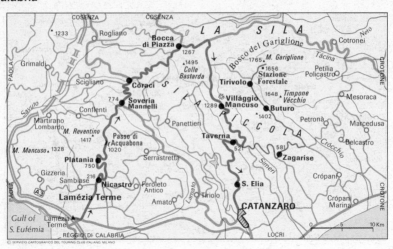

4. La Sila Piccola

marble *Pietà* and a bas-relief with the figure of Christ, both by A. Gagini. ☐

Practical information ⎯⎯⎯⎯⎯⎯⎯

≋

ⓘ p. Nettuno, ☎ 21759.

Hotels:
★★★ *Nettuno,* p. Nettuno, ☎ 25371, 45 rm closed 16 Sep-31 May,70,000; bkf: 5,000.
★★★ *Ulivi,* v. Moro 1, ☎ 21487, 50 rm ⌕ ▒ & ⊗ closed Oct-Apr. No restaurant, 75,000.

⚿ *Glauco,* SS 106 at 166-km marker, 85 pl, ☎ 25533; *Le Giare,* SS 106 at 166.5-km marker, 36 pl, ☎ 25279.

SPEZZANO ALBANESE

Cosenza 49, Catanzaro 142, Rome 477 km
Pop. 7,161 ⊠ 87019 ☎ 0981   B2-3

Spezzano Albanese, a hilly town in the mountains of Spezzano in the lower valley of the Crati, owes its name to the fact that a settlement of Albanians was established here in the 16C. There are thermal springs and a pretty park 5 km NW. ☐

Practical information ⎯⎯⎯⎯⎯⎯⎯

♨ ☎ 953096 (Jun-mid-Oct).

TERME LUIGIANE

Cosenza 57, Catanzaro 110, Rome 475 km
Pop. 139 ⊠ 87020 ☎ 0982   A-B3

Terme Luigiane consists of four springs, one cold and the others warm. 2 km away is the beach of **Guardia Piemontese Lido**. The village of **Guardia Piemontese** is up above on a hill. The origin of the name of the village is most interesting and goes back

Albanian villages

Although Calabria is historically a land of invasions, it has also been a land of refuge. Spezzano Albanese, Vaccarizzo Albanese, Santa Sofia d'Epire... over seventy Albanian villages are nestled to this day in the mountains of Sila, northeast of Cosenza. They are inhabited by descendants of Albanian refugees who fled Turkish invasions of their country in the 15C. The Aragonians gave the Albanians land in Calabria where they settled between 1450 and 1550, sheltered from clashes with the local population. Protected by their isolation, these orthodox communities have preserved their customs and their religious practices. Mass is said in Greek, but popular religious songs are sung in Albanian. Certain rites recall the primitive church: baptism by immersion, communion with bread and wine. Albanian marriages and Easter are cause for massive folk celebrations during which embroidered costumes based on 15C designs are still worn.

to the Middle Ages when, in France, a religious body was formed called the Waldenses or Vaudois (1176). They were persecuted and took refuge in Piedmont, where they were again persecuted. They fled to Calabria where they became known as the Piedmontese. Even in Calabria they were persecuted. In 1561 Cardinal Ghisleri (later Pius V) organized a crusade against them and the survivors escaped to this mountain village where their descendants still live. ☐

Practical information

⚓ ☎ 94054 (May-Oct).
ℹ v. S. Lucia, ☎ 94056.

Hotel:
★★★ *Grand Hotel delle Terme,* v. delle Terme, ☎ 94475, 128 rm Ⓟ ⬚ ⬚ ⬚ ✧ closed 6 Oct-24 May, 60,000. Rest, ♦♦♦ *Orsa Maggiore* Regional cuisine: pasta in Sila manner, Mount Pollino mushrooms, 20/85,000.

TIRIOLO

Catanzaro 17, Rome 605 km
Pop. 4,340 ⊠ 88056 ☎ 0961   B4

Even for this part of the world Tiriolo is unusually situated on top of a southern spur of the Sila Piccola with a view of two seas. The traditional costumes called *pacchiane* are very colourful and the shops sell handmade silk scarves called *ivariacali.* The best view is from the top of **Mt. Tiriolo** (3,000 ft) twenty minutes away.   ☐

Practical information

ℹ p. Italia.

Restaurant:
♦♦ *Autostello,* v. Mazzini 284, ☎ 991005, closed Tue. Regional cuisine, 16/25,000.

TREBISACCE

Cosenza 86, Catanzaro 183, Rome 484 km
Pop. 7,972 ⊠ 87075 ☎ 0981   B2

With the building of a railway line along the coast (1866-76) the towns that in the past were built on the hills for safety tended to split into two; part of the population returning to live by the sea. Slowly, these towns on the sea surpassed their inland mother towns. Trebisacce is an example of this development. **Marina di Amendolara** is 9.5 km N and **Villapiana Lido** is 7 km S. These two pleasant resorts have long sandy beaches on the Gulf of Taranto.   ☐

Practical information

TREBISACCE
≋
ℹ v. Lutri 363, ☎ 57187.

Hotel:
★★ *Stellato,* lungomare Ovest 7, ☎ 51546, 21 rm Ⓟ ✧ closed Oct-Apr, 50,000; bkf: 6,000.

⚓ *Pignagrande,* nr Canale Monaco, 75 pl, ☎ 51994.

Recommended
Farm vacations: *Azienda Torre Albidona,* at Marina di Albidona, ☎ 51290.

Environs

VILLAPIANA LIDO, ⊠ 87070, ☎ 0981, 7 km S.
≋
ℹ v. delle Rose, ☎ 56132.

TROPEA

Catanzaro 83, Rome 636 km
Pop. 6,841 ⊠ 88038 ☎ 0963   A5

It is said that the name of the town comes from the Greek verb *tropein,* meaning to *turn* or *turn around,* referring to the round mass on which Tropea is built and from which it has a splendid view of the sea and sandy beaches below.

▶ The **cathedral★** (11C-12C) is in a small square; inside are many works of art including a *Black Crucifixion* (16C), a statue of the *Madonna del Popolo* by Montorsoli (1555) and a *Madonna of Rumania* (14C) in the Byzantine style. ▶ In the other churches, **S. Francesco,** the **Cappuccini,** the **Annunziata,** are 16C paintings and sculptures. ▶ **S. Maria dell'Isola,** formerly a medieval Benedictine church, stands on a large rock near the beach.   ☐

Practical information

TROPEA
≋
ℹ v. Stazione 10, ☎ 61475.

Hotels:
★★★ *Rocca Nettuno,* contrada Nunziata, ☎ 61612, 282 rm ⬚ ⬚ ✧ 1/2 Pens. Overlooking the sea in a park full of flowers, 190,000.
★★★ *Virgilio,* v. Tondo, ☎ 61978, 48 rm Ⓟ ✧ 72,000; bkf: 4,000.

⚓ *Marina del Convento,* at Marina del Convento, 133 pl, ☎ 62501; *Marina dell'Isola,* at Marina dell'Isola, 188 pl, ☎ 61970; *Paradise,* nr La Grazia, 140 pl, ☎ 62577.

Recommended
Farm vacations: *Azienda Conte Ruggero,* at Santa Domenica-Ricadi, ☎ 69029.
Marina: ☎ 61104.
Vacation villages: *Villaggio Sabbie Bianche* (Jun-Sep); information: *Vacanze,* at Milan, ☎ 02/85391.

Environs

CAPO VATICANO, ⊠ 88030, 12 km SW.

Hotels:
★★★ *Baia del Capo,* ☎ 63170, 30 rm Ⓟ ⬚ ⬚ ✧ ⬚ ✧ closed 11 Oct-24 May, 40,000; bkf: 5,000.
★★ *Punta Faro,* ☎ 63139, 25 rm Ⓟ ⬚ ⬚ closed Oct-May 45,000.
★ *Costa Azzurra,* ☎ 63109, 21 rm Ⓟ ⬚ ⬚ ✧ closed Oct-Apr, 45,000; bkf: 6,000.

VIBO VALENTIA

Catanzaro 64, Rome 613 km
Pop. 32,400 ⊠ 88018 ☎ 0963   A-B5

Vibo Valentia is a lovely town near the sea with much of interest for a visitor.

▶ The **State Archaeological Museum** *(9 a.m.-1 p.m.; also Tue, Thu and Sat 3-5 p.m.; closed Mon)* has finds from the Greek site of **Hipponion** and the Roman site of **Valentia** which include ceramics, terra-cottas and bronzes. ▶ The Baroque **Duomo** has a rebuilt altar from Serra San Bruno (→) and three 16C statues by Antonello Gagini. ▶ The church of **S. Michele** (17C) is a Renaissance building of the Tuscan type. There is a **castle** on a hillock where once stood the **acropolis of Hipponion** and the remains of its walls can be seen near the cemetery. ▶ There is a splendid view★ of the Tyrrhenian coast from Cape Palinuro to the Etna volcano from the Belvedere; nearby, in an enclosure, are the remains of a Doric temple (6C-5C BC). ▶ Near S. Aloe some Roman baths have recently been uncovered; they have coloured mosaic pavements with figures. ▶ The seaside resort of **Vibo Marina** is 10 km N. ▶ The **Diocesan Museum,** in the Episcopal Palace *(visits by request)* at **Mileto** *(12 km S),* has sculpture and bas-reliefs from 14C-17C tombs.   ☐

Practical information

VIBO VALENTIA
ℹ p. Diaz, ☎ 42008.

Hotel:
★★★★ *501 Hotel,* at Madonnella, ☎ 43951, 124 rm ⬚ ⬚ ✧ Pens. 100,000. Rest. ♦ By swimming pool, 15/25,000.

⅄ *Eden Park,* at Porto Salvo, ☎ 271027; *Lido degli Aranci,* at Bivona, ☎ 271141.

Recommended
Cycling: *G.S. Castagna,* v. dei Basiliani 13, ☎ 43382.
Events: six-day *Musical Festival of Vibo* (Jun); *Vibonese August Festival; International Medical Convention.*

VIBO MARINA, ⊠ 88019, ☎ 0963, 10 km N.
≈

Restaurant:
♦♦ *Maria Rosa,* v. Toscana 13/15, ☎ 240538, closed 20 Dec-15 Jan and Sun in winter.   Seafood: scampi, sea salad, risotto alla pescatora, 25/40,000.

Recommended
Marina: ☎ 240004.

For help in understanding terms when visiting museums or other sites, see the *Art and Architectural Terms Guide* at the end of the Practical Holiday Guide.

VILLA SAN GIOVANNI

Reggio di Calabria 15, Catanzaro 150, Rome 694 km
Pop. 12,605 ⊠ 89018 ☎ 0965   A6

Completely rebuilt after the 1908 earthquake, all that remains of old Villa San Giovanni are the ruins of an 18C fort and a 16C palace.   It is an important rail and shipping centre for communications with Sicily.   ☐

Practical information _____

≈
ℹ ☎ 751160.
⛴ car ferries for Messina, ☎ 751026, daily ferry departures connecting with principal train arrivals, *Caronte,* ☎ 756725 (daily departures every 30 mn).

Hotels:
★★★★ *Piccolo Hotel,* p. Stazione 1, ☎ 751410, 64 rm ℗ 74,800; bkf: 6,000.   Rest. ♦♦♦ Seafood: risotto di Mare, swordfish, 25/30,000.
★★★ *Altafiumara,* at Santa Trada di Cannitello, ☎ 759061, 36 rm ℗ ⋘ ⊗ ▭ ⌁ 105,000.

Campania

▶ The most frequently visited sites in Campania are Mt. Vesuvius, Pompeii and Herculaneum: the volcano for the fascination and heady sense of danger associated with a menacing natural force, the two dead cities for the wealth of information they impart about everyday life in ancient times, as well as for their reminder of the sudden force with which life can be ended. These are only a sampling of the famous sites around Naples. Cumae, Pozzuoli, Capo Miseno, Baia, Mergellina and Sorrento are ancient and picturesque and the islands of Ischia and Capri sit beautifully in the Tyrrhenian Sea. Naples itself defies summation, with its magnificent site and turbulent past. From the 13C, Naples was the foremost city in Italy. It is no longer the capital of a kingdom, but it abundantly rewards visitors who take the time to probe the myriad layers of its cultural and artistic riches. The landscape, architecture and people of Campania place it among the most interesting regions of Italy. Along the coast beyond Punta di Campanella lie the resort towns of Positano, Amalfi and Ravello, with white-washed, typically Mediterranean houses, verdant terraces and architectural details that betray a long history of Eastern influence. On the plains of the Sele, roses bloom among the Doric columns of the Greek temples to Poseidon. The Cilento coast and the Gulf of Policastro seem to be bathed in marine light filtered through the olive groves. □

● Don't miss

In Naples★★: Castel Nuovo★★, the Duomo★★, S. Lorenzo Maggiore★★, the Museo Archeologico Nazionale★★, the Museo and Galleria di Capodimonte★★, the Certosa★★ and the Museo Nazionale di S. Martino★★. In the surrounding area: the Piscina Mirabile★★ in Bàcoli; Pozzuoli★ with the Sol-

fatara★★; Sorrento★; the island of Ischia★; Capri★★ and the Grotta Azzurra★★; Ercolano (Herculaneum)★★ and Pompeii★★; the view★★ from the crater★ of Vesuvius. In Amalfi★: the Chiostro del Paradiso★ and the coast including Positano★; the Arch of Trajan★★ in Benevento★; the Reggia★★ and its park★★ in Caserta★; Paestum★★; Ravello★ and the Villa Rufolo★★; the Duomo★★ in Salerno★.

● Brief regional history

8C BC-5C AD
Greeks, Etruscans, Samnites and Romans. *C.* 750 BC the Chalcideans, after first settling on the island of **Pitecusa** (Ischia), founded **Cuma,** the first city of Greater Greece (Magna Grecia). ● Other **Greek colonies** on the Italian mainland were **Parthenope** (680 BC) and, on the same site but later, **Neapo-**

The Samnites

The inhabitants of the back-country fought the Roman legions long and hard, and it was only after numerous and costly military expeditions that these peasants were held to their own territories. The mountain people known as Samnites were hard men who were skilled in the use of weapons. They would periodically move down the barren slopes of their regions to pillage and conquer land more fertile than their own, thus sowing terror among the more peaceful populations in the lowlands and on the coast. Overpopulation was a constant problem for the Samnites and often led to periods of starvation. In extreme cases, they would practice the Sacred Spring, pledging to the God of War everything that would be produced the following spring: crops, children, etc. Upon reaching maturity, the child was sent off to find a new group to which to belong. Geographical conditions haven't changed in the Apennine mountains since ancient times and neither have economic conditions. Even recently, the area around Naples has sent waves of immigrants off to distant shores, especially America.

---

lis (Naples, 470 BC), **Dicearchia** (Pozzuoli, 531 BC), **Posidonia** (Paestum, *c.* 600 BC) founded by the Sybarites and **Elea** (540 BC) founded by the Phocians. ● At the same time the **Etruscans** expanded southwards on the fertile interior plain and founded **Capua** in the 6C. ● The **Samnites**, an Italic tribe, were in the bordering mountains. ● **Capua** ceded to Rome in exchange for its protection in 330 BC. The defense of Campania was one of the principal reasons for the **Samnite Wars** and the **Romanization** of the region. ● Regional partition under the Emperor Augustus (1C) united **Campania** with Latium. Campania was much loved by the emperors for the beauty of its towns and countryside.

6C-11C

Lombard Benevento, Amalfi as marine republic. After the fall of the Roman Empire the **Goths** conquered **Giustiniano.** Conflict continued between the coast, which remained tenaciously Byzantine, and

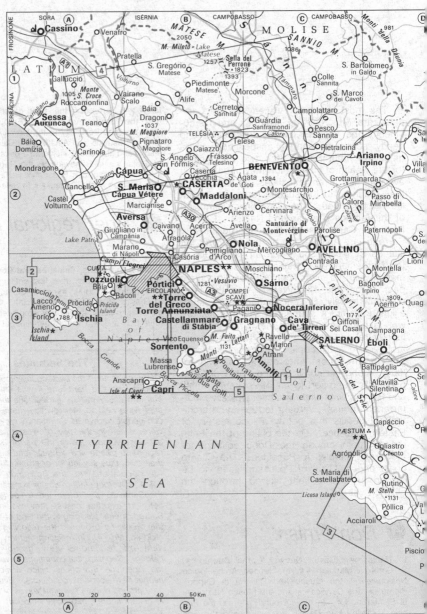

© SERVIZIO CARTOGRAFICO DEL TOURING CLUB ITALIANO, MILANO

the mountains, where the Lombards had established a southern **duchy** in **Benevento** (570). ● The Lombards of Benevento also absorbed **Salerno,** which eventually became an independent principality. ● Another principality was established in **Capua,** which in 900 extended its domains to include Benevento. ● The first known document in the Italian language records evidence about a land ownership dispute in Capua. This is the **Carta Capuana** of 960. ● The Byzantine duchy of **Naples,** meanwhile, acquired increasing autonomy, while **Amalfi,** having repulsed the Lombards, enjoyed a period of success (9C-11C) through intensive overseas trade; Amalfi was the first of the Italian **marine republics.** Her ships sailed the Mediterranean from Constantinople to Spain, from Syria to the shores of Africa, and her merchants had warehouses and quarters in many ports. ● Naples, in return for help against the Lombards, ceded the **county of Aversa** to the Norman **Rainulfo Drengot** in 1030. ● This was the first territory established by the Norman warrior-adventurers outside France. ● The **Normans** achieved increasing importance in the turbulent events of medieval Italy, and in the course of only a few decades became the rulers of the region (**Capua,** 1062; **Salerno,** 1070; **Amalfi,** 1137; **Naples,** 1139) and of the whole of **southern Italy.**

Arch of Trajan in Benevento

Facts and figures

Location: *The coastal strip is level, but it also contains the volcanic regions of the Campi Flegrei and Vesuvius (4,203 ft). The mountainous interior has complex geography. The Tyrrhenian coastline is more varied than other regions and presents, in the adjacent bays of Naples and Sorrento, a celebrated landscape. The Sorrento view is especially striking, with the islands of Ischia and Capri and the backdrop of Vesuvius, which has been without its once characteristic plume of smoke since the eruption of 1944.*
Area: *13,595 sq km.*
Climate: *Mediterranean, mild on the coast, more rigorous in the uplands. Naples, the Amalfi coast and Sorrento, Capri and Ischia are also winter resorts.*
Population: *5,563,230 inhabitants, second region in Italy by number and first by density, more than one-fifth live in Naples, third largest city in Italy.*
Administration: *Former capital of the southern kingdom, Naples is now the regional capital. The capitals of the other four provinces are Avellino, Benevento, Caserta and Salerno.*

Duomo in Amalfi

Palazzo Reale in Caserta

Temple of Neptune in Paestum

12C-19C
The kingdom. From this point the history of the region and its chief city is the history of the king-dom — called, according to the period, the **Kingdom of Sicily, of Naples** or of the **Two Sicilies,** but known to contemporaries simply as 'the Kingdom', the largest political entity in Italy until unification in the 19C. It included modern Abruzzi, Molise, Apulia, Basilicata, Calabria and Sicily. ● Naples passed from the **Normans** to the **Hohenstaufen** emperors and subsequently (1266) to the **Angevin dynasty,** whose founder, Charles of Anjou, was the brother of Louis IX of France (St. Louis). In 1442 the throne passed to the house of **Aragon,** descendants of an illegitimate branch of the ruling house of Spain. ● Naples alternated between French and Spanish rule until the early 16C, when Spain gained definitive possession, placing the kingdom under the rule of **viceroys.** It has been calculated that a quarter of the territory was owned by the church and that nine-tenths of the rest was sold off in fief to refill the depleted coffers of Spain. ● Spanish rule was disturbed by a **rebellion** in 1647-8 because of a tax on fresh fruit. The revolt was led by a young fishmonger, Tommaso Aniello **(Masaniello),** and paved the way for the 'Duke of the Republic', the French Henry of Lorraine, **Duke of Guise.** ● Naples was occupied by **Austria** during the War of Spanish Succession (1713) and later (Peace of Vienna, 1734) assigned to the Bourbon **Charles III.** ● In 1799, the **Repubblica Partenopea** was proclaimed in Naples (the original settlement of Naples was called Parthenope; Neapolis meant 'new town'). Six months later **Cardinal Ruffo's** Sanfedistas put the **Bourbons** back on the throne. ● Under the Napoleonic Empire, Naples was ruled by **Joseph Bonaparte** (1806-8) and **Joachim Murat** (1808-15). ● **Garibaldi** entered Naples on 7 September 1860. The annexation of the southern kingdom to the Kingdom of Sardinia was confirmed by **plebiscite.**

 Practical information

Information: tourist offices in principal towns and regions.

SOS: public emergency service, ☎ 113; police emergency, ☎ 112; road emergency *ACI,* ☎ 116.

Weather: forecast, ☎ 191; roads open and closed, ☎ 194 or *(ACI)* 06/4212; snow information, ☎ 081/974974 (Naples, ☎ 162); shipping forecast, ☎ 196.

Vacation villages: *TCI* village (→ Cilento Coast), information at Milan, ☎ 02/85261; Bari, ☎ 080/365140; at Rome, ☎ 06/6874432; at Turin, ☎ 011/540177.

Farm vacations: regional Agriturist association, at Naples, v. A. Vespucci 9, ☎ 081/225250.

Fairs and markets: commercial events at *Mostra d'Oltremare* in Naples.

Events: at Naples: opera season at *Teatro San Carlo,* concerts at *Accademia Musicale;* various theatres in the city; *Festa di Piedigrotta* and *Naples song festival, Festa di San Gennaro, Festa della Madonna del Carmine;* nativity scenes and other festivals at Christmas. Classical theatre in *Teatro Antico* at Pompeii and the archaeological area at Paestum; *Wagner concerts* in garden of *Villa Rufolo* at Ravello; *international open-air ballet festival and piano festival* at Amalfi; opera and theatre season at *Roman theatre* at Benevento; shows and concerts at Reggia di Caserta; classical music concerts in *cloister of S. Francesco, international film festival* at Sorrento; *8- and 16-mm film festival* at Salerno; *children's film festival* at

Giffoni Valle Piana (→ Salerno); *summer festival* and *Disfida dei Trombonieri* at Cava de'Tirreni; *S. Paolino lily festival* at Nola; *summer festival* and *Torneo dei Quartieri* at Sessa Aurunca; *obelisk festival* at Mirabella, Eclano (→ Mirabella Pass); *carnival* at Capua. *Holy Week processions* at Mirabella Eclano, on the island of Prócida, at Sessa Aurunca and Sorrento. Sporting events include: horse racing (trots and gallops) at *Ippodromo di Agnano* (→ Campi Flegrei); national equestrian competition at *Parco della Reggia* at Caserta; *sailing regattas* at Sorrento (Aug).

Nature parks: Serre Persano (→ Eboli) conservation areas. Monti Alburni and Vesuvius national parks have been proposed.

Conservation: *WWF* regional office in Naples, Riviera di Chaia 200 (Villa Pignatelli), ☎ 081/684043; branches in: Avellino, v. Colombo 32, ☎ 0825/22675; Caserta, p. Marconi 9, ☎ 0823/322795; Vesuvius/Herculaneum, v. Panoramica 108, ☎ 081/489884; Salerno, v. Manganario 89, ☎ 089/7331890 (work-camps in places of natural interest; Green Guards: surveillance of Neapolitan parks by children). *LIPU* branches: Naples, v. Loggia dei Pisani 13, ☎ 081/5511651 (courses and bird-watching centres in Capri, Monte Epomeo and Monte Faito, Ischia); Salerno, ☎ 089/241140, office near *Somerset House*, v. Diaz 53, ☎ 089/239914 (*Hera Argentina* bird-watching centre in Paestum; bird-watching courses in the *WWF* sanctuary in Serre Persano); Caserta, near Biblioteca Comunale, v. Roma 89 (excursions and bird-watching in the Matese Mountains).

Zoos and theme parks: aquarium, zoo and *Edenlandia* theme park, at Naples.

Excursions: areas of particular interest for excursions (as well as the classic one, Vesuvius) include: the Sorrento peninsula; the Monti Picenti in Irpinia and the Monti Alburni in the Sele Valley, opposite Éboli; no long-distance excursions are indicated, information: *CAI* Naples, Castel dell'Ovo, ☎ 081/404421; Cava de'Tirreni, corso Italia 153.

Cycling: assistance and information from cycling groups affiliated with *UDACE* (86) in all parts of region. The following are suggested itineraries over 100 km: Naples-Sorrento (via Pórtici, Ercolano, Torre del Greco, Pompeii, Castellammare); Paestum-Sapri (via Agropoli, Castellabate, Marina d'Ascea, Palinuro, Marina di Camerota, Policastro); Padula-Montevergine (via Avellino, Éboli, Castelcivita); Caserta-Benevento (via Piedimonte Matese, Cerreto Sannita, Pontelandolfo); in Irpinia from Lake Laceno to Materdómini (via Bagnoli Irpino, Serino, Avellino, Sant'Angelo dei Lombardi).

Horseback riding: *Federazione Italiana Sport Equestri*, regional committee in Naples, v. Ruggieri 12/B, ☎ 081/7609379; riding school in Agnano Terme (→ Campi Flegrei); centre at Pontetalone (→ Capua), v. Ponte Pellegrino 69, ☎ 0823/878107 (riding courses, excursions lasting several days; some accommodation, own camp site, associate of *ANTE*); associated centres at Benevento.

Earthquake

This word has a sinister ring for Italians. On 23 November 1980, at 7:35 in the evening, when the nation was at its Sunday supper, the whole country trembled. The epicentre was about 30 km underground, between the upper valleys of the Ofanto and the Sele, and the towns of Sant'Angelo dei Lombardi and Laviano. Three thousand people were killed, and damage was inflicted on a region of 6 million inhabitants. Avellino, Sant'Angelo dei Lombardi, Solofra, Bagnoli Irpino and Ariano are just a few of the places where the effects of this disaster can be seen; the old town in Naples suffered considerable artistic and architectural losses.

Pizza

Alexandre Dumas the elder, on returning from Naples (he had been expelled by the Bourbon police) wrote that 'pizza is made with the same dough as bread. It varies in diameter according to the price. A two centesimi pizza is enough for one, if you pay two soldi it will feed an entire family...' Today the pizza is not just Neapolitan, and indeed not just Italian. It existed in Naples even before the tomato arrived from America. The classic Neapolitan versions, known all over the world, are the Margherita, in which the bread crust, baked in a wood-fired oven, is covered with mozzarella cheese, tomato sauce and basil, and the Napoletana, in which anchovies are added to the above ingredients. It would be impossible to list all the types of pizza available; the range at any Italian pizzeria would foil the attempt, particularly if the pizzarolo (pizza maker) is imaginative. Obviously, there are excellent pizzas and modest pizzas; bad pizzas are rare. They are often eaten with white wine, but also, although 'historically' it is not a suitable match, with beer.

Castel Volturno, Melizzano (→ Telese, Matese). Racecourses: *Villa Glori*, at Agnano Terme (→ Campi Flegrei), v. Ippodromo, ☎ 081/7601660; *Cirigliano*, at Aversa, v. Olimpico, ☎ 081/8111022.

Canoeing: *Federazione italiana canoa-kayak*, affiliated schools at Bàcoli (→ Campi Flegrei) and Posillipo (→ Naples).

Sailing: *Lega Navale*, at Naples, v. Molosiglio, ☎ 081/314057 or 5511806; at Salerno, p. Concordia (marina), ☎ 089/226924; at Naples: *Federazione Italiana Vela*, v. Molosiglio, ☎ 081/5510433; *Centro Vela UISP, Nautic Coop*, p. Amedeo 15, ☎ 081/415371 or 415447.

Water skiing: *Federazione Italiano Sci Nautico*, at Naples, p. Leonardo da Vinci, ☎ 081/36070; affiliated school at Pozzuoli.

Skindiving: at Naples, p. Santa Maria degli Angeli 11 (Pizzofalcone), ☎ 081/417579; at Salerno, v. Porto traversa Marcina, ☎ 089/236043; at Sapri, v. Verdi 1, ☎ 0973/392650; Santa Maria di Castellabate (→ Cilento Coast), v. Marina, ☎ 0974/961069.

Skiing: at Piano Laceno (→ Bagnoli Irpino) and Campolaspierto (→ Serino).

Golf: at Arco Felice (→ Naples).

Archery: *Comitato Regionale Fitarco*, at Naples, v. D'Alessandro 3/A, ☎ 081/7600311; affiliated society at Naples, Pórtici (→ Bay of Naples), Salerno.

Flying: aeroclub *Terra di Lavoro*, at Capua, v. Aeroporto, ☎ 0823/963430; at Naples, *Aeroporto Capodichino*, ☎ 081/7805697; at Salerno, *Aeroporto Pontecagnano*, ☎ 089/301186.

Caving: Grotte di Pertosa, Grotta di Castelcivita, Grotta Azzurra in Capri, Grotta di Smeraldo or di Amalfi, marine caves on Cilento coast, information: *Comitato Grotte Pertosa*, ☎ 0975/37037; town hall in Castelcivita, ☎ 0828/975009, tourist offices at Capri, ☎ 081/8370686, Amalfi, ☎ 089/872619, Palinuro, ☎ 0974/931121, Sapri, ☎ 0973/392061. *Gruppo grotte CAI*, at Naples, v. Bonito 19, ☎ 081/404421 (exploration of man-made underground passages in town).

Fishing: *Federazione Italiana Pesca Sportiva*, at Avellino, v. Don Minzoni 3; at Capua, v. Appia 61, ☎ 0823/963530; at Caserta, corso Trieste 169, ☎ 0823/325014; at Naples, p. Santa Maria degli Angeli 11 (Pizzofalcone), ☎ 081/417579; at Salerno, corso Garibaldi 215. For fishing conditions (permitted stretches of water, prohibitions, etc) inquire at local branch concerned.

● *Towns and places*

ALIFE

Caserta 39, Naples 72, Rome 186 km
Pop. 6,472 ⊠ 81011 ☎ 0823   B1

The **plan** of Alife is that of a Roman military encampment, almost entirely protected by an ancient wall. The **cathedral** (rebuilt 17C) has a 9C crypt supported by Roman columns. Outside the walls is a Roman mausoleum, transformed in the 13C into the chapel of **S. Giovanni Gerosolimitano** (St. John of Jerusalem) now a war memorial chapel.   □

AMALFI*

Salerno 24, Naples 62, Rome 272 km
Pop. 6,007 ⊠ 84011 ☎ 089   C3

Amalfi was one of the Italian marine republics that wrote a chapter of Mediterranean and European history. This coastal town with narrow streets and ancient passageways is set on terraces between the mountains and the sea.

▶ Near the shore is the p. Flavio Gioia (a citizen of Amalfi credited with inventing the compass). ▶ Nearby are remains of the **arsenal** of the marine republic. ▶ The **Duomo★**, at the top of a flight of steps, was founded in the 9C, rebuilt in the Arab-Norman style of Sicily in 1203 and rebuilt again in the 18C. The façade was refurbished in the 19C; the **campanile★**, topped with Arab turrets and arches, dates from 1180-1276; the central portal in the Gothic porch contains a bronze **door** cast in Constantinople *c.* 1066; the interior has been restored to reveal earlier construction. In the sanctuary are candelabra; in the crypt, with the supposed relics of the Apostle Andrew, are statues including one by Bernini. The Cappella del Crocifisso, with elements from the 13C church, is on the l.-hand aisle. ▶ Access to the **Chiostro del Paradiso★** *(9 a.m.-7 p.m.)* is through the l.-hand end of the portico of the Duomo; interlaced arches (1266-8) surround a small space planted with palm trees; it was once a cemetery for the nobility and distinguished citizens of Amalfi. ▶ The **Museo Civico** in the municipio *(8 a.m.-2 p.m.; Sat 8 a.m.-12 noon; closed Sun and hols; telephone in advance)* displays the **Tavole Amalfitane**, a codex of maritime law which was valid in the Mediterranean until the 17C. ▶ There are 13C **cloisters** *(visits permitted)* in the Luna and Cappuccini hotels; the veranda of the latter has a **view★** of the town and coast. ▶ The waterfalls of the **Valle delle Mulini** (mills) above Amalfi feed the oldest paper mills in Europe: there is a small **Museo della Carta** *(paper, Tue, Thu and Sat 10 a.m.-1 p.m.)*; one hr's walk to the **Mulino Rovinato**.   □

Practical information ‾‾‾‾‾‾‾‾‾‾‾‾‾

≋
ⓘ corso Romano 19, ☎ 872619 or 871107.
⚤ boats for Salerno, Positano and Capri (Jul-Aug); hydrofoils daily in summer to Salerno, Sapri, Positano, Capri and Naples; *Scarano Navigazione,* ☎ 225322; motor boats to the Grotta di Smeraldo.

Hotels:
★★★★★ *Santa Caterina,* v. Nazionale 9, ☎ 871012, 70 rm ℙ ⦓ ▭ 310,000.
★★★★★ *Saraceno,* v. Augustariccio 25, ☎ 872601, 56 rm ℙ ⬜ ⊗ ▭ closed Nov-Mar except New Years. Complex in oriental style sloping down to sea, 240,000.
★★★★ *Cappuccini Convento,* v. Annunziatella 46, ☎ 871008, 39 rm ℙ ⦓ ⬜ 100,000; bkf: 10,000.
★★★★ *Excelsior,* at Palavena, ☎ 871344, 100 rm ℙ ⦓ ⬜ ▭ closed Nov-Mar, 89,000; bkf: 15,000.

★★★★ *Luna,* v. Comite 19, ☎ 871002, 45 rm ℙ ⦓ ⬜ ⅄ ▭ 13C convent on a crag above sea, 100,000; bkf: 9,000.
★★★ *Aurora,* v. Protontini 7, ☎ 871209, 31 rm ℙ ⬜ closed 16 Oct-31 Mar, 74,500; bkf: 6,000.
★★★ *Bussola,* lungomare dei Cavalieri 16, ☎ 871131, 65 rm ℙ 72,000; bkf: 6,000.
★★★ *Cavalieri,* v. Comite 26, ☎ 871333, 70 rm ℙ ⦓ ⬜ 71,000; bkf: 10,000.
★★★ *Residence,* v. Repubbliche Marinare 9, ☎ 871183, 26 rm ⦓ ⅄ ⊗ closed Nov-Easter, 65,000; bkf: 6,000.
Lidomare, largo Piccolomini 9, ☎ 871332, 13 rm ℙ No restaurant, 50,000; bkf: 6,000.

Restaurants:
♦♦ *Caravella,* v. Camera 12, ☎ 871029, closed Tue and 10-30 Nov. Rooms decorated with mythical scenes. Regional cuisine: squid all'amalfitana, mozzarella in carozza, 15/28,000.
♦♦ *Marinella,* lungomare dei Cavalieri 1, ☎ 871043, closed Nov and 11 Jan-31 Mar and Fri in Oct. By sea with terrace and bathing facilities. Regional cuisine: stuffed pancakes, seafood soup, crayfish, 20/35,000.
♦ *Taverna del Doge,* p. Duomo 6, ☎ 872303, closed Mon in winter and Feb. Next to Duomo, furnished in marine taverna style. Regional cuisine: linguine with crayfish, stuffed shellfish, 16/30,000.

Recommended
Events: *international open-air ballet festival;* concerts in the *Chiostro del Paradiso; theatre and folk events* (Jul-Aug).
Marina: ☎ 871366.

The AMALFI COAST

From Sorrento to Salerno *(98 km, 1 day; map 1)*

This itinerary largely explores the territory of the old marine republic, which stretched from Positano to Cetara, and to the Monti Lattari watershed. Amalfi's commercial success may have begun with the export of Lombard slaves from the same tribes that harried the remaining Byzantines along the jagged and inaccessible coastline. Houses are built one above the other in villages with twisting streets. The land is cultivated on laboriously constructed terraces; these fishing and wine-growing villages have 'one foot in a boat and the other in the vineyard.'

▶ The departure point is **Sorrento** (→) on the N side of the Sorrento peninsula. **Massa Lubrense** sits on a rolling plain. The Baroque church of S. Maria delle Grazie has an 18C majolica pavement in the transept. 2 km away, through citrus and olive groves, is the fishing village of **Marina della Lobra.** ▶ The high coast road goes on to **Términi,** on the Amalfi side of the peninsula. ▶ **Santa'Agata sui Due Golfi** (17C altar of polychrome marble, semi-precious stones and mother-of-pearl in the Florentine manner in the 16C parish church) owes its name to its site on the bays of Naples and Salerno. ▶ The road presents a succession of wonderful views passing through **Positano** (→); **Praiano;** the ravine of the **Furore Valley★;** the entrance to the **Grotta di Smeraldo,** where light filtered through the water creates an unearthly atmosphere (elevator or stairs; *Mar-May 9 a.m.-5 p.m.; Jun-Sep 8.30 a.m.-6 p.m.; Oct-Feb 10 a.m.-4 p.m.);* **Conca dei Marini** and **Véttica.** ▶ The road then climbs through meadows and chestnut groves to the **Agérola** plateau; splendid **terrace** with fine view★ in **San Lazzaro.** ▶ Back on the coast, the route proceeds through **Amalfi** (→) and **Atrani** (→) then into the Monti Lattari to **Ravello** (→), then into the Monti Lattari to the **Valico di Chiunzi .** ▶ Crossing the coast through the Tramonti Valley through chestnut woods, the same route arrives at the citrus groves and vineyards of the lower ter-

1. The Amalfi Coast

races. ▶ The majolica dome of the church of S. Maria a Mare dominates picturesque **Maiori**; the little **museum** has an unusual 15C alabaster altar frontal in the English style. ▶ Back briefly in the Amalfi direction the road reaches Minori and the ruins of a 1C **Roman villa** *(caretaker, 9 a.m.-12 noon and 4-6 or 7 p.m.)* with a **museum of antiquities.** ▶ From Maiori along the splendid coast to **Cetara, Marina di Vietri** *(1.2 km)* to **Raito**, where the **Museo della Ceramica Vietrense** from the 17C to the present is in a tower in the park of Villa Guariglia *(9 a.m.-1 p.m. Thu and Sat; in spring and summer also 5-7 p.m.; closed Mon)* and **Vietri sul Mare,** then on to **Salerno** (→). □

Practical information _____

AGEROLA, ✉ 80051, ☎ 081.
ℹ at Pianillo, v. della Vittoria, ☎ 8791064.

CETARA, ✉ 84010, ☎ 089.
≋

Hotel:
★★★ *Cetus,* ☎ 261388, 40 rm ⓟ 63,000.

MAIORI, ✉ 84010, ☎ 089.
≋

ℹ v. Capone, ☎ 877452.
🚢 Salerno-Capri hydrofoils in summer.

Hotels:
★★★★ *Reginna Palace,* v. Colombo, ☎ 851200, 67 rm ⚱ ▤ ⚲ closed Nov-Mar, 140,000.
★★★ *Panorama,* v. S. Tecla 8, ☎ 877202, 79 rm ⓟ ♿ ⚲ closed Nov-Easter, 70,000; bkf: 8,000.
★★★ *San Francesco,* v. S. Tecla 8, ☎ 877070, 44 rm ⓟ ⚱ closed 16 Oct-14 Mar, 55,000; bkf: 6,000.
★★★ *San Pietro,* v. Nuova Chiunzi 139, ☎ 851095, 40 rm ⓟ ⚱ ⚲ ⸖ closed 1 Nov-14 Mar, 62,000; bkf: 10,000.

MARIA DEL CANTONE, 11 km SE, ✉ 80068, ☎ 081.
≋

🚢 boats daily to Capri, Positano and Amalfi in summer.

Restaurant:·
♦♦ *Taverna del Capitano,* ☎ 8081028, closed 16 Oct-14 Mar. Fine seafood, 25/35,000.

MASSA LUBRENSE, ✉ 80061, ☎ 081.
ℹ v. Filangeri 2, ☎ 8789123.

Hotels:
★★★★ *Delfino,* at Marciano, v. Nastro d'Oro 2,

☎ 8789261, 49 rm ⓟ ⚱ ⚲ ▥ ⚲ ▤ closed Oct-Mar, 86,000.
★★★ *Bellavista-Francischiello,* v. Partenope 26, ☎ 8789181, 28 rm ⓟ ⚱ ♿ ▤ 45,000; bkf: 5,000.
★★ *Maria,* rotabile Massa-Turro 58, ☎ 8789163, 30 rm ⓟ ⚱ ⚲ ▤ closed Nov-Mar, 33,500; bkf: 4,500. Rest. ♦♦♦ *Maria di Francischiello* closed Fri. Among gardens, olive and citrus groves. Regional cuisine: spaghetti with clams, fritto all'Italiana, Lacryma Christi del Vesuvio wine, 25/35,000.

⚿ *Villa Lubrense,* v. Partenope 31, 200 pl, ☎ 8772140 (all year).

MINORI, ✉ 84010, ☎ 089.
≋

ℹ v. Roma, ☎ 877087.

Hotel:
★★★ *Villa Romana,* corso Vittorio Emanuele 90, ☎ 877237, 60 rm ⓟ ⚲ closed Nov-Feb, 45,000; bkf: 6,000.

PRAIANO, ✉ 84010, ☎ 089.

ℹ at Véttica Maggiore, v. Nazionale, ☎ 874456.

Hotels:
★★★ *Nettuno,* at Véttica Maggiore, v. Nazionale 147, ☎ 874007, 58 rm ⓟ ⚱ ⚲ ♿ closed Nov-Feb, 69,000.
★★★ *Tramonto d'Oro,* v. Véttica Maggiore, v. Capriglione 89, ☎ 874008, 40 rm ⓟ ⚱ ♿ ▤ 72,000; bkf: 8,000.

Restaurant:
♦♦ *Brace,* at Véttica Maggiore, v. Capriglione, ☎ 874226, closed Wed in winter. Large summer terrace with view of Positano, Isola dei Galli, and, on fine days, the Faraglioni on Capri. Regional cuisine: braised, grilled or baked fish, frittura mista, 30/40,000.

Recommended
Youth hostel: *Ostello dei Galli,* at Véttica Maggiore, v. Capriglione, ☎ 874093.

SAN LAZZARO, ✉ 800051, ☎ 081.

⚿ *Beata Solitudo,* p. Gen. Avitabile 2, 30 pl, ☎ 8025048 (all year).

SANT'AGATA SUI DUE GOLFI, ✉ 80064, ☎ 081.

Hotels:
★★★ *Due Golfi,* v. Nastro Azzurro 2, ☎ 8780004, 56 rm ⚱ ▤ ⸖ closed Nov-Mar, 42,000; bkf: 5,000.

★★★ *Montana,* v. Torricella 2/A, ☎ 8780126, 50 rm Ⓟ ⏴
ὅ ⅋ closed Nov-Mar, 50,000; bkf: 7,500.

Restaurant:
● ♦♦♦ *Don Alfonso 1890,* corso S. Agata 11,
☎ 8780026, closed Sun eve, Mon and Jan-Feb. Well furnished and equipped, managed by a sommelier couple. Regional cuisine: maccaroni with artichoke and sausage, shellfish all'acqua pazza, 45/60,000.

Ⓐ *Nocelleto,* v. Reola 12, 30 pl, ☎ 8780302.

VETTICA, ✉ 84011, ☎ 089.

Restaurant:
♦ *Ciccio, Cielo-Mare-Terra,* v. Nazionale ☎ 871030,
closed Tue in winter and Feb. Regional cuisine,
20/30,000.

VIETRI SUL MARE, ✉ 84019, ☎ 089.
≈
ⓘ p. Matteotti, ☎ 211548.

Hotels:
★★★★ *Lloyd's Baia,* v. De Marinis 2, ☎ 210145, 111 rm
Ⓟ ◲ 145,000.
★★★★ *Raito,* at Raito, ☎ 210033, 52 rm Ⓟ ⏴ ҉ 80,000;
bkf: 7,000.
★★★ *Bristol,* at Marina, v. Colombo 2, ☎ 210216, 22 rm
Ⓟ ⏴ ⅋ 47,000; bkf: 6,000.
★★★ *Lucertola,* at Marina, v. Colombo 29, ☎ 210837,
30 rm Ⓟ ⏴ ὅ ⅋ 46,000; bkf: 7,000.
★★★ *Voce del Mare,* v. Costiera Amalfitana, ☎ 210080,
25 rm Ⓟ closed Nov, 48,000; bkf: 6,000.

Recommended
Craft workshops: *Santoriello,* at Raito, v. Fontanalimite 18,
☎ 210912 and *Solimene,* v. Madonna degli Angeli 5/7,
☎ 210243 (ceramics).

ARIANO IRPINO

Avellino 49, Naples 105, Rome 294 km
Pop. 22,735 ✉ 83031 ☎ 0825   D2

Ariano Irpino was damaged in the earthquake of
1980. It spans three hills, with views of central Irpinia. On a hill are the remains of a **castle** whose corner towers have Norman foundations. There are
16C elements in the façade of the **cathedral.**   ▯

ATRANI

Salerno 23, Naples 35, Rome 242 km
Pop. 1,103 ✉ 84010 ☎ 089   C3

Atrani sits between high cliffs at the mouth of the Dragone torrent. The village is an intricate web of steps
and little bridges, with occasional shady patches out
of the brilliant Amalfi light. Gardens flourish among
the white-washed houses.

▶ Atrani was the seat of the nobility of the Amalfi
Republic; the doges were elected in **S. Salvatore de'Bi-
reto.** The church has a bronze **door**★ (1087) cast in
Constantinople *(apply to sacristan)* and, inside, a 12C
screen. ▶ The collegiate church of **S. Maria Maddalena**
(13C, altered) dominates the village.   ▯

Practical information _____

Restaurant:
♦ *Arcate,* v. Di Benedetto 4, ☎ 871367, closed Mon and
Dec-Feb. Sea view. Regional cuisine: bucatini alla sco-
gliera, linguine capriccio, 20/35,000.

> For the translation of a name of a meat, a fish or a
> vegetable, for the composition of a dish or a sauce,
> see the *Menu Guide* at the end of the Practical Holi-
> day Guide; it lists the most common culinary terms.

AVELLINO

Naples 56, Rome 245, Milan 811 km
Pop. 56,744 ✉ 83100 ☎ 0825   C2

The **centre** of this modern-looking town is the p. della
Libertà which joins the main street (corso Vittorio
Emanuele) at the **Villa Comunale.**

▶ The **Museo Irpino** *(8:30 a.m.-2 p.m.; Mon and Fri also
4:30-7 p.m.; Sat 8:30 a.m.-2 p.m.; closed Sun and hols)*
documents Irpinia's past — Avellino is the regional capital — from the neolithic to the Roman period. Archaeological finds include **wooden statuettes** of the Italic type,
from the sanctuary of the goddess Mefite in the Ansanto
Valley, and a 1C BC circular marble altar from *Abellinum;*
works of art include 17C-18C paintings of the Neapolitan
school, porcelain and an 18C crèche. ▶ In the old
town in the p. Amendola are the **Torre del Orologio**
(clock tower), a 17C monument to the Hapsburg Emper-
or Charles II and the **Palazzo della Dogana.** ▶ In the
v. Umberto I is the Baroque **Fontana di Constantino-
poli.** ▶ The **Duomo,** a 12C foundation rebuilt in Neoclassical style, has 16C choir stalls, a tabernacle with 16C
reliefs and a Romanesque crypt. ▶ The adjacent **Museo
Diocesano** *(9 a.m.-1 p.m.; Tue, Thu and Sat also 4-8 p.m.)*
displays works of art recovered from regional churches
after the 1980 earthquake including a 12C **crucifix** from
Mirabella. ▶ The **excavations** of Roman *Abellinum* are
at the E edge of town: houses, parts of the baths and the
amphitheatre have been unearthed. ▶ 20 km away is the
sanctuary of **Montevergine** (→).   ▯

Practical information _____

ⓘ p. della Libertà 50/51, ☎ 35175.
🚂 ☎ 626031.
🚌 from p. Macello and from A16 access point.
Car rental: *Avis,* v. Italia 151/153, ☎ 33345.

Hotel:
★★★★ *Jolly,* v. Tuoro Cappuccini 97/A, ☎ 25922, 74 rm
Ⓟ 110,000; bkf: 18,000.

Restaurant:
● ♦♦♦ *Caveja,* v. Tuoro Cappuccini 48, ☎ 38277,
closed Mon and Aug. Emilian cuisine: gramigna with
sausage, capelletti al ragù, ventre di Venere, 25/40,000.

Recommended
Craft workshops: *C. Castagnetti,* at Montefusco,
p. Castello, ☎ 964024 (embroidery).
Wine: *Mastroberardino,* at Atripalda, v. Manfredi 87/89,
☎ 626123 (Greco di Tufo and Taurasi wines).

AVERSA

Caserta 18, Naples 19, Rome 217 km
Pop. 56, 936 ✉ 81301 ☎ 081   B2

The inland plain just behind Naples, the Terra di
Lavoro, has always been renowned for its fruit,
cereals and wine. Lavoro in the name is not connected with labour, as one might expect, but comes from
Terra Leboriae, land of the Leborini, the tribe who
lived here in antiquity. Aversa is the birthplace of
the composer Domenico Cimarosa (1749-1801).

▶ The elliptical **old town** is complicated, with concentric and radial streets and charming nooks and cran-
nies. ▶ Notable features of the **Duomo** (11C, rebuilt
18C) are the three apses and the octagonal dome of
Norman-Arab design; the campanile (1499) incorporates
ancient marbles from Atella. The ambulatory has medieval sculpture along its walls; in the fourth chapel on the l.
is a wooden crucifix in the Catalan style (*c.* 1250). ▶ The
church of the **Annunciata,** in a courtyard near the 17C
Porta Napoli, has several paintings of the Neapolitan
school. ▶ The **Museo di S. Francesco** has a collec-

tion of carvings in wood and stone (13C-14C), paintings (14C-16C) and other *objets d'art* from the diocese. ☐

Queen Jane

In the countryside of Aversa, if grains refuse to sprout or if trees do not bear fruit, it is said that Queen Jane (Riggina Giuvanna) has passed by. Although the papal court of Avignon absolved her, the people of Aversa have not forgiven this devil incarnate who was executed in 1345 for the murder of her husband, King Andrew of Hungary. The peasants believe that good King Andrew is still lying in the moats of the castle and that the queen, a truly evil spirit, still wanders through the countryside, sowing ruin and destruction in her wake.

Peaches of Campania

The area between Giugliano and Aversa is known as the ploughing land, a fertile patch covered with grains, fruit, orchards and vine. Harvest fever hits every season. In the summer, after the grain harvest, the peaches are ready to be picked. It's difficult to maneuver through the gigantic fruit orchards which are closed off by curtains of poplars and elms and where the intertwined branches of the trees are laden with fruits. Peaches ripen quickly, so the villages in the area build counters and stalls decorated with peach tree branches. Crates full of heavy and succulent peaches are stacked in trucks which speed them away towards markets all over Italy and Germany.

Practical information _____

ⓘ v. Botticelli, ☎ 8902936.

Recommended
Cycling: *GS Aversa*, v. Matilde Serao 12, ☎ 8112391.
Horse racing: *Cirigliano*, v. Olimpico, ☎ 8111022.

BAGNOLI IRPINO

Avellino 39, Naples 100, Rome 289 km
Pop. 3,851 ✉ 83043 ☎ 0827   D3

Bagnoli Irpino is on the wooded slopes of the Cervialto at the head of the Calore Valley.

▶ The **parish church** has wood carvings and a 17C intaglio choir. ▶ There is skiiing at **Piano Laceno** (3,421 ft; *8 km SE*). ▶ Near **Montella** *(6.7 km W)* are the monastery and church of **S. Francesco a Folloni** (16C-17C, under restoration). ☐

Practical information _____

Environs

PIANO LACENO, ✉ 83043, ☎ 0827.
ƒ ski lifts, cross-country skiing, ski instruction.
ⓘ *Direzione Impianti Laceno*, ☎ 68057.

Hotel:
★★★ *Quattro Camini*, ☎ 68086, 52 rm 🅿 ⬭ 🕸 ☐ ⤴
closed Apr-Jun and 16 Sep-19 Dec, 45,000.

⛺ *Monte Rajamagra*, 48 pl, ☎ 68057 (all year).

BAIA*

Naples 22, Rome 239 km
✉ 80070 ☎ 081   A3

The thermal springs of Baia were well-known to the ancient Romans. They were mentioned by the writer Martial, and the emperors had a residence here.

▶ The **Parco Archeologico★** *(9 a.m.-2:45 and 6:20 p.m. according to season; closed Mon)* is an architectural complex that includes the imperial palace, dating from the 1C-4C. It is divided into three principal sectors: in the **Settore di Sosandra** are three terraces, containing, from the top, a rest area, a theatre-grotto (once dedicated to the nymphs that supposedly dwelt in its spring) and the great bath, *(piscina)* known as the **Bagno di Sosandra.** The **Settore di Mercurio,** wrongly called the Temple of Mercury, was almost certainly a thermal bath. The **Settore di Venere** is a vast terraced complex. ▶ The so-called **Temple of Venus,** almost opposite the jetty, is an octagonal building topped with picturesque vegetation and is also part of the *palatium.* ▶ The so-called **Temple of Diana** is a great domed circular hall. ☐

Thermal cures of Baia

In ancient times visitors came to Baia to enjoy the mild climate and the beautiful lido. Baia was mostly a famous spa. Its warm waters and steam were piped through sophisticated installations into public baths and special rooms in villas and had therapeutic uses. Documents and monuments from the period show that Baia was known for its sudatio (or sweat cure), which was considered a panacea against all ills at the time. Pliny and Celsius exalt the miraculous virtues of these steam baths which were fed by volcanic steam. In the 16C, Don Pedro of Aragon had an inscription placed in Stufe de Nerone which is still a sudotorium. The inscription is a long list of all the ailments treated with steam and the specific procedures to follow for each ailment. While Neapolitan medical tradition sang the praises of the 'miraculous' sweat cure, the school of Salerno was completely hostile to this kind of treatment. This divergence of professional opinion soon turned into bitter jealousy between the two groups of doctors. Some doctors even tried to poison the waters. An unexplained phenomenon has deteriorated the shoreline and most of the small villages of antiquity have disappeared under twelve feet of water. Today, the few springs that haven't disappeared are still used by the inhabitants.

BAIA DOMIZIA

Caserta 54, Naples 67, Rome 167 km
Pop. 204 ✉ 81030 ☎ 0823   A2

The sandy shore on the l. of the mouth of the Garigliano is densely covered with **pine woods.** 5 km inland, at **Céllole,** is the church of S. Marco, Romanesque in origin (9C-13C) with frescos. 7 km away, on the other side of the Garigliano, near the via Appia, are the **ruins of Minturnae.** ☐

Practical information _____

BAIA DOMIZIA
≈
ⓘ *Domizia Travel*, ☎ 930021.

Hotels:
★★★★ *Domizia Palace,* v. dei Tamerici, ☎ 930100, 110 rm 🅿 🛇 ₩ 🖵 closed Nov-Mar, 110,000; bkf: 15,000.
★★★ *Baia,* at Baia Domizia Sud, v. dell'Erica, ☎ 721344, 56 rm 🅿 🛇 ₩ ⛱ 🏊 closed 1 Oct-9 May, 83,000; bkf: 8,000.

⚓ *Baia Domizia,* 900 pl, ☎ 930164.

Environs
CELLOLE, ✉ 81030, ☎ 0823.

Recommended
Wines: *Villa Matilde estate,* v. Domiziana at the 4.7-km marker, ☎ 932088 (Falernian wine; reserve in advance).

BATTIPAGLIA

Salerno 21, Naples 77, Rome 284 km
Pop. 41,883 ✉ 84091 ☎ 0828   C-D3

Resting on the edge of the plain of Sele Battipaglia was a settlement where the Bourbon King Ferdinand II sheltered earthquake victims from Melfi in Basilicata. **Buffalo** are bred here to produce famous mozzarella cheese.   □

Practical information _____

Hotels:
★★★ *Commercio,* SS 18 improvement route, ☎ 71321, 81 rm 🅿 ₩ ⛱ 48,000; bkf: 10,000.
★★ *Etap Hotel Club Paestum,* in Spineta Nuova, ☎ 624121, 304 rm 🅿 🖵 🏊 66,000; bkf: 6,000.

⚓ *Lido Mediterraneo,* at Lido Lago, v. Litoranea, 80 pl, ☎ 624097; *Maldive First Class,* v. Litoranea, 100 pl, ☎ 624103.

Recommended
♥ **cheese:** *Valtusciano cheese factory,* v. Belvedere 353, ☎ 71309 (reserve in advance).

BENEVENTO*

Naples 62, Rome 228, Milan 849 km
Pop. 63,456 ✉ 82100 ☎ 0824   C2

The Romans defeated Pyrrhus, King of Epirus, near Beneventum in 275 BC. It was Pyrrhus whose victories cost so much that they could be counted as losses. The area was originally called Maleventum (ill wind); the Romans changed it to Beneventum (fair wind). The city sits surrounded by wooded peaks at the confluence of the Sabato and the Calore. Roman columns, tombstones and milestones sometimes appear embedded in the walls of the houses. Earthquakes and bombing (1943) failed to destroy the historic charm of the town. The well-known liqueur, Strega, is produced at Benevento.

▶ The **Duomo★** (C2) was almost completely destroyed by WW II bombing, but the original façade (13C), the campanile (1279) with Roman marbles, the central portal and the late 6C crypt survived. ▶ Fragments of the **bronze door★** of the Duomo and illuminated manuscripts are displayed in the **Museo Diocesano** in the archbishop's palace *(on request, ☎ 29773).* ▶ The v. C. Torre (C2) passes under the imperial Roman **Arco del Sacramento.** ▶ The **Roman theatre★** *(9 a.m.-sunset)* from the reign of Hadrian (2C) has survived in part. ▶ The **Port'Arsa** (C1) is a gateway in the medieval town wall; to its r. is the **Torre della Catena,** the remains of a Lombard fortress. ▶ The **Ponte Leproso** (C1) carried the via Appia over the Sàbato in Roman times. ▶ The v. S. Lorenzo, with a statue of the sacred Egyptian **bull Apis** from an ancient temple of Isis, leads to the Neo-

classical church of the **Madonna delle Grazie** (B1) with a venerated wooden Madonna (16C). ▶ The v. Posillipo, on the bank of the Calore, passes the remains of the **Roman baths** (B2). ▶ **Old town E of the Duomo.** There are remains of 14C frescos in the manner of Giotto in the monastery of **S. Francesco** and parts of an 11C fresco in the large cloister with Roman columns. ▶ The **Arch of Trajan★★** (B-C3) dedicated in 114, is perhaps the finest of the Roman arches, certainly the most famous in the town. ▶ The church of **S. Sofia★** (C3) was part of a Benedictine abbey founded by the Lombards (760); the 12C portal is framed by two Roman columns; the interior is unusual: hexagon, decagon and star join under the dome. In the apses are remains of 8C frescos. In the ancient monastery around the 12C **cloister★** is the **Museo del Sannio★** (C3, Samnite museum, *9 a.m.-1 p.m.; closed Sun and hols);* the archaeological section contains Samnite finds from the necropolises of *Caudium* (Montesarchio), Greco-Italic ceramics, classical marbles, Egyptian and neo-Egyption statues from the temple of Isis; the medieval and modern art section★ includes medieval sculpture, decorative arts and a gallery with paintings by Roman and Neapolitan masters of the 17C-18C as well as contemporary works; the numismatic section has gold coins from Benevento's period as a principality. ▶ The **Rocca dei Rettori** (C3), built by Pope John XXII (1321) over a Lombard fortress and a Roman building, houses the **Sezione Storico del Museo del Sannio** *(9 a.m.-1 p.m.; closed Sun and hols).* This houses documents and memorabilia from the history of Benevento and Samnium as well as popular art. ▶ The **Villa Comunale** (public park) (C3) looks over the Sàbato Valley.   □

Practical information _____

ℹ️ v. Sala 31 (C3 off map, along v. Perasso), ☎ 21960 (head office), v. Giustiniani 36, ☎ 25424 (information).
🚂 (A1), ☎ 21015.
🚌 from p. S. Maria and v. delle Poste (C2).

Hotels:
★★★★ *President,* v. Perasso 1 (C3 a), ☎ 21000, 76 rm 🅿 74,000; bkf: 3,500.
★★★ *Cittadella,* in Piano Cappelle, ☎ 51917, 53 rm 🅿 ₩ 52,000; bkf: 5,000.

Restaurant:
♦♦ *Pedicini,* v. Grimoaldo Re 16 (B2 b), ☎ 21731, closed Mon, Aug and Christmas. Regional cuisine: fusilli, homemade fettuccine, capriccio sannita, 15/25,000.

Recommended
Events: *town show* (Sep); *opera and theatre seasons in the Teatro Romano (Jul).*
Horseback riding: *Associazione Sannita Sport Equestre,* v. Giustiniani 8; *Fontana Morena,* contrada S. Vitale 42, ☎ 54114 (associate of *ANTE*).
Sports centre: ☎ 21945.
Tennis: v. Atlantici, ☎ 29920.
♥ **gastronomy:** mountain salami and hams, hazelnuts, nougat.

CAMPI FLEGREI

From Naples *(93 km, 1 day; map 2)*

When Greek colonists landed on this coast they thought the Campi Flegrei (burning fields) must have been the site of the mythological battle between the Titans and the gods. The region is volcanic, with low craters broken by volcanic activity. The hills are varied in form with occasional intensely coloured lakes. Chestnut woods and vines cover the fertile terrain.

▶ The route departs from **Naples** (→). ▶ **Agnano Terme** is a spa on the edge of a crater drained of its lake just over a century ago. ▶ In the crater is the **Bosco degli Astroni,** a forest of ilex, chestnut, oak, elm and poplar,

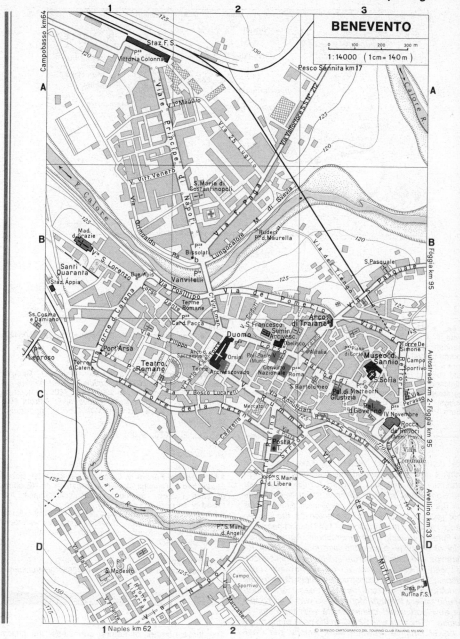

BENEVENTO

0   100   200   300 m

1 : 14000   (1cm = 140 m)

with lakes and abundant wildlife *(toll)*. ▶ From **Pozzuoli** (→) there are boat services to the islands of **Prócida** (→) and **Ischia** (→). ▶ A short detour leads to **Lake Averno**★; the Roman general Agrippa built a military harbour on the lake (1C) and linked it to the sea by a canal. ▶ After **Baia** (→) the route continues to the fishing village of **Bàcoli**. **Cento Camerelle**★ *(caretaker at v. Camerelle 161)* is a remarkable system of reser-

voirs that supplied a Roman villa; the **Piscina Mirabile**★★ *(caretaker at v. Greco 16)* is the largest of the ancient systems. A dike leads from the coastal lagoon of **Lake Miseno** and the port of Miseno to the village of **Miseno** with noteworthy Roman remains, including the ruins of the Villa of Lucullus. This lake and harbour were the most important Tyrrhenian military harbour of the Augustan era. ▶ **Monte di Prócida** has magnificent

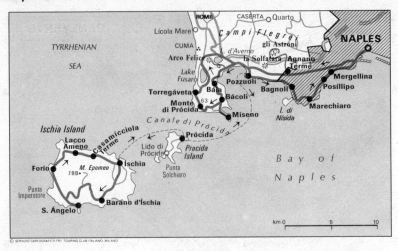

2. Campi Flegrei

views. ▶ The route continues around **Lake Fusaro** to **Cuma** (→) and returns to Pozzuoli via the **Montagna Spaccata**, a deep cutting made by the Romans to accommodate the via Campana. ▶ From Pozzuoli to the **Solfatara★★** *(7 a.m.-sunset; guide advisable):* craters of a dormant volcano (diameter 2,526 ft). Phenomena typical of a volcano in this state include fumaroles, crevices emitting steam and boiling mud, carbon dioxide and mineral springs. ▶ Beyond **Bagnoli** the route runs through **Marechiaro, Posillipo** and **Mergellina** back to Naples. □

Lake Averno

The dense and dark waters of Lake Averno lie within a deep crater and at one time emitted devilish vapours. The site was devoted to minor divinities, and Homer had his hero Ulysses travel here to consult the Tieresias goddess. Virgil sent Enea to this spot (guided by Sibyl and protected by the Golden Bough) to enter the Kingdom of the Dead in search of her father. Braving local superstitions, Agrippa, strategist of Octavius, turned the lake into a harbour for warships and called it Portus Julius. It was connected with these a via a canal through Lake Lucun. Timber for construction sites and repair workshops came from nearby trees. An underground gallery through Monte Grillo was built so that the new port could communicate with the coast of Cumae. The year was 37 BC, at the peak of the deadly power struggle between Mark Antony and Octavius. With the development of Misena and Pozzuoli, Portus Julius was abandoned and the lake regained its mysterious solitude.

Practical information ――――――――――

AGNANO TERME, ⊠ 80125, ☎ 081.
⚓ ☎ 7602122 (all year).

Hotel:
★★★★ *San Germano,* v. Beccadelli 41, ☎ 7605422, 103 rm ℗ ⬚ ⬚ ⬚ ⬚ 140,000.

Recommended
Horseback riding: *Centro ippico Agnano,* v. Circumvallazione 12/D, ☎ 7601757; *Scuola Napoletana di Equitazione,* v. Beccadelli 37, ☎ 7603619 or 7609200 (instruction); *Centro Astroni Turismo Equestre,* v. Astroni 402, ☎ 7261409. Horse racing at *Villa Glori,* v. Ippodromo, ☎ 7601660.

BACOLI, ⊠ 80070, ☎ 081.
≋
ℹ v. Ercole 2.

Restaurants:
♦♦♦ *Arturo al Fusaro,* v. Cuma 322, ☎ 8543130, closed Easter and Christmas. In villa with garden on NE shore of Lake Fusaro. Seafood: crayfish californiana, fish grilled or en papillote, 50/60,000.
♦♦♦ *Misenetta,* v. Lungolago 2, ☎ 8679169, closed Mon, Aug and Christmas. Seaside restaurant with summer terrace. Seafood: prawn risotto, mixed shellfish au gratin, 25/45,000.

Recommended
Canoeing: *Canoa Club Napoli,* ☎ 8670864 (instruction).

The isle of CAPRI★★

B4

The large number of natural curiosities, the charm of the countryside, the architecture of the towns, the Mediterranean flora and fauna and the quality of the light are among the features of this little block of limestone less than 5 miles long that have attracted flocks of visitors since the early 19C.

▶ Visitors arrive at **Marina Grande** (A2-3). At the end of the beach are the ruins of the **Palazzo a Mare** (A2) and beyond it, the ruins known as the **Bagni di Tiberio** (baths of Tiberius) (A2). ▶ The **Grotta Azzurra★★** (Blue Grotto); (A1; *25 mn by motorboat, 1.5 hr by rowboat, visits*

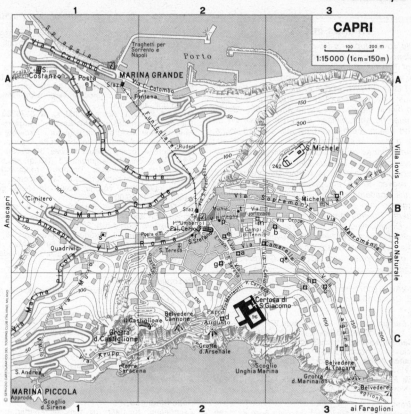

in fishing boats 9 a.m.-1 hr before sunset) is illuminated by sunlight filtered and diffused through the seawater. There is a funicular *(5 mn)* to Capri and a tour of the island by motorboat passing between the Fraglioni (B3) every morning at 9 *(2 hr)*. ▶ **Capri** (B3) is the principal town. The **piazzetta** is closed off like a courtyard; the surrounding district is medieval: arches, shady vaults, sunlit white walls, arcades, terraces, pergolas, surprising views everywhere. To one side of the square are the domes of the church of **S. Stefano** (rebuilt 17C). ▶ The 14C Carthusian monastery of **S. Giacomo★** (B3, *9 a.m.-2 p.m.; Sun and hols 9 a.m.-1 p.m.*) is the most important piece of architecture on Capri. The small cloister is 15C; the large, 16C. The complex contains a **museum** that includes four Roman statues recovered from the Grotta Azzurra. It takes 45 mn to reach the excavations at the **Villa Jovis★** *(9 a.m.-1 hr before sunset; closed Mon)*, the palace where the misanthropic Emperor Tiberius spent his final decade. The ruins include a magnificent **loggia★★**. It takes 30 mn to reach the **Arco Naturale★**, a rock arch, and the **Grotta di Matromània** (B3), dedicated in ancient times to the cult of Cybele; 20 mn to the **Belvedere di Tragara** (B3), to the r. of which are the strangely misshapen rocks of the **Fraglioni★★**; rare blue lizards live on the third island, Scopola. ▶ Between Capri and **Marina Piccola** (B2) are the Parco Augusto and the **via Krupp★**, winding up the cliff, with magnificent views. ▶ In the little town of **Anacapri** (A1) is the 18C church of **S. Michele** *(summer 9 a.m.-6 p.m.; winter 10 a.m.-3 p.m.)*, which has a majolica **pavement★** with a representation of *Earthly Paradise* (1761). 10 mn away is the **Villa of S. Michele** (A2, *sum-*

mer 9 a.m.-6 p.m.; winter 10 a.m.-3 p.m.), built for the Swedish writer and physician Axel Munthe whose book, *The Story of San Michele* has had unparalleled success), with 17C furniture, antiques, famous garden, view★. Other fine views are available from the summit of **M. Solaro★★** (1,932 ft, B2, *chair lift*); from the 14C sanctuary and hermitage of **S. Maria Cetrella★** (1,424 ft, B2, *20 mn*) and from the **Torre di Damecuta★** (A1), en route to which are the ruins of an **imperial Roman villa**.   □

Practical information

🚢 several ferries per day from Naples (Molo Beverello) to Marina Grande *(c. 1.5 hr direct or with stops at Sorrento and Massa Lubrense)*; from Sorrento *(c. 40 mn)*; from Castellamare di Stàbia; daily crossings in summer from Salerno, Amalfi, Positano, Marina del Cantone; several crossings per week from Ischia; weekly crossings from Prócida; car ferry from Naples (reserved for island residents in summer); *Caremar*, ☎ 081/8370700 (departures from Naples and Sorrento); *Navigazione Libera del Golfo*, ☎ 081/8370819 (departures from Naples, Sorrento, Castellamare di Stàbia, Ischia, Prócida), *GRU.SO.N*, ☎ 081/87811430 (departures from Sorrento), *Scarano*, ☎ 089/225322 (departures from Salerno, Positano, Amalfi); several hydrofoils per day from Naples (Mergellina and Molo Beverello) to Marina Grande *(c. 40 mn)* and from Sorrento *(c. 15 mn)*; daily from Salerno, Amalfi, Positano; *Caremar* (departures from Naples); *Alilauro*, ☎ 081/8771506 (departures from Sorrento); *SNAV*, ☎ 081/660444 (departures from Naples), *Scarano* (departures from Salerno, Amalfi, Positano).

Tiberius in Capri

The Villa Jovis *(Jupiter's House)*, now in ruins, stood on a glorious site on the island of Capri. It was the home of Tiberius, Roman Emperor, and most powerful man in the world. He was the son by the first husband of Livia Drusilla, who later married the Emperor Augustus. He was adopted by Augustus and succeeded him in the year 14 at the age of 56. Seven years later he shut himself away on Capri 'on an enclosed beach, surrounded by tall, pointed rocks, and by a deep sea.' Thus Suetonius, senator and historian, reported on the reclusive retirement of intelligent and cultivated Tiberius Claudius Nero. Suetonius produced a portrait in rather sombre colours: 'Capri proved to be the place of execution, from which the condemned, after long and cruel torture, were thrown into the sea under his eyes and on his orders.' Tiberius stayed in the Villa Jovis for ten years. On returning from one of his rare journeys to the capital he died at Miseno, in Lucullus's villa, probably of a heart attack, but possibly suffocated on the orders of his nephew and successor, Caligula.

ANACAPRI, ⊠ 80071, ☎ 081.
ⓘ v. G. Orlandi 19/a, ☎ 8371524.

Hotels:
★★★★ *Europa Palace,* v. Capodimonte 2/B, ☎ 8370955, 103 rm Ⓟ ⬚ ⓑ ⊟ closed Nov-Easter, 21,000.
★★★ *San Michele,* v. Orlandi 3, ☎ 8371427, 56 rm Ⓟ ⬚ ⅏ ⌒ closed Nov-Mar, 95,000.
★★ *Bianca Maria,* v. Orlandi, ☎ 8371000, 17 rm ⅏ closed Nov-Mar. No restaurant, 70,000; bkf: 10,000.
★★ *Villa Patrizia,* v. Pagliaro 55, ☎ 8371014, 40 rm ⬚ closed Nov-Mar. No restaurant, 75,000.

Restaurant:
● ♦ *Gelsomina alla Migliara,* v. Migliara 6, ☎ 8371499, closed Tue. Set in open countryside with terrace, vegetable garden, orchard; can be reached on foot only. Mixed regional cuisine: ravioli alla caprese, rabbit chasseur, 25/35,000.

Recommended
Excursions: to Mt. Solaro by chair lift (12 mn), departures from p. della Vittoria.

CAPRI, ⊠ 80073, ☎ 081.
ⓘ p. Umberto I (B2), ☎ 8370686.

Hotels:
★★★★★ *G. H. Quisisana,* v. Camerelle 2 (B2 a), ☎ 8370708, 142 rm ≼ ⬚ ⅏ ⊟ ⌒ closed Nov-Mar, 344,000.
★★★★ *A Paziella,* v. Giuliani 4 (B3 b), ☎ 8370044, 20 rm ≼ ⬚ ⅏ No restaurant, 170,000.
★★★★ *Luna,* v. Matteotti 3 (C2 d), ☎ 8370433, 48 rm ≼ ⬚ ⊟ closed Nov-Mar. Furnished in 19C style with terraced gardens, 199,000; bkf: 15,000.
★★★★ *Palma,* v. Vittorio Emanuele 39 (B2 e), ☎ 8370133, 80 rm ⬚ closed Nov-Mar, 262,000.
★★★★ *Punta Tragara,* v. Tragara 57 (C3 f), ☎ 8370844, 41 rm ≼ ⬚ ⬚ ⅏ closed 16 Oct-14 Apr, 132,000.
★★★★ *Regina Cristina,* v. Serena 20 (B2 g), ☎ 8370744, 55 rm ⬚ ⬚ ⅏ 143,000.
★★★★ *Scalinatella,* v. Tragara 8 (C3 c), ☎ 8370633, 30 rm ≼ ⬚ ⬚ ⊟ closed 1 Nov-19 Mar. No restaurant, 360,000.
★★★ *Pineta,* v. Tragara 6 (C3 h), ☎ 8370644, 54 rm ≼ ⬚ ⬚ closed Nov-Mar. No restaurant, 190,000.
★★★ *Vega,* v. Occhio Marino 8 (C3 i), ☎ 8370481, 23 rm ≼ ⬚ ⊟ closed Nov-Mar. No restaurant, 120,000.
★★★ *Villa delle Sirene,* v. Camerelle 51 (B2-3 1), ☎ 8370102, 35 rm ≼ ⬚ ⬚ ⌒ closed Nov-Mar, 132,000.

★★ *Florida,* v. Fuorlovado 34 (B2 m), ☎ 8370710, 19 rm Ⓟ ⬚ ⓑ No restaurant, 66,000.
★★ *Villa Sarah,* v. Tiberio 3/A (B3 n), ☎ 8370689, 28 rm ⬚ ⬚ closed Nov-Easter. No restaurant, 80,000.

Restaurants:
● ♦♦♦ *Capannina,* v. delle Botteghe 12 bis (B2 p), ☎ 8370732, closed Wed except Aug and 10 Nov-15 Mar. Romantic atmosphere, careful service. Excellent regional cuisine: gnocchi verdi with salmon, fish mixed grill, 35/45,000.
● ♦♦♦ *Pigna,* v. Roma 30 (B1 s), ☎ 8370280, closed Tue except summer and Nov-Easter. Large room with veranda, pine wood and citrus grove. Excellent regional and international cuisine: linguine Grotta Azzurra, crayfish luna caprese, locally produced wines, 30/45,000.
♦♦♦ *Faraglioni,* v. Camerelle 75 (B3 q), ☎ 8370320, closed Mon and Nov-Mar. Windowed room and terrace facing countryside and Certosa di San Giacomo. Regional and international cuisine: crayish in shells, grilled or baked fish, 35/50,000.
♦♦ *Gemma,* v. Madre Serafina 6 (B2 r), ☎ 8370461, closed Mon and Nov. Terrace with view. Regional cuisine: lobsters, grilled fish, 20/35,000.
♦ *O' Saraceno,* v. Gradoni Sopramonte 8 (B2 t), ☎ 8377511, closed Tue and 15 Jan-10 Mar. Regional cuisine: ravioli alla caprese, squid, homemade wines, 20/35,000.

Recommended
Events: New Year festival; classical ballet in the Certosa di San Giacomo.

MARINA GRANDE, ⊠ 80070, ☎ 081.
≋
ⓘ Banchina del porto (A1), ☎ 8370634.

Restaurant:
♦ *Paolino,* v. Palazzo a Mare 11, ☎ 8376102, closed Wed and Nov-Feb. Near Roman ruins in country, garden with lemon pergola. Regional cuisine: rabbit alla Michelina, grilled mozzarella, homemade wines, 35/50,000.

Recommended
Excursions: to Capri by funicular, departures every 15 mn (bus after 10 p.m.).
Marina: ☎ 8370226.

CAPUA

Caserta 12, Naples 25, Rome 201 km
Pop. 18,224 ⊠ 81043 ☎ 0823   B2

Capua occupies an important place in the history of Italy. It sits in a loop of the Volturno where the via Appia crossed the river at *Casilinum*, the former river port of Capua, now Santa Maria Capua Vétere (→), from which the new Capua took its name. The Lombards, who built the Duomo, settled here after ancient Capua had been burned down by the Saracens in 841. Buildings in the Catalan style are evidence of Spanish rule (15C); such as the Palazzo Antignano which houses the Museo Campano (B2). After an earthquake in 1465 the fortifications were reinforced by the Spaniards; Charles V's perimeter wall was strengthened with polygonal bastions and extended towards the apex of the loop (A1) and on the plain to the S (C1-3).

► The town has many attractive features. There are busts of divinities in the **Palazzo del Municipio** in the central p. dei Giudici (B2) that came from the Roman amphitheatre in Santa Maria Capua Vétere. An interesting church is **S. Eligio** (B2), rebuilt in the 18C; the **Arco di S. Eligio** dates from the 13C. ► The **Palazzo Fieramosca** (B2) is 14C with Gothic portal and windows. ► The corso Appio (B-C2-3), the main street, follows the route of the via Appia; at one end is the 16C church of **S. Annunziata** (C3, the interior has a Baroque

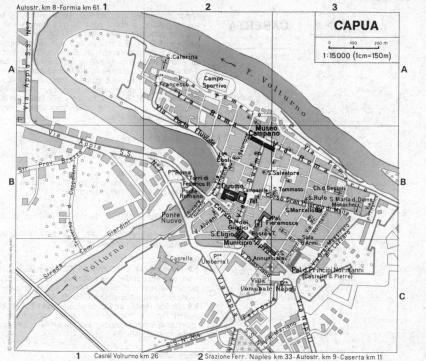

CAPUA

0   100   200 m

1:15000 (1cm=150m)

1   Castél Volturno km 26   2 Stazione Ferr. Naples km 33 - Autostr. km 9 - Caserta km 11

gallery over the chapels and a wooden ceiling with 17C paintings); at the other, the **Roman bridge** over the Volturno (B2), with the two towers of the **Porta di Federico II**. ▶ The **Duomo★**, founded in the 9C, was rebuilt in the 12C and the 18C, and finally repaired after war damage. It has an atrium with 3C Corinthian columns; inside is a 13C paschal candelabrum. ▶ There are Romanesque bas-reliefs around the portal of **S. Marcello** (B3, 12C). ▶ The **Museo Campano★** (B2, *9 a.m.-2 p.m.; Sun 9 a.m.-1 p.m.; closed Mon and midweek hols*) is important both for its Italian and Roman antiquities and for the medieval section. Outstanding items include about 200 **'madri'★** (*Deae Matres;* mother-goddesses), votive statues in tufa (7C-1C BC), **mosaic★** from the temple of Diana Tifatina; statues and sculpture from the Porta di Federico II and a detached fresco of the *Ascension* (13C).

Environs

▶ 5 km NE, the basilica of **S. Angelo in Fórmis★★** (1073) belonged to the monks of Monte Cassino. The portico has arabesque arches, campanile with mullioned windows, and a St. Michael★ in the portal lunette. The finest items are the 11C **frescos** inside the basilica *(if closed apply to caretaker)*. The frescos, by local masters steeped in the Byzantine tradition, are key works of early Italian painting. ☐

Practical information

ⓘ p. dei Giudici (B2), ☎ 963930.

Hotel:
★★★ *Mediterraneo*, v. Falco 26, ☎ 961575, 36 rm Ⓟ ♨ 🖾 38,000; bkf: 5,000.

The Roses of Capua

Famous throughout the world in ancient times, the district of Seplasia, in Capua, specialized in making perfumes. Great quantities of wild roses were used to distill the perfume because their scent was stronger than that of cultured roses. In spring, the wild roses bloomed and covered large parts of the countryside. The roses of Capua were the most renowned in Italy along with those of Peneste and Paestum. Sweet clover from Campania (with its saffron aroma) was also very popular and crowns were woven with its branches.

Recommended

Events: *Capua carnival; Luglio a Capua* (Jul; shows and ballet); *S. Lazzaro fair* (Dec).
Flying: *Terra di lavoro,* v. Aeroporto, ☎ 963430.
Horseback riding: *Fontana Pila,* in Pontelatone *(14 km N),* v. Ponte Pellegrino 69, ☎ 878107 (associate of ANTE).

CASERTA*

Naples 28, Rome 192, Milan 760 km
Pop. 65,332 ⊠ 81100 ☎ 0823   B2

The palace in Caserta was started for the Bourbon King, Charles III, in 1752. The exterior was completed in 1774, the interior 100 years later. The façade is 810 ft long and conceals 1,200 rooms, 1,790 windows and 94 staircases. An aqueduct brought water

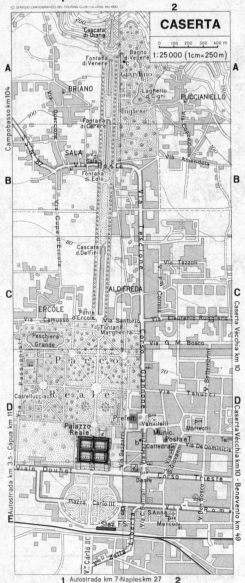

© SERVIZIO CARTOGRAFICO DEL TOURING CLUB ITALIANO, MILANO

CASERTA

0 100 200 300 400 m

1:25 000 (1cm=250m)

1 Autostrada km 7-Naples km 27   2

Appartamento Vecchio, an 18C crèche with 1,200 figures, an art gallery, a room containing a Vanvitelli museum and the exquisite court theatre (1769). ▶ The splendid park★★ (A-D1-2; *9 a.m.-2.30 or 7 p.m. according to season; also by car except on Sun and hols*) has fountains and waterfalls extending up the hill; the **Cascata Grande★** with sculptures of **Diana and Actaeon** (A1) and the **English Garden** (A2, *guided visits in groups*) are key features in this incomparable complex. ▶ 3 km NW, in **San Léucio**, Ferdinand IV set up a silk factory (18C) with the intention of building a model town as an example of enlightened industrialism.   □

Practical information ─────────────────

i corso Trieste (E2), ☎ 321137; Palazzo Reale (D1), ☎ 322233 (head office).
▭▭ (E1), ☎ 327170.
▭▭ from the p. Garibaldi and the v. Roma.
Car rental: *Avis,* railway station, ☎ 443756.

Hotels:
★★★★ *Jolly,* v. Vittorio Veneto 9 (E1-2 a), ☎ 325222, 92 rm Ⓟ 111,000.
★★★ *Centrale,* v. Roma 170, ☎ 321855, 41 rm Ⓟ ♿ ✖
No restaurant, 58,000; bkf: 5,500.

Restaurants:
♦♦ *Massa 1848,* v. Mazzini 55 (D2 b), ☎ 327315, closed Mon, eve except Sat and 5-20 Aug. In 18C palazzo with garden service in summer. Mixed cuisine: linguine baked en papillote, rigatoni antica Caserta, 25/55,000.
♦♦ *Mulini Reali,* at Ponte di Sala (A1-2), ☎ 301842, closed Tue. In old mill with period furnishings. Mixed regional cuisine: tagliatelle alla carmelitana, grilled fish al salmoriglio, 25/45,000.

Recommended
Cycling: *Amici del Pedale,* at Portico di Caserta *(6 km SW)*, p. Rimembranze 5.
Events: *shows and concerts* in the Reggia; *national equestrian competition* (May, Parco della Reggia).
Sports centre: v. Medaglie d'Oro, ☎ 325994.

CASERTA VECCHIA*

Caserta 10, Naples 38, Rome 202 km
Pop. 289 ⊠ 81020 ☎ 0823   B2

This was Caserta before Charles III built his palace in the present town of Caserta (→), 10 km away. It is a charming **medieval town,** founded by Lombards, on a hill and facing the plain.

▶ The **cathedral★**, completed in 1153, is a fascinating mixture of Apulian-Romanesque, Arabic and Benedictine elements; the motif of interlocking arches runs through the façade, **campanile★** (1234 complex decoration, supported by a pointed arch), sides, transept ends and octagonal lantern (13C, decorated with polychrome incrustations). Inside are antique columns; the **pulpit★** was rebuilt in the 17C using a 13C mosaic ambo. ▶ Behind the r.-hand side is the small Gothic church of the **Annunciata.** ▶ On the edge of the town, which has several medieval houses, are the ruins of the **castle,** possibly 9C in origin, with a sturdy round tower.   □

Practical information ─────────────────

Restaurant:
● ♦♦ *Castellana,* v. Torre 4, ☎ 371230, closed Mon. Medieval walls, rural decoration, large pergola. Regional cuisine: orecchiette, wild boar, scamorza cheese, 20/30,000.

Recommended
Events: *Settembre al Borgo* (Sep; theatre, music, dance).

to the palace and gardens. The architect was Luigi Vanvitelli (d. 1773, he was the son of a Dutch artist, Van Witel, who lived in Rome). The modern town grew up around the palace.

▶ The **Palazzo Reale★★** (D1, *9 a.m.-1:30 p.m.; closed Mon*) is arranged on a rectangular plan around four courtyards; the lower vestibule★, the main staircase★ and the upper vestibule★ make up a striking architectural entity; the charm of the apartments lies in their Neoclassical decoration, furnishings and equipment and their reminder of court life. The visit includes: the Royal Apartments, the Appartamento Nuovo, the Appartamento del Re, the

CASTELLAMMARE DI STABIA

Naples 29, Rome 238 km
Pop. 68,928 ⊠ 80053 ☎ 081   B3

The mineral **springs** at Castellamare di Stabia were used for curative purposes by the Romans and recommended by the 1C Greek physician, Galen. Twenty-eight in number, they feed the **Antiche Terme** and the **Nuove Terme Stabiana.**

▶ The centre of this industrial town is the p. Giovanni XXIII, which contains the **Duomo** (16C rebuilt) and the **Chiesa del Gesù** (1615). The **Villa Comunale** is a park with a view of the bay and Vesuvius. ▶ The **Antiquarium Stabiano** (v. M. Mario 2, *9 a.m.-2 p.m.; Sun and hols 9 a.m.-1 p.m.; closed Mon*) displays material from the Roman excavations: frescos, sculpture and bronze. ▶ Above the town a **road with fine views★** passes the medieval castle that gave the town its name. ▶ 20 mn to the NE on the Varano hill, **excavations** of Roman *Stabia*, destroyed in the eruption of Vesuvius in AD 79, have revealed the **Villa of Ariadne**, with a painting of Ariadne and Dionysos in the *triclinium* (dining room), and another **Roman villa** with two peristyles and traces of decorative paintwork in the rooms.   □

Practical information _____

≋
⚓ (Apr-Nov), ☎ 8714422.
ⓘ p. Matteotti, ☎ 8711334.
⛴ ferries to Capri and Ischia, ☎ 8714048.
Hotels:
★★★ *Congressi,* v. Puglie 45, ☎ 8711206 Ⓟ ⋒ 42,000.
★★★ *Medusa,* Passeggiata Archeologica 5, ☎ 8712800, 54 rm Ⓟ ⚲ ⋒ ⚘ 58,000; bkf: 7,000.
Restaurant:
♦ *Tolino,* lungomare Garibaldi 10, ☎ 8711607, closed Sat. Regional cuisine: spaghetti scogliera, scampi alla provenzale, 13/25,000.

Recommended
Excursions: to Mt. Faito (3,609 ft) by cableway (8 mn).
Marina: ☎ 8711077, *Circolo velico* (sailing club), ☎ 8711678.

CASTEL VOLTURNO

Caserta 36, Naples 42, Rome 191 km
Pop. 8,934 ⊠ 81030 ☎ 0823   A2

Castel Volturno is to the l. of the mouth of the Volturno; the residential and holiday area is between the sea and the pines. The region is noted for its buffalo mozzarella.   □

Practical information _____

Hotel:
★★★ *Perla,* SS Domiziana at 38.3-km marker, ☎ 5093166, 51 rm Ⓟ ⋒ ⚘ 35,000; bkf: 5,000.
⚲ *Laila,* at Pineta Grande, v. Bernardino, ☎ 851720 (all year).

Recommended
Sports centre: *Pinetamare,* Villaggio Coppola, ☎ 858901 (indoor swimming pool, instruction).
Horseback riding: *Circolo ippico Pinetamare,* Villaggio Coppola, ☎ 5094075 (associate of ANTE).

> In preparing for your trip, consult the pages pertaining to the regions. You will find there the description of the region you wish to visit, as well as a list of sites that must be seen, a brief history and practical information.

Buffaloes of Volturno

Large herds of buffalo roam freely in the wet flatlands at the mouth of the Volturno River. The herds belong to the large farms known as pagliara. Those in charge of watching the buffalo herds have followed a strict daily routine for generations. Some herders work only during the day, others only at night. Other people specialize in milking the buffalo while others make the cheese, the famous mozzarella. Each animal has been classified and each given a special name of its own. Every morning, the herder calls out each buffalo by name. A moment later, a mother runs up with her calf. After the calf has suckled his mother, the rest of her milk is extracted and used to make cheese.

CAVA DE' TIRRENI

Salerno 7, Naples 45, Rome 254 km
Pop. 51,342 ⊠ 84013 ☎ 089   C3

Apart from the picturesque **Borgo Scacciaventi** on the edge of the old town, the most important site in Cava de'Tirreni is the **Abbazia della Trinità di Cava★**, on a crag 3.8 km SW near Corpo di Cava. The abbey was founded in 1011 and almost completely rebuilt in the 18C *(9 a.m.-12 noon; Sun and hols 8:30-10:30 a.m. except during services and at special periods; guided tour)*. In the **church** are a mosaic candelabrum and a marble portal with intaglio wooden door (16C) in the r. transept. The visit includes the following parts of the **Benedictine monastery:** chapter house; small **cloister★** with twin columns and raised arches (12C); two small chapels with interesting furnishings; the 12C crypt known as the Lombard cemetery; the **museum** in three late 13C rooms, with a collection of archaeological items, sculpture, painting of the 17C-18C Neapolitan school and some illuminated manuscripts.   □

Practical information _____

ⓘ p. Duomo, ☎ 341572.

Hotels:
★★★★ *Scalapolatiello,* at Corpo di Cava, ☎ 463911, 52 rm Ⓟ ⋒ ⚘ ▭ 65,000; bkf: 5,000.
★★★★ *Victoria Maiorino,* corso Mazzini 4, ☎ 465048, 61 rm Ⓟ ⋒ ⟋ 60,000; bkf: 4,000.

Recommended
Bowls: at Corpo di Cava, ☎ 461715.
Events: *castle festival* (week after Feast of Corpus Christi); *Disfida dei Trombonieri* (trombone competition; last Sat and Sun in Jun), ☎ 342010.
Farm vacations: *Azienda Saura,* ☎ 66563.
Horseback riding: *Club ippico Le Ginestre,* v. N. Pastore 1.

The CILENTO COAST

From Agropoli to Sapri *(115 km, 1 day; map 3)*

The ruins of ancient Velia are the focal point of this itinerary. The rest of the route keeps to the coast of the promontory between the Gulf of Salerno and the Gulf of Policastro, a Mediterranean landscape of steep cliffs, green valleys, twisted olive trees and the sun glinting on the sea.

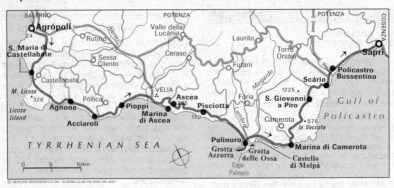

3. The Cilento Coast

▶ In ancient **Agrópoli**, the ruins of a castle, high above the sea, are a reminder of the Byzantine origins of the region. ▶ After a time inland, the route returns to the sea at **Santa Maria di Castellabate**, a seaport, with the church of S. Maria Assunta dating from the 12C (marine underwater park in the sea). ▶ **Acciaroli** was dear to Hemingway. ▶ The **Velia archaeological site★** *(9 a.m.-1 hr before sunset)* is reached after leaving the coast to cross the River Aletto. It was founded by the Phocians, Greeks from Asia Minor (540 BC); excavations are proceeding; so far revealed are a stretch of wall and a bath-house with a mosaic of dolphins*in the S quarter (on the level area beyond the railway). The street then climbs to the **agora** (market, rebuilt 3C BC) via the paved v. di Porta Rosa★; the **Porta Rosa★** (4C BC) is in a cutting below the ridge of the hill. It is the unique example of Greek architecture with a complete curved arch; on the **acropolis**, dominated by a medieval Angevin tower, are the base of a temple (early 5C BC), a building designed like a theatre (early 4C BC), and, on the S side, the wall of the *temenos★* or sacred enclosure with *stoá* (portico) of the Hellenistic period. On the acropolis, the **Museo di Velia** is housed in the tower, the palatine chapel (11C) and two religious buildings in an olive grove. ▶ A short diversion leads to the resort of **Marina di Ascea**. ▶ After Ascea come **Pisciotto** and **Palinuro**: Palinurus, Aeneas' helmsman, fell into the sea and swam to the shore: he was killed by the Lucani and supposedly buried here; Virgil, recording the legend, wrote *'aeternum locus Palinuri nomen habebit'* (this place will always bear the name of Palinurus). An **antiquarium** is being prepared to display artifacts from 6C BC necropolises. There is a view from the lighthouse on the point of the promontory *(2 km);* 10 mn by boat to the **Grotta Azzurra**, and around the promontory (numerous other caves) to the **Grotta delle Ossa**, with stalagmites and stalactites and walls in which are embedded prehistoric human and animal bones. Finally to the **arco naturale**, a natural rock arch at the mouth of the Mingardo. These last points can also be reached from the coast road, where the itinerary continues. ▶ After **Marina di Camerota**, amid rocks, in which is the Grotta della Cala, the route turns inland for the last time to return to the sea on the Gulf of Policastro, at **Scario**, from which it proceeds along the coast to **Sapri** (→). □

Practical information _____

ACCIAROLI, ⊠ 84041, ☎ 0974.
≋

Hotel:
★★★ *Playa,* v. Nicotera 135, ☎ 904002, 77 rm P ⋙ ✦ ✦ closed Oct-May, 43,000; bkf: 4,000.

Restaurant:
♦♦ *Grigliaro,* ☎ 905025, closed Nov-Dec. Summer service under pergola. Regional cuisine: seafood salad, squid and octopus casserole, 23/35,000.

AGROPOLI, ⊠ 84043, ☎ 0974.
≋
ⓘ v. S. Marco, ☎ 824885.

Hotels:
★★★ *Carola,* v. Pisacane 1, ☎ 823005, 34 rm P ⋙ ✦ closed Nov, 42,000.
★★★ *Mare,* v. Risorgimento, ☎ 823666, 48 rm P ⋙ ✦ 47,000; bkf: 6,000.
★★ *Serenella,* v. S. Marco, ☎ 823333, 32 rm P ⋙ ✦ 37,500; bkf: 4,000.

Restaurants:
♦♦♦ *U Saracino,* v. Trentova, ☎ 824063, closed Tue and Nov. Very large, large garden and dancing in open air. Regional cuisine: seafood risotto, fish baked en papillote, 38/45,000.
♦♦ *Ceppo,* v. Madonna del Carmine 31, ☎ 824308, closed Wed and Sep-Oct. Family management. Mixed regional cuisine: tubettino with fish sauce, stuffed squid, 30/50,000.

⚓ *Arco delle Rose,* contrada Isca, Paestum-Agrópoli coast road, 40 pl, ☎ 838227.

Recommended
Events: *Sagra del pesce azzurro* (fishing festival, Aug 24).

CAPRIOLI, ⊠ 84040, ☎ 0974, 6 km N of Palinuro.

Hotel:
★★★ *Stella del Sud,* ☎ 976090, 76 rm ⋙ ⅙ ⌂ ⋗ closed 1 Oct-24 May, 68,500.

⚓ *Baia del Silenzio,* v. Valle di Marco 78, 74 pl, ☎ 976079.

MARINA DI ASCEA, ⊠ 84058, ☎ 0974.
≋
ⓘ v. Oberdan, ☎ 971230.

Hotel:
★★ *Zia Adelina,* v. Oberdan 83, ☎ 971079, 18 rm P ⋙ ✦ 28,500; bkf: 4,000.

△ *Palme,* at Fiumarella, 150 pl, ☎ 971036.

MARINA DI CAMEROTA, ⊠ 84059, ☎ 0974.
≋
ⓘ at Porto Piccolo, ☎ 93256.

Hotels:
★★★ *Baia delle Sirene,* ☎ 932236, 72 rm ℗ ⬙ ⅋ ⬚ ⌁
closed Oct-May except at Easter and Christmas, 70,000.
★★ *Bolivar,* v. Bolivar, ☎ 932036, 21 rm ℗ closed
20 Dec-6 Jul, 27,000; bkf: 4,000.

Restaurant:
◆ *Valentone,* p. S. Domenico 5, ☎ 932004, closed Sun,
Oct-Easter. Family-style trattoria in typical
square. Regional cuisine: ciambotta, grilled swordfish,
18/25,000.

△ *Isola,* contrada Sirene, SS 562 at 9.4-km marker,
536 pl, ☎ 932230; *Happy,* at Cala d'Arconte, SS 562
at 8.2-km marker, 400 pl, ☎ 932326; *Mingardo,* at Torre
Mingardo, SS 562 at 2.9-km marker, 180 pl, ☎ 931391;
Sirene, contrada Sirene, SS 562 at the 9.5-km marker,
☎ 932338.

Recommended
Vacation villages: *Villaggio TCI* (closed Oct-May), infor-
mation at Milan, ☎ 02/85261; at Bari, ☎ 080/365140; at
Rome, ☎ 06/6874432; at Turin, ☎ 011/540177.

PALINURO, ⊠ 84064, ☎ 0974.
≋
ⓘ p. Virgilio 21, ☎ 931121.

Hotels:
★★★★ *Saline,* ☎ 931112, 57 rm ℗ ⬙ ⬚ ⌁ closed Oct-
Mar, 80,000; bkf: 8,000.
★★★ *King's Residence,* Piano Faracchio, ☎ 931324,
78 rm ℗ ⌖ ◷ ⬙ ⬚ closed Oct-Mar, 80,000; bkf: 8,000.
★★★ *Torre,* v. Porto 5, ☎ 931107, 34 rm ℗ ◷ ⬙ ⅋
closed 1 Oct-24 May, 53,500.
★★ *Lido Ficocella,* v. Ficocella, ☎ 931051, 32 rm ℗ ⌖ ⅋
closed Oct-Mar, 40,500; bkf: 6,000.
△ *Arco Naturale,* at Mingardo-Molpa, 340 pl, ☎ 931157;
Marbella Club, at Piana Mingardo, 200 pl, ☎ 931003;
Saline, at Saline, ☎ 931220.

Recommended
Boat trips: to Grotta Azzurra and other caves along
promontory, *Cooperativa pescatori,* ☎ 931233.
Marina: ☎ 931233.

SANTA MARIA DI CASTELLABATE, ⊠ 84072, ☎ 0974.
≋
ⓘ v. Marina.

Hotels:
★★★★ *Castelsandra,* at Monte Liscosa (5 km S),
☎ 966021, 118 rm ℗ ⌖ ◷ ⬙ ⅋ ⬚ ⌁ closed Nov-
Mar, 102,000.
★★★ *Approdo,* at San Marco, v. Porto 49, ☎ 966001,
52 rm ℗ ◷ ⬚ closed Oct-Mar, 51,000; bkf: 7,000. Rest.
◆◆◆ Facing harbour and sea. Regional cuisine: seafood, trenette with scampi, 20/25,000.
★★★ *G. H. Santa Maria,* v. Velia, ☎ 961001, 61 rm ℗ ⬙
⅋ closed Oct-Mar, 56,000; bkf: 4,500.
★★★ *Punta Licosa,* at Ogliastro Marina (8 km S),
v. Licosa, ☎ 963024, 66 rm ℗ ⬙ ⬚ ⌁ closed Oct-May,
80,000; bkf: 10,000.
★★ *Sonia,* v. Marina 25, ☎ 961172, 25 rm ℗ ⅋ closed
1 Nov-15 Dec, 40,000; bkf: 5,000.

Restaurant:
◆◆ *Due Fratelli,* v. S. Andrea, ☎ 961188, closed Wed and
Nov. Seafood, 20/35,000.

△ *Trezene,* 200 pl, ☎ 965013.

Recommended
Skindiving: Centro subacqeo, v. Marina, ☎ 961069.

SCARIO, ⊠ 84070, ☎ 0974.
≋

Hotel:
★★ *Approdo,* v. Nazionale 10, ☎ 986070, 25 rm ℗ ⬙ ⅋
closed Oct-Mar, 37,000; bkf: 7,000.

△ *Lanterna,* at Faro, 80 pl.

CONTURSI TERME

Salerno 54, Naples 107, Rome 313 km
Pop. 3,044 ⊠ 84024 ☎ 0828   D3

Contursi Terme is an ancient hilltop town. Its mineral springs feed the **Bagni di Contursi** near the Oliveto
bridge *(5 km N)* and the **Bagni Forlenza** near the
bridge over the Sele.   □

Practical information

♨ (Jun-Oct) at Bagni Contursi: Terme Capasso,
☎ 995034, Terme Cappetta, ☎ 991258, Terme Rosapepe,
☎ 995019; at Bagni Forlenza: Terme Forlenza, ☎ 991140;
Parco delle Querce, ☎ 991047.
ⓘ municipio, ☎ 991013.

Hotels:
★★★ *Parco delle Querce,* at Ponte Mefita, ☎ 991047,
64 rm ℗ ◷ ⬙ ⅋ ⬚ 27,000; bkf: 4,000.
★★ *Terme Forlenza,* at Bagni Forlenza, ☎ 991140, 63 rm
℗ ⬙ ⅋ ⬚ 30,000; bkf: 3,500.

CUMA*

Naples 20, Rome 238 km
⊠ 80070 ☎ 081   A3
See map on page 152.

Cumae was one of the holiest places of antiquity. Devotees flocked to hear the oracles of the
Cumaean Sibyllae. 'The great flank of the Euboean
cliff is dug out like a cave, a hundred broad passages
lead to it, a hundred doors, from which the answers
of the Sybil sound forth in as many voices.' Virgil's
description shows how the echo from the manmade
cave (5C BC) was exploited. Cumae was founded by
Greek colonists in the 8C BC and was a thriving
regional capital until conquered by the Romans in
334 BC. The city never regained its former dominance and was sacked by Saracens in 915.

▶ The **Arco Felice★** (B3) is an arch from a brick aqueduct; it frames a view★ of the acropolis with the sea
in the background. ▶ The arched perimeter of the
amphitheatre (B2), built in the early imperial period, has
survived. ▶ On the steep sides of the **acropolis** (A1,
9 a.m.-2:45 and 6:10 p.m.; closed Mon) are remains of the
5C Greek walls. ▶ The **Cave of the Cumaean Sybil★**
(B1) is a gallery nearly 150 yds long, trapezoidal in cross-
section, a Greek excavation dating from the 6C-5C BC;
the room at the end was Sybil's prophecy cham-
ber. ▶ Following the **via Sacra:** the **Roman crypt** (A1-2)
of the Augustan period tunnels through the hill; the
Temple of Apollo (A1-2) has the original Greek and Samnite base and remains of Augustan columns; the **Temple
of Jupiter** (A1) was founded by Greeks, rebuilt by Augustus, then turned into a Christian basilica (5C-6C). It is on
the uppermost terrace of the acropolis; there is a view★
to the Gaeta promontory, including the Pontine islands
and the Monti Aurunci.   □

EBOLI

Salerno 29, Naples 86, Rome 292 km
Pop. 32,299 ⊠ 84025 ☎ 0825   D3

Eboli has a **medieval centre,** high on a hill above the
plain of the Sele. The basilica of **S. Pietro alli Marmi**
has Norman elements (11C) and simple columns

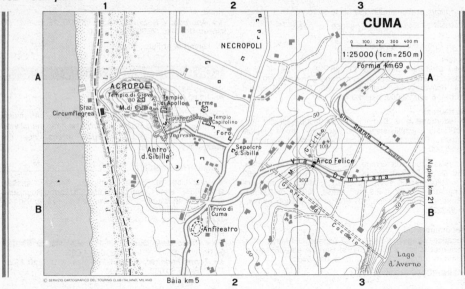

inside. The 18C **collegiate church** has a *Pietà* dating from 1698. ☐

Practical information _____

Hotel:
★★★ *Grazia*, SS 19, ☎ 38038, 47 rm ℗ ♨ ⑂ 44,000; bkf: 5,000.

⚑ *Paestum*, at Foce Sele, 600 pl, ☎ 691003.

Recommended
Nature park: *Serre Persano sanctuaries (c. 6 km E)*, closed Jul-Aug, visits Wed and Sun at 10 a.m. and 2 p.m.; groups on Sat, reserve in advance, ☎ 48078.

ERCOLANO**

Naples 10, Rome 224 km
Pop. 61,033 ⊠ 80056 ☎ 081 B3

Ercolano, known to the Romans as Herculaneum, was buried by the eruption of Vesuvius in 79. The avalanche of mud that covered Herculaneum to a depth of 40 ft hardened and made excavation, which is still continuing, extremely difficult. The layout of the town, perched on a promontory above the shoreline, was typically Roman and regular. The houses are similar to those at Pompeii, but with a greater variety. The patrician villas, with loggias and verandas facing the sea, reveal a high degree of sophistication.

▶ The entrance to the **excavations** (A3, *9 a.m.-2:45 and 6:20 p.m.; closed Mon*) allows a view of the entire site. The ruins include mosaics, paintings, statues and decorated rooms. ▶ The most important features are: in Cardo (street running N-S) IV, the **House of the Mosaic Atrium★** (C2); the **House of the Wooden Partition★** (C2); the **Samnite House★** (C2), of pre-Roman type; the **baths★★** (B-C1-2); the **House of Neptune and Amphitrite★** (B2) with, next to it, the best-preserved shop in the town; the **House of the Bicentenary★★** (B2). In Cardo V, the **Palaestra★★** (B3) with a magnificent bronze fountain;

the **House of the Deer★★** (D2) one of the most lavish and sumptuous, with two marble groups of deer being attacked by dogs★ in the *triclinium* (dining room) and a statue of the drunken Hercules★; the **House of the Relief of Telephus★** (D3); the **House of the Gem★** (D3) and the **Terme Suburbane★★** (D3). ☐

Practical information _____

Restaurant:
♦♦ *Piadina*, v. Cozzolino 10, ☎ 7717141, closed Tue. Mixed regional cuisine: grilled bream, sea bass or mixed meats, 20/25,000.

Recommended
Cycling: *G. S. Pedale Ercolanese*, contrada Patacca 60, ☎ 7713425.

The island of ISCHIA

A3

Archaeology has confirmed the traditional date of Greek colonization of Ischia (*Pithecusa* to the Greeks) as 775 BC, the earliest colonization in Italy. The coastline is jagged, the soil fertile and the climate gentle. Ischia is the largest island in the Bay of Naples. It is volcanic, as is evident from the fumaroles and numerous thermal springs. The description follows the road that runs round the island.

▶ **Ischia** (A3), the principal centre on the island at the NE extremity, is made up of **Ischia Porto** and Ischia Ponte. In the former, the inner basin of the harbour is a volcanic crater which was joined to the sea by a canal in 1854. ▶ The lively v. Roma, with cafés, restaurants and shops, and its continuation, the corso V. Colonna, lead to the fishing village of **Ischia Ponte**. The Ponte Aragonese (1438) leads to the small castle island *(Mar-Oct; elevator)* with the ruins of the cathedral (14C frescos in the crypt); the 18C church of the Immacolata; a convent with interesting cemetery and the 16C hexagonal church of S. Pietro a Pantaniello. On the summit is the **castle** *(not open to public)*, parts of which are old and parts rebuilt. ▶ 1.5 km

ERCOLANO

0 10 20 30 40 m

1:2000 (1cm = 20 m)

© SERVIZIO CARTOGRAFICO DEL TOURING CLUB ITALIANO, MILANO

along the road is a fine view from the **Belvedere di Carta-romana** (A3). ▶ On the N coast is **Casamicciola Terme** (A2) with a spa fed by the waters of the Gurgitello and the Rita. ▶ In the piazza of **Lacco Ameno** (A1), famous for its radioactive mineral **springs**, is the sanctuary of **S. Restituita** which consists of two churches. The smaller was built in the 11C over an early Christian basilica of which remains have been found under the church; there is a

museum with Bronze age and Byzantine finds and Greek ceramic kilns and workshops (7C-2C BC) under the church-yard. 1.5 km W is the **Lido di San Montano**. ▶ The town of **Forio** (A1) offers a magnificent **view★** of the esplanade of Madonna del Soccorso: the church of **S. Maria di Loreto** (14C, redesigned in Baroque style) has lavish polychrome marble decoration; the **Torrione**, a 15C cylindrical tower, was part of the defensive system against pirates; there are numerous mineral **springs** and fine **beaches** (S. Francesco and Citara). ▶ **Sant'Angelo** (B2) is a charming fishing village with terraces of multicoloured houses *(closed to motor vehicles)* joined to the promontory by an isthmus; the radioactive mineral **springs** rise near **Maronti beach** (B2). ▶ **Monte Epomeo** (2,585 ft), the highest point on the island, can be climbed *(1 hr)* from **Fontana** (B2). ▶ **Barono d'Ischia** is an agricultural town above a valley of vineyards. □

Practical information ───────────

🚢 passenger and car ferries several times a day to Ischia Porto, often stopping at Prócida; from Naples (Molo Beverello, *c.* 1 hr 20 mn) and from Pozzuoli (*c.* 1 hr); several crossings per week in summer from Capri, Sorrento and Castellammare di Stàbia, information, *Caremar,* ☎ 081/991781 and *Libera Navigazione Lauro,* ☎ 081/991889 (departures from Naples and Pozzuoli); *Navigazione Libera del Golfo,* ☎ 081/320763 (departures from Capri, Castellammare di Stàbia and Sorrento); *Navigazione Basso Lazio,* ☎ 0771/267090 (departures from Pozzuoli, also for Casamicciola); *GRU.SO.N.,* ☎ 081/8781143 (departures from Sorrento). Several hydrofoil departures a day from Naples (Mergellina and Molo Beverello) to Ischia Porto (*c.* 40 mn); daily crossings from Anzio, Ponza, Ventotiene (→ Lazio), information, *Caremar,* (departures from Naples); *Alilauro,* ☎ 081/991888; *SNAV,* ☎ 081/660444 (departures from Naples and Anzio).

BARANO D'ISCHIA, ⊠ 80070, ☎ 081.
≋ at Lido dei Maronti.
♨ (May-Oct), spa facilities attached to hotels.

Hotels:
★★★ *St. Raphael Terme,* at Tescaccio, ☎ 990922, 27 rm ≼ 🏧 ☐ closed 1 Nov-14 Mar, 65,000; bkf: 9,000.
★★★ *Villa San Giorgio,* at Lido dei Maronti, v. Maronti 42, ☎ 990098, 34 rm 🅿 ≼ 🏧 ☐ closed Nov-Mar, 95,000; bkf: 8,000.
⚓ *Mirage,* at Lido dei Maronti, v. Maronti 19, 76 pl, ☎ 990551 (all year).

CASAMICCIOLA TERME, ⊠ 80074, ☎ 081.
≋
♨ (Apr-Oct), *Terme Belliazzi,* ☎ 994580 and spa facilities attached to hotels.
ℹ *Viaggi AVET,* p. Marina 24, ☎ 994441.

Hotels:
★★★★ *Cristallo Palace & Terme,* v. Eddomade 1, ☎ 994377, 77 rm 🅿 ≼ 🏧 ☐ closed Nov-Mar, 71,000.
★★★★ *Terme Manzi,* p. Bagni 4, ☎ 994722, 62 rm 🅿 🏧 ☐ ✏ closed 11 Oct-9 Apr, 100,000; bkf: 12,000.
★★★ *Approdo,* v. Eddomade 19, ☎ 994077, 33 rm 🅿 ≼ ✏ ☐ closed 16 Oct-31 Mar, 82,000.
★★★ *Elma,* corso Vittorio Emanuele, ☎ 994122, 68 rm 🅿 ≼ 🏧 ✏ Pens. Closed Nov-Easter, 115,000.

FORIO, ⊠ 80075, ☎ 081.
≋
♨ (Apr-Oct), *Terme Poseidon,* ☎ 997122 and spa facilities attached to hotels.

Hotels:
★★★ *Parco Maria,* at Cuotto, v. per Citara 212, ☎ 907322, 68 rm ≼ 🏧 ☐ closed 26 Nov-28 Feb except Christmas, 62,000; bkf: 10,000.
★★★ *Parco Regine,* v. per Citara 2, ☎ 907366, 50 rm 🅿 🏧 ≼ 65,000.
★★★ *Splendid,* v. Statale 270 30, ☎ 987374, 40 rm 🅿 🏧 ≼ ☐ closed Nov-Mar, 61,000; bkf: 7,000.

Restaurant:
◆◆◆ *Romantica,* v. Marina 46, ☎ 997345, closed Wed. Typical Ischia restaurant. Mixed regional cuisine, 30/40,000.

Looking for a locality? Consult the index at the back of the book.

Recommended
Events: *Ischia Jazz* (Sep).

ISCHIA, ⊠ 80077, ☎ 081.
≋
♨ *Terme Comunali,* ☎ 981025 (all year); spa facilities attached to hotels.
ℹ at the harbour (p. Trieste), ☎ 991146.

Hotels:
★★★★★ *Excelsior,* at Ischia Porto, v. Gianturco 19, ☎ 991522, 72 rm 🅿 ≼ 🏧 ☐ Pens. Closed 6 Oct-24 Apr. Former private villa in an ancient park, 230,000.
★★★★ *Alexander,* at Ischia Porto, lungomare Colombo 3, ☎ 993597, 91 rm 🅿 🏧 ✐ ☐ closed 26 Oct-4 Apr, 107,000; bkf: 12,000.
★★★★ *Continental Terme,* at Ischia Porto, v. M. Mazzella 74, ☎ 991588, 218 rm 🅿 🏧 ☐ ✏ closed 1 Nov-9 Apr, 148,000.
★★★★ *G. H. Punta Molino Terme,* at Ischia Porto, lungomare Colombo, ☎ 991544, 88 rm 🅿 ≼ 🏧 ☐ closed 2 Nov-9 Apr, 205,000; bkf: 20,000.
★★★★ *Hermitage e Park Terme,* at Ischia Porto, v. L. Mazzella 67, ☎ 992395, 98 rm 🅿 ≼ 🏧 ✐ ☐ ✏ Pens. Closed 1 Nov-19 Mar, 107,000.
★★★★ *Jolly delle Terme,* at Ischia Porto, v. De Luca 42, ☎ 991744, 208 rm 🅿 ≼ 🏧 ☐ closed Nov-Feb, 225,000.
★★★★ *Mare Blu,* at Ischia Ponte, v. Pontano 40, ☎ 982555, 40 rm 🏧 ✐ ☐ closed 26 Oct-14 Apr, 126,000.
★★★ *Bellevue,* at Ischia Porto, v. Morgioni 83, ☎ 991851, 37 rm 🏧 ☐ closed 1 Nov-14 Mar, 60,000; bkf: 10,000.
★★★ *Central Park,* at Ischia Porto, v. De Luca 6, ☎ 993517, 44 rm 🅿 🏧 ♿ ☐ ✏ closed Nov-Mar, 75,000; bkf: 10,000.
★★★ *Flora,* at Ischia Porto, v. De Luca 95, ☎ 991502, 68 rm 🅿 ≼ ☐ closed 1 Nov-14 Mar, 57,500.
★★★ *Nuovo Lido,* at Ischia Porto, v. Gianturco 33, ☎ 991550, 39 rm 🅿 🏧 ☐ closed Nov-Mar, 72,000; bkf: 9,000.
★★ *Villa Diana,* at Ischia Porto, v. Colonna 212, ☎ 991795, 25 rm ✐ closed Nov-Mar, 60,000.

Restaurants:
◆◆◆ *Damiani,* at Ischia Porto, v. Nuova Circonvallazione, ☎ 983032, closed Mon-Fri noon, Oct-Mar. Regional cuisine: taglierini al limone, baked white bream, 30/60,000.
◆◆◆ *Gennaro,* at Ischia Porto, v. Porto 66, ☎ 992917, closed Tue and 1 Nov-14 Mar. Regional cuisine: rigatoni 2000, Ischia white wines, 25/55,000.
◆◆◆ *Giardino Eden,* at Ischia Ponte, v. Nuova Cartoromana 50, ☎ 993909, closed Oct-Apr. By the sea with garden-terrace, thermal baths, pier solarium. Mixed cuisine: seafood, homemade gnocchi, 35/60,000.

⚓ *Isola d'Ischia,* at Ischia Porto, v. Foschini, 100 pl, ☎ 991449.

Recommended
Marina: ☎ 991417.
Tennis: lungomare Colombo, ☎ 993486; v. Spinavola, ☎ 987547; corso Colonna, ☎ 982289.

LACCO AMENO, ⊠ 80076, ☎ 081.
≋
♨ (Apr-Oct), spa facilities attached to hotels.

Hotels:
★★★★★ *Regina Isabella e Royal Sporting,* p. S. Restituta, ☎ 994322, 134 rm 🅿 🏧 ☐ ✏ closed Nov-Mar. Complex of buildings framed by rocks, 276,000; bkf: 22,000.
★★★★ *Parco Michelangelo Terme,* v. Provinciale Fango, ☎ 995134, 70 rm 🅿 ≼ 🏧 closed Nov-Mar, 148,000.
★★★★ *Terme La Reginella,* p. S. Restituta, ☎ 994300, 50 rm 🅿 🏧 ♿ ☐ ✏ Pens. Closed 26 Oct-9 Mar, 175,000.
★★★★ *Terme San Montano,* at Monte Vico, ☎ 994033, 65 rm 🅿 ≼ ≼ 🏧 ✏ closed 21 Oct-9 Apr, 170,000; bkf: 19,000.
★★★ *Villa Svizzera,* v. Lungomare, ☎ 994263, 20 rm 🅿 🏧 ☐ closed 26 Oct-24 Apr, 78,000; bkf: 9,000.

Recommended
Events: *Premio Rizzoli di Cinematografia* (film award, Jun).
Marina: ☎ 991417.

SANT'ANGELO, ✉ 80070, ☎ 081.

≋ (Mar-Oct), *Termi Apollon*, ☎ 999272; *Terme Linda*, ☎ 999202 and spa facilities attached to hotels.

Hotels:
★★★ *Miramare*, v. Com. Maddalena 67, ☎ 999219, 68 rm ℗ ≼ ⛰ ▱ ⏚ closed 1 Nov-14 Mar, 96,000; bkf: 10,000.
★★★ *Palma*, v. Com. Maddalena 15, ☎ 999215, 51 rm ℗ ≼ ⛰ ⁓ ▱ Pens. Closed 1 Nov-14 Mar, 85,000.
★★★ *San Michele*, v. S. Angelo, ☎ 999276, 62 rm ≼ ⛰ ⛰ ▱ closed 1 Nov-19 Mar, 100,000; bkf: 11,000.

Restaurant:
♦♦ *Pescatore*, p. O. Troia, ☎ 999206, closed 20 Dec-28 Feb. Lively trattoria, family-run, in piazzetta in summer. Regional cuisine: fried and grilled fish, eggplant alla parmigiana, 25/45,000.

MATERDOMINI

Avellino 58, Naples 114, Rome 303 km
Pop. 633 ✉ 83040 ☎ 0827   D3

Materdomini sits among oak woods on a ridge at the head of the Sele Valley. It is a pilgrimage site.

▶ The sanctuary of **S. Gerardo Maiella** or S. Maria Materdómini, destroyed by earthquake, took over the monastery of the Redemptorists where St. Gerard Majella (a patron of women in childbirth) died (1755). Adjacent is the modern **church** (1976). ▶ 6 km downhill above **Caposele** are collection and pumping equipment for the **Apulian aqueduct** that carried the waters of the River Sele, which flows into the Tyrrhenian sea, to the Adriatic side of the peninsula. □

Il MATESE

From motorway service station at Caianello to Capua
(152 km, 1 day; map 4)

The Matese is a massif extending from Campania to Molise, bounded on the Campanian side by the higher reaches of the Volturno and its tributary the Calore; its highest peak is Mt. Miletto (6,726 ft). The countryside is varied, with rolling plains and gentle slopes. On the Campanian side are 7,500 acres of forest, principally beech, and meadows covered with wildflowers. The last bears were killed a century ago, but there are still wolves, foxes, weasels, badgers and squirrels; eagles nest on the rocky cliffs of the higher summits. There are other birds of prey, as well as lapwing, coots and other waterfowl by the rivers. This itinerary explores the Campanian side (→ Molise).

▶ The departure point is the **Caianello** service station on the Rome-Naples motorway. ▶ Beyond **Vairano Scalo** and **Vairano Patenora** a brief detour to the r. reaches the ruined **Abbazia della Ferrara**, founded by Cistercians in the 12C; the chapel in the pilgrimage church has a fresco showing Byzantine influence. ▶ After crossing the Volturno and passing through **Alife** (→) the route reaches **Piedimonte Matese**, which has interesting buildings: the church of S. Tommaso with Gothic portal; the small church of S. Biagio with mid-15C frescos; the Santuario della Annunciata with stucco, gilded altars and 17C-18C paintings; the 18C basilica of S. Maria Maggiore and the Palazzo Ducale. ▶ This is the beginning of the mountain section which passes through **San Gregorio Matese** and the **Passo di Miralago** (3,615 ft); a short detour leads to **Lake Matese**, the **Sella del Perrone** and the **Bocca della Selva** (4,570 ft) below Mt. Mutria (ski lifts). ▶ Of the towns and villages encountered on the descent to the Calore Valley — **Pietraroia**, **Cusano Mutri** and **Cerreto Sannita** — the last is notable for its regular 17C layout and Baroque buildings full of character. ▶ **Guardia Sanframondi** lies below the remains of an ancient castle; the **museum** by the Santuario della Assunta *(ask at Casa dei Filippini)* displays reliquaries, silver, paintings, sculpture and polychrome papier-mâché statues. ▶ **Telese**, in a circle of wooded hills, is a thermal spa; 2 km W are the remains of *Telesia*, originally Samnite, later a Roman colony; remains of walls, circus, theatre and spa facilities have survived from the Roman period. ▶ The route crosses the Volturno and climbs to **Caiazzo**, a small town

4. Il Matese

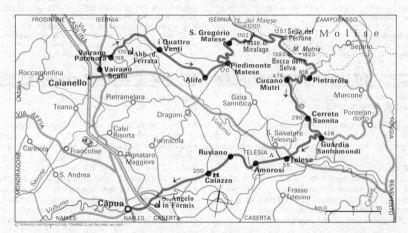

with rococo façades in the main street. ▶ The tour ends in **Capua** (→), reached by way of the basilica of **S. Angelo in Formis★★** (→ Capua). ☐

Practical information _____

BOCCA DELLA SELVA, ⊠ 82033, ☎ 0823.
⌇ ski lifts.
ⓘ at Matese, ☎ 911845.
CERRETO SANNITA, ⊠ 82032, ☎ 0824.

Recommended
Craft workshops: *Barbieri*, at San Lorenzello, v. P. Fusco 6, ☎ 861337 (ceramics).
GUARDI SANFRAMONDI, ⊠ 82034, ☎ 0824.

Recommended
Craft workshops: *Morelli*, at Pontelandolfo, v. S. Rocco, ☎ 851302 (weaving of blankets and carpets).
TELESE, ⊠ 82037, ☎ 0824.
♨ (mid-Jun-mid-Oct), ☎ 976016.

Hotel:
★★★★ *G. H. Telese-Minieri*, ☎ 940500, 76 rm ℗ ▥ ₺ ☞ ✆ closed 15 Dec-15 Jan. 19C building near spa, 55,600. Rest. ♦♦♦ *Terrazza* closed Tue and Nov. Italian and international cuisine: pancakes del Grand Hotel, beef Wellington, 25/45,000.

Recommended
Bowling: v. Cerretto 108, ☎ 976353.
Horseback riding: *Assocazione Torello*, at Melizzano *(13 km SW)*, ☎ 970826 (associate of *ANTE*).

MERCOGLIANO

Avellino 7, Naples 53, Rome 242 km
Pop. 7,190 ⊠ 83013 ☎ 0825   C2

Near Mercogliano on the old road to Avellino is the **Palazzo Abbaziale di Loreto**, octagonal in plan (1749). This was the winter quarters of the monks of the Santuario di Montevérgine (→). In the **pharmacy** are more than 300 majolica vases; the archives contain documents on the history of the region. ☐

Practical information _____

Hotel:
★★★ *Mercurio*, v. S. Modestino 42, ☎ 647149, 58 rm ℗ ⅍ ✍ ⤴ 45,000.

Restaurant:
♦♦ *Girarrosto*, v. S. Modestino 44, ☎ 647049, closed Tue except summer. Spacious with good views. Regional cuisine: various fish dishes, grilled meat, 18/40,000.

Recommended
Excursions: to Montevergine by funicular (7 mn).
Swimming: v. Romiro Marcone, ☎ 647653.

MONDRAGONE

Caserta 44, Naples 55, Rome 178 km
Pop. 21,473 ⊠ 81034 ☎ 0823   A2

A little to the N of Mondragone near ancient *Sinuessa*, the Roman via Appia left the Tyrrhenian coast and swung towards Apulia. Traces of the **Roman town** can be seen (wall, aqueduct), some on the sea bed and best seen through the clear waters in the early morning. The waters in the nearby spa of **Le Vagnole** are the *Aquae Sinuessanae*, well known to the Romans. On Mt. Petrino are remains of a Norman **castle**. There is a wonderful view from the summit of the **Màssico** (2,667 ft; *4 hr on foot*). ☐

Practical information _____

♨ (Jun-Sep), ☎ 772131.
⚐ *Splendid Park*, at Le Vagnole, v. Domiziana, at the 14.4-km marker, 36 pl, ☎ 772048.

MONTESARCHIO

Benevento 18, Naples 48, Rome 223 km
Pop. 11,366 ⊠ 82016 ☎ 0824   C2

The centre of Montesarchio lies at the foot of a hill on which is a 15C **castle** with towers in which many were imprisoned during the Risorgimento. The plain is the Valle Caudina. **Arpaia** is 8.5 km SW. A road with fine views *(13.5 km)* runs through pine and fir woods and it is possible to reach the summit of **Mt. Taburno** (4,573 ft; *1 hr on foot*), covered by dense forest. ☐

Practical information _____

Hotel:
★★★★ *Cristina Park Hotel*, v. Benevento 102, ☎ 835888, 16 rm ℗ ▥ ☞ 51,500; bkf: 4,000.

Restaurant:
♦♦ *Dante's Tavern*, p. Poerio 83/86, closed Wed and Aug. Rural and comfortable. Mixed cuisine: sea bass with red pepper, rib of beef with pimento purée, 25/45,000.

MONTEVERGINE SANCTUARY

Avellino 19, Naples 53, Rome 242 km
⊠ 83010 ☎ 0825   C2

This celebrated pilgrimage church rests on a rocky spur at the head of a ravine. It was founded *c.* 1118 and still attracts large numbers of pilgrims.

▶ Most of the buildings of the Benedictine **sanctuary** date from the 17C, but they include a modern basilica (1961); there is a **view★** of the Avellino Valley from the piazzale. ▶ The painting of the *Madonna di Montevérgine* is above the throne of the Madonna with marbles, bas-reliefs and bronze and silver statues in the sanctuary of the modern basilica. ▶ This leads to the **old church**, originally Gothic, rebuilt in the Baroque style in the 17C; it has a late 13C mosaic *baldacchino* (altar canopy). ▶ Major exhibits in the **Museo dell'Abbazia** *(9 a.m.-12 noon and 4-6 p.m.)* are the abbot's throne★ (13C) and the *Madonna di S. Guglielmo★* (12C). ▶ In the **monastery** *(women not admitted; students only)*, the visit includes the 18C chapterhouse, night chapel (1632), refectory (18C) and meteorological observatory. ▶ There is also a permanent exhibition of **crèches** from all over the world and an exhibition of **historical and artistic memorabilia** from the sanctuary. ▶ There is a famous view★ of the Gulf of Naples from the summit of Montevergine. ☐

NAPLES**

Rome 217, Milan 782 km
Pop. 1,208,545 ⊠ 80100 ☎ 081   B3

Naples, magnificently sited, enjoys blue skies, clear air and Vesuvius as a backdrop. The volcano is responsible for the high quality of the local farmland. Its population density is 6,723 inhabitants per sq mile (the next highest, Milan, has only 3,740 inhabitants/sq mile). Naples has been a regional capital since the 12C. Neapolitans are reputed to have the qualities of theatricality, irony, festivity and discontent. This may explain why Naples has produced many of Italy's great thinkers and philosophers. The city is lively and colourful, with magnificent museums, the San Carlo opera house, countless churches and corners full of character hidden away on the sea-front, around the harbour and in the heart of the city.

▶ The name comes from the Greek: *Neapolis* (new town), which presupposes (although there is no agreement about this point) the existence of an old town, called *Parthenope*, possibly a 9C BC settlement on the slopes of Pizzofalcone (E-F3-4). ▶ The subsequent *Neapolis*, Greek and later Roman, developed on three levels (C4-5, largely around the present Duomo) and two of the three *decumani* (main streets) parallel to the sea followed the line of the present v. Tribunali and v. di S. Biagio dei Librai (or Spaccanapoli). ▶ The city expanded: in the Norman period the Castel dell'Ovo (F4) was built as the palace of Roger II, and under the Angevins (13C) the Castel Nuovo (E4) by the harbour was constructed. ▶ The Bourbon viceroy Pedro di Toledo (1532-53) extended the walls to include the fortress of S. Elmo (D3) and increased the urban area by about one-third, building in Montecalvazio W of the v. Toledo (D-E4). ▶ The return of the Bourbons (1815) was celebrated by the opening of the Foro Ferdinandeo (p. Plebiscito, E4). ▶ After the cholera epidemic of 1884, the most crowded and dilapidated urban districts were demolished, and the straight line of the Rettifilo, or corso Umberto I (C5), was drawn. ▶ Modern expansion, restricted by the site, has profoundly changed the face of the city; the maritime suburb of S. Lucia (E4) has become the cosmopolitan area containing the luxury hotels; the Carità district (D4) is an administrative and commercial area; the Vómero (D2), traditional home of the middle class, is now a city within a city; densely packed districts extend W on the Posillipo hill, Fuorigrotta and Bagnoli and to the E in Capodichino, Poggioreale and Barra.

▶ **From the harbour to the Museo Nazionale.** ▶ The **harbour** is one of the most important in the Mediterranean; the **Stazione Marittima** (E5) is on the Angevin breakwater; to the N are the rococo church of the **Immacolatella** (18C) and quays for ferries to Sicily and Sardinia (D5); to the S is the **Beverello quay** (E4), departure point for boats to islands in the Bay. ▶ At the far end of the p. Municipio, the 19C **Palazzo del Municipio** incorporates the 16C church of **S. Giacomo degli Spagnoli** (tomb of Pedro di Toledo). ▶ The **Castel Nuovo**★★ (E4), or Maschio Angioino because of its Angevin origins (1279-82), was rebuilt by Alfonso I of Aragon (15C) with Catalan and Tuscan artisans. It is trapezoid in plan with cylindrical towers. The entrance, between two towers, is the **Arco di Trionfo**★, a 15C work by several sculptors. The finest of the reliefs is the **Triumph of Alfonso I**★. Inside the 14C **Cappella Palatina** is the only surviving section of the Angevin palace, with a Madonna (1474) over the Renaissance portal, and the **Sala dei Baroni** *(sometimes closed, permission from municipio, Segretaria del Sindaco)*. ▶ In the **p. del Plebiscito** (E4) the elliptical curves of the colonnades meet at the Neoclassical church of **S. Francesco di Paola** with a large dome (1817-46); the equestrian statue of Charles III is by Canova; the other represents Ferdinand I. ▶ The **Palazzo Reale**★ (B4), which faces the church, was built in 1600-2, renovated and extended in 1743-8 and subsequently reorganized and rebuilt. The visit *(9 a.m.-1.30 p.m.; Sun and hols 9 a.m.-1 p.m.; closed Mon)* includes the courtyard, the grand staircase (in hall at its foot is a bronze **door**★ from Castel Nuovo by the Parisian sculptor Guillaume le Moine, 1468), the **Appartamento Storico**, with rooms containing 18C-19C furniture, tapestries, porcelain, objets d'art, paintings and frescos of the 17C-18C Neapolitan school and the **Teatro di Corte** (1768). ▶ The **Teatro S. Carlo** (E4, *9 a.m.-12 noon*) dates from 1737, but was rebuilt in Neoclassical style in the 19C. ▶ Opposite is the entry to the **Galleria Umberto** (E4); (late 19C), a popular meeting-place. ▶ The **via Toledo** (E-C4), main artery of old Naples and a favourite place for strollers, climbs from the p. Trieste e Trento (E4) to the Museo Archeologico Nazionale, passing the churches of **S. Nicola alla Carità**, 17C, with paintings by 18C masters, and **Spirito Santo** (C4), rebuilt in the 18C (various

works of art inside). ▶ The **Pinacoteca dell'Accademia di Belle Arti** (C4, v. Bellini 36; *closed for reorganization*) contains works principally by 19C southern Italian artists. ▶ The **Museo Archeologico Nazionale**★★ (C4; *9 a.m.-2 p.m.; Sun and hols 9 a.m.-1 p.m.; closed Mon; some sections closed for reorganization*) is one of the most important in the world. It was established by Charles III to house the Farnese collection inherited from his mother as well as artifacts from Pompeii and Herculaneum in a late 16C building that had been a cavalry barracks and was later occupied by the university. Roman replicas of Greek sculpture from towns buried by the eruption of Vesuvius were one of the great sources of knowledge about Greek art before the discovery of the rare originals. The mosaics, paintings (the best of the painting from Pompeii is here) and minor collections complete a marvelous picture of classical antiquity. The number of works, arranged in more than one hundred rooms, is vast. On the ground floor, **marble sculptures** include: the *Tyrannicides*, a 5C BC funerary stele★; an *Athena* of the school of Phidias; *Eurydice and Hermes*★★, Augustan replica of the original of the school of Phidias; the *Aphrodite of the Gardens*★; the best replica of the famous *Doryphorus*★★ by Polycleitus; *Diomedes* from Cumae★; the *Palestrita*★; the *Venus Callipyge*★ from a Hellenistic original; a bronze statue of *Hercules*; the *Farnese Hercules*★; the torsos of *Ares*★ and *Aphrodite*★; *Psyche*★ from Capua; *Venus* from Capua★; the *Farnese bull*★★, the largest group of sculpture to have survived from antiquity; *Diana of Ephesus*★; the *Seated Matron*★ considered to be Agrippina; bust of *Caracalla*★; bronze horse's head, perhaps 3C BC; *Fondi Augustus*★; portait of *Homer*★ and the *Herm of Euripides*★. **Paintings and mosaics**★ in the mezzanine include the *Battle of Issus*★, a mosaic based on an Alexandrian painting of unique historical and artistic value; other mosaics★ from Pompeii include *Consulting the Sorceress*★, *Plato and Pupils in the Garden of the Academy*★; portrait of a *woman*★; *Cat Catching a Quail*★ and the statue of a *Dancing Faun*★, also from Pompeii. On the first floor are the *Farnese Atlas*★, a Hellenistic sculpture; a room with works of art and objects found in the 18C in the **Villa dei Papiri**★ in Herculaneum; the sculptures of the original of the school of *Sleeping Satyr*★, *Drunken Silenus*★ and *Hermes Resting*★ and the portrait said to be of Seneca★. The **painting collection**★ includes wall painting from Pompeii, Herculaneum and Stabia (including the *Funeral Dance*★ from Ruvo; *knuckle-bone players*★, neo-Attic in style; *Pasquius Proculus and His Wife*); the **collection of objects** includes: two gladiators' helmets★, a blue glass vase★, a table service of 115 pieces from the house of Menander in Pompeii and the *Tazza Farnese*★★, a cup made of veined sardonyx; **small bronzes**★ of interest for the history of costume and private life in ancient times, still lifes and paintings of gardens★. ▶ The **technology section**★ is being reorganized. The **collections of vases**★ from Campania and Apulia and Etruscan and Attic vases are on the second floor *(open to students on request)*.

▶ **Old Naples.** The oldest part of the city lies E of the v. Toledo, extending as far as the Porta Capuana (B5). It is full of important churches and patrician palazzi (the expansion of the city by the viceroy Pedro di Toledo also had the political objective of encouraging the unreliable nobility of the kingdom to live in the capital by making room for their residences in the old centre). ▶ In the v. Medina e Monteoliveto are the **chiesa dell'Incoronata** (D4) with 14C-15C frescos in its two Gothic aisles; the church of **S. Maria la Nova** (D4), 16C with two Renaissance cloisters in the former monastery and the **Palazzo Gravina**★ (D4), in the Tuscan Renaissance style. ▶ The nearby church of **S. Anna dei Lombardi**★ (D4; *generally closed p.m.*) is practically a museum of Renaissance sculpture. Works include a marble **altarpiece** (1489); a terra-cotta *Pietà* (1492); *Nativity*★ (1475); the **Tomb of Mary of Aragon**★; frescos by Giorgio Vasari and inlaid stalls★ in the old sacristy. ▶ **Spaccanapoli** (v. B. Croce and v. S. Biagio dei Librai) follows the line of an old street and contains some famous churches and ancient palazzi, including the **Palazzo Filomarino**, where the his-

torian Benedetto Croce (1866-1952) lived and died. ▶ The interior of **Il Gesù Nuovo** (C4), with lavish coloured marble, is an example of Neapolitan Baroque. ▶ **S. Chiara★** (C4), restored to its original Provençale-Gothic appearance (1310-28), is one of the major monuments of medieval Naples; in the bright interior are the **tomb of Mary of Valois★** (1333-8) and remains of the monument to **Robert I of Anjou** (1343-5). ▶ Adjacent are the **Convento dei Minori**, with fine portal★ leading to the choir, and the **Chiostro delle Clarisse★** *(8:30 a.m.-12:30 p.m. and 4-6:30 p.m.)* with a rustic garden designed in 1742: the perimeter walls, benches and pillars are covered with majolica tiles representing landscapes. ▶ St. Thomas Aquinas taught and Pontano and Giordano Bruno studied in the monastery attached to the church of **S. Domenico Maggiore★** (C4); there are frescos dating from *c.* 1308 inside the church (originally 14C); the 13C *Crucifixion★* which is said to have spoken to St. Thomas Aquinas and a *Descent from the Cross* are in the Cappellone del Crocifisso. ▶ The neighbouring **Cappella Sansevera** *(entrance at v. De Sanctis 19; 10:30 a.m.-5 p.m.; Sun and hols 10:30 a.m.-1:30 p.m.; closed Mon)*, with 18C coloured marble decoration, is famous for the virtuosity of the statues of *Disillusion, Modesty* and *Veiled Christ★* (1735). ▶ **S. Angelo a Nilo** (C4), in a piazzetta with an ancient statue representing the river, contains the **tomb of Cardinal Rinaldo Brancaccio★** by Donatello, Michelozzo and Pagno di Lapo Portigiani (1426-8). ▶ Another interesting street is the **via Tribunali**, also a former *decumanus.* ▶ **S. Pietro a Maiella** (C4) is a 14C Gothic church; there are fine paintings in the austere interior. ▶ The humanist Giovano Pontano commissioned the elegant **Cappella Pontano,** with numerous Latin inscriptions both outside and inside, in 1492. ▶ **S. Paolo Maggiore** (C5; 1583-1603) is at the top of a flight of steps in the piazzetta S. Gaetano, the site of the Graeco-Roman forum; the interior is rich in marble inlay and frescos *(visits a.m., apply to priests).* ▶ The author, Giovanni Boccaccio (1313-1375), employed in Naples by a branch of a Florentine business, saw the girl he immortalized as Fiammetta in the church of **S. Lorenzo Maggiore★★** (C5), a notable example of 14C architecture; the apse is the work of French Provenal Gothic masters. The interior houses a 14C *Crucifixion* panel and the Gothic tomb of **Catherine of Austria★**; the 18C cloister leads to Greek, Roman and medieval **excavations** *(in course of arrangement).* ▶ The interior of the **chiesa dei Girolamini** (16C-17C) is an interesting example of Baroque decoration, although damaged; there is a small **picture gallery** *(9 a.m.-12 noon and 4-8 p.m.; temporarily under restoration).* ▶ The 17C **chiesa del Monte della Misericordia** contains sculptures and paintings; the **pinacoteca,** with paintings of the Neapolitan school of the Pio Monte di Misericordia, is closed for restoration. ▶ The **via del Duomo** follows a *cardo* of the Graeco-Roman city. ▶ The Renaissance **Palazzo Duomo★** (C5; 1560-90) houses the **Museo Civico Filangieri** *(9 a.m.-2 p.m.; Sun and hols 9 a.m.-1 p.m.; closed Mon),* with a fine collection of Neapolitan paintings, Italian and Spanish weapons (16C-18C), European and oriental porcelain and ceramics and 16C embroidery. ▶ **S. Giorgio Maggiore** (C5), rebuilt in the 17C, has retained the apse of the original 4C-5C early Christian building by the entrance. ▶ The **Duomo★★** (C5), despite alterations, has maintained its Gothic 13C interior, with pointed arches and piers incorporating 110 antique columns. The third chapel in the r. aisle is the **Cappella di S. Gennaro** *(8 a.m.-12 noon)* 17C, with bronze grille, frescos, silver altar-frontal dating from 1695, statue of St. Januarius, the miraculous phials of blood and the saint's head in a 14C French reliquary. An *Assunta★* by Perugino and pupils is in the second chapel in the r.-hand transept; there are frescos from the late 13C-16C, a 13C mosaic pavement, a 14C Sienese altarpiece and two Minutolo tombs in the **Cappella Minutolo** *(if closed, ask in sacristy)* and a 14C fresco of the *Tree of Jesse* in the second chapel in the l.-hand transept. The entrance to the church of **S. Restituta★**, the first Christian basilica in Naples (4C, rebuilt after the earthquake of 1688), is in the l.-hand aisle; in the 5C **baptistery** are

remains of **mosaics★** of the same period; in the sixth chapel in the l.-hand aisle is a mosaic, *Madonna with Saints* (1322). ▶ Two churches have the title **S. Maria Donnaregina★** (B5); one is Baroque (1649) with polychrome marble and frescos *(closed for restoration);* the other, an example of Franciscan medieval Gothic, contains the **tomb of Queen Mary of Hungary★** (1326) and, in the monks' choir, **frescos★** dating from the early 14C. ▶ At the E extremity of old Naples is the **Castello Capuano★** or Vicaria (C5), Norman, extended by the Swedes, the royal palace until the 15C; the **Porta Capuana★** (B5), built in 1484, a Renaissance masterpiece and **S. Giovanni a Carbonara★** (B5), reached by a flight of 18C steps, founded in 1343, rebuilt in the early 15C, then altered and extended *(under restoration);* it has notable sculptures, such as the Miroballo monument★ (16C), the **monument to King Ladislas★** (1428) and the tomb of **Gianni Caracciolo★,** one of the lovers of Queen Joan II, who had him stabbed to death. ▶ Finally, in the Rettifilo, is the church of **S. Pietro Martire** (D5) with a portrait of **St. Vincent Ferrer★** (*c.* 1460).

▶ **Capodimonte, the Certosa di S. Martino and the Floridiana.** ▶ The **Museo e Galleria di Capodimonte★★** (A4; *9 a.m.-2 p.m.; Sun and hols 9 a.m.-1 p.m.; closed Mon)* is in the 18C royal palace of Capodimonte. The **Galleria Nazionale** collection is built around paintings and *objets d'art* owned by the Farnese Dukes of Parma and is one of the most important collections of paintings in Italy. A brief list of selected masterpieces will give an impression of its scope: *St. Louis of Toulouse Crowning Robert of Anjou King of Naples★★* by Simone Martini; *Crucifixion★★* by Masaccio; *Transfiguration★★* by Giovanni Bellini; *La Zingarella★★* by Correggio; *Paul III with Nephews Ottavio and Alessandro Farnese★★* by Titian; *The Blind Leading the Blind★* by Pieter Bruegel and the *Flagellation★★* and the *Seven Works of Mercy★★* by Caravaggio. Other sections include the **Galleria dell'Ottocento,** with 18C Neapolitan paintings; the **Appartamento Storico e Museo** with porcelain and majolica and the vast De Ciccio★ collection, including Pollaiolo's *David★* among the Renaissance bronzes and the **Salottino di Porcellana★★** (1757-9), a masterpiece of Capodimonte porcelain from the Portici palace. In the **park** *(9 a.m.-sunset)* is the Capodimonte porcelain factory (in production from 1743-59). ▶ The **Certosa di S. Martino★★** (D3), on a spur of the Vómero hill is the most complete expression of 17C Neapolitan Baroque. It houses the **Museo Nazionale di S. Martino★★** *(9 a.m.-2 p.m.; Sun and hols 9:30 a.m.-1 p.m.; closed Mon; some sections closed for reorganization).* The **church,** with splendid inlaid marble, is in itself a gallery of 17C Neapolitan painting *(Descent from the Cross★* by M. Stanzione, *Twelve Prophets★* by Ribera, frescos★ and *Washing of Feet★* by Caracciolo, 17C carved choir★). The rooms of the **monastery** are interesting; the *Triumph of Judith★* by Luca Giordano is in the vault of the treasury chapel. The museum includes the **Sezione Navale; Ricordi Storici del Regno di Napoli** (history of the Kingdom of Naples, with the famous *Tavola Strozzi★,* a view of 15C Naples, and the **belvedere★** with a view of the city and the Bay); the **Sezione Topografica Napoletana** (views of Naples; maps); the **Sezione Feste e Costumi;** the **Sezione Presepiale** (crèches, including the famous **Cuciniello crèche★**) and on the other side of the **Chiostro Grande★** the pinacoteca, the sculpture section, the **Sezione di Arti Minori** and monastery records. There is a splendid **view★** from the square in front. ▶ Above the Certosa is **Castel S. Elmo,** a massive star-shaped fortress, rebuilt in the 16C. ▶ Ferdinand I presented the villa (D2; 1817-9,) known as **Floridiana★** to his wife Lucia Partanna, Duchess of Floridia. The **park** *(9 a.m.-sunset)* is famous for its camellias; the Neoclassical palazzo houses the **Museo Nazionale della Ceramica Duca di Martina★** *(9 a.m.-2 p.m.; Sun and hols 9 a.m.-1 p.m.; closed Mon),* an incomparable collection of porcelain and majolica by the principal European and oriental manufacturers, with a collection of minor art such as walking sticks, snuff-boxes, keys, glass and enamels. There is a superb **view★** from the esplanade behind the palazzina.

▶ **The Riviera.** ▶ The v. N. Sauro (E-F4) is the first section of the **sea-front road**★★ which continues as far as Mergellina. The **Porto di S.** Lucia (F4) has a breakwater leading to the **Borgo Marinaro** and the **Castel dell'Ovo** (originally 12C; the present building dates from the 17C) on the site of the Villa of Lucullus. ▶ On the **Riviera di Chiaia** (E2-3), in a park, is the **Museo Principe Diego Aragona Pignatelli Cortes** (E2; *9 a.m.-2 p.m.; Sun and hols 9 a.m.-1 p.m.; closed Mon*), which has maintained the character of the original patrician residence; the garden contains the **Museo delle Carrozze** (carriages). ▶ The gardens of the **Villa Comunale**★ separate the Riviera di Chiaia from the **via Caracciolo**★ and contain the **Acquario**★ (E2; *9 a.m.-5 p.m.; Sun and hols 10 a.m.-8 p.m.*). ▶ At the end of the Riviera di Chiaia is the church of **S.** Maria di Piedigrotta (F1), dating from the 13C, with a 14C Sienese wooden Madonna; the piazza in front of it is crowded for the **festival** held every 7 September. ▶ Nearby are the **Parco Virgiliano** *(9 a.m.-sunset)* and the so-called **Tomb of Virgil** (F1; *9 a.m.-2 p.m.*), actually a Roman *columbarium.* ▶ The v. Caracciolo leads to one of the most poetic sites in Naples, the Bay of **Mergellina** (F1). ▶ **S. Maria del Parto** (set on a terrace with view from top of a flight of steps) contains the tomb of the Neapolitan humanist poet Jacopo Sannazaro and the *Diavolo di Mergellina,* a 16C painting showing St. Michael overthrowing the devil. ▶ A crossroads on the **via di Posillipo**★ is the departure point for walks in the enchanting part of the town known as **Posillipo**★, a hilly promontory that separates the Bay of Naples from that of Pozzuoli. Posillipo is central to Neapolitan song — its name comes from the Greek and means 'which soothes pain'. ▶ The via di Posillipo leads to the **Capo di Posillipo,** with a cluster of houses by the sea and a little harbour, also to the fishing village of **Marechiaro,** sheer above the sea. Finally, on the Bay of Pozzuoli side, is the **island of Nisida,** a volcanic crater linked to the mainland by a causeway. ▶ The views and glimpses of the countryside are fascinating throughout this area, but perhaps the finest Neapolitan **view**★★ is from the belvedere of the **Eremo dei Camàldoli** (1,503 ft), the highest point of the Campi Flegrei, NW of the Vómero (A1 exit; *9 a.m.-1 p.m. and 5-8 p.m.*). The view includes the Bay of Naples, the Bay of Gaeta, Vesuvius and the Lattari Mountains with the Matese in the distance. □

Practical information

ⓘ v. Partenope 10/A (F3), ☎ 418988; ☎ 761202 (head office); Stazione Centrale (C6), ☎ 268779 (information); Capodichino, v. Ruffo di Calabria, ☎ 7805761; p. Plebiscito, Palazzo Reale (E4), ☎ 419744; p. del Gesù Nuovo (C4), ☎ 323328; hydrofoil station in Mergellina (F1), ☎ 660816.
✈ *Napoli Capodichino* ☎ 7805763; city bus no. 14 (red and black) from Stazione Centrale; *Alitalia,* v. S. Giacomo 32 (D4), ☎ 325325.
🚃 (C6), ☎ 264644; *Circumvesuviana,* ☎ 7792444.
🚌 from Porta Capuana (B5), p. Garibaldi (C5-6), v. Libroia (C2), v. Marina Nuova (D5), v. Marittima (D5), v. M. Spadaro (C4), v. Pisanelli (C4), Porta Vesuviana (C6).
⚓ ferries and hydrofoils to Capri, Ischia, Prócida, Sorrento, Positano, Amalfi, information: *Caremar,* ☎ 313882; *Navigazione Libera del Golfo,* ☎ 320763; *SNAV,* ☎ 660444, *Alilauro,* ☎ 684288; *Libera Navigazione Lauro,* ☎ 313236; car ferries to Cagliari; Palermo and Tunis; Syracuse and Malta; Messina, Milazzo and the Aeolian islands; Tripoli via Catania, information: *Tirrenia Navigazione,* ☎ 7201111; *Siremar,* ☎ 312112.
Car rental: *Avis,* reservation centre, ☎ 7901174; station, ☎ 284041; airport, ☎ 7805790; *Hertz,* reservation centre, ☎ 400400; p. Garibaldi 69, ☎ 206228; airport, ☎ 7802971; *Maggiore,* v. Cervantes 92, ☎ 324308; station, ☎ 287858; airport, ☎ 7803011.

Hotels:
★★★★★ *Excelsior,* v. Partenope 48 (F4 a), ☎ 417111, 145 rm Ⓟ ≼ 345,000. Rest. ● ◆◆◆◆ *Casanova Grill* Distinguished and subtly designed. Creative cuisine:

Naples

The cult of the Nativity began in Naples c. 1000. At first, a few men disguised themselves as animals on Christmas night and walked through the church towards the altar from which came the voices of the angels and the cries of a newborn infant. It wasn't until the 13C that earthenware statues replaced the actors. The Neapolitan nativity scene is a grandiose construction, rich with vivid details. It can easily cover 250 sq ft and include as many as hundreds of characters. The figurines are carved out of clay, then painted with care and hyperrealist precision. The same is true for the clothes and accessories which became ethnographic objects. At the center of the nativity scene is a rock masso on the sides of which flow rivers. Peasants and shepherds loaded with fruit, vegetables and fowl move towards the tip of the rock where the Nativity scene itself is placed. Angels, shepherds and musicians who have come from the Abruzzi are also placed on top of the rock. Further in the distance are the Three Wise Men. Above the Holy Family, a little to the side, the whole population of Naples is represented. It moves forward, half-naked, ready for a royal feast in an immense cornucopia. This scene alone can take up to two-thirds of the Neapolitan nativity scene. There are fish, barrels of wine, tripes, onion garlands and mozzarella. All the details that symbolize the goodness of Neapolitan life are included.

Neapolitan songs

Neapolitans have fine singing voices. Neapolitan songs have always been inspired by daily life in nearby villages or ports. The rhythm is sometimes frenetic, resembling the beat of the local dances it accompanied in the past. At other times, the songs are filled with the sighs of a young lover who has lost his love or with the immigrant's nostalgia for the country he has left behind. The singer plays a mandolin or accordion, while his female companion uses the castagnettes or tambourine. Visitors to Naples are well acquainted with these ambling musicians who move from table to table in local restaurants. The visitor will recognize many of these Neapolitan songs, since they have been one of the city's main exports for decades. Every year on 7 September, fans of the bel canto flock to the city to gather on piazza de Piedigrotta for the song festival and competition.

prawns with salmon, fried fish with sea lettuce soufflé, 85/95,000.
★★★★★ *Vesuvio,* v. Partenope 45 (F4 b), ☎ 417044, 170 rm Ⓟ ≼ ⚓ 218,000.
★★★★ *Britannique,* corso Vittorio Emanuele 133 (E2 c), ☎ 660933, 86 rm Ⓟ ≼ 🕍 150,000; bkf: 11,000.
★★★★ *Jolly Ambassadors,* v. Medina 70 (D4 d), ☎ 416000, 278 rm Ⓟ ≼ 165,000.
★★★★ *Miramare,* v. Sauro 24 (E4 e), ☎ 427388, 29 rm Ⓟ ⚓ No restaurant, 135,000.
★★★★ *Paradiso,* v. Catullo 11 (F1 f), ☎ 660233, 74 rm Ⓟ ≼ 140,000.
★★★★ *Royal,* v. Partenope 38 (F3 g), ☎ 400244, 300 rm Ⓟ ≼ 🖂 190,000.
★★★★ *Santa Lucia,* v. Partenope 46 (F4 h), ☎ 416566, 130 rm Ⓟ ≼ No restaurant, 147,000.

★★★ *MotelAgip,* at Secondigliano, SS 7 at 25-km marker, ☎ 7540560, 57 rm P ⌂ 97,000.
★★★ *Palace,* p. Garibaldi 9 (C6 i), ☎ 267044, 102 rm P 85,000.
★★★ *Splendid,* v. Manzoni 96, ☎ 645462, 45 rm P ⌂ ♨ ॐ 59,000.

San Gennaro

In the Duomo in Naples the chapel of S. Gennaro is the third in the r.-hand aisle. Adorned with frescos by Domenichino, it was built in the 17C to fulfil a vow made during the plagues of 1526-9. The saint-bishop of Benevento was decapitated in Pozzuoli in 305. While the body was being taken from Pozzuoli to Naples, the blood liquified, and this phenomenon is said to be repeated twice each year, in May and September. The cult of S. Gennaro spread throughout 7C Byzantine Naples, when the protection of the martyr was invoked against the eruption of Vesuvius in 685. During a Lombard siege (831) of the city, the body of S. Gennaro, kept in the catacombs outside the walls, was taken to Benevento by the Lombards. The head remained in Naples, but the body was brought back in the late 15C. The blood is the most important relic, however, and for Neapolitans the miracle of the blood confirms ongoing protection by their saint and his approval of events. The event is still anxiously awaited and greeted with unrestrained joy. It is a demonstration of faith, as well as of a superstition that seems southern, difficult to understand, but profoundly human.

Restaurants:

● ◆◆◆◆ *Sacrestia,* v. Orazio 116 (F1 r), ☎ 664186, closed Sun in Jul, Wed and Aug. Former villa with diverting frescos, 17C ecclesiastical furnishings. Excellent regional cuisine: scazzette frà Leopoldo, gamberoni del Priore, 35/50,000.
● ◆◆◆ *Cantinella,* v. Cuma 42 (E4 e), ☎ 404884, closed Sun, Easter, Aug and Christmas. In fine position by sea. Excellent regional and Italian cuisine: risotto allo champagne, penne with vodka or salmon, 35/50,000.
● ◆◆◆ *Ciro e Santa Brigida,* v. S. Brigida 71/4 (D-E4 m), ☎ 324072, closed Sun and Aug. In the forefront of Neapolitan restaurants. Regional cuisine: penne with eggplant and mozzarella, pignatiello e vavella, 30/40,000.
● ◆◆◆ *Don Salvatore,* v. Mergellina 5 (F1 p), ☎ 681817, closed Wed. Charming rooms on site where founder used to draw up his fishing boats. Seafood: linguine Cosa Nostra, rigatoni a mammà, 30/45,000.
● ◆◆◆ *Giuseppone a Mare,* at Capo Posillipo, v. Russo 13, ☎ 7696002, closed Sun and Christmas. On seafront overlooking harbour, originally 19C tavern. Seafood: fish grilled or baked in paper, spigola puteolana, 30/50,000.
◆◆◆ *Fazenda,* v. Marechiaro 58/A, ☎ 7691297, closed Sun and 10-25 Aug. Pleasant terrace-garden with view of bay and Capri. Mixed regional cuisine: grilled fish or meat, fritto misto all'italiana, 35/50,000.
◆◆◆ *Gallo Nero,* v. Tasso 466 (E1 q), ☎ 643012, closed Sun eve, Mon, noon Tue-Fri and Aug. In 19C villa with period furniture and summer terrace. Mixed Italian cuisine: risotto with radicchio, octopus salad alla pirata, 35/45,000.
◆◆◆ *Harry's Bar,* v. Lucilio 11 (F4 h), ☎ 407810, closed Sun and Aug. Elegant, open until small hours. Mixed cuisine: salmon and caviar risotto, crayfish alla Luciana, 30/38,000.
◆◆ *Rosiello a Posillipo,* v. S. Strato 10, ☎ 7691288, closed Wed and 10-20 Aug. On estate with vineyard; with flowered terrace overlooking bay and Capri. Sea-

food: tagliolini with artichokes or broccoli, polipo al pignatiello, homemade wines, 35/45,000.
◆◆◆ *San Carlo,* v. Cesario Console 18/19 (E4 s), ☎ 417206, closed Sun and Aug. Seafood: baked fish alla termolese, grilled crayfish, 40/50,000.
◆◆◆ *Sierra,* at Posillipo, v. Virgilio 1, ☎ 7694700, closed Mon. Fine terrace and view. Regional and Italian cuisine: penne alla sangiovannara, veal with pimentos, 25/55,000.
◆◆ *Sbrescia,* at Posillipo, rampe S. Antonio, ☎ 669140, closed Mon. Fine view of bay, local character enhanced by fish tanks. Sea food: grilled crayfish, clams, 25/40,000.
◆◆ *Umberto,* v. Alabardieri 30 (E3 t), ☎ 418555, closed Wed and Aug. Traditional family-run, with band in evenings. Mixed regional cuisine: seafood risotto, involtini di vitello, 20/30,000.
◆ *Cinquantatré,* p. Dante 53 (C4 l), ☎ 341124, closed Thu, Sun eve and Sep. In popular and lively square, with food cooked in the open, relaxed Neapolitan atmosphere with dining outside in summer. Mixed regional cuisine: poached octopus, braciola al ragù, 25/40,000.
◆ *Dante e Beatrice,* p. Dante 44 (C4 n), ☎ 349905, closed Wed and 20-30 Aug. Authentic Neapolitan trattoria. Regional cuisine: zuppa di soffrito, sausages and broccoli, 18/30,000.

⚓ *Città di Napoli,* at Agnano Terme, v. Giochi Mediterraneo 75, 200 pl, ☎ 7605169 (all year).

Recommended

Amusement park: *Edenlandia,* v. Kennedy, ☎ 619711.
Archery: *Arcieria Partenopea,* v. Terracina 125, ☎ 634834; *Compagnia Arcieri Artemide,* v. Gemito, ☎ 657970.
Boat trips: from Mergellina to Castel dell'Ovo and Capo Posillipo (May-Oct), ☎ 661434.
Botanical garden: v. Foria 223 (A-B5), ☎ 449759.
Canoeing: *Circolo nautico Posillipo,* v. Posillipo 5, ☎ 7691133 (instruction).
Clay pigeon shooting: *Società Partenopea,* v. Domiziana 63, ☎ 7606000.
Events: opera and music at the *Teatro San Carlo* (E4), ☎ 426518 and at the *Accademia* and the *Auditorio RAI,* theatre in numerous city venues; *Festa di Piedigrotta* and *Neapolitan song festival* (Sep); *feast of S. Gennaro* (May-Sep), *feast of the Madonna del Carmine* (16 Jul); crèche displays and other Christmas festivities; tomb decoration for Good Friday; public procession through the city centre at Easter.
Fairs and markets: *commercial events* at *Mostra d'Oltremare,* ☎ 7258111.
Fencing: *Accademia Nazionale,* stadio Collana, v. Ribera, ☎ 643178.
Flying club: *Aeroporto Capodichino,* ☎ 7805697.
Golf: *Club Napoli,* at Arco Felice *(19 km W),* v. Campiglione 11.
Guided tours: half-day tours of city are organized by *Tourcar,* ☎ 320429 (also Naples at night) and by *Cimatours,* ☎ 201052; tours of the environs and islands (Pompeii, Vesuvius, Capri, etc) are also organized by *CIT,* ☎ 325424-322960 (information from travel agents); tourist offices organize guided tours to individual sights Sunday a.m. according to monthly calendar, ☎ 406289.
Horse racing: *ippodromo di Agnano* (→ Campi Flegrei), ☎ 7601660.
Marinas: Mergellina, Manzi, Posillipo, Santa Lucia, Molosiglio, ☎ 206231.
Motocross: *Terzigno* track in Terzigno *(29 km SE);* management *Moto club Napoli,* ☎ 7532406.
Sailing: *Lega Navale,* v. Molosiglio, ☎ 314057 or 5511806; *Nautic Coop,* p. Amedeo 15 *(Centro Vela UISP),* ☎ 415371 or 415447.
Sports centre: v. Giochi del Mediterraneo, ☎ 7609573.
Swimming: v. Bernini (D2), ☎ 658553; *Piscina Olimpionica,* at Mostra d'Oltremare.
Technical tourism: *Osservatorio Astronomico,* v. Moiariello 13 (A4), ☎ 440101 (by appointment).
Tennis: v. Giochi del Mediterraneo, ☎ 7603912.

Yacht club: *Canottieri Savoia,* Banchina S. Lucia, ☎ 418038.
Youth hostel: *Ostello Mergellina,* at Piedigrotta, salita Piedigrotta 23, ☎ 685346.
Zoos: *Acquario e Stazione Zoologica,* v. Caracciolo (E2), ☎ 406222 (closed Mon); *Giardino zoologico,* v. Kennedy, ☎ 615943.

The bay of NAPLES

From Naples to Capri *(54 km and ferry, 1 day; map 5)*

This itinerary examines the Bay of Naples in detail. The itinerary around the Campi Flegrei (→) complements this one.

▶ The E coastal district of S. Giovanni a Teduccio is the departure point from **Naples** (→). The first railway in Italy ran between Naples and **Pòrtici** in 1839; it was used by the monarch to reach the Palazzo Reale, commissioned by Charles of Bourbon in 1738 and surrounded by a fine park. The **Museo Nazionale Ferroviario** (railway museum; *wkdays 9 a.m.-7 p.m.*) is still in Pòrtici. ▶ It is followed immediately by **Ercolano** (→) from which the climb to **Vesuvius** (→) begins. ▶ On descending from the volcano it is possible to go straight to **Torre del Greco;** the **Museo del Corallo** *(9 a.m.-1 p.m.; closed Sun and hols)* shows carving of coral, lava, pink shells, sardonyx, carnelian, striped shells, mother-of-pearl and ivory, for which the area is famous. ▶ At **Torre Annunziata** are excavations of a **Roman villa** which probably belonged to Poppaea, the wife of Nero *(guided tours, 9 a.m.-2:45-6:20 p.m, according to season).* The mineral springs are used in the **Terme Vesuviane Nunziante.** ▶ The route leaves **Pompeii Scavi** (→) on the l. and climbs from **Castellammare di Stàbia** (→) to **Monte Faìto** *(also by cableway, 8 mn)* along a road with hairpin turns; there is an exceptional view★ from the belve-

dere (3,445 ft). ▶ The route returns to the sea at **Vico Equense** (→) and continues along the Sorrento peninsula to **Meta,** on a ridge among citrus groves; there is another fine view, this time of the plain of Sorrento from the square outside the 18C church of the Madonna del Lauro. ▶ Hydrofoils or ferries for the island of **Capri** (→) leave from the **Marina Piccola** in Sorrento. ☐

Practical information ─────────────

META, ✉ 80062, ☎ 081.
≋

Hotel:
★★ *Giosué a Mare,* v. Marina 2, ☎ 8786685, 25 rm ℗ 33,500.

Recommended
Marina: at Piano di Sorrento, ☎ 8788338.

PORTICI, ✉ 80055, ☎ 081.
≋

Recommended
Archery: *Compagnia Arcieri S. Ciro di Pòrtici,* v. A. Diaz 120 (Palazzo Attanasio).
Botanical garden: v. Università 100, ☎ 274256.

TORRE ANNUNZIATA, ✉ 80058, ☎ 081.
≋
⚓ (Jun-Oct), ☎ 8611285.

Hotels:
★★★ *Motel Pavesi,* service area, Torre Annunziata E at 21-km marker on the A3 autostrada, ☎ 8611401, 31 rm, 44,000.
★★ *Giara,* v. Panoramica 6, ☎ 8581117, 18 rm ℗ ⚏ ▭ closed Christmas, 40,000; bkf: 5,000.

5. The Bay of Naples

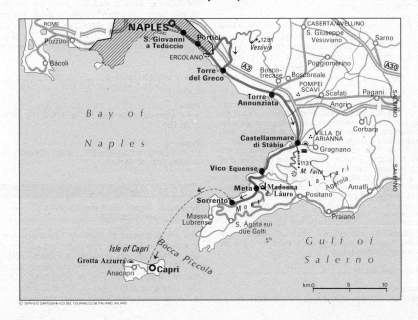

© SERVIZIO CARTOGRAFICO DEL TOURING CLUB ITALIANO, MILANO

⚑ *Ginevra,* v. Torrette di Siena 56, ☎ 8622345.

Recommended
Cycling: *G. S. Catapano,* v. Antonio Vignas 138, ☎ 8614246.

TORRE DEL GRECO, ⊠ 80059, ☎ 081.
≋
ℹ v. Marconi 14 (stazione Circumvesuviana), ☎ 8814676.

Hotel:
★★★★ *Sakura,* v. De Nicola 26, ☎ 8810602, 72 rm P ⬥
🅟 ♿ ⧆ 109,000.

Restaurant:
♦♦ *Settebello,* at Santa Maria la Bruna *(5 km S),* v. Litoranea 13, ☎ 8831893, closed Tue. Large veranda overlooking sea. Regional cuisine: seaweed fritters, fish baked, fried or grilled with mint sauce, 20/40,000.

⚑ *Pineta Vesuvius,* at Camaldoli della Torre, v. Agnano, ☎ 8833407 (all year).

NOCERA INFERIORE

Salerno 15, Naples 34, Rome 253 km
Pop. 46,759 ⊠ 84014 ☎ 081   C3

Nocera Inferiore contains the 14C church of **S. Antonio,** which stands at the top of a flight of steps (painting by Andrea da Salerno inside). In the adjacent convent is the **Museo dell'Agro Nocerino** *(8 a.m.-2 p.m. and 5-8 p.m.)* housing funerary artifacts from *Nuceria* (6C-5C BC) and from Samnite *Nuceria Alfaterna* (4C-3C BC). 13 km in the direction of Salerno in **Nocera Superiore** in the S. Maria Maggiore district is the church of the **Rotonda★,** an early Christian baptistery probably dating from the 6C; it has a surprising interior *(caretaker at v. Mazzini 39)* with circular aisle and a ring of thirty twin columns with classical capitals and a central domed space with baptismal font surrounded by an iconostasis with columns.▯

NOLA

Naples 28, Rome 247 km
Pop. 31,738 ⊠ 80035 ☎ 081   B-C2

In the year 14 Augustus died at Nola, in the house of his ancestors. Bishop Paulinus (4C-5C) is said to have invented bells, called *nolae* or *campanae,* in the Middle Ages from Nola and Campania. Pomponio de Algerio was born in Nola and executed as a Protestant in Rome in a cauldron of boiling oil and pitch in 1556.

▶ The **Duomo** is Neoclassical with an ancient crypt. ▶ The Baroque church of **S. Felice** replaced the 14C building, parts of which are now included in the adjacent monastery. ▶ The 14C church of **S. Biagio** or della Misericordia has a Gothic arch and small Romano-Gothic campanile. ▶ The **Palazzo Orsini** (1461) incorporates material from the Roman amphitheatre. ▶ The 16C **Palazzo Covoni** has Roman marbles in the basement. ▶ 2 km N is **Cimitile** with a group of early Christian and medieval buidings: the complex of **basilicas★** *(Tue, Thu and Sun 9 a.m.-12 noon and 2-5 p.m.)* includes the basilica of S. Felice in Pincis (4C, four-sided portico with 5C mosaics, traces of 9C-12C sculptures and frescos); the chapel of S. Giovanni with 14C frescos; the basilica dei SS. Martiri, with frescos. Parts of a pagan *hypogeum* have been discovered by excavation; the finds are shown in a small **antiquarium.**   ▯

Practical information ――――――――――

Recommended
♥ **lily festival:** 22 June or following Sun, ☎ 8231540.

San Paolino

On a June day of an unknown year in the 5C, eight men of Nola received their bishop, Paolino, on the beach of Torre Annunziata with bunches of lilies. He was returning from Africa, where he had traveled to offer himself as hostage to ransom the son of a widow of Nola. The young man had been taken into slavery by the Vandals. The bishop (later Saint Paolino) died on 22 June 431. Almost immediately a ritual symbolizing his triumphal reception started in the town. Lilies were replaced by floral staves, eight in number and one for each of the original delegates (a gardener, a grocer, a tavern-keeper, a baker, a butcher, a smith, a confectioner and a tailor). Naturally, the guilds felt a sense of competition. The floral staffs grew into wooden towers so tall that they could not be taken into the church and, from the late 16C, had to be blessed in the square. The ceremony is still performed on the Sunday after June 22. Eight painted towers up to 100 ft high are carried swaying in procession through the streets, accompanied by fanfare and fireworks.

PADULA

Salerno 105, Naples 161, Rome 368 km
Pop. 5,763 ⊠ 84034 ☎ 0975   E4

Padula houses the **Certosa di S. Lorenzo★** *(9 a.m.-1 hr before sunset),* which is an example of sumptuous Southern Baroque (17C-18C). It was started in the 14C and completed in the 19C. The **church** contains 16C stalls; the spacious **chiostro grande** has two rows of arches; other outstanding features are the **library** and an **elliptical staircase★.** The complex houses the **Museo Archeologico della Lucania Occidentale** *(9 a.m.-1 p.m. and 4 p.m.-1 hr before sunset)* with finds from tombs in the Sala Consilina in Padula. 1 km NW are the ruins of the early Christian baptistery of **S. Giovanni in Fonte** (5C-6C) with an immersion font fed by a spring and now used for trout breeding. 11.5 km SE is Montesano sulla Marcellana with the **Terme di Montesano.**   ▯

Practical information ――――――――――

PADULA

Hotel:
★★★ *Certosa,* v. Certosa 57, ☎ 77046, 33 rm P ♿ ⧆
🅟 35,000.

Environs
MONTESANO SULLA MARCELLANA, ⊠ 84033, ☎ 0975.
♨ (May-Oct), ☎ 861049.

PAESTUM**

Salerno 36, Naples 92, Rome 305 km
Pop. 181 ⊠ 84063 ☎ 0828   C-D4

The Greek temples of Paestum have remained largely intact, gleaming in light reflected off the nearby sea. Paestum was originally a Sybarite colony (late 7C BC) called Poseidonia, for the god of the sea, as the sea was the basis of its prosperity. The Lucanians conquered the town (*c.* 400 BC), it then became a Roman colony (273 BC) under the name of Paes-

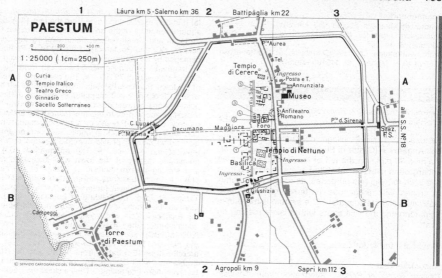

PAESTUM

1:25000 (1cm=250m)

① Curia
② Tempio Italico
③ Teatro Greco
④ Ginnasio
⑤ Sacello Sotterraneo

Láura km 5 - Salerno km 36

Battipáglia km 22

P.ta Aurea

Tempio di Cerere

Ingresso
Posta e T.
Annunziata

Museo

Anfiteatro Romano

P.ta d. Sirena

Decumano Maggiore

Foro

Tempio di Nettuno

Ingresso

Basilica

Ingresso

Giustizia

Campeggi

Torre di Paestum

© SERVIZIO CARTOGRAFICO DEL TOURING CLUB ITALIANO, MILANO

2 Agropoli km 9   Sapri km 112 3

tum. From the 9C to the 18C it remained isolated among forests and malarial swamps.

▶ The **monument and excavation area** *(9 a.m.-sunset)* is to the r. inside the **Porta Aurea** (A2). ▶ There are three Greek temples: the **Basilica**★ (B2), dating from the mid-6C BC, is the oldest temple on Paestum; the **Temple of Neptune**★★ (B2) or Poseidonion (450 BC) is practically intact as far as the external shell is concerned and considered by some to be the most beautiful Doric temple of antiquity; standing apart from the others is the smaller **Temple of Ceres**★ (A2), late 6C BC, probably dedicated to Athena. ▶ The Roman **forum** (A2) occupies the site of the Greek *agora* (market place); a building that may have been the **curia** (court) has survived, remains of the **baths**, the **Italic temple** (273 BC, altered 80 BC), perhaps the **Comitium** and the **amphitheatre**. ▶ The **via Sacra**, a processional road (A-B2), ran alongside a residential quarter; at the side of the *decumanus maximus* (A2) is what may have been the **gymnasium** and a sacred area with an **underground shrine**★ (6C). ▶ The **museum**★★ (A3; *9 a.m.-1 hr before sunset; closed Mon)* complements the visit. The most important features are: archaic **metopes**★★ from the *thesauros* and **metopes**★★ from the major temple (late 6C BC), both from the sanctuary of Hera at the mouth of the Sele; the seated clay statue of **Zeus**★★ (mid-6C BC); eight bronze hydras★ (mid-6C BC) and the painted slabs of the **Tomb of the Divers**★, a rare example of Greek painting. ▶ The **chiesa dell'Annunziata** (A3) is a proto-Roman basilica. ▶ The surrounding **walls** *(4.7 km long)* were rebuilt by the Lucanians and Romans. ▶ On the right bank off the Sele *(11 km)* are the modest remains of the **Sanctuary of Hera**, the foundations of which date from the 7C BC. ▶ 37 km NE *(13.5 km N of Roccadàspide)* are the **Caves of Castelcivita** *(Apr-Sep 8 a.m-9 p.m.; Oct-Mar Thu and Sun 6-7 p.m.; other days by appointment)*. □

Practical information

≋

ℹ v. Nazionale (A3), ☎ 811016.

Hotels:
★★★ *Calypso,* at Licinella, ☎ 811031, 30 rm P ⚓ ⋙ & 55,000; bkf: 5,000.
★★★ *Martini,* on archaeological site (B2 a), ☎ 811020, 27 rm P ⋙ & ⋘ 50,000; bkf: 6,000.

★★★ *Palme,* at Laura, ☎ 851025, 50 rm P ⚓ ⋙ ▱ ⁄° closed Nov-Feb, 53,000; bkf: 8,000.
★★★ *Park Hotel,* coast road to Agrópoli, ☎ 811134, 28 rm P ⚓ ⋙ & ⁄° 58,000; bkf: 4,000.
★★ *Cristallo,* at Laura, ☎ 851077, 18 rm P ⋙ 30,000; bkf: 3,000.
★★ *Villa Rita,* v. Principe di Piemonte (B2 b), ☎ 811081, 13 rm P ⚓ ⋙ ⋘ closed 1 Nov-14 Mar. No restaurant, 40,000; bkf: 5,500.

Restaurant:
◆◆◆ *Nettuno,* v. Principe di Piemonte 1 (B2 c), ☎ 811028, closed Mon except summer. Terrace with fine views. Mixed cuisine: pancakes, baked or fried fish, roast or grilled meat, 20/45,000.

⚓ *Mare Pineta,* at Sterpina, v. Ponte di Ferro, 200 pl, ☎ 811086; *Nettuno,* at Laura, v. Pagliaio della Madonna, 100 pl, ☎ 851042 (all year).

Recommended
Caving: *Grotta di Castelcivita (37 km NE);* inquire at the Comune, ☎ 975009.
Events: concerts, ballet and classical shows on the archaeological site (Jul-Aug, occasional).
Farm vacations: *Azienda La Vigna,* at Ogliastro Cilento *(12 km SE),* ☎ 0974/833271.

PASSO DI MIRABELLA

Avellino 34, Naples 90, Rome 279 km
Pop. 1012 ✉ 83030 ☎ 0825   D2

Passo di Mirabella is a village on the pass of the same name on the SS Benevento-Foggia at the Calore/Ufita watershed. W of the village are the **Aeclanum excavations,** a Samnite then a Roman city, destroyed in the 7C AD, including ruins of houses, a peristyle, part of the fortifications and baths. Various materials are on display in a pavilion. □

Practical information _____

Hotel:
★★★ *Aeclanum,* v. Nazionale 32, ☎ 449065, 43 rm P ⋙ ▱ closed Easter and Christmas, 40,000; bkf: 3,000.

Recommended
Events: at Mirabella Eclano *(2.5 km SW), Good Friday procession; Feast of the Obelisk* (third Sun in Sep), Comune, ☎ 447057.
Craft workshops: *A. De Dominicis* at Fontanarosa *(6.5 km S)*, v. Monaca, ☎ 445100 (stone).

PERTOSA

Salerno 71, Naples 127, Rome 332 km
Pop. 906 ⊠ 84030 ☎ 0975   D-E4

Pertosa is a small village containing the **Grotta dell'Angelo**★★ (Grotta di Pertosa; *visit lasting c. 1 hr; 9 a.m.-5.30 p.m.*) on the left of the Tànagro. It is an underground riverbed, inhabited in the neolithic period and used for religious purposes; its rooms have natural arches with arabesque patterns; galleries have stalactites and stalagmites. The system is more than 2 km long and the visit starts with a lake-crossing on a raft.   □

Practical information _____

Recommended
Caving: *Grotta di Pertosa*; information from *Comitato Grotte*, ☎ 37037.

POMPEII EXCAVATIONS**

Naples 24, Rome 237 km
⊠ 80045 ☎ 081   B3

Roman houses in Pompeii were built around a square courtyard *(atrium)*, in which was the *impluvium* (cistern) for collecting rainwater. Opposite the entrance was the *tablinum* (dining and sitting room); the bedrooms *(cubicula)* were at the sides, as were the store-rooms *(cellae)*. This simple dwelling was later elaborated to include a Hellenistic peristyle, with colonnades encircling the garden *(viridarium)*; off this opened the *triclinium* (dining room tranferred from the *tablinum)* and rooms for domestic and reception purposes *(oeci; exedrae)*. The rooms in the façade were used as shops; the second floor, which most houses had, accommodated lodgers or slaves. The internal walls were decorated with tempera or encaustic (colours mixed with wax and applied warm) pictures, in which four phases are distinguished: the first style, with stucco ornamentation (Samnite period) imitating marble; the second style, architectural (1C BC) in which false perspectives frame compositions with figures; the third style, with Egyptian traits (imperial era to 52), in which the architectural features, executed with great delicacy, have an ornamental purpose, and the fourth style, ornamental (62-79) in which the painted figures are enclosed within complex and whimsical architectural designs. The urban pattern of *insulae* bordered by streets and alleys, not all occupied by a single *domus* (house), does not have the lucid regularity of strict Roman planning (Pompeii is Oscan in origin). The ancient town, which occupied a modest area around the *forum* and was elliptical in plan, was extended with the aim of rationalization, but involved compromise, as still happens today. The visit is moving and often surprising, however much is known in advance, and demonstrates what a wealth of knowledge about the Roman world and its culture was preserved for us by this town's tragedy.

▶ The excavations *(9 a.m.-1 hr before sunset)* have so far (the first explorations date from the mid-18C) exposed about three-fifths of the area of the city, of mixed Oscan, Etruscan and Greek culture, taken over by the Samnites (late 5C BC) and Roman only from 80 BC. Pompeii was damaged by an earthquake in 62 AD, before being buried by fragments of pumice *(lapilli)* and ash from the explosion of Vesuvius in 79 AD. ▶ The ruins give a clear idea of the town: the paved streets show the marks left by cartwheels; footpaths and stepping stones for pedestrians; painted signs between residential houses indicate hostels *(hospitia)*, shops *(tabernae)*, inns *(cauponae)* and the *thermopolia* or bars. Painted or scratched inscriptions support various candidates in public elections or announce gladiatorial shows; phallic symbols abound to ward off envy or the evil eye. ▶ The **antiquarium** (C3) documents the history of the town with excavated material and striking **plaster casts**★ of victims of the catastrophe. ▶ Public buildings and areas of particular interest include the rectangular **forum**★★ (C3) with the base of the Temple of Jove; the **Building of Eumachia**, used by the *fullones* (bleachers, dyers and cloth manufacturers) and the **Basilica**★ from which justice and public affairs were administered; the **Teatro Grande**★★ (C4) Hellenistic (200-150 BC), subsequently enlarged, on the slope of the hill; the **Teatro Piccolo**★★ (C4); the oldest known ampitheatre★ (B6) dating from 80 BC and the **Thermae Stabianae**★★ (B-C4). ▶ The private houses are possibly even more interesting. They include the **House of the Menander**★ (C5) with lavish frescos; the **House of Lorieus Tibertinus**★ (B5) with *triclinium* decorated with episodes from the *Iliad* and the *Labours of Hercules*; the **Villa of Julia Felix**★ (B6) which includes, next to the proprietor's house, a public bath, rented accommodation, and shops; the magnificent **House of the Vetii**★★ (B3) in which the *triclinium*★ is decorated with some of the finest paintings of antiquity; the **Casa degli Amorini Dorati**★ (B3); the **House of the Faun**★ (B3); the **House of the Tragic Poet**, an example of a middle class house (in the pavement of the threshold is a mosaic of a growling dog, with the inscription *cave canem:* beware of the dog). ▶ The charming, suburban **via dei Sepolcri**★ leads to the **Villa di Diomedes**★ (B1). ▶ Outside the main area of the excavations is the **Villa dei Misteri**★★ (A1), perhaps the finest building in Pompeii; the enormous painting by a 1C Campanian artist on the walls of one of the rooms shows **initiation into the mysteries of Dionysos**★★. ▶ In the modern village of **Pompeii** is the sanctuary of the **Madonna del Rosario** (1891), a pilgrimage church.   □

Practical information _____

ℹ v. Sacra 1, ☎ 8631041; office on the excavation site, ☎ 8610913.

Hotels:
★★★ *Villa Laura*, v. delle Salle 13, ☎ 8631024, 20 rm ℗ ⋘ ⋙ No restaurant, 68,000; bkf: 5,000.
★★ *Europa*, v. de Fusco 30, ☎ 8632190, 28 rm ℗ No restaurant, 40,000; bkf: 5,500.
★★ *Villa dei Misteri*, v. Villa dei Misteri 1 (C2 a), ☎ 8613593, 41 rm ℗ ⋘ & ⋙ 35,000; bkf: 4,000.

Restaurant:
♦♦♦ *Zi' Caterina*, v. Roma 20, ☎ 8631263, closed Tue and Christmas. Mixed regional cuisine: grilled fish or meat, grilled crayfish, 25/45,000.

⚠ *Spartacus*, v. Plinio, 90 pl, ☎ 8614901 (all year).

Recommended
Events: classical plays in the ancient theatre (Jul-Aug).

POSITANO*

Salerno 40, Naples 57, Rome 266 km
Pop. 3,581 ⊠ 84017 ☎ 089   B3

Positano looks onto a small bay and has a pleasant beach backed by mountain buttresses. The houses

Sports in Pompeii

Inhabitants of ancient Pompeii often gathered at the palestre (an open-air gymnasium) to exercise. However, most of them enjoyed sitting in the shade of the amphitheatre, urging the team of their choice to victory. Fiercely loyal to their own team, Pompeians showed little fair play for the opposing team. Angry verbal outbursts sometimes degenerated into scenes. This was the case in 59 BC. Visitors from Nocera were showing great enthusiasm for their team during a gladiator tournament. The Pompeians cheered for their own team. Insults flew, then rocks. Finally, weapons were drawn! Tacitus recalls the tragedy and said that many Nucerians were wounded, some killed. News of the brawl reached Rome and the Senate took severe sanctions. Those responsible for the outbreak of violence — at least those who were identified — were exiled. The city of Pompeii was forbidden to put on any games for a period of ten years. Violence at sporting events is nothing new!

are built on terraces, among gardens. Palme and citrus groves form white cubes, each with a canopy over the entrance.

▶ In the lower part of the town the short beach is dominated by the parish church of **S. Maria Assunta** with its majolica dome; there is a 12C painting in Byzantine style on the high altar. ▶ The **belvedere** above the town and a little way along the Sorrento road offers a magnificent view. ☐

Practical information ─────────────

≋
ℹ v. del Saracino, ☎ 875067.
🚢 boats and hydrofoils to Amalfi, Salerno and Capri in summer, *Scarano Navigazione*, ☎ 225322.

Hotels:
★★★★★ *San Pietro,* v. Laurito 2, ☎ 875455, 59 rm ℙ ⊰ 🝔 ♨ ⟡ ᐃ ⟋❀ closed 6 Nov-19 Mar. Sheer above the sea, connected to two idyllic beaches by elevator, 420,000.
★★★★★ *Royal,* v. Colombo 30, ☎ 875066, 60 rm ℙ ⊰ 🝔 ❀ ⟋ closed 1 Nov-20 Dec. 19C villa with antique furnishings, 360,000.
★★★★ *Royal,* v. Pasitea 102, ☎ 875000, 65 rm ℙ ⊰ 🝔 ♨ ⟋ closed 6 Oct-14 Apr, 138,000; bkf: 11,000.
★★★ *Ancora,* v. Colombo 36, ☎ 875318, 18 rm ℙ ⊰ 🝔 closed 21 Oct-Easter, 85,000; bkf: 7,000.
★★★ *Buca di Bacco e Buca Residence,* v. Rampa Teglia 8, ☎ 875699, 55 rm ⊰ closed Nov-Easter, 107,000; bkf: 8,500.
★★★ *Casa Albertina,* v. della Tavolozza 4, ☎ 875143, 21 rm ℙ ⊰ ❀ 80,000; bkf: 8,000.
★★★ *Marincanto,* v. Colombo, ☎ 875130, 23 rm ℙ ⊰ ♨ ❀ closed 16 Oct-31 Mar. No restaurant, 75,000; bkf: 6,000.
★★★ *Savoia,* v. Colombo 73, ☎ 875003, 44 rm ⊰ ❀ closed 16 Oct-31 Mar. No restaurant, 70,000; bkf: 6,000.

Restaurants:
♦ *Cambusa,* p. Vespucci, ☎ 875432, closed Nov-Dec. Veranda overlooking beach. Mixed regional cuisine: fish mixed grill, seafood sauté, frittata paesane, 25/35,000.
♦ *Vincenzo,* closed Sun and Mon in winter. Mixed regional cuisine: anchovy pie, involtini with peas, 25/30,000.

Recommended
Discothèque: *La Fregata Blue Angels,* v. del Saracino, ☎ 875778.
Events: picture shows in summer; chamber music concerts (Sep).

POZZUOLI*

Naples 13, Rome 235 km
Pop. 71,052 ⊠ 80078 ☎ 081   A3

Pozzuoli is affected by bradyseism, a rhythmic rise and fall of the earth's crust, imperceptible as it occurs. However, holes made by shellfish in the columns of the Serapeum show how the ground level has changed. The picturesque alleyways around the district of Terra, the acropolis of the Graeco-Roman town, are now depopulated and closed off because of the increasingly marked effect of geophysical tension.

▶ The **Serapeum★** (A1), partially submerged, was in fact the *macellum* or public market of imperial Roman *Puteoli*; the sixteen Corinthian columns with holes supported a dome. ▶ A Roman temple of the first imperial period originally served as the **Duomo** (B1); it was rebuilt in the 17C and a fire in 1964 revealed the earlier structure. Excavations are still under way, but have already established that the podium includes remains of a tufa temple of the Republican period, identified as the *Capitolium* of the first Roman colony (194 BC). ▶ The **Flavian Amphitheatre★** (A2; *9 a.m.- 2:45-6 p.m. according to season*), one of the largest to have survived, was built in the 1C. It was used for *naumachiae* (mock naval battles), combat and wild animal hunts; a visit to the **substructure** gives a view of the shafts used for bringing the beasts' cages into the arena. ▶ The traditional name of the **Temple of Neptune** (A1) is used for what are actually the remains of thermal baths. The **Temple of Diana**, not far away, is the ruins of a *nymphaeum* (grotto with spring dedicated to tutelary nymph). ▶ From the p. Capomazza (A1), at the entrance to the v. Celle, it is possible to see a section of the **Necropolis of Puteoli**, with a long series of tombs; another part of the necropolis can be seen a little further on in the San Vito area. ▶ Water from various thermal springs is used to feed the **Terme Puteolane** and the **Terme La Salute** *(temporarily closed)*; there is a thermal swimming pool near the **Parco Averno** (along the v. Domiziana, A1). ☐

Practical information ─────────────

≋
ℹ v. Campi Flegrei 3 (A1), ☎ 8672419.
🚢 several car ferry sailings daily to Prócida (→) and Ischia (→).

Hotel:
★★ *Mini Hotel,* SS Domiziana at 61.7-km marker, ☎ 8672223, 18 rm ℙ ⊰ 🝔 ♨ 🝔 38,000.
⚓ *Vulcana Solfatara,* at Solfatara, v. Domiziana at 60-km marker, 100 pl,☎ 8673413.

Recommended
Marina: ☎ 8671160.
Water skiing: *Sci nautico Partenopeo,* Lake Averno, ☎ 8663526.

The island of PROCIDA

Naples 24, Rome 247 km
Pop. 10,565 ⊠ 80079 ☎ 081   A3

Procida is a volcanic island with a steep, jagged coastline, vineyards and citrus groves. It is *c.* 2.5 miles long.

▶ The principal town, also called **Procida** is picturesque with brightly painted houses and a **castle** (now a prison) on a promontory. ▶ **Terra Murata** is the highest point on the island. The church of **S. Michele** has a ceiling painting. ▶ **Marina di Chiaiolella** is attractive; the **Tavola del Re** *(2 km)* offers a fine view from Solchiaro point; opposite, linked by a pier-acqueduct, is the **islet of Vivara** with

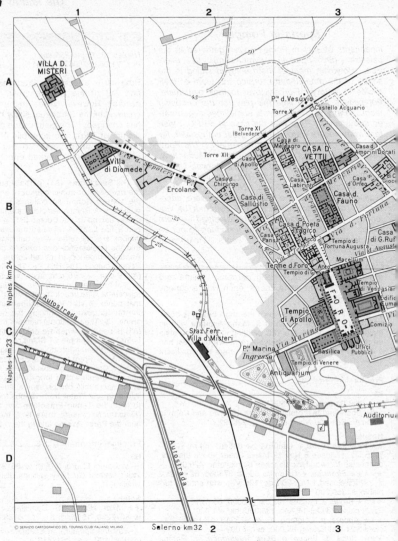

dense olive groves. ▶ The Ciraccio and Ciraciello beaches make up the **Lido di Prócida.** ▶ A boat trip around the island lasts 3 hours. □

Practical information

🚢 passenger and car ferries several times daily day from Naples-Molo Beverello (*c.* 1 hr 10 mn), Pozzuoli (*c.* 30 mn), Ischia; weekly service from Capri, information, *Caremar,* ☎ 081/8967280; *Libera Navigazione Lauro,* ☎ 081/313236 (departures from Naples, Pozzuoli, Ischia); *Navigazione Libera del Golfo,* ☎ 081/8370819 (departures from Capri); several hydrofoils daily from Naples (Mergellina and Molo Beverello, *c.* 30 mn) and from Ischia-Cesamicciola (*c.* 10 mn), information, *Caremar; SNAV,* ☎ 081/660444 (also departures from Ischia).

Restaurant:
♦ *Crescenzo,* v. Chiaisella 28, ☎ 8967255, closed Nov-Mar. Seafood, 30/35,000.

⚓ *Punta Serra,* at Punta Serra, 50 pl, ☎ 8969540.

Recommended
Events: procession on Good Friday.

RAVELLO*

Salerno 27, Naples 66, Rome 276 km
Pop. 2,317 ☒ 84010 ☎ 089   C3

Ravello sits perched on a high buttress of rock sticking out into the sea between two small valleys and full of intense colours and melancholy ruined palaces. Ravello was given its characteristic Norman-Saracen stamp by rich merchant families who, in the 13C and earlier, traded with Sicily and the eastern Mediterranean.

4   **5**   **6**

POMPEI

0   50   100   150 m

1:8000 (1cm=80m)

▶ The centre of Ravello is the p. Vescovado (B2), where cars may be parked. ▶ The **Duomo★** (B2) was founded in 1086, rebuilt in the 12C and 18C; features include the bronze **door★** (1179) and the 13C campanile topped with intricate arches. Inside are a **pulpit★** decorated with mosaic and reliefs (1272) and an **ambo★** dating from *c.* 1130. ▶ Part of the garden of the **Villa Rufolo★★** (C2; *9:30 a.m.-sunset*) is on the p. Vescovado; fascinating among the Norman-Saracen buildings (13C) is the **courtyard★**, resembling a small cloister; there is an **antiquarium** in rooms adjacent to the villa; the **garden★** has exotic plants and a view from the terrace. ▶ Interesting churches are **S. Maria a Gradillo** (B2), late 12C, and **S. Giovanni del Toro** (B2; *caretaker at no. 50*) with its 12C **ambo★**, a 14C stucco relief of St. Catherine and 14C frescos in the chapels and crypt. ▶ Past the church of **S. Francesco** (C2), with its white Gothic cloister, is the **Villa Cimbrone★** (D1). Its courtyard incorporates ancient fragments; at the end of the garden is the **Belvedere Cim-**

brone★★, a terrace at the end of the rocky spur offering an incomparable view of coast and gulf. ▶ 1.3 km NW is **Scala** (A1), with works of art in the Duomo including a pulpit, a panel painting of the *Crucifixion* (1260), the Gothic Coppola tomb (stucco, 1399) and a treasury. □

Practical information ─────────

ⓘ p. Vescovado (B2), ☎ 857096; at Scala, near Municipio, ☎ 857325.

Hotels:
★★★★★ *Palumbo*, v. Toro 28 (B2 a), ☎ 857244, 21 rm Ⓟ ⌇ ⌂ ⋒ 300,000; bkf: 18,000. Rest. ◆◆◆ *Confalone* Refined and romantic, built on ruins of Confalone. Italian and international cuisine: scamponi alla Confalone, curried crayfish, homemade wines, 45/65,000.
★★★ *Caruso Belvedere*, v. Toro 52 (B2 b), ☎ 857111, 26 rm Ⓟ ⌇ ⌂ ⋒ closed 10 Jan-28 Feb, 80,000.

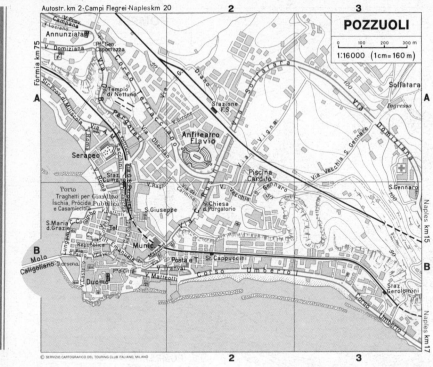

Autostr. km 2-Campi Flegrei-Naples km 20

POZZUOLI

0   100   200   300 m

1:16000 (1cm=160 m)

★★★ *Rufolo,* v. S. Francesco 3 (C2 c), ☎ 857133, 30 rm ℗
⟨ ⟨ ⟨ ⟨⟨⟨ ⊟ 80,000; bkf: 10,000.
★★ *Graal,* v. della Repubblica 8 (B2 d), ☎ 857222, 30 rm
⟨⟨⟨ ⊟ 50,000; bkf: 6,000.
★★ *Parsifal,* v. D'Anna 5 (A2 e), ☎ 857144, 19 rm ⟨ ⟨⟨⟨
closed 6 Oct-31 Mar, 51,000; bkf: 6,000.

Restaurants:
♦♦ *Cumpà Cosimo,* v. Roma 44 (B2 f), ☎ 857156, closed
Mon in winter. Trattoria with family atmosphere. Regional cuisine: pancakes, cannelloni, grilled meat or fish,
homemade wines, 18/25,000.
♦♦ *Garden,* v. Chiunzi 4 (B2 g), ☎ 857226, closed Tue in
winter. Spacious with shady terrace and view. Regional cuisine: pancakes, stewed or fried fish, scallops with
mushrooms, 20/28,000.

Recommended
Events: Wagnerian concerts in *Villa Rufolo* (summer).

ROCCAMONFINA

Caserta 46, Naples 79, Rome 190 km
Pop. 3,817 ⊠ 81035 ☎ 0823   A1

Roccamonfina is set among chestnut woods on the
slopes of an extinct volcano between the Garigliano
plain and that of the Volturno.

▶ The site of the sanctuary of **S. Maria dei Làttani**
(2.5 km) is isolated. The church is Gothic with a 15C
fresco inside; the painted stone Madonna, in a Baroque chapel, dates from the 11C. In the piazza are a
15C convent and another arcaded convent with Gothic
cloister (1440) inside.   □

SALA CONSILINA

Salerno 93, Naples 144, Rome 350 km
Pop. 12,442 ⊠ 84036 ☎ 0975   E4

From Sala Consilina the narrow Vallo di Diano can be
seen, the drained bed of an ancient lake stretching for
37 km between the mountains of the Tànagro Valley.

▶ 8 km away is **Teggiano**, a picturesque medieval town
on an isolated hill; its 14C-15C **castle** has been altered;
the **cathedral** has 13C portals, an ambo with reliefs dating
from 1271 and 14C sculptures. Marbles of the Roman
and medieval periods are shown in the former church of
S. Pietro *(Tue, Thu and Sat 5-10 p.m.; Wed, Fri and Sun
9 a.m.-2 p.m.).* ▶ **Atena Lucana** *(11 km)* is on the site of
ancient *Atina;* there are remains of stone walls. An antiquarium is in preparation. ▶ In the church of S. Antonio
(16C-18C) in *Polla (20 km)* are a crucifix (1635) and a
17C carved choir.   □

Practical information _____

Hotel:
★★ *Pergola,* at Trinità, ☎ 45054, 28 rm ℗ 36,000;
bkf: 6,000.

SALERNO*

Naples 56, Rome 262, Milan 829 km
Pop. 156,921 ⊠ 84100 ☎ 089   C3

See map on page 172.

Salerno had a distinguished medieval school of medicine; some of its precepts are still current. Its
renown started in the early 9C. Greek and Arab

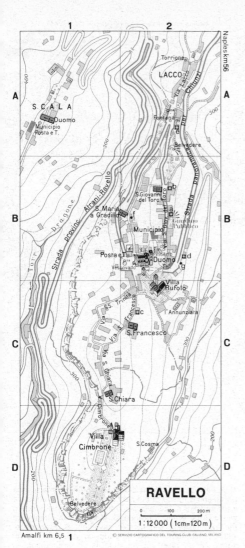

Naples km 56

RAVELLO

0   100   200 m

1 : 12 000 (1cm=120 m)

Amalfi km 6,5 **1**

© SERVIZIO CARTOGRAFICO DEL TOURING CLUB ITALIANO, MILANO

---

palatine church; the campanile is Lombard and the interior frescos date from the 11C. ▶ The **Duomo★★** (B2) was commissioned by Robert Guiscard when Salerno was the capital of the Norman domains. The 12C **campanile★**, topped with interlaced arches, is at the side; ancient columns, Islamic arches and the loggia in the **atrium★** bear witness to the numerous influences that met in Norman culture; the Romanesque portal has a **bronze door★** from Constantinople (1099). The interior contains fine works of art: two mosaic **amboes★★** (13C on the r.; 12C on the l.) which rest on the **iconostasis★** (1175); mosaics in the r.-hand apse where Pope Gregory VII is buried, in the vault of the l.-hand apse and on the marble framework of the high altar; monument to **Margaret of Anjou★** (15C) and Baroque crypt with reliquary of Matthew the Evangelist. ▶ The **Museo del Duomo** *(9:30 a.m.-2:30 p.m., currently closed)* contains, among other things, two excellent pieces: the **Exultet★**, a 13C illuminated manuscript, and a 12C ivory **altar frontal★**. ▶ The **Museo Provinciale** *(B3; 9:30 a.m.-1 p.m. and 5-8 p.m.; Sun and hols 9 a.m.-1 p.m. and 5-7 p.m.)*, in the former abbey of S. Benedetto, has an interesting regional archaeological collection, including a 1C BC Italic bronze head of *Apollo★*. ▶ The **medieval aqueduct** (A-B3), Lombard and Norman, has arches on many levels. ▶ Beyond the *planum montis* quarter, where the medical school was located, is the 15C church of **S. Maria delle Grazie** (A1) with a painting dating from 1493 and, in the former sacristy, a **pinacoteca-museo** *(7 a.m.-1 p.m. and 4-8 p.m.)* with 17C-19C Neapolitan pictures, wooden statues and church furnishings. ▶ The town is dominated by the **Castello di Arechi** (A1), Byzantine, Lombard and Norman, with superb views and a collection of 8C-19C ceramics *(9 a.m.-1 p.m. and 3-6 p.m.)*. ▶ The **lungomare Trieste** (B-C2-4), lined with palms, offers views of the gulf.

Environs

▶ Artifacts from the Iron Age necropolises (9C BC) discovered in **Pontecagnano** *(11 km SE)* are shown in the **Museo Nazionale dell'Agro Picentino** *(9 a.m.-2 p.m.; Sun and hols 9 a.m.-1 p.m.; closed Mon).* □

Practical information

ℹ p. Ferrovia (C4), ☎ 231432; v. Velia 15 (B3; head office), ☎ 224322; p. Amendola 8 (B2), ☎ 224744.

🚃 (C4-5), ☎ 231415.

🚢 from p. della Concordia and corso Garibaldi (C4).

🛥 daily boat and hydrofoil service to Amalfi, Positano and Capri in summer; hydrofoil in season to Maratea and Naples, *Scarano Navigazione,* ☎ 225322.

Car rental: *Avis,* corso Garibaldi 144, ☎ 229686; *Maggiore,* station, p. Ferrovia 3, ☎ 229588.

Hotels:
★★★★ *Jolly delle Palme,* lungomare Trieste 1 (B1 a), ☎ 225222, 105 rm Ⓟ 139,000.
★★★ *Fiorenza,* v. Trento 145, ☎ 351160, 30 rm Ⓟ No restaurant, 67,000; bkf: 5,000.
★★★ *Plaza,* p. Vittorio Veneto 42 (C4 b), ☎ 224477, 42 rm Ⓟ ⊗ No restaurant, 68,000; bkf: 5,000.

Restaurants:
♦♦♦ *Nicola dei Principati,* corso Garibaldi 201 (B3 d), ☎ 225435, closed Sat. Regional cuisine: linguine with scampi; stewed or grilled mixed fish, 18/32,000.
♦♦ *Vicolo delle Neve,* vicolo della Neve 24 (B2 e), ☎ 225705, closed Wed and noon. Turn-of-the-century rooms in an alleyway. Regional cuisine: pasta and beans, salt cod alla pizzaiola, 15/25,000.
♦ *Brace,* lungomare Trieste 13 (B1 c), ☎ 225159, closed Sun and Christmas. Regional cuisine: penne with salmon, baked or grilled fish, grilled meat and cheese, 25/40,000.

Recommended
Archery: *Compagnia Arcieri Cadim Style,* traversa Villa Marina 6, ☎ 323642 or 35540.
Cycling: *Cicli Rauler,* v. Berta 13, ☎ 238048; *Cicli De Simone,* largo Prato 21.

---

medical ideas were melded here, and the school's teaching spread to the West where it was known as the *civitas Hippocratica* (city of Hippocrates); it was one of the rare medieval institutions to include women among its students and teachers. Suppressed by Joachim Murat in 1812, it was by then a pale shadow of its former self. The town stands on a slope facing the sea.

▶ The **via dei Mercanti** (B2-3), narrow, twisting and rich in atmosphere, is the main axis of the old town. In its early stages and in the districts immediately adjacent the buildings are largely of the Lombard period. ▶ They include the **Chiesa del Crocifisso** (B3), 10C-11C *(restored)* with antique columns in the nave, 15C frescos in the apse and 13C frescos in the crypt; the church of **S. Giorgio** (B2, *in a side street*), Baroque, with frescos from 1675; the **Arco di Arechi** (B2), a surviving feature of an 8C building. ▶ **S. Pietro a Corte** *(vicolo Adalberga)* is the former

Events: concert seasons at *Teatro Verdi,* ☎ 226985; summer theatre and classical ballet, at the *Torre Acarnale; 8 and 16 mm film festival* (Oct); *children's cinema festival,* at Giffoni Valle Piana, ☎ 868544 (Jul-Aug).
Flying: *Aeroporto Pontecagnano,* ☎ 301186.
Marina: ☎ 224544.
Sailing: *Lega Navale,* p. Concordia (marina), ☎ 226924.
Tennis: lungomare Marconi, ☎ 238900.
Youth hostel: *Ostello Irno,* lungomare Marconi 34 (C4-5), ☎ 238520.

SANT'AGATA DE' GOTI

Benevento 35, Naples 48, Rome 267 km
Pop. 11,286 ☒ 82019 ☎ 0823   B-C2

In the 6C, Goths defeated at Vesuvius were allowed to settle here in what had originally been a Samnite village; however, *de' Goti* was added much later. The site is best seen from the W: a compact group of grey and ochre buildings, medieval in appearance, against the surrounding green; above the roofs, not too steeply pitched, rise the campanile and majolica cupola of the Duomo.

▶ The **Duomo** dates from the 12C and was rebuilt in the 18C; the vestibule has Corinthian capitals; in the presbytery are parts of a medieval mosaic pavement and there are remains of 14C frescos in the crypt. ▶ Other notable

churches are the **Annunziata,** Gothic, with a Renaissance portal and a fresco of the *Last Judgment* on the entrance wall, parts of a 15C altarpiece and, in a chapel, modern windows by Bruno Cassinari; **S. Menna,** with remains of the 12C building and mosaic pavement **S. Francesco,** with Gothic tomb (14C) of Ludovico Artus, the local count. ▶ A diocesan museum is in preparation in S. Maria del Carmine.   ☐

Practical information _____

ℹ p. Municipio 4.

SANTA MARIA CAPUA VETERE

Caserta 7, Naples 20, Rome 206 km
Pop. 32,052 ☒ 81055 ☎ 0823   B2

Santa Maria Capua Vetere is the city where Hannibal's soldiers are said to have been so softened by good living that they never won another battle. The original rectangular layout is almost indecipherable, but the v. A. Moro and v. Caserta follow the line of the Appian Way, which ran through the Roman city.

▶ The **Duomo,** founded in the 5C, later altered, has antique columns from Roman buildings and fine works of art in its interior. ▶ The **amphitheatre★** dates from the 1C and was restored in the 2C; it is one of the most impressive to have survived *(9 a.m.-4 or 6 p.m.; closed*

4 5 Avellino km34

A

B

Baripaglia km 20 - Paestum km 36

Lido

4 5

Mon). ▶ In the adjacent garden *(permission from Soprintendenza Archeologica in Naples)* is an **antiquarium**. ▶ The 2C-3C **Mithraeum★** *(guided tour by caretaker of amphitheatre)* is one of the best preserved places of worship of the Persian god Mithras; the tunnel-vaulted ceiling of the subterranean hall is painted with stars; the rear wall has a fresco of Mithras killing a bull and the side walls are decorated with initiation scenes. ▶ Only one of the original three arches of the **Arco di Adriano** on the via Appia remains. ▶ The two **Roman tombs** on the Strada Statale to Caserta are known as the **Carceri Vecchie** and **La Conocchia**. ▶ There are beautiful **mosaics★** (early 6C) on a dark blue background in chapel of S. Matrona in the **parish church** in **San Prisco** *(2 km NE)*. □

Practical information
ⓘ v. Mazzocchi 143.

Hotel:
★★★ *Milano,* v. De Gasperi 98/100, ☎ 843323, 30 rm Ⓟ
⅋ No restaurant, 40,000.

SANT'ANGELO DEI LOMBARDI

Avellino 45, Naples 101, Rome 290 km
Pop. 5,402 ⊠ 83054 ☎ 0827　　　　　D2

Sant'Angelo was damaged by an earthquake in 1980 and, at the time of writing, is still being rebuilt.

▶ The 16C **Cathedral** with a late Renaissance portal is undergoing restoration. ▶ The **Casa Ceceri** and other private buildings, with Renaissance portals and loggias, will be rebuilt retaining as much as possible their their original architecture and setting. ▶ The abbey of **S. Guglielmo al Goleto** *(8 km SW)* was founded as the abbey of Montevérgine in the 12C. It was badly damaged in the earthquake, but parts of the main church and the small church *(under restoration)* have survived. The Benedictine library (in rebuilt premises) contains statues and architectural fragments recovered after the earthquake, here and in Sant'Angelo. □

Practical information

Recommended
Craft workshops: *M. Marena,* at Sant'Andrea di Conza *(30 km SE),* v. S. Lorenzo 7, ☎ 55135 (wrought iron).

SAPRI

Salerno 157, Naples 201, Rome 407 km
Pop. 7,319 ⊠ 84073 ☎ 0973　　　　　E5

Sapri is the place where Carlo Pisacane's 300 men landed in 1857 on their ill-fated mission during the Risorgimento. They are commemorated by an **obelisk** at the end of the **lungomare,** facing the Gulf of Policastro. □

Practical information

≋
ⓘ municipio, ☎ 392460.

Hotel:
★★ *Tirreno,* corso Italia 73, ☎ 391157, 55 rm Ⓟ ⅋ closed Oct-Apr, 41,000; bkf: 6,000.

Restaurant:
♦ *Oriente,* lungomare Italia 79, ☎ 391290, closed Mon except summer. By sea with fine view. Regional cuisine: seafood risotto, mixed grills, 20/25,000.

Recommended
Marina: ☎ 392115.
Skindiving: *Centro Santacroce,* v. Verdi 1, ☎ 392650.

SARNO

Salerno 24, Naples 32, Rome 255 km
Pop. 30,648 ⊠ 84087 ☎ 081　　　　　C3

There are important excavations near Sarno, which have uncovered a pre-Roman sanctuary and a 2C BC Hellenistic theatre. Materials from necropolises and pre-Roman sanctuaries in the area are on display in the **Museo della Valle del Sarno** *(10 a.m.-4 p.m.; entrance behind the convent).* □

SERINO

Avellino 12, Naples 68, Rome 257 km
Pop. 7,178 ⊠ 82028 ☎ 0825　　　　　C3

Serino is a scattered community that rests among luxuriant chestnut woods. It is a pleasant place to visit.

▶ A road with alternating open views and stretches in the forest leads to the **Piano di Verteglia,** pleasant routes to Terminio peak (5,890 ft); on the way up, a side road leads off to **Campolaspierto** *(4 km;* 4,600 ft; ski lift, winter sports). ▶ 6 km S is **Solofra** with the Palazzo Ducale (late 16C) and the 16C church of S. Michele (under restoration) with Baroque façade, carved ceilings and 17C pictures. □

Practical information

SERINO

Hotel:
★★★ *Eden Park Hotel,* at Sala, v. Turci 12, ☎ 594173, 29 rm Ⓟ 🅰 ⫰ ⫰ 🏷 47,600; bkf: 7,000.

Environs

CAMPOLASPIERTO, ✉ 83048, ☎ 827.
⚡ ski lifts.
🛈 nr municipio of Montella, ☎ 0827/61168.

SESSA AURUNCA

Caserta 44, Naples 58, Rome 179 km
Pop. 24,395 ✉ 81037 ☎ 0823   A1

Sessa Aurunca is on the site of ancient *Suessa,* in a natural amphitheatre on a volcanic ridge.

▶ The 12C Romanesque **Duomo**★ in the centre of town incorporates materials from Roman buildings; the interior has mosaic pavement (12C); the **pulpit**★ (13C) and paschal candelabrum are also covered with mosaics. ▶ Near the park are the **ruins** of a theatre and imperial Roman baths. ▶ At the top of the town is the ruined medieval **castle** with square tower. ▶ 3.5 km SW in charming natural surroundings is the Roman **Ponte degli Aurinci**★, a bridge with twenty-one brick arches. ▶ **Carinola** *(10 km SE)* has 15C Catalan-Gothic buildings (some in ruins), a crumbling castle, the **Chiesa dell'Annunziata** with Renaissance portal and 15C frescos and a late 11C Romanesque **cathedral** with triple-arched atrium. Beyond Sessa Aurunca *(4 km)* near **Ventaroli** is the isolated Romanesque church of **S. Maria,** with 12C and 15C frescos *(keys from police in Carnola).* ☐

Practical information

Recommended
Events: *Good Friday procession; Estate Sessana* (summer festival, concerts, crafts in piazza); *Torneo dei Quartieri* (Sep).
Farm vacations: *Azienda Arianova,* at San Castrese, ☎ 706249.

SORRENTO*

Naples 47, Rome 257 km
Pop. 17,601 ✉ 80067 ☎ 081   B3

Sorrento, birthplace of the poet Torquato Tasso, is set on a tufa terrace bordered with ravines, high above the sea in the Bay of Naples.

▶ The centre of the town is the **piazza Tasso;** a terrace overlooks the ravine running down to the Marina Piccola. ▶ The basilica of **S. Antonio** was based on a 14C oratory; an 11C portal is on one side. ▶ In front of the **Duomo** (rebuilt 15C) is an unusual campanile supported by an arch with four antique columns; inside there is a **choir,** a fine specimen of Sorrento inlaid woodwork. ▶ The **Sedile Dominiova** is a 15C loggia with a 17C dome in typical Neapolitan coloured majolica; the local nobility was divided into two *sedili* (political factions). ▶ The 16C **walls** are interrupted by the remains of a **Roman arch** at the top of the town. ▶ Near the entrance to the **Villa Comunale,** a park with palm trees on a terrace overlooking the sea, is the church of **S. Francesco;** the **cloister** has interlaced arches (14C). ▶ The 18C palazzo of the same name houses the **Museo Correale di Terranova**★ *(closed for restoration)* with an interesting collection of 17C-18C decorative art. ▶ **Marina Piccola** is the harbour, **Marina Grande** an inlet with beach. ▶ It takes *1 hour* by boat from the Marina Piccola to the **Punta del Capo**★ where there are Roman ruins which may be those of the villa of Pollio Felix and the **Bagno della Regina Giovanna** (Queen Joan's bath), a

mirror of water in the rocks with remains of walls. Punta del Capo can also be reached on land by first climbing to the village of **Capo di Sorrento** *(2.8 km)* and then following a lane *(15 mn).* ☐

Practical information

≋
🛈 v. L. De Maio 35, ☎ 8782104 or 8781115.
🚢 boats to Naples, Capri and Ischia, *GRU.SO.N,* ☎ 8781430; hydrofoils for Capri and Naples (in summer), *Alilauro,* ☎ 8771506.
Car rental: *Avis,* corso Italia 155, ☎ 8782459.

Hotels:
★★★★ *Bristol,* v. Capo 22, ☎ 8784522, 132 rm Ⓟ ⫰ ⫰ ⫰
▭ 120,000.
★★★★ *Cocumella,* at Sant'Agnello, v. Cocumella 7, ☎ 8782933, 50 rm Ⓟ 🅰 ⫰ ⫰ ▭ 🏷 Former 16C Jesuit residence recently restored, 160,000.
★★★★ *Continental,* p. della Vittoria, ☎ 8781476, 80 rm Ⓟ 🏷 closed Nov-Mar, 125,000.
★★★★ *Excelsior Vittoria,* p. Tasso 34, ☎ 8781900, 125 rm Ⓟ ⫰ 🅰 ⫰ ⫰ ▭ 19C villa sheer above sea with elevator to beach, 205,000.
★★★★ *G. H. Ambasciatori,* v. Califano 18/20, ☎ 8782025, 103 rm Ⓟ ⫰ ⫰ ▭ 102,000; bkf: 13,000.
★★★★ *G. H. Flora,* corso Italia 248, ☎ 8782520, 85 rm Ⓟ ⫰ ▭ closed 16 Nov-28 Feb except Christmas, 110,000.
★★★★ *G. H. Royal,* v. Correale 42, ☎ 8781920, 96 rm Ⓟ ⫰ ⫰ ▭ closed 16 Nov-14 Mar, 125,000; bkf: 13,000.
★★★★ *Parco dei Principi,* v. Rota 1, ☎ 8784644, 173 rm Ⓟ ⫰ 🅰 ⫰ ⫰ 🛁 ▭ closed 16 Nov-31 Mar. Complex made up of 18C villa and futuristic building, 192,000; bkf: 16,000.
★★★ *G. H. Capodimonte,* v. Capo 14, ☎ 8784067, 131 rm Ⓟ ⫰ ⫰ ▭ closed 16 Nov-14 Mar, 96,000; bkf: 13,000.
★★★ *G. H. Cesare Augusto,* v. degli Aranci 108, ☎ 8782700, 120 rm ⫰ ▭ 110,000; bkf: 12,000.
★★★ *Central,* corso Italia 254, ☎ 8783674, 58 rm Ⓟ ⫰ 🏷 ▭ 🏷 74,000.
★★★ *Gran Paradiso,* v. Catigliano 9, ☎ 8782911, 83 rm Ⓟ ⫰ 🅰 ⫰ ⫰ ▭ closed Nov-Mar, 88,000.
★★★ *Solara,* v. Capo 118, ☎ 8783122, 40 rm Ⓟ ⫰ ⫰ ▭ closed Nov-Mar, 63,000.
★★ *Desirée,* v. Capo 31 bis, ☎ 8781563, 22 rm Ⓟ ⫰ ⫰ ⫰ ⫰ closed Nov-Mar. No restaurant, 50,000.
★★ *Minervetta,* v. Capo 25, ☎ 8781098, 12 rm Ⓟ ⫰ 42,000; bkf: 6,000.
★★ *Tonnarella,* v. Capo 31, ☎ 8781153, 16 rm Ⓟ ⫰ ⫰ ⫰ closed Dec-Feb, 48,000.

Restaurants:
● ◆◆◆ *Favorita-'o Parrucchiano,* corso Italia 71/73, ☎ 8781321, closed Wed except summer. Long tradition with vaults and antique furniture, elegant garden. Regional cuisine: cannelloni, fish stewed or grilled, homemade wines, 20/30,000.
◆◆◆ *Cavallino Bianco,* v. Correale 11/A, ☎ 8785809, closed Tue and 15 Dec-15 Jan. Open kitchen, fireplace, meals outside in large garden. International cuisine: crêpes al formaggio, scampi or crayfish all'americana, dishes cooked at table, 23/40,000.

🍴 *Nube d'Argento,* v. Capo 21, 150 pl, ☎ 8781344 (all year); *Santa Fortunata-Campogaio,* v. Capo 39/A, 600 pl, ☎ 8782405.

Recommended
Craft workshops: *Notturno,* v. Fuori Mura 33, ☎ 8783239 (art inlay).
Events: *Good Friday processions; international film competition; sailing regattas* (Aug hol).
Marina: ☎ 8781108.
Youth hostel: *Ostello Surriento,* v. Capasso 5, ☎ 8781783.

Be advised that hotels and restaurants in this Guide have perhaps changed addresses; prices indicated are also subject to modifications.

TEANO

Caserta 33, Naples 66, Rome 197 km
Pop. 14,523 ✉ 81057 ☎ 0823   A1

The exact site of the encounter between Garibaldi and Victor Emmanuel II is subject to dispute, but nevertheless is commemorated by a **stele** about 4 km along the Caianello Road.

▶ The 12C **Duomo**, with antique columns and a campanile incorporating Roman marbles, has a pulpit made of 13C materials and a 14C panel painting of the *Crucifixion;* the crypt of S. Paride houses a **museum** of Roman, medieval and modern marbles. ▶ The **Loggione** is a medieval building with large Gothic vault. ▶ The impressive ruins of the **Roman theatre** are in Le Grotte. ▶ 8 km SE beyond the Romanesque basilica of **S. Paride** (founded 13C) is **Calva Vecchia**. The cathedral has elements of a 9C building and a crypt with ancient columns *(keys from house next door);* the ruined castle is 15C. **Excavations** in ancient *Cales* have revealed remains of an amphitheatre, theatre and parts of baths and a temple. ☐

VALLO DELLA LUCANIA

Salerno 91, Naples 147, Rome 354 km
Pop. 7,957 ✉ 84078 ☎ 0974   D5

Vallo della Lucania is the major agricultural and commercial centre of the Cilento. It sits on a spur in a valley covered with dense olive groves.

▶ The church of **S. Maria delle Grazie** has an altarpiece from 1530 and a painting from 1515. ▶ The **Museo Diocesano** contains 15C-16C paintings and liturgical objects including a 14C Sienese chalice and an ivory casket from the Embriachi workshop. ▶ 10.5 km by road and 30 mn on foot leads to the **Santuario della Madonna di Novi Vélia** (5,594 ft), which affords a panoramic **view**★. ☐

Practical information _____

Hotel:
★★ *Mimi,* v. Nazionale 157, ☎ 4302, 24 rm Ⓟ ⏦
⏦ 29,500.

VESUVIUS

Naples 24, Rome 248 km
4,190 ft   B3

Vesuvius is not the largest volcano in the world, perhaps not even the one that has caused the most suffering, but it is surely the most famous. The eruption of 79, which buried Pompeii, Herculaneum and Stabia, made Vesuvius part of the heritage of classical culture. Its smoke plumes ceased in 1944, depriving Naples of one of its most striking visual features, the black plume above the mountain. The truncated cone that is so familiar in profile is Mt. Somma, with the Punta del Nasone as its highest point (3,714 ft); a smaller cone, Vesuvius proper, rises from the floor of the Somma crater reaching a height of 4,190 ft; this was formed by the eruption of 79; between the cone of Vesuvius and the Somma is a valley known as the Atrio del Cavallo in the N section and the Valle dell'Inferno in the E. For a time the volcano remained quiescent, and in the 16C woods grew right to the summit; an eruption in 1631 sent lava as far as the sea; another in 1794 destroyed Torre del Greco.

▶ The **Strada del Vesuvio** *(13 km)* climbs from **Pugliano** through orchards, vineyards and sheets of cooled lava, first to the **Osservatorio Vesuviano** (1,998 ft, fine view★ from the square of the coast and the side of the mountain)

then to a crossroads from which a road leads to the **Valle dei Gigante** (3,337 ft); from here it is possible to walk in 20 mn to the crater along the NW side. Finally, the road reaches the **chair lift station** (2,474 ft). ▶ An ascent to the **crater**★ takes 6 mn by chair lift *(9 a.m.-between 4:30 and 7 pm, according to season; closed 5-30 Nov)* over the steep, lava-covered slope; from the upper station (3,799 ft) a path leads to the **edge of the crater,** which is almost 2,000 ft in diameter; a guide accompanies groups around the crater; only a few fumaroles betray that the volcano is active; the **view**★★ extends from Gaeta to Capri. ☐

Vineyards of Campania

Visitors driving through the countryside of Campania often see a peasant pushing a light plow that is pulled by a donkey or a mare. Making slow progress, he digs into the fertile ground where cereal or vegetables quickly grow between high rows of vine that are intertwined like garlands. Every village makes its own wine, each famous in its own way. Horace was proud of the Ager Fabernus wines of which Faberne is the most well-known. On the slopes of Mount Vesuvius, growing is a very serious and careful affair and in the past, peasants greeted each other with: 'May the vine grow!' On the wall of a house in Pompeii, a painter has drawn Vesuvius, dedicated to Bacchus, and turned it into a bunch of ripe grapes.

The eruption of Vesuvius

On the warm, clear morning of 24 August 79 Pliny the Elder was in Miseno, in command of the naval squadron, with his nephew (Pliny the Younger) who wrote two letters to Tacitus describing what had happened. A cloud shaped like an umbrella pine appeared over the bay and blotted out the sun. The admiral moved the fleet towards Herculaneum (Ercolano), but was unable to go ashore; he went on to Stabiae (Castellammare di Stàbia), but after landing, died on the beach, suffocated by the ash and smoke. Not until late on the 26th did a feeble light reappear. The basalt plug of the cone of the volcano had burst; lava and rock were thrown hundreds of feet into the air and fell back to earth like an apocalyptic bombardment, followed by a thick cloud of glowing pumice. Pompeii was buried to a depth of six feet. During the night the internal walls of the volcanic cone collapsed, causing further explosions, earthquakes, steam, ash and dust spread over the town to a depth of several more feet. Herculaneum was flooded by a torrent of superheated mud. This had advanced relatively slowly, and many people had been able to escape. Pompeii had been taken by surprise; more than 2,000 were dead. Some had been killed by falling rocks in the early stages; most suffocated in the smoke or gas.

VICO EQUENSE

Naples 36, Rome 248 km
Pop. 17,808 ✉ 80069 ☎ 081   B3

Vico Equense lies in a fine position on a tufa promontory of the N coast of the Sorrento peninsula, with the beaches of **Marina di Vico, Capo la Gala** and **Marina di Equa** at its feet. The Baroque façade of the 14C Gothic **Cathedral** looks over a little terrace high above the sea; in the interior *(apply to caretaker)* are frescos and panels in Byzantine style, paintings and a 14C sarcophagus. An **antiquarium** *(9 a.m.-1 p.m. and 6-8 p.m.; winter 9 a.m.-2 p.m.)* displays archaeological material recovered from a 7C-5C BC necropolis in the urban area. □

Practical information ⎯⎯⎯⎯⎯⎯⎯⎯

≋
⚓ (Jun-Oct), Scraio, ☎ 8798283.

⏸ v. Umberto I, ☎ 8798342.

Hotels:
★★★★ *Capo La Gala*, SS Sorrentina at 14-km marker, ☎ 8798278, 18 rm P ⟵ ⌇ ∰ ⚘ ⊡ closed Nov-Easter, 140,000.
★★★ *Aequa*, v. Filangieri 46, ☎ 8798000, 57 rm P ⟵ ∰ 75,000.

Restaurant:
♦♦ *Pizza a Metro*, v. Nicotera 10, ☎ 8798309. Mixed cuisine: misto Gigino, paglia e fieno, 25/50,000.

⚐ *Seiano Spiaggia*, at Marina di Equa, 170 pl, ☎ 8798165.

Emilia-Romagna

Emilia-Romagna stretches from the Adriatic Sea to within 22 km of the Mediterranean. Although it existed in Roman times, it was not given its present form until 1947 when Emilia and Romagna were joined. What constitutes this region is a combination of history and arbitrary decision-making. A Roman, Marcus Emilius Lepidus, traced a route — the ancient via Emilia — from what is now Piacenza to what is now Rimini. Most of the region's major cities (with the exception of Ferrara and Ravenna) are along this route, now paralleled by a highway that cuts straight through the region, dividing it roughly in two. Although this region is very flat, there are hills and long valleys to the right of this highway. The flatlands have been intensively cultivated since Roman times and now produce grain, sugar beet, grapes, livestock and fruit. Automobile, metal-working and chemical plants also give the region an industrial base. Through the reclamation of marshy land, sandy beaches on the Adriatic now offer lovely resorts. Links to the past are ever-present. Emilia-Romagna can claim a vital artistic heritage that includes the Byzantine mosaics at Ravenna and the Romanesque cathedrals at Parma, Piacenza and Ferrara. It also produced three outstanding sculptors: Wiligelmus of Modena, Benedetto Antelami of Parma and the unknown master who was responsible for the *Reliefs of the Months* at Ferrara. Bologna has been a spectacular centre of art since medieval times and Rimini and Ferrara testify to the influence of the Renaissance. The more mundane art of cuisine is also well-represented in this region, which offers excellent Parmesan cheese, prosciutto and, of course, marvelous pasta. Although the bustle of modernity is evident in Emilia-Romagna, the visitor may still find the variety that makes the region enchanting. □

 ## Don't miss

At Bologna★★: S. Petronio★★; the Pinacoteca Nazionale★★; S. Domenico★★ containing the tomb★★ of St. Dominic; S. Francesco★★ and the Madonna di S. Luca★ on the Guardia hill. At Ferrara★★: the Cathedral★★; the Palazzo Schifanoia★★ and frescos★★ in the Sala dei Mesi; the Palazzo di Ludovico il Moro★★ and the Palazzo dei Diamanti★★. At Modena★: the Duomo★★ and the Galleria Estense★★. At Parma★★: the Duomo★★; the Baptistery★★; the frescos★★ by Correggio in S. Giovanni Evangelista★; the Galleria Nazionale★★ and the Camera di S. Paolo★★ decorated by Correggio. At Piacenza★: 'Il Gothico'★★ (Palazzo Comunale) and the Farnese equestrian statues★★. At Ravenna★★: S. Vitale★★ (mosaics★★); the Mausoleum of Galla Placidia★★(mosaics★★); the throne of Maximian★★ in the Museo Arcivescovile★; S. Apollinare Nuovo★★ (mosaics★★); S. Apollinare in Classe★★. At Rimini★: the Tempio Malatestiano★★ and the Arch of Augustus★. Among the smaller cities with their artistic riches, special mention should be made of the Basilica★★ at Pomposa★.

piazza Matteotti in Castell'Arquato   Castello Estense in Ferrara

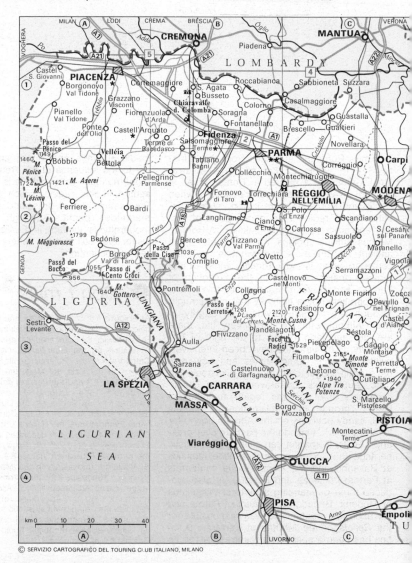

© SERVIZIO CARTOGRAFICO DEL TOURING CLUB ITALIANO, MILANO

Duomo and Baptistery in Parma   **cathedral in Ferrara**

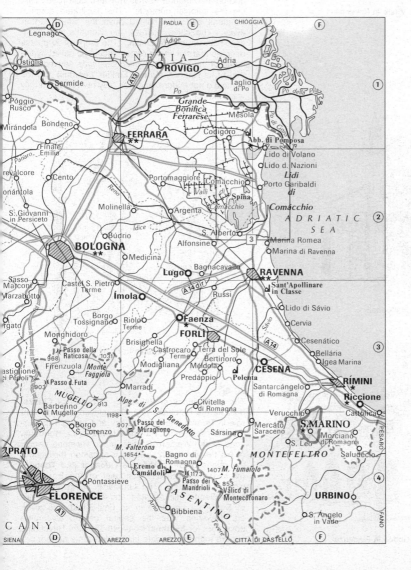

S. Vitale in Ravenna

● *Brief regional history*

6C BC-4C AD

Etruscans, Gauls and Romans. The Etruscans cross-ed the Apennines, probably from Asia Minor (although their origins have not been firmly estab-lished) to colonize the Po Valley at the end of the 6C BC. ● Archaeological excavations have reveal-ed important Etruscan artifacts (they were particu-larly good at metal-working) at **Marzabotto** near Bolo-gna and in the Ferrara region, especially at **Spina,** a lively port noted for its trade with the Greeks in ancient times. ● The devastating invasion of the Gauls came in the 4C BC, followed by the Roman conquest and subsequent colonization (2C BC). The Romans populated their colonies, cultivated the land and created market towns; they also built roads link-ing the colonial outposts. This facilitated commu-nications and also helped push the Gauls farther away. The cities built by the Romans still exist, especially on the **Via Emilia.** The Emperor Augustus decreed that the whole region should be called by the name of the Via Emilia (which itself was derived from that of its planner, **Marcus Emilius Lepidus**), but the name did not endure, and was only revived when Italy was reunified.

Duomo in Modena

S. Petronio in Bologna

il Gotico in Piacenza

5C-8C

The ascendancy of Ravenna. The port of **Classe,** built by the Emperor Augustus, played an important role in Roman imperial strategy and brought its sur-rounding settlement, Ravenna, to the fore. **Honorius,** head of the Western Empire, made Ravenna capital of his Empire in 402, and so it remained throughout the reigns of the barbarians **Odoacer** and **Theodo-ric** and the Byzantine conquest of the E part of what is now Italy. The Lombards came after 568, but Ravenna still resisted and became the centre of Byzantine presence in an Emilia that was divid-ed. Ravenna was the capital of the Byzantine governors (or **Exarchs**) from 540-751, and Ravenna's superb monuments date largely from this period.

Rocca in Fontanellato

Palazzo Bevilacqua in Bologna

9C-13C

Bishops, independent city-states and emperors. In 754, at the request of the papacy, the Franks, under **Pepin** the Short, moved in to take over the territory of the **Exarchs** which was once again being threatened by the Lombards. Pepin gave this territory to the papacy and the acquisition was the first territorial basis of the **papal states.** ● **Charlemagne,** son of Pepin, continued his father's fight against the Lombards and, after his victory, accepted the Lombard kings' crown of iron. ● By the first half of the 12C, several cities — **Bologna, Modena, Reggio, Parma** and **Piacenza** — had become independent city-states that had to protect themselves not only against the popes (whose supporters were the Guelphs) but against the emperors whose partisans were the Ghibellines. They also had to defend themselves against other city-states. This period was one of almost constant bloodshed. ● Finally, in 1248, Emperor Frederick II, long master of the region, was beaten at **Parma;** his son was made a lifetime captive in Bologna the year after.

13C-16C

The feudal domains. After Frederick's defeat and death, the Western Empire was forced to give up its designs on N Italy, and, in Emilia, the city-states became feudal lordships. ● In **Parma** and **Piacenza** the Visconti family held sway and these two cities leaned towards Lombardy. **Ferrara** (1240) and then **Modena** and **Reggio** went to the **Este** family (1288-90); **Bologna** had a brief spell under the **Pepoli** family (14C), and a century later was the domain of the **Bentivoglio;** in **Rimini** it was the **Malatesta** family; in **Ravenna** the **da Polenta.** ● In Romagna the old rule of the Church was revitalized by Cardinal **Albernoz** (1353-67). ● Later Romagna was the focus of the expansionist intentions of Venice and Florence, but **Cesare Borgia** was able to carve out a personal dominion in Florence where he was made Duke of Romagna by Pope Alexander VI. ● At Cesare Borgia's death in battle (1503), Pope Julius II finally managed to return Romagna to the **papal states.**

16C-18C

Duchies and legations. In the second half of the 16C the region began to enjoy an almost undisturbed peace for some 200 years. ● The papal states (the E parts of Emilia were known as **Legations,** as they were governed by papal legates) took over **Ferrara** in 1598, ending its glorious Renaissance years under the Este family. Only the **Duchies** of Parma, Piacenza, Modena and Reggio remained outside direct papal control. ● In 1545, Pope **Paul III** gave **Parma** and **Piacenza** to his son, **Pier Luigi Farnese,** whose family kept the duchy until 1731 when **Elisabetta Farnese,** the wife of King Philip V of Spain, managed to have it assigned to one of her sons. It thus passed to the house of **Bourbon-Parma.** ● **Modena and Reggio** remained in the hands of the **Este** family, which, having lost Ferrara, made Modena its capital. ● The marriage of a niece of Francesco III d'Este to the son of Maria Theresa of Austria (18C) prepared the way for the **Austria-Este** line to take control.

19C-20C

Napoleon, Restoration, the Risorgimento. Modena, Reggio, Bologna and Ferrara, feeling the threat of French arms, united to form what later became part of Napoleon's **Italian empire,** the **Repubblica Cisalpina.** ● The **Congress of Vienna** (1815) restored the 18C status quo, whereby the region was divided into duchies and papal legations, with one exception: the **Duchy of Parma and Piacenza** was assigned to the Austrian **Marie Louise,** former Empress and wife of Napoleon. ● Early agitation for Italian unity foun-

S. Apollinare in Classe in Ravenna

dered in 1848, but during the second war of independence (1859) the duchies and the legations rebeled and united under **Luigi Carlo Farini** (at which point the region revived the old Roman name of **Emilia**); the region allied itself briefly to the **Kingdom of Sardinia** (18 March 1860) before becoming part of the Kingdom of Italy. ● **Romagna** — the southernmost part of the region — and **Emilia** were joined in 1947, under the terms of the Republican Constitution.

abbey of Pomposa

● *Practical information*

Information: tourist offices in district capitals and principal centres.

SOS: public emergency services, ☎ 113; police emergency, ☎ 112; road assistance *(ACI)*, ☎ 116.

Weather: forecast, ☎ 191; road and traffic conditions, ☎ 194 or *ACI,* ☎ 06/4212; snow bulletins, ☎ 162; shipping forecast, ☎ 196.

Farm vacations: *Associazione regionale Agriturist,* at Bologna, v. Lame 15, ☎ 051/233321.

Events: art exhibits and music festival, at Bologna; opera season at the Teatro Regio, at Parma; international Verdi singing competition, at Busseto; *international ballet festival,* at Comacchio; *international organ festival, music festival,* opera and ballet seasons, at Ravenna; *festival of young voices,* at Castrocaro Terme; *music and European film festivals,* at Rimini; *international detective film festival (Mystfest),* at Cattolica; *independent film festival,* at Poretta Terme; *international theatre festival,* in the piazza of Santarcangelo di Romagna; modern ceramic arts competition, at Faenza; international numismatic conference, at Riccione; art competition, at Marina di Ravenna; Palio di San Giorgio, at Ferrara; investiture of the Capitani Regenti and the *Palio della Balestra* (crossbow), at San Marino.

Fairs: *International Children's Book Fair,* at Bologna; *Fiera di Forlì;* international food preserving technology fair,

Quota 600 and traders' fair, at Parma; exhibition and fair for the vacation and recreation industry, and for telecommunications, at Piacenza; international conferences for pig farmers and ornithologists, at Reggio nell'Emilia; hotel exhibition and boat show, at Rimini; antique fair and exhibition, at Cesenàtico; regular antique fairs, at Modena and Ravenna.

Nature parks: *Riserva dei Sassi di Roccamalatina* (→ Vignola); *Riserva delle Salse di Nirano* (→ Modena); *Parco dei Boschi di Carrega;* nature reserve at Punta Alberete (→ Ravenna); Gran Bosco della Mésola; nature-reserve in valleys of the Argenta and Marmorta; nature reserve on Mt. Fuso (→ Parma); nature reserve at Foce di Volano; nature reserve with picnic areas, at Brisighella; nature reserve and zoo at Cervia.

Ecology: *WWF* regional office, at Bologna, v. Savenella 13, ☎ 051/332233; branches at: Piacenza, v. Scalabrini 19, ☎ 0523/21624; Parma, p. Garibaldi (centro civico), ☎ 0521/206990; Reggio nell'Emilia, v. Isonzo 72, ☎ 0522/40339; Modena, corso Canal Grande 17, ☎ 059/222161; Finale Emilia, v.Trento-Trieste 14, ☎ 0535/25108; Rimini, v. Cavalieri 12, ☎ 0541/52530; Ferrara, v. Ariosto 88, ☎ 0532/34771; Ravenna, v. Mentana 19, ☎ 0544/33081; Forlì, corso Garibaldi 17, ☎ 0543/21635; Faenza, corso Garibaldi 2, ☎ 0546/26490 (excursions and courses in natural history). *LIPU,* Parma (national headquarters), v. S. Tiburzio 5, ☎ 0521/33414-27116, p. Garibaldi (centro civico), ☎ 0521/31113 (courses and excursions in spring to the *Parco del Tizzo;* visits by appointment to the *Oasi del Cavaliere d'Italia,* at Trescasali); Ferrara, v. delle Chiodare 3/5 (visits to the *Oasi di Bosco Forte* in the communes of Comacchio and Argenta); Bologna, v. Zamboni 59, ☎ 051/244552; Modena, corso Canal Grande 17 (centre for sightings of peregrin falcons); Reggio nell'Emilia, v. Isonzo 72, ☎ 0522/40339.

Excursions: sign-posted long-distance itineraries: *Grande Escursione Apenninica,* through the Parmesan, Reggiano and Modenese Apennines (11 stages, from the Passo dei Due Santi to Pracchia; Apr to late autumn, → Tuscany, section on excursions). Information: *CAI,* divisions at: Carpi, v. Brennero, ☎ 059/682759; Castelnovo ne' Monti, Isolato Maest 21/A, ☎ 0522/811939; Forlì, v. Flavio 4; Imola, v. Emilia 147; Modena, v. Caselline 11; Parma, v. Ospizi Civili 6, ☎ 0521/282344; Piacenza, v. S. Vincenzo 2, ☎ 0523/28847; Reggio nell'Emilia, corso Garibaldi 14, ☎ 0522/36685. *ARCI-UISP:* Reggio nell'Emilia, v. Isonzo 72, ☎ 0522/44935; Modena, v. Mala-

Facts and figures

Location: *Emilia-Romagna comprises the S section of the Po plain (from a point a little upriver of Piacenza to the Adriatic Sea) and the N slopes of the Apennines, but neither the N bank of the Po nor the mountain peaks to the S coincide precisely with the administrative boundaries of the region.*

Area: *22,122 sq km.*

Climate: *A typically continental climate, with hot summers and cold winters, frequent rain in autumn (also snow) and in spring. The Adriatic, which borders the E part of the region, is not a moderating influence on the wide variations in the weather.*

Population: *3,952,304 inhabitants.*

Administrative organization: *The regional capital is Bologna, and the provincial capitals are Ferrara, Forlì, Modena, Parma, Piacenza, Ravenna and Reggio nell'Emilia. In Romagna, near the border with the Marches and not far from the sea, is the old independent Republic of San Marino, one of the two sovereign states lying within Italian territory (the other being the Vatican).*

goli 6, ☎ 059/225641. Travel for young people: *Centro turistico giovanile*, Reggionell'Emilia, v. Isonzo 72, ☎ 0522/42990; *GEAS*, Sassuolo, v. Parco 4, ☎ 0536/862677.

Cycling: assistance and information from various cycling organizations affiliated to *UDACE* (249) throughout region. The *TCI* cycling map *Ferrara e il Po* gives details of itineraries along valley and hill routes (Ferrara circuits) and an itinerary between the Panaro and Po Rivers (Bondeno circuit). Among the numerous cycling events organized each year are: the Italian youth championship, at Cattolica (May); Milano-Santarcangelo di Romagna (beginning May, 4 days); Parma-coast (Jun).

Horseback riding: *Federazione Italiana Sport Equestre*, regional committee at Parma, v. Padre Onorio 18, ☎ 0521/38850; centres associated with *ANTE* throughout region.

Instruction: ceramics: *M. Morigi* art and ceramics workshop, at Faenza, p. S. Domenico 1, ☎ 0546/29940 (week-long courses in decorative techniques, including majolica, for beginners and experts); *E. Galassi*, at Faenza, v. Castellina, ☎ 0546/661655 (two-week courses for beginners and experts, Japanese techniques); *C. Matteini* ceramics workshop at Medicina, v. Piave 485, ☎ 051/850345-477725 (week-long courses). Mosaics: *Centro internazionale di studi per l'insegnamento del mosaico*, at Ravenna, at tourist office, v. S. Vitale 2, ☎ 0544/35755 (two-week summer courses at Lido Adriano). Music: *Circolo ocarinistico budriese* (ocarina-playing), at Budrio, v. Golinelli 5, ☎ 051/801057.

Sailing: *Lega Navale*: Marina di Ravenna, molo Dalmazia 89, ☎ 0544/430513; Bellaria-Igea Marina, v. Abbazia, ☎ 0541/44478; *UISP* sailing centres at Bologna and Ravenna.

Canoeing: *Federazione Italiana Canoa-kayak*, affiliated schools at Bologna, Modena and Parma; *On the Beach Kayak School*, at Modena, v. Mascarella 36, ☎ 059/217956 (courses and practice in rafting, river descents in rubber dinghies).

Water-skiing: *Federazione italiana* at Boretto (→ Guastalla), Colorno, Sissa (→ Colorno).

Motor-racing: *Dino Ferrari*, at Imola, ☎ 0542/31444; *Santamonica*, at Misano Adriatico, ☎ 0541/615159; *San Cristoforo*, at Varano de' Melegari, ☎ 0525/52238; *Ferrari*, at Fiorano Modenese (→ Modena), at Spezzano, ☎ 059/843650.

Motocross: *Baldasserona*, at San Marino; track: *G. Costa*, at Serramazzoni.

Golf: Chiesa Nuova di Monte San Pietro (→ Bologna, 18 holes).

Tennis: summer centres (two-week courses) at: Lizzano in Belvedere, ☎ 0534/51032; and Séstola ☎ 0536/62380; Pievepélago, ☎ 0536/71358; Serramazzoni, ☎ 0536/952224; information, *Società sportiva Luigi Orsini*, at Rome, ☎ 06/390064.

Fencing: international summer centres for men and women at: Lizzano in Belvedere and at Zocca. Information, *Federazione Italiana Scherma*, at Rome, ☎ 06/36851.

Flying: *G. Bortolotti*, at Bologna airport, ☎ 051/400337 (also gliding); at Carpi, at Budrione airport, ☎ 0531/660080; at Ferrara airport, ☎ 0532/91655; *Centro studi volo a vela padano* (gliding), at Aguscello (→ Ferrara), ☎ 0532/418550; *G. Ridolfi*, at Forlì airport, ☎ 0543/780242 (also gliding); *F. Baracca* at Lugo, at Villa San Martino, ☎ 0545/23338; at Modena airport, v. Marzaglia, ☎ 059/389090; *G. Bolla*, at Parma airport *N. Palli*, ☎ 0521/90204 (also gliding); *F. Baracca*, at Ravenna airport, v. Dismano, ☎ 0544/497644 (also gliding); at Reggio nell'Emilia, v. Vertoiba 1, ☎ 0522/511650; at Rimini airport *Miramare*, ☎ 0541/373301.

Fishing: *Federazione Italiana Pesca Sportiva*: at Bologna, v. Rizzoli 7, ☎ 051/224640-235878; Ferrara, v. Cortevecchia 67, ☎ 0532/25568; Forlì Ginnasio Sportivo, v. Libert,

The navel of Venus and Emilian cuisine

In a famous poem by Tassoni, the Secchia Rapita (stolen bucket), there is an essential piece of information: '... the inn-keeper, who was cross-eyed and Bolognese, learned the art of making tortellini by imitating the navel of Venus'. Indeed, the sheets of fresh pasta from which tortellini (and also tagliatelle, lasagne and parpadelle) are made form one of the three pillars on which the gastronomic delights of this region rest. The second is its sauces, well seasoned, rich in body and flavour and perfectly accompanied by grated parmesan, the king of Italian cheeses, savoured by Boccaccio and Montaigne. The third pillar is pork — cured ham from Langhirano, salami from Felino, culatello from Zibello, mortadella from Bologna and zampone from Modena. Culatello (pork rump cured like ham) was on the menu at the marriage feast of Count Andrea Rossi and Giovanna Sanseverino in 1322. There are those who claim to discern certain fine differences between the cuisine of Emilia and that of Romagna (where tortellini are called cappelletti): Emilian cooking, it is said, is gentle and persuasive like the Emilians themselves; while that of Romagna is rougher and more aggressive. Whether such differences exist or not, Emilian-Romagnese cooking is appreciated by all those who are lucky enough to taste it.

Zampone

Gioacchino Rossini, who came from Pésaro and was a gourmand of the first order, praised zampone and lambrusco in the following terms: 'I received the zampone and ate it,/ I received the lambrusco and drank it./ The food was exquisite, worthy of Rossini,/ the wine was worthy of the gods of Homer.' Zampone is a traditional specialty of Modena: it consists of pig's trotter boned and pared down to the skin, then stuffed with coarsely minced pork and delicately seasoned with spices. It is an absolute necessity for New Year's Eve, gently simmered in water for several hours and served with lentils. This dish is thought to have been invented in the second half of the 18C by one Giuseppe Bellentani, a charcutier from Modena. But there is another story. In the winter of 1510-11 the impetuous Pope Julius II ordered a siege to be laid on the town of Miràndola. As the siege went on (so long that the pope himself went to the town) the besieged citizens, on the point of starvation, decided to make use of every last piece of slaughtered pig, rolled it into sausages and came up with zampone. Despite this, the town surrendered.

☎ 0543/25696; Modena, v. L. Poletti 4, ☎ 059/214372; Parma, v. N. Sauro 5, ☎ 0521/29451; Piacenza, v. Mazzini 58, ☎ 0523/36892; Ravenna, v. Zirardini 14, ☎ 0544/322292; Reggio nell'Emilia, v. G. Castello 8, ☎ 0522/39984. For fishing conditions (permits and terms, prohibited stretches of river, etc.) apply to appropriate regional division.

Hang gliding: *Federazione Italiana Deltaplano*, information, ☎ 015/538703; affiliated schools at Imola, Modena, Parma, Riccione.

Amusement parks: *Fiabilandia* and *Italia in miniatura*, at Rimini.

● Towns and places

Bolognese and Modenese APENNINES

From Bologna to Pavullo nel Frignano *(139 km, 1 day; map 1)*

By and large the Bolognese Apennines are of modest altitude, except in the upper reaches of the valley of the River Silla and that of the River Dardagna where the Corno alle Scale reaches 6,380 ft; yet this area offers a wide range of excursions and itineraries, and summer vacations in the fresh alpine air in the midst of forests. The Modenese Apennines, corresponding roughly to the Frignano region, are probably the most beautiful part of the Apennine chain in Emilia, where the highest and most majestic peaks of the northern Apennines (Mt. Cimone rises to 7,101 ft) are found. This is a very popular area for vacations, with an excellent choice of hotels, and offers not only fine landscapes but a visit to the archaeological excavation of an Etruscan city near Marzabotto.

▶ From **Bologna** (→) the road to the S follows the wide valley of the River Reno. ▶ At **Pontecchio Marconi** the **Mausoleo di Guglielmo Marconi** (built in 1941) contains the tomb of this renowned scientist who carried out some of the first experiments in radio transmission (1895) in the **Villa Grifone**, which stands above this site. ▶ After **Sasso Marconi** the valley of the Reno narrows. ▶ **Marzabotto** was the tragic site of a Nazi massacre in 1944. 500 m from the town, on the v. Porrettana, is a large **archaeological site** *(9 a.m.-12 noon; 3 p.m.-1 hr before sunset; closed Mon)* which has uncovered the remains of an Etruscan city founded in the 6C BC and destroyed by the Gauls some two centuries later. An interesting **museum** displays the results of the dig. ▶ After **Vergato** the itinerary leaves the valley floor to take a road over valleys and ridges to **Castel d'Aiano**, before descending the Silla Valley (panorama). ▶ At **Lizzano in Belvedere**, a summer vacation centre and the departure point for excursions to Mt. Nuda (5,992 ft), there is an extraordinary 8C-10C pre-Romanesque construction called **La Rotonda**. ▶ From **Vidiciàtico**, on the watershed between

the Reno and the Panaro, it is worth climbing up to the **Madonna dell'Acero★**, a wonderful wooded spot with rustic sanctuary, and then on to **Baggioledo,** a ski centre. From here one can continue on to **Lake Scaffaiolo,** beneath the Corno alle Scale. ▶ Having descended into the valley of the Leo, the road then climbs to **Fanano,** beneath the Libro Aperto (6,353 ft); the church of **S. Silvestro** here retains some of its Romanesque and Renaissance elements. ▶ Crossing the slopes of Mt. Cimone, one comes to **Séstola,** surrounded by greenery and the largest vacation resort in this part of the Apennines. From Séstola one can reach *(9 km)* **Ninfa Lake,** set among larch woods; a detour away from the road to the lake leads to the cablecar to **Pian Cavallaro** beneath the peak of Mt. Cimone (far-ranging panorama). ▶ The road then descends through woods and, having crossed the River Scoltenna, joins the SS 12 to Abetone (→), which then crosses the Apennines, connecting Modena to Lucca. ▶ From Pavulla nel Frignano there is an interesting detour to the **Castello di Montecuccolo,** birthplace of a famous Italian general, Raimondo Montecuccoli (1609-80). The houses gathered at the foot of the castle still have their picturesque old doorways and chimneys. □

Practical information

FANANO, 2,099 ft, ✉ 41021, ☎ 0536.
ⅹ ski lifts, cross-country skiing, instruction.
ⓘ ☎ 68825.

LIZZANO IN BELVEDERE, 2,099 ft, ✉ 40042, ☎ 0534.
ⅹ ski lifts, cross-country routes, instruction at Corne alle Scale-Val Carlina.
ⓘ p. Marconi, ☎ 51052; at Vidiciàtico, v. Mercanti, ☎ 53159.

Hotels:
★★★ *Montegrande,* at Vidiciàtico, v. Marconi 27, ☎ 53210, 10 rm ⓟ ⌘ closed May and Nov, 45,000; bkf: 5,000.
★★★ *Piccolo Hotel,* p. Marconi 4, ☎ 51107, 22 rm ⌘ closed 1-25 Oct, 50,000; bkf: 4,000.

Recommended

Fencing: *centro internationale estivo* (women); information: *Federazione italiana scherma,* Rome, ☎ 06/36851.
Tennis: *centro federale estivo* (two-week courses); information: *Società sportiva L. Orsini,* Rome, ☎ 06/390064.

1. Bolognese and Modenese Apennines

PAVULLA NEL FRIGNANO, ⊠ 41026, ☎ 0536.
① p. S. Bartolomeo, ☎ 20358.

Hotels:
★★★ *Ferro di Cavallo,* v. Bellini 4, ☎ 20098, 19 rm P ⚒ 48,000; bkf:8,000.
★★★ *Vandelli,* v. Giardini Sud 7, ☎ 20288, 21 rm P ⚒ Ġ ⚗ 45,000; bkf: 5,000.

Restaurant:
♦ *Parco Corsini,* v. Martiri 11, ☎ 20129, closed Mon and 15-30 Jun. Regional cuisine: pappardelle verde, lasagne with porcini, 20/25,000.

Recommended
Clay pigeon shooting: at Polinago, v. del Brutto, ☎ 47016.
Horseback riding: *Oasi,* v. Miceno 50, ☎ 51099.

SASSO MARCONI, ⊠ 40037, ☎ 051.

Hotel:
★★ *Bettola,* v. Porrettana 361, ☎ 841376, 20 rm P closed 1-15 Jan and 1-15 Jul, 45,000; bkf: 6,000.

⚓ ★★★ *Piccolo Paradiso,* at Leona, 247 pl, ☎ 842680 (all year).

Recommended
Horseback riding: *Ca' Brusa* riding club, v. Val di Setta; *Allevamento Tivirolo,* v. Pieve del Pino 9 (associate of ANTE).

SESTOLA, 3,345 ft, ⊠ 41029, ☎ 0536.
⚡ cable car, ski lifts, instruction.
① p. Passerini 18, ☎ 82324.

Hotels:
★★★★ *San Marco,* v. delle Rose 2, ☎ 62330, 42 rm P ⚓ ⚒ ⚗ ⚲ closed 16 Mar-14 Jun and 16 Sep-19 Dec, 75,000; bkf: 8,000.
★★★ *Cristallo* p. Passerini 34, ☎ 62551, 27 rm P ⚔ ⚒ closed 16 Apr-14 Jun and 16 Sep-14 Nov, 50,000; bkf: 8,000.
★★★ *Tirolo,* v. delle Rose, ☎ 62523, 40 rm P ⚓ ⚒ ⚲ closed 1 Apr-19 Jun and 11 Sep-19 Dec, 45,000; bkf: 4,000.
★★ *Capriolo,* v. Statale Ovest 42, ☎ 62325, 26 rm P ⚒ closed May-Jun and Oct-Nov, 48,000; bkf: 6,000.

Restaurant:
♦♦♦ *San Rocco,* corso Umberto I 17, ☎ 62382, closed Mon and Oct-Nov. In elegant hotel. Regional cuisine: ricotta cannelloni in salsa rosa, pancakes stuffed with ham and béchamel sauce, 25/45,000.

Recommended
Horseback riding: *Centro ippico Sestolese,* ☎ 82046.
Tennis: *centro federale estivo* (two-week courses); information: Società sportiva L. Orsini, Rome, ☎ 06/390064.

ARGENTA

Ferrara 34, Bologna 50, Milan 261 km
Pop. 23,744 ⊠ 44011 ☎ 0532   E2

Argenta is an agricultural and industrial town in a fertile area of reclaimed land on the l. bank of the River Reno. Its name is that of the tax that inhabitants had to pay to the bishops of Ravenna.·

▶ Of particular note is the church of **S. Domenico** (built end 15C-16C), containing 16C frescos and other works of art. ▶ 1 km W of the centre, on the other side of the Reno, the small parish church of **S. Giorgio** is all that remains of the old town of Argenta, destroyed by an earthquake in 1624. Of Byzantine origin, only one of its original three aisles remains; the Romanesque portal (1122) is particularly fine. ▶ S of Argenta, near Campotta, is the park of the Argenta and Marmorta Valley, noted for its birdlife *(information at town hall,* ☎ *854328).* □

Practical information _____

Restaurants:
● ♦♦♦ *Trigabolo,* p. Garibaldi, ☎ 804121, closed Mon

eve, Tue, Jan and Jul. In town square, unexpected and secluded. Excellent creative cuisine: pancakes with gorgonzola and pistachio nuts, partridge in brandy, 50/60,000.
♦ *Spaventapasseri,* at Anita, v. Morelli 1, ☎ 801220, closed Mon eve, Tue and 10 Jan-15 Feb. Regional cuisine: pappardelle with hare, grilled eel, 16/30,000.

Terme di BACEDASCO

Piacenza 34, Bologna 135, Milan 100 km
⊠ 29010 ☎ 0523   B1-2

Terme di Bacedasso is an establishment with thermal springs, set in a large **park,** closed to traffic *(connected by special railway).* In the middle of the park is the **'Wilhelm Körner' Thermal Centre,** which offers mud treatment and baths.   □

Practical information _____

☘ (Mar-Nov), ☎ 895410.

Hotel:
★★★ *Cortina,* at Cortina Vecchia, ☎ 948101, 52 rm P ⚔ Ġ ⚗ closed 1 Nov-19 Mar, 40,000.

Restaurant:
♦♦ *Giovanni,* at Cortina Vecchia, ☎ 948304, closed Tue, Jan and Aug. Regional Emilian cuisine, 30/40,000.

BAGNACAVALLO

Ravenna 19, Bologna 63, Milan 273 km
Pop. 17,362 ⊠ 48012 ☎ 0545   E2

The peculiar name of this small town in the Romagnese plain has always aroused curiosity: it appears to owe its origin to a spring which, on account of its medicinal qualities, was used for bathing horses. Situated on the l. bank of the Canale Naviglio in a prosperous agricultural and industrial area, Bagnacavallo retains numerous indications of its noble medieval past among its arcaded streets and fine palaces. It was also the scene of a noted event of modern Italian history when, in the spring of 1898, popular movements against the increases in the price of grain and taxation erupted into violent rioting.

▶ The abbey of **S. Michele,** attributed to Bramante (rebuilt 1584-1622), retains the polygonal apse, with its Gothic windows, of the earlier 15C building. It houses a painting by Bartolomeo Ramenghi (1484-1542; a prime figure of the Mannerist school of Bologna, known as 'Il Bagnacavallo'). ▶ Of particular interest is the elliptically shaped **Piazza Nuova** (1759), a rare example of a market for both fish and meat. ▶ Just NW of the town is the parish church of **S. Pietro in Sylvis★,** built in the Ravenna tradition and probably dating from the 7C.   □

BAGNO DI ROMAGNA

Forlì 56, Bologna 125, Milan 346 km
Pop. 6,333 ⊠ 47021 ☎ 0543   E4

Ever since the Roman age, this has been a thermal spa where rheumatism and arthritis have been treated. The verdant valley of the Salvio is an agreeable place to stay. In the small town square is the beautiful basilica of **S. Maria Assunta.** Inside, there are several notable paintings of the Tuscan school *(The Madonna of the Assumption and Saints, Madonna and Child).* The 16C **Palazzo Pretorio** is decorated with numerous coats of arms and Florentine standards recalling Florentine occupation (1404).   □

Practical information

⚓ (Mar-Nov), ☎ 911046.
ⓘ p. S. Maria 1, ☎ 911046; winter, ☎ 911026.

Hotels:
★★★★ *G.H. Terme Roseo,* p. Ricasoli 2, ☎ 911016, 62 rm Ⓟ ⌘ ⌷ closed Dec-Feb, 65,000.
★★★★ *Tosco Romagnolo,* p. Dante 2, ☎ 911260, 51 rm ⊞ Ⓟ ⌘ ⌷ closed 5 Nov-Easter, 70,000; bkf: 10,000. Rest. ● ♦♦♦ *Paolo Teverini* Excellent cuisine, 35/50,000.
★★★ *Euroterme,* v. Lungo Savio 2, ☎ 917979, 183 rm Ⓟ ⊞ ⌷ ⌘ ⌷ closed Dec-Feb, 75,000.
★★ *Balneum,* v. Lungo Savio 17, ☎ 911085, 40 rm Ⓟ ⊞ ⌘ closed 10 Jan-28 Feb and 20 Nov-15 Dec, 46,000; bkf: 4,000.

BARDI

Parma 62, Bologna 163, Milan 139 km
Pop. 2,831 ⊠ 43032 ☎ 0525   A2

Bardi is a resort in the Parmesan Apennines, in a beautiful position on the flank of Mt. Crodolo that drops down into the valley of the River Ceno.

▶ The parish church contains the *Marriage of St. Catherine,* the first known work of Parmigianino. ▶ The **castle** rises up from an outcropping of red and green stone; originally built before the 10C, the present structure dates back to the 13C-14C *(for access, apply to the caretaker).* ▶ 8.5 km N is the **Pellizzone Pass** (3,375 ft, *ski lift*) leading to the Val d'Arda.   ▢

BERCETO

Parma 53, Bologna 156, Milan 165 km
Pop. 3,079 ⊠ 43042 ☎ 0525   B2

Berceto is a quiet resort in the Parmesan Apennines on the road to Cisa.

▶ The Romanesque church of **S. Moderanno** (13C) is interesting, with a curious **animal sculpture** on the façade. ▶ In the town many of the houses have Renaissance portals and windows. ▶ 8.5 km SW, having passed a luxuriant pine forest and the **Fonti di S. Moderanno** (mineral springs) on the l., the road reaches the **Cisa Pass** (3,407 ft), crossing between the valleys of the Rivers Taro and Magra; this marks the boundary between the provinces of Parma (Emilia) and Massa Carrara (Tuscany).   ▢

Practical information

Hotels:
★★★ *Poggio,* v. Nazionale 14, ☎ 60088, 30 rm Ⓟ ⌷ ⊞ ⌷ closed Nov-Mar except Christmas, 44,000; bkf: 5,000.
★★ *Vittoria-da Rino,* p. Micheli 11, ☎ 64306, 15 rm Ⓟ ⌘ closed 21 Dec-28 Feb, 32,000; bkf: 6,000. Rest. ♦ closed Mon and 20 Dec-Jan. Regional cuisine, 25/40,000.

Ⓐ ★★ *Pianelli,* at Poggio, v. Nazionale 109, 180 pl, ☎ 64521 (all year).

Recommended
Excursions: to Cisa Pass via the Fonti di S. Moderanno, ☎ 64218.
Farm vacations: *Azienda Castoglio,* at Valmozzola, ☎ 98173.

BERTINORO

Forlì 14, Bologna 77, Milan 296 km
Pop. 8,069 ⊠ 47032 ☎ 0543   E3

This picturesque little town, on the slope of a steep hill that dominates the Romagnese plain, bears innu-

merable marks of its rich historic past. Walls built on the orders of Pope Alexander VI and narrow medieval streets witnessed the departure of warlike Countess Aldruda Frangipane on her quest to raise the siege of Ancona by the Archbishop of Magonza (1174); the Ghibelline rule of the Mainardi, whose expulsion (1294) is mentioned by Dante; the enthronement of the new Count of Romagna, Amerigo di Chalux (1318); Cardinal Albornoz, who had the bishop's see transferred to Bertinoro from the ruined Forlimpópoli; the rule of the Ordelaffi, the Malaspina, and Lionello Pio da Carpi, and then, in 1580, of the papal states.

▶ The **Piazza della Libertà** is flanked by the **cathedral** (rebuilt end·16C) and the **Palazzo Comunale**, originally built in the 14C by the Ordelaffi but heavily restored. At the end of the piazza is the **Colonna dell'Ospitalità** (the 'Column of Hospitality' or 'Column of Rings', 13C, rebuilt 1926). ▶ 6 km W is **Fratta Terme**, a thermal spa.   ▢

Practical information

BERTINORO

Hotel:
★★★ *Panorama,* p. Libertà 11, ☎ 445465, 16 rm ⌷ ⌷ ⊞ ⌷ ⌘ closed Dec-Feb. No restaurant, 50,000.

Recommended
Wine: Enoteca *Cà de Bé,* p. del Comune, ☎ 445303; *Fattoria Paradiso,* v. Palmeggiana 285, ☎ 445044 (Sangiovese wine).

Environs

FRATTA TERME, ⊠ 47030, ☎ 0543.
⚓ (Mar-Nov), ☎ 460617.

BOBBIO

Piacenza 45, Bologna 196, Milan 110 km
Pop. 4,110 ⊠ 29022 ☎ 0523   A2

Bobbio is an important commercial centre in the Trebbia Valley (Piacentine Apennines), famous for the historic abbey of St. Colombanus. The **abbazia di S. Colombano** was founded in 612 by an Irish monk who had previously established churches and monasteries in Gaul and Germania and moved to Italy under the protection of the Lombard king. A few years later the abbey joined the Benedictine order and, along with Montecassino, became an important cultural centre in the early medieval period, noted in particular for its schools, scriptorium and manuscripts (dispersed in 18C).

▶ The **church** was rebuilt in the 15C-17C, but retains its 11C Romanesque campanile. The interior has 16C decoration; in the crypt, there are parts of the 12C mosaic floor and a sarcophagus of St. Colombanus (1480). Next to the abbey is the **museum** *(open Sun; appointments for other days,* ☎ *936018),* which contains sculptural remains of the original church, the church treasure, sculpture, and paintings of the Lombardy school. ▶ In the irregularly shaped p. del Duomo, bordered by old houses with columned porticoes, is the **Duomo,** Romanesque in origin but altered many times. ▶ Around the v. Genova are medieval houses with porticos and the **Palazzo del Tribunale** (15C). ▶ The town is dominated by a **castle,** built in 1440. ▶ Spanning the River Trebbia is the bridge of St. Colombanus, known as the **Ponte Gobbo** ('humpback or Devil's bridge'), with Roman and medieval features. ▶ 2.5 km S, at the river's edge, are the **Terme di Bobbio** (thermal spas). ▶ At 12.5 km the **Pénice Pass** (3,768 ft) connects the Trebbia Valley to the valley of the Stàffora. A 3 km road leads to the top of Mt. Pénice (4,788 ft), passing a radio-TV transmitting station. At the summit is the **Sanctuario della Madonna** and a striking panorama. ◻

Practical information ─────────

🛒 (May-Oct), ☎ 936250.
⛷ ski lifts and instruction at Pénice Pass.
ⓘ p. S. Francesco, ☎ 936178.

Hotel:
★★ *Piacentino*, p. S. Francesco 19, ☎ 936266, 20 rm Ⓟ ♿ ⌘ 40,000; bkf: 6,000.

Restaurant:
♦ *Cacciatori*, contrada di Porta Agazza 7, ☎ 936267, closed Wed and Jan-Mar. Regional cuisine: taglierini with nettles, snails alla bobbiese (in season), 24/33,000.

🅰 *Ponte Gobbo Terme*, at San Martino, 110 pl, ☎ 936927.

BOLOGNA*

Milan 210, Rome 380 km
Pop. 447,971 ✉ 40100 ☎ 051   D2

One of the routes which has always linked N Italy to central Italy through the Apennines reaches the plain between the Reno and the Savena. Very early on, the site was occupied and has had successive waves of population, as archaeological finds have shown. During the 6C BC, seeking to conquer the rich plain of the Po, the Etruscans founded Felsina. Three centuries later, the Romans crossed the Apennines, drove out the Gauls who had replaced the Etruscans and installed their own soldiers, merchants, farmers and citizens and renamed the settlement Bononia. The decline of the Roman Empire and the aggressiveness of the barbarians weakened the rich city, but faithful to its Roman heritage, its citizens, wanting power and liberty, founded one of the first independent city-states (11C) and challenged and often defeated both the Emperors Barbarossa and Frederick II, as well as duchies and papal states. After the 14C, however, the city could no longer resist repeated attacks from the outside or its internecine disputes and Bologna went the way of many neighbouring cities: it was conquered, sold and finally submitted to the rule of the papal states in 1513. In the following centuries, popular uprisings were both frequent and bitter. Caught up in the movement for national unity, the city became part of the Italian Kingdom in 1859. The constitution of 1947 made Bologna the capital of Emilia-Romagna, as it is the agricultural, commercial and industrial centre of the region and has kept its role as the centre of communications, first with the arrival of the railway, then with the autostrada. Visitors from all over the world frequent its trade fairs and exhibits. There is a lively cultural life: a leading newspaper and high quality books are published here; concerts and theatre are widely attended by the local populace (there is a first-class music conservatory), and the university — the oldest in Europe — attracts many foreign students and is particularly known for its school of medicine and the Rizzoli Institute of Orthopedics.

▶ The **Piazza Maggiore★** (D4) forms the focal point of the town. It is bordered by the austere façade of the church of S. Petronio; the Palazzo dei Podestà; the **Palazzo Comunale**; the **Palazzo dei Banchi** by Vignola (1568, so called for the moneylenders' booths once located here); and the crenellated **Palazzo dei Notai** (14C-15C). ▶ **S. Petronio★★** (D4), dedicated to one of the city's patron saints, St. Petronius, bishop here in the 5C, is one of the greatest achievements of Italian Gothic archi-

tecture. Building began in 1390 and work continued until 1659 and is still not complete. The **middle portal★★** of the façade is a masterpiece by Jacopo della Quercia (1425-38); of particular note are the ten biblical stories on the pilasters★. The sculptures on the other two portals are 16C. To the l. and r. are marble alcoves containing 15C busts of saints, prophets and sibyls. The **interior** is a simple and majestic Gothic structure, 432 ft long and 185 ft wide. Two sessions of the Council of Trent were held in S. Petronio (transferred here in 1547 because of plague), and it was here that Pope Clement VII crowned Charles V emperor of Germany and Rome in 1530. On the floor of the l.-hand aisle, leading to the façade, is the **meridian line** traced in 1655 by Cassini along the 60th meridian. There is a hole in the vaulted ceiling to admit the sun's rays. Among the works of art in the chapels are: in the fourth chapel to the r., beautiful stained glass by Jacob of Ulm (1464-6); in the sixth, *S. Girolamo★* by Lorenzo Costa; the eighth, enclosed by a remarkable marble balustrade (1525), has a marble reredos (decorative screen) designed by Vignola (1550) and fine inlaid **stalls★** (1521); in the ninth, a statue of St. Anthony of Padua attributed to Sansovino (16C) and, on the walls, the *Miracles of the Saints* by Girolamo da Treviso (1526); in the first chapel to the l., frescos by Giovanni da Modena (1420); in the fourth, **frescos★** by Giovanni da Modena and his studio (1410-15); in the fifth, the *Martyrdom of St. Sebastian★*, Emilian school (15C); in the seventh, *Madonna and Saints★* by Lorenzo Costa (1492); in the eighth, *S. Rocco* by Parmigianino. In the sanctuary, above the main altar, is the magnificent apse designed by Vignola; the organ on the r. is probably the oldest in Italy (1470-5). To the l. of the sanctuary is the **museum** of church treasures *(10 a.m.-12:30 p.m.; closed Tue and Thu)*. ▶ The **Palazzo del Podestà** (D4), medieval in origin, was rebuilt in Renaissance style after 1484; rising above the building is its crenellated tower, the **Torre dell'Arengo** (1212, whose bell has tolled for the most important events in the city since 1453). ▶ The **Palazzo Comunale★** (D3), an impressive brick building, was constructed out of two distinct structures (l., 13C; r., 15C). Connecting the two is the magnificent **portal** designed by Galeazzo Alessi in 1555; on the balcony above stands a statue of Pope Gregory XIII. Higher up, to the l., is a *Madonna and Saints★*, and remarkable terra-cottas by Nicolò dell'Arca (1478). From the impressive **courtyard** inside a fine staircase of shallow steps, attributed to Bramante, leads up to the first floor, where one can visit *(apply to the staff)* a number of rooms, among which are the **Sala d'Ercole** (Hercules), the **Sala Farnese** and the reception room. On the second floor the **Municipal Art Collection** *(9 a.m-2 p.m; Sun 9 a.m.-12:30 p.m.; closed Tue and wkday public hols)* consists mainly of paintings of the Bologna school (14C-15C) as well as items in majolica and glass. ▶ Adjoining the p. Maggiore is the **Piazza del Nettuno**, opened in 1564 as the site of the famous Neptune Fountain, the **Fontana del Nettuno★★** (D3), with its bronze statue by Giambologna (1556). ▶ On the E side of the piazza is the crenellated **Palazzo di Re Enzo** (1246), named after Enzo, son of Frederick II. ▶ The imposing **Palazzo dell'Archiginnasio** (D4), built in 1563, and until 1803 the site of the university, today houses the municipal library *(wkdays 9 a.m.-7:45 p.m.)*. Inside, at the far side of the elegant courtyard with its coats of arms of teachers and scholars of the university, is the 16C church of **S. Maria dei Bulgari**, with remnants of frescos by Bartolomea Cesi; on the first floor is the famous **Teatro Anatomico** (17C-18C, restored). ▶ The **Museo Civico Archeologico★** (D4; *9 a.m.-2 p.m.; Sun 9 a.m.-12:30 p.m.; closed Mon and wkday public hols)* is particularly interesting for its prehistoric, Etruscan, Roman and medieval collections. Among them are artifacts from Villanovan tombs: burial urns in terra-cotta or bronze; bronze brooches, razors, sword-fittings★ and pottery. From Etruscan tombs: bronze figurines, votive offerings, Greek and Etruscan vases and the bronze **situla★** from the Certosa. In the Greek section: the *Head of Minerva★*, a Roman copy of a Greek Head of Athena Lemnia attributed to Phidias; and among the

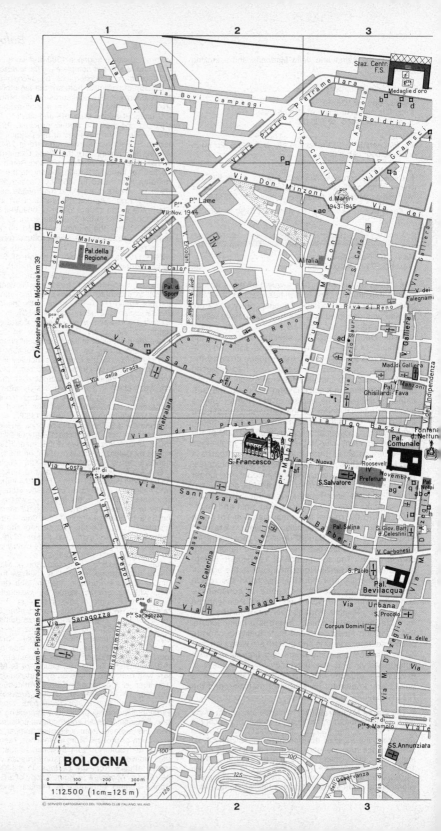

BOLOGNA

0   100   200   300 m

1:12.500 (1cm = 125 m)

© SERVIZIO CARTOGRAFICO DEL TOURING CLUB ITALIANO, MILANO

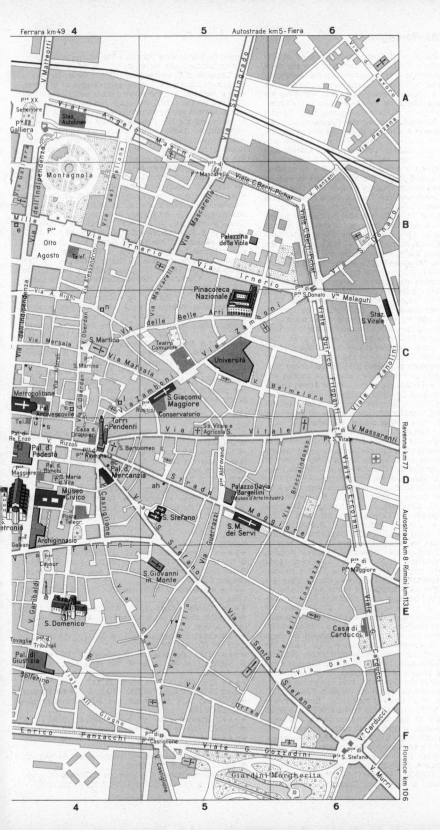

attic vases, the 'Cup of Codrus'★ in the style of Phidias. ▶ Nearby is the Baroque church of S. **Maria della Vita** (D4), housing a fine terra-cotta of the *Pietà*★ by Nicolò dell'Arca. ▶ From the p. del Nettuno, take the **via Rizzoli** (D4), a popular meeting-place and venue for the evening *passeggiata* (a few Roman remains in the underpass), to reach the p. di Porta Ravegnana (D4). Of note here is the Renaissance **casa dei Drappieri**; also the two **leaning towers**★, symbols of the city and among the very few of the numerous medieval towers to have survived. The highest (320 ft) is the **Torre degli Asinelli**, built in the early 12C; from the top there is a magnificent panorama★ over the entire city *(accessible by climbing 498 steps; 9 a.m.-6 p.m.)*. The earlier **Torre Garisenda** (late 11C) is referred to in Dante's *Inferno*. ▶ One of the main streets which lead from the p. di Porta Ravegnana is the **via Zamboni** (C 4-5-6), with porticos along its length and fine palazzi of 16C-18C. No. 20 is the **Palazzo Salem-Magnani**, with a reception room decorated with scenes of the foundation of Rome★, by the Carracci (1588-91, *apply to the Credito Romagnolo*). ▶ The point where the v. Zamboni joins the p. di Porta Ravegnana is the site of the church of **S. Giacomo Maggiore**★ (C5) which, though much altered, retains its Romanesque-Gothic character. The interior is Renaissance and Baroque, with a number of works of art, including the **Bentivoglio tomb**★, by Jacopo della Quercia and his studio (1435). The **Bentivoglio Chapel**★★, consecrated in 1486, has frescos by Lorenzo Costa and a painting by Fr. Francia. The **oratoria di S. Cecilia** *(apply to the sacristy)* is decorated with ten frescos★ (the *Lives of St. Cecilia and St. Valerian*) by Fr. Francia, Lorenzo Costa and their pupils. ▶ On the r. of the church the former Augustine monastery is now the home of the **Conservatorio di Musica** (C5), famed for the celebrated musicians and composers who have studied and taught here. ▶ Further on, to the l., is the **Teatro Comunale** (C5), designed by Antonio Bibiena and opened in 1763. ▶ Still in the v. Zamboni, at no. 33, is the main **university** building, transferred here from the Archiginnasio in 1803. ▶ The **Pinacoteca Nazionale**★★ (C5; *9 a.m.-2 p.m.; Sun and hols 9 a.m.-1 p.m.; closed Mon)* houses an important collection of Bolognese paintings of 14C-18C. Among the most notable paintings: *St. George and the Dragon*★ by Vitale da Bologna; the *Victory of St. James at the Battle of Clavijo*★★ by Jacopino da Bologna; a large polyptych of the *Virgin Enthroned and Four Saints*★, signed by Giotto; the *Merchants' Altarpiece*★ by Francesco del Cossa; a polyptych★ by the Vivarini; the *Ecstasy of St. Cecilia*★ by Raphael; the *Madonna and St. Margaret*★ by Parmigianino; the *Pietà of the Mendicants*★★, *Samson Victorious*★★, *Portrait of His Mother*★★ by Guido Reni. ▶ Returning to the p. di Porta Ravegnana, take the **Strada Maggiore** (D 4-5-6), another picturesque thoroughfare flanked by medieval houses, palazzi and churches. ▶ The Gothic church of S. **Maria dei Servi**★ (D5; begun 1346, completed 16C) is situated behind **four porticos**★. In the Gothic interior there are frescos by Vitale da Bologna and, in the third chapel on the r., a splendid painting of the *Madonna Enthroned*★★ by Cimabue. ▶ In the v. S. Stefano (D4-E5, from the p. di Porta Ravegnana) is the **Palazzo della Mercanzia**★ (D4), one of the most elegant of Bologna's medieval buildings. ▶ Further on is a cluster of medieval buildings dedicated to St. Stephen, **S. Stefano**★ (D5). Facing the piazza are: the church of SS. Vitale and Agricola, probably 5C, rebuilt 8C and again in the 11C in Romanesque form; the polygonal church of S. Sepolcro, or Calvario, 12C; and the church of the Crocifisso, 11C. From the church of S. Sepolcro one can reach the cortile di Pilato, a 12C courtyard with an 8C basin at the centre. Beyond this is the entrance to the chiesa della Trinità (13C) and a small **museum** *(apply to the caretaker)* containing paintings, sculpture and work in gold. ▶ In the S part of the city, in p. S. Domenico, is the large church of **S. Domenico**★★ (E4) — one of the prettiest in Bologna, with its two canopied tombs of the 13C-14C and two 7C columns. Built by the Dominicans, 1221-33, it was reduced to its present size in 1728-32. On the l. of the simple 13C façade (restored) is the elegant **Cappella Ghisilardi** de-

signed by Baldassarre Peruzzi. The interior of S. Domenico is adorned with works of art. In the r.-hand aisle, the **Cappella di S. Domenico**★ (1605, a fresco by Reni in the apse) contains the famous **sarcophagus of St. Dominic**★★: the tomb and the reliefs are the work of the pupils of Nicola Pisano (1267); the cover and the statues of the patron saints★ are by Nicolò dell'Arca (1473); the angel★ to the r. and the SS. Petronius★ and Proculus★ are by Michelangelo (1494); behind the sarcophagus, the **reliquary**★ containing the head of St. Dominic is by Jacopo Roseto (1383). The other chapels and the transepts contain a number of works of art by Filippino Lippi (the *Marriage of St. Catherine*★), by Guercino *(St. Thomas Aquinas)*, by Giunta Pisano *(Crucifixion*★), by Calvaert, Cesi, the Carracci, Guido Reni and others. In the **museum**, reached via the sacristy, there is a bust of St. Dominic★ in terra-cotta by Nicolò d'Arca. ▶ Nearby is the **Palazzo Bevilacqua**★ (E3), an elegant example of early Renaissance architecture. ▶ In the W part of the town is the church of **S. Francesco**★★ (D2), built 1236-63 and showing the influence of the French Gothic style (the façade was restored following damage in World War II). The splendid interior contains a Gothic **reredos**★ by Pier Paolo Masegne (1392); along the walls are Renaissance tombs. ▶ The **Chiesa Metropolitana**★ (C4) is the cathedral of Bologna, of very early origins and rebuilt in the 17C-18C. ▶ Behind the cathedral is an interesting **medieval quarter**★, much of which has survived intact. ▶ The **via Galliera**★ (C-B3) is one of the most architecturally impressive in Bologna, flanked by palazzi (15C-18C). ▶ Situated on a hill to the S of the city, the church of **S. Michele in Bosco**★ has a fine Renaissance façade (1523), attributed to B. Peruzzi and B. Rossetti, and an interesting **cloister** with frescos, said to be by the Carracci. The monastery next to the church is now occupied by the Rizzoli Institute of Orthopedics. There is a fine panorama of Bologna from here. ▶ Another view★ is offered at the sanctuary of the **Madonna di S. Luca**★. □

Practical information

ⓘ p. del Nettuno (D3), ☎ 239660; railway station (A3), ☎ 246541.

✈ *Guglielmo Marconi*, at Borgo Panigale, ☎ 311576; *Alitalia*, v. Marconi 34 (B3), ☎ 522250 (bus No. 91 from the railway station).

▨▨▨ (A3), ☎ 246490.

▨▨▨ from Stazione Autolinee (A4), ☎ 248374.

Car rental: *Avis*, v. Amendola 14, ☎ 551528, airport, ☎ 380754; *Hertz*, v. Masini 4, ☎ 366918, airport, ☎ 311811; *Maggiore*, v. dei Mille 11/E, ☎ 248235, airport, ☎ 311552.

Hotels:

★★★★★ *Royal Hotel Carlton,* v. Montebello 8 (B3 a), ☎ 554141, 250 rm P ⌂ ⊛ 260,000. Rest. ● ◆◆◆◆ *Royal Grill* ☎ 249368, closed Sun and Aug. Excellent regional cuisine, 45/65,000.

★★★★ *Alexander,* v. Pietramellara 47 (A3 b), ☎ 270924, 108 rm P closed Aug, 121,000.

★★★★ *Corona d'Oro 1890,* v. Oberdan 12 (C4 c), ☎ 236456, 35 rm P ⌂ closed Jul-Aug. No restaurant, 130,000.

★★★★ *Crest,* p. Costituzione 1, ☎ 372172, 163 rm P ⌂ ⌂ ▭ 175,000; bkf: 15,000.

★★★★ *Etap Bologna,* v. Pietramellara 59 (A3 d), ☎ 558558, 244 rm P ⌂ ⊛ No restaurant, 153,000; bkf: 13,000.

★★★★ *G.H. Elite,* v. Saffi 36, ☎ 437417, 86 rm P ⌂ ⊛ closed 25 Jul-25 Aug, 174,000. Rest. ● ◆◆◆◆ *Cordon Bleu* closed Sun, Mon noon and Aug. Excellent cuisine, 50/70,000.

★★★★ *Internationale,* v. Indipendenza 60 (B4 e), ☎ 262685, 140 rm P ⌂ No restaurant, 178,000.

★★★★ *Jolly,* p. XX Settembre 2 (A3 f), ☎ 264405, 176 rm, 195,000.

★★★★ *Milano Excelsior,* v. Pietramellara 51 (A3 g), ☎ 239442, 78 rm P 170,000.

★★★★ *Novotel Bologna,* at Villanova di Castenaso, v. Villanova 31, ☎ 781414, 204 rm P ⌂ ⌂ ▭ ⌂ 180,000.

★★★ *City Hotel,* v. Magenta 10, ☎ 372676, 50 rm P ⌂ No restaurant, 85,000; bkf: 7,000.

★★★ *Commercianti,* v. Pignattari 11 (D3 h), ☎ 233052, 35 rm P ♿ No restaurant, 85,000; bkf: 9,000.

★★★ *Fiera,* v. Stalingrado 82, ☎ 377735, 93 rm P 85,000; bkf: 8,000.

★★★ *Maggiore,* v. Emilia Ponente 62, ☎ 381634, 60 rm P ⚘ closed Aug and Christmas. No restaurant, 79,000; bkf: 7,000.

★★★ *MotelAgip,* at Borgo Panigale, v. Lepido 203, ☎ 401131, 64 rm P106,000.

★★★ *Roma,* v. D'Azeglio 9 (D3 i), ☎ 274400, 81 rm P ♿ 85,000; bkf: 8,000.

★★★ *San Donato,* v. Zamboni 16 (C4 l), ☎ 235397, 60 rm P ⚘ closed Aug, 110,000.

★★★ *San Felice,* v. Riva Reno 2 (C1 m), ☎ 5547457, 36 rm P ⚘ No restaurant, 110,000.

★★★ *San Giorgio,* v. delle Moline 17 (C4 n), ☎ 238435, 30 rm P ⚘ No restaurant, 110,000.

★★ *Astoria,* v. F.lli Rosselli 14 (A-B2 p), ☎ 521410, 38 rm P ⌂ ⚘ No restaurant, 62,000; bkf: 5,000.

★★ *Orologio,* v. IV Novembre 10 (D3 q), ☎ 231253, 32 rm P No restaurant, 62,000; bkf: 8,000.

Restaurants:

● ◆◆◆◆ *Notai,* v. de' Pignattari 1 (D3-4 ab), ☎ 228694, closed Sun and Aug. Elegant, in a 14C palazzo. Outstanding creative cuisine: tortelloni with mushrooms, scampi in cream, 40/60,000.

● ◆◆◆◆ *Pappagallo,* p. Mercanzia 3/C (D4 ac), ☎ 232807, closed Sun eve, Mon and Aug. New version of a former glory. Excellent creative cuisine: tortellini in salso primavera, turkey petroniana with truffles, 55/85,000.

● ◆◆◆ *Dante,* v. Belvedere 2/B (C3 t), ☎ 224464, closed Mon, Tue noon, Aug and Dec. In a 14C building (national monument). Outstanding Italian and international cuisine: risotto with scampi, kidneys with mushrooms, 50/65,000.

● ◆◆◆ *Franco Rossi,* v. delle Donzelle 1/A (C4 v), ☎ 279959, closed Sun and Jul. Refined tone. Regional and international cuisine: tagliatele, gnocchetti verdi, 30/45,000.

● ◆◆◆ *Rosteria Luciano,* v. Sauro 19 (C3 ad), ☎ 231249, closed Tue eve, Wed, Aug and Christmas. Beautiful in every particular. Excellent cuisine: tortellini petroniano, armonie dell'appennino, 40/55,000.

◆◆◆ *Bacco-Villa Orsi,* at Funo di Argelato, ☎ 862451, closed Sat, Sun and Aug. 18C villa with fine park. Regional and Italian cuisine: lamb with juniper berries, meat braised in wine, 30/40,000.

◆◆◆ *Bitone,* v. Emilia Levante 111, ☎ 546110, closed Mon, Tue and Aug. Service in open air in summer. Regional and Italian cuisine: tortellini goccia d'oro, cutlet alla bolognese, 36/46,000.

◆◆◆ *Brunetti,* v. Caduti di Cefalonia 5 (D4 s), ☎ 234441, closed Sun eve and Mon. Regional cuisine: tagliatelle with lemon, tortelloni, 25/40,000.

◆◆◆ *Solito Posto,* v. Turati 112, ☎ 410415, closed Tue, Aug and Christmas. 18C inn elegantly restored. Neapolitan and Spanish cuisine: spaghetti scogliera, maccaroni with broccoli, 35/40,000.

◆◆◆ *Tartufo,* v. del Porto 34 (B3 ae), ☎ 521350, closed Sun, Sat in summer and Aug. Outdoor service in summer. Umbrian cuisine: strangozzi alla spoletina, lamb in dripping with truffles, 35/45,000.

◆◆◆ *Tre Frecce,* strade Maggiore 19 (D5 ah), ☎ 234621, closed Sun eve, Mon and Aug. In a 13C palace. Creative cuisine: pappardelle with duck, guinea fowl with grapes, 40/60,000.

◆◆ *Antica Osteria Romagnola,* v. Rialto 13 (E5 r), ☎ 263699, closed Mon and Aug. 17C, with charming courtyard. Mixed cuisine: ravioli alla fonduta, deviled scampi, 24/40,000.

◆◆ *Antica Trattoria del Cacciatore,* v. Caduti di Casteldebole 25, ☎ 564203, closed Mon, Jan and Aug. Summer garden and veranda. Creative cuisine: risotto with nettles and strawberries, breast of pheasant al Nebbiolo, 29/38,000.

◆◆ *Duttour Balanzon,* v. Fossalta 3 (C-D4 u), ☎ 232098,

closed Fri eve and Sat. Regional cuisine: tortellini alla bolognese, lasagne verdi al forno, 22/30,000.

◆◆ *Paolo,* p. Unità 9/D, ☎ 357858, closed Tue, Fri eve, Jan and Jul. Pergola for meals outdoors. Regional cuisine: tagliatelle alla bolognese, tortellini in brodo, 22/25,000.

◆◆ *Sandro al Navile,* v. Sostegno 15, ☎ 6343100, closed Sun and Aug. Covered terrace and piano bar. Regional cuisine: pancakes with truffles, roast kid, 30/40,000.

◆◆ *Tavernetta-San Francesco,* p. Malpighi 12 (D2 af), ☎ 236947, closed Sun and Aug. 13C building tastefully renovated. Italian and international cuisine: tortelli alla fonduta, venison with blueberries, 40/50,000.

◆◆ *Trattoria Battibecco,* v. Battibecco 4/B (D3 ag), ☎ 275845, closed Sat, Sun and 20 Jul-20 Aug. Regional and international cuisine: gnocchi with nuts, deviled prawns, homemade Sangiorese, 30/50,000.

Recommended

Archery: *Compagnia arcieri del Reno,* v. Zampieri 3, ☎ 367127.

Botanical gardens: v. Irnerio 42, ☎ 234376.

Bowling: v. Costa 169, ☎ 411817.

Canoeing: *Canoa club Progetta Delta,* v. Toscana 9/C, ☎ 482280 or 442442.

Clay pigeon shooting: at Casalecchio di Reno, ☎ 571118.

Conference centre: p. Costituzione 5, ☎ 503331.

Craft workshops: *Prato,* v. Caldarese 1/D, ☎ 239593 (wrought-iron).

Cycling: *Rolo Sport,* v. Zamboni 16, ☎ 338404.

Discothèque: *Variety,* v. Rotta 10, ☎ 562656.

Events: *Bologna Music Festival* (Apr-Jun); art exhibits (co-ordinating organization, ☎ 517118).

Fairs: at trade fair centre (Quartiere Fieristico): *trade fair* (early Jun); *children's book fair* (Mar-Apr); *camping fair* (Jan-Feb); *perfume fair* (Apr) and various other specialist fairs.

Flying club: *G. Bortolotti,* v. Aeroporto 38, ☎ 400337 (also gliding).

Golf: at Chiesa Nuova di Monte San Pietro, ☎ 969100 (18 holes).

Guided tours: guides through tourist information bureau, ☎ 239660.

Horseback riding: *Gruppo emiliano sport equestri,* at San Lazzaro di Sàvena, v. Jussi 140, ☎ 468452.

Horse racing: *Arcoveggio,* v. Corticelli 104, ☎ 353561 or 371505.

Instruction: *Ocarina club,* at Budrio, v. Golinelli 5, ☎ 801057 (music).

Sailing school: *Vela UISP,* v. Pilastro 8 (at *Record Sport*).

Spelunking: Grotta della Spigola, Grotta Novella and Grotta Calindri (at San Lazzaro di Sàvena); information and reservations: *Gruppo speleologico CAI,* v. Indipendenza 2, ☎ 234856.

Sports centre: p. Azzarita 8 (BC1-2), ☎ 557283.

BORGO VAL DI TARO

Parma 65, Bologna 163, Milan 172 km
Pop. 7,337 ✉ 43043 ☎ 0525   A2

Borgo Val di Taro is the principal town of the Taro Valley and a summer resort, with a famous mushroom market. The old part of the town retains its original rectangular street-plan, and there are still remains of its **walls** and **castle**.

▶ The church of **S. Domenico,** late 15C, has a detached fresco and paintings of the 16C-17C. ▶ 14 km NW, in a fold in the Taro Valley at the foot of Mt. Pelpi, lies **Bedonia,** a popular summer holiday centre. On the San Marco Pass is the **Seminario,** containing an interesting natural history and archaeological collection and an **art gallery.** Next to it is the modern sanctuary of the **Madonna di S. Marco.** □

The arrow (→) is a reference to another entry.

Practical information ——————————

Restaurant:
♦ **Firenze,** p. Verdi 3, ☎ 96478, closed Fri and Nov. Regional cuisine: tortelli alla parmigiana, mushroom risotto, 25/30,000.

Recommended
Children's facilities: *Il Bosco,* at Tarsogno, Pisa, ☎ 050/550010 (4-12 yrs; open Jul-Aug).
Events: *Valtarese gastronomic fair* (Sep).
Horseback riding: *Amici del Cavallo,* v. Nazionale (associate of *ANTE*).

BRISIGHELLA

Ravenna 43, Bologna 62, Milan 278 km
Pop. 8,224 ✉ 48013 ☎ 0546   E3

Dominated by three rocky outcroppings and located at the head of the Lamone Valley, this is an active commercial and agricultural centre with a thermal spa. On one of these outcroppings is the **Torre dell'Orologio** (1290, rebuilt 19C); on another, the 14C **fortress,** enlarged by the Venetians in the 16C, housing the **Museo del Lavoro Contadino,** a museum of agriculture and folk-craft of the Lamone Valley and surrounding regions *(usually open Sat p.m. and Sun a.m.).*

▶ The church of **S. Maria degli Angeli,** built 1518-25, contains a fine painting on wood by Marco Palmezzano. ▶ The Neoclassical town hall also contains the **Museo Civico della Val Lamone,** of particular interest for its collection of artifacts from the pre-Roman necropolis of San Martino in Gattara. ▶ On higher ground is the picturesque **via del Borgo** (or 'degli Asini') covered and lined by arcades. ▶ 1.5 km toward Marradi is the Romanesque parish church of **S. Giovanni in Ottavo** (or 'del Tho'), so called because it stands at the eighth mile from Faenza in the direction of Tuscany.   ☐

Practical information ——————————

♨ (Apr-Oct), ☎ 81068.
ⓘ p. Stazione, ☎ 81166.

Hotels:
★★★ **Meridiana,** v. delle Terme 19, ☎ 81590, 56 rm Ⓟ ⬛
♨ closed Nov-Apr, 42,000; bkf: 5,000.
★★★ **Terme,** v. delle Terme 37, ☎ 81144, 56 rm Ⓟ ≮ ⬧
⬛ ⌖ ఈ ♨ closed Nov-Apr, 45,000; bkf: 5,000.
★★ **Gigiolé,** p. Carducci 5, ☎ 81209, 17 rm closed Feb-Mar, 35,000; bkf: 5,000. Rest. ● ♦♦ closed Mon. Outstanding Romagnese and creative cuisine, 30/40,000.

Restaurant:
♦♦♦ **Osteria la Grotta,** v. Metelli 1, ☎ 81829, closed Tue, Jan and Jun. In a cave. Creative cuisine: ravioli with chicory, tortellini with pheasant,13/23,000.

Recommended
Nature park: *G. Gatta,* ☎ 81468 (picnic areas).

BUSSETO

Parma 37, Bologna 128, Milan 93 km
Pop. 7,422 ✉ 43011 ☎ 0524   B1

Everything in this ancient town on the Emilian plain speaks of Italy's most popular musician. 'The swan of Busseto', as Giuseppe Verdi was called, has not totally eclipsed the older and glorious past of this town, the capital of the tiny state of Pallavicino. From the 10C to 1588, when it became part of the Duchy of Parma, Busseto had its moments of splendour, above all in the 15C, at the time of Orlando the Magnificent, as well as the 16C when Pallavicino

played host at a meeting between Emperor Charles V and Pope Paul III.

▶ In the central p. Verdi stand the old **Palazzo del Comune** (15C) and the **fortress** (built 1250, rebuilt 16C), which houses the town hall and the **Teatro Verdi** *(9:30 a.m.-12 noon and 3-6:30 p.m. or 2-5:30 p.m.).* On the opposite side is the parish church of **S. Bartolomeo** (rebuilt 1436, much altered in the 18C). The Gothic façade has a fine portal; inside, frescos by Michelangelo Anselmi (1537-8). ▶ On the edge of the town is the **Villa Pallavicino,** with rooms decorated with frescos and stuccos (16C-18C). The villa also contains the **Museo Civico** (paintings, ceramics, furniture, sculpture) and a series of rooms devoted to Verdi. ▶ Almost in front of the villa is the church of **S. Maria degli Angeli,** a Gothic building of 1472; inside is a terra-cotta *Pietà*★ by Guido Mazzoni. ▶ 4 km NE, set in a luxuriant park, is the **Villa Verdi di Sant'Agata** *(9 a.m.-12 noon and 3-9 p.m. Apr-Oct; closed Mon),* built by Verdi in 1849 and where he lived and composed some of his most famous works; Verdi's private rooms are carefully preserved and contain the furniture from the hotel room in Milan where he died. ▶ 4 km SE is **Róncole Verdi,** where one can visit the humble **birthplace** of Verdi and the church of **S. Michele,** containing the organ on which he played.   ☐

Verdi at Busseto

Giuseppe Verdi was born at Le Roncole, an outlying part of Busseto, in 1813 when it was still part of the duchy of Parma and Piacenza. His father was a modest trader in food and wine, his mother a spinner. The parish priest of Roncole taught him to read and write: an old organist imbued him with the love of music. A wine merchant, Antonio Barezzi (whose daughter, Margherita, Verdi was later to marry), helped him enter the music school connected to the cathedral of Busseto. When he was fifteen, he played his own overture in public at a performance of Rossini's Barbiere di Siviglia in Busseto. Sent to Milan by Barezzi, he tried in vain to be admitted to the Conservatory of Music and so studied privately for several years. Returning to Busseto, he was made conductor of the local orchestra. At the same time, he began to compose the music for Oberto, Conte di Bonifacio, his first opera. In September 1838, he returned to Milan, a city under Austrian rule, with his wife and their young son, both of whom were to die a short while later. In the same year, his first opera was performed at La Scala with some success. After remarrying — his second wife was the celebrated opera singer Giuseppina Strepponi — in Paris in 1859, he bought a house for her at Sant'Agata, a few miles from the town, a property which he enlarged as his fame increased, and it was here that he composed his greatest works. His birthplace in Le Roncole, the small theatre at Busseto and his villa at Sant'Agata are all moving places to visit.

Practical information ——————————

ⓘ at Teatro Verdi, ☎ 92487.

Hotel:
★★★ **Due Foscari,** p. Rossi 15, ☎ 92337, 18 rm Ⓟ ⬛ ⬧
closed 20 Jul-20 Aug, 53,000.

Restaurants:
● ♦♦♦ **Guareschi,** at Róncole Verdi, v. Processione 160, ☎ 92495, closed Fri, eve in Jul and 20 Dec-28 Feb. Graceful and comfortable, on edge of Guareschi estate. Parmesan cuisine: cannelloni with ricotta, duck alla carbonara, 33/43,000.

◆◆◆ **Cavallino Bianco,** at Polésine Parmense, v. Sbrisi 2, ☎ 96136, closed Tue and Aug. Views of countryside on banks of the Po. Excellent cuisine: malfatti with fresh mushrooms, risotto alla Massimo, 20/35,000.
◆◆◆ **Colombo,** at Santa Franca (3 km), v. Mogadiscio 110, ☎ 98114, closed Mon eve, Tue, Jan and Jul. Food shop attached. Regional cuisine: salted meats, beef in oil, homemade wines, 21/37,000.
◆◆◆ **Ugo,** v. Mozart 3, ☎ 92307, closed Mon, Tue and Jan. Regional cuisine: casseroled guinea fowl, tripe alla parmigiana, 25/35,000.

Recommended
Events: *Verdi international singing competition* (Jul); *carnival.*

CARPI

Modena 18, Bologna 62, Milan 176 km
Pop. 60,595 ⊠ 41012 ☎ 059   C2

Once noted for an ancient local industry — the production of *truciolo* (fine strips of willow used to make hats) — Carpi has adapted to changing times by becoming an important hosiery centre. The Carpi of the past is symbolized by the Castello dei Pio, seat of that noble Modenese family which made Carpi the centre of its domain from 1327-1525. The most illustrious member of the family, Alberto the Learned, a pupil of Aldo Manuzio and patron of Ariosto, transformed the town into one of the focal points of Renaissance culture.

▶ The vast **piazza dei Martiri** is bordered on one side by the fifty-two arches of the imposing **Portico Lungo** (1505), 689 ft long. Here also are the cathedral and the Castello dei Pio. ▶ The **cathedral,** begun in 1514 by Baldassarre Peruzzi, was completed in 1667. ▶ The **Castello dei Pio★** is a massive structure, complete with towers (14C-17C). Dominating the façade is the 17C **Torre dell'Orologio,** beneath which one has to pass in order to reach the Renaissance **courtyard,** designed by Bramante. An impressive staircase leads up to the **Museo Civico** *(May-Oct wkdays 4-7 p.m.; Sun and hols 10:30 a.m.-12:30 p.m. and 4-7 p.m.; other months apply to the management).* Of particular note: the chapel, with early Renaissance frescos; the 'La Stanza Ornata' room, with its magnificent ceiling; the adjacent room in the Passerino tower, with Lombard frescos of the 15C; the 'Salone dei Mori', with perspective frescos. The museum's painting collection comprises primarily works of the Emilian and Venetian schools. In one room there is the **Museo della Xilografia** (woodblock printing), with works by Ugo da Carpi (16C) as well as modern and contemporary artists. ▶ The parish church of **S. Maria,** or 'della Sagra', originally 8C, was partially destroyed in 1515, after which it received its present Renaissance façade by Peruzzi; it contains a 12C pulpit, Romanesque frescos, the 14C tomb of Manfredo Pio (the first lord of Carpi), and 15C frescos (in the chapels of SS. Martino and Caterina). ▶ Another interesting church is **S. Nicolò,** a harmonious Renaissance building, completed in 1516 by Peruzzi.   ☐

Practical information _____

Hotel:
★★★★ **Touring,** v. Dallai 1, ☎ 686111, 70 rm Ⓟ ⏣ ♿ closed 1-25 Aug, 130,000; bkf: 10,000.

Restaurant:
◆◆◆ **Magnani,** v. Bellantanina 6, ☎ 686094, closed Sat eve, Sun and Aug. Modenese cuisine: tortelloni with pumpkin, rabbit chasseur, 25/30,000.

Recommended
Flying club: at Budrione, v. Grilli, ☎ 660080.
Wine: *cantina sociale* (co-operative wine-growers associa-

tions), at Santa Croce, SS Correggio 35, ☎ 664007; *cantina sociale,* at Sorbara, ☎ 909103 (Lambrusco).

CASTELL'ARQUATO*

Piacenza 33, Bologna 134, Milan 96 km
Pop. 4,512 ⊠ 29014 ☎ 0523   A-B1

Situated in the foothills of the Piacentine Apennines on a hillside strewn with fossilized shells, at the point where the River Arda empties into the plain, Castell'Arquato must be one of the loveliest medieval villages in Emilia-Romagna. Originally a Roman camp set up to defend the road from Fidenza to Velleia, it later became the possession of the bishops of Piacenza, then (13C) an independent city-state, then the feudal domain first of the Viscontis, then of the Sforzas. It was conquered and occupied by several condottieri, notably il Piccinino, il Colleoni and Gian Giacomo Trivulzio. When the last of the Sforzas died in 1707, it became part of the duchy of Parma and Piacenza. Entering the town and climbing the steep, winding alleys between the medieval houses is, in a way, a passage through time.

▶ On the beautiful **piazza Matteotti★,** at the top of the hill, stands the Palazzo Pretorio, the collegiate church and the remains of a fortress. ▶ The **Palazzo Pretorio,** fortified with crenellated battlements and a tower, was built on the Gothic model (1293-14C); the exterior staircase and loggia are 15C. ▶ The **Collegiata★** is 12C Romanesque, with a fine apsidal exterior and, on the l. side, a loggia with ogive arches. Inside are the baptistery, with 8C font, and the Gothic chapel of S. Caterina with 15C frescos (much restored). Next to the church is a picturesque cloister and the **Museo della Collegiata** *(apply to the caretaker),* containing Roman and Romanesque artifacts, sculptures and paintings. The **archives** have a collection of parchment documents from 1120 onward and 16C and 17C antiphonaries. ▶ The **fortress★,** which still has its original crenellated towers, was built by the city-state of Piacenza in 1343. ▶ In the v. Remondini the 16C Farnese Tower houses the **Museo Geologico** *(open Sun p.m.; other times,* ☎ *803724),* with Pliocene and Pleistocene fossils found locally; on the ground floor are mementos of the librettist Luigi Illica, who was born in Castell'Arquato.

Environs

▶ **Vigolo Marchese** *(7 km NW)* has two medieval monuments: a Romanesque **parish church** (11C) and a **baptistery** (1008), with a font made from a Roman capital. ▶ 5 km S, the 16C parish church of **Lugagnano Val d'Arda** has a *Supper in Emmaus* by Luigi Crespi.   ☐

Practical information _____

Ⓘ v. Remondini 1 ☎ 803091.

Restaurants:
◆◆◆ **Rocca-da Franco,** v. Asilo 4, ☎ 803154, closed Wed, Jan and Jul. Piacentine cuisine: baked pancakes, meat roast in paper, 25/35,000.
◆◆ **Faccini,** at S. Antonio, ☎ 896340, closed Wed and Jul. Piacentine cuisine: pappardelle with rabbit, tortelli with pumpkin, homemade wines, 22/28,000.

CASTELNOVO NE' MONTI

Reggio nell'Emilia 44, Bologna 108, Milan 180 km
Pop. 9,509 ⊠ 42035 ☎ 0522   B-C2-3

Situated at the foot of the Pietra di Bismántova and dominating the Secchia Valley, this resort in the Reggiano Apennines attracts many Florentines. There is an **old centre** (above which is a castle) and an extensive modern development which stretches out along the road that climbs from Reggio to the Cerreto Pass. A pleasant excursion *(5 km by car)* leads to the **Pietra di Bismántova** (3,434 ft), a spectacularly steep mountain with overhangs and a flat top, noted by Dante; beneath the E face is the **Eremo**, a small 17C church, recently renovated (detached frescos dating from 1422), and a Benedictine monastery. From the summit *(30 mn walk)* there is a magnificent panorama★. 2 km from **Cervarezza** *(11 km SW)* there is a well-known mineral spring.   ☐

Practical information ──────────────

Hotel:
★★ *Bismantova*, v. Roma 73, ☎ 812218, 18 rm ✅ closed Oct, 45,000; bkf: 6,000. Rest. ♦ closed Tue and Oct. Regional cuisine, 20/30,000.

Recommended
Farm vacations: *Unicoper Turist*, at Unione Cooperative, p. Matteotti 4/A, ☎ 812798.
Swimming: ☎ 812655.

CASTEL SAN PIETRO TERME

Bologna 23, Milan 235 km
Pop. 16,090 ⊠ 40024 ☎ 051   D3

In the 12C, this small town developed as a stronghold for the Bolognese in their confrontations with Imola, and in 1338 it sheltered the University of Bologna during an interdiction. Today it is known for its thermal waters. The parish church of **S. Maria Maggiore** (14C, altered several times) is of interest.   ☐

Practical information ──────────────

♨ (mid-Mar-mid-Dec), ☎ 941247.
ℹ v. Terme 150, ☎ 941457.

Hotel:
★★★ **Nuova Italia**, v. Cavour 73, ☎ 941932, 30 rm ᕦ ✅ No restaurant, 85,000.

Restaurant:
♦♦ *Bussola*, at Liano, ☎ 941697, closed Mon and Sep. Seafood: linguine with scampi, sea-bass baked in paper, 30/40,000.

Recommended
Bowling: v. Terme 740, ☎ 942504.
Horseback riding: *Ghisiola*, at Gallo, v. Stanzani, ☎ 941612 (associate of *ANTE*).
Swimming: v. Terme 840, ☎ 942042 (also tennis, ☎ 942630).

CASTIGLIONE DEI PEPOLI

Bologna 55, Milan 252 km
Pop. 6,047 ⊠ 40035 ☎ 0534   D3

Situated among woods of chestnut trees and firs in the valley of the River Brasimone and on the road to the Montepiano Pass, this is an agricultural centre and a popular resort of the Bolognese Apennines.

▶ The **Palazzo dei Pépoli** (now the town hall), rebuilt in the 16C, recalls the feudal lordship of the Pépoli family, which was to survive until 1797, and which provided a place where gentlemen could duel unhindered. ▶ 4 km W is the huge, artificial **Lake Brasimone**. ▶ 8 km SE, the **Santuario di Boccadirio**, rebuilt 18C-19C, houses a terracotta *Madonna* attributed to Andrea della Robbia (1505). ☐

Looking for a locality? Consult the index at the back of the book.

Practical information ──────────────

ℹ p. Liberto 10, ☎ 91081.

Hotel:
★★ *Roncobilaccio*, at Roncobilaccio, nr exit from autostrada, ☎ 97577, 86 rm ℙ ⊰ ▩ ⚄ ᕦ 90,000; bkf: 7,000.

CASTLES NEAR PARMA

From Parma to Reggio nell'Emilia *(102 km, 1 day; map 2)*

In the foothills of the Apennines around Parma are numerous castles. Some occupy strategic positions at the head of a valley, at the crossing of a river or overlooking a road. Merchants traveling by caravan had to buy the right of passage to protect themselves against bands of brigands who roamed these mountains. Other castles belonged to noble families who derived power and wealth from the fields and cities of the plain. The castle provided them with refuge from foreign incursions, the attacks of neighbours, revolts in the cities and the plague. Game was abundant in the woods, enabling the nobles to hunt, a favourite pastime during the Middle Ages.

▶ Leaving **Leaving Parma** (→) on the Fornovo road and traveling as far as **Collecchio**, situated at the foot of the first hills which rise to the r. of the River Taro, the route arrives at the Romanesque parish church of **S. Prospero** (12C), much restored. ▶ Passing through **Sala Baganza** and crossing the River Baganza is the village of **Felino**, famous for its sausages. A little farther is the **Castello di Felino**, standing on the crest of a hill; rebuilt in the 15C, it is still encircled by a deep moat. ▶ From **Pilastro** a short detour leads to **Torrechiara**, a village at the foot of the **Castello di Torrechiara★**, an imposing and picturesque structure built by Pier Maria Rossi (1448-60), with a set of three ramparts and angular watchtowers. Inside *(summer 9 a.m.-1 p.m. and 3:30-6:30 p.m.; winter 9 a.m.-1 p.m. and 2-4 p.m.; Sun and hols 9 a.m.-1 p.m.; closed Mon)* are beautifully decorated rooms, in particular the sala dei Giocolieri and the **golden room**, with frescos by Benedetto Bembo. ▶ Crossing the Parma River the route comes to **Traversetolo** and **Montechiarugolo**, a village dominated by a majestic **castle** surrounded by a moat, with tall towers and a courtyard. Inside *(access permitted)* there are various rooms with frescos of the 15C, 16C and 18C. ▶ Crossing the Enza River the road arrives at **Montecchio Emilia** and follows the river to **San Polo d'Enza** and **Ciano d'Enza**. Here, it turns l. into the hills in the direction of Canossa. ▶ The climb through the clay hills leads beneath the **Castello di Rossena**, perched on its rocky outcrop. ▶ The road now passes through an area of limestone from which the ruins of the **Castello di Canossa** rise on an isolated crag *(accessible by steep slope cut with steps; apply to caretaker; 9 a.m.-12 noon and 3-6:30 p.m.; closed Mon)*. Built c. 940 by Azza Adalberto, the castle was completely destroyed by the townspeople of Reggio in 1255. It was reconstructed several times and then destroyed again. At Canossa the most famous episode in the fight between the empire and the papacy took place in 1077. The Emperor Henry IV, having fought Pope Gregory VII in the War of the Investiture, had been excommunicated. He came to Canossa to seek the pope's pardon, as the pope was, at the time, the guest of the Countess Matilda of Tuscany, the great-granddaughter of the castle's founder. From 24-27 January, the emperor stayed in the first set of ramparts, dressed in red wool and barefoot in the snow. On the evening of the third day, he was finally received by the pope and allowed to return to the church. He never forgot the humiliation and sought revenge by attempting to lay siege to the castle in vain. A small **museum** contains objects excavated from the castle. ▶ Crossing a bleak ridge with extensive views, the road drops down to **Quattro Castella**, named after the four castles that once

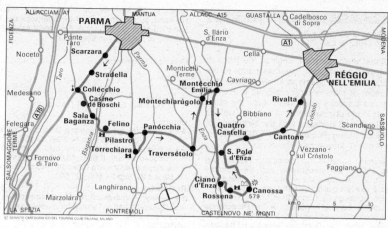

2. Castles near Parma

stood in this area (of these only one has survived); the parish church retains some Romanesque features. ▶ The road now leads toward Scandiano, where it turns l. at **Cantone** to cross the plain to **Reggio** (→). □

Practical information

COLLECCHIO, ⊠ 43044, ☎ 0521.

Restaurant:
● ♦♦♦♦ **Villa Maria Luigi-da Ceci**, v. Galaverna 28, ☎ 805489, closed Thu, Jan and Aug. In 18C villa, formerly the Grand Duke's hunting lodge, fine summer terrace. Outstanding Parmesan and international cuisine: fettucine ai porcini, risotto with stuffed quail, 35/50,000.
♦♦♦ **Cavalli-il Baule**, at Cavalli, ☎ 804110, closed Sun, Tue eve, 25 Jan-10 Feb and 15-30 Aug. Formerly coaching inn. Regional cuisine: anolini in brodo, boeuf en croûte, 23/30,000.

FELINO, ⊠ 43035, ☎ 0521.

Restaurant:
♦♦♦ **Hostaria del Castello**, v. Castello 200/A, ☎ 831142, closed Mon and 1 Jan-15 Mar. In partially restored 9C castle. Parmesan cuisine: tagliolini with lemon, tortellacci with artichoke, 25/35000.

MONTECCHIO EMILIA, ⊠ 42027, ☎ 0522.

Recommended
Cheese: *Antico Caseificio*, at Aiola, ☎ 871115 (by appointment).

MONTECHIARUGOLO, ⊠ 43022, ☎ 0521.

Hotel:
★★★ **Rose**, at Monticelli Terme, v. Montepelato Nord, ☎ 65521, 87 rm Ⓟ 🗄 🌐 🎾 ▭ closed 16 Dec-14 Mar, 60,000.

SALA BAGANZA, ⊠ 43038, ☎ 0521.

Recommended
Nature park: *Boschi di Carrega*, head office at Centro Parco R. Levati, ☎ 833440.

> For the translation of a name of a meat, a fish or a vegetable, for the composition of a dish or a sauce, see the *Menu Guide* at the end of the Practical Holiday Guide; it lists the most common culinary terms.

CASTROCARO TERME

Forlì 11, Bologna 74, Milan 293 km
Pop. 5,093 ⊠ 47011 ☎ 0543   E3

Dominated by the remains of a fortress, this is a popular thermal spa situated at the foot of the Montone Valley on the road from Forlì to the Muraglione Pass. It is the capital of the commune of Castrocaro and Terra del Sole (→), to which it is connected by an avenue 1.5 km long.

▶ In the **Parco delle Terme** are various sports facilities and a pavilion (Padiglione dei Divertimenti) where artistic events are held. ▶ In the old, higher part of the town is the 11C church of **S. Nicolò**, with a late Gothic interior and 15C frescos. ▶ Higher still is the baptistery of **S. Giovanni**, probably 8C, built on a circular plan and containing a Byzantine tomb and the majestic ruins of a **fortress**. □

Practical information

⌖ (Apr-Nov), ☎ 767122.
ⓘ v. Garibaldi 50, ☎ 767162.

Hotels:
★★★★ **G.H. Terme**, v. Roma 2, ☎ 767114, 100 rm Ⓟ 🌐 ⚘ closed 1 Nov-14 Apr, 90,000; bkf: 8,000.
★★★ **Ariston**, v. Dante 13, ☎ 767312, 48 rm 🌐 closed Dec-Mar, 50,000; bkf: 4,000.
★★★ **Eden**, v. Samorì 11, ☎ 767600, 32 rm Ⓟ ≼ 🌐 🎾 closed Dec-Mar, 48,000; bkf: 4,000.

Restaurant:
● ♦♦♦ **Frasca**, v. Matteotti 38, ☎ 767471, closed Tue, 2-20 Jan and 1-15 Jun. In house with beautiful garden and a winery. Outstanding creative cuisine: mezzolune with asparagus, rabbit stuffed with herbs, 45/80,000.
⚓ ★★ **Terme**, v. Conti 1, 40 pl, ☎ 767558.

Recommended
Conference centre: v. Marconi, ☎ 767776 or 767125.
Events: *song festival* (Festival delle voci nuove) at Padiglione dei Divertimenti (Sep); *Palio di S. Reparata* (Sep).

> Be advised that hotels and restaurants in this Guide have perhaps changed addresses; prices indicated are also subject to modifications.

CENTO

Ferrara 34, Bologna 33, Milan 207 km
Pop. 29,300 ⊠ 44042 ☎ 051   D2

This agricultural town, on the l. bank of the Reno in the heart of the Emilian plain, owes its name to the number 100, but no one seems to know whether this was the number of plots of land assigned to Roman settlers, as one tradition would have it, or the number of houses in the original town. The town, with its old streets flanked by porticos, was the birthplace of one of the great Italian painters of the 17C: Giovanni Francesco Barbieri, known as Il Guercino.

► The p. Guercino contains the crenellated **Palazzo del Governatore** (1502), the **clocktower**, and the **Palazzo Comunale** (1612). ► The nave of the 17C **chiesa del Rosario** has a painted ceiling by Guercino *(Assumption)*; there are also paintings by Guercino in the second chapel to the l., built at his own expense. ► The **Pinacoteca Civica** *(9-12 noon; Sun and hols 9:30 a.m.-1 p.m.; closed Mon)* contains work by Guercino (detached frescos, altarpieces), Ludovico Carracci and others of the Emilian school. ► 2 km on the other side of the Reno is **Pieve di Cento**; the **collegiate church** here has its original campanile and polygonal apse; inside, 16C-17C paintings, among which are an *Assumption* by Guido Reni (apse) and an *Annunciation* by Guercino (second altar to the l.). □
Practical information _____

Hotel:
★★★ **Europa,** v. IV Novembre 16, ☎ 903319, 44 rm P 60,000; bkf: 6,000.

Lake CERRETO

Reggio nell'Emilia 79, Bologna 144, Milan 228 km
4,408 ft ⊠ 42030 ☎ 0522   B3

Surrounded by beech woods and stocked with abundant trout, this small lake in the Reggiano Apennines was probably formed by a glacier. Falling within the commune of Collagna, at the foot of Mt. La Nuda (6,212 ft), this area is well equipped for both summer vacations and winter sports. □

Practical information _____

⚐ ski lifts, cross-country skiing, instruction.
ⓘ at Collagna, ☎ 898121.

Hotel:
★★★★ **Sport,** v. Belfiore 1, ☎ 898211, 80 rm P ⚐ ⚏ ⚓
⚆ Pens. closed May and 15 Sep-1 Dec, 60,000.

CERVIA

Ravenna 22, Bologna 96, Milan 307 km
Pop. 24,813 ⊠ 48015 ☎ 0544   F3

The old town, on the Adriatic, was once a rival to Ravenna and in the 6C the seat of one of the principal bishoprics of Romagna. Now nothing remains except the small church dedicated to the Madonna della Neve; Cérvia was abandoned and destroyed when the area in which it was built *(3 km from the sea)* was deemed too unhealthy to live in. The present town was founded in 1698 and built following designs by the Roman Bellardino Berti.

► An important seaside resort and thermal spa, Cérvia is situated near a huge **salt marsh.** ► To the N, beyond the **Canale delle Saline,** is **Milano Marittima,** a seaside centre also specializing in thermal cures. It was built in 1912 in a **pine forest.** ► To the SE, on the edge of the forest and facing the beach, is the more recent **Pina-**

rella. ► 2.5 km NW, on the l. of the main road to Ravenna, is the sanctuary of the **Madonna del Pino,** 15C Lombard-style portal; inside, the *Madonna of the Pine,* a painting of the 15C Venetian school. □

Practical information _____

CERVIA
≋
⚓ (May-Oct), ☎ 992221.
ⓘ p. Garibaldi 8, ☎ 971013 (seasonal).

Hotels:
★★★ **Beau Rivage,** lungomare Deledda 116, ☎ 971010, 50 rm P closed 16 Sep-14 May, 65,000; bkf: 8,000.
★★★ **Bristol,** lungomare D'Annunzio 22, ☎ 71518, 51 rm P ⚏ closed 21 Sep-9 May, 40,000; bkf: 4,000.
★★★ **Strand,** lungomare Deledda 104, ☎ 72325, 33 rm P ⚏ closed 21 Sep-24 May, 35,000.

Restaurant:
♦♦ **Genny,** v. Volturno 2, ☎ 71427, closed Sun eve, Mon and 15 Sep-31 Jan. Terrace for meals in open air. Seafood: spaghetti with fish, cuttlefish with mushrooms, 40/50,000.

Recommended
Children's facilities: *Villa Irma,* ☎ 992054, management, at Bergamo, ☎ 035/260477 (5-12 yrs; open mid-Jan-Apr).
Cycling: *Aquilotti,* corso Mazzini 37, ☎ 71954.
Events: *ceremony of the Marriage to the Sea* (Ascension); *Feast of St. Lawrence* (Aug).
Horseback riding: *circolo ippico cervese,* ☎ 949303.
Nature park: v. G. di Vittorio, ☎ 973613 (9 a.m.-sunset).

Environs

MILAN MARITTIMA, ⊠ 48016, ☎ 0544.
≋
ⓘ v. Romagna 107, ☎ 993435.

Hotels:
★★★★★ **Exclusive Waldorf,** VII Traversa 17, ☎ 994343, 24 rm P ⚏ ⚏ closed Oct-Apr, 120,000; bkf: 20,000.
★★★★ **Bellevue Beach,** XIX Traversa, ☎ 994233, 70 rm P ⚏ closed 16 Sep-14 May, 100,000; bkf: 15,000.
★★★★ **Doge,** v. 2 Giugno 36, ☎ 992071, 78 rm P ⚏ ⚏ ⚏ closed 26 Sep-9 May, 85,000; bkf: 12,000.
★★★★ **Mare e Pineta,** v. Dante 36, ☎ 992262, 197 rm P ⚏ ⚏ closed 21 Sep-14 May, 180,000; bkf: 15,000.
★★★ **Acapulco,** v. VI Traversa 19, ☎ 992396, 55 rm P ⚏ ⚏ closed 16 Sep-14 May, 65,000; bkf: 8,000.
★★★ **Kent,** v. 2 Giugno 142, ☎ 992048, 45 rm P ⚏ closed 21 Sep-9 May, 65,000; bkf: 9,000.
★★★ **Monaco,** XV Traversa 11, ☎ 994400, 50 rm P ⚏ closed Oct-Apr, 58,000; bkf: 8,000.
★★★ **Savini,** XVIII Traversa 14, ☎ 994219, 64 rm P ⚏ closed 16 Sep-14 May, 65,000; bkf: 10,000.
★★★ **Silver,** v. Spalato 10, ☎ 992312, 52 rm P ⚏ closed 26 Sep-9 May, 50,000; bkf: 6,000.
★★★ **Sorriso,** VIII Traversa 19, ☎ 994063, 34 rm P ⚏ ⚏ closed Oct-Apr, 70,000; bkf: 15,000.
★★ **Fiora,** v. Dante 42, ☎ 991209, 35 rm P ⚏ ⚏ closed 1 Nov-10 Dec, 50,000; bkf: 5,000.

Recommended
Clay pigeon shooting: v. Stazzone 5, ☎ 992563.
Sailing: v. 2 Giugno, ☎ 993377.
Young people's facilities: *Mariscivolo,* v. Zara, ☎ 993134.

PINARELLA, ⊠ 48015, ☎ 0544.
≋
ⓘ v. Emilia, ☎ 987254 (seasonal).

Hotels:
★★★ **Antares,** v. Italia 282, ☎ 987497, 30 rm P ⚏ ⚏ closed 21 Sep-14 May, 45,000; bkf: 8,000.
★★ **Everest,** v. Italia 230, ☎ 987214, 42 rm P ⚏ ⚏ closed 21 Sep-14 May, 40,000; bkf: 3,500.

⚑ ★★★ **Adriatico,** v. Pinarella 30, 380 pl, ☎ 71537.

CESENA

Forlì 19, Bologna 89, Milan 300 km
Pop. 90,005 ⊠ 47023 ☎ 0547   F3

Set in the heart of Romagna on the r. bank of the River Savio and on the old Via Emilia, overlooking the plain, but also on the first gentle slopes of the Apennines, Cesena is an ancient city. (Its name is perhaps Etruscan.) Its brief but glorious rule by the Malatesta family has left an indelible mark on the city, despite successive rounds of architectural renovation. All the new buildings are integrated into the old, with the result that the town centre today is a most extraordinary architectural mixture. Specialized and intensive agriculture, vineyards which produce Sangiovese and Albana wines of the highest quality, and the agricultural machine industry have made Cesena the prosperous town it is today.

▶ At the centre of the town, in p. Bufalini 2, in the 'Palazzo delle Scuole', is the **Biblioteca Malatestiana★** *(winter 9 a.m.-1 p.m. and 3-7 or 8 p.m. Sat; closed Sun and Mon a.m.; summer Tue-Sat 8 a.m.-1 p.m., Mon 4-8 p.m.; Sun and hols 10 a.m.-12 noon; individual visitors should apply to the caretaker).* Perfectly preserved, this is one of the oldest monastic classical libraries in existence. Built under the patronage of Malatesta Novello by Matteo Nuti (1452), it shows Florentine taste in its Renaissance style. Its reading room is a long room with three aisles, and the collection includes a large number of illuminated manuscripts. ▶ A little beyond this, in the corso Mazzini, the **cathedral** stands as a faithful representative, after careful restoration, of its original Gothic structure. Inside are several Renaissance altars. ▶ In p. del Popolo, with its fountain (1583), rises the picturesque fortress, the **Rocca Malatestiana**, with its long walls, corner turrets and dungeon. Built on the Garampo hill by Galeotto Malatesta (14C) it was extensively rebuilt after 1466 by Matteo Nuti. Stretching around the courtyard is the **Museo della Civiltà Contadina** *(rural life; 9 a.m.-12 noon and 4-7:30 p.m. or 9:30 a.m-12 noon and 3-4:30 p.m. winter; closed Mon).* ▶ 2 km SE is the old Benedictine abbey of the **Madonna del Monte★** (founded 12C, rebuilt 15C-16C) with the *Presentation to the Temple★* by Francia and an impressive collection of **ex-voto offerings★** of both anthropological and artistic interest.   ☐

Practical information ────────────────

Hotels:
★★★★ *Casali,* v. Croce 81, ☎ 22745, 38 rm ℗ 〰 ᶜ 79,000; bkf: 5,000.
★★★★ *Meeting Hotel,* v. Romea 545, ☎ 333160, 26 rm ℗ 〰 ⌘ No restaurant, 75,000; bkf: 6,500.

Restaurant:
◆◆◆ *Gianni,* v. dell'Amore 9, ☎ 21328, closed Thu. Summer terrace. Regional and international cuisine: tagliolini with shrimps, risotto alla marinara, 29/40,000.

Recommended
Events: *week-long festival of crafts and agriculture,* ☎ 22073 (end Aug-Sep).
Farm vacations: *Podere Bettina,* at Trebbo di Roversano, v. Comunale di Roversano, ☎ 346556.
Horse racing: trotting, ☎ 333148.

COLORNO

Parma 15, Bologna 104, Milan 130 km
Pop. 7,289 ⊠ 43052 ☎ 0521   B1

This pretty, ancient town, located at the confluence of the Lonro Canal and the Parma River, belonged first to the Sanseverino, then to the Farnese families. It still retains much of the atmosphere of that time. Barbara Sanseverino, the famous Marchesa of Colorno, written about by Tasso, suffered torture and death for the part she played in a plot against the Farnese Duke of Parma (1612). It was then that the old Sanseverino fortress was seized by the Farnese and, in the decades that followed, transformed into an imposing ducal palace (used as a summer residence) in a magnificent park (largely ruined during World War II) where the Dukes of Parma held sumptuous feasts and hunting parties.

▶ The **Palazzo Ducale**, standing on the piazza by the bridge over the River Parma, is fortified with corner turrets and contains several splendid rooms on the piano nobile *(open during town festivals; other times arrange with caretaker).* The Orangery, a hothouse for citrus plants, houses a **Museo Etnografico della Civiltà Contadina** (rural-life museum). ▶ Behind the palace is the ducal church of **S. Liborio,** designed by Petitot (1796).   ☐

Practical information ────────────────

ⓘ at Palazzo Ducale.

Restaurant:
● ◆◆◆ *Stendhal,* at Sacca, ☎ 815493, closed Tue and Jul-Aug. Fine garden for meals in the open air. Parmesan cuisine: tortelli with herbs, mushroom risotto, homemade wines, 25/40,000.

Recommended
Water skiing: *Motonautica parmense,* at Sacca, v. Alzaia, ☎ 815885; *Sci nautico Torricelle,* at Sissa, ☎ 879827.

COMACCHIO

Ferrara 52, Bologna 93, Milan 298 km
Pop. 21,349 ⊠ 44022 ☎ 0533   E2

Comacchio is situated on a group of thirteen small islands in a marshy valley of the same name. When at its height in late medieval times, it was Florentine and its fleet rivaled that of Venice. The town was completely destroyed by the Venetians and nothing remains of its medieval and Renaissance architecture: every building in Comacchio today was constructed after its revival in the 17C. The town was cut off from the mainland by water until 1821, when a road built on dykes connected it to Ostellato. Since then, the draining and reclamation of the region has transformed the countryside around the lagoon. Over time, bridges fell into ruin, many of the canals dried up, and the inhabitants' lives, formerly almost entirely based on fishing and especially eel-trapping, turned towards agriculture and the tourist trade which developed in the new resorts that sprang up along the coast.

▶ The main feature of the town is the **Trepponti** (three bridges, 1634). This unique construction by Luca Danesi provides a picturesque solution to the problem of crossing four canals with five converging footpaths. ▶ The **Loggiato dei Cappuccini** was built in 1647 to connect the town to the sanctuary of S. Maria in Aula Regia. Nearby is the **Museo Mariano di Arte Sacra Contemporanea** *(8 a.m.-12 noon and 3-7 p.m.)*   ☐

Practical information ────────────────

Recommended
Cycling: *Boldrini,* v. Fogli 71, ☎ 81004.
Events: *international ballet festival* (Jul-Aug).

┌─────────────────────────────────────┐
│ Send us your comments and suggestions; we will │
│ use them in the next edition. │
└─────────────────────────────────────┘

Eels from Comacchio

The flat, salty landscape of Comacchio, its glassy waters spiked with reeds, is famous for its eels. The 'Valli di Comacchio', today no longer the marshy expanses that they once were before the massive agrarian drainage program, correspond to some degree to the position of the Po delta during Roman times. At that time, sea water seeped into the land and, during medieval times, it became a valuable source of food. Young eels swim into the ponds and lagoons, grow and fatten; the adults leave to reproduce, but their journeys are carefully regulated by watergates. When the sea causes a current of salt water to flow into the ponds in autumn, the outward procession of the eels is arrested and they are caught. Eel fishing is particularly successful on stormy nights. In Comacchio, eels are made into soup, grilled or cooked on a spit.

The COMACCHIO VALLEYS

From Comacchio to Mésola *(84 km, 1 day; map 3)*

The Comacchio Valleys (a term that here indicates

3. The Comacchio Valleys

salt marshes and entrophied lagoons rather than the valleys of flowing rivers) at one time occupied an extensive area of the E and S parts of the Ferrara province, corresponding to the strip of the Adriatic coast through which the Po flowed into the sea in ancient times. The origin of these valleys is not ancient: they were formed in the late medieval and Renaissance periods through progessive subsidence of the soil. A massive drainage program, begun in the 1950s, has reclaimed thousands of acres and has radically transformed the landscape as well as the economic outlook of the local people. This intervention has given rise to bitter controversy, with one body of opinion in favour of preserving the marshes, be it for their scientific or ecological significance, their touristic value, their economic potential (fish-farming), or for their function in controlling flood water, as sea-defenses and in safe-guarding the water table. This itinerary shows the marshes as they once were, as well as some of the areas that have been drained, and indicates the main cultural sites and nature reserves.

▶ Leaving **Comacchio** (→) near the Trepponti and the Ferrara road to the r., the route follows a straight road across flat, drained land. On the r. are the excavations of the site of the Graeco-Etruscan city of **Spina** (6C-3C BC); valuable artifacts from the tombs here are kept in the archaeological museum at Ferrara *(guided tours at Spina in summer, ☎ 81234).* ▶ Continuing through this silent and remote landscape: on the r. is drained land; on the l., the mirror-like surface of the lagoon. ▶ Passing through **Sant'Alberto** and **Mandriole**, a short detour leads on the l. to the **memorial to Anita Garibaldi**, Garibaldi's wife, who died at the nearby farmhouse, **Fattoria Bastogi**, on 4 August 1849. ▶ Turning down the 'Strada Romea' (a name recalling that this was a medieval pilgrimage route; *romeus* meant a pilgrim going to Rome) and continuing through **Porto Garibaldi**, a fishing town and seaside resort, the route leads to **Volano** with a fine view of the lagoon known as the Valle Bertuzzi. ▶ From Volano the route turns W to the Strada Romea, which leads to a Benedictine monastery, the **abbazia di Pomposa★**, recognizable from a distance by its campanile. This is one of the great works of Romanesque architecture. Probably founded in the 7C, it was an important cultural centre during medieval times; the 15C saw the beginning of its decline and, in the 17C, it was abandoned because of malaria. The group of buildings comprises the basilica with its campanile, the Palazzo della Ragione and the remains of the monastery. The **Basilica★★**, in the style of Ravenna, dates back to the 8C-9C; it was extended in the late 10C-early 11C; the atrium was added at that time. The **campanile★**, built in Lombard style in 1063, rises to a height of 157 ft. The interior has a nave and two aisles with Roman and Byzantine columns and a raised sanctuary. On the walls are 14C frescos of the Bologna school; the frescos in the apse are by Vitale di Bologna (1351). All that is left of the monastery are the **Sala del Capitolo**, with early 14C frescos, and the refectory, also with frescos (1316-20) by a Riminese master. In another room is the small **Museo Pomposiano**. Opposite the basilica is the **Palazzo della Ragione** (11C), from which the abbot administered justice. ▶ A few km to the NE on the Strada Romea is the **Gran Bosco della Mésola**, a large area of scrub and woodland stretching between the Po and Taglio della Falce; deer are protected here *(Sun and hols 8 a.m.-sunset).* ▶ Continuing on the road that follows the Po di Goro to the fishing village of **Goro** and **Gorino Ferrarese**, the route passes through countryside with a quality entirely its own. ▶ The final destination on the itinerary is **Mésola**, back on the Strada Romea; here is the interesting **Castello della Robinie** (1579-83) of Alfonso II d'Este, Duke of Ferrara, later used as a summer residence and hunting lodge. □

Practical information
MESOLA, ✉ 44026, ☎ 0533.

Hotel:
★★ *Felice,* v. XXV Aprile 64, ☎ 99180, 35 rm Ⓟ ⌁ 38,000.

Recommended
Nature park: *Gran Bosco della Mésola* (toll payable for cars; access also on foot; bicycles available for rent). Information: *Corpo forestale,* ☎ 794028.

VOLANO, ✉ 44021, ☎ 0533.

Recommended
Excursions: to Po Delta (→ Porto Tolle, Venetia) with motor vessel *Eridano,* ☎ 0542/49351.

CORNIGLIO

Parma 50, Bologna 146, Milan 172 km
Pop. 3,190 ✉ 43021 ☎ 0521   B2

Corniglio is a resort surrounded by chestnut forests in the valley of the River Parma. This is the departure point for excursions along the chain of mountains that marks the Apennine watershed, and to places such as **Lagdei** *(14.2 km)* and **Prato Spilla** *(30 km),* which also have facilities for winter sports. From Lagdei, by mule-track *(45 mn)* or by chair lift, it is possible to reach **Lake Santo,** on the NE slope of Mt. Marmagna (ski slopes).   ▫

Practical information
⚞ ski lifts, cross-country skiing at Lagdei and Prato Spilla.

CORREGGIO

Reggio nell'Emilia 17, Bologna 59, Milan 166 km
Pop. 19,761 ✉ 42015 ☎ 0522   C2

The ancient landscape here is covered by thin strips of farm land isolated between marshes and woods. On these bands of soil, called *corrigiae,* rose the first settlement. Set in the midst of the plain between Carpi and Reggio, this is one of the many Italian towns which had their moments of glory; from 1452, when the town became a countship, until 1635, when it became part of the Duchy of Modena, this was the seat of the da Correggio family who also briefly held sway over Reggio and Parma. The poetess Veronica Gambara was a Countess of Correggio and the court played host to numerous celebrated poets and men of letters, including Ariosto, Tasso, Aretino, Bembo and Molza. It was during these years of splendour that the painter Antonio Allegri (later known as Correggio) was born here.

▶ On the wide corso Cavour stands the town's most important monument: the **Palazzo dei Principi.** Built by craftsmen from Ferrara *c.* 1500 on the site of an earlier building, it has an elegant marble gateway and a porticoed courtyard. Inside, the **Museo Civico** *(being reorganized; for access apply to the caretaker of the palazzo)* contains Flemish tapestries, prints and paintings, including the *Head of Christ★* by Mantegna. ▶ Also of interest is the basilica of **S. Quirino,** built in the 16C based on a design attributed to Vignola, with a 14C campanile (once the tower of a fortress), and the church of **S. Francesco** (1470). ▶ 5.5 km S lies **S. Martino in Rio,** with its impressive **fortress** (now the town hall) which contains the Gothic chapel of S. Giovanni and fine rooms with ceilings covered with painted panels (14C-17C).   ▫

Don't forget to consult the Practical Holiday Guide: it can help in solving many problems.

Practical information

Recommended
Cycling: *Polisportivo Correggio,* v. Carlo V 4, ☎ 693724.

CORTEMAGGIORE

Piacenza 20, Bologna 137, Milan 84 km
Pop. 4,754 ✉ 29016 ☎ 0523   A-B1

On the l. bank of the River Arda, known as *Curtis Major* during the Carolingian period, Cortemaggiore was rebuilt to its present symmetrical plan at the end of the 15C by the Pallavicino family who came to settle here from their native Busseto. The town is known as one of Italy's most important oil centres since the discovery of oil and natural gas in 1949.

▶ In the central piazza stands the collegiate church of **S. Maria delle Grazie,** begun in 1481 but with a modern façade. Its Gothic interior contains two tombs of the Pallavicino (1499) by Lombard sculptors and polyptych panels by Mazzola. ▶ In the Gothic-Renaissance church of S. Francesco (1490), the chapel of **S. Anna** has frescos by Pordenone (1530); in the aisle opposite there is a *Deposition* by the same artist. In the convent next door are late 16C frescos.   ▫

Practical information
ⓘ v. Brigheti 2, ☎ 839080.

Restaurant:
● ◆◆◆ *Valentino,* at Caorso, v. Roma 29/B, ☎ 821233, closed Mon and Aug. Authentic rustic setting. Excellent Piacentine and Italian cuisine: risotto with frogs, horse rosticciano, homemade wines, 45/60,000.

FAENZA*

Ravenna 31, Bologna 49, Milan 264 km
Pop. 54,922 ✉ 48018 ☎ 0546   E3

The people of Faenza, which reached its artistic apogee in the 15C-16C, created a pottery industry that made this Romagnese town famous throughout Europe: its majolica wares were exported to Germany, Holland, England and France, and gave rise to the French word *faïence,* subsequently adopted by English. The tradition is kept alive today through the activity of the Museo delle Ceramiche, which continues to produce ceramics and organizes a competition and other events.

▶ The **piazza del Popolo,** bordered on two sides by porticos and galleries, and the adjoining **piazza della Libertà** form the centre of the town. These are divided by the Via Emilia which, under the names corso Mazzini and corso Saffi, cross the town from the NW-SE. ▶ On the p. del Popolo stands the **Palazzo del Podestà,** enlarged in 1256 but partially abandoned since; also the **Palazzo del Municipio,** formerly called the 'Palazzo del Popolo', which retains little of its original 13C structure other than a section of its battlements. ▶ The p. della Libertà is dominated by the imposing form of the **cathedral★,** one of the most important architectural works of the Renaissance in Romagna. It was begun in 1474 based on designs by Giuliano da Maiano, and completed in the 16C; the marble facing on the façade was never completed. The interior, in a pure Tuscan style, contains various works of art of the 15C-16C, among which are the two **tombs★** of SS. Terenzio and Emiliano by the 15C Tuscan school, and the tomb of S. Savino★ by Benedetto da Maiano. Among the paintings is a *Madonna and Child with Saints,* one of the best works by Innocenzo da Imola (1526). ▶ The **Pinacoteca★,** at no. 1 v. S. Maria dell'Angelo *(9 a.m.-1:30 p.m.; closed Sun),* contains paintings of the Faentine and Romagnese schools of the 14C-19C, and of the Bologna school of the 16C-18C, as well as a statue in wood of *S. Girolamo*★ by Donatello, a marble bust of *S. Giovannino*★ by Rossellino, and a terra-cotta *(Madonna and Child with the Two SS. Giovanni*★) by Alfonso Lombardi. ▶ The **modern art section** of the gallery at corso Matteotti 2 *(9:30 a.m.-12:30 p.m. Wed, Thu and Sat)* has paintings by Fattori, Spadini, Signorini, Carena, De Pisis, Morandi and sculptures by Rodin and Martini. The **Museo delle Ceramiche**★ *(9:30 a.m.-6 p.m. summer; 9:30 a.m.-1 p.m. and 2:30-5:30 p.m. winter; Sun and hols 9 a.m.-1 p.m.; closed Mon)* at no. 2 v. Campidori provides a unique centre for the exhibit and study of ceramics of every period and country, from prehistoric and pre-Columbian pottery to Renaissance majolica ware as well as works by Chagall, Léger, Matisse, Picasso and Rouault. ▶ The church of **S. Maria Vecchia** (rebuilt 17C) has a beautiful 8C octagonal **campanile**★. ▶ On the other side of the River Lamone, in the medieval quarter of Borgo Durbecco, is the 13C **chiesa della Commenda**, which contains charming frescos by Girolamo da Treviso the Younger (1533). ▶ On the side of the town facing Forlì stands the **Porta delle Chiavi**; this gate is the sole reminder of the medieval walls built by the Manfredi family.   □

Practical information _____

ⓘ voltone Molinella, ☎ 25231.

Hotel:
★★★ *Vittoria*, v. Garibaldi 23, ☎ 21508, 47 rm Ⓟ ⏺ ⟡ closed 1-20 Aug, 54,000; bkf: 6,000.

Restaurant:
⏺ ◆◆◆ *Amici Miei*, corso Mazzini 54, ☎ 661600, closed Mon and 15-30 Aug. In basement of Gessi palazzo. Excellent regional cuisine: risotto nel pane, tortelloni with asparagus, 40/50,000.

Recommended
Craft workshops: *Carf*, v. Boaria 46, ☎ 620567; *Zauli*, v. della Croce 6, ☎ 22123; *Geminiani*, v. Pasolini 21, ☎ 26566 (ceramics).
Events: *international contemporary ceramics competition* (Palazzo delle Esposizioni, corso Mazzini 92, Jun-Sep); *Palio del Niballo* (4th Sun in Jun); *Festa Nott de' bisó* (eve Epiphany); *100 km walk of il Passatore* (May).

FERRARA**

Bologna 47, Milan 252, Rome 425 km
Pop. 147,328 ⊠ 44100 ☎ 0532   D-E1
See map on page 202.

Ferrara's origins are obscure. It sprang up on the Adriatic coast not far from the Po Delta, a position that gave it an advantage in both river- and seaborne commerce and the ability to challenge both Venice and Ravenna. Although it became a free state in the 12C, it only began to acquire the status of a commercial city a century later when the Este family came to power. Then it became an immense building site where the best architects of the time could express themselves. Painters and sculptors also arrived in Ferrara to decorate the new buildings; they opened schools and trained a future generation of artists. The brilliant and cultivated Niccolò II (1338-88) encouraged musicians and poets, and invited Petrarch to Ferrara. Among the illustrious guests were Ariosto (1474-1523), who wrote *Orlando Furioso* there, and Tasso (1544-95), *Jerusalem Delivered*. Albert I founded the university. At the end of the 15C, Ercole I (1471-1505) had the city rebuilt and it became one of the most beautiful in Europe. Alfonso I (1505-34) married Lucretia Borgia, which also contributed to the splendour of the court of Ferrara. The family forged alliances with the

greatest powers of Europe: Ercole II (1534-89) married Renata da Francia, daughter of Louis XII, King of France. Later the power of Ferrara began to decline. The open-handedness of its princes emptied the treasury and made tax increases inevitable; thus burdened, the people became uneasy. At the same time, the war had undermined the leaders' power; moreover, Renata da Francia received Calvin and his ideas: in 1598, Cesare of Este had to leave the city and transport his court to Modena, while Clement VIII attached Ferrara to the papal states. Abandoned by its princes the city was without resources, and other inhabitants deserted it as well. The streets were invaded by weeds to the extent that Stendhal could write in 1817: 'The Papal legations could feed half a cavalry regiment on the grass that grows in the streets'. The prosperous and populous city of today owes its riches to modern reclamation methods that have permitted the once-solitary wastelands — flooded by salt water and invaded by malaria — that surrounded the city to be drained and cultivated. The success of these methods has made Ferrara a leading fruit producer and exporter. Its monuments continue to bear witness to the contribution made to European culture by the Este family.

▶ The **cathedral**★★ (D4) in the p. della Cattedrale is the largest medieval building in the city. It was built 12C-14C in Romanesque-Gothic style; the **façade** represents a fusion of the two styles, with the sober Romanesque aspect of the original structure set against intricate Gothic sculpture and ornamentation added in the 13C-14C. The **middle portal** (*c.* 1135) and the **porch** are decorated with interesting sculptures. On the r.-hand side, the lower section of which is concealed behind a 15C portico of shops (called the **Loggia dei Merciai**), stands the massive marble **campanile**★ (1451-1596), built according to a classical design, probably by Leon Battista Alberti. The **interior** (altered 18C, decorated late 19C) contains works by Garofalo, Guercino, Francia and del Bastianino (fresco of the *Last Judgment*★ in the apse), and two 15C bronze statues (*St. Maurelius*★ and *St. George*★) by Paris. ▶ The **Museo del Duomo** *(10 a.m.-12 noon and 3-5 p.m. summer or 4-6 p.m. winter; closed Sun and hols)*, located above the narthex of the cathedral, contains important works of art, among which are *St. George*★ and *The Annunciation*★, temperas by Cosmè Tura; *Madonna of the Pomegranates*★★ and *St. Maurelius*★, 16C sculptures by Jacopo della Quercia; eight 16C tapestries and twelve marble *Reliefs of the Months* (late 12C). ▶ Opposite the cathedral is the **Palazzo Comunale** (C4), formerly the ducal palace of the Este family, built in the 13C and subsequently much altered. The **piazza Municipio**, reached by way of the Vòlto del Cavallo, was once the courtyard of the palazzo and still has several Renaissance windows and an original outside **staircase** (1481). ▶ Close by is the **Castello Estense** (C4), rising in its impressive bulk from the moat that surrounds it. It is built as a square, with massive towers at each corner, and represents an admirable combination of medieval military architecture and the classical style of 16C civil architecture. Inside *(9:30 a.m.-12:30 p.m. and 3-6 p.m. or 2-5 p.m. Sep-Mar; closed Mon)*, besides the 15C courtyard, one can visit several rooms with frescos by Bastianino and the **Salone dei Giochi**★, with interesting frescos by the Filippi depicting various athletic feats; the elegant chapel of Renata di Francia (Renée de France), the wife of Ercole II d'Este and an ardent supporter of Calvinism (this is one of the few Protestant chapels to have escaped the Counter-Reformation). The **dungeons** witnessed the tragic end to the love of Parisina Malatesta, wife of Niccolò III, her stepson Ugo, both of whom were incarcerated here before being executed (1425). Leading from the Castello Estense is the **corso della Giovecca** (C-D4-6), one of the prettiest and most animated streets of the city. It was part of the 'Addizione Erculea' (the urban development project of Ercole I, planned and carried out by Biagio Rossetti in 1492). Along the street are the **Church of the Teatini** (at the third altar on the l., *Presentation at the Temple*★ by Guercino) and notable palazzi, including the **Palazzina di Marfisa d'Este**★ (D5) dating from 1559; inside *(9 a.m.-12:30 p.m. and 3-6 p.m. or 2-5 p.m. Oct-Mar; Sun and hols 9 a.m.-12:30 p.m.)* there are rooms with ceilings painted in the grotesque style by the Filippi. ▶ The nearby **via Savonarola** (D5) was the focal point of early Ferrarese Renaissance noble architecture: at no. 9 is the **Palazzo Pareschi,** now the main building of the university, but formerly belonging to the Este family and sometimes called the Palazzo di Renata di Francia, who lived here; no. 30 is the **Casa Romei**★ *(8:30 a.m.-12:30 p.m. and 3-6:30 p.m. or 3-5 p.m. Oct-Apr; closed Mon)*, a typical aristocratic house of the 15C, built with two picturesque courtyards and various rooms containing frescos. ▶ The church of **S. Francesco** (D5), medieval in origin but altered in 1494 by Biagio Rossetti, contains fine works of art of the 15C-16C. ▶ Another church rebuilt by Rossetti is **S. Maria in Vade** (E5). ▶ Still another palace reconstructed by Rossetti (1466-93) is the **Palazzo Schifanoia**★★, also of the Este family, and the earliest example of Renaissance architecture in Ferrara. Its magnificent marble **entrance** was designed by Francesco del Cossa. The interior, housing the **Museo Civico** *(9 a.m.-7 p.m.)*, includes the **Sala dei Mesi,** decorated with superb frescos★★ (scenes from the life of Borso d'Este and an allegory of the months), the work of Cossa, de' Roberti and other artists of the Ferrarese school of the late 15C; in the other rooms, the museum's collection (bronzes, ceramics, coins, medals, precious stones, paintings) is displayed. ▶ On the v. XX Settembre (E-F4-5), laid out in the early 15C, stands the 15C **house of Biagio Rossetti** (F5), the architect who built most of the city's great monuments. At no. 124 v. XX Settembre is the **Palazzo di Ludovico il Moro**★ (E-F5), Rossetti's unfinished masterpiece built for the ambassador of Ercole I to the court of the Duchy of Milan, for whom it is named. It opens onto a magnificent **courtyard**★, and a room on the ground floor contains delightful **frescos** by Garofalo (16C). The piano nobile houses the **Museo Archeologico Nazionale**★ *(9 a.m.-2 p.m.; May-Sep 9 a.m.-6 p.m.; Sun and hols 9 a.m.-2 p.m.; closed Mon)* with its collection of pottery★ from the mausoleum of Spina (6C-3C BC) which was discovered as a result of the drainage work in the Comacchio Valleys (→). ▶ The **via delle Volte**★ is the most typical and best preserved of Ferrara's streets of the 14C-early 15C. ▶ The **corso Ercole I d'Este**★ (A-C4) is, by contrast, the main artery of the 'Addizione Erculea', with its numerous 15C palazzi, among which are the Palazzo Turchi-di Bagno (B4), the nearby Palazzo dei Diamanti (→), and the **Palazzo Prosperi-Sacrati**★ (B4; 15C-16C), noted for its splendid portal (1506-16). ▶ The **Palazzo dei Diamanti**★★ (B4), which takes its name from the diamond-shaped indentations decorating its façade, was begun by Rossetti in 1492 and completed in the late 15C. This houses the **Pinacoteca Nazionale**★ *(9 a.m.-2 p.m.; Sun and hols 9 a.m.-1 p.m.; closed Mon)*, an important collection of paintings, mainly by Ferrarese artists of the 14C and onward, with particular emphasis on those of the 16C. Besides the paintings of de' Roberti, Cosmè Tura, Dossi and Garofalo (including the splendid polyptych of the *Madonna and Saints*★, begun by Garofalo and completed by Dosso Dossi), there are also a Mantegna *(Christ and the Virgin*★), a *Madonna and Child* by Gentile da Fabriano, an *Adoration of the Magi* by Giovanni Bellini, and an *Assumption of the Virgin* by Carpaccio. On the ground floor is the **Galleria Civica d'Arte Moderna** *(9:30 a.m.-1 p.m. and 3-6:30 p.m.; summer 9 a.m.-1 p.m. and 4-7 p.m.)* which contains an important collection of works by Italian and foreign artists. The **Museo Boldini e dell'Ottocento Ferrarese** (B4-5; *winter 9:30 a.m.-1 p.m. and 3-6:30 p.m.; summer 9 a.m.-1 p.m. and 4-7 p.m.)* contains a comprehensive record of the Ferrarese painter Giovanni Boldini and others. ▶ Nearby is the huge, tree-shaded **piazza Ariostea** (B5), bordered by notable Renaissance palazzi: at no. 10 is the Palazzo Rondinelli; at no. 11, the Palazzo Bevilacqua. ▶ In one

of the most evocative quarters of old Ferrara is the Benedictine monastery of **S. Antonio in Polesine** (E-F5; *wkdays 9-11:30 a.m. and 3-5 p.m.*), founded in 1294 and altered a number of times since; the **coro delle Monache**★ (the nuns' choir) contains groups of 13C-15C frescos. ▶ The **house of Ludovico Ariosto,** which the poet bought as his residence, today serves as municipal offices. □

Practical information _____

ⓘ largo Castello 22 (C4), ☎ 35017.

🚌 (B1-2), ☎ 37649.

🚃 from p. Stazione (B1-2) and rampari S. Paolo (D2-3).

Hotels:
★★★★ **Astra,** v. Cavour 55 (C3 a), ☎ 26234, 77 rm Ⓟ 108,000; bkf: 10,000.
★★★★ **Ripagrande,** v. Ripagrande 21 (D3 b), ☎ 34733, 40 rm Ⓟ 120,000; bkf: 15,000.
★★★ **Europa,** corso Giovecca 49 (C4 c), ☎ 21438, 46 rm Ⓟ 🏛 closed Aug. 17C palazzo with frescoed rooms and paintings donated by Napoleon, 59,000; bkf: 8,000.
★★★ **Touring:** v. Cavour 11 (C4 d), ☎ 37522, 39 rm Ⓟ No restaurant, 62,000; bkf: 6:000.

Restaurants:
♦♦♦ **Buca San Domenico,** p. Sacrati 22 (C3 f), ☎ 37006, closed Mon and Jul. In 14C building. Ferrarese cuisine: mushroom risotto, grilled meat, 25/35,000.
♦♦♦ **Grotta Azzurra-da Giovanni,** p. Sacrati 43 (C3 g), ☎ 37320, closed Sun and 1-15 Jul. Ferrarese cuisine: pasticcio alla ferrarese, bolliti misti, 25/35,000.
♦♦♦ **Provvidenza,** corso Ercole I d'Este 92 (A4 h), ☎ 21937, closed Mon. Outdoor service in summer. Ferrarese cuisine: pasta with truffles, charcoal grilled eel, homemade wines, 18/25,000.
● ♦♦ **Vecchia Chitarra,** v. Ravenna 13 (F5 i), ☎ 62204, closed Tue. Capricious and imaginative. Ferrarese cuisine: eel and salt cod, oxtail in red wine, 25/35,000.
♦ **Aldobrando,** corso Porta Mare 45 (B5 e), ☎ 37186, closed Sat eve, Sun and Aug. Ferrarese cuisine: tortellini with cream, bollito misto, 18/22,000.

🅐 *Estense,* v. Porta Catena 118, NE zone, ☎ 52791 (all year).

Recommended
Cycling: *UDACE,* v. Cairoli 6, ☎ 47719.
Events: *Palio di San Giorgio* (last Sun in May); *Premio Letterario-Giornalistico Estense* (award for literature/journalism; Sep).
Flying: v. Aeroporto, ☎ 91655 (powered flight); *Centro studi di Volo a Vela Padano,* at Aguscello, v. Prati Vecchi, ☎ 418550 (gliding).
Horseback riding: *Centro ippico Barbantini,* v. Argine Po 20, ☎ 724081; *Associazione ippica estense,* v. del Gorgo 10, ☎ 60242.
Horse racing: (F3), v. Ippodromo; *Concorso ippico nazionale* (Sep).
Motorcycling: racetrack at v. Porta Catena 73 (A3), ☎ 54394 *(Centro specializzazione ciclismo,* ☎ 52649).
Youth hostel: *Ostello Estense,* v. Benvenuto Tisi da Garafolo 5, ☎ 21098.

FIDENZA

Parma 23, Bologna 116, Milan 103 km
Pop. 23,510 ⊠ 43036 ☎ 0524   B1

Situated on the Via Emilia beside the River Storone, Fidenza was founded as a Roman colony (1C BC) and became the township of *Fidentia* before being completely destroyed in the 3C at the time that S. Donnino, the Christian soldier, was decapitated. Rebuilt in the 9C, it bore the name Borgo San Donnino until 1927, when it was given its original Roman name once again.

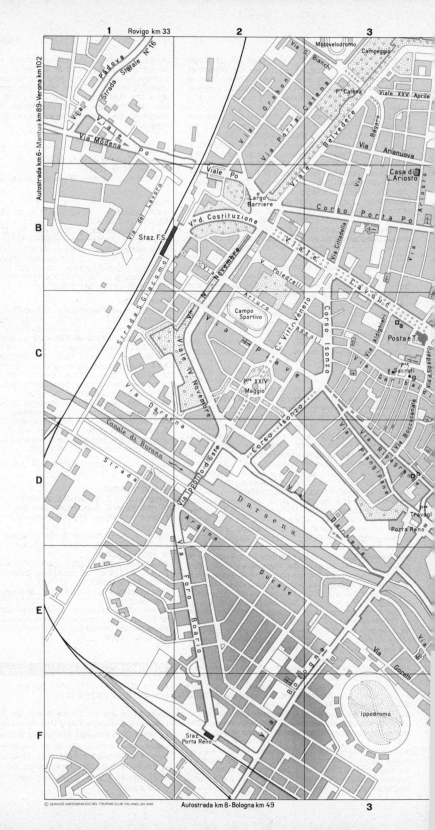

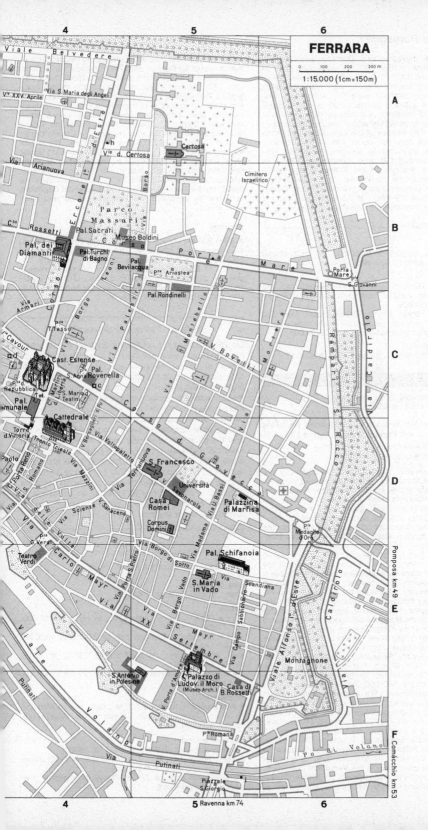

FERRARA

0   100   200   300 m
1:15.000 (1cm=150m)

Viale   Belvedere

Via S. Maria degli Angeli

V.^{le} XXV. Aprile

Certosa

•h

V^{le} d. Certosa

Via   Arianuova

Cimitero
Israelitico

A

Parco
Massari

C 50

Rossetti

Pal. Sacrati

Museo Boldini

Pal. dei
Diamanti

Pal. Turchi
di Bagno

Pal.
Bevilacqua

P.za
Ariostea

Porta
Mare

Porta
Mare

p.le
S. Giovanni

B

Via
Armari

Pal. Rondinelli

P.za
T. Tasso

V. Bovelli

p.^{za}
Cavour

•d

Cast. Estense

Pal.

S. Anna Rovorella

•c

R.^a d.
Repubblica

Tel.

S. Maria d.
Teatini

Pal.
munale

Cattedrale

Torre
d. Vittoria

Trento Trieste

C

Corso   d.   Giovecca

Paolo

S. Francesco

Università

Casa
Romei

Palazzina
di Marfisa

Corpus
Domini

p.le
Medaglie
d'Oro

D

Teatro
Verdi

Pal. Schifanoia

S. Maria
in Vado

Scandiana

E

Montagnone

S. Antonio
in Polesine

Palazzo di
Ludov. il Moro
(Museo Arch.)

Casa di
B. Rossetti

P.za Romana

P o   d i   V o l a n o

F

Via   Putinati

P.le
S. Giorgio

Ravenna km 74

Pomposa km 49

Comacchio km 53

4   5   6

▶ The **Duomo★**, dedicated to S. Donnino, was begun in Romanesque style in the 12C but was completed in Gothic style in the 13C. The magnificent façade, standing between two square towers, was never completed, but the lower sections have fine sculptural ornamentation★; the splendid middle portal is by sculptors of the school of Antelami (the statues of Ezekiel and David may be by Antelami himself). The interior contains a series of late 13C **frescos** of the *Last Judgment* (in the apse); the **crypt** has the burial urn of S. Donnino, with bas-reliefs attributed to Giovanni Pietro da Rho (15C). ▶ Opposite the Duomo, beneath the **Porta di S. Donnino**, are vestiges of the **Roman bridge** which took the Via Emilia over the Storone. ▶ On the p. Garibaldi in the town centre stands the Gothic **Palazzo Comunale** (late 13C, now restored). ▶ 6.5 km NW is **Castione Marchesi**, with a Romanesque abbey church (11C-12C). □

Practical information ――――――――――――

Hotel:
★★★ *Astoria*, v. Gandolfi 5, ☎ 524314, 30 rm Ⓟ closed Aug. No restaurant, 50,000; bkf: 5,000.

Restaurants:
♦♦ *Astoria*, v. Gandolfi 7, ☎ 524588, closed Mon and 1-15 Aug. Italian cuisine: tortelli with ricotta, tagliatelle with porcini, 20/30,000.
♦♦ *Duomo*, v. Micheli 27, ☎ 524268, closed Mon and Aug. Regional cuisine: pappardelle with hare sauce, tripe alla parmigiana, homemade wines, 20/30,000.

Recommended
Cycling: *G.S. Cicli Aimi*, v. Berenini 175, ☎ 524017.

FORLÌ

Bologna 63, Milan 282, Rome 347 km
Pop. 110,943 ⊠ 47100 ☎ 0543   E3

Situated on the Via Emilia and surrounded by fertile farmland, Forlì — the Roman town of *Forum Livii* — is one of the principal towns of Romagna. The hub of its historic centre is largely 17C-18C.

▶ On the spacious p. A. Saffi, at the centre of the city, are the **Palazzo del Municipio**, extensively altered over the years (the present façade is 19C); the Gothic **Palazzo del Podestà**; the **Palazzina degli Albertini** (end 15C); and the Romanesque church of S. Mercuriale. ▶ **S. Mercuriale★**(12C-13C) has a marble portal with a fine 13C relief of the *Vision and Adoration of the Magi★* (beneath the lunette). The church contains the **Tomb of Barbara Manfredi★**, who died in 1466, an early work by Francesco di Simone called Ferrucci of Fiesole, and also a votive tablet by Palmezzano. On the r. side of the church are the massive and elegant **campanile★**, built in 1180 (246 ft high), and a beautiful 14C cloister, all that remains of the former monastery. ▶ Facing the p. Ordelaffi are the **Palazzo Paulucci Piazza** (the Prefecture), 17C, and the Neoclassical **Duomo** (1841); inside, beneath the cupola of the 17C chapel of the Madonna del Fuoco, is a fine fresco *(The Assumption★)* by Carlo Cignani, who worked here for 25 years (1681-1706); at the far end of the l.-hand aisle is a large Romanesque crucifix. ▶ No. 72 corso della Repubblica houses the **Pinacoteca and Musei Comunali** *(9 a.m.-2 p.m.; Sun 10 a.m.-1 p.m.; closed Sat)*. The former is of particular interest for its collection of Romagnese paintings of the 14C-16C, including works by Palmezzano (*Annunciation★*), Fra Angelico (*Nativity★* and *Agony in the Garden★*), Lorenzo di Credi (*Portrait of a Lady★*),Guercino (*Annunciation★* and *St. John the Baptist★*) and Melozzo da Forlì (the so-called *Pestapepe★*, now the sign of a pharmacy, traditionally attributed to him). Among the sculptures are: a bust of *Pino III Ordelaffi*, attributed to Pollaiolo, the Amanni sarcophagus★ by Antonio and Bernardo Rossellino, and *Hebe* del Canova. On the upper floor is the **Verzocchi Collection**, comprising 70 pieces of contemporary art (Carrà, Campigli, De Pisis, Sironi) mainly devoted to the merits of

work. On the next floor is the interesting **Pedriali Collection** of works by Flemish artists (van Goyen, van Ostade, Hobbema) and Italian artists (Sebastiano Ricci, Ciardi, Fattori). The building is also the home of the **Museo Etnografico Romagnolo**. ▶ The **Rocca di Ravaldino**, at the end of the corso Diaz, is an impressive fortress on a quadrangular plan, with round corner towers and a squat dungeon. Built in the 14C and enlarged in the 15C, it endured the famous siege by the army of Cesare Borgia against Caterina Sforza, widow of Girolamo Riario and the seigneur of Imola (→). Her son, Giovanni dalle Bande Nere, was born here in 1498. ▶ The church of S. Maria dei Servi was originally built in the 12C (note the portal), but completely refurbished in the 18C; it contains the **Numai tomb★** (1502) and the 14C **Cappella del Capitolo★** enlivened by frescos of the Riminese school and other local artists.

Environs

▶ 8 km E is the church of S. Maria delle Grazie di Fornò, an unusual piece of circular architecture built in the late 15C. Inside: a fine Renaissance marble relief (*The Trinity★*). ▶ 8 km SE in the direction of Cesena, **Forlimpópoli** has an impressive **rocca** of the 14C-15C, and a **collegiate church** (S. Rufillo) dating from the end of the 14C, with a much older apse, possibly 5C. □

Stefano Pelloni, il Passatore

On 25 January 1851, in Forlimpópoli, at a time when the Legations were still part of the Papal States, a group of fifteen outlaws, led by Stefano Pelloni, took possession of the town gates and the garrison, blockaded the audience, actors and gendarmes in the theatre where a performance was taking place, and then systematically relieved the houses of the rich of their possessions. By this time, Stefano Pelloni, known as 'il Passatore', had escaped from prison; he and his gang terrorized the whole of Romagna with violence, highway robbery and pillage on a grand scale. No one was able to put a stop to his activities, until, two months after his bold coup in Forlimpópoli, he fell into a trap devised by Captain Michele Zambelli: il Passatore was killed in an exchange of gunfire. He died at the age of twenty-seven; but his name lives on in legend.

Practical information ――――――――――――

ⓘ corso della Repubblica 23, ☎ 25545.
✈ ☎ 780525.
⟳ ☎ 32329.
⟳ from p. Saffi, ☎ 25604.

Hotels:
★★★★ *Città*, v. Fortis 8, ☎ 28297, 55 rm Ⓟ ♨ 105,000; bkf: 7,000.
★★★★ *Principe*, v. Bologna 153, ☎ 34531, 46 rm Ⓟ ♨ 90,000; bkf: 6,000.
★★★ *Masini*, corso Garibaldi 28, ☎ 28072, 42 rm Ⓟ 45,000; bkf: 4,000.
★★★ *Vittorino*, v. Baratti 4, ☎ 24393, 21 rm Ⓟ 43,000; bkf: 3,000.

Restaurant:
♦ *A m'arcord*, v. Solferino 1/3, ☎ 27349, closed Wed and 15-30 Jul. Summer garden. Italian cuisine: strozzapreti, risotto, 20/35,000.

Recommended
Cycling: *G.S. Valli*, v. Bologna 43/C, ☎ 29769.
Events: *Festa della Madonna del Fuoco* (4 Feb); *Sagra della Segavecchia*, at Forlimpópoli.
Fairs: *Fiera di Forlì*, ☎ 724780 (May); *international bird-lovers'exhibition* (Sep).

Flying: *G. Ridolfi,* ☎ 780242 or 781577 (also gliding).
Swimming: v. Turati, ☎ 67317.
Wine: *Ca' del Sanzves,* outlet of organization representing all Romagnese wines, at Predappio Alta, p. Cavour 18, ☎ 922410.

FORNOVO DI TARO

Parma 23, Bologna 119, Milan 145 km
Pop. 5,993 ⊠ 43045 ☎ 0525   B2

Situated on the Taro River, at the base of the first foothills of the Parmesan Apennines, Fornovo — the Roman Forum Novum — is famous as the site of the battle between the armies of the Italian League and the French under Charles VIII on 6 July 1495.

▶ The façade of the Romanesque **parish church** (11C) has some notable 13C sculptures on the r.-hand side in an apsidal niche; inside, there is a marble relief of the *Story of St. Margaret* by the school of Antelami. ▶ 10 km S, just off the road to Calenzano, **Bardone** has a parish church with numerous sculptures.   ☐

Practical information ⎯⎯⎯⎯⎯⎯⎯⎯⎯⎯⎯⎯⎯⎯

Recommended
Motor racing: *San Cristoforo track,* at Varano de' Melegari, ☎ 53238.

FRASSINORO

Modena 65, Bologna 104, Milan 235 km
Pop. 2,729 ⊠ 41044 ☎ 0536   C3

Nestling in a sunny spot in the Modenese Apennines, Frassinoro is a year-round vacation centre.

▶ The **parish church** is built on the remains of a Benedictine abbey, of which only a few traces have survived (in the campanile, the presbytery and the interior of the church). ▶ 9.5 km SW of the outlying village of Piandelagotti, on the other side of the Apennine watershed at **Foce,** or the Foce delle Radici Pass (5,015 ft), where there are ski slopes and an excellent view, lies the solitary village of **San Pellegrino in Alpe,** in the Garfagnana chain in Tuscany, huddling around the **sanctuary** of S. Pellegrino (inside, the tomb of Matteo Civitali, 15C). From here there is a splendid **panorama★** over the Garfagnana and the Apuan Alps.   ☐

Practical information ⎯⎯⎯⎯⎯⎯⎯⎯⎯⎯⎯⎯⎯⎯

⤓ ski lifts, cross-country routes, instruction at Piandelagotti.
ⓘ v. Roma; at Piandelagotti, v. Lunardi, ☎ 967079.

GUALTIERI

Reggio nell'Emilia 25, Bologna 90, Milan 152 km
Pop. 6,131 ⊠ 42044 ☎ 0522   C1

Only 2 km from the Po River, this town has suffered from fearful flooding in recent years. It had a brief spell of political and architectural glory as a result of a drainage program carried out by Cornelio Bentivoglio (1560-1604); in return, the Duke of Modena gave him feudal rights over the area in 1567. After the Bentivoglio line died out (1634), this town assumed the modest role of a small provincial centre, always at the mercy of the capricious Po. During the great flood of 1755, the Palazzo Bentivoglio was partially demolished in order to provide materials for the construction of a new dyke.

▶ The beautiful p. Bentivoglio, with a garden in the centre, is lined on three sides by 17C **porticos** and domi-

nated by the **Torre del Comune.** Next door is the collegiate church of **S. Maria della Neve,** rebuilt in the late 18C after a flood. ▶ The fourth side of the piazza is occupied by the **Palazzo Bentivoglio,** begun at the end of the 16C by Aleotti. ▶ 10 km W, in the central square of **Brescello,** is a statue of Duke Ercole II by Jacopo Sansovino (1533).   ☐

Practical information ⎯⎯⎯⎯⎯⎯⎯⎯⎯⎯⎯⎯⎯⎯

Hotel:
★★★ **Ligabue,** p. IV Novembre, ☎ 834153, 37 rm Ⓟ ⌗
closed Aug, 60,000; bkf: 8,000.

GUASTALLA

Reggio nell'Emilia 28, Bologna 91, Milan 156 km
Pop. 13,442 ⊠ 42016 ☎ 0522   C1

Today this quiet little town, set on the r. bank of the Po River, has flourishing industries based on metal working, engineering, wood and food products; but it was not always so. The town is believed to have been founded in 603 by Agilulfo, as a Lombard military outpost; hence the name of *Wartstall,* which later became *Guardistallum.* In the 14C-15C it became the seat of the Counts of Torelli, and later became a part of the Gonzaga family's domains. Finally, when Ferrante II became a duke, it became the capital of his duchy. When this dynasty died out in 1746, the Treaty of Aquisgrana assigned the town to the Duchy of Parma and, like many other urban centres of the Po Valley, it ceased to play a leading role in the history of the region.

▶ In the central p. Mazzini is the bronze **statue of Ferrante I Gonzaga** by Leone Leoni (1564). There is also the 16C **Palazzo Gonzaga,** a bare semblance of its former self, and the **cathedral** (16C, rebuilt 18C-19C). ▶ No. 54 corso Garibaldi is the **Biblioteca Maldotti,** a library of some 60,000 volumes and a small **museum** *(3-7 p.m.; closed Sat and Sun)* containing coins, paintings and Gonzaga documents. ▶ 3 km SW is **Gualtieri** (→).   ☐

Practical information ⎯⎯⎯⎯⎯⎯⎯⎯⎯⎯⎯⎯⎯⎯

Restaurants:
◆ **Faro,** v. Po 17, ☎ 825897, closed Wed. Terrace on the Po. Regional cuisine: tortelli with pumpkin, river fish, 20/30,000.
◆ **Rina,** v. Po 40, ☎ 824580, closed Mon, Tue noon and Jul. Fine open-air terrace. Seafood: spaghetti with clams, mixed grill, 20/30,000.

Recommended
Water skiing: *Club Boretto Po,* at Boretto, ☎ 686828 or 686110 (Po lido).
Youth hostel: *Ostello Guastalla,* v. Lido Po 11/13, ☎ 824915.

IMOLA

Bologna 33, Milan 249 km
Pop. 61,169 ⊠ 40026 ☎ 0542   E3

On a site which is probably Etruscan in origin, Cornelius Sylla founded the *Forum Cornelii* in 82 BC to make the Roman presence felt in N Italy at a time of internal struggles. The city has kept its rectangular plan of the Roman period and is the first Romagnese city on the Via Emilia. Throughout the Middle Ages, the city was ravaged by long wars between neighbouring cities and torn by civil war. Relatively peaceful times finally came with the Alidosi family (1341-1424). Next came the rule of the Viscontis as Imola was included (along with Forlì) in the dowry given by Galeazzo

Maria to his daughter Caterina for her marriage to Girola Riario. When her husband died in 1488, Caterina ruled Imola and Forlì alone and defended them heroically against the army of Cesare Borgia. During the drive for unity (Risorgimento), it was the first large commune to be taken over by the Socialists (1896). Today, it is a modern city, the hub of the automobile world because of its nearby international car racing track.

▶ In the p. Matteotti in the centre of the town are the **Palazzo Sersanti**, a fine Renaissance building designed by Giorgio Fiorentino for Girolamo Riario, and the **Palazzo Comunale**, formerly the seigneurial palace, rebuilt in the 18C. ▶ The **Via Emilia** runs right through the entire town, dividing it into two almost equal parts and forming the main artery. At the corner of the v. Orsini stands the **Palazzo della Volpe** (1482), perhaps by Giorgio Fiorentino; opposite is the 18C **Farmacia dell'Ospedale**, with a collection of more than 400 ceramic pots from Imola and Faenza. The **Palazzo dei Musei** at no. 80 houses collections belonging to the city, including the library and the archives. The **Pinacoteca** *(9 a.m.-12:30 p.m. and 2:30-6 p.m.; closed Sat)* contains pictures of the Romagnese, Ferrarese and Bolognese schools of 15C-18C. ▶ In the Bishop's Palace, opposite the Duomo, is the **Museo Diocesano** *(9:30 a.m.-12 noon Tue and Thu; apply to the director)*. The apartment of Pius IX, once the Bishop of Imola, has illuminated manuscripts of the 13C-15C and paintings of the Venetian and Emilian schools. ▶ The **castle**, built in 1259 and fortified by Gian Galeazzo Visconti (1472-3) and again in 1499 when the town was threatened by Cesare Borgia, is flanked by four large cylindrical corner towers. It has an imposing set of walls and, inside, a dungeon and an open gallery with Bramantian-style arcades *(summer, Thu and Sat 9 a.m.-12 noon and 3:30-6:30 p.m.; Sun 3:30-6:30 p.m.; winter Sat and Sun only)*. There is a civic collection of antique arms and an exhibition on the evolution of the castle and a collection of medieval pottery. ▶ On the p. Bianconcini are the **Montanara Gate**, all that remains of the city walls, and the **chiesa dell'Osservanza**. Built c. 1473, this church has a façade containing late Renaissance tombs and, inside, 15C paintings; the front of the tribune of Pope Julius II is original, erected at the beginning of the 16C to mark the days that he spent in Imola (there is a reconstruction of it in a small garden outside).

Environs

▶ 3 km along the Via Emilia towards Bologna is the **santuario della Madonna del Piratello**. Built in 1491 and restored in the 19C, it still has an elegant altar canopy and a 15C *Madonna* in stone. ▶ 8 km W is the old fortified village of **Dozza**, notable also for the numerous modern paintings that decorate the walls of the houses. Above the village stands a fine **fortress**, rebuilt 15C-16C; inside *(10 a.m.-12 noon and 2-5 p.m. or 3-6 p.m.; Sun and hols 10 a.m.-1 p.m. and 2-6 p.m. or 3-7 p.m.; closed Mon)* is the **Museo della Civiltà Contadina**, an ethnological museum on rural life. □

Practical information ─────────────

IMOLA

Hotels:
★★★★ *Olimpia*, v. Pisacane 69, ☎ 24130, 80 rm Ⓟ ☼ 75,000; bkf: 8,000.
★★★ *Molino Rosso*, statale Selice 49, ☎ 31240, 82 rm Ⓟ ⚒ ☼ closed Christmas, 100,000; bkf: 8,000.

Restaurants:
● ♦♦♦♦♦ *San Domenico*, v. G. Sacchi 1, ☎ 29000, closed Mon. Refined and artistic. Outstanding cuisine: riso mantecato, crayfish with artichokes, 65/85,000.
♦♦♦ *Naldi*, v. Santerno 13, ☎ 29581, closed Sun. Creative cuisine: garganelli with fresh tomato and basil, rabbit with honey and white wine, 25/40,000.

♦♦♦ *Zio*, v. Nardozzi 14, ☎ 35274, closed Sat and Sun eves. Regional cuisine: tortelloni, tagliatelle, 18/28,000.

Recommended
Archery: *Compagnia Arcieri del Santerno*, v. Petrarca 12, ☎ 22388.
Fair: *Fiera del Santerno* (end Aug-Sep).
Hang gliding: schools: *Imola Delta*, v. Gherardi 11/A, ☎ 40876; *Fletcher Lind*, v. Brodolini 10, ☎ 31266.
Horseback riding: *Centro ippico Imolese*, v. Ascari 9, ☎ 40108 or 34230 (associate of *ANTE*).

Environs

DOZZA, ⊠ 40050, ☎ 0542.

Restaurant:
♦♦♦ *Canè*, v. XX Settembre 19, ☎ 88120, closed Mon. Regional cuisine, 20/30,000.

Recommended
Wine: Enoteca Regionale, v. Rocca Sforzesca, ☎ 88089.

LUGO

Ravenna 25, Bologna 55, Milan 266 km
Pop. 33,947 ⊠ 48022 ☎ 0545   E2

On the Romagnese plain between the Rivers Santerno and Senio, not a trace of the vast area of woodland that once existed remains today, yet wood (*lucus* in Latin) gave Lugo its name. The modern Lugo is an important commercial centre, known particularly for its agriculture. One of its celebrated sons was the World War I Italian flying ace, Francesco Baracca.

▶ The **castle**, now the town hall, has kept its original 14C dungeon and N wall; the remainder was rebuilt in the 16C. Inside, the **Sala Baracca** exhibits a collection of mementos of the pilot, killed at Montello in 1918. ▶ Opposite the castle is the rectangular market place, surrounded by the arcades of the **Paviglione** (1783-1889). ▶ The collegiate church of **S. Francesco**, rebuilt in the 18C, still retains some of its original Romanesque structure (r.-hand side) and an ogival portal of the 13C. ▶ 3.5 km NW toward Ca' di Lugo is the graceful **chiesa dell'Ascensione** (1534) with frescos of the 16C Ferrarese school. □

Practical information ─────────────

ℹ️ largo Relencini 13, ☎ 25043.

Hotels:
★★★★ *Ala d'Oro*, corso Matteotti 56, ☎ 22388, 38 rm Ⓟ 58,000; bkf: 6,000.
★★★★ *San Francesco*, v. Amendola 14, ☎ 22324, 30 rm Ⓟ ⚒ ⚘ 80,000;bkf: 7,000.

Restaurants:
● ♦♦♦ *Meridiano-da Mario*, v. De Brozzi 94, ☎ 24111, closed Mon and 1-25 Aug. In fin-de-siècle patrician's house with a country setting. Excellent cuisine: garganelli with shellfish and sausage, tortelli with nettles, 25/40,000.
● ♦♦♦ *Tino*, at Massa Lombarda, v. Torchi 24, ☎ 81317, closed Mon. Excellent regional cuisine, 30/50,000.

Recommended
Clay pigeon shooting: at Villa San Martino, v. Rio Fantino, ☎ 21120.
Flying club: *F. Baracca*, at Villa San Martino, ☎ 23338.

MEDICINA

Bologna 25, Milan 235 km
Pop. 12,449 ⊠ 40059 ☎ 051   E2

This town has a spectacular silhouette from a distance: towers and campaniles, domes, turrets and terraces. It had a degree of administrative and economic autonomy, especially during the 17C-18C, during which it underwent extensive architectural renovation, resulting in the noble appearance it partially retains today.

▶ On the p. Garibaldi rises the solitary **campanile★** (masterpiece (1752-77) of Carlo Francesco Dotti) of the parish church of **S. Mamante** (1734-9). ▶ In v. Saffi, ending at the 17C church of **SS. Francesco e Anna**, stands the **Porticone**, a Neoclassical building. ▶ Also of note, at no. 1 v. Pillio, is the **Palazzo della Partecipanza**, the former seat of the commune, with a magnificent staircase. ▶ Next to the **Torre dell'Orologio** (decorated with the city's heraldic emblems and flagstones inscribed with verses by Dante) is the former 18C **Palazzo del Podestà**, a shadow of its former glory. ▶ In the v. della Libertà, which terminates at the picturesque 18C **chiesa dell'Assunta** (or 'del Crocifisso'), stands the 16C-17C **Palazzo Comunale**, with modern additions; from the 16C-18C this was a Carmelite monastery, a centre of philosophical, musical and artistic activity. ☐

Practical information _____

Recommended
Craft workshops: *C. Matteini*, v. Piave 485, ☎ 850345-477725 (pottery).

MELDOLA

Forli 12, Bologna 75, Milan 294 km
Pop. 9,117 ⊠ 47014 ☎ 0543   E3

The picturesque ruins of the 12C castle which was fought over through the centuries by the Ordelaffi and Malatesta families, Cesare Borgia and the Venetians, and which then belonged to the Aldobrandini and the Doria Pamphili, dominate this ancient town of the upper Romagnese plain, on the left bank of the River Ronco. Once a flourishing silk market and a centre of silk production, Méldola was the home of Felici Orsini, the Italian patriot guillotined in Paris in 1858 following an unsuccessful attempt to assassinate Napoleon III, who stood in the way of Italy's independence.

▶ At the centre of the town is the charming p. F. Orsini, on which are the 17C **Palazzo Comunale**, with its tower, and the **Palazzo Aldobrandini Pamphili**, with its loggia, as well as the **house of Felice Orsini**. ▶ A little further along v. Cavour is the **Ospedale**, rebuilt in the 16C-17C following designs by G.B. Aleotti; the chapel contains a series of 16C frescos of the Forli school (restored). ☐

MIRANDOLA

Modena 31, Bologna 71, Milan 202 km
Pop. 21,979 ⊠ 41037 ☎ 0535   D1

Mirandola's most famous son, a man of encyclopaedic learning and prodigious memory whose powers have become proverbial, was Giovanni Pico della Mirandola, born here in 1463, the illustrious scion of the feudal family which held sway over this district from 1115-1707. The city is in the northernmost part of the lower Modenese plain as it reaches the Po, in a landscape dominated until the 18C by the huge, unbroken stretches of marshy plain. Its advantageous location — on the ancient Roman route between Modena and Verona — helped Mirandola's development as a fortress-capital. Today it is a flourishing agricultural town, with only a few architectural reminders of its great historic past.

▶ On the aptly named p. Grande stand the porticoed **Palazzo del Comune**, restored to its Renaissance form,

and a few remains of the **Castello dei Pico**, destroyed in an explosion in 1714. ▶ The Gothic church of **S. Francesco** (15C) contains a number of tombs of the Pico family (14C-15C), including that of Prendiparte, a work by Paolo di Jacobello delle Masegne (1394). ▶ In v. Verdi is the small **Museo Civico**, part of the public library, containing paintings, portraits of the Pico family and medals. ▶ In p. Conciliazione is the **collegiate church**, built in an ogival form in 1447 (restored).

Environs

▶ 6 km NE at **Quarántoli** is the parish church of **S. Maria della Neve** (possibly 9C, rebuilt 12C, partially restored); inside are two columns in the form of a male figure by the school of Wiligelmos. ▶ 12 km E, **San Felice sul Panáro** has a castle built by the Este family in 1340 containing a collection of archaeological finds *(ask at the Biblioteca Comunale).* ☐

Practical information _____

Hotel:
★★★ *Pico*, v. Statale Sud 12, ☎ 20050, 26 rm ℗ ⑄ ⑆ closed Aug, 69,000; bkf: 5,000.

Restaurant:
♦♦♦ *Castello*, p. Marconi 10, ☎ 22918, closed Mon and Aug. In restored 18C building. Italian cuisine: tortellini in brodo, escalope alla boscaiola, 25/30,000.

MODENA*

Bologna 39, Milan 170, Rome 405 km
Pop. 178,985 ⊠ 41100 ☎ 059   C2

Before its Roman column was erected in 183 BC, the site of Modena had been occupied by the Etruscans, then by the Gauls. Its key position on the Via Emilia made it the focal point of many decisive military operations in Roman times. At the end of the Roman Empire, the waves of invasion and the floods led the population to take refuge in a fortress in neighbouring Lombardy. Only the bishop and several other members of the clergy stayed on to protect the relics of their patron saint, S. Geminiano. Due to their presence, the city was able, little by little, to replace its population, and by 1106 the relics of the patron saint could be protected in the newly built Duomo. Modena became an independent city-state c. 1135 and, for protection, walls were built around the city. To compete with Bologna, its great enemy and rival, Modena created a university in 1182. The animosity between the two cities caused bitter fighting, but Modena's hopes for precedence were destroyed when the Bolognese took prisoner the son of Emperor Frederick II, Modena's main ally. After an unsettling period of external and civil wars, the city chose to be governed by the House of Este whose fortunes it would in any case have shared. When Cesare of Este was forced to leave Ferrara, he went to Modena which became the capital of his dukedom. After the Napoleonic wars, the Austrians installed on the ducal throne Francesco IV, a descendant on his mother's side of the Dukes of Modena but also a Hapsburg. After many tribulations, his family was able to stay in power until 1860 when the city became part of the Kingdom of Italy. The city entered the industrial era very rapidly and its automobile industry (especially the manufacture of the Ferrari and Maserati) enjoys enormous prestige. Yet Modena has not abandoned its agriculture, until recently its main source of revenue. In the surrounding plain, animal husbandry,

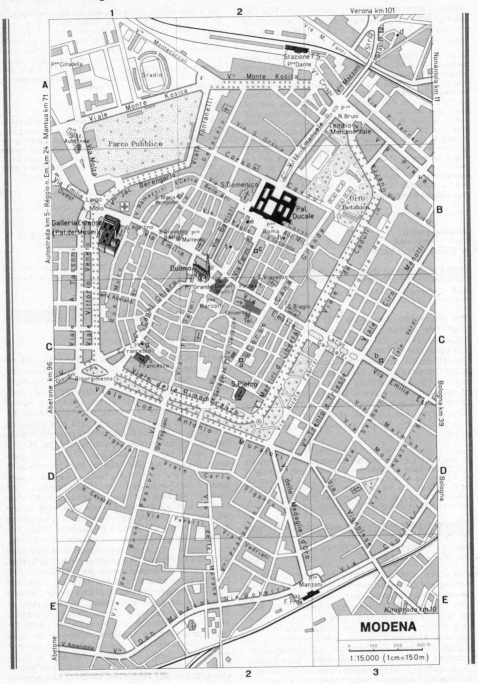

MODENA

0   100   200   300 m

1:15.000 (1cm=150m)

grain cultivation and the production of the well-known Lambrusco wine are widespread. The city is enlivened by the presence of a military academy, which offers parades and other ceremonies along with the schooling of future military men. The tourist will take pleasure in a visit to the city and its monuments, which contain highly interesting works of art.

▶ On the **piazza Grande** (B-C2), in the centre of town, is the Duomo; its apses and the Torre della Ghirlandina form a monumental whole. ▶ The porticoed building with a clocktower in the middle is the **Palazzo Comunale** (1194, but completely rebuilt 1624). A staircase leads up from the courtyard *(entrance at no. 20 v. Scudari)* to the upper floor where there are some interesting rooms with 15C coffered ceilings and frescos, transferred to canvas, by Nicolò dell'Abate. ▶ The 12C **Duomo**★★ (B2), the centrepiece of Modena's architectural heritage, is attributed to Lombard Lanfranco. He was assisted by Wiligelmo, the acknowledged master of Romanesque architecture in N Italy. On the three-part façade are extremely interesting **bas-reliefs**★ (depicting stories from Genesis) by Wiligelmo, some of the earliest examples of Romanesque sculpture. Also by Wiligelmo is the panel to the l. and above the central portal which depicts the prophets Enoch and Elijah holding an inscription showing the founding date of the church and the name of the sculptor. On the r.-hand side of the Duomo are the Romanesque **Porta dei Principi**, decorated with reliefs, and the elaborate **Porta Regia**, a Gothic work (1178) with bas-reliefs by Agostino di Duccio (the life of S. Geminiano, 1442). Another portal, decorated with sculpture, is on the l.-hand side of the building. Near the dome stands the beautiful campanile, called the **Ghirlandina**★, symbol of the city, soaring to 288 ft. It owes its name to the 'garland' of columns which embellish its crown (1319). The wooden pail which inspired Tassino is here. Inside the red brick **interior**, at the end of the nave, is a fine **tribuna**★ (screen) with reliefs depicting the Passion by Anselmo da Campione (1180); in the middle of the l.-hand aisle is a **pulpit** by Arrigo da Campione (1322). The large **crypt** contains the tomb of S. Geminiano and, to the r., the group of five polychrome statues in terra-cotta, known as the *Madonna della Pappa*★, by Guido Mazzoni (1480). ▶ The **Via Emilia** (B-C1-2) is lined by porticos and is a favourite venue for the evening *passegiata* (promenade). Here too is the 18C church of **S. Giovanni Battista** (B1-2), which contains another fine polychrome group in terra-cotta by Guido Mazzoni *(The Deposition from the Cross*★). ▶ The impressive **Palazzo dei Musei** (B1), built in 1753 to serve as an arsenal, today contains the city's collections, the most important of which are the Galleria Estense and the Biblioteca Estense. The **Galleria Estense**★★ *(wkdays 9 a.m.-2 p.m.; Sun and hols 9 a.m.-1 p.m.; closed Mon)* contains a collection of works by the Emilian and Venetian schools of the 14C-17C, among which are a *St. Anthony*★ by Cosmè Tura, three *Saints*★ by Veronese, a small triptych, painted on both sides, a youthful masterpiece by El Greco★, a *Madonna and Child with Saints*★ by Dosso Dossi, the *Madonna Campori*★ by Correggio and the *Portrait of Francesco I d'Este*★ by Velasquez. The **Museo Estense**, which forms part of the gallery, has an extensive collection of coins and **medals**★ by Pisanello, Renaissance bronzes and sculptures, ivories, furniture, pottery, glass and crystal ware — and, above all, a bust of *Francesco I d'Este*★★ by Bernini. The **Biblioteca Estense**★ *(10 a.m.-1 p.m.; closed Sun and hols)* is one of Europe's richest libraries, containing an extraordinary collection of illuminated books from Italy and abroad, among which is the famous **Bible of Borso d'Este**★, brilliantly illuminated by Taddeo Crivelli and others (15C). ▶ The nearby church of **S. Maria Pomposa** (B1-2) was rebuilt between 1717-19 on the initiative of its provost, the historian and man of letters, Ludovico Antonio Muratori. ▶ The house next door, no. 1 v. della Pomposa, is where Muratori (d. 1750) lived the last 34 years of his life; it now houses the **Aedes Muratoriana** *(wkdays 9 a.m.-12 noon and 5-7:30 p.m.)*, which brings together his historical and critical works as well as various mementos. ▶ The **Palazzo Ducale**★ (B2), the former palace of the Este family, and one of the largest in Italy, was begun in 1629; it is now the Military Academy *(not open to the public)*. ▶ On the corso Canal Grande, one of the most beautiful streets in the city, are the **Teatro Comunale** (1841) and, opposite,

the **house of Ciro Menotti**. ▶ A bit further are the church of **S. Vincenzo** (C2) and the Modenese Pantheon of the Este family. ▶ The church of **S. Pietro** (C2), which once formed part of a Benedictine monastery, rebuilt 1476-1505, contains attractive paintings.

Environs

▶ 3 km along the Via Emilia toward Bologna is **Castelfranco Emilia**, whose parish church contains a *Madonna of the Assumption*★ by Guido Reni. ▶ A few km further to the S lies **San Cesario sul Panáro** (→).   □

Ferrari

At Maranello, a small vilage near Modena, on the Abetone road, Ferrari Automobili was founded in 1945. Today it produces 2,500 cars a year; everyone a masterpiece of design and engineering. (In 1984, the racing-car division was transferred to a separate unit at Fiorano, next to the local test-track.) The first vehicle to carry the name of Ferrari was the 125 S with a twelve-cylinder engine (V-12). Its first race was on 11 May 1947, on the Piacenza track, with Franco Cortese as driver. It did not finish the race. Four years later, F. Gonzales, driving a Ferrari 375 F1, won the British Grand Prix, beating Alfa Romeo for the first time. 'Wept for joy', wrote Enzo Ferrari, who had been a driver for Alfa Romeo (in the famous 'Ferrari stable') during the 1920s. Enzo Ferrari left Alfa Romeo in 1939 to return to Modena, his home base, to try his luck at making an automobile that could better the Alfa. It was twelve years before his dream was realized. Today, these superb machines from Maranello, adorned with a black coat on a yellow background (the crest of the old' Ferrari stable'), are probably the most famous cars in the world.

The war of the bucket

In a room in the campanile of the Duomo of Modena, the so-called Ghirlandina, a wooden bucket hangs from the ceiling. This is said to be the one that the Modenese seized from the Bolognese after the battle of Zappolino on 15 November 1325, an insignificant episode in the perennial local strife of the medieval period. In the 17C, the Modenese writer Alessandro Tassoni used this as the inspiration for his mock-heroic poem La Secchia Rapita ('The Stolen Bucket'), which has as its hero the Count di Culagno, courageous when he ran no risks but terrified when he encountered them — 'philosopher, poet and bigot'. This is a yarn about an absurd enterprise to steal the bucket ('even Helen of Troy was kidnapped with less effort'), and about a war which achieves nothing. But through it, Tassoni reveals the bitterness of a man with fierce civic pride, whose homeland was then under Spanish domination.

Practical information

ℹ corso Canal Grande 1/A (C2), ☎ 222482; autostrada del Sole, service area at Secchia, ☎ 518177.
🚂 (A2-3), ☎ 218226.
🚌 from the Stazione Autolinee (A1).
Car rental: Avis, v. Malmusi 26, ☎ 230096; Hertz, v. Canaletto 60, ☎ 315344.

Hotels:

★★★★ *Canalgrande,* corso Canal Grande 6 (C2 a), ☎ 217160, 78 rm P ⑭ ⌘ 137,000; bkf: 12,000.

★★★★ *Fini,* v. Emilia Est 441, ☎ 238091, 93 rm P closed Aug and Christmas. No restaurant: 152,000; bkf: 14,000.

★★★★ *Palace Hotel,* v. Emilia Est 27 (C3 b), ☎ 236090, 53 rm P ⓹ ⌘ closed Aug and Christmas, 122,000; bkf: 8,000.

★★★ *Eden,* v. Emilia Ovest 666, ☎ 335660, 76 rm P ⑭ ⓹ No restaurant, 80,000.

★★★ *MotelAgip,* at Secchia, ☎ 518221, 184 rm P ⓹ 69,000; bkf: 10,000.

★★★ *Ritz,* v. Rainusso 108, ☎ 338090, 144 rm P 75,000; bkf: 6,000.

★★★ *Roma,* v. Farini 44 (B2 c), ☎ 222218, 53 rm P No restaurant, 68,000; bkf: 6,000.

Restaurants:

● ♦♦♦♦ *Fini,* p. S. Francesco (C1 g), ☎ 214250, closed Mon, Tue, Aug and Christmas. In the great tradition, elegant but relaxed atmosphere. Outstanding cuisine: pasticcio with tortellini, fritto misto all italiana, 40/48,000.

♦♦♦ *Bianca,* v. Spaccini 24 (A3 d), ☎ 311524, closed Sat noon, Sun and Aug. Fine garden and summer pergola. Modenese cuisine: tortellini in brodo,tortelloni with pumpkin, 30/35,000.

♦♦♦ *Borso d'Este,* p. Roma 5 (B2 e), ☎ 214114, closed Sun and Aug. Creative cuisine: gnocchi soufflé, risotto with asparagus, 30/45,000.

♦♦♦ *Oreste,* p. Roma 31 (B2 h), ☎ 243324, closed Sun eve, Wed and Jul. Regional cuisine: gramigna with sausages, bollito misto modenese, 23/37,000.

♦♦ *Enzo,* v. Coltellini 17 (B2 f), ☎ 225177, closed Sat. Modenese cuisine: tagliatelle, stuffed pig's trotter, 20/25,000.

⚔ *International,* at Bruciata, strada Cave Ramo 113, ☎ 332252.

Recommended

Botanical garden: (B3), ☎ 236132.

Canoeing: v. Ruffini 13/A, ☎ 219814.

Cheese: *Quattro Madonne,* at Lascignana; and *Bellaria,* at San Martino di Mugnano (Parmesan cheese).

Flying: v. Marzaglia, ☎ 389090.

Hang gliding: *Jonathan Livingstone,* v. Ferrari 33, ☎ 238269.

Horse racing: ☎ 309102 (trotting, spring season).

Motor racing: *Ferrari track,* at Spezzano, v. Agazzotti, ☎ 843650.

Nature park: *Riserva della Salse di Nirano,* at Fiorano Modenese, ☎ 0536/830262.

Technical tourism: visits to the *Maserati* factory, v. Menotti 322, ☎ 217160 (write in advance to: Direzione Maserati, Hotel Canalgrande, corso Canal Grande 6); and to the *Masetti* workshop, Rua Freda 21, ☎ 217431 (string instruments).

Wine: visits to the *Cantina sociale Castelvetro,* at Formigne, v. Pascoli 4, ☎ 558112 (Lambrusco).

♥ gastronomy: mortadella, zampone (stuffed pigs' trotters); herbal vinegar; amaretti (macaroons); liqueurs.

MODIGLIANA

Forlì 34, Bologna 69, Milan 284 km
Pop. 4,870 ⊠ 47015 ☎ 0546   E3

Situated in the foothills of the Apennines a few km from Faenza, at the confluence of three rivers (the Acerreta, Tramazzo and Ibola), the town belongs to the part of Romagna which was Tuscan until 1926. This was once the domain of the Counts Guidi di Pistoia. In 1377, they surrendered to Florence. From that time, the town's future was linked to that of Tuscany.

▶ In **Modigliana Nuova,** between the Acerreta and the Tramazzo, are the **Duomo,** containing a 16C *Annunciation* and a *S. Girolamo* by Sigismondo Foschi; the **Capella di Gesù Morto,** the old crypt of the Duomo, containing seven

15C wooden statues depicting the *Lamentations over the Body of Christ;* the **Episcopio,** with four lunettes by Silvestre Lega, a native of Modigliana *(Plague, Famine, War and Earthquake).* ▶ On the other side of the Tramazzo is the **Tribuna,** a semi-circular tower which was part of the old defensive wall of the castle. ▶ Beyond this is **Modigliana Vecchia,** where the former **Palazzo dei Conti Guidi** serves as the municipal library. ▶ At no. 30 v. Garibaldi is the **house of Don Giovanni Verità,** where Garibaldi was sheltered in 1849 during his flight, and which is now the home of the **Museo Storico Risorgimentale** containing various mementos of Garibaldi as well as paintings by Sivestro Lega. ▶ On the hill to the l. stand the imposing ruins of the **Roccaccia,** the castle of the Guidi; on the hill to the r. is the old Capuchin convent.   ☐

Practical information _____

Restaurant:

♦♦ *Solieri,* v. Garibaldi 32, ☎ 92493, closed Tue. Italian cuisine: strozzapreti with mushrooms, wood pigeon with mushrooms, 25/35,000.

MONTEFIORINO

Modena 54, Bologna 93, Milan 206 km
Pop. 2,565 ⊠ 41045 ☎ 0536   C3

In a superb position on a spur between the rushing Rivers Dolo and Dragone, Montefiorino is a town which evokes the memory of one of the major episodes of World War II involving the Emilian resistance movement. Today it has largely been rebuilt and is a popular place for summer vacations. On the heights is the **rocca,** now the town hall, a massive building of the 13C, much altered. At **Rubbiano,** 2.5 km W, there is an 11C Romanesque church.   ☐

NONANTOLA

Modena 10, Bologna 34, Milan 180 km
Pop. 10,482 ⊠ 41015 ☎ 059   D2

This town, on the Modena plain and r. bank of the Panáro, is famous for its Benedictine abbey. ▶ Founded in the 8C by the Lombards and altered over the centuries, the abbey was restored to its 12C condition in 1913-21. It enjoyed great wealth and fame in the Middle Ages, becoming a centre of culture and, in the 15C, acquired its own printing workshop in which the famous *Brevario Romano,* illustrated with woodblock prints, was produced in 1480. The present abbey **church,** in Lombard-Romanesque style, dates back to the 12C; the **portal** has reliefs by the school of Wiligelmo (1121); the interior contains a polyptych by Michele di Matteo (1460). In the **treasury** *(open by appointment,* ☎ 549025) are priceless illuminated manuscripts, 10C and 12C reliquaries and parchments. Nearby is the parish church of **S. Michele Arcangelo,** rebuilt in the 11C, and now partially restored. Above the town are two **towers:** the clocktower, built by the Modenesi in 1261, and the Rocca, built by the Bolognesi in 1307.   ☐

Practical information _____

Restaurant:

♦ *Osteria di Rubbiara,* at Rubbiara, ☎ 549019, closed Sun eve, Tue, 1-5 Jan and Aug. Regional cuisine: tortellini in brodo, roast guinea fowl, homemade wines, 16/22,000.

PARMA**

Bologna 90, Milan 125, Rome 458 km
Pop. 177,062 ⊠ 43100 ☎ 0521   B2

The second city of Emilia Romagna after Bologna, Parma is on the plain and also on the ancient Via Emilia, where the two rivers that cross the region meet. It became a Roman colony in 183 BC. Both Caesar and Augustus gave the town their names — Julio-Augusto — at the end of the 1C BC. Parma met the same fate as other cities which were in the path of constant invasions. After a period of decline, it came back under the influence of the Byzantine Empire in the 6C. In the 11C it was a Ghibelline city. Parma was torn by wars with its neighbours. It came under the rule of the Visconti in the 14C. After a short spell under the Sforzas, and later the French, Parma became part of the papal states (1521). Alessandro Farnese, Pope Paul III, created a small duchy in 1545 and gave it to Piero Luigi Farnese, one of his children; Parma became its capital. For almost two centuries — until 1731 — the Farnese family governed the duchy; commerce was protected by favourable legislation, while artists, poets and musicians brought their lustre to the court. At the death of the last of the Farneses (1731) the duchy was given to Charles I of Spain and, one year later, to Austria. In 1748, with the peace of Aquisgrana, the duchy was returned to the Bourbons of Spain, and a new dynasty installed itself on the ducal throne with Philip of Bourbon. On the advice of his minister, du Tillot, Philip brought the city into the cultural and artistic mainstream of Europe. During the French Revolution and the Napoleonic Empire, Parma and Piacenza came under French rule. In 1815, the Empress Marie Louise was granted the two cities as well as Guastella. She was a wise and moderate ruler until her death in 1847, when power returned once again to the Bourbons. They lost it only 13 years later when the city became part of the Kingdom of Italy. It was the reigning families who made Italy what it is today: the Farnese gave a taste for architectural and artistic beauty, the Bourbons, the grandeur of the Spanish court; Marie Louise, a passion for music. Today Parma is a prosperous industrial and agricultural city. Its intellectual and artistic life is evident in the activities of its university, its concerts and opera.
▶ In its calm and beauty, the **piazza del Duomo** has retained its medieval character. ▶ The **Duomo★★** (C4) is one of the great monuments of 12C Romanesque architecture. The middle **portal,** with its projecting porch, is the work of Giambone da Bissone (1281), with bas-reliefs depicting the months of the year around the arch. To the r. of the façade the Gothic **campanile,** built 1284-94, soars to 208 ft. The interior comprises a nave and two aisles supported by pillars with splendid capitals and raised triforium and sanctuary built over the crypt. The walls of the nave are decorated with 16C frescos; those in the fourth chapel r. and the fifth l. are 15C. In the cupola is the *Assumption of the Virgin★★,* a magnificent fresco by Correggio (1526-30). On the wall of the r. transept is the *Descent from the Cross★* (1178) by Benedetto Antelami, one of the great works of Italian sculpture. In the sanctuary is the **bishop's throne★,** white marble carved in high relief also by Antelami (12C). In the vast **crypt** are interesting fragments of mosaics from the Early Christian era. ▶ The **Baptistery★★** is a remarkable Romanesque-Gothic building (1196-1260) on an octagonal plan. The **reliefs★** on the three portals and the decorative frieze and the **statues★** in the niches, also by Antelami and his school, are among the most expressive Romanesque sculptures in Italy. The interior *(9 a.m.-12 noon*

and 3-7 or 5 p.m. winter) contains more reliefs and, in particular, twelve stelae★★ in high relief representing the months of the year, all by Antelami. In the lunettes and in the cupola are Byzantine frescos and traces of earlier decoration. ▶ Behind the Duomo is the church of **S. Giovanni Evangelista★** (C4), completely rebuilt 1498-1510; it contains **frescos** by Correggio★★, (*Vision of St. John,* in the cupola; *Evangelists and Doctors of the Church,* in the spandrels; *St. John writing the Revelations,* in a lunette of the l. transept). **Frescos** by Parmigianino are also noteworthy (*Saints,* under the arches of the first, second and fourth chapels to the l.). ▶ Adjacent is the **monastery,** with its three 15C cloisters. Behind it is **Storica Farmacia di S. Giovanni Evangelista** (C4; *9 a.m.-2 p.m; Sun and hols 9 a.m.-1 p.m.; closed Mon),* the old Benedictine pharmacy founded in 1201 which continued to operate until 1881 (restored 1951). The frescos are 16C and the furniture and shelves 16C-18C; there are 192 15C-17C ceramic pots. ▶ P. Garibaldi (C3) is the centre of the modern city, with the **Palazzo del Governatore** (1760) and its **clocktower,** and the **Palazzo del Municipio** (1673), to the r. of which is the former **Palazzo del Capitano del Popolo** (13C). ▶ In strada Garibaldi (B-C3) is the **Teatro Regio,** built at Marie Louise's instigation in Neoclassical style and opened in 1829 with Bellini's *Zaira.* ▶ Opposite is the **Madonna della Steccata★,** a splendid Renaissance church showing the influence of Bramante (1521-39). The interior contains frescos of the Parmesan school, notable among which are those by Parmigianino around the arch of the main altar; to the l. of the entrance is the **Memorial to Count Neipperg,** a general who became the morganatic husband of Marie Louise, a work by Lorenzo Bartolini (1841); the crypt contains tombs of the Dukes of Parma; there is also a fine sacristy★ decorated with wood carving. ▶ The Neoclassical Palazzo di Riserva houses the **Museo Civico Glauco Lombardi** (C3; *9:30 a.m.-12:30 p.m. and 4-6 p.m. or 3-5 p.m. winter; closed Mon)* which has an important collection of records and mementos of the rule of the Bourbons, Napoleon and Marie Louise. ▶ The **Palazzo della Pilotta** (B3) is a huge building put up by the Farnese 1583-1622 but unfinished; its name comes from the game *pelota* which was played in one of the courtyards. Today it is the home of the Museo Archeologico Nazionale, the Galleria Nazionale, the Teatro Farnese, the Biblioteca Palatina and the Museo Nazionale Bodoni. ▶ The **Museo Archeologico Nazionale★** (*9 a.m.-2 p.m.; Sun and hols 9 a.m.-1 p.m.; closed Mon)* was founded by the Bourbon Philip I in 1760 to accommodate the finds of the excavations at Velleia (→ The Foothills of the Piacentine Apennines), and is one of the first museums of its kind in Italy; it contains artifacts from excavations throughout W Emilia as well as sculpture from the Farnese and Gonzaga collections, a collection of artifacts from ancient Egypt, Greek vases, and Etruscan bronzes and funerary urns. ▶ The **Galleria Nazionale★★** (*9 a.m.-2 p.m.; Sun and hols 9 a.m.-1 p.m.; closed Mon)* is noted for its collection of paintings by Parmesan artists from the 15C-18C, but it also has a cross-section of other Italian painting. The following are to be found here: paintings of the 15C-16C Emilian school; pre-Renaissance Tuscan and Venetian painting; the splendid *Enthroned Madonna with Child and Saints★★,* and other works by Cima da Conegliano; a sketch of the *Head of a Young Girl★★* by Leonardo da Vinci; and works by Correggio which occupy four rooms (of special note: the *Madonna of S. Girolamo★★,* a detached fresco of the *Madonna della Scala★★,* the *Madonna della Scodella★★,* a *Coronation of the Virgin★★* and an *Annunciation★★).* Also of note are the *Turkish Slave Girl★★* and the *Self-Portrait★* by Parmigianino, paintings by Holbein the Younger (*Erasmus★★*) and by Murillo. There are also works by the Tuscan and Venetian Mannerists, by the Carracci, and one by El Greco; as well as 17C and 18C French and Venetian paintings. ▶ The **Teatro Farnese** (*9 a.m.-2 p.m.; Sun and hols 9 a.m.-1 p.m.; closed Mon),* constructed in 1618, was one of the first purpose-built theatres in Europe and for a long time was the largest in the world. Modeled on the Palladian Teatro Olimpico at Vincenza, designed for movable sets and with a huge mobile stage, it was virtually destroyed by bombing in 1944 but has been recently restored. ▶ Nearby is the **Biblioteca Palatina** *(8:30 a.m.-1:30 p.m.)*, a library of some 555,000 volumes, and the **Museo Nazionale Bodoni**, devoted to the art of printing *(9 a.m.-12 noon; closed Sat).* ▶ By way of the strada Melloni, one can reach the **Camera di S. Paolo**★★ (B3; *9 a.m.-2 p.m.; Sun and hols 9 a.m.-1 p.m.; closed Mon)*, once the refectory in the apartments of the Abbess of the Convent of S. Paolo and decorated by Correggio in 1518; on the vault, a trompe-l'oeil pergola with putti and, in the lunettes, monochrome compositions on classical themes. ▶ In the beautiful **Parco Ducale**, laid out in 1560, with its many trees and statues, is the **Palazzo Ducale** (A-B2), built for Ottavio Farnese in 1564 by Giovanni Boscoli and enlarged in 1767 by Petitot. It is now the headquarters of the Carabinieri; visitors should apply to the duty officer *(8:30 a.m.-12:30 p.m.).* ▶ The **university** (C3), one of the oldest in Italy, is in the street of that name, an imposing 16C building attributed to Alessi and Vignola. ▶ Other places to visit include: the **house of Toscanini** (B2; *9 a.m.-12 noon, by appointment,* ☎ *208855; closed Mon)*; the **Pinacoteca Stuard** (C-D3; *wkdays 8:30 a.m.-12 noon and 3-5 p.m.; closed Sat)*, which contains pre-Renaissance Tuscan and 17C and 18C Italian paintings; and the **Museo di Arte Cinese**, a collection of Chinese art, at the Istituto Saveriano in v. San Martino (F8; *9 a.m.-12 noon and 3-6 p.m.; closed Mon and Tue)*.

Environs

▶ 4 km NE is the **Certosa di Parma** *(8 a.m.-6 p.m. or 4 p.m. winter).* Founded in 1285 and altered several times, this Carthusian charterhouse was suppressed in 1769 and today serves as a reeducation centre. It gave its name to Stendhal's famous novel *The Charterhouse of Parma.* The church (1673) is of interest. ▶ 6 km SW one passes through Vicofértile, which has an interesting parish church, **S. Geminiano**, a typical Romanesque rural building. ▶ 17.5 km S, on the road to Langhirano, is the **Castello di Torrechiara**. ☐

Practical information

ℹ p. Duomo 5 (C4), ☎ 34735.
🚃 (A3), ☎ 771118.
🚌 from station at v. Toschi (B3), ☎ 52841.
Car rental: *Avis,* v. Fratti 24, ☎ 772418; *Hertz,* v. Mentana 124, ☎ 32481; *Maggiore,* v. Brescia 7, ☎ 76880.

Hotels:

★★★★ *Palace Hotel Maria Luigia,* v. Mentana 140 (B4 a), ☎ 281032, 105 rm ℙ 180,000. Rest. ◆◆◆ *Maxim's* closed Sun and Aug. Creative cuisine, 40/60,000.
★★★★ *Park Hotel Stendhal,* v. Bodoni (B3 b), ☎ 208057, 62 rm ℙ 122,000; bkf: 12,000. Rest. ◆◆◆ *Pilotta* closed Sun eve, Mon and Aug. Regional cuisine, 27/35,000.
★★★★ *Park Hotel Toscanini,* v. Toscanini 4/A (C3 c), ☎ 29141, 48 rm ℙ 102,000; bkf: 12,000. Rest. ◆◆◆ *Torrente* closed Sun and Jul. Parmesan cuisine, 23/33,000.
★★★ *Button,* Borgo S. Vitale 7 (C3 d), ☎ 208039, 41 rm ℙ closed 15 Jul-15 Aug. No restaurant, 65,000.
★★★ *Daniel,* v. Gramsci 16, ☎ 995147, closed Aug and Christmas, 32 rm ℙ 69,000; bkf: 7,000. Rest. ◆◆◆ *Cocchi* ☎ 91990, closed Sat. Parmesan cuisine, 25/40,000.

Restaurants

● ◆◆◆ *Greppia,* v. Garibaldi 39 (B3 f), ☎ 33686, closed Thu, Fri, Jul and Christmas. Small restaurant, tastefully modernized and managed with character. Excellent regional cuisine: tagliolini with lemon, pasticcio with radicchio, 40/50,000.
● ◆◆◆ *Parizzi,* v. Repubblica 71, (D5 g), ☎ 285952, closed Sun eve, Mon and Jul-Aug. Run by an able couple. Parmesan cuisine: tortelli with herbs, bigarade of duck, 35/45,000.
◆◆ *Canon d'Or,* v. Sauro 3 (C-D3 e), ☎ 285234, closed Sat, Sun and 15 Aug-15 Sep. Decorated with Verdi

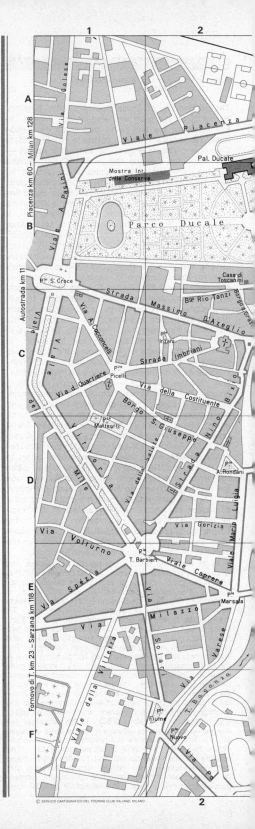

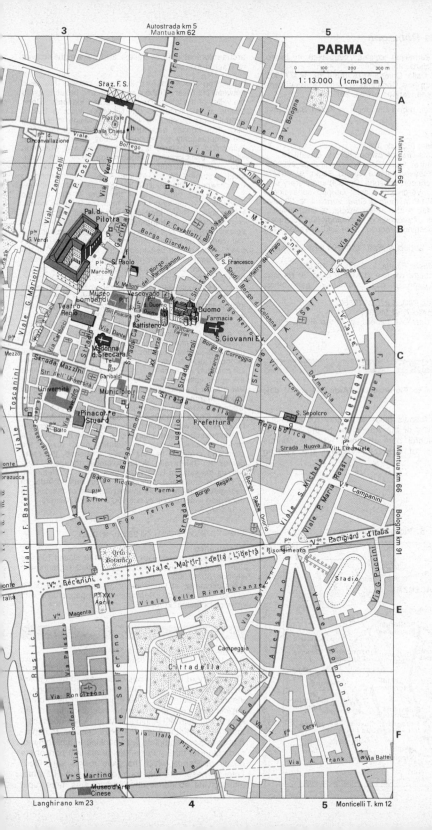

PARMA

0   100   200   300 m

1 : 13.000   (1cm=130 m)

A

Mantua km 66

Staz. F.S.

Piazzale
Dalla Chiesa

Pⁿ d.
Circonvallazione

Viale

Borrego

Viale

Viale

Via Trento

Via P. Toschi

Via G. Verdi

Via G. Verdi

Via Zanardelli

Pⁿ
G. Verdi

B

Pal. d.
Pilotta

d.

S. Paolo

Marconi

Museo
Lombardi

Teatro
Regio

Battistero

Madonna
d. Steccata

Garibaldi

Università

Municipio

Pinacot.ᵉᵉ
Stuard

C

Via G. Marotti

Via Cavallotti

Borgo Giordani

V. Melloni

Vescovado

Duomo

Farmacia

S.Giovanni Ev.

Viale P. Palermo

Via Bologna

Viale Antonio

Via Triesti

Borgo Naviglio

Pⁿ
S. Francesco

S. Anna

V. Studi

V. Pietro del Prato

Borgo Retro

Borgo di Colonne

Borgo Riccio

Borgo di Correggio

A.

Saffi

Pⁿ
S. Allende

Viale

F.

Mentana

Fratti

Tanara

Medaglia

S. Sepolcro

Mantua km 66

Bologna km 91

Prefettura

Repubblica

Strada Nuova Vitt. Emanuele

Strada Mazzini

Str. dell'Università

Strada Cairoli

Via C. Corsi

Via Dalmazia

Viale S. Michele

Viale P. Maria Rossi

V.le Campanini

D

Str. Pisacane

V. Dante

Viale Card. Ferrari

Borgo della

Str. Petrarca

Str. Felino

Borgo Riccio
da Parma

Pⁿ
S. Fiora

Borgo Regale

Borgo Felino

Borgo Pietro

Borgo Onorio

Pⁿ
V.le Partigiani d'Italia

Risorgimento

Mezzo

Orto
Botanico

V.le Berenini

Pⁿ XXV
Aprile

V.le Magenta

Viale Martiri della Libertà

Viale delle Rimembranze

E

Stadio

Via G. Puccini

Viale F. Basetti

Viale G. Toscanini

Viale F. Rustici

Via G. Conforti

Via Palestro

Via Solferino

Via Rondizzoni

Campeggio

Cittadella

Alessandro

Pescara

Viale

Pomponio

Totti

F

Via Italo

Pizzi

Via A. Frank

F.lli Cervi

Via Battei

V.le S. Martino

Museo d'Arte
Cinese

memorabilia. Parmesan cuisine: cappalletti in brodo, tripe alla parmigiana, 25/40,000.
♦♦ ***Puglia,*** p. Dalla Chiesa 15/A (A3-4 h), ☎ 772605, closed Wed, Aug and Christmas. Apulian cuisine: orrechiette alla barese, various roasts, 20/25,000.

⛺ ★★ *Cittadella,* parco Cittadella, v. Passo Buole (E4), 30 pl, ☎ 581546.

Recommended
Botanical garden: (E3), ☎ 33524.
Canoeing: *Scuola Gruppo canoa UISP,* v. Basetti 12.
Conference centre: *Aurea Parma,* v. Verdi 2, ☎ 282090.
Events: opera season, at the Teatro Regio, ☎ 795678 (end Jan-Apr); concert seasons (Oct-Jul) and literary season (Oct-May). Verdi enthusiasts: Gruppo appassionati Verdiani, ☎ 29514; *Instituto di Studi Verdiani,* ☎ 286044.
Fairs: at trade fair centre at Baganzola, ☎ 9961: *international exhibition of preserving technology* (Oct, biennial); *Quota 600* (Apennine produce, Sep) and a *traders' fair* (Oct).
Flying: *G. Bolla,* airport *N. Palli,* ☎ 90204 (also gliding; air show in Jul).
Hang gliding: *libero Parma,* v. Genni, ☎ 481654.
Nature park: nature reserve at *Monte Fuso,* at Neviano degli Arduini, open all day, information: park office, ☎ 54841.
Sports centre: v. Pellico 22, ☎ 795662.
Squash: v. Rapallo 7, ☎ 992961.
Youth hostel: *Ostello Cittadella,* v. Passo Buole 7 (E4), ☎ 581546.

PIACENTINE APENNINES

From Piacenza to Fiorenzuola d'Arda *(98 km, 1 day; map 5)*

This itinerary follows quiet secondary roads among the first foothills of the Apennines to the S of Piacenza, a beautiful part of Emilia with the curious reconstructions of Grazzano Visconti, the startling archaeological digs at Velleia and the unique appeal of Castell'Arquato.

▶ Leaving **Piacenza** (→), the route crosses the plain between the Rivers Trebbia and Nure, and heads towards the valley of the latter to reach **Grazzano Visconti.** Here, beside a 14C castle, Count Giuseppe Visconti built a faithful reconstruction of a medieval village in the late 19C. The houses, accurately built in 14C and 15C style, are picturesquely set among patches of green. In the Palazzetto Podestarile is a craft school and workshop with an exhibition of wrought-iron work and furniture. During the summer festival the women dress in local costumes of the Middle Ages. ▶ Returning to **Podenzano** (castle rebuilt in the 16C), the route continues E. ▶ On the other side of the Nure is **San Giorgio Piacentino,** dominated by the high tower of its castle. ▶ Continuing S, the landscape remains flat but then becomes more hilly at **Gropparello.** ▶ Set in this rolling landscape, **Velleia** is one of the most important archaeological centres in Emilia, and certainly the most evocative. *Veleia* (which belonged to the Ligurian tribe of the *Eleates*) became a flourishing Roman town which reached its apogee during the 1C and was destroyed, probably by a barbarian invasion, in the 4C or 5C. Discovered in 1747, excavation and restoration have been going on since 1760 *(9 a.m.-1 hr before sunset).* The remains include the forum, with its portico and the buildings which surrounded it, of which one is the basilica, as well as baths and private dwellings. The **antiquarium** *(9 a.m.-1 hr before sunset; Sat 9 a.m.-2 p.m.; Sun 9 a.m.-4 p.m.; closed Tue)* contains artifacts discovered in the latest excavations, but the major finds (including the famous Trajan *tabula alimentaria*) are in the archaeological museum in Parma (→). ▶ The route leads down into the upper valley of the Arda River and skirts **Lugagnano Val d'Arda** (→ Castell'Arquato) in following the road to **Vigolo Marchese** (→ Castell'Arquato). Here, a r. turn leads to **Castell'Arquato** (→). ▶ A secondary road leads through **Costa Stradivari** and **Bacedasco Alto** to **Vigoleno,** a village with crenellated walls and castle turrets, and a Romanesque parish church of S. Giorgio that retains a strong medieval flavour. ▶ Heading down toward the plain and crossing the Via Emilia at **Alseso,** the route comes to **Chiaravalle della Colomba** (founded 1135), with its magnificent Gothic **cloister**★ (13C). ▶ Returning to the Via Emilia and turning r. is **Fiorenzuola d'Arda;** its **collegiate church,** rebuilt toward the end of the 15C, is decorated with frescos by late 15C Lombard painters. □

5. Piacentine Apennines

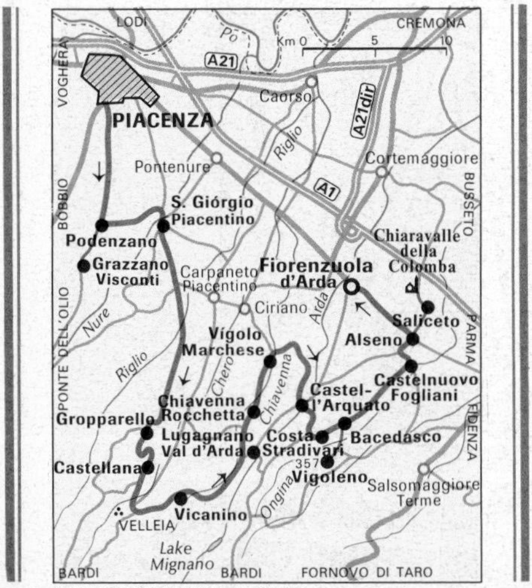

Practical information

GRAZZANO VISCONTI, ✉ 29020, ☎ 0523.

Restaurants:
♦♦♦ **Biscione,** p. del Biscione, ☎ 870149, closed Tue and Jan. Regional cuisine: risotto with truffles, taglierini with salmon, 30/40,000.
♦♦ ***Coccinella,*** at Vigolzone, v. Celaschi 2, ☎ 870627, closed Mon and Jul. Regional cuisine: pappardelle with artichokes, game, 20/30,000.

PIACENZA*

Bologna 150, Milan 67, Rome 514 km
Pop. 107,617 ✉ 29100 ☎ 0523 A1

The history of Piacenza has been marked by its proximity to the River Po. First, as a Roman colony, it insured the defense of the Emilian plain by protecting the river crossings from the incursions first of the Gauls, and then of Hannibal. As an independent city-state in the Middle Ages, Piacenza became an important river port, complete with banking establishments and colourful fairs. Pope Paul III made it part of the duchy of Parma which he gave to his son, Piero Luigi Farnese. Its fate then followed that of Parma, although its economic development was more rapid and intense because of its proximity to Lombardy. The Lombardian influence also made itself felt in the local dialect and cuisine. The city's industrial base has been reinforced in modern times by the discovery of oil and natural gas nearby. Piacenza, however, is altogether Emilian in the sense that it still has links to farming and the land. Because of its industrial development, the city has grown rapidly and suburbs have sprung up. Yet the city centre still retains the plan of a Roman fortified camp, its streets at right angles to each other; the medieval part of the city, surrounded by ramparts, is reflected in the narrow winding lanes lined with churches, palaces and other old buildings. The traces left by the magnificent Farnese family have not been eradicated by modern developments in Piacenza.

▶ The p. dei Cavalli (B 2-3) is dominated by the palazzo called il Gotico★★, the seat of the city-state. This splendid example of Lombard-Gothic civic architecture (1280) rises over a deep portico of two aisles, and the upper part, in red brick, decorated with elegant arched windows, is crowned with a Ghibelline crenellation and three turrets, the central one of which houses the historic bell used to summon the populace on important occasions. In front of the palazzo are the two bronze equestrian statues of the Farnese★★ (Alessandro and his son Rannucci), masterpieces by Francesco Mochi (1620-5), which gave the piazza its name. ▶ On the SE side of the piazza is the church of S. Francesco (B3), begun in 1278; this contains noteworthy sculptures (1470-80) by the school of Amadeo in the lunette of the middle portal. ▶ The Duomo★ (B3, 1122-1233) is a good example of Romanesque architecture; on the façade are three projecting portals, the work of the schools of Wiligelmo and Niccolò (12C). The campanile (1333) is 232 ft high. The triforium and the vaulting are Gothic. The frescos in the cupola depicting prophets, Sibyls and scenes from the life of Christ are mainly by Guercino. ▶ Near the Duomo is the ancient church of S. Savino★ (B4), dedicated to the patron saint of the city. Remodeled in Romanesque style in 1107, and altered and restored several times since, it now has a Baroque façade. The interior retains its original basilican form. The floor of the crypt is covered with a mosaic★ depicting the signs of the zodiac (12C). ▶ Another fine Romanesque basilica lies not far from the Duomo: the church of S. Antonio★ (B3), rebuilt in the 11C in the form of a Greek cross which was modified to a Latin cross, after moving the façade to the back of the transept in the 13C. An elegant Gothic atrium, known as the Paradiso, was added to the earlier façade in 1350; inside the atrium a stone tablet records the meeting between messengers of the Lombard League and Frederick Barbarossa in 1183 which established the basis for the peace treaty of Constance. ▶ The church of the Madonna di Capagna★ (A1) is a fine example of Renaissance architecture; built 1522-8 by the Piacentine architect Alessio Tramello, its interior is in the form of a Greek cross with a cupola; it contains a wealth of decoration from the 16C-18C, and works by various artists including Guercino and Pordenone, who was responsible for the fine frescos. ▶ To the N of the p. dei Cavalli stand the Romanesque church of S. Eufemia (A2, 11C) and the Renaissance church of S. Sisto★ (A2). The latter is by Alessio Tramello, built 1499-1511; the interior is a harmonious fusion of straight architectural lines and the decorative elements. ▶ The imposing Palazzo Farnese (A3) on the p. Cittadella is a late Renaissance building begun in 1558 and continued by Vignola (1564) but never finished (to the l.,the remains of the 13C Rocca Viscontea). The palazzo now houses the state archives and the Museo Civico, with its collection of Roman and prehistoric archaeological artifacts, medieval and modern sculpture, paintings, miniatures, goldwork and carriages. ▶ The Galleria Ricci-Oddi (B-C2, summer 10 a.m.-12 noon and 3-6 p.m.; winter 2-4 p.m.; closed Mon and p.m. Mar-Apr) contains over 700 works by Italian artists of the 19C and 20C; of particular note are the rooms devoted to the Tuscan macchiaiole (impressionists) and Fontanesi.

Environs

▶ 2.5 km along the Via Emilia in the direction of Parma is the Collegio Alberoni, founded in 1732, with a Galleria d'Arte★ (Sun 3-6 p.m.), containing an Ecce Homo★ by Antonello da Messina. □

The Farnese

The central square of Piacenza is called the Piazza dei Cavalli after the two magnificent equestrian statues to be found there. These statues are of Duke Alessandro Farnese and his son Ranuccio I and were both the work of Francesco Mochi in the first quarter of the 17C. Farnese is a family name of considerable import in Italian history, politics and culture, particularly in Piacenza and Parma. The family had already distinguished itself by the 12C when its name was taken from the Castello di Farneto near Orvieto. At the end of the 15C, Alessandro Farnese (not the same Alessandro as in the Piazza dei Cavalli), a man of great artistic taste and understanding despite his somewhat disorderly life, was made cardinal by the Borgia Pope Alessandro VI, who enjoyed an intimacy with his sister. He built a large and splendid palazzo in Rome, now the French Embassy, to which Michelangelo added the final touches; then he was made Pope (Paul III) at the age of sixty-seven. He convened the Council of Trent, approved the Jesuit Order, reorganized the Inquisition and commissioned Michelangelo to do the frescos in the Sistine Chapel. Before entering the Church, he had had four sons: in 1545 he made one of them, Pier Luigi Farnese, the Duke of Parma and Piacenza, cities that were then Church territory. Two years later the new duke was assassinated in Piacenza following a series of questionable deeds in which Emperor Charles V (father-in-law of Pier Luigi's son, Ottavio) had a hand. It was the son of Ottavio, Alessandro, the third Duke, a Hapsburg through his mother's line, who was the subject of Mochi's statue. He was one of the great military leaders of the 17C. At the time that the male line ceased, the daughter of Duke Odoardo II, Elisabetta Farnese, was performing her role as the energetic second wife of Philip V of Spain, the first Bourbon on that throne. By political cunning, she managed to have her ancestral duchy conferred on her two sons: first to Don Carlos (later King of Naples and, later still, King of Spain), and then to Don Filippo, to whom the people of Parma owe the Museo di Antichità, the Biblioteca Palatina and the Galleria Nazionale.

Practical information _____

ⓘ p. dei Mercanti (B2), ☎ 29324.
🚂 (B4), ☎ 20637.
🚌 from p. Cittadella, ☎ 37245, and from p. Casali (A3), ☎ 38149.

Hotels:
★★★★ G.A. Roma, v. Cittadella 14 (B2-3 a), ☎ 23201, 90 rm Ⓟ 占 ※ 100,000; bkf: 9,000.
★★★ Nazionale, v. Genova 33 (C1 b), ☎ 754000, 74 rm Ⓟ No restaurant, 52,000; bkf: 5,000.

Restaurants:
● ♦♦♦ Antica Osteria del Teatro, v. Verdi 16 (B2 c), ☎ 23777, closed Sun and Aug. In 15C building in histor-

ic centre. Creative cuisine: sea bass in lettuce leaves, scampi fritters, 45/60,000.
♦♦ *Ginetto,* p. S. Antonio 8 (B3 d), ☎ 35785, closed Sun, Aug and Christmas. Piacentine cuisine: tortelli with greens, risotto with truffles, 25/35,000.
♦♦ *Gotico,* p. Cavalli 26 (B2-3 e), ☎ 21940, closed Sun and Aug. Piacentine cuisine: tortelli, pappardelle, 25/35,000.

Recommended
Fairs: *national exhibition of vacations and recreation* (Apr); *radio and telecommunications* (Sep); *agricultural engineering* (Oct), ☎ 60620.
Gastronomic specialties: coppe, pancetta, sausages and other pork charcuterie.
Horseback riding: *circolo ippico piacentino,* v. Trebbia 68, ☎ 40287 (riding school).
Sports centre: (C2), ☎ 24312.
Swimming: v. Casella, ☎ 70028 (indoor pool).
Youth hostel: *Ostello Meridiana,* at Ponte dell'Olio, at Monte Santo, ☎ 87934.

PIEVEPELAGO

Modena 80, Bologna 100, Milan 259 km
Pop. 2,335 ✉ 41027 ☎ 0536   C3

In a fold in the valley of the River Scoltenna, a few km from Abetone, among forests of chestnut, beech and fir trees, lies Pievepélago, a popular vacation resort in the Modenese Apennines. 4.5 km NE, on the road to Séstola (at the start of which is a **medieval bridge** over the Scoltenna) is **Riolunato,** a popular ski resort and summer vacation spot.   ☐

Practical information ⎯⎯⎯⎯⎯⎯⎯⎯

⚡ ski lifts, instruction at Sant'Anna Pélago and at Riolunato.
ⓘ v. Costa 25, ☎ 71304.

Hotel:
★★ *Bucaneve,* v. Giardini 31, ☎ 71383, 16 rm Ⓟ ⏝ ⌇ closed 15-30 Jun and 15-30 Nov, 45,000; bkf: 4,000.

Recommended
Swimming: ☎ 71372.
Tennis: *Centro Federale Estivo,* v. Roma, ☎ 71358 or 71376.

Palaces and castles of the PO

From Fidenza to Modena *(138 km, 1 day; map 4)*
See map on page 218.

In the heart of the luxuriant Emilian countryside, rarely straying far from the River Po, whose presence is almost always felt even if not actually seen, this itinerary unravels the thread of history that runs through towns that enjoyed brief periods of artistic and political eminence.

▶ From **Fidenza** (→) the route heads over the Autostrada del Sole. ▶ At the centre of **Soragna,** on the l. bank of the Stirone, is a massive square **rocca,** transformed (16C-18C) into a sumptuous residence by the Meli Lupi family. Inside *(summer 9 a.m.-12 noon and 3-7 p.m; winter 9 a.m.-12 p.m. and 2-5 p.m.; closed Mon and Tue except public hols, when it closes the following day)* are various rooms and galleries decorated with stuccos and frescos and containing paintings and other works of art. ▶ Crossing the Stirone the route heads SE toward **Fontanellato,** whose **rocca** is one of the best preserved and most interesting in Emilia. Built as a fortress by

the Sanvitale family in the early 15C, it was converted into a residence in the 16C-17C. Inside *(winter 9:30 a.m.-12:30 p.m. and 3 p.m.-6 p.m.; summer 9 a.m.-12:30 p.m. and 3:30-7 p.m.; closed Mon)* are a number of rooms with furniture, arms and paintings, and one with a vaulted fresco ceiling painted by the twenty-year-old Parmigianino (*Actaeon Surprising Diana at Her Bath★*). The **camera ottica** is a curiosity with its optical games and mirrors. ▶ **San Secondo Parmense** still retains some of the original **rocca,** built c. 1440 by Pier Maria Rossi for his wife, Antonia Torelli. A sumptuous salon, with a late 16C fireplace, contains interesting frescos from the same period. ▶ A long, straight road, which crosses the Stirone, leads to **Roccabianca,** the site of another **castle** built in the 15C by Pier Maria Rossi, this time for his mistress Bianca Pellegrini, hence the present name of both the castle and the village. ▶ Staying to the S of the Po, which at this point marks the boundary with Lombardy, the route crosses the Taro to **Colorno** (→). ▶ From here, it continues E parallel to the river before reaching **Brescello,** then **Gualtieri** (→) and **Guastalla** (→). A short excursion leads to **Luzzara,** on the Po. In the p. Castello are the 17C parish church and the 16C **Palazzo della Macina,** once the residence of the

Turin ‧ Autostrada ‧ Aprile ‧ A ‧ Madonna di Campagna ‧ S. Sepolcro ‧ Str. Stat. N.º 10 ‧ Pⁱᵉ Torino ‧ Via Giuseppe ‧ B ‧ XXIV ‧ Via Morigi ‧ Maggio ‧ C ‧ **PIACENZA** ‧ 0 100 200 300 m ‧ 1 : 17.000 (1 cm = 170 m) ‧ **1** Bóbbio km 46 · Genoa km

Gonzaga family. The former convent at **Villasuperiore** houses the **Museo dei pittori naïf** *(wkdays 9 a.m.-12 noon and 3-6 p.m.; closed Mon).* ▶ Returning to Guastalla, take the road to Modena. ▶ **Novellara,** today a major industrial and agricultural centre, was once the domain of a collateral branch of the Gonzaga family (1371-1737). In the large main piazza stand the collegiate church of **S. Stefano,** 16C with a 17C façade, and the **castle,** built by the Novellara Gozagas in the 14C-15C. This is the home of the small **Museo Gonzaga** containing detached frescos of the 13C and 16C, paintings and majolica ware *(9 a.m.-12 noon),* and a **Museo della Civiltà Contadina** (rural life). ▶ Heading SE once more in the direction of Modena, the route comes to **Correggio** (→) and then, crossing the Modena-Brenner autostrada, **Carpi** (→), from which Modena lies to the S. □

Practical information

FONTANELLATO, ⊠ 43012, ☎ 0521.

Restaurant:
♦♦ *Tre Pozzi,* at Sanguinaro, ☎ 874347, closed Mon and 20 Jul-20 Aug. Regional cuisine: beef with pepper, carpaccio parmigiana, 25/35,000.

SORANGNA, ⊠ 43019, ☎ 0524.

Recommended
Events: Giostra dei nasi (tournament) and *Feste del Culatello* (ham) *e del Grana* (Parmesan cheese) (May).

POLENTA

Forlì 20, Bologna 83, Milan 302 km
Pop. 52 ⊠ 47032 ☎ 0543   E3

Standing among cypress trees in an evocative setting, a few km from Bertinoro (→), the **church of Polenta,** dedicated to S. Donato, was visited by Dante and Francesca da Rimini and praised by Carducci. Probably built in the 9C-10C, the church was restored in the 18C and 19C. On a hill nearby can be seen the ruins of the **castle,** built 958-1047 and owned by the Da Polenta family, the lords of Ravenna who are known for their hospitality to Dante. □

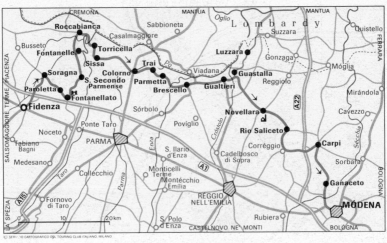

4. Palaces and castles of the Po

PORRETTA TERME

Bologna 60, Milan 261 km
Pop. 4,981 ⊠ *40046* ☎ *0534*   C3

Toward the middle of the 13C this town began to develop in the upper valley of the River Reno. Taking the name **Bagni della Porretta,** from 1471-1797 it was the domain of the Ranuzzi family, and it was members of this family who, as naturalists and physicians, first developed the town as a spa. At **Riola** *(12.5 km N),* also on the Reno, a **church** by the Finnish designer Alvar Aalto (1978) is an interesting example of modern ecclesiastical architecture.   □

Practical information _____

⚓ (all year), ☎ 22062.
ⓘ p. Libertà 75, ☎ 22021.

Hotels:
★★★★ *Santoli,* v. Roma 3, ☎ 23206, 48 rm Ⓟ ⑭ ⅄ ⅏
⊠ 100,000.
★★★★ *Sassocardo,* v. della Piscina 2, ☎ 23075, 60 rm
Ⓟ ⑭ closed Nov-Mar, 90,000; bkf: 5,000.

Recommended
Events: *summer music season* (Jun-Sep); *international independent film festival* (Oct).
Swimming: ☎ 22024.

RAVENNA**

Bologna 74, Milan 295, Rome 362 km
Pop. 136,786 ⊠ *48100* ☎ *0544*   F2

Although Ravenna is now situated inland, until the beginning of the Middle Ages it was directly on the seacoast. Little is known about its ancient history. One theory is that it was founded by the Greeks as a commercial outpost for trade with the Etruscans and other peoples of the region. In the 2C BC, the Romans made it a fortified camp, and

its ships plied the Adriatic Sea. In the same century Apollinarus converted its inhabitants to Christianity, and in the 4C AD the city became a bishopric. During the troubled period of invasions and counter-invasions, Ravenna's isolated position in the middle of a lagoon protected it while its naval strength enabled the city to control the Adriatic. Because of these advantages, Honorius, the Emperor of the West, chose it as the capital of the Western Roman Empire (402). To house the emperor, his court and administration, huge buildings were constructed. Galla Placidia (450), the 'barbarians' Odoacro and Theodoric (493-526) embellished the city with splendid civil and religious structures. Conquered by the Byzantine Greeks in 540, Ravenna had a power she never was to enjoy again, under the reign of Justinian and Theodora. At the end of the Exarchate, the city began its slow decline. It was first brought under the rule of the da Polenta family (1272-1441), then Venice and finally became part of the papal states in 1509. Conquered several times thereafter and impoverished, the once great city hardly played a role after the 16C. With the silting over of the Po, Ravenna was no longer a seacoast city and her port was closed. Since World War II, Ravenna has been given a new lease on life. It has become an important industrial complex, based on the discovery of natural gas in the region. Due to the construction of the Canal of Porto Corsino, its port has been reopened, and although other cities on the coast of the Adriatic have developed as tourist centres — with consequent growth of income and employment — it is Ravenna itself which arouses the greatest interest. Many tourists come to visit the religious monuments of the city, especially its mosaics which have preserved a remarkable freshness. Because it represents a synthesis of East and West as well as the heritage of Byzantium and Rome, and was the disseminator of earliest Christianity, a visit to Ravenna is a profoundly moving experience.

▶ The basilica of **S. Vitale★★** (B2; *summer 8:30 a.m.-7:30 p.m.; winter 8:30 a.m.-5:30 p.m.),* one of the outstanding examples of Early Christian art in Italy, was begun in 525 and consecrated in 547. It is on an octagonal plan, crowned with a cupola, and has a cylindrical campanile. The interior★, of exceptional beauty, has wonderful **mosaics★★** in excellent condition. Executed in the mid-6C, they generally have a classical form, with the exception of two panels on the lateral walls of the apse (*Justinian and His Court*★ to the l., and *Theodora and Her Court*★ to the r.) which are in true Byzantine style. ▶ Superb mosaics are also found in the neighbouring **Mausoleo di Galla Placidia★★** (B2), a chapel in the form of a Latin cross, built *c.* mid-5C, perhaps by the Roman Empress herself. These **mosaics★★**, made before 450, are almost certainly the oldest in Ravenna and, with their distinctive naturalism, belong firmly in the camp of classical art. ▶ The **Museo Nazionale★** (B2; *8:30 a.m.-1:30 p.m.; closed Mon),* occupying part of the old Benedictine monastery next to S. Vitale, is of particular interest for its collections of artifacts from the Roman and early Christian periods. ▶ Beside the **Duomo** (C2), rebuilt in Baroque style in the 18C (fine 10C cylindrical campanile and, inside, an impressive 6C **pulpit★** built for Archbishop Agnellus), is the **Battistero Neoniano★★** (or 'degli Ortodossi', *9 a.m.-12 noon and 2:30-6 or 5 p.m. in winter; Sun and hols 9 a.m.-12 noon).* This simple 5C octagonal building contains beautiful **mosaics★★**, dating from after 450, partly reworked. ▶ Nearby, the **Museo Arcivescovile** (*9 a.m.-12 noon and 2:30-6 or 5 p.m. winter; Sun and hols 9 a.m.-1 p.m.; closed Tue*) contains the celebrated *Throne of Maximian*★★, one of the greatest works of ivory sculpture, a masterpiece by Alexandrine artists of the 6C. ▶ Rivaling S. Vitale in the beauty of its mosaics, the church of **S. Apollinare Nuovo★★** (C4) was built by Theodoric at the beginning of the 6C for the Arians; the elegant cylindrical campanile is 9C. The interior (*8 a.m.-12 noon and 2-5 or 6 or 7 p.m., according to the time of year*) is in basilical form with a nave and two aisles. The walls of the nave are decorated with **mosaics★★** which are divided into three parts: those at the top, in a style that is still classical, are early 6C; those at the bottom, with the wonderful **processions** (*Martyrs Going from Ravenna toward Christ Surrounded by Angels*★, and *Virgins Preceded by the Magi Going from Classe toward the Madonna and Child among Angels*★) in Byzantine style dating from the mid-6C. ▶ Nearby is the **Palazzo di Theodorico** (C4), an unusual building from the late 7C-early 8C. ▶ The **Battistero degli Ariani** (B3; *8:30 a.m.-12:30 p.m. and 2:30-5:30 or 7 p.m.),* early 6C, contains a fine mosaic (*Baptism of Christ* and a *Procession of the Apostles*). ▶ Beside this is the **chiesa dello Spirito Santo**, altered in the 16C and restored; this was the old Arian cathedral of the time of Theodoric. ▶ On the p. S. Francesco, to the l. of the 5C church of **S. Francesco** (C3; rebuilt in the 10C when the campanile was added and subsequently further altered and restored) is **Dante's tomb★** (*7 a.m.-7 p.m. or 9 a.m.-12 noon and 2-5 p.m. winter);* Dante came to Ravenna in about 1317 and died here on 14 September 1321. The exterior structure was built in 1780, sheltering the old sarcophagus on which Pietro Lombardo carved an effigy of the poet in 1483. ▶ Also of interest is the church of **S. Giovanni Evangelista★** (B4), built on the instructions of Galla Placidia in the 5C and restored after World War II; it has an attractive Gothic portal★ in marble and a square 10C campanile (the upper part is 14C). ▶ The church of **S. Maria in Porto** (C4; *7 a.m.-12 noon and 3-7 p.m.)* is late Renaissance and contains fine paintings. It adjoins a former monastery, the Monasterio dei Canonici Lateranensi, part of which is the **Logetta Lombardesca★** (early 16C), looking out over the public gardens; it also has a beautiful Renaissance cloister★. The monastery now houses the **Pinacoteca Comunale** (C4; *9 a.m.-1 p.m. and 2:30-5:30 p.m.; closed Mon),* containing paintings of the Emilian, Tuscan and Venetian schools of the 14C-17C,

including a *Crucifixion*★ by Lorenzo Monaco; among the sculptures is the famous effigy of **Guidarello Guidarelli★** (1525) by Tullio Lombardo. ▶ 2 km from the centre of the city, leaving by the 16C Porta Serrata, is the **Mausoleo di Teodorico★** (A4; *8:30 a.m.-7:30 p.m. summer, 8:30 a.m.-1:30 p.m. winter).* This unusual, solitary monument, with its backdrop of cypresses, was begun in 520 by the Gothic king Theodoric, who was interred here after his death in 526. Built of great blocks of Istrian stone, laid without mortar on the outside, the interior is crowned by a cupola hollowed out of a single limestone monolith. ▶ 5 km along the main road to Rimini is the basilica of **S. Apollinare in Classe★★**, consecrated in 549, the only surviving building of the city of Classe, the old port of Ravenna. Entered through a narthex, flanked by the 10C cylindrical campanile, the impressive interior (*7:30 a.m.-12 noon and 2-6:30 p.m. summer; 8 a.m.-12 noon and 2-5 p.m. or 7:30 p.m. winter*) has a nave and two aisles with an elevated sanctuary decorated by 6C and 7C **mosaics★★**. S of the basilica, the ancient **pineta di Classe**, a pine forest praised by Dante and Byron, stretches toward the sea. ▢

Galla Placidia

Galla Placidia was the daughter of Theodosius I, in one sense the last Roman Emperor, since it was he who divided the empire in two, giving his son Arcadius the E and his other son, Honorius, the W. The W lasted but a 100 years, while the E, which became the Byzantine Empire, lasted a thousand. Galla Placidia was twenty years old when the the Visigoth Alaric I sacked Rome and took her prisoner. Four years later she was married to Alaric's successor, Ataulfo, who was later assassinated. She was then allowed to leave the 'barbarians' and took refuge with her brother Honorius. When she was twenty-seven, she married a general of the Empire, and succeeded in having him proclaimed co-emperor with Constantine III. She was then widowed a second time, and on the death of Honorius had her own son, Valentinian III, placed on the imperial throne of the W. Daughter, sister, wife and mother of emperors, she now exercised the power of a regent. She died, aged sixty, in Rome in 450. It is not certain that it was Galla Placidia herself who instigated the construction of the famous Mausoleum of Galla Placidia in Ravenna. In fact, she was buried in Rome. The mosaics in this small mausoleum, delicately illuminated by the blue and gold light that filters through the sheets of alabaster in the windows, are almost certainly the oldest in Ravenna, a city renowned for its mosaics.

Practical information

ℹ p. S. Francesco 7 (C3), ☎ 36129; v. S. Vitale 2 (B2), ☎ 35404; Mausoleo di Teodorico (A4), ☎ 31282 (seasonal).
🚍 (B4), ☎ 36450.
🚃 from railway station (B4).
Car rental: *Avis,* v. Trieste 25, ☎ 420581; *Hertz,* v. Alighieri 20, ☎ 33674; *Maggiore,* v. Alighieri 40, ☎ 31078.

Hotels:
★★★★ *Bisanzio,* v. Salara 30 (B3 a), ☎ 27111, 36 rm ⟨⟩ closed 15 Dec-15 Jan. No restaurant, 131,000; bkf: 7,000.
★★★★ *Jolly Mameli,* p. Mameli 1 (B4 b), ☎ 35762, 75 rm ℗ 145,000.
★★★ *Centrale Byron,* v. IV Novembre 14 (B3 c), ☎ 33479, 57 rm ⌖ No restaurant, 61,000; bkf: 4,500.
★★★ *Romea,* v. Romea Sud 1, ☎ 61247, 39 rm ℗ ⟨⟩ 63,000; bkf: 5,200.

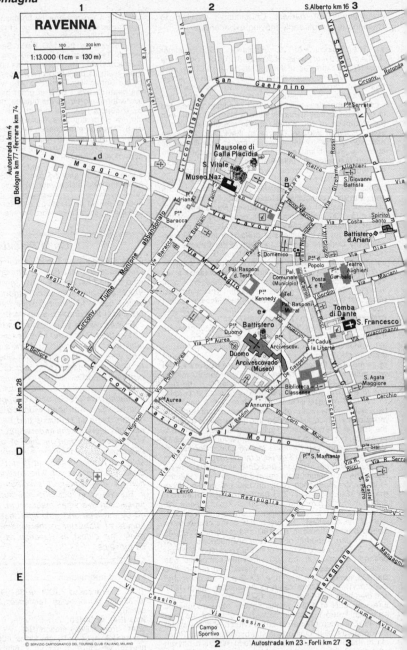

RAVENNA

0   100   200 km

1:13.000 (1cm = 130 m)

© SERVIZIO CARTOGRAFICO DEL TOURING CLUB ITALIANO, MILANO

Restaurants:
◆◆◆ *Bella Venezia*, v. IV Novembre 16 (B3 c). ☎ 22746, closed Sun and 20 Dec-20 Jan.   Italian cuisine: steak with vegetables, snails, 30/40,000.
◆◆◆ *Coq qui Rit*, v. Romea Nord 262, ☎ 451044, closed

Mon.   In large park, service in open air in summer.   Italian cuisine: garganelli with speck, pancakes with melted cheese, 25/40,000.
◆◆◆ *Tre Spade*, v. Rasponi 35 (C2 e), ☎ 32382, closed

4 Chióggia km 96

Mausoleo
di Teodorico

4 S.Apollinare in Classe km 5
Cesena km 32-Rimini km 51

Mon and Jul-Aug. Modern cuisine: garganello with shallots, pigeon with juniper berries, 30/40,000.
◆◆ *Gallo*, v. Maggiore 87 (B1 d), ☎ 23775, closed Mon eve, Tue, 20 May-10 Jun and Christmas. Regional cuisine: tortellacci with cream and ham, pappardelle with hare, 25/35,000.

⚥ ★★★ *Adriano*, at Punta Marina, v. dei Campeggi 7, 1,037 pl, ☎ 437230.

Recommended
Antiques: market every 3rd wkend of month, in p. Garibaldi.
Archery: *Compagnia Arcieri della Costa*, v. Nizza 13, ☎ 460073; *Compagnia Arcieri Bizantini*, v. Battuzzi 79, ☎ 460185.
Craft workshops: *Studio Il Mosaico*, v. Argentario 22, ☎ 36090; *Gruppo Mosaicisti*, v. Fiandrini, ☎ 34799; *Studio F. Carrara*, v. Mariani 9, ☎ 31226 (mosaics).
Cycling: *GS Cicloamatori*, v. Carso 32, ☎ 401649.
Events: *international festival of organ concerts* (San Vitale, Jul-Aug); *jazz concerts, opera and ballet season*, at the Rocca Brancaleone (Jul); *Dante festival* (Sep).
Flying: *F. Baracca airport*, v. Dismano 160, ☎ 497644 (also gliding).
Horseback riding: *Associazione ippica ravennate*, v. Stadio, ☎ 422048.
Nature park: *Oasi di Punta Alberete*, information, *WWF Ravenna*, v. Mentana 19, ☎ 33081.
Sailing school: *Vela Vacanze T.S.T.*, v. Gulli 51.
Wine: Enoteca *Ca' de vin*, v. Ricci 24 (C3), ☎ 30163.
Youth hostel: *Ostello Dante*, v. Aurelio Nicolodi 12, ☎ 420405.

REGGIO NELL'EMILIA

Bologna 63, Milan 147, Rome 443 km
Pop. 131,075 ⊠ 42100 ☎ 0522   C2

To every Italian, Reggio nell'Emilia is the city of the tricolour flag. It was here, in the Palazzo Comunale, that in January 1797 the Congress of the cities of Emilia, recently united as the Cispadane Republic, chose as its own standard the tricolour which was then to become the national flag. It is also the birthplace of Ariosto (1474-1533), author of *Orlando Furioso*.

▶ On the S side of the large p. Prampolini (B2) is the **Palazzo Comunale**, begun in 1414, altered several times and now bearing the mark of the 18C; it contains the **Sala del Tricolore**, once the Council Chamber. To the l. is the 15C **Torre del Comune**. ▶ On the E side is the **Duomo** (B2), founded in the 9C, rebuilt in the 13C, but considerably altered since. The Romanesque façade was to be given a marble facing in the 16C, the work of Prospero Spani, but the lower half was never completed. Inside are numerous tombs by Benedetto and Prospero Spani and an *Assumption and Saints* by Guercino. ▶ Behind the apse of the Duomo is the church of **S. Prospero** (B2), founded in the 10C and rebuilt 1514-27; the façade is 18C. Inside, in the transept, sculpted tombs by the Spani; in the sanctuary, frescos by Camillo Procaccini. ▶ In corso Garibaldi, opposite the former **Palazzo Ducale** (1784-1839), stands the sanctuary of the **Madonna della Ghiara**★ (B1), dating from the early 17C. The impressive interior, in the form of a Greek cross, is decorated with frescos by the Bolognese school of the 17C, depicting scenes from the Old Testament; in the l. wing is *Christ on the Cross Consoled by Angels*, by Guercino (1624). ▶ In the p. Cavour (B2) is the **Teatro Municipale**, inaugurated in 1857. ▶ Alongside the theatre are the **Musei Civici** (B2; *Sun 10:30 a.m.-12:30 p.m. and 4-6 p.m.; wkdays 8:30 a.m.-12:30 p.m.; Tue and Fri 4-6 p.m.; closed Mon*) which comprise: the **Museo Spallanzani di Storia Naturale**, begun in 1799 with the collection of Lazzaro Spallanzani; the **Museo del Risorgimento della Resistenza**; the **Museo Archeologico**, containing the Chierici collection, on the prehistory of the Po Valley; and the **Galleria d'Arte Antonio Fontanesi**, with works by Emilian painters. ▶ The **Galleria Parmeggiani**★ (B 1-2, *closed for restoration*) contains works by Spanish, Flemish and Italian artists.

REGGIO NELL'EMILIA

0   100   200   300 m

1 : 17.000   (1 cm=170 m)

Environs

▶ 3 km SE on the Via Emilia in the direction of Modena is the villa **Il Mauriziano**, which Ariosto frequently visited as a guest of his cousins, the Malaguzzi. ▶ 12.5 km SE on the Via Emilia lies **Rubiera**. An interesting Romanesque church, **SS. Faustino e Giovita** *(restored)*, is 3 km to the N; inside there is a fine painting by the school of Garofalo. ▶ 19.5 km NE is **Novellara** (→ Palaces and Castles of the Po). □

Practical information

ⓘ p. Battisti 4 (B2), ☎ 43370.

🚋 (B3), ☎ 39650.

🚌 from the new Autostazione (A2), ☎ 31667.

Hotels:
★★★★ *G.H. Astoria*, v. Nobili 2 (A2 a), ☎ 35245, 112 rm Ⓟ 120,000; bkf: 10,000. Rest. ♦♦♦ *Girarrosto* closed Sun, Aug and Christmas. Regional cuisine: gramigna with sausage, stuffed pig's trotter, 30/40,000.
★★★ *Posta*, p. Battisti 4 (B2 b), ☎ 32944, 45 rm Ⓟ ⊗ closed Aug. No restaurant, 70,000; bkf: 9,000.
★★★ *San Marco*, p. Marconi 1 (B3 c), ☎ 35364, 52 rm, closed Aug and Christmas. No restaurant, 70,000.
★★★ *Scudo d'Italia*, v. Vescovado 5 (B2 d), ☎ 34345, 33 rm Ⓟ closed Aug, 67,000; bkf: 8,000.

Restaurants:
♦♦♦ *Zucca*, p. Fontanesi 1 (C2 e), ☎ 485718, closed Sun and 20 Jul-20 Aug. Reggian cuisine: tortelli with pumpkin, gnocchi with gorgonzola, 23/36,000.
♦ *Cinque Pini-da Pelati*, v. Martiri di Cervarolo 46, ☎ 553663, closed Wed and Aug. Reggian cuisine: tortelli with herbs, roast meats, 25/35,000.

Recommended

Bowling: v. Sant'Ambrogio-Rivalta, ☎ 560164.
Clay pigeon shooting: v. Montessori, ☎ 52553.
Events: *international congress of pig breeders* (Apr); ornithologists (Nov); *international chess tournament* (Dec-Jan).
Flying club: v. Vertoiba 1, ☎ 511650.
Horseback riding: *Circolo equitazione Reggio Emilia*, via Tassoni 146, ☎ 569400 (riding school).
Ice skating: v. Zandonai, ☎ 73247.
Sports centre: v. Guasco 8 (B1), ☎ 47295.
Wine: visits to the *Cantine cooperative riunite*, v. Gramsci 54, ☎ 30341 (by appointment).

RICCIONE*

Forlì 60, Bologna 123, Rome 327 km
Pop. 32,069 ⊠ 47036 ☎ 0541   F3

This was a quiet fishing port on the Romagnese riviera until 1890; now it is one of the major and most elegant seaside resorts of the Adriatic, with an abundance of greenery.

▶ On the seafront is the interesting **Aquarium dei Delfini** (dolphins). ▶ Near the Biblioteca Civica, v. Sirtori 7, is an **antiquarium** *(☎ 600504)*, a collection of prehistoric and Roman artifacts from the region. ▶ In a small park, at v. Torino 14, are the **Terme di Riccione**. ▶ 18 km SW is **Montefiore Conca**, an attractive town set on a hilltop dominating the valley of the Conca and at the foot of the imposing 14C **fortress** of the Malatestas from which there are magnificent views★ over the Adriatic coast. ▶ 19 km S is **Saludecio**, a picturesque fortified town, with magnificent views, which retains a medieval character with ruined walls and 14C gates. ☐

Practical information

≋ (Mar-Nov), ☎ 602201.
ⓘ p. Ceccarini 10 (palazzo del Turismo), ☎ 43361.
🚌 ☎ 600417.

Hotels:
★★★★ **Abner's,** lungomare della Repubblica, ☎ 600601, 50 rm ℗ ৬ 130,000; bkf: 12,000.
★★★★ **Alexandra Plaza,** v. Torino 61, ☎ 610344, 60 rm ℗ ⚏ ৬ ⊠ closed Oct-Mar, 100,000; bkf: 10,000.
★★★★ **Augustus,** v. Oberdan 18, ☎ 43434, 48 rm ℗ ⚏ ⊠ closed 1 Nov-14 Mar, 130,000.
★★★★ **Baltic,** p. Di Vittorio 1, ☎ 600966, 72 rm ℗ ⚏ ৬ 75,000; bkf: 5,000.
★★★★ **Promenade,** v. Milano 67, ☎ 600852, 39 rm ℗ ⚏ closed Oct-Apr, 100,000; bkf: 7,000.
★★★★ **Savioli Spiaggia,** v. D'Annunzio 6, ☎ 43253, 100 rm ℗ ⚏ ⊠ closed 16 Oct-Easter, 140,000; bkf: 15,000.
★★★ **Anna,** v. Trento-Trieste 48, ☎ 601503, 36 rm ℗ ⚏ closed 1 Oct-14 Apr, 69,000; bkf: 5,000.
★★★ **Campidoglio,** lungomare della Repubblica, ☎ 601565, 45 rm ℗ ⚏ closed Oct-Easter, 60,000.
★★★ **Carlton,** v. Gramsci 83, ☎ 601033, 38 rm ℗ ⚏ ⚒ closed 26 Sep-14 May, 60,000.
★★★ **Clipper,** lungomare Costituzione 21, ☎ 642525, 51 rm ℗ closed Oct-Apr, 60,000.
★★★ **Club Hotel,** v. D'Annunzio 58, ☎ 42105, 68 rm ℗ ⚏ closed Oct-Apr, 55,000.
★★★ **Gemma,** v. D'Annunzio, ☎ 43251, 41 rm ℗ ⚏ ৬ ⊠ closed 16 Oct-9 Feb, 60,000.
★★★ **Romagna,** v. Gramsci 64, ☎ 600604, 50 rm ℗ ⚏ closed 16 Sep-19 May, 58,000; bkf: 6,000.
★★★ **Savoia,** v. Ceccarini 29, ☎ 601244, 37 rm ℗ closed Oct-Mar. No restaurant, 90,000.
★★★ **Select,** v. Gramsci 89, ☎ 600613, 42 rm ℗ ⚏ ⚒ closed 21 Sep-19 May, 70,000; bkf: 5,000.
★★ **Petronio,** v. Goldoni 9, ☎ 641111, 36 rm ℗ ⚏ closed 1 Oct-9 May, 40,000.

Restaurants:
♦♦♦ **Pescatore,** v. Nievo 11, ☎ 42526, closed Tue and Nov-Dec. Summer pergola. Seafood: penne with scampi, risotto alla crema di mare, 35/50,000.
♦♦♦ **Punta de l'Est,** v. Emilia 73, ☎ 42448, closed Mon and Oct-Dec. Cool garden for summer. Italian and international cuisine: seafood risotto, grilled fish, 25/40,000.
♦♦ **Fino,** v. Galli 1, ☎ 43326, closed Wed and Oct. Terrace with sea view. Seafood: tagliatelle with sole, tagliolini with squid, 35/45,000.
♦♦ **Gambero Rosso,** molo di Levante, ☎ 41200, closed Tue and 1 Jan-14 Feb. Two terraces with sea views. Seafood: tagliatelle with sole, crayfish, lobster, 28/35,000.
⚼ ★★★ **Alberello,** v. Torino 80, 330 pl, ☎ 615402.

Recommended
Cycling: rentals at v. Vespucci, v. Milano (near v. Ceccarini), v. F.lli Cervi, at the port-canal.
Discothèque: Savioli, v. Dante, ☎ 41705.
Events: national theatre prize (Jun); international philately exhibition (end Aug); national numismatic conference (early Sep); concerts, exhibitions and sports meetings during the summer season.
Excursions: along the coast with the motor vessel Marinella, molo Nord, ☎ 48656.
Go-cart: track at v. Nazionale Adriatica 75, ☎ 641726.
Hang gliding: Delta club Cassini, via Piave 13, ☎ 43149.
Marina: The port-canal only accommodates boats that draw less than 1.80 m (5ft 10 in); harbourmaster, ☎ 602608.
Nature park: Aquarium dei delfini, lungomare Repubblica, ☎ 601712.

RIMINI*

Forli 49, Bologna 112, Milan 330 km
Pop. 129,506 ⊠ 47037 ☎ 0541 F3

The Roman *Ariminum,* at the crossroads of the Via Emilia, the Via Flaminia and the Via Popilia, became the centre of the Byzantine *Sentapolo* after 567 AD. An independent city-state in the 12C, it belonged to the Malatesta family from the 13C onwards. Under Sigismondo (1417-68), it reached the heights of its power. Dante wrote about the loves of Francesca Malatesta in *The Divine Comedy* (Hell, fifth canto). In 1509, Rimini became part of the papal states. Capital of the department of the Rubicon during the French Revolution and the Napoleonic Empire, the city was returned to church rule in 1816 and in 1860 was annexed to the Kingdom of Italy. Tourists enjoy the beaches of Rimini Marina as well as the port. Promenades reveal the monuments that the powerful lords of Rimini, the Romans and Sigismondo built in the old city.

▶ The historic centre of the city is the p. Cavour, with its statue of Paul V (1613) and a 16C fountain. On one side of the piazza are: the 17C **Palazzo Comunale,** restored following damage during World War II; the **Palazzo dell'Arengo,** built in 1204 and subsequently remodeled (there are two detached frescos of the 14C-16C in the large salon); and the Gothic **Palazzo del Podestà,** housing the **Museo delle Arti Primitivi** *(visits by appointment, 8:30 a.m.-1 p.m.,* ☎ *23667).* ▶ One end of the piazza is closed off by the 19C Teatro Comunale, behind which is the p. Malatesta, on which stand the remains, now restored, of the **Castel Sigismondo,** built in 1446 with the help of Brunelleschi. ▶ The outstanding monument of the city is the **Tempio Malatestiano★★,** one of the major architectural accomplishments of the Renaissance. The church (restored after World War II) dates back to the 13C, but was almost completely rebuilt 1447-60 for Sigismondo Malatesta as a monument to his own power and glory. The magnificent unfinished **façade,** inspired by a Roman triumphal arch, is the work of Leon Battista Alberti. The interior was partially rebuilt by the Veronese artist Matteo de' Pasti. To the r. of the entrance is the tomb of Sigismondo Malatesta. On the r. side, in the Capella delle Reliquie, is a detached fresco by Piero della Francesca (1451) depicting *Sigismondo before His Patron Saint★★* (note Castel Sigismondo in the background). In the second chapel is the **tomb of Isotta degli Atti★,** third wife of Sigismondo, and a **crucifix★★** attributed to Giotto. In the first chapel to the l. is the **Arca degli antenati e dei discendenti★,** an ancestral tomb decorated by Agostino di Duccio (1454). ▶ The **Arco di Augusto,** the oldest surviving Roman arch (with a medieval crenellation), was built in 27 BC in honour of Augustus who restored the Via Flaminia, which meets the Via Emilia at this point. ▶ The corso d'Agusto, the N-S axis of the city, leads from the Arco d'Augusto through the p. Tre Martiri (on the site of the old Roman forum where Caesar, after crossing the Rubicon, is said to have given a speech to encourage his troops), passes to one side of the central p. Cavour (→) and ends at the **Ponte di Tiberio★,** over the River Marecchia, which was begun by Augustus and finished by Tiberius (14-21 AD). ▶ Beyond the bridge is the 16C church of **S.Giuliano,** containing an altarpiece by Veronese (*The Martyrdom of S.Giuliano★*). ▶ In the church of **S.Agostino,** a Romanesque-Gothic construction of 1247 with a fine **campanile★,** there are **frescos★** by the Riminese school of the 14C. ▶ Also of interest is the **Pinacoteca Comunale,** temporarily housed in the Biblioteca Civica in v. Gambalunga 27 *(9.30 a.m.-12.30 p.m.; closed Mon),* and noted for its *Pietà★* by Giovanni Bellini and a painting by Ghirlandaio (*Saints★*).

Environs

▶ 3 km SW, in the Covignano Pass, is the church of the **Madonna delle Grazie**, built in the 14C and with a 16C façade and 17C portico. Opposite the church is the **Museo delle Grazie** *(visits by appointment,* ☎ *751061),* with an interesting ethnological collection. A little way off, set in a park, is the **Stabilimento termale Galvanina**, a thermal spa which has a beautiful 16C fountain. ☐

Practical information ——————————

RIMINI

≋

♨ *Istituto Talassoterapico* (Jun-Sep), ☎ 370503; *La Galvanina* (Jun-Sep), ☎ 751315.

ⓘ p. Battisti, ☎ 27927; Parco Indipendenza, ☎ 24511.
✈ at Miramare, *Aeradria,* ☎ 373132; *Alitalia,* ☎ 370017. City bus No. 9 from the train station.
🚂🚌 ☎ 53512.
🚌 from largo Clementini and p. Malatesta.
Car rental: *Avis,* v. Trieste 16, ☎ 51256; *Hertz,* v. Trieste 16/A, ☎ 25440, airport, ☎ 35108.
Hotels:
★★★★★ *Grand Hotel,* parco Indipendenza, ☎ 24211, 121 rm Ⓟ ₩ ♿ 🖵 ⤢ closed 1 Nov-14 Jan. Art Nouveau building in an age-old park, 315,000.
★★★★ *Bellevue,* p. Kennedy 12, ☎ 54116, 66 rm Ⓟ No restaurant, 138,000.
★★★★ *Imperiale,* v. Vespucci 16, ☎ 52255, 64 rm Ⓟ ₩ 🖵 210,000.
★★★★ *Waldorf,* v. Vespucci 28, ☎ 54725, 60 rm Ⓟ ₩ 🖵 140,000; bkf: 8,000.
★★★ *Admiral,* v. Regina Elena 67, ☎ 381771, 90 rm Ⓟ ♿ closed 20 Dec-20 Jan, 75,000; bkf: 6,000.
★★★ *Ariminum,* v. Regina Elena 159, ☎ 380472, 47 rm Ⓟ ₩ ♿ closed Oct-Mar, 64,000.
★★★ *Diplomat,* v. Regina Elena 70, ☎ 380011, 67 rm Ⓟ closed Dec, 75,000; bkf: 8,000.
★★★ *Duomo,* v. G. Bruno 28, ☎ 24215, 46 rm Ⓟ No restaurant, 75,000; bkf: 6,000.
★★★ *Lotus,* v. Rovani 3, ☎ 381680, 46 rm Ⓟ ₩ 🖵 closed 1 Oct-14 Jun, 65,000; bkf: 3,500.
★★★ *Villa Rosa Riviera,* v. Vespucci 71, ☎ 22506, 51 rm Ⓟ ♿ closed Oct-Easter. No restaurant, 78,000.
★★★ *Villa Verde,* v. Vespucci 38, ☎ 24742, 35 rm Ⓟ ₩ ⤢ 74,000; bkf: 5,000.
★★ *Atlas,* v. Regina Elena 74, ☎ 380561, 66 rm Ⓟ ₩ closed Oct-Apr, 41,000; bkf: 4,000.
★★ *Costa del Sole,* at Rivabella, v. Toscanelli 1/A, ☎ 50373, 38 rm Ⓟ ₩ closed 1 Oct-14 Apr, 51,000; bkf: 5,000.
★★ *Nancy,* v. Leopardi 11, ☎ 381731, 30 rm Ⓟ closed Oct-Apr, 50,000.
★★ *Rondinella,* v. Neri 3, ☎ 380567, 31 rm Ⓟ ₩ closed 16 Oct-Easter, 45,000; bkf: 4,000.

Restaurants:
♦♦♦ *Belvedere,* molo di Levante, ☎ 50178, closed Mon except summer and 20 Sep-20 Mar. Fine views of sea. Seafood: fish risotto, brodetto, 35/50,000.
● ♦ *Zio,* v. S. Chiara 16/18, ☎ 52325, closed Wed and Jul. Plain and pleasingly furnished with antiques. Seafood: tagliolini with clam sauce, brodetto alla marinara, 30/40,000.

⚠ ★★★ *Italia,* at Viserba, v. Toscanelli 112, 320 pl, ☎ 738682.

Recommended
Amusement parks: *Fiabilandia,* at Rivazzurra, ☎ 372064; *Italia in miniatura,* at Viserba, v. Popilia 239, ☎ 734406.
Baseball: stadium at v. Nuova Circonvallazione, ☎ 740355.
Clay pigeon shooting: at Vergiano, v. S. Giustina 387, ☎ 727180.
Discothèque: *Altro Mondo,* at Miramare, v. Flaminia 358, ☎ 375151.
Events: *festival of music,* at the Tempio Malatestiano (Sep); *European film festival* (Sep); *national equestrian competition* (Jul); a variety of *artistic, cultural and sporting events* during the vacation season.

Fairs: *hotel exhibitions* (Feb and Dec); *nautical show* (Mar), *craft exhibition* (Jul), ☎ 773553.
Flying club: Miramare airport, ☎ 373301.
Marina: ☎ 50211.
Sailing school: *Club Nautico,* p. Boscovich 12, ☎ 26520.
Sports centre: v. Flaminia 28, ☎ 704194.
Wine: Enoteca *Chesa de Vein,* v. Dante 18, ☎ 54180.
Youth hostel: *Ostello Urland,* at Miramare, v. Flaminia 300, ☎ 33216.

Environs

MIRAMARE, ✉ 47045, 6 km SE.
Hotels:
★★★ *Coronado-Airport,* v. Flaminia 390, ☎ 33161, 25 rm Ⓟ ₩ ⤢ 78,000; bkf: 7,000.
★★★ *Miramare et de la Ville,* v. Oliveti 93, ☎ 372510, 60 rm Ⓟ ⤢ closed 1 Oct-9 Apr, 55,000; bkf: 5,000.
★★★ *Touring,* v. Regina Margherita 82, ☎ 33005, 86 rm Ⓟ ₩ closed 16 Oct-4 Apr, 60,000.

RIVAZZURRA, ✉ 47037, 6 km SE.
Hotels:
★★★ *Grand Meeting,* v. Regina Margherita 46, ☎ 32123, 40 rm Ⓟ ₩ closed 1 Oct-14 Apr, 60,000; bkf: 8,000.
★★ *Christian,* v. Lecce 4, ☎ 370915, 44 rm Ⓟ ₩ 🖵 closed 11 Oct-31 Mar, 50,000; bkf: 5,000.

TORRE PEDRERA, ✉ 47040, 7 km NW.
Hotels:
★★★ *El Cid,* v. Tocra 5, ☎ 721285, 55 rm Ⓟ ₩ ⤢ closed 26 Sep-9 May, 60,000; bkf: 7,000.
★★ *Doge,* v. Salvador 156, ☎ 720170, 50 rm Ⓟ closed Oct-Apr, 50,000; bkf: 8,000.
★★ *Du Lac,* v. Lago Tana, ☎ 720462, 52 rm Ⓟ ₩ ⤢ closed 21 Sep-9 May, 50,000; bkf: 6,000.

VISERBA, ✉ 47049, 4 km NW.
Hotel:
★★★ *Byron,* v. Dati 88, ☎ 738161, 39 rm Ⓟ 🖵 closed Oct-Apr except Easter, 64,000.

VISERBELLA, ✉ 47049, 5 km NW.
Hotels:
★★★ *Sirio,* v. Spina 3, ☎ 734639, 45 rm Ⓟ ⪦ ₩ ⤢ 🖵 ⤢ closed 21 Sep-9 May, 60,000.
★★ *Palos,* v. Porto Palos 154, ☎ 721015, 34 rm Ⓟ ₩ closed 21 Sep-11 May, 49,000; bkf: 5,000.

RIOLO TERME

Ravenna 48, Bologna 49, Milan 265 km
Pop. 4,760 ✉ 48025 ☎ 0546   E3

Riolo Terme was a **medieval centre** and now is surrounded by 15C ramparts in the valley of the River Senio, with a popular and modern **thermal spa**. ☐

Practical information ——————————
♨ (May-Oct), ☎ 71045.
ⓘ corso Matteotti 40, ☎ 71044.
Hotel:
★★★ *Italia,* v. Belvedere 6, ☎ 70270, 36 rm Ⓟ ₩ closed Nov-Feb except 16-31 Dec, 45,000; bkf: 3,000.

Recommended
Events: *exhibition of painting and ceramics* (Aug-Sep); gastronomic festival during the Ferragosto Riolese (mid-Aug).

RIVIERA OF ROMAGNA AND FERRARA

F2-3

The Romagnese coastline, with its natural extension to the N in the Ferrarese and Comacchio beaches, is Italy's biggest seaside development for the tourists. From the Gabicce promontory, which marks the S limit and the boundary with the coastline of the Marches, to the area around the Po delta in the N, there is a virtually uninterrupted ribbon of seaside resorts, fronting onto beaches that are both long and wide, with fine sand, sloping gently to the sea. In the summer, a festive atmosphere reigns.

▶ **Cattolica**, an important seaside resort as well as fishing harbour, is on a wide bay, with the Gabicce promontory marking its southernmost point. The resort zone, stretching over more than a mile, is criss-crossed by shady avenues. In v. Carlo Marx there are the remains of a **Roman building** of the First Empire; in p. Repubblica there is a small **archaeological museum**. ▶ **Misano Adriatico**, a quiet spot between the resorts of Cattolica and Riccione, has a fine sand beach. ▶ **Bellaria** is one of the main resorts of the Romagnese Riviera, but is also a fishing **port-canal** at the mouth of the River Uso which separates it from **Igea Marina**, with its dunes and **pine forest**. ▶ **San Mauro a Mare** is between Bellaria and the mouth of the Rubicon. In the main centre of this commune, **San Mauro Pascoli**, 7 km inland, is the **birthplace** of the poet Giovanni Pascoli, whose house contains a small museum and a library. ▶ **Gatteo a Mare** is a seaside resort near the Rubicon, connected to Cesenàtico by a beautiful avenue that follows the coastline. ▶ **Cesenàtico**, founded in 1302 by the Cesenati as a military port, was (and still is) a major fishing port before it developed into one of the most well-known seaside resorts of Romagna. The old part of town is situated around the picturesque **port-canal**. The modern section stretches to the S of the extensive dockyard. An interesting **Aquarium dei Delfini** is located in the Vena Mazzarini, a lateral branch of the port. ▶ **Lido di Sàvio** is a recent seaside development situated between Milano Marittima (to the S) and the mouth of the Savio. On the other side of the river is the **Lido di Classe**. At **Savio** *(7 km inland), in a restaurant called La Gramadora, there is a museum of mechanical musical instruments (visits by appointment,* ☎ *60530).* ▶ **Marina di Ravenna**, near the celebrated pine forest, the **Pineta di Ravenna**, is at the mouth of the Candiano canal, which connects the port to Ravenna. To the N of the canal is **Porto Corsini**, after Pope Clement XII (Corsini) who built it in 1736. The beach of **Punta Marina** stretches out to the S, with its **spa**; further S is **Lido Adriano**. To the N of Porto Corsini, on the edge of the **Pineta di San Vitale**, is the beach of **Marina Romea.** ▶ **Lidi Ferraresi**, or Lidi di Commachio, are the names given to the tourist development comprising seven seaside resorts which stretch for 20 km to the E and NE of the **Valli di Comacchio**: Lido di Spina, Lido degli **Estensi**, the most developed of the resorts, **Porto Garibaldi**, Lido degli Scacchi, Lido di Pomposa, Lido delle **Nazione** and, separated and a little further N, **Lido di Volano**. Most of the beaches are near large pine groves. □

Practical information _____

BELLARIA-IGEA MARINA, ⊠ 47041 (Bellaria), ⊠ 47044 (Igea Marina), ☎ 0541.
≋

ⓘ at Bellaria, palazzo del Turismo, v. Leonardo da Vinci, ☎ 44574; at Igea Marina, v. Pinzon, ☎ 630052 (in season only).

Hotels:

★★★★ *Elisabeth*, v. Rovereto 11, ☎ 44119, 50 rm P ⊟ ⁄° closed 11 Oct-31 Mar, 70,000.

★★★ *Ermitage*, v. Ala 11, ☎ 47633, 60 rm P ⊟ ⁄° closed 1 Oct-14 May, 70,000.

★★★ *Gambrinus*, v. Panzini 101, ☎ 49421, 63 rm P ⊰ ⊗ ⊟ closed Oct-Apr, 65,000; bkf: 10,000.

★★★ *Globus*, v. Pinzon 193, ☎ 631195, 57 rm P ◐ closed 26 Sep-9 May, 40,000; bkf: 5,000.

★★★ *K 2*, v. Pinzon 212, ☎ 630064, 55 rm ⊗ closed Oct-Apr, 36,000; bkf: 5,000.

★★★ *Miramare*, lungomare Colombo 37, ☎ 44131, 64 rm P ⋘ ◐ ⊟ closed 1 Oct-14 May, 55,000; bkf: 5,000.

★★★ *Nautic*, v. Panzini 128, ☎ 47437, 30 rm P ⋘ ⊗ ⊟ closed 21 Sep-14 May, 50,000; bkf: 5,000.

★★★ *Touring*, v. Pinzon 217, ☎ 631619, 31 rm P ⋘ ⊗ ⊟ closed 20 Sep-22 May. No restaurant, 63,000; bkf: 9,000.

★★ *Strand*, v. Pinzon 161, ☎ 630126, 33 rm P closed Oct-Apr, 40,000; bkf: 7,000.

★★ *Victoria*, v. Pinzon 246, ☎ 630253, 30 rm P ⊰ ⋘ ⊗ closed 16 Sep-14 May, 40,000.

Restaurant:

◆ *Tolmino*, v. Pinzon 8, ☎ 44031, closed Mon and Nov-Dec. Seafood: tagliatelle with cuttlefish, crabs with sauce, 20/30,000.

🅐 ★★★ *Riccardo*, v. Pinzon 308, 185 pl, ☎ 630273.

Recommended
Marina: *Lega Navale*, ☎ 44478; *Circolo nautico*, ☎ 49838.
Tennis: v. Bellini, ☎ 47357.

CATTOLICA, ⊠ 47033, ☎ 0541.
≋

ⓘ p. Nettuno, ☎ 963341.

Hotels:

★★★★★ *Caravelle*, v. Padova 6, ☎ 962416, 45 rm P ⋘ ⊟ ⁄° closed Oct-Apr, 130,000.

★★★★ *Negresco*, v. del Turismo 10, ☎ 963282, 75 rm P ⊟ closed Oct-Apr, 76,000; bkf: 9,000.

★★★★ *Victoria Palace*, v. Carducci 24, ☎ 962921, 88 rm P ⋘ closed Oct-Apr, 131,500; bkf: 5,000.

★★★ *Astoria*, v. Carducci 22, ☎ 961328, 70 rm P closed Oct-Apr, 66,000; bkf: 9,000.

★★★ *Diplomat*, v. del Turismo 9, ☎ 967442, 64 rm P ◐ ⁄° closed 16 Sep-24 May, 60,000; bkf: 15,000.

★★★ *Europa Monetti*, v. Curiel 39, ☎ 961159, 77 rm P ⊟ closed 21 Sep-9 May, 70,000; bkf: 5,000.

★★★ *Maxim*, v. Facchini 7, ☎ 967650, 55 rm P ⊗ closed 21 Sep-26 May, 47,000; bkf: 3,000.

★★★ *Regina Vanni*, v. Carducci 40, ☎ 961167, 62 rm P ⋘ ⊗ closed 1 Oct-9 May, 60,000; bkf: 8,000.

★★★ *Villa Ombrosa*, v. del Prete 61, ☎ 961064, 30 rm P ⋘ Pens. closed 1 Oct-14 May, 42,000.

Restaurant:

◆◆◆ *Lampara*, p. Darsena, ☎ 963296, closed Tue and 20 Oct-30 Jan. Shady terrace with sea view. Seafood: risotto aurora, fish cannelloni, 30/50,000.

Recommended
Events: *Mystfest*, international festival of detective films (Jun), ☎ 967802.
Tennis: v. Donizetti, ☎ 967558.

CESENATICO, ⊠ 47042, ☎ 0547.
≋

ⓘ palazzo del Turismo, v. Roma 112, ☎ 80091.

Hotels:

★★★ *Britannia*, v. Carducci 129, ☎ 80041, 44 rm P ⋘ ⊟ closed 14 Sep-24 May, 74,000; bkf: 11,000.

★★★ *Des Bains*, v. dei Mille 52, ☎ 81119, 30 rm P closed 1 Oct-9 May, 50,000; bkf: 5,000.

★★★ *Esplanade*, v. Carducci 120, ☎ 82405, 70 rm P closed 26 Sep-14 May, 65,000; bkf: 7,000.

★★★ *Internazionale*, v. Ferrara 7, ☎ 80231, 51 rm P ⊟ ⁄° closed May, 60,000.

★★★ *Nuovo Renzo*, at Zadina Pineta, v. dei Pini 49, ☎ 82316, 25 rm P ◔ ⋘ ⊗ Pens. closed Oct-Apr, 43,500.

★★★ *Roxy*, v. Carducci 90, ☎ 82004, 40 rm P ⋘ ⊗ ⊟ ◐ closed 21 Sep-19 May, 48,000; bkf: 5,000.

★★★ *Royal*, at Valverde, v. Carducci 292, ☎ 86140, 70 rm P ◐ closed 21 Sep- 14 May, 46,000; bkf: 6,000.

★★★ *San Pietro*, v. Carducci 194, ☎ 82496, 80 rm P ⋘ ⊟ closed Oct-9 May, 60,000; bkf: 6,000.

★★★ *Torino*, v. Carducci 55, ☎ 80044, 45 rm P ⊟ closed Sep-14 May, 62,000; bkf: 5,000.

★★ *Caesar*, at Valverde, v. Carducci 290, ☎ 86500, 55 rm P ⊟ ⁄° Pens. closed Oct-Apr, 60,000.

★★ *Domus Mea*, v. del Fortino 7, ☎ 82119, 29 rm ⋘ closed Oct-Apr. No restaurant, 55,000.

★★ *New Bristol*, v. del Fortino 9, ☎ 80047, 56 rm ⋘ ⊗ closed 21 Sep-19 May, 40,000.

★★ ***Residence,*** at Valverde, v. Tiziano 34, ☎ 87170, 40 rm [P] 🌳 ▭ Pens. closed 16 Sep-14 May, 49,500.

Restaurants:

● ♦♦♦ ***Gambero Rosso,*** molo di Levante 21, ☎ 81260, closed Tue except summer and Nov-Feb. Terrace on the sea. Excellent seafood: macaroni with cuttlefish, poached octopus, 35/50.000.

♦♦ ***Punta Nord,*** v. Cavour 12, ☎ 81446, closed Wed and 15-30 Sep. Seafood: taglioni with fish ragù, fritto misto mare, 25/30,000.

♦♦ ***Teresina,*** v. Trento, ☎ 81108, closed Wed except summer and Jan. Terrace with sea view. Seafood: tagliolini with cuttlefish ink, fried dishes, 35/45,000.

♦♦ ***Trattoria del Gallo,*** v. Baldini 21, ☎ 81067, closed Wed and Oct-Nov. Seafood: spaghetti with clams and orange, polenta with cuttlefish, 40/55,000.

Recommended

Events: *antiques fair* (Jul); *Festa di Garibaldi* (early Aug).
Marina: ☎ 81094.
Technical tourism: *Ferroni* printing house, v. Fiorentini 55, ☎ 80377 (pictures printed by traditional Romagnese process); *Briganti* workshop, at Bagnarola, v. Cesenàtico 880, ☎ 311151 (oak barrels).
Wine: Enoteca *Domus Popilia-Ca' del Pasador,* v. Mazzini 180, ☎ 76548.

GATTEO A MARE, ⊠ 47043, ☎ 0541.

≋

ⓘ p. della Libertà, ☎ 86083.

Hotel:

★★ ***Simon,*** v. Matteotti 41, ☎ 85224, 47 rm [P] ▭ 🎾 closed 21 Sep-9 Oct and 31 Oct-28 Feb, 60,000; bkf: 3,500.

⛺ ★★★ *Delle Rose,* SS 16 at 186-km marker, 400 pl, ☎ 86213.

LIDO ADRIANO, ⊠ 48020, ☎ 0544.

≋

ⓘ v. Parini, ☎ 494086.

Recommended

Skating: v. Tasso 77, ☎ 494110.

LIDO DEGLI ESTENSI, ⊠ 44024, ☎ 0533.

≋

ⓘ v. Carducci 147, ☎ 327464.

Hotels:

★★★ ***Conca del Lido,*** v. Pascoli 42, ☎ 327459, 63 rm [P] ▭ closed Oct-Apr, 42,000; bkf: 5,000.

★★★ ***Tropicana,*** v. Foscolo 2, ☎ 327301, 65 rm [P] 🌳 ▭ closed Oct-Easter, 53,500, bkf: 6,000.

Restaurant:

♦♦♦ ***Casa Bianca,*** strada Romea 35, ☎ 327460, closed Tue and 2-30 Jan. In a pine wood. Mixed cuisine: seafood risotto, game with polenta, 25/30,000.

LIDO DEGLI SCACCHI, ⊠ 44020, ☎ 0533.

≋

ⓘ v. Montenero, ☎ 380342 (in season only).

LIDO DELLE NAZIONI, ⊠ 44020, ☎ 0533.

≋

ⓘ ☎ 89068 (in season only).

Hotel:

★★★ ***Quadrifoglio,*** v. Inghilterra 2, ☎ 39185, 68 rm [P] 🌳 ♿ ▭ closed 16 Oct-31 Mar, 55,000; bkf: 6,000.

⛺ ★★★★ *Tahiti,* v. Libia 133, 460 pl, ☎ 39500.

Recommended

Young people's activities: birdwatching on horseback, apply to the tourist village *Spiaggia Romea,* v. Oasi 2, ☎ 355130.

LIDO DI POMPOSA, ⊠ 44020, ☎ 0533.

≋

ⓘ v. Dolomiti, ☎ 380228 (in season only).

Hotel:

★★ ***Lido,*** v. Mare Adriatico 23, ☎ 88136, 44 rm [P] closed 21 Sep-Easter, 41,500.

⛺ ★★★ *Tre Moschettieri,* v. Acciaiuoli, 731 pl, ☎ 380376.

LIDO DI SAVIO, ⊠ 48020, ☎ 0544.

≋

ⓘ v. Romagna 166, ☎ 949063 (in season only).

Hotels:

★★★ ***Adler,*** at Lido di Classe, v. Caboto 121, ☎ 939216, 76 rm [P] 🌳 🚫 ▭ closed Oct-Apr, 43,000; bkf: 6,000.

★★★ ***Astor,*** at Lido di Classe, v. F.lli Vivaldi 94, ☎ 939437, 24 rm [P] 🌳 closed 21 Sep-19 May, 45,000; bkf: 8,000.

★★★ ***Concord,*** v. Russi 1, ☎ 949115, 55 rm [P] 🌳 ▭ 🎾 closed 16 Sep-19 May, 51,000; bkf: 4,000.

★★★ ***Mediterraneo,*** v. Sarsina 11, ☎ 949018, 80 rm [P] 🌳 closed 16 Sep-14 May, 50,000.

★★★ ***Rossi's,*** v. Lavezzola 2, ☎ 949001, 35 rm [P] 🌳 closed 1 Oct-14 May, 50,000; bkf: 12,000.

★★ ***Asiago Beach,*** v. Romagna 217, ☎ 949187, 40 rm [P] 🌳 🎾 closed Nov-Mar, 44,000; bkf: 7,000.

LIDO DI SPINA, ⊠ 44024, ☎ 0533.

≋

ⓘ ☎ 330250 (in season only).

Hotels:

★★★ ***Caravel,*** v. Leonardo 56, ☎ 330106, 22 rm [P] 🌳 ♿ closed Christmas, 49,000; bkf: 7,000.

★★★ ***Continental,*** v. Tintoretto 19, ☎ 330120, 41 rm [P] 🌳 closed 1 Oct- 19 May, 50,000; bkf: 6,000.

LIDO DI VOLANO, ⊠ 44020, ☎ 0533.

≋

ⓘ v. Imperiale 11, ☎ 85115 (in season only).

Recommended

Nature park: *Foce di Volano* nature reserve, information at FAI Milan, ☎ 02/4693693.

MARINA DI RAVENNA, ⊠ 48023, ☎ 0544.

≋

ⓘ v. delle Nazioni 159, ☎ 430117.

Hotels:

★★★★ ***Park Hotel Ravenna,*** v. delle Nazioni 181, ☎ 431743, 146 rm [P] 🌳 ▭ 🎾 closed Nov-Mar, 155,000.

★★★ ***Bermuda,*** v. della Pace 363, ☎ 430560, 17 rm 🌳 🚫 closed 20 Dec-31 Jan, 38,000; bkf: 6,000.

★★★ ***Maddalena,*** v. delle Nazioni 345, ☎ 430431, 32 rm 🌳 closed 15 Oct-15 Nov, 38,000; bkf: 4,000.

★★★ ***Marepineta,*** v. delle Nazioni 215, ☎ 430147, 54 rm [P] 🌳 closed 16 Nov-28 Feb, 46,000.

★★ ***Belvedere,*** v. Lungomare 59, ☎ 430113, 36 rm [P] 🌳 closed 15 Dec-15 Feb, 46,000.

⛺ ★★★ *Piomboni,* v. delle Pace 421, 490 pl, ☎ 430230.

Recommended

Events: *national painting contest* (end Aug-Sep).
Horseback riding: *Gruppo ippico La Piallassa,* v. Trieste, ☎ 431880 (associate of *ANTE*).
Marina: (Porto Corsini) *Circolo motovelico,* ☎ 431162; *Circolo velico,* ☎ 430513; *Centro velico Punta Marina,* ☎ 437153.
Sailing school: *Lega Navale,* molo Dalmazia 89, ☎ 430513.

MARINA ROMEA, ⊠ 48023, ☎ 0544.

≋

ⓘ v. Italia 112, ☎ 446035.

Hotels:

★★★ ***Colombia,*** v. Italia 70, ☎ 446038, 44 rm [P] 🌳 ▭ closed Oct-Mar, 50,000; bkf: 5,000.

★★★ ***Corallo,*** v. Italia 102, ☎ 446107, 82 rm 🌳 ▭ closed Sep-May, 54,000; bkf: 6,000.

★★★ ***Royal,*** v. Ferrara 25, ☎ 446227, 40 rm [P] 🌳 closed 16 Sep-30 Apr, 46,000; bkf: 5,000.

MISANO ADRIATICO, ⊠ 47046, ☎ 0541.

≋

ⓘ v. Platani 22, ☎ 615520.

Hotels:

★★★★ ***Gala,*** v. Pascoli 8, ☎ 615109, 27 rm [P] 🌳 ♿ closed Oct-Apr, 90,000; bkf: 10,000.

★★★ **Savoia,** v. della Repubblica 1, ☎ 615319, 85 rm Ⓟ
🦌 closed Oct-Easter, 55,000; bkf: 5,000.

Recommended
Horseback riding: *Batex ranch,* v. Settembrini 51.
Marina: *Yachting club Porto Verde,* ☎ 614503.
Motor racing: *Santamonica* track; management, *Automotorsport,* ☎ 615159.

PORTO GARIBALDI, ⊠ 44029, ☎ 0533.
≋
ℹ v. dei Mille, ☎ 327580 (in season only).

Restaurants:
● ♦♦♦ **Sambuco,** v. Caduti del Mare 30, ☎ 327478, closed Mon and 10 Nov-10 Dec. Elegant and secluded, shaded by leafy elders in summer. Excellent seafood: spaghetti with clams, scampi kebab, 50/60,000.
♦♦ **Europa,** p. 5 Maggio, ☎ 327362, closed Fri and Sep. Facing the sea. Seafood: fritto misto, grilled fish, 35/40,000.

PUNTA MARINA, ⊠ 48020, ☎ 0544.
≋
⚓ (May-Oct), ☎ 437222.
ℹ v. delle Fontana 4, ☎ 437312.

SAN MAURO A MARE, ⊠ 47030, ☎ 0541.
≋
ℹ p. C. Battisti 4, ☎ 49344.

SAVIO, ⊠ 48020, ☎ 0544.

Restaurant:
♦♦♦ **Gramadora,** SS Adriatica at 163-km marker, ☎ 60530, closed Mon and Jan. Mixed cuisine: penne all'arrabbiata, grilled meat, 30/40,000.

SALSOMAGGIORE TERME*

Parma 32, Bologna 129, Milan 113 km
Pop. 18,035 ⊠ 43039 ☎ 0524   B1-2

One of the most celebrated spas in Italy, it sits in a verdant setting in the lower foothills of the Parmesan Apennines.

▶ Its **waters** have been appreciated since ancient times (drainage channels existed in 2C BC) as a source of salt, and have been used as a thermal cure since the middle of the last century. Cures are offered by the **Terme Bezieri**, an Art Nouveau building (1923), the modern **Terme Zoia** and several hotels. ▶ The main recreational spot is the **Poggio Diana**, a hilltop garden equipped with sports facilities.

Environs

▶ 5.5 km E is **Tabiano Bagni**, another spa. ▶ 3.3 km NW, on the strada Salsediana, is **Scipione**, a fortified village on a pass, with a castle dating from the 12C. ▶ At 5.5 km, turning I. toward Tabiano, is **Bargone**, with another castle dating from the 12C. ▶ 1 km W, on the other side of the River Stirone, is **Vigoleno**, a village which has preserved its medieval architecture, and a 12C castle and Romanesque parish church. ☐

Practical information _____

SALSOMAGGIORE TERME
⚓ (all year), ☎ 78201.
ℹ v. Romagnosi 7, ☎ 78265.

Hotels:
★★★★★ (L) **Grand Hotel & Milano,** v. Dante 1, ☎ 770141, 119 rm Ⓟ ░ 🗔 closed 11 Nov-31 Mar. Art Nouveau building with some fine public rooms, 180,000.
★★★★ **Cristallo,** v. Matteotti 5 bis, ☎ 77241, 73 rm Ⓟ ░ closed Dec-Mar except Christmas, 85,000.
★★★★ **Excelsior,** v. Berenini 3, ☎ 70641, 54 rm Ⓟ 🦌 Pens. closed 11 Nov-19 Apr, 70,000.
★★★★ **G.A. Centrale Bagni,** largo Roma 4, ☎ 771142, 93 rm Ⓟ ░ closed Nov-Apr, 80,000; bkf: 6,500.

★★★★ **G.H. Porro,** v. Porro 10, ☎ 78221, 85 rm Ⓟ ░ ░░
🗔 Pens. closed Jan-Feb, 118,000.
★★★★ **Roma,** v. Mascagni 10, ☎ 71171, 24 rm Ⓟ ░ &. closed 16 Nov-31 Mar, 64,000.
★★★ **Brescia,** v. Romagnosi 1, ☎ 72117, 32 rm 🦌 closed Dec-Mar, 45,000; bkf: 5,000.
★★★ **De la Ville,** p. Garibaldi 1, ☎ 72126, 40 rm 🦌 closed 21 Dec-14 Mar, 44,000; bkf: 4,000.
★★★ **Suisse,** v. Porro 5, ☎ 79077, 23 rm Ⓟ ░░ 🦌 closed 11 Nov-19 Mar, 53,000; bkf: 5,000.
★★★ **Valentini,** v. Porro 10, ☎ 78251, 127 rm Ⓟ ░ ░░ 🗔 Pens. closed 21 Nov-9 Mar, 78,000.
★★★ **Villa Fiorita,** v. Milano 2, ☎ 77842, 43 rm Ⓟ ░░ closed 1 Nov-24 Apr, 50,000; bkf: 5,000.
★★ **Rex Egisto Jr,** v. Porro 37, ☎ 71281, 27 rm Ⓟ ░░ 🦌 closed Dec-Feb, 41,000; bkf: 5,000.

Restaurants:
♦♦♦ **Tartufo,** v. Marconi 32, ☎ 72296, closed Mon and Feb. Flower garden and belvedere terrace. Outstanding cuisine: cappelletti with truffles, stuffed chicken alla parmigiana, 35/45,000.
♦♦♦ **Vecchio Parco,** v. Parma 95, ☎ 71292, closed Tue and Jan. Former country house in ancient park. Regional cuisine: cheese pancakes, escalope forestiera, 28/35,000.

⚘ ★★★ *Arizona,* v. Tabiano 40, 250 pl, ☎ 66141.

Recommended
Events: *musical, cinematographic, cultural and sporting events,* particularly in spring and autumn.
Farm vacations: *Azienda Antica Torre Congelasio,* ☎ 70425.
Swimming: v. Porro, ☎ 79495.

Environs

TABIANO BAGNI, ⊠ 43030, ☎ 0524.
⚓ (Mar-Nov), ☎ 66221.
ℹ v. delle Fonti 1, ☎ 66245 (in season only).

Hotels:
★★★★ **Farnese,** v. Terme 1, ☎ 66127, 60 rm Ⓟ ░ &. closed 21 Nov-31 Mar, 40,500; bkf: 6,000.
★★★★ **G.A. Astro** v. Castello 2, ☎ 66523, 113 rm Ⓟ 120,000; bkf: 10,000.
★★★ **Pandos,** v. delle Fonti 15, ☎ 66234, 63 rm Ⓟ ░ ░░ closed 5 Nov-31 Mar, 49,000; bkf: 7,000.
★★★ **Napoleon,** v. Terme 11 bis, ☎ 66621, 48 rm Ⓟ 🦌 closed Dec-Feb, 48,000; bkf: 5,000.
★★★ **Rossini,** v. delle Fonti 10, ☎ 66425, 57 rm Ⓟ ░ ░░ closed Dec-Feb, 40,000; bkf: 3,000.

SAN CESARIO SUL PANARO

Modena 17, Bologna 27, Milan 187 km
Pop. 4,975 ⊠ 41018 ☎ 059   C2

The village is on the r. bank of the River Panàro, amid vineyards and orchards.

▶ It has a 15C crenellated tower (**Torre dell'Orologio**), and the remains of a medieval fortress. There is also the parish church of **S. Cesario★**, an important Romanesque building of the 12C, with traces of the earlier 10C-11C church, once part of a Benedictine monastery. The campanile dates from 1544. The interior has a nave and two aisles, with fine capitals, the work of Antonio Begarelli (1525) and a tomb of Count Gian Boschetti. ▶ Beside the church is the **Palazzo dei Boschetti** (15C-18C) with a large park. ☐

Practical information _____

Recommended
Clay pigeon shooting: v. per Spilamberto, ☎ 930105.

Looking for a locality? Consult the index at the back of the book.

SAN MARINO*

Bologna 139, Milan 357, Rome 355 km
Pop. 4,516 ⊠ 47031 ☎ 0541   F4

Travelers heading S by road or rail from Emilia-Romagna toward the Marches or heading N on the same route will at once notice Mt. Titano (2,456 ft), a distinctive outcrop of the Apennines at the southernmost end of the Po plain. On the gently sloping extremities of this mountain lies San Marino, the capital of the oldest republic in Europe. According to tradition, it was founded at the beginning of the 4C by Marino, a stonemason from the Dalmatian island of Arbe (today called Rab), fleeing from persecution by Diocletian with his companion Leo (said to be the founder of neighbouring San Leo). Already a free city-state by the 11C, with its status acknowledged even by Napoleon and the Council of Vienna, this tiny republic of some 25 sq. mi. has succeeded in retaining its independence and its own republican institutions to this day. It is therefore not just a historical curiosity, with its own stamps and coinage, but also a symbol of political freedom. Nowadays it is also the focus of considerable tourist attention.

▶ Entering the city by the Porta di S. Francesco (A1; 1451), the visitor immediately sees the church of **S. Francesco,** which, although redone in the 17C-18C, preserves traces of its original 14C construction. In the building next door is a small **pinacoteca** *(for admission times, → the Museo e Pinacoteca di Stato),* which contains an *Adoration of the Magi,* an early 15C fresco by painters from the Marches; *The Stigmata of St. Francis*★ by Guercino; and a *St. Francis* by Titian. ▶ V. Carducci, which connects the piazzetta del Titano to the 15C Porta della Rupe, is lined with elegant houses of the 16C - 17C. One of these, Palazzo Valloni (no. 141), houses the **Museo e Pinacoteca di Stato** (A1, *open 25 Jun-23 Nov; 8 a.m.-8 p.m.* or *8:30 a.m.-12:45 p.m.* and *2:45-5:30,*

SAN MARINO

0   100   200 m

1 : 14.000 (1 cm = 140 m)

2

6:30 or *7 p.m., according to the time of year),* containing paintings (including works by Guercino, Tintoretto and Domenichino); prehistoric, Etruscan and Roman artifacts; Italo-Greek and Egyptian pottery and figurines; and mementos of Garibaldi. ▶ The hub of the city is the **Piazza della Libertà** (A1), with a panoramic view of the Apennines. At one end is the **Palazzo Pubblico,** or Palazzo del Governo, built at the end of the last century in a 14C Gothic style and inaugurated with a famous speech by Giosuè Carducci; it has a magnificent interior. ▶ A little above the piazza is the Neoclassical basilica of **S. Marino** (1836). ▶ On the very top of Mt. Titano, overlooking the plain, are the three towers of San Marino *(for admission times, → the Museo e Pinacoteca di Stato).* The first, known as the **Rocca,** or Guaita, (A2), dates from the 11C, but was rebuilt in the 15C; the second, **Cesta** (B2), was built in the 13C on a peak 2,420 ft high, offering a vast panorama★, and contains a collection of weapons, the **Museo delle Armi Antichi;** the third, **Montale,** also 13C, is an isolated spot, surrounded by oak scrub. ▶ At the foot of Mt. Titano and at the point of access to San Marino at **Borgo Maggiore** is the old Mercatale which dates from the 12C and is still an important commercial centre. This is also the site of the **Musei delle Armi da Fuoco, Numismatico Filatelico e Postale.** □

Practical information

① palazzo del Turismo (A1), ☎ 992101; at Dogana, ☎ 905414.

Hotels:
★★★★ **G. H. S. Marino,** v. Onofri 31 (A-B2 a), ☎ 992401, 59 rm ℗ ⊰ 戍 closed 16 Nov-14 Mar, 68,000; bkf: 6,000.
★★★★ **Joli San Marino,** v. F. d'Urbino 233 (B2 b), ☎ 991009, 24 rm ℗ ⅋ closed 20 Dec-20 Feb, 49,000; bkf: 5,000.
★★★★ **Titano,** contrada del Collegio 21, (A1 c), ☎ 991006, 50 rm ℗ ⊰ closed 16 Nov-14 Mar, 52,000; bkf: 5,500.
★★★ **Diamond,** contrada del Collegio (A1-2 d), ☎ 991003, 7 rm closed Nov-Feb, 46,000.
★★★ **Excelsior,** v. Istriani (B2 e), ☎ 991940, 26 rm ℗ ⊰ ⊞ 43,000; bkf: 4,000.
★★★ **Quercia Antica,** v. Cella Bella 241 (B2 f), ☎ 991257, 27 rm ℗ ⊰ 45,000; bkf: 4,000.
★★ **Tre Penne,** v. Lapicidi Marini (A2 g), ☎ 992437, 12 rm, 45,000; bkf: 6,000.

Restaurants:
♦♦♦ **Righi-la Taverna,** p. Libertà (A1 i), ☎ 991196, closed Wed and Christmas-15 Feb. Regional cuisine: tortellacci with butter and sage, strozzapreti al sugo matto, 20/35,000.
♦ **Buca San Francesco,** p. Feretrano 3 (A1 h), ☎ 991462, closed Fri in winter and 15 Nov-15 Dec. Regional cuisine: lasagne verde al forno, escalope with cheese, 15/20,000.
⚓ **Murata,** at Murata, v. del Serrone 594/65, 120 pl (open all year), ☎ 991299.

Recommended
Clay pigeon shooting: at Murata, ☎ 991290.
Conference centre: v. Kennedy, ☎ 991421.
Events: *ceremonial investiture of the Capitani Reggenti and historical procession* (1 Apr and 1 Oct); *Palio della Balestra Antica* (3 Sep, anniversary of the foundation of the republic).
Motocross: *Baldasserona* track, at Borgo Maggiore, ☎ 902606; *Federazione Motociclistica,* ☎ 902653.
Swimming: at Borgo Maggiore, v. Tavolucci, ☎ 903354.

SANTARCANGELO DI ROMAGNA

Forlì 38, Bologna 104, Milan 315 km
Pop. 16,277 ⊠ 47038 ☎ 0541   F3

On the S edges of the Romagnese plain, this small town consists of a modern quarter, on the plain, and a medieval quarter, on a hilltop called the Monte di

Giove (288 ft). The medieval section is still virtually intact, with winding alleyways, arches and old windows.

▶ In p. Ganganelli, the traditional site of the market, is the **triumphal arch** erected in 1772 in honour of Pope Clement XIV, who was born here; also, the Neoclassical Palazzo Comunale. ▶ Higher up, on the l., is the 18C **collegiate church**, containing a fine polyptych by Jacobello da Bonomo (1385), and paintings by Guido Cagnacci (17C), a local painter. ▶ On the crest of the hill is the quadrilateral **rocca**, with corner towers, built by the Malatesta family in the 13C-14C. Inside *(Jun-Sep, Tue, Thu and Sat 10 a.m.-12 noon and 4-7 p.m.)*, where the tragedy of Dante's Paolo and Francesca is said to have taken place, there are rooms furnished with well-preserved 17C furniture. ▶ On the slopes of the hilltop are a number of manmade **caves**, supposedly dug by monks during the Byzantine period *(for admission, ☎ 624103)*. ▶ At v. Montevecchi 41 is a folk museum, the **Museo degli Usi e Costumi della Gente Romagnola** *(9 a.m.-12 noon and 4-6 p.m.; Sat 9 a.m.-12 noon and 3-7 p.m.; Sun and hols 3-7 p.m.; closed Mon)*.

Environs

▶ About 1 km along the road to Novafeltria is the church of **S. Michele**, an early Christian building of the 6C, one of the few surviving examples of Ravenna architecture in S Romagna. ▶ 12 km SW is **San Giovanni in Galilea**, in a superb panoramic position on a hill, inhabited even during prehistoric times. The **Castello Malatestiano** (13C-15C) houses the **Museo Archeologico**, containing mainly prehistoric and Roman artifacts *(for admission see caretaker in v. Castello)*. ☐

Practical information ⁄⁄

Restaurant:
♦ **Zaghini,** p. Gramsci 14, ☎ 626136, closed Mon except summer. Regional cuisine: cannelloni, rabbit in porchetta, 17/30,000.

Recommended
Events: *international theatre festival,* in the piazza, ☎ 626480 (Jul).

SARSINA

Forli 49, Bologna 115, Rome 303 km
Pop. 4,042 ⊠ 47027 ☎ 0547   E4

The ancient ruins and pointed pyramids of the tombs here still speak of the town's past as the old capital of the Umbrians, on the N slopes of the Apennines, in the valley of the River Savio. Conquered by the Romans in 266 BC, Sarsina was the birthplace (254 BC) of Plautus, the great comic poet and playwright.

▶ Overlooking the p. Plauto, which corresponds to the **forum** of the Roman city (remains are visible nearby), is the **cathedral**, originally Romanesque but subsequently remodeled. ▶ Of particular interest is the **Museo Archeologico Sarsinate** *(summer 9 a.m.-1 p.m. and 3-6 p.m.; winter 9 a.m.-2 p.m.; Sun and hols 9 a.m.-1 p.m.; closed Mon)*, which contains artifacts from excavations of the ancient city, among which are the famous pointed Roman **tombs★** of the 1C BC. One of these tombs has been reconstructed in the Parco della Rimembranza, on the main road. ☐

Practical information _____

Hotel:
★★ **Piano,** v. S. Martino 691, ☎ 94848, 15 rm ℗ 🔍 🎖
🍽 ☐ ⤴ closed 1-15 Oct, 39,000; bkf: 2,500.

Recommended
Events: *performances from the classics in honour of Plautus* (Jul-Aug); *Sagra di S. Vinicio* (end Aug).

SASSUOLO

Modena 17, Bologna 56, Milan 187 km
Pop. 39,718 ⊠ 41049 ☎ 0536   C2

The ceramics industry, and in particular the production of **tiles,** has given impetus to the recent industrial growth of this town.

▶ In v. Cavallotti is the **Mostra Permanente della Ceramica Italiana** *(8:30 a.m.-12:30 p.m. and 2:30-6:30 p.m.; closed Sun and hols)*. ▶ On the site of the old fortress stands the magnificent **Palazzo degli Estensi**, now the Military Academy of Modena, built in the 17C by Bartolomeo Avanzini. ▶ 3 km S is the spa **Terme della Salvarola**. ☐

Practical information _____

♨ (Apr-Nov), at Terme della Salvarola, ☎ 872115.

SCANDIANO

Reggio nell'Emilia 12, Bologna 64, Milan 162 km
Pop. 21, 615 ⊠ 42019 ☎ 0522   C2

This charming little town, with its silhouette of towers and castle set against the backdrop of hills, is famous for having been the feudal domain of the Boiardo family, whose most renowned son was Matteo Maria Boiardo, author of *L'Orlando Innamorato*. The Italian physiologist, Lazzaro Spallanzani, was also born here.

▶ The town grew around the **rocca** built in 1262 by Gilberto Fogliani and rebuilt during the Renaissance by Giovanni Boiardo. Giulio Boiardo commissioned Nicolò dell'Abate to paint the castle's frescos in 1540 (*Verses from the Aeneid* and others), which were detached in 1772 and taken to Modena, where they can be seen in the Galleria Estense. ☐

Practical information _____

Restaurant:
♦♦ **Portone,** p. Boiardo 4, ☎ 855985, closed Tue, 15 Jul-15 Aug and Christmas. Italian cuisine: cappalletti in brodo, guinea fowl in balsam vinegar, 35/45,000.

TERRA DEL SOLE

Forli 9, Bologna 72, Milan 291 km
⊠ 47010 ☎ 0543   E3

This citadel was founded in 1564 on the instructions of Cosimo I. It is at the extreme NE borders of the Tuscan Grand Duchy and still retains its original form and almost all of its surrounding 16C **walls**. Additional passages were made through the walls in the late 19C to complement the original two gates, Romana and Fiorentina, which are surmounted by two **castles**, del Capitano di Piazza and del Capitano dell'Artiglieria. In the central p. Garibaldi are the church of **S. Reparata** (1594), the **Palazzo del Provveditore,** with its pure Tuscan lines, and, opposite, the **Palazzo dei Commissari,** designed by Buontalenti. A road connects Terra del Sole to Castrocaro Terme (→), the seat of this commune. ☐

Practical information _____

Recommended
Farm vacations: *Podere Orto Pantani,* v. Sacco e Vanzetti, ☎ 767501.

VERUCCHIO

Forlì 52, Bologna 125, Milan 336 km
Pop. 6,525 ⊠ 47040 ☎ 0541   F3-4

Formerly called the 'eyes' of Romagna; because of its altitude, it was an ideal place from which to survey the countryside during troubled times. It is from this precipitous height *(verucca)* that the powerful Malesta family came. They were to descend from here to Rimini.

▶ On an isolated crag stands the **Rocca Malatestiana,** restored in 1449 by Sigismondo, overlord of Rimini, *(summer 9 a.m.-12 noon and 2-7 p.m.; winter Sun only 10 a.m.-12 noon and 2-6 p.m.).* In the central room is an interesting museum, the **Museo Preistorico e Lapidario.** ▶ The collegiate church of **SS. Martino e Francesco d'Assisi** contains a 14C crucifix of the Rimini school. ▶ 1 km S of the nearby **Villa Verucchio** is the old Franciscan **monastery** which, according to tradition, was founded by St. Francis himself in 1215; in the cloister, towering above the walls of the buildings, stands the huge **cypress tree★**, said to have been planted by St. Francis (several botanists believe it to pre-date him). □

Practical information _____

Restaurants:
● ◆◆ *Rò e Buni,* at Villa Verucchio, v. Mulino Bianco, ☎ 678484, closed Mon, Jul-Aug at noon, Jan and Sep-Oct. In a 16C mill turned into an authentic rural trattoria. Excellent regional cuisine: shin of mutton, kebabs, 20/25,000.
◆ *Zanni,* at Villa Verucchio, v. Casale 171, ☎ 678449, closed Fri. Regional cuisine: strozzapreti, mixed grills, 20/26,000.

VIGNOLA

Modena 22, Bologna 33, Milan 192 km
Pop. 19,906 ⊠ 41058 ☎ 059   C2

One of the most beautiful castles in Emilia, built 1401-35, dominates this town at the point where the River Panàro drops down to the plain of Modena. This was the birthplace of the great 16C architect Jacopo Barozzi, known as Il Vignola, and the historian Ludovico Antonio Muratori. Today, it is famous for its cherries.

▶ Inside the **rocca** *(wkdays 9 a.m.-12 noon and 3-6 p.m.; Sun and hols 10 a.m.-12 noon and 3-6 p.m.; closed Mon)* is a chapel and several rooms with 15C **frescos;** out of

the courtyard rises a tall **tower,** a relic of the earlier castle, which was built here to survey the surrounding lands in defense of the territory belonging to the abbey of Nonantola (→). ▶ The **Palazzo Boncompagni** (16C-17C) is famous for its internal ovoid **staircase.** ▶ 2 km W on the road to Marano sul Panàro is an old Romanesque **parish church,** restored. ▶ 12 km SW, in a panoramic position overlooking the valley of the Panàro, lies **Guiglia,** a country vacation spot. □

Practical information _____

VIGNOLA

Restaurant:
◆◆◆ *Sagittario,* at Campiglio, ☎ 772747, closed Tue-Wed. Regional cuisine: penne with asparagus, ravioli with gorgonzola and walnuts, 20/25,000.

Environs

GUIGLIA, ⊠ 41052, ☎ 059.

Recommended
Nature park: *Riserva dei Sassi di Roccamalatina,* offices in the town hall, ☎ 792412. □

ZOCCA

Modena 48, Bologna 57, Milan 218 km
Pop. 4,164 ⊠ 41059 ☎ 059   C3

On the spur that separates the valley of the Panàro from that of the Samoggia, set among chestnut trees, this is a summer vacation centre in the Modenese Apennines.

▶ About 8 km NW, near Rocca Malatina, are the **Sassi della Rocca,** giant yellow sandstone monoliths, resembling turrets as a result of water erosion. Some 2 km further is **Pieve Trebbio** where there is the fine Romanesque church of **S. Giovanni Battista** (9C-10C) and an octagonal baptistery. □

Practical information _____

ⓘ Palazzo comunale, ☎ 987073.

Hotel:
★★★ *Joli,* v. della Pineta 20, ☎ 987429, 37 rm ℗ ⋵ ⋙ &. ⊗ closed Sep-Oct, 45,000; bkf: 5,000.
⚠ ★★★ *Montequestiolo,* v. Montequestiolo 184, 77 pl, ☎ 987764 (all year).

Recommended
Fencing: *Centro sportivo estivo internationale* (men); information: *Federazione italiana Scherma,* Rome ☎ 06/36851.

Florence

▶ Florence, in the fertile valley of the Arno, lies on both banks of the river, at the foot of the Fiesole hills. The meaning of its name — City of Flowers — is very appropriate, because flowers grow in abundance in its gardens and fields. Originally Florence was confined within two circles of walls (the inner built *c.* 800 AD and the outer in medieval times) of which only a few towers remain. The city has long since spread beyond these and, with its river, bridges, cupolas, market places, fine squares, streets and boulevards, it is a marvelous sight, especially if seen from the Piazzale Michelangelo, the highest point of the Viale dei Colli. Near the Ponte Vecchio — the oldest bridge in Florence (1345) — the banks of the Arno are lined with goldsmiths', silversmiths' and jewelers' shops as well as with those of craftsmen working in leather, skins, embroidery, straw and carved furniture — all trades for which the skilled artisans of the city are renowned. From the 12C to the 15C Florence surpassed architecturally every other city in Italy, and it was only after the monk-reformer Savonarola (1452-98) denounced the profligacy of its rulers that a decline set in and the leadership of the arts passed to Rome. During these three hundred years some of the greatest architects of all time lived in Florence — men like Arnolfo di Cambio (the Duomo), Giotto (the Campanile), Michelozzo (the Medici Palace), Alberti (the Rucellai Palace) and above all Brunelleschi (the vast span of the dome of S. Maria del Fiore) — and worked on the great masterpieces which are the glory of the city today. Englishmen of rank and substance, doing the grand tour in the 18C, were the first to discover the splendour of Florence and the pleasure of living in this imposing city of old stone, among the cypress, pine and olive of the surrounding hills from which the ever-changing Arno flows down. Since then the whole world has followed, and tourism is the city's principal industry. ☐

● Don't miss

Piazza del Duomo★ with S. Maria del Fiore★★, the Baptistery★★ and the Campanile★★. Piazza della Signoria★★ and the Palazzo Vecchio★★. The Galleria degli Uffizi★★. S. Lorenzo★★ and the Cappelle Medicee★★. The Ponte Vecchio★★, the Palazzo Pitti★★ and its collections, the Boboli Gardens★★, S. Spirito★★, the Masaccio frescos★★ in S. Maria del Carmine★, the Palazzo Strozzi★★, S. Maria Novella★★, the Museo S. Marco or dell'Angelico★★, Michelangelo's David★★ in the Galleria dell'Accademia★, the Museo Nazionale del Bargello★★, S. Croce★★ and the Cappella Pazzi★, S. Miniato al Monte★★ and the view of Florence from the piazzale Michelangelo.

Facts and figures

Location: Capital of the region of Tuscany, 275 km from Rome and 300 km from Milan.
Area and Population: The city administration extends over an area of 102.41 sq km with a population of 440,910 inhabitants.
Postal code: 50100.
Dialing code: 055.

232

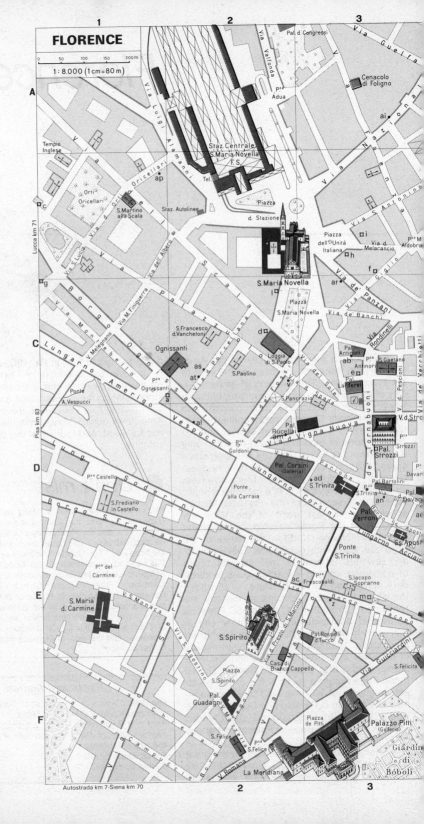

FLORENCE

0 50 100 150 200 m

1:8.000 (1cm=80m)

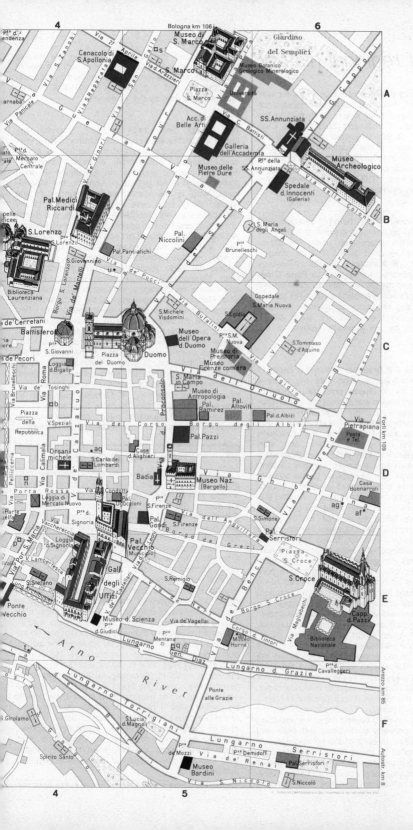

● *Brief regional history*

1C BC-5C AD

Florentia. The old **Roman colony** of Florentia was on a site on which there had been settlements since the dawn of history. After it was destroyed in the Civil War between Marius and Sulla, Julius Caesar rebuilt it, in 59 BC, to protect the ford of the Arno. ● The square of the Roman town extended from the N side of the Duomo to the middle of the piazza della Signoria, and from the via Tornabuoni to the via del Proconsolo. The pattern of streets in the centre still follows the Roman grid.

6C-11C

Medieval Florence. After being besieged and sacked during the barbarian invasions of Italy, Florence rose to some importance under the **Carolingians** and was included in the Tuscan margravate (princedom). ● **Matilda,** Countess of Tuscany (1046-1115), bequeathed her estates to **Pope Gregory VII** in 1077, and the papacy claimed them on her death. As a result Florence became a source of conflict between popes and emperors or between **Guelphs** and **Ghibellines,** as their followers were called, and was plagued by the constant feuding of the two sides.

12C-15C

The comune and the republic. After the death of Matilda, the Florentines declared their city to be a **comune,** headed by an elected **podestà** (Captain of the People). They waged war against the feudal landlords whose castles were in the neighbourhood, forcing them to become citizens of Florence and to live for a certain time each year in the city. Gradually they threw off the rule of the emperor and, after the death of Frederick II, they proclaimed Florence a **republic.** ● The executive power, formerly residing in the podestà, was now transferred to the **priori** (a governing group of eight elected members) and to the **gonfaloniere** (the chief magistrate). Around this time Florence, which had been a Guelph city, siding with the pope ever since the days of Matilda, joined with others to form the **Tuscan League,** which fought against Ghibelline (pro-emperor) towns like Pisa and Siena. The Florentines, who were great traders, now formed themselves into **guilds** to which anyone wanting to hold public office had to belong. As a consequence a class of rich burghers came into being which soon divested the nobles of power and brought the city to the brink of civil war. The aristocrats and the populace which sided with them, became known as the **Blacks** (Neri) and the rich merchant class, which ran the government, the **Whites** (Bianchi). ● **Dante,** the great poet, who was a White, was elected a priore in the government which exiled the Black leaders. These went to Rome and appealed to the pope who was always ready to interfere in the affairs of the city. On the pretext of restoring order, the pontiff sent the French Prince Charles of Valois with an army into Florence. The Blacks followed, the government was overthrown and the priori, including Dante, had their property confiscated and were sent into perpetual exile. In spite of the fighting and suffering brought about by these feuds, Florence grew in splendour and prosperity as Florentine merchants visited foreign countries and established banks everywhere. ● Fine churches, palaces and libraries were built and the city soon became the leading centre of arts and letters in Europe. On the eve of the **Plague of 1348** (so vividly described by **Boccaccio**), the city had a population of 120,000. It was reduced by a third by the epidemic.

15C & 16C

The Medici. From 1414 to 1527, Florence was governed by the **Medici,** a rich banking family, and under them the city attained the summit of splendour. **Cosimo I** (1389-1464), a princely merchant, was very popular and rose to a position of great power, but it is his grandson, **Lorenzo the Magnificent,** who is the most famous member of the family. ● Lorenzo was even more lavish in his patronage than his grandfather had been, and it was under him and his successors that Florence became the leading Italian city of art and letters. ● Between 1420 and 1470, the greatest painters and sculptors in Italy, men like **Leonardo, Michelangelo,** the Lippis, Andrea del Sarto, Paolo Uccello, Fra Angelico, Botticelli, **Masaccio,** Antonio Pollaiolo, Benozzo Gozzoli and Andrea del Castagno, to mention but a few, were all in Florence working alongside the great architects whose names have already been mentioned. Two years after the death of Lorenzo, his son **Piero II** was forced to flee by **Fra Savonarola,** a reforming monk, and a new republican regime was proclaimed. The friar was overthrown and burnt at the stake, in the piazza della Signoria in 1498, and although the republic lasted for a further short period, this final outburst of democracy was quickly crushed when the imperial troops entered the city. ● Florence ceased to be independent and in 1532 became the capital of the **Grand-Duchy of Tuscany,** ruled once again by the Medici family who had now become Grand-Dukes.

The nose of David

The David which Michelangelo carved between 1501 and 1504 is today in the Galleria della Accademia and a copy stands on its original position, to the side of the door of the Palazzo della Signoria. According to Giorgio Vasari (1511-74), the art historian, the trustees responsible for the upkeep of the Duomo had in their yard a piece of marble nearly 18 ft long which a certain master Simone da Fiesole had ruined while attempting to carve it into a giant for the cathedral. Michelangelo asked if he could have it, 'thinking that anything he did with it would be better than leaving it unused'. The great sculptor carved his David as a symbol of the justice and energy of the government of Florence — then a republic after having expelled the Medici. When the figure was installed on its site and the sculptor was working on the scaffolding, the Gonfalonier, Pier Soderini, the highest authority in the republic and therefore the patron, appeared with his nose in the air and, while praising the statue, said to Michelangelo that 'it seemed to him that the nose of the figure was too big'. Michelangelo, who, when working for a client knew how to be patient, took a handful of marble dust and pretended to chisel away at the nose of David, allowing dust to trickle out of his hand. When the supposed finishing touch was complete, the Gonfalonier said, 'it pleases me more, you have given him life'. Vasari also tells that this unequalled masterpiece cost four hundred scudi.

16C-20C
Later Florentine history. The first of the Grand-Dukes was named **Cosimo,** like his ancestor who had established the Medici dynasty a century before, and the Grand-Duchy was ruled by members of the Medici family, almost without interruption, for a period of nearly two-and-a-half centuries. It was a time of stagnation, of decline, but also one of peace. ● In the end Florence and the Grand-Duchy were annexed by the French Empire (1808). ● In 1859 the city was united with Piedmont, and, from 1865 to 1871, until it was possible to move the seat of government to Rome, Florence became the capital of Italy. In the Second World War, South African troops reached the outskirts of the city on 4 August 1944, and on the 11th the Allies took Florence. ● The great monuments, most of which lie north of the river, escaped undamaged because, although the Germans held the north bank, the Allies deliberately refrained from shelling it. ● To hold up the Allied advance, the Germans blew up all the bridges over the Arno except the Ponte Vecchio but, to prevent it being crossed, they mined all the bank around it. The Allies crossed nevertheless, using mine detectors, and in the ensuing blasts most of the old city on the north bank around the Ponte Vecchio and many houses on the south side were destroyed or severely damaged. On the south side, much of **via de' Guicciardini,** from the Pitti Palace to the river, and the whole of the **famous view** looking up the river to the Ponte Vecchio, with the medieval houses reflected in the water, are gone forever, along with three towers. On the north side, the **Torre degli Amedei,** one of the best preserved of the Florentine towers, was destroyed. Among the palazzi lost were the **Acciaoli,** the **De Angelis** and the old houses around the Piazza del Pesce, right up to the church of S. Stefano. The calamities undergone by this marvelous city were not over when the war ended. In 1966 a disastrous flood once more caused severe damage to its artistic heritage. It has been possible to make good much of the damage, but there is still much restoration work to be done.

In the poets' footsteps

'I will sit on the left bank of the Arno, facing the Orient. This is where one finds the widest and most pleasant perspective.' So speaks Alfredo, the hero of Alfred de Musset's Lorenzaccio. *Musset was not the only writer seduced by Florence's charms. After a visit to the city in 1898, Rainer Maria Rilke decided to devote himself to poetry. Dostoïevsky spent a year writing* The Idiot *at 22, via Guicciardin. At number 16 on the same street once stood the house in which Machiavelli spent all his life. The Marquis de Sade preferred the enchanting Boboli Gardens to Florence's women whom he considered 'arrogant, impertinent, ugly, dirty and gluttonous'. The French writer Giono liked the city's boutiques and bistros as did D. H. Lawrence who wrote: 'The piazza della Signoria is the perfect centre of the human world'. Elizabeth Barrett Browning was laid to rest in the city's English cemetery and Stendhal's shadow still haunts the Colomero theatre. More recently, E. M. Forster's novel set in turn-of-the-century Florence inspired the film* Room With a View.

▶ Galleria dell'ACCADEMIA*
v. Ricasoli 60   A5

Established for study purposes in 1784 by Grand-Duke Pietro Leopoldo of Lorraine, who endowed the Accademia and its drawing schools with a number of old paintings, the Galleria *(presently being partly rearranged; 9 a.m.-2 p.m.; hols 9 a.m.-1 p.m.; closed Mon)* has an extensive collection of Florentine paintings from the 13C-19C which in several ways complements that of the Uffizi. However, it is not this heritage, nor the two works by **Botticelli,** that draw the huge crowds of visitors. These come, quite rightly, to see an extraordinary group of **Michelangelo** sculptures. There are seven in all, of varied provenance, and the most admired of them is *David*★★, the most famous male nude in the history of art, which exudes a calm and powerful beauty. It is a large statue (the figure is 13 ft 5 in high), which originally stood in front of the Palazzo Vecchio. However, in the last century it was transferred here to protect it from the weather and a copy has been placed on its original site in the square. In deciding at the beginning of the 16C to place it in the piazza della Signoria, the Florentine Republic made it the symbol of the city ready to defend itself against any enemy. The other works by Michelangelo comprise his unfinished *statue of St. Matthew,* which was intended for S. Maria del Fiore, the beautiful Palestrina Pietà★, and the four *Prisoners*★, which are finished only in part. It is precisely this unfinished quality which conveys to the viewer the sense of the struggle of form, i.e., that which is human and spiritual, to free itself from the dull matter that imprisons it. Among the Galleria's other treasures, there is the front of a marriage chest from a Florentine noble's house, the 15C *Adimari cassone,* on which is depicted an elegant and joyous wedding.   □

The Accademia della Crusca

The Accademia della Crusca, *one of the most famous of the many Italian academies, was founded in Florence in 1582 and is still in existence.* Crusca *means the bran that remains after the sifting of the flour. The Academy aimed at purifying and cultivating the Italian language and literature. Its coat of arms were a bolter with the motto, 'Pick the finest flower', where the word flower has a triple meaning — the literal one, the flour without the bran and the flower of the Italian language. Regarding this last meaning, the academicians, after 30 years' work, published in 1612 their great* Dictionary of the Academicians of the Crusca, *which still remains a model for works of its kind and on which the French Academy modeled its dictionary.*

▶ La BADIA*
v. del Proconsolo   D5

This is the church of an old Benedictine abbey dating back to the 10C. It retains, however, none of its original structure and little of the many transformations it underwent from the 13C onward. In its present form it dates largely from its extensive rebuilding in the 17C, when even its orientation was changed. It is entered from the v. del Proconsolo through a rich portal, with an enamelled terra-cotta tympanum. This leads to a portico and a small courtyard. Up to this point, each feature has been Renaissance, but before entering the church, to the r. there is a full view of the beautiful medieval (part Romanesque, part Gothic) campanile★ and spire. The quiet, sumptuous interior contains works such as Filippino Lippi's *Appearance of the Madonna to St. Bernard★*, one of the finest Florentine paintings of the 15C, and the *Monument to Ugo★*, Margrave of Tuscany (benefactor of the Badia and therefore of the city in the early 11C), which Florence commissioned from Mino da Fiesole in the 15C. The charming **chiostro degli Aranci** is entered from the sacristy and has an enchanting fresco cycle by the Portuguese artist Giovanni di Consalvo (15C) in the upper loggia depicting *The Life of St. Benedict.* □

▶ BAPTISTERY**
(Il Battistero)
p. S. Giovanni   C4

From the 12C onward the towns and villages which Florence gradually brought under its own rule were obliged to offer candles to the *Battistero* (Baptistery) on the feast of St. John and this ritual perhaps explains the extent to which the city identified with this much-loved monument. Its administration and care was entrusted to a powerful merchant corporation, and it is this which has been responsible for the splendid building.

▶ The octagonal ground plan may pre-date the existing structure and go back as far as the 5C, but the Baptistery, as it now appears with its white-and-green marble facing, geometrical areas and classical windows, dates from the 11C. ▶ The **bronze doors★★** are an outstanding feature. The **south door★** (the entrance) has 28 quatrefoil compartments with reliefs by Andrea Pisano,perhaps the greatest sculptor of the 14C. The *Life of Christ*, which is depicted on the leaves of the **north door★**, is by Lorenzo Ghiberti, and the east door, facing the cathedral, with Old Testament scenes, is the famous **Paradise Door**, Ghiberti's masterpiece, which comprises not only the ten panels but the magnificently decorated architrave and door jambs. The use of perspective in the scenes and the highly refined decorative approach make this one of the high points of the Florentine Renaissance. ▶ The **interior** is also outstandingly beautiful *(9 a.m.-12:30 p.m. and 2:30-5:30 p.m. or 5 p.m. winter)*. On the ground floor there is a tier of columns and marble pilasters and above there is a loggia with paired windows. Above this there is an attic storey with panels and a pointed dome with Byzantine-style **mosaics**. The walls are faced with marble in two colours and the finely inlaid pavement displays oriental motifs. ▶ The tall 15C *tomb of the anti-Pope John XXIII★* (deposed by the Council of Constance and later Cardinal of Florence) at the side of the Baptistery is by Donatello and Michelozzo. □

The doors of the Baptistery

'In the said year of 1330', wrote the chronicler Giovanni Villani, 'the metal doors of Santo Giovanni began to be made. They were very beautiful and of marvelous work and cost. The figures, by master Andrea Pisano, were first formed in wax and finally, after being cleaned and gilded, were cast in a furnace by Venetian masters. And we, the Guild of the merchants of the Calimala, guardians of San Giovanni, were responsible and I was the official to have the

said work done.' This was the door facing the Bigallo, with the Life of the Baptist. Seventy years later, in 1401, the Guild of the Calimala announced a competition for the second door, the north one, requiring each of the competitors to produce a Sacrifice of Isaac. Seven artists took part, including Lorenzo Ghiberti, who at twenty-three was the youngest, Filippo Brunelleschi, Jacopo della Quercia, Niccolò d'Arezzo and Niccolò Lamberti. The test pieces submitted by Brunelleschi and Ghiberti, who won, are still in the Bargello and they were judged by thirty-four experts drawn from all ranks of citizens. The competition was of 'capital importance for the history of art, since it heralded the beginning of a new epoch' (L. H. Heydenreich). Ghiberti worked on this door from 1402-25. He was then commissioned to do the third door and worked on it from 1425-52, thus spending half a century on the Baptistery doors. The choice of which Bible episodes were to be illustrated was made after consulting various well-known humanists; it was not an easy choice since these famous men often failed to agree among themselves. In his Commentaries Ghiberti states that 'it is the most singular work that I have produced and with every art and measure and ingenuity it has been finished. It was supposed to be the south door but it pleases me greatly that it was placed in the position of honour, opposite the cathedral, where the doors of Andrea Pisano originally were'. Michelangelo said it was worthy of Paradise and it is in fact known today as the Porta del Paradiso.

▶ BIBLIOTECA LAURENZIANA**
p. S. Lorenzo 9   C4

The Biblioteca Laurenziana *(wkdays 9 a.m.-5 p.m.; closed Mon)* is approached from a large **cloister★** (1475), which is an elegant example of the luminous tranquility of the architecture of the century of Brunelleschi. This restful harmony is in marked contrast to the **library**, which was designed by Michelangelo in collaboration with Vasari and Ammannati (vestibule). In the **vestibule** the architecture of Michelangelo provided an outlet for his genius as a sculptor; the walls of the high but narrow room are transformed into a plastic space with strong chiaroscuro effects, articulated by paired columns, frames, cornices, projecting consoles and niches within aedicules. The staircase itself is magnificent, with the curving steps of the central flight ascending like dark waves of stone. The long rectangular **room** to which the staircase leads was designed by Michelangelo right down to the coffered wooden ceiling and the benches and reading desks. The inlaid white-and-red floor is also 16C. Valuable **manuscripts** from the Library collections, begun by Cosimo il Vecchio (15C) and continued by the later Medici, are displayed on the desks. □

▶ The BOBOLI GARDENS**
(Il giardino di Boboli)
p. de' Pitti   F3

Extending over eleven acres and occupying a hilltop position with views over the city and its surroundings, these magnificent gardens *(summer 9 a.m.-7 p.m.;*

winter 9 a.m.-4:30 p.m.) lie behind the Palazzo Pitti. The overall impression is of the refined integration of art and nature. Grottos, fountains, statues, resting places, secluded paths and grand avenues are all in close harmony with the green backdrop of ilexes, cypresses, pines, plane-trees, laurel hedges, lemon trees and green recesses. The vegetation is chosen by man, controlled and cared for as just another element in a landscape that is not natural, but designed.

▶ Some of its well-known features include the **Grotta del Buontalenti** (1588), which is decorated with frescos, statues including Giambologna's *Venus*, fountains and shells. The dramatic 17C **amphitheatre** was the scene of festivals under the Medici and the House of Lorraine and is now used in the summer for staging open-air entertainments. The large **Neptune Pool** has a central rock crowned by a statue of the God of the Sea (1565). ▶ At the top is the **Giardino del Cavaliere** (view★) and behind this a Neoclassical villa houses the **Museo delle Porcellane★** *(Tue, Thu and Sat 9 a.m.-2 p.m.)*. This has an outstanding collection of pieces from such famous factories as Sèvres, Meissen and Doccia. ▶ A straight avenue, the **Viottolone**, leads down to the fascinating **piazzale dell'Isolotto** which has, at its centre, a copy of Giambologna's *Fountain of Oceanus* (the original of the great statue is in the Museo Nazionale del Bargello). ☐

▶ **Il CAMPANILE★★**

p. S. Giovanni   C4

So splendid is the result that the twenty-five years which it took the Florentines to complete the campanile do not seem a long time. Work began in 1334 under the direction of Giotto and then continued under Andrea Pisano and finally Francesco Talenti. It is 286 ft 9 in high and square in ground plan, with corner buttresses that rise as far as the uppermost cornice. The entire structure is faced with inlaid and carved bands and panels of green, white and pink marble, displaying an unparalleled grace and yet, at the same time, vigour. Cornices mark the divisions.between the five storeys and the topmost of these is taller than the others, emphasizing their slenderness.

▶ The ground storey is decorated with two bands, one above the other, of rectangular compartments, each of which contains relief panels carved by 14C sculptors *(copies, the originals are in the Museo dell'Opera del Duomo)*. ▶ The second storey has two rows of niches; the upper ones are blind, the lower ones contain statues of Prophets and Sybils *(also copies, originals in the same museum)*. ▶ The next two storeys are pierced by pairs of tall pointed windows and the top storey has four large triple windows. ▶ A staircase of 414 steps climbs up to the **terrace** *(8:30 a.m.-12:30 p.m. and 2:30-5:30 p.m. or 5 p.m. winter)*, which offers an extensive view★ over the city. ▶ The reliefs and statues which adorn the panels and niches are the work of three great Florentine sculptors: Andrea Pisano (responsible for the extraordinary images★ celebrating the works and arts of man), Luca della Robbia and Donatello. The involvement of so much genius has meant that the Campanile, spare and elegant inside as well as out, is quite rightly regarded as the finest in Italy. ☐

▶ **CAPPELLE MEDICEE★★**

p. di Madonna degli Aldobrandini   B4

The entrance leads into a vast crypt *(9 a.m.-7 p.m.; hols 9 a.m.-1 p.m.; closed Mon)*, with the tomb slabs of members of the Medici family set into the pavement. It is possible to climb to the Baroque **cappella dei Principi**, a grandiose, domed chapel of somewhat gloomy opulence which contains the monumental sarcophagi of the Grand-Dukes of Tuscany. A corridor leads off from here to the **New Sacristy★★**, a funerary chapel begun by Michelangelo in 1521 and completed by Vasari and Ammannati around 1555. The high, square room is vaulted by a coffered dome with compartments radiating out from the centre. Dark ribs and piers of pietra serena stand out sharply against the pale plaster of the wall and the marble facing of the lower section. On one side there is a square recess with an altar while on the opposite wall, above the long, simple coffin of Lorenzo the Magnificent and his brother Giovanni, there is Michelangelo's splendid sculpture, the *Madonna and Child★*. On the other two sides are the two famous *Medici Tombs★★* carved by Michelangelo in the decade before his final departure from Florence in 1534. One represents Lorenzo, Duke of Urbino, in a thoughtful pose, with the figures of **Dawn** and **Dusk** reclining on the sarcophagus before him. The other is Giuliano, Duke of Nemours, who is depicted as a young warrior in armour, with the figures of **Day** and **Night**, again reclining on the sarcophagus in front. The figures of the two Medici, set in niches in the wall, symbolize thought and action in man, while the other four figures, masterpieces at the very pinnacle of Italian sculpture, are allegories for the threatening and disturbing passage of time. To the l. of the altar *(access for groups of no more than twelve people; book at entrance)* there is a cycle of wall drawings, attributed to Michelangelo, which was only discovered in 1975-76. ☐

▶ **CASA BUONARROTI**

v. Ghibellina 70   D6

Michelangelo bought this house *(9 a.m.-2 p.m.; hols 9 a.m.-1 p.m.; closed Tue)* for a nephew and it was turned into a museum during the last century. The house was decorated by Florentine artists in the 17C; besides mementos of the Buonarroti family, its 16 rooms house their archaeological, mineral and numismatic collections — together with works acclaiming Michelangelo by artists from various periods. However, the heart of the museum is directly connected with Michelangelo himself and, in particular, with two important reliefs carved in his youth, the *Battle between Lapiths and Centaurs★* and the splendid *Madonna and Child★*, known as the *Madonna of the Steps* (1490-2), his oldest surviving carving and one which already shows his formidable personality. ☐

▶ **CASA DI DANTE**

v. S. Margherita 1   D5

Roman Florence with its regular grid of streets lies to the S of the Duomo and it is here that the **Casa degli Alighieri,** supposedly the birthplace of Dante, stands *(intensive restoration between 1875-1910)*. The **museum** contains mementos of Dante and exhibits relating to the city at the time of Dante and the places of his exile. ☐

▶ **Le CASCINE***
at end of Lungarno Amerigo Vespucci   C1

This is a beautiful park that extends over nearly 300 acres and for some 3 km along the right bank of the Arno as far as the confluence with the Mugnone. It was originally a Medici estate but at the beginning of the 19C it was set aside as a public park.

▶ In the middle of the park there are modern sports facilities (gallop, race track, pallone court, speedway, shooting range, swimming pool, tennis courts), all of which attract large numbers of visitors. ▶ At the confluence of the two rivers there is the *Monumento all'Indiano,* which commemorates a young Maharajah, who was cremated here according to Brahminic tradition. A festive note, which is not out of place in this theatrical setting, is the traditional **Festa del Grillo,** held each Ascension Day. A recent change has ensured that the small caged song birds are no longer carried home by children to listen to their singing, but are quickly released back into the wild.   □

▶ **CENACOLO DEL GHIRLANDAIO***
Borgognissanti 42   C1

A Renaissance cloister *(9:30 a.m.-12:30 p.m. and 4-8 p.m. or 3-6 p.m.; hols 9 a.m.-12 noon)* leads to the former **refectory** of the convent of Ognissanti. There are a number of works of art including Botticelli's beautiful fresco of *St. Augustine in his Study*★ and Domenico Ghirlandaio's famous *Cenacolo*★, a spacious and serene work in which even the minor details are depicted with virtuoso skill. Frescos by Domenico and Davide Ghirlandaio can also be seen in Vespucci Chapel in the attached **church,** which was extensively rebuilt in the 17C.   □

▶ **CENACOLO DI FOLIGNO**
v. Faenza 42   A3

There were many cenacles in Florence, but then there were just as many monasteries, each with its refectory, and if these were decorated with paintings then the subject matter was inevitably the Last Supper *(cenacolo).*

▶ The Franciscan convent of S. Onofrio (or Foligno) has a large **cenacolo**★ from the end of the 15C by Perugino and his assistants *(9 a.m.-2 p.m.; hols 9 a.m.-1 p.m.).* Perugino's concern here was to give breadth to the scene and to immerse it in an atmosphere of ecstasy. Hence, an aisle of pillars seen in perspective opens to reveal a clear, almost Umbrian landscape of soft lines suffused with a calm and diffuse light.   □

▶ **CENACOLO DI SAN SALVI**
v. S. Salvi 16, suburb of Madonnone, near v. Aretina

The former abbey of San Salvi, now a museum, has an important collection of 16C works. In the refectory there is Andrea del Sarto's famous *Last Supper*★, which depicts the dramatic moment when Christ reveals that one of his disciples will betray him. The tabernacolo del Madonnone is in the same part of the city, at the corner of the v. Aretina and the v. S. Salvi. There are many other similar shrines in the streets of Florence and they form a characteristic part of the old city.   □

▶ **CENACOLO DI SANTO SPIRITO**
p. S. Spirito   F2

The refectory *(9 a.m.-2 p.m.; hols 8 a.m.-1 p.m.; closed Mon)* of the former Augustinian monastery of S. Spirito still stands, but only a few fragments of Andrea Orcagna's great pictorial cycle (*c.* 1360), which once decorated the end wall, remain. In the upper part there is still a large *Crucifixion*★ but little of the *Last Supper* survives. The Cenacolo houses the Salvatore Romano Foundation which, in addition to detached frescos, has a collection of furniture, architectural fragments and important pieces of Romanesque and Renaissance sculpture.   □

▶ **CENACOLO DI S. APOLLONIA***
v. XXVII aprile 1   A4-5

The refectory of the former convent of S. Apollonia, of the strict Camaldolese order, was decorated by one of the greatest Florentine painters of the 15C, Andrea del Castagno *(9 a.m.-2 p.m.; hols 9 a.m.-1 p.m.; closed Mon).* There are a number of frescos, the most important of which is the *Last Supper*★★, as well as drawings and other works by the same artist.□

▶ **CHIOSTRO DELLO SCALZO**
v. Cavour 69   B4

The 16C cloister of the Scalzo *(9 a.m.-2 p.m.; hols 9 a.m.-1 p.m.;closed Mon)* is worth a visit for the monochrome frescos which decorate its walls. They depict scenes from the *Life of the Baptist*★ and were painted by Andrea de Sarto in 1514-26 for the Confraternity of St. John the Baptist, known as the Scalzo because during processions the bearer of the cross wore no shoes.   □

▶ **Galleria CORSINI**
v. Parione 11   D2-3

This is the most important private art collection in Florence *(closed at present).* It is housed in the city's finest 17C palace, the Palazzo Corsini, which stands close to the Arno. The works have not been arranged within the gallery on historical criteria or by type but, as was usual in old private collections, according to personal taste, since the paintings were intended for decoration. Here art is an ornament to the house and the house itself is a splendid residence, with monumental staircases that are among the finest in Florence and rooms such as the dramatic 18C white room and the sumptuous bedchamber. Most of the works are from the 15C-17C and one 16C panel is of particular interest for its view of the piazza della Signoria.   □

▶ **FORTE BELVEDERE***
along Costa S. Giorgio   F4

Since its fairly recent restoration and opening to the public, the Belvedere Fort has become one of the most popular attractions for both tourists and Florentines alike. Major art exhibitions are held in it. Built in 1590-5 by Bernardo Buontalenti, architect and sculptor, the Fort is laid out in the **form of a star** with massive bastions set at different levels, and it dominates Florence on one side and the hills which ring the city to the S on the other. The attractions offered by its **views★**, the light and the air are added to by an elegant **Palazzetto,** also built by Buontalenti, which stands in the centre of the fortress.   □

▶ **LOGGIA DEL BIGALLO**
p. S. Giovanni   C4

The marble Loggia was built in 1352-8 for the Compagnia della Misericordia and it comprises two arcades at right angles to each other which are richly decorated with reliefs and closed off with railings. On the upper storey there are beautiful paired trefoil windows and three 14C tabernacles. The name Bigallo is derived from another old Florentine company, which merged with the Misericordia in 1425. Abandoned children were rescued by the organization and displayed in the loggia to attract the charity of the public. The **Museo del Bigallo** *(2:30-7 p.m.; closed Sun; entered from p. S. Giovanni)* contains many fine works, including a detached fresco dating from 1342 which, in its lower section, provides the oldest known view of Florence.

▶ **LOGGIA DEI LANZI***
p. della Signoria   D4

This tall, vast Gothic building (known also as the Loggia della Signoria or dell'Orcagna after the architect wrongly supposed to have designed it) forms a noble backdrop to the p. della Signoria. It was built (1376-80) to the plans of Benci di Cione and Simone Talenti for the Comune of Florence. Later Cosimo I de' Medici used the Loggia to house his Lance-Knights, a guard of German mercenary soldiers, and it is from these that it takes its name of Dei Lanzi. It is now a museum filled with statues which include two 16C masterpieces — Giambologna's marble group, the *Rape of the Sabine Women★*, and Benvenuto Cellini's bronze *Perseus*.   □

▶ **MUSEO ARCHEOLOGICO***
v. della Colonna 36   A-B6

The museum *(9 a.m.-2 p.m.; hols 9 a.m.-1 p.m.; closed Mon)* is particularly important for the light it sheds on Etruscan art and civilization, but it also has collections of Egyptian, Greek and Roman antiquities. Unfortunately, the damage caused by the disastrous flood of the Arno in November 1966 has still not been repaired and much of the material is not on show.

▶ Important exhibits include the *François Krater★*, a fine archaic Attic vase (6C BC) recovered from an Etruscan tomb near Chiusi; the *Chimera★* (5C BC), a splendid Etruscan bronze found at Arezzo in the middle of the 16C; the *Sarcophagus of Larthia Seianti★*, a polychrome Etruscan terra-cotta with the figure of a young woman looking at herself in a mirror (3C-2C BC); the *Arringatore★*, a Roman funerary statue; and the *Ancella★*, a polychrome Egyptian wooden maidservant (c. 2400 BC).   □

▶ **MUSEO BARDINI***
p. dei Mozzi 1   F5

The museum's collections *(9 a.m.-2 p.m.; hols 8 a.m.-1 p.m.; closed Wed)* occupy twenty rooms and stem from an extensive and valuable bequest made to the city of Florence by a great antiquarian in the 1920s.

▶ It is a varied collection, covering paintings, furniture, ceramics, tapestries and weapons, and ranging from antiquity to the Baroque. Artists that are represented include major figures such as Tino di Camaino (14C), with a marble group, *Charity★*. Other exhibits are of interest for their origin, like a magnificent 16C **Persian carpet,** or because of their association with everyday life, like some **15C chests** with gilded plaster. ▶ On the second floor, the **Galleria Corsi** *(open on request)* has more than 600 works of art from between the 12C and the 19C.   □

▶ **MUSEO BOTANICO**
v. La Pira   A5-6

The central **Herbarium** has nearly 4 million specimens and there is also a collection of over 6,000 samples of wood, making this one of the most important botanical collections in Italy *(Mon, Wed, Fri and 1st Sun in month from Oct-Jun, 9 a.m.-12 noon)*. It also has interesting **15C&18C herbaria** as well as a tropical herbarium. The attached **Botanical Garden** (entrance v. Micheli 3) is the former *Giardino dei semplici*, founded in 1545 by Cosimo I, and it has quite a few trees that are now several centuries old.   □

▶ **MUSEO DEL BARGELLO****
v. del Proconsolo   D5

The museum is housed in the massive **Palazzo del Podestà★** or del Bargello, which was built in the middle of the 13C by the people of Florence for their captain *(9 a.m.-2 p.m.; Sun 9 a.m.-1 p.m.; closed Mon)*. In the 15C it became the residence of the Podestà and it was extended and raised at the same time. In 1574, the *Capitano di Giustizia* (or *bargello,* the chief of police) was installed in the palace and the interior was altered, part of it being turned into prisons. These were removed in 1857.

▶ The heart of its interesting collections is devoted to 14C-17C Tuscan sculpture, but it also contains coins, medals, majolica, gold, fabrics, seals, ivories, weapons and other *objets d'art* (a total of some 30,000 items). ▶ Under the arcades of the **courtyard★** (external staircase and walls covered with old coats-of-arms), there are 16C statues, including Giambologna's gigantic *Oceanus,* which was originally in the Bòboli Gardens, and curiosities such as the 17C Canon of St. Paul, decorated with a large head of the saint. ▶ In the hall on the ground floor are several works by major 16C artists (including Benvenuto Cellini) and four masterpieces by Michelangelo: a highly polished *Bacchus drunk★* with a mischievous faun; a serene Apollo or *David★★*, a vibrant tondo, the *Madonna and Child with St. John★*, and the intense bust of *Brutus★★*. ▶ On the first floor, in a tall, light hall, there is a veritable treasury of 15C Florentine sculpture, beginning with the **panels★★** submitted by Brunelleschi and Ghiberti for the competition of 1401 for the second of the Baptistery's doors, and continuing with statues and reliefs by Agostino di Duccio, Desiderio da Settignano and Luca della Robbia. However, the major figure here is Donatello, who is represented by his famous *St. George★★* (until the last century this was in a tabernacle at Orsanmichele) and the splendid bronze *David*★★, the first Renaissance nude, commissioned by Cosimo de' Medici. ▶ In the porch, at the top of the stairs, there are bronzes by Giambologna. ▶ The second floor has Della Robbia terra-cottas and masterpieces of Florentine sculpture from the second half of the 15C by artists such as Verrocchio and Antonio Pollaiolo. ▶ There is also a collection of **bronzes** which bears witness to the fondness of the rich collectors of the Renaissance and the 17C for this genre. □

▶ MUSEO DELLE PIETRE DURE
v. degli Alfani 78   B5

The museum *(wkdays 9 a.m.-1 p.m.)* attached to the famous Opificio (established in 1588) which was responsible for the decoration of the Chapel of the Princes (→ Cappelle Medicee) is primarily devoted to works from the 18C-19C in semi-precious stones, scagliola (plasterwork imitating stone) and painting on stone. There is also an interesting collection of old tools and work benches from the Opificio and samples of rare stones. Today the Institute is also an important centre for restoration. □

▶ MUSEO DELL'OPERA DEL DUOMO*
p. del Duomo 9   C5

The importance of this modestly sized but quite extraordinary museum *(9:30 a.m.-1 p.m. and 3-6 p.m. or 2-5:30 p.m. winter; hols 10 a.m.-1 p.m.)*, which is essential for an understanding of Florentine sculpture, has recently been even further increased by the transfer to it of Donatello's dramatic wooden *Magdalene* (from the Baptistery), Michelangelo's marble *Pietà* (from S. Maria del Fiore) and the first restored **panels** from Ghiberti's Paradise Door. There are a number of other major attractions, including the **model of the dome** by Brunelleschi; the statues which decorated the 14C façade of the Duomo until the 16C (for example Arnolfo di Cambio's majestic *Madonna and Child*★); the precious gilded and enamelled silver altar from the Baptistery (the sculptural ornament is by Verrocchio and others); statues from the niches on the Campanile, including the lifelike figure of the *Prophet Habakkuk*★, known as *lo Zuccone*, by Donatello and the superb 14C panels, again removed from the Campanile, by Andrea Pisano, depicting Ploughing, Weaving, Navigation and other human activities. The two famous *Cantorie*★★ by Donatello and Luca della Robbia, previously in the Duomo, occupy a separate room. □

▶ MUSEO DEL TEMPIO ISRAELITICO
v. Farini 4

Anyone looking down on the city from above, from the piazzale Michelangelo, for example, would immediately notice the green dome of the **synagogue** near the tree-lined p. d'Azeglio. The synagogue itself was built in the 19C in moresque style and the nearby museum *(Sun and Thu 9 a.m.-1 p.m.; Mon and Wed 2-5 p.m.; winter Sun, Mon and Wed 10 a.m.-1 p.m.)* has a collection of ancient codices, parchments and other objects connected with Jewish culture. □

▶ MUSEO DI ANTROPOLOGIA
v. del Proconsolo 12   C-D5

The museum *(open 1st and 2nd Sun of month; school groups: Wed, Fri 9 a.m.-1 p.m.)* is housed in the Palazzo Nonfinito, which was begun in 1593 by the innovatory Buontalenti but never completed. Buontalenti was, however, responsible for the windows with their scrolled pediments. Its collections cover the civilizations of Africa, Asia, the Americas and Oceania; there are pictures from Ethiopia, amulets from Zimbabwe, hunting and fishing implements from Lapland, dried human heads decorated with feathers from South America, idols and weapons from Malaya, sterns and prows from Polynesian ships and porcelain and lacquer from the Far East. □

▶ MUSEO DI MINERALOGIA
v. La Pira 4   A5-6

One of this museum's exhibits is a topaz from Brazil weighing 333 lb. It has a series of regional collections including a particularly good one for the island of Elba, with a series of superb tourmalines *(9 a.m.-12 noon and 3-6 p.m. Sun and hols apart from 1st Sun of month).* □

▶ MUSEO DI SAN MARCO**
p. S. Marco 3   A5

The plan of this **convent** *(9 a.m.-2 p.m.; hols 9 a.m.-1 p.m.; closed Mon),* which was rebuilt in 1437-52 by Michelozzo for Cosimo il Vecchio, is very simple. All the main rooms are on the ground floor and are grouped around the cloister beside the church, with the cells of the friars and the library being on the upper floor. What makes it important in artistic terms is the works it contains. There are nearly one hundred panels (of varied origin) and frescos by Fra' Angelico (a friar of the convent) and his school.
▶ The Pilgrim's Hospice contains a *Deposition*★ (1435-40), with an interesting background; the large *Tabernacle of the Linaioli*★★, with a Madonna and Child and Angels playing musical instruments (1433), and a marble frame designed by Ghiberti; a splendid *Last Judgment* (*c.* 1430). ▶ The chapterhouse has a large fresco of the *Crucifixion*★★, and on the first floor, facing the top of the staircase, there is an *Annunciation*★★, one of Fra' Angelico's finest works which has the timorous figures of the Virgin and the Angel set in an architectural framework of rarefied elegance. ▶ After this come the **cells**, each of which has a fresco exhorting the friars to spiritual retirement. ▶ At the end of a corridor there is a set of rooms with mementos of the most famous of the convent's priors, **Girolamo Savonarola**. ▶ The **library** is one of the purest of Renaissance designs, with two airy arcades supported by slender, white columns. □

▶ MUSEO FIRENZE COM'ERA
v. dell'Oriuolo 24   C5

What did the Medici villas look like at the end of the 16C? What did the city centre look like before the thoughtless destruction at the end of the last century? How has the city developed with the passage of time? This is the museum *(9 a.m.-2 p.m.; hols 8 a.m.-1 p.m.; closed Thu)* to answer these questions with photographs, paintings, drawings, prints and plans which record the city and the various aspects of its life from the 15C to the present. Note the group of works by O. Rosai.

▶ **MUSEO HORNE**
v. dei Benci 6   E5

Housed in a 15C palazzo, the collection *(9 a.m.-2 p.m.; closed Sat and the 1st, 2nd and 4th Sun of month)* was assembled by an English scholar and presented to the state. It includes sculptures, paintings, furniture and antiquities (largely domestic objects). Among the paintings there are works by Giotto (*St. Stephen★*), Lorenzetti, Sassetta, F.Lippi, D.Dossi and Beccafumi. There is also a fine collection of drawings by artists such as Michelangelo, Raphael, Poussin, Gainsborough and Constable.

▶ **MUSEO STIBBERT***
v. Stibbert 26

Antique weapons and armour★ from both East and West form the bulk of the material exhibited in the sixty rooms of the museum *(9 a.m.-2 p.m.; hols 9 a.m.-1 p.m.; closed Thu)*, which originates from the extensive collection of the Garibaldian hero, Federico Stibbert. There is an arresting procession of 14 knights and 14 foot soldiers with Italian, German, Spanish and Saracen weapons and armour of the 16C. The interesting collections of *objets d'art* range over almost every period and country.

▶ **MUSEO ZOOLOGICO LA SPECOLA**
v. Romana 17   D3

The museum *(Tue 9 a.m.-12 noon; Sat, for the wax museum 2-5 p.m.; Sun 9 a.m.-12 noon)* is housed in the Palazzo Torrigiani. On the ground floor there is a vivarium with reptiles and amphibians, while on the first floor the **Tribuna di Galileo** is a semicircular room built by the last Grand-Duke of Tuscany in 1841. It is decorated with mosaics and frescos celebrating the scientists of Florence. On the second floor a series of over 500 cases houses a collection of **anatomical models and pieces** made of coloured wax between 1775 and 1814. This final section is also the most interesting, since it documents the activities and aims of the museum's old wax modeling workshop. There are a number of pieces modeled in the 17C by Gaetano Zumbo, including *The Corruption of Bodies*, which were not produced for study purposes but out of a gloomy and characteristic taste for the depiction of the macabre.

▶ **ORSANMICHELE***
v. de' Calzaiuoli   D4

Built as a loggia to serve as a grain market in 1337, the Orsanmichele later became the site for Andrea Orcagna's large, highly ornate marble tabernacle and, in 1380, its arcades were filled in by a screen of splendid Gothic windows and two upper storeys were added. These were intended as a store for grain and the ground floor as a place of worship. Another

unusual and interesting feature of the building is the series of statues of the patron saints of the guilds placed in niches on all the external pillars. Carved by famous artists, they document the development of Florentine sculpture between the 14C and the 16C. They include *St. John the Baptist* and the *Incredulity of St. Thomas★* by Verrocchio; *St. Luke* by Giambologna; and *Four Soldier Saints★* by Nanni di Banco. There is also a fine **bas-relief** by Donatello and a *Madonna and Child* by Luca della Robbia. Inside, in addition to Andrea Orcagna's **tabernacle** of 1349-59 *(coin-operated light)* and the **14C panel** on the altar within it, there is one rather unusual feature for a church — the outlet chutes for the granary on the two upper floors.

▶ **PALAZZO DAVANZATI***
p. Davanzati   D3

This 14C palace has a rusticated ground floor, a 16C loggia and a narrow, irregularly shaped courtyard with a projecting staircase. It houses the **Museo dell'Antica Casa Fiorentina** *(guided tours; 9 a.m.-2 p.m.; summer 9 a.m.-1 p.m.; closed Mon)* with its interesting collections of works of art, furniture, fabrics, tapestries, lace, and domestic objects from the 14C-18C. These are all set against the background of a comfortable house, with rooms that have been lived in and decorated by their former owners.

▶ **PALAZZO DI PARTE GUELFA**
p. di Parte Guelfa   D4

Altered several times over the centuries, it was originally, in the 14C, an awesome centre of political power, the seat of the Guelph party, the faction of the aristocrats and rich citizens who opposed the democratization of Florentine public life. The classical first floor windows facing the v. delle Terme and the v. di Capaccio are, like the **Audience Room** inside, the work of Brunelleschi. Vasari designed the gracious **loggetta.**

▶ **PALAZZO GUADAGNI***
p. S. Spirito 10   F2

A magnificent palace from the early 16C. The well-balanced façade has sturdy corner pilasters and rusticated openings, surmounted by a grand loggia, the columns of which support the projecting roof.

▶ **PALAZZO MEDICI-RICCARDI****
v. Cavour   B4

Built by Michelozzo for Cosimo il Vecchio between 1444-64, it was enlarged a couple of centuries later by the new owners, the Riccardi family. It is a splendid Renaissance palace and the first to be built in Florence as a nobleman's seat.

▶ The exterior is rusticated on the ground floor, smooth on the upper ones, and in the arches of the ground floor it has the two famous **windows**, attributed to Michelangelo, which have served as a model to countless other buildings. ▶ Inside, there is a splendid arcaded **courtyard,** which broke new ground in its airiness and geometrical spaciousness. From here it is possible to climb to the fine **chapel** *(9 a.m.-12:30 p.m. and 3-5 p.m.; Sun 9 a.m.-12 noon; closed Wed)*, which was designed by Michelozzo right down to the compartments of the marble pavement, the magnificent coffered wooden ceiling and the splendid stalls. It is decorated with a famous **fresco** by Benozzo Gozzoli, which depicts the *Journey of the Magi to Bethlehem*. The various figures are portraits of members of the Medici family, including Lorenzo the Magnificent, who is the youth on a white horse. ▶ In another part of the palace, there is a long 17C **gallery** *(same opening times as the chapel)*, decorated with stuccos and mirrors, with its vault frescoed by Luca Giordano's *Apotheosis of the Medici*. □

▶ **PALAZZO PAZZI-QUARATESI***

v. del Proconsolo 10   D5

An elegant Renaissance palace built by Giuliano da Maiano (1462-72), the façade has a superb row of **double windows** on the upper floors and a rusticated ground floor. There is also a fine **courtyard** with arcades supported by columns with excellent capitals, above which there is a storey with another set of double windows, and the whole is crowned by a light loggia. □

▶ **PALAZZO PITTI****

p. de' Pitti   F2-3

The monumental **Palazzo**, behind which the Bóboli Gardens (→) extend, is the result of a long period of building. It was begun, in the mid-15C and possibly to a design by Brunelleschi, as the residence of the rich Florentine merchant Luca Pitti. A century later it was acquired by the Medici and gradually extended towards the rear with the construction of a vast courtyard (Ammannati, 1570) and then at the front, where the rusticated façade extends for more than 650 ft (17C). Finally, in 1783, the two wings (the *rondòs*) were added on the vast piazza laid out on the slope of the Bóboli hill.

▶ Externally, the architecture is simple but grand; inside the rooms are of extraordinary splendour and in their dazzling richness the opulent and refined taste of the Grand-Dukes who made it their palace appears to be crystallized. ▶ Priceless art collections assembled over the centuries by various members of the house of Medici form the core of the material in the Galleria Palatina and the Museo d'Argenti, which, together with the Galleria d'Arte Moderna and the Collezione Contini Bonacossi, are housed in the palace. ▶ The **Galleria Pitti** or Palatina *(9 a.m.-2 p.m.; hols 9 a.m.-1 p.m.; closed Mon)* contains both Italian and foreign works from the 15C-18C and it is not arranged along the lines of a modern museum but retains, at least in part, its original character as the gallery of a prince. **Raphael** and **Titian** are both represented by serenely beautiful and mature masterpieces. These include: Titian's *Concert*★★, *La Bella*★★ and *Gentleman*★★, *La velata*★★, the *Madonna del Granduca*★★, and the *Madonna della Seggiola*★★ by Raphael; the *Three Ages of Man*★★ (unknown artist, possibly Giorgione); *Luigi Cornaro*★ by Tintoretto; *Sleeping Amore* by Caravaggio; *Return From the Fields*★ and *The Four Philosophers*★ by Rubens; Velazquez's *Philip IV of Spain*★; and *Portrait of Cardinal Bentivoglio*★★ by Van Dyck. ▶ The **Galleria d'Arte Moderna** *(9 a.m.-2 p.m.; Sun 9 a.m.-1 p.m.; closed Mon)* was moved here at the beginning of this century and it offers a comprehensive survey of 19C-20C Italian — particularly Tuscan — painting. At its core there is a strong collection of works by the **Macchiaioli**, a group of Florentine artists painting between 1855-60. ▶ The **Museo degli Argenti** *(Wed and*

Fri *9 a.m.-2 p.m.; hols 9 a.m.-1 p.m.)* houses diverse collections of objects made out of precious metals, semi-precious stones, crystal, ivory and so on. ▶ The Neoclassical Meridiana, the residence of the first King of Italy during the years when Florence was the capital (1865-71), now houses the paintings, sculptures and *objets d'art* of the **Collezione Contini Bonacossi**★ *(book to visit, apply at the Uffizi)*, and as a result the Pitti has been enriched by masterpieces by artists such as Duccio di Boninsegna, Veronese and Goya. ▶ The Meridiana also contains the interesting **Museo dei Costumi** *(Wed, Thu, Sat 9 a.m.-2 p.m.)* which exhibits costumes from different periods by rotation. □

The birth of opera

When the French writer Stendhal, who had accompanied Napoleon's Army into Italy, first heard at Novara Cimarosa's Matrimonio Segreto, he wrote: 'My one desire in life now is to live in Italy and listen to operatic music'. Opera arose in Florence around 1600 when an aristocratic circle of musicians and literary men known as the Camerata Fiorentina attempted to revive principles of Greek drama in a new declamatory style called recitative. The leaders were the composers Jacopo Peri and Giulio Caccini, and the poet, Ottavio Rinuccini. The first known opera is Dafne (1597), by Peri and Rinuccini, and the first of which the music completely survives is Euridice, by the same two. This opera, which was performed at the Pitti Palace on the occasion of the marriage by proxy of Maria de'Medici with Henry IV, King of France, had a prologue and six scenes, and its composer, Peri, sang the leading role of Orfeo. Shortly afterwards, Caccini, who was listed on the Medici pay roll as receiving sixteen ducats, wheras Peri received only six, composed his own Euridice, and this opera was also performed at the Pitti at the end of 1602. So the birth of opera was immediately followed by the lively artistic rivalry which has accompanied it ever since.

▶ **PALAZZO RUCELLAI***

v. della Vigna Nuova 18   D3

One of the most refined architectural masterpieces of the Florentine Renaissance, it was built 1446-51 by Bernardo Rossellino to a design by Leon Battista Alberti. The **façade** is articulated by a series of classical pilasters and horizontally by two prominent cornices. The entire surface is lightly rusticated and gives the appearance of a dense mesh of lines cut into the stone in a complex pattern. Across the street, there is an annex to the palace, the beautiful **Loggia**★, again designed by Alberti. In the nearby v. della Spada, in the **Cappella Rucellai** *(apply to the warden of the palace for access, 8 a.m.-1:15 p.m. and 3-8 p.m.)*, there is another example of Alberti's work, the **Edicola del Santo Sepolcro**★, a splendid shrine of polychrome marbles. □

▶ **PALAZZO STROZZI****

p. Strozzi   D3

Built as a residence for the Strozzi family it more than fulfilled the ambitious and explicit intention of Filippo Strozzi who commissioned it in order to ensure the fame of his family 'in Italy and beyond'. It was begun by Benedetto da Maiano (1489) and continued by Cronaca (1497-1504). There is a fine **courtyard** and the outer walls are deeply rusticated. The famous projecting **cornice** rests on the walls rather like a 'crown of nobility on the forehead of a *nouveau riche*' (Piero Bargellini). Today the palace is used for the staging of major exhibitions and events. ☐

▶ PALAZZO VECCHIO**

p. della Signoria   E4-5

The vertical emphasis of its stone walls is unbroken by the slender cornice marking the first floor, which is pierced by paired windows set in semicircular arches with marble dressings. Above this there is a high battlemented gallery for the guard and a tower ending in a room for the watch, and, above this, a bell chamber. According to tradition, the Palazzo Vecchio was built by Arnolfo di Cambio, extended in the course of the 14C and again in later centuries. Inside it is Renaissance and late Renaissance in style and dates from the second half of the 16C in response to the princely requirements of the Medici, who had left the Palazzo Medici-Riccardi (→) but who had not yet made the Palazzo Pitti (→) their sole residence. The alterations were largely the work of Giorgio Vasari, the favourite architect of Cosimo I.

▶ It now serves as the municipio and is only open to visitors in part *(9 a.m.-7 p.m.; hols 8 a.m.-1 p.m.; closed Sat).* ▶ After crossing the **courtyard** (rebuilt by Michelozzo in 1470 and stuccoed and frescoed in 1556), the visitor enters a hall with a staircase which leads to the upper floors. On the first floor there is the large **Salone dei Cinquecento★**, now full of statues including Michelangelo's marble **Victory★** and vaulted by a superb ceiling with gilded panels and paintings celebrating the glory of Florence and the Medici. A small windowless room, the **Studiolo★** of Francesco I, leads off the Salone. This marvelously decorated room (second half of the 16C) is covered with frescos, oils and bronze statuettes by Giambologna. ▶ There are then a number of rooms named after various members of the Medici family, from Cosimo il Vecchio to Cosimo I, and they contain an endless sequence of splendid paintings. ▶ Equally ornate rooms are to be found on the mezzanine and the second floor, and they include the **Sala dei Gigli★** and the **Sala dell'Udienza★**, as well as a loggia with a fine view over the SE part of the city. ☐

▶ PIAZZA DELLA SIGNORIA**

                                                              D4

Always crowded with both Florentines and tourists from all parts of the world, the piazza has a number of features of architectural interest. These include not only the massive bulk of the **Palazzo Vecchio** (→) and the vaulting arcades of the **Loggia dei Lanzi** (→), but also a number of other old buildings, particularly on the east side of the square. At its heart is the 16C **Fountain of Neptune.** The god himself is at the centre of the basin, but in artistic terms it is the nymphs, satyrs and fauns which are the most striking feature. On one side there is the equestrian monument to Cosimo I de' Medici (Giambologna, 1594) and on the other the sculptures standing in front of the entrance to the Palazzo Vecchio, including the gigantic *David* (copy of Michelangelo's original). ☐

▶ PIAZZALE MICHELANGELO**

From p. F. Ferrucci, along v. Michelangelo

Roads have climbed up into the hills surrounding Florence for hundreds of years, but it was only in the 19C after the unification of Italy that the famous **viale dei Colli** was laid out and built for the specific purpose of offering Florentines and visitors alike an incomparable scenic route. The road, which is named in turn after Michelangelo, Galileo and Machiavelli, curves along the slopes of the hills for some 6 km and long sections are cloaked by the lush vegetation. The **piazzale Michelangelo** lies along this route, on the hill of S. Miniato, and it is one of the best known, most enchanting and popular of the vantage points offering a view over the city and the basin in which it lies. At its centre, a monument displays copies of Michelangelo's works (G. Poggi, 1870) but has little intrinsic worth of its own. ☐

A historical and artistic heritage

Obviously, there is more to see in Florence than just famous museums and monuments, churches and palaces. It would be foolish to omit the pleasure of wandering about, crossing and recrossing the Arno and strolling along the streets and through the piazzas, discovering new views, typical corners, luxury boutiques and old shops. However, when visiting such major thoroughfares as the **via Maggio,** **de' Calzaiuoli, Por S. Maria** *or* **de' Tornabuoni,** *it is important to remember that the soul of Florence is no less present in some relatively peripheral spot, such as the* **mercatino di S. Piero** *or the seats of the tree-lined* **p. d'Azeglio.** *The city has an immense artistic and historical heritage; parts of it are required viewing for any visitor, others depend upon personal interests. The required category includes sites such as the* **p. della Signoria** *and the* **Ponte Vecchio** *and, above all, that extraordinary group formed by the* **Duomo, Baptistery, Campanile** *and the* **Loggia del Bigallo,** *together with the exhibits in the* **Museo dell'Opera del Duomo.** *The single most outstanding strand running through Florentine architecture is the series of buildings by Brunelleschi, including the dome of the cathedral and the* **Palazzo Pitti.** *There are many famous collections of paintings, only two of which are housed in the* **Uffizi** *and the* **Galleria Palatina.** *In short, days in Florence should be divided between the wealth of sights offered by a guide and personal interests, avoiding the impossible desire to see everything. No one, however, should fail to take in the extraordinary view of the city from the* **balustrades of the piazzale Michelangelo** *or from the bastions of the* **Forte di Belvedere.**

▶ PONTE SANTA TRINITA*

end of v. Tornabuoni   D3

The people of Florence decided to rebuild the 16C Ponte a Santa Trinità, which was destroyed in 1944 by retreating German troops, exactly as it had been and using the old materials. As a result, it is still possible to see one of Bartolomeo Ammannati's masterpieces, although possibly based on designs of Michelangelo, and admire the unusual, flattened curve of its arches. From its parapet there are splendid views of the banks of the Arno, the Ponte Vecchio and the hill of S. Miniato. ▫

▶ PONTE VECCHIO*

E3-4

This is perhaps the one structure most closely associated in people's minds with the city of Florence. It has never simply been a means of crossing the Arno and a bridge may have existed here in Roman times. It was already known as the Ponte Vecchio in 966, and when it was rebuilt in 1345 it became a commercial thoroughfare with a double row of shops (from the 16C reserved for goldsmiths') and a place to linger, with its two central terraces offering fine views. The distinctive, projecting additions to the back of the shops began to appear as far back as the 15C. In 1565 Cosimo I had the enclosed and rather severe **Corridoio Vasariano** built above the shops on the upstream side to connect the Uffizi and the Pitti *(guided tours, book in advance, Wed, Fri and Sun 9:30 a.m.; apply to the Uffizi).* The bridge crosses the Arno at the level of the via Por Santa Maria and the via Guicciardini, two medieval streets which the Germans destroyed in 1944 to prevent the bridge from being used. ▫

▶ La ROTONDA

p. Brunelleschi   B5

After its rediscovery in the 1930s, the oratory of **S. Maria degli Agnoli** has been cleared of other buildings and extensively restored. It is one of Brunelleschi's unfinished works and has an octagonal ground plan and chapels with two apses on each side corresponding to the 16 faces of the exterior. ▫

▶ SAN FELICE

p. S. Felice   F2

San Felice is a medieval church rebuilt several times (14C, 15C and 16C), with a fine 15C façade, including a portal with ornately carved doors. The second half of the **interior** retains part of its 15C structure, with tie-beams, and has a large painted **Crucifix** from the Giotto workshop. ▫

▶ SAN FIRENZE

p. S. Firenze   D5

This is one of the few examples of Baroque architecture in the city. The massive façade stands at the top of a dramatic flight of steps and is divided into three sections, which originally corresponded to (from l. to r.) a church, convent and oratory, all belonging to the Oratorians; the last two now house the courts. The 17C interior of the **church** consists of a tall, light single aisle with a fine carved and gilded ceiling and large oval reliefs on the walls. The former **convent** has an open-air staircase supported by three arches, and the old oratory has a graceful 18C **cantoria.** ▫

▶ SAN LEONARDO IN ARCETRI

from Forte Belvedere along v. S. Leonardo

This Romanesque church on the hilltop of the v. S. Leonardo houses a 13C **pulpit**, decorated with very beautiful bas-reliefs. ▫

▶ SAN LORENZO

p. S. Lorenzo   B4

Designed by Brunelleschi, San Lorenzo's interior was completed after the architect's death by one of his pupils while the exterior was left unfinished. It is one of the greatest masterpieces of 15C Florentine architecture. The well-balanced interior is divided into a nave and two aisles. There are two **pulpits★** with bronze bas-reliefs designed by Donatello and completed by his pupils, and a famous *Annunciation★* painted by Filippo Lippi.

▶ Brunelleschi and Donatello were responsible for the **Sagrestia Vecchia★★** *(entered from the l. transept),* one of the greatest achievements of the Renaissance. Brunelleschi designed the actual room (1429), and from 1443 Donatello and his pupils worked on the painted stucco medallions in the pendentives *(Life of St. John★),* the figures of the *Evangelists★* which decorate the tondi of the lunettes, and the terra-cotta **reliefs★** above the doors at the sides of the apsidal chapel and the bronze **leaves★** of the two doors. The extraordinary **tomb of Giovanni and Piero de' Medici★**, a porphyry sarcophagus with bronze plant ornament, is by Verrocchio. ▶ It was the Medici who financed the building of the church and it contains tombs of various members of the family. ▫

▶ SAN MARCO

p. S. Marco   A5

The **church** is admittedly not on a par with the attached convent (→ Museo di San Marco), partly because after Michelozzo rebuilt it in the 15C a number of rather awkward alterations were carried out. Inside there are 16C bronze **statues** by Giambologna; an 8C **mosaic** of the Madonna in prayer; a **Crucifix** by the school of Giotto and an altarpiece of the Madonna and Saints by Fra'Bartolomeo. ▫

▶ SAN MINIATO AL MONTE**

from p. F. Ferrucci, along v. Michelangelo and v. Galileo

After the Baptistery (→), this church is undoubtedly the finest example of Romanesque architecture in Florence. It stands at the top of a pleasant hill, up which the viale Michelangelo winds, and its splendid **façade** covered with a beautifully ordered pattern of two-coloured marble looks across to Florence. On the ground floor there is·a classical arcade of five blind arches and the pediment is crowned by an eagle, the symbol of the merchant corporation entrusted with looking after this church by the city.

▶ **Inside** it has a raised sanctuary, beneath which there is a fascinating crypt, and it is a blaze of colour, in part due to restoration during the 19C. Among its finest features are the pavement in the nave, with **panels★** of inlaid marble (1207), and the old **pulpit★**, decorated with carved figures. The elegant Renaissance **Cappella del Crocifisso** (Michelozzo, 1448) stands at the end of the nave and has a vault of glazed terra-cotta (Luca della

Robbia). Another pure Renaissance component is the **Cappella del Cardinale del Portogallo★**, built by Antonio Manetti (1466), with **tondi★** by Luca della Robbia in the vault. The tomb of the cardinal is by Antonio Rossellino (1461). □

San Miniato al Monte

▶ **SAN SALVATORE AL MONTE**
from p. F. Ferrucci, along v. le Michelangelo

The **church,** which Michelangelo called 'the beautiful villa', stands behind the piazzale Michelangelo amid cypresses. Built by Cronaca (1499), it displays simple, straightforward Renaissance forms and a sober and charming interior which contains a number of 15C altarpieces and a terra-cotta by Luca della Robbia. The 15C **convent** has an unusual cloister. □

▶ **SANTA CROCE****
p. S. Croce   E6

The polychrome marble façade was added in the last century and the basilica dominates one of the city's largest piazzas, in a quarter that is still popular today. A Franciscan church, it was begun at the end of the 13C, at the time of Dante, and its Gothic **interior** still clearly bears the stamp of that extraordinary phase in Florentine civilization, with its octagonal pillars and Gothic arches dividing it into a nave and two aisles.

▶ There is an even greater concentration of memorials and works of art here than in other Florentine churches and in the r. aisle there are tombs or funerary monuments to figures such as Michelangelo, Dante, Machiavelli and the composer Gioaccino Rossini. ▶ 14C painting and Renaissance sculpture are well-represented, the finest pieces of sculpture being the *Tomb of Leonardo Bruni★★* (r. aisle), in which Bernardo Rossellino established the model for Florentine tombs of the 15C, and two works by Donatello, the delicate and precious high-relief of the *Annunciation★* (r. aisle) and a powerfully realistic wooden *Crucifix★* (end of l. transept). ▶ It also contains Giotto's frescos★ in the **Cappella Peruzzi** (to the r. of the sanctuary) and the *Life of St. Francis★★* in the adjacent Cappella Bardi. ▶ The **Museo dell'Opera di S. Croce★** *(9 a.m.-12:30 p.m. and 3-6:30 p.m. or 5 p.m.*

winter; closed Wed) is entered from the arcade on the r. of the cloister beside the church and occupies the former refectory of the convent and adjacent rooms. It contains numerous Florentine masterpieces, including a bronze *St. Louis★* by Donatello and Cimabue's extraordinary 13C *Crucifix★*, which was badly damaged in the floods of 1966. ▶ At the end of the cloister there is a superb 15C **portal★** by Giuliano da Maiano, preceded by a portico of six columns. This leads into the **interior★★** of the **Cappella dei Pazzi** *(same opening times as museum)*, one of Brunelleschi's masterpieces, which was built in 1443-6. Its white walls are articulated by a pure and harmonious rhythm of pilaster strips, beams, windows, arches, roundels and cornices picked out in pietra serena, crowned by a ribbed dome with a central lantern and oculi. The decorative features include **polychrome** medallions by Luca della Robbia. □

▶ **SANTA FELICITA**
v. Guicciardini   F3

Rebuilt by Ruggeri in 1736, the church contains two strikingly beautiful **paintings★** by Pontormo (16C) in the **Cappella Barbadori,** attributed to Brunelleschi. One unusual feature is that the **Corridoio Vasariano** (→ the Ponte Vecchio), which runs above the tall external portico (also by Vasari, retained by Ruggeri), is connected to the church and there is a box opposite the high altar in which the family of the Grand-Duke could attend services. □

▶ **SANTA MARIA DEL CARMINE***
p. del Carmine   E1

In 1425 Felice Brancacci, a silk merchant, commissioned Masaccio to paint the **frescos★★** in what is now the most famous chapel in Florence. The church itself is of medieval origin but was rebuilt after a fire in 1771. Masolino da Panicale worked alongside Masaccio and half a century later Filippino Lippi continued the cycle that they had left unfinished. It is, however, the scenes painted by Masaccio, for example the *Expulsion of Adam and Eve From Paradise* or the *Tribute Money*, that open up new approaches to painting. □

▶ **SANTA MARIA DEL FIORE****
p. S. Giovanni   C4

The Duomo, begun in 1296 by Arnolfo del Cambio and continued by F. Buontalenti, although not completed during the 14C, is the most typically Florentine of the city's monuments — even its name, 'fiore' refers to the city. In particular, Brunelleschi's extraordinary **dome★** which was added between 1418 and 1436 and which both crowns the cathedral and marks its completion, has always stood for Florence, its art and its spirit. Still capable of exciting awe today, the dome consists of two interconnected shells, the inner one of which is covered by a 16C fresco. The outer one, built of red brick and white ribs, is crowned by a high lantern (351 ft) and rises 'magnificent and swelling', as Brunelleschi wished, to dominate the city. However, it is the cathedral in its entirety that stands as the most impressive piece of architecture in Florence, not least because its immense bulk is splendidly clad in marble (extended to the façade in the last century), a 14C reworking of the green-and-white geometrical patterns on Romanesque churches but here with the addition of a warm pink. The tribunes, which display a lively handling of space, are particularly fine.

The Duomo, Santa Maria del Fiore

▶ The famous **Porta della Mandorla** (15C), with an elegant gable containing a high-relief, is on the l. side. ▶ Over the centuries, numerous works of art have been placed in the solemn **interior,** which is divided into a nave and two aisles by arcades of high Gothic arches on pillars extending as far as the grand octagon crowned by the dome. ▶ The majority of the works are by 15C artists. Paolo Uccello and Andrea del Castagno painted the **frescos★★** on the wall of the l. aisle depicting two condottieri on horseback. Luca della Robbia produced the **terra-cottas★** which decorate the lunettes above the doors to the two sacristies. Lorenzo Ghiberti designed the **stained glass** for the high rose-window and the bronze **urn★** beneath the altar of the central chapel of the middle tribune. The sumptuous inlaid marble pavement dates from the 16C onward. □

▶ SANTA MARIA MADDALENA DE'PAZZI*
v. Borgo Pinti 58   C6

The Renaissance **church** was rebuilt by Giuliano da Sangallo (1445-1516, architect and sculptor) in 1492 and is preceded by a fine arcaded 16C **courtyard** which has recently been well restored. In the **chapterhouse** of the adjacent monastery, Perugino painted an ecstatic *Crucifixion and Saints* on the end wall (1493-6). It is arranged as three scenes divided by arches and in the background there is a sweeping, gentle landscape suffused with light *(9 a.m.-12 noon and 5-7 p.m.).* □

▶ SANTA MARIA MAGGIORE
corner of v. de' Vecchietti and v. di Cerretani   C3-4

One of the oldest churches in Florence (pre-11C, rebuilt 13C), its dark, atmospheric interior contains fragments of medieval frescos and an extraordinary 13C gilded polychrome bas-relief in wood of the *Madonna and Child Enthroned★.* On the outside of the bell tower, near the top and facing the v. de' Cerretani, there is a bust of a Roman matron, which has been nicknamed **Berta** by the people of Florence. □

▶ SANTA MARIA NOVELLA**
p. S. Maria Novella   B2-3

According to tradition this Dominican church was designed by two members of the order and begun in 1268. In any event, with its large, severe interior, it is a masterpiece of Florentine Gothic. The superb Renaissance **façade★**, begun in 1430, was continued in 1456-70 by Leon Battista Alberti at the request of the rich merchant Giovanni Rucellai. In building it, Alberti reworked in large measure elements that were already present in the city's Romanesque churches, among them the facing of two-coloured marble geometrical patterns, the blind arcades and the green half-columns. However, the innovations that he introduced, such as the elegant portal, the fantastic volutes, and the inlaid decoration incorporating the arms of the Rucellai, are outstanding.

Santa Maria Novella

▶ The **interior** has a nave and two aisles with pillars in a mixture of styles and it also contains numerous works of art. There is a powerful Masaccio fresco, the *Trinity, the Virgin and Donors★★*, a wooden *Crucifix★* by Brunelleschi and a large panel painting of the *Cross★★* by Giotto. Of particular interest is the fresco cycle of the *Story of the Virgin and St. John the Baptist★* by Domenico Ghirlandaio, which covers the apse walls and which displays views of Florence and its people at the time of Lorenzo the Magnificent. ▶ The cloisters *(9 a.m.-7 p.m.; hols 9 a.m.-1 p.m.; closed Fri)* are entered through the Baroque portal to the l. of the façade. The first, the broad **Chiostro Verde,** is 14C and on the walls of its arcades it has restored **frescos★** by 15C artists, the most important of whom is Paolo Uccello. ▶ Frescos from the previous century (Andrea da Firenze) devoted to the glory of the church and the Dominican order cover the interior of the **Cappellone degli Spagnoli★** (Spanish chapel), the former chapterhouse of the convent which opens off the north side of the cloister. ▶ Finally, behind the chapel, there is the quiet **Chiostrino dei Morti,** which contains old tombstones and 14C frescos. It is one of the most atmospheric corners of Florence. □

▶ SANT'AMBROGIO
at end of v. Pietrapiana   D6

Rebuilt several times, Sant'Ambrogio is like a pattern book of various architectural styles. However, it remains important for the works of art that it contains. The **Cappella del Miracolo** is perhaps the most interesting part of the church with both a fresco by Cosimo Rosselli, which gives a view of the edge of Florence in the 15C, and a magnificent marble **tabernacle**, one of the finest pieces by the sculptor Mino da Fiesole (15C). ▯

▶ SANTA TRINITA*
p. S. Trinita D3

Although it has a Baroque façade built by Buontalenti (1594), it is its 14C interior that makes it one of the most beautiful Gothic churches in the city. There are major works by a number of 15C Florentine artists, including Lorenzo Monaco, Luca della Robbia and Ghirlandaio. The first of these painted an enchanting triptych of the *Annunciation*★ and the second built the marble *Federighi tomb*, which is decorated by a superb ceramic frame. Ghirlandaio, as well as painting the altarpiece the *Adoration of the Shepherds*★, also frescoed the famous **Cappella Sassetti** (coin-operated light). This is of particular interest for the portraits of late 15C figures, particularly members of the Medici court, as well as views of such monuments and parts of Florence as the Loggia dei Lanzi, the Palazzo Vecchio and the p. S. Trinita as they then were. ▯

▶ SANTI APOSTOLI
from Borgo SS. Apostoli E3

The old church of the Holy Apostles, which stands in a small piazza surrounded by ancient houses, was built in the 11C. It has a beautiful Renaissance door, the work of Rovezzano. Its Romanesque interior, with its green marble columns, shows that Florence before the comune already had monuments of great beauty.

▶ SANTISSIMA ANNUNZIATA*
p. della SS. Annunziata A6

It is not difficult to imagine the importance of this church in a city which until 1750 began the new year on 25 March, the day of the Annunciation, rather than 1 January, and it is still outstanding amongst Florentine churches for the splendour of its decoration. It was an extremely wealthy sanctuary and in the 17C it contained several thousand votive offerings as well as hundreds of wax statues depicting famous and powerful figures who, by these portraits, placed themselves under the protection of the Madonna. This unusual assemblage also filled the enormous adjacent cloister but unfortunately it has completely vanished. Rebuilt by Michelozzo and then altered, the church's main interest now is its 15C-16C **frescos**★ (Rosso Fiorentino, Pontormo, Andrea del Sarto, Alessio Baldovinetti, Cosimo Rosselli), which decorate the atrium (known as the **Chiostrino dei Voti**), and the Renaissance paintings in its interior. The **sanctuary**, a grand classical rotonda, is largely the work of Leon Battista Alberti (15C) and, as a design, the impression that it makes, to echo the judgment given in Florence at the time of its building, is to be 'capricious and difficult'. ▯

▶ SANTO SPIRITO**
p. S. Spirito E2

The architects who continued the work of Brunelleschi in the course of the 15C did not follow his designs to the letter when rebuilding this Augustinian church. The magical harmony of the interior, however, clearly displays the stamp of his genius and if the Renaissance stands for elegance, harmony and rhythm of form, then this is certainly one of its supreme expressions.

▶ The paintings inside are superb. There is a *Madonna Enthroned and Saints*★ (r. arm of the transept, 5th chapel) by Filippino Lippi. Other works include Sansovino's carvings in white marble (15C) in the **Cappella Corbinelli** (l. arm of the transept). The l. aisle leads into a **vestibule**★ (15C) with a superb coffered barrel vault supported by columns and then into a fine octagonal Renaissance **sacristy**★ by Giuliano da Sangallo. ▶ To the l. of the church is the Cenacolo di S. Spirito (→). ▯

▶ SPEDALE DEGLI INNOCENTI*
p. della SS. Annunziata B6

This enormous hospital was built in the 15C to house abandoned children. It is arranged around large courtyards and stands on the **piazza SS. Annunziata**★ at the top of a flight of steps (the other two sides of the square are flanked by 16C arcades). It is fronted by Brunelleschi's splendid **Loggia**★, one of the earliest examples of Renaissance architecture (1419). The beautiful harmony of its broad arches and slender columns was enhanced in the second half of the 15C by ten enamelled terra-cotta **tondi**★ by Andrea della Robbia, depicting swaddled babies. 15C-16C works form the bulk of the **collection** of detached frescos arranged in the first floor corridors and in the **Gallery** *(summer 9 a.m.-7 p.m.; winter and hols 9 a.m.-1 p.m.; closed Wed)*. There is an *Adoration of the Magi*★ by Ghirlandaio, as well as some sculptures, furniture and paintings from other centuries, ranging from the 14C-18C. ▯

▶ UFFIZI**
p. degli Uffizi 6 E4

The **Palazzo** with portico and loggia was built in 1560-80 by Giorgio Vasari in order to provide Cosimo I with a single building to house the numerous central offices of the Grand-Duchy. As early as the end of the 16C this administrative function was complemented by another, totally different one, as the Medici began to transform the top floor into a place to house and display their important art collections.

▶ The heritage that can be admired today in the **Galleria degli Uffizi** *(9 a.m.-2 p.m.; summer 9 a.m.-7 p.m.; hols 9 a.m.-1 p.m.; closed Mon)* is therefore the result of a process of acquisition, selection and rearrangement stretching over several centuries and consists mostly of antique sculpture and paintings ranging from the 13C-18C. These latter works cover both Italian and foreign painting but first and foremost they provide an extraordinary and comprehensive survey of the Florentine school from Cimabue (13C) to Bronzino (16C). The Corridoio Vasariano houses the **Collection of Self-Portraits** *(guided tour, book in advance, Wed, Fri and Sun 9:30 a.m.)*, which includes quite a number of more recent paintings. ▯

Uffizi and Palazzo Vecchio

▶ **VIA DE' TORNABUONI***

C-D3

This, the most elegant and famous of Florence's streets, runs from the p. Antinori, which takes its name from the splendid **palazzo** built between 1461-66, possibly by Giuliano da Maiano, to the marvelous Ponte S. Trinita (→). The street is flanked by some of the city's most beautiful buildings, such as the Palazzo Strozzi (→). Before it reaches the end of the bridge, the street crosses the p. S. Trinita. At its centre this square has a tall granite column with a statue of Justice, and it is ringed by monumental buildings like the 16C classical façade of the Palazzo Bartolini Salimbeni and that of the church (→) from which the square takes its name. However, the via de' Tornabuoni is known mainly as a meeting place and, above all, for its exclusive and sophisticated shops, whose windows display goods made by the world's leaders of fashion.   □

● *Practical information*

Information: v. Manzoni 16, ☎ 2478141; v. Tornabuoni 15 (C-D3), ☎ 216544 (main office), ☎ 217459.

✈ at Pisa ☎ 050/28088; at Perétola ☎ 370123. *Alitalia,* ☎ 373498. *Alitalia,* lungarno Acciaioli 10-12 (E4), ☎ 2788/263051.

🚂 (A-B2), ☎ 278785; *Firenze Rifredi,* ☎ 411138.

🚌 from p. della Stazione and adjoining piazze.
Car rental: *Avis,* Borgognissanti 128r, ☎ 213629; *Hertz,* v. Maso Finiguerra 33r, ☎ 298205; *Maggiore,* v. Maso Finiguerra 11r, ☎ 210238.

SOS: public emergency service, ☎ 113; police emergency, ☎ 112; medical service, ☎ 477891; ambulances, ☎ 212222, ☎ 215555; chemists' shops open on holidays, ☎ 192; state police, ☎ 49771; municipal police, ☎ 352141; fire brigade, ☎ 222222; traffic service *ACI,*

☎ 116. Offices for telegrams and trunk and international telephone calls (information: ☎ 160): *Palazzo delle Poste,* v. Pellicceria (D6, open 24 hours); inside *S. Maria Novella* station, telegram office open 24 hours, public telephone booth open 7:30 a.m.-9:30 p.m., telegram dictation service, ☎ 186.

Weather: forecast, ☎ 2691; road conditions, ☎ 2692.

Fairs and markets: *international handicrafts exhibition and market,* Fortezza da Basso, ☎ 470991 (Apr-beginning of May); *international antiques exhibition,* ☎ 282283 (Sep-Oct, odd-numbered years, Palazzo Strozzi); numerous other exhibitions (gift articles, gold works, furniture) at the *Palazzo degli Affari,* ☎ 27731 and Fortezza da Basso; *Florence trade fair,* ☎ 215867 (Jan and Sep; leather and other animal skins).

Events: *Scoppio del Carro,* a festival held in courtyard of Santa Maria del Fiore (Easter); *Festa del Grillo,* a fair in the Cascine (Ascension Day); football matches played in historical costumes in p. della Signoria (Jun); *Festa delle Rificolone* (7 Sep); exhibitions of plants and flowers in loggia of the Uffizi (end of Apr); displays of irises and roses near p. Michelangelo (May); ready-to-wear fashion shows in spring and autumn (*Pitti Moda,* Florence institute for Italian fashions, ☎ 219331-211732); *Florence Music Festival,* ☎ 22791 (end of Apr-beginning of Jul; *Teatro Comunale, Teatro della Pergola, Giardino di Bòboli*); opera season (autumn) and symphony season (Jan-Apr) at *Teatro Comunale,* ☎ 2779313; at *villa Poggio Imperiale* and *Teatro della Pergola,* ☎ 2479651 (autumn-spring; Amici della musica,* ☎ 607440); drama seasons at *Teatro della Pergola* and various other theatres in city; *Florence summer;* art exhibitions at palazzi: *Pitti, Medici-Riccardi, Strozzi* and at *Forte di Belvedere; festival dei popoli,* ☎ 294353 (social documentary films; Nov-Dec); *Florence Festival of independent films* (Apr-Jun)at *Palazzo dei Congressi.*

Nature conservation: regional office of *WWF,* v. S. Gallo 32, ☎ 476079; *Amici della bicicletta,* v. Fortini 35, ☎ 686467; *LIPU,* v. S. Gallo 32, ☎ 474013 (birdwatching courses); *Italia Nostra,* v. Gramsci 9/A, ☎ 2479213.

Botanical garden: *Giardino dei Semplici,* v. Micheli 3 (A6), ☎ 284696 (Mon-Wed, 9 a.m.-12 noon).

Guided tours: *Cooperativa Giotto,* v. Gramsci 9/A, ☎ 2478188; coach trips organized by *CIT,* ☎ 2943046-284145 and other agencies (day trips also include some environs); daily visits to Florentine villas (Apr-Jun p.m.) and to Chianti estates (Sep-Oct; Tue, Thu and Sat), trips to Pisa, Siena and San Gimignano organized by *Agriturist,* p. S. Firenze 3 (D5), ☎ 287838.

Horseback riding: *Centro ippico toscano,* at Cascine, v. Vespucci 5/a, ☎ 372621 (riding school); *Centro ippico La Torre,* v. dei Serragli 144 (associate of *ANTE*); *Scuola di equitazione fiorentina,* v. Benivieni 9, ☎ 632718; *Country riding club,* at Scandicci *(6 km SW),* at Badia a Settimo, v.di Grioli, ☎ 790277.

Instruction: courses in acting, elocution, mime, clowning: *Theatrical college,* v. Alfani 84, ☎ 215543 (15 Oct-15 Jun, Mon-Thu; international courses for advanced drama students are held at theatre from mid-Aug-Sep); monthly courses in restoring pictures, antique woodwork and ceramics, courses in painting and antique dealing: *Istituto per l'arte e il restauro,* borgo S. Croce 10 (Palazzo Spinelli), ☎ 244809; courses in classical, modern and Oriental dancing (for adults and children aged 5 and above): *Centro studi danza,* p. Signoria 7, ☎ 218672; courses in Italian language and culture for foreigners: *Koiné,* v. de' Pandolfini 27, ☎ 265088 (language courses held in summer at Cortona and Orbetello); *Centro di cultura per stranieri Lorenzo de'Medici,* p. delle Pallotole 1, ☎ 283142; *Scuola Leonardo da Vinci,* v.Brunelleschi 4, ☎ 924247 (also courses in handicraft).

Children's facilities: courses in dancing and acting, *Accademia dei piccoli,* v. Alfani 81, ☎ 283137.

Sailing: *Lega Navale,* v. dei Bardi 5, ☎ 217015 (courses in sailing and navigation); *Centro nautico italiano,* p. della Signoria 31r, ☎ 287045 (cruising courses in the Tuscan Archipelago, the Adriatic and the Eastern Mediterranean).

Canoeing: *Società canottieri comunali,* lungarno Ferrucci 6, ☎ 6812151.

Skindiving: *Federazione Italiana,* v. Nazionale 23, ☎ 218967; *Centro tecnico subacqueo,* v. Giuliani 209, ☎ 451475; *gruppo subacqueo Centostelle,* v. Fortezza 9r, ☎ 483832.

Swimming: *Amici del nuote,* v. del Romito 38, ☎ 483951; *Costoli,* v.Paoli, ☎ 675744; *Micropiscina Isolotto,* v. Bandinelli 61, ☎ 703760; *Tropos,* v. Orcagna 20/A, ☎ 671581 (courses in swimming and skindiving); *Centro sportivo fiorentino,* v. Bardazzi 15, ☎ 430703 (also sauna and gymnasium); *Rari Nantes Florentia,* lungarno Ferrucci 24, ☎ 6812141 (swimming, diving, water polo); *Bellariva,* lungarno Colombo 6, ☎ 677521; *Le Pavoniere,* at Cascione, v. degli Olmi, ☎ 367506.

Golf: *Golf club Ugolino,* at Gràssina *(7 km SE),* strada Chiantigiana-Impruneta, ☎ 2051009.

Flying: *Perétola civilian airport,* ☎ 370313.

Fishing: *Federazione italiana pesca sportiva,* v. de' Neri 6, ☎ 214073 (information on fishing conditions).

Archery: *Compagnia Arcieri Ugo di Toscana,* v. dei Pandolfini 16, ☎ 2340792.

Clay pigeon shooting: p. delle Cascine, ☎ 360052.

Fencing: *Circolo scherma Firenze,* v. Fiume 5, ☎ 282250.

Motorcycling: *Moto club Firenze,* v. Fosso Macinante 13, ☎ 356659; Crossodromo di Polcanto, at Borgo S. Lorenzo *(28 km NE).*

Parachuting: *Associazione aeronautica militare,* v. I. da Diacceto 1-3/B, ☎ 287426.

Tennis: *Circolo tennis alle Cascine,* ☎ 356651; *Assi Giglio Rosso,* v. Michelangiolo 61, ☎ 6812686; *Tennis club Rifredi,* v. Facibeni, ☎ 432552; *Il Poggetto,* v. M. Mercati 24/B, ☎ 460127 (also swimming pool, skating, bowling); Piazzale Michelangiolo, ☎ 6811880; *Affrico,* v. M. Fanti 20, ☎ 600845.

● Hotels

★★★★★ **Excelsior Italie,** p. Ognissanti 3 (C1-2 a), ☎ 264201, 205 rm Ⓟ ⅋ 487,000; bkf: 21,000.
★★★★★ **G.H. Villa Cora,** v. Machiavelli 18, ☎ 2298451, 48 rm Ⓟ ⚘ ⚏ ⅋ ⛟ 19C villa in Neoclassical style, 356,000; bkf: 16,000.
★★★★★ **Regency,** p. D'Azeglio 3, ☎ 245247, 38 rm Ⓟ ⚏ ⅋ Two villas, former residence of senior officials when Florence was capital of Italy, 413,000. Rest. ◆◆◆ *Relais le Jardin* closed Sun. Quality Tuscan cuisine, 50/65,000.
★★★★★ **Savoy,** p. della Repubblica 7 (C4 b), ☎ 283313, 101 rm Ⓟ 454,000; bkf: 20,000.
★★★★★ **Villa Medici,** v. il Prato 42 (B1 c), ☎ 261331, 107 rm Ⓟ ⅋ ⛁ 450,000; bkf: 15,000.
★★★★ **Alexander,** v. Guidoni 101, ☎ 4378951, 88 rm Ⓟ ⚏ ⛟ 180,000; bkf: 10,000.
★★★★ **Anglo-American,** v. Garibaldi 9, ☎ 282114, 118 rm Ⓟ ⚏ ⅋ 236,000.
★★★★ **Croce di Malta,** v. della Scala 7 (C2 d), ☎ 282600, 98 rm Ⓟ ⚏ ⅋ ⛁ 205,000.
★★★★ **De la Ville,** p. Antinori 1 (C3 e), ☎ 261805, 75 rm Ⓟ ⛁ 240,000.
★★★★ **Etap Hotel Astoria,** v. del Giglio 9 (B3 f), ☎ 298095, 90 rm Ⓟ ⅋ 235,000.
★★★★ **Executive,** v. Curtatone 5 (B-C1 g), ☎ 217451, 40 rm Ⓟ No restaurant, 215,000.
★★★★ **G.H. Baglioni,** p. Unità Italiana 6 (B3 h), ☎ 218441, 195 rm Ⓟ ⅋ 245,000.
★★★★ **G.H. Majestic,** v. Melarancio 1 (B3 i), ☎ 264021, 103 rm Ⓟ 205,000; bkf: 18,000.

★★★★ **G.H. Minerva,** p. S. Maria Novella 16 (C21), ☎ 284555, 112 rm Ⓟ ⅋ ⛁ 205,000; bkf: 16,000.
★★★★ **Jolly Carlton,** p. Vittorio Veneto 4/A, ☎ 2770, 167 rm Ⓟ ⛁ 225,000.
★★★★ **Kraft,** v. Solferino 2, ☎ 284273, 68 rm Ⓟ ⅋ ⛁ 205,000; bkf: 16,000.
★★★★ **Londra,** v. J. da Diacceto 18, ☎ 262791, 107 rm Ⓟ ⅋ 205,000; bkf: 16,000.
★★★★ **Lungarno,** borgo S. Jacopo 14 (E3 m), ☎ 264211, 71 rm Ⓟ No restaurant, 190,000; bkf: 12,000.
★★★★ **Michelangelo,** v. F.lli Rosselli 2, ☎ 278711, 138 rm Ⓟ 180,000.
★★★★ **Monginevro,** v. di Novoli 59, ☎ 431441, 127 rm Ⓟ ⛟ 160,000.
★★★★ **Montebello Splendid,** v. Montebello 60, ☎ 298051, 41 rm Ⓟ ⚏ ⅋240,000.
★★★★ **Pierre,** v. Lamberti 5 (D4 n), ☎ 216218, 39 rm Ⓟ ⅋ No restaurant, 200,000; bkf: 15,000.
★★★★ **Plaza Hotel Lucchesi,** lungarno Zecca Vecchia 38, ☎ 264141, 104 rm Ⓟ ⅋ 230,000.
★★★★ **Signoria,** v. delle Terme 1 (E4 p), ☎ 214530, 27 rm Ⓟ No restaurant, 195,000.
★★★★ **Villa Belvedere,** v. B. Castelli 3, ☎ 222501, 27 rm Ⓟ ⚘ ⅋ ⛟ closed Dec-Feb. No restaurant, 156,000; bkf: 12,000.
★★★★ **Villa Carlotta,** v. Michele di Lando 3, ☎ 220530, 26 rm Ⓟ ⚘ 227,000.
★★★★ **Ville sull'Arno,** lungarno Colombo 5, ☎ 670971, 47rm Ⓟ ⅋ ⛁ No restaurant, 173,000; bkf: 12,000.
★★★ **Astor,** v. Milton 41, ☎ 483391, 25 rm Ⓟ ⅋ 91,000.
★★★ **Auto Hotel Park,** v. Valdegola 1, ☎ 431771, 114 rm Ⓟ ⅋ 104,000; bkf: 9,000.
★★★ **Balestri,** p. Mentana 7 (E5 q), ☎ 214743, 50 rm Ⓟ ⛟ closed 1 Dec-14 Mar. No restaurant, 96,000; bkf: 12,000.
★★★ **Capitol,** v. Amendola 34, ☎ 675201, 88 rm Ⓟ ⅋ ⛟ 125,000.
★★★ **Columbus,** lungarno Colombo 22/A, ☎ 677251, 100 rm Ⓟ 97,000; bkf: 9,000.
★★★ **Concorde,** v. L. Gori 10, ☎ 373551, 101 rm Ⓟ ⅋ 92,000; bkf: 8,000.
★★★ **Fleming,** v. Guidoni 87, ☎ 4376939, 100 rm ⅋ ⛟ No restaurant, 103,000; bkf: 7,000.
★★★ **Franchi,** v. Sgambati 28, ☎ 372563, 35 rm Ⓟ No restaurant, 92,000; bkf: 9,000.
★★★ **Golf,** v. F.lli Rosselli 56, ☎ 293088, 39 rm Ⓟ ⅋ ⛟ No restaurant, 100,000; bkf: 10,000.
★★★ **Jane,** v. Orcagna 56, ☎ 677382, 28 rm Ⓟ ⚏ ⛟ No restaurant, 63,000; bkf: 7,000.
★★★ **Mediterraneo,** lungarno del Tempio 42, ☎ 672241, 340 rm Ⓟ ⚏ 80,000.
★★★ **Residenza,** v. Tornabuoni 8 (D3 r), ☎ 284197, 24 rm Ⓟ 101,000; bkf: 10,000.
★★ **Orcagna,** v. Orcagna 57, ☎ 675959, 18 rm Ⓟ ⚏ No restaurant, 70,000.
★★ **Splendor,** v. S. Gallo 30 (A5 s), ☎ 483427, 31 rm Ⓟ No restaurant, 58,000; bkf: 10,000.

● Restaurants

● ◆◆◆◆ **Enoteca Pinchiorri,** v. Ghibellina 87 (D6 ag), ☎ 242777, closed Sun, Mon noon, Aug and Christmas. Located in Palazzo Ciofi; garden and well-stocked wine cellar. Creative cuisine: maltagliati with duck sauce and black olives; scampi tails with diced tomato, 100/120,000.
● ◆◆◆◆ **Oliviero,** v. delle Terme 51r (D3 an), ☎ 287643, closed noon, Sun and Aug. Refined, elegant furnishings. Regional and international cuisine: pasta cardinale, soufflé arlecchino, 50/60,000.
● ◆◆◆◆ **Sabatini,** v. de' Panzini 9/A (C3 ar), ☎ 211559, closed Mon. Traditional society rendezvous, refined service. Regional and international cuisine: spaghetti cooked at table, ribollita, 45/70,000.
● ◆◆◆ **Dino,** v. Ghibellina 51r (D6 af) ☎ 241452, closed

Sun eve, Mon and Aug. Old wine shop, converted into a lively trattoria. Regional and creative cuisine: crostini di bosco, braised beef Granduca, 25/35,000.
● ♦♦♦ *13 Gobbi,* v. del Porcellana 9r (C2 at), ☎ 298769, closed Sun, Mon and Jul-Aug. Traditional restaurant and beer-house. Regional cuisine: pappardelle with mushrooms, 30/40,000.

Florentine cooking

Florence offers many specialties including bean soup in which garden and mountain herbs have been cooked in oil; lamb, veal and chicken fricassee; tripe with parmesan and tomatoes; fritto misto, made with brains croquettes, calf sweetbread, artichokes, zucchinis, lamb chops, all rolled in flour and egg yolks and golden fried in oil. Fegatelli a la Florentine are pieces of pork-liver rolled in chopped fennel flowers, stuffed into casings and then baked, grilled or skewered.

♦♦♦ *Alfredo sull'Arno,* v. dei Bardi 46r (E4 t), ☎ 283808, closed Sun and Jul. Terrace overlooking Arno with view of Ponte Vecchio. Regional and Italian cuisine: pappardelle with wild boar, curried scampi, 25/35,000.
♦♦♦ *Barrino,* v. de' Biffi 2r (B4 u), ☎ 215180, closed Sun and Aug. Spectacular site. Italian and creative cuisine: asparagus ravioli, crayfish tiepidi with chervil, 40/50,000.
♦♦♦ *Cantinetta Antinori,* p. Antinori 3 (C3 ab), ☎ 292234, closed Sat, Sun, Easter, Aug, and Christmas. Small tables in the palazzo Antinori. Regional cuisine: pappa al pomodoro, homemade spezzatino, 35/45,000.
♦♦♦ *Dante — al Lume di Candela,* v. delle Terme 23r (D3 ae), ☎ 294566, closed Sun and 15-31 Aug. English-inspired style. Regional and international cuisine: pasta cardinale, escalope Jean Bart, 35/50,000.
♦♦♦ *Harry's Bar,* lungarno Vespucci 22r (D2 al), ☎ 296700, closed Sun and Dec-Jan. Elegant atmosphere of a grand café and an English club. Italian and international cuisine: smoked veal, taglierini al gratin, pasta casereccia, 40/50,000.
♦♦♦ *Latini,* v. Palchetti 6r (D2 am), ☎ 210916, closed Mon, Tue noon, 15-31 Jul and Christmas. Tastefully converted in former stables of palazzo Rucellai Regional cuisine: pappa al pomodoro, roast rabbit, 30/40,000.
♦♦♦ *Otello,* v. degli Orti Oricellari 36r (B1 ap), ☎ 215819, closed Tue. Near S. Maria Novella station. Regional cuisine: mixed grill from the spit, wild boar maremmana, 35/50,000.
♦♦♦ *Paoli,* v. Tavolini 12r (D4 aq), ☎ 216215, closed Tue. 14C Florentine interior. Regional cuisine: penne strascicate, tiramis, 25/45,000.
♦♦♦ *Pierot,* p. Gaddi 25 r, ☎ 702100, closed Sun and 15-31 Jul. Seafood: sea bass in foil, stewed squid, 25/40,000.
♦♦ *Buca Mario,* p. Ottaviani 16r (C2 v), ☎ 214179, closed Wed, Thu noon, and 10-30 Jul. Regional cuisine: pappa al pomodoro, stew alla toscana, 30/45,000.
♦♦ *Cammillo,* borgo S. Jacopo 57r (E3 z), ☎ 212427, closed Wed, Thu, Aug and Dec-Jan. Regional and Emilian cuisine: curried tortellini, homemade tagliatelle, homemade wines, 40/60,000.
♦♦ *Coco Lezzone,* v. Parioncino 26r (D3 ad), ☎ 287178, closed Sat and Sun in summer, Mon and Tue eve in winter and Jul-Aug. May have to share table with strangers. Regional cuisine: tomatoes in oil, escalopes with globe artichokes, 30/45,000.
♦♦ *Fagioli,* corso dei Tintori 47r (E5 ah), ☎ 244285, closed Sat, Sun and Aug. Simple trattoria, managed with care. Regional cuisine: tomatoes cooked in oil, roast meat dishes, 20/30,000.
♦♦ *Fonticine,* v. Nazionale 79r (A3 ai), ☎ 282106, closed Sat and Jul-Aug. In courtyard with pergola. Regional and Emilian cuisine: roast or grilled meat, tripe alla fiorentina, 30/45,000.

♦ *Cantinone del Gallo Nero,* v. S. Spirito 6r (E2-3 ac), ☎ 218898, closed Mon, noon on hols and Aug. Typical 14C wine cellar. Regional cuisine: kidney beans all'uccelletto with sausage, garlic toast with black cabbage and kidney beans, 15/25,000.
♦ *Sostanza,* v. del Porcellana 25r (C2 as), ☎ 212691, closed Sat eve, Sun and Aug. This old trattoria, now almost an institution, has a marble bar-counter and large communal tables. Regional cuisine: tripe alla fiorentina, roast pigeon, 30/35,000.

 # Recommended

Auction houses: rooms for international auctions and exhibitions, v. Maggio 11, ☎ 293000-282905; *Pitti auction house,* v. Maggio 15, ☎ 296382; *Pandolfini auction house,* Borgo degli Albizi 26, ☎ 2340888; *Sotheby's Italia,* v. G. Capponi 26, ☎ 2479021.
Craft workshops: *Agnoletti jeweler's shop,* v. Tesi 65, ☎ 240810 (advance booking); semi-precious stones and mosaics at *Paci,* v. S. Monaca 13, ☎ 212168 and *Chiasso,* degli Altouiti 1/3 (D-E3), ☎ 263662; bronzes at *Ciulli,* v. della Fonderia 51, ☎ 221156 (advance booking) and *Banchi,* v. dei Serragli 10, ☎ 294694; picture restoration at *Garosi,* p. Mercato Nuovo (D4), ☎ 263348 (advance booking); crystal restoration and antique glass at *Locchi,* v. Burchiello 10, ☎ 2298371; metal desk furniture at *Cavari,* v. D'Annunzio 19, ☎ 675425; furnishings at *Carretti,* v. Presto di S. Martino 8/10 (E2), ☎ 287967; wrought iron at *Giachetti,* v. Toscanella 3/5 (E3), ☎ 218567.
Cycling: *Ciao e Basta agency,* v. Alamanni corner of p. Stazione (B2), ☎ 213307-263985 (office).
Discothèques: *Giab Jim,* v. Sassetti (D3), ☎ 282018.

Arts and crafts in Florence

From the Middle Ages until recently, Florence gained its wealth with the wool and silk industries. Today, only one textile plant is still in operation. However, Florence's arts and crafts have acquired an international reputation. Marble and stone carving is also an important activity and Florence's sculptors have extraordinary talents. The ceramics industry began developing at the beginning of the 18C in a factory in Doccia near Florence. Since then, the factory has expanded and now produces porcelain and earthenware dishes as well as electrical and laboratory equipment.

Entertainment information: cinemas, ☎ 198; theatres, exhibitions, concerts, etc. are listed in the monthly, *Firenze Spettacolo,* in the daily, *La Nazione,* in the *Carnet del Turista* booklet, published by the *Chiavi d'Oro* association of hotel porters (published weekly in summer, distributed free of charge at hotels with three or more stars).
Palazzetto dello sport: v. B. Dei 56, ☎ 417004.
Palazzo dei congressi: Pratello Orsini 1 (v. Valfonda) (A2-3), ☎ 262242.
Race courses: *Ippodromo Le Cascine,* p. delle Cascine, ☎ 353394 (galloping); *Ippodromo delle Mulina,* at Cascine, v. del Pégaso, ☎ 411130 (trotting).
Shopping: best shopping streets: v. Calzaiuoli, v. de' Cerretani, v. Panzani, Borgo S. Lorenzo, v. de' Martelli and other streets around the Duomo; v. Roma, v. Calimala and Por S. Maria in city centre; Borgo S. Jacopo, v. Maggio and v. Guicciardini on left bank of Arno. Jewelers' shops, cut stones and pearls in workshops on Ponte Vecchio; leather goods, purses, straw hats at the stalls under-

neath Uffizi, at Porcellino market and markets around S. Lorenzo and S. Croce (more luxury items are to be found in historical city centre and near school of leatherworking at S. Croce); linen embroidery in various shops in Por S. Maria, v. Porta Rossa, v. Calimala; antiques, paintings and *objets d'art* in streets along Arno; modern handicrafts in areas adjoining Ponte Vecchio; old books, fashion in v. Tornabuoni, v. Strozzi and adjoining streets; miniature handicraft products in quarters around S. Croce and S. Lorenzo and in narrow streets on left bank of Arno. **Wines:** *Murga wine cellar,* p. S. Maria Novella 15r, ☎ 293149.
Youth hostel: *Ostello Europa-Villa Camerata,* v. Righi 2/4, ☎ 601451.
♥ historic café: *Caffè pasticceria Rivoire,* v. Vacchereccia 4r (p. della Signoria); pasticceria: *zuccotto* (ice-cream cake), *pan di ramerino* (rosemary bread), *bomboloni* (doughnuts), *brigidini* (aniseed wafers), pancakes and various kinds of flat loaves.

● *Environs*

Villa di ARTIMINO

Florence 21 km
Pop. 158 ⊠ 50040 ☎ 055

The numerous Medici pleasure villas were all built in particularly beautiful sites between the mid-15C and the late 16C. From the Villa d'Artimino, built for Grand-Duke Ferdinando I on the flat part of a hill *(Tue 8 a.m.-12 noon and 2-6 p.m.)*, there is an extensive view of the valley of the Arno, including Florence, and also of Prato, Pistoia and the surrounding hills. This is also one of the most architecturally beautiful villas (designed by B. Buontalenti, 1594) and appears as a broad, white building, with powerful sloping corner buttresses. In front it has a staircase which leads to a monumental open entrance loggia on the first floor. The roof is oddly decorated by a forest of chimneys. Inside there is an **Etruscan archaeological museum** with finds from nearby Comeana *(Sat 3:30-6:30 p.m., Sun 9 a.m.-12 noon, Mon 9 a.m.-12 noon and 3-6:30 p.m.; on other days, advance booking,* ☎ 871002). ▫

Practical information _____

Restaurants:
♦♦♦ *Biagio Pignatta,* ☎ 8718081, closed Wed. In old stables of Medici villa of La Ferdinanda. Regional and creative cuisine: pancakes Caterina dè Medici,leg of pork with apple sauce, 25/45,000.
♦♦♦ *Delfina,* v. della Chiesa, 1 ☎ 8718074, closed Mon eve, Tue, 1-10 Jan, and Aug. In converted lodge, terraces overlooking countryside and Medici villa of La Ferdinanda. Regional cuisine: soup La Ferdinanda, nettle risotto, 30/40,000.

CALENZANO

Florence 13 km
Pop. 14,202 ⊠ 50041 ☎ 055

This was once a farming area, but has now been developed and has become quite industrialized. There is a charming medieval **village of Castello,** which stands in a defensive position on a hill surrounded by old walls with a gatehouse tower. At

v. Firenze 12 there is a **museum of toy soldiers** and historical statuettes *(9 a.m.-12 noon on weekdays; 9:30 a.m.-12:30 p.m. on hols).* The **Villa Fritelli** is a fine example of Art Nouveau architecture. ▫

Practical information _____

Hotel:
★★★★ *First,* v. Ciolli 5, ☎ 8876042, 116 rm ℗ ⅏ ⅙ ▣ ⌀ 130,000; bkf: 10,000.
Restaurant:
♦♦ *Terrazza,* v. del Castello 25, ☎ 8879078, closed Sun, Mon and Aug. Old trattoria built from walls of 14C Guelph castle with view of Florence. Regional and Italian cuisine: tagliatelle with mushrooms, gran pezzo spit-roasted, 19/35,000.

Villa di CASTELLO

Florence 6 km
⊠ 50141 ☎ 055

The **Villa** was owned by a branch of the Medici family as early as 1480, when it housed works such as Botticelli's *Primavera.* The building is notable for its Renaissance architecture and the 17C-18C frescos decorating the rooms. Today the **Accademia della Crusca** *(apply to the warden)* is housed here. The magnificent terraced **garden**★ *(9 a.m.-4:30 p.m.; 6:30 p.m. in summer)* is the oldest Italian-style garden (16C) and has statues, fountains and waterworks. Strange groups of animals carved in stone and marble of various colours (Giambologna) occupy the artifical grotto at the end of the central avenue. The terrace leads up to the park where there is another bizarre 16C work: a colossal figure known as Gennaio (January), which is by Ammannati. ▫

La CERTOSA DEL GALLUZZO

Florence 5 km
⊠ 50124 ☎ 055

Set in the hills S of Florence, the **Certosa del Galluzzo** *(guided tours of the charterhouse every 30 mns, 9 a.m.-12 noon and 4-7 p.m., 3-5 p.m. in winter)* was built in 1341 thanks to the munificence of the Acciaiuoli, an important family of Florentine bankers. **Funerary monuments** and fine tomb slabs of members of the family are to be found in the underground chapels of the **church;** these works of art (14C-16C) are among the attractions of this imposing

---

Florence's villas

The patrician villas around Florence exude a nostalgic charm. While many of these villas are privately owned, the Italian government has bought a few and opened them up to visitors. Poggio a Caiano was built in 1679 for Lorenzo the Magnificent and features magnificent frescos by Filippino Lippi, Pontono, Franciatigio, Andrea del Sarto and Allon. The Villa di Castella holds two surprises for the visitor: a grotto with stone animals and beautiful fountains, both of which were described by Montaigne. The nearby castle of the Brunelleschi family, la Petraia, houses the Venus by Jean de Bologne. Boccaccio set many of the stories of his Decameron in the garden of the Villa Palmieri in Fiesole.

complex. There are splendid carved and inlaid 16C walnut **choir stalls** in the **monks' choir** of the same church. The entrance courtyard and the various **cloisters** are charming, particularly the **Chiostro Grande**, with its 66 Della Robbia terra-cotta heads. Each of the minute, attractive houses where the monks live has a loggia and a small garden. For those who appreciate genuine liqueurs, the monastery's inevitable pharmacy has some tempting items on offer. The *Passion of Christ* by Pontormo is among the works in the beautiful **picture gallery** housed in the Gothic **Palazzo degli Studi**.

Practical information ———————————

Restaurant:
♦♦♦ *Certosa,* v. Cassia 1, ☎ 2047109, closed Tue in winter. Cheerful setting with music, dancing and open-air grilling on summer evenings. Regional cuisine: tagliatelle moscovita, gran pezzo, 25/40,000.

FIESOLE*

Florence 8 km
Pop. 14,899 ⊠ 50014 ☎ 055

A must for anybody making the trip from Florence is the ancient **Badia Fiesolana**, rebuilt in 1456 in Renaissance form; the marvelous original Romanesque façade, faced in marble and decorated with inlaid geometrical motifs, was incorporated in the later structure. Fiesole itself occupies a hill with two peaks. In the environs of Florence there is no locality more celebrated for its beauty, whether due to the charm of the countryside and the site or because of its many historical and cultural associations. The long rectangular section of Etruscan **wall** on the north slope of the hill is built of massive squared cyclopean blocks laid one above the other to a height of 13 ft and is a reminder that the town was here before the Romans appeared inthe Arno valley. The splendid nearby **theatre** is, however, Roman (from the Empire), and was rediscovered in the 19C after being buried for centuries.

▶ An **archaeological museum**★ preserves many finds from that distant era *(the entrance to archaeological zone is in v. G. Dupré; 9 a.m.-7 p.m.; 10 a.m.-4 p.m. in winter; closed Mon).* On the other hand, the **Duomo**★, with its fine Romanesque interior, frescos by Cosimo Rosselli and 15C sculptures in the **Cappella Salutati**★, dates back to the Middle Ages and the Renaissance. However, the most fascinating area is undoubtedly the high ground once occupied by the Etruscan acropolis and where the small Gothic church of **S. Francesco**★ now stands. The tranquil cloisters of an old monastery are to be found beside the church. Along the street leading from the central piazza there is an esplanade with a parapet offering an enchanting **view** of Florence. ☐

Practical information ———————————

ⓘ p. Mino da Fiesole 45, ☎ 598720.

Hotels:
L★★★★★ **Villa San Michele**, v. Doccia 4, ☎ 59451, 28 rm ℗ ⟨ ⌂ ♨ ▱ Pens. closed 16 Nov-14 Mar. 15C building with a façade by Michelangelo, 375,000.
★★★ *Aurora*, p. Mino 39, ☎ 59100, 26 rm ℗ ⟨ ♨ No restaurant, 110,000; bkf: 10,500.
★★ *Villa Bonelli*, v. Poeti 1, ☎ 59513, 23 rm ℗ 70,000.

Restaurants:
♦♦♦ *Lance,* at San Domenico, v. Mantellini 2/B, ☎ 599308, closed Mon, Tue noon and Jan. In country with fine views. Regional and Italian cuisine: tagliatelle cardinale, noodles with salmon, 30/40,000.

♦♦ *Cave di Maiano,* at Maiano, ☎ 59133, closed Sun eve, Thu and Aug. Views, terrace and garden. Regional cuisine: tomatoes cooked with oil, green tortelloni with cream, 30/42,000.

⚐ ★★★ *Panoramico,* at Prato ai Pini, v. Peramonda 1, 480 pl, ☎ 599069 (all year).

Recommended
Events: *Estate Fiesolana* (summer festival: concerts, ballets, plays, cinema; Jun-Aug).
Music school: *S. Domenico* (musical education centre for adults and children), v. delle Fontanelle 24, ☎ 599994.

IMPRUNETA

Florence 13 km
Pop. 14,832 ⊠ 50023 ☎ 055

Impruneta is a rich farming town situated on a hill between the Greve and the Ema in the green countryside to the S of Florence, and it is famous for its traditional **Fiera di S. Luca** (mid-Oct). It produces good wines (close to Chianti) and its terra-cotta and brick **kilns** have a long tradition — Brunelleschi used them during the building of the dome of S. Maria del Fiore. **S. Maria dell'Impruneta**★ is a famous and very old basilica (11C), which has been rebuilt several times. Outside, features include the battlemented 13C campanile and the 17C portico, which precedes the simple façade. Inside, two ornate 15C chapels (attributed to Michelozzo) stand in front of the sanctuary. These are the **Cappella della Croce**★ and the **Cappella della Madonna**★ and their ceilings and friezes are splendidly decorated with terra-cottas by Luca della Robbia, who was also responsible for the statues. The church and its splendid works of art suffered serious damage during the war. They have been repaired with great care. ☐

Practical information ———————————

♨ (May-Dec) at Falciani *(7 km E)*, ☎ 2020090.

Restaurants:
♦♦ *Falciani*, at Ponte dei Falciani, v. Cassia 245, ☎ 2020091, closed Tue. In spacious villa with verandas. Regional and Emilian cuisine: rotolo al forno, shin of beef, raw beef, 30/40,000.
♦♦♦ *Tre Pini*, at Pozzolatico, ☎ 208065, closed Mon and Jan-Feb. Elegant room, originally an old farmhouse. Regional and international cuisine: risotto al funghetto, chicken baked in a brick, Chianti, 25/40,000.

Villa della PETRAIA

Florence 6 km
⊠ 50100 ☎ 055

Giambologna's famous bronze statue of the goddess **Venus** emerging from the sea and wringing out her hair stands here, in the **terraced garden** of the villa, at the centre of a splendid Renaissance fountain by Tribolo and surrounded by dolphins, putti and fauns. The view of Florence and of the Arno valley from the vast 17C **garden** is superb. As for the **Villa** itself *(9 a.m.-2 p.m.; closed Mon),* it is a 16C building by Buontalenti with spacious furnishings (Empire style and Louis XV) in the spacious apartments and public rooms. However, the most magnificent feature is the courtyard decorated with **frescos**★ (by Volterrano, 1648), which celebrate figures and episodes in the history of the Medici. ☐

Bianca Capello

The second Grand-Duke of Tuscany, Francesco I Medici, and his wife, Bianca Cappello, died within hours of each other on the 19 and 20 October 1587, supposedly of malaria, in the villa Poggio a Caiano which the architect Giuliano da Sangallo had built for Lorenzo the Magnificent. The coincidence of the almost simultaneous deaths has given rise to the story that it was a case of poisoning gone wrong and that the intended victim was Cardinal Ferdinando de' Medici, who was hated by Bianca, and who became third Grand-Duke. Bianca was thirty-nine when she died and Francesco forty-seven. He was not a bad Grand-Duke in a period of absolutism and economic decline. He enlarged Livorno and its port, encouraged the cultivation of mulberries (for silk), attempted to reclaim the Maremma marshes and to exploit the copper of Montecatini, but he was of mediocre intellect, frivolous and pleasure-seeking, and posterity has been more interested in his wife. Bianca came from a family of Venetian patricians whose origins went back to the 9C. She was extremely beautiful and at 15 she eloped with Pietro Buonaventuri, a Florentine gentleman. This provoked not just a scandal, but a diplomatic incident between Venice and the Grand-Duchy. Once married to Buonaventuri, Bianca became the mistress of Francesco, not yet Grand-Duke and married to the daughter of the Emperor Maximilian II. Buonaventuri was murdered, Francesco was widowed and Bianca, the secret mistress, became the official one and finally the legitimate wife. The Capello family and the Venetian Signoria accepted the situation and the associated honours, hoping for political advantages. The couple had no children, but in the life story of this headstrong Venetian girl there were two feigned pregnancies and births. Three centuries later, Vittorio Emanuele II and his mistress, the Contessa di Mirafiori (called by the people Bela Rosin or Pretty Rosie) stayed in the same apartment, on the first floor of the Villa Poggio a Caiano. Crowned heads do not worry about ghosts.

Villa di POGGIO A CAIANO

Florence 17 km
Pop. 6,749 ⊠ 50046 ☎ 055

There is no more architecturally beautiful Medici villa than this 15C gem designed by Giuliano da Sangallo for Lorenzo the Magnificent. The villa *(wkdays 9 a.m.-1:30 p.m.; hols 9 a.m.-12:30 p.m.; gardens 9 a.m.-4:30 p.m. or 6 p.m. depending on season; closed Mon)*, set within an extensive ring of walls reinforced by massive corner towers, appears for what it is — a grand and elegant residence. The façade has a classical entrance loggia, with columns and pilasters surmounted by a **terra-cotta frieze** covered with bas-reliefs and by a tympanum with the Medici coat-of-arms. The finest room in the sumptuous **interior** is the **Salone** decorated by the greatest 16C Florentine artists, including Andrea del Sarto and Pontormo, with frescos whose subjects, though taken from Roman history, are meant to glorify the Medici. Outside the walls there are the stables, and the extensive garden continued as an immense park which reached as far as the Arno. The nearby estate provided the villa with food of every kind and in this paradise the relaxed life of the Medici court unfolded: a sequence of banquets, cavalcades, hunting with falcons, jousts and masques. ▯

SESTO FIORENTINO

Florence 9 km
Pop. 45,061 ⊠ 50019 ☎ 055

The **Museo delle Porcellane di Doccia** *(9:30 a.m.-1 p.m. and 3:30-6:30 p.m.)* takes its name from the nearby original site of the famous Ginori factory. However, the factory has now been moved to Sesto after having operated at Doccia for over two centuries. It is an interesting collection which documents the factory's products from 1737 to the present. Porcelain is a feature of Sesto Fiorentino, a small prosperous industrial town. For example, the nearby village of **Colonnata** has an 18C porcelain altar in the church of S. Romolo and a number of porcelain tombs in the cemetery. Not far away at **Quinto** is the imposing Etruscan **tomb** (7C BC) of **Montaguola★** *(apply at v. Fratelli Rosselli 95; Sat and Sun 10 a.m.-1 p.m.; in summer also Tue and Thu).* ▯

Practical information

Hotel:
★★★★ **MotelAgip,** Firenze Mare, Autostrada del Sole junction, ☎ 4211881, 164 rm Ⓟ ⅋ 160,000.

SETTIGNANO

Florence 6 km
⊠ 50135 ☎ 055

On a hill cloaked in cypresses and olives and scattered with famous villas, the delightful village of Settignano dominates the Mensola valley and looks down on the basin in which Florence lies *(view from broad terrace of p. Desiderio)*. The beautiful 15C parish **church** has a serene Renaissance interior and some fine works of art. Among the surrounding villas are the 17C **Villa Gamberaia** with a splendid Italian garden; **Capponcina,** which belonged to D'Annunzio and **I Tatti,** in which Bernard Berenson assembled his famous art collection *(closed)* and which today houses Harvard University's Centre for Renaissance History. ▯

Friuli - Venezia Giulia

▶ Situated on an outlying limb of Italy almost on the border with Yugoslavia, Trieste is the provincial capital of Friuli. Collio, the Carso plateau, Gorizia and Trieste became part of Italy when the Republic was created. They were the remains of a much larger area called Venezia Giulia which had been under Italian rule during the two previous wars. Time has healed the wounds of war and Italy's border is now considered one of the most open in the world. Italy's side of the green and rocky Carso plateau is riddled with strange caves. Trieste is a fascinating and unique city with a windy, sunny climate. The sea dominates the city and ships have left from here to all corners of the world. In Friuli are the steep-walled mountains of la Carnia and the Alpine ridge of the Monte Croce Pass which runs from the Comelico Valley to Tarvisio. There are also high pasture lands dotted with stalls and barns (*stavoli* and *staipe* in local dialect), as well as the hills of Tagliamento. Upstream from the rivers with their large shingle beds are the barren grasslands of the *magredis*. Downstream, land reclamation has turned lower Friuli into one vast stretch of corn fields. Rustling poplars and campaniles peer out above the corn. The whole area is border territory; political boundaries and commercial routes criss-cross the region, giving it an international character. Events and people have mingled here since prehistoric times. Celts, Istrians, Romans, Lombards, Avars, Slovenian colonists, German nobles, Byzantine prelates, Venetian aristocrats, Danubian merchants: all have left their mark on Friuli. These 'visitors' influenced local architecture: verandas and *carnielle*, Carinzian houses with pavilion roofs, the courtyards of the lowlands, Slavonic Mediterranean stone houses on the Carso plateau and the large houses of wood and swamp reeds of the lagoon fishermen. ☐

 Don't miss

Aquileia★, its Basilica★★ and the excavations of the Roman town; Cividale del Friuli★ and the stuccos★★ in the medieval Tempietto★; picturesque Grado★, situated between the sea and the lagoon; the Venetian fortified town of Palmanova; the Villa Manin★ at Passariano; the coastline around Trieste★; S. Giusto★★; the piazza della Libertà★★ and Tiepolo's frescos★ in the Archbishop's Palace at Udine.

Facts and figures

Location: *This is Italy's northeasternmost region, E of the Tagliamento and Livenza Rivers and N of the Adriatic Sea. It was formed when Venezia Giulia, which first became part of Italy between the two world wars, was joined to the 'Patria del Friuli'. The name Friuli comes from* Forum Iulii *(Julius' Forum), the ancient name of the town of Cividale, founded by Julius Caesar.*
Area: *7,846 sq km.*
Climate: *Continental; however, an unpleasant feature of Trieste during the winter is the violent, cold wind known as the* bora.
Population: *1,228,180 inhabitants, including a minority of Slavs (just over 50,000).*
Administration: *The northeasterly region has its own constitution; its capital is Trieste. Other provincial capitals are Gorizia, Pordenone and Udine.*

● *Brief regional history*

2000-3C BC

Venetian and Istrian fortified villages. Known as *castellieri*, these villages are found on high ground, surrounded by dry stone walls or ramparts. They mark the presence of early civilization from the middle of the Bronze Age. However, there is no clear indication as to who built them. ● The area was later settled by the **Veneti** and **Istrians.** ● The Celts began to infiltrate the area in the 4C BC, giving their name **(carni)** to Carnia.

3C BC-5C AD

The Romans. Romans carried out military expeditions into **Istria** to ensure control of the area (3C-2C BC). They conquered the local population, including the **Carni** (115 BC). The Romans' main contribution was the colony of **Aquileia** (181 BC). ● Other early Roman settlements included **Cividale, Zuglio** and **Trieste.** ● The region then became part of a larger territory founded under Augurtus and known as *Venetia et Histria*.

6C-10C

The Lombards and the Franks. In 553, the church of **Aquileia** aligned itself against **Byzantum** which had conquered Italy. It was during this period that the local bishop assumed the title of **Patriarch.** ● For strategic reasons, **Cividale** had become the most important town in the region. ● The **Lombard** invasion of Italy began in Friuli in 568. ● The 6C also saw the beginning of the influx of **Slavs** who later worked the most difficult lands, explaining the presence of Slavic speakers near towns where Italian was spoken. ● The **Franks,** who followed the Lombards, feudalized the area (late 8C).

basilica in Aquileia

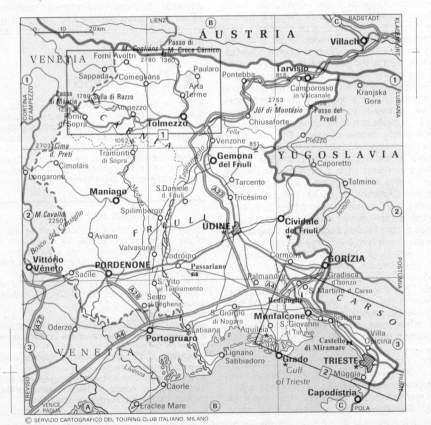

11C-14C
The Aquilean patriarchy. Charlemagne began donating funds to the patriarchy, thus contributing to its economic rise. The church had fought to recapture Friuli and the **Patriarch Poppone** (1019-45) rebuilt the basilica in Aquilea. ● In 1077, Emperor **Henry IV** granted the **territory of the counts of Friuli** to the patriarch, thus giving him temporal power over the area. ● The patriarchy was one of the pillars of the imperial faction in Italy. **Bertolds di Andechs** (1218-51), the last of the Ghibelline patriarchs, moved the patriarchal seat to **Udine**, and from then on the town began its commercial expansion and development. ● As the Venetians gained power, that of the patriarchy waned. The Venetians cast a greedy eye on Friuli's **commercial routes.** ● Following a war between Venice and the Empire in the 15C, Venice won power over almost the entire **patriarchy.** ● The then small town of **Trieste** placed itself under the protection of the **Duke of Austria** (a Hapsburg) in the late 14C, in order to safeguard its commercial interests.

15C-18C
Venice and the Hapsburgs. Although the Venetian government did not allow the local nobility to participate in politics, **Friuli** was faithful to Venice until the end of the Republic (1797). ● The **Hapsburgs** were becoming an increasing threat in the E and finally **absorbed the territories of the counts of Duino** in the 15C and that of the **counts of Gorizia** in the 16C. ● The Venetians fortified **Gradisca** as their E bastion against both the Empire and the Turks. It eventually fell, however, and they built **Palmanova** in 1593. ● The Hapsburgs, especially under **Maria Theresa,** developed **Trieste** as a port and commercial centre. ● Following the upheavals of the Napoleonic wars, the whole region came under **Austrian rule** (1815).

p. della Liberta in Udine

19C-20C
Italy's E borders. Friuli and Venetia both became part of Italy in 1866. ● The last hundred years of Austrian control over **Trieste** marked the high point of the city's economic expansion. ● Italy's main goal in World War I was to regain control of the area, which was then called **Venezia Giulia** (Gorizia, Triestes and Istria). Between 1915-17, some of the war's bloodiest battles were fought on nearly the same spots as in 1866. ● Between the two wars, a great number

of **Slavic minority groups** moved into Italy. ● After World War II **Istria** and most of **Gorizia** were handed over to Yugoslavia. ● The **autonomous region** of Friuli-Venezia Giulia was set up in 1964, with Trieste as its provincial capital.

S. Giusto in Trieste

● *Practical information*

Information: *Azienda Regionale per la Promozione Turistica,* at Trieste, v. G. Rossini 6, at Trieste, ☎ 040/60336.

SOS: emergency assistance, ☎ 113; police emergency, ☎ 112; *ACI* breakdown service, ☎ 116.

Weather: forecast, ☎ 040/2211 for Trieste, ☎ 1911, for Gorizia and Udine, ☎ 191; road conditions, ☎ 040/2214 or 06/4212, for Gorizia, Trieste and Udine, ☎ 194; snow bulletin, ☎ 040/2232, for Trieste and Udine, ☎ 162; shipping forecast, ☎ 040/2216, for Gorizia, Trieste and Udine, ☎ 196.

The eastern hills

The gentle, rolling countryside that stretches SE from Tarcento to Gorizia is the area where Friuli's fine white wines are produced (although good red wines are also plentiful). The region is divided into two official wine-producing areas: Colli Orientali del Friuli and Collio Goriziano. The Tokay vine is predominant and Friuli is its most natural habitat. The local aperitif is a tajut de tocai (or glass of Tokay), a delicate, dry wine with a slight taste of bitter almonds. Another vine, the Picolit, produces a wine of rare elegance, made only in limited quantities. An interesting itinerary for the wine lover (as well as its own scenic merits) starts in Tarcento and goes through Cormons (grape festival and Collio wine tasting in September) and on through Gorizia. There are inviting vineyards on the left all along this route.

Farm vacations: *Associazione regionale Agriturist,* v. Moro 18, at Udine, ☎ 0432/295294.

Festivals: *international folklore festival* and *choir and violin contest,* at Gorizia; *opera season* and *festival,* at Teatro Verdi, at Trieste.

Fairs: *international trade fairs* at Gorizia, Pordenone and Trieste.

Nature parks: information about Isonzo and Stella nature reserves at Trieste, ☎ 040/7702843. For Carso nature reserve (→ San Dorligo della Valle): *Azienda regionale delle Foreste,* at Udine, v. Manzini 41, ☎ 0432/294711 (information and guided tours).

Nature conservation: *WWF Delegazione regionale,* at Udine, v. Odorico da Pordenone 3, ☎ 0432/290895 (visits to Marano lagoon reserves and Miramare marine nature reserve: → il Carso); *Servizio Beni ambienti e cultu-*

rali della Regione, at Trieste, v. Carducci 6, ☎ 040/7355, *LIPU,* at Trieste, v. Alpi Giulie 13, ☎ 040/828709 (birdwatching courses).

Mountaineering: *CAI* schools: at Trieste, v. Machiavelli 17, ☎ 040/60317; at Pordenone, v. Odorico (Ariston building); at Tolmezzo, v. Patriarca della Torre 5; at Cividale, v. Borgo S. Pietro 4; at Udine, v. Odorico da Pordenone 3, ☎ 0432/504290.

Skiing: in Carnic area; summer skiing at Sella Nevea *(71 km NE of Udine),* ☎ 0433/54015 (Rifugio Giberti); cross-country skiing at Tarvisio.

Golf: at Fagagna (→ Udine) and Trieste (9 holes).

Caving: *S. Giusto,* at Trieste, v. S. Spiridione 1, ☎ 040/64303; *E. Boegan CAI,* at Trieste, v. Machiavelli 17, ☎ 040/60317.

● *Towns and places*

AQUILEIA*

Udine 36, Trieste 45, Milan 374 km
Pop 3,424 ✉ 33051 ☎ 0431   B3

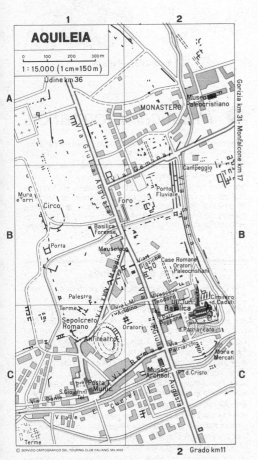

Now only a modest agricultural settlement in the flat countryside leading down to the Grado lagoon, Aquileia has great historical significance. It was witness to two periods of economic prosperity and intense artistic activity. Founded in 181 BC, the colony of Aquileia was the capital of *Venetia et Histria* under Augustus. During imperial Rome, Aquileia was a nerve centre for trade between the Adriatic and the N; it also produced craft work in glass, amber, and in precious and semi-precious stones. The province was abandoned during the barbarian era but flourished once more under the Patriarchate. The basilica was rebuilt by the Patriarch Poppone in the 11C and still is, today, a powerful evocation of the town's cultural and political importance, which came to an end when the patriarchal seat was transferred to Udine in the 13C. The most striking artistic feature, however, is the strong mosaic tradition which developed from the Hellenistic-Roman era to the early Christian centuries.

▶ V. Giulia Augusta, a stretch of the main road from Grado to Udine (C2-A1), runs straight through town, conveniently linking the museums, excavations and various other sights. ▶ The **Basilica★** (C2) is a splendid Romanesque building. It is joined to the church of the Pagani (9C) and the ruins of the baptistery (5C) by a portico. Its campanile has an octagonal spire and is the earliest example of many others of its kind throughout Friuli and Istria. ▶ Although the basilica seems uniform on the outside, the building and the works of art inside span a period of over a thousand years. It was built on the remains of early Christian basilicas dating back to the 4C. ·The 14C alterations were made following an earthquake. The various phases of the church's troubled history can be clearly seen in its solemn **interior★★**. The pointed arches above the columns are the result of Gothic restoration work: the ribbed ceiling was added in 1526; the **mosaic pavement★★** depicting allegorical figures within geometric shapes is the largest and most beautiful early Christian mosaic in the West and formed part of the 4C basilica. At the far end of the r.-hand aisle is the Gothic chapel of St. Ambrose, containing four large sarcophagi, the tombs of the patriarchs. The altarpiece is by Pellegrino di San Daniele (1503), and the room on the r. of the chapel contains a late 15C *Pietà* of the German school. In the chapel of S. Pietro is a group of frescos. The Renaissance **tribune★** in the centre of the staircase leading to the sanctuary and the altar of the Holy Sacrament on the l. are both by Bernardino da Bissone; the apse contains 11C Romanesque frescos. Part of a mosaic from the late 5C can be seen to the r. of the central altar. The **crypt** beneath the presbytery contains late 12C frescos★. ▶ At the near end of the nave is the entrance to the **Cripta degli Scavi★** (excavations; *9 a.m.-2 p.m.; 9 a.m.-1 p.m. Sun and hols; closed Mon; the ticket can also be used for the Museo Archeologico).* ▶ The **via Sacra★** is lined with cypress trees and flanked by capitals and architectural remains (B2). It runs alongside the excavations of the Roman river port on the Natissa. ▶ The **Museo Paleocristiano★** (A2; *9 a.m.-2 p.m.; Sun and hols 9 a.m.-1 p.m.; closed Mon*) is connected to a large Christian basilica (5C). Its remarkable mosaic floor can be seen from the first floor of the museum. ▶ The next part of the Roman Aquileia tour leads to v. Patriarca Poppone (C2), where excavations have uncovered a group of **houses** from the Roman town (mosaic floors, wells and two early Christian oratories). ▶ The **Museo Archeologico★** in v. Roma (C2; *9 a.m.-2 p.m.; Sun and hols 9 a.m.-1 p.m.; closed Mon*) displays most of the material from the archaeological sites, including collections of glass, amber and engraved stones and fine local marble funerary busts, including the portrait of an old man carved in the 1C BC. ▶ Next to the v. Giulia Augusta are the **excavations of the forum** (B1-2). The forum's basilica is currently being excavated. ▶ In the fields lies a **Roman cemetery** *(key at v. XXIV Maggio 17)* with family tombs dating from the 1C-4C. ☐

Practical information ⎯⎯⎯⎯⎯⎯

ⓘ p. Basilica (B-C2), ☎ 91087.

⋏★★★★ *Belvedere Pineta,* at Belvedere, ☎ 91007.

Recommended
Cycling: *G.S. Cais* at Cervignano del Friuli, v. Torino 22, ☎ 33252.
Wines: Visits to the E. Friuli cooperative wine store at Cervignano del Friuli, v. Aquileia 65, ☎ 32110 and to the *Distilleria Roppa,* v. Stabile 34, ☎ 32560.

AVIANO

Pordenone 13, Trieste 126, Milan 356 km
Pop. 8,532 ⊠ 33081 ☎ 0434   A2

Located in the flatlands of Pordenone, at the foot of Mt. Cavallo, the present military airport was first used in World War I. ▶ In the village of **Castello di Aviano** lie the ruins of an ancient castle, and in the church of **S. Giuliana** (13C-16C) the visitor can find a group of frescos begun in the 13C *(ask at parish church).* Recent excavations have uncovered tools from the late paleolithic era at **Piancavallo** *(c. 4,100 ft).* ☐

Practical information ⎯⎯⎯⎯⎯⎯

AVIANO
ⓘ v. S. Giorgio, ☎ 651888.

Restaurant:
◆ *Stella,* at Costa, v. Zovenzoni 41, ☎ 651098, closed Tue and Sep-Oct. Near Santuario della Madonna di Piancavallo. Italian cuisine: dumplings, deviled chicken, 14/17,000.

Recommended
Events: aerial display at the airfield (end Jun).
Hang gliding: *M. Cavallo* school, v. M. Cavallo 27, ☎ 551334.

Environs

PIANCAVALLO, ⊠ 33081, ☎ 0434.
� ski lifts, cross-country skiing, instruction, skating.
ⓘ ☎ 655191.

Hotel:
★★ *Regina,* p. della Puppa, ☎ 655166, 47 rm Ⓟ ⌕ ⅋ ⚘ closed 15 May-15 Jun and Oct-Nov, 40,000; bkf: 4,000.

La CARNIA

From Tolmezzo *(130 km, 1 day; map 1)*

While the peaks in the area seem low (the highest is Mt. Cogliàns, 9,120 ft), this is an alpine region. Mountain vegetation can be found here at much lower altitudes than usual. This is caused by above normal rainfall and heavy cloud cover. Local traditional architecture consists of 17C houses with verandas and of 18C houses with paired central windows. The traditional hearth or *carniello* is a type of arched extension of the ground floor of the house with benches for people to sit around the fire. The name **Càrnia** originated with the Celtic people who moved into the area *c.* 4C BC.

▶ From the Carni capital of **Tolmezzo** (→), the road leads up through the broad Tagiamento Valley. ▶ The 16C parish church at **Villa Santina** includes remains of an older building. ▶ In **Ampezzo** there are still a few houses in the Carnic style. ▶ Leaving the Tagliamento behind and moving up through the wild, narrow Lumiei River Valley, there is the **Buso bridge★** with a view of the Lumiei gorge. ▶ The man-made **Lake Sauris** is nestled in the mountains at **La Maina** (3,356 ft). ▶ The hamlets of **Sauris di Sopra** (4,593 ft) and **Sauris di Sotto** (3,976 ft) lie peacefully amid the woods and meadows and contain picturesque houses and 15C houses featuring Gothic altarpieces. ▶ Beyond the two passes lies **Sella di Razzo** (5,774 ft), and after a steep climb to a green plateau, **Forcella Lavardet** (5,059 ft) and the Pesarina Valley. ▶ **Prato Carnico** (2,251 ft) is a holiday resort. ▶ The Pesarina Valley runs into the **Canale di Gorto.** ▶ Beyond **Comeglians** is **Sella Valcada** (3,146 ft), located in a beautiful meadow. From there, the road on the l. leads to **Ravascletto** (3,117 ft), a resort with winter sports facilities. ▶ **Paluzzo** is located in another of the Tagliamento valleys known as the **Canale di San Pietro.** ▶ Continue through the valleys and climb to **Forcella di Liùs** (3,313 ft); then come down to **Paularo** (2,126 ft) where old style Carnic Alpo architecture can still be found: the Casa Gerometta (1591) and the Palazzo Fabiani (18C). ▶ The **Canale di Incaroio** goes through to **Lambrugno** and back into the Canale di San Pietro at Zuglio. ▶ **Zuglio** is built on the site of the Roman colony of *Julium Carnicum,* the Carni capital: the forum, basilica, baths and traces of other buildings remain. The parish church of **S. Pietro di Carnia** (Gothic, 14C) overlooks the village. ▶ A detour leads to the thermal spa of **Arta Terme** (1,453 ft). From there, the lower valley of the But River leads back to Tolmezzo. ☐

Practical information ⎯⎯⎯⎯⎯⎯

AMPEZZO, ⊠ 33021, ☎ 0433.
⌕ski lifts, cross-country skiing.
ⓘ municipio, ☎ 80173.

Hotel:
★★ *Colmajer,* v. Nazionale 5, ☎ 80219, 23 rm, Ⓟ ⅋ closed Nov, 48,000.

ARTA TERME, ⊠ 33022, ☎ 0433.
⚓ (May-Oct), ☎ 92022.
ⓘ ☎ 92002.

Hotels:
★★★ *Fonte,* v. Avosacco 38, ☎ 92105, 28 rm Ⓟ ⚿ ⅋ closed Oct-Apr, 55,000.

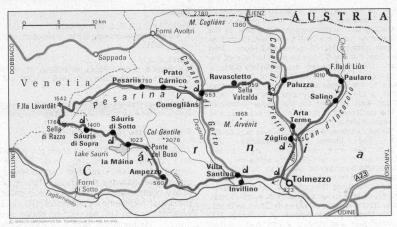

© SERVIZIO CARTOGRAFICO DEL TOURING CLUB ITALIANO, MILANO

1. La Carnia

★★★ *Gardel,* at Piano d'Arta, v. Marconi 63, ☎ 92588, 51 rm ℗ ▨ ⊗closed Nov-Dec, 50,000.
★★★ *Salon,* at Piano d'Arta, v. Casaletto 37, ☎ 92003, 26 rm ℗ ▨ closed Nov-Dec, 55,000; bkf: 5,000.

RAVASCLETTO, ⊠ 33020, ☎ 0433.
⚐ cableway, ski lifts, cross-country skiing, instruction, skating, ski jumps.
ℹ at the cableway station, ☎ 66035.

Hotels:
★★★ *Valcalda,* v. Edelweiss 8/10, ☎ 66220, 32 rm ℗ ▨ ⊗ closed May and Nov, 50,000; bkf: 5,000.
★★ *Perla,* v. S. Spirito 43, ☎ 66039, 41 rm ℗ ▨ & ⊗ closed 21 Sep-30 Nov and 1 May-14 Jun, 42,000; bkf: 5,000.

SAURIS DI SOTO, ⊠ 33020, ☎ 0433.
⚐ ski lifts, cross-country skiing, instruction.
ℹ ☎ 86076.

Recommended
Gastronomic specialties: smoked hams.

VILLA SANTINA, ⊠ 33029, ☎ 0433.

Recommended
Crafts workshops: visits to the Tessitura Carnica (textile gallery), v. Nazionale 14, ☎ 74129 or 74529.

II CARSO

Round trip from Trieste *(123 km, 1 day; map 2)*

Most of this vast geological formation lies outside Italy. The small part that remains is the steep ledge above the sea that links Trieste to the rest of Italy like a corridor. The name may be of Celtic origin and means 'land of rock': bare, fragmented, cracked limestone. The region includes some strange geological phenomena. For example, the 95 km-long Timave River runs underground for 40 km and surfaces at S.Giovanni al Timavo with a volume twenty-five times as great as when it disappeared. This is typical of the underground activity in the Carso plateau: tunnels, caves, abysses, sinkholes and underground springs and rivers. Under the surface lies a fantastic world of stalactites and stalagmites of rare colour

and transparency. The recommended itinerary explores the plateau and returns along the coastline.

▶ Traveling SE from Trieste (→), climb to the plateau via **San Dorligo della Valle** and **Sant'Antonio in Bosco.** ▶ Then proceed along the plateau, passing **Padriciano** (with a 795-ft-deep cave at the bottom of which is a metereological station which studies underground atmospheric conditions). The next stop is Trebiciano, with one of the deepest caves in the area (1,045 ft). ▶ Beyond **Villa Opicina** (1,050 ft, splendid view of Trieste and the gulf from the piazzale dell'Obelisco), at Borgo Grotta Gigante, is the entrance to the **Grotte Gigante★** *(group visits every half hr; summer 9 a.m.-12 noon and 2-4 p.m.; winter 9:30-11:30 a.m. and 2:30-4:30 p.m.; closed Mon except hols.).* ▶ Take a detour to the r. to reach **Rupingrande** (1,015 ft): craftwork, costumes and furniture on sale at the **Casa Carsica** *(wkends 11:30 a.m.-12:30 p.m. and 2-5 or 7 p.m. summer).* Further on is the **Manrupino Sanctuary** with a 16C church next to the modern sanctuary. ▶ Back on to the SS 202, continue along the plateau to Sistiana and the motorway, exiting at the signal box at Redipuglia. ▶ The **Redipuglia war cemetery** is the final resting place for 100,000 men of the Third Army (two museums with war memorials). ▶ Next, cross the Isonzo, and beyond **Sagrado** is **Gradisca d'Isonzo** (→). ▶ Back over the Isonzo, a short detour from **San Martino del Carso** leads to **M. San Michele,** the S. stronghold of the Austrian defense which was captured in 1916. ▶ Go through **Doberdò del Lago** and reach **Monfalcone** (→). ▶ To get back to Trieste, take the coastal road (SS 14). ▶ At **Duino,** which slopes down towards the small harbour, is the Castel Nuovo, the ruins of the Castello Vecchio and the landscape which inspired Rainer Maria Rilke's *Duino Elegies (boat trips to the inlets below the castles).* ▶ **Sistiena** is set in an enchanting rocky inlet, surrounded by thick woods. ▶ At **Gri** is the **Castello di Miramare** (→ Trieste), with its marvelous park.
▶ Re-enter Trieste via the waterfront at **Barcola.** ▢

Practical information

BARCOLA (comune di Trieste), ⊠ 34136, ☎ 040.

Restaurant:
♦♦ *Squero,* v. Miramare 42, ☎ 410884, closed Mon and Jan-Feb. Seafood, 20/30,000.

DUINO, ⊠ 34013, ☎ 040.

≋

ⓘ Duino Sud autostrada service area, ☎ 208281.

Hotel:
★★★ *MotelAgip,* near autostrada, ☎ 208273, 80 rm Ⓟ & 80,000.

Recommended
Technical tourism: visits to the *Cava Romana* (marble and stone), at Aurisina, v. Cave 29, ☎ 200101.

GRIGNANO, ⊠ 34014, ☎ 040.

≋

Hotel:
★★★★ *Adriatico Palace,* v. Grignano 9, ☎ 224241, 102 rm Ⓟ & ⌂ ⌀ closed 11 Oct-31 Mar, 145,000.

Recommended
Nature park: *Marino di Miramare,* ☎ 224147 (land section open daily; visits to the underwater section: Apr-Oct; on Sat, advance booking necessary).
Youth hostel: *Ostello Tergeste,* v. Miramare 331, ☎ 224102.

SAGRADO, ⊠ 34078, ☎ 0481.

Restaurant:
● ♦♦ *Bella Trieste,* v. Dante 130, ☎ 99127, closed Mon eve, Tue and Jul. Small garden with fountain. Mixed regional cuisine: tagliatelle with mushrooms, risotto with asparagus, 30/35,000.

SAN DORLIGO DELLA VALLE, ⊠ 34018, ☎ 040.

Recommended
Horseback riding: *Scuderia della Rosandra,* at Bagnoli della Rosandra, ☎ 2284843.
Nature park: del Carso (Val Rosandra), municipio, ☎ 228110.

SISTIANA, ⊠ 34019, ☎ 040.

≋

ⓘ at Trieste, ☎ 420182; road toward Sistiana Mare, ☎ 299166.

Hotels:
★★★ *Posta,* ☎ 299103, 30 rm Ⓟ ⌀ closed Sat and Sun Oct-May and Dec-Jan. No restaurant, 66,000; bkf: 5,500.

★★ *Villa Pia,* v. Sistiana 55/C, ☎ 299237, 12 rm Ⓟ ⏠ & closed 20 Dec-31 Jan, 45,000.

VILLA OPICINA, ⊠ 34016, ☎ 040.

Hotel:
★★ *Daneu,* v. Nazionale 194, ☎ 214214, 17 rm Ⓟ ⏠ ⌀ 46,000; bkf: 4,000.

⚒ ★★★★ *Pian del Grisa,* SS 202 at 15.2-km marker, 390 pl, ☎ 213142.

CIVIDALE DEL FRIULI*

Udine 17, Trieste 65, Milan 394 km
Pop. 11,187 ⊠ 33043 ☎ 0432   C2

The Palazzo Pretorio (home of the Republic of Venice's representatives) was designed along classical lines by Palladio. Cividale was the capital of the first Lombard duchy in Italy. King Alboino gave it to his nephew and the town became known as *Civitas*. The rare remains of the early medieval Lombard civilization which can still be found in Cividale are of exceptional interest. In 737, Callisto (then Patriarch of Aquileia) took over Cividale and made it a seat for the long line of patriarchs who were to follow. The seat of the patriarchs was finally moved to Udine in the 13C. The *Messa dello Spadone* (Mass of the Sword) which is celebrated in the cathedral at Epiphany is an old tradition from the patriarchal ceremonies of the Middle Ages.

▶ At the centre of the old town is the historic p. del Duomo (B2),as well as the **Museo Archeologico,** the **Palazzo Pretorio** (late 16C) and the **Palazzo Comunale** (14C-16C) with its Gothic arcades. ▶ The **Duomo★** (B2) was begun in 1457 in the Venetian-Gothic style, but some Renaissance additions were made by Pietro Lombardo in the 16C. The interior contains some remarkable pieces, especially the early 13C embossed silver **altarpiece★** on the high altar. In the r.-hand aisle is the entrance to the **Museo Cristiano,** which contains two extraordinary pieces: the octagonal Callisto **baptistery★★** (8C) and **Duke Ratchi's altar** (8C). ▶ The **Museo Archeologico Nazionale★** (A-B2; *9 a.m.-1:45 p.m.; Sun and hols 9 a.m.-12:45*

2. Il Carso

1 Tarcento km 27   2   Caporetto km 27

A

Udine km 17

CIVIDALE DEL FRIULI

0 100 200 m
1 : 13.000 (1cm=130m)

© SERVIZIO CARTOGRAFICO DEL TOURING CLUB ITALIANO, MILANO

2   Cormons km 17

Recommended
Caves: visits to the grotta di S. Silvestro all'Antro, ☎ 726026.
Events: *Messa dello Spadone,* in the Duomo, and *historical procession* (Sun preceding or following Epiphany).
Gastronomic specialties: *gubana,* a local confection.
Horseback riding: *Associazione Forum Iulii,* v. Gemona 131, ☎ 715202.
Wines: visits to the *Rodaro* vineyard, ☎ 730865.

CORMONS

Gorizia 13, Trieste 49, Milan 384 km
Pop. 7,792 ⊠ 34071 ☎ 0481   C2

Cormons was once the hub of Collio, a vast region of vine-covered slopes, with orchards, beech trees and oaks. Only the southernmost part is still within Italy.

▶ In the historic town centre, part of the double medieval ramparts are still standing. They surround the **Duomo** of St. Adalbert, rebuilt 18C. ▶ There are other remains of the medieval ramparts in v. Cancelleria Vecchia, beside the 16C Palazzo Neuhaus, including a late medieval cylindrical **tower.** ▶ P. Libertà contains some fine 17C-18C buildings. ▶ Apparently, the town's name is pre-Roman in origin and means 'weasel country'. ▶ There is a splendid view stretching from the Alpi Giulie down to the Istrian coastline, from the summit of **Mt. Quarin.** ☐

Practical information _____

Restaurant:
♦♦♦ *Felcaro,* v. S. Giovanni 45, ☎ 60214, closed Mon and Sep-Oct. Regional cuisine: risotto with herbs, tagliatelle with hare gravy, 22/35,000.

Recommended
Cycling: *Ciclistica Cormonese,* p. XXIV Maggio 27, ☎ 60460.
Farm vacations: *Azienda la Subida,* at Monte 22, ☎ 60531 (restaurant open to the public, some accommodation).
Horseback riding: *La Subida Vacanze Natura,* ☎ 60531.
Wines: grape festival and Collio wine tasting (Sep). Visits to the *Cantina Produttori del Collio e dell'Isonzo,* v. Mariano 31, ☎ 60579.

FORNI DI SOPRA

Udine 95, Trieste 165, Milan 418 km
2,975 ft pop. 1,280 ⊠ 33024 ☎ 0433   A1

Forni di Sopra is a small Carnian community located amid the Dolomites.

▶ The **parish church** in **Cella** contains carved wooden altars, including one by Domenico da Tolmezzo; in the nearby 15C church of **St. Florian** are frescos by Giovanni da Tolmezzo and a polyptych painted in 1480. ▶ The church of S. Giacomo at **Vico** (15C) includes a Gothic portal, traces of outside frescos and a tall campanile. ☐

Practical information _____

♒ ski lifts, cross-country skiing, instruction, skating.
ⓘ v. Cadore 1, ☎ 88024.

Hotels:
★★ *Edelweiss,* at Vico, v. Nazionale 11, ☎ 88017, 23 rm Ⓟ ⌖ ⋙ ⌘ closed Oct-Nov, 48,000; bkf: 5,000.
★★ *Posta,* at Vico, v. Nazionale 94, ☎ 88014, 40 rm Ⓟ ⌖ ⋙ closed 1 Apr-14 Jun and 16 Oct-14 Dec, 47,000.
★★ *Villa Alpina,* at Vico, v. Madonna della Salute 8, ☎ 88120, 34 rm Ⓟ ⌖ ⋙ ⌘ closed 1 Oct-19 Dec and 21 Apr-31 May, 44,000; bkf: 5,000.

▲ ★ *Tornerai,* at Stinsans, v. Nazionale, ☎ 88035.

Recommended
Swimming: ☎ 88056 (indoor pool and sauna).

p.m.; closed Mon) has a large Lombard exhibit: weapons, tools, utensils, necklaces from Lombard tombs, jewelry including crosses, brooches and some manuscripts. ▶ The 14C church of **S. Francesco** (B2) contains some 14C and 15C frescos. ▶ In the medieval quarter of Borgo Brossana, on a steep slope above the Natisone, is the church of **Tempietto Longobardo★** (8C), one of the most interesting early medieval monuments in the area (A2; *9 a.m.-12 noon and 2-5 p.m.; Sun and hols 9 a.m.-1 p.m.; closed Mon; apply to the caretaker, v. Monastero Maggiore 7).* ☐

The Lombards

Described as fiercer than the fiercest Teutons, the Lombards entered Byzantine Italy in the spring of 568. Led by their king, Alboino, they came with 40,000 able-bodied men, plus women and children, slaves, livestock and wagons. The Lombards were Teutons from Scandinavia who had made their way to the lower Danube. They easily conquered Italy and, until their defeat by the Franks (774), they ruled over a peninsula divided between Lombardy and Romania. King Alboino gave Cividale to his nephew Gisulfo and it became the first seat of the Lombard Duchy in Italy. The Lombards stayed in power for two centuries and Cividale bears the most significant traces of their presence.

Practical information _____

ⓘ largo Boiani 4, ☎ 731398.

Hotel:
★★ *Castello,* v. del Castello 18, ☎ 734015, 10 rm Ⓟ ⌖ ⌂ ⋙ ⌘ closed Feb, 50,000; bkf: 4,000.

Restaurants:
♦♦ *Fortino,* v. Carlo Alberto 46 (A2 a), ☎ 731217, closed Mon eve, Tue and Jun. Regional cuisine: tagliatelle alla vigliacca, beef musetto and turnips brovada, 22/25,000.
♦♦ *Frasca,* v. De Rubeis 10 (A2 b), ☎ 731270, closed Sun eve and Mon. Regional cuisine: tagliatelle with truffles, dumplings, 20/35,000.

GEMONA DEL FRIULI

Udine 25, Trieste 98, Milan 404 km
Pop. 11,050 ⊠ 33013 ☎ 0432   B2

Gemona del Friuli belongs to the past. The once-beautiful ancient village located between the harsh mountains of Glémina and the Colle del Castello was severely damaged by the 1976 earthquake (as were many other parts of Friuli). The restoration work has not completely recaptured the past, yet the Romanesque-Gothic **Duomo** *(nearly rebuilt)* is of special interest (an enormous statue of **St. Christopher,** dated 1331, is on the façade). A street flanked by old arcades leads from the Duomo to the **Palazzo del Comune,** built in the Renaissance style of Lombardy (1502). The **castle** on the hill was already in ruins before the earthquake.   □

Practical information _____

⚠ ★ *Ai Pioppi* v. del Bersaglio 44, ☎ 981276.

GORIZIA

Trieste 45, Milan 388, Rome 650 km
Pop 41,413 ⊠ 34170 ☎ 0481   C2

Located at the foot of the Colle del Castello, near the Isonzo, the town has retained its 19C garden city atmosphere. As Italy's easternmost point, it is now a border town. Nova Gorica (Yugoslavia) is 'just across the road', as they say locally.

▶ The centre of the town is dominated by the Colle del Castello, and it is here that the **piazza della Vittoria,** the Baroque church of **S. Ignazio** (1654-1757) and the 18C **fountain of Neptune** are found. ▶ The **Duomo** was begun in the 14C (remains from this period can be seen in the apse), but has been altered several times. ▶ The hill upon which the castle stands is surrounded by fortifications built by the Venetians in 1509. A gate (1660) leads into the **Borgo Castello,** with Venetian-style houses. At no. 15, the **Museo di Storia e Arte** *(10 a.m.-12 noon and 3-6 p.m.; closed Mon)* specializes in folklore, history, art (18C-19C Gorizian pottery and glass, textiles and sacred robes) and archaeology. The **castle★** dates from the 12C, but has been extended at various times, up to the end of the 18C. It was the home of the counts of Gorizia, imperial feudal lords and fierce enemies of the Venetians. The rooms *(9 a.m.-12 noon and 2 or 3-5 p.m.; closed Mon)* contain 16C and 17C furniture and pictures. From the fortifications there is a splendid view over the battlefields of the Isonzo and the Carso plateau. ▶ The Palazzo Attems (1745), in p. De Amicis, houses the **Musei Provinciali** *(9 or 10 a.m.-12 noon and 3-6 p.m.; closed Mon)* including a WWI museum and an art gallery (altarpiece★ by A. Guardi, 1746, and works by local artists from the 18C to the present).

Environs

▶ Gorizia is a good starting point for a visit to the WWI battlefields in the Carso plateau and middle Isonzo areas. Here, the twelve bloody battles of the Isonzo were fought. ▶ 4.5 km NW is the **Military Cemetery of Oslàvia,** within view of Mt. Sabotino, the N stronghold of the Austrian defense of Gorizia. ▶ Fine view★ from **Mt. Calvario** (Podgora), 5.4 km away through the Vallone delle Acque. ▶ At **Mt. San Michele,** S stronghold of the Austrian defense of Gorizia, there is a museum *(16 km along the Trieste SS, r. at the Devetachi junction, then r. again at the S. Martino junction).*   □

> Send us your comments and suggestions; we will
> use them in the next edition.

Practical information _____

ℹ Galleria del Corso 100/E, ☎ 83870.
✈ at Ronchi dei Legionari, ☎ 777001; *Alitalia,* corso Italia 60, ☎ 84266.
🚊 ☎ 22171.
🚌 from v. IX Agosto 13, ☎ 84566; from Poste Centrali, ☎ 80013.

Hotels:
★★★ *Palace,* corso Italia 63, ☎ 82166, 70 rm ℗ �& 68,000; bkf: 7,000.
★★ *Motel Nanut,* v. Trieste 118, ☎ 20595, 29 rm ℗ ⋙ ⊗ 🖃 ⋌ closed Aug, 43,500.

Restaurants:
● ♦♦♦ *Castello Formentini,* at San Floriano del Collio, p. Libertà 3, ☎ 884034, closed Mon and Jan. In 15C castle with period furnishings. Regional cuisine: meats alla pietra, medieval banquet on Sat eve, 30/40,000.
♦♦♦ *Lanterna d'Oro,* borgo Castello 20, ☎ 85565, closed Sun eve, Mon and Jan. Regional cuisine: spinach pastry, pancake pie with pork and truffle, 20/40,000.

Recommended
Archery: *Compagnia Arcieri goriziana,* v. Rismondo 2, ☎ 84531; *Compagnia Arcieri Isonzo,* v. Fatebenefratelli 26, ☎ 31463; *Fitarco,* corso Verdi 139 ☎ 85115.
Events: *international folklore parade* (Aug); *international competition in choir singing and violin* (Sep).
Festivals and markets: *Gorizia festival* (May-Jun.); *Salone dell'Arredamento* (furniture; late Oct-early Nov); *antiques market,* in the Giardini Pubblici (third Sun of each month).
Flying: v. Trieste 300, ☎ 20744.
Purchases: iron ware, light fittings, gold, fabrics.
Sports centre: v. Madonnina del Fante, ☎ 390784.
Swimming: v. Campagnuzza 4, ☎ 22215.

GRADISCA D'ISONZO

Gorizia 12, Trieste 42, Milan 378 km
Pop. 6,209 ⊠ 34072 ☎ 0481   C2-3

The name is of Slavic origin and alludes to a 10C-11C 'fort'. The Venetians built a fortress here in 1473 to keep out the counts of Gorizia who supported the Empire, as well as to ward off Turkish invasions. The town has a definite Venetian air about it and still looks like a fortified city with its parallel streets linked by tiny Venetian 'calle' (narrow streets). In 1500, Leonardo da Vinci was consulted regarding military operations. Nevertheless, in 1509, the fortress was captured by Maximilian of Hapsburg and remained in the hands of the Hapsburgs until World War I.

▶ The remaining towers, bastions and gates of the **town walls** date from the same era as the castle. ▶ The Loggia dei Mercanti in v. C.Battisti houses the **Lapidario** *(9 a.m.-12 noon; apply to caretaker other times),* which contains inscriptions, reliefs and Roman and Venetian architectural remains. ▶ The Palazzo Torriani houses the **Galleria Regionale d'Arte Contemporanea Luigi Spazzapan,** with works by this artist (born in Gradisca) and other Friulian modern artists.   □

Practical information _____

ℹ v. M. Ciotti (Palazzo Torriani), ☎ 99217.

Restaurant:
♦ *Commercio,* v. della Campagnola 6, ☎ 99358, closed Sun eve, Mon, Feb, and Aug. Regional cuisine: pancakes with radishes, shank of pork, 16/28,000.

Recommended
Clay pigeon shooting: v. lungo Isonzo, ☎ 99632.
Wines: *La Serenissima* regional wine cellar, in the Palazzo Torriani, ☎ 99528 (wine show and competition in May); visits to the *M.Felluga* cellars, v. Gorizia 121, ☎ 99164.

GRADO*

Gorizia 42, Trieste 54, Milan 385 km
Pop. 9,639 ✉ 34073 ☎ 0431   B-C3

Situated on an island between the lagoon and the sea, Grado gets its name from the gentle slope of its beach. The exquisite beach and healthy climate inspired the Florentine doctor, Giuseppe Barellai, to open a seaside home for sick children. The home was taken over by Austrian hotelkeepers in 1873. Guests came by train as far as Cervignano, then completed the journey by coach and ferry. Consequently, a busy seaside resort with villas and gardens was built around the ancient centre of town with its narrow streets, small squares and early Christian churches. It is here that Aquileians took refuge when they fought Attila in 451.

▶ The **S. Eufemia★** (B1-2) basilica is not much changed since Bishop Elia consecrated it in 579. It was built with material salvaged mainly from the Roman era, including remains of a 4C-5C basilica. The 15C **campanile** features a statue of St. Michael. Inside are a magnificent **mosaic★** floor (6C) and 15C frescos and paintings in the apse. ▶ The **Lapidario** (to the r. of the basilica, *8 a.m.-7 p.m.*) has Roman inscriptions and altars, fragments of early Christian and medieval sculpture. ▶ Also worth noting is **S. Maria delle Grazie** (B1) with its mosaic floor. ▶ There is a splendid view of the Trieste riviera from the **lungomare Nazario Sauro** (B1) which runs along the embankment. ▶ The **Parco delle Rose** contains an impressive variety of roses. ▶ A 30-minute motorboat ride to the island in the lagoon offers the **Shrine of S. Maria di Barbana**, featuring a wooden Byzantine *Madonna*. ▶ On the **lagoon**, are a few fishermen's huts made from marsh grass, with steep roofs and a door which doubles as a chimney. ☐

Practical information _____

≋
⚓ (Apr-Oct), ☎ 82821.
ⓘ v. Dante Alighieri 72 (B3), ☎ 80035.

▬ motorboat service in the lagoon and to the shrine of S. Maria di Barbana.

Hotels:
★★★★ *Antica Villa Bernt*, v. Colombo 5 (B2 a), ☎ 82516, 39 rm 🅿 ≴ ♨ closed Nov-Easter, 128,000.
★★★ *Eden*, v. Polo 2 (A-B3 b), ☎ 80136, 39 rm 🅿 ≴ ♨ closed 1 Nov-Easter, 50,000; bkf: 5,500.
★★★ *Mar della Plata*, v. Andromeda 5, ☎ 81081, 35 rm 🅿 ♨ ⅙ closed 26 Sep-14 May, 70,000; bkf: 6,000.
★★★ *Plaza*, v. Pegaso 1, ☎ 82082, 45 rm ♨ ⅙ ☒ closed Nov-Apr, 64,000.
★★★ *Rialto*, v. del Turismo 2, ☎ 81181, 40 rm 🅿 ♨ ⅌ ⌀ closed Nov-Mar, 80,000; bkf: 7,000.
★★ *Cristina*, v. Martiri della Libertà 11, ☎ 80989, 26 rm 🅿 ♨ closed Oct-Mar, 44,000; bkf: 5,000.
★★ *Friuli*, riva Foscolo 14 (B3 c), ☎ 80841, 45 rm 🅿 ≴ closed Oct-Apr, 55,000; bkf: 6,000.
★★ *Lido*, v. Morosini 12 (B2 d), ☎ 80420, 31 rm ♨ ⌀ closed Oct-Apr, 47,500.

Restaurants:
♦ *Colussi*, p. Carpaccio 1 (B2 e), ☎ 80471, closed Mon and 15 Nov-15 Dec. Seafood: gilt-head sea bream al cartoccio, grilled fish, 20/35,000.
♦ *Nico*, v. Marina 10, ☎ 80470, closed Thu. Seafood: bucatini with lobster, soused sardines, 30/40,000.

⚹ ★★★★ *Europa*, at Punta Spin, v. Rotta Primero, 1040 pl, ☎ 80877.

Recommended
Canoeing: *Canottieri Ausonia* school, darsena Torpediniere, ☎ 80305.
Conference centre: Palazzo dei Congressi, v. Italia 2 (B3), ☎ 82741.
Events: *procession to the Barbana shrine* (first Sun in Jul).
Purchases: rag dolls and toys.
Sailing: riva Brioni, ☎ 81271.
Tennis: ☎ 81344.

LATISANA

Udine 41, Trieste 80, Milan 337 km
Pop. 10,708 ✉ 33053 ☎ 0431   B3

Latisana was once a port on the l. bank of the Tagliamento where the road from Venice to Trieste crosses

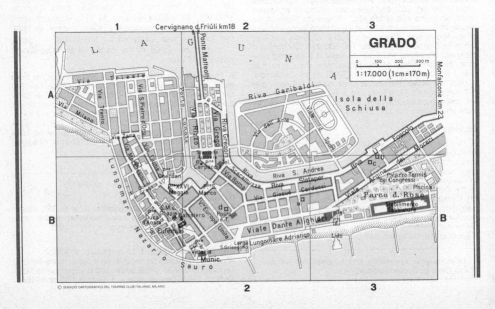

the river. Today it is a prosperous agricultural centre in the reclaimed territory of lower Friuli. The **Duomo,** which was once the abbey parish church, contains an altarpiece by Veronese, *Baptism of Jesus*★, and a wooden crucifix dating from 1566. ☐

Practical information

Hotel:
★★ *Bella Venezia,* parco Gaspari, ☎ 59637, 22 rm ℗ ⋙ ⅁ 68,000; bkf: 8,000. *Rest.* ◆◆◆ Garden service in summer. Mixed regional cuisine: linguine with spider crab, dried salt cod, 25/35,000.

Restaurant:
◆◆◆ *Sot la Nape,* v. Marconi 59, ☎ 50310, closed Tue, Jan and Sep. Mixed cuisine: fish terrine, charcoal grilled meats, 25/45,000.

LIGNANO SABBIADORO

Udine 59, Trieste 100, Milan 358 km
Pop. 5,594 ⊠ 33054 ☎ 0431   B3

Lignano Sabbiadoro is an area of beaches and pine groves surrounded by lagoons. This newly built resort located on the strip of sand enclosing the lagoon includes three centres, **Sabbiadoro, Pineta** and **Riviera.** ▶ The **Marano lagoon** and the Grado lagoon further E are both located in the hollow between the Tagliamento and Isonzo deltas, with offshore islands between Lignano and Grado (intensive fishing in the Valle del Pesce Azzurro). On the N shore lies the picturesque fishing village of **Marano Lagunare** *(39 km from Lignano Sabbiadoro by road, 8 km by boat).* ☐

Practical information

⚓ (mid-May-Sep), ☎ 422217.
ⓘ v. Latisana 42, ☎ 71821; at Lignano Pineta, v. a Mare, ☎ 42169 (summer).

Hotels:
★★★★ *Eurotel Lignano Riviera,* calle Mendelssohn 13, ☎ 428992, 93 rm ℗ ⋙ ⅁ ⌂ closed 21 Sep-14 May, 90,000; bkf: 9,000.
★★★★ *Greif,* arco del Grecale 23, ☎ 422261, 69 rm ℗ ⋙ ⌖ ⌂ closed 16 Sep-19 May, 128,500.
★★★ *Atlantic,* lungomare Trieste 160, ☎ 71101, 68 rm ℗ ⋙ closed 21 Sep-19 May, 71,000; bkf: 9,000.
★★★ *Bellavista,* lungomare Trieste 70, ☎ 71313, 48 rm ℗ ⋙ closed Oct-Apr, 82,000.
★★★ *Bristol,* lungomare Trieste 132, ☎ 73131, 59 rm ℗ ⋙ ⌖ closed Oct-Apr, 69,000; bkf: 7,000.
★★★ *Columbus,* lungomare Trieste 22, ☎ 71516, 60 rm ℗ closed 1 Oct-14 Apr, 60,000; bkf: 5,000.
★★★ *Meridianus,* v. della Musica, ☎ 428561, 90 rm ℗ ⋙ ⅁ ⌂ Pens. closed 26 Sep-19 May, 75,500.
★★★ *Park Hotel,* v. delle Palme 41/43, ☎ 422380, 44 rm ℗ ⋙ ⌂ closed 21 Sep-14 May, 70,000; bkf: 7,000.
★★ *Ambra,* lungomare Trieste 124, ☎ 71027, 43 rm ℗ ⋙ ⌖ closed Oct-Apr, 44,000.
★★ *Astoria,* lungomare Trieste 150, ☎ 71315, 37 rm ℗ ⋙ closed Oct-Easter, 52,000; bkf: 7,000.
★★ *Bellevue,* arco del Libeccio 37, ☎ 428521, 26 rm ℗ ⋙ ⌖ closed 16 Sep-31 May. No restaurant, 43,000.
★★ *Martini,* v. delle Palme 47, ☎ 422666, 41 rm ℗ ⋙ ⌂ closed 16 Sep-14 May, 50,000; bkf: 5,000.
★★ *Olympia,* v. delle Palme 54, ☎ 422468, 51 rm ℗ ⋙ ⌂ closed 16 Sep-19 May, 50,000; bkf: 5,500.

Restaurant:
◆◆◆ *Bidin,* v. Europa 1, ☎ 71988, closed Wed except summer and Nov. Mixed cuisine: cheese pancakes, turbot with green pepper, 22/35,000.

⚱ ★★ *Sabbiadoro,* v. Sabbiadoro, ☎ 71455; ★★ *Pino Mare,* at Lignano Riviera, v. Adriatico, ☎ 428512.

Recommended
Children's facilities: *Adriatico* children's residence, lungomare Trieste 140, ☎ 71877; management, ☎ 040/414915 (children aged 3-12 yrs, open Jun-Sep).
Clay pigeon shooting: v. Lovato 34, ☎ 70435.
Cycling: *S.C. Lignano,* v. Latisana 165, ☎ 81166.
Horseback riding: *Centro ippico,* ☎ 70237.
Marina: Darsena Sabbiadoro, ☎ 71821; Porto di Punta Faro-Torremare, ☎ 70315; at Lignano Riviera, Darsena Marina 1, ☎ 428524.
Young people's facilities: *Acqua Splash* (waterchutes, swimming pools with wave machine), v. Europa, ☎ 428826.

MONFALCONE

Gorizia 24, Trieste 30, Milan 380 km
Pop. 29,783 ⊠ 34074 ☎ 0481   B-C3

The shingle used for many buildings in Trieste and its harbour was once dug from the shores of the Gulf of Panzano. The Cosulich brothers of Trieste established their shipyard in the resulting basins in 1907. This was the beginning of the Monfalcone shipbuilding industry, which developed into a warship and merchant vessel yard when the region became part of Italy. The *Saturnia* and the *Vulcania,* famous names from the legendary era of oceanliners, were both launched here.

▶ The **shipyards,** now part of *Italcantieri,* are still crucial to the local economy. ▶ At the foot of the hill, near the remains of a pre-Roman fortified village, are traces of an ancient settlement. ▶ The **Roman baths,** mentioned by Pliny, are close to Mt. Sant'Antonio. ☐

Practical information

≋ at Lido di Panzano, Marina Iulia and Lido di Staranzano.
✈ at Ronchi dei Legionari, ☎ 777001.

Hotels:
★★★ *Excelsior,* v. Arena 4, ☎ 72893, 46 rm. No restaurant, 57,000; bkf: 5,000.
★★★ *Sam,* v. Cosulich 3, ☎ 73471, 66 rm ℗ No restaurant, 76,000; bkf: 6,000.

Restaurants:
● ◆◆◆ *Bruno,* v. Cosulich 1, ☎ 72903, closed Sat noon, Sun and Jul-Aug. Seafood: boreto soup, turbot al Sauvignon, 25/40,000.
◆◆◆ *Hannibal,* v. Bagni, ☎ 470112, closed Mon and Jan. Mixed cuisine: scampi ravioli, fish al cartoccio, 45/55,000.

⚱ ★★★★ *Albatros,* at Marina Iulia, 336 pl, ☎ 40561.

Recommended
Marina: Bacino di Panzano, *Società Vela O. Cosulich,* ☎ 711325; *Centro motovelico Hannibal,* ☎ 73032.
Sailing: *Tito Nordio Hannibal,* v. Bagni, ☎ 75192.
Water skiing: *Sci nautico California,* on Canale Lisert.

MUGGIA

Trieste 12, Milan 423 km
Pop. 13,795 ⊠ 34015 ☎ 040   C3

This small seaside town facing Trieste features a central piazza so Venetian in character that it could easily be the setting for a Goldoni play. His plays have in fact been performed here. This square is the heart of the old town, located behind the small harbour and encircled by ramparts. The Venetian atmosphere is a reflection of the town's history. Muggia remained faithful to Venice from the time when a mutual pact, aimed at keeping the sea free from pirates as far as Rovigno, was signed (1202).

▶ The 15C **Duomo** (of 13C origin) has a Gothic façade. ▶ Of interest too is the Gothic church of **S. Francesco**, the only one of its kind in the whole region of Trieste. ▶ 2 km away, on the hill overlooking the town, is **Muggia Vecchia**. The sanctuary is a rural Romanesque church and affords a fine view of Trieste. ▶ 3 km away, near Santa Barbara, are the remains of a prehistoric fortress, used until the medieval period. ☐

Practical information ─────────────

≋
ⓘ corso Puccini 6, ☎ 273259.

Hotels:
★★ *Lido*, v. Battisti 22, ☎ 273338, 46 rm Ⓟ ≼ ⌇ 65,000.
★★ *Sole*, at Lazzaretto (4 km W), ☎ 271106, 23 rm Ⓟ ⌇
⍿ ⌇ ⊠ closed 10 Jan-15 Feb, 57,000; bkf: 3,500.

Recommended
Clay pigeon shooting: v. Trieste, ☎ 274345.
Events: *Muggia carnival* with decorated boats from Venice.
Marina: sailing club, ☎ 272416.

PALMANOVA

Udine 20, Trieste 51, Milan 361 km
Pop. 5,576 ⊠ 33057 ☎ 0432 .   B2-3

Disastrous Turkish invasions swept through Friuli, and the Hapsburgs also bore down on this open border of the Republic of Venice. When the Venetians lost their stronghold at Gradisca (→), they decided to build a fortress in the lowlands of Friuli, and the first stone was laid on 7 October 1593. This fortress town (named Palma by the Venetians, after the old village of Palmada; Napoleon added the 'nova' when he extended it) reflects both the late Renaissance concept of the 'ideal town' and that of fortification following advances in artillery.

▶ The town is designed geometrically; star-shaped, with nine points of bastions, casemates, bulwarks, curtains and lunettes; six wide streets radiate from the **piazza Grande** (three of them lead to the **gates** designed by Vincenzo Scamozzi) which is hexagonal and contains a Venetian column and 17C statues. ▶ The **Duomo** in the square is the work of either Longhena or Scamozzi (1615). ▶ No. 4 Borgo Udine houses the **Museo Storico** *(10 a.m.-12 noon; closed Mon)* with relics from the Venetian and Napoleonic eras. ☐

Practical information ─────────────

Hotel:
★★ *Roma*, borgo Cividale 27, ☎ 928472, 36 rm Ⓟ ⍿
⌇ 37,500.

Restaurant:
♦ *Buona Vite-da Baffo*, borgo Cividale 30, ☎ 928508, closed Tue and Aug. Regional cuisine: pasta alla contadina, fillets of meat, 20/45,000.

Recommended
Canoeing: at San Giorgio di Nogaro *(13 km SW)*, v. Libertà 1, ☎ 0431/65211.

PASSARIANO

Udine 27, Trieste 74, Milan 354 km
Pop. 226 ⊠ 33033 ☎ 0432   B2

The few houses are grouped around the grandiose **Villa Manin★**, a typically large and sumptuous 18C building designed along the classical lines inspired by Palladio. It was originally a 16C country house, and Ludovico Manin, the last Doge of Venice, had it enlarged for his own purposes. Napoleon signed the

treaty of Campoformio there in 1797, marking the end of the Republic of Venice. The interior has vast rooms covered with frescos *(9:30 a.m.-12:30 p.m. and 2-5 p.m. or 3-6 p.m.; closed Mon)*. The large and attractive park *(summer Sun 9:30 a.m.-12:30 p.m. and 3-6 p.m.; also Thu and Sat p.m.)* was a celebrated rural haven in the 18C.   ☐

Practical information ─────────────

Restaurants:
● ♦♦♦ *Toni*, at Gradiscutta di Varmo, v. Sentinis 1, ☎ 778003, closed Mon and 15 Jul-15 Aug. Meals served on veranda in summer. Regional cuisine: masurin al spet and polenta zale te golose, spit-roasted duck, 22/32,000.
♦♦♦ *Doge*, v. dei Dogi, ☎ 906591, closed Mon. In barchessa of Villa Manin. Regional cuisine: dumplings Manin, meats al limone with cheese sauce, 25/35,000.
♦♦♦ *Toni*, at Gradiscutta di Varmo, v. Sentinis 1, ☎ 778003, closed Mon and 15 Jul-15 Aug. Meals served on veranda in summer. Regional cuisine: masurin al spet and polenta zale te golose, spit-roasted duck, 22/32,000.

Recommended
♥ **crafts:** permanent exhibition at Villa Manin, ☎ 904547.

PONTEBBA

Udine 65, Trieste 136, Milan 442 km
Pop. 2,449 ⊠ 33016 ☎ 0428   B1

Pontebba is a holiday resort in the countryside near La Càrnia. As early as the 2C there was a customs house for goods passing from Illyria to Italy here. The local fair (8 Sep) was begun by Bertrando, Patriarch of Aquileia, in 1342.

▶ Next to the Gothic church of **S. Maria Maggiore** (1504) is a tall campanile. The church has a richly carved, gilded altar (1517) and a *Madonna and Saints* by Palma il Giovane (1624). ▶ A winding, scenic road leads to the **Pramollo Pass** (5,092 ft; *12.5 km N*) which connects Italy to Austria.   ☐

Practical information ─────────────

⌇ ski lifts at Studena Alta, skating.

PORDENONE

Trieste 106, Milan 343, Rome 605 km
Pop. 51,795 ⊠ 33170 ☎ 0434   A2

Pordenone is an ancient and refined town centre, clearly Venetian in character. Nevertheless, it is the lively, flourishing heart of the biggest industrial centre in Friuli and has been since the second half of the last century. The economic expansion of the last few decades (it is the provincial capital) has caused the built-up areas to spread in every direction, far beyond the old town walls, which are no longer standing. Once called *Portus Naonis*, i.e., the port on the Naone (later known as Noncello), it was the terminal for journeys via inland waters, between the W lowlands of Friuli and the lagoons of Venetia. Today, it is one of the chief manufacturing centres for electrical household appliances.

▶ **Corso Vittorio Emanuele** (A1-B2), the main street of the old town, is flanked by beautiful arcaded Gothic, Renaissance and Baroque houses. On the façade of several buildings, one can still see traces of the old decorative fresco work; those of no. 52) are by Giovanni Antonio de Sacchis, a distinguished early 16C painter, known locally as Il Pordenone. ▶ The **Museo Civico** (B2), housed in the 17C Palazzo Ricchieri (no. 51 corso Vittorio Emanuele; *9:30 a.m.-12:30 p.m. and 3-6:30*

Maniago km 26 **1** **2**

Treviso km 58

allo Stadio

Porcia

PORDENONE

0   100   200   300   400 m
1:18.000   (1 cm = m 180)

© SERVIZIO CARTOGRAFICO DEL TOURING CLUB ITALIANO, MILANO

Autostrada km 2 - Udine km 49
Autostrada-Portogruaro km 27

---

p.m.; closed Mon) contains wooden sculptures from Friuli; works by painters from Friuli and Venetia, including the *S. Gottardo* altarpiece, the *Finding of the True Cross* and the *Country Dance*, all by Il Pordenone; contemporary paintings, sculpture and graphics. ▶ The **Palazzo Comunale** (B2) is a 14C Gothic building featuring a portico at ground level with three arches and a projecting tower designed by Amalteo (16C); the clock dates from the same period. ▶ The **Duomo** (B2) is late Gothic (15C) with a modern façade, although the portal is by Pilacorte (1511). It also has a beautiful campanile with decorative brickwork (1219-1417); inside are works by Fogolino, Pilacorte and il Pordenone, an altarpiece depicting the *Madonna della Misericordia★* and frescos on the pilasters of the cupola and in the vestry. ▶ The former church of **S. Francesco** (B2), a 15C cloistered building, is now used for exhibitions. ▶ The **chiesa del Cristo**, or S. Maria degli Angeli (B2), has a fine marble portal designed by Pilacorte (1510); inside, there are still traces of 14C frescos and also a 16C wooden crucifix. ▶ Also of interest is the **Museo di Storia Naturale** (B2; *9 a.m.-12 noon and 3-6 p.m.; 9 am.-12 noon Sun; closed Mon*). ▶ Excavations in the suburb of Torre have revealed Roman buildings; findings from this site will be exhibited in an archaeological museum now being built in the castle of the counts of Ragogna. □

Practical information ───────

ⓘ p. della Motta 13 (B2), ☎ 24218; v. Beato Odorico 7 (A1), ☎ 27977.
🚂 (B1), ☎ 22616.
🚌 departures from p. Risorgimento (A2).
Car rental: *Avis*, v. Grigoletti, ☎ 30025.

Hotels:
★★★★ *Villa Ottoboni*, v. Aprile (A1 a), ☎ 21967, 72 rm Ⓟ 𝟨 𝒮 closed Aug and Christmas, 106,000.
★★★ *Residence Italia*, p. Costantini 6 (A2 b), ☎ 27821, 54 rm Ⓟ 𝒮 No restaurant, 70,000.

Restaurant:
◆◆◆ *Noncello*, v. Marconi 34 (A1-2 c), ☎ 253814, closed Sun and Aug. Venetian cuisine: pappardelle with duck sauce, shank of veal, 25/38,000.

Recommended
Bowling: v. Musile, ☎ 43252.
Fairs: *international trade fair* (Sep); *national ham radio fair* (Apr); *arts and crafts fair* (Dec), Ente Fiera, ☎ 255651.
Hockey and skating: v. Molinari (A2), ☎ 28338.
Sports centre: v. Rosselli, ☎ 31332.
Swimming: v. Treviso, ☎ 962004.
Technical tourism: visits to the *Battiston* marble and onyx works, at Zóppola, ☎ 97549; and to the *Alexander* works (cutlery manufacture), at Maniago, v. Industria 1, ☎ 0427/72538.
Wines: visits to the *Casarsa la Delizia* wine cooperative, at Casarsa della Delizia, v. Udine 24, ☎ 869564; and to *Friulvini*, at Zóppola, ☎ 979274.

SACILE

Pordenone 12, Trieste 125, Milan 331 km
Pop. 16,530 ✉ 33077 ☎ 0434   A2

This town is built on two large islands carved out by the meandering Livenza River. The old town centre is made up of arcaded streets flanked by dignified Venetian-style houses. It deserves its title as 'garden of the Serenissima'.

▶ Looking at the different architectural styles, it is still possible to discern traces of long-standing wealth and the cultural preoccupations of the Humanist era, when the presence of schools and teachers transformed the town into a 'second Padua'. ▶ The 14C **Loggia Comunale** has been rebuilt a number of times and was used as a theatre for a short time. ▶ The Gothic **Duomo** (15C) has a 16C campanile. Inside is a *Madonna of the Rosary* by Palma il Giovane and a rare tombstone depicting the burial of David (1454), who was a son of the Turkish sultan Murad II. ▶ In the hall of the **Palazzo Flangini-Biglia** (15C-16C; v. Cavour) are six frescos illustrating the deeds of a local family, by F.Montemezzano, an artist of the Veronese school. □

Practical information ───────

Restaurant:
◆ *Sfriso*, p. del Popolo 47, ☎ 71110. Regional cuisine: pasticcio di lasagne al forno, polenta and poultry, 20/25,000.

Recommended
Events: ancient *Festival of the Osei* (Sun after Aug hol).

SAN DANIELE DEL FRIULI

Udine 23, Trieste 92, Milan 371 km
Pop. 7,118 ✉ 33038 ☎ 0432   B2

An exquisite local ham, called 'sandaniele', matures well in the local climate. The ham is manufactured on the hill in buildings with high windows with slits to allow the mountain breeze to filter through and dry out the tens of thousands of pork legs hanging on wooden frames. This little town on a hill, huddled around its cathedral, exudes old-world Venetian charm, though it was badly damaged by an earthquake.

▶ In the upper part of the town is the **Duomo**, featuring a sumptuous façade adorned with 18C statues, the 18C **Palazzo del Monte di Pietà** and the ancient **Palazzo del Municipio**. ▶ The **Civica Biblioteca Guarneriana** (named after Guarnerio D'Artegna, who made the first gift to the library in 1466) contains a number of books and illuminated manuscripts. ▶ The late Gothic former church of

S. Antonio Abate (15C; *restored*) has a fine portal and rose window and contains frescos by Pellegrino da San Daniele (1498-1522). ▶ The **Museo del Territorio** contains numerous works of art including archaeological finds, detached frescos, jewelry, a wooden altarpiece, a 15C polychrome and the *Trinità* by Pordenone (1535). ▶ From the esplanade, with its tower and the few remains of the **castle**, there is a fine view over the whole amphitheatre and its castles, the plains of Friuli and the Giulian Alps. □

Practical information ——————————————

Restaurant:
♦ *Alfio*, v. Osoppo 95, ☎ 957380; closed Mon eve, Tue and Jul. Regional cuisine: pumpkin dumplings; venison in wine sauce, 20/30,000.

Recommended
Flying: *Associazione volovelistica Rivoli di Osoppo* (gliding), at Rivoli, v. Molino del Cucco 20, ☎ 986250.
Gastronomic specialties: San Daniele ham (traditional drying houses); festival in late Aug.

SAN VITO AL TAGLIAMENTO

Pordenone 19, Trieste 109, Milan 339 km
Pop. 12,224 ⊠ 33078 ☎ 0434   B3

Three gates and the remains of the surrounding walls bear witness to the historical significance of this site, which became one of the castles of the patriarchs of Aquileia in the 10C.

▶ The **Duomo** was rebuilt in 1745. Next to it stands a **campanile** with a Romanesque base and Renaissance top. ▶ The **Torre Raimonda** houses a **municipal museum** (*inquire in municipio*) containing prehistoric and Roman exhibits, including findings from the San Valentino necropolis of the early Veneti (9C-7C BC). ▶ The **Museo della Vita Contadina del Friuli Occidentale** (rural life) at v. Falcon Vial 12, (*all visits are accompanied, reserve in advance*) contains tools, furniture and crafts.   □

Practical information ——————————————

Hotel:
★★ *Angelina*, v. Madonna di Rosa 8, ☎ 80217, 24 rm ⓟ ⫩ closed Aug and Christmas, 36,500.

Restaurant:
♦♦ *Griglia d'Oro*, at Rosa, v. della Dogana 2, ☎ 80301, closed Sun eve, Tue, Jan and Aug. Italian cuisine: risotto with poppy seeds, pappardelle with pheasant, 25/50,000.

SESTO AL REGHENA

Pordenone 23, Trieste 107, Milan 333 km
Pop. 5,313 ⊠ 33079 ☎ 0434   A-B3

The abbey of **S. Maria in Sylvis** (a powerful Benedictine monastery, founded in the 8C) overlooks the is village. It played an important part in the political life of the region.

▶ The sturdy **tower** which serves as an entrance to the abbey is the only one of seven to have survived. The watch tower (12C) has been turned into a **campanile**. The abbey chancellery is now a school and the abbot's house is currently the town hall. ▶ The Romanesque-Byzantine **Basilica** (12C-13C) has been restored. There are frescos (some of them in the style of Giotto) inside the basilica; in the large crypt beneath the presbytery are **St. Anastasia's urn** (8C) and a 13C relief of the *Annunciation*. ▶ The 18C **Villa Fabbris-Fancella** can also be found in the village.   □

> Don't forget to consult the Practical Holiday Guide: it can help in solving many problems. •

SPILIMBERGO

Pordenone 32, Trieste 98, Milan 364 km
Pop. 11,107 ⊠ 33097 ☎ 0427   A-B2

This little town is located on a terrace on the r. bank of the Tagliamento and is typical of the rural communities in the area, and of Venetia in general. It was badly damaged by the earthquake of 1976. In the 11C, immigrants from Switzerland ruled the fief.

▶ The Gothic **Duomo** (begun in 1284) is on the outskirts of the town towards the Tagliamento River. It has a fine portal by Zenone da Campione (1376) on the l. side; inside are the Carmine chapel with marble decorations by Pilacorte (1498); an **organ★** with case and doors painted by Pordenone (16C); 14C-15C frescos in the apses and the crypt; and 15C statues and sculptures. ▶ The restored **castle** consists of a group of Gothic and Renaissance buildings, including the **Palazzo Dipinto**, whose façade is decorated with late 15C frescos. ▶ **Clauzetto** (*19 km N*) is a holiday resort in the Carnic pre-Alps, near the **Pradis ravine** and the Grotte Verdi (Green Grottos). □

Practical information ——————————————

ⓘ v. Piave, ☎ 2274.

Hotel:
★★ *Michielini*, v. Barbacane 3, ☎ 2150, 39 rm ⓟ ⫩ 37,000.

Recommended
Archery: *Compagnia Arcieri Theodoro dal Borlus*, v. Udine 14, ☎ 40126.
Horseback riding: *Cellina Trekking Club*, at Vivaro, v. Roma 8.
Spelunking: visits to the Pradis ravine; caretaker on duty; information from the *Gruppo speleologico*, ☎ 80329.

TARVISIO

Udine 98, Trieste 169, Milan 471 km
2,400 ft pop. 6,060 ⊠ 33018 ☎ 0428   C1

Located at Italy's farthest NE point on the border with Austria and Yugoslavia, Tarvisio is a pleasant holiday resort.

▶ 5 km from Valbruna, in the **Valbruna-Monte Santo di Lussari** area, there is a funicular to the **Monte Lussari shrine** (14C). ▶ Just outside Tarvisio, at the customs checkpoint of Coccau, there is a small 13C **church** in which some interesting 13C-14C frescos were discovered in 1958. ▶ The two **Fusine lakes** (*10.5 km*) near the Yugoslavian border are worth a detour. **Lake Inferiore★** (3,031 ft) is enchanting with its crystal-clear water, against a background of white mountain peaks and dark fir woods. This area, including the state-owned Fusine Forest, the upper valleys of Dogna and Fella, extending as far as the border between the Pramollo and Predil passes, will soon be part of the 100,000 acre **Tarvisiano National Park**, now in preparation. Nearby are the ski resorts of **Camporosso in Valcanale** (*3 km W*) and **Fusine in Valromana** (*8 km E*).   □

Practical information ——————————————

⛷ ski lifts, cross-country skiing (over 70 km), instruction, skating, ski jumps.
ⓘ v. Roma 10, ☎ 2135.

Hotels:
★★★ *Nevada*, v. Kugj 4, ☎ 2332, 60 rm ⓟ ⫩ closed Nov-Dec, 58,000; bkf: 6,000.
★★ *Friuli*, v. Vittorio Veneto 104, ☎ 2016, 38 rm ⓟ ⫩ ⅙ closed Nov, 50,000; bkf: 5,000.
★★ *Sport Hotel Bellavista*, at Camporosso in Valcanale, v. Sella 17, ☎ 63025, 34 rm ⓟ ⫩ 51,000; bkf: 5,000.

Restaurant:
♦ *Italia,* v. Roma 103, ☎ 2041, closed Wed and 15 Oct-15 Nov. Regional cuisine: spit-roasted loin of pork, braised beef, 20/30,000.

▲ ★ *Da Cesco,* at Camporosso in Valcanale, v. Alpi Giulie 63, 12 pl, ☎ 2254 (all year).

TOLMEZZO

Udine 52, Trieste 121, Milan 427 km
Pop. 10,503 ⊠ 33028 ☎ 0433　　　　　　　　B1

The mountains of La Càrnia loom large behind this picturesque old-world town, which is the centre of the region.

▶ The elegant 18C Palazzo Campeis houses the **Museo Carnico delle Arti e Tradizioni Popolari** *(summer 9 a.m.-12 noon and 3-6 p.m.; winter 2:30-5:30 p.m.; closed Tue)* which illustrates the life, costumes, agriculture and crafts of Càrnia. ▶ The **Duomo** (1764) contains 16C sculptures, marble altars and 18C altarpieces. ▶ Industrialization came early to the area. Jacopo Linussio set up a **textile mill** as early as the 18C, still in existence. It consists of an 18C villa with two arcaded wings and other industrial buildings. ▶ In the But Valley, 400 steps lead up to the parish church of **S. Maria oltre But** (13C, rebuilt in the 17C). It was built on remains of Roman and medieval foundations.　　　　　　□

Practical information _____

⚑ ski lifts, cross-country skiing, instruction at Sella Chianzutan *(14 km SW).*

Hotels:
★★★ *Cimenti,* v. della Vittoria 28, ☎ 43069, 19 rm Ⓟ ⚬ closed Jul, 62,000; bkf: 5,000.
★★★ *Roma,* p. XX Settembre 14, ☎ 20281, 34 rm Ⓟ 48,000. Rest. ♦♦♦ Closed Mon and Oct. Regional cuisine: pasta, pumpkin dumplings, game, 35/50,000.

Recommended
Motocross track: *Sorgenti,* at Bordano, management: *Autocross Carnico,* at Impronzo, ☎ 97245.
Swimming: v. Val di Goito, ☎ 40624.

TRICESIMO

Udine 11, Trieste 83, Milan 389 km
Pop. 6,673 ⊠ 33019 ☎ 0432　　　　　　　　B2

Ad tricesium lapidem, i.e., at the thirteenth milestone from Aquileia, on the road to Norico, was the Roman *mansio,* situated in the moraine amphitheatre of the Tagliamento. The r.-hand side of the 18C **parish church** in Tricesimo features a marble portal carved by Bernardino da Bissone (1505).　　　　　　□

Practical information _____

TRICESIMO

Hotel:
★★★★ *Boschetti,* p. Mazzini 10, ☎ 851230, 32 rm Ⓟ closed Aug, 80,000; bkf: 9,000. Rest. ● ♦♦♦♦ closed Mon and Aug. Creative regional cuisine: terrine with liver and red chicory, tagliata al Refosco, 50/70,000.

Environs

TARCENTO, ⊠ 33017, ☎ 0432, 8 km N.
ⓘ v. Pretura Vecchia, ☎ 785392.

Recommended
Spelunking: guided tours of the Villanova caves, *Gruppo Esploratori Lusevera,* ☎ 787020 or 787030.

TRIESTE*

Milan 410, Rome 670 km
Pop. 246,305 ⊠ 34100 ☎ 040　　　　　　　　C3

In 1719, Charles VI of Hapsburg conferred the status of 'free port' on the village of about 600 houses grouped around the Colle di S. Giusto and its church. This was intended as a hostile act towards Venice, which claimed sovereignty over the Adriatic Sea. It also marked the rise of the future great city which would stretch from the sea up to the chalky Carso plateau and to the border between the Italian- and Slavic- speaking areas. Although the city is in Italy, it is imbued with the essence of Italian, Slavic and middle-European cultures. While this combination is sometimes discordant, it has always been productive. Trieste is an open, receptive and civilized city. As central Europe's 'window to the Mediterranean', it has become a major trading centre, creating important E-W links. In *Il mio Carso* (1912), the local author Scipio Slataper wrote: 'Trieste's history is inextricably tied to its harbour. We were a small community of pirate fishermen, we succeeded in using Rome and Austria, we fought and held back the others... The sun shines high and clear above the sea and the city. The shores of Trieste awake full of movement and colour, and our ships lift their anchors and sail off towards Salonika and Bombay'. By the end of World War I, the people of Trieste obtained the union with Italy for which they had fought so heroically. The union was once again placed in jeopardy at the end of World War II and the city is now in a precarious position in the face of restructured international trade.

▶ The centre of the city is the **piazza Unità d'Italia** (C2-3), which opens on to the beach and is popular with strollers. Its present appearance dates from the second half of the 19C, but there are still a few 18C elements: the Baroque Palazzo Pitteri, Charles VI's column and the fountain showing the Four Continents and the Angel of Commerce. The **Caffè degli Specchi** (opened in 1840) is one of the oldest in the city and serves as a reminder of the importance of café life in 19C Trieste. ▶ The square looks out toward the sea and harbour. Behind the square is the Colle di S. Giusto (C3), the original site of the town and the Roman colony of *Tergeste,* which dates from to the end of the 1C BC. The town did not spread beyond the hill until the 18C. Once occupied by salt works, today it is referred to as 'new town' or 'borgo teresiano' (B3). Uniformity and a Neoclassical style are evident along the **Canal Grande** (B3), with the façade of the church of **S. Antonio Nuovo** (19C) as a backdrop. When the town had spread out over most of the plain, it began to expand uphill again. ▶ Monuments and places of interest branch out from p. Unità in three directions: towards the Colle di S. Giusto; E; and along the harbour.

▶ Behind p. **Unità d'Italia** (C3) is the 11C Romanesque church of **S. Silvestro** and the Baroque church of **S. Maria Maggiore** (17C). Behind the latter, sheltered by the hill and surrounded by old houses is the **Arco di Ricardo** (C3), once the gateway into the walled city at the time of Augustus. ▶ Further on is the **early Christian basilica** (no. 11 v. Madonna del Mare, C2; *Wed 10 a.m.-12 noon; apply in advance to the Superintendent of Monuments,* ☎ *422806)* which contains monochrome and polychrome mosaics. ▶ At the bottom of v. del Teatro Romano (C3) are the amphitheatre and the remains of the stage of the ancient town of *Tergeste.* ▶ The v. Capitolina (C3-4), which leads to the Colle S. Giusto and also runs alongside the **Parco delle Rimembranze,** affords a spectacular

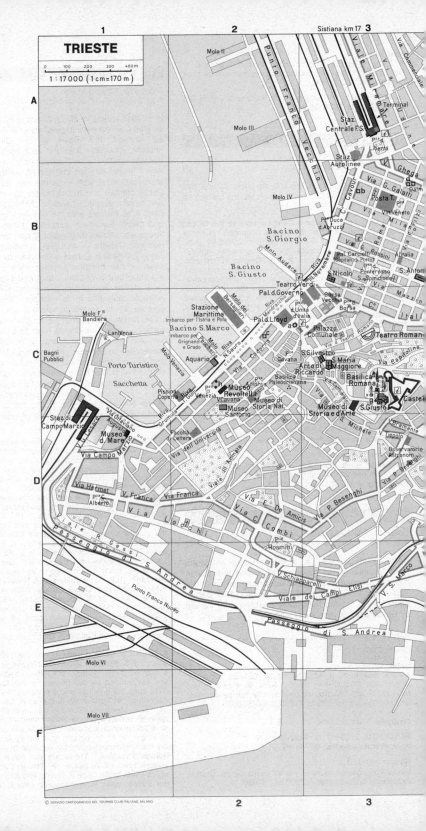

TRIESTE

0 100 200 300 400m

1:17000 (1cm=170 m)

Sistiana km 17

Molo II

Molo III

Molo IV

Punto Franco Vecchio

Staz.
Centrale F.S.

Terminal

Liberta

Staz.
Autolinee

Ghega

Via G. Galatti

Via Cavour

Posta 1.

P°°
Duca
d.Abruzzi

VIII Veneto

Milano

Via Rossini

Attilia

Bacino
S.Giorgio

Molo Audace

Pal. Carciotti
(Capitan.di Porto)

S.Nicolo

Congresso
S.Spiridione

S.Anton

Bacino
S.Giusto

Teatro Verdi

Pal. d.Governo

Borsa
Vecchia

Mazzin

Italy

Molo F.lli
Bandiera

Lanterna

Molo dei
Bersaglieri

Stazione
Marittima
Imbarco per l'Istria e Pola

Bacino S.Marco
Imbarco per Passeggeri
Grignano e Grado

Pal.d.Lloyd

P°
d.Unita
d'Italia

Borsa

Palazzo
Comunale

Teatro Roman

Bagni
Pubblici

Porto Turistico

Sacchetta

Molo Venezia

Aquario

Cadorna

Cavana

S.Silvestro

S.Maria
Maggiore

Via Capitolina

Arco di
Riccardo

Basilica
Paleocristiana

Basilica
Romana

Piscina
Coperta

Museo
Revoltella

V.Cavana

Museo di
Storia Nat.

Castel

Staz.di
Campo Marzio

Via Ottaviano
Augusto

Museo
d. Mare

Via Campo Marzio

Facoltà
di Lettere

Museo
Sartorio

Museo di
Storia e d'Arte

S.Giusto

Michele

V. Tiepolo

V.Bramante

Osservatorio
Astronom.

Via Hermet

V. Franca

Via Franca

Viale di Acmara

Via dell'Università

P°°S.
Alberto

Viale R. Gessi

Passeggio di S. Andrea

Via F. De Amicis

Via C. Combi

Via P. Besenghi

P°
Rosmini

Punto Franco Nuovo

Schiapparelli

Viale dei Campi Elisi

Passeggio di S. Andrea

Molo VI

Molo VII

SCÓRCOLA

Via C. Cantù

Via Commerciale

Via dell'Alpina

Fiume

P.ta Scórcola

Martiri Libertà

Via Fabio

Severo

Università

P.zza
Europa

Via A. Valerio

150

Postúmia km 51 (Valico di Ferneti)
Fiume km 76 (Valico di Pese)

Museo d.
Risorgimento
Casa d.
Combattente
Oberdan
Pal. d.
Regione

Pal. di
Giustizia

Via del Corgneo

Via G. Marconi

Giardino
Pubblico

Via Giulia

Rotonda
d.Boschetto

Via Giulia

P.zza d.
Volontari
Giuliani

50

Sinagoga

Via C. Battisti

Viale XX Settembre

Politeama
Rossetti

Orto
Botanico

Boschetto

100

B

Teatro
Eden

Via della Ginnastica

Via R. Timeus

Rossetti

C. Marcheselli

150

CHIADINO

Via

C

Museo
Purgo

P.ta
S.Giovanni

Via Carducci

P.ta
Goldoni

Italia

G. Pascoli

Largo d.
Barriera
Vecchia

V. Capitolina

P.za
Garibaldi

Tel.

Via Tel.

Via Matteotti

Via dei Piccardi

Via Domenico Rossetti

D

Via S. Marco

V. Madonnina

Via d. Bosco

sovino

Via di Servola

S.Giacomo

P.za di
Perugino

Via P. Revoltella

Via P. Vergerio

Via P. Revoltella

Fiera
Campionaria

D' Alviano

Caduti sul Lavoro

Via d. Orlandini

P.za dei
Pestalozzi

Viale G. D'Annunzio

Viale dei Mulini a vento

P.za dei
Foraggi

Viale d. Ippodromo

Piazzale
De Gasperi

Via C. Cumano

Sistiana km 32 - Fiume km 76 (Valico di Pese)

Ippodromo

Via di Servola

Via B. Orlandini

Via Zanetti

Via Lorenzetti

Via dei Mulini

SS. N. 202

Gall. di Chiárbola

Strada di Fiume

100

Via Barriera Vecchia d'Alviano

CHIÁRBOLA

Gall. di Montebello

50

V. Doda

Piazzale
Autostrada

Via Tiziano

Via Carpaccio

Via Sidoni

Palazzetto
dello
Sport

50

P.za
Baiamonti

F

Via Capodistria

Via Baiamonti

view. ▶ At the top of the hill is the **piazza delle Catte-drale★** (C3). It contains a column with the melon and halberd which are the city's symbols. Notice the **Altar of the Third Army** and the ruins of the **basilica** from the **Roman forum** (2C) and of the **Capitoline Temple** (1C). ▶ The cathedral of **S. Giusto★★** (C3) was begun in the 14C, when two already existing buildings were joined. The Romanesque façade has a large, 14C Gothic rose window, while the pillars of the central portal are Roman funerary steles; the 14C **campanile**, which incorporates the remains of the propylaeum of a Roman temple, also has a niche containing a 13C statue of S. Giusto (a 3C Christian martyr). Inside, in the r.-hand apses are 13C frescos and a remarkable mosaic of Christ with S. Giusto and S. Servulo (late 14C); in the l.-hand apse is an enthroned **Madonna with the Infant Jesus** and the Archangels Michael and Gabriel, with the Twelve Apostles below, plus 12C **mosaics★**. To the r. of S. Giusto is the small 15C Gothic church of **S. Michele al Carnale.** ▶ The **Museo di Storia ed Arte** (C3; *9 a.m.-1 p.m.*) contains some important collections, mainly archaeological; remarkable finds from caves and prehistoric fortified villages and in particular from the necropolis of S. Lucia di Tolmino; **Greek and Italiot vases★** and earthenware from Tarentum plus **274 drawings★** by G.B. Tiepolo. ▶ The **castle★** (C3), built between 1470-1630 on the site of an earlier Venetian castle, houses the **museum** *(9 a.m.-2 p.m.; 9 a.m.-1 p.m. wkends; closed Mon).* It contains furniture from various eras and a collection of ancient weapons★.

▶ **E of p. Unità d'Italia.** ▶ **Piazza della Borsa** (C3), along with the **Tergesteo**, the Neoclassical **Borsa Vecchia** (Old Stock Exchange) and the **Borsa**, is the traditional centre of commercial activity. ▶ The nearby **Teatro G. Verdi** (C3; 1801) has always been the centre of the city's musical and cultural activities. *(The Museo Teatrale is open Tue and Thu 9 a.m.-1 p.m. and during performance intermissions; closed Mon.)* ▶ Corso Italia (C3-4) which joins the centre of town with the areas E, leads to the **Civico Museo Morpurgo** (C4; *9 a.m.-1 p.m.; closed Mon)* which contains collections of historical documents and traditional costumes from Trieste, along with pictures, sculptures and prints and furniture from a 19C house. ▶ **Via Carducci** (B-C4) is one of the liveliest streets in the city. It connects with v. XX Settembre, a popular place for strollers. At no. 35 is the **Teatro Eden** (B4), a remarkable example of G. Sommaruga's Art Nouveau style (1906). ▶ **Piazza Oberdan** stands on the site of the Grand Barracks, where Guglielmo Oberdan, an Italian nationalist, was hanged in 1882. The Casa del Combattente, at v. XXIV Maggio 4, also houses the **Museo del Risorgimento** *(9 a.m.-1 p.m.; closed Mon),* with exhibits on the history of Trieste and Italy.

▶ **The harbour.** ▶ The **port** of Trieste, the third largest in the Mediterranean, stretches from Bàrcola in the N down to the S slope of the Gulf of Muggia. ▶ By the waterfront to the r. of the p. Unità d'Italia is the **Molo Audace** (B2), a traditional place for strolls (at the end, a splendid view of the city). ▶ Next to the **fish market** (C2) is the **salt water Aquarium** *(9 a.m.-1 or 7 p.m.; closed Mon)* which contains fish and marine life from the Adriatic, also a tropical fish section. ▶ The **Museo Revoltella★** in p. Venezia (C2; entrance at v. Diaz 27; *9 a.m.-1 p.m.; wkends 10 a.m.-1 p.m.; closed Mon)* still looks like a luxurious 19C residence with lavish *fin de siècle* furnishings, paintings and 19C sculptures by Canova, Bartolini, Angelica Kauffman, Hayez and the Indunos, plus Venetian school works by local artists. The Gallery of Modern Art is being moved to a new location. ▶ The **Museo Sartorio** (C2; *9 a.m.-1 p.m.; closed Mon),* housed in an 18C building, is an interesting example of a wealthy residence of the end of the last century; the pottery collection★ includes Italian and European majolica and china from the 15C-19C, plus local pottery; also paintings from the 14C-18C, Cretan-Venetian and Slavic icons; rooms and furnishings in Neoclassical and other styles, from neo-Gothic to Biedermeier. ▶ The **Museo del Mare★** (D1; *9 a.m.-1 p.m.; closed Mon)* deals mainly with the city's maritime past and the history of its shipyards; one section is dedicated to fish from the Adriatic. ▶ Old locomotives

and other railway exhibits, plus models, are on view at the **Museo Ferroviario** (C-D1; *9 a.m.-1 p.m.).* ▶ The **Museo della Resistenza** (Resistance Museum) is in the **Risiera di S. Sabba**, the former Nazi extermination camp (S part of city, Ratto Pileria 1, entrance along the SS to Pola; *10 a.m.-1:30 p.m. winter; 10 a.m.-7:30 p.m. summer; 9 a.m.-1 p.m. wkends; closed Mon).*

Environs

▶ There is a magnificent view of the gulf from the **Faro della Vittoria**, on a small hill above Barcola *(3 km N).* ▶ The **Castello di Miramare** *(7 km N)* has a museum *(9 a.m.-2 p.m.; 9 a.m.-1 p.m. wkends; closed Mon)* and a magnificent park *(9 a.m.-sunset).* ▶ **Villa Opicina** *(9 km, funicular with fine views from the p. Oberdan, B4)* and the **Grotta Gigante** *(12.5 km)* are also interesting. ▶ **Val Rosandra** *(10 km SE)* is an unusual area of the Carso. □

Practical information

ⓘ v. Rossini 6 (B3), ☎ 60336; at Castello di S. Giusto (C3), ☎ 750002; at the station (A3), ☎ 420182.
✈ at Ronchi dei Legionari, ☎ 0481/777001; *Alitalia, Agenzia Cosulich,* p. S. Antonio 1 (B3), ☎ 680170; bus from v. Miramare (A3), ☎ 422711.
🚂 (A3), ☎ 418207; Stazione Trieste-Villa Opicina, ☎ 211682 (trains to Yugoslavia).
🚍 departures from the coach station (A-B3), ☎ 61080.
⛴ to Istria and Pola and to Grignano and Grado, *Lloyd Triestino,* ☎ 7785428 or 7785205.
Car rental: *Avis,* v. S. Nicolò 12, ☎ 68243, airport, ☎ 777085; *Hertz,* v. Mazzini 1, ☎ 60650, airport, ☎ 777600; *Maggiore,* station, v. Miramare 2, ☎ 421323.

Hotels:
★★★★ *G. H. Duchi d'Aosta,* p. Unità d'Italia 2 (C2 a), ☎ 62081, 52 rm ℗ ♿ 175,000. Rest. ● ♦♦♦ **Harry's Grill** Regional and international cuisine: baked sea bass, filets of salmon with globe artichokes, 45/70,000.
★★★★ *Jolly Cavour,* corso Cavour 7 (B3 b), ☎ 7694, 177 rm ℗ 153,000.
★★★★ *Savoia Excelsior,* riva del Mandracchio 4 (C2 c), ☎ 7690, 156 rm ℗ ⚅ ⚟ 195,000.
★★★ *Colombia,* v. della Geppa 18 (B3 d), ☎ 69434, 40 rm ℗ ♿ No restaurant, 86,000; bkf: 6,500.
★★★ *San Giusto,* v. C. Belli 3 (D4 e), ☎ 764824, 48 rm. No restaurant, 84,000.
★★ *Abbazia,* v. della Geppa 20 (B3 d), ☎ 61330, 21 rm ♿ No restaurant, 74,000; bkf: 6,000.

Miramare

Set in a green park overlooking the deep blue Gulf of Trieste, Miramare is like a fairy-tale castle. Architecturally, it is part of that curious eclectic style so popular in the 19C. It was built for Archduke Maximilian (brother of Emperor Franz Joseph) who had been exiled from power. When Napoleon III took Trieste from the Hapsburgs in 1859, he arranged for Maximilian to be given the title of Emperor of Mexico and installed him there in 1864. Miramare had not yet been finished when Maximilian left for Mexico — he lived in the Castelletto at the upper end of the park. Three years later, Maximilian faced a firing squad on Benito Juarez's orders. His wife Charlotte, daughter of King Leopold I of Belgium, slowly sank into insanity at Miramare.

Restaurants:

● ♦♦♦ *Antica Trattoria Suban,* v. Comici 2, ☎ 4368, closed Tue, Aug and Christmas. With fine summer garden. Regional cuisine: fritters alla mandriera, eggs all'istriana with truffles, 30/50,000.
♦♦♦ *Bottega del Vino,* p. Cattedrale 3 (C3 g), ☎ 733235, closed Tue and Jan. Overlooking city and surrounding

Trieste and its writers

Trieste's history and unique geographical location have made it a meeting-place for a number of different cultures. While this may have occasionally troubled its inhabitants, many artists have found this melting-pot atmosphere inspiring. In recent history, Trieste has made a distinctive contribution to Italian literature and culture through the work of the poet Umberto Saba (1883-1957) and the novelists Scipio Slataper and Italo Svevo. Slataper died at the age of twenty-seven during the battle of Podgora in 1915. His memoirs of childhood and adolescence (Il mio Carso, 1912) show a passion for Italy and Trieste, without rejecting the central European and Slavic elements which permeated the society in which he grew up. A businessman from Trieste, Ettore Schmitz took on the pen-name of Italo Svevo (1861-1928) and became one of Italy's most brilliant novelists. His works (A Life, 1892, Senility, 1898 and Confessions of Zeno, 1923) have been more widely read since WWII than when they were first published and now occupy an essential place in the history of the modern novel.

area; dancing in evenings. Regional and international cuisine: fritters with salmon, shank of veal, 25/40,000.

♦♦♦ *Bragozzo*, riva Sauro 22 (C2 h), ☎ 303001, closed Sun, Mon and Christmas. Terrace in summer. Seafood: ravioli Miramare, fish baked in foil, 30/45,000.

♦♦♦ *Buffet Benedetto*, v. Ottobre 19 (B4 i), ☎ 61655, closed Mon and Aug. Regional cuisine: cheese dumplings, wholegrain pappardelle, 25/35,000.

♦♦♦ *Granzo*, p. Venezia 7 (C2 h), ☎ 306788, closed Wed. Mixed cuisine: seafood risotto, mushroom dumplings, 30/35,000.

♦♦ *Adriatico*, v. S. Lazzaro 7 (C4 f), ☎ 65680, closed Mon and Aug. Mixed regional cuisine: fritters, gilthead fish baked in foil, 25/40,000.

Recommended

Archery: *Compagnia Arcieri Trieste*, v. dei Pellegrini 22, ☎ 910219.

Baseball: baseball field and instruction, Prosecco, ☎ 225922; *Federazione Italiana*, v. Severo 14, ☎ 60629.

Botanical gardens: v. Marchesetti 2, ☎ 726839 (closed Mon); *Carsiana* botanical garden on the Gabrovizza-Sgonico road, ☎ 820002 (May-Sep; Sun 10 a.m.-12.30 p.m., Sat 5-7 p.m.).

Ceramics: *Ars cretaria*, v. Settefontane 25/B, ☎ 391335.

Cycling: *Pedale triestino*, v. Toti 15/B, ☎ 729312.

Events: *opera season* (Oct-May), *operetta festival* (Jul-Aug) and *symphony concerts*, at the Teatro Verdi, ☎ 62931; *drama season* (Jan-May), at the Teatro Stabile, ☎ 567507; *drama, ballet, and other art forms*, at the Castello di S. Giusto (Jul-Aug); *sound and light show* at the Castello di Miramare (Jul-Aug); *harness racing season*, at the Ippodromo di Montebello; *sailing and speedboat races*.

Fairs: *international trade fair* (Jun); *boat show* (Mar) and other specialized exhibitions in the exhibition district (D-E6), ☎ 392961.

Golf: at Padriciano, ☎ 226159 (9 holes).

Guided tours: molo Bersaglieri 3, ☎ 305050.

Historical cafés: *Caffè San Marco*, v. Battisti 18 (B4), ☎ 727216; *Caffè degli Specchi*, p. Unità d'Italia (C-D3); *Caffè Tommaseo*, rive III Novembre 5 (B3).

Horseback riding: *Centro ippico*, strada nuova per Opicina 12; *Circolo ippico triestino*, SS 202, ☎ 211724 (riding school).

Horse racing: race course: di Montebello, p. De Gasperi 4 (E5-6), ☎ 393176.

Liqueurs: visits to the *Stock* factories, v. L. Stock 2, ☎ 7350.

Marina: *Sacchetta Yachtclub Adriaco*, ☎ 305567; *Società triestina Vela*, ☎ 306327.

Sailing: *Lega Navale*, v. Geppa 6, ☎ 69145.

Spelunking: visits to the Grotta del Gigante; information from Borgo Grotta Gigante, ☎ 227312; at Trieste, *CAI commissione grotte*, ☎ 60317.

Sports centre: v. Chiarbola 906 (F5), ☎ 730481.

Swimming: riva Gulli 3 (C2), ☎ 306024.

Wines: wine shop at the Castello di S. Giusto (C3), ☎ 733235.

Zoological gardens: Acquario, Riva Sauro 1 (C2), ☎ 306201.

UDINE*

Trieste 70, Milan 380, Rome 639 km
Pop. 101,179 ⊠ 33100 ☎ 0432   **B2**

The small mound of glacier deposit in the middle of the city rises to no more than 85 ft, but it provides a commanding view over the plain and the ring of alpine foothills. This was a fine place for setting up lookouts, fortifications and armed men, hence the castle, built here when the Hungarians overran the region. Their horses were so swift that folk tradition speaks of an 'ogre with seven-league boots'. *Udene*, the name of the castle, appears in 10C documents following the Hungarian incursions. Count Gorizia, deputy for the Patriarch of Aquileia, was the political authority in Friuli and sat in judgment twice a year. Patriarch Bertoldo di Andechs preferred Udine to Cividale and gave the city the right to hold markets and the privilege of citizenship. Tuscan markets were quick to take him up on the offer. From then on, Udine's power increased as the capital of Friuli. There is a Venetian atmosphere about the city, especially in the p. della Libertà. The 'Friuli homeland' belonged to Venice from 1420 onwards. Only a few reminders of the patriarchal period survive.

▶ The monumental **piazza della Libertà★★** is the main feature of the historical city centre; the castle which towers above it introduces the onlooker to the Venetian architectural style. ▶ The **Palazzo del Comune★** is a Gothic-Venetian structure, with a portico and a loggia between two arched windows in a two-colour stone façade; the Madonna in the r.-hand corner niche is by B. Bon (1448). ▶ In the centre of the **S. Giovanni portico★** (16C, Bernardino da Morcote) is a triumphal arch giving access to what was then the chapel of S. Giovanni, now the war memorial. On the **Torre dell'Orologio** (1527), the lion of St. Mark and two Moors strike the hours. ▶ From the piazza the street leads to the **Arco Bollani** (1556, designed by Palladio). The hill can be climbed from here. ▶ The site on which the patriarchs' castle stood is occupied today by a large 16C building which looks like a sumptuous palazzo (**castello★**, B2). It houses the **Musei Civici** and the **Galleries of History and Art★** *(closed for restoration)*. The museum features paintings by Friuli artists; the paintings in the Parlamento★ room include some by Tiepolo. ▶ The large square of the castle extends sideways in front of the building. In it is a reconstruction (1931) of the **Casa delle Contadinanza** (16C), and beyond the 16C Venetian arch are the 15C **Casa della Confraternita** and the church of **S. Maria di Castello** (B2). ▶ The façade and sides of the **Duomo★** (C2), refurbished in the 18C, still show remnants of the original 14C Gothic building. It contains paintings by Tiepolo (first altar on r.: SS. Trinità; second altar on r.: SS. Ermagore and Fortunato; Resurrection and frescos in the SS. Sacramento chapel), inlay-work pulpit and two organs. To the l. of the sanctuary is the entrance to the **Museo del Tesoro** *(Tue, Thu, Sat 9 a.m.-12 noon)*: the first of the museum's three rooms is the 14C chapel of S. Nicolò dei Fabbri with frescos by Vitale da Bologna. ▶ The 18C **Oratorio della Purità** to the r. of the Duomo *(facing sacristy)* contains paintings by Giambat-

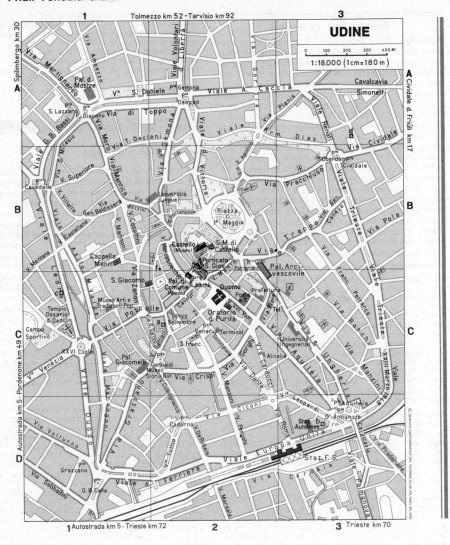

tista Tiepolo and by his son Giandomenico. ▶ The imposing **Palazzo Arcivescovile** (B-C2; *9 a.m.-12 noon; closed
wkends and hols*) contains interesting **frescos** by Tiepolo
on the vaulted ceiling of the main staircase and in the
gallery. ▶ The former church of **S. Francesco** (C2) has
been restored to its original 13C form and is now used for
art exhibitions. ▶ The 17C Palazzo Giacomelli houses
the **Museo Friulano di Storia Naturale** *(10 a.m.-12 noon
and 2-4 p.m.; 9:30 a.m.-12:30 p.m. Sun and hols).* ▶
Facing p. Matteotti is the elegant, Lombardesque façade
of **S. Giacomo** (C1-2). ▶ The **Museo Friulano delle Arti
e Tradizioni Popolari** is housed in the Baroque Palazzo
Gorgo-Maniago (C1, *9 a.m.-12:30 p.m. and 3-6 p.m.; closed Sun p.m. and Mon*). It contains folk art and other
exhibits from the 18C to the present. ▶ The **Manin
Chapel** (see sacristan of SS. Redentore in the nearby v.
Mantica) is an 18C building. ▶ The Palazzo delle Mostre
(exhibition hall: C1) also houses the **Galleria di Arte
Moderna** *(9 a.m.-12:30 p.m. and 3-6 p.m.; closed Sun*

p.m. and Mon) with works by 20C artists, mainly from
Friuli and Trieste. □

Practical information _____

ⓘ v. dei Missionari 2 (C3), ☎ 295972.
✈ at Ronchi dei Legionari, ☎ 777001; *Alitalia*, v. Carducci 26, ☎ 294601; buses depart from v. Savorgana 18,
☎ 92923.
🚍 (D2-3), ☎ 208969.
🚌 from bus station (D3), ☎ 203941.
Car rental: *Avis,* v. Europa Unita 23, ☎ 501149; *Hertz,*
v. Europa Unita 127, ☎ 503403; *Maggiore,* v. Europa
Unita 26, ☎ 290956.

Hotels:
★★★★ *Astoria Italia,* p. XX Settembre 24 (C2 a),
☎ 505091, 80 rm ℗ 125,000; bkf: 11,000.
★★★ *Casa Bianca,* v. Podgora 16, ☎ 35612, 50 rm ℗ ♿
🍴 closed Christmas. No restaurant, 70,000; bkf: 6,000.

★★★ *Continental,* via Tricesimo 73, ☎ 46969, 60 rm P ⨀ 65,000; bkf:8,000.
★★★ *Cristallo,* p. D'Annunzio 43 (D3 b), ☎ 205921, 81 rm P 66,500.
★★★ *Friuli,* v. Ledra 24 (C1 c), ☎ 34351, 100 rm P ⅙ 71,000; bkf: 7,000.
★★★ *President,* v. Duino (A3 d), ☎ 292905, 67 rm P ⅙ ⚘ 70,000; bkf: 8,000.

Restaurants:
● ♦♦♦ *Buona Vite,* v. Treppo 10 (B2-3 e), ☎ 21053, closed Sun eve, Mon and Aug. Near Palazzo Arcivescovile. Mixed cuisine: orata bream, liver alla veneziana, 30/40,000.
♦♦♦ *La' di Moret,* v. Tricesimo 276, ☎ 471930. Regional and Italian cuisine:fish from Adriatic, goulash alla friulana with dumplings, 25/40,000.
♦♦ *Antica Maddalena,* v. Pellicerrie 4 (B2 f), ☎ 25111, closed Sun and 10-31 Aug. Mixed cuisine: thinly sliced fresh salmon with rucola salad, tagliata alla Maddalena, 25/35,000.
♦♦ *Vedova,* v. Tavagnacco 9, ☎ 470291, closed Sun eve, Mon and Aug. Managed by same family for three generations. Regional cuisine: risotto with game, pappardelle, pasta al salmi, homemade wines, 21/31,000.

Recommended
Archery: *Compagnia Arcieri Udine,* v. Latisana 17, ☎ 479738.
Events: *students' drama competition* (Apr); concerts and plays at the Palazzo delle Mostre (A1).
Fairs and markets: in the fairground district (Torreano di Martignacco, NW outskirts): international exhibition of chairs (May) and various other displays of goods, ☎ 400041.
Golf: at Fagagna *(13 km NW),* ☎ 800418 (9 holes).
Horseback riding: at Manzano *(16 km SE),* v. Casali Birri 4, ☎ 750475.
Liqueurs: visits to the *Grappa Nonno* factory, Pavia di Udine *(10 km SE),* at Percoto, v. Aquileia 104, ☎ 676333.
Motocross track: at Faédis *(15 km NE),* club management p. 1 Maggio.
Sports hall: v. Marangoni 6, ☎ 203576.

Swimming: v. Ampezzo 4, ☎ 26967.

VALVASONE

Pordenone 20, Trieste 79, Milan 363 km
Pop. 1,982 ✉ 33098 ☎ 0434   A-B2

The village's main attraction is the ancient centre, with its galleried streets and remains of the town walls.

▶ The entrance to the village is by way of a gate with numerous towers. The 13C **castle** consists of a few buildings grouped around a small courtyard. It has been rebuilt several times and is now being restored. ▶ The neo-Gothic church of **Corpo di Cristo** contains the only surviving 16C Venetian school **organ★** (1532). ▶ During the 16C, the village was home to Erasmo di Valvason, the most renowned Friulian writer of the times. Milton was certainly acquainted with his *Angeleida,* a poem about the good and faithful angels and the fall of Lucifer.   □

VENZONE

Udine 33, Trieste 104, Milan 410 km
Pop. 2,389 ✉ 33010 ☎ 0432   B1

The 1976 earthquake almost completely destroyed Venzone; the remains of the 13C wall formerly surrounded a very beautiful old village in the Tagliamente Valley.

▶ A few walls and arches survive from the Gothic **Duomo,** a masterpiece which may be the work of Giovanni Griglio (1338). ▶ Corpses mummified by a natural process are housed in a temporary building in the small square in front of the Duomo: they date from the 17C-19C. ▶ The **Palazzo Comunale** is a fine structure with a long portico on the ground floor, an outdoor staircase and double-arched windows. Built between 1390-1410, it was rebuilt and restored after World War II.   □

Latium

▶ The city of Rome is surrounded by the Roman Campagna, for a long time a desolate and empty area, now heavily cultivated, although still only sparsely inhabited. The region of Latium is much larger than the Roman Campagna, but it is difficult to characterize simply. Once the Fiora has been crossed in the north or the Garigliano in the south, the call of the eternal city becomes so strong that it engulfs everything. The landscape, towns and styles of art included within this area are extremely varied and fascinating. The beaches on the Tyrrhenian Sea are rich in monuments of ancient history, recalling Greek merchants at Santa Severa (Pyrgi), Paul of Tarsus at the Tiber mouth, Aeneas at Lavinium, Ulysses at Circeo and Saracen pirates at Garigliano. There are also the charming Castelli Romani, the hills, woods, and volcanic lakes where the popes and Roman princes spent time in their 16C villas. The entire territory of Latium to the r. of the Tiber formed S Etruria; the most interesting sites of this first great Italian civilization are Tarquinia and Cervéteri, followed by Veii and Vulci. Rome's contribution is felt everywhere: in the marble monuments (many reused in later buildings), and especially in Ostia, a cosmopolitan city of merchants that grew thanks to the import trade to the great imperial capital, and in the Villa of Hadrian, the dream of a cultivated man immersed in Greek culture, leader of a vast empire of which he visited every corner. Later, the Romanesque and medieval periods were times of intense creativity in this region. The famous classically in-spired Romanesque portico of the cathedral at Civita Castellana seems to foreshadow the Renaissance. A similar idealized vision of the past influenced skilled marble workers known as the Cosmati. Medieval architecture is superbly represented in the churches of Tuscania and the section around the piazzetta S. Pellegrino in Viterbo, while the French Gothic style brought by the Cistercian order is found almost exclusively in Italy in the abbeys of Fossanova and Casamari. The Renaissance produced elegant fortresses. The great architect Vignola built his masterpieces in the gardens of the Villa Lante at Bagnaia and in the Palazzo Farnese in Caprarola. Among so many riches, mention must still be made of the strange and disturbing colossal statues of animals erected by Vicino Orsini in Bomarzo park and the glittering cascades of the Aniene falls at Tivoli. □

 ## Don't miss

Alatri★, the Acropolis★★; Anagni★, the Cathedral★★; Caprarola, the Farnese Palace★★; the church★★ at the Abbey of Casamari★; Cerveteri★, the Etruscan necropolis★★; the excavations of Ostia Antica★★; near Priverno, the Abbey of Fossanova★★; Subiaco, the monastery of S. Benedict★★; Tarquinia★, the Museo Nazionale Tarquiniese★★ in the Palazzo Vitelleschi★★, and the Etruscan necropolis★★; Tivoli, the Villa D'Este★★ and garden★★, the Aniene falls★★ in the Villa Gregoriana★★, and the nearby Villa of Hadrian ★★; Tuscania★, S. Pietro★★; Viterbo★, the Papal Palace★★ and loggia★★, the medieval quarter★★, and nearby the monster park at Bomarzo★.

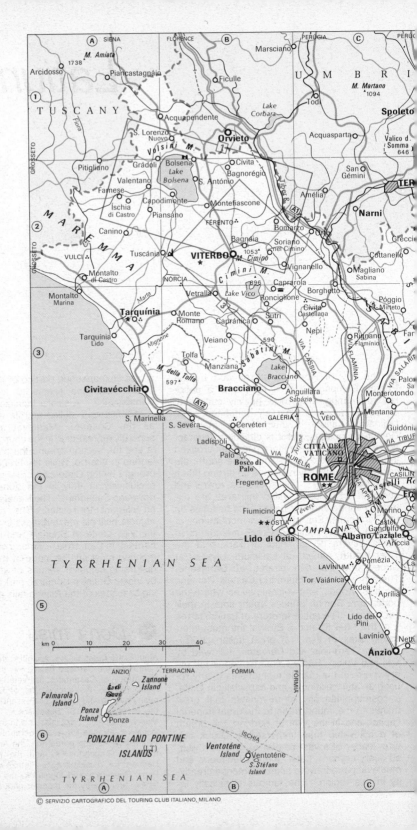

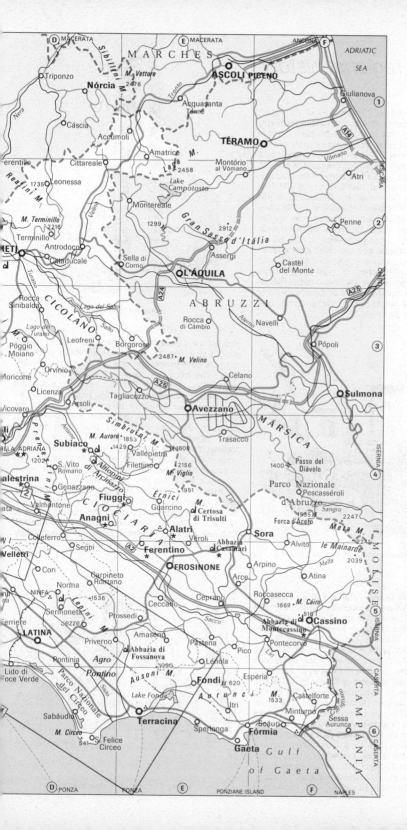

MARCHES

ADRIATIC
SEA

Triponzo
Nórcia M. Vettore 2476
Cáscia
Accumoli
Amatrice
Cittareale
erentillo
Leonessa 1735
Nera
Reafini M.
M. Terminillo 2216
Terminillo
Antrodoco
ETI
Cittaducale
Sella di Corno

ASCOLI PICENO
Acquasanta Terme
Montório al Vómano
Atri
TÉRAMO
Lake Campotosto
Montereale
1299
Gran Sasso d'Itália 2912
Assergi
Castèl del Monte
L'AQUILA

Giulianova 1
A14
PESCARA
Vómano
Penne 2

ABRUZZI

Rocca Sinibalda
Lago del Salto
CICOLANO
Lago del Turano
Póggio Moiano
Leofreni
Borgorose
Sallo
2487 M. Velino
Orvinio
Moricone
Licenza
Arsoli
Tagliacozzo
Vicovaro
li
Simbruini M.
M. Aurora 1853
1429
Subiaco
VILLA ADRIANA
1202
S. Vito Romano
Altipiani di Arcinazzo
alestrina
Genazzano
1951
Fiuggi
Anagni
Colleferro
Velletri
Cori
Segni
Ferentino
Carpineto Romano
NINFA
Norma
1536
Sermoneta
Prossedi
Sezze
Ceccano
erriere
LATINA
Priverno
Amaseno
Pastena
Pontínia
Abbazia di Fossanova
Agro
Pico
Pontino
1090
Lido di oce Verde
Parco Nazionale del Circeo
Sabáudia
Ausoni M.
Lake Fondi
Fondi
Terracina
Sperlonga
M. Circeo
S. Felice Circeo
541
Gaeta

Rocca di Cámbio
Navelli
Aterno
Pópoli 3
Celano
A25
A24
A25
CHIETI
Sulmona
Avezzano
MARSICA
Trasacco
Passo del Diávolo 1400
Parco Nazionale d'Abruzzo
Pescasséroli
Sangro
Forca d'Acero (535)
Meta M. 2247
le Mainarde 2241
2039
Alvito
Mella
Atina
MOLIS E
ISERNIA 4
Sora
Arpino
Arce
Roccasecca
M. Cáiro 1669
516
Abbazia di Montecassino
Cassino 5
CASERTA
Pontecorvo
Lénola
Espéria
Castelforte
Minturno
M. 1533
Itri
Scáuri
FÓRMIA
Gulf
Aurunci M.
CAMPANIA
Sessa Aurunca 6
CASERTA

of Gaeta

D MACERATA
E MACERATA
ANCONA F
D PONZA
PONZA
E PONZIANE ISLAND
F NAPLES
PONZA

A2
Ciociaria
Érnici
Guarcino
Certosa di Trisulti
Alatri
Vèroli
Abbazia di Casamari
FROSINONE
Ceprano
Sacco
Lepini M.
Lini
1608
Vallepietra
Filettino 2156
M. Viglio
Aniene
Prenestini M.
Sisto

● *Brief regional history*

cathedral in Anagni

8C BC-5C AD

Etruscans, Latins, Rome. The history of the region is mostly tied to that of Rome. ● **Latium** (probably derived from *latus:* wide open) was the plain I. of the Tiber and the Alban Hills; the league of Latin villages centred on **Alba Longa.** The area was inhabited by a different Italic people who played their part in building Rome. The **Hernici, Aequi** and **Volsci** were also Italic peoples who inhabited the Sacco and Liri Valleys. ● R. of the Tiber dwelt the **Etruscans,** at Veii and Tarquinia. ● Rome was founded in 754 BC, and grew slowly. In 493 BC, a defensive alliance against the Latin cities was made; Etruscan Veii was taken and destroyed after a ten-year siege in 396 BC; in 338 BC the **Latin League** was dissolved after a rebellion, and the Volsci became subjects in 329 BC with the conquest of **Priverno.** It was only in the 4C BC that the region was finally united under Roman rule. ● Under Augustus *Latium et Campania* up to the Tiber formed a single region, the remainder was part of *Etruria* and *Samnium.*

medieval quarter of Viterbo

against the power of the papacy, sometimes deeply caught up in the flow of European history (as in the struggle over investiture between popes and emperors). The emperors came to Rome armed for their coronation. Otho of Freising, who accompanied **Frederick I Barbarossa** in 1155, noted that the air of Latium was *'Lethifera et pestilens'.* During the 12C, the city of Rome controlled the countryside, although the free cities did their best to stop this. **Viterbo, Corneto** (modern Tarquinia), **Tivoli, Velletri, Terracina** and **Anagni** are examples of rebellious cities. ● Some of the ancient families regained influence in the feudal period. These **barons** wielded influence when the papal see was transferred to Avignon (1309-77), although **Cardinal Albornoz** (1353-77) worked to restore the prestige of the Holy See and prepared the way for the popes' return to Rome. ● The noble families (such as the **Caetani, Colonna, Orsini,** and **Savelli**) were only brought under the church's control after long struggles.

6C-16C

Church's temporal power. Rome lost its status as imperial capital under Diocletian (284-305). The Western Roman Empire collapsed in 476; after the brief interlude of the Barbarian kingdoms and the terrible **Gothic wars** (535-53), Latium fell under Byzantine rule in the **Duchy of Rome.** ● The 6C-7C were marked by constant wars between Lombards and Byzantines, but also saw the foundation of the abbey at **Montecassino** by Benedict of Nursia (6C). ● Following the decline of Byzantine power, **the church** sought to assert its own political power. The donation of **Sutri** in 728 by the Lombard Liutprand laid the foundations of the **'Patrimony of St. Peter',** and successive **donations by the Franks** (8C) shifted temporal power, although this was only finally consolidated with the general 16C settlement of the peninsula. ● Between 870 and 910 the **Saracens** had a raiding base at the mouth of the **Garigliano.** Through the centuries, local forces of various kinds have stood

Abbey of Fossanova near Priverno

17C-19C

Papal states. Once the Farnese **Duchy of Castro** was absorbed in 1649, the history of Latium coincided with that of the papal states, disturbed only by the **French occupation** at the end of the 18C and beginning of the 19C. ● **Brigands** were a permanent feature of the area. One of the most famous was Michele Pezza da Itri, otherwise known as **Fra' Diavolo.** He was a popular figure and a Sanfedista guerilla and was hanged at Naples in 1806.

S. Maria Maggiore in Ferentino

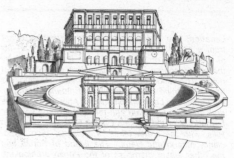

Palazzo Farnese in Caprarola

Resistance

During the night of 21 January 1944, Anglo-American troops landed at Anzio and Nettuno. Blocked by the Germans, they held firm and resisted enemy attacks for four months. Finally, on 25 May, the Allies coming from Cassino met up with the group for the general offensive that culminated in the liberation of Rome on 4 June 1944. A chapel that depicts the Allied operations in Italy between 1943-45 overlooks the site. The 90,000 graves of Allied and German soldiers stand as a permanent witness to the violence of the battles which raged in the area.

19C-20C

The end of the church's temporal power and the Italian state. Due to annexation and plebiscites, the only territory remaining under the church's rule in 1860 was Latium (its boundaries much narrower than today's). ● The defeat of Napoleon III, who had been the guarantor of the church's temporal power, set the scene for the **union of Rome and Latium with Italy** on 20th September 1870. ● The 1860-70 boundaries were enlarged by adding the region of Rieti in 1923 and in 1927 by the addition of a southern zone including **Gaeta**, formerly part of the Napoleonic kingdom. ● The *campagna Romana* (or Roman countryside) came into use again only after 1870. Latium stayed a desolate pastoral area replete with malaria until the land reclamation and agricultural improvements of the 20C. ● In 1871, the pope's right of free exercise of his spiritual power and the extra-territorial status of the Vatican were unilaterally recognized by the Italian state. The links between the pope and the Italian state were not, however, resolved until the **Lateran Pact** of 1929, when the **Vatican City** was recognized as a state.

● *Practical information*

Information: tourist offices in district capitals and principal centres.

SOS: public emergency services, ☎ 113; police emergency, ☎ 112; *ACI* (assistance on the road), ☎ 116.

Weather: forecasts, ☎ 1911; road conditions, ☎ 194 or from *ACI*, ☎ 06/4212; shipping forecast, ☎ 06/6514, for Latina, Formia, Rome and Civitavecchia, ☎ 196; snow report, ☎ 075/992992.

Farm vacations: *Agriturist* regional association, at Rome, corso Vittorio Emanuele II 101, ☎ 06/6512342.

Events and festivals: procession of the *Santa Rosa machine,* at Viterbo; procession of the *Corpus Domini flower arrangement,* at Genzano di Roma; *commemoration of the first Franciscan dwelling,* at Greccio; *festival of hood-wearers,* at Gràdoli; *mid-May festival,* at Acquapendente; *eight-day medieval festival* and *display of bells,* at Orte; *carnival,* at Ronciglione; *festivals of amateur film and folklore,* at Alatri; *opera season,* at Cervéteri and at Civitavecchia; *wine festival,* at Montefiascone; *festival of chestnuts,* at Soriano in Cimino.

Nature parks: *Parco Nazionale del Circeo,* main office and management at Sabaudia, v. Carlo Alberto 107, ☎ 0773/57251; *Parco Suburbano Marturanum* (→ Viterbo); *Ninfa* nature reserve; *Bosco di Palo* animal reserve; *Macchiatonda* regional reserve; *Piano Sant'Angelo* nature reserve; *Vulci* nature reserve; *Gallese* nature reserve (→ Viterbo). The following are being set up: the *Appennino-Monti Simbruini* nature park; the suburban nature parks of Castelli Romani and Valle del Treja; the *Pineta di Castelfusano* urban park. Information at *Ufficio Parchi della Regione Lazio,* at Rome, v. C. Colombo 212, ☎ 06/5110843.

Rocca in Civita Castellana

Facts and figures

Location: The region occupies the Tyrrhenian coast from a point E of the Argentario promontory as far as the mouth of the Garigliano. It is crossed by the lower course of the Tiber, Italy's third largest river. The landscape is very varied, including the harsh Apennine zone, a number of mountain ranges, the undulating Latin Maremma and Ager romanus, the drained Pomptine plain and the four strange volcanic formations of the Volsini, Cimini, Sabatini and Alban Hills, with the crater lakes of Bolsena, Vico, Bracciano, Albano and Nemi. The island of Ponza and the other lesser members of the Ponza archipelago also form part of the region.
Area: 17,203 sq km.
Climate: The climate is basically Mediterranean, varying with altitude. Summer on the coast is hot, spring and autumn delightful.
Population: 5,056,119, the third largest region of Italy; more than half inhabit the city of Rome.
Administration: Rome is both capital of the Republic and regional capital. The four other provincial capitals are Viterbo and Rieti to the N of Rome and Frosinone and Latina to the S.

The wine of the Castelli

When Cyneas (ambassador for Pyrrhus) came to Rome by the Appian Way, he saw vines growing over the trees in the Alban Hills and remarked disdainfully that the vines seemed to be crucified on the trees, like wicked sons. The vines of the Alban Hills and the Castelli Romani are no longer grown 'spindle-wise', four vines planted in a square, their supporting canes tied together at the top, as they still were at the beginning of the century. However, the wine they produce is still renowned. The area immediately SE of Rome is divided into the pleasant hills of Castelli Romani, Frascati, stretching as far as Rocca Priora and Zagarolo, and Colli Albani, around the volcanic crater lakes of Albano and Nemi. The principle vines are Malvasia (bianca di Candia, del Lazio, bianca lunga, Istriana) and Trebbiano (toscano, giallo, di Velletri, romagnolo). The vintages are Colli Albani, Colli Lanuvini, Cori Bianco, Frascati. The latter is the best known since it found a place in the cellars of Buckingham Palace some sixty years ago. Other vintages include Marino, Montecompatri, Velletri Bianco, and Zagarolo. All are white wines with the exception of Velletri Rosso, a ruby wine which matures very well.

The Pontins Marshes

The reclamation project of the Pontins marshes had two basic goals. The first was to clean up and fertilize the marshlands. The other was to populate the area. This great project took place actively between 1928-32 and included setting up drinking water, irrigating and constructing cities like Latina, Sabaudia, Pontinia and Aprilia. Today, due to its proximity to the capital (and its 3 million consumers), the Latinia region produces great quantities of wheat, beets, fruit, flowers, fern plants and dairy products.

Animal and amusement parks: La Selva animal park, at Paliano (→ Fiuggi).

Conservation: WWF Delegazione Lazio, at Rome, v. Mercadante 10, ☎ 06/8440108 (management regional nature reserves, summer work camps at Castelporziano estate); local branches at: Viterbo, ☎ 0761/263120; Rieti, ☎ 0746/483012; Latina, v. delle Grotte; Alatri, ☎ 0775/45831. LIPU Latina, corso Matteotti 169, ☎ 0773/484993 (birdwatching courses at Parco del Circeo in spring and autumn, in Lepini Mountains in summer; nature study at Maiella, Jun, Aug and Sep; nature observation trips by bicycle); local branches at: Frosinone, v. Monteverdi 35, ☎ 0775/81175; Terracina, ☎ 0773/727117; Sora, p. Risorgimento 17, ☎ 0776/831168 (nature walks, birdwatching courses).

Excursions: specially marked long routes: trekking, at Selva del Lamone in southern Etruria (in 5 stages from Farnese, recommended in spring); Alta Via dei Lepini (c. 70 km, 4 days' walking, recommended in Mar-Oct); information from CAI, at Alatri, v. delle Grotte; at Guarcino, ☎ 0775/499806; at Frosinone, v. S. Simeone 5, ☎ 0775/852103; at Latina, v Don Morosini 87; at Rieti, v. Pennina 28; at Rome, v. Ripetta 42, ☎ 06/6561011; at Sora, v. Borgo S. Rocco 2; La Montagna, at Rome, v. M. Colonna 44, ☎ 06/351549 or 315948.

Cycling: assistance and information from cycling groups affiliated to UDACE (74), which are to be found all over the region.

Horseback riding: Federazione italiana sport equestri (regional committee), at Rome, v. Flaminia Nuova 213, ☎ 06/3278547; riding school, at Rocca di Papa; clubs associated with ANTE: Buttero Fontana nuova, at Sacrofano, ☎ 06/9036057 or 9036040; Centro Ippico di Cornazzano, v. Braccianese, ☎ 06/694014 (trekking in Manziana forest and around Bracciano Lake, some accommodation available); Monte del Pavone, at Campagnano di Roma, SS Cassia 31, ☎ 06/9041906 (trekking to Lake Vico and along v. Clodia); riding clubs associated with ANTE are to be found in all the provinces.

Young peoples' activities: guided tours of Parco Nazionale del Circeo, on foot, bicycle, horseback, by canoe, by boat; visits to Zannone island; summer camps (10-15 days) for boys aged 8-17: Cooperativa Melacotogna, at Sabaudia, p. Comune 2, ☎ 0773/55046; holidays for skin divers and tourists, at Ventotene (Ponziane archipelago), organized by Club Ventotene, v. Roma 13, ☎ 0771/877469; Nuova Compagnia delle Indie, hotel and sailing instruction, v. Olivi 37, ☎ 0771/85185.

Canoeing: Italian federation of canoe-kayak, at Rome, v. Tiziano 70, ☎ 06/390954; affiliated school at Subiaco.

Water skiing: Italian federation of water skiing, affiliated schools at Castel Gandolfo and at Sperlonga.

Sailing: Lega Navale, at Anzio, v. Riviera Zanardelli 24, ☎ 06/9845345; at Lido di Ostia, lungomare Duilio 36, ☎ 06/5626709; sailing schools at Sabaudia (nautical club of Lega Navale di Roma), at Bracciano and at Formia.

Skiing: main skiing resorts in this region are: Terminillo, Campo Staffi (→ plateaus of Arcinazzo), Monte Livata (→ Subiaco).

Golf: at Fiuggi and Marina di Velca (→ Tarquinia).

Flying: Ciociaria Airport, ☎ 0776/728259; at Latina, p. del Popolo 27, ☎ 0773/499806; at Viterbo, ☎ 0761/250510.

Fishing: Federazione italiana pesca sportiva, branches at: Frosinone, v. Marconi 12, ☎ 0775/851010; Cisterna di Latina, v. Nigra 10; Rieti, v. Cavour 14/16; Viterbo, v. delle Volta Buia 20. Apply for information on waters where fishing is forbidden, permission required, etc.

Hang gliding: Federazione italiana Volo Libero, information, ☎ 015/538703, at Rieti and Viterbo (instruction).

Gliding: Aeroclub Centrale di Volo a Vela, at Rieti, v. Rosatelli, ☎ 0746/43127 or 42138 (Italian gliding championships and other gliding events).

● *Towns and places*

ACQUAPENDENTE

Viterbo 50, Rome 131 km
Pop. 5,881 ⊠ 01021 ☎ 0763   B1

The upper portion of the Romanesque cathedral of **S. Sepolcro** (12C) in Acquapendente was rebuilt in the 18C. Two **bas-reliefs** from the school of Agostino de Duccio are set into the steps leading to the sanctuary. The crypt is from the 9C with frescos, and the chapel below houses the **relics** believed to have come from the Pretorium at Jerusalem. 8 km away along the v. Cassia is **San Lorenzo Nuovo**, an 18C town with an octagonal fortress.   □

Practical information _____

Recommended
Events: *mid-May festival*, with displays of large floral panels, inquire at Comune, ☎ 74008.

ALATRI*

Frosinone 13, Rome 93 km
Pop. 23,335 ⊠ 03011 ☎ 0775   E4

Alatri is an ancient city of medieval appearance that sits on an olive-covered slope of the Ernici hills. Its fortified acropolis may be the most beautiful in Italy. The polygonal city-walls overlook a typical landscape.

▶ The city entrance is marked by the massive stones of the **Cyclopean walls** that encircle the hill. They may date back to the 4C BC. Two of the five gates are well preserved, particularly the impressive **Areopagus gate★** (the City or Great Gate) reached by a series of steps. ▶ At the top of the **Acropolis★★** is a huge open space covered with trees, from where there is a superb view★. On this square stand the **Duomo**, with an impressive 15C façade, and the bishop's palace beneath a squat campanile. The church of **S. Maria Maggiore★** (originally Romanesque, heavily rebuilt in the 13C) overlooks the piazza of the same name. The Romanesque-Gothic façade contains a rose-window, while the campanile has two rows of double-lighted windows. Inside is a painted wooden sculpture of the *Madonna of Constantinople★* of the 12C-13C. ▶ The Gothic façade of the church of **S. Francesco** (13C) has a rose-window similar to that of S. Maria Maggiore. The medieval church of **S. Silvestro** on the edge of the city contains 13C-14C frescos. ▶ The city streets have retained their 12C appearance; the most notable of the medieval buildings is the **Palazzo Gottifredi**, a 13C Gothic building. ▶ 8 km away is **Collepardo**, which is surrounded by an area dotted with caves (the Grotta dei Bambocci). 6.5 km farther is the **Trisulti Charterhouse** (13C, restored 17C and 18C).   □

Practical information _____

ⓘ Palazzo Comunale, v. C. Battisti, ☎ 45748.

Hotels:
★★★ *Aletrium*, v. Stazione 273, ☎ 440005, 36 rm ℗ ≮ ₩ ⚄ 38,000; bkf: 6,000.
★ *Rosetta*, v. Duomo 31, ☎ 450068, 12 rm ⚄ ₩ closed Nov and Christmas, 27,000; bkf: 3,500. Rest. ♦ closed Fri. In sight of Acropoli. Regional cuisine: lasagne with ricotta, rabbit with olives, 16/26,000.

Recommended
Caves: visits to *Grotta Regina Margherita*, at Collepardo, ☎ 47021.

Events: *festival of amateur films* (Jun); *folklore festival* (Aug).

ALBANO LAZIALE

Rome 24 km
Pop. 28,519 ⊠ 00041 ☎ 06   C4-5

One of the Castelli Romani stands on the slopes of the Alban hills near a lake. The road from Rome leads to p. Mazzini.

▶ In p. Mazzini a **belvedere terrace** offers a superb view over the **Villa Comunale**, which stands on the site of one of Pompey's villas. ▶ Steps lead up to the Baroque **Duomo;** inside the columns of the original 4C basilica are preserved. ▶ The church of **S. Pietro** (6C) stands amid the ruins of ancient baths off the corso Matteotti, which runs straight through the town. In v. Saffi are the monumental remains of the **Porta Pretoria★**, the gate of a military camp built under Septimius Severus (2C-3C). ▶ To visit the church of **S. Maria della Rotonda★**, the **Cisternone★**, and the **Tomb of the Horatii**, apply at the Museo Civico (☎ *9323490*). The church is built in the nymphaeum of an ancient Roman villa. It has a circular plan with four niches and an elegant dome. Next to it is a 13C Romanesque campanile. ▶ The **Cisternone** is an underground cistern built by Septemius Severus for the military camp and was excavated from the rock. ▶ The **Tomb of the Horatii and Curiatii★** is a majestic tomb dating from the last days of the Roman Republic, named after the heroes of a famous duel. ▶ The **Museo Civico** *(8:30 a.m.-12:30 p.m. and 3:30-7:30 p.m. Mon, Wed and Thu; Jul and Aug 8:30 a.m.-2 p.m.; closed 2nd and 3rd Sun of month)* is in the Villa Ferraioli and contains prehistoric, Etruscan and Roman exhibits. ▶ At the top of the city stand the impressive ruins of a 3C **amphitheatre**.   □

Practical information _____

ⓘ v. Olivella 2, ☎ 9321323 or 9320298.

Hotel:
★★ *Miralago*, v. dei Cappuccini, ☎ 9321018, 35 rm ℗ ≮ ⚄ ₩ ⚄closed Nov, 57,000; bkf: 6,000.

AMATRICE

Rieti 65, Rome 144 km
Pop. 3,257 ⊠ 02012 ☎ 0746   E1

This little town, now isolated amid the hills, was probably designed by Cola dell'Amatrice after 1529. Its streets are laid out on a regular plan.

▶ In the town centre stands the 13C **Civic Tower.** ▶ The Romanesque-Gothic church of **S. Francesco** has a fine marble door and a rose-window. Inside is a 17C altar with a Gothic reliquary. ▶ 5 km E lies the man-made **Lake Scandarello.** ▶ 6 km E of **Molletano** is the **shrine of the Passatora Icon**, with 15C and 16C frescos. ▶ 21 km E along v. Salaria is **Cittareale.** This town was built by Charles of Anjou in 1261; it is dominated by a 15C castle.   □

Practical information _____

AMATRICE
ⓘ v. Madonna della Porta 15, ☎ 85249.

Hotel:
★★★ *Castagneto*, v. del Castagneto 9, ☎ 85224, 26 rm ℗ ≮ ⚄ ₩ ⚄ 50,000; bkf: 3,000.

Environs

CITTAREALE, 3,156 ft, ⊠ 02010, ☎ 0746, 21 km W.
⍧ ski lifts at Selva Rotunda, downhill slope at Caituro.
ⓘ municipio, ☎ 947032.

ANAGNI*

Frosinone 22, Rome 65 km
Pop. 18,975 ⊠ 03012 ☎ 0775   D-E4

The fine view of Anagni from the v. Casilina reveals
its strong medieval atmosphere. The town straddles
a long, narrow hill and is surrounded by walls (visible
from v. Piscina, B2 and v. Dante, B3).

▶ The hill is reached by a winding road which comes
out into v. Regina Margherita (A1). · ▶ Through the Porta
Cerere is v. Vittorio Emanuele II, which runs the length of
the town. There are numerous medieval houses along
this street, including the **Casa Barnekow** (A2), owned by
the municipality since the 14C. It has an external staircase surmounted by two arches and a balcony. The
façade was decorated by the Swedish painter Baron Barnekow in the middle of the 19C. ▶ In front of this building stands the Romanesque campanile of the church
of **S. Andrea** (A1-2), which contains a precious 14C triptych. ▶ P. Cavour (B2) is the town centre. ▶ A little farther is the austere 13C **Palazzo Comunale**, originally
built in the 12C and restored many times. The **Palace of
Boniface VIII** (B3) stands in the open area known as the
'Caetani quarter'. It was built by Gregory IX and has a
large loggia with two arches and double-lighted windows. Some of the rooms feature frescos and can be
visited. ▶ In p. Innocenzo III (B3) is the l. side of the
Cathedral★★ (A-B3), which stands alone at the top of
the city. This Romanesque building occupies the site of

the ancient acropolis; in front of the façade with its triple
entrance stands the heavy campanile (12C). The floor
of the cathedral is decorated with Cosmati mosaic work,
while the tabernacle★ on the altar and the candelabrum★
are by Vassalletto (1263). The crypt★★ has a Cosmati-
work floor and 13C frescos★ and leads into the chapel
of Thomas à Becket (also decorated in 13C frescos). A
small **museum** *(apply to parish priest, 9 a.m.- 12 noon and
3-5 p.m.)* contains some gold vessels and vestments,
some of them given by Boniface VIII.   ☐

Practical information

ⓘ p. Innocenzo III (B3), ☎ 727852.

Hotels:
★★★ *Coccinella,* contrada Collacciano 23, ☎ 78133,
50 rm ℗ ⚲ ▥ ⚑ ▱ ♪ 43,000; bkf: 5,000.
★★★ *Motel Pavesi,* Macchia Ovest service area, autostrada to Naples, ☎ 78104, 24 rm ♿ ⚑ 54,000.

Restaurant:
♦ *Gallo,* v. Vittorio Emanuele (B2 a), ☎ 727309, closed
Jun and Aug-Sep. View of Sacco Valley. Regional cuisine: tagliatelle alla ciociara, beef roulades alla campagnola, 23/30,000.

ANTRODOCO

Rieti 23, Rome 101 km
Pop. 3,026 ⊠ 02013 ☎ 0746   D2

Antrodoco lies at the foot of Mt. Giano amid green,
wooded slopes. At the entrance to the town stands
the Romanesque church of **S. Maria extra Moenia**
(12C). Its 9C baptistery contains 15C and 16C
frescos. On the edge of town are the **Baths of**

Antrodoco, currently being restored, and upstream lie the **Velino gorges★**, a wild and narrow stretch of road 14 km long between Terminillo and Mt. Giano. Along the L'Aquila road are the rocky **Antrodoco gorges★**, which lie between Mt. Giano and Mt. Serrone. □

Practical information

Restaurant:
♦ *Dionisio,* v. Marmorale 70, ☎ 56264 closed Tue and Sep. Italian cuisine: stockfish with chestnuts, liver sausage, 20/30,000.

ANZIO

Rome 57 km
Pop. 28,901 ⊠ 00042 ☎ 06   C5

The Cape of Anzio is a limestone promontory that juts out of the monotonous sandy coastline S of the Tiber estuary. The town lies at the bottom of a hill. The **Anzio Lido** is divided by the breakwater that separates the Riviera di Ponente and Riviera di Levante. The beaches of **Lavinio** and **Lido di Enea** on the N coast are outstanding. The **Caves of Nero** are found on the Riviera di Ponente. A little farther, toward the lighthouse, are the ruins of **Nero's villa.** On top of a rise on the site of ancient Antium, the remains of the defenses and of an imperial theatre can be found. □

Practical information
ANZIO
≋
ⓘ riviera Zanardelli 105, ☎ 9846119.
⚓ daily ferry, Jun-Sep: *Caremar,* ☎ 9831231; hydroplane, twice daily, more frequently in Jul and Aug: *SNAV,* ☎ 9845085 or 9848320.
Hotel:
★★★★ *G.H. dei Cesari,* v. Mantova 3, ☎ 9874751, 108 rm Ⓟ ⑯ ⚃ ⚘ ▧ 130,000; bkf: 3,500.
Restaurant:
♦ *Romolo al Porto,* v. Porto Innocenziano 20, ☎ 9844079, closed Wed and Dec-Jan. Seaside setting near castle. Seafood: pasta tubes stuffed with fish, oysters, 25/45,000.
Recommended
Events: *Festa del Mare* (30 Jun); sailing races.
Marina: ☎ 9844683; *Circolo della vela di Roma,* ☎ 9846019; *Circolo Canottieri Tevere Remo,* ☎ 9830470.
Sailing: *Lega Navale,* riviera Zanardelli 24, ☎ 9845345 (instruction).
Windsurfing: moletto Pamphili, ☎ 9831338.

Environs
LAVINIO, ⊠ 00040, ☎ 06, 7 km NW.
Hotel:
★★★ *Sirenetta,* passeggiata delle Sirene 42, ☎ 9820273, 30 rm Ⓟ ⚃ ⚘ closed 16 Oct-Mar, 66,000; bkf: 5,000.

AQUINO

Frosinone 42, Rome 125 km
Pop. 5,172 ⊠ 03031 ☎ 0776   F5

The great Dominican friar, St. Thomas Aquinas, was the third son of Count Landolfo, the medieval feudal lord of this area. Aquino lies in the Liri Valley and is the only flatland in this part of Latium. It has a medieval atmosphere and features Roman ruins.

▶ The church of S. **Maria della Libera** incorporates pieces of Roman masonry and was built in 1125. It has a 12C mosaic lunette above the door★, beneath the portico. ▶ Next to it is a Roman monument known as the **Arch of Marcus Antonius**, almost submerged in the canal. ▶ From the ancient v. Latina, the Roman **gate of** S. **Lorenzo** can be seen. ▶ The ruins of ancient **Aquinum** are in the nearby countryside (theatre, amphitheatre and remains of walls). □

Practical information

Recommended
Flying: *Ciocaria airport,* ☎ 728259.

The ARCINAZZO PLATEAU

Rome 87 km
Pop. 243 ⊠ 00020 ☎ 0775   D-E4

Between the Ernici and Affilani hills lies a karstic basin *c.* 3 km long and 1.5 km wide. It forms an undulating landscape of knolls and fields, dotted with sinkholes. **Trevi del Lazio,** 7 km away, and **Filettino,** 17 km away, are attractive villages in the upper Aniene Valley. In the Simbrivio Valley, 14 km away, lies **Vallepietra;** beneath a rock-wall stands the shrine of **SS. Trinità,** with 12C frescos. □

Practical information
ARCINAZZO
Hotel:
★★★ *Caminetto,* v. Sublacense, ☎ 59096, 54 rm Ⓟ ⑯ ▣ ⚘ closed Jan, 60,000. Rest. ♦♦♦ closed Tue in winter. Regional cuisine: pastry cake with grilled veal, cornmeal with sausage and spuntature, 25/30,000.
Recommended
Tennis: v. Provinciale, ☎ 59242.

Environs
CAMPO STAFFI, ⊠ 03010 (at Filettino), ☎ 0775, 30 km NE.
𝄐 ski lifts, instruction.
ⓘ *Impianti Turistici Invernali,* ☎ 528923.

ARICCIA

Rome 25 km
Pop. 15,716 ⊠ 00040 ☎ 06   C4-5

Ariccia is entered by the historic **Ariccia bridge,** a viaduct 328 yards long and 194 ft high which spans a great ravine, formed by an ancient volcanic crater. The bridge was built by Pius IX in 1854 and rebuilt after the war; it offers a superb view over the grounds of the Villa Chigi and the whole of the Appian Way.

▶ The town centre is p. della Repubblica★, designed by Bernini and adorned with two fountains. The majestic **Palazzo Chigi** stands on the piazza; it is a castle with four towers and has a fine park. The round, domed church of S. **Maria dell'Assunzione★** (1664) is also on the square. ▶ 1 km along the Appian Way is the 17C church of **S. Maria di Galloro,** with a façade by Bernini. □

Practical information
ⓘ at Albano Laziale, ☎ 9321323.
Recommended
Go-cart track: v. Vallericcia, ☎ 9343130.

ARPINO

Frosinone 31, Rome 114 km
Pop. 7,940 ⊠ 03033 ☎ 0776   F5

This hilltop town overlooks the Liri Valley. The p. del Municipio is particularly interesting and occupies the site of the ancient **Roman forum.** There are two monuments to Gaius Marius and Cicero, both one-time citizens of Arpinum. 3 km N are the remains of the ancient town **(Civitavecchia).** Long stretches of walls, several towers and an arched gate★ cover a scenic hill.   □

Practical information ─────────

Hotel:
★★★ *Sunrise Crest,* at Civitavecchia, ☎ 848901, closed Nov-Easter, 16 rm Ⓟ ⋐ ⚲ ⫸ ☒ ✎ 35,000; bkf: 4,000.

Restaurant:
♦♦ *Mingone,* at Carnello, ☎ 86140, closed Mon. On Fibreno River. Mixed cuisine: spaghetti with crayfish, young lamb, 18/28,000.

ATINA

Frosinone 50, Rome 148 km
1,608 ft, pop. 4,860 ⊠ 03042 ☎ 0776   F5

The **Museo Comunale** *(9 a.m.-12 noon and 3:30-6 p.m. hols)* is located in the 14C Palazzo Cantelmi and contains archaeological finds from Atina and the surrounding valley, as well as medieval finds and detached 14C frescos. 12 km NE lies **Picinisco,** in unspoiled countryside on the edge of Abruzzi National Park (→ Abruzzi). 12 km farther is **Prati di Mezzo** in the heart of the Mainarde. 15 km N lies Fibreno Lake.   □

Practical information ─────────

⚡ ski lifts, instruction at Forca d'Acero Pass *(33 km N).*
ⓘ corso Munazio Planco 251, ☎ 60379.

Recommended
Cycling: *GS Cicli Rosa,* v. Casino Pica, ☎ 60127.
Horseback riding: *Circolo Atina,* at Ponte Melfa, ☎ 60266 or 60172 (associate of *ANTE).*

BOLSENA

Viterbo 31, Rome 138 km
Pop. 4,042 ⊠ 01023 ☎ 0761   B1-2

Bolsena is a **medieval town** that lies in the basin of Lake Bolsena, with its modern section stretching out along the shore.

▶ The town centre is p. Matteotti, with the 13C church of **S. Francesco,** which has a fine Gothic door and the remains of frescos inside. ▶ A red stone gate next to the church leads into the medieval quarter. ▶ The Romanesque church of **S. Cristina★** (11C) has a Renaissance façade, with doors decorated with Della Robbia lunettes. The interior is decorated with many frescos and contains the Capella del Miracolo, where the miracle of the eucharistic blood took place in 1263. Adjoining the church is the **Grotta di S. Cristina,** part of a Christian catacomb. ▶ The city is dominated by a picturesque 13C-14C **castle** with angular towers. *C.* 1 km away are the ruins of the Roman city of **Volsinii,** with a stretch of Etruscan city-walls.   □

For the translation of a name of a meat, a fish or a vegetable, for the composition of a dish or a sauce, see the *Menu Guide* at the end of the Practical Holiday Guide; it lists the most common culinary terms.

Practical information ─────────

ⓘ p. Matteotti, ☎ 989923.

Hotels:
★★★ *Columbus Hotel del Lago,* v. Colesanti 27, ☎ 98009, 38 rm Ⓟ ⚲ ⋐ ✎ closed Nov-Feb, 72,000.
★★★ *Moderno,* v. Roma 2, ☎ 988001, 35 rm Ⓟ ⚲ ⋌ 52,000; bkf: 6,000.

Restaurant:
♦ *Picchietto,* v. Porta Fiorentina 15, ☎ 98158, closed Mon and 15-30 Sep. Seafood: ricotta cheese and spinach tortelloni, whitefish with green sauce, homemade wines, 14/20,000.

⚓ *Lido,* v. Cassia at 111-km marker, 600 pl, ☎ 98258.

Recommended
Boat trips: to Bisentina Island and Capodimonte (tours round the lake by request), ☎ 98213.
Events: *Mysteries of Santa Cristina* (Jul, sacred commemoration in costume), Comune, ☎ 98601.
Farm vacations: *Azienda Sant'Antonio,* at Sant'Antonio Valdilago, ☎ 98195.

Lake BOLSENA

Round trip from Viterbo *(97 km, 1 day; map 1)*

In his 'Inferno', Dante mentions a gluttonous poet who is fasting and is 'purged of Bolsena eels and of vernaccia wine'. There are still eels in the lake, as well as pike, carp and whitefish. Vines cover the terraced slopes of the basin, interspersed with olive groves and patches of oak and chestnut forest. This is the largest of Italy's volcanic lakes and has two islands, almost certainly the remains of volcanic cones, covered with Mediterranean scrub brush. This peaceful trip around the lake offers many attractions.

▶ The trip starts at **Viterbo** (→). ▶ The archaeological area of **Ferento★,** an Etruscan town which flourished under the Romans, has an interesting theatre from the age of Augustus and ruins of baths *(usually open a.m.; closed Mon).* The nearby cliffs contain Etruscan and Roman tombs. ▶ **Bagnoregio** is a gracious and quiet town. St. Bonaventure was born here, and there is a 14C church of St. Augustine. Nearby **Civita di Bagnoregio★** (→) features unusual countryside. ▶ The route then turns toward the lake, descending round gentle bends among olive trees with superb views before reaching the shores of **Lake Bolsena.** ▶ Beyond a hill covered with vineyards and olive trees is **Gràdoli.** It lies on a hill between two deep valleys and is dominated by the great Palazzo Farnese (16C). ▶ Continuing around the lake the route arrives at **Valentano,** partly surrounded by walls and towers. ▶ Next is **Capodimonte** along a marvelous stretch of road which descends the lake and follows its shores through dense olive groves. The town lies on a rocky hill and contains a Farnese castle, built by Antonio da Sangallo il Giovane (16C). ▶ Also on the lakeshore is **Marta,** a medieval town that sits at the mouth where the Marta River empties into the lake. The route then leads to **Montefiascone** (→) where it picks up the via Cassia to return to Viterbo.   □

Practical information ─────────

GRADOLI, ⊠ 01010, ☎ 0761.

Recommended
Events: *Festa degli Incappucciati per Carnevale* (hood-wearers' festival), ☎ 456082.

For help in understanding terms when visiting museums or other sites, see the *Art and Architectural Terms Guide* at the end of the Practical Holiday Guide.

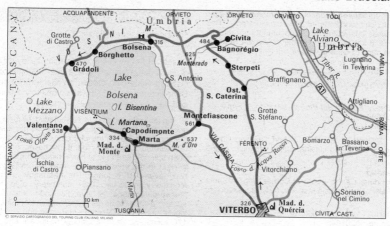

1. Lake Bolsena

Amalasuntha

The ghost of Amalasuntha still haunts the ruins and oaks of the deserted island on Lake Bolsena, where her husband, Theodahad, had her throat cut while she was taking a bath. This was no crime of passion, but a political assassination. The daughter of Theoderic the Great, King of the Goths and Italy, she was an educated and lively woman, perhaps even beautiful; as queen mother, she ruled the kingdom on behalf of her son Athalaric during eight difficult years. Theoderic the Ostrogoth had conquered Italy by the sword, and preserved a delicate balance between the Romans and the Goths. Where her father had managed to hold these forces in tension, Amalasuntha could not. The two groups differed both in culture and in faith; the Goths were Arian Christians, impatient of any obstacle to their power. When Athalaric died of consumption, Amalasuntha tried to retain her power by marrying her cousin Theodahad. Her efforts met with only limited success; Theodahad had her locked up in the island castle in 535, and shortly afterward assassinated her. This gave Justinian, the Eastern Roman emperor, his excuse to reconquer the peninsula, unleashing the Gothic wars (535-53) which devastated Italy and wiped out the Gothic power.

BOMARZO

Viterbo 19, Rome 92 km
Pop. 1,459 ✉ *01020* ☎ *0761*   B-C2

Bomarzo sits prettily on a hilltop overlooking the Tiber Valley. The large **Palazzo Orsini** is a remarkable 16C building reached by a very steep street leading out of the central piazzetta. It consists of two blocks joined by terraces and other buildings. One wing is occupied by the municipio, and contains a state-room with a great fresco by Anton Angelo Bonifazi *(8 a.m.-2 p.m. hols)*. The **Parco dei Mostri**★ is on the slopes of a natural amphitheatre just outside the town. It is a monumental complex created by Vicino Orsini between 1552 and 1580, with gigantic figures of monstrous and fantastic animals carved in the rock and hidden here and there in the beautiful terraced park sloping down to the bottom of the valley.   □

Practical information _____

Recommended
Amusement park: *Parco dei Mostri*, ☎ 424029.
Farm vacations: administration, at Pomigliozzo, ☎ 42381.

Lake BRACCIANO

B3

This lake forms almost a perfect circle. The N shores are wooded, with a few settlements, and the S shores are marshy. A **scenic route** leads around the lake.

▶ The little town of **Bracciano** contains the lovely **Castello Orsini-Odescalchi**★ *(9 a.m.-12 noon and 3-6 p.m.; winter 10 a.m.-12 noon and 3-5 p.m.; closed Mon)*, which was built by the Orsini during the second half of the 15C. It is a fine example both of military architecture and of a noble house (apartments of Charles VIII with period furniture). The majestic round towers mark out the pentagonal layout (from the battlement walk, a fantastic view★ over the lake). A 16C gate leads into the courtyard, with colonnade and loggia and a magnificent outer staircase leading to the upper floors (frescos and works of art). ▶ **Anguillara Sabazia** features a medieval castle and the remains of a Roman villa from the middle of the 1C BC. ▶ **Trevignano Romano** (possibly the ancient *Sabatia* mentioned by Roman writers) lies on a little peninsula, where the ruins of an Orsini castle stand. Nearby at Olivetello and Poggio delle Ginestre are some **Etruscan chamber tombs**. Their finds are in the Palazzo Comunale in Trevignano. ▶ High above the lake is **Manziana**, beautifully located at the foot of the wooded Mt. Calvario. ▶ On the S shore of the lake is the village of **Vigna**

di Valle with its **Museo Storico dell'Aeronautica** *(winter 8 a.m.-4 p.m.; summer 9 a.m.-6 p.m.; closed Mon).* This museum houses interesting relics, documents and historic aircraft. ▶ 8 km farther along the v. Claudia Braccianese are the **ruins of Galeria,** an ancient Roman town. ☐

Practical information —————————————

ANGUILLARA SABAZIA, ✉ 00061, ☎ 06.

Hotel:
★★★ *Residence Poggio dei Pini,* ☎ 9018241, 60 rm ℗ ⑂ ⑄ ✑ 60,000.

Restaurant:
♦ *Zaira,* v. Belloni, ☎ 9018082, closed Tue and Christmas. Lake view. Mixed cuisine: grilled whitefish, grilled meats, 15/25,000.

Recommended
Horseback riding: *Centro ippico di Cornazzano,* at Santa Maria di Galéria, v. Braccianese, ☎ 694014, (associate of *ANTE).*

BAGNI DI STIGLIANO, ✉ 00060, ☎ 06.
⌇ (Jun-Sep), ☎ 9020164.

BRACCIANO, ✉ 00062, ☎ 06.
ⓘ v. Claudia 58, ☎ 9023664.
⏧ boat trips on lake, ☎ 6794595.

⚓ *Roma Flash Sporting,* v. Settevene Palo at 19.8-km marker, 150 pl, ☎ 5023669.

Recommended
Flying: *Associazione Vela Sabazia,* strada Circumlacuale 31, ☎ 9022804.
Horseback riding: *Crazy Horse* at Pisciatelli; *Equestrian Country Sports,* at Piane Roma (associates of *ANTE).*

MANZIANA, ✉ 00066, ☎ 06.

Hotel:
★★★ *Etruschi,* v. Roma 101, ☎ 9026082, 50 rm ℗ ⌂ ⑄ ✑ closed Jan-Feb, 55,000; bkf: 5,000.

Recommended
Horseback riding: *Scurella La Mola,* ☎ 9026157 (associate of *ANTE).*

CAPRAROLA

Viterbo 18, Rome 72 km
Pop. 4,886 ✉ 01032 ☎ 0761   B2-3

Caprarola is beautifully located on the SE slope of the Cimini hills and is dominated by the **Palazzo Farnese★★** *(9 a.m.-4 p.m. or 7 p.m.; closed Mon),* on the site of a fort built by Cardinal Alessandro Farnese (1559-75). It is one of the most important buildings of the 16C and is approached by a pair of elliptical ramps. The façade has two orders above the ground storey, with a loggia on the piano nobile. Inside is a superb round colonnaded **courtyard★.** The famous **scala regia★** supported by columns leads up to the apartments decorated with stucco and frescos depicting the achievements of the Farnese family (partly the work of the Zuccari). The loggia affords an exceptional **view★** stretching from the fortress of Narni at Terminillo to Sabina. Behind the palace is a **park** with terraces, gardens, fountains and a lovely lodge. ☐

Practical information —————————————

Hotel:
★★ *Bella Venere,* on Vico Lake, ☎ 646453, 14 rm ℗ ⑄ ✑ ⚘ Pens. closed Nov and Christmas, 40,000.

Send us your comments and suggestions; we will use them in the next edition.

CASAMARI ABBEY*

Frosinone 14, Rome 98 km
✉ 03020 ☎ 0775   E4-5

Casamari Abbey lies in a charming valley with a backdrop of distant hills. It is a fine example of French-inspired Cistercian Gothic architecture. Founded by Benedictines in 1035, it was completely rebuilt in 1140 and has recently been fully restored.

▶ The **abbot's lodging** is surmounted by a loggia; next door is the monastic liqueur still. ▶ At the lower end of the courtyard stands the **church★★** (1217) with an elaborate Gothic entrance. The three naves of the interior are a splendid example of harmonious Gothic architecture. ▶ Next to the entrance is the **refectory,** a large hall with two naves 121 ft long. The **pharmacy** is outside the monastery gate. ▶ The monastery also houses a **Museo-pinacoteca** *(9 a.m.-12 noon and 3:30 p.m.-sunset; a monk acts as guide),* which contains archaeological finds from **Cereatae Marianae** and some 16C and 17C paintings. ▶ The **cloister** is square and surrounded by a colonnade of slender columns with capitals of varied shape. ▶ The **chapter-house★** has three naves with clustered columns. ☐

CASSINO

Frosinone 53, Rome 130 km
Pop. 33,157 ✉ 03043 ☎ 0776   F5

An abbey stands on a hill, at the foot of which lies Cassino, which was completely rebuilt after the Second World War.

▶ SE of town is the **archaeological area,** along v. Casilina. Here are a **tomb** attributed to the Ummidia family, a large cruciform building from the 1C and a **theatre** from the time of Augustus, now partially hidden by modern buildings. Parts of the road and walls of the Roman city, which was built on terraces cut into the hill, can also be seen. ▶ Near the Cappella del Crocifisso is the **Museo Archeologico Nazionale** *(9 a.m.-1 hr before sunset)* which houses exhibits from the Cassino area and information on the monuments of the ancient city. S of the city are the **Terme Varroniane,** an area with natural springs among weeping willows. Nearby are the remains of a bathhouse identified as part of the villa of Marcus Tercentius Varro. ▶ The SS 149 leads to the abbey of Montecassino offering lovely views of the city and plain. The road skirts the 10C Rocca Janula and the Polish military cemetery hidden among the cypresses and passes a stretch of polygonal wall before reaching the great **abbey of Montecassino★** standing alone on the mountaintop *(8 a.m.-12:30 p.m. and 3-7 or 6 p.m. winter).* ▶ This is the headquarters of the order and the most renowned of all Benedictine abbeys. It was founded by Benedict of Nursia in 529, was destroyed several times, but has always been rebuilt. During the Middle Ages it was a centre of Western culture, and much of the literature and learning of the ancient world was preserved by its monks. On 15 February 1944 it was completely destroyed by violent Allied air bombardment. It was faithfully reconstructed after the war. ▶ The buidings form a large irregular rectangle comprising cloisters, church and the monastery itself. The entrance leads into three **cloisters** opening into one another. The middle cloister dates from 1595 (superb **view★** from the balcony) and opens into the **cloister of the Benefactors,** designed by Antonio da Sangallo. ▶ This leads to the **basilica** with bronze doors by P. Canonica (1951; central door contains panels cast in Constantinople in 11C). The interior was reconstructed to the 18C drawings of C. Fanzago. Frescos by P. Annigoni adorn the entrance wall and the dome (1978); below the high altar is the tomb of St. Benedict, with the remains of the saint and of his sister St. Scholastica. ▶ On the l. of the cloister of the Benefactors is the **museum**

(9 a.m.-12:30 p.m. and 3:15-6:30 p.m.). It contains sketches of the vanished frescos, documents and vestments, and the treasury contains some fine reliquaries. ▶ The **crypt** survived the bombing and is decorated by German monks from the Beuron school (1913). □

Practical information _____

ⓘ v. Condotti 6, ☎ 21292.
Car rental: *Maggiore*, v. Pascoli 102, ☎ 25090.

Hotels:
★★★★ *Forum Palace*, v. Casilina Nord ☎ 481211, 104 rm ℗ ▨ & 57,000; bkf: 7,000.
★★★ *Pace*, v. Abruzzi 8, ☎ 22288, 60 rm ℗ 38,000.

Recommended
Cycling: *GS Rinascita Cassino*, v. Molise 9, ☎ 23296.

CASTELLI ROMANI

Round trip from Rome *(104 km, 1 day; map 2)*

Castelli Romani (Roman castles) were castles that belonged to the popes and Roman patrician families. They include Frascati, Grottaferrata, Marino, Castel Gandolfo, Albano, Ariccia, Genzano, Nemi, Rocca di Papa, Rocca Priora, Montecómpatri, Monte Porzio Catone and Colonna. They lie scattered across the slopes of the Alban hills, an isolated volcanic range, the highest peak of which is Mt. Cavo at 3,114 ft. The landscape is enchanting and varied, with sloping vineyards and olive groves, green chestnut forests and crater lakes. The air is pure and sparkling.

▶ Leaving **Rome** the route starts on the ring road and then the Autostrada del Sole heading toward Naples as far as the **San Cesareo junction**. This is the start of the tour. ▶ **Montecompatri** (1,890 ft) is a picturesque town which clings to a hill. ▶ At **Monte Pozio Catone**, amid olive groves, there is a superb view★ from the main square. The route then proceeds toward **Frascati** (→). ▶ The ruins of **Tusculum**★, an ancient Latin city, include the remains of the amphitheatre, the theatre, the forum, the villa of Cicero and a cistern of the archaic

period (possibly 6C-5C BC). There is a fine view★ from the top of the acropolis hill. ▶ From **Grottaferrata** (→) the route climbs to Rocca di Papa, with the ancient quarter of the 'Bavarians' at the top of the town. The church of the Assumption contains a 14C Madonna. ▶ **Rocca di Papa** lies on the slope of **Mt. Cavo**★; from here a private toll road leads to the summit. The former 18C convent (now an inn) occupies the site of the temple of Jupiter Latialis and affords superb views★. ▶ Continuing through **Nemi** (→) and **Velletri** (→), the route comes to **Lanuvio** on a ridge on the S edge of the Alban hills. Here are walls and towers of the medieval town, the 15C Palazzo Colonna and Roman remains of the Temple of Hercules, the acropolis and the temple of Juno Sospes. ▶ The route now turns back toward Rome. ▶ **Genzano di Roma** lies on the outer slope of the crater that contains Lake Nemi. From p. Frasconi the v. Berardi leads to terraces above the plain, climbing to the churches of S. Maria della Cima and the 'Infiorata', so named for the bright floral compositions that cover the entire street during the Corpus Christi procession. The route then continues through **Ariccia**, (→), **Albano Laziale** (→) and comes to **Castel Gandolfo** on the W edge of Lake Albano. Here, in p. del Plebiscito★, Bernini's influence can be seen in the fountain and the church of St. Thomas (1661). The Palazzo Pontificio was begun by Maderno in 1624 for Urban VIII; it joins the villa Barberini, and its park stretches as far as Albano, taking in the remains of Domitian's villa. This is the pope's summer residence and enjoys extraterritorial status *(visits not permitted; special permit required for villa Barberini)*. The little belvedere on the p. del Palazzo has a view of **Lake Albano**. ▶ The route then descends to the shores of the lake. Its elliptical shape is due to the fact that it consists of two volcanic craters. ▶ In **Marino**, the fontana dei Mori in p. Matteotti flows with the famed Castelli wine (but only on festival day, the first Sun of Oct). Among interesting buildings here are the 17C church of S. Barnaba, the 16C Palazzo Colonna (a terrace on the r. side affords a glimpse of the Acqua Ferentina Valley and the quarries of Peperino) and the church of the Madonna del Rosario (1713; inside Dominican convent), whose round interior is Baroque. ▶ The route completes the circuit of Lake Albano and returns by the v. Appia to **Rome**. □

2. Castelli Romani

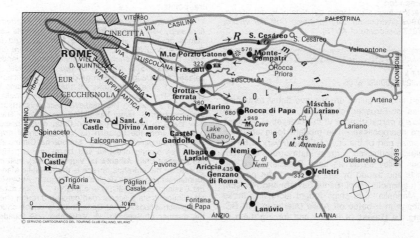

© SERVIZIO CARTOGRAFICO DEL TOURING CLUB ITALIANO, MILANO

Practical information _____

CASTEL GANDOLFO, ⊠ 00040, ☎ 06.
ⓘ p. della Libertà 6, ☎ 9360340 (seasonal); at Albano Laziale, ☎ 9321323.

Recommended
Water ski skiing: *Water Ski Castelgandolfo*, v. Spiaggia del Lago 46, ☎ 9360047.

GENZANO DI ROMA, ⊠ 00045, ☎ 06.
ⓘ at Albano Laziale, ☎ 9321323.

Hotel:
★★ *Villa Robinia*, v. F.lli Rosselli 25, ☎ 9396409, 30 rm ℗ ▥ ⚒ 40,000; bkf: 5,000.

Restaurant:
♦♦ *Bracconiere*, p. Frasconi 16, ☎ 9396621, closed Wed. With a winter garden. Regional and Italian cuisine: scampi risotto, venison, 30/40,000.

Recommended
Events: *Corpus Domini floral procession* (Jun).
Horseback riding: *Quarto della Mandorla*, at Pozzo Bonelli, ☎ 9373111 (associate of *ANTE*).

MARINO, ⊠ 00047, ☎ 06.
ⓘ p. Matteotti 1, ☎ 9385555.

Restaurant:
♦♦ *Vigneto*, v. dei Laghi, ☎ 9387034, closed Tue. Among woods and vineyards, garden with pergolas. Mixed regional cuisine: spaghetti capriccio, cornmeal alla spianatora, 22/26,000.

Recommended
Events: *grape festival*, with a parade of floats bearing symbolic figures (1st Sun in Oct).

MONTE PORZIO CATONE, ⊠ 00040, ☎ 06.

Hotel:
★★★ *Giovannella*, p. Trieste 1, ☎ 9449038, 43 rm ℗ ▥ 60,000; bkf: 4,500.

Restaurant:
● ♦♦♦ *Fontana Candida da Micara*, v. Fontana Candida 5, ☎ 9449614, closed Tue and 5-25 Aug. Grill and veranda. Regional and creative cuisine: penne cardinale, veal with nuts, 30/45,000.

Recommended
♥ wine: *Costantini* cellar, v. Frascati Colonna 29 (Frascati).

ROCCA DI PAPA, ⊠ 00040, ☎ 06.
ⓘ at Albano Laziale, ☎ 9321323.

Hotel:
★★★ *Europa*, p. Repubblica 20, ☎ 949361, 38 rm, closed Nov-Mar, 56,000; bkf: 6,000.

Recommended
Horseback riding: *Club ippico del Vivaro*, v. del Vivaro, ☎ 9467003 (instruction); *Circolo ippico Colli del Vivaro*, ☎ 9467017 (associate of *ANTE*).

CERVETERI*

Rome 44 km
Pop. 13,929 ⊠ 00052 ☎ 06   B4

Cerveteri and Tarquinia are the two finest remaining examples of Etruscan civilization. Of course they only show a partial glimpse of this civilization because both are necropolises. The modern town occupies only a small part of the city of *Caere* (*Kysry* in Etruscan), which controlled a great state stretching from the Tiber Valley as far as Lake Bracciano and the Tolfa hills and traded by sea from its three ports at *Alsium* (Ladispoli), *Pyrgi* (Santa Severa) and *Punicum* (Santa Marinella). Its ships fought alongside those of Carthage in a battle off Alalia (Aleria) in 540 BC, defeating the Greeks of Phocis and forcing them to

abandon Corsica, one of the decisive events in the history of the ancient Mediterranean. **Caere** finally submitted to Rome in 358 BC. The tombs in the necropolis range from the 7C to the 1C BC and include shaft, pit and chamber tombs; the most typical type is the great round tumulus, sometimes more than 100 ft in diameter, raised on a base containing chambers cut into the rock and modelled on Etruscan houses.

▶ The medieval town occupies a hilltop and surrounds the fortified **Castello**; the curtain wall on the tree-lined piazza contains portions of the Etruscan walls. ▶ From here it is possible to see the 13C Rocca or fortress, the **Palazzo Ruspoli** (16C) and the modern church of **S. Maria**, with a 12C Romanesque church behind it forming the transept. ▶ The **Rocca** contains the **Museo Nazionale Cerite** *(May-Sep 9 a.m.-12 noon and 4-7 p.m.; other months 9 a.m.-4 p.m.; closed Mon)*, with finds from the 9C BC to the 1C BC. There are remains from the necropolises of the area and Villanova funerary urns, archaic Greek pottery, Attic and Etruscan and wooden and bronze furniture. ▶ The **Etruscan necropolis★★** at the colle della Banditaccia 2 km away *(9 a.m.-1 hr before sunset; closed Mon)* is a huge and impressive complex. There are a great many tombs; of particular note is the **tomba dei Rilievi★★★**, a chamber tomb with polychrome stucco depicting everyday articles and the **tomba G. Moretti★**. The route along v. Sepolcrale is most impressive. ▶ There are other isolated necropolises in the countryside. The Sorbo necropolis contains the **Regolini Galassi** tomb, named after its discoverer; the remarkable treasure from this tomb is displayed in the Vatican. ▶ On the coast is **Cerenova-Marina di Cerveteri**, a seaside resort.   ☐

Practical information _____

Recommended
Events: *festival of the Stations of the Cross* (Good Friday); opera season (Aug); *grape festival* (last Sun in Aug).

The CIMINI MOUNTAINS

From Viterbo *(110 km, 1 day; map 3)*

The gentle contours of these hills were formed long ago by volcanic action. They reach their apex at Mt. Cimino (3,455 ft). The great oak and chestnut forests and beech woods of Mt. Cimino are the remnants of the *Cimina Silva*, which for a time prevented the Romans from expanding into Umbria. The traces of man's colonization of the area add to its natural appeal; it can be visited from a number of central points.

▶ This itinerary starts at Viterbo (→). ▶ A wooded road flanked by villas leads to **Bagnaia** where the **Villa Lante★** stands above the village *(guided tours at fixed times: 9 a.m.-4 or 7:30 p.m. depending on season; closed Mon)*. This late Renaissance masterpiece of landscaping (Vignola, 1578) consists of two symmetrical, small palaces and a superb Italian garden★ with fountains and a park. ▶ The route turns off the road toward **Vitorchiano**. The town is enclosed by fortified walls and overlooks a ravine. The medieval section is intact, and the church of S. Maria has a fine campanile. The way now leads to **Bomarzo** (→) and **Chia**, where some fine paintings from the Lorenzo da Viterbo school are preserved in the parish church. ▶ **Soriano nel Cimino** stands on a rise among chestnut and hazel groves. Here is the **Palazzo Chigi-Albani★** by Vignola (1562), built in two blocks; on the entrance terrace is the fantastic Mannerist fountain known as the Regina delle Acque. Above looms the Castello Orsini (13C, now a prison). ▶ The ascent of **Mt. Cimino** is via a scenic road passing through chestnut and beech woods. ▶ At **Canepina** is a parish church in the manner of Sangallo. ▶ **Vallerano** was founded by

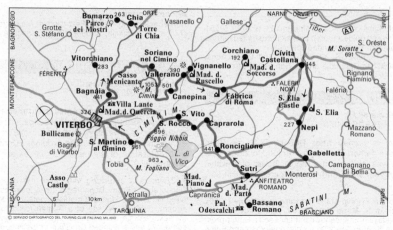

3. The Cimini Mountains

the Etruscans and retains some medieval sections, as well as the 17C shrine of the **Madonna del Ruscello**. ▶ **Vignanello** occupies a rocky rise with a fine view over the Tiber Valley. ▶ The collegiate church of **Fabrica di Roma** contains some 16C frescos. ▶ Farther on, the route passes **Corchiano**, **Falerii Novi** and **Civita Castellana**. ▶ **Castel Sant'Elia** is another old town, with the **basilica of S. Elia★** *(keys from municipio)* standing at the bottom of a steep valley, framed by cypresses. It is an outstanding 11C work, with a cycle of 12C frescos of Byzantine inspiration. ▶ The medieval town of **Nepi** is partly surrounded by thick walls and is noteworthy for the ruins of the fortress (Rocca), the Palazzo Comunale by A. da Sangallo the younger and the cathedral with its 12C portico and crypt. ▶ **Bassano Romano** also retains a medieval flavour. The route continues to **Sutri** (→) and **Ronciglione** on the SE slope of the crater that forms Lake Vico. The medieval section and the gate both show 16C and 18C influence. ▶ **Lake Vico** is set among quiet wooded shores and lies in the bottom of a volcanic crater. ▶ **Caprarola** (→) is the artistic highpoint of the trip. ▶ The last stop is at **San Martino al Cimino**, with the charming 13C church of **S. Martin**, which was built by the Cistercians of Pontigny. A short road leads back to **Viterbo**. □

Practical information ⎯⎯⎯⎯⎯⎯⎯⎯

CORCHIANO, ⊠ 01030, ☎ 0761.

Recommended
Nature park: *Piano Sant'Angelo* nature reserve, information at *WWF Italia*, ☎ 06/854892.

RONCIGLIONE, ⊠ 01037, ☎ 0761.
ⓘ corso Umberto 22, ☎ 625460.

Hotels:
★★★ **Sans Soucis,** at Punta del Lago, v. dei Noccioleti 18, ☎ 612052, 24 rm Ⓟ ⚲ ⊞ 51,500; bkf: 7,000.
★★★ **Vecchio Mulino,** p. Principe di Piemonte, ☎ 625011, 27 rm, closed 1-15 Nov, 52,000; bkf: 4,500.
★★ **Cardinale,** strada Cimina, ☎ 625188, 20 rm Ⓟ ⊞ ⚹ closed Nov, 45,000; bkf: 7,000. Rest. ● ◆◆◆ closed Mon. On the lake. Italian cuisine: red chicory risotto and pasticcio, escalopes alla perpetua, 28/40,000.

Recommended
Events: carnival with parades and horse races, Comune, ☎ 626877.

SAN MARTINO AL CIMINO, ⊠ 01030, ☎ 0761.

Hotel:
★★★★ **Balletti Park Hotel,** v. Umbria 2/A, ☎ 29777, 136 rm Ⓟ ⊞ ⚹ ⊞ 〰 102,000; bkf: 10,000. Rest. ◆◆◆ *Cavaliere* Italian cuisine: pancakes with cheese, tournedos of veal alla zingara, Est Est Est di Montefiascone wine, 25/35,000.

SORIANO NEL CIMINO, ⊠ 01038, ☎ 0761.
ⓘ v. S. Maria 28, ☎ 729001.

Hotels:
★★★ **Bastia,** v. Giovanni XXIII 45, ☎ 729062, 39 rm Ⓟ ⊞ ⚹ 49,000; bkf: 5,000.
★★★ **Oleandri,** v. Battisti 51, ☎ 729009, 16 rm Ⓟ ⚹ ⊞ ⚹ closed Dec, 45,000.

Recommended
Events: festival of chestnuts, with archery tournament and competition held in costume (Oct).
♥ **gastronomy:** boletus mushrooms, ewe's cheese, ham, local confectionery.

CIRCEO NATIONAL PARK

D6

This park includes territory from Latina, Sabaudia and S. Felice Circeo (*c.* 80 sq km). It comprises the **promontory of Mt. Circeo**, the **dunes** between the Pomptine lakes and the sea, **Lake Sabaudia** and an area of scrub brush near Sabaudia itself. The park was created in 1934 to conserve the vegetation of the area and what remained of the surrounding forests following agricultural reclamation. It is an area of great natural interest and diversity. The N slopes of the mountains are covered with forests of ilex, cork oak and scrub brush. The rocky precipices offer superb views★ over the sea, the lakes and the Pomptine plain. The lake★ has a tropical atmosphere, with its thousands of water birds and densely wooded shores concealing picturesque Roman ruins. Wild boar and fallow deer roam these woods. Migrating flocks of thrush and woodcock fly over in autumn, and turtle doves, cuckoos and quails in spring. □

Practical information ──────────────

ⓘ office at Sabaudia, v. Carlo Alberto 107, ☎ 0773/57251 (information and guided tours); access unrestricted, spring and late autumn recommended for visits.
🚌 from Rome-EUR, ☎ 06/57531 and from Latina, ☎ 0773/80647 to Sabaudia and to San Felice Circeo.

CITTADUCALE

Rieti 10, Rome 88 km
Pop. 5,750 ⊠ 02015 ☎ 0746   D2

This town is named after Robert, Duke of Calabria, whose father, Charles of Anjou, founded it in 1309. It was laid out on a regular street plan within the rectangular **walls** and **towers,** parts of which survive.

▶ In the p. del Popolo stand the **torre municipale** (1580), the church of **S. Maria del Popolo,** with a late Romanesque façade, a Romanesque campanile and a Gothic presbytery, and **S. Agostino** with a polygonal apse and a fine late Gothic portal (1450). ▶ 5.5 km away on the Salaria road are the **Terme di Cotilia.**   □

Practical information ──────────────

♨ (Jun-Oct), at Terme di Cotilia, ☎ 693036.
ⓘ corso Mazzini 106.

CIVITA CASTELLANA

Viterbo 35, Rome 53 km
Pop. 15,736 ⊠ 01033 ☎ 0761   C3

This town stands on the site of **Falerii Veteres,** capital of the Falisci, occupying a flat stratum of porous rock between the gorges of two small rivers. Its main feature, however, is the high medieval town itself. The kaolin and silicaceous sands and clays found locally caused the pottery industry to flourish. The first workshop opened in 1792.

▶ The Romanesque parts of the **cathedral★** (12C, apse and campanile) are remarkable. Note the **portico★** with its columns and architrave and its great central arch, the work of the Roman marble-workers Iacopo di Lorenzo and Cosma (1210), which seem to hint at the coming Renaissance, linking the classical tradition with its humanist revival centuries later. A number of ancient pieces and works of art decorate the 18C interior and the crypt. ▶ The perfect pentagonal **fortress★** (begun by Antonio da Sangallo il Vecchio in 1494 and finished by Antonio da Sangallo il Giovane for Julius II) contains the **Museo Archeologico dell'Agro Falisco** *(9 a.m.-1 p.m.; closed Mon),* with funeral items from the necropolis of Falerii and other exhibits. ▶ 6 km away is **Falerii Novi★,** the city built in 241 BC, after the Romans had destroyed the rebellious city of *Falerii Veteres* and forced its inhabitants to occupy a less easily defensible site. This was abandoned in the 8C in favour of the older site. The remains of the **fortified enclosure** form one of the largest such examples, with its 50 towers and 9 gates. Inside the walls lay the **porta di Giove** (Jupiter Gate) is the Romanesque church of **S. Maria di Falleri★** (12C). ▶ Corchiano, 9 km away, features the church of S. Biagio with frescos by Lorenzo da Viterbo (15C) and Antonio da Viterbo.   □

Practical information ──────────────

Restaurant:
♦ **Mignolò,** v. Ferretti 101, ☎ 53465, closed Jun and 15-30 Aug. Near medieval town centre. Mixed regional cuisine: fettuccine with mazzancolle prawns, wild boar chops, 17/23,000.

Recommended
Horseback riding: *Horse Raid Club,* at Mazzano Romano *(17 km S),* v. Cassia, ☎ 06/9049062 (associate of *ANTE*).

CIVITA DI BAGNOREGIO

Viterbo 28, Rome 109 km
Pop. 26 ⊠ 01022 ☎ 0761   B1-2

A languishing air pervades this dying medieval town, set in a strange eroded landscape. The town's population is dwindling and the porous rock ledge on which the town is built is eroding. Consolidation and restoration of the medieval houses are currently underway.

▶ There is a surprising view from the belvedere★ in Bagnoregio. From Bagnoregio, this town can be entered via a footbridge and medieval gate. ▶ On its small square, perhaps the site of a Roman forum, stands the medieval church of **S. Donato,** with a 16C façade, a 12C campanile and a wooden Crucifix★ of the school of Donatello.   □

CIVITAVECCHIA

Rome 71 km
Pop. 50,076 ⊠ 00053 ☎ 0766   A3

This modern city is the main port of Latium. When Trajan built the port it was called *Centumcellae.* The **Roman basin** with remains of partially restored warehouses forms the N part of the modern port. The Saracens held the port for some twenty years from 828, when the inhabitants fled to the hills. According to local lore it was an old sailor, Leander, who advised the people to return to the sea. He dispensed his advice under a large oak tree. The oak stands on the city's coat of arms between the letters O and C, standing for *'ottimo consiglio',* best advice.

▶ **Fort Michelangelo★,** overlooking the port, is a fine Renaissance work. Begun by Bramante, it was continued by Antonio da Sangallo il Giovane. Michelangelo built the octagonal keep. ▶ The small 18C palace built by Clement XIII for the garrison command houses the **Museo Nazionale Archeologico** *(9 a.m.-2 p.m.; closed Mon),* with exhibits from the area and from neighbouring necropolises and towns (including Roman copies of the portrait of Socrates, the *Venus of Cnidos* and the *Diadumeno* from the port of *Centumcellae).* ▶ Stendhal lived here as French consul from 1821 until just before his death in 1842. ▶ The **Terme Taurine,** 4.5 km away, are actually the remains of a Roman villa built to use the warm springs, with hot and cold baths, a library, and large cisterns. Nearby are the two warm springs called **Fonti della Ficoncella.**   □

Practical information ──────────────

ⓘ v. Garibaldi 42, ☎ 25348.
🚂 ☎ 24975.
🚢 ferries to Sardinia: to Golfo Aranci, several sailings daily, journey c. 8.5 hrs, *State Railways,* ☎ 23273; to Olbia, c. 7 hrs; Cagliari, c. 13 hrs, Arbatax, c. 9 hrs, *Tirrenia,* ☎ 28801.

Hotel:
★★★★ **Sunbay Park Hotel,** v. Aurelia Sud, ☎ 22801, 59 rm ℗ ⚏ ⅙ ▤ 110,000; bkf: 6,000.

Restaurant:
♦ **Trattoria del Gobbo,** lungoporto Gramsci 29/35, ☎ 23163, closed Wed and 1-15 Oct. Regional seafood: scampi al gratin, grilled mazzancolle prawns, 20/30,000.

Recommended
Craft workshops: *I Mascherari,* p. Leandra 13, ☎ 22520 (ceramic masks, mirrors); *Bartolozzi,* at Tolfa *(22 km NE),* v. Roma 75, ☎ 92420 (saddlery).
Cycling: *Portuali,* v. 24 Maggio 2, ☎ 25563.
Events: opera season at the Teatro Estivo in the Forte Michelangelo; *Cristo Morto procession* (Apr); boat races.
Marina: ☎ 20250; *Lega Navale,* ☎ 20374.

FARFA

Rieti 37, Rome 55 km
Pop. 71 ⊠ 02032 ☎ 0765 C3

The **abbey** at Farfa was one of the most important religious and cultural centres during the middle ages *(guided tours, 9:30 a.m.-12 noon and 3:30-6 p.m.; hols, every 30 mn).* It was founded in the 6C and its influence was felt mostly in the 9C and the 11C. Many famous codices were written in the *scriptorium,* dating from the 11C. A 15C gate leads into the court, with a great fortified tower. The **church** was reconstructed in the second half of the 15C; it has a nave and two aisles with columns taken from Roman buildings. The coffered ceiling dates from the 15C; frescos are by a master of the 16C Flemish school, Gentileschi, and the school of the Zuccari (16C-17C). The Romanesque **campanile** contains frescos dating perhaps from the start of the 11C. The Lombard cloister has Romanesque features. The great 16C cloister leads to the Carolingian **crypt,** with a Roman **sarcophagus★** (2C). The **library** includes 20,000 books, among them illuminated choir-books from the 16C-17C. Next to the abbey is the little medieval town with rows of houses, which have been largely rebuilt. 2 km NW is **Fonte di Farfa.** □

FERENTINO*

Frosinone 12, Rome 75 km
Pop. 18,397 ⊠ 03013 ☎ 0775 E4-5

Ferentino stands on a hill overlooking the Sacco Valley and still preserves the original design of its Hernici inhabitants. It was incorporated into the late Roman republic and today features a juxtaposition of Roman remains, Romanesque and Gothic monuments and medieval buildings.

▶ The **acropolis★** stands on the summit, supported by strong pre-Roman walls, partly rebuilt under Sulla. ▶ The Romanesque **cathedral★** (11C) stands in an open space. It was rebuilt in the 17C and restored at the beginning of this century. It features Cosmati pavements★ (sanctuary 1116, nave and aisles 1203) and a 13C tabernacle (on the high altar). The apses and campanile can be seen from the courtyard of the bishop's palace, occupying the site of a temple. ▶ The **Roman market place** of the Republican period consists of a great hall adjoined by five shops with colonnades *(apply at municipio).* ▶ The **palazzo dei Cavalieri Gaudenti** dates from the 13C and has a portico with pointed double arches; the **palace of Innocent III** has a fine portal. ▶ The church of **S. Maria Maggiore★** is in the Cisterian Gothic style (1150); its W door dates from the first half of the 13C. There is a tall transept and octagonal lantern below the dome above the crossing, a nave and two aisles. ▶ Next to the Romanesque-Gothic church of **S. Francesco** (13C) stands the little **Museo Civico** *(apply to municipio)* with Roman exhibits and Romanesque bas-reliefs. ▶ The **polygonal city-walls** (5C-2C BC; the upper portion is medieval) are broken by the **Porta Sanguinaria★,** or Bloody Gate, near which are the remains of a great Roman theatre (perhaps 2C) and the **porta di Casamari.** Outside this second gate is a large rock carved with the **will of Aulus Quintilius,** a man of Trajan's time who left his worldly goods to the city. ▶ The **Baths of Pompey** stand in a park on v. Casilina, heading towards Frosinone. □

Practical information

♆ (Jun-mid-Oct), ☎ 394114.
ℹ p. Matteotti.

Hotel:
★★★ ***Bassetto,*** v. Casilina Sud, ☎ 394931, 72 rm Ⓟ ♨ ♿ ✗ 68,000; bkf: 6,000. Rest. ♦♦♦ Regional and Italian cuisine: crepes with cheese, rigatoni with artichoke, 25/35,000.

FIUGGI*

Frosinone 32, Rome 82 km
Pop. 7,855 ☎ 0775 E4

Boniface VIII used to send his servants to Fiuggi to bring him water to treat the infectious disease which had stricken him. Michelangelo was also cured here and wrote to friends in praise of the waters. The climate is fresh, dry and breezy in summer, and green trees surround this spot high on the Ernici Mountains facing down the Sacco Valley.

▶ There are two distinct towns: **Fiuggi Città,** which stands on a rise with a medieval centre and steep, narrow streets and contains a former casino (1910) in art nouveau style; and **Fiuggi Fonte,** in a pleasant wooded valley. ▶ The health-giving waters flow from two springs, the **Polla di Bonifacio VIII** and the **Polle anticolane.** ▶ 4.5 km SE is **Lake Canterno.** ▶ **Fumone,** 12 km away, is a pretty town on a hill. Here, Pope Celestine V died in an ancient fortress after abdicating his throne. ▶ 25 km away is the **La Selva Nature Park,** 115 acres of woods and glades and pools densely populated by birds. □

Practical information

FIUGGI CITTA, ⊠ 03014.
♆ (Apr-Nov), ☎ 54341.

Hotel:
★★ ***Anticoli,*** v. Verghetti 70, ☎ 55667, 18 rm Ⓟ ⋞ ♨ closed Dec, 46,000.

FIUGGI FONTE, ⊠ 03015.
ℹ at Fiuggi Fonte, p. Frascara 4, ☎ 55019 (in season); v. Gorizia 4, ☎ 55446.

Hotels:
★★★★ ***Silva Hotel Splendid,*** corso Nuova Italia 40, ☎ 55791, 120 rm Ⓟ ♨ ♿ ▭ closed Nov-Apr, 130,000; bkf: 12,000.
★★★★ ***Vallombrosa & Majestic,*** v. Vecchia Fiuggi 209, ☎ 55531, 80 rm Ⓟ ♨ ▭ closed Oct-Apr, 170,000; bkf: 9,000.
★★★★ ***Villa Igea,*** corso Nuova Italia 32, ☎ 55435, 65 rm Ⓟ ♨ ✗ ▭ closed 16 Oct-30 Apr, 115,000; bkf: 8,000.
★★★ ***Alfieri,*** v. Fonte Anticolana, ☎ 55646, 40 rm Ⓟ ♨ closed Nov-Apr, 48,000; bkf: 6,000.
★★★ ***Astoria,*** v. Prenestina 105, ☎ 55046, 56 rm Ⓟ ♨ closed 16 Oct-Apr, 60,000.
★★★ ***Casina dello Stadio e del Golf,*** v. IV Giugno 19, ☎ 55027, 49 rm Ⓟ ✗ closed Nov-Mar, 54,000; bkf: 5,000.
★★★ ***Fiuggi Terme,*** v. Prenestina 9, ☎ 55212, 53 rm Ⓟ ♨ ✗ ▭ ⚲ closed 2 Nov-14 Dec and 6 Jan-Mar, 59,000; bkf: 8,000.
★★★ ***Mondial Park Hotel,*** v. S. Emiliano 82, ☎ 55848, 43 rm Ⓟ ♨ ♿ ▭ closed Nov-Mar, 60,000; bkf: 7,000.
★★ ***Edison,*** v. De Medici 33, ☎ 55875, 24 rm Ⓟ ♨ ♿ closed Nov-Mar, 43,000; bkf: 3,000.
★★ ***Sorrentino,*** v. Diaz 532, ☎ 55220, 45 rm Ⓟ ♨ ♿ ✗ closed 11 Oct-Apr, 40,000; bkf: 8,000.

⚐ *Fiuggi*, v. del Campo Sportivo, 150 pl, ☎ 54420.

Recommended
Events: *tourist film festival* (Jun); Fiuggi prize for literature (Jul) and various other cultural and artistic events.
Golf: superstrada Anticolana, ☎ 55250 (9 holes).
Nature park: *La Selva*, at Paliano (informatiion and guided tours). ☎ 533177 or 533288.

FONDI

Latina 57, Rome 127 km
Pop. 29,126 ⊠ 04022 ☎ 0771   E6

Fondi lies on a plain of citrus groves at the edge of the Aurunci hills, near Lake Fondi. It still preserves a rectangular street plan and **Roman walls**, which were fortified in the 14C. The E-W road (corso Appio Claudio) is where the v. Appia crossed the town.

▶ **S. Maria Assunta**, rebuilt at the end of the 15C, has a campanile with double windows and, in the Gothic interior, two Renaissance ambos, 16C paintings and a fine tabernacle (1491). ▶ The cathedral of **S. Pietro**★ is 14C and has Roman foundations. In its Gothic interior is a Cosmati pulpit★ (1286). ▶ Beside the rugged **castle** is the **Palazzo del Principe**★, a fine building with examples of Durazzo Anjou and Catalan Gothic work, double windows, and a porticoed court with gallery, an external staircase and loggia. ▶ The **cloister** of the church of S. Francesco (incorporated into the municipio) features Roman statues and architectural fragments. ▶ The **Lido di Fondi** is 15 km away, on a shore with pines and dunes.   ▫

Practical information ⎯⎯⎯⎯⎯⎯⎯⎯⎯

ⓘ v. S. Francesco d'Assisi 8, ☎ 503477.

Restaurant:
♦ *'Ndino*, v. Garibaldi 46, ☎ 531210, closed Mon and Christmas. Mixed regional cuisine: taglionii with scampi, shellfish with tomato and beans, 25/35,000.

FORMIA

Latina 76, Rome 153 km
Pop. 31,448 ⊠ 04023 ☎ 0771   E-F6

This little town on the Gulf of Gaeta consists of two surviving medieval towns: **rione Mola** (with its church of S. Giovanni Battista and the Torre di Mola, the surviving part of the 13C Anjou castle) and picturesque **rione di Castelleone** (with its 14C octagonal Torre di S. Erasmo).

▶ There are many Roman remains because this was a famous resort in Roman times: fragments of columns in p. della Vittoria; the buildings now beneath the garden known as the **villa Comunale**; and the remains of the so-called **villa of Cicero** on the shore. ▶ Some of the Roman material found locally is exhibited in the **Antiquarium** *(9 a.m.-2 p.m.; closed Mon).* ▶ There are two beaches, the **Riviera di Levante** and the **Riviera di Ponente**, also known as Vendicio. ▶ 2 km NW on the v. Appia is a Roman ruin called the **tomb of Cicero**. He was murdered by supporters of Mark Anthony in 43 BC near Formia. ▶ **Itri**, 8.6 km away, contains the medieval church of S. Angelo, a crenellated castle and the house of the famous bandit Michele Pezza, known as Fra' Diavolo (1771-1806).   ▫

Practical information ⎯⎯⎯⎯⎯⎯⎯⎯⎯

≋
ⓘ v. Unità d'Italia 30, ☎ 21490.
⚓ ferries: *Caremar*, ☎ 461600; hydroplanes: *Società Navigazione Basso Lazio*, ☎ 267090; *Linee Assenso*, ☎ 23110 (to Ponza and Ventotene).

Hotels:
★★★★ *Castello Miramare*, v. Balze di Pagnano, ☎ 24238, 11 rm ℗ ⅀ ⛳ ⑅ ⤴ closed Nov, 93,500; bkf: 13,000.
★★★★ *G.A. Miramare*, v. Appia lato Napoli 44, ☎ 267181, 90 rm ℗ ⑅ ⊗ ▣ 93,500; bkf: 13,000.
★★★ *Bajamar*, at Marina di Santo Janni, lungomare Santo Janni, ☎ 28063, 48 rm ℗ ⑅ 62,000; bkf: 6,500.
★★★ *Caposele*, v. Porto Caposele, ☎ 23230, 52 rm ℗ ⅀ ⑅ ▣ ⤴ 60,500; bkf: 7,000.
★★★ *Fagiano Palace*, v. Appia lato Napoli 54, ☎ 266681, 95 rm ℗ ⑅ ⊗ ▣ ⤴ 60,000; bkf: 9,000.

Restaurant:
♦♦♦ *Italo*, v. Unità d'Italia, ☎ 21529, closed Mon and Christmas. Seaside,with a lively and festive atmosphere. Regional seafood: oyster risotto, cassuola alla formiana, 25/50,000.

⚐ *Gianola*, at Gianola, v. delle Vigne, 300 pl, ☎ 270223.

Recommended
Craft workshops: *Artigianato Itrano*, at Itri *(9 km NW)*, v. Baldo 65, ☎ 209737 (ceramics).
Cycling: *G.S. Cicloamatori*, v. Pietra Erta, ☎ 28325.
Marina: ☎ 21552.
Sailing: *Circolo nautico Caposele*, ☎ 21454.
Sports: *Scuola nazionale*, v. Appia lato Napoli, ☎ 24585; *CONI*, ☎ 21542.

FRASCATI

Rome 20 km
Pop. 19,222 ⊠ 00044 ☎ 06   C4

When *Tusculum* was destroyed, the survivors took refuge around the ancient churches of S. Maria and S. Sebastiano in Frascata, named from the right of *frasca*, gathering branches for fodder. This town is possibly the best known of the *Castelli Romani* (→). Goethe described its 'endless horizon, with a view of Rome in the plain and the sea beyond'.

▶ The best viewpoint is **p. Marconi**★, with the villa Aldobrandini as backdrop, and the **municipal park**, formerly belonging to the villa Torlonia, with its **theatre of water** (a waterfall designed by C. Maderno). ▶ The façade of the cathedral (16C-17C) is by Girolamo Fontana (1700) and the interior, in the shape of a Greek cross, is by O. Mascherino (1598). ▶ Fontana was also responsible for the fountain nearby with its triple arcade. ▶ The **Gesù church** is attributed to Pietro da Cortona (17C) and contains frescos by A. Pozzo. ▶ The **fortress**, which now serves as the bishop's palace, retains its medieval angular towers and square keep. ▶ The most charming feature of the town is its **noble houses**. The **villa Aldobrandini**★ was designed by B. Della Porta, C. Maderno and Giovanni Fontana (17C). It includes a superb **park**★ *(hols 9 a.m.-1 p.m.; apply to tourist office)* with oak woods dotted with statues, grottos, terraces and fountains. The **villa Falconieri** (16C, later enlarged by Borromini) and **villa Mondragone** (16C) cannot be visited. ▶ 1 km away is **Cappuccini** with the church of S. Francesco (1575) which contains paintings by Giulio Romano and Pomarancio and the tomb of Cardinal Massaia, Ethiopian missionary and explorer. The convent next door houses an **Ethiopian museum** *(visit by request).*   ▫

Practical information ⎯⎯⎯⎯⎯⎯⎯⎯⎯

ⓘ p. Marconi 1, ☎ 9420331.

Hotel:
★★ *Eden Tuscolano*, v. Tuscolana, ☎ 9420488, 32 rm ℗ ⑅ ⅃ 51,000; bkf:5,000.

Restaurants:
♦♦♦ *Cacciani*, v. Diaz 13, ☎ 9420378, closed Tue. Fine summer terrace. Regional cuisine: young lamb alla cacciatora, devilled chicken, 30/40,000.
♦♦♦ *Spartaco*, v. Letizia Bonaparte 1, ☎ 9420431, closed Tue. With large veranda, flower-decorated terrac-

es and garden. Regional and Italian cuisine: sirloin steak all'arancia, meat fillet with pineapple, 25/35,000.

Recommended
Rugby: v. di Villa Borghese 4, ☎ 9425321.

FREGENE

Rome 31 km
Pop. 2,660 ✉ 00050 ☎ 06   B4

A thick forest of umbrella pines comes down to the beach where Fregene sits and runs N of the Tiber mouth.   ☐

Practical information ⎯⎯⎯⎯⎯⎯⎯⎯⎯⎯
≋
ⓘ v. Castellamare 58, ☎ 6460596.

Hotel:
★★★ *Conchiglia,* lungomare Ponente 4, ☎ 6460229, 36 rm
ⓟ ⸬ ⅋ 73,000; bkf: 9,000.

FROSINONE

Rome 85, Milan 650 km
Pop. 45,271 ✉ 03100 ☎ 0775   E5

The modern town is the capital of the Ciociaria and stretches from the old town on top of the hill down to the plain.

▶ From piazzale Vittorio Veneto is a **view**★ over the Sacco Valley and the Lepini and Ernici hills. ▶ The site of Frusino, a Volscian and later Roman city, is marked by a few ruins in the plain by the River Cosa, including those of the amphitheatre. ▶ 28 km SE are the **caves of Pástena**★ *(guided tours; 9:30 a.m.-3:20 p.m. winter; 8:30-1 hr before sunset summer),* which branch in two. The upper part is divided into chambers rich in mineral deposits, the lower part into a number of lakes.   ☐

Sandals

The province of Frosinone is still popularly known as 'Ciociaria', from ciocia, the leather sandals worn by peasants who came to the markets of Rome and by shepherds who came to play the bagpipes at Christmas. Relief engravings on the column of Trajan reveal that these sandals used to be common among many of the Apennine highlanders and are directly descended from ancient Roman dress. They consist of a leather sole with a turned-up tip fastened to the feet by leather straps which are wound thirteen times around the leg, either on strips of cloth or on white cloth legging. Today, they are only found on the statues of shepherds around creches and on folk-dancers.

Practical information ⎯⎯⎯⎯⎯⎯⎯⎯⎯⎯
ⓘ p. De Matthaeis (Edera skyscraper), ☎ 872526; Macchia service area (autostrada A2), ☎ 78817.
🚃 ☎ 80368.
🚌 from railway station, ☎ 80647.
Car rental: *Maggiore,* v. De Matthaeis 31, ☎ 872460.

Hotels:
★★★★ *Henry,* v. Piave 10, ☎ 854321, 63 rm ⓟ ⅋ ⅋ 115,000; bkf: 9,000.
★★★ *Cesari,* v. Refice 137, ☎ 81581, 56 rm ⓟ 62,000. Rest. ♦♦♦ 25/40,000.
★★★ *Palombella,* v. Maria 234, ☎ 872163, 34 rm ⓟ ⸬ ⅋ ⅋ 55,000; bkf: 6,000.

Restaurant:
♦♦♦ *Quadrato,* p. De Matthaeis 53, ☎ 874474, closed Sun. Italian and some international dishes: dumplings alla caprese, pappardelle alla pizzaiola, 20/35,000.

Recommended
Caves: *Grotta di Pàstena,* ☎ 0776/546322.
Clay pigeon shooting: v. Selva di Polledrane, ☎ 84514.
Sports hall: v. Martiri di Vallerotonda.

GAETA

Latina 70, Rome 141 km
Pop. 23,950 ✉ 04024 ☎ 0771   E-F6

Gaeta is a beautiful site with charming Mediterranean architecture, narrow valleys and arched balconies. This historic port, described by Cicero, was a stronghold. It was besieged fourteen times and is directly tied to the history of the southern kingdom. With the advent of the Thousand and the surrender of Capua (2 November 1860), 12,000 Bourbon troops with 300 cannon shut themselves up in Gaeta, where Francis II (last king of Naples) had already retired with his family, his court, his ministers and the diplomatic corps. The siege came to an end four months later. Virgil called the city *Caieta,* after Aeneas' nurse who was buried there. Strabo thought the name was associated with the Greek *kaietas,* a cavity, referring to the caves along the coast.

▶ The modern city lies on the isthmus (B2) joining the coast to Mt. Orlando (C3) and the **ancient city** on the narrow peninsula (B-C4) which projects to the E. ▶ The oldest part of the **cathedral** (C4) is the **campanile**★, completed in 1276, with interlaced arches, inlaid majolica plates, turrets and Romanesque arabesques. The interior is Neoclassical, with an inlaid choir (16C) and a 17C crypt. The **Diocesan Museum** next door *(apply at cathedral)* contains sculptures and architectural fragments from the old church and other churches and paintings including a *Pieta*★ by Quentin Metsys. ▶ The **Museo del Centro storico culturale Gaeta** in the Palazzo De Vio *(5-9 p.m.; Sun also 9 a.m.-12 noon)* features archaeological finds, detached frescos and paintings and the standard used at the battle of Lepanto. ▶ The **castle** (C4) at the top of the picturesque **medieval quarter** has two gates. ▶ The church of the **SS. Annunziata** (B4; 1320, rebuilt in the 17C) has a fine Baroque façade and houses a polyptych by Andrea da Salerno and the **Grotta d'Oro**★ or chapel of the Immaculate Conception, a Renaissance work with nineteen paintings by Criscuolo. Pius IX retired here during the revolutionary year of 1848, together with the Grand-Duke of Tuscany and Ferdinand II Bourbon, to meditate upon the dogma of the Immaculate Conception. ▶ A scenic route leads to the top of Mt. Orlando, to the **mausoleum of Lucius Munatius Plancus**★, one of Caesar's generals (C3): there is a superb view★. ▶ At the SW edge of the mountain which delimits the **beach of Sérapo** (B1-2) is the **sanctuary of the Montagna Spaccata**★ or broken hill (C2; *8 a.m.-1 p.m. and 3-8 p.m. summer; 8 a.m.-12 noon and 2:30-5 p.m. winter).* To the r. of the church of the Trinity a fissure (produced according to legend by the earthquake which accompanied Christ's death) leads up to the **Cappella del Crocifisso** on a rock. In front of the church of the Trinity, a rocky stairway leads down to the **Grotta del Turco** (C3). From the church of the Scalzi (A2) v. Atratina leads to the ruins of the **mausoleum of Lucius Sempronius Atratinus,** prefect under Mark Antony.   ☐

Practical information ⎯⎯⎯⎯⎯⎯⎯⎯⎯⎯
≋
ⓘ p. Traniello 19 (B-C4), ☎ 462767.

GAETA

0   100   200   300 m
1 : 18.000 (1 cm = 180 m)

© SERVIZIO CARTOGRAFICO DEL TOURING CLUB ITALIANO, MILANO

Hotels:
★★★ *Flamingo,* corso Italia 109 (B1 a), ☎ 442038, 51 rm P ⫶ ▭ 72,000; bkf: 6,000.
★★★ *Ninfeo,* v. Flacca, ☎ 463088, 41 rm P ⫶ ⫶ ⫶ 76,000; bkf: 8,000.
★★★ *Serapo,* v. Firenze 11 (B2 b), ☎ 460092, 176 rm P ⫶ ⫶ ▭ ⫶ 72,000; bkf: 5,000.
★★★ *Summit,* v. Flacca, ☎ 463087, 83 rm P ⫶ ⫶ ⫶ ⫶ closed Nov-Easter, 71,500.

Restaurant:
♦ *Taverna del Marinaio,* v. Faustina 36 (B4 c), ☎ 461342, closed Wed. With summer terrace. Regional cuisine: shellfish au gratin, baked fish, 20/30,000.

Recommended
Cycling: *G. S. Ciclistico Gaeta,* v. Europa 49/F, ☎ 464588.
Marina: ☎ 460088; *Club nautico,* ☎ 460448.

GRECCIO

Rieti 13, Rome 94 km
Pop. 1,511 ⊠ 02040 ☎ 0746   C2

2 km out of Greccio a **Franciscan monastery**★ clings to the rock amid the ilex forests. The most interesting sections of the monastery *(summer*

7:30 a.m.-12 noon and 4-8 p.m.; winter 8 a.m.-12 noon and 3-6 p.m., accompanied by a friar) are the **chapel** cut into the rock, where St. Francis started the tradition of the Christmas creche (1223), St. Francis' dormitory, the 13C chapel of S. Bonaventure, the neighbouring **oratory of St. Francis** (with its 14C copy of the lost portrait of the saint wiping away his tears) and the dormitory of S.Bonaventure (with its bare wooden cells). From the loggia there is a fine view over the Reatine basin.   □

Practical information _____

Restaurant:
♦♦ *Nido del Corvo,* v. del Forno 15, ☎ 753181. Regional cuisine, 25/32,000.

Recommended
Events: commemoration of the first Franciscan dwelling, ☎ 750124.

Be advised that hotels and restaurants in this Guide have perhaps changed addresses; prices indicated are also subject to modifications.

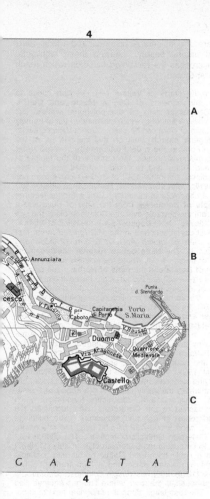

4

Grottaferrata is one of the Castelli Romani (→) and is famous for its Greek **abbey★**, which is still inhabited by Basilian monks. It was founded by St. Nilus in 1004 on the ruins of a Roman villa. At the end of the 15C Cardinal Giuliano della Rovere surrounded it with a wall, towers and moats, giving it the appearance of a fortress (work by Baccio Pontelli and Giuliano da Sangallo).

▶ The first courtyard leads through an inner court into the **museum** *(9 a.m.-12 noon and 4:30-6 p.m.; Sun 9 a.m.-12 noon and 4-6 p.m.; closed Mon)* with ancient marbles (Attic funerary stele★ of the 5C BC), medieval sculptures, vestments and precious manuscripts in the library. ▶ In the second court is the church of **S. Maria** (consecrated in 1024). The 13C campanile has triple windows, the **entrance★** to the narthex has inlaid wooden doors and a mosaic in the lunette (11C-12C); the basilica interior has a Cosmati pavement that contrasts with its 16C wooden ceiling. Above the triumphal arch is a 13C mosaic of the **Pentecost★**. The **chapel of S. Nilus★** contains frescos by Domenichino (1610). ▶ 3 km along v. Anagnina toward Rome is the huge underground palaeo-Christian cemetery known as the **catacombs ad Decimum** (3C-5C; *hols 10 a.m.-12 noon and 4-7 p.m. or 3-5 p.m. winter*). □

Practical information _____

ⓘ at Frascati, ☎ 9420331.

Hotel:
★★★ **Residenza Villaferrata,** v. Tuscolana 287, ☎ 9458820, 62 rm Ⓟ 🔶 🏧 🅱 🖃 74,000.

Restaurants:
♦♦♦ **Fico,** v. Anagnina 86, ☎ 9459214, closed Wed and Aug. In a villa with verandas, garden and pinewood. Regional cuisine: grilled kid, chicken a panzanella, 30/40,000.
♦♦ **Taverna dello Spuntino,** v. Cicerone 22, ☎ 9459366, closed Wed and Jul-Aug. Typical cantina of the Castelli Romani. Regional cuisine: ravioloni di ricotta and spinach, roast suckling pig, 25/40,000.

GUARCINO

Frosinone 22, Rome 91 km
Pop. 1,824 🖂 03016 ☎ 0775   E4

Guarcino sits on the slopes of the Ernici hills and has a fine **medieval section.** There is skiing at **Campocatino**, 18 km N. □

Practical information _____

Environs

CAMPOCATINO, 🖂 03016, ☎ 0775.
⛷ ski lifts, instruction.
ⓘ *Società Cristallo,* ☎ 441272.

ISCHIA DI CASTRO

Viterbo 41, Rome 122 km
Pop. 2,717 🖂 01010 ☎ 0761   A2

The **Palazzo Ducale** in Ischia di Castro dates from the Renaissance and was perhaps designed by Antonio da Sangallo il Giovane. The **Museo Archeologico P. Lotti** in the municipio contains finds from the Etruscan necropolis at Castro. □

Greccio, St. Francis and the Creche

In 1217, St. Francis of Assisi settled on Mt. Lacerone above Greccio in the Reatino. Six years later, the Christmas Mass of 1223 was celebrated next to a manger in a cave in the woods, surrounded by a live ox and ass. Giovanni Vellita, a landowner who had helped Francis, claimed to have seen a baby lying in the manger, Francis take it reverently in his arms, and the baby wake and smile. So, it is said, began the tradition of the Christmas creche. The oldest surviving example of such a creche dates from the end of the 13C. This is the group of statues which consists of the Three Kings, Joseph, the ox and the ass made by Arnolfo di Cambio and kept in the basilica of Santa Maria Maggiore in Rome. A relic said to be of the true creche is also located there.

GROTTAFERRATA

Rome 20 km
Pop. 15,537 🖂 00046 ☎ 06   C4

In preparing for your trip, consult the pages pertaining to the regions. You will find there the description of the region you wish to visit, as well as a list of sites that must be seen, a brief history and practical information.

298 *Latium*

LATINA

Rome 70, Milan 650 km
Pop. 96,163 ✉ 04100 ☎ 0773   D5

Latina was founded in 1932 as the administrative centre of the Pomptine plain which was then being reclaimed and cultivated. Industrial growth followed, and the town became the second largest city in Latium. 7 km away is the **Lido di Latina** on a long stretch of coast. ☐

Practical information

ⓘ v. Duca del Mare 19, ☎ 498711; Comune, ☎ 480878. 🚂 ☎ 43130.
🚌 from v. Pio VI, ☎ 493067.
Car rental: *Avis,* v. Tucci 34, ☎ 495956.

Hotel:
★★★ *De la Ville,* v. Canova 12, ☎ 498921, 68 rm Ⓟ ≋
🅿 85,000; bkf: 7,500.

Restaurants:
● ♦♦♦ *Fioretto,* v. dell'Agorà 81, ☎ 495273, closed Mon, Aug and Christmas. In classical building with veranda and fireplace, meticulous management and summer garden. Mixed cuisine: cicche del nonno, meat filet in red wine, 20/30,000.
♦♦ *Giggetto,* v. Litoreana, ☎ 20007, closed Tue, Mon eve in winter and Sep. Fine summer garden. Italian cuisine: cornmeal with sauce, scamorza alla brace, 25/35,000.
⚓ *Pineta Rio Martino,* at Borgo Grappa, ☎ 20367.

Recommended
Archery: *Compagnia Arcieri Latina,* v. Amaseno 6, ☎ 491692.
Craft workshops: *V. Bono,* v. Isonzo 194, ☎ 241776 (copper and brass).
Flying: p. del Popolo 27, ☎ 499806.
Horseback riding: at Tor Tre Ponti, ☎ 43248 (associate of *ANTE*).

LEONESSA

Rieti 35, Rome 116 km
Pop. 3,005 ✉ 02016 ☎ 0746   D2

Leonessa lies on the N slope of the Reatine hills. Around the piazza are **medieval houses** with low porches and noble **palaces** (16C-17C) run along straight, parallel streets. The town was founded in 1228. There is skiing on the slopes of **Mt. Tillia** and at **Campo Stella** *(6 km SE).* ☐

Practical information

🎿 cable car and ski lifts at Mt. Tillia; ski lifts at Campo Stella.
ⓘ municipio, ☎ 932115.

Hotel:
★★★ *Torre,* v. Crispi 2, ☎ 932167, 48 rm Ⓟ ⚓ ≋ 65,000; bkf: 7,000.

Recommended
Gastronomic specialties: black truffles and food grown in the forest.

LEPINI MOUNTAINS TO CIRCEO

From Velletri to San Felice Circeo *(114 km, 1 day; map 4)*

The Lepini hills run more or less parallel to the coast. They overlook the Pomptine plain, for centuries an inhospitable marsh. Some of the mountain towns are of considerable historical and artistic interest and natural beauty. Leaving these highlights, the tour crosses the reclaimed flatlands which reach the sea at Circeo.

▶ The route starts at **Velletri** (→). ▶ **Cori** clings to a ridge and consists of **Cori a Monte** and **Cori a Valle.** Several portions of the polygonal **walls**★ (5C BC), originally 2 km long, which surrounded the extremely ancient town of *Cora* can be seen. Cori a Valle contains: the **collegiate church,** built on the foundations of the temple of Fortune, the **v. del Porticato**★, a covered street between medieval houses, the remains of the temple of Castor and Pollux and two little churches side by side (one medieval, the other 15C) of S. Oliva *(keys from bar beside walls),* with 16C frescos, Renaissance cloister and a small archaeological museum. Cori a Monte features the **temple of Hercules**★ from the time of Sulla and a view★ from the piazzale over the Pomptine plain, the sea and the Circeo. ▶ At **Doganella** are the **ruins of Ninfa**★, a medieval city abandoned in the 17C *(guided tours, first Sat and Sun of month Apr-Oct 9 a.m.-12 noon and 2:30-6 p.m.).* The **Ninfa nature reserve** shelters many species of birds. ▶ The route then climbs to the medieval town of **Norma** and the **ruins of Norba.** The polygonal walls★ (4C BC) are 2.5 km long; inside them are the remains of temples and dwellings laid out in a regular pattern. ▶ **Sezze** has the remains of megalithic walls from the 4C BC, an interesting cathedral in mixed architectural styles, and an Antiquarium *(hols 10 a.m.-12 noon)* with prehistoric exhibits, archaic pottery and Roman mosaics. ▶ **Priverno** stands on three hills in the Amaseno Valley and has a charming central piazza with a Gothic Palazzo Comunale (13C-14C, later altered), with portico and double windows, and the Cistercian Gothic cathedral (13C). The church of S. Benedetto dates from the 9C and contains frescos from various periods. At the point where the valley opens is the **abbey of Fossanova**★★. This was a 9C Benedictine foundation, which in 1135 passed to the Cistercians, who reclaimed the land and rebuilt church and monastery. The buildings *(9 a.m.-12 noon and 3-7:30 or 5:30 p.m.)* are fine examples of Cistercian Gothic architecture. The church was the first to be built in the Cistercian style in Italy (1178-87) and has a richly decorated Gothic portal with a simple nave and two aisles inside and a high transept. The **cloister**★ (1280-1300) has double columns. Upstairs, in the guest-house, is the room where Thomas Aquinas died (1274). The road leads along the shoreline next to imperial Roman ruins of the so-called **villa of Domitian.** The route then crosses the Circeo promontory on the landward side among oaks, finishing at **San Felice Circeo** (→). ☐

Practical information

CORI, ✉ 04010, ☎ 06.

Restaurant:
♦♦ *Pigna,* v. delle Grazie 9, ☎ 9678083, closed Tue and Jul. Regional cuisine: penne all'arrabbiata, chicken alla cacciatora, 20/35,000.

Recommended
Archery: *Compagnia Arcieri Cora,* v. Roma 31, ☎ 9679493.

PRIVERNO, ✉ 04015, ☎ 0773.
ⓘ p. Vittorio Emanuele, ☎ 96230.

Restaurant:
♦ *Griglia,* at Ceriara, ☎ 924015, closed Jun and Aug. Regional cuisine: fresh pasta, meat on grill, 20/25,000.

Recommended
Craft workshops: *M. Ioteri,* v. Monti Lepini, ☎ 924011 (ceramics).

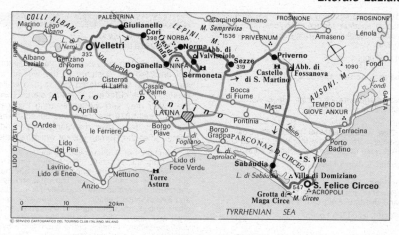

4. Lepini Mountains to Circeo

ROVINE DI NINFA

Recommended
Nature park: *Ninfa reserve,* reservations at WWF Latium, ☎ 06/8440108, or *LIPU Latina,* ☎ 0773/484993.

LIDO DI OSTIA

Rome 31 km
Pop. 85,043 ⊠ 00122 ☎ 06   B4-5

The wide beaches on the Roman seashore stretch to the l. of the Tiber. In the S are the oaks and pines of the **park of Castle Fusano★**. Further S along the shore is the scrub and forest of the **Castelporziano estate,** partly state-owned.   ☐

Practical information ————————————

≈
ⓘ p. Stazione 34, ☎ 5627892.

Hotel:
★★★ **Ping Pong,** lungomare Toscanelli 84, ☎ 5602767, 21 rm ё 68,000; bkf: 6,000.

Restaurant:
♦♦ **Ferrantelli,** v. Claudio 7/9, ☎ 5625751, closed Mon. Regional cuisine: cannelloni with fish, fettuccine al salmone, 30/45,000.

⚓ *Castelfusano Country Club,* at Castel Fusano, 1,000 pl, ☎ 5662394 (all year).

Recommended
Horseback riding: *Circolo La Mandria,* v. del Circuito di Castelfusano, ☎ 5670130, (associate of *ANTE*).
Sailing: *Lega Navale,* lungomare Duilio 36, ☎ 5626709 (instruction).
Young peoples' facilities: summer work camps organized by *WWF Latium,* at Castelporziano, ☎ 8440108.

LITORALE LAZIALE

This itinerary visits the coast of Latium on the Tyrrhenian Sea. It features a number of beaches which provide an almost uninterrupted succession of resorts.

▶ Starting from the r. bank of the Tiber, there are two shallow curves on the sandy coast, the first ending in Cape Linaro, beyond which lies Civitavecchia, and the second ending at the promontory of Argentario in Tuscany. The border of Latium is a few km down the coast. ▶ In the first stretch, the most important resort is **Fiumicino.** 3 km along the v. Portuense is the hexagonal basin of the **port of Trajan** (113) where remains of warehouses, porticos and baths line the shore. The port of Trajan was built to replace the port of Claudius (which had become silted up) and a number of Roman ships have been discovered. These are now in the **museum** *(9 a.m.-2 p.m.).* 3.5 km along the Ostia road is the **necropolis of the Isola Sacra** or Holy Island *(9 a.m.-1 hr before sunset).* ▶ Continuing NW along the coast the route reaches **Fregene** (→), **Palo, Ladispoli** and **Santa Severa.** Near a picturesque castle are the remains of **Pyrgi.** The porous rock foundations of two temples (5C BC) and remains of the walls of the later Roman colony (3C) are visible. The finds are in the **Antiquarium** *(Tue, Thu, Sat 9 a.m.-1 p.m.).* A little farther is **Santa Marinella** with the 15C Odescalchi castle. ▶ Beyond Cape Linaro and the beaches of **Civitavecchia** (→) are **Tarquinia, Lido** (→ Tarquinia) and **Montalto Marina.** ▶ Starting from the l. bank of the Tiber the route comes to **Lido di Ostia** (→) and **Tor Vaianica.** 6 km inland are the ruins of **Lavinium** *(visit by permit from Soprintendenza archeologica del Lazio).* 11 km E is **Ardea** with Palazzo Cesarini Sforza (16C), a 14C parish church and Roman and pre-Roman remains; a short distance away is the **Amici di Manzu' collection** *(9 a.m.-1:30 p.m.; closed Mon).* SE of the Anzio hill the coast forms three gulfs. The first contains **Anzio** (→), **Nettuno** (→), the beaches of **Latina** (→) and **Sabaudia** (→). ▶ In the second are **San Felice Circeo** (→), **Terracina** (→), **Lido di Fondi** and **Sperlonga** (→). ▶ In the third (between the hill of **Gaeta** (→) and the mouth of the Garigliano) are **Formia** (→), **Scauri** and **Marina di Minturno.** ☐

Practical information ————————————

FIUMICINO, ⊠ 00054, ☎ 06.

Restaurant:
● ♦♦♦ **Bastianelli al Molo,** v. Torre Clementina 312,

☎ 6440118.   Closed Mon and Aug-Sep.   Facing the sea, with agreeable summer terrace.   Regional and creative cuisine: bavette noodles with young squid, fish with fennel, 35/50,000.

LADISPOLI, ⊠ 00055, ☎ 06.
≋
ⓘ v. Duca degli Abruzzi 149/B, ☎ 9913049.

Hotel:
★★★ *Villa Margherita*, v. Duca degli Abruzzi 147, ☎ 9929089, 79 rm P ₩ 62,000.

Restaurant:
◆◆ *Sora Olga*, v. Odescalchi 99, ☎ 9929088, closed Wed except summer.   Veranda and fireplace.   Mixed cuisine: filet with red wine, mushrooms in season, 20/32,000.

⚓ *La Torretta*, v. Torre Flavia, 180 pl, ☎ 9926380.

Recommended
Events: *festival of artichokes* (Apr).
Nature park: *Bosco di Palo* nature reserve (→).

LIDO DI FONDI, ⊠ 04020, ☎ 0771.
≋
⚓ *Fondi*, v. Flacca, ☎ 555029; *Sant'Anastasia,* v. Sant'Anastasia 43, 400 pl, ☎ 59254.

MARINA DI MINTURNO, ⊠ 04020, ☎ 0771.
≋

Hotel:
★★★ *Villa Edy*, v. Lungomare 315, ☎ 680808, 20 rm P ₩ & 60,000; bkf: 7,000.

MONTALTO MARINA, ⊠ 01014, ☎ 0766.
≋

Hotel:
★★★ *Enterprise*, v. dei Tamerici 32, ☎ 820337, 76 rm P ₩ ▭ 66,000; bkf: 6,000.

⚓ *Torraccio*, v. Aurelia, 507 pl, ☎ 820077.

SANTA MARINELLA, ⊠ 00058, ☎ 0766.
≋
ⓘ v. Aurelia, corner of v. della Libertà, ☎ 737376.

Hotel:
★★★ *Najadi*, lungomare Marconi 23, ☎ 737019, 25 rm P ⅋ closed Nov, 65,000; bkf: 5,000.

⚓ *Marinella*, v. Aurelia, ☎ 736147.

Recommended
Marina: ☎ 710484.
Nature park: *Macchiatonda regional reserve*, information from *WWF Latium*, ☎ 06/8440108.

SANTA SEVERA, ⊠ 00050, ☎ 0766.
≋

Hotels:
★★★ *Fenici*, v. della Monacella 35, ☎ 740851, 28 rm P ⅋ 75,000; bkf: 8,000.
★★★ *Pino al Mare*, lungomare Pyrgi 32, ☎ 740027, 49 rm P ₩ ⅋ closed Christmas, 60,000; bkf: 5,000.
★★ *Pyrgi Mare*, lungomare Pyrgi 15, ☎ 740783, 36 rm P ₩ closed Jan, Nov and Christmas-New Year, 50,000; bkf: 8,000.

SCAURI, ⊠ 04028, ☎ 0771.
≋
ⓘ v. Marconi 23, ☎ 683400.

Restaurant:
◆ *Grappolo d'Oro*, v. Sebastiano 240, ☎ 682571, closed Sat except Jul-Aug.   Mixed cuisine: spaghetti with small clams, mixed fried fish, 20/25,000.

For the translation of a name of a meat, a fish or a vegetable, for the composition of a dish or a sauce, see the *Menu Guide* at the end of the Practical Holiday Guide; it lists the most common culinary terms.

MINTURNO

Latina 89, Rome 159 km
Pop. 17,418 ⊠ 04026 ☎ 0771   F6

In one of his last canvases, the painter Antonio Mancini depicted the costume of the women from this area: a white veil bordered with lace, a white blouse pleated at the cuffs and a scarlet skirt.   Even today, the visitor may see women wearing that same costume.   Until 1879 the town was called *Traetto* (after the nearby ferry over the Garigliano).   Today, it is named after the Roman colony which resettled here.

▶ The church of **S. Pietro** with its atrium and campanile dates from the 11C-14C.   The interior has a nave and two aisles with columns, some Roman, a 13C pulpit★ and 15C frescos in the choir.   ▶ The vault and apse of the church of the **Annunziata** (originally 14C) contain Gothic and Renaissance frescos.   ▶ 5 km away, near the Garigliano bridge, are some **ruins of Minturnae**, an Ausonian town and later a Roman colony: the arches of an aqueduct, the theatre, remains of the forum and a bath-house, and some Ausonian and Roman walls.   The Antiquarium *(9 a.m.-1 hr before sunset; closed Mon)* features marble statuary and other archaeological finds.   ▶ 17 km NE are the warm springs of the **Terma di Suio.**   □

Practical information ――――――――――――
MINTURNO

Recommended
Events: summer drama season in *Teatro Romano.*

Environs
TERME DI SUIO, ⊠ 04020, ☎ 0771.
♨ (Jun-Oct), *Terme Caracciolo Forte*, ☎ 672222.

MONTALTO DI CASTRO

Viterbo 50, Rome 114 km
Pop. 6,755 ⊠ 01014 ☎ 0766   A2

Parts of the ancient city walls and a **medieval town** lie on the border of the Tuscan and Latin Maremmas.   **Montalto Marina** is on the coast.   □

Practical information ――――――――――――
♨ (all year), at Musignano *(15 km NE)*, ☎ 437681.
Hotel:
★★★ *Vulci*, v. Aurelia, ☎ 89065, 26 rm P ₩ & ⅋ ⚘ closed Christmas, 54,000; bkf: 4,000.

MONTEFIASCONE

Viterbo 16, Rome 98 km
Pop.12,575 ⊠ 01027 ☎ 0761   B2

The octagonal **cathedral** attributed to Sammicheli (1519) stands at the top of Montefiascone.   The majestic cupola was added by Fontana in the 17C.   From the top of the hill is a view★ over Lake Bolsena, the secondary crater and the picturesque ruins of the **fortress** which housed a number of popes between the 14C and 15C.   The tombstone of the triple *Est!* (from which the wine takes its name) can be found in **S. Flaviano★**, an unusual Roman-

---

Be advised that hotels and restaurants in this Guide have perhaps changed addresses; prices indicated are also subject to modifications.

Est, est, est

In the Middle Ages, a German prelate of the Fugger Augsburg family went on a trip to Italy and became a keen connoisseur of local cuisine. He got into the habit of sending his manservant ahead to find the better inns and mark them with the designation est (meaning Vinum est bonum *or the wine is good). At Montefiascone, the servant found the wine so delicious that he wrote* est, est, est. *The master, who no doubt shared his servant's opinion, drank so much of the wine that he died. He was buried in the nearby church of San Flaviano. On his tombstone is a Latin inscription which translates: 'It is because of too much* est, est, est *that my master Jean Fugger is dead'. To this day, the local white wine has kept the name.*

esque church (12C, later reordered) on the Orvieto road. It consists of two superimposed churches. □

Practical information ————————

ⓘ v. Verentana 4, ☎ 86040.

Restaurant:
♦ *Dante,* v. Nazionale, ☎ 86015, closed Tue. Mixed cuisine: cannelloni all'etrusca, fried pike, 25/30,000.

⚱ *Amalasunta,* at Prato Roncone, v. Lago 77, 170 pl, ☎ 85294.

Recommended
Cycling: *G. S. Caprio,* v. Pini.
Wines: wine festival with various artistic, sporting and folk events (Aug), ☎ 84567.

NEMI

Rome 33 km
Pop. 1,509 ✉ 00040 ☎ 06   C4

This is one of the Castelli Romani (→). *Nemus Dianae* was the sacred grove after which the site is named. The Renaissance **Palazzo Ruspoli** in the central square has a round medieval tower. The two famous 'ships of Nemi', highly ornate floating platforms from the time of Caligula, were probably related to the cult of Diana. Discovered in 1928, the platforms were burnt in 1944. Models of these and other finds are displayed in the **Museo Nemorense** *(under renovation).* The remains of the sanctuary of Diana are nearby. □

Practical information ————————

ⓘ at Albano Laziale, ☎ 9321323.

Recommended
Events: *strawberry festival* (early Jun).

NETTUNO

Rome 60 km
Pop. 30,924 ✉ 00048 ☎ 06   C5

Winding alleys thread through the **medieval town,** which is partly enclosed by walls with round towers. The square **fort** with its rectangular ramparts may be the work of Antonio da Sangallo il Vecchio (1503). The shrine of **S. Maria Goretti** contains the mortal remains of this girl who was canonized in 1950. At **Torre Astura** 12 km SE, the remains of a

Roman villa believed to have belonged to Cicero can be seen. □

Practical information ————————

≋
ⓘ at Anzio, ☎ 9846119.

Hotels:
★★★ **Astura,** lungomare Matteotti 79, ☎ 9803343, 55 rm ⸙ ⚘ 50,000; bkf: 6,000.
★★★ **Scacciapensieri,** largo Giovanni XXIII 9, ☎ 9802428, 59 rm Ⓟ ⚘ 68,000; bkf: 4,000.

Restaurant:
♦ *Torre Astura,* at Acciarella, ☎ 452000, closed Tue and Jul. Regional cuisine, 15/25,000.

⚱ *Isola Verde,* at La Campana, v. Nettunese, 850 pl, ☎ 9871072 (all year).

Recommended
Baseball: v. Cisterna, ☎ 9805719.
Swimming: v. Nettunense, ☎ 9830146.

NORCHIA*

Viterbo 23, Rome 83 km   B2

Norchia is the site of the Etruscan city of *Orcla* which flourished between the 4C and 3C BC. Today the silent ruins of a medieval **castle** and of the parish church of **S. Pietro** (12C) greet the visitor. The unusual **necropolis** features monumental Etruscan tombs cut into the porous rock on the sides of the trenches, some with sculpted façades. Follow the *fossi di Pile* to reach the **Tomb of the Three Heads.** The Biedano Valley behind the castle contains the **Lattanzi tomb** with two superimposed porticos and the **Cava Buia,** which is a stretch of the **v. Clodia,** and the ruins of a bridge. S of the village is the **Torraccia,** the remains of a Roman mausoleum. □

ORTE

Viterbo 29, Rome 78 km
Pop. 8,027 ✉ 01028 ☎ 0761   C2

This ancient town of Etruscan origin lies in a curve of the Tiber Valley on a small rise. The **medieval town** was well preserved, but has suffered from modern development. The Romanesque church of **S. Silvestro** with a fine 16C campanile stands in a pretty piazzetta. Inside is the **Diocesan Museum of Sacred Art** *(apply to cathedral clergy),* with paintings of the Viterbo and Tuscan schools of the 13C-15C, processional crosses and a fine Byzantine Madonna, a fragment of an 8C mosaic. 8 km SW is **Vasanello,** a picturesque town famous for its pottery; it features the churches of **S. Maria Assunta** with 13C frescos and **S. Salvatore** with an elegant 13C campanile★. □

Practical information ————————

Recommended
Events: *eight-day medieval fair* and *festival of bells* (early Sep).

OSTIA ANTICA**

Rome 24 km
Pop. 3,949 ✉ 00050 ☎ 06   B4

With the first explorations at Pompeii in the 18C the shape of a typical Hellenistic Roman House came to light. The excavations at Ostia, which began in the

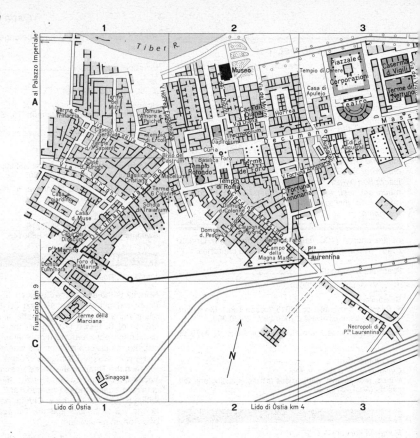

Lido di Ostia   **1**   **2**   Lido di Ostia km 4   **3**

early 19C, gave a more complete picture of Roman life. Ostia was a large town, centre of the Roman grain trade, a cosmopolitan city of traders and businessmen with up to 100,000 inhabitants. Archaeologists discovered the organization of public and private life, the construction of multi-storeyed dwellings and rented flats curiously reminiscent of modern buildings.

▶ In town, the **castle** (A6) is one of the earliest and finest examples of Renaissance military architecture (Baccio Pontelli 1483-86); the Papal apartments contain the **Museo della Rocca** of historical interest *(closed for restoration).* ▶ The excavations (A5) can be entered by the **decumanus maximus** or main EW axis of the ancient city. Along the route, or close by, are the following major monuments: the **baths of Neptune** (A3), with fine mosaics, the **barracks of the Vigili** (A3), the v. della Fontana with shops and the *caupona* (inn) of Fortunata; the pavement mosaic has an inscription inviting the customer to drink. ▶ The Augustan **theatre** was reconstructed under Septimius Severus (A3). ▶ Behind the theatre is the **piazzale delle Corporazione** (A3), its shipping companies, traders' and artisans' premises designated by signs on the mosaic pavement of the portico. Later, the v. dei Molini diverges, flanked by grain warehouses. This is crossed by the v. di Diana (A2) lined with several-storeyed terraces; the **House of Diana** has a balcony projecting from its façade. The *decumanus* opens finally into the **Forum** (A-B2), the city centre, with the **Capitolium** built by Hadrian, the **temple of Roma and Augustus** (1C), the **Forum baths,** the **Basilica,** and the **Round Temple** (3C). ▶ At the *Castrum* crossroads, the *decumanus*

bends, forming a U with the **v. della Foce** (A1). The area between the two streets contains the house of the Muses (B1) and the house of the Faces, both with fine paintings and mosaics. ▶ In the **v. degli Horrea Epagathiana** (A2) is a great commercial house. ▶ S of the first stretch of the *decumana* is the **House of Fortuna Annonaria** (B2-3), a noble house of the late imperial period. The **Domus dei Pesci** (B2) in v. Caupona was inhabited by Christians. ▶ Outside the city is the **Synagogue** (C1), the earliest place of Jewish worship in the West. ▶ The **Museo Ostiense** (A2; *9 a.m.-2 p.m.)* features exhibits of finds from the excavations and from the territory of Ostia and is an excellent complement to a visit to the ruins. ☐

Practical information _____

Restaurant:
♦♦ *Sbarco di Enea,* v. dei Romagnoli 675 (A5 a), ☎ 5650034, closed Mon and Feb. Fine summer pergola. Mixed cuisine: pennette with salmon, risotto pescatora, 25/35000.

⚑ *Capitol,* v. di Castelfusano 195, ☎ 5662720 (all year).

PALESTRINA*

Rome 38 km
Pop. 14,337 ☒ 00035 ☎ 06   D4

See map on page 304.

The sanctuary of Fortuna Primigenia (or Praenestina) was named after the city of Praeneste from which the modern name derives. It had been a place of worship for probably a century when, in 82 BC, Sulla

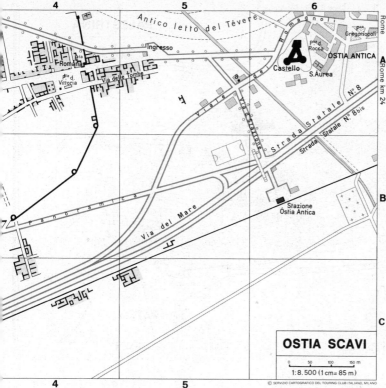

OSTIA SCAVI

0   50   100   150 m
1:8.500 (1 cm= 85 m)

© SERVIZIO CARTOGRAFICO DEL TOURING CLUB ITALIANO, MILANO

punished the city which had supported Marius by destroying it and removing its colonial status. He rebuilt the temple, however, and in the 4C AD it was still in use. The little town which occupies the site today preserves the ancient complex.

▶ The **cathedral** stands in p. Regina Margherita (B2) the site of the pre-Sullan Forum of Praeneste. Rebuilt in the 12C, the church has a medieval façade and campanile. Traces of the ancient building on which it is built are still visible. ▶ The **Area sacra** *(under restoration),* a basilica cut into the slope of a hill, can be reached from the piazza. The **Atrio delle Sorti** (B2), a cave carved into the rock and extended with walls, is nearby. It contains a **mosaic★** pavement depicting the sea-bed (1C BC). ▶ At the E end is the great **apsidal hall** (B2), perhaps the shrine of an oriental cult. ▶ The **sanctuary★** is higher up (above v. del Borgo). Two great ramps converged here, leading to the **terrazza degli Emicicli.** The terrace above is the **terrazzo dei Fornici,** the rear walls of which are decorated alternately with doors and arches framed by half-columns. Further up still is the **terrazza della Cortina** which is very steep and surrounded by porticos. The sanctuary complex can be entered from p. della Cortina (B2; *9 a.m.-1 hr before sunset; Jun-Aug up to 7:30, closed Mon).* The highest part of the sanctuary is now occupied by the **Palazzo Barberini** (1640). It houses the **Museo Archeologico Prenestino★** (A-B2; *same times as sanctuary).* The rooms, some decorated with frescos by the Zuccari, contain precious finds from Praenestine territory, fragments of the sanctuary itself, and a reconstruction of the complex, bronze mirrors★, and the great mosaic of the **Nile in Flood★** (perhaps 1C BC), a copy of

an Alexandrian painting. ▶ 4 km away is **Castel San Pietro Romano,** whose polygonal wall encircling the acropolis of Praeneste has been preserved. There is a superb view★. □

Practical information

♨ (Jun-Oct), ☎ 9557901.
ⓘ p. Regina Margherita (B2).

Restaurants:
● ♦♦♦ *Vecchia Osteria,* at Làbico, v. Casilina, ☎ 9510032. An old postal stopping-place, prettily restored. Excellent creative cuisine, 40/45,000.
♦♦ *Stella,* p. della Liberazione 3 (B1 a), ☎ 9558367. Italian cuisine: pappardelle with hare, chicken Nerone, 16/22,000.

Recommended
♥ crafts: embroidery, copper and ironwork.

Forest of PALO

B4

The Bosco di Palo **(nature reserve)** has been set up on the site of the Etruscan *Alsium* at Palo on the coast. It is managed by the *World Wildlife Fund,* and has extremely interesting flora and fauna *(guided tours).* Near **Castello Odescalchi** *(no visits),* beneath the **Villa La Posta,** are the remains of a large **Roman villa★** *(no visits),* richly decorated with mosaics (3C-4C). □

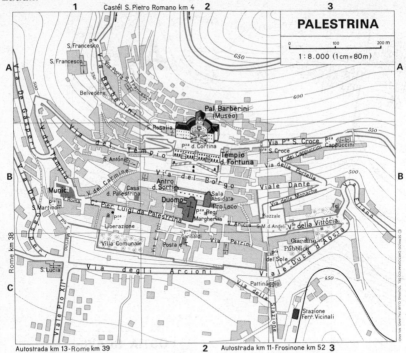

PALESTRINA

0   100   200 m

1 : 8.000 (1cm=80m)

Castél S. Pietro Romano km 4 2 3

Autostrada km 13-Rome km 39 2 Autostrada km 11-Frosinone km 52 3

Practical information

ⓘ open Sep-May, visits on Thu and Sun (10 a.m. and 2 p.m.); group visits on Sat can be booked in advance at *Guardia dell'Oasi,* ☎ 06/9911641.

PONZA ISLAND

Latina 89, Rome 159 km
Pop. 3,203 ✉ 04027 ☎ 0771   A-B6

This is the largest island in the **Ponza archipelago,** which consists of two groups of volcanic islands (Ponza, Gavi, Zannone and Palmarola to the W, Ventatene and Santo Stefano to the E). The island is 8 km long and its shores are broken by banks of coloured volcanic rock alternating with inlets and beaches. The main town is **Ponza,** encircling the port. 1 km W is the beach of **Chiaia di Luna.** There is a motorboat tour around the island (5-6 hrs). 7.3 km away by boat is the **island of Palmarola,** with spectacular cliffs. ☐

Practical information

⛴ ferries from Formia (2.5 hrs); Terracina (2.5 hrs); Anzio (3 hrs); motorship from San Felice Circeo (1 hr); ferry from Formia to Ventotene, *c.* 2 hrs.
≋ v. Roma 3, ☎ 80031; at Ventotene, p. Castello, ☎ 85193.

Hotels:
★★★★ *Chiaia di Luna,* contrada Chiaia di Luna, ☎ 80133, 65 rm Ⓟ ⟨ ⟨ ☒ closed Nov-Apr, 84,000; bkf: 18,000.
★★★ *Baia,* v. Nuova 16, ☎ 80045, 22 rm ⟨ ☒ closed 21 Sep-31 May. No restaurant, 75,000.

★★★ *Cernia,* v. Panoramica, ☎ 80412, 50 rm Ⓟ ⟨ ⟨ ☒ ☒ ⸰° closed Nov-Mar. No restaurant, 78,000; bkf: 9,000.

Restaurants:
◆◆ *Mimi,* v. Dietro la Chiesa, ☎ 80338, open in season. Regional cuisine: oysters Palmarola, baked fish, 40/55,000.
◆ *Amedeo all'Aragosta,* p. Pisacane 13, ☎ 80102. Campanian cuisine: potato gattò, stuffed peperoni, 30/40,000.
◆ *Eéa,* v. Umberto I, ☎ 80100, closed Oct-May. Regional cuisine: pickled anchovies, spaghetti with crawfish, 25/40,000.

Recommended
Boat trips: to islands of Palmarola and Zannone, trip around the island of Ponza: boat rental in harbour.
Young peoples' facilities: week-long holidays for divers and trippers, *Club Ventotene,* v. Roma 13, ☎ 85085 (in Rome ☎ 06/877469); hostel combined with a sailing school, *Nuova Compagnia delle Indie,* v. Olivi 37, ☎ 85185 (in Rome, ☎ 06/679091).

RIETI

Rome 80, Milan 565 km
Pop. 43,632 ✉ 02100 ☎ 0746   D2

The adjoining p. Vittorio Emanuele and C. Battisti (B1) form the city centre. The **Palazzo Comunale** houses the **Museo Civico** *(8:30 a.m.-1:30 p.m.; closed hols):* prehistoric finds, Roman and medieval sculptures, processional crosses, goldwork, paintings from the 13C to 19C, and Canova's original cast of Hebe. The second piazza contains the **Palazzo della Prefettura** (B1), with a double loggia (1596) on its side, and the **cathedral★** (12C-13C, restored in the

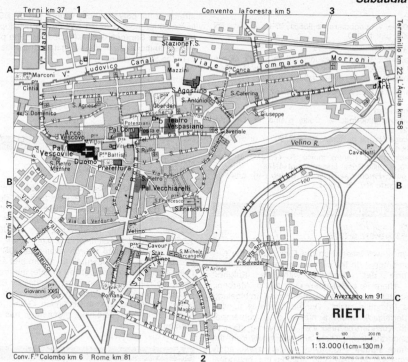

Terni km 37 **1**

Convento laForesta km 5 **3**

Conv. F.^{le} Colombo km 6   Rome km 81   **2**

RIETI

0   100   200 m

1:13.000 (1cm=130m)

© SERVIZIO CARTOGRAFICO DEL TOURING CLUB ITALIANO, MILANO

17C) with Romanesque campanile, interesting works of art and a 12C crypt. The adjoining baptistery houses the **Treasury Museum** *(apply to sacristy; Tue and Thu 10 a.m.-12 noon, Sat and Sun 4-6 p.m.)* with works from the cathedral and other churches of the Reatino. Next door is the **bishop's palace★**, joined by the papal loggia (1288) which opens on the ground floor into the portico of the **volte del Vescovado★** (13C) and the raised bridge known as the **arco del Vescovo★** (13C). Other interesting churches are **S. Agostino** (A2) with 13C-14C exterior and **S. Francesco** (B2) *(closed for restoration)*. The 13C **walls** can be seen in the N span from the **Porta Cintia** (A1) to the **Porta d'Arci** (A3).

Environs

▶ 2 km away on v. Salaria toward Rome is **Fonte Cottarella**. ▶ There are Franciscan religious houses at **Fonte Colombo** *(5.5 km SW);* **La Foresta** *(5 km N);* **Poggio Bustone** *(19 km N)* and **Greccia** (→).   □

Practical information _____

⚓ (Jun-Oct), ☎ 41155.
ℹ v. Cintia 87 (B1), ☎ 41146; p. Vittorio Emanuele II 18 (B1), ☎ 43220.
🚂 (A2), ☎ 43143.
🚌 from railway station, ☎ 44382.

Hotels:
★★★ *Miramonti,* p. Oberdan 5 (A2 b), ☎ 41333, 30 rm. No restaurant, 66,000.
★★★ *Quattro Stagioni,* p. Battisti 14 (B1 a), ☎ 43306, 38 rm 🅿 ⚒ 60,000; bkf: 8,000.

★★ *Massimo D'Azeglio,* v. Canali 4 (A1 c), ☎ 41710, 32 rm ⚒ No restaurant, 32,000.

Restaurant:
♦♦♦ *Checco - al Calice d'Oro,* v. Marchetti 10 (A2 b), ☎ 44271, closed Mon and Aug. Comfortable rooms with paintings by well-known artists. Regional cuisine: linguine alla pecorara, fregnacce pancakes alla sabinese, 25/35,000.

Recommended
Events: *festival of the Sun* (Jul).
Farm vacations: *Cooperativa Vallecceriola,* at Contigliano, ☎ 756440.
Flying: *Centrale di Volo a Vela* (gliding), v. Rosatelli, ☎ 43127-42138; *Aeroclub della Sabina,* ☎ 43637 (Italian gliding championships in Aug, and other gliding events).
Swimming: v. Madonna del Cuore; v. dello Sport.

Latina 24, Rome 96 km
Pop. 13,012 ✉ 04016 ☎ 0773   D6

This modern little town stands between two sections of Lake Sabaudia. There are resorts on the shore and S of the lake at **Baia d'Argento**. The **Circeo National Park** lies behind. 4 km away at Molella are the **Springs of Lucullus**.   □

Practical information _____

ℹ p. del Comune 18, ☎ 55046.
≈

Hotel:
★★★★ *Dune*, v. Lungomare, ☎ 55551, 77 rm Ⓟ ⌕ ⋙ ▣ ◢◉ 110,000; bkf: 15,000.

Restaurant:
◆ *Pineta*, corso Vittorio Emanuele 110, ☎ 55053; closed Tue and 20 Dec-20 Jan. Fine garden and pergola. Seafood: lobster tagliatelle, grilled fish, 22/40,000.

⚓ *Sabaudia*, in Sant'Andrea, 250 pl, ☎ 57757.

Recommended
Clay pigeon shooting: v. Colle d'Alba di Levante, ☎ 50242.
Flying: *Lega Navale di Roma*, ☎ 06/6780017 or 6780070 (instruction).
Horseback riding: *Centro ippico S. Giorgio*, at Baia d'Argento, v. delle Rose, (associate of *ANTE*).
Nature park: *Parco Nazionale del Circeo* (→), office at v. Carlo Alberto 107, ☎ 57251.

SAN FELICE CIRCEO

Latina 33, Rome 106 km
Pop. 7,963 ⊠ 04017 ☎ 0773   D6

The town is well located on the E slopes of the Circeo promontory. In the central square is the medieval **Torre dei Templari** with its **Knights' House.** There is a **Belvedere★** in the p. Marconi: views stretch out as far as the Ponza archipelago and the Pomptine plain. On the beach is a cave *(visits permitted)* where a human skull contemporary with Neanderthal man was discovered (next to the Neanderthal Inn). There are also views from the **Semaphore station** 4 km away *(military zone: apply for permission to visit)*; this adjoins the polygonal **walls** of the acropolis of the ancient *Circei* (4C-3C BC). 2.5 km away is the **grotta delle Capre** cave. 3 km along the high road on the S slope of the promontory is the **Torre Cervia lighthouse. Torre Paola**, built by Paul III, is 7 km away at the W end of the Circeo, by the Roman outlet for Lake Sabaudia. The sea is reached at the **Caves of Circe the Witch.**   □

Practical information

≋
ℹ️ p. Lanzuisi 4, ☎ 527770; lungomare, ☎ 527013.
⛴ daily motorship to Ponza (Jun-Sep), 1 hr, *Tala Mata Navigazione*, ☎ 528809.

Hotel:
★★★ *Punta Rossa*, at Quarto Caldo, v. delle Batterie 37, ☎ 528069, 40 rm Ⓟ ⌕ ⌕ ⋙ ⋙ ▣ Pens. closed Nov-May, 150,000.

Recommended
Caves: *Grotta Guattari* (inside grounds of Hotel Neanderthal), lungomare Circe 33, ☎ 5280126.
Discothèque: *Nautilus Club*, v. Bergamini 1, ☎ 527821.
Marina: *Circeo Yacht Vela Club*, ☎ 527033.

SEGNI

Rome 57 km
Pop. 8,434 ⊠ 00037 ☎ 06   D5

Segni's **cathedral** (originally Romanesque but rebuilt in the 17C) contains a *Madonna and Saints* by Pietro da Cortona. On top of the hill is the **acropolis** and the 3C BC enclosure of a temple (perhaps the *Capitolium*) built of polygonal blocks. The larger enclosure is now occupied by the **church of S. Pietro**, 13C with frescos from the 13C to the 16C. Behind the church is a 3C BC circular **cistern★**. The best preserved

stretch of the **polygonal city walls★** (6C-5C BC; 2 km in circumference) is to the NW on the hill-slope, with the famous **Saracen Gate★** (footpath). The **passeggiata Pianillo** leads to the summit, with a wide view★ over the Sacco valley.   □

Practical information

Hotel:
★★ *Pace*, v. Cappuccini 9, ☎ 9767084, 45 rm Ⓟ ⋙ ⋘ 35,000; bkf: 4,000.

SERMONETA

Latina 17, Rome 74 km
Pop. 6,545 ⊠ 04010 ☎ 0773   D5

This medieval town stands on a ridge of the Lepini hills, overlooked by the majestic **castello dei Caetani★**. Built by local lords, it dates from the first half of the 13C and was later extended and altered *(groups, 11:30 a.m.-12:30 p.m.; hols 10:30 a.m.-12:30 p.m. and 3-7 p.m. or 2-5 p.m. winter; closed Thu)*. The **collegiate church** retains its 13C Cistercian Gothic style. It features an atrium and a magnificent Romanesque campanile. Inside, the first chapel on the r. has a *Madonna degli Angeli* by Benozzo Gozzoli. 3 km NE along the Sezze road is the **abbey of Valvisciolo**, a Cistercian Gothic building from 1240. The adjoining monastery has a 13C **cloister★**.   □

SORA

Frosinone 30, Rome 114 km
Pop. 26,248 ⊠ 03039 ☎ 0776   F4

Sora's **cathedral** was consecrated in 1155, rebuilt in the Cistercian style, and reordered in the 17C. It still has its Romanesque portal and campanile. The interior (restored in the Gothic manner) features a 15C wooden triptych. Beneath the building are the remains of a Roman temple from the end of the 4C BC. 6.6 km away is the **Island of Liri** with the 11C church of S. Domenico (Gothic interior and crypt with Roman capitals); and the Liri falls★ (Valcatoio and Cascata Grande); a little further on, by Anitrella (13 km), are the **Anitrella falls.** 8.5 km NE is the pretty village of **Càmpoli Appennino★**.   □

Practical information

Hotel:
★★★ *Motel Valentino*, v. Napoli 56, ☎ 831071, 70 rm Ⓟ 50,000; bkf: 5,000.

Recommended
Cycling: *G. S Cicilistico Sora*, v. Balbo 35, ☎ 831977.

SPERLONGA

Latina 57, Rome 127 km
Pop. 3,838 ⊠ 04029 ☎ 0771   E6

The ancient part of Sperlonga is huddled on a precipitous ledge over the sea. Its white houses are connected by alleys and steps. Below lies the lovely **Angolo** beach fringed with olive trees. 1 km away is the **cave of Tiberius★**, a large cavity open to the sea which was once part of Tiberius' sumptuous villa. The cave was decorated with Hellenistic sculptures of Homeric subjects. Over 10,000 fragments have been found and are now exhibited in the nearby **Museo Nazionale Archeologico di Sperlonga** *(9 a.m.-1 hr before sunset).* ☐

Practical information _____

≋

ⓘ p. Europa, ☎ 54796.

Hotel:
★★★ *Motel Miralago,* v. Flacca, ☎ 54129, 22 rm Ⓟ ⪡ 𝔐 ⅋ closed Christmas, 52,000; bkf: 5,000.

Restaurant:
♦♦♦ *Laocoonte - da Rocco,* v. Colombo 4, ☎ 54122, closed Mon. Terrace facing the sea. Seafood: clams al salmone, linguine agli scampi, 30/50,000.

⚓ *Nord Sud,* v. Flacca, 247 pl, ☎ 54255.

Recommended
Marina: at Gaeta, ☎ 460088.
Water skiing: *Sci Club Laghetto,* SS Flacca, ☎ 54042.
Wind surfing: *Associazione tavola a vela,* p. della Repubblica 3, ☎ 723340.
Youth hostels: *Ostello Marina degli Ulivi,* contrada Fiorelle, ☎ 54416.

SUBIACO*

Rome 70 km
Pop. 8,993 ✉ 00028 ☎ 0774   D4

'Nero was dining in a villa called Sublaqueum by the Simbruine lake, when all of a sudden tables and food were struck by lightning' (Tacitus). It was Nero who created the lake (Stagno Simtruina) by damming the flow of the Aniene; the villa gave birth to the town (Subiaco, from Sublaqueum) where the slaves employed on the great construction projects lived. Nearly five hundred years later, Benedict of Nursia came here to seek peace away from Rome.

▶ The city is entered by the **medieval hump-backed bridge** over the Aniene. ▶ Beyond is the church of **S. Francesco** (1327) with frescos attributed to Sodoma and a triptych by Antoniazzo Romano (1467). ▶ The monasteries are reached by the Vallepietra road which skirts the ruins of **Nero's villa.** ▶ The only survivor of the thirteen foundations set up by Benedict of Nursia in the area is the **monastery of St. Scholastica★** *(9 a.m.-12 noon and 4-7 p.m.; hols 8-9:45 a.m. and 11 a.m.-12 noon and 4-7 p.m. or 3:30-6:30 p.m. winter; a monk acts as guide).* It is possible to visit the cloisters: the first cloister has a garden, the second is Gothic with a great flamboyant **arch★** surmounted by the **campanile★** (1052), the third **cloister★**, with its slender marble columns, some paired, and fine capitals is the work of the Cosmati (beginning of the 13C); the **church** of St. Scholastica (sister of St. Benedict) has a 13C façade over the second cloister, whilst the interior is 18C by G. Quarenghi. ▶ The **monastery of St. Benedict** or **Sacred Cave★★** *(9 a.m.-12 noon and 3-6:30 p.m. from Easter to Sep; 5:30 other months)* was built at the end of the 12C over the cave where Benedict spent the first years of his monastic life. A path leads to the group of buildings which cling to the rock. There are 15C Umbrian frescos in the passages leading to the **upper church★** (mid 14C), which has a number of rooms with 14C Sienese frescos and Umbrian-Marches frescos of 1430, and a 13C pulpit. The **lower church★★** consists of a number of chapels with 13C frescos (largely the work of the master Consolo), 14C Sienese frescos, and 15C frescos in the **chapel of St. Gregory.** This finally leads into the Sacred Cave in which Benedict lived. A painting of **St. Francis★** was done in 1223 when the saint was in Subiaco. ☐

Benedict of Nursia

Benedict and his twin sister Scholastica were born c. 480 in Nursia (modern Norcia) in Umbria. Benedict left his studies in Rome for the wastelands of Subiaco. Thirty years later, he traveled to Montecassino and helped to build the most famous of all Benedictine monasteries. Monastic life in the west, both in centuries past and today, was shaped by Benedict. In his day some monks lived in solitude (the hermits or anchorites). Others (cenobitic monks) lived the common life. The Rule of Benedict, the foundation of western monastic life, deals with the latter. The monastery was seen as a community which provided for the physical and spiritual needs of its members. According to Benedict, it should be located in a solitary place and was conceived as a city, surrounded by walls, with a church, oratory, dormitories, cells for guests, pilgrims and the poor, a refectory, kitchen, cellar, garden, mill, workshops, library and scriptorium where books were produced. The surrounding land was to be cultivated for food. The abbot was elected for life; the community was egalitarian and rules prescribed a simple life of manual work, study and prayer. Benedict died at Montecassino at the age of sixty-seven, forty days after his sister Scholastica, and was buried beneath the altar of John the Baptist, on the site of the altar of Apollo in the great temple he had demolished. Benedict's disciple Maurus took an autograph copy of the Rule to France, while a second was copied by Abbot Teodemaro in the 8C and was later given to Charlemagne.

Practical information _____

⚡ ski lifts, skating at Monte Livata *(15 km E).*
ⓘ v. Cadorna 59, ☎ 85397.

Hotel:
★★ *Belvedere,* v. dei Monasteri 33, ☎ 85531, 20 rm Ⓟ 𝔐 ⅋ 36,000.

Restaurant:
♦♦ *Genziana,* at Monte Livata, v. dei Boschi 16, ☎ 86100, closed Tue, 1 Sep-20 Dec and 25 Apr-30 Jun. Near ski slopes. Regional cuisine: fettuccine alla ciociara, dumplings, 17/25,000.

Recommended
Canoeing: *Scuola Canoanium Club,* v. Dante Alighieri 34, ☎ 83419 (06/7980840 in Rome).

SUTRI

Viterbo 28, Rome 53 km
Pop. 3,631 ✉ 01015 ☎ 0761   B3

This picturesque town located on a rocky ridge consists of dark medieval and Renaissance houses, narrow streets, the Etruscan city walls and various ruins.

▶ The **cathedral** retains its original Romanesque campanile, portal and Cosmati paving. ▶ On v. Cassia is the **Roman amphitheatre★**, probably from the 1C BC, entirely cut from the rock. ▶ A short distance away is the shrine of the **Madonna del Parto** *(keys from municipio),* which was converted in the Middle Ages into Christian worship. ☐

Practical information _____

ⓘ p. del Comune 31, ☎ 68330 (eve only).

TARQUINIA*

Viterbo 42, Rome 96 km
Pop. 13,368 ☒ 01016 ☎ 0766   A3

This Etruscan city (Tarquinia is the Latin name) was known in the Latin Maremma as *La Civita*. The city enjoyed great cultural power and influence. By the end of the 4C, it was absorbed by Rome. It had apparently been founded in the 13C or 12C BC (though the earliest archeological evidence dates from the 9C) by Tarchon, son or brother of Tyrrhenus, the eponymous ancestor of the Etruscans. Modern Tarquinia (known until 1922 as Corneto) was created in the 7C when the survivors of a malaria epidemic moved to a hill near the Etruscan site. The necropolis was mainly excavated in the last century. 2,000 tombs were already known by 1839. Three times as many (though only a small proportion of these with paintings) have been identified in recent work by the Fondazione Lerici. The tombs (7C to the Roman period) are underground chamber-tombs, and dot the countryside E of the city. Most of the decorations depict funeral games, banquets, and dances in honour of the departed.

▶ In the p. Cavour at the entrance to the city is the splendid Renaissance Gothic shape of the **Palazzo Vitelleschi★** (B2; 1436-39), with a superb **court★** enclosed on two sides by a double order of arches surmounted **with** loggias. ▶ Here is housed the **Museo Nazionale Tarquiniese★★** *(May-Sep 9 a.m.-2 p.m. and 4-7 p.m.; other months 9 a.m.-2 p.m.; closed Mon)*, one of the largest collections of Etruscan antiquities, figured funeral stones,

sarcophagi, sculptures and paintings, furniture from the archaic necropolis, funeral goods from the 7C and 6C BC, precious painted **vases★** both Greek and local, a high relief of **two horses★** from a terra-cotta frieze, bronze objects, and the **complete cycles of paintings★** from various tombs removed for conservation. These include the tomb of the chariot race, the triclinium, the ship, the Olympiads, the funeral couch, and the black sow. The Vitelleschi chapel with wooden coffered ceiling and 15C frescos is also on view. ▶ The **cathedral** (A2) has noteworthy frescos★ by Pastura (1509). Next to the castle with ruins of the medieval enceinte is the Romanesque church of **S. Maria di Castello★** (A1; *attendant in the neighbouring house*), with a simple façade and basilica plan, Cosmati paving and pulpit, and a tabernacle of 1166. ▶ Piazza Matteotti (A-B2) has a fine position on the hill-top, an 18C fountain and the **Palazzo Municipale,** in which portions of Roman building work are visible, particularly at the rear. ▶ The **medieval quarter** in the N of the city is picturesque with its churches, towers and old houses. Among these are the church of **S. Martino** (A2; 13C) and the Romanesque-Gothic church of the SS. Anunziata (A2; 12C-13C). ▶ The church of **S. Francesco** (B3) is Romanesque and Gothic, with a 14C campanile. ▶ The Romanesque church of **S. Maria di Valverde** (B1; *apply to the cathedral clergy*) has a Byzantine style Madonna in marble from the 15C. ▶ The **Etruscan necropolis★★** *(apply to the museum; May-Sep 9 a.m.-1 hr before sunset; other months 9 a.m.-2 p.m.; closed Mon; only 4 tombs visited each day in rotation)* is 4 km away on the hill of Monterazzi. The most interesting tombs are those of the Augurs (mid-6C BC), of the Baron (6C-5C BC), Hunting and Fishing (2nd half of the 6C BC), the Mushrooms (6C BC), the Jugglers (end 6C BC), the Lionesses (end 5C BC), the Leopards (5C BC), of Orcus (4C-3C BC) and the Bulls. ▶ 6 km away on the coast is **Tarquinia Lido;** to the S the remains of **Porta Clementina,**

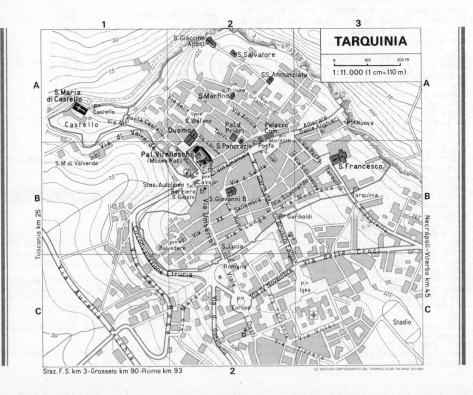

TARQUINIA

0   100   200 m
1:11.000 (1 cm=110 m)

an ancient Roman port, where excavations have brought to light part of the Roman colony of the **Etruscan port** (6C BC), and of a **sanctuary** visited by Greeks. N of the Lido is **Marina di Velca**. □

Practical information _____

📖 p. Cavour 1 (B2), ☎ 856384.

Hotels:
★★★★ *G. H. Helios*, at Tarquinia Lido, v. Porto Clementino, ☎ 88617, 95 rm ℗ ✿ 🖃 105,000.
★★★ *Tarconte, v. della Tuscia 19* (C2 a), ☎ 856002, 53 rm ℗ ૐ 63,000.
★★ *Velcamare*, at Tarquinia Lido, v. degli Argonauti 1, ☎ 88024, 20 rm ℗ 🏊 ૐ ✿ closed 5 Nov-30 Jan, 65,000. Rest. ♦♦ closed Tue. Mixed regional cuisine: crawfish in green sauce, roast lamb, 25/35,000.

Restaurant:
♦♦ *Antico Ristorante Giudizi*, p. Cavour (B2 b), ☎ 855061, closed Mon. In a former 13th-century monastery. Mixed regional cuisine: risotto alla pescatora, roast lamb, 25/35,000.

⚓ *Europing Tarquinia*, at Riva dei Tarquini, v. Aurelia, 500 pl, ☎ 814010; *Tuscia Tirrenica*, at Tarquinia Lido, v. Aurelia, 480 pl, ☎ 88294.

Recommended
Cycling: *G. S. Amatori*, v. Umberto I 7, ☎ 856544.
Golf: at Marina Velca, ☎ 812109 (*7 km SE*, 9 holes, also swimming pool and tennis).
Visits to workshops: *Etrusco Ludens*, v. Granari 18, ☎ 855175 (ceramics).

TERMINILLO

Rieti 21, Rome 99 km
                                                        D2

The ski resorts on the slopes of Terminillo are **Pian de' Valli** and **Campoforogna**. There is a chair lift to **Terminiletto** with a fantastic view★. □

Practical information _____

PIAN DE' VALLI, ✉ 02017, ☎ 0746.
☃ cableway, chair lift, ski lifts, downhill slopes at Pian dè Valli and Campoforogna (instruction).
📖 v. Covemese, ☎ 61121.

Hotels:
★★★★ *Cristallo*, v. dei Licheni, ☎ 61112, 50 rm ℗ ᧒ ✿ closed Sep-Jun and 20 Dec-10 Apr, 105,000; bkf: 10,000.
★★★★ *Togo Palace*, p. Zamboni 10, ☎ 61271, 43 rm ℗ ૐ closed 6 Sep-14 Dec and 21 Apr-30 Jun, 90,000; bkf: 8,000.
★★ *Bucaneve*, v. degli Appennini 76, ☎ 61237, 16 rm ℗ ⚞ ᧒ ✿ closed 1 Sep-19 Dec and 11 Apr-30 Jun, 33,000.

Recommended
Youth hostel: *Ostello della Neve*, at Terminillo Anello Panoramico, ☎ 61169.

TERRACINA

Latina 39, Rome 109 km
Pop. 37,596 ✉ 04019 ☎ 0773   E6
See map on page 310.

Legend states that the city was founded by Spartans unable to endure the Lycurgan legislation. Etruscan expansion may be indicated by the name of the site (from Tarcina), while the Volsci who held it for a century called it by the name of their protector deity *Anxur*. It was taken by the Romans in 406 BC. The landscape makes it easy to imagine traces of the Romans, but the town itself is stamped with the architecture of the Gothic period (13C-14C).

▶ **Piazza del Municipio**★(B2), centre of the medieval city, is on the site of the ancient forum of the Republican city, and still has its original Roman paving stones. ▶ Facing onto the square is the **cathedral**★ (B1-2), on the ruins of the great temple; it has a **portico**★ with lovely 12C frieze and mosaic. The **campanile**★ is 13C, and the interior, reworked in the 18C, retains a fine mosaic pavement of the 12C-13C, a superb **ambo**★ and a Paschal candlestick★. ▶ The grain tower, forming part of the municipio, houses the **Museo Archeologico**, with Roman exhibits (B2; *May-Sep 9 a.m.-1 p.m. and 5-7 p.m.; closed Mon; other months 9 a.m.-2 p.m.; closed holidays*). ▶ Opposite the town hall is a portico which formed the *Porticus post scaenam* of the theatre. Up the salita dell'Annunziata (B2) is one of the arches which led into the forum, and the forum basilica close by. ▶ The summit of Mt. Sant'Angelo is reached by a scenic route some 3 km long crossing the **acropolis walls**. Here is the **Temple of Jupiter Anxur**★ (B3) built in the 1C BC. The platform and foundations survive. □

Practical information _____

〰
📖 v. Lungo Linea 156 (B2), ☎ 727759.
⛴ daily ferry to Ponza, twice daily in Jul and Aug, Linee Mazzella, ☎ 0771/80261.

Hotels:
★★★ *G. H. L'Approdo*, lungomare Circe (C2 a), ☎ 727671, 52 rm ℗ ᧒ 🏊 80,500.
★★★ *G. H. Palace*, lungomare Matteotti 2 (C3 b), ☎ 752585, 73 rm ℗ 52,000; bkf: 7,000.
★★★ *Riva Gaia*, v. Friuli-Venezia Giulia 10, ☎ 730166, 70 rm ℗ 🏊 ⚞ closed Dec-Feb, 53,000; bkf: 6,000.
★★★ *River*, at Porto Badino, ☎ 730681, 94 rm ℗ 🏊 ✿ 🖃 closed Oct-Mar, 65,000; bkf: 6,500.

Restaurants:
♦♦♦ *Capannina*, v. Appia (C3 c), ☎ 752539, closed Jun and 1-20 Dec. Overlooking the bay on one side and the temple of Jove Anxur on the other. Mixed cuisine: risotto alla pescatora, grilled meats, 30/40,000.
♦♦♦ *Hostaria Porto Salvo*, v. Appia (B-C3 d), ☎ 726251. Closed Mon and Nov. By the sea. Seafood: seasonal risotto, foil-wrapped fish, 35/50,000.
♦♦ *Miramare*, lungomare Circe 32 (C1 e), ☎ 727332, closed Tue and 20 Nov-31 Jan. Large veranda, a few steps from the beach. Mixed regional cuisine: tagliolini noodles with scampi, langouste all'americana, 25/35,000.

⚓ *Europa*, at Acqua Santa, v. Appia, 180 pl, ☎ 726523.

Recommended
Marina: ☎ 727238.
Tennis: v. Valle d'Aosta, ☎ 730693; v. Badino, ☎ 71516; v. Guardiola, ☎ 792194.

TIVOLI*

Rome 31 km
Pop. 52,237 ✉ 00019 ☎ 0774   D4

So numerous were the villas here, according to Horace, that 'the Tiburtine soil no longer has any ploughland'. At that time none of the three villas which today form the principal attraction of the place, the villa of Hadrian (→), the villa d'Este, or the Gregoriana, were in existence. These three make a fascinating tour illustrating the use of nature in architecture.

▶ The church of **S. Maria Maggiore** (C1) rebuilt in the 16C has a Gothic portal and rose window, and a Cosmati pavement inside. R. of the church façade is the entrance to the **villa d'Este**★★ (B-C1; *9 a.m.-1 hr before sunset; closed Mon*). This was built in the 16C for Cardinal Ippolito II d'Este by Pirro Ligorio, who also designed the park and some of the fountains. The rooms of the palace are decorated with 16C Roman school frescos. The loggia on the façade has a wonderful view over the **gar-**

TERRACINA

0   100   200   300 m

1:16.000 (1 cm = 160 m)

den★★, descending in symmetrical terraces, with stunning planting and remarkable fountains. The staircase leads down to the **fontana del Bicchierone** by Bernini and the **viale delle 100 fontane**, their waters shooting up among the statues, and to the **fontana dell'Ovato;** thence to the **Rometta,** a reproduction in miniature of the ancient sites of Rome, the **fontana dei Draghi,** the **fontana dell'Organo idraulico,** ending in the square of the **rotunda of Cypresses.** ▶ The church of S. **Pietro alla Carità** (B1), originally 5C, has a nave and two aisles with antique columns placed here in the 12C. ▶ The charming v. Campitelli leads into p. del Colonnato, with its Romanesque church of S. **Silvestro** (B1). ▶ V. del Colle winds between ancient remains and medieval houses to the **cathedral** (B1-2), with a portico of 1650 and a fine campanile. Inside is a large 13C **wooden statue★** of the Deposition and the precious triptych★ of the *Saviour between the Virgin and St. John,* 12C *(covered, notify in advance).* ▶ Go by v. San Valerio through the medieval houses and v. della Sibilla to the two Acropolis temples, interesting both in architecture and in their situation. The **temple of Vesta** (A2-3), entered from the restaurant, stands on the rocky brow overlooking the valley of waterfalls; it is an elegant circular building with ten Corinthian columns of the late Republican period. Next to it is the **temple of the Tiburtine Sibyl,** rectangular with four Ionic columns at the front. ▶ The entrance to the **Villa Gregoriana** (A-B3; *8:30-1 hr before sunset)* is in largo S. Angelo. The lovely park encloses the famous water-

falls★★ of the Aniene, falling in a drop of 525 ft. Descend to the upper viewpoint of the **Grande Cascata,** thence to the **Sibyls' cave,** the lesser falls and the Bernini falls. There is a remarkable view of the falls from the middle viewpoint at the Grande Cascata★. ▶ The ruins of the Roman amphitheatre (2C) are overlooked by the **Rocca Pia** (C2), a massive fortress with four crenellated towers built by Pius II in the 15C.

Environs

▶ Follow the v. Quintilio Varo (A3), skirting the falls, through an olive grove, to the church of S. **Maria Quintiliolo.** Near the church are the ruins of the villa of Quintilius Varo. ▶ 6 km away is the **Villa of Hadrian** (→). ▶ 8 km along the v. Tiburtina are the **Baths of Tivoli;** the waters have been known since Roman times and are now exploited in the **Terme Acque Albule,** set in lovely countryside. □

Practical information

ℹ giardino Garibaldi (C1), ☎ 21249.

Restaurant:
♦♦ *Cinque Statue,* largo S. Angelo 1 (B3 a), ☎ 20366, closed Fri and 15-30 Aug. Open-air service in summer. Regional cuisine: roast piglet, young lamb grilled, 25/40.000.

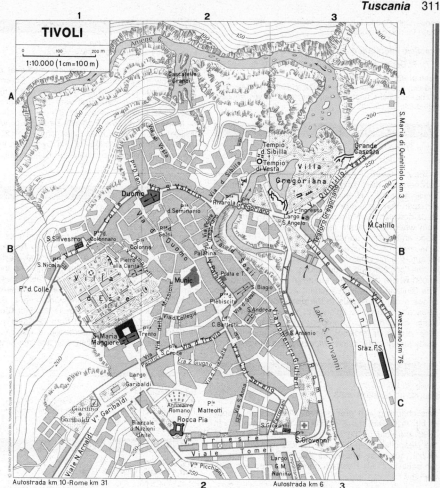

TIVOLI

1:10.000 (1cm=100 m)

0 — 100 — 200 m

Aniene R.

Cascatelle Grandi

Tempio d.Sibilla
Tempio di Vesta

Grande Cascata

Villa Gregoriana

Duomo

d.Seminario

Rivarola

Ingresso
Largo a
S.Angelo

M.Catillo

S.Silvestro
P.za d. Colonnato

P.za d. Selci

S.Nicola
P.za V.
Colonna

S.Pietro alla Carità

P.za Palatina

Posta e T.

S.Biagio

P.za d.Colle

Villa d'Este

Munic.

Plebiscito

S.Andrea
C.Battisti

Via d.Collegio

S.Antonio

Lake S. Giovanni

S.Maria Maggiore

P.za Trento

Via di Trevio

S.Ceppe

Via 2 Giugno

Via d. Sosii

Via Domenico Giuliani

Staz. F.S.

Largo
Garibaldi

Giardino
Garibaldi
V.le Garibaldi

Anfiteatro
Romano

P.le Matteotti

Rocca Pia

Piazzale
d. Nazioni Unite

S.Giovanni

S.Giovanni

V.le Trieste

Viale Tomei

V.le Picchieri

Largo G.M. Nanino

Autostrada km 10 - Rome km 31

Autostrada km 6

S. Maria di Quintiliolo km 3

Avezzano km 76

Tratto Gregoriano

Via Mazzini

Via Valeria

© ISTITUTO CARTOGRAFICO DEL TOURING CLUB ITALIANO, MILANO

⛺ *Chalet del Fiume,* at Reali, v. Tiburtina Valeria, ☎ 20709 (all year).

Recommended
Horseback riding: *Centro ippico Tivoli,* v. Parmegiani 4, ☎ 28578 or 22689.

BAGNI DI TIVOLI, ⊠ 00011, ☎ 0774.
♨ (Feb-mid Dec), ☎ 529012.

TUSCANIA

Viterbo 23, Rome 89 km
Pop. 7,432 ⊠ 01017 ☎ 0761   A-B2

The city stands on a tufa shelf bordered by deep ravines, breathing the air of the Maremma, the air, as Curzio Malaparte wrote, of 'the true Tuscany, ancient spring of our Etruscan forebears'.

▶ The damage caused in the city by the earthquake of 1971 has almost been repaired. ▶ The city is still surrounded by its **medieval walls** with square, round and polygonal towers. Its finest monument is the Roman-esque and Lombard church of **S. Pietro★★** on the edge of the town outside the Viterbo gate, on the top of a hill on the site of the Etruscan acropolis. The church stands on a grassy square, with remains of two medieval towers and the bishop's palace. Built in the 8C, it has a 13C facade with a portal surmounted by a small loggia and a large rose-window. The interior is stately with a nave and two aisles, and 12C frescos along the walls of the sanctuary and apse. ▶ At the foot of the same slope is the superb church of **S. Maria Maggiore★**, in Romanesque style with Gothic influence. It has a Romanesque bell-tower and a facade similar to that of S. Pietro, with three doors, a small loggia and rose-window. The decoration of the sides and apse is remarkable. Inside there is a fine 12C ambo and a huge 14C fresco of the *Last Judgment* on the apse wall. ▶ The church and monastic buildings of **S. Maria del Riposo** outside the walls now form the **Museo Nazionale Etrusco** *(9 a.m.-1:30 p.m. and 2:30-7 p.m. in spring/summer; other months 9 a.m.-4 p.m.; closed Mon),* with terra-cotta sarcophagi (2C-1C BC) and a splendid collection of pottery (12C-17C) found in the wells of medieval houses. ▶ The **cathedral** has a 16C facade and was rebuilt in the 18C; inside are a number of works of art. ▶ **S. Maria della Rosa** (14C) is Romanesque with Gothic influence, and has an altar-piece by Giulio Pierino d'Amelia (1581). ☐

Practical information —————————————

ℹ p. F. Basile, ☎ 436196; at Tarquinia, ☎ 0766/856384.

Restaurant:
♦ *Gallo,* v. del Gallo 24, ☎ 435028, closed Tue. Regional cuisine: penne pasta al salmone, pappardelle noodles with duck, 20/25,000.

The VEIO RUINS

Rome 20 km
C3-4

In the old town of Isola Farnese, situated on a cliff between two deep ravines, are a 15C church and a medieval castle. N and E of the town lie the ruins of Etruscan Veii, once a powerful rival to Rome. A road leads down to the Mola channel by a pretty waterfall, from where a footpath leads to a terrace on which stood an Etruscan sanctuary *(May-Sep 9 a.m.-7 p.m.; other months Tue-Fri 10 a.m.-2 p.m.; Sat and hols 10 a.m.-6 p.m.; closed Mon).* Visible are the remains of the *piscina* and foundations of the temple of Apollo where the famous statue of Apollo now in the Villa Giulia in Rome was found. Across the Formello bridge a dirt road leads to the **ponte Sodo**, a 6C BC Etruscan gallery. A little way off is the **Campana tomb**, a 7C-6C BC chamber-tomb. There are two lions on either side of the entrance and frescos inside *(apply to the ticket-office near the sanctuary).* ☐

VELLETRI

Rome 38 km
Pop. 42,432 ⊠ 00049 ☎ 06
D5

This charming and gracious town stands on a spur of Mt. Artemisio, the S bastion of the Alban hills. In 1799, the year of the Sanfedista resurgence against the Neapolitan Republic, the famous bandit Michele Pezza, otherwise known as Fra' Diavolo, acting for the occasion as a Bourbon general, arrived and took the city.

▶ The city centre is p. Cairoli, dominated by the Romanesque-Gothic **Torre del Trivio**. ▶ The **Museo Civico** *(Tue, Thu and Sat 9-11:30 a.m.; Thu also 4-6:30 p.m.)* is housed in the imposing **Palazzo del Comune** (1573-90) with a portico to Vignola's design. Among the exhibits is a Roman **sarcophagus★** (193) with scenes of the Labours of Hercules. ▶ On the edge of the city is the **cathedral**, a 4C building refaced in the 17C. Inside are the high altar tabernacle. 14C and 15C frescos in the apse and the crypt. The chapter-house contains a small **museum** *(Tue, Thu and Sat 3:30-6 p.m.; holidays 9 a.m.-12 noon),* with two Madonnas by Antoniazzo Romano and one by Gentile da Fabriani. ☐

Practical information —————————————

ℹ v. dei Volsci 2, ☎ 9630896.

Recommended
Visits to workshops: *Bottega del Tarlo,* contrada Colle Piombo 24, ☎ 9614300 (wooden objects, furnishings).

In preparing for your trip, consult the pages pertaining to the regions. You will find there the description of the region you wish to visit, as well as a list of sites that must be seen, a brief history and practical information.

VEROLI

Frosinone 14, Rome 97 km
Pop. 18,854 ⊠ 03029 ☎ 0775
E4-5

This ancient town has a pleasing **medieval quarter** and a few monuments; the church of **S. Erasmo** with Romanesque portico of three arcades and campanile; the Romanesque **cathedral** with an elegant façade and some precious treasures inside; the church of **S. Maria Salome**, the medieval structure of which is visible inside; the Romanesque chapel of **S. Maria dei Franconi**; the remains of the Cyclopean **walls** of the ancient Ernician city, and the ruins of the **castle of S. Leucio.** ☐

VETRALLA

Viterbo 13, Rome 68 km
Pop. 10,895 ⊠ 01019 ☎ 0761
B3

This town on the slopes of the Cimini hills retains some of its medieval character. The Romanesque church of **S. Francesco** has a fine portal and remarkable apses; inside the columns of the nave have ornate capitals. There are also frescos of various periods and a crypt. The 18C **cathedral** has a 12C *Madonna* painted on wood and a Baroque choir and organ. 17 km away is the **San Giovenale archeological zone,** reached from La Cassia at Cura di Vetralla. Here are an acropolis, a 12C castle, the foundations of an Etruscan city and many tumulus tombs. ☐

Practical information —————————————

Restaurant:
♦ *Pino Solitario,* v. Cassia 299, ☎ 471045, closed Fri. Italian cuisine: penne noodles all'arrabbiata, rabbit in wine sauce, 20/25,000.

VILLA ADRIANA**

Rome 28 km
Pop. 10,091 ⊠ 00010 ☎ 0774
D4

Hadrian was a native Spaniard from Baetica, of a family originally from Picenum, and a man steeped in Greek culture. He is one of the most fascinating characters among the Roman emperors. He was forty-one when he succeeded his fellow-countryman Trajan (117) at a time when the empire had reached its greatest territorial expansion. He reigned twenty-one years, of which the first part was almost entirely spent in a series of inspections of all the subject provinces. All his work can be seen as an attempt to forge a common destiny and identity for the diverse peoples brought by the course of history within the Roman ambit. Hadrian's villa at Tivoli (→) reflects in some degree the character of the man. It was begun about the time he came to the throne and finished about the time when he ended his travels (118-130); the grounds contain reproductions or souvenirs of monuments and places he had admired in the East.

▶ The huge **villa** — nearly one km divides the Greek theatre (A1) from the nymphaeum of Canopus (F2) — was sacked during the Middle Ages. Today it is an **archeological park** where the ruins combine with the charm of the site to make it a fascinating visit *(9 a.m.-1 hr before sunset; closed Mon).* Visit the **Museo didattico** (explanatory exhibition) and the **plastico della villa,** the sculpture exhibition (C1) before visiting the actual remains. ▶ The

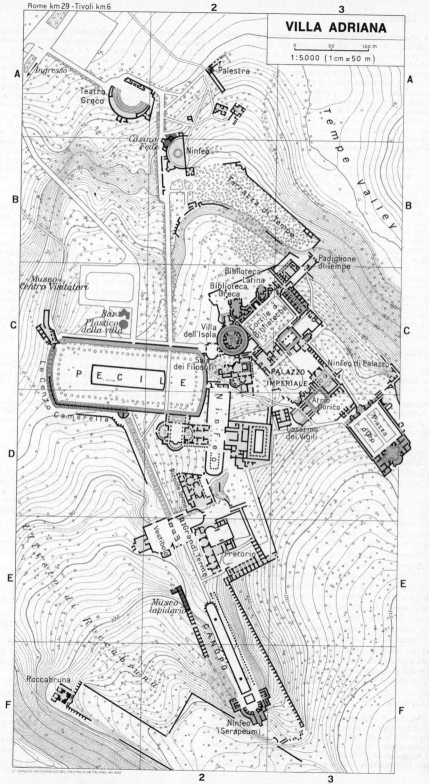

2   3

VILLA ADRIANA

0   50   100 m

1:5.000 (1 cm = 50 m)

A   Ingresso   Palestra   A

Teatro
Greco

Casino
Fede   Ninfeo

Terrazza di Tempe

T
e
m
p
e

V
a
l
l
e
y

B   B

Padiglione
di Tempe

Museo-
Centro Visitatori   Biblioteca
Latina
Biblioteca
Greca   Cortile d.
Biblioteca

C   Plastico
Bar
della villa   Villa
dell'Isola   C

Ninfeo di Palazzo

Sala
dei Filosofi   PALAZZO
IMPERIALE

P E C I L E   Atrio
Dorico   Piazza
d'Oro

Le Cento Camerelle   Ninfeo   Caserma
dei Vigili

D   D

Piccole terme

Valletto di Roccabruna   Grandi Terme
Vestibolo

Pretorio

E   E

Museo
lapidario   C A N O P O

F   Roccabruna   F

Ninfeo
(Serapeum)

2   3

Pecile arcaded court (C1-2) enclosed a garden and pool, and has been tentatively identified with the famous *Stoa Poikile* in Athens.   ▶ The **villa dell'Isola** is a round building with a columned portico, with a circular canal around a little island.   ▶ Beyond a large **nymphaeum** (D2) are the ruins of the **Little Baths** (D2) and **Great Baths** (E2). The latter have an interesting *frigidarium* with an adjoining room with a very fine stuccoed ceiling.   ▶ The little artificial **Canopus** valley (E-F2), named after the Canopus canal in the Nile delta, is crossed by a canal with casts of statues and replaced columns on its banks.   At the end is the **Nymphaeum** or temple of Serapis (F2).   Close by is the Antiquarium or **Museo lapidario** (E2), with finds from recent excavations and sculptures, including the *4 Caryatids* and an *Amazon★*, copy of a work of Pheidias.   ▶ The ruins of the **Imperial Palace** occupy 12.5 acres and are divided into three groups of private rooms and audience rooms around three peristyles.   These latter are: the **cortile delle biblioteche** (D2-3): the two several-storeyed buildings known as the Greek library and Latin library are thought to be *triclinia* with towers; the **Palace peristyle**; and the **piazza d'Oro** (D3), surrounded by 60 columns, and with a remarkable octagonal hall with curved sides, alternately concave and convex, a motif found again in the Baroque period, at the end.   ▶ The **Pavilion of Tempe** (B3) is a three-storeyed belvedere at the edge of the charming **terrace of Tempe**, shaded by a wood and looking out over the **valley of Tempe**, dug out of the tufa. The name comes from the vale of Tempe in Thessaly between Mt. Olympus and Mt. Ossa, the beauty of which was sung by Virgil.   ▶ In the area around the **Nymphaeum** is the 18C **Casino Fede** (B2).   Farther on is the Greek theatre (A1) covered in grass.   ☐

Practical information ⎯⎯⎯⎯⎯⎯⎯⎯

Hotel:
★★★ *Motel River,* at Pontelucano, v. Tiburtina, ☎ 528281, 44 rm ℙ 🅿 🏖 60,000; bkf: 5,000.

Restaurant:
♦♦ *Adriano,* v. Villa Adriana 222, ☎ 529174, closed Mon and Aug.   Opposite the Villa Adriana.   Regional cuisine: saltimbocca rolled veal, chicken alla diavola, 25/30,000.

VITERBO*

Rome 75, Milan 510 km
Pop. 58,156 ⊠ 01100 ☎ 0761   B2

When the Venetians Matteo and Nicolo' Polo passed through Acre on their way back from their voyage to the Great Khan, and when they passed through once more on a later voyage East with their young brother Marco, they visited the church legate there, Teobaldo da Piacenza, seeking papal letters in reply to the messages they had brought from the Mongol emperor.   Since the see of Rome was vacant, they obtained these from the Bishop of Acre, and it was only later on their journey that 'news came that the legate they had left in Acre had been proclaimed Pope'.   This was Gregory X, elected in one of the most famous conclaves in history, which took place in Viterbo in the papal palace.   It lasted two years and ten months.   The city's papal period lasted little more than twenty years (1257-81); the popes had retired there distrusting their natural seat at Rome.   The city is one of the most beautiful in Italy, retaining a magical medieval air, enclosed within a triangle of sturdy walls.

▶ The church of **S. Angelo** stands on **p. del Plebiscita** (D2) in the city centre, where stands the **Palazzo dei Priori** with a 15C façade, inner court with fountain and 15C-16C frescos inside.   ▶ In p. della Morte is a 13C fountain and the **loggia of St. Thomas** (C1), which houses the **Museo delle Confraternite** *(10 a.m.-1 p.m. and 3-6:30 p.m.;*

closed Mon, Sun p. m. and winter).   ▶ The 15C **Palazzo Farnese** (C1) is on the other side of the raised cathedral bridge.   ▶ **P. San Lorenzo★** is a superb medieval square (C1) with papal palace and the cathedral.   ▶ The 12C **cathedral** (C1) has a Renaissance façade and a 14C campanile with striped two-coloured stonework.   It contains a *Madonna della Carbonara★* painted at the end of the 12C.   ▶ The **papal palace★★** (C1; 1255-66) is typical of the Viterban Gothic style, and has a **loggia★★** with delicate interlaced arches, and the hall where the famous conclave that elected Gregory X took place.   ▶ **S. Maria Nuova** (C2) is a 12C Romanesque church with a 15C pulpit inserted in a corner of the façade.   The **medieval quarter★★** is the most picturesque part of the city, being an almost intact 13C quarter with towers, steep houses, raised walkways, outer stairs and mullioned windows.   Across it runs the **v. San Pellegrino★**, with the charming **piazzetta San Pellegrino★**, containing its patronal church and the austere 13C Alessandri palace.   ▶ SE of the p. del Plebiscito is a fine medieval house, the **Casa Poscia** (C2) with an outer stair on a flying arch; the **Fontana Grande★**, loveliest of Viterbo's many fountains, and the **Porta Romana** (1653) behind the Romanesque church of **S. Sisto**.   ▶ The quarters to the N of the p. Plebiscito contain the little quatrefoil church of **S. Maria della Salute** (B-C2), the 11C **S. Giovanni in Zoccoli** (B3), the **shrine of S. Rosa**, where the body of this popular Viterban saint, whose house is nearby, is preserved, and the Gothic church of **S. Francesco** (A2) with interesting medieval funeral monuments in the transept, among them the *tomb of Hadrian V★*, the first work of Arnolfo di Cambio (13C).   ▶ The **medieval walls** (11C-13C) run along viale R. Capocci (A-C3) from the Porta Romana to the Porta Fiorentina; there are 7 city gates.   Halfway down the street is the church of **S. Maria della Verità★★** (C3), with the Mazzatosta chapel decorated with fine frescos of the *Life of the Virgin★* by Lorenzo da Viterbo and assistants (1469).   ▶ The former monastery has a Gothic **cloister★** (13C-14C) and houses the **Museo Civico★** (B-C3; *Apr-Sep 8:30 a.m.-1:30 p.m. and 3:30-6 p.m.; other months and hols 9 a.m.-1:30 p.m.*), with an archeological section devoted to finds from the Etruscan necropolises of the Viterbese and a gallery with paintings by Antoniazzo Romano, Vitale da Bologna and Sano di Pietro, and della Robbia ceramics.

Environs

▶ 3 km away is **S. Maria della Quercia★**, an elegant Renaissance work (1470-1525).   The adjoining **museum** *(apply to parish priest)* has a collection of *ex voto* offerings from 1490 painted on wood.   The monastic buildings include a **cloister★** in two styles, Gothic and 16C.   ☐

Practical information

♨ (three buildings with separate entrances) at Bagni di Viterbo *(4 km E)*, ☎ 226666.
ℹ p. dei Caduti 16 (B2), ☎ 234795; p. Verdi 4/A (B2-3), ☎ 226666.
🚂 (A2), ☎ 30955.
🚌 from the Autostazione, v. Trento (A2), ☎ 38837.

Hotels:
★★★★ *Mini Palace Hotel,* v. S. Maria della Grotticella 2, ☎ 239742, 38 rm ℙ 90,000.
★★★ *Leon d'Oro,* v. della Cava 36 (B2 a), ☎ 235954, 44 rm ℙ 🏖 closed 23 Dec-20 Feb, 55,000; bkf: 6,000.
★★ *Tuscia,* v. Cairoli 41 (B2 b), ☎ 223377, 48 rm ℙ No restaurant, 45,000; bkf: 6,000.

Restaurants:
♦ *Biscetti,* at Bagnaia, v. Gandin 11/A, ☎ 288252, closed Thu and Jul.   Regional cuisine, 25/35,000.
♦ *Scaletta,* v. Marconi 41 (B2 c), ☎ 30003, closed Mon, Aug and Christmas.   Italian cuisine: penne noodles al brandy, veal alla spingarda, 20/30,000.
♦ *Tre Re,* v. Macel Gattesco 3 (B2 d), ☎ 234619, closed Thu and Aug.   Regional cuisine: chicory acquacotta, chicken viterbese, 20/25,000.

VITERBO

0   100   200 m

1:10 000 (1 cm=100 m)

© SERVIZIO CARTOGRAFICO DEL TOURING CLUB ITALIANO, MILANO

Recommended

Events: *Trasporto della Macchina di Santa Rosa,* 3 Sep; baroque festival (Jun-Jul); exhibition of antiques, at Palazzo dei Papi (Oct-Nov).

Flying club: ☎ 250510.

Hang gliding: *Scuola Delta 1,* v. Po 18, ☎ 220838.

Motocross: *Tuscia Nord* racing track, management at *Moto club Massantini,* ☎ 221375.

Nature parks: *Parco Suburbano Marturanum,* office at Barbarano Romano *(28 km S),* ☎ 474601;

Gallese nature reserve *(31 km E),* information from *WWF Viterbo,* ☎ 263120 or Rome, ☎ 06/8440108.

Visits to workshops: *Zucchetti* laboratory, p. Schiaccirici 1, ☎ 235996 (gold, silver and pewter).

In preparing for your trip, consult the pages pertaining to the regions. You will find there the description of the region you wish to visit, as well as a list of sites that must be seen, a brief history and practical information.

The VULCI EXCAVATIONS

Rome 126 km

A2

Among poplars, willow trees and oaks there stand the **Abbadia**★, which is a medieval castle, and the **di Vulci**★ bridge, a hazardously constructed Etruscan-Roman bridge (6-3C BC), to which the Romans added three arches. The **Museo Nazionale di Vulci**★ *(9 a.m.-1 p.m. and 4-7 p.m. summer; 10 a.m.-4 p.m. winter; closed Mon)* is in the castle. It has collections of Villanovian culture, Etruscan and Attic ceramics, burial objects (the **corredo Panatenaica**★, late 7-6C BC), and Etruscan and Roman architectural fragments. A little way away are the **Vulci excavations.** Vulci was a famous Etruscan city, a small part of which has been explored (Etruscan-Roman dwellings and a temple) and **burial mounds.** The following tombs are open to the public *(inquire at museum):* the **Tomba François** (4-2C BC) and the **Tomba delle Iscrizioni** (4-3C). ☐

Practical information ─────────────

Recommended

Nature park: *Vulci* nature reserve, information from *WWF Lazio,* ☎ 06/8440108.

Liguria ●

▶ A great diversity of coastline, vegetation and inhabitants contributes to Liguria's well-deserved reputation as the Italian Riviera. Visitors are captivated by the area's fascinating and vivid history, as well as by the beauty of its landscape. The mouth of every river hides a small harbour and buildings offer delightful architectural details. It was at the end of the 16C that the noble families of the Republic of Genoa (the 'magnifici' or 'magnificent ones') began to establish the superb Mannerist villas that dot the region. While the well-to-do at the end of the 19C still had the space for costly architecture, they no longer had the taste for it. The building boom in the last twenty or thirty years has created an architectural style that begs to be tolerated more than appreciated. When Eugenio Montale, a Genoese, wrote about the area earlier in this century, there were 'only a few red brick houses in the hospitable valley, by the shore'. Things have changed since then, yet the visitor can still hear '...the distant beating of the sea beyond the branches of the trees'. Behind the coastline, the steep slopes of the Apennines and the Maritime Alps are covered with lavender, basil and rosemary, along with olive, walnut and chestnut trees. This is the rural aspect of a seafaring people equally at home at sea or on land. Many of the Ligurians who make their living from the sea take time out to relax by growing vegetables on a scrap of land. On the other end of the spectrum, Liguria is also the base for a high-tech flower industry: enormous greenhouses that produce carnations and chrysanthemums with the precision of a computerized production line. The area's rich agricultural history has left a legacy of high terraces of vines, ancient fruiting olive trees and marvelous country houses. Strangely enough, the roads around Genoa seem to invite the driver to bypass the town. That would be a mistake for Genoa is the key to understanding the whole region. Early Genoese traders extended their routes to the Middle East, Greece and as far as the Crimea. They sailed everywhere: Christopher Columbus was born in Genoa. The Genoese were also great businessmen and quickly adapted to the Industrial Revolution and more recent developments. Genoa boasts large steel mills and an airport built over the sea. Genoa's history owes more to specific individuals than to public institutions. The Ligurians remain a strongly individualistic people who are self-sufficient and put great value in professionalism and dignity. Genoa is a great mirror for all those things the visitor can love and admire about Liguria: the warm and friendly atmosphere, the colourful architecture, the artistic individuality, the presence of the sea and the distinctive character of the people. □

● Don't miss

In Genoa★★, the cathedral of S. Lorenzo★★ and its treasury★★, the 16C via Garibaldi★★, one of the finest in Italy, containing the galleries housed in the Palazzo Bianco★ and the Palazzo Rosso★, the Museo E. Chiossone★ of oriental art and the Anita Garibaldi promenade★ by the sea at Nervi★. Portofino★★ is enchantingly elegant. San Remo★★ is noted for its climate. The Hanbury Gardens★★, not far from the French border, are marvelous. Maritime Liguria is well represented by picturesque Camogli, Portovenere★ and the bleaker coast of the Cinque Terre.

● Brief regional history

5C BC-5C AD
Ligurians and Romans. The ancient Greeks knew the Ligurians for their primitive way of life, the boldness of their navigation and piracy and their courage in war. ● They settled from the Varo to the Serchio in the Apennines and in the Alps from the Rodano to the Po. **Genoa** emerged as a centre of Mediterranean trade in the late 5C BC. ● The Roman conquest began in the 3C BC and was long and hard: allies of Rome were the **Genoese Ligurians,** while the **Ingauni Ligurians** (from present-day Albania) were their implacable enemies. ● **Romanization** was completed in the 1C AD.

6C-12C
From the Roman Empire to the city-states. In Liguria the historical process was similar to that in other Italian regions: first the Lombards, then the Franks and then **urban expansion** under the rule of the bishops. As a maritime region, Liguria remained Byzantine for longer *than other Italian regions* (the Lombard Rotari took Genoa in 641); later there were numerous **raids** by marauding Saracens and Normans.

S. Matteo in Genoa

12C-14C
The city-state of Genoa and the sea. The Genoese city-state was a union of 'compagne' or companies of soldiers. ● 'Compagna' was also the name of the Genoese company formed to undertake high-risk commercial ventures at sea, all of which con-

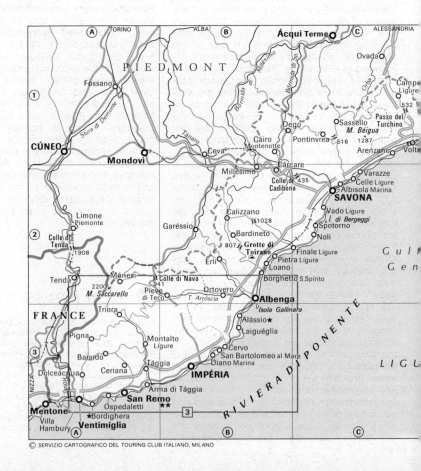

© SERVIZIO CARTOGRAFICO DEL TOURING CLUB ITALIANO, MILANO

tributed to the formation of the **maritime republic** of Genoa. ● No less important was Genoa's involvement in the **Crusades:** setting up overseas bases, barracks, stores, warehouses and taking over islands; the maritime republic prospered through its colonial outposts. ● Pisa and Venice were the competitors and bitter enemies of the Genoese. ● **Pisa** was defeated in a decisive naval battle at **La Meloria,** the rock outside Genoa, in 1284. ● Another battle at **Curzola,** an island in the Adriatic (1298), seemed to signal Genoese superiority in the rivalry with **Venice.** ● This was the battle in which **Marco Polo** is said to have been captured and taken as a prisoner to Genoa, where he dictated *Il Milione* to a fellow prisoner, Rustichello da Pisa. ● At its moment of maximum power (12C-14C) Genoa owned **Corsica,** participated in a condominium in Sardinia, operated harbours and warehouses in North Africa and possessed landing places in Syria, along with Aegean bridgeheads in Lemnos, Scios and Smyrna. The Pera quarter of Constantinople and Caffa, in the Crimea, were thriving Genoese colonies. ● In the meantime (12C-14C) the **Rivieras** were conquered, removing the vassals and subduing the communities. ● Subduing the Ponente was more difficult than subduing the Levante, but finally Genoa was able to indicate the limits of its territory on treaties with

the phrase from Nice to Portovenere. ● **Nice** fell to Savoy in 1388, but from the 13C the history of Liguria was the history of Genoa.

Portofino

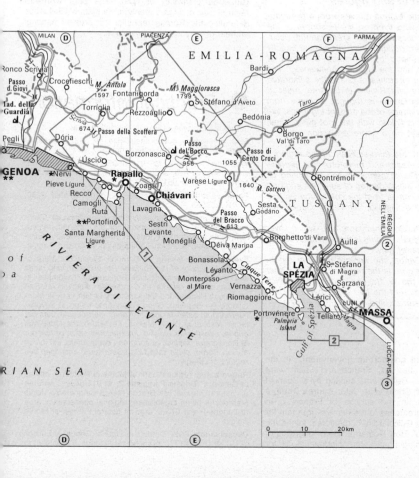

14C-15C
External rule. The extraordinary energy concentrated in the maritime city produced friction and difficulties. ● Bloody **internal conflicts** flared up between the noble families (Fieschi, Doria, Adorno, Fregoso, Spinola) and cut across power struggles on the Italian and European stages. ● This led to a series of large-scale revolts and successive periods of **external rule** by foreign powers, almost always resulting in rebellions on the Rivieras, into which malcontents were driven. ● In 1311 the Emperor Henry VII became overlord of the city and was succeeded a little later by Roberto d'Angiò. ● In 1339 **Simone Boccanegra,** the first Doge, was installed. ● Then came other outside rulers for longer or shorter periods, with short intervals of autonomy for Genoa. In 1353 Giovanni Visconti was installed and the struggle with Venice was concluded in the battle of **Chioggia** (1381), from which Genoa emerged vanquished; in 1396, Charles VI of France ruled Genoa; then the Marquis of Monferrato (1409), Filippo Maria Visconti (1421), Charles VII of France (1458), Francesco Sforza (1466), Ludovico il Moro (1468) and Louis XII of France (1499).

Facts and figures

Location: The name Liguria derives from a pre-Indo-European people who lived on the N shores of the Tyrrhenian Sea, in a rather larger area than that occupied by the modern region, which fits almost exactly into the area bounded by the steep S slopes of the Maritime Alps and the Ligurian Apennines. The two corresponding stretches of coast, the celebrated Riviera di Ponente and Riviera di Levante, meet at Genoa. The Latin Genua is thought to come from the Leopontine language of the ancient Ligurians; like Geneva the word is linked with the root genu, knee; both towns are set on a shore projection which is shaped like a knee.
Area: 5,416 sq km, the third-smallest Italian region.
Climate: Mediterranean, and therefore mild, particularly on the coast, with certain oases combining an even temperature, a high degree of sunshine and protection by the mountains from the cold of the Po Valley: Nervi, the gulf of Tigullio, San Remo, Ospedaletti and Bordighera.
Population: 1,778,024 inhabitants, of which over 700,000 live in Genoa. Liguria is the third most densely populated region of Italy.
Administration: Genoa, the ancient maritime republic, Italy's premier port, is the regional capital. Other provinces are, in the W, Savona and Imperia, which arose from the union of the two small towns of Oneglia and Porto Maurizio, and, in the E, La Spezia.

16C-18C
Andrea Doria and aristocratic government. In the first decades of the 16C France and Spain went to war over Italy. Genoa was sacked by a Spanish army in 1522. ● Some years later **Andrea Doria,** a Genoese admiral in the service of Francis I, to impose his own greatness in the name of freedom for the fatherland, as Guicciardini commented, joined the party of Charles V, Holy Roman Emperor and King of Spain, thus obtaining a guarantee of independence for

the Republic. ● On 13 September 1528 he declared himself ruler of Genoa and endowed the city with a constitution which retained power in the hands of the nobility. ● This aristocratic **oligarchy** lasted until the French Revolution: there was a decline in commerce, but Genoa remained powerful in the field of **international finance.** ● Peace was disturbed from time to time. Two particular incidents should be noted: the pointless bombardment of Genoa by Louis XIV's troops (1684) and the Austrian occupation of 1746. In 1768, **Corsica,** the last Genoese colonial possession, was sold to France, following a rebellion led by the Corsican patriot Pasquale Paoli.

19C-20C
Rule by Sardinia and Italy. In the period after the French Revolution, Liguria was annexed to France, under Napoleon. ● At the Congress of Vienna (1815), Genoa was assigned to rule by Savoy under Sardinia and known as the **Duchy of Genoa** (from the second half of the 16C Savoy owned **Oneglia** in Liguria). ● Genoa, republican and revolutionary as she was, did not take kindly to this treatment. ● However, Ligurian revolutionary energy was soon channeled toward the great objective of national unity. Ligurians took a prominent part in the events of the Risorgimento, notably the Genoese **Giuseppe Mazzini** and Giuseppe Garibaldi of Nice. The poet **Goffredo Mameli** also deserves mention; he died in 1849 while defending the Roman republic, the present national anthem of Italy is his composition.

 Practical information

Information: tourist offices in principal towns.

SOS: emergency public assistance, ☎ 113; emergency police, ☎ 112; accident emergency ACI, ☎ 116.

Weather: forecast, ☎ 010/5605; road information, ☎ 010/5606 or ACI, ☎ 06/4212; shipping forecast, ☎ 196; snow warning, ☎ 051/992992.

Farm vacations: at Genoa, v. degli Orefici 7/30, ☎ 010/206563.

Fairs and markets: Salone Nautico Internazionale, Tecn-hotel-Interfood-Bibe (equipment for the catering, restaurant, wine and drinks trades) in autumn at Genoa; Euroflora at Genoa; occasional antiques fair at Arma di Taggia.

Events: fishing festival at Camogli; Fiesta del Mare at Levanto; Regatta of the Maritime Republics, rowing races and events associated with Christopher Columbus at Genoa; district regatta at Ventimiglia; festivals at San Michele di Pagana and the sanctuary of Our Lady in Montallegro (→ Rapallo); Good Friday procession at Savona; international ballet festival at Nervi; international chamber music festival at Diano Marina; Festival of the Little Wall and jazz festival at Alassio; international salon of humour at Bordighera; festival of song and songwriters' exhibition at San Remo; cycle race Milan-San Remo and deep-sea regatta at Giraglia.

Nature parks: regional park of Monte di Portofino, offices at Genoa, v. Brigate Partigiane 2, ☎ 010/5485. An area of natural interest at Bracco-Mesco-Cinqueterre-Monte Marcello is being established; regional conservancy area at Langhe-Piana Crixia; area of natural interest at Monte Beigua.

Conservation: WWF districts in Liguria: Genoa, v. Luccoli 17/10, ☎ 010/281775; branches at Albenga, v. Pontelungo

87; La Spezia, v. Volturno 14, ☎ 0187/515759; Portofino, v. Colombo 1; Savona, v. Untoria 14r; Tigullio-Lavagna, p. Cordviola 18. *LIPU* Genoa, Passo dell'Osservatorio 1; ☎ 010/217326 (excursions and observation trips); Lèrici, v. Matteotti 17, ☎ 0187/968956. Italia Nostra, regional council at Genoa, salita S. Matteo 19/13, ☎ 281500. *FAI* (owns some wooded areas at Monte di Portofino) Milan, ☎ 02/4693693.

Excursions: marked long distance routes: Monte Liguri old road (420 km in all, 4 provincial sections, 44 stopping places); *CAI* network of marked paths in the Cinque Terre; information: *CAI* branches at Bordighera, corso Italia 50; Chiàvari, p. Matteotti 22; Genoa, p. Luccoli 2/5; Imperia-Oneglia, p. U. Calvi; La Spezia, v. Carpenino 43; San Remo, p. Cassini 13; Sarzana, p. Firmafede 13; Savona, p. Diaz; Ventimiglia, p. XX Settembre 6.

Bougainvillea

In spring the walls of the gardens and villages of the Riviera are covered with bougainvillea flowers in vivid shades ranging from deep pink to purple. This is a comparatively recent sight; the plant was not imported to Europe until the second half of the 18C. It was discovered and classified by Philibert Commerson, who in 1766-9 made a voyage of exploration around the world under the command of Louis-Antoine de Bougainville. The naturalist named the beautiful climbing plant after the commander of the expedition, thus assuring him greater fame than his importance as a navigator had earned him.

Cycling: assistance and information for cycling groups affiliated to *UDACE;* cycling itineraries organized in the province of Imperia (information from tourist office, ☎ 0183/24947).

Horseback riding: *Federazione Italiana Sport Equestri,* regional committee at Genoa, v. Montallegro 28/B, ☎ 010/316873; centres associated with *ANTE* at Genoa, Masone and Montoggio (→ Genoa), Andora S. Pietro, Bassana di San Remo, Castelnuovo Magra (→ Gulf of La Spezia), Plodio Valle (→ Savona), Rivarola Carasco (→ Chiàvari), Val Durasca (→ La Spezia).

Canoeing: at San Remo, ☎ 0184/86546 (instruction); Sestri Levante, ☎ 0185/43464.

Hang gliding: at Genoa, ☎ 010/459678 (instruction); Savona, ☎ 019/26663; Cengio (→ Savona), ☎ 019/554903.

Children's facilities: day-care at Bordighera, Nervi-S, Ilario and Borzonasca (→ Chiàvari); *mini garden zoo* at Ameglia (→ Gulf of La Spezia); *parco-zoo* at Giovo Ligure (→ Sassello).

Water skiing: *Federazione Italiana Sci Nautico,* affiliated societies at Alassio and La Spezia; practice and racing at Albisola Marina, Arenzano, Laigueglia, Santa Margherita Ligure, Portofino, Rapallo and Sestri Levante.

Skindiving: *Federazione Italiana Pesca Sportiva e Attività Sub-acquee,* at Genoa, Galleria Mazzini 7/1, ☎ 010/587730; La Spezia, v. V. Veneto 173, ☎ 0187/511026; instruction at Chiàvari, Genoa, La Spezia, Rapallo, Recco; international sub-aqua centre at Nervi.

Sailing: *Federazione Italiana Vela,* at Genoa, v. Brigata Bisagno 2/17, ☎ 010/565723; regional committee at Alassio, *Circolo Nautico al Mare,* Porticciolo Luca Ferrari, ☎ 0182/42516; *Lega Navale Italiana* (instruction in sailing and navigation, canoeing, fishing), branches at Chiàvari, Cogoleto (→ Arenzano), Genoa, Genoa Nervi, Genoa Quinto, Genoa Sestri, Imperia, La Spezia, Rapallo, Santa Margherita Ligure, Savona and Sestri Levante.

The cuisine

The scent of Mediterranean herbs — basil, marjoram — and the savour of olive oil are the basis of Genoese or Ligurian cuisine, in which experts see similarities with Moorish, Sicilian and Spanish cooking. Basil is used in pesto, related to the Provençal pistou, a mixture of pine nuts, cheese, oil and garlic worked together in a mortar, and used among other things to season lasagne, which in Liguria is made with extremely thin pasta squares. Pansoti, or ravioli with a vegetable filling, is seasoned with a walnut sauce. Traditionally 'poor' fish are used such as anchovies with lemon, stuffed anchovies or soused bream (scabecio). Difficult to find, but memorable, are dishes prepared from dried or salt cod, historic dishes recalling times when endemic Mediterranean famines were beaten by this first industrial method of food preservation. Very rare now is mosciame, filet of dolphin dried in the sun and cut into the thinnest of slices. This delicacy is prepared on board small boats and sold in the carugi, the small alleyways of the towns and villages; today it is usually made with tuna. Stuffed vegetables (the pulp of onions, eggplants, tomatoes and peppers is scooped out, enriched with other ingredients, flavoured with marjoram and replaced) are Ligurian specialties. So are savoury cakes, among which the queen is the pasqualina (Easter cake), made of thirty-three sheets of pasta dough, one for each year of Christ's life. The cappon magro — a lavish pyramid of fish and vegetables with spectacular decoration served on Christmas Eve — gloriously unites the two ancient well-springs of the region's food: the sea and the rich countryside.

Lo sciacchetrà

This is a variety of Cinque Terre white wine. It is golden to amber in colour, pleasantly flavoured and highly alcoholic, available in dry, medium and sweet versions; it is also extremely rare, as the entire area permitted to use the Cinque Terre DOC label covers fewer than 350 acres. The name comes from the two Ligurian words sciac *to crush and* trac *to pull, because the ancient method of vinification for making sweet wines was to draw freshly pressed grape juice from the vat after only twenty-four hours. Like the white Cinque Terre, the Cinque Terre Sciacchetrà is made from 60 percent Bosco grapes and the rest from Albarola or Vermentino grapes. The vineyards are steep and sunny, situated on the cliffs between Monterosso and La Spezia.*

Golf: at Arenzano (18 holes); at Garlenda (18 holes) (→ Albenga); at Rapallo (18 holes); at San Remo (18 holes).

Flying: Genoa Sestri, C. Colombo Airport, ☎ 010/607727; Luni, at airport, v. Alta Vecchia, ☎ 0187/673180 (flying instruction, parachuting, model aircraft); *Villanova di Albenga* (→ Albenga) *Airport,* ☎ 0182/58019.

Archaeology and caving: *Gruppi Archeologici d'Italia (CAI),* at Genoa, v. Ponte dell'Ammiraglio 64/10; *Gruppo speleologico CAI di Imperia,* p. Ulisse Calvi 8 PO Box 58 (exploring organization in Ligurian Alps); caving trips at Toirano (→ Loano) and Borgio-Verezzi (→ Pietra Ligure).

Towns and places

ALASSIO*

Savona 51, Genoa 98, Milan 221 km
Pop. 12,690 ⊠ 17021 ☎ 0182   B3

Alassio has a long, splendid quartz beach, the finest in Liguria, a mild, dry climate, green orchards and olive groves which once ran right down to the sea. If Alassio is able to survive on its own resources today it owes this in large measure to English tourists, who were the first to discover it at the end of the last century. The villas and gardens at the foot of the hills still evoke the elegant atmosphere of those years.

▶ Celebrities are at home here. Near the palazzo in which Napoleon spent a night are the **Chaplin gardens** and the famous *muretto* (little wall) with autographs in clay of many film stars and singers. ▶ The surrounding roads are busy until late at night, particularly the **budello** (alley) known as the via XX Settembre, which runs through the centre parallel to the shoreline, and the **passeggiata Italia**. An interesting building is the parish church of **S. Ambrogio**, with a 16C portal and campanile. The little Romanesque church of **S. Croce** commands a fine view at the beginning of the Roman road which leads to Albenga (→). ▶ Excursions can be made to **Madonna della Guardia** and to the **island of Gallinara** *(in summer by boat)*. □

Practical information _____

≈
ⓘ palazzo Hambury, v. Gibb, ☎ 40346.
Car rental: *Avis*, v. Gibb 16, ☎ 40234 (Apr-Oct); *Hertz*, v. Mazzini 55, ☎ 43382.

Hotels:
★★★★ *Ambassador*, corso Europa 64, ☎ 43957, 47 rm ℗ closed 21 Oct-31 Mar, 90,000.
★★★★ *Diana*, v. Garibaldi 110, ☎ 42701, 77 rm ℗ ➘ ⌂ closed 23 Nov-30 Jan, 145,000; bkf: 14,000.
★★★★ *Europa e Concordia*, p. Partigiani 1, ☎ 43324, 70 rm ℗ ⚄ closed 16 Oct-14 Mar, 90,000; bkf: 7,000.
★★★★ *G. H. Méditerranée*, v. Roma 63, ☎ 42564, 76 rm ℗ ⚄ ♿ closed 16 Oct-Easter, 97,000; bkf: 10,000.
★★★★ *Spiaggia*, v. Roma 78, ☎ 43403, 83 rm ℗ closed 20 Oct-20 Dec, 170,000; bkf: 15,000.
★★★ *Enrico*, v. Dante 368, ☎ 40000, 33 rm ℗ closed Oct, 60,000; bkf: 7,000.
★★★ *Firenze*, v. Dante 35, ☎ 43239, 24 rm ℗ ⚄ closed 7 Jan-16 Apr and 30 Oct-20 Dec, 71,000.
★★★ *Majestic*, v. L. da Vinci 300, ☎ 42721, 77 rm ℗ closed 13 Oct-14 Apr, 72,000; bkf: 6,000.
★★★ *Toscana*, v. F. Gioia 4, ☎ 40657, 65 rm ℗ closed 30 Oct-20 Dec, 71,000.
★★ *Eden*, passeggiata Cadorna 20, ☎ 40281, 29 rm ℗ closed Nov-Jan, 40,000; bkf: 4,000.

Restaurants:
● ♦♦♦ *Palma*, v. Cavour 5, ☎ 40314, closed Tue and 4 Nov-20 Dec. Well managed. Excellent creative cuisine: sea bass with artichokes and grapes, sole with basil, 40/60,000.
♦♦ *Torcia*, v. Torino 72, ☎ 42413, closed Wed and 30 Oct-28 Dec. Maritime atmosphere. Mixed cuisine: maccheroncini isola Gallinara, tagliolino with salmon, 20/40,000.
♦♦ *Vigna*, at Solva, v. Lepanto 2, ☎ 43301, closed Wed and 10 Oct-20 Dec. Terrace with fine view. Regional cuisine: bucantini with scampi, gnocchi with pesto, 35,000.
♦ *Liggia*, v. Aleramo 3, ☎ 469076, closed Mon and 7 Jan-7 Mar. Fine summer terrace overlooking countryside. Regional cuisine: pansoti with walnut sauce, fresh pasta, 35/45,000.

▲ ★★ *Monti e Mare International Resort*, Monti region, v. Aurelia at 619.5-km marker, 209 pl, ☎ 43036; ★★

Vedetta Est, Monti region, v. Aurelia at 621.3-km marker, 100 pl, ☎ 42407 (all year).
Recommended
Cycling: *Arcobaleno Cicli Prato*, v. Massabò 6, ☎ 42587.
Events: *Muretto festival* (Aug); *jazz festival* (Sep).
Marina: Capo Santa Croce, ☎ 40861, *Al Mare yacht club*, ☎ 42516.
Sport: horseback riding and golf at Garlenda *(17 km NW)*; aeronautical club at Villanova d'Albenga *(13 km NW)* (→ Albenga); water-skiing at *Miniature club*, v. Loreto 7, ☎ 42815; tennis at Villa Michelangelo, ☎ 40174.

ALBENGA

Savona 44, Genoa 90, Milan 213 km
Pop. 21,805 ⊠ 17031 ☎ 0182   B2

The historic town centre of Albenga is plainly of Roman origin. However, the Roman site in the plain was only founded after the destruction of the ancient and powerful *Albium Ingaunum*, the capital of the Ligurian Ingauni, which stood on the heights nearby. The settlement grew steadily for over 2,000 years, and its main thoroughfares and medieval walls still follow the original Roman layout. The ancient town is still the nerve centre of the community, even though the built-up area has expanded massively toward the sea because of the move from the country to the town and also because industry has developed in association with the market gardening practised in what is the largest alluvial plain in coastal Liguria.

▶ Most of the public and private monuments date from the medieval revival between the 12C and the 15C, when Albenga was a free city-state and its inhabitants were amassing wealth through trade. The 14C **Palazzo Vecchio del Comune** opens on to the v. Ricci and is flanked by a large tower with paired windows. It houses the **Civico Museo Ingauno** *(9 or 10 a.m.-12 noon and 3-6 p.m.; closed Mon)*, with remains and finds from the pre-Roman and medieval periods. ▶ The loggia leads into the 5C **baptistery★**, which is the oldest monument in Albenga and the most important early Christian building in Liguria *(same opening hours as museum)*. The octagonal interior has a splendid late 5C mosaic and beautiful Lombard decoration. ▶ The **cathedral of S. Michele★** stands beside the baptistery on the piazza of the same name. The church, on which some complex and much-debated restoration work has been carried out, shows traces of the previous early Christian basilica (5C-8C), which was largely rebuilt in the Romanesque-Gothic period (11C-13C). The fine **campanile★** (1390), together with the **Torre del Municipio**, completes the striking triumvirate of towers, referred to as 'Government', 'Justice' and 'Prayer'. ▶ The fine **Palazzo Peloso-Cepolla** stands at the S end of p. S. Michele. Medieval in origin, it is crowned by a tower, as are many of the town's palazzi. It contains the **Museo Navale Romano** *(9 a.m.-12 noon and 3-6 p.m.)*, established to preserve the remains of a 1C BC Roman ship with its cargo of wine amphoras and also to house the Centre for Experimental Underwater Archaeology, which co-ordinates research all over Italy. ▶ The small **piazza dei Leoni**, behind the apse of the Cathedral, is surrounded by medieval houses of the Costa family, grouped around a typical battlemented tower dating from 1300. This piazza forms one of the most charming parts of Albenga. The three Renaissance stone lions which decorate the piazza were originally from Rome. At the W end of the piazza, the **Palazzo Costa del Carretto di Balestrino**, built in the 16C in the area of the medieval shoemakers' market, houses the town's principal Roman inscriptions.

Environs

▶ 4 km N is the Romanesque-Gothic church of **S. Giorgio di Campochiesa** (12C-13C), with late-medieval frescos; 6.5 km W is the walled village of **Villanova d'Albenga,** the largest and most complex of the villages which the city-state of Albenga founded for defensive purposes in the 13C. ☐

Amphoras from the Roman galley at Albenga

In February 1950 Professor Nino Lamboglia orga-nized the excavation of the remains of a Roman trading galley lying in 130 ft of water off Albenga. The recovery vessel Artiglio caused some damage, but brought ashore many wine amphoras of the type known as Dressel 1, seven bronze helmets, examples of weapons for defense against pirates (very active in the 1C BC, as the wreck of the vessel shows) and black glazed pottery. The hull was over 130 ft long and loaded with a thousand amphoras. These finds are now exhibited in the extremely interesting Museo Navale Romano in the Palazzo Peloso-Cepolla in Albenga. This first experiment led to a spate of submarine archaeology, extensively developed by the use of underwater techniques and suitable methods. The coast of the Mediterranean is strewn with numerous relics bearing witness to the heavy marine traffic of ancient times, as well as to the risks of navigation. Research has revealed some unusual facts; for example, a powerful family of senatorial rank, whose stamp on the amphoras was Ses, short for Sestius, shipped wine to Sardinia, Liguria and the French and Spanish coasts from its vast agricultural estates at Cosa (Ansedonia). Following the trail of the amphoras it is known that from Narbonne in Gaul the Italian wine passed down the Garonne and arrived at Bordeaux, from which port some of it was shipped to Britain. Although Bordeaux is today the centre of the world's greatest wine-growing region, under the Romans the inhabitants of Gaul were forbidden to cul-tivate the vine.

Practical information _____

≈ v. Martiri della Libertà 17, ☎ 50475.

Hotel:
★★★ **Sole Mare,** lungomare Colombo 15, ☎ 52752, 28 rm ⛟ ⚘ 52,000; bkf: 6,000.

▲ ★★ *Delfino,* Vadino region, v. Aurelia 23, 120 pl, ☎ 51998 (all year); ★★ *Sole,* Vadino region, v. Miche-langelo 17, 50 pl, ☎ 51957; ★ *Mauro,* Lionetta region, v. dell'Apparizione 1, 110 pl, ☎ 52615.

Recommended
Aeroclub: *Villanova d'Albenga Airport,* ☎ 58919 (season-al).
Bowling: p. Corridoni, ☎ 52241.
Golf: at Garlenda, ☎ 580012 (18 holes).
Horseback riding: at Garlenda, v. Piani Romani 2, ☎ 580387.
Tennis: v. Olimpia, ☎ 53826; v. Vecchia Morello, ☎ 52642.

In preparing for your trip, consult the pages pertain-ing to the regions. You will find there the descrip-tion of the region you wish to visit, as well as a list of sites that must be seen, a brief history and practi-cal information.

Savona 3, Genoa 43, Milan 167 km
Pop. 6,146 ⊠ 17012 ☎ 019   C2

Albisola Marina is the rare example which demon-strates that tourism can coexist with the ancient tra-ditions of craftsmanship. One such tradition is the **ceramic work** for which this small town is still justly famous. That fame reached its peak from the 17C onwards, when the Conrado brothers left here to set up the celebrated Névers potteries in France. There are a large number of ceramic workshops along v. Aurelia, and, in homage to the art of ceramics, some well-known modern painters and sculptors (Sassu, Capogrossi, Crippa, Fontana) have contribut-ed to the large multi-coloured slabs in the pavement of the **lungomare degli Artisti.** Local ceramics are exhibited annually at the **Villa Durazzo Faraggiana,** and the Museo Mario Trucco is being established at **Albisola Superiore** for ceramics. ☐

Practical information _____

≈ water-skiing.
ⓘ v. dell'Oratorio 2 (nr parish church), ☎ 481648; at Albi-sola Capo, corso Ferrari 160/b, ☎ 41313 (seasonal).

Hotels:
★★★★ *Park Hotel,* at Albisola Capo, v. Alba Docilia 3, ☎ 42355, 11 rm ⓟ 59,000; bkf: 8,000.
★★★ *Corallo,* v. Repetto 116, ☎ 481784, 22 rm ⓟ ⚘ ⚘ closed 15 Nov-15 Mar, 60,000; bkf: 8,000.

Restaurants:
◆◆◆ *Cambusiere,* v. Repetto 82/86, ☎ 481663, closed Mon and 15 Jan-15 Feb. In former monastery with sum-mer pergola. Excellent seafood: cuttlefish risotto, spag-hetti with crayfish, 25/50,000.
◆◆◆ *Mario-ai Cacciatori,* corso Bigliati 70, ☎ 481640, closed Tue eve, Wed and Aug. Summer terrace. Sea-food: trenette with pesto, cuttlefish with artichokes, 20/32,000.
◆◆◆ *Pescatori-da Gianni,* corso Bigliati 82/r, ☎ 481200, closed Tue and 10 Nov-15 Dec. Tuscan cuisine: risotto alla risacca, red mullet livornese, homemade Chianti, 25/40,000.

Recommended
Clay pigeon shooting: *Priamo club,* at Albisola Superiore, v. alla Pace 68,☎ 482285.
Cycling: *Velo Club Albisola,* at Albisola Superiore, v. Ita-lia 1.
Swimming: corso Bigliati, ☎ 481270.
Tennis: at Albisola Superiore, v. del Cantan, ☎ 40277; pri-vate road off corso Mazzini, ☎ 41620.

Savona 59, Genoa 102, Milan 225 km
Pop. 6,110 ⊠ 17020 ☎ 0182   B3

This modern resort conceals the traces of the old town centre, which was abandoned by its inhabitants in the 16C after being reduced to a bleak and marshy stretch of land. However, one of the most important medieval complexes in the Ponente stands on a hill 2 km from the sea. It includes the striking remains of a 12C-13C castle and the fine Romanesque-Gothic church of **Ss. Giacomo e Filippo,** flanked by a battle-mented gatehouse tower which functions as a cam-panile. At the foot of the hill, the so-called Roman bridge (ten arches, in fact medieval) spans the Mérula River. ☐

Practical information

≋
[i] v. Fontana 9, ☎ 85796.

Hotels:
★★★ **Liliana,** at Marina di Andora, v. del Poggio 23, ☎ 85083, 35 rm [P] 🏨 closed 16 Oct-31 Mar, 41,000; bkf: 6,000.
★★ **Pigna,** at Marina di Andora, v. del Poggio 1, ☎ 85231, 20 rm [P] ≮ closed Oct-Mar, 35,000; bkf: 5,000.

Restaurant:
◆◆◆ **Rocce di Pinamare,** v. Aurelia 39, ☎ 85223, closed Wed and Nov. On shore with little beach, swimming pool, tennis court and terrace. Regional cuisine: trenette with pesto, fish or meat grilled over olive wood, 35/50,000.

⚓ ★★ **Mare e Sole,** v. Aurelia, ☎ 85008.

Recommended
Bowling: v. M. Polo 20, ☎ 88823.
Horseback riding: *Club Ippico Andora,* at Andora San Pietro, v. Duomo 2, ☎ 80188 (associate of *ANTE*).
Marina: yacht club, ☎ 86548.

The Ligurian APENNINES

From Sestri Levante to Recco *(224 km, 1 day; map 1)*

The area between Monte Góttero and Monte Antola in E Liguria is bisected by a multitude of valleys and covered by a chestnut woodland. In the past it was held by the most powerful of Genoa's families (first the Fieschi, then the Doria), and its strategic importance lay in the fact that a major communications route to the Po Valley ran through it, Parma being three days by mule across the Cento Croci Pass. A

1. The Ligurian Apennines

© SERVIZIO CARTOGRAFICO DEL TOURING CLUB ITALIANO, MILANO

social system based upon independent production was active in all these valleys and the key element in its economy was the chestnut tree. Its methods survived into the middle of the last century but they have now been overwhelmed by the development of new industries for the extraction of raw materials and energy and by the even more pervasive influence of the tourist industry.

▶ From **Sestri Levante** (→), the via Aurelia is followed across the **del Bracco Pass** (2,010 ft) as far as Carródano, a crucial junction at the crossroads of the SS 566, the Apennine road. This road goes up the valley of the Vara, passing through San Pietro Vara. ▶ **Varese Ligure,** founded by the Fieschi for defense and trade, has two centres. **Borgo Rotondo,** the older of the two (14C), lies behind the 15C castle and has an unusual oval plan, surrounded by a screen of rustic houses. **Borgo Nuovo** (16C), on the other hand, has a linear layout. ▶ A considerable collection of items relating to the ethnography of the mountain region is housed in the **Càssego** elementary school, which stands in the road leading over the Bocco Pass. ▶ From the **Bocco Pass** (3,135 ft) it is possible to reach the beech-wood on **Monte del Zatta** (4,605 ft), which has many ancient trees and species of Mediterranean flora in the undergrowth. ▶ Passing through **Santa Maria del Taro** (fine medieval bridge) and Pontestrambo and turning l., the road leads up to the Penna Pass across the Chiodo Mountains and then descends to the Aveto basin. ▶ **Santo Stefano d'Aveto** (3,335 ft) is a popular resort, both in summer and winter, and preserves some medieval remains, including the ruins of the **Malaspina castle.** ▶ Further down, in the **Rezzoaglio** district, another tourist resort, there are some rustic houses with stone decorations by local masons. ▶ Passing from the Aveto to the Trebbia Valley, the inhabitants of **Fontanigorda** were once woodcutters and gatherers of mushrooms. Now they are among the pioneers of a revival of traditional Apennine husbandry, which had virtually disappeared. ▶ At the bottom of the Trebbia Valley, into which the SS 45 descends, is the **sanctuary of Nostra Signora di Montebruno,** built in 1486 as a result of a legendary apparition of the Virgin Mary. This shrine is a pilgrimage site, and boasts among its votive offerings some pieces of cable taken from the galleys of Andrea Doria. ▶ In 1547 the Doria family took over the now ruined Fieschi castle at **Torriglia.** Here too, on the important route to Piacenza, the Doria have left their mark, shrewdly promoting commerce in the village. ▶ The **Scoffera** pass (2,210 ft) leads to **Gattorno.** ▶ **Uscio** has historically been a place of transit for both trade and the seasonal movement of livestock between Fontanabuona and the Recco valley (→). From Uscio the road leads down to the sea amid olives and chestnuts. ▶ **Workshops to visit** include the **Neive** wrought-iron works at **Bargagli** *(6 km from Scoffera Pass, v. Partigiani 9,* ☎ *010/906131)* and the **Leverone** pottery works at **Ferrada di Mocònesi** *(3 km from Gattorna, v. Colombo 24/a).* ☐

Practical information

CARRODANO, ✉ 19020, ☎ 0187.

⚓ ★★ **Bracchetto Vetta,** v. Aurelia at 444.5-km marker, 50 pl, ☎ 893331 (all year).

SANTO STEFANO D'AVETO, ✉ 16049, ☎ 0185.
⚡ cable car to Monte Bue, ski lifts, cross-country skiing, ski school.
[i] p. del Popolo 1, ☎ 98046.

Hotels:
★★★ **Groppo Rosso,** v. Badinelli 1, ☎ 98054, 39 rm [P] 🏨 ♨ 36,000.
★★★ **Leon d'Oro,** v. Razzetti 52, ☎ 98073, 37 rm, closed Nov, 50,000.

Recommended
Bowling: covered bowling green and tennis court in v. Badinelli.

SESTA-GODANO, ⊠ 19020, ☎ 0187.

⚠ ★★★ *River Vara*, at Pian di Suina, 200 pl, ☎ 891457 (all year).

VARESE LIGURE, ⊠ 19028, ☎ 0187.

Hotel:
★★★ *Posta*, p. Marconi 16, ☎ 842115, 27 rm P ⋙ 🕭 ✷ 38,000; bkf: 3,500.

ARENZANO

Genoa 22, Milan 151 km
Pop. 11,257 ⊠ 16011 ☎ 010   C1

The sweep of the sea-front, with its pines, palms and tamarisks bears witness to the mild climate of this health and seaside resort. The medieval town centre has disappeared, but there is a spectacular **Grand Hotel** (1915), and, as elsewhere in the Ponente, there are numerous elegant villas. Even more common are the second homes of people from Lombardy, Piedmont and Genoa. These houses have by now almost entirely swallowed up the large pine forest at Cape San Martino. There are some more good sand and shingle beaches at **Cogoleto** *(5 km)*, a seaside village which preserves some old features and is said to be the birthplace of Christopher Columbus. ☐

Practical information _____
ARENZANO

≋
ⓘ former railway station, ☎ 9127581.

Hotels:
★★★★ *G. H. Arenzano*, v. Stati Uniti 4, ☎ 9126351, 60 rm P ⋙ ⊑ 95,000.
★★★ *Ena*, v. Matteotti 12, ☎ 9123139, 25 rm ⋙ closed Christmas, 49,000; bkf: 6,000.
★★★ *Miramare*, corso Matteotti 138, ☎ 9127325, 40 rm P ≼ closed 15 Dec-15 Jan, 50,000; bkf: 6,000.

Restaurant:
♦♦ *Lazzaro e Gabriella*, v. S. M. Rapallo 14, ☎ 9124259, closed Mon and 15 Dec-15 Jan. Seafood: crêpes with anchovies in parsley sauce, ravioli in bream sauce, 30/50,000.

Recommended
Golf: at Pineta di Arenzano, p. del Golf 2, ☎ 9127296 (18 holes).
Horseback riding: v. Aurelia 21, ☎ 9110616.
Marina: ☎ 9123251.
Sailing instruction: *Lega Navale*, at Cogoleto, v. Rati 48, ☎ 9181839 (also fishing lessons).
Swimming pool: ☎ 9126322.
Tennis: v. Terralba 69, ☎ 9127228; v. della Colletta, ☎ 9111846.

Environs
CAMPO LIGURE, ⊠ 16013, ☎ 010, 25 km N.

Recommended
Craft workshops: *Filigree Artists' Studio*, v. Don Minzoni 58, ☎ 921381 (filigree work).
Farm vacations: *Azienda Prato Rondanino*, ☎ 921398.

BONASSOLA

La Spezia 42, Genoa 83, Milan 218 km
Pop. 1,150 ⊠ 19011 ☎ 0187   E2

Surrounded by vineyards and olive groves, Bonassola faces a small open bay with sandy shores. In the past, this exposed position made the town an easy target for pirate raids, so much so that a mutual aid society was formed to ransom the inhabitants who

had been kidnapped. Today, the same bay attracts tourists. Red Lévanto marble is mined in the **quarries** (visits by prior permission) at **La Grande** *(1 hr)*. ☐

Practical information _____

≋
ⓘ municipio, ☎ 813460.

Hotel:
★★★ *Rose*, v. Garibaldi 8, ☎ 813713, 30 rm ✷ closed 21 Oct-19 Mar, 45,000; bkf: 4,000.

Recommended
Farm vacations: *Villaggio La Francesca*, ☎ 228277.

BORDIGHERA*

Imperia 37, Genoa 155, Milan 278 km
Pop. 11,754 ⊠ 18012 ☎ 0184   A3

Doctor Antonio, a novel by Giovanni Ruffini set in Bordighera, was published in Britain in 1855 and from then on this small Ligurian town contained a flourishing British colony, which, at the end of the century, actually outnumbered the local population. Bordighera was one of the first places on the Riviera to attract English tourists and from that day to this, it has — to a greater extent than other similar towns — continued to be a well-ordered and elegant health resort and watering place. More profound transformations have resulted from other factors. For example, the local agriculture has been converted to flower-growing, and this has led to the disappearance of the famous citrus groves in the Borghetto Valley. The beautiful Monte Nero pine forest, today a municipal park, has remained intact.

▶ The **old town** has retained its 15C layout to a large extent. At the end of the cape is the symbol of the town: the modest church of **S. Ampello**, the legendary home of the 5C hermit saint. ▶ To the W, above the beach, is the **lungomare Argentina★**, a splendid panoramic walk with a view of the French Côte d'Azur. The **via Romana**, at the foot of the hills surrounded by villas, hotels and gardens, is one of the principal arteries of the modern town. In a side street, the **Museo Bicknell** *(9 a.m.-1 p.m.; Sat 10 a.m.-12 noon and 3:30-6:30 p.m.; closed Sun, Mon and hols)* houses the International Institute of Ligurian Studies and shows plaster casts of the prehistoric Rupestrian incisions of Mount Bego (France). ☐

Practical information _____

≋
ⓘ v. Roberto 1 (palazzo del Parco), ☎ 262322.

Hotels:
★★★★ *G. H. Cap Ampelio*, v. Virgilio 5/11, ☎ 264333, 104 rm P ≼ ⋒ ⋙ 🕭 ⊑ closed 20 Nov-20 Dec, 137,000; bkf: 11,800.
★★★★ *G. H. del Mare*, v. Portico della Punta 34, ☎ 262201, 107 rm P ≼ ⋙ 🕭 ⊑ ∿ closed Oct-22 Dec, 180,000; bkf: 15,000.
★★★ *Britannique & Jolie*, v. Regina Margherita 35, ☎ 261464, 56 rm P ⋙ closed 20 Sep-20 Dec, 82,000; bkf: 5,000.
★★★ *Centrohotel*, p. Eroi della Libert 10, ☎ 265265, 35 rm P ⊑ closed Nov. No restaurant, 70,000; bkf: 7,000.
★★★ *Fiori*, v. Arziglia 38, ☎ 262287, 21 rm P ≼ No restaurant, 55,000; bkf: 5,000.
★★★ *Florida*, v. Vittorio Emanuele 310, ☎ 263545, 83 rm P closed 7 Oct-21 Dec, 80,000; bkf: 8,000.
★★★ *Lucciola*, v. Regina Margherita 49, ☎ 266651, 15 rm ⋙ closed May and 24 Oct-20 Dec, 38,000; bkf: 3,800.
★★★ *Mar Ligure*, v. Aurelia Ponente 22, ☎ 262341, 37 rm P ⋙ ✷ 70,000; bkf: 3,000.

★★★ *Mirelia,* v. Balbo 7, ☎ 262351, 14 rm P 🖭 closed 25 Oct-22 Dec, 50,000; bkf: 5,000.
★★★ *Parigi,* lungomare Argentina 18, ☎ 261406, 41 rm P ≶ 🖭 ⅋ closed 1 Nov-20 Dec, 95,000; bkf: 1,000.
★★★ *Villa Elisa,* v. Romana 70, ☎ 261313, 34 rm P 🖭 closed 15 Oct-20 Dec, 75,000.

Restaurants:
♦♦♦ *Reserve Tastevin,* v. Arziglia 20, ☎ 261322, closed Mon and 30 Oct-20 Dec. Terrace with view and bathing facilities. Excellent seafood: frittura del golfo, pescatrice with myrtle, 30/50,000.
♦♦♦ *Chaudron,* p. Bengasi 2, ☎ 263592, closed Mon, 15-31 Jan and 15-30 Jun. In the French style. International, predominantly French cuisine: coquilles St. Jacques au gratin, Sisteron lamb, 40/50,000.

Recommended
Children's facilities: *Piccolo Nido* children's home, v. Romana 51, ☎ 263556 (children up to 11 years, all year).
Cycling: *GS Ford chic Patrizia,* v. Ferrara 10.
Events: *international exhibition of humour* (Jul-Aug).
Tennis: v. Stoppani 7, ☎ 261661.
Wines: *Enoteca del Dolceacqua,* at Dolceacqua *(9 km N),* v. Roma 33, ☎ 36180.

CAMOGLI

Genoa 21, Milan 162 km
Pop. 6,560 ✉ 16032 ☎ 0185   D2

The men of the Ligurian coast have always been sailors. Today it is still easy to imagine the period when this area, full of women who were 'neither widows nor brides', was known as 'casa della mogli' (wives home). Tourism has not altered the structure and character of the streets around the old village of Isola, neither has it erased the memory of the glorious seafaring traditions of Camogli's sailors, who, in the 19C, leased out their sailing ships to half of Europe and built a fleet twice as large as that of Hamburg.

▶ The compact, fortified town centre has tall, narrow houses with **multi-coloured** façades, narrow alleyways and steep steps. This central part faces the old **harbour,** which is protected by a massive 17C harbour wall. ▶ The **parish church** and, further uphill, the **castel Dragone** which rises steeply above the sea are both originally 12C. The castle houses the **Tyrrhenian Aquarium** *(10 a.m.-12 noon and 3-7 p.m.).* ▶ Many families from Camogli have donated mementos, relics and documents from the age of sailing ships to the **Museo marinaro Gio Bono Ferrari** *(Wed, Sat and hols, 9 a.m.-12 noon and 4-7 p.m.).* The exhibits include engravings, paintings, nautical instruments, ships in bottles and votive offerings.

Environs

▶ Starting from Camogli, the Portofino promontory can be explored on foot: San Rocco is easily reached and from there it is possible to climb to **Portofino Vetta★** or descend to **Punta Chiappa,** going past the small Romanesque church of **S. Nicolò di Capodimonte.** It was to this church, which rises steeply above the rocks, that the sailors who had escaped the dangers of their voyages brought their votive offerings. ▶ **San Fruttuoso** is more easily accessible by boat *(all year).* This small village clusters around the abbey of **S. Fruttuoso di Capodimonte★** (13C). This was built by the Doria family beside the 10C church and originally stood on rocky spurs which emerged from the sea.   ◻

Practical information
CAMOGLI
≋
ⅈ v. ♦♦ Settembre 33r, ☎ 771066.

Hotel:
★★★★ *Cenobio dei Dogi,* v. Cuneo 34, ☎ 770041, 88 rm P ≶ 🝆 🖭 ⊡ ⚹ closed 7 Jan-28 Feb. Former cus-

toms post set amid conifers and flowers, overlooking the sea between castle at Camogli and headland of San Fruttuoso, 25/50,000.

Restaurants:
♦♦♦ *Gattonero,* p. Colombo 32, ☎ 770242, closed Thu and Jan. Open-air service in summer. Seafood: trofiette with pesto, pappardelle Elio, 25/50,000.
♦♦♦ *Rosa,* largo Casabona 11, ☎ 771088, closed Tue, Nov-Dec and Feb. High above sea with terrace overlooking bay. Seafood: pansoti with walnuts, fritto misto, 40/55,000.
♦♦♦ *Vento Ariel,* calata Porto Franco 1, ☎ 771080, closed Wed and Feb. Veranda overlooking little harbour. Seafood: trenette with pesto, flambed prawns or crayfish, 35/50,000.

Recommended
Boat trips: to San Fruttuoso, *Battelli Golfo Paradiso,* ☎ 772091.
Events: *festival of fish* (2nd Sun in May); *Stella Maris procession* (beginning of Aug).
Marina: ☎ 770032.
Swimming: on road through Ruta.

Environs

PORTOFINO VETTA, ✉ 16030, 6 km SE.

Hotel:
★★★★ *Portofino Vetta,* v. Gaggini 8, ☎ 772281, 12 rm P ≶ 🝆 🖭 🍽 closed Feb and Nov. Includes museum of Byzantine, Romanesque, Gothic and Renaissance frescos, 127,000. Rest.● ♦♦♦♦ 30/40,000.

CELLE LIGURE

Savona 8, Genoa 39, Milan 162 km
Pop. 4,805 ✉ 17015 ☎ 019   C2

The houses in the centre of Celle, a typical example of a long narrow coastal village, were at one time separated from the seashore and the gardens by the railway and the via Aurelia. However, the railway has been moved uphill and this has meant that the town centre is no longer so cut off from the sea. To the E, on the other hand, the **Piani** district extends unimpeded, with hotels, villas and blocks of flats. Further uphill, the parish church of **S. Michele,** which once stood on its own, is now surrounded by buildings. Inside the church, which has a fine campanile (13C-14C), there are 17C-18C Ligurian paintings and sculptures and a 16C polyptych. At **Pecorile** there is the house where Francesco della Rovere, later Pope Sixtus IV, was born in 1414.   ◻

Practical information
≋
ⅈ largo Giolitti 7, ☎ 990021.

Hotels:
★★★★ *Riviera,* v. Colla 55, ☎ 990541, 52 rm 🖭 ⚹ closed 1 Nov-15 Dec, 65,000; bkf: 5,000.
★★★★ *San Michele,* at Piani, ☎ 990017, 57 rm P 🖭 ⊡ closed Oct-May, 75,000; bkf: 9,000.
★★★ *Ancora,* v. De Amicis 3, ☎ 990052, 41 rm P 🝆 🖭 closed Oct-Mar, 55,000.

Restaurant:
● ♦♦♦ *Villa Alta,* v. Aurelia 1/A, ☎ 990939, closed Tue and 7 Jan-28 Feb. In elegant old villa with terraces overlooking sea and garden. Excellent international cuisine: fillet of sole Bercy, lobster Thermidor, 50/60,000.
⚞ ★ *Casarino,* at Presane, v. Aurelia 8, 76 pl, ☎ 990896 (all year).

Recommended
Sailing: ☎ 990448 (instruction).
Tennis: v. Torino, ☎ 991771; v. Pescetto 24, ☎ 990869.

CERIANA

Imperia 33, Genoa 149, Milan 276 km
Pop. 1,348 ⊠ 18034 ☎ 0184   A3

Ceriana has expanded slowly up the mountain and today is one of the most typical compact inland villages in Liguria, with its old houses set in rising circles and a charming tangle of alleyways, flights of steps and passageways.

▶ The **parish church** is Baroque, with a fine 16C wooden altar, but more striking is the group formed by the Romanesque church of **S. Spirito** (12C, altered) in the lower part of the village and the 17C oratory of **S. Caterina**, which displays the influence of Borromini.   ◻

CERVO

Imperia 10, Genoa 196, Milan 228 km
Pop. 1,281 ⊠ 18010 ☎ 0183   B3

In the late 17C and early 18C coral fishing in the seas of Corsica and Sardinia was still one of the most profitable activities for local people. Some of this money was used to build the church of **S. Giovanni Battista★**, known as 'corallina', a major example of Ligurian Baroque; it still makes a striking impression as it rises out of the old village sheer above the sea. In the upper section, below the castle, is the fascinating **medieval village**, with closely-packed groups of houses. In the lower part of the village are some fine **Baroque palazzi**, a sign of the growth of the community in the 17C.   ◻

Practical information
≋
ⓘ v. Aurelia, ☎ 408197.

Restaurant:
◆◆◆ **San Giorgio**, v. Volta 19, ☎ 400175, closed Tue, 10 Jan-25 Feb and 10-25 Dec. Tranquil with outdoor service in summer. Regional cuisine: trenette with pesto, fritto misto, 25/45,000.

⚘ ★ **Lino**, v. N. Sauro 4, 102 pl, ☎ 400087.

Recommended
Events: *international festival of chamber music* (Jul-Aug).
Tennis: v. Torrente Steria, ☎ 402392.

CHIAVARI

Genoa 42, Milan 173 km
Pop. 29,502 ⊠ 16043 ☎ 0185   E2

Chiavari has always had a reputation as a hardworking and thrifty town. Its present prosperity is based on tourism, light industry and crafts ('campanino' chairs, macram), but it still owes a great deal to the enterprise of the citizens of the town who emigrated to South America in the second half of the 19C and returned wealthy and eager for status. From then on the town grew considerably, to an extent which might make it seem colourless and anonymous to the superficial observer. In fact it has a highly original personality derived from the fusion of 19C and medieval elements. In the 16C Chiavari's fortifications were counted among the finest in Europe, and the layout of the town was considered an ideal model.

▶ From the 14C the town had two main axes: the longitudinal 'straight alley' **(v. Martiri della Liberazione)**, the show street, flanked with porticos, and the street running at right angles to it from the parish church to the citadel **(v. S. Giovanni-v. della Cittadella)**. This was the commercial, religious and civic heart of the town and shows the importance of spatial relationships in its social life.
▶ Until the late 17C Chiavari, subordinate to Genoa and conscious of the need for disciplined urban design, opted for architectural sobriety, with the exception of certain buildings in the oldest part of the town. The most important of these are the citadel (all that remains is a tower in the **Palace of Justice**, in the piazza Mazzini) and the parish church of **S. Giovanni Battista** (1182). ▶ In the 17C-18C, a period of autonomy and great prosperity, the churches of S. Giovanni Battista, **S. Franceso** and S. **Giacomo** were rebuilt, and the **santuario di Nostra Signora**, the present cathedral, was built (the marble pronaos was an addition of 1841-1907). ▶ The town walls were also partially demolished and most of the noble residences built or extended: the **Palazzo Torriglia**, the **Palazzo Rocca** (soon to house the Civico Museo Archeologico), the **Palazzo Marana**. ▶ Modern urban expansion began in the 19C. Streets leading towards the coast were opened up, but they followed the principle of axes intersecting at right angles which had been established in the older part of the town.

Environs

▶ The **basilica dei Fieschi★** *(in San Salvatore district, 4.5 km NE)* is one of the largest and best-preserved Romanesque-Gothic buildings in Liguria, built in 1245-52 for Pope Innocent IV Fieschi. It has a façade with black-and-white bands, a large marble rose-window and a massive crossing tower. ▶ The **santuario della Madonna delle Grazie** *(on road to Rapallo, about 4 km)* dates from *c.* 1430, with 16C frescos. ▶ The **abbazia di Borzone** *(c. 20 km N)* is a fine 13C Romanesque church.

Practical information ———————

CHIAVARI
≋ corso Assarotti 1, ☎ 310241.

Hotels:
★★★★ **Giardini**, v. Vinelli 9, ☎ 313951, 72 rm Ⓟ ⌖ 85,000; bkf: 8,000.
★★★★ **Santa Maria**, v. Tito Groppo 29, ☎ 309621, 34 rm Ⓟ ⚏ closed 20 Oct-20 Dec, 62,000; bkf: 7,000.
★★★ **Mignon**, v. Salietti 7, ☎ 309420, 32 rm ⚏ 53,000; breakfast 4,000.

Restaurants:
◆◆◆ **Copetin**, p. Gagliardo 16, ☎ 309064, closed Tue eve, Wed, Dec and Jan. Pleasant summer veranda overlooking sea. Excellent seafood: spaghetti with fish sauce, scampi Copetin, 35/60,000
◆◆◆ **Lord Nelson Pub**, corso Valparaiso 27, ☎ 302595, closed Mon and 5 Nov-6 Dec. English-inspired, on promenade. Excellent seafood: tagliolini with crayfish, champagne risotto, 55/75,000.

⚘ ★★ *Chiavari al Mare*, v. Preli 30, 50 pl, ☎ 304633.

Recommended
Bowling: *Italian bowls union*, p. Sanfroni 4, ☎ 310432.
Children's facilities: *Temossi* children's home, at Temossi Borzonasca *(23 km N)*, v. Comunale, ☎ 341024 (children aged 4-12; open Jun-Sep).
Craft workshops: *Citi*, v. Franceschi 14, ☎ 309670 (beechwood chairs).
Events: Display of Orchids (held Feb of odd-numbered years); *Tigullio nautical contest* (Sep).
Horseback riding: Rivarola Carasco, v. Veneto 212, ☎ 382304 (associate of *ANTE*); *Boschetto Horse-Riding Club*, salita Ceiva, ☎ 301785 (instruction).
Marina: ☎ 3161.
Sailing: *Lega Navale*, marina box 51, ☎ 301769 (instruction, also navigationand rowing).
Swimming: nr Stabilimenti Lido, ☎ 311898.
Tennis: v. Preli 20, ☎ 304471.

For help in understanding terms when visiting museums or other sites, see the *Art and Architectural Terms Guide* at the end of the Practical Holiday Guide.

Environs

LEIVI, ⊠ 16040, 6 km N.

Restaurants:
● ◆◆◆ *Ca' Peo*, v. dei Caduti 80, ☎ 319090, closed Mon, Tue noon and Nov. Regional cuisine, 40/55,000.
◆◆ *Pepen*, largo Marconi 1, ☎ 319010, closed Tue, Mon eve in winter and Oct. Regional and Emilian cuisine, 27,000.

The CINQUE TERRE

E-F2

The Cinque Terre are five little villages at the ends of narrow valleys cutting through the steep coastal range. Their houses rise in tiers on the cliffs, the alleyways are narrow, with flights of steps, and boats are pulled up on to the tiny spaces left by the sea. This would be one of the wildest landscapes in Liguria, if it were not for the green terraced slopes of the ancient vineyards.

▶ Only the outer villages of the Cinque Terre (Monterosso and Riomaggiore) are easily reached by car, but it is precisely this restriction which makes them so fascinating. They can be reached by boat, by train, or by walking from one to the next along the 'sentiero azzurro' (blue path) high on the hill. ▶ **Monterosso al Mare** is the most important centre and the only one with a broad, sandy beach. It has vestiges of old walls, towers and bastions, a fine parish church with 14C façade and a convent possessing interesting paintings. ▶ **Vernazza's** beach was long ago washed away by the sea; the village itself, in wonderful condition, is like a wedge pushed into the rocky coast: old houses are set one above the other and steps lead down the only street to the little harbour and the piazza in which the fine **Gothic parish church** stands. ▶ **Corniglia** is even more cramped and looks out over the sea from a promontory on the edge of a little valley of vines. The austere 14C **parish church** with marble rose-window is one of the most interesting Ligurian Gothic buildings in the Cinque Terre. ▶ The narrow gorge of **Manarola** ends in a rocky promontory and a harbour so tiny that the boats have to be pulled out of the water on to a jetty. ▶ The **'via dell'amore'** leads high above the sea to **Riomaggiore**, built between extensive vineyards and olive groves in the valley of the River Maior. This village too has a 14C parish church (façade rebuilt in 1870). **Walks** include path no. 1 *(along ridge, marked in red paint)*: Portovenere - Campiglia - Foce Drignana - Levanto; path no. 2 *(along coast, marked in blue paint)*: Portovenere - Campiglia - Riomaggiore -Corniglia - Vernazza - Monterosso - Lvanto *(information in Levanto, p. Colombo 12, ☎ 0187/807175 and La Spezia, Club Alpino Italiano, v. Carpenino 43).* □

Practical information ⎯⎯⎯⎯⎯⎯⎯⎯

MANAROLA, ⊠ 19010, ☎ 0187.

Restaurants:
◆ *Marina Piccola*, v. Discovolo 38, ☎ 920103, closed Thu and Jan-Feb. By sea with olive garden; fine views. Seafood: risotto marinara, grilled fish, 20/35,000.
◆ *Porticciolo*, v. Discovolo 178, ☎ 920083, closed Wed. Regional cuisine: risotto alla marinara, lasagne al pesto, 15/20,000.

MONTEROSSO AL MARE, ⊠ 19016, ☎ 0187.
≋ v. Fegina (below station), ☎ 817506.
⬛ seasonal La Spezia - Portofino.

Hotel:
★★★★ *Porto Roca*, v. Corone 1, ☎ 817502, 43 rm ⬧ ⬭ ⬭⬭⬭ closed Nov-Mar, 110,000.

Restaurants:
◆◆ *Gigante*, v. IV Novembre 9, ☎ 817401, closed Tue and 15 Mar-15 Oct. Regional cuisine: spaghetti with steamed octopus, fusilli in conger eel sauce, 20/30,000.

◆ *Pozzo*, v. Roma 24, ☎ 817575, closed Mon and Nov. Seafood: grilled scampi, fish soups, 25/35,000.

Recommended
Sport: *Sailing club*, ☎ 817484; sports centre, p. Garibaldi 3, ☎ 817253.

RIOMAGGIORE, ⊠ 19017, ☎ 0187.

Hotel:
★★★ *Due Gemelli*, at Campi, v. Litoranea 1, ☎ 920111, 18 rm ℗ ⬭ ⬭ ⬭ closed Christmas, 45,000; bkf: 5,000.

VERNAZZA, ⊠ 19018, ☎ 0187.

Restaurant:
◆ *Gianni Franzi*, v. Visconti 2, ☎ 812228, closed Wed and 10 Jan-10 Mar. Near harbour, with terrace overlooking sea. Seafood: penne with scampi, pasta with pesto, 20/40,000.

DEIVA MARINA

La Spezia 52, Genoa 67, Milan 202 km
Pop. 1,606 ⊠ 19013 ☎ 0187   E2

Deiva Marina has a fine sand and gravel beach that attracts a large number of summer visitors. In **Framura** *(11 km E)* among pines and olives high above the sea, the campanile of the parish church is a 13C fortified tower. □

Practical information ⎯⎯⎯⎯⎯⎯⎯⎯

≋
ⓘ corso Italia 4, ☎ 815811.

Hotels:
★★★ *Clelia*, corso Italia 23, ☎ 815827, 24 rm ℗ ⬭⬭⬭ ⬭ closed 15 Oct-20 Dec and 15 Jan-15 Mar, 46,000; bkf: 7,000.
★★ *Riviera Giardino*, at Fornace, ☎ 815805, 28 rm ℗ ⬭⬭⬭ closed Oct-Easter, 42,000; bkf: 6,000.

Restaurant:
◆◆◆ *Maestrale*, v. XX Settembre 8, ☎ 815850, closed Wed and 10 Nov-10 Dec. Seafood, 20/30,000.

⬭ ★★★ *Costabella*, at Ghiaia, 150 pl, ☎ 815948.

DIANO MARINA

Imperia 7, Genoa 109, Milan 232 km
Pop. 6,911 ⊠ 18013 ☎ 0183   B3

In the late 18C Diano was the collective name of a community controlled from the mountain centre of Castello. The Diano region was the first in Liguria to specialize in the cultivation of olives, trading with the shepherds of the republic of Mendàtica in Piedmont and with the coastal centres of Porto Maurizio and Albenga. Then the railway and the coast road cut off the inland areas and made Diano Marina the most important settlement, and it opted to make a living from tourism.

▶ The centre, rebuilt after the earthquake of 1887, is typical of a late 19C small town. ▶ Since the Second World War new tourist developments have merged Diano Marina and **San Bartolomeo al Mare** in a somewhat messy way, but the latter district has two small areas which still show signs of medieval planning. ▶ Olive oil is produced in the valley, and there are many country villages in which the use of nets for collecting the fruit is common. ▶ The historic centre of **Diano Castello** *(2 km inland)* has retained the character of an old walled village. □

Practical information ⎯⎯⎯⎯⎯⎯⎯⎯

DIANO MARINA
≋
ⓘ Giardini Ardissone, ☎ 496956.

Hotels:

★★★★ *G. H. Diana Majestic,* v. Oleandri 15, ☎ 495445, 80 rm P ░ ☐ closed Nov-Mar, 115,000; bkf: 15,000.
★★★ *Caravelle,* v. Sausette 24, ☎ 496033, 48 rm P ░ ░ ☐ ,℗ closed 11 Oct-30 Apr, 79,000.
★★★ *Palace,* v. Torino 2, ☎ 495479, 46 rm P closed Nov-Christmas, 72,000; bkf: 9,000.
★★★ *Torino,* v. Milano 42, ☎ 495108, 63 rm P ░ ☐ closed 1 Nov-31 Dec, 72,000; bkf: 6,000.

⚖ *Edy,* v. Diano Calderina, 120 pl, ☎ 497040 (all year);
★ *Diana,* v. dei Sori, 130 pl, ☎ 495302 (all year).

Recommended

Events: *international festival of chamber music.*
Marina: ☎ 496112; *Club del Mare,* ☎ 496144.
Tennis: at Prato Fiorito, ☎ 403648.
♥ olive oil: can be bought direct from the various oil presses or, further inland, from farmers.

Environs

SAN BARTOLOMEO AL MARE, ⊠ 18016, ☎ 0183.
≋
ⓘ v. Aurelia, ☎ 400200.

Hotels:

★★★ *Bergamo,* v. Aurelia 9, ☎ 400060, 46 rm P ░ ⬙ ☐ closed Nov-Mar, 50,000; bkf: 4,000.
★★★ *Piccolo Hotel le Palme,* v. Colombo 5, ☎ 400758, 26 rm P ░ closed 1 Oct-1 Jan, 48,000.

⚖ ★ *Rosa,* v. al Santuario 4, 150 pl, ☎ 400473 (all year).

Recommended

Swimming and **tennis:** v. Martiri della Libertà 33, ☎ 401155.

Il FINALE

C2

The beautiful whitish-pink or orange colour of many buildings in Genoa is due to the famous 'Finale stone', the pride of that extraordinary geological zone where ancient outcrops of limestone rich in marine sediment create a fascinating landscape of deep, narrow valleys with numerous caves once inhabited by prehistoric man. In these dry, warm surroundings live a number of rare European reptiles. The flora too is unusual with many rare species. A network of regional parks is planned for the area's protection.

▶ Il Finale includes the town of **Finale Ligure,** made up of the three settlements of Borgo, Marina and Pia, numerous other tiny villages and the important coastal centre of **Varigotti.** ▶ **Finalborgo** is the most interesting of the historic centres of Finale Ligure. Its 15C **walls** are still intact and within them the symmetrical layout shows that Finalborgo was built as a medieval 'new town', under strict planning supervision. Various **palazzi** (15C-18C) are a reminder of the 250 years of prosperous stability enjoyed by Finalborgo as capital of il Finale and focal point of the Spanish domains in N Italy. The Baroque collegiate church of **S. Biagio** is particularly rich in works of art. The Dominican convent of **S. Caterina** (14C-15C) houses the new **Museo Civico** *(winter 9 a.m.-12 noon and 2:30-4:30 p.m.; summer 10 a.m.-12 noon and 3-6 p.m.; wkends 9 a.m.-12 noon; closed Mon),* with exhibits on the palaeontology and natural history of il Finale and its caves. ▶ Above the town are the fine, imposing ruins of **Castel Gavone;** not far from here is the church of **Nostra Signora di Loreto,** a Renaissance building on the model of the Portinari chapel in S. Eustorgio in Milan. ▶ **Finale Marina** is a typical linear coastal village, with an avenue of palms by its sandy beach. The historic centre has 16C-18C palazzi; Finale Marina was an important commercial centre in this period. The fortress dates from the 14C. ▶ A little to the SE, on the other side of Cape Caprazoppa, is the **Arene Candide** cave *(not open to public),* the scene of exceptional prehistoric

finds. ▶ **Finale Pia** grew up around the abbey of S. Maria di Pia (12C, rebuilt in 18C) and does not have a particularly coherent historic centre. Interesting features are the Benedictine **abbey,** a fine 16C building adjacent to S. Maria *(visit by request),* and a few km away, the half-abandoned village of **Calvisio,** one of the oldest inland centres of il Finale, with typical large ashlar houses. ▶ **Varigotti,** a 14C fishing village, now a seaside resort, has many old houses with typical Ligurian terraced roofs. The church of **S. Lorenzo Vecchio,** on a crag overhanging the sea, dates from the early Middle Ages. ☐

Practical information

FINALE LIGURE, ⊠ 17024, ☎ 019.
≋
ⓘ v. S. Pietro 14, ☎ 692581; Varigotti branch office, v. Aurelia 79, ☎ 698013.

Hotels:

★★★★ *Moroni,* v. delle Palme 38, ☎ 692222, 113 rm P ⬙ 95,000; bkf: 10,000.
★★★★ *Residenza Punta Est,* v. Aurelia 1, ☎ 600611, 38 rm P ⬙ ░ ⬙ ☐ closed Oct-Apr, 100,000.
★★★ *Colibri,* v. Colombo 57, ☎ 692681, 41 rm P closed 16 Oct-31 Mar, 80,000; bkf: 9,000.

Restaurants:

♦♦♦ *Torchi,* at Finalborgo, v. dell'Annunziata 12, ☎ 690531, closed Tue and 9 Jan-9 Mar. In former oil-mill. Mixed cuisine: ravioli with prawn sauce, trenette with pesto, 30/45,000.
♦♦ *Osteria del Castel Gavone,* at Perti, ☎ 692277, closed Tue and 10-30 Jan. On terrace looking out over il Finale and sea. Regional and Italian cuisine: gnocchi alla piemontese, buridda, 18/25,000.

Recommended

Archery: *Il Finale archery group,* v. Pertica 45.
Horseback riding: at Prato del Signore, v. Calice, ☎ 691650 (instruction).
Marina: yacht club, ☎ 601697.

VARIGOTTI, ⊠ 17029, 5 km E.

Restaurant:

♦ *Muraglia-Conchiglia d'Oro,* v. Aurelia 133, ☎ 698015, closed Wed, Tue, Oct-May and 1 Dec-7 Jan. Seafood, 30/50,000.

⚖ ★ *Eurocamping Calvisso,* v. Calviso 37, 150 pl, ☎ 601240; ★ *San Martino,* at Mamie, 130 pl, ☎ 698250 (all year).

GENOA**

(Genova)

Milan 145, Rome 501 km
Pop. 746,785 ⊠ 16100 ☎ 010   C-D1-2

Genoa was built a little at a time, as can be seen from the gradual way in which its streets developed over the ages and the slow extension of the town walls as a result of political and economic change. Today Genoa is sadly neglected by tourists, who tend to skirt its edges on their way to somewhere else. It is not easy to say why tourists avoid Genoa, whether it is because of the specific geography of the region, shortage of space or the nature of the inhabitants, who are reputed to be greedy, as they have always been merchants, financiers and conquerors. 'A royal city... magnificent men, magnificent walls' was Petrarch's view, but in the 19C another illustrious visitor, Stendhal, complained that Genoa was 'only interested in business' and was to a large extent just a 'labyrinth of streets four feet wide'. Contrasting opinions of a city of contrasts. Genoa still bursts with vital-

The homeland of Columbus

Ruined and ivy-clad, in the piazza Dante in old Genoa, near the porta Soprana, is the house in which Christopher Columbus spent his childhood. (The house was rebuilt in the 18C.) But where was the navigator born? For centuries people have tried to prove that it was not in Genoa, and the question has filled hundreds of erudite volumes. By tradition he was Ligurian at least, if not from Genoa then from Savona, Cogoleto, Nervi, Quinto or Bogliasco, or even Piacenza, or Costello di Cuccaro in Monferrato. But there are other strange theories: some have identified him with the Levantine corsair Giorgio Paleologo Bissipat, in French service in the 15C; a 17C English work said he was 'born in England but lived in Genoa', another suggestion is that he was French, or was confused with a corsair called Coullon. According to Salvador de Madariaga he was a Jewish convert of Spanish origin forced by racial persecution to emigrate to Liguria; other Spaniards have maintained that he was from Estremadura, Galicia or Catalonia; two Corsicans attempted to demonstrate that he was born at Calvi on their island; and the Italian patriot Agostino Ruffini, while a refugee in Ferney, met a Monsieur Colomb who thought that Columbus was born in Geneva. The family was from Mocónesi in the valley of Fontanabuona, from which they moved down to the city. Domenico, the father of Christopher, was born in Quinto and became a weaver before being appointed custodian of the porta dell'Olivella in Genoa. The Genoese chronicler Antonio Gallo was certainly right when he wrote that the navigator 'was born in Genoa of plebeian parents'. The admiral himself, in the Mayorazgo, a sort of will in favour of his son Diego, which he dictated in Seville in 1498 before setting off on his third ocean voyage, categorically declared 'I was born in Genoa'.

ity and contradictions: it no longer knows whether to expand, in which case more space will be needed for development, or whether it should cut back its marine and industrial activities. It has all the characteristics of a great modern metropolis and yet there is nowhere in Italy quite like it; for Genoa's run-down urban centre, laden with history, still preserves the colourful, exotic atmosphere and bustle of an ancient sea port.

▶ **Early building on the coast.** ▶ Coming down from the Piazza Principe railway station (AB 2) Genoa resembles the main streets of an early coastal town; this is a part of Genoa that has always belonged to working people and its tiny, narrow streets are full of life and colour. ▶ The **via di Pré** begins at a group of Romanesque-Gothic buildings consisting of the **church of S. Giovanni di Pré** (12C-14C) and the **loggia dei Cavalieri Gerosolimitani** or Commendatory (12C-16C, restored) which accommodated pilgrims about to set off for the Holy Land. Today it is a lively, dirty and disreputable part of town. ▶ The **via del Campo** (B-C3) is much the same, leading past the 12C city walls through the **porta dei Vacca**, the work of Lombard masons (a guild which settled in Genoa and worked here for centuries). ▶ Here, near the city's first cathedral, **S. Siro** (C3; rebuilt in the 16C-17C), and along the v. Fossatello and the v. S. Luca (a stretch of the **'carrugio dritto'**, straight road), the buildings were organized around the little squares of the merchant nobility, making a compact 13C suburb. Here there are austere residential towers and the sumptuous palazzi of the Pallavicini, Pinelli, Centurione, Grimaldi and Spinola families. ▶ The

two last-named families at various times from the 16C-18C owned the most notable patrician residence in the district, which today houses the **Galleria Nazionale di Palazzo Spinola**★ (C3; *9 a.m.-4 p.m.; Sun 9 a.m.-1 p.m.; closed Mon*). The original bequest included not only fine furniture and household objects, but also an extremely valuable collection of art, of which the most striking are a sculpture by Giovanni Pisano and pictures by Antonello da Messina, Joos van Cleve, Bernardo Strozzi and Van Dyck. ▶ At the intersection of the v. S. Luca and the axis made up by the v. Orefici-v. Luccoli, the **piazza Banchi** (C3) was the commercial and urban centre until the 18C. The new layout of the old moneychangers' square, the rebuilding of **San Pietro** and the building of a new and more spacious **Loggia dei Mercanti** (restored) were among the most significant of the profound urban changes that took place in the 16C, when expanding financial activity and international popularity made the city more susceptible to diverse cultural experience. ▶ The v. Ponte Reale connects the piazza Banchi to the **Ripa** (now v. Sottoripa, on the **piazza Caricamento**, C3), the old commercial dock and coastal road with stalls and shops of most kinds, particularly those concerned with boatbuilding and ships' instruments. This was the site of the 'Palazzo del Mare', later called **Palazzo S. Giorgio** (C3) because it housed the bank of the same name, a partially Gothic (1260), partially Renaissance (1571) building. The Ripa has gradually lost its original contact with the sea, but admirable work in the late 19C restored great vitality (characteristic shops, restaurants) to the area, which to some extent still conveys the ancient fascination of the maritime republic. ▶ The v. Turati leads to the **piazza Cavour** (D3), with a 13C building in the corner by the v. del Molo. At the end of the v. del Molo there is a section of 15C walls, pierced by the **porta del Molo** or porta Siberia (D2), a remarkable piece of military architecture (G. Alessi, 1553) with two façades: a great gate on the city side and a forbidding stronghold on the side that looks towards the sea.

▶ **The old centre.** ▶ The castle hill is the site of Genoa's oldest urban settlement (6C BC), bounded to the N by the natural hollow of the *chiavica* (sewer; now the v. Giustiniani). In the 9C-10C, the existing town (*civitas*) was already enclosed by a ring wall which had developed along the line of the same *chiavica* (above the Ripa) and the fortified hill (*castrum*) on which the bishop's palace was built. Lower down the church of **S. Maria di Castello**★ (D3), which once served as a second cathedral, was rebuilt in plain Romanesque style by Lombard masons in the 12C, then decorated and extended by the addition of the convent and the two cloisters in the 15C (*visit on request during daylight hours, guided by a monk*) and finally completed in 1513 (sanctuary, apses). The interior has been restored. This church is one of the most important religious monuments in Genoa and also contains fine works of art, some of which are in the **museum** in the convent (*Wed, Sat and Sun 8 a.m.-12 noon; and 3-6 p.m.*). ▶ On the street which runs down the hill is the proud **Torre degli Embriaci** (D3), a particularly striking monument to feudal rule by the family of the same name and the only surviving evidence of a statute of 1296 limiting the height of private towers in Genoa. ▶ Over the centuries the district enclosed within the first walls was taken over by artisans and small businessmen, becoming increasingly working-class. The homes of the feudal and commercial nobility, established in the 12C, still show medieval characteristics: the great social changes of the 16C made little difference to the appearance of the palazzi of the privileged nobility. ▶ Religious and monastic architecture are also well represented. The Romanesque church of **S. Cosimo** (D3), late 11C, is the only church in Genoa in which the original shallow apses have survived. ▶ Through sections less typical of the town, passing the p. S. Giorgio (D3; *site of original market by harbour in 11C*) and the **v. di Canneto il Lungo** (D3; with many medieval houses and Renaissance portals with reliefs) is the 12C Romanesque church of **S. Donato**★ (D3); parts of this church have been restored, but the portal is original, as is the fine octagonal campanile. ▶ Finally, **S. Agostino** (D4) is a 13C Gothic church, rebuilt and restored after bomb damage in 1943, with a notable **campanile★** and **two cloisters.** The first, triangular, dates from the 14C-15C and is being restored. The second, rectangular and larger, is 18C and has been reorganized to accommodate the **Museo di Architettura e Scultura Ligure** *(wkdays 9 a.m.-1:15 p.m. and 3-6 p.m.),* which has a huge collection on the development of representational art in Genoa from the high Middle Ages to the 18C. The finest item in the collection is the **tomb of Margaret of Brabant** (wife of Henry VII) by Giovanni Pisano. ▶ From the p. Sarzano, site of the campo Sarzano until the 17C-18C, a fine example of an open public space suitable for demonstrations and parades, the street leads to the striking twin towers of the 12C **porta di S. Andrea** or **porta Soprana★** (D4), on the site of a 9C predecessor, important as the gateway to the Roman road to the Near East.

▶ **Genoa's medieval political and religious centre.** ▶ Along the via Soprana from porta Soprana is the area which in the late 11C was the political and religious centre of the city, behind the commercial axis, the 'carrugio dritto' (v. S. Luca and v. Canneto il Curto); here, in the 16C, the Genoese oligarchy built their magnificent residences. ▶ On one side of the p. Matteotti (D4), a 19C open space, is the 16C **church of Il Gesù,** with a sumptuous Baroque interior in lavish polychrome marble; the pictures are some of the most important to be found in any church in Genoa (particularly the two paintings by Rubens behind the high altar and in the third chapel on the l.). The **Palazzo Ducale** is on the other side of the square; its Neoclassical façade was the final stage of a late 18C reconstruction of the palazzo, which was originally planned and built in the late 16C and early 17C during one of the most radical phases of urban change. The remains of the medieval town hall are incorporated in the left wing. ▶ The cathedral of **S. Lorenzo★★** (D3) is in a 19C square and was built over many centuries (the high altar (on the site of an earlier sanctuary) was consecrated in 1118 and the last campanile was completed in 1522. The black-and-white striped façade, typical of high Tyrrhenian architecture, is articulated with lavish portals in the French Gothic style (13C) and is decorated at its extremities by two lions on columns. In the interior are three striking decorative cycles: the frescos in the Cappella Lercari (on the l. of the sanctuary) by G. B. Castello and L. Cambiaso (1565); the frescos in the choir by L. Tavarone (1624); and the Cappella di S. Giovanni Battista★ (1451-65), designed by D. Gagini, a pupil of Brunelleschi. There is a fine collection in the **Museo del Tesoro di S. Lorenzo★** *(9:30-11:45 a.m. and 3-5.45 p.m.; closed wkends and Mon),* remarkable both for its quality and for the advanced principles underlying its organization. ▶ The streets to the l. and r. of the cathedral give an interesting view of social and civic history. ▶ The v. S. Lorenzo (D3) was built in the last century to link the 19C town with the harbour; it ruined the homogeneity of the older part of the town by cutting both the financial district and the political and religious quarter off from the working-class area around the castle by orientating them more to the N, towards the 'new road'. ▶ The streets on the opposite side of the church, behind the **Palazzo Ducale,** were the quarter in which the rich guilds settled and in which the wealthiest Genoese families built their homes in the 16C. The v. Indoratori and the v. Orefici are a reminder of the work of the ancient goldsmiths' guilds, who achieved enormous prosperity at this time. In these streets and in the v. Scurreria, p. Campetto, p. Soziglia and v. Luccoli (C3-4) are the major palazzi, often with decorated façades and magnificent carved portals. For example, at no. 2 v. Indoratori, the **portal** of the Palazzo Valdettaro-Fieschi is among the most interesting (by G. Gagini, *c.* 1460). Also striking is the way in which the **Palazzo Imperiale** (C3), built for the family of the same name, makes good use of the perspective afforded by the v. Scurreria, which was built in the 16C and forms the main approach to the entrance portal. ▶ An interesting clue to the nature of urban Genoa in the Middle Ages

and the Renaissance is the absence of a main city square. Community life was focused on the private 'curias', small squares enclosed by tall houses, with porticos, sometimes defensive towers and a family church. The **piazza S. Matteo★★** (C-D4), residence of the Doria faction from the 12C-17C, has retained its medieval appearance almost intact. On one side is the Romanesque-Gothic church of **S. Matteo,** founded in 1125, with a black-and-white façade dating from 1278, a crypt containing the tomb of Andrea Doria and a cloister dating from 1310. All round the square, forming an incomparable scenic group, are the **houses★** of Branca, Domenicaccio (13C), Lamba (13C) and Costantino Doria (15C), all with black-and-white bands, fine portals, mullioned windows and loggias.

▶ **The Strade Nuove.** ▶ From the 16C-19C a new axis tangential to the old town shifted the focus of the city away from the quays and warehouses of the harbour. Today the area around these 'new streets' *(strade nuove)* running from the p. Fontane Marose to the p. Acquaverde is one of the most impressive and elegant in the town. ▶ In the 19C the via XXV Aprile (CD4) was built to link this district and the new centre in the **piazza De Ferrari** (D4), a vast modern square with impressive Neoclassical buildings, including the ruins of the **Teatro Carlo Felice** (1828, awaiting rebuilding) and the palazzo which houses the **Accademia Ligustica di Belle Arti** and the **Pinacoteca dell'Accademia** *(wkdays 9 a.m.-1 p.m.),* with 16C-17C works of the Genoese school. ▶ In the **piazza Fontane Marose** (C4), the loveliness of the Gothic windows and the black-and-white façade of the **Palazzo Spinola** anticipate the splendour of the 16C patrician residences in the next section of the strada nuova. ▶ 'One of the most beautiful streets in the world' wrote Stendhal in 1837, with architecture which is 'courageous, rich in arches and columns, magnificent and light-hearted': this is the **via Garibaldi★★** (C4), originally called Strada Nuova dei Palazzi and a superlative example of 16C European town planning. It is a straight street divided into building plots one opposite the other, sold by auction to six of the noblest Genoese families. The Strada Nuova was conceived as a controlled outlet for the urge to erect magnificent buildings suited to the new way of life and to the power of the ruling oligarchy. In the first decade of the second half of the 16C, thirteen sumptuous palazzi were built, each with a courtyard and magnificent frescoed rooms. The most interesting are the **Carrega-Cataldi,** no. 4, the **Spinola,** no. 5 and the **Podestà,** no. 7. No. 9, the **Palazzo Municipale★** (C4), built 1565-79 by the extremely wealthy Nicolò Grimaldi, called 'il monarca', principal creditor of King Philip II of Spain, breaks the logical organization of the street: it is a large building with a rectangular courtyard and a façade three times longer than those of the palazzi built before it. ▶ The street ends in two more large palazzi, one opposite the other. No. 11 is the **Palazzo Bianco** (C4), with a neoclassical façade; it houses one of the city's most important art collections, the **Galleria di Palazzo Bianco** *(9 a.m.-1:15 p.m. and 3-6 p.m.; Sun 9:15 a.m.-12:45 p.m.; closed Mon).* The gallery has works by Genoese painters from the 15C-16C, 17C Spanish artists and painters of the Flemish school, as well as canvases by Pontormo and Palma Vecchio. No. 18 is the 17C, baroque **Palazzo Rosso** (C4), with two piani nobili and spacious loggias in the courtyard, and it also houses a fine art gallery, the **Galleria di Palazzo Rosso★** *(for opening times see Palazzo Bianco).* The collection consists mainly of works by Italian and Genoese painters of the late 15C-16C, along with numerous **portraits★** of the nobility painted by Van Dyck while staying in Genoa; original furnishings. ▶ The v. **Cairoli** (B-C3) was built in 1786 to connect the Strada Nuova and the Strada Balbi, and for this reason was called 'Strada Nuovissima'. It was the first attempt to join the roads coming in from the E and W extremities of the town and relate them to the historic centre. Building proceeded according to the same logic as had been used in the Strada Nuova: numerous aristocratic residences were built opposite each other along the street. ▶ In the nearby v. Lomellini is the **birthplace of Giuseppe Mazzini** (B3), which contains libraries, archives

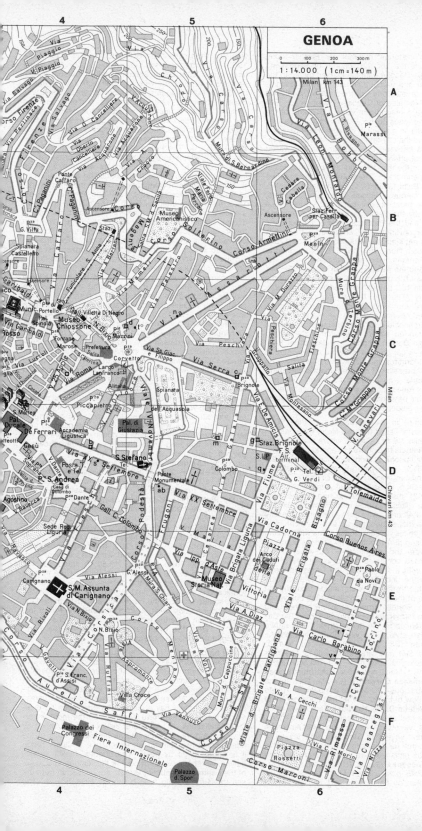

and collections of historical material. ▶ Further along the strade nuove is the 16C-17C church of **Santissima Annunziata★** (B3). Despite damage caused by fire in the Second World War and partial destruction of the decoration, the church is still one of the most typical rich and magnificent examples of Genoese Baroque. ▶ The final section of these magnificent streets consists of the **v. Balbi** (B2-3) and leads to the Piazza Principe railway station. It was built as a result of an agreement between the Balbi family and the city fathers aimed at the improvement of the roads between the harbour and the walled city and is the final attempt at planned growth made in old Genoa, which in the late 19C was still confined within its late medieval perimeter. The street was the residential district of the Balbi family (with seven palazzi), interspersed with numerous religious buildings (convents, churches). ▶ The most notable buildings among those originally planned by the Balbi are the **Palazzo Durazzo Pallavicini** (1618) and the **Palazzo Reale★**; the former's original modest proportions were enlivened with portals and loggias: the great staircase was acquired later (1780); the so-called Palazzo Reale (B2-3) is 17C, redesigned in the 18C by C. Fontana, who was responsible for the double staircase and the hanging garden looking out over the Porto Vecchio. The piano nobile, a splendid example of the interior of an 18C patrican residence, accommodates an **Art Gallery** *(Tue and Thu 10 a.m.-1 p.m.; Sun and hols 9 a.m.-12 noon)* with paintings, Baroque sculpture, tapestries and oriental ceramics. ▶ Another excellent example of architecture for the nobility of the period is in the area intended as an extension of the strade nuove: the **Palazzo Doria Pamphili** or **Palazzo del Principe★** (B1), which — cut off as it is by the railway station and the Stazione Marittima and subdivided into flats — no longer gives the impression of coherent mannerism intended by Andrea Doria, who between 1529 and 1547 had the whole complex redesigned in a style of princely splendour to celebrate his personal fame and as a fitting palace in which to receive emperors (Charles V) and kings.

▶ **The modern city.** In the second half of the 19C a road system was established that ran along the coast on the slopes of the hills NE of the town, where upper middle class residential districts had started to spring up. ▶ The so-called **Circonvallazione a Monte**, which starts at the p. Acquaverde (AB2), winds high above the city, almost always with magnificent views, as far as the p. Manin (B6). The first section, corso U. Bassi, ends at the **Castello d'Albertis** (A2), the most striking neo-Renaissance building in Genoa. This was built in 1886 by the explorer captain E. A. d'Albertis, who presented it to the city along with all the rich ethnographic and nautical treasures he collected on his voyages; these items will form the nucleus of the Museo di Archeologia ed Etnografia *(opening soon)*. ▶ From the magnificent 17C **Albergo dei Poveri** (A3), the road continues to the esplanade of the **Castelletto** (B4), with a fine view★; the Castelletto was for four centuries the nerve centre of the city's fortifications. It is possible to reach the esplanade from the old town by using one of the two lifts available; the one which leaves from the p. Portello arrives at a fine *art nouveau* station. ▶ A little farther, in the corso Solferino, the Circonvallazione is flanked by the dense growth of a **public park** in the English style. The villa Gruber houses the **American Museum** (B5; *9:30 a.m.-12 noon and 3-5:30 p.m.; closed Sun a.m. and Mon*) with a fine pre-Columbian archaeological collection. ▶ From here, along the corso Armellini, p. Manin and the v. Assarotti, the road descends to the **piazza Corvetto★** (C4-5). The 'serene strength' of the spacious 19C square is now lost, ruined by the ceaseless flow of traffic. What has survived is the fine view of the **Villetta Di Negro public park** (C4), which was originally planned as a botanical garden and therefore has a great variety of exotic and Mediterranean shrubs and plants. Lovers of Stendhal, who stayed in the Villetta, will search for it in vain, as it was destroyed in an air raid. It was replaced by a small palazzo housing the **Museo A. Chiossone★** *(9 a.m.-1:15 p.m. and 3-6 p.m.; Sun 9:15 a.m.-12:45 p.m.; closed Mon)*, which has an interesting collection on Far Eastern art and civilization

from the third millennium BC to the second half of the 19C. ▶ On the opposite side of the p. Corvetto is the large public park called **Spianata dell'Acquasola** (C-D5) on the site of ramparts where plague victims were buried in 1657. The v. Quattro Novembre which flanks it was once a tree-lined street for carriages, partially raised on arches. Today it marks the edge of the new commercial and office district of Piccapietra (C-D4), where a little beyond the Ponte Monumentale the street skirts the apse of the 12C-14C Romanesque-Gothic church of **S. Stefano★** (D5). ▶ The **Ponte Monumentale** (1895) crosses the v. XX Settembre, the elegant and lively artery of the modern city. ▶ The corso Podestà and the v. Alessi lead to the p. Carignano (E4), containing the basilica of **S. Maria Assunta in Carignano★**, one of the finest works of Galeazzo Alessi, started *c.* 1550 and not finished until 1602, thirty years after his death. The basilica is built on a square cross plan, with a central dome and four corner domes, making the interior spacious and light. The twin towers are a notable feature of the façade. ▶ The **Circonvallazione a Mare**, made up of the corso Quadrio and the corso Saffi, runs high above the rocky coast, first skirting the medieval walls of the Grazie church, then the little port of Duca degli Abruzzi and the vast artificial embankment occupied by the halls of the **International Fair** (F4-5). After this it turns inland as far as the modern **piazza della Vittoria** (E5-6), a huge and striking space with a central triumphal arch which serves as a war memorial (1931). On one side of the square, with entrance from the v. Brigata Liguria, is the **Museo di Storia Naturale G. Doria★** (natural history; E5; *9 a.m.-12 noon and 3-5:30 p.m.; closed Mon and Fri*), with a largely zoological collection. ▶ Near the far a long **Marine Promenade★** begins with the corso Marconi (F6), broad and planted with flowers, which runs high above the coast as the corso Italia to the picturesque little port of **Boccadasse**.

▶ **The forts.** ▶ In 1626-33 Genoa built a powerful system of defensive walls, which ran along the ridge of the mountain amphitheatre surrounding the city. The building of the so-called 'new wall' was not just a fine piece of military engineering, but became a dominant feature of the town: from that time onward Genoa was often shown in painted panoramas as an urbanized arc of coast enclosed within a mountainous triangle with fortified ramparts at key points. ▶ A walk along the walls and fortresses provides a view of the impressive surviving fortifications and the city from above. ▶ It is also possible to go up to the **Righi★** (991 ft; *funicular railway from Largo della Zecca;* B3), the traditional method of reaching this spectacular viewpoint. ▶ The nearby *(keep r. on v. del Peralto)* **Forte Castellaccio** (1,188 ft; *military, visit by permission only*) has existed since the 13C. It featured in the struggles between the Guelphs and the Ghibellines, was rebuilt in the 19C and enclosed within a circle of ramparts. ▶ The **Forte Sperone** (1,680 ft) stands on the summit of the Monte Peralto, the N point of the triangle of the new wall, and was the defensive core of the 17C fortifications. ▶ On the next stretch, the great square block of the **Forte Begato** (1,549 ft; *military, visit by permission only*), which completes the trio of fortresses which were the focal points of the defensive system. ▶ Then the road descends rapidly to the **Forte Tenaglia** (709 ft), now abandoned.

▶ **The harbour.** ▶ Splendidly equipped at the end of the 12C, the harbour has mirrored the changing fortunes of the city through the centuries and bears clear signs of a long series of functions and transformations. Today it is the largest in Italy and the second largest in the Mediterranean after Marseilles. Any visitor wishing to understand Genoa must pay a visit to the port, even if he restricts himself to the **Porto Vecchio** and the most important installations. ▶ A general view can be obtained by driving along the sopraelevata as far as the halls of the International Fair, but for an experience at closer range it is better to go by boat. The bridges, moles, quays, basins, warehouses and of course the famous 16C tower of the **Lanterna,** symbol of Genoa, are best seen from the sea *(boat trip leaving from ponte dei Mille,* B1). ▶ The

Staglieno cemetery★ *(8 a.m.-5 p.m.)* is in the v. Bobbio (A-B4) in the Bisagno Valley. Famous for its flowers and lavish monuments (rather than for the severe tomb of Mazzini), the cemetery has become a sort of tourist legend, a characteristic feature of the city along with the harbour and the lantern. □

Practical information _____

GENOA

ℹ v. Roma 11/3-4 (C4), ☎ 581407; Principe station (A-B2), ☎ 262633; Brignole station (D6), ☎ 562056; *C. Colombo Airport*, ☎ 420341; v. Porta degli Archi 10/5 (D4), ☎ 541541.

✈ *C. Colombo International Airport*, at Sestri Ponente, ☎ 60071; *Alitalia*, v. XII Ottobre 188r (C4-5), ☎ 531091; city terminal, p. Vittoria 32r (E5-6), ☎ 581316.

🚂 Porta Principe (A-B2), ☎ 262455; Brignole (D6), ☎ 586350; Sanpierdarena, ☎ 459728; Sestri Ponente, ☎ 673088; Voltri, ☎ 631555.

🚌 from p. Vittoria 32r (E5-6), ☎ 313851.

⛴ car ferry to Sardinia, Sicily, Corsica, Tunisia and Spain, information: *Corsica Line* and *Sardinia Ferries*, p. Dante 5/A (D4), ☎ 593301; *Coastal shipping lines*, v. D'Annunzio 5r (D4), ☎ 54831 or 587851 (nights); *Tirrenia*, ponte Colombo, ☎ 258041.
Car rental: *Avis*, v. Balbi 190r, ☎ 255598, airport, ☎ 607280; *Hertz*, v. delle Casacce 3, ☎ 564412, airport, ☎ 607422; *Maggiore*, Booking Centre, ☎ 881421, P. P. station, ☎ 255342, airport, ☎ 605912.

Hotels:
★★★★★ **Colombia**, v. Balbi 40 (B2 a), ☎ 261841, 172 rm ℙ 240,000; bkf: 16,000.
★★★★ **Bristol Palace**, v. XX Settembre 35 (D4 b), ☎ 592541, 133 rm. No restaurant, 171,000.
★★★★ **Nuovo Astoria**, p. Brignole 4 (C5 c), ☎ 873316, 73 rm ℙ 👌 No restaurant, 109,000.
★★★★ **Plaza**, v. Martin Piaggio 11 (C4-5 d), ☎ 893641, 97 rm ℙ 179,000; bkf: 11,000.
★★★★ **Savoia Majestic**, v. Arsenale di Terra (A2 e), ☎ 261641, 111 rm ℙ 👌 194,000; bkf: 12,000.
★★★ **Agnello d'Oro**, v. delle Monachette 6 (B2 f), ☎ 262084, 40 rm, 70,000; bkf: 8,500.
★★★ **Brignole**, v. del Corallo 13r (D5-6 g), ☎ 561651, 26 rm ℙ No restaurant, 81,000; bkf: 8,000.
★★★ **City**, v. S. Sebastiano 6 (C4 h), ☎ 592595, 71 rm ℙ No restaurant, 130,000.
★★★ **Londra & Continental**, v. Arsenale di Terra 5 (A-B2 i), ☎ 261641, 48 rm ℙ 👌 126,000; bkf: 12,000.
★★★ **Rio**, v. Ponte Calvi 5 (C3 l), ☎ 290551, 46 rm ℙ 🦮 closed Christmas, 69,000.
★★★ **Viale Sauli**, v. Sauli 5 (D5 m), ☎ 561397, 49 rm. No restaurant, 85,000; bkf: 4,000.

Restaurants:
● ♦♦♦ **Gran Gotto**, v. Fiume 11/r (D6 q), ☎ 564344, closed Sat noon, hols except Christmas noon and Aug. Quiet and refined. Excellent regional cuisine: tagliolini with prawns, dried cod accomodato, 40/50,000.
♦♦♦ **Primo Piano**, v. XX Settembre 36 (D4 s), ☎ 540284, closed Sun and Aug. Quality regional cuisine: trenette al pesto, pappardelle with mushrooms, 30/50,000.
♦♦♦ **Saint Cyr**, p. Marsala 8/r (C5 t), ☎ 886897, closed Sat, Sun, Aug-Sep and Christmas. Piedmontese cuisine: rice with fonduta, timballo arlecchino, 35/45,000.
♦♦♦ **Santa**, vico Indoratori 1/r (C4 u), ☎ 293613, closed Sun and Aug. Typical Ligurian trattoria. Regional cuisine: pansoti, barnzino alla ligure, 30/35,000.
♦♦♦ **Svizzero**, v. della Libertà 113/r (E-F6 v), ☎ 590481, closed Sun and 10-31 Aug. International cuisine: tagliatelle cossica, risotto Pojarski, 30/35,000.
♦♦♦ **Zeffirino**, v. XX Settembre 20 (D5 ab), ☎ 595939, closed Wed. Mixed cuisine: sea bream in foil, fritto misto pesce, 30/70,000.
♦♦ **Cardinali**, v. Assarotti 60/r (C5 n), ☎ 870380, closed Sun and 10-25 Aug. International cuisine: trofiette al pesto, crêpes flambées, 40/50,000.
♦♦ **Michele**, v. della Libertà 41/r (E6 r), ☎ 593671, closed Sun except summer and 1-20 Sep. Rebuilt rustic taverna;

summer service outdoors. Mixed cuisine: risotto alla Vernaccia, date-shell and crayfish soup, 25/40,000.
♦♦ **Trattoria del Mario**, v. Conservatori del Mare 35 (C3 z), ☎ 298467, closed Sat and 10-20 Aug. In 13C loggia. Regional cuisine: homemade lasagne, dried cod stew, 25/40,000.
♦ **Franco**, archivolto Mongiardino 2/r (D3 p), ☎ 203614, closed Sun and 20 Jul-20 Sep. Small trattoria. Mixed cuisine: taglierini verdi with crayfish sauce, game and mushrooms, 30/35,000.

▲ ★★★★ *Caravan Park La Vesima* at Voltri, v. Aurelia at 547-km marker, 250 pl, ☎ 635772 (all year); ★★ *Villa Masnata*, v. di Creto 119 toward Montoggio, 100 pl, ☎ 803311.

Recommended
Archery: *Associazione genovese arcieri*, v. Borsieri 3/7, ☎ 490057; *Compagnia arcieri genovesi*, v. Acquarone 30/3, ☎ 294787.
Auction houses: p. Rossetti 34, ☎ 586233; v. Puccini 25r, ☎ 671074.
Bowling: p. Rizzolio, ☎ 466671; v. Serra 6/E (C5), ☎ 590793; v. Gobetti 8/A, ☎ 314102; salita S. Rocco 32 (A1), ☎ 256317.
Cycling: *Quinto al mare cycling enthusiasts*, p. S. Pietro 3r; *Alta Val Bisagno sports club*, v. Benedetto da Porto 2/A (A1), ☎ 804771.
Events: *rowing competition* between the districts (29 Jun); *Colombian fair* (6-12 Oct); *regatta of the old maritime republics* (held every four years, in Genoa in 1990); opera season at the *Teatro Margherita*, ☎ 591697 or 589321.
Exhibitions: *International Nautical Exhibition, Tecnhotel-Interfood-Bibe* (hotel amenities, refreshments, wines and other beverages) in autumn; other shows (flower shows, gift exhibitions, caravan shows, etc) in spring; every 5 years (the next will be in 1991) there is an *exhibition of ornamental plants*. Exhibition organization, p. Kennedy (F4-5), ☎ 53911.
Flying: *Genova Sestri, C. Colombo Airport*, ☎ 607727 (powered flight).
Guided tours: by bus *(Artebus)* at 2:30 or 3:30 p.m. depending on season (c. 3 hrs), inquire at *AMT* (A-B2), p. Acquaverde *(kiosk)*, ☎ 261550; trips to the harbour by motorboat (c. 1 hr), departing from calata degli Zingari, inquire at *Cooperativa battellieri* kiosk at Ponte dei Mille maritime station (B1), ☎ 265712.
Hang gliding: *Volo libero Genova*, ☎ 459678 (instruction).
Horseback riding: *Ligurian horse-riding club*, v. Bosco 57/7 (D5), ☎ 588872 or 587216; *Pratorondadino farm*, at Masone (16 km N of Voltri), ☎ 921398; *Pony trekking group*, at Montoggio (26 km N), v. Monte Moro 1.
Marina: *Duca degli Abruzzi* and, to the W, the *Festri Ponente* harbour, for both, ☎ 267451.
Sailing: *Lega Navale*, p. Kennedy (F5), ☎ 542067; *Quinto al Mare*, v. Maiorana 6r, ☎ 331863; Sestri Ponente, v. L. Librario, ☎ 621702 (also canoeing and angling).
Skindiving: *Federation of Sport Fishing*, Galleria Mazzini 7/1, ☎ 587730 (instruction).
Swimming: at Voltri, p. Villa Giusti, ☎ 630497; at Multedo, v. Reggio 13, ☎ 689253; at Rivarolo, p. Guerra 1, ☎ 447945; at Stadio del Nuoto, v. O. De Gaspari 39, ☎ 368409.
Wines: p. Colombo 13r (D5), ☎ 561329.
Youth hostel: *Ostello del Mare*, v. V. Maggio 79, ☎ 387370.
♥ cafés: *Caffè pasticceria Klainguti*, v. Soziglia 98r, ☎ 296502; *Confetteria Romanengo*, v. Soziglia 74/76r, ☎ 297869.

Environs

ALBARO, ✉ 16100, 4 km toward Rapallo.

Restaurants:
♦♦♦ **Vittorio al Mare**, belvedere Firpo 1-Boccadasse, ☎ 312872, closed Mon. Terrace with sea view. Seafood: sea bream in foil, sea bass Ligurian style, 50/65,000.
♦♦♦ **Gheise**, v. Boccadasse 29/n, ☎ 310097, closed Mon and 25 Jul-31 Aug. Summer garden. Mixed cuisine: trofiette al pesto, gnocchi parigina, 25/40,000.

QUARTO DEI MILLE, ⊠ 16148, 7 km toward Rapallo.

Restaurant:
● ♦♦♦ *Antica Osteria del Bai,* v. Quarto 12, ☎ 387478, closed Mon and Jul-Aug. In former coastal fortress, veranda overlooking sea. Seafood: tagliolini with scampi, trofie, 30/50,000.

QUINTO AL MARE, ⊠ 16166, 9 km toward Rapallo.

Restaurant:
♦ *Cicchetti 1860,* v. Giannelli 41/r, ☎ 331641, closed Tue and Aug. Seafood: lasagne al pesto, dried cod alla genovese, 28/35,000.

SAMPIERDARENA, ⊠ 16149, 5 km toward Savona.

Restaurant:
♦♦♦ *Torre del Mangia,* p. Montano 24/r, ☎ 465607, closed Mon and Aug. In period palazzo. Mixed cuisine: pappardelle al pesto, chicken in a brick, 35/45,000.

SESTRI PONENTE, ⊠ 16154, 10 km toward Savona.

Restaurant:
♦ *Toe Drue,* v. Corsi 44, ☎ 671100, closed Sun noon, Mon and Aug. Regional cuisine: pansoti, trenette al pesto, 35/40,000.

IMPERIA

Genoa 114, Milan 239, Rome 615 km
Pop. 41,368 ⊠ 18100 ☎ 0183   B3

In reality, Imperia is two towns, Oneglia and Porto Mauririo. Its unification is purely administrative and it will probably never be a homogeneous urban unit. The two original centres look quite distinct: they have separate histories and were subject to different territorial authorities. Porto Maurizio, with its old town set on a hill, is essentially a tourist town and was linked historically to Genoa. 'Piedmontese' Oneglia, with its porticoed streets set at right angles, was traditonaly subject to Savoy; today it is an industrial centre (oil refineries, pasta factories, pharmaceutical companies).

▶ The medieval centre of **Porto Maurizio,** sited on a sea-promontory, has remained almost intact. The town consists of groups of tall buildings facing two streets on different levels; they include harmonious 17C-18C **palazzi,** plain outside but with sumptuous interiors. ▶ The Neoclassical **Duomo** (B2), with its remarkable proportions, rises from the surrounding buildings like a combined symbol of prosperity and progress. ▶ In front of it, in the former Palazzo Communale, is the **Museo Navale del Ponente Ligure** *(Tue 9-11 a.m.; Wed and Sat 5:30-7:30 p.m.)* and the **Pinacoteca Civica** *(closed at present).* ▶ Economic and urban development in Oneglia began in the second half of the 19C and the buildings in the central district date from that time. There are significant exceptions: the palazzo (1466) in which Andrea Doria was born, the Baroque collegiate church of **S. Giovanni Battista** (B6), started in 1739, and the 18C **Piarist College.** ▶ The **harbour** is the main port of W Liguria.

Environs

▶ **Lucinasco** *(15 km from Oneglia)* contains the fine church of the **Maddalena** (1401-30). ▶ **Montegrazie** *(9 km from Porto Maurizio)* lies near the **sanctuary of Nostra Signora delle Grazie** (1450), containing the most important 15C frescos in the region.   □

Practical information ——————

≋
ⓘ v. Matteotti 54 bis (A3), ☎ 24947; v. Matteotti 22 (A2), ☎ 60730.
🚂 at Oneglia (A6), ☎ 20375; at Porto Maurizio (A2-3), ☎ 650560.
🚌 at Oneglia, from p. dell'Unità Nazionale (A6).

Hotels:
★★★ *Centro,* at Oneglia, p. Unità Nazionale 4 (A6 a), ☎ 273771, 21 rm ⅄ No restaurant, 71,000.
★★★ *Corallo,* at Porto Maurizio, corso Garibaldi 29 (B2 b), ☎ 61980, 42 rm Ⓟ ✗ 77,000.
★★★ *Croce di Malta,* at Porto Maurizio, v. Scarincio 142 (B2 c), ☎ 63847, 42 rm Ⓟ 🍴 ⅄ 80,000; bkf: 7,000.

Restaurants:
● ♦♦♦ *Nannina,* at Porto Maurizio, v. Matteotti 58 (A4 f), ☎ 20208, closed Sun eve, Mon and Feb. Sea

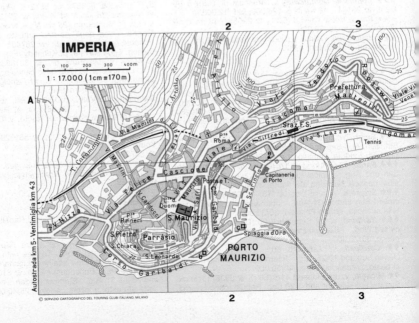

view. Excellent regional cuisine, some French dishes: sciancui al pesto, red mullet in abito verde, 40/65,000.
◆◆◆ *Lanterna Blu-da Tonino,* at Porto Maurizio, v. Scarincio 32 (A-B2 e), ☎ 63859, closed Wed and Nov. In harbour area. Seafood: linguine with crab, seaweed pappardelle with botarga and scampi, 50/85,000.
◆◆◆ *Salvo-Cacciatori,* at Oneglia, v. Vieusseux 12 (A6 g), ☎ 23763, closed Mon and Nov. Seafood: risotto with crayfish, spaghetti with red mullet sauce, 25/40,000.
◆◆◆ *Taverna del Borgo Antico,* at Porto Maurizio, lungomare Colombo 114, ☎ 61062, closed Mon. Seafood: cuttlefish ink risotto, novellini with rosemary, 60/70,000.
◆ *Chez Braccioforte,* at Oneglia, calata G. B. Cuneo 33 (B6 d), ☎ 24752, closed Mon and 6-31 Jan. Regional cuisine: dried cod, cuttlefish buridda, 20/40,000.

⚐ ★ *De Wijnstok,* at Garbella, v. Poggi 4, 85 pl, ☎ 64986 (all year); ★ *Eucalyptus,* at Porto Maurizio, v. D'Annunzio 20, ☎ 61534 (all year).

Recommended
Archery: *S. Camillo archery group,* v. Europa 26, ☎ 22277.
Events: sailing, rowing and motorboat competitions (Jul-Aug); international chess festival (Sep).
Marina: at Porto Maurizio, *Imperia Mare,* ☎ 650246.
Sailing: *Yacht club,* v. Scarincio 124 (B2), ☎ 61866; *Nautical Society,* v. Scarincio 128/a, ☎ 60679 (instruction).
Swimming: v. S. Lazzaro, ☎ 650353.
Tennis: v. S. Lazzaro (A3), ☎ 650244.
♥ factory visits: *F.lli Carli oil mill,* v. Garessio 11, ☎ 27101; *Agnesi* pasta factory and attached *Pasta Museum,* at Pontedassio *(8 km N),* strada Col di Nava, ☎ 64617.

LAIGUEGLIA

Savona 55, Genoa 101, Milan 224 km
Pop. 2,592 ✉ 17020 ☎ 0182   B3

Laigueglia's beach continues from Alassio (→). Facing it are 17C-18C palazzi and little squares in which goods were unloaded, showing the role played by maritime commerce and coral fishing after the inhabitants left Andora (→).

▶ The village still looks like an old Ligurian maritime and commercial centre, huddled around the fine, striking Baroque church of **S. Matteo.** ▶ **Colla Micheri** *(3 km),* a tiny country village among the olives, is the property of the Norwegian ethnologist Thor Heyerdahl (famous for the *Kon-Tiki expedition,* 1947), who restored it and now lives there permanently.   □

Practical information ─────────────

≈
ⓘ v. Milano 33, ☎ 49059.

Hotels:
★★★★ *Splendid,* p. Badarò 3, ☎ 49325, 50 rm 🅿 ⚙ ঐ
▭ closed Oct-Mar, 100,000; bkf: 10,000.
★★★ *Mediterraneo,* v. Doria 18, ☎ 49240, 35 rm 🅿 ⚙ closed 10 Oct-22 Dec and Easter-20 May, 50,000; bkf: 5,000.
★★★ *Villa Ida,* v. Roma 90, ☎ 49042, 33 rm 🅿 ⚙ ঐ closed Oct-Easter, 50,000; bkf: 5,000.

Restaurant:
◆◆◆ *Vascello Fantasma,* v. Dante 105, ☎ 49847, closed Wed and 20 Nov-10 Dec. In period palazzo: outdoor service in summer. Regional cuisine: chicche al pesto, pescata del nostromo, 35/50,000.

⚐ ★ *San Sebastiano,* v. S. Sebastiano 23, ☎ 49420.

Recommended
Events: cycling trophy competed for at opening of season (Feb).
Sailing: *Aquilia yacht club,* ☎ 49157 (also water-skiing and surfing).
Tennis: at Fonte del Faro, ☎ 49248.

LA SPEZIA

Genoa 99, Milan 220, Rome 418 km
Pop. 112,606 ✉ 19100 ☎ 0187   F2

La Spezia is a 19C town: in the early part of that century it had fewer than the 4,000 souls recorded by the 16C chronicler Giustiniani. A profound change occurred as a result of the transfer of the naval dockyard from Genoa and the construction of the

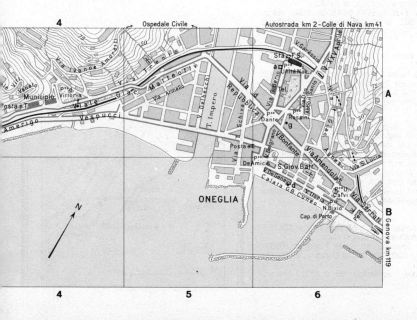

4   Ospedale Civile   Autostrada km 2 - Colle di Nava km 41

ONEGLIA

N

A

B

Genova km 119

4   5   6

arsenal in 1869, on the instructions of Cavour. The military administration not only started an industry which at the time was among the most important in Italy, but initiated complete replanning of the town and industrialization of the entire district.

▶ Little remains of the medieval town, which was at the foot of the Poggio, around the present v. del Prione. ▶ The only exception is the **Castel S. Giorgio**, which dominates the town with its massive bulk; it consists of the original 13C section (with rounded bastions) and the 17C extension (with angular bastions). ▶ The church of **S. Maria Assunta** dates from the 13C, but has been rebuilt on a number of occasions and has a modern façade. In the interior is a polychrome **terra-cotta** by Andrea Della Robbia. ▶ The most interesting part of the town grew up in the second half of the 19C, coincidental with the importance and strategic role bestowed on La Spezia by the arsenal. The spacious perspectives of the new tree-lined streets, set at right angles to each other, make a network following the line of the **corso Cavour**, still one of the principal arteries of the town. The **Musei Civici** *(9 a.m.-1 p.m.; closed Sun p.m. and Mon)* is at v. Curtatone 9 and has a notable archaeological section with a collection of the famous stele from the plain of Luni and prehistoric and Roman material from **Luni.** ▶ The **via Domenico Chiodo** (D3) links the 19C and modern cities; the centre moved E in the 1920s, developing the plain of Migliarina. ▶ The entrance to the **Arsenal** *(open Sun nearest to March 19; otherwise Mon-Fri to groups only with permission from Direzione generale)* is in the p. Chiodo. Some of the interior (largely rebuilt after bombing) is very interesting: for example the craft and machine shops and the sail-loft with stores. The dry docks, extremely advanced for their time and exceeded in size only by those in Toulon, were admired by the English and taken as a model for the construction of Kiel by the Prussians. To the l. of the entrance is the **Museo Navale** *(9 a.m.-12 noon and 2-6 p.m.; closed Sun, Mon and Fri)* with a fine collection of naval relics, arms and models. □

Practical information ───────────

ⓘ v. Mazzini 47, ☎ 36000; v. Italia 221, ☎ 21294.
🚂 ☎ 35373.
🚌 from p. Chiodo.
⛴ boat trips in the Gulf, passengers' landing stage at Morin, ☎ 28066; ferry to Corsica, ☎ 21282.
Car rental: *Avis*, v. Frat. Rosselli 86/88, ☎ 33345; *Hertz*, v. S. Bartolomeo 665, ☎ 516712; *Maggiore*, v. Rattazzi 17, ☎ 33387.

Hotels:
★★★★ *Jolly del Golfo*, v. XX Settembre 2, ☎ 27200, 110 rm ⌧ 130,000.
★★★★ *Residence Hotel*, v. Tino 62, ☎ 504141, 50 rm Ⓟ ⟨⟩ ⅄ ⌧ No restaurant, 115,000.
★★★ *Genova*, v. F.lli Rosselli 84, ☎ 30372, 29 rm ⟨⟩ ⅄ No restaurant, 67,000; bkf: 7,000.

Restaurants:
◆◆◆ *Locandina*, v. Sapri 10, ☎ 27499, closed Mon and Aug. Spacious and well-furnished. Mixed cuisine: risotto in cuttlefish ink, stewed red mullet, 50/60,000.
◆◆◆ *Posta*, v. Don Minzoni 24, ☎ 34419, closed Sat, Sun and Aug. Regional and international cuisine: date shell soup, pappardelle Breton, 25/35,000.
◆◆ *Rossetto*, v. dei Colli 107, ☎ 31121, closed Tue and Sep. Regional and Italian cuisine: mesciua, pappardelle with hare sauce, 40/50,000.

Recommended
Bowling: *Italian bowling union*, v. Veneto 173, ☎ 505189.
Events: *Maritime festival* (1st Sun in Aug).
Horseback riding: *Spezzina club*, v. dei Pioppi, ☎ 705331 (instruction); *Riding club Follo*, at Val Durasca, ☎ 700163 (associate of *ANTE*).
Sailing: *Lega Navale*, v. Amendola 196, ☎ 31303 (instruction).

Skindiving: *Spezia sub*, p. Saint Bon, ☎ 511026 (instruction).
Swimming: v. Fieschi, ☎ 28186.
Tennis: v. S. Verrerio 33/a, ☎ 503557.
Water-skiing: *Bronzi water-skiing*, v. Rebocco 55; *La Spezia motorboat club*, v. della Marina 224, ☎ 50401.

Gulf of LA SPEZIA

Around La Spezia *(73 km, 1 day; map 2)*

The area immediately around La Spezia is industrialized, but the natural and historical attractions of countryside and coast have long attracted tourists. Beyond Montemarcello a long alluvial plain opens up towards Tuscany. The Magra plain corresponds substantially to the plain of Luni, a large, strategically important region, which was for many centuries a historical entity taking its origin from the Roman colony of Luni. These 30,000 acres of flood plain, which include the junction of two recently completed motorways, are also the largest single commercial and industrial complex in Liguria. The 'golden hinterland' of La Spezia seems destined for exceptional economic development.

▶ The road between **La Spezia** (→) and beautiful **Lérici** (→) runs along unspoiled coast with high, whitish-grey cliffs and Aleppo pines. ▶ **Tellaro**, a little village on a rocky spur, descends in steps towards the sea. ▶ **Montemarcello**, to which a fine road with a splendid view climbs from Lérici, is laid out with streets at right angles, an unusual feature in old hill settlements. ▶ Beyond the punta Bianca, at the mouth of the river, is **Bocca di Magra**, which was of strategic importance until the last war. Since then it has been a famous tourist centre and also has a reputation for attracting intellectuals. ▶ 'Witness Luni and Urbisaglia, how they have declined', wrote Dante. In the 14C **Luni** could well be cited as an example of decay. The former Roman colony flourished until the 13C, when the silting up of the port and other events including the transfer of the bishop's seat to Sarzana condemned it to rapid decline. **Archaeological excavations** have brought to light remains of the forum, monuments, houses and an amphitheatre with seats for 6,000 spec-

2. Gulf of La Spezia

© SERVIZIO CARTOGRAFICO DEL TOURING CLUB ITALIANO, MILANO

tators. Many of the finds are in the **Museo Nazionale Lunense** *(9 a.m.-12 noon and 2-5 p.m. or 4-7 p.m.; closed Mon).* ▶ **Castelnuovo Magra** is of considerable interest. It is set on the ridge of a hill and its focal points are the church and the 13C palazzo that housed the bishops of Sarzana at the time of the struggle between the Guelphs and the Ghibellines. In the parish church are a painting attributed to Brueghel and a Crucifixion by the school of Van Dyck. ▶ The Via Aurelia leads to **Sarzana** (→), and from here it is possible to return to La Spezia. □

Practical information _____

AMEGLIA, ⊠ 19031, 3.5 km N of Bocca di Magra.

Hotels:
★★★★ *Paracucchi-Locanda dell'Angelo,* v. XXV Aprile 60, ☎ 64391, 37 rm Ⓟ ⌕ ⅏ 120,000; bkf: 13,000. Rest.
● ♦♦♦ Exceptional cuisine, 50/70,000.
★★★ *Ala Bianca,* v. Camisano 94/96, ☎ 65080, 26 rm ⅏ ❀ closed Nov, 53,000; bkf: 7,000.

BOCCA DI MAGRA, ⊠ 19030, ☎ 0187.

Restaurants:
♦♦ *Capannina-da Ciccio,* v. Fabricotti 71, ☎ 65568, closed Tue and Nov. Fine view and outdoor service in summer. Mixed cuisine: salt cod alla genovese, cima ripiena, 30/45,000.
♦♦ *Ferrara,* v. della Pace 54, ☎ 65082, closed Mon and 15 Jan-15 Feb. Quiet and rural, near River Magra. Mixed cuisine: sautéed penne, lasagne al pesto, 25/35,000.

CASTELNUOVO MAGRA, ⊠ 19030, ☎ 0187.

Recommended
Horseback riding: *Ufficio Tecnico Comunale* (associate of *ANTE*).

FIUMARETTA DI AMEGLIA, ⊠ 19031, 4 km S of Ameglia.

Restaurant:
♦♦ *Sergiunca,* v. Litoranea 104, ☎ 64459, closed Mon. Refurbished rural premises, piano music at weekends. Seafood: penne with scampi, spaghetti alla corsara, 30/32,000.

Recommended
Children's facilities: *Miniature garden and zoo,* at Ameglia, ☎ 65892 (closed Mon).

LUNI, ⊠ 19034, ☎ 0187.

Recommended
Flying: *Lunense Piero Lombardi flying club,* at airport, ☎ 673180 (instruction; model aircraft; parachuting).

TELLARO, ⊠ 19030, ☎ 0187.

Hotels:
★★★★ *Nido,* v. Fiascherino 75, ☎ 967286, 36 rm Ⓟ ⌕ ⌕ ⅏ ❀ closed 11 Oct-31 Mar, 75,000; bkf: 11,000.
★★ *Miramare,* v. Fiascherino 22, ☎ 967589, 18 rm Ⓟ ⌕⌕ ⅏ closed 1 Oct-30 Nov and 16 Feb-31 Mar, 30,000; bkf: 5,000.
⚐ ★★ Gianna, v. Fiascherino, ☎ 966411.

LAVAGNA

Genoa 44, Milan 176 km
Pop. 13,436 ⊠ 16033 ☎ 0185   E2

'Between Siestri and Chiavari a raging torrent of great beauty descends to the sea,' wrote Dante. He was describing the Entella, which flows into the sea between Chiavari and Lavagna, now a single conurbation. But despite this spatial and economic link, Lavagna still has many distinctive characteristics: the slate mines and above all a fine medieval **centre. Cavi** has bathing facilities and a beach. 4 km away is the **basilica dei Fieschi** (Chiavari →).   □

Slates and slate

It is well known that masters and scholars write on slate. Slate is a form of black stone, known in Italian as ardesia or lavagna. Lavagna is also the name of a village in the Riviera di Levante to the left of the mouth of the Entella River. This old village, called Levannia in ancient times, is very picturesque, though obscured by modern buildings on the sea front. In the 11C it became the seat of a powerful family and ruled other villages on the coast and in the interior. The counts of Lavagna were the Fieschi, an important family which produced seventy-two cardinals and, in the 13C, two popes, Innocent IV and Hadrian V. The first was uncle of the second and between them they built the Gothic basilica of the Fieschi, a short distance from the coast. This fine monument, like other old Ligurian churches, has a characteristic tower over the crossing, an architectural feature of French origin. Slate is mined above all in the Monte San Giacomo area and was exported as far as California. In Liguria it is used, cut very thin, to cover roofs and also, though in this case black marble is preferred, for the door frames still seen in the narrow carugi (alleyways) of the Riviera villages, and for decorative bas-reliefs, frequently of St. George killing the dragon. George, probably a Christian martyred in Palestine in the early 4C, was transformed by legend into a warrior who fought a dragon to rescue a king's daughter and has always been a popular figure in Liguria; the red cross of St. George on a white background is the coat of arms of Genoa. However, in 1961 he was removed from the list of saints, during the reign of Pope John XXIII.

Practical information _____

LAVAGNA
≋
ⓘ p. della Libertà 46, ☎ 392797.

Hotels:
★★★ *Admiral Lido,* v. dei Devoto 89, ☎ 306072, 22 rm ⌕ ❀ ⌧ closed Oct-Feb, 53,000; bkf: 5,000.
★★★ *Tigullio,* v. Matteotti 3, ☎ 392965, 37 rm Ⓟ ⅏ closed Nov-Mar, 52,000; bkf: 4,000.

Restaurant:
♦♦♦ *Gabbiano,* v. S. Benedetto 26, ☎ 390228, closed Mon except summer, 15 Jan-1 Feb. and 15 Nov-15 Dec. Mixed cuisine: mesciua, tortelli with asparagus, 30/45000.

⚐ ★★ *International,* at Madonna della Neve, 64 pl, ☎ 302274.

Recommended
Events: *Torta dei Fieschi,* a commemorative festival (Aug).
Horseback riding: *Club Area Verde,* v. dei Devoto 13, ☎ 305626 (associate of *ANTE*).
Marina: ☎ 312626.
Motorboats: *Union Yacht Brokers,* p. Milano 9, ☎ 314021.
Sports: *Parco del Tigullio* sports complex, with swimming pool, bowling, clubhouse, ☎ 39058 and tennis courts, ☎ 390969.
♥ **quarries:** guided tours of slate quarries of Valfontanabuona, Consorzio Assolipidei, Cicagna, ☎ 92311.

Environs

CAVI, ⊠ 16030, 4 km toward Sestri Levante.
Hotels:
★★★ *Maggi,* v. Vercelli 9, ☎ 390474, 24 rm Ⓟ ⌕ closed Oct, 60,000.

★★★ **Park Hotel,** v. Aurelia 2242, ☎ 390131, 47 rm Ⓟ ⚏
closed Oct-Feb, 50,000; bkf: 5,000.

Restaurant:
◆◆ **Cantinna,** v. Torrente Barassi 8, ☎ 390394,
closed Tue and 1-20 Feb. Rural yet refined, in an old
cellar. Seafood: pansoti, capponadda, homemade wines,
25/40,000.

LERICI

La Spezia 10, Genoa 107, Milan 224 km
Pop. 13,579 ⊠ 19032 ☎ 0187   F2-3

Shelley was shipwrecked and drowned in these
waters and so the Golfo dei Poeti was rechristened in
honour of him and his friend Byron. Lérici has been
a tourist attraction for a century, and there have been
many other illustrious visitors (Böcklin, Mantegazza,
Benelli, D. H. Lawrence), but its prime concern is still
to preserve the memory of the two poets and the
romantic atmosphere for which their era was famous.

▶ Chaotic building development has spoiled the town's
original appearance, although it has been retained in part
in the older area near the sea with its **brightly coloured
houses.** ▶ The towering **castle★,** apparently carved
out of the cliff, a 13C Pisan building extended by the
Genoese, is a fine example of medieval military architecture *(lift from v. Mazzini; 8:30 or 9:30 a.m.-12:30 p.m.
and 2-7 or 3:30-8:30 p.m.; winter, Sat, Sun and hols
8:30 a.m.-12:30 p.m. and 2-5:30 p.m.).* ▶ Also worth
seeing is the 17C parish church of **S. Francesco** in the old
quarter to the N around the v. Cavour. ▶ In **San Terenzo**
(2 km) is the **Villa Magni,** where Shelley lived, with a collection devoted to the poet. ▶ **Fiascherino** *(4 km)* has
a fine beach set among the rocks. Farther on is **Tellaro;**
from here the old salt road leads to **Montemarcello**
(→ Gulf of La Spezia).   ☐

Practical information _____

≋
Ⓘ v. Roma 47, ☎ 967346.
🚆 to La Spezia and Portovénere.

Hotels:
★★★ **Europe,** v. Carpanini 1, ☎ 967800, 33 rm Ⓟ ⚄ ◁ ⚏
🏊 No restaurant, 75,000; bkf: 8,000.
★★★ **Florida,** lungomare Biaggini 35, ☎ 967344, 32 rm
Ⓟ 🏊 closed 20 Dec-15 Jan. No restaurant, 66,000;
bkf: 6,500.
★★★ **Venere Azzurra,** lungomare Biaggini 29, ☎ 965334,
22 rm. No restaurant, 72,000.

Restaurants:
◆◆◆ **Griglia,** at S. Terenzo, v. Meneghetti 14, ☎ 970665,
closed Tue, Feb and Nov. On the promenade. Seafood:
seafood risotto, penne with fish pesto, 25/35,000.
● ◆◆ **Conchiglia,** p. del Molo 3, ☎ 967334, closed Wed
and Christmas. Excellent seafood: apribocca di Massimo, prawn risotto, 30/40,000.
◆◆ **Paolino,** v. S. Francesco 14, ☎ 967801, closed
Mon. Seafood: sautéed penne with date shells, fritto
misto, 20/35,000.
◆ **Palmira,** at S. Terenzo, v. Trogo 13, ☎ 971094, closed
Wed, Sep-Oct and Dec-Jan. Seafood: penne alla pescatora, gnocchi al pesto, 30/35,000.

⚐ ★★ **Maralunga,** Lerici-Tellaro road, ☎ 966589.

Recommended
Boat trips: to Portovénere and Cinque Terre, ☎ 900785
(winter), ☎ 967676 (summer).
Marina: *Yacht club,* ☎ 966770.
Swimming: at Venere Azzurra.
Tennis: ☎ 967282.

_____
| Don't forget to consult the Practical Holiday Guide: it
| can help in solving many problems.
_____

LEVANTO

La Spezia 36, Genoa 83, Milan 218 km
Pop. 6,438 ⊠ 19015 ☎ 0187   E2

Tourism has changed the original rural and seafaring
role of the village and has brought about a recent
surge in building. The importance and autonomy that
Lévanto enjoyed under the Republic of Genoa has not
yet been completely obliterated.

▶ The town faces a fine, broad, sandy **beach.** ▶ The
historic centre has interesting domestic medieval architecture: the **Casa Restani,** a rare example of a 13C-14C
Ligurian merchant's house, the 13C **Loggia del Comune**
and the **Casa del Capitano del Popolo** (which houses
a permanent exhibition on local history). ▶ Also worth
seeing is the Gothic parish church of **S. Andrea** (13C-15C)
with typical black-and-white banded façade. Inside are
two fine **paintings★** by C. Braccesco (1485).   ☐

Practical information _____

≋
Ⓘ p. Colombo, ☎ 808125.

Hotels:
★★★ **Carla,** v. Martiri della Libertà 28, ☎ 808275, 36 rm
Ⓟ closed 1-20 Dec and 10 Jan-10 Mar, 42,000.
★★★ **Dora,** v. Martiri della Libertà 27, ☎ 808318, 37 rm
Ⓟ closed 16 Oct-28 Feb, 42,000; bkf: 5,000.

Restaurants:
◆◆ **Giada del Mesco,** v. Panoramica del Mesco 16,
☎ 808705, closed Tue. In the countryside. International
cuisine: lasagnette ai gamberetti, paella valenciana, homemade wines, 25/40,000.
◆ **Gritta,** v. Vallesanta, ☎ 808593, closed Wed and
Oct-Mar. Trattoria on beach, summer terrace with sea
view. Seafood: trofie al pesto, pesce alla genovese,
22/34,000.
◆ **Hostaria da Franco,** v. Olivi 6 (private road), ☎ 808647,
closed Mon and 1 Nov-15 Nov. Lively with summer terrace. Mixed cuisine: shellfish Nettuno, maccheroni del
poeta, 25/40,000.

⚐ ★★ **Albero d'Oro,** at Albero d'Oro, 60 pl, ☎ 800400.

Recommended
Clay pigeon shooting: ☎ 808076.
Cycling: *Genoa Club Lévanto,* p. Staglieno 23, ☎ 808160;
Lévanto cycling club, corso Roma 1, ☎ 808297.
Events: *Maritime festival* (25 Jul).
Swimming: managed by tourist office, ☎ 808125.

LOANO

Savona 33, Genoa 79, Milan 202 km
Pop. 12,256 ⊠ 17025 ☎ 019   B2

A flat site and fine beaches have encouraged both
tourism and the erection of a large number of enormous buildings that have swamped the historic centre. However, some buildings dating from the enlightened rule of the Dorias still remain. The grand and
austere **Palazzo Comunale** was built by the Dorias
in the 16C. In the interior is a large fragment of 3C
Roman **mosaic** pavement.

Environs

▶ The **Toirano caves** *(5.8 km)* are famous for stalactite
and stalagmite formations and also for exceptional prehistoric finds. Most important is the **grotta della Bàsura★**
or **della Strega** *(guided tour; 9:30-11:30 a.m. and 2:30-5
or 6 p.m.).* There is a **Museo preistorico della Val Vara-
tella** in the piazzale.   ☐

Practical information

LOANO

≋

Ⓘ corso Europa 19, ☎ 669918.

Hotels:
★★★★ **Garden Lido,** lungomare Sauro 9, ☎ 669666, 95 rm Ⓟ ≼ ⨌ ✕ ⌷ closed 1 Nov-21 Dec, 76,000.
★★★ **Continental,** v. Carducci 1, ☎ 668592, 72 rm Ⓟ ⨌ closed 1 Oct-21 Dec, 45,000.
★★★ **Villa Mary,** v. Minniti 6, ☎ 668368, 27 rm Ⓟ ⨌ ✕ closed 1 Oct-21 Dec, 30,000; bkf: 4,000.

Restaurant:
♦♦ **Vecchio Camino,** corso Europa 35, ☎ 668037, closed Wed and Oct. Regional and Italian cuisine: homemade penne, trenette al pesto, 25/30,000.

Ⓐ ★ *Holiday,* v. Bulaxe 18, 63 pl, ☎ 666148 (all year).

Recommended
Marina: ☎ 668836.
Sports hall: ☎ 666033 (indoor swimming pool).
Tennis: v. Aurelia 92, ☎ 669055.

Environs

TOIRANO, ⊠ 17020, ☎ 0182, 6 km E.
Recommended
Tennis: v. Mainero, ☎ 98115.
♥ caves: group tours (fee) of *Grotta della Basura* and the lower *Grotta di S. Lucia, Toirano cave authority,* ☎ 98062.

MONEGLIA

Genoa 61, Milan 193 km
Pop. 2,781 ⊠ 16030 ☎ 0185   E2

The original layout of this village along a little bay protected on both sides by ruined castles is partially preserved. Below the **Castello di Monleone** is the important church of **S. Giorgio,** with 15C cloister. ☐

Practical information

≋

Hotel:
★★★ **Leopold,** v. La Secca 5, ☎ 49240, 19 rm Ⓟ ≼ ⬙ ⨌ closed 10 Oct-20 Dec, 43,000; bkf: 6,000.

Restaurant:
♦♦ **Ruota,** at Lemeglio, ☎ 49565, closed Wed in winter and Nov. In countryside with fine view from garden terrace. Seafood: risotto, fish stewed, grilled or in foil, 50/55,000.

Ⓐ ★★★★ *Smeraldo,* at Preata, ☎ 49375.

Colle di NAVA

Imperia 37, Genoa 121, Milan 244 km
Pop. 71 ⊠ 18020 ☎ 0183   A-B2

This pass at the centre of a system of forts is a grassy hollow facing the Arroscia valley. The N slope runs down to the Tànaro basin (Piedmont). The region is noted for its lavender plantations. ☐

Practical information

COLLE DI NAVA

Hotel:
★★★ **Colle di Nava-Lorenzina,** v. Nazionale 65, ☎ 38923, 34 rm Ⓟ ⨌ closed 1 Nov-10 Dec, 46,000; bkf: 4,000.

> Looking for a locality? Consult the index at the back of the book.

Environs

PONTE DI NAVA, ⊠ 12070, ☎ 0174, 4 km N.
Hotel:
★ **Ponte di Nava,** v. Nazionale 32, ☎ 51924, 18 rm Ⓟ ⨌ ✕ closed 7-22 Jan and 15-30 Jun, 36,000; bkf: 4,000. Rest. ♦♦ **Beppe** closed Wed. Piedmontese cuisine, 20/35,000.

NERVI*

Genoa 10, Milan 147 km
Pop. 13,000 ⊠ 16167 ☎ 010   D1-2

Set at the E extremity of Greater Genoa, Nervi's principal attraction is the modern district, which has retained the grandeur and elegance which made it famous as a winter resort at the turn of the century: large hotels and villas, gardens and roads lined with palms.

▶ The **viale delle Palme** is the principal street in modern Nervi and it still has the feel of tourism in the *belle époque.* ▶ Not far off, at the edge of the historic centre overlooking the small harbour, is the 13C church of **S. Siro.** ▶ Along the sea front runs the **passeggiata Anita Garibaldi★,** high above the rocks and waves, flanked by the luxuriant **Parco Municipale★** *(8 a.m.-dusk),* formed from the grounds of the Gropallo and Serra villas. ▶ The villa Serra houses the **Galleria d'Arte Moderna** *(9 a.m.-1 p.m. and 3-6 p.m.; wkends 9:15 a.m.-12:45 p.m.; closed Mon),* with many 19C-20C Italian works. ▶ The **Museo Luxoro** *(for opening times see gallery)* has a varied collection, including decorative arts. ▶ **Bogliasco,** just to the E, has a tiny beach among the rocks. ☐

Practical information

NERVI

≋

Ⓘ p. Pittaluga 4, ☎ 321504.

Hotels:
★★★★ **Astor,** v. delle Palme 16, ☎ 328325, 55 rm Ⓟ ⨌ ⬙ ✕ 145,000; bkf: 8,000.
★★★ **Marinella,** passeggiata Garibaldi 18, ☎ 321429, 12 rm ≼ ⬙ 54,000; bkf: 4,500.

Recommended
Children's facilities: Sant'Ilario children's home, v. S. Ilario 92, ☎ 321593 (children from 2-10; all year).
Events: *international festival of ballet* (Jul), ☎ 542792; open-air opera season.
Sailing instruction: Lega Navale, Torre Gropallo, passeggiata Garibaldi, ☎ 585824.
Skindiving: *international sub aqua centre,* v. Ardizzone 4 (instruction).
Swimming: v. Caboto 23r, ☎ 326678.

Environs

BOGLIASCO, ⊠ 16031, ☎ 010, 3 km.
≋
Ⓘ v. Mazzini 28, ☎ 3470429.

NOLI

Savona 15, Genoa 64, Milan 187 km
Pop. 3,185 ⊠ 17026 ☎ 019   C2

Every family rich enough to provide Genoa with an armed galley had the right to build a tower and by the 14C Noli, which had been a prosperous free republic since 1193, had 72 of them. The 12-14C town within the defensive walls has survived almost intact. The little town combines the attractions of a seaside resort with many artistic and historical features, all of which make it one of the most interesting places in the Riviera di Ponente.

▶ Fishing is a flourishing industry here, and in the early morning the nets are hauled ashore in front of the ancient arcades of the corso Italia. ▶ The **Palazzo del Comune**, with its high crenellated 13C tower, is the earliest surviving urban architectural feature of any size. ▶ Another characteristic building is the very high, trapezoid **Torre del Canto**, near the section of wall destroyed by the railway crossing. ▶ The **Cathedral** (13C, altered in 16C) is interesting, but the most important religious building in the town is certainly the proto-Romanesque church of **S. Paragorio★** (11C, restored; *daily except Mon*). At the side is a portal with 14C Gothic porch, in the interior a wooden throne (1239), a restored font, a 12C wooden crucifix and remains of 14C-15C frescos. ▶ The town is dominated by the enormous, ruined **Castello Ursino** (12C), from which a curtain wall with towers and wall walks descends. □

Practical information —————————

~
ⓘ corso Italia 8, ☎ 748931.

Hotel:
★★★ *Gino,* v. Defferrari 6, ☎ 748957, 19 rm ⓟ ░ ₺ closed 10 Oct-5 Dec, 60,000.

Recommended
Cycling: *Nolese sports ground,* v. Manzoni 14.
Events: *Regatta dei Rioni,* day and night (2nd Sun in Sep).
Sailing: *Lega Navale,* v. Aurelia Levante, ☎ 748335; *Noli Sailing Club,* Chiariventi region, ☎ 748335.
Swimming: at Bagni Nirvana.
Tennis: v. 25 Aprile, ☎ 748639.

OSPEDALETTI

Imperia 31, Genoa 151, Milan 274 km
Pop. 3,225 ⊠ 18014 ☎ 0184   A3

Ospedaletti makes its living from growing flowers and tourism, in the best tradition of the Riviera dei Fiori. There is one difference, however: it has managed to retain, despite changed building styles, its characteristic appearance and a sense of being at one with its surroundings. Pines, eucalyptus and palms shelter the fine promenade, the **corso Regina Margherita★**. At Coldirodi (*6 km*) is the **Pinacoteca Rambaldi** (*by prior arrangement with Biblioteca Comunale di San Remo,* ☎ 80304, *8:30 a.m.-7:30 p.m.*) with 15C-19C paintings. □

Practical information —————————

~
ⓘ v. Regina Margherita 1, ☎ 59085.

Hotels:
★★★ *Firenze,* corso Regina Margherita 97, ☎ 59221, 32 rm ⓟ ₺ 60,000; bkf: 6,000.
★★★ *Floreal,* corso Regina Margherita 83, ☎ 59638, 26 rm, closed 3-30 Nov, 49,000; bkf: 5,000.
★★★ *Madison,* v. Aurelia Levante 1, ☎ 59713, 40 rm ⓟ � ₺ 85,000; bkf: 6,000.

Recommended
Archery: *Archery club,* strada Vallagrande 9, ☎ 59725.
Swimming: at Rocce del Capo and Capo Nero.

PEGLI

Genoa 10, Milan 152 km
Pop. 37,000 ⊠ 16155 ☎ 010   D1

Pegli, at the W end of Greater Genoa, used to be a smart winter and summer resort, frequented by half

the aristocracy of Europe, but it has long since lost that status due to its proximity to expanding Genoa.

▶ The **Villa Durazzo Pallavicini** stands in a luxuriant park★, laid out in the 19C on the model of literary and dramatic predecessors, and houses the **Museo Civico di Archeologia Ligure** (*9 a.m.-1:15 p.m. and 3-6 p.m.; Sun 9:15 a.m.-12:45 p.m.; closed Mon*), with palaeontological and archaeological finds from various parts of Liguria. ▶ The 16C **Villa Doria** houses the **Museo Civico Navale** (*9 a.m.-12:45 p.m. and 3-6 p.m.; Sun 9:15 a.m.-12:45 p.m.; closed Mon*), a maritime museum concentrating mainly on Liguria and Italy. □

Practical information —————————

Hotel:
★★★ *G. H. Méditerranée,* v. Lungomare 69, ☎ 683041, 72 rm ⓟ ⌕ ░ ₺ ▭ 89,000; bkf: 7,000.

PIETRA LIGURE

Savona 30, Genoa 77, Milan 200 km
Pop. 10,144 ⊠ 17027 ☎ 019   BC2

The 'pietra' is the rock on which the medieval **castle** stands. Old houses and 17C palaces in the **old town**, SW of the castle, have been protected from recent extensive building projects. There is a fine beach, making it a much-frequented resort. The 18C parish church of **S. Nicolò di Bari** is worth a visit. **Borgio-Verezzi** (*2 km*) has a beach and the interesting Borgio caves (*9-11:30 a.m. and 3-5 p.m.*).□

Practical information —————————

PIETRA LIGURE

~
ⓘ p. Martiri della Libertà 31, ☎ 645222.

Hotels:
★★★★ *Paco,* v. Crispi 63, ☎ 645015, 44 rm ⓟ ⌕ ░ ▭ ℗ closed 16 Oct-31 Mar, 70,000; bkf: 6,000.
★★★★ *Royal,* v. Don Bado 129, ☎ 647192, 102 rm ⓟ closed 20 Oct-15 Dec, 70,000; bkf: 6,000.
★★★ *Azucena,* v. Repubblica 76, ☎ 645058, 28 rm ⓟ ░ ░ closed Oct-Nov, 46,000; bkf: 7,000.
★★★ *Capri,* v. Repubblica 132, ☎ 612716, 38 rm ⓟ ░ ░ closed 15 Oct-20 Dec, 35,000; bkf: 5,000.
▲ ★★★ *Fiori,* v. Riviera, 250 pl, ☎ 645636; ★★★ *Pian dei Boschi,* v. Riviera 82, 240 pl, ☎ 645425 (all year).

Recommended
Tennis: v. Soccorso 19, ☎ 645393.
Windsurfing: *Windsurf Centre,* v. don G. Bado, ☎ 645454.

Environs
BORGIO-VEREZZI, ⊠ 17022, ☎ 019, 2 km NE.
~

Recommended
Caves: visit to the **Grotta Valdemino** (fee, closed Tue), information from the *Gruppo Grotte Borgio Verezzi* near cave or from municipio, ☎ 610454.

PIEVE LIGURE

Genoa 16, Milan 151 km
Pop. 2,706 ⊠ 16030 ☎ 010   D2

Pieve Ligure is a quiet resort with rocks and high cliffs, set among olive groves and fields of cultivated flowers. Oil used to be produced in substantial quantities, cattle were raised and timber was felled in the woods for the small shipyards in the area. The 17C parish church of **S. Michele** has a façade with lavish stucco decoration. □

Practical information _____

≋

Restaurant:
♦♦ *Picco,* at Pieve Alta, v. alla Chiesa 56, ☎ 3460234, closed Tue and 15 Jan-8 Feb. Terrace with fine view. Seafood: pansoti, farfalle with olive cream, 22/30,000.

PIGNA

Imperia 56, Genoa 174, Milan 297 km
Pop. 1,194 ⊠ 18037 ☎ 0184   A3

Huddled in concentric circles around a promontory, this ancient and picturesque village resembles a pine-cone (*pigna* means pine-cone) from a distance. Note the narrow, sunken alleyways known as *chibi* with their vaults, passages and archways running between the medieval houses. ▶ There are interesting ruins of the Romanesque church of **S. Tommaso** (12C) and a fine parish church of **S. Michele,** with large 15C rose window. ▶ The **piazza Castello★,** an open square with excellent views, sits high above town. ☐

Practical information _____

♨ (May-Sep), ☎ 201195.

The valleys of the PONENTE

From San Remo to Albenga *(131 km, 1 day; map 3)*

The Argentina and Arroscia Valleys, in W Liguria, were important centres on the ancient salt roads to Piedmont. Today they encourage tourism and have set up commercial and industrial enterprises to slow down population loss. The countryside, towns and villages have survived to a large extent unchanged because the economy is still highly dependent upon agriculture. Afforestation has been abandoned, and instead farmers concentrate on the specialized farm-

ing typical of the coastal plain, as well as the cultivation of olives and vines. Cattle farming has been reintroduced in the Arroscia Valley, using modern methods, but also relying on the natural cycle of moving the cattle to and fro from high summer pastures to low seaside areas with the changing seasons.

▶ From **San Remo** the route climbs to **Ceriana** (→) and then, among vineyards and olive groves, to **Baiardo.** The compact medieval centre on the little hill is dominated by the ruins of the ancient church of **S. Nicolò,** which towers up on a site with a wonderful view; the church lost its roof in the earthquake of 1887. On Ascension Day the inhabitants celebrate the 'Festa della barca' (boat festival) and sing of the tragic death of a young girl who loved a sailor. ▶ The first water mills are sited in the Argentina Valley on the road to **Badalucco,** ancient home of the counts of Ventimiglia. ▶ **Montalto Ligure,** which appears dramatically on a bend, has an ancient medieval fortress; especially interesting is the central part of the building, where there are numerous carved portals. ▶ The road continues not far from the coast, flanked by **woods** (in the past the region supplied large quantities of timber to Genoese shipyards) and by half-deserted villages. ▶ **Triora,** a lively and complex town, dominates the high valley. It has many historic buildings: about ten churches and oratories, more than five castles and fortresses, stretches of wall with three of the original gates and four fountains. There are also numerous alleyways, squares and carved portals. In the past Triora was a prosperous farming town (thanks to the provisions of the famous 16C 'statutes'). There was a famous witches' trial here in 1588. ▶ Beyond the **Teglia Pass** (4,550 ft) the road descends to the Arroscia Valley, above which stands the striking 15C sanctuary of **Nostra Signora del Sepolcro.** ▶ **Pieve di Teco** was the feudal stronghold of the valley and a commercial centre at the point at which some of the most important salt and cattle routes converge. The 14C-15C linear urban structure has been maintained almost intact. ▶ Just outside **Ranzo** is the important but isolated **S. Pantaleo,** rebuilt in the 15C on the site of an 11C proto-Romanesque church. ▶ Finally the road leads down to Ortovero and the plain of **Albenga** (→), through fields and orchards. ☐

3. The valleys of the Ponente

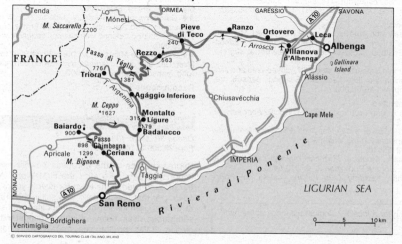

© SERVIZIO CARTOGRAFICO DEL TOURING CLUB ITALIANO, MILANO

Practical information

MONESI DI TRIORA, 4,530 ft, ☒ 18025, ☎ 0183, 22 km NW of Pieve di Teco.
⚡ Ski lifts, instruction, ice skating.
ⓘ Mónersi sports centre, ☎ 38522.

PIEVE DI TECO, ☒ 18026, ☎ 0183.
ⓘ p. Brunengo, ☎ 36453.

Recommended
Events: procession through S. Sebastiano (20 Jan).
♥ gastronomy: olive oil and mushrooms.

TRIORA, ☒ 18010, ☎ 0184.

Hotel:
★★ *Colomba d'Oro*, corso Italia 66, ☎ 94051, 28 rm ℙ ⚡ ⚂ ♿ ᴄ closed 15 Oct-1 May, 38,000; bkf: 4,000.

PORTOFINO**

Genoa 36, Milan 171 km
Pop. 710 ☒ 16034 ☎ 0185   D2

The ancient 'Portus Delphini' mentioned by Pliny was the home of coral fishermen. The houses still look as they used to and the exterior of the village has not changed, but since the famous piazzetta and the little harbour became the haunt of the international jet set the restored houses sell for enormous prices and traditional trades have vanished. The extraordinary natural environment has remained; it is considered the most important unspoiled promontory on the entire Ligurian coast.

▶ Cars are not allowed in the centre of the village *(car park just outside)*. The **harbour** is surrounded by a fine group of typical **Ligurian houses**, restored, with original polychrome decoration. ▶ A climb to the 16C **fortress of S. Giorgio** *(9 a.m.-12 noon and 3-6 p.m.)* offers a fine **panoramic view**★ of the bay from the little square in front of the nearby church, or a little higher up, from the lighthouse on the **punta del Capo**★. ▶ There are fine walks on the **Portofino promontory** (Camogli →). □

Practical information

≋
ⓘ v. Roma 35-37, ☎ 69024.

Hotels:
★★★★★ *Splendido*, v. Baratta 13, ☎ 69551, 65 rm ℙ ⚡ ⚂ ₩ ☒ ↗ closed 29 Oct-27 Mar. Fine villa converted into a hotel in splendid park, 383,000; bkf: 24,000.
★★★★ *Nazionale*, v. Roma 2, ☎ 69575, 42 rm, closed Jan-Feb. No restaurant, 114,000; bkf: 8,000.
★★ *Eden*, vico Dritto 18, ☎ 69091, 12 rm ℙ ₩ 95,000.

Restaurants:
♦♦ *U Batti*, vico Nuovo 17, ☎ 69379, closed Mon and Christmas. Tiny trattoria with maritime atmosphere. Seafood: tagliatelle al pesto, scampi al segreto, 30/50,000.
♦ *Stella*, molo Umberto I 3, ☎ 69007, closed Wed and Jan-Mar. Facing the little harbour. Seafood: pansoti, trenette genovesi, 25/50,000.

Recommended
Boat trip: to San Fruttuoso (20 mn), *Tigullio boat service*, ☎ 265712.
Events: *St. George's day festivities* (23 Apr); *international sailing regattas* (spring, summer).
Marina: ☎ 69040.
Natural park: *Monte di Portofino regional park*, office at Genoa, v. Brigate Partigiane 2, ☎ 010/5485.
Yacht club: *Yachting Club Italiano*, calata del Porto, ☎ 69298.

| Looking for a locality? Consult the index at the back of the book. |

PORTOVENERE

La Spezia 12, Genoa 114, Milan 232 km
Pop. 4,763 ☒ 19025 ☎ 0187   F2-3

Portovenere was originally a favoured commercial port and Genoese guardian of the gulf, much more important than La Spezia in the late 15C. The past military and naval role of this ancient and fascinating little town still shows in its compact, almost fortified layout. Times have changed, however, and Portovenere's modern invaders, the tourists, are no longer in danger of slipping off rocks wickedly smeared with tallow, as happened to imprudent Pisan and Aragonese attackers in 1421.

▶ 'The churches of Liguria, like ships ready to be launched'; the fine little black-and-white church of **S. Pietro** (6C, rebuilt 13C) stands on a lonely promontory and recalls Cardarelli's lines. ▶ Nearby, a steep flight of steps leads down to the **Arpaia cave**, beloved of Byron.' ▶ The original linear layout of the village, winding along a single narrow street, can be seen clearly from the church. ▶ The compact group of polychrome **houses and towers** opens on to the **Doria quay**★ and the port with its narrow alleyways (easy to barricade in case of attack). ▶ The fine Romanesque collegiate church of **S. Lorenzo** has 15C-16C paintings and sculptures and a small but lavish museum and treasury. ▶ The town is dominated by the Genoese **castle**, rebuilt between the 16C-17C *(10 a.m.-12 noon and 2-6 p.m.)*. ▶ A boat trip to the **Palmaria islands** is recommended, including **Tino** and **Tinetto**, with caves, remains of prehistoric settlements and a ruined monastery. □

Practical information

≋
ⓘ p. Bastreri 1 (at edge of built-up area), ☎ 900691.
🚢 in season there are trips to La Spezia and Portofino, ☎ 900785.

Hotels:
★★★★ *Royal Sporting*, v. dell'Olivo 345, ☎ 900326, 62 rm ℙ ₩ ☒ ↗ closed Nov-Mar, 140,000; bkf: 10,000.
★★★ *Baia*, at Le Grazie, v. Lungomare Est 111, ☎ 900797, 42 rm ⚡ ❀ ☒ 60,000; bkf: 7,000.
★★★ *San Pietro*, v. Capellini 177, ☎ 900616, 31 rm ⚡ ⚂ ❀ closed 21 Dec-15 Mar, 64,000; bkf: 7,000.

Restaurants:
● ♦♦♦ *Taverna del Corsaro*, passeggiata Doria 102, ☎ 900622, closed Thu, 15-31 Jan and 1-15 Jun. On tip of peninsula with veranda overlooking bay and island of Palmaria. Excellent seafood: tagliolini with scampi, buridda S. Pietro, 25/40,000.
♦♦ *Gambero*, at Le Grazie, v. Libertà 143, ☎ 900325, closed Mon and Jan-Feb. By harbour in this old fishing village. Seafood: penne with scampi, spaghetti with crab, 18/35,000.
♦♦ *Gavitello-da Mario*, calata Doria 20, ☎ 900215, closed Mon, Dec and Jan. Veranda overlooking harbour. Seafood: pansoti, scampi, 30/45,000.

Recommended
Marina: ☎ 900768.

RAPALLO*

Genoa 30, Milan 163 km
Pop. 29,309 ☒ 16035 ☎ 0185   D1-2

Representatives of the European powers signed an important treaty here after the First World War and Ezra Pound lived in the town for twenty years prior to 1945. At that time Rapallo was still in the first phase of its long domination by cosmopolitan tourism, with sumptuous villas, hotels of international standing and elegant cafés on the sea front. Today, after the boom in the 60s, it is the largest and best-equipped holiday resort on the Riviera di Levante, but it is also an example of uncontrolled building development, which has effectively destroyed the town.

▶ There is a fine collection of lace, for which Rapallo was famous, in the **Museo Civico** *(9 a.m.-12 noon; closed wkends)*, near the 17C **Oratorio dei Bianchi.** The remains of the **historic centre** are squeezed between these two buildings, the parish church and the sea; it includes some old houses, fine arcades and a very lively market. ▶ There is a pretty town bandstand in the little square which opens on to the **Vittorio Veneto★** promenade. Here are the cafés, palms, flowers and the little 16C **castle** on a rock by the sea which is a well-known Rapallo landmark. ▶ To find a little peace and quiet amid the olive groves, go up to the **Santuario di Montallegro** (cable car). ▶ To the E is the little beach at **Zoagli** (→). ▶ To the W, on the road to Santa Margherita (→) and Portofino (→), the village of **San Michele di Pagana** has maintained its ancient appearance and in the church is a 17C painting by A. Van Dyck. □

Practical information _____

RAPALLO
≋
Ⓘ v. Diaz 9, ☎ 51282.

Hotels:
★★★★ *Eurotel Rapallo,* v. Aurelia Ponente 22, ☎ 60981, 64 rm Ⓟ ⧫ ẘ ₺ ⊡ 120,000.
★★★★ *Rosabianca,* lungomare Vittorio Veneto 42, ☎ 52262, 18 rm Ⓟ ⧫ ₺ 12,000; bkf: 8,000.
★★★ *Bel Soggiorno,* v. Gramsci 10, ☎ 50927, 24 rm Ⓟ ⧫ ẘ closed 1 Nov-20 Dec, 75,000; bkf: 5,000.
★★★ *Cuba e Milton,* at S. Michele di Pagana, v. Pagana 160, ☎ 50610, 30 rm Ⓟ ⧫ ẘ closed 1 Nov-20 Dec, 70,000; bkf: 7,000.
★★★ *Moderno e Reale,* v. Gramsci 6, ☎ 50601, 49 rm ⧫ ẘ ₺ 77,000; bkf: 8,000.
★★ *Stella,* v. Aurelia Ponente 10, ☎ 50368, 31 rm Ⓟ 50,000; bkf: 5,000.
★★ *Vittoria,* v. S. Filippo Neri 11, ☎ 54838, 40 rm Ⓟ closed 20 Oct-20 Dec, 43,000; bkf: 4,000.

Restaurant:
♦♦♦ *Elite,* v. Milite Ignoto 19, ☎ 50551, closed Thu and Nov. Regional cuisine: trofie al pesto, pansoti, 20/30,000.

⚠ ★ *Rapallo,* at Santa Margherita del Campo, v. S. Lazzaro 4/D, 119 pl, ☎ 60260.

Recommended
Cablecar excursions: Montallegro (from v. Betti).
Events: *cartoonists' exhibition* (odd-numbered years); *traditional festival* at Santuario di Nostra Signora di Montallegro (Jul) and at *San Michele di Pagana* (Sep).
Golf: v. Mameli 377, ☎ 50210 (18 holes).
Horseback riding: *Rapallo riding club,* v. Santa Maria Campo 196, ☎ 50462 (instruction).
Marina: international private marina, ☎ 6891; public marina, ☎ 55253.
Sailing: *Rapallo club,* at San Massimo Chiapparolo, ☎ 50750.
Swimming: at San Pietro di Novella, ☎ 50797.
Tennis: ☎ 61119.

Environs

SAN MASSIMO, ⊠ 16035, 4 km W.

Restaurant:
♦♦ *Gianco,* ☎ 56189, closed Wed, Thu noon and 2 Nov-22 Dec. Unusual collection of original works by famous cartoonists. Regional cuisine: chestnut fettucine with pesto, stoccafisso accomodato, 20/30,000.

┌─────────────────────────────────┐
│ Send us your comments and suggestions; we will │
│ use them in the next edition. │
└─────────────────────────────────┘

RECCO

Genoa 19, Milan 160 km
Pop. 10,794 ⊠ 16036 ☎ 0185   D2

The town of Recco, entirely rebuilt after bombing in the Second World War, has become a seaside holiday, craft and industrial centre and has almost completely relinquished its traditional seafaring and commercial activities. **Sori** *(c. 4 km E),* in a little inlet on the golfo Paradiso, has an interesting 17C parish church. □

Practical information _____

RECCO
≋

Hotels:
★★ *Elena,* v. Garibaldi 5, ☎ 74022, 31 rm Ⓟ ⧫ 59,000; bkf: 8,000.
★★ *Oasi,* v. Roma 278, ☎ 74128, 14 rm Ⓟ ẘ closed Jan-Feb and Jul, 50,000. Rest. ● ♦♦♦ *Manuelina* closed Wed. Excellent regional cuisine, 45/75,000.

Restaurants:
♦♦♦ *Vittoriö,* v. Roma 160, ☎ 74029, closed Thu. Run by same family for three generations. Regional cuisine: trofie matte, mesciua, 25/50,000.
♦♦♦ *Vitturin,* v. del Giustiniani 50, ☎ 731225, closed Mon. Mixed cuisine: trofiette al pesto, fish fritto misto, 30/50,000.

Recommended
Marina: *Yacht club,* ☎ 74357.
Swimming: lungomare Bettolo, ☎ 75311.

Environs

SORI, ⊠ 16030, ☎ 0185, 4 km W.
≋
Ⓘ v. Stagno, ☎ 700681.

Recommended
Swimming: ☎ 700112.

RIVIERA DI LEVANTE

D-F2-3

The whole of Liguria is squeezed between the Apennines and the sea, but this is particularly true of the strip of coast between Genoa and la Magra. The Riviera di Levante has coasts which are often rocky and barren, as on the promontory of **Portofino** (→) and in the **Cinque Terre** (→). Exceptions are the plains of **Chiavari** (→) and la Magra. There are no major inlets except the Gulf of La Spezia and no long sandy beaches. The landscape is extremely varied. The area has characteristic villages with diffuse centres such as **Recco** (→) and **Sestri Levante** (→), set among luxuriant olives, citrus fruits, ilexes, agaves and other exotic plants. Elsewhere, especially in the far E, the villages are compact, often isolated and built on rocks, in picturesque and wild surroundings, in which man has carved out a place for himself among the vines and olives. □

RIVIERA DI PONENTE

A-C1-3

Unlike the Riviera di Levante, the Riviera di Ponente (from Genoa to the French frontier) has expanded as a result of urbanization in the hinterland. Furthermore, specialization in agricultural and marine activities brought about greater opportunities for contact and cross-fertilizing links between the littoral and the interior, resulting in reciprocal enrichment of the two cultures. The coast is a narrow strip cut off by the mountains, with many rocky promontories, broad inlets and sandy coves; the varied landscape and mild climate have attracted both summer and winter visitors. An example of this is **San Remo** (→), the main centre of the Riviera dei Fiori between **Ventimiglia** (→) and **Imperia** (→), famous for the intensive cultivation of flowers. Even toward the valleys of Piedmont, however, many centres have maintained their former appearance and enough economic vitality to avoid loss of population. □

RUTA

Genoa 28, Milan 164 km
Pop. 800 ⊠ 16030 ☎ 0185 D2

This small village consists of villas and houses scattered among the pines and chestnuts and has expanded little since 1885, when Friedrich Nietzsche stayed here. Now as then it is a useful centre for visits to Camogli (→) and the Portofino promontory. □

Practical information

ℹ at Camogli.

Recommended
Excursions: to Portofino Vetta (road toll).

SAN REMO**

Imperia 25, Genoa 141, Milan 262 km
Pop. 62,131 ⊠ 18038 ☎ 0184 A3

It was not by chance that in 1860 the first hotel built here was called the 'Londra'. This was the period in which British 'gentlemen-tourists', attracted by an exceptionally mild climate and the romantic fascination of the countryside, started to frequent the Riviera and San Remo in particular. Then came Maria Alexandrovna, consort of Tsar Alexander II, and Prince Friedrich Wilhelm of Germany, followed by the flower of the European aristocracy. Between the late 19C and the Second World War, San Remo built hotels, villas, the casino (which still hands out billions of lire), sports facilities, the cable car to Monte Bignone (in its time the longest in the world, now under reconstruction) and parks and gardens everywhere. In the meantime agriculture has given way to the cultivation of flowers, radically changing the hilly countryside (now criss-crossed with geometrical lines of greenhouses and nurseries) and making San Remo Italy's most important flower market.

▶ The medieval centre, the **Pigna,** still fascinating despite change and deterioration, climbs in concentric circles towards the **piazza Castello** in a labyrinth of alleyways, flights of steps, covered passages and little squares. ▶ In the upper town, the **Santuario della Madonna della Costa** (17C-18C) faces a terrace with a fine view. ▶ Below it, the irregular piazza Eroi Sanremesi, in which is the Romanesque and Gothic cathedral of **S. Siro** (13C), links the old and new towns. ▶ The main modern artery is the **corso Matteotti,** with luxury shops and cafés; it runs from the **Palazzo Borea d'Olmo** (15C-16C, restored), the most important secular building, and the famous **Casinò Municipale** (1904-6). ▶ The Russian Orthodox church of **S. Basilio,** with onion domes, a reminder of the Empress Alexandrovna's stay, is in a little square near the sea. The church stands at one end of the **corso Imperatrice★**, an elegant seaside promenade, flanked with palms presented to the town by the Empress herself. To the r. is the fine **parco Marsaglia.** ▶ A little farther on the **corso degli Inglesi** climbs between villas and gardens. ▶ In the E part of the town the **corso Trento e Trieste★** leads to the public gardens of the Villa Comunale. ▶ Early risers and insomniacs should not miss the spectacular opening of business in the **flower market,** at dawn, in the hall between the p. Colombo and the corso Garibaldi.

Environs

▶ **Mt. Bignone** (4,262 ft; 12.4 km; cable car is under reconstruction) is covered with pinewoods and offers a fine panorama★. ▶ **Bussana Vecchia** *(8 km)* has a colony of artists living among the ruins of this village, which was destroyed by the earthquake of 1887. □

Practical information

≋

ℹ largo Nuvoloni, ☎ 85615; office at *Coldirodi autostrada junction,* ☎ 530350.
🚆 ☎ 80172.
Car rental: *Avis,* corso Imperatrice 96, ☎ 73897 (Apr-Oct); *Hertz,* v. XX Settembre 17, ☎ 85618; *Maggiore,* railway station, p. Colombo 19, ☎ 85165.

Hotels:
★★★★★ ***Royal,*** corso Imperatrice 80, ☎ 79991, 143 rm Ⓟ ♨ ♿ ▭ 🎾 closed 10 Oct-20 Dec. International reputation with public rooms and bedrooms in period style, 280,000; bkf: 15,000.
★★★★ ***Des Etrangers,*** corso Garibaldi 82, ☎ 79951, 100 rm Ⓟ ♨ ♿ ▭ closed 4 Nov-20 Dec, 111,000; bkf: 12,000.
★★★★ ***G. H. Londra,*** corso Matuzia 2, ☎ 79961, 140 rm Ⓟ ♨ ▭ closed 1 Nov-20 Dec, 158,000.
★★★★ ***Méditerranée,*** corso Cavallotti 76, ☎ 75601, 63 rm Ⓟ ♨ ♿ ▭ 135,000; bkf: 12,000.
★★★★ ***Miramare Continental Palace,*** corso Matuzia 9, ☎ 882381, 57 rm Ⓟ ⚘ ♨ ♿ ▭ 🎾 closed 21 Sep-19 Dec, 140,000; bkf: 10,000.
★★★★ ***Nyala,*** strada Solaro 143, ☎ 63405, 36 rm Ⓟ ⚘ ♨ 132,000; bkf: 13,000.
★★★★ ***Parco,*** corso Mazzini 401, ☎ 66222, 36 rm Ⓟ ⚘ ♨ ✗ ▭ closed 16 Nov-20 Jan, 79,000; bkf: 7,000.
★★★ ***Ariston Montecarlo,*** corso Mazzini 507, ☎ 889255, 52 rm Ⓟ ⚘ ♨ ▭ 80,000; bkf: 7,000.
★★★ ***Bobby Motel,*** corso Marconi 208, ☎ 60255, 75 rm Ⓟ ⚘ ♨ ♿ ▭ closed 25 Oct-20 Dec, 80,000; bkf: 6,000.
★★★ ***Napoleon,*** corso Marconi 56, ☎ 62244, 28 rm Ⓟ ⚘ ♨ closed 15 Nov-15 Dec. No restaurant, 90,000; bkf: 8,000.
★★★ ***Paradiso,*** v. Roccasterone 12, ☎ 85112, 41 rm Ⓟ ⚘ ⛱ ♨ closed 1 Nov-19 Dec, 83,000; bkf: 7,000.
★★★ ***Villa Maria,*** corso Nuvoloni 30, ☎ 882882, 19 rm Ⓟ ⛱ ♨ ♿ 83,000; bkf: 7,000.
★★★ ***Ville & Tivoli,*** corso Matuzia 187, ☎ 61661, 46 rm Ⓟ ✗ 72,000; bkf: 6,000.
★★ ***Centrale,*** v. Roma 16, ☎ 883696, 45 rm Ⓟ ✗ closed Nov. No restaurant, 60,000; bkf: 5,000.

Restaurants:
● ♦♦♦♦ ***Rendez-Vous,*** v. Matteotti 126, ☎ 85609, closed Sun, Mon eve. Classical and elegant. Mixed cuisine: crayfish risotto, fish brodetto, 25/45,000.
♦♦♦ ***Caravella-ai Pesci Vivi,*** giardini Vittorio Veneto 1, ☎ 80902, closed Mon, Tue eve and 14 Nov-22 Dec. Pleasant maritime surroundings with terrace with sea view. Seafood: prawns Caravella, special fried dishes, 35/50,000.
♦♦♦ ***Pesce d'Oro,*** corso Cavallotti 300, ☎ 66332, closed Sun and 15 Feb-15 Mar. Quietly elegant with fine veranda. Mixed cuisine: seafood zuppetta, green lasagnette al pesto, 45/55,000.
♦♦ ***Marinaio-da Carluccio,*** v. Gaudio 28, ☎ 84978, closed Mon and 10 Oct-30 Nov. Small establishment by fish market. Seafood: spaghetti alla botarga, shellfish, 50/70,000.
♦ ***Porto - da Nicò,*** p. Bresca 9, ☎ 84144, closed Thu and 1 Nov-20 Dec. Long-established fishermen's trat-

toria between harbour and fish market. Seafood: spaghetti, penne Nicò, 35/40,000.

⚠ ★ *San Remo*, at Pian di Poma, v. Tiro a Volo 3, ☎ 60635 (all year).

Recommended
Canoeing: *San Remo canoeing school*, v. Matteotti, ☎ 86546.
Casinò Municipale: ☎ 79901.
Discothèque: *Nabila*, Giardina Vittorio Veneto 74, ☎ 80959.
Events: *Song festival*, with songs by well-known composers; *international gathering of composers and conductors; men's fashion shows; parade of flower floats* (last Sun in Jan); *display of handicrafts* (end of Aug); *Milan-San Remo cycle race* (Mar); *sea regatta* (Giraglia).
Golf: v. Campo Golf 59, ☎ 67093 (18 holes).
Horseback riding: *horse-riding club*, v. Solaro 127, ☎ 60770 (instruction); *Speron d'oro Turismo Equestre*, at Bussana *(6 km E)*, v. delle Fonti, ☎ 52255 or 52256 (associate of *ANTE*).
Marina: ☎ 8861.
Swimming: corso Cavallotti; at Capo Nero (Olympic pool).
Tennis: corso Maturia 18, ☎ 61776.
Yacht club: *Yachtclub Sanremo*, molo Levante quay, ☎ 85760.

SANTA MARGHERITA LIGURE*

Genoa 31, Milan 166 km
Pop. 12,316 ⊠ 16038 ☎ 0185   D2

The hill between the two inlets formerly separated the towns of Corte (by the harbour) and Pescino; the latter grew considerably in the 19C to cope with the first wealthy visitors, which gradually ousted marine and agricultural activities. Extensive building has changed the face of the town, which has nevertheless retained some of its former refinement and charm.

▶ From the p. Vittorio Veneto the **seaside promenade**, shaded with palm and ilex, ends with the houses grouped around the old port. ▶ On the hill, the large **Villa Durazzo Centurione** (16C) is set in the **parco comunale** *(8:30 a.m.-6:30 p.m.);* its paths are paved with little black-and-white flags and there are also statues and fountains in a wooded setting full of exotic plants. ▶ **Paraggi** *(about 4 km)* on the panoramic road to Portofino (→) is an ancient village of fishermen and millers, in an exquisite bay, today an elegant tourist resort.   ☐

Practical information _____

≋
ℹ v. XXV Aprile 2/B, ☎ 287485.
Car rental: *Avis*, v. Solimano 20, ☎ 86833 (Apr-Oct).

Hotels:
★★★★★ *Imperial Palace*, v. Pagana 19, ☎ 288991, 106 rm P ⫫ 🕭 🖃 ⁓ closed Nov-Mar. Former private mansion, furnishings mostly 17C, 348,000.
★★★★ *G. H. Miramare*, v. Milite Ignoto 30, ☎ 287013, 81 rm P ⫫ 🕭 🖃 Art Nouveau with tropical garden, 260,000.
★★★★ *Laurin*, lungomare Marconi 3, ☎ 289971, 41 rm P 🕭 closed Jan-Mar, 140,000; bkf: 13,000.
★★★★ *Metropole a Santa Margherita*, v. Pagana 2, ☎ 286134, 48 rm P ⫫ 🕭 closed 1 Nov-20 Dec, 98,000; bkf: 9,000.
★★★★ *Park Hotel Suisse*, v. Favale 31, ☎ 289571, 75 rm P ⫫ ⫫ 🕭 🖃 175,000; bkf: 9,000.
★★★★ *Regina Elena*, v. Milite Ignoto 44, ☎ 287003, 86 rm P ⫫ 🕭 148,000; bkf: 13,000.
★★★ *Argentina*, at Paraggi, ☎ 286708, 13 rm P closed Nov-Feb, 50,000; bkf: 10,000.
★★★ *Minerva*, v. Maragliano 34/D, ☎ 286073, 40 rm P ⫫ 🕭 closed 5 Nov-20 Dec, 77,000.
★★★ *Vela*, corso N. Cuneo 19/21, ☎ 286039, 16 rm P ⫫ 🕭 ⁓ closed Feb and Nov, 95,000; bkf: 8,000.

★★ *Villa Anita*, v. Tigullio 10, ☎ 286543, 12 rm P ⫫ 🕭 ⁓ closed 20 Oct-20 Dec, 50,000; bkf: 6,500.

Restaurants:
♦♦♦ *Cesarina*, v. Mameli 2/C, ☎ 286059, closed Wed and Feb-Mar. Regional cuisine: taglierini with fish sauce, octopus with potatoes, 50/60,000.
♦♦♦ *Paraggi*, at Paraggi, v. Lungomare, ☎ 289961, closed 1 Nov-19 Mar. In small hotel with private beach facing little bay. Mixed cuisine: riso certosina, spaghetti in foil, 60/90,000.
♦ *Ancora*, v. Maragliano 7, ☎ 280559, closed Mon and 15 Dec-28 Feb. Family-run trattoria. Seafood: taglierini with red mullet, scampi alla paolin, 35/50,000.

Recommended
Bicycle rental: outside tourist office.
Discothèques: *Covo di Nord Est*, lungomare Rossetti 1, ☎ 286558 (closed Mon); *Carillon*, at Paraggi *(3 km S)*, ☎ 286721.
Events: *spring festival* (Mar); *national award for figurative painting* (Aug).
Marina: ☎ 287029.
Sailing: *Lega Navale*, calata Porto, ☎ 88575 (also skin-diving).
Tennis: corso G. Matteotti, ☎ 286523.
Water-skiing: at *G. Hotel Miramare*, ☎ 287013.
Yacht club: *Yachtclub Tigullio*, calata Porto 21, ☎ 86889.

SARZANA

La Spezia 17, Genoa 102, Milan 219 km
Pop. 19,242 ⊠ 19038 ☎ 0187   F2

Sarzana today is a commercial flower-growing centre, a focal point for the surrounding agricultural areas and a link between La Spezia and Versilia. None of this is new; the town is set in the borderlands of Liguria and Tuscany, a melting-pot of culture and tradition, and has always been important in the economy, politics and strategy of the region. 'Cannons are firing from the mountains of Sarzano': this event narrated in a partisan song must have recurred frequently from the 15C, when Genoa and Florence were fighting for the region.

▶ The **historic centre** runs along the axis of the ancient via Francigena (v. Mazzini, v. Bertoloni), which connected Rome with Flanders. Almost all the most important palaces (rebuilt in 18C-19C) are on this main road or the p. Matteotti. ▶ The oldest building is the church of **S. Andrea**, perhaps 11C, which from 1204 was the town baptistery and seat of municipal jurisdiction. ▶ The Romanesque-Gothic **cathedral★** was founded in the 13C, when Sarzana replaced Luni as seat of the bishop, and was then extended and altered, particularly in the 15C, under the Sarzanese Pope Nicholas V. In the interior are two 15C works by Riccomanni and Guglielmo's **Crucifixion★** of 1138, the oldest such painted cross and the model for subsequent Tuscan and Umbrian works of this kind. ▶ A little beyond the 19C **Teatro degli Impavidi** (with fine *art nouveau* gate) the road rises to the **Cittadella**, a powerful fortress constructed in the 15C by Lorenzo the Magnificent. ▶ The **fortezza di Sarzanello** *(2 km, on the hill)* was built from the 14C-16C on a knoll looking out over the plain of Luni. ▶ The beach of **Marinella** di Sarzana *(14 km)* is visited on the Gulf of La Spezia itinerary (→).   ☐

Practical information _____

Hotel:
★★★★ *MotelAgip*, circonvallazione Aurelia 32, ☎ 621491, 51 rm P 🕭 ⁓ 85,000.

Restaurants:
♦♦ *Galletto*, v. Mazzini 28, ☎ 620041, closed Mon and Nov. Mixed cuisine: spaghetti with salmon, scampi with cognac, 35/45,000.

♦♦ *Girarrosto-da Paolo,* v. dei Molini 138, ☎ 621088, closed Wed and 1-20 Sep. On edge of town, toward the hills, garden. Italian cuisine: gnocchi al pesto, pappardelle in hare sauce, 12/22,000.
♦ *Scaletta,* at Bradia 5, ☎ 620585, closed Tue, Sep and Christmas. Long-established family trattoria. Regional cuisine: homemade tagliatelle, dried cod, 13/20,000.

⚠ ★★ *Mirafiume,* at Battifollo, 70 pl, ☎ 620690.

SASSELLO

Savona 27, Genoa 73, Milan 162 km
Pop. 1,938 ⊠ 17046 ☎ 019   C1

The only signs in Sassello of pre-industrial development under Genoese rule are a few ruined ironworks and the 17C design of the town. Today it lives mainly on tourism and is famous for two specialties: amaretti (macaroons) and canestrelli (a type of bun).

▶ Some ruins and the **Torre dei Saraceni** remain of the 12C-15C feudal fortifications. ▶ Interesting and in good condition, however, are the six 19C **forts** to the S which dominate the 1,693 ft **colle del Giovo,** a level area popular with visitors.   ☐

Practical information _____

✝ ski lifts at Alberola.

Recommended
Children's facilities: zoo at Giovo Ligure *(11 km SW),* ☎ 705012 (8 a.m.-7:30 p.m.).
♥ pastries: macaroons and canestrelli buns.

SAVONA

Genoa 46, Milan 170, Rome 531 km
Pop. 74,129 ⊠ 17100 ☎ 019   C2

For years Savona has been the most important ferry port for cars and trucks in the Mediterranean. Ease of communication with Turin has earned the town the name 'port of Piedmont', but in fact this is less than it deserves, as the port complex of Savona and Vado has a turnover in excess of 15 million tons. A large proportion of this is in oil and coal, and the handling facilities for these materials are among the most extensive in Italy and indeed in Europe. There are also older industries in the town and surrounding area (in the metallurgical sector, for example), which recent developments have not entirely eliminated. On the other hand, the scale of dock and industrial activity sometimes diminishes the importance of historical and cultural events to which the town bears eloquent witness.

▶ The old centre is bounded by fortifications showing contrasting aspects of the town's history. ▶ On the hill to the S the impressive **Fortezza del Priamar** (C-D2), built 1542-3 by the Republic of Genoa on the ruins of an entire district of the town, is a reminder of Savona's unwilling submission to its more powerful rival. In 1830-1 Giuseppe Mazzini was imprisoned here. ▶ On the other hand, the 14C **Torre di Leon Pancaldo** (C2) in the old harbour not only commemorates the Savonese navigator and companion of Magellan, but also the ancient della Quarda district, which at the time of the town's greatest expansion was the home of the rich merchant classes. ▶ The **via Paleocapa** (C2) starts at the tower; it is the principal artery of the town and a reference point for visits to the historic centre. The finest examples of medieval urban architecture are on the l. in the street running parallel to the port. ▶ The **Pinacoteca Civica★** is housed in a palazzo (no. 7) in the via Quarda Superiore (C2; *winter 10 a.m.-12 noon and 3-6 p.m.; summer 4-7:30 p.m.; closed Mon and Sep),* with works by Taddeo di Bartolo, L. Brea,

Donato de'Bardi *(Crucifixion),* G. Mazone, V. Foppa *(Madonna and Saints)* and of the 17C Genoese school. ▶ In the v. Pia, the splendid **Palazzo della Rovere** (C2), an incomplete work by Giuliano da Sangallo (1495), shows the Renaissance tendency to rebuild by the laborious insertion of new sections into the hitherto compact texture of the group. ▶ The 14C **Palazzo degli Anziani** (with 17C façade) is the only surviving medieval building facing the old harbour, and the Corsi, Guarnieri and del Brandale towers (C2) are 12C. The **Duomo** (C2) was built in the late 16C on the site of an earlier church. The interior is more interesting than the exterior (the façade is 19C); there are fine works of art, furnishings from the old cathedral and other important ecclesiastical buildings, in particular some Renaissance sculptures and the wooden choir dating from the early 16C. ▶ A triptych by L. Brea (1495) and a panel painting by Tuccio d'Andrea are housed with the cathedral treasure in the **Museo Diocesano** *(Thu and Sun p.m.; group bookings,* ☎ *25960).* To the r. of the cathedral are a cloister and the **Cappella Sistina** *(apply in the Duomo),* commissioned by Sixtus IV in the 15C as a mausoleum for his parents. ▶ A little farther on, in the oratorio of **S. Maria di Castello** (C2; *wkends 8:30-10 a.m.)* is a large polyptych by V. Foppa and L. Brea *(Madonna and Saints★),* important in the history of Ligurian figurative art during the Renaissance. ▶ The most interesting feature in the district to the r. of the v. Paleocapa is the **Teatro Comunale Chiabrera** (C2) in Neoclassical style (1850-3). This is the monumental focal point of the piazza Diaz, on the border between the old walled town and the area of 19C urban expansion of th "Piedmontese type', i.e. organized on a strict network of right angles.

Environs

▶ 6 km W along the Aurelia is **Vado Ligure,** the Roman *Vada Sabatia,* now an important industrial centre in an anchorage equipped with modern wharfs for handling oil, chemicals and coal. ▶ 7 km N is the **santuario di Nostra Signora di Misericordia** (16C-17C), with works by O. Borgianni, del Domenichino and the school of Bernini, also 16C-20C vestments and gold vessels.   ☐

Practical information _____

SAVONA
ⓘ v. Paleocapa 9 (C2), ☎ 25305.
▨▨▨ (C1), ☎ 806969.
▨▨▨ from p. del Popolo (C2) and the railway station; *Riviera coach lines,* ☎ 21879.
Car rental: *Avis,* v. Famagosta 1, ☎ 20976.

Hotels:
★★★★ *Riviera Suisse,* v. Paleocapa 24 (C2 a), ☎ 20683, 70 rm Ⓟ ♿ ⚘ closed Christmas. No restaurant, 80,000; bkf: 7,000.
★★★ *Ariston,* v. Giordano 11r (D1 b), ☎ 805633, 16 rm Ⓟ No restaurant, 75,000.

Restaurants:
♦♦ *Due Corsari,* v. S. Lorenzo 2r (B2 c), ☎ 26320, closed Wed. Mixed cuisine, some international dishes: seafood or cuttlefish ink risotto, charcoal-grilled fish, 20/30,000.
♦♦ *Sole,* v. Stalingrado 66, ☎ 862177, closed Wed and 10-30 Sep. Regional cuisine: trenette al pesto, cima ripiena, 15/26,000.

Recommended
Bowling: v. Brignoni 3 (C2), ☎ 20373.
Cycling: *G. S. Torretta,* v. Quarda Superiore 37r (C2); *G. S. Poggio Savona,* v. XX Settembre 44r (C2), ☎ 26360.
Events: *Good Friday procession* with a parade of wooden statues (even-numbered years).
Factory visits: *Bormioli glassworks,* at Altare *(14 km W),* v. Paleologo 16, ☎ 58254.
Hang gliding: *Pro delta* hang gliding school, v. Giachero 20/1, ☎ 26663; *Ali bianche* school, at Cengio *(32 km NW along Mondovi-Savona road),* v. 25 Aprile 4/1, ☎ 554903.
Horseback riding: *Plodiese horse-riding assocation,* at Plodio Valle *(24 km NW);* v. Niprati 12, ☎ 518976 (associate of *ANTE).*

Santuario km 6 1 2 Genoa km 46 3

LAVAGNOLA

SAVONA

0   200   400 m

1:24.000 (1cm=240 m)

Impéria km 73 1 2

© SERVIZIO CARTOGRAFICO DEL TOURING CLUB ITALIANO, MILANO

Sailing: *Lega Navale,* Porticciolo Miramare, ☎ 34392 (also motorboat club).
Swimming: v. Eroe dei due Mondi (C3), ☎ 37772.
♥ confections: sour orange candied or preserved in liquer, macaroons.

Environs
ZINOLA, ⊠ 17049, 4 km SW.

Hotels:
★★★ *Mare,* v. Nizza 89r, ☎ 862263, 42 rm ℗ ⚈ ὅ 59,000; bkf: 6,000.
★★★ *MotelAgip,* v. Nizza 62, ☎ 861961, 60 rm ℗ ∉ 96,000.

△ ★★★★ *Buggi International,* v. N.S. del Monte 15, 500 pl, ☎ 860120 (all year); ★★ *Victoria,* v. Nizza 99, 60 pl, ☎ 881439 (all year).

> For the translation of a name of a meat, a fish or a vegetable, for the composition of a dish or a sauce, see the *Menu Guide* at the end of the Practical Holiday Guide; it lists the most common culinary terms.

SESTRI LEVANTE

Genoa 50, Milan 183 km
Pop. 21,388 ⊠ 16039 ☎ 0185   E2

In the 16C the chronicler Giustiniani wrote enthusiastically of Sestri's facilities — in those days the Apennine road for the Po Valley was a vital artery and Sestri was its principal port. More recently, expansion of the coastal communications system has led to the establishment of shipyards and iron and steel works. Thus today the town is a tourist resort and at the same time an industrial centre of long standing.

▶ Hans Christian Andersen called the Gulf of Sestri the 'bay of fairy tales'. It has bathing facilities, a marina and a pleasing **seaside promenade.** The greatest expansion has been in the modern town. ▶ From the piazza Matteotti, the original medieval core, the road climbs along the Isola promontory to the fine Romanesque church of **S. Nicolò** (12C, altered). A little farther on is the **parco dell'albergo dei Castelli** (*summer 8 a.m.-12 noon and 2-7 p.m.; winter wknds only*). G. Marconi conducted his first short-wave experiments at the highest point. ▶ The heart of the **historic centre** is around the v. XXV Aprile and the v. Cappuccini, with the **Galleria Rizzi** *(guided tour, Thu, wkends 3-6 p.m.)*; works by various painters. ▶ The side streets run down to the *'Baia del Silenzio'*, a secluded and charming inlet with some old houses. ▶ The typical Mediterranean maquis and pines of the Monte Castello on the **Manara point** are worth a visit. ▶ Beyond the point, at **Riva-Trigoso** *(3 km)*, is a modern shipyard. ☐

Practical information

≋
ⓘ v. XX Settembre 33, ☎ 41422.

Hotels:
★★★★★ *G. H. dei Castelli,* v. Penisola 26, ☎ 41044, 45 rm Ⓟ ≶ ⚲ ⚜ ὅ closed 11 Oct-9 May. Dating from the Middle Ages, standing in large park; seashore and natural swimming pool reached by lift, 202,000; bkf: 13,000.
★★★★ *G. H. Villa Balbi,* v. Rimenbranza 1, ☎ 42941, 100 rm Ⓟ ⚜ ☳ closed 5 Oct-14 Apr. 17C palazzo; swimming pool with heated seawater, 135,000; bkf: 15,000.
★★★★ *Vis à Vis,* v. della Chiusa 28, ☎ 42661, 48 rm Ⓟ ≶ ⚲ ⚜ ☳ closed 20 Oct-20 Dec, 105,000.
★★★ *Celeste,* lungomare Descalzo 14, ☎ 41166, 29 rm ≶ closed 1 Oct-31 Dec, 55,000; bkf: 7,000.
★★★ *Due Mari,* vico Coro 18, ☎ 42697, 26 rm ⚜ closed 5 Nov-20 Dec, 60,000; bkf: 7,000.
★★★ *Helvetia,* v. Cappuccini 43, ☎ 41175, 28 rm Ⓟ ≶ ⚲ ⚜ closed 1 Nov-28 Feb, 60,000; bkf: 9,000.

Restaurants:
◆◆◆ *Sant'Anna,* lungomare Descalzo 60, ☎ 41004, closed Thu and 5 Jan-5 Feb. Fine sea view. Seafood: crayfish and date-shell soup, spaghetti brezza marina, 30/45,000.
◆◆ *Portobello,* v. Portobello 16, ☎ 41566, closed Mon and Jan. In 18C palazzo with stucco ceilings and Gothic windows; summer terrace by sea. Mixed cuisine: spaghetti with crabs, trenette al pesto, 25/35,000.

⚠ ★★★★ *Tigullio,* v. Sara 111/A, 200 pl, ☎ 47257 (all year); ★★★ *Trigoso,* at Riva-Trigoso, v. Aurelia 251/A, 320 pl, ☎ 41047 (all year).

Recommended
Canoeing: *Tigullio canoeing centre,* ☎ 43464 (instruction).
Cycling: *Pedale Sestrese,* v. Dante 87/89, ☎ 41679.
Sailing: *Lega Navale,* v. Portobello 2, ☎ 44810.
Tennis: v. alla Fattoria, ☎ 42677; v. Fabbrica Valle, ☎ 43235.
Yacht club: *Sestri Levante yacht club,* p. del Porto 26/a, ☎ 42935.

SPOTORNO

Savona 15, Genoa 61, Milan 184 km
Pop. 4,594 ⊠ 17028 ☎ 019   C2

The large buildings on the sea front, down below and now in the hills as well, have smothered the historic centre of Spotorno to the extent that it has become unrecognizable, that it was once a typical linear coastal settlement. A trip can be made by sea to the **isolotto di Bergeggi,** once lighthouse of the Roman port of Vada Sabatia (→ Savona) and then a monastery *(ruins not open to public).* The sea bed here has been called the most beautiful in Liguria and plans are afoot to turn it into an underwater park. ☐

Practical information

SPOTORNO
≋
ⓘ v. Aurelia 43, ☎ 745128.

Hotels:
★★★★ *Royal,* lungomare Kennedy 125, ☎ 745074,

100 rm Ⓟ ⚜ ὅ ☳ closed 13 Oct-17 May, 130,000; bkf: 9,000.
★★★ *Ligure,* p. della Vittoria 1, ☎ 745118, 37 rm, closed Nov-Easter, 63,000; bkf: 8,000.
★★★ *Miramare,* v. Aurelia 70, ☎ 745116, 30 rm Ⓟ ≶ ⚜ ὅ closed Oct-Easter, 49,000; bkf: 9,000.
★★★ *Pineta,* v. Provinciale Pineta 2, ☎ 745412, 30 rm Ⓟ ≶ ⚲ ⚜ closed Oct-Easter, 50,000; bkf: 5,000.
★★★ *Zunino,* v. Serra 23, ☎ 745441, 29 rm Ⓟ ⚜ ⚸ closed 10 Oct-20 Dec, 54,000.
★ *Inglese,* v. Laiolo 47, ☎ 745432; 18 rm Ⓟ ⚲ ⚜ closed Oct-Mar. No restaurant, 44,000.

⚠ ★ *Rustia,* at Prelo, v. alla Torre 2, 150 pl, ☎ 745042.

Recommended
Bowls: indoor bowling alley, ☎ 745094.
Sailing: *Lega Navale,* ☎ 745280.
Tennis: v. Serra, ☎ 745843; v. Maremma, ☎ 746547.

Environs

BERGEGGI, ⊠ 17042, 4 km NE.

Restaurant:
◆◆◆ *Claudio,* v. XXV Aprile 37, ☎ 744750, closed Mon and Jan-Feb. High above the sea, with summer terrace. Regional cuisine: menu based on seasonal fish and produce, 35/55,000.

TAGGIA

Imperia 20, Genoa 136, Milan 259 km
Pop. 14,646 ⊠ 18011 ☎ 0184   A-B3

There is now practically no break between the large historic centre of Taggia, one of the most interesting on the Riviera di Ponente, and the modern coastal district of Arma. To a certain extent this restores the status quo, since in the Middle Ages the people of Taggia abandoned the coast to avoid Saracen raids.

▶ The convent of **S. Domenico**★ *(on l. at edge of town),* founded in 1490, was for three centuries the main centre of culture and art in W Liguria. In the Gothic church (restored) are some fine **paintings** by L. Brea *(1a, 2a and 3a in the r. chapel; high altar; l. altar in the sanctuary).* The convent has a 15C cloister leading to a refectory and a chapter house with frescos by Canavesio (1482). There is a small **museum** showing 12C-17C works. ▶ Within the town walls numerous 14C-17C **palaces** dominate the historic v. Soleri and, above all, the v. Dalmazzo; they look medieval, with vaulting, buttresses and portals in decorated slate. ▶ Outside the walls are the Romanesque church of the **Madonna del Canneto** (12C) with frescos by G. Cambiaso and a magnificent medieval **bridge.** ☐

Practical information

Environs

ARMA DI TAGGIA
≋
ⓘ villa Boselli, ☎ 43733.

Hotel:
★★★★ *Vittoria Grattacielo,* v. Lungomare, ☎ 43495, 77 rm Ⓟ ≶ ⚜ ☳ closed 16 Oct-Christmas, 119,000.

Restaurants:
◆◆ *Club,* at Castellaro, v. Provinciale 1, ☎ 45502, closed Mon noon and Oct-Nov. Quiet room with fireplace. Regional and Italian cuisine: green vegetable ravioli, girello with mushrooms, 45/55,000.
◆ *Saraceno,* v. Lungomare 17, ☎ 43288, closed Mon and 15 Oct-22 Dec. Seafood: spaghetti in conger eel sauce, fillet and entrecôte, 25/40,000.

Recommended
Cycling: *G. S. Pedale Azzurro,* at Riva Ligure, v. Martiri della Libertà 10.
Events: *Festival of St. Benedict* (2nd Sun in Feb).
Tennis: v. Lungomare, ☎ 42059.

♥ second-hand market: v. Solari colonnade (last Sun in month).

VARAZZE

Savona 12, Genoa 35, Milan 158 km
Pop. 14,807 ⊠ 17019 ☎ 019   C2

Varazza is known for its fine **beach;** there are also shipyards, and the town is still expanding (into the hills, as there is no more room on the plain). Some **picturesque corners** and fine monuments in the historic centre have survived. The collegiate church of **S. Ambrogio** (16C) has a fine Romano-Gothic campanile. The façade of the former Romanesque church of **S. Ambrogio** (12C-13C) is incorporated in a section of the old town walls. ☐

Practical information ――――――――――

≋
ⓘ v. Nazioni Unite, ☎ 97298.

Hotels:
★★★★ *Chico,* at Piani d'Invrea, strada Romana 63, ☎ 96491, 45 rm Ⓟ ≼ 𝓦 ⌘ ▭ closed Christmas-Jan, 80,000; bkf: 5,000.
★★★★ *Cristallo,* v. Cilea 4, ☎ 97264, 47 rm Ⓟ 𝓦 closed Nov-Dec, 60,000; bkf: 5,000.
★★★★ *Savoy,* lungomare Marconi 4, ☎ 97056, 46 rm Ⓟ closed 1 Oct-14 May, 80,000; bkf: 8,000.
★★★ *Ariston,* v. Villagrande 16, ☎ 97371, 29 rm Ⓟ 𝓦 closed Nov, 52,000; bkf: 5,000.
★★★ *Genovese-Villa Elena,* v. Coda 16, ☎ 97526, 40 rm Ⓟ 𝓦 closed 1 Oct-20 Dec, 53,000; bkf: 5,000.
★ *Villa Centa,* v. XXIV Aprile 33, ☎ 95702, 24 rm 𝓦 closed Oct-Nov, 15,000.

Restaurant:
♦♦♦ *Cavetto,* p. S. Caterina 7, ☎ 97311, closed Thu and 1-15 Nov. Seafood: fish ravioli, pansoti with walnut sauce, 30/45,000.

Recommended
Marina: ☎ 97271.

VENTIMIGLIA

Imperia 41, Genoa 159, Milan 282 km
Pop. 25,978 ⊠ 18039 ☎ 0184   A3

Ventimiglia stands at the crossroads of the old Roman road to France and the ancient salt road to Piedmont and was for centuries the centre of trade and traffic in the busy extreme W of Liguria, before Genoa cut it off from the hinterland, reducing it to the status of a frontier town. Modern Ventimiglia, on the coastal plain, has grown out of all proportion. It makes a living from tourism and the cultivation of flowers, but it is above all a commercial centre, aimed specifically at French customers. In contrast the historic centre, effectively cut off and abandoned on the r. bank of the Roia, has been allowed to fall into disrepair, despite its considerable cultural interest.

▶ The **Roman remains** of **Albintimilium** *(E of present town)* are some of the most important in Liguria. The 2C **theatre** gives an idea of its prosperity under the Empire. ▶ The most sizeable and architecturally complete area of the old town is the **piazza della Cattedrale,** bounded on the l. by the 17C convent of the canonesses. The Romanesque **cathedral** (11C-13C) has a Gothic portal dating from 1222 and a Carolingian crypt with pre-Romanesque sculptures *(apply to priest,* ☎ 351813). The octagonal **baptistery** (11C) has old baths for baptism by immersion and remains of Lombard sculptures. ▶ The narrow streets of the built-up area

around the Mille lead via vaulted passages and medieval sections to the Romanesque church of **S. Michele** (11C-13C, crypt). Nearby is a hospital specializing in the cure of erysipelas. ▶ In the extreme E of the town the **spianata del Cavo** offers an extensive view.

Environs

▶ At **Mórtola Inferiore** *(5.7 km)* is the **Hanbury garden** *(10 a.m.-4 p.m.),* the largest botanical garden in Italy and one of the most celebrated in the world. ▶ Also interesting are the **Ponte San Ludovico** *(7.7 km)* and the **Balzi Rossi**★ (red cliffs; *9 a.m.-12:30 p.m. and 2-5 or 6:30 p.m. or 4-7 p.m.*), a rocky stretch of coast with large caves in which exceptional prehistoric remains have been found (Neanderthal and Cro-Magnon man). There is a small **museum** showing some of the material. ☐

Practical information ――――――――――

VENTIMIGLIA
≋
ⓘ v. Cavour 61, ☎ 351183.

Hotel:
★★ *Sole e Mare,* v. Marconi 12, ☎ 351855, 28 rm Ⓟ ≼ 𝓦 ⌘ closed 15 Nov-15 Dec, 48,000; bkf: 5,000.

Restaurant:
♦♦ *Cuneo,* v. Aprosio 16, ☎ 33576, closed Tue eve, Wed and 25 Jun-25 Jul. Mixed cuisine: tagliatelli with prawns, ossobuco, 25/45,000.

⅄ ★★ *Riviera Flowers,* at San Lorenzo, v. S. Anna 164, 45 pl, ☎ 33820; ★ *Roma,* v. Peglia 5, 50 pl, ☎ 33580 (all year).

Recommended
Botanical gardens: *Giardino Hanbury,* at Mórtola Inferiore, ☎ 39507.
Cycling: *Interciclo Olmo,* corso Genova 56/F, ☎ 34937; *Ventimiglia cycling club,* corso Genova 112, ☎ 352879.
Events: *flower competition* (Jun); *festival of ancient music* (Jul); *historic procession and regatta contest* between the town's districts (Aug); *exhibition of flowers and plants* for export to Vallecrosia (Dec-Jan).
Swimming: at Vallecrosia, c. Col. Aprosio 518, ☎ 292288.
Tennis: v. Peglia 1 bis, ☎ 355224.

Environs

CASTEL D'APPIO, 5 km NW.

Hotel:
★★★ *Riserva,* ☎ 39533, 29 rm Ⓟ ≼ ⚄ 𝓦 ⌘ ⌀ closed 21 Sep-14 Dec and 7 Jan-Easter, 80,000. Rest. ♦♦ Seafood: homemade verdoni, flambéed prawn kebabs, 25/40,000.

ZOAGLI

Genoa 35, Milan 177 km
Pop. 2,326 ⊠ 16030 ☎ 0185   E2

Zoagli is a secluded village on a little plain between hills with olive trees facing a small **beach** under a railway viaduct. It is the starting point of a **marine promenade** cut in the rocks. ☐

Practical information ――――――――――

≋
ⓘ p. S. Martino 8, ☎ 59127.

Hotel:
★★★★★ *G. H. Bristol,* v. Aurelia Orientale 369, ☎ 273313, 93 rm Ⓟ ≼ 𝓦⅃ ▭ closed 1 Nov-19 Dec. Built at beginning of 20C and recently restored, the Bristol is at once elegant and modern, 357,000.

Recommended
Craft workshops: *Cordani,* v. Aurelia 104, ☎ 259022 (velvet).

Lombardy

▶ The lakes of Lombardy are an unforgettable feature of the Italian landscape. Their shining waters are surrounded by classical villas in gardens of azaleas, old fishing villages, towns in wild landscapes and the echo of the battles of the past. Milan is perhaps more famous for *La Scala* than for commerce. However, its location and the absence of amenities have compelled its inhabitants to put all their energies into work, production, exchange and stress. Milan is a city whose attractions are man-made. It is a city of art, one of the major ones, and a formidable producer of culture. The gilded statue of the Madonna on top of the 18C spire of the Gothic Duomo is the geometrical and emotional centre of the city; few buildings have broken with the convention that nothing should be higher. From the terrace of the Duomo it is possible to see almost all of Lombardy: from the opulent green of the plain to the mountains in the north. Almost everywhere are the brooding glories of the Romanesque, the expressive force of humble brick, the proud town halls of the medieval period, the acerbic touch of the Renaissance and cobbled streets shaded by severe palazzi. □

Don't miss

In Milan★★: the Duomo★★; the Pinacoteca di Brera★★; the Castello Sforzesco★★ including Michelangelo's *Rondanini Pietà*★★, S. Maria delle Grazie★★ and Leonardo's *Last Supper*★★; S. Ambrogio★★; S. Lorenzo Maggiore★★; the Cappella Portinari★★ in S. Eustorgio★. In Bergamo★★: the old town with S. Maria Maggiore★★ and the Cappella Colleoni★★; the Pinacoteca dell'Accademia Carrara★★. In Brescia★: the Pinacoteca Tosio Martinengo★★ and the Rotonda★. In Capo di Ponte: the Parco Nazionale delle Incisioni Rupestri★ (rock carvings). In Castiglione Olona★: frescos★★ by Masolino da Panicale in the collegiate church★ and the Baptistery★★. The Certosa★ di Pavia. Above Civate, S. Pietro al Monte★★. In Como★: the Duomo★★ and, on the splendid lake, Bellagia★; the Villa Carlotta★ at Cadenabbia; S. Maria del Tiglio★ at Gravedona. In Cremona★: the Duomo★★. On the Lombardy bank of Lake Garda, Gardone★ and Sirmione★. In Lodi★: l'Incoronata★★. In Mantua★★: S. Andrea★★; the Palazzo Ducale★★ with Mantegna's Camera degli Sposi★★, the Palazzo Te★★. In Pavia★: S. Michele★★, the Castello Visconteo★★ and S. Pietro in Ciel d'Oro★★. The 16C town of Sabbioneta★, the Piazza Ducale★★ in Vigevano★.

Facts and figures

Location: *Lombardy occupies the plain of the Po N of the river between Lake Maggiore and the Ticino in the W, and Lake Garda and the Mincio in the E, as well as the corresponding pre-alpine and alpine valleys. In addition, Lombardy extends S of the Po to the area around Mantua and into the Oltrepò Pavese, a pre-Apennine triangle between Piedmont and Emilia. The Lomellina, on the right bank of the Ticino, is part of Lombardy and was formerly in the Duchy of Milan, whereas the Swiss canton of Ticino split off in the 15C-16C.*
Area: *23,834 sq km.*
Climate: *Moderate, with local variations caused by the altitude, the lakes and hours of sunshine, giving rise to winter climates on Lakes Como, Iseo and Garda; windy summers in the strip at the foot of the mountains; areas that are very hot in the summer on the plain, with correspondingly dense autumn mists and low winter temperatures. The countryside is beautiful and varied, hemmed with mountains enjoying clear weather in all seasons.*
Population: *8,891,318 inhabitants of whom more than 1.5 million live in Milan. Lombardy is the largest Italian region by size and the second largest by density of population.*
Administration: *The regional capital is Milan; the other eight provinces are Bergamo, Brescia, Como, Cremona, Mantua, Pavia, Sondrio and Varese.*

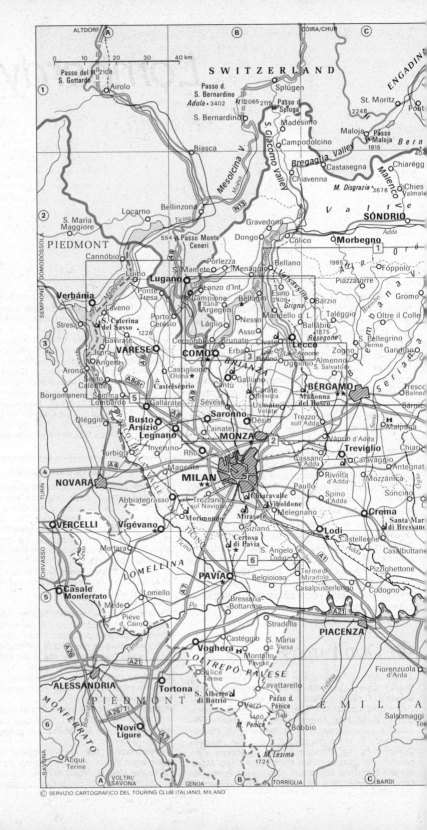

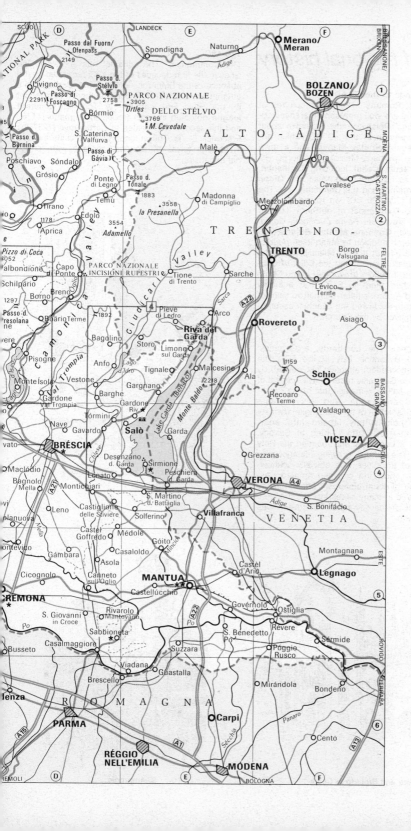

● *Brief regional history*

From the beginnings to the 5C AD

Prehistory, Gauls, Romans. Prehistoric cultures of the Neolithic period are well represented archaeologically in this region. Relatively little is known about the **Etruscan expansion** in the 7C BC, which advanced as far as modern-day Mantua and a town known as Melpum (perhaps Melzo). ● The 6C BC saw an influx of **Gauls (Celts)**, including the **Insubri**, who are thought to have founded Milan, the **Orobi**, who founded Bergamo, and the **Cenomani.** ● The **Roman conquest** (224-220 BC) led to the development in **Cisalpine Gaul** (most of northern Italy) of such modern-day towns as **Pavia** *(Ticinum)*, **Como,** **Lodi** *(Laus Pompeia)*, **Cremona, Mantua, Brescia** *(Brixia)*, and **Bergamo,** in addition to **Milan** itself *(Mediolanum)*. ● At the end of the 3C **Milan** became the capital of the Western Empire, and the **Edict of Constantine,** conceding freedom of worship to the Christians, was published there in 313. The authority wielded by Bishop Ambrose (later the patron saint of Milan) in the 4C foreshadowed the eventual assumption of temporal power by the Church.

6C-11C

Early Middle Ages. The **Lombards,** a Germanic people, occupied Byzantine Italy in the 5C. The Lombards were succeeded, although not ousted, by the **Franks,** another Germanic race. Pavia, capital of the Lombard King Alboin, remained that of the Frankish Emperor **Charlemagne** and his successors. ● At the dissolution of the Carolingian dynasty (Charlemagne's heirs), Italy lapsed into anarchy. ● In the mid-10C, **Otto I,** King of Saxony, assumed control of Lombardy and founded the **Holy Roman Empire.** The bishops' growing influence over the government of the cities was officially acknowledged when Otto, now the crowned emperor, established the order of **count-bishops.** The autonomy of the cities evolved in many cases into the independence and power of the city-state, whose aim was territorial expansion.

12C-13C

The Communes. The **consuls'** rule spread to the cities in the first decades of the 12C, facilitated by the absence of the Emperor. ● **Frederick Barbarossa's** attempt to re-establish imperial authority was fought by the cities and leagues. ● The first **Lombard league** defeated imperial troops at **Legnano** (1176), and the second was beaten at **Cortenuova** (1237) by Frederick II. ● The autonomy of the cities evolved in various forms of *signoria*, charged with territorial expansion.

Piazza Vecchia in Bergamo

Duomo and Broletto in Como

S. Ambrogio

Palazzo ducale in Mantua

of peace in Italy, the Sforza duchy, from the Alps to the Cisa, from Novara to Parma, exemplified the politics of balance and the new intellectual and artistic order of the Renaissance.

16C-18C
Spain and Austria. The arrival of **Charles VIII** of France in Naples marked the beginning of a long period of foreign occupation in the peninsula. ● The Duchy of Milan, occupied by Louis XII of France in 1499, was hotly contested. Finally, victory went to **Charles V,** Holy Roman Emperor and King of Spain. ● **Lombardy,** with the exception of the area controlled by Venice, **Bellinzona, Locarno** and **Lugano** (Swiss from 1502 to 1514) and the **Valtellina** (under Swiss rule from 1512 to 1797), was governed by the Spanish from 1535 to 1714, but was also progressively eroded by the province and ruling house of **Savoy,** which advanced from the Sesia to the Ticino. ● In 1714, after the War of Spanish Succession, which placed a Bourbon on the throne of Spain, Lombardy passed to the Austrian Hapsburgs.

14C-15C
Milan, the Visconti and the Sforzas. The **Torriani** family, rulers of Milan, controlled large areas of Lombardy under the feudal system until, at the Battle of **Desio** in 1277, they were defeated by **Ottone Visconti,** founder of another feudal dynasty. ● For a century and a half there after, Lombardy (except for Mantua, which from 1238 to 1708 led a separate existence under the **Gonzagas**) was ruled by the **Visconti,** with **Milan** as the capital. ● **Gian Galeazzo Visconti,** Duke of Lombardy from 1397, extended his power over half of Italy, and his death in 1402 almost brought down the state. ● **Filippo Maria Visconti** regained many territories, but **Brescia, Bergamo** and **Crema** were taken by the Venetians and remained under the rule of Venice until the fall of the Venetian Republic in 1797. ● Francesco Sforza, a *condottiere* (chief of a band of soldiers of fortune) and son-in-law and heir of Filippo Maria Visconti, became Duke of Milan after the brief interlude of the **Ambrosian Republic.** ● In the second half of the 15C, a rare period

1797-1859
The Napoleonic era and the rise of Italian unity. Napoleon I, as General Bonaparte, created the **Cispadan Republic** in 1797 (with the tricolor as its flag), of which Lombardy was part. Napoleon soon transformed the republic into a kingdom, assumed the iron crown of the kings of Italy and appointed his stepson Eugène Beauharnais (the Empress Josephine's son) as viceroy in Milan. ● At the collapse of Napoleon's rule in 1814, the Austrians returned and Lombardy became part of **Lombardy-Venetia.** ● Fledgling patriotic movements, whose revolts were quickly crushed, nevertheless grew in strength and coalesced into the **Risorgimento** (resurgence) offically formed in 1831. In 1848, a broad-based insurrection led by the Duke of Savoy (who also enjoyed the title of King of Sardinia) marked the end of Austrian domination. ● The **Kingdom of Italy** was proclaimed in 1861, with Turin as its capital. When, in 1870, Rome was designated capital of Italy, Italian unity had finally been accomplished.

Certosa di Pavia

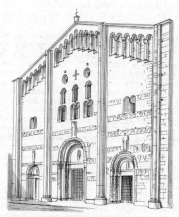

S. Michele in Pavia

Practical information

toric Zoo, at Rivolta d'Adda; zoo and amusement park, at Cogliate (→ Saronno); safari park, at Pombio (→ Somma Lombardo).

Information: tourist offices in district capitals and principal centres; *TCI* tourist information service, at Milan, corso Italia 10, ☎ 02/8526225.

SOS: public emergency services, ☎ 113; police emergency, ☎ 112; *ACI* (assistance on the road), ☎ 116.

Weather: forecasts, ☎ 1911; road conditions, ☎ 194 or from *ACI*, ☎ 06/4212; snow forecasts, ☎ 02/67509 or from Milan, ☎ 1911 194 162; avalanche warnings, at Sondrio, ☎ 0342/901657; weather bulletin from Cisalpine Geophysical Centre, at Varese, ☎ 0332/237021.

Farm vacations: *Agriturist* regional association, at Milan, v. Isonzo 27, ☎ 02/5468387.

Fairs and markets: *Grande Fiera d'Aprile* and similar events take place in market quarter of Milan; antiques market at Sabbioneta; periodic antique markets at Bergamo, Castiglione Olona, and Desenzano del Garda.

The terragne and the wines of the Valtellina

'They make strong wine in abundance,' wrote Leonardo da Vinci of the Valtellinese. The valley of the Adda runs from E to W and, on the sunnier northern side, vines flourish on terragne, terraces on steep slopes, which require hard and patient tilling. The region is subdivided into four: Sassella for grapes grown between Castione and Sondrio, Grumello between Sondrio and Montagna, Inferno between Poggiridenti and Trevisio, and Valgella between Chiuro and Teglio. Valtellina wines are made from the Chiavennasca grape (local name for the Nebiolo), with some Brugnola, Merlot, Pignola Valtellinese, Pinot Noir and Rossola grapes. The wine is bright red in colour, dry in flavour and needs to be at least 1 year old before drinking, but is even better after two or three. For Valtellina Superiore at least 95 per cent of Chiavennasca grapes must be used. It must age for two years and is at its best after six. The colour is deep ruby red; the taste is dry, velvety and balanced.

Events: *Triennale* exhibition and *La Scala* opera season, at Milan; *International Piano Festival*, at Bergamo; *International Fair of Contemporary Music*, at Brescia; and *September in Sabbioneta festival.*

Naturel parks: *Parco Nazionale dello Stelvio* has its main office at Bormio, v. Monte Braulio 56, ☎ 0342/901582; *Forest Administration*, at Temù, ☎ 0364/76361, and at Uzza Valfurva, ☎ 0342/945676; information centre at Isolaccia Valdidentro (Bormio) and Sondalo. *Regional parks:* Colli di Bergamo (→ Bergamo), Serio (→ Bergamo), Adamello (→ Breno), Pineta di Appiano Gentile e Tradate (→ Como), Montevecchia and the Curone Valley (→ Montevecchia), Mincio (→ Mantua), North Adda (→ Trezzo sull'Adda), South Adda (→ Lodi), Lambro Valley (→ Seregno), Groane (→ Milan), Campo dei Fiori (→ Varese); Lombard Regional Park in the Ticino Valley; animal sanctuary at Piani Resinelli (→ Ballabio). There are regional nature reserves at Monticchie (→ Lodi), Le Bine (→ Asola), Vanzago (the *WWF* forest) (→ Milan), Valpredina (→ Bergamo) and an animal sanctuary at Bassone-Torbiere di Albate (→ Como).

Animal parks and amusement parks: *Al Mulino* zoo, at Antegnate (→ Soncino); *Minitalia* park, at Capriate S. Gervasio (→ Bergamo); *Orobica* animal park, at Bergamo; *Le Cornelle* animal park, at Valbrembo (→ Bergamo); *Prehis-*

Nature conservation: *WWF Lombardia* has its main office at Milan, v. Monte Grappa 2, ☎ 02/6556810 (summer work camps and outdoor and adventure camps at the Parco dello Stelvio and other places of natural interest; excursions and guided visits to nature reserves). Its local offices are at: Milan, v. Mazzini 20, ☎ 02/800830; Bergamo, p. Goisis 6, ☎ 035/226038; Brescia-Mompiano, v. Dabbeni 33A, ☎ 030/383440; Como, v. Vittorio Emanuele 98, ☎ 031/273428; *Archeo club*, at Cremona, v. S. Lorenzo 2, ☎ 0372/21874; *WWF Groane*, at Cogliate, largo Follini 25, ☎ 02/9660069; *WWF Lario Orientale* has branches at Lecco, v. Dante 21; Mantova, largo 24 Maggio 12; Pavia, v. Brigate Pavia 7, ☎ 0382/465315; Sondri, v. Longoni 31, ☎ 0342/210042; Varese, p. Monte Grappa (Torre Civica), ☎ 0332/285676. *LIPU* has branches at Milan, v. Settembrini 27, ☎ 02/6700353; Mantova-Carbonara di Po, v. Provinciale Ferrarese 21, ☎ 0386/41221; Pavia, v. Chinaglia 12, ☎ 0382/302289; Varese, p. Monte Grappa (Torre Civica), ☎ 0332/285676; Brescia, v. Ozanam 4, (near the Natural Science Museum) ☎ 030/29831 (birdwatching expeditions, excursions, and walks). *Italia Nostra* has a regional council at Bergamo, v. Pignolo 88, ☎ 035/224802 and a branch office at Milan, v. Pellico 1, ☎ 02/871924 (a project for 'bringing the forest into the city' organizes voluntary work and summer work camps for young people; office at Cascino S. Romano, v. Novara 340, ☎ 02/4522401).

Walking tours: long-distance cross-country walks S of the Alps include: *Via dei Monti Lariani* along the W shore of Lake Como (130 km from Cernobia; 6 overnight stops; open Apr-Oct); *Sentiero delle Orobie* (50 km, 6 overnight stops in mountain huts; Jul-Sep); area of the Alps: *Sentiero Roma*, runs across the Badile and Disgrazia ranges as far as Chiesa Valmalenco (7 overnight stops; mid-Jul-mid-Sep); *Alta Via della Valmalenco*, along the slopes of Disgrazia and Bernina ranges (110 km; 8 nights; mid-Jul-mid-Sep). Information: local branches of *CAI* and mountain guides in the towns concerned (→ mountain climbing); and, in Milan: *Federazione italiana escursionismo*, v. Valtellina 46, ☎ 02/6882076; *Lo Zodiaco*, v. Pisacane 44, ☎ 02/2870056; *Spazi d'avventura di P. Rava*, p. Leonardo da Vinci 3, ☎ 02/292118; *Centro milanese per lo sport e la ricreazione*, corso di Porta Romana 116/A, ☎ 02/5450548; and *Trekking Italia*, corso di Porta Vittoria 56, ☎ 02/5459521.

Cycling: assistance and information from bicycling groups affiliated with *UDACE* (506) throughout Lombardy. The *TCI* provides cycling itineraries for Ticino Park, outskirts of Milan, the Adda, Bergamo, upper and lower Varesotto and Lodi. Bicycling tours of ecological interest are run by *Lega Ambiente di Milano*, v. Adige 11, ☎ 02/5456551.

River trips: the motor boat *Stradivari* cruises along the Po from Cremona: inquire from *Società di Navigazione Interna*, corso Vittorio Emanuele 17, ☎ 0372/25546. For guided cruises down the Naviglio Grande as far as the Ticino regional park (Jul-Sep) ask at the *Palace of Tourism*, at Milan, v. Marconi 1, ☎ 02/809662; reservations, ☎ 02/62083122.

Lake cruises: public steamship service on Lakes Maggiore, Garda, and Como, at Milan, v. Ariosto 21, ☎ 02/4812086 (also summer cruises); local offices: for Lake Maggiore, Arona, v. F. Baracca 1, ☎ 0322/46651; for Lake Garda, Desenzano del Garda, p. Matteotti 2, ☎ 030/9141321; and for Lake Como, Como, p. Volta 44, ☎ 031/273324 and 260234. Cruises on Lake Iseo: Lovere-Costa Volpino, v. Nazionale 24, ☎ 035/971483.

Art and handicraft courses: ceramics: *Vacanze con la ceramica*, at Gombito (33 km NE of Cremona), v. Delmati 2, ☎ 0374/69107; classes in hand weaving: *F. Paravicini dal Verme*, Torre degli Alberi (7 km NE of Zavattarello in the Pavian part of the Oltrepò); drawing and engraving: *Centro culturale*, at Osmate, (3 km NE of Comabbio), v. Maggiore 18, ☎ 0331/953412. Milan offers courses in:

weaving, dyeing, and tapestry-making: *Studio di tessitura di P. Besana*, v. Crespi 7, ☎ 02/8354801; painting: *Atelier di pittura*, Naviglio Grande towpath 66, ☎ 02/8327552 (classes in self-expression); painting on fabrics: *G. Fantini*, v. Suzzani 12, ☎ 02/6437707 (also embroidery and leatherwork); cookery: *Cooperativa Papavero*, corso Porta Ticinese 56, ☎ 02/8325952, and *Scuola di cucina*, corso Monforte 15, ☎ 02/799204.

Canoeing: *Federazione italiana canoa-kayak* has schools at Cremona, Legnano, Milan, Palazzolo sull'Oglio (→ Chiari), and Sesto Calende (→ itinerary for Lake Maggiore).

Water skiing: *Italian federation of water skiing*, at Milan, v. Piranesi 44/B, ☎ 02/7381120.

Sailing: *Lega Navale*, at Milan, corso di Porta Romana 17, ☎ 02/879762 and at Varese, p. Giovanni XXIII 11, ☎ 0332/230275; marina at Dervio, ☎ 0341/850672 (→ Colico); also in Milan: *Centro vélico Caprera*, corso Italia 10, ☎ 02/808428 and *Centro velico d'altura*, v. Ajaccio 13, ☎ 02/745578.

Skiing: main skiing resorts are in the Como area S of the Alps, in the valleys in Bergamo and Brescia provinces, and in Valchiavenna and Valtellina. Summer skiing may be possible at the Passo dello Stelvio (→ Bormio and Santa Caterina Valfurva), Chiesa in Valmalenco, Livigno, and Ponte di Legno.

Golf: many golf courses throughout Lombardy, concentrated mainly in the provinces of Bergamo, Como, and Milan; practice courses at Milan, Peschiera Borromeo (→ Milan), and Olgiate Olona (→ Busto Arsizio).

Flying: flying clubs: at Bergamo, *G. Taramelli* airport, ☎ 035/297062; at Brescia airport, v. Olivari, ☎ 030/901101 or 902364; at Como, v. Masia 44, ☎ 031/559882; at Cremona, *Migliaro* airport, ☎ 0372/31555 (parachuting and flying of model aircraft also possible); at Bresso airport, ☎ 02/6140878; at Varese, *A. Ferrarin* airport, ☎ 0331/864128 and *Siai-Marchetti* airport, ☎ 0331/946151.

Pot-holing: *Gruppo Grotte Milano CAI*, v. Foscolo 3, ☎ 02/8059191 (courses in pot-holing; information available Tue after 9 p.m.); *Le Nottole*, Bergamo, v. Colleoni 21, ☎ 035/225114, (winter courses and summer camps); fully equipped pot-holing sites at Alpe del Vicer (→ Erba), Rescia (→ Porlezza), San Pellegrino Terme (→ La Val Brembana) and Sedrina (→ Bergamo).

Fishing: *Federazione italiana pesca sportiva* branches at: Bergamo, v. Scotti 11, ☎ 035/232586; Brescia, v. S. Zeno 69, ☎ 030/52396, Como, v. Volta 65, ☎ 031/272559; Cremona, p. Zaccaria 6, ☎ 0372/23425; Mantua, v. Mazzini 18; Milan, v. Abruzzi 79, ☎ 02/2043952 and v. Rivoli 4, ☎ 02/865666; Pavia, v. Frank 11, ☎ 0382/37233; Sondrio, v. Dante 17; and Varese, v. S. D'Acquisto 2, ☎ 0332/280386. Apply to the appropriate branch for information on waters where fishing is forbidden, permission required, etc.

Mountain climbing: for information contact CAI branch offices at: Bergamo, v. Ghislanzoni 15, ☎ 035/244273; Bormio, v. De Simoni 42; Brescia, p. Vescovado 3, ☎ 030/48426; Chiesa in Valmalenco (near the tourist office), ☎ 0342/451150; Como, v. Volta 56, ☎ 031/264177; Edolo, v. della Chiesa; Lecco, v. Roma 51; Lovere, v. XX Settembre; Milan, v. Pellico 6, ☎ 02/808421; and Sondrio, v. Trieste 27. Guides' offices are at: Lecco, v. Caprera 3, ☎ 0341/590140; Chiesa in Valmalenco, v. Milano 6 (near Valmturist); Bormio, v. Stelvio 10, ☎ 0342/901116; and near the tourist office at Santa Caterina Valfurva, ☎ 0342/935598.

Bowls: *Unione bocciofila italiana* at: Milan, p. Lugano 9, ☎ 02/371143; Bergamo, v. Fossoli 2, ☎ 035/216122; Brescia, v. Castelli 24, ☎ 030/381817; Como, v. Canturina 207, ☎ 031/503764; Varese, v. Maspero 8,- ☎ 0332/242129. *Federazione italiana Bocce*, Pavia, v. Ponte Vecchio 1, ☎ 0382/24372. *Società bocciofila mantovana*, v. Te 25, ☎ 0376/324620.

Hang gliding: information from *Italian federation*, ☎ 015/538703; affiliated schools at Cólico, Fino Mornasco (→ Como), Laveno, Lentate sul Séveso (→ Cantù), Mapello (→ Bergamo), Milan and Varese.

Horseback riding: *Federazione italiana sport equestri* (regional committee) at Milan, v. Piranesi 44/B, ☎ 02/7384615; many centres associated with *ANTE* throughout Lombardy. Race courses include: *Ippodromo e Trottatoio S. Siro*, at Milan, ☎ 02/4084350; *Ippodromo di Mirabello*, at Monza; and *Ippodromo delle Bettole*, at Varese, v. Ippodromo, ☎ 0332/282516.

Ballooning: *Club Aerostatico Italiano*, at Milan, v. Alserio 23, ☎ 02/603485.

Tennis: summer centre, at Brallo di Pregola, ☎ 0383/50632 (→ L'Oltrepò Pavese).

Risotto alla milanese and other Lombard rice dishes

Risotto alla milanese *is the best-known rice dish of the region. Milan is surrounded by rice fields, but it is not known when cultivation started. Some scholars contend that the grain spread from SE Asia to Egypt, and was then brought by Arabs to Sicily. As long ago as 1475 the duke of Milan promised to supply 12 sacks of rice each week to the duke of Ferrara. Details of the recipe for risotto can produce fierce argument. The classic version uses rice gently fried with butter and onions, then cooked in an open pan with meat stock, marrow and saffron. Butter and grated parmesan cheese are mixed in just before the risotto is served. The basic dish is often served as a bed for* osso bucco, *another classic Milanese dish. Osso bucco is slices of veal shin braised with lemon rind, rosemary, sage and parsley. Risotto al salto is traditionally enjoyed as an after-theatre supper: partly cooked* risotto *is left to cool, then sliced thin and fried in butter. Lombardy has many* risotti: *the Certosa version, invented by Carthusian monks, with freshwater crayfish; a version from Monza, with sausage; another from Comasco using perch; from the Lomellina with frogs; and the Mantuan version, called* alla pilota, *that is prepared by workers employed to husk the rice, a process known as* pilatura.

Panettone

This traditional Christmas cake is now so widely available that many people may not realize that it is a Milanese invention — or rather, a sentimental institution. The ingredients are constant: flour, yeast, butter, egg yolks, sugar, candied peel and raisins. One slice used to be saved at Christmas to be eaten stale at the feast of San Biagio, the 3 February.

Gliding: *Milan gliding club*, at Alzate Brianza (→ Como), ☎ 031/630960; *Upper Lombardy gliding club and study centre for gliding in mountain areas*, P. Contri airport, Calcinate del Pesce (→ Varese), ☎ 0332/310073; *Alpine gliding club* and *Alpine gliding association*, Valbrembo (→ Bergamo) airport, ☎ 035/631093 or 613293; *Milano-Bresso gliding academy*, Bresso airport, v. Monteceneri 36, *Migliaro* airport, Cremona, ☎ 0372/31555; at Voghera-Rivanazzo, v. Baracca 8, ☎ 0383/91500.

● *Towns and places*

The ABBEYS OF THE MILAN AREA

In the 12C the French Cistercian monks of Clairvaux and Morimond were given land in the plain of Milan where they founded the abbeys of Chiaravalle and Morimondo. The rules of the order demand simplicity in architecture and decoration. Above all, the rule insists on work. The Cistercian community changed the area by draining the marshes and developing agricultural techniques (including *marcite*), which were then taken up and improved by the farmers throughout the region.

▶ All the abbeys are on the plain S of Milan, a short distance from the city. Directions: for Chiaravalle and Viboldone *(12.6 km)* porta Romana-corso Lodi; for Mirasole *(10 km)* porta Vigentina-v. Ripamonti; for Morimondo *(22 km)* v. Lorenteggio-nuova Vigevanese. ▶ Notable features of the **abbey of Chiaravalle★** are the sacristy, the cemetery and the remains of the cloister (13C), but above all the **church** dating from 1172-1221, in the French Gothic style, with characteristic tapering, arcaded tower. Inside *(9 a.m.-12 noon and 2-5 p.m.)* are frescos of the school of Giotto (14C) and the 17C Flemish school, a carved wooden choir (17C) and a Luini Madonna. ▶ The **abbey of Morimondo** has a church in good condition (1186-1292; restored). Remains of the chapterhouse and the cloister may also be visited. ▶ The **abbey of Viboldone★** (12C-13C) has a Gothic church with fine façade dating from 1348. In the interior are **frescos★** of the school of Giotto. ▶ In the **abbey of Mirasole** (13C) are a 14C-15C church with 13C campanile and 15C cloister. ☐

The marcite

This phenomenon, a characteristic of the plain of Milan, is now infrequently seen, but was important in establishing agricultural prosperity in the Po area. Marcita is derived from the Latin pratum marcitum, meaning grassland covered by water which is not quite stagnant, and is applied to meadows that are flooded in winter but irrigated normally in the summer. The system requires precision in the distribution of water. Early improvements were attributed to the teaching of St.Benedict, and in the 13C the monks at the abbey of Viboldone introduced the refinement of allowing a thin layer of water to spread over the land, thus increasing productivity: the grass grew continuously, and it was possible to mow seven to ten times a year. The scientific basis of marcite is obvious. Springs abound on the left bank of the Po, extending from Piedmont to Venetia. Their waters remain several degrees above zero even during winter frosts, and prevent the ground they cover from freezing.

Practical information ————————

CHIARAVALLE, ⊠ 20139, ☎ 02.

Restaurant:
♦♦♦ *Antica Trattoria San Bernardo*, v. S. Bernardo 36, ☎ 5398735, closed Sun eve, Mon and Aug. Formerly part of neighbouring abbey, with summer garden. Italian and regional cuisine: olivette mantovana, cassoeula, 35/65,000.

VIBOLDONE, ⊠ 20098, ☎ 02.

Restaurant:
● ♦♦♦ *Antica Osteria Rampina*, at Cascina Rampina, v. Emilia, ☎ 9833273, closed Wed. 16C inn with stables, tastefully rebuilt without altering original lines; fine inside garden. Creative cuisine: risotto with herbs, gnocchi with mint, 40/55,000.

ABBIATEGRASSO

Milan 23 km
Pop. 27,401 ⊠ 20081 ☎ 02   A-B4

The moat of the Visconti castle built when the principal town of the Valle Grassa became an important commercial centre can still be seen, as can the Naviglio Grande (canal), which carried goods from Milan, Pavia and Lake Maggiore to the docks in Abbiategrasso. The town, enriched by fertile soil and trade, was built in style, as shown by the church and the houses commissioned by the nobility. Abbiategrasso is still one of the major industrial and agricultural centres of the plain of Milan.

▶ The **castle** (1882) is being restored. It houses a museum and a library. ▶ The basilica of **S. Maria Nuova★** has an elegant arcaded **portico★** (15C).The magnificent **arcade★** is the work of Bramante (1497). ☐

Practical information ————————————

Restaurant:
● ♦♦♦ *Antica Osteria del Ponte*, at Cassinetta di Lugagnano *(3 km N)*, p. Negri 9, ☎ 9420034, closed Sun, Mon, Jan and Aug. The exterior and romantic site are all that remain of an old country inn; interior is refined with antique furnishings and fire place. Outstanding creative cuisine: daily sample menu and à la carte selection, 90/100,000.

Recommended
Cycling: *CTA Abbiategrasso*, v. Mazzini 50, ☎ 9463491.

The central section of the ADDA

map 2

Among the most interesting features of the region are evidence of material culture and early **industrialization** in Italy. There are wonderful historic buildings, set in green **countryside**.

▶ **Rivolta d'Adda** has a fine 11C **basilica**. **Parco Zoo della Preistoria** is SW of the town, with life-size models of prehistoric animals *(Mar-Nov daily, 9 a.m.-dusk)*. ▶ The Borromeo residences are in **Cassano d'Adda** and contain a medieval **castle** and 18C **villa**. ▶ The **Palazzo Melzi d'Eril** (15C-17C) in **Vaprio d'Adda** was the home of Leonardo da Vinci. ▶ The **castle** in **Trezzo sull'Adda** was a stronghold within the Milanese defensive system. Below the castle is the Taccano central hydroelectric station (1906), art nouveau in style, and the most striking of the hydroelectric stations built in Lombardy in the first quarter of the 20C. ▶ Not far away, at **Crespi d'Adda**, is an important example of a 19C Italian artisans' village built around textile mills (1878). ▶ It is worth a trip to **Paderno d'Adda** to see the elegant iron **bridge** dating from 1889. ☐

For help in understanding terms when visiting museums or other sites, see the *Art and Architectural Terms Guide* at the end of the Practical Holiday Guide.

Practical information

CASSANO D'ADDA, ⊠ 20062, ☎ 0363.

Hotel:
★★★ *Julia,* v. Isola Ponti 23, ☎ 62154, 37 rm ⓟ ⚘ 𝟶𝟶 𝕝
🖾 55,000; bkf: 5,000.

Recommended
Archery: *Compagnia arcieri Osio,* v. Volta 27, ☎ 65037.

RIVOLTA D'ADDA, ⊠ 26027, ☎ 0363.

Restaurant:
♦♦ *Capanno,* v. Pontevecchio 21, ☎ 78024, closed Mon eve, Tue and 7 Jan-6 Feb. Small zoo and play area for children. Italian cuisine: costata Cavour, 25/30,000.

Recommended
Animal park: *Parco Zoo Safari della preistoria,* at Fornarello, v. Ponte Vecchio 21, ☎ 78184.
Cycling: *V. C. Rivoltana,* v. Filzi 27, ☎ 78152.

TREZZO SULL'ADDA, ⊠ 20056, ☎ 02.

Recommended
Nature park: *Parco naturale regionale dell'Adda Nord,* Villa Comunale, ☎ 90939674 (13,950 acres).

ALMENNO SAN SALVATORE

Bergamo 12, Milan 54 km
Pop. 5,278 ⊠ 24031 ☎ 035   C3

When Venice destroyed this ancient town at the foot of the Imagna Valley in 1443, only two churches were left standing. They are now the main monuments.

▶ The church of **Madonna del Castello** is decorated with frescos in its 15C Gothic interior. ▶ The Romanesque church of **S. Giorgio** (12C) has 12C-16C frescos. ▶ The **parish church** in the next village, **Almenno San Bartolomeo,** has interesting paintings. ▶ 3 km SW is the notable Romanesque church of **S. Tomaso in Lémine**★ or S. Tomè *(keys in house next door),* dating from the 13C. ☐

Practical information

Recommended
Golf: at Almenno S. Bartolomeo, v. Longoni 21, ☎ 640028/640707 (18 holes, closed Mon and Jan).

Lakes ANNONE AND PUSIANO

map 3

These are small lakes on the plain of Erba, between the moraines deposited by the glaciers of the Adda. Fine old mansions are now surrounded by little modern houses in **Bosisio** on the shores of Lake Eupili (Pusiano). ☐

Practical information

ANNONE DI BRIANZA, ⊠ 22048, ☎ 0341.

Recommended
Golf: *Royal Sant'Anna,* ☎ 57751 (9 holes).

PUSIANO, ⊠ 22030, ☎ 031.

Recommended
Water-skiing: *Ski Club Nautico Pusiano, v. Zoli 27,* ☎ 656726.

APRICA

Sondrio 31, Milan 157 km
3,845 ft pop. 1,564 ⊠ 23031 ☎ 0342   D2

Aprica, set among woods on the pass of the same name between Valtellina and Valcamonica, is a popular holiday and winter sports resort, crowded with hotels, time-shares and shops. ☐

Practical information

𝟧 cableway, cable car, ski lift, ski instruction, skating.
ⓘ corso Roma, ☎ 746113.

Hotels:
★★★★ *Park Hotel Bozzi,* v. Europa 18, ☎ 746169, 46 rm ⓟ 𝟶𝟶 ⤴ closed Sep-Oct and 16 Apr-Jun, 120,000.
★★★ *Cristallo,* v. Europa 37, ☎ 746159, 33 rm ⓟ 𝟶𝟶 closed May-19 Jun and 21 Sep-Nov, 54,000; bkf: 7,000.
★★★ *Eden,* v. Adamello 31, ☎ 746253, 21 rm ⓟ 𝟶𝟶 ♿ closed 21 Sep-Nov and 21 Apr-Jun, 54,000; bkf: 8,000.
★★★ *Larice Bianco,* v. Adamello, ☎ 746275, 25 rm ⓟ 𝟶𝟶 closed May-20 Jun and Oct-Nov, 50,000; bkf: 7,000.
★★★ *Sport,* v. Europa 106, ☎ 746134, 20 rm ⓟ 50,000; bkf: 6,000.
★★ *Serenella,* v. Europa 112, ☎ 746066, 26 rm ⓟ 𝟶𝟶 closed Easter-Jun and Sep-Christmas, 40,000; bkf: 4,000.

Restaurants:
♦♦ *Arrigo,* v. Roma 266, ☎ 746131, closed Tue, Oct-Nov and May-Jun except wkends and hols. Regional cuisine: pancakes, risotto, game with polenta, 25/35,000.
♦ *Barbasch,* v. Valtellina 35, ☎ 746210, closed Wed. Regional and Italian cuisine: gnocchetti verdi, tagliata alla Robespierre, 25/30,000.

⚠ ★★★ *Aprica,* at S. Pietro Aprica, v. Nazionale, 85 pl, ☎ 746784 (all year).

Recommended
Children's facilities: *Biancaneve children's residence,* v. Italia 55, ☎ 746521 (children 4-14 years; closed Oct-mid-Dec and May).
Swimming pool: v. Maiorca, ☎ 747034 (summer only).
Tennis: ☎ 747089.

ASOLA

Mantua 37, Milan 118 km
Pop. 8,687 ⊠ 46041 ☎ 0376   D5

A small agricultural town on the left bank of the Chiese, it is ancient in origin and quadrilateral in plan, with straight roads. Under Venetian rule from 1440, Asola has retained some elegant buildings from the period, including the parish church of **S. Andrea** (1472-1514), containing many works of art (the organ and pulpit are decorated with a notable **picture cycle**★ by Romanino). ☐

Practical information

BARCHI, ⊠ 46040, 4 km S.

Hotel:
★ *Rinascente:* v. Parma 160, ☎ 710340, 10 rm ⓟ 𝟶𝟶 𝟶 38,000; bkf: 2,000. Rest. ♦ closed Wed. Family-run trattoria. Mantuan and Italian cuisine: pumpkin tortelli, venison with bilberries, home-produced Lambrusco wines, 25/30,000.

CANNETO SULL'OGLIO, ⊠ 46013, 10 km SW.

Restaurants:
♦♦♦ *Pescatore,* at Runate, ☎ 70304, closed Mon, Tue, Jan and Aug. Rural elegance; summer service on veranda facing garden. Excellent Mantuan and creative cuisine: risotto alla pilota, baked hock with porcini, 45/55,000.
♦ *Torre,* p. Matteotti 5, ☎ 70121, closed Wed and

Aug. Mantuan cuisine: pike Gonzaga, pheasant with cream, 25/35,000.

Recommended
Nature park: *Le Bine nature reserve* (Comune di Acquanegra sul Chiese e Calvatone), open Sep-Jun, information *WWF Lombardia,* ☎ 02/6556810.

BAGOLINO

Brescia 61, Milan 154 km
Pop. 4,142 ⊠ 25070 ☎ 0365   D3

This small town in the valley of the Càffaro has fascinating streets, a 15C **church** with frescos by Giovan Pietro da Cemmo (1486) and an ancient, untranslatable dialect. The town is famous for its carnival, with elaborate dancing under the arcades, bizarre costumes and traditional music. There is skiing at **Val Dorizzo** (3,760 ft) and **Gaver** (4,957 ft).   ▢

Practical information _____

⸕ departure point for skiing in the Valle Dorizzo (*7.5 km N;* ski lifts, ski school) and in Gaver (*13 km N;* ski lifts, downhill skiing, ski school).

⚠ ★★★ *Pian d'Oneda,* at Ponte Càffaro, v. Pian d'Oneda 4, 120 pl, ☎ 990365.

Recommended
Events: *carnival* in costume, ☎ 99283.

BALLABIO

Como 36, Milan 64 km
Pop. 2,108 ⊠ 22040 ☎ 0341   B-C3

This village on the mountain stream that runs down from the Grigna Meridionale (→ Le Grigne and Il Resegone) is the first important resort in Valsàssina and the first approach to the Lecchesi Mountains. The **Piani Resinelli** (3,989 ft) is a vast plateau dotted with winter sports resorts. It is a base for excursions to the Grigna Meridionale and the **Parco Valentino,** with forests of beech, larch, fir and birch.   ▢

Practical information _____

⸕ at Piani Resinelli (*8 km W*); ski lifts, ski school.
ⓘ at Lecco, v. Nazario Sauro 6, ☎ 362360.

⚠ ★★★ *Grigna,* at Basilio, v. Provinciale, 100 pl, ☎ 530475 (all year).

Recommended
Nature park: *Piani Resinelli* animal reserve (car toll); including *Parco Valentino* (300 acres, pedestrians only).

BELLAGIO*

Como 30, Milan 78 km
Pop. 3,138 ⊠ 22021 ☎ 031   B3

Bellagio's position at the apex of the Como triangle, on a promontory dividing the two branches of Lake Como, provides magnificent views. The town is very attractive with narrow arched streets. It is surrounded by parkland attached to the large hotels and patrician villas that make this an elegant resort.

▶ The Romanesque church of **S. Giacomo** (12C, restored) is of interest. ▶ The park of the 18C **Villa Serbelloni★** (guided tour 10 a.m. and 4 p.m.; closed Mon) occupies almost all the top of the promontory. ▶ In **Loppia,** the **Villa Melzi★** (entrance near the Lido; Mar-Oct 9 a.m.-12:30 p.m. and 2:30-6 p.m.; summer 9 a.m.-

6:30 p.m.) has a magnificent park containing interesting archaeological finds, as well as a Chinese pagoda in the early 19C style. There is a noteworthy **art collection** in the palazzo (1810). ▶ The **Villa Giulia** (18C; *private*) on the road to Lecco was the residence of Leopold I, King of the Belgians.   ▢

Practical information _____

ⓘ lungolago, ☎ 950294.
⛴ boats and hydrofoils; car ferry from Varenna and Cadenabbia, ☎ 950180.

Hotels:
★★★★★ **G. H. Villa Serbelloni,** v. Roma 1, ☎ 950216, 82 rm ℗ ⬩ ⬩ ⬩ ⬩ ⬩ ⬩ closed 11 Oct-9 Apr. Fin-de-siècle villa with huge park on lake, 280,000; bkf: 10,000.
★★★ **Du Lac,** p. Mazzini 32, ☎ 950320, 49 rm ℗ ⬩ closed 16 Oct-14 Apr, 77,000; bkf: 8,000.
★★★ **Florence,** p. Mazzini 14, ☎ 950342, 46 rm ℗ ⬩ ⬩ closed 16 Oct-19 Apr, 86,000; bkf: 6,000.
★★ **Fiorini,** v. Vitali 2, ☎ 950392, 14 rm ℗ ⬩ ⬩ closed Jan, 50,000; bkf: 5,000.
★★ **Perlo-Panorama,** at Mulini del Perlo, v. Valassina 180, ☎ 950229, 14 rm ℗ ⬩ ⬩ ⬩ closed 10 Nov-30 Apr, 55,000; bkf: 7,000. Rest. ♦♦♦ closed Thu except Jun-Sep. Regional cuisine, 25/35,000.

Restaurants:
♦♦ **Pergola,** at Pescallo, ☎ 950263, closed Tue and Dec-28 Feb. With lake view and some accommodation. Regional cuisine: panzerotti, grilled or baked lake fish, 20/35,000.
♦ **Bilacus,** v. Serbelloni 32, ☎ 950480, closed Mon and 15 Mar-Oct. Mixed cuisine: ravioli montanara, lavarello Beatrice, 17/32,000.

Recommended
Craft workshops: *Tacchi,* v. Garibaldi, ☎ 950836 (wooden objects).
Marina: ☎ 950201.
Tennis: ☎ 950492.
Water skiing: *Sci nautico Bellagio,* at Punta Spartivento, ☎ 951394.

BERGAMO**

Milan 50, Rome 605 km
Pop. 121,033 ⊠ 24100 ☎ 035   C3

Bergamo is neatly divided into two. The more striking part is the upper town (Bergamo Alta), distinctive for its beautifully preserved old centre and commanding position. Despite active industry and commerce, the lower town (Bergamo Bassa) is not as impressive. In the upper town the two main squares with their magnificent buildings outclass attempts at modern urban planning. Bergamo was a rich and powerful commune ruled for more than three centuries by Venice. It is also the city of music and Donizetti, of the *Risorgimento* and Garibaldi's men (180 of the Thousand were from Bergamo), and of the *Commedia dell'Arte*. Together with its surrounding communities, Bergamo today has a higher concentration of residential and industrial buildings than almost anywhere else in Lombardy.

▶ **Bergamo Bassa.** Between 1914 and 1934 a new urban nucleus (the present town centre) was constructed on the grounds where S. Alexander's Fair had been held for centuries; the new area was built to blend with existing buildings. ▶ The focal point was the expanse of the p. Matteotti and p. V. Veneto (D3), which face each other across the **Sentierone** (D3), a broad, tree-lined and arcaded street where the people of Bergamo love to stroll. ▶ The 18C **Teatro Donizetti** (D3) is on the p. Matteotti; the theatre was restored and extended in 1964 (the façade dates from 1897-8). The 17C church of **S. Bar-**

tolomeo (D4), which has a magnificent altarpiece by Lorenzo Lotto (1516), is on the same square. ► The streets leading up to Bergamo Alta are the v. S. Alessandro and the v. Pignolo, named for the quarters in which they start; the modern link is the v. Vittorio Emanuele II. ► The v. S. Alessandro (C-D2) twists its way up the hill between villas and gardens, passing the church of S. Alessandro in Colonna (D2), rebuilt in the 18C and rich in works of art, and the 16C church of S.Benedetto (C2), which has a pleasing Renaissance façade with brick decoration and a frescoed cloister. The v. Pignolo★ (B-C4), flanked by 16C-18C palazzi, rises to the Porta S. Agostino (→). At the intersection with the v. Tasso is the 16C church of S. Spirito (C4) with paintings by Lotto, Previtali and. Bergognone. Next comes the church of S. Bernardino in Pignolo (B4) with an altarpiece★ by Lotto (1521) in the apse. Other works of art including a Trinity by Lotto and a *Christ Bearing the Cross*★ by Costa are to be found in the sacristy *(open during services; notice required,* ☎ *237887)* of the church of S. Alessandro della Croce (B4). ► The v. S. Tomaso (B4) on the r. rises between old houses to the Neoclassical Palazzo dell'Accademia (1805-10), which houses one of the most important museums in Italy, the Pinacoteca dell'Accademia Carrara★★ (A4; *9.30 a.m.-12.30 p.m. and 2.30-5.30 p.m.*).

► Bergamo Alta. It is possible to go to the upper town on the funicular (B2) from the v. V. Emanuele, but the main way in is through the Porta S. Agostino (A4), one of four gates in the 16C walls★ (the Porta S. Giacomo (B2) is also remarkable). ► The v. Porta Dipinta runs uphill from the former church of S. Agostino (14C; A3; 14C-15C frescos inside). The street is steep and twisting, lined with palazzi and old houses; it ends in the p. Mercato delle Scarpe (B2), an important medieval centre for trade and exchange and the site of the upper station of the funicular (in a 14C building with terrace with fine views). On the way are the Romanesque church of S. Michele al Pozzo Bianco (A3), which is 12C-15C with 12C-14C frescos, and Neoclassical S. Andrea (B3; altarpiece★ by Moretto). ► To the r. is the park of the 14C Rocca (fortress; A3; *under restoration).* On the esplanade is the Museo del Risorgimento e della Resistenza *(closed for restoration).* ► The v. Gombito leads to the austere 12C Torre di Gombito (A-B2), first of the handsome group of buildings set around the two central squares of the upper town. ► The Piazza Vecchia★ (A2) contains the principal secular buildings. On the NE side is the 17C Palazzo della Biblioteca, in the centre the 16C fountain, and on the SW side the Palazzo della Ragione★ (12C), the former Palazzo del Comune, open and arcaded on the ground floor and flanked on the r. by the massive Torre Civica (12C). Inside *(open only when exhibitions are in progress)* is a large room with 14C-15C frescos, including one by Bramante (1477). ► Through the arcade is the p. del Duomo (B2), an asymmetrical space surrounded by the most important ecclesiastical buildings. ► The Duomo (B2) was rebuilt in the 17C and has a 19C façade. ► The church of S. Maria Maggiore★★ (B2) is a complex, austere Romanesque basilica dating from the 12C. The lack of a façade is compensated for by the magnificent marble porch by Giovanni da Campione (1350-3) on the portal leading into the l.-hand transept. Campione was also responsible for the second portal on the l. and another leading into the r. transept (with porch). Notable exterior features are the Renaissance Sagrestia Nuova (new sacristy; 1491), the apse, the campanile (14C-16C), an arcaded fountain and the quatrefoil church of S. Croce (11C). The interior of the basilica *(7:30 a.m.-12:30 p.m. and 6-6:30 p.m.)* was refurbished in the 16C-17C. The gilded and stuccoed walls are decorated with Tuscan (16C) and Flemish (17C) tapestries. There is also a Baroque confessional (1704), a magnificent inlaid★★ wooden choir, partly designed by Lotto (1522-55) and finally, the tomb of Donizetti (1855) and other monuments. ► Next to the church is the Cappella Colleoni★★ (B2), built by the celebrated condottiero (soldier of fortune) in the service of the Venetian Republic for his tomb. The chapel (1476), a gem in terms of architecture and decoration, is one of the most important

Renaissance works in Lombardy. Inside *(9 a.m.-12 noon and 3-6 p.m.)* are the tombs of Colleoni★ and his daughter Medea★; in the lunettes under the dome and the votive chapel are frescos★ by Tiepolo (1733). ► The octagonal baptistery on the NW side of the square has an elegant gallery and columns in red Verona marble decorated with statues by Campionese masters (14C). It is a 19C reconstruction of the original building (1340). ► At v. Donizetti 3 (B2) in the Renaissance Casa dell Arciprete (1520) is the Museo Diocesano d'Arte Sacra *(notice required,* ☎ 211001). ► The Palazzo della Misericordia (15C-17C) houses the Museo Donizettiano (B2; 9 a.m.-12 noon and 2-6 p.m.; closed Sat, Sun and hols), displaying memorabilia of Bergamo's great opera composer. ► To the W is the p. Mascheroni (A1), with the remains of the 14C Citadel, which leads to the Piazzale Colle Aperto and the 16C Porta S. Alessandro, opening on to the hill footpath. In the square begins the Viale delle Mura (A-B1-3), a path that winds gently down the fortified walls.

Environs

► S. Vigilio (from Porta S. Alessandro, A1; 1,513 ft) is on a hill with remains of a castle and a magnificent view. On the slope is the birthplace of Donizetti (A1; *Jun and Sep, Sat and Sun 10 a.m.-12 noon and 3-6 p.m.).* ► Ponterànica *(7 km N)* has a parish church with altarpiece★ by Lotto (1526). ► Sotto il Monte Giovanni XXIII *(16 km W),* was renamed after the Pope John XXIII (Angelo Roncalli, 1881-1963), who was born in the district of Brusicco; his birthplace may be visited *(8 a.m.-12 noon and 2-7 p.m.; 6 p.m. in winter).* ► Dàlmine *(8 km SE)* has extensive iron and steel works and an unusual Museo del Presepio (cradles; *Dec-Jan 2-5 p.m., Sun and hols, 2-7 p.m.; other months Sun 2-7 p.m.).* ► 13.5 km W is Pontida with the historic abbey (11C) where the members of the Lombard league opposed to Frederick Barbarossa met in 1167. □

Arlecchino

At the heart of the Commedia dell'Arte lies the contrast between the Magnifico and the Zanni. Magnifico, or Pantalone, is a Venetian character and Zanni, the servant, is from Bergamo. Over the years the Zanni multiplied: Arlecchino (Harlequin), the masked figure who passed from the theatre to the carnival (not the other way round), is one of these Zanni. In one of the first pictorial records of the figure of Arlecchino, a series of French engravings illustrating a performance in Paris by Italian players in the late 16C, Arlecchino appears with many patches on his coat and not in the elegant, multicoloured clothes featured in 18C stylizations. Tristano Martinelli was a famous Arlecchino among early commedia dell'arte players. He travelled to Paris at the request of Henry IV and Queen Maria de'Medici. The story is told of his encounter with the king: when the king rose from his throne, the actor quickly sat down, turned to the king and said 'Arlecchino, you have come to entertain me. I am pleased and promise to protect you and give you a large pension'. Martinelli knew how to play Arlecchino both on stage and off.

Practical information

BERGAMO
ⓘ v. Vittorio Emanuele 4 (C3), ☎ 242226; v. Vittorio Emanuele 20 (C2-3), ☎ 210204; p. Vecchia 9 (A2), ☎ 232730 (seasonal).
✈ Orio al Serio ☎ 312315; *Alitalia,* v. Casalino 5, ☎ 224425; bus from the station (E4) stops at the Porta Nuova (D3).
🚆 (E4), ☎ 247624.

BERGAMO

0   50   100   200   300 m

1 : 12.000 (1 cm = 120 m)

© SERVIZIO CARTOGRAFICO DEL TOURING CLUB ITALIANO, MILANO

from station in p. Marconi (E4), ☎ 248150.
Car rental: *Avis*, airport, ☎ 310192; *Hertz*, v. Camozzi 38, ☎ 248186, airport, ☎ 311258; *Maggiore*, v. Locatelli 45, ☎ 213350, airport, ☎ 212231.

Hotels:
★★★★ *Cristallo Palace*, v. Ambiveri 35, ☎ 311211, 90 rm Ⓟ ら ⛾ 154,000.
★★★★ *Excelsior San Marco*, p. della Repubblica 6 (C3a), ☎ 232132, 151 rm Ⓟ 152,000; bkf: 13,000. Rest. ◆◆◆
Tino Fontana ☎ 215321, closed Fri. Regional cuisine, 35/55,000.
★★★ *Arli*, largo Porta Nuova 12 (D3b), ☎ 222014, 48 rm Ⓟ ら No restaurant, 69,000; bkf: 6,000.
★★★ *Cappello d'Oro e del Moro*, v. Giovanni XXIII 12 (D3c), ☎ 232503, 78 rm Ⓟ ら 68,500; bkf: 8,000.
★★★ *Città dei Mille*, v. Autostrada 3/C (F3d), ☎ 221010, 40 rm Ⓟ ⛾ No restaurant, 72,000; bkf: 9,000.
★★ *Agnello d'Oro*, v. Gombito 22 (A-B2e), ☎ 249883, 20 rm, 49,000; bkf: 5,000. Rest. ◆◆◆ closed Mon and 2 Jan-2 Feb. Artistic atmosphere. Excellent regional cuisine: casonsei, stracotto, 30/35,000.

Restaurants:
● ◆◆◆ *Antico Ristorante dell'Angelo*, v. Borgo S. Caterina 55 (A5 f), ☎ 237103, closed Mon and Aug. 17C inn with courtyard-garden. Outstanding cuisine: chestnut tagliatelle, zuppa di porcini, lobster with beurre blanc, 40/55,000.
◆◆◆ *Taverna del Colleoni*, p. Vecchia 7 (A2 l), ☎ 232596, closed Wed and Jan-Feb. In palazzo in monumental square with Renaissance decorations and summer service in open air. Regional cuisine: tournedos Donizetti, filet of ox, 37/55,000.
◆◆◆ *Vittorio*, v. Giovanni XXIII 21 (D4 n), ☎ 218060, closed Wed and Aug. Summer service in open air. Seafood: crêpes with salmon, turbot with orange, crayfish with vegetables, Friulian wines, 50/70,000.
◆◆ *Gourmet*, v. S. Vigilio 1 (A1 g), ☎ 256110, closed Tue. Garden in summer and some accommodation. Creative Italian cuisine: tagliatelle al cuore di capesante, scamorza ravioli with asparagus, 45/55,000.
◆◆ *Lio Pellegrini*, v. S. Tomaso 47 (B4 h), ☎ 247813, closed Mon, Tue noon, Jan and Aug. Under arches of 16C sacristy. Tuscan cuisine: pappardelle with fresh mushrooms, infarinata, 30/65,000.
◆◆ *Ol Giopi e la Margi*, v. Borgo Palazzo 25/G (C5 i), ☎ 242366, closed Mon and 25 Jul-25 Aug. Under brick arches in old palazzo. Regional cuisine: stracotto, bocconcini with mushrooms, 22/30,000.
◆◆ *Pianone*, v. al Pianone 21, ☎ 216016, closed Wed and Jan-Feb. Outside old town, terrace with fine view. Regional and Italian cuisine: casonsei with capon and pistachio nuts, sea-bass steak en croûte, 30/40,000.
◆ *Trattoria del Teatro*, p. Mascheroni 3 (A1 m), ☎ 238862, closed Mon. 19C trattoria. Regional cuisine: braised snails, rabbit or kid with polenta, 20/27,000.
◆ *Valletta*, v. Castagneta 19, ☎ 239587, closed Sun eve, Mon and Aug. Regional cuisine: foiade with mushrooms, wild boar with chestnuts, 25/40,000.

Recommended
Aeroclub: at Orio al Serio, *G. Taramelli airport*, ☎ 297062; alpine gliding club, at Valbrembo airport, ☎ 631093 or 613293.
Archery: *Compagnia Arcieri Bartolomeo Colleoni*, v. Statuto 19/F, ☎ 244698.
Botanical gardens: *Scaletta di Colle Aperto* (Al), ☎ 212034.
Bowling: v. Fossoli 1 (A5), ☎ 233659.
Caving: visits to *Grotta delle Meraviglie*, at Sedrina *(14 km N)*, May-Oct, 1st and 3rd Sun in month; book with *Le Nottole Gruppo Speleologico* (caving club), ☎ 235114.
Children's facilities: *Parco-Fauna Orobica* (animal park), p. Brigata Legnano 12 (A3), ☎ 247116; *Le Cornelle* (animal park), at Valbrembo, ☎ 630422 (closed Mon and winter); *Parco Minitalia*, at Capriate San Gervasio, ☎ 02/9090169.
Crafts: wrought iron, embossed copper, turned wood: permanent craft show at p. Vecchia 6 (A2), ☎ 239869.

Events: *International piano festival*, Teatro Donizetti (D3), ☎ 249631 (May-Jun, with Brescia).
Golf: at Chiuduno *(16 km SW)*, v. Montebello 4, ☎ 838600 (9 holes); at Almenno San Salvatore *(12 km NW*, 18 holes).
Hang gliding: *Scuola Delta di Maffi*, at Mapello *(11 km W)*, v. XXIV Maggio 1, ☎ 909607.
Horseback riding: *Centro Ippico Bergamasco*, at Brusaporto, v. per Albano, ☎ 681205 (riding school); *Azienda Agricola Cirocchi*, at Terno d'Isola, v. Medolago 32, ☎ 904082; *Cascina Grumello*, at Nese-Alzano Lombardo, ☎ 510060 (associate of *ANTE*); *Centro Equitazione Bergamasco*, at Seriate, ☎ 295441.
Ice Skating: p. Fiera, ☎ 220197.
Natural parks: *Parco Regionale dei Colli di Bergamo*, office, v. Pradello 12, ☎ 225589; *Parco Regionale del Serio*, office at Romano di Lombardia *(25 km SE)* town hall, ☎ 036/910661; *Riserva Naturale Regionale della Valpredina*, at Cenate di Sopra *(15 km E)*, reservations: *WWF Lombardia*, ☎ 02/653251 or 6556810.
Palazzo dello sport: v. Battisti 4 (B5), ☎ 210001.
Wine: Enoteca, v. Locatelli 24/b (BC2-3), ☎ 222181.
Youth hostel: *Ostello E.P.T.*, v. G. Ferraris 1, ☎ 342349.
♥ antiques: *Mercantico* in upper town on 3rd Sun of month; bar: *Bar del Tasso*, p. Vecchia 3 (A2), ☎ 237966.

Environs

ZINGONIA, ⊠ 24040, 15 km SE.

Hotel:
★★★★ *G. H. Zingonia*, corso Europa 4, ☎ 883225, 100 rm Ⓟ ⋙ ⛾ closed 1-25 Aug, 111,000.

The BERGAMO VALLEYS

From Lóvere to Bellano *(164 km, 1 day; map 1)*

The Alpi Orobie, the mountain chain at the head of the Bergamo Valleys, separating them from the Valtellina, take their name from the Orobi, a Celtic subtribe that stamped an identity on the area, forging a link between Bergamo and the surrounding countryside, or 'Bergamasca', as some of the residents still call it. This itinerary, between Lake Iseo and Lake Como, or between the Oglio and the Adda, is a way of getting to know the beautiful pre-alpine countryside of the Seriana, Brembana and Valsàssina Valleys.

▶ From **Lóvere** (→) the route leads to **Boario Terme** in the lower Valcamónica, an old market town and depot for iron from the Val di Scalve, now principally known as a spa. Life in the town revolves around the **Parco delle Fonti**, with spa and sports facilities. ▶ Entering the v. Mala, which climbs the lower Val di Scalve, the contrast with the gentle countryside of the Valcamónica becomes marked after the little spa centre of **Angolo Terme**. The road runs into a steep, wild **gorge** between rocky cliffs overhanging the swirling waters of the river Dezzo. ▶ From **Dezzo di Scalve** the route climbs to the **Passo della Presolana** (4,255 ft, → Val Seriana), then descends to **Clusone** (→). ▶ **Oltre il Colle** (3,543 ft), in a broad hollow at the head of the Valserina, surrounded by mountains rising above 6,500 ft, is a famous ski resort. ▶ **Serina** is a summer resort in the valley of the same name; during the 16C-18C, under Venetian rule, it was the principal town of the upper Brembana Valley and the centre of prosperous wool and iron industries. It is the birthplace of the great 16C Venetian painter Palma Vecchio, who painted the fine altarpiece in the parish church. ▶ In **Zogno**, principal town of the lower Brembana Valley, is the **Museo della Valle** *(9 a.m.-12 noon and 2-5 p.m.; closed Mon)* with objects, tools, furniture and reconstructed rooms illustrating the traditional culture of the valleys. ▶ The road continues by way of **Brembilla**, a timber-producing centre in the valley of the same name, and **Vedeseta**, a quiet little country town in the Taleggio Valley. ▶ From here the route crosses the meadows of the **Culmine di San Pietro** (4,167 ft) and climbs the Valsàs-

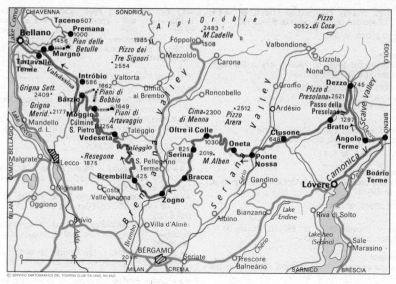

1. The Bergamo Valleys

sina to **Barzio** (2,523 ft), in a broad valley dominated by the Grigne (cable car to the **Piani di Bobbio** (5,531 ft) and cableway *(from Moggio, 4 km)* to the **Piani di Artavaggio** (5,249 ft)). ▶ The historic capital of the Valsàssina is **Intròbio**, where a massive 11C tower recalls the rule of the Grigioni. ▶ Near **Taceno** are the springs of **Tartavalle Terme**. The **Pian delle Betulle** (5,013 ft) are worth a detour *(cableway from Margno, 2.5 km)*, as is the little town of **Premana** *(11.5 km)*, known for cutlery and scissors, heritage of an ancient tradition of iron-making. The **Museo Comunale** *(partly under reconstruction; Apr-Oct, Sat and Sun 3-6 p.m.; other months, groups only,* ☎ *0341/890242)* has interesting exhibits on rural culture and crafts. ▶ At the end of the Valsàssina on the shores of Lake Como is elegant **Bellano**, with a spectacular **gorge** on the Pioverna. □

Practical information _____

BARZIO, ✉ 22040, ☎ 0341.
✦ cable car, ski lifts, downhill skiing, ski school at Piani di Bobbio.
ⓘ p. Garibaldi 10, ☎ 996255.

Hotel:
★★★★ **G. H. Ballestrin,** v. Coldogna 1, ☎ 996111, 50 rm Ⓟ ⛲ ☒ ♨ ☒ closed Oct-Christmas and Easter-May, 95,000; bkf: 10,000.

BELLANO, ✉ 22051, ☎ 0341.
≋
ⓘ v. Manzoni 1, ☎ 820044.
⛴ hydrofoils to Bellagio, Tremezzo and Lenno.

Hotel:
★★★ **Meridiana,** v. Carlo Alberto 19, ☎ 821126, 42 rm Ⓟ ♨ ♿ closed Christmas, 55,000; bkf: 5,000.

___

Be advised that hotels and restaurants in this Guide have perhaps changed addresses; prices indicated are also subject to modifications.

Recommended
Marina: ☎ 820528.

BOARIO TERME, ✉ 25041, ☎ 0364.
⚕ (all year), ☎ 531242; at Angolo Terme *(3 km;* May-Oct), ☎ 54012.
ⓘ p. Einaudi 2, ☎ 531609.

Hotels:
★★★★ **G. H. Boario e delle Terme,** v. Manzoni 2, ☎ 531061, 77 rm Ⓟ ♨ ♿ ☒ ♨ closed 16 Oct-14 May, 80,000.
★★★ **Rizzi,** v. Carducci 9, ☎ 50617, 55 rm Ⓟ ♨ closed 11 Oct-14 May,75,000; bkf: 7,000.
★★★ **Alpinisti,** corso Italia 85, ☎ 51161, 36 rm Ⓟ ♨ closed 11 Oct-31 Mar, 49,500; bkf: 5,000.
★★★ **Bossi,** v. Manzoni 22, ☎ 531057, 55 rm Ⓟ ♨ closed Nov-Mar, 70,000; bkf: 6,000.
★★★ **Brescia,** corso Zanardelli 6, ☎ 531409; 50 rm Ⓟ ♿ closed Jan, 70,000; bkf: 4,000.
★★★ **Mina,** corso Italia 56, ☎ 531098, 27 rm Ⓟ ♨ ♨ closed Nov-Mar, 50,000; bkf: 3,000.
★★★ **San Martino,** v. S. Martino 28, ☎ 531209, 36 rm Ⓟ ♨ ♿ ♨ 50,000; bkf: 4,000.

Restaurant:
♦ **Mignon,** v. Manifattura 29, ☎ 531043, closed Sun and 15 Jul-15 Aug. Regional cuisine: tagliatelli with mushrooms and salmon, rustin negà, 25/35,000.

Recommended
Cycling: A. S. Boario, v. Manifattura, ☎ 50777.
Events: concerts, theatre and fashion shows in the Parco delle Fonti.
Swimming: ☎ 533796 (in the Stadio Comunale).

CREMENO, 2 km S of Barzio.
✦ cableway, ski lifts and ski school at Piani di Artavaggio.
ⓘ town hall, ☎ 996113; at Moggio, p. Pradello 1, ☎ 998147.

Hotel:
★★★★ **Clubino,** v. Combi 15, ☎ 996145, 22 rm Ⓟ ♨ ♨

◫ closed Oct, 95,000; bkf: 10,000. Rest. ● ◆◆◆
closed Tue.   Excellent regional cuisine, 30/45,000.

INTROBIO, ⊠ 22040, ☎ 0341.

Recommended
Cheese: *Cadermatori dairy*, ☎ 980324; *Mauri Formaggi*
dairy, at Pasturo *(3 km S)*, ☎ 955244.

OLTRE IL COLLE, ⊠ 24013, ☎ 0345.
⚡ ski lifts, downhill skiing, ski school, skating.
ℹ v. Roma 50, ☎ 95088.

Hotel:
★★★ *Manenti*, v. Roma 29, ☎ 95005, 32 rm ℗ ⋘ ⅏
close 1 Oct-20 Nov, 45,000; bkf: 6,000.

PREMANA, ⊠ 22050, ☎ 0341.

Recommended
Crafts: scissors and cutlery manufacture, information at
municipio, ☎ 890127.

TACENO, ⊠ 22040, ☎ 0341.

Hotel:
★★ *Savoia*, v. Provinciale 1, ☎ 880120, 40 rm ℗ ⋘
closed Oct-Apr, 57,000; bkf: 4,000.

Recommended
Excursions: by cableway from Margno *(2.5 km)* to the
Pian delle Betulle (5,013 ft), ☎ 840020.

ZOGNO, ⊠ 24019, ☎ 0345.

Hotel:
★★ *Gianni*, at Ambria, v. Tiolo 37, ☎ 91093, 9 rm ℗ ⅏
28,000. Rest. ◆ closed Mon and 1-20 Sep. Regional
cuisine, 15/25,000.

BORMIO

Sondrio 65, Milan 202 km
Pop. 4,105 ⊠ 23032 ☎ 0342   D1

In the 15C-16C Bormio was a way-station on the *via
imperiale*, which connected Venice to northern Europe
through the high Fraele pass, avoiding Hapsburg territory. The town was granted many privileges and
monopolies and enjoyed a long period of prosperity
until the marked weather change, known as the 'little
ice age', in the 17C led travelers to prefer lower
alpine passes. Bormio's fortunes revived with tourism, which encouraged the development of the old
spas (mentioned in the 6C and modern ski resorts,
now among the most important in the Alps. In the
summer of 1987 there was a landslide in the Valtellina which blocked access to Bormio. It can be entered by a high alpine pass in good weather, but in winter must be entered from Switzerland. Italian authorities are at work on a new road at the time of publication.

▶ The medieval **old town** reveals some of the splendour
of the past. ▶ The Romanesque church of **S. Vitale**
has 14C-16C frescos. ▶ Next to the **collegiate church,**
rebuilt in the 17C, is a loggia in which justice used to be
administered. ▶ Also of interest are the interior of the
church of **S. Ignazio** (17C) and the 14C **Santuario del
Crocifisso**, with 15C-16C frescos. ▶ At v. Braulio 56 is
the Visitors' Centre for the **Parco dello Stelvio**, a national
park covering 342,500 acres in the Ortles-Cevedale group,
one of the great attractions of the region (→ Trentino
Alto Adige).

Environs

▶ **Bagni di Bormio** (4,324 ft; *4 km beside the Stelvio road*)
is made up of the Bagni Nuovi *(not in use)* and the Bagni
Vecchi. ▶ Near **Cepina** (3,743 ft; *3 km SW*) are mineral
springs (Fonte Levissima). ▶ A road *(10 km)* and a cable-

way lead to **Bormio 2000** (6,381 ft), an ultra-modern
skiing centre, and a cableway also runs to **Cima Bianca**
(9,882 ft), from which there is a magnificent
view★. ▶ **Cancano II** (6,234 ft) and **San Giacomo**
(6,056 ft) are reservoirs built for hydroelectric purposes
(20 km; difficult road).   ◻

Practical information _____

BORMIO
⚓ (all year), ☎ 901325; at Bagni di Bormio *(4 km N*, Dec-
mid-May and late-June-Oct), ☎ 901131.
⚡ cableways from Vallecetta, cable cars from Ciuk, chair
lifts, ski lifts, downhill skiing, ski school, skating, summer
skiing at the Passo dello Stelvio (→).
ℹ v. Stelvio 10, ☎ 903300.

Hotels:
★★★★ *Palace Hotel*, v. Milano 52, ☎ 903131, 80 rm ℗
⋘ ⅏ ▱ ⌖ closed 16 Sep-30 Nov and 15 Apr-14 Jun,
230,000; bkf: 12,000.
★★★ *Alù*, v. Btg. Morbegno 20, ☎ 904504, 30 rm ℗ ⌕
⋘ ♿ ⅏ closed 16 Sep-3 Dec and 21 Apr-30 Jun, 70,000;
bkf: 6,000.
★★★ *Astoria Hotel Majori*, v. Roma 73, ☎ 904451, 44 rm
℗ closed 16 Sep-30 Nov and 1 May-9 Jun, 68,000;
bkf: 5,000.
★★★ *Baita dei Pini*, v. alla Funivia, ☎ 904346, 46 rm ℗
⋘ closed 21 Sep-30 Nov and 21 Apr-14 Jun, 72,000;
bkf: 9,000.
★★★ *Larice Bianco*, v. Funivia 10, ☎ 904693, 45 rm ℗ ⋘
⅏ closed 1 Oct-Nov and May-14 Jun, 72,000; bkf: 9,000.
★★★ *Nazionale*, v. al Forte 14, ☎ 903361, 48 rm ℗ ⋘ ♿
closed 16 Oct-30 Nov and 1-14 May, 62,000; bkf: 6,500.
★★★ *Posta*, v. Roma 66, ☎ 904753, 55 rm ℗ ⅏ closed
16 Sep-30 Nov and 16 Apr-30 Jun, 72,000; bkf: 9,500.
★★★ *Rezia*, v. Milano 9, ☎ 904721, 42 rm ℗ ⋘ ⅏ clo-
sed 20 Apr-25 Jun, 73,000; bkf: 7,000.
★★★ *San Lorenzo*, v. S. Lorenzo 2, ☎ 904604, 38 rm ℗
⅏ closed Oct-Nov and May-14 Jun, 60,000; bkf: 5,000.
★★★ *Stelvio*, v. della Vittoria 36, ☎ 901130, 39 rm ℗
60,000; bkf: 5,000.
★★ *Cervo*, v. Don Peccedi 5, ☎ 904744, 23 rm ℗ closed
Oct- Nov and May, 43,000; bkf: 5,000.
★★ *Dante*, v. Trieste 2, ☎ 901329, 19 rm ℗ ⅏ closed
21 Sep-30 Nov and 1 May-14 Jun, 43,000; bkf: 5,000.
★★ *Everest*, v. S. Barbara 11, ☎ 901291, 26 rm ℗ ⋘ ⅏
closed 1 Oct-19 Dec and 1 Apr-19 Jun, 46,000; bkf: 5,000.
★★ *Genzianella*, v. Zandilla 6, ☎ 904485, 42 rm ℗ ⋘ ♿
closed 10 May-20 Jun and 10 Oct-30 Nov, 43,000;
bkf: 5,000.
★★ *Vallecetta*, v. Milano 107, ☎ 904587, 39 rm ℗ ⋘ ♿
closed Oct-Nov and May, 43,000; bkf: 5,000.

Restaurants:
◆◆◆ *Baiona*, v. per S. Pietro, ☎ 904243, closed Mon,
May-15 Jun and Oct-Nov. Surprise menus, with specialties of the valley predominating, 32/38,000.
◆◆ *Kuerc*, p. Cavour 8, ☎ 904738, closed Wed, May
and Oct-Nov. Regional cuisine: malfatti Kuerc, sciatt with
salad, 20/25,000.

⛺ ★★★ *Cima Piazzi*, at Tola, v. Nazionale, 80 pl,
☎ 950298 (all year).

Recommended
Alpine guides: v. Stelvio 10, ☎ 901116 (mountaineering
school, guided tours of the Parco dello Stelvio).
Archery: *Compagnia arcieri Bormio*, v. Funivie 43,
☎ 901895.
Excursions: *cableway to Cima Bianca* (9,881 ft),
☎ 905082.
Natural parks: *Parco Nazionale dello Stelvio*, v. Monte
Braulio 56, ☎ 901582 (office); *Rezia* botanical garden
at Rovinaccia-Bormio.

For the translation of a name of a meat, a fish or a
vegetable, for the composition of a dish or a sauce,
see the *Menu Guide* at the end of the Practical Holiday Guide; it lists the most common culinary terms.

Environs

BORMIO 2000, ⊠ 23032, ☎ 0342, 9 km S.

Hotel:
★★★ *Girasole 2000,* ☎ 901081, 50 rm Ⓟ ⬧ ⬧ closed 11 Sep-30 Nov and 20 Apr-30 Jun, 57,000.

CEPINA, ⊠ 23020, ☎ 0342, 5 km S.

Restaurant:
♦♦ *Fiorella,* v. Nazionale 8, ☎ 950310, closed Wed, 15-30 Jun and 15 Oct-15 Nov. Regional cuisine, 25/35,000.

CIUK, ⊠ 23030, 5 km SE.

Hotel:
★★ *Baita de Mario,* ☎ 901424, 21 rm Ⓟ ⬧ ⬧ ⬧ ⬧ closed 21 Sep-Nov and 26 Apr-Jun, 40,000; bkf: 4,500. Rest. ♦♦ Regional cuisine, 20/32,000.

BORNO

Brescia 76, Milan 117 km
2,992 ft pop. 2,762 ⊠ 25,042 ☎ 0364   D3

A ski and health resort between the Val di Scalve and the Valcamónica, on a **plateau** surrounded by woods. From Ossimo Inferiore *(2.5 km)* there is a detour to the 15C **Convento dell'Annunciata,** with two magnificent cloisters dating from 1485 and a church with 15C frescos. □

Practical information _____

⚡ cable car, ski lifts, downhill skiing, ski school, skating on Lake Giall.
ⓘ v. Giardini 8, ☎ 41022.

Restaurant:
♦ *Belvedere,* v. Giardini 30, ☎ 41052, closed Wed and 10-30 Sep. Regional and Italian cuisine: pancakes alla valdostana, gnocco malfatto, 17/40,000.

⚴ ★★ *Boscoblù,* at Le Ogne, v. Funivia 41, 280 pl, ☎ 41386 (all year).

The BREMBANA VALLEY

map 1

A 16C Venetian historian described the Brembo as a threatening, hostile river, that 'disdains to carry boats...and is even too proud to drive mills'. Three centuries later, when the Val Brembana became one of the principal centres of the Lombardy textile industry, the river had to submit to the new machines' need for power. Today industry is not so important in the region, and tourism has taken over. A magnificent road, following the old Priula, (one of the main lines of communication with central Europe from the 16C), makes it easy to reach the many tourist resorts, even in the high valley known as Oltre il Giogo.

▶ **Serina** (→ the Bergama Valleys) is the principal centre in the upper Brembana Valley. ▶ **San Pellegrino Terme,** in the central valley, is one of the most famous thermal spas in Italy; it has villas and palazzi in art nouveau style (the Grand Hotel, *closed at time of publication,* the Palazzo della Fonte, and the magnificent **Casino** dating from 1905), which are used for congresses, concerts, theatrical presentations and gala evenings. There is a fine view from **San Pellegrino Vetta** (2,838 ft, *funicular)* and from there it is possible to go on to **Dossena** *(10 km NW)* with a *Beheading of John the Baptist*★ by Veronese in the parish church. ▶ The road leads up the Val Taleggio (where a famous cheese is made) and passes through the narrow and picturesque **Enna gorge** before reaching the straggling village of **Taleggio.** ▶ **Piazzatorre** (2,848 ft) is an important tourist

centre in the Mezzoldo valley. ▶ **Branzi** (2,867 ft), at the confluence of the three branches of the Brembo, is also a busy ski resort (famous for a superb cheese). ▶ The principal centre in the high valley is **Fóppolo** (4,947 ft), the best-known and best-equipped winter sports resort in the Bergamo region. □

Practical information _____

BRANZI, ⊠ 24010, ☎ 0345.
⚡ chair lift, ski lift, downhill skiing, and ski school at Carona.
ⓘ p. Vittorio Emanuele 3/B, ☎ 71189.

Recommended
Excursions: ski and mountaineering journeys from *Fratelli Calvi rifugio,* ☎ 77047.

FOPPOLO, ⊠ 24010, ☎ 0345.
⚡ ski lifts, downhill skiing, ski school, skating.
ⓘ p. Paese, ☎ 74101.

Hotel:
★★★ *Des Alpes,* v. Cortivo 9, ☎ 74037, 30 rm Ⓟ ⬧ closed Sep-7 Dec and 21 Apr-Jun, 55,000; bkf: 7,000.

PIAZZATORRE, ⊠ 24010, ☎ 0345.
⚡ cable car, ski lifts, downhill skiing, ski school.
ⓘ municipio, ☎ 85056.

Hotel:
★★ *Milano,* v. Centro 13, ☎ 85027, 29 rm Ⓟ 40,000.

Recommended
Skating: *Palazzo del Ghiaccio,* at Rossanella.

SAN PELLEGRINO TERME, ⊠ 24016, ☎ 0345.
⚡ (May-Sep), ☎ 21355.
ⓘ v. B. Tasso 1, ☎ 21020.

Hotels:
★★★★ *Terme,* p. della Fonte, ☎ 21125, 50 rm Ⓟ ⬧ ⬧ closed 16 Sep-14 Jun, 64,000; bkf: 5,000.
★★★ *Bigio,* v. Matteotti 2, ☎ 21058, 52 rm Ⓟ ⬧ ⬧ closed Oct-May, 48,000; bkf: 5,000.
★★★ *Centrale,* v. Papa Giovanni 65, ☎ 21008, 30 rm Ⓟ ⬧ 42,000; bkf:4,000.
★★★ *Ruspinella,* v. De'Medici 47, ☎ 21333, 20 rm Ⓟ ⬧ ⬧ closed 15 Sep-1 Oct, 40,000.

Recommended
Caving: visits to *Grotta del Sogno,* at S. Pellegrino Vetta (mid-Jun-mid-Sep); *Gruppo Grotte,* v. Caffi 1, ☎ 21018.
Clay pigeon shooting: at Poggio Balconcello, ☎ 21467.
Events: congresses, concerts, gala evenings at Casino Municipale.
Spa visits: S. Pellegrino, at Ruspino (*2 km;* thermal and drinking water), ☎ 21355/21160 (reservations).
Swimming: *Natatoria Termale,* v. Mazzoni, ☎ 22455.

TALEGGIO, ⊠ 24010, ☎ 0345.

Hotels:
★★ *Miravalle,* at Olda, v. Costa 72, ☎ 47022, 10 rm Ⓟ ⬧ ⬧ closed 15-31 Jan, 30,000; bkf: 5,000.
★★ *Salute,* at Olda, v. Roma 73, ☎ 47006, 36 rm Ⓟ ⬧ ⬧ 30,000; bkf: 5,000.

BRENO

Brescia 69, Milan 112 km
Pop. 5,748 ⊠ 25043 ☎ 0364   D3

Breno, in the central Valcamónica, was an important stop on the road linking Venice with Protestant Germany, a route bitterly contested during the Thirty Years War. Modern industrial and commercial development owe much to this crucial position, which in the past compelled Breno to build fortifications among the most formidable in the valley.

▶ The impressive medieval **castle** (12C), high on a mound, has towers and crenellated walls. ▶ The church of **S. Antonio** (14C-15C) has an interesting fresco by Romanino (1535).

Environs

▶ In **Cividate Camuno** *(4 km SW)*, the old Roman capital of the valley, is the **Museo Archeologico della Valcamónica** *(9 a.m.-2 p.m.; Sun 9 a.m.-1 p.m.; closed Mon)*. ▶ The Strada delle Tre Valli climbs to the **Passo di Croce Domínii** (6,207 ft) between steep alpine meadows; wonderful view of the mountains. □

Practical information ────────────

ⓘ v. Garibaldi, ☎ 22970.

Hotel:
★★★ **Castello**, v. Belvedere 10, ☎ 21421, 42 rm Ⓟ 50,000.

Recommended
Horseback riding: *Centro Ippico*, v. Spinera (associate of *ANTE*).
Natural park: *Parco Naturale Regionale dell'Adamello*, Comunità Montana Val Camonica, v. Moro, ☎ 22573.

BRESCIA*

Milan 93, Rome 538 km
Pop. 204,278 ⊠ 25100 ☎ 030   D4
See map on page 372.

For centuries, iron and the arms factories of the lower Trompia Valley made Brescia rich. Today the city's economy is based more than ever on the ironworks in that same valley (still producing weapons exported throughout the world) and on the more recent development, around the town centre, of metal, textile and food industries. Brescia is demographically and economically second only to Milan in the region. Modern districts have adopted the right-angled street layout of Roman Brixia. In the older centre of the town, art and architecture recall the past in medieval, Renaissance and 19C districts.

▶ The **piazza del Foro** (B4) was the centre of the Roman town, and the excavated remains make up the most important Roman archaeological complex in Lombardy. It includes the ruins of the **Theatre**, the remains of the Curia and the E portico of the Forum, and the **Tempio Capitolino★** *(9 a.m.- 12 noon and 2-5 p.m.; closed Mon)*, built by the Emperor Vespasian in 73 AD and partially restored in the first half of the 19C. The remains of an earlier (1C BC) Republican temple can be seen beneath the pronaos. ▶ Behind the temple is a modern building containing the **Museo Romano★**; in its collection are a bronze **Winged Victory★** (1C AD) and six Roman heads, also in bronze, dating from the 2C-3C. The monastic complex of **S. Salvatore-S. Giulia** (B5; *closed for restoration*) included queens and empresses among women who took the veil. The 16C former church of **S. Giulia** used to house the **Museo dell'Età Christiana★** (Christian antiquities), with a lavish collection of sculpture and objects from the early Christian era to the Renaissance. The most valuable pieces are provisionally exhibited in the Pinacoteca Tosio Martinengo (→ below) until the Museo della Città is established in the S. Salvatore-S. Giulia complex, also intended to house material from the Museo Romano. Also closed is the **Galleria d'Arte Moderna**, situated in another monastery. Although they are under restoration, it is possible to visit the two most important churches in the monastic complex *(Mon only, with permission from the Direzione dei Musei, v. M.da Barco 1, ☎ 59120)*. The basilica of **S. Salvatore★**, a magnificent 9C building, has Romanesque columns with fine capitals (6C-8C) and walls decorated with 8C-14C frescos and stucco (frescos by Romanino in the chapel of S.Obizio). The Romanesque church of **S. Maria in Solario★** (12C) has a polygonal lantern. The former p. del Duomo, now piazza Paolo VI (B-C4), with an 18C fountain, is the architectural heart of the city, bounded on the

E by ecclesiastical and secular buildings (the Rotonda, the Duomo Nuovo and the Broletto). ▶ The **Rotonda★** (C4; *apply to the sexton in the Duomo Nuovo*) or Duomo Vecchio is a fine example of a centrally planned Romanesque church, built in the 12C above the former basilica of S. Maria Maggiore (6C-7C). The portal at the front was rebuilt in the 18C after the collapse of the campanile. The **interior★**, plain and austere, consists of a central space above which is a huge hemispherical vault on massive piers with raised circular ambulatory. The raised sanctuary was added in the 15C; it houses the **treasure** *(rarely exhibited)* and paintings by Moretto *(Assumption★, S. Luke★*). In the upper ambulatory are two tombs carved by Campionese masters (14C) and remains of Roman mosaic pavements. In the **crypt** (11C) are remains of Byzantine-style frescos of the 12C-14C. ▶ The **Duomo Nuovo** (B-C4) is a superb example of Mannerist architecture. It was started in 1604 but not completed until the 18C. The high dome, designed by Cagnola, was added in 1825. Outstanding among the various works of art in the interior are a picture by Moretto *(Sacrifice of Isaac★)* and the tomb of **S. Apollonio and S. Filastro**, dating from 1510. ▶ The Romanesque-Gothic **Palazzo del Broletto★** (B4) was built between 1187 and 1230 and is one of the most interesting in Lombardy, with mullioned windows in the façade and the delightful **Loggia delle Grida** *(restored)*. It has a partly arcaded courtyard with a fine 17C fountain. Beside it, austere, crenellated and in ashlar, is the **Torre del Popolo** (11C) or **Tor del Pegol**, as Brescians call it. ▶ The **Piazza della Loggia★** (B3) is close by. It was the historic and administrative centre of the town from the late 15C. It is dominated by the Palazzo del Comune or **Loggia★** (B3), an impressive Renaissance building of extraordinary grace and balance, built between 1492 and 1574, with contributions from the major artists and architects of the period, including Sansovino and Palladio. ▶ All the buildings around the square bear the stamp of Venetian-Lombardy Renaissance art. The **Monte di Pietà** (B3) has elegant little balconies. The arcades on the E side lead to the v. X Giornate and v. Zanardelli, forming a busy covered walk. ▶ Not far away is the church of **S. Giovanni Evangelista** (B3), rebuilt in the 15C, with an interior altered in the 16C and **paintings★** by Moretto and Romanino. ▶ Other works★ by Moretto and Romanino (in addition to 13C-15C frescos) are to be found in the Romanesque-Gothic church of **S. Francesco** (C3), dating from 1265. ▶ The church of **S. Maria dei Miracoli** (C3), rebuilt inside, has a lavish 15C-16C marble façade. ▶ There are notable paintings★ by Moretto and Romanino in the church of **S. Nazario e S. Celso** (C2), which also contains an altarpiece depicting *The Risen Christ, Annunciation and Saints★★*, a youthful masterpiece by Titian. ▶ From the modern **Piazza della Vittoria** (C3), laid out in 1932, the arcades lead to the v. Moretto (C3-4), flanked with Baroque palazzi. ▶ The church of **S. Alessandro** (C4) has an Annunciation attributed to Bellini. ▶ A little beyond is the 16C church of **S. Angela Merici** (C4; rebuilt), containing pictures by Tintoretto, Paolo da Cailina the Younger, F. Bassano the Younger, G. C. Procaccini, Palma Giovane and others. ▶ In the 16C Palazzo Martinengo da Barco is the **Pinacoteca Tosio Martinengo★★** (C4; *9 a.m.-12 noon and 2-5 p.m.; closed Mon)*, important for Renaissance painting by local artists. ▶ The church of **S. Clemente** (C4; *if closed ask at v. S. Clemente 6*) has numerous paintings★ by Moretto and Romanino. ▶ The Colle Cidneo is laid out as a public park and taken up to a large extent by the massive **Castle** (B4), rebuilt in the 16C; it contains the **Museo del Risorgimento** *(9 a.m.-12 noon and 2-5 p.m.; closed Mon)*. ▶ The Via Panoramica (B6) climbs to **Mt. Maddalena** *(7 km; 2,870 ft)* with a **view★** of the mountains, Lake Garda and the plain. ▶ 3 km E is the 18C church of **Madonna del Patrocinio**, with a collection of 18C ex-votos. ▶ 9.5 km E is **Botticino**, noted in the Roman period for its marble, which was used to build all the major monuments in Brescia. □

Practical information

ⓘ corso Zanardelli 34 (C4), ☎ 43418; motorway toll Brescia Centro, ☎ 346142 (May-Sep).
🚄 (D2), ☎ 52449.
🚌 from railway station, p. Ovest (D2-3).

Car rental: *Avis*, v. XX Settembre 2, ☎ 295474; *Hertz*, v. XXV Aprile 12, ☎ 45132; *Maggiore*, railway station, ☎ 49268.

Hotels:
★★★★★ *Vittoria*, v. X Giornate 20, ☎ 280061, 65 rm, 190,000.
★★★★ *Ambasciatori*, v. C. di Rosa 90/92, ☎ 308461, 67 rm ℗ ⴆ 80,000; bkf: 6,000.
★★★★ *Igea*, v. della Stazione 15 (C-D2a), ☎ 44221, 72 rm ℗ ⌘ 83,000; bkf: 5,000.
★★★★ *Master*, v. Apollonio 72 (A4b), ☎ 294191, 76 rm ℗ ⌘ ⴆ 120,000; bkf: 10,000.
★★★ *Alabarda*, v. Labirinto 6, ☎ 341065, 28 rm ℗ ⌘ 65,000; bkf: 5,000.
★★★ *Capri*, v. S. Eufemia 37, ☎ 360149, 21 rm ℗ closed 15-30 Jul. No restaurant, 55,000; bkf: 6,000.
★★★ Industria, v. Orzinuovi 58, ☎ 340521, 70 rm ℗ ⌘ 60,000; bkf: 5,000.

Restaurants:
♦♦♦ *Sosta*, v. S. Martino della Battaglia 20 (C4 e), ☎ 295603, closed Mon and Aug. Elegant surroundings in former stables of Palazzo Martinengo Colleoni. Regional cuisine: risotto with lemon, tortelloni di magro with basil cream, 40/60,000.
♦♦♦ *Stretta*, v. Stretta 63, ☎ 302786, closed Mon. Regional and international cuisine: gnocchetti al Gorgonzola, casonsei, piatto del re, 35/55,000.
♦♦ *Palazzo Caprioli*, v. Capriolo 46/A (B3 d), ☎ 296847, closed Mon and Aug. In rebuilt palazzo. International cuisine: menu based on seasonal produce, 30/45,000.
♦ *Castello Malvezzi*, at Mompiano, v. Colle S. Giuseppe 1, ☎ 391701, closed Sun eve and Mon. In 16C house. Italian and international cuisine: risotto with nettles, veal in truffle cream, 40/55,000.
♦ *Loggia*, v. S. Faustino 34 (B3 c), ☎ 48135, closed Sun and 1-25 Aug. Seafood: spaghetti with crab meat, porcini, 30/45,000.
♦ *Vedetta*, v. Buttafuoco 21, ☎ 54296, closed Wed. Pleasing views. Regional cuisine: tagliatelle with porcini, baked kid, 30/45,000.

Recommended

Bowling: v. B. Castelli 24, ☎ 392827.
Events: *International Piano Competition* and *International Festival of Contemporary Music* (May-Jun, with Bergamo); theatre and concert seasons in the Teatro Grande (C3-4), ☎ 59448.
Flying club: *Ghedi Aeroporto* v. Olivari, ☎ 901101; *Montichiari Aeroporto* ☎ 964355.
Golf: *Golf Club Franciacorta*, at Nigoline di Cortefranca, ☎ 9484167 (18 holes).
Horseback riding: *Società della Cavallerizza*, v. Chiappa 15, ☎ 361005; *Società Ippica Franciacorta*, at Passirano, ☎ 653610 (associate of *ANTE*).
Palazzetto dello sport: v. Orzinuovi, ☎ 340477.
Squash: *Squash Centre*, at Bovezzo, v. Vernazza 3, ☎ 2711342.
Swimming: v. Piave (D6), ☎ 362638; at Mompiano, ☎ 303007.

Santa Maria di BRESSANORO

Cremona 29, Milan 57 km

The finest feature of this church, which is among the oldest in the Cremona area, having been rebuilt by Bianca Maria Visconti in 1460, is the magnificent **interior**, with decorative brickwork and frescos. ☐

BRIANZA

From Monza to Como (62 km, 1 day; map 2)
See map on page 374.

Brianza is an extensive, hilly territory between the Lariano triangle and the Monza region, between the Seveso and the Adda. It still has some of the character of old Brianza, where refined villas are numerous and pleasant, lived in by delightful people, and the land is fertile, as a visitor wrote in 1794. However, the 'garden of Lombardy' and its rich culture (particularly the 16C-17C villas) are today menaced by dense urban and industrial expansion, the result of impulsive development in the post-war period.

▶ The itinerary starts at **Monza** (→). ▶ At Merate are the **Villa Belgioioso** (17C-18C), one of the finest in the area with a splendid garden, and the **Astronomical Observatory** *(visits on first Thu of month, provided it is not a hol, 2-5 p.m., ☎ 592035)*, one of the most important in Italy. 3 km SE is the 17C **santuario della Madonna del Bosco**, from which it is possible to climb to **Imbersago**, noted for the ingenious **ferry** over the Adda, driven by a mechanism said to have been designed by Leonardo da Vinci. ▶ A little farther, a diversion to the r. leads to the hill of **Montevecchia** (1,572 ft) with a fine view. ▶ In the environs of **Carate Brianza** are numerous old industrial buildings, evidence of important textile works in past centuries. ▶ **Agliate** is a tiny village, set around the exceptional proto-Romanesque basilica of **S. Pietro★** (9C-11C) and the contemporary **baptistery★**. ▶ According to tradition, **Giussano** was the birthplace of the military commander Alberto, who led the Lombard Compagnia della Morte to victory against Frederick Barbarossa at the Battle of Legnano in 1176. ▶ **Inverigo**, known as the pearl of Brianza, has a distinguished Neoclassical villa called the **Rotonda** (1813) and, facing the rough **giants' ladder**, the beautiful **Villa Crivelli** (17C-18C) flanked with cypresses and dominated by a statue of Hercules. ▶ From **Alzate Brianza**, with many villas and a medieval tower, the route continues through **Galliano** (→), **Cantu** (→) and **Como** (→). ☐

Practical information

ALZATE BRIANZA, ✉ 22040, ☎ 031.

Hotel:
★★★★ *Villa Odescalchi*, v. Anzani 12, ☎ 630822, 25 rm ℗ ⌘ 🖻 ✍ 98,000; bkf: 10,000.

Recommended

Flying club: at Verzago, ☎ 630960 (gliding).
Horseback riding: *Centro ippico Brianza*, ☎ 630448 (associate of *ANTE*).

CARATE BRIANZA, ✉ 20048, ☎ 0362.

Hotel:
★★★ *Tosi*, v. Valassina 2, ☎ 903891, 32 rm ℗ ✍ 60,000; bkf: 7,000.

Recommended

Wines: *Enopolio italiano*, at Seregno, v. Liguria 5, ☎ 230879.

INVERIGO, ✉ 22044, ☎ 031.

Hotel:
★★★ *Bosco Marino*, v. Corridoni 13, ☎ 607117, 38 rm ℗ ⌘ ✍ closed Christmas, 60,000; bkf: 5,000.

MERATE, ✉ 22055, ☎ 039.

Recommended

Observatory: *Osservatorio Astronomico*, ☎ 592035 (each 1st non-hol Fri in month; 2 p.m.-5 p.m.).
Wines: *Rocca enoselezioni* (wine retail outlet), at Casatenovo (9 km W), v. Parini 23, ☎ 931196.

1° SERVIZIO CARTOGRAFICO DEL TOURING CLUB ITALIANO, MILANO

MONTEVECCHIA, ⊠ 22052, ☎ 039.

Restaurant:
● ♦♦♦ *Eremo della Priora*, at Missaglia, v. Pianeta IV, ☎ 949351, closed Mon and Aug. In 16C building that may have been a monastery; site is secluded, with magnificent vegetation, park with botanical garden. Friuli cuisine: frico alla carnica, wild boar with bilberry sauce, 55/60,000.

Recommended
Nature parks: for regions of Montevecchia and Valle del Curone, municipio, ☎ 593154.

USMATE, ⊠ 20040, ☎ 039.

Restaurant:
♦♦♦ *Chiodo*, v. Michelangelo 1, ☎ 674275; closed Wed and Aug. Verdant rural site. Creative cuisine: salmon alla parigiana, prawns with pink pepper, 35/50,000.

In preparing for your trip, consult the pages pertaining to the regions. You will find there the description of the region you wish to visit, as well as a list of sites that must be seen, a brief history and practical information.

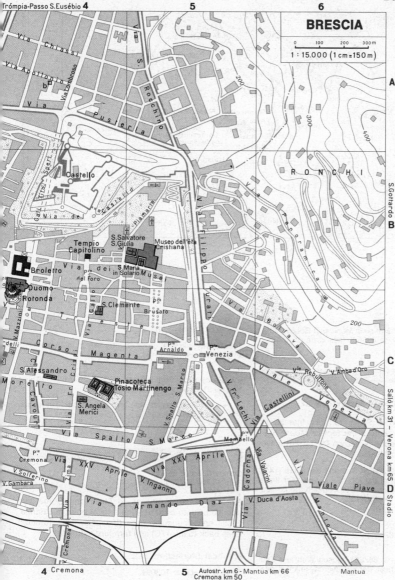

Trómpia-Passo S.Eusébio **4**   **5**   **6**

BRESCIA

0   100   200   300m

1 : 15.000 (1 cm=150 m)

A

R O N C H I

B

S.Gottardo

Castello

Tempio
Capitolino
S.Salvatore
S.Giulia
Museo dell'età
Cristiana
Broletto
Via dei
del foro
S.Maria
in Solario Musei
Duomo
Rotonda
S.Clemente
Brusato

C

Salò km 31 - Verona km 65

Corso
delli
Magenta
Arnaldo
Venezia
S.Alessandro
Moretto
Pinacoteca
Tosio Martinengo
S.Angela
Merici
Castellini
Venezia
V.le Rebuffone
V.Amba d'Oro

Spalto
S.Marco
Mombello

D

Stadio

Cremona
XXV Aprile
XXV Aprile
V.Inganni
Viale
Piave
Via
Armando Diaz
V. Duca d'Aosta
V.Solferino
V.Gambara

4 Cremona   **5** Autostr. km 6 - Mantua km 66
Cremona km 50   Mantua

BUSTO ARSIZIO

Varese 26, Milan 35 km
Pop. 79,085 ⊠ 21052 ☎ 0331   A4

In the 19C the revolution in the textile industry made
this the 'Manchester of Italy'. Even in the 14C the
village artisans wove cloth of famous quality, which
they sold at Milan. Today Busto Arsizio (which, with
Legnano (→) and Castellanza, forms one of the major
conurbations of the plain of Padua) remains one of
the most important textile centres in Italy.

▶ In the old town the church of **S. Maria di Piazza★**
(1521) is a Renaissance gem. Inside, the high drum of
the dome is decorated with late 16C statues; numerous
paintings are in the interior.   □

Practical information _____

Hotel:
★★★ *Astoria,* v. Duca d'Aosta 14, ☎ 636422; 46 rm Ⓟ
& ⊗ 65,000; bkf: 5,000.

Recommended
Golf: *Idea Verde* practice course, at Olgiate Olona
(3 km E), ☎ 629483.

2. Brianza

Horseback riding: *Stud farm della Monica*, at Robecchetto con Induno *(13 km SW)*, ☎ 898680 (associate of *ANTE*).

CAMPIONE D'ITALIA

Como 25, Milan 72 km
Pop. 2,254 ⊠ 22060 ☎ 004191 (Lugano network)   B3

A strip of Italian land in Swiss territory that is on the banks of Lake Lugano at the foot of Mount Sighignola. Campione today is known for an attractive Casino, the nearest to Milan.

▶ The lively Baroque façade of **S. Maria dei Ghirli** (14C, rebuilt in the 18C) is set at the top of a spectacular flight of steps and looks out over the lake; beneath the portico are frescos dating from the 15C-16C.   □

Practical information _____

ⓘ v. Volta 16, ☎ 688182.

Restaurant:
♦♦ *Taverna*, p. Roma, ☎ 687201, closed Wed and Thu noon. Italian cuisine: river perch Taverna, involtini alla crema, 40/65,000.

Recommended
Casino: p. Milano, ☎ 687921.
Tennis: sports centre, at Groscio, ☎ 686360.

CAMPODOLCINO

Sondrio 72, Milan 135 km
3,515 ft pop. 1,217 ⊠ 23021 ☎ 0343   B1

A small **upland plain** in the rugged valley of S. Giacomo, before the road climbs steeply into a desolate alpine landscape. A cableway climbs to the **Alpe Motta** (5,659 ft), a broad upland valley between Campodolcino and Madesimo.   □

Practical information _____

≴ cableway, ski lifts, cross-country skiing, instruction.
ⓘ p. Municipio, ☎ 50137.

Hotel:
★★ *Europa*, v. Corti 93, ☎ 50022, 26 rm ℗ closed 16 Sep-31 Oct and May, 36,000.

⚐ ★★★ *Campodolcino*, at Corti, strada per Starleggia, 167 pl, ☎ 50097 (all year).

CANTU

Como 10, Milan 36 km
Pop. 36,804 ⊠ 22063 ☎ 031   B3

Although ease of access to Milan and Como has deprived Cantu of its role as a focal point in Brianza, it still has flourishing **lace** (the pillow-lace tradition goes back to the 17C) and **furniture** industries.   □

Practical information _____

ⓘ p. Marconi, ☎ 703094.

Hotels:
★★★★ *Canturio*, v. Vergani 28, ☎ 703035, 28 rm ℗ ⅙ ⌽ closed Aug and Christmas. No restaurant, 87,000; bkf: 7,000.
★★★ *Sigma*, v. Grandi 32, ☎ 710589, 40 rm ℗ ⅙ closed Aug, 80,000; bkf: 6,000.

Restaurants:
● ♦♦♦ *Querce*, at Mirabello *(3 km)*, ☎ 731336, closed Tue and Aug. In a wood with terrace and garden. Excellent creative cuisine: pancakes with salmon, mushrooms and truffles (in season), 30/45,000.
♦♦ *Trattoria Fossano*, at Vighizzolo, v. Fossano 68, ☎ 730601, closed Tue and Jul. Seafood: risotto mare, salmon taglione, 30/45,000.
♦ *Scaletta*, v. Milano 30, ☎ 703540, closed Tue and Aug. Italian cuisine: fresh pasta, saddle of veal bordolese, 20/28,000.

Recommended

Furniture: numerous permanent exhibitions; visits to *Arts Institute*, v. Andina, ☎ 701100.
Hang gliding: *Scuola Ostini delta sport*, at Lentate sul Seveso, v. Colombo 5, ☎ 0362/563117.
Horseback riding: *Ipporonco club*, at Cabiate, v. Ronco Bigin; *Ranch Due Olmi*, at Mariano Comense, v. Arosio (associate of *ANTE*); *Ippica Comense*, v. per Alzate 15, ☎ 712820.
Rowing: at Cucciago, *Pallacanestro Cantù*, ☎ 787344 or 787244.

CAPO DI PONTE

Brescia 79, Milan 124 km
Pop. 2,375 ⊠ 25044 ☎ 0364   D2-3

Sandstone smoothed by glaciers during the Pleistocene Age provided the 'blank slate' on which the alpine Camuni tribe inscribed their history. The graffiti of the Valcamònica are the richest specimens of rock inscription in Italy, running from the Neolithic to the Iron Age. With rare expressive force they depict hunting and war, agriculture and cattle-breeding, family life, metal-working, tools and weapons, religious and social customs.

▶ The **Centro Camuno di Studi Preistorici** in Capo di Ponte has a specialist library. ▶ Around the village is the **Parco Nazionale delle Incisioni Rupestri★** *(9 a.m.-sunset; closed Mon)*, with numerous incised rocks, of which about 100 are at **Naquane**, site of the great rock of Naquane★, with 876 figures (a guide is indispensible to locate and decipher the incisions). ▶ Above the village is the notable small Romanesque parish church of **S. Siro★** *(keys from the priest in Cemmo)*, 12C. ▶ 2 km N is the 11C Romanesque church of **San Salvatore★** *(keys from the house next door)*.   ◻

Practical information

ⓘ v. Briscioli, ☎ 42080.

CARAVAGGIO

Bergamo 23, Milan 37 km
Pop. 13,932 ⊠ 24030 ☎ 0363   C4

The painter Caravaggio (1573-1610, real name Michelangelo Merisi) was born here and adopted the town's name as his own. Caravaggio's notoriety gives this prosperous agricultural and industrial centre on the Lombardy plain a touch of profane glory on top of the religious fame it enjoys because of the venerable sanctuary 2 km from the town. Under the high altar of the **santuario della Madonna di Caravaggio** (1451, extended 16C-18C) is the supposedly miraculous spring that gushed forth from the place where the Virgin Mary appeared to a peasant woman. It attracts pilgrims all year round.   ◻

Practical information

Hotel:
★★★ **Verri**, at Santuario, v. Beata Vergine 4, ☎ 84622, 35 rm ℗ ⌸ ⅙ 42,000; bkf: 4,500.

Restaurant:
◆◆◆ **Dé Firem Röstec,** at Santuario, ☎ 84380, closed Wed and 1-15 Aug. Regional cuisine: tagliatelle with salmon, risotto with porcini and truffles, 18/50,000.

For help in understanding terms when visiting museums or other sites, see the *Art and Architectural Terms Guide* at the end of the Practical Holiday Guide.

CASTELSEPRIO

Varese 14, Milan 39 km
Pop. 1,079 ⊠ 21050 ☎ 0331   A3

Castelseprio is in a strategic position on a road that, even in Roman times, was one of the most important to the Alps. In the Middle Ages it became a mainstay of the Po Valley defensive system (under Byzantine, Lombard and French rule) until 1287, when Ottone Visconti destroyed it. The church of **S. Maria Foris Portas★** *(11 a.m.-5 p.m; closed Mon; keys from the caretaker)* is an unusual 7C-8C building; in the interior there is an extraordinary **fresco** cycle (6C-8C or 9C), painted by an oriental master in the Romano-Hellenistic tradition.   ◻

CASTIGLIONE DELLE STIVIERE

Mantua 37, Milan 122 km
Pop. 15,707 ⊠ 46043 ☎ 0376   D4

This is the birthplace of St.Aloysius Gonzaga (1568-91) and the home of the Red Cross, which was conceived by the Swiss Henri Dunant while helping the wounded on the battlefield of Solferino.

▶ A **sanctuary** (16C-18C) is dedicated to St.Aloysius, as is the **Museo Storico Aloisiano** *(9-11 a.m. and 3-5 or 6 p.m.)*, with ecclesiastical objects, furniture and picture gallery. The International Museum of the Red Cross (**Museo Internazionale della Croce Rossa**) is in the Palazzo Trineri-Longhi *(9 a.m.-12 noon and 3-5:30 or 7 p.m; closed Mon)*. 7.2 km SE is **Solferino**, site of Napoleon III's victory over the Austrians on 24 June, 1859; **Museo Storico** *(daily, closed Mon, opening times vary according to the time of year; from Nov to Feb, consult curator)* and the little church of S. Pietro which is used as an **ossuary** (→ also San Martino della Battaglia).   ◻

Practical information

CASTIGLIONE DELLE STIVIERE

Restaurants:
◆◆◆ **Tomasi**, at Grole *(3 km)*, v. Solferino 77, ☎ 630873, closed Sun and Aug. In villa with garden. Italian cuisine: sfogliatelle with cheese, salmon en croûte, 30/50,000.
◆◆ **Hostaria Viola**, v. Verdi 32, ☎ 638277, closed Mon, Easter and Christmas. Fine Mantuan cuisine: agnoli, pumpkin tortelli, 25/35,000.

Environs

SOLFERINO, ⊠ 46040, ☎ 0376, 7 km SE.

Hotel:
★★ **Spia d'Italia**, v. Ossario 2, ☎ 854041, 14 rm ℗ ⅋ 48,000. Rest. ◆◆ closed Tue. Regional cuisine, 20/30,000.

Restaurant:
◆ **Piccola Vedetta Lombarda**, v. Barche 34, ☎ 854085, closed Fri. Regional cuisine: ass stracotto with polenta, proprietor's red and white wines, 15/35,000.

CASTIGLIONE OLONA*

Varese 9, Milan 46 km
Pop. 7,275 ⊠ 21043 ☎ 0331   A-B3

This rural centre in the wooded Olona Valley was long viewed as a Tuscan enclave in Lombard territory. The town owes its Renaissance grandeur to Cardinal Castiglioni, a free-spending patron who, in the first half of the 15C (just before his death at the age of 93), built almost the entire town.

▶ The **Palazzo Branda Castiglioni,** the cardinal's residence, has a 14C wing, with loggia, and another 15C, with carved portal and windows decorated with terracotta. Inside are *(2.30-5 p.m.; Sat, Sun and hols also 10 a.m.-12.30 p.m.; closed Mon)* halls and rooms with stucco and frescos. ▶ Nearby is the **Chiesa di Villa★,** a church built 1430-41 in the manner of Brunelleschi. The façade is divided into three by pilasters: in the centre is a decorated portal, and on either side colossal statues of St. Antony Abbot and St. Christopher, works of a Veneto-Lombard master. In the interior is the tomb of Count G. Castiglioni. ▶ The Gothic **collegiate church★** (1421), set on a mound, dominates the little town. The carved portal dates from 1428. Inside *(for opening times see Palazzo Branda Castiglioni; Apr-Sep also 10 a.m.-12:30 p.m. daily except Mon)* is the cardinal's tomb, Veneto-Lombard school. There are noteworthy frescos in the **polygonal apse★★.** In the nearby **baptistery★★** is a cycle of **frescos★★** (1435) on the life of St. John. □

Practical information _____

Recommended
Antiques market: in historical centre every first Sun in month, ☎ 857121.
Archery: *Società arcieri,* v. P. Schiavo 53, ☎ 850225.
Motocross: *Impianto Somadeo,* managed by Moto Club Somadeo.

CERTOSA DI PAVIA*

Pavia 8, Milan 27 km
Pop. 2,890 ⊠ 27012 ☎ 0382   B5

The unfinished façade of the church is decorated with dazzling Candoglia and Carrara marble, carved with remarkable sensitivity. Especially striking at Certosa is the contrast between the opulent exterior and the controlled, balanced interior. Here Gian Galeazzo Visconti built in addition to the funerary monuments of himself and his wife, a Carthusian monastery *(certosa)* at the edge of the park of Pavia castle, 'as solemn and notable as possible'. The monastery took more than two centuries to complete from the laying of the foundation stone in August 1396; it displays all the currents of the Lombard Renaissance.

▶ The tour of the charterhouse is guided by a monk *(9-11.30 a.m. and 2:30-6 p.m. or 5 p.m. Mar, Apr, Sep, Oct; 4.30 p.m. in winter; closed Mon but not hols).* In the entrance courtyard is the **Foresteria★** (hostelry; 1625), which stands at r. angles to the ornate **façade★★** of the church (late 15C-mid-16C). ▶ The **church,** transitional in style between Gothic and Renaissance, was completed in 1473. The nave and aisles of the interior are closed off from the transept by a superb 17C grille and flanked by chapels containing fine **paintings★** and **frescos★** by Perugino (15C), Bergognone (15C) and Crespi (17C). There are bronze **candelabra★** by A. Fontana (1580), effigies of **Beatrice d'Este** and **Ludovico il Moro★** by C. Solari (1487), a 15C ivory **triptych★** *(being restored),* wooden choir stalls★ (1498); and the **tomb of Gian Galeazzo Visconti★** (1487). ▶ A door with delightful carvings leads into the **Little Cloister** (1462-72), which has arcades decorated with terra-cotta and a good view of the r. flank of the church. ▶ The monks' cells are arranged around the **Great Cloister.** □

Practical information _____

Restaurant:
♦♦♦ *Vecchio Mulino,* v. Monumento 5, ☎ 925894, closed Sun eve, Mon, Jan and Aug. Old country building adjacent to the Certosa; summer veranda. Regional cuisine: risotto with frogs, tagliatelle with rabbit, 35/60,000.

Recommended
Liqueurs: *Gra Car,* v. Certosa 42, ☎ 925547 (old distillery, using herbs).
Wines: Enoteca Lombarda, in the Certosa.

CHIARI

Brescia 25, Milan 82 km
Pop. 16,585 ⊠ 25032 ☎ 030   C4

Industry and modern building have not destroyed the medieval old town. Behind the 15C **Duomo** (rebuilt 18C) is the church of **S. Maria Maggiore,** also 15C, with 18C façade. The **Pinacoteca Repossi** *(9 a.m.-12:30 p.m. and 2:30-6 p.m.; closed hols and Mon),* with 15C-19C paintings and a notable collection of prints and engravings, is attached to the **Biblioteca Morcelliana** (displaying a theological treatise, the *Secunda Secundae* by Thomas Aquinas, printed in 1467) and the **Biblioteca Comunale.** □

Practical information _____

CHIARI

Restaurant:
♦♦♦ *Zucca,* v. Andreoli 10, ☎ 711739, closed Mon and Aug. Italian cuisine: tagliolini with lemon, scamponi, 20/30,000.

Recommended
Canoeing: at Palazzolo sull'Oglio *(9 km NE),* Canoa club, v. Britannici 1, ☎ 731762.
Wines: at Rovato, Bresciano DOC wine show (Oct); at Erbusco *(10 km NE),* visits to the Longhi de Carli cellar (Franciacorta), ☎ 7267097.

Environs

ROVATO, ⊠ 25038, 7 km NE.

Restaurants:
● ♦♦ *Tortuga:* v. Angelini 12, ☎ 722980, closed Mon, 1-20 Jan and Aug. Excellent cuisine, 45/60,000.
♦♦ *Due Colombe,* v. Bonomelli 17, ☎ 721534, closed Sun and Aug. Italian cuisine: strozzapreti, chicory soup, 30/40,000.

CHIAVENNA

Sondrio 60, Milan 119 km
Pop. 7,687 ⊠ 23022 ☎ 0343   B2

Surrounded by wild mountains, Chiavenna place was once the *chiave* (key) on the Splügen pass. Frederick Barbarossa stopped here, and Swiss from the Grisons occupied the territory, making it their principal base beyond the Alps, and holding it until the late 18C.

▶ In the centre are still many noble 16C-17C **palazzi.** ▶ The church of **S. Lorenzo** (rebuilt after 1538) with 18C four-sided portico and free-standing campanile has a Romanesque font (1156) and a rich **treasury,** with a 12C gospel. ▶ The **Paradiso** rock, on which a castle once stood, now has an archaeological and botanical garden *(2-5 p.m.; Sat and Sun 2-6 p.m.; closed Mon).* ▶ In this region the **crotti** (natural caves) are used as cellars. □

Practical information _____

ⓘ Stazione FS, ☎ 33442.

Hotels:
★★★ *Conradi,* p. Verdi 10, ☎ 32300, 34 rm Ⓟ 46,000.
★★★ *Crimea,* v. Pratogiano 16, ☎ 34343, 36 rm Ⓟ closed 22 Sep-10 Oct, 55,000; bkf: 6,000.

Restaurant:
♦♦ *Cenacolo,* v. Pedretti 16, ☎ 32123, closed Tue eve,

Wed and Jun. Regional cuisine: bresaola, costini al lavecc, 21/35,000.

Recommended
Wines: Festival of the *crotti* (Sep).
▼ inns: *Crotto Refrigerio,* ☎ 34175; *Crotto Ombra,* ☎ 34138 (Pratogiano).

CHIESA IN VALMALENCO

Sondrio 14, Milan 152 km
Pop. 2,847 ✉ 23023 ☎ 0342   C2

The soft local ollare stone takes its name from *olla,* a pot; it is used for making containers and decorative objects as well as houses and roofs. Chiesa is the major centre in Valtellina for this soapstone industry.

▶ From the village with the **Museo della Valmalenco** *(Jul and Aug daily; 5:30-7:30 p.m.; other months Sat p.m.),* there is a magnificent view of the Bernina and Disgrazia groups and of Pizzo Scalino, centres for excursions and climbs. ▶ It is possible to go up to **Alpe Palù** (6,594 ft; *cableway).* ▶ 3.6 km E, **Caspoggio** (3,595 ft) is a holiday and winter sports resort. ▶ 12 km, **Chiareggio** (5,289 ft) is an alpine village in sight of the Disgrazia. ▶ 8 km away is the charming valley of **Franscia** (4,927 ft).   □

Practical information _____

CHIESA IN VALMALENCO
⌁ cableway, ski lifts, cross-country skiing 40 km, instruction, summer skiing at the Entova Scerscen rifugio.
ⓘ p. SS. Giacomo e Filippo 1, ☎ 451150.
🚌 to Sondrio, ☎ 451280; from Sondrio, ☎ 212055.
Hotels:
★★★ *Betulla,* v. Funivia 52/A, ☎ 451100, 31 rm Ⓟ ﹐ closed 1 Oct-31 Nov and 1 May-20 Jun. No restaurant, 46,000.
★★★ *Chalet Rezia,* v. Marconi 27, ☎ 451271, 33 rm Ⓟ ﹐ closed 16 Sep-19 Dec and 21 Apr-14 Jun, 50,000; bkf: 5,000.
★★★ *Tremoggia,* v. Bernina 4, ☎ 451106, 35 rm Ⓟ ﹐ closed 21 Sep-30 Nov and 21 Apr-14 Jun, 50,000; bkf: 5,000.
★★ *Lanterna,* v. Bernina 88, ☎ 451438, 20 rm Ⓟ closed 1 Oct-4 Dec and 1 May-30 Jun, 38,000; bkf: 3,000.
★★ *Pigna d'Oro,* v. Funivia 13, ☎ 451401, 22 rm ﹐ closed Sep-Nov and May-Jun, 35,000; bkf: 5,000.
Restaurant:
◆ *Castel,* at Costi, ☎ 451355, closed Thu, 16 Sep-30 Nov and 16 Apr-14 Jun. Regional cuisine: risotto with mushrooms, carpaccio, 30/45,000.

Recommended
Alpine guides: *Casa delle guide alpine Valmalenco,* information office, ☎ 451150; *P. Masa* head guide, ☎ 352016 (alpine climbs, instruction in rock-climbing and climbing on ice, trekking along the Alta Via della Valmalenco).
Excursions: by cableway to Lake Palù, ☎ 451284.
Palazzotto dello sport: in Comune, ☎ 451114.
▼ pietra ollare (soapstone): visit to caves and production facilities: *Gaggi,* v. Roma 2, ☎ 451283; *Bagiolo,* v. Marconi 35, ☎ 451266.

Environs

CASPOGGIO, ✉ 23020, ☎ 0342, 3 km E.
⌁ chair lifts, ski lifts, ski instruction, skating.
ⓘ municipio, ☎ 451135 (in season).

CIVATE

Como 24, Milan 51 km
Pop. 3,183 ✉ 22040 ☎ 0341   B3

The simple, 11C church of **S. Pietro al Monte**★★ *(1hr 15 min by mule-track from Civate; keys with*

the caretaker at Civate) is one of the most distinctive examples of Romanesque architecture in Lombardy. Inside are a fine 11C **ciborium,** decorated with stucco and bas-reliefs★, and **frescos**★in Byzantine style. In front of the church is the 11C oratory of **S. Benedetto.**   □

Practical information _____

Restaurant:
◆ *Cascina Edvige,* at Roncaglio 11, ☎ 550350, closed Tue and Aug. Rural restaurant in old farmhouse. Italian cuisine: fresh pasta, brasato al Barolo, 20/30,000.
△ ★★ *2 Lakes,* at Isella, v. al Lago, 160 pl, ☎ 550101.

CLUSONE

Bergamo 34, Milan 80 km
Pop. 8,048 ✉ 24033 ☎ 0346   C3

Between the Seriana and Borlezza Valleys (which descend toward Lake Iseo) lies a plateau. This is the site of Clusone, main centre of the Seriana Valley and an important tourist resort. In the old town, where much medieval architecture survives, there are relics of the time when Clusone was the seat of the *nobile patrizio,* the Venetian magistrate of the region.

▶ The tower of the 15C Palazzo Comunale has an elaborate **astronomical** clock (1583), the invention of a local craftsman. ▶ To the l. of the tower the way leads to the basilica of **S. Maria Assunta** (late 17C), which has 17C sculpture and interesting paintings of the Venetian school. ▶ Opposite, on the façade of the oratorio dei Disciplini (15C) is a renowned fresco of the *Triumph of Death*★ (1485).   □

Practical information _____

⌁ cross-country skiing at La Spessa and Pianone, ski instruction.
ⓘ p. dell'Orologio 21, ☎ 21113.
△ ★★ *Clusone Pineta,* at Fiorine, v. Valflex, 340 pl, ☎ 22144 (all year).

COLICO

Como 69, Milan 97 km
Pop. 5,533 ✉ 22050 ☎ 0341   B2

Colico is a large village in the extreme N of the eastern shore of Lake Como. Here the road divides, one section leading to Valtellina, the other to the Splügen pass and the Engadine. 4 km N is a haven for flowers and wild life: **Pian di Spagna,** where there is a colony of royal swans. 6 km S is the **abbey of Piona** (11C) on a peninsula separating Lake Como from the Laghetto di Piona, former refuge of pirates and brigands. The church has frescos in the Byzantine style and a fine Romanesque-Gothic **cloister** (1257). □

Practical information _____

≋
ⓘ v. Nazionale 122, ☎ 940468.
⛵ boats and hydrofoils, ☎ 940815.

Hotels:
★★★ *Risi,* lungolago Polti 1, ☎ 940123, 64 rm, closed Oct-Feb, 50,000; bkf: 5,000. Rest. ◆◆◆ closed Nov-Feb. Regional cuisine: river perch dorato with pilau rice, lavarello mugnaia, 20/25,000.
★★ *Gigi,* v. Legnone 4, ☎ 940268, 14 rm Ⓟ closed 15-31 May and 15-30 Nov, 48,000; bkf: 6,000. Rest. ☎ 940703, closed Thu, May and Nov. Regional and

Italian cuisine: pappardelle with mushrooms, poultry with polenta, 29/30,000.

⚐ ★★ *Baia di Piona*, at Laghetto, v. Nazionale Sud, 31 pl, ☎ 941473.

Recommended
Hang gliding: *Scuola Volario*, v. Nazionale Nord 33, ☎ 940425.
Sailing: base of the *Lega Navale of Milan* (→ Dervio), at S. Cecilia *(10.5 km SW)*, ☎ 850672 (Mar-Oct, introductory sailing courses and courses for experienced sailors).

COMO*

Milan 45, Rome 630 km
Pop. 94,634 ✉ 22100 ☎ 031   B3

High above the city like a sentinel stands the Baradello tower *(torre)*, a reminder of bloody rivalry with Milan in the period when Como sided 'with the strong, and abandoned the League'. Como gained protection from Frederick Barbarossa, then, in 1183, its independence. The former Roman outpost soon fell to the duchy of Milan. Inventiveness, enterprise, tenacity and a capacity for hard work restored in other fields the prestige that Como had been denied on the political scene. Como and the surrounding

area produced master builders who spread the Lombard style of architecture from the medieval period and beyond in Italy and abroad. In the first decades of the 20C, it was in Como that contemporary Italian architecture produced some of its most important buildings. The city is above all renowned for silk manufacturing and trading which formed the basis of its economy from the 16C onwards.

▶ The 11C church of **S. Abbondio★** (C2) is a fine example of Lombard Romanesque architecture, with an impressive façade and apse flanked by two bell towers. Inside are pleasing frescos by 17C Lombard painters. ▶ The **city walls** built by Frederick Barbarossa (the entire W side and other shorter stretches have survived) follow the layout of the Roman city. Within this area, the medieval **old town** still clearly shows the rectilinear plan of the Roman camp. ▶ It is possible to enter the **Porta Torre** (B2-3), a rare example of Romanesque military architecture. ▶ Not far away is the **Museo Civico** (B3; *8:30 a.m.-12 noon and 2-5 p.m., or 2:30-5:30 p.m. in summer; Sun 9.15 a.m.-12 noon; closed Mon*) with exhibits on archaeology and local history. ▶ The p. S. Fedele (B2), the ancient and charming centre of city life, is surrounded by medieval houses with low arcades; the basilica of **S. Fedele** (12C), the town's first cathedral, has an interesting polygonal apse topped with a small balcony and flanked by a portal decorated with sculpture. The principal axis of the old town leads along the v. Vittorio

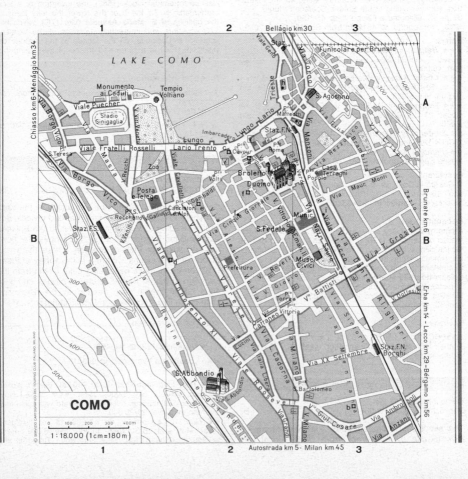

Emanuele (B2-3) and past the arcades of the v. Plinio (A2). ▶ Between the two streets is the **piazza del Duomo,** the most imposing of the city's squares. ▶ The tall, severe, **Torre del Comune** (1215; restored) rises above the **palazzo del Broletto★** (B2), a Romanesque-Gothic building contemporary with the tower, with pilastered portico and polychrome marble façade (15C). ▶ The **Duomo★★**, next to the Broletto, is a typical Lombard Renaissance building. It was begun in 1396 but not finished until the 17C. The cupola was added in 1744. The two 16C statues on either side of the portal represent the Elder and the Younger Pliny (the Roman historians), who were born in Como. In the interior are fine 16C Flemish and Ferrara **tapestries;** on the altars, bas-reliefs and paintings. ▶ The **casa dei Terragni** (A-B3) is an example of functionalist architecture, the work of the architect G. Terragni (1932-6). ▶ A little farther, between the hill and the lake, is the 14C church of **S. Agostino** (A3), a Gothic building with Romanesque carved portal and in the interior, 15C-17C frescos and paintings. ▶ In the p. Matteotti is the beginning of the **Lungolario** (A3), a tree-lined walk that skirts the harbour and the modern p. Cavour and leads to the public park containing the **Tempio Voltiano** (A1; *10 a.m.-12 noon and 3-6 p.m.; closed Mon*) dating from 1927, a museum displaying memorabilia relating to Alessandro Volta (1745-1827), inventor of the electric battery, who was born and died in Como. ▶ The v. Borgo Vico (B1-2) runs through a district known for its fine Neoclassical villas, the most striking of which is the Villa Olmo, by S. Cantoni (1782-97), where exhibitions, congresses and concerts are now held. ▶ 3 km away, with an impressive view, are the remains of the **Castello Baradello,** built in 1158 by Barbarossa and dismantled by the Spanish in the 16C. A detour can be made to **S. Carpaforo** (11C-12C). ▶ **Brunate** *(funicular, 6 km by road),* a summer resort on a wooded plateau, looks out over the city and the lake. □

Practical information

COMO

ℹ p. Cavour (A2), ☎ 262091; p. Cavour 33 ☎ 265592.
🚆 (B1), ☎ 261494; Railways Nord Milan: stations Camerlata, ☎ 501595; Borghi (C3), ☎ 266314; Lago (A3), ☎ 266313.
🚌 from p. Matteotti, p. del Popolo and portici Plinio, ☎ 73133.
⛴ boats and hydrofoils (A2), ☎ 260234.
Car rental: *Avis,* v. Manzoni 18, ☎ 266174; *Hertz,* v. Masia 77, ☎ 551307.

Hotels:
★★★★ ***Barchetta Excelsior,*** p. Cavour 1 (A2 a), ☎ 266531, 59 rm Ⓟ ♿ 148,000; bkf: 12,000.
★★★★ ***Como,*** v. Mentana 28 (C3 b), ☎ 266173, 72 rm Ⓟ ♿ closed Christmas. No restaurant, 100,000; bkf: 8,500.
★★★★ ***Metropole & Suisse,*** p. Cavour 19 (A2 c), ☎ 269444, 70 rm Ⓟ No restaurant, 110,000; bkf: 13,000.
★★★★ ***Villa Flori,*** v. Cernobbio 12, ☎ 557642, 42 rm Ⓟ ♿ closed 15 Dec-20 Jan. No restaurant, 110,000; bkf: 8,000.
★★★ ***Continental,*** v. Innocenzo XI 15 (B2 d), ☎ 260485, 66 rm Ⓟ 89,000.
★★★ ***Plinius,*** v. Garibaldi 33 (B2 e), ☎ 273067, 31 rm Ⓟ closed Dec-Feb. No restaurant, 80,500; bkf: 7,000.
★★ ***Tre Re,*** v. Boldoni 20 (B2 f), ☎ 265374, 32 rm Ⓟ closed 15 Dec-5 Jan, 68,000: bkf: 7,000.

Restaurants:
♦♦♦ ***Fiorentina,*** v. Carso 69, ☎ 271042, closed Wed and Dec. Garden for meals. Italian cuisine: tortellachi with mushrooms, bocconcini with mushrooms, 30/45,000.
♦♦♦ ***Hosterietta,*** lungolario Trieste 54 (A2 h), ☎ 275312, closed Mon. Terrace facing lake. Regional cuisine: risotto with mushrooms, spaghetti in foil, 30/45,000.
♦♦♦ ***Imbarcadero,*** p. Cavour 20 (A2 c), ☎ 277341, closed 1-15 Jan. Can be very crowded in season. Italian cuisine: lavarello with butter and sage, chateaubriand, 23/45,000.
♦♦♦ ***Pizzi,*** v. Geno 12, ☎ 266100, closed Thu and New Year's Day. Lake views in summer. Regional cuisine: gnocchetti verdi, lavarello with butter and sage, 30/45,000.
♦♦♦ ***Sant'Anna,*** at Camerlata, v. Turati 3, ☎ 505266, closed Fri, Sat noon and 25 Jul-25 Aug. Italian cuisine: tagliolini with Alba truffle, baked fillet with herbs, 35/60,000.
♦♦♦ ***Trattoria del Gesumin,*** v. V. Giornate 44 (B2 l), ☎ 266030, closed Sun and Aug. Attractive setting in old inn. Italian cuisine: porcini omelette, guinea fowl with herbs, 45/60,000.
● ♦♦ ***Angela,*** v. Foscolo 16 (A3 g), ☎ 263460, closed Mon and Aug. In a former monastery. Piedmontese cuisine: homemade tagliatelle, bagna cauda, 35/45,000.
♦♦ ***Silenzio,*** v. Lecco 25 (B3 i), ☎ 260298, closed Sat and Aug. Regional cuisine: missoltitt, soused agoni, 25/30,000.

⛺ ★★ *International,* at Breccia, v. Cecilio, 200 pl, ☎ 501636.

Recommended
Aeroclub: v. Marsia 44, ☎ 559882.
Archery: *Compagnia arcieri cumacini,* v. Indipendenza 20, ☎ 262295.
Cycling: *Cral Banco Lariano,* v. Cavour 15, ☎ 271356.
Events: *Motonautica del Lario,* a 100-mile boat race (1st Sun in Oct).
Excursions: at Brunate, cable railway (A2), ☎ 269311.
Golf: *Villa d'Este,* at Montorfano, ☎ 200200 (18 holes); *Monticello,* at Cassina Rizzardi, v. Volta 4, ☎ 928055 (18 + 18 holes); *La Pinetina,* at Appiano Gentile, ☎ 933202 (18 holes); at Carimate, v. Airoldi 2, ☎ 790226 (18 holes).
Hang gliding: *Week End's Fly,* at Fino Mornasco, v. Roma 22, ☎ 929019.
Horseback riding: *Centro equitazione Lariano,* at Lurate Caccivio, v. Plinio 45, ☎ 491352; *Dany Ranch,* at Lurago Marinone (18 km SW), v. della Pace 5, ☎ 935183 (associate of *ANTE*); *Centro equitazione Comasco,* at Grandate, ☎ 450235.
Ice skating: Breccia, ☎ 505118.
Marina: ☎ 277318.
Natural parks: *Pineta di Appiano Gentile e Tradate* is a regional park at Castelnuovo Bozzente, municipio, ☎ 9882203; *Oasi Torbiere di Albate,* closed mid-Jun-Aug, reservations at *WWF Lombardia,* ☎ 02/653251.
Silk: visits to *Centro della seta,* ☎ 288111, factory at Grandate (*6 km SE,* exit from the autostrada), ☎ 4521102 (closed Sun and Mon a.m.); *Seteria Ratti,* Villa Sucota (road to Cernobbio), ☎ 233111, factory at Guanzate *(14 km S),* ☎ 233111 (Tue-Sat).
Sports hall: Muggiò, ☎ 503744.
Swimming: Muggiò, ☎ 559986.
Tennis: *Camerlata,* v. Belvedere 15, ☎ 501947 (also skating).
Water skiing: Lecco (→), Lake Como.
Youth hostel: *Ostello Villa Olmo,* v. Bellinzona 2, ☎ 558722.

Environs

CAMNAGO VOLTA, ✉ 22030, 3 km E.

Restaurant:
♦♦♦ ***Navedano,*** v. Pannilani, ☎ 261080, closed Tue and 15-30 Aug. In the hills, with garden and fine summer terrace. Italian cuisine: spaghetti with salmon and caviar, gnocchetti with porcini, 35/50,000.

Lake COMO

From Lecco *(119 km, 1 day; map 3)*

Since the time of Pliny the Younger (1C AD) this pre-alpine glacial basin has often been hailed as the most beautiful lake in the world. Enthusiasm for Lake Como stems from a pleasing interaction of geographical and human elements. Lake Como has three roughly equal arms: Como to the SW, Lecco to the

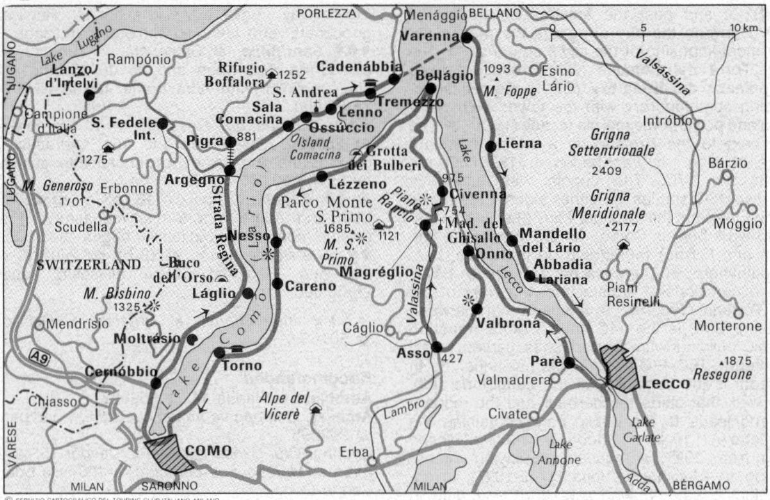

3. Lake Como

SE and Colico to the N. These arms are enclosed by shores that never seem too steep or too flat, in a landscape of rare variety and balance. Ancient transit routes have laid down successive layers of culture and settlement that have enriched life on the lake shore and enhanced the diversity of the environment. The fascination of lake Como lies not just in the aristocratic villas with luxuriant parks lining roads and reaching to the water with their jetties, but also in picturesque villages so steeped in history that they seem like marine republics in miniature.

▶ From **Lecco** (→) the road leads to **Onno,** an outlying district of Oliveto Lario on the W bank of the Lecco arm of the lake, then rises to **Valbrona,** a scattered community in the valley of the same name, with view of the lake and the Grigne Mountains. ▶ **Magreglio,** the principal summer resort, is the starting point for excursions to the **Ghisallo** pass (2,474 ft; *wonderful views*★) on which is the santuario della **Madonna del Ghisallo,** patroness of cyclists; to **Piano Rancio** (3,199 ft) and **Parco Monte San Primo** (3,839 ft), a small, grassy valley surrounded by woods, from which it takes 1 hr 30 mn to walk to the **Monte San Primo** (5,512 ft; *superb view*★). ▶ Beyond the little summer resort of **Civenna,** almost overhanging the lake, the road descends to **Ballagio** (→). ▶ From **Lézzeno,** on the E shore of the Como arm, boat trips are available to the **Bulberi grotto** (Villa district). ▶ **Nesso** is famous for a picturesque **gorge** and waterfall. There is an interesting little church of **S. Martino** (12C) in the **Careno** district. ▶ The parish church of **S. Tecla,** on the lake in **Torno,** is worth a visit, with Gothic portal and rose-window dating from 1480; also the church of **S. Giovanni** (14C), with Romanesque campanile and Renaissance portal. **Villa Pliniana** *(private; visible from the lake),* built by Count Anguissola in 1573, is remarkable for a strange, intermittent waterfall in the grounds, which was described by Pliny the Elder in his *Natural History.* ▶ From Como (→) the road leads to **Cernobbio** and the spacious grounds of the **Villa d'Este,** now one of the most luxurious hotels in Europe. A twisting road climbs to **Monte Bisbino** (4,360 ft; *fine view*★). Follow the line of the old **strada Regina,** which runs between the villas facing the lake, past the resorts of **Moltrasio** (from which it is possible to climb to the 11C church of **S. Marta**) and **Laglio,** departure point for excursions to the cave called **Buco dell'Orso** *(c.* 2,000 ft; *ask at town hall).* ▶ From **Argegno** it is possible to climb the Intelvi valley (→ Lanzo d'Intelvi); cableway to **Pigra** (2,890 ft) on a plateau with fine view of the lake. ▶ Opposite **Sala Comacina** is the **island of Comacina,** the only one in the lake, with the church of **S. Giovanni** (15C). Along the road are numerous Romanesque buildings: the little church of **S. Maria Maddalena** in **Ossuccio** has an unusual bell tower with Gothic brick bell chamber; the church of **S. Andrea** (11C) in **Casanova;** the 11C-12C crypt in the parish church and an 11C baptistery in **Lenno.** ▶ **Tremezzo** is an elegant resort in sight of the Bellagio promontory. Just outside the town is the entrance to the magnificent **Villa Carlotta**★ *(Apr-Sep 9 a.m.-6 p.m.; Mar and Oct 9-11:30 a.m. and 2-6:30 p.m.),* dating from 1747, famous for its large park on the lake (displays of azaleas and rhododendrons) and for the works of art in the villa. ▶ From **Cadenabbia,** a resort, a ferry crosses to **Varenna,** a picturesque town on a ridge of Monte Foppe on the E shore of the lake. The 14C parish church of **S. Giorgio** has 14C-16C frescos and paintings; picturesque ruins of the Castello di Vezio. ▶ On the E shore of the lake, more wooded and with a less favourable climate, there are fewer villas and holiday resorts. Exceptions are **Lierna** and the industrial centre of **Mandello del Lario,** at the foot of the Grigne mountains, now almost amalgamated with nearby **Abbadia Lariana.** □

Practical information

ABBADIA LARIANA, ⊠ 22050, ☎ 0341.

▲ ★★★ *Spiaggia,* v. Torrente Zerbo 5, 80 pl, ☎ 731621.

ARGEGNO, ⊠ 22010, ☎ 031.

≋

boats and hydrofoils, ☎ 821229.

Recommended
Excursions: cableway to Pigra (2,890 ft), ☎ 821344.

CADENABBIA, ⊠ 22011, ☎ 0344.
≋
ℹ v. Regina 1, ☎ 40393.
⛴ boats, car ferry for Bellagio and Varenna, ☎ 40479.

Hotel:
★★★ ***Britannia Excelsior,*** v. Regina 41, ☎ 40413, 152 rm 🅿 ☀ ⚘ ♿ 📺 closed Nov-Mar, 75,000.

CERNOBBIO, ⊠ 22012, ☎ 031.
ℹ v. Regina 33/b, ☎ 510198.
⛴ boats, ☎ 510094.

Hotels:
★★★★★ ***G. H. Villa d'Este,*** v. Regina 40, ☎ 511471, 182 rm 🅿 ⚘ 📺 🎾 ⛳ (18) closed Nov-Mar. Splendid Renaissance villa in an old park, 500,000.
★★★★ ***Regina Olga-Reine du Lac,*** v. Regina 18, ☎ 510171, 67 rm 🅿 ⚘ ♿ 📺 132,000; bkf: 15,000.
★★★ ***Asnigo,*** p. S. Stefano, ☎ 510062, 30 rm 🅿 ☀ ⚘ ♿ 📺 92,000; bkf: 9,000.
★★★ ***Miralago,*** p. Risorgimento 1, ☎ 510125, 30 rm, closed Nov-14 Mar, 75,000.

Recommended
Cycling: *Ciclistica Cernobbio,* v. Regina, ☎ 511663.
Water skiing: *Sci club Villa d'Este,* v. Regina 40, ☎ 511471.

LAGLIO, ⊠ 22010, ☎ 031.

Hotel:
★★★★ ***Plinio-Casa Svizzera,*** v. Regina 101, ☎ 400135, 25 rm 🅿 ☀ ♿ ❄ 150,000.

LENNO, ⊠ 22016, ☎ 0344.
⛴ boats and hydrofoils.

Hotel:
★★★ ***San Giorgio,*** v. Regina 81, ☎ 40415, 29 rm 🅿 ☀ ⚘ ❄ 🎾 closed 6 Oct-14 Apr, 80,000; bkf: 7,000.

Recommended
Water skiing: *Idrosciatori Isola,* at Ossuccio *(2 km),* v. Regina 80, ☎ 55142.

LEZZENO, ⊠ 22025, ☎ 031.

Restaurant:
♦♦ ***Crotto del Misto,*** at Crotto 10, ☎ 914495, closed Tue except summer and Dec-Feb. Lake view, terrace and harbour. Cuisine of lake fish: coregone in pastry with black butter, Como filets with orange, home-produced wines, 30/40,000.

Recommended
Visits to boatyards: *Molinari shipyards,* ☎ 914533; *Mostes,* ☎ 914560 (motorboat yards).
Water skiing: *Jolly racing club,* v. Sossana 2, ☎ 914645; *Morgan skiing club,* at Crotto, ☎ 914541.

LIERNA, ⊠ 22050, ☎ 0341.

Restaurant:
♦♦♦ ***Crotto,*** v. Ducale 42, ☎ 740134, closed Tue and Oct. Regional cuisine: vegetable pancakes, gnocchetti with vegetables, charcoal-grilled fish and meat, 27/35,000.

MAGREGLIO, ⊠ 22030, ☎ 031.
⛷ ski lifts and ski instruction at Piano Rancio and Parco Monte San Primo.
ℹ v. Adua, ☎ 965325.

MANDELLO DEL LARI, ⊠ 22054, ☎ 0341.
≋
ℹ at Lecco, ☎ 362360.

Recommended
Marina: *Lega Navale,* ☎ 730355.

MENAGGIO, ⊠ 22017 ☎ 0344, 4 km N of Cadenabbia.
≋
ℹ p. Garibaldi 8, ☎ 32334.
⛴ hydrofoil for Como, Bellagio and Bellano; car ferry to Varenna.

Hotels:
★★★★ ***G. H. Victoria,*** v. Castelli 7, ☎ 32003, 53 rm 🅿 ⚘ ❄ 📺 closed Jan, 130,000; bkf: 13,000.
★★★ ***Bellavista,*** v. IV Novembre 21, ☎ 32136, 37 rm 🅿 ☀ closed 16 Oct-31 Mar, 63,000; bkf: 6,000.
★★ ***Miralogo,*** at Nobiallo, v. Diaz. 32, ☎ 32363, 26 rm 🅿 ⚘ ♿ closed 1 Nov-15 Mar, 50,000; bkf: 4,000.

Restaurant:
♦ ***Paolino,*** p. Cavour 4, ☎ 32335, closed Tue and Nov. Regional cuisine: risotto alla paesana, gnocchi alla parigina, lake fish, 28/40,000.

Recommended
Bowls: ☎ 32259.
Golf: *Golf club Menaggio e Cadenabbia,* at Gràndola *(3.5 km),* v. Golf 12, ☎ 32103 (closed Dec-Feb; 18 holes).
Youth hostel: *Ostello La Primula,* v. IV Novembre 38, ☎ 32356.

MOLTRASIO, ⊠ 22010, ☎ 031.
≋

Hotels:
★★★ ***Caramazza,*** v. Besana 50, ☎ 290050, 19 rm 🅿 ☀ ⚘ closed 26 Oct-24 Mar, 72,000; bkf: 7,000.
★★ ***Posta,*** p. S. Rocco 5, ☎ 290280, 20 rm, closed Jan-Feb, 60,000; bkf: 4,500.

SALA COMACINA, ⊠ 22010, ☎ 0344.

Restaurants:
♦♦ ***Locanda dell'Isola,*** at Isola Comacina, ☎ 55083, closed Tue except mid-Jun-mid-Sep and Nov-Feb. Romantic rural setting on island in lake. Regional cuisine: single menu, cooked and served with a flourish, 56/58,000.
♦♦ ***Taverna Bleu,*** v. Puricelli 4, ☎ 55107, closed Tue and 1-20 Sep. Garden with lake view. Cuisine of lake fish: risotto with river perch, agoni and lavarelli with butter and sage, 25/30,000.

TORNO, ⊠ 22020, ☎ 031.

Restaurants:
♦♦♦ ***Vapore,*** v. Plinio 20, ☎ 419311, closed Wed and Nov-Feb. Terrace for summer service; some accommodation. Italian cuisine: tagliolini ai porcini, baked lavarello, 25/40,000.
♦♦ ***Taverne du Clochard,*** v. Poggi 27, ☎ 419022, closed Mon, wkday noon and 15 Jan-15 Feb. In small villa on a promontory with fine views of lake. International cuisine: trout with pink pepper, grilled entrecote with herbs, 32/38,000.

TREMEZZO, ⊠ 22019, ☎ 0344.
ℹ p. Trieste 3, ☎ 40493.
⛴ boats and hydrofoils, ☎ 40457.

Hotels:
★★★★ ***Bazzoni et Du Lac,*** v. Regina 26, ☎ 40403, 125 rm ☀ ❄ closed Nov-Mar, 100,000; bkf: 6,000.
★★★★ ***G. H. Tremezzo,*** v. Regina 8, ☎ 40446, 105 rm 🅿 ☀ ⚘ 📺 🎾 ⛳ (18) closed Nov-Mar, 126,000; bkf: 12,000.

Restaurant:
● ♦♦♦ ***Veluu,*** v. Rogaro 11, ☎ 40510, closed Tue and Nov-Feb. Rural with magnificent views. Italian cuisine: lake fish, baked lamb and kid, 30/45,000.

⛺ ★★★ *Degli Ulivi,* at Bolvedro, v. Sala 18, 80 pl, ☎ 40161.

Recommended
Visits to boatyards: *Abate,* ☎ 40122 (motorboats).

VARENNA, ⊠ 22050, ☎ 0341.
ℹ v. Venini 6, ☎ 830367.
⛴ car ferry for Bellagio, Menaggio and Cadenabbia, ☎ 830270.

Hotels:
★★★★ ***Du Lac,*** v. del Prestino 4, ☎ 830238, 18 rm 🅿 ☀ ⚘ closed 2-31 Jan, 105,000; bkf: 9,000.

★★★★ *Royal Victoria,* p. S. Giorgio 5, ☎ 830102, 45 rm 🌾 🎯 80,000; bkf: 7,000.

Restaurant:
● ♦ *Montecodeno,* v. Croce, ☎ 830123, closed Tue and Feb. Traditional rustic restaurant, service in open air in summer. Seafood; soused fish, fish pâté, penne with smoked trout, 30/45,000.

Recommended
Marina: *Club nautico,* v. Lido 1, ☎ 830272.

CREMA

Cremona 39, Milan 44 km
Pop. 34,287 ⊠ 26013 ☎ 0373   C4

Perched on Fulcheria, an island of rock amid swamps and marshes, Crema has been a free municipality since the 11C. A textile industry founded by monks dominated the local economy for centuries. Crema was destroyed by Frederick Barbarossa, but eventually found stability under Venice, of which it was for centuries an enclave within the Duchy of Milan. The old town within the walls was built in that period.

▶ The nucleus of the town was the **piazza del Duomo,** surrounded by arcaded buildings and dominated by the **Duomo★** (A2), Lombard Gothic, built 1284-1341; the false façade with two side windows open to the sky is an unusual interpretation of a model common in the plain of the Po. The interior, redesigned in the 18C, contains works by a 15C Crema painter, Civerchio. Opposite the church is the **Palazzo del Comune** (1525), which bears the stamp of the Venetian Renaissance. ▶ There are numerous interesting 16C-18C palazzi scattered around the old town, as well as the Baroque church of **SS. Trinità** (A1; 1739) with two vigorous façades and an elegant campanile. ▶ The Renaissance church of **S. Maria della Croce** *(1 km)* is built in the style of Bramante. ⬜

Practical information _____

Hotel:
★★★★ *Palace,* v. Cresmiero 10 (B1 a), ☎ 814487, 46 rm 🅿 🎯 🍽 closed 1-15 Aug. No restaurant, 88,000; bkf: 7,000.

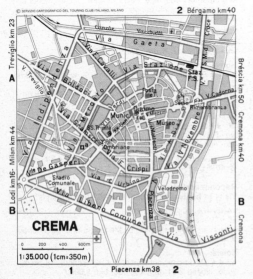

CREMA
0   200   400   600m
1:35.000 (1cm=350m)
1   Piacenza km38   2

Restaurants:
♦♦♦ *Barbarossa,* v. Cresmiero 6 (B1 a), ☎ 81864, closed Thu and Aug. Italian cuisine: gnocchetti del buongustaio, medallions of veal with celery, 25/35,000.
♦♦ *Guada 'l Canal,* at San Stefano, v. Crocicchio, ☎ 200133, closed Sun eve, Mon and Aug. In old farm house on bank of Vacchelli canal. Creative cuisine: prawn risotto, saddle of rabbit with basil, 35/50,000.
♦ *Benpensata,* at Ombrianio *(4 km W),* v. R. Ceri 81, ☎ 30193, closed Mon eve, Tue and Aug. Regional cuisine: risotto Mariuccia, pisarei e fasoi, tortelli alla cremasca, 25/45,000.

Recommended
Horseback riding: *Tenuta Corti,* at Pieranica (10 km NW), ☎ 71274 (associate of *ANTE).*

CREMONA*

Milan 81, Rome 516 km
Pop. 79,370 ⊠ 26100 ☎ 0372   D5

A tenacious appetite for freedom helped Cremona to hold back the Lombards for 65 years and to resist any kind of domination, although it always remained within the Duchy of Milan. Its wealth and strength have always been derived from a crucial position near rivers and principal roads, but especially from the soil, which is moist, loamy and fertile. The landscape around Cremona is dominated by dairy farms. The people of Cremona established a flourishing agricultural industry, cultivated the art of gastronomy, and achieved fame for the mysterious sensitivity with which they were able to fashion fine woods to make stringed instruments of unsurpassed sonority.

▶ The **piazza del Comune★★** (B2; the civic, religious and artistic centre) is marked from afar by the **Torrazzo★,** the tallest campanile in Italy (364 ft), which was built in two phases (the base in 1267; the Gothic arched top section from 1287 to the early 14C); on the side facing the square is a 16C clock, with 17C face *(Sun 10 a.m.-12 noon and 3 p.m.-dusk).* It is worth climbing the 487 steps for the view which extends as far as the Alps and the Apennines. ▶ The **Torrazzo** is connected to the cathedral by the **portico della Bertazzola** (1525); beneath the loggia are marbles and 14C sarcophagi. ▶ The **Duomo★★** (B2) is a group of 12C-14C Romanesque buildings, onto which Gothic, Renaissance and Baroque features have been grafted. An example of this mixture of styles is the main **façade★,** with a striking marble frieze showing **agricultural tasks.** The **interior★** is architecturally austere but has lavish decoration, including five Flemish **tapestries** of the story of Samson. The walls of the nave and central apse are decorated with a **fresco★★** cycle by various Lombard and Veneto painters of the 16C (including B. Boccaccino, G. Romanino and Pordenone; the two **pulpits★** in front of the sanctuary have reliefs attributed to G. A. Piatti and G. A. Amadeo (15C). ▶ The octagonal Romanesque **Baptistery★** (B2) is on the S side of the square (1167, rebuilt in the 16C); inside, beneath a slate dome, is a 16C font. The red-brick façades of the civic buildings form a symbolic counterpoint to the white marble of the religious monuments. ▶ The **Loggia dei Militi** (B-C2) was built in 1292 for meetings of the town's military commanders. ▶ Next to it is the **Palazzo del Comune★** (D2) dating from 1206-47 (restored), ancient seat of city government (also called palazzo dei Nobili or dei Ghibellini to distinguish it from the **palazzo dei Guelfi** →); on a room inside *(9 a.m.-12 noon and 3-5 p.m.; Sat and Sun a.m. only)* four magnificent violins are on display, masterpieces of violin-makers A. Amati (1566), N. Amati (1658), A. Stradivari (1715) and G. Guarneri (1734). ▶ The noble violin-making tradition is kept alive by the **Istituto Professionale Liutario e del Legno,** housed in the modern Palazzo del Arte (C2). ▶ Not far away is the 16C church of **S. Pie-**

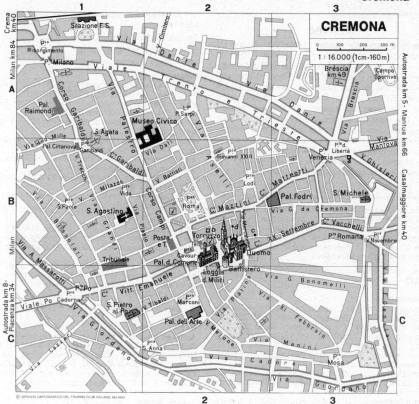

tro al Po (C1), notable for charming pictorial decoration in the interior. ▶ Visitors interested in the old violin-makers, particularly Stradivari, should visit the **Museo Stradivariano** at v. Palestro 17 (A1), in the 16C Palazzo Affaitati, opening times same as the **Museo Civico★** (*9:30 a.m.-12:30 p.m. and 3-6 p.m.; Sun a.m. only, closed Mon*) with various collections and an art gallery with medieval frescos and Italian painting from the 15C to the present day (in particular of the Cremona school). ▶ Other aristocratic Renaissance palazzi are to be found in the old town, including the **Palazzo Raimondi** (A1), dating from 1496, with a fine façade and picturesque courtyard; the palazzo houses the international violin-making school. ▶ Not far away is the **Palazzo dei Guelfi** or di Cittanova (B1), dating from 1256, with Gothic portico, merlons and three-arched windows. ▶ A little farther is the Gothic façade of the church of **S. Agostini★** (B1; *1345, much restored*). ▶ Away from the historic centre, toward the walls, are the 16C **Palazzo Fodri** (B2-3) with elegant façade and pretty courtyard, and the Romanesque church of **S. Michele** (B3; 12C).

Environs

▶ The church of **S. Sigismondo** (*2.5 km beyond the porta Romana*, B3), rebuilt after 1463, and lavishly decorated with 16C painting and frescos of the Cremona school; Bianca Maria and Francesco Sforza were married here in 1441. ▶ The **Museo della Civiltà Contadina** near

the Cascina Cambonino (*v. Castelleone 51, main road to Milan; 9 a.m.-12:30 p.m. and 3-6 p.m.; Sun 9:30 a.m.-12:30 p.m.; closed Mon*). ▶ At **Piádena** (*30 km towards Mantua*) is the **Museo Civico 'Platina'** (*9:30 a.m.-12:30 p.m. and 3:30-6:30 p.m., by arrangement, not Tue and Sat a.m.,* ☎ *0375 98125 or in the town hall, closed Sat p.m. and Sun*), with finds from the neolithic and Lombard periods. □

Practical information ⎯⎯⎯⎯⎯⎯⎯⎯

CREMONA

🛈 p. del Comune 8 (B2), ☎ 23233.
🚄 (A1), ☎ 22237.
🚌 from p. Marconi (C2).

Hotels:

★★★★ **Continental,** p. Libertà 26 (B3 a), ☎ 434141, 57 rm Ⓟ ♿ ⊘ 95,000; bkf: 8,000.
★★★ **Astoria,** v. Bordigallo 19 (B2 b), ☎ 30260, 32 rm Ⓟ No restaurant, 45,000.

Restaurants:

♦♦♦♦ **Ceresole,** v. Ceresole 4 (B2 c), ☎ 23322, closed Sun eve, Mon, Jan and Aug. Regional and Italian cuisine: risotto with eel, sea bass with cardoons, 35/50,000.
♦♦ **Dordoni,** v. del Sale 58, ☎ 22703, closed Mon eve, Tue, Jan and Aug. Italian cuisine: ricotta sfogliatina, potato gnocchi, 20/30,000.

Torrone

Lombardy's exquisite nougat confection bears no resemblance to the 'tower' suggested by its name. Nevertheless, the nougat has some connection with a tower. In 1441 Duke Filippo Maria Visconti gave the city of Cremona as dowry to his daughter Bianca Maria on her marriage to Francesco Sforza, the powerful captain of soldiers of fortune. The dessert at the wedding banquet paid homage to Cremona: it was a monumental confection of egg whites, honey and toasted almonds in the shape of the great bell tower, (364 ft high) of the Cremona Duomo. It is well known, however, that the bell tower in Cremona is called not torrone but torrazzo.

♦ **Alba,** v. Persico 40, ☎ 433700, closed Sun, Mon, 25 Jul-20 Aug and Christmas. Italian cuisine: gnocchetti verdi with gorgonzola, meat braised in Barolo, 18/25,000.
♦ **Cigno,** vicolo Cigno 7 (B2 d), ☎ 21361, closed Sun. In middle of old town. Regional cuisine: black spaghetti, tagliolini with truffles, 28/42,000.

⚐ ☆☆ *Parco Po,* v. Lungo Po Europa 12/A, 109 pl, ☎ 27137.

Recommended
Canoeing: instruction at *Canoa club,* v. Lago Gerundo 28, ☎ 37570; *Canottieri L. Bissolati,* v. Riglio 12, ☎ 28540.
Cycling: *Cicloamatori,* v. G. da Cremona 46, ☎ 23340.
Flying club: *Migliaro airport,* ☎ 31555 (also gliding, parachuting, model aircraft).
Gastronomic specialties: torrone (nougat), mustard, butter, cheese and pork sausages.
Horseback riding: *Allevatori e Possessori Equini,* v. Solferino 33; *Azienda agricola Borlenga,* at Pieve d'Olmi, v. Tidolo (associate of *ANTE*).
Palestra Spettacolo: v. Postumia (3A), ☎ 430238 (sports).
River trips: on the Po on the *Stradivari* (Apr-Oct), Società di Navigazione Interna, corso Vittorio Emanuele 17 (C1-2), ☎ 25546.
Stringed instruments: *Scuola di Liuteria,* corso Garibaldi 178, ☎ 38689 (to visit reserve in advance); *Ente Triennale internazionale strumenti ad arco,* v. Bella Rocca 25, ☎ 21454 (organizers of autumn festival held every three years with concerts and exhibitions of bowed instruments); *Associazioni liutai,* V. Vacchelli 7, ☎ 22087, p. Lodi 3, ☎ 34947; p. Cavour 5, ☎ 28301.

Environs
SAN FELICE, 4 km E.

Hotel:
MotelAgip, v. Passalombardo 1, ☎ 434101, 77 rm ℙ 𝕎 85,000.

DESENZANO DEL GARDA

Brescia 28, Milan 118 km
Pop. 20,090 ⊠ 25015 ☎ 030   D-E4

Desenzano is the main harbour for navigation on Lake Garda. Once Garda's principal cereal market was here and the little town was the port for the sailing barges that plied between the various lake centres.

▶ The old part of the town is dominated by the 14C-15C **Castello** and looks out over the old **harbour** on the lakeside. ▶ Behind the harbour is the **piazza Malvezzi,** long and narrow, with arcades, the commercial centre of the town. Close by is the **Duomo** (16C) which has a *Last Supper* by Gian Battist Tiepolo (1696-1770). ▶ In the v. degli Scavi are the ruins of a 4C **Roman villa** *(9 a.m.*

to *1 hr before dusk; closed Mon),* with polychrome mosaic pavements.   □

Practical information
ⓘ p. Matteotti 27, ☎ 9141510.
⛴ boats and hydrofoils, ☎ 9141321.

Hotels:
★★★★ *City,* v. Sauro 29, ☎ 9142248, 32 rm ℙ 𝕎 ⅍ closed Christmas. No restaurant, 70,000; bkf: 9,000.
★★★★ *Park Hotel,* lungolago Battisti 17, ☎ 9143494, 65 rm ℙ ≮ 𝕎 ⅍ 70,000; bkf: 9,000.
★★★★ *Tripoli,* p. Matteotti 18, ☎ 9141305, 24 rm ≮ No restaurant, 70,000; bkf: 9,000.
★★★★ *Villa Rosa,* lungolago Battisti 89, ☎ 9141974, 38 rm ℙ 𝕎 ⅍ ⁂ 65,000; bkf: 8,000.
★★★ *Benaco,* v. Cavour 30, ☎ 9141710, 25 rm ℙ 𝕎 ⅍ ▣ closed Nov-Feb, 50,000; bkf: 7,000.
★★★ *Piccola Vela,* v. Dal Molin, ☎ 9141134, 34 rm ℙ 𝕎 ⁂ ▣ closed Feb, 55,000.
★★★ *Piroscafo,* v. Porto Vecchio 11, ☎ 9141128, 32 rm ⁂ 55,000; bkf: 7,000.

Restaurants:
♦♦♦ *Esplanade,* v. Lario 10, ☎ 9143361, closed Wed. Lake view with beach and landing stage. Italian cuisine: sea bream with porcini, sea bass with herbs, 38/55,000.
♦♦ *Taverna Tre Corone,* v. Stretta Castello 16, ☎ 9141962, closed Tue and 5-30 Dec. Creative cuisine: spaghetti al cartoccio, pork in milk with prunes and honey, 25/40,000.

⚐ ★★★★ *Vò,* v. Vò 4, 133 pl, ☎ 9141357.

Recommended
Antiques market: p. Malvezzi, 1st Sun of every month.
Golf: *Gardagolf,* at Soiano del Lago, ☎ 674116 (18 holes).
Horseback riding: *Centro ippico West Garda,* at Padenghe sul Garda *(6 km N),* v. Prais, ☎ 917383; *Scuderia Amadei,* at Bedizzole *(14 km NE, turnoff to Padenghe),* v. Fusina 6, ☎ 674227 (associate of *ANTE*).
Marina: ☎ 9141151.
Sailing school: *Fraglia della vela,* v. Porto Maratona, ☎ 9143343.
Tennis: v. Dal Molino, ☎ 9140400.

EDOLO

Brescia 99, Milan 141 km
Pop. 4,483 ⊠ 25048 ☎ 0364   D2

Throughout the Middle Ages and the Renaissance Edolo was famous for the manufacture of weapons and armour. Its mines produce much of the ore required by the ancient and still flourishing Valcamónica iron industry. The church of S. **Giovanni Battista** (15C-16C) has interesting 16C frescos.   □

Practical information
ⓘ p. Martiri della Libertà 2, ☎ 71065.

Hotel:
★★★ *Larici,* p. Martiri della Libertà 18, ☎ 71006, 21 rm, closed Nov, 45,000; bkf: 5,000.

⚐ ★★★ *Adamello,* at Nembra, 60 pl, ☎ 71694 (all year).

ERBA

Como 14, Milan 44 km
Pop. 16,318 ⊠ 22036 ☎ 031   B3

Erba is an attractive agricultural and industrial centre in the hills of Brianza.

▶ Little remains of the medieval town. ▶ The church of S. **Eufemia** has a Romanesque campanile with mullioned windows. ▶ A long flight of steps leads to the open-air **Teatro Licinium** (1926), surrounded by greenery. ▶ 2.5 km away is the **Buco del Piombo,** a deep open cave in a vertical rock face, accessible for about 400 yds *(May-Oct, ask at the Comune, ☎ 641006).* □

Practical information _____

ℹ Villa Mainoni (municipio), ☎ 641006.

Hotels:
★★★★★ *Castello di Pomerio,* v. Como 5, ☎ 611516, 58 rm Ⓟ ♨ ♿ ☒ ↗ Medieval manor, with 14C frescos and large windows opening onto the garden, 200,000.
★★★ *Erba,* v. Milano 12/D, ☎ 640681, 21 rm Ⓟ 60,000; bkf: 4,000.

Restaurants:
● ♦♦♦ *Cantuccio,* at Albavilla *(4 km W),* v. Dante 34, ☎ 612736, closed Mon. Old country house in centre of village. Italian cuisine: taglioni with porcini, breast of duck in raspberry vinegar, 35/50,000.
♦ *Cavenaghi,* p. Vittorio Veneto 10, ☎ 641243, closed Fri and 18 Jul-10 Aug. Traditional trattoria. Regional cuisine: cassouela, rostisciada, 20/30,000.

Recommended
Caves: visits to *Buco del Piombo,* from Alpe del Vicerè *(8 km NE, by way of Albavilla),* Jul-Sep, municipio, ☎ 641006.
Horseback riding: Centro ippico ANTE Alpe del Viceré, at Albavilla *(4 km E).*
Tennis: v. Garibaldi, ☎ 642425.

ESINO LARIO

Como 63, Milan 111 km
2,985 ft pop. 805 ☒ 22050 ☎ 0341   B3

This winter sports resort lies in a valley above the central basin of Lake Como. Fossils, archaeological finds and tools are displayed in the **Museo Civico delle Grigne** *(open Jul and Aug a.m., Sat and Sun also p.m.; for other months, ask at municipio).* 3 km SE is the **Alpe Cainallo** (4,165 ft), an undulating plateau with a view of the Grigne Mountains. □

Practical information _____

⛷ ski lifts and skiing instruction at Alpe Cainallo.
ℹ Grigne cableway, ☎ 860050.

GALLARATE

Varese 19, Milan 40 km
Pop. 46,865 ☒ 21013 ☎ 0331   A3-4

There are two interesting churches in this busy town: 12C Romanesque **S. Pietro** and the Baroque **S. Maria Assunta,** with 15C campanile and 17C painting. The **Museo Archeologico Storico Artistico** *(Tue-Fri 3-5 p.m.; Sat 9 a.m.-12 noon; Sun 10 a.m.-12 noon,* ☎ 795092 or 899281) displays a collection of prehistoric material from the Golasecca civilization. The **Civica Galleria d'Arte Moderna** *(10 a.m.-12 noon; closed Mon)* has about 400 works by contemporary painters and sculptors. 6.5 km away is **Malpensa (Milan) International Airport.** Nearby is the **Museo Aeronautico Caproni-Taliedo** *(under reorganization),* with aircraft from 1908 to the present. □

Practical information _____

Hotels:
★★★★ *Cardano,* at Cardano al Campo, v. Campo 10, ☎ 261011, 32 rm Ⓟ ♨ ♿ No restaurant, 103,000; bkf: 10,000.
★★★ *Astoria,* p. Risorgimento 9/A, ☎ 791043, 50 rm Ⓟ ♿ ♨ 66,000; bkf: 6,000.

Restaurants:
♦♦♦ *Risorgimento,* p. Risorgimento 8, ☎ 793594, closed Sun and Aug. Regional fish cuisine: ravioli in truffle cream, sea bass alla Damiano, 34/40,000.
♦ *Saverio,* corso Sempione 99, ☎ 791508, closed Mon and Aug. Terrace in summer. Italian cuisine: penne with onions, mezzemaniche with herbs, 30/35,000.

Recommended
Motocross: *MV Agusta* motor circuit, at Ciglione Malpensa, run *by Moto club Gallarate.*

GALLIANO

Como 11, Milan 37 km
Pop. 225 ☒ 22030 ☎ 031   B3

The 10C-11C Romanesque basilica and baptistery are among the earliest in Lombardy. The basilica of **S. Vincenzo★,** possibly 5C in origin and rebuilt in 1007 by Ariberto da Intimiano, has a façade in rough stone and an austere interior *(apply to the caretaker at v. S. Vincenzo 10; 9 a.m.-12 noon and 2-6 p.m.).* The walls of the nave and apse have extraordinary **frescos★★,** (1007-9), Carolingian-Ottonian in inspiration and considered to be among the finest and largest specimens of early art in Lombardy. To the r. of the basilica is the baptistery of **S. Giovanni★,** one of the oldest in Lombardy (possibly second half of 10C), quatrefoil in plan, with women's galleries and dome. □

GANDINO

Bergamo 24, Milan 71 km
Pop. 5,719 ☒ 24024 ☎ 035   C3

The Baroque basilica of **S. Maria Assunta** (17C) has a sumptuously decorated interior. The **Museo della Basilica** *(apply to the sacristan at v. Loverini 2)* exhibits an interesting collection of sacred art. □

Practical information _____

Recommended
Events: traditional *Corpus Domini procession* (2nd Thu after Pentecost).
Hang gliding: *Scuola Monte Farno,* v. Rottini 14, ☎ 93637.

Lake GARDA

From Sirmione to Salò *(149 km, 1 day; map 4)*

Looking at Lake Garda from the hills at the S end, its origins are clear: the glacial moraine formed a barrier upstream of the plain, behind which the lake formed. Hence, the outline of the lake is narrow in the N, with steep, mountainous slopes like a fjord, and in the S so wide that it is almost like a sea. Along the S banks the landscape and climate are typically those of the Po valley, whereas Goethe's 'land where the lemon tree blooms' begins farther N, where the lake becomes narrower. Today, olives are cultivated in the almost Mediterranean climate that is due to the regulatory effect of the deep water (on the E banks and at the S extremity (→)in Veneto and Trentino-Alto Adige).

▶ Travelling up the W shore from **Sirmione** (→) and **Desenzano** (→), through the wine-growing hills of the Valténesi, the route arrives at **Manerba del Garda** on a promontory ending in the picturesque **Rocca,** on a peak above the lake. A little further on, near the 12C Roman-

4. Lake Garda

esque **parish church** (rebuilt 16C) is the **Museo Archeo-logico della Valténesi** *(Jul-Sep 9 a.m.-12 noon and 3-7 p.m.; other months apply to the caretaker)* with finds from the Neolithic to the Middle Ages. ▶ To the N, past the Romanesque-Gothic sanctuary of the **Madonna del Carmine** (15C frescos) is **San Felice del Benaco**, a farming and tourist centre on the Punta Portese promontory, which marks the S extremity of the gulf of Salò; in the **parish church** is an altarpiece by Romanino. ▶ **Gardone Riviera** (→) marks the beginning of the Brescia bank, with houses, villas, and gardens luxuriant with evergreens. ▶ In the resort of **Maderno**, once famous for paper mills, the 12C church of **S. Andrea** is an interesting example of Romanesque architecture. Maderno and **Toscolano**, the Roman *Benacum* now make up a single municipality. ▶ **Gargnano** has the typical charm of the older lakeside resorts, with its little harbour, venerable streets and noble villas. ▶ **Campione del Garda** was once an industrial centre. A cotton mill (in the grounds of which is the 18C villa Archetti) and workers' village now stand abandoned. ▶ The lake banks here are rough and rocky, with no room for settlements. Thus, the old part of **Pieve di Tremósine**, high on a rock overhanging the lake, commands exceptional views. ▶ **Limone sul Garda** is on a little islet, huddled beneath rock walls covered with lemon groves. ▶ A little before **Riva del Garda** (→ in Trentino-Alto Adige) a road turns off to **Pieve di Ledro** on the little lake of **Ledro**. Here are the substantial remains of a Bronze Age lake dwelling, submerged but still visible on the E bank. ▶ A column at the **Colle Santo Stefano**, above **Bezzecca** marks the spot where Garibaldi, after defeating the Austrians in August 1866, received notice of the armistice and the order to abandon the confines of the Trentino. ▶ The road reaches **Storo**, then **Ponte Cáffaro** and the **Lake Idro** (→) and then passes below the picturesque **Rocca d'Anfo**. This stronghold was a strategic Venetian garrison in the 15C, was later conquered by the French and the Austrians, and finally was taken by Garibaldi who, in 1866, set up his headquarters here. ▶ **Vestone** is an ancient centre of agricultural equipment production. ▶ The Sabbia valley is most noted for indus-

try. **Vobarno**, which formerly provided the Venetian fleet with rivets and anchors, still has a specialist iron and steel industry. ▶ The road rejoins Lake Garda at **Salò** (→). □

Practical information ────────────

GARGNANO, ⊠ 25084, ☎ 0365.
ⓘ p. Feltrinelli 1, ☎ 71222.
⚓ boats and hydrofoils.

Hotels:
★★★ *Bartabel*, v. Roma 39, ☎ 71330, 11 rm ⁙ 38,000; bkf: 4,000.
★★★ *Livia*, at Villa, v. Libertà 42, ☎ 71235, 25 rm ⬛ ⬛ closed 16 Oct-14 Mar, 44,000; bkf: 8,000.
★★★ *Palazzina*, at Villa, v. Libertà 10, ☎ 71118, 25 rm ℗ ⬛ ⁙ ⬛ closed Oct-Mar, 50,000; bkf: 6,000.

Restaurant:
● ♦♦♦ *Tortuga*, v. XXIV Maggio 5, ☎ 71251, closed Mon eve except Jun-Sep, Tue and 1 Feb-15 Mar. Creative cuisine: capriccio of fresh pasta with mushrooms, capponcello with lettuce and peas, 40/55,000.

Recommended
Events: 100 Miglia del Garda sailing regatta *(early Sep)*.
Golf: *Golf club Bogliaco*, ☎ 643006 (9 holes).
Marina: *Circolo della vela*, at Bogliaco, ☎ 71028.

LIMONE SUL GARDA, ⊠ 25010, ☎ 0365.
ⓘ v. Comboni 15, ☎ 954070.
⚓ boats and hydrofoils.

Hotels:
★★★★ *Capo Reamol*, v. IV Novembre 92, ☎ 954040, 61 rm ℗ ⬛ ⬛ closed Nov-Easter, 81,000; bkf: 15,000.
★★★★ *Panorama*, v. IV Novembre 86, ☎ 954028, 69 rm ℗ ⬛ ⬛ ⁂ closed Nov-Feb, 60,000.
★★★ *Astor*, v. IV Novembre 76, ☎ 954092, 50 rm ℗ ⁙ ⬛ closed Nov-Mar, 57,000.
★★★ *Lido*, v. IV Novembre 36, 26 rm ℗ ⬛ ⬛ ⬛ closed 16 Oct-9 May, 56,000.
★★★ *Pergola*, v. IV Novembre 66, ☎ 954002, 37 rm ℗ ⬛ ⬛ closed Nov-Mar, 57,000.
★★★ *Saturno*, v. Einaudi 4, ☎ 954076, 70 rm ℗ ⬛ ⁙ ⬛ ⁂ closed Nov-Mar, 50,000.
⚠ ★★ *Garda*, at Fasse, v. IV Novembre 10, 190 pl, ☎ 954550.

Recommended
Surfing: ☎ 954266 (instruction).
Tennis: v. IV Novembre 36, ☎ 954468.

MANERBA DEL GARDA, ⊠ 25080, ☎ 0365.
≋

Hotel:
★★★ *Quiete*, v. del Rio 92, ☎ 653156, 29 rm ℗ ⬛ ⬛ ⁂ closed Nov-Mar, 40,000; bkf: 6,000.
⚠ ★★ *San Biagio*, at Belvedere, v. Cavalle, 190 pl, ☎ 653046.

SAN FELICE DEL BENACO, ⊠ 25010, ☎ 0365.
≋

Hotels:
★★★ *Garden*, at Portese, v. delle Magnolie 10, ☎ 41489, 29 rm ℗ ⁙ ⬛ closed Oct-Mar, 54,000; bkf: 7,000.
★★★ *Piero Bella*, at Portese, v. Preone 6, ☎ 62040, 24 rm ℗ ⬛ ⁙ ⁂ closed 15 Oct-31 Jan, 45,000; bkf: 7,000.
⚠ ★★★★ *Ideal Molino*, at Macina, v. Gardiolo 1, 83 pl, ☎ 62023; ★★★ *Europa-Silvella*, v. Silvella, 290 pl, ☎ 651095.

TOSCOLANO MADERNO, ⊠ 25080, ☎ 0365.
≋
ⓘ lungolago Zanardelli 18, ☎ 641330.
⚓ boats and hydrofoils; car ferry to Torri del Benaco (7-14 trips per day), ☎ 641389.

Hotels:
★★★ *Benaco*, lungolago Zanardelli 30, ☎ 641110, 35 rm ℗ ⬛ ⬛ ⁂ closed Oct-Mar, 57,000; bkf: 7,000.

★★★ *Milano,* v. Lungolago 12, ☎ 641223, 34 rm P ⚏ closed Oct-Mar, 65,000; bkf: 8,000.
★★ *Eden,* p. S. Marco 27, ☎ 641305, 28 rm P ⚏ closed 11 Oct-31 Mar, 31,000; bkf: 4,000.

Restaurant:
◆◆◆ *Milani,* v. Statale 1, ☎ 641042, closed Mon except Jun-Sep and Nov-Feb. Regional cuisine: fresh pasta, charcoal-grilled meat and fish, 25/50,000.

⚠ ★★★ *Foce,* v. Religione 64, 529 pl, ☎ 641372 (all year).

TREMOSINE, ⊠ 25010, ☎ 0365.
ⓘ at Pieve, p. G. Marconi, ☎ 953185.

Hotels:
★★★ *Faver,* at Voltino, v. Volta 15, ☎ 954354, 21 rm P ⚏ ⚘ ⌂ ♨ closed Dec-Feb except Christmas, 60,000.
★★★ *Paradiso,* at Pieve, v. Europa 19, ☎ 953012, 14 rm P ⚜ ⚍ ⚏ ⚘ ⌂ closed 16 Oct-Easter, 55,000.
★★★ *Pineta Campi,* at Campi, ☎ 957036, 66 rm P ⚜ ⚍ ⚏ ⌂ ♨ closed 1 Nov-19 Mar, 45,000; bkf: 6,000.

GARDONE RIVIERA*

Brescia 33, Milan 129 km
Pop. 2,516 ⊠ 25083 ☎ 0365   E4

Vittoriale, villa of the writer Gabriele D'Annunzio (1863-1938), has been described as 'not a house to live in, but a stage to speak on'. The extraordinary house and its magnificent garden stand above quiet, elegant Gardone Riviera, the busiest and most famous resort on the Brescia side of the lake.

▶ Villas and hotels are set among luxuriant vegetation. Cafés and shops line the **lakeside,** with its view of the Isola di Garda. The **Hruska botanical gardens** *(Mar-Oct 8:30 a.m.-dusk)* and the **Parco comunale della villa Alba** are attractive. ▶ In Gardone di Sopra is **Vittoriale degli Italiani** *(8:30 a.m.-12 noon and 2-5 p.m.; closes later in summer),* the final home of D'Annunzio (designed by G. C. Maroni), an eclectic complex of buildings and gardens. As well as the poet's house, opulent and oriental in feeling, interesting features include D'Annunzio's mausoleum; the open-air theatre (the *Parlaggio,* as the writer called it); the prow of the cruiser *Puglia* (on the hillside); the *Búccari* motor torpedo boat; and a display of vintage cars. There is also a **museum** with documents and memorabilia relating to the colourful life, works and exploits of D'Annunzio.   ▫

Practical information _____

GARDONE RIVIERA

ⓘ corso della Repubblica 35, ☎ 20347.
⛴ boats and hydrofoils.

Hotels:
★★★★ *Grand Hotel,* corso Zanardelli 72, ☎ 20261, 180 rm P ⚏ ⚐ ⌂ closed 11 Oct-14 Apr, 186,000.
★★★ *Monte Baldo,* corso Zanardelli 100, ☎ 20951, 46 rm P ⚏ ⌂ closed Oct-Apr, 72,000; bkf: 8,000.
★★ *Bellevue,* corso Zanardelli 81/83, ☎ 20235, 31 rm P ⚜ ⚏ closed 11 Oct-31 Mar, 50,000; bkf: 6,000.

Restaurants:
● ◆◆◆ *Villa Fiordaliso,* corso Zanardelli 132, ☎ 20158. Art nouveau villa. Excellent creative cuisine: scampi tails with peppers, veal chops with escarole and peas, 50/55,000.
◆◆ *Al Lago,* v. Statale, ☎ 20387, closed Mon and 1 Jan-15 Feb. Summer service on lakeside terrace. Regional cuisine: homemade pasta, maccheroncini alla bizzarra, 25/35,000.

Environs

FASANO, ⊠ 25080, 3 km NE.

Hotels:
★★★★ *G. H. Fasano,* corso Zanardelli 160, ☎ 21051,

77 rm P ⚏ ⚐ ⌂ ♨ closed Oct-Apr. Originally a hunting lodge, 144,000; bkf: 18,000.
★★★ *Riccio,* corso Zanardelli 206, ☎ 21987, 26 rm P ⚏ ⚘ closed 1 Oct-14 May, 54,000; bkf: 9,000.
★★★ *Villa del Sogno,* corso Zanardelli 107, ☎ 20228, 25 rm P ⚜ ⚐ ⚏ ⚘ ⌂ closed Oct-Mar, 110,000.

Recommended
Tennis: sports club, v. Roma, ☎ 22123.

GRAVEDONA

Como 52, Milan 100 km
Pop. 2,741 ⊠ 22015 ☎ 0344   B2

Gravedona is the former capital of the Tre Pievi (the three parishes of Gravelona, Sorico and Dorigo), which united to resist the Visconti and Sforza forces during the feudal era.

▶ The church of **S. Maria del Tiglio**★ is an unusual Lombard Romanesque building showing Burgundian influence. Built in the 12C, it was clad with light and dark bands of stone; the campanile (with square base and octagonal top) projects from the façade. Inside *(apply to the sacristan in the adjacent basilica of S. Vincenzo)* are a large Romanesque carved wood Crucifix and remains of 12C-14C frescos. ▶ Also of interest is the church of **S. Maria delle Grazie** (1467), with cloister, marble portals and 16C frescos. ▶ In **Calozzo** (6.5 km SW) is an unusual **Museo delle barche lariane** (Museum of Lake Como boats; *Sat and Sun 10 a.m.-12 noon and 2-5 p.m.).* ▶ In **Peglio** (6 km N) the 17C church is decorated with Flemish paintings.   ▫

Practical information _____

≋
ⓘ v. Sabbati.
⛴ boats and hydrofoils.

Hotel:
★★ *Turismo,* v. Regina 17, ☎ 85227, 12 rm P ⚏ closed Dec-Feb, 50,000; bkf: 5,000.

⚠ ★★ *Serenella,* at Torretta, v. Scuri 6, 48 pl, ☎ 80060.

Recommended
Sailing instruction: *Centro diffusione vela,* at Serenella, ☎ 80045.
Youth hostel: *Ostello Domaso,* at Domaso, v. Case Sparse 4, ☎ 85192.

Le GRIGNE AND IL RESEGONE

                                                              B-C3

Lecco (→) is surrounded by a severe, mountainous landscape. The dominant feature N of the Grigne group is the Valsassina. On the **Grignone** or Grigna settentrionale (7,900 ft), according to legend, a beautiful but cruel warrior maiden was changed into a rock for killing a knight who was in love with her. The **Grignetta** or Grigna meridionale (7,165 ft) and the **S. Martino-Coltiglione** (6,152 ft), the other peaks in the group, have rugged slopes, difficult for climbers. E of the town is the **Resegone** (6,152 ft), unmistakable with the row of little peaks that give it a sawtooth profile.   ▫

GROSIO

Sondrio 41, Milan 174 km
Pop. 4,800 ⊠ 23033 ☎ 0342   E4

The magnificent, ruined 14C **castello** of the noble house of Visconti still dominates the countryside. In the park that surrounds it *(wkdays,* ☎ *845047)* are noteworthy prehistoric **rock carvings** (3C-2C BC). Interesting features of the town are the 17C church of **S. Giuseppe,** with impressive façade and interior rich in works of art; and the ancient church of **S. Giorgio,** with a carved wood altarpiece, painted and gilded (1494), with 15C-16C frescos. □

Practical information _____

Hotel:
★★★ **Sassella,** v. Roma 2, ☎ 845140, 20 rm, 51,500. Rest. ● ♦♦♦ closed Mon except summer. Excellent Valtellina cuisine, 25/30,000.

Recommended
Events: *Corpus Domini* processions, ☎ 845123.

Lake IDRO

D-E3

Entirely surrounded by mountains, the highest prealpine lake in Italy (a fjord in the Pleistocene sea) is used today for irrigation and as a source of hydroelectric power. The 10-km lake is also a popular spot for anglers, although the trout are less numerous than they used to be. **Crone,** principal community of **Idro,** is on the E bank; **Anfo is** on the opposite bank. □

Practical information _____

IDRO, ⊠ 25074, ☎ 0365.
≋
ⓘ v. Trento, ☎ 83224.

Restaurant:
● ♦♦♦ **Girelli Benedetto,** at Barghe, v. Nazionale 17, ☎ 84140, closed Tue, Christmas, Easter and 15 Jun-15 Jul. Well run, with attention to detail. Outstanding regional cuisine: casonsei, polenta taragna, 45/50,000.

⚠ ★★★★ *Rio Vantone,* at Vantone, v. Capovalle, 250 pl, ☎ 83125 (all year).

Lake ISEO

D3

Originally this beautiful lake basin was a gulf of the Pleistocene sea. It was formed, like all the lakes in Lombardy, by the raising of the plain and by glacial moraine deposits. The climate is mild, and olives and vines grow on the steep banks. The lake has an atmosphere and colouring all its own, rich in contrasts. Monte Isola is the largest, highest island in all the Italian lakes.

▶ In **Iseo,** on the SE bank, is the 12C parish church of **S. Andrea** with a 14C campanile in the centre of the façade. ▶ **Sale Marasino,** with traditional fishing net and woollen blanket industries, faces the central section of the lake, which is dominated by Monte Isola. ▶ **Monte Isola** might have been designed to attract romantic painters, who have visited it in large numbers: the island is high and wooded, with rustic fishing villages and even a ruined castle, the **Rocca Martinengo.** ▶ **Pisogne** is an old village with porticoed houses; 16C **frescos**★★ in the charming 15C church of **S. Maria della Neve.** From here it is possible to climb to **Fraine** (2,687 ft), where there are fine views, or to **Alpiaz-M.Campione** (3,609 ft), a ski resort. ▶ From **Lovere** (→) the road runs along the lake to **Sàrnico,** at SW extremity, inhabited since prehistoric times and noted for centuries for its fine sandstone. □

Practical information _____

ALPIAZ MONTE CAMPIONE, ⊠ 25040 (at Artogne), 18 km NE of Pisogne.
ⵗ chair lifts, ski lifts, skiing instruction, ice skating.
ⓘ ALPIAZ S.A. Monte Campione, ☎ 560721.

Recommended
Sports hall: ☎ 560721 (indoor swimming pool, tennis).

ISEO, ⊠ 25049, ☎ 030.
≋
ⓘ lungolago Marconi 2, ☎ 980209.
⛴ boats.

Hotel:
★★★ **Moselli,** at Pilzone, v. Fenice 17, ☎ 980001, 30 rm Ⓟ ⬜ closed Nov, 34,000; bkf: 6,500.

Restaurants:
● ♦♦♦ **Fenice,** at Pilzone, v. Fenice 21, ☎ 981565, closed Thu and 15-31 Aug. Small taverna with wines on sale. Italian cuisine: risotto with porcini or asparagus tips, lake fish, 40/55,000.
♦♦♦ **Punta-da Dino,** at Clusane, ☎ 989037, closed Wed and 1-25 Nov. Cuisine of lake fish: baked stuffed tench with polenta, grilled perch and coregone, 20/30,000.
♦♦ **Gallo Rosso,** vicolo Nulli 11, ☎ 980505, closed Thu and 1-10 Aug. Well-kept rural restaurant, with fireplace and grill. Italian cuisine: penne del Gallo, grilled lake fish and meat, 30/45,000.
⚠ ★★ *Sassabanek,* v. Colombera 1, 200 pl, ☎ 980300.

Recommended
Golf: *Franciacorta* (Brescia →; 18 holes).
Marina: *Circolo velico Pilzone,* ☎ 981163.
Sports centre: at Sassabanek (swimming pool, tennis, sailing instruction).

MONTE ISOLA, ⊠ 25050, ☎ 030.
ⓘ at Iseo, lungolago Marconi 2, ☎ 980209; at Sulzano, ☎ 985283 (seasonal).
⛴ from Iseo, Sàrnico and other centres on the lake for Siviano, Sensole, Peschiera and Carzano; ferries from Sulzano, Sale Masrasino and Tavérnola.

Restaurant:
♦♦ *Trattoria del Pesce,* at Peschiera Maraglio, v. Tempini 5, ☎ 988137, closed Tue. Traditional restaurant in ancient building. Cuisine of lake fish: lasagne al forno, fried, grilled or baked fish, Franciacorta Pinot wine, 20/30,000.

Recommended
Bicycle rental: p. di Peschiera Maraglio and at Sensole.

PISOGNE, ⊠ 25055, ☎ 0364.
ⓘ corso Nave Corriera 15/b, ☎ 8219.
⛴ boats.

Hotel:
Tre Stelle, v. Zanardelli 11, ☎ 8254, 20 rm Ⓟ 39,000; bkf: 8,000.

⚠ ★★★ *Eden,* at Goia, v. Piangrande 3, 80 pl, ☎ 8050 (all year).

SARNICO, ⊠ 24067, ☎ 035.
ⓘ v. Parigi 2, ☎ 910469.
⛴ boats.

Hotels:
★★★★ *Cantiere,* v. Monte Grappa 2, ☎ 910091, 25 rm Ⓟ ⬜ ⚿ closed 26 Dec-25 Jan, 70,000; bkf: 10,000.
★★ *Turistico del Sebino,* p. Besenzoni 1, ☎ 910043, 23 rm ⬙ 40,000; bkf: 5,000.

⚠ ★★ *Lido di Nettuno,* v. Predore 33, 170 pl, ☎ 910402.

Recommended
Tennis: v. Garibaldi, ☎ 910461.
Water skiing: *Sci club Sebino,* v. Predore Lido Cadè, ☎ 911165.

LAKES MAGGIORE AND LUGANO

From Varese *(119 km, 1 day; map 5)*

Lake Maggiore (Verbano) and lake Lugano (Ceresio) are in the territory of Milan, which also includes the Varesotto, the area of Lombardy between the two lakes. Since 1927 this has been the centre of the province of Varese, the most heavily industrialized in Italy (specializing in textiles and machinery) and one of the richest. Industry and urbanization have cut into tourism, although until the 1920s luxury tourism gave the region a certain lustre and scattered great hotels and villas over the hills and shores of Lake Maggiore. (For the W bank → Piedmont).

▶ The itinerary begins at **Varese** (→). ▶ In **Bisuschio** the **Villa Cicogna Mozzoni** *(from Easter to the first Sun in Nov, 9 a.m.-12 noon and 2-6 p.m.)* is a typical country residence of the 16C nobility (in the portico and on the façade, 15C frescos; Italianate terraced garden). ▶ **Porto Ceresio**, on one of the S arms of Lake Lugano, is a holiday resort and transit point for Switzerland. ▶ The road continues by the lake through **Brusimpiano** and **Lavena to Ponte Tresa**; from here only a short diversion is necessary to get to **Ghirla**, on the little lake of the same name amid the greenery of Valganna; in nearby **Ganna** are the ruins of **San Gemolo** priory (11C). ▶ The road rejoins the NE shore of Lake Maggiore at **Luino**. This old village has characteristic palazzi, particularly in the N by the lakeside; in the church of the **Madonna del Carmine** (15C) are 17C frescos, and in **S. Pietro**, by the cemetery, is an *Adoration of the Magi* attributed to B. Luini. ▶ The road skirts **Porto Valtravaglia**, then continues to **Laveno**, a popular resort also noted for ceramics manufacture. It is a lake port and has a railway station and for some time was an important centre on the route to l'Ossola (→ Piedmont) on the other side of Lake Maggiore. ▶ A little farther, near **Leggiuno**, is the sanctuary of **S. Caterina del**

Sasso, a group of ecclesiastical buildings which grew up in the 13C around the cave of a hermit-saint. On a spur above the lake, at the foot of an overhanging wall of rock, this is one of the most popular religious centres on Lake Maggiore. ▶ The road continues by **Ispra** to **Angera**, home of the Maggiore fleet and military base for the control of the lake and the Sempione road. On the promontory that dominates the little town and the bay is the **Rocca** *(end Mar-end Oct, 9 a.m.-12 noon and 1:30-5:30 p.m.)*, the stronghold in succession of the Torriani, Visconti and Borromeo families. Various rooms in the old keep and 13C palazzo are open to the public, including the immense sala della Giustizia, with a cycle of 14C frescos celebrating the exploits of Ottone Visconti against the Torriani. ▶ At **Sesto Calende** the **Museo Archeologico** *(8:30 a.m.-12:30 p.m. and 2:30-4:30 p.m.; Sun 10 a.m.-12 noon and 3-7 p.m.; closed Mon)* has an extensive collection of finds from the Golasecca culture (from the village of the same name 3.5 km S in the Ticino, where Iron Age tombs lavishly endowed with artefacts have been excavated. N of the town is the church of **S. Donato**, built in the 9C and subsequently altered. There are 15C-16C frescos and a large crypt. ▶ Passing by **Comabbio**, between the lakes of Comabbio and Monate, the road continues to **Biandronno**, on Lake Varese. From here boats ply to the **Isolino Virginia**, a former lake village. ▶ On the N shore of the lake is **Gavirate**, where macaroons are a local delicacy. In nearby Voltorre, the church of **S. Michele** has a Romanesque **cloister**★ (11C-12C). ▶ From Gavirate the road leads back to Varese.

Practical information

ANGERA, ⊠ 21021, ☎ 0331.
≋
ℹ p. Garibaldi 14, ☎ 930168.
⛴ boats and hydrofoils.

Hotels:
★★★ *Conca Azzurra*, at Ranco, v. Alberto 53, ☎ 969526, 20 rm Ⓟ ⚜ ⛵ closed Jan-Feb, 70,000; bkf: 8,000. Rest. ♦♦♦ closed Fri (Oct-May). Quality cuisine, 25/40,000.
★★ *Lido*, v. Libertà 11, ☎ 930232, 18 rm Ⓟ ⚜ ⅏ closed Dec, 60,000; bkf: 6,000.

Restaurant:
● ♦♦♦ *Sole*, p. Venezia 5, ☎ 969507, closed Mon eve, Tue and 1 Jan-12 Feb. Painstaking attention to detail, lake views, lido and swimming area. Excellent creative cuisine: armonie del lago, involtini of lavarello with balsam vinegar, 48/60,000.
⚓ ★★ *Citta di Angera*, v. Bruschera al Lago, 380 pl, ☎ 930736 (all year).

Recommended
Water skiing: *Sci nautico Angera,* at Tognoli, ☎ 930893.

COMABBIO, ⊠ 21020, ☎ 0331.

Restaurant:
♦♦♦ *Cesarino*, v. Labiena 65, ☎ 979072, closed Wed, Feb and Aug. Comfortable, with lake view. Regional cuisine: terrine of tagliatelle with truffles, dishes cooked at table, 30/55,000.

Recommended
Children's facilities: courses in painting and woodwork at Centro culturale Cascina S. Vitale, at Osmate *(3 km),* v. Maggiore 18, ☎ 953412.

GAVIRATE, ⊠ 21026, ☎ 0332.
ℹ p. Matteotti (municipal palazzo), ☎ 743108.
⚓ *Lido*, lungolago Virginia 7, 76 pl, ☎ 744707 (all year).

ISPRA, ⊠ 21027, ☎ 0332.
≋

Hotel:
★★★ *Europa*, v. Verbano 19, ☎ 780184, 40 rm Ⓟ closed Jan-15 Feb, 63,000; bkf: 5,000.

5. Lakes Maggiore and Lugano

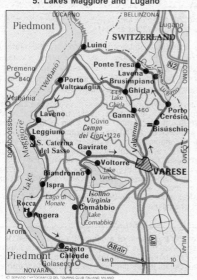

△ ★★ *International Ispra,* v. Carducci, 200 pl, ✆ 780458.

Recommended
Swimming pool: at Lavoraccio (road to Laveno), ✆ 780391.

LAVENA-PONTE-TRESA, ✉ 21037, ✆ 0332.

≈

Hotel:
★★ *Du Lac,* at Lavena, v. Ungheria 19, ✆ 550308, 23 rm P ⋚ 50,000; bkf: 5,000.

△ ★★ *International Camping,* at Ponte Tresa, v. Marconi 16, 160 pl, ✆ 550117 (all year).

LAVENO, ✉ 21014, ✆ 0332.

≈

ⓘ Palazzo Comunale, ✆ 666666.
⎯ hydrofoils and car ferry (every half-hour) to Intra, ✆ 667128.

Hotel:
★★★ *Moderno,* v. Garibaldi 15, ✆ 668373, 14 rm P closed Jan-Feb. No restaurant, 63,000.

Restaurant:
♦♦ *Scoiattolo,* v. Monteggia 20, ✆ 668253, closed Mon and 7 Jan-1 Feb. Fine views, terrace for eating outdoors in summer. Regional cuisine: pasta della mamma, grilled meat and fish, 20/35,000.

Recommended
Craft workshops: *Dal Santo* workshop, v. XXV Aprile 79; *La Torre,* v. Martiri della Libertà 6; *Albino Reggioni,* at Mombello, ✆ 668596; *Bottega Costantini,* ✆ 668238 (ceramics).
Cycling: *U.C. Lavenese,* at Mombello, v. Garibaldi 65, ✆ 667454.
Excursions: by cable car to Poggio S. Elma (3,000 ft).
Hang gliding: instruction at *Icaro school,* at Mombello, v. Luino 3, ✆ 21014.
Motocross: *Scag,* at Mombello; *Moto club Laveno,* v. Saggiano 57.

LUINO, ✉ 21016, ✆ 0332.

≈

ⓘ v. Dante Alighieri 6, ✆ 530019.
⎯ boats and hydrofoils.

Hotel:
★★★★ *Camin,* v. Dante 35, ✆ 530118, 13 rm P ⋚ ℏ closed 15 Dec-7 Mar, 110,000; bkf: 12,000.

Restaurant:
♦ *Due Scale,* p. Libertà 30, ✆ 530396, closed Fri. In rebuilt 18C building. Regional cuisine: risotto with frogs or strawberries, river perch, 25/40,000.

△ ★★★ *Parkcamping,* at Maccagno Inferiore *(5 km N),* 100 pl, ✆ 560203 (all year).

Recommended
Marina: *Lido,* ✆ 531250.
Swimming pool: at Paù, v. Lugano, ✆ 531706.

PORTO VALTRAVAGLIA, ✉ 21010, ✆ 0332.

≈

Hotel:
★★ *Cacciatore,* v. Varese 4, ✆ 547531, 26 rm P ⋚ ℏ closed 2 Jan-20 Mar, 47,000; bkf: 3,000.

SESTO CALENDE, ✉ 21018, ✆ 0331.
ⓘ v. Italia 3, ✆ 923329.

Hotel:
★★★ *Tre Re,* p. Garibaldi 25, ✆ 924229, 36 rm, closed 1 Dec-28 Feb, 62,000.

Restaurant:
♦♦♦ *Mosè,* at Lisanza, v. Ponzello 14, ✆ 910210, closed Mon eve, Tue, Jan and Aug. Large fireplaces and garden. Creative cuisine: gnocchetti with pesto and prawns, John Dory with pink peppercorns, 35/55,000.

Recommended
Canoeing: at *Circolo sestese,* p. C. da Sesto, ✆ 923309 (instruction).
Children's facilities: *La Filanda* children's residence at Golasecca, v. Matteotti 24, ✆ 02/6599145 (children 3-12 yr; all year).

LANZO D'INTELVI

Como 35, Milan 83 km
Pop. 1,470 ✉ 22024, ✆ 031   B3

Lanzo, on a plateau surrounded by woods, is the picturesque centre of the Val d'Intelvi, which rises from Argegno on Lake Como. 1.6 km away is the **Belvedere**★ (2,995 ft), a terrace offering a view of Lake Lugano. 6 km away is **Monte Sighignola** (4,272 ft) with views and ski facilities.   □

Practical information

LANZO D'INTELVI
♯ ski lifts on Monte Sighignola, cross-country skiing, skiing instruction.
ⓘ municipio, ✆ 840143.

Hotels:
★★★★ *Belvedere,* at Belvedere, v. Poletti 27, ✆ 840122, 36 rm P ⋚ ℏ ℇ ⋝ (9) closed Nov, 80,000.
★★★★ *Park Hotel Villa Violet,* at Belvedere, v. Poletti 29, ✆ 840139, 31 rm P ⋚ ℏ closed 16 Sep-14 Jun, 95,000.
★★ *Funicolare Miralago,* p. Belvedere, ✆ 840212, 20 rm P ⋚ ℍ closed Nov, 55,000; bkf: 4,000.
△ ★★ *Pian delle Noci,* at Pradale, 183 pl, ✆ 840179 (all year).

Recommended
Golf: ✆ 840169 (closed Oct-Apr; 9 holes).
Tennis: v. Poletti, ✆ 840136.

Environs

SAN FEDELE INTELVI, ✉ 22028, 7 km SE.

Hotel:
★★ *Villa Simplicitas,* at Simplicitas, ✆ 831132, 10 rm P ℍ ⋚ closed Dec-Feb. Splendid residence with 19C furnishings, 80,000; bkf: 10,000.

LECCO

Como 29, Milan 56 km
Pop. 50,685 ✉ 22053 ✆ 0341   B-C3

The foundries of Lecco, powered by the waters of the river Adda, produce iron. The industry was well-established in the 17C, but greatly expanded in the second half of the 19C, when the widespread silk industry was ruined by a silk-worm disease.

► Many distinguished visitors have praised the **Ponte Vecchio** over the Adda, built by Azzone Visconti (1336-8). It is a symbol of this town at the E extremity of Lake Como. ► The **Villa Manzoni** (in the Caleotto district) is named for the poet Alessandro Manzoni (1785-1873) who spent much time at Lecco. His play, *I Promessi Sposi,* is set in the town. The villa displays documents and memorabilia relating to Manzoni's life. ► **Piani d'Erna** (4,360 ft; *cableway from Malnago, 5 km away)* is a wooded plateau on the slopes of the Resegone. ► In **Vercurago** *(4.3 km SE)* are the ruins of a castle.   □

For the translation of a name of a meat, a fish or a vegetable, for the composition of a dish or a sauce, see the *Menu Guide* at the end of the Practical Holiday Guide; it lists the most common culinary terms.

Practical information

≋
ⓘ v. Sauro 6, ☎ 362360.
🚃 ☎ 364130.
🚗 ☎ 364036.

Hotels:
★★★★ *Griso*, at Malgrate, v. Provinciale 51, ☎ 375235, 41 rm Ⓟ ⚡ ⚙ ⊟ 110,000; bkf: 10,000. Rest. ● ◆◆◆◆ Outstanding creative cuisine, 48/73,000.
★★★ *Dom Abbondio*, p. Era 10, ☎ 366315, 19 rm Ⓟ closed Aug, 64,000.
★★★ *Promessi Sposi*, at Malgrate, v. Italia 4, ☎ 364089, 38 rm Ⓟ ⚡ ⚙ 70,000; bkf: 4,000. Rest. ◆◆ *Giovannino* 25/45,000.
★★ *Croce di Malta*, v. Roma 41, ☎ 363134, 48 rm Ⓟ 59,000; bkf: 4,000.

Restaurants:
◆◆◆ *Granaio*, vicolo del Torchio 1, ☎ 362396, closed Tue and Aug. Modern and efficient, family management. Fine cuisine, with international dishes: risotto with champagne or mushrooms, granaroli with onion cream or contadina, 30/50,000.
◆◆◆ *Les Paysans*, lungolario Piave 14, ☎ 369233, closed Mon, Tue noon, Christmas, May and Oct. Very atmospheric, summer service on floral terrace. Excellent creative cuisine: menu according to season and market availability, 30/55,000.
◆◆ *Don Rodrigo*, at Maggianico, corso E. Filiberto 112, ☎ 421100, closed Thu and Aug. Italian cuisine: pancakes, cannelloni, mixed roast meats, 20/26,000.

⚓ ★ *Rivabella*, at Chiuso, v. alla Spiaggia 35, 93 pl, ☎ 421143.

Recommended

Excursions: to Piani d'Erna (4,360 ft; skiing instruction, ski lifts) by cable car from Malnago.
Golf: *Royal Sant'Anna*, at Annone Brianza (→), ☎ 577551.
Marina: *Lecco rowing club*, ☎ 364273.
Mountaineering: *Casa delle Guide di Lecco*, v. Caprera 3, ☎ 590140 (courses in mountaineering, Alpine skiing); *Società escursionisti lecchesi*, v. Roma 5, ☎ 373330; *CAI Lecco*, v. Roma 51, ☎ 363588.
Skindiving: *Lecco diving club*, v. Risorgimento 46, ☎ 374160-367182 (instruction).
Swimming: sports facilities at Bione, ☎ 374144 (also tennis).
Water skiing: *Sci nautico Lago di Lecco*, at Malgrate, v. Italia 4, ☎ 364223; *Club nautico Garlate*, at Garlate, v. Statale 88, ☎ 680020; *Centro nautico Moregallo*, at Moregallo, ☎ 581024.

LEGNANO

Milan 27 km
Pop. 48,974 ✉ 20025 ☎ 0331   A-B4

Legnano is the site of the battle where, in 1176, the Lombard League put Frederick Barbarossa to rout.

▶ Legnano has a fine basilica of **S. Magno** (1504) with an altarpiece (1523) and frescos. ▶ In the **Castellanza** district is the **Museo d'Arte Moderna** of the Fondazione Pagani *(9:30 or 10 a.m.-12 noon and 3-6 p.m.)*, with open-air exhibition in a large park of sculpture and mosaic work by contemporary Italian and foreign artists.   □

Practical information

Hotel:
★★★ *2C*, v. Colli di S. Erasmo 51, ☎ 440159, 24 rm Ⓟ ⚙ ⚙ closed Aug. No restaurant, 61,500.

Restaurant:
◆◆◆ *Botte*, v. XXIX Maggio 35, ☎ 548173, closed Mon and Aug. Excellent cuisine, 35/40,000.

Recommended

Canoeing: *Gruppo canoe Legnano*, v. Berchet 41, ☎ 542859 (instruction).
Events: *Sagra del Carroccio festival* (end May), ☎ 546445.

LIVIGNO

Sondrio 103, Milan 240 km
Pop. 3,552 ✉ 23030 ☎ 0342   D1

Once most of the houses in Livigno were made of wood and, to reduce the risk of fire, the village spread out for kilometres along the road through the broad valley of the Spöl (a tributary of the river Inn, N of the alpine watershed and outside customs jurisdiction). The village is now an internationally known skiing centre. On the road to Bormio is **Trepalle** (6,818 ft), one of the highest villages in Europe.   □

Practical information

𝄢 cable cars, ski lifts, instruction, skating, summer skiing on Diavolezza glacier (in Swiss territory).
ⓘ municipio, ☎ 996379.

Hotels:
★★★★ *Intermonti*, v. Gerus 17, ☎ 996331, 175 rm Ⓟ ⚓ ⚙ ⊟ closed Oct and Easter-May, 85,000; bkf: 7,000.
★★★ *Bucaneve*, v. Nazionale 6, ☎ 996201, 38 rm Ⓟ ⚙ ⊟ ⚙ closed 1 May-9 Jun and 11 Oct-31 Nov, 55,000; bkf: 7,000.
★★★ *Concordia*, v. Plan 20, ☎ 996061, 40 rm Ⓟ ⚓ 58,000.
★★★ *Paré*, v. Gerus 3, ☎ 996263, 40 rm Ⓟ ⚡ ⚙ ⚙ ⊟ closed 1 Oct-30 Nov and May, 62,000; bkf: 7,000.
★★ *Augusta*, v. Rasia 60, ☎ 996163, 22 rm Ⓟ ⚡ ⚙ closed 16 Sep-30 Nov and 16 Apr-30 Jun, 40,000.
★★ *Steinbock*, v. Rin 11, ☎ 996268, 9 rm ⚙ closed 1 May-15 Jun and Nov, 44,000; bkf: 4,000. Rest. ◆◆ Comfortable, mountain style. Regional cuisine: slinzega of venison, venison chasseur with polenta, 15/25,000.

Restaurants:
◆◆◆ *Vecchia Lanterna*, v. Ostaria 17, ☎ 996103, closed Wed off season, May and Nov. Typical mountain restaurant. Regional cuisine: pappardelle with porcini, gypsy kebabs, 20/30,000.
◆◆ *Stua*, v. Teola, ☎ 996585; closed May-Jun and Oct-Nov. Regional and Italian cuisine: tagliatelle with botarga, fonduta, 18/23,000.

Recommended

Alpine guides: *Casa delle guide*, v. Milano 6, ☎ 451573.
Swimming: indoor swimming pool, ☎ 996278.

LODI*

Milan 31 km
Pop. 42,847 ✉ 20075 ☎ 0371   C4-5

Lodi is a market town and port on the Adda River at one end of the Milanese lowlands. Livestock, agriculture and dairy farming are the principal economic resources of the area.

▶ The **Piazza della Vittoria** (A-B1) is the largest and most important urban space, the heart of the new town built by Frederick Barbarossa in the 12C after the destruction of a neighbouring town of Roman origin *(Laus Pompeia)*. It is paved, and entirely surrounded by arcades and contains numerous important ecclesiastical and secular buildings. ▶ The façade of the 12C Romanesque **Duomo★** (A1) was rebuilt with Gothic and Renaissance elements. The interior (restored) has 14C-16C frescos in good condition, a 13C statue of S.Bassiano in copper and 16C altarpieces and marquetry. ▶ To the l. of the Duomo is the Baroque façade of the **Broletto** (municipal palace; A1), its arcade surmounted by a large loggia (18C). The arcade gives access to the p. Broletto, onto which the

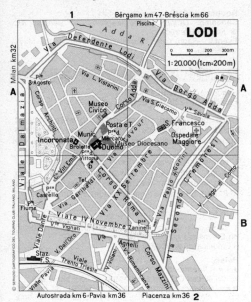

1 Bérgamo km47-Bréscia km66

LODI

0   100   200   300m

1:20.000 (1cm≈200m)

Milan km32

Autostrada km6-Pavia km36   Piacenza km36   **2**

older part of the building (13C) faces. ▶ Not far away is the church of the **Incoronata★★**, a gem of Lombard Renaissance architecture in the manner of Bramante. The octagonal interior with segmented dome is on two levels (the decorations on the lower level date from the 16C). There are **pictures** by Bergognone on either side of the second altar on the r. ▶ The **Museo Civico** (A1; *Sun 3:30-6:30 p.m.; other days by request 8:30 a.m.-12 noon and 2:30-6 p.m.; closed Mon*) has an archaeological collection and a picture gallery, but especially an interesting collection of ceramics, with specimens documenting the activities of Lodi manufacturers in the 18C. ▶ The Gothic church of **S. Francesco** (A2) is 13C and has a façade with rose window. ▶ 6.2 km W is **Lodi Vecchio**, on the site of the original Roman town destroyed by the Milanese in the 12C. Only the basilica of **S. Bassiano★** survived. It is 4C in origin with a Gothic false façade; 14C frescos inside. □

Practical information ———————

ℹ municipio (A1), ☎ 55255 extension 272.

Hotel:
★★★ *Europa*, v. Pavia 5, ☎ 35215, 44 rm Ⓟ ⌘ closed Christmas. No restaurant, 65,000; bkf: 7,000.

Restaurants:
♦♦♦ *Isola Caprera*, v. Isola Caprera 14 (A2 a), ☎ 63316, closed Tue and Jul-Aug. On bank of the Adda, with garden. Italian cuisine: pancakes with gorgonzola, trout, game, 25/35,000.
♦♦♦ *Quinta*, p. della Vittoria 20 (B1 b), ☎ 64232, closed Mon and 15-30 Aug. Skilfully run by two brothers. Regional cuisine: risotto mantecato, pasta al mascarpone, 25/25,000.
♦ *Trattoria Sobacchi*, v. Pavia 76, ☎ 35041, closed Mon eve, Tue, Aug and Christmas. Pleasant family trattoria with long tradition. Regional cuisine: risotto mantecato, polenta with braised filet, 25/35,000.

Recommended
Cycling: *U. C. Lodi*, v. Marsala 60 (B1), ☎ 65908.
Flying club: *Aeroclub di Lodi*, at S.Colombano al Lambro *(15 km S)*, ☎ 89238.

Horseback riding: *La Fornace*, at Zelo Buon Persico *(16 km N)* SS. Paullese, ☎ 02/9065016.
Natural park: regional park of *Adda Sud*, v. Zalli 5, ☎ 36047; regional nature reserve of *Monticchie*, guided tours, reservations from *WWF Basso Lodigiano*, ☎ 0377/33001 or *WWF Lombardia*, ☎ 02/6556810.
Wines: *De Tomi*, corso Vittorio Emanuele 32 (B1), ☎ 52786.

LOMELLO

Pavia 33, Milan 62 km
Pop. 2,523 ☒ 27034 ☎ 0382   A5

Lomello has been an active agricultural centre since ancient times.

▶ The baptistery of **S. Giovanni ad Fontes★**, originally 5C and restored in the 8C, has survived from the Lombard period. The interior is on the plan of a Greek cross, with octagonal dome, remains of the original paving and font for baptism by immersion. ▶ Also of interest is the Romanesque church of **S. Maria Maggiore★** (11C), a charming brick building. The interior is assymetrical. ▶ 11 km E is the **Castello di Scaldasole** (12C-15C), with four corner towers and a courtyard in the style of Bramante. □

LONATO

Brescia 23, Milan 120 km
Pop. 10,785 ☒ 25017 ☎ 030   D-E4

Lonato is a pleasing little town with fine architecture. Napoleon defeated the Austrians here with great brilliance in 1796. Lonato gained further fame among historians after the discovery of substantial remains of a lake civilization commonly known as the Polada culture.

▶ The **Casa del Podestà** *(Mon-Fri 2:30-6 p.m.)*, restored to its original 15C form and enclosed within the walls of a Visconti stronghold, has a library with valuable incunabula and manuscripts (16C-20C). □

Practical information ———————

Hotel:
★★★ *Rustichello*, v. Roma 48, ☎ 9130107, 10 rm Ⓟ 卌 42,000; bkf: 3,000.

Recommended
Motocross: *La Piana*, at Campanoli, management at Manerba del Garda, v. Trieste 15, ☎ 0365/53163.

LOVERE

Bergamo 41, Milan 86 km
Pop. 6,049 ☒ 24065 ☎ 035   D3

This little town at the N end of Lake Iseo and the end of the Valcamonica is an important resort, as well as a centre of iron and steel and light engineering industries. A reminder of the times in which it was heavily fortified and of strategic importance and also a flourishing agricultural market town is provided by the medieval centre, with traces of the old fortifications and buildings.

▶ It is imperative to visit the **Galleria dell'Accademia Tadini** *(May-Sep; Sun and hols 10 a.m.-12 noon and 3-6 p.m.; p.m. only on weekdays)*, with an important picture gallery and collection of porcelain, and the church of **S. Maria in Valvendra** (1473-83), with a magnificent interior rich in works of art. □

Practical information

p. Vittorio Emanuele 2, ☎ 962488.
🚤 boats, ☎ 971483.

Hotels:
★★★ *Sant'Antonio,* p. XIII Martiri 2, ☎ 961523, 22 rm ℗ & ❀ 47,000, bkf: 5,000.
★★ *Castello,* v. del Santo, ☎ 960228, 20 rm ℗ ⅋ ◬ ⬛ ❀ 32,000. Rest. ♦ *Due Ruote* closed Mon in winter. Abruzzi cuisine, 20/35,000.
★★ *Moderno,* p. XIII Martiri 21, ☎ 960607; 18 rm ⅋ & closed Christmas; 45,000; bkf: 4,000.

Recommended
Marina: *Circolo nautico,* ☎ 960466.
Sailing instruction: *Associazione nautica Alto Sebino,* v. del Centreve, ☎ 960235; *Associazione nautica Sebino,* at Montécolo, ☎ 985196 (cruises, international sailing regattas).

MADESIMO

Sondrio 79, Milan 142 km
Pop. 687 ⊠ 23024 ☎ 0343   B1

Madesimo is a flourishing winter sports centre known since 1612 for curative springs. Near **Pianazzo** (3 km) is a waterfall, the **Cascata dello Scalcoggia,** which falls 525 ft. There are fine ski slopes on the **Pizzo Groppera** (9,462 ft); ski lifts to Alpe Motta (→ Campodolcino).   □

Practical information

⚞ cable cars, ski lifts, cross-country skiing, instruction, tobogganing slopes, ice skating.
v. Carducci, ☎ 53015.

Hotels:
★★★★ *Cascata et Cristallo,* v. Carducci 2, ☎ 53108, 80 rm ℗ ⬛ ⬛ 110,000; bkf: 10,000.
★★★ *Meridiana,* v. Carducci 8, ☎ 53160, 25 rm ℗ ⬛ closed 16 Sep-29 Oct and 6 May-14 Jun, 60,000; bkf: 8,000.
★★★ *Emet,* v. Carducci 28, ☎ 53395, 33 rm ℗ ❀ closed Sep-Nov and May-Jun, 68,000; bkf: 7,000.

Restaurant:
♦♦ *Osteria Vegia,* v. Cascata 7, ☎ 53335, closed Mon, May-Jun and Sep-Oct. Historic restaurant dating from 18C. Regional cuisine: bresaola, polenta tragna, 25/30,000.

MALPAGA CASTLE

Bergamo 14, Milan 51 km
                    C4

This 14C **castle**★ *(Sun 2:30-5:30 p.m.; other days by appointment,* ☎ 840003) has a cycle of **frescos** dating from 1520 commemorating the life and deeds of the condottiere, Bartolomeo Colleoni, who lived in a splendid round of feasts, tournaments and hunts, along with his retinue of 800 knights.   □

MANTUA★★

(Mantova)

Milan 147, Rome 472 km
Pop. 59,592 ⊠ 46100 ☎ 0376   E5

The Roman poet Virgil was born close to Mantova or 'Mantua, rich in ancestors' as he called the city in 70 BC. (The village of his birth, then called Andes, still exists under the commemorative name of Pietole Virgilio.) In the late 12C-early 13C the city, by now

Isabella d'Este

Daughter of the Duke of Ferrara, Ercole d'Este, Isabella d'Este is commemorated in the vast Gonzaga palace at Mantua. She lived in this apartment as the wife of the Marquis Francesco II Gonzaga, ruler of Mantua, to whom she was married for sixteen years after being engaged for ten. Widowed, Isabella moved in 1519 to an apartment on the ground floor of the palace, where she had her celebrated gabinetti, including study and music room. They can still be visited today, although the magnificent works of art which she commissioned have been removed. She was a highly intelligent woman, well-read and cultivated. She enjoyed being surrounded by men of letters and corresponded with the greatest artists. She was also involved in politics in defence of herself and her family in tempestuous times. She died in 1539 at the age of seventy-five, remembered as 'the fount and origin of all that is finest in Italy', as good as she was beautiful.

a free commune, drained the marshes that surrounded it and erected majestic buildings. For 300 years, from 1328, Mantua was governed by the Gonzaga family, victors in a bloody power struggle that had been waged for two centuries. From the 14C-17C Mantua was a political centre of international significance, seat of one of the most splendid courts in Europe and rich in art and culture. The magnificent buildings in the centre date from this period, protected by ancient streets charming in their tranquility, where palazzi and the plain houses of modern Mantua look over the calm waters of the river.

▶ For many centuries the **Piazza Sordello**★ (B3-4) has been the centre of the city's artistic and political life; it retains the fascination and grandeur of the medieval period. ▶ The NE extremity is formed by the 18C façade of the **Duomo**★ (B4), rebuilt in the 16C (the Romanesque campanile and parts of the original Gothic building have survived). The huge, beautifully balanced interior (1545) was inspired by the basilicas of ancient Rome. Notable features are a 5C Christian sarcophagus, remains of 13C frescos in the baptistery and a large fresco by D. Fetti. The 15C **Cappella dell'Incoronata** can be reached from the l. aisle. ▶ The **Palazzo Ducale**★★ (B4; *guided tour lasting approximately 1.5 hr; weekdays 9 a.m.-2 p.m., Sun and hols 9 a.m.-1 p.m.; closed Mon)* is an impressive complex covering almost an acre. The buildings were erected and altered over centuries (13C-18C) to accommodate the court of the Gonzaga. The more than 450 rooms contain well-organized and valuable collections of paintings (including Rubens' *Duchi e Duchesse Gonzaga*★), Greek and Roman sculpture, Roman sarcophagi and inscriptions, medieval and Renaissance sculpture (including a *bust of Francesco Gonzaga*★ attributed to Andrea Mantegna). The most interesting rooms are: the **appartamento degli Arazzi,** displaying a set of nine Flemish tapestries woven to cartoons by Raphael; the **appartamento Ducale** (16C-17C) with decorated and inlaid ceilings; the **appartamento dei Nani** (dwarfs; 17C), with stairs, rooms and even a chapel in miniature; the **appartamento delle Metamorfosi** (17C) with decoration inspired by the works of Ovid; **la Rustica** (16C); the **galleria della Mostra,** intended for exhibitions of treasures from the palace, with balconies facing the 16C **cortile della Cavallerizza;** and the **sala di Manto,** one of the grandest in the palace (probably 16C), which is named after a mythical female founder of the city. Particularly important here are fragments of **frescos** painted by Pisanello, probably in 1446-7. The stairway of Aeneas *(scalone di Enea)* leads to the **Castello di S. Giorgio,** looking out over a courtyard surrounded by elegant arcades. In a corner tower is the famous **camera degli Sposi**★★, one of the most important sites in Italian painting, with a fresco cycle dedicated by Mantegna to the Marchese Ludovico Gonzaga and his family. *(To avoid microclimatic variations that could damage the pictures, which have recently undergone delicate restoration, access to the room is permitted only to small groups for a few minutes at a time.)* On the second floor of the castle are the **jails** in which political prisoners were confined. The **gabinetti Isabelliani**★ (the rooms of Isabella d'Este, wife of Francesco II Gonzaga, near the Cortile d'Onore), with magnificent inlaid and gilded ceilings (15C), are under partial restoration. ▶ Pass through the arcades from the p. Sordello to the adjacent **piazza del Broletto**, with 15C façade (rebuilt) and the high square tower of the palazzo del **Broletto** (C3) or del Podestà (13C), the former seat of government. There is a 13C statue of Virgil, *Mantuanus poetarum clarissimus* ('most famous poet of Mantua') in a niche on the façade. ▶ The **Piazza delle Erbe**★ (C3) is the second architectural, civic and religious centre of the old town. ▶ The 13C **Palazzo della Ragione** (C3; restored) has a 15C arcade. On the r. is the **Torre dell'Orlogio** (clock tower) built in 1473. ▶ The Romanesque **Rotonda di S. Lorenzo**★ (C3), at the level where the whole square was formerly set, was commissioned in the 11C by the Countess Matilda di Canossa. The interior of the rotunda is supported on ten massive columns with a hemispherical dome. ▶ The NW side of the piazza is dominated by the dome of the basilica of **S. Andrea**★★ (B-C3), rising above the old arcaded houses. The basilica, a major example of Renaissance ecclesiastical architecture, was designed in 1470 and built in the 15C-17C. The Baroque dome is an 18C addition. The Neoclassical façade looking on to the p. Mantegna was inspired by Roman triumphal arches; a 16C portal, carved in lavish detail, opens into the vestibule, with coffered ceiling; the adjacent Gothic campanile (1413) was part of an earlier church. The **interior**★ has a broad single aisle and tunnel vaulting. In side chapels are the tomb of Mantegna, with paintings by his pupils. ▶ The old town contains other monuments and distinguished buildings, such as the elegant **Teatro Scientifico**★ (1769; C4) in the Palazzo del Accademia Virgiliana *(weekdays 9 a.m.- 12 noon and 3:30-6 p.m.);* the 14C Gothic church of **S. Francesco** (B2) with frescos by Tommaso di Modena (14C), not far from the Neoclassical Palazzo d'Arco (B2); the **house of Giulio Romano** (D2), designed by the artist himself; the vigorous 17C **Palazzo di Giustizia**★ (D2); **Mantegna's house** (D2), possibly designed by the artist himself; the restrained church of **S. Sebastiano**★ (E2; *for visits ask at the Palazzo Te; Tue and Sat 9:30 a.m.-12 noon and 2:30-5 p.m.),* built in 1460 and now used as a memorial chapel for war dead; and finally, set slightly apart, the 13C Gothic church of **S. Maria di Gradaro** (E4), with interesting remains of Byzantine frescos. ▶ The **Palazzo Te**★★ *(E-F2; Apr-Oct 9:30 a.m.-12:30 p.m. and 2:30-5:30 p.m. or until 5 p.m. from Oct-Nov to Mar; closed Mon)* takes its name from the old suburb of Teieto. This magnificent Renaissance (16C) villa, in unusually good condition, was built as a rural retreat for Federico II Gonzaga. Particularly interesting among numerous rooms are the **Sala dei Cavalli;** the **Sala di Psiche,** with mythological scenes painted on vault and walls; the **sala di Fetonte** or delle Aquile, with a ceiling fresco by Giulio Romano and stucco by Francesco Primaticcio (1504-70); the **sala dei Giganti,** illustrated by the Fall of the Titans Struck by Jove's Thunderbolt, painted in fresco on the ceiling and walls in a single impressive sweep, which creates a spectacular effect.

Environs

▶ 7.3 km to the N is the **Bosco della Fontana,** formerly the Gonzagas' hunting grounds. ▶ The church of **S. Maria degli Angeli** (4 km W) is in Lombardy Gothic style (1429). ▶ The sanctuary of **S. Maria delle Grazie** (9 km W) was endowed by Francis I Gonzaga in thanksgiving for Mantua's liberation from the plague; it was built in the 14C-15C and is a popular place of pilgrimage. On

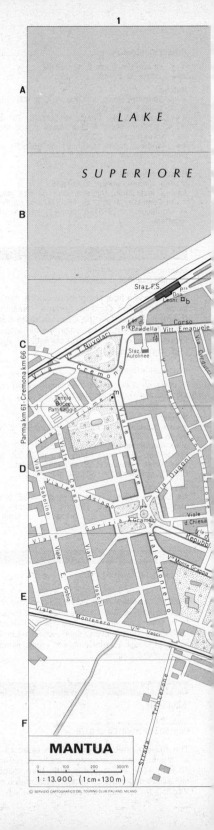

MANTUA

0   100   200   300m

1 : 13.000   (1 cm = 130 m)

© SERVIZIO CARTOGRAFICO DEL TOURING CLUB ITALIANO, MILANO

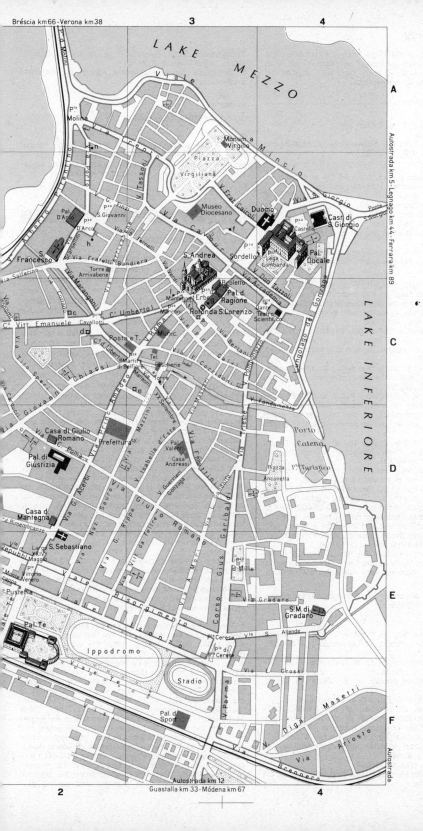

15 August (Feast of the Virgin Mary's Assumption into heaven) the traditional *madonnari* exhibition is held here: sacred scenes are drawn on the asphalt in chalk. ▶ 33 km away, **Sabbioneta** (→).   ☐

Practical information _____

MANTUA
ⓘ p. Mantegna 6 (C3), ☎ 350681.
▤▥ (C1), ☎ 321647.
☞▦ departures from the Autostazione, v. Mutilati and Caduti del Lavoro (D1), ☎ 327237.

Hotels:
★★★★ *San Lorenzo,* p. Concordia 14 (C3 a), ☎ 327153, 42 rm ℗ ✹ No restaurant, 120,000; bkf: 15,000.
★★★ *Apollo,* p. Don Leoni 17 (C1 b), ☎ 350522, 35 rm ℗ No restaurant, 73,000; bkf: 8,000.
★★★ *Dante,* v. Corrado 54 (C2 c), ☎ 326425, 40 rm ℗ No restuarant, 73,000; bkf: 7,500.
★★★ *Italia,* p. Cavallotti 8 (C2 d), ☎ 322609, 34 rm ℗ 73,000; bkf: 8,000.
★★★ *Mantegna,* v. Filzi 10 (C3 e), ☎ 350315, 37 rm ℗ closed Christmas. No restaurant, 73,000; bkf: 7,000.

Restaurants:
● ◆◆◆◆ *Cigno,* p. C. d'Arco 1 (B2 h), ☎ 327101, closed Mon, Tue eve and Aug. In 16C palazzo with some ceilings and friezes of the period. Outstanding regional cuisine: risotto alla pilota, maltagliati with kidney beans, stracotto alla mantovana, 40/55,000.
◆◆◆◆ *San Gervasio,* v. S. Gervasio 13 (A2 n), ☎ 350504, closed Wed and Aug. In ancient palazzo with 14C and 17C ceilings. Italian cuisine: savarin of prawns, steak florentine, 30/45,000.
◆◆◆ *Campana,* v. S. Maria Nuova 10, ☎ 325679, closed Fri and Aug. Regional cuisine: pumpkin tortelli, fish in green sauce, 25/35,000.
◆◆◆ *Garibaldini,* v. S. Longino 7 (C3 l), ☎ 329237, closed Fri and 1-20 Aug. In a 16C house with a long tradition; fireplace and period rooms, plus cool summer courtyard. Regional cuisine: risotto picon, agnoli in brodo, 35/45,000.
◆◆◆ *Ritzino,* v. Piave 2 (D1 m), ☎ 326474, closed Mon. Art nouveau décor. Regional cuisine: pappardelle, grilled fish, 20/40,000.
● ◆◆ *Cento Rampini,* p. delle Erbe 11 (C3 g), ☎ 366349, closed Mon, Sun eve in summer and 1-20 Aug. Charming, under the arcade of the Palazzo della Regione, with service in square in summer. Regional cuisine: pumpkin tortelli, pike in sauce, horse stracotto, 20/30,000.
◆◆ *Aquila Nigra-la Ducale,* vicolo Bonacolsi 4 (B3 f), ☎ 350651, closed Sun eve and Mon. In a former convent. Regional and Italian cuisine: gnocchetti with nettles, fried brains and artichokes, 25/40,000.
◆◆ *Franco,* v. Peschiera 28 (C3 i), ☎ 362784, closed Mon and Sep. Refined family atmosphere. Regional cuisine: pumpkin tortelli, gnochetti verdi, stracotto with polenta, 25/35,000.
▲ ★ *Sparafucile,* at Lunetta San Gioregio, strada Legnaghese 2, 45 pl, ☎ 372465.

Recommended
Boat trips: on the Po, on the Mincio and the Venice lagoon: *Andes motorships,* at Governolo *(16 km SE),* ☎ 668110-668240.
Bowling: *Bocciodromo europeo,* at Guidizzolo *(28 km NE),* v. H. Dunant 14, ☎ 819144.
Canoeing: *Canottieri Mincio,* v. S. Maria 15 (B2-3), ☎ 325276.
Cycling: *Polisportiva Te Brunetti,* v. Semeghini 8.
Events: exhibition of antiques at the Palazzo della Ragione (Oct); exhibition-market of antique books and prints (May and Sep): organizing office, ☎ 323849.
Guided tours: Associazione guide turistiche, ☎ 368917.
Natural park: *Mincio regional park,* v. P. Amedeo 30, ☎ 320541 (33,874 acres).
Sports hall: v. Te (F3), ☎ 368084.
Visits to boatyards: *Mendes Baratti* yard, at Rivalta on the Mincio (riverboats).

Youth hostel: *Ostello Sparafucile,* at Lunetta San Giorgio, strada Legnaghese,☎ 322415.
♥ pasticceria: torta di tagliatelle, sbrisolona, and other local delicacies.

Environs
GOITO, ☒ 46044, 15 km NW.

Restaurant:
● ◆◆◆ *Bersagliere,* v. Goitese 360, ☎ 60007, closed Mon, Jan and Aug. Secluded atmosphere with veranda facing the Mincio. Outstanding regional cuisine: tagliatelle with duck sauce, snail risotto, 45/55,000.

MILAN**

Rome 575 km
Pop. 1,561,438 ☒ 20100 ☎ 02   B4

Milan is concerned with production, renewal, movement and experiment. It was always a working-class as well as a middle-class city; today it is also cosmopolitan, modern and efficient. The Milanese, however, are still influenced by the Lombard characteristic of shifting from the practical to the romantic when things get difficult. Modern-day Milano is still a 19C town, built on a human scale. Its potential is not fully exploited, and it does not always provide the infrastructure and services, the quality and variety of cultural and entertainment facilities that a successful industrial, commercial and financial image demands. A popular saying often heard among the Milanese is 'to do or to undo, either is work.'

▶ In the decade after the unification of Italy, Milan was seized by building fever. Before this, the city had consisted of a compact centre within a circle of canals with a characteristic Roman pattern of streets modified in the Middle Ages as well as a series of linear villages (with open spaces, gardens and numerous convents) in the strip bounded by the rampart of the 16C Spanish walls, by then used as a footpath and customs barrier. Isolated in the NW were the great castle, now a barracks, and the piazza d'Armi and the adjacent arena, which served as a sports and amusement ground. In the NE was the 15C poor house (lazzaretto), which had been turned over to commercial and artisan activities. Outside, around the walls that followed the municipal administrative boundaries, was the commune known as *Corpi Santi,* which was to be annexed in 1873. Onto this framework, which had developed over the centuries by a process of continuous but rebuilding and replacement (which is why there are no districts that can properly be called medieval, 16C, 18C and so on) were superimposed new building projects and alterations that, over the span of a century, have made Milan look as it does today.

▶ **The centre between the piazza del Duomo, La Scala and the piazza San Babila.** ▶ The first town plan dates from 1884. Before this, in 1865, the complex of the **piazza del Duomo** (DE-4), geometric centre and heart of the inner city, had been completed at the price of the destruction of an entire district and the appropriation of almost half the money available from public funds. ▶ The final stages of the long building history of the **Duomo★★** (D4), which was started in 1386 under Gian Galeazzo Visconti, were tackled in 1887. After St. Peter's in Rome and Seville cathedral, it is the largest church in the Roman Catholic world, and the largest and most complex Gothic building in Italy. Numerous Lombard, Campionese, French and German architects directed the work over the centuries. Finally (15C-16C) Italians took over. Particularly striking are the masses of white marble (best appreciated from the adjacent p. Reale), articulated with pilasters and soaring skyward in flights of flying buttresses, 125 spires (completed in 1887) and thousands of statues. ▶ The cathedral is a forest of architecture and sculpture where it is possible to wander by climbing to the **terrazzi**★ *(entrance outside the Duomo; elevator or steps; 9 a.m.-5:30 p.m.; Oct-Feb, 9 a.m.-4:30 p.m.)*. In clear weather the view extends over the city to the plain and the Alps, and it is possible to admire from close quarters the **lantern**★, topped with a tall spire (356 ft) with the gilded statue of the **Madonnina**. The façade was completed in 1813, with variants on the original design; it is Baroque to the first tier of windows, but returned to Gothic forms for the upper parts. The five portals are 16C, but have bronze doors by 20C artists. The dim light that penetrates the great Gothic windows, with old (15C-16C) and modern **stained glass,** gives an air of mystery and solemnity to the vast interior. Noteworthy among the many works of art are: **the tomb of Gian Giacomo Medici**★ by L. Leoni (1563); a magnificent **choir**★ in inlaid walnut (1572-1620); and the **casket of S. Carlo Borromeo,** by F. M. Richini (1606), in which are the remains of St. Charles Borromeo, archbishop of Milan. ▶ Nearby is the **treasury**★, with precious ivories, silver and gold from the 4C-17C. ▶ Building in the cathedral and along the centuries are documented in the **Museo del Duomo**★, on the l. of the Palazzo Reale (E4; *9:30 a.m.-12:30 p.m. and 3-6 p.m.; closed Mon)*: glass, tapestries, paintings and drawings, vestments, models and plans are on display, along with an exceptional collection of Lombard Gothic, French and Rhenish sculpture from the 14C-15C and Lombard sculpture to the present day. ▶ The **Palazzo Reale** (E4), the 14C former ducal palace, later residence of the Spanish and Austrian governor has been rebuilt to the original Neoclassical design (1778). The interior is no longer as richly decorated as it used to be (having been destroyed by bombing) and is used for public functions. The **Civico Museo d'Arte Contemporanea** *(9:30 a.m.-12:30 p.m. and 2:30-5:15 p.m.; closed Mon)* has two sections showing the most important 20C movements in Italian art in the years after the Second World War. ▶ Leave via the v. Pecorari exit and visit the adjacent church of **S. Gottardo in Corte,** notable for its fine 13C octagonal **campanile**★. ▶ The **p. Fontana** (DE-4) takes its name from the fountain built in 1782 by the architect Piermarini, who was also responsible for the façade of the **Palazzo Arcivescovile** (E4), with parts of the original 12C building to the N and W; inside is a fine Mannerist **courtyard**★ with rustication. ▶ Opposite the Duomo is an equestrian statue of Victor Emmanuel II (by E. Rosa, 1896), behind which the **piazza Mercanti**★ (D4) opens out; it is the only surviving corner of medieval Milan. Isolated between the square and the v. Mercanti is the **Palazzo della Ragione**★ or Broletto Nuovo (1233) on a raised arcade; the second floor was added in the 18C. In a niche on the side overlooking the square is a fine Romanesque **relief**★ of the school of Antelami (13C) representing a *podestà* (governor) on horseback. Opposite this is the **loggia degli Osii** (1316) with black and white marble and two open galleries, flanking the **Palazzo delle Scuole Palatine** (1645); on the other side is the **casa Panigarola** (15C), while on the v. Mercanti is the **Palazzo dei Giureconsulti** (1564). Return to the N side of the p. del Duomo under the imposing arch of the **Galleria Vittorio Emanuele II**★(D4), built 1865-77; the two covered ways under an iron and glass roof, intersecting in the piazzetta called the **Ottagono,** have been called 'Milan's drawing room'. ▶ On the l. of the piazza della Scala is the **Teatro alla Scala**★, a restrained Neoclassical building (1778) that at the time of building was most celebrated for its fine interior. Today it is one of the glories of Milan, Italy's major opera house, and one of the greatest in the world. The adjacent **Museo Teatrale** *(9 a.m.-12 noon and 2-6 p.m.; Sun and hols May-Oct 9:30 a.m.-12 noon and 2:30-6 p.m.)* houses an important collection of memorabilia and documents on the history of the theatre and operatic art. ▶ Opposite the theatre is the 19C façade of the **Palazzo Marino** (D4), the town hall started in 1553 in Mannerist style, which has been authentically preserved in the elegant **cortile d'onore**★ (court of honour), with rear façade on the p. S. Fedele (D4). The

piazza is named after the church of **S. Fedele,** started in 1569 and completed in the 19C. ▶ Not far away in the street of the same name is the **casa degli Omenoni**★, called after the large, melancholy caryatids, the work (1565) of Leone Leoni, sculptor to Emperor Charles V and Philip II, who lived (1509-90) and had his studio here. ▶ At the end of this short street is the p. Belgioioso, onto which looks the Neoclassical **Palazzo Belgioioso** (D4; 1781), and the house of the poet Alessandro Manzoni, which houses the **Museo Manzoniano** and the Centro Nazionale di Studi Manzoniani *(Tue to Fri 9 a.m.-12 noon and 2-4 p.m.; Wed till 5 p.m.)*. ▶ The v. Morone leads back to the **via Manzoni,** one of the most elegant and stylish streets in Milan, flanked by Neoclassical palazzi and terminating in the N with the Porta Nuova (C5). At no. 12 is the **Museo Poldi-Pezzoli**★ (D4; *9:30 a.m.-12:30 p.m. and 2:30-6 p.m.; Sat and Sun until 5:30; Thu also 9-11 p.m., exc Aug; Apr-Sep Sun a.m. only; closed Mon)*, formerly a valuable private collection, then bequeathed to the city, together with the palace, by the art collector G. G. Poldi-Pezzoli. The collection includes antique weapons and armour★, 16C-19C clocks, gold, enamels, glass, porcelain, bronze, furniture, textiles (notably a Persian carpet★ dating from 1522 and a Flemish tapestry★ of 1602) and lace. The paintings include masterpieces★ by Pollaiolo, Botticelli, Piero della Francesca, Mantegna, Foppa and Guardi. ▶ The 19C **via Montenapoleone** (B5), flanked with Neoclassical palazzi, has gradually become Milan's most luxurious shop window, with shops selling antiques, fashionable clothes and luxury items. ▶ In the v. S. Andrea (D5), a side street, is the 16C Palazzo Morando-Bolognini, which houses the **Museo di Storia Contemporanea** *(9.30 a.m.-12:30 p.m. and 2:30-5:30 p.m.; closed Mon)* and the **Museo di Milano.** ▶ The **Piazza S. Babila** (D5) is called after the Romanesque **church** of the same name (11C; badly restored in the 19C); the square dates from the late 1930s and is surrounded by office buildings and finance houses; it is one of the key points for the busy traffic of the town. ▶ Return to the Duomo via the **corso Vittorio Emanuele II** (D4-5), also rebuilt after the Second World War and full of elegant shops, including the great department stores, to which Gabriele d'Annunzio gave the name 'La Rinascente' because they had been rebuilt after a fire.

▶ **From the Brera to Porta Venezia and Porta Vittoria.** ▶ From the piazza della Scala proceed by the v. Verdi, with the baroque church of **S. Giuseppe** (1630), to the 19C **via Brera** (A-B4), once heart of the artists' quarter and still endowed with fine art shops and galleries. At no. 28 is the **Accademia di Belle Arti,** in the same 17C palazzo that houses the important **Pinacoteca di Brera**★★ (C4; *9 a.m.-1 p.m.; Sun 9 a.m.-1 p.m.; under reconstruction and restoration)*, which is approached through the **courtyard** dominated by a bronze statue of Napoleon by Canova. The Pinacoteca is a cultural institution of European rank; the collections include: detached frescos of the 15C-16C Lombard school; 18C Italian primitives; 15C-16C Venetian paintings (including **masterpieces**★★ by Tintoretto, Mantegna, Giovanni and Gentile Bellini); 15C-17C Lombard painting; 15C-16C Emilian painting (including a *Madonna Enthroned and Saints*★★); central Italian paintings (including **masterpieces**★★ by Piero della Francesca and Raphael); 17C-19C Italian painting; finally, in a new wing, 20C Italian works. ▶ Behind the Brera, in the Neoclassical Palazzo Moriggia in the v. Borgonuovo, is the **Civico Museo del Risorgimento** (C4; *9:30 a.m.-12:30 p.m. and 2:30-5:30 p.m.; closed Mon)*, with documentary and pictorial records on the history of Italy from the 18C to 1870. ▶ The church of **S. Simpliciano**★ (C3) is the former *Basilica Virginum,* founded in the 4C by St. Ambrose and completed by his successor Simpliciano. Parts of the perimeter walls (discovered during restoration) have survived of the original church; the façade, lantern and campanile were rebuilt in the 12C, then restored. In the interior, the apse is decorated with a large **fresco**★ by Bergognone (c. 1515). To the r. of the church is the former **convent** *(apply to the porter's*

Stendhal in Milan

Henri Beyle (later to achieve fame as a novelist under the pseudonym Stendhal) arrived in Milan in June 1800, as a private in Napoleon's army. He was seventeen years old, and having grown up in the provinces (Grenoble) and been disappointed by a stay in Paris, was fascinated by Milan. The same year, the youth achieved the provisional rank of second lieutenant in the Sixth Dragoons; he had a fine uniform and a sabre, but garrison life, which kept him away from Milan, bored him. He returned to Grenoble and resigned. Stendhal visited Milan in 1811 and 1813, and in 1814 returned to stay, except for intermittent journeys, until 1821. These years made him a true Milanese. He was much involved in Milan's literary world in these years, but left Milan in 1821 because of unrequited love. He returned only once, in 1827, but the Austrian police ordered him to leave the city within 12 hours. Reporting to Vienna, the chief of police said of Stendhal's work that it 'not only propounds the most pernicious political principles, but has also compromised with lies and calumnies the good reputation of many persons in this province and other Italians'.

lodge at no. 6), with two cloisters; the *chiostro grande★* (16C), is particularly fine.

▶ Also important is the church of **S. Marco** (C4), founded in 1254 and often restored; in the interior are notable marble tombs and 14C frescos. ▶ The v. Fatebenefratelli (C4-5), where the old circle of canals used to be (they were covered over in the 1920s), leads to the modern p. Cavour (C5); on the l. is the v. Turati (B-C5), also modern, with the former palazzi of the Montecatini, by G. Ponti (1938-51) in the first section of the street. In the v. Moscova is the 16C church of **S. Angelo** (B-C4), with a typical Lombard Mannerist façade (started in the 17C) and a lavishly decorated interior. ▶ The second part of the v. Turati (at no. 34 is the **Palazzo della Permanente**, used for art exhibitions) leads to the enormous **piazza della Repubblica** (B5), seething with traffic, surrounded by luxury hotels and dominated by two skyscrapers; until the late thirties it was the p. della Stazione Centrale. ▶ The present **Stazione Centrale** (A6), built 1925-31 to plans dating from 1912, is on the vast p. Duca d'Aosta. The building is a mixture of art nouveau and other styles, overburdened with sculptural ornament; the bold metal roofing of the arrival hall gives a magnificent effect. ▶ At the NW corner of the square is the unmistakable, extremely elegant Pirelli **skyscraper**, the tallest in Milan (417 ft), built 1955-60 and now housing regional government offices. ▶ The v. Vitruvio (A-B6) leads to the **corso Buenos Aires** (B-C6), the major business thoroughfare. At the beginning of this street, near the Porta Venezia (Neoclassical gatehouse, 1828) was the **Lazzaretto** (poor house), pulled down *c.* 1880 and divided into small building plots. ▶ The urban landscape changes considerably towards the centre by the wide **corso Venezia** (C5-6), flanked by parks and as it continues toward the p. S. Babila, running between noble, austere palazzi. ▶ The **Giardini Pubblici** (B-C5-6) are not extensive, but offer a pleasing variety of trees, clearings, paths, water and monuments. On the corso Venezia side are the **Planetario** (C6; *Tue and Thu 9 p.m.; Sat and Sun 3-4:30 p.m.; closed Jul-Sep*), which offers lectures and demonstrations, and the **Museo Civico di Storia Naturale★** (C5; *9:30 a.m.-12:30 p.m. and 2.30-5.30 p.m. or 2-5 p.m. Nov-Feb; closed Mon*). ▶ At the opposite end of the park is the 18C **Palazzo Dugnani** (C5). Inside (*office hours*) is a room with frescos★ by Tiepolo, as well

as the **Museo del Cinema.** ▶ The v. Palestro leads to the **Villa Reale★** now **Comunale** (C5), one of the finest examples of Neoclassical architecture in Milan. The villa was built in 1790 with the courtyard on the street side; the façade forms the background to a charming garden in the English style. It now houses the **Galleria d'Arte Moderna★** (*9:30 a.m.-12 noon and 2:30-5:30 p.m.; closed Tue*), which has 35 galleries showing a collection of Neoclassical, Romantic and modern art, mainly from Lombardy; also three collections of 19C-20C Italian and French art. The activities of the gallery are associated with those of the **Padiglione d'Arte Contemporanea**, an outstanding example of Italian architecture from the 1950s, built 1948-54 within the perimeter of the old stables of the villa. It now displays significant works of contemporary Italian art. ▶ The shady, tree-lined v. Marina (C5) meets the **via del Conservatorio** (D6) near the **Palazzo del Senato**. Next to the **Conservatorio Giuseppe Verdi**, in the former Lateran monastery, is the church of **S. Maria della Passione**, the second-largest in Milan after the Cathedral. It was started in 1486 and finally completed with a Baroque façade in 1729; the dome dates from 1530. In the interior are notable paintings. The adjacent **Museo della Basilica** (*10 a.m.-12 noon and 3-5:30 p.m.; Sun and hols p.m. only*) displays other interesting 17C Lombard work and fine frescos. ▶ Nearby, opposite the oppressive Palazzo di Giustizia (1940), is the church of **S. Pietro in Gessate** (E5; 15C), in transitional style between Gothic and Renaissance. Inside are important frescos and paintings of the 15C Lombard school. ▶ In the v. Besana (E6) is the **Rotonda**, built 1698-1725 as a cemetery for the Ospedale (hospital) Maggiore; eight segments of a circle surround a former church now used for exhibitions. ▶ The **corso di P. Vittoria** passes the 18C **Palazzo Sormani-Andreani** (E5), which houses the Biblioteca Comunale Centrale and leads to the **Largo Augusto** (E5) with the 17C colonna del Verziere (column). ▶ The Baroque **Palazzo Durini** stands in the street of the same name (D5), with other noble buildings including the 17C **Casa Toscanini**.

▶ **From the centre to the Ticino harbour area and the porta Romana.** ▶ On the S side of the p. del Duomo are two buildings with loggias (1939) flanking the entrance to the modern p. Diaz, from which it is not far to the church of **S. Maria presso S. Satiro★** (E4), one of the finest Renaissance buildings in Milan (restored, particularly in the 19C). The **Cappella della Pietà★** (9C, with Renaissance additions) and the campanile (10C) are evidence of the original foundation by Archbishop Ansperto. The asymmetry and modest proportions of the interior are compensated for by the illusion of perspective created by the celebrated *false sanctuary★* behind the high altar. The octagonal **baptistery★** is the work of Bramante; it is decorated with a frieze by A. De Fondutis (15C), who was also responsible for the *Pietà* in the chapel of the same name. ▶ The heart of old Milan was the Roman forum, on the site of which now stands the palazzo built in 1609 for Federico Borromeo. It houses two important cultural institutions, both bequeathed by the cardinal: the Biblioteca and the **Pinacoteca Ambrosiana★** (E4; *9:30 a.m.-5 p.m.; closed Sat*). The latter has a well-organized collection from the enormous original estate, including works particularly of the Lombard and Venetian schools and drawings by great masters (including masterpieces★★ by Leonardo, Raphael and Caravaggio). ▶ The church of **S. Sebastiano★** (E4) was built at the city's expense in thanksgiving for the end of the plague in 1576. The protracted nature of the work (from 1577-17C) meant considerable alteration of the original design. ▶ The via **Torino** (E3-4) and its continuation, the corso di Porta Ticinese (E-F3), are extremely busy streets crowded with shops which become less elegant and more down-to-earth the farther away they are from the centre of town. ▶ The basilica of **S. Lorenzo Maggiore★★** (E3) faces a churchyard bounded by 16 Roman **columns★** of the imperial period (from a temple sited elsewhere) and its essential features are a late-16C church, which included and restored a 4C-5C early Christian building that had already been rebuilt to a Romanesque design in the 12C. It is considered to be the most important evidence of Roman and early Christian Milan. The basilica consists of a centrally-planned main building, with dome and a series of minor buildings from various periods, radiating from the sides and back of the church. The most attractive and valuable late-Romanesque section is the octagonal **Cappella di S. Aquilino** on the r., with 4C **mosaics★** and a 3C sarcophagus. The apse of S. Lorenzo faces the **Parco delle Basiliche** (E-F3), a pompous name for a long stretch of green ending in the basilica of **S. Eustorgio★** (F3), one of the most distinguished medieval buildings in Milan. Complex and stratified in organization, it includes 7C fragments and parts of the Romanesque ossuary (11C-12C) incorporated in the course of alterations and successive additions that continued until the late-15C. The entire façade and other elements were rebuilt in 1862-5. Beside the apse is the tall **campanile★** (1297-1309). The interior is flanked with chapels containing various tombs and 14C-15C frescos. The gem in this basilica is the **Cappella Portinari★★** behind the apse. It is a Renaissance work of Tuscan inspiration (1466), with a procession of **angels★** in coloured stucco on the drum of the dome; the same artist's masterpiece is undoubtedly the **frescos★★** (1468) on the upper part of the walls, with scenes from the life of St.Peter the Martyr, whose remains are in a **sarcophagus★★** (1339). ▶ At the end of the corso di Porta Ticinese is the gate of the same name (F3), near to which is the **Darsena**, a dock built by the Spaniards in the 17C. The river Olona (now underground) and the **Naviglio Grande** (coming from the Ticino, built in the 12C-13C) flow into it, and the Naviglio di Pavia (which rejoins the Ticino S of Pavia, built by the Visconti and the Sforzas in the 14C-15C) and the Ticinello flow out of it. ▶ In the 15C there were so many pilgrims to the ancient church of S. Celso, said to be the scene of miracles performed by the Madonna, that it became necessary to build a sanctuary. The building of **S. Maria dei Miracoli** or **presso S. Celso★** (F4) started in 1490 and continued for more than a century. The church contains significant works of art, including paintings★. ▶ The corso Italia (E-F4), in which is the church of **S. Paolo** with 17C façade by Campi *(10 a.m.-12:30 p.m. and 3-7 p.m.; closed Mon a.m.)*, leads to the modern p. Missori and to the first section of the fine corso di Porta Romana, dominated by the high and unusual mass of the skyscraper called **Torre Velasca** (E4) with protruding upper section. Built in 1950-1, it is considered to be a synthesis and manifesto of post-war Italian architecture. ▶ The basilica of **S. Nazaro Maggiore★** (E4) is one of the four churches outside the walls founded by St. Ambrose (386). The original cruciform building was rebuilt in the 11C, altered on numerous occasions, and recently restored. In front of the church is the **Cappella Trivulzio★**, the imposing and austere funerary chapel of the Trivulzio family, containing the sarcophagus of Giacomo Trivulzio (1512-20). ▶ The former **Ospedale Maggiore★** (E4-5), also called Ca'Granda, is set on the largo Richini and the v. Festa del Perdono. It was founded in 1456 by Francesco Sforza and his wife Bianca Maria and enlarged in the 17C-18C. For some time it has housed the arts faculty of the **Università Statale**. The r. wing is a transitional Gothic-Renaissance design, with arcade and an upper floor with fine mullioned windows with two lights. The other wing and the imposing **courtyard★** were added in the 17C. ▶ At the end of the v. Festa del Perdono is the p. S. Stefano (E5), one of the corners of which is formed by two historic churches, both rebuilt: 16C-17C **S. Stefano Maggiore** and 17C-18C **S. Bernardino alle Ossa**, named for the ossuary chapel lined with human bones from the city cemeteries razed in the 17C.

▶ **From the centre to the Magenta and Sempione areas.** ▶ The **piazza Cordusio** (D4) was built between 1889 and 1901 as the financial centre of the city. Nearby are the **Palazzo Clerici** (D4; *visits by permission of the*

La Scala

On 3 August, 1778, the Empress Maria Theresa inaugurated the Teatro Ducale, already called alla Scala because it was on the site of the church of S. Maria alla Scala. The theatre was built to replace the former Ducal Theatre, which had been razed by fire 2 years earlier on the last night of the pre-Lenten carnival. The curtain of the new theatre portrayed Apollo showing Good Taste fleeing from Vice to the muses of the theatre. It was a splendid occasion. All the Milanese nobility were present. The theatre was in fact owned by the government and members of the nobility who were boxholders. An opera-goer who was present at the opening noted, 'the design has succeeded so well that wherever one faces one seems to be at the centre of things, able to see everything which is happening'.

ISPI secretariat, ☎ 878266) with a splendid tapestry gallery adorned with frescos★ by Tiepolo and the **Palazzo Borromeo** (E3; *visits by permission*) with 15C Gothic frescos★. In the corso Magenta (D2-3) are the important remains of the ancient **Monastero Maggiore★** (D3), with the 16C church of S. Maurizio (fine interior; *Wed 9:30 a.m.-12 noon and 3-6 p.m.; in summer also other weekdays, a.m. only*) completely covered in frescos by various artists (**frescos★★** on the rood screen and scenes from the life of St.Catherine). ▶ The **Museo Archeologico** (D3; *9.30 a.m.-12:30 p.m. and 2:30-5:30 p.m.; closed Tue*) occupies the rooms of the former monastery and houses the Greek, Etruscan and Roman sections of the Civiche Raccolte Archeologiche (the others are in the Castello Sforzesco); outstanding among the finds in the Roman section is the so-called **Parabiago patera★** (4C AD), a silver-gilt plate with a representation of the triumph of Cybele. ▶ Opposite the rococo façade (1752-63) of the **Palazzo Litta**, the v. S. Agnese leads to the **piazza S. Ambrogio** (D-E2-3); in which there are many impressive buildings including the **Università Cattolica del Sacro Cuore** (largely modern, with two fine **cloisters**), the heterogeneous **Tempio della Vittoria** (1930) dedicated to Milanese war dead and at the end the most famous example of medieval ecclesiastical architecture in Milan, the basilica of **S. Ambrogio★★** (E2-3), founded in 386 by Bishop Ambrose under the name *Basilica Martyrum* over the tomb of Sts. Gervase and Protase. Ambrose himself was buried here in 397. The present building looks Romanesque as a result of considerable alteration and rebuilding from 9C-late 12C, but its appearance has also been affected by modern restoration and refurbishment felt by some to be excessive. A rectangular **atrium** with arcades (built after 1080) conceals the **façade★** from the street. The campanile on the r. is 9C; that on the l., 12C. The **interior** has broad rib vaulting and women's galleries over the side aisles, a deep apse and sanctuary raised above the crypt and topped with a lantern. Features include the **pulpit** on the l. of the nave, made up of 11C fragments, and the **ciborium★** decorated with Lombard-Byzantine coloured stucco (10C) above the magnificent **altar frontal★★** or altare d'Oro (golden altar), the work of Carolingian goldsmiths (*c.* 835). In the apse are a magnificent inlaid wooden choir and a mosaic dating partly from the 4C-8C and remade in the 18C-20C. The church also has frescos and paintings. The remains of St. Ambrose, St. Gervase and St. Protase are in a modern urn in the **crypt**. The r. aisle leads to the **Sacello di S. Vittore in Ciel d'Oro★** (4C), with 5C mosaics *(closed for restoration)*. The l. aisle leads out under the **portico della Canonica★** (15C; rebuilt after bombing). ▶ The 16C basilica of **S.ʾVittorio al Corpo** (E2) is not far down the v. S. Vittore. The church was rebuilt on the site of an early Christian church. The interesting interior contains many late 16C works of art. ▶ The Olivetan convent was attached to the church, also 16C with two splendid

MILAN

0   100   200   300 400m

1:20.000 (1cm=200m)

© SERVIZIO CARTOGRAFICO DEL TOURING CLUB ITALIANO; MILANO

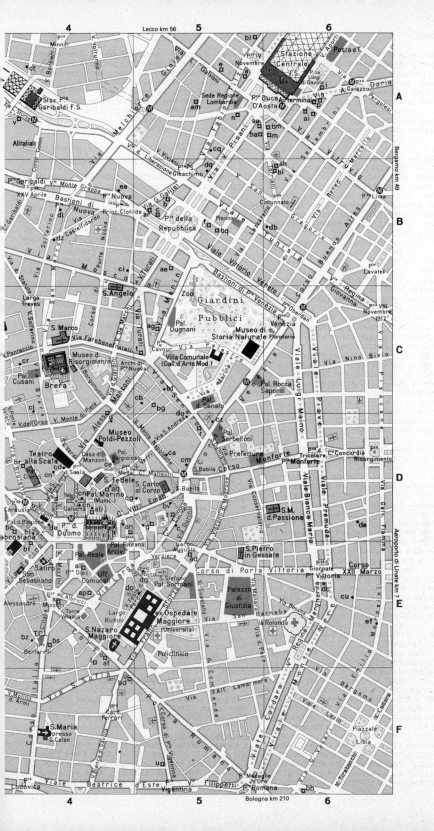

cloisters★. The rooms of the former convent (restored) accommodate part of the **Museo Nazionale della Scienza e della Tecnica Leonardo da Vinci★** (E2; *9 a.m.-5 p.m.; closed Mon.* except *hols*), which also occupies two adjacent buildings; it has an interesting collection documenting the origins and development of scientific thought and technical progress. The majority of the sections (*not all always accessible*) are in the former convent, notably the **Galleria di Leonardo da Vinci**, which is devoted to his scientific work, and the **Civico Museo Navale Didattico** (*9:30 a.m.-12:20 p.m. and 2:30-5:15 p.m.; closed Mon*). The other two spacious buildings house the sections devoted to rail transport (with 20 locomotives) and air and sea travel (with aeroplanes, the training ship *Ebe* and the bridge of the Atlantic liner *Conte Biancamano*). ▶ The v. Zenale leads to a square in front of the church of **S. Maria delle Grazie★★** (D2). The finest example in Milan of the transitional period from late Gothic to Renaissance is the apse or **Tribuna★** (added in 1492 to the original building of 1466-90). From the outside the church looks like a cube with three apses, topped with a polygonal lantern with gallery, but the most notable feature is the **interior★★**, where a white dome soars above four magnificent arches. Access to the lovely **chiostrino★★** is through the apse. ▶ In the square beside the church is the entrance to the refectory of the Dominican monastery (*closed for restoration at the time of writing*) on the walls of which Leonardo da Vinci painted his fresco of *The Last Supper★★* 1495-7. Unfortunately the painting is in a condition of grave deterioration. ▶ After crossing the neat and ordered district of Magenta, around the v. Boccaccio (D2), set apart for middle-class accommodation in the town plan of 1889, it is possible to climb the tree-lined v. XX Settembre to the **Parco★** (B-C2-3), laid out in the English style in 1893 on the site of the parade ground of the Castello Sforzesco. The parade ground was moved further W to the site now occupied by the Fiera di Milano (B-C1), used for Italy's principal marketing show. ▶ On the SE side of the park is the **Palazzo dell'Arte** (C2), which houses a theatre, the Mostra Triennale d'Arte Decorativa and other exhibitions. ▶ On the NW side, at the centre of a vast piazza, is the **Arco della Pace** (C2), a Neoclassical arch built in 1807 to honour Napoleon, then dedicated to Francis I of Austria, and finally to Italian independence. ▶ The other notable example of Neoclassical architecture of the Napoleonic period is the **Arena Civica** (B-C3) on the NE side of the park. ▶ Nearby is the **Acquario Civico** (v. Gadio 2, C3; *9 a.m.-12 noon and 2-5 p.m.; closed Mon*). ▶ The **Castello Sforzesco★★** (C-D3) was commissioned by Francesco Sforza in the 15C on the site of an earlier 14C fortress and became the increasingly magnificent residence of the lords of Milan until the 16C, when it was turned back into a heavily fortified citadel under the Spanish. From 1893 it was radically restored. Today the castle is a square with brick windows and crenellated corner towers, surrounded by a moat. Inside is a courtyard or parade ground, with three buildings at the rear: on the l., the **Rocchetta**, a kind of citadel around a courtyard; in the centre the tower of **Bona di Savoia** (1476); and on the r. the **Palazzo della Corte Ducale**. The castle houses numerous cultural institutions (libraries, historical archives and the **Raccolta delle Stampe A.** Bertarelli (prints; *8.45 a.m.-12 noon and 2:30-4:15 p.m.; Wed until 5 p.m.; closed Sat, Sun and hols*) and an impressive and well-organized museum complex. ▶ The **Musei del Castello★★** (*9.30 a.m.-12:30 p.m. and 2:30-5:30 p.m.; closed Mon*) are arranged in various buildings. The Palazzo della Corte Ducale houses the **Civiche Raccolte d'Arte Antica**, which includes sculpture from the early Christian era to the 16C (notably the **Pietà Rondanini★★** by Michelangelo; a collection of **furniture★** and other 15C-18C art and an excellent **Pinacoteca★★** covering paintings up to the 18C). The rooms in the Rocchetta contain the **Civiche Raccolte d'Arte Applicata**, including ceramics, gold, musical instruments, vestments and textiles (notably **12 tapestries of the months★** made in Vigevano in 1503; *not usually on show*) and 18C-19C costume. The basement of the Rocchetta contains the

Civiche Raccolte Archeologiche e Numismatiche (archaeology and coins) with the prehistoric and Egyptian sections of the Museo Archeologico and a fine medal collection (*open for academic research*). ▶ In front of the castle are the two semicircular arms of the Neoclassical **Foro Buonaparte** (C-D3), the Largo Cairoli and the v. Dante showing the broad sweep of the 19C town plan, intended to provide a link between the centre and the now isolated area of the military fortress. □

Leonardo da Vinci's machines

Leonardo da Vinci arrived in Milan from Florence in 1482, thirty years old and famous. In a letter to Duke Ludovico il Moro, Leonardo introduced himself as a 'master and manufacturer of instruments of war', as well as architect, hydraulic engineer, sculptor and painter. He remained in the service of Ludovico until Louis XII of France invaded the duchy in 1499. After sojourns in various Italian cities he returned to Milan in June 1506 and stayed there, under the protection of the French governor Charles d'Amboise and Louis XII for a total of a quarter century. The Museo Nazionale della Scienza e della Tecnica in the former monastery of San Vittore has a vast collection on the great master as a scientist, technician, inventor and student of nature. The most popular exhibits are the explanatory models of his machines and instruments, created from drawings in his scientific monographs (many from the Codice Atlantico preserved in the Biblioteca Ambrosiana), inventions perhaps intended to please or amaze Ludovico and which gave Leonardo his reputation as a genius ahead of his time, anticipating many inventions such as submarines, tanks, helicopters, gliders, machine guns, diving suits and the parachute.

Practical information

MILAN

ⓘ Palazzo del Turismo, v. Marconi 1 (E4), ☎ 809662; Stazione Centrale (A6), ☎ 6690532; Linate Airport, ☎ 744065; Galleria Vittorio Emanuele, corner of p. della Scala (D4), ☎ 870545; sports information, ☎ 801466.
✈ Forlanini International Airport; Malpensa International Airport, nr Gallarate; general information from S.E.A., ☎ 74852200, *Alitalia*, v. Albricci 5 (E4) and corso Como 15 (A4), ☎ 62811; bus to Linate and Malpensa, from p. Luigi di Savoia (E side of Stazione Centrale, A6), to Linate from p. S. Babila (D5).
🚍 (A6), ☎ 67500; Porta Garibaldi (A4), ☎ 6552078; Ferrovie Nord Milano, Milano Nord station (D2), ☎ 800517.
🚌 destinations and points of departure are listed in a booklet distributed at tourist offices, ☎ 809662.
Car rental: *Avis*, v. Filzi 43 and p. Diaz 6, ☎ 6981, Stazione Centrale, ☎ 6690280, Linate, ☎ 6598151, Malpensa, ☎ 868019; *Hertz*, p. Duca d'Aosta 9, ☎ 717214, Stazione Centrale, ☎ 6690061, Linate, ☎ 7384580, Malpensa, ☎ 868001; *Maggiore*, booking office, ☎ 5243846, Stazione Centrale, ☎ 6690934, Linate, ☎ 717210, Malpensa, ☎ 868036.

Hotels:
L★★★★★ *Excelsior Gallia*, p. Duca d'Aosta 9 (A5 a), ☎ 6277, 266 rm Ⓟ A luxury palace in the grand tradition, with some furniture in period style; includes a modern fitness centre, 403,000.
L★★★★★ *G.H. Brun*, v. Caldera 2, ☎ 45271, 330 rm Ⓟ ⬛ 📺 ✐ 285,000. Rest. ♦♦♦ *Ascot* closed Sun. Excellent cuisine, 55/90,000.
L★★★★★ *Palace*, p. della Repubblica 20 (B5 f), ☎ 6336, 203 rm Ⓟ ⅙ 370,000; bkf: 18,000. Rest. ♦♦♦♦ *Casanova Grill* ☎ 650803, closed Sat. Creative cuisine, 65/85,000.
L★★★★★ *Principe di Savoia*, p. della Repubblica 17 (B5 b), ☎ 6230, 302 rm Ⓟ 487,500; bkf: 21,000.

★★★★★ *Duca di Milano*, p. della Repubblica 13 (B5 c), ☎ 6284, 60 rm P ⬛ ⅄ closed Aug, 416,600; bkf: 20,000.

★★★★★ *Grand Hotel et de Milan*, v. Manzoni 29 (C-D4 d), ☎ 870757, 105 rm. Old-style tradition and modern comfort, in the elegant and fashionable heart of the city, 300,000; bkf: 15,000.

★★★★★ *Milano Hilton*, v. Galvani 12 (A5 e), ☎ 6983, 347 rm P ⅄ 368,000; bkf: 20,500. Rest. ◆◆◆◆ *Giuseppe* Creative cuisine, 43/57,000.

★★★★ *Accademia*, v. Certosa 68, ☎ 3271841, 48 rm P ⅏ No restaurant, 190,000; bkf: 10,000.

★★★★ *Anderson*, p. Luigi di Savoia 20 (A6 i), ☎ 6690141, 102 rm P closed Aug. No restaurant, 180,000; bkf: 12,000.

★★★★ *Ascot*, v. Lentasio (E4 l), ☎ 862946, 57 rm P ⅏ closed Aug and Christmas. No restaurant, 175,000; bkf: 12,500.

★★★★ *Atlantic*, v. Torriani 24 (A6 m), ☎ 6691941, 62 rm P ⬛ ⅄ closed 1-28 Aug. No restaurant, 235,000.

★★★★ *Auriga*, v. Pirelli 7 (A5 n), ☎ 6592851, 65 rm ⅏ closed Aug and Christmas. No restaurant, 150,000; bkf: 10,000.

★★★★ *Bristol*, v. Scarlatti 32 (A6 p), ☎ 6694141, 71 rm P ⅏ closed Aug. No restaurant, 173,000; bkf: 10,000.

★★★★ *Capitol*, v. Cimarosa 6 (D1 q), ☎ 4988851, 96 rm P ⅏ 198,000.

★★★★ *Carlton Senato*, v. Senato 5 (D5 r), ☎ 798583, 79 rm P closed Aug, 180,000; bkf: 12,500.

★★★★ *Cavalieri*, p. Missori 1 (E4 s), ☎ 8857, 169 rm P No restaurant, 202,000.

★★★★ *Cavour*, v. Fatebenefratelli 21 (C4-5 t), ☎ 650983, 113 rm ⅄ 150,000; bkf: 10,000.

★★★★ *Concorde*, v. Petrocchi 1, ☎ 2895853, 84 rm P ⅏ closed 1-20 Aug. No restaurant, 195,000.

★★★★ *Crivi's*, corso di Poreta Vigentina 46 (F5 u), ☎ 5463341, 69 rm P ⬛ ⅄ closed Aug and Christmas. No restaurant, 166,000; bkf: 13,000.

★★★★ *De la Ville*, v. Hoepli 6 (D4 aq), ☎ 867651, 105 rm P ⅏ No restaurant, 200,000; bkf: 14,000.

★★★★ *Duomo*, v. S. Raffaele 1 (D4 ab), ☎ 8833, 161 rm P ⅄ ⅏ closed Aug, 270,000; bkf: 13,000.

★★★★ *Executive*, v. Sturzo 45 (A4 v), ☎ 6294, 420 rm P ⅄ 250,000.

★★★★ *Galileo*, corso Europa 9 (D5 z), ☎ 7743, 71 rm P ⅏ 300,000.

★★★★ *G.H. Fieramilano*, v. Boezio 20 (B1 ac), ☎ 3105, 238 rm P ⅏ 260,000; bkf: 22,000.

★★★★ *G.H. Rosa*, v. Pattari 5 (D4 an), ☎ 8831, 163 rm P 250,000.

★★★★ *Jolly President*, largo Augusto 10 (E5 ad), ☎ 7746, 201 rm P 260,000. Rest. ◆◆◆ *7746* Lombard cuisine, 50/70,000.

★★★★ *Jolly Touring*, v. Tarchetti 2 (B5 ae), ☎ 6335, 270 rm, 220,000.

★★★★ *Lloyd*, corso di Porta Romana 48 (E4 af), ☎ 867971, 52 rm P ⬛ No restaurant, 190,000; bkf: 12,000.

★★★★ *Manin*, v. Manin 7 (C5 ag), ☎ 6596511, 110 rm P ⬛ closed Aug and Christmas, 177,000; bkf: 15,000. Rest. ◆◆◆ *Bettolino* closed Sat and Sun. Good Lombard cuisine, 40/55,000.

★★★★ *Mediolanum*, v. Macchi 1 (B6 ah), ☎ 6705312, 52 rm P ⅏ No restaurant, 194,000.

★★★★ *Michelangelo*, v. Scarlatti 33 (A6 ai), ☎ 6755, 278 rm P 320,000.

★★★★ *Plaza*, p. Diaz 3 (E4 al), ☎ 8058452, 118 rm ⅄ ⅏ closed Aug. No restaurant, 250,000.

★★★★ *Raffaello*, v. Certosa 108, ☎ 3270146, 109 rm P ⬛ No restaurant, 150,000; bkf: 10,000.

★★★★ *Royal*, v. Cardano 1 (A5 am), ☎ 6709151, 110 rm P ⅏ closed Christmas, 160,000.

★★★★ *Rubens*, v. Rubens 21, ☎ 405051, 76 rm P ⅏ closed Aug. No restaurant, 190,000.

★★★★ *Select*, v. Baracchini 12 (E4 ap), ☎ 8843, 140 rm. No restaurant, 250,000; bkf: 15,000.

★★★★ *Splendido*, v. Doria 4 (A6 p), ☎ 2050, 156 rm P 250,000.

★★★★ *Windsor*, v. Galilei 2 (B5 ar), ☎ 6346, 114 rm P ⅄ No restaurant, 162,000.

★★★ *Adriatico*, v. Conca del Naviglio 20 (F3 as), ☎ 8324141, 105 rm P closed Aug. No restaurant, 109,000; bkf: 8,000.

★★★ *Ambasciatori*, galleria del Corso 3 (D5 g), ☎ 790241, 86 rm P No restaurant, 115,000.

★★★ *Ariosto*, v. Ariosto 22 (C1 at), ☎ 490995, 53 rm P ⬛ ⅄ No restaurant, 119,000; bkf: 8,000.

★★★ *Astoria*, v. Murillo 9, ☎ 4046646, 75 rm P ⅏ 150,000.

★★★ *Augustus*, v. Torriani 29, (A5 au), ☎ 6575741, 56 rm P ⅄ No restaurant, 140,000.

★★★ *Domus*, p. Gerusalemme 6 (A1-2 av), ☎ 3490251, 87 rm P ⅏ No restaurant, 107,000; bkf: 12,000.

★★★ *Este*, v. Bligny 23, ☎ 5461041, 54 rm P ⅄ 101,000; bkf : 11,000.

★★★ *Europeo*, v. Canonica 38 (B2 az), ☎ 3314751, 45 rm P ⬛ ⅏ ⬜ closed Aug and Christmas. No restaurant, 150,000.

★★★ *F.i.n.i. Motel*, v. del Mare 93, ☎ 8464041, 78 rm P ⅏ No restaurant, 104,000; bkf: 8,000.

★★★ *Flora*, v. Torriani 23 (A5 ba), ☎ 650242, 45 rm ⅏ No restaurant, 104,000; bkf: 12,000.

★★★ *Florida*, v. Lepetit 33 (A6 ai), ☎ 6705921, 52 rm. No restaurant, 112,000; bkf: 8,000.

★★★ *Gamma*, v. V.Peroni 85, ☎ 214116, 55 rm P closed Aug. No restaurant, 105,000; bkf: 8,000.

★★★ *Gran Duca di York*, v. Moneta 1/A (D4 bc), ☎ 874863, 33 rm P ⅄ closed Aug. No restaurant, 110,000; bkf: 9,000.

★★★ *Imperial*, corso di Porta Romana 68 (F4-5 bd), ☎ 5468421, 37 rm ⅏ closed Aug. No restaurant, 110,000; bkf: 10,000.

★★★ *Lancaster*, v. Sangiorgio 16 (B-C1 be), ☎ 344705, 29 rm P ⅏ closed 25 Jul-25 Aug and Christmas. No restaurant, 143,000.

★★★ *Lombardia*, v. Lombardia 74, ☎ 2824938, 69 rm P 126,000.

★★★ *Lord Internazionale*, v. Spadari 11 (D-E4 bf), ☎ 8693028, 46 rm P No restaurant, 107,000; bkf: 8,000.

★★★ *Manzoni*, v. S. Spirito 20 (C5 bg), ☎ 705697, 52 rm P ⅏ No restaurant, 118,000; bkf: 10,000.

★★★ *Mediterraneo*, v. Muratori 14 (F6 bh), ☎ 5488151, 93 rm P closed Aug. No restaurant, 112,000; bkf: 7,500.

★★★ *Mennini*, v. Torriani 14 (B6 bi), ☎ 6690951, 72 rm, closed Aug. No restaurant, 135,000; bkf: 12,000.

★★★ *Molise*, v. Cadibona 2/A, ☎ 5464249, 32 rm P ⅏ closed Aug and Christmas. No restaurant, 102,000; bkf: 9,000.

★★★ *New York*, v. Pirelli 5 (A5 n), ☎ 650551, 71 rm P closed Aug and Christmas. No restaurant, 111,000.

★★★ *San Carlo*, v. Torriani 28 (A6 bm), ☎ 203022, 64 rm P No restaurant, 125,000.

★★★ *San Guido*, v. Farini 1/A (A3 bn), ☎ 6552238, 31 rm P No restaurant, 80,000; bkf: 7,000.

★★★ *Sant'Ambroeus*, v. Papiniano 14 (E1 bp), ☎ 4697451, 52 rm P ⅏ closed Jul-Aug and Christmas. No restaurant, 110,000; bkf: 10,000.

★★★ *Sempione*, v. F. Aprile 11 (B5 bq), ☎ 6570323, 40 rm P 110,000; bkf: 8,000.

★★★ *Star*, v. dei Bossi 5 (D4 br), ☎ 871703, 28 rm P closed Aug and Christmas. No restaurant, 95,000; bkf: 8,500.

★★★ *Tourist*, v. F. Testi 300, ☎ 6437777, 85 rm P closed Aug, 138,000.

★★★ *Zefiro*, v. Gallina 12, ☎ 7384253, 55 rm ⅏ closed Aug and Christmas. No restaurant, 99,000; bkf: 9,000.

★★★ *Zurigo*, corso Italia 11/A (E4 bs), ☎ 808909, 41 rm P ⅄ closed Christmas. No restaurant, 115,000; bkf: 7,000.

★★ *Corallo*, v. Cesena 20, ☎ 312747, 36 rm P ⅏ No restaurant, 76,500; bkf: 9,000.

★★ *Motel dei Fiori*, v. Renzo e Lucia 14, ☎ 8436441, 55 rm P ⅄ No restaurant, 77,000.

Restaurants:

● ◆◆◆◆ *El Toulà*, p. P. Ferrari 6 (D4 cd), ☎ 870302, closed Sun, Aug and Christmas. Fine décor, stylish service. Excellent Venetian and international cuisine: risotto with cuttlefish ink, saddle of lamb with mentuccia, 55/90,000.

● ◆◆◆◆ *Giannino*, v. Sciesa 8 (E6 cu), ☎ 5452948, closed

Sun and Jul-Aug. Elegant and famous. Excellent Italian cuisine: bream and sea bass in foil, fritto misto mare, 55/80,000.

● ♦♦♦♦ *Gualtiero Marchesi,* v. Bonvesin de la Riva 9, ☎ 741246, closed Sun, hols, Mon noon and Aug. Stylish rooms, intimate atmosphere. Outstanding individual cuisine: riso manrecato with herbs and scampi tails, raviolo aperto, 70/110,000.

● ♦♦♦♦ *Savini,* galleria Vittorio Emanuele (D4 cn), ☎ 8058343, closed Sun and Aug. Fashionable venue for society, business people and visitors to La Scala. Outstanding regional cuisine: sea bass in foil, cutlets and osso bucco alla milanese, 60/80,000.

● ♦♦♦♦ *Scaletta,* p. Stazione Genova 3 (FL dv), ☎ 8350290, closed Sun, Mon, Aug, Christmas and Easter. Small and exclusive, American bar in entrance. Outstanding creative Italian cuisine: tripe in aspic, terrine of cabbage and asparagus, 75/80,000.

♦♦♦♦ *Biffi Scala,* v. Filodrammatici 2 (D4 cd), ☎ 876332, closed Sun and Aug. Elegant 'after-theatre' style. Regional and international cuisine: risotto alla milanese, tournedos Scala or Rossini or Indian, 45/65,000.

♦♦♦♦ *Saint Andrews,* v. S. Andrea 23 (C-D5 du), ☎ 793132, closed Sun and Aug. Elegant, English in style. Excellent regional and Italian cuisine: pennette with cheese and pepper; sea bass stuffed with vegetables, 80/100,000.

● ♦♦♦ *Aimo e Nadia,* v. Montecuccoli 6, ☎ 416886, closed Sat noon, Sun and Aug. Fine summer garden. Creative cuisine: rucola gnocchi, stuffed squid, 45/90,000.

● ♦♦♦ *Berti,* v. Algarotti 20, ☎ 6081696, closed Sun and Christmas. Classic rooms in old style and garden with pergola. Fine regional and Italian cuisine: rigatoni del curato, marenghi meneghina, 35/40,000.

● ♦♦♦ *Canoviano,* v. Hoepli 6 (D4 aq), ☎ 8058472, closed Sun, Mon noon and Aug. Mirrors, columns and bright colours, more functional than intimate; elegant service. Excellent regional and innovative cuisine: marbré of rabbit; agnolotti with duck, 60/75,000.

● ♦♦♦ *Cucina di Edgardo il Montacino,* v. Valenza 17, ☎ 8321926, closed Sun. Tasteful and elegant. Quality Italian and creative cuisine: risotto al Brunello, crema contadina, 45/55,000.

● ♦♦♦ *Don Lisander,* v. Manzoni 12/A (D4 d), ☎ 790130, closed Sun, in summer also Sat eve, Aug 15, and Christmas. Attractive summer garden and classical restaurant in ancient Trivulzio chapel. Excellent creative cuisine: trout ravioli, sea bass with thyme, 60/80,000.

● ♦♦♦ *Elo-Wué,* v. Sabatelli 1 (B2 cp), ☎ 3315666, closed Sun, Mon noon and Aug. Pleasant Italian Chinese atmosphere. Excellent Chinese cuisine: nuvoletti, soya spaghetti, paradise prawns, 35/45,000.

● ♦♦♦ *Hong Kong,* v. Schiaparelli 5, ☎ 6890645, closed Mon and Aug. One of the best Chinese restaurants in Italy. Cantonese and Szechwan cuisine: ravioli in various forms, piquant scampi with onions, 50/65,000.

● ♦♦♦ *Osteria del Binari,* v. Tortona 1 (F2 dh), ☎ 8399428, closed Sun and Aug. Old Milan atmosphere with garden and bowls. Quality Italian cuisine: panzerotti piacentina, timballe of agnolotti with truffles, 30/45,000.

● ♦♦♦ *Peck,* v. V. Hugo 4 (D4 bf), ☎ 876774, closed Sun and Jul. Typical modern restaurant. Excellent Italian cuisine: house pâté, turbot with porcini, sea bass steak with date-shells, 40/60,000.

● ♦♦♦ *Tre Pini,* v. Morgagni 19, ☎ 6896464, closed Fri noon, Sat and Aug. In villa with fine garden; rustic veranda with fireplace and grill opening on to a green terrace with fountains. Excellent Italian cuisine: tufoli primaverili, osso bucco alla milanese with risotto (Buon Ricordo dish), 35/45,000.

♦♦♦ *Alfio-Cavour,* v. Senato 31 (C5 bt), ☎ 780731, closed Sat, Sun noon, Aug and Christmas. Elegant restaurant with open kitchen, conservatory. Good Italian cuisine: risotto with mushrooms, portafoglio Cavour, 40/70,000.

♦♦♦ *Arabesque,* corso Vittorio Emanuele 34 (D5 bv), ☎ 798791, closed Tue. Set on various levels, conser-

vatory and art-nouveau décor. Italian cuisine: pancakes with herbs, lasagnette with vegetable cream, 20/35,000.

♦♦♦ *Bagutta,* v. Bagutta 14 (D5 ca), ☎ 702767, closed Sun, Aug and Christmas. Restaurant with frescos and decorations in small historic street; summer meals in open air; literary prize of the same name is awarded here. Italian cuisine: tagliatelle al salmone, black cabbage soup, 40/60,000.

♦♦♦ *Bice,* v. Borgospesso 12 (C5 cb), ☎ 702572, closed Mon, Jul-Aug and Christmas. Refined version of original trattoria which was one of the bridgeheads of the Tuscan culinary invasion of Milan. Tuscan cuisine: ribollita, meat balls and kidney beans, stracotto alla toscana with polenta, 45/70,000.

♦♦♦ *Boeucc,* p. Belgioioso 2 (D4 ce), ☎ 792880, closed Sat and Sun noon. In former stables of Palazzo Belgioioso, summer service in internal arcade. Regional cuisine: raviolini with scampi and crayfish, fettuccine with nettles and porcini, 35/45,000.

♦♦♦ *Calajunco,* v. Stoppani 5, ☎ 2046003, closed Sat noon, Sun, Aug and Christmas. Elegant and comfortable. Seafood: eolina; conchiglia del pescatore, involtino of swordfish, 55/70,000.

♦♦♦ *Cascina Corba,* v. dei Gigli 14, ☎ 4158977, closed Sun eve, Mon and Aug. Refined rural furnishings with fireplace, surrounded by enclosed garden for meals in open air. Italian cuisine: pasta capriccio, fish cooked in various ways, 30/45,000.

♦♦♦ *Cassina de Pomm,* v. M. Gioia 194, ☎ 6081448, closed Sun and Aug. Refined with summer garden. Regional cuisine, some international dishes: tortelloni without meat, rustin negaa, 40/45,000.

♦♦♦ *Charleston,* p. Liberty 8 (D4-5 cg), ☎ 798631, closed Sat noon, Mon and Aug. In fine period palazzo, lively in evening. Italian cuisine: fresh pasta, spaghetti with fresh spring vegetables, 25/35,000.

♦♦♦ *Cinque Terre,* v. Appiani 9 (B4 ci), ☎ 651650, closed Sun and Aug. Views of romantic area from which it takes its name. Ligurian cuisine: trenette with pesto, pansoti in walnut sauce, prawns in champagne, 33/48,000.

♦♦♦ *Ciovassino,* v. Ciovassino 5 (C-D4 cl), ☎ 8053868, closed Sat noon, Sun and Aug. In Bohemian Brera quarter; old style bar. Creative cuisine: carrot gnocchi with amaretto, tagliata of swordfish with chives, 30/40,000.

♦♦♦ *Crispi,* corso Venezia 3 (D5 cm), ☎ 782010, closed Sat and Aug. Modern and stylish; fine internal garden; open into the small hours. Interesting regional and international cuisine: white and green lasagne, filet Café de Paris, 35/50,000.

♦♦♦ *Down Town Restaurant,* galleria Vittorio Emanuele (D4 cn), ☎ 800148, closed Mon. Elegant and painstaking, garden in the Galleria. Regional cuisine: risotto alla Milanese, baked slices of Scottish beef, 40/45,000.

♦♦♦ *Endo,* v. Filzi 8 (A5 cq), ☎ 6595017, closed Sun and Aug. Elegant, with typical Japanese furnishings. Fine Japanese cuisine: raw fish, sliced meats with a selection of vegetable cooked at the table, 50/80,000.

♦♦♦ *Franco il Contadino,* v. Fiori Chiari 20 (C4 cr), ☎ 808153, closed Tue and Jul. Typical old building in the Brera district. Regional cuisine: tagliolini with seafood, tagliata del contadino, hare in a rich wine sauce, 32/45,000.

♦♦♦ *Giordano,* v. Torti 3 (E3 cv), ☎ 8350824, closed Sun and Aug. Modern rural style, on two floors. Bolognese cuisine: tortellini or passatelli in brodo, fritto misto emiliana, 25/30,000.

♦♦♦ *Girarrosto-da Cesarina,* corso Venezia 31 (D5 cz), ☎ 700481, closed Sat, Sun noon, Aug and Christmas. The Tuscan proprietors have created a comfortable restaurant. Tuscan and Italian cuisine: ricotta tortellini, penne alla toscana, 35/45,000.

♦♦♦ *Lino Buriassi,* v. Lecco 15 (B6 db), ☎ 228227, closed Sat noon, Sun and Aug. Panelled walls and illuminated mirrors. Creative cuisine: spaghetti in foil, tortelli with truffles, 35/48,000.

♦♦♦ *Magic Restaurant,* v. Foscolo 1 (D4 ab), ☎ 800148, closed Mon. Modern and efficent self-service restaurant. Regional and Italian cuisine: fixed menu, as much as you wish, 30/40,000.

◆◆◆ **Marino al Conte Ugolino,** p. Beccaria 6 (D5 g), ☎ 876134, closed Sun and Aug. Tuscan atmosphere and cuisine: risotto with porcini, prawns Conte, 30/50,000.
◆◆◆ **Mercante,** p. dei Mercanti 17 (D4 de), ☎ 8052198, closed Sun and Aug. Mezzanine facing charming little square. Regional and Italian cuisine: cheese pancakes, pappardelle with herbs, 25/35,000.
◆◆◆ **Montecristo,** v. Prina 17 (B2 df), ☎ 312760, closed Tue and Sat noon. Light and beautifully equipped, but little space between tables. Seafood: fried scampi, fish mixed grill, sea bass in foil, 40/60,000.
◆◆◆ **'Nderre a la Lanze,** p. S. Stefano 10 (E5 dg), ☎ 873494, closed Mon and Aug. Recalls Apulia in its pleasant furnishings. Apulian fish cuisine: spaghetti with seafood or lobster, mixed grills, 40/50,000.
◆◆◆ **Osteria del Vecchio Canneto,** v. Solferino 56 (B4 dl), ☎ 6598498, closed Sun, Mon noon and Aug. Unusual taverna: seaside-rural, music and folklore. Various fixed price menus from noon (recommended) to eve. Abruzzi fish cuisine: seafood lasagnette, fish brodetto pescarese, 23/45,000.
◆◆◆ **Osteria la Lanterna,** v. Novati 2 (E3 di), ☎ 879435, closed Sat noon, Sun and Aug. Elegant split-level restaurant in former stable. Quality creative cuisine: risotto with asparagus and champagne, crêpes with chives, fillet with juniper berries, 50/60,000.
◆◆◆ **Pantera,** v. Festa del Perdono 12 (D5 dc), ☎ 8057374, closed Tue and Aug. Regional and Tuscan cuisine: gnocchi, osso bucco, 25/50,000.
◆◆◆ **Peschereccio,** Foro Buonaparte 62 (C3 dp), ☎ 861418, closed Mon, Tue noon, Aug and Christmas. Tempting display of fish and seafood. Fish cuisine: tagliolini uovo di riccio, risotto black or with scampi and small scallops, 40/55,000.
◆◆◆ **Porto,** p. Cantore (F2 dr), ☎ 8321481, closed Sun, Mon noon, and Aug. In the old Porta Genova customshouse, with fine summer garden. Seafood: risotto del capitano, sea bream with pink peppercorns, 50/55,000.
◆◆◆ **Replay,** p. Pattari 2 (D4 an), ☎ 8059409, closed Tue and Aug. For quick snacks or after-theatre suppers. Italian cuisine: steak tartare or with scamorza or grilled meats, 25/35,000.
◆◆◆ **Riccione,** v. Taramelli 70, ☎ 6086807, closed Mon. Spacious, with marine décor. Quality seafood: risotto and fresh pasta with various fish sauces, fish fritti misti, 50/70,000.
◆◆◆ **Romani,** v. Trebazio 3 (B1 ds), ☎ 340738, closed Sat noon, Sun and Aug. On first floor of Piaggio skyscraper; somewhat English impression. Italian and international cuisine: mixed smoked fish, risotto with porcini and bilberries, 25/60,000.
◆◆◆ **San Vito-da Nino,** v. S. Vito 5 (E3 dt), ☎ 8377029, closed Mon, Aug and Christmas. Tiny restaurant, intimate and pleasant. Regional and Italian cuisine: maccheroncini and gingilli with truffles, fritto misto italiano, 55/65,000.
◆◆◆ **Taverna del Gran Sasso,** p. Principessa Clotilde 10 (B9 ea), ☎ 6597578, closed Fri noon, and Aug. Rural, range of fixed-pice menus. Abruzzi cuisine: Abruzzi pancakes with cheese; chicken arrabbiata, 20/38,000.
◆◆◆ **Torre del Mangia,** v. Procaccini 37 (A2 ed), ☎ 314871, closed Sun eve, Mon, Aug and Christmas. Lively, attentive service. Quality Tuscan cuisine: crostini alla toscana, tagliolini with crab, 30/45,000.
◆◆◆ **Vecchia Viscontea,** v. Giannone 10 (B2 eh), ☎ 3315372, closed Sat, Sun noon and Aug. In old building with art-nouveau furnishings and fine covered garden. Italian cuisine: salmon and pistacchio pâté, orecchiette rucola, 30/40,000.
● ◆◆ **Antica Trattoria della Pesa,** v. Pasubio 10 (A-B3 bu), ☎ 6555741, closed Sun, Aug, Christmas and Easter. Authentic old-style atmosphere, Milanese simplicity. Regional cuisine: tripe in brodo, cassoeula, rostisciada with polenta, 35/40,000.
● ◆◆ **Gran San Bernardo,** v. Borgese 14, ☎ 3319000, closed Sun, 15 Jul-30 Aug and 22 Dec-19 Jan. Known for the proven tradition associated with its owner. Excellent regional cuisine: osso bucco with herbs, garlic and lemon, tripe and onion stew with cheese, 40/45,000.

◆◆ **Assassino,** v. Amedei 8 (E4 bz), ☎ 8056144, closed Tue and Christmas. Under arches of private palazzo, popular with sportsmen. Regional cuisine: tagliolini scampi, ravioli with butter and truffles, grilled samponi, 30/55,000.
◆◆ **Brasera Meneghina,** v. Circo 10 (E3 cf), ☎ 808108, closed Fri, Sat noon and Aug. Authentic old Milanese tavern dating from 17C. Regional cuisine: cassoeula, osso bucco, rostin negaa, 40/45,000.
◆◆ **Casa Fontana 23 Risotti,** p. Carbonari 5, ☎ 6892684, closed Sat noon, Mon and Aug. Family trattoria. Italian cuisine: 23 risottos, kidneys in brandy, 35/45,000.
◆◆ **Franca-Paola-Lele,** v. Certosa 235, ☎ 305238, closed Sat, Sun, Mon eve and Aug. Tiny family-run establishment, with very carefully chosen oils, charcuterie, cheese and wines. Excellent regional and Venetian cuisine: according to season and market availability: lasagne, duck with bilberries, 50/70,000.
◆◆ **Gianni e Dorina-Pontremolese,** v. G. Pepe 38 (A4 ct), ☎ 606340, closed Sat noon, Sun and Aug. Tiny establishment with little garden. Tuscan cuisine: testaroli al pesto, lasagnette with chestnuts and ricotta, 35/50,000.
◆◆ **Hostaria del Cenacolo,** v. Archimede 12 (D6 da), ☎ 5458962, closed Sat noon, Sun and Aug. Spacious trattoria with service in garden in summer. Regional cuisine: penne with onions, pappardelle with yellow peppers, 35/45,000.
◆◆ **Masuelli-San Marco,** v. Umbria 80, ☎ 584138, closed Sun, Mon noon and Sep. In operation since the twenties under same family management. Regional cuisine: mondeghili, tagliatelle al Barolo, stracotto al Barolo, 25/30,000.
◆◆ **Palio,** v. Cenisio 37 (A1-2 dm), ☎ 3453687, closed Sat and Aug. Pleasant trattoria in Tuscan rustic style. Italian cuisine: penne all'arrabbiata, tagliata of green pepper, 25/35,000.
◆◆ **Porta Rossa,** v. Locatelli 2 (B5 dq), ☎ 6705932, closed Mon, Easter and Christmas. Decorated with ceramics, paintings, curios and has a convivial cellar. Apulian cuisine: orecchiette, pasta and chick peas, pappardelle with cream and ham, 20/40,000.
◆◆ **Solferino,** v. Castelfidardo 2 (B4 dz), ☎ 6599886, closed Sat noon, Sun and Aug. Small, elegant and fashionable. Regional and Italian cuisine: fried risotto, mezzemaniche, 30/50,000.
◆◆ **Taverna della Trisa,** v. Ferruccio 1 (B2 eb), ☎ 341304, closed Mon and Sun alternately and Aug. Quiet rural atmosphere; small, cool garden. Trentino cuisine: canederli, strangolapreti, 35/45,000.
◆◆ **Tavolozza,** v. Solari 7 (F2 ec), ☎ 8390084, closed Tue and Jul. Recently rebuilt, with fireplace and fine pergola for summer. Regional cuisine: fresh salmon marinated in coriander, tagliata with rucola, 30/45,000.
◆◆ **Trattoria della Pesa-Rino,** v. Morosini 12 (E6 ef), ☎ 5452906, closed Wed and Aug. Regional and Italian cuisine: gnocchetti verdi, veal smitaine, 30/45,000.
◆◆ **Ungherese,** largo La Foppa 5 (B3 eg), ☎ 6599487, closed Sun, Aug and Christmas. International cuisine: goulash, sauerkraut kolozsvàr, 15/20,000.
◆ **Matteoni,** p. V. Giornate 6 (E6 dc), ☎ 588293, closed Sun and Jul-Aug. Tuscan trattoria. Tuscan cuisine: ribollita, macaroni with rabbit, 30/40,000.
◆ **Pechino,** v. Conisio 7 (A2 dn), ☎ 384668, closed Mon, Jul-Aug and Christmas. Simple and secluded, Western in style but with Chinese lamps and decorations. Peking Chinese cuisine: prawns with ginger, tea-smoked duck, 25/35,000.

⚠ ★★ *AGIP Metanopoli,* at San Donato Milanese, v. Emilia, 97 pl, ☎ 5272159 (all year); ★★ *Il Bareggino,* at Bareggio, v. Corbettina, 350 pl, ☎ 9014417 (all year).

Recommended

Archery: *Compagnia arcieri Conte Biancamano,* v. Frugoni 20/2; *Fitarco,* v. Brenta 33, ☎ 5392354.
Auction houses: *Geri,* corso Venezia 10 (D5), ☎ 702939; *Finarte,* p. Bossi 4 (D4), ☎ 877041; *Christie's Italy,* v. Borgogna 9 (D5), ☎ 794712; *Sotheby's,* v. Mascagni 15/2 (D5-6), ☎ 794609.
Bicycle-racing track: *Vigorelli,* v. Arona 15, ☎ 3311513.

Bowling: *Centro XXV Aprile*, v. Cimabue 24, ☎ 322689; *Forza e Coraggio*, v. Gallura 8, ☎ 563130.

Canoeing: instruction given at *Circolo kajak canoa*, p. Novelli 8, ☎ 717168; *Canoa club Milano*, v. San Martino 5, ☎ 6080620; *Centro propaganda canoa*, v. Piolti De Bianchi 4, ☎ 7426771.

Children's facilities: courses in free expression at *Atelier di pittura*, alzai Naviglio Grande 65, ☎ 8327552; guitar courses at *Accademia chitarra classica*, v. Corridoni 34, ☎ 680076 (Sun, free of charge).

Clay pigeon shooting: v. Macconago 50, ☎ 5394037.

Conference centre: at Assago, *Milanofiori*, ☎ 824791.

Events: opera season at La Scala, ☎ 807041; concerts at La Scala, Conservatorio all'Angelicum, ☎ 6592748; triennial exhibition at the palazzo dell'Arte in the park (C2), ☎ 862441; *Festa dei Navigli* (boating festival, 1st Sun in Jun); *Fiera degli Oh bei Oh bei* (6-8 Dec) in p. S. Ambrogio (D-E2-3) and surrounding area.

Excursions: to lakes of Lombardy by bus, motorboat and ferry; departures daily (Apr-early Oct) from p. Castello (Autostradale, ☎ 801161) and from Stazione Centrale, galleria delle Carrozze (*C.I.T.*, ☎ 202677).

Exhibitions and markets: in the exhibition district: *Grande Fiera d'Aprile*, ☎ 3453251 and 80 other specialist shows of various kinds (cinema, sport, tourism, fashion and so on), ☎ 4997336. Antiques market at alzaia Naviglio Grande (last Sun of every month); market at v. Armorari (coins and stamps, every hol a.m.); Sinigaglia fair (bric-à-brac, second-hand clothes, etc.) every Sat.

Fencing: regional committee, v. Piranesi 44, ☎ 7381282; practice and courses of instruction: *Mangiarotti*, ☎ 6551188; *Palalido*, ☎ 366100; *Centro Saini*, ☎ 7380841; *Forza e Coraggio*, ☎ 563130.

Flying: *Milano-Bresso* airport, ☎ 6140878 (panoramic flights, ☎ 6102428); *Accademia volovelistica* (gliding), at Bresso, v. Monteceneri 36; *Club aerostatico italiano* (lighter-than-air aircraft), v. Alserio 23, ☎ 603485 (flight in a hot-air balloon).

Golf: *Barlassina*, at Birago di Camnago, ☎ 560621 (18 holes); *Golf club Milano*, at Monza, ☎ 039/303081 (18 holes); *Le Rovedine*, at Noverasco d'Opera, 5242730 (9 holes); *Molinetto*, at Cernusco sul Naviglio, ☎ 9238500 (18 holes); *Zoate*, at Zoate, ☎ 9060015 (18 holes). Practice ranges: *Golf Milan School*, v. Brioschi 62, ☎ 8464762; at Peschiera Borromeo, v. Lombardia, ☎ 5471859; v. Buozzi 4/c, ☎ 5470581.

Guided tours: by bus departing from p. Duomo (Piazzetta Reale, E4) at 9 a.m. and 2:30 p.m. except Mon; Nov-Mar a.m. only. Reservations at hotels, travel agencies and *Società Autostradale*, ☎ 801161. Free guided tours of monuments, museums, exhibitions (in Milan and Lombardy): ask at tourist offices, ☎ 809662. *Società guide Milano* (association of Milan guides), ☎ 863210.

Hang gliding: *Scuola Albatros*, v. F. Filzi, ☎ 655716.

Horseback riding: *Centro ippico lombardo*, v. Fetonte 21, ☎ 4084270 (associate of *ANTE*); *Centro ippico milanese*, v. Macconago 20, ☎ 5392013; *Gruppo ippico Ticino*, Boffalora beyond Ticino, v. Dante 13, ☎ 9754102.

Ice skating: v. Piranesi 14, ☎ 7398 (Sep-May); ice rink at *Centro Saini*, v. Corelli 136, ☎ 7380841 (also beginners' artificial ski slope).

Natural parks: *Groane regional park*, at Cesate, v. Piave 5, ☎ 9942329; *Valle del Lambro regional park*, at Triuggio, municipio, ☎ 0362/931217; *Vanzago WWF regional forest reserve*, information and visits, ☎ 6556810-653251.

Palazzo del turismo: v. Marconi 1 (E4), ☎ 809662.

Race course: *San Siro* race course and trotting track, v. Trenno, ☎ 4084350 (information on trotting races, ☎ 4521851).

River trips: along the Naviglio Grande as far as Parco del Ticino (→), Jul-Sep; information, ☎ 809662, reservations, ☎ 6208-3122.

Sailing: *Lega Navale*, corso di Porta Romana 17, ☎ 879762; base at Dervio (→ Lake Como); *Centro velico Caprera*, corso Italia 10, ☎ 808428 (courses in sailing and navigation on the open sea, May-Nov, → Sardinia, La Maddalena); *Centro velico d'altura*, v. Ajaccio 13, ☎ 745578; *Velamare*, alzaia Naviglio Grande 12, ☎ 8321739 (two-week courses with a base in Sardinia);

Centro nautico Utopia, v. De Cristoforis 5, ☎ 654037 (introductory courses, basic cruising, and cruising by the islands of Palmaria and Elba); *Horca Myseria*, v. Pelitti 1, ☎ 2552585.

Skindiving: *Federazione italiana attività subacquee*, v. Piranesi 44/B, ☎ 774781; courses held by *CUS Milano*, v. Monteverdi 18, ☎ 278529.

Sports facilities: *Palalido*, p. Stuparich, ☎ 366100.

Stock exchange: visits to the Borsa Valori (stock exchange), p. degli Affari 6 (D3), ☎ 8534-4229 (reserve well in advance).

Windsurfing: Idroscalo, ☎ 7560190.

Wines: wine cellars in v. Poggibonsi 14, ☎ 4078461; v. S. Marco 2, ☎ 6599650; v. Morosini 19, ☎ 573826; v. Speronari 4, ☎ 808698; v. S. Gottardo 13, ☎ 8351239; v. Pasubio 6/8, ☎ 664246; v. Solferino 42, ☎ 665736.

Young people's facilities: courses in off-road driving, *Federazione italiana fuoristrada*, v. Campania 4, ☎ 230018; courses in racing and rallying, *Scuola piloti Milano*, at Cerro Maggiore (25 km NW), v. Brunelleschi 10, ☎ 0331/592395.

Youth hostel: *Ostello Pietro Rotta*, v. Martino Bassi 2, ☎ 367095.

♥ **shopping:** elegant shops in the area around v. Dante, v. Manzoni, corso Vittorio Emanuele and corso Venezia; antique shops and art galleries mainly near to v. Montenapoleone and v. Brera.

Environs

ASSAGO-MILANOFIORI, ✉ 20090, 9 km SW.

Hotel:
★★★★ *Milanofiori*, ☎ 82221, 255 rm ℗ ⋒ 230,000.

OPERA ✉ 20090, 10 km S.

Hotel:
★★★★ *Sporting*, v. Sporting Mirasole 56, ☎ 5241577, 84 rm ℗ & 155,000; bkf: 10,000.

SAN DONATO MILANESE, ✉ 20097, 8 km SE.

Hotel:
★★★★ *MotelAgip*, Metanopoli Autosole junction, ☎ 512941, 275 rm ℗ & 149,000. Rest. ♦♦♦ *Executive* closed Sat, Sun, Christmas and Jul-Aug. Excellent cuisine, 40/60,000.

SEGRATE-MILANO 2, ✉ 20090, 10 km E.

Hotel:
★★★★ *Jolly Milano 2*, v. F.lli Cervi, ☎ 21606, 149 rm ℗ 198,000.

MONTICHIARI

Brescia 20, Milan 112 km
Pop. 15,718 ✉ 25018, ☎ 030   D4

Near Montichiari, an active agricultural and industrial centre on the bank of the Chiese River, the countryside becomes progressively more varied as it approaches the slopes of the amphitheatre formed by the Garda moraine.

▶ The town is dominated by the dome of the 18C **parish church**, which has an important painting of the *Last Supper* by Romanino, and by the ruins of a multi-turreted **castle.** ▶ Also striking is the 12C Romanesque church of **S. Pancrazio,** isolated on a hill with splendid views.   ☐

MONZA*

Milan 15 km
Pop. 122,476 ✉ 20052 ☎ 039   B4

The Lombard queen Theodolinda established her court at Monza in the 6C AD. She is entombed in the Duomo, where 15C frescos also illustrate her life. The 9C iron crown of the kings of Italy, supposed-

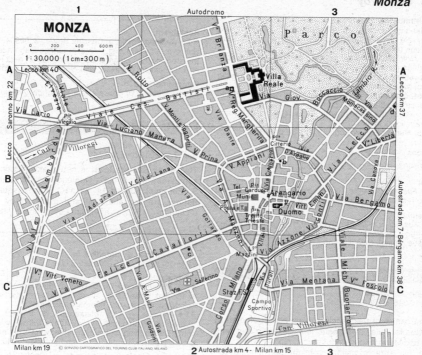

MONZA

0   200   400   600 m

1 : 30.000 (1 cm = 300 m)

ly forged from an nail used in Christ's Crucifixion, is kept here in the chapel of Theodolinda. It was used at coronations from the 13C. Napoleon wore the crown in 1805. Monza was also the scene of the assassination of King Umberto I by the anarchist Gaetano Bresci in 1900.

▶ Modern industrial Monza (the third city of Lombardy) is now part of the Milan conurbation. Nevertheless the **old town** remains distinctive. ▶ At the centre of the p. Roma is the former **Palazzo Comunale** or **Arengario** (B2-3; 13C), now the **Museo Archeologico** *(under restoration)*. ▶ The principal ecclesiastical building is the **Duomo★** (B3), 13C-14C Gothic. The façade, adorned with bands of white and green marble, is a superb example of Campionese architecture. Inside (altered in the 17C-18C), the **Cappella di Teodolinda★** (visit combined with the Treasury) is decorated with frescos (1444) and the **iron crown★** is kept in the tabernacle. The church **treasure★**, exhibited in the **Museo Serpero** *(9 a.m.-12 noon and 3-5 p.m.; closed Sun a.m. and Mon)*, is most important (items from the 5C-9C). ▶ Not far from the old town is the **Villa Reale** (A2), a Neoclassical complex built in 1777-80 for the Archduke Ferdinand of Austria. Particularly fine is the central building overlooking the garden *(9 a.m.-7 p.m.)*. One wing houses the **Pinacoteca** *(under restoration)* with 15C-20C works. The villa is surrounded by an extensive **park★★** (A2-3; *7 a.m.-5 or 8.30 p.m. according to the month)* laid out in 1806 with flowerbeds, glades, wilder areas, paths, houses and dairy farms, now to a large extent occupied by sports grounds and the celebrated **Autodromo**, the motor-racing track where international events are held. □

The arrow (→) is a reference to another entry.

Practical information ⎯⎯⎯⎯⎯⎯⎯⎯

MONZA

ℹ p. Carducci (B2), ☎ 323222.
Car rental: *Maggiore,* v. Villoresi 4, ☎ 361478.

Hotel:
★★★ ***De la Ville,*** v. Regina Margherita 15 (A2 a), ☎ 382581, 55 rm Ⓟ closed Aug and Christmas, 115,000; bkf: 9,000.

Restaurants:
● ◆◆◆◆ ***Saint Georges Premier,*** Villa Reale, ☎ 320600, closed Tue. 18C hunting lodge with large veranda. International cuisine: pancakes, scampi in sauce, bollito gigante, 30/55,000.
◆◆◆ ***Grazie,*** v. Lecco 84 (A3 d), ☎ 387650, closed Wed and 10-31 Aug. Rebuilt period villa with summer service under canopies. Creative cuisine: tagliolini in crayfish sauce, risottino all ambrosiana, 40/45,000.
◆◆◆ ***Olivo,*** at S. Fruttuoso (3 km SW), v. Risorgimento 1, ☎ 742845, closed Sun eve, Mon and Aug. Elegant and spacious, with little park for summer meals. Regional cuisine: gnocchi verdi piemontesi, sea bass in white wine with black olives, 30/45,000.
◆◆ ***Cigno Blu,*** v. Cavallotti (C2 c), ☎ 365379, closed Wed. Urban restaurant with relaxed atmosphere. Regional cuisine: risotto with crayfish, poached capesanti, 23/35,000.
◆ ***Antica Trattoria dell'Uva,*** p. Carrobiolo 2 (B3 b), ☎ 323825, closed Fri and Aug. Trattoria with traditional atmosphere. Regional cuisine: homemade pasta, game with polenta, 22/30,000.

⛺ ★★ *Autodromo,* in the park of the Villa Reale, 200 pl, ☎ 387771.

Recommended
Events: international car *(Formula 1 Grand Prix)* and motorcycle races at the Autodromo; international furniture exhibition (Sep).
Golf: *Golf club Milano,* in the park of Villa Reale, ☎ 303084 (18 + 9 holes).
Horse racing: *Ippodromo di Mirabello,* Centro ippico in the park of Villa Reale, ☎ 366351.
Motor-racing track: in the park of Villa Reale, ☎ 329866 (entrance fee, 8 a.m.-6:30 p.m.).
Polo: field in the park of Villa Reale, *Polo club Monza,* v. Mirabello, ☎ 320670.
Wines: *Meregalli,* v. Visconti 43 (BC 3), ☎ 384220.

Environs

CANONICA DI TRIUGGIO, ⊠ 20050, ☎ 0362, 10 km N.

Hotel:
★★★ *Fossati,* v. Conte Taverna 20, ☎ 970401, 45 rm P ⅏ No restaurant, 80,000; bkf: 6,000.

Restaurant:
♦♦♦ *Fossati,* v. Filiberto 1, ☎ 970212, closed Mon, Jan and Aug. Regional cuisine: risotto alla milanese with sausage, guinea fowl alla creta, 30/40,000.

MORBEGNO

Sondrio 25, Milan 113 km
Pop. 10,345 ⊠ 23017 ☎ 0342　　　　　　　　　　C2

At the centre of the Valtellina plain and the mouth of the Gerola Valley, Morbegno is engaged in mechanical, textile and food industries. A celebrated livestock fair attracts visitors from the surrounding valleys, but it is less important than formerly.

▶ Notable features of the old town include: the Baroque church of **S. Giovanni Battista,** with frescos and paintings (18C); the 14C church of **S. Antonio,** with a sculpted *Pietà* and 16C frescos; the **santuario dell'Assunta** (15C-16C), with gilded polychrome altarpiece (1526) and the 18C **Palazzo Malacrida,** with large frescoed rooms. □

Practical information ──────────

Hotels:
★★★ *Bellevue,* at Regoledo, ☎ 635108, 39 rm P ⅏ 🅱 ⅏ 48,000; bkf: 4,000.
★★★ *Margna,* v. Margna 24, ☎ 610377, 38 rm P ⅏ 🅱 ⅏ 45,000; bkf: 5,000.

Restaurant:
♦♦♦ *Vecchio Ristorante Fiume,* contrada Cima alle Case 3, ☎ 610248, closed Tue, Wed and 15 Jun-15 Jul. Regional cuisine: penne del contadino, soused trout, escalope with bitto cheese, 25/40,000.

MORTARA

Pavia 37, Milan 47 km
Pop. 14,599 ⊠ 27036 ☎ 0384　　　　　　　　　　A5

This town, which has some interesting works of art, is prosperous and industrialized, the capital of the Lomellina rice-growing area.

▶ The Gothic church of **S. Lorenzo** (1375-80) has two fine portals (one side was rebuilt during restoration in 1916) with rectangular frames decorated in terra cotta. Inside are 17C paintings. ▶ 1.5 km away is the abbey of **S. Albino,** founded in the 5C and rebuilt in the 16C. Tradition has it that it was also rebuilt in 774 by Charlemagne as a Frankish burial ground after a battle against the Lombards. ▶ 19 km towards Alessandria, at **Sartirana Lomellina,** is an imposing 14C-15C **castle**★, extended in the 17C, with moat and high square tower. □

Practical information ──────────

Restaurant:
♦♦♦ *Cascina Bovile,* at Cascina Bovile, ☎ 99904, closed Sun eve, Mon and Aug. Ancient farmhouse in rice fields transformed into elegant restaurant. Good regional cuisine: pancakes, pheasant with cloves, 50,000 (minimum).

Recommended
Events: *Festival of goose salami (sagra del salame d'oca)* (last Sun in Sep).

OGGIONO

Como 25, Milan 48 km
Pop. 7,288 ⊠ 22048 ☎ 0341　　　　　　　　　　B3

This small Brianza town is near **Lake Annone** (→), sometimes called Lake Oggiono. In the church of **S. Eufemia,** flanked by an 11C Romanesque **baptistery,** are an altarpiece and a fresco by Marco d'Oggiono, who was a pupil of Leonardo da Vinci. □

Practical information ──────────

Hotel:
★★★ *Fattorie di Stendhal,* v. Dante 16, ☎ 576561, 21 rm P 🅱 ⅏ ⅏ 75,000; bkf: 5,000.

Restaurants:
♦♦♦ *Peschereccio,* at Bevera di Sirtori, v. Lecco 26, ☎ 955330, closed Tue. Tuscan cuisine: risotto with cuttlefish ink, tagliata alla fiorentina, 35/45,000.
♦♦♦ *Pierino,* v. XXIV Maggio 36, ☎ 956020, closed Sun eve, Mon, Jan and Aug. Veranda with view and garden. Outstanding regional and creative cuisine: monkfish tails in tomato with pâté brise and prawns, 28/40,000.
⋏ ★★ *4 Stagioni,* at Imberido, v. Dante 21, 120 pl, ☎ 577022 (all year).

L'OLTREPO PAVESE

From Pavia *(187 km, 1 day; map 6)*

The hills rise gently from the plain, then sharpen into the first spurs of the Apennines, where oak and chestnut woods give way to conifers and pasture land. Agricultural mechanization is impossible or at best difficult in these mountain uplands. Little profit can be made from cultivating the small parcels of land, and the population is declining. Young people migrate to the plain. In the strip of land at the foot of the hills, however, the vine still reigns supreme, and this part of the Oltrepò now makes up about half the wine-producing area of Lombardy.

▶ The departure point is **Pavia** (→). The Romanesque former church of S. Marcello di Montalino (12C) marks the site of the oldest settlement in **Stradella,** a town known for accordions and fine wines (with neighbouring Broni). ▶ The road proceeds through luxuriant vines to **Santa Maria della Versa,** with well-equipped cellars producing fine sparkling wines. ▶ **Lake Trebecco** is artificial, used for aquatic sports. ▶ In **Zavattarello** in the high Tidone Valley are the ruins of the ancient Dal Verme castle named after the lords of the valley. ▶ The town of **Varzi** is renowned for its excellent salami. When the Malaspina family were the feudal lords here (12C), Varzi controlled merchant traffic along the Apennine road from Genoa to Milan. The medieval old town has narrow streets, low arcades, towers and passages. ▶ After **San Pietro Casasco,** at **Piazza,** the road for the **Pénice** pass (→ Bobbio in Emilia-Romagna) branches off to the l. while this route continues along the W slopes of Mt. Pénice via **Brallo di Pregola** (3,120 ft) and over the pass of the same name, between the slopes of the Stàffora and Trebbia. ▶ The road follows the first of the two. **Santa Margherita di Stàffora** is dominated by a hill with the remains

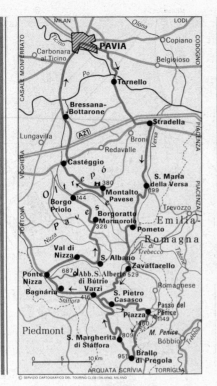

6. L'Oltrepo Pavese

of a castle and a church. ▶ After Varzi, from which the road proceeds to **Bagnaria**, the route turns off for the abbey of **Sant'Alberto di Butrio** on a hillock between dense woods. Founded by a hermit in the 11C, the abbey became powerful in the 12C-14C. Still to be seen are the remains of towers, cloisters and walls, and three little Romanesque churches with 15C frescos. ▶ Minor roads skirt **Borgoratto Mormorolo** and **Borgo Priolo** then the route reaches **Montalto Pavese**; on a hillock is a late-16C castle with gardens in the Italian style. ▶ In the wine-growing centre of **Casteggio**, where the road returns to the plain, the rebuilt **Civico Museo Archeologico** *(Sun 3-6 p.m.; Tue and Fri 9 a.m.-12 noon)* displays Roman finds from the Roman town of *Clastidium* and the surrounding area. ▶ The road crosses the Po and the Ticino to return to **Pavia**. □

Practical information _____

BRALLO DI PREGOLA, ⊠ 27050, ☎ 0383.
↡ ski lifts at Brallo and Cima Colletta.
ⓘ v. della Pineta, ☎ 500221.
Recommended
Tennis: *Centro federale estivo,* ☎ 50632.

PASSO DEL PÉNICE, 3,760 ft.
↡ ski lifts, skiing instruction.
ⓘ Mencónico municipio *(9 km W),* ☎ 0383/574001; at Bobbio *(12 km SE),* p. S. Francesco, ☎ 0523/936178.

RECOARO DI BRONI, ⊠ 27043, 5 km E of Stradella.
♨ (May-Oct), ☎ 51305.

SANTA MARGHERITA DI STAFFORA, ⊠ 27050, ☎ 0383.
⚸ ★★★ *Alta Valle Staffora,* at Sala, Pian del Lago, 200 pl, ☎ 50148 (all year).

SANTA MARIA DELLA VERSA, ⊠ 27047, ☎ 0385.

Restaurant:
♦ *Hostaria il Casale,* at Il Casale 2, ☎ 79108, closed Jun-Jul. Pleasantly green courtyard. Italian cuisine: stracotto with red wine, quails in Pinot, Oltrepò Pavese wines, 25/32,000.
Recommended
Wines: exhibition of Oltrepò sparkling wines (Jun).

STRADELLA, ⊠ 27049, ☎ 0385.

Hotel:
★ *Gallo,* v. Parea 7, ☎ 48323, 19 rm Ⓟ closed Aug, 36,000. Rest. ♦ closed Mon, 20/25,000.
Recommended
Accordion making: visits to the *Dallapè Mariano & figli* accordion workshop, v. Mazzini 14/16, ☎ 48627 (reservations advisable).

VARZI, ⊠ 27057, ☎ 0383.

Restaurant:
♦ *Corona,* p. Fiera 19, ☎ 52043, closed Mon and Nov. Italian cuisine: risotto with mushrooms, baked breast of veal, 22/33,000.
Recommended
Gastronomic specialties: salami, white truffles.

ZAVATTARELLO, ⊠ 27059, ☎ 0383.
Recommended
Botanical garden: *Pietra Corva alpine botanical garden,* at Romagnese *(8 km SE),* ☎ 0383/580054 (open Apr-Oct, in bloom May-Jun).

ORZINUOVI

Brescia 29, Milan 65 km
Pop. 10,144 ⊠ 25034 ☎ 030   C4

Less than 1 km from Soncino, on the opposite bank of the River Oglio, the military outpost of Orzinuovi (founded late 12C) used to guard Brescia. The **castle** ruins are all that remain of a massive defensive system built in the 16C. The **old town** consists of rectangular blocks arranged around a square. □

Practical information _____

Recommended
Cycling: *Pedale orceano,* v. Cossali 40, ☎ 941707.

PAVIA*

Milan 34, Rome 565 km
Pop. 83,960 ⊠ 27100 ☎ 0382   B5

Pavia stands among the rice-fields of the Lomellina, the vineyards of the Oltrepò and the meadows of the Po Valley and has always been involved with agriculture and associated trades. Its buildings of red brick and sandstone and low houses are arranged tidily on the pattern of the old Roman town. For more than five centuries Pavia remained confined within medieval walls, then expanded significantly in the course of industrial development in late 19C and early 20C. Pavia still maintains the style of an ancient (14C) university city of undisputed excellence.

▶ The **piazza della Vittoria** (C2-3), the old market place, is surrounded by arcades and 14C-15C houses. On the S side is the Palazzo del Comune or **Broletto** (C2; 12C) with loggia (1563) in the façade (rebuilt 19C) and a court-

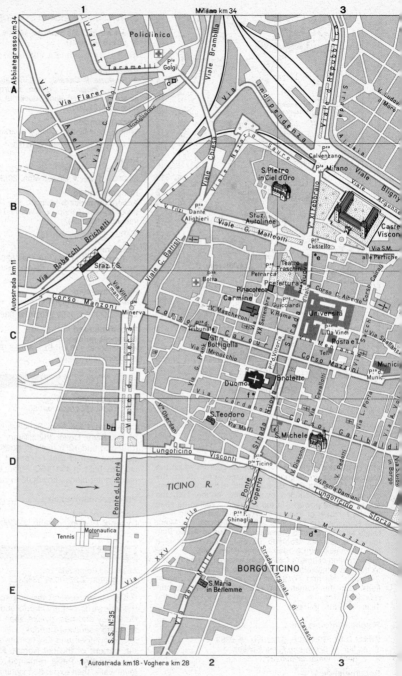

yard (12C-15C) overlooking the Duomo. ▶ The façade of the cathedral faces the **piazza del Duomo** (C2), dominated by the massive **Torre Civica** (11C) and decorated with the **Regisole** (sun god on horseback), a modern reconstruction of an imperial Roman statue. The **Duomo★** (C2) was started in 1488 and completed in 1936 (transepts). The interior is a complex design on a Greek cross plan, topped with an octagonal dome of exceptional

PAVIA

0   100   200   300m

1 : 15.000 (1cm=150m)

Milan/km 35

A

B

C

E

Lodi/km 36

Cremona km 75 - Autostrada km 19 - Piacenza km 52

© SERVIZIO CARTOGRAFICO DEL TOURING CLUB ITALIANO, MILANO

1944. ▶ Beyond the river, in Borgo Ticino, is the Romanesque church of **S. Maria in Betlemme** (E2; 12C). The basilica of **S. Michele★★** (D3) is a masterpiece of Lombard Romanesque architecture, rebuilt in the 12C. The superb **façade** is lightened in the upper part by an elegant gallery and decorated in the lower part, above the lavish portals, with horizontal bands with fantastic figures in bas-relief. Kings and emperors (from Berengarius to Henry II of Sassonia) were crowned in the basilica, which is rich in works of art, including a crucifix in silver leaf (10C), reliefs by Campionese masters (1383; on the high altar) and a 15C fresco. ▶ From the little Romanesque church of **S. Teodoro** (D2; 12C) with a 16C veduta of Pavia and its towers, pass through ancient streets to the corso Cavour, near the Renaissance **Palazzo Carminali Bottigella** (C2; 15C) with decorated façade. ▶ Farther on is the exuberant Gothic church of **S. Maria del Carmine** (C2), dating from 1390, with 15C-16C frescos and sculptures. ▶ Return to the Strada Nuova and follow it N, skirting the Neoclassical building of the **university** (C3), an extremely old foundation (10C-11C), reorganized by the Visconti in 1361, and famous for academic distinction. The university operates at the highest level and has faculties and research institutes of international rank. In the town various colleges house university students; most famous is the **Collegio Borromeo** (D4), founded by St. Charles Borromeo and built between 1564 and 1585. ▶ Still on the Strada Nuova, onto which faces the 17C **Teatro Fraschini** (B3), pass to the piazzale del **Castelleo Visconteo★★** (B3), a handsome 14C secular building. The imposing brick quadrilateral enclosing a broad arcaded **courtyard★** was commissioned by Galeazzo Visconti in 1365 (the N side was destroyed by the French in 1527, two years after the battle of Pavia at which Francis I of France was defeated). The castle houses the **Museo Civico** *(Apr, Jun and Sep 10 a.m.-12 noon and 2:30-5 p.m, or 2-4 p.m. in Feb, Mar, Oct and Nov; other months 9 a.m.-1 p.m.; closed Mon)* and the **Pinacoteca★** with 12C-17C exhibits. ▶ Not far away is the church of **S. Pietro in Ciel d'Oro★★** (B2-3), a gem of Lombard Romanesque. Tombs in the church include those of Severinus Boethius (480-524), philosopher and statesman, and of St. Augustine on the high altar, in the Gothic **arca di S. Agostino★** (1362). ▶ 20 km away is **San Lanfranco;** in the church (12C-13C) is the finely carved **arca di Lanfranco★** (cenotaph; 1488). ▶ **Certosa di Pavia** (Carthusian monastery; →). ▶ 14 km E is **Belgioioso,** with a 14C Visconti castle and an 18C villa.

Zuppa alla pavese

Eggs are poached in broth, and the dish is completed with sippets and grated parmesan cheese. It is said that the soup was created by a confused Pavese farmer's wife who saw Francis I, King of France, arriving at her house, battle-weary and famished after the disastrous battle of Pavia in 1525. She rapidly prepared soup, slices of bread and cheese, and fried eggs, then put them all into the same tureen. It is doubtful that this happened because it was recorded at the time that the king fought for quite some time, then his horse was wounded and he fell to the ground; he was then taken by five soldiers who did not recognize him, but when the viceroy of Naples arrived unexpectedly he recognized the king and took him prisoner. Francis surrendered and was taken to the Rocca di Pizzighettone.

Practical information

PAVIA
ⓘ corso Garibaldi 1 (D3), ☎ 22156.
🚂 (B1), ☎ 23000.
🚌 from p. Castello (B3) and p. Stazione FS (C-B1).

breadth (fourth broadest in Italy). ▶ The **Strada Nuova,** main artery of the city, links the Castello (→) to the distinctive **Ponte Coperto** (D2), rebuilt with variations on the 14C original, which was destroyed by bombing in

Hotels:
★★★★ *Ariston,* v. Scopoli 10/D (C4 a), ☎ 34334, 60 rm
P & closed Christmas, 74,000; bkf: 7,000.
★★★★ *Palace,* v. della Libertà 89 (D1 b), ☎ 27441, 53 rm
P 82,000; bkf: 6,000.
★★★★ *Rosengarten,* p. Policlinico 19 (A2 c), ☎ 27701,
84 rm P closed Aug, 74,000; bkf: 7,000.

Restaurants:
● ♦♦♦ *Locanda Vecchia Pavia,* v. Cardinal Riboldi 2
(C2 f), ☎ 304132, closed Mon, Jan and Aug. In ancient
Casa Cairoli, with fin-de-siècle furnishings. Creative cui-
sine: risotto with truffled kidneys, sole in sweet and sour
sauce, 35/55,000.
♦♦♦ *Bixio,* p. Castello 1 (B3 e), ☎ 25343, closed Sun eve,
Mon and Aug, 25/40,000.
♦ *Antica Osteria del Previ,* v. Milazzo 65 (E3 d), ☎ 26203,
closed Wed and Nov. Regional cuisine: risotto with
vegetables or sausage, freshwater fish cooked in various
ways, 20/30,000.

⚠ ★★★ *Ticino,* at Bagni Chiosso, v. Mascherpa 10, 70 pl,
☎ 20015.

Recommended
Cycling: *Velo club Pavia,* v. Tasso 41 (B4).
Events: *motorboat race* from Pavia to Venice, from the
River Ticino to the River Po and the Venice lagoon (Jun).
Horseback riding: *Ippica pavese,* v. Guffanti 28, ☎ 29366
(instruction).
Motorboats: *Motonautica pavese,* strada Canarazzo 9
(E1), ☎ 30459.
Natural parks: regional park of Valle del Ticino (→),
☎ 02/9794401; WWF Pavia, ☎ 465315.
Rowing: *C.U.S. sezione canottaggio,* v. Folla di Sotto,
☎ 27422; *Canottieri Ticino,* lungoticino Calvi (D1),
☎ 31263.
Sports centre: v. Treves (B4), ☎ 475411.
Swimming: indoor swimming pool, v. Resistenza 2 (DE4),
☎ 32367.
Wines: *Bolis,* corso Manzoni 27 (C1), ☎ 35575.

Environs

BEREGUARDO, ⊠ 27021, 14 km NW.

Restaurant:
● ♦♦♦ *Zelata,* at Zelata, p. della Chiesa 17, ☎ 928178,
closed Sun eve, Mon and Aug. Elegant and secluded. Quality Italian cuisine: ravioloni imperiale, guinea
fowl with green peppercorns, 50/55,000.

CASSININO, 4 km N.

Restaurant:
● ♦♦♦ *Cassinino,* ☎ 422097, closed Wed and
27 Dec-20 Jan. Tiny, exclusive and elegant restaurant. Excellent Italian cuisine: varies according to morning's shopping; fish or rucola risotto, sea bass carpaccio, 40/60,000.

PARASACCO DI ZERBOLO, ⊠ 27020, 19 km W.

Restaurant:
♦ *Da Nicola,* ☎ 83027, closed Wed. Country trattoria
with garden. Regional cuisine: pancakes, pheasant in
foil, 16/28,000.

PIZZIGHETTONE

Cremona 25, Milan 64 km
Pop. 7,131 ⊠ 26026 ☎ 0372   C5

12C refugees from Lodi Vecchio, which had been destroyed by the Milanese, found hospitality in this agricultural village on the Adda. They rebuilt the church
of **S. Bassano.** The façade has a rose window and
there are interesting 14C reliefs in the interior. The
little town has 16C **ramparts** and the medieval **tower,**
square and crenellated, in which Francis I of France
was held prisoner after the battle of Pavia (1525).   □

Practical information

Restaurants:
● ♦♦♦ *Albergo del Sole,* at Malo, v. Trabattoni 22,
☎ 58142, closed Sun eve, Mon, Jan and Aug. Historic
establishment refurbished with good taste. Outstanding
Italian cuisine: stracotto with polenta, liver with grapes,
40/55,000.
♦ *Leon d'Oro,* at Malco, v. Dante 81, ☎ 58149, closed
Wed, Jan and Aug. Small trattoria. Regional cuisine: onion purée with raspadura, salmon with pink peppercorns, 28/40,000.

PONTE DI LEGNO

Brescia 118, Milan 167 km
4,125 ft pop. 2,068 ⊠ 25056 ☎ 0364   D2

Ponte di Legno, Temù (→) and the Tonale pass make
up an important winter sports area in the high Valcamonica. It is possible to go by chair lift or road
(18 km) to the **Rifugio Corno d'Aola** (6,398 ft) with
view over the Adamello and Ortles. 17.3 km away
is the **passo di Gavia** (8,599 ft) through the Valfurva
(→ Santa Caterina Valfurva).   □

Practical information
℥ chair lifts, ski lifts, cross-country skiing, skiing instruction, artificial ski jump, summer skiing in the Presena glacier (→ passo del Tonale, Trentino).
ℹ corso Milano, ☎ 91122.
🚌 from the Autostazione, ☎ 91136.

Hotels:
★★★★ *Mirella,* v. Roma 21, ☎ 91661, 61 rm P ♨ & ≋
⌂ ⌇ closed Oct-Nov and May, 110,000; bkf: 9,000.
★★★ *Mignon,* v. Corno d'Aola 11, ☎ 91195, 27 rm P ♨
62,000; bkf: 6,000.
★★ *Bleis,* v. Corno d'Aola 4, ☎ 91316, 13 rm P ♨ ≋
closed Oct-Nov and May, 42,000; bkf: 5,000.

Restaurant:
♦♦ *Maniero,* v. Roma 54, ☎ 92314, closed Mon and
Nov. Italian cuisine: strozzapreti with Gorgonzola, veni-
son steak with butter and rosemary, 21/35,000.

Recommended
Children's facilities: *I Folletti* children's residence,
v. Piazza 4, ☎ 91234-91538 (open mid-Jun-early Sep and
Christmas hols).
Golf: corso Milano 41, ☎ 91122 (open Jul and Aug;
9 holes).
Swimming pool: v. Venezia, ☎ 91618 (with sauna).
Young people's facilities: *Scuola italiana sledog* (sled-
dog racing), at Ca' de Foi, Milan office, ☎ 02/653451.

PORLEZZA

Como 43, Milan 95 km
Pop. 3,681 ⊠ 22018 ☎ 0344   B2

The people of Porlezza go to work in Switzerland and
the Swiss come to Porlezza for their vacations. This
ancient village stands at the E end of Lake Lugano,
amid austere but picturesque mountains. 4.3 km S
are the **grotte di Rescia** *(ask at campsite),* little galleried caves with petrification and a waterfall
below. The **Val Cavargna** is wild and little-visited.   □

Practical information
🚢 boats to Lugano.

Hotel:
★★ *Regina,* p. Matteotti 11, ☎ 61228, 24 rm, closed
12 Jan-20 Feb, 45,000; bkf: 6,000.

⚠ ★★★ *International Sport,* towards Osteno, 650 pl,
☎ 61852 (all year).

Recommended
Caves: visits to the caves of Rescia (*4.5 km S,* Apr-Oct), warden's office at campsite opposite, ☎ 65240.

REVERE

Mantua 35, Milan 210 km
Pop. 2,838 ⊠ 46036 ☎ 0386   F5

On the right bank of the Po, this agricultural and commercial centre has a fine **Palazzo Ducale,** built 1450-60 by the Gonzaga family, rulers of Mantua. It houses the **Museo del Po,** with material on successive river civilizations. On the opposite bank is **Ostiglia** (→).   □

Practical information _____

Restaurant:
● ◆◆◆ *Tartufo,* v. Guido Rossa 13, ☎ 46404, closed Thu, Jun-Jul. Family atmosphere, with fireplace. Regional cuisine: pappardelle with duck, fried frogs, 25/35,000.

SABBIONETA*

Mantua 33, Milan 142 km
Pop. 4,764 ⊠ 46018 ☎ 0375   D5

In the 16C this Mantuan village was transformed into a little Athens: centre of enlightenment and seat of a collateral branch of the Gonzagas. It also became a 'new town', an ideal urban space, planned and rebuilt by the ruling Duke Vespasiano Gonzago. The fortifications, the palazzi, the rational quality of the original plan (which included a district set aside for the Jews who formed the backbone of the town's economy) provide one of the most interesting examples of Renaissance town planning.

▶ The town is enclosed within hexagonal 16C walls, with corner bulwarks and a network of streets at right angles, centred on the axes of the principal Roman streets. Two squares contain the palazzi (open *10:30 a.m.-12:30 p.m. and 3-6:30 p.m., or 2-6:30 p.m. Nov-Feb; closed Mon); ask at the Pro Loco tourist office, A1-2.* ▶ The town centre is the **piazza Ducale** (A1-2), surrounded by arcaded buildings. ▶ The **Palazzo Ducale★** (A1), built in 1568, is a solid construction on two floors with a covered terrace on the roof. The rooms have carved and painted wooden ceilings. The stucco busts exhibited in the Galleria degli Antenati and the four wooden equestrian statues in the guard room represent ancestors of the Gonzagas. ▶ In the church of the **Incoronata** (A1; 1588) is the mausoleum of Duke Vespasiano Gonzaga (1592); the bronze **statue★** of the duke (1588), originally in the town square, was placed in the church after his death. ▶ In the via Gonzaga is the elegant **Teatro Olimpico★** (A1), masterpiece of the architect Vincenzo Scamozzi (1552-1616), who designed it in only ten days in 1588 and completed the building before the end of 1590. The interior is rectangular, with tiered seating and loggia, decorated with frescos by painters of the Venetian school. ▶ The long brick arcade of the **Galleria degli Antichi★** (A-B1), dating from 1584, in which Vespasiano Gonzaga arranged a collection of ancient statues (transferred to Mantua at the command of Maria Theresa of Austria in 1774), forms one side of the p. Castello, corresponding to the former piazza d'Armi. The gallery is linked to the **Palazzo del Giardino★** (B1) built in 1584 for Vespasiano in his old age, plain outside but decorated inside with frescos, stucco and grotesque figures.   □

Practical information _____

ⓘ v. V. Gonzaga 31 (A1-2), ☎ 52039.

Restaurants:
◆◆◆ *Parco Cappuccini,* at Vigoreto, v. Santuario, ☎ 52005, closed Mon, Wed eve and Christmas-Jan. In 19C villa with fine park. Regional cuisine: risotto with salami, grilled meat and fish, 20/30,000.
◆◆ *Nizzoli,* at Dosolo, v. Garibaldi 18, ☎ 89150, closed Wed and 1-15 Nov. Regional cuisine: frog risotto, snails alla mantovana, 25/35,000.

Recommended
Events: antiques market in the palazzo Ducale, in the palazzo del Giardino, and in the Galleria degli Antichi (mid-Apr-mid-May); *Sabbioneta September,* classical plays at the Teatro Olimpico and exhibitions.
Guided tours: fee charged, information, ☎ 52039 (closed Mon).

SALICE TERME

Pavia 38, Milan 72 km
Pop. 742 ⊠ 27056 ☎ 0383   B6

The heart of this village is the magnificent **park** surrounding the **thermal springs** that give Salice Terme its name.   □

Practical information _____

♨ (Mar-Nov), ☎ 91203.
ⓘ v. Marconi 8, ☎ 91207.

Hotels:
★★★★ *President Hotel Terme,* v. Fermi 5, ☎ 91491, 95 rm Ⓟ 86,000; bkf: 8,000.
★★★ *Angolo,* v. delle Terme 147, ☎ 91316, 14 rm Ⓟ 45,000.

Restaurants:
◆◆◆ *Caminetto,* v. Battisti 11, ☎ 91391, closed Mon and Jan. Regional and Italian cuisine: taglioni with salmon, nettle soup, 35/40,000.
◆◆ *Guado,* v. delle Terme 59, ☎ 91223, closed Wed and 20 Nov-15 Dec. Regional cuisine: malfatti, mixed roasts, 30/40,000.

Recommended
Horseback riding: *Centro ippico,* v. Galbicella 18, ☎ 91513.
Swimming: v. Principale 65, ☎ 91642 (also tennis courts).

SABBIONETA

0   100   200   300m
1 : 14.000 (1cm = 140m)

Parma km 29   2

SALO

Brescia 31, Milan 126 km
Pop. 10,279 ⊠ 25087 ☎ 0365   D-E4

Mussolini's puppet republic took its name from this town in 1943. Salo is the most populous Garda town, on green hills around a narrow inlet. Its Fascist association largely forgotten, Salo is a lively and elegant tourist resort of great distinction.

▶ The 16C **Palazzo del Magnifica Patria** by the lakeside is used by the local authorities. It is part of a group of old buildings, including one that houses the **Ateneo di Salò** (founded in 1560), a library of thousands of books, incunabula and manuscripts, and the **Museo del Nastro Azzurro** *(Apr-Oct, Sat and Sun 10 a.m.-12 noon)*, with memorabilia, documents and weapons from the Napoleonic period to the Second World War resistance. ▶ The Duomo (Gothic, 15C), with fine 16C portals, has numerous works of art in the interior, including paintings and a Gothic altarpiece dating from 1510.   □

Practical information ─────────────
ⓘ lungolago Zanardelli 61, ☎ 21423.
🚢 boats and hydrofoils, ☎ 21591.

Hotels:
★★★★ **Astoria**, at Barbarano (2.5 km), v. Spiaggia d'Oro 1, ☎ 20761, 95 rm ℗ 🔍 ♨ 🔥 ⊘ 🖭 ⛱ ✒/ (18) 110,000.
★★★★ **Duomo**, lungolago Zanardelli, ☎ 21026, 22 rm ℗ 🔥 112,000.
★★★★ **Laurin**, v. Landi 9, ☎ 22022, 40 rm ℗ ♨ ⊠ closed 20 Dec-31 Jan, 119,000; bkf: 10,000. Rest. ♦♦♦ Excellent cuisine, 50/70,000.
★★★★ **Spiaggia d'Oro**, at Barbarano *(2.5 km)* v. Spiaggia d'Oro, ☎ 20764, 31 rm ℗ 🔍 ♨ 🔥 ⊠ ⛱ ✒/ (18) closed 1 Nov-14 Mar, 145,000.
★★★ **Benaco**, lungolago Zanardelli 44, ☎ 20308, 22 rm 🔥 58,000; bkf: 7,000.
★★★ **Vigna**, lungolago Zanardelli 413, ☎ 20516, 22 rm ℗ closed 21 Oct-28 Feb, 49,000; bkf: 4,000.

Recommended
Golf: at Bogliaco (*13 km NE*; → Lake Garda itinerary).
Horseback riding: *G.S. milanese sul Garda*, at Villanuova sul Clisi, v. Pier 12 (associate of *ANTE*).
Marina: *Club nautico*, ☎ 43443; *Canottieri Garda*, ☎ 43245.
Swimming pool: sports complex with indoor swimming pool and tennis court at Rimbalzello Park, v. Montessori, ☎ 40030.

SAN BENEDETTO PO

Mantua 21, Milan 179 km
Pop. 8,004 ⊠ 46027 ☎ 0376   E5

The town grew up around the abbey of Polirone, which was founded in the 10C by Countess Matilda Canossa. The countess's sarcophagus is in the former abbey church of S. Benedetto, although her remains were transferred to St. Peter's in Rome during the 17C.

▶ The present church of **S. Benedetto** was rebuilt in 1544-7. Inside are 16C terra-cotta statues, paintings, wooden choir stalls dating from the 16C and the sarcophagus of Countess Matilda (in the atrium of the sacristy). The 10C Cappella dell'Immacolata has a 12C mosaic pavement. All that remains of the ancient monastery are the infirmary (15C), the refectory (1478) and three cloisters. In the cloister of S. Simone is the **Museo Civico Polironiano**, with furniture and objects documenting the material culture of the Po Valley *(10 a.m.-12 noon and 1:30-5 p.m. Mar-May or 4-7 p.m. Jul-Oct; closed Mon and winter)*. ▶ 8.3 km SW is **Pegognaga**, with fine Romanesque church of **S. Lorenzo★** (11C). 15 km SW **Gonzaga**, the village that gave its name to the lords of

Mantua, has a charming **arcaded square** dominated by a 15C tower.   □

Practical information ─────────────
Recommended
Events: Thousand-year Fair (*Fiera Millenaria;* a gypsy gathering) at Gonzaga (first 10 days of Sep).
Motocross stadium: *F.lli Rossetti*, at Quistello, sports management, ☎ 618661, information, ☎ 619406.

SAN MARTINO DELLA BATTAGLIA

Brescia 35, Milan 125 km
Pop. 695 ⊠ 25010 ☎ 030   E4

24 June 1853 was a bad day for the Austrians. Attacked on a broad front (here by the Piedmontese and at Solferino by the French) and caught by a violent thunderstorm, *i Alman* as Victor Emmanuel II called them, had to retreat. The victory is recalled by memorials at both places, but particularly in San Martino (for Solferino → Castiglione della Stiviere).

▶ The village is dominated by a **tower** *(every a.m. and p.m. except Tue; hours subject to seasonal variation)* dating from 1893, decorated inside with pictures and sculptures relating to the battle. ▶ Other memorabilia and documents are to be found in the nearby small **Museo della Battaglia**, and the ossuary in a little Romanesque church contains the remains of thousands of the fallen.   □

SANTA CATERINA VALFURVA

Sondrio 77, Milan 214 km
5,700 ft, pop. 147 ⊠ 23030, ☎ 0342   D1

Amid dense coniferous woods in Valfurva where the Forno and Gavia Valleys meet, Santa Caterina Valfurva is a popular winter sports resort and a centre for mountaineering in the alpine Ortles Cevedale. 8 km NW is **San Nicolò** with a small **Museo Vallivo** *(in season, Tue, Thur, Sat and Sun 4-6:30 p.m.).* There is a chair lift to the **Plaghera plateau** (6,890-7,546 ft). 13 km from the **passo di Gavia** from where it is 1 hour's walk to the **belvedere** (8,261 ft) with a magnificent view★.   □

Practical information ─────────────
🎿 chair lift, ski lifts, cross-country skiing, skiing instruction, ice skating; summer skiing in Passo dello Stelvio (→ Trentino-Alto Adige), ☎ 935550.
ⓘ p. Migliavacca, ☎ 935598.

Hotels:
★★★ **Tre Baite**, ☎ 935545, 25 rm ℗ closed 6 Sep-5 Dec and Easter-30 Jun, 55,000; bkf: 5,000.
★★ **Pedranzini**, p. Migliavacca 5, ☎ 935525, 22 rm ℗ ♨ 45,000.

Recommended
Alpine guides: guides' office at information office, chief guide, ☎ 935562; Casati rifugio, ☎ 935507.

SANT'ANGELO LODIGIANO

Milan 32 km
Pop. 11,255 ⊠ 20079 ☎ 0371   B5

At the centre of the town is the **Castello Visconteo**, a massive block with turrets, crenellations and keep (14C, restored 20C). The interior houses various museums: the **Museo Morando Bolognini** *(guided tour Sun and hols 2:30-6:30 p.m.; closed Aug and*

1 Nov-15 Mar) with antique furniture, weapons and paintings; the **Museo Nazionale del Pane** (bread; *same hours as above)*; the **Museo Lombardo di Storia dell'Agricoltura** (history of agriculture; *Thu 9:30 a.m.-12:30 p.m.; Sun 2:30-5 p.m.; closed as the other museums)* with implements from neolithic times to the present day and various documents. ☐

Practical information

Recommended
Horseback riding: *Centro ippico La Madonnina,* at Graffignana, v. Miradolo 18 (associate of *ANTE)*.

SARONNO

Varese 29, Milan 26 km
Pop. 37,538 ⊠ 21047 ☎ 02   B4

Saronno is noted for *amaretti* (macaroons) and *amaretto* (liqueur). In art, however, it is also important: the santuario della **Madonna dei Miracoli★** was started in 1493 and completed in 1596-1612. The interior has a large dome with masterly frescos (*Concerto d'Angeli★*, 1534); the Madonna chapel is decorated with exceptional **frescos★** (1521-31). ☐

Practical information

SARONNO

Hotel:
★★★★ *Motel Pioppeto,* ☎ 9603345, 33 rm ℗ ⚏ & No restaurant, 63,000; bkf: 5,000.

Restaurants:
♦♦♦ *Rotonda-Mezzaluna,* v. Lazzaroni 25, ☎ 9601101, closed Mon. Regional cuisine: taglioni with artichoke cream, swordfish with porcini, 25/40,000.
♦ *Dino,* p. Santuario 8, ☎ 9600358, closed Fri and Aug. Apulian cuisine: spaghetti vigliacca, involtini pugliese, 25/35,000.

Recommended
Children's facilities: zoo and amusement park, at Cogliate, v. Diaz 23, ☎ 9660048.

Environs

GERENZANO, ⊠ 21040, 4 km NW.

Hotel:
★★★★ *Concorde,* v. Clerici 97/AB, ☎ 9682317, 42 rm ℗ ⚐ No restaurant, 84,000; bkf: 11,000.

Restaurant:
♦♦♦ *Croce d'Oro,* v. Clerici 97, ☎ 9689550, closed Sun eve, Mon, Aug and Christmas. In villa with garden. Quality cuisine: homemade pasta, chicken with mushrooms, 25/45,000.

SERIANA VALLEY

C3

Seriana is the most important valley in the Bergamo region, broad and almost a plain in its lower part, steep and wild up above. With rich water, minerals, grazing and agricultural resources, wool, cotton and silk weaving, the valley thrives on agriculture and industry. Today in the lower part of the valley towns form a continuous urban belt. In the high valley, too, tourist and residential buildings thrust as far as the foothills of the Dolomitic Presolana massif.

▶ On a plateau between the Seriana and Brembana Valleys, near Bergamo and Milan, **Selvino** (3,156 ft) is a popular tourist resort. Skiing facilities are located mainly around **Monte Poieto**. A branch of the Seriana Valley rises E of the **Clusone** (→) basin to the Presolana

pass. ▶ **Rovetta** (2,159 ft) has rustic, open-galleried houses and is a summer holiday centre. The **Casa Fantoni** *(June-Sep 3-5 p.m.; closed Wed)* houses a museum devoted to the local Fantoni family of carvers and sculptors (17C-18C). ▶ **Castione della Presolana** (2,854 ft) combines with the municipalities of **Bratto** (3,304 ft) and **Dorga** (3,280 ft) and the winter sports area of **Mt. Pora** to make up one of the best-equipped and popular tourist complexes in the Bergamo region. In the **parish church** of Castione are a pulpit and a choir by the Fantoni family; in the centre the elegant **Palazzo Comunale** (16C-17C) has a Venetian look. ▶ Hotels and skiing facilities are also to be found at the **passo della Presolana** (4,255 ft), departure point for the Dolomitic massif of the same name, through rocky walls, ledges and gorges to an area that is also interesting from the botanical point of view. ▶ In the high Serio Valley **Gromo** (2,218 ft) exploits the beautiful open spaces of the woods and grasslands of the **Spiazzi** (3,937 ft), much visited by trippers and skiers. ▶ In the last basin of the valley the scattered municipality of **Valbondione** is a winter sports centre and base for trips to the Orobie Alps. ☐

Practical information

CASTIONE DELLA PRESOLANA, ⊠ 24020, ☎ 0346.
⚡ ski lifts, cross-country skiing and instruction at Mt. Pora.
ⓘ v. Vittorio Emanuele, ☎ 60039; at Bratto, v.Donizetti, ☎ 31146.

Hotels:
★★★★ *Milano,* at Bratto, v. Pellico 3, ☎ 31211, 50 rm ℗ ⚐ ⚏ ⚐ closed 20 Oct-30 Nov, 45,000; bkf: 5,000. Rest.
♦♦♦ *Caminone* closed Mon. Regional cuisine, 25/30,000.
★★★★ *Presolana,* at Dorga, v. Santuario 35, ☎ 30198, 51 rm ℗ ⚐ ⚏ ℘ 50,000; bkf: 6,000.
★★ *Aurora,* at S. Antonio, ☎ 60004, 25 rm ℗ ⚐ ℘ closed Sep, 30,000; bkf: 4,000.

Restaurant:
♦♦♦ *Cascina delle Noci,* at Bratto, v. Provinciale 22, ☎ 31251, closed Mon (and Mon-Fri, Feb-May). In old farmhouse in the fields. Regional cuisine: casonsei, porcini parcels, baked rabbit, 25/35,000.

Recommended
Sports centre: v. Cluren, ☎ 60085.

GROMO, ⊠ 24020, ☎ 0346.
⚡ ski lifts, ice skating at Spiazzi *(6.5 km E);* ski lifts at Valcanale *(9.5 km SW);* instruction at Spiazzi and Valcanale.
ⓘ municipio, ☎ 41128

PASSO DELLA PRESOLANA, ⊠ 24020, ☎ 0346.
⚡ ski lifts, cross-country skiing, instruction, skating; ski lifts, instruction at Còlere (spring skiing at the Albani rifugio, ☎ 51105).
ⓘ at Castione *(7 km SE),* p. Roma, ☎ 60039; at Còlere *(8 km N),* v. Tortola, ☎ 54051.

ROVETTA, ⊠ 24020, ☎ 0346.

Hotel:
★★ *Sant'Ambroeus,* at Conca Verde, v. De Gasperi 39, ☎ 71228, 23 rm ℗ ⚐ 32,000; bkf: 3,000.

SELVINO, ⊠ 24020, ☎ 035.
⚡ cableway from Albino, ☎ 751408, cableway, ski lifts, summer skiing school on artificial slope at Aviàtico.
ⓘ municipio, ☎ 761362.

Hotels:
★★★ *Aquila,* v. Monte Grappa 17, ☎ 761000, 22 rm ⚐ ⚏ 38,000; bkf: 4,000.
★★★ *Elvezia,* v. Usignolo 2, ☎ 761058, 17 rm ℗ ⚐ ⚏ closed Sep, 40,000.

Recommended
Swimming: v. Miramonti, ☎ 761673 (also tennis club).

VALBONDIONE, ⊠ 24020, ☎ 0346.
⚡ cableway, ski lifts, instruction, skating at Lizzola.

ⓘ v. S. Lorenzo, ☎ 44018.

Å ★★★ *Valbondione*, v. Casa Corti, 3,250 pl, ☎ 44088 (all year).

SIRMIONE*

Brescia 38, Milano 127 km
Pop. 4,567 ⊠ 25019 ☎ 030   E4

The name of Catullus is often heard and seen in this enchanting little town, which the Roman poet chose as his place of residence. Sirmione is set on the slender peninsula in Lake Garda that separates the bays of Desenzano and Peschiera. The town's strategic importance is quickly seen from the 13C fortress (one of the most imposing and impressive on Garda) and the large harbour built to shelter the Scaligera fleet that controlled the settlements on shore. The site, varied and with many charming features within a small area, is one of the most beautiful in Lombardy.

▶ The **Rocca Scaligera★** *(summer 9 a.m.-1 p.m. and 2:30-6:30 p.m.; winter 9 a.m.-2 p.m.; closed non-hol Mon or Tue)*, a stronghold built in the 13C, is on the edge of town. Entirely surrounded by water, it has several towers, a double crenellated wall and an extraordinary fortified harbour. ▶ The old part of Sirmione (pedestrian precinct), beyond the 14C gate beside the fortress, still looks like a typical medieval Garda town. ▶ The church of **S. Maria Maggiore** (15C) has 15C-16C frescos. ▶ The oldest church is **S. Pietro in Mavino**, high on the promontory, originally 8C but rebuilt 11C-14C. It contains 13C-16C frescos. ▶ A miniature railway links the town with the tip of the peninsula, where the archaeological area known as **Grotte di Catullo★** is situated *(9 a.m. to 2 hrs before sunset; closed non-hol Mon or Tue)*. It is doubtful that Catullus ever entered the caves, however, excavations have brought to light impressive remains (including fragments of frescos) of a **Roman villa** of the imperial period, the largest in N Italy.   ☐

Practical information

SIRMIONE
⚓ Mar-Nov, ☎ 916044.
ⓘ v. Marconi 8, ☎ 916114; at Colombare, ☎ 919322 (during the season).
⚓ boats and hydrofoil.
Car rental: *Hertz*, at Brescia, ☎ 45132.

Hotels:
★★★★★ **G.H. Terme**, v. Marconi 1, ☎ 916261, 57 rm Ⓟ 🅦 ❧ ☐ closed 26 Oct-31 Mar, 180,000; bkf: 16,000.
★★★★★ **Villa Cortine Palace**, v. Grotte 12, ☎ 916021, 54 rm Ⓟ ❧ ◳ 🅦 ☐ ↗ closed 26 Oct-31 Mar. 19C villa in a park sloping down towards the lake, 234,000; bkf: 20,000.
★★★★ **Broglia**, v. Piana 36, ☎ 916305, 40 rm Ⓟ 🅦 ☐ closed Nov-Easter, 95,000; bkf: 9,000.
★★★★ **Continental**, v. Punta Staffalo 7/9, ☎ 916031, 53 rm Ⓟ 🅦 ☐ closed 1 Dec-28 Feb, 112,000; bkf: 9,000.
★★★★ **Flaminia**, p. Flaminia 8, ☎ 916078, 49 rm Ⓟ closed 1 Nov-28 Feb. No restaurant, 78,000.
★★★★ **Ideal**, v. Catullo 23, ☎ 916020, 25 rm Ⓟ 🅦 closed Nov-Feb, 70,000; bkf: 7,000.
★★★★ **Olivi**, v. S. Pietro 3, ☎ 916110, 60 rm Ⓟ ◳ 🅦 ☐ closed 21 Dec-31 Jan, 90,000; bkf: 12,000.
★★★★ **Sirmione**, p. Castello, ☎ 916331, 76 rm Ⓟ 🅦 ☐ closed Nov-Mar, 100,000; bkf: 9,000.
★★★ **Brunella**, v. Catullo 29, ☎ 916115, 20 rm Ⓟ ◳ 🅦 closed 1 Nov-30 Mar, 70,000; bkf: 6,000.
★★★ **Fonte Boiola**, v. Marconi 4, ☎ 916431, 60 rm Ⓟ 🅦 ❧ closed 11 Nov-30 Mar, 65,000; bkf: 8,000.
★★★ **Golf & Suisse**, v. XXV Aprile, ☎ 916176, 30 rm Ⓟ 🅦 ☐ closed 1 Nov-28 Feb. No restaurant, 63,000; bkf: 6,000.
★★★ **Miramar**, v. XXV Aprile 22, ☎ 916239, 30 rm Ⓟ 🅦 closed 1 Nov-9 Mar, 58,000; bkf: 6,000.

★★★ **Paül**, v. XXV Aprile 26, ☎ 916077, 21 rm Ⓟ 🅦 ❧ closed 11 Nov-31 Mar. No restaurant, 57,000; bkf: 6,000.
★★ **Mirabello**, v. XXV Aprile 100, ☎ 9196163, 42 rm Ⓟ 🅦 closed 16 Oct-30 Apr. No restaurant, 45,000; bkf: 5,000.

Restaurants:
● ◆◆◆ **Grifone**, v. delle Bisse 5, ☎ 916097, closed Wed and 1 Nov-10 Mar. Excellent regional cuisine: fresh pasta, grilled lake or sea fish, 20/35,000.
◆◆◆ **Antica Taverna del Marinaio**, v. Casello 20, ☎ 916056, closed Mon and Nov-Feb. Attractive summer terrace. Seafood: taglioni capriccio, trittico di mare, trout carpaccio with rucola, 25/35,000.
Å ★★★ *Sirmione*, at Colombare, v. Sirmioncino 9, 190 pl, ☎ 919045.

Recommended
Congress centre: p. Europa 1, ☎ 916114.
Cycling: *Polisportiva Sirmionese*, p. Flaminia.
Excursions: tourist railway from the historic town centre to the *grotte di Catullo*, ☎ 9196660 (open in good weather).
Marina: *La Darsena*, ☎ 9196072.
Tennis: lungolago Diaz 3; at Colombare, v. Coorti Romane 2.
Windsurfing: instruction, ☎ 9196130 or 916208.

Environs

COLOMBARE, ⊠ 25010, 3.5 km S.

Hotels:
★★★ **Europa**, v. Liguria 5, ☎ 919047, 25 rm Ⓟ 🅦 ☐ closed 11 Dec-28 Feb, 60,000; bkf: 8,000.
★★★ **Florida**, v. Colombare 91, ☎ 919018, 28 rm Ⓟ 🅦 ☐ closed 1 Nov-9 Mar, 60,000; bkf: 6,000.

Restaurant:
◆◆◆ **Griglia-da Carlo**, v. IV Novembre 14, ☎ 919223, closed Tue and 6 Jan-14 Feb. Trattoria with grill and view from terrace. Regional cuisine: tagliatelle with tench, Garda eel kebab, 27/35,000.

LUGANA, 4 km S.

Hotel:
Nuova Lugana, v. Verona 69/71, ☎ 919003, 14 rm Ⓟ 🅦 closed 15 Nov-10 Dec, 55,000; bkf: 8,000.

Restaurants:
● ◆◆◆◆ **Trattoria Vecchia Laguna**, p. Vecchia Lugana 1, ☎ 919012, closed Mon eve, Tue, Jan and Nov. Elegant restaurant in old inn, with lakeside terrace. Outstanding creative cuisine: seasonal menu: Garda eel, trout with olives, escalope with tarragon, 35/55,000.
◆◆ **Campagnola**, v. Verona 83, ☎ 9196009, closed Fri and Jan. In small modern villa with veranda-garden. Regional fish cuisine: pappardelle with game, corregone alla pescatore with polenta, 30/45,000.

SOMMA LOMBARDO

Varese 22, Milan 49 km
Pop. 16,935 ⊠ 21019 ☎ 0331   A3-4

This is a woollen industry centre, near heathland and pinewoods, with a large **Visconti castle** (rebuilt 15C, later altered). 2 km to **Arsago Seprio** with Romanesque basilica of **S. Vittore★** (9C) and adjacent polygonal **baptistery★** (11C-12C).   ☐

Practical information

Restaurant:
◆◆ **Pio**, at Coarezza, ☎ 256667, closed Wed, Jan and Aug. On the bank of the Ticino. Regional cuisine: taglione with salmon, gnocchi with gorgonzola, 35/45,000.

Recommended
Children's facilities: *Safari park*, at Pombia, SS. del Sempione, ☎ 956439 (closed Tue except hols).

Horseback riding: *Riding club,* corso Europa 44 (associate of *ANTE;* → Ticino park).
Motocross: *De Maria* motocross facilities, at Arsago Seprio; *moto club,* v. G. d'Annunzio 1, ☎ 253868.

SONCINO

Cremona 35, Milan 62 km
Pop. 7,248 ⊠ 26029 ☎ 0374   C6

This Po Valley centre by the river Olio is surrounded by ancient walls and was defended by a fortress, the **Rocca** *(Sat and Sun 10 a.m.-12 noon and 4-7 p.m. or 3-6 p.m.; other days 9 a.m.-12 noon, reserve at tourist office),* built 1473-5 by Galeazzo Maria Sforza and one of the most important and best preserved in Lombardy. It is square in plan, with four imposing towers, crenellated walls and a moat. The old town has many old houses on low arcades. Ten minutes away is the Renaissance church of **S. Maria delle Grazie** (1492-1528); in the interior, polychrome terra cotta friezes and frescos dating from the 16C.   ☐

Practical information ———————————
ⓘ p. Garibaldi, ☎ 85333.
Restaurants:
◆◆◆ *Lame Pendenti,* v. Brescia 23, ☎ 85797, closed Tue and 15 Jan-15 Feb. In green fields running down to the Olio. Regional cuisine: maccheroni contadina, porcini and truffles, 25/40,000.
◆ *Antica Rocca,* v. Battista 1, ☎ 85672, closed Mon and 10-31 Jul. Regional cuisine: fettucine with porcini, salt cod alla vicenta, 25/35,000.
Recommended
Children's facilities: *Al Mulino zoo,* at Antegnate, ☎ 0363/997309.

SONDALO

Sondrio 47, Milan 180 km
Pop. 5,231 ⊠ 23035 ☎ 0342   D2

Sondalo is a small spa town in the high Valtellina, dominated by former sanatoriums on heights above the town. Interesting features are the 17C **parish church** and the church of **S. Maria** (rebuilt 18C), with Romanesque campanile and 14C-16C frescos.   ☐

Practical information ———————————
ⓘ v. Vanoni 32, ☎ 801127.
Hotel:
★★★ *Alpi,* v. Bolladore 19, ☎ 802170, 15 rm ℙ ⴜ closed 20 Sep-10 Oct, 45,000.

⚓ ★★★ *Città di Sondalo,* at Bolladore, v. Verdi, 78 pl.

SONDRIO

Milan 133, Rome 708 km
Pop. 22,840 ⊠ 23100 ☎ 0342   C2

Sondrio is the capital of the Valtellina. The history of the region gives the lie to the image of a closed alpine world keeping itself to itself. Like the Valchiavenna (also part of the ancient province of Sondrio), the high valley of the Adda saw a constant flow of troops, pilgrims, merchants, monarchs and courtiers over the centuries. From the earliest times, the stream of men and merchandise along the transalpine routes encouraged the development of a rich and lively culture, which was also stimulated by political and religious conflicts and by effort to overcome the difficul-

ties posed by the natural surroundings. The history is palpable today along the roads of the lower valleys, dotted with enterprises large and small, and flanked by slopes laboriously terraced for the cultivation of vines. The summer of 1987 saw heavy flooding and landslides in the Sondrio region. Before planning a trip to the region it would be wise to contact Italian authorities.

▶ Sondrio is predominantly modern. ▶ The **old town** is set around the p. Campello, with a **collegiate church** (18C) and the 16C **Palazzo Pretorio,** now the town hall. ▶ In the v. IV Novembre is an interesting **Museo Valtellinese di Storia e Arte** (history and art; *9 a.m.-12 noon and 3-6 p.m.; closed Sat and Sun).*

Environs
Ponte in Valtellina (1,591 ft; 10.5 km) is reached on the strada dei Castelli which runs across the hill between vines and fruit trees and provides excellent views. Ponte is noted for vines, apples and the manufacture of local carpets known as *pezzotti.* Another notable feature is the Gothic **parish church** (14C, with portal frescos and furnishings from the 15C-16C).   ☐

Practical information ———————————
ⓘ p. Garibaldi 28, ☎ 214463.
🚌 ☎ 212237.
🚕 from p. Bertacchi.
Hotels:
★★★★ *Posta,* p. Garibaldi 19, ☎ 211222, 43 rm ℙ ⴜ 84,000; bkf: 7,500. Rest. ● ◆◆◆ *Sozzani* closed Sun and Aug. Quality Valtellina cuisine, 27/36,000.
★★★ *Campelli,* at Moia, ☎ 510662, 20 rm ℙ ⴜ closed Aug, 60,000; bkf: 4,000.
★★★ *Europa,* lungomàllero Cadorna 27, ☎ 211444, 43 rm ℙ 63,000; bkf: 8,000.
Restaurants:
◆◆ *Fermata,* v. dello Stadio 112, ☎ 218481, closed Tue. Regional and Italian cuisine: agnolotti, fresh pasta, fileto alpino, 20/30,000.
◆◆ *Trippi-Grumello,* v. Nazionale 23, ☎ 212447, closed Mon and Nov. Regional cuisine: gnocchetti engadinesi, 30/40,000.

⚓ *Castelletto,* at Castelletto, v. Orobie 1, 120 pl, ☎ 216016.
Recommended
Handicrafts: patchwork carpets (rustic carpets of wool and cotton) at Arigna; at Albaredo on the way to San Marco is the *Cooperativa la Lum,* ☎ 611595; Valtellina mountain community council at Morbegno, p. Bossi, ☎ 613124.
Sports centre: p. Merizzi, ☎ 214470.
♥ cheeses: *bitto, scimudin* and others from the high valleys.

SUZZARA

Mantua 21, Milan 167 km
Pop. 18,511 ⊠ 46029 ☎ 0376   E5

Suzzara was Mantua's principal outpost on the Po, an island among the rivers of the flood plain. The **old town** still looks like a Po valley agricultural centre, with low brick houses and broad arcaded streets. A crenellated 13C **tower** is the only remaining feature of the original fortress. **Galleria Civica d'Arte Contemporanea** *(Sun and hols, Apr-Sep 10:30 a.m.-12:30 p.m. and 4-7 p.m. or 3-6 p.m. in other months; wkdays p.m. only; closed Mon).*   ☐

The arrow (→) is a reference to another entry.

Practical information _____

Hotel:
★★ *Cavallino Bianco,* v. Luppi Menotti 11/A,
☎ 531676, 18 rm, closed Aug, 48,000. Rest. ● ◆◆◆
closed Sat. Creative cuisine, 20/30,000.

TEGLIO

Sondrio 20, Milan 153 km
Pop. 5,187 ✉ 23036 ☎ 0342   D2

Artistic and architectural evidence of Teglio's antiquity
are still apparent in the **old town.** The 15C **parish
church** has a Gothic portal and valuable furniture;
the church of **S. Lorenzo** has 16C tombs and frescos. Outstanding is the 16C **Palazzo Besta** *(May-
Sep 9 a.m.-12 noon and 2:30-5:30 p.m.; other months
9 a.m.-2 p.m.; Sun and hols 9 a.m.-1 p.m.; closed
Mon),* a fine example of a Renaissance residence in
the Valtellina, with portal, arcaded courtyard and loggia, furniture and frescos.   □

Practical information _____

ʒ cableway, ski lifts, cross-country skiing and skiing instruction at Prato Valentino.
ⓘ v. Valtellina 7, ☎ 780038.

Hotel:
★★ *Meden,* v. Roma 29, ☎ 780080, 38 rm Ⓟ ﷺ ⊗
42,000; bkf: 3,000.

Restaurants:
◆◆ *Corna-da Paola,* at San Giacomo, ☎ 785070,
closed Mon. Rustic atmosphere. Regional cuisine: tagliatelle with chamois, polenta taragna, 25/40,000.
◆ *Combolo,* v. Roma 5, ☎ 780083, closed Tue. Regional cuisine: tagliatelle with chamois, polenta taragna,
25/40,000.

Recommended
Gastronomic specialty: cheeses and *bresaola* (dried
beef).

TICINO PARK

A3-4-5 B4-5

The Ticino Valley Natural Park is an undulating strip
of about 225,000 acres running along the river from
Sesto Calende to its confluence with the Po. Four
regions can be distinguished: the **river valley** itself,
the most interesting landscape, accessible only on
foot or by boat; the **flood plain** (S of the Villoresi
canal) with agriculture, towns and industry; the **dry
plateau** (N of the Villoresi), with heath, poor agricultural land and industry; and the **pre-alpine hills** in the
N, less urbanized and another interesting landscape.□

Practical information _____

ⓘ park society at Magenta, v. IV Giugno 80,
☎ 02/9794401 (organized excursions). *TCI* information
leaflets on the *Parco del Ticino* (tours and stays in natural
surroundings; cycling tours).

Recommended
Horseback riding: at Sesona di Vergiate, *La Garzonera*
horse-riding club, ☎ 0331/947376; at Casorate Sempione, *Le Querce,* v. Ronchetto 8, ☎ 0331/295430; *Scude-*
ria Felli, v. Sempione 24, ☎ 0331/296630.

> For the translation of a name of a meat, a fish or a
> vegetable, for the composition of a dish or a sauce,
> see the *Menu Guide* at the end of the Practical Holi-
> day Guide; it lists the most common culinary terms.

TIGNALE

Brescia 56, Milan 152 km
Pop. 1,269 ✉ 25010 ☎ 0365   E3

Tignale has excellent views★ over Lake Garda, from
a cultivated plateau with olives and fruit trees. For
an even more extensive view climb to the sanctuary
of the **Madonna di Monte Castello** (2,267 ft; *1.5 km*),
13C-14C, rebuilt.   □

TIRANO

Sondrio 27, Milan 160 km
Pop. 8,906 ✉ 23037 ☎ 0342   D2

On 19 July 1620 the religious and political revolt
against Grison (Swiss) domination broke out here in a
conflict so brutal as to pass into history as the Holy
Massacre of the Valtellina. This town at the end of
the Poschiavina valley played a major role then as
now. In the 17C it had more than 5,000 inhabitants, was prosperous, and boasted a famous sanctuary next to which the most important fair in the valley took place, as it still does today.

▶ In the old town are the parish church of **S. Martino**
(15C) and the late 16C **Palazzo Salis,** one of the finest in
the Valtellina, with two rugged towers, fine baroque portal
and rooms decorated with frescos. ▶ In the municipality of Madonna di Tirano *(1.5 km)* is the **santuario della
Madonna,** a Renaissance building started in
1505. Notable exterior features are the façade portal
(1530), the side portals (1506), the apse and the high
campanile (1578). In the stuccoed interior (1590-1608) is
an outstanding organ (1617).   □

Practical information _____

ⓘ p. Basilica, ☎ 701181 (in season).

Restaurant:
◆◆ *Bernina,* p. Stazione, ☎ 01302, closed Sun. In a
small hotel next to the station. Regional and Italian cuisine: manfrigoli, mushroom pancakes, 20/30,000.

Recommended
Cycling: *Pedale tiranese,* v. Pedrotti, ☎ 701432.

TRESCORE BALNEARIO

Bergamo 14, Milan 60 km
890 ft pop. 6,657 ✉ 24069 ☎ 035   C3

The ancient thermal springs in this little town were
brought back into use in the 15C by the *condottiere*
Bartolomeo Colleoni and enjoyed in the 19C by Giuseppe Garibaldi. In the park of the 18C Villa Suardi
is the 14C church of **S. Barbara,** with **frescos** dating
from 1524. The **Villa Terzi** in the suburb of Canton,
is a notable Baroque building, with sculpture, frescos
and a wooden roof.   □

Practical information _____

♨ (Mar-Dec), ☎ 940425.
ʒ ski lifts at Colli di S. Fermo.
ⓘ *Terme di Trescore,* ☎ 940425.

Hotel:
★★ *Torre,* p. Cavour 26, ☎ 941365, 30 rm Ⓟ ﷺ ⊗
43,000; bkf: 4,000.

Restaurant:
◆ *Cascina,* v. Nazionale 11, ☎ 940138, closed Mon,
1-15 Jan and Aug. Rural atmosphere, with small selection of vintage wines on sale and some accommoda-

tion. Creative Italian cuisine: tagliolini with grapes, stewed ass, 20/40,000.

TREVIGLIO

Bergamo 20, Milan 36 km
Pop. 25,668 ⊠ 24047 ☎ 0363   C4

From the 15C-18C the river here formed a border between the Duchy of Milan and the Venetian Republic. The flat land of the **Gera d'Adda** centres around the ancient city of Trevoglio, important for silk manufacture. The church of **S. Martino** (15C-16C, altered 18C) with Gothic campanile has an **altarpiece★** dating from 1485. 5 km NE is **Brignano Gera d'Adda** with the Visconti **castle** rebuilt in the Baroque era and one of the most important and best-preserved 18C Milanese country houses. ☐

Practical information _____

Hotel:
★★★ *Lepre*, v. Caravaggio 37, ☎ 48233, 64 rm ⓅⓌ ⚹ ▭ ⌇ 42,000; bkf: 4,000.

Restaurant:
◆◆◆ *Taverna Colleoni*, v. Portaluppi 75, ☎ 43384, closed Mon and Aug. Regional cuisine: tajarin, agnolotti, 30/45,000.

VARESE

Milan 52, Rome 627 km
Pop. 90,396 ⊠ 21100 ☎ 0332   A3

In the early 19C Varese was studded with palazzi and villas, the result of the building fever of the two preceding centuries. The bulk of the Palazzo Estense dominated the gentle landscape, and the surrounding hills were crowned with *castellanze*, noble residences with parks and gardens. Even then Varese was a resort favoured by the nobility, and later by the Milanese and Lombard middle classes. Today many parts of the Varese area, once famous for their beauty, have changed as a result of urbanization and industrialization, and the capital itself looks predominantly modern.

▶ The basilica of **S. Vittore** (1580-1615) has a tall Baroque campanile (1617-73); the Neoclassical façade dates from 1791. ▶ Behind the campanile is the baptistery of **S. Giovanni**, Romanesque-Gothic (12C-13C); inside are a 13C font and remains of 14C-15C frescos. ▶ The **Palazzo Estense★** or Ducale, now the town hall, was built 1766-8 for Francesco III d'Este, Duke of Modena, lord of Varese and governor of Lombardy. The interior is a fine example of the architectural and decorative style known as *barochetto teresiano*, particularly in the stately Salone Estense. The **giardini pubblici★** (public gardens) are attached to the park of the **Villa Mirabello** (18C-19C), which houses the **Musei Civici** (*9:30 a.m.-12:30 p.m. and 2-5:30 p.m.; closed Sun p.m. and Mon*). The collections include historical, archaeological and scientific exhibits, and an art gallery with 17C-20C works and two notable fresco fragments from S. Maria Foris Portas in Castelseprio (→).

Environs

▶ The **Sacro Monte★** (*8 km*, 2,887 ft) is a place of pilgrimage. The itinerary includes 14 chapels with frescos and terra cotta statues illustrating the mysteries of the Rosary in allegorical language and style. The *via sacra* finally reaches the **santuario di S. Maria** or del Sacro Monte di Varese (rebuilt 16C-17C) in which is a 14C statue of the Virgin. ▶ **Monte Campo dei Fiori** (4,022 ft) is a holiday area in a position commanding wonderful views in the mountains between Lake Varese and the Valcuvia. The former Campo dei Fiori Grand Hotel (3,389 ft; *11.5 km NW*) is in art nouveau style. ☐

Practical information _____

ⓘ p. M. Grappa 5, ☎ 283604; v. Ippodromo 9, ☎ 284624. ▩ ☎ 286705; Ferrovie Nord Milano, ☎ 284174. ▤ from bus station in p. Kennedy.
Car rental: *Avis*, p. della Repubblica 11, ☎ 239333; *Maggiore*, v. Ortello 5, ☎ 233228.

Hotels:
★★★★ *City*, v. Medaglie d'Oro 35, ☎ 281304, 47 rm Ⓟ ⓺ No restaurant, 108,000; bkf: 10,000.
★★★★ *Crystal*, v. Speroni 10, ☎ 231145, 45 rm. No restaurant, 108,000; bkf: 10,000.
★★★★ *Palace Hotel*, v. Manara 11, ☎ 312600, 106 rm Ⓟ Ⓦ ⌇ 145,000; bkf: 12,000.
★★★ *Acquario*, v. Giusti 7, ☎ 260550, 41 rm Ⓟ No restaurant, 68,000.
★★★ *Motor Hotel Varese Lago*, at Bobbiate, v. Macchi 61, ☎ 310022, 34 rm Ⓟ Ⓦ ⓺ No restaurant, 69,000; bkf: 7,000.

Restaurants:
◆◆◆ *Lago Maggiore*, v. Carrobbio 19, ☎ 231183, closed Sun, Christmas and 1-15 Jul. Excellent creative cuisine: reginette with peppers and basil, sea bass with raw fennel, 35/60,000.
◆◆◆ *Vittorio*, p. Beccaria 1, ☎ 234312, closed Fri. Italian and international cuisine: pancakes Vittorio, flambéed scampi and steak, game with polenta, 20/35,000.
◆◆ *Gestore*, vicolo Scuole 3, ☎ 236404, closed Sun and Jul-Aug. Rural trattoria. Regional cuisine: seasonal menus on various themes, 30/40,000.

⚹ ★★★ *Famiglia*, at Malnate, v. Nizza 2, 100 pl, ☎ 427696 (all year).

Recommended
Conference centre: *Villa Ponti*, at Biumo Superiore, ☎ 239130.
Events: horse-racing season at the *Ippodromo delle Bèttole* (Jun-Aug); *Tre Valle Varesine* bicycle race (Aug).
Flying: *Aeroclub volovelistico*, at Calcinate del Pesce; *P.Contri* airport, ☎ 310073; at Venegono Inferiore, *A.Ferrarin* airport, ☎ 864128; at Vergiate, *Siai Marchetti* airport, ☎ 946151.
Golf: *Golf club Varese*, at Luvinate, v. Vittorio Veneto 32, ☎ 229302 (18 holes).
Hang gliding: *Scuola Fantinato-Fontana*, v. Fra' Galgario 14, ☎ 231658.
Horseback riding: *Centro ippico Seprio*, Cascina Tuss, at Gornate Olona, ☎ 0331/850100.
Ice skating: v. Albani 33, ☎ 241300.
Natural park: *Campo dei Fiori regional natural park*, offices at the Amministrazione Provinciale, ☎ 281100.
Race course: delle Bèttole, ☎ 282516.
Sailing: *Lega Navale*, v. Giovanni XXIII 11, ☎ 230275.
Sports centre: at Masnago, v. Manin, ☎ 227661.
Swimming: v. Copelli, ☎ 230200; at Lido della Schiranna, v. Canottieri, ☎ 310418.
Tennis: v. Ippodromo 9, ☎ 240097.
Visits to technical facilities: visits to the *Schiaparelli Astronomical Observatory*, the *Pre-Alpine Botanical Garden* and the *Centre of Botanical Studies*, Campo dei Fiori, ☎ 229162-235491 (astronomical observations Sat. eve, reserve in advance).

VIGEVANO*

Pavia 34, Milan 36 km
Pop. 64,179 ⊠ 27029 ☎ 0381   A4

Vigevano used to be a country town with a compact circular layout, isolated in the reclaimed land of the plain on the edge of the Lomellina. Over the centuries, Renaissance architecture and town planning

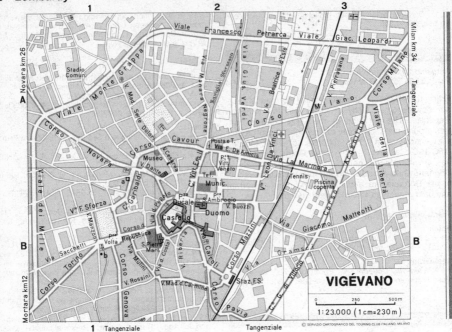

VIGÉVANO

0   250   500 m

1:23.000 (1 cm=230 m)

© SERVIZIO CARTOGRAFICO DEL TOURING CLUB ITALIANO, MILANO

defined the space in the centre of the town, which is now organized around one of the most beautiful squares in Italy. In addition the rapid development of the footwear industry contributed to the industrialization of this former agricultural centre.

▶ The **piazza Ducale★★** (B2) was the first complete realization of the idea of the Renaissance square, laid out 1492-4 for Duke Ludovico il Moro to create a courtyard for the castle beyond a flight of steps in the SW corner. The present appearance of the entrance was finally settled at the end of the 17C when the steps were removed, the arcade was completed, and the front of the **Duomo** (B2) was hidden behind a pleasing concave façade, set asymmetrically in relation to the square. Inside the church (rebuilt 16C) are 16C paintings. Interesting Vigevano tapestries are exhibited in the **Museo del Tesoro** (*Sun 3-5 p.m.*). ▶ The high telescope **tower** (*Sat and Sun 10 a.m.-12:30 p.m. and 3-6:30 p.m.*) gives access to the courtyard of the **Castello** (B2; *closed for restoration*) built by the Visconti and turned into a ducal residence by the Sforzas (15C). A long, raised, covered way protected by high crenellations links the castle to the Rocca Vecchia or Bergonzone. ▶ S beyond the castle is the Gothic church of **S. Pietro Martire** (B1-2; 14C-15C). □

Practical information

Hotels:
★★★★ *Diamanti,* at Garlasco, v. L. da Vinci 59, ☎ 822777, 39 rm ℗ & ✆ closed Aug. No restaurant, 77,000; bkf: 7,000.
★★★ *Europa,* v. Trivulzio 8 (B1 a), ☎ 75156, 39 rm ℗ ✆ closed 1-25 Aug. No restaurant, 70,000; bkf: 5,000.

Restaurants:
♦♦♦ *Rotonde,* at Garlasco, v. L. da Vinci, ☎ 821171, closed Mon and Aug. Italian cuisine, some international dishes; risotto garlaschese or with porcini, pancakes, 25/35,000.

♦ *Caravel,* v. Pompei 6 (B1 b), ☎ 84371, closed Mon and Aug. Italian cuisine: grilled meat and fish, 20/26,000.
Recommended
Golf: v. Chiotola 49, ☎ 76872 (9 holes).

VOGHERA

Pavia 28, Milan 62 km
Pop. 42,306 ⊠ 27058 ☎ 0383   B5

The old town is enclosed within a ring road that follows the line of walls knocked down in the 19C. It has an ordered and dignified look that seems typically Piedmontese, although until the unification of Italy Voghera was in fact a provincial capital under Savoyard rule.

▶ In the central p. V. Emanuele II is the collegiate church of **S. Lorenzo,** rebuilt in the 17C. ▶ The **castello,** with rectangular entrance tower, has traces of Galeazzo Visconti's extensions built 1367-72. ▶ The 12C Romanesque church of **S. Flavio e S. Giorgio** (or Chiesa Rossa; *caretaker at v. Tempio Sacrario 4*) is the memorial chapel of the Italian cavalry. ▶ 4 km SE, the **Sforzesca** (1486) is the largest and most important of the model farms built by Duke Lodovico il Moro on his agricultural estates. Leonardo da Vinci also spent some time experimenting with hydraulics here. □

Practical information

Hotel:
★★★ *Domus,* v. Matteotti 40, ☎ 49630, 27 rm, 60,000; bkf: 6,000.

Restaurants:
♦♦♦ *Castello di San Gaudenzio,* at San Gaudenzio, ☎ 75025, closed Tue. In a 15C castle surrounded by a beautiful park. Quality cuisine: taglierini castellana, frog brodetto, 25/40,000.

♦ *Cristina,* v. Ricotti 36, ☎ 48436, closed Sat eve, Sun and Aug. Italian cuisine: ravíoli al brasato, baked kid, 15/22,000.

Recommended
Flying club: *Aeroclub M. Resta,* at Rivanazzano,

v. Baracca 8, ☎ 91500 (also gliding, parachuting, model aircraft).

Wines: visits to *Carlo Boatti,* v. S. Lazzaro 5, ☎ 89144 (the wines include Barbera and Bonarda).

The Marches

The towns and villages of the Marches nestle amid hills and valleys that sweep from the Apennines down to the shores of the Adriatic. Vines, olive groves and fields of maize and barley spread over hillocks and ridges, extending almost as far as the beaches that border the Marches. The name Marches is derived from the German *marka,* meaning boundary line. The term was used in Italy from the early feudal period (10C) to denote the imperial regions of the Marca di Camerino and the Marca di Fermo, which were held as buffers against barbarian invasion. The history of the Marches, like that of most of Italy, is intricate and turbulent. The great warrior families of the feudal era, such as the Montefeltri and the Da Varani, left a rich architectural legacy of fortresses built by the greatest architects of their day. The artists of the region, including the Renaissance masters Bramante and Raphael among many others, immeasurably enriched Italy's artistic heritage. Industry and agriculture today are the mainstays of the region. The varied coastline, known as the Marches Riviera, attracts tourists to its fashionable beaches. The history, beauty and spiritual character of the Marches is most perfectly preserved in the city of Urbino. More than a city, Urbino is itself a work of art. To many artists of the Renaissance, Urbino embodied an ideal city and, indeed, it is represented as such in paintings of that period.   ☐

● Don't miss

In Ancona★, S. Ciriaco★★, S. Maria della Piazza★ and the Museo Nazionale delle Marche★; in Ascoli Piceno★, S. Francesco★★; in Fano, the arch of Augustus★★; in Fermo, the Piazza del Popolo★ and the Duomo★; in Jesi★, the Palazzo della Signoria★; in Loreto★, the Santuario della Santa Casa★★; in Pesaro★, the Palazzo Ducale★ and the Musei Civici★; in Portonovo, S. Maria★; in Urbino★★,the Palazzo Ducale with the Galleria Nazionale delle Marche★★.

● Brief regional history

8C BC-5C AD
Piceni, Celts, Romans. The region of the Marches abounds in evidence of palaeolithic, neolithic and early Iron-Age occupation. The **Piceni** culture flourished here as early as the 8C BC. These Italic or Illyrian tribes took their name from their totem, the *picu* (modern Italian *picchio* or woodpecker). ● In the early 4C BC **Sicilian Greeks** founded a colony at **Ancona,** and **Celts** *(galli senoni)* established themselves in the territory between Rimini and the Esino. ● In 299 BC the **Romans** forged an alliance with the Piceni, but eventually won control of their lands. ● Roman colonies in the Marches included modern-day **Fermo** *(Firmum),* **Potenza Picena** *(Potentia),* **Osimo** *(Auximum)* and **Pesaro** *(Pisaurum).* ● The Carthaginian general **Hasdrubal** was defeated and killed at the river **Metaurus** (now Metauro) in 207 BC as he was bringing reinforcements to his brother Hannibal. ● The last great Italic revolt against the Romans, in 90-89 BC, started at the town of **Ascoli Piceno** (then *Asculum*) with the murder of a Roman proconsul and ended in the siege of the town. ● During the course of the repartition of Italy by the Emperor Augustus in the 1C BC, the region now known as the Marches was divided between *Picenum* in the S and *Umbria* in the N.

6C-13C
The five coastal cities and the Marches. The region was buffeted as much by **Frankish (Gothic) infiltration** from the N of Italy (535-553) as by barbarian invasions. ● **Lombard** expansion downward from the N regions in the late 6C compelled the inhabitants of the Marches, including many **Byzantine settlers,** to

retreat to the five coastal cities *(pentapoli marittimi):* Rimini, Pesaro, Fano, Senigallia and Ancona. These were eventually entrusted by the Frankish (Holy Roman) Emperors **Pepin** and **Charlemagne** to the rule of the **Pope.** ● In the 10C, feudal territories corresponding to **Camerino, Ancona** and **Fermo** were grouped under the Frankish name of **Marches** (boundaries). ● During the first half of the 12C, a rebellion led by Ancona resulted in the reorganization of the cities of the Marches into **free communes.** By and large, the communes remained allied with the Pope rather than with the Holy Roman Emperor; however, lukewarm support for the government of the day was grounds for 13C popes to complain of the 'fickleness of the people of the Marches'.

15C-16C

The Warlords of the Marches. During the feudal period, the N area of the Marches enjoyed stability under the rule of two great lordly families. ● The **Malatestas'** territories at the point of their greatest power (15C) extended to **Ancona** and included

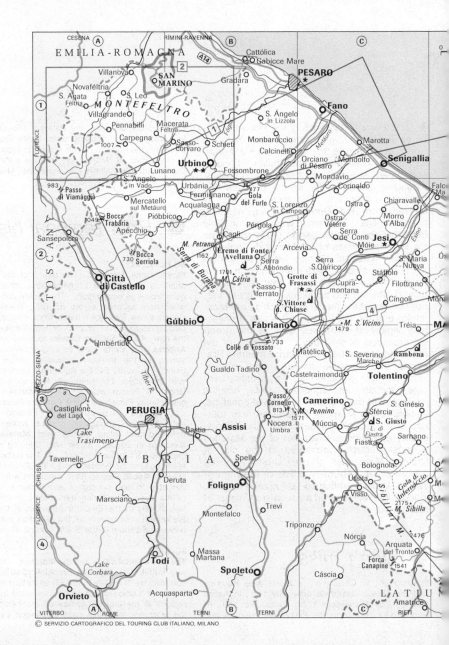

© SERVIZIO CARTOGRAFICO DEL TOURING CLUB ITALIANO, MILANO

Pesaro. ● The **Montefeltri** were given the city of Urbino by the Emperor Frederick Barbarossa in 1155. ● Urbino, Cagli and Fossombrone were splendidly embellished during the Renaissance first by the Montefeltri then by the **Della Rovere** family, into whose hands they had fallen. The Della Rovere also absorbed **Pesaro** in the early 16C. ● The **Da Verano** family ruled **Camerino** for three centuries, until 1540. ● In the 15C **Francesco Sforza** laid claim to lands in the central N Marches but abandoned them in 1447 for the richer prize of the duchy of Milan. ● In the early years of the 16C the Marches were pawns in the ambitious but fruitless struggle for power of **Duke Valentine,** son of the Borgia Pope Alexander VI.

16C-19C
The Papal States and the Kingdom of Italy. The church never completely relinquished its claim to the Marches. ● After the Renaissance, the commune of **Ancona** became the principal papal port on the Adriatic, and in 1631 the papal states absorbed the duchy of Urbino when the Della Rovere family died out. ● The Emperor **Napoleon** interrupted papal government from 1797 to 1815. ● At **Tolentino** on 19 February 1797, Cardinal Mattei signed the infamous **Bonaparte Treaty** *(trattato col Bonaparte)* on behalf of the Pope. The most memorable clause of this document ceded thousands of priceless manuscripts and works of art, which left for Paris in a long string of carriages. ● The army, led by **Joachim Murat,** King of Naples and brother-in-law of Napoleon, was defeated by Austrian forces near Tolentino in May 1815. Murat thereby lost not only the battle but also his southern kingdom together with the hope — expressed only a month earlier in his **Proclamation of Rimini** — of uniting Italy under his leadership. ● The Marches remained under papal rule until 1860, when the **Piedmontese army** loyal to the princely house of Savoy (soon to be the royal house of a united Italy) defeated the papal troops at **Castelfiardo.** ● Union of the Marches with the kingdom of Vittorio Emanuele II was confirmed by a **plebiscite** the following November.

S. Ciriaco in Ancona

Facts and figures

Location: *The region is quadrilateral and runs from the Adriatic coast in the E to the Apennines. It is contained by the rivers Foglia and Tronto. Rugged toward the mountains, the countryside becomes increasingly gentle as the hills roll down to the sea; there is no maritime plain.*
Area: *9,694 sq km.*
Climate: *Mediterranean, modified by varied topography. The Adriatic coast of Italy is cooler than the Tyrrhenian.*
Population: *1,420,829 inhabitants.*
Administration: *Ancona is the regional capital; the other three provinces are Pesaro with Urbino N of Ancona, and Macerata and Ascoli Piceno in the S.*

Map labels:

10 · 20 · (D) · 30 · 40 km

D R I A T I C
S E A
(1)

a
a ANCONA ★
S.Maria di Portonovo
572 · M. Conero
Camerano
Numana
(2)

stelfidardo — Porto Recanati
★ Loreto
canati
siano — Porto Potenza Picena
Potenza Picena
Potenza
RATA S.Cláudio al Chienti
Civitanova Marche
Porto Sant'Elpídio
Corridónia
bb. di iastra
Lido di Fermo
S. Elpidio a Mare
Porto San Giórgio
giórgio
Fermo ★
Torre di Palme
(3)
Monterubbiano
Servigliano
Montefiore d'Aso
Cupra Marittima
Ripatransone
Grottammare
dola
S. Benedetto del Tronto
Offida
Porto Áscoli
rtino
ASCOLI PICENO ★
naco
sia
Alba Adriática (4)
A14
Tronto
Acquasanta Terme
Giulianova
TERAMO
A B R U Z Z I
(D)
PESCARA

Palazzo Ducale in Urbino

Cagliostro

The self-styled Count Alessandro Cagliostro (really Giuseppe Balsamo of Palermo) was a many-faceted character: a monk who renounced his religious calling in Caltagirone, a forger in Rome, a magnificent marquis in Naples. In London in 1776 Cagliostro adopted Freemasonry, assumed his imposing title and achieved notoriety as a chemist, doctor, sage and prophet. He settled in Paris in 1785, where he reached the peak of his fortunes. Here he invented an Egyptian rite of Freemasonry, while his wife Lorenza Feliciani fascinated society with her charm. Cagliostro became embroiled in the affair of Queen Marie Antoinette's diamond necklace, the colossal swindle that further undermined the French monarchy on the eve of the Revolution. This was his downfall: he ended up in the Bastille, was released, but had to leave Paris. The erstwhile count scurried from one country to another, pursued by rumours and threats. He managed to persuade the prince-bishop of Trent of his repentance, and the bishop put in a good word in Rome. Cagliostro struggled along but, having attempted to found a Masonic Lodge using his Egyptian rite, he was again imprisoned — this time by the Inquisition — and condemned to death. Lorenza, contrite, confessed all. In 1790 the pope commuted the sentence to life imprisonment, and the 70-year-old intriguer was confined to the fortress of S. Leo in Montefeltro. He died in prison 5 years later.

● Practical information

Information: tourist offices in principal towns.

Emergency services: public emergency service, ☎ 113; emergency police, ☎ 112; emergency road services *ACI,* ☎ 116.

Weather: forecasts, ☎ 071/991991; state of roads, ☎ 071/994994, ☎ 06/4212 *(ACI);* snow information, ☎ 071/992992; shipping forecast, ☎ 196.

Farm vacations: *Regional Agriturist Association,* at Ancona, corso Mazzini 107, ☎ 071/201763.

Festivals: *jousting tournament* at Ascoli Piceno; *carnival* at Fano; *biennial festival of humour in art* at Tolentino; *Rossini opera festival and international film festival* at Pesaro; *opera season* at the Sferisterio di Macrata; *international polyphonic choir festival* at Fano; *international sacred music festival* at Loreto; *international young musicians' festival* and *Leopardi celebrations* at Recanati.

Events: *Salone Nautico dell'Adriatico* (boats) and *Fiera Internazionale della Pesca* (fishing) at Ancona; *Mostra Internazionale della Calzatura* (footwear) at Civitanova Marche; *Mostra Mercato dell'Antiquariato* (antiques) at Pennabilli; *Mostra Mercato d'Arte, Antiquariato e Artigianato Artistico* (art,antiques and crafts) at Sarnano; *Mostra dell'Artigianato Artistico* (crafts) at Urbino; occasional *antiques market* at Fano.

Nature parks: *Riserva della Montagna di Torricchio* (→ Camerino); *Riserva dell'Abazzia di Fiastra* (→ Macerata).

Ecology: *WWF,* at Ancona, v. Marconi 103, ☎ 071/203634; other offices: at Jesi, p. della Repubblica 9/C; at Macerata, v. F. Crispi 113, ☎ 0733/40485; at Pesaro, v. Meucci 21 (trips, ecological surveillance, wildlife recovery centre). *LIPU,* at Ancona and Pesaro, ☎ 0721/452734 (birdwatching centres at Monte Paganuccio, work camps).

Rambling and hiking: itinerary from Cónero (Portonovo) to Sibillini (Visso) along footpaths and tracks (8 stages), from Mar-Nov; information from *CAI* branches: at Ancona, v. Cialdini 29 A/B; at Ascoli Piceno, corso Mazzini 81; at Camerino, v. C. Lilli 15; at Fermo, v. Perpenti 10; at Jesi, p. della Repubblica, ☎ 0731/52001; at Macerata, p. Veneto 14; at Pesaro, v. Battisti 9, ☎ 0721/30849; at S. Severino Marche, v. del Popolo 39. *Il Pungitopo,* at Ancona, v. Goito 3, ☎ 071/55250.

Brodetto

Brodetto *is the traditional Adriatic fish soup that is served from Trieste to Pescara. Variations on the theme are endless. In Romagna they claim that every beach has its own version.* Brodetto has seven homes in the Marches: S. Benedetto, Porto S. Giorgio, Porto Recanati, Numana, Ancona, Falconara and Senigallia. Purists argue over whether shellfish may be included. The brodetto *of the Marches includes red and grey mullet, sole, gurnard, cuttlefish and baby squid. The steaming fish broth — enriched with oil, onions, herbs, garlic and seasonings — is ladled over sliced bread. The Cónero promontory forms a border between two major brodetto camps: south of Cónero the fish is floured, which thickens the soup, saffron is used and the slices of bread are toasted; to the north they don't flour the fish, a dash of vinegar is added and the untoasted bread is rubbed with garlic.*

Cycling: information from cycling clubs affiliated with UDACE (96) throughout region; inland and hill circuits, leaving from and returning to coast.

Horseback riding: *Federazione Italiana Sport Equestri,* regional committee at Parma, v. Padre Onorio 18, ☎ 0521/38850; equestrian centres at Ancona, Camerano and Sirolo (→ Il Cónero; associates of *ANTE),* at Fabriano, Macerata, Maiolo (→ S. Leo), Matelica, Senigallia and Urbania.

Sailing: *Lega Navale,* at Ancona, v. Mattei, ☎ 071/22506; at Pesaro, v. Fra i Due Porti 2, ☎ 0721/33964; at Porto

S. Giorgio, sea front, ☎ 734/378705; at Porto Sant'Elpidio (→ Sant'Elpidio a Mare), v. Trieste 18; sailing school, at Civitanova Marche, Grottammare, Senigallia.

Caving: *Gruppo Spelologico Marchigiano CAI.*

Skindiving: centres in Ancona and Pesaro.

Winter sports: areas with reasonably extensive facilities are concentrated principally in the provinces of Macerata, Pesaro and Urbino.

Motocross: facilities in Cingoli, Esantoglia (→ Matelica), Grottazzolina (→ Fermo), Piani di Apiro (→ Cingoli),

S. Severino Marche; tracks at Agugliano (→ Ancona), Civitanova Marche and Pergola.

Hang gliding: *Italian federation,* information, ☎ 015/538703; affiliated schools at Ascoli Piceno and Jesi.

Flying: *Aeroclub Ancona-Falconara Marittima,* at airport, ☎ 071/202890; *Pesaro-Fano Airport,* ☎ 0721/82941.

Fishing: *Federazione Itaiana Pesca Sportiva,* at Ascoli Piceno, v. XX Settembre 3, ☎ 0736/65295; at Macerata, v. Crescimbeni 39, ☎ 0733/45976; at Pesaro, v. Panoramica 15, ☎ 0721/24682. For fishing conditions (permitted stretches of water, prohibitions, etc.) inquire at federal sections.

● Towns and places

ACQUASANTA TERME

Ascoli Piceno 20, Ancona 142, Rome 171 km
Pop. 4,111 ✉ 63041 ☎ 0736   D4

Acquasanta Terme in the Tronto Valley has been noted since Roman times for its thermal springs. The springs are used for the treatment of arthritis, respiratory problems and digestive ailments. There are 16C houses in the main street, the corso Schiavi. In the **Palazzo Municipale** and the church of **S. Maria Maddalena** are some noteworthy paintings.   ☐

Practical information

 (May-Oct), ☎ 98268.
ⓘ v. Salaria 2, ☎ 98291.

Recommended
Caving: visits to *Grotte di Acquasanta,* inside the *Stabilimento Termale* (Jul-Oct), ☎ 98268 or 98269.

ANCONA*

Rome 290, Milan 425 km
Pop. 105,657 ✉ 60100 ☎ 071   D2

The Roman historian Pliny the Elder wrote that 'the colony of Ancona is sited on the Cónero promontory near to a sharp bend in the coast, like an elbow...': Ancona is derived from the Greek *ankòn,* which means elbow. The basilica of S. Ciriaco, the town's main monument, was built at the heart of the ancient Piceni settlement on the Guasco hill. The church dates from the 11C and is a beacon for travelers arriving from the north, gleaming above the port to which the town owes its existence.

▶ On the narrow strip of level ground alongside the harbour are the piazza della Repubblica and piazza Kennedy (B2-3), separated by the church of **SS. Sacramento** (16C-18C) at the bustling heart of the town. Here the corsi Mazzini, Garibaldi and Stamira converge. They link the harbour area with the straight viale della Vittoria, which cuts through the modern town to the War Memorial and the **Passetto** (C6). ▶ Just N of the p. della Repubblica is the **Loggia dei Mercanti★** (B2), its Venetian-Gothic façade decorated with statues. ▶ The v. della Loggia leads to the church of **S. Maria della Piazza★** (B3), built in the 13C over earlier 5C-6C buildings; the balconied Romanesque façade★ dates from 1210-25; in the interior, in the crypt are remains of the earlier churches, with fine mosaics. ▶ The picturesque **piazza del Plebiscito** is flanked by a 16C tower and the **Palazzo del Governo,**

dating from 1484 and designed by Francesco di Giorgio Martini, with an arcaded courtyard reached by a Renaissance arch. ▶ In the same square is the 17C church of **S. Domenico** (B3), with an impressive double flight of steps; in the interior, in the apse, are a *Crucifixion★* by Titian and an *Annunciation* by Guercino. ▶ The v. Pizzecolli (B3) leads up the hill and contains the few old buildings that survived the many air raids on Ancona. ▶ At no. 17 is the 16C Palazzo Bosdari, which houses the **Pinacoteca Civica** and the **Galleria d'Arte Moderna** *(10 a.m.-7 p.m.; Sun and hols 9 a.m.-1 p.m.; closed Mon),* with works by Carlo Crivelli, Titian, Lotto, Andrea del Sarto, Pomarancio, Guercino, and, among the moderns, Cassinari and Guidi. ▶ The church of **S. Francesco delle Scale** (B3), rebuilt in the 18C, has a flight of steps in front of it and a magnificent Venetian-Gothic portal★ and a Lotto altarpiece in the interior. ▶ On the p. Stracca (view of the harbour) is the **Palazzo degli Anziani,** with 13C, Romanesque-Gothic and 15C elements. ▶ A little beyond is the Palazzo Ferretti (16C), which houses the **Museo Nazionale delle Marche★** (A3); the collection consists primarily of archaeological finds from the Palaeolithic to the Roman era: artifacts from Piceni tombs (8C-5C BC), Attic red-figure vases★, oriental ivories, objects from Celtic and Etruscan tombs and gilded bronze statuettes from the 1C AD. ▶ The v. Giovanni XXIII climbs to the basilica of **S. Ciriaco★★,** emblem of the town (A3). Built between the 11C-13C, it is Romanesque with Byzantine and Gothic elements and dominated by a fine 13C dome. The façade, with rose window, has a Gothic **portal★** with 13C reliefs and a fine porch supported on stone lions. The interior is on a Greek cross plan, with three naves separated by Roman columns with Byzantine capitals; in the l. arm is an altar by Vanvitelli; at the end of the church is a tomb by Giovanni da Traù (1509); in the r. arm are 12C painted panels. The crypt gives access to the remains of a 6C church. ▶ L. of the basilica is the **Diocesan Museum** *(closed for restoration)* with early Christian and medieval finds from various churches in Ancona and the 4C tomb of Flavio Gorgonio★. ▶ By the harbour are the elegant *Arch of Trajan★ (Arco di Traiano,* A2), by Apollodorus of Damascus (115 AD), and the **Arco Clementino,** built by Vanvitelli (1738) in honour of Pope Clement XII. ▶ The S section of the harbour is protected by the five-sided **Mole Vanvitelliana** (C1-2) or Lazzaretto, started in 1733 to Vanvitelli's design and surrounded by a canal over which two bridges lead; it served as barracks, prison and warehouse. ▶ Close by is the Baroque **Porta Pia,** dedicated to Pope Pius VI (1789). ▶ A striking feature of the **corso Mazzini** (B-C3), which runs through the modern part of the town and contains shops and other facilities, is the **Fontana del Calamo** or delle 13 Cannelle (B3), dating from 1560. In the neighbouring p. Roma (C3) is the 18C **Fontana dei Cavalli.** ▶ → Il Conero.   ☐

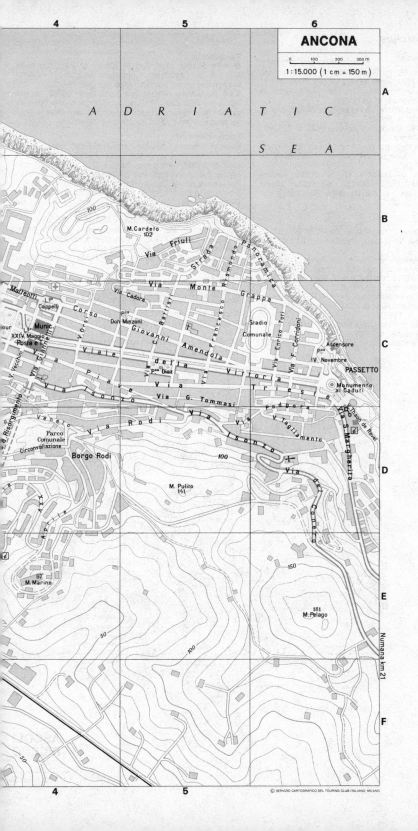

ANCONA

0 100 200 300 m

1:15.000 (1 cm = 150 m)

A D R I A T I C

S E A

M.Cardeto
102

Via Friuli

Strada panoramica

Via Monte Grappa

Matteotti

L.go
Cappelli

Corso

Via Cadore

P.za
Don Minzoni

Giovanni Amendola

Munic.

XXIV Maggio
Posta e T.

Viale

della

Vittoria

Via Enrico Toti

Via F. Corridoni

Stadio
Comunale

Ascensore

P.za
IV Novembre

PASSETTO

Piave

Via

P.za Diaz

Via

Via

Trieste

Monumento
ai Caduti

Via G. Tommasi

Via Isonzo

Via Rodi

Via Padova

V Tagliamento

Via S. Margherita

Thaon de Revel

Veneto

Via del Risorgimento

Parco
Comunale
Circonvallazione

Borgo Rodi

Via Rodi

Isonzo

100

Via del Conero

D

M. Pulito
141

Aprile

XXV

97
M. Marino

150

181
M.Pelago

E

50

100

Numana km 21

50

F

4   5   6

Practical information

ℹ corso Stamira 60, (p. Roma, C3), ☎ 29882, railway station (E1), ☎ 41703; v. M. Marini 14 (E4, head office), ☎ 28313; v. Thaon de Revel (D6), ☎ 34938; Stazione Marittima (B2, seasonal), ☎ 201183.
✈ at Falconara Marittima (13 km NW), ☎ 56257; *Alitalia,* p. Roma 21 (B-C3), ☎ 58892.
🚌 (E1), ☎ 43330; Stazione Marittima (B2), ☎ 202069.
🚎 from p. Stamira (C3) and p. Cavour (C3-4).
⛴ (B2), ferries to Yugoslavia and Greece (car ferries); *Linea Adriatica di Navigazione,* box stazione Marittima, ☎ 51334.
Car rental: *Avis,* v. Marconi 17, ☎ 50369; airport, ☎ 935064; *Hertz,* v. Flaminia 32, ☎ 43439; airport, ☎ 41314; *Maggiore,* v. Martiri della Repubblica 51, ☎ 82753; airport, ☎ 82753.

Hotels:

★★★★ *G.H. Palace,* lungomare Vanvitelli 24 (B3 a), ☎ 201813, 41 rm P closed Christmas, 110,000; bkf: 10,000.
★★★★ *G.H. Passetto,* v. Thaon de Revel 1 (D6 b), ☎ 31307, 45 rm P ⟨ ⚘ 〰 125,000. Rest. ● ♦♦♦ p. IV Novembre 1, ☎ 33214, closed Wed. Elegant, with terrace overlooking the sea. Regional seafood: sweet-sour millerighe, monkfish in potacchio, 35/50,000.
★★★★ *Jolly Miramare,* Rupi di XXIX Settembre 14 (C2 c), ☎ 201171, 89 rm P 120,000.
★★★★ *MotelAgip,* at Palombina Nuova *(8 km W),* v. Flaminia at 293-km marker, ☎ 888241, 51 rm P ⅙ 48,000.
★★★ *G.H. Roma e Pace,* v. Leopardi 1 (C3 d), ☎ 202007, 74 rm, 72,000.

Restaurants:

● ♦♦♦ *Miscia,* Molo Sud 44 (D1 e), ☎ 201376, closed Sun eve and Christmas. Furnished like a ship. Regional seafood: grilled scampi, large fish grill, 65/70,000.
♦♦♦ *Moretta,* p. Plebiscito 52 (B3 f), ☎ 58382, closed Sun and 10-20 Aug. 17C palazzo; elegant, with open-air service in summer. Regional seafood: tagliatelle in oyster sauce, dried cod all'anconetana, 30/40,000.

Recommended

Events: *Salone Nautico dell'Adriatico* (boat show, Apr); *Fiera Internazionale della Pesca* (fishing fair, Jun), ☎ 54364; *sailing regattas.*
Flying: *Falconara Marittima airport,* ☎ 202890.
Horseback riding: *Gruppo Ippico Anconetano,* v. Vittoria 7 (Parco della Cittadella), ☎ 988188 (associate of *ANTE*).
Motocross track: *La Chiusa,* at Agugliano *(16 km SW),* La Chiusa district, ☎ 907804.
Sailing: *Lega Navale,* at Zipa, v. Mattei, ☎ 22506.
Skindiving: *Centro Attività Subacquee,* v. Cialdini 24/I, ☎ 50300; *Kamaros Sub,* v. Fortunato 5, ☎ 26558.
Sports hall: v. Vittorio Veneto, ☎ 53644.
Swimming: v. Thaon de Revel, ☎ 31348; v. Vallemiano, ☎ 896968.

ARCEVIA

Ancona 67, Rome 240 km
Pop. 6,317 ☒ 60011 ☎ 0731   B-C2

Arcevia is a small town with fine views, set on a spur in the upper Misa valley. The **medieval area** is within

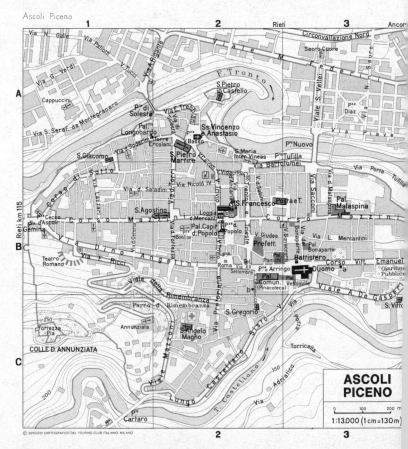

ASCOLI
PICENO

0   100   200 m
1:13.000 (1cm=130m)

the ancient **town walls.** Remains of the **Rocca** are in the beautiful Leopardi Gardens. The 17C collegiate church of **S. Medardo** has two works by Luca Signorelli and an altarpiece by Giovanni della Robbia, also Gothic wooden choir-stalls dating from 1490. Nearby is the 15C **cloister** of S. Francesco. □

Practical information ───────────────────

ℹ corso Mazzini 22, ☎ 9126.

Hotels:

★★★ *Park Hotel Arcevia,* v. Roma 1, ☎ 9595, 38 rm P ⌕ ▥ closed Nov, 45,000; bkf: 4,000.

★★★ *Terrazze,* v. Rocchi 24, ☎ 9391, 61 rm P ▥ ₺ ⌘ ▣ ﾟ closed 15 Jan-20 Feb, 54,000; bkf: 5,000.

ASCOLI PICENO*

Ancona 121, Rome 190, Milan 548 km
Pop. 53,988 ⊠ 63100 ☎ 0736   D4

This stately town is set on a green, sheltered plain at the confluence of the rivers Tronto and Castellano. It is still medieval in layout, with certain areas based on an earlier Roman plan. The Renaissance town was superimposed in the 15C-16C, preserving and enriching the earlier architecture, both ecclesiastical and secular. The austere but spacious design is enhanced by the colour of the local travertine stone. Ascoli's favourable position on the Roman salt road was always helpful to the town's economy.

▶ The centre of the town is the **piazza del Popolo★** (B2) with crenellated and arcaded Renaissance buildings. ▶ The 13C **Palazzo dei Capitani del Popolo** has been much altered (in particular by Cola dell'Amatrice in the 16C); it has a 13C tower, a massive portal beneath a monument to Pope Paul III (1549) and a fine Renaissance courtyard with arcades and balconies. ▶ The Gothic church of **S. Francesco★★** (B2) was started in 1258, consecrated more than a century later and completed in the 16C. It has a magnificent Gothic portal surmounted by the monument to Pope Julius II (1506). The church façade has three Venetian-Gothic portals, interior with nave and two aisles and a fine apse with niche chapels

and women's gallery. Beside it is the **Loggia dei Mercanti★**, dating from 1513. ▶ To the l. of the church, the 16C **Chiostro Maggiore** (now a public market) and the 13C **Chiostro Minore** can be reached from the v. Ceci. ▶ The other major town square is the **Arringo★** (B2-3), opening onto the old salt road which crosses the city: this square contains the Duomo, the bishop's palace, the Palazzo Comunale and the Palazzo Panichi. ▶ The **Duomo** (B3) was rebuilt in the late 15C; the unfinished façade is the work of Cola dell'Amatrice (1539). In the interior the crypt of the medieval building has survived (11C-12C); the Gothic carved choir stalls are of interest. The Cappella del Sacramento (r. aisle) contains a large **altarpiece★** by Carlo Crivelli (1473), a tabernacle designed by Giorgio Vasari (1573) and the silver frontal (14C), consisting of 27 panels presenting episodes from the life of Christ. ▶ Beside the Duomo is the octagonal 12C **baptistery★**. ▶ The **bishop's palace** (B2-3) is an 18C adaptation of earlier buildings (15C-16C); it houses the **Museo Diocesano** *(10 a.m.-12 noon; closed Sun).* ▶ The **Palazzo Comunale** (B2) houses the **Pinacoteca Civica** *(10 a.m.-1 p.m. and 4:30-6:30 p.m. in summer; 8 a.m.-1 p.m. in winter; Sun and hols 10 a.m.-12 noon).* The most important exhibit is a cope★ used by Pope Nicholas IV in the 13C; also paintings by Crivelli, Amatrice, Titian, Guercino, Carracci, Sassoferrato, Reni and Giordano. ▶ The Palazzo Panichi (B2) houses the **Museo Archeologico** *(9 a.m.-5:30 p.m.; Sun and hols 10 a.m.-1 p.m.),* with prehistoric Italic and Roman exhibits. ▶ In the nearby v. Bonaparte (B3) is the elegant 16C **Palazzetto Bonaparte.** ▶ The church of **S. Pietro Martire** (A2) is a Gothic building started *c.* 1280 and completed in the first half of the 14C; the portal on the l. side dates from 1523. ▶ Next to it is the Romanesque church of **S. Vincenzo e S. Anastasio★** (11C) extended in the 13C-14C, with fine Gothic portal and campanile with mullioned windows; the 6C crypt contains remains of 14C frescos. ▶ The **Via di Solestà★** (A2), flanked with towers and medieval houses partly rebuilt in the 16C, leads to the Ponte di Solestà★ (A1), a Roman bridge dating from the early imperial period and spanning the Tronto with a single arch. Before the bridge is the **Porta di Solestà** (1230) flanked by medieval buildings and high towers. ▶ In the **via dei Soderini** (A1) are the tall and elegant **Torre Ercolani** (11C-12C), flanked by the **Palazzetto Longobardo,** dating from the same period, and the church of **S. Giacomo** (13C-14C) with a decorated portal and campanile. ▶ **S. Maria inter Vineas** (A2) overlooks a quiet little square; it is a 12C-13C building with a fine campanile with mullioned windows. In the interior are 13C-14C frescos. ▶ In the v. Bartolomei (quay) is the **Porta Tufilla** (A3), dating from 1553. ▶ The central **corso Mazzini** (B1-2-3), which runs through the town parallel to the salt road, contains two medieval towers, the church of **S. Agostino,** with 15C façade and portal dating from 1547 and, E of the p. del Popolo, the **Palazzo Malaspina** (B3), with ashlar portals and loggias above. It houses the **Civica Galleria d'Arte Contemporanea** *(10 a.m.-1 p.m. and 4:30-6:30 p.m. in summer; 9 a.m.-1 p.m. in winter; 10 a.m.-1 p.m.; Sun and hols 10 a.m.-12 noon).* ▶ At the E end of the town, near the ruined **Ponte di Cecco** is the **Forte Malatesta** (C4), built by Galeotto Malatesta in 1349 and later rebuilt. ▶ The other town fortress is the **Fortezza Pia** (C1), built on the site of an earlier Piceni structure by Pope Pius IV in 1560. ▶ At the foot of the hill are the ruins of the **Roman theatre** (B1) and the p. Cecco d'Ascoli (B1), at the end of which is the little **Porta Gemina,** a Roman gate dating from the 1C BC, under which the salt road passed. ▶ The **Colle San Marco** (11.5 km S) affords a panoramic view over the town and the Tronto Valley to the sea. □

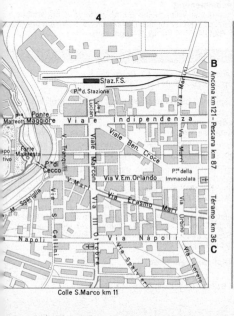

Colle S.Marco km 11

Practical information ───────────────────

ℹ corso Mazzini 229 (B3), ☎ 51115; v. del Trivio 1, ☎ 53045.

🚂 (B4), ☎ 50172.

🚌 from the p. Stazione (B4) and the p. Basso (A2).

Hotels:
★★★★ **Marche,** v. Kennedy 34, ☎ 45475, 32 rm ✧ closed Aug, 60,000.
★★★ **Pennile,** v. Spalvieri, ☎ 41645, 33 rm P ⌕ ⌂ ✧ No restaurant, 60,000; bkf: 3,000.

Restaurants:
♦♦♦ **Gallo d'Oro,** corso Vittorio Emanuele 13 (B3 a), ☎ 53520, closed Mon and Christmas. Modern with well-stocked wine cellar. Regional cuisine: timballetto piceno, macaroni montanara, 20/30,000.
♦♦ **Tornasacco,** v. Tornasacco 31 (B2 b), ☎ 54151, closed Fri and Jun. Three rooms in old and well-equipped wine cellar. Regional cuisine: pasta sheets, rigatoni with calf offal, 20/30,000.
♦ **Guerriero,** v. Mari 38, ☎ 41908, closed Sun eve, Mon, Jul-Aug and Christmas. Italian cuisine: ravioli with cream, grilled scamorza with Parma ham, 20/30,000.

Recommended
Cycling: G.S. Ciclistico, v. Piemonte 10, ☎ 45600.
Events: jousting in 15C costume (1st Sun in Aug); public carnival.
Hang gliding: Monti Sibillini school, ☎ 45995.
Technical tourism: visits to Coccetti workshop, at Force, v. Falconieri 7, ☎ 73195 (copper).
Youth hostel: Ostello de' Longobardi, v. Soderini 26 (A1), ☎ 50007.

CAGLI

Pesaro 61, Ancona 114, Rome 241 km
Pop. 9,553 ✉ 61043 ☎ 0721   B2

Cagli is on the Roman via Flaminia, on a spur of M. Petrano, surrounded by woods, vines and orchards.

▶ Features include the **Roman bridge** that leads into the town, the 13C-15C **Palazzo Comunale,** the **Duomo,** rebuilt in the late 18C after an earthquake, and the churches of **S. Francesco** (Romanesque-Gothic), **S. Angelo** (14C) and **S. Giovanni Battista.** ▶ The **Rocca** built in 1481 by Francesco di Giorgio Martini is in the upper part of the old town. ▶ Parts of the medieval **town walls** remain. □

Practical information _____

ⓘ v. Alessandri 4, ☎ 787457.

Hotel:
★★ **Pineta,** v. della Vittoria 15, ☎ 787387, 33 rm P ⌕ ⌂ ✧ 35,000; bkf: 2,000.

Recommended
Cycling: G.S. Mastini, v. S.Pietro 2.

CAMERINO

Macerata 48, Ancona 93, Rome 207 km
Pop. 7,850 ✉ 62032 ☎ 0737   C3

Camerino lies along a hill between the Potenza and Chienti Valleys, within the wide sweep of gentle hills below the harsher Apennine valleys. A university town and an archbishopric, Camerino was a stronghold of the Da Varano family during the feudal era (14C-16C).

▶ The 19C **Duomo** soars above the central **piazza Cavour,** which boasts a statue of Pope Sixtus V (1587). The 16C **Archbishop's Palace** houses the interesting **Diocesan Museum** (Tue and Sat 10 a.m.-1 p.m., ☎ 2611); the former **Palazzo Ducale** (now the university) has an arcaded courtyard leading to a terrace with magni-

ficent view of the **Botanical Gardens.** ▶ The **Pinacoteca Museo Civico** in the 13C former church of S. Francesco (Jul-Sep 9 a.m.-12 noon and 4-7 p.m.; Sat a.m. only; other months apply to director's office) shows frescos and paintings dating from the 14C-16C and Graeco-Roman antiquities. ▶ In the large church of **S. Venanzio,** rebuilt in 1875, is a notably lavish Gothic portal★. 3.5 km E in a wooded valley is the **Convento dei Cappuccini** (Capuchin convent) dating from 1530 with a majolica altarpiece by Mattia della Robbia and an interesting **Museo Etnografico Religioso.** □

Practical information _____

ⓘ vico del Comune 4, ☎ 2534.

Hotel:
★★★ **Tourist,** v. Favorino 72, ☎ 3451, 52 rm P ✧ 48,000.

Recommended
Botanical garden: v. Pontoni 5 (closed Sat, Sun and hols).
Events: historic procession and fencing tournament (second half of May); various shows at the Rocca (mid-Jul-Aug).
Nature park: Riserva della Montagna di Torricchio (14 km SW), apply to the university for information on visits, ☎ 2527.
Tennis: borgo San Giorgio, ☎ 36973.

CASTELFIDARDO

Ancona 21, Rome 299 km
Pop. 14,535 ✉ 60022 ☎ 071   D2

Castelfidardo sits on a hill, with fine views over the sea and countryside, including the Aspio and Musone Valleys. Its main industry is accordion manufacture.

▶ During the feudal period the town was ruled by the Malatestas and the Sforzas. Historical features are the **medieval walls,** the **Palazzo Comunale** and the 16C **Convento degli Agostiniani** (Augustinian convent). ▶ In the town hall is the **Museo della Fisarmonica** (accordion museum) (9 a.m.-12 noon and 3.30-7 p.m.). ▶ The clash between the Piedmontese and papal troops in 1860 is commemorated by a **park** with pines and cypresses. □

Practical information _____

Recommended
▼ccordions: visits to the S.E.M. factory, v. Squartabue, ☎ 977681 (Mon-Fri); and Titano Victoria, IV Novembre 61, ☎ 780004 (Mon-Fri; by arrangement).

CINGOLI

Macerata 29, Ancona 52, Rome 250 km
Pop. 10,240 ✉ 62011 ☎ 0733   C2

A splendid hilltop position has earned Cingoli the title of 'balcony of the Marches'; the view★ from the **Belvedere** (behind the apse of S. Francesco) stretches as far as the Adriatic. The little town is quiet and secluded, surrounded by walls and with irregular topography.

▶ Historic buildings from the medieval to the Baroque period show its former importance. The Palazzo Municipale houses the **Museo Civico** (inquire at library, v. Mazzini 1) with prehistoric, Roman and medieval exhibits. ▶ In the 13C church of **S. Nicolò** is a Madonna and Saints★ by Lotto. ▶ Outside the Porta Pia is the Romanesque-Gothic church of **S. Esuperanzio** with numerous 15C-16C frescos and important works including a Scourging of Sebastian by Piombo. □

Practical information _____

ⓘ v. L. Ferri 4, ☎ 612444; p. Vittorio Emanuele I, ☎ 612411 (seasonal).

Hotels:

★★★ *Antica Taverna alla Selva,* at San Vittore, v. Cicerone 1, ☎ 617119, 10 rm P ▥ ▭ ,⁄º closed Jan, 35,000; bkf: 5,000.

★★★ *Diana,* v. Cavour 21, ☎ 612313, 15 rm P closed Oct and Christmas, 43,000; bkf: 6,000.

★★★ *Miramonti,* v. dei Cerquatti 31, ☎ 612239, 25 rm P ⫟ ⚲ ▥ ⬦ ,⁄º closed Nov, 41,000; bkf: 6,000.

Recommended

Motocross: *Titoni* track, v. Pian dei Conti, ☎ 612493; *Moto Club Fagioli,* ☎ 612595; *Apiro* track, at Piani di Apiro (11 km W); *Moto Club Sassaroli,* ☎ 611111.

CIVITANOVA MARCHE

Macerata 27, Ancona 47, Rome 270 km
Pop. 36,311 ✉ 62012 ☎ 0733   D2-3

Civitanova Marche is an industrial town (shoe manufacturing) and seaside resort. On a little hill 4 km NW, partly enclosed within 15C walls, is **Civitanova Alta,** which originally sheltered refugees from coastal settlements destroyed by the Goths. In the former Palazzo Comunale is a small **Galleria d'Arte Moderna.** 8 km away is **S. Maria a Piè di Chienti** or dell'Annunciata, a 9C church with two women's galleries. □

Practical information _____

≋
ⓘ p. XX Settembre (in town hall), ☎ 73967; at Civitanova Alta, p. Libertà, ☎ 79189.

Hotels:

★★★★ *Miramare,* v. Matteotti 1, ☎ 770888, 64 rm P ▥ ♿ ⬦ ⬦ 90,000; bkf: 7,000. Rest. ♦♦♦ *Ciacco* closed Sun. Reminiscent of English twenties style. Creative cuisine: sample menu according to season and market availability, 35/55,000.

★★★★ *Villa Eugenia,* v. Villa Eugenia, ☎ 72422, 33 rm P ▥ closed 15-30 Sep and Christmas, 73,000; bkf: 6,000.

★★★ *Sant'Elena,* at Fontespina, v. IV Novembre 124, 39 rm P ▥ closed Oct-Mar, 55,000; bkf: 6,000.

Restaurant:

♦♦♦ *Piccolo Mondo,* v. Dalmazia 52, ☎ 74700, closed Mon and Jan. Elegant, rustic style, quiet atmosphere. Seafood, 40/60,000.

Recommended

Clay pigeon shooting: v. Ippodromo 7, ☎ 72630.
Events: *Mostra Internazionale della Calzatura,* ☎ 772744 (Jan and Jun, footwear show).
Motocross: Track at *Le Grazie,* ☎ 72950.
Sailing: sailing club, N. Molo, ☎ 73687 and 75692.

Il CONERO

                                                            D2

The Cónero promontory is almost an island, with magnificent views, thick woods and cliffs dropping to the sea. The flora is particularly interesting, some of it rare. Holm oak, arbutus and lentiscus mingle with maple, service trees and oak. Birds include peregrine falcon and sand martins, and migrant species in season.

▶ **Camerano,** in the Aspio Valley, has two interesting churches: **S. Francesco,** with Gothic portal and Baroque interior, and the **parish church** with *Madonna and Child,* a youthful work by Carlo Maratta (1625-1713), who was born in the town. ▶ **Portonovo** is a seaside resort in attractive surroundings. At the end of the road that climbs the mountain ridge is **S. Maria di Portonovo★,** a Romanesque church (11C) in delightful surroundings *(inquire at the house next door).* **Sirolo** is on the slopes

of Monte Conero. **Numana** is on the site of an important Graeco-Roman centre; archaeological finds from local excavations are shown in the **Antiquarium** *(9 a.m.-2 p.m.; Sun and hols 9 a.m.-1 p.m.; closed Mon; in summer also 4-7:30 p.m.).* There is a fine polychrome wooden **Crucifixion** (possibly Byzantine,13C-14C) in the modern sanctuary in the square. Boat trips can be made to the **Due Sorelle** rocks. ▶ At **Badia di S. Pietro,** once a hermitage, parts of the original buildings (11C-13C) can be seen. □

Practical information _____

ASPIO TERME, 3 km NW of Camerano.
⚘ (mid-May-Oct), ☎ 95691.

Hotel:

★★★ *Palace del Cónero,* SS 16 at 309-km marker, ☎ 7108312, 51 rm P ▥ ♿ 80,000.

CAMERANO, ✉ 60021, ☎ 0171.

Recommended

Horseback riding: *Centro Ippico del Cónero,* at Varano (5 km N), v. Burànico 199, ☎ 804569.
Wine: *Vinimarc plant,* ☎ 731319; *Cónero municipal cellars,* v. Direttissima del Cónero 47, ☎ 731023.

NUMANA, ✉ 60026, ☎ 071.

ⓘ p. Santuario, ☎ 936142 (seasonal).

Hotels:

★★★★ *Numana Palace,* at Marcelli, v. Litorana 10, ☎ 930155, 102 rm P ▭ ,⁄º closed 16 Sep-14 May, 100,000.

★★★ *Baby Gigli,* at Marcelli, v. Litorana, ☎ 930186, 21 rm P closed Oct-May. No restaurant, 70,000; bkf: 5,500.

★★★ *Eden Gigli,* v. Morelli 11, ☎ 936182, 30 rm P ⚲ ▥ ♿ ▭ ,⁄º closed Nov-Feb, 70,000.

★★★ *Fior di Mare,* v. Colombo 14, ☎ 936614, 45 rm P ⚲ ⬦ closed 21 Sep-19 May, 78,000; bkf: 6,000.

★★★ *Sorriso,* v. del Golfo, ☎ 936175, 38 rm P ▥ ⬦ closed 1 Oct-14 May, 71,000; bkf: 6,000.

Restaurant:

♦♦ *Zi' Nene,* at Marcelli, v. Litorana 230, ☎ 930159, closed Mon. Farmhouse with summer service under a pergola. Regional cuisine: pasta and kidney beans with pork rinds and garlic toast, potato gnocchi with duck sauce, 40/50,000.

⚘ ★★★★ *Numana Blu,* at Marcelli, 607 pl, ☎ 930863.

Recommended

Marina: *Circolo nautico,* ☎ 936096 or 937212.

PORTONOVO, ✉ 60020, ☎ 071.

Hotels:

★★★ *Emilia,* v. Poggio 149, ☎ 801117, 30 rm P ⫟ ⚲ ▥ ♿ ▭ ,⁄º closed Dec-Feb, 73,000; bkf: 7,000. Rest. ♦♦♦ ☎ 801145, closed Mon and 15 Dec-31 Jan. On slopes of Monte Conero, rising steeply out of the sea. Local seafood: dumplings with scampi, dried cod all'anconetana, 35/50,000.

★★★ *Excelsior la Fonte,* ☎ 801125, 63 rm P ▥ ⬦ ▭ ,⁄º closed Nov-Apr, 66,000.

★★★ *Fortino Napoleonico,* v. Poggio 166, ☎ 801124, 30 rm P ▥ ♿ 75,000; bkf: 10,000.

⚘ ★★★ *Torre,* 180 pl, ☎ 801038.

SIROLO, ✉ 60020, ☎ 071.
ⓘ p. Vittorio Veneto, ☎ 936141.

Hotels:

★★★ *Conchiglia Verde,* v. Giovanni XXIII 12, ☎ 936888, 28 rm P ▥ ▭ No restaurant, 68,000; bkf: 5,000.

★★★ *Monteconero,* v. Monteconero 26, ☎ 936122, 41 rm P ▥ ▭ ,⁄º closed 10 Jan-28 Feb, 65,000.

★★ *Beatrice,* v. Vallone 1, ☎ 936301, 27 rm P ▥ ⬦ 50,000.

Recommended

Farm vacations: *Azienda il Ritorno,* ☎ 937214.
Horseback riding: *Riding Club Le Azalee,* v. della Molinella (associate of *ANTE*).

CORINALDO

Ancona 47, Rome 316 km
Pop. 5,382 ✉ 0013 ☎ 071   C2

Corinaldo is a picturesque little town on a hill among the famous Verdicchio vineyards, between the Cesano and Nevola valleys. It has 14C-15C **walls**★ in exceptional condition, with gates, towers and ramparts. The **birthplace of S. Maria Goretti** (1890-1902) and the crypt dedicated to her in the church **dell'Addolorata** attract pilgrims all year long. □

Practical information ————————————
ℹ️ v. del Corso 10.

Restaurant:
◆ *Bellavista,* v. dei Capuccini 9, ☎ 67073, closed Fri in winter. Simple and informal. Regional cuisine: fresh pasta, pancakes, mixed grilled meats, 18/20,000.

CUPRA MARITTIMA

Ascoli Piceno 41, Ancona 80, Rome 234 km
Pop. 4,366 ✉ 63012 ☎ 0735   D3

Cupra Marittima is a small coastal centre with modern section and medieval town on the high ground above it. A lane between two rows of pines leads to the old town, **Cupra Alta**★, surrounded by walls built by Francesco Sforza in the 15C. In the higher part is the church of **S. Maria in Castello,** with a Romanesque portal. The **Pineta dei Pignotti** (pine wood), reached by a road with fine views, overlooks the sea. 12 km NW, on a raised site, is **Montefiore dell'Aso,** with medieval ring walls and, in the collegiate church of S. Lucia, sections of a Crivelli altarpiece★.   □

Practical information ————————————
≋
ℹ️ v. Vittorio Emanuele 11, ☎ 77145.

Hotels:
★★★ *Europa:* v. Gramsci 18, ☎ 778033, 25 rm 🅿️ ♨ closed 15-30 Oct, 35,000; bkf: 3,000.
★★ *Sans Souci,* lungomare Sauro 68, ☎ 777192, 20 rm 🅿️ closed Oct-Feb, 34,000; bkf: 7,000.

⚠ ★★★ *Led Zeppelin,* at Boccabianca, 700 pl, ☎ 778125 (all year); ★★★ *Verde Cupra,* v. S.Silvestro 37, 160 pl, ☎ 777666 (all year).

Recommended
Events: *Mostra Internazionale di Malacologia* (shell exhibition, Jul); secretariat, ☎ 890667.

FABRIANO

Ancona 72, Rome 216 km
Pop. 28,809 ✉ 60044 ☎ 0732   B2-3

Papermaking was developed at Fabriano in the 12C; by the 14C-15C the town supported 40 papermills. The industry, rooted here in ancient times, still flourishes today.

▶ This ancient and rich tradition is documented in the **Museo della Carta e della Filigrana** (C1; paper and watermarks; *9 a.m.-12 noon and 3-6 p.m.;Sun and hols 9 a.m.-12:30 p.m.; closed Mon*) in the former monastery of S. Domenico (next to the 14C **church**). ▶ The old town is medieval in layout, on higher ground, around the **piazza del Comune**★ (B1-2). The square has a monumental fountain dating from 1285-1351, the **Palazzo del Podestà** (1255, governor's palace, with mullioned windows and

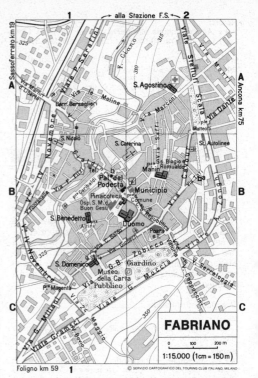

FABRIANO

0   100   200 m
1:15.000 (1cm = 150m)

Foligno km 59

merlons) and the **Palazzo Vescovile** (bishop's palace, 16C-17C). Under the arches of the latter is the way to the **Pinacoteca Comunale** *(art gallery; 9 a.m.-12 noon; summer also 3-6 p.m.; closed Mon)* with 14C-15C paintings by local artists. ▶ Nearby, opposite the Ospedale di S. Maria del Buon Gesù (1456) is the **Duomo** (B1-2), founded in the 14C, but largely rebuilt in 1617; inside are 14C frescos depicting the life of St. Lawrence. On the l. is a 14C-15C cloister. ▶ Also interesting are the churches of **S. Biagio e S. Romualdo** (B2) (15C rebuilt 18C) and **S. Agostino** (A2), with 14C frescos in the interior *(information from the rectory).* ▶ From **Poggio San Romualdo** *(20 km NE)* it is not far to the abbey of **Val di Castro,** founded in the 10C (the 13C church and parts of the monastery have survived). The splendid **Grotte de Frasassi**★ (caves) are 18 km N (→ La Terra del Verdicchio).   □

Practical information ————————————

ℹ️ p. del Comune 42, ☎ 5387.
Car rental: *Avis,* p. del Comune 7, ☎ 22522; *Hertz,* v. Campo Sportivo 2, ☎ 24176.

Hotel:
★★★★ *Janus Hotel Fabriano,* p. Matteotti 45 (B2 a), ☎ 4191, 83 rm 🅿️ ♨ closed Aug, 90,000; bkf: 5,000.

Restaurant:
◆ *Pollo,* v. Corridoni 22 (B1 b), ☎ 24584, closed Tue and Aug. Near piazza del Comune. Regional cuisine: polenta with game, roast meats, 18/30,000.

Recommended
Horseback riding: Fattoria *La Quercia d'Oro,* at Canapegna (associate of *ANTE*); *Circolo Ippico Fabrianese,* at Brosciano, ☎ 23079.

FALCONARA MARITTIMA

Ancona 10, Rome 280 km
Pop. 30,361 ⊠ 60015 ☎ 071   D2

Falconara Marittima thrives on modern industry: oil refining, chemical and mechanical plants. The castle and the church of **S. Maria delle Grazie,** with Gothic portal, have survived in the old town, **Falconara Alta** *(2 km into the interior).* 2 km N is the **Rocca Priora,** a large medieval fortress. 3 km away the **Paese dei Bimbi** is a children's amusement park with zoo.   □

Practical information _____

≋
ℹ v. Cavour 3, ☎ 910458.
✈ Ancona-Falconara, ☎ 56257.

Hotels:
★★★ **Touring,** v. degli Spagnoli, ☎ 913000, 80 rm P ⊟ 60,000; bkf:3,000. Rest. ♦♦♦ *Ilario* v. Tito Speri 2, ☎ 9170678, closed Sun eve, Mon and Jun. Regional cuisine, 25/45,000.
★★ **Avion,** v. Caserme 6, ☎ 9170444, 37 rm P ▥ ✻ ⌇ 50,000; bkf:4,000.

Restaurant:
● ♦♦♦ *Villa Amalia,* v. degli Spagnoli 4, ☎ 912045, closed Tue and 15 Sep-15 Jun. In villa with large veranda giving onto a cool garden. Regional seafood: tagliolini with oysters, dried cod all'anconetana, 35/45,000.

Recommended
Children's facilities: *Paese dei Bimbi,* v. Barcaglione, ☎ 911312 (amusement park and zoo).
Clay pigeon shooting: v. Monti e Tognetti, ☎ 911648.
Cycling: *Velo Club,* v. Molise 5, ☎ 9171596.
Flying club: airport, ☎ 202890.

FANO*

Pesaro 12, Ancona 65, Rome 290 km
Pop. 52,295 ⊠ 61032
☎ 0721   C1

See map on page 436.

The town covers a broad tract of land between the mouth of the Metauro and the Porto canal; it grew up around the regular layout of the original Roman colony. From the 13C to the mid-15C Fano prospered under the Malatestas. The name is derived from a temple of Fortuna *(fanum fortunae).*
▶ The 16C **Fontana della Fortuna** adorns the central p. XX Settembre (B-C2), in front of the Romanesque-Gothic **Palazzo della Ragione★.** ▶ A Renaissance arcade leads to the courtyard of the **Palazzo Malatesta,** (15C-16C). The palazzo houses the collections of the **Museo Civico** and **Pinacoteca** (art gallery) *(10 a.m.-12 noon and 4-7 p.m.; winter 10 a.m.- 12 noon; closed p.m. Sun and hols, and Mon)* with local finds from the Neolithic to Roman periods; Malatesta medals★ by Matteo De'Pasti, paintings including a *Guardian Angel★* by Guercino, *Annunciation★* by Guido Reni, an altarpiece★ by Giambono (*c.* 1420), ceramics from the 14C-18C, and modern paintings. ▶ The **Malatesta tombs★** are under the portico of the former church of S. Francesco (B-C2). Pandolfo III died in 1427, Paola Bianca, his wife, in 1398. ▶ **S. Maria Nuova** (C2) has a 16C portico and portal; the interior features 18C stucco and a *Madonna and Saints* by Perugino, possibly with the assistance of the young Raphael. In the via Arco d'Augusto (B1-2) are the Gothic church of **S. Domenico** (future Diocesan Museum) and the **cathedral,** with 12C Romanesque façade (in the interior are a reconstructed pulpit with Romanesque carvings and reliefs and the Cappella Nolfi, decorated by Domenichino in 1623). At the

end of the street is the **Arco d'Augusto★★** (1C BC) (B-C1), erected on the Roman via Flaminia. The Renaissance façade of the adjacent church of **S. Michele★** (1495) features a bas-relief depicting the arch. ▶ The viale delle Rimembranze (B1) runs along the **Augustan walls.** ▶ The **Rocca Malatestiana** (B1-2) was built (1438-52) for Sigismondo Malatesta, later extended and altered. ▶ **S. Pietro ad Vallum** (B2) is a fine Baroque church. ▶ **S. Paterniano** (C2), mid-16C with Renaissance cloister, is attributed to Jacopo Sansovino. ▶ 5.5 km SW is the **Eremo di Monte Giove,** a former monastery in a commanding position with fine view★ of the Metauro valley and the Apennines.   □

Practical information _____

FANO
♨ (May-Oct), at Carignano Terme *(10 km W),* ☎ 885128.
ℹ v. C. Battisti 40 (B3), ☎ 82534; v. Cairoli 108, ☎ 866645 (A1, seasonal); at Torrette, ☎ 884779 (seasonal).
Car rental: *Maggiore* (near Snam Progetti), ☎ 881786.

Hotels:
★★★★ *G.H. Elisabeth:* v. Carducci 12 (A1 a), ☎ 878241, 37 rm P ▥ 115,000; bkf: 7,000.
★★★ *Corallo,* v. Leonardo da Vinci 3 (B3 b), ☎ 878200, 22 rm P ✻ closed Christmas, 48,000; bkf: 5,000.
★★★ *Excelsior,* v. Simonetti 17 (A1 c), ☎ 82558, 30 rm P closed 16 Sep-14 Jun, 52,000; bkf: 8,000.
★★ *Marina,* v. Adriatico 15 (B3 d), ☎ 82157, 40 rm P closed Oct-Mar, 40,000; bkf: 5,000.

Restaurants:
♦♦♦ *Quinta,* v. Adriatico 42 (A2 e), ☎ 878043, closed Sun and Aug. In converted fishermen's cottages. Seafood: passatelli in fish broth, tagliatelle in fish sauce, 30/40,000.
♦♦♦ *Tutta Frusaglia,* v. Buozzi 75 (B1 f) ☎ 82006, closed Wed. Elegant, rustic style. Regional seafood: noodles with olives, Adriatico roast, 18/30,000.

▲ ★★★ *Mare Blu,* at Torrette, SS Adriatica at the 256-km marker, 200 pl, ☎ 884389; ★★★ *Stella Maris,* at Torrette, v. Cappellini 5, 282 pl, ☎ 884231.

Recommended
Bowling: p. Malatesta 1, ☎ 878334.
Cycling: *G.S. Ciclistico Fano,* v. Nicol da Fano 6.
Events: *Fano carnival* (Feb); *Incontri Internazionali di Cori Polifonici* (choral competitions; Jun); *Summer carnival* and *Festival of Festivals* (Jul); *Rassegna Regionale dell'Artigianato Orafo* (regional goldsmiths' fair; Jul); theatre and music in the *Corte Malatestiana,* organ recitals in *S. Paterniano* (Jul and Aug).
Flying club: airport, v. della Colonna, ☎ 82941.
Go-karting: v. del Bersaglio, ☎ 82805.
Guided tours: inland centres (Jun and Sep); agencies: *Amadei,* ☎ 84211; *Adria,* ☎ 82855.
Technical tourism: visits to *COILSE co-operative* (textiles of various kinds, old hand-looms), v. Gasparoli 60, ☎ 876208.
♥ antiques market: second week of the month in the former church of S. Domenico (B2).

Environs

CARTOCETO, ⊠ 61030, 18 km SW.

Restaurant:
♦♦♦ *Symposium - Quatro Stagioni,* v. Cartoceto 38, ☎ 898320, closed Sun eve, Mon and winter. Rustic exterior, sophisticated interior. Regional and Italian cuisine: vol au vent with chicken liver, tagliatelle with truffles, 40/50,000.

SALTARA, ⊠ 61030, 15 km SW.

Restaurant:
♦♦♦ *Posta Vecchia,* at Calcinelli, v. Flaminia 18/20, ☎ 897800, closed Mon. Rustic yet elegant; central fireplace. Regional cuisine: ravioli with truffle ricotta, stuffed rabbit, 30/40,000.

FANO

0　100　　200 m

1 : 15.000　(1cm = 150 m)

ADRIATIC

SEA

Foligno km 133　　Autostrada km 3

© SERVIZIO CARTOGRAFICO DEL TOURING CLUB ITALIANO, MILANO

FERMO*

Ascoli Piceno 66, Ancona 69, Rome 258 km
Pop. 35,137 ✉ 63023 ☎ 0734　　　　　　　　D3

The town is attractively placed on a hill commanding wonderful views, on the spur between the Tenna and Ete Vivo valleys. A striking feature is the 13C Duomo on the Girfalco esplanade, above the steep alleyways of the medieval town.

▶ In the **piazza del Popolo★** (A-B3) are the Baroque **Palazzo degli Studi,** with a library established in 1688, and the 16C **Palazzo dei Priori,** containing the **Pinacoteca Civica** *(weekdays 9 a.m.-12 noon and 5-8 p.m.),* with a fine collection of paintings, particularly of the Venetian and Marche schools. ▶ The **Duomo★** (A-B2) is 5C in origin, rebuilt in the 13C; in the interior are the outstanding remains of a 5C mosaic pavement and, in the sacristy, St. Thomas Becket's **chasuble★** of 12C English manufacture using gold and silk fabric made by Arab weavers in Spain. There is a wonderful view from the esplanade, which is laid out as a garden. ▶ The corso Cefalonia and the corso Cavour (A2), the principal arteries of the

city, contain some fine palaces including the 16C **Palazzo Azzolino** by Antonio da Sangallo the Younger; as well as the 14C **Monte di Pietà** and the 13C **Torre Matteucci,** now in ruins. ▶ On the largo Fogliani (B1) is the church of **S. Zenone,** with Romanesque portal dating from 1186. ▶ Nearby, in the v. Firmiano, is the church of **S. Pietro,** with portal built in 1251. ▶ Near the Gothic church of **S. Domenico** (B3) is the **Roman cistern,** an enormous complex (30 underground rooms) built in 41-60 AD to conserve and purify the water *(inquire at the Azienda di Soggiorno).* ▶ The Romanesque-Gothic church of **S. Agostino** (A-B1) and the Gothic church of **S. Francesco** (A3) are also interesting. ☐

Practical information

ℹ️ palazzo del Comune (A3), ☎ 23205.

Restaurant:
♦ **Nasò,** v. Crollalanza 45 (B3 a), ☎ 29100, closed Mon. Pleasant rural style. Regional cuisine: yellow and green noodles sibillina, lamb fermanella, 20/28,000.

⚠ ★★★★ *Spinnaker,* at Santa Maria a Mare, 570 pl, ☎ 52412.

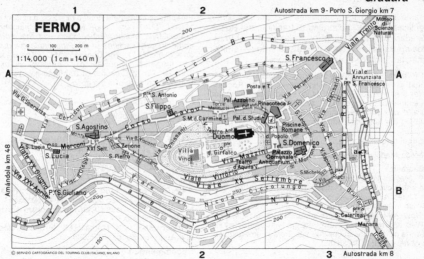

Recommended
Events: traditional *Piceni Festival,* at Monterubbiano (*14 km S;* Jun at Whitsuntide), Comune, ☎ 59125.
Farm vacations: information from office for economic development (Sviluppo Economico del Comune), ☎ 213273.
Motocross: *Monterosato di Fermo* track, at Monterosato, ☎ 219480, run by the *Moto Club Ippogrifo,* ☎ 219966; *Catini* track, at Grottazzolina (14 km SW), run by the *Moto Club Azzolino,* v. Valdete, ☎ 52011 and 52208.
Swimming: v. Beni, ☎ 215311.

FOSSOMBRONE

Pesaro 37, Ancona 87, Rome 262 km
Pop. 10,079 ⊠ 61034 ☎ 0721   B1

The via Flaminia runs through this former Roman township of *Forum Sempronii* on the flood plain of the Metauro. The surrounding area is thickly wooded, with many picturesque and hard-to-reach places that once attracted hermitages and monasteries.

▶ The town nestles at the foot of a hill on which are the remains of the **Rocca Malatestiana** (round tower; 13C-15C). Some Gothic houses and alleyways of the old town have survived, and there are numerous ducal residences, including those of the Montefeltri and the Della Rovere. ▶ The **Corte Bassa** and the **Palazzo Ducale** (or Corto Rossa) no longer have their original furnishings. The **Corte Alta,** built in the 13C for the Malatestas, restored and extended in 1466-70, houses the **Museo Civico A. Vernacecci** *(to visit inquire at the Biblioteca Passionei (library), v. Torricelli 2),* with archaeological material from prehistoric times to the Roman period and Renaissance exhibits. ▶ In the 16C Palazzo Pergamino, in the street of the same name, are the **Quadreria Cesarini** (art gallery) and the **Pinacoteca Comunale** *(to visit inquire at the Biblioteca Passionei).* □

Practical information _____

Recommended
Craft workshops: visits to *Gaudenzi* workshops, at Fratte Rosa (16 km SE), v. Terrecotte 6, ☎ 777138 (inquire in advance; terra-cotta); *Gasparucci* workshops, at Sant' Ippolito (8 km E), v. Raffaello 86, ☎ 728421 (bamboo furniture).

GABICCE MARE

Pesaro 16, Ancona 93, Rome 317 km
Pop. 5,591 ⊠ 61011 ☎ 0541   B1

The fishing boats in this **canal port** provide touches of colour. Gabicce is the northernmost Marche resort; the Tavollo River is the regional boundary.   □

Practical information _____

≋
ℹ v. della Vittoria 41, ☎ 961375.

Hotels:
★★★★ *Alexander,* v. Panoramica 35, ☎ 961166, 50 rm Ⓟ ⬚ ㊉ ⌧ closed Oct-Apr, 50,000; bkf: 5,000.
★★★ *Capo Est,* at Vallugola, v. Panoramica 123, ☎ 963333, 90 rm Ⓟ ≮ ⚲ ⬚ ⟋ closed 16 Sep-14 May. Modern building on hill, with elevator to beach and marina, 180,000.
★★★ *Bellavista,* v. Giardini Unità d'Italia, ☎ 961640, 58 rm Ⓟ ⬚ closed 26 Sep-14 Apr, 52,000; bkf: 6,000.
★★★ *Maiestic,* v. Balneare 10, ☎ 961274, 55 rm Ⓟ ⬚ ⌧ closed Oct-Apr, 50,000; bkf: 7,000.
★★★ *Nobel,* v. Vittorio Veneto 99, ☎ 961039, 41 rm Ⓟ ㊉ Pens. closed 1 Oct-14 May, 55,000.
★★ *Giovanna Regina,* v. Vittorio Veneto 173, ☎ 961181, 43 rm Ⓟ ⬚ closed 21 Sep-30 Apr, 51,000; bkf: 5,000.
★ *Ambra,* v. Vittorio Veneto 15, ☎ 961366, 44 rm Ⓟ closed Oct-Apr, 39,000.

Restaurant:
◆◆ *Grottino,* at Gabicce Monte, p. Valbruna 3, ☎ 962595, closed Wed and Jan-15 Feb. Summer service on terrace facing the sea. Seafood: risotto and tagliatelle alla marinara, fritto misto, 30/40,000.

Recommended
Marina: Delegazione di Spiaggia, ☎ 967463.
Tennis: v. Panoramica, ☎ 962405.

GRADARA

Pesaro 15, Ancona 89, Rome 316 km
Pop. 2,424 ⊠ 61012 ☎ 0541   B1

The 13C Rocca (keep) and the turreted wall surrounding the town, which is set on a hill dominating the area between the Apennines and the sea, offer magnificent views. According to tradition, the Rocca at Gradara was the setting for the tragic tale of Francesca da Rimini, related in Dante's Inferno (→ Emilia, Romagna, Sant' Arcangelo di Romagne).

▶ It is possible to **walk** around the walls as far as the highest tower and there is a fine view. ▶ The **Rocca★** *(winter 9 a.m.-2 p.m., closed Mon; summer 3-8 p.m., but check summer opening times, ☎ 964181)* dates from the 13C and was extended and restored by Giovanni Sforza in 1494. It is furnished with period pieces. □

Practical information _____

ℹ borgo Mancini (outside the walls), ☎ 964115.

Restaurants:
♦♦♦ *Mastin Vecchio,* v. Dante 5, ☎ 964024, closed Mon and Nov. Medieval-style between walls of old castle. Mixed regional cuisine: tagliatelle alla malatestiana, crawfish in bellavista, 25/35,000.
♦♦ *Hosteria la Botte,* p. IV Novembre 11, ☎ 964404, closed Wed and Nov. 15C surroundings with arched vaults and wine cellar. Italian cuisine: spaghetti in green sauce, filet of meat in foil, 25/38,000.

GROTTAMMARE

Ascoli Piceno 37, Ancona 84, Rome 230 km
Pop. 11,344 ✉ 63013 ☎ 0735　　　　　　　　D3

Grottammare is a seaside resort at the foot of a hill, site of a medieval town. It was the birthplace of the 16C Pope Sixtus V whose sister had the church of **S. Lucia** built in his memory (1597). A narrow street climbs to the remains of the 14C **castle;** excellent view. 1 km SW is the Romanesque church of **S. Martino,** perhaps built on the remains of a temple to Cupra, a goddess of Eastern origin. □

Practical information _____

≋
ℹ p. Martiri Triestini 5, ☎ 631087.

Hotel:
★★★ *Roma,* lungomare De Gasperi 16, ☎ 631145, 60 rm Ⓟ ▥ ⁓ closed 16 Sep-31 May, 55,000; bkf: 5,000.

⚑ ★★★ *Don Diego,* lungomare De Gasperi, 285 pl, ☎ 60261.

Recommended
Sailing school: *Club Ischia Cultura e Sport,* at Ischia, v. Foscolo 43 (*UISP* sailing and windsurfing league).

JESI*

Ancona 29, Rome 260 km
Pop. 40,946 ✉ 60035 ☎ 0731　　　　　　　　C2

Jesi, on the left bank of the Esino, is enclosed within 14C town walls in extremely good condition. On St. Stephen's Day 1194, Costanza of Sicily, wife of the Holy Roman Emperor Henry VI, sheltering under an awning in the market place while on her way to Palermo, gave birth to her only son, the future Emperor Frederick II, who was generous to the town where he had been born with so little ceremony.

▶ The **Palazzo della Signoria★,** designed by Francesco di Giorgio Martini (1486-98), houses the **Museo Archeologico** *(weekdays 9 a.m.-12 noon and 4-6 p.m.; winter 3:30-6:30 p.m.; Sat 9 a.m.-1 p.m.; 1st and 3rd Sun of month 10 a.m.-12 noon),* with archaeological finds, 15C-16C sculptures and 18C ceramics *(to be transferred to the Palazzo Pianetti).* ▶ The **Palazzo Pianetti,** 18C with rococo **gallery** and stucco decoration, houses the

Pinacoteca Comunale (9.30 a.m.-12.30 p.m. and 4-7 p.m.; closed Sun p.m. and Mon), with **paintings★** by Lotto. *(The Museo Archeologico and the modern and contemporary sections of the Pinacoteca are due for re-arrangement.)* ▶ The **Duomo** is 18C. The elegant **Teatro Pergolesi** *(inquiries to caretaker)* is also late 18C. ▶ The 13C church of **S. Marco** has 14C frescos★ of the Rimini school in the apse. □

Practical information _____

ℹ p. della Repubblica 9, ☎ 52712.

Hotels:
★★★★ *Federico II,* v. Ancona 10, ☎ 543631, 80 rm Ⓟ ▥ ⓓ ▤ ⁓ 110,000; bkf: 7,000.
★★★ *Italia,* v. Trieste 28, ☎ 4844, 13 rm Ⓟ ▥ ⁓ closed Aug, 80,000; bkf: 5,000.

Restaurants:
♦♦♦ *Galeazzi,* v. Mura Occidentali 5, ☎ 57944, closed Mon and Aug. Near piazza della Repubblica. Regional cuisine: flaky pastry with cream, pasta squares with ricotta, 18/26,000.
♦ *Ippocampo,* v. S. Marcello 86, ☎ 57487, closed Mon and Aug. Seafood, 40/45,000.

Recommended
Farm vacations: *Azienda Santoni,* at San Maurizio, ☎ 6770.
Hang gliding: *Delta Club Jesi,* v. Raffaello 55, ☎ 3335.
Horseback riding: *Circolo Ippico Lo Sperone,* v. Piandelmedico 51, ☎ 58545 and 60035.
Wines: visits to Verdicchio producers' cooperative, at Montecarotto *(18 km W),* v. Piandole 7/A, ☎ 89245.

LIDO DI FERMO

Ascoli Piceno 62, Ancona 60, Rome 254 km
Pop. 2,432 ✉ 63010 ☎ 0734　　　　　　　　D3

Lido Di Fermo is a seaside resort with a splendid stretch of sand. On the hills behind the village, on the road to Fermo, is **Capodarco,** a quiet little place with wonderful views. □

Practical information _____

≋
ℹ v. Lido, ☎ 50471 (seasonal).

LORETO*

Ancona 25, Rome 288 km
Pop. 10,603 ✉ 60025 ☎ 071　　　　　　　　D2

Loreto is famous as the sanctuary of the Virgin Mary's house. Tradition holds that the house was transported by angels from Nazareth to Loreto by way of Dalmatia. Whatever the facts may be, a small brick dwelling, lavishly adorned over the centuries, has been preserved in the *Sanctuary of the Holy House (Santa Casa)* since the end of the 13C. It is believed that the house might have been shipped from the Holy Land during the Crusades. The name of Loreto is derived from the laurel grove *(lauretum)* where the *Santa Casa* came to rest.

▶ The great sweep of the **piazza della Madonna★** is a fitting setting for the **Santuario della Casa.** The sanctuary was begun as a Gothic design in 1468 and continued by the Renaissance architects Giuliano da Maiano, Baccio Pontelli, Giuliano di Sangallo, Francesco di Giorgio Martini, Bramante, Andrea Sansovino and Antonio da Sangallo the Younger. The façade and the three bronze **doors★** are late Renaissance, and the campanile is by Vanvitelli. ▶ There are some notable works inside: the **screen★** of the Santa Casa (which is below the dome) has statues and reliefs executed in the 16C; 15C **frescos★**

the dome of the sacristy of St. Mark (at the end of the r. aisle) and in the sacristy of St. John. ▶ Adjacent to the basilica is the **Sala di Pomarancio**, named after the artist who painted the vault with frescos of episodes from the life of Mary, Prophets and Sybils★ (1610). ▶ The **Museo Pinacoteca** (museum and art gallery) is in the Palazzo Apostolico *(9 a.m.-1 p.m. and 3-6 p.m., closed Fri, Aug 15, Christmas, Easter and 1 May);* displays include **paintings★** by Lotto and a collection of pharmaceutical **ceramics★.** ⊓

Practical information _____

ℹ v. G.Solari 3, ☎ 977139.

Hotels:
★★★ *Bellevue & Marchigiano,* p. Squarcia 14, ☎ 970165, 70 rm ℗ ≼ ▒ ⅙ 65,000.
★★★ **Giardinetto,** corso Boccalini 10, ☎ 977135, 76 rm ℗ 51,000; bkf:8,000.

Restaurant:
◆◆◆ *Orlando Barabani,* v. Villa Costantina 91, ☎ 977696, closed Wed, Jul and Christmas. Regional and Italian cuisine: noodles in venison stew, pigeon, 20/30,000.

Recommended
Archery: *Compagnia Arcieri Loreto,* v. Gatti 15, ☎ 977880.
Events: *Rassegna Internazionale di Cappelle Musicali* (concerts of sacred music, Easter week, ☎ 970414); *folk festival* (Jul).
Tennis: v. Gatti, ☎ 976353.

MACERATA

Ancona 49, Roma 245, Milan 475 km
Pop. 43,703 ✉ 62100 ☎ 0733   D2-3
See map on page 440.

Macerata is a town that cultivates the land, producing gardens and flowers. The surrounding area is fertile, rich and well-cultivated, and Macerata has a lordly elegance. Large sections of the 16C town walls have survived alongside remains of the earlier Roman city of *Helvia Ricina.*

▶ At the heart of the town is the p. della Libertà (A2), with the **Palazzo del Comune,** in the atrium and courtyard of which are Roman statues and tombstones from *Helvia Ricina;* the Renaissance **Loggia dei Mercanti** (1505); the **Palazzo della Prefettura,** 16C with parts of a 13C building and a fine portal dating from 1509. Opposite the Palazzo Comunale is the **University,** founded in 1540, and next to this the Baroque church of **S. Paolo.** At the end of the square are the 18C Teatro Comunale Rossi and the 16C **Torre dell'Orologio** (clock tower). Nearby, in the corso Matteotti (A2), are the 16C Palazzo Mozzi and Palazzo Rotelli-Lazzarini. ▶ The **Duomo** (A3) is an 18C building with incomplete façade, and 15C campanile. ▶ In the same square is the 18C sanctuary of the **Madonna della Misericordia,** decorated with stucco, marble, intaglio, paintings and wrought iron. ▶ S of the Duomo, by the old walls, is the **Sferisterio** (arena) (A-B3); *ask the caretaker* ☎ *40735)* built 1820-30 for the game of *pallone.* ▶ At v. Pantaleoni 4 (B3) is the **Museo Tipologico del Presepio** (crèches; *ask in advance* ☎ *49035;* 4,000 exhibits from the 18C to the present day). ▶ The **Pinacoteca Civica** (B2; *9 a.m.-1 p.m., in Jul and Aug also 5-7 p.m.; closed Mon)* includes paintings from the 14C-19C; attached to it are the **Museo Civico,** with Piceni and Roman finds and a good local collection (including photographs), and the **Museo delle Carrozze** (carriages). On the first floor of the same building, in frescoed 18C rooms, are the **Biblioteca Comunale,** with a fine collection of early printed books (incunabula) and illuminated manuscripts and the **Museo Marchigiano del Risorgimento e della Resistenza** (Marche Museum of the Risorgimento and the Resistance).

Environs

▶ About 4 km NW is **Villa Potenza,** on the site of *Helvia Ricina,* the Roman town destroyed by the Visigoths in the 5C-6C; the surviving inhabitants may have founded Recanati and Macerata; extensive ruins of the 2C AD Roman theatre. ▶ Not far beyond the Porta Picena (B3; *2 km)* is the 16C sanctuary of **S. Maria delle Vergini,** on a Greek cross plan with octagonal dome. Proceeding SE, the road descends to the SS 485. Turning l. and l. again and continuing straight for about 8 km is the Romanesque church of **S. Claudio al Chienti★** (12C), in fact two churches one above the other. ▶ 10 km down the SS 78 in the direction of Ascoli Piceno, just before the junction for Urbisaglia, is the interesting 12C abbey of **Chiaravalle di Fiastra;** the church, with frescos (15C-17C) and a 15C cloister have survived. Nearby are remains of the Roman *Urbs Salvia* (1C BC) with an impressive **amphitheatre** (2C AD). ⊓

Practical information _____

ℹ p. della Libertà 12 (A2), ☎ 45807; v. Garibaldi 87 (A1; head office), ☎ 40449.
🚌 (C3), ☎ 424016.
🚈 Giardini Diaz (A-B1).

Hotels:
★★★ **Centrale,** v. Armaroli 98 (A2 a), ☎ 47276, 21 rm ℗ No restaurant, 55,000.
★★★ **MotelAgip,** v. Roma 149/B, ☎ 34248, 51 rm ℗ ⅋ 100,000.
★★★ **Piaggia,** v. S. Maria della Porta 18 (A-B2 b), ☎ 40387, 25 rm ℗ ⅋ No restaurant, 52,000.
★★★ **Roganti,** at Montecassiano *(5 km N),* SS 77 at 97-km marker, ☎ 598639, 61 rm ℗ ▒ ⅋ 60,000; bkf: 5,000.

Restaurant:
● ◆◆◆ *Secondo,* v. Pescharia Vecchia 26 (A3 c), ☎ 44912, closed Mon and Aug. Rustic style, with massive tables. Regional and Italian cuisine: green ravioli with cream of mushroom, ricotta crêpes, 25/35,000.

Recommended
Archery: *Compagnia Arcieri del Melograno,* at Pollenza *(11 km SW),* v. Cantagallo 1/A, ☎ 519477.
Bowling: v. Giuliozzi 17/A, ☎ 31547.
Clay pigeon shooting: at Corridonia *(10 km SE),* v. Crocifisso, ☎ 433695.
Events: *opera season* in the Sferisterio arena (Jul), inquiries, ☎ 40735.
Horseback riding: *Centro Equestre Casal Lornano,* at Lornano (associate of *ANTE*).
Horse racing: *Ippodromo San Paolo,* at Montegiorgio *(30 km SE),* Piane di Montegiorgio, ☎ 0734/68727.
Nature park: *Riserva dell'Abbazia di Fiastra (12 km SW),* managed by *WWF,* ☎ 40735.
Swimming: v. Don Bosco 34, ☎ 49961.
Technical tourism: visits to *Borgani* brass and wind instrument workshops, v. Ancona 7, ☎ 425585 (reserve in advance); visits to *Salva* wicker and straw workshops, at Mogliano *(20 km S),* contrada Santa Caterina 2, ☎ 556460.

MAROTTA

Pesaro 25, Ancona 37, Rome 306 km
Pop. 4,804 ✉ 61035 ☎ 0721   C1

Marotta is a resort with a long, narrow beach, part of Fano (→) and Mondolfo. **Mondolfo** *(6 km inland)* is set on a hill with fine views and has a medieval centre within double walls rebuilt in the 16C; an interesting church of **S. Agostino** with 13C foundations, rebuilt in the 16C. ⊓

Practical information _____

MAROTTA
≋

MACERATA

1:11.000 (1cm=110m)
0   100   200 m

© SERVIZIO CARTOGRAFICO DEL TOURING CLUB ITALIANO, MILANO

ⓘ v. Carducci, ☎ 96591 (seasonal).

Hotels:
★★★ *Imperial*, v. Fa di Bruno 119, ☎ 96145, 36 rm Ⓟ ⚱
❀ closed 1 Oct-19 May, 51,000.
★★★ *Levante*, lungomare Colombo, ☎ 96647, 36 rm ⚱
45,000; bkf: 5,500.
★★ *Caravel*, v. Fa di Bruno 135, ☎ 96670, 32 rm Ⓟ ⚱
closed 1 Oct-14 May, 40,000.

Environs

MONDOLFO, ✉ 61037, ☎ 0721, 6 km SW.

Recommended
Archery: *Compagnia Arcieri della Rovere*, v. Gramsci
52.

MATELICA

Macerata 45, Ancona 77, Rome 225 km
Pop. 10,082 ✉ 62024 ☎ 0737   C3

Matelica is set on a spur in the upper Esino Valley. Its layout is medieval, and parts of the town
walls as well as palazzi and churches have survived
from various periods. The town was once famous
for wool processing and tanning. Matelica now thrives on a variety of light industries.

▶ In the central p. Enrico Mattei, with a 17C fountain, are
the 15C **Palazzo Ottoni**, the **Palazzo Pretorio**, dating from
1270, with the **Torre Civica** (tower), the 16C **Loggia degli
Ottoni**, the **Palazzo Salta** and the Baroque **chiesa del
Suffragio**. ▶ Not far away is the **cathedral**, with campanile dating from 1474. The church of **S. Francesco** has

a 15C triptych by Gentile da Fabriano, as well as several other noteworthy paintings. ▶ The **Museo Piersanti**
*(10 a.m.-12 noon and 5-7 p.m. in summer; 4-6 p.m. in win-
ter; closed Mon)* at v. Umberto I 11 has an exceptional
collection of 15C Marche paintings; together with tapestries, carpets, furniture and silver to designs by the followers of Raphael, Barocci and Guercino.   □

Practical information _____

ⓘ p. E. Mattei 3, ☎ 85671.

Hotel:
★★★ *MotelAgip*, SS 256 at the 29-km marker, ☎ 84781,
16 rm Ⓟ 53,500.

Recommended
Horseback riding: *Centro Ippico Mucucci*, at Passo
Gabella, ☎ 804722 (associate of *ANTE*).
Motocross: *Libana Ripetti* track, at Esanatoglia *(6 km W)*,
☎ 89330; *Moto Club Esanatoglia*, v. Battisti 3, ☎ 89108.

METAURO VALLEY

From Fano to Urbino *(105 km, 1 day; map 1)*

The Metauro River flows into the sea a little SE of
Fano, at Madonna del Ponte; the name of the river is
remembered for the battle here in 207 BC when the
Carthaginian general Hasdrubal was defeated and
killed. This itinerary is of great scenic interest, particularly in the spectacular Furlo gorge, and fascinating
culturally because of the historic sites through which
it passes.

1. Metauro Valley

▶ From Fano (→) the route climbs the Metauro valley, following the Roman via Flaminia passing through countryside that is at first gentle but that becomes harsher higher in the Apennines. ▶ Beyond **Fossombrone** (→) the route passes into the narrow Candigliano valley and the **Furlo gorge★**; this section is made easier by the tunnel (Latin *forulus;* Furlo is a corruption of this) built by the Emperor Vespasian in 76-77 AD (inscription above NE entrance). ▶ Passing the church of **S. Vincenzo al Furlo**, part of an 8C abbey, rebuilt 1271, the route continues to **Acqualagna**, one of the major centres for white truffles. ▶ It continues across some of the wildest and most beautiful gorges in the Apennines, past the ancient abbey of Naro on the l. ▶ Beyond an extremely narrow gorge★ *(2 km long)* bristling with rocky pinnacles, the road emerges in the Pióbbico valley. ▶ **Pióbbico** is dominated by the **Castello Brancaleoni**, built in the 13C and transformed in the 16C into a splendid Renaissance residence; fine view of the medieval village. ▶ From Pióbbico at Apécchio the road follows the course of the Biscubio through an attractive gorge★ *(about 5 km long),* with peaks rising to form one of the most interesting ravines in the central Apennines. ▶ The route touches **Sant'Andrea** (near little Romanesque church of same name is the **cave of S. Ubaldo**; the saint was a bishop of Gubbio who retired to this cave in 1125 where he lived the rest of his life as a hermit) and continues to the medieval town of Apcchio, amid oak and pine woods. ▶ The road returns to the Metauro valley and strikes N across empty hills to the small plateau where **Sant'Angelo in Vado** stands. This Roman town was destroyed by the Goths but rapidly re-established under its present name (in honour of the Archangel Michael and called 'in Vado' because it is near a ford, Latin *vadum*); the historic centre is intact. ▶ The itinerary continues E to **Urbania** (→), then **Fermignano**, with a Roman bridge and medieval tower in its historic centre. There is a fine view over Urbino to the Apennines, and it is possible to go up *(3 km)* to the **Serra Alta**, a wooded hill with tourist centre. ▶ A road with fine views descends to **Urbino** (→). ☐

Practical information

ACQUALAGNA, ✉ 61041, ☎ 0721.

Hotel:
★★★ *Ginestra*, at Furlo, v. Flaminia 7, ☎ 70013, 10 rm Ⓟ ⦿ ⌕ 🖂 ⌕ 48,000; bkf: 5,000.

Recommended
Bowling: v. del Candigliano, ☎ 79231.
♥ gastronomy: white truffles.

FERMIGNANO, ✉ 61033, ☎ 0722.

Hotel:
★★★ *Serra Alta*, at Serra Alta, ☎ 54173, 12 rm Ⓟ ⦿ 🖂 51,000.

PIOBBICO, ✉ 61046, ☎ 0722.

Hotel:
★★★ *Trota Blu*, v. S. Maria 15, ☎ 9209, 49 rm Ⓟ ⦿ closed Nov, 43,000; bkf: 5,000.

SANT'ANGELO IN VADO, ✉ 61048, ☎ 0722.

Restaurant:
♦ *Lucia*, v. Nazionale Sud, ☎ 8245, closed Tue and 20 Sep-10 Oct. Regional cuisine: cannelloni (with white truffles in season), bacon in porchetta, 20/40,000.

II MONTEFELTRO

From Urbino *(161 km, 1 day; map 2)*

The broad, green vistas of Montefeltro sweep right down to Urbino, dominated by the massif of Monte Carpegna, the highest peak. This historic region (the boundaries do not correspond to the present administrative area) has many interesting features apart from its varied countryside scattered with fortified villages and castles.

▶ After leaving **Urbino** (→) the road winds among cultivated fields to the Foglia valley at **Schieti**. ▶ It then climbs to **Sassocorvaro** dominated by the unusual ship-shaped **Rocca degli Ubaldini** *(Jun-Sep 9:30 a.m.-12:30 p.m. and 3:30-6:30 p.m.; closed Mon; in other months apply to the Comune* ☎ *0722/76148).* ▶ **Macerata Feltria** has a medieval core set on a crag above a plateau (remains of walls), with a modern area below (*Crucifixion* by Carlo di Camerino, 1396, in the parish church). ▶ A road with interesting views, always in sight of the flat peak of the Carpegna, connects the Foglia and Conca valleys to reach **Monte Cerignone** (1,732 ft) at the foot of Monte Faggiola. ▶ **Villagrande** (3,002 ft) is protected by a rocky crag on which are the ruins of the **Castello di Montecpiolo**. ▶ There follows a rapid descent through pleasantly rolling countryside, past the church of the **Madonna di Pugliano** and arriving, with magnificent views of Verucchio and San Marino, at **San Leo** (→). ▶ At **Villanova** the road enters the Marecchia valley, which climbs via **Secchiano** to **Novafeltria**. ▶ From here a detour of 12.2 km along a road with magnificent views leads to **Sant'Agata Feltria**, with the **Rocca Fregoso**, an impressive piece of military architecture by Francesco di Giorgio Martini. From Novafeltria again the route climbs to **Pennabilli**, in a valley between two rocky peaks. On one of these is a ruined Malatesta fortress; on the other the historic centre of Pennabilli, with the church of S. Agostino (15C-17C) and the **Museo Diocesano** *(inquire in the Curia or the Seminario).* ▶ **Carpegna** is on the S slopes of the wooded mountain of the same name. In the centre is the Renaissance Palazzo Carpegna; the little church of S. Sisto, by the cemetery, has a Romanesque crypt. From the summit of **Carpegna** (4,642 ft), reached by a forest road open to cars for the first 3 km only, there is a superb

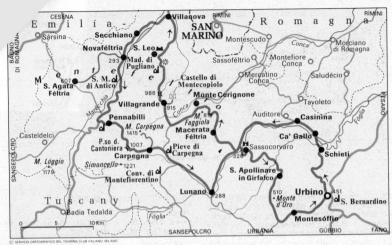

2. Il Montefeltro

© SERVIZIO CARTOGRAFICO DEL TOURING CLUB ITALIANO, MILANO

view★. ▶ The 14C **Pieve di Campagna** (parish church) is on the Lunano road. ▶ From Lunano, which is again in the Foglia valley, the road returns to **Sassocorvaro** (→) and then runs between gentle hills via **Montesoffio** back to **Urbino** (→). □

Practical information

CARPEGNA, ✉ 61021, ☎ 0722.
ℹ p. dei Conti 1, ☎ 77153.

Hotels:
★★ *Ulisse,* v. Amaducci 16, ☎ 77119, 39 rm Ⓟ ♿ 40,000; bkf: 5,000.
★ *Onelia,* v. Amaducci 42/C, ☎ 77175, 16 rm ♨ ⚄ closed 16 Oct-30 Apr, 35,000.

⚐ ★★ *Paradiso,* at Troticoltura, v. Paradiso, ☎ 77122 (all year).

PENNABILLI, ✉ 61016, ☎ 0541.

Hotel:
★★ *Parco,* v. Marconi 14, ☎ 918446, 22 rm Ⓟ ⚄ ♨ closed 6 Nov-31 Mar and Christmas, 38,000; bkf: 3,000.

Recommended
Events: *Mostra Mercato Nazionale dell'Antiquariato* (antiques fair and show), ☎ 918534 (Jun-Jul).

MORRO D'ALBA

Ancona 29, Rome 272 km
Pop. 1,770 ✉ 60030 ☎ 0731   C2

This is a village with a small but fascinating old centre, enclosed within 15C **walls★**, with arcaded houses on the slope above them. There are lookout points on the six pentagonal towers. □

OFFIDA

Ascoli Piceno 23, Ancona 110, Rome 214 km
Pop. 5,448 ✉ 63035 ☎ 0736   D4

Offida lies on the watershed between Tesino and Tronto, at the centre of a broad hilly strip of well-cultivated land. It is noted for vineyards and bobbin-lace manufacture.

▶ Parts of the **walls** (14C-15C) and traces of a 15C **Rocca**, a small rectangular fortress with two cylindrical towers, have survived. ▶ The 15C **Palazzo Comunale★** (14C tower) faces the triangular p. Vittorio Emanuele II. The Palazzo Comunale houses the **Museo Civico Archeologico** *(10 a.m.-12:30 p.m. and 3-8 p.m. in summer; other seasons inquire at museum).* ▶ The church of **S. Maria della Rocca** stands on a hillock; it is an impressive 14C Romanesque-Gothic building, with 14C frescos. □

Practical information

ℹ v. Roma 20.

OSIMO

Ancona 18, Rome 279 km
Pop. 26,402 ✉ 60027 ☎ 071   D2

Osimo, between the rivers Aspio and Musone, stands on a hill with views over the sea and the upper Musone valley. Osimo began as the Roman town of *Auximum.*

▶ The **Palazzo Comunale,** which dates from the second half of the 17C, features Roman statues and a 15C altarpiece by A. and B. Vivarini. ▶ The **Duomo** was first built in the 8C and rebuilt in the 13C, but has been frequently remodeled over the centuries. ▶ In the adjacent **baptistery** *(apply to the sacristan)* are bronze fonts★ dating from 1627. ▶ The sanctuary of **S. Giuseppe da Copertino** has an apse from the 14C building; the interior is 18C. ▶ Below the E side of the wall the Roman ruins of the **Fonte Magna** can be seen. ▶ The gardens in the p. Gramsci offer a magnificent **view★** from the Titano to the Sibillini, including Càtria, Cingoli, the Gran Sasso and the sea. □

Practical information

ℹ v. Cinque Torri, ☎ 72440.

Hotel:
★★★ *Fonte,* v. Fontemagna 117, ☎ 714767, 40 rm Ⓟ ⚄ 60,000; bkf: 4,000.

Recommended
Tennis: v. Olimpia, ☎ 714562.

OSTRA

Ancona 40, Rome 279 km
Pop. 5,910 ⊠ 60010 ☎ 071   C2

Ostra, high above the Misa valley, is largely surrounded by 14C-15C walls reinforced with towers; the town centre is still medieval in appearance. In the piazza is the **Torre Civica**, 15C in plan. On the way into the village, the 18C santuario della **Madonna della Rosa** contains numerous ex-voto offerings, including Turkish banners.   □

Practical information —————————

Hotel:
★★★ *Cantinella,* v. Matteotti 44, ☎ 68081, 21 rm P ⚱
❦ 35,000; bkf: 2,000.

⚔ *Ostrense,* v. Matteotti 47, 40 pl, ☎ 68106.

Recommended
Cycling: *G.S. Pro Loco Ostra,* v. Don Minzoni 1, ☎ 68508.
Wines: visits to the *Vinicola Colli Marchigiani cellar,* at Pianello, SS Arceviese at 12-km marker, ☎ 688030.

OSTRA VETERE

Ancona 47, Rome 282 km
Pop. 3,481 ⊠ 60010 ☎ 071   C2

Ostra Vetere is a picturesque medieval village, with terraces linked by pathways and flights of steps, on a hill between the Misa valley and that of its tributary, the Nevola. Fine buildings include the church of **S. Severo,** with 13C Romanesque portal, the **Palazzo De Poccianibus** (15C) and the medieval **Porta Pesa** in the town walls.   □

Practical information —————————

Recommended
Wines: visits to *Fratelli Bucci cellars,* v. Cona 30, ☎ 96179 (Verdicchio wine; reserve in advance).

PERGOLA

Pesaro 60, Ancona 65, Rome 251 km
Pop. 7,708 ⊠ 61045 ☎ 0721   B2

This medieval town, at the confluence of the Cinisco and Cesano rivers, is in sight of the mountain ranges culminating in the Monte Cátria. The **Duomo** has a 15C Gothic reliquary and a 14C painting of the Crucifixion. Other interesting churches are the Gothic **S. Francesco** and **S. Giacomo,** 13C in origin with a Baroque interior.

Environs

▶ **Frontone** *(12 km SW)* has a Malatesta **Rocca** (keep) which has been partly restored. ▶ The **10C monastery Fonte Avellana** *(18 km SW)* on the slopes of Monte Cátria, set in deep forest, was founded by S. Romualdo *c.* 980 and rebuilt several times between 1050 and the first decades of the 14C. Dante stayed here. The Romanesque-Gothic **church** is built over an 11C crypt. The S. Pier Damiani hall, the cloister and the chapterhouse are open to visitors; the writing desk at which classical texts were copied is also on display. A good road leads *(14 km)* up to the hermitage on the peak of **Monte Cátria** (5,580 ft), from which there is a magnificent view★.   □

Practical information —————————

PERGOLA
ⓘ corso Matteotti 63, ☎ 774496.

Recommended
Motocross: p. G. Fulvi, ☎ 778274.

Environs

FRONTONE, ⊠ 61040, ☎ 0721, 12 km SW.
⚐ cable car, ski lifts, downhill skiing, instruction.
ⓘ p. Municipio, ☎ 786107.

PESARO*

Ancona 60, Rome 310, Milan 360 km
Pop. 90,667 ⊠ 61100 ☎ 0721   D2-3

Pesaro grew up on either side of the estuary at the mouth of the river Foglia, with the S. Bartolo hills to the NW and the Ardizio hills in the SE. Its elegant buildings and layout reflect a grand past (the city was ruled by the Malatestas, the Sforzas and the Della Rovere).

▶ The **old town** retains some of its 16C character. In the central **piazza del Popolo** (D2-3, with its 17C **Fontana dei Tritoni,** is the 15C **Palazzo Ducale★** (D2), built by Alessandro Sforza. The Renaissance building is set around a splendid courtyard. Some of the lavishly decorated rooms are open to the public *(guided tour, Thu 4:30 p.m.).* ▶ Nearby is the 13C **Santuario della Madonna delle Grazie** (D3) with fine Gothic portal and 14C-15C frescos. ▶ Behind the church is the **Rocca Costanza** (D3), a splendid example of 15C military architecture, once used as a prison. ▶ The **cathedral** (D3) has a plain 13C façade with Gothic portal. ▶ In the adjacent **birthplace of the composer Rossini** is a museum of posters, printed matter and portraits associated with the composer *(10 a.m.-12 noon and 4-6 p.m. Apr-Oct; Sun and hols 10 a.m.-12 noon).* ▶ In the Palazzo Toschi-Mosca (D-C3) are the **Musei Civici★,** which includes the Pinacoteca (art gallery) and the Museo delle Ceramiche *(9 a.m.-12:30 p.m. and 4-7 p.m. or 2-4:30 p.m. in winter; closed Sun p.m. and Mon a.m.).* The **Pinacoteca** has works by Venetian, Tuscan and Bolognese artists, including Giovanni Bellini's *Coronation of the Virgin Mary★★ and a Head of John the Baptist★* by Marco Zoppo. The **Museo delle Ceramiche** is one of the most important in Italy for its exhibits from the most important Renaissance and Baroque workshops (Urbino, Castel Durante, Pesaro, Faenza, Derita, Castelli, Gubbio). ▶ The church of **S. Agostino** (C2) has a lavish Venetian-Gothic portal dating from 1413 and, inside, 15C-16C wood carving. ▶ Nearby, the **chiesetta del Nome di Dio** (D2) has a fine interior with 17C decorations *(Thu 10 a.m.-12 noon, apply to the caretaker).* ▶ The **Museo Archeologico Oliveriano** *(D2; weekdays 4-7 p.m.; winter on request, weekdays 9:30 a.m.-12:30 p.m., apply at the library)* displays artifacts from prehistoric tombs in Pesaro and the Novilara necropolises; bronzes (including ornaments from a Greek vase★); coins; inscriptions; vases, glass and ivories. ▶ Beside the museum, in the Palazzo Machirelli, is the **Conservatorio Rossini** (D2), founded with a bequest from the composer. ▶ The **Marina** is reached from the town centre by the p. della Repubblica (D3). The promenades that run along 3 km of sandy beach start in the piazzale della Libertà.

Environs

▶ A road with magnificent views leads to Gabicce, and from there a track through the pine forests goes on *(5.6 km)* to the **Imperiale★,** a residence in a spacious park built by Alessandro Sforza (1469-72) and later enlarged by the Della Rovere *(not open to the public).* ▶ **Novilara** *(7 km S)* is a village on a vine-covered hill, renowned for its Piceni necropolises (displayed in the Museo Oliveriano in Pesaro); walls and ruins of a Della Rovere castle (16C-17C).   □

Practical information —————————
≋

v. Mazzolari 4 (D3), ☎ 30258; v. Rossini 41 (D3), ☎ 63690; p. della Libertà (C3), ☎ 69341.

(E1), ☎ 3309.

p. Matteotti (D3), ☎ 34768.

Car rental: *Avis*, p. degli Innocenti 29, ☎ 61893.

Hotels:

★★★★ *Savoy,* v. Repubblica 22 (C3 a), ☎ 67440, 54 rm P ⌂ ⚏ 90,000; bkf: 9,000.

★★★★ *Vittoria,* p. Libertà 2 (C3 b), ☎ 34343, 27 rm P ⌂ 150,000; bkf: 10,000.

★★★ *Atlantic,* v. Trieste 365 (B2 c), ☎ 61911, 40 rm P ⌂ closed 21 Sep-14 May, 52,000; bkf: 6,000.

★★★ *Baltic,* v. Trieste 36 (D4 d), ☎ 67150, 55 rm P closed Oct-9 May, 52,000; bkf: 4,000.

★★★ *Bussola,* lungomare Sauro 43 (D4 e), ☎ 64937, 24 rm ⌖ closed Oct-Apr, 50,000; bkf: 5,000.

★★★ *Diplomatic,* v. Parigi 2, ☎ 21677, 46 rm P ⌂ ⌖ ☒ closed 16 Sep-9 Jun, 50,000.

★★★ *Due Pavoni,* v. Fiume 79 (B2 f), ☎ 69017; 48 rm P ⚏ ⌖ 55,000; bkf: 5,000.

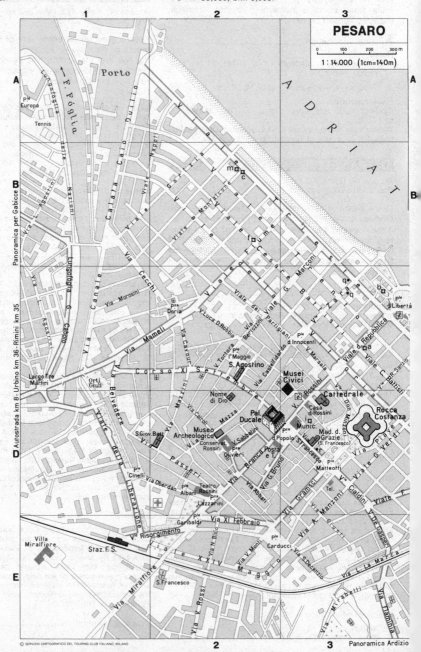

PESARO

0   100   200   300 m
1:14.000 (1cm=140m)

© SERVIZIO CARTOGRAFICO DEL TOURING CLUB ITALIANO, MILANO

Panoramica Ardizio

★★★ *Excelsior*, v. Marco Polo 35 (C4 g), ☎ 32720, 80 rm ⊡ Pens. Closed 11 Oct-31 Mar, 40,000.
★★★ *Flying*, v. Verdi 129 (C4 h), ☎ 69219, 27 rm Ⓟ closed Oct-Mar, 51,000; bkf: 6,000.
★★★ *Mamiani*, largo Mamiani 24 (D3 i), ☎ 35541, 40 rm Ⓟ ◿ ⊗ No restaurant, 54,000; bkf: 6,000.
★★★ *Mediterraneo Ricci*, v. Trieste 199 (C4 1), ☎ 31556, 42 rm Ⓟ ⚑ closed 1 Dec-15 Jan, 55,000; bkf: 6,000.
★★★ *Nettuno*, v. Trieste 367 (B1 m), ☎ 61879, 65 rm Ⓟ ⚑ ᵭ ⊡ closed Oct-Apr, 51,000; bkf: 8,000.
★★★ *President's*, lungomare Sauro 33 (C4 n), ☎ 32976, 50 rm Ⓟ closed Oct-Apr, 51,000; bkf: 6,000.
★★★ *Spiaggia*, v. Trieste 76 (D4 p), ☎ 32516, 74 rm Ⓟ ⚑ ⊡ closed 1 Oct-14 May, 50,000; bkf: 6,000.

Restaurants:
● ♦♦♦ *Carlo*, v. Trieste 265 (C3 q), ☎ 31453, closed 11 Oct-9 May. Romantic service in garden on summer evenings. Seafood: polenta with seafood, stew pesarese, 20/45,000.

● ♦♦♦ *Scudiero*, v. Baldassini 2 (D3 r), ☎ 64107, closed Thu and Jul. Elegant and rustic beneath splendid 15C vaults of Palazzo Baldassini. Mixed regional cuisine: white risotto with clams, meat dishes, truffles (in season), 35/50,000.
♦♦♦ *Nuovo Carlo*, v. Zara 54 (C3 q), ☎ 68984, closed Mon and Nov-Feb. Mixed regional cuisine: duck with dumplings, sole marinara rosa, 20/45,000.

4

Gioachino Rossini was born here

The composer's birthplace (brick façade, arched doorway and tiny balcony with straight rails) is at 34 in the street quite properly called G.Rossini. The plaque says that he was born on 29 February 1792, a leap year, and spells his first name with double c, though Rossini himself preferred to spell it with one. His father was a horn player in bands and orchestras and also a 'public trumpeter' (town crier). His mother was a singer in provincial opera houses. Rossini composed his first opera, La Cambiale di Matrimonio, at the age of eighteen to fill a gap in the programme for the Teatro San Moisé in Venice. The work was performed on 3 November 1810 and repeated thirty times; Rossini was paid 40 scudi. Only six years later, Duke Francesco Sforza Cesarini offered the young composer 400 scudi for Almaviva Ossia l'Inutile Precauzione, which became The Barber of Seville (premiered at the Teatro di Torre Argentina in Rome). When the philosopher Hegel heard it in Vienna he wrote, 'I have listened to the Barber for a second time and I fear that my taste must be somewhat depraved, because this Figaro seems more attractive to me than Mozart's.' William Tell, produced on 3 August 1829 at the Paris Opéra, was the last music Rossini wrote for the theatre. He lived for thirty-nine more years and died in Paris. He was buried in the cemetery of Père Lachaise, next to Bellini and Chopin. In 1887 his remains were taken to the church of S. Croce in Florence, to lie among those of the great men of Italy.

⚑ ★★★ *Campo Norina*, at Fosso Sejore, v. Marina Ardizia 181, 160 pl, ☎ 55792; ★★ *Marinella*, at Fosse Sejore, SS 16 at 244-km marker, ☎ 55795; ★★ *Panorama*, at Fiorenzuola di Focara, strada Panoramica, 150 pl, ☎ 208145.

Recommended
Baseball: courts at v. Nanterre and v. Strasburgo, ☎ 451251; *Baseball Club*, v. Battisti 155, ☎ 63413.
Cycling: *G.S. Brancorsini*, v. Lombardia 19.
Events: *Esposizione Marche Musicali e Festival Nazionale dei Gruppi d'Arte Drammatica* (Apr-May; music and drama); *Mostra del Mobile* (May; furniture); *Mostra Internazionale del Nuovo Cinema* (Jun; new films); *Rossini Opera Festival* (Aug-Sep).
Flying club: *Fano airport*, ☎ 82491.
Sailing school: *Lega Navale*, v. Fra i Due Porti 2, ☎ 33964.
Skating: v. Toscanini, ☎ 452232.
Skindiving: *Centro Ricerche Attività Subacquee*, v. Canale 16.
Sports hall: v. Partigiani 22, ☎ 32636.
Swimming pools: *Baia Flaminia*, ☎ 22841 (also tennis courts); v. della Vittoria, ☎ 32735; v. Togliatti, ☎ 452388.
Technical tourism: beaten and enameled copper, jewelry: visits to *Studio Cellini*, Villa Fastiggi, v. Montanelli 68, ☎ 604466 (reserve in advance).
Water sports: *Club Nautico*, v. Fra i Due Porte 2, ☎ 33964.
Youth Hostel: *Ostello Ardizio*, strada Panoramica dell'Ardizio, ☎ 55798.

PORTO POTENZA PICENA

Macerata 34, Ancona 40, Rome 277 km
Pop. 5,988 ⊠ 62016 ☎ 0733   D2

Porto Potenza Picena is a small seaside resort between the mouths of the Potenza and Chienti

4

rivers. Near the remains of the 16C fortress built against raids by barbarian pirates is the modern parish church, in which is displayed a painting by Pomarancio. 8 km inland, on a hill, stands **Potenza Picena**, with some fine buildings within its medieval walls. □

Practical information _____

Recommended
Bowling: v. Alvata, ☎ 688034.

PORTO RECANATI

Macerata 29, Ancona 30, Rome 287 km
Pop. 7,673 ⊠ 62017 ☎ 071　　　　　　　　D2

Porto Recanati is a seaside resort N of the mouth of the Potenza, within sight of the Cnero promontory. The little town is built along the line of the sea, with fine streets and a **castle** in good condition. The castle was built in the 15C as a defense against the pirates who preyed on the coast. It is a good departure point for Loreto (→) and Recanati (→). □

Practical information _____

≋
ⓘ corso Matteotti 111, ☎ 9799084.

Hotels:
★★★ **Bianchi Nicola,** p. Bracondi 1, ☎ 9799016, 17 rm Ⓟ closed Christmas-Feb, 48,000; bkf: 4,000.
★★★ **Bianchi Vincenzo e Grattacielo,** v. Garibaldi 15, ☎ 9798060, 63 rm ⌖ closed Nov-Feb, 50,000; bkf: 4,000.
★★★ **Brigantino,** v. Scarfiotti 10, ☎ 976686, 66 rm Ⓟ ▣ closed 16 Sep-30 Apr, 45,000; bkf: 5,000.
★★★ **Giannino,** v. Colombo 23, ☎ 9799289, 40 rm Ⓟ closed 15 Dec-15 Jan, 40,000; bkf: 4,000.
★★★ **Mondial, v. Europa 2,** ☎ 9796272, 50 rm Ⓟ ⌖ closed Christmas, 50,000; bkf: 4,000.
▲ ★★★ **Bellamare,** at Lido Scossicci, strada Numana, 549 pl, ☎ 976628; ★★★ **Medusa,** at Lido Scossicci, 580 pl, ☎ 976670.

PORTO SAN GIORGIO

Ascoli Piceno 60, Ancona 62, Rome 252 km
Pop. 15,642 ⊠ 63017 ☎ 0734　　　　　　　D3

Formerly the port of Fermo, now Porto San Giorgio is an active fishing centre. The 13C **Rocca** with towers and an imposing keep has survived. 6 km S is **Torre di Palme,** strikingly set on a hill, with some medieval churches. □

Practical information _____

PORTO SAN GIORGIO
≋
ⓘ v. Oberdan 4, ☎ 4375.

Hotels:
★★★★ **Timone,** v. Kennedy 61, ☎ 49536, 85 rm Ⓟ ⌖ 75,000; bkf: 6,000.
★★★ **Rosa,** lungomare Gramsci 163, ☎ 378485, 23 rm Ⓟ closed Nov-Mar. No restaurant, 54,000.
★★★ **Tritone,** v. S. Martino 26, ☎ 377104, 36 rm Ⓟ ▦ 55,000; bkf: 5,000.
★★ **Riviera,** v. S. Martino 22, ☎ 377004, 33 rm Ⓟ closed Nov-Apr, 42,000; bkf: 5,000.

Restaurants:
♦♦♦ *Davide,* v. Mazzini 102, ☎ 377700, closed Mon except summer, Nov and Christmas. Regional seafood: cicche pirata, Adriatico grill, 18/30,000.
♦ *Cascina,* contrada S. Nicola 13, ☎ 379926, closed Mon and 1-15 Oct. Italian cuisine: pancakes with gratinéed ricotta, pork loin with citrus sauce, 20/30,000.

Recommended
Sailing school: *Lega Navale,* lungomare, ☎ 378705.
Tennis: v. Vittoria, ☎ 4703.

Environs

TORRE DI PALME, ⊠ 63010, ☎ 0734, 6 km S.
⚓ (Jun-Sep), ☎ 53106.

Recanati, Leopardi

Recanati is famous for figs and charcuterie, and for Giacomo Leopardi (b. 1798), poet of suffering and pessimism. His 'wild native city' is in fact a beautiful little town, civilized, and with clear skies; his 'town tower', 13C, crenellated, where 'the hours ring out' is in the central square; his 'ancient tower' of the Passero Solitario is the campanile of the Gothic church of S. Agostino. The Leopardis' 'ancestral palace' faces the road now called Sabato del Villaggio. The palace library, which witnessed much of the poet's anguish and emotion, has a low, frescoed ceiling lined with shelves and books; light is reflected from the windows that open onto the square. The oldest son of Count Monaldo and his wife Adelaide (he was a man of letters, politically a survivor, imprudent in the handling of his fortune; she aware of the necessity of restoring her husband's estates) passed long days in avid study here. Precocious and a gifted linguist, Giacomo Leopardi translated the first book of Horace's Odes at the age of eleven; at twelve he filled an exercise book with twenty Latin dissertations. These manuscripts, in a childish hand, are displayed in the library; its windows look onto the house of 'cheerful, pensive' Silvia, who was in fact Teresa Fattorini, daughter of the family's coachman.

RECANATI

Macerata 21, Ancona 38, Rome 271 km
Pop. 18,860 ⊠ 62019 ☎ 071　　　　　　　D2

The town is spread along a hill in the ridge between the Musone and Potenza valleys and looks out over an expanse of countryside. The landscape features in the work of the poet Giacomo Leopardi, who was born here in 1798. Also born in Recanati was the great tenor Gigli (1890-1957).

▶ The **Palazzo Comunale** is in the central p. Leopardi, dominated by the crenellated **Torre del Borgo** (12C). The Palazzo Comunale houses the **Pinacoteca Civica** (10 a.m.-1 p.m. and 4-7 p.m.; closed Sun p.m. and Mon); among the exhibits are paintings by Lorenzo Lotto (altarpiece★, Annunciation★, Transfiguration). Also in the Palazzo Comunale is the **Museo Beniamino Gigli,** with memorabilia of the singer. ▶ There is a Lotto fresco in the church of **S. Domenico.** ▶ The town's most attractive feature is the **piazzetta del Sabato del Villaggio,** in which stands the 18C **Palazzo Leopardi,** the poet's birthplace, containing his library with memorabilia and manuscripts *(9 a.m.-12 noon; spring-autumn 3-6 p.m., winter*

3-7 p.m.; summer 3-5 p.m.). ▶ Near the cathedral, in the 14C Bishop's Residence (Episcopio), is the **Museo Diocesano** with a fine collection of paintings, sculpture and archaeological finds *(Sun and hols 10:30 a.m.-12:30 p.m.; other days ask the sacristan).* ☐

Practical information _____

ⓘ p. G. Leopardi, ☎ 981242.

Hotel:
★★ *Ginestra,* v. Calcagni 2, ☎ 980355, 27 rm Ⓟ ⌦
closed Jun, 43,000; bkf: 3,000.

Restaurant:
◆ *Cantina di Palazzo Bello,* SS 77, ☎ 9841605. Rustic, with a cool garden and some accommodation. Italian cuisine: cannelloni with cream and peas, pigeon in wine sauce, 20/30,000.

Recommended
Events: *Rassegna Internazionale Giovani Musicisti* (young musicians' festival; Apr); *Fiera di S. Vita* (fair; mid-June); *Celebrazioni Leopardiane* (late Jun).

RIPATRANSONE

Ascoli Piceni 37, Ancona 97, Rome 243 km
Pop. 4,335 ⊠ 63038 ☎ 0735   D3

Ripatrasone spreads along the chain of hills that divides the Menocchia and Tesino Valleys. **Ring walls** reinforced with towers preserve the little town's medieval appearance. There are some notable palazzi, a 16C **cathedral** and the **Museo Civico Archeologico** *(10 a.m.-12 noon and 4-7 p.m.)* in the 17C Palazzo Municipale. In the 17C **Palazzo Bonomi-Gera** are the **Gipsoteca 'Uno Gera'** (plaster casts) and the **Pinacoteca Civica,** with paintings from the 15C to the present day, engravings, drawings by G.B. Piranesi, ceramics and local memorabilia. ☐

Practical information _____

Hotel:
★★ *Piceno,* v. Leopardi 12, ☎ 9418, 28 rm, closed Oct, 40,000.

SAN BENEDETTO DEL TRONTO

Ascoli Piceni 32, Ancona 89, Rome 225 km
Pop. 45,104 ⊠ 63039 ☎ 0735   D3-4

This is one of the major seaside resorts in the central Adriatic and an important **fishing port** with a lively fish market. The old centre consists of the **Castello,** with 14C hexagonal tower, and a number of narrow, twisting streets lined with brick houses. The broad beach is flanked by a magnificent **promenade★** shaded with palms, pines and oleanders, which stretches S for 4 km. Near the fish market is the **Museo Ittico** with fossil finds and an aquarium *(summer 9 a.m.-12 noon and 4-8 p.m.; winter Tue, Thu, Sat and Sun only).* ☐

Practical information _____

≈
ⓘ v. C. Colombo 3/5, ☎ 2237; at Porto d'Ascoli, ☎ 659229; at railway station, ☎ 4436 (both seasonal).

Hotels:
★★★★ *Roxy,* v. Buozzi 6, ☎ 4441, 74 rm Ⓟ ⌂ ♿ ⌦ ⌧
104,000; bkf: 7,000.
★★★★ *Sabbiadoro,* lungomare Marconi 46, ☎ 81911, 64 rm Ⓟ ⌦ Pens. closed 16 Sep-24 May, 60,000.
★★★★ *Solarium,* v. Europa 102, ☎ 81713, 55 rm Ⓟ closed 20 Sep-20 Oct and New Year's Day, 60,000; bkf: 6,000.

★★★ *Girasole,* v. Europa 126, ☎ 82162, 32 rm Ⓟ ⌒⌒
closed 16 Sep-14 May, 50,000; bkf: 4,000.
★★★ *San Giorgio,* v. De Gasperi 36, ☎ 84692, 27 rm Ⓟ
⌦ 45,000; bkf: 3,000.
★★★ *Sydney,* lungomare Marconi, ☎ 81910, 30 rm Ⓟ ⌦
closed 21 Sep-31 May, 45,000; bkf: 4,000.
★★★ *Touring Residence,* v. Curzi 29, ☎ 60647, 20 rm Ⓟ
No restaurant, 51,000; bkf: 5,000.
★★ *Elisabetta,* v. Clotilde di Savoia 10, ☎ 81758, 49 rm
⌦ closed 16 Sep-19 May, 45,000; bkf: 5,000.

Restaurants:
◆◆◆ *Angelici,* v. Piemonte 1, ☎ 84674, closed Mon and 20 Dec-25 Jan. Windows looking onto garden (in which there is open-air service in summer). Regional seafood: seafood risotto, fried food Adriatico, 25/30,000.
◆◆ *Stalla,* v. Marinuccia 35, ☎ 4933, closed Mon. Former stable, on a hill with large terrace overlooking town and sea. Regional cuisine: polenta with sausage, olives all'ascolana, crema fritta, homemade wines, 17/21,000.
◆ *Zodiaco,* lungomare Marconi 1 ☎ 82010, closed Mon and Nov-Feb. On sea front. Regional seafood: pappardelle with fish and basil sauce, guazzetto, 25/35,000.

Recommended
Bowling: v. degli Oleandri, ☎ 60444.
Discothèque: *Atlantide,* v. dei Tigli, ☎ 60632.
Marina: *Circolo Nautico,* ☎ 5615.

Environs

PORTO D'ASCOLI, ⊠ 63037, 4 km S.

Hotels:
★★★★ *Ambassador,* v. Cimarosa 5, ☎ 659443, 63 rm Ⓟ
⌂ ⌦ ⌧ ⌒⌒ closed Oct-Apr, 80,000; bkf: 9,000.
★★★★ *International,* v. Rinascimento 45, ☎ 650241, 50 rm Ⓟ ⌂ ⌧ closed Oct-Apr, 65,000; bkf: 7,000.
★★★ *Panama,* v. Puccini 3, ☎ 659844, 44 rm Ⓟ ⌂ ⌦ ⌧
closed Oct-Apr, 45,000; bkf: 4,000.
★★★ *President,* v. S. Francesco 14, ☎ 650838, 52 rm Ⓟ
⌂ ⌒⌒ closed 16 Sep-24 May, 45,000; bkf: 4,000.

Restaurant:
◆◆ *Mattia,* v. Fratelli Cervi 20, ☎ 659597, closed Mon and Dec. In villa with garden. Seafood: risotto alla marinara, grilled fish, 23/45,000.

Recommended
Bowling: v. Sgattoni, ☎ 657995.
Swimming pool: v. dei Mille, ☎ 650283.

SAN GINESIO

Macerata 31, Ancona 81, Rome 232 km
Pop. 4,151 ⊠ 62026 ☎ 0733   C3

San Ginesio is a walled town in a commanding position on the Fiastrella River. Surrounded by a defensive wall with towers dating from the 14C-15C, San Ginesio is generally medieval in appearance.

▶ Near the Porta Picena is the **Ospedale dei Pellegrini** (pilgrims' hospital), a rustic 13C building with portico and loggia. In the **piazza Gentili** is the **Collegiate Church,** with a Romanesque foundation and late Gothic façade and campanile, the upper part of which was rebuilt to a Baroque design. There are 14C-15C frescos in the church crypt. ▶ A **Museo Pinacoteca** has been established in the former church of S. Sebastiano, behind the apse of the Collegiate Church *(Mon, Wed, Fri 5:30-6:30 p.m.).* ☐

Practical information _____

ⓘ p. A. Gentile, ☎ 666014.

Hotel:
★★ *Miramarche,* v. Trensano 25, ☎ 666243, 27 rm Ⓟ ⌂
⌦ closed 15-30 Oct, 33,000; bkf: 3,000.

SAN LEO

Pesaro 68, Ancona 142, Rome 322 km
Pop. 2,623 ✉ 61018 ☎ 0541   A1

San Leo is a typical medieval Montefeltro town, on an enormous rock mass above steep cliffs overhanging the lower reaches of the Marecchia. The important Romanesque churches and massive fortress make the town centre artistically interesting.

▶ The **parish church** is a pre-Romanesque rustic building dating from the 8C-9C, with 11C additions. The 12C **Duomo** is in the same square, possibly built on the ruins of a Roman temple, with an imposing Romanesque-Gothic interior. The bell tower offers an exceptional view★ down to the coastal towns and the sea. ▶ The **Forte★** (fortress) *(9 a.m.-12 noon and 2-6 p.m. or 7 p.m. in summer)* is set on the highest point of the rock (2,096 ft), in an impregnable position, with majestic cylindrical towers. Machiavelli thought it the finest example he knew of a military fortress. In 1795 Cagliostro died here, in a cell known as *il pozzetto* (the shaft). ▶ Less than 2 km N is the monastery of **S. Igne**, founded by Saint Francis of Assisi in 1213.   ☐

Practical information ―――――――――――

ⓘ p. Dante, ☎ 916231.

Recommended
Horseback riding: *Circolo Ippico Montefeltro,* Maiolo (10 km SW; associate of *ANTE*).

SAN SEVERINO MARCHE

Macerata 26, Ancona 69, Rome 229 km
Pop. 13,114 ✉ 62027 ☎ 0733   C3

This is a picturesque little town in the Potenza Valley, built on the site of Roman *Septempeda,* of which there are reminders in the area. San Severino Marche was the birthplace of the physician and anatomist Bartolomeo Eustachi (1500-74) whose name is commemorated in the tubes he first described between the pharynx and the eardrum. The town is dominated by its old centre *(il Castello)* on the peak of Montenero, from which there is a magnificent view of the surrounding hills.

▶ The modern centre of the town is the arcaded **piazza del Popolo;** in it are the **Palazzo dei Governatori** (16C) and the **Palazzo Servanzi Collio** (16C, with remains of sculpture and Roman inscriptions in the atrium) and the **chiesa della Misericordia,** containing pictures by Pomarancio and frescos by Salimbeni. ▶ The **cathedral** has a Gothic portal in brick dating from 1473 and a Romanesque-Gothic campanile; various works of art inside. ▶ The v. Salimbeni contains some fine palazzi, including, at no. 40, the 15C Palazzo Tacchi-Venturi, which houses the **Museo Archeologico** and the **Pinacoteca** *(9 a.m.-1 p.m. and 4:30-6:30 p.m.; closed Mon and p.m. from Oct-Jun).* The museum contains Roman and Piceni finds, and the art gallery has a fine collection including works by Pinturicchio, Crivelli and the brothers Salimbeni, who were born here. At v. Bigioli 126 is the **Museo della Civiltà Contadina** *(weekdays 8 a.m.-2 p.m.).* ▶ After the Porta Romana the road climbs to the heart of the **Castello,** with some fine buildings. The **Duomo Vecchio,** facing a 14C tower, has a fine façade and 14C campanile; in the interior are a fine inlaid wood choir★ dating from 1483 and the remains of frescos by Salimbeni.   ☐

Practical information ―――――――――――

ⓘ p. del Popolo, ☎ 638414.

Restaurant:
♦ **Due Torre - da Giovanna,** v. S. Francesco 21, ☎ 638347, closed Mon except summer. Near the castle. Regional cuisine: four-vegetable rigatoncini, pasta cubes with garlic, 25/35,000.

Recommended
Events: *Presepio Vivente delle Marche* (living crèche festival in local period costume; in the Castello on Feast of the Epiphany, 6 Jan).
Motocross: *S. Pacifico* track, ☎ 639328, managed by *Moto Club Settempedano,* v. della Mura Orientali, ☎ 638020.

SANT'ELPIDIO A MARE

Ascoli Piceno 77, Ancona 57, Rome 268 km
Pop. 15,158 ✉ 63019 ☎ 0734   D3

Despite its name, Sant'Elpidio a Mare is inland; it stands within its original ring of medieval walls. The late-16C **chiesa della Misericordia** is in the central square. **Porto Sant'Elpidio,** 9 km away, is a seaside resort.   ☐

Practical information ―――――――――――

Recommended
Events: *Re-enactment of historic events in costume,* ☎ 858406 (town hall; Aug).

Environs

PORTO SANT'ELPIDIO, ✉ 63018, ☎ 0734, 9.5 km E.
≋
ⓘ v. Umberto I, ☎ 992198.

Recommended
Sailing school: *Lega Navale,* v. Trieste 18.

SASSOFERRATO

Ancona 72, Rome 234 km
Pop. 7,303 ✉ 60047 ☎ 0732   B2

Sassoferrato is in a harsh, mountainous district at the point where the Sanguirone and the Marena flow into the Sentino. The town consists of a modern low section and a medieval old town high on a hill. It developed in the 11C near the ruins of ancient Umbrian-Roman *Sentinum,* the remains of which can be seen E of the town.

▶ The main building in the low town is the church of **S. Maria del Piano,** rebuilt in the 16C, with a fine brick façade dating from 1618. ▶ The older part of the town is about 2 km away by a steep road flanked with cypresses. Just outside the town is the **Casa Maggiore dei Francescani,** with frescoed cloister, and the Gothic church of **S. Francesco** (13C-14C). The 15C **Palazzo Oliva** is in the central p. Matteotti; the palazzo houses the Biblioteca Comunale and the Istituto Internazionale di Studi Piceni. In the same square is the **Palazzo dei Priori,** dating from the 14C-16C, which houses the **Museo Civico** *(Mar-Jun 9:30 a.m.-12:30 p.m. and 3-6 p.m.; Jul-Sep 9:30 a.m.-12:30 p.m. and 4-7 p.m.).* ▶ In the **Palazzo Montanari,** in the street of the same name, is the **Museo dell'Arte e delle Tradizioni Populari** *(same opening times as the Museo Civico).* The **Galleria d'Arte Contemporanea** has a collection of pictures, sculpture and graphics. ▶ In the church and monastery of S. Chiara are frescos and two Madonnas by G.B. Salvi, known as il Sassoferrato, who was born here in 1609. ▶ About 2 km E of the lower town is the church of **S. Croce,** possibly built in the early 12C, partly with materials recovered from nearby *Sentinum;* fine interior with nave and two aisles with 14C frescos. ☐

Practical information ————————————

ⓘ v. C. Battisti 13, ☎ 95214.

SENIGALLIA

Ancona 28, Rome 297 km
Pop. 40,475 ⊠ 60019 ☎ 071   C1

Senigallia spreads along the coast at the mouth of the River Misa; it is a modern seaside resort. The old town, still partly walled, is inland.

▶ The **piazza del Duca,** with its fine **Fontana dei Leoni** (1596), is dominated by the massive **Rocca** (1480) built to a design by Baccio Pontelli for Giovanni della Rovere; it houses the **Mostra Permanente di Centri Storici delle Marche** (Marche history) and the Centro di Documentazioni e Ricerche (documents and research). In the same square are the **Palazzo del Duca** (16C, former ducal residence) and the 15C **Palazzo Baviera** (noteworthy 16C stucco decoration of 6 rooms on the upper floor with scenes from ancient history, myth and the Bible). ▶ Also of interest in the p. del Foro Annonario are the **Foro** in Neoclassical style (19C) and, in the Lungomisia, the **Portici Ercolani** (18C). ▶ The 16C **Palazzo Mastai** houses the **Museo Pio IX,** with memorabilia of the pope who was born here in 1792, and the **Pinacoteca d'Arte Sacra** *(weekdays, Jun-Sep 10 a.m.-12 noon and 4-7 p.m.).* ▶ 3 km away, on the cemetery hill, is the Renaissance church of **S. Maria delle Grazie,** dating from 1491; there is a Madonna and Saints by Perugino in the interior (1489). The adjacent monastery, with two elegant cloisters, houses the **Centro di Ricerca, Studio e Documentazione sulla Storia dell'Agricoltura e dell'Ambiente Rurale delle Marche** (agricultural and rural museum; Oct-May 9 a.m.-12 noon; Jul-mid-Sep 9 a.m.-12 noon and 4-7:30 p.m.).

Practical information ————————————

≋
ⓘ p. Morandi, palazzo del Turismo, ☎ 62150.

Hotels:
★★★★ *G.H. Excelsior,* lungomare Alighieri 150, ☎ 61491, 89 rm Ⓟ ▥ closed Oct-Apr, 75,000; bkf: 6,000.
★★★★ *Ritz,* lungomare Alighieri 142, ☎ 63563, 150 rm Ⓟ ఉ ✑ ▭ ⁓ closed 21 Sep-May, 80,000; bkf: 6,000.
★★★ *Baltic,* lungomare Alighieri 66, ☎ 63229, 70 rm Ⓟ closed 21 Sep-24 May, 60,000; bkf: 4,000.
★★★ *City,* lungomare Alighieri 12, ☎ 63464, 60 rm ఉ 65,000; bkf: 5,000.
★★★ *Cristallo,* lungomare Alighieri 2, ☎ 62919, 60 rm Ⓟ ▥ closed Oct-May, 60,000; bkf: 4,000.
★★★ *Diana,* lungomare Leonardo da Vinci 81/A, ☎ 62698, 63 rm Ⓟ ▥ ✑ closed 21 Sep-19 May, 44,000; bkf: 5,000.
★★★ *Europa,* lungomare Alighieri 110, ☎ 63800, 60 rm, closed 11 Sep-31 May, 65,000; bkf: 5,000.
★★★ *International,* lungomare Mameli 44, ☎ 60549, 60 rm Ⓟ ▥ ✑ closed Oct-Mar, 53,500; bkf: 5,000.
★★★ *Metropol,* lungomare Leonardo da Vinci 11, ☎ 65576, 65 rm Ⓟ ▭ ⁓ closed 21 Sep-21 May, 66,000; bkf: 9,000.
★★★ *Palace,* p. della Libertà 7, ☎ 63453, 57 rm, closed Nov, 65,000; bkf: 5,000.

Restaurant:
♦♦ *Albatros Riccardone's,* v. Rieti 69, ☎ 64762, closed Mon in winter and Nov-Dec. Mixed regional cuisine: tagliolini bianco mare, baked turbot, 35/45,000.

⚓ ★★★★ *Liana,* lungomare Leonardo da Vinci 54, ☎ 62881; ★★★★ *Summerland,* v. Podesti 236, 193 pl, ☎ 62933.

Recommended
Horseback riding: *Centro Equestre L'Airone,* strada Squartagallo 126, (associate of ANTE).
Motocross: at Sant'Angelo, *La Fossa del Diavolo,* ☎ 661086.
Sailing school: *Club Nautico,* dockyard, ☎ 64849.
Swimming pool: *Residence Vivere Verde,* town hall, ☎ 6629288.
Tennis: lungomare Alighieri 56, ☎ 62804.

SERVIGLIANO

Ascoli Piceno 49, Ancona 85, Rome 224 km
Pop. 2,351 ⊠ 63029 ☎ 0734   D3

The interesting 18C town of Servigliano is near the confluence of the Tenna and the Salino; it is square in layout, according to the town-planning ideas of its time. In the piazzale Leopardi is the church of **S. Maria del Piano,** in which there are wood sculptures and frescos. ☐

The SIBILLINI MOUNTAINS

From Macerato to Ascoli Piceno *(186 km, 1 day; map 3)*

The Sibillini are an Apennine group running from N to S on the borders of the Marche and Umbria with summits higher than 6,500 ft. The slopes are thickly wooded with oak and chestnut; gorges are pierced by rushing mountain streams. There are remote lakes and old monastery churches. The peaks used to provide pasture for herds in the summer; now they are enlivened by summer vacationers and skiers.

▶ From Macerata (→) the road leads to the **Passo di Tréia** (from which it is worth a detour to **Tréia,** →) and continues SW. ▶ A short diversion climbs to the abbey of **Santa Maria di Rambona,** 11C-12C in origin, with a noteworthy crypt. ▶ From **Tolentino** (→), on the l. bank of the Chienti, the route turns into the Potenza valley at **San Severino Marche** (→). ▶ It passes through rolling hills to **Castelraimondo** and climbs the ridge between the Chienti and Potenza Valleys, with panoramic views, to **Camerino** (→). ▶ At **Sfercia** it returns to the floor of the valley, crosses the Chienti and climbs to San Maroto, with its Romanesque church of **S. Giusto**★ (13C), circular in layout. ▶ An undulating road leads to the **Fiastra** hill, with the interesting 15C church of **S. Paolo** on the **Lago di Fiastra.** The road continues through an alpine landscape towards the highest community in the Marche, **Bolognola.** ▶ A twisting road with fine views runs along the side of the Pizzo di Meta to **Sarnano.** This medieval town with steep, narrow streets ends in a square containing the church of S. Maria Assunta (13C; late 15C frescos) and old public buildings; there is an interesting art gallery in the town hall. ▶ **Amàndola,** in the Tenna Valley within sight of the Sibillini, has fine 15C churches. A detour *(8 km NE)* leads to the abbey of **S. Rufino e S. Vitale** (13C). The Palazzo Comunale in **Montefortino** houses an art gallery with 15C-18C works *(apply to the caretaker).* 6.5 km farther, in a charming site, is the 17C **santuario della Madonna dell'Ambro.** Also interesting, in the heart of the Sibillini, is the **Gola del Infernaccio**★, divided by the River Tenna. ▶ In the upper Aso Valley, **Montemónaco** has the two churches of S. Benedetto and S. Biagio (15C-16C), joined together and backing on to the walls of the castle. It is possible to go by car *(12 km)* on a road with fine views up to the summit of Mt.Sibilla (7,135 ft) with its famous cave and a mountain hut; fine views★ to the Gran Sasso and the sea. ▶ Returning to the main road, past a ridge with extensive views over a majestic sweep of mountains to the Gran Sasso, the road descends to the Tronto Valley and **Ascoli Piceno** (→). ☐

3. The Sibillini Mountains

Practical information

AMANDOLA, ⊠ 63021, ☎ 0736.
ⓘ ☎ 97291.

Hotel:
★★★ **G.H. Paradiso,** p. Umberto I 7, ☎ 97168, 40 rm Ⓟ ⸖
🄐 ᨆᨆ 🄶 ✆ ⫯ 45,000; bkf: 4,000.

Recommended
Craft workshops: *Fabrizi,* v. Pignotto 7, ☎ 97408 (furniture made from precious woods).

CASTELRAIMONDO, ⊠ 62022, ☎ 0737.

Hotel:
★★ **Bellavista,** v. S. Anna 11, ☎ 470469, 25 rm Ⓟ 🄐 ᨆᨆ
🄶 ✆ closed Christmas, 44,000; bkf: 5,000.

Recommended
Cycling: *G.S. Folgore,* corso Italia 55.

FIASTRA, ⊠ 62033, ☎ 0737.

🄐 *Al Lago,* at San Lorenzo al Lago, ☎ 52295.

MONTEFORTINO, ⊠ 63047, ☎ 0736.

Hotel:
★★ **Montazzolino Residence,** v. Montazzolino 1,
☎ 969135, 25 rm ᨆᨆ closed New Year to Easter, 40,000.

SARNANO, ⊠ 62028, ☎ 0733.
⌇ (Jun-Sep), ☎ 667144.
⚡ cableway, cable car, ski lifts, downhill skiing and ski school at Sasso Tetto-Maddalena and in Bolognola.
ⓘ v. Rimembranza, ☎ 667144; p. Perfetti, ☎ 667195 (head office).

Hotels:
★★ **Eden,** v. De Gasperi 26, ☎ 667123, 37 rm Ⓟ 🄐 ᨆᨆ
✆ closed 1 Nov-10 Dec, 45,000; bkf: 4,000.
★★ **Terme,** p. Libertà 82, ☎ 667166, 26 rm ✆ closed Mar and 10 Oct-20 Nov, 44,000; bkf: 3,000. Rest. ♦ *Girarrosto* 20/30,000.

🄐 ★★★ *4 Stagioni,* at Forseneta, 210 pl, ☎ 665147 (all year).

Recommended
Events: *Mostra Mercato d'Arte, Antiquariato e Artigianato Artistico* (May-Jun; art, antiques and crafts show and market).
Swimming pool: largo S. Agostino, ☎ 662127.

TOLENTINO

Macerata 19, Ancona 70, Rome 229 km
Pop. 18,234 ⊠ 62029 ☎ 0733   C3

Tolentino is in the Chienti Valley, surrounded by green hills. The landscape is charming with the peaks of the Sibillini Mountains in the background. The town gave its name to Napoleon's treaty with Pope Pius VI in 1791.

▶ The most striking building is the basilica of **S. Nicola da Tolentino★**, a place of pilgrimage dating from the 13C-14C. The Baroque façade has a late Gothic **portal★** with 15C reliefs and statues. The coffered ceiling dates from 1628. Works of art in the church include a painting by Guercino (St.Anne) and a relief attributed to Rossellino. At the end of the nave on the right is the entrance to the **Cappellone di S. Nicola**, decorated with magnificent **frescos★** by the anonymous Tolentino master (beyond the chapel is the 13C-14C cloister). The chapel of SS. Braccia gives access to the **Museo delle Ceramiche** (works from Albisola, Nova, Castelli), and to the other museums attached to the basilica, the **Galleria degli Ex-voto** (1493-1870), the **Museo dell'Opera,** which contains fine silver, woodwork and vestments, and the **Museo Civico,** with artifacts from prehistoric and Roman tombs. ▶ The **Duomo** was originally built in the 8C-9C; it contains a 4C AD sarcophagus. ▶ The **Palazzo Parasini-Bezzi** (v. della Pace 20) saw the signing of the Treaty of Tolentino. It now houses the **Museo Internazionale della Caricatura** *(9 a.m.-12:30 p.m. and 4-6:30 or 8 p.m.).*

Environs

▶ There is an oak wood at the **Terme di Santa Lucia** *(3.5 km NE).* ▶ The **Castello della Rancia★** *(6.5 km along the main road to Macerata, then turn r.)* was a Benedictine foundation, extended in the mid-14C. ▶ 10 km NE is **S. Maria di Rambona** (→ Sibillini Mountains). ☐

Practical information

TOLENTINO
ⓘ p. Libertà 17-18, ☎ 973002.

Hotel:
★★★ *Motel 77,* v. Buozzi 72, ☎ 91471, 49 rm Ⓟ 55,000.

Recommended

Events: *Biennale Internazionale dell'Umorismo nell'Arte* (humour in art; Sep; odd-numbered years); in S. Nicola complex: *Festival Organistico* (Jun; organ music) and *Esposizione dell'Editoria Marchigiana* (Marche publishing; Sep).
Tennis: v. Santini, ☎ 972696.
Wine: visits to *Claudi* cellars at Serrapetrone (10 km SW), p. S. Maria 13, ☎ 908101. (Vernaccia; reserve in advance).

Environs

TERME DI SANTA LUCIA, ✉ 62029, ☎ 0733, 3.5 km NW. ♨ (May-Oct), ☎ 91227.

TREIA

Macerata 16, Ancona 63, Rome 247 km
Pop. 8,992 ✉ 62010 ☎ 0733   C2-3

Treia is medieval in origin, set on a ridge in the central Potenza Valley. The town walls have towers and gates, and there are other impressive old buildings in the quiet streets. The striking **piazza della Repubblica** is open toward the valley. The Palazzo Comunale dates from the 16C-17C.   □

URBANIA

Pesaro 52, Ancona 116, Rome 254 km
Pop. 6,340 ✉ 61049 ☎ 0722   B2

Urbania is in a narrow loop in the centre of the upper Metauro Valley, in pleasant countryside. It is the former Castel Durante, summer residence of the dukes of Urbino. It was renowned in the 16C for majolica production. Urbania took its present name from Pope Urban VIII in 1636. The old town is typically medieval and 15C.

▶ The **Palazzo Ducale** is a massive brick building dating from the late 13C, but rebuilt in the 15C and 16C. It houses **museums,** the **Pinacoteca** and the former **Biblioteca Ducale** (ducal library), now town hall *(open afternoons and by request),* with collections of engravings and drawings and numerous incunabula; a section featuring local ceramics; a collection of 16C and 17C Marche pictures and 14C frescos. ▶ Other interesting features are the 16C **Palazzo Comunale;** the Baroque **cathedral** which contains various paintings including a Crucifixion★ dating from 1320; the fine late Baroque church of **S. Francesco;** the **Oratorio del Corpus Domini** which contains 16C paintings and frescos; the medieval convent of the Poor Clares (feminine counterparts of the Franciscans) with the 13C church of **S. Chiara.** ▶ On the SS 73 bis, in the direction of Sant'Angelo in Vado, is the Parco Ducale or **Barco,** the hunting ground of the dukes of Urbino. A large villa and church have survived.   □

Practical information

ℹ municipio.

Recommended

Horseback riding: *Allevamento Ca' Mangano,* v. Porticelle (associate of *ANTE*); *Centro Ippico,* at Palazzina, ☎ 618233.
Swimming pool: at Parco, ☎ 61640.

URBINO**

Pesaro 35, Ancona 103, Rome 271 km
Pop. 15,905 ✉ 61029 ☎ 0722   B1

Urbino was the perfect Renaissance city. The artists Raphael and Bramante were born there. The city was ruled by the Montefeltro family from 1213; the

URBINO

0   50   100   150 m
1:10.000 (1cm=100m)

Stazione F.S. km 3

most famous of the line was the exemplary 15C Renaissance prince Duke Federico da Montefeltro. A most difficult site was selected for the Palazzo Ducale, but the brilliant architect Luciano Laurana managed to turn it into an advantage. The loggia flanked with towers is an unparalleled architectural invention. Other artists who worked on the project, contributed works or gave advice included Piero della Francesca, Paolo Uccello and Sandro Botticelli. It has been said that the palace is like a city and the city like a palace. This seems a fitting description for this civilized, cultivated and surprising town in the beautiful Marche countryside.

▶ The **Palazzo Ducale★★** (B1-2) is the work of Laurana, who was commissioned in 1465 to extend the old building with mullioned windows on the p. Rinascimento. Laurana focused the interior on a splendid courtyard and opened up the downhill elevation with the loggia and towers★; Francesco di Giorgio Martini designed the two wings on the piazza Duca Federico, and Genga was probably responsible for the top floor, which now houses the **Galleria Nazionale delle Marche★★** *(9 a.m.-2 p.m. and 3-7 p.m.; Sun and hols 9 a.m.-1 p.m.; closed Mon),* which is included in a visit to the Palazzo. A monumental **staircase★** leads from Laurana's **courtyard★** to the loggia. The beautiful rooms have handsome capitals, fireplaces and intarsia doors. The works of art have been re-organized

Duke Federico's study

The Duke's study (studiolo) is perhaps the most beautiful room in the Ducal Palace at Urbino, a building ranked among the most brilliant examples of Italian Renaissance architecture. An intarsia (inlaid wood) picture in the study portrays the builder, Duke Federico di Montefeltro, carrying a lance pointing to the ground, symbolizing that war is over and peace and study may begin. The picture is the key both to the study and to the duke's life. The room is lined with inlaid wood trompe l'oeil to a height of about 2 metres. The intarsia, by the foremost artists of the day, including Botticelli, suggests furnishings and cupboards with incredible virtuosity. Objects appear to have been left on the seats or are glimpsed through half-open doors: armour that the Duke has cast off the better to devote himself to the humanities, books, musical instruments, a parrot in a cage, a clock, an armillary sphere. A basket of fruit and a squirrel appear on a balcony in a series of arches apparently opening onto the outside world. Portraits of famous men formerly looked down from between the top of the woodwork and the ceiling. The paintings were removed and vandalized in the 17C, although some of them still survive in Paris. The subjects and the Latin dedication to each, of which transcriptions have survived, allow a glimpse of the cultural breadth of the man who commissioned them. A contemporary biographer of the duke recorded that Federico's own portrait was included (this painting is still in the palace): 'lifelike, and lacking nothing but his spirit'. The spirit of the duke and that of Renaissance Italy are still alive in this study.

in chronological order according to the phases in which the Palazzo was built. Masterpieces include: the *Flagellation*★★ and the *Madonna di Senigallia*★★ by Piero della Francesca; the *Studiolo del Duca Federico*★, with intarsia work probably designed by Botticelli and the fourteen *tavolette*★★; portraits of distinguished men by Giusto di Gand and P. Berruguete; the *Perdono* chapel★ and the delle Muse temple; a portrait of *Federico da Montefeltro and his son Guidobaldo*★, by P. Berruguete; the frieze of *putti*★ (cherubs) by D. Rosselli, above a fireplace; the intarsia doors★ designed by Laurana and the *Veduta della Città Ideale* (view of the ideal city — actually Urbino) attributed to him; the *Communion of the Apostles*★ by Giusto di Gand; the *Miracle of the Host*★ by Paolo Uccello; the *Portrait of a Lady called 'La Muta' by Raphael; the Salvator Mundi*★ attributed to Bramantino; a *Last Supper*★ by Titian. ▶ In the piazza Rinascimento opposite the Palazzo is the Gothic church of **S. Domenico** (B2; 14C); the lunette with *Madonna and Saints*★ by Luca della Robbia formerly above the portal is now in the Palazzo. ▶ The **Duomo** (B1-2) was rebuilt to a Neoclassical design by Valadier; one of the paintings inside is a *Last Supper*★ by Barocci. ▶ The collection in the **Museo del Duomo 'Albani'** (*9 a.m.-12:30 p.m. and 3-7 p.m.*) includes a 13C bronze lectern in the English style and a Paschal candelabrum★ in bronze, possibly designed by Francesco di Giorgio Martini. ▶ The oratory of **S. Giovanni Battista**★ (B1; *10 a.m.-12:30 p.m. and 3-5 p.m.*) is completely decorated with frescos★ (*Life of St. John and Crucifixion* by I. and L. Salimbeni, 1416); the adjacent oratory of **S. Giuseppe** (*opening times same as oratory, above*) contains F. Brandani's stucco *Nativity*★ (1522). ▶ In the v. Raffaello (A1) are the 14C church of **S. Francesco** and **Raphael's house** (*9 a.m.-1 p.m. and 3-7 p.m.; winter, Sun and holidays 9 a.m.-1 p.m.*). ▶ There is a sweeping view★ from the piazzale Roma (A1). ▶ The fortified **walls** dating from 1507 are best viewed from the viale Buozzi (AB1). The 15C **For-**

tezza Albornoz *(Apr-Sep 10 a.m.-12 noon and 5-8 p.m.)* is in the walls. ▶ 2.5 km E, Federico da Montefeltro and his son Guidobaldo are buried in the harmonious Renaissance church of **S. Bernardino degli Zoccolanti** by Francesco di Giorgio Martini (1491). ▶ The church of the **Madonna dell'Homo** 1.5 km NW *(keys in the house next door)* contains notable 15C frescos.   □

Practical information _____

ⓘ p. Duca Federico 37, (B2), ☎ 2613.
▨ (C2, off map), ☎ 328767.
▥ from piazzale Mercatale (B1).

Hotels:
★★★ *Montefeltro*, v. Piansevero 2, ☎ 328324, 65 rm ⪡ ⌗ closed 15 Dec-15 Jan, 51,000; bkf: 5,000.
★★★ *Piero della Francesca*, v. Comandino 53, ☎ 328427, 84 rm. No restaurant, 51,000.
★★ *Due Querce*, v. della Stazione 35, ☎ 2509, 13 rm Ⓟ ⛟ 40,000; bkf: 5,000.

Restaurants:
♦♦ *Nuovo Coppiere*, v. Porta Maja 20 (B2 a), ☎ 320092, closed Wed and Feb. Italian cuisine: asparagus risotto, boned guinea fowl with stuffing, 25/40,000.
♦ *Vecchia Fornarina*, v. Mazzini 14 (B1 b), ☎ 320007, closed Mon and 1-15 Jan. Regional cuisine: nest of pomfret, rabbit in porchetta, 20/30,000.

△ ★★★ *Pineta*, at Bassa Cesana, v. S. Donato, 130 pl, ☎ 4710.

Recommended
Botanical gardens: v. Bramante 28 (A1), ☎ 2428.
Events: theatrical performances, art exhibitions and open-air concerts in S. Domenico (various venues, Jul-Aug); ancient music courses in S. Domenico (Jul); *Mostra Nazionale dell'Artigianato Artistico* (arts and crafts; Aug); historic procession in costume (Aug); *Festa dell'Aquilone* (kite festival; 1st Sun in Sep).
Swimming pool: at Varrea, ☎ 329045 (also gymnasium and bowling green).

USSITA

Macerata 72, Ancona 132, Rome 184 km
Pop. 460 ▨ 62030 ☎ 0737   C4

Ussita is a mountain community at the heart of the Sibillini Mountains, consisting of scattered hamlets in a lovely valley below Monte Bove. The principal village, **Pieve**, has a 14C church.   □

Practical information _____

𝄢 cableway, ski lifts, ski school at Frontignano.
ⓘ p. XI Febbraio, ☎ 99124; at Frontignano, *Sport Neve*, ☎ 91024.

Hotel:
★★ *Ussita*, p. dei Cavillari, ☎ 99171, 24 rm Ⓟ ⚹ closed Sep-Oct, 44,000; bkf: 4,000.

VERDICCHIO COUNTRY

From Senigallia to Ancona *(206 km, 2 days; map 4)*

This hilly countryside south of Corinaldo and Pergola produces the white wine known as Verdicchio. This itinerary from Senigallia to Ancona includes Fabriano and Jesi. Its principal attractions are the scenery, the attractive Apennine gorges of Frasassi and the gentle Marche countryside.

▶ From **Senigallia** (→) the route leads by the road on the l. of the Misa to **Brugnetto**, passing **Corinaldo** on a hill on the ridge between the Rivers Cesano and Nevola. ▶ **Mondàvio** is a picturesque walled town; the Rocca (1482-92) houses a museum of historical

4. Verdicchio Country

tableaux. ▶ In **Orciano di Pesaro** is the Renaissance church of S. Maria Nuova★, with a fine portal and elegant interior. ▶ Back to San Michele, then on to **San Lorenzo in Campo** in the Cesano Valley, a medieval town with an archaeological museum and a museum of African ethnography in the Palazzo delle Rovere *(apply at the Pro Loco)*. The old church of **S. Lorenzo** was part of a Benedictine abbey (8C-13C); there is an **antiquarium** attached to it *(apply to the parish priest)*. ▶ The road climbs the Cesano valley, which gradually becomes narrower, running through oak woods. From **Pérgola** (→) the route proceeds via **Serra Sant'Abbondio** to the **Eremo i Fonte Avellana** (→ Pérgola). ▶ Next are **Sassoferrato** (→) and **Fabriano** (→). ▶ After passing through the **Frasassi gorge** the road goes on to the **Grotte di Frasassi**, in the Sentino Valley, a system of caves with vast chambers, stalactites and stalagmites *(guided tours; in summer every 10-15 mns, 8 a.m.-8 p.m.; winter 11:30 a.m.-3:30 p.m.)*. ▶ Close by is the church of **S. Vittore delle Chiuse★**, an unusual 11C Romanesque building showing Byzantine influence, with a charming interior. ▶ In the Esino Valley the route passes through the **della Rossa gorge** between high limestone cliffs, and climbs to **Serra San Quirico** (9,884 ft) where odd, vaulted streets have been formed by houses built against the castle wall. ▶ At **Móie** there is the fine 12C Romanesque church of S. Maria. ▶ The route crosses the Esino and climbs to **Maiolatti Spontini** with remains of 15C walls; the town is of interest to music lovers for the tomb of the conductor and composer Gaspare Spontini (in the church of S. Giovanni and a museum containing manuscripts and memorabilia of the composer, who was born here. ▶ **Cupramontana,** an old town on a rise, and **Stáffolo,** walled and medieval (13C Romanesque portal, 15C-16C paintings in the parish church), are set amid the luxuriant vineyards that produce Verdicchio. ▶ From **Jesi** (→), the route passes **Santa Maria Nuova** and continues along a road with fine views from the Esino to the Musone Valley and on to **Osimo** (→). ▶ Finally it reaches **Ancona** (→) on the shores of the Adriatic. □

Practical information _____

CUPRAMONTANA, ⊠ 60034, ☎ 0731.
🛈 p. Cavour, ☎ 78302.
Hotel:
★★★ *Park,* v. Ferranti 12, ☎ 78272, 34 rm ℗ ⚲ 34,000.

GROTTE DI FRASASSI, ⊠ 60040, ☎ 0732.
🛈 consorzio Grotte di Frasassi, ☎ 90080.

SAN LORENZO IN CAMPO, ⊠ 61047, ☎ 0721.
Hotel:
★★★ *Giardino,* v. Mattei 4, ☎ 76803, 25 rm ℗ ⚲ ⌧ ▭

Verdicchio

This is a white wine, of pale straw colour, with a delicate bouquet, dry, and with a slightly bitter aftertaste. It is made from the grape of the same name, with the addition of up to 15 percent of the Trebbiano and Malvasia Toscane varieties. It goes well with the fish soups of the region. A historian called it 'clear as the sun and excellent in virtue'. Verdicchio was known to Alaric the Goth who, on his way to the sack of Rome in 410, took from Corinaldo 'forty barrels, as he deemed that there was nothing better than the said Verdicchio for health and warlike vigour'. Corinaldo is still, along with twenty-two other places, in the Verdicchio production area of Castelli di Iesi. An area to the S, extending from Fabriano to Camerino, produces Verdicchio di Matelica.

closed Christmas, 48,000. Rest. ● ♦♦ ☎ 76032, closed Fri eve and Christmas. Regional and Italian cuisine: mezzelune with courgettes, stuffed dumplings, 25/40,000.

SANTA VITTORE DELLE CHIUSE, ⊠ 60040, ☎ 0732.
🏕 (Apr-Nov), ☎ 90012.
Hotel:
★★★ *Terme San Vittore,* ☎ 90012, 49 rm ℗ ⚲ closed Dec-Mar, 48,000.

SERRA SAN QUIRICO, ⊠ 60048, ☎ 0732.
🏕 ★★ *Minicamping Sant'Elia,* at Sant'Elia, 15 pl, ☎ 74057.

VISSO

Macerata 67, Ancona 118, Rome 179 km
Pop. 1,414 ⊠ 62039 ☎ 0737 C4

Visso is almost on the border with Umbria, in a hollow in the upper Nera Valley at a point where five small valleys meet. Green pastures alternate with wooded areas in a high mountain landscape, making the town a pleasant holiday centre and a base for trips into the Sibillini Mountains.

▶ The central **piazza Martiri Vissani** and the adjacent **piazza Capuzi** are surrounded with 15C-16C houses and palazzi, the most striking of which is the **Palazzo del Governatore.** ▶ Next to it is the collegiate church of

S. Maria, 12C-14C with a lavish 13C portal and polygonal apse with mullioned windows; in the interior are 15C-16C frescos and paintings. ▶ The 14C church of **S. Agostino** is now used as a **Museo-Pinacoteca** *(apply to the parish priest).* ▶ The Gothic church of **S. Francesco** contains a 16C wooden tabernacle. ▶ 9.5 km along the main road to Camerino is the **Santuario di Macereto** (3,274 ft), an elegant building in the manner of Bramante. □

Practical information _____

ⓘ p. Umberto I, ☎ 9239 (seasonal).

Molise

▶ The region of Molise begins shortly before the mouth of the River Trigno on the Adriatic coast. Pliny, the Roman historian, wrote that in his time this river had many ports, and it is still navigable in its lower reaches by small craft. A little farther into Molise is Térmoli, set on a promontory with a fishing harbour at its feet. The historical past of the region is evident in the town's Romanesque Duomo and the towers of the castle wall built by Frederick II. From the mouth of the Fortore River the Gargano promontory may be seen thrusting out in the sea, but here it is already Apulia, the Molise border being defined by an obscure mountain stream called the Saccione. The coastline is short (scarcely 30 km long) and the land stretches back inland to the Apennine watershed and even beyond. The flatlands at the head of the Rivers Trigno, Tappino and Fortore were the historical centre of the county of Molise, which gave its name to the region. Vines and olives (Horace praised Venafro's olive oil), grains and vegetables, sheep and goats: Molise is still a land of hardworking country folk and shepherds, as it has always been. Although the region is small, the landscape is beautiful and there are many works of art and architecture to delight the visitor and to suggest links with other cultures, regions and styles — the Romanesque abbey of S. Mario di Canneto, for example, lonely among the olives in the Trigno Valley, or the 9C fresco cycle in the crypt of S. Vicenzo al Volturno, enigmatic pictures which art historians link directly with the Benedictine miniatures of the period. □

● Don't miss

The two capitals, Campobasso and Isernia. The remains of ancient Larinum, at Larino; the theatre in the ruins of a Samnite city in Pietrabbondante; the ruins of the Roman city of Saepinum; the Duomo★ in Térmoli; the abbey of S. Vincenzo in Volturno.

● Brief regional history

10C-4C BC
The Samnites. According to Strabo, the Roman historian, and this opinion is generally held to be correct, this **Italic** tribe was Sabine in origin. ● The **Sabines,** under pressure from persistent attacks by the Umbrians, dedicated all the boys born in a certain year to Mars. When these young men came of age they set off to the South, guided by an ox. When they reached the territory of the **Opici** they sacrificed the beast and settled there. ● The mountainous area bounded by Latium, Basilicata and Apulia became the **Samnite** homeland, and this **Samnia** corresponds to a large extent with present-day Molise. ● The Samnites founded **Boiano, Sepino, Trivento** and **Isernia.** ● The **Pentri** and **Caraceni** were the Samnite tribes in the territory of Molise; community of language between tribes and the rest of the population was reinforced by common **sanctuaries** and the political federation of the **city-states**. ● Attracted by the rich plain of Campania and by the void left by the decline of Etruscan hegemony, they expanded downwards into **Campania** (in the 5C) where they built **Capua** and **Cuma.** ● This expansion brought them into conflict with the Romans.

3C BC-5C AD
The Roman era. Of all the Italic peoples, the Samnites were the ones who put up the greatest resistance to the **Roman** conquest of Italy. Although they were finally overcome by the might of the legions, they did

at one time heavily defeat the Romans near the town of *Caudium* — an historical event that is still remembered. In the early days of Rome captured prisoners were put in yokes carved for a pair of oxen. Later, symbolically, conquered armies were made to file under a 'yoke' made of three spears, two upright and one horizontal. ● Not far from Caudium there is a narrow mountain pass which today is called the Valley of Arpaia. It was here, in 321 BC, that the Roman army under the consuls (generals) T. Veturius Calvinus and Sp. Postumius was trapped by the Samnites. The mountaineers sealed both entrances to the gorge and as they controlled all the surrounding heights the Romans had to choose between annihilation or surrender. They chose the latter course. The Samnites decided that they should be humiliated in the same way that they humiliated others and set up a yoke of spears and made them pass under it. From then on the expression 'to pass through the Caudine Forks' (from the name of the gorge) came to have the same meaning as 'to pass under the yoke' both signifying 'to be utterly defeated'. ● Other Roman armies were sent against the Samnites and defeated them but were unable to subdue them and time and again they rose in revolt against the imperial might. Inevitably however Romanization proceeded, though slowly. ● Under the Emperor Caesar Augustus, Molise was included in the territory known as *Samnium*, and among the Roman cities in it were the present **Isernia, Boiano, Triventa, Sepina** and **Larino**. ● The capital of Molise today, **Campobasso**, is more recent, probably having been founded by the Lombards.

6C-11C

The name Molise. The **Byzantines,** powerful at sea, defended this fragment of the Adriatic coast and the hinterland against the **Lombards** with great tenacity, but the latter prevailed, added the territory to the **duchy of Benevento** and established the **stewardship of Boiano.** ● When the **Normans** first appeared in southern Italy, the local leaders formed 'the council of Molise', the first historical mention of the region, linked with a castle in Molise, a village between Torella and Duronia. ● The origin of the name is obscure, however, but seems to be associated with one of the dominant families of the early medieval period.

Bells

Agnone is bell country, or, more precisely, bell-founding country. The forges still use traditional wood fires and terra-cotta moulds. Each bell takes four to six months to make, is tuned to a particular note and given a name of its own (la Pierpaola, la Giovanna, la Gloriosa). Even bells in the distant Buddhist monasteries of Asia come from Molise, as do those of the basilica of S. Paolo fuori le Mura in Rome and the cathedral in Buenos Aires. The sacred mingles with the profane: the little bells for the World Cup in football are also cast in Molise.

13C-19C

Part of the southern kingdom. In time, the region's affairs merged with those of the kingdom of southern Italy, with which Molise was associated from then on until 1860, when the country was unified. An important date is 1221, when **Frederick II** of Sweden defeated **Tomaso, Conte di Celano e del Molise,** who had opposed the empire. ● In the 15C small groups of **Albanian** immigrants established colonies in Ururi,

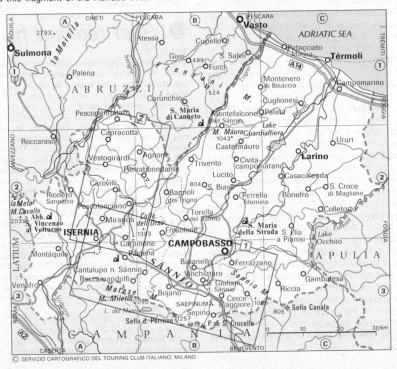

© SERVIZIO CARTOGRAFICO DEL TOURING CLUB ITALIANO, MILANO

Campomarino, Montecilfone, Portocannone and Santa Croce di Magliano. ● In the early 16C the **county of Molise** was added to the Capitanata (Apulia), where it remained under the joint rule of Spain and the Bourbon kingdom. ● Molise became a province, with **Campobasso** as its capital, in 1807 when **Giuseppe,** Napoleon Bonaparte's brother, was King of Naples. ● It became a region in 1963, detached from Abruzzi. In 1970 a second province was constituted, with **Isernia** as its capital.

Facts and figures

Location: Almost quadrilateral in shape, between Abruzzi, Campania, Apulia and the Adriatic, Molise is mostly hilly or mountainous. The Apennine watershed runs through it and part of the region drains into the Tyrrhenian Sea.
Area: 4,438 sq km, the second smallest Italian region.
Climate: Campobasso is on roughly the same line of latitude as Portovecchio (in Corsica) and Barcelona, but the whole Adriatic coast of Italy is cooler than the Tyrrhenian. Summer heat on the coast is mitigated by altitude in the interior.
Population: 331,670 inhabitants, the second least populated region of Italy.
Administration: Campobasso is the regional capital, the other provincial capital is Isernia.

 ## Practical information

Information: tourist offices in principal towns and other localities.

SOS: emergency services, ☎ 113; police emergency, ☎ 112; road emergency, *ACI*, ☎ 116.

Weather: forecast, ☎ 0874/991991 (Campobasso district, ☎ 191); roads open and closed, ☎ 0874/994994 (Campobasso district, ☎ 194) or *ACI*, ☎ 06/4212; snow information, ☎ 085/992992; boating information, ☎ 085/996996.

Farm vacations: *Associazione Regionale Agriturist*, at Campobasso, v. Cavour 18, ☎ 0874/92912.

Molise cuisine

Experts consider Molise cuisine to be the same as that of Abruzzi, with some signs of influence from Apulia or Naples. It has some distinctive touches, however. Nirvi e musse is an hors d'oeuvre served in Campobasso, a kind of brawn made from a calf's head; cacio e uova in the Matese is lamb cooked in an earthenware pot with oil and herbs. At the end of the cooking period eggs beaten with sheep's cheese are added — the flavour is controlled by the sharpness of the cheese. Tircinelli are grilled meat-balls of lamb's intestines, also with sheep's cheese. Sweets include cavagnoli, pancakes with honey, and picellati, based on breadcrumbs, with grape must, honey, walnuts and almonds. Capracotta lentils vie for the title of best in Italy with those from Castelluccio, in Umbria. Molise has had a reputation for fine olive oil since Roman times (it was mentioned as an ingredient in a dish enjoyed by the poet Horace) and it is still produced in small quantities, but all of extra-virgin quality. Delicious dishes based on snails are served in Venafro.

Events: *Mystery procession* on Corpus Christi Day, at Campobasso; *Stations of the Cross and processions* at night on Christmas Eve, at Agnone; *festival of S.Pardo,* at Larino; *grain festival,* at Jelsi; *fish festival,* at Térmoli; *craft show,* at Isernia.

Nature parks: Molise section (province of Isernia) of the *Parco Nazionale d'Abruzzo* (→ Abruzzi), head office in Rome, v. del Curato 6, ☎ 06/6543584, Pescassroli office, ☎ 0863/91315.

Excursions: areas of particular interest for excursions are Molise slopes of *Parco Nazionale d'Abruzzo* and Monti del Matese (no indicated long-distance routes). *CAI,* at Campobasso, v. Cardarelli 59; *Cooperative Turistica,* at Pizzone.

Horseback riding: centre at Isernia (associate of *ANTE*).

Skiing: Campitello Matese (alpine and cross-country skiing; alpine ski itineraries); cross-country skiing at Capracotta in the Molise Apennines.

Fishing: *Federazione Italiana Pesca Sportiva*, at Campobasso, v. Monforte 16, ☎ 0874/95025; at Isernia, v. Berta, ☎ 0865/3932. For fishing conditions (agreed waters, prohibitions, etc) inquire at local office responsible.

 ## Towns and places

BAGNOLI DEL TRIGNO

Isernia 39, Campobasso 42, Rome 216 km
Pop. 1,342 ✉ 86091 ☎ 0874   B2

Bagnoli del Trigno, called 'the pearl of Molise', is in the enclosed Trigno Valley amid charming countryside set in an immense mass of limestone with tapering mountains.

▶ At the top of an impressive crag is the austere Sanfelice **castle,** guarding the village and the valley. ▶ In the narrow space between the bulk of the castle and a harsh spur of rock is the parish church of **S. Silvestro** with a fine Romanesque portal; a flight of steps leads to the campanile, strikingly sited on the spur. Rock, castle, houses and church make an impressive ensemble.

Environs

▶ A road offering fine views of the deep Trigno Valley leads to **Duronia** (*8.5 km;* 3,012 ft). Its name is based on the tradition (as yet unproven) that it was built on the remains of the Samnite city of *Duronia,* destroyed by the Romans in 293 BC. Nearby, on the hill called **Civita** are remains of megalithic walls where there is a fine view of the Maiella, a mountain chain with Mt. Corno and Mt. Amarco as its highest peaks.   ☐

For help in understanding terms when visiting museums or other sites, see the *Art and Architectural Terms Guide* at the end of the Practical Holiday Guide.

CAMPITELLO MATESE

Campobasso 43, Rome 216 km
Pop. 45 ⊠ 86027 (S. Massimo) ☎ 0874   B3

Campitello Matese is a recently established resort, an attractive centre for visiting the mountains of the **Matese,** one of the most important limestone massifs in Italy in area (more than 1,000 sq km) and height and for the large numbers of streams and rivers which flow from it. The natural surroundings are not entirely unspoiled, but further into the Matese the landscape becomes more wild and attractive: quiet meadows and dense woods, grazing land with shepherds, wild and deserted ravines and gorges, rivers, mountain streams and caves. There are many points affording fine views. From the **Rifugio Guerino Jezza,** on the edge of the village, there is a relatively easy climb to **Mt. Miletto** (6,726 ft, *c. 1 hr*), the highest peak in the Matese, which dominates the countryside and may be Livy's *Tifernus Mons,* scene of the Samnites' last, desperate resistance.   □

Practical information ———————————————

⚡ ski lifts, cross-country skiing, instruction.
ⓘ at Campitello Duemila, ☎ 784156.

Hotel:
★★★ *Kristiania,* ☎ 784107, 63 rm ℗ ⌂ ঌ 🐾 ⛵ ◯ ♨ closed 15-31 May and 15-30 Sep, 80,000.

CAMPOBASSO

Rome 225, Milan 740 km
Pop. 49,412 ⊠ 86100 ☎ 0874   B3

It is worth visiting Campobasso on the day of the feast of Corpus Christi seven weeks after Easter for the *Sagra dei Misteri,* a procession which mingles religion and folklore and in which the local shepherds and their flocks take part. The most striking features are the 'machines', strange, heavy twisted metal structures made in 1740 by Paolo Saverio di Zinno. There used to be eighteen, now there are only twelve. The others were damaged by time and weather, and no one was willing or able to repair them. Little children take up positions on these contraptions, at various levels and in various poses. They are in costume and carry props representing Biblical scenes and scenes from the lives of the saints. The machines wobble perilously through the town, carried on sturdy wooden platforms. The procession is accompanied by a band, and the sound of the instruments is superimposed on the buzz of the crowd, the bleating of the sheep and often the tears of a frightened 'angel' on one of the machines.

▶ The town is in two parts: the new town on the plain and the old town on the hill dominated by the massive castle. The old town has the more interesting monuments. ▶ The **Castello Monforte** (A1), used in part as a war memorial, is square and severe and dates in its present form from 1549, but was originally Lombard; there is a fine view from the piazza in front of it. ▶ A little farther down are two 13C churches, **S. Giorgio** (A1) with a plain façade with striking carved lunette and **S. Bartolomeo** (A1) with a fine central portal. ▶ The old town is well worth visiting at random, climbing up and down the numerous steps which make up the majority of its narrow streets and alleyways. ▶ The **via S. Antonio Abate** (A-B1) is particularly interesting. At the end of it, in the **church** of the same name (1572), there are some fine wooden altars and pictures by F. Guarino. ▶ The **Museo Permanente del Presepio** (C1) in the new town has a collection of

miniature crèches from Italy and elsewhere; the oldest exhibits date from the 18C *(visits in p.m., at least three days' notice required,* ☎ *93672).*

Environs

▶ **Ferazzano** (2,861 ft), 4 km SE, stands on a pine-clad hill: the 13C **pulpit** in the parish church dell'Assunta, with Romanesque portal, is very fine. There is an exceptional view from the 15C **castle.** ▶ 13 km NW is **S. Maria della Strada;** its 12C Romanesque church has a façade with reliefs and a 15C Gothic tomb in the interior. ▶ 14 km NW is **San Giovanni in Galdo;** nearby, in Colle Rimontato *(2 km)* are interesting remains of a 2C BC **Italic temple.** ▶ 19.6 km N is **Petrella Tiferina;** its parish church of **S. Giorgio** (1165) is a fine Romanesque building.   □

Practical information ———————————————

ⓘ p. della Vittoria 14 (C1), ☎ 95662.
🚎 (B2), ☎ 92785.
🚌 from corso Bucci (B2) and p. delle Repubblica.

Hotels:
★★★★ *Roxy,* p. Savoia 7 (C1a), ☎ 91741, 72 rm ℗ 70,000; bkf: 5,000.
★★★ *Skanderbeg,* v. Novelli 3/B (B2-3b), ☎ 93341, 68 rm ℗ 🐾 54,000; bkf: 3,000. Rest. ◆◆◆ *Griglia* Modern, elegant, equipped for conferences. Regional cuisine: bucatini all'amatriciana, spring pancakes, saltimbocca alla romana, 10/24,000.

Restaurants:
◆◆◆ *Potestà,* vicolo Persichillo 3 (A2d), ☎ 311101, closed Sun and Aug. 17C building, carefully furnished and equipped. Regional cuisine: homemade dumplings, baked pumpkin with macaroni, 30/40,000.
● ◆◆ *Abruzzese,* p. Battisti 12 (B2c), closed Sun. Regional cuisine: pacchiarotti, mbanniccia, roast kid or lamb, 25/35,000.

Recommended
Archery: *Compagnia Arcieri Cristian,* v. Verga 7, ☎ 90796.
Clay pigeon shooting: at Madonnella, contrada S. Vito, ☎ 95346.
Events: *Sagra dei Misteri* procession on Corpus Christi Day *(Jun); Grain festival,* at Jelsi *(19 km SE, Jul),* ☎ 710134.
Farm vacations: information from *Comunità Montana del Fortore Molisano,* at Riccia *(28 km SE),* v. Capello 18, ☎ 71279.
Swimming: Villa Comunale, ☎ 9091.
Tennis: Villa Comunale, ☎ 92248 (also bowls).

ISERNIA

Campobasso 51, Rome 175, Milan 740 km
Pop. 20,777 ⊠ 86170 ☎ 0865   A2

Isernia is a modern version of *Aesernia* (used by the Romans for the city of the Pentri tribe of Samnites), which in its turn derives from the Oscan (the Samnite language) word *aiser* (god). An ancient town, then, but not thought to be older than many others until recent discoveries suggested that it could be the oldest town in Europe, or to be more precise, the oldest recorded human settlement in Europe. In La Pineta traces of human activity going back at least 730,000 years have been found. Hundreds of elephant and bison bones and clear proof of the use of fire suggest the existence of a permanent camp of ancient hunters to which palaeontologists have given the name *homo aeserniensis,* despite the lack of specific remains.

▶ The town is set on a spur of travertine rock between the Rivers Crápino and Sordo, overlooking an extensive valley. ▶ The **cathedral,** destroyed by an earthquake in the early 19C, has been rebuilt to a Neoclassical design

Trivento km 51

Termoli km 70

Foggia km 88

CAMPOBASSO

0   100   200   300 m

1:13.000 (1cm = 130 m)

Isérnia km 50 - Benevento km 64   2

© SERVIZIO CARTOGRAFICO DEL TOURING CLUB ITALIANO, MILANO

(1837); inside are an altar, four statues and a base from the pagan temple (3C-BC), on the remains of which the first cathedral was built; in the sacristy is a relic of the head of S. Nicandro. ► In the p. S. Maria the church of **S. Maria Assunta** is under restoration. It was destroyed by heavy shelling in 1943; the Romanesque campanile (1015) and the portal are intact. In the adjacent former convent is the **Museo Civico**, with archaeological finds from the Samnite and Roman periods (there is a curious memorial stone with a depiction of an ass being loaded with its pack saddle) and palaeolithic finds awaiting definitive arrangement. ► The interesting 14C **Fontana delle Fraterna** is built partly of ancient Roman materials; it has six arches supported on slender columns. ► In Quadrella are remains of a **Roman bridge** and an archaeological site. ► A museum and an archaeological site open to the public are planned in La Pineta, where the extensive **palaeolithic finds** already mentioned were made. □

Practical information ——————————

ISERNIA
ℹ️ v. Farinacci 9, ☎ 59590.
🚂 ☎ 50921.
🚌 from p. Stazione and p. Veneziale.

Hotels:
★★★ *Sayonara,* v. Berta 131, ☎ 50992, 31 rm ℗ ⚇ 34,500; bkf: 6,000.
★★★ *Tequila,* v. S. Lazzaro 85, ☎ 51346, 69 rm ℗ ⚇ ও ⚇ ▱ 46,000; bkf: 6,000.
★★ *Emma,* contrada Valgianese, ☎ 26386, 20 rm ℗ ⚇ ⚇ 33,000; bkf: 2,000.

Restaurant:
♦ *Taverna Valgianese,* corso Marcelli 186, ☎ 3976, closed Sun, Easter, 1 Aug-5 Sep and Christmas. Regional cuisine: tacconelle with beans, maccheroni alla chitarra, Abruzzi wines, 18/25,000.

Recommended
Events: *craft show* (lace, textiles, terra-cotta), last wk in Jun.
Horseback riding: *Centro Ippico Molisano,* at Breccelle, ☎ 3830 (associate of *ANTE*).
Sports centre: v. Giovanni XXIII.
Technical tourism: visits to *V. Di Clemente* workshops, v. Libero Testa 256/A, ☎ 3345 (copper, brass, embossed silver); *Coltellerie Molise,* at Frosolone *(32 km E),* v. Silva 1/7, ☎ 0874/89207 (cutlery); *E. di Fiore* workshops, at Scàpoli *(23 km NE),* Fonte Costanzo 30, ☎ 954357 (bagpipe manufacture).

Environs

PESCHE, ✉ 86090, 5 km toward Vasto.

Hotel:
★★★ *Santa Maria del Bagno,* contrada S. Sebastiano 29, ☎ 29143, 45 rm ℗ ⚇ ➿ 45,000; bkf: 5,000.

LARINO

Campobasso 54, Rome 280 km
Pop. 8,034 ✉ 86035 ☎ 0874   C2

The Feast of San Pardo is celebrated on the fourth Sunday in May. About fifty ox carts, lavishly decorated with flowers and sheets of precious ancient cloth woven by local craftsmen, parade through the streets. In the evening, in the torchlit piazzettas, streets and alleys of the town, the notes of the 'carrese', an ancient song associated with the pastoral tradition of Molise, can be heard.

▶ Larino, set among olive groves on a hill on the r. of the Biferno River, is an agricultural centre in which some traces of the medieval town have survived. The courtyard of the **Casa Saracina** is particularly charming. ▶ The 14C **cathedral** has a lavish Gothic portal in the façade and a rose window of the Apulian type; the portal on the r. side is Romanesque. ▶ W of the town are remains of Roman *Larinum* (wall, parts of 1C-2C amphitheatre and villa). Various finds, including notable polychrome pavement **mosaics★** are on display in the **Palazzo Ducale,** now the town hall (p. del Duomo).   ▢

Practical information —————————————

ⓘ Palazzo Ducale, ☎ 822265.
Hotel:
★★★ *Campitelli,* v. Mazzini, ☎ 822666, 20 rm ⌦ 60,000; bkf: 5,000.

Recommended
Events: *Feast of S. Pardo* (25-27 May) with parade of floral floats and torchlight procession.

Ancient SAMNIUM

From Campobasso to Isernia *(70 km, 1 day; map 1)*

Recent research suggests that the Samnites, best known for their ferocious resistance to Roman rule in the three Samnite Wars, did not cease to exist once they ceased to resist. They were not just warriors and rough shepherds, but men who created a civilization which established a dense network of little towns and a defensive system of massive fortresses, as well as a number of sanctuaries. This itinerary goes into the heart of Samnium, with three crucial stops: mythical Aquilonia, rich Sepino and Boiano, the capital of the Samnite Pentri tribe.

▶ From **Campobosso** (→) the route leads SW to the turning (on the r.) for **Baranello,** a village with a small Museo Civico (European and non-European porcelain and vases from various periods, bronzes and ivories, statues and paintings). On **Mt. Vairano** above the town are interesting remains of a fortified Samnite settlement (125 acres

in area, enclosed in more than 3,000 yards of wall, at some points over six feet high; three gates; 3C-2C BC vase kilns). ▶ The itinerary continues to the **Monteverde crossroads,** then turns l., and runs on at a considerable height through scenery with splendid views (the Matese mountains; the Maiella range on the r.; towns and villages perched on hills and rocky outcrops on the l.). ▶ Having passed through Cercepiccola, the route climbs to **Cercemaggiore** where, on nearby Mt. Saraceno (3,563 ft), there are some prehistoric settlements known as Le Fate caves and the remains of Samnite fortifications. ▶ From the first junction mentioned the road goes down to **Cercepiccola** and **San Giuliano del Sannio** with splendid views all along the way. ▶ S to the junction, then r. for **Sepino** (→), from which turn N for ancient *Saepinum* (→ Sepino). The SS N 17 leads NW along a series of straight stretches across the plain N of the Matese mountains. ▶ At the Epitaffio junction, a l. turn leads *(3.5 km)* to **Campochiaro,** near which is **Civitella,** with an ancient Samnite sanctuary (notable temple, one of the largest in Samnium). ▶ **Boiano** was also a Samnite settlement (the ancient name *Bovianum* is derived from the ox market which was held here). Near the village is the source of the Biferno. ▶ There is a fine view★ of the valley from **Civita Superiore** *(4 km SE)* and also remains of Samnite walls and of a Lombard castle. ▶ The route continues toward Isernia, at the junction taking the road to the r. It has splendid views and, thrusting into the Matese, climbs through San Massimo then in sweeping curves to **Campitello Matese** (→). ▶ There again it follows the Strada Statale and after a l. turn reaches **Roccamandolfi,** where rich and elaborate traditional female costumes have survived. ▶ The Strada Statale leads on to **Isernia** (→).   ▢

Practical information —————————————

CANTALUPO NEL SANNIO, ✉ 86092, ☎ 0865.

Restaurant:
♦♦ *Riccio,* v. Biferno 30, ☎ 814246, closed Mon and 15-30 Jun. Country trattoria. Regional cuisine: penne alla contadina, orechiette al ragù, Abruzzi wines, 20/25,000.

VINCHIATURO, ✉ 86019, ☎ 0874.

Restaurant:
♦♦ *Cupolette,* contrada S. Maria delle Macchia 6, ☎ 34521. Spacious rooms in tourist village with swimming pool, tennis and bowls. Regional cuisine: dumpling ragout, salt cod with walnuts, 24/30,000.

Ancient Samnium

SEPINO

Campobasso 25, Rome 248 km
Pop. 2,426 ⊠ 86017 ☎ 0874   B3

Sàipins, Saepinum, Sepino: three centres which grew up one after the other, almost on each others' ruins; the persistence of the name also suggests continuous settlement for almost twenty-four centuries. This tenacity is perhaps explained by the fact that the sheep route from Pescasséroli to Apulia passed through here. The area was thus the obligatory toll-house for traffic (especially when flocks were being moved in spring and autumn) between Pentri Samnium and Apulia, Campania and Sabina.

▶ The present town is set on a hill. In the older part is a **campanile** with a surprising onion dome in pierced wrought iron. ▶ There is a notable collection of ex votos in the collegiate church of **S. Cristina.** ▶ 3.3 km N is the village of **Altilia** (with rural houses some of which date from the 18C), on the site of Roman Saepinum. Archaeological **excavations** have exposed a large part of the ancient settlement, and the principal buildings, mingling with the country houses, make a charming ensemble. Notable sites are: a stretch of wall (over 1,000 yards in length) with twenty-seven towers and four gates (the **Porta di Boiano** has an interesting inscription on its base inviting the townsfolk not to rob the shepherds and not to exploit the fact that they are passing through); the **theatre,** which has survived in excellent condition, with an entrance which led outside the town's walls to admit shepherds and merchants encamped outside it; numerous houses and shops, an olive press with storage wells, hydraulic mill, a Samnite cistern and the basilica, baths and forum. Outside the walls is the Numisi tomb, in the form of an altar, and the mausoleum of G. Ennius Marsus. ▶ On the **Terravecchia** hill a short distance away are remains of a gigantic wall with three gates indicating the site of ancient Samnite *Sàipins,* destroyed by the Romans in 293 BC.   ▢

Church of S. MARIA DI CANNETO

Campobasso 74, Rome 223 km   B1

This church stands in isolation by the broad River Trigno in an extensive olive grove. The monastery, mentioned in 944 as a dependency of Montecassino, was destroyed after 1474. The 13C **church,** despite the damage caused by clumsy restoration in the 1930s, is interesting for various reasons. In the interior are a rectangular pulpit (1223) with saints and symbols; a medieval bas-relief of the *Last Supper* and the *Madonna del Canneto,* a polychrome wooden statue (15C). The campanile dates from 1329. On the r.-hand side are remains of a 3C-4C **Roman villa,** with a fine polychrome mosaic pavement.

Environs

▶ *C.* 20 km S, after a steep climb, is **Trivento,** the *Terventum* of the Pentri Samnite tribe. The oldest part of the little town, set on a hill, is linked to the modern area by a flight of 200 steps; the **cathedral** has been rebuilt on various occasions and has a fine 18C marble altar and the extremely interesting crypt★ of S. Casto, built in the 11C using disparate architectural elements recovered from elsewhere, in particular the memorial stone of a priestess of Diana, a fact which reinforces the theory that the cathedral was built on the site of a pagan temple. *C.* 14 km S of the town, a steep road leads to **Pietracupa** (2,280 ft); the name reflects its situation on an isolated rocky outcrop. Nearby is an interesting ancient cave settlement. The church hollowed out of the rock is particularly striking.   ▢

S. VINCENZO AL VOLTURNO

Isernia 31, Rome 181 km   A2

In an enchanting location, with the Mainarde mountains as a beautiful backdrop, what in the 8C-9C must have been a genuine and flourishing Benedictine **'monastic city'** has been partially but accurately rebuilt. It was almost completely destroyed in the disastrous earthquake of 1349, but the establishment had already had to suffer a great deal: other earthquakes and repeated Saracen raids, the most serious of which led to the death of 900 of the 1,000 monks who formed the community and to the burning and destruction of ten of the eleven churches completed at the time. Thus what can be seen today can only suggest the grandeur of the past.

▶ Large parts of the **monastery** (founded 8C) and the 13C **church** (the area around the sanctuary is particularly fine) have been rebuilt. ▶ The most interesting part of the building, which has survived almost intact, is the 9C **crypt of S. Lorenzo★** *(apply to custodian of abbey).* Its vaults and walls are completely covered with fine frescos, many of which are still in good condition. Their anonymous artists belonged to a local school, and comparable work is only to be found in contemporary Benedictine miniature painting. ▶ 4.7 km from the junction of the lane leading to the abbey and the Strada Statale is the Romanesque church of the **Madonna delle Grotte,** with interesting frescos.   ▢

TERMOLI

Campobasso 68, Rome 300 km
Pop. 24,119 ⊠ 86039 ☎ 0875   C1

Termoli has a busy fishing industry and falls neatly into two sections. The older part is medieval and set on a promontory, with a labyrinth of streets and alleyways. The **Duomo,** possibly built in the 6C on the ruins of an earlier Roman temple, was rebuilt in the Romanesque style of Pisa and Apulia in the 12C and has since been altered; interesting mosaic pavements of oriental inspiration in the crypt (10C-11C). The **castle** is the surviving part of the massive fortifications built by Frederick II in 1247 to defend the port.   ▢

Practical information _____

ⓘ p. Melchiorre Bega, ☎ 2754.
🚢 motor boats (daily, every 1.5 hr) and hydrofoils (in summer, every 45 mns) to the Trémiti islands; *Adriatica,* ☎ 2429; *Navigazione Libera del Golfo,* ☎ 4859. There is also a service to Vasto and Ortona.

Hotels:
★★★★ *Corona,* v. Milano 2/A, ☎ 2241, 39 rm Ⓟ 🐾 100,000; bkf: 5,000. Rest. ♦♦♦ *Bel Ami* closed Sun except Aug and Christmas. Elegant art nouveau decor. Seafood: fusili with fish sauce, prawn kebabs, 30/50,000.
★★★ *Glower,* SS 16 at 538.6-km marker, ☎ 52121, 33 rm Ⓟ closed Oct-May, 56,000; bkf: 3,600.
★★★ *Rosary,* lungomare Colombo, ☎ 2557, 72 rm Ⓟ ⓺ closed Dec-Jan, 65,000; bkf: 5,000.
★★★ *Savoia,* corso Nazionale 115, ☎ 2375, 35 rm Ⓟ closed Christmas, 48,500; bkf: 5,000.

Restaurants:
● ♦♦♦ *Squaloblù,* v. De Gasperi 49, ☎ 83203, closed Mon, 20-31 Oct and Christmas. Seaside restaurant, pleasant surroundings, garden in summer. Excellent seafood: fish pancakes, stuffed shellfish au gratin, 30/35,000.
♦♦♦ *Torre Saracena,* SS Adriatica, ☎ 3318, closed Mon and 15 Oct-15 Nov. Refurbished

Saracen coastal tower, fine views and terrace overlooking lido. Fine quality seafood: squid kebabs, stuffed mussels, moscardini in purgatorio, 30/40,000.
♦♦ *Drago*, v. Vittorio Emanuele III 58, ☎ 71139, closed Wed, Sun eve in winter and 1-20 Feb. Seafood: tubetti with mussels, black risotto, brodetto, 30/45,000.

⚓ *Cala Saracena*, v. Europa 2, 120 pl, ☎ 52193.

Recommended
Discothèque: *Torre Saracena*, v. Europa 2, ☎ 3318 (closed Oct-Apr).
Events: *Térmoli summer festival* (including fishing festival, Aug).
Marina: Ufficio Marittimo, ☎ 2484.
Sailing school: *Circolo Vela Surf*, v. Rio Vivo, ☎ 84582.
Swimming pool: ☎ 71547.

The TRIGNO AND THE SANGRO

From Isernia *(121 km, 1 day; map 2)*

The itinerary moves between the Valleys of the Trigno and the Sangro, crossing and recrossing ridges and peaks and giving an insight into a part of Molise which is not particularly well known, but has a number of historic, artistic and architectural monuments, and above all magnificent countryside and views. The villages and towns are all at heights between 2,600 and 4,600 ft. Pietrabbondante alone would justify the journey for the chance of sitting in the Samnite theatre and admiring both the wonderful ancient building and

The Trigno and the Sangro

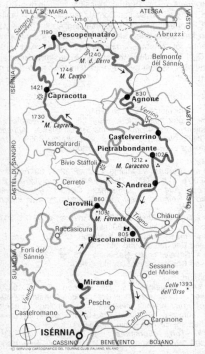

the semicircle of glorious mountains which seem to mirror the theatre on an enormous scale.

▶ The route sets off from **Isernia** (→) towards the NW on the SS 17, then turns r. at the first junction. ▶ **Carovilli** is set on a crag at the foot of Mt. Ferrante (3,448 ft) and has remains of a small Samnite temple halfway up the hill. ▶ The road then climbs rapidly to the **Stffoli** junction, on a rolling plain, and proceeds to the NW. ▶ **Capracotta** (4,662 ft; one of the highest towns in Italy; it can have as much as 16 ft of snow) is sunk in meadows and pine trees. On fine days there is a magnificent view of the Adriatic, the Maiella and the Sangro Valley from the top of the Grilli. Near the town is Monte Cavallerizzo, with remains of Samnite walls. Nearby is **Fonte Romita**, where the "tavola di Agnone" was found, written in Oscan characters (the language of the Samnites) and now in the British Museum in London. ▶ Still climbing rapidly, with fine views, the road reaches **Pescopennataro**, dominating the Sangro Valley on a rocky spur on the edge of the pine forests (*pesco*, common in Molise and Abruzzi place names, means rock, crag). ▶ The road then descends SE to **Agnone** on a hill surrounded by woods. ▶ This was the "Athens of Samnium". It is famous for bell production and has an interesting old town in which some houses show strong Venetian influence, the result of immigration from Venice in ancient times. This may also explain the local cult of S. Mark; fine 18C polychrome wooden statues in the parish church of **S. Emidio** (1443), which also has a little museum with a collection of stone weapons. ▶ After an easy descent the road goes through the **Selvapiana forest**. ▶ **Pietrabbondante** seems threatened by the enormous rocks which hang out above it. It contains the remains of a Samnite city, probably a centre of the Pentri Samnite tribe; a little to the S, at the foot of Mt. Caraceno (3,976 ft), the base of a large temple, remains of a minor temple, arcades, shops and a **theatre★** hollowed out of the hill have survived. The countryside is attractive and the view magnificent. ▶ **Pescolanciano** had a famous porcelain factory in the 18C (according to tradition the artisans of Capodimonte set it on fire once they had found out its secrets by trickery). It is surrounded by woods, dominated by a castle and near the "great sheep road" used for spring and autumn flock movement. Remains of walls are evidence of the existence of an ancient Samnite settlement. ▶ The final leg leads back to Isernia. ☐

Practical information ──────────

AGNONE, ✉ 86081, ☎ 0865.

Restaurant:
♦ *Buoni Amici:* corso Vittorio Emanuele 39, ☎ 77882, closed Tue. Regional cuisine: brawn, Santè soup, sagne and tacconi, 20/25,000.

Recommended
Events: *Via Crucis Vivente* (Apr); *Festival of the Madonna del Carmine with procession and fireworks (Jul)*; procession at night (24 Dec), town hall, ☎ 78207.
Technical tourism: visits to *Pontificia Fonderia Campane Marinelli*, v. Felice D'Onofrio, ☎ 78235 (bell foundry, other bronze castings); *Ceramiche La Giara*, corso Vittorio Emanuele 251, ☎ 77278 (ceramics).

CAPRACOTTA, ✉ 86082, ☎ 0865.

⚲ cross-country skiing.

Restaurant:
♦ *Vittoria:* corso S. Antonio 79, ☎ 94205, closed 15-31 Oct and 15-30 Nov. Mountain restaurant with wooden tables. Regional cuisine: maccheroni alla chitarra, grilled lamb, sausages with polenta, 18/25,000.

PIETRABBONDANTE, ✉ 86085, ☎ 0865.

Recommended
Archery: *Compagnia Arcieri Carecini*, corso Sannitico 70, ☎ 76157.

Events: *theatre season* in the Samnite theatre (Jul-Aug).

VENAFRO

Isernia 22, Campobasso 73, Rome 154 km
Pop. 9,106 ✉ 86079 ☎ 0865   A3

This little town is strikingly situated at the foot of Mt. Santa Croce in the central Volturno valley, on the westernmost border of Molise.

▶ The **cathedral** is a 15C Gothic rebuilding of an earlier Romanesque church; the apses★ were built from stones of the imperial period. ▶ The **Palazzo Caracciolo** was built in the 15C for residential and defensive purposes and has fine portals. ▶ There are seven English alabaster panels in the **chiesa dell'Annunziata** (1387). ▶ The medieval **castle** has maintained its original complex layout despite much tampering. ▶ The remains of *Venafrum*, originally a Samnite then a Roman city, famous even in ancient times for its olive oil and as a holiday resort (mentioned by Cicero, Horace and Pliny, among others) are near the station (**amphitheatre**) and the **Terme di S. Aniello**, a little above the town. This latter site contains a **theatre** and a fine **aqueduct**, which brought water for a distance of more than 30 km, from the source of the Volturno, near the present abbey of S. Vincenzo (→). ▶ A **Museo Archeologico** (*in preparation; v.* Garibaldi) will show archaeological material from *Venafrum*, including an 'edict of the Venafrum aqueduct' and other inscriptions, parts of an olive press and a reconstruction of a hydraulic wheel, a Venus and other sculptures.   □

Practical information ⎯⎯⎯⎯⎯⎯⎯⎯⎯⎯

Hotel:
★★ **Motel Dora**, at Pozzilli, SS 85, ☎ 972115, 16 rm Ⓟ Ⓟ ⌷ closed Christmas and Easter, 32,000.

Piedmont

▶ Although it has no coastline, Piedmont offers many other kinds of scenery lying as it does within the great sweep of the Alps and their succession of rugged, crystalline peaks. Glaciers shimmer against the clear blue skies, forming the backdrop to the plain through which flows the Po River. The valleys gradually deepen as they cut into the mountains, and the vegetation and landscapes become alpine. This region was long isolated, but new life has been brought to it by tourism and the skiing offered by its year-round snow. On the right bank of the Po, extending to the Maritime Alps, is the hilly countryside of Monferrato and Langhe with castles and vineyards that are a riot of soft greens, burnt yellows and hints of red. Elsewhere, the area reached by the glaciers during the quaternary period is now a gentle countryside of moraine deposits covered with moorland greens, which lose their vividness on the plain. To the E, where the Po Valley broadens out, the still waters of rice fields in springtime reflect poplars, clouds and the occasional blue heron. The famous lakes of N Italy nestle at the foot of the Alps; Lake Orta and the W half of Lake Maggiore lie within Piedmont, and the mild climate allows palms to grow and magnolias to bloom in the gardens of the old villas scattered along their shores. Turin both dominates and encapsulates the region. It stands on the Po, with hills rising on the opposite bank to a backdrop of distant mountains. A capital for four centuries, Turin is at once refined and industrial, dynastic and middle-class, and its arcaded streets bring a touch of humanity to the rational, regular grid of its typical Roman street plan. As the centre of the Kingdom of Savoy, it guided the yearnings of Italian unity down a road that was both feasible and liberal. Aristocratic and bourgeois, it fostered the Industrial Revolution in Italy; working-class, it has set social transformation in motion. The approach of the Turin political Left is imbued with a tradition in which class-consciousness goes hand in hand with a pride in craftsmanship and manufacture. Turin is a city of many tantalizing faces. Piedmont has an enormous and varied cultural heritage. Some elements result almost from chance, such as the Egyptian Museum at Turin which is matched only in Egypt itself. Others shed a fascinating light on Italian art such as the courtly frescos at Manta, the Gothic church of S. Andrea at Vercelli and the popular art of the Sacro Monte in Varallo. In Turin, the bold innovations attempted by Antonelli and Nervi, both of whom were engineers, demonstrate the difficulty in architecture of separating engineering and art. This issue had already been raised by Fra Guarini (1604-83), the master of architectural fantasy, in Turin, and by Filippo Juvara (18C) in Stupinigi. Guarini came from Modena and Juvara from Messina, but their work in Piedmont symbolizes the region's importance as a stimulus to all of Italy and a melting pot of ideas, even though geographically it is far from the centre. □

● Don't miss

Egyptian museum ★★, the Savoy gallery ★★, the Royal Armoury ★★, the Chapel of the Holy Shroud ★, and San Lorenzo ★ in Turin; San Andrea ★★ in Vercelli; Stresa ★ and the Borromean Islands ★★ at Lake Maggiore; the Villa Reale ★ at Stupinigi; Sacra di San Michele ★; the Monte Rosa in Alagna Valsesia and Macugnaga.

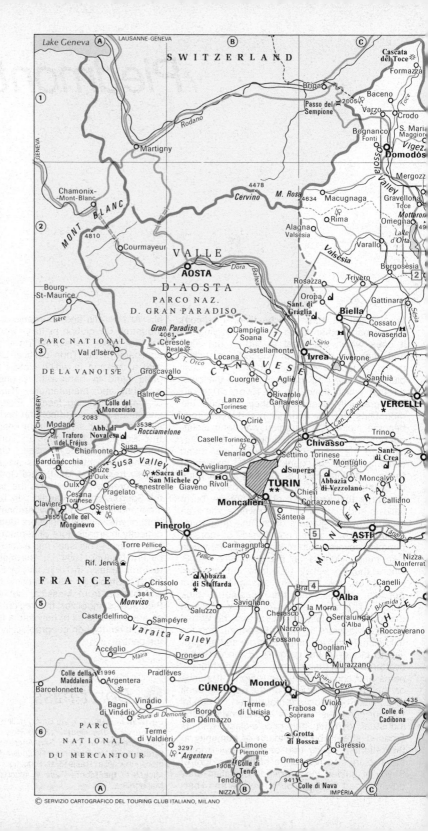

● Brief regional history

5C BC-5C AD

Ligurians, Gauls and Romans. Piedmont was the original home of the Ligurians. During the middle of the 1st millennium BC, the Gauls headed E and settled here. ● By the beginning of the Punic Wars, the territory under Rome's rule formed an enclave S of the Po, along the lower edge of the Dora Baltea, from **Eporedia** (Ivrea) to **Pollentia** (Pollenzo). ● The result was the Roman occupation and conquest of Transalpine Gaul (France).

5C-15C

Feudal lords. Charlemagne and his Franks, at war with the Lombards, crossed the Susa Valley and entered Italy in 773. ● During the crisis of the Carolingian Empire, after the death of Charlemagne, three great feudal territories were formed: the **marquisates of Turin, Ivrea and Monferrato.** ● In 1045, the Turin territory, stretching from Monginevro to the Sea of Albenga, was inherited by **Adelaide de Susa** who brought it as part of her dowry on her marriage to **Oddone of Savoy.** This marriage was a turning point in Italian history. The place of the Savoy family in Italy had been assured by Oddone's father, **Humbert the White-Handed,** who had been awarded alpine fiefdoms in recognition of his military feats. The family was to retain substantial political force until the end of World War II. ● The feudal dominions were eventually divided, and the Savoy family split into many different branches. ● In communard times, **Asti, Tortona, Vercelli, Novara and Alessandria** were part of the Lombard Anti-imperial League; Alessandria (named after Pope Alexander III) had been built in haste at the intersection of the Rivers Tanaro and Bormida to hold off the imperial forces coming in from the Susa Valley. ● Piedmont's political map was still considerably fragmented in the 14C and 15C. It included the **counties of Savoy, Tenda and Nizza; the marquisates of Saluzzo and Monferrato;** and the **principality of Savoy-Acaia.** A further branch of the Savoys held Turin, Chieri, Pinerolo and Savigliano. The **County of Asti** formed part of the dowry of Valentina Visconti, daughter of Gian Galeazzo Visconti, Duke of Milan, when she married the Duke of Orleans. During **Gian Galeazzo Visconti's** lifetime (d. 1402), the duchy of Milan extended into what is now W Piedmont, including **Novara, Vercelli and Alessandria.** ● Amedeo VIII of Savoy, created duke by the Germanic Emperor Sigismund in the first half of the 15C, was able to reunite the fragmented dominions that accounted for a considerable part of today's Piedmont.

16C-18C

The Savoy family. Political intrigues among the opposing European powers dominating Italy (France, Spain and Austria) fostered a gradual increase in the Savoy family's power. ● The duchy of Savoy almost disappeared in the foreign wars fought on Italian soil between 1494, when Charles VIII of France invaded Italy, and 1559, date of the treaty of Cateau-Cambrésis, which marked the end of French, Spanish and English claims to Italian territory. ● **Emanuele Filiberto** of Savoy, in return for service to the Hapsburgs, was granted the duchy that had once belonged to his father. Establishing the capital in Turin,

Emanuele Filiberto firmly set the dynasty's sights on Italy. ● **Carlo Emanuele I** of Savoy ceded transalpine land to Henry IV of France in exchange for the marquisate of Saluzzo in 1601. The **marquisate of Monferrato** was recognized as Savoy territory in 1714. ● In 1713, the treaty of Utrecht put an end to the War of Spanish Succession and **Vittorio Amedeo II** of Savoy was named King of Sicily (in 1720, Sicily was exchanged for Sardinia). ● Napoleon's armies, in the aftermath of the French Revolution, upset Italy's political geography, but also provided some of the ideas that later inspired the forces of the **Risorgimento** (national resurgence).

S. Andrea in Vercelli

19C-20C
Piedmont and Italy. Piedmont was absorbed into the Napoleonic Empire, but with the systematization of Europe in 1815, the Savoy family was restored to power. ● **The Kingdom of Sardinia** (later known as Piedmont) included Savoy, the county of Nizza, Sardinia and Liguria, in addition to the Piedmont area, which extended as far as the Ticino River and towns beyond the Po River, right to the border of the duchy of Parma. ● On the Italian peninsula, Piedmont was renowned for its well-trained army, rapid economic development and liberal political orientation after the European revolutions of 1848 (especially under the leadership of **Camillo Benso Conte di Cavour**, the architect of Italian unity). ● After the second war of independence against Austria in 1859, in which Cavour and **Vittorio Emanuele II's** Piedmont were supported by Napoleon III, the **Kingdom of Italy** was proclaimed on 14 May 1861 in a temporary pavilion erected in the courtyard of Turin's Carignano Palace, the seat of Parliament. **Turin** remained the country's capital until 1865. ● **Savoy** and **Nizza** were made part of France in accordance with conditions laid

down by the 1859 alliance; as Savoie and Nice they remain French to this day. ● The Piedmont region was extended as a result of a redefinition of boundaries that took place after the Second World War.

abbey of Staffarda

● *Practical information*

Information: tourist offices in main centres and principal localities; *Servizio Informazioni Turistiche TCI,* at Turin, p. Solferino 3/bis.
SOS: public emergency aid, ☎ 113; immediate police intervention, ☎ 112; highway patrol ACI, ☎ 116.
Weather: forecasts, ☎ 011/57601; road conditions, ☎ 011/5711, or ACI, ☎ 02/4212; snow reports, ☎ 011/5731 (from Turin, ☎ 162).
Vacation villages: *Club Mediterranée,* at Sestriere (open Dec-Apr); *Hotel-Villaggio Valtur,* at San Sicario, *Cesana Torinese* (open Jun-Aug and Dec-Apr).
Festivals: *historical carnival* at Ivrea; *competition and wine festival* at Asti; *joust* at Cento Torri; *music festival* at Stresa; *International Motorcycle Rally* at Castellazzo Bormida.
Events: *white truffles fair* at Alba; *wine fairs* at various localities in Monferrato and Langhe; *exhibition of antique furniture* at Saluzzo; *antique markets* at Casale and Nizza Monferrato; *exhibition of silverware* at Alessandria; at Turin: *Automobile and Industrial Vehicle Show;* vacation, tourism, sports and leisure exhibits; mountaineering and climbing shows; *horse racing,* v. Rocciamelene 3, ☎ 011/9651356.
Parks and reserves: *Gran Paradiso National Park* (partly in Valle d'Aosta region), at Turin, v. della Rocca 47, ☎ 011/871187 (headquarters), at Noasca, ☎ 0124/90001 and Ronco Canavese, ☎ 0124/87103 (visitors centres open Jul-Aug); *Alta Valle Pesio Natural Park* (→ Cuneo); *Palanfrè Woods and Lakes Natural Reserve* (→ Limone Piemonte); *Argentera Natural Park* (→ Terme di Valdieri); *Veglia Alps Natural Park* (→ Varzo); *Valle del Ticino Natural Park* (→ Novara); *Orsiera-Rocciavrè Natural Park* (→ Fenestrelle); *Val Troncea Natural Park* (→ Pragelato); *Gran Bosco di Salbertrand Natural Park* (→ Oulx); *La Mandria Regional Park* (→ Turin); *Alta Valsesia Natural Park* (→ Varallo Sesia); *Lame del Sesia Natural Park, Isolone Oldenico* and *Garzaia Villarboit Special Nature Reserves* (→ Vercelli); *Capanne di Marcarolo Natural Park* (→ Gavi).

Environmental protection: *World Wildlife Fund Piedmont Delegation,* at Turin, v. Livorno 18/A, ☎ 011/486434, other offices: at Turin, corso Regina Margherita 139/A, ☎ 011/534255, at Novara, v. S. di Santarosa 18, ☎ 0321/28841 (summer work camps in regional natural parks , accommodation in shelters), at Alessandria, v. del Vescovado 10; *Biella,* at Cossato, v. Mendola, at Pinerolo, v. Brignone 1; *International League for the Protection of Birds,* at Asti, p. Leonardo da Vinci 1 (offices at Nizza Monferrato, v. S. Giulia, ☎ 0141/701116, exhibition of birds nests). *Crava animal preserves,* at Cuneo, v. Roma 50, ☎ 0171/491495 (→ Mondovi); at Racconigi, *Cascina Stramiano reserve for the reintroduction of native white storks,* ☎ 0321/28841 (birdwatching classes, oversees Agognate forest); at Turin, v. Bari 21, ☎ 011/487051 (birdwatching and naturalist photography classes); *Italia Nostra,* at Turin, v. Massena 71, ☎ 011/500056.

Technical tourism: oenology, at Alba, Barbaresco, Canelli, Santo Stefano Belbo, Gavi, Monforte d'Alba, Castiglione Falletto, Gallo d'Alba (→ Le Langhe); Castelnuovo Don Bosco, Pessione (→ Chieri). Musical instruments workshop, at Quarna di Sotto (→ Omegna); wood-carving, school, at Mélezet (→ Bardonecchia); artisanal foundry, at Valduggia (→ Borgosesia); modern tapestry workshop, at Asti; hat factory, at Alessandria; typography workshop, at Turin (technical manuals and rare books); *associazione regionale Agriturist,* at Turin, v XX Settembre 2, ☎ 011/513297.

Rambling and hiking: outstanding long-distance trails in alpine country: itineraries with stopovers in Grande Traversate in Alps (stopovers in Alagna Valsesia, Ceresole Reale, Crissolo, *Q. Sella shelter,* at Monviso, ☎ 0175/94943, Certosa di Pesio, Susa; open mid-Jul-Sep); in Apennines, last section of Europeo E itinerary from Gavi (Apr-Oct), information: CAI offices at Acqui Terme, v. Monteverde 44, Alessandria, v. Mazzini 58, Asti, corso della Vittoria 50, Bardonecchia, p. don Vachet 1, Biella, v. P. Micca 13, Cuneo, v. Allione 1, Domodossola, v. Capis 2/4, Garessio, p. Balilla, Ivrea, casella postale 50, Macugnaga (inquire at tourist office); Mondovi, v. Beccaria 26, Novara, v. Cavallotti 11, Ovada (inquire at SOMS, v. Piave), Pinerolo, v. Sommeiller 26, Saluzzo, Palazzo di Città 29, Turin, v. Barbaroux 1, Varallo, v. Durio 14 and Vercelli, v. Stara 1. *Italian Excursion Federation,* at Turin, Cibrario 33, ☎ 011/740011; *Ente, Gran Paradiso National Park,* at Turin, v. della Rocca 47, ☎ 011/871187; GTA promotion committee, at Turin, v. Barbaroux 1, ☎ 011/514477; *Trekking International,* at Turin, v. G. F. Re 78, ☎ 011/793023; *Gruppo Guide Aria di Montagna,* 10010 Cascinette d'Ivrea.

Mountaineering: tourists can climb Mt. Rosa from Alagna Valsesia and Nacugnaga; ski-mountaineering routes start at Argentera, Dardonecchia, Entracque, Garessio, Limone Piemonte, Macugnaga, Oropa, Sestriere, in Ossola and Varaita valleys; 34 CAI shelters linked by telephone; mountaineering classes in Bardonecchia and Macugnaga, information: CAI offices, at Bardonecchia, p. Don Vachet 1, Biella, v. Micca 13, ☎ 015/21234, Cuneo, v. Allione 1, ☎ 0171/67998, Domodossola, v. Capis 2/4, Garessio, p. Balilla, Macugnaga (inquire at tourist office ☎ 0324/65119), Varallo, v. Durio 14 ☎ 0163/51530, *Centro Alpinismo Valle Ossola,* at Domodossola, Premosello Chiovenda, ☎ 0324/88237; at Villadossola (7 km S of Domodossola) ☎ 0324/522530 (alpine guides), at Gravellona Toce ☎ 0323/846325 (week-long trips, classes on technical climbing); 'Great crossing' of solan, Verbanese and Cusian Alps, information at Novara, ☎ 0321/23398 or 22214; *Cooperativa Guide Alpi Marittime,* at Cuneo, corso Marconi 8, ☎ 0171/54896; *Gruppo Guide Aria di Montagna,* 10010 Cascinette d'Ivrea.

Cycling: information and assistance can be obtained from UDACE-affiliated cycling groups (197 altogether) throughout the region; TCI bicycle touring maps: routes in Canavese and Alessandrino and from Sesia to Monferrato.

Horseback riding: *Italian Federation of Equestrian Sports,* at Turin, corso Duca degli Abruzzi 72, ☎ 011/540309; ANTE, at Candelo (→ Biella), Tenuta La Mandria, ☎ 015/53078; riding centres, at Bossolasco (→ Le Langhe itinerary), Capriata d'Orba (→ Novi Ligure), Cas-

Piedmontese wines

Land given over to viticulture has shrunk over the years to 70,000 hectares, 90 percent of which is on sloping hillsides. The 405 million hectolitres of wine produced annually account for 6 percent of total world production. 50 percent of all regulated DOC (denominazione di origine controllata) wines - 12 percent of world production - are white Moscato Asti, sweet Asti and sparkling Asti. Nevertheless, the region is especially known for its red wines. Of the five regulated and guaranteed DOCG wines (all reds) two are Piedmontese: Barbaresco and Barolo. Even as far back as the 13C-14C, Pietro de Crescenzi, a Bolognese student of agriculture, congratulated the Monferrato peasants on their expert grape cultivation. At that time, the a spanna method was introduced, in which vines were tied to poles and pruned. Later, in Novara, the spanna became the name of Piedmont's principal vineyards, the Nebbiolo. The wine that bears the name of this celebrated vineyard, Nebbiolo, is highly recommended. Gattinara, a fine red wine with a bouquet likened to violets from the Navarese hills surrounding Gattinara, contended for the title of the best wine in Italy against the renowned Barolo made from Barbaresco, Roero and the rare Carema grapes. Another curiosity of the region is that the wine known as Dolcetto (from dolce, meaning sweet) is not even a little sweet; in fact, its smooth, dry taste can sometimes conceal a touch of bitterness. The grapes plucked from the vineyards are, nevertheless, sweet. Barbera, formerly one of the best known and widely appreciated wines, has recently declined in popularity - like certain other Italian reds - while the white Cortese are increasingly appreciated by winelovers. The region of production includes upper and lower Monferrato; the hills south of the Po which continue right down to the Maritime Alps (some of which are known as the Langhe). The wines produced there are Barbera, Dolcetto, Freisa, Grignolino, Brachetto, Barolo, Nebbiolo, Moscato, Asti and Cortese. Also noteworthy are the wines of the upper Eporediese at the edge of the Valle d'Aosta (Carema), the Canavese (Erbaluce di Caluso), the Vercelli and Novaran pre-Alps and the hills of Chierese and the Colli Tortonesi.

Breadsticks

In 1643, the Florentine Abbot Vincenzo Rucellai was amazed 'by bread as long as an arm and ever so thin'. He might have been referring to the breadsticks that the French call les petits bâtons de Turin and that Napoleon enjoyed. A legend dates their invention to 1679 by a baker called Antonio Brunero, and another gives their creation to a court doctor, anxious to promote the good health of the young Duke Vittorio Amedeo II (later the first king of his line), who asked a baker to prepare gherse, very thin oblong loaves of bread. From ghersa came the diminutive ghersin, which eventually became grissino. These thin breadsticks are found not only in Piedmont, but throughout Italy: hand-worked, irregular, long, lightly sprinkled with flour and baked until thoroughly crisp. Whatever their origin, their role in the Piemont diet is firmly established.

Walser

Near Mt. Rosa, in the high Gressoney, Formazza and Anzasca (Macugnaga) valleys and in Alagna (Valsesia), Rima San Giuseppe and Rimella, many villages are linguistic islands of German speakers. The villagers, known as 'walser', are descended from immigrants from the high Rodano valley, Vallese (hence their name). Thought to have originally been nomadic shepherds in the summertime, the Walser settled in northern Italy during the Middle Ages. Their towns are noteworthy for beautiful, functional wooden houses built upon stone foundations, one of which - in Alagna Valsesia - has been converted into the Walser Museum. The local dialect remains quite distinct.

Vermouth

Vermouth is derived from the German wermuth *meaning bitter. It is an aromatic wine made from a recipe of Vittorio Emanuele II's cook, by steeping thirteen ingredients (including cassia wood, angelica, gentian and spices) in a generous quantity of white wine. It was first concocted in the very heart of Turin, at the corner of P. Castello and v. Barbaroux, in 1786 under the reign of Vittorio Amedeo III. Antonio Benedetto Carpano, the inventor, sold vermouth in the square. Vermouth may be sweet, dry or bitter; red or white. A Carpano variant is called* punt e mes *which in Piedmontese dialect means a point and a half, an expression supposedly taken from a slip of the tongue made by a money broker when his listing fell a point and a half: when he ordered his apéritif his mind was elsewhere and he pronounced these very words. The bartender, of course, immediately understood what was wanted. Dry vermouth is used in making Martini cocktails, which get their name not from a vermouth brand name, as is commonly believed, but from a legendary bartender, Martinez, who worked in New Orleans, Chicago, Boston or somewhere else altogether in the 19C.*

Facts and figures

Location: *The original name* Pedemontium *(at the foot of the mountains) appeared only around the middle of the 13C and indicated a small tract of flat land between the rivers Po and Sangone SW of Turin. The area grew with the state of Savoy's expansion beyond the Alps. In the region surrounded by the great W cirque of the Alps, there are more mountains and hills than plains, although the latter are historically richer and more densely populated.*
Area: *25,399 sq km, the second largest Italian region.*
Climate: *Continental, with cold winters and hot summers and wide temperature variations at different altitudes. The countryside is popular with tourists especially during the spring and autumn.*
Population: *4,431,064 inhabitants, of whom a quarter live in Turin.*
Administration: *The regional capital, Turin, is where the Savoy dynasty established the seat of government in the 16C; the other provinces are Alessandria, Asti, Cuneo, Novara and Vercelli.*

telletto Ticino (→ Novara), Castiglione d'Asti and Cerreto d'Asti (→ Asti), Mottalciata (→ Vercelli), Pinerolo, Prato Nevoso (→ Fabrosa Soprana).
Lake trips: Lake Maggiore at Arona, v. F. Baracca 1, ☎ 0322/46651 (tourist trips and summer evening cruises).
Instructional courses: *Bottega del Telaio,* at Turin, v. Buozzi 2, ☎ 011/539691 (private classes in weaving), *Scuola di arte e pittura di Lella Burzio,* at Turin, p. Statuto 11, ☎ 011/548358 (painting, graphics and applied arts).
Youth activities: *CTS,* at Turin, v. Alfieri 17 ☎ 011/535966, Novara corso XXIII Marzo 126, ☎ 0321/399572 (travel and tourism aid); *CAI,* at Turin ☎ 011/537983 or 546031, Alessandria, ☎ 0131/321313, Bardonecchia, ☎ 0122/99163 (summer classes and excursions); *Est Monte Rosa,* at Domodossola ☎ 0324/40338, Macugnaga ☎ 0324/65059 (ski lessons off marked runs), ARCI, at Turin, ☎ 011/885067 or 8396696, Alessandria, ☎ 0131/53253, Asti, ☎ 0141/32555, Cuneo, ☎ 0171/63678, Novara, ☎ 0321/20023, Vercelli, ☎ 0161/26378; *Cooperative guide Alpi Marittime,* at Cuneo, ☎ 0171/54896 (skiing off marked runs, rock and ice-climbing, excursions for naturalists and photographers, dangerous work on bridges, roads and bell towers).

Bagna cauda

Cauda *is the Piedmontese dialect word for hot (*caldo *in Italian). This recipe involves simmering a mixture of oil, minced garlic, anchovies and other ingredients. The resulting sauce is a kind of fondue in which are dipped prepared vegetables and regional sausages. In the classic Piedmontese preparation, the bagna cauda is the only pot on the table. In a more sophisticated version, each guest has an individual terra-cotta bowl kept hot over an alcohol burner. Copious and robust regional red wines cool the palate. The bagna cauda is one of the few traditional Piedmont dishes that calls for oil: Piedmont is on the 'butter side' of the line that divides the Mediterranean oil civilization from the northern continental butter civilization.*

Aquatic sports: *Italian Federation of Water Skiing,* at Avigliana, Omegna, Turin, Verbania Pallanza; novices can practice on Lakes Maggiore, Mergozzo, Orta, Viverone and Avigliana.
Boating and sailing: tourist ports at Cannero Riviera, Cannobio and Verbania on Lake Maggiore; at Orta San Giulio on Lake Orta; *boating league* has offices at Arona, corso Europa 26 and Turin, corso Unione Sovietica 316, ☎ 011/530979 (sailing and boating classes); practice on Lakes Maggiore, Orta, Viverone and Avigliana.
Canoeing: *Italian Federation,* at Cuneo, corso IV Novembre 29, ☎ 011/54529; canoe races at Ivrea, Omegna, Turin, Verbania and Island of Vocca (→ Varallo).
Winter sports: Alagna Valsesia (summertime glacier skiing at Indren and Bors); Bardonecchia (summer skiing at Sommeiller Pass); Cesana Torinese-San Sicario; Claviere; Formazza, Ossola (summertime glacier skiing at Siedel); Limone Piemonte; Macugnaga (summer skiing at Moro Pass); Sauze d'Oulx (50 km of cross-country ski trails in Oulx); Sestriere.
Golf: at Avigliana (18 holes), Claviere (9 holes), Fiano Torinese (→ Turin), Magnano (→ Biella), Premeno (9 holes) (→ High Lake Maggiore), Sestriere (18 holes), Turin, Valenza, Vezzo (9 holes) (→ Stresa).
Aerial sports: *aeroclub,* at Alessandria, v. Milite Ignoto, ☎ 031/323296, Biella-Cerrione ☎ 015/21167; *Aeroporto F. Cappa,* at Casale Monferrato, ☎ 0142/2556; Cuneo-Levaldigi, ☎ 0172/374132 (also hang-gliding and parachuting), *Aeroporto Carlo del Prete,* at Vercelli ☎ 0161/53791; gliding club, at Novi Ligure airport, ☎ 0143/71898; Ita-

lian Federation of Hang-gliding, ☎ 015/538703 (information), affiliated schools at Asti, Burolo (→ Ivrea), Candelo (→ Vercelli), Cuneo, Macugnaga, Mondovi and Turin. Cuneo-Levaldigi Airclub, at airport, ☎ 0172/374132 (hot-air balloons); Sport Promotion, at Turin, v. Palladio 1, ☎ 011/832805.
Spelunking: CAI speleological groups, at Biella, v. P. Micca 13; Alpi Marittime, at Cuneo, p. Galimberti 13, Novara, v. Cavallotti 11, Turin, subalpine gallery 30, ☎ 011/537983 (courses on speleology Jan-May); outfitted speleological trips at Bossea (→ Frabosa Soprana), Villanova Mondovi and Crissolo.
Clay pigeon shooting: at Turin, strada Bramafame 41, ☎ 011/254137; at Asti, Valmanera ☎ 0141/271807; at Pecetto di Valenza (5 km SE of Valenza) ☎ 0131/970114.
Fishing: Italian Fishing Federation, at Alessandria, v. Tortona 41, ☎ 0131/65264, Asti, palazzo della Provincia, Cuneo, corso Dante 21, ☎ 0171/61422, Novara, v. Lombardo 3 ☎ 0321/30354; Turin, v. Giolitti 24, ☎ 011/546732 (regional office); Vercelli, p. Roma 36, ☎ 0161/60492 (for fishing conditions, permitted and prohibited zones, etc.).
Car and motorcycle racing: Alfa Romeo car racing, at Balocco (→ Vercelli); car racing, at Lombardore (→ Turin); motorcycle racetrack, at Maggiora (→ Borgomanero).
Motocross: trails, at Casale Monferrato, Lombardore (→ Turin), Maggiora (→ Borgomanero), San Salvatore Monferrato (→ Alessandria).
Bowling: Italian Bowling Association, at Alessandria, v. Pontida 96, ☎ 0131/53074, Asti, v. Mameli 32, Biella, v. Micca 30, Casale Monferrato, v. Visconti 2, ☎ 0142/2504, Cuneo, corso IV Novembre 29, ☎ 0171/54529, Novara, v. Brera B, Vercelli, v. Dalmazia 22, Turin, corso Stati Uniti 10, ☎ 011/534382, v. Beaumont 2 ☎ 541571, corso Re Umberto, ☎ 546311. Indoor bowling alleys at Asti, v. del Bosco 2, ☎ 0141/34350, Biella, v. Macallè, ☎ 015/401982, Moncalieri, (Vallese region), ☎ 011/641695, Novara, v. Kennedy 32, ☎ 0321/452894, Turin, lungodora Colletta 53, ☎ 011/2743275.
Zoos and amusement parks: Langhe Safari Park, at Murazzano (→ Langhe itinerary); Crava Morozzo Nature Preserve (→ Mondovi); Villa Pallavicino Zoological Park, at Stresa; La Torbiera Zoo, at Agrate Conturbia; Castelbeltame Zoo (→ Novara); Sergio Martinat zoological gardens, at Pinerolo.

Truffles and other delicacies

White truffles with their firm texture, delicate flavor and pungent smell are most abundant in Alba (the most important truffle market in Italy), but can also be found outside of Langhe in various parts of Monferrato and Astigiano. A traditional Piedmontese way of eating these delicacies involves slicing them on to a fresh salad and adding a dressing made of sieved hard-boiled eggs mixed with oil and vinegar, salt, mustard and anchovy paste. A classic regional dish is jugged rabbit, which calls for the animal to be marinated for at least two days, then braised in its own blood and spiced with Barbera or Dolcetto wine along with aromatic herbs and various spices. Monferrato and Langhe offer a Piedmontese specialty of mixed boiled meat. It boasts seven different cuts of veal, seven 'ornaments' (ox tail and tongue, head and leg of veal, chicken broth, pork sausages and meatloaf), seven greens and three sauces (green, red and mustard). In Alba, the Piedmontese mixed-fry platter calls for at least twelve savoury ingredients: veal and lamb cutlets, brains and giblets, greens, various croquettes and even certain sweet ingredients which are found in the sweet semolina- or macaroon-based fry platters. Fish stuffed with minced macaroons, peaches, sugar and eggs, soaked in white Canelli wine and baked is considered to be a typically Piedmontese dessert; there is also zabaglione which takes its name from S. Giovanni Baglione, patron saint of pastry shops, venerated in Turin's S. Tomaso church. A lawyer, Count Giuseppe Barbaroux, Minister of Justice under Carlo Alberto, is taken to be the inventor of the delicious and hearty cannelloni alla Barbaroux; Bela Rosin, mistress and later wife of Vittorio Emanuele II, gave her name to the egg dish alla Bela Rosin, which is simply hard-boiled eggs halved and covered with mayonnaise.

● Towns and places

ACQUI TERME

Alessandria 33, Turin 106, Milan 130 km
Pop. 21,414 ⊠ 15011 ☎ 0144   C-D5

The sulphurous waters of Acqui Terme flow from the great Lake of Sorgenti and the springs of Acqua Marcia. During the Roman conquests in the 2C BC, the native Ligurians were almost entirely wiped out. Acqui Terme has always been renowned for its thermal waters and celebrated throughout history by poets and writers. The capital of Alto Monferrato since the 13C and once a French stronghold, the town is today an important commercial and political centre.

▶ Not far away is the Carlo Alberto bridge in which can be seen the ruins of a Roman **aqueduct**; the town, nonetheless, has a distinctly medieval aura. The **cathedral** dates from the 11C but the apse and part of the belfry are the only reminders of this period. An exquisite Renaissance marble portal (1481) leads to a 16C hall lined with columns. The presbytery hides a remarkable crypt. To the r. of the church is a magnificent 14C cloister with Roman relics. ▶ The **Castello dei Paleologhi**, like the cathedral, dates from the 11C; it was destroyed and

rebuilt in the 16C and later restored anew in the 18C. It houses the **Civic Archaeological Museum** (Wed, Thu, Sat 9 a.m.-12 noon and 4-7 p.m.; Sun 9:30 a.m.-12 noon; telephone in advance, ☎ 57555), worth visiting for its splendid Roman relics. ▶ Although the basilica of **S. Pietro** (10C-11C) is even older, the apse is all that survives from the earlier period. ▶ The **Bollente** is a classical pavilion designed by Ceruti (1870) to shelter the hot springs. The bubbling water, with a constant temperature of 75º, gushes out at the rate of 500 l/mn. ▶ The thermal springs are renowned for their therapeutic properties; the **Nuove Terme** (all year) is in the centre of the town, the **Antiche Terme** (closed Oct-Apr) is on the other side of the River Bormida.   □

Practical information _____

⚓ ☎ 52106.
ℹ corso Bagni 9, ☎ 52142.
🚂 ☎ 52583.

Hotels:
★★★ **Ariston,** p. Matteotti 13, ☎ 52996, 36 rm P closed 12 Dec-15 Jan, 50,000; bkf: 5,000.
★★★ **Pineta,** strada della Salita 1, ☎ 50688, 100 rm P ⚐ ⊠ closed Nov-Mar, 42,000; bkf: 4,000.

Restaurant:
♦♦ *Carlo Parisio,* v. Mazzini 14, ☎ 56650, closed Mon and Jun-Jul. Run by a man of artistic talent. Regional cuisine: wild game, mushrooms and truffles, 22/35,000.

Recommended
Horseback riding: circonvallazione Valoria 17, ☎ 55688.
Tennis: v. Micheli, ☎ 52052.
Wine: regional wine shop in Palazzo Robellini, p. Levi 7, ☎ 55966.

AGLIE

Turin 34, Milan 142 km
Pop. 2,575 ✉ 10011 ☎ 0124   B3

The church of **S. Marta,** ornately Baroque in style but with a contrasting triangular belfry, is one of Aglie's many architectural treasures. More famous is the **Castello Ducale** (17C-18C), 'bold, sturdy and rugged', in the words of the Italian poet Guido Gozzano. It is more of a fortress than a palace and its monumental front steps lead to the entrance of a large natural park; it is the only castle in the region open to the public *(on special occasions).* The **villa Meleto** *(15 mn walk)* is known for its garish interior. 'A vulgar old mansion is all it would have been', wrote Gozzano, 'if I had not filled it with my curios and odds and ends'.   □

AGRATE

Novara 29, Milan 60, Turin 124 km
Pop. 414 ✉ 28010 ☎ 0322   D2-3

Agrate is one of two major towns in this primarily agricultural area of Agrate Conturbia. It was already an important fortified town in the 10C. Its most renowned and interesting monument is a 9C-12C baptistery. This elliptical edifice has an octagonal Romanesque dome with graceful arches and blind trefoil windows.   □

Practical information _____

Recommended
Animal park: *La Torbiera,* v. Borgoticino-Agrate, ☎ 802136 (closed Fri and Jan-Feb).

ALAGNA VALSESIA

Vercelli 101, Milan 141, Turin 155 km
3,908 ft pop. 431 ✉ 13021 ☎ 0163   B-C2

From the lookout point of the Turlo Pass, the Valsesia Valley must have looked like paradise to the Germans who migrated here during the 13C and 14C. Pastures, forests and rivers offer unequaled scenic beauty. Shepherds, who spoke a Germanic dialect, had very little contact with the outside world until the 17C, when the exploitation of the area's gold mines forced them to confront social and economic realities. The tourist industry began in the mid-19C, and Mt. Rosa later became one of the first ski resorts.

▶ The **Walser Museum** is a typical wooden house dating from 1628 *(Aug 2-6 p.m.; Jul Sat and Sun; other months telephone in advance, ☎ 91326).* This little museum has furniture, objects, tools and instruments dating from the 17C. Like other Valsesian houses, the Museo Walser has balconies on three sides.   □

Environs

▶ 2.5 km away is the **Riva Valdobbia.** The façade of its 15C church is covered with frescos by Melchiorre d'Errico (1597). ▶ The **Sesia waterfalls** are nearby. ▶ The **punta Indren** *(cablecar)* on Mt. Rosa between the Indren and Bors glaciers (ideal for summer skiing) offers a stunning view of the valley. Adventurous sightseers can hike across the glacier, arriving after an hour's climb at the **Rifugio Gnifetti** or continue as far as the **Rifugio Margherita,** the highest point in Europe.   □

Practical information _____

↕ cablecar at Mt. Rosa goes to Alagna-Zaroltu-Bocchetta-Punta Indren; ski lifts, cross-country skiing, summer skiing on Indren and Bors glaciers, ☎ 91333.
ℹ p. della Chiesa, ☎ 91118.

Hotel:
★★★★ *Cristallo,* p. degli Alberghi, ☎ 91285, 29 rm
ℙ 74,000.

Recommended
Alpine guides: at Centro, ☎ 91310.
♥ gastronomy: honey, mortadella, salami *d'la duja;* handicrafts: lace, woodwork.

ALBA

Turin 59, Cuneo 62, Milan 155 km
Pop. 31,182 ✉ 12051 ☎ 0173   C5

Alba is the cultural, social and economic centre of Langhe, rich in history and reputed to be the wine and truffle capital. The local economy is fueled mainly by wine-growers and truffle hunters, although candy and clothes are also produced here. The last decade has seen an important increase in industrial and commercial activity, attracting workers and leading to the construction of a new city near the historical centre.

▶ Fortlike houses and tower homes are characteristic of Alba. ▶ In corso Cavour, the most interesting of the houses is the **Casa Riva** (no. 13), which has preserved a good deal of its medieval appearance. ▶ In v. Vittorio Emanuele, the **Casa Fontana** (no. 11) is decorated with a *cotto* frieze of dancing figures— a notable example of rich figurative production in local brick. ▶ Of the forty towers that once dotted Alba's skyline, only thirteen are still standing. Three are in the heart of the city on the **piazza Risorgimento,** which in 1800 was linked to the ancient piazza delle Erbe, forming a spacious open area around the cathedral. ▶ This latter, dedicated to **S. Lorenzo,** was rebuilt in a Gothic-Lombard style in the 15C; frequently restored, the façade was refinished for the last time in 1800. Inside is an impressive choir stall dating from 1512. The mullioned 13C campanile encloses the original 11C Romanesque tower. ▶ On the piazza Risorgimento is the town hall whose Council Hall is decorated with interesting paintings of the *Madonna with the infant Jesus and Saints* by Macrino d'Alba and numerous Renaissance depictions of churches and palaces influenced by the Umbrian schools and the followers of Ghirlandaio. ▶ Other works by Macrino can be seen on the altar and in the presbytery of the church of **S. Giovanni Battista,** in which can also be found a 1377 painting by Barnaba da Modena. ▶ Also interesting are the Gothic church of **S. Domenico** (13C-14C), with a simple façade boasting an elegant splayed portal, and the small Baroque **Maddalena Church,** reconstructed by B.A. Vittone c. 1749. With its rustic *cotto* façade and elliptical floor plan, this church is the best local example of 17C architecture. ▶ At v. Paruzza 1/A, the **Museo Civico** *(9 a.m.-12 noon; Thu and Sat also 3-6 p.m.; other days inquire at adjoining library; closed Mon and hols)* displays prehistoric and Roman finds.   □

Practical information

ALBA

ⓘ v. Vittorio Emanuele 19, ☎ 497118; *Alba Manifestazioni*, p. Risorgimento, ☎ 362807.

Hotels:
★★★ *Motel Alba,* corso Asti 5, ☎ 363251, 34 rm Ⓟ ⬚ ▣ 57,000; bkf: 6,000.
★★★ *Savona,* v. Roma 1, ☎ 42381, 104 rm Ⓟ ᕼ 60,000; bkf: 6,000.

Restaurants:
◆◆◆ *Beppe,* corso Coppino 20, ☎ 43983, closed Tue and Jul. Regional cuisine: tajarin d'la magna, wild game, Langhe wines, 30/45,000.
● ◆◆ *Capannina,* borgo Moretta, ☎ 43952, closed Mon. Traditional ambiance in old farmhouse. Regional cuisine: raw meat all'albese, tajarin, 20/35,000.
◆◆ *Daniel's al Pesco Fiorito,* corso Canale 28, ☎ 43969, closed Tue and Aug. Regional cuisine: gnocchi al Castelmagno, finanziera Cavour, homemade brandy, 25/35,000.

Recommended
Events: *Centro Torri Joust and donkey competition* (Oct); *truffle festival* at S. Martino (Nov).
Fair: *national truffle fair* (Oct).
Sports field: v. Toti 3, ☎ 30090.
Swimming: v. Tanaro 10, ☎ 43318.
Wine: *Pio Cesare,* v. Cesare Balbo 6, ☎ 42407 and *Angelo Gaja,* at Barbaresco, v. Torino 36, ☎ 635158; *wine outlet* at Barolo, ☎ 56277; *wine shop* at Novello (→ Le Langhe).

Environs
GUARENE, ⊠ 12050, 5 km N.

Restaurant:
◆◆◆ *Villa,* at Castelrotto, v. Provinciale 74, ☎ 36149, closed Sun eve, Mon and Jan. Terrace with view and garden. Refined regional cuisine, 40/55,000.

NEIVE, ⊠ 12057, 12 km NE.

Restaurant:
◆◆◆ *Contea,* p. Cocito 8, ☎ 67126, closed Sun eve except in Oct-Nov and Tue. Hospitable atmosphere in seignorial 17C building. Regional cuisine: cold tagliolini with egg yolks, sott paletta ed bocin, 30/45,000.

ALESSANDRIA

Turin 90, Milan 95, Rome 563 km
Pop. 98,595 ⊠ 15100 ☎ 0131   D4

Alessandria was an important military stronghold until the last century. The Citadel, which dates from 1700, still hosts a military detachment. The tree-lined boulevards around the town are called spalti, the name of a race organized to celebrate the 100 cannons added to the city's already formidable defense force in 1856. Appropriately enough, the city was named after Pope Alexander III, the warrior-pope who led the local populace against the Emperor Frederick Barbarossa in the 12C.

▶ In the old part of the city, medieval remnants are still evident, but its most noble artistic elements are in the 18C Baroque style. ▶ The oldest monuments are the two 15C Gothic churches, **S. Maria del Carmine** and **S. Maria di Castello.** ▶ In the p. della Libertà stands a fine example of Baroque architecture, the **Palazzo della Prefettura,** built by B. Alfieri (1730-33). ▶ On the S side of the same piazza, the **Palazzo del Municipio** (1775-1826) with its graceful archways boasts an ingenious three-quadrant clock. ▶ Not far away, the Neoclassical cathedral (renovated 1810-79) is topped by a lofty octagonal cupola, adorned with twenty-four statues of the city's patron saints. ▶ The **Civic Museum** and **Pinacoteca** (art gallery) housed in the same palace *(visits by appointment only,* ☎ 54681; *9 a.m.-12 noon and 2:45-6 p.m.; closed Sat,*

Sun and Mon a.m.) exhibit modest but nonetheless interesting collections.

Environs

▶ **Marengo** *(4.7 km SE)* is the site of Napoleon's victory over the Austrians in 1800. In the **Villa Marengo** *(caretaker, Oct-May 2:30-5:30 p.m.; hols 10 a.m.-12 noon and 2:30-5:30 p.m.; Jun-Sep 4-7 p.m.; hols 9:30 a.m.-12 noon and 4-7 p.m; closed Mon),* built in 1847, is the **Battle Museum** with documents, relics and a large animated relief model.   ☐

Practical information

ⓘ v. Savona 6, ☎ 51021.
▬▬ ☎ 42221.
▭▭ from railway station and p. Garibaldi.

Hotels:
★★★★ *Due Buoi Rossi,* v. Cavour 32, ☎ 445252, 65 rm Ⓟ ᕼ 165,000. Rest. ● ◆◆◆ closed Fri eve, Sat, Aug and Christmas. Regional and international cuisine: truffle fondue, Red Ox cutlets, 30/50,000.
★★★ *Domus,* v. Castellani 12, ☎ 43305, 27 rm Ⓟ ᕼ No restaurant, 72,000.
★★★ *Europa,* v. Palestro 1, ☎ 446226, 33 rm Ⓟ ⌇ 68,000; bkf: 7,500.

Restaurant:
◆◆◆ *Grappolo,* v. Casale 28, ☎ 53217, closed Mon eve, Tue, Jan and Aug. Regional cuisine: braised meat al Barolo, wild game, 25/35,000.

⚠ ★★★ *Valmilara,* at Valmadonna, 120 pl., ☎ 50725 (all year).

Recommended
Archery: *Compagnia archieri Città della paglia,* v. Marengo 106, ☎ 65173.
Events: *National Silverware Show* (Sep-Oct); *Bordino Car Show* (Jun); *Madonnina dei Centauri International Motorcycle Rally* at Castellazzo Bormida (2nd Sun in Jul).
Horseback riding: strada vecchia Bagliani, ☎ 68006 or 40784.
Motocross: at San Salvatore Monferrato, *Val Dolenga* (run by Moto club Mirabello) and *T. De Michelis* (run by Moto club G. Corsico,* ☎ 33209).
▼ hats: *Borsalino* hat factory, at (6 km SE), Spinetta Marengo ☎ 61880.

ARONA

Novara 38, Milan 64, Turin 116 km
Pop. 16,290 ⊠ 28041 ☎ 0322   D2

When Frederick Barbarossa destroyed Milan in 1162, many families took refuge in Arona, an old town on the SW bank of Lake Maggiore. For more than 600 years, Arona was subject to the dukes of Lombardy; eventually, it became an important trading harbour. The city combines a lovely natural environment with a beautiful, intact, historical centre.

▶ From the **lungolago,** there is a fine view of the Rocca di Angera (→ Lombardy, Lake Maggiore). ▶ In the lower city, it is imperative to see the Gothic portico to the 15C **Casa del Podesta** (governor's residence). ▶ In the upper city are two important churches: **S. Martiri,** whose apse shelters a 15C painting of the *Madonna,* and **S. Maria** (built 15C-17C, later restored) with a polyptych by G. Ferrari (15C). ▶ 2.5 km away is the square dominated by **S. Carlone★,** an immense statue in bronze and copper of Saint Charles Borromeo, born to a prominent local family and Archbishop of Milan at the age of twenty-two. The tall statue was begun in 1614 and finished in 1694. It is possible to climb the interior staircase *(8 a.m.-12 noon and 2-6 or 7 p.m. summer; closed Nov and Wed in winter).*   ☐

Practical information _____

① p. Stazione 4, ☎ 3601.
⛴ boats and hydrofoils to Stresa and Locarno,
☎ 42352.

Hotels:
★★★★ *Atlantic,* v. Repubblica 124, ☎ 46521, 78 rm ♿ ⚗
110,000; bkf: 10,000.
★★★★ *Rocca,* v. Verbano 1, ☎ 3637, 64 rm Ⓟ ≮ 108,000.
★★★ *Florida,* p. del Popolo 32, ☎ 46212, 25 rm ⚗
closed 15 Nov-Jan. No restaurant, 59,000.

Restaurants:
◆◆◆ *Barcaiolo,* p. del Popolo 23, ☎ 3388, closed Wed
and 20 Jul-20 Aug. Traditional tavern in 14C
palazzo. Regional and Italian cuisine: mocetta, paniscia, 30/45,000.
◆◆◆ *Taverna del Pittore,* p. del Popolo 39, ☎ 3366,
closed Mon, Jan, Jun and Christmas. In 17C palazzo
with view of lake and Rocca di Angera. Creative cuisine:
pigeon galantine with truffles, scampi ragout with beans
and peas, 45/60,000.
◆◆ *Vecchia Arona,* lungolago Marconi 17, ☎ 42469,
closed Fri, Jun and Nov. Creative cuisine: menu
depends on seasonal availability of foods, 35/50,000.

Recommended
Fair: *Fair of Lake Maggiore,* ☎ 3600, (late May-Jun).
Sailing: *Lega Navale,* corso Europa 26.
Sports centre: v. Cadorna (swimming and tennis).
♥ shopping: ceramics, pastries.

For the translation of a name of a meat, a fish or a
vegetable, for the composition of a dish or a sauce,
see the *Menu Guide* at the end of the Practical Holiday Guide; it lists the most common culinary terms.

ASTI*

Turin 54, Milan 130, Rome 599 km
Pop. 76,365 ⊠ 14100 ☎ 0141   C4

Built of red brick and yellow tufa, Asti lies amid the
green, vine-clad hills of Monferrato. A sense of austerity hovers over this city, its past heavy with strategic purpose. Continually agitated by family rivalries
and coveted by foreign powers, Asti was fortified with
'hundred tower' houses. The city became wealthy in
the 12C as its trade increased and it remains wealthy
today, thanks to the bounty of nature. Despite Baroque influence, Asti retains a medieval flavour, and
despite industrial development, it remains primarily
an important agricultural centre. The tranquil streets
come spectacularly alive during Jousting Contests
(said to date back even farther than those held
in Siena) and innumerable historical, artistic and gastronomic festivals. In the market square, the hum of
many local dialects testifies to this N region's agricultural debt to immigrants from the S.
▶ One main street intersects the whole of the old city
centre (B1-3). It was the Roman road and the medieval
Contrada Maestra, the principal lifeline of urban development. Asti renamed this road in honour of its most illustrious citizen, the tragic poet Vittorio Alfieri (1749-1803),
and gave the same name to the largest piazza (B2)
through which it passes. ▶ At one end of the street is
the monumental complex, S. Pietro (A3). The Romanesque **baptistery** is an octagonal structure built in the 12C,
when knights of the Order of St. John of Jerusalem established their headquarters in Asti. Next door is the for-

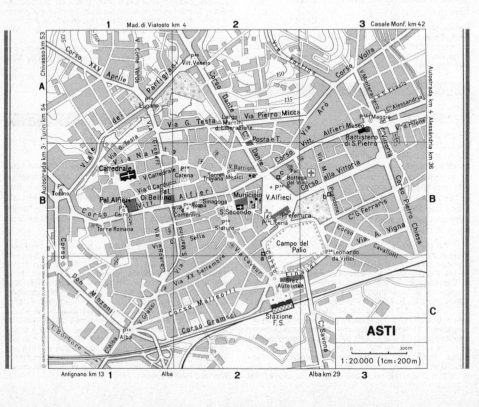

mer Gothic-Renaissance church of **S. Pietro in Consavia** (15C), whose windows and cornices are adorned with *cotto* friezes. Inside are 17C frescos and a marble bas-relief of 1300. Housed in the former Pilgrims' Hospital is the **Museo Archeologico** *(caretaker; 9 a.m.-12 noon and 3-6 p.m.; Sun 10 a.m.-12 noon; closed Mon).* ► Beyond p. Alfieri lies the medieval quarter known as the **Recinto dei Nobili,** where the predominant architectural features are the fortress-house and the tower-house, with brick and tufa façades. ► Many of the towers for which Asti was famous have been demolished, but some still remain and are exceptional: **Torre Romana** (B1), originally built in the Roman era and added to the 11C-12C, the 13C **Torre dei Comentini** (B2) and the **Torre Troyana** (B2). Slender and elegant, attached to the Palazzo Troya in p. Medici, this last is perhaps the most beautiful. ► The adjoining Romanesque-Gothic church of **S. Secondo**★ (B3; 13C-15C) has three portals in its façade; the rich beauty of the 18C chapel is underlined by 15C frescos and Renaissance polyptychs, one of which is attributed to Gandolfino d'Asti, a local artist influenced by the Flemish school. In this church on the first Tuesday in May, the civil authorities make a solemn offering of a cream-coloured flag to the patron saint. This banner goes to the winner of the spectacular horse race held in September (accompanied by a grand parade) in the huge Campo del Palio (BC 2-3). ► The **cathedral** (B1) is a vast Romanesque-Gothic edifice (1309-54); outside on the r. wall is a **protiro**★ in a flowery Gothic style (1450). Inside are three lofty naves frescoed in the 18C and altarpieces from the 15C-16C. ► In corso V. Alfieri, two palaces exemplify the work of Benedetto Alfieri, an architect who renovated the city during the 18C. At corso V. Alfieri 357, the **Bellino Palace** (B1) houses the **Risorgimento Museum** and the 18C-19C **Pinacoteca** *(9 a.m.-12 noon and 3-6 p.m.; Sun 10 a.m.-12 noon; closed Mon).* No. 375, the **Alfieri Palace** (B1), in which the poet Alfieri (cousin of the architect) was born and lived, is currently the seat of the National Centre for Alfieri Studies as well as a small museum *(10 a.m.-12 noon and 3:30-5:30 p.m.; Sat and hols 10 a.m.-12 noon; closed Mon).* □

Practical information ───────────────

ASTI
ⓘ p. Alfieri 34 (B2), ☎ 50357.
🚂 (C2), ☎ 50311.
🚌 from bus station, p. Medaglie d'Oro (C2).

Hotels:
★★★★ **Aleramo,** v. Emanuele Filiberto 13 (B2 a), ☎ 55661, 38 rm Ⓟ No restaurant, 98,000.
★★★ **Lis,** v. Fratelli Rosselli 10 (B3 b), ☎ 55051, 35 rm Ⓟ ⌘ No restaurant, 60,000; bkf: 4,000.
★★ **Reale,** p. Alfieri 6 (B2 c), ☎ 50240, 27 rm Ⓟ 50,000; bkf: 6,000.

Restaurants:
● ♦♦♦ **Gener Neuv,** lungotanaro 4, ☎ 57270, closed Sun eve, Mon and Aug. On shore of the Tanaro. Regional cuisine: rabbit in white wine, finanziera, 40/60,000.
♦♦♦ **Vicoletto,** vicolo Anfossi 6 (B2 f), ☎ 52114, closed Mon and Aug. Regional cuisine: tajarin, grilled goat meat, 30,000.
♦♦ **Falcone Vecchio,** v. S. Secondo 8 (B2 d), ☎ 53106, closed Mon and Aug. Dates from late 17C. Regional cuisine: bagna cauda, goose salami, homemade Barbera and Grignolino wines, 30/40,000.
♦♦ **Grotta,** corso Torino 366, ☎ 214168, closed Mon eve, Tue and Jul-Aug. Regional cuisine: meat ravioli, pork sausages with polenta, 25/35,000.
♦ **Piuma d'Oro,** v. Battisti 18, (B2 e) ☎ 32059, closed Mon. In old palazzo. Regional cuisine: potato gnocchi, braised meat al Barolo, 30,000.

⚠ ★★ *Umberto Cagni,* at Valmanera, 110 pl, ☎ 271238.

Recommended
Craft workshops: *Arazzeria Scassa,* ☎ 271352 (tapestries).

Cycling: *Pedale Sandamianese,* v. S. Marzanotto 270, ☎ 75393.
Events: *Asti Competition* (mid-Sep); *Douja d'Or wine festival* (Sep); *Festival of feasts* (Sep, Jan); *Astiteatro,* ☎ 3991.
Fairs and markets: *Fiera d'Asti* (May); *truffle exhibition/market* (Nov).
Farm vacations: *Podere La Piazza,* at Santa Margherita, ☎ 96267.
Hang gliding: *I Corvi,* v. Cagna 22, ☎ 968385.
Horseback riding: *Asti Country Club,* at Castiglione d'Asti, Centro Residenziale, ☎ 206106; *Il Cavalcavalli,* at Cerreto d'Asti, ☎ 0142/945361 (associate of *ANTE*).
Wine: regional wine outlet at Costigliole d'Asti, ☎ 966289.

Environs

VALLE BENEDETTA, 4 km NW.

Hotel:
★★★★ **Hasta Hotel,** strada Vallebenedetta 25, ☎ 213312, 26 rm Ⓟ ⌘ 🔥 ♨ ✐ closed Jan, 110,000; bkf: 6,000.

AVIGLIANA

Turin 25, Milan 161 km
Pop. 9,259 ⊠ 10051 ☎ 011   A-B4

Avigliana is a favourite destination for visitors from Turin, who are attracted by its beauty and lovely view of the lake. Perhaps for similar reasons, Avigliana was chosen by the Savoys (until 1416) as their preferred residence. Their influence fostered the arts and led to economic prosperity. A mint was built in Avigliana and the city remained an important centre of exchange for many years.

► In the old city centre are many interesting medieval houses with porticos. Of particular interest are the **Casa della Porta Ferrata** (v. Omonima), with Gothic archways and mullioned vaults, and **Casa dei Savoia** (15C, v. XX Settembre). ► The Romanesque-Gothic church of **S. Giovanni** (13C-14C) contains valuable polyptychs by D. Ferrari (1511) and his followers. ► **S. Pietro** (10C-11C) is also Romanesque-Gothic; it was remodeled in the 15C *(caretaker at no. 22 on same street).* ► There is a splendid view from atop the **Rocca** overlooking the city.

Environs

► Worth visiting are the glacier-fed **Avigliana Lakes** (**Grande and Piccolo**) 2 km from Avigliana in their natural park surroundings. The lakes are open to the public for sports activities. ► **S. Antonio di Ranverso**★ *(4 km from town)* is an important medieval (12C-15C) abbey attesting to the influence of the French Gothic style upon the region. Inside are frescos by G. Jaquerio (15C) and an altarpiece by Defentente Ferrari (16C), but the church is closed temporarily for restoration. The abbey was founded by the Hospitalers of St. Antony, who cared for those afflicted with St. Antony's fire, now known as ergotism. This agonizing and often crippling disease was caused by eating fungus-infected grain. ► **La Sacra di San Michele** (→). □

Practical information ───────────────

ⓘ corso Laghi 33, ☎ 938650.

Restaurant:
♦♦♦ **Maiana,** at Meana, ☎ 938805, closed Sun eve, Mon, Jan and Aug. Garden and terrace overlooking lake. Regional cuisine: taglionlini, scaloppine alla finanziera, 50/60,000.

⚠ ★★ *King,* at Prefetti, strada Giaveno-Sant'Ambrogio, 100 pl, ☎ 930389 (all year).

Recommended
Cycling: *Velo Club Vallesusa* at Sant'Ambrogio, v. Antica di Francia 1, ☎ 9688214.
Golf: *Le Fronde,* v. S. Agostino 68, ☎ 938053 (18 holes).

Horseback riding: *Manus Club,* at Almese, ☎ 9359866; at Buttigliera Alta, v. Reano, ☎ 932741.
Nature parks: at Avigliana Lakes and Palude Marshes.
Tennis: ☎ 938104; sports centre with swimming pool, ☎ 9359245.
Water skiing: *Circolo nautico Avigliana,* corso Laghi 296, ☎ 9312578; *Sport Nautici Avigliana,* v. Monginevro 30, ☎ 938270.
Windsurfing: *Circolo nautico Oasi,* corso Laghi 292, ☎ 9312301.

BARDONECCHIA

Turin 90, Milan 226 km
4,305 ft pop. 3,328 ⌧ 10052 ☎ 0122   A4

A summer health resort and winter sports centre with an international clientele, Bardonecchia is situated at the end of the Susa Valley, near the Frejus Transalpine Tunnel, Italy's Link with W Europe. The area became a sports haven as far back as 1932; today it hosts a prestigious and highly competitive ski team. Near the church is the **Museo Civico** with an interesting ethnographic collection. **Mélezet** *(2.5 km)* was home to an art school (15C-18C) whose fame spread far beyond the Alps; today, a wood-carving school keeps the artistic tradition alive.   ☐

Practical information _____

↧ chair lifts, cross-country trails, instruction, skating, summer skiing at Sommeiller Pass.
ⓘ p. Europa 15, ☎ 99032.

Hotels:
★★★★ **G.H. Riky,** v. della Vittoria 22, ☎ 9353, 74 rm ℗ ⌂ closed Easter-Jul and Sep-Christmas, 105,000.
★★★ **Betulla,** v. della Vittoria 4, ☎ 9846, 40 rm ℗ closed May-14 Jun and 16 Sep-19 Dec, 59,000; bkf: 5,000.
★★★ **Des Geneys-Splendid,** v. Einaudi 21, ☎ 99001, 58 rm ℗ ⌂ ⌲ closed 16 Apr-Jul and Sep-14 Dec, 79,000; bkf: 6,000.
★ **Quiete,** v. S. Francesco 26, ☎ 9859, 15 rm ⌲ ⌂ ⚐ closed Sep. No restaurant, 47,000.
⚠ ★★ *Bokki,* at Mélezet, 265 pl, ☎ 99893 (all year).

Recommended
Alpine guides: *A. Re,* ☎ 901373 (head guide); *R. Pirona,* ☎ 9347 (rock climbing).
Archery: *Compagnia arcieri Bardonecchia,* p. Des Ambrois 1, ☎ 99070.
Craft workshops: *Bruno Blanc,* ☎ 99197 (wood carving)
Excursions: to Sommeiller Pass, *Società Va. Ro.,* v. P. Micca 42, ☎ 99484 (Jul-Sep).
Tennis: v. Mélezet 1, ☎ 99829.

BIELLA

Vercelli 41, Turin 74, Milan 102 km
Pop. 52,779 ⌧ 13051 ☎ 015   C3

A 12C bishop of Vercelli decided to counter the growing power of the congregation of S. Stefano's church (in the town of Bugello on the plains) by founding a town on the Piazzo's higher ground and granting privileges and franchises to the new inhabitants. Since that time Biella has had two centres. For three centuries the lower town of Biella Piano, built around an ancient Roman site, waned in importance while the upper town (Biella Piazzo) became a civic and mercantile centre. Then in the 1600s, the lower town underwent an economic boom and regained its pre-eminence. Indeed, at the beginning of the 1800s the tanning and textile industries (the latter of which brought Biella international fame)

became the focal point for all production along the Cervo River's banks.

▶ On the large tree-lined central square in **Biella Piano** is the neo-Gothic façade (1826) of the 15C **Cathedral,** which was largely reconstructed in the 1700s. To the l. of the cathedral lies the city's pride: the small 9C-10C pre-Romanesque **Baptistery,** with cupola and four apses decorated with vaulted niches. Nearby, the elegant Romanesque **campanile** is all that remains of the church of S. Stefano, demolished in 1872. ▶ Despite its modern appearance (1882), the 16C **S. Sebastiano** is an important example of Lombard Renaissance architecture. The interior is richly embellished with paintings and a fine wooden **choir**★ by G. Mellis (1546). ▶ The lower city boasts two noteworthy museums. At v. P. Micca 38 is the **Museo Civico** *(Sat 8:30 a.m.-12 noon; Tue also 2:30-6:30 p.m.)* with a collection of archaeological finds, paintings and glass. The **Alpine Troop Museum** at v. Delleani 33 *(4-7 p.m.; closed wkends)* contains documents as well as relics of war. ▶ Along the banks of the Cervo River are typical 19C factories which harness the river to drive their machines. ▶ In **Biella Piazzo** *(can be reached by cable car)* the **piazza Cisterna,** for centuries the city's commercial centre, is especially worth visiting. 16C arcaded buildings stand on the N edge of the piazza with the **Cisterna Palace.** In a small adjoining piazza is the late Romanesque **S. Giacomo** with a 13C campanile. Other 15C-16C palazzos can be seen in the neighbouring streets and squares. A graceful octagonal **tower,** built in 1519 on a palace roof by Sebastiano Ferrero, is visible from afar. ▶ In **Candelo** *(5 km S)* is the medieval refuge of **Ricetto** with towers, turreted walls and a palace. ▶ 6 km NW is **Pollone** (→ il Biellese).   ☐

Practical information _____

Hotels:
★★★★ **Astoria,** v. Roma 9, ☎ 20545, 50 rm ℗ No restaurant, 115,000.
★★★★ **Augustus,** v. Italia 54, ☎ 27554, 36 rm ℗ ⚐ No restaurant, 100,000.
★★★ **Michelangelo,** p. Adua 5, ☎ 21270, 19 rm ⚐ No restaurant, 90,000.

Restaurants:
◆◆◆ **Bagatto,** v. Repubblica 45, ☎ 28671, closed Tue and Aug. Regional and Italian cuisine: fresh pasta, trout, 27/40,000.
◆◆◆ **Prinz Grill,** v. Torino 14, ☎ 30302, closed Sun, Jan and Aug. Italian cuisine: grilled fish and meat, mushrooms and truffles (seasonal), 35/50,000.

Recommended
Cycling: *Cicli Pinella,* v. Sella 22/A, ☎ 666396.
Flying: at Cerrione *(12 km S),* ☎ 21167.
Golf: *Le Betulle,* at Magnano *(19 km SW),* ☎ 679151.
Hang gliding: *I Barbagianni,* at Candelo, v. S. Sebastiano 42, ☎ 538703 (instruction).
Horseback riding: *Tenuta La Mandria,* at Candelo, ☎ 539306 (daily or weekly excursions in Bielle Alps and nr Serra Lakes).
Swimming: v. Macallè, ☎ 402808.

Il BIELLESE

From Ivrea to Biella *(123 km, 1 day; map 1)*

Il Biellese is a colourful mountain region. Its industry is based on a long tradition of textile manufacturing; mountain streams provide the energy to turn the wheels in the mills. Today more than ever the region's economy is concentrated in the textile sector and this is one of the most highly industrialized areas in Italy. Now that factories no longer depend on water for power, the flatlands below the mountains are also increasingly being developed in the search for additional work space.

1. Il Biellese

St. Eusebio, Bishop of Vercelli, who was responsible for bringing the black wood statue of the **Madonna** (believed to be the work of Luke the Evangelist) from Jerusalem. The statue now stands in the original chapel of **Chiesa Vecchia** (old church) where it is honoured by thousands of faithful. Behind the ancient structures is the imposing **Chiesa Nuova** (new church; 1895-1960). On a hill to the SW are nineteen chapels (of which twelve were constructed 1620-1720) with terra-cotta groups and frescos illustrating the life of the Virgin Mary. ▶ **Rosazza** is a resort with unusual neo-Gothic architecture. The **Panoramica Zegna★**, one of the most beautiful roads through the Alps, begins at this point. E. Zegna, a textile magnate, provided both the idea and money for this road. The route climbs to the **Bielmonte** ski station and ends in **Trivero**, an active and renowned wool textile centre propitiously situated in the Sessera basin. ▶ A pleasant hill road leads to **Mosso Santa Maria**, a lovely town in the midst of a dense forest, which actually marks the border to a zone where some of the most important and characteristic examples of Biellese industrial archaeology have been found. ▶ **Pettinengo** was formerly a wool-working town (12C). It is known as Biellese's balcony because of its advantageous position on the sloping sides of the Mount Rubello Valley. Tradition has it that the mountain streams flowed red with blood after a battle in 1307 in which heretics were defeated. ▶ The route ends in **Biella** (→). □

Practical information _____

BIELMONTE, 4,977 ft, ✉ 13059 (Lora), ☎ 015.
✦ ski lifts, cross-country skiing, instruction.

BORGOFRANCO D'IVREA, ✉ 10013, ☎ 0125.

Restaurant:
◆◆◆ *Casa Vicina,* at Ivozio, ☎ 752180, closed Wed, Jan and Nov. Summer dining on terrace. Regional and Italian cuisine: meat ravioli, varied rice dishes, 25/40,000.

OROPA, 2,809 ft, ✉ 13060 ☎ 015.
✦ cable cars at Lake Mucrone and Lake Mucrone-Anticima, cabin-lifts, cross-country skiing, instruction.
ⓘ Azienda Funivie Oropa, ☎ 55114.

Restaurant:
◆ *Fornace,* v. Santuario Oropa 480, ☎ 55122, closed Wed in winter. Regional cuisine: crêpes alla montanara, chamois in civet, 25,000.

SORDEVOLO, ✉ 13050, ☎ 015.

Recommended
Events: *Passion Play* (late Jun-mid-Sep, generally every Sun; every 5 yrs: next in 1990).

TRIVERO, ✉ 13059 ☎ 015.

Hotel:
★★ *Monte Rubello,* at Centro Zegna, ☎ 75047, 20 rm, 46,000.

BORGOMANERO

Novara 32, Milan 70, Turin 106 km
Pop. 19,385 ✉ 28021 ☎ 0322   C-D2

Located in upper Novarese, Borgomanero is an industrial and commercial centre known mainly for textile manufacturing. The past is evident in the town's rectilinear layout, the 12C-13C Baroque **parochial church** and the Romanesque church of **S. Leonardo**. □

Practical information _____

BORGOMANERO

Hotel:
★★★ *Ramosecco,* v. Matteotti 1, ☎ 81479, 40 rm Ⓟ ⁂ closed Dec-Jan and Jul, 62,000.

▶ The itinerary starts at Ivrea (→). The hilly countryside NE of Ivrea is dotted with lakes; of particular interest is **Lake Sirio,** surrounded by forests and dominated by an 18C hermitage in which the playwright (and Verdi's librettist) Arrigo Boito and the actress Eleonora Duse lived. ▶ In **Montalto Dora,** the massive 15C castle is a typical medieval military structure. ▶ **Borgofranco d'Ivrea,** a chemical-producing centre, boasts an ancient quarter with 15C houses. ▶ The climb on roads lined with chestnut trees to **Croce Serra** is beautiful and the town offers a magnificent view of the Canavese and Biellese regions. A fine view of the wooded Elvo basin can be seen on the way down. ▶ **Netro** is an old metalworking centre, which was one of the main producers of arms during the Napoleonic era and World War I. It has rustic houses with wooden porticos built into the terraced hill. ▶ From **Graglia,** a quiet vacation village, there is a road to the **Santuario di Graglia** (1659-1760), the destination of pilgrims honouring the Madonna di Loreto. ▶ **Sordévolo,** a cotton- and wool-manufacturing centre, is famous for a passion play *(Passione di Cristo)* staged every five years (last performance was 1985) from the end of June to mid-September, with the participation of the whole community. ▶ **Pollone** has sumptuous villas and splendid gardens, and nearby lies the entrance to the **Parco della Burcina★,** created in 1849, with lush vegetation and interesting botanical specimens. ▶ A winding road leads to the **Santuario della Madonna di Oropa★,** a large complex built primarily to shelter the poor. This 17C-18C Baroque structure encompasses three superimposed piazzas with porticos, staircases and balustrades. One of the most important destinations for pilgrims in Italy, the sanctuary was founded in the 14C by

Restaurants:
● ◆◆◆ *Pinocchio,* v. Matteotti 147, ☎ 82273, closed Mon, Jul-Aug and Christmas. Regional and creative cuisine: veal with thyme, tapulon with polenta, 40/60,000.
◆◆◆ *San Pietro,* p. Martiri 6, ☎ 82285, closed Wed and Aug. With garden and pergola. Mixed cuisine: tortelloni, fish and meat dishes, 18/35,000.

Recommended
Auto racing: at Maggiora *(5 km W),* v. Don Minzoni 8, ☎ 87346.
Events: at Romagnano Sesia *(14 km SW),* religious performances in Holy week (only certain yrs).
Motocross: *M. Del Balmone,* at Maggiora, *Unione Sportiva Maggiorese,* p. Antonelli 2, ☎ 87220.

Environs

SORISO, ⊠ 28018, 9 km NW.

Restaurant:
● ◆◆◆ *Soriso,* v. Roma 18/20, ☎ 983228, closed Mon, Tue noon, Jan-Feb and Aug. Excellent creative cuisine, 70/90,000.

BORGOSESIA

Vercelli 49, Milan 91, Turin 107 km
Pop. 15,688 ⊠ 13011 ☎ 0163   C2

Borgosesia lies in the wide industrial basin of lower Valsesia where rivers and roads form a latticework. Economically, this important textile centre is a part of the industrial zone of Biellese, but it is situated in a valley where ancient folkloric traditions are maintained, such as the **Mercu Scuret,** a carnival held on Ash Wednesday. Textiles, clothes, furniture and handicrafts from the valley are housed in the **Museo del Folclore Valsesiano** *(Sun 3-6 p.m.; Sat also 9 a.m.-noon; otherwise by appointment,* ☎ *22205).*

Environs

▶ **Valduggia** *(5.3 km)* was the home of the painter Gaudenzio Ferrari; hanging in the parish church are his *Natività,* a triptych by Lanino and a painting by Morazzone. ▶ **Quarona** *(5.2 km)* has an interesting pre-Romanesque church, **S. Giovanni sul Monte,** with 13C-16C frescos. □

Practical information ―――――――

⬚ v. Sesone 6.

Hotel:
★★★ *Campagnola,* v. Varallo 244, ☎ 22676, 27 rm ℗ ⌂
⌕ 59,000; bkf: 7,000.

Restaurant:
◆ *Reale,* p. Cavour 12, ☎ 22262, closed Fri and Jul-Aug. Italian cuisine: salmon tagliolini, braised somarello in Barolo wine sauce, 25,000.

Recommended
Archery: *Compagnia arcieri Valsesia,* v. Mazzini 26, ☎ 23279.
♥ bells: visit bell foundries at Valdugia *(5.3 km W).*

BORROMEAN ISLANDS*

On Lake Maggiore between Stresa and Baveno
Pop. 159 ⊠ 28049 ☎ 0323   D2

To appreciate the art of Baroque gardens, it is imperative to visit Isola Bella, the largest of the three Borromean Islands. It is not surprising that this island, originally called Isabella in honour of Carlo III Borromeo's wife, eventually acquired this more appropriate name.

▶ **Isola Bella★★** is almost entirely occupied by the grand 17C **Borromeo Palace★** *(guided tours 19 Mar-31 Oct 9 a.m.-12 noon and 1:30-5 p.m.).* The sumptuous interior includes furniture, paintings (by Tempesta, G. B. Tiepolo, L. Giordano and others) and a gallery with 17C **Flemish tapestries★.** Underground are **grottos★** lined with tufa, shells and marble. The splendid **garden★** contains many rare plants, graceful statues and fountains, which majestically cover ten descending terraces. On the highest terrace stands the **theatre,** an ornate stone construction crowned with a large unicorn copied from the Borromeo family's coat of arms. The terrace offers a magnificent view★ of the lake. ▶ **Isola dei Pescatori★** shelters an ancient, rustic village with tiny narrow streets. ▶ **Isola Madre** is the site of another 18C Borromeo palace, surrounded by noteworthy **Botanical Gardens** *(19 Mar-31 Oct 9 a.m.-12 noon and 1:30-5 p.m.).*   □

Practical information ―――――――

⛴ boat service from Stresa, Baveno and Verbania; hydrofoils and motorboats.

Restaurants:
◆◆ *Verbano,* at Isola dei Pescatori, v. Ugo Ara 2, ☎ 30408, closed 9 Dec-9 Mar. 19C villa with garden. Seafood: fresh-water fish, rice with filet of Persian fish, 25/35,000.
◆ *Belvedere,* at Isola dei Pescatori, v. di Mezzo, ☎ 30047, closed Wed except Jul-Aug and 15 Oct-1 Apr. Seafood: fresh-water fish, grilled coregonids, 20/30,000.
◆ *Elvezia,* at Isola Bella, v. Vittorio Emanuele 18, ☎ 30043, closed Nov-Mar. Seafood: fresh-water fish, Persian fish alla Borromea, 20/40,000.

Recommended
♥ botanical gardens: at Isola Madre, ☎ 31261; camelia exhibition (Apr).

BOSCO MARENGO

Alessandria 13, Milan 103, Turin 104 km
Pop 2,459 ⊠ 15062 ☎ 0131   D5

The history of Bosco Marengo is filled with illustrious personalities: the Emperors Teodorico and Ottone II, the Viscontis, the Savoys, the Colleonis, the Bonapartes and Pope Pius V. The city's major monument was built in honour of this pope. The Renaissance church of **S. Croce** has a 16C wooden choir stall, paintings by Giorgio Vasari and Pius V's **mausoleum★** *(caretaker; 9 a.m.-12 noon and 3-5 p.m.).*   □

BRA

Cuneo 46, Turin 56, Milan 170 km
Pop. 26,453 ⊠ 12042 ☎ 0172   B-C5

Bra was founded *c.* 1000 as a refuge for the inhabitants of the Roman town of *Pollentia* (now Pollenzo), which had been laid waste by barbarian raids. Today, its dominant style is Baroque. The leather industry that supported numerous tanneries in the 19C has given way to other kinds of production.

▶ In the irregularly shaped p. Caduti per la Libertà (dominated by the extremely Baroque church of **S. Andrea**) the Baroque **Palazzo Civico** (civic palace), attributed to Vittone, should be visited. ▶ Nearby is the Gothic **Casa Traversa.** ▶ The church of **S. Chiara,** with a rococo façade was also built by Vittone. ▶ The **Museo Civico** *(3-6 p.m.; closed Mon)* offers archaeological remains from Pollentia as well as a natural history section. ▶ 5 km away, at **Pollenzo** it is possible to see the site of ancient Pollentia and the **Castello Reale,** part of which dates from the 14C.   □

Practical information _____

Hotels:
★★★ *Badellino*, p. XX Settembre 4, ☎ 412950, 22 rm P
closed Aug, 40,000; bkf: 3,000.
★★★ *Cavalieri*, p. Carlo Alberto 27, ☎ 43304, 30 rm P &
No restaurant, 50,000; bkf: 4,000.

Restaurant:
♦♦ *Castello*, at Santa Vittoria d'Alba, v. Cagna 4,
☎ 47147, closed Wed, Jan and Jul-Aug. In renovated
castle with medieval tower open to public. Regional and
Italian cuisine: maltagliti with leeks, mixed wild game,
20/35,000.

Recommended:
Cycling: *Associazione Ciclistica Bra*, corso IV Novembre
7, ☎ 411573.
Wine: *Cinzano wine cellars*, ☎ 47041 (guided tours).

CANELLI

Asti 28, Turin 84, Milan 131 km
Pop. 10,634 ⊠ 14053 ☎ 0141   C5

Canelli is the heart of the Asti region, source of the
famous sparkling wine. It has myriad **vineyards** and
sits on a labyrinth of wine cellars.   □

Practical information _____

Hotels:
★★★ *Asti*, v. Risorgimento 44/B, ☎ 834220, 24 rm P ♨
closed Aug, no restaurant, 46,000; bkf: 5,500.
★★★ *Grappolo d'Oro*, v. Risorgimento 21, ☎ 833812,
16 rm P 40,000.

Restaurant:
● ♦♦♦ *Guido*, at Castigliole d'Asti, p. Umberto I 27,
☎ 966012, closed Sun and hols. Elegant atmosphere. Refined regional cuisine: spinach flan with fondue, mushroom polenta, 90/120,000.

Recommended
Wine: *Bosca*, v. Cavia del Lavoro C. Bosca 2, ☎ 83250
(reservations); *Gancia*, v. Libertà 16, ☎ 8301 *(reservations, Tue and Thu)*; *Cantine sociali*, v. Loazzolo 12,
☎ 833347 or 831828; *Moscato d'Asti* and *Asti Spumante*,
frazione Marsini 12, ☎ 840419.

CASALE MONFERRATO

Alessandria 30, Turin 70, Milan 75 km
Pop. 41,161 ⊠ 15033 ☎ 0142   C-D4

Casale Monferrato mixes medieval monuments with
the smokestacks of factories. Between these two
starkly contrasting architectural styles, the city has
managed to preserve fascinating elements attesting
to its historical vicissitudes: from fiefdom to Monferrato's Renaissance capital and from one of Italy's best
protected military strongholds to one of Piedmont's
most Baroque bourgeois and mercantile cities.

▶ The graceful and ornate façade of **S. Caterina's** church,
designed by G.B. Scapitta and considered to be a masterpiece of the Casalese Baroque period (c. 1725), faces
the **p. Castello** and the 16C fortress. ▶ The **Torre civica**,
rebuilt by Matteo Sammicheli in 1512, is one of the city's
landmarks. ▶ The 12C-13C **Duomo** has been completely
restored. The **narthex** demonstrates a middle-eastern
influence; the 12C Romanesque silver crucifix attests to
the richness of the original ornaments. ▶ **S. Domenico** is
a Lombard late Gothic church (1472), with a heavy stone
portal (1505). ▶ **S. Filippo Neri** is Baroque (1667) and
its austere façade contrasts strikingly with the sumptuous
interior. ▶ The splendid frescoed ceiling above the
stairway in the **Palazzo Gozzani di Treville** by G.B. Sca-

pitta (1714) must be seen. An elegant entrance hall
opens on a magnificent courtyard. ▶ In the v. Alessandria, formerly the Jewish ghetto, the 1595 **synagogue** with
its wood and stucco decorations (18C-19C) and the
adjoining **Museo Israelitico** *(hols 10 a.m.-12 noon and
3-5 p.m.)* are interesting. ▶ In the same street, the
Palazzo di Anna d'Alençon has a delightful plant-filled
15C courtyard with late-Gothic archways. On the second
floor is a painting of the Marquis of Monferrato on a wood-
en ceiling.   □

Practical information _____

Hotels:
★★★ *Castello di San Giorgio*, at San Giorgio Monferrato,
v. Cavalli d'Olivola 3, ☎ 806203, 11 rm P ∰ ♨ ♨ closed
1-20 Aug. Medieval castle in park, 120,000; bkf: 10,000.
★★★ *Garden*, v. Montebello 1, ☎ 71701, 55 rm P ♨
closed Aug, 70,000.
★★ *Principe*, v. Cavour 55, ☎ 2019, 30 rm P closed
Aug, 50,000.

Restaurants:
● ♦♦♦ *Torre*, v. D. Garoglio 3, ☎ 70295, closed Wed and
1-20 Aug. Beautiful view and attentive service. Creative
cuisine: goose liver with salted butter, tagliolini with aromatic herbs, 30/45,000.
♦♦♦ *Alfeo*, p. Battisti 32, ☎ 2493, closed Mon and
Aug. Seafood: linguine with lobster, fish with salt and
champagne, 25/40,000.

Recommended
Cycling: *G.S. Cinghiale*, v. Gioberti 2, ☎ 54051.
Flying: *F. Capra Airport*, SS Alessandria, ☎ 2556.
Motocross: *Belvedere track*, operated by *Motoclub Italo
Palli*, ☎ 808241 or 808158.
Motorboating: *Associazione casalese*, strada Rolasco,
☎ 808133.
Young people's activities: *Orienteering Casale*, v.
O. Capello 38 (nature sports).
♥ antiques: at Pavia, market every 2nd Sun of month.

CASTELLAMONTE

Turin 38, Milan 131 km
Pop. 9,085 ⊠ 10081 ☎ 0124   B3

The ancient castle from which the town took its name
is no longer standing, nor is the Romanesque parish
church that was demolished to make way for an unusual **basilica** designed by Antonelli. Construction was
begun in 1842 but left unfinished because of a bitter
controversy. Castellamonte's only monument is the
ancient **ceramics** workshop that still produces heavy
wood-burning stoves.   □

Practical information _____

Hotel:
★★★ *Tre Re*, p. Martiri Libertà 27, ☎ 585470, 15 rm P
♨ 50,000.

CERESOLE REALE

Turin 80, Milan 176 km
Pop. 191 ⊠ 10080 ☎ 0124   B3

Vittorio Emanuele II is said to have liked this alpine
resort near an artificial lake, surrounded by green
forests and rocky terrain. The hunting trails are perfect for excursions in the adjacent **Parco del Gran
Paradiso** (→ Valle d'Aosta) where it is common to
cross paths with mountain goats. It is possible to
climb to the **Rifugio Leonesi**, the **Rifugio Jervis**, the
Rifugio Città di Chivasso or the **Nivolet Pass** (→ in
Valle d'Aosta, Valsavarenche).   □

Practical information _____

ⓘ ☎ 95186.

Recommended
Excursions: *Parco del Gran Paradiso,* ☎ 95186.
Young peoples' activities: *Centri Rousseau,* at Milan,
v. Vico 10, ☎ 02/468496 (information).

CESANA TORINESE

Turin 88, Milan 224 km
4,442 ft pop. 946 ⊠ 10054 ☎ 0122　　　　　A4

A renowned vacation and winter sports centre,
Cesana Torinese is located at the junction of a number of important roads linking the Chisone and Susa
Valleys close to the French border and the region
of Monginevro.

▶ This ancient village with a 12C **parish church** has had
a troubled past because of its strategic position; in the
1700s it was sacked and destroyed by the
French. ▶ Cesana Torinese has had many illustrious
inhabitants: Vittorio Alfieri wrote several tragedies here
and Paul Cézanne's ancestors came from this village
from which they later took their name. ▶ The **Via Lattea
Ovest resort** is accessible by the chair-lift leading up to
the Colle Bercia where this ski resort meets with the Claviere resort. ▶ On the other side of the valley *(5 km),*
another ski resort has been built on the slopes of Mt. Fraiteve above **San Sicario** and is linked to the **Via Lattea Est
resort.**　　　　　　　　　　　　　　　　□

Practical information _____

CESANA TORINESE
⚐ ski lifts, cross-country skiing, instruction.
ⓘ at Claviere, ☎ 878856; nr bus station, ☎ 89202.

Hotel:
★★ *Chaberton,* v. Roma 10, ☎ 89147, 9 rm ℗ ⚏ clos-
ed May and Nov, 46,000; bkf: 7,000. Rest. ◆◆ closed
Tue. Regional cuisine, 20/40,000.

Environs

SAN SICARIO, 5,151 ft, 5 km NE.
⚐ ski lifts, cross-country skiing, instruction.
ⓘ *Sansicario Ski,* p. Amedeo, ☎ 89489.

Hotel:
★★★★ *Rio Envers,* ☎ 811333, 45 rm ℗ ≼ ⚘ closed
Dec 21-Apr 10, 130,000.

Recommended
Horseback riding: *Circolo Ippico S. Sicario,* ☎ 89238.
Swimming: indoor pool in shopping centre (also tennis).
Vacation village: *Hotel-Villaggio Valtur,* ☎ 811222 (closed
May and Sep-Nov).

CHERASCO

Cuneo 45, Turin 57, Milan 174 km
Pop. 6,302 ⊠ 12062 ☎ 0172　　　　　　B5

Cherasco was formerly a military stronghold. Its
streets are laid out on a regular plan with perpendicular intersections often flanked by porticos and civil
and religious structures. The imposing Viale Napoleonico, lined with tall plane trees, leads to the
Visconte Castle. Cherasco was once considered an
ideal setting for diplomatic and military talks and it
was here that the European plenipotentiary ended
the struggle for control over Monferrato in 1631. The
Turin court and magistrates took refuge here during
the 1706 siege of Turin and in 1796 an armistice
was signed here between Vittorio Amedeo II and
the French.

▶ The beautiful façade of the 12C-13C Romanesque
church of **S. Pietro** has loggias decorated with majolica sculptures. ▶ **S. Maria del Popolo's** (1702) façade
is large and Baroque; its interior is magnificent, as is its
octagonal dome. ▶ The **Museo G. B. Adriani** *(first Sun
of month 9:30 a.m.-12 noon; other times inquire at municipio,* ☎ *48498)* houses impressive numismatic and medal
collections.　　　　　　　　　　　　　　□

Practical information _____

Restaurant:
◆ *Vittorio Veneto-da Aldo,* v. Salmatoris 13, ☎ 48003,
closed Wed and 20 Aug-10 Sep. Regional cuisine: fresh
tagliolini with truffles, rabbit with juniper, 20/30,000.

CHIERI

Turin 15, Milan 159 km
Pop. 30,885 ⊠ 10023 ☎ 011　　　　　　B-C4

In the 15C, Chieri's textile industries produced
100,000 articles per year; fustian cloth-makers had
their own guild and the special plant called 'woad'
was cultivated in the countryside to create blue
dyes. The town preserves a number of historical and
artistic remains from that time.

▶ The **Duomo** (1435) in the city centre is one of the best
examples of Piedmontese Gothic architecture; to its r. lies
the 12C-15C Romanesque-Gothic **Baptistery** with campanile. On the façade is a gabled portal; inside is a beautiful
Gothic carved wooden choir stall (15C-16C). ▶ **S. Domenico** (14C-15C) preserves some of its Gothic form; its
polygonal apse and campanile are of interest. **S. Giorgo**
(15C) is a mixture of architectural styles because of an
18C restructuring. ▶ 5 km S at **Pessione** is the **Museo
di Storia dell'Enologia** (wine history) near the Martini e
Rossi plant *(open daily; reservations,* ☎ *57451).*　　□

Practical information _____

Hotel:
★★ *Tre Re,* corso Torino 64, ☎ 9478383, 30 rm ℗ ⚘ closed Jul-Aug, 60,000; bkf: 5,000.

CHIOMONTE

Turin 61, Milan 201 km
2,460 ft pop. 1,053 ⊠ 10050 ☎ 0122　　　　A4

Chiomonte is a vacation spot and winter sports
centre that owes its popularity to the slopes of
Pian del Fràis. The 13C church of **S. Caterina** and
the 10C-17C church of **Assunta,** with a Romanesque
campanile, recall the city's ancient roots. Nearby is
the **Forte di Exilles,** a border fortress until 1713. It
served for many years as the prison for the mysterious Man in the Iron Mask.　　　　　　□

Practical information _____

⚐ ski lifts at Fràis and Pian Mesdi; cross-country skiing,
instruction at Pian des Fràis.
ⓘ municipio, ☎ 54104.

CHIVASSO

Turin 23, Milan 120 km
Pop. 25,985 ⊠ 10034 ☎ 011　　　　　　C4

Chivasso was once the capital of Monferrato, but now
is within the Turin metropolis. It remains an important commercial and industrial crossroads (e.g., beef
market, automobile production). In the 15C, Chivasso had one of the first Piedmont printing indus-

tries. The Cavour canal (inaugurated 1866) begins here, linking the Rivers Po and Ticino to irrigate the Vercellese, Novarese and Lomellina regions.

▶ The 15C **Duomo** has an unusual cornice that accentuates the Gothic high portal that takes up much of the façade; inside is a 16C painting, *Descent From the Cross* by Defendente Ferrari who was a native of Chivasso. □

Practical information —————————

Hotels:
★★★ *Europa*, p. d'Armi 5, ☎ 9102025, 32 rm Ⓟ No restaurant, 55,000; bkf: 6,000.
★★ *Centauro*, v. Torino 90, ☎ 9102169, 12 rm Ⓟ closed 1-25 Aug, 50,000; bkf: 4,000.

Recommended
Pastry shop: *Nocciolini* (sweet macaroons and cakes).

CIRIE

Turin 21, Milan 144 km
Pop. 18,720 ⊠ 10073 ☎ 011   B3-4

Cirie lies at the mouth of the Lanzo Valley (→). In the 16C, it was the fiefdom of the d'Oria family from Doria. The family later changed their name to Doria, which holds an honoured place in Italian history. Cirie is an important industrial and agricultural centre in the plain of Turin.

▶ The 13C-14C Gothic **Duomo** has a striking portal and campanile; inside are paintings by Ferrari and Giovenone the Elder (1535). ▶ **S. Martino di Liramo**, a 10C-11C Romanesque church, is also interesting. □

Practical information —————————

Restaurant:
♦♦♦ *Mario*, corso Martiri della Libertà 41, ☎ 9203490, closed Mon eve, Tue and Aug-Sep. Regional cuisine: finanziera, homemade puddings, 22/40,000.

CLAVIERE

Turin 94, Milan 230 km
5,774 ft pop. 171 ⊠ 10050 ☎ 0122   A4

Situated on the French border, Claviere was one of the first Italian winter resorts, created in the early 1900s when skiing was still new. Partly destroyed in World War II, the resort was rebuilt and now hosts a panoply of services, while complementing the Cesana Torinese resort (→). □

Practical information —————————

⚡ ski lifts, cross-country skiing, instruction, skating.
ⓘ in the Statale, ☎ 878856.

Hotel:
★★ *Bes*, v. Nazionale 18, ☎ 878805, 9 rm ⊗ closed 15 May-15 June and 15 Oct-15 Nov, 55,000.

Recommended
Golf: ☎ 878917 (9 holes).
Swimming: v. Nazionale (also tennis).

CRISSOLO

Cuneo 64, Turin 85, Milan 235 km
4,324 ft pop. 309 ⊠ 12030 ☎ 0175   A-B5

Monviso, the isolated pyramidal mountain, was admired by the Romans for its massiveness and majesty and because the Po River has its source in the lofty peak. To climb to the **Piano del Re** where the Po is

a mountain stream, a trail begins at Crissolo, a winter resort at the foot of Monviso. ▶ A mule trail leads *(25 mn)* to the **Grotta del Rio Martino** with calcium formations *(guide and light are obligatory).* □

Practical information —————————

⚡ instruction, ski lifts at Pian Giasset and Piano del Re.

Restaurant:
♦ *Polo Nord*, v. Provinciale 26, ☎ 94908, closed Thu and Oct-Nov. Regional cuisine: trout from the Po, bagna cauda, 16/21,000.

Recommended
Caving: guided tours of *Grotta del Rio Martino dal Pian Giasset, Hotel Bucaneve, v. Umberto 10, ☎ 94948 (information).

CUNEO

Turin 84, Milan 250, Rome 631 km
Pop. 56,091 ⊠ 12100 ☎ 0171   B6

Cuneo's site on a high terrace between the Stura di Demonte and Gesso streams made it a strategically important but isolated city from its earliest days in the 12C. The city was often beseiged by invading armies. Although Cuneo does not have a strong artistic and cultural heritage, it is proud of its tradition of courage and civic consciousness. These two qualities made it one of the most active antifascist centres in Italy.

▶ Confined for centuries behind battlemented walls, Cuneo began to expand in the Napoleonic era. ▶ Between the old and new cities is the enormous **piazza Duccio Galimberti** (named after the leader of the partisan struggle who was murdered in 1944) with 19C palaces with graceful arcades. This is the city's hub and main market area. ▶ Emblematic of the city's monuments is the former church of **S. Francesco**, a Gothic edifice with a richly decorated portal, which now houses the **Museo Civico** *(8:30 a.m.-12:30 p.m. and 2:30 p.m.-6:30 p.m.; closed Sat p.m., Sun and Mon).* ▶ Two other important churches are **S. Croce** (1709-15) with a unique concave façade and **S. Ambrogio** (1703-43); both were designed by F. Gallo (1703-43). ▶ Tree-lined promenades replaced the city ramparts, which were destroyed in the 19C. They afford a splendid view of the city and its surroundings. At the extreme NE end of the city, on viale degli Angeli, is the striking **monument to the Resistance** built by U. Mastroianni in 1969. □

Practical information —————————

CUNEO
ⓘ corso Nizza 17, ☎ 3258.
🚂 ☎ 3681.
🚌 from bus station in p. Torino.

Hotels:
★★★ *Principe*, v. Cavour 1, ☎ 3355, 40 rm Ⓟ No restaurant, 60,000; bkf: 7,000.
★★★ *Royal Superga*, v. Pascal 3, ☎ 3223, 30 rm Ⓟ No restaurant, 58,000; bkf: 6,000.
★ *Ligure*, v. Savigliano 11, ☎ 61942, 26 rm ⊗ closed 10-31 Jan, 25/30,000; bkf: 3,000.

Restaurants:
● ♦♦♦ *Rododendro*, at San Giacomo di Boves, ☎ 880372, closed Sun eve, Mon, Tue noon and Aug. Refined, in a mountain villa. Creative cuisine: salted salmon, roasted goat, 60/80,000.
● ♦♦♦ *Tre Citroni*, v. Bonelli 2, ☎ 62048, closed Wed, 15-30 Jun and 15-30 Sep. Regional and Italian cuisine: fondued tagliatelle with truffles, rice mantecato, 30/40,000.
♦♦♦ *Basin*, contrada Mondovi 2, ☎ 61962, closed Thu, 1-15 Jan and 15 Aug. Mixed cuisine: soufflé with parmigiano and truffles, tagliolini with green shrimp, 30/40,000.

◆◆◆ **Plat d'Etain,** corso Giolitti 18, ☎ 61918, closed Mon and Jun-Jul. Currently under complete renovation. French cuisine: terrine maison à l'armagnac, veal rognon in porto, 45/65,000.

⚓ ★★ *Bisalta,* at San Rocco Castagnaretta, v. S. Maurizio 33, 200 pl, ☎ 491334 (all year).

Recommended
Archery: v. Porta Mondovi 11; *Federazione Italiana,* v. Schiapparelli 20, ☎ 65652.
Cycling: *Sport Cuneo,* frazione Ronchi 74, ☎ 61821.
Fairs and markets: *Animal show and market* (Mar); *cattle show* (Nov); *snail fair* at San Dalmazzo (Dec).
Flying: at Levaldigi *(21 km N),* ☎ 374132 (also gliding, airballons and parachuting).
Hang gliding: *Flyers,* corso Francia 86, ☎ 491751 (instruction).
Sports: p. Martiri della Libertà (playing field); *Federazione Italiana,* corso IV Novembre 29, ☎ 54529.
♥ gastronomy: *cuneesi al rum* (chocolate-covered meringues).

Environs

CHIUSA DI PESIO, 690 ft, ✉ 12013, 15 km SE.
⑆ ski lifts, cross-country skiing, instruction.
ⓘ municipio, ☎ 734009.

Recommended
Park: *Alta Valle Pesio,* v. S. Anna 13, ☎ 734021 (office).

CUORGNE

Turin 40, Milan 137 km
Pop. 10,346 ✉ 10082 ☎ 0124   B3

Cuorgne is a town of low houses overshadowed by two medieval towers. They are symbols of a feudal epoch that was torn by a long popular revolt known as *tuchinaggio.* Cuorgne was actively involved in this revolt, but was not among the victors. *C.* 1000 King Arduino, the first King of Italy, was supposed to have spent some time in a Gothic **house** with *cotto* decoration (v. Arduino 27). 7 km from Cuorgne is the **Santuario di Belmonte;** it was rebuilt in the 19C.   ▢

Practical information _____

Hotel:
★★★ *Astoria,* v. Don Minzoni 5, ☎ 666001, 24 rm Ⓟ closed Feb, 47,500.

DOMODOSSOLA

Novara 91, Milan 121, Turin 187 km
892 ft pop. 20,129 ✉ 28037 ☎ 0324   C1

In 1908, the Sempione Tunnel opened a direct line of communication between W and SE Europe. The legendary Orient Express promptly adopted this route for its Paris-Istanbul journey. Domodossola had previously been the Ossola (→) region's main centre and an outpost on the Sempione road until the end of the Roman era. It grew in importance in the 1800s because of the Napoleonic road which passed through the town, but its real growth arrived with the Transalpine railroad line. Its industrial activities are now closely linked to international commercial traffic.

▶ The irregularly shaped **piazza del Mercato** is bordered by delightful 15C-16C houses with porticos and loggias. ▶ Two small museums *(currently under renovation)* are housed in the 16C-17C **Palazzo Silva** and the **Palazzo di S. Francesco.** The latter contains remains of the 14C church of the same name.   ▢

Practical information _____

⑆ ski lifts, cross-country skiing, instruction at Alpe Lusentino *(10 km W); Sciovie Lusentino Moncucco,* ☎ 42722 (information).
▄▄▄ ☎ 42533; transport service for cars through Sempione Tunnel (runs more frequently from Iselle, *18 km N),* ☎ 42055.

Hotels:
★★★ *Motel Europa,* at Calice, ☎ 42116, 36 rm Ⓟ ⚿ ㋡ closed Nov. No restaurant, 60,000; bkf: 6,000.
★★ *Sempione,* v. Galletti 53, ☎ 43869, 30 rm Ⓟ closed 15 Aug and Christmas, 54,000; bkf: 5,000.

Restaurants:
◆ *Piemonte-da Sciolla,* p. Convenzione 4, ☎ 42633, closed Wed, Jan and Aug-Sep. Regional cuisine: tortelloni with nuts, veal with greens, 18/25,000.
◆ *Trattoria Romana Chez Tullio,* v. Binda 69, ☎ 43685, closed Sun eve, Mon and Jul. Mixed cuisine: grilled meat and fish, lampada dishes, 25/30,000.

Recommended
Cycling: *G.S. Cicloamatori,* v. Cavalieri di Vittorio Veneto 2, ☎ 53387.

DRONERO

Cuneo 19, Turin 82, Milan 228 km
Pop. 7,129 ✉ 12025 ☎ 0171   B5

Dronero, although a lively industrial and agricultural centre, has never been able to develop the **Maira Valley,** one of the most beautiful, but also one of the poorest, Piedmontese valleys. Emigration has been so extensive that the valley is now sometimes called the 'valley of silence'. Dronero's 15C Gothic **parish church** has a lovely doorway. 2.4 km away, the 12C church of **S. Costanzo sul Monte★** has three apses and the lantern from the original Romanesque structure *(inquire at adjoining farmhouse).*   ▢

Practical information _____

Hotel:
★★ *Tripoli,* v. Roma 15, ☎ 918088, 31 rm, 39,500.

Recommended
Technical tourism: Fabbriche Riunite, ☎ 918106 (hobby products).

FENESTRELLE

Turin 69, Milan 219 km
3,786 ft pop. 775 ✉ 10060 ☎ 0121   A4

Fenestrelle is a small vacation and winter sports centre in the Chisone Valley. It boasts an ancient dungeon and interesting old houses. A covered stairway with some 4,000 steps links the sturdy 17C buildings constructed by the French and those added later by the Savoys. Within the complex, a massive structure follows the ridge of the mountain; it is called the **Forte di Fenestrelle.**   ▢

Practical information _____

⑆
⚓ ★★★ *Serre Marie,* SS 23 at 71-km marker, 170 pl, ☎ 83982 (all year).

Recommended
Park: *Orsiera-Rocciavrè,* at Pra Catinat *(8 km E),* ☎ 83757.

┌─────────────────────────────────────┐
│ Send us your comments and suggestions; we will │
│ use them in the next edition. │
└─────────────────────────────────────┘

FOSSANO

Cuneo 25, Turin 70, Milan 191 km
Pop. 23,420 ⊠ 12045 ☎ 0172   B5

Situated on the edge of the high Famolasco plateau, Fossano overlooks the corso della Stura di
Demonte. Its **historical centre** is interesting. From
the v. Marconi al Borgo S. Antonio there is a lovely
view of the city's two main monuments: the **Castello
dei principi d'Acaia,** a rectangular fortress with tall
angular towers (1324-32), and the Baroque church of
SS. Trinità, one of the finest works of Francesco Gallo
(1730-8). The church has a graceful, frescoed campanile. Gallo also designed the **Ospedale Maggiore
SS. Trinità,** similar in style to the city's churches.
11 km E is **Bene Vagienna,** a medieval village built on
a hillside; close by are remains of a Roman settlement, including a theatre.   ◻

Practical information _____

Hotel:
★★★ *Castello d'Acaja,* corso Emanuele Filiberto 32,
☎ 61555, 32 rm ℗ ⚹ closed Aug, 60,000; bkf: 8,000.

Restaurants:
● ◆◆◆ *Apollo,* v. Regina Elena 19, ☎ 62417, closed
Mon eve, Tue and Jul. Italian cuisine with a few Cilano
dishes: nettle pie, wild boar in red wine, 25/50,000.
◆◆◆ *Sant'Antonio-da Regis,* v. Palocca 7, ☎ 60197,
closed Mon and 1-15 Aug. Regional cuisine: filet with
hazelnuts, wild game in civet, 20/30,000.

FRABOSA SOPRANA

Cuneo 31, Turin 96, Milan 228 km
2,923 ft pop. 1,190 ⊠ 12082 ☎ 0174   B-C6

Frabosa Soprana is the most important vacation and
winter sports resort in the Monregalesi Valley; it
has a wide range of slopes, excellent facilities and
roads. Near Bossea, the **Grotta di Bossea★** *(guided
tours 10 a.m.-12 noon and 2-6 p.m.)* is one of Italy's most fabulous caves with myriad rock formations,
vast internal chambers, waterfalls and underground
lakes.   ◻

Practical information _____

FRABOSA SOPRANA
⚶ ski lifts, cross-country skiing, instruction, skating.
ⓘ p. del Municipio, ☎ 34010.

Hotels:
★★★ *Bossea,* p. Umberto I 5, ☎ 34012, 29 rm, closed
1 Oct-19 Dec and Easter-14 Jun, 50,000; bkf: 4,500.
★★★ *Excelsior,* p. Marconi 9, ☎ 34006, 62 rm ℗ ⅏
closed 25 Sep-22 Dec and 10 Apr-1 Jun, 50,000; bkf:
4,000.
★★★ *Gildo,* v. Vittorio Emanuele 39, ☎ 34009, 18 rm ℗
⅏ closed 15 Apr-1 Jun and 30 Sep-20 Dec, 50,000;
bkf: 5,000.
★★★ *Miramonti,* v. Roma, ☎ 344533, 48 rm ℗ ⚹ ⅏ ⌖
closed 1 Apr-15 Jun and 25 Sep-20 Dec, 45,000; bkf:
4,000.

Recommended
Caving: guided tour of *Grotta di Bossea* (Oct-Apr; reservations required), ☎ 349128 or 349129.

Environs
ARTESINA, 4,262 ft, ⊠ 12083, 12 km SW.
⚶ ski lifts, instruction.
ⓘ ☎ 334264.

PRATO NEVOSO, 5,577 ft, ⊠ 12083, 14 km S.
⚶ ski lifts, cross-country skiing, instruction.
ⓘ v. Galassia, ☎ 334133.

Recommended
Horseback riding: *Centro Sportivo Prato Nevoso,*
v. Galassia 4, ☎ 334133 (associate of *ANTE*).

GARESSIO

Cuneo 73, Turin 115, Milan 239 km
2,037 ft pop. 4,300 ⊠ 12070 ☎ 0174   C6

Garessio lies at the E limit of the Cunese Alps in the
upper Tànaro Valley. Surrounded by dense forests
of chestnut trees, it is a vacation centre popular for
its mineral cures in the waters of the S. Bernardo and
other streams in the vicinity. There are modern ski
facilities at **Garessio 2000** on the slopes of Mt. Anto-
roto.   ◻

Practical information _____

⚶ ski lifts, cross-country skiing, instruction.
♨ (Jun-Sep), ☎ 81101
ⓘ corso Paolini, ☎ 81122.

Hotels:
★★★ *Ramo Verde,* v. Nazionale 108, ☎ 81075, 23 rm ℗
⅏ closed Christmas, 45,000; bkf: 4,000.
★★ *Ponte Rosa,* v. Fasiani 1, ☎ 81007, 35 rm ℗ ⅏
closed 9 Jan-1 Mar and 14 Oct-1 Dec, 31,000; bkf: 5,000.
⚠ ★ *Relax Montano,* at Sant'Orsola, v. Regina Margherita, 44 pl, ☎ 81122 (all year).

GATTINARA

Vercelli 34, Milan 79, Turin 91 km
Pop. 9,297 ⊠ 13045 ☎ 0163   C3

Gattinara sits in the hills in the Sesia area. Grape-
vines, part of the Nebbiolo vineyards, source of
the Nebbiolo red wines, cover the area. The parish
church of **S. Pietro,** rebuilt in the 19C, still has
its beautiful 15C Romanesque-Gothic façade. 11 km
away to the SW in **Rovasenda** is a superb castle
with a 13C tower and 15C trappings.   ◻

Practical information _____

Hotel:
★★ *Impero,* corso Garibaldi 81, ☎ 833232, 20 rm ⅏ closed Aug, 45,000; bkf: 5,000.

Restaurant:
◆◆◆ *Dui Camin,* corso Garibaldi 165, ☎ 834446, closed
Mon, Jan and Aug. International cuisine: carpaccio with
rucola, black rice with cuttlefish, 35/45,000.

GAVI

Alessandria 33, Milan 97, Turin 136 km
Pop. 4,490 ⊠ 15066 ☎ 0143   D5

Gavi is a wine-producing centre in the Lemme Valley. It was under Genovese rule for almost six centuries, thus the town has distinctively Ligurian characteristics. The 12C Romanesque church of **S. Gia-
como★,** made of local sandstone, has a sculpted portal; its octagonal lantern has a Baroque elevated section which serves as a campanile. The **Portino** has
a 13C turreted portal and there is a remarkable
16C-17C **Forte Genovese** *(9 a.m.-12:30 p.m. and
2-4 p.m.; closed Sun p.m. and Mon).*   ◻

Practical information _____

Restaurants:
◆◆◆ *Cantine del Gavi,* v. Mameli 50, ☎ 642458, closed Mon and 1-15 Jul. Near Romanesque Parrocchiale. Regional cuisine: cappellacci with herbs, wild game, homemade wines, 30/40,000.
◆ *Castello,* p. Dante 13, ☎ 642794, closed Fri and Christmas. Regional cuisine: lasagna Zerbetta, fagottino Gavina, 20/30,000.
◆ *Marietto,* at Rovereto *(5 km NW)* ☎ 682118, closed Mon, Jan and 1-15 Jul. Regional cuisine, 22/28,000.

Recommended
Cycling: *Zerbo Sport,* p. della Chiesa 9/R, ☎ 642774.
Park: *Capanne di Marcarolo,* ☎ 684131 or ☎ 684220 (information).
Wine: *Villa Giustiniana wine cellars,* frazione Rovereto, ☎ 682132; *cantine sociali,* at Maddalena, ☎ 642786.

IVREA

Turin 50, Milan 115 km
Pop. 27,577 ⊠ 10015 ☎ 0125   C3

'Ivrea la bella' still looks much as it has always done. The red towers of King Arduino contrast with the dark towers of Camillo and Adriano Olivetti. The city is a rare example of how pride in the past and an enlightened entrepreneur can work together to preserve character. The famous Carnival, with its red berets and 'battle of the oranges', is reminiscent of earlier popular libertarian struggles. The medieval centre stands as a testament to a specific turning point in the city's political history. Ivrea is, and has always been, the capital of the Canavese region, where the expanse of the plain meets the majestic Alps. Economically important in ancient times, the area underwent early industrialization. Adriano Olivetti, leader of the industrial conglomerate started by his father Camillo, worked hard to further social, political and cultural projects in this area during the 1950s and 1960s, making Ivrea into one of the most active intellectual centres in Italy.

▶ **Piazza Vittorio Emanuele** (A1) in the heart of the old city is divided by the Roman road *Eporedia* (v. Arduino and v. Palestro). In medieval times these axes divided the city into thirds. ▶ The **Duomo** (A1) was transformed in the 18C and only the campanile, lantern and crypt remain from the original Romanesque building from the era of Bishop Warmondo (10C), when Ivrea was the site of King Arduino's throne. Two 16C paintings by D. Ferrari hang in the sacristy. ▶ The square bulk of the Sabaudo **Castello** (A1), begun in 1358, is an impressive sight. Standing guard at the four corners are the famous red towers (one of which was truncated by an explosion in the 17C), which offer splendid views. ▶ In v. Palestro is the piazza Ottinetti (A2), a large rectangle surrounded in by buildings (1843). At no. 18 on the same street, the **P.A. Garda Civic Museum** *(9:30 a.m.-12 noon and 3-6:30 p.m., Sat until 7:30 p.m.; closed Sun and Mon)* displays Eastern art, pre-Romanesque and Romanesque relics and frescos from 15C-17C houses. An art, history and folklore museum, the Museo Canavesano, is under construction. ▶ The Romanesque **S. Stefano tower** (B2), dating from 1041, is all that remains of an abbey destroyed by the French in 1558. ▶ From the tower, there is a walk along the river (following corso Umberto I). Beyond the Ponte Nuovo (B1) lies a more recent urban expansion zone. The **Olivetti** complex, with production, residential and service units (v. Jervis, B1), is a significant example of Italian architecture from 1930-60. ▶ The nearby church of **S. Bernardino** has frescos by Spanzotti (*c.* 1500).   □

Practical information _____

ℹ (A2) corso Vercelli 1, ☎ 424005.
🚍 from bus station (B1), ☎ 49049.
Car rental: *Avis,* corso Nigra 78, ☎ 422091.

Hotels:
★★★★ *Serra,* corso Botta 30 (A2 a), ☎ 44341, 54 rm ℗ 🅿 ⊠ No restaurant, 131,000.
★★★ *Eden,* corso d'Azeglio 67, ☎ 49190, 36 rm ℗ No restaurant, 63,000; bkf: 5,500.
★★★ *Moro,* corso d'Azeglio 43 (A2 b), ☎ 40170, 33 rm ℗ No restaurant, 62,000.
★★★ *Ritz,* at Banchette, ☎ 424148, 40 rm ℗ No restaurant, 79,000; bkf: 6,000.
★★★ *Sirio,* at Lake Sirio, ☎ 424247, 38 rm ℗ ≼ ⚒ ⅃ No restaurant, 79,000; bkf: 6,500.

Restaurant:
◆ *Moro,* corso d'Azeglio 41 (A2 b),☎ 423136, closed Sun in Nov-Feb and Christmas. Regional and Italian cuisine: meat ravioli with nuts, pappardelle with wild boar or hare, 20/32,000.

⚲ ★★★ *San Michele Lago,* v. Lago S. Michele 13, 45 pl, ☎ 40868.

Recommended
Archery : *Compagnia arcieri del Canavese,* corso Vercelli 74, ☎ 49022.
Canoeing: *Canoa Club Ivrea,* v. S. Grato 11, ☎ 46251 (instruction).
Events: *Historical carnival* and *battle of the oranges.*
Hang gliding: *Arcobaleno,* at Burolo *(5 km NE),* v. Asilo 23, ☎ 577488 (instruction).
Wine: *Enoteca Eporediese di Ferrando,* corso Cavour 9, ☎ 422383; regional wine shop at Carema *(15 km N).*

LAKE MAGGIORE AND LAKE ORTA

From Arona *(90 km; 1 day; map 2)*

At the narrowest point of the great furrow dug out by glaciers in the depths of the Ticino Valley, the cities of Arona and Angera are so close that they virtually merge into one town. These Piedmontese banks of Lake Maggiore are markedly different from those in Lombardy. Whereas the Lombardy shoreline offers a panorama of gently rolling hills, the Piedmontese

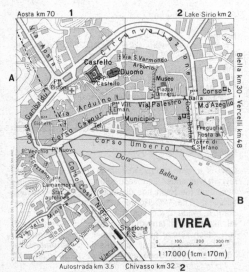

Aosta km 70   **1**   **2** Lake Sirio km 2

A

B

IVREA

0   100   200   300 m
1 : 17,000 (1cm = 170m)

Autostrada km 3.5   Chivasso km 32 **2**

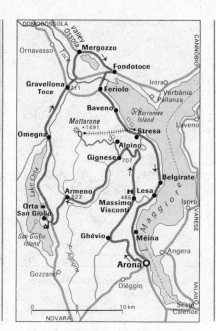

2. Lake Maggiore and Lake Orta

many and Queen Victoria. From the **lungolago** (view) there is a short climb to the piazza to visit the octagonal Renaissance **baptistery** with restored 15C-16C frescos and the **parish church** with an 11C-12C façade and campanile. ▶ The route then follows the lake shore to **Stresa** (→) and continues to **Belgirate,** a health resort nestled in verdant surroundings. In 1858, Garibaldi, Cavour, Manzoni and d'Azeglio came here for a memorable regatta organized by Italy's first rowing club. ▶ Finally, the route passes through **Lesa** and **Meina** on the way back to **Arona.** □

Practical information _____

ALPINO, ✉ 28040, ☎ 0323.

Hotel:
★★★ **Alpino Fiorente,** ☎ 20103, 39 rm P ≮ ♧ ▩ closed 1 Sep-14 Jun, 65,000; bkf: 5,000.

BAVENO, ✉ 28042, ☎ 0323.
ℹ p. Dante 5, ☎ 24632.
⛴ p. Imbarcadero, ☎ 23552.

Hotels:
★★★★ **Lido Palace Hotel Baveno,** v. Sempione 22, ☎ 24444, 100 rm P ▩ ☐ ↗ ≮ closed Nov-Feb, 100,000; bkf: 14,000.
★★★★ **Splendid,** v. Sempione 12, ☎ 24383, 120 rm P ▩ ☐ ↗ closed 26 Oct-27 Mar, 110,000; bkf: 6,500.
★★★ **Romagna,** v. Sempione 21, ☎ 24879, 18 rm P ≮ closed Dec-Feb, 70,000; bkf: 5,000.
⚲ ★★ **Lido,** v. Piave 66, 66 pl, ☎ 24775.

BELGIRATE, ✉ 28040, ☎ 0322.
ℹ v. Sempione 53, ☎ 7494 (seasonal).
⛴ boats and hydrofoils.

Hotels:
★★★★ **Milano,** v. Sempione 4, ☎ 76525, 52 rm P ≮ ᵬ 105,000. Rest. ♦♦♦ Veranda with lake view. Mixed cuisine: salmon in cartoccio, coppa Guja, 25/40,000.
★★★★ **Villa Carlotta,** v. Sempione 119, ☎ 76461, 110 rm P ≮ ▩ ᵬ ⚭ ☐ ↗ 115,000. Rest. ♦♦♦ Overlooks the lake; summer dining in garden. Mixed cuisine: gnocchetti soufflé with mushrooms, filet of beef with celery, 25/40,000.

Recommended
Tennis: v. Quattro Novembre 58, ☎ 7403.
Water skiing: across from *Hotel Villa Carlotta.*

FERIOLO, ✉ 28040, ☎ 0323.

Hotels:
★★★ **Carillon,** SS del Sempione, ☎ 28115, 26 rm P ▩ closed Oct-Easter. No restaurant, 60,000; bkf: 5,000.
★★ **Serenella,** v. 42 Martiri 5, ☎ 28112, 15 rm P ▩ closed 2 Jan-28 Feb, 48,000; bkf: 5,000.
⚲ ★★ **Conca d'Oro,** v. 42 Martiri, 230 pl, ☎ 28116.

FONDOTOCE, ✉ 28040, ☎ 0323.

⚲ ★★ **Isolino,** v. per Feriolo 25, 752 pl, ☎ 496080;
★★ **Quiete,** v. Turati 72, 180 pl, ☎ 496013.

Recommended
Horseback riding: *Associazione Ippica Verbano,* v. Piano Grande 14, ☎ 496040.

GIGNESE, ✉ 28040, ☎ 0323.

Restaurant:
♦♦♦ **Bardelli,** at Vezzo, ☎ 20329, closed Mon and Nov-Feb except hols. Gracious villa with summer dining in garden. Italian cuisine: gnocchi with gorgonzola, chifferoni regina, 25/40,000.
⚲ ★★ **7 Camini,** road to il Mottarone, 140 pl, ☎ 20183 (all year).

side is shadowed by the Matterhorn and other peaks. The nearby small Lake Orta is surrounded by forests with wild and melancholy beauty.

▶ From **Arona** (→) the route passes to **Ghevio.** Here it is possible to climb to **Massino Visconti,** the site of a 13C **Castello.** The ancient church of **S. Michele** with a Romanesque campanile is close by. ▶ In **Gignese** there is a curious **Umbrella Museum,** and in **Alpino the Giardino Alpinia** (alpine garden; *closed Nov-Apr).* Continuing to climb, the route follows a detour along the crest of **Mt. Mottarone,** which in the 19C was used by many climbers headed for Lake Orta. Today it is frequented by skiers. ▶ The route descends toward **Armeno** and **Orta San Giulio,** the major tourist centre and health resort on Lake Orta; it contains an old wealthy area with picturesque, elegant buildings (mostly Baroque). Especially worth seeing is the **Palazzo della Comunità** (1582) which stands on the central piazza near the lake. ▶ Here there is an interesting climb to **Sacro Monte** with a remarkable sanctuary dedicated to S. Francesco with twenty 16C-18C chapels adorned with frescos and terra-cotta sculptures. It is possible to take a boat to visit the island of **San Giulio★.** It contains a very old **basilica** (first rebuilt in 11C-12C and restored later), inside of which are a sculpted Romanesque ambo and 15C-16C frescos. ▶ The road climbs again toward **Omegna** (→) and then descends into the Toce Valley to **Gravellona Toce,** a commercial and industrial centre at the base of the Ossola Valley. ▶ To the l. of the river, the health resort of **Mergozzo** is known for its spring of the same name and its solitary lake which is separated from Lake Maggiore by a narrow plain. ▶ Beyond **Fondotoce** is **Feriolo** on the banks of Lake Maggiore. ▶ **Baveno** is one of the most important tourist centres in Verbano. **Borromeo** is full of elegant architecture and in the 19C hosted many illustrious visitors such as the Emperor Frederick III of Ger-

---

If you enjoy sports, consult the pages pertaining to the regions; there you will find addresses for practicing your favorite sport.

LESA, ⊠ 28040, ☎ 0322.

Recommended
Swimming: v. Davicini, ☎ 7367 (also tennis).

MEINA, ⊠ 28046, ☎ 0322.
≋

Hotels:
★★★ *Villa Paradiso,* v. Sempione 125, ☎ 65652, 40 rm P closed Nov-Feb, 58,000; bkf: 6,000.
★★ *Bel Sit,* v. Sempione 76, ☎ 6483, 12 rm P ∰ ※ closed 1 Nov-10 Dec, 38,000; bkf: 3,500.

Restaurant:
♦♦♦ *Piccola Baita,* at Fosseno, ☎ 589813, closed Mon. Italian cuisine, some international dishes: onion soup (order in advance), faraona with cherry, 30/50,000.

Recommended
Sports: *water sports centre,* at Lido di Meina, v. Sempione 106, ☎ 6326; tennis, ☎ 65616.

MERGOZZO, ⊠ 28040, ☎ 0323.

Restaurant:
♦♦ *Ancienne Auberge,* at Bracchio, ☎ 80122, closed Wed and Oct. French cuisine: escargots bourguignonne, coq au vin, 25/35,000.

MOTTARONE, 4,662 ft, ⊠ 28040 (Gignese), ☎ 0323.
↯ ski lifts, instruction.
ℹ tourist offices at Stresa (→).

Hotel:
★★ *Miramonti,* ☎ 24822, 12 rm ≮ ※ closed 16 Sep-30 Nov and Easter-30 Jun, 50,000; bkf: 4,000.

Restaurant:
♦♦ *Eden,* ☎ 24873, closed 15 Oct-15 Nov. Italian cuisine: scallopine with mushrooms, wild game, 30,000.

ORTA SAN GIULIO, ⊠ 28016, ☎ 0322.
≋
ℹ p. Motta 26, ☎ 90355.

Hotel:
★★★★ *San Rocco,* v. Gippini da Verona 11, ☎ 90222, 38 rm P ≮ ∰ ⬚ Recently renovated 17C convent, 125,000.

Restaurant:
♦♦ *Sacro Monte,* v. Sacro Monte 5, ☎ 90220, closed Tue and 5-30 Jan. Near Sacro Monte Sanctuary. Italian cuisine: truffled delicacies, taglierini al pesto, 20/40,000.

⚐ ★★ *Orta,* at Bagnera, v. Domodossola 28, 140 pl, ☎ 90267 (all year).

Recommended
Events: *Ortafiore* (Apr); *Cusiano ancient music festival* (Jun).
Tennis: v. Panoramica, ☎ 90293.
♥ shopping: speciality pastries, wrought iron.

The valleys of upper LAKE MAGGIORE

From Pallanza to Domodossola *(68 km, 1 day; map 3)*

Lake Maggiore has a generally mild climate and on the most sheltered parts of the Piedmontese shore olive, cedar, lemon and orange trees and some rare plants abound. Many imposing villas, some of which date from the 1800s, dot the central part of Piedmontese Verbano, particularly the area around Stresa and Pallanza. These houses built by the Borromean aristocracy are fanciful and exotic. They were designed to be accessible by road rather than water, therefore they are open, surrounded by parks that were planned not to isolate or hide them, but to provide decorative settings. In the mid-19C, the road along the lake's W bank carried heavy traffic to Domodossola and Sempione. In later years, this main artery fur-

3. The valleys of upper Lake Maggiore

thered tourist development in adjacent Ossola valleys such as Vigezzo.

▶ The itinerary starts at the promontory of the N Borromean gulf with the towns of **Pallanza** and **Intra** (→ Verbania). ▶ From Intra, the views become more beautiful as the road climbs to **Premeno,** a summer vacation and winter sports centre in a pretty hollow with a view of the lake. ▶ The coastal road continues on to **Ghiffa,** a summer vacation town with many elegant villas perched on its verdant hillside, and then to **Cannero Riviera,** with a mild climate and Mediterranean-type vegetation. ▶ Nearby is the 19C villa where Massimo d'Azeglio wrote his memoirs (1798-1866, author, politician and leading figure in Risorgimento). ▶ A 10-minute boat ride goes to the **Castelli di Cannero,** picturesque ruins of two medieval castles on a rocky island. ▶ **Cannobio,** the last of the Italian towns on the lake situated at the base of the Cannobina Valley, is a renowned tourist centre. ▶ The late 16C **Santuario della Pietà** stands alongside the coastal road flanked by porticos and ancient palazzetti; its octagonal dome dates from 1601; its altarpiece was painted by G. Ferrari. ▶ The **Cannobina Valley** is quite steep, its walls covered with chestnut and beech trees; it connects the lake region with the Vigezzo Valley. To the r. is the **Orrido di S. Anna,** a deep rocky gorge chiseled out by the waters of the Cannobino stream. ▶ Climbing out of the valley, the route passes Finero and continues on to **Piano di Sale** and the **Vigezzo Valley.** ▶ The descent starts in a forested area and leads to **Malesco,** another vacation resort. ▶ Next is **Santa Maria Maggiore,** a resort situated in a beautiful hollow surrounded by fir trees with a **Museo dello Spazzacamino** *(p.m. in summer; other seasons inquire at Azienda di Soggiorno; groups only),* which documents the old craftsmen who plied their trade from town to town in the valley. ▶ The route follows the valley back to **Domodossola** (→). ▢

Practical information

CANNERO RIVIERA, ⊠ 28051, ☎ 0323.
≋
🚢 boats and hydrofoils.

Hotel:
★★★ *Cannero,* lungolago 2, ☎ 788046, 32 rm P 🔍 ሬ 🖾
↗ closed 1 Nov-19 Mar, 64,000.

⚐ ★★ *Lido,* v. dei Tigli, 95 pl, ☎ 788176.

CANNOBIO, 🖂 28052, ☎ 0323.
≋
ⓘ v. Veneto 4 (off highway), ☎ 71212.
🛥 boats and hydrofoils.

Hotel:
★★ *Lago,* at Carmine Inf., v. Nazionale 2, ☎ 71395, 10 rm
P ⅏ ⅏ closed Nov-Feb, 47,000; bkf: 6,000.

⚐ ★★ *Campagna,* v. Casali Darbedo 22, 101 pl, ☎ 70100;
★★ *Internazionale Paradiso,* v. Nazionale 12/A, 100 pl,
☎ 71227.

Recommended
Cycling: *G.S. Cannobio,* v. Sasso Carmine 12.
Events: *Fish festival* (2nd Sat in Jul).
Marina: ☎ 71212.
Tennis: v. Vittorio Veneto; v. Nazionale.

GHIFFA, 🖂 28055, ☎ 0323.

Hotel:
★★★ *Ghiffa,* v. Belvedere 88/90, ☎ 59285, 26 rm P ⅏ ሬ
closed Oct-Mar, 70,000; bkf: 9,000.

PIANCAVALLO, 4,078 ft, 🖂 28050.
⛷ ski lifts, cross-country skiing, instruction.
ⓘ *Sciovie Piancavallo-Zeda,* at Premeno, corso Italia 3,
☎ 47197.

PREMENO, 🖂 28057 ☎ 0323.
ⓘ at Verbania Pallanza (→).

Hotel:
★★ *Premeno,* v. Bonomi 29, ☎ 47021, 60 rm P ⅚ 🔍 ⅏
🖾 closed Oct-Easter, 58,000; bkf: 6,000.

Recommended
Golf: v. Pineta 1, ☎ 47100 (9 holes).

SANTA MARIA MAGGIORE, 2,677 ft, 🖂 28038, ☎ 0324.
⛷ cablecar from Prestinone to Piana di Vigezzo; ski lifts,
cross-country skiing at Piana di Vigezzo; ski lifts at Druogno; ski lifts, cross-country skiing at Malesco; *Centro del
fondo* with long nature trails at Santa Maria Maggiore;
nordic ski school at Malesco, ☎ 92387; instruction at Cra-
veggia; skating at Druogno and Malesco.
ⓘ v. Domodossola 3, ☎ 9091.

Recommended
Horseback riding: at Pineta, ☎ 92376.
Swimming: at Pineta (also tennis).

Le LANGHE

From Bra to Alba *(109 km, 1 day; map 4)*

The Langhe landscape is rich in contrasts, from the
mosaic-like vineyards and bare fields in the 'Langa
domestica' basin to the barren outlines of the high
'Langa selvaggia' which seems to have been hewn
with a hatchet. The sense of unity in the natural surroundings is nevertheless profound: the dense pattern of landmarks weaves together the countryside,
the towns and the roads traced out along the narrow
hillcrests (the *langhe*) carved by erosion. This itinerary, offering interesting sites and gastronomic pleasures, winds from Bra to Alba mostly along the hills,
affording beautiful vistas.

▶ From **Bra** (→), the road passes through **Cherasco** (→)
to reach **Narzole** where graves from the Iron Age have
been discovered *(in township of Golasecca).* ▶ **La Morra**
has a medieval section; the town still boasts remnants of
its ancient walls. Halfway up the hill, the local ethnological **museo** is housed *(8 a.m.-12 noon and 2-6 p.m.;
closed Sat and Sun)* in the **Abbazia dell'Annuziata.**

4. Le Langhe

▶ **Monforte d'Alba,** known for Barolo wine, is also popular for its health resort facilities. ▶ **Dogliani** is the
largest town in the Monregalese Langa; it has an interesting medieval quarter and is known for an excellent Dolcetto wine. ▶ **Belvedere Langhe** offers splendid views.
▶ Nearby, **Murazzano** affords another fine view. ▶ The
route continues over the **Bossola** Pass, the gateway to
Bossolasco, which is one of the most frequently visited towns in the Langhe, beautifully situated on a ridge
between the Rivers Belbo and Rea. The town has an
unusual main thoroughfare, with store signs painted by
contemporary artists. ▶ The route then continues to **Serravalle Langhe,** a health resort with several medieval buildings. ▶ **Serralunga d'Alba** is known for wine production and a beautifully restored 13C **Castello**★, one of the
finest Piedmontese examples of hilltop castles
*(9 a.m.-12 noon and 2:30-7 p.m summer; 2-5 p.m. winter;
closed Mon).* ▶ Another of the oldest and most important castles in the Langhe is in **Grinzane Cavour: Castello Cavour** is an imposing edifice from the 13C, rebuilt
in the 1600s. It was the home of Camillo di Cavour (**wine
museum;** *guided tours 9:30-11:30 a.m. and 3-6 p.m.; closed
Tue).* ▶ The route goes through **Diano d'Alba** and
ends in **Alba** (→). ☐

Practical information _____

BOSSOLASCO, 🖂 12060, ☎ 0173.

Restaurant:
◆◆◆ *Bellavista,* v. Umberto I 10, ☎ 793102, closed Tue
and Easter. Fireplace and veranda. Regional cuisine:
gnocchi, tagliatelle, 25/35,000.

Recommended
Horseback riding: *Castelleri Sporting Club,* ☎ 793368
(associate of *ANTE*).

DOGLIANI, ⊠ 12063, ☎ 0173.

Recommended
Wine: Wine shop *(bottega)*.

GRINZANE CAVOUR, ⊠ 12060, ☎ 0173.

Restaurant:
♦♦♦ *Castello,* ☎ 62159, closed Tue and Jan. In 13C castle that also houses Piedmont regional wine outlet. Regional cuisine: rabbit with pepperoni, pheasant, 30/34,000.

Recommended
Wine: regional wine outlet at Castello, ☎ 62159.
♥ liqueur: *Grappa Montanero, distilleries,* at Gallo d'Alba, ☎ 62014.

LA MORRA, ⊠ 12064, ☎ 0173.

Restaurant:
● ♦♦♦ *Belvedere,* p. Castello 5, ☎ 50190, closed Sun eve, Mon and 1 Jan-15 Feb. Historic building with exceptional view onto Langhe. Regional cuisine: wild game, stuffed fish, 35,000.

Recommended
Wine: communal cellars (Cantina comunale).

MONFORTE D'ALBA, ⊠ 12065, ☎ 0173.

Hotel:
★ *Giardino-da Felicin,* v. Vallada 18, ☎ 78225, 11 rm ℙ ≮ ♤ ▥ closed Jan-Feb, 35,000. Rest. ● ♦♦♦ closed Wed. Good regional cuisine, 20/40,000.

Restaurant:
♦ *Grappolo d'Oro,* p. Umberto I 4, ☎ 78293, closed Tue. Overlooks vine-covered hills. Regional cuisine: fresh pasta, wild game and truffles, 30,000.

Recommended
Wine: *Nebbiolo* and Barolo cellars, at Bussia 48, ☎ 78150, Bricco Rocche cellars at Castiglione Falbetto *(7 km N),* v. Alba-Monforte 55, ☎ 62867.

MURAZZANO, ⊠ 12060, ☎ 0173.

Recommended
Young peoples' activities: *Langhe Safari park,* at Rea, ☎ 791142 (closed Dec-Feb except hols).

The LANZO VALLEYS

A-B3-4

The Stura di Lanzo (Lanzo opening) is made up of three valleys: Stura di Ala, Stura di Val Grande and Stura di Viù. This area must once have been much greener and more wooded, for its forests have supplied fuel to forges and foundries for centuries. Throughout the Lanzo valleys, the iron industry was a boon to the inhabitants, who might otherwise have been forced to emigrate because of the harsh agricultural conditions. Today, the mines are closed and only quarries are still in operation. Agriculture is languishing and emigration has started, but tourism remains a strong element in the area's economy.

► **Lanzo Torinese** is the main centre in the three valleys. Its medieval quarter winds through narrow streets and arches known as *chintane*. Nearby, a hump-backed bridge, the **Ponte del Diavolo,** spans the gorge. ► The **Valle di Viù** is a vacation resort, the **Colle del Lis** and the **Alpe Bianca** (at Tornetti) are winter sports areas. ► Farther on, the **S. Giulio** chapel near Forno, perhaps from the 11C, is decorated with frescos. **Usseglio** (4,150 ft) is another vacation and winter sports area. The route climbs to **Margone** and the artificial Lake **Malcaiussià** at the foot of the Rocciamelone. **Pian Benot** is frequented by skiers. ► In the **Val di Ala,** on the promontory dividing it from the Val Grande, lies **Céres,** a very popular health resort (one of the many in this area). Near its municipio is the **Museo delle Genti delle Valli di Lanzo** (museum

of people of valley; *by appointment,* ☎ 53455). ► **Ala di Stura** (3,543 ft) is the valley's most important vacation centre with skiing at **Pian Belfé. Balme** (4,698 ft) is the highest town in the Lanzo valleys. In 1874, Italy's first large-scale mountain expedition left from Balme to climb Uia di Mondrone. From the magnificent **Piano della Mussa★** (5,742 ft) the view extends over green forests cloaking the mountainside to the bottom of the valley; wonderful mountain excursions begin here. ► In the basin at the bottom of **Val Grande** is **Groscavallo,** another starting point for excursions.   ☐

Practical information _____

ALA DI STURA, ⊠ 10070, ☎ 0123.
ℨ ski lifts, cross-country skiing, instruction, skating.
ⓘ p. Centrale 43, ☎ 55192.

Hotel:
★★★ *G.H. Ala di Stura,* v. Pian del Tetto 2, ☎ 55189, 22 rm ℙ ≮ ▥ ❦ closed Nov, 40,000; bkf: 5,000.

LANZO TORINESE, ⊠ 10074, ☎ 0123.

Hotel:
★★ *Piemonte,* v. Umberto 23, ☎ 29461, 32 rm ℙ ▥ ❦ 55,000.

Recommended
Tennis: v. Matteotti 3, ☎ 29089; regione Grange, ☎ 28279.

USSEGLIO, ⊠ 10070, ☎ 0123.
ℨ ski lifts, instruction at Pian Benot, cross-country skiing on Piano di Usseglio.
ⓘ *Sciovie Usseglio,* ☎ 83731.

VIÙ, ⊠ 10070, ☎ 0123.
ℨ ski lifts, instruction at Lis Pass and at Tornetti.
ⓘ municipio, ☎ 6101.

⋏ ★★ *Tre Frei,* at Versino Fucine, 124 pl, ☎ 6114.

LIMONE PIEMONTE

Cuneo 26, Turin 121, Milan 243 km
3,300 ft pop.1,709 ⊠ 12015 ☎ 0171   B6

Limone Piemonte has been a well-known ski centre for many years. It lies just N of the Maritime Alps ridge and Mediterranean winds bring humid air and clouds over the rock masses, which assure that there is always a lot of snow. It has good facilities and slopes of varying difficulty. In the old town, the Gothic church of **S. Pietro in Vincoli** (1363) has a Romanesque 12C campanile.   ☐

Practical information _____

LIMONE PIEMONTE
ℨ ski lifts, cross-country, skiing, instruction, skating.
ⓘ v. Roma 30, ☎ 92101.

Hotels:
★★★ *Principe,* v. Genova 45, ☎ 92389, 42 rm ℙ ▥ ❦ closed 7 Sep-30 Nov and 16 Apr-30 Jun, 70,000.
★★★ *Touring,* v. Roma 4, ☎ 92393, 33 rm ℙ closed 1 Sep-19 Dec and Easter-30 Jun, 55,000; bkf: 7,000.
★★★ *Tripoli-La Margherita,* v. Valbusa 11, ☎ 92397, 33 rm ℙ ▥ ≮ closed 11 Apr-19 Dec, 59,000; bkf: 6,000.

Restaurant:
♦♦♦ *Mac Miche,* v. Roma 64, ☎ 92449, closed Mon eve, Tue, 15 Jun-10 Jul and 2 Nov-2 Dec. Old style tavern. Regional cuisine: whipped spicy maccheroncini, stuffed trout, 30/45,000.

⋏ ★★★ *Luis Matlas,* corso Torino 39, 100 pl, ☎ 927565 (all year).

Recommended
Swimming: at Cros (outdoor pool reached by chairlift).

Environs

COLLE DI TENDA, 6 km S.

Hotel:
★★★ *Tre Amis,* ☎ 928175, 69 rm ⌘ ⊟ Pens. closed 15 Dec-10 Apr, 60,000.

VERNANTE, 2,621 ft, ⊠ 12019, 7 km N.
⚡ ski lifts, cross-country skiing.
ⓘ municipio, ☎ 920104.

Recommended
Park: *Palanfre Forest and Lake Reserve,* at Renetta, ☎ 920220.

Terme di LURISIA

Cuneo 22, Turin 94, Milan 226 km
2,297 ft ⊠ 12088 ☎ 0174   B6

Marie Curie (1867-1934), suffering from the effects of radiation caused by her work, investigated the curative powers of the Lurisian waters. She did not know that the spring that gushes from the mountain is high in radioactivity — higher than any other tested area in the world. There is a cablecar from Lurisia to **Colle Pigna** (4,938 ft), a popular ski peak. **Certosa di Pesio** is primarily a summer vacation area but also offers winter sports. ☐

Practical information _____

♨ (Jun-Sep), ☎ 683223.
⚡ ski lifts, instruction, skating.
ⓘ v. Radium 10, ☎ 650119.

Hotels:
★★★ *G.A. Radium,* v. delle Terme, ☎ 683324, 72 rm ℗ ⚏
⚄ ⌘ ⌁ closed 1 Oct-14 Dec and 16 Apr-14 May, 48,000; bkf: 8,000.
★★ *Scoiattolo,* v. Viglioni, ☎ 683103, 22 rm ℗ ⚄ ⚏ closed Oct, 45,000; bkf: 5,000.

△ ★★ *Lurisia,* v. Morté 1, 82 pl, ☎ 683480 (all year).

MACUGNAGA

Novara 108, Milan 139, Turin 182 km
4,354 ft pop. 711 ⊠ 28030 ☎ 0324   C2

Macugnaga in the upper Anzasca (or Ossola) Valley at the foot of Mt. Rosa offers summer and winter skiing, excursions and hiking. It is a wild and beautiful alpine landscape. As in Valsesia and Gressoney, the language and customs of the German Walsers (who colonized the area around Mt. Rosa in the 13C-14C) are still prevalent today.

▶ An ancient alpine hut houses a small historical and ethnographic museum *(Jul 3-7 p.m., also 10 a.m.-12 noon in Aug; other times make appointment at town hall,* ☎ *65009).* ▶ From the **Belvedere★★**, a restaurant-lodge reached by chair lift, there is a magnificent view of Mt. Rosa. Higher up is the **Rifugio Zamboni Zappa** (6,775 ft), below the Punta Dufour, and even higher is **Piani Alti di Rosareccio** (7,218 ft). ▶ The **M. Moro Pass** (9,410 ft) leading to the Saas Valley (Switzerland) offers a magnificent view★. The Camosci crossing begins at the pass and continues to the top of Roffel and to Rifugio E. Sella. ☐

Practical information _____

⚡ Alpe Bill cablecar, ski lifts, cross-country skiing, instruction, skating, hockey, summer skiing at Moro Pass (also cross-country), ☎ 65217.
ⓘ at Staffa, p. del Municipio, ☎ 65119.

Hotels:
★★ *Cristallo,* at Pecetto, ☎ 65139, 21 rm ℗ ⚄ ⚏ ⚄ closed 1 May-14 Jun and 1 Oct-19 Dec, 52,000.
★★ *Nordend,* at Staffa, v. Jacchetti 32, ☎ 65102, 16 rm ⌘ closed Sep-14 Dec and 16 Apr-Jun, 55,000. Rest.
● ♦♦♦ closed Tue. Regional and Italian cuisine: homemade pasta, bolliti, 30/38,000.
★★ *Nuovo Pecetto,* at Pecetto, ☎ 65025, 18 rm ℗ ⚄ ⚏ closed 21 Sep-Nov and May, 52,000.
★★ *Zumstein,* at Staffa, v. Faggi Bile 15, ☎ 65118, 44 rm ℗ ⚄ ⚏ closed May and Oct-Nov, 60,000; bkf: 6,000.

Restaurant:
♦♦ *Chez Felice,* at Staffa, v. alle Ville 14, ☎ 65229, closed Thu. Italian cuisine: chicken with pepperoni, stuffed turkey, 20/30,000.

△ ★★ *Sporting Centre,* at Testa, 35 pl, ☎ 65489.

Recommended
Alpine guides: L. Pironi, at Pecetto, ☎ 65549.
Hang gliding: *Monte Rosa* school (nr ski school), ☎ 02/3492851.
Young peoples' activities: beginner and advanced courses in mountaineering, *CAI Macugnaga Monte Rosa,* ☎ 65119 (tourist office).

MONDOVI

Cuneo 27, Turin 80, Milan 212 km
Pop. 22,458 ⊠ 12084 ☎ 0174   B6

Mondovi took its name originally from Monte Vico, where rebels fleeing the Bishop of Asti took refuge in 1198. Since 1290 the inhabitants have called themselves Monregalesi because at that time the city bought its autonomy, thereby acquiring the right to call the town *Mons Regalis* (royal mountain). Mondovi's autonomy was short-lived; for the next several centuries it was overrun by one ruler after another. Nonetheless it remained a lively cultural and economic centre. In 1472, the first book to be printed in Piedmont came from Mondovi presses. In the 16C, it had many active industries, including woolworking, leather-tanning, paper-making, hat-making, carpet-weaving, candle- and candy-making. Today, commerce and industry still exist, but Mondovi likes to be known as the 'city of study' and maintains scholarly traditions.

▶ The city is divided into two sections: the ancient part, called **Piazza,** lies high above the Ellero Valley and the newer part, called **Breo,** runs along the river's edge. In the 19C, the section by the river became the centre for the heavier industries and remains today the commercial and industrial centre. ▶ In Breo, places of interest include the church of **S. Filippo** (1757) by the Monregalese Francesco Gallo, one of the city's great 18C renovators, and the 17C church of **SS. Pietro e Paolo** with a cupola by B.A. Vittone (1755) and a highly ornate Baroque façade — its bells are rung on the hour. ▶ The upper city has many valuable monuments. Its remarkable mixture of historical and architectural styles is evidence of the town's rapid development. ▶ The Baroque **Missione** church (1679), decorated with important frescos by the Jesuit A. Pozzo, has a raised balcony overlooking **piazza Maggiore**, the old town centre. This square is bordered by 15C-16C houses with porticos. ▶ The **cathedral** (1763), designed by F. Gallo, has a monumental sandstone façade. ▶ The esplanade in the **Belvedere gardens★** offers a splendid view of the town. ▶ The tower that can be seen from the city centre is the 14C **Torre dei Bressani.**

Environs

▶ The extremely religious Duke Carlo Emanuele I wanted the **Santuario di Vicoforte★** *(7 km)* to be of exceptional size and beauty. It is a grandiose monument — one of the largest in Piedmont. Work began in 1596 under the direction of A. Vittozzi, but it was not completed until 1884. Its extraordinary cupola★ (1728-33) is F. Gallo's most daring accomplishment. □

Practical information

ⓘ p. Mellano 6/A, ☎ 47140.

Hotel:
★★★ *Europa*, v. Torino 29, ☎ 44388, 20 rm P ♨ No restaurant, 56,000; bkf: 6,000.

Restaurant:
♦♦ *Tre Limoni d'Oro*, p. Battisti 2, ☎ 40333, closed Mon. Regional cuisine: braised meat al Barolo, wild boar in civet, 17/37,000.

⚠ ★★ *Rio della Plata*, at Vicoforte, SS 28, 60 pl, ☎ 63195 (all year).

Recommended
Caving: visits to Dossi cave leaving from Villanova Mondovi, ☎ 699081.
Cycling: *G.S. Valeo*, corso Francia 4, ☎ 46341.
Hang gliding: *Delta Club Mondovi*, p. Maggiore 18, ☎ 42037 (instruction).
Park: naturalist oasis at Crava *(9 km NW)*, marked trails and observation posts, *LIPU*, ☎ 0171/491772 or 491495.

Northern MONFERRATO

From Asti *(108 km, 1 day; map 5)*

It is difficult to define the natural borders of Monferrato in the vast hilly terrain lying between the Po River and the N spurs of Piedmont. Its internal divisions are more historical than geographical, and Monferrato has played a leading role in the region's history. The poet Carducci (1835-1907) defined Monferrato as, 'exultant in castles and vineyards below Aleramo'. As the official poet of Italian unity, he tried in vain to unite this state politically. Long, bitter struggles for autonomy have marked the population deeply. These struggles accentuated the region's isolat-

ed nature, which is still evident in its dealings with the rest of Piedmont. In the past, Monferrato was dotted with castles and economic enclaves of every type of social group. Despite many changes, the region remains a land of wine and truffles. Thus, its attractions include not only culture and environment, but also gastronomy. This itinerary, beginning and ending in Asti, goes through the Stura Valley.

▶ From **Asti** (→) the route leads to **Calliano**, with its extremely old church of **S. Pietro**. ▶ Next is **Moncalvo**, an agricultural marketing centre with huge communal wine cellars. Moncalvo takes pride in being called the smallest city in Italy. The painter Moncalvo is buried in the 12C-14C church of **S. Francesco**; the church also has a painting by Macrino d'Alba. ▶ On a hill is the **Santuario di Crea**, the legendary refuge of Saint Eusebius, Bishop of Vercelli, who fled here from Aryan heretics. Its 12C Romanesque church has often been renovated and has a Baroque façade (1608-12). The interior, decorated with 15C frescos, contains the reputedly miraculous 14C wooden statue of the Madonna di Crea. A small museum displays votive offerings. The complex includes twenty-three chapels and five hermitages scattered in the woods. There are sculptures by Tabacchetti (16C-17C) and paintings by Moncalvo represent the *Mysteries of the Rosary*. ▶ The route leads to **Murisengo**, dominated by a castle in which Silvio Pellico (1789-1854) wrote his patriotic tragedy, *Francesca da Rimini*. In Murisengo's **parish church** is one of the best examples of Piedmontese rococo art. ▶ In **Montiglio**, gypsum is mined and processed. The town is famous for its steep, narrow streets as well as the most extensive series of 14C frescos (in the castle chapel) surviving in Piedmont. ▶ After Montiglio, the route leads to **Cocconato** where, on the second-to-last Sunday in September, there is an ancient Mule Race with 300 participants in 13C dress. ▶ **Vezzolano Abbey★** is a wonderful example of Romanesque and Gothic art. The small 12C church★★ is especially interesting *(caretaker; closed Mon and Fri p.m.);* its design shows traces of French influence and the magnificent façade has beautiful sculptures. The **cloisters** are decorated with unusual 14C frescos and the chapter house is also noteworthy. ▶ Beyond **Albugnano** and its ancient houses lies **Castelnuovo Don Bosco**, a wine centre renowned for its wicker furniture. St. John was born near this town (1815-88; founder of the Salesian Brothers, a religious society for the education of boys); it is possible to visit his birthplace *(9 a.m.-12 noon and 2-6 p.m.)* in **Colle Don Bosco** *(4 km)*. ▶ Near the ancient town of **Cortazzone**, the Romanesque church of **S. Secondo★** has three apses and massive pillars with capitals in the form of animals. ▶ The route heads back to Asti through **Baldichieri d'Asti**. □

5. Northern Monferrato

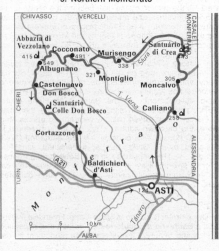

Practical information

CASTELNUOVO DON BOSCO, ⊠ 14022, ☎ 011.

Recommended
Wine: regional wine shop (also at Moncucco, *6 km NW*); *Freisa communal cellars*, v. S. Giovanni 6, ☎ 9876117.

COCCONATO, ⊠ 14023, ☎ 0141.

Hotel:
★ *Cannon d'Oro*, p. Cavour 19, ☎ 485024, 12 rm P ♨ closed 10-31 Jan, 37,000. Rest. ♦ closed Tue. Regional cuisine, 15/45,000.

MONCALVO, ⊠ 14036, ☎ 0141.

Restaurants:
♦♦ *Tre Re*, p. Romita 5, ☎ 91125, closed Mon eve, Tue and Jul. Rustic atmosphere in former post office. Regional cuisine: meat ravioli, braised meat al Barolo, 25/40,000.
♦ *Centrale*, p. Carlo Alberto 24, ☎ 91126, closed Mon, Christmas, New Year and Jul. Part of castle overlooking hills. Regional cuisine: meat ravioli, roast cotechino, 20/30,000.

Recommended
Events: *truffle fair (Oct).*
Wine: regional wine shop.

PENANGO, ⊠ 14030, ☎ 0141.

Hotel:
★★★★ *Locanda del Sant'Uffizio,* at Cioccaro, ☎ 91271,
20 rm 🅿 ⌗ ◁ ▣ ⸰̸ closed Jan and Aug, 100,000; bkf:
15,000. Rest. ● ◆◆◆ *Beppe* closed Tue. 17C building
with garden. Regional cuisine: gnocchetti stuffed with
fondue, filet in casserole with fondue and truffles, 70,000.

PORTOCOMARO, ⊠ 14037, ☎ 0141.
Recommended
Wine: regional wine shop.

MOUNT ROSA*

15,204 ft   B-C2

'Mount Rosa is a great boulder; the summits run to
the right and to the left as far as the eye can
see'. So said visionary poet Dino Campana
(1885-1932). The first men to climb the peak must
have seen it exactly that way as they laboured up
the mountainside, at the same time trying to ignore
the popular legends that the peaks were inhabited by
demons, witches and dragons. The second highest
mountain in Europe, Mt. Rosa has eight adjacent
summits; it extends from the Colle del Teodulo to the
M. Moro Pass and is situated at the junction of several valleys: Ayas, Gressoney (→ Valle d'Aosta), Valsesia (→ Alagna Valsesia), Anzasca (→ Macugnaga)
and Mattertal (in Switzerland). Enormous glaciers
feed the waterways that determine the landscape
of regions such as Biellese, Valsesia and Ossola. □

NIZZA MONFERRATO

Asti 28, Turin 83, Milan 120 km
Pop. 10,212 ⊠ 14049 ☎ 0141   C5

Nizza Monferrato lies near the Belbo Valley, where
the hills are covered with vineyards. Winemaking is
the region's main industry, taking the place of the
once-important textile industry. Near the Bersano
wine-producing facilities is the **Museo Bersano delle
Contadinerie** *(hols 9-11 a.m. and 3-5 p.m. Apr-Sep;
Sat and hols a.m. by appointment, ☎ 721273)* with
an interesting collection of wine presses and old and
new wine-making implements. □

Practical information ―――――――――――
ℹ ☎ 721753.

Restaurant:
◆◆◆ *Trattoria Savona,* v. Carlo Alberto 127, ☎ 721573,
closed Wed. Regional cuisine: tagliolini with mushrooms,
wild game, 30,000.

⚲ ★★★ *Antica Contea,* at Bricco Morone, v. Albera 44,
☎ 62100 (all year).

Recommended
Events: *Nizza Village Joust (Jun).*
Wine: regional wine shop in castle at Quaranti *(12 km SE).*
♥ antiques: antiques market every 3rd Sun of month in p.
Garibaldi below the Foro Pio Corsi.

NOVARA

Milan 50, Turin 95, Rome 625 km
Pop. 102,279 ⊠ 28100 ☎ 0321   D3

The 19C architect Alessandro Antonelli praised two
particular structures: the Turin mole and the Novara

cupola. The two structures are somewhat similar
and may give the impression that Novara has a more
Piedmontese character than it really does. In reality, the city's closest historical ties were with Lombardy. Situated between two opposing political and
military regimes, Novara often served as a battle-
ground. Novara today appears quite up-to-date, but
the **historical centre** is full of Neoclassical, medieval,
Renaissance and Baroque structures.

▶ The S side of the p. della Repubblica is bordered by the
Duomo (B2), a Neoclassical edifice by A. Antonelli (1869);
its faade is in the form of a high vestibule in front of
which is a four-sided portico. Of the original Romanesque church all that remains are the chapel of S. Siro
(next to sacristy) decorated with **Gothic and Romanesque
frescos★** and the 15C cloister. Inside are a painting by
G. Ferrari (16C, second altar on r.) and frescos by Lanino
and Giovenone. 16C Flemish **tapestries★**, among the
church's treasures, are exhibited on solemn occasions. ▶ The baptistery★ is one of the most important
examples of primitive Christian architecture in the Po
region. The polygonal structure, built in the 5C, was probably enlarged toward the end of the 10C; its pre-Romanesque **frescos★** illustrating scenes from the Apocalypse
(revealing Carolingian as well as Byzantine influence) may
date from the same period. ▶ The porticos on the N side
of the piazza lead to **Broletto** (B2), a vast courtyard
surrounded by medieval buildings. Near the entrance
stands the 14C-15C **Palazzo del Podestà** (governor's
palace); opposite is the 13C **Palazzo del Comune** and on
the r. the 13C-15C **Palazzo dei Paratici** (guildhall) with an
18C portico. Here also are the **Galleria d'Arte Moderna**
and the **Museo Civico** *(10 a.m.-12 noon and 3-6 p.m.,
2-5 p.m. winter; closed Mon),* displaying local archaeological artifacts and Piedmontese painting and sculpture from
the 15C-18C. ▶ In p. Martiri della Libertà (B2), near the
remains of the **Castello Sforzesco,** are two Neoclassical
buildings, the **Teatro Coccia** (1886) and the **Palazzo del
Mercato** (1840). ▶ In the distance looms the dome of
the basilica of **S. Gaudenzio**; it is not surprising that Antonelli's masterpiece has become the symbol of Novara. It
can be seen from every part of the city as well as from
the surrounding countryside. It is mannerist in style and
of grandiose proportions; it has a Baroque campanile and
its daring **cupola** (1888) soars to 397 ft. The late Renaissance interior, in the form of a latin cross, is richly decorated with works of art including a sumptuous Baroque
chapel (1674-1711) and a **polyptych★** by G. Ferrari
(1516). ▶ At v. Canobio 6 is a 15C gatehouse (**Casa
della Porta;** B3); (B3) with windows framed in
cotto. ▶ 7.4 km NE at **Galliate** is the 15C Castello
Sforzesco. ▶ The Benedictine abbey at **San Nazzaro
Sesia** *(17 km W)* was rebuilt and fortified in the 15C. □

Practical information ――――――――――
ℹ corso Cavour 2 (B2), ☎ 23398.
🚃 (A3), ☎ 28759, *Ferrovie Nord Milano* (A2-3),
☎ 474094.
Car rental: *Maggiore,* corso Vercelli 9, ☎ 455182.

Hotels:
★★★★ *Italia,* v. Solaroli 8 (B2 a), ☎ 399316, 40 rm
🅿 120,000.
★★★★ *Rotonda,* rotonda d'Azeglio 6 (B-C2 b), ☎ 23691,
26 rm 🅿 ⚐ 90,000; bkf: 7,000.
★★★ *Europa,* corso Cavallotti 38/A (B3 c), ☎ 30240,
60 rm 🅿 ⚐ 60,000.
★★★ *Maya,* v. Boggiani 54 (C2 d), ☎ 452722, 94 rm 🅿 ♿
⚐ 70,000.

Restaurants:
◆◆◆ *Caglieri,* v. Tadini 12 (C2 e), ☎ 456373, closed
Fri and Aug. Outdoor summer dining. Regional cuisine:
paniscia, Novarese fried meat, 20/30,000.
◆◆◆ *Giorgio,* v. delle Grazie 2 (B1 g), ☎ 27647, closed
Mon, Tue noon and 1-15 Sep. Seafood: penna pasta
with seppia black sauce, gilthead fish with cartoccio,
35,000.

1 Autostr. km 5 - Borgomanero km 32   Autostrada km 3 ▴ Arona km 38 **3**

NOVARA

0   250   500 m
1 : 25.000 (1cm = 250m)

RomagnanoSesia km 30

2   3   Mortara km 24

♦♦♦ *Moroni,* v. Solaroli 6 (B2 a), ☎ 29278, closed Mon eve, Tue and Aug. Mixed cuisine: taglierini ai porcini, veal scottadito, 25/35,000.
♦♦ *Cupola,* v. Ferraris 14 (C1 f), ☎ 33337, closed Sat and 15-31 Jul. Regional cuisine: crêpes with Gorgonzola, donkey stufato, 18/22,000.
♦ *Terrazza dell'Autogrill,* Milan-Turin expressway (Novara station), ☎ 390591. Italian cuisine: cooked ham with pistachio paste, cream with crunchy almonds, 20/40,000.

Recommended
Events: *crafts fair* (Apr-May).
Horseback riding: *Club ippico Ticino,* at Castelletto Ticino *(32 km N),* v. Glisente 29, ☎ 0331/920187 (associate of *ANTE*).
Nature park: animal reserve at Casalbeltrame *(15 km W),* information at town hall, ☎ 83154 and at Parco Lame del Sesia office (→ Vercelli), ☎ 0161/73112.
Sports: hockey field in Agogna region, *Federazione Italiana,* v. Monteverdi 2.

NOVI LIGURE

Alessandria 23, Milan 87, Turin 125 km
Pop. 31,201 ⊠ 15067 ☎ 0143   D5

For almost four centuries, Novi Ligure was the most important centre 'beyond the yoke' *(oltregiogo),* the area of Genoese influence on the N side of the Ligurian Apennines. The people speak a dialect similar to that of Genoa and the **historic centre** is marked by Ligurian styles. In the oratory of the 15C-16C church

of **S. Maria Maddalena,** a group of eight terra-cotta figures dates from the 16C. The church also contains an imposing Calvary, composed of twenty-one wooden statues and two life-size horses.   □

Practical information

Hotel:
★★ *Corona,* corso Marenco 11, ☎ 2019, closed Aug and Christmas, 12 rm Ⓟ ⌘ 38,000; bkf: 5,000. Rest. ♦♦♦ closed Mon. Italian cuisine: rigatoni with four cheeses, fagottino with mushrooms, homemade Dolcetto wines, 25/30,000.

Recommended
Hang gliding: *Aeroclub Fulvio Padova,* at airport, ☎ 71898.
Horseback riding: *Western Men,* at Capriate d'Orba *(12 km W),* v. Brizzoleri 58, ☎ 46119; *Centro ippico Valdorba,* strada Novi Ligure-Ovada, ☎ 46592 (associate of *ANTE*).
Sports: *Palezzetto dello sport,* v. Crispi, ☎ 743388.

OLEGGIO

Novara 17, Milan 63, Turin 107 km
Pop 11,240 ⊠ 28047 ☎ 0321   D3

Oleggio contains the 10C-11C Romanesque church of **S. Michele**★ with a simple stone façade embellished with pilasters, arches and rustic apses. Inside are 10C-13C **frescos.** The church rests in the town's cemetery.   □

Practical information _____

Recommended
Park: *Valle del Ticino,* v. Garibaldi 12, ☎ 93028 (office).

OMEGNA

Novara 54, Milan 93, Turin 129 km
Pop. 16,264 ⊠ 28026 ☎ 0323   C2

Omegna was one of the major Piedmontese centres of antifascist activity during World War II. Today, the city built on Lake Orta is an industrial and commercial centre, although it preserves vestiges of the medieval and Renaissance eras.

▶ The **Casa dei Bazzetta de Vemania** was built during the Middle Ages and remodeled in the 16C. The Romanesque 13C collegiate church of **S. Ambrogio** has also been significantly altered.   ☐

Practical information _____

Hotels:
★★★ *Croce Bianca,* v. Mazzini 2, ☎ 642163, 36 rm ℗ �&
⌘ closed 2-31 Jan, 70,000; bkf: 5,000.
★★ *Pagoda,* v. De Amicis 23, ☎ 62344, 11 rm ℗ ⌘
45,000; bkf: 5,500.
Recommended
Canoeing: Canottieri Omegna, lungolago Buozzi,
☎ 881539 (instruction).
Tennis: v. Parogno 5, ☎ 61377.
Water skiing: *Sci Club Omegna,* lungolago Buozzi 3/B,
☎ 642781, v. Novara, ☎ 61636; *Sci Nautico Cusio,*
v. Cavallotti 33, ☎ 61365; *nautical centre,* v. Rosselli 15.
♥ musical instruments: *Fabbrica Italiana di Strumenti musicali,* at Quarna Sotto *(7 km W),* v. Rampone,
☎ 826134; historical museum near municipio, ☎ 826117 (by appointment).

ORMEA

Cuneo 84, Turin 126, Milan 250 km
2,415 ft pop. 2,591 ⊠ 12078 ☎ 0174   B-C6

Ormea is a summer vacation resort in the upper Tanaro Valley along a road through the Nava hills. It has an interesting **medieval sector** with 14C-16C houses.   ☐

Practical information _____

⚡ ski lifts, cross-country skiing.
ⓘ municipio, ☎ 51101.

Hotels:
★★ *Italia,* v. Gen. Cagna 43, ☎ 51147, 39 rm ℗ 38,000;
bkf: 5,000.
★★ *San Carlo,* at Cantarana, v. Nazionale 23, ☎ 51917,
37 rm ℗ ⌂ ⌐ closed Jan-Mar and Nov, 45,000; bkf:
6,000.

OSSOLA

C1-2

The Ossola region covers the wide Toce basin with some 20 valleys whose rivers join the main waterway. From 1943 to 1945, it was the site of heavy fighting. The alpine landscape, abounding in pastures and forests, is particularly lush owing to the damp climate and a plethora of rivers and streams. The abundance of water has also led to heavy industrial development. Mining industries have a long local history: evidence suggests that iron was mined in the area as early as the 14C. Quar-

ries flourish, and chemical and mechanical technologies are gaining footholds. Development has been encouraged by the construction of a series of dams for the production of hydroelectric power.

▶ From **Domodossola** (→), this itinerary climbs through a narrow wooded valley to **Bognanco Fonti,** a vacation centre renowned for its thermal baths. ▶ In the **Divedro Valley,** perhaps the most interesting valley in Ossola, crisscrossed by roads and railways leading to Sempione, is the agricultural centre of **Varzo** (1,863 ft), a resort and starting point for excursions. From here, it is possible to climb to the **Veglia Alps Natural Park** in a hollow surrounded by high peaks. ▶ Another noteworthy tourist and health resort is **Bagni di Crodo** in the **Antigorio Valley,** which boasts three cold-water mineral springs. ▶ At the foot of the Dévero Valley, **Baceno** (2,149 ft) is a base for the ski area of **Alpe Dévero** (5,351 ft), a broad plain surrounded by the Cervandone and Rossa peaks. Perched on a rocky spur above the Dévero River the 14C-16C Romanesque **parish church** of Baceno is Ossola's principal religious monument. Its lovely façade has three 16C portals; inside are frescos and a carved wooden altar ornament of the 16C Swiss school. ▶ Leaving Baceno, the route enters the **Formazza Valley,** with verdant pastures and forests surrounded by rocky mountains. **Formazza** (4,199 ft) is the main centre for climbs to the beautiful **Toce Cascades**★ *(hols Jun-Sep).*   ☐

Practical information _____

BACENO, ⊠ 28031, ☎ 0324.
⚡ cablecar to Alpe Dévero, ski lifts, cross-country skiing, instruction in Alpe Dévero.
ⓘ *Sciovie Alpe Dévero,* ☎ 619106.

FORMAZZA, ⊠ 28030, ☎ 0324.
⚡ ski lifts, at Ponte and Valdo, cross-country skiing, instruction, skating, summer skiing on Camasci glacier (*CAI* shelter).
ⓘ municipio, ☎ 63059.

⚑ ★★ *Val Formazza,* 75 pl, ☎ 63069 (all year).

VARZO, ⊠ 28039, ☎ 0324.
⚡ ski lifts, cross-country skiing, instruction at San Domenico.
ⓘ *San Domenico Neve,* ☎ 72466.

Recommended
Alpine excursions: *Centro Alpinismo Valle Ossola,* at Premosello Chiovenda *(17 km S of Domodossola),*
☎ 0325/88237; at Villadossola *(7 km S of Domodossola),*
☎ 0324/52530; at Gravellona Tuce, ☎ 0323/846325.
Nature park: *Veglia Alps,* v. Castelli 2, ☎ 45391.

OULX

Turin 78, Milan 218 km
3,609 ft pop. 2,119 ⊠ 10056 ☎ 0122   A4

Surrounded by high mountains, Oulx is a vacation resort in the Dora Riparia Valley. Its **old centre** is interesting and in the Middle Ages the town was one of Delfinato's cultural centres and the site of bloody battles between local people and French invaders.   ☐

Practical information _____

⚡ cross-country skiing, ski lifts, instruction at Beaulard
(7 km W).
ⓘ p. Garambois, ☎ 831213.

Recommended
Nature park: *Gran Bosco Reserve,* at Salbertrand *(6 km NE).*

Be advised that hotels and restaurants in this Guide have perhaps changed addresses; prices indicated are also subject to modifications.

OVADA

Alessandria 33, Milan 114, Turin 125 km
Pop. 12,707 ⊠ 15076 ☎ 0143   D5

Ovada is a commercial centre with a highway and railway crossing in the Orba Valley. Its command over communications routes stems from a long history of wars and disputes during Genoese attempts to gain control over the area. The town retains its densely fortified **old city centre** marked by Ligurian shapes, colours and styles.

Environs

▶ 7.5 km away is **Lerma** with the 15C Spinola Castle. ▶ 17 km along the Turchino road is **Campo Ligure** with the 15C Palazzo Spinola and a **museum** specializing in filigree *(3-6 p.m.; 9 a.m.-12 noon wkends; closed Mon)*.   □

Practical information

Hotel:
★★★ *Vittoria,* v. Voltri 27/D, ☎ 80331, 29 rm Ⓟ ⌂ 55,000; bkf: 6,000.
Restaurants:
◆◆◆ *Pietro,* p. Mazzini 5, ☎ 80457, closed Mon, Jan and Jul. Regional and Ligurian cuisine: pappardelle alla boscaiola, pasqualina torte, 20/37,000.
◆◆ *Volpina,* strada Volpina 1, ☎ 86008, closed Sun eve, Mon, Christmas and 1-15 Aug. Restored villa in park. Italian cuisine: sorpresa di bosco, scrigno di venere, 35/50,000.

PINEROLO

Turin 37, Milan 185 km
Pop. 36,364 ⊠ 10064 ☎ 0121   A-B4

In the 14C and 15C under the Acaia family (a branch of the Savoys), Pinerolo was known for art and culture. Later it became an important centre for printing, and still later a French economic and military stronghold. The French significantly changed the face of the city during the second half of the 17C by turning it into an impregnable fortress. In the process, they demolished a great deal of the city's artistic patrimony.

▶ The **Duomo,** renovated in Gothic style (15C-16C), has a fine portal with high gables and an imposing campanile. ▶ **S. Maurizio,** a church on a hill overlooking the town, is late Gothic (1470). ▶ Most noteworthy of the 15C-16C houses is the **Casa del Senato.** ▶ **Museo Nazionale dell'Arma di Cavalleria** (National Cavalry Museum; *9-11:15 a.m. and 3-5:15 p.m.; closed Sun p.m., Mon and Thu)* displays arms, uniforms and trophies and has historical archives and an interesting library.   □

Practical information

ⓘ palazzo Vittone, ☎ 74477.
Restaurant:
◆ *Gargota-Sansossi,* p. Frajria 15, ☎ 73420, closed Wed and Jul. Regional cuisine: rabbit in white wine, roast goat, 25,000.

Recommended
Horseback riding: *Gruppo ippico ricreativo,* at Abbadia Alpina, v. Valmaggi 15, ☎ 201256 (associate of *ANTE).*
Park: *S. Martinat* zoological gardens, v. Gorizia 4, ☎ 74434 (by appointment).

Looking for a locality? Consult the index at the back of the book.

PRADLEVES

Cuneo 24, Turin 96, Milan 239 km
Pop. 411 ⊠ 12027 ☎ 0171   A-B6

The Grana Valley, where this vacation village nestles, is one of the liveliest of the Italian Provenal minority communities. The 'Movement for Autonomy of the Provenal Civilization in Alpine Coumboscuro' was started here in 1976. 13 km away at the bottom of the valley is the **Sanctuary of S. Magno,** built in 1710 around a 15C chapel. In the hamlet of Santa Lucia is **Monterosso Grana** and the **Coumboscuro Ethnographic Museum** *(8 a.m.-12 noon and 2-6 p.m.; upon request,* ☎ *98771).*   □

PRAGELATO

Turin 80, Milan 220 km
5,000 ft pop. 495 ⊠ 10060 ☎ 0122   A4

Pragelato is a popular summer vacation and winter sports centre in the upper Chisone Valley. It contains numerous slopes and lift facilities that go as high as 6,562 feet.   □

Practical information

ϟ ski lifts, cross-country skiing, instruction, skating.
ⓘ p. Lantelme, ☎ 78844.
Recommended
Gastronomic specialties: local honey.
Nature park: *Val Troncea,* office at Traverses, v. S. Lorenzo 23, ☎ 78849.
Sports centre: v. Albergian, ☎ 78870.

RIVALTA SCRIVIA

Alessandria 28, Milan 80, Turin 119 km
Pop. 306 ⊠ 15050 ☎ 0131   D5

In the 12C-13C, the Cistercian abbey of **S. Maria** in Rivalta Scrivia was of great importance. Only the **sala capitolare** part of the **cloister** and the Gothic **church** (influenced by 12C-13C French styles) remain; the church has three naves and many 15C-16C frescos.   □

ROCCAVERANO

Asti 51, Turin 106, Milan 157 km
Pop. 747 ⊠ 14050 ☎ 0144   C5

One of the Langhe's summer vacation centres, Roccaverano has a **church** inspired by Bramantesca (1509) and the remains of what appears to have been a 13C castle.   □

Practical information

Restaurant:
◆ *Aurora,* v. Bruno 1, ☎ 93023, closed Tue and 15 Jan-15 Mar. Regional cuisine: roast with toasted hazelnuts, formaggetta di Roccaverano, 18/32,000.

Recommended
Gastronomic specialties: locally produced *robiole* cheese.

La SACRA DI SAN MICHELE*

Turin 38, Milan 178 km   B4

On the summit of Mount Pirchiriano overlooking the Susa Valley and the road to Moncenisio stands an abbey — imposing, austere and almost menacing. Built right into the mountain, its harsh architectural forms rise to more than 3,281 feet. There may have been a Lombardian Oratory dedicated to S. Michele on the mountain before the first part of the present church was erected in 998. Frequent pilgrimages brought fame to the fortified abbey, which became so wealthy and powerful that by the 11C it controlled 176 churches in Italy, France and Spain. The abbey was repeatedly assaulted and sacked and began declining in the 14C, until in 1622 it was abandoned. Having fallen into ruin, it was restored by the architect-restorer A. d'Andrade between 1889 and 1939.

▶ Beyond the structure known as the **Sepolcro dei Monaci** (11C), an outdoor staircase leads to the first entrance at the foot of the ponderous construction topped by the church's apse *(9 a.m.-12 noon and 2-5 p.m. winter; 2-7 p.m. summer; ring at door).* ▶ Inside, the **Scalone dei Morti** staircase is 'steep and irregular under the very high and ancient vaults, blackened by time and the destructive air' (as described by Massimo d'Azeglio). There is an extraordinarily sculpted Romanesque **porta dello Zodiaco★** which leads to the Gothic portal on the r.-hand side of the church. ▶ The restored **church★** has a luminous Romanesque-Gothic (12C-13C) interior with paintings and frescos from the 15C-16C as well as modern Savoy tombs. It is possible to visit the **crypt** with its three small chapels (9C or 10C, 11C-12C). The **belvedere** to the l. of the church offers a splendid view★. ◻

Cuneo 31, Turin 52, Milan 202 km
Pop. 16,472 ⊠ 12037 ☎ 0175   B5

The commercial and agricultural city of Saluzzo has recently begun spreading onto the plain, but in the area in the hills there remain superb historical and artistic treasures. Between the 14C and 16C, the Marquisate of Saluzzo was a political and commercial hub for the whole of the SW Alps region, as well as a lively cultural centre. Intellectuals and artists of great distinction frequented Ludovico II's court (1475-1504). During his thirty years' reign, Ludovico founded a school of surgery, promulgated sanitary statutes, constructed churches and palaces, commissioned works of art, drew up plans for developing an urban centre, encouraged printing, favoured the use

1 : 25.000 (1cm=250m)

of the vernacular languages and even dug the first alpine tunnel through Monviso to facilitate trade with France.

▶ The still-intact medieval quarter is of a rare and measured architectural balance. Each step reveals the refined and cultured community that existed here in the 14C-15C. ▶ The only important monument lying outside the walls is the **cathedral** (B2), a late Gothic structure (1491-1501) containing many noteworthy works of art. ▶ Within the walls, the **Casa Cavassa★** (B1) is an uncommon example of a Renaissance seigneurial residence; it is now a museum *(Apr.-Sep. 9 a.m.-12 noon and 3-6 p.m.; other months 9 a.m.-12:15 p.m. and 2-5:15 p.m.).* The rich marble portal of **M. Sammicheli** (1523) opens to a lovely courtyard with porticos supported by columns and loggias. The rooms are decorated with works including exquisite carved wooden choir stalls from the 15C and a painting of the Madonna della Misericordia★ believed to be the work of Maestro d'Elva (1499). The remains of two distinguished local citizens, Silvio Pellico and the renowned printer G. B. Bodoni, also rest here. The belvedere offers a fine view★. ▶ Nearby, in an adjacent small piazza dominated by the high Torre Comunale (1460) is the austere 14C-15C Gothic church of **S. Giovanni★** (B1). Its green stone apse is elegant and contains a carved wooden choir stall (15C) and Ludovico II's sepulchre, the work of B. Briosco and other Lombardian sculptors (begun in the 16C). The sculpture of the marquis is a remarkable example of plastic portraiture from the 1500s. Across the Gothic cloister is the chapter house, where Galeazzo Cavassa's mausoleum is an example of M. Sammicheli's exquisite Renaissance craft. ▶ Particularly picturesque is the street known as **Salita al Castello** (B1-2) which leads to the ancient castle of the Marquises of Saluzzo (13C), now a prison. The street is lined with 15C houses, many rebuilt in the 16C.

Environs

▶ The **Castello di Manta** *(4 km S)* is a 14C fortress that became a seigneurial residence in the 15C *(visits by appointment, ☎ 87822; 10 a.m.-12:30 p.m. and 2:30-5 p.m.; closed Mon).* It contains important **frescos★** by Giacomo Jaquerio and his assistants (1418-30) depicting French courtly themes. ▶ The Cistercian **Staffarda abbey★** *(10 km N)* is an important example of Romanesque architecture; the apse is remarkable for its strong Gothic influence. ◻

Practical information ⎯⎯⎯⎯⎯⎯⎯

ℹ municipio (A1), ☎ 45551.

Hotel:
★★★ *Astor,* 39, p. Garibaldi (A-B2a), ☎ 45506, 28 rm. No restaurant, 57,000; bkf: 6,000.

Restaurants:
♦♦♦ *Taverna di Porti Scür,* v. Volta 14 (B2c), ☎ 41961, closed Mon, Jan and Aug. Regional and Italian cuisine: gnocchi val Varaita, lamb with curry sauce, 30/60,000.
♦ *Perpoin,* v. Spielberg 19 (B2b), ☎ 42552, closed Tue, Sun in Jul and 15-30 Aug. Regional cuisine: batsoà, panzerotti fondue with butter and sage, homemade wines, 30,000.

Recommended
Events: *National Exhibition - Antique Show; National Horse Competition* (Sep).
Handicrafts: artisanal furniture, wrought iron and pewter objects.

Turin 20, Milan 160 km
Pop. 10,279 ⊠ 10026 ☎ 011   B4

Camillo Cavour is buried in the parish church at the entrance to the park surrounding the 18C **Villa Cavour**

(9 a.m.-12 noon and 2-5 or 6 p.m.; closed Mon). The villa has an interesting museum with a collection of relics and mementos of the state of Turin. □

Practical information ────────────

Restaurant:
♦♦ *Andrea*, v. Torino 48, ☎ 9492783, closed Tue and Aug. Regional cuisine: wild game, mushrooms, truffles, 35/40,000.

SANTHIA

Vercelli 20, Turin 55, Milan 93 km
Pop. 9,464 ⊠ 13048 ☎ 0161   C3

Santhia is an important crossroads as well as an agricultural and commercial centre on the Vercello plain. It has a **historical centre** of medieval origin. The **parish church** has a Romanesque campanile and a polyptych by Giovenone or Lanino (1531). □

Practical information ────────────

Restaurant:
♦♦♦ *San Massimo*, nuova variante SS 143, ☎ 94617, closed Fri. Regional cuisine: paniscia, tench in vinegar, 20/35,000.

SAUZE D'OULX

Turin 83, Milan 218 km
4,951 ft pop. 971 ⊠ 10050 ☎ 0122   A4

This well-established summer and winter resort, one of the first ski stations in Italy, is under constant development (to the detriment of the scenery). With neighbouring **Sportinia**, the area has turned into an impressive ski complex, especially now that it has been linked with Sestriere (→), whose lift facilities open up the slopes of Mt. Triplex. □

Practical information ────────────

⌇ ski lifts, cross-country skiing, instruction, skating.
ⓘ p. Assietta, ☎ 85009.
Hotels:
★★★ *G. H. Palace*, p. III Reggimento Alpini, ☎ 85222, 60 rm Ⓟ closed 11 Sep-Nov and May-15 Jun, 73,500.
★★★ *Splendid*, v. Clotes 71, ☎ 85463, 36 rm ⅏ ♿ closed Sep-19 Dec and 16 Apr-Jun, 80,000; bkf: 6,000.
★★ *Gran Baita*, villaggio Alpino 21, ☎ 85183, 29 rm Ⓟ ⅏ ♨ closed Sep-Nov and Easter-Jun, 60,000; bkf: 3,000.
★ *Assietta*, p. Assietta 4, ☎ 85180, 20 rm Ⓟ ⚘ closed Sep-Nov and May-Jun. No restaurant, 34,000.
Restaurant:
♦♦♦ *Capricorno*, at Les Clotes, ☎ 85273, closed 16 Sep-Nov and May-15 Jun. Rustic and elegant mountain chalet in a pine forest. Regional and Italian cuisine: polenta with cheeses, turkey with myrtle and rosemary, 30/50,000.

Recommended
Horseback riding: at Gran Villair.
Tennis: v. Genevris, ☎ 85319.

SAVIGLIANO

Cuneo 33, Turin 61, Milan 201 km
Pop. 18,823 ⊠ 12038 ☎ 0172   B5

Savigliano is an industrial and agricultural centre that is developing rapidly to maintain its reputation as the hub of Cuneo communication. Expansion has not affected the historical centre. The abbey church of **S. Pietro dei Cassinesi** (16C-17C) has a Gothic inte-

rior decorated in Baroque style and the church of **S. Andrea** is Baroque. These are the area's two most important religious monuments. The **Palazzo Cravetta** (late 16C) has a lovely Renaissance courtyard.

Environs
▶ 7.2 km N is **Cavallermaggiore** with a church of the Fraternity of the Holy Cross and the church of S. Bernardino designed by F. Gallo (1743). ▶ **Racconigi** *(14 km N)* is dominated by the huge **Castello reale** (royal castle; *administrative authorization needed to visit*) built between 1676 and 1842, surrounded by a now derelict park. □

Practical information ────────────

Hotel:
★★★ *Gran Baita*, v. Cuneo 23, ☎ 32060, 16 rm Ⓟ ⅏ ⚘ 45,000; bkf: 6,000.

SERRAVALLE SCRIVIA

Alessandria 29, Milan 88, Turin 131 km
Pop. 6,203 ⊠ 15069 ☎ 0143   D5

A crossroads for automobile and train traffic, Serravalle Scrivia lies at the junction of the Scrivia River and a plain. 25 km away is the site of the ancient Roman town of *Libarna*, which was most probably the centre of Liguria in the 2C. The settlement, now well-preserved ruins, was a Roman military outpost on the v. Postumia and flourished as a trading centre during the Roman Empire. Still evident are remains of an amphitheatre, a theatre, houses, roads and tombs. □

SESTRIERE*

Turin 90, Milan 240 km
6,677 ft pop. 802 ⊠ 10058 ☎ 0122   A4

The two famous tower-hotels, at the pass between the Chisone and Dora Riparia Valleys, symbolize this winter sports resort, one of the most famous and popular in Europe. There is always plenty of snow, thanks to snowmaking machines. The slopes are connected with those of **Sauze d'Oulx** (→) and other valley resorts, offering hundreds of miles of ski runs. □

Practical information ────────────

⌇ cablecars for Mounts Fraiteve, Sises and Banchetta, ski lifts, cross-country skiing, instruction, skating.
ⓘ p. Agnelli, ☎ 76045.

Hotels:
★★★★ *Cristallo*, v. Pinerolo 5, ☎ 77234, 72 rm Ⓟ closed 11 Apr-30 Nov, 142,000: bkf: 12,000.
★★★★ *G.H. Sestriere*, v. Assietta 1, ☎ 76476, 97 rm Ⓟ ⅏ closed 1 Apr-19 Dec, 157,500.
★★★★ *Principi di Piemonte*, v. Sauze, ☎ 7941, 94 rm Ⓟ ⅏ ⚘ closed 1 Apr-23 Nov, 150,000.
★★★ *Olimpic*, v. Monterotta 9, ☎ 77344, 29 rm Ⓟ closed 26 Aug-Nov and May-9 Jul, 60,000; bkf: 6,000.
★★★ *Sud-Ovest*, v. Monterotta 17, ☎ 77393, 17 rm Ⓟ ♿ closed May-Jun and Sep-Oct, 78,000; bkf: 7,000.

Restaurants:
♦♦♦ *Last Tango*, v. La Gleisa 12, ☎ 76337, closed Tue and Nov. Italian cuisine: gnocchi alla Parigina, trout with almonds, 26/38,000.
♦ *Baita*, v. Louset 4/A, ☎ 77496, closed Tue and May. Regional cuisine: cheese ravioli, polenta with meat, 20/35,000.

⋏ ★ *Chisonetto*, at Borgata Sestriere, v. al Colle 11, 150 pl, ☎ 77546 (all year).

Recommended
Golf: v. Colle, ☎ 76276 (18 holes).
Horseback riding: ☎ 70109.
Skating : at Panettone, p. Kandahar, ☎ 77396.
Swimming : at Borgata (indoor pool).
Tennis: *Sporting Sestriere,* ☎ 76276.
Vacation village: *Club Méditerranée,* ☎ 77123 (closed May-Nov).

SEZZADIO

Alessandria 20, Turin 110, Milan 115 km
Pop. 1,554 ⊠ 15079 ☎ 0131   D5

The abbey of **S. Giustina** at Sezzadio was at the height of its power in the 12C-13C. The Romanesque church *(3-7 p.m.)* was built *c.* 722 and rebuilt in 1030. It has a massive tower (15C). There are 14C-15C frescos in the apse and a monochrome mosaic in the crypt.   □

STRESA*

Novara 55, Milan 80, Turin 134 km
Pop. 5,097 ⊠ 28049 ☎ 0323   D2

In Stresa, parks and shaded gardens with lush Mediterranean vegetation camouflage grand villas and hotels. Architectural styles are eclectic, but the buildings still clearly belong to a single period. Between the 1800s and the early 1900s, the transformation of Stresa reached its zenith and the town prided itself on the most elegant lakeside drive in Verbano. A few eccentricities in no way detract from the effect: near the entrance of the Villa Pallavicino, for instance, animals and birds (pheasants, deer, kangaroos and ostriches) roam wild in an unusual zoological garden *(open to visitors).*

▶ The **lungolago★** (drive along the lake) offers wonderful sightseeing, with woods and gardens on one side and the lake and the Borromean Islands (→) on the other. ▶ Near p. Marconi are a landing-stage and the Neoclassical parish church of S. Ambrogio (late 18C). Behind the church, the **Villa Ducale**, the oldest villa in Stresa (1770), is where the philosopher Rosmini died; it houses the **Centro Studi Rosminiani** *(8:30 a.m.-12 noon and 2:30-6:30 p.m.; closed wkends and Aug).* Close by, a modern, well-equipped conference centre hosts international conventions and expositions.   □

Practical information _____

≋
ⓘ p. Europa 1, ☎ 30150.
🚂🚂 ☎ 30472.
🚢 boats and hydrofoils to Arona and Locarno, ☎ 30393; boats and motorboats to Borromean Islands (Isola Bella, ☎ 30556; Isola Madre, ☎ 31261; Isola dei Pescatori, ☎ 30392); *Stresa Boat Cooperative,* ☎ 30316.
Car rental: *Avis,* v. Sempione Nord, 37, ☎ 30544; *Maggiore,* corso Umberto 14, ☎ 30252.

Hotels:
★★★★★ *Des Iles Borromées,* corso Umberto 67, ☎ 30431, 166 rm Ⓟ ≼ ⑭ 🖵 ⌐ 19C building in park facing lake, 322,000; bkf: 17,000.
★★★★ *Astoria,* corso Umberto 31, ☎ 32566, 98 rm Ⓟ ⑭ 🖵 ⌐ closed Nov-19 Mar, 165,000.
★★★★ *Bristol,* corso Umberto 73, ☎ 32601, 250 rm Ⓟ ≼ ⑭ 🖵 ⌐ closed Dec-19 Mar, 165,000.
★★★★ *Milano au Lac,* p. Marconi, ☎ 31190, 80 rm Ⓟ ≼ closed Nov-27 Mar, 96,000; bkf: 10,000.
★★★★ *Palma,* v. Duchessa di Genova, ☎ 32401, 128 rm Ⓟ ≼ ⑭ 🕭 🖵 closed 16 Nov-14 Mar, 130,000; bkf: 12,000.
★★★★ *Speranza du Lac,* p. Marconi, ☎ 31178, 87 rm Ⓟ ≼ 🕭 closed Nov-27 Mar, 96,000; bkf: 10,000.

★★★★ *Villa Aminta,* v. Sempione Nord 123, ☎ 32444, 65 rm Ⓟ ≼ ⑭ 🖵 ⌐ closed Jan-Feb, 130,000.
★★★ *Moderno,* v. Cavour 33, ☎ 30468, 53 rm Ⓟ closed Nov-Feb, 72,000; bkf: 7,000.
★★★ *Primavera,* v. Cavour 39, ☎ 31286, 31 rm Ⓟ 🕭 closed Jan-Feb. No restaurant, 54,000; bkf: 4,000.
★★★ *Royal,* v. Sempione, ☎ 32777, 45 rm Ⓟ ≼ ⑭ ⌁ closed Nov-Mar, 75,000; bkf: 8,000.
★★★ *Torre,* v. Sempione 45, ☎ 32555, 44 rm Ⓟ ⑭ closed 16 Oct-Easter, 70,000.

Restaurants:
◆◆◆ *Emiliano,* corso Italia 48, ☎ 31396, closed Tue and 10 Nov-20 Dec. Creative cuisine: potato tortelli, bass with fig leaves, 50/90,000.
◆◆ *Barchetta,* v. Garibaldi 10, ☎ 30205, closed Wed. Italian cuisine: cannelloni, nodini, 25/35,000.
◆◆ *Chandelle,* at Carciano, v. Sempione 23, ☎ 30097, closed Mon and 6 Jan-6 Feb. International cuisine: paella valenciana, bouillabaisse (order by phone), 30/45,000.
◆ *Luina,* v. Garibaldi 21, ☎ 30285, closed Wed and Nov-12 Mar. Mixed cuisine: ravioli with cream, sole with sage, 25/40,000.

Recommended
Boat trips: to the Borromean Islands (guided tours).
Botanical gardens: *Alpinia,* at Alpino.
Convention Centre: p. Europa 3.
Events: *international music festival,* ☎ 31095 (Aug).
Excursions: by cablecar to Alpino and Mottarone, ☎ 24172; by road 10 km.
Gastronomic specialties: pastries, liver sausage *(mortadelle di fegato).*
Golf: at Vezzo *(5 km SW),* v. Panorama, ☎ 20101 or 20642 (9 holes).
Horseback riding: *Piccolo Ranch,* v. Prato Piano Magognino, ☎ 32130.
Yacht club: *Verbano Yachtclub,* v. Sempione 68, ☎ 30555 or 31382.
Zoological park: *Villa Pallavicino,* v. Sempione 61, ☎ 32407.

SUSA

Turin 54, Milan 190 km
Pop. 7,128 ⊠ 10059 ☎ 0122   A4

The Susa Valley becomes increasingly steep as it climbs toward the corso della Dora, taking on a typically alpine aspect. The roads uniting Piedmont to France diverge here on the way to Monginevro and Moncenisio. Known as the 'key to Italy', Susa was razed first by the Emperor Constantine and later by Barbarossa, and it was occupied in between by the Saracens. Being a crossroads also bestowed some advantages on the city, and Susa's economy is still buoyed by the merchants who have been flocking to this area since Roman times. The monuments dotting the city attest to its wealth in the Roman era.

▶ The **Arco di Augusto★** (Arch of Augustus), a square barrel-vault supported by Corinthian columns, was erected in honour of this Roman Emperor by the King of the Cozis in 8 BC. The bas-relief represents the alliance made between Emperor Augustus and the local sovereign. ▶ Traces of the ancient walls can still be seen, as well as part of a 2C amphitheatre. The **Due Porte** (Two Gates), marble barrel-vaults, were probably part of a Roman aqueduct. ▶ The **Porta Savoia**, originally Roman, was altered in the Middle Ages; it abuts the façade of the **cathedral★**, the city's main medieval monument which was erected in Graeco-Byzantine style in the 11C and often remodeled. History books attest that the church was built in honour of S. Giusto, a monk at the Novalesa convent, who was martyred by the Saracens in 906. There is an imposing Romanesque **campanile** (11C) on the r. side of the church and, in the interior, a triptych attributed to Bergognone and a 16C wooden statue said to depict the Marquise Adelaide di Susa. A precious Flemish triptych (1358) in the chapel to the r. is unfortunately rarely displayed. ▶ The Romanesque-Gothic church of **S. Francesco** was begun (according to legend) in the 13C to comply with the will of Saint Francis of Assisi who passed through Susa in 1213. ▶ On a promontory overlooking the city is the Castello dei Marchesi Arduinici (10C, but often rebuilt) with the **Museo Civico** *(summer 3:30-5:30 p.m.; hols also 9:30-11:30 a.m.; closed Mon; winter Thu and Sun 2:30-4:30 p.m.).* ▶ 8 km away, the Benedictine **Novalesa Abbey**, founded in 726, was destroyed by the Saracens and rebuilt only to be ruined again in the 19C and finally entrusted to the Benedictine Order in 1972. The most interesting building is the chapel of S. Eldrado (10C) with 12C frescos which were partly destroyed in the 19C. ☐

The man in the iron mask

He was held prisoner, treated benignly, yet forced to hide his face behind an iron-framed mask covered with velvet. One prison in which he was held from 1680-1687 was the Forte di Exilles on the Dora Riparia near Susa. Transferred to a fortress on the island of Sainte Marguerite off the coast of Cannes, France, and finally to the Bastille, the man in the iron mask died in 1700. His personal effects and all prison records concerning him were destroyed. His identity has never been plausibly solved. Historians and amateurs point the finger at dozens of different figures, including one of Louis XIV's supposed stepbrothers, the result of Anne of Austria's adultery. Other candidates include Ercole Mattioli and Eustache Douger. The latter, a valet, was arrested in Dunkerque, but no one knows why. He had perhaps found out about the secret treaty of Dover between Louis XIV and Carlo II, or, as manservant to Nicolas Fouquet, Louis' disgraced Minister of Finance, maybe he had learned dangerous secrets concerning the king's origins. As secretary to the Duke of Mantua, Mattioli had arranged for the Casale fortress to be handed over to Louis XIV in exchange for the sum of a hundred thousand scudi. As he was concluding the secret deal, someone passed on the information to foreign court officials. The mystery may never be solved.

Practical information ⎯⎯⎯⎯⎯⎯

ⓘ corso Inghilterra 39, ☎ 2222.

Hotel:
★★★ *Napoleon,* v. Mazzini 44, ☎ 2704, 40 rm Ⓟ closed Jan, 55,000; bkf: 7,000.

Restaurant:
◆ *Pesce,* v. Monte Grappa 25, ☎ 2476, closed Thu and Oct. Italian cuisine: cannelloni, game, 20/30,000.

Recommended
Nature park: guided automobile tours in *Orrido di Chianocco reserve (11 km E),* information from *Comunità Montana Bassa Valle Susa,* at Bussoleno *(8 km E),* v. Traforo 62 or from *Comune di Chianocco,* ☎ 49734.
Swimming: v. Berenfelz (also tennis).

TERME DI VALDIERI

Cuneo 33, Turin 127, Milan 249 km
⊠ 12010 ☎ 0171   A-B6

Terme di Valdieri is a thermal spring and vacation spot in the upper Gesso Valley with scenery dominated by the rugged Serra dell'Argentera Mountains. ☐

Practical information ⎯⎯⎯⎯⎯⎯
⚓ (Jun-Sep), ☎ 97106.

TORRE PELLICE

Turin 51, Milan 201 km
1,693 ft pop. 4,568 ⊠ 10066 ☎ 0121   A5

Torre Pellice has been called the 'Italian Geneva'. The affinity lies not only in a certain order and austerity, but also in their roles as centres of Protestantism. The Walsers (who settled the Pinerolese valleys from the 14C) followed the Reformation of 1532. It took three centuries of bloody battles before the Savoys accorded freedom of religion to this tenacious community who contributed greatly in social and economic terms to the Pellice Valley.

▶ A general synod of the community is held in the **Casa Valdese** every summer. The library has over 50,000 volumes and specializes in Protestantism. ▶ A **museum** *(Mon and Thu 4-7 p.m.; Sun 10 a.m.-12:30 p.m. and 4-7:30 p.m.)* exhibits mementos and relics from the 16C-17C religious wars. ☐

Practical information ⎯⎯⎯⎯⎯⎯
🎿 cross-country skiing, skiing camps at Mt. Vandalino.
ⓘ v. Caduti per la Libertà 2/B, ☎ 91875.

Hotel:
★★★★ *Gilly,* corso Lombardini 1, ☎ 932477, 60 rm Ⓟ ⚜
☒ closed Christmas, 100,000; bkf: 9,000.

⚠ ★ *Cairo,* v. Dante 19, 80 pl, ☎ 932060 (all year).

Recommended
Skating: v. Filatoio 8, ☎ 91246.
Tennis: v. Dante, ☎ 91563.

TORTONA

Alessandria 21, Milan 73, Turin 112 km
Pop. 28,753 ⊠ 15057 ☎ 0131   D4

At the foot of the Ligurian Apennines, near Scrivia, Tortona was a centre of exchange until the Romans built roads connecting other cities. From this point, Tortona had a lively but tortuous history: subjected to innumerable sieges, destructions and occupations, the city nevertheless remained powerful and its citizens had a reputation for wisdom.

▶ The oldest monument in the city is the 13C-14C church of **S. Maria Canale** with a simple Romanesque-Gothic façade. ▶ The Baroque church of **S. Matteo** has preserved a painting by Barnaba da Modena (14C). ▶ In the austere **Palazzo Guidobono**, erected in the 15C in Gothic style with spacious porticos, is the **Museo Civico** (see Library director) which has a collection of Roman artifacts including an exquisite marble sarcophagus decorated with pagan symbols, as well as medieval art. ▶ The church of **S. Maria** in Rivalta Scrivia (→) is also interesting. ☐

Practical information ⎯⎯⎯⎯⎯⎯
TORTONA

Hotels:
★★ *Aurora,* SS per Genova 13, ☎ 861188, 18 rm Ⓟ ⚜ ⏚
closed Aug, 50,000; bkf: 8,000. Rest. ◆◆◆ *Girarrosto*
closed Mon, Aug and Dec. Regional and Italian cuisine:
fagotini, malfatti, 30/50,000.
★★ *Oasi,* SS per Voghera 85, ☎ 861356, 27 rm Ⓟ ⚒
closed Christmas, 51,000; bkf: 6,000.

Restaurant:
● ◆◆◆ *Cavallino San Marziano,* corso Romita 83,
☎ 861750, closed Mon, Christmas and 20 Jul-

20 Aug. Regional and creative cuisine: pappardelle all'aja, filet with champagne vinegar, 28/45,000.

Environs

MOBISAGGIO, 5 km S.

Restaurant:
♦ *Montecarlo,* ☎ 879114, closed Tue and Aug. Regional cuisine: ravioli di stufato, malfatti with butter, 25/40,000.

TURIN**

(Torino)

Milan 140, Rome 653 km
Pop. 1,069,013 ⊠ 10100 ☎ 011   B4

Turin has a rectilinear lay-out that seems to emulate American cities, but a glance at the façades, roofs and squares shows at once the French influence on these surroundings. Although the city seems severe, uniform and grey, it is nonetheless multifaceted and swarming with contrasts. Some say that Turin equals Fiat, and the automobile manufacturer certainly plays an important role in the city's development. Turin has many other sides, however. It has a long-standing military tradition, years as the seat of government of the ruling Savoy family (but fewer as the capital city of Italy), Baroque architecture, a collection of Egyptian art and artifacts that ranks second only to Cairo's, a highly cultural and scientific publishing industry, an important university and a long and spirited theatrical tradition. Turin is a city of picturesque boutiques and cafés, and mountains that form a majestic background at the far ends of long boulevards. These attractions should bury the image of Turin as a squalid, gloomy town; visitors can discover the brighter side of this important city, described by the writer Guido Gozzano as 'a bit provincial, old and new / attired, still, in Parisian garb'.
▶ **The ancient quarter.** ▶ A tour of Turin should start at the **piazza Castello** (B3), the heart of the city's oldest quarter where its historical and artistic strains mingle. The main entrance to the Roman bull-fighting arena stood on the site of the present-day piazza. Under the porticos, the Baratti café and pastry shop is the most famous of the numerous spots to sit back and watch the passing scene; it preserves all the elegant charm of the *belle époque*. ▶ For an idea of the piazza's original shape, it should be viewed from v. Roma (facing the Palazzo Reale) and visualized as closed off on the r.-hand side by the **Palazzo Madama**★★, which now stands alone. Until the 17C, the W façade of this palazzo looked on to a rectangular piazza (decorated with porticos by A. Vitozzi in 1584) while its noble bastions rose to the E. The building blends many different styles and eras. It incorporates the remains of a Roman gate that was transformed during the Middle Ages into a castle that, in turn, was enlarged in the 15C by the Savoy family. In the 17C, the palace was the residence of Maria Cristina of France, widow of one ruler and regent for his successor, her son. She was known in the French manner as Madame Royale, and the palace still honours her with the name. The Baroque **façade**★ was added in 1721 by Filippo Juvarra, who also designed the atrium and the magnificent staircase. ▶ The **Museo Civico di Arte Antica**★ (Civic Museum of Antiquities) is housed here *(9 a.m.-7 p.m.; Sun 10 a.m.-1 p.m. and 2-7 p.m.; closed Mon and hols)* and contains interesting art collections from Piedmont (and elsewhere) from the Middle Ages to the 19C. Among the most important works are *Portrait of a Man*★★ by Antonello da Messina and pages from the celebrated Book of Hours, the *Très Belles Heures of Jean, Duke of Berry*★★, illuminated in the 14C-15C by

Sindone and Guarini

In the mid 15C, the supposed shroud of Jesus, the 'sindone' (a cloth measuring more than 4 yards long and showing an imprint of a human body both front and back) was brought to Ludovico di Savoia. He placed it in a chapel erected for that purpose in Chambéry (now capital of the Savoie province of France). In 1578, Emanuele Filiberto brought the shroud to Turin where he had established the house of Savoy's seat. Since 1694, the cloth has been preserved in the S. Sindone chapel. This architectural masterpiece, situated behind the presbytery of Turin cathedral, was designed by the architect and priest, Guarino Guarini (1604-83). According to one commentator, 'his plans were based on serious calculations, but nevertheless seemed thoroughly audacious'. This genius of the Baroque period greatly appreciated Gothic styles as well as Arab architecture, which he most probably saw in Spain. Buildings in Messina, Lisbon, Paris and Prague were all built from his designs. His major works, however, are in Turin. Summoned here by Duke Carlo Emanuele II, Guarini was designated the court's official engineer and mathematician. The façade of the Carignano Palace, the church of the Theatine Fathers of S. Lorenzo (of whom he was one) and the Sindone chapel — crowned with an unusual cupola — are ample testimony to his genius.

The first Fiat

The first Italian car had a collapsible roof and rear seats where passengers had to sit facing each other. It resembled the horse-drawn cart in many ways: it could boast only 3 1/2 HP and could not exceed 35 km/h. The model was designed by the engineer Aristide Faccioli. In July 1899, a few well-to-do citizens of Turin, fascinated by this new means of transportation, founded the Fabbrica Italiana Automobili Torino (FIAT). One of them, Giovanni Agnelli, was later to head this automobile empire. He set his sights on a location, corso Dante, near the Po River and built the first Fiat factory. In the meantime, the group bought out the Ceirano automobile company which had made Faccioli's first model and went into production right away. During the first years, 50 cars rolled out of the tiny factory. One of these original models is on display in Turin's Automobile Museum.

van Eyck and his school *(displayed in photo reproduction).* ▶ The church of **S. Lorenzo**★ (B3; minus the façade), built 1668-80 by G. Guarini, is a work of Baroque genius. Guarini's complex and ornate architectural style is seen in the richly decorated polychrome interior and even more so in the daring cupola. ▶ Wrought-iron gates separate the p. Castello from the p. Reale's four-sided courtyard, in which stands the **Palazzo Reale**★ (B3), the Savoy royal palace *(winter 9 a.m.-12 noon and 2-4 p.m.; summer 9 a.m.-12:30 p.m. and 3-5 p.m.; Fri and hols 9 a.m.-12:30 p.m.; closed Mon).* Built 1646-60, its façade is angular and austere and its inner courtyard verges on a military style. On the other hand, typically for Turin, the inside reveals an atmosphere of luxury with sumptuous 17C-19C furnishings. Among the most remarkable works are the curious Chinese cabinet *(gabinetto)* and the so-called 'scissor stairs' (between the first and second floors). Behind the palace, it is possible

to take summer walks in the royal gardens
(9 a.m.-7 p.m.). In the former conservatory, a Museum of
Antiquities is being built; in the Palazzo dell'Accademia
delle Scienze is a museum with archaeological finds
dating from the prehistoric era to the coming of the
barbarians. ▶ To the r. of the royal palace, the **Arme-
ria Reale★★** (Royal Armoury; *temporarily closed*) has one
of the greatest European collections of arms and armour
mostly from the 16C-19C. ▶ To the l. of the royal
palace, under a portico is the 18C Palazzo Chiablese
(B3) which houses an interesting **Museo del Cinema**
*(10 a.m.-12 noon and 3-6:30 and 8:30-11 p.m.; access
to projection rooms at 4 and 9:25 p.m.; museum closed
during projection hours; closed Mon).* ▶ This is the
edge of the Roman and medieval zone and the **Duomo★**
(B3) marks the transition from the remote past to the
17C. Its façade is 100 percent Renaissance (the only
example of its kind in Turin) and dates from 1491-8. The
foreboding **Cappella della S. Sindone★** *(7 a.m.-12 noon
and 3-7 p.m.; closed Mon and p.m. on hols),* another masterpiece of Guarini (1668-94), is made from black marble
and topped by an extraordinary cupola. It stands at the
exact spot where the church's apse meets the wall of the
Palazzo Reale. In the chapel is the famous Turin Shroud
which was supposed to have been draped over Christ's
body when he was taken off the cross; it is rarely exposed
to the public. ▶ Little remains from the Roman era: the
ruins of a **theatre** (B3) dating from the 1C, parts of city
walls, a stretch of a paved Roman road and the turreted mass of the 1C **Porta Palatina★** (A3; one of the most
ancient, grandiose and best-preserved examples of such
a gateway). ▶ The reconstruction projects and urban
renewals carried out since the 17C have virtually effaced
the medieval city. Its narrow alleys must not have differed greatly from De Amicis' description of 'tall, lugubrious
houses divided by a narrow streak of sky' or from the buildings found between v. Garibaldi (B2) and p. della Repubblica (A3). ▶ From p. Duomo, v. IV Marzo (in which stand
two partly restored medieval houses with *cotto* cornices)
angles off in the direction of **piazza Palazzo di Città** (B2),
formerly the piazza delle Erbe, a market square that was
the heart of the medieval town. It was built in the 1700s
and is dominated by the 17C façade of the **Palazzo di
Città,** which is now the city hall. ▶ This piazza can also
be reached by v. Garibaldi (tortuous and crumbling in the
Middle Ages and spectacularly straightened in the first
half of the 18C), as well as by v. Palazzo di Città
(also straightened). Along **via Garibaldi** stand the church
of the **SS. Trinità** (B3) by A. Vittozzi (1606), decorated
inside with marble (1718), and the church of the **SS. Martiri** (B2), designed by Pellegrini in 1577, which is flanked
by the 17C Baroque **Cappella dei Banchieri i e Mercanti**
(bankers and merchants; *hols 10 a.m.-12 noon; Tue and
Sat 2:30-6 p.m.).* The **v. Palazzo di Città** leads part way
into the small piazza in which stands the magnificent
church of **Corpus Domini** (B2). This austere edifice was
erected according to Vittozzi's plans (1609-71) to commemorate the miracle in 1453 when a consecrated wafer
fell from a stolen vessel and then rose to heaven, glowing
brightly. ▶ V. Milano bears traces of the Middle Ages
and leads to the 13C-14C Gothic church of **S. Domenico**
(A2; seriously damaged in the 18C when a section of the
nave was eliminated because 'half of it was in the
way' according to Juvarra's street-straightening project);
it was restored at the beginning of the 20C. ▶ Near the
remains of a Roman wall stands the ancient **Santuario
della Consolata★** (A2); already in the 4C an image of the
Virgin was venerated at this spot. Its present appearance is the result of numerous transformations between
1678 (by Guarini) and the early 1900s (with emphasis on
the interior).

▶ **Expansion in 17C-18C.** SW of p. Castello, the present-day **via Roma** (B3; originally via Nuova) was the axis
of the first urban expansion beyond the ancient Roman
boundaries. In 1619, Carlo Emanuele I, the ruler of Turin
and 'too narrow-minded for the mélange of people who
hoped to stay there', imprisoned the architect Castellamonte for having proposed a plan to construct a new
area of town. ▶ The heart of this addition would have

TURIN

0 100 200 300 400 500m

1:20.000 (1cm=200 m)

been the **piazza S. Carlo** (C2), a large rectangle border-ed by palaces, porticos and the churches of **S. Cristina** (Juvarra directed work on the Baroque façade, 1715-18) and **S. Carlo**. In the centre is a statue of Duke **Emanuele Filiberto** symbolically sheathing his sword after the battle of S. Quintino (1557), thus marking the end of much bloodshed and the beginning of reconstruction. The monument (familiarly referred to as *caval 'd brons*) is a fine example of 19C equestrian statuary (C. Marocchetti, 1838) and one of the city's symbols. ► In the 17C church of **S. Teresa** (B2; located on street bearing the same name) is a rich altar by Juvarra (1735). ► On the streets running between the two main piazzas of the time (Castello and S. Carlo), Guarini's whimsical spirit ruled. There were setbacks however: the great oval cupola of **S. Filippo Neri** (B3) collapsed in 1714, destroying the entire nave. The present-day structure is primarily the work of Juvarra (1730-72). ► The nearby **Palazzo dell'Accademia delle Scienze** (B3) is again the work of Guarini (1678). The façade reveals the architect's inter-est in fanciful forms, but maintains a certain nobility and austerity (as was only fitting for the College of Nobles of the Society of Jesus which was lodged here). Today, the palace houses two of Turin's most important museums: the Egyptian Museum and the Sabauda Gallery. The **Egyptian Museum**★★ *(9 a.m.-1:30 p.m.; hols 9 a.m.-1 p.m.; closed Mon)*, one of the greatest in the world for the wealth of its collections, offers a sweep-ing view of ancient Egyptian civilization. Among other art objects, the museum features sarcophagi, mummies, vases, statuettes, weapons, manuscripts on papyrus (including *The Book of the Dead*) and paintings. The museum has become famous for some of the objects it displays: the archeological pieces found in the tomb of the couple Kha and Merit (15C BC), the statue of *Pharaoh Ramses II*★ (13C BC) and the small Ellesija temple★ with its rock drawings (15C BC). ► The **Sabauda Gallery**★★ *(same opening hrs as Egyptian Museum)* is outstanding, displaying paintings by 15C and 16C Piedmontese artists, several masterpieces of Tuscan and Venetian painting (*Virgin and Child surrounded by angels*★ by Fra Angelico; *Tobie and the angel*★ by Pollaiolo; *Eleonora of Toledo*★ by Bronzino; *Madonna with saints*★ by Mantegna; *the Last Supper with Simon*★ by Veronese; *Shepherds in worship*★ by Savoldo; *Scenes of Torino*★ by Bellotto), as well as a series of rare Flemish and Dutch paintings (*Saint Francis with stigmata*★★ by Jan van Eyck; *Visitation*★ by Roger van der Weyden; *Passion*★ by Hans Memling; *the three sons of Charles the 1st of Britain*★ by van Dyck; *Old man sleeping*★ by Rembrandt). The **Gualino collec-tion** is also displayed in this gallery: it includes Italian paint-ings, Chinese sculptures and medieval furniture. ► On one side of the harmonious Guarini-like piazza stands the **Palazzo Carignano** (B3; 1679-85) with its façade 'red as old mahogany stained with fire', another of Guarini's u-nique Baroque creations. This palazzo overflows with Piedmontese history: within its walls Carlo Alberto (1798) and Vittorio Emanuele II (1829) were born, the Reign of Italy was proclaimed (1861), the first national parliament was held *(visits to assembly hall)* and it now houses the **Museo Nazionale del Risorgimento** *(9 a.m.-6 p.m.; hols 9 a.m.-12 noon; closed Mon)*. It is natural to follow a visit to this palazzo with a stop at the old Cambio restaurant in the piazza where, for more than fifteen years, Cavour ate pastries at a table that even today is reserved in his name. ► **Via Po** (B3, C3-4) is the axis along which the new quarter added in 1675 was oriented. It was the first major exception to the city's ancient r.-angled layout. ► The only monument of note here is the **Palazzo dell'Università** (B3), completed in 1720 under the direction of M. Garove. Apart from this, there is little to disturb the architectural uniformity and precise organiza-tion of the long broad street. The avenue is lined with aristocratic palaces originally built according to an exact social stratification: under the porticos were the shops, on the first floor ('the noble storey') the proprietor's family, and on the other floors, apartments to rent. ► The **Mole Antonelliana** (B4) was originally planned as a synagogue by A. Antonelli in 1863, but was later bought by the city,

which completed construction in 1897. The strange and daring structure was originally built entirely of brick; it has an enormous square cupola with a spire. In its time, it was the tallest building in the world. There is an eleva-tor to a panoramic terrace *(9 a.m.-7 p.m.)*. ► The **Acca-demia Albertina** (C3) dates from the city's second expan-sion. Built in the 17C, the palazzo now houses the **Galle-ria dell'Accademia Albertina** *(hols 10 a.m.-12 noon)* with a display of 17C pictorial works. ► Nearby is the **piazza Carlo Emanuele II** (C3; known as Carlina) which was intended to be the heart of the new quarter in the 17C. In a setting of architectural unity, the beautiful palazzi har-monize with the gracious church of **S. Croce** (1718-30; the campanile and façade were added later) designed by Juvarra. **Via del Carmine** (A2), starting in p. Savoia, was the main axis of the third urban expansion, planned by Juvarra in 1714. In anticipation of later architec-tural trends, elegance and severity are the dominant fea-tures of this quarter. These did not, however, rule out daring projects like the **Carmine Church**, with its light and airy nave. ► Turin could not expand farther from the SW corner of the Roman quadrilateral until the second half of the 19C. It was at this spot that Emanuele Filiberto erect-ed an imposing pentagonal fortress, the so-called **Citta-della** (B1; designed by F. Paciotto), only the massive outline of which remains today. It is the site of the Museo Storico Nazionale dell'**Artiglieria** (artillery; *Tue and Thu 9 a.m.-1:45 p.m.; Sat and Sun, 9 a.m.-12:30 p.m.)*. ► Nearby, in v. Guicciardini, is the **Museo Pietro Micca** (B1; *9 a.m.-12 noon and 3-6 p.m.; Sun and Jul-Aug 9 a.m.-2 p.m.; closed Mon)*, which allows access into the underside of the Turin fortifications that have been preserved virtually intact. The extensive network linking miles of underground passageways and galleries at times extends over several storeys. Only part of it can be visited, but it is possible to see the spot where the Turin hero Pietro Micca, a simple soldier, sacrificed him-self by lighting gunpowder and going up in flames with the fort during the siege of 1706.

19C-20C. The main boulevards encircling the historical centre between the Dora, the Po and the two railroad sta-tions were built in the first half of the 19C when the bas-tions, having been partially destroyed by the French and later by the Savoys, no longer served any real pur-pose. The Cittadella too was torn down in 1856-7, strip-ping Turin of its image as a fortified military town and allow-ing it to expand freely. ► **Via Micca** (B2-3) was the last urban planning project in the old centre, which is clear from the way it cuts across the otherwise r.-angled layout of the streets. ► The **19C ring road** starting at the **Porta Nuova** railroad station (C2) is one of the most impressive from the last century (1860-8). Along this road is the **piazza Carlo Felice** (1823-55) with lush greenery and elegant porticos. To the W, **corso Vittorio Emanuele II** leads to a square bearing the same name. Two steps away, the **Galleria d'Arte Moderna**★ (C1) has one of the most important modern art collections in Italy *(closed for repairs)*. ► N on corso Inghilterra and corso Principe Eugenio is the **piazza Statuto** (A1), constructed in 1864 to complete the symmetrical series of four monumental entrances to the city. ► The **piazza della Repubblica** (A3; 1814) was supposed to serve the same function, but with more pomp and circumstance. The **Porta Palazzo** (as it is called by locals) is the city's biggest and busiest square and hosts permanent boutiques and temporary stalls (including the famous **Balòn** flea market held every Sat a.m.). ► It lies near the old working-class neigh-bourhood of **Borgo Dora**, which was built around the first industrial plants that used the river's hydraulic energy to drive their machines. It was no accident that the famous religious institution **Piccola Casa della Provvidenza** (A2), dedicated to the poor, opened its doors in this area: already in 1851, 20,000 people lived in this impover-ished area. ► Far along the ring road is the corso Mau-rizio. On the l. is the **piazza Vittorio Veneto** (C4), a large rectangular square that gently slopes down to the Po, designed in 1828 by G. Frizzi, an architect from Lugano. In the 17C p. Castello and v. Po, there is a fine view of the Napoleonic bridge (the first brick bridge to be built in the city, 1810-15) and the hills beyond. On the other side of the bridge, the Neoclassical church of **Gran Madre di Dio** (C4) was erected in 1831 to commemorate the return of the Savoy family at the end of the French occupation of 1814. The hilly scenery can be viewed even more clearly from the **Monte dei Cappuccini** (D4), on which stands a simple 16C church by A. Vittozzi, **S. Maria del Monte**. Next to it is the **Museo Nazionale della Montagna Duca degli Abruzzi** *(winter 8:45 a.m.-12 noon and 2:45-6:15 p.m.; other months 8:45 a.m.-12:15 p.m. and 2:45-6:15 p.m.)*. Between corso M. D'Azeglio and the river is the magnificent **Valentino Park** (D-F3; opened to public in 1856), considered one of the most beautiful in Italy; it has the reputation of being a very romantic setting and is a worthy spot to end a trip through 19C Turin. Two monumental architectural complexes contribute to this feeling. The **Valentino Castle** (E3), built in 1630-60 by Carlo di Castellamonte, was based on 16C French castles. During its period of splendour, it was the seat of the court and the scene of sumptuous public festivals, tournaments and jousts. There is also a **Borgo Medievale** (medieval city; F3), with faithful reconstructions of medieval Valdostan and Piedmontese buildings. ▶ At the edge of the park, the huge **Palazzo Torino Esposizioni** is a significant example of Turin architecture during the 20C when the city experienced an industrial and demographic explosion. ▶ All that the contemporary city has to offer is closely linked to the world of industrial production: the **Museo dell'Automobile C. Biscaretti di Ruffia★** at corso Unità d'Italia 10 *(winter 10 a.m.-12:30 p.m. and 3-5:30 p.m.; closed Mon and Tue; summer 9:30 a.m.-12:30 p.m. and 3-7 p.m.; closed Mon)* and, in the same street, the now classic **Palazzo del Lavoro** (labour) by P.L. Nervi (1959) and the old **Fiat Lingotto** track (v. Nizza), built 1915-18 with what were then highly advanced materials; it was the indoor car-testing ground for years.

Environs

▶ The **Basilica di Superga★** *(10 km)* on top of a neighbouring hill was built by F. Juvarra (1731) for Vittorio Amedeo II. It has a large Corinthian vestibule and a high cupola. The interior is magnificent, boasting canvases and high reliefs. In the crypt *(summer 8 a.m.-12:30 p.m. and 2-7 p.m; winter 9 a.m.-12:30 p.m. and 2-5 p.m.)* are the tombs of the Savoys. ▶ The wooded **Colle della Maddalena** *(9.5 km)* has become the Parco della Rimembranza (remembrance). ▶ The **Villa reale di Stupinigi★**, surrounded by a vast park *(10.6 km along corso Stupinigi; 10 a.m.-12:30 p.m. and 2-5 p.m.; summer 10 a.m.-12:30 p.m. and 3-6 p.m.; closed Mon and Fri)*, was built by Juvarra (1730). Inside is the **Museo d'Arte e di Ammobiliamento.** ▶ At Moncalieri *(8.6 km SE)*, an industrial town on the Po River, is the **Castello Reale** of the Savoys (built 1260, rebuilt in 1400s and extended in 17C-18C), Vittorio Emanuele II's favourite residence. ▶ **Rivoli** *(13.5 km W)*, now an industrial centre, was the medieval site of the Savoy court. Here are the **Casa del Conte Verde** (Amedeo VI), erected in the 14C or 15C, and the **castle** of the Savoys, built partly under Juvarra's direction in the 18C. ☐

Practical information ⎯⎯⎯⎯⎯⎯⎯⎯

TURIN
ℹ️ v. Roma 226 (C2), ☎ 535181; *Porta Nuova station*, ☎ 531327; p. Solferino 3/bis (B2), ☎ 540177 (B2).
✈ at Caselle, international airport, 15 km N, ☎ 5778361; Alitalia, v. Lagrange 35 (C2), ☎ 55911; bus for airport, corso Inghilterra (B1).
🚂 *Porta Nuova* (CD 2), ☎ 517551.
🚌 from bus station corner of corso Inghilterra and corso Vittorio Emanuele (B1).
Car rental: *Avis*, corso Turati 15, ☎ 501107, at station, ☎ 659800, at airport, ☎ 4701528; *Hertz*, corso Marconi 19, ☎ 6504504, at station, ☎ 659658, at airport, ☎ 4701103; *Maggiore*, reservation centre at station, ☎ 6503013, at airport, ☎ 4701929.

Hotels:
★★★★ *Concord,* v. Lagrange 47 (C2a), ☎ 5576756, 139 rm 🅿 ⬥ 179,000.
★★★★ *G.H. Sitea,* v. Carlo Alberto 35 (C3b), ☎ 5570171, 120 rm 🅿 ⬥ 180,000; bkf: 13,000.
★★★★ *Jolly Ambasciatori,* corso Vittorio Emanuele II 104 (B-C1c), ☎ 5752, 197 rm 🅿 180,000.
★★★★ *Jolly Ligure,* p. Carlo Felice 85 (C2d), ☎ 55641, 156 rm 🅿 226,000. Rest. ◆◆◆ *Birichino* Creative cuisine, 40/55,000.
★★★★ *Jolly Principi di Piemonte,* v. Gobetti 15 (C2e), ☎ 519693, 107 rm, 226,000. Rest. ● ◆◆◆ *Gentilom* Regional cuisine, 40/55,000.
★★★★ *Majestic,* corso Vittorio Emanuele 54 (C2f), ☎ 539153, 159 rm 🅿 No restaurant, 170,000.
★★★★ *Royal,* corso Regina Margherita 249, ☎ 748444, 65 rm 🅿 ⏧ closed 1-25 Aug. No restaurant, 130,000; bkf: 9,000.
★★★★ *Turin Palace,* v. Sacchi 8 (C2g), ☎ 515511, 125 rm 🅿 ⬥ 230,000; bkf: 18,000.
★★★★ *Villa Sassi,* strada Traforo del Pino 47, ☎ 890556, 12 rm 🅿 〰 🔍 ⏧ closed Aug. 18C villa in large park, 230,000; bkf: 15,000. Rest. ● ◆◆◆ *El Toulà* closed Sun and Aug. International cuisine: green rice with champagne, tegoline alla cardinale, 60/80,000.
★★★ *Bramante,* v. Genova 2, ☎ 697997, 42 rm 🅿 83,000; bkf: 5,000.
★★★ *Dock Milano,* v. Cernaia 46 (B1h), ☎ 512622, 69 rm 🅿 80,000; bkf: 5,000.
★★★ *Genio,* corso Vittorio Emanuele II 47 (C-D2i), ☎ 6505771, 82 rm 🅿 ⬥ No restaurant, 82,000; bkf: 9,000.
★★★ *Giotto,* v. Giotto 27 (F21), ☎ 637172, 45 rm 🅿 ⬥ 86,000; bkf: 7,000.
★★★ *Goya Residence,* v. Principe Amedeo 41 bis (C3-4m), ☎ 874951, 31 rm 🅿 ⬥ closed 1-25 Aug. No restaurant, 77,000; bkf: 7,000.
★★★ *Lancaster,* corso Turati 8 (E1n), ☎ 501720, 75 rm, closed 10-31 Aug. No restaurant, 82,000.
★★★ *President,* v. Cecchi 67, ☎ 859555, 72 rm 🅿 〰 No restaurant, 96,000; bkf: 8,500.
★★★ *Roma & Rocca Cavour,* p. Carlo Felice 60 (C2p), ☎ 518137, 93 rm 🅿 No restaurant, 79,000; bkf: 7,000.
★★★ *Stazione & Genova,* v. Sacchi 14/B (D2q), ☎ 545323, 45 rm 🅿 ⬥ 〰 No restaurant, 102,000.
★★ *Cairo,* v. La Loggia 6, ☎ 352003, 35 rm 🅿 〰 No restaurant, 60,000.
★★ *Cristallo,* corso Traiano 28/9, ☎ 618383, 20 rm 🅿 〰 ⬥ closed August. No restaurant, 59,000; bkf: 5,000.

Restaurants:
● ◆◆◆◆ *Cambio,* p. Carignano 2 (B3t), ☎ 546690, closed Sun and 28 Jul-30 Aug. Historical building with original furnishings. Excellent cuisine, 40/55,000.
● ◆◆◆◆ *Vecchia Lanterna,* corso Re Umberto 21 (C2af), ☎ 537047, closed Sat noon, Sun and Aug. Quiet and elegant. Regional and international cuisine: duck ravioli, venison with polenta, 50/70,000.
● ◆◆◆ *Due Lampioni,* v. Carlo Alberto 45 (C3v), ☎ 555292, closed Sun and 31 Jul-25 Aug. Creative regional and international cuisine: lasagne alle capesante gratiné, shrimp with rucola and porcini mushrooms, 40/60,000.
● ◆◆◆ *Montecarlo,* v. S. Francesco da Paola 37 (C3ab), ☎ 541234, closed Sat noon, Sun, Jul or Aug. Creative cuisine: seaweed with clams, duck with myrtle, 40/50,000.
◆◆◆ *Bue Rosso,* corso Casale 10 (C4s), ☎ 830753, closed Mon and Aug. Rustic elegance, dinners with live entertainment. Italian cuisine: braised meat, wild game, 30/40,000.
◆◆◆ *Capannina,* v. Donati 1 (C1u), ☎ 545405, closed Sun and Aug. Regional cuisine: stew al Barolo, mushrooms and truffles, 25/40,000.
◆◆◆ *Cloche,* strada Traforo del Pino 106, ☎ 894213, closed Mon. With sheltered terrace. Regional cuisine: gnocchi with fontina cheese, guinea fowl with grapes, 35/60,000.
◆◆◆ *Gatto Nero,* corso Turati 14 (E1z), ☎ 590477, closed Sun and Aug. Tuscan cuisine: tortellini with cream, tagliolini with greens, 40/60,000.
◆◆◆ *Smarrita,* corso Unione Sovietica 244, ☎ 390657,

closed Mon and Aug. Creative cuisine: fish ravioli with pine nut sauce, scampi with peas, 35/70,000.
♦♦ *Camin,* corso Francia 339/D, ☎ 24033, closed Sun and Aug. Italian cuisine: guinea fowl stuffed with artichokes, turkey with pomegranate, 30/40,000.
♦♦ *Ciacolon,* v. XXV Aprile 11, ☎ 6610911, closed Sun eve, Mon and Aug. Venetian cuisine: rice with radishes, guinea fowl in peverada, 30,000.
♦♦ *Mara e Felice,* v. Foglizzo 8, ☎ 731719, closed Sat noon, Sun and Aug. Mixed cuisine: tagliolini with salmon, baked lamb, 35/50,000.
♦ *Antica Trattoria Parigi,* corso Rosselli 83, ☎ 592593, closed Wed, Sun eve and Aug. Regional cuisine: homemade pasta, roasts, 20/23,000.
♦ *Buca di San Francesco,* v. S. Francesco da Paola 27 (C3r), ☎ 544576, closed Mon, 1-10 Jan and 15 Jul-18 Aug. Italian cuisine: mozzarella fagottini all'ortolana, lombatina luculliana, 20/33,000.
♦ *Buco,* v. Lombriasco 4, ☎ 442210, closed Sun and 10-25 Aug. Regional cuisine: green Valdostan gnocchetti, rabbit canavesana, 26/35,000.
♦ *Fontana dei Francesi,* strada Pecetto 123, ☎ 8610397, closed Tue and 2-31 Jan. Possibility of outdoor dining. Regional and Italian cuisine: panissa, wild game, 20/30,000.
♦ *Mina,* v. Ellero 36, ☎ 6963608, closed Mon and Aug. Summer terrace. Regional cuisine: paupiettes with truffles, mushrooms in padella, homemade wines, 30/40,000.
♦ *Ostu Bacu,* corso Vercelli 226, ☎ 264579, closed Sun and 20 Jul-20 Aug. Renovated restaurant. Regional cuisine: homemade tagliatelle, snails with green sauce, 30/40,000.
♦ *San Giors,* v. Borgo Dora 3 (A3 ac), ☎ 5211256, closed Mon, Tue and Jun-Jul. Regional cuisine: fondue with truffles, bagna cauda, 35/40,000.
♦ *Spada Reale,* v. Principe Amedeo 53 (C4 ad), ☎ 832835, closed Sun, Christmas, Easter and 20 Jul-25 Aug. Tuscan and Italian cuisine: garmucia, cheese ravioli with nut sauce, 17/28,000.
♦ *Tre Galline,* v. Bellezia 37 (A2 ae), ☎ 546833, closed Mon and Aug. Regional cuisine: bagna cauda, hare in civet, 20/35,000.

⅄ ★★ *Riviera sul Po,* at Fioccardo, corso Moncalieri 422, 40 pl, ☎ 6611485 (all year); ★*Villa Rey,* strada Val S. Martino Sup. 27, 105 pl, ☎ 878670.

Recommended
Archery: *Compagnia arcieri Alpignano* v. Ventimiglia 166, ☎ 635214.
Auction house: *Galleria Sant'Agostino,* corso Siccardi 15, ☎ 535963.
Automobile racing: at Lombardore (20 km NE), ☎ 9886028.
Canoeing: *Associazione piemontese canoa,* ☎ 593762; *Canottieri Armida,* v. Virgilio 45, ☎ 659219; *Amici del fiume,* corso Moncalieri 19, ☎ 688890.
Cycling: *Amici del pedale,* v. Rismondi 15, ☎ 6066356.
Discothèques: *Pick up,* v. Barge 8, ☎ 4472204; *Patio,* corso Moncalieri 346/14, ☎ 6965383.
Events: *Lyric Season* at *Teatro Regio* (B3), ☎ 548000; *Torino Exhibition Complex,* at Valentino (F2), ☎ 6569: *Automobile Show* (bi-annual, Apr-May, alternating with *Industrial Vehicle Show*); *Vacation, Tourism, Sports and Leisure Exhibition* (Feb-Mar); *Europa Camping Cars and Tents* (Sep); *Mountain and Climbing Exhibition* (Oct); *Automotor* (Oct); *New Technology and Innovations Exhibition* (Oct-Nov).
Flying: strada Berlia 500, ☎ 790916.
Gastronomic specialties: *grissini* (breadsticks), pastries made with cream and liqueur, *giandujotti* (Turin chocolate speciality), caramels, candied chestnuts.
Golf: corso Unione Sovietica 506/A, ☎ 343975; at Fiano *(23 km NW), Golf Torino,* v. Grange 137, ☎ 9235440; *La Mandria,* ☎ 9235719.
Guided tours: guides at information office, v. Roma 226, ☎ 535181 (reserve beforehand).
Hang gliding: *Aerodelta,* v. Gatti 8, ☎ 721525; *Volo Torino,* v. Salbertrand 48, ☎ 752073.

Horseback riding: *Gimmy and his horses,* strada vicinale del Meisino 33, ☎ 890865 (associate of *ANTE*).
Horse racing: at Vinovo *(15 km S),* v. Rocciamelone 3, ☎ 9651356.
Motocross: at Lombardore *(20 km NE),* ☎ 9886819.
Regional park: *La Mandria,* office at Venaria *(9 km N),* v. C. Emanuele II 256, ☎ 490025 (bicycle rental at Ponte Verde except Mon and Tue; bus departures from station at v. Fiocchetto).
Shopping: clothes shopping in downtown boutiques on v. Roma and v. Garibaldi; antiques and old books in p. S. Carlo, v. Po and v. Maria Vittoria; *Balôn* flea market in p. Repubblica.
Skating: v. Petrarca 39, ☎ 6569.
Skindiving: v. Pomba 24, ☎ 546732 (instruction).
♥ rare books: *A. Tallone,* at Alpignano *(15 km W),* v. Diaz 9, ☎ 9676455 (hand-printed).

Environs

CASELLE TORINESE, ✉ 10072, 14 km N.

Hotel:
★★★ *Jet,* v. della Zecca 9, ☎ 993733, 68 rm Ⓟ ⑊ ♿ closed Aug, 92,500; bkf: 6,000. Rest. ♦♦♦ *Antica Zecca* closed Mon. In renovated 16C monastery. Creative cuisine: corn flour tagliolini, ⊅Persian fish with saffron, 38/60,000.

CASTIGLIONE TORINESE, ✉ 10090, 14 km NE.

Restaurant:
● ♦♦♦ *Villa Monfort's,* v. del Luogo 29, ☎ 9606214, closed Sun, Mon, Jan and Aug. Refined atmosphere in 17C villa. International and regional cuisine: fiananziera, Boves cake, 50/60,000.

MONCALIERI, ✉ 10024, ☎ 011, 9 km SE.

Hotel:
★★★ *Darsena,* strada Torino 29, ☎ 642448, 25 rm Ⓟ ⑊ 78,000; bkf: 7,000.

Restaurants:
♦♦ *Cà Mia,* strada Revigliasco 138, ☎ 641638, closed Tue and Aug. Regional cuisine: tortelloni with asparagus tips, wild game, 35/40,000.
♦ *Rosa Rossa,* v. Carlo Alberto 5, ☎ 645873, closed Sun eve, Mon and Aug. Regional cuisine: finanziera, stew, 25/35,000.

Recommended
Cycling: *G.S. Moncalierese,* v. Roma 23, ☎ 6403095.
Water skiing: *Circolo Nautico Marco Merlo,* v. Rocchetto 16, ☎ 761000; *Lo Ski Nautique,* corso Appio Claudio 207, ☎ 710704.

RIVOLI, ✉ 10098, ☎ 011, 14 km W.

Restaurant:
♦♦♦ *Nazionale,* corso Francia 4, ☎ 9580275, closed Sat and Aug. Italian cuisine: fresh pasta, fish and meat, 25/40,000.

SAN GILLIO, ☎ 10040, 18 km NW.

Restaurant:
● ♦♦♦♦ *Rosa d'Oro,* v. Balbo 1, ☎ 9840890, closed Sun eve, Mon, Aug, noon, 26-30 Dec and 2 Jan-2 Feb. With lovely garden. Regional and international cuisine: chicken alla Marengo, filet of wild boar, 25/38,000.

STUPINIGI, ✉ 10040, ☎ 011, 10 km S.

Restaurant:
♦♦♦ *Cascine,* on road to Orbassano, ☎ 9002581, closed Mon, Oct-Apr and 15-31 Aug. With park and small lake. Italian cuisine: fettuccine primaverili, medieval roast, 26/38,000.

For help in understanding terms when visiting museums or other sites, see the *Art and Architectural Terms Guide* at the end of the Practical Holiday Guide.

VALENZA

Alessandria 13, Milan 84, Turin 102 km
Pop. 22,365 ☒ 15048 ☎ 0131   D4

Overlooking the Po River, Valenza is at the extreme E boundary of Monferrato and was an important military stronghold until the Napoleonic era. Toward the middle of the 19C, it developed an industry of **artisanal goldsmithing,** which was later perfected through industrial techniques and has brought the city international acclaim.   □

Practical information ────────────
⚓ (May-Sep), ☎ 975253.

Recommended
Events: permanent display of gold and silver jewelry at p. Don Minzoni 1, ☎ 953643; display of Valenzano jewelry (Oct).
Golf: v. Astigliano 44, ☎ 93425 or 954778.

VARAITA VALLEY

A-B5

In the lowlands are orchards, pastures and tracts of woodland. In the upper valley, dense forests stand against a backdrop of majestic alpine scenery. The Varaita Valley is situated in the SW Alps where even now a French Provençal dialect is spoken and Languedocian traditions are respected. The landscape's nobility is deceptive; life in this area has always been hard. From the 12C to the 17C, these valleys were the site of much bloodshed and ferocious religious persecution.

▶ The main centre is **Sampéyre,** a vacation resort. Part of the parish church of **SS. Pietro e Paolo** dates from the 15C. Near the secondary school is the **Museo Civico,** devoted to the history and ethnology of the area *(open summer).* ▶ **Casteldelfino,** another vacation centre, was the hub of ancient Castellata. ▶ **Pontechianale,** at the top of the valley, is a winter sports centre and starting point for expeditions to the top of Monviso.   □

Practical information ────────────
CASTELDELFINO, 4,252 ft, ☒ 12020, ☎ 0175.
⚡ ski lifts, cross-country skiing, instruction.

PONTECHIANALE, 5,295 ft, ☒ 12020, ☎ 0175.
⚡ ski lifts, cross-country skiing, instruction.

SAMPEYRE, 3,202 ft, ☒ 12020 ☎ 0175.
⚡ ski lifts, cross-country skiing (at Frassino as well, *9 km E),* instruction, skating.
ⓘ *Comunità Montana,* p. della Vittoria 52, ☎ 96152.

Hotels:
★★ *Amici,* at Rore, ☎ 96119, 11 rm ℗ ᚑ ⌘ closed Oct, 23,000.
★★ *Monte Nebin,* v. Cavour 26, ☎ 96112, 64 rm ℗ closed Oct-Nov and May-Jun, 42,000; bkf: 4,000.

⚠ ★★★ *Valvaraita,* at Fiandrini, 100 pl, ☎ 96258 (all year).

                    ▾

VARALLO

Vercelli 62, Milan 105, Turin 121 km
1,476 ft pop. 8,245 ☒ 13019 ☎ 0163   C2

Bernardino Caimi (late 15C), pastor of S. Sepolcro, did not live long enough to see the result of the project for which he had fought: the reproduction of the Holy Places of Palestine for the faithful who could not make the long pilgrimage to the Holy Land. The project was eventually completed after almost two centu-

ries, although the end result was not exactly as Caimi had imagined. Pushed by the church authorities, the artists working on the project recast the original idea, using visual and dramatic representation as a means of communicating with the masses. Between the 15C and 17C, the Sacro Monte de Varallo, which drew crowds of worshippers, was a driving force in cultural and artistic evolution.

▶ Varallo's central piazza is dominated by the church of **S. Gaudenzio** (restored 1710), totally surrounded by an elegant gallery; inside is a polyptych by G. Ferrari. ▶ The **Palazzo dei Musei** *(summer 10 a.m.-12 noon and 3-6 p.m.; closed Fri; winter on request)* has a picture gallery with works by regional painters such as G. Ferrari and Tanzio da Varallo, as well as a natural history museum. ▶ At the foot of the hill leading to Sacro Monte stands the church of **S. Maria delle Grazie,** built in 1487-1501 according to Caimi's plan. Inside is an admirable series of frescos by G. Ferrari *(The Life and Passion of Christ★,* 1513). ▶ The impressive religious complex of **Sacro Monte★** dominates the city to the E. Its forty-four chapels, known as the New Jerusalem, are scattered about the wooded plain. The 600 statues and 400 fresco figures making up the representation are the work of numerous artists: P. Tibaldi and G. Alessi (architecture); G. Ferrari, G. Tabacchetti and G. d'Errico (sculptures); and G. Ferrari, Morazzone, Tanzio da Varallo and others (paintings). ▶ 1.5 km away, the chapel of the **Madonna di Loreto** (16C) has lively frescos.   □

Practical information ────────────
⚡ ski lifts at Tapone di Camasco *(7 km NE).*
ⓘ corner of corso Roma and p. Garibaldi, ☎ 51280.

Hotel:
★ *Casa del Pellegrino,* at Sacro Monte, ☎ 51656, 21 rm ⚞ ᚑ ⌘ closed Nov-Feb, 40,000; bkf: 5,000.

Restaurants:
♦♦ *Sacro Monte,* at Sacro Monte, ☎ 51189, closed Nov-Feb. Regional and Italian cuisine: lasagnette alla Valsesiana, polenta and merluzzo, 20/30,000.
♦ *Delzano,* at Crosa 8, ☎ 51439, closed Mon and 1-15 Sep. Regional and international cuisine: tajarin with herbs, paella vallenciana, 20/35,000.

⚠ ★★ *Valsesia,* at Valmaggia, 40 pl, ☎ 52307 (all year).

Recommended
Canoeing: *Centro canoa Valsesia,* at Vocca *(6 km W),* office at Milan, v. Lomellina 46, ☎ 02/7388685.
Nature park: *Alta Valsesia,* office at Comunità Montana Valsesia, v. Franzoni 2, ☎ 51555.
♥ lace and fine products: boutique near Palazzo dei Musei, v. Don Maio, ☎ 51338.

VERBANIA

Novara 70, Milan 95, Turin 146 km
Pop. 32,165 ☒ 28048 (Pallanza) or 28044 (Intra) ☎ 0323
                    D2

In 1939, Pallanza and Intra united to form the community of Verbania and since that time the towns have physically merged. In a sense, Verbania has a single body but two souls. The town of Pallanza, facing the idyllic Borromean Gulf, guards the opulent yet discreet charm of the aristocratic vacation resorts dating from the last century. The villas and grand hotels are surrounded by lush parks and gardens. The city of Intra, also a major lakeside resort, has seen constant growth in industrial development; its strength has always been in textiles; the first Italian mechanized cotton-spinning mill was built here.

▶ In the centre of **Pallanza,** the 18C Palazzo Dugnani houses the **Museo del Paesaggio** and the **Museo Sto-**

rico Artistico del Verbano *(Apr-Oct 10 a.m.-12 noon and 3-6 p.m.; closed Mon; Nov-Mar wkends 10 a.m.-12 noon and 3-5 p.m.).* ▶ In v. Azari, the 16C church of **Madonna di Campagna** shows the influence of the Renaissance architect Bramante; inside are frescos by B. Lanino and C. Procaccini. ▶ The lakeside drive offers a view of the gulf and the Borromean Islands (→). ▶ Past Castagnola point is **Villa Taranto★**. Its splendid botanical gardens were designed by a Scotsman, Captain Neil MacEacharn, and boast innumerable terraces, fountains, basins, cascades and nearly 2,000 species of plants; from March to October the gardens are resplendent with flowers in full bloom. ▶ On the summit of the promontory is the 11C-12C Romanesque church of **S. Remigio** with frescos from the same period and a 16C portico. ▶ In this fairly modern town the landing-stage is typical of late 19C architectural styles. ▶ **Isola Madre** can be visited by boat (→ Borromean Islands).   ☐

Practical information

ⓘ at Pallanza, corso Zannitello, ☎ 42976.

🚢 boats and hydrofoils; car ferry every 20 mns from Intra to Laveno, ☎ 44007.

Hotels:
★★★★ *G.H. Majestic,* at Pallanza, v. Vittorio Veneto 32, ☎ 504305, 119 rm Ⓟ ⌂ ⌀ ▤ ⁀ closed 16 Oct-31 Mar, 160,000; bkf: 12,000. Rest. ◆◆◆ *Beola* ☎ 504202, closed Wed. Garden along lake shore. Italian and some international cuisine: Florentine fish, cooked pigeon, 30/50,000.
★★★ *Astor,* at Pallanza, v. Vittorio Veneto 17, ☎ 504261, 52 rm Ⓟ ⌂ ⌀ closed 16 Oct-14 Mar, 75,000; bkf: 8,500.
★★★ *Belvedere,* at Pallanza, v. Magnolie 6, ☎ 503202, 58 rm ⌇ closed Oct-Mar, 70,000; bkf: 5,000.
★★★ *Miralago,* at Intra, corso Mameli 173, ☎ 44080, 41 rm Ⓟ ⌇ 665,000; bkf: 5,000.
★★★ *San Gottardo,* at Pallanza, v. Magnolie 6, ☎ 504465, 40 rm ⌇ closed Nov-Feb, 70,000; bkf: 5,000.
★★ *Italia,* at Pallanza, v. Magnolie 10, ☎ 503206, 14 rm ⌇ closed 11 Nov-14 Mar, 55,000; bkf: 4,500.

Restaurants:
● ◆◆◆ *Milano,* at Pallanza, corso Zanitello 2, ☎ 506816, closed Tue, Jan and Jun. Terrace overlooking lake. Creative cuisine: green gnocchi, freshwater fish, 30/45,000.
◆◆◆ *Torchio,* at Pallanza, v. Manzoni 20, ☎ 503352, closed Mon, Jun and Dec. In historical centre. Regional and international cuisine: pennette di Vittorino, filet of coregone alla Verbano, 30/45,000.

Recommended
Archery: *Compagnia arcieri Val Grande,* at Intra, vicolo del Forte 29, ☎ 43376.
Boat trips: to Isola Madre, ☎ 503220 (departures from Pallanza every 30 mns).
Canoeing: *Polisportiva Verbano,* at Intra, v. De Lorenzi 12, ☎ 501429; *Canottieri Intra,* v. Ticino 4, ☎ 42136.
Marina: ☎ 5421.
Tennis: at Pallanza, v. Piave, ☎ 503341; at Intra, rione Fornace 8, ☎ 41039.
Waterskiing: *Club nautico Mergozzo,* at Pallanza, v. alla Castagnola 25; boating office at Mergozzo Lake, Fondotoce, v. Turati, ☎ 496330.

VERCELLI*

Milan 75, Turin 80, Rome 618 km
Pop. 52,123 ⊠ 13100 ☎ 0161   C3

Vercelli is Europe's rice capital, but its agricultural celebrity tends to obscure its noble past. In the 4C, a bishop, Eusebius, founded the first Piedmontese bishopric here, and between the 12C and 13C the community built one of the first Gothic churches in Italy and one of the first universities in Piedmont. Rice-growing came a little later, but developed rapidly. In the 18C, the fields between Sesia and

Dora Balteo were already being cultivated. Further expansion was made possible thanks to the Cavour canal (→ Chivasso) and better agricultural technology. Today, rice is the only foodstuff produced here.

▶ The **Basilica of S. Andrea★★** (A2) is one of the earliest examples of Italian Gothic architecture. The façade is broken by several loggias, portals and **sculpted lunettes★** attributed to Antelami and his school (13C). There are tall towers on either side and, to the r., noteworthy buttresses, climbing arches, a small loggia, an octagonal lantern and a 14C-15C campanile. The interior is pure Gothic with a ribbed vault above groups of slender columns dividing the three naves; in the second chapel to the r. of the main chapel is the 13C Gothic tomb of the abbot Tommaso Gallo with reliefs and frescos from the 14C. Leaving the church and descending to the l., there are the remaining buildings of the 13C abbey: the cloisters, the chapter house, the sacristy and the parlour. ▶ Nearby is the **cathedral** (A2), rebuilt in the 16C over the remains of St. Eusebius's primitive Christian basilica (5C); it was significantly remodeled in the 18C. Behind it stands a 12C Romanesque campanile. It contains a very rich Treasury *(temporarily closed to public)* and an important chapter library with valuable manuscripts including the so-called Gospel of St. Eusebius (4C) and the Sassone Code also known as Vercelli's Book, perhaps the oldest example of English poetry (11C). ▶ A few civil buildings remain from the Renaissance. One is the **Casa Alciati** (15C), which is near the Baroque **Palazzo Langosco,** site of the **Museo Leone** (B2; *Tue and Thu Apr-mid-Nov 3-5:30 p.m.; winter by appointment every day 10 a.m.-12 noon; closed Sat).* The museum exhibits historical curios concerning Vercelli and various art collections. ▶ Near p. Cavour (B2), a square surrounded by very old porticos in the old city centre, stand the medieval towers of Angelo and Città. ▶ Nearby the **Palazzo Centori** (B3) has a 15C courtyard★ inspired by Bramante. ▶ The **Museo Borgogna★** (B3; *Tue and Thu 3-5 p.m.; Sun 10 a.m.-12:30 p.m.; other days by appointment)* is the second largest regional picture gallery. It contains works by local Renaissance painters such as D. and G. Ferrari, Lanino, Giovenone, Sodoma and Spanzotti, as well as by painters of the Lombardian, Venetian, Central Italian, Provençal, Flemish and Dutch schools. ▶ The former church of **S. Chiara** (B3), the most complete and characteristically Baroque edifice in the city (built 1754 by B.A. Vittone), is part of a monumental complex that was restored in 1967 and converted into a cultural centre. ▶ A series of **frescos★** by G. Ferrari (1529-34), one of the finest Renaissance works in N Italy, is in the 16C church of **S. Cristoforo** (B2).   ☐

Practical information

ⓘ v. Garibaldi 90 (A-B2), ☎ 64631.
🚃 (A1-2) ☎ 65078.
🚌 from station at corso Gastaldi 3 (A1).

Hotels:
★★★ *Europa,* v. Santarosa 16 (B2 a), ☎ 66847, 23 rm ⌀ closed Aug, 65,000; bkf: 3,000. Rest. ◆◆◆ closed Mon and 1-20 Jul. Regional and Italian cuisine: paniscia, wild game, 18/30,000.
★★★ *Modo,* p. Medaglie d'Oro 21, ☎ 57481, 32 rm Ⓟ 73,000; bkf: 6,000.

Restaurant:
◆◆ *Paiolo,* v. Garibaldi 74 (B2 b), ☎ 53577, closed Thu and 10 Jul-10 Aug. Regional and Italian cuisine: tortelloni di magro, cod in green sauce, 25/30,000.

Recommended
Automobile racing: *Alfa Romeo,* at Balocco *(19 km NW).*
Cycling: *G.S. Agraria,* p. Vittoria 3, ☎ 60002; *Velo Club Vercelli,* v. Mucrone 1.
Events: *Good Friday evening car procession; International Music Competition* (Oct) and *Viottiano Festival* (Oct-Dec); *guided tours by air* (May-Jun).

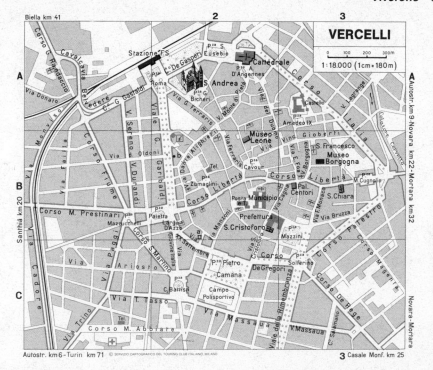

Biella km 41

VERCELLI

0   100   200   300m
1:18.000 (1cm=180m)

Autostr. km 6 – Turin km 71 © SERVIZIO CARTOGRAFICO DEL TOURING CLUB ITALIANO, MILANO

3 Casale Monf. km 25

Flying: *Carlo del Prete Airport,* ☎ 53791; *Aeroclub M. Rigazio,* ☎ 60106.
Horseback riding: *Club Ippico del Mompolino,* at Mottalciata *(29 km NW),* ☎ 857155 (associate of *ANTE*).
Nature park: *Lame del Sesia, Riserve Naturali Speciali Isolone Oldenico* and *Garzaia Villarboit,* office at Albano Vercellese *(13 km N),* v. Cappellania 4, ☎ 73112 (guided tours only, by reservation Mon-Fri).
Technical tourism: visits to mercantile exchange Borsa merci (rice), v. Zumaglini 4, ☎ 5981 (call in advance).

VINADIO

Cuneo 35, Turin 130, Milan 252 km
2,966 ft pop. 871 ⊠ 12010 ☎ 0171   A6

Imposing fortifications separate the valley from the Stura River. Carlo Alberto ordered the construction of Vinadio's defense, turning it into a military stronghold that was coveted by the French. Today, the town is a quiet vacation centre. The hamlet of **Bagni di Vinadio** is a summer health resort offering mineral water cures.   □

Practical information _____

BAGNI DI VINADIO 10 km W.
⚐ ski lifts, cross-country skiing.
⚕ (Jun-Sep), ☎ 95821.

VIVERONE

Vercelli 32, Turin 59, Milan 97 km
Pop. 1,414 ⊠ 13040 ☎ 0161   C3

Viverone is a vacation centre on the way to Ivrea, near the little Lake Viverone which offers boating and fishing. The lake is fed by underwater springs.   □

Practical information _____

≋
ⓘ v. Lido, ☎ 98644.

Hotels:
★★★ *Lido,* v. al Lido 28, ☎ 98024, 26 rm ℗ ⠿ 55,000; bkf: 8,000.
★★★ *Marina,* at Comuna, ☎ 98079, 20 rm ℗ ⠿ ⌘ ⊠ ✗ closed 3-31 Jan, 60,000; bkf: 5,000.
★★★ *Royal,* v. Lungolago 19, ☎ 98038, 32 rm ℗ ♿ 55,000; bkf: 5,000.

⚐ ★★ *Internazionale del Sole,* at Comuna, 220 pl, ☎ 98169.

Recommended
Swimming: v. Provinciale, ☎ 98163.
Waterskiing: *Le ski nautique,* lungolago P. Becco, ☎ 98420.
Wine: Serra regional wine outlet at Castello di Roppolo.
Young people's activities: sailboat races (ages 7-14) organized by *Lega Navale di Torino,* ☎ 011/530979.

Rome

Walking through Rome is unlike walking through any other city in the world. Walking through Rome means strolling through time. Close to 3,000 years of history are inscribed on the banks of the Tiber River and around the famous seven hills. Both glorious success and shameful defeat have left visible traces throughout the city. The visitor will quickly realize that there is no one single Rome, but that the city is a synthesis of its history: antique Rome, Christian Rome, Renaissance Rome, Baroque Rome and modern Rome. The visitor will discover all these facets of the city and will learn how the city has always adapted and survived these major changes. It is the Romans who make Rome what it is. They love to talk and are curious about all the events that happen in their streets. The small cafés with their inimitable espresso are always full late into the night. Every holiday means crowded streets and new shows. Rome's famous movie studio, Cinecitta, created a new approach to cinema after the war, and its actors and directors are known around the world. Romans are very much concerned by appearances. Italian fashion enhances women's beauty, and men all over Europe are happy to wear clothes made in Italy. Jewelry designers today are as imaginative as those who designed jewels for the wealthy women of Rome's imperial court. Modern Roman architects and furniture designers have had a broad influence which emphasizes harmony of form and daring colour schemes. Nowhere more than in Rome will the visitor to Italy get a sense of the continuity of Italian civilization. In the streets or on the piazzas, in the gardens and churches or in front of palaces, the visitor will understand why Rome has always considered itself a capital, eternally renewing herself and finding strength in her rich past. □

Facts and figures

Location: *Rome is capital of the Italian Republic and principal town of the province of Latium. It is 575 km from Milan, 280 km from Florence and 220 km from Naples.*
Area and population: *Rome covers an area of 1507.60 sq km with 2,830,650 inhabitants.*
Postal code: *00100.*
Telephone dialing code: *06.*

● Don't miss

Buildings of the Roman period: the Colosseum★★, the Arch of Constantine★★, Trajan's Column★★, the Roman Forum with the Basilica of Maxentius★★ and the Arch of Titus★★, the Palatine★★, Marcus Aurelius' Column★★, the Pantheon, the Ara Pacis Augustae★★, the Baths of Caracalla★★ and the Via Appia Antica. Museums: the Galleria Doria-Pamphili★★, the Galleria Borghese★★, the Museo Nazionale di Villa Giulia and the Museo Nazionale Romano★★. Churches, palaces and squares: il Gesù★★, S. Maria Sopra Minerva★★, S. Maria del Popolo★★, S. Agnese★★, S. Costanza★★, S. Maria degli Angeli★★, S. Maria Maggiore★★, S. Giovanni in Laterano★★, S. Lorenzo fuori le Mura★★ with cloister★★, S. Maria in Trastevere★★, Bramante's Tempietto★★ in S. Pietro in Montorio★★, the Palazzo Venezia★★, the Palazzo della Cancelleria★★, the Palazzo Farnese★★, the Palazzo Barberini★★, La Farnesina★★, Castel Sant'Angelo★★, Piazza del Campidoglio★★ with the Palazzi dei Musei Capitolano★★ and dei Conservatori★★, the piazza Navona★★ and the piazza del Quirinale★★. Also the Trevi Fountain★★, the Porta Pia★★, the Pincio★★ and the Villa Borghese★★. In Vatican City: St. Peter's Basilica★★ and Square★★, Vatican Museums and Galleries★★ with Raphael's Stanze★★ and the Sistine Chapel★★, the Pinacoteca★★. The great panorama★★ of Rome from the esplanade of the Victory Beacon on the Gianicolo.

510

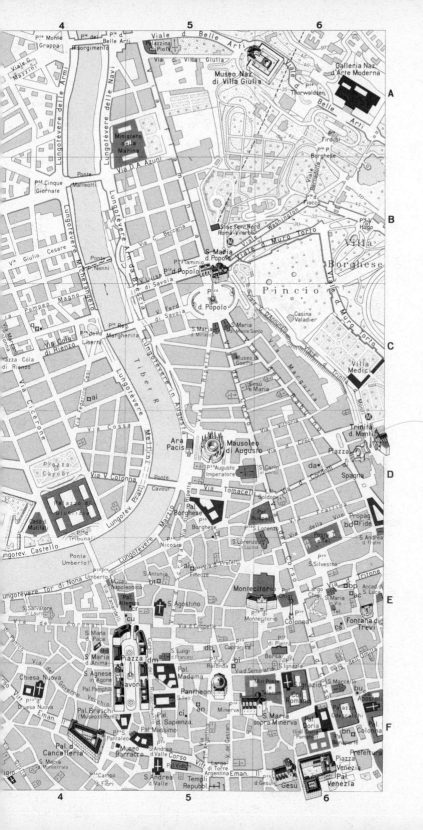

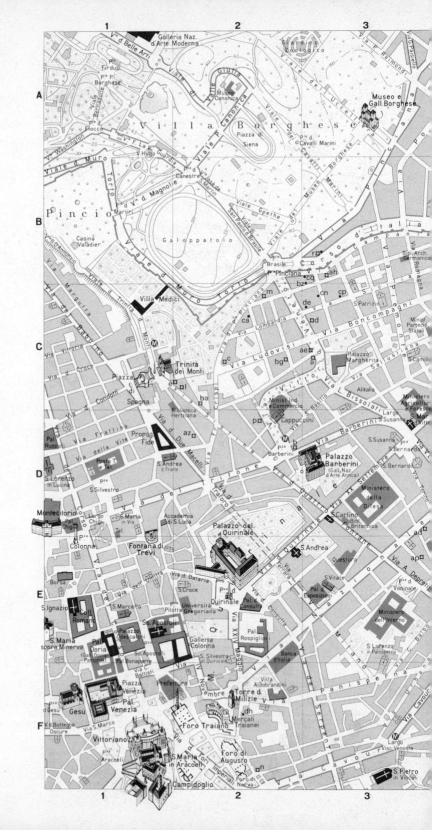

512

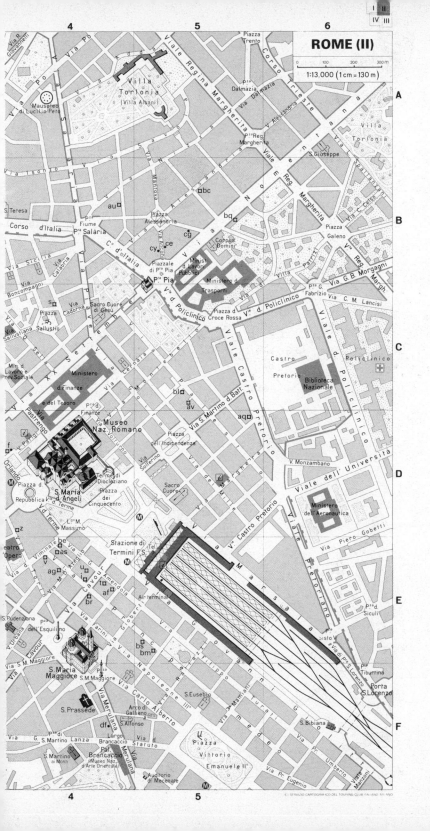

ROME (II)

1:13,000 (1 cm = 130 m)

A

Villa Torlonia (Villa Albani)

Villa Torlonia

Mausoleo di Lucilio Peto

P.za Trento

Corso Trieste

Piazza Dalmazia

Via Dalmazia

Via Alessandria

S. Giuseppe

Viale Regina Margherita

bc

au

Corso d'Italia

P.za Salaria

P.za Fiume

Piazza Alessandria

bq

V.le Reg. Margherita

Piazza Galeno

V.le G.B. Morgagni

B

Via Stelto

Via Calabria

C.so d'Italia

cg

cy ce

Ministero del Lavoro Pubblici

Corpus Domini

Villa

P.za G. Fabrizio

Via C.M. Lancisi

Via Boncompagni

Piazzale di P.ta Pia

P.ta Pia

Ministero dei Trasporti

Via di Policlinico

Piazza d. Croce Rossa

V.le d. Policlinico

C

Sacro Cuore di Gesù

Piazza Cadorna

Via Sallustiana

Sallustio

Min. d. Lavoro e Prev. Sociale

Ministero d. Finanze e del Tesoro

bl

av

Castro Pretorio

Biblioteca Nazionale

Policlinico

Via Castro Pretorio

Viale di Policlinico

Pastrengo

P.za Finanze

Museo Naz. Romano

aq

Via S. Martino d. Batt.

D

Orlando

Termе di Diocleziano

Piazza dell'Indipendenza

Piazza dei Cinquecento

Sacro Cuore

V. Monzambano

Viale dell'Università

Ministero dell'Aeronautica

S. Maria d. Angeli

Piazza d. Repubblica

Terme

L.go M. Massimo

M

z

Stazione di Termini F.S.

Via Castro Pretorio

Viale Pretoriano

Via Piero Gobetti

Teatro d. Opera

be

as

ag

af

br

Air terminal

M

Via Marsala

E

P.za Siculi

S. Pudenziana

dell'Esquilino

Via Cavour

bs

bm

Sisto V

Via di P.ta S. Lorenzo

Tiburtina

Porta S. Lorenzo

S. Maria Maggiore

S.M. Maggiore

S. Eusebio

S. Prassede

Arco di Gallieno

S. Alfonso

S. Bibiana

F

df

Via Merulana

Largo Brancaccio

P.za di S. Martino Lanza

S. Martino ai Monti

Pal. Brancaccio (Museo Naz. d'Arte Orientale)

Piazza Vittorio Emanuele II

Auditorio di Mecenate

Via Pr. Eugenio

Viale Manzoni

M

4   5   6

514

ROME (III)

1:13.000 (1 cm = 130 m)

0   100   200   300 m

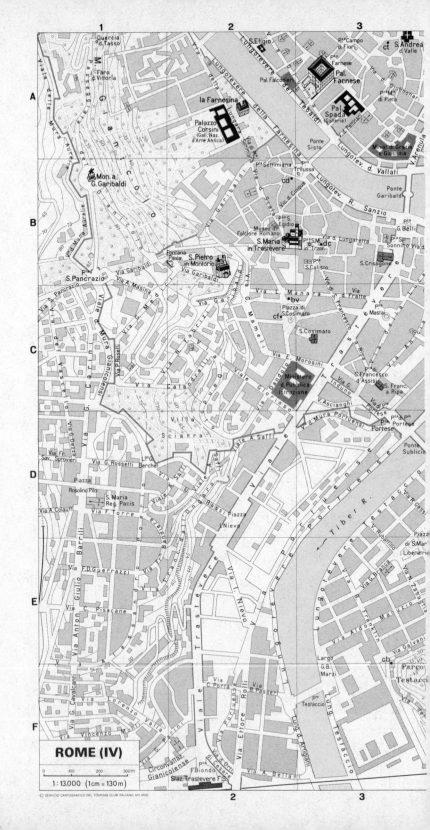

ROME (IV)

0 100 200 300m

1:13.000 (1cm = 130 m)

© SERVIZIO CARTOGRAFICO DEL TOURING CLUB ITALIANO, MILANO

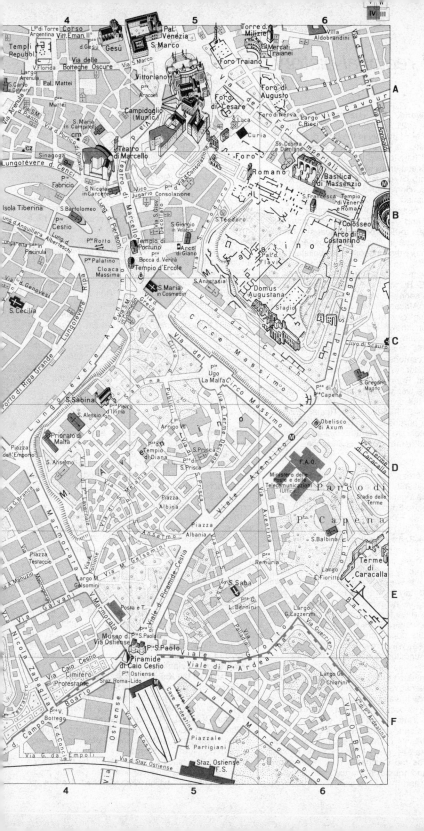

Brief regional history

Water service in imperial Rome

Throughout the Roman countryside are the large arcs of aqueducts which brought water to Rome from the Apennine Mountains. The water was actually a public service and was paid for by the government. The fourteen aqueducts brought some one billion liters of water daily into the 247 water towers of the city before sending them to the various public fountains or to the baths in large houses via a system of large lead canals. Private service was limited to the ground floors of the more well-to-do citizens. Whole sections of the city never received running water and everyone was supposed to keep some water on hand in case of fire. Surplus water was channeled into the sewer network which drained the lower portions of the city that often flooded and could become health hazards. Today, near the Ponte Rotto, are the remnants of an arc 15 feet in diameter through which the cloaca maxima spilled out into the Tiber. Nonetheless, this great underground network developed by Agrippa did not bring cleanliness and comfort to all the inhabitants of Rome. There were only a few toilets in the better neighborhoods along the water network. The public utility company set up a few of these latrines all over the city. They were decorated and had a row of seats. Users would stay and chat and the latrines quickly became part of the daily routine of any well-to-do Roman. Others would simply use pots which were occasionally collected by fertilizer merchants or simply emptied at the local dump.

8C BC-3C AD

Rome rules the world. The legendary date for the founding of Rome is 21 April 754 BC, when **Romulus** traced the perimeter of the city in the form of a square on the **Palatine hill.** ● Actually, the **Latins** are said to have arrived in Italy toward the end of the second millenium and their numerous hill-top settlements gradually coalesced into city-states, the greatest of which was Rome. Its dominant position was assured by its geographical situation — it was within easy reach of the sea and commanded the crossing of the Tiber. ● At the end of the 7C BC it was governed by kings (some said to have been Etruscans). Under them Rome advanced in civilization, prosperity and size. After a century the kingdom was abolished and an aristocratic republican constitution set up. ● Rome conquered the surrounding province of **Latium** in the 4C BC and the **Italian peninsula** in 270 BC. After a series of wars with Carthage, capital of the North African Phoenician Empire, Rome became the ruling city of the Mediterranean and finally of the then known world. ● **Augustus,** the first Emperor, is said to have 'found a city of brick and left it — at his death — a city of marble', but it really took two centuries more to build the imperial capital. ● Later, in 272 AD, the Emperor **Aurelianus** surrounded Rome with walls — a sure sign of decline. Rome was, indeed, soon to lose its role as the centre of the civilized world. ● The Emperor **Diocletian** (284-305) divided the Roman Empire, for administrative purposes, into two parts (East and West) and the Emperor **Constantine** moved the imperial throne to the Eastern capital of Byzance.

4C-14C

The sign of the cross. Constantine the Great was converted to Christianity by the appearance in the sky of a cross with the legend — by this sign you will conquer — and, with the **Edict of Milan** (313), he decreed toleration for all the Christians throughout Europe. Later (in 334) Christianity became the official religion of the Roman Empire and soon the great **basilicas** started to be built. ● The Empire was to end in 476, but even before this date the city had twice been captured by Barbarians (Goths in 410 and Vandals in 445). It was the armies of the Eastern Empire that freed Italy from these invaders, but as a result Rome became no more than another Byzantine city in an Italy ruled from Constantinople. ● Two centuries later, however, Rome was the centre of the temporal rule of the popes, and in 800 **Charlemagne,** King of the Franks, was crowned in Rome with the title of Caesar Augustus, Emperor of the West, by Pope Leo III. By this coronation the destinies of the two great institutions of church and state were to be inextricably interwoven with many important future consequences. ● It was **Leo IV,** in 847, who walled that part of Rome he occupied against the Barbarians, thus creating the **Vatican.** ● In the medieval city of Rome, which was smaller and had less than a twentieth of the inhabitants of imperial Rome, the marble and mosaic workers — many from the same families — were known as the **Cosmati.** They made pavements, pulpits and tombs in marble, with inlays of coloured stones, and they were also sculptors. The chief figures producing frescos and mosaic work were **Filippo Rusuti** and **Jacopo Torriti,** while **Pietro Cavallini** (1273-1308) was the leader of the Roman school that contributed much to the birth of Italian painting. ● During the same period, a **Comune** was established on the **Capitoline** hill (1143-4) and became a third force between the popes and the great feudal families. Emperors came from Germany to be crowned, and pilgrims thronged the Holy City, centre of Christianity, for the first **Jubilee,** proclaimed by **Boniface VIII** in 1300. ● This was followed by a period known as the **Babylonian captivity** (1309-77) when the popes left Rome for Avignon, in France, and the city declined once more.

15C-18C

Capital of the arts. On their return from Avignon the popes chose to live on the **Vatican** hill rather than in the Lateran, next to the crumbling Constantine basilica of St. Peter, already a thousand years old. In the 15C the temporal power of the popes, within the structure of the Italian regional states, was consolidated as a **principality,** stretching from the Po to the boundaries of the Kingdom of Southern Italy (with the exception of Florence and Tuscany). ● The humanistic renewal of the arts, started in Florence, reached Rome. ● With the elevation to the throne of Peter of **Julius II** (1503), Rome's great season as capital of the arts exploded into being. **Bramante, Raphael** and **Michelangelo,** among many others, were working in Rome, and masterpiece followed masterpiece. ● The **'sack of Rome'** (1527) by Charles V's Protestant soldiers did little more than create a pause in the movement, which re-established itself in the new cultural atmosphere and was rapidly absorbed into the spirit of the Catholic **Counter-Reformation** (concluding in the Council of Trent, 1563). ● In the second half of the 16C buildings erected by the great late Renaissance **architects** confirmed the monumental character of the city; town planning was carried out on lines laid down by **Sixtus V** (1585-90). The **papal state** kept out of European wars. During this time **Caravaggio** was producing paintings of genius, and a little later the new **St. Peter's** was consecrated by **Urban VIII** (1626). It is a church that embodies the lavish and imaginative ideas of the **Baroque**. ● In the wake of the Baroque, the 18C added the final touches to the image of the city (Trevi Fountain, Trinità dei Monti (Spanish) steps), while in the cultural climate of the Enlightenment interest in the **Roman art of antiquity** revived, as well as interest in conservation. (Winckelmann developed his doctrines of classical art in Rome.) Admirers and men of letters streamed into the city from all over Europe.

Discovery of the Laocoon

In the 15C and 16C, peasants plowing their fields near Rome would often find a vase or statue. Merchants were eager to see such finds and would buy them for rich collectons. On 14 January 1506, in a vineyard where the baths of Titus have been located, a farmer found a group of statues depicting Laocoon and his two sons being attacked by serpents. People flocked to see the find and Felix de Fredi, the man who had found the statues, became the hero of the day. Michelangelo, Sangallo and other artists admired the work, which had been famous among the ancients and about which Pliny had spoken. The statues referred to an episode of the Trojan War in which Laocoon, priest of Apollo, was strangled along with his two sons by serpents sent by Minerva because he had wanted to stop the Trojans from letting the Greek's wooden horse into the city. Pope Jules II bought the find for 600 ducats and placed it prominently in the Vatican collection.

19C-20C
Capital of Italy. Temporal dominion was interrupted for the first time by the **French** with the first proclamation of the Republic in Rome (1798-9) and the deportation of Pius VI. ● **Pius VII,** elected in Venice (1800), entered Rome, but in 1809 **Napoleon** made Rome, which he had never seen, the second city of the Empire and proclaimed his son King of Rome. ● With the **Restoration** (1814), Pius VII returned to Rome. ● In 1849 the short-lived **Roman Republic** was proclaimed, inspired by Giuseppe Mazzini and defended by **Garibaldi** against **Napoleon III's** expeditionary force. ● On 20 September 1870 the Italian Bersaglieri soldiers entered Rome by the **Porta Pia.** ● On 1 July 1871 the city became the capital of Italy. The quarrel between the papacy and the Italian government over who should rule Rome was resolved by the **Lateran Treaty** (1929), which was signed by **Cardinal Gaspari,** on behalf of the pope, and **Benito Mussolini,** as Plenipotentiary for Italy. The latter recognized the sovereignty of the Vatican, while the Holy See acquiesced to the occupation of the rest of the former papal states.

▶ ABBAZIA TRE FONTANE
NW of EUR

The abbey stands at the place where St. Paul was beheaded. According to tradition three fountains sprang up at the points where his head rebounded, and three churches were built here. In the courtyard at the entrance to the abbey is the medieval church of **S. Vincenzo e S. Anastasio** (1221) with the octagonal church of **S. Maria Scala Coeli,** rebuilt in 1583 by G. Della Porta, on its r. The **three fountains** are in the adjacent church of **S. Paolo alle Tre Fontane,** rebuilt in 1599, again by Della Porta. ◻

▶ Via APPIA ANTICA**
from porta S. Sebastiano   III F4

The Old Appian Way is the consular road built in 312 BC by the censor Appius Claudius to link Rome with southern Italy. Its suburban stretch is one of the most picturesque in Rome *(by car, one way from the catacombs of S. Callisto to the Casal Rotondo).* Starting at the **Porta S. Sebastiano** (→) the route reaches the **catacombs of San Callisto** (→) beyond the 17C church of **Domine quo vadis** where, according to tradition, Jesus appeared to St. Peter. Further on is the church of **S. Sebastiano** (→) and near it the **via delle Sette Chiese** strikes off W to cross the v. Ardeatina not far from the **Fosse Ardeatine,** which is now an offical memorial to 335 Italians shot in reprisals by the Germans on 14 March 1944. A little further along the via delle Sette Chiese are the gigantic **Catacombs of Domitilla★** *(8:30 a.m.-12 noon and 2:30-5 p.m.; closed Tue),* originally hypogeums (underground rooms) on the Flavian estate. The visit includes: the basilica built in the 4C over the tomb of S. Nereo and S. Achilleo; the Flavian hypogeum (2C) and parts of the burial area with 3C-4C Christian frescos. Returning past the via Appia Antica, beyond the extensive ruins of the **Circus of Maxentius** (309), the road reaches the famous **tomb of Cecilia Metella★** *(9 a.m.-1:30 p.m.; Sun 9 a.m.-12:30 p.m.; closed Mon),* a cylindrical tomb of a daughter-in-law of Crassus, the triumvir, which dates from the final decades of the Republic. It is here that the **ancient section of the Appian Way★★** begins, with stretches of the old paving and remains of ancient tombs on both sides, framed in cypresses and umbrella pines. The **Casal Rotondo** *(after the 7-km marker)* is a large cylindrical tomb of the Augustan era with a house and olive garden on top of it. A little further on, at Frattocchie, the old road joins the Appia Nuova. ◻

tomb of Cecilia Metella

▶ ARCH OF CONSTANTINE**

near the Colosseum   III B2

This is the last triumphal monument of the classical era, built in 315 to celebrate Constantine's victory over Maxentius near Ponte Milvio (312). The eight columns surrounding the three arches date from the time of Domitian (81-96); the friezes and relief medallions were originally made for temples of Trajan, Hadrian and Marcus Aurelius and when compared with the reliefs made for the monument, they reveal the changing taste that had taken place in the world of art.   □

Arch of Constantine and Colosseum

▶ BASILICA OF MAXENTIUS**
(Basilica di Massenzio)

on N side of Forum Romanum   III A1-2

The three enormous **arches** with octagonal panels that remain rise to a height of over 80 ft. They represent only a third (one of the side aisles) of the building started by Maxentius (306-312) and completed by his rival Constantine. The entire building was 263 ft by 197 ft, and the nave 114 ft high. Excessively shallow foundations in unstable ground caused the building to collapse in the late Middle Ages. The head of the colossal statue of the Emperor **Constantine**, with its large staring eyes, is now in the courtyard of the Palazzo dei Conservatori in Campidoglio (→). The bronze sheets on the roof were removed and used for the roof of the first basilica of St. Peter.   □

▶ BATHS OF CARACALLA**

in Porta Capena park   III D-E2

Baths had a place in the life of ancient Rome for which it is difficult to find modern parallels. Under the Empire they were the preferred daily meeting place, and a great deal of effort was put into their construction, both in Rome and in the provinces. The first major Roman baths were those built by Agrippa in the area of the Campus Martius (25 BC). Even in ancient times the baths inaugurated by Caracalla in 216 and further elaborated by his successors were considered the most magnificent yet seen. Because they were so large (they could accommodate more than 1,600 people) they were built on the edge of the city and fed by the Acqua Marcia. The pavements of the exedrae were covered with marbles and polychrome mosaics of athletes preparing to compete. Sculpture on a large scale (including the Farnese Hercules, the Farnese Flora and the Belvedere Torso) decorated the niches of the major rooms. The majestic **ruins** are still the best source of information about the character of

such buildings, their organization and the ingenuity with which architectural and technical problems were solved. As well as rooms for bathing the complex included gymnasia, libraries, meeting rooms and gardens *(9 a.m.-1 hr before sunset; Sun, Mon and hols 9 a.m.-1 p.m.).*   □

▶ BATHS OF DIOCLETIAN*
(Terme di Diocleziano)

p. della Repubblica and p. dei Cinquecento   II D4

The porticoed palaces (late 19C) following the curve of the piazza (formerly p. dell'Esedra) run round the edge of the central semicircle of one side of the **Baths of Diocletian★**. Important ruins of them remain today. They were built by Maximian and Diocletian between 298 and 306 and originally occupied an area of about 33 acres.

▶ The church of **S. Maria degli Angeli★★**, for which Michelangelo adapted the *tepidarium* (the warm room) of the Baths, was rebuilt by Vanvitelli (1749), who altered the orientation. A circular vestibule leads to the **transept** (the nave in Michelangelo's version) where it is difficult to decide whether to admire the strength of the great Florentine's design or the majesty of late imperial Roman architecture; Vanvitelli's apse occupies the site of a frigidarium (cooling room). ▶ The **Museo Nazionale Romano★★** *(entrance at p. dei Cinquecento 79; 9 a.m.-1 p.m.; closed Mon; not all open to public)* occupies some rooms of the baths and a Carthusian convent was established in the enormous ruins in the 16C. ▶ This major archaeological museum, one of the few which, as well as Roman and Hellenistic works and Roman copies of Greek works, also has some Greek originals, is based around the **Ludovisi collection★**, started in the 17C by Cardinal Ludovico Ludovisi. ▶ **Greek and Hellenistic originals** include the **Ludovisi throne** with a bas-relief, perhaps of the birth of Venus, a 5C BC Italiot work; a torso of a *young athlete★★* (5C BC); the *Niobid* from the Orti Sallustiani★★ (5C BC); a *young girl running★* (4C BC); *Paetus and his wife Arria killing themselves★*, of the school of Pergamon (3C BC); the *Venus of Cyrene★★*, Hellenistic; the *Young Man Ephebus of Subiaco★★*, Hellenistic; *Boy with a Staff★*, Hellenistic bronze; *Boxer Resting★*, Hellenistic bronze; the delicate *Maiden of Anzio★*, Hellenistic; *Maiden sitting on a Rock★*, Hellenistic; *Orestes and Electra★* signed by Menelaus (1C BC). ▶ There are also excellent copies of Phidias' *Athene Parthenos; Satyr Pouring Wine★*, after Praxitiles; the *Ares Ludovisi★*, after Lysippos; the *Tiber Apollo* from a 5C Greek original; a statue of *Hera* from a 5C Greek original; the *Discobolos* from the Castel Parziano★★ and the *Discobolos Lancelotti★★*, a replica of a bronze by Myron; *Amazon charging a Barbarian★*, school of Pergamon; *Head of a Dying Persian★*, school of Pergamon; the *Apollo* of Anzio, Hellenistic school; a *Girl on a Throne★*, Hellenistic school; and the *Sleeping Hermaphrodite★*, Hellenistic school. ▶ The collection includes fine **Roman works** as well, such as a *Head of Hera★*, in neo-Attic style (1C); a marble altar with plane fronds and bucranes★ (1C); *Augustus as High Priest★*; the altar of Ostia★ with reliefs of Roman legends (124); imperial portrait busts of *Nero★*, *Vespasian★* and *Hadrian★*; bust of a *bearded personage★* (3C); **Sarcophagi** with scenes of a *battle between the Romans and Barbarians★* (3C), and *pastoral scenes★* (3C), and the sarcophagus of Acilia★ (3C). ▶ There are rooms housing **stucco★** and **wall paintings★** from a building of the Augustan age discovered in the Farnesina; finally, the frescoed room from the **Villa of Livia at Prima Porta★★** has been reconstructed in its entirety; it is decorated with a marvelous continuous representation of a fruit and flower garden. ▶ Inscriptions, ancient statues, reliefs and steles are also to be found in the great Carthusian **cloister** surrounded by monks' cells, beautiful architecture traditionally attributed to Michelangelo (1565).   □

▶ CAPITOLINE HILL*
(Il Campidoglio) IV A5

This smallest and most famous of the seven hills of Rome rises about 150 ft above the Forum. In ancient times its relative isolation made it an ideal site for the *arx* (or citadel) which was located between its northern peak (now the site of the church of S. Maria in Aracoeli) and the Temple of Jove, the most venerated in the city, on its southern peak (on the r. of the piazza del Campidoglio, which occupies the dip between the two). In time the buildings on the hill fell into disrepair, and stone was taken away for use elsewhere. After the Sack of Rome (1527), Pope Paul III decided that the area should be revitalized and started by ordering Michelangelo to replace the equestrian statue of Marcus Aurelius which had survived in the Lateran because it was thought to represent the Christian Emperor Constantine. Michelangelo did not approve of the plan, but allowed himself to be persuaded to provide a base for the statue, which finally made an ideal centrepiece for the marvelous square which he designed in 1536, universally recognized as his architectural masterpiece. It was completed in the 17C by others who did not completely respect his original intentions. The **Cordonata★** (or ramp) conceived by Michelangelo leads up to the **piazza del Campidoglio★★**. On the balustrade at the top are two statues of the **Dioscuri** and other statues, trophies and columns from the imperial period. The statue of **Marcus Aurelius★★**, a 2C work, is at present being restored. On the two sides of the square are the Palazzo dei Conservatori (on the r.) and the Palazzo Nuovo (on the l.), symmetrical, with majestic façades framing the **Palazzo Senatorio,** which is built over the **Tabularium** (in which the State archives are kept; its arcaded gallery can be seen at the rear of the present building). The Palazzo Senatorio was started in 1541 to plans by Michelangelo (steps★) and was completed in 1605 by Giacomo Della Porta and Girolamo Rainaldi, who altered the original façade design. The **torre capitolina** above the building (M. Longhi the Elder, 1578-82) no longer contains the famous bell; it used to be rung to summon public assemblies, but was removed in the 13C. There is a statue of **Julius Caesar★** dating from the period of Trajan in the council chamber.

▶ The two **Capitoline Museums** came into being when Sixtus IV presented a set of classical bronze statues to the people of Rome in 1471. They include the famous *She-Wolf* and are the oldest public collection in the world. ▶ The **Palazzo Nuovo★★**, built faithfully by Rainaldi (1655) to Michelangelo's dignified design, houses the **Museo Capitolino★** *(9 a.m.-2 p.m.; Tue and Thu also 5-8 p.m.; Sat also 8:30-11 p.m.; Sun and hols 9 a.m.-1 p.m.; closed Mon).* Important ancient marbles are exhibited here in an exemplary Neoclassical setting: the Amendola★ sarcophagus (2C); the mosaic of the *Four Doves★* from the Villa of Hadrian; the *Capitoline Venus★,* Hellenistic in origin; two reliefs from the period of Hadrian of *Perseus freeing Andromeda★* and *Selene and Endymion★;* 64 busts★ of Emperors and Empresses in the **Sala degli Imperatori** and 79 busts★ of philosophers and men of letters; *The Old and the Young Centaur★* of the period of Hadrian; the *Wounded Amazon★,* the *Boy with a Goose★,* the *Dying Gaul★, Amor and Psyche★* and the *Resting Satyr★,* all Roman reproductions of Greek or Hellenistic originals. ▶ The façade of the enormous **Palazzo dei Conservatori★★** is identical with that of the Palazzo Nuovo; it was built by Giacomo Della Porta (1568) to Michelangelo's design. The route through the museum

takes in sumptuous rooms and important and varied works of art *(opening times same as for Museo Capitolino)* such as Arnolfo di Cambio's statue of Carlo d'Angiò★ on the staircase; statues of Urban VIII★ (Bernini) and Innocent X★ (Algardi), the *Spinario,* or *Boy Pulling a Thorn From his Foot★* (bronze, 1C BC), the bronze portrait known as *Junius Brutus★,* the *Capitoline She-Wolf★* (an Etruscan bronze from Veii, 6C-5C BC, with twins added by Pollaiolo) and *9 Roman Scenes★* by Gaspare Vanvitelli in the **Sale dei Conservatori★.** Graeco-Roman statues in the **Museo del Palazzo dei Conservatori★** include the *Esquiline Venus★* (1C BC), a headless statue of a *Girl wearing a peplum★* (Greek style, 5C BC), a 5C stele of a *Girl with a Dove★,* Roman litter★ with ornamental bronzes (1C), a colossal head of *Constantine★* and this is merely a selection of the magnificent pieces on display. In the Passage of the Roman Wall one side is built out of the remains of the **Temple of Capitoline Jove** (6C), the principal place of worship of the Roman era. Exhibits in the **Pinacoteca Capitolina★** include: *Woman Taken in Adultery★* by Palma Vecchio, *Baptism of Christ★★* by Titian, *Man with a Crossbow★* by Lotto, *Mary Magdalene★* by Tintoretto, 2 double portraits★ by Van Dyck, *Romulus and Remus fed by the Wolf★* by Rubens, *Portrait of a Man★* by Velasquez, *Gypsy Fortune-Teller★* and *St. John the Baptist★★* by Caravaggio, *S. Petronilla★* by Guercino and precious porcelain★ from Sassonia, Capodimonte and other 18C factories. ▶ There is access to the terrace which provides the best **view★★ of the Forum Romanum** (→) from the side of the Palazzo Senatorio. ▶ In the Middle Ages, the elders met to discuss public affairs in the church of **S. Maria in Aracoeli★** with its plain brick façade. It can be reached by monumental steps from the foot of the hill or by a flight of steps to the right of the Palazzo Nuovo. The early Christian basilica occupied the site on which the Sibyl (woman oracle) predicted the coming of Christ to Augustus; it was rebuilt in Romanesque-Gothic style by the Franciscans in the mid-13C. On the Baroque high altar is a 10C **Madonna★** of the Roman school; other works include Donatello's tomb slab for G. Crivelli★ (1432), the *Life of S. Bernardino* frescos by Pinturicchio (*c.* 1485), a *Madonna and Saints★* by Pietro Cavallini and *St. Antony of Padua* by Benezzo Gozzoli (*c.* 1449). □

▶ CASA DEL BURCARDO
v. del Sudario 44 I F5

This building in the German Gothic style was commissioned in 1503 by Johann Burckhardt of Strasbourg and houses the **Raccolta Teatrale** (theatrical museum; *9 a.m.-1:30 p.m.; closed Thu and Aug)* with prints, masks, marionettes, costumes and ancient terra-cotta statuettes documenting the history of the theatre. □

▶ CASTEL SANT'ANGELO**
lungotevere Castello I D-E3-4

The original grandiose **mausoleum** commissioned (135-9) by the Emperor Hadrian for himself and his successors became a fortress less than a century later when Aurelian (271) transformed it into a fortified bridgehead on the right bank of the Tiber, a function which it also retained under the popes (it was connected to the Vatican Palace by a covered way, the *passetto*).

▶ The outer wall (with the exception of Sangallo's **corner ramparts,** built under Alexander VI) is that of the original square base dating from the period of Hadrian, and the **round tower,** in blocks of travertine and peperino (volcanic rock), is also Roman. It was later surrounded with a curtain wall which included the loggia of Julius II. ▶ At the top of the keep was a bronze quadriga driven by the Emperor Hadrian. This has been replaced by Verschaffelt's **angel** (1753), a reminder of the angel who appeared on the top of the keep to Gregory the Great in 590 while he was passing in procession to pray for the end of the plague. The **Campana della Misericordia**, beside the angel, was rung to announce executions. ▶ The castle now houses the **Museo Nazionale di Castel S. Angelo** *(9 a.m.-1 p.m.; Sun and hols 9 a.m.-12 noon; closed Mon)*, one of Rome's most striking museums. It gives a clear view of the history of the castle and has fine *objets d'art* and furniture. ▶ Particularly important are the apartments of the Renaissance popes and the prisons, including Cagliostro's cell.   ☐

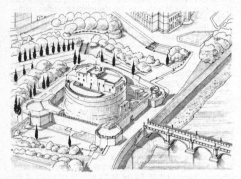

Castel Sant'Angelo

▶ CATACOMBS OF SAN CALLISTO*
along via Appia Antica from Porta S. Sebastiano   III F4

These important ancient Roman catacombs *(8:30 a.m.-12 noon and 2:30-5 pm; closed Wed)* date from the 2C and were the burial ground of several popes in the 3C. *(Groups can be taken by a guide to visit oldest part of burial complex.)* Only the **papal crypt** (3C), the **crypt** containing the tomb of S. Cecilia (with 7C-8C frescos), the 5 Cubiculi of the Sacraments (with important early Christian frescos) and the crypt of Pope Eusebius (4C) can be visited. The **oratory of S. Sisto and S. Cecilia**, a small basilica with three apses, is at the end of an avenue of cypresses.   ☐

▶ COLOSSEUM**
                                              III B2

The building was started by Vespasian (72) because Augustus' amphitheatre in the Campus Martius had been destroyed in the great fire of 64, under Nero. The Colosseum was opened by Titus in 80 (5,000 wild animals were killed in the opening games which lasted for 100 days), and the third Flavian Emperor, Domitian, added the fourth storey. The correct name of the building is **Flavian Amphitheatre** *(9 a.m.-1 hr before dusk; Sun and hols 9 a.m.-1 p.m.)*.

▶ One third of the **ellipse**, more than 1640 ft in circumference, is intact. During the games, a special detachment of sailors from the navy was laid on to spread out sails to protect spectators from the hot Roman sun. The brackets used to support the poles are still visible, on the walls of the fourth level, and the rings through which they fitted into the cornice. ▶ The 50,000 spectators able to attend the games were admitted to the interior tiers by 80

numbered arches. Entry was free. The imperial stand and seats reserved for senators, priests, magistrates and vestal virgins were on the podium; the **cavea** (seats) were divided into three tiers, the first reserved for the knights and the second for Roman citizens, while others stood on the third tier or the terrace above it. ▶ In the **arena** (249 ft by 151 ft) 30 counterweighted hoists were used to bring animals and men up from the subterranean passages to the games, which were notoriously cruel. It was also po⌐sible to bring up scenery representing woods or hills during the proceedings. The amphitheatre was restored c. 230 by Alexander Severus after extensive storm damage. In 249, at the celebrations for the millennium of Rome, 2,500 gladiators fought simultaneously. Gladiatorial games were finally prohibited by an edict of Honorius in 404, after a monk, Telemachus, had thrown himself into the arena to stop the fighting and been massacred by the crowd. Other games and combats between wild beasts continued for another century and a half. ▶ The tradition that the Colosseum was the scene of the martyrdom of early Christians seems to be unfounded.   ☐

The catacombs
The Roman catacombs form an underground city of over 600 acres. The name comes from the Greek prefix kata (down) and the Gallic word cumba (hollow), denoting an underground cave. Cremation was customary throughout the Roman Empire, but the Christians refused this because they thought it would make it impossible for the resurrection of the flesh of the Last Judgment. Cremated remains were placed in tombs which were protected as sacred by Roman law and at first the Christians also placed the bodies of their dead in them. Later, with persecution, came underground burial, and tunnels were dug out of the tufa of the Roman countryside. The catacombs are complex labyrinths of underground galleries (ambulacra) with burial places (cubicula) superimposed and dug out wherever there was space, even in the chapels, under the steps, in the pavement, as well as along the walls of the ambulacri. Christian painting was born in the decoration of the catacombs. After the fall of the Roman Empire the remains of martyrs were transferred to the churches inside the walls (on one occasion two thousand corpses were moved) and the catacombs fell into disuse.

▶ DOMUS AUREA
on the Oppian hill   III A2-3

In July 64 there was a great fire in Rome and two-thirds of the city was reduced to ashes. It was said that the reigning Emperor, Nero, had been responsible for the fire which he watched, from a distance, reciting poems (fiddling while Rome burnt), but modern historians rather doubt this story. Nero put the blame on the Christians who he set about persecuting with extreme cruelty. He rebuilt Rome with great magnificence and reared for himself, on the Oppian hill, an immense palace named, from the profusion of its golden ornaments, the *Domus Aurea* (Golden House; *closed at present)*. This palace was later buried by the building of the baths of Trajan. The **ruins** now consist of a series of enormous rooms, still partially decorated with stucco and paintings. The finest are the room with the gilded vault and the octagonal one.   ☐

► **EUR**
v. Cristoforo Colombo   III F3

This acronym is formed from Esposizione Universale di Roma, designed in the late thirties and due for completion in 1942, but prevented by the Second World War. The complex covers a vast area on the l. bank of the Tiber, S of the city. Monumental buildings in thirties style rub shoulders with interesting modern ones; some government offices are housed here.

► Striking among the more recent buildings is the **Palazzo dello Sport**, while enormous edifices such as the **Palazzo della Civiltà del Lavoro**, commonly called the 'square Colosseum' because of its peculiar arches, survive from the original project. ► The **abbazia delle Tre Fontane** (→) is sited near EUR, and the complex itself includes the **Museo Preistorico ed Etnografico Luigi Pigorini★** (→), the **Museo dell'Alto Medioevo** (→), the **Museo Nazionale delle Arti e Tradizioni Popolari** (→) and the **Museo della Civiltà Romana★** (→).   □

► **La FARNESINA★★**
v. della Lungara   IV A2

Dinner was served to guests from solid gold and silver vessels which were then thrown from the terraces into the Tiber with extravagant abandon (but then fished out again in specially provided nets). This is one of the many stories told about Agostino Chigi, astute businessman and banker to Julius II. Popes, cardinals, princes and artists visited Chigi's **villa** standing between the via della Lungara and the Tiber. It acquired the name Farnesina (to distinguish it from the larger Palazzo Farnese) when it became the property of Cardinal Alessandro Farnese in 1580.

► The villa, with two side sections framing a central gallery, was designed by Baldassarre Peruzzi (1508-11) and is one of the masterpieces of the Renaissance *(wkdays 9 a.m.-1 p.m.)*. ► In the vault of the ground floor gallery is Raphael's fresco (with the assistance of Giulio Romano, F. Penni and Giovanni da Udine) of the *Legend of Cupid and Psyche★★* as told by Apuleius. Another room has Raphael's fresco of *Galatea★★* (1511), *Constellations* by B. Peruzzi, *Polyphemus* and *Scenes from Ovid's Metamorphoses* by Sebastiano del Piombo. On the upper floor is the **Salone** with *trompe-l'oeil* views of Rome and mythological subjects by Peruzzi and others; the *Wedding of Alexander and Roxana★* in the bedroom is by Sodoma (1512). ► The villa houses the **Gabinetto Nazionale dei Disegni e delle Stampe** (prints and drawings; *periodic exhibitions*).   □

► **FORI IMPERIALI★**
v. dei Fori Imperiali   III A1-2

At the end of the Republican period Rome was the chief city of the interior Mediterranean basin. The central nucleus of urban and social life, the Forum Romanum (→), was beginning to seem unduly cramped. Thus, various Emperors built the forums now known as the **Fori Imperiali** to the N of the Forum Romanum. These consisted of a succession of squares surrounded by arcades, basilicas and temples, intended as much for use at key moments in public life as to establish an adequate image for the city which ruled the known world. They were completed in the following order: Forum of Caesar (54-46 BC); Forum of Augustus (31-2 BC); Forum of Vespasian (69-75 AD); Forum of Nerva (92 AD) and finally, not by chance at the moment of maximum imperial

expansion, the Forum of Trajan (113 AD). After the imperial period such practices as placing new buildings on the site of ancient monuments, re-using walls which were still intact, adapting columns and capitals for other purposes or taking away stone which had already been dressed made the area into a picturesque quarter in which elements of imperial architecture sporadically came to the surface, to be lovingly measured and studied in the Renaissance period.

► In 1932-3 the via dei Fori Imperiali (III A1-2) was laid out in a straight line from p. Venezia to the Colosseum. While this brought to light some of the ancient Roman ruins, it buried the rest under the bed of the new road. There is now a debate in progress about whether the road should be removed so that excavations can start again. ► In the **Forum of Caesar** (III A1; *closed for work*), built in commemoration of the victory at Pharsalus, are three Corinthian columns from the **Temple of Venus Genetrix** (46 BC, rebuilt in 113), the ruins of a late imperial arch and the remains of the **Basilica Argentaria** (a sort of ancient Roman Stock Exchange). ► The **Forum of Augustus★** (III A1; *entrance from p. del Grillo; closed at present*) has a rusticated wall supporting the high podium with steps and three Corinthian columns of the **Temple of Mars Ultor** (the Forum was built to commemorate the Battle of Philippi, at which Octavian avenged the death of Caesar). On the l. of the Forum is the **Casa dei Cavalieri di Rodi** (Knights of the Order of St. John of Jerusalem), a medieval seat of the Order, rebuilt in the 15C. ► The **Colonnacce** (two Corinthian columns from the fortifying wall) remain of the **Forum of Nerva** (III A1; *closed at present*) or Forum Transitorium, so called because it links the Forum of Augustus and the Forum of Vespasian (this latter was cut in two by the v. dei Fori Imperiali). ► Toward the end of the Fori Imperiali, beyond the Basilica of Maxentius (→), are the apses with coffered arches and some columns of the **Temple of Venus and Rome** (III B2), built by Hadrian in 135.   □

► **FORO ITALICO**
along viale Angelico and lungotevere Cadorna   I A-B2

This modern sports complex at the foot of the Monte Mario, also called **Campo della Farnesina**, includes among other things the **Stadio dei Marmi** (1932), with tiers decorated with statues of athletes. This is an architectural style not without documentary interest. The modern **Stadio Olimpico**, built for the Olympic Games of 1960, is also part of the complex.   □

► **FORO ROMANO★★**
main entrance from via dei Fori Imperiali   IV A-B5-6

'These buildings', complained Stendhal, 'famous throughout the world, have been stripped of their ornaments and so seem ruined from top to bottom. Then, to make matters worse, the Forum became a cattle market under the ignoble name of Campo Vaccino (cows field). It would be more accurate to say pastureland and stone quarry in an abandoned valley, between the Capitoline, Palatine, Viminal and Quirinal hills.

► The Roman Forum was one of the cradles of Western civilization and the centre of life in ancient Rome. There is a fine **view★★** of the ruins from the churchyard of **S. Luca e S. Martina** (with dome★ by Pietro da Cortona, 1635-50). On the r. is the Capitoline Hill (→) with the Tabularium and below it the twelve columns of the **Portico degli Dei Consenti** (Portal of the Assenting Gods), three columns of the Temple of Vespasian and eight of the temple of Saturn and the green slopes of the Palatine (→); a little further away are the Arch of Titus (with a single opening), the Arch of Septimus Severus (with three openings) and the remains of the Curia. ▶ To one side, below the church of S. Giuseppe dei Falegnami, is the entrance to the **Mamertine prison**, the prison of the Roman state. ▶ The following is a recommended route for a visit to the various parts of the Forum: from the entrance in the v. dei Fori Imperiali, the route leads first to the r. in the direction of the Capitoline Hill, then to the l., toward the Arch of Titus *(9 a.m.-1 hr before dusk; Sun and hols 9 a.m.-1 p.m.; closed Tue)*. ▶ The **Basilica Emilia**, a great hall of which the coloured marble pavement and bases of columns have survived, was, like all the basilicas, intended for merchants, for the tribunes' sessions and as a general meeting-place. ▶ The **Curia★** has been restored to its form under Diocletian; it was the seat of the Senate. In the interior are the **Plutei of Trajan★**, sculpted balustrades which perhaps decorated the tribune of the Rostra. ▶ In front of the Curia is the **Lapis Niger**, a square slab of black marble, covering what the ancients held to be the **Tomb of Romulus**: the inscriptions on the stele are the earliest written record of the Latin language (6C-5C BC). ▶ The **Arch of Septimus Severus★** (203) shows the conquest of Mesopotamia in relief. To the l. of the arch are the **Rostra**, the orator's tribune (338 BC, rebuilt by Caesar) decorated with the beaks *(rostra)* of the ships captured at the battle of Antium. ▶ In front of the Rostra, paved in travertino, is the **Piazza del Foro** with the **Column of Phocas**, set up in honour of the centurion Phocas, who seized the throne of Byzantium. It was the last monument to be placed in the Forum (608). ▶ A little further on, under a canopy, a puteal (stone curb surrounding a well) marks the site of the *Lacus Curtius*, the gulf in which Marcus Curtius sacrificed himself (he threw himself, armed and on horseback, into the abyss because an oracle held that it would close only if it swallowed up the city's most precious treasure). ▶ The state treasure was kept in the **Temple of Saturn★**, on a high podium with eight Ionic columns from the 3C restoration. ▶ This is the beginning of the **Via Sacra**, paved with polygonal flags, which crosses the Forum from E to W. ▶ The podium pavement with gaming boards and bases of the arch pilasters has survived in the **Basilica Julia** (Julius Caesar, 55-44 BC, rebuilt by Diocletian). ▶ Only three extremely elegant Corinthian columns with entablature (supporting platforms) remain from the **Temple of the Dioscuri★**, dedicated to Castor and Pollux in 484 BC, who according to legend appeared to fight at the side of the Romans at the battle of Lake Regillus against the Latins (496 BC). ▶ The church of **S. Maria Antiqua★** is a 6C adaptation of an imperial building; the bands of 6C-8C frescos★ in the interior *(closed at present)* are important in the history of painting. ▶ The **Fountain of the Nymph Juturna** is a square basin at which legend has it that the Dioscuri watered their horses after the battle of Lake Regillus. ▶ In front of the podium which is the only remaining section of the **Temple of Caesar** built by Octavian, a semicircle with an altar at its centre, is the place where the body of Caesar was cremated on 19 March 44 BC. ▶ The circular **Temple of Vesta** has been partially reconstructed with fragments from the age of Severus. It was here that the eternal sacred flame burned, guarded by virgin priestesses who lived in the **House of the Vestals★** behind it. This had a two-storey portico with a large central courtyard with gardens and pools. ▶ The **Regia** was by tradition the house of the second King of Rome, Numa Pompilius, and later the residence of the Pontifex Maximus (high priest). It housed the state archives and the Sacrarium of Mars, in which were the shields which providentially fell from the sky and spears which trembled at the outbreak of war. ▶ Still on the v. Sacra is the **Temple of Antoninus and Faustina★** dedicated to the imperial couple (2C), with ten Corinthian columns from the pronaos on the podium and the church of **S. Lorenzo in Miranda**, with Baroque façade (1602). ▶ To the r. of the temple, in the **Archaic Necropolis**, are a series of pit and trench tombs (9C-6C BC),

contemporary with the origins of Rome. ▶ A portal with the original bronze door framed by two porphyry columns formed part of a circular building considered to be the **Temple of Romulus** (not the founder of the city but the son of Maxentius): it was probably the vestibule of the Forum of Peace or of Vespasian. It now houses a large 18C Neapolitan Nativity and is in front of the hall in which the church of **S. Cosma and S. Damiano** was established in the 6C, rebuilt in the 17C. There are 6C mosaics★ in the apse. At its side are the magnificent ruins of the **basilica of Maxentius★★** (→), and a little beyond, the church of **S. Francesca Romana**, dating from the 10C, but much restored. The façade is Baroque (C. Lombardi, 1615), and the campanile 12C; in the interior are the *Confessio* in polychrome marble designed by Bernini and a 12C mosaic *(Madonna Enthroned with Saints★*, in the vault of the apse); in the sacristy is a 6C painting of the *Madonna and Child★*. The former convent houses the **Antiquarium Forense** *(9 a.m.-6 p.m.; closed Tue)* containing material from the ancient necropolis and marble from the buildings in the Forum. ▶ At the highest point of the v. Sacra is the elegant **Arch of Titus★★**, built in 81 BC to commemorate the victory in Judaea. The **two reliefs★** inside the single opening of the arch are splendid examples of Roman sculpture. ☐

▶ FORUM OF TRAJAN*
(Foro di Traiano)   IV A5-6

This magnificent final product of town planning in imperial Rome was the work of the architect Apollodorus of Damascus who, to realize his imposing spatial concepts, leveled part of the Quirinal hill. The **Forum of Trajan** consisted of an enormous **square**, bounded on the N (on the Quirinal side) by the semicircles of the Market of Trajan. At the W end is the basilica Ulpia. Immediately behind this soared Trajan's column, between the Greek and Latin libraries, and, further on again, in an arcaded courtyard, the Temple of Trajan.

▶ The central section of the **Basilica Ulpia**, with four rows of reconstructed columns, has survived *(closed at present)*, along with **Trajan's Column★★**. The column was dedicated in 113, is 98 ft high, and stands on a base containing the famous tomb of the Emperor. The entire shaft is decorated with a frieze presenting a continous narrative of the Dacian campaign. This is a masterpiece of Roman sculpture, formerly easily visible from the libraries on either side. A spiral staircase carved in the marble of the interior leads to the top, where the statue of St. Peter was placed in 1587. ▶ In front of the Forum are the two churches of **S. Nome di Maria** (Holy Name of Mary; 1738) and **S. Maria di Loreto**, Renaissance (started by Antonio da Sangallo the Younger in 1507). ▶ The **markets of Trajan★** (v. IV Novembre 94; *9 a.m.-2 p.m.; Sun and hols 9 a.m.-1 p.m.; summer also 4-7 p.m. Tue, Thu and Sat; closed Mon)*, also by Apollodorus of Damascus, are a vast exedra (porch) on the slopes of the Quirinal, with two tiers of shops and a third tier with terrace. Behind the exedra is the via Biberatica, also flanked with shops; the large covered hall above two floors of shops may have housed a bazaar. ▶ At the top of the hill is the **Torre delle Milizie** (Soldiers' Tower). ☐

▶ GALLERIA BORGHESE**
in grounds of Villa Borghese   II A3

The gallery is in the **Casino Borghese**, built for Cardinal Scipio Borghese, the 'darling of Rome', nephew of Paul V, in 1618 by the Dutch architect Vasanzio to house the collection the Cardinal and the Pope had amassed. The building is at the E end of the Villa Borghese (→).

▶ The collection is now organized with sculpture in the museum and painting in the gallery or *quadreria (under restoration; visits in summer and autumn in groups, ground floor or museum only)*. ▶ The most famous piece in the museum is Canova's statue of *Pauline Bonaparte*★★, the sister of Napoleon, wife of Prince Camillo Borghese (who in 1823 acquired Correggio's *Danae* in Paris). There are also masterpieces by Bernini *(David with the Sling*★, 1623, the face is a self-portrait; *Apollo and Daphne*★, *Rape of Proserpine*★ and *Truth revealed by Time*★) as well as classical works like the *Dancing Faun*★ from an original by Lysippos and fragments of Roman mosaic pavement (4C) with scenes of gladiatorial combat and hunting★. ▶ In the gallery there is a *Holy Family*★ by Fra Bartolomeo; *Descent From the Cross*★★, *Portrait of Lady With Unicorn*★ and *Portrait of a Man*★★ by Raphael; *Crucifixion and Two Saints*★ by Pinturicchio; *Venus and Cupid*★ by Cranach; *Madonna and Child with Saints*★ and *Self-Portrait*★ by Lotto; *Tobias and the Angel*★ by Savoldo; *Madonna of the Serpent*★★, *David with the Head of Goliath*★, *Boy Crowned with Ivy*★★, *Boy with a Basket of Fruit*★★ by Caravaggio; *Diana the Huntress*★ by Domenichino; 2 busts of *Cardinal Borghese*★ and three self-portraits by Bernini; *Adoration of the Shepherds*★ and *Last Supper*★ by Jacopo Bassano; *St. Stephen*★ by Francia; *Circe the Magician*★ by Dosso Dossi; *Danae*★★ by Correggio; *Sacred and Profane Love*★★ and *Venus Blindfolding Cupid*★ by Titian; *Preaching of the Baptist*★ by Veronese; *Madonna*★★ by Giovanni Bellini; *Portrait of a Man*★★ by Antonello da Messir a and *Portrait of a Woman* by Carpaccio. ▢

▶ GALLERIA COLONNA*
v. della Pilotta 17   II E2

This is an important example of a Roman patrician's collection displayed in a magnificent hall and minor rooms *(9 a.m.-1 p.m.; closed Aug)*. Outstanding among the 15C-18C paintings are the *Madonna and Child*★ by Stefano da Zevio, *Cupid and Satyr*★ by Bronzino, *Portrait of a Gentleman*★ by Veronese and *Narcissus at the Pool*★ by Tintoretto. Note also the *Greedy Peasant* (by Carracci or Passarotti), various other 17C paintings and a series of landscapes by G. Dughet, van Bloemen, P. Brill and Lorenese.   ▢

▶ GALLERIA ACCADEMIA S. LUCA
p. dell'Accademia 77   I E6

The collection *(Mon, Tue, Fri and last Sun in month 10 a.m.-1 p.m.)* housed in the 16C **Palazzo Carpegna**, with porch and elliptical staircase by Borromini, was formed in the 18C from bequests and gifts from its own academicians. It contains works by Italian and foreign artists, of which the most striking are a *Child*★, fragment of a fresco by Raphael, the *Annunciation to the Shepherds*★ by Jacopo Bassano and Rubens' *Nymphs Crowning Abundance*★.   ▢

▶ GALLERIA ARTE MODERNA*
viale delle Belle Arti 131   I A6

This is the major Italian collection of 19C-20C art *(9 a.m.-2 p.m.; Sun and hols 9 a.m.-1 p.m.; closed Mon)*. Recent acquisitions have to some extent filled gaps left when the collection was first started (for the Esposizione di Roma in 1881) and during the first decades of its existence.

▶ **19C Italian art** is represented by Neoclassical works (including sculpture by Canova), Romantic works, the Neapolitan school, the Tuscan artists known as the Macchiaioli, northern Italian landscape painters, painters showing French influence or connected with Realism or the social art of the latter part of the century, Divisionism and Neo-Impressionism; also sculpture by Vincenzo, Gemito and Medardo Rosso. ▶ The **20C** is represented by Futurism, paintings by Modigliani and Gino Rossi, pittura metafisica and the 'Novocento', the Roman school, sculpture by Manzù and Marino Marini, also more recent artists (Guttuso, Afro, Vedova, Viani and many others). Works by **foreign artists** include names of the calibre of Courbet, Cézanne, Degas, Monet, van Gogh, Klimt, Rodin, Klee, Kandinsky, Mirò, Utrillo, Ernst, Pollock, Moore and Giacometti.   ▢

Reading the stones

It is called the Colosseum because of its size or because there used to be a colossal statue of Nero next to it. In any case Nero never received the salute of the gladiators from the imperial podium since the amphitheatre was built by Vespasian after his death in 72 AD and inaugurated by Titus eight years later. It is a four-storeyed building, the three lower storeys have arches supported by pilasters (rectangular columns engaged in the wall), and the fourth has a solid wall. The pilasters have bases (as in Greek architecture) supporting a cornice over the keystones and marking the division of the floors. However, with an invention unthinkable in the architectural system which it was imitating, the three Greek orders (Doric, Ionic, Corinthian) were placed one above the other 'logically' in respect of the proportions. On the fourth floor, with a solid wall, slender pilasters of composite order were used. The Colosseum started to fall into disrepair with the earthquakes of 442 and 508; the partial collapse of two rows of arches in the earthquake of 851 marked the end. The fallen stones were used in new buildings and the entire complex was looted despite the saying 'When the Colosseum falls, Rome falls'. Such looting was forbidden in 1750 by Pope Benedict XIV, and what was left behind was evidently enough to save Rome. Apart from the popular saying, the existence of this enormous building had important stylistic consequences. At the time of the Renaissance it was the most famous of the remaining ancient monuments and therefore a useful source of information. A reading of the style of the building (the fusion of Roman and Greek building systems, the logical superimposition of the architectural orders) governed the language of architecture from Leon Battista Alberti until the Neoclassical period.

▶ GALLERIA DORIA-PAMPHILI**
p. del Collegio Romano 1A   I F6

Both the **collection** and the **interior** of the palazzo give a vivid impression of affluent Roman life in the 17C; it is the most important patrician collection to have remained in the possession of the family who assembled it. The core of the collection was amassed by Olimpia Maidalchini, sister-in-law of Pope Innocent X Pamphili (1644-55).

▶ The 15C-17C paintings are shown in rooms with magnificent 18C decoration and in the courtyard loggia *(Tue,*

Fri, Sat and Sun 10 a.m.-1 p.m.). Masterpieces include: *Double Portrait★* by Raphael, *St. Jerome★* by Lotto, *Herodias★* by Titian, *St. Roch and the Angel★* by Saraceni, *Mary Magdalene★* and *Rest During the Flight to Egypt★★* by Caravaggio, *Jesus Pays Tribute★* and *Concert★* by Mattia Preti, bust of *Olimpia Maidalchini★* by Algardi, *Herminia and Tancred★* by Guercino, *Birth and Marriage of the Virgin★* by Giovanni di Paolo, *Adoration of the Shepherds* by Parmigiano, *Portrait of a Franciscan★* by Rubens, *Battle in the Bay of Naples★* by Pieter Brueghel, *Portrait of Innocent X★* by Velazquez, bust of *Innocent X★★* by Bernini, five *Landscapes With Figures* by Lorenese, *Flight Into Egypt★* by Annibale Carracci and *Landscape★* by Salvator Rosa. ▶ There are also numerous other works of art (F. Lippi, S. del Piombo, Lotto, Beccafumi) in the private★ apartments *(guided visit, same days as gallery, 10:30 a.m. and 12:30 p.m.)*. Kaiser Wilhelm II remarked when staying here that he would not be able to return the hospitality in equivalent surroundings. □

Pilgrims in Rome

From the dawn of Christianity, Christians came to Rome to affirm their faith. They came to visit the few buildings in which the first Christians had brought together the relics of the martyrs in spite of imperial wrath. Crusaders would also stop in Rome before continuing their journey. It was in the 15C that pilgrimages to Rome became popular. Christians would come from all over to visit St. Peter's tomb. Christmas and Easter were celebrated with increasing pomp as were the jubilees. In 1300, Pope Bonifacio VIII proclaimed the jubilee year and dispensed indulgences and remission of sins to all those who would visit the basilicas, confess their sins and perform communion. To receive all these visitors and facilitate access to the Vatican, Nicolas V (1447-55) built bridges, an avenue through the old city (for processions), and piazzas so the faithful could gather. The massive numbers of pilgrims created major logistical problems (as they do today in Mecca). At first, pilgrims would lodge with friends or in small inns north of the city. The religious orders then added hospices to their convents to greet the visitors. Foreign countries followed suit by building dormitories, refectories, hospitals and even cemeteries. So were built the Saxon Holy-Ghost Hospital, San Giovanni of the Genovese in the Trastevere district, Saint-Jacques of the Spanish and others. Inns would greet visitors near the bridges and the port. On the papal route, the Campo dei Fiori became a gathering spot for foreigners. Signs offered lodging, currency exchange, cart rentals. Those more well-to-do travelers prefered the better known inns where they could find comfort and good food such as the Orso (founded in 1460) near the Tiber on the via di Monte Brianzo. Today, religious establishments still receive members of the clergy and groups of pilgrims who visit Rome.

▶ Il GESU**

p. del Gesù   I F6

This **church** has a single aisle flanked by chapels and the altar tomb of St. Ignatius Loyola. It is the principal ecclesiastical building of the Jesuit Order in Rome, and both in its architecture and in the sumptuousness of its decorations it is the prototype of Catholic places of worship at the time of the Counter-Reformation. It is Vignola's principal Mannerist work (1568), completed by Della Porta, who was responsible for the façade (1575) and the dome. In the interior are frescos of the *Triumph of the Name of Jesus★* by Baciccia (1669-83) and the *Chapel of St. Ignatius Loyola★* by Andrea Pozzo (1696-1700). The lapis lazuli globe in the Trinity group above the altar was made from the largest known block of this material. □

▶ Il GHETTO

IV A-B4

The area between the Tiber and the portico di Ottavia (→) was bounded by a wall with three gates; Roman Jews were compelled to live here, with severe restrictions, from the 16C-19C. The space in front of the church of S. Maria del Pianto is still known as the 'piazza Giuda'. The modern **synagogue** (1904) is on the lungotevere dei Cenci. □

▶ Il GIANICOLO*

IV A-B1

This attractive green hill on the r. bank of the Tiber is associated with Garibaldi's defense of the Roman Republic against Oudinot's French troops (1849). From the **Fontana Paola** (IV B2), with its majestic demonstration of architecture at the time of Paul V (1612) the road climbs to the **piazzale** containing the Garibaldi monument where there is also a magnificent view★ of the city. A little farther an even fuller view★★ can be seen from the *Faro della Vittoria* (Beacon of Victory). In the park there is the stump of **Tasso's oak**, which was struck by lightning. Tasso, the poet (1544-95), used to enjoy its shade. (→) **S. Onofrio** and **S. Pietro in Montorio**. □

▶ L'ISOLA TIBERINA

IV B4

This island in a bend of the Tiber is a picturesque feature of the city's landscape. In the days of imperial Rome it was made to look like a ship by means of a facing of travertine rock. It was also linked with Aesculapius, the god of healing, to whom it is sacred: the prow of the marble ship had a serpent, the symbol of the god, carved on it. The island is linked to the l. bank by the **Ponte Fabricio** (62 BC), now the oldest bridge in Rome (with the exception of the Ponte Milvio), and to the r. bank by the Ponte Cestio. On the island is a hospital with a church dedicated to **S. Giovanni Calibata**, almost opposite **S. Bartolomeo,** another ancient church rebuilt in the 17C. □

▶ MAUSOLEUM OF AUGUSTUS*

between v. del Corso and v. di Ripetta   I D5

The tomb of the first Roman Emperor and principal members of the Julian-Claudian family was started in 29 BC, after the conquest of Egypt. It is in the form of an Etruscan tumulus tomb. Its marble was stripped off in the Middle Ages and it was used as a fortress and for other purposes until 1936. It has a circular base (295 ft in diameter) with a tumulus in the shape of a truncated cone, on top of which stood a statue of the Emperor. Inside *(closed at present)* were circular passageways with a crypt for funerary urns at the centre. Next to it, protected by a modern glass structure, the **Ara pacis Augustae★★** (Altar of Peace of Augustus) has been reconstructed (1938) from original fragments and copies of missing pieces *(9 a.m.-2 p.m.; Sun and hols 9 a.m.-1 p.m.; summer also 4-7 p.m. Tue, Thu and Sat; closed Mon)*. The altar is enclosed in marble with **reliefs★** (fertile earth, imperial procession with Augustus and members of his family), examples of the solemn dignity of official Augustan sculpture. The altar was set up in 13C-9C BC to celebrate peace and stability in the Augustan world. ◻

▶ MONTECITORIO*

p. di Montecitorio   I E5-6

According to an ancient Roman custom, votes were cast here, and the place became known as *mons ad acceptandis suffragis* (the place where votes were taken); this became *monte accettorio,* later corrupted to Montecitorio. Pope Pius VI, in 1792, erected the Egyptian **obelisk** of Psammetichus II (6C BC), which had been brought to Rome by Augustus. The superb **palazzo,** seat of the Chamber of Deputies since 1870, was started by Bernini in 1650 and completed by Carlo Fontana in 1694 for Innocent XII, who located the law courts there. At one time the numbers of the public lottery were called out on the long balcony. The **parliamentary chamber** is in the rear section of the palazzo, which faces p. del Parlamento. ◻

▶ MUSEO ARTE ORIENTALE

v. Merulana 248   III A4

The collection in the Palazzo Brancaccio *(9 a.m.-1 p.m.; closed Mon)* is based largely on excavations in Asia by the Istituto Italiano per il Medio Oriente. It includes sections on Iranian, Chinese, Indian, Tibetan, Nepalese and Thai art and other valuable material, including Islamic **ceramics★** from Iran (9C-18C) and a collection of Chinese, Japanese and Korean **Buddhist bronzes★.** Also in the **v. Merulana,** a long, straight street built in the late 16C to connect S. Maria Maggiore and S. Giovanni in Laterano, is the **Auditorio di Mecenate** (Auditorium of Maecenas; III A4; *open to students only; apply at Direzione Musei, p. Campitelli 7),* an Augustan nymphaeum with apses and paintings of landscapes and gardens. ◻

▶ MUSEO BARRACCO★

corso Vittorio Emanuele II   I F4-5

The **Farnesina ai Baullari★,** a Renaissance palazzo attributed to Antonio Sangallo the Younger, is also called the *Piccola Farnesina* (but the lilies on the string course are those of France, not of the Farnese family). The museum *(9 a.m.-2 p.m.; Tue and Thu also 5-8 p.m.; Sun 9 a.m.-1 p.m.; closed Mon)* was presented to the city by Baron Giovanni Barracco and consists of a small but valuable collection of **ancient**

sculpture from the Near East and the Roman age, with rare originals such as an Egyptian bas-relief★ of *Nofer* (a court functionary, 3rd Dynasty), a head of a *priest★* of the Egyptian Roman period, 5C BC, a head of a *Greek youth,* a head of *Marsyas* which is a copy of one by Myron, a head of *Apollo* in the manner of Praxiteles and a statuette of *Hercules★* after Polykleitos. ◻

▶ MUSEO DEL FOLCLORE

p. S. Egidio 1B   IV B2

This museum is housed in the austere and ancient monastery of the Discalced or Barefooted Carmelites and includes costumes from Latium, pictures of popular festivals, a model of the studio of the Roman poet Trilussa (Carlo Alberto Salustri) and Ettore Roesler Franz's watercolours that catch a flavour of a Rome which has now disappeared *(9 a.m.-2 p.m.; Sun and hols 9 a.m.-1 p.m.; Tue and Thu also 5-8 p.m.; closed Mon).*

▶ MUSEO DELLA CIVILTA ROMANA*

at EUR, p. G. Agnelli

This museum houses an important collection of objects illustrating all aspects of Roman culture by means of plaster casts and models *(under restoration).* Of special interest is the large **model★** of Rome at the time of Constantine (4C; *9 a.m.-1:30 p.m. and 4-7 p.m. Tue and Thu; Sun 9 a.m.-1 p.m.).* ◻

▶ MUSEO DELLA FANTERIA

p. S. Croce in Gerusalemme 9   III B6

This distinctive **military collection** *(Tue, Thu and Sat 10 a.m.-12 noon; closed Aug)* consists of relics, banners, reproductions of uniforms, historical documents and ancient weapons from the Risorgimento and recent wars. ◻

▶ MUSEO DELL'ALTO MEDIOEVO

at EUR, viale Lincoln 1

This museum houses material from the 4C-10C *(9 a.m.-2 p.m.; Sun and hols 9 a.m.-1 p.m.; closed Mon).* It includes treasure from the **Lombard burial sites** at Nocera Umbra and Castel Trosino (near Ascoli Piceno), fragments of sculpture and architectural decoration from central Italy, finds from the Etruscan grave in S. Cornelio (near Veio) and Coptic (Egyptian) fabrics and reliefs. ◻

▶ MUSEO DELLE ARTI E TRADIZIONI POPOLARI

at EUR, p. Marconi 8

In this museum is lavish documentation *(9 a.m.-2 p.m.; Sun and hols 9 a.m.-1 p.m.; closed Mon; only partially open to public)* on folklore, traditions and popular art from all Italian regions, arranged in categories: cycle of the year, cycle of human life, home, agricultural and pastoral life, life at sea, town life, popular art, dance, music and song, costume and popular religion. Only part of the material is on show, although there are occasionally exhibitions featuring the museum's treasures. □

▶ MUSEO DI GOETHE

v. del Corso 18   I C5

'Yes, at last I am in this capital of the world' (Goethe, 1786). The house in which the poet lived during his stay in Rome (1786-8) exhibits a collection of paintings, graphics, manuscripts and books recalling his Italian journey and the cultural atmosphere of the late 18C *(10 a.m.-1 p.m. and 4-7 p.m.; closed Thu p.m. and Mon).* □

▶ MUSEO DI VILLA GIULIA**

viale delle Belle Arti   I A5-6

The suburban **villa of Julius III★**, built in 1551-3 by Vignola with a façade by Ammannati and a courtyard with loggia over the **nyphaeum,** houses the largest museum of **Etruscan art** in existence. The collection includes exceptional archaeological material from S. Etruria and from non-Etruscan territories in Latium and Umbria. The thirty-four rooms, arranged by modern topographical methods, are dedicated to finds from Vulci (archaic statue of a *Centaur★* and of a *Man Astride a Sea Monster★*, 6C BC); from Cervéteri (reconstructed tomb in the basement); from the territory of Tarquin; from Veio (statues of *Apollo★* and *Hercules With the Hind★★* and a *Goddess With Child* from the Temple of Apollo, works by Vulca and masterpieces of 6C BC Etruscan sculpture); and from Caere (sarcophagus in the oriental style from a 6C BC tomb, portrait of a man, Etrusco-Roman, *Sarcophagus of a Husband and Wife★*, famous masterpiece of Etruscan sculpture 6C BC). There are sections for bronze (fine series of **cistas★** or cylindrical boxes in layers of copper for toilet items); ancient wood, glass and terra-cotta; ceramics in the **Castellani collection** (including all types of Greek and Etrusco-Italic ceramics from the 8C BC to the late Hellenistic era and a group of Attic red-figure vases by famous masters); grave finds from Faliscan and Campanian burial grounds; material from the temple at Falerii Vatres★; material from Etruscan and Etrusco-Italic centres around and S of Rome; burial items from two Barberini and Bernardini tombs in oriental style (two **Pectorals★★** or large buckles decorated with cats' heads, chimeras and sphinxes and bronze mirrors and cistas from Praeneste including the celebrated 4C BC **Ficorini Cista★**); weapons, gold objects and vases from Umbrian sites. □

▶ MUSEO ETNOGRAFICO PIGORINI*

at EUR, p. Marconi 1

This is one of the largest collections of its kind in Europe *(9 a.m.-2 p.m.; Sun and hols 9 a.m.-1 p.m.; closed Mon)* and consists of two distinct sections. The **prehistoric section** shows material on Latium and its palaeolithic, neolithic, and bronze age

cultures, as well as finds from various sites in the eastern Mediterranean, including the Italian excavations in Crete. The **ethnographic section** houses rooms devoted to African art and musical instruments, the culture of the Americas with pre-Columbian archaeological material and a show of Peruvian textiles. □

▶ MUSEO GRANATIERI SARDEGNA

p. S. Croce in Gerusalemme 7   III B6

This museum contains relics, memorabilia, documents, sculpture and weapons recalling the traditions of the Reggimento Sabaudo delle Guardie (1659, Savoy Guard Regiment), which in 1861 became the Brigata Granatieri di Sardegna (Sardinian Brigade of Guards; *Thu and Sun 10 a.m.-12 noon; closed mid-Jul to late Aug).* □

▶ MUSEO STRUMENTI MUSICALI

p. S. Croce in Gerusalemme 9A   III B6

At present the museum consists of 18 rooms *(9 a.m.-2 p.m.; Sun 9 a.m.-1 p.m.; closed Mon)* showing 850 of more than 3,000 **musical instruments** in the collection. Instruments exhibited include some from outside Europe, popular Italian and foreign instruments, mechanical and cylinder, disc and punched tape, and a vast collection of chamber and concert instruments from the medieval, Renaissance and Baroque periods. Notable features include a German **harpsichord★** dating from 1537, the famous **Barberini harp★** and the pianoforte built in 1722 by its inventor Bartolomeo Cristofori. □

▶ PALATINE HILL**
(Il Palatino)   IV B-C5-6

'This is an extraordinary place. We went to the Palatine and climbed towards the Emperor's palace' wrote the German historian Gregorovius one evening in 1853, 'its gigantic columns, arches and ruins rise above the swaying trees... Here the world was ruled, squandered, given away in a single night. Now it is silent and dead, and nothing can be heard but the lamenting owl, flying around the arching vaults...'. It is strange that this otherwise austere historian allowed himself to be thus carried away to the extent of imagining the emperors like Russian princes in a *belle époque* casino. The ruins do stimulate the imagination; by tradition this area is *Roma quadrata,* named and defended by Romulus, the city's founder. In imperial Rome it was the official seat of the Emperors, the nerve centre of a world of 54 million inhabitants, few by modern standards, but a significant proportion of the population of the then world, extending from the Atlantic to the Euphrates, from the Sahara to the Danube.

▶ The visit *(some areas closed for consolidation and restoration)* is a natural continuation from the Roman Forum. ▶ The enormous Italian garden known as the **Orti Farnesiani★,** in front of the 16C Farnese villa, is above the ruins of the **Palace of Tiberius;** the podium of the **Temple of Cybele** remains (the enthroned statue is under an arch of the *Domus Tiberiana*); nearby are remains of 9C-8C BC **huts,** more or less the period of the legendary foundation of Rome. ► The **House of Livia★** *(apply to caretaker)* was probably not the residence of Augustus' wife, but remains a typical example of a rich Roman's house, with fine pictorial decoration in the rooms around the square atrium. ► The **Cryptoporticus** dates from the period of Nero and runs along one side of the Palace of Tiberius; it may have linked the palaces of Augustus and Tiberius with the **Domus Aurea** (→). A flight of steps leads to the **Flavian Palace** (Domitian, late 1C) and among the impressive ruins are the **Aula Regia** (throne room), **Basilica** (hall of imperial justice), the **Lararium,** the **Peristyle** and the **Triclinium.** The **Domus Augustana★** (Domitian) was the private area of the imperial residence and developed on two terraces, one on top of the hill and the other on the slope down to the Circus Maximus; some of the numerous rooms have been incorporated into the convent building housing the **Antiquarium del Palatino** *(closed),* which contains among other things the famous **graffito★** of a youth worshipping a crucified man with the head of an ass. ► Nearby are the **Stadium★** of Domitian and, further to the E, the **baths** and the **Domus Severiana★** *(partially closed for work)* and other buildings affording a good view of the valley containing the **Circus Maximus,** the perimeter of which can easily be discerned. ► From the terrace there is a fine **view★** of the archaeological site between the Circus, the Baths of Caracalla (→) and the Aventine hill facing the Tiber. ☐

► **PALAZZINA DI PIO IV**

v. Flaminia   I A5

The lower section, probably designed by Vignola (1552), was part of a public fountain of the Acqua Vergine. Pius IV presented the building to his nephew Borromeo (St. Charles) who had the elegant upper floor added by Pirro Ligorio. ☐

► **PALAZZO BARBERINI★★**

v. 4 Fontane 13   II D3

This **palazzo★★** (1625-33) is considered to be the 'key to the Baroque'. Following an initial idea by Carlo Maderno, it was built for Urban VIII by the two major architects of the 17C, Bernini and Borromini, who at that time still enjoyed swapping ideas and 'inventions'; their bitter rivalry began when Borromini began to feel inferior.

► Borromini was responsible for the **elliptical flight of steps** below the portico; Bernini designed the porticoed **façade,** topped by a double closed loggia between two projecting sections, the **staircase,** the façade on the v. Barberini and the internal decoration. ► The **gallery** *(9 a.m.-2 p.m.; Sun and hols 9 a.m.-1 p.m.),* which still occupies some of the rooms on the first floor decorated with 17C-18C frescos, is complementary to the one in the Palazzo Corsini (→); it contains 13C-16C painting and some sculpture. The collection consists of Italian and foreign masterpieces: *Life of Christ★* by G. Baronzio, *Madonna and Child★* by the maestro of the Palazzo Venezia, *Madonna and Child★* and *Annunciation★* by Filippo Lippi, *Mary Magdalene★* by Piero di Cosimo, *La Fornarina★★* by Raphael, *Portrait of Stefano Colonna★* by Bronzino, *Portrait of a Gentleman★* by Bartolomeo Veneto, *Madonna With Child and Saints* by Lotto, *Christ and the Woman Taken in Adultery★* by Tintoretto, *Adoration of the Shepherds★* and *Baptism of Christ★* by El Greco, *Judith and Holofernes★* by Caravaggio, *Expulsion From the Temple* by Valentin, *Resurrection of Lazarus★* by Mattia Preti, *Agar and the Angel★* and *Bacchanalia★* by Poussin, *Scourging of Christ★* and *Et in Arcadia Ego*

by Guercino, *Pietà* by Baciccia, *Portrait of Henry VIII★* by H. Holbein and *Portrait of Erasmus of Rotterdam★* by Q. Metsys. ► There are also lavish rococo decoration and works by 18C Italian painters in the **Barberini Apartments** on the second floor, 18C French works from the **Cervinara bequest** and the section devoted to **Arti Decorative del Settecento** (furniture, porcelain, costume). ☐

► **PALAZZO BRASCHI★**

p. S. Pantaleo 10   I F4-5

The last palace built in Rome for a papal family, the nephews of Pius VI Braschi, dates from after 1792; the rear façade gives on to the piazza containing the most famous of the sarcastic 'talking statues', **Pasquino.** The **museum** *(9 a.m.-2 p.m.; Tue and Thu also 5-8 p.m.; Sun 9 a.m.-1 p.m.; closed Mon)* offers a chance to enjoy the 'Rome which is no more', the city as it was before the demolitions and changes of modern times began. The collection includes watercolours and oils by E. Roesler Franz, water-colours and drawings by Pinelli, detached frescos, statues of the *Baptism of Christ★* by F. Mochi (1634) and ceramics. There are also carriages, state coaches and Pius IX's train. ☐

Pasquino and the pasquinade

In English a pasquinade means a lampoon or a political squib, having ridicule as its object. Its origin can be found in Rome, where the statue of Pasquino stands besides the Palazzo Braschi, in the piazza Pasquino. It was put there originally by Cardinal Carafa and its name comes from the schoolmaster near whose house it was dug up. The statue, which is mutilated, is said to represent a gladiator, or the hero Ajax, supporting Menelaus. A festival in its honour was held once a year and the public was asked, to encourage learning, to write polished Latin verses and place them on the statue. Later however it came to be associated with a tailor celebrated for the gibes he hurled at every turn, and it became customary to affix to it political verses in Italian directed at prominent personages. Still later, the satires developed into a form of question and answer. On an ancient statue of Mars, called Marforio, which stood nearby, people would append questions on current affairs and prominent matters of the day and witty replies would appear promptly on the statue of Pasquino.

► **PALAZZO CORSINI★**

v. della Lungara   IV A2

This palace, majestic and sombre, is the work of Ferdinando Fuga (1736). It stands on the site of an earlier 15C building; in the 17C it housed Queen Christina of Sweden and her academy of men of letters and poets. Many of them, the year after the queen's death (1689), were followers of Arcadia, another academy, founded by Canon Giovanni Maria Crescimbeni to 'stamp out bad taste', which met on the nearby Gianicolo hill, in the Bosco Parrasio. The French General Duphot lived here in the late 18C; he was engaged to Pauline Bonaparte and his murder in a riot (1797) provoked the French occupation of the city and the exile of Pius VI. Today it houses the **Accademia dei Lincei** (of the lynxes, symbols of keen-eyed research), founded in 1603 by Prince Federico Cesi, and a section of the **Galleria Nazionale di Arte Antica** which complements the one in the Palazzo Barberini (→). The **collection** *(9 a.m.-7 p.m.; Mon and Sat 9 a.m.-2 p.m.; Sun 9 a.m.-1 p.m.)* of 17C-18C Italian and foreign works (Flemish, Dutch and French) includes a triptych★ by Beato Angelico, Caravaggio's *St. John the Baptist*★ and Guido Reni's *Salome*★. □

▶ **PALAZZO PALLAVICINI** ,
v. XXIV Maggio 43   II E2

This 17C palazzo was owned by Cardinal Mazzarin for a time. It was built by Vasanzio (the Dutch architect Jan van Santen) opposite the Quirinale, on the site of the Baths of Constantine, for Scipione Borghese, the nephew of Pope Paul V. On the ceiling of the **Casino** *(10 a.m.-12 noon and 3-5 p.m. on first of each month)* is Guido Reni's celebrated fresco of *Aurora*★ (1614).   □

▶ **PALAZZO SPADA***
p. Capo di Ferro 3   IV A3

This 16C palazzo has lavish decoration and stucco (statues, reliefs, medallions, festoons) by Giulio Mazzoni on the façade and in the courtyard.

▶ On the ground floor *(apply to caretaker)*, is a **gallery**★ with columns, a short corridor brilliantly made to look enormous by skillful *trompe l'oeil* perspective, the work of Giovanni Maria da Bitonto, traditionally attributed to Borromini. ▶ The **Galleria Spada** houses a number of 16C-17C works *(9 a.m.-2 p.m.; Sun and hols 9 a.m.-1 p.m.; closed Mon)*, a typical 17C patrician collection including *Musician*★ by Titian, *Portrait of Cardinal Bernardino Spada*★ (who initiated the collection) by Guido Reni and *Portrait of a Cardinal*★ by Rubens. □

▶ **PALAZZO VENEZIA***
p. Venezia   II F1

The elevation of this crenellated palazzo, with large cruciform windows in the piano nobile, is sometimes attributed to Alberti. It was commissioned by the Venetian Cardinal Pietro Barbo (later Paul II) *c.* 1455. From the 16C-18C it was the residence of the Venetian ambassador, then the ambassador of the Austrian Empire; during the Fascist regime it was used by Mussolini.

▶ It now houses the **Museo di Palazzo Venezia**★ *(9 a.m.-2 p.m.; Sun and hols 9 a.m.-1 p.m.; closed Mon; parts under reconstruction)* a huge collection of mainly applied art outstanding in which are a 14C embroidered cope★, the 13C enamel of the *Pantocrater*★, the triptych of *Alba Fucens*★ (14C) and the statue of a *Pope*★ by Arnolfo di Cambio. ▶ The basilica of **San Marco**, with a Renaissance façade on the piazza San Marco is part of the palazzo; in the apse is a 9C mosaic★ and in the sacristy is a **tabernacle for holy oil**★ perhaps by A. Bregno and Giovanni Dalmata (15C). ▶ The **Palazzetto Venezia** (1455-69) was formerly in the Palazzo Venezia, but was moved to its present position to open up the view to the **Monument of Vittorio Emanuele II** (→). □

▶ **The PANTHEON***
p. della Rotonda   I F5

The Pantheon was built by Marcus Agrippa, son-in-law of Augustus, in 27 BC and dedicated to 'all the gods' (as the Greek name suggests). Despite sacking and looting, it still looks as it did when restored under Hadrian; the bronze ceiling of the portico was melted down by Pope Urban VIII Barberini to make the baldacchino (projecting canopy) in St. Peter's, which provoked Pasquino's famous remark 'what the Barbarians didn't do, the Barberini did'. The Pantheon was dedicated to the worship of the Madonna and Martyrs in 609.

▶ The **piazza** in which it stands, with its 16C **fountain** (G. Della Porta) topped with an Egyptian obelisk, is one of the most picturesque parts of Rome. ▶ The Pantheon's **pronaos** (space in front enclosed by a portico) has 16 monolithic columns in red-and-grey granite; beyond it is the portal with ancient bronze door leading to the **interior**★★ *(9 a.m.-1 p.m. and 2-5 p.m.; Sun 9 a.m.-1 p.m.; closed Mon)*. The alternating niches and aedicules (recesses) and the coffers in the arches — all plain and majestic — have been much imitated since the 16C. ▶ Vittorio Emanuele II, Umberto I and Queen Margherita are buried here, as is Raphael, in an aedicule with a Madonna by Lorenzetto. ▶ There is a fresco of the *Annunciation* attributed to Melozzo da Forli. □

The obelisks of Rome

It was the Greeks, when they arrived in Egypt and were amazed by that ancient civilization, mysterious and impressive, who invented the name obelisk, or 'spit'. The Romans were also impressed by the culture of the Nile and when the country became one of their provinces many obelisks were brought to Rome. From the 16C to the early 18C popes had them set up where they are today. The first was the one known as Flaminio in the piazza del Popolo. It was an obelisk from Heliopolis, of the time of the nineteenth dynasty, which Augustus had brought to Rome to decorate the centre of the Circus Maximus. Domenico Fontana moved it in 1585 on the orders of Sixtus V. The next year it was the turn of the obelisk in St. Peter's Square. The undertaking of moving it to the middle of the square was complex: it took four months' work by nine hundred workers. At the crucial moment when it was to be placed upright, Pope Sixtus, who was present, told the crowd of onlookers to observe silence with death as a punishment for anyone breaking it. However, something threatened to go wrong in the complex apparatus of winches, scaffolding and ropes which Fontana had prepared, and under the enormous weight the hemp ropes were beginning to stretch. It was then that a Ligurian seaman took the risk of breaking the papal ban, and yelled 'water on the ropes', a sound piece of advice. A little later, in 1588, the obelisk in the piazza S. Giovanni in Laterano was put in place. It is over 100 ft high, made of red granite and the largest of the Roman obelisks. It is also the oldest. It was raised by Pharoah Thothmes III before the temple of Ammon in Thebes almost fifteen centuries before Christ. Constans, the son of Constantine, had it brought to Rome for the Circus Maximus in 357, on a specially built boat, and it was found, broken into three, the year before its new siting. The obelisk in the piazza della Minerva, dating from the 6C BC, came from the Temple of Isis in the Campus

Martius and was set up again in 1687; Bernini designed the elephant which supports it and Urban VIII added the inscription which explains its allegorical significance; a robust mind is needed to sustain solid wisdom. The obelisk erected in 1711 in the piazza del Pantheon also came from the Temple of Isis. Various other obelisks were set up in the late 18C by Pius VI: the one in the piazza della Trinità dei Monti, which is a Roman imitation from the Gardens of Sallust near the Porta Salaria, that of Psammetico II (6C BC) in the piazza Montecitorio which Augustus had brought from Heliopolis to act as the gnomon (column) of a massive sundial, of which vestiges still exist, and two twins which used to stand at the entrance of the Mausoleum of Augustus and which are now to be found in the piazza dell'Esquilino and the piazza del Quirinale. Finally, in 1822, Pius VII placed the Pincio obelisk. It was raised by the Emperor Hadrian in honour of his favourite, the boy Antinous; it was found in the 16C outside the Porta Maggiore.

▶ **PIAZZA BOCCA DELLA VERITA**

IV B5

This is a square with various Roman and medieval monuments on the site of the ancient Forum Boarium, near the Tiber. In the garden with a fine Baroque fountain (1715) are the **Temple of Portunus★** (god of harbours), usually called the Temple of Fortuna Virilis (1C BC) and the contemporary circular **Temple of Hercules★** (wrongly called Temple of Vesta). To the l. of the Teatro Marcello, and at r. angles to it, is the **Casa dei Crescenzi** (also called Casa di Coladi Rienzo), probably the remains of a guard tower at a Tiber crossing. It dates from the 12C and is an example of medieval construction using elements recovered from ancient buildings. At the E extremity of the piazza is the **Arch of Janus** dating from the age of Constantine (4C); it formed a covered passage at a crossroads. Near the piazza are the churches of **S. Giorgio in Velabro** (→) and **S. Maria in Cosmedin** (→). □

▶ **PIAZZA CAVALIERI DI MALTA***

IV D4

When the Venetian Cardinal Giovan Battista Rezzonico entrusted the design of the square, the villa and the church of the Roman priory to his fellow townsman Giovan Battista Piranesi, Vanvitelli, even though he was a friend, was scandalized: Piranesi was mad, so it was said, and madmen were not allowed to be architects. Despite all this, the **piazza★** designed by the great engraver, visionary Baroque interpreter of Roman ruins, is an exquisite space decorated with steles and trophies and framed with cypresses.

▶ On the r. is the monumental entrance (also by Piranesi) to the **Villa del Priorato** *(visit by prior permission of the Order, v. Condotti 68)*. On looking through a keyhole in the door, it is possible to see the dome of St. Peter's, 2 km away. ▶ Access to the extremely elegant church of **S. Maria del Priorato** (Piranesi, 1765) is through the garden. C. Brandi said that Piranesi's decorative handwriting 'seems to have absorbed the light of the Roman sun'. □

Seeing Rome

'To see Rome', announced Stendhal, you need two or three of the best maps of the town, bought on the Corso and 'a carriage with good horses.' Rome has a number of centres, the River Tiber runs through it and it is built on hills, the last spurs of the Campagna Romana. To the right of the river are the Monte Vaticano and the Gianicolo; to the left, in the direction of the flow of the river, the Pincio, the Quirinale, the Viminale, the Esquilino, the Campidoglio, the Palatino, the Celio and the Aventino. There are two bends in the Tiber, the first to the W and the second to the E, on the stretch of the river within the Aurelian walls. This irregular late imperial circle of fortifications contains (with the exception of the Vatican) almost all the important historical and cultural sites in Rome. (The modern metropolis is obviously much larger.) The piazza Venezia and the Campidoglio are placed nearly at the centre of the second loop and are an ideal starting point for learning the topography of the city. The area S of the piazza Venezia and the Campidoglio has the most ancient ruins and monuments. There are also extensive green areas skillfully blending marble with nature: the Forum Romanum between the Campidoglio and the Colosseum, the Fori Imperiali between the valley of the Forum Romanum and the slopes of the Quirinale, the Palatino with the imperial palaces and to the S, the green spaces between the Aventino and the Celio contain the massive ruins of the Baths of Caracalla. On the left bank of the first Tiber bend is the beautiful Baroque and Renaissance centre, with the piazza Navona and the Pantheon. The straight line of the via del Corso is the principal axis of the modern centre, running from the p. Venezia and the Porta Flaminia or del Popolo. 'No city', wrote an 18C guide, 'has an entrance as remarkable as that provided by the Porta del Popolo. The obelisk, the three great streets and the two churches are a magnificent sight, a brilliant introduction to the city of Rome'. The Corso runs down to the via dei Condotti. This is one of the streets which form a square making up the commercial centre and leads to the piazza di Spagna at the foot of the hill served by the magnificent Spanish steps. Not much remains of Rome's marvelous green belt, but spaces (in particular the park of the Villa Borghese just outside the Aurelian wall) are a characteristic feature of the city. On the right bank of the Tiber is the Mausoleum of Hadrian, which later became the Castel Sant'Angelo, and the picturesque district of Trastevere, where, it is said, the real Romans live.

▶ **PIAZZA COLONNA**

I E6

Piazza Colonna is bounded on the E side by the v. del Corso (beyond which is the early 20C **Galleria Colonna**) with the **Palazzo Chigi**, started by C. Maderno (housing the Presidenza del Consiglio dei Ministri), and the 19C **Palazzo Wedekind**, which has 16 columns of the Augustan age, taken from the Etruscan town of Veio, in its portico. The piazza takes its name from the **Column of Marcus Aurelius★★**, erected in imitation of the Column of Trajan (→ Forum of Trajan) between 176 and 193. It has reliefs illustrating the imperial wars against the Germans and Sarmatians spiraling to the full height of the shaft (88 ft); Sixtus V had the base refurbished and placed the statue of St. Paul on the top. From nearby Largo Chigi, the busy v. del Tritone, famous for its deluxe shops, goes up to the Piazza Barberini (→ Palazzo Barberini), linking the city centre with the higher part. □

▶ PIAZZA DEL POPOLO*
I C5

Giuseppe Valadier's design (1816-20) of this oval urban space with **semicircles** decorated with statues and fountains was the last mark made on the layout of the city by the popes. It was very successful and much admired and took intelligent account of existing buildings, integrating them effectively.

▶ The **Porta del Popolo** was built by Nanni di Baccio Bigio (1565) and Bernini added the internal façade (1655); adjacent is the Renaissance church of **S. Maria del Popolo**★★ (→). ▶ The Egyptian **Flaminian Obelisk** was placed in the middle of the square by Sixtus V (1589) and Valadier added the basins and lions to the base. ▶ The two twin churches, on a central plan, marking the entrance to the trio of famous streets (v. del Babuino, v. del Corso and v. di Ripetta) leading to the city centre, are **S. Maria dei Miracoli** (1679) with circular interior and **S. Maria di Montesanto** (1675) with elliptical interior; they were started by C. Rainaldi and completed by Bernini and C. Fontana. □

▶ PIAZZA DI SPAGNA*
I D6

This famous square was the romantic centre of 19C Rome. It gets its name from the Spanish Embassy and is the site of the **barcaccia**, Pietro Bernini's fountain (1629), a replica of the boat which once used the Ripetta, the Tiber harbour, now disappeared.

▶ The **v. del Babuino** (one of the Baroque trio of streets) begins at the N end. It is, with the parallel **v. Margutta**, the centre of the antiques and art trade. To the W is the **v. dei Condotti** (→) and to the S Bernini's **Palazzo Propaganda Fide**★ (→ Renaissance and Baroque Palazzi). At no. 25 is the **Keats and Shelley Memorial House** *(9 a.m.-1 p.m. and 2:30-6 p.m. in summer; closed Sat and Sun)* with memorabilia and portraits of the two poets. ▶ The focal point of the piazza is the magnificent **Trinità dei Monti**★ (Spanish) steps leading to the church of the same name on the hill, a late example of Roman Baroque (Francesco de Sanctis, 1723-6). □

▶ PIAZZA NAVONA**
I E-F4-5

Some consider this to be the most beautiful square in Rome, and it is certainly true that the sweep of its buildings, following the elongated ellipse of the Stadium of Domitian, is splendid in its architectural harmony. There are three fountains (Fontana del Nettuno in the N, with 19C sculpture, the Fontana dei Fiumi in the centre and the Fontana del Moro, designed by Bernini, in the S). The Fontana dei Fiumi (Bernini, 1651) has an obelisk which is an imitation of an Egyptian one. On the rocks supporting it are allegorical figures of the Nile, the Ganges, the Danube and the River Plate, Baroque allusions to the four parts of the known world. Opposite, Borromini com-

pleted in 1657 the church of **S. Agnese in Agone**★, started by Rainaldi in 1652. It stands on the site where the thirteen-year old Virgin and martyr was exposed naked in the pillory and had her body miraculously covered by her hair. The **interior** *(10 a.m.-6 p.m.; Sun 11 a.m.-12 noon; closed Aug),* on a Greek cross plan, is a sumptuous example of Baroque furnishings; in the basement *(by request)* are ruins of the **Roman stadium.** □

piazza Navona

The Neopolitan and the Ticinese in piazza Navona

There was no love lost between Francesco Borromini from Bissone, a Swiss, and Gian Lorenzo Bernini, of Naples, incomparable masters of the Baroque and the two greatest architects of the 17C. In the piazza Navona the Fontana dei Fiumi with the Roman obelisk from the Circus of Maxentius on top of the hollow rock is the work of Bernini; opposite, the façade of the church of S. Agnese in Agone, concave with twin campaniles, is by Borromini. The gestures of the statues are interpreted as a silent but trenchant polemic. Bernini's statue, representing the River Plate, is raising its hand as if to ward off the collapse of Borromini's church façade, and his Nile statue hides his head in order not to see Borromini's 'errors of style'. On the other hand, Borromini's St. Agnes, at the foot of the right-hand campanile, reassuringly keeps her hand on her breast as a sign of faith that the church would not collapse. An anecdote adds that Borromini's supporters were sure that the obelisk on the fountain, weighing down heavily on the empty space, must have wobbled, and that Bernini, during the night, had it supported with four ropes. Both fountain and church are two marvelous notes in the harmonious complex of the piazza which, with its buildings on the perimeter of the stadium of Domitian (Navona, from agonis from campus agonis, field of competitions), is one of the most beautiful achievements of Baroque architecture.

▶ Il PINCIO*
II B1

'Sitting under the trees in the Pincio, full of the song of the cicadas, we enjoy the delights of a fresh breeze from the sea...', thus wrote Stendhal

(1828). The architect Giuseppe Valadier laid out the public **park** (and built the Neoclassical **Casina Valadier**) on the hill where old Roman noble families like the Domiti and the Pinci (from whom the name is derived) had their villas. There is a wonderful **view★★** of the city from the terrace above the p. del Popolo. ▫

▶ PORTA MAGGIORE*
p. di Porta Maggiore   III B6

The Porta Maggiore was formed by the archways carrying a double aqueduct at the time of Claudius (52). Aurelian included it in his fortifying walls. On the outside of the gate is the tomb of the baker **M. Virgilio Eurisace** (1C BC), with openings representing the mouths of an oven. Against the railway embankment is the entrance (v. Prenestina 17) to the **Basilica di Porta Maggiore** (1C), the subterranean sanctuary of a mystic sect, decorated with magnificent stucco★ *(students' visits by permission of Soprintendenza, p. delle Finanze 1).* ▫

▶ PORTA PIA**
at end of v. XX Settembre   II B-C5

Now isolated from the Aurelian wall in which it was a gate, this is the last architectural work by Michelangelo (1561-4), commissioned by Pius V to make a monumental beginning to the v. Nomentana (the layout of this street is by Vespignani, 1864). On the l. is the 'breach' through which Italian troops entered Rome on 20 September 1870. It houses the **Museo Storico dei Bersaglieri** *(Tue and Thu 9 a.m.-1 p.m.).* ▫

▶ PORTA SAN PAOLO*
                            IV E5

This is the ancient *Porta Ostiensis* in the Aurelian wall. The inner side, with two arches, dates from the time of Aurelian, but the outside, with one arch between two crenellated half-cylindrical towers, dates from the time of Honorius (started in the 5C).

▶ It houses the **Museo della Via Ostiense** *(9 a.m.-1 p.m.; closed Mon).* ▶ Beyond the gate is the **Pyramid of Caius Cestius★**, the tomb of the praetor and tribune of the people, who died in 12 BC. It is clearly influenced by the exoticism of Egypt, which had recently been conquered. ▶ Inside the wall, on the r. of the gate, is the **Protestant Cemetery** where Shelley and Keats are buried. ▶ Beyond the cemetery is the park and **Monte Testaccio**, a mound formed by broken fragments of wine and oil amphoras from the Tiber landing stage. ▫

▶ PORTA SAN SEBASTIANO*
                            III F4

This is the opening in the Aurelian wall on to the v. Appia Antica★★ (→). It was rebuilt in the 5C and restored in the 6C by Belisarius and has one arch between two crenellated towers. Inside is the **Museo delle Mura**, which gives access to **Passeggiata sulle Mura** (footpath ending at v. Cristoforo Colombo; *9 a.m.-1 p.m.; Tue and Thu also 4-7 p.m.; closed Mon).* The **Arch of Drusus**, inside the gate, carried the aqueduct which fed the Baths of Caracalla. ▫

▶ PORTICO DI OTTAVIA
v. del Portico di Ottavia   IV A4

The portico was named after Augustus' sister in whose honour the Emperor rebuilt (23 BC) the earlier porticus of Q. Cecilius Metellus. It enclosed a temple area with a double row of columns decorated with statues and including a library. The **propylaeum** at the entrance has five Corinthian columns and now forms the porch of the church of **S. Angelo in Pescheria**; it was part of a later rebuilding by Septimus Severus and Caracalla (203). The adjacent quarter was the Jewish **ghetto** (→). ▫

▶ Il QUIRINALE*
p. del Quirinale   II E2

Students of Roman urban development attach great importance to Gregory XIII's decision in 1574 to build the papal summer residence among Cardinal Ippolito d'Este's vineyards on the highest of the seven hills of Rome. Previous popes had been preoccupied with the Borgo, with the streets between the city and the Vatican, with the spaces within the bend of the Tiber and with the routes out to S. Giovanni in Laterano and the p. del Popolo. With Gregory XIII interest and planning policy turned to the hills, away from the city. The **p. del Quirinale★★** contains the statue of the *Dioscuri*, Castor and Pollux, a Roman replica of a 6C-5C BC Greek original. In its centre is the slender **obelisk** from the Mausoleum of Augustus and around it stands the **Palazzo della Consulta** (F. Fuga, 1734) and the **Palazzo del Quirinale★**, on which various architects worked, including Bernini and, in the 18C, F. Fuga. Formerly the papal summer residence, it was the royal residence from 1870-1946 and is now the residence of the President of the Italian Republic. Inside *(permission from Servizio Intendenza della Presidenza della Repubblica, v. Dataria 96)* are splendid rooms, tapestries, vases and furniture. Outstanding features are the fresco of *Christ in Glory with Angels★* by Melozzo da Forlì (on the staircase), the Salone dei Corazzieri and the Cappella Paolina, with superb stucco. ▫

▶ RENAISSANCE AND BAROQUE PALAZZI

'In Rome everything should be sought out calmly.' This was Winckelmann's sage advice. The most beautiful Roman finds reward patient searching. In a stroll through the area of central Rome W of the v. del Corso, bounded by the great bend in the Tiber between the ponte Cavour (I D5) and the ponte Sisto (IV A3), there are a wealth of important buildings and the palazzi (listed here in chronological order) can be seen in the context of other visits.

▶ The Roman Renaissance palazzo has Florentine ancestry. This is clear in the **Palazzo della Cancellieria★★** (I F4; 1483-1517) with lightly rusticated façade, articulated with pilaster strips in the upper storeys; it was probably the work of Andrea Bregno. Bramante may also have been involved; the superb courtyard★ is definitely his work. The nearby **piazza Campo dei Fiori**, the place of execution, where Giordano Bruno was burned, is now the most popular market in the city centre. ▶ A Florentine, Antonio da Sangallo the Younger, started the stupendous **Palazzo Farnese★★** for Cardinal Farnese (later Pope

Paul III) in 1514 (IV A3; *houses the French Embassy; not open to public),* which was then continued by Michelangelo (1546), who was responsible for the architectural energy of the façade windows and cornices. Da Sangallo's **vestibule★** is an example of Renaissance Neoclassical ideas. The two upper storeys of the **courtyard★** are by Michelangelo, while the **gallery★** on the first floor has frescos by Carracci (in piazza in front are two fountains built of huge granite basins from the Baths of Caracalla). ▶ The façade (1515) of the **Palazzo Vidoni** (I F5) in the v. del Sudario may be a product of Raphael's architectural genius (the Casa del Burcardo (→) is in the same street). ▶ Near **S. Andrea della Valle** (→) is the **Palazzo Massimo alle Colonne★** (I F5), a masterpiece of the Sienese architect Baldassarre Peruzzi (1532-6); the rusticated façade is broken by a portico with six columns. The stucco decoration★ on the portico and the upper storey is also by Peruzzi. ▶ The **Palazzo Borghese★** (I D5), started in 1560, possibly to a design by Vignola, is a fine example of a late Renaissance elevation, and in the courtyard is a Baroque grotto (G.P. Schor and C. Rainaldi; the palazzo was completed by F. Ponzio in 1605-14). ▶ The same mixture of Renaissance and Baroque is found in the **Palazzo Madama★** (I F5; *houses the Senate),* formerly Medici, 16C, but with a mid-17C Baroque façade. ▶ A more imposing example of Baroque, however, is the **Palazzo di Propaganda Fide★** (I D6) in which the two major 17C architects met: Bernini (the elevation on p. di Spagna; 1627) and Borromini (in lively façade on v. di Propaganda). ▶ Finally the **Palazzo della Sapienza** (I F5) shows Baroque imagination of the highest originality; in Giacomo Della Porta's **courtyard★** is the **dome★** with magnificent spiral lantern of Borromini's **Cappelle di S. Ivo** (1660). ▶ A reasonable route between the palazzi mentioned would be as follows: Borghese, Propaganda Fide, Madama, Sapienza, Massimo, Cancelleria, Vidoni, and Farnese. □

▶ **REPUBLICAN TEMPLES**

largo di Torre Argentina   I F5

Excavations have revealed **4 temples** of the Republican age in the square containing the **Teatro Argentina,** one of the most important in papal Rome. There are three rectangular and one circular temple; the latter is known to have been erected in 101 BC by Quintus Lutatius Catullus in memory of the battle of Vercelli and to 'the good luck of this day'. □

▶ **SAINT PETER'S IN THE VATICAN★★**

II E1-2

The largest church in Christendom, the heart of the Catholic world, was built by Constantine in the early 4C on the site where, according to tradition, St. Peter was buried. This tradition was recently confirmed by the discovery of a Greek inscription saying 'Peter is here' on an ancient wall of the Vatican grotto.

▶ The complex building is surprising in its coherence. The early Christian basilica consecrated by Pope Silvester (while still incomplete) in 326 had a nave and four aisles, with transept and portico in front of the façade; a thousand years later it was falling into disrepair and Nicholas V entrusted Bernardo Rossellino with the rebuilding project in 1452. Little progress was made, and finally Julius II brought in Bramante, a revolutionary moment for architecture (1506). ▶ Bramante wanted to work on a Greek cross plan and to set 'the Pantheon above the basilica of Maxentius'. To this end he built the four piers and the arches of the dome, winning the title of 'the demolisher' by pulling down the ancient church. ▶ He was followed by Giuliano da Sangallo, Raphael and Baldassarre Peruzzi; Antonio da Sangallo

the Younger hesitated between Bramante's central plan and a longer nave on the Latin cross design. ▶ Michelangelo intervened in 1546, stamping his genius on Bramante's initial concept, but the dome was completed, with an elliptical outline, by Domenico Fontana and Giacomo Della Porta (1589). ▶ Carlo Maderna, commissioned by Paul V, extended the rear arm, thus confirming the Latin cross design, and built the façade. ▶ The church was consecrated by Urban VIII on 18 November 1626, the day on which the Constantinian basilica had been blessed thirteen centuries before. ▶ Bernini laid out the magnificent **piazza★★** with two **semicircles** with 284 columns and 88 pilasters in 1656-67; the Egyptian **obelisk★** was erected in 1586 (between this and the two 17C **fountains** two circular stones indicate the points at which the quadruple colonnade of each of the arms of Bernini's ellipse look like a single line). ▶ Above the r.-hand colonnade, at the end of which is the **bronze doorway** leading to the Vatican, is the 16C complex of the **Palazzi Apostolici★**. In the impressive **façade** (376 ft long by 149 ft wide) is the window used for papal blessings. ▶ Five openings lead into the **atrium:** above the central opening is the famous mosaic of *Christ walking on the water,* the *Navicella,* designed by Giotto; at the r.-hand end beyond a door is Bernini's equestrian statue of *Constantine* (1670). Five bronze doors lead into the basilica; the central one is by **Filarete** (1433-45); the last one on the l. is the **Porta della Morte★** (G. Manzù, 1964); and the last on the r. is the **Porta Santa,** walled up and only opened in jubilee years. ▶ The **interior** defies description; it is the largest church in Christendom (610 ft long and 451 ft wide at the transepts), but this is only clear on examination of detail; the space has a harmony equal to its size, organized with great lucidity around the **dome★★** (height 435 ft, diameter 139 ft). There are numerous masterpieces among the works of art. Particularly notable are the bronze statues of *St. Peter Enthroned★* attributed to Arnolfo di Cambio (last pier on the r. in the nave); the bronze *baldacchino★* by Bernini (1633) above the papal altar; in the r. aisle is the *Pietà★★,* a youthful work by Michelangelo; in the r. transept Canova's *Monument of Clement XIII★;* on the Tribune the *Chair of St. Peter★* (Bernini, 1656), between Bernini's *Monument of Urban VIII* and that of *Paul III* (Gugliemo Della Porta); the marble relief of *St. Leo Arresting the Progress of Attila★* by A. Algardi (1646; *on the altar of St. Leo the Great);* in the l. aisle the *Monument of Innocent VIII★* by Antonio Pollaiolo (1498). ▶ The **Treasury★** *(9 a.m.-1 p.m.; summer 9 a.m.-6 p.m.)* contains, among other things, the **cross★** of the Emperor of the East Justinian II (6C); the **Dalmatic★** (regal vestment) said to be Charlemagne's (in fact 11C); the *Tomb of Sixtus IV★* by Pollaiolo; the *Sarcophagus of Junius Bassus★*(4C). ▶ Other works of art can be found in the **Vatican Grottos★** *(7 a.m.-5 p.m.)* under the nave, between the floor of the Constantinian basilica and the present one. The collection includes a mosaic medallion with a *Bust of an Angel★* attributed to Giotto and Arnolfo di Cambio's *Boniface VIII★.* ▶ It is possible to climb the **dome★** *(9 a.m.-5 p.m.; summer 9 a.m.-6 p.m.; lift to terrace above nave).* The roof of the basilica provides a wonderful view of the dome; the first and second circular galleries give fine views of the interior of the church, from the loggia (537 steps from the pavement of the basilica) there is a sweeping **view★** of the palazzi, the Vatican gardens and the city. □

▶ **SAN CARLO AL CORSO**

v. del Corso   I D5-6

This Baroque church has a nave and two aisles, apses, ambulatory (unique in Rome) and a magnificent **dome** (by Pietro da Cortona. It was the Roman church of the Lombards and was built by Onorio and Martino Longhi (1612-72). The interior has lavish marble, stucco and frescos with, on the high altar, a painting by Maratta of the *Glory of S. Ambrogio and S. Carlo,* patron saints of Milan. □

▶ **SAN CARLO QUATTRO FONTANE***

v. del Quirinale   II D3

The **four fountains** are in the four rounded-off corners of this crossroads typical of Sixtus V's Rome, looking toward the Porta Pia and the Esquiline, Quirinal and Trinità dei Monti obelisks. The **church**, founded in 1638, is attached to the convent on which Borromini worked until 1634 (cloister★). The church itself is the first work realized completely by the architect, while the façade was his last (built in 1667, the year he committed suicide). The **interior** *(wkdays, p.m. only)*, on an oval plan, has the dimensions of one of the pillars of the dome of St. Peter's.   □

▶ **SAN CLEMENTE****

p. S. Clemente   III B3

This magnificent medieval basilica is a typical example of the stratification of architecture in Rome. The present **church** was commissioned by Paschal II (1108) to be built on the ruins of an early Christian basilica (4C) destroyed by the Normans in 1084. The 12C **porch** has four ancient Ionic columns and the interior has a nave and two aisles on Roman columns. It has in the ceiling vault a mosaic of the *Triumph of the Cross★★* (12C Roman school). A screen★ (partly 6C) surrounds the sanctuary; the high altar and episcopal throne date from the 12C. At the head of the l.-hand aisle is the **cappella di S. Caterina di Alessandria** decorated with **frescos★** by Masolino da Panicale (*c.* 1430). The **lower church** can be reached from the sacristy *(9 a.m.-12 noon and 3:30-6:30 p.m.)* which contains 6C-12C frescos. There are remains from the time of the Roman Republic and a 2C mithraeum (temple to the sun God Mithras) under the apse.   □

▶ **SAN FRANCESCO A RIPA**

in Trastevere   IV C3

The finest feature of this Baroque **church** (1689) is Bernini's statue of *Lodovica Albertoni★* (1674). In the convent *(apply at sacristy)* is the **cell** inhabited by St. Francis, with a 13C painting★ of him.   □

▶ **SAN GIORGIO IN VELABRO**

near p. Bocca della Verità   IV B5

This church may date from the 6C. Its portico and campanile are Romanesque (12C), the interior columns Roman. Near the campanile is the small, ornate **Arco degli Argentari**, built in honour of the Emperor Septimus Severus by moneychangers (3C).□

▶ **SAN GIOVANNI A PORTA LATINA**

near v. di Porta Latina   III E4

Modern restoration has maintained the medieval appearance of this 5C **church**, rebuilt in the 8C. The portico and campanile are Romanesque. Inside it has a series of 12C frescos. Just before it is the octagonal oratory of **S. Giovanni in Oleo** (1509, with additions by Borromini) on the spot where tradi-

tion maintains that the Evangelist emerged unscathed from torture by boiling oil. Further on is the **Porta Latina**, a gate pierced in the Aurelian Wall by Belisarius (6C).   □

▶ **SAN GIOVANNI DEI FIORENTINI**

v. Giulia   I E3

Leo X Medici wanted to build this church for his fellow citizens and all the major architects of the period submitted plans. Jacopo Sansovino's were chosen (*c.* 1520). Antonio da Sangallo the Younger, Giacomo Della Porta and Alessandro Galilei were also subsequently involved (1734).   □

▶ **SAN GIOVANNI IN LATERANO****

p. S. Giovanni in Laterano   III C4-5

'The entire site', said a 17C historian, 'could not 'satisfy the artist', at that time Borromini, who in the final rebuilding (1646-9) of Rome's cathedral found that he was required to retain, at the specific wish of Innocent X, the existing early Christian basilican design with nave and four aisles. The Emperor Constantine himself presented the property of the Plautius Lateranus family to the Christians, and the thirty-second pope, S. Melchiades, built a church on the site in 311-14. It remained the seat of the popes from then until the move to Avignon in 1309.
▶ In the **p. S. Giovanni in Laterano**, in which the Theban **obelisk** was set up in 1588 (the highest and oldest in Rome), are the **Palazzo del Laterano** (Domenico Fontana, 1586), the baptistery and the **side façade** (D. Fontana, 1586) of the basilica with two 14C campaniles. The **main façade**, on the p. di Porta S. Giovanni, is the work of Alessandro Galilei (1735). ▶ The church contains many distinguished works, including the ancient statue of Constantine (in the portico) and the **bronze doors** from the Curia in the central portal. In the **interior★** by Borromini notable features are the 16C wooden ceiling★, the fresco attributed to Giotto showing Boniface VIII proclaiming the Jubilee in 1300 and the Gothic tabernacle (1367) with frescos attributed to Barna da Siena (1368). ▶ The **Museo del Tesoro** has a 13C-14C processional cross★ and a cross★ by Nicola da Guardiagrele (1451). ▶ The exquisite **cloister★★** with plain and twisted columns is the work of the Vassalletti (1215-32). ▶ The baptistery of **S. Giovanni★**, built by Sixtus III (5C), was rebuilt by Urban VIII in 1637; its central plan was a tribute to Constantine and the prototype of Christian buildings. The octagonal interior at its centre two sets of columns with an architrave supporting the dome; one of the four surrounding chapels has a bronze door dating from 1196 and 5C mosaics. ▶ A 16C building opposite the Palazzo del Laterano contains the **Scala Santa** *(7 a.m.-12 noon and 3:30-7 p.m.)*, which tradition says was brought to Rome by St. Helena from Pontius Pilate's house in Jerusalem. From the upper terrace it is possible to see, through a grill, the **Cappella del Sancta Sanctorum★**, the remains of the ancient papal palace, with Cosmati-work mosaics (1278), paintings and ancient reliquaries.   □

▶ **SAN GREGORIO MAGNO**

p. S. Gregorio   III C2

Even before he became pope in 575, Gregory the Great had transformed his house into a monastery with attached church. The present **church** has a Baroque façade (G.B. Soria, 1629-33) and 18C interior. In the **Chapel of St. Gregory** at the end of the r. aisle is his episcopal throne. On the l. of the church, in a little square with cypress trees, are three plain **chapels★** *(closed for restoration):* the one on the r. and the one in the middle have frescos by Guido Reni (the second also has frescos by Domenichino); the chapel on the l. contains the stone table on which St. Gregory himself served twelve poor people with food each day. ◻

▶ SAN LORENZO FUORI LE MURA**
from piazzale Sixtus V along v. Tiburtina   II E6

This **church** was founded by Constantine (330) on the site of the martyrdom of St. Laurence and is one of the seven pilgrimage churches of Rome. The present building is in the form created by Honorius III (13C), who joined the church built by Hadrian I (8C) end to end with the earlier church restored by Pelagius II in the 6C.

▶ The **campanile** is Romanesque (12C); the **portico★** (1220) has ancient columns with architrave and 12C-13C frescos and leads to the interior with a nave and two aisles, again with ancient columns. ▶ The raised sanctuary is the Constantinian basilica, with a women's gallery added by Pelagius II; within the triumphal arch is a 6C mosaic of *Christ with Saints★*; the episcopal throne★ (13C) breaks the run of marble stalls in the choir. ▶ Medieval inscriptions and remains of sculpture surround the late 12C Romanesque **cloister.** ◻

▶ SAN LORENZO IN LUCINA
. p. S. Lorenzo in Lucina   I D-E 5-6

The 3C Spaniard Lorenzo, treasurer of the Roman church, died as a martyr on the gridiron and, according to tradition, parts of this object are contained in the 17C interior of this **church,** built in the 4C on the site of the house of the matron Lucina. The portico and campanile are 12C; on the high altar is *Christ Crucified* by Guido Reni.

▶ SAN LUIGI DEI FRANCESI*
p. S. Luigi dei Francesi   I E5

The façade of this **church,** which belongs to France and was built in 1518-89, may be the work of Giacomo Della Porta. The interior has lavish 18C decoration. In the second chapel on the r. are frescos *(Life of St. Cecilia)* by Domenichino and in the second chapel on the l. three masterpieces by Caravaggio: *Call of St. Matthew★★, St. Matthew and the Angel★* and *Martyrdom of St. Matthew★* (1598-1601). These works were commissioned by Cardinal Mathieu Cointrel, who was so puzzled by their 'realism' and 'vulgarity' that the first and third were taken back and altered while being painted, and *St. Matthew and the Angel* was the second version of the same subject, after the first had been rejected. ◻

▶ SAN MARTINO AI MONTI
v. Lanza   II F4

The Romanesque **apse** of this **church** is behind one of the two medieval towers (of the Capocci and the Graziani) which mark the way up the Esqui-

line. This 4C, early Christian foundation was totally rebuilt by Pietro da Cortona (1635-76). Interior **frescos** include some fine work by G. Dughet and two of documentary interest, one showing the interior of St. Peter's as a Constantinian basilica and one of S. Giovanni in Laterano before it was rebuilt by Borromini. ◻

▶ SAN NICOLA IN CARCERE
v. Teatro di Marcello   II B4

This church with an elegant late 16C façade by G. Della Porta is on the site of the Roman **Forum Holitorium** (the vegetable market). It is built on the remains of three **temples,** from which various columns were incorporated along the sides. There is a *Trinità* by Guercino in the interior. Opposite the church are a small 13C house and the columns of a **portico** of the Augustan era. ◻

▶ SAN PAOLO FUORI LE MURA**
from porta S. Paolo along v. Ostiense   IV E5

A fire on the night of 15 July 1823 destroyed the **basilica** built by Constantine on the site of the Apostle's tomb, the most beautiful of all the Roman churches and one of the four patriarchal basilicas. Immediate rebuilding left what is effectively a model of the original. Inside, decorated according to the eclectic style of the period, are **bronze doors★** from the original basilica (1070); on Arnolfo di Cambio's Gothic high altar (13C) is a paschal candlestick★ by the Vassalletti (12C-13C); the mosaic of *Christ with Four Saints★* in the apse is by Venetian artists (*c.* 1220). The splendid **cloisters★★**, with arches on coupled columns, are by the Vassalletti (1214) and lead to a small **picture gallery** *(8:30-11:30 a.m. and 3:30-6:30 p.m.).* ◻

▶ SAN PIETRO IN MONTORIO*
v. Garibaldi   IV B2

There is a sensational **view★** of Rome from the piazzale. The Renaissance **church** (perhaps by Baccio Pontelli, 15C) is on the site traditionally held to be that of the crucifixion of St. Peter. In the interior is Sebastiano da Piombo's *Scourging of Christ.* The most famous architectural feature of the church is in the little courtyard to the r. (the original plan foresaw a circular courtyard). It is **Bramante's Tempietto★★** (1502), a small centrally planned building with a ring of sixteen Doric columns and a dome, in which Bramante expressed completely, for the first time, the spatial concepts of the Renaissance. A hole in the floor of the chapel underneath is supposed to have been the one in which the cross on which St. Peter was crucified was stuck. ◻

▶ SAN PIETRO IN VINCOLI*
from v. Cavour along steps by S. Francesco di Paola   II F3

This **church** dates from the 5C and was restored in the 18C. It was built to house the chains *(vincula)* which bound the Apostle Peter. In the **interior,** with a nave and two aisles and ancient columns, is the

Mausoleum of Julius II★, a realization (completed by pupils) of the most modest of six plans drawn up by Michelangelo for the tomb and rejected by Leo X. Michelangelo planned 40 statues. Of those completed, some are now in Paris and Florence. All that remain here are the magnificent *Moses* (1514-16) and the figures of *Leah* and *Rachel,* completed by Raffaello da Montelupo. □

▶ **SAN SABA**
v. S. Saba   IV E5

This church is on the site on the Aventine of the house of Silvia, the sainted mother of Gregory the Great. It was founded in the 7C by Palestinian monks and named after a monk from Cappadocia (6C) who was one of the organizers and leaders of Eastern monasticism. The church was rebuilt in 1205 and subsequently much altered. The façade has a Cosmati-work **portal** and 15C **loggia**; the interior has three naves and two aisles with ancient columns, Cosmati-work and remains of some frescos (8C-10C) removed from the underground **Oratorio di S. Silvia** (6C). □

▶ **SAN SEBASTIANO***
from porta S. Sebastiano along v. Appia Antica   III F4

This **church** was founded in the 4C and rebuilt in the 17C by F. Ponzio and G. Vasanzio. In the **Cappella delle Reliquie** are one of the arrows from the martyrdom of St. Sebastian and the stone with Christ's footprint from the spot at which he met St. Peter (→ Via Appia Antica). From the atrium it is possible to go down to the **catacombs** with galleries on four levels *(winter 8:30 or 9 a.m.-12 noon and 2:30-5 p.m.; closed Thu; guided by a monk).* The visit usually includes, on the second level: the **Crypt of St. Sebastian;** the 3C **Triclia** or room with funeral benches, with graffiti invoking St. Peter and St. Paul; the **Platonia** or mausoleum of St. Quirinus (5C) and the **Chapel of Honorius III** with 13C frescos. □

▶ **SANTA BALBINA**
in Porta Capena park   III D2

This little **church** dates from the 5C and is set among remains of imperial and medieval buildings; in the centre of the nave is the refurbished *schola cantorum.* There is a Cosmati-work throne in the nave and, in the niches along the walls, 9C-14C frescos. Around the **Porta Capena park★** is the green area, thickly planted with holm oaks and Italian pines, surrounding the **Baths of Caracalla★★** (→). □

▶ **SANTA CECILIA IN TRASTEVERE***
p. S. Cecilia   IV C4

This **church** stands on the site of Saint Cecilia's martyrdom. It dates from earlier than the 5C, was rebuilt in the 9C and refurbished in various ways in the 18C; there is a courtyard with a garden in front of the Baroque façade (F. Fuga) with a 12C portico; the campanile dates from 1113. Inside a **Gothic tabernacle★**

by Arnolfo di Cambio (1283) covers the high altar under which is the statue of *St. Cecilia★* by Stefano Maderno (1600) showing her body as found when her tomb was opened in 1599. The great **mosaic** in the vault of the apse (9C) shows the Redeemer with other saints, Cecilia and her betrothed Valerian and, with a square nimbus (the early Christian convention for those portrayed when still alive), Pope Paschal I. From the crypt it is possible to go down *(10 a.m.-12 noon wkdays)* to the **Roman remains** under the church. In the adjacent enclosed convent the monks' choir contains the monumental fresco of the *Last Judgment★*, a masterpiece by Pietro Cavallini (13C; *Tue and Thu 10 a.m.-12 noon).* □

▶ **SANTA COSTANZA★★**
from porta Pia along v. Nomentana   II B5

The building *(visit accompanied by custodian of catacombs of S. Agnese)* dates from the 4C and was originally the mausoleum of Costanza and Elena, daughters of Constantine. It was then made into a **baptistery** and adapted to a **church** in the 13C. Inside is a circular aisle and high dome and excellent 4C **mosaics★★** with symbolic scenes of the grape harvest and Bacchic motifs in the vault of the aisle. The ruins of the basilica built by Costanza and dedicated to St. Agnes are near this church. □

▶ **SANTA CROCE***
p. S. Croce in Gerusalemme   III B6

This church was originally built by St. Helena to house the relic of the True Cross (*c.* 320). The impressive 18C **façade,** the oval **atrium** and the Baroque interior date from rebuilding (1743) at the time of Benedict XIV; the Romanesque **campanile** dates from 1144. Fine features of the church include a Cosmati-work pavement, a fresco of the *Legend of the True Cross★* attributed to Antoniazzo Romano (*c.* 1492), the tomb of Cardinal Quinones by J. Sansovino and, in the chapel of St. Helena, a **mosaic★** probably designed by Melozzo da Forli. Access to the **Cappella delle Reliquie** *(apply to sacristan)* is from the l. aisle. □

▶ **SANT'AGNESE★★**
from porta Pia along v. Nomentana   II B5

St. Agnes, denounced as a Christian to the Prefect of Rome by one of her rejected suitors, was shut up in a brothel and then beheaded at the age of thirteen (*c.* 304). The **church** was built shortly after as a small sanctuary above the catacombs where the saint was buried; was rebuilt in the 7C; then restored on numerous occasions. The **interior** has a nave and two aisles separated by Roman columns (the wooden ceiling dates from the early 17C). There is a splendid **mosaic** set in a gold background in the vault of the apse showing the saint with two popes (625-638). From the narthex it is possible to go down to the **Catacombs of S. Agnese** *(10 a.m.-12 noon and 3-6 p.m.; closed Sun and hol a.m.),* which are in good condition and pre-4C in places. □

▶ **SANT'AGOSTINO***

p. S. Agostino   I E5

This Renaissance **church** (Giacomo da Pietrasanta, 1479-83) with an interior refurbished in 1760 by Luigi Vanvitelli contains three major works of art: Jacopo Sansovino's **Madonna del Parto★** (1521), Raphael's *Prophet Isaiah★★* (1512) and Caravaggio's *Madonna dei Pellegrini★★ (Our Lady of Loreto;* 1605).   ☐

▶ **SANTA MARIA DELL'ANIMA**

near p. Navona   I E4

This early 16C **church** of the German Catholics has a plain Renaissance **façade★** attributed to Giuliano da Sangallo. Inside *(8 a.m.-1 p.m. and 4-7 p.m.; Sun 8 a.m.-1 p.m.; ring at v. della Pace 20)* the tomb of Adrian VI, until John Paul II the last non-Italian Pope (d. 1523), was designed by B. Peruzzi; there is a painting by Giulio Romano over the high altar.   ☐

▶ **SANTA MARIA DELLA PACE***

vicolo della Pace   I E4

There are three very good artistic reasons for seeking out this little church in a secluded corner near the p. Navona. The first is to see Pietro da Cortona's curved **façade** (1656-9) and the exquisite **polygonal piazzetta** into which it fits so perfectly, creating a wonderful Baroque space; the second is to visit the inside of the church (B. Pontelli, *c.* 1480; *Sun 11 a.m.; other days inquire at v. Arco delle Pace 5, 9 a.m.-12 noon and 4-6 p.m.)* and admire the *Sybils★★* painted by Raphael (1514) on the arch of the r.-hand chapel; the third is to visit the **cloister★★** *(v. Arco della Pace 5)*, Bramante's first work in Rome (1504).   ☐

▶ **SANTA MARIA DELLA VITTORIA***

v. XX Settembre   II D3

This Baroque **church** (C. Maderno, 1608-20; façade by G.B. Soria, 1626) owes its name to a small image of the Virgin (now lost) found among the rubbish of the castle of Pilsen and to which the Catholic soldiers of Ferdinand II attributed their victory over Protestant Prague. A more serious claim to fame is the **Cappella Cornaro** with Bernini's marble group of the *Ecstasy of St. Theresa★★* (1646), much admired by Stendhal, and about which the friar accompanying him and his guests said: 'It's a pity that this statue can easily bring profane love to mind'.   ☐

▶ **SANTA MARIA DEL POPOLO****

p. del Popolo   I B5

The interior of this beautiful **church** (rebuilt in 1477, perhaps by B. Pontelli and A. Bregno who were certainly responsible for the façade) is, despite the Baroque superstructure (by Bernini), essentially Renaissance in character. It houses numerous works: in the first chapel on the r., frescos and altarpiece by Pinturicchio; in the apse, by Bramante, are more frescos by Pinturicchio, two tombs by A. Sansovino and a 12C *Madonna★* on the altar; in the chapel on the l. of

the apse are two masterpieces by Caravaggio (*Conversion of St. Paul★★* and *Crucifixion of St. Peter★★).* The artistic heart of the church is the **Cappella Chigi★**, lucidly designed by Raphael; on the altar is the *Birth of the Virgin* by Sebastiano del Piombo and in the corners, four statues of prophets (*Jonah★* and *Elijah★* by Lorenzetto to designs by Raphael; *Habakkuk* and *Daniel* by Bernini). The church was originally a chapel built to celebrate the liberation of the Holy Sepulchre by the Crusaders (1099), but according to tradition it came into being to exorcise the ghost of Nero, buried here in his family vault.   ☐

▶ **SANTA MARIA IN CAMPITELLI**

p. Campitelli   IV A4

The **interior★** of Carlo Rainaldi's **church** (1667), in a typical 17C Roman square, is considered a major masterpiece of Roman Baroque. It was commissioned by Alexander VII, redeeming his promise to the people to build a church to house the *Madonna in Portico* (an 11C enamel in Franco-Rhenish style now on high altar), held to have stopped the plague of 1656. Nearby is the **Palazzo Mattei** (C. Maderno, 1598-1611) with a fine **courtyard** with statues and ancient reliefs, which houses the **Museo degli Strumenti di Riproduzione del Suono** (sound reproduction; *wkdays 9 a.m.-1:30 p.m.)*. Finally the **Fontana delle Tartarughe★** in the p. Mattei was designed by Giacomo Della Porta (1581-4).   ☐

▶ **SANTA MARIA IN COSMEDIN***

p. Bocca della Verità   IV C5

The **mask** beneath the portico is the 'Bocca della Verità' (Mouth of Truth; hence the name of the square), popularly supposed to bite the hands of liars. The **church** is a magnificent example of medieval architecture. It dates from the 6C, and in the 8C it was given to Greek refugees from iconoclastic persecution, who decorated it (*cosmedin* means decoration). The Romanesque **campanile★** was added in the course of 12C restoration and is one of the most beautiful of its period in Rome. The **interior,** with a nave and two aisles separated by ancient columns, has been restored to the 8C design: pavement, paschal candelabrum, episcopal throne and ciborium are the work of the Cosmati (11C-12C). There is a fragment of **mosaic★** dating from 706 in the sacristy.   ☐

▶ **SANTA MARIA IN DOMINICA***

p. della Navicella   III C3

The 16C **Fontana della Navicella** in the square at the top of the Caelian hill is a replica of an ancient votive ship. The **church** (the name may be derived from the adjective *dominicum,* of the Lord, used in the early Christian centuries to indicate places of worship) was rebuilt in the 9C by Paschal I and again in the 16C. The interior, with a nave and two aisles separated by ancient columns, contains 9C mosaics (on the triumphal arch and in the apse); the Renaissance frieze below the coffered ceiling (1556) is the work of Perin del Vaga.   ☐

▶ **SANTA MARIA IN TRASTEVERE****
p. S. Maria in Trastevere   IV B2

There is a 17C **fountain** in this piazza, which also has the first **church** in Rome to be dedicated to the mother of Christ (4C), rebuilt in 1130-43. It has a **portico** in front of the **façade** (12C-13C mosaics) and a Romanesque **campanile**. The **interior**, with nave and two aisles, has ancient columns and a Cosmatiwork pavement. The wooden **ceiling** was designed by Domenichino (also responsible for the central painting of the *Assumption*). In the sanctuary the point is indicated at which, according to tradition, a fountain of oil flowed on the day of Christ's birth. The triumphal arch and the vault of the apse are decorated with large **mosaics★** (1140) and under these are six panels of the *Life of Mary★★*, the work of Pietro Cavallini (*c.* 1291).   □

▶ **SANTA MARIA IN VALLICELLA***
p. della Chiesa Nuova   I F4

This church was built for St. Philip Neri, who is buried here. It was started in 1575 and concluded to designs by Martino Longhi the Elder *c.* 1583. The façade is by F. Rughesi (1605) and the lavish **interior** contains frescos by Pietro da Cortona and *Madonna with Angels★* and two other pictures of *Saints★* by Rubens (1608). Access to the rooms in which St. Philip Neri lived is from the sacristy. On the l. of the church is a superb piece of Baroque architecture, Borromini's façade of the **Oratorio dei Filippini★** (1640).   □

▶ **SANTA MARIA MAGGIORE****
p. S. Maria Maggiore   II E-F4

By foundation this is the most recent of the four great patriarchal basilicas of Rome (the others are San Pietro in Vaticano and San Paolo Fuori le Mura, linked with the places of martyrdom of the two Apostles, and San Giovanni in Laterano, the oldest by some years), but it is the only one in which the **early Christian** design has survived. It is believed to have been founded by Sixtus III shortly after the Council of Ephesus (431). In the 13C the apse was rebuilt, in the 17C the rear façade was added and in the following century the main façade was added (F. Fuga, 1750); the campanile to the r. of it dates from 1337. Important features of the **interior★** are the 5C **mosaics★** above the columns and on the triumphal arch; the mosaic of the *Coronation of the Virgin★* by Jacopo Torriti (1295) in the apse; the lavish **Sistine Chapel★** by Fontana (1586), who was also responsible for the two tombs below the altar; the **Oratorio del Presepio** with a group of statues by Arnolfo di Cambio and the **Cappella Paolina★** by F. Ponzio (1611) with a 13C **Madonna★** of Byzantine appearance.   □

▶ **SANTA MARIA SOPRA MINERVA****
p. della Minerva   I F5-6

The **elephant** supporting the Egyptian **obelisk** (6C BC) was designed by Bernini. The **church★★**, built on the ruins of a temple of Minerva, was rebuilt in

Gothic style by Dominicans *c.* 1280. It is the only church in this style in Rome. Its fine collection includes an altarpiece and frescos★ by Filippino Lippi (in the **Cappella Carafa**) and Michelangelo's statue of *Christ With the Cross★* (1521). Fra Angelico is buried here, and behind the sacristy is the chapel built in 1637 using the walls of the room in which St. Catherine died in 1380, with frescos by Antoniazzo Romano and pupils (1482).   □

▶ **SANT'ANDREA AL QUIRINALE***
v. del Quirinale   II E2

When Cardinal Camillo Pamphili, nephew of Innocent X, entrusted the building of this **church** to Bernini, the great Baroque genius did something that had never been done before: he chose an elliptical plan for the interior, placing the minor axis between the entrance and the altar. The result is one of the architectural masterpieces of Rome (1658-70; *closed Tue; open a.m. only in Aug*).   □

▶ **SANT'ANDREA DELLE FRATTE**
v. S. Andrea delle Fratte   I D-E6

Borromini added the unusual **campanile** (best seen from start of rise in v. Capo le Case), the elliptical **apse** and the incomplete **dome** to this 12C church in the course of its 17C rebuilding. Bernini's two **angels** by the high altar were intended for the Ponte Sant'Angelo. They were acquired by Cardinal Rospigliosi, the nephew of Clement IX, and placed here in 1729.   □

▶ **SANT'ANDREA DELLA VALLE***
corso Vittorio Emanuele II   I F5

The first plans for this church (1591) were by Father Francesco Grimaldi and Giacomo Della Porta; the project was taken up and completed by Maderno in 1625, who was responsible for the **dome** (the highest in Rome after St. Peter's); the **façade** was finally added by Carlo Rainaldi in 1665. Notable among the **frescos** in the fine Baroque **interior** are those by Lanfranco, including the *Gloria del Paradiso* (1625, in the dome), by Domenichino (the *Evangelists★*) and by Mattia Preti (*Martyrdom of St. Andrew*, in the apse, 1651).   □

▶ **SANTA PRASSEDE***
v. S. Martino ai Monti   II F4

The 'garden of Paradise' (the name comes from the mosaics) in this church is the **Cappella di S. Zenone★★**, one of the most important examples of 9C Byzantine art in Rome, built by Paschal I as a mausoleum for his mother Theodora. The shaft of a column brought from Jerusalem in 1223 is said to be that at which Christ was scourged. Paschal I was also responsible for the **church** (822; frequently restored) and the 9C **mosaics★** that have survived (in the sanctuary), as well as an attractive **crypt** *(apply to priest)*.   □

▶ **SANTA PUDENZIANA**

p. dell'Esquilino   II E4

This church dating from the 4C-early 5C has fine mosaics★ (late 4C) in the apse, with the *Redeemer Enthroned* and a symbolic representation of Jerusalem.   □

▶ **SANTA SABINA**★★

p. Pietro d'Illiria   IV C4

This isolated church on the Aventine is the best example of an early Christian basilica in Rome and restoration has preserved its serene and glowing atmosphere. It is probably built over the house of the matron Sabina (though she is not the saint of the title). The portal in the vestibule has the famous 5C **wooden door★**, carved with scenes from the Old and New Testaments. In the **interior** with a nave and two aisles and arches with columns, above the portal, is an inscription in gold letters on an azure background flanked by two figures★. There are also remains of 5C mosaics. There is a 13C **cloister** in the convent.   □

▶ **SANT'ELIGIO DEGLI OREFICI**★

lungotevere dei Tebaldi   I F4

The **interior**, a Greek cross on a square with a hemispherical dome *(caretaker at v. S. Eligio 9)*, shows Raphael's customary architectural lucidity. The titular saint, Eligius, was a goldsmith, then a minister of the Merovingian kings (6C-7C).   □

▶ **SANTI APOSTOLI**★

p. Ss. Apostoli   I F6

This **basilica** (founded in the 6C and rebuilt in 1702) has a 2C Roman relief with an **imperial eagle★** in the vestibule. In the splendid Baroque interior are Baciccia's fresco (1707, in the vault) of the *Triumph of the Franciscan Order* and the *Monument of Clement XIV*★ by Canova (1789).   □

▶ **SANTI GIOVANNI E PAOLO**★

at end of v. S. Paolo della Croce   III C2

The façade is 5C; the portico with antique columns, the Romanesque campanile★ and the fine apse are 12C; the best view of the apse is from the Clivo di Scauro. The church was founded in the 4C and built over the house of the titular martyrs, victims of the persecution of Julian the Apostate. In the **basement★** *(8-11:30 a.m. and 4-6:30 p.m.; closed Sun a.m. and hols)* are rooms from a Roman palace, a Christian house and an oratory, with 2C-3C frescos.   □

▶ **SANT'IGNAZIO**★

p. S. Ignazio   I F6

The **piazza** in front of the church, one of the most refined examples of 18C architecture, is the work of Filippo Raguzzini (1727-8). The solemn and magni-ficent Jesuit **church** (1626-50, designed by Maderno) has a single aisle, and its interior marble decoration and frescos are a fine example of the architecture of the order. The fresco in the vault of the *Triumph of St. Ignatius★* by Father Andrea Pozzo is famous for its perspective effects (a disc in the pavement indicates the point from which it should be viewed); the same artist is responsible for the **perspective** painting which simulates the nonexistent dome.   □

▶ **SANTI NEREO E ACHILLEO**

v. delle Terme di Caracalla   III D2-3

This church was restored in the 16C, masking its early Christian origins. A 9C **mosaic** has survived on the triumphal arch; the choir and sanctuary screen are Cosmati work (13C).   □

Postwar Italian cinema

One of Italy's most famous exports in the last forty years has been its incredible output of motion pictures. The movie industry had its share of successes before the war under the watchful eye of Mussolini: studios were built (Rome's Cinecitta), epics were made, stars were born! It was not until after World War II, however, that Italian cinema flourished and acquired its overwhelming international reputation. The watershed film was Roberto Rossellini's Rome Open City (1944) which told the story of Romans struggling during the last days of German occupation. Shot on a shoestring under the noses of retreating German troops, the film launched Anna Magnani's career and created a sensation in movie theaters around the world. A new stark style was born: Italian Neo-Realism. Doing away with elaborate studio sets and glamourous lighting, filmmakers like Rossellini, Vittorio de Sica (The Bicycle Thief), Federico Fellini (Nights of Cabiria) and Luchino Visconti focused on Italy's common people as they rebuilt their war-torn country. Although the movement's heyday was mostly over by the mid-1950s, it had lasting effects on later Italian filmmakers such as Bernardo Bertolucci and Michelangelo Antonioni. It also left a strong mark on foreign directors in France (Truffaut, Godard), Great Britain (Lindsay Anderson) and the United States (John Cassavettes).

▶ **SANTI QUATTRO CORONATI**★

from v. S. Quattro Coronati   III B3

Two courtyards of the monastery that played host to popes and emperors lead to this **church**, early Christian in origin (4C). The **interior** has a nave and two aisles separated by ancient granite columns, with women's galleries and Cosmati-work pavement (13C); the apse has 17C frescos. The **cloister** with coupled columns (1220-43), reached from the l.-hand aisle, is the work of Roman marble craftsmen. On leaving the church it is possible to visit the **Cappella di S. Silvestro★** *(apply for key at monastery)*, decorated with frescos dating from 1246.   □

▶ SANT'ONOFRIO
along the Gianicolo footpath   I F2

Torquato Tasso died at the age of fifty in the monastery of S. Onofrio (25 April 1595) while Pope Clement VIII was preparing to crown him on the Capitoline with a wreath of laurels because of the excellence of his poetry. There is a small **Tasso museum** in the rooms now occupied by the Equestrian Order of the Holy Sepulchre in Jerusalem *(office hrs)*. The **church** (1419, since restored) is at the top of a flight of steps with a fine view. There are three frescos by Domenichino on the r. below the portico; in the interior are an *Annunciation* by Antoniazzo Romano and frescos by Peruzzi (1503).   ☐

▶ SANTO STEFANO ROTONDO*
v. S. Stefano Rotondo 7   III C3

This is one of the older circular churches (5C) with circular aisles in the interior separated by ancient columns *(under restoration)*. The thirty-four 16C-17C frescos of *Martyrdom* (by Pomarancio and others) are of iconographic interest, being examples of Counter-Reformation painting. In the basement remains of a **Roman barracks** with **mithraeum** (2C-3C) have been discovered.   ☐

▶ THEATRE OF MARCELLUS*
v. Teatro di Marcello   IV B4

In Rome the tragedies of Ennius and the comedies of Terence and Plautus were performed in temporary wooden theatres. It was not until 55 BC that Pompey commissioned the first stone theatre. The **Theatre of Marcellus** was started by Julius Caesar and completed by Augustus (13-11 BC). It is dedicated to Claudius Marcellus, who died at the age of twenty. The exterior semicircle, with arches with two superimposed rows of Doric and Ionic columns, is the first example of architectural articulation of this kind, repeated in the Colosseum and finally adopted by Renaissance architects. Toward the middle of the 12C the Fabi family had their castle built here and in the 16C the Savelli family commissioned Peruzzi to build the two floors of the **palazzo** that now occupies the site. The ancient building is still a major example of a Roman theatre, however. The three columns on the r. of the theatre are the remains of the **Temple of Apollo**, rebuilt under Augustus.   ☐

▶ TIBER BRIDGES
(ponti sul Tevere)

Between the Foro Italico (upstream) and S. Paolo Fuori le Mura (downstream) there are **twenty-two bridges** over the Tiber. Four of these are of particular interest.

▶ In the N, at the end of the v. Flaminia (I A5), is the **Ponte Milvio** which featured in the famous battle against Maxentius (312) when the Cross appeared to Constantine. Four of the 2C BC Roman arches have survived, and it is guarded by a 15C watchtower. ▶ Opposite the Castel Sant'Angelo (→) is the **Ponte S. Angelo★** (I E3), built by Hadrian to give access to his mausoleum; for centuries it was the principal link between the Vatican and the city

centre. In 1669 Bernini designed the balustrade with ten statues of **angels★**, bearing the symbols of the passion, sculpted by pupils of Bernini (two angels by Bernini himself originally intended for the bridge are in S. Andrea delle Fratte (→). ▶ Further downstream the **Ponte Fabricio** or dei Quattro Capi (IV B4), between the l. bank of the Tiber and the Isola Tiberina (→), dates from 62 BC. ▶ Close by the Ponte Palatino (IV B4) are the picturesque ruins of the **Ponte Rotto**, downstream of the Isola Tiberina. It is the surviving arch of a bridge destroyed in 1598: the arch is supported on piles from the Roman Pons Aemilius, completed in 142 BC, the first in Rome with masonry arches.   ☐

▶ TRASTEVERE
IV B-C2-4

This most 'Roman' of all the districts of Rome is on the r. bank of the Tiber, between the Ponte Sisto and the Ponte Sublicio, on the convex side of the bend opposite the Isola Tiberina. The **architecture** is as full of humorous touches as the language of the inhabitants. Monuments include: **Santa Maria in Trastevere★★** (→); **Santa Cecilia in Trastevere★** (→); **San Francesco a Ripa** (→); **Museo di Folclore** (→); **Palazzo Corsini★** (→) with the Galleria Nazionale d'Arte Antica★ and **La Farnesina★★** (→). There is a picturesque second-hand **market** at Porta Portese (IV D3) on Sunday mornings. Behind are the green slopes of the **Gianicolo★** (→) with **Sant'Onofrio** (→) and **San Pietro in Montorio★** (→).   ☐

Caffé Greco

Coffee and other beverages are served in the padded rooms of the Caffé Greco (v. Condotti 86). It is called Greek because it was started by a clever Levantine (taken to be a Greek) on its present site in 1760. The custom of drinking coffee came from the Turkish end of the Mediterranean, and it was an Armenian who opened, around this time, the first café in Paris. Goethe and Gogol, Stendhal and Wagner, Baudelaire and Liszt were among the many famous visitors to this meeting-place of intellectuals and ordinary people, and Guttusi painted a famous canvas of it as it was during the 19C.

▶ The TREVI FOUNTAIN
I E6

This splendid fountain is the final performance by the Acqua Vergine, restored to Rome by Nicholas V in 1453. He repaired the damage which for eight centuries had blocked and interrupted its flow. The 15C fountain was demolished at the time of Urban VIII, but less than a century later Clement XII commissioned a new fountain from Nicola Salvi who, incorporating part of the side of the **Palazzo Poli,** realized his fantastic masterpiece from 1732-51; it was completed by dal Bracci under Clement XIII. The fascinating composition consists of rocks, tritons and the **chariot of Neptune** drawn by sea-horses, and indeed includes the rushing of the water. It is a superb farewell from the Baroque imagination. By tradition, throwing a coin into this fountain ensures a return to Rome.   ☐

▶ **TRINITA DEI MONTI***
up the Spanish Steps from p. di Spagna   II C1-2

The p. **Trinità dei Monti★** provides a splendid view of the city. The **church** with a narrow façade between two bell towers (C. Maderno, 1585) was commissioned by Louis XII of France (building from 1502). It contains two notable 16C frescos by Daniele da Volterra, *Assumption* and *Descent From the Cross★*. □

Trinita dei Monti

▶ **The VATICAN****
                                    I D-E1-2

Vatican City, a sovereign state by virtue of the Lateran Treaty (1929), covers 110 acres, including St. Peter's (→) and St. Peter's Square (→), the Apostolic Palaces and the Vatican gardens, the basilicas of S. Maria Maggiore, S. Giovanni in Laterano and S. Paolo Fuori le Mura, and some palazzi also enjoy extraterritoriality vis-à-vis the Italian state. In the mid-9C Pope Leo IV surrounded the Vatican hill on the r. of the Tiber with a solid wall with twenty four towers to protect the basilica built by Constantine over the tomb of the Apostle Peter against Saracen raids: this old Vatican City had the same boundaries as the present Vatican City. In 1337, on the return from Avignon, the popes began to live in the *Palazzi Apostolici*, which became a complex of 1,400 halls, rooms and chapels covering an area of fourteen acres. With Martin V (Oddone Colonna, 1417) the papacy returned to one of the great Roman families which had held it in the Middle Ages. They wanted to be remembered for having restored the damage caused by time in a city that was full of ruins and memories, but that now, due to the absence of the popes in Avignon, was in a worse state of dereliction than ever. The past, too, was beginning to be seen in a different light and not simply as an easy source of marble. Martin V was followed by other popes from princely Roman families, but above all by popes of humanist culture. Extension and embellishment of the Vatican palaces was started by Nicholas V in 1450. He said 'the faith of the people is reinforced and consolidated by fine buildings which seem like monuments created by God himself... the world

will embrace faith with the most profound devotion'. This is the key to the artistic policy constantly followed from the throne of Peter and which, stimulated by the happy surge of creativity in the 16C-17C, has left the stunning miracles of St. Peter's and the Apostolic Palaces (due particularly to Alexander VI, Julius II, Leo X, Paul III and Urban VIII), and the entire heritage of ecclesiastical buildings in the city as it appears today.

The conclave

When the papal throne is vacant and the conclave is taking place, the faithful gather in St. Peter's Square and look to the right, above the roof of the Sistine chapel, for the colour of the smoke produced by burning the cardinals' voting slips. If the prescribed majority of two-thirds has not been reached, damp straw is mixed with the papers to produce black smoke. White smoke indicates that a pope has been chosen. In our century this has occurred eight times: producing Pius X, Benedict XV, Pius XI, Pius XII, John XXIII, Paul VI, John Paul I and John Paul II, the first non-Italian pope since Hadrian VI in the 16C. A cardinal, or a member of the Sacred College of Cardinals, is elected by his peers; it was Nicholas II, in the mid-11C, who assured the cardinals' preponderance in the election of the pope, but the last pope who was not a cardinal was Urban VI in the 14C. The conclave (from the Latin cum clave, meaning with a key), the name for the meeting in a locked room of the cardinals to elect a pope, was instituted in 1271 at the suggestion of St. Bonaventura as a result of a vacancy on the throne of Peter which, after the death of Clement IV, had lasted for three years. It was sanctioned in 1274 by Gregory X. The cardinals meet twice a day to cast their votes and count them until one of them reaches the prescribed majority. The number of electors has varied considerably over the ages. In 1586 Sixtus V decided that the sacred College should consist of 70 cardinals, and John XXIII, in 1960, increased the number to 85. Since then the number of cardinals has been further increased as the church expanded throughout the world. A few minutes after the definitive scrutiny, the first cardinal of the order of deacons looks out of the central window of the nine in the façade of the basilica of St. Peter to announce the name of the chosen cardinal starting with the words (in Latin), 'I have joyful tidings to announce. We have a pope'.

▶ The **organization of the museums,** however (by Clement XIV, Pius VI, Pius VII and Gregory XVI), was the fruit of critical reflection in the second half of the 18C and the first half of the 19C. The collections were rearranged and new ones established and there was some new building, including the **audience hall★** by P.L. Nervi, 1971. ▶ Visits to the **Vatican museums and galleries** *(9 a.m.-2 p.m.; 9 a.m.-5 p.m. at Easter and Jul-Sep; Sat always 9 a.m.-2 p.m.; final admission 1 hr before closing time; closed on religious feast days and Sun except last of month)* are programmed according to 4 obligatory itineraries, from which it is possible to choose at the entrance. To visit the **Vatican Necropolis★** under the Vatican grottos and the basilica of St. Peter, including the sacred area of the Apostle's tomb, apply to the Ufficio Scavi della Reverenda Fabbrica di S. Pietro *(wkdays 9 a.m.-12 noon and 2-5 p.m.).* ▶ The collections are housed in the Apostolic Palace and the buildings and wings around the Cortile della Pigna, the Cortile della Biblioteca and the Cortile del Belvedere, the result of centuries of building activity since Bramante's original arrangement, of fundamental importance for the history of 16C architecture. ▶ The following list of treasures contains only the principal works. The **Museo Gregoriano Egizio★** (founded by Gregory XVI, 1839) contains important documentation on ancient Egyptian art and civilization. ▶ The **Museo Chiarmonti**, arranged by Canova, which occupies the **Galleria Chiaramonti** (a long gallery built by Bramante), the **Galleria Lapidaria** *(not open to public)* and the Neoclassical **Braccio Nuovo** (new wing) complete the Museo Pio-Clementino's classical collection; outstanding items include: the *Prima Porta Augustus★*, bust of *Caesar★*, *Wounded Amazon★*, Roman replica of the Greek original by Kresilas (430 BC) and a colossal Roman statue of the *Nile* (1C). The **Museo Pio-Clementino★** has especially works of Greek and Roman sculpture. Items in the numerous rooms, some of great interest in themselves, include: *Apoxyomenos★* (The Scraper), Roman copy of a bronze by Lysippos; in the **Cortile Ottagono** *Apollo Belvedere★*, Greek in origin, 4C; *Hermes★*, copied under Hadrian, and the famous *Laocöon★★*, a late Hellenistic work from Rhodes; *Meleager★*, probably by Scopa; *Sleeping Ariadne★*; the Centocelle *Eros★*, *Apollo Sauroctonos★*, by Praxiteles; *Wounded Amazon★*, by Phidias; Roman portrait group★ (known as *Cato and Porcia*); the *Boy Caracalla★* and *Trajan★*; the *Cnidos Venus★*, replica of Praxitiles, and the *Belvedere torso★★* by Apollonius (1C BC); in the **Rotonda★**, a fine Neoclassical room (1780) is an ancient mosaic with *Centaurs, Tritons and Nereids★*, a statue of a *goddess★* of Greek origin (5C) and the *Juno Sospita* (2C); finally two porphyry sarcophagi of *St. Helen★* and *Constantia★* (4C). ▶ The **Museo Gregoriano Etrusco★** (Gregory XVI, 1837; *Mon and Fri only*) shows material excavated from Etruscan sites in the S, including grave items from the *Regolini-Galassi tomb★★* (Cervéteri, 7C BC), the *Todi Mars★* (5C BC), statues and portrait busts★ in terra-cotta, fragments of a horse's head from the Parthenon and a very full collection of Greek, Italian and Etruscan *vases★*; in the **Sala della Biga** is the 1C BC biga (two-horse chariot), a Greek *Dionysus★* and one of the replicas of Myron's *Discobolos★*. ▶ Other classical works are to be found in the six sections of the **Galleria dei Candelabri**. ▶ The **tapestries★** of the *Life of Christ* woven in Brussels by Pieter van Aelst to cartoons by pupils of Raphael (not to be confused with the Raphael tapestries, → below) and other fine tapestries are exhibited in the **Galleria degli Arazzi**. ▶ **Maps★** of the Italian regions and plans of Civitavecchia, Genoa, Venice and Ancona by Father Ignazio Danti (1580-3) decorate the long **Galleria delle Carte Geographiche**. ▶ The masterly **Stanze of Raphael★★** certainly offer one of the most intense emotional experiences in a visit to the Vatican. In the **Stanza dell 'Incendio di Borgo** (painted 1514-17) the hand of Raphael can only be detected in the *Incendio di Borgo★* section, the other frescos are by pupils; the **Stanza della Segnatura★★** (1509-11) may well be entirely the work of Raphael; it includes the *Dispute on the Holy Sacrament★★*, the *School of Athens★★* and the *Parnassus★*; the **Stanza di Eliodoro★** also entirely by Raphael (1512-14) with the *Mass of Bolsena★★* (referring to a miracle which occurred in 1283, but Julius II is present in the fresco); *Leo Repulsing Attila★* with a clear allusion to contemporary defense of Italy by the popes and the *Deliverance of St. Peter★★*. The **Sala di Costantino** was frescoed after the death of Raphael by Giulio Romano and F. Penni. ▶ The loggias of the Cortile di S. Damaso were started by Bramante for Julius II and completed by Raphael under Leo X; the **Loggia di Raffaello★**, on the upper floor, is decorated with stories from the Old and New Testaments designed by Raphael and executed by his pupils, Giulio Romano, F. Penni and Perin del Vaga (stucco and grotesques by Giovanni da Udine between the frames and on the walls). ▶ Access to the **Cappella di Niccolò V**, with delicate 15C **frescos★★** by Beato Angelico (1448-50), is from the Sala di Costantino via the **Sala dei Chiaroscuri** (frescos by the Zuccari, 1582) in which is the wooden **model** of Michel-

angelo's dome for St. Peter's (1561). ▶ Pinturicchio and his pupils decorated the **Appartamento Borgia★** (1432-95), lived in by Alexander VI; the finest features of these magnificent specimens of late 15C taste are the *Sibyl and Prophets★* in the lunettes of the **Sala delle Sibille** (pupils), the **Sala dei Misteri della Fede★** (attributed to Pinturicchio) and above all the **Sala della Vita dei Santi★★**, considered to be Raphael's masterpiece. ▶ The rooms of the Borgia apartments mark the beginning of the **Collezione d'Arte Religiosa Moderna★** (1973), occupying fifty-five rooms with painting, sculpture and graphics by important artists from many countries (including Matisse, Rouault, Chagall, Klee, Kandinsky, Moore, Ben Shahn, Dali, Picasso, Ensor, Orozco, to name but some of the non-Italian artists). ▶ The second (only in terms of the order of the exhibitions) great moment in the Vatican visit is the **Cappella Sistina★★** (Sistine Chapel), seat of the conclaves for papal elections, commissioned by Sixtus IV (1475-81). Major Tuscan and Umbrian painters of the late 15C executed the twelve frescos on the side walls which juxtapose, with considerable theolo-

Raphael

Julius II Della Rovere, when elected pope, did not want to live in the Borgia apartments in the Vatican where (according to notes left by his chamberlain) everything reminded him of his predecessor Pope Alexander VI Borgia, 'a man he hated and called by foul names'. Julius therefore prepared to move to apartments on the floor above and decided to have them completely redecorated. He was never to live in them as he died before the work was finished, but the frescos there are among the greatest paintings of all time. It was, according to Vasari the chronicler, Bramante of Urbino, then painting in the Vatican, who contacted Raphael, a distant relative of his and a man who came from the same provincial town, and told him that 'the Pope has certain rooms to be repainted and on which you could well set to work and show how good you are'. Raphael, at the time, was working in Florence, with Michelangelo and Leonardo da Vinci. He came at once to Rome and after he had done a test (the frescos on the arch of the Stanza della Segnatura), the pope in 1509 entrusted him with the whole work. Thus the famous stanze (rooms) of Raphael in the Vatican. The amount of work produced by the artist during the next two years was prodigious. The first room he did, the Stanza della Segnatura (so called because it contained the seals, library and study of Julius II), has the famous School of Athens fresco in which he portrayed himself, according to Vasari, as 'a person with a youthful face and modest appearance, as seen in a mirror'. While working on a wall in the second room (called the Stanza di Eliodoro) on a fresco showing Pope Leo the Great confronting, in 452 AD, Attila the Hun who was threatening to sack the Eternal City, Julius II died. In his preliminary sketch Raphael had given Leo the Great the face of Julius II. He now changed this and gave Leo the Great the face of the new pope, Leo X. Raphael is one of the most celebrated painters of all time and his work in the Vatican must be considered as almost unrivaled. In spite of his short life (he died at 37), critics consider Raphael to be not only a marvelous creator of classical composition, but an artist who saw beyond his time and who influenced all the great painters to come, men like Titian, Correggio, Rubens and Rembrandt, the Romanticists and even the Moderns of today.

gical skill, scenes from the lives of Moses and Christ (1481-3). Distinguished among them are *Moses' Journey to Egypt*★ (Perugino and Pinturicchio), *The Burning Bush*★★ (Botticelli), the *Punishment of Korah, Dathan and Abiram*★★ (Botticelli), the *Death of Moses*★ (Luca Signorelli), the *Temptation of Christ*★★ (Botticelli), the *Calling of Peter and Andrew*★ (Ghirlandaio) and *Christ Giving the Keys to Peter*★★ (Perugino assisted by Signorelli); fresco artists not mentioned above include Cosimo Rosselli and Piero di Cosimo. In 1508 Julius II entrusted Michelangelo with the decoration of the vault lunettes; he completed the work in 1512 *(under restoration)*. The **frescos of Michelangelo**★★, framed by magnificent architectural painting, deal, in nine pictures of stories of the Creation, with the spiritual events of human life. Twelve magnificent figures (seven prophets and five sibyls) see the Redemption to come and twenty splendid naked figures show how stories of the distant past have a message for the world today. Twenty-three years later Michelangelo returned to the Sistine Chapel to paint the *Last Judgment*★★ on the back wall for Paul III (destroying two scenes from the 15C cycle in the process). In preparing the wall Michelangelo gave it a slope intended to prevent the accumulation of dust (but which increased deposits from the smoke of candles and incense). This enormous fresco, with the damned falling to the l. and the elect rising to heaven on the r. (on the skin of the flayed St. Bartholomew is a self-portrait of Michelangelo) and the great figure of Christ in Judgment at the centre, is a dramatic vision of human destiny which merits the adjective 'apocalyptic': Paul III fell to his knees when he saw the completed fresco. When the Council of Trent pronounced a vague condemnation of the *Judgment* of Michelangelo and in general of all improper pictures in churches (1563) Michelangelo was already dead. Pius IV ordered that some of the nude figures be clothed. The unfortunate painter who received the commission was Daniele da Volterra, who became known as the 'breeches-maker'. ▶ The **Biblioteca Apostolica** was established by Nicholas V and placed in its present magnificent sequence of rooms by Sixtus V (D. Fontana, 1588). Distinguished features are the Augustan mural of the *Aldobrandini Marriage*★; gilded **glass**★ from the catacombs in the **Museo Sacro** (Benedict XIV, 1756); the great **Salone Sistino**★, created as a reading room by Sixtus V; and the 17C arrangement in Valadier's showcases of Etrus-

---

The Vatican library

In the 15C, Rome was one of the foremost centers of intellectual life in Europe. Popes and cardinals were, for the most part, very learned men. Their collection of manuscripts, which was increased by gifts and legacies, created the core of the Vatican library. Teams of copiers, illustrators, translators and binders created precious volumes that were stored in well-guarded rooms. Merchants from Sienna and Florence supplied new texts at high prices. From Genoa came Greek manuscripts that ships brought back from the East. As early as 1467, German printers came to Rome and produced religious, legal and common books in their workshops. Sixtus IV put Niccolo Fieschi in charge of the Vatican archives and library. The latter undertook the construction of new buildings, and books were stored in a more sumptuous decor: marble floors and columns taken from ancient monuments, gilt, Venetian glass, frescos and paintings by the best artists. The volumes were lent to prelates, visiting ecclesiastics and members of literary circles (which were numerous in Rome). Platin, a famous humanist born in Cremona in 1421, became the first official librarian in 1478.

---

can, Roman and medieval material in the **Museo Profano della Biblioteca**. ▶ The **Pinacoteca**★★ (picture gallery) is in the gardens, in a relatively modern building. Masterpieces are exhibited in eighteen rooms. Some of the pictures were recovered by Canova from France after the Congress of Vienna, where they had gone as a result of a clause in the Treaty of Tolentino (1797). Notable are the *Stefaneschi Triptych*★ by Giotto and pupils; *Christ Before Pilate*★ by Pietro Lorenzetti; *Redeemer*★ by Simone Martini; *Madonna of the Magnificat*★ by Bernardo Daddi; *Stories from the Life of St. Nicholas* by Gentile da Fabriano; *Stories from the Life of St. Nicholas* by Gentile da Fabriano; *Madonna and Child with Saints*★ by Fra Angelico; *Coronation of Mary*★ by Filippo Lippi; *Sixtus IV and Platina*★ and *Angel Musicians*★ by Melozzo da Forli; *Miracles of St. Vincent Ferrer*★ by Ercole de'Roberti; *Madonna and Saints*★ by Perugino; an important group of works by Raphael: *Coronation of Mary*★ and predella with the *Mysteries*★ (1503), *Transfiguration*★★ (his last work), the *Madonna of Foligno*★★ (1512), the predella of the *Theological Virtues*★ and the famous **ten tapestries**★ woven in Brussels by Pieter van Aelst to cartoons by Raphael (1515-16); *St. Jerome*★ by Leonardo da Vinci; *Madonna of S. Niccolò dei Frari*★ by Titian; *Descent From the Cross*★★ by Caravaggio; *Communion of St. Jerome*★ by Domenichino and *Clement IX* by Carlo Maratta. ▶ Other new buildings house the **Museo Gregoriano Profano**★ (copy of Myron's *Athene and Marsyas*★ group; *Sophocles*★, *Medea and the Pleiades*, neo-Attic works); the **Museo Pio Cristiano**★ in which is the famous statue of the *Good Shepherd* (perhaps 3C) and the **Museo Missionario-Etnologico**★ *(Wed and Sat only)*. ▶ Finally, the **Museo delle Carrozze** (carriages; *Sat only*) is below the Giardino Quadrato. □

▶ **VIA DEI CONDOTTI**

I D6

The *condotti* are the conduits of the Acqua Vergine that finally brought water from these ancient springs to the centre of Rome. The *Scalinata della Trinità dei Monti* (Spanish Steps) and the church of the same name form a magnificent backdrop to this street which, with the parallel **v. Borgognona** and **v. Frattina**, forms the area containing Rome's most elegant clothing and jewelry shops. At one end is the 17C church, with elliptical interior, of **Santa Trinità**, and at the other the ancient **Caffè Greco**★, established in 1760; its interesting interior décor has survived almost intact. □

▶ **VIA DEL CORSO***

I C-F5-6

This is the principal artery of Rome, running straight and level from the p. Venezia to the p. del Popolo. It forms the axis of the city centre and is flanked with palazzi and churches dating from the late 16C to the 18C. The name (corso means race) derives from the festive horse races held here from the 15C-19C. The 'barberi' races were famous. (The horses were from Barbary in N Africa and were run without jockeys.) The races were banned in 1882 after two people had been knocked down, a by no means infrequent occurrence. □

▶ **VIA DI PORTA SAN SEBASTIANO***

III E-F3-4

This street has many interesting archaeological and ecclesiastical features. Immediately on the r. is the little church of **San Cesareo in Palatio★** *(9 a.m.-12 noon and 3-5 p.m.)* with notable 13C Cosmati-work furnishings and frescos and mosaics by the Cavalier d'Arpino in the apse; in the basement are remains of a 2C Roman room with mosaic pavement and of an earlier church (8C). At no. 8 is the 15C **Casina del Cardinal Bessarione** *(closed for restoration).* Immediately beyond this (no. 9) is the entrance to the **Sepolcro degli Scipioni★** *(9 a.m.-2 p.m.; Sun and hols 9 a.m.-1 p.m.; also 4-8 p.m. in summer, Tue, Thu and Sat; closed Mon),* a 3C BC family tomb under a Roman house of the imperial period. Nearby are a columbarium and a small catacomb; in the park *(accompanied by caretaker)* is the **Columbarium of Pompono Hylas** with burial niches decorated with stucco and paintings. ☐

▶ **VIA GIULIA**

I F3-4 and IV A2-3

Julius II ordered that this street should be pierced in the early 16C, paving the way for Renaissance town planning in Rome, and even though it has declined to some extent, its architectural grandeur remains. It contains the **Palazzo Falconieri** (no. 1), 16C, with a loggia by Borromini (on the lungotevere); the **Palazzo Sacchetti** (no. 66) by Antonio da Sangallo the Younger; and the church of **San Giovanni dei Fiorentini** (→). Nearby are the church of **S. Eligio degli Orefici** (→), the **Palazzo Farnese** (→) and the **Palazzo Spada** (→). ☐

▶ **VIA NAZIONALE**

II E2-3

The v. Nazionale starts at the p. della Repubblica with the ruins of the Baths of Diocletian (→) and is the principal line of communication between the Stazione Termini and the city centre, where the Vittorio Emanuele monument (→) gleams white at the end of the staight street. About halfway up the street on the r. a staircase goes down to the early Christian façade of the church of **S. Vitale**, restored in 1475. In the interior are frescos by the Cavalier d'Arpino and G. Dughet. ☐

▶ **VIA VENETO***

II C-D2-3

The roaring night life of the Fifties made this the most famous street in Rome, particularly for foreigners. Its full name is v. Vittorio Veneto and it is broad and tree-lined, with numerous hotels, shops, meeting places and deluxe cafés. It runs in broad curves from the p. Barberini to the Porta Pinciana, through the area which was once the park of the Villa Ludovisi.

▶ At the beginning of the street is the **Fontana delle Api** by Bernini (1644). ▶ A little beyond, at the top of a double flight of steps, is the church of the **Cappuccini**, or S. Maria della Concezione (1626), with paintings by Guido Reni, Gherardo delle Notti, G. Lanfranco and Domenichino. The five underground chapels *(May-Oct 9 a.m.-12 noon and 3-6:30 p.m.)* are lined in a somewhat macabre fashion with the skeletons and bones of 4,000 monks. ▶ At the second bend is the **Palazzo Margherita**, formerly residence of Queen Margherita, and now the home of the United States Embassy. ☐

▶ **VILLA BORGHESE****

II A-B1-3

The Villa Borghese, which has a 6-km perimeter, is the largest and most beautiful public park in Rome. It was created by Cardinal Scipio Borghese, nephew of Paul V, in the early 17C, altered at the end of the next century and then enlarged by Luigi Canina in the early 19C. Among the greenery on an island in the **Giardino del Lago** is a little Greek temple built in the late 18C; tall pines shade the **Piazza di Siena★**, used for equestrian events; the Fortezzuola is built like a medieval castle and houses the **Museo Canonica** *(Thu and Sun 9 a.m.-1 p.m.; closed Aug)* with sculpture in the form of originals and plaster casts. ☐

▶ **VILLA MADAMA***

along viale Angelico and l. on v. di Villa Madama III A-B2

This villa was designed by Raphael (1517) for Cardinal Giulio de' Medici, later Pope Clement VII, and then altered by Antonio da Sangallo the Younger. The Madama of its title was Margherita of Hapsburg (natural daughter of Charles V and wife of Ottavio Farnese), to whom it belonged. The splendid **loggia★** on the inside is decorated with excellent stucco by Giovanni da Udine and pictures by Giulio Romano *(visits by permission of Presidenza del Consiglio dei Ministri and Ministero degli Esteri).* ☐

▶ **VILLA MEDICI***

viale della Trinità dei Monti II C1

Built in 1544 by the Florentine architect Annibale Lippi for Cardinal Ricci, it passed to the Medici family in 1576. Napoleon moved the **Académie Française,** founded by Louis XIV in 1666, here in 1803. The lavish internal **façade★** looks over a charming **park** decorated with ancient statues *(guided tours of park, Tue and Thu 9 a.m.-1 p.m.).* ☐

▶ **Il VITTORIANO***

p. Venezia II F1

This enormous monument in white Botticino marble, classical in inspiration, was built to designs by G. Sacconi from 1885-1911 and dedicated to Victor Emmanuel II (represented in the equestrian statue) in celebration of the achievement of Italian unity. After the First World War the **Remains of the Unknown Soldier★** were placed on the **Altare della Patria,** below the figure of Rome. The monument houses the **Museo Centrale del Risorgimento** *(entrance on r.-hand side; generally closed; ☎ 6793598)* and the **Museo Sacrario delle Bandiere della Marina Militare** *(9:30 a.m.-1:30 p.m.)* with naval banners and Luigi Rizzo's motor-torpedo boat. ☐

▶ **ZOOLOGICAL GARDEN***

at N extremity of Villa Borghese II A-B 1-2

The most important zoo in Italy *(8 a.m.-6 p.m. summer or 5 p.m. winter),* it occupies 30 acres in the grounds of the **Villa Borghese** (→). The zoo is arranged to reflect the animals' natural surroundings as much as possible. ☐

● *Practical information*

Information: v. Parigi 11 (II D4), ☎ 461851; *Centro Assistenza Turisti*, v. Parigi 5, ☎ 463748; Stazione Termini (railway station) (II E5), ☎ 465461; autostrada A1 (service area Salaria Ovest), ☎ 6919958, and A2 (service area Frascati Est), ☎ 9464341; *Aeroporto Fiumicino*, ☎ 6011 255; *TCI*, v. Ovidio 7/A (I D3), ☎ 6874432.

 Leonardo da Vinci (international), at Fiumicino, ☎ 60121; *Ciampino* (charter flights), ☎ 4694; dell'Urbe (tourist), v. Salaria 825, ☎ 8120571; *Alitalia*, v. Bissolati 13 (II C3), ☎ 46881 or 5456; *EUR*, p. G. Pastore, ☎ 54442151. Bus to *Fiumicino* from v. Giolitti (II E5) *(South Stazione Termini)*, ☎ 464613; to *Ciampino*, metropolitana from *Stazione Termini* to Cinecittà, buses from there to airport.

🚊 Stazione Termini (II E5), ☎ 4775; Stazione Tiburtina, ☎ 4956626. Delay information service, ☎ 464466.

🚌 from v. Castro Pretorio (II D4); v. Lepanto (I B3); Stazione metropolitana EUR-Fermi; p. dei Cinquecento (II D4); p. Flaminio (I B5); v. Gaeta (II C5); v. Giolitti (II E5); p. M. Fanti (II E5); p. di Cinecittà; v. Vicenza (II D5), ☎ 57531.

Car rental: *Avis*, v. Tiburtina 1231/A, ☎ 43696, reservations, ☎ 47011; *Hertz*, v. L. da Vinci 421, ☎ 51711, reservations, ☎ 547991; *Maggiore*, v. di Villa Massimo 13, ☎ 866956, reservations, ☎ 851620.

SOS: public emergency services, ☎ 113; police emergency, ☎ 112; guardia medica, ☎ 4756741; ambulance, ☎ 5100; duty pharmacist, ☎ 1921/5; state police, ☎ 4686; city police, ☎ 67691; fire brigade, ☎ 44444; *ACI* call-out, ☎ 116; post and telegrams: information, ☎ 160; post centre, p. S. Silvestro (II D1), ☎ 6771 (8:30 a.m.-8 p.m.); telegrams: p. S. Silvestro, ☎ 6795530 (24-hour services); telegrams taken on the telephone, ☎ 6790623); dictated telegrams, ☎ 186.

Weather: forecast, ☎ 1911; roads open or closed, ☎ 194 or *ACI*, ☎ 4212; snow information, ☎ 162; shipping forecast, 196.

Farm vacations: *Azienda Cacciarella*, v. Braccianese at 3.5-km marker, ☎ 311881.

Events: opera season at *Teatro dell'Opera*, ☎ 461755; summer opera and concerts at *Terme di Caracalla;* theatre at *Teatro Stabile*, ☎ 6798569 and in several other theatres in Rome; concerts in hall of *Accademia di Santa Cecilia*, ☎ 6541044 and in halls of *Palazzo Pio, RAI, Pontificio Istituto di Musica Sacra.* Religious events include: meeting of the faithful in St. Peter's Square for *Papal Blessing at Easter;* solemn service in St. Peter's for *feast of St. Peter and St. Paul;* feast of *Immaculate Conception* (8 Dec); *Christmas service; Feast of St. John* and *'de Noantri' festival* (Trastevere, mid-Jul), with illuminations, games, stalls. *Spring festival and azalea show* on Scalinata della Trinità dei Monti (Spanish Steps, Apr); *Mostra delle Rose* (rose show) in Valle Murgia (May-Jun); International conventions and events in *Palazzo dei Congressi* in EUR, ☎ 5912755. *Concorso Ippico Internationale* (horse show), p. di Siena (Apr-May); important annual sporting events in various Roman venues.

Conservation: *WWF* national office, v. Salaria 290, ☎ 852492 or 854892; Latium branch, v. Mercadante 10, ☎ 8440108; *LIPU* v. Radiotelegrafisti 70, ☎ 388703; *Italia Nostra*, v. Porpora 22, ☎ 856765.

Guided tours: organized by *Carrani*, ☎ 486947; *CIT*, ☎ 47941; *ATAC*, ☎ 4695; coach tours, daily departures 8-9 a.m. and 2-3 p.m.; night tours of illuminated monuments and theatres, etc; tour to Castel Gandolfo, the Castelli Romani and Tivoli, day and evening. Organized tour of the Vatican City: notification in advance to Ufficio Informazioni Pellegrini e Turisti in p. S. Pietro (St. Peter's Square; on the l. of the basilica).

Horseback riding: *Federazione Italiana Sport Equestri*, v. Tiziano 70, ☎ 3960626; *Società Ippica Romana*, v. Monte Farnesina 30, ☎ 3966386; *Pony Club*, v. dei Campi Sportivi 43, ☎ 879709; *Lazio Equitazione*, v. Pilsudski 25, ☎ 3966136 or 3962223; *ANTE*, largo Messico 13, ☎ 864053; *Appia Antica*, v. Appia Nuova at 16.5-km marker, ☎ 600197; *Porta Medaglia*, v. Torre S. Anastasia 81, ☎ 6009424; *Agricolandia*, v. R. Cappelli 94, ☎ 3270139; *Il Negretto*, v. dei Cocchieri 9, ☎ 5581825; *Centro di Equitazione di Campagna*, v. Nomentana 1563, ☎ 6100108; *Circolo Ippico S. Nicola*, v. Braccianese at 1-km marker, ☎ 6170071; *Circolo Ippico Monti della Camera*, v. Cavalier d'Arpino 39, ☎ 9035000; *Centro Valle dell Aniene*, v. Tor Cervara 57 (v. Tiburtina at 8-km marker).

River trips: Tiber boat trips from ponte Marconi (3:30 p.m.) to Ostia Antica, with visit to excavations: agency *Tourvisa*, ☎ 4950722.

Arts and crafts: instruction in history and theory of restoration, art courses: *Centro Culturale Cembalo Borghese*, largo Fontanella Borghese 19, ☎ 6790620 or 6876542; weaving, dying and printing on fabric: *Associazione Culturale Graf-Tex*, v. del Cardello 14, ☎ 486970.

Sailing: *Lega Navale*, v. XXIV Maggio 11, ☎ 6784706 or 6780070 (nautical centres in Sabaudia and Ferrara); *Vela Sub*, v. Tuscolana 55, ☎ 341218 or 3494470 (regatta racing); *Circolo Velico Ventotene* and *Nuova Compagnia delle Indie* (→ Isola di Ponza, Latium), v. Frangipane 30, ☎ 6790901 or 877569 (wk stays, hostel combined with sailing school); *Vela Blu Roma*, v. Spadini 15 (ARCI Vela).

Special children's facilities: adventure trips: *CTS*, v. Nazionale 66, ☎ 479931; *Nouvelles Frontières*, v. del Divino Amore 18, ☎ 3602452; *La Montagna*, v. M. Colonna 44, ☎ 351549 or 315948; *Avventure nel Mondo*, v. Cino da Pistoia 7, ☎ 5819400.

Canoeing: *Canoa Club EUR*, v. Sardegna 22, ☎ 4952893.

Swimming: *Foro Italico*, lungotevere Maresciallo Cadorna, ☎ 3608591 (indoor pool, ☎ 3601498); *Piscina Coperta*, v. Stadio Flaminio, ☎ 399812; *Piscina delle Rose*, at EUR, v. America, ☎ 5926717.

Skindiving: *Gruppo Leone Marino*, p. Martiri di Belfiore 4, ☎ 3565804 (instruction).

Golf: *Federazione Italiana*, v. Flaminia 388, ☎ 394641; *Circolo del Golf di Roma*, v. Acqua Santa 3 (Appia Nuova), ☎ 783407 or 7886154; *Golf Club Fioranello* at Santa Maria della Mole, ☎ 608291; *Olgiata Golf Club*, v. Olgiata 15, ☎ 3789141.

Flying: *Aeroporto dell Urbe*, v. Salaria 825, ☎ 8105952 (power flights and gliding).

Fishing: *Federazione Italiana Pesca Sportiva*, p. Emporio 16/A, ☎ 5755253 (information on fishing conditions).

Hang gliding: *Volo Libero Roma*, corso Trieste 50, ☎ 8444269; *Delta Club Roma*, v. Cassiodoro 1/A, ☎ 3279883.

Fencing: *Palestra di Scherma*, v. Sannio, ☎ 776537.

Tennis: *Foro Italico*, v. Gladiatori, ☎ 3619021.

Clay pigeon shooting: v. di Trigoria at 7.5-km marker, ☎ 6490109; v. Vajna, ☎ 8722088; at Ponte Galeria, v. Malnome, ☎ 6471140; at Fiumicino, v. M. Spinoncia, ☎ 6453917.

Archery: *Fitarco*, v. Poggi d'Oro 5, ☎ 7941044; *Compagnia Arcieri Il Sagittario*, v. S. Tommaso d'Aquino 40, ☎ 3595604; *Compagnia Arcieri Romani*, v. G.B. Martini 13, ☎ 864823.

Cycling: at EUR, v. della Tecnica, ☎ 5925997 (Olympic track).

Looking for a locality? Consult the index at the back of the book.

● *Hotels*

★★★★★ *Ambasciatori Palace,* v. Vittorio Veneto 70 (II C3 a), ☎ 47493, 149 rm P 417,000.

★★★★★ *Bernini Bristol,* p. Barberini 23 (II D2 b), ☎ 463051, 126 rm P & ⁂ 350,000; bkf: 18,000.

★★★★★ *Cavalieri Hilton,* v. Cadlolo 101, ☎ 3151, 387 rm P ⚭ ▥ & ▭ ⁓ 350,000. Rest. ● ◆◆◆◆ *Pergola* closed noon, Sun and Jan. Excellent cuisine, 65/90,000.

★★★★★ *Eden,* v. Ludovisi 49 (II C2 c), ☎ 4743551, 110 rm P & ⁂ 353,500; bkf: 15,000.

★★★★★ *Excelsior,* v. Vittorio Veneto 125 (II C3 d), ☎ 4707, 394 rm P 458,000; bkf: 21,000.

★★★★★ *Hassler Villa Medici,* p. Trinit dei Monti 6 (II C1-2 e), ☎ 6792651, 103 rm P ▥ ⁂ Classical elegance and spectacular roof-garden, 480,000; bkf: 20,000.

★★★★★ *Lord Byron,* v. De Notaris 5, ☎ 3609541, 50 rm P ⚭ ▥ 380,000; bkf: 16,500. Rest. ● ◆◆◆◆ *Relais le Jardin* closed Sun. Excellent creative cuisine, 80/100,000.

★★★★★ *Grand Hotel et de Rome,* v. V.E. Orlando 3 (II D3-4 f), ☎ 4709, 175 rm, 464,000; bkf: 22,000. Rest. ◆◆◆◆ *Rallye* 60/85,000.

★★★★ *Aldrovandi Palace Hotel,* v. Aldrovandi 15, ☎ 841091, 140 rm P ▥ 247,000.

★★★★ *Atlante Garden,* v. Crescenzio 78 (I D2 g), ☎ 6530341, 50 rm. Free transport to and from airport, 290,000.

★★★★ *Atlante Star,* v. Vitelleschi 34 (I D3 h), ☎ 6564196, 100 rm P Free transport to and from airport, 290,000.

★★★★ *Atlantico,* v. Cavour 23 (II E4 i), ☎ 485951, 83 rm P & ⁂ No restaurant, 166,000.

★★★★ *Borromini,* v. Lisbona 7, ☎ 841321, 84 rm P ⁂ No restaurant, 210,000; bkf: 15,000.

★★★★ *Claridge,* v. Liegi 62, ☎ 868556, 88 rm P 195,000.

★★★★ *De la Ville,* v. Sistina 67/71 (II C2 l), ☎ 6733, 197 rm P 291,000.

★★★★ *Eliseo,* v. Porta Pinciana 30 (II C2 m), ☎ 460556, 53 rm P ⁂ 244,000.

★★★★ *Forum,* v. Tor de' Conti 25 (II F2 n), ☎ 6792446, 79 rm P ⁂ 275,000; bkf: 16,000.

★★★★ *Holiday Inn, - EUR Parco dei Medici,* v. Castello della Magliana 65, ☎ 5475, 331 rm P ▥ ▭ ⁓ 208,000; bkf: 13,000.

★★★★ *Imperiale,* v. Vittorio Veneto 24 (II D2 p), ☎ 4756351, 85 rm P & ⁂ 216,000.

★★★★ *Jolly Leonardo da Vinci,* v. dei Gracchi 324 (I C4 q), ☎ 39680, 245 rm P ⁂ 210,000.

★★★★ *Jolly Via Veneto,* corso Italia 1 (II B3 r), ☎ 8495, 200 rm P 245,000. Rest. ◆◆◆ *Garden* 40/45,000.

★★★★ *Londra & Cargill,* p. Sallustio 18 (II C4 s), ☎ 473871, 105 rm P ⁂ 240,000.

★★★★ *Massimo D'Azeglio,* v. Cavour 18 (II E4 t), ☎ 460646, 210 rm P & ⁂ 192,000.

★★★★ *Mediterraneo,* v. Cavour 15 (II E4 u), ☎ 464051, 272 rm P & ⁂ 224,000.

★★★★ *Metropole,* v. P. Amedeo 3 (II E4 v), ☎ 4774, 285 rm P ⁂ 200,000.

★★★★ *Mondial,* v. Torino 127 (II D4 z), ☎ 272861, 77 rm P ⁂ No restaurant, 223,000.

★★★★ *Napoleon,* p. Vittorio Emanuele 105 (III A4 ab), ☎ 737646, 80 rm ⁂ P ⁂ No restaurant, 132,000; bkf: 11,000.

★★★★ *Nazioni,* v. Poli 7 (I E6 ac), ☎ 6792441, 75 rm P & ⁂ No restaurant, 260,000.

★★★★ *Parco dei Principi,* v. Frescobaldi 5, ☎ 841071, 203 rm P ▥ ⁂ ▭ 290,000.

★★★★ *President,* v. Emanuele Filiberto 173 (III B5 ay), ☎ 770121, 180 rm P & No restaurant, 188,000.

★★★★ *Quirinale,* v. Nazionale (II D3 ad), ☎ 4707, 193 rm P ▥ 220,000.

★★★★ *Regina Carlton,* v. Vittorio Veneto 72 (II C3 ae), ☎ 476851, 132 rm P ⁂ 240,000; bkf: 10,000.

★★★★ *Residence Palace,* v. Archimede 69, ☎ 878341, 191 rm P & 140,000.

★★★★ *San Giorgio,* v. Amendola 61 (II E4 af), ☎ 4751341, 186 rm P & ⁂ No restaurant, 166,000.

★★★★ *Shangri La' Corsetti,* v. Algeria 141, ☎ 5916441, 52 rm P ⚭ ▥ ⁂ 190,000; bkf: 9,000.

★★★★ *Universo,* v. P. Amedeo 5 (II E4 ag), ☎ 476811, 225 rm P & 224,500.

★★★★ *Victoria,* v. Campania 41 (II B3 ah), ☎ 473931, 115 rm P & 230,000; bkf: 10,000.

★★★★ *Villa Pamphili,* v. della Nocetta 105, ☎ 5862, 253 rm P ▥ & ▭ ⁓ 190,000.

★★★★ *Visconti Palace,* v. F. Cesi 37 (I C4 ai), ☎ 3684, 247 rm P ⁂ No restaurant, 220,000.

★★★ *Adriano,* v. Pallacorda 2 (I E5 al), ☎ 6542451, 84 rm P ⁂ No restaurant, 82,000.

★★★ *Aranci,* v. Oriani 11, ☎ 870202, 42 rm P ▥ ⁂ 130,000.

★★★ *Arcangelo,* v. Boezio 15 (I D3 am), ☎ 6874143, 30 rm P ⁂ No restaurant, 129,000.

★★★ *Bologna,* v. S. Chiara 4/A (I F5 an), ☎ 6568951, 117 rm. No restaurant, 144,000.

★★★ *Britannia,* v. Napoli 64 (II E3 ap), ☎ 463153, 32 rm P ▥ No restaurant, 183,000.

★★★ *Canada,* v. Vicenza 58 (II D5 aq), ☎ 4957385, 62 rm ⁂ No restaurant, 130,000.

★★★ *Conciliazione,* v. Borgo Pio 164 (I D2 ar), ☎ 6567910, 65 rm ⁂ No restaurant, 88,000; bkf: 6,000.

★★★ *Diana,* v. P. Amedeo 4 (II E4 as), ☎ 4751541, 187 rm P 130,000.

★★★ *Edera,* v. Poliziano 75 (III B4 at), ☎ 738355, 42 rm P ▥ ⁂ No restaurant, 130,000.

★★★ *Fiume,* v. Brescia 5 (II B4 au), ☎ 866772, 60 rm ⁂ No restaurant, 95,000; bkf: 6,500.

★★★ *Galileo,* v. Palestro 33 (II C5 av), ☎ 485817, 38 rm P No restaurant, 83,000; bkf: 8,000.

★★★ *Gregoriana,* v. Gregoriana 18 (II D2 az), ☎ 6794269, 19 rm P & No restaurant, 160,000.

★★★ *Internazionale,* v. Sistina 79 (II C2 ba), ☎ 6793047, 38 rm ⁂ No restaurant, 210,000.

★★★ *Lloyd,* v. Alessandria 110/A (II B5 bc), ☎ 850432, 53 rm P No restaurant, 95,000; bkf: 7,000.

★★★ *Madrid,* v. Mario De' Fiori 93 (I D6 bd), ☎ 6791249, 24 rm P No restaurant, 130,000.

★★★ *Nord Nuova Roma,* v. Amendola 3 (II E4 be), ☎ 465441, 159 rm P ⁂ No restaurant, 130,000.

★★★ *Piccadilly,* v. Magna Grecia 122 (III D5 bf), ☎ 777017, 55 rm P No restaurant, 118,000.

★★★ *Residenza,* v. Emilia 22 (II C2 bg), ☎ 4744480, 29 rm P No restaurant, 122,000.

★★★ *Rivoli,* v. Taramelli 7, ☎ 870141, 55 rm P ▥ ⁂ 130,000.

★★★ *Sant'Anna,* v. Borgo Pio 134 (I D2 bh), ☎ 6541602, 18 rm P & No restaurant, 130,000.

★★★ *Senato,* p. della Rotonda 73 (I E-F5 bi), ☎ 6793231, 51 rm P ⁂ No restaurant, 90,000.

★★★ *Siviglia,* v. Gaeta 12 (II C5 bl), ☎ 4750424, 41 rm ⁂ No restaurant, 113,000.

★★★ *Terminal,* v. P. Amedeo 103 (II E5 bm), ☎ 734041, 35 rm P ⁂ No restaurant, 97,000; bkf: 8,000.

★★★ *Tre Api,* v. del Mancino 12 (I F6 bn), ☎ 6783500, 24 rm. No restaurant, 140,000.

★★★ *Tritone,* v. del Tritone 210 (I E6 bp), ☎ 6789444, 43 rm ⁂ No restaurant, 156,000.

★★★ *Villa del Parco,* v. Nomentana 110, ☎ 865611, 25 rm ▥ No restaurant, 118,000.

★★★ *Villa Florence,* v. Nomentana 28 (II B5 bq), ☎ 8442841, 33 rm P ▥ & ⁂ No restaurant, 120,000; bkf: 12,000.

★★ *Giardino d'Europa,* v. Lucrezia Romana 95, ☎ 743142, 46 rm P ▥ 78,000; bkf: 7,000.

★★ *Giglio,* v. P. Amedeo 14 (II E4 br), ☎ 460219, 22 rm P 83,000.

★★ *Igea,* v. P. Amedeo 97 (II E5 bs), ☎ 7311212, 42 rm ⁂ No restaurant, 60,000; bkf: 5,000.

★★ *Portoghesi,* v. dei Portoghesi 1 (I E5 bt), ☎ 6564231, 27 rm P No restaurant, 91,000.

Be advised that hotels and restaurants in this Guide have perhaps changed addresses; prices indicated are also subject to modifications.

Restaurants

Roman cuisine is said to follow the traditional cooking of the shepherds and farmers who originally inhabited the region and as such is considered to be simple, tasty, but without frills. One speciality is bruschetta slices of homemade bread toasted on the grill, soaked in oil and scattered with garlic. Spaghetti is served all'amatriciana, that is, flavoured with lard, streaky bacon, white wine, tomato and piquant pepper, and covered with ripe sheep's cheese. Gnocchi alla Romana are generally eaten on Thursday. Internationally, alla Romana means discs of semolina baked in the oven, but in Rome itself, it means discs of potato flour served with a meat stew or a tomato and basil sauce. There is roast spring lamb, served with artichokes, prepared alla giuda (in the Jewish way), a technique which came from the ghetto. The artichokes must be globe variety, stripped of their spines. Coda alla vaccinara is a dish invented in the trattorias around the slaughter-house, which used otherwise unsaleable cuts of meat: the tail is prepared in a stew of aromatic herbs, sultana grapes, pine nuts and bitter chocolate. This is only a selection of the many delicious dishes.

● ♦♦♦♦ *El Toulà*, v. della Lupa 29/B (I D-E5 cl), ☎ 6781196, closed Sat noon, Sun and Aug. Refined and elegant. Good international and Venetian cuisine: cuttlefish ink risotto, beef baked in paper with artichokes, 60/80,000.

● ♦♦♦♦ *Sans Souci*, v. Sicilia 20 (II C3 de), ☎ 493504, closed Mon and Aug. Excellent international cuisine: shrimp mousse, bresaola with grapefruit and fines herbes, 60/95,000.

● ♦♦♦ *Alberto Ciarla*, p. S. Cosimato 40 (IV C2 bv), ☎ 5818668, closed Sun, Aug and Dec. Choice of several 'guided' menus. Creative seafood: raw fish hors d'oeuvres, bombolotti sparaceddo, 70/80,000.

● ♦♦♦ *Piperno*, v. Monte de' Cenci 9 (IV A-B4 cz), ☎ 6540629, closed Sun eve, Mon, Easter, Aug and Christmas. Service in romantic square in summer. Interesting regional cuisine: ricotta and spinach ravioli, oxtail ragout, 45/65,000.

● ♦♦♦ *Severino a Piazza Zama*, p. Zama 5/C (III E5 dg), ☎ 7553901, closed Sun eve, Mon, Aug and Christmas. Open-air service in summer. Excellent regional cuisine: taglierini rosa, saltimbocca alla Romana, 30/50,000.

♦♦♦ *Andrea*, v. Sardegna 28 (II B-C2-3 bz), ☎ 493707, closed Sun and Aug. Near v. Veneto. Creative cuisine: oyster risotto, liver with grapes, 40/56,000.

♦♦♦ *Aurora 10 - da Pino il Sommelier*, v. Aurora 10 (II C2 ca), ☎ 4742779, closed Mon and 20 Jul-10 Aug. Guitar music in evenings. Italian and international cuisine: risotto with chicory, bucatini all'amatriciana, 35/45,000.

♦♦♦ *Checco er Carrettiere*, v. Benedetta 10 (IV B2 cd), ☎ 5817018, closed Sun eve, Mon and Aug-Sep. Typical Trastevere restaurant. Regional cuisine: spaghetti alla carrettiera, ossobuco alla romana, 40/60,000.

♦♦♦ *Chianti*, v. Ancona 17 (II B5 ce), ☎ 856731, closed Sun and Aug. Tuscan rural atmosphere, long under same management. Tuscan cuisine: noodles with hare, tagliatelle montanara, 30/45,000.

♦♦♦ *Coriolano*, v. Ancona 14 (II B5 cy), ☎ 8449501, closed Sun, Easter, Aug and Christmas. Refined atmosphere. Regional and Italian cuisine: ravioli with ricotta and spinach, braised meat al Barbaresco, 50/80,000.

♦♦♦ *Corsetti - il Galeone*, p. S. Cosimato 27 (IV C2 cf), ☎ 5816311, closed Wed. Mixed cuisine: fish risotto, pancakes with ricotta and spinach, barbecued fish, 30/40,000.

♦♦♦ *Drappo*, vicolo del Malpasso 9 (I F3 ch), ☎ 6877365, closed Sun and Aug. Romantic, with close attention to detail. Sardinian cuisine: tallarinus al fiore sardo, veal with mullet roe, Sardinian wines, 35,000.

♦♦♦ *Eau Vive*, v. Monterone 85 (I F5 ci), ☎ 6541095, closed Sun and Aug. In 16C palazzo, run by nuns. French and international cuisine: escargots bourguignonne, noix de veau flambée à l'armagnac, 25/40,000.

♦♦♦ *Giovanni*, v. Marche 64 (II C3 cn), ☎ 493576, closed Fri eve, Sat and Aug. Careful family management. Good mixed cuisine: agnolotti, cuttlefish, Marche wines, 35/55,000.

♦♦♦ *Girarrosto Fiorentino*, v. Sicilia 46 (II C3 cp), ☎ 460660, closed Fri. Tuscan cuisine: lasagnette with ham, chicken toscana, kid on the spit, 40/55,000.

♦♦♦ *Mastrostefano*, p. Navona 94 (I E-F5 dm), ☎ 6541669, closed Mon. Service on terrace in pleasant square in summer. Regional cuisine: cream of noodle soup with shrimps and chicory, roast spring lamb, artichokes alla giuda, 40/60,000.

♦♦♦ *Pancrazio*, p. del Biscione 92/94 (IV A3 ct), ☎ 6561246, closed Wed and Aug. Reconstruction of a Roman tavern on remains of ancient theatre, the Teatro di Pompeio. Regional and Italian: mullet baked in paper, 28/45,000.

♦♦♦ *Passetto*, v. Zanardelli 14 (I E4-5 cu), ☎ 6540569, closed Sun. Long tradition and good service. Fine Italian cuisine: risotto with truffles, 40/65,000.

♦♦♦ *Pierdonati*, v. della Conciliazione 39 (I E2 cv), ☎ 6543557, closed Thu and Aug. Italian cuisine: pappardelle, linguine all'Ortolana, 30/45,000.

♦♦♦ *Ranieri*, v. Mario de' Fiori 26 (I D6 da), ☎ 6786505, closed Sun. Founded in 1849; rooms in Louis Quinze style. Italian and international cuisine: homemade cannelloni, gnochetti gratinati, 40/75,000.

♦♦♦ *Sabatini in Trastevere*, p. S. Maria in Trastevere 13 (IV B3 dc), ☎ 582026, closed Wed. Service in square in summer. Roman and fish cuisine: linguine with shrimps and squid, tonnarelli alla ciociara, 35/60,000.

♦♦♦ *Scoglio di Frisio*, v. Merulana 256 (II F4 df), ☎ 734619, closed noon, Sun in summer and Mon in winter. Neapolitan atmosphere, with band. Neapolitan seafood: risotto, deviled oysters and mussels, 28/38,000.

♦♦♦ *Taverna Giulia*, vicolo dell'Oro 23 (I E3 di), ☎ 6569768, closed Sun and Aug. In ancient palazzetto with small garden for summer. Genoese and Italian cuisine: pansoti in walnut sauce, trenette with pesto, 40/50,000.

● ♦♦ *Checchino dal 1887*, v. Monte Testaccio 30 (IV E-F3 cb), ☎ 576318, closed Sun eve, Mon, Aug and Christmas. In front of old slaughterhouse, cellars can be visited, family management for many generations. Excellent Roman cuisine: rigatoni can pajata, tonnarelli with oxtail sauce, 35/50,000.

● ♦♦ *Majella*, p. S. Apollinare 45/46 (I E5 cr), ☎ 6564174, closed Sun. Attractive summer service in piazza. Regional and Italian seafood: trenette with black Norcia truffles, tonnarelli with clams, 40/55,000.

● ♦♦ *Moro*, vicolo delle Bollette 13 (I E6 cs), ☎ 6783495, closed Sun and Aug. Traditional Roman trattoria, run by two generations of same family. Regional cuisine: artichokes alla romana, shrimps alla Moro, 35/70,000.

♦♦ *Abruzzi*, v. del Vaccaro 1 (I F6 bu), ☎ 6793897, closed Sat and Aug. Cuisine from Abruzzi and Latium: tonarelli abruzzese, bucatini all'amatriciana, roast pig, 25/35,000.

♦♦ *Girarrosto Toscano*, v. Campania 29 (II B2-3 cq), ☎ 493759, closed Wed. Tuscan and Italian cuisine: Tuscan hors d'oeuvres, tagliolini with salmon and caviar, 40/60,000.

♦♦ *Tana del Grillo - da Ferrarese*, salita del Grillo 6/B (II F2 dh), ☎ 6798705, closed Sun, 1 Aug-15 Sep and Christmas. Fine Ferrara cuisine: pumpkin cappellacci, trolley of mixed boiled dishes, 40/55,000.

♦ *Costa Balena*, v. Messina 5/7 (II B5 cg), ☎ 857686, closed Sun and 10-31 Aug. Seafood: cuttle-fish ink risotto

or shrimp cream, tagliolini with scampi and caviare, 28/45,000.
♦ *Giggetto,* v. del Portico d'Ottavia 21/A (IV A4 cm), ☎ 6561105, closed Mon and Jul. In old Jewish ghetto. Regional cuisine: rice alla pescatora, rigatoni alla pajata, 18/45,000.
♦ *Rosetta,* v. della Rosetta 9 (I E5 db), ☎ 6561002, closed Sun, Mon noon and Aug. Crowded restaurant not far from Pantheon. Seafood: crayfish, tonnarelli, turbot with oysters, 60/90,000.

⚠ *Happy,* at Prima Porta, v. Prato della Corte 1915, 160 pl, ☎ 6422401; *Roma,* v. Aurelia 831, ☎ 6223018 (all year); *Seven Hills,* at Giustiniana, v. Cassia 1216, ☎ 3765571.

● *Recommended*

Auction houses: *Christie's,* p. Navona 114 (I E-F5), ☎ 6564032; *Finarte,* v. Margutta 54 (I C6), ☎ 6786557; *Galleria Borghese,* v. di Ripetta (I C5), ☎ 6876458; *Galleria d'Arte L'Antonina,* p. di Spagna 93 (I D6), ☎ 6792064; *Galleria dei Cosmati,* v. V. Colonna 11 (I D4), ☎ 3611141; *Romana Aste,* v. del Babuino 96 (I C6), ☎ 6790192; *Sotheby Parke Bernet Italia,* p. di Spagna 90 (I D6), ☎ 6781798.

Bicycle rental: *Bicinoleggio,* lungotevere Marzio (I D-E5), ☎ 6573394; *Collalpi,* ☎ 6541084 (near p. di Spagna, I D6).

Botanical gardens: largo Cristina di Svezia 24 (IV A2), ☎ 6544140.

Conference centres: *Palazzo dei Congressi,* at EUR, ☎ 5912735; *CIR (Centro Internazionale Roma),* v. Aurelia 619, ☎ 3874.

Craft workshops: *C. Meloni,* v. di Bravetta 342, ☎ 6253578 (mosaics); *F. M. Franchi,* v. del Piede 21, ☎ 6789116 (original gold work); *V. Mortet,* v. dei Portoghesi 18, ☎ 6561629 (gold and silver work; book in advance); *V. M. De Marchi,* v. Divino Amore 2, ☎ 6798787 (metal, enamel); *Vetro Creare,* p. S. Salvatore, Lauro, ☎ 6547634 (glassware); *Sartoria 1220,* v. Calisti 92, ☎ 6244954 (period theatrical costumes); *Quero,* v. della Lungaretta 65, ☎ 5892350 (leather goods); *Gianni e Vittorio,* v. Liegi 42, ☎ 861809 (leather goods).

Discothèques: *Bella Blu,* v. Luciani 21, ☎ 3608840; *Hysteria,* v. Giovannelli 3 (II A4), ☎ 864587.

Fairs and markets: *Settimana del Mobile Antico* (antique furniture), v. dei Coronari (I E4); spring and autumn *Fiere d'Arte* (art fairs), v. Margutta; *Fiera da Roma* (May-Jun), ☎ 5138141; *Natale Oggi* show and market (Dec); *Tevere Expo-Mostra delle Regioni d'Italia* (Jun-Jul, along the Tiber).

Horse racing: *Capannelle,* v. Appia Nuova 1255, ☎ 7994359; *Tor di Valle,* v. del Mare at the 9.3-km marker, ☎ 5924205; military racecourse *Tor di Quinto,* ☎ 3274622.

Motor racing: at Vallelunga, v. Cassia at 34.5-km marker, ☎ 9041027.

Shows: cinema information, ☎ 198; information on cinema, theatre, events, exhibitions, concerts, etc in *Carnet,* issued monthly by tourist offices, in local pages of daily newspapers and in *Carnet del Turista,* edited by porters' association of *Hotel Chiavi d'Oro* (weekly in summer, distributed free in hotels with three or more stars).

Sports complexes: *Acquacetosa,* v. dei Campi Sportivi 50, ☎ 879248; *Tre Fontane,* v. delle Tre Fontane, ☎ 5926386.

Sports hall: p. Apollodoro 10, ☎ 390874 (near Olympic Village); at EUR, Palazzo dello Sport, ☎ 5925107.

Wine: *Costantini,* p. Cavour 16/B, ☎ 388588; *Quadrozzi,* v. Manzoni 26/B, ☎ 576768; *Trimani,* v. Goito 20, ☎ 4755851.

Youth hostels: *Ostello del Foro Italico,* v. delle Olimpiadi 61, ☎ 3964709.

Zoos: Giardino Zoologico (II A2-3), ☎ 870564; Zoo Safari Fiumicino, v. Portuense 2178, ☎ 601961 or 6011188.

♥ café: *Caffè Greco,* v. Condotti 86 (I D6); pastry: maritozzi (oval brioches with sweet filling), ricotta tart; shopping: international shops in and around v. Veneto; clothes, furs, gold and deluxe items around v. Condotti; art galleries and antique shops in v. del Babuino, v. Margutta and around p. di Spagna; bric-à-brac, smaller antiques and second-hand furniture in shops in old town, around Campo dei Fiori and (especially for books) p. Navona. Porta Portese second-hand market at Trastevere (Sun a.m.); clothes market in v. Sannio (S. Giovanni); flower and fruit markets in p. Vittorio. Principal shopping streets include: v. Nazionale, v. del Tritone and corso Vittorio Emanuele, in city centre; v. Cola di Rienzo and v. Ottaviano, in Prati district (near Vatican); beginning of v. Appia Nuova, Porta S. Giovanni; so-called African streets (v. Libia, v. Somalia, etc.) in Nomentano district.

The arrow (→) is a reference to another entry.

Sardinia

▶ A turning point in the history of Sardinia occurred in 1950 when for the first time there was not one single case of malaria reported during the previous twelve months. This confirmed the success of the post-war Italian government's program to rid the island forever of this scourge, but the results went far beyond the humanitarian reasons for which the campaign had originally been undertaken. For when the sickness was eliminated, Prince Karim Aga Khan IV, who had long understood the latent possibilities of the island as a tourist attraction, invented the 'Costa Smeralda' (Emerald Coast), creating in the NE of the island, where previously there had been a wilderness, a large tourist centre with hotels, restaurants, marinas, shopping areas, nightclubs and other entertainments. Sardinia was launched as a holiday resort. This brought about further improvements since the Italian government, faced with the fact that thousands wanted to visit the island each summer and that communications were inadequate, had to remedy the situation. More steamer and airline services, new airports and roads followed, and soon what had been an isolated agricultural and pastoral community was brought into the 20C. The standard of living rose and things were improving for everybody. Strangely enough, in spite of the island's wild beauty, Sardinia had long been ignored by travelers visiting the Italian peninsula. There was one exception to this rule—D.H. Lawrence, who wrote *Sea and Sardinia* about the island. The island's prehistoric past struck the same chord in him that the Mexico of the Aztecs was to do later. Perceptively he was to say that Sardinia 'which is unlike any other place on earth, was nevertheless inside the net of European civilization, but it hasn't been dragged ashore yet to join the rest of Europe.' Today Sardinia is indeed a part of Europe, but all that fascinated Lawrence about it is still there: endless horizons, rocky escarpments that crop up all over the island, wild mountains covered in dense brushwood, clear lakes with flamingos flying over them, ancient ruins and prehistoric monuments. ☐

● Don't miss

The cathedral★ and the Museo Nazionale Archeologico★ at Cagliari; the Losa nurag★ at Abbasanta; the cathedral★ at Alghero and at Capo Caccia, the grotto of Neptune★★; the nurag Su Nuraxi★ at Barumini; the church of St. Peter★ near Bosa; the cathedral★ at Iglesias; the majestic church of S. Giusta★ near Oristano as well as the ruins of Tharros★; the church of S. Antioco di Bisarcio★ near Ozieri; the church of S. Gavino★ at Porto Torres; the ruins of Nora★ at Pula; the Duomo★ and the Museo G. A. Sanna★ at Sassari and nearby the S. Trinita di Saccargia★; the Santu Antine nurag★ at Torralba and S. Pietro di Sorres★ nearby. Porto Cervo and the Costa Smeralda; the islands of La Maddalena and Caprera★.

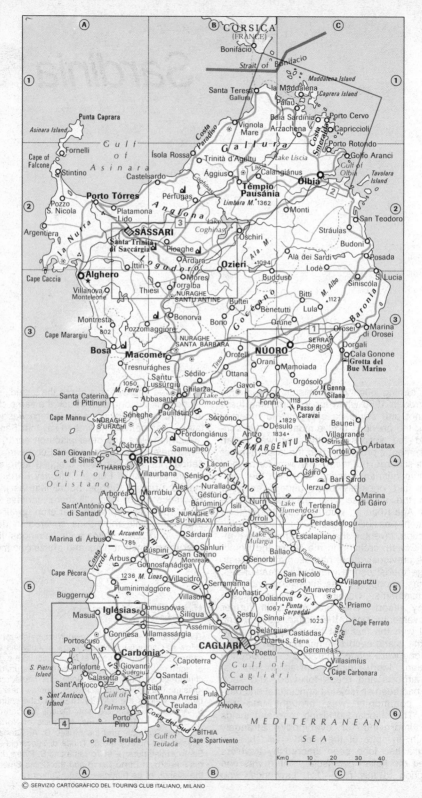

● *Brief regional history*

15C-6C BC
Nurags. **Nurags** are the round towers which abound on the island and date from ancient times. They are built of stone and consist of two or three storeys reached by a spiral staircase. Their original purpose is not known, nor is there much known about their builders, but they seem to have been a **palaeolithic people.** ● The highest point of the nurag culture was reached between 900 and 500 BC when the tribal society began to be ruled by an aristocratic **elite** and **trading** developed with other Mediterranean societies.

6C BC-5C AD
Carthaginians and Romans. The **Greeks,** who had several colonies in Sardinia, lost control of the E Mediterranean to the **Carthaginians** and the **Etruscans** at the battle of **Alalia** (537 BC) off Corsica. ● In sharing the spoils, the Carthaginians won control of Sardinia and began exploiting its mineral resources and building a series of fortifications like the one that may still be seen at **Mt. Sirai.** ● Three centuries later the Carthaginians were replaced by the Romans who had defeated them in the Punic Wars. ● Roman ruins may be seen all over the island and notably at **Turris Libysonis (Porto Torres), Karalis (Cagliari),** Nora and Tharros.

5C-12C
The giudicati, Genoa and Pisa. In the 5C AD Sardinia was invaded by the **Vandals.**● The **Eastern Roman Empire** (the Byzantines) reconquered the island and fought off an attempt by the **Longobards** to occupy it. ● Because Sardinia is a long way from Byzantium the islanders gradually obtained their freedom and they divided the country into four giudicati (kingdoms)—**Cagliari, Torres, Arborea** and **Gallura.** ● At the same time the **Moors** were looting the Christian countries in the Mediterranean, and Sardinia did not escape their attention. They tried to invade the island, but **Genoa** and **Pisa,** maritime republics with strong fleets, intervened. ● They rid Sardinia of the Moors, but gradually took it over themselves. The Sardinians in the N were ruled by the Genoese and those in the S by the Pisans. Minerals, grain, cattle, cheeses, skins, salt, honey and coral were exported from the island.

13C-17C
Spain. In 1297 **Pope Boniface VIII** nominated **King James of Aragon** ruler of an imaginary **Kingdom of Sardinia and Corsica.** He was thus giving the **Aragonese** the right to conquer the island from the Genoese, the Pisans, the **comune of Sassari** and the descendants of the rulers of the **giudicato of Arborea** who resided at **Oristano.** ● The attempt was delayed until 1323-26 and introduced a period of violence with rebellions, fierce fighting, sackings and looting which lasted for 150 years and caused a severe decline in population. ● When the kingdoms of Aragon and Castile united in the 15C to form the **Kingdom of Spain,** Sardinia was governed, like most other Spanish possessions, by a viceroy. Every ten years a **parliament** met, comprised of nobility and clergy, and formulated a series of requests which were forwarded to Madrid. Any requests that might have reduced the island's contribution in taxes and exports were ignored.

SS. Trinita di Saccargia near Sassari

S. Pietro in Bosa

The Sardinian language

The Sardinian language developed directly from Latin, but because of the island's history has been much influenced by the language's of its many occupants. Philologists usually divide Sardinian into three distinct groups: campidanese, *spoken in the southern plains,* nuorese, *spoken in central Sardinia, and* logudorese, *spoken on the western seaboard. These differences, however, are minor and the Sardinian language is basically the same throughout the island. It has retained certain Latin words that other Latin languages discarded long ago, and the languages spoken by foreign invaders have also filtered into it, particularly Spanish. In spite of the absorption of foreign words, Sardinian remains a genuine language.*

18C-20C

Kingdom of Sardinia and Italy. Spanish domination of Sardinia ended at the beginning of the 17C with the **War of the Spanish Succession.** ● The **Congress of London** (1718) gave the crown of the Kingdom of Sicily and Sardinia to the **Dukes of Savoy,** a title they held until 1861 when Sardinia became part of the newly formed **Kingdom of Italy.** ● In 1948 Sardinia became an **autonomous region** of the Republic of Italy.

Mamuthones

Mamuthones is the name given to the strange masks worn at the Carnival of Mamoiada in Barbagia. For centuries this festival took place at the New Year, when according to popular belief the devil appeared. The masks originally had devilish features and were called Maimones, meaning devil in Sardinian. The name later changed to Mamuthones and came to denote all the masks at the festival. Their appearance on 17 January, the day of S. Antonio Abate, marks the carnival's start and it concludes on Shrove Tuesday with a grand procession led by the mamuthones. The masked participants are usually attired in sheepskins, under which they wear a brown velvet suit. They have clusters of sheep's bells on their shoulders and wear the bisera (a black wooden mask) on their faces. They move along in the procession keeping step and accompanied by the issocadores, unmasked members of the group who wear caps held in position by a handkerchief passed over the top of the head and tied underneath the chin; they also carry the tocca, a piece of rope which they swing about trying to lasso the spectators. This gesture is symbolic and represents the temptings of the devil.

 Practical information

Information: tourist offices in provincial capitals and other chief towns.

SOS: public emergency service, ☎ 113; police emergency, ☎ 112; ACI breakdown services, ☎ 116.

Weather: forecast, ☎ 070/5551 (from Cagliari area, ☎ 1911); road conditions, ☎ 070/5554 (from Cagliari area, ☎ 194) or from ACI, ☎ 06/4212; sea conditions, ☎ 070/5556 (from Cagliari, Olbia and Sassari areas, ☎ 196).

Maritime services: Italian State Railways Ferries (passengers, cars, trains): several daily departures from Civitavecchia to Golfo Aranci (c. 8.5 hrs), information and reservations: at Cagliari, ☎ 070/656293, at Oristano, ☎ 0783/72270, at Sassari, ☎ 079/260362. Tirrenia (passengers and cars): ferries leave several times a day from Genoa for Porto Torres and Olbia (c. 12.5 hrs) and several times a week for Arbatax and Cagliari (c. 18 hrs), several times a week from Leghorn to Porto Torres (c. 11.5 hrs) and to Cagliari (c. 17 hrs), daily services from Civitavecchia to Olbia (c. 7 hrs) and to Cagliari (c. 13 hrs) twice a week for Arbatax (c. 9 hrs) twice a week from Naples to Cagliari (c. 15 hrs) weekly services from Palermo and Trapani to Cagliari (c. 10/12 hrs) twice weekly services from Tunis to Cagliari (via Trapani, c. 21 hrs) daily services from Bonifacio (Corsica) to La Maddalena (c. 2.5 hrs) and several daily departures to Santa Teresa Gallura (c. 1 hr), information at: Naples, ☎ 081/7201111, Civita-

vecchia, ☎ 0766/28801, Genoa, 010/26981, Leghorn, ☎ 0586/34732, Cagliari, ☎ 070/666065, Olbia, ☎ 0789/22482, Porto Torres, ☎ 079/514600. Sardinia Ferries: daily ferries from Leghorn to Olbia (c. 9 hrs), information: at Leghorn, ☎ 0586/31001, at Olbia, ☎ 0789/25200. Ferry Line: several ferry crossings a week from Genoa to Cagliari and Olbia, information: at Cagliari, ☎ 070/668121. Grandi Traghetti: ferry departures several times a week during summer from Genoa to Porto Torres, information: at Genoa, ☎ 010/589331. Compagnia Marittima Tolone-Sardegna: weekly services during summer from Toulon (France) to Porto Torres, information: at Porto Torres, ☎ 079/514477.

Air services: direct daily flights from Rome, Milan, Pisa and Genoa for Cagliari, Alghero and Olbia with connections to other airports on island, information: Alitalia, at Rome, ☎ 06/5456, at Milan, ☎ 02/2838; Alisarda, at Olbia, ☎ 0789/52600.

Farm vacations: Associazione regionale Agriturist (c/o Federazione Agricoltori), at Cagliari, v. Trieste 6, ☎ 070/668330.

Vacation villages: TCI Village, at La Maddalena, information: at Milan, ☎ 02/852672, at Rome, ☎ 06/6874432, at Turin, ☎ 011/540177; Club Méditerranée, at Caprera (→ La Maddalena Archipelago) and at Santa Teresa di Gallura, information: at Milan, ☎ 02/778663, at Rome, ☎ 06/4745951; Valtur Village, at Santo Stefano island (La Maddalena Archipelago), information: at Milan, ☎ 02/791733, at Rome, ☎ 06/6784588; Telis and Cala Moresca Villages, at Arbatax, information: Vacanze, at Milan, ☎ 02/85391.

Fairs: Sardinia Trade Fair, at Cagliari.

Sardinian cuisine

The Sardinian language differs radically from Italian and makes comprehension of Sardinian dishes difficult for the tourist. The best known dishes are, therefore, described so that eating in Sardinia can be a pleasure. Culingiones (known also as culuriones in Nuoro and as angiulottus in Oliena) are ravioli filled with fresh sheep's milk cheese; is malloreddus is a Sardinian variety of gnocchi; sa fregula is a local variation of the Arab couscous. Coccois de gerda are buns filled with pork and salted cheese; la lepudrida Cagliaritana is a meat and vegetable soup; pane frattau is a soup with grated cheese and grated Sardinian bread, pane carrasau, which is as thin as a sheet of paper. Coiettos means small quails but they are actually rolls of cabbage with meat stuffing; tacculas are thrush boiled and packed with myrtle leaves into cloth bags and left for a few days before they are eaten. Cordula are grilled giblets of lamb or kid; is pardulas are Easter sweetmeats made from pasta shaped into small baskets that are filled with fresh cheese perfumed with saffron, baked and then covered before serving with honey. Sebadas too are covered in honey and filled with cheese, but instead of being baked they are fried in oil; suspirus, gueffus and candelaus are sweets with almonds.

Events: Festivals of S. Efisio, of the Sea, of S. Maria di Bonaria, of S. Saturnino, at Cagliari; Sartiglia Horse Race, at Oristano; Sardinian Cavalcade and Procession of the Candlesticks, at Sassari; Festivities of the Redeemer, at Nuoro; many other religious festivals with displays of traditional costumes of the Nuoro region, at Fonni, Orgosolo, Mamoiada (→ Le Barbagie and Il Gennargentu); March of the Mamuthones, at Mamoiada; traditional cavalcade, at Sedilo (→ Abbasanta); Lunissanti ceremony, at Castelsardo; Procession of S. Maria del Mare, at Bosa Marina.

Nature parks: *WWF Mount Arcosu Reserve* (→ Cagliari) and *Turri 'E Seu Reserve* (→ Oristano); Pond of Sale Porcus Reserve (→ Oristano). The creation of regional parks in the Gennargentu and Sinis Mountains is under consideration.

Conservation: *WWF Sardinia*, at Cagliari, v. del Mercato Vecchio 15, ☎ 070/670308: at Oristano, v. Canalis 20, ☎ 0783/71447; at Nuoro, v. Gramsci 6, ☎ 0784/30206; at Carbonia, v. Catania 5, ☎ 0781/674389; at Sassari, p. Tola 43, ☎ 079/290008; at Ozieri, v. Tripoli, ☎ 079/788135; at Olbia, v. S. Sera 27/B, ☎ 0789/26289 (management of Mt. Arcosu and Turri 'E Seu reserves, summer working camps in Sardinian deer regions). *LIPU*, at Cagliari, v. L. Alagon 21, ☎ 070/494971 (camps for hawk-watching on San Pietro Island; visit to marshlands in Cagliari region); at Oristano, v. Deledda 2 (guided tours of pond at Sale Porcus in autumn and spring; bird-watching at Mari e Pauli pond with possibility of room and board for students and keen bird-watchers); at Alghero, p. del Molo 2, ☎ 079/952885 (excursions to nature reserves).

Excursions: horseback rides across island from Cala Gonone to Capo Mannu in twelve stages across the Gennargentu; horseback rides through the Sopramonte from Oliena to Orosei in 4 stages, *CAI Cagliari*, v. Piccioni, ☎ 070/667877; *Sardegna da Scoprire* (Discover Sardinia), at Nuoro, v. Dante 29, ☎ 0784/30400 (rural journeys by boat or car; also archaeology and caving); *Cooperativa Enis*, at Oliena, v. Aspromonte 8, ☎ 0784/288365 (sea excursions from Nuoro); *La Montagna*, at Rome, v. M. Colonna 44, ☎ 06/351549.

Cycling: information: from cycling clubs affiliated with *UDACE* (19) found in provinces of Cagliari and Nuoro; cost of shipping bicycle on ferry is reasonable and it is not easy to rent bicycles on island. *Marco Polo Cycling Vacations Cooperative*, ☎ 06/8393525 (itineraries planned across SW of island).

Horseback riding: *Federazione Italiana Sport Equestri*, at Oristano, ☎ 0783/35389, affiliated schools at Cagliari, Oristano and Sassari; centres offering excursions, day cross-country rides with overnight accommodation, at Oliena (→ Nuoro) and Arborea (associates of *ANTE*); hippodromes, at Cagliari, at Chilivani (churches of the Logudoro) and at Sassari.

Sailing: *Centro Velico Caprera*, at La Maddalena; *Lega Navale*, at Alghero and at Poetto (→ Cagliari); *Centri ARCI Vela*, at Cagliari and at San Vero Milis (→ Oristano); windsurfing school, at Porto Cervo (→ La Costa Smeralda and la Gallura).

Skindiving: *Centro Sub Tavolara*, at Porto San Paolo (→ Olbia).

Canoeing: *Italian Canoe-Kayak Federation*, instruction at Cagliari, Oristano and Sant' Antioco (→ Il Sulcis and the southern islands).

Skiing: ski lifts at Gennargentu (→ La Barbagia and il Gennargentu).

La Vernaccia

La Vernaccia di Oristano *is the best known Sardinian wine and should not be confused with the two Vernacce found on the mainland, the Vernaccia di Serrapetrona from the Marches region and Vernaccia di San Gimignano in Tuscany. The Sardinian Vernaccia is a white wine, or rather a golden-coloured nectar, subtle and warm with a perfume of almond blossoms. The Superiore must be kept for at least three years before bottling. There are also a Liquoroso Dolce and a Liquoroso Secco; the first is an excellent dessert wine and the second is an aperitif. The ordinary Vernaccia di Oristano is normally served with fish and is wonderful when accompanied by a Sardinian lobster.*

Facts and figures

Location: *With a coastline nearly 1,900 km long, Sardinia is the second largest island in the Mediterranean, as well as the second largest Italian island. Its mountains are of average height with the highest peak being Gennargentu at 6,000 ft. The landscape is rugged and rocky with sparse vegetation.*
Area: *24,089 sq km, which makes Sardinia the third largest Italian region.*
Climate: *Wholly Mediterranean. The N tip of the island is roughly on the same latitude as Mt. Circeo in Latium and its S point is on the same latitude as Catanzaro in Calabria. The summer is dry, and the rains come at the end of autumn and again between February and April, with a dry period in January known as le secche.*
Population: *1,617,265 inhabitants.*
Administration: *Sardinia is an autonomous region and Cagliari is its capital; there are three provincial capitals—Nuoro, Oristano and Sassari.*

Golf: at Porto Cervo (→ La Costa Smeralda and la Gallura); at Santa Margherita di Pula (the ruins of Nora).

Flying: *Alghero-Fertilia Flying Club,* at airport, ☎ 079/935081; at Cagliari-Elmas airport, ☎ 070/240153 (also parachuting and model flying); at Olbia-Costa Smeralda airport, ☎ 0789/69000; at Oristano airport, ☎ 0783/73511 (also parachuting).

Fishing: *Federazione Italiana Pesca Sportiva*, at Cagliari, v. Elmas, ☎ 070/290077 (information on fishing conditions, prohibited areas, permitted zones, etc.).

 # Towns and places

ABBASANTA

Oristano 35, Porto Torres 100, Cagliari 128 km
Pop. 2,446 ⊠ 09030 ☎ 0785   B3-4

Abbasanta is a dialectical form of Acquasanta (holy water) and the town's name perhaps derives from a health-giving spring in the vicinity. Its houses are built in black basalt that is transported from the plateau above the town.

▶ The **Losa nurag★** *(inquire at municipio)* is 2 km SW; it is one of the best preserved nurags and originally had three storeys. It is surrounded by other towers all enclosed in a fortified curtain-wall; the complex was built starting in the Bronze Age (*c.* 800 BC) and was finished *c.* 600 BC. ▶ In nearby **Paulilatino** *(7 km SW),* there are other nurag remains and near the small church of S. Cristina, a **nurag temple with a well★**. ▶ **Lake Omodeo** *(10 km E)* is a man-made dam, and the Romanesque-Gothic church of S. Pietro★ (13C-14C) that stood on its site was completely removed to nearby **Zuri**. In the parish house at **Tadasuni** there is a remarkable collection of 360 Sardinian musical instruments *(telephone before visiting,* ☎ *50113).*

Practical information ───────────

Environs
PAULILATINO, ⊠ 09030, ☎ 0785, 7 km SW.

Recommended
Craft workshops: *Istituto Sardo Organizzazione Lavoro Artigiano* (carpets, tapestries, carved furniture, objects in iron, all for sale).
SEDILO, ⊠ 09076, ☎ 0785, 14 km NE.

Recommended
Craft workshops: *Sardatappeti* cooperative at Madonnina, ☎ 59125 (hand-woven material).
Events: *procession of riders* (Jul), Comune, ☎ 59028.

ALGHERO*

Sassari 35, Porto Torres 35, Cagliari 227 km
Pop. 37,398 ⊠ 07041 ☎ 079   A3

Alghero was originally a fort on the W coast of the island, but it became more important as an outpost of the Aragonese maritime empire. It is now the fourth largest city in Sardinia. The Catalonians came to Alghero in the 14C and the people today still speak Catalan and jealously preserve this language.

▶ The seafront road follows the old 15C Spanish **ramparts** from Torre Sulis to Porta a Mare (B1). ▶ The **old town** (B1) has frequently arched cobbled streets and is more Spanish than Italian. ▶ The 16C **Casa Doria** at v. Principe Umberto II (B1) has Catalan-Gothic windows and a Renaissance portal. ▶ All that remains of the original Catalan-Gothic 16C **cathedral★** (B1), now rebuilt, is the octagonal campanile with a majolica tiled gable and the apse. ▶ Inside the church of **S. Francesco** (B1, 14C-15C) is a Gothic presbytery with a cross vault. The octagonal campanile can be seen from the adjacent small cloister.

Environs

▶ On a lovely bay 13 km away **Porto Conte★** has some fine beaches. The road to Porto Conte passes the **Palmavera nurag** *(see caretaker in nearby farmhouse);* this is a complex structure protected by towers and standing near the ruins of a nurag village. ▶ A bit farther on the road is **Capo Caccia★** *(25 km from Alghero)*, which rises vertically out of the sea, offering magnificent views. More than 600 steps, hand-cut out of the rock lead down to the **grotta di Nettuno★★** *(summer 9 a.m.-7 p.m.; winter 9 a.m.-2 p.m.; with guide)* which contains a lake and large chambers with fantastic stalactites and stalagmites. It is possible to visit the grotto directly by sea from Alghero, passing the **island of Foradada★**, which is crossed at sea level by a natural gallery, and the **cala d'Inferno★**, a narrow rocky corridor upon which the sea breaks. ▶ The ancient **cemetery of Anghelu Rui**, with thirty-six prehistoric tombs, is 17 km N. ▶ **Porto Ferro** is 22 km away on a lonely inlet N of Capo Caccia. ☐

Practical information ───────────

ALGHERO
≋
🛈 p. Porta Terra 9 (B1), ☎ 979054.
✈ at Fertilia, ☎ 935033; *Alitalia,* corso Vittorio Emanuele II (B1-2), ☎ 979395 (provides bus to airport).
Car rental: *Avis,* p. Sulis 7, ☎ 979577, at airport, ☎ 935064; *Hertz,* at airport, ☎ 935054; *Maggiore,* p. Sulis, ☎ 979375, at airport, ☎ 935045.

Hotels:
★★★ *Calabona,* at Calabona, ☎ 975728, 113 rm Ⓟ ▨ closed Nov-Easter, 84,000; bkf: 8,000.
★★★ *Continental,* v. Kennedy 66 (C2 a), ☎ 975250, 32 rm Ⓟ ▥ closed Nov-Easter. No restaurant, 57,000; bkf: 6,000.
★★★ *El Balear,* lungomare Dante 32 (C2 b), ☎ 975229, 57 rm ▥ closed 16 Oct-14 Apr, 49,500; bkf: 7,000.
★★★ *Margherita,* v. Sassari 70 (B2 c), ☎ 976417, 64 rm Ⓟ ⚹ ⊗ Pens. 56,000.
★★★ *Villa Las Tronas,* lungomare Valencia 1 (C2 d), ☎ 975390, 30 rm Ⓟ ⚹ ◁ ⚘ ⊗ ☐ Former private residence, sits like a castle on an outcrop of rock, 120,000; bkf: 9,000.
★ *Milano,* v. Banyolas 13 (C2 e), ☎ 979531, 25 rm, closed 21 Oct-19 Apr. No restaurant, 37,000; bkf: 4,000.

Restaurants:
♦♦♦ *Tuguri,* v. Maiorca 57 (Bl i), ☎ 976772, closed Sun and 15 Nov-15 Dec. In historical centre of town in 15C renovated building. Regional cuisine: malloreddus all'antica, seafood, lamb or pork on spit, 20/27,000.

◆◆ **Pavone,** p. Sulis 3/4 (Bl g), ☎ 979584, closed Wed, Christmas and Jan. Intimate and tastefully furnished. Seafood: spaghetti with crabs, salted red mullet and bass in Vernaccia wine sauce, 25/45,000.
◆ **Dieci Metri,** v. Adami 37 (Bl f), ☎ 979023, closed Mon and 10 Jan-28 Feb. Dieci metri (ten meters) from piazza in historical centre. Regional cuisine with fish fillings, bass in Vernaccia wine sauce, 22/30,000.
◆ **Pietro,** v. Machin 20 (Bl h), ☎ 979645, closed Wed and Dec. Near 14C church of S. Francesco. Regional cuisine: rigatoni in salmon sauce, grilled scampi, 18/25,000.

⚐ *Mariposa,* at Lido San Giovanni, v. Lido 22, 287 pl, ☎ 950360.

Recommended
Archery: *Compagnia Arcieri Corax,* v. Togliatti 27, ☎ 978228.
Bicycle rental: v. Lamarmora 34, ☎ 952386; v. Vittorio Veneto 90, ☎ 977182; v. Brigata Sassari 50/A, ☎ 951140.
Flying: Aeroclub, at *Fertilia Airport,* ☎ 935081.
Marina: *Capitaneria di porto,* ☎ 953174; *Yacht Club Alghero,* ☎ 952074.
Sailing: *Lega Navale,* Banchina el Porto (instruction).
Wines: visit to *Sella e Mosca* Wine Growers, at I Piani, ☎ 951281 or 951282 (reserve in advance).
Youth hostel: *Ostello dei Giuliani,* at Fertilia, v. Zara 1.

Environs

FERTILIA, ⊠ 07040, 6 km NW.

Hotel:
★★★ **Punta Negra,** ☎ 930222, 94 rm Ⓟ ⅏ ▭ ⤴ closed Oct-Apr, 83,500; bkf: 10,000

PORTO CONTE, ⊠ 07041, ☎ 079, 13 km NW.

Hotels:
★★★★ **El Faro,** ☎ 942010, 92 rm Ⓟ ⋦ ⚲ ⅏ ▭ closed Nov-Mar. Modern hotel with terrace sloping down to breakwater, 156,000.
★★★ **Corte Rosada,** ☎ 942038, 160 rm Ⓟ ⚲ ⅏ ⅏ ▭ ⤴ closed 16 Nov-14 Apr, 82,600; bkf: 15,000.
★★★ **Porto Conte,** ☎ 942035, 151 rm Ⓟ ⅏ ▭ ⤴ closed Nov-Mar, 80,000; bkf: 7,000.

ARBATAX

Nuoro 94, Cagliari 145, Olbia 182 km
Pop. 1,419 ⊠ 08041 ☎ 0782   C4

The **red rocks** of Arbatax rise out of the blue sea near the jetty and in the inlets around Cape Bellavista and Frailis. The rocks contain crystals of red felspar that cause their colour. From the lighthouse 25 km away at Cape Bellavista there is a superb view of the sea. The village of **Santa Maria Navarrese,** in an inlet facing the island of Ogliastra, is 12.4 km N. 23 km NW, there is a splendid view of the Ogliastra area from the **Genna Arramene Pass.**   □

Practical information _____

🚢 in summer ferries leave twice a week for Genoa, Civitavecchia and Olbia and once a week for Cagliari; *Tirrenia,* ☎ 667067.

Hotels:
★★★ **La Bitta,** v. Porto Frailis, ☎ 667080, 28 rm Ⓟ ⚲ ⅏ 39,200; bkf: 4,000. Rest. ◆ Regional cuisine: spaghetti alla bottarga, maloreddus, grilled fish or meat.
★★★ **Villaggio Saraceno,** at Baia di S. Gemiliano, ☎ 667318, 93 rm Ⓟ ⅏ ⅏ ▭ ⤴ closed Oct.-19 May, 66,000; bkf: 6,500.

> If you enjoy sports, consult the pages pertaining to the regions; there you will find addresses for practicing your favorite sport.

Recommended
Cycling: *G.S. Loi,* p. dei Caduti 6, ☎ 622249.
Horseback riding: *centro Sportivo,* at Tortoli, v. Umberto I 190 (associate of *ANTE*).
Marina: ☎ 667093.
Vacation villages: *Telis* and *Cala Moresca* (closed Oct-May), information: *Vacanze,* at Milan, ☎ 02/85391.

ARBOREA

Oristano 16, Cagliari 85, Porto Torres 154 km
Pop. 3,494 ⊠ 09092 ☎ 0783   A4

Arborea is a modern town surrounded by a vast zone of reclaimed land (50,000 acres) near the S coast of the Gulf of Oristano. This land is used for growing rice, grape vines and grazing. Architecturally the town is a mixture of the Liberty and Neo-Gothic styles that were fashionable when it was built in 1928.   □

Practical information _____

Hotel:
★★★ **Ala Birdi,** strada a Mare 24, ☎ 800268, 26 rm Ⓟ ⚲ ⅏ ▭ ⤴ 74,800; bkf: 7,000.

⚐ ★★**S'Ena Arrubia,** at S'Ena Arrubia, strada a Mare 29, 353 pl, ☎ 800552.

Recommended
Horseback riding: *Ala Birdi,* strada a Mare 24, ☎ 800268 (various excursions including 7 day tours of Sardinia with overnight accommodation available; associate of *ANTE*).

BARBAGIE AND GENNARGENTU

From Nuoro to Lanusei *(172 km, 1 day; map 1)*

There are 10 million sheep in Italy and 3 million of them are in Sardinia. The old pastoral way of life is still much in evidence despite the continuing transformation of the island. In the Barbagie region many characteristics of much earlier times remain because the region was isolated for so long. It is this that makes a visit here so interesting. In these remote uplands, far from the W coast of the island and separated from the E by a chain of mountains, the population strenuously resisted invading Carthaginians, Romans and Spaniards; even Christianity didn't penetrate here until the 6C. The Gennargentu (meaning silver gate) range consists of a series of bare peaks, all more or less of the same height (the highest is Punta La Marmora at 6,000 ft), crossed, as are the hills below them, by deep and often wide ravines. In La Barbagia territory the villages are isolated and the shepherds are away six months of the year in the higher pastures. It is divided into four parts: Barbagia di Ollolai, N of the Gennargentu; Mandrolisai to the W; Barbagia di Belvi to the S and Barbagia di Seùlo, still further S. In the past, Barbagia street vendors were a familiar sight throughout Sardinia. They were men who with a horse and cart wandered all over the island and were to be found in markets at all the traditional village festivals. They sold crockery and wooden spoons, chests which also served as benches, fabrics, chestnuts and nougat.

▶ The itinerary starts at **Nuoro** and heads S through oak and chestnut forests to **Mamoiada,** an isolated agricultural and pastoral village famous for the procession of the *mamuthones.* ▶ It then continues to **Fonni,** which at 3,581 ft is the highest inhabited settlement in the island. Its late-Baroque church of the Madonna dei Martiri has some 17C-19C paintings and sculptures. ▶ From

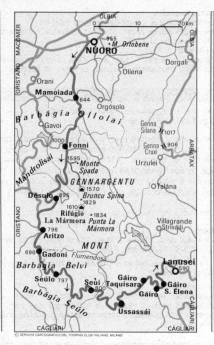

1. Barbagie and Gennargentu

Fonni, two excursions can be made to **Mount Spada** and to the **Gennargentu.** Mount Spada *(8 km SE of Fonni)* has a fully equipped skiing centre. The route to the Gennargentu arrives first at the **Bruncu Spina restaurant,** an hour from the top of the **Bruncu Spina** mountain. Another hour's drive down the mountain ends at the **Refugio La Marmora,** where the route climbs again to the top of **Punta La Marmora** (6,020 ft), the highest peak on the island with a magnificent view across Sardinia. Moufflons (Sardinian wild sheep) live on these slopes, as do vultures and many other wild creatures. ► After these excursions, the route ambles from Fonni through the wild valley of the River Bau until it reaches **Desulo.** In Desulo, there is an interesting parish church with a carved wooden pulpit and a polychrome statue. ► **Aritzo** is next with some old Barbarician stone houses and a parish church with two lovely 15C statues. ► Farther on lies **Gadoni,** a mining village on the S point of Barbagia di Belvì. ► Crossing a rugged and stony landscape where the rocky soil has been terraced to grow vines, the route comes to **Seulo** and then **Seui,** a town with an agricultural museum, **Museo della Civiltà Contadina** *(open p.m. Sun and hols),* divided in two sections, one located in the former Spanish jail and the other in the municipio. The museum documents the pastoral and mining activities of the region. ► The route leads through **Ussassai, Gairo Scalo,** the old village of **Gairo,** abandoned because of danger of landslides, to **Gairo S. Elena** and ends in **Lanusei.** □

Practical information _____

ARITZO, ☒ 08031, ☎ 0784.

Restaurant:
♦♦♦ **Sa Muvara,** at Funtana Rubia, ☎ 629336, closed

Mon except summer and 5 Nov-15 Dec. In modern tourist complex with tennis and conference rooms. Regional cuisine: salamis, boar on a spit, 18/30,000.

Recommended
Events: *Festival of chestnuts and hazelnuts* (folklore, local craftsmanship, Jul), comune, ☎ 629223.

FONNI, ☒ 08023, ☎ 0784.

Recommended
Events: *Festival of Virgin of Martyrs* (Thu-Sun of Pentecost); of *Nostra Signora del Monte* (17 Sep) and of *S. Cristoforo* (3rd Sun in Sep).

AMOIADA, ☒ 08024, ☎ 0784.

Recommended
Events: *Procession of the mamuthones* during feast of S. Antonio Abate (17 Jan) and at Carnival.
Horseback riding: *Società Ippica,* v. Indipendenza 22 (associate of *ANTE*).

MONTE SPADA, 5,233 ft, ☒ 08023, ☎ 0784.
ᔕ ski lifts, instruction.
ⓘ *Sporting Club Ispada,* ☎ 57285.

Hotel:
★★★★ **Sporting Club,** ☎ 57154, 49 rm 🅿 🔥 ♨ 🔲 🎿 55,700; bkf: 7,500.

SADALI, ☒ 08030, ☎ 0782.

Recommended
Caving: *Is Janas* grotto, ☎ 59094 (local guide).
Horseback riding: *Associazione Turistica Pro Loco,* p. Chiesa, ☎ 59094 (associate of *ANTE*).

BARI SARDO

Nuoro 91, Cagliari 129, Olbia 187 km
Pop. 3,820 ☒ 08042 ☎ 0782   C4

Bari Sardo is set in lovely, unspoiled countryside facing the sea with red rocks and sandy inlets. Nearby, in the hilly Ogliastro, there are **nurags** and **domus de janas** (literally 'witches' houses', actually primitive tombs dug out of rock). 405 km away is **Torre di Bari,** a town facing the sea and built around an old fort which protected the coast from pirate attacks. 14 km S is **Marina di Gairo.** □

BARUMINI

Cagliari 61, Porto Torres 215, Olbia 239 km
Pop. 1,528 ☒ 09021 ☎ 070   B4

The most conspicuous feature of the area around Barumini is the mass of the Giara di Gésturi plain. Nearby are the Su Nuraxi nurags, comprising a fortress and village overlooking the flatlands of Marmilla.

► In Barumini, some parts of the original 16C parish church still survive. Inside are fine 14C-15C Sardinian and Catalan paintings. ► 1 km W of the village is **Su Nuraxi** *(9 a.m.-12 noon and 2-5 p.m.; summer 3-7 p.m.).* This is a huge fortress built with large uncemented blocks of stone. It has a central tower (13C-9C BC) and is enclosed by a rectangular line of walls with four more towers, one on each corner. In the 8C-6C BC the fortress was surrounded by yet another series of walls and towers. The **nurag village** that lies against the fort on its E side is made up of 50 stone huts (8C BC). A good view of this amazing prehistoric work, built by men who had only stone tools, is possible from the top of the central tower. In the 6C BC the Carthaginians stormed and occupied the fortress, but the village seems to have been inhabited until Roman times. ► The **Giara di Gésturi** plain extends across the land for some 12 km and is covered in brushwood and fields. It can be reached from the village of **Gésturi,** 4.5 km N of Barumini. A few wild Sardinian horses live on the plain. ▶ The church of S. Pietro, at **Villamar** *(10 km S),* is a perfect example of Sardinian Romanesque architecture (14C); inside is a 15C ikon. Many of the village houses have recently painted **murals,** fine specimens of popular art. □

Practical information ─────────

Restaurant:
◆ *Zia Annetta,* v. Tuveri 8, ☎ 9368006. Regional cuisine: ravioli with ricotta and spinach, malloreddus, 15/20,000.

Recommended
Cycling: *G. S. Villamar,* at Villamar, v. Lussu 8, ☎ 9309045.

BENETUTTI

Sarrari 83, Porto Torres 102, Cagliari 194 km
Pop. 2,329 ⊠ 07010 ☎ 079   B3

Benetutti is built on granite in the high valley of the Tirso.

▶ The **parish church** contains four paintings describing the Invention of the Cross by a disciple of the Master of Ozieri (c. 1540). ▶ In the countryside are some **round megalithic stones** and the **dolmen of Monte Maone.** ▶ 6 km SW are the **Aurora Baths** with a curative mineral spring. They are not far from the older **Baths of S. Saturnino,** which took their name from a small Romanesque church nearby. When this church was rebuilt the remains of some Roman baths were found underneath it.   □

Practical information ─────────

TERME AURORA, ⊠ 07010, ☎ 079, 6 km SW.
⚓ *Aurora Thermal Baths,* ☎ 796871 (closed Nov-Apr); *Thermal Baths di San Saturnino,* ☎ 795579 (closed Nov-May).

Hotel:
★★★ *Terme Aurora,* ☎ 796871, 66 rm ⚕ ⚘ ▣ ✐ closed 6 Nov-30 Apr, 40,000; bkf: 5,000.

BONO

Sassari 78, Porto Torres 97, Cagliari 172 km
Pop. 4,044 ⊠ 07011 ☎ 079   B3

Bono is located at the foot of Mount Rasu (4,130 ft) and is the centre of the wooded, alpine region of Goceano. 8 km SW the hamlet of **Burgos** lies beneath the ruins of the **castle of Goceano** (or of Burgos) which was built in the 11C. 13 km S the SS 128 b offers a good view of a **medieval bridge.** Sardinian thoroughbred horses are raised among the ilex and the oak of the **forest of Burgos,** 18 km NW.   □

BONORVA

Sassari 52, Porto Torres 71, Cagliari 162 km
Pop. 4,960 ⊠ 07012 ☎ 079   B3

Bonorva is a small town containing a lovely archaeological garden, which is near a spring.

▶ The **parish church** retains part of its original 16C Aragonese-Gothic structure. 6 km SW is the 12C church of **S. Nicolo di Trullas.** It has a small loggia and a fine apse and reveals Tuscan and Lombard influences. ▶ 9 km E is the prehistoric burial ground of **S. Andria Priu★** in a region of extinct volcanos. The tombs, called *domus de janas,* were dug out of the rock between 3,000 and 1,800 BC. They form a

series of chambers and the one called **the tomb of the Chief** has 18 rooms. The top of the rock has a strange shape and is known as **the bull.** The shape is natural, but some see a ritualistic significance in the fact that the burial site is beneath it.   □

BOSA

Nuoro 83, Porto Torres 85, Cagliari 174 km
Pop. 8,675 ⊠ 08013 ☎ 0785   A3

Bosa lies in a charming bay on the banks of the Temo. The river is partly navigable but has a tendency to silt up, causing, on several occasions, disastrous flooding in the town.

▶ The **Castle of Serravalla,** overlooking the town with its austere walls and towers, was built by the Genoese Malaspina family in 1112; in its chapel are frescos from the Aragonese period *(contact caretaker at v. Ultima Costa 12,* ☎ *33030).* ▶ At the foot of the castle, in the medieval part of the town known as **Sa Costa,** many of the houses have been dug out of the hillside. ▶ Near the bridge on the opposite side of the river (the l., the city centre is on the r.) the small 15C church of **San Antonio** has a Gothic-Aragonese façade. On the banks of the river, further down, some old tanneries, called **Sas Conzas,** date back to the 18C. ▶ The most important site in the region is the church of **S. Pietro★** *(2 km E).* Parts of its nave date from the 12C and its apse and campanile were built in the 13C. The façade and the first four extensions behind it, in Gothic-Burgundian style, are 14C. ▶ **Bosa Marina,** 2.4 km away, has a pier linking the beach with a rocky island called **Isola Rossa** where there is a 16C tower.   □

Practical information ─────────

BOSA
ⓘ v. Azuni, ☎ 373580.

BOSA MARINA, ⊠ 08013, ☎ 0785, 2.4 km SW.
≋

Hotel:
★★★ *Gabbiano,* v. Mediterraneo, ☎ 374123, 15 rm ⚘ 42,000; bkf: 4,000. Rest. ◆◆ Regional cuisine, 25/40,000.

Recommended
Events: *Procession of S. Maria del Mare* (1st Sun in Aug).
Marina: ☎ 373419.

BUDONI

Olbia 37, Nuoro 67, Cagliari 248 km
Pop. 3,189 ⊠ 08020 ☎ 0784   C2

Budoni is a tourist resort at the mouth of the Budoni River. In spring oleanders bloom in the riverbed.   □

Practical information ─────────

Hotel:
★★★ *Motel Isabella,* v. Nazionale 75, ☎ 844048, 30 rm ℗ ⚕ ✐ closed 5 Oct-5 Nov, 50,000. Rest. ◆◆◆ closed Oct. Regional cuisine: malloreddus, lobster catalan style, 20/30,000.

⚠ ★★★ *Malamuri,* at Agrustos, 200 pl, ☎ 846007.

CAGLIARI*

Porto Torres 229, Olbia 270 km
Pop. 225,009 ⊠ 09100 ☎ 070   B5

Cagliari, surrounded by beaches and lagoons, is the natural port for S Sardinia, the most prosperous

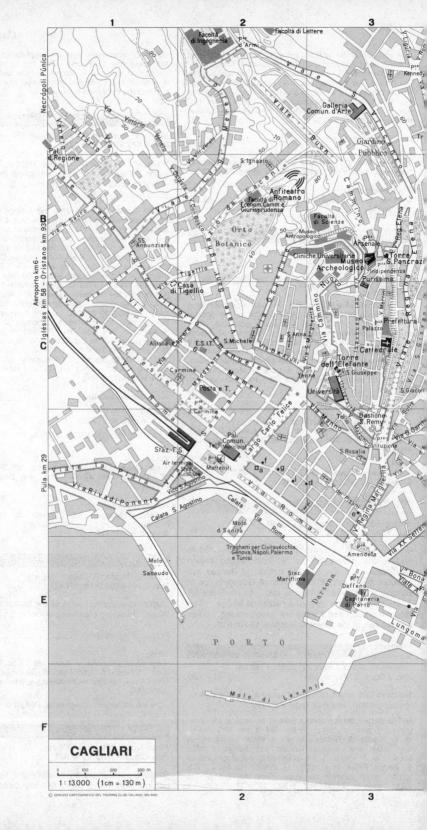

CAGLIARI

0   100   200   300 m

1 : 13 000 (1cm = 130 m)

© SERVIZIO CARTOGRAFICO DEL TOURING CLUB ITALIANO, MILANO

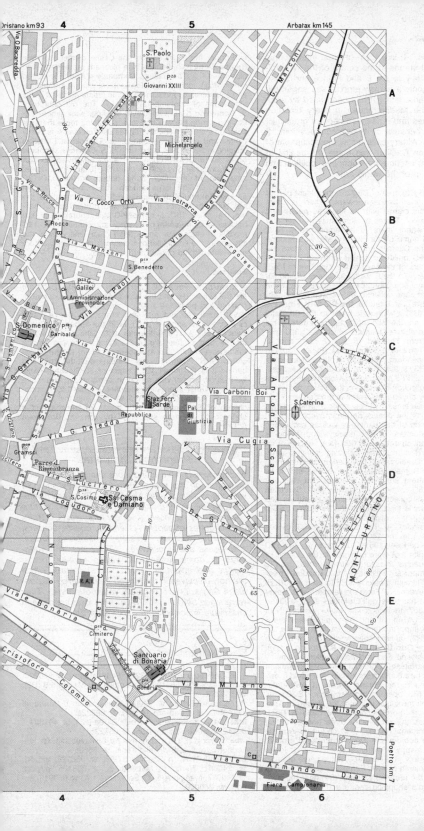

part of the island. It is a town of great international importance for it stands at the centre of the W Mediterranean, with Italy to the E and France and Spain to the W, while only a narrow strip of sea separates it from the African coast. It has been used by shipping crossing the Mediterranean in every direction from ancient times and it has also been of great military importance because of its strategic position. It has served as a military base for all the occupants of the island. When Cagliari was made the capital of Sardinia it had to assume the economic, political and cultural leadership of the whole area.

▶ The **Castello** (B-C3) area of Cagliari, the oldest part of the city, is surrounded by Pisan towers. There is a hint of Spain about this district with its flowered **patios** and ceramic decorations. Traces of Rome may be seen NW of the Castello where there is an amphitheatre (B2), while the original name of the city, *Kàralis*, was Phoenician. Between the Castello and the port (E2) there are many fine 18C-19C buildings similar to those in Genoa and Turin, reminders of the days of the Kingdom of Piedmont and Sardinia. To the E, as far as Mount Urpino (D-E6), there are many fine churches and sanctuaries, while the large industrial zone occupies the W area by the saltworks of Santa Gilla. ▶ **Castello, the Old City.** From the p. dell' Arsenale (B3) a wide gate leads to the **Citadella dei Musei,** built on the site of a Spanish fort. This houses the **Museo di Arte Orientale** which has 1,300 specimens mostly from Thailand *(8 a.m.-1 p.m. and 4-7 p.m.).* ▶ The **Torre di S. Pancrazio★** (Pisan, 1305) in the nearby p. Indipendenza houses the **Museo Nazionale Archeologico★** (B3; *9 a.m.-2 p.m. and 2:30-5 p.m.; Sun 9 a.m.-1 p.m. and 2:30-5 p.m.; closed Mon*), which has the most important collection of relics on the island and which must be visited by anyone interested in the Sardinian culture of pre-Roman times. It has objects from archaic burial sites such as the **domus de janas** (witch's house) and from the tombs of the giants, as well as prehistoric nurag bronze statuettes. It also displays copper ingots marked in Minoan characters (3,000 BC), articles from Phoenician and Roman times including jewelry, amulets and bronzes, Greek vases, Egyptian ornaments and a large collection of Roman glassware★. In the Pinacoteca (picture gallery) there are Pisan, Sienese and Genoese paintings, 15C-16C works by Spanish and Sardinian artists and a small collection of Sardinian costumes and articles. ▶ Nearby is the church of the **Purissima** (B-C3) in 17C Gothic-Aragonese style *(for visit ring at no. 130 at the Istituto Magistrale).* ▶ The **Cathedral★** (C3; *closed for repairs*) dates from the 14C but was largely rebuilt in the Baroque style between 1660-1702; inside are two 13C Romanesque pulpits that were originally in the duomo of Pisa. A small **museum** *(closed because of theft)* used to house the most important articles of the Cathedral's treasure including a Flemish triptych★ said to be the work of Roger van der Weyden. ▶ From the **rampart of S. Remy** (D3), not far from the **torre dell'Elefante★** (C3), a Pisan construction of 1307, there is a fine view★, especially at sunset, over the city, the gulf and the small lakes to the E and W. ▶ Other important points of interest include the **Amphitheatre★** (B2), almost entirely dug out of rock in 2C AD; the nearby **Orto Botanico** (B2; *8 a.m.-2 p.m.; Sat 8 a.m.-12 noon; closed Sun and hols*), which has many specimens of Sardinian, Corsican and Mediterranean plants, as well as rare plants from all over the world growing in the open air; the **Museo Sardo di Antropologia ed Etnologia** (B3; *open on request 9 a.m.-12:30 p.m., ☎ 653839*) and, in the same building, the **Museo di Anatomia** with waxwork reproductions. The **Casa di Tigellio** (C1-2) encloses the remains of three houses dating from the time of imperial Rome. ▶ Much further W is the **necropoli punica occidentale** (Phoenician burial ground) of Kàralis (A1 off map) with many ancient tombs, while the **Grotta della Vipera** (v. S. Avendrace) is the name given to the Roman mausoleum of Atilia Pompilia. ▶ The **modern area** consists of the arcaded **v. Roma** (D2) near the port, which is the town's shopping centre and meeting place,

and under the rocky spur of the Castle district the **viale Regina Elena** (C3), flanked by a pleasant promenade with pine trees. ▶ The **Galleria Comunale d'Arte** (A3; *closed temporarily*), lodged in a Neoclassical villa, has paintings and sculptures by modern Sardinian artists and also holds exhibitions of contemporary art. ▶ The old church of **S. Domenico** (C4), a medieval building, was almost destroyed during the war and is now nothing more than the crypt of a modern church; its beautiful **cloister★** is partly Gothic and partly Renaissance. ▶ The oldest Christian building in Sardinia is the church of **S. Cosma e Damiano** or S. Saturno (D4; *open Sun a.m., otherwise contact parish priest at S. Lucifero church*). It has a 6C dome; only one of the four arms added in the 11C-12C remains. ▶ The large modern basilica (19C) known as the **Santuario di Bonària** (F5) is dedicated to the Madonna, patron of the island and protectress of sailors. A small 15C Aragonese-Gothic church near the basilica has a **museum** of ex-votos and contains 18C-19C models of ships *(visit on request).* ▶ A fine view of the city and of the small lake of Molentargius is possible from the **Monte Urpino** public gardens (D-E6).

Environs

▶ 5 km SE is **Poetto,** Cagliari's beach resort. Behind it are the salt-works and the **lake of Molentargius,** a nature reserve and protected area. A museum devoted to Sardinian rural life and arts and crafts, **Sa dom'e Farra** *(9 a.m.-1 p.m. and 4-8 p.m.),* is in the suburb of **Quarti Sant'Elena.** ▶ The **salt-works of S. Gilla** *(10 km W)* on the SE part of the lake of the same name are among the largest in Italy. ▶ At **Assémini** *(10 km W)* the parish church of S. Pietro is in the Aragonese-Gothic style and behind it is the small 12C chapel of **S. Giovanni** *(keys with parish priest)* with an onion dome in the Byzantine style. ▶ Other interesting churches are the 14C Romanesque **S. Maria★** at Uta *(22.5 km NW)* and the 13C-14C church of **S. Pantaleo★** with traces of frescos and a shrine with columns supported by lions at Dolianova *(20 km NE).*   ☐

Prehistoric statuettes

Archaeologists have found more than 500 prehistoric statuettes on the island. Even today they astonish with the vigour of their execution. They are invaluable for the light they shed on prehistoric culture because they represent a variety of subjects. There are statuettes of people—chieftains, priests, soldiers, shepherds, farmers, artisans, aristocratic ladies, priestesses and housewives. There are also statuettes of domestic animals, village houses, boats, nurags and enigmatic gods. The statuettes, which are now displayed in the Museo Archeologico Nazionale in Cagliari, were originally votive offerings. They were made between 9C-7C BC from local copper and cassiterite imported from Cornwall or Etruria.

Practical information

CAGLIARI
ⓘ p. Deffenu 9 (E3), ☎ 663207; *Elmas Airport,* ☎ 240200; v. Mameli 97, ☎ 664195 (head office); p. Matteotti 9 (D2), ☎ 669255.
✈ *Cagliari Elmas,* ☎ 240047; buses from p. Matteotti (D2); *Alitalia,* v. Caprera 14 (C1), ☎ 669221.
▤ (D1-2), ☎ 656293; *Ferrovie Sarde* (C5), ☎ 491304.
🚌 from bus station (C2), ☎ 657236.
⚓ *Tirrenia* (E2-3), car ferries for Civitavecchia, Genoa, Leghorn, Naples, Sicily and Tunis, ☎ 666065.
Car rental: *Avis,* v. Sonnino 87/89, ☎ 668128, airport, ☎ 240081; *Hertz,* p. Matteotti 8, ☎ 668105, airport, ☎ 240037; *Maggiore,* v. XX Settembre 1/A, ☎ 650919, airport, ☎ 240069.

Hotels:
★★★ *Italia,* v. Sardegna 31 (D2 a), ☎ 656832, 118 rm ⌗
No restaurant, 73,000.
★★★ *Mediterraneo,* lungomare Colombo 46 (F4 b),
☎ 301271, 136 rm P 𝟰𝟰𝟰 ⅙ 104,000; bkf: 11,500.
★★★ *Solemar,* v. Diaz 146 (F5-6 c), ☎ 306211, 42 rm P
⌗ No restaurant, 85,000.
★★ *MotelAgip,* circonvallazione Pirri, ☎ 561645, 57 rm
63,500; bkf: 11,000.

Restaurants:
● ◆◆◆ *Corsaro,* v. Regina Margherita 28 (D3 e),
☎ 664318, closed Tue. Elegant dining room displaying
Sardinian arts and crafts. Regional cuisine: fregula with
mussels, tagliatelle with lobster sauce, 35/50,000.
◆◆◆ *Antica Hostaria,* v. Cavour 60 (D2-3 d), ☎ 665870,
closed Sun and Aug. Pleasant dining room with picture
collection. Regional cuisine: malloreddus alla campidanese, fregula with crabs, 30/40,000.
◆◆◆ *Pineta,* v. della Pineta 108 (F6 h), ☎ 303313, closed
Mon and Sep. Lively and modern, with adjacent pizzeria. Italian cuisine: malloreddus, risotto quattro gusti,
30/40,000.
◆◆ *Italia,* v. Sardegna 30 (D2 f), ☎ 657987, closed Sun
and 20 Dec-20 Jan. Modern, with fish displayed in glass
tanks. Seafood: spaghetti in lobster sauce, fregula with
eel, 15/30,000.
◆◆ *Rosetta,* v. Sardegna 44 (D2 g), ☎ 663131, closed
Mon and 1-15 Jul, 20/35,000.
◆ *Lillicu,* v. Sardegna 78 (D2 i), ☎ 652970, closed Sun
and 10 Aug-1 Sep, 20/25,000.

🜊 ★ *Pini e Mare,* at Quartu S. Elena, ☎ 805216.

Recommended
Archery: *Compagnia Arcieri Nuragici,* p. Sirio 4,
☎ 370129 or 4792545.
Botanical gardens: (B2), ☎ 657651 (closed Sun and hols).
Canoeing: *Scuola Canottieri Ichnusa,* calata dei Trinitari
14, ☎ 300226.
Conference centre: *Palazzo dei Congressi,* v. Diaz 221,
☎ 300788.
Craft workshops: *G. Puddu,* at Pirri, v. Principe di Pie-
monte 2, ☎ 560657 (inlaid woodwork).
Cycling: *C.S. Monia Flor,* v. Monia 77, ☎ 650216.
Events: *Festival of S. Efisio* (1 May, Sardinian folklore);
Feste del Mare (1st Sun in Apr); *Festa di S. Maria di Bona-*
ria (Jul); *Festival of S. Saturnino* (last Sun in Oct).
Fairs and markets: *Fiera Campionaria della Sardegna* (F6;
May), ☎ 302225.
Flying: *Cagliari Elmas Airport,* ☎ 240153.
Hippodrome: v. Poetto, ☎ 371294.
Horseback riding: *Società ippica Cagliari,* v. Poetto,
☎ 373863 (instruction).
Nature reserves: *Monte Arcosu Reserve (20 km W),* infor-
mation and visits from *WWF Sardinia,* ☎ 670308 or official
in charge of reserve, ☎ 493778.
Sailing: *Sardegna,* v. Trento 8, ☎ 663201 *(ARCI Vela)* (in-
struction).
Sports centre: *Palazzetto dello Sport,* v. Rockefeller,
☎ 301665.
Swimming: v. Diaz 133, ☎ 301749; v. Diaz 213,
☎ 301750; v. Monte Mixi, ☎ 301611; v. Colombo 137,
☎ 300286 (pools).
♥ shopping: inlaid furniture, masks, filigreed gold.

Environs

ASSEMINI, ⊠ 09032, ☎ 070, 14 km NW.

Recommended
Craft workshops: *S. Farci,* v. Sardegna 115
(S. Andrea district), ☎ 941125; *L. Nioi,* v. Carmine 91,
☎ 941224 (ceramics).

CALA MOSCA, 5 km SE.

Hotel:
★★★ *Capo Sant'Elia,* v. Calamosca 50, ☎ 370252, 47 rm
P 𝟰𝟰𝟰 ⅙ 74,000; bkf: 6,000.

POETTO, ⊠ 09100, ☎ 070, 5 km SE.
≈

Restaurants:
● ◆◆◆ *Corsaro a Poetto,* at Marina Piccola, ☎ 370295,
closed winter. Service on terrace facing sea. Seafood:
tagliatelle and lobster sauce, pane frattau, 35/50,000.
◆◆◆ *Ottagono,* v. Lungomare, ☎ 372879, closed
Tue. On coast with tank with rare fish. Regional seafood: risotto with lobster sauce, grilled crayfish,
35/50,000.

Recommended
Marina: *Yacht Club Cagliari,* ☎ 370350.
Sailing: *Lega Navale,* v. marina Piccola, ☎ 370380 (in-
struction).

CASTELSARDO

Sassari 32, Porto Torres 34, Cagliari 243 km
Pop. 5,241 ⊠ 07031 ☎ 079   A-B2

Castelsardo is magnificently situated, lying on a rocky
ledge sloping down to the sea in front of the Gulf of
Asinara. Behind it are 13C ramparts and in the distance the Gallura Mountains. At one time it was a
fortress of the powerful Genovese Doria family, who
are said to have founded it in 1102. It received its
present name in 1767, when it was incorporated into
the kingdom of Savoy.

▶ Winding streets in the **old town** lead to the fortifications and the terraces of the **Castle,** which has a splendid
view★ over the town and sea. ▶ The **Cathedral,** which
still shows traces of its 16C Gothic origins, has a slim
campanile that ends in a small glazed cupola; inside is a
15C ikon of *Madonna degli Angeli★* by the Maestro
of Castelsardo.

Environs

▶ 21 km E are the medicinal springs of **Terme di Castel-**
doria in the Coghinas Valley at the foot of a hill surmounted by the ruins of a Doria castle. ▶ The Romanesque
13C Pisan church of **Nostra Signora de Tergu** *(10.5 km S)*
was formerly a Benedictine monastery. ▶ On the road to
Bulzi, prehistoric tombs, **domus de janas** have been dug
in the rocky mass known as **l'Elefante★** *(2.5 km).* At
Sédini *(15.3 km)* a large **domus de janas★,** cut out of
the rock and comprising five rooms has been consecrated and turned into the Gothic-Aragonese church of
S. Andrea (1517). ▶ Past Bulzi, the 13C Pisan church of
S. Pietro di Simbranos★ has a façade with black and
white bands and inside a 12C Crucifixion★ in wood.   ☐

Practical information ────────────────────

CASTELSARDO
≈

ⓘ v. del Bastione 5, ☎ 470585.

Hotels:
★★★ *Baia Ostina,* at Cala Ostina, ☎ 470223, 120 rm 𝟰𝟰𝟰
⊠ ⌗ closed Oct-Apr, 65,000; bkf: 7,500.
★★★ *Riviera,* v. Lungomare Anglona 1, ☎ 470143, 26 rm
P ⌗ 41,600; bkf: 5,000. Rest. ◆◆ *Fofo* closed Wed in
winter. Regional cuisine, 18/35,000.

Restaurants:
◆ *Guardiola,* v. del Bastione 4, ☎ 470755, closed
Mon. On fortifications of old Genoese Doria fort with
small summer garden. Seafood, 30/35,000.
◆ *Sa Ferula,* at Le Bagnu, ☎ 474049, closed Wed
and Oct. View over sea and service outside in summer. Regional cuisine: risotto, penne, grilled fish,
18/29,000.

Recommended
Events: *Procession del Lunissantu* (Easter Mon,
Comune, ☎ 470138).
Marina: ☎ 470916.

Environs

TERME DI CASTELDORIA, ✉ 07039, ☎ 079, 21 km E. ♨ (Apr-Nov), ☎ 585601.

COSTA DEL SUD

B6

Costa del Sud is a recently created name for an area of sun and sea, luxuriant and untouched landscape and small beaches following one another in deep bays separated by rocky spurs. This is the coast of S Sardinia, between the headland of the torre di Chia and the port of Teulada, where the jagged Capes of Malfatano and Spartivento extend into the sea.

▶ Only a few ruins are left, near the **tower of Chia**, of the ancient Phoenician and Roman city of **Bithia**. ▶ 20 km W of Porto Teulada, **Porto Pino**, near Punta Menga, lies in an inlet on a sandy neck of land where pines grow among large lakes. ▶ The Phoenician-Carthaginian archaeological site of **Pani Loriga**, which dates from 7C BC, is inland on a height SW of **Santadi**, 20 km N of Teulada. There are fortifications on top of the hill, a shrine, traces of a wall and houses, a burial site, a pit where incineration took place and Carthaginian tombs with several cells. ☐

Practical information ————————————

TEULADA, ✉ 09019, ☎ 070. ⓘ p. Mazzini, ☎ 922032.

COSTA PARADISO

Sassari 75, Porto Torres 77 km
Pop. 18 ✉ 07038 ☎ 079   B1-2

Costa Paradiso, on the NW coast of Sardinia, is a series of sandy bays and small inlets with reddish rocks out to sea and an expanse of brushwood inland. 12 km SW along the coast is **Costa dei Tinnari**, a village of fishermen, and **Isola Rossa** is 3 km further on. Going NE is **Portobello di Gallura** *(18 km)* and **Vignola Mare** *(18.5 km)*. ☐

Practical information ————————————

≋ ⓘ at Trinità D'Agultu, v. Vittorio Emanuele 59, ☎ 681141.

Hotel:
★★★ *Li Rosi Marini,* ☎ 689731, 30 rm Ⓟ ≸ ▥ ▤ ✍ closed 16 Oct-31 Mar, 70,000; bkf: 9,000.

La COSTA SMERALDA

From Olbia to Santa Teresa Gallura *(101 km, 1 day; map 2)*

The Costa Smeralda, about 30 km of enchanting coastline NE of Olbia, has now attained worldwide renown. Yet it was little more than twenty years ago that the Aga Khan, a group of international financiers and the Italian government decided to develop what was then a wild and deserted stretch of the Gallura coastline into a fashionable seaside resort. They were most successful and they kept to certain standards: buildings had to be in the Sardinian manner or in other Mediterranean styles. The elements of a first-class tourist resort followed with splendid hotels, marinas, restaurants, nightclubs, deluxe shops and boutiques. There are also many residential villages and hotels.

▶ The itinerary mostly follows the coast, but when there are no roads by the sea the route turns inland. Leaving **Olbia** (→), following the N side of the Gulf of Olbia the route passes the **Lido di Pittulongu** and arrives at **Golfo Aranci** (→). It next follows the Gulf of Marinella, in typically Mediterranean country, with cliffs and dry brushwood on land and small promontories projecting out to sea. ▶ At the tip of one of these promontories is **Punta della Volpe** and **Porto Rotondo**, an exclusive and recently created resort. Follow the road along the **Costa Smeralda**, by the shores of the **Gulf of Cugnana**, the **Cala di Volpe**, **Punta Capaccia** and **Golfo Pero**; everywhere there are fine beaches, separated by rocky spurs, all housing luxurious coastal resorts. ▶ The chief of these is **Porto Cervo** with a small square facing the old port. It is famous for its deluxe hotels and shops. ▶ Farther on is another new resort, **Baia Sardinia**. ▶ Now proceed along the E side of the Gulf of Arzachena, turning inland to **Arzachena** itself, which is an important farming town. The **tombs of the giants of Capichera** are nearby *(5 km)* on the road to Luogosanto. These prehistoric monuments comprise a single large oval façade with dolmens, and further on *(8 km)* is the **burial ground of Li Muri**, with dolmens set out in a circle. Another excursion off this route would lead to **Mount Moro** *(22 km)*; from its summit there is a splendid view of the whole Costa Smeralda. ▶ This itinerary goes back to the sea at **Palau** (→), which faces La Maddalena Islands (→ La Maddalena Archipelago). The road then turns inland to Santa Teresa Gallura and returns to the coast at one point only, **Porto Pozzo**. The route ends at **Santa Teresa Gallura**. ☐

Practical information ————————————

ARZACHENA, ✉ 07021, ☎ 0789. ⓘ p. Risorgimento, ☎ 82624.

Hotels:
★★★ *Baja,* at Cannigione, ☎ 88010, 54 rm Ⓟ ▥ ▤ ✍ closed 11 Oct-14 May, 64,000; bkf: 7,000.
★★★ *Rocce Sarde,* at San Pantaleo, ☎ 65265, 72 rm Ⓟ ≸ ▥ ▤ ✍ closed 21 Oct-31 Mar, 95,000; bkf: 10,000.

Restaurant:
◆◆◆ *Grazia Deledda,* ☎ 98990, closed Jan. On road to coast. Regional cuisine: zuppa alle sarde, pane frattau, spigola in wine sauce, 60/80,000.

⚐ ★★★ *Isuledda,* at Cannigione, 900 pl, ☎ 86003.

BAIA SARDINIA, ✉ 07021, ☎ 0789.
≋

Hotels:
★★★★ *Bisaccia,* ☎ 99002, 62 rm Ⓟ ≸ ◈ ▤ closed 16 Oct-31 Mar, 112,500; bkf: 9,000. Rest. Regional cuisine: salted or grilled fish, roast lamb or kid.
★★★★ *Mon Repos-Hermitage,* v. Emilia, ☎ 99093, 40 rm Ⓟ ▥ ◈ ▤ closed 11 Oct-9 Mar, 85,500; bkf: 10,000.
★★★ *Punta Est,* ☎ 99028, 49 rm Ⓟ ▥ ▤ ✍ closed 21 Oct-24 Apr, 85,000; bkf: 10,000.
★★★ *Ringo,* at Cala Bitta, ☎ 99024, 113 rm Ⓟ ▥ ▤ ✍ closed 1 Oct-2 May, 81,000; bkf: 8,500.
★★★ *Smeraldo Beach,* ☎ 99046, 132 rm Ⓟ ▥ ▤ closed Oct-Apr, 113,400; bkf: 10,000.

CALA DI VOLPE, ✉ 07020, ☎ 0789.
≋

Hotels:
L★★★★★ *Cala di Volpe,* ☎ 96083, 123 rm Ⓟ ≸ ◈ ▥ ◈ ▤ ✍ Pens. closed 1 Oct-14 May. Laid out as an old village, 460,000.
L★★★★★ *Romazzino,* at Romazzino, ☎ 96020, 90 rm Ⓟ ≸ ◈ ▥ ◈ ▤ ✍ Pens. closed 16 Oct-14 May. Sardinian style, with lawns running down to beach, 438,000.
★★★ *Nibaru,* ☎ 96038, 45 rm Ⓟ ◈ ⚅ ◈ ▤ ✍ (18) closed Oct-Apr, 94,300; bkf: 12,000.

PORTO CERVO, ✉ 07020, ☎ 0789.
≋
ⓘ *Società Alberghiera Costa Smeralda,* ☎ 94000.

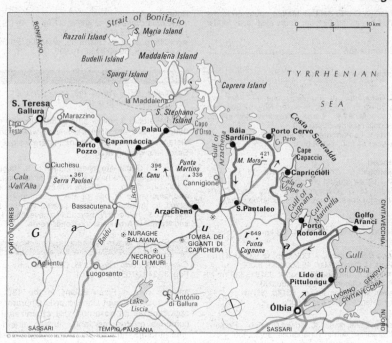

2. La Costa Smeralda

Hotels:
L★★★★★ *Pitrizza,* at Liscia di Vacca, ☎ 91500, 28 rm ℗
⟨ ⟨ ⋘ ⫸ ⬒ Pens. closed 1 Oct-14 May.　Sardinian villas among rocks and greenery, 462,000.
★★★★★ *Cervo,* ☎ 92003, 93 rm ⫸ ⬒ closed Nov-Mar, 558,000; bkf: 21,000.
★★★★ *Cervo Tennis Club,* ☎ 92244, 16 rm ⋘ ⫸ ⬒ ⫽ No restaurant, 209,000; bkf: 17,500.
★★★★ *Ginestre,* ☎ 92030, 63 rm ℗ ⟨ ⋘ ⫸ ⬒ ⫽ closed Oct-Mar, 230,000; bkf: 16,000.
★★★★ *Luci di la Muntagna,* ☎ 92051, 70 rm ℗ ⟨ ⋘ ⬒ closed 11 Oct-31 Mar, 126,400; bkf: 12,000.
★★★ *Balocco,* ☎ 91555, 30 rm ℗ ⟨ ⋘ ⫸ ⬒ ⫽ closed 16 Oct-Easter.　No restaurant, 135,000; bkf: 10,000.

Restaurant:
♦♦♦ *Fattoria,* at Golfo Pervero, ☎ 92214, closed Mon except summer and 20 Oct-20 Mar.　Large fireplace and fine terrace.　Regional cuisine: zuppa quata, grilled fish, pork or lamb, 25/35,000.

Recommended
Golf: *Pevero Golf Club,* ☎ 96072 (18 holes).
Marina: ☎ 94498; *Yacht Club Costa Smeralda,* ☎ 91332.
Windsurfing: *Windsurfing Sardinia,* ☎ 704001, at Milan, ☎ 02/3453680.

PORTO ROTONDO, ⊠ 07026, ☎ 0789.
≈

Hotels:
★★★★★ *Sporting Hotel,* ☎ 34005, 27 rm ℗ ⟨ ⟨ ⋘ ⬒ ⫸ ⬒ Pens. closed 6 Oct-14 May, 344,000.
★★★ *Abi d'Oru,* in Gulf of Marinella, ☎ 32001, 66 rm ℗ ⟨ ⟨ ⫽ closed 6 Oct-14 May, 170,000; bkf: 12,000.

★★★ *San Marco,* ☎ 34108, 28 rm ℗ ⫸ closed 16 Oct-31 Mar. No restaurant, 130,400; bkf: 20,000.

Recommended
Marina: *Yacht Club Porto Rotondo,* ☎ 34010 or 34145.

DORGALI

Nuoro 32, Olbia 114, Cagliari 213 km
Pop. 7,733 ⊠ 08022 ☎ 0784　　　　　　　C3

Dorgali is a small city where it is still possible to see women wearing the traditional Sardinian costume.　In the city centre are workshops where skilled artisans produce fine gold and silverware, leather goods and ceramics.

▶ Prehistoric, Roman and early medieval finds from Serra Orrios are on display in the **Museo Civico Archeologico** *(9 a.m.-1 p.m. and 4-7 p.m.; closed Oct-Apr).*　▶ 10 km NW, beyond the **man-made lake** in the narrows of the river **Cedrino,** is the site of the **Serra Orrios nurag village** where the remains of about 70 stone huts and two small temples have been excavated.　▶ 7 km N in a huge chamber of the **grotto of Ispinigoli** *(9 a.m.-1 p.m. and 3-5 p.m. or 6 p.m. in summer; closed mid Oct-late Mar)* there is a stalagmite rising to 125 ft and a series of galleries with dazzlingly beautiful coloured walls.　▶ A road winds along a ridge of the rocks, offering splendid views of the Sopramonte and the wild valleys that slope down from the Gennargentu.　20 km S is a construction hut at **Genna Silana.**　▶ 9.3 km farther is the small port of **Cala Gonone;** nearby are the **Arvu nurags** which stand in the middle of a neolithic village of some 100 stone huts.　To the S the famous **Grotto del Bue Marino** opens on to the sea and may be visited by boat *(inquire at local tourist office).* ☐

Practical information _____

DORGALI
ⓘ v. Lamarmora 181, ☎ 96243.

Hotels:
★★★ *Su Gologone,* at Su Gologone *(17 km W),* ☎ 287575, 33 rm Ⓟ ⚱ ⚱⚱ 🗔 ⤴ closed Nov, 52,000; bkf: 7,000. Rest. ● ♦♦♦ Large fireplace in dining room. Regional cuisine, 20/30,000.
★★ *Querceto,* v. Lamarmora 4, ☎ 96509, 20 rm Ⓟ ⚱⚱ ⤴ closed Oct-Mar, 41,000; bkf: 6,000.

Recommended
Craft workshops: G. Cherchi, at Orosei *(21 km NE),* v. Matteotti 1 (straw-stuffed chairs).
Events: *Festa di S. Giuseppe* and *Arts and Crafts Exhibition* (Aug); *Orosei Arts & Crafts Exhibition (Jul).*

Environs

CALA GONONE, ✉ 08022, ☎ 0784, 9.3 km E.

Hotels:
★★★ *Mastino-Delle Grazie,* v. Colombo, ☎ 93150, 41 rm Ⓟ ⚵ ⚱ closed 11 Oct-19 Mar, 45,000; bkf: 6,000.
★★★ *Palmasera,* v. del Bue Marino, ☎ 93191, 320 rm Ⓟ ⚱⚱ ⚵ 🗔 ⤴ Pens. closed Nov.-Mar, 150,000.
★★ *Miramare,* v. Lungomare, ☎ 93140, 38 rm Ⓟ ⚵ ⚱⚱ closed Oct-Easter, 42,000; bkf: 5,000.

Restaurant:
♦ *Su Recreu,* p. Doria, ☎ 93135, closed Oct-Feb. Regional seafood: shellfish, fish in wine sauce, 30/35,000.

⚓ ★★★ *Cala Gonone,* v. Collodi 1, 400 pl, ☎ 93165.

Nuoro 40, Olbia 145, Cagliari 158 km
Pop. 3,619 ✉ 08020 ☎ 0784　　　　　　B3

Gavoi, surrounded by wooded hills, has houses built of granite. It has a 17C late-Gothic church, **S. Gavino,** with a tabernacle and pulpit made by local artists in the 18C. The small church of **S. Antioco** is covered in ex-voto filigreed ornamental work in silver and gold. 2 km S is the man-made Guzana Lake. ☐

Practical information _____

ⓘ v. Roma, ☎ 53400.

Restaurant:
♦ *Gusana,* at Gusana, ☎ 53000, closed Oct. On Lake Gusana. Regional cuisine: pane frattau, braised eel, 16/20,000.

Recommended
Horseback riding: *Società ippica Gavoese,* p. S. Croce (associate of *ANTE).*

Olbia 19, Sassari 122, Cagliari 304 km
Pop. 1,901 ✉ 07020 ☎ 0789　　　　　　C2

Golfo Aranci is an arrival point in Sardinia because the *Italian Railways* ferries from Civitavecchia dock here. The surroundings are of unsurpassed beauty.☐

Practical information _____

≈
ⓘ at Olbia, ☎ 21453.
⛴ several daily crossings *(c.* 8 hrs) from Civitavecchia by car ferries of the *Italian State Railways.* Bookings at Cagliari, ☎ 070/656293.

Hotels:
★★★ *Baia Caddinas,* ☎ 46898, 47 rm ⚱⚱ ⚶ 🗔 ⤴ closed 1 Oct-14 May, 82,600; bkf: 15,000.
★★★ *Margherita,* v. Liberta 59, ☎ 46906, 26 rm Ⓟ ⚱⚱ ⚵ No restaurant, 69,000; bkf: 10,000.

Cagliari 61, Porto Torres 183, Olbia 228 km
Pop. 13,683 ✉ 09036 ☎ 070　　　　　A-B5

Guspini sits in a hollow among the hills of the Campidano. There are olive trees everywhere and in the distance the Arburese Mountains are visible. This is Sardinia's mining area.

▶ The 15C Gothic-Aragonese church of **S. Nicola di Mira** in the village centre has a rosette on its façade and inside a 16C *Crucifixion.* ▶ 8.5 km NW the **Montevecchio lead and zinc mine** is one of the most important on the island; its installations occupy several acres of the countryside. ▶ 18 km NW, beyond Montevecchio, is the sea and **Marina di Arbus** and the **Costa Verde.** ☐

Cagliari 56, Porto Torres 235, Olbia 280 km
Pop. 30,241 ✉ 09016 ☎ 0781　　　　　　A5

Iglesias was a Pisan colony in the 13C and the Pisan soldier, Count Ugolino della Gherardesca, was appointed as its governor. He organized it like the comunes on the mainland. It was already, in his time, an important mining area. Count Gherardesca was later to organize a conspiracy against the Republic. He was executed and then immortalized by Dante in his *Inferno.*

▶ The **Castello di Salvaterra** with its towers and sloping walls with crenellated battlements stands on top of a hill dominating the town. ▶ The **Cathedral** has a Romanesque-Gothic façade (1288), but its interior is 16C Aragonese-Gothic. ▶ The church of **S. Francesco** (15C-16C) has a single nave supported by large transverse arches. ▶ The **Museo di Mineralogia** *(opening shortly,* ☎ 22502) has over 8,000 specimens of rocks, minerals, fossils and other material from the nurag era. ▶ The church of **Nostra Signora di Valverde** (13C) near the cemetery has a presbytery with an Aragonese-Gothic dome (1592).

Environs

▶ The **Grotta di S. Giovanni** *(13.6 km E)* is entered through a steep wall. ▶ An excursion to **Fluminimaggiore** *(25 km)* and **Buggerru** *(40 km)* crosses wild, alpine territory scattered with disused mines. After **S. Angelo** is the **Roman temple of Antas** (3C AD) dedicated to *Sardus Pater* (the Sardinian Father God). It was built over an earlier Phoenician shrine dedicated to the god *Sid-Addir.* Six fallen pillars at the front of the shrine have been raised. After Fluminimaggiore the road arrives at the coast by **Portixeddu** beach and follows the coast to the deep bay where Buggerru stands. ▶ V Il Sulcis. ☐

Practical information _____

Recommended
Cycling: *G. S. Cicli Cherri,* v. Cagliari 39.

Cagliari 67, Nuoro 120, Porto Torres 208 km
Pop. 3,227 ✉ 08033 ☎ 0782　　　　　　B4

Isili is perhaps best known for the nearby splendid nurag **is Paras.** This nurag has the tallest *tholus* (prehistoric circular tomb) ever discovered. The town also contains the white church of **S. Giuseppe Calasanzio**, a fine example of Sardinian provincial architecture. ☐

LACONI

Cagliari 86, Nuoro 101, Porto Torres 189 km
Pop. 2,595 ✉ 08034 ☎ 0782   B4

Laconi sits on the edge of the central Sardinian plain near the Giara di Gesturi plateau in a region rich in prehistoric monuments. The Palazzo Comunale has a collection of over 50 **menhir-statues** dating from 3,000 BC. Above the town in a beautiful **park★** are the remains of a medieval **castle** with a tower and an Aragonese-Gothic hall. ☐

Practical information

Restaurant:
◆ **Sardegna,** corso Garibaldi 97, ☎ 869033. Regional cuisine, 15/25,000.

LA MADDALENA ARCHIPELAGO

C1

The Maddalena Archipelago lies just off the N tip of Sardinia. These seven windswept islands are: Maddalena, Carrera and Santo Stefano to the SE; Spargi, Budelli, Razzoli and Santa Maria to the NW. The granite cliffs of these islands have been smoothed and rounded by the wind and the sea; the vegetation is sparse and the coasts are rocky, with small inlets and beaches. In 1793, Napoleon, then a Corsican captain of artillery in the French army, landed at the head of a small group of French and Corsican forces on the island of Santo Stefano after crossing the straits from Bonifacio in Corsica, and set about shelling La Maddalena. However, Domenico Millelire, a Sardinian naval captain on Maddalena, replied with a barrage of fire against the French and eventually put Napoleon to flight. He was the first to receive the Medal of Valour of the newly formed Kingdom of Piedmont and Sardinia.

▶ The small town of **La Maddalena**, by the port of **Cala Gavetta**, is the only urban centre of any importance on the islands. ▶ The **Museo Archeologico Navale** at Ricciolina *(9 a.m.-1 p.m.; closed Sun)* has on display objects from the cargo of an ancient Roman freight vessel that foundered between the islands of La Maddalena and Spargi in 2C BC. ▶ Across the canal named **Passo della Moneta** is the **island of Caprera★**. Giuseppe Garibaldi, the Liberator of Italy, bought half of it in 1855 and retired there. After ten years a group of his English admirers bought and offered him the other half of the island. It is possible to visit **Garibaldi's house** *(9 a.m.-1:30 p.m.; Sun and hols 9 a.m.-12:30 p.m.)*, which is as he left it when he died there on 2 June 1882. Nearby is his simple granite **tomb.** ☐

Practical information

LA MADDALENA, ✉ 07024, ☎ 0789.
♨
🛈 v. XX Settembre 24, ☎ 736321.
⚓ *Tirrenia,* ☎ 737660 (car ferry services to La Maddalena several times a day from Palau, daily from Santa Teresa Gallura and daily [except Sun] from Bonifacio in Corsica).

Hotel:
★★ **Nido d'Aquila,** v. Litoranea, ☎ 722130, 24 rm Ⓟ ≪ 🦢 ᨏ ◇ closed Christmas. No restaurant, 65,000.

Restaurant:
◆ **Grotta da Setteotto,** v. Principe di Napoli 3, ☎ 737228, closed Mon and 15 Oct-15 Nov. Seafood: lobster soup, fish in wine sauce, 25/35,000.

Å ★ *La Maddalena, at Moneta, 146 pl, ☎ 738333.*

Recommended
Marina: ☎ 737095.
Sailing: *Centro Velico Caprera*, at Punta Coda, ☎ 738529, at Milan, ☎ 02/808428 (instruction, long-distance cruises and navigation).
Vacation villages: *Villageo, TCI*, at Punta Cannone (closed Oct-May), information: at Milan, ☎ 02/852672, at Rome, ☎ 06/6874432, at Turin, ☎ 011/540177; *Club Méditerranée*, at Caprera (closed Oct-May), information: at Milan, ☎ 02/778663, at Rome, ☎ 06/4745951; *Valtur Villages*, at Santo Stefano Island (closed Oct-May), information: at Milan, ☎ 02/791733, at Rome, ☎ 06/6784588.

LANUSEI

Nuoro 76, Cagliari 145, Olbia 189 km
Pop. 6,315 ✉ 08045 ☎ 0782   C4

Lanusei is in the woods of the Ogliastra surrounded by mountains and affords a glimpse of the sea. 21.5 km NW is **Lake Alto del Flumendosa**, which was created by damming a river. There is a forest road around its shores that offers many splendid views. ☐

Practical information

Hotel:
★★★ **Villa Selene,** at Coroddis, ☎ 42471, 61 rm Ⓟ ≼ 🦢 ᨏ & 🖃 ᨏ 55,000; bkf: 6,000.

Å★ *Selene*, at Selene, 60 pl, ☎ 41058.

Recommended
Farm vacations: *Azienda Taccu*, at Loceri *(9 km SE)*, ☎ 42696.

Churches of the LOGUDORO

From Sassari *(117 km, 1 day; map 3)*

During the Middle Ages Sardinia was under the suzerainty of the Eastern Empire. Byzantium was too far away to govern the island, however, and divided it into four *giudicati*, or kingdoms, each with a feudal overlord. Logudoro was one of these giudicati. This itinerary traces the architectural history of Logudoro, emphasizing the Pisan and Lombard influences on the Romanesque style.

▶ Leaving Sassari (→) the first objective is **SS. Trinità di Saccargia★**, a Pisan-Romanesque church and one of the most famous on the island. The building with a campanile★ is all that remains of an ancient abbey consecrated in 1116. Its Pisan origins can be seen in the arches of the façade and the black-and-white dressed stone. A series of frescos by a 14C Abruzzi painter can be admired in the apse. ▶ Another Pisan-Romanesque church is that of **S. Michele di Salvénero**, built in the 12C; the village that gave its name to the church no longer exists. **S. Antonio di Salvénero**, also Pisan as can be observed from the red-and-white front, was renovated by the Aragonese. ▶ In nearby **Ploaghe**, a **Pinacoteca** has Tuscan, Flemish, Spanish and Sardinian paintings *(for visit see parish priest)*. ▶ The large Romanesque church of **S. Maria del Regno★**, a 12C building with a dark granite façade, is at **Ardara**, the old capital of the Logudoro region. ▶ The church of **S. Antioco di Bisarcio★** *(caretaker in nearby village)* is a 12C-13C construction that was once the cathedral of the old diocese of Bisarcio. ▶ The

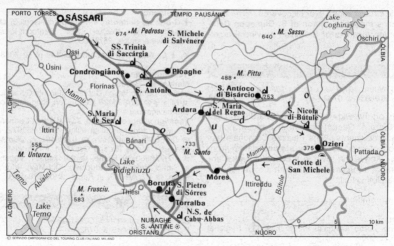

3. Churches of the Logudoro

small church of **S. Nicola di Bùtule,** a 13C-14C Romanesque-Gothic edifice near a medieval village which has disappeared, is next. After this the route arrives at **Ozieri.** This picturesque town in a hollow is the chief town of the Logudoro district. In the sacristy of its **Cathedral** there is an altarpiece painting by the 16C painter known as the Maestro di Ozieri. The church of **S. Lucia** has a Spanish *Crucifixion★* from the 14C. A former Franciscan convent now houses a **museo** with finds from neolithic and Roman sites *(9 a.m.-1 p.m. and 4-9 p.m.; closed Sun p.m. and Mon).* The front of the high school has a large mural by Aligi Sassu, a Sardinian artist. The **grotta of S. Michele** *(caretaker, 9 a.m.-12 noon and 4-7 p.m.)* is an ancient burial ground where many ceramics and other interesting prehistoric material have been found. ▶ The itinerary now leads to Torralba where the Romanesque church of **Nostra Signora di Cabu Abbas** dates from the 12C-13C. Nearby is the famous **nurag Santu Antine★**, which is one of the principal attractions of this route *(→ Torralba).* ▶ The church of **S. Pietro di Sorres✝**, on an isolated height to the N, is a 13C example of Sardinian Romanesque architecture, influenced by the Pisan style. It has the characteristic black-and-white façade and inside are a Romanesque altar, a pulpit with Gothic ornaments and a 16C wooden statue of the Madonna. The elegant, ancient priests' house by the church and the Benedictine monastery close by have been partly renovated. ▶ The Carlo Felice superstrada leads back to Sassari. □

Practical information _____

CODRONGIÀNOS, ⊠ 07040, ☎ 079, 5 km SW of SS. Trinita di Saccargia.

Restaurant:
♦♦ *Saccargia,* ☎ 435071, closed Mon. Regional cuisine, 18/25,000.

OZIERI, ⊠ 07014, ☎ 079.

Recommended
Hippodrome: at Chilivani *(10 km NW),* ☎ 758812.

MACOMER

Nuoro 54, Porto Torres 87, Cagliari 141 km
Pop. 11,231 ⊠ 08015 ☎ 0785   A-B3

Macomer sits on a basalt ledge at the extreme S end of the Campeda plain. In this highest and most central part of the island the **landscape** is grandiose, especially at sunset. The view includes the immense Abbasanta plateau, the granite mountains of the Barbàgie, the ridge of the Gennargentu and, far away beyond Nuoro, the pale peaks of the Oliena Mountains.

▶ The **S. Barbara nurag** is 7 km N, and 12 km W is the village of **Sindia** with a small church, **S. Pietro** (12C Romanesque). Nearby *(4 km)* is the abbey of **S. Maria di Corte,** built by the Cistercians in 1147. ▶ At **Silanus** *(12 km E),* the Romanesque church of **S. Sabina** (11C) is unusually constructed with three vaulted chambers. Not far from the church is a prehistoric **nurag** with a well and a giants' tomb. □

Practical information _____

Hotel:
★★★ *MotelAgip,* corso Umberto, ☎ 71066, 96 rm ℗ 50,200; bkf: 11,000.

Recommended
Horseback riding: *Centro Ippico,* v. E. Lussu, ☎ 70241; *Associazione Ippica Bortigalese,* at Bortigali *(8 km NE),* ☎ 80579 (associate of *ANTE).*

MANDAS

Cagliari 55, Porto Torres 222, Olbia 246 km
Pop. 2,775 ⊠ 09042 ☎ 070   B4-5

Mandas is a small town with a 16C parish church that retains part of its Gothic-Aragonese structure.

▶ 6 km N is the **Giara di Serri,** a basalt rock plateau. It is rich in archaeological remains because it was used by

Stone Age people as a place for religious festivals. It offers a remarkable view over the Mandas region and the Giara di Gesturi, and it is possible to see as far as the Gennargentu. □

MURAVERA

Cagliari 65, Olbia 253, Porto Torres 288 km
Pop. 4,922 ⊠ 09043 ☎ 070   C5

Muravera, standing a little back from the coast near the Flumendosa land reclamation zone, is an orange and lemon centre. From a rocky spur 10 km S, the **Torre Salinas** overlooks the coast and **Lake Colostrai. Costa Rei** is 25 km S beyond Cape Ferrato. The sheep-folds in the hills are mostly in ruins. □

Practical information _____

ⓘ v. Europa 22, ☎ 993760.

Hotel:
★★ *Colostrai Residence,* at Torre Salinas *(10 km S),* ☎ 993496, 31 rm Ⓟ △ ᵚᵚᵚ ⅌ closed 20 Dec-20 Jan, 54,000; bkf: 7,000.

▲ ★★*Torre Salinas,* at Torre Salinas, 120 pl, ☎ 99632.

The ruins of NORA*

Cagliari 32 km
                                                        B6

Nora disappeared in the 8C. Before its disappearance it was a prosperous Phoenician town, then a Carthaginian town and finally a Roman town.

▶ The **ruins of Nora** may be seen on a small neck of land at Cape Pula *(9 a.m.-1 p.m. and 2 p.m.-sunset).* The **tower of Coltellazzo** (16C) is at the end of the isthmus. In the ancient city's remains are part of a burial ground, a Carthaginian temple to their chief goddess, Ashtart or Tanit, a Roman theatre, four separate Roman baths, houses, paved streets and sidewalks with mosaics. Part of the city is now submerged, but when the weather is fine it is possible to see through the clear water the remains of the old city. ▶ The church of **S. Efisio,** a Romanesque building from the end of the 11C, is close to where the isthmus joins the mainland. ▶ The town of **Pula** is 3 km NW and 5.5 km farther is the fashionable seaside resort of **Santa Margherita** with fine beaches and a pine forest. □

Practical information _____

SANTA MARGHERITA, ⊠ 09010, ☎ 070, 8 km SW.
≈

Hotels:
★★★★ *Castello,* ☎ 921520, 142 rm Ⓟ ᵚᵚᵚ ᕱ ᘍ ☑ ⅌ closed Nov-Mar, 280,800; bkf: 23,000.
★★★★ *Flamingo,* ☎ 9208361, 122 rm Ⓟ △ ᵚᵚᵚ ᕱ ☑ ⅌ closed 11 Oct-9 May, 90,500; bkf: 10,000.
★★★★ *Is Morus,* ☎ 921434, 89 rm Ⓟ △ ᵚᵚᵚ ᘍ ☑ ⅌ ⎚ (18) closed 11 Oct-Easter, 240,000; bkf: 20,000.
★★★ *Mare e Pineta,* ☎ 9209407, 60 rm Ⓟ △ ᵚᵚᵚ ᕱ ☑ ⅌ closed 11 Oct-9 May, 57,800; bkf: 8,000.

Restaurant:
◆◆◆ *Urru,* v. Tirso, ☎ 921491, closed Mon except summer. Regional cuisine: ravioli and ricotta, maloreddus, grilled fish, 20/35,000.

Recommended
Golf: at Lo Molas, ☎ 9209062 (18 holes).

┌──┐
│ For the translation of a name of a meat, a fish or a │
│ vegetable, for the composition of a dish or a sauce, │
│ see the *Menu Guide* at the end of the Practical Holi- │
│ day Guide; it lists the most common culinary terms. │
└──┘

NUORO

Olbia 105, Porto Torres 135, Cagliari 180 km
Pop. 36,848 ⊠ 08100 ☎ 0784   B-C3

Nuoro, situated on a granite ridge at the foot of Mt. Ortobene, has retained all the traditions and cultural values of this inland region of Sardinia, but it also clearly shows signs of the transformation and modernization that the island has been undergoing.

▶ There is a fine 17C painting of *The Death of Christ* by A. Tiarini in the **Duomo** (B3). ▶ The piazza Satta (B3) is named after the poet Sebastiano Satta, a native of Nuoro; there are stone blocks, sculptures and reproductions of nurag bronzes in it. Not far from the piazza is the **house of Grazia Deledda,** the Italian novelist who won the Nobel Prize and who is a native of Nuoro. The house has been turned into a **museum** *(9 a.m.-1 p.m. and 3-7 p.m.; 6 p.m.-winter; closed Sun p.m. and Mon).* ▶ The **Civico Museo Speleo-Archeologico** (B3; *closed for reorganization)* has items of paleontology, speleology and archaeology from the neolithic period to the Middle Ages. ▶ The public gardens, with a splendid view over the city from the top of the **hill of S. Onofrio** (B3), contain the **Museo della Vita e delle Tradizioni popolari sarde** *(9 a.m.-1 p.m. and 3-7 p.m., closed Sun p.m. and Mon).* This museum displays traditional Sardinian clothing, fabrics, utensils, ornaments, amulets, arms and furniture, as well as 17C Spanish furniture and musical instruments.

Environs

▶ The tomb of Grazia Deledda (1871-1936) is in the church of **Nostra Signora della Solitudine,** 1.5 km E at the end of a cypress-lined avenue. Twenty minutes farther is the small church of the **Madonna di Valverde** near springs and two **domus de janas** dug out of the granite. ▶ 8 km along the route is **Monte Ortobene** (3,420 ft) with slopes covered in ilexes, cork-trees, Spanish oaks and mastic trees. The **statue of the Redeemer** stands on the top of the peak and from beneath this monument there is a magnificent view of the surrounding landscape. ▶ **Punta Corrasi** (5,240 ft), the highest peak in the **Supramonte** chain, is nearby and offers some splendid views. ▶ Below it are Oliena *(11.8 km SE)* and Orgosolo *(29.4 km S).* **Oliena** has narrow, winding streets and traditional Sardinian houses with small courtyards, outside stairways, pergolas and a variety of tiles on the roofs. The section known as **Sa Tiria** came into existence in the 17C when the inhabitants of a village called Locoe abandoned it and sought refuge in Oliena because of the incursions they were subjected to by the people of Orgosolo. ▶ **Orgosolo** is a town of shepherds, with ancient stone houses that have been recently decorated with murals, often of a political character. ▶ To the N on the road to Bitti in a wood of cork-trees is the **nurag village of Noddule,** which has round prehistoric Sardinian huts and rectangular ones from the Roman period. All the huts have been built with stone taken from the ruins of the main nurag standing in the centre. ▶ **Sarule** is 24 km SW. Here, by road for 4 km and then on foot, amid ilexes and ferns, it is possible to climb to the sanctuary of the **Madonna di Gonare,** one of the most venerated on the island. ▶ → Barbagie and Gennargentu. □

Practical information _____

NUORO
ⓘ p. d'Italia 19 (A2), ☎ 30083.
▨▨▨ *Ferrovia Sarde* (B1), ☎ 30115.
▨▨▨ from bus station (B3), ☎ 32201.
Car rental: *Maggiore,* v. Convento 32, ☎ 30461.

Hotels:
★★★★ *Grazia Deledda,* v. Lamarmora 175 (B1 c), ☎ 31257, 74 rm Ⓟ 63,000; bkf: 6,000.
★★★ *Grillo,* v. Melas 15 (B2-3 b), ☎ 32005, 46 rm ᕱ 36,400; bkf: 3,000. Rest. ◆◆◆ *Nuovo Grillo* Regional

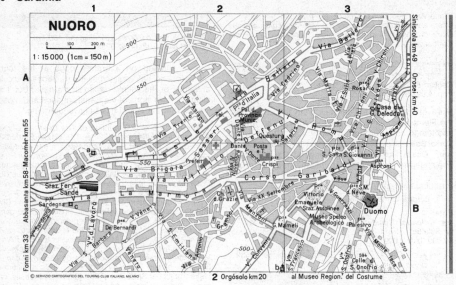

NUORO

0   100   200 m

1 : 15 000 (1cm = 150m)

2 Orgósolo km 20   al Museo Region. del Costume

© SERVIZIO CARTOGRAFICO DEL TOURING CLUB ITALIANO, MILANO

cuisine: ravioli di ricotta, malloreddus, pane frattau, roast cheeses, 14/22,000.

★★★ *MotelAgip*, v. Trieste (B1 a), ☎ 34071, 51 rm P 彩 50,200; bkf: 9,000.

★★★ *Sandalia*, v. Einaudi, ☎ 38353, 49 rm P ♨ & 彩 50,200; bkf: 4,000.

Restaurant:
◆ *Canne al Vento*, v. Repubblica 66, ☎ 201762, closed Sun except summer. Regional cuisine: ravioli di ricotta, pork and various roasts, 20/25,000.

Recommended
Events: *Festival of the Redeemer* (last Sun in Aug).
Horseback riding: *Gruppo Ippico Nuorese*, v. Ciusa 14 (associate of *ANTE*).
Tennis: *Campo Farcena*, at Monte Ortobene, ☎ 35478 (also swimming).

Environs

MONTE ORTOBENE, ⊠ 08200, ☎ 0784, 8 km E.

Hotel:
★★ *Fratelli Sacchi*, ☎ 31200, 23 rm P ♨ 35,400; bkf: 4,200. Rest. ◆◆◆ closed Mon except summer. Regional cuisine: ravioli busa, pane frattau, trout in red Vernaccia wine, 20/30,000.

OLIENA, ⊠ 08025, ☎ 0784, 11.8 km SE.

Recommended
Craft workshops: *A. Fele*, corso Deledda 3, ☎ 287654 (embroidery).
Horseback riding: *Su Gologone*, ☎ 287512 (excursions in Barbagia; horseback rides across island from one coast to the other; overnight accommodation; associate of *ANTE*).

OLBIA

Sassari 103, Cagliari 268 km
Pop. 32,633 ⊠ 07026 ☎ 0789   C2

Olbia is a modern city and the Sardinian port closest to the Italian mainland. It has a magnificent church, **S. Simplicio★** (11C-12C), with a Pisan façade and

three naves. It is possible to go by boat from **Porto San Paolo** *(14 km SW)* to the island of **Tavolara**. It is uninhabited and arid, but it has some pleasant creeks which are good for scuba diving.   □

Practical information _____

ⓘ v. Catello Piro 5, ☎ 21453.

✈ *Costa Smeralda (4 km SE)*, ☎ 69228 (buses from piazza Regina Margheritaz; *Alisarda*, corso Umberto I 195/C, ☎ 52600.

⚓ car ferries leave several times a day in summer for Civitavecchia and Genoa and once a day for Leghorn and Piombino: *Tirrenia*, ☎ 22482; *Sardinia Ferries*, ☎ 25200; *Ferry Line*, at Cagliari, ☎ 070/668121.
Car rental: *Avis*, v. Genova 67, ☎ 22420; *Hertz*, v. Regina Elena 34, ☎ 21274, at airport, ☎ 69389; *Maggiore*, at station, ☎ 22131, at airport, ☎ 69457.

Hotels:
★★★ *Mediterraneo*, v. Montello 3, ☎ 24173, 80 rm 彩 68,000; bkf: 6,000.
★★★ *Royal*, v. Moro, ☎ 50253, 65 rm P ♨ ▭ 85,000; bkf: 7,000.

Restaurant:
● ◆◆◆ *Gallura*, corso Umberto 145, ☎ 24648. Picturesque surroundings. Seafood: rice with cuttlefish, spigola with onions, 20/40,000.

⚲ ★★★ *Cugnana*, at Cugnana, 450 pl, ☎ 33184.

Recommended
Flying: *Aeroclub Costa Smeralda*, at airport, ☎ 69000.
Marina: ☎ 21243.
Skindiving: *Centro Sub Tavolara*, at Porto San Paolo *(14 km SE)*, v. Traversa Faro, ☎ 40360.

ORISTANO

Cagliari 95, Porto Torres 135, Olbia 180 km
Pop. 30,397 ⊠ 09170 ☎ 0783   A-B4

Eleonora di Arborea was one of the few women in Sardinian history who rose to great power. In the 14C she was a *giudice*, the ruler of the *giudicato* of

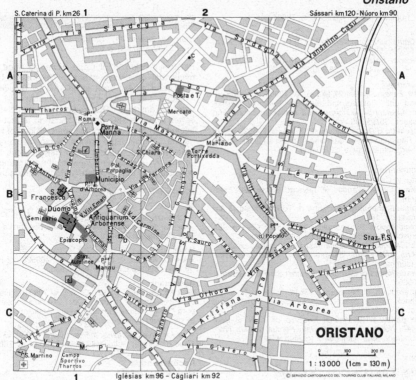

S. Caterina di P. km 26 **1** · **2** · Sássari km 120 - Núoro km 90

ORISTANO

0   100   200 m

1 : 13 000 (1 cm = 130 m)

© SERVIZIO CARTOGRAFICO DEL TOURING CLUB ITALIANO, MILANO

Iglésias km 96 - Cágliari km 92

Arborea. She wielded much influence on the events of her time and the future of the island. The capital of the giudicato was Oristano. The ancient Carthaginian and Roman settlement of Tharros (which has been excavated) is nearby, as are other important archaeological sites.

▶ **Piazza Roma** (A1), Oristano's shopping centre, is near the **torre di S. Cristoforo★** (1291), once part of the city's fortifications. ▶ There is an 18C statue of Eleonora in the **piazza de Arborea** (B1). Her so-called **house** at v. Parpaglia 8/12 (B1) was built long after her death (16C). ▶ The **Antiquarium Arborense** (B1; *9 a.m.-12 noon and 4:30-7 p.m.; winter 3:30-5:30 p.m.; closed Sat p.m. Sun and hols*) has neolithic and nurag relics (bronzes, arms, ceramics), Carthaginian artifacts (glassware, goldplate), Roman antiques and 16C Sardinian paintings. ▶ The **Duomo** (B1), rebuilt in the 18C-19C, has a 14C campanile and many splendid works of art inside. Among them are a polychrome wooden statue of the Virgin★ by Nino Pisano (14C); a 14C marble statue of the Madonna on the high altar and a large painting by S. Conca. The chancel leads to the sacristy with access to the old chancel; here there is a small museum displaying illuminated books and manuscripts of great antiquity. ▶ The v. Duomo leads to the church of **S. Francesco**, which was rebuilt in the 19C. Inside are a Crucifixion★ (15C Spanish school), an altar picture of *S. Francis Receiving the Stigmata★* (16C) and a marble statue of *Santo Vescovo★* by Nino Pisano (16C).

Environs

▶ **Marina di Torre Grande** *(8.5 km W)* has a superb beach on the gulf coast. The Romanesque 12C church

of **S. Giusta★**, near the small lake of the same name (3 km S), is one of the finest in the region. ▶ **Cabras** is a fishing village *(7.6 km NW)* on the shores of Lake Cabras with, to the W, the Sinis Peninsula where aquatic birds fly over the cane-brakes and migratory ones come to nest. To fish here, the local people use boats called *fassonis* made of cane and rushes. Farther on at **San Salvatore** there is a primitive **shrine** *(Tue, Thu and Sat 9 a.m.-12 noon and 4-7 p.m.)* which was in use from prehistoric to early Christian times. The church of **S. Giovanni in Sinis** (11C) is farther along the Sinis Peninsula. It has a Byzantine dome with arches perhaps dating from the 6C. Immediately afterward, on a neck of land called the Cape of St. Mark that marks the N limit of the Gulf of Oristano in a beautiful, wild and deserted landscape, are the **ruins of Tharros★** (20 km from Oristano). The city rests partly under the sea, but much that is on land has been excavated. It was, in succession, Phoenician, Carthaginian and Roman and although some of the ruins of the houses are difficult to date, the Roman layout of streets and squares stands out clearly. To the N is a **tophet** (Phoenician altar on which first-born children were sacrificed). ▶ In September migrating flamingos stop on the waters of the small **Lake of Sale Porcus** in the **Nature Reserve of San Vero Milis** *(22 km NW; LIPU arranges organized excursions, consult your travel office).* ▶ **Fordongianus** *(26 km NE)*, in antiquity *Forum Traiani*, on the l. bank of the Tirso River, has curative mineral springs. ☐

Practical information

ORISTANO
ⓘ v. Cagliari 278 (C1), ☎ 74191.
🚞 (B3), ☎ 72270 also (advance bookings for *Italian State Railway Ferries*).

from v. Cagliari 189 (C1), ☎ 78001.

Hotels:
★★★ *Cama,* v. Vittorio Veneto 119 (B3 a), ☎ 74374, 54 rm Ⓟ ❀ 57,000; bkf: 6,000.
★★ *Piccolo Hotel,* v. Martignano 19 (B1 b), ☎ 71500, 16 rm ❀ No restaurant, 38,200; bkf: 3,300.

Restaurants:
● ♦♦♦ *Faro,* v. Bellini 27 (A2 c), ☎ 70002, closed Sun, Jan and Jul. Refined and elegant. Regional cuisine: gnocchi country style, striped red mullet in tomato and wine sauce, 35/55,000.
♦♦ *Forchetta d'Oro,* v. Giovanni XXIII 8, ☎ 70462, closed Sun. Regional cuisine: penne with cuttlefish black sauce, bass campidanese style, 20/30,000.

Recommended
Bowling: v. Cagliari 1, ☎ 212220.
Canoeing: *Circolo Nautico,* v. Levanto 84, ☎ 22027 (instruction).
Clay pigeon shooting: at Marina di Torre Grande *(8 km W),* strada no. 18.
Craft workshops: *Su Torbasciu,* at Mogoro *(35 km SE),* v. Gramsci 1, ☎ 87581 (tapestries and carpets).
Events: *Sartiglia Horse Race* (last Sun and Wed of Carnival); *Arts and Crafts Exhibition* and *Food and Wine Show* (summer).
Farm vacations: *Cooperativa Allevatrici Sarde,* v. Giotto 4, ☎ 418066.
Flying: areoclub, at Fenosu, ☎ 73511.
Horseback riding: *Società Oristanese di Equitazione,* v. Verdi 23, ☎ 212438 (instruction).
Nature parks: *WWF Animal Reserve of Turri 'E Seu,* ☎ 71447; *Nature Reserve of Sale Porcus (22 km NW); LIPU Oristano,* ☎ v. Deledda 2 (guided visit).

Environs
CABRAS, ⊠ 09072, ☎ 0783, 7.6 km NW.

Recommended
Events: *San Salvatore Festival* (Sep), ☎ 290524.

MARINA DI TORRE GRANDE, ⊠ 09170, ☎ 0783, 8.5 km W.
≋
Hotel:
★★★ *Sole,* ☎ 22000, 54 rm Ⓟ ⅏ ὕ ⊡ ⁀ closed Oct-Mar, 70,000; bkf: 7,000.

⚑ ★★ *Oristano-Torregrande,* v. Stella Maris 8, 133 pl, ☎ 22008.

Recommended
Marina: Ufficio Marittimo locale, ☎ 72262.
Youth hostel: *Ostello Eleonora d'Arborea,* v. dei Pescatori 31, ☎ 22097.

SAN VERO MILIS, ⊠ 09070, ☎ 0783, 14 km N.

Recommended
Horseback riding: *Associazione turistica Pro Loco,* v. Eleonora 51; *Associazione Ippica Sanverese,* v. S. Barbara 31 (associates of *ANTE*).
Windsurfing: *Associazione nautica Capu Mannu,* v. Del Bianco *(ARCI Vela).*

OTTANA

Nuoro 29, Olbia 134, Cagliari 155 km
Pop. 2,697 ⊠ 08020 ☎ 0784   B3

Ottana was a town of farmers and shepherds until the arrival of a chemical plant. At the end of the village is the church of **S. Nicola**★ (1140-50), a typical Romanesque-Pisan construction. Inside is a fine altar picture (1338-44). ☐

PALAU

Olbia 40, Sassari 117, Cagliari 325 km
Pop. 2,532 ⊠ 07020 ☎ 0789   C1

Palau lies 6 km W of Capo d'Orso, a huge granite mass that resembles a bear. This resemblance is mentioned as far back as 2C AD by Claudius Ptolemaeus, the most famous geographer and astronomer of antiquity. The region was completely deserted until the 18C when it began to attract visitors because of the beauty of the nearby island of La Maddalena. Similar large granite masses can be seen at Baia Nelson *(3 km)* and Porto Rafael, along the NW coast. An outstanding view of the surroundings is possible from the belvedere at Punta Sardegna. ☐

Practical information ────────────

≋
ⓘ v. Nazionale 94, ☎ 709570.
⛴ car ferries leave several times a day for La Maddalena *Tirrenia,* ☎ 709270.

Hotel:
★★★ *La Roccia,* v. dei Mille 15, ☎ 709528, 22 rm Ⓟ ⅏ ❀ No restaurant, 53,000; bkf: 4,500.

Restaurant:
● ♦♦♦ *Franco,* v. Capo d'Orso 1, ☎ 709310, closed Mon except summer and Dec. Terrace overlooking port. Regional cuisine: salmon and sofficini potatoes, filet steak and asparagus, 35/60,000.

⚑ ★★★ *Baia Saraceno,* at Ponta Nera, 248 pl, ☎ 709403; *Capo d'Orso,* at Golfo delle Saline, 500 pl, ☎ 708182.

Recommended
Marina: ☎ 709419.

PLATAMONA LIDO

Porto Torres 7, Sassari 16, Cagliari 225 km
Pop. 44 ⊠ 07037 ☎ 079   A2

Platamona Lido lies on the Gulf of Asinara surrounded by a pine forest, with Lake Platamona to its rear. It is the seaside resort of the people of Sassari and its beach, together with the beach of **Marina di Sorso,** is some 15 km long. 6.5 km SE, the church of **S. Michele of Plaianu** has one long, narrow nave. ☐

Practical information ────────────

Hotel:
★★★ *Golfo,* ☎ 310319, 60 rm Ⓟ ⅏ ὕ ⊡ ⁀ closed Oct-Mar, 52,000; bkf: 8,000.

Restaurant:
♦♦ *Ernesto,* v. degli Oleandri, ☎ 310205, closed Mon in winter and 15 Dec-15 Jan. Regional cuisine: fish roasted, grilled or in wine sauce, roast piglet, 25/35,000.

⚑ ★★★ *Cristina,* 400 pl, ☎ 310230.

PORTO TORRES

Sassari 19, Cagliari 229 km
Pop. 21,295 ⊠ 07046 ☎ 079   A2

Near Rome in the remains of the old port of Ostia, there is a mosaic of the Forum of the Corporations recalling the ships from Porto Torres that already, 2,000 years ago, were carrying grain from the plain of Nurra in Sardinia across to Italy. Porto Torres at that time was a Roman colony and the most important port in N Sardinia.

▶ Porto Torres still retains many traces of the Roman period. The **Palazzo di re Barbaro** is actually the remains of an old roman spa. Many finds are displayed in the nearby museum, the **Antiquarium** *(9 a.m.-1 p.m.; closed Sun and Mon).* On the Turritano River there is a **Roman bridge** with seven arches, and other **relics** are at v. Ponte Romano. ▶ The most important monument in the city and one of the most imposing in Sardinia is the 11C Pisan cathedral known as the Basilica of **S. Gavino**★. It has an unusual layout. In the crypt of the basilica are Roman sarcophagi of the 3C-4C.　☐

Practical information _____

≋
ℹ️ Torre Aragonese, at the port.
🚢 car ferries daily for Genoa (c. 12 hrs); weekly sailings for Toulon, France (Apr-Sep, c. 11 hrs); several times a week for Leghorn (c. 11 hrs), information: *Tirrenia,* ☎ 514107; *Sarda Viaggi,* ☎ 514485, *Compagnia Marittima Tolone-Sardegna,* ☎ 514477; *Grandi Traghetti,* at Genoa, ☎ 010/589331.

Hotels:
★★★ *Casa,* v. Petrarca 8, ☎ 514288, 55 rm 🍴 46,700; bkf: 5,000.
★★★ *Libyssonis,* at Serra dei Pozzi, ☎ 501613, 43 rm Ⓟ ♨ 🖂 ♪ 53,600; bkf: 5,000.

Recommended
Youth hostel: *Ostello Balai,* v. Lungomare 91, ☎ 502761.

SANLURI

Cagliari, 43, Porto Torres 184, Olbia 240 km
Pop. 8,439 ⊠ 09025 ☎ 070　　　　　　　　　B5

Sanluri stands at the E end of the Campidano, which is the name given to the plain that goes from the Cagliari Gulf to the Oristano Gulf. The Carthaginians deforested this wide expanse of land to grow wheat on it and turned it into the granary it has remained ever since. In the 18C, the port authorities in Marseilles classified Sardinia as the fifth most important Mediterranean producer of cereals and this no doubt was because of the exports of grain from the Campidano.

▶ The 14C **castle** in the centre of town has much of historical interest. Some objects may be seen in the **Museo Duca d'Aosta** housed in the castle *(private collection, must book in advance to visit,* ☎ 9307105; *winter Sat 3-5:30 p.m.; summer also Mon and Wed).* ▶ The Romanesque-Gothic church of **S. Gregorio** (14C) is at **Sàrdara,** 9 km NW of Sanluri. N of Sàrdara near the small church of S. Anastasia is a **nurag** temple and a well (10C BC; *contact municipio).* The Baths of Sàrdara, with healing spring waters, are in a wooded depression 3.2 km away. ▶ Near **Villanovaforru** *(11 km N),* the fortified **nurag village** of **Genna Maria** is of considerable interest; Stone Age, Carthaginian and Roman finds may be seen in the **Museo Archeologico** *(9 a.m.-1 p.m. and 3:30-5:30 or 6:30 p.m.; closed Mon)* on the main square.　☐

Practical information _____
SANLURI

Hotel:
★★ *Motel Ichnusa,* SS 131 at 42.2-km marker, ☎ 9307073, 18 rm Ⓟ 🍴 37,500; bkf: 2,500.

Environs

SARDARA , ⊠ 09030, ☎ 070, 9 km NW.
♨ (May-Nov), ☎ 934025.

Recommended
Craft workshops: *Su Cauru,* v. Fontana Nuova 1, ☎ 934368 (tapestries and carpets).

SANTA CATERINA DI PITTINURI

Oristano 26, Cagliari 118, Porto Torres 135 km
Pop. 304 ⊠ 09073 ☎ 0785　　　　　　　　A3-4

Santa Caterina di Pittinuri is a small seaside resort in a rocky bay beneath a Spanish tower. 3.5 km S near Fanne Massa are the ruins of an aqueduct and of the acropolis of **Cornus,** which was a Carthaginian and then a Roman colony. Near the region of Columbaris are the remains of a very early Christian church (3C-5C). Archaeological finds from this region are displayed in the **Antiquarium** in a former convent at Cuglieri *(14.5 km NE).*　☐

Practical information _____

Hotel:
★★ *Baia,* ☎ 38105, 24 rm Ⓟ ♨ ♨ 🍴 47,000.

Recommended
Children's facilities: *Centri Rousseau,* at Is Arenas *(6 km S),* information at Milan, v. Vico 10, ☎ 02/468496 (camping).

SANTA TERESA GALLURA

Olbia 61, Sassari 99, Cagliari 329 km
Pop. 3,960 ⊠ 07028 ☎ 0789　　　　　　　　B1

Santa Teresa Gallura, on a rocky point facing the Strait of Bonifacio, is laid out like a chessboard with streets crossing each other at right angles. It was founded in 1808 by the House of Savoy to try and put a stop to smuggling from Corsica. The Piedmontese officer, Francesco Maria Magnon, who designed it was later to be murdered. It is now one of the most important Sardinian tourist resorts.

▶ The bay of **Porto Longone** lies below Santa Teresa. ▶ From the **Torre di Longonsardo** (16C Aragonese) there is a magnificent view over the sea, the beach of Rena Bianca and, in the distance, the white coast of Corsica. ▶ A winding road leads to Capo Testa; some of the caves here were used 2,000 years ago by the Romans. The prospect from Capo Testa is striking indeed, with views over the Strait of Bonifacio. ▶ → La Costa Smeralda.　☐

Practical information _____

≋
ℹ️ p. Vittorio Emanuele, ☎ 754127.
🚢 Several daily sailings in summer to Bonifacio, Corsica and to La Maddalena (except Sun in winter), *Tirrenia,* ☎ 754156.
Car rental: *Hertz,* v. M. Teresa 29, ☎ 754247.

Hotels:
★★★ *Belvedere,* p. della Libertà 2, ☎ 754160, 22 rm ♨ 🍴 closed Christmas, 51,000; bkf: 6,500.
★★★ *Capo Testa e dei Due Mori,* at Capo Testa *(3 km),* ☎ 754334, 115 rm ♨ ♨ 🍴 🖂 closed Oct-May, 80,000; bkf: 5,000.
★★★ *Esit Miramare,* p. della Libertà 6, ☎ 754103, 14 rm Ⓟ ♨ closed 21 Oct-14 May, 52,000; bkf: 6,000.
★★★ *Li Nibbari,* at La Testa, ☎ 754453, 37 rm Ⓟ ♨ 🖂 ♪ closed Oct-May, 58,000; bkf: 7,000.
★★★ *Shardana,* at Santa Reparata, ☎ 754031, 51 rm Ⓟ ♨ ♨ 🖂 ♪ closed Oct-May, 86,000; bkf: 10,000.
★★ *Marinaro,* v. Angioy 48, ☎ 754112, 20 rm 🍴 closed Oct-Mar, 44,000; bkf: 8,000.

Restaurant:
● ♦ *Canne al Vento,* v. Nazionale 23, ☎ 754219, closed Sat in winter and Oct-Nov. Regional cuisine: risotto with shellfish, fish in wine sauce, 20/30,000.

⚠ ★★★ *Arcobaleno,* at Porto Pozzo, 400 pl, ☎ 752040.

Recommended
Events: *National Horse Riding Competition* (Sep).
Marina: ☎ 754602.
Vacation villages: *Club Méditerranée* (closed Oct-May), information at Milan, ☎ 02/778663, at Rome, ☎ 06/4745951.
♥ discothèque: *Ottagono,* at La Testa, ☎ 754139.

SAN TEODORO

Olbia 29, Nuoro 79, Cagliari 258 km
Pop. 2,158 ⊠ 08020 ☎ 0784   C2

San Teodoro lies to the S of the beach of **La Cinta,** separated by a small expanse of brushwood from Lake San Teodoro. The region has fruit and olive groves; other beaches include **Cala d'Ambra** and **Isuledda.**   □

Practical information _____

≋
ⓘ v. Tirreno 3, ☎ 865767.

Hotel:
★★★ *Bungalow Hotel,* v. Cala d'Ambra 3, ☎ 865786, 118 rm Ⓟ ▩ 🛁 ⚄ ✉ ♨ closed 16 Oct-14 May, 65,000; 7,000.

⚠ ★★★ *Eucaliptus,* v. del Tirreno, 150 pl, ☎ 865796.

SANTU LUSSURGIU

Oristano 32, Porto Torres 112, Cagliari 125 km
Pop. 2,981 ⊠ 09075 ☎ 0783   A3

Santu Lussurgiu lies among olive and chestnut trees inside a depression in the earth of volcanic origin. Its main activity is sheep farming.

▶ 605 km away, the village of **San Leonardo de Siete Fuentes** lies in a wooded valley with seven springs that are always the same temperature. Its parish church was built in the 12C in Pisan-Romanesque style and enlarged during the following two centuries. ▶ At **Bonàrcado** *(8.5 km S)* are the Romanesque church of **S. Maria** (12C-13C) and the Byzantine shrine of the **Madonna di Bonacattu.** ▶ At **Milis** *(5.7 km S)* is the Romanesque church of **S. Paolo** (12C-13C).   □

Practical information _____
SANTU LUSSURGIU

Recommended
Horseback riding: *Circolo Ippico,* v. S. Pietro 3, ☎ 550720 (associate of *ANTE*).

MILIS, ⊠ 09070, ☎ 0783, 14 km S.

Recommended
Events: *Festival of S. Sebastiano* (Jan), ☎ 51232.

SASSARI

Porto Torres 19, Olbia 103, Cagliari 210 km
Pop. 119,781 ⊠ 07100 ☎ 079   A-B2

On the third Sunday in May a festival takes place in Sassari: the Cavalcata Sarda or Sardinian Cavalcade. It is the greatest festival held in Sardinia. People come from all over the island and both men and women wear their traditional costumes,

which differ from town to town, but are all equally picturesque, bringing colour and gaiety to the streets in the lovely Sardinian spring. The women of Desulo wear red, blue and yellow, while the men, all shepherds, wear traditional black waistcoats and white trousers. The girls from Oliena wear blue vaporous blouses and shawls embroidered in silk and gold. Soldiers, police and officials from all parts of the island are decked out in splendid uniforms, proudly displaying rows of medals, while their wives wear necklaces, earrings and holy medals. In the evening everybody meets in the piazza d'Italia for the public ball where the men and the women, forming separate circles, move slowly and solemnly to the music of the *launeddas,* shepherds flutes with three reeds, similar to the ones played by Virgil's pipers 2,000 years before. The pervading quality is Mediterranean, traditional and of ancient times, as if Sardinia, just on this one day of the year, wanted to remember her past.

▶ Sassari is a modern city and the second most important one on the island. Its centre is grouped around the **piazza d'Italia** (C2) and the adjoining **piazza Cavallino de Honestis.** ▶ The **Museo G. A. Sanna★** (C3; *9 a.m.-2 p.m.; Sun and hols 9 a.m.-1 p.m.; closed Mon*) is divided into three sections: archaeology, art, and ethnography. The first, perhaps the most important, has many Stone Age finds, 9C-7C BC nurag statuettes and Carthaginian and Roman material. In the second section *(presently being reorganized)* there are many fine paintings including a 13C Sardinian *Crucifixion,* a *Madonna* by B. Vivarini (1473), a *Portrait of a Woman* possibly by Piero di Cosimo, a *Madonna with Grapes* attributed to Mabuse and a *Portrait of a Lady* by Sustermans. The ethnographic section is devoted to Sardinian folklore and has collections of costumes, carpets, looms, utensils and recordings of traditional music. ▶ The **Permanent Exhibition of Sardinian Arts and Crafts** is in the **public garden** (C2). ▶ The **corso Vittorio Emanuele** (B1-2) crosses the oldest part of the town where houses are of the Gothic-Catalan type (15C-16C). ▶ The **Duomo★** (B1) is a picturesque structure renovated many times between the 13C-18C; a touch of the exotic results from the small carvings on the portal of the façade. In the Gothic interior are a *Madonna del Bosco* by a 14C Sienese painter. Past the Aragonese 15C chapel is the **Museo del Tesoro del Duomo** with many paintings, a 15C Catalan banner, *Madonna dell'Umiltà* by C. van Loo, a 17C silver statue by S. Gavino, 12C-13C vestments and sacred vessels. ▶ The church of **S. Maria di Betlem** (B-C1) has a 12C Romanesque façade and a Gothic interior. It contains several 17C statues in wood and a 13C *Madonna and Child;* in the adjoining cloister the **Fonte Brigliadore** (14C) has heads of bronze monsters. ▶ From the church of the S. Trinità steps lead down to the **Fonte Rosello,** elegant fountain built by the Genose in 1606 with statues on the corners symbolizing the four seasons.

Environs

▶ 11 km NW is the prehistoric sanctuary of **Monte d'Accoddi★.** This is a raised platform that looks like a truncated pyramid and resembles similar constructions, called ziggurats, in ancient Mesopotamia. The structure is unique in Sardinia and indeed in the Mediterranean. It probably had a temple on its summit and possibly a statue of the deity, and it goes back to the megalithic epoch. Near it are the remains of stone huts, two menhirs, two sacrificial tables and a round stone probably connected with the cult of some god. ▶ → Churches of the Logudoro.   □

Practical information _____
SASSARI
ⓘ p. d'Italia 19 (C2), ☎ 233751; v. Caprera 36, ☎ 233729 (head office).

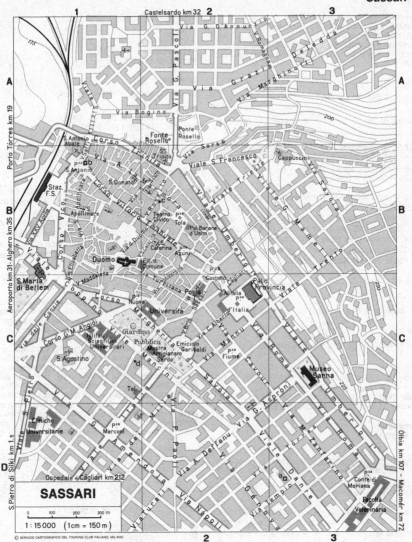

SASSARI

0   100   200   300 m

1 : 15 000   (1cm = 150 m)

© SERVIZIO CARTOGRAFICO DEL TOURING CLUB ITALIANO, MILANO

✈ at Fertilia *(30 km SW); Alitalia,* v. Cagliari 30 (C2), ☎ 234498 (bus to airport).

🚂 (B1), ☎ 260362 (also advance bookings for Italian Railways Ferries).

🚌 from Emiciclo Garibaldi (C2), ☎ 231449.

Car rental: *Avis,* v. Mazzini 2, ☎ 235547; *Hertz,* v. Spano 1/3, ☎ 236715; *Maggiore,* v. Italia 3/A, ☎ 235507.

Hotels:

★★★★ *Grazia Deledda,* v. Dante 47 (D3a), ☎ 271235, 139 rm Ⓟ 109,000; bkf: 10,000. Rest. ♦♦♦ Regional cuisine: penne or rigatoni with artichokes, gnocchi alla campidanese, 30/40,000.

★★★ *MotelAgip,* at Serra Secca, ☎ 271440, 57 rm Ⓟ 77,800; bkf: 11,000.

★★ *Giusy,* p. S. Antonio 21 (B1b), ☎ 233327, 23 rm ⌂ closed Christmas. No restaurant, 44,000.

Restaurants:

♦♦ *Tre Stelle,* v. Porcellana 6 (C1d), ☎ 232431, closed Sun and Aug. Regional cuisine: rice and shellfish, lamb on the spit, 25/30,000.

♦ *Assassino-da Tomaso,* v. Ospizio Cappuccini 1 (B2c), ☎ 235041, closed Sun and Jul-Aug. Typical Sardinian trattoria. Regional cuisine: gnocchi with boar sauce, risotto gallurese, 15/20,000.

Recommended

Craft workshops: *V. Marini,* v. Sardegna 42/A, ☎ 292836 (jewelry, goldwork); *F. Scarrellati,* Stradabuddi region, ☎ 399928 (ceramics).

Events: *Cavalcata Sarda Festival* (3rd Sun in May); *Procession of the Candelieri* (14 Aug); *Holy Week Procession; Sassari in May celebrations; Palio Citta di Sassari* (Aug bank hol) and *National Horse Riding Trials.*

Fairs: *Fiera Campionaria of Sassari,* ☎ 274591.

Hippodrome: *Pinna*, at Rizzeddu.
Horseback riding: *Società ippica Sassarese*, v. Umberto I, ☎ 235470 (instruction).
Sports centre: Palazzetto dello sport, v. Coradduzza.
▼ exhibits: Permanent Exhibition at Artigianato Pavilion, v. Mancini (C2).

Environs

OTTAVA, ⊠ 07040, 10 km NW.

Hotel:
★★★ *Marini*, ☎ 20716, 31 rm [P] ✗ 48,000; bkf: 3,000.

Nuoro 46, Olbia 57, Cagliari 228 km
Pop. 9,226 ⊠ 08029 ☎ 0784   C3

Siniscola is a country town that sits among almond trees at the foot of Mount Albo some way from the coast. Small seaside communities exist nearby. 6.5 km NE in a small bay is **La Caletta** where 3C Roman ruins have been discovered. 6 km E is **S. Lucia** near a pine forest and **Capo Comino** and the rocks of **isola Ruia** are farther S.   □

Practical information ——————————
SINISCOLA

⚓ ★★★ *Selema*, at S. Lucia, 300 pl, ☎ 819068.

Environs

LA CALETTA, ⊠ 08029, ☎ 0784, 605 km NE.
≋

Hotels:
★★★ *Caletta*, v. Cagliari 14, ☎ 810077, 111 rm ░ ▣ closed 11 Oct-9 May, 55,000; bkf: 5,000.
★★★ *Villa Pozzi*, v. Cagliari 8, ☎ 810275, 48 rm [P] ░ ♿ ✗ ✗ closed 11 Oct-9 May, 42,000; bkf: 5,000.

Recommended
Marina: ☎ 810137.

Nuoro 70, Cagliari 124, Porto Torres 155 km
Pop. 2,117 ⊠ 08038 ☎ 0784   B4

Sorgono is in the Barbagie region and the chief town of the area known as Mandrolisai. It sits in the centre of the island on the W slopes of the Gennargentu among hills covered with forests.   □

Porto Torres 29, Sassari 48, Cagliari 258 km
Pop. 695 ⊠ 07040 ☎ 079   A2

Stintino lies at the tip of the peninsula that forms the W arm of the Asinara Gulf at the top of Sardinia. From the town there is a magnificent view of the bay. At the end of the peninsula and facing it is the island of Asinara. This is separated from Stintino by the narrow canal of Falcone. Stintino was founded in 1896 when the government of Italy decided to turn the island of Asinara into a penal colony. The shepherds and fishermen of Asinara were removed and resettled in Stintino. Today it is a seaside resort and several interesting excursions may be made from it, including one to the 16C **tower of Falcone**. To visit Asinara, government permission is required.   □

Practical information ——————————
STINTINO

Recommended
Marina: ☎ 523381.

Environs

CAPO FALCONE, ⊠ 07040, ☎ 079, 5 km N.

Hotel:
★★★ *Roccaruja*, ☎ 527100, 103 rm [P] ≷ ░ ▣ ✗ closed Oct-Mar, 110,200; bkf: 13,200.

From Iglesias *(99 km, 1 day; map 4)*

Although this SE corner of Sardinia, near the mouths of the Rivers Iglesiente and Sulcis, is among the wildest in the island, it is also, because of its mineral resources, among the richest. It was here that the Stone Age communities learned to use iron and bronze, and it was because of these minerals that the Phoenicians came, followed by all the other conquerors over the centuries. There are two main islands off this coast, Sant'Antioco and San Pietro. The islanders are mostly farmers and fishermen.
▶ Immediately to the W of **Iglesias** (→), where the itinerary begins, are the **installations of the Monteroni mine** and the **Masùa mine**. ▶ Close to the small village of Sirai is a Phoenician-Carthaginian fortress *(8 a.m.-sunset)* with Stone Age huts, tombs and a sacrificial table on which infanticide was performed. Passing **Carbonia**, a mining town, the route leads to **Tratalias** with a Pisan-Romanesque church, **S. Maria** (1213). ▶ Following the shores of **Lake Monte Pranu** on its S side, the route arrives at **Giba**. Here the route turns W toward the bridge to the island of **Sant'Antioco**, whose parish church is 12C Byzantine. Recent excavations near this church have unearthed a Phoenician sanctuary. Its finds are now in the **Antiquarium** *(9 a.m.-12 noon and 2 p.m.-sunset)*. ▶ Beyond the town of **Calasetta**, a ferry goes to

4. Il Sulcis

the **island of San Pietro** and its main town of Carloforte. ▶ The route crosses the hilly island to its W point, **Sandalo,** and then goes back to Carloforte for the ferry to **Portovesme.** From here the route goes to **Portoscuso,** the site of the **nurag village of Seruci,** and ends back in Iglesias. ☐

Practical information —————

CALASETTA, ⊠ 09011, ☎ 0781.
≋
ⓘ p. Municipio, ☎ 88534.
⛴ several daily crossings by car ferry to Carloforte on island of S. Pietro (*c.* 30 mns).

Hotel:
★★★ *Stella del Sud,* spiaggia Grande, ☎ 88488, 50 rm Ⓟ ⓓ ⌇ ▭ ⌁ closed 15 Jan-10 Mar and 15 Oct-15 Dec, 49,200; bkf: 7,000.

Restaurant:
♦♦ *Torre,* v. Marconi 1, ☎ 88466, closed Mon and Oct. In a Saracen tower. Seafood: bass in broth, dorado alla marinara, 20/30,000.

CARLOFORTE, ⊠ 09014, ☎ 0781.
≋
⛴ several daily crossings by car ferry from Portovesme-Portoscuso (*c.* 40 mns) and from Calasetta (*c.* 30 mns).
ⓘ corso Repubblica 1, ☎ 854009.

Hotel:
★★ *Paola,* at Tacca Rossa *(3 km),* ☎ 854898, 18 rm Ⓟ ⌂ ⌁ closed Nov-Apr, 38,000; bkf: 4,000.

Restaurant:
♦ *Nicolo,* corso Cavour 32, ☎ 854048, closed Fri in winter. Traditional trattoria. Seafood: pasta with vegetable sauce, lobster, grilled fish, 25/30,000.

Recommended
Marina: ☎ 854023; *Carloforte Yacht Club,* ☎ 854067.

GONNESA, ⊠ 09010, ☎ 0781, 9 km SW.

Recommended
Motocross: *Gonnesa Track* (motorclub).

PORTOSCUSO, ⊠ 09010, ☎ 0781.
≋
ⓘ p. Municipio Vecchio, ☎ 509504.
⛴ several car ferry crossings daily from Portovesme to Carloforte.

Hotels:
★★ *Costa del Sol,* v. Deledda 8, ☎ 508123, 132 rm Ⓟ ⌁ ⓓ ⌁ 42,000; bkf: 3,000.
★★ *Mistral,* v. De Gasperi 1, ☎ 509230, 10 rm ⌇ 30,000; bkf: 3,500.

Recommended
Marina: ☎ 509114.

SANT'ANTIOCO, ⊠ 09017, ☎ 0781.
≋
ⓘ p. De Gasperi, ☎ 82031.

Hotel:
★★ *Moderno,* v. Nazionale 82, ☎ 83105, 10 rm Ⓟ ⌁ ⌇ closed 20 Dec-15 Jan, 36,000; bkf: 4,000.

Restaurant:
♦♦ *Nicola,* lungomare Vespucci 37, ☎ 83286, closed Tue in winter and Oct. Regional cuisine: spaghetti and shellfish, risotto with mussels, 20/25,000.

⚠ ★★★*Tonnara,* at Calasapone, 220 pl, ☎ 83803.

Recommended
Canoeing: *Circolo Nautico S. Antioco,* lungomare Colombo (instruction).
Events: *Festival of S. Antioco.*
Marina: ☎ 83071.

TEMPIO PAUSANIA

Olbia 45, Sassari 69, Cagliari 253 km
Pop. 13,472 ⊠ 07029 ☎ 079   B2

Tempio Pausania, on a tableland, is the chief town of the Gallura region.

▶ The **Cathedral** in piazza S. Pietro still has its 14C portal and campanile. ▶ There is a scenic route that leads to the mineral springs of **Fonti Rinaggiu.** ▶ The **Maiori nurag** is 2 km N. ▶ 16 km SE is Punta Balistreri on the long ridge of **Monte Limbara.** From here there is a splendid view over the whole of N Sardinia. ▶ The town of **Aggius,** 6.2 km NW, is surrounded by granite cliffs with torrents flowing below them. ▶ The **Capitza park★** is very beautiful with cork-tree forests, Mediterranean brushwood and many rocks. Not far is the **Valle della Luna★** with enormous rocky masses that originated in the glacial era. ☐

Practical information —————

ⓘ p. Gallura 2, ☎ 631273.

Hotel:
★★★ *Petit Hotel,* p. De Gasperi 9, ☎ 631134, 42 rm Ⓟ ⌁ ⌇ 55,000; bkf: 4,000.

TORRALBA

Sassari 36, Porto Torres 55, Cagliari 175 km
Pop. 1,137 ⊠ 07048 ☎ 079   B3

Torralba is an agricultural village 4 km from the **Valley of the Nurags.** The **Santu Antine nurag★** is an imposing megalithic monument. Its massive central tower, in the form of a cone, is surrounded by a triangular defensive wall with three towers, one on each corner. Dating the monument was not easy, but experts now agree that it was built between 1500-1300 BC. It was in use until medieval times. It is estimated that there are between 7-8,000 megalithic nurag monuments in Sardinia, which gives some indication of the organization of this prehistoric society. ☐

VILLASIMIUS

Cagliari 50, Porto Torres 273, Olbia 296 km
Pop. 2,456 ⊠ 09049 ☎ 070   C6

Villasimius is a few km inland from the coast, with the small Carbonara Gulf to the E and the much larger Cagliari Gulf to the W. There are many fine beaches in its vicinity. Along the peninsula toward Capo Carbonara is the **torre S. Caterina** *(5.3 km),* which faces the small **Isola dei Cavoli** in the imposing Cagliari Gulf. ☐

Practical information —————

Hotels:
★★★★ *Grand Hotel Capo Boi,* at Capo Boi *(9 km W),* ☎ 791515, 190 rm Ⓟ ⌁ ⌂ ⓓ ⌇ ▭ ⌁ closed 1 Oct-19 May, 200,000; bkf: 20,000.
★★★ *Cormoran,* 3 km toward Cagliari, ☎ 791401, 66 rm Ⓟ ⌂ ⓓ ⌇ ▭ ⌁ closed 1 Oct-24 May, 117,400; bkf: 8,000.

Restaurant:
♦ *Stella d'Oro,* v. Vittorio Emanuele 21, ☎ 791255. Regional cuisine, 20/25,000.

⚠ ★★ *Spiaggia del Riso,* at Campu Lungu, 258 pl, ☎ 797150.

Recommended
Marina: *Circolo Nautico Il Porticciolo,* ☎ 797120.

Sicily

▶ Sicily offers golden orange groves; Mount Etna, with its plume of smoke and snowy slopes; crooked silhouettes of sycamore trees against blue skies; Doric columns rising on rocky spurs; the indigo sea; the pale ochre fields and the sun streaming down on it all. That such a land should have been coveted and invaded by outsiders over the centuries is hardly surprising. From ancient times, the invaders came from all sides of the Mediterranean and from the distant north. Many, perhaps, came only to plunder, but once tasting the sweetness of this land, they could never abandon it. Thus, the history of Sicily is marked by Greeks, Carthaginians, Romans, Moors, Normans, Angevins, Aragonese, Hapsburgs and Bourbons. Sicily today is an amalgam of all these various artistic and architectural influences that have been absorbed, creating something Sicilian. For example, in Palermo, Monreale, Trapani and Catania the beautiful buildings of the Norman era have been perfectly blended with Byzantine and Saracen styles. It has been said that Sicily is Italy, but at a faster tempo. The Italian propensity for pomp and pageantry is evident on the island on a grand scale and confirms what Goethe said, 'Without seeing Sicily, one cannot get a clear idea of what Italy is'. For most people Sicily remains the land of *la dolce vita*. Homer told the story of the Lotophagi who inhabited the island 'long, long ago'. All new arrivals were made to eat of the lotus tree and at once forgot their homes and lost all desire to return to their native lands. And so it happened that Ulysses and his men, weary after so much wandering, put into Sicily where the sailors refused, in spite of their leader's entreaties, to go to sea again. They had reached an earthly paradise and were going no farther. After seeing this wonderful island, the visitor can understand. □

● Don't miss

At Palermo★★, la Martorana★★ with its mosaics★★ and campanile★★; the Cathedral★★; the mosaics★★ of the Palatine Chapel★★ in the Palazzo dei Normani★; S. Giovanni degli Eremiti★★; the Museo Archeologico★★; the Parco della Favorita★★. Nearby, at Monreale★, the Duomo★★ with its mosaics★★ and cloister★★. At Agrigento★★, the archaeological tour★★, the regional archaeological museum★★, the temple of Concordia★★ and the temple of Juno★★. The city of Catania★★. At Cefalu★, the mosaics★★ of the Cathedral★★; at Gela★, the Greek fortifications of Capo Soprano★★; at Piazza Armerina★, the Roman villa of the Casale★★ with its mosaic floors★★; at Segesta★, the temple★★. At Syracuse★★, the Duomo★★, the archaeological park of the Neapoli★★, the Greek theatre★★, the stone quarries of the Paradiso★★, the regional museum★★ and the Castello Eurialo★★. At Taormina★★, the Greek theatre★★. The excursions on Mount Etna★ and the Lipari Islands★.

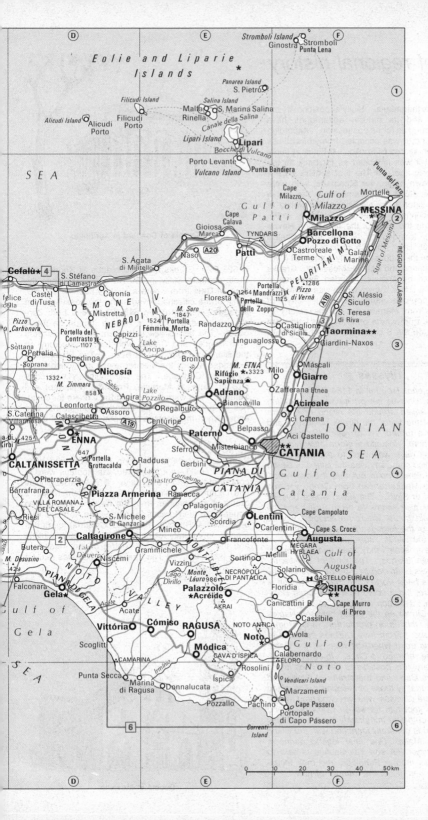

● Brief regional history

Temple of Concord in Agrigento

8C-4C BC
Greeks and Carthaginians. Sicily's position in the Mediterranean and its natural advantages have caused many struggles for its possession. According to Homeric legend, it was occupied in mythical times by herds of oxen sacred to Apollo. ● Finds at burial sites prove that it was inhabited as far back as the **upper palaeolithic age.** ● The first settlers were a people of unknown origin, the **Sicanians,** who were followed by the **Siculi,** who came from the Italian peninsula, and signs have also been discovered of Cretan and Mycenaean influence. ● Greek settlements followed in the 8C BC, the first being **Naxos** (Giardini-Naxos), founded by Greeks from Chalcis in Euboea in 735 BC. The Chalcidians established other colonies on the E coast of Sicily, **Leontinoi** (Lentini), **Catana** (Catania) and **Zancle** (Messina). Greeks from Corinth, led by Archias, founded **Syracuse** in 734 BC on the SE coast, a town which was to become the most populous and powerful city of Sicily. Greeks from **Megara** set up the colony of **Megara Hyblaia,** from where other settlers later went on to establish, on the S coast, the city of **Selinunte**

in 628 BC. Greeks from the islands of Rhodes and Crete came to Sicily in 689 BC and established the town of **Gela** from where a century later, in 581 BC, some of the citizens moved along the coast to found **Akragas** (Agrigento). In 648 BC Greeks from Zancle organized a colony at **Himera** (Imera) on the N coast. The last Greek settlement was by pioneers from Rhodes and Cnidos who formed a colony on the island of **Lipari** in 580 BC. ● The Phoenicians expanded across the Mediterranean and founded the colony of Carthage. The Carthaginians had colonies in Sicily at **Marsala, Panormo** (Palermo) and **Solunto.** The were at war with the Greeks for centuries for possession of the island, a conflict that only ended when the Romans took possession of it in the 3C BC.

3C BC-5C AD
Romans. Once Pyrrhus, King of Epirus, had been defeated and Taranto captured, the Romans were in control of the whole of S Italy. ● The Carthaginians had captured Messina, expelling the **Mamertines,** a group of mercenaries from the Italian mainland who appealed to the Romans for help. The Romans, with a garrison at Rhegion (Reggio di Calabria) found this a good opportunity for dealing with the Carthaginians and the long struggle for control of the Mediterranean broke out. ● The **First Punic War** was really a

---

Ulysses

According to legend, Troy fell in 1184 BC and it was at that time that Ulysses set off for home. Leaving Asia Minor he sailed around the island of Cythera (now Cerigo), at the tip of the Greek peninsula, and then should have turned NW to reach the island of Ithaca, his kingdom. Instead a storm blew him and his men for nine days westward to the land of the lotus-eaters, which some say was the island of Gerba off Tunis, while others point out that if blown westward across the Mediterranean from Cerigo you run into the E coast of Sicily. The place where Ulysses met the Cyclops also seems to be in Sicily, and the island 'full of wild goats' where he landed could be Favignana, one of the Aegadeans. Aeolia, the island of the king of the winds, 'surrounded by a wall of cliffs impossible to scale', may have been Stromboli, one of the Lipari Islands. The land of the Lestrigons, where Ulysses arrived in a port surrounded by rocks, may have been Porto degli Infreschi, which is by Cape Palinuro, but it could also have been Bonifacio in Corsica. Tradition refers to the kingdom of Circe as Cape Circeo on the coast between Naples and Rome, but this is a promontory and Homer refers to an island. From here Ulysses sailed W to some mysterious point where he reached the Gates of Hades, but he returned to Circe. In attempting to follow his itinerary, it is possible to identify the island of the Sirens as Capri and the straits of Scylla and Charybdis are certainly those of Messina. The island of Ogygia, where Ulysses was wrecked and where Queen Calypso kept him for seven years promising him perpetual youth and immortality if he would stay with her forever, is generally identified with the island of Gozo, near Malta. One final legend connects Ulysses with Italy. His son Telemachus is said to have married his mother Penelope and their incestuous offspring was Italus, the founder of Italy.

Duomo in Messina

struggle for the possession of Sicily and ended with a Roman naval victory near the **Aegadian islands** in 241 BC. ● Syracuse at first had been an ally of Rome, but then went over to the Carthaginian side. It was captured in 212 BC after a siege in which **Archimedes** invented a number of military machines that postponed the fall of his native city. ● The subsequent decline of the flourishing cities in Sicily was not due to misgovernment by the Romans; malaria was its cause in Selinunte and Leontinoi, while Syracuse, Gela and Agrigento declined in importance chiefly because many of its citizens moved to the interior where life was less dangerous than on the coast.

piazza del Duomo in Catania

5C-13C
Byzantines, Arabs, Normans and Swabians. After the decline of Rome, the **Vandals** and **Goths** came to Sicily, but did not stay long. ● The **Byzantines** who followed them stayed for three centuries. ● The **Arabs** took seventy-five years to conquer the island and were then defeated by the **Normans,** who were followed by the **Swabians.** ● **Roger I** conquered the island for the Normans (1061-91), and his son, **Roger II,** was crowned **King of Sicily** in the duomo of **Palermo** in 1130. ● One of the greatest eras for the island was when the Holy Roman Emperor **Frederick II** held court in Palermo, where he too had been crowned King of Sicily in 1198. ● His son **Manfred,**

Duomo in Monreale

cathedral in Palermo

however, was excommunicated by the Pope (who gave his dominion to Charles of Anjou) and killed at the **Battle of Benevento** (1266). ● With Charles I the short Angevin occupation of Sicily began.

13C-17C
Jurisdiction of Spain. Charles of Anjou and his French troops mismanaged the government and at Easter 1282 a popular revolution broke out. This revolution, known as the **'Sicilian Vespers',** celebrated in many plays as well as in the opera by Verdi, is still regarded as a symbolic event in Italian history. ● A republic was proclaimed and the island asked for the intervention of **Peter of Aragon.** Sicily was attached in 1130 to the republic of Naples and the two became the **Kingdom of the Two Sicilies,** which passed to the crown of Aragon and, on the union of Castile and Aragon, to **Spain.** It was governed by a Spanish **viceroy** from 1415-1712.

18C-20C
Part of Italy. After remaining the property of the **Austrians** and the **Bourbons** successively (with a brief interlude of French rule from 1806-15), Sicily, captured by **Garibaldi,** was annexed to a united Italy on the accession of **King Victor Emmanuel** in 1860.

Sicilian puppets

Sicilian puppets are three ft high and operated by strings from above. The stories enacted by Sicilian puppets are mainly about Charlemagne or the Knights of the Round Table or French paladins like Roland fighting the Moors. In this they differ from puppets in N Italy and other countries, whose stories have more to do with whacking an opponent to the merriment of the audience, and are similar to the Guignol puppet shows of France or the Punch and Judy shows of Britain. The Sicilian puppet show is full of magnificence and colour; the women wear bright silk clothes and the men shining tin armour and helmets with visors. A cunning string arrangement enables them to unsheath their swords and engage in furious duelling and this is the play's highlight. Originally the pupari (puppet showmen) went from village to village across Sicily with their puppets and equipment on a cart, but now most major cities have their own playhouse called the 'Opera dei Pupi'. The plays are always crowded as they have always been very popular in Sicily.

Practical information

Information: tourist offices in provincial capitals and other principal towns.

SOS: public emergency services, ☎ 113; police emergency, ☎ 112; road emergency *ACI*, ☎ 116.

Weather: forecasts, ☎ 095/976976, from W Sicily, ☎ 091/976976, from provincial capitals (except Caltanissetta and Enna), ☎ 191; road conditions, ☎ 095/975000, from W Sicily, ☎ 091/975000, *ACI*, ☎ 06/4212, from provincial capitals (except Caltanissetta, Enna and Ragusa), ☎ 194; sea conditions, ☎ 095/977977, from Sicily, ☎ 091/977977, from provincial capitals (except Caltanissetta, Enna and Syracuse), ☎ 196.

Air services: Rome-Palermo, 7/10 flights daily (*c.* 1 hr); Milan-Palermo, 2/4 direct flights daily (*c.* 1.5 hrs); Naples-Palermo, 1 direct flight daily (*c.* 45 mn); Pisa-Palermo, 1 direct flight daily (*c.* 1 hr); Cagliari-Palermo, 1 flight daily (*c.* 1 hr); Genoa-Palermo, 1 direct flight daily (*c.* 2.5 hrs); Bologna-Palermo, 1 direct flight daily (*c.* 1.5 hrs); Rome-Catania, 6/7 flights daily (*c.* 1 hr); Milan-Catania, 5/6 direct flights daily (*c.* 1.5 hrs); Bologna-Catania, 3 direct flights daily (*c.* 1.5 hrs); Naples-Catania, 1 direct flight daily (*c.* 50 mn); Pisa-Catania, 1 direct flight daily (*c.* 1.5 hrs); Roma-Trapani, 1 direct flight daily (*c.* 1 hr); Milan-Trapani, 1 direct flight Sun from late May-Sep (*c.* 1.5 hrs); Rome-Palermo-Trapani-Pantelleria, daily flights increased during summer (*c.* 35 mn from Palermo to Pantelleria); information, *Alitalia*, at Rome, ☎ 06/5456, at Milan, ☎ 02/2838.

Rail services: fast trains Rome-Palermo (*c.* 12 hrs) and Rome-Catania (*c.* 10 hrs); express services with sleepers Milan-Palermo, Milan-Catania-Syracuse (*c.* 21 hrs); express services with sleepers Turin-Palermo, Turin-Syracuse (*c.* 22/23 hrs); express service with sleepers Venice-Palermo-Syracuse (*c.* 22 hrs).

Maritime services: *Tirrenia Navigazione*, car ferries: Naples-Palermo, daily (*c.* 9/10 hrs); Naples-Catania, weekly (*c.* 15 hrs); Naples-Syracuse, weekly (*c.* 19 hrs); Genoa-Palermo, 4 weekly (*c.* 23 hrs); Cagliari-Palermo, weekly (*c.* 12.5 hrs); Cagliari-Trapani, weekly (*c.* 11 hrs); Reggio Calabria-Catania, 3 weekly (*c.* 3 hrs); Reggio Calabria-Syracuse, 3 weekly (*c.* 7 hrs); information, at Milan, ☎ 02/809466, at Rome, ☎ 06/732141, at Genoa, ☎ 010/26981, at Naples, ☎ 081/7201111. *Siremar:* Naples-Lipari Islands-Milazzo, weekly Nov-Mar, 2 weekly Apr, May and Oct, 3 weekly Jun-Sep (*c.* 15/18 hrs); information, at Milazzo, ☎ 090/9283242. *Grandi Traghetti:* Genoa-Palermo, 3 weekly (*c.* 22 hrs); Leghorn-Palermo, 3 weekly (*c.* 18 hrs; no sailings in Aug), information, at Genoa, ☎ 010/589331. *State Railways,* passengers and cars: Villa San Giovanni-Messina, regular departures connecting all main train services (*c.* 35 mn); Reggio Calabria-Messina, 2 daily (*c.* 55 mn), information, at Messina, ☎ 090/773811. *Caronte:* Villa San Giovanni-Messina, uninterrupted services in summer (*c.* 15 mn), information, at Messina, ☎ 090/44982, at Villa San Giovanni, ☎ 0965/756725. *Aliscafi SNAV* (hydrofoil): Reggio Calabria-Messina, several daily (*c.* 15 mn); Reggio Calabria-Lipari Islands, 2 daily summer (2/4 hrs); Naples-Ustica-Palermo, 3 weekly summer (*c.* 5 hrs); Naples-Lipari Islands, daily summer (*c.* 5 hrs), information, at Messina, ☎ 090/364044, at Naples, ☎ 081/660444, at Reggio Calabria, ☎ 0965/29568.

Vacation villages: *Club Méditerranée*, at Camarina and at Cefalù, information, at Milan, ☎ 02/778663, at Rome, ☎ 06/4745951; *Villaggi Valtur*, at Brùcoli (→ Augusta) and at Finale di Pollina (→ Cefalù), information, at Milan, ☎ 02/791733, at Rome, ☎ 06/6784588; *Villaggio L'Approdo di Ulisse*, at Favignana (→ Aegadean Islands), information, *Vacanze*, at Milan, ☎ 02/85391.

Farm vacations: *Associazione Regionale Agriturist*, at Palermo, v. Alessio di Giovanni 14, ☎ 091/296666.

Fairs and markets: *International Mediterranean Trade Fair* and *Mediterranean Wine Exhibition*, at Palermo; *Mediterranean Wines Exhibition*, at Marsala; *trade fair*, at Messina; *leisure exhibition* and *grapes and wine show*, at Catania; *Central Sicily Trade Fair*, at Caltanissetta; *Agricultural and Arts and Crafts Fair and Market*, at Ribera (→ La Costa Agrigentina).

Marzipan

Until quite recently in Palermo the head of the family would go every Sunday morning to the monastery of the Martorana to buy small cakes, shaped like fruit, made from a paste of ground almonds, sugar and spices by the nuns. Almond paste, known as pasta reale, was also called pasta di Martorana, corrupted into marzipan. Confectioners all over the world now make cakes and sweets of marzipan in every imaginable shape and form. In Sicily a marzipan lamb, filled with quince jam, is the classic Easter sweet. Cannolo, another traditional Sicilian dessert, is eaten at the time of Carnival. The almond paste is cooked in the oven and then filled with sugared ricotta and pistachio and covered with grated candied fruit. The best Sicilian dessert is the cassata Siciliana. The basis for this sweet is Pan di Spagna — a paste cooked with flour, sugar, yolk of eggs and cream; covered with sugared ricotta and spiced with cinammon, vanilla, chocolate and pistachio. A layer of icing is placed over the top of the sweet and this in turn is decorated with candied fruit and marzipan. The word cassata has also been defined as 'a Neapolitan ice cream of fruit and nuts'. This has nothing to do with the traditional Sicilian cassata, except perhaps that Sicilian ice creams are also delicious.

Marsala

Iotalinum, Tauromenium, Inicynium, Pollio, Biblinum, Potulanum, Mamertinum — these were the names of Sicilian wines in ancient times and they were famous throughout the Mediterranean and the favourite of Julius Caesar. In more recent times the robust Sicilian wines were used for blending with other wines and few were sold under their own name except the well-known Corvo di Casteldaccia. Now, however, because the Italian government is grading wines and wineproducing regions, Sicilian wines are coming back into their own and there are at least a dozen widely known brands. One Sicilian wine that is world-famous is Marsala, the sweet aperitif wine which is also drunk with dessert. Marsala is a dark, fortified wine made from grapes grown between Palermo and Messina. It was originally produced by an Englishman named John Woodhouse who was in Trapani in 1773 to buy almond husks to make caustic soda. He realized that he might use Sicilian wines to produce a competitor, in Britain, with port from Portugal and sherry from Spain. He set up a laboratory at Cannizzo, near Marsala, and eventually was successful — Marsala became popular in Britain. Today Marsala is produced in three distinctive tastes, called Gold, Amber and Ruby.

Nature parks: *Parco Regionale dell'Etna* (→ Palermo); other parks are being set up in Madonie and Nebrodi Mountains.

Facts and figures

Location: *Sicily is the largest island in the Mediterranean and also the most southern region of Italy. At its nearest point, in the Straits of Messina, it is less than two miles from the Italian mainland. The island is, for the most part, a plateau some 500 ft above sealevel. In the N and centre are mountains of which the chief ranges are the Nebrodi and the Madonie, reaching heights of 6,500 ft. The great volcano of Etna, the largest active volcano in Europe, reaches 10,968 ft. The only extensive plain is that of Catania in the E, while the largest rivers are the Simeto, Cantara, Platani and Salso. The name of Sicily can be found in Homer, although there have been other names such as Sicania and Trinacria, this last alluding to the triangular shape of the island. Included as parts of the region of Sicily are the islands of Ustica, Pantelleria, Lampedusa and Linosa, as well as the Lipari (Eolie) group and the Aegadean (Egadi) group.*
Area: *25,708 sq km, the largest region in Italy.*
Climate: *The island is famous for its blue skies and mild temperature in winter, but it can be very hot in summer.*
Population: *5,006,684 inhabitants, of which nearly a fifth live in Catania and Palermo.*
Administration: *An autonomous region with the provincial capital at Palermo. The other 8 provinces are Agrigento, Caltanissetta, Catania, Enna, Messina, Ragusa, Syracuse and Trapani.*

Conservation: *WWF Delegation for Sicily,* at Palermo, v. P. Calvi 2/H, ☎ 091/322169; branch at Agrigento, v. Diodoro Siculo 8/C (summer work camps at Siculiana). *WWF Delegation for E Sicily,* at Catania, v. delle Acacie 14, ☎ 095/382380; branches at: Syracuse, corso Timoleonte 125, ☎ 0931/65305; Milazzo, p. Cesare Battisti 19, ☎ 090/9982196; Enna, v. delle Muse 6, ☎ 0935/42342; Giradini-Naxos, v. Larunchi 11, ☎ 0942/51271; Niscemi, v. del Popolo 6, ☎ 0933/951961 (summer work camps on Mount Etna; centre for recuperating wildlife at Catania). *LIPU* branches at: Palermo, v. P. Paternostro 43, ☎ 091/581323 (for excursions in Madonie Mountains park, ☎ 091/420708); Messina, v. Libertà 19, ☎ 090/362869 (birds-of-prey-watching on Mounts Peloritani and Nébrodi in spring); Alcamo, v. Ugo Manno 71, ☎ 0924/20542 (excursions to nature reserve *Lo zingaro* of Castellamare del Golfo, salt-works of Trapani and Stagnone Lake of Marsala); Syracuse, ☎ 0931/31922 (birdwatching on River Ciane, salt-works of Syracuse and Vindicari nature park); Caltanissetta, v. Re d'Italia 18, ☎ 0934/28002 (birdwatching on Lakes Soprano, Biviere and Pergusa); Catania, v. Ventimiglia 84, ☎ 095/402067 (excursions to springs of River Simeto and Etna nature park).

Events: opera season at *Teatro Masimo,* season of plays at *Teatro Biondo,* puppet (pupi) shows at *Teatro Bradamante, Festival of S. Rosalia,* at Palermo; season of concerts and season of plays, *Procession of Giants, Good Friday Processions of the Vascelluzzo and of the Vara,* at Messina; opera season at *Teatro Bellini,* season of plays at *Teatro Stabile, Festival of S. Agata,* at Catania; *Festival of the Flowering Almond Tree, Folklore Festival and Pageant, Festivals of S. Gerlando* and of *S. Calogero, Pirandello Week,* at Agrigento; classical plays at *Teatro Greco, International Festival of Music* and *Open Air Opera Season, Festivals of S. Lucia* and *S. Sebastiano,* at Syracuse; *Festivals of S. George* and of *S. Giovanni Battista,* at Ragusa; *Holy Week Processions* and summer theatre season at *Castello di Lombardia,* at Enna; *Processions of Holy Week Thursday* and *Good Friday, Christmas in*

Two Nobel Prize winners

The Nobel Prize is considered to be the highest award a writer can receive. It was established in 1901 and has been given, with a few interruptions, every year since. Italy has received four Nobel Prizes — the first went to Carducci in 1906, the second to Grazia Deledda, the Sardinian novelist, in 1926, the third to Luigi Pirandello in 1934 and the fourth to Salvatore Quasimodo in 1959. Since the last two are Sicilians, this means that of four of Italy's Nobel Prizewinning writers, two came from Sicily. Pirandello (1867-1936) was born into a well-to-do family in Agrigento. He began his remarkable career with short stories which were published in Italian magazines. When his novels began to make money and things became a little easier, his troubles were not over — his wife, Maria Antonietta, went mad and in a fit of jealousy attacked him with a knife. Later still, when in his fifties, he began to write for the theatre; he again met with success. Because of the experimental nature of certain of his plays he has been called the inventor of modern drama. All modern playwrights are indebted to him. Salvatore Quasimodo (1901-1968) came from a completely different milieu; his father was a poorly paid station-master who was posted from one small Sicilian town to another, at the whim of the railway authorities. In 1908 an earthquake destroyed Messina and Quasimodo senior was sent there at once. A truck was shunted in for them and the family huddled together in it while the father went out and tried to start up the trains. The poet was only seven at the time, but this experience marked him for life and clearly influences his poetry. It came up again even in his conversation — the lunar landscape, the 75,000 dead, when minor tremors still continued to shake the region and the troops shot looters out of hand. At 18, Quasimodo went to Rome and got a job as a state employee, writing poetry in his spare time. It was his fellow-Sicilian, Elio Vittorini, who helped him get his work published and introduced him to the Italian literary circles of the time. He finally gave up his job to edit a magazine and to translate Shakespeare and Greek classics since he had taught himself English and Greek as a young man. His poetry is about the plight of man, his history and his fate in a disruptive world. His fame in Italy gradually spread abroad, and the voice of the Sicilian poet became a major European one.

Piazza, Nisseno September, at Caltanissetta; *Good Friday Procession of the Mysteries, Trapani Musical July,* at Trapani; *Carnival* and puppet (pupi) show, at Acireale; religious ceremonies according to Greek rite, at Piana degli Albanesi (→ Palermo); *Palio dei Normanni* (Race of the Normans) in Piazza Armerina; *Ball of the Cordella,* at Petralia Sottana; *Ceramics Biennale, Festival of S. Giacomo, Festival of Madonna del Ponte,* at Caltagirone; *Folklore Representation of the Diavolata,* at Adrano; *Dawn Ceremony,* at Castelvetrano; classical plays, at Segesta. Sporting events include: *International Tennis Championships, Florio Car Racing, International Horse Show,* at Palermo; *International Scuba Diving Meeting,* at Ustica; *Mediterranean Grand Prix,* at Pergusa race track; *Trapani-Erice Uphill Car Race; International Skating Competitions* and basketball games, at Capo d'Orlando.

Excursions: areas of special interest are the Etna region (with a climb to crater of the volcano from Nicolosi and

Rifugio Sapienza on the S side, from pine forest of Linguaglossa' on the E side; hiking in the Alcantara Valley with departures from Taormina, Francavilla and Randazzo; late spring-autumn), the Nebrodi Mountains (from Pass della Portella di Femmina Morta to the summit, or from Randazzo and Trearie through the Foresta Vecchia), the Madonie Mountains (marked paths from Piano Battaglia and Rifurgio Marini or Piano Zucchi), the Palermitano Mountains (paths from Piana degli Albanesi to Pizzo Mirabella, to Portella Garrone, to Pizzo Pélavet), information, *CAI Catania*, v. Vecchia Ognina 169, ☎ 095/387674; Linguaglossa, p. Municipio; Messina, v. Natoli 20, ☎ 090/2961196; Palermo, v. Agrigento 30, ☎ 091/6256587 or 6254352; Petralia Sottana, v. Garibaldi 252/e; *Centro Turistico Giovanile*, Palermo, v. Sammartino 79, ☎ 091/332209.

Cycling: help and information can be obtained from cycling groups belonging to *UDACE* (89) throughout region; many itineraries along coast or in the interior lasting several days (very hot in summer).

Horseback riding: *Federazione Italiana sport equestri*, at Catania, v. S. Euplio 134, ☎ 095/325415 (regional committee; instruction at Catania and Palermo). Centres associated with *ANTE* at Castelvetrano, Catania, Cefalù, Palermo, San Giovanni La Punta (→ Mount Etna).

Sailing: *Lega Navale*, at Syracuse, p. Lepanto 24, ☎ 0931/69147; at Trapani, v. Duca d'Aosta, ☎ 0923/29200; at Ponterchiano (→ Messina) and at Palermo.

Canoeing: *Italian canoe-kayak federation*, affiliated schools at Augusta, Catania, Palermo and Syracuse.

Skiing: ski lifts up Etna (from Nicolosi and Linguaglossa) and on Madonie range nr Piano Battaglia.

Caving: numerous caves to be explored: grotto of Addaura at Mondello; grotto of Bue Marino at Filicudi, grotto of Cavallo at Vulcano, grotto of Genovese on Lévanzo Island, grotto of Acqua and grotto of Pastizza on Ustica Island, information, *Soprintendenza alle Antichità*, at Palermo, v. Bara all'Olivella 24, ☎ 091/580642; Lipari Island tourist office, ☎ 090/9811410, Vulcano, ☎ 090/9852028, Ustica, ☎ 091/841190; caretaker at grotto of Genovese, ☎ 0923/924104.

Fishing: *Federazione Italiana pesca sportiva*, at Agrigento, v. Atenea 131, ☎ 0922/25634; Catania, v. C. Vivante 24/A, ☎ 095/446292; Milazzo, p. Mazzini 7; Palermo, v. Terra Santa 93, ☎ 091/302302; Ragusa, v. Italia 115; Trapani, v. Martogna 45; Syracuse, v. Sacramento 41, ☎ 0931/721265. For fishing regulations (permitted and prohibited waters, etc.) apply to relevant federal departments.

Hang gliding: *Italian Federation of Hang Gliding*, ☎ 015/538703; affiliated schools at Fiumefreddo (→ Giardini-Naxos), Palermo, Patti.

Flying: *Catania Aeroclub*, at *Fontanarossa Airport*, ☎ 095/341027; at Palermo, *Boccadifalco Airport*, ☎ 091/421488.

Gliding: *Centro Volo a Vela Siciliano*, at Palermo, v. Leonardo da Vinci 367.

Zoos: *Parco zoo di Sicilia*, at Paterno; aquariums at Messina and Syracuse.

Archery: *Fitarco*, at Messina, v. Patti 32, ☎ 090/58005; affiliated associations at Messina, Palermo and Trapani.

● *Towns and places*

ACI CASTELLO

Catania 9, Palermo 217, Rome 757 km
Pop. 14,844 ⊠ 95021 ☎ 095   F4

Aci Castello is dominated by its Norman **castle,** built from black lava and sitting on a basalt cliff over the sea. It was erected in 1076.

▶ 2 km N the village of **Aci Trezza** is where the Sicilian novelist Giovanni Verga situated his saga of a sea-going family, *I Malavoglia*. Off the coast lie the *faraglioni*, also called the **islands of the Cyclops**, the big rocks which the giant Polyphemus is supposed to have hurled after the ship of the fleeing Ulysses. They rest peacefully now in front of the beautiful beach of **Lido dei Ciclopi.**   ☐

Practical information _____
ACI CASTELLO

Hotels:
★★★★ *Catania Sheraton Hotel,* nr Cannizzazo, v. A. da Messina 45, ☎ 631557, 167 rm ℗ 𝕃 ⌀ ☒ 167,000.
★★★★ *Grand Hôtel Baia Verde,* nr Cannizzazo, v. Musco 8/10, ☎ 491522, 127 rm ℗ 𝕃 ⌀ ☒ ⤴ 170,000.

Restaurant:
◆◆◆ *Villa delle Rose,* v. XXI Aprile 79, ☎ 637420, closed Mon and Nov. Opens into park. Regional cuisine: risotto with shellfish sauce, pappardelle, 28/45,000.

Environs

ACI TREZZA, ⊠ 95026, ☎ 095, 2 km N.

ⓘ v. Provinciale 214, ☎ 636074.

Hotels:
★★★★ *Faraglioni,* lungomare dei Ciclopi 115, ☎ 636744, 82 rm ℗ 83,000; bkf: 6,000.
★★★ *Malavoglia,* v. Provinciale 3, ☎ 636711, 83 rm ℗ ⤴ ☒ ⤴ 78,000; bkf: 8,000.

△ ★★ *Galatea,* v. Livorno 168, 60 pl, ☎ 636015.

ACIREALE

Catania 16, Palermo 225, Rome 749 km
Pop. 48,036 ⊠ 95024 ☎ 095   F3

Galatea was one of the Nereids, who, according to Greek legend, spurned the advances of the ugly giant Polyphemus and fell in love with the beautiful youth Acis, whereupon the jealous giant crushed the boy to death under a huge rock. Galatea threw herself into the sea and Acis was turned into the river of the same name which was straight and fast (*Acis* in Greek means arrow). Some identify it with the Fiumefreddo River in Sicily and the name of the hapless lover is still attached to certain places at the foot of Etna, among them Aci Castello (→) and Acireale, a large town with Baroque architecture lying among citrus farms on the edge of a lava ridge overlooking the sea.

▶ The centre of town is the piazza del Duomo; the **Duomo** has a Baroque portal on its modern Gothic façade and its frescoed interior has a rich chapel with a silver statue of its patron saint, S. Venera (1651). Close by are the basilica of **Ss. Pietro e Pado** and the **Palazzo Comunale**, both 16C. ▶ The 17C church of **S. Sebastiano**, in the p. Vigo, has a highly ornate Baroque façade with a balustrade crowned with statues (1754). The nearby **Palazzo Pennisi di Floristella** contains a numismatic collection with interesting ancient Greek and Sicilian coins. ▶ A mint, a picture gallery with 17C-18C paintings and an archaeological museum (with Roman bust of *Julius Caesar*) are housed in the **Pinacoteca dell'Accademia Zelantea** (*10 a.m.-1 p.m. and 3-6 p.m.; summer 4-7 p.m.; Sat. 10 a.m.-1 p.m.; closed Sun*). ▶ The Sicilian puppets, with stories of the paladins in the local version, may be seen at the **Teatro del Folclore** (v. Alessi 9). ▶ From the **Villa**

Belvedere Public Gardens in the N of the city is a magnificent view of the sea and Mount Etna. ▶ There is another park on the other side of town which contains the **Terme di S. Venera** with baths and mineral springs. ▶ The 16C **strada delle Chiazzette** *(1.8 km)* is a footpath that leads, amid lush vegetation, to the little fishing village of **Santa Maria la Scala**. ▶ There is a splendid view from the belvedere of **Santa Caterina**, 1 km S. ▶ The **Riviera dei Limoni** (lemons), with the fishing villages of Santa Tecla, Stazzo and Pozzillo, is N *(7 km along provincial road to Riposto).* ▶ The **Riviera dei Ciclopi** is 7 km S (→ Aci Castello); it is also possible to go there by boat from Santa Maria la Scala.   ☐

Practical information ─────────────

♨ (annual), ☎ 601508.
ℹ corso Umberto 179, ☎ 604521.

Hotels:
★★★ *Grande Albergo Maugeri,* p. Garibaldi, ☎ 608666, 40 rm ℙ 61,000.
★★★ *Park Hotel Capomulini,* at Capo Mulini, SS 14 at 85 km marker, ☎ 877511, 105 rm ℙ ▨ ▤ closed Nov-14 Mar, 57,000; bkf: 7,000.
★★★ *Santa Tecla Palace,* at Santa Tecla, v. Balestrate, ☎ 604933, 240 rm ℙ ▨ ♨ ▤ ⌖ 120,000.

Restaurants:
♦♦♦ *Panoramico,* at Santa Maria Ammalati, v. Jonio 12, ☎ 885291, closed Fri, Aug and Nov. Etna, the coast and the Straits are visible. Regional cuisine: spaghetti with cuttle-fish sauce, canelloni with veal stuffing, 25/40,000.

Å ★★★ *Al Yag,* at Pozzillo, v. Altarellazzo, 331 pl, ☎ 871666 (all year).

Recommended
Farm vacations: *Azienda Russo Rocca,* at Giarre *(13.5 km N),* ☎ 931259.
Marina: at Santa Maria La Scala.

ADRANO

Catania 33, Palermo 176, Rome 799 km
Pop. 34,308 ⌧ 95031 ☎ 095   E3

Adrano lies on a lava plateau dominating the valley of the Simeto River on the SW side of Etna. Around it 'the black magpie laughs in the orange groves' (Quasimodo, the Sicilian Nobel Prize-winning poet).

▶ Adrano's square **Norman castle** (11C, altered 14C) houses the **Museo Archeologico** *(9 a.m.-1:30 p.m.; Sun 9 a.m.-12:30 p.m.; closed Mon)* with prehistoric material and remains of the old Greek city of *Adranon.* ▶ Along the v. Roma is the monastery of **S. Lucia**; it was built between the 15C-17C and has a church with a tall façade. ▶ W of town are Greek columns, remains of a temple, as well as remains of the walls of **Adranon** (4C BC). ▶ 7 km SW is an experimental **solar energy plant**. ☐

Practical information ─────────────

ℹ v. Spampinato 31, ☎ 681938.

Recommended
Events: *Diavolata* (Easter), Comune, ☎ 681405.

The AEGADEAN ISLANDS
(Le isole Egadi)

               A1 and A3

In 1874, the Florio family of Palermo bought the Aegadean Islands, including all fishing rights, from the Pallavicini-Rusconi family of Genoa for 2 million lire. This archipelago, on the W point of Sicily, comprises three major islands, Favignana, Levanzo and Marettimo, and two small ones, Formica and Maraone. It was around these islands that the fleets of Carthage and Rome met in 241 BC for the famous naval battle which was to decide the First Punic War.

▶ **Favignana**, the largest of the group, is a bare island that grows a small amount of wheat and some vines. There are a number of forts above the small port. ▶ Going around the island by boat it is possible to see some grottos, a few cliffs, the islets of Galera and Galeotta and the beach of Calagrande. ▶ The tuna caught in the local *tonnara* (fishing ground), the largest in Sicily, is cured on Favignana and on Galeotta. ▶ **Levanzo**, with high cliffs, is famous for its fine cave art in the **grotta del Genovese★**; there are paintings and drawings of men and animals dating from the palaeolithic and neolithic periods. ▶ **Marettimo** rises to 2,250 ft with Mount Falcone; there are many beautiful caves along its coasts and its clear waters are ideal for skindiving. ☐

Practical information ─────────────

⛴ in summer several sailings daily from Trapani to Favignana (*c.* 50 mn) and Levanzo and one daily to Marettimo; daily hydrofoil services from Trapani to Favignana and Levanzo (*c.* 15 mn) and Marettimo (30 mn); regular services between islands. Siremar: at Trapani, ☎ 0923/40515, at Favignana, ☎ 0923/921368, at Levanzo, ☎ 0923/924003, at Marettimo, ☎ 0923/923144; *Traghetti delle Isole,* at Trapani, ☎ 0923/22467.

FAVIGNANA, ⌧ 91023, ☎ 0923.
≋
ℹ p. Matrice, ☎ 921647.

Hotel:
★ *Egadi,* v. Colombo 17/18, ☎ 921232, 12 rm 30,000; bkf: 3,500.

Å★★★ *Egad,* at Arena, 140 pl, ☎ 921555.

Recommended
Vacation villages: *L'Approdo di Ulisse,* closed Oct-May, information, *Vacanze,* at Milan, ☎ 02/85391.

LEVANZO, ⌧ 91010, ☎ 0923.
≋

Restaurants:
♦♦ *Nautilus,* v. Pietre Varate 2, ☎ 924008, closed Oct-Jun. Looks down on the sea. Seafood: risotto alla marinara, stuffed cuttle-fish, 20/30,000.
♦ *Paradiso,* v. Calvario 133, ☎ 924090. Near grotta Genovese. Seafood: spaghetti alla siciliana, swordfish, 19/25,000.

Recommended
Caving: visit to grotta Genovese (caretaker on landing-stage), ☎ 924104.

La costa AGRIGENTINA

From Sciacca to Licata *(122 km, 1 day; map 1)*
The Agrigento coast is sometimes called 'African Sicily' in allusion to the heat of summer and to stress that it is not the same as the rest of the island or Italy. The coast mounts to a hilly tableland given over, almost exclusively, to the cultivation of cereals. On the *latifondi* (as the large farms are called), there is not a tree in sight; everything is either green or yellow, according to season, and the landscape is only broken by the emergence here and there of white or black rocks. The beauty of the region has been praised by the poets of ancient times, like Pindar and Virgil, and by modern poets, like Salvatore Quasimodo.

▶ From **Sciacca** (→) the itinerary goes, climbing hills until arriving at **Caltabellotta** (3,100 ft), up the slopes of the Sicani Mountains. This town was built against rocky hills, which were previously used as prehistoric burial sites. A *Descent from the Cross*, a grandiose group in polychrome

1. La costa Agrigentina

terra-cotta by A. Ferraro (1552), may be seen in its church of **S. Agostino**. A scenic route then rises beneath the **Hermitage of S. Pellegrino** and descends among the gorges of the plain of La Matrice; here are the Gothic church of **S. Salvatore** and the **Chiesa Madre**. A rocky escarpment behind the church offers a splendid view★ over the Verdura Valley; some steps lead up a crag to a Norman-Saracen **castle** where again there is a marvelous view★ of the surrounding landscape. Excavation in the area *(taking place at present)* has unearthed the remains of the Hellenized Sicilian town of **Triokala**. ▶ **Ribera**, which looks out over the sea, was founded in the 16C; it was the birthplace of Francesco Crispi (1819-1901), Italian patriot and collaborator of Garibaldi and Mazzini. ▶ **Seccagrande** is a nearby seaside resort. To the l. of the mouth of the Platani River, high on a plateau straight above the sea, are the **ruins of Heracleia Minoa** *(9 a.m.-1hr before sunset)*, which may have been a colony of Selinus, at first bearing the name of Minoa, but which was seized *c.* 500 BC by Euryleon, a Spartan, who gave it the name of Heracleia. It was later occupied by the Carthaginian general Hanno in 260 BC and was the scene of the defeat of the Carthaginian fleet in 256 BC. It was still flourishing in Cicero's time. It is possible to see the walls, the towers and the gate of the town, as well as the theatre (3C BC) and part of the town itself (4C BC). The **Antiquarium** *(9 a.m.-2 p.m.; Sun 9 a.m.-1 p.m.)* contains much documentation on the city. ▶ From **Montallegro** it is possible to climb *(20 mn)* to the remains of its old town, which was abandoned in the 18C because of lack of water; cacti and aloes now grow among the deserted ruins. ▶ **Siculiana** is overshadowed by its 13C castle and the mass of its large Baroque Chiesa Matrice (church with font). ▶ **Porto Empedocle** is the port of **Agrigento** (→). It is the embarkation point for the island of Lampedusa and the birthplace of Pirandello, who is buried here under his favourite pine tree facing the sea. The house where he was born has been turned into a museum. ▶ The route continues to **Palma di Montechiaro**, a town laid out like a chessboard and founded in 1637 by Carlo Tomasi di Lampedusa, ancestor of the author of *Il Gattopardo (The Leopard)*, who situated part of the work in the town, changing its name to Donnafugata. The picturesque 14C **castle of Montechiaro** is some distance away on a spur facing the sea; also nearby is **Marina di Palma**. ▶ Continuing along the main coastal road, which sometimes moves inland over a plain devoted to market gardening, the route reaches the city of **Licata** (→). □

Practical information ————————

ERACLEA MINOA, ⊠ 92011, ☎ 0922.

▲★★★ *Eraclea Minoa*, at Capo Bianco, 70 pl, ☎ 847310.

PORTO EMPEDOCLE, ⊠ 92014, ☎ 0922.
≋

🚢 daily summer sailings to Lampedusa (*c.* 9 hrs) and to Linosa (*c.* 6.5 hrs), *Siremar*, ☎ 66683 or 66685.

Hotels:
★★★★ *Pini*, SS 115, ☎ 64844, 138 rm Ⓟ ♨ ♿ ⊠
✓° 88,500.
★★★ *Tiziana Residence*, SS 115, ☎ 67363, 75 rm Ⓟ ♨
♿ ⊠ 62,000; bkf: 9,000.

Recommended
Cycling: *G.S. Ciclistico Amatoriale*, v. Granet 2.
Marina: *Club Nautico Punta Piccola*, ☎ 67198.

RIBERA, ⊠ 92016, ☎ 0925.

Hotel:
★★★ *Miravalle*, ☎ 61383, 38 rm Ⓟ 47,500.

Recommended
Fairs and markets: *Agricultural and Artisan Fair and Market with Wine and Food Competition* (Apr-May).

SICULIANA, ⊠ 92010, ☎ 0922.

▲ ★★★ *Herbesso*, at Siculiana Marina, ☎ 815722.

AGRIGENTO★★

Palermo 125, Rome 932, Milan 1,507 km
Pop. 52,156 ⊠ 92100 ☎ 922   C4

'Agrigento, loveliest of mortal cities', Pindar wrote, and Virgil added, 'a beautiful city with stout walls'. It was, however, Pirandello who wrote the most enthusiastically about Agrigento, not surprisingly as it was his native city. 'Agrigento,' he said, 'is where people eat as if they were having their last meal on earth; on the other hand, they build their houses as if they were going to live in them for ever', and he added, 'in other cities, between December and February you have fog, ice and, at best, a pale ray of sunshine, here the almond trees are in full flower, warmed by the breath of the African sea'. The town's history can be gauged from its previous names: called *Akragas* by the Greeks, *Agrigentum* by the Romans, *Karkint* by the Arabs, *Girgentum* by the Byzantines, later changed

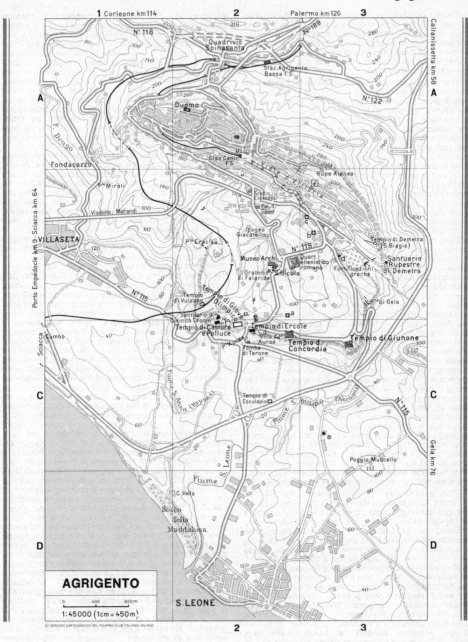

AGRIGENTO

0   400   800 m

1:45 000 (1cm = 450 m)

© SERVIZIO CARTOGRAFICO DEL TOURING CLUB ITALIANO, MILANO

to *Girgenti* when Italian replaced Latin in official documents and finally, in 1927, changed by the Italian government to Agrigento. The city was founded in 582 BC by Greeks from nearby Gela and in time it became one of the richest and most splendid cities of the ancient world. It was destroyed by the Carthaginians in 405 BC, who also massacred the inhabitants; some 70 years later it was rebuilt, but never regained its former greatness. Visitors to Agrigento go mainly to see its magnificent buildings and the fabulous ruins of the Hellenic city; it can truly be said that nowhere else, not even in Greece itself, are so many glorious monuments bearing witness to the greatness of classical Greece to be found in one place as at Agrigento.

▶ The old medieval city, situated around the Duomo, lies on top of a hill facing the sea (Al-2). On its l. is the more modern part of town (A2-B3); farther l. and closer to the sea are the ruins of Akragas, the ancient Greek town where the tall marble columns of a series of temples stand (C2-3) among other ancient monuments and sites that are presently being excavated. ▶ The crowded and picturesque **medieval part of the city** starts at p. Marconi (A2) and p. Aldo Moro, which separate it from the modern city. P. Aldo Moro leads to **via Atenea,** the main thoroughfare that runs through to p. Pirandello. ▶ Along v. Atenea is the **Palazzo Celauro,** the headquarters of the Sicilian Centre for Prehistoric Studies, with a permanent **informative exhibition** of Sicilian palaeontology and palaeoanthropology *(wkdays 9 a.m.-1 p.m.).* ▶ In p. Purgatorio is the Baroque **Purgatorio church** with a series of statues representing the Virtues, said to be by the Sicilian sculptor Giacomo Serpotta (1656-1732) who has decorated many churches in his native Palermo. ▶ To the l. of the church is the entrance to a series of grottos *(closed at writing for safety reasons)* which were used for filtering the water supply to the ancient city and also as a burial ground. ▶ In p. Pirandello, the **Museo Civico** *(9 a.m.-2 p.m.: closed Mon)* is being reorganized; it has a picture gallery with 14C-18C paintings and medieval sculptures. ▶ From here v. Fodera leads to the ancient abbey of **S. Spirito★** (founded late 13C and looted on several occasions), with a church with delicate stuccos attributed to Serpotta *(caretaker at no. 2, in front).* ▶ There are elements of primitive architecture in the cloister and halls of the old abbey. ▶ Down v. Fedora and along v. Atenea to v. Mateotti, through some winding narrow streets is the Gothic church of **S. Maria dei Greci** *(caretaker at v. S. Alfonso 8).* ▶ It is built on a 5C BC Doric temple and, inside the church, parts of the columns of the temple are clearly visible. ▶ The **Duomo★** (A2), with fine campanile, dates from the 11C, but has been renovated several times; it is still undergoing repairs following the 1966 earthquake. It is most interesting architecturally and has many fine frescos. It also contains a curious acoustic phenomenon, for near the cornice of the apse it is possible to hear clearly the whispers of people at the entrance to the church. ▶ The **Episcopal Seminary** (17C-18C) in front of the Duomo has a fine colonnaded loggia. ▶ The **viale della Vittoria** (B2), which starts in p. Marconi, runs in a straight line through the modern part of town; it offers splendid views of the valley of the temples and the sea. ▶ There is an even better view from the **Rupe Atenea** (B3); this rocky mass was part of the walls that surrounded the town in classical times.

▶ **The ancient city.** From p. Marconi the SS 118 (v. Crispi) leads down to the valley of the temples to the piazzale *(parking)* in front of the enclosure of the temple of Olympic Zeus. Passing the three main temples and rejoining the SS 118 constitutes a **walk around the ancient monuments★★.** It allows visits to the following major sites: ▶ the small medieval church of **S. Biagio** (B3) is built over the inner part of a temple of Demetra (480-460 BC); the pronaos can clearly be seen at the back of the church. There is also a fine view over the valley of the Akragas River. ▶ Nearby is the **sanctuary of Demetra and Persephone** (B3), probably the oldest (7C BC) sacred remains in Agrigento. The site was a sacred Sicanian one before the Greeks substituted Demetra for their Earth goddess; it comprises two grottos. ▶ Behind it are important **remains of Greek fortifications** (B3). ▶ The **Hellenic-Roman quarter★** (B2-3; *9 a.m.-1 hr before sunset; closed Sun)* gives a realistic idea of what it was like to live in a city of the ancient world. Originally, houses in Agrigento were built without any special plan, according to where water was obtainable. When this quarter was built in the 4C BC, however, town planning had already come into being and the houses had to be built on straight lines. In many of them there are remains of paintings or floor mosaics. ▶ The church of **S. Nicola★** was built in the 13C by the Normans over what was originally a Greek sanctuary, then a Hellenist and Roman one. In spite of some renovation, it still preserves

its character. The famous **sarcophagus of Phaedra** can be seen in the second chapel on the r. It is a delicate 2C-3C Roman work, inspired by an earlier Greek one, with decorations recounting the myth of Hyppolitus and Phaedra. ▶ There is a fine view★ of the temples from the piazzale. ▶ The **oratory of Phalaris★** (B2) is a small Greek temple which was part of the larger one over which the church has been built. ▶ The **Museo Archeologico Regionale★★** (B2; *9 a.m.-2 p.m.; Sun 9 a.m.-1 p.m.; closed Mon)* has many important collections divided into two sections; one about Agrigento and the other about the provinces of Agrigento and Caltanissetta. Among items that must be seen are the **telamone★** (male sculpted figure used as a pillar to support entablature), a survival from the temple of Olympic Zeus; **finds★** from the sites excavated in the Hellenic-Roman quarter; the marble statue of a boy called *Efebo★,* done *c.* 470 BC and of a sobriety rivaling the sculpture of Greece itself; the charming statuette of a *Sitting Venus★* from the Hellenic period and a *cratere★* (vase) from the 5C BC with designs featuring the War of the Amazons. One room houses important material from the **Museo Diocesano★,** including two Byzantine reliquaries (13C), church vestments and pieces of detached mediaeval frescos. ▶ A little farther N is the **Giacatello Burial Ground** (B2), a large chamber dug out of rock and supported by pilasters, which was probably a water reservoir originally. ▶ The **Temple of Olympic Zeus★** (B-C2), which was built after the victory over the Carthaginians at Himera (480 BC), was destroyed by an earthquake. It was the largest temple in Sicily and did not have the usual circle of pillars, but instead was surrounded by a wall in which were fitted half-columns alternating with telamons; there were thirty-eight of these statues holding up the main beams of the temple; half were of bearded men, the other of young boys, and they followed each other in succession. ▶ Immediately W of the temple are a large number of ruins of sacred places (B-C2) with altars, foundations of temples and enclosures, all of which belonged to the **sanctuary of the Goddesses of the Infernal Regions★** (Demeter and Persephone, who spent six months in Hades and six on Olympus). Also here are the four pillars of the **temple to the Dioscuri★** (5C BC; Castor and Pollux); the entablement was rebuilt and dates from Hellenic-Roman times. This striking group of columns, reproduced world-wide in photographs, is one of the best-known pictures of Greek antiquities and of Agrigento's monuments. Other celebrated temples lie to the E on a rocky escarpment. ▶ The **temple of Hercules** (C2) must be considered the oldest Greek temple in Agrigento (built *c.* late 6C BC). It had a portico with six pillars and was surrounded by a series of columns standing isolated from the walls. Eight of these fallen pillars were re-erected in 1923. ▶ The **Villa Aurea** (C2), with a beautiful garden of lush vegetation, is on the edge of a vast burial ground which comprises the Roman **Giambertoni necropolis** (3C-2C BC), a series of Christian catacombs **(grotte di Fragapane)** and a Christian burial ground from Byzantine times. ▶ The **temple of Concord★★** was built in the 5C BC. It was magnificent, with a series of thirty-four pillars, and it is well preserved because it was turned into a Christian church near the end of the 6C. Its name is quite arbitrary and was given because of a tablet with this word found on it during the Roman period. In fact it is believed to have been dedicated to Castor and Pollux. ▶ The **temple of Juno★★** (C3) stands lonely and majestic at the extreme end of the ridge; it was built at the same time as the temple of Concord and has the same form and structure. The columns on the N side are practically intact. ▶ Other worthy sights are the **Porta di Gela** (B3), through which passed a road dug out of the rock; the **tomb of Theron** (C2), a Roman mausoleum of the 1C and the **temple of Asklepios** (C2), on the Akragas River, which is 5C BC. Here, also, is a splendid view.

Environs

▶ **San Leone** (D2), 7 km S, is Agrigento's seaside resort; it was here that the port of the ancient city was located. ▶ The small town of **Naro,** 35 km E, contains a 13C castle (castello di Chiaramonte) and many Baroque churches (the 17C chiesa Matrice has works by the Gaginis, the family of sculptors); near the Canal Baglio *(10 mn)* is the Grotto of Marvels, an old Christian burial ground *(guide from municipio)*. ► 33 km NW, **Sant'Angelo Muxaro** dates from the pre-Greek epoch; on the side of a hill are tholos (dome-shaped tombs) and a number of small grottos (8C-7C BC). □

Practical information

AGRIGENTO
ⓘ v. della Vittoria 255 (B3), ☎ 26922; p. Vittorio Emanuele 33 (A2; head office), ☎ 20391; p. A. Moro 5 (A2; information), ☎ 20454.
🚂 (A2), ☎ 29007.
🚌 from p. Stazione (A2); v. Favara Vecchia; p. Vittoria.
⚓ from Porto Empédocle (→) for Linosa and Lampedusa.

Hotels:
★★★★ *Villa Athena,* v. dei Templi (B2a), ☎ 23833, 41 rm Ⓟ ⋯ ✖ 🖵 100,000.
★★★ *Colleverde,* v. dei Templi (B3b), ☎ 29555, 31 rm Ⓟ ⋯ 53,000; bkf: 5,000.
★★★ *Valle,* v. dei Templi (B3c), ☎ 26966, 89 rm Ⓟ ⅙ ⅙ 76,000.

Restaurants:
♦♦♦ *Vigneto,* v. Cavalieri Magazzeni 11 (C3e), ☎ 44319, closed Tue and 1-15 Nov. Terrace looking out over valley of the temples. Regional cuisine: cavatelli Maria Grazia, roasted capon, 12/29,000.
♦ *Caprice,* v. Panoramica dei Templi 51 (B3d), ☎ 26469, closed Fri and 1-15 Feb. Regional cuisine: spaghetti lupara, meat on spit, 25/35,000.

▲ ★★★ *Internazionale San Leone,* at San Leone, 120 pl, ☎ 46121.

Recommended
Events: *Festival of the Almond Trees; Folklore Festival and Pageant* (Feb.); *Festivals of S. Gerlando* (16 Jun) and *S. Calogero* (Jul); *Pirandello Week* (Jul-Aug).
Tennis: v. S. Vito; v. De Gasperi, ☎ 20005.

Environs

VILLAGGIO MOSE, 8 km SE.
Hotels:
★★★★ *Jolly dei Templi,* parco Angeli, ☎ 76144, 146 rm Ⓟ 🖵 120,000. Rest. ● ♦♦♦♦*Pirandello,* Regional cuisine: cappellini Gattopardo, escalopes Dioscuri, 31/41,000.
♦♦♦ *Tre Torri,* SS 115, ☎ 76733, 74 rm Ⓟ 🖵 62,000; bkf: 7,000.

L'ALTOPIANO CENTRALE

From Enna *(165 km, 1 day; map 2)*
See map on page 592.

A Sicilian proverb states that summer begins in January and winter in August. Autumn doesn't exist and is referred to simply as 'when it gets cool'. Spring too is just that part of the year when the fields are green and full of flowers, before the heat arrives and everything turns to the colour of ochre. Then, in the words of the Sicilian novelist Giovanni Verga, 'the sun beats fiercely down from straight above your head on the wide empty fields, and the only noise is that of the crickets'.

► This itinerary around the central plateau starts at Enna (→). From Enna it leads to **Pergusa** and follows the perfect oval of **Lake Pergusa**, with its many cane-brakes frequented by a wide variety of birds. On the S side of the lake is a cave which, it is said, leads to the infernal regions. It was near here that Persephone was gathering flowers when Hades, the god who reigns over the dead, seized her and carried her off in his chariot... down

the cave, to his underground kingdom where she became his bride. ► As the route proceeds, the monotony of the hills is relieved by the large forest of Bellia where pine, eucalyptus, cypress and acacia grow side by side in profusion. It then comes to the town of **Piazza Armerina★** (→) and the **Casale roman Villa★★** (→ Piazza Armerina). ► Farther on, taking at Gigliotto the fork to the l., the route reaches **San Michele di Ganzaria,** a 15C town where, on a hill, it is possible to see the ruins of the palace of its founder, a nobleman of the Spanish-Sicilian Gravina family. ► After visiting **Caltagirone** (→) the route returns to the Gigliotto crossroads and from there rises to the basin of the Gela River and **Mazzarino.** Here, in the Carmelite church is a painting of Mattia Preti (1613-99), the Calabrian painter much influenced by Caravaggio; in the Capuchin church is a 17C tabernacle decorated with ivory, ebony, mother-of-pearl, bone, coral and tortoiseshell. ► The route now moves on through an area with numerous sulphur mines (many of which are no longer worked) and passes **Barrafranca** and **Pietraperzia** (the name of this village — meaning pierced stone — comes perhaps from a nearby cliff which is pierced with sepulchral chambers of prehistoric times) until it arrives at **Caltanissetta** (→), the last stop before proceeding back to **Enna,** which is not far away. □

Practical information

PERGUSA, ✉ 94010, ☎ 0935.

Hotels:
★★★ *Park Hotel La Giara,* v. Nazionale 125, ☎ 42287, 20 rm Ⓟ ⅃ ⋯ ✖ 🖵 43,000; bkf: 4,500.
★★★ *Riviera,* ☎ 32627, 26 rm Ⓟ ⋯ ✖ 🖵 44,000; bkf: 5,000.

Recommended
Race track: *Pergusa Race Track,* ☎ 36069 (Mediterranean Grand Prix, Jul and other races Mar and Oct).

AUGUSTA

Syracuse 32, Palermo 250, Rome 804 km
Pop. 39,515 ✉ 96011 ☎ 0931   F3-4

Augusta, a port and an industrial centre, is really an island joined to Sicily by a number of bridges. Its **castle,** which was built when the town was founded (by Frederick II in 1232), is now a prison. The **Duomo** was finished in 1769 and the severe Palazzo Comunale in 1699. 7 km away is the picturesque Bay of Brucoli. 10.5 km away are the **ruins of Megara Hyblaea** (→). □

Practical information

Hotel:
★★ *Villa dei Cesari,* at Monte Tauro, ☎ 983311, 24 rm Ⓟ ⋯ ✖ 34,000.

▲ *A'Massaria,* at Monte Tauro, 150 pl, ☎ 983078 (all year).

Recommended
Canoeing: *Club Nuoto Augusta,* v. Capitaneria 2, ☎ 975595.
Cycling: *G.S. Amatori Augusta,* v. Italia 99, ☎ 991777.
Tennis: at Balate, ☎ 992277.
Vacation villages: *Valtur,* at Brùcoli *(7 km NW),* closed Nov-Apr, information, at Milan, ☎ 02/791733, at Rome, ☎ 06/6784588.

2. L'Altopiano Centrale

© SERVIZIO CARTOGRAFICO DEL TOURING CLUB ITALIANO, MILANO

CALTAGIRONE

Catania 67, Palermo 200, Rome 830 km
Pop. 37,034 ⊠ 95041 ☎ 0933   D4

Caltagirone, built on three hillocks, has all the characteristics of a Baroque, 17C Sicilian town because it was completely rebuilt in 1693 after a terrible earthquake. It is famous for its *azulejos* (Spanish style glazed tiles) which are used to embellish the fronts of local houses. It is also the birthplace of the ruling Italian party, the Christian Democrats, because it was here that its founder, Don Luigi Sturzo, was born.

▶ The centre of town is p. Umberto I (A-B1) where the palazzetto della **Corte Capitaniale**★ (16C-17C) houses a permanent **ceramics exhibit** *(9 a.m.-1 p.m. and 4-8:30 p.m.)*. ▶ In p. del Municipio (A1) is the **galleria Luigi Sturzo,** an animated meeting place pleasingly decorated with glazed tiles and mosaics. ▶ The Baroque church of **Gesu** (A1-2) has some rich marble work inside and a *Nativity* by Polidoro da Caravaggio (16C). ▶ The Norman church of **S. Giacomo** (A1) was rebuilt 1694-1708; it contains sculpture by the Gaginis and a silver reliquary with the relics of the saint. ▶ A long **staircase** (142 steps), decorated with coloured tiles, leads to the 17C church of **S. Maria del Monte** (A1). The steps are decorated with coloured lanterns during the religious festivities of 20-31 May and 24-25 July. The church itself houses the highly venerated 13C painting of the *Madonna of Conadomini*. ▶ The church of **S. Giorgio** (A2), easily recognizable because of its medieval campanile, has a painting on wood of the *Trinity*★, which could be by Rogier van der Weyden (15C). ▶ The **Museo Civico** (B1; *9 a.m.-2 p.m.; Sun 10 a.m.-12 noon; closed Mon)*, formerly a Bourbon prison, contains interesting archaeological finds, as well as Norman, Swabian and Aragonese parchments and old manuscripts. ▶ By the **Teatrino,** with steps and parapets decorated with coloured tiles (1792), is the **Museo Nazionale della Ceramica**★ (B2;

9:30 a.m.-2 p.m.; Sun 9 a.m.-1 p.m.; closed Mon) with material illustrating the history of Sicilian ceramics. ▶ The **Sicilian Ethnological Museum** is near the former church of S. Nicola (A1; *telephone before visiting,* ☎ 25520). ▶ The church of **S. Maria di Gesu** (D2) has a statue of the *Madonna della Catena* by Antonello Gagini. ▶ **Mount S. Ippolito,** 1 km E, is the site of a prehistoric burial ground with many tombs dug from rock. □

Practical information ⎯⎯⎯⎯⎯⎯⎯

ℹ Palazzo della Corte Capitaniale (A1), ☎ 22539.

Hotel:
★★★ **Grand Hotel Villa San Mauro,** v. Portosalvo 18 (D1 a), ☎ 26500, 92 rm ℗ ⚹ ▤ 75,000; bkf: 8,000.

Recommended
Craft workshops: *Judice,* v. Fontanelli 19, ☎ 22207 (ceramics).
Events: *Sicilian Ceramics Exhibition,* Palazzo del Bonaiuto; *Festival of San Giacomo* (Jul); *Festival of Madonna del Ponte* (Aug), information from Comune, ☎ 23744.

CALTANISSETTA

Palermo 128, Rome 875, Milan 1,450 km
Pop. 61,731 ⊠ 93100 ☎ 0934   D4

In the heartland of Sicily among hills, valleys and mountain ridges, Caltanissetta is the centre of the island's mining industry (sulphur, potash and magnesium). It is a very old town, originally called Nissa, which the Arabs prefaced with the word *kalat* (castle); thus Caltanissetta.

▶ P. Garibaldi (B2), the town's centre, is dominated by the church of **S. Sebastian,** the Baroque **Duomo** (1570-1622), with a painting of the *Madonna del Carmelo* by Paladini, and the **municipio.** ▶ The 17C Jesuit church of **S. Agata,**

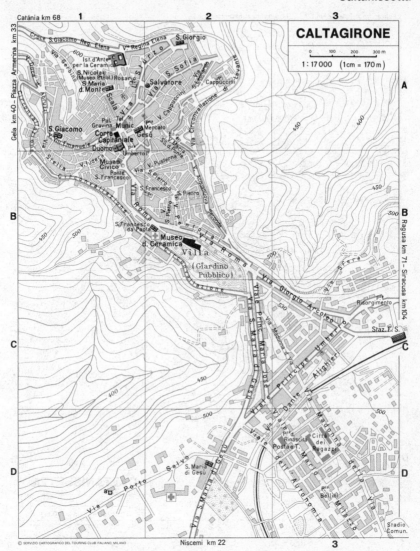

CALTAGIRONE

0   100   200   300 m

1 : 17 000   (1cm = 170 m)

Gela km 40 – Piazza Armerina km 33

Ragusa km 71 – Siracusa km 104

© SERVIZIO CARTOGRAFICO DEL TOURING CLUB ITALIANO, MILANO   Niscemi km 22   3

in corso Umberto I, the city's main thoroughfare, has a rich interior with marble work and sculpted wood. ▶ The grandiose **Palazzo Moncada** was never finished. ▶ Another painting by Paladini, *Madonna of the Rosary,* can be seen in the 17C church of **S. Domenico** (B3). ▶ The **Museo Civico** (v. N. Colaianni; C1; 9 a.m.-1:30 p.m.; *closed Sun*) has collections of archaeological finds from the surrounding district including a small terra-cotta model of a temple★ from the 6C BC. ▶ A number of statues representing the *Mysteries of Christ's Passion* are kept beneath the church of S. Pio X, also in v. N. Colaianni (☎ 31280, *during school yr*). The **Museo Mineralogico** (viale della Regione 77) has collections on minerals and palaeontology. ▶ From the **Villa Amedeo Public Gardens** (D1) there is a splendid view of the surrounding countryside. ▶ E of town, on top of a peculiarly shaped rock, is the former church of **S. Maria degli Angeli** with a 13C Gothic portal and the ruins of the Norman or Arab **Castello di Pietrarossa.**

Environs

▶ 3 km away on the road encircling the town, the remains of the **Abbey of S. Spirito,** founded after the victory of the Normans over the Arabs and consecrated in 1153, still show the Romanesque church with 14C frescos and a beautiful baptismal basin. ▶ 2 km N is a magnificent view across central Sicily from the top of **Mount S. Giuliano** (2,385 ft). Here also is a large statue of Christ. ▶ 6 km along the road to Enna is an **archaeological park** *(caretaker)* on **Mount Sabucina.** Traces of a Sicilian-Greek village have been unearthed from the 6C-4C BC. The site was already occupied in prehistoric times and some round circular huts from this period may also be seen. ▶ 10 km SW near **Vassallaggi** are remains

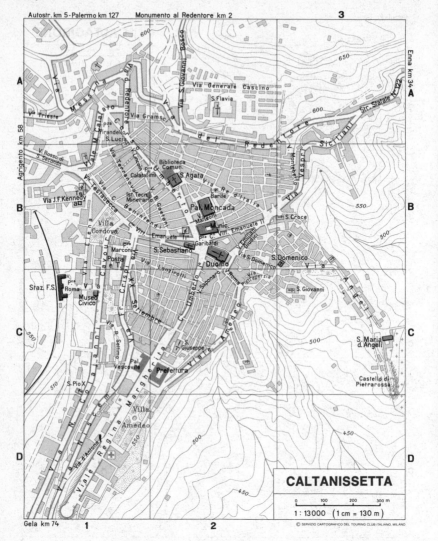

Autostr. km 5-Palermo km 127   Monumento al Redentore km 2   **3**

Agrigento km 58

Enna km 34

Gela km 74   **1**   **2**

CALTANISSETTA

0   100   200   300 m

1 : 13000 (1 cm = 130 m)

© SERVIZIO CARTOGRAFICO DEL TOURING CLUB ITALIANO, MILANO

---

of a wall that circled a Greek town, and ruins of a Greek temple (5C BC). ▶ **Gibil-Gabib,** 5 km S, is another hill which served as a prehistoric and Greek burial ground (with tombs dug out of the rock), and it is also possible to see the ruins of a fortification with two towers.   The name ot the hill comes from the Arabic and means 'mountain of death'.   □

Practical information

ℹ️   corso Vittorio Emanuele 109 (B2; head office), ☎ 21731; v. Conte Testasecca, corner v. Kennedy (B1), ☎ 21089.
🚂 (C1), ☎ 25242.
🚌   from v. Catania (B1 off map).

Hotel:
★★★ **Diprima,** v. Kennedy 16 (B1 a), ☎ 21688, 106 rm ℗ 55,000.

Restaurant:
♦♦♦ *Cortese,* corso Sicilia 166, ☎ 31686, closed Mon and Aug.   Regional cuisine: cavati alla siciliana, pasta con sarde, 20/27,000.

Recommended
Clay pigeon shooting: at Torretta, ☎ 68123.
Events: *Holy Week Thursday and Good Friday Processions; Christmas in Piazza* (creche with live actors); *September Nisseno* (folklore festival).
Fairs and markets: *Agricultural and Industrial Fair of Central Sicily* (May), ☎ 22400.
Swimming: v. Rochester, ☎ 20443.
♥ wine: *Regaleali,* at Vallelunga Pratameno *(51 km NW),* ☎ 0921/52522 (telephone before visiting).

Don't forget to consult the Practical Holiday Guide: it can help in solving many problems.

The ruins of CAMARINA

Ragusa 33, Palermo 249 km

D5-6

Camarina, a colony of Syracuse at the mouth of the Ippari River, was founded in 598 BC and was razed by the Romans in 258 BC. There are still traces of the **wall** that surrounded the town, remains of the **port-canal**, ruins of streets and houses and part of a temple to Athena near which there is a museum. Nearby are splendid beaches. □

Practical information

Recommended
Vacation villages: *Club Méditerranée* (closed Oct-Mar), information, at Milan, ☎ 02/77866, at Rome, ☎ 06/4745951.

CAPO D'ORLANDO

Messina 103, Palermo 149, Rome 760 km
Pop. 10,849 ☒ 98071 ☎ 0941   D-E2

Capo d'Orlando sits at the foot of a headland on top of which a **sanctuary** (1598) and the ruins of a 13C **castle** look out to sea. □

Practical information

ⅈ v. Vittorio Veneto 54, ☎ 902471.
≋
⛴ hydrofoil departures several times weekly in summer for Lipari and Vulcano; *SNAV*, at Messina, ☎ 090/364044.

Hotels:
★★★ *Tartaruga*, at San Gregorio, ☎ 955013, 38 rm ⌘ ▣ closed Nov-10 Dec, 60,000; bkf: 8,000.
★★ *Bristol*, v. Umberto 37, ☎ 901390, 75 rm ℗ ⌘ 40,000; bkf: 4,000.

Recommended
Events: international skating tournaments and basketball competitions.

CASTEL DI TUSA

Messina 157, Palermo 78, Rome 829 km
Pop. 633 ☒ 98070 ☎ 0921   D3

Olive trees grow about the ruins of the old castle from which this seaside resort takes its name. 4 km away is the **ancient town of Halaesa** (founded 403 BC), with square towers and walls and the remains of a theatre and an agora. The site may be visited *(winter 9 a.m.-2 p.m.; summer until 1 hr before sunset; closed Mon)*. Local handmade ceramics are on display on the road leading to **Santo Stefano di Camastra,** 11.5 km E. □

Practical information

⚐ ★★ *Lo Scoglio*, SS 113 at 164.4-km marker, 150 pl, ☎ 34345.

Environs

SANTO STEFANO DI CAMASTRA, ☒ 98077, ☎ 0921, 11.5 km E.

Recommended
Craft workshops: *SUIR*, v. Nazionale, ☎ 31630 (telephone before visiting).

> Looking for a locality? Consult the index at the back of the book.

CASTELLAMMARE DEL GOLFO

Trapani 38, Palermo 61, Rome 968 km
Pop. 14,318 ☒ 91014 ☎ 0924   A3

Castellammare del Golfo occupies the site of the old port of Segesta (→), probably the best-known Sicilian city when Greek settlers began arriving on the island. The **castle** with a round tower was rebuilt by the Aragonese in the 14C-15C. It lies out in the sea, joined to the town by a bridge. The mineral baths known as the **Terme Segestane** are 7 km S, near the Caldo River. 9 km NW around the gulf is **Scopello,** a village of fishermen and farm labourers, on a picturesque point surrounded by the sea breaking over the black rocks emerging from its clear waters. □

Practical information

♨ Terme Segestane, Jun-Oct, ☎ 25458.

⚐ ★★★ *Baia di Guidaloca*, at Scopello, 200 pl, ☎ 56022; ★★★ *Nausicaa*, at Forgia, 100 pl, ☎ 33030.

Recommended
Events: *Agosto Castellammarese*, with Sicilian song festival.
Tennis: v. Duchessa 36, ☎ 32196.

CASTELVETRANO

Trapani 57, Palermo 104, Rome 1,011 km
Pop. 31,645 ☒ 91022 ☎ 0924   A3

Castelvetrano contains an elegant **fountain of the Nymph** (1615), which stands before the campanile of the **chiesa Madre** (16C) with a battlemented front and, inside, stuccos by G. Serpotta (17C). In the **municipio** *(Thu 9 a.m.-1 p.m.)* is a museum with an archaeological collection, pictures by 16C-17C Sicilian painters, and sculptures, including a *Madonna with Child* by Francesco Laurana and Pietro da Bonitate. The famous statue known as the *Ephebe of Selinunte*★, a beautiful 5C BC bronze of a boy, was once stolen from here and, since being found has been moved to the National Archaeological Museum of Palermo. In the church of **S. Domenico** *(usually closed)* are some remarkable stucco decorations and interesting 15C frescos. In the church of **S. Giovanni**, rebuilt at the end of the 17C, is an engaging statue of *St. John the Baptist* by Antonello Gagini (1522).

Environs

▶ 3.5 km S, the Norman church of **SS. Trinità di Delia** (12C) has a Moorish dome. ▶ 13.5 km S is **Selinunte★★** (→). ▶ SW is **Campobello di Mazara** with an **agricultural museum** (☎ 0294/47100 or contact the Comune) and farther on, 11.5 km from Castelvetrano, is the **Rocche di Cusa** where it is still possible to see the excavations into the tufa made by the inhabitants of Selinunte when they were extracting stone to build their city. ▶ 26 km N is **Salemi** where, in Frederick II's castle, is the **Museo del Risorgimento** *(a.m. only)*, devoted to the 19C movement to liberate Italy. It was here that on 14 May 1860 Garibaldi proclaimed himself, in the name of the King of Italy, dictator of Sicily. ▶ The newly built town of **Gibellina Nuova** is near Salemi; it was constructed 20 km from the old town after this was destroyed in the earthquake of 1968. The **N. Soldano Museum of Contemporary Art and Sculpture** is near the school and the **Ethnographic and Anthropological Museum** *(only wkdays, a.m.)* is in the vicinity. □

See map on page 598.

Practical information _____

CASTELVETRANO
ℹ corso Vittorio Emanuele 102, ☎ 41015.

Hotel:
★★★ *Selinus,* v. Bonsignore 22, ☎ 41104, 48 rm Ⓟ ⌀ 42,000; bkf: 7,000.

Recommended
Horseback riding: *Circolo ippico Castelvetranese,* ☎ 43381 (associate of *ANTE*).

Environs

GIBELLINA NUOVA, ✉ 91018, ☎ 0924, 19 km N.

Recommended
Events: *Bread, Confectionery and Agricultural Produce Fair* (Jan-Feb).

CASTROREALE TERME

Messina 50, Palermo 182, Rome 715 km
Pop. 3,824 ✉ 98050 ☎ 090   F2

The **waters** from the mineral springs of Ciappazzi and Fonte di Venere are said to have curative powers and **bathing** in the blue sea of the gulf, in front of the Lipari Islands, also has a restorative effect. 2.5 km W near **San Biagio** is a **Roman villa** (1C) with mosaic floors. At **Castroreale**, 14.5 km away on the slopes of the Peloritan Mountains, there are splendid views over the surrounding countryside. There are also, in the chiesa Matrice and in the church of S. Agata, some handsome works of the 16C sculptor Antonello Gagini.   ☐

Practical information _____
⚤☎ 9781078.

Hotels:
★★ *Belvedere,* v. Nazionale 132, ☎ 9781338, 27 rm Ⓟ ⌀ 35,500; bkf: 4,000.
★★ *Gabbiano,* v. Marchesana, ☎ 9781385, 30 rm Ⓟ ⌀ ⌀ closed Oct-May, 40,000; bkf: 4,000.

Recommended
Youth hostel: *Ostello delle Aquile,* salita Frederico II d'Aragona, ☎ 9761247.

CATANIA**

Palermo 202, Rome 763, Milan 1,338 km
Pop. 380,370 ✉ 95100 ☎ 095   F4
See map on page 598.

Catania's main street, v. Etnea, has a view of Mt. Etna. There has always been a close association between this city and the volcano. Catania has a modern layout, with streets running at r. angles, as on a chessboard. This was the work of a remarkable Palermo architect, Giovanni Battista Vaccarini (1702-68), who was given the task of rebuilding the city after it had been destroyed in the terrible earthquake of 1693. Thus it appears that Catania is an 18C Baroque town, whereas it is one of the oldest cities in Sicily. It was among the first colonies that the Greeks founded in the 8C BC and today it is the capital of E Sicily and Palermo's great rival. It has a busy port, some important industrial centres and an active business community, all of which explain why it has been called the 'Milan of the South'. Because it is surrounded by Sicily's largest and most fertile plain, however, Catania remains essentially an agricultural town, the chief supplier of produce on the island. In spring, when the orange groves are in flow-

er, their perfume reaches across the city and Catania's oranges are said to be among the finest in the world.

▶ In **p. del Duomo★** (D3), the **fountain of the Elephant** (G.B. Vaccarini, 1736) was inspired by the one of Minerva, by Bernini, in Rome. In fact, Vaccarini and his followers were much influenced by Roman Baroque in rebuilding the town. The obelisk comes from Aswân in ancient Egypt, and the elephant that supports it is also very old, dating from the Byzantine rule of the island when, it is said, a sorcerer gave it to the city, assuring the population that it would protect it from the dangers of the volcano. What is certain is that it was in the piazza del Duomo in 1239, during the reign of Frederick II and it has now come to symbolize the town. ▶ The **Duomo's★** façade is also by Vaccarini and of the original 11C-12C Norman church there remain the apse, the transept and the **chapel of the Madonna,** which has two ancient tombs, one with the remains of six Aragonese kings and princes, the other with those of Constance of Aragon. In the r. apse of the Duomo is the **Chapel of St. Agatha★,** the patron saint of the city; it contains a rich **treasure** *(on view only during festivities in honour of saint).* In the sacristy is a fresco by G. Platania (1679) showing the city under the 1669 eruption of Etna. ▶ The **church of St. Agatha** (D3) is next to the Duomo and the **Palazzo del Municipio** is nearby; both were constructed by Vaccarini. To the r. of the Duomo, the former **Seminary** dates from the 18C. ▶ V. Vittorio Emanuele 56 is the **Collegio Cutelli,** which has an elegant courtyard (also by Vaccarini). ▶ The **Porta Uzeda** (D-E3; 1696), which leads to the port, is on p. del Duomo and on the other side of the square is **via Etnea** (A-D3), the city's busiest street. This leads to **p. dell' Università** (D3). In this Baroque piazza are the **Palazzo San Giuliano** (1745) and the university buildings. **P. Stesicoro** (C3) contains the ruins of a **Roman amphitheatre** from the 2C. Behind the amphitheatre, in p. S. Carcere (C3), is the **church of S. Carcere** with a 12C portal belonging originally to the Duomo. The church was built over the Roman prison in which St. Agatha was confined before being martyred. ▶ Farther N, in the public gardens of the **Villa Bellini★** (B-C2-3) are lofty trees which offer restful shade. ▶ There are also many interesting monuments and buildings in the districts on the W side of p. del Duomo. ▶ The imposing and sinister mass of the **Ursino Castle** (E3), built by Frederick II (1239-50, rebuilt 15C), houses the **Museo Civico★** *(9 a.m.-2 p.m.; Sun 9 a.m.-12.30 p.m.)* with collections of archaeological remains, ancient and modern art, including ivories, terracottas, bronzes and arms. Among the more remarkable exhibits are a statue of the head of a Greek boy★ (6C BC), a statue of a Greek girl★ (5C BC), the marble torso of a Roman emperor★, a *St. Christopher★* by P. Novelli (17C) and a *Madonna and Child★* by Antonello de Saliba (1466-1535, nephew of Antonello da Messina). The museum also has collections of old Sicilian, Greek and Roman coins, 14C tarot cards, Limoges enamels, 16C Amati violins, 17C creches, costumes, vestments, embroidery and 16C-17C fans. ▶ **Piazza Mazzini** (D-E3) is surrounded by a colonnade whose marble pillars were originally part of a Romanesque basilica that lies underneath the convent of S. Agostino. ▶ Nearby, in p. S. Francesco 3, is the house where the composer Vincenzo Bellini was born; it has been turned into the **Bellini Museum** *(9 a.m.-1.30 p.m.; Sun 9 a.m.-1 p.m.)* and has documents, autographs, pictures and scores of operas by the famous Catanian composer. The opera house (D-4), which was opened in 1890 with a performance of *Norma,* is named after Bellini. ▶ The **Roman theatre** (D2-3), which is nearby at v. Vittorio Emanuele 266 *(9 a.m.-sunset; closed Mon),* was most likely built in the 5C BC, but was remodeled by the Romans. The corridors leading to the steps, the central section and part of the orchestra with marble floors are all clearly visible; close by is the **Odeon,** a small Roman theatre where rehearsals of the chorus and other repetitions took place. ▶ In p. S. Francesco is the church of **S. Francesco d'Assisi all' Immacolata** with a beautiful Baroque façade. Along **v. dei Crociferi★** (D3) are a number of sumptuous churches; especially **S. Benedetto** (1704-13), the **chiesa dei Gesuiti** and **S. Giuliano** (Vaccarini, 1760). ▶ Farther W is the vast church of **S. Niccolo★** (D2), the largest in Sicily, with a façade that has never been completed. Seven of the eleven carved and richly painted and ornamented candelabra, carried with lighted candles in the procession on the festival of St. Agatha, are kept in this church; its interior is white and bare, but it has some large 17C-19C paintings on its altars, a carved and decorated choir and a rococo sacristy. There is a splendid view over the city from the dome *(see sacristan)*. ▶ On the l. of the church is a former Benedictine convent, also very large; it was rebuilt in the 17C around two fine courtyards with loggias. ▶ The church of **S. Maria del Gesù** (B2) is some distance from the city centre but interesting because of its painting of the *Madonna★* by Antonello Gagini. ▶ The **Palazzo delle Scienze** (A-B4; corso Italia 55) houses a number of university institutes which have mineralogical, geological and vulcanological museums. ▶ 3 km S is **Lido Plaia,** a long, sandy beach lined with pines. □

Vincenzo Bellini

Vincenzo Bellini (1801-35), the Italian operatic composer, was born in Catania of a family of musicians. His father was a church organist and a harpsichord teacher. Vincenzo began his studies at five and could compose at seven. When he was seventeen, several Catanian patrician families joined to provide money to enable him to continue his studies in Naples. The German writer, Heinrich Heine, wrote in Florentine Nights *that Bellini was 'effeminate in his manners, poetic, ethereal. He seemed to be perpetually sighing. Few women could refuse him their favours'. Some of Bellini's early operas were performed in Naples without causing much notice, but when* La Sonnambula, *which he had written on Lake Como in the villa of his mistress, Giuditta Turina, was put on in Milan in 1833 it received a standing ovation.* Norma, *equally successful, followed. The composer then moved to Paris and when* I Puritani *had its premiere there in 1835, it too had an enthusiastic reception. A few months later Bellini was taken suddenly ill and died in a Paris suburb. He was only thirty-four. His popularity has always been enormous. His remains had to wait forty years before they were finally brought home from Paris to his native Catania in 1876.*

Practical information

ℹ largo Paisiello 5 (C3), ☎ 312124.
✈ at Fontanarossa, ☎ 340937; city bus no. 24 from railway station; *Alitalia,* corso Sicilia 111 (C4), ☎ 327555.
🚆 (C5), ☎ 531625, *Circumetnea,* ☎ 434365; Stazione Porto (E4), ☎ 531402.
🚌 from ETNA bus station, ☎ 532716.
⛴ car ferries several times weekly for Reggio di Calabria, weekly for Naples; services to Malta and North Africa; *Tirrenia Navigazione,* ☎ 316394.
Car rental: *Avis,* v. San Giuseppe Larena 87, ☎ 347975, v. F. de Roberto 10, ☎ 374905, at airport, ☎ 340500; *Hertz,* v. Toselli 45, ☎ 322560, at airport, ☎ 341595; *Maggiore,* p. G. Verga 48 ☎ 310002, p. Gioeni 6, ☎ 338306, at airport, ☎ 340594.

Hotels:
★★★★ ***Central Palace,*** v. Etnea 218 (C3 a), ☎ 325344, 111 rm Ⓟ ❄ 134,000.
★★★★ ***Excelsior,*** p. Verga 39 (B4 b), ☎ 325733, 163 rm ♿ 164,000.
★★★★ ***Jolly Trinacria,*** p. Trento 13 (B3 c), ☎ 316933, 159 rm Ⓟ 150,000.
★★★ ***Gelso Bianco,*** on motorway to Palermo, ☎ 345657, 90 rm Ⓟ ♨ ♿ ❄ 🏊 🎾 70,000; bkf: 7,500.
★★★ ***Nettuno,*** v. di Lauria 121, ☎ 493533, 84 rm Ⓟ ♿ ❄ 🏊 117,000.

Restaurants:
● ♦♦♦ ***Siciliana,*** v. Marco Polo 52/A, ☎ 370003, closed Sun eve and Mon. In a former villa with lovely garden. Regional cuisine: rigatoni alla Norma, risotto alla pescatora, 32/45,000.
♦♦♦ ***Costa Azzurra,*** v. de Cristofaro 4, ☎ 494920, closed Mon and Aug. Windows and terrace looking over the sea. Regional cuisine: Bucatini Alioto, fritto misto, 35/50,000.
♦ ***Commercio,*** v. Riso 8/10 (A-B4 d), ☎ 447289, closed Sat and Aug. Mixed cuisine: sarde a beccafico, swordfish, 20/25,000.
♦ ***Pagano,*** v. De Roberto 37 (B4 e), ☎ 322720, closed Sun and Aug. Long tradition. Regional cuisine: pasta with anchovies, escalopes alla siciliana, 17/25,000.

⛺ ★★ *Jonio,* at Ognina, v. Villini a Mare 2, 136 pl, ☎ 491139 (all year).

Recommended
Canoeing: *Circolo Canottieri Jonica,* v. Alagona 2, ☎ 491364.
Craft workshops: *M. Patané,* SS 121 at 9-km marker, ☎ 391182 (mosaics).
Events: opera and musical season at *Teatro Bellini,* ☎ 312020; theatrical season at *Stabile Theatre,* ☎ 354466; *Festival of St. Agatha* with procession.
Fairs and markets: *Free Time Fair* (May); *Grapes and Wines Fair* (Sep).
Flying: Fontanarossa Airport, ☎ 341027.
Horseback riding: *Società Catanese di Equitazione,* at Boschetto Plaia, ☎ 345678; *Associazione Regionale per il Turismo Equestre,* at Coda Volpe, ☎ 339088.
Swimming: v. Kennedy, ☎ 340362; v. Riso 11/19, ☎ 437487.
♥ botanical garden: v. Etnea 397 (A-B2-2; wkdays 8 a.m.-2 p.m.).

CEFALU*

Palermo 70, Rome 839 km
Pop. 13,962 ✉ 90015 ☎ 0921 D3

Cefalu, on the N coast, lies at the foot of a rocky spur surrounded by the Madonian peaks. While remaining a fishing village, it has also recently developed into a resort because of its beautiful beach. The name *cefalu* comes from the Greek *cephale,* meaning head, and refers to the large rock above the city. This town is at least 25 centuries old.

▶ The **cathedral** is the most Norman and Romanesque of Sicilian churches and would not look out of place in France, but it is also an example of that astonishing fusion of Europe, Africa and the East that the Norman kings of Sicily were masters at carrying out. It was built by Roger II in 1131, following a vow he had made when caught in a storm at sea, although the church took nearly a century to complete. It has a sober façade and the nave and the vaults of the choir are 13C. The two towers are typically Norman. In 1471 Ambrogio da Como added a portico to the façade. In the interior everything has been conceived for the purpose of raising man towards God, towards Christ Pantocrator who stands surrounded by the Virgin, the Archangels and the Apostles. This truly marvelous Byzantine **mosaic** dates from 1148. The other mosaics are later ones (13C). In the r. nave is a *Madonna* by Antonello Gagini (1533). ▶ From p. del Duomo, with its palm trees and ochre-coloured houses, v. Mandralisca leads to the **Museum Mandralisca** *(9.30 a.m.-12 noon and 3.30-6 p.m.; Sun 9.30 a.m.-12 noon)* with its famous *Portrait of a Man* by Antonello da Messina (1470), a decorated 4C BC vase with the red figure of a fisherman and many other Greek ceramics. ▶ At corso Ruggero 75 is the **Osterio Magno,**

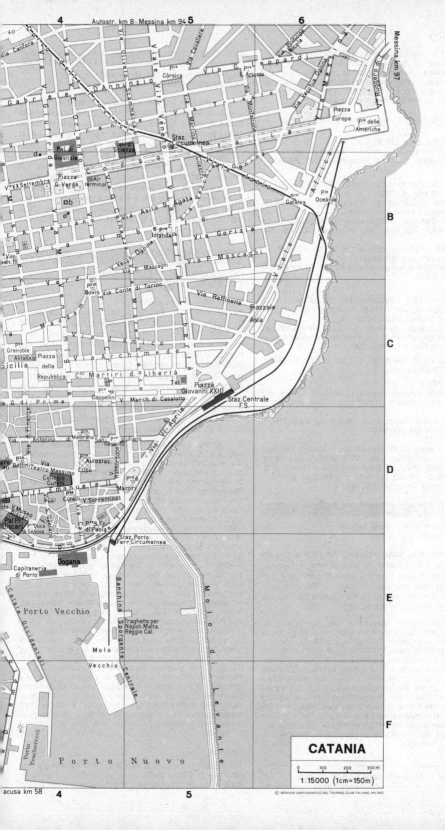

CATANIA

0   100   200   300 m

1:15000 (1cm=150m)

© SERVIZIO CARTOGRAFICO DEL TOURING CLUB ITALIANO, MILANO

the ruins of an old palace of King Roger. ▶ In p. Garibaldi and along the coast N of town are the ruins of some old **fortifications**. ▶ It is possible to get to the top of the rock that overlooks the town by taking the vicolo Saraceni which starts at the corso Ruggero. It's an hour's walk, but there is a wonderful view from the summit. ☐

Practical information _____

≋
🛈 v. Amendola 2, ☎ 21050.
⛴ hydrofoil service several times weekly in summer for Lipari and Vulcano; *SNAV*, at Messina, ☎ 090/364044.

Hotels:
★★★ *Baia del Capitano*, ☎ 20003, 34 rm [P] ▥ ⌂ ⚲
closed Nov-14 Mar, 66,000.
★★★ *Calette*, at Caldura, ☎ 24144, 50 rm [P] ▥ ⚲ ⌂
closed Nov-Apr, 79,000; bkf: 11,000.
★★★ *Santa Dominga*, v. Gibilmanna 18, ☎ 21081, 56 rm
[P] ⚲ closed Nov-Mar. No restaurant, 53,000; bkf: 4,000.
★★★ *Tourist*, lungomare Colombo, ☎ 21750, 46 rm [P] ⚲
⌂ closed 21 Nov.-30 Apr, 70,000.
★★ *Riva del Sole*, v. Lungomare, ☎ 21230, 28 rm [P] ▥ ⚲
45,000; bkf: 6,000.

Restaurants:
♦♦ *Brace*, v. XXV Novembre 10, ☎ 23570, closed noon, Mon and Jan. Mixed cuisine: rigatoni with nut sauce, roast meat and fish, 16/30,000.
♦ *Gabbiano*, lungomare Giardina 17, ☎ 21495, closed Wed. Regional cuisine: maccheroni and sardine sauce, escalopes alla Siciliana, 20/35,000.

Å ★★★ *Costa Ponente*, SS 113 at 190.3-km marker, 350 pl, ☎ 20085 (all year).

Recommended
Events: *Cefalù Summer Festival* (traditional dances and festivities, yacht racing); *international philatelic show* (summer).
Horseback riding: *Vallegrande Ranch*, at Vallegrande, ☎ 21805 (associate of *ANTE*).
Marina: ☎ 21580.
Vacation villages: *Club Mediterranée*, closed Oct-Apr, information, at Milan, ☎ 02/778663, at Rome, ☎ 06/4745951; *Hotel Villaggio Valtur*, at Finale di Pollina *(13 km E)*, closed Oct-Apr., information, at Milan, ☎ 02/791733, at Rome, ☎ 06/6784588.

CENTURIPE

Enna 59, Palermo 192, Rome 810 km
Pop. 6,749 ⊠ 94010 ☎ 0935   E4

Centuripe is on a ridge between the Rivers Simeto and Dittaino with Etna in its background. Because of its wonderful view over the plain of Catania it has been called 'the balcony of Sicily'. The site was inhabited before the arrival of the Greeks by peoples of the Sicanian race in the 9C BC.

▶ The **Archaeological Museum** in the municipio *(a.m. only, office hrs)* has finds from local sites that include architectural fragments, Roman and Hellenic statues, vases and fictile figurines (3C-1C BC). ▶ On the outskirts of town are traces of the ancient city. ▶ There is a belvedere in the piazzale with a superb view★ of Etna and all the surrounding countryside. Also in the piazzale is a mausoleum of the imperial period which is called locally the **castle of Corradino**. ▶ In **Vallone Difesa** a building with a colonnade from Roman times may have been the seat of the *Augustales* (College of Priests). ▶ In the district of **Panneria** are ruins of an ancient **Greek house** and in the Bagni Valley ruins of a sumptuous building that housed Roman baths. ☐

The arrow (→) is a reference to another entry.

COMISO

Ragusa 16, Palermo 251, Rome 868 km
Pop. 28,866 ⊠ 97013 ☎ 0932   E5

The spring that fed the 2C **Roman baths** now gushes into a covered basin behind the modern **Fountain of Diana** in the p. del Municipio; the remains of these baths may be seen under this municipio *(inquire at Comune)*. The mosaic floor of the baths has been set up on a wall in the public library. Both the **chiesa Madre** and the **church of SS. Annunziata** have tall façades and splendid domes. There are 16C altars and the **tomb of Naselli** (1517) in the **church of S. Francesco**. The tomb may be the work of Antonello Gagini. The truncated octagonal tower of a 14C castle contains a Byzantine baptistery with 14C frescos. ☐

ENNA*

Palermo 135, Rome 846, Milan 1,421 km
Pop. 28,415 ⊠ 94100 ☎ 0935   D4

Enna, one of the oldest cities on the island, was *Henna* until the Middle Ages. Then, because of its castle, it became *Castrum Hennae* (the castle of Enna); the Arabs wrote this as *Casr Iani*, which in turn was interpreted as Castrogiovanni. This was the name by which the town was known for centuries until Mussolini changed it back to Enna. The Greek poet Callimachus called the town 'the navel of Sicily', but it is usually called 'the belvedere of Sicily'. This seems more appropriate since from its rocky summit there is a stupendous view over the valley of the Dittaino River. Enna, on a prosperous plateau (3,000 ft), is the highest capital in Italy.

▶ On one side of the central **p. Vittorio Emanuele** (A2) the church of **S. Francesco** has a 15C campanile; in its interior is a 14C wooden painted *Crucifixion* and a painting of the *Manifestation of Christ to the Magi*, which may be by the Flemish artist Simon of Wobreck. ▶ The myth of Persephone (she personifies the seasonal changes and the disappearance of vegetation) is supposed to have taken place by the shore of nearby Lake Pergusa and a copy of Bernini's famous sculpture representing this episode has been erected over a fountain in **p. Crispi** (A2). From here also is a splendid view★ over Calascibetta, the Madonie Mountains and Etna. ▶ **V. Roma** (A-B1-3), the town's main street, rises gently starting from p. Vittorio Emanuele. ▶ The **Duomo** (A3) is a 14C building; its interior has Gothic arches, contains sculptures from different periods, two statues of the Annunciation, one on each side of the portal and richly decorated ceilings in wood. ▶ The nearby **Museo Alessi** (A3; *9 a.m.-12.30 p.m. Tue, Thu-Sat; Jun-Sep daily)* houses the treasure of the Duomo which includes articles in gold, precious church vessels, Graeco-Roman collections, Byzantine paintings and prints. ▶ Six of the twenty towers of the **Castello di Lombardia**★ (A3) are still standing; it is one of the most imposing buildings of its kind in Sicily. It was originally built by the Byzantines, but the Normans and Swabians enlarged it; it contains ruins of a residence of Frederick III of Aragon and, from its tower, called the Eagle or Pisan tower, there is an extensive view★ over the surrounding countryside. ▶ On the city's outskirts, on a rise in the public gardens, the octagonal tower that Frederick II built in the 13C (B1) should be visited.

Environs

▶ The Lake of Pergusa is 10 km S. ▶ 7 km along a scenic route is **Calascibetta**. It is in the form of a horseshoe on a rock full of caves. In the sacristy of the **chiesa**

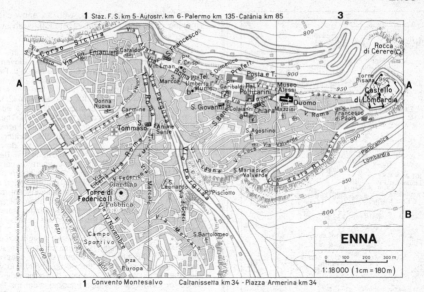

1 Staz. F. S. km 5-Autostr. km 6-Palermo km 135-Catánia km 85   **3**

ENNA

0   100   200   300 m

1:18000 (1cm = 180 m)

1 Convento Montesalvo   Caltanissetta km 34 - Piazza Armerina km 34

Matrice (13C) is a 13C Bible in handwritten Gothic characters. The marble group representing the *Annunciation* in the **Carmelite church** is attributed to A. Gagini. In the **Capuchin church** is an *Adoration of the Magi* by F. Paladini. □

Practical information _____

ⓘ p. Garibaldi (A2), ☎ 21184; p. Colaianni (A2), ☎ 26119. ▨ ☎ 21960.
🚌 from v. Diaz (A-B1), ☎ 21902.

Hotel:
★★★ *Sicilia,* p. Colaianni 7 (A2 a), ☎ 21127, 60 rm Ⓟ ⅙ No restaurant, 45,000.

Restaurants:
♦ *Centrale,* p. VI Dicembre 9 (A2 b), ☎ 21025, closed Sat and Oct. Regional cuisine: pappardelle, falsomagro, 15/25,000.
♦ *Fontana,* v. Volturo 6 (A2 c), ☎ 25465, closed Sun except summer and Christmas. Regional cuisine: cavatelli alla Siciliana, roast lamb, 18/25,000.

Recommended
Craft workshops: *G. Fornasier,* at Sant'Anna, v. Michelangelo, ☎ 29425 (mosaics).
Evens: *Holy Week Procession;* summer theatre in Castello di Lombardia.
Swimming: at Sant'Anna, ☎ 29875.

ERICE*

Trapani 13, Palermo 96, Rome 1,003 km
Pop. 26,804 ⊠ 91016 ☎ 0923   A2

On a hill NW of Trapani, Erice, known as 'the sentinel of the West' was a town of great fame and importance in antiquity and a sacred place of worship. It was then called **Eryx.** When the Phoenicians arrived, they worshipped Astarte here, and the Greeks that followed built a magnificent temple to Aphrodite. Later, Romans and Christians followed. In 1167, when Roger the Norman took the town from the Arabs, he re-named it Monte San Giuliano and that it remained until 1934.

▶ The **walls** of the town (well-preserved, especially on the NE side) are of megalithic blocks (5C BC) in the lower part and Norman in the upper part, as are the three gates. ▶ The **chiesa Matrice★** (1314) has an isolated **campanile★** (1312); inside are 15C-16C chapels and a statue of the Virgin (1469), attributed to Francesco Laurana. ▶ The **Museo Comunal A. Cordici** *(9 a.m.-2 p.m. and 3-5 p.m.; Sat 9 a.m.-2 p.m.; Sun 9 a.m.-1 p.m.)* has some interesting collections of ancient finds (prehistoric, Phoenician, Greek, Roman), 17C-19C paintings and local crafts (creches, wax images of the Madonna, silverware). It also has an *Annunciation★* by Antonello Gagini (1525). ▶ The church of **S. Giovanni Battista** stands isolated among cypress trees; it has a 12C portal and in its interior 15C-16C sculpture, including a *St. John the Evangelist* by Antonello Gagini (1531). ▶ The **garden of Balio** is on top of the hill where the temple of Venus once stood; to the r. is the **castello Pepoli,** and at the end of a narrow street, the **castello di Venere** (12C-13C), inside of which are the remains of an ancient temple to Venus and a sacred well. ▶ From **viali dei Cappuccini** and the surrounding pine forest there are magnificent views★ of the Aegadean Islands, Trapani and the sea. □

Practical information _____

ⓘ v. Conte Pepoli 55, ☎ 869388.

Hotels:
★★★★ *Ermione,* v. Pineta Comunale 43, ☎ 869138, 48 rm Ⓟ ▨ ⅙ 🖵 74,000.
★★★ *Moderno,* v. Vittorio Emanuele 63, ☎ 869300, 26 rm Ⓟ ⅙ 70,000; bkf: 5,000.

Restaurants:
● ♦♦ *Taverna di Re Aceste,* v. Conte Pepoli, ☎ 869084, closed Wed and Nov. A renovated old tavern. Regional cuisine: rigatoni all'ericiana, grilled fish, 25/30,000.
♦♦ *Ciclope,* v. Nunzio Nasi 45, ☎ 869183, closed Tue except summer and Oct-Feb. Overlooks sea and coast. Regional cuisine: risotto with shellfish, lobster on spit, 20/30,000.

Recommended
Events: *Erice Summer Festival;* Trapani-Erice uphill car racing (May).

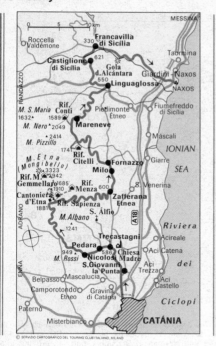

3. Mount Etna

Mount ETNA*

From Catania to Giardini-Naxos *(130 km, 1 day; map 3)*

Mount Etna, the largest and most active volcano in Europe, is in the province of Catania on the E coast of Sicily. (Its name comes from the Greek *aipho* meaning I burn.) The volcano is in the shape of a truncated cone and it rises to 10,758 ft; it has as many as 200 craters. On the W side the symmetry of its slope is interrupted by a deep gully known as the Valle del Bove. There are three distinct zones of vegetation. Most of the highest region, down to a level of 7,000 ft, is barren except for stunted alpine shrub and is usually covered in snow and ashes. The next zone is one of forests, the upper part of which is covered with birch trees, while the lower reaches — to 6,000 ft — are dense with evergreens and chestnuts. The lowest region, which extends up 3,000 ft, has the splendid fertility natural to volcanic soil. Here olives, vines and all kinds of vegetables flourish and the slopes are dotted everywhere with populous towns and villas. It is said that the volcano has erupted more than 135 times during the period since records have been kept (*c.* 500 BC), and some of these eruptions have been very serious. Catania was destroyed by an eruption in 1169 and again in 1669 when a great abyss, 12 miles long, opened up in the side of the mountain and lava poured down to the coast. In 1917, an eruption of lava was thrown

2,700 ft into the sky. Etna, with its snow-capped, smoking peak and luxuriant vegetation, is an awe-inspiring sight.

▶ **Catania** (→) is a natural starting point for this itinerary. ▶ At 1,150 ft is the village of **San Giovanni La Punta.** ▶ At **Trecastagni** (1,920 ft), the beautiful Renaissance **chiesa Madre** is probably the work of Antonello Gagini; it sits on a height which offers a fine view★ of the coast. ▶ **Pedara** is at 1,450 ft. ▶ At **Nicolosi** (2,300 ft), there is an office where it is possible to hire a guide to go up the mountain (*groups only,* ☎ *914209*). ▶ The route circles the **Rossi Mountains** and, passing the **Ferrandina** and **Serra la Nave** forests, reaches the **parking area** (6,170 ft). Here there is a stupendous view down the mountain and over the sea. ▶ Above is the **Refugio Albergo Sapienza** (6,266 ft), from where a cable-car ascends to 8,530 ft; at this point there is a service that leads farther up the **side of the crater★** (*c. 2.5 hrs for this trip, including return*). The incandescent magma that often rises from inside the volcano often obliges the authorities to change the sides from which the crater may be approached. From the top of Etna it is possible to see the whole of Sicily and, when it is clear, the distant island of Malta. ▶ It is also possible to take a **night excursion** to the top from the Rifugio Sapienza and see the sunrise (*departure 2:30-3 a.m.*). ▶ The best time to observe the **eruptions**, when material is thrown up to 600 ft in the air and small amounts of hot lava flow down the sides, is at sunset or dawn. ▶ It is also possible, from the Rifugio Sapienza, after a two hours' walk, to reach the **Rifugio Gino Menza** (5,528 ft). This is the starting point for visits and crossings of the **valle del Bove** (*6 hrs*). ▶ Proceeding from the parking area, the route crosses the ridge of the **Silvestri Mountains** and comes to **Zafferana Etnea** (1,885 ft), located among the abundant vegetation on the Ionian side of the volcano. ▶ Farther on, past **Milo** and **Fornazzo** (2,756 ft), the route begins to climb again, near the Cubania forest, to the **Rifugio Citelli** (5,712 ft; *closed at present*), from where, passing the **Rifugio Conti** (5,210 ft), the road leads to **Mareneve** and then descends through a pine forest to **Linguaglossa** (1,800 ft). ▶ The route now leaves Etna and crosses a series of low hills to arrive at **Castiglione di Sicilia** (2,037 ft), an old town with a 16C church. It lies on a rocky spur and looks out over the Alcantara Valley. ▶ From **Francavilla di Sicilia,** passing through orchards and orange groves, the route reaches the sea. ▶ At a certain point on the SS 185, by the spot where cars park, it is possible to go down a stony slope (*advise wearing bathing suit and rubber-soled shoes*) to the **Alcantara** gorge, which the river has dug out of the lava. There is a spectacular view of foaming waters rushing down through tall volcanic walls, with layers of basalt in different colours. ▶ The itinerary ends at **Giardini-Naxos** (→). ☐

Practical information _____

[i] at Catania, largo Paisiello 5, ☎ 095/312124; *CAI Catania*, v. Vecchia Ognina 169, ☎ 095/387674; *Funivia dell'Etna-SITAS* (office for guided climb of volcano), at Nicolosi, p. Vittorio Emanuele 45, ☎ 095/914209 (at cable-car point, ☎ 914141).

LINGUAGLOSSA, ⬚ 95015, ☎ 095.
✶ ski lifts, cross-country skiing and instruction at Mareneve.

[i] *STAR*, v. Roma 334, ☎ 643180 (excursions on Etna).

MILO, ⬚ 95010, ☎ 095.

⚠ ★★ *Mareneve*, at Piano Grande, v. Bosco 30, ☎ 951396 (all year).

NICOLOSI, ⬚ 95030, ☎ 095.
✶ Etna cableway, ski lifts, cross-country skiing, instruction.

Hotels:
★★★ *Biancaneve,* v. Etnea 163, ☎ 911176, 69 rm Ⓟ ▭ ⤳ 46,000; bkf: 7,000.
★★★ *Gemmellaro,* ☎ 911060, 44 rm Ⓟ ⤸ 42,000; bkf: 5,000.

Recommended
Excursions: by cable-car and special transport from Rifugio Sapienza (☎ 911062) to crater; also night excursions (2.30-3 a.m.), information, ☎ 914209.

SAN GIOVANNI LA PUNTA, ⊠ 95037, ☎ 095.
Ⓘ p. Municipio 1, ☎ 822604.

Hotel:
★★★ *Ares,* ☎ 827373, 35 rm Ⓟ 〰 59,000; bkf: 3,000.

Restaurant:
◆◆◆ *Nuovo Calatino,* v. della Regione 62, ☎ 822005, closed Tue. Regional cuisine: rigatoni alla Norma, escalopes Sicilian fashion, 25/30,000.

Recommended
Horseback riding: *Centro Ippico 31º Cavalleria,* v. Piave 1, ☎ 611955 (associate of *ANTE*).

ZAFFERANA ETNEA, ⊠ 95019, ☎ 095.

Hotel:
★★★ *Primavera dell'Etna,* strada per l'Etna, ☎ 951582, 53 rm Ⓟ ⚲ ≮ 〰 35,000; bkf: 4,500.

GELA*

Caltanissetta 74, Palermo 206, Rome 868 km
Pop. 77,230 ⊠ 93012 ☎ 0933   D5

Gela is on the S coast and was founded in 1230 by the Emperor Frederick II who named it Terranova. It was only in 1928 that it took the name of Gela because of an ancient Greek town of this name that had once existed nearby. This original Gela was founded by Rhodians and Cretans in 690 BC and rapidly grew in importance, its most flourishing period being the reign of Hippocrates. Modern Gela has little to connect it with the ancient old one beyond its site. It has a petrochemical plant, cotton and woolen manufacturers, sardine and tuna fisheries and trades in agricultural produce, wine and sulphur.

▶ The **Museo Regionale Archeologico★** *(9 a.m.-2 p.m.; Sun 9 a.m.-1 p.m.; closed Mon)* has collections of finds from sites near Gela and others in the province of Caltanissetta. The most beautiful is the **head of a horse★** in terra-cotta (5C BC) and there are also decorations from ancient temples, sarcophagi, Attic vases and collections of ancient coins. ▶ From the piazza at the side of the museum is a view over the most recent archaeological **excavations** in a part of the old city known as **Timoleonteo** (4C BC). A number of houses and shops have been unearthed. Close by, to the S, in the **Parco delle Rimembranza** are the foundations of a Doric temple dedicated to Athena (6C BC) and the remains of another temple, of which a column is still standing (5C BC). ▶ The **Greek baths,** near the hospital, were a public establishment in the 4C BC. ▶ The **fortifications of Capo Soprano★★** *(9 a.m.-1 hr before sunset)* are part of a wall which at one time encircled the whole hill of Gela; part of them have been excavated. ▶ 8 km toward Syracuse is **Lake Biviere.** ▶ 17 km N is **Lake Disueri,** which is an artificial reservoir; on the sides of the surrounding rocky heights is one of the largest early Sicilian burial grounds and, farther N on **Mount Bubonia,** archaeologists have identified a primitive Sicilian centre that was later taken over by the Greeks. ▶ 21 km N, **Butera** is a picturesque village on a rocky crest locking out over the plain of Gela, with an 11C castle and a palazzo comunale with a 14C portal. N of the village, in the **Piano della Fiera** district, there is an early Sicilian-Greek burial ground. ▶ 21 km W, on the coast, the **castle of Falconara** (14C) rises in front of the sea with a park at its back.   ▯

Practical information _____

≋
Ⓘ v. Navarra Bresmes, ☎ 913788.
Car rental: *Maggiore,* v. G. Verga 100, ☎ 911009.

Hotel:
★★★ *MotelAgip,* SS 117 bis at SS 115 crossing, ☎ 911579, 91 rm Ⓟ 66,500; bkf: 3,500.

Recommended
Marina: ☎ 917755.
Events: *Gela Summer Festival* (arts and traditional displays).
Clay pigeon shooting: v. Guarnaccia 11, ☎ 911171.

GIARDINI-NAXOS

Messina 51, Palermo 257, Rome 726 km
Pop. 8,551 ⊠ 98035 ☎ 0942   F3

Naxos was the first Greek colony in Sicily, founded in 735 BC. In its **archaeological park** *(9 a.m.-1 hr before sunset; closed Mon),* which extends along the course of the S. Venera stream, are the remains of a city wall made of basalt blocks, as well as the ruins of some houses with potters' ovens. The **Museo Archeologico di Naxos** *(9 a.m.-2 p.m.; Sun 9 a.m.-1 p.m.; closed Mon)* contains much interesting material, especially concerning the making of Chalcidean vases. There is a view★ of the beautiful coast, Etna and Taormina.   ▯

Practical information _____

≋
Ⓘ v. Tysandros, ☎ 51010.

Hotels:
★★★ *Arathena Rocks,* v. Calcide Eubea 55, ☎ 51349, 49 rm ⚲ Ⓟ 〰 ▤ ♪ Pens. Closed Nov-Mar. Located in a small bay, 68,000.
★★★ *Assinos,* at Alcantara, v. Nazionale 33, ☎ 50181, 62 rm Ⓟ 〰 ⚬ ▤ ♪ 43,500; bkf: 8,000.
★★★ *Holiday Naxion,* v. Jannuzzo, ☎ 51931, 310 rm Ⓟ 〰 ⚬ ⚶ ▤ ♪ closed Jan-Feb, 94,000; bkf: 11,500.
★★★ *Kalos,* v. Calcide Eubea 29, ☎ 52116, 27 rm ⚲ 〰 closed Nov-Mar, 55,000; bkf: 6,000.
★★ *Sirenetta,* v. Naxos ☎ 54267, 15 rm closed Dec-Jan, 33,000; bkf: 5,000.

Restaurant:
◆◆◆ *Cambusa,* v. Schisò 3, ☎ 51437, closed Tue, 15-31 Jan and 1-15 Dec. Veranda opening on to sea. Seafood: spaghetti with cuttle-fish sauce, swordfish on spit, 20/35,000.

Recommended
Craft workshops: *Patané,* v. Regina Margherita 111, ☎ 51149 (wrought iron).
Hang gliding: *Etna Delta,* at Fiumefreddo di Sicilia, ☎ 095/641692 (instruction).
Marina: ☎ 51911.
♥ discothèque: *Marabù,* at Jannuzzo, ☎ 54076 (summer only); *Taitù,* v. Vulcano, ☎ 51407 (winter only).

GIOIOSA MAREA

Messina 87, Palermo 148, Rome 759 km
Pop. 6,373 ⊠ 98063 ☎ 0941   E2

Gioiosa Marea's beautiful beach has a background of luxuriant vegetation and there are many rocks and grottoes in the sea. From the abandoned **Gioiosa Guardia,** two hours away on the mountain of Cape Calavà, there is a magnificent view of the N coast and the Lipari Islands.   ▯

Practical information _____

≋
Ⓘ v. Umberto I 197, ☎ 301211.

Hotel:
★★★ *Capo Skino Park Hotel,* at Capo Skino, ☎ 301167, 88 rm Ⓟ 〰 ▤ ♪ closed Nov, 50,000; bkf: 6,500.

⛺ ★★ *Cicero,* at San Giorgio, 420 pl, ☎ 39295.

The island of LAMPEDUSA

Agrigento 231, Palermo 356, Rome 1,163 km
Pop. 4,172 ✉ 92010 ☎ 0922 B6

Lampedusa is closer to Tunisia (113 km) than to Sicily (205 km). It has a rocky coast and traces of prehistoric buildings, although the island remained uninhabited until 1843 when the Bourbon King Ferdinand settled a small community on it. Its surface is 20 sq km and its maximum height 433 ft. □

Practical information

≋

ℹ *Agenzia Le Pelagie,* v. Roma 155, ☎ 970170.
✈ ☎ 970006; *Ati,* ☎ 970299.
⛴ daily summer sailings from Porto Empedock (*c.* 9 hrs), *Siremar,* ☎ 970003.

Hotel:
★★ ***Vega,*** v. Roma 19, ☎ 970099, 13 rm closed 20 Dec-20 Jan. No restaurant, 40,000.

Restaurants:
♦♦ ***Gemelli,*** v. Cala Pisana 2, ☎ 970699, closed Oct-May. Seafood, 20/35,000.
♦ ***Da Tommasino,*** v. Lido Azzurro 13, ☎ 970316, closed Mon and Nov. Seafood: spaghetti with anchovy sauce, red mullet, 20/30,000.

⛺ ★ *La Roccia,* 250 pl, ☎ 970055 (all year).

LENTINI

Syracuse 46, Palermo 238, Rome 735 km
Pop. 30,982 ✉ 96016 ☎ 095 E4

Lentini's **chiesa Madre,** on the N slopes of the Iblei Mountains, encloses a 3C Christian burial ground and contains an 11C Byzantine ikon of the Madonna. The **archaeological museum** *(9 a.m.-2 p.m.: closed Mon)* has material from the early Sicilian, Classical Greek and Hellenistic Greek periods of ancient *Leontinoi,* which was located in the S. Mauro Valley *(access by car from Carlentini).* Excavations there have unearthed the S gate and parts of the wall that encircled the citadel. In the same valley is the Swabian **Castellaccio** and the **cave of the Crucifixion** with Byzantine frescos. 26 km W is **Militello in Val di Catania** facing the Catanian plain and Etna. Its **Museo di S. Nicola** has some art that was originally in the local churches. □

LICATA

Agrigento 44, Palermo 172, Rome 901 km
Pop. 42,242 ✉ 92027 ☎ 0922 C5

After destroying Gela in 282 BC, the tyrant *Phintias* founded a town that he named after himself and settled there the survivors from Gela. Licata, on the S coast at the mouth of the Salso River, is supposedly this same town, and the ruins of Phintias can be seen in the grounds of the 16C **Castel S. Angelo,** on a hill W of Licata. The **Museo Civico** *(wkdays 9 a.m.-2 p.m.)* displays many archaeological finds, mostly material from burial grounds in the surroundings, dating from prehistoric times to the 3C BC. □

Practical information

Hotel:
★★★ ***Faro,*** v. Dogana 6, ☎ 862526, 30 rm 🅿 47,500.

Restaurant:
♦ ***Logico,*** v. Lido 5, ☎ 862122, closed Mon and Sep. Seafood: risotto marinara, lobster, 20/25,000.

The island of LINOSA

Agrigento 183, Palermo 308, Rome 1,115 km
Pop. 409 ✉ 92010 ☎ 0922 C5

Linosa is a volcanic island (Mount Vulcano rises to 640 ft) of little more than 5 sq km with no springs and little vegetation beyond brushwood. With the islands of Lampione and Lampedusa it forms the Pelagian group, administered from Agrigento. Its 409 inhabitants, grouped on the island's S coast, live from farming and fishing. □

Practical information

⛴ daily sailings from Porto Empedocle (*c.* 6.5 hrs) and daily connections with Lampedusa; *Siremar,* ☎ 972062.

The LIPARI ISLANDS*

(Le isole Eolie)

D-E-F1/E2

In the ancient world these islands were supposed to have been ruled by Aeolus who, according to Homer and Virgil, was given power over the winds by Zeus, and they were therefore called the Aeolian Islands. They are a mountainous group, with a healthy climate and fertile soil, and the inhabitants grow grapes, figs, olives and corn and export pumice-stone, sulphur, nitre, soda, capers and fish. The islands were a Carthaginian naval station during the Punic Wars until their capture by the Romans in 252 BC.

▶ The seven **Lipari Islands,** as they are known today, lie off the NE coast of Sicily in the Tyrrhenian Sea. They are: Vulcano, Lipari, Salina, Filicudi, Alicudi, Panarea and Stromboli.

▶ **Lipari.** This is the largest island, with a rocky coast and a rugged interior that culminates in Mt. Chirica (2,000 ft) and Mt. S. Angelo (1,950 ft). ▶ The picturesque town of **Lipari,** in the island's centre, contains the island's port and the beach of Marina Lunga to the N and the hydrofoil landing and the beach of Marina Corta to the S. ▶ The Spanish fortifications (16C) of the **castle**★ have, along with medieval towers (13C), an older Greek tower (4C-3C BC); until the 17C they enclosed the whole town. ▶ There is a Norman cathedral with Baroque interior containing a silver 17C statue of its patron, S. Bartolo and a 15C Madonna painted on wood. ▶ At the **excavation site,** the various layers unearthed have revealed oval cabins of the early Bronze Age (17C-15C BC) and middle Bronze Age (14C-13C BC), remains of other huts of the early Iron Age (11C-9C BC) and buildings of the Greek period. ▶ The **Museo Eoliano**★ *(9 a.m.-2 p.m.; Sun 9 a.m.-1 p.m.; closed Mon)* is the 17C Palazzo Vescovile to the r. of the cathedral, and in another building on its l. It displays finds tracing the history of the island's inhabitants from prehistoric times, mainly using material found at the sites at the castle and in the Diana district. On display are Mycenean ceramics imported from Greece, ceramics from Greek, Roman and medieval times found on the smaller islands, material from burial grounds on Lipari and at Milazzo, on Sicily, and also finds from underwater explorations. A section of the museum devoted to **volcanology** is housed opposite in 15C-16C houses. ▶ Behind the church of Madonna delle Grazie, in the **archaeological park of the castle,** Greek and Roman sarcophagi have been set up, using material found at the Diana site. ▶ In the **archaeological park of Diana** (W of the castle), which includes part of the Greek fortifications, is a Roman burial ground. From **Canneto,** 3.5 km N on an inlet on the

E coast, it is possible to visit the **Forgia Vecchia**, with pumice-stone caves and a mass of obsidian known as **Rocche Rosse★**. ▶ Completing the circuit of the island leads to **Acquacalda** and **Quattropani**. It is also possible to tour around the island by boat. ▶ At the belvedere of **Quattrocchi** is a splendid view over the sea and the island of Vulcano in the distance. 3.2 km NW is the central plateau called **Piano Conte**, with white houses and vineyards. This is near *(30 mn)* the **Baths of S. Calogero**. ▶ **Bagno Secco** contains fumaroles (holes in the rock) issuing hot vapour.

▶ **Vulcano.** A short isthmus links Vulcano to **Vulcanello**; with **Porto Ponente** on one side and **Porto Levante** on the other. In the latter are fumaroles, small mud and sulphur cones boiling over and similar eruptions and rumblings under the clear waters of the sea. ▶ In the sea is the **Faraglione della Fabbrica**, a large rock with grottos from which alum is dug. There is a good view★ from **Vulcanello**, which came into existence with its first eruption in 183 BC. ▶ S of the isthmus is the **large crater** of Vulcano (1,280 ft; *climb c. 40 mn*); the volcano's opening is 1,640 ft wide. There is also a splendid view of all the islands, the Sicilian coast and Etna. On the SE of the island, white steam and sulphur fumes rise from the plane of the **grandi Fumarole**. ▶ On the W coast, during a tour by boat, it is possible to see the **Grotta del Cavallo**.

▶ **Salina.** This is the second largest island; also the most fertile, producing good wine. It is also the highest (Fossa delle Felci, 3,156 ft). ▶ **Santa Marina Salina** is half way along the beach on the E side; **Lingua** in by the lagoon that gave its name to the island; **Malfa** is a picturesque port on the N side; **Leni**, among vineyards, is on a slope of the Fossa delle Felci and **Rinella** is a fishing village on the S coast. In the interior is the **sanctuary of the Madonna del Terzito**.

▶ **Panarea.** This island contains a prehistoric village of oval cabins dating from 14C-13C BC *(see caretaker)*. There are three small villages on beautiful Panarea: **Iditella**, **San Pietro** and **Drauto**, which rest among greenery on the slopes of Timpone del Corvo (1,380 ft). To the NE, the large volcanic rock of **Basiluzzo** rises out of the sea; it is only inhabited during caper harvest.

▶ **Stromboli.** This island has three villages: Piscità, Ficogrande and San Vincenzo. They are on the NE coast, their white Mediterranean houses surrounded by palm trees, olive groves and citrus trees. The island is the only one of the Lipari group to have a large active volcano. ▶ Along the coast small beaches are succeeded by rocky spurs, some of which contain caves *(to the NW grotta di Eolo)*. ▶ The crater of the volcano *(3 hrs climb, must have authorized guide)*, at 2,460 ft, is filled with molten lava in active periods that erupts on the slope of the **Sciara del Fuoco★**. The best view of this is from the observatory at the **Punta Labronzo**. The sight, at night, is magnificent. ▶ It is possible to go to Sciara di Fuoco by boat *(c. 25 mn)* and watch the descending molten lava flow into the sea. Special night excursions are available. ▶ **Ginostra** is a tiny village on the NW side of the island that can be reached from the port of **Pertuso** *(1 hr by boat from Stromboli town)*. ▶ **Strombolicchio** is a needle-like rock of basalt rising (183 ft) out of the sea; a stairway excavated inside allows a climb to a platform and lighthouse at the top *(20 mn by boat from Stromboli town)*.

▶ **Filicudi.** This is a rocky cone rising from the sea that in antiquity was called *Phoenicusa;* its modern name recalls the ferns *(felci)* that grow abundantly on it. It has two ports, **Porto** and **Pecorini**, and a third village, **Val di Chiesa**. At Capo Graziano there is a **prehistoric village** with round cabins from the Bronze Age (18C-13C BC; *see caretaker)*. ▶ A boat excursion around the island reveals a large rock, **La Canna** (232 ft), and the **Bue Marino** cave with marvelous displays of reflected light.

▶ **Alicudi.** This was previously called *Ericusa* because of the heather *(erica)* that covers it. Its houses are dotted along the beach and on the slope of Timpone della Montagnola (2,214 ft). Lobster fishing is the main activity. □

Practical information

🚢 Several regular daily sailings by boat and ferry from Milazzo for Vulcano, Lipari and Salina; 3 weekly for Filicudi and Alicudi; 2 weekly winter and 3 weekly summer from Naples, *Siremar*, Milazzo, ☎ 090/9283242, Naples, ☎ 081/312109, Alicudi, ☎ 090/9812370, Filicudi Porto, ☎ 090/9844194, Lipari, ☎ 090/9812200, Santa Marina Salina, ☎ 090/9843004, Stromboli, ☎ 090/986016, Vulcano, ☎ 090/9852149; *LEM Travel*, Milazzo, ☎ 090/9282073. Hydrofoil: several daily from Milazzo to Vulcano, Lipari and Salina; several daily summer for Panarea and Stromboli, several weekly for Filicudi and Alicudi; from Messina, 2 daily summer for Lipari, Vulcano, Panarea, Stromboli and Salina; from Reggio di Calabria, 2 daily summer for Lipari, Vulcano and Salina; from Naples, daily summer for Stromboli, Panarea, Lipari, Vulcano and Salina; from Palermo, several weekly summer for Lipari and Vulcano, for Milazzo departure, *CO.VE.MAR,* ☎ 9281213 and *Siremar;* for other departures, *SNAV,* Messina, ☎ 090/364044.

FILICUDI, ✉ 98050, ☎ 090.
≋

Recommended
Caving: *grotta del Bue Marino,* boat from Filicudi Porto (*c.* 1 hr), ☎ 9811410.

LIPARI, ✉ 98055, ☎ 090.
≋
ℹ corso Vittorio Emanuele 239, ☎ 9811580; at Marina Corta, ☎ 9811108 (seasonal).

Hotels:
★★★ *Gattopardo Park Hotel,* v. Diana, ☎ 9811035, 53 rm 〰 ⚘ 65,000; bkf: 6,000.
★★★ *Giardino sul Mare,* v. Maddalena 65, ☎ 9811004, 30 rm ≼ 🛥 🖵 closed Nov-19 Mar, 65,000; bkf : 7,000.
★★★ *Rocce Azzurre,* porto delle Genti, ☎ 9811582, 33 rm, closed Nov-Easter, 61,000; bkf: 9,000.
★★ *Augustus,* v. Ausonia 16/18, ☎ 9811232, 32 rm ℗ 〰 ⚘ closed Dec-15 Jan. No restaurant, 49,000; bkf: 6,000.
★★ *Villa Diana,* ☎ 9811403, 13 rm ℗ 〰 closed Nov-Feb, 40,000; bkf: 5,200.

Restaurants:
● ♦♦♦ *Filippino,* p. Municipio ☎ 9811002, closed Mon except summer and Nov-Dec. Country setting with terrace. Seafood: risotto with cuttle-fish, lobster, 25/35,000.
♦ *'E Pulera,* stradale Nuovo, ☎ 9811158, closed noon and Nov-May. Garden; orchestra in evening. Regional cuisine: risotto, roast lamb, 28/38,000.

Recommended
Events: *Eoliana Summer* with theatre, sport and traditional performances.
Marina: ☎ 9811402.
Sport: *Centro Sportivo,* v. Garibaldi 69, ☎ 9811309.

PANAREA, ✉ 98050, ☎ 090.
≋

Hotel:
★★ *Lisca Bianca,* ☎ 9812422, 29 rm ≼ closed Nov-Easter. No restaurant, 48,000.

SALINA, ✉ 98050, ☎ 090.
≋

Hotels:
★★ *Ariana,* at Leni, v. Rotabile 11, ☎ 9842075, 15 rm, closed 16 Oct-Easter, 47,000.
★★ *Punta Scario,* at Malfa, v. Scalo 4, ☎ 9844139, 17 rm ≼ 〰 ⚘ closed Oct-May, 39,000.

Restaurant:
♦ *Marinara,* at Santa Marina Salina, ☎ 9843022. Seafood: pasta con sarde, fish fry, 20/25,000.

Recommended
♥ wine: *Hauner Farm,* at Santa Maria Salina, ☎ 9843141 (Lipari Malmsey wine).

STROMBOLI, ☎ 98050, ☎ 090.
≋

ⓘ at Picogrande, ☎ 986023 (seasonal).

Hotel:
★★★ *Sciara Residence,* v. Cincotta, ☎ 98604, 75 rm ⬩
〰 & ▤ ⌇ closed Oct-Mar, 140,000.

VULCANO, ☎ 98050, ☎ 090.
≋

ⓘ at Porto di Ponente, ☎ 9852028 (seasonal).

Hotels:
★★★ *Archipelago,* at Vulcanello, ☎ 9852002, 80 rm ⬩ ℗
〰 ▤ Pens. Closed Oct-Apr, 75,000.
★★★ *Eolian Hotel,* at Porto di Ponente, ☎ 9852152, 80 rm
℗ ⬩ 〰 Pens. Closed Oct-14 May, 102,000.
★★★ *Garden Vulcano,* at Porto di Ponente, ☎ 9852069,
30 rm ℗ ⬩ 〰 closed 16 Oct-31 Mar, 70,000; bkf: 7,000.

Recommended
Caving: *grotta del Cavallo* (by boat, *c.* 1.5 hrs).

Le MADONIE

From Cefalu to Termini Imerese *(149 km, 1 day; map 4)*

Le Madonie is a part of the mountain chain that runs
along the N coast, from the Straits of Messina to the
mouth of the Torto River, in the Gulf of Termini Imerese. The other two parts are the Peloritani Mountains and Nebrodi. Le Madonie is the most W part
and has the tallest peaks, with Pizzo Carbonara
(6,500 ft), Pizzo Antenna (6,485 ft) and Pizzo Palermo
(6,415 ft). These are the highest mountains on Sicily
after Etna. They tower above the coast, covered in
pine, beech and chestnut, until toward the top, they
flatten out into bare plateaus.

► The itinerary starts at **Cefalu** (→) and, passing olive
groves and forests of beech and chestnut, arrives at the
sanctuary of Gibilmanna where it is possible to see Pizzo
S. Angelo (3,550 ft). ► In the valley of the Castelbuono
stream, the village of **Isnello** lies beneath the ruins of an
old castle, and its churches (chiesa Madre, S. Michele and
Rosario) contain 15C-16C sculpture and paintings. ► **Castelbuono,** in a green hollow at the foot of
Pizzo Carbonara, has a fine **Matrice Vecchia★** church
with 14C-17C frescos and a large polyptych (16C) attributed to Antonello De Saliba. The **chapel of S. Anna★**, in
the **castle** of Ventimiglia *(see caretaker),* has some beautiful stucco decorations, the work of Giuseppe and Giacomo Serpotta (1683). The **Museo Civico F. Mina
Palumbo** has, among much else, a herbarium with samples of the flora of Madonie, and the churches of Matrice
Nuova and S. Francesco have 16C paintings and sculpture. ► The route now leads up to **Rifugio Crispi** on the
Sempria plateau (4,600 ft; *10 km S).* ► Passing **Geraci
Siculo,** the route circles the Madonie and arrives at, on
their S side, **Petralia Soprana,** with a chiesa Matrice
containing a lovely *Crucifixion* by Fra'Umile di Petralia
(17C). From the Baroque church of S. Maria di Loreto
there is a good view★ over the Madonie and Nebrodi
ranges and Etna. ► At **Petralia Sottana** is a chiesa
Matrice with a pretty campanile. It has a 15C portal
and an 11C bronze chandelier of Arab origin. ► **Polizzi
Generosa** has a **Flemish tryptych★** in its chiesa
Madre. ► The route proceeds around Mt. San Salvatore and rises to **piano Battaglia** (5,400 ft), the only
site in Sicily equipped for winter sports, apart from
Etna. ► Now descending, the route arrives at **piano Zucchi,** surrounded by pine and beech near the Rifugio Orestano. ► It continues down the mountain to **Collesano,**
once more on the Tyrrhenian side, beneath Mt. Cucullo
(4,675 ft) and facing the valley of the Roccella
stream. ► The route continues along the valley to the
coast at **Campofelice di Roccella,** a town founded in the
16C (**La Roccella** was the name of an ancient town on the
beach, where there is still a 13C **fort** built over an Arab
one). ► The road follows the sea to **Buonfornello,** from
where there is a drive to the **ruins of Himera.** This city
was founded by Greeks from Zancle (Messina) in 648 BC

4. Le Madonie

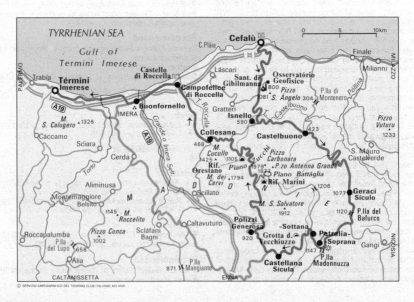

and destroyed by the Carthaginians in 409 BC. The ruins of a **Doric temple** (480 BC) are still visible and finds are exhibited in an **Antiquarium** at the site. ▶ Still following the coast the itinerary ends at **Termini Imerese** (→). □

Practical information _____

GIBILMANNA, ⊠ 90010, ☎ 0921.

Recommended
Farm vacations: *Fattoria Pianetti,* ☎ 21890.

PETRALIA SOTTANA, ⊠ 90027, ☎ 0921.
ℹ v. Carapezza 10, ☎ 41680.

Recommended
Events: *dance of the cordella* (Sep).

PIANO BATTAGLIA, ⊠ 90027, ☎ 0921.
⚡ ski lifts.
ℹ at Petralia Sottana (→).

PIANO ZUCCHI, ⊠ 90010, ☎ 0921.

Hotel:
★★ *Montanina,* corso Vittorio Emanuele 18, ☎ 62030, 42 rm ⬡ P ♻ ⚒ ⚒ 47,500; bkf: 5,000.

Restaurant:
◆◆ *Rifugio Orestano,* ☎ 22637. Near ski lifts. Regional cuisine: pennette with mushrooms, roast veal, 20/25,000.

POLIZZI GENEROSA, ⊠ 90028, ☎ 0921.
ℹ v. Carlo V, ☎ 49932.

MARSALA

Trapani 30, Palermo 124, Rome 1,031 km
Pop. 79,877 ⊠ 91025 ☎ 0923   A3

Marsala was originally a Carthaginian stronghold, founded in 397 BC. It resisted many attacks, but eventually fell to the Romans in 241 BC after a siege lasting 10 years. When the Saracens occupied Sicily, they developed and rebuilt Marsala, turning it into an important port. They also changed its name. Until then it had been *Lilybeum,* it now became *Marsa Ali* (*Marsa* in Arabic means port and *Ali* is the son-in-law of the Prophet). There are salt mines and marble caves near the city, which, along with agricultural produce and olive oil, also makes a well-known fortified dessert wine. It was at Marsala that Garibaldi landed with his 'thousand' in 1860, liberating Sicily and eventually the whole peninsula during the Italian War of Independence.

▶ In the city centre of p. della Repubblica is the 18C **Loggia** or Palazzo Comunale and the Baroque **chiesa Madre** with 16C marble sculptures of the school of A. Gagini. A **museum** *(9 a.m.-1 p.m. and 4-6 p.m.; closed Mon)* at the back of the church displays some magnificent **Flemish tapestries★** depicting the war of the Emperor Titus in Judaea, the gift of Phillip II of Spain. ▶ The convent of **S. Pietro** has a tower with tiled gables and a tiled gallery; the interior of its church is sumptuous. The **Pinacoteca civica** *(9 a.m.-1 p.m. and 4-6:30 p.m.; Sun 9 a.m.-1 p.m.)* has more than 500 works by modern artists and a **Garibaldi Museum.** ▶ From the small church of **S. Giovanni** it is possible to visit a grotto *(caretaker,* ☎ 959751) — perhaps an early Christian baptistery — originally this was the place of residence of a Sibyl who uttered her prophesies gazing in the waters of the well. ▶ The **Museo di Capo Lilibeo** *(9 a.m.-1 p.m. and 4:30-6:30 p.m.)* houses the remains and a rebuilt model of an ancient *liburna,* a Phoenician war ship of the 3C BC. ▶ The **insula romana★** *(9 a.m.-12 noon and 2 p.m.-1 hr before sunset, see caretaker)* contains excavated 3C ruins, among which are small baths with coloured mosaic floors. □

Practical information _____

ℹ v. Garibaldi 45, ☎ 958097.
🚢 daily hydrofoil departures for Trapani and Pantelleria, *Traghetti delle Isole* (Island Car Ferries), ☎ 22467; sailings for the Aegadean Islands, ☎ 959060.

Hotels:
★★★ *Cap 3,000,* v. Trapani 161, ☎ 989055, 50 rm P ⬡ ⌂ 64,000; bkf: 3,500.
★★★ *MotelAgip,* v. Mazara 14, ☎ 999166, 41 rm P ⚒ 58,000.
★★★ *President,* v. Bixio 1, ☎ 999333, 68 rm ⚒ ⬡ 76,500; bkf: 7,000.
★★★ *Stella d'Italia,* v. Rapisardi 7, ☎ 953003, 51 rm P 57,000.

Restaurant:
◆◆◆ *Zio Ciccio,* lungomare Mediterraneo 211, ☎ 981962, closed Mon except summer. Windows opening on to sea. Regional cuisine: spaghetti with lobster, grilled fish, 30/35,000.

Recommended
Wines: *Mediterranean Wines Fair* (permanent wine exhibition, May-Sep), ☎ 999445; visit *Florio* wine establishment, v. Florio 1, ☎ 999222.

MAZARA DEL VALLO

Trapani 52, Palermo 127, Rome 1,034 km
Pop. 45,747 ⊠ 91026 ☎ 0923   A-B4

Mazara del Vallo has one of the busiest fishing ports on the island. In the picturesque centre of the city, the **p. della Repubblica** is dominated by the 17C **Seminario, Palazzo Vescovile** and the cathedral. Among the **Cathedral's** many sculptures is a grandiose group representing *Christ's Transfiguration* by Antonino Gagini (1537). The nearby church of **S. Caterina** was designed by Antonello Gagini (1524), a relative of Antonino. The **public gardens,** on the coast, go as far as the busy **canal port** in the estuary of the Mazaro River. The **Museo Civico** *(8 a.m.-2 p.m.; Tue and Fri also 3:30-6:30 p.m.; closed Sun)* in the 16C **Palazzo dei Cavalieri di Malta** has archaeological material from the Roman period and an important collection of paintings. **S. Nicolo Regale★** is a small Norman church built to a 12C square plan; in a basement in front of the church is a late Roman mosaic floor *(Sun 10 a.m.-1 p.m.: contact tourist office).* In the **old section of the city** the 16C church of **S. Michele,** the church of **S. Veneranda** and the **Casa Scuderi** are interesting. □

Practical information _____

ℹ p. della Repubblica, ☎ 941727.

Hotel:
★★★ *Hopps,* v. Hopps 29, ☎ 946133, 240 rm P ⚒ ⬡ ⌂ 63,000; bkf: 6,000.

Restaurant:
◆◆ *La Bettola,* corso Diaz 20, ☎ 946203, closed Mon except Jul-Aug. Regional cuisine: orecchiette, involtini alla siciliana, 20/30,000.

Recommended
Cycling: A.C. Mazara, v. Val di Mazara 82, ☎ 947534.
Events: *Festival of St. Vitus* (last Sun in Aug).

The ruins of MEGARA HYBLAEA

Syracuse 20, Palermo 249, Rome 803 km
                                                F5

This ancient Greek colony was situated on a plain by the sea, near the Gulf of Augusta on the Ionian side of the island. Archaeologists have found and excavated the ruins of the central part of the city, including the **agora**, the **temples**, the **sanctuaries**, the **baths** and the 3C BC fortifications. Some material is on display in the small **Antiquarium**. □

MESSINA*

Palermo 240, Rome 672, Milan 1,247 km
Pop. 263,294 ⊠ 98100 ☎ 090   F2

In the piazza del Duomo at noon, everyone looks at the campanile where there is a colossal Strasburg astronomical clock (1933) with automated figures. These represent the days of the week, the four ages of man and Biblical scenes. The lion was once Messina's emblem, thus one comes to life and roars every noon. At the same time the hour is sounded by two feminine figures, representing Dina and Clarenza, heroines who, during the popular revolution known as the Sicilian Vespers (1282), saved the city from the French by raising the alarm at night. The clock is huge (diameter 16.5 ft) with a mechanism with 35 revolving wheels. On 28 December 1908 an earthquake lasting 30 seconds, followed by a tidal wave 20 ft high, destroyed 91 percent of Messina and killed 60,000 of its inhabitants. Nothing was left of the old buildings dating back, in some cases, to Zancle (8C BC) or to the Roman Messina that Cicero called a *civitas maxima et locupletissima* (a huge and rich city). Today Messina is a modern city, with wide streets and low houses, planned to resist further earthquakes. It is the port of entry to Sicily from the Italian peninsula and the main concern of its inhabitants seems to be about when a bridge will be built over the straits.

▶ The city's main thoroughfare is the v. Garibaldi. The **piazza Unita d'Italia** (B2-3) is a square with a **Fountain of Neptune★** (1557), the work of the Florentine Montorsoli. Beyond is a height that offers a magnificent view of the other side of the straits — the Aspromonte and the town of Villa San Giovanni, in Calabria. ▶ In the gardens of the nearby **Villa Mazzini**, the **Acquario Comunale** *(Tue, Thu, Sat and Sun 9 a.m.-1:30 p.m.)* has displays of fish from the straits and the Mediterranean. ▶ The **Orion Fountain★**, also by a Montorsoli, is in p. del Duomo (C2). ▶ The **Duomo** (C2) is a careful copy of the old one that was destroyed in the earthquake. The lower part of the façade, with mosaic ornamentation and reliefs, is the oldest; the Gothic portals at the front are also old, while those on the side are 15C. Among the works of art inside are a statue of *St. John the Baptist* by Antonello Gagini (1525) and the *De Tabiatis★* by the Sienese Goro di Gregorio (1333). The rich **treasure** *(not on display at present)* has many precious items including a golden coverlet encrusted with precious stones and a silver vessel that is carried in the procession of Corpus Domini. ▶ *Don Giovanni d'Austria*, the winner at the Battle of Lepanto, returned to Messina with his fleet after the defeat of the Turks; his statue stands in the small square near the church of **SS. Annunziata dei Catalani★**. ▶ This was erected during the 12C and a façade was added in the 13C. ▶ The **Museo Zoologico Cambria** (D2; *9 a.m.-12:30 p.m.; telephone before visiting, ☎ 771177)* has interesting collections on insects, reptiles and vertebrates. ▶ The most important museum in the city is the **Museo Regionale★** (on coast road by lighthouse, from A3; *9 a.m.-2 p.m.; Sun 9 a.m.-1 p.m. summer also Tue, Thu and Sat 3-6 p.m. or 4-7 p.m.)*. ▶ Its archaeological section is at present being re-organized; the section on medieval and modern art outlines the city's art history and has many masterpieces. Among these are *Madonna degli Storpi★*, a sculpture by Goro di Gregorio (1333); a **polyptych of S. Gregorio★★**, by Antonello da Messina

Antonello da Messina

Antonello da Messina (1414-79) was Sicily's greatest painter and one of the major Italian artists of the Cinquecento. He was the only Italian to be influenced by the Flemish methods of painting which he learned from the van Eycks, and he introduced their technique into Italy. Antonello left Messina for Naples when very young and he is supposed to have been a pupil there of Colantonio. There is no reason to suppose he visited Flanders because there were Flemish artists in S Italy. His mature style combines Flemish detail with Italian breadth of form. In 1475-6 he was in Venice where he painted the S. Cassiano altarpiece (now known only from copies and fragments in Vienna), in which he was one of the first artists to treat the picture space as a continuation of real space so that the spectator is drawn into the scene. As well as a pioneer in oil technique, he was known as a great portrait painter and his virtuoso style influenced his contemporary Venetian painters. His paintings that survive are scattered around Europe and America. In Sicily three of his works remain: the portrait of a man with an enigmatic smile in the Mandralisca Museum in Cefalù; a polyptych of St. Gregory in the Museo Regionale of Messina and a painting of the Annunciation in the Palazzo Abatellis in Palermo. There is a marvelous self-portrait of Antonello in the National Gallery in London — a picture of a clean-shaven young man, in his early thirties, with a firm, unsmiling mouth and thick eyebrows. He is wearing a coat buttoned up to the neck and a peakless round felt cap. His head is turned slightly to the left, and the black eyes look straight at the viewer.

(1473); *Presentation of Christ in the Temple* and the *Universal Judgment*, by Girolamo Aliprandi (1519); *Scilla★*, the original from the fountain of Neptune, by Montorsoli and *Adoration of the Shepherds* and *Resurrection of Lazarus*, by Caravaggio, which he did while in Messina between 1608-9. ▶ The boulevards known as the **Circonvallazione a monte** encircle a hill W of the city; there are magnificent views here, especially from viale Principe Umberto (B-C1-2); this avenue passes the **tempio votivo di Cristo Re** (B-C2), the **sanctuary of Montalto** (C1-2) and the **botanical gardens** (C1).

Environs

▶ The road along the sea (from A3) to the Peloritan Mountains leads to **Ganzirri** *(10 km)*, a fishing village near Lake **Pantano Grande**; to **Granatari** *(12.5 km)*, near **Pantano Piccolo**, where, dividing, it goes either to **Lido Mortelle** *(14 km)* or to the **Cape Peloro lighthouse**. ▶ Encircling the Peloritan Mountains *(55 km)*, the road arrives at **Scala**, where a path goes *(20 mn)* to the ruins of the church of **S. Maria della Scala** (13C). The road then leads, offering splendid views★ to the watershed of **Portella San Rizzo**. From here there is a scenic route over the ridge to the **sanctuary of Dinamare**, with a view★ of Mount Antennamare (3,675 ft); the descent, with views over Milazzo and the Lipari Islands, goes to **Ponte Gallo** where, joining the coast road, it arrives at Lido Mortelle. □

Practical information

MESSINA
ℹ️ p. Republica (D3), ☎ 7770731; v. Calabria (D3, head office), ☎ 775356; p. Cairoli 45 (D2), ☎ 2933541.
🚂 (D3), ☎ 775234.
🚌 *AST*, from v. S.M. Alemanna (D2), ☎ 2937548; *SAIS*, p. della Repubblica (D1), ☎ 771914.
⛴ continuous car and cycle ferries for Villa San Giovanni and Reggio di Calabria: *state railways*, ☎ 773811;

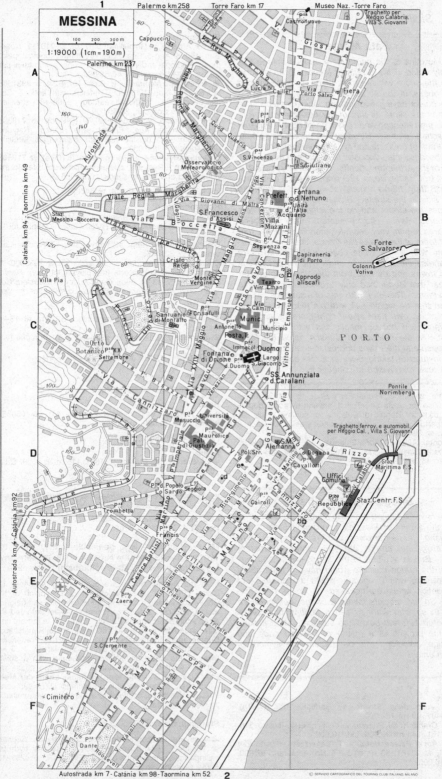

MESSINA

0 100 200 300 m

1:19000 (1cm = 190 m)

Palermo km 237

Cappuccini

PORTO

Forte
S. Salvatore

Colonna
Votiva

Pontile
Norimberga

© SERVIZIO CARTOGRAFICO DEL TOURING CLUB ITALIANO, MILANO

Fata Morgana

Fata Morgana *is the name for a curious mirage frequently noted in the Straits of Messina. An observer on the shore will see men, ships, streets, palaces and houses, in the air or the sea, or sometimes the same object having two images, one inverted. The cause is the same as that of the desert mirage; it is due to the reflection and refraction of light in unusual atmospheric states. However, the people living near the Straits of Messina call the phenomenon Fata Morgana because it is supposed to be caused by the fairy (fata) of the Arthurian legends. A local story tells that Roger I of Hauteville, a 12C Norman king, after subduing S Italy, found himself facing Messina from the other side of the straits. Sicilian refugees urged him to cross the straits and rid the island of its Moslem occupants. While he hesitated, Fata Morgana appeared to him, very beautiful, standing with her feet in the foam of the waves like Venus, and she presented him with a fine white coach which would carry him across the straits. To show him her power she made towns and palaces from the other side appear so near that Roger had only to put out his hand to touch them. The king, who was of a cautious nature, replied that he would sail with his men for Sicily in ships of his own fleet at the right moment, and that he would win not by magic, but with the help of Christ. At the mention of Christ's name the fairy, the coach and the towns and palaces all disappeared and, instead of taking Sicily in a few days, the Normans took thirty years to conquer it.*

Caronte, ☎ 44982; *Tourist Ferry Boat,* ☎ 41415 (departures also for Malta and Tunis); several hydrofoil departures daily for Reggio di Calabria, in summer, daily for the Lipari Islands, in summer, several weekly for Naples: *SNAV,* ☎ 364044.
Car rental: *Avis,* v. Vittorio Emanuele 35, ☎ 58404; *Hertz,* v. Vittorio Emanuele 113, ☎ 363740; *Maggiore,* v. Cannizzaro 46, ☎ 775476.

Bridge over the Straits

There have been long-standing plans to build a bridge over the Straits of Messina, connecting Sicily to the mainland. At its narrowest point (the village of Torre di Faro), the straits are only three kilometers wide. But, in addition to the strong winds and currents, the bridge builders would have to think about the tremors which regularly shake the ground, not to mention actual earthquakes. A bridge or a tunnel? So far, officials favour a bridge, but there are also those who want to see a floating tube-tunnel anchored 120 feet below the surface. Most Italians see the project as a matter of national pride and prestige. Wouldn't this be the ultimate symbol of Italian unity?

Hotels:
★★★ *Jolly dello Stretto,* v. Garibaldi 126 (C2-3a), ☎ 43401, 99 rm 122,000.
★★★ *Grand Hotel Riviera,* v. della Libertà, isolato 516, ☎ 57101, 144 rm 90,000; bkf: 10,000.
★★★ *Royal Palace Hotel,* v. T. Cannizzaro, isolato 224 (E3-b), ☎ 21161, 83 rm P & ⍥ No restaurant, 97,000; bkf: 10,000.

Restaurants:
♦♦♦♦ *Alberto,* v. Ghibellina 95 (D2d), ☎ 710711, closed Sun and 5 Aug-5 Sep. Deluxe interior, original paintings. Regional and international cuisine: spaghetti al cartoccio, grilled swordfish, 40/55,000.
● ♦♦♦ *Pippo Nunnari,* v. U. Bassi 157 (E2f), ☎ 2931568, closed Thu and 1-15 Jul. Refined with antique Sicilian decoration. Regional seafood: risotto with shellfish, small lobsters on spit, 28/40,000.
♦♦♦ *Agostino,* v. Maddalena 70 (D-E2c), ☎ 718396, closed Mon and Aug. English style, refined. Regional and international cuisine: rice with strawberries, fettucine with salmon, 40/60,000.
♦ *Donna Giovanna,* v. Risorgimento 16 (D2e), ☎ 718503, closed Sun. Regional cuisine: maccheroni alla Norma, babbalucci and tomato sauce, 20/28,000.

⚠ ★ *Il Peloritano,* at Rodia, ☎ 848021.

Recommended
Aquarium: *Acquario Comunale,* Villa Mazzini (B2).
Archery: *Compagnia Arcieri Toxon Club,* v. Cappuccini 13, ☎ 40022.
Clay pigeon shooting: at Torre Faro, v. Vecchia Lanterna 2, ☎ 321486.
Cycling: *G.S. Boncoddo,* v. S. Cecilia 28, ☎ 2938000.
Events: seasonal concerts and plays (Oct-May); *Parade of the Giants* (13-14 Aug); *Good Friday Procession; Corpus Christi Procession of the Vascelluzzo and of the Vara* (15 Aug).
Fairs: trade fair (Aug), ☎ 364011.
Sailing: *Vela Mare,* at Ponterchiano, SS 114 at 13-km marker.
Swimming: v. Salandra, ☎ 2924480; v. C. Pompea (villa Pace), ☎ 393182.
♥ *botanical gardens:* v. P. Castelli 2 (C1).

Environs

CONTEMPLAZIONE, ⊠ 98010, 6 km N.

Hotel:
★★★ *Paradis,* v. Consolare Pompea 441, ☎ 650682, 92 rm P ⍥ 70,000; bkf: 6,000.

PISTUNIA, ⊠ 98013, 6 km S.

Hotel:
★★★ *Europa,* SS 114, ☎ 2711601, 115 rm P ⌕ ⍥ ⌂ ⌙ 76,000; bkf: 8,600.

MILAZZO

Messina 41, Palermo 209, Rome 713 km
Pop. 31,497 ⊠ 98057 ☎ 090   F2

Milazzo lies on a long **peninsula** that juts into the Tyrrhenian Sea from the N coast. The **modern** town faces the sea by the **Marina Garibaldi** promenade.

▶ In the **Duomo Nuovo** are paintings by Antonello De Saliba (16C). ▶ The **municipio** has a tryptych of the Gagini school and souvenirs of the Garibaldi campaign (it ended, in Sicily, at Milazzo where Garibaldi defeated the Neapolitan Bourbons on 20 July 1860). ▶ In the **old** city, surrounded by a **Spanish 16C wall**, are a Renaissance **Duomo** and a formidable **castle**, enlarged by Frederick II in the 13C and completed by the Spaniards. ▶ 6 km away is the Capo di Milazzo **lighthouse** with a splendid view★ of the Lipari Islands, the Sicilian coast and Etna. 12 km S is the town of **Santa Lucia del Mela,** which has some interesting buildings (17C cathedral, Palazzo Vescovile, castle) and a Seminario with valuable articles in its library.   ☐

Practical information _____

🚢 several departures daily for Lipari Islands: *Siremar,* ☎ 9283242; *LEM Travel,* ☎ 9284091; several hydrofoil sailings for Lipari Islands daily: *CO.VE.MAR,* ☎ 9281213; *SNAV* Messina, ☎ 364044.

Hotels:
★★★ *Eolian Inn Park Hotel,* v. Cappuccini, ☎ 9286133, 250 rm P ⫤ ⚲ ♨ ⊠ ⤳ closed 16 Nov-14 Mar, 87,000; bkf: 13,000.
★★★ *Residenzial,* p. Nastasi, ☎ 9283292, 69 rm P ⌁ closed Nov-Mar, 70,000; bkf: 5,000.
★★★ *Silvanetta Palace Hotel,* v. Nazionale, ☎ 9281633, 110 rm P ♨ ⌁ ⊠ ⤳ 65,000; bkf: 8,000.
★★ *Mignon Riviera,* v. Tono 68, ☎ 9283150, 10 rm P ♨ ⌁ closed 16 Nov-14 Mar, 37,000; bkf: 3,000.

Restaurant:
◆◆◆ *Al Covo del Pirata,* v. Marina Garibaldi, ☎ 9284437, closed Wed. Faces the sea. Regional cuisine: fettuccine alla brasaiola, meat on spit, 22/32,000.

⚿ ★★ *Sayonara,* at Gronda, 250 pl, ☎ 9283647.

Recommended
Marina: ☎ 9281110.

MODICA

Ragusa 15, Palermo 282, Rome 883 km
Pop. 48, 542 ⊠ 97015 ☎ 0932   E5

Ancient Motyka was built on the slopes of a hill and today it still may be divided into upper Modica, on top of the hill, and lower Modica, at its base. The town produces nuts and oil.

▶ In **lower Modica**, the **Carmelite church** has a 15C Gothic portal and an *Annunciation* by Antonello Gagini. ▶ The **S. Maria di Betlem** church has an unusual chapel and the 17C church of **S. Pietro** has an imposing façade. ▶ The **Museo Civico** *(8 a.m.-2 p.m.; closed Sun)* in a former convent houses palaeolithic, neolithic, Greek and early Christian material, as well as fossils and 18C-19C paintings. In an annex is the **Museo Ibleo di arti e tradizioni popolari** which contains farm and artisan implements. ▶ The 17C church of **S. Giorgio★**, the pride of **upper Modica** is at the top of 250 steps. It has an elegant campanile. ▶ 11.6 km S is **Scicli**, with some fine 18C houses and Baroque churches; 5 km farther is the **santuario of S. Maria delle Milizie.**   ☐

Practical information ⎯⎯⎯⎯⎯⎯

Hotel:
★★★ *Motel di Modica,* corso Umberto, ☎ 941022, 40 rm P 38,000; bkf: 4,000.

Recommended
Cycling: *G.S. della Contea di Modica,* v. Regina Margherita 13, ☎ 946251.
Tennis: SS 115 at 338-km marker, ☎ 904013.

MONREALE*

Palermo 8, Rome 915 km
Pop. 24, 492 ⊠ 90046 ☎ 091   B2

Goethe praised the road that leads from Palermo to Monreale. 'It is', he wrote in *Travels in Italy,* 'a wide road, lined with trees, sloping gently, full of fountains, some with jets, others flowing, but all beautifully decorated with ornaments and friezes'. It was also on this road that the Sicilian Vespers broke out.

▶ Monreale's **cathedral★★** is one of the most magnificent ever built. It remains in its original state. Its façade stands between two towers (one incomplete); the knockers on the bronze door of the portal in the 17C porch are by Bonanno Pisano (1186); on the l. side of the church, under a 15C porch by Gagini, there is another portal with a bronze door by Barisano da Trani (1179). Inside *(7 a.m.-12.30 p.m. and 3-6.30 p.m.),* the cathedral seems to sparkle with the gold of its mosaics; in the sanctuary Arab stalactites descend from the ceiling and the walls, where the mosaics end, are cov-

ered in marble. The **mosaic work** is 12C-13C and depicts events from both the Old and New Testaments. Of interest, too, are the sarcophagi of William I and William II, the 15C chapel of St. Benedict and a 16C Crucifixion. It is possible to view the **Treasure** *(9 a.m.-12.30 p.m. and 3-6 p.m.).* There is a splendid **view★** from the steps in front of the church *(180 steps).* ▶ The **cloister★★** *(winter 9 a.m.-2.30 p.m.; summer 9 a.m.-12.30 p.m. and 4-7 p.m.; Sun 9 a.m.-12.30 p.m.; closed Mon)* was built at the same time as the cathedral; it is surrounded by a portico with narrow arches and a double line of pilasters. In one corner is a fountain. ▶ At **San Cipirello** archaeologists have unearthed the remains of the ancient town of *Ietum* (4C BC), destroyed in the 13C. Some colossal statues have been found near the theatre; they have been placed in the **Museo Civico** *(9 a.m.-12 noon and 4-6 p.m.; Sun 9 a.m.-12 noon; closed Mon).*   ☐

Practical information ⎯⎯⎯⎯⎯⎯

Hotel:
★★★ *Carrubella Park Hotel,* corso Umberto I, ☎ 413187, 30 rm ⚲ P ⫤ 53,000; bkf: 6,000.

Restaurant:
● ◆◆ *La Botte,* SS 186, ☎ 414051, closed Mon and Aug-Sep. Fine veranda for open-air dining in summer. Regional cuisine: gnocchi bava, involtini, 23/28,000.

NICOSIA

Enna 48, Palermo 150, Rome 867 km
Pop. 15,592 ⊠ 94014 ☎ 0935   D3

Nicosia is built on rocky hills nearly 3,000 ft above sea level; during the Norman period, the city was populated with immigrants from Lombardy and Piedmont and to this day the local dialect preserves some Gallic and Italic forms. There are tombs of Crusaders in the region and salt mines and sulphur springs nearby.

▶ The **14C cathedral** has a splendid façade, a Gothic portal with rosette and a fine **campanile.** Inside are many wonderful works of art, including a *Crucifixion* by Fra' Umile di Petralfa (17C). ▶ In the church of **S. Maria Maggiore** are a polyptych by Antonello Gagini (1512) and the throne of Charles V on which he was supposed to have sat when he visited the town in 1535. ▶ 10 km NW is **Sperlinga,** a typical Sicilian village. It has some troglodyte houses. During the Sicilian Vespers the townspeople did not massacre the French, but allowed them to take refuge in the castle and it is still possible to see on its walls the Latin inscription 'Quod Siculis placuit, sola Sperlinga negavit', which means 'Only Sperlinga refused to do what the rest of Sicily did'.   ☐

Practical information ⎯⎯⎯⎯⎯⎯

Hotel:
★★★ *Pineta,* at San Paolo, ☎ 47002, 48 rm P ⫤ 45,000; bkf: 5,000.

NOTO*

Syracuse 32, Palermo 299, Rome 858 km
Pop. 22,844 ⊠ 96017 ☎ 0931   E5

On 11 January 1693 an earthquake practically destroyed SE Sicily. Completely razed were: Catania, Lentini, Augusta, Syracuse, Noto, Ragusa and about 60 smaller localities. One direct consequence was that the Baroque style played the dominant part in the rebuilding.

▶ Noto's main street **corso Vittorio Emanuele★** (B-C1-3). It widens into three piazzas from where steps rise into the higher parts of town. ▶ Along the corso, starting at the porta Nazionale, is **piazza Immacolata** (C3) from

NOTO

0   75   150 m
1 : 13 000 (1cm = 130 m)

Noto Antica km 16

Ragusa km 53   Siracusa km 32   Staz. F.S. km 1.3   Siracusa km 32

where steps lead to the **chiesa dell'Immacolata** and the **convento del SS. Salvatore.** ▶ In this last is the **Museo Civico** *(9 a.m.-1 p.m.)*, which has archaeological sections with material from prehistoric, Greek (small statuettes of Demeter and Kore from the ruins of a temple) and medieval periods (material from the Norman abbey of S. Lucia del Mendolo and the ruins of ancient Noto), as well as a modern section in a room of the nearby former monastery of S. Chiara. ▶ Next is **piazza del Municipio** (C2) with the elegant **Palazzo Ducezio★** (v. Sinatra, 18C) and the steps that lead to the **Duomo** (B2), with a grandiose 17C façade and the silver urn of its patron saint, S. Corrado Confalonieri. ▶ Near the Duomo, other major buildings are the **Palazzo Vescovile** and the **Palazzo dei Principi di Villadorata.** ▶ Continuing along the corso, after the **chiesa del Collegio** (attributed to R. Gagliardi), is **Piazza XXIV Maggio** (B2), containing the church of **S. Domenico** by R. Gagliardi and a former Dominican convent. ▶ Parallel to the corso, higher up the hill, the **via Cavour** (B2-3) also a many 18C palaces, churches and convents. ▶ In the upper part of town, the Baroque church of the **Crucifixion** (B2) has a *Madonna and Child* by Francesco Laurana (1471). 21 km S, the town of **Pachino** and the seaside resorts of **Marzamemi** and **Portopalo** are on the extreme SW tip of Sicily.   □

Practical information _____

Restaurant:
♦ *Trieste*, v. Napoli 17/21 (C3 a), ☎ 835495, closed Mon and 5-20 Sep. Regional cuisine: lobster, veal escalope with peas, 15/20,000.

NOTO VALLEY, IBLEI MOUNTAINS

From Syracuse to Noto *(216 km, 1 day; map 6)*

Sicily was divided into three parts during the Arab occupation, each called a valley, their borders meeting at Mt. Altesina (3,900 ft). They were the Mazara Valley to the W, the Demone Valley to the NE and the Noto Valley. The Iblei plateau is occupied mostly by the Noto Valley, between the wide plain of Catania and the smaller one of Gela. Mt. Lauro (3,235 ft) stands at its centre, its volcanic slopes scarred by riverbeds, and cliffs often pierced by prehistoric burial caves. The vegetation is sometimes scrub with brushwood, sometimes forests with myrtle, mastic, arbutus, laurel, pine, juniper and carob. The landscape is sometimes rough, sometimes gentle, the horizons always wide and distant.

▶ Leaving **Syracuse** (→) and going S among the citrus groves and the olive trees, the itinerary passes the Anapo and Ciane Rivers. ▶ **Cassibile** is where, on 3 September 1943, an armistice was signed between the Allies and Italy. ▶ **Avola** was built after the 1693 earthquake to a hexagonal plan, with five piazzas set out like a cross, to replace **Avola Vecchia,** the ruins of which are 8.5 km N. ▶ From **Noto** (→) the route heads for the sea and arrives at **Noto Marina** with a beach that extends as far as the site of the old Greek city of **Eloro.** Here it is possible to see a considerable part of the old 6C-5C BC fortifications, a **sanctuary** dedicated to Demeter with a temple and a roofed colonnade and a monument called **la Pizzuta**

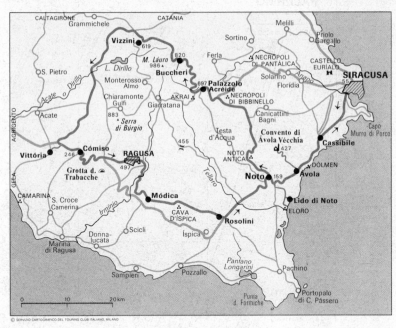

6. Noto Valley, Iblei Mountains

that stands over an ancient burial ground. ▶ Returning to Noto the route goes on to the ruins of **Noto Antica,** also abandoned after the earthquake of 1693. It is still possible to see the shattered walls and the ruins of porta Reale and of the castle. ▶ The **Palazzolo Acreide** (→) and the ruins of the Greek Acrai are also interesting. The route now enters the heart of the Iblei Mountains. ▶ **Buccheri** (2,700 ft) is renowned for its clear air and fresh waters; **Vizzini** (2,030 ft) is a picturesque village on a rocky spur, where Giovanni Verga, the Sicilian novelist, placed the story of *Mastro Don Gesualdo.* It is said that this village was the site of Verga's famous short story *Cavalleria Rusticana,* from which Mascagni composed his opera. ▶ The route travels along the plateau toward its S side, passing the cities of **Vittoria** (→), **Comiso** (→), **Ragusa** (→) and **Modica** (→). ▶ The **Cava d'Ispica** is a deep gully cut from the limestone; it is narrow and primitive and has been inhabited from prehistoric times. It has early burial grounds, troglodyte dwellings, Christian catacombs and Byzantine cliff chapels *(accompanied by guide; inquire at houses near beginning of gorge by bridge over main road).* Interesting are the **cave of S. Nicola,** with traces of Byzantine frescos, the **catacomb of the Larderia,** the cliff sanctuary of **Grotta di S. Maria, u campusantu,** a Christian burial ground, **urutti caruti,** or troglodyte grottos, the grottos **a-bbizzaria** and **urutti Giardina** and the **Castello.** The route ends at Noto. □

Practical information _____

FONTANE BIANCHE ✉ 96010, ☎ 0931, 4 km SE of Cassibile.

Hotel:
★★★ *Fontane Bianche,* v. Mazzaro 1, ☎ 790611, 170 rm Ⓟ ✗ ◢ 60,000; bkf: 5,000.

Restaurant:
♦ *Spiaggetta,* v. dei Lidi 473, ☎ 790334, closed Tue in winter and 1-26 Nov. Seafood: risotto alla pescatora, grilled fish, 18/25,000.

⅄ ★★ *Fontane Bianche,* ☎ 790333.

Recommended
Farm vacations: *Azienda Rinaura,* ☎ 721224.

ROSOLINI, ✉ 96019, ☎ 0931, 12 km E.

Hotel:
★★ *Villa Marina,* v. Granati Nuovi 1, ☎ 856246, 38 rm Ⓟ ◢ 32,000.

PALAZZOLO ACREIDE*

Syracuse 43, Palermo 263, Rome 869 km
Pop. 10,003 ✉ 96010 ☎ 0931   E5

Palazzo Acreide had to be almost entirely rebuilt after the earthquake of 1693 and its architecture is mostly 18C Baroque. The **Church of the Immaculate Conception** *(to visit contact college behind church)* has a *Madonna with Child*★ by Francesco Laurana (15C). Churches of particular interest are **S. Paolo, l'Annunziata** and, in p. del Popolo, **S. Sebastiano.**

▶ Valuable finds from the city's surroundings which were formerly displayed in the **Palazzo Iudica** have been removed for cataloging and will soon be housed elsewhere. Also closed for re-organization is the **Casa-Museo di Antonino Uccello;** it has interesting material on Sicilian customs and traditions. The most interesting visit is the **archaeological area** of the ancient city of Akrai. This town was founded by people from Syracuse in 664 BC and razed by the Moors *(9 a.m.-sunset;*

PALERMO

1:15 000   (1 cm = 150 m)

0   100   200   300 m

Autostrada km 12

A

Via L. Ariosto
Via E. Notarbartolo
Via Roma
Via Duca d. Verdura
P.za Gentile
Ass. Reg. d. Turismo
Staz. Notarbartolo F.S.
Via L. Da Vinci
Via O. Costantino
Giardino Inglese
Villa Gallidoro
Villa Gonzaga
Villa Bordonaro
Via della Libertà
Villa d. Giardino
Via P. Crispi
Via d. Croci

B

Via Malaspina
Terrasanta
P.za D. Siculo
P.za Busacca
Via G. Aurispa
Via Gen. Cantore
Via C. Cusmano
Via Siracusa
Villa Trabia
Via Carini
P.za Mordini
F. Crispi
Alitalia
Via Mazzini
Via P. Nasce
Via XX Settembre
Via O. Sella
Via Archimede
Via R. Carbi
Via della Libertà

C

Villa Malfitano
Via Serradifalco
Via Parlatore
Via Dante
Viale A. Veneziano
P.za Virgilio
Via Marconi
Via Dante
Via Dante
V. Latini
Via P. Palermostro
P.za di Giosta
S. Oliva
Amendola
S. Francesco di Paola
S. Francesco di Paola
Via Stabile
P.za Ungheria
Quattro C. di Campo
Galleria Arte Moderna
Politeama
P.za Ruggero Settimo
Castelnuovo
Via Libertà
g

D

P.za Principe di Camporeale
Via Whitaker
Via Margherita
Via Bagnera
Corso Finocchiaro Aprile
Via Re Federico
Via Cluverio
Via Goethe
Villa Filippina
P.za N. Turrisi
P.za Vitt. Eman. Orlando
P.za Carini
Pal. di Giustizia
Via A. Volturno
Via Pignatelli Aragona
Teatro Massimo
P.za Ver.
P.za d. Stigma

E

Zisa
P.za V. Cantù
Via Guglielmo il Buono
V. Confessa Giuditta
Via Zisa
Vicolo Zisa
Via C. Lascaris
P.za Amedeo
Via d'Ossuna
P.za Cuccia
Noviziato
Via S. Agostino
P.za Monte di P.
P.za Beati Paoli
P.za Ingastone
Via d'Osuna
Via G. Mosca
Peranni
Via Papireto
Cattedrale
Cattedrale
P.za dei 7 Ang.
P.za d. Cattedrale
Arcivescovile
Museo Diocesano
Pal. Sclafani
Via Vittorio Emanuele
Villa Bonanno

F

Via Cipressi
Via G. Mosca
Convento d. Cappuccini
Piazza Danisinni
Via Colonna Rotta
Nuava
Pal. d. Normanni
(Cappella Palatina)
P.za d. Vittoria
S. Giova.
P.za del Parlamento
Via di Castro.
Corso Ruggero
Via Pindemonte
Via Cappuccini
Via Calatafimi
Corso P. Prisani
P.za d. Pinta d. Castro
Indipendenza
Pal. Orleans (Residenza Regione Siciliana)
Parco d'Orleans
S. Giov. d. Eremiti
V. Benedettini
V. Vanni
P.za Montalto
Cuba

closed Mon). It is still possible to see the auditorium, the orchestra and remains of the stage of its 3C BC **theatre★**; close by is the **council chamber** of the Senate with a tiered circle of seats. Two **stone quarries**, in back of the theatre, were turned into dwelling-places and also used as burial sites in the later Byzantine-Christian epoch. ▶ Outside the excavation area is the **Temple of Aphrodite** and, beyond it, the **agora**. ▶ Another stone quarry is known as the **Templi Ferali** and has many niches that received offerings in memory of dead heroes *(accompanied by caretaker).* The **Santoni★** are some primitive sculptures (3C BC) located in a valley E of the hill, which were made in honour of Cybele, mother of the gods *(accompanied by caretaker).* ▶ A **scenic route** goes around the Acremonte hill. ☐

Practical information ─────────────────

Restaurant:
◆ *La Trota,* at Pianetta, ☎ 875694, closed Mon and Nov. Regional cuisine: tagliatelle alla Laura, trout, 15/20,000.

⚐ *La Torre-Elio Vittorini,* at Torre Judica, ☎ 872322 (all year).

PALERMO**

Rome 908, Milan 1,483 km
Pop. 712,342 ⊠ 90100 ☎ 091   B2

The name Palermo comes from the Greek *Panormos,* meaning 'all port' and in ancient times the port went much farther inland than it does today. The Greeks, however, never held the city, which was founded as a trading post by the Phoenicians in 8C BC. It is located on the N coastal plain of the Conca d'Oro, a bay of the Tyrrhenian Sea. Palermo became a stronghold of the Carthaginians until their defeat in the Punic Wars, when it became Roman, in 254 BC. Thereafter it was occupied by the Vandals (440), Belisarius and the Byzantines (535) and the Arabs (831), who held it for 240 years. This was Palermo's most glorious period — they made it the capital of Sicily and one of their Empire's chief cities and trading centres. 'Whoever visited Palermo in the 10C', writes the modern historian Denis Mack Smith, 'was impressed by the fact that this large city had a population composed of Greeks, Lombards, Jews, Slavs, Berbers, Persians, Tartars and Negroes, as well as Arabs'. Arab contemporary historians were constantly extolling its beauty. One Bagdad merchant writes of hundreds of minarets and mosques, 'more than he had seen even in Cordoba', and mentions a population of 1,300,000 which, even if exaggerated, would make it the largest city in the world for that time after Byzantium (Constantinople). In 1072 the Norman Roger II took Palermo and wrested Sicily from the Moors. Roger got more money from Palermo than his Norman relatives got from England. The Spaniards and the Bourbons came later and turned the city, in the 17C-18C, into a Baroque one; this is now the predominant, architectural face of Palermo, but its Arab-Norman past remains very much in evidence.
▶ The two main thoroughfares of via Cavour and via Volturno (C4-D3) divide the city into two parts with, to the N, by the **port**, the **modern city** with large rectangular buildings separated by wide streets, and, to the S, the **old city,** which was once surrounded by medieval and Spanish walls. Two Spanish viceroys, during development projects, cut two **major arteries** through the old town: the Duke of Toledo, in 1565-66, built the **via Vittorio Emmanuele** which runs from the marina (D5) to the Palazzo dei

Normanni (F3). The Marquis de Maqueda in 1598-1601 laid out the **via Maqueda** (F5-D4), which runs perpendicular to the first street and bisects it as it runs toward the sea. ▶ The two streets, which cross each other at p. Vigliena or **Quattro Canti★** (E4), once the city centre, divide the old town into **four sections,** all roughly the same size. All monuments and places of interest are therefore listed in accordance with these four sections, followed by those in the new city and the environs. The starting point is p. Quattro Canti, with elegant Baroque buildings, fountains and statues (1609-20). ▶ The wide and crowded **v. Roma,** running parallel across the town with v. Marqueda, was built later to link the railway station (F5) with the new city.
▶ **NW section of old city.** ▶ The grandiose **cathedral★★** (E3), at the end of a verdant piazza, is a monument that must be considered in detail because its history is complex, with many alterations from the time when it was first erected in 1185 to its rebuilding with a dome by the architect Fuga (1781-1804). The **loggia dell'Incoronata** (12C), l. of the façade (14C-15C), was reconstructed in the 15C. On the r. is a **portal** in a flowery Catalan-Gothic style; the cross-vaulted arches of the **three apses,** between two turrets, retain some of the tendencies of the Norman period. The cathedral's interior is Neoclassical and contains the famous **imperial and royal tombs★** of Henry VI, Frederick II, Constance and Roger II and a **reliquary** in silver (1631) with the relics of S. Rosalia, patron saint of Palermo. The **treasure** *(7 a.m.-12 noon and 4-7 p.m.)* is full of precious objects, including the **golden tiara** of Constance of Aragon, wife of Frederick II. In the sacristy is a *Madonna* by Antonello Gagini (1503), the eldest of this family of Palermo sculptors. A sacristan accompanies visitors to the church's 12C **crypt.** ▶ The **Diocesan Museum** (E3), in the Arch-Episcopal Palace, is open only to students *(inquire of secretarial service).* It contains some eminent 12C works of sacred art, among them a tryptych of the Sicilian school, *Coronation of the Virgin★* (1419), a 16C Venetian school *Head of St. John the Baptist★,* marble tiles from the cathedral's apse, a *Holy Family Flight into Egypt★* and the tombstone of the *Young Cavalier★* by Francesco Laurana, as well as many gold vessels, church vestments and tapestries. ▶ The 16C church of **S. Agostino** (D4) has many decorations by Giacomo Serpotta, the Palermo master of stucco ornamentation (between the Baroque and the rococo). ▶ The **Teatro Massimo** (D3), Palermo's opera house, on the line dividing the old town from the new one, is presently closed for redecoration and the opera season is being held at the Politeama theatre.

─────────────────

The marionettes of Palermo

The marionettes of Palermo are part of a tradition which goes back to the Middle Ages. The figures are almost three feet tall, they wear painted faces, shining armor and helmets, and their swords continuously swing to and fro. They almost always represent the same characters. The story goes something like this: Rinaldo or Orlando must avenge an insult to their honor. Each character raises his arm emphatically as a signal to the audience that he's about to speak (although the characters' comments are practically interchangeable). The marionettes' "handler" uses the same voice as he moves from one character to the other. With the help of a debonnaire Charlemagne surrounded by different creatures (monsters, giants, dragons, witches, fairies, etc.) the paladins always end up defeating their enemies.

─────────────────

▶ **NE section of old city.** ▶ The following churches are on or near v. Vittorio Emanuele: **St. Matthew's** (E4), a Baroque church built in 1663, with marble work and four statues by Serpotta; **St. Anthony's** (D5), with 12C elements (leaving by its l. door leads to **Boccheria vecchia,**

Palermo's oldest market); **S. Maria di Porto Salvo** (D5; *open only Sun*), which was originally Renaissance, but renovated in the 16C in Gothic-Catalan style, and **S. Maria della Catena★** (D5-6), a church poised between the Renaissance and Gothic-Catalan styles. ▶ **S. Domenico** (D4-5), in the piazza of the same name that contains a column to the Immaculate Conception (1727), is a church that was rebuilt in the Baroque style. It houses tombs of some notable Sicilians; it also has sculptures by Antonello Gagini and some of his followers. ▶ From its 13C cloister, on the l. is the **Risorgimento Museum** *(Mon, Wed and Fri 9 a.m.-1 p.m.; contact secretariat of Società Italiana di Storia Patria).* ▶ The **oratory of the Rosary of S. Domenico** (D4-5), in back of the church of the same name *(v. Bambinai 4; contact caretaker at no. 16),* is a marvel of **stucco ornamentation** inside, all elegance and gracefulness, the work of Giacomo Serpotta. It also contains many fine paintings, including some by Luca Giordano, a Neapolitan, and Pietro Novelli, considered the greatest Sicilian painter of the 17C. A *Madonna del Rosario,* on the altar, is by van Dyck. ▶ Other fine stucco decorations by Serpotta are the **Oratory of S. Zita★** (D4; *8 a.m.-12 noon and 4-6 p.m.; caretaker at v. Valverde 3 or at parish church of S. Mamiliano in v. Squarcialupo).* ▶ The church of **S. Giorgio dei Genovesi** (C-D5; *closed for repairs)* was built at the end of the 16C by Genoese businessmen living in Palermo. ▶ The **Museo Archeologico★★** (D4; *9 a.m.-1:30 p.m.; Tue and Thu also 3-6 p.m.; Sun 9 a.m.-1 p.m.*) is in a former 16C convent. Outstanding among its many large collections are **prehistoric Sicilian sculptures★★** from the site at Selinus, including in particular three **metopes★★** (panels) from temple C (6C BC), two **half metopes** from temple F (5C BC) and, best known of all, the four **metopes** from temple E (460-450 BC). There are also rainwater basins in the shape of the head of a lion★ from the temple of Himera (5C BC); the *Ram of Syracuse★,* a Hellenistic work from the 3C BC; *Hercules Overpowering a stag★,* a Roman copy from Pompeii of the original 4C Greek one; a *Satyr Pouring out to drink★,* another Roman copy of an original Greek sculpture; a fragment from the frieze of the Parthenon and an Etruscan collection, with finds from excavations at Chiusi, in Tuscany. ▶ In the same piazza of the museum is the fine Baroque façade of the church **dell'Olivella** (1598), which has interesting statues and paintings. ▶ To the r. of the church stands the Neoclassical oratory of S. Filippo Neri (Venanzio Marvuglia, 1769). ▶ **SW section of old city.** ▶ The rich Baroque church of **S. Giuseppe dei Teatini★** (E4; *closed for restoration),* built in 1612, is topped with a dome and has a marvelous profusion of marble, stucco and frescos inside. ▶ **Il Gesù★** (E4) is typical Sicilian Baroque and excels in marquetry and polychrome marble work. ▶ The church of **S. Antonino** (F5), in the piazza of the same name, has a wooden Crucifixion by Fra' Umile da Petralia (1639). ▶ The **Palazzo Sclafani★** (E3), beside the **Villa Bonanno** and its garden of palms, has a façade with high crossed arches and is a fine example of lay Gothic architecture. ▶ The imposing mass of the **Palace of the Normans★** (F3) is on the other side of the Villa Bonanno; it was originally built by the Arabs and then transformed in the 12C into a royal palace by Roger II. Later, under Frederick II it became a cultural centre renowned throughout Europe. On the second floor, the **Palatine Chapel★★** *(9 a.m.-1 p.m. and 3-5 p.m.; sometimes closes at 10:30 a.m.; Sun 9 a.m.-1 p.m.),* dedicated to St. Peter, is the greatest example of the peculiar, composite architectural style that flourished in Sicily under the Normans. All forms of Mediterranean architecture are assembled in this church, begun by Roger II in 1132 and consecrated in 1140. It is basically Romanesque, but some ancient Roman columns support the pointed arches that divide the chapel into three naves, mosaics cover the floor, and the walls, in their lower parts, are covered with precious marble, while the extraordinary ceiling, in carved wood with cavities and pendants, is Moorish. Byzantium is also present, with the dome and the walls of the apses and the naves covered in marvelous **mosaics★★** that, against a background of gold, depict scenes from the

Bible. Near the high altar is an ambo★ on columns with mosaics and a 12C Easter candelabrum★. In the **royal apartments** *(Mon, Fri and Sat 9 a.m.-12.30 p.m.)* are the **hall of Hercules** (also called the hall of Parliament because the regional assembly meets in it) and the **hall of King Roger★** with mosaics depicting a hunting scene (*c.* 1170). ▶ The Norman church of **S. Giovanni degli Eremiti★★** in a pleasant garden (F3; *9 a.m.-2 p.m.; Sun 8:30 a.m.-12:30 p.m.),* is one of the most picturesque buildings in the city with five small red domes on top of its square mass. It was Roger II who wished it to be like this and it is proof of how strong, at the time, Arab influence was architecturally. In the garden of exotic plants is a beautiful 12C **cloister★** with double columns. ▶ **SE section of old city.** ▶ **Piazza Pretoria** (E4), near p. Quattro Canti, is almost entirely occupied by the monumental **Fontana pretoria★,** covered with statues of monsters, birds and marine divinities; it is the work of the Florentines F. Camilliani and M. Naccherino (1555-75) and was originally intended for a Florentine villa. ▶ In nearby p. Bellini, the church of **St. Catherine,** with marble carvings, reliefs and intarsia work and frescos, is a fine example of Sicilian 18C Baroque. ▶ In front of it, on some elevated ground surrounded by palms are la Martorana and **S. Cataldo★** (E4); this last church is unaltered; its crenellation and three small red domes demonstrate Arab influence, while its bare interior is pure Norman (*c.* 1160). ▶ **La Martorana★** or church of S. Maria dell'Ammiraglio is another glorious monument from the Norman period. It was erected in 1143, partly altered in the 16C-17C when a Baroque façade was added and has an elegant campanile ornamented with slender columns. The interior, originally in the form of a Greek cross (with arms of equal length), was transformed into a Latin one by extending, in the 17C, the church's western side; at the entrance, on the r., is a mosaic depicting King Roger being crowned by Jesus, while on the l., a mosaic shows his faithful Admiral Giorgio of Antioch at the feet of Mary. Inside, the church is resplendent with marvelous mosaics in the purest Byzantine style (12C). ▶ The **oratorio di S. Lorenzo★** (E5; v. Immacolatella 5; *open Sun a.m. or see caretaker)* has stucco work showing scenes from the lives of Saints Lawrence and Francis of Assisi, as well as statues and other ornamentation, all the work of Giacomo Serpotta. Because of the vivacity and maturity of style, the interior of this church is considered his greatest masterpiece. The *Nativity of Jesus★,* a painting by Caravaggio which was on the altar but stolen in 1969, has still not been recovered. ▶ **S. Francesco d'Assisi★** (E5) is a Gothic church with three naves; its two minor ones have a series of Gothic or Renaissance chapels; the arch★ of the fourth chapel on the l. is the work of Francesco Laurana and Pietro de Bonitate (1468). There are eight allegorical statues by Serpotta (1723) in the central nave; also in the apse is a sumptuous 17C chapel of the Immaculate Conception and there are choir stalls in carved wood with the presbytery. ▶ The **Palazzo Mirto,** close at hand (E5; *9 a.m.-1.30 p.m.; Sun 9 a.m.-12:30 p.m.; Wed and Thu also 3-4:30 p.m.; closed Mon),* has 17C decorations, tapestries and fittings.

▶ The **Palazzo Chiaramonte★** (D6) is in the vast p. Marina which also has, in its centre, the **giardino Garibaldi,** with palm trees, giant magnolias and many rare plants. The palazzo, compact and severe, is a fine example of Sicilian medieval architecture; it was at one time seat of the tribunal of the Inquisition. ▶ The **International Marionette Museum** *(D6; Mon, Wed and Fri 10 a.m.-12:30 p.m. and 5-7 p.m.)* has, along with Sicilian puppets, specimens of those used in the Neapolitan theatre and marionettes used in many other countries. ▶ The church of S. Maria degli Angeli, called **La Gancia** (E5-6), was built in the 15C. It has a sober façade with two Gothic portals and inside are two tondi (paintings in circular form) of the *Annunciation★* by Antonello Gagini. ▶ The **Palazzo Abatellis★** (E6), a fine building with features ranging from Gothic Catalan to Renaissance (1495), houses the **Galleria Regionale della Sicilia★** *(9 a.m.-1.30 p.m.; also 3-6 p.m. Tue and Thu; Sun 9 a.m.-1 p.m.; closed Mon),* an

Saint Rosalie in Palermo

*In 1664, during an outbreak of the plague, a man griev-
ing the loss of his 15-year-old wife wandered onto the
slopes of the Monte Pellegrino. At the entrance of a
cave, he suddenly saw a very beautiful woman who
told him to gather the bones buried inside the cave
and give them proper burial. She assured him that
if he did this, the outbreak of the plague would
stop. The prophecy came true and ever since then,
the people of Palermo have honored Saint Rosalie
with all due pomp and circumstance. In the 18C,
fantastic celebrations were devoted to Saint Rosalie. Clothed in magnificent garments, the saint's statue was set in a decor built on a gigantic float in the
form of a Roman ship. On the "ship's" bow sat an
orchestra. The float was pulled by a group of mules
led by superbly dressed lackeys. The team was surrounded by soldiers and preceded by a master of
ceremonies on horseback with a company of dragoons. On the first day, the procession would leave
from the beach and would finally reach the Cassaro
— Corso Vittorio Emmanuel. Fireworks were set off
in front of the royal palace. On the second and third
days, there were horse races. On the fourth day, a
procession led by the viceroy and the nobility would
reach the cathedral which had been transformed into
a palace of light: fragments of mirrors were mixed
with silver and gold paper and lit by thousands of
candles. On the fifth day, the final procession would
move toward the cathedral with a large silver statue
of the saint carried by leading townspeople.*

important gallery with many masterpieces. Among them
are a marvelous *Annunciation*★★ by Antonello da Messina, as well as his painting of *Three Saints*★, also
a beautiful bust of *Eleanor of Aragon*, sculpted by Francesco Laurana (1430-1502), the famous *'Triumph of
Death'*, a 15C fresco that used to be in the Palazzo Sclafani, the *Madonna del Latte*★ by Giovanni di Nicola and a
rare Malaga vase★. ▶ At **Foro Umberto I** (D-E6) is the
sea front and the famous promenade with a view of the
gulf. ▶ Behind the promenade is **piazza della Kalsa** with
the church of **S. Teresa**, a 17C Baroque building designed by G. Amato. The church of **La Magione** (E5) is
remarkable for its sober Norman lines; it was built in 1150
and was part of a Cistercian monastery. ▶ The **Palazzo
Aiutamicristo** (E5), which preserves some parts of its original structure (built by M. Carnelivari, 1490-95), is on
v. Garibaldi, at the end of which is the **Porta di Termini**. This is the gate through which Garibaldi and his
troops entered the city on 27 May 1860, on his way to
uniting Italy in the name of the King of Piedmont.
▶ **The New City and Mount Pellegrino.** ▶ In piazza
Ruggero Settimo, the **Galleria d'Arte Moderna E. Res-
tivo** (C3); *(9 a.m.-1 p.m.; Tue and Thu saw 4:30-7:30 p.m.)*
features the work of 19C and 20C painters and sculptors
from Naples and Sicily, among them Tosi, Severini,
Casorati, Campigli, Carrà, Sironi, Pirandello and Guttuso. ▶ The elegant **viale della Libertà**★, with its many
fine houses and gardens (B3), starts in the piazza in
front of the museum. ▶ The Villa Zito, with the Fondazione Mormino (A2), has an **archaeological museum**
(9 a.m.-1 p.m. and 3-5 p.m.; closed Sat p.m. and Sun) with
collections of Greek ceramics, pottery from ancient Sicilian burial grounds and a numismatic collection from the
time of the Kings of Aragon to those of the Bourbons. ▶ At the foot of Mt. Pellegrino, the magnificent
Parco della Favorita★★ (from A2) was created by the
Bourbon King Ferdinand when the French forced him
out of Naples and he was obliged to come to live in
Sicily. The strange **Palazzina Cinese**, in which the Neoclassical and the Oriental are hybridized, was partly de-

signed by King Ferdinand himself at the beginning of the
19C; it was his favourite residence as it was also of
his wife, Maria Caroline *(because of repairs, only certain
rooms may be visited; contact Museo Pitrè).*
▶ **The Muséo Etnografico Pitrè** is alongside the Palazzina
*(8:30 a.m.-1:30 p.m. and 3-5 p.m.; Sun 9 a.m.-1 p.m.;
closed Friday a.m. and hol).* It displays much material relating to the traditional customs and way of life in Sicily;
among the many objects are a puppet theatre, statues of
shepherds and figurines by G. Matera. ▶ The outline of
Mt. Pellegrino is forever associated with Palermo; it rises
to 2,000 ft and up it *(13 km N)* is the **sanctuary of S. Rosalia**★ (1,400 ft). The saint, daughter of Duke Sinbaldo, retired to a grotto here and died in it, after a life of penitence, in 1166. After miraculously ridding the city of a
plague in 1624, the people of Palermo adopted her as
their patron saint. It is still possible to see the building
where there was a monastery, as well as the grotto-chap-
el, where a miraculous spring of water still erupts; a road
leads to the nearby colossal statue of the saint, overlooking the town, and there is a belvedere with a magnificent view of the city, the coast and the sea.
▶ **The city's southern and western surroundings.** ▶ The beautiful gardens of the **Villa Giulia** or
Flora★, with one side overlooking the sea, were designed in 1777 and are adorned with several lovely fountains. The **Orto Botanico**★ (E-F6) is right beside them;
it is considered one of the finest botanical gardens in
Europe and has specimens of flora from all parts of
the world *(8:30 a.m.-12:30 p.m.; Sat 8:30-11 a.m.; closed
Sun).* In the S part of town is the church of **S. Giovanni
dei Lebbrosi**, which was built in 1070 (corso dei Mille 384;
see caretaker). Next to it are the **ponte dell'Ammiraglio**, a bridge built in 1113, and the **church of S. Spirito**★, in the precincts of the cemetery of S. Orsola
(9-11 a.m.). The church is a square edifice, dating from
the 12C with a splendid interior that has the cross before
which began the anti-Angevin French revolt known as the
Sicilian Vespers on 31 March 1282. Up the slopes of
Mt. Grifone, a road leads to the monastery of S. Maria di
Gesù where, behind the small cemetery, is the church of
S. Maria di Gesù★; the statue of the Virgin, on its N portal, and the S portal itself, are the work of the Gaginis. In
the convent is a belvedere with a marvelous view★ over
Palermo and its bay *(visit accompanied by friar).* ▶ In
the W part of the city is the castle of la **Zisa**★ (D1),
which was built in the 12C by the Norman Kings, William I
and William II, in the Moorish style. In the manner of
the Moors, great attention was paid to the interior decoration and it had mosaics, fountains and other ornamentation *(closed for repairs).* ▶ The **Capuchin Convent** (E-
F1) is famous for its catacombs where, in long corridors, hanging up along the walls, are nearly 8,000 mummies and skeletons of the citizens of Palermo put there
between 1600 and 1881; the exceptional dryness of the
air is responsible for the unusual state of preservation
*(9 a.m.-12 noon and 3:30-5 p.m.; Sun only foreigners
admitted).* ▶ The **Cuba Pavilion**★ (F1) was originally part
of a park of William II (1180) and was much influenced by
the Moorish architecture of the time; it is awaiting repairs
and is now in the courtyard of a barracks *(inquire at guard-
room at entrance).*

Environs

▶ 11 km NW (from A2) is the fashionable seaside resort of
Mondello, next to a fishing village. Near the **punta Priola**
are a number of grottos of prehistoric interest, in particular the **grotta Addaura** *(2 km)* with palaeolithic graffiti. ▶ The nobles of Palermo used to build their villas
at **Bagheria** *(15 km E)* during the 17C and 18C. Architecturally, **villa Valguarnera** (1721) is considered the most
beautiful, but the best known is certainly the **villa Palagonia** *(9 a.m.-12:30 p.m. and 4-6 p.m.);* it was built in 1715
by Francesco Ferdinando Gravina, Prince of Palagonia,
but in spite of its fine architecture, it is best known for its
extraordinary statues of monsters, animals, hunchbacks,
dwarfs, musicians, punchinellos, Turks, beggars, cripples
and the deformed of every kind. It seems that the
Prince, mad with jealousy at the behaviour of his young

and pretty wife, whom he accused, rightly or wrongly, of having numerous lovers, locked her away in the villa and gave to many of the statues the faces of her alleged lovers. Goethe, who visited the villa, says that he felt himself 'surrounded by madness'. ▶ The **Palazzo Cattolica** (on SS 113; *wkdays 9 a.m.-1 p.m.)* at Bagheria has a collection of the paintings of Renato Guttuso, who was born in the town in 1912, as well as works of other contemporary artists. ▶ *C.* 27 km S of Bagheria is **Bagni Cefalà**, the remains of some baths built by the Arabs in the 11C. ▶ **Soluntò★** is magnificently situated on a spur of Mt. Catalfano *(18 km E of Palermo);* the Phoenicians built here one of their first trading posts on the island but the **ruins** *(9 a.m.-1 hr before sunset; closed Mon)* are those of the town during its Hellenic-Roman period (4C-2C BC). A number of streets leave the main thoroughfare and go up the slope, sometimes with steps; there are remains of houses and the so-called gymnasium, probably only a house with a portico and an atrium. There is also a theatre and a council chamber; the objects found are on display in an **antiquarium**. There is also a good view from the site. ▶ 23.5 km S is **Piana degli Albanesi,** a town inhabited by the most important group of Albanian emigrants in Sicily. In the 15C church of **S. Demetrio,** as well as in the church of S. Giorgio, the Greek Orthodox rites are used and sumptuous, traditional costumes are worn for weddings or special feast days. ▶ The town of **Carini** lies among the hills to the W of Palermo, on a height beneath Mt. Saraceno which towers above the Gulf of Palermo and the orange groves of the plain. It contains a 12C-14C **castle** and a 15C legend about a murdered chatelaine. ▶ At **Terrasini,** by the sea 15 km W of Carini, there is an interesting **Museo di Storia Naturale** *(9 a.m.-1 p.m. and 3-6 p.m.)* and a **Museum of the Sicilian Cart** *(in Palzzo Daumale on sea front; telephone before visiting, ☎ 8882767).* □

The Sicilian cart

The Sicilian carretto or cart now has its own museum in the Palazzo d'Aumale, on the Lungomare di Terrasini, not far from Palermo. It is the standard peasant cart, with two wheels and long shafts, used for everyday tasks. On special occasions it is fitted with highly decorated sides, and the horse is dressed in a sparkling tinselled harness with coloured pennants and plumes. The decorations are done by local artists — often the village blacksmith — and the themes on the sides usually revolve around three subjects: Garibaldi landing on the island in 1860 and chasing out the Bourbons; the life of a well-known saint or the story of one of Charlemagne's Paladins, most often Roland, fighting the Moors. The origins of this custom are not easy to trace, but it is certainly not older than a century, for when Garibaldi came to liberate the island there were no carts because there were no roads for them to move on. Goods were carried by mule pack over sheep tracks and mountain paths. It was probably the building of roads that caused the peasants, delighted to use a more efficient form of transport, to show their pleasure by decorating their new carts with bright pictures.

Practical information

PALERMO

ⓘ p. Castelnuovo 35 (C3), ☎ 583847; v. Notarbartolo 9/B (A2), ☎ 6256263; aeroporto Punta Raisi, ☎ 591405.
✈ at Punta Ràisi *(31 km NW),* ☎ 591278; buses from p. Ruggero Settimo (C3); *Alitalia,* v. Mazzini 59 (B3), ☎ 6019111.
▰▰▰ (F5), ☎ 6161806.
▰▰▰ from v. Balsamo (F5), *SAIS,* ☎ 6166027; *Segesta,*

☎ 297163; from Stazione Lolli (C2), *AST,* ☎ 266743; from v. Lincoln (E6), *Cuffaro,* ☎ 6161510.
▰▰ car ferries to Ustica, *Siremar,* ☎ 582403; for Naples, Cagliari, Genoa and Leghorn, Tunis, *Tirrenia,* ☎ 582733 and *Grandi Traghetti,* ☎ 587801; several hydrofoil services weekly in summer for Ustica, *SNAV,* ☎ 329990.
Car rental: *Avis,* v. Principe Scordia 12/14, ☎ 586940, at airport, ☎ 591684; *Hertz,* v. Messina 7/E, ☎ 331668, at airport, ☎ 591682; *Maggiore,* v. Agrigento 27/33, ☎ 297128, at airport, ☎ 591681.

Hotels:
★★★★★ *Grand Hotel Villa Igiea,* at Acquasanta, v. Belmonte 43, ☎ 543744, 119 rm ◪ Ⓟ ⌂ ▣ ☞ 300,000; bkf: 18,000.
★★★★ *Grand Hotel et des Palmes,* v. Roma 398 (C4a), ☎ 583933, 188 rm Ⓟ ☜ 125,000.
★★★★ *Jolly del Foro Italico,* v. Foro Italico 22 (E6 b), ☎ 6165090, 290 rm Ⓟ ⌂ ▣ 130,000. Rest. ◆◆◆ *Ai Paladini* Regional and international cuisine: linguine Favignana, involtini Ruggero, 35/45,000.
★★★★ *Politeama Palace,* p. Settimo 15 (C3c), ☎ 322777, 102 rm Ⓟ ☜ 98,000; bkf: 8,000.
★★★★ *President,* v. Crispi 230 (B4d), ☎ 580733, 129 rm Ⓟ ☜ 98,000; bkf: 8,000.
★★★ *Europa,* v. Agrigento 3 (B3e), ☎ 266673, 73 rm Ⓟ 78,000; bkf: 7,000.
★★ *Villa Archirafi,* v. Archirafi 10 (F6f), ☎ 285827, 32 rm Ⓟ ⌂ No restaurant, 45,000; bkf: 5,000.

Restaurants:
● ◆◆◆◆ *Charleston,* p. Ungheria 30 (C3h), ☎ 321366, closed Sun and 15 Jun-15 Sep. Elegant and refined with impeccable service. Regional and international cuisine: gramigna Lido, roast swordfish, 45/65,000.
● ◆◆◆ *Gourmand's,* v. Libertà 37/E (B3i), ☎ 323431, closed Sun and 10-25 Aug. Comfortable and modern, with good service. Regional and international cuisine: troccole, fettucine Nelson, 35/55,000.
● ◆◆◆ *Scuderia,* v. del Fante 9, ☎ 520323, closed Sun eve. Full of flowers, overlooks racecourse, pleasant garden. Regional cuisine: spaghetti lampara, bucatini freschi, 30/45,000.
◆◆◆ *Chamade,* v. Torrearsa 24 (B3g), ☎ 322204, closed Mon and 20 May-30 Sep. Classical and elegant. Regional and international cuisine: fettucine with salmon, marinated perch, 30/45,000.
◆◆◆ *Friend's Bar,* v. Brunelleschi 138, ☎ 201401, closed Mon and Aug. Garden in summer. Regional cuisine: risotto al pesto ericino, lobster with orange, 30/40,000.
◆◆◆ *Trittico,* v. U. Giordano, ☎ 294809, closed Sun. Garden in summer. Regional cuisine: sole, red mullet, 35/50,000.
◆◆ *Spano,* v. Messina Marine 22, ☎ 470025, closed Mon. Seafood: risotto with shellfish, swordfish, 20/30,000.

⅄ ★★ *Trinacria,* at Sferracavallo, v. Barcarello, ☎ 530590.

Recommended
Archery: Società *CSEN,* v. Vanvitelli 2, ☎ 334180; Compagnia *Arcieri Grifoni di Sicilia,* v. Serradifalco 78, ☎ 563066.
Botanical gardens: (E-F-6), ☎ 6161493.
Canoeing: *Canottieri Trinacria,*v. Stabile 221, ☎ 230991.
Craft workshops: G. *D'Ignoto,* v. del Medico 9, ☎ 200292 (papier maché); *Argento,* v. Vittorio Emanuele 455 (puppets); G. *Spatafora,* v. Bambinai 10, ☎ 211482 (waxwork).
Events: opera season at *Politeama Theatre,* ☎ 331826; season of orchestral music *(Church Music Festival* in Nov); plays at *Teatro Biondo,* ☎ 588755; open-air theatre at *Villa Castelnuovo; Opera dei Pupi* at *Bradamante Theatre,* ☎ 296929; *Festival of Santa Rosalia* (11-15 Jul); international tennis tournaments (Oct.).
Fairs: *Mediterranean Trade Fair* (May-Jun), ☎ 543755.
Fencing: *Accademia Palermitana,* v. Siracusa 12, ☎ 584712.
Flying: aeroclub, at *Boccadifalco Airport,* ☎ 421488; gliding, at *Centro Volo a Vela,* v. Leonardo da Vinci 67.

Hang gliding: *Condor Club School,* v. Terrasanta 65, ☎ 546668.
Horseback riding: *SPE-SECEP,* v. Diana 4 (Parco della Favorita), ☎ 513935; *Cooperativa il Bosco,* v. Magnada 110, ☎ 232159 or 277209 or 283019 (associate of *ANTE*).
Horse racing: *Alla Favorita Hippodrome,* v. del Fante 9, ☎ 510462.
Nature parks: *Etna nature park,* information from *Azienda Foreste Demaniali,* v. Libertà 97, ☎ 404387.
Sailing: *Il Salpancore,* v. M. Stabile 213, ☎ 331055.
Swimming: v. P di Paterno 128; v. Fante 11, ☎ 510558; *Scuola Nuoto di Palermo,* v. Strasburgo 540.
Wine: *Medivini (Mediterranean Wine Exhibition,* Oct), ☎ 543755; *Miceli,* v. Generale Streva 18/A, ☎ 325966.
♥ guided tours: daily (9 a.m. and 2 p.m.), ☎ 586333.

Environs

BAGHERIA, ⊠ 90011, ☎ 091.
Hotel:
★★★ *'A Zabara,* SS 113 at 246-km marker, ☎ 937104, 66 rm Ⓟ ⌷ ⁓ 83,000; bkf: 5,000.

Restaurant:
♦ *Osteria Don Ciccio,* v. Stazione 8, ☎ 934366, closed Sun eve and Mon. Regional cuisine: pasta with sardine sauce, grilled cuttlefish, 15/20,000.

MONDELLO, ⊠ 90151, ☎ 091, 11 km NW.
≋
Ⓘ at Palermo, v. Belmonte 43, ☎ 540122.

Hotels:
★★★★ *Mondello Palace,* v. Principe di Scalea, ☎ 450001, 83 rm Ⓟ ⌷ ⅍ ⌷ 120,000; bkf: 15,000.
★★★ *Splendid La Torre,* at Piano Gallo, ☎ 450222, 177 rm Ⓟ ⌷ ⅍ ⌷ ⁓ Pens. 95,000.
★★ *Esplanade,* v. Gallo 22, ☎ 450003, 32 rm Ⓟ ⅍ 46,000; bkf: 5,000.

Restaurants:
● ♦♦♦♦ *Charleston-le Terrazze,* v. Regina Elena, ☎ 450171, closed 9 Sep-14 Jun. Summer location of restaurant of same name in Palermo, elegant terrazzo overlooking the sea. Fine quality cuisine: ariccola cartoccio, Sicilian veal escalopes, 45/70,000.
♦♦♦ *Chamade Mare,* v. Regina Elena 43, ☎ 450512, closed 1 Nov-9 Jun. Elegant villa with large garden. Regional and international cuisine: ravioli with salmon, swordfish, 40/60,000.
♦ *Gambero Rosso,* v. Piano Gallo 30/32, ☎ 454685, closed Mon and 15-30 Nov. Seafood: risotto with shellfish sauce, swordfish, 15/35,000.

Recommended
Caving: visit to Addaura Cave, contact Soprintendenza alle Antichità, at Palermo, v. Bara 24, ☎ 580642.
Marina: ☎ 450182; *Windsurfing Club,* ☎ 454034.

PIANA DEGLI ALBANESI, ⊠ 90037, ☎ 091, 23.5 km S.

Recommended
Events: Greek Orthodox services on important feast days, information, Comune, ☎ 771043.

SOLUNTO, ⊠ 90017, ☎ 091, 18 km E.
Hotel:
★★★ *Zagarella & Sea Palace,* at Solanto, v. Nazionale 55, ☎ 937077, 414 rm Ⓟ ⌷ ⌷ ⁓ 90,000.

PANTALICA BURIAL GROUND*

Syracuse 48, Palermo 275, Rome 871 km

E5

Pantalica is the largest of the Sicilian rock burial grounds and is located on a plateau between two deep gullies — the Anano and the Calcinara. Of the primitive Sicilian centre of the 13C-8C BC there remain the ruins of the **Anaktoron,** also called the Palace of the Prince (12C-11C BC), and the 5,000

cave tombs excavated from the limestone rock. Small niches for statuettes and troglodite village remains show that the site was occupied by Christian communities during the first centuries of the Middle Ages. □

The island of PANTELLERIA

Trapani 143, Palermo 248, Rome 1,149 km
Pop. 7,815 ⊠ 91017 ☎ 0923   A3 and A6

Pantelleria is the largest of the small islands that form part of the territories administered from Sicily. It is a volcanic island and its mountain slopes are forested. Vines, olives, capers and other sub-tropical fruit are grown. Sheep are also reared in the valleys.

▶ The capital of the island is **Pantelleria,** situated around the port beneath an old castle. Around the island are *dammusi,* traditional stone dwellings with domed roofs. ▶ On the S slopes of the **Cuddie Rosse** are the archaeological remains of the fortified neolithic village of **Mursia.** ▶ Nearby, at **Sesi,** there are domed megalithic funeral monuments which recall the nuraghi of Sardinia. ▶ A road goes around the island more or less close to the coast. ▶ It is also possible to go around the island by boat, stopping at some of the many inlets and visiting some of the numerous caves. □

Practical information

≋
Ⓘ v. S. Nicola, ☎ 911838.
✈ *(4 km SE),* ☎ 911172; *Alitalia,* v. Borgo Italia, ☎ 911078.
⇌ daily summer sailings from Trapani (*c.* 4.5 hrs) and weekly from Marsala (4 hrs), *Siremar,* ☎ 911104 at Trapani, ☎ 40515; *Traghetti delle Isole,* at Trapani, ☎ 22467 (departures also from Marsala).

Hotels:
★★★ *Cossyra,* at Mursia, ☎ 911154, 80 rm Ⓟ ⌷ ⌷ ⁓ closed 6 Nov-26 May, 80,000; bkf: 6,000.
★★★ *Porto,* v. Borgo Italia, ☎ 911257, 43 rm ⅍ closed Nov-May. No restaurant, 60,000.
★★ *Turistico Residenziale,* at Bue Marino, ☎ 911054, 28 rm ⋚ ⌷ ⌷ No restaurant, 41,000.

Restaurant:
♦ *Bartolo-Miramare,* v. Catania 4, ☎ 911428, closed Nov-Feb. Seafood: spaghetti with fish, fried and grilled fish, 18/25,000.

Recommended
Horseback riding: *Centro Ippico,* at Scauri Basso, ☎ 916364.
Marina: ☎ 916222.

PATERNO

Catania 20 km, Palermo 204, Rome 786 km
Pop. 46,540 ⊠ 95047 ☎ 095   E4

Paterno lies near the base of Mt. Etna, NW of Catania. It is a busy country town with a trade in wine, flax, olive oil and oranges. From a basalt cliff above the city there is a good view over the valley of the Simeto River. Paterno is built over the site of the Greek town of *Hybla Major* and has mineral springs that date back to antiquity. Its 11C Norman **castle** (rebuilt 13C; *see caretaker*) has some fine halls with windows with two lights. Norman, too, is its church of **S. Maria dell'Alto.** There is also a French-Gothic church of **S. Francesco.** Nearby, the church of **St. Mary of the Valley of Josaphat** has a 14C Gothic portal and a 15C ceiling. □

Practical information ―――――――――

Recommended
Zoo: *Parco zoo di Sicilia,* Valcorrente exit on SS Catania-Paterno, ☎ 918057.

PATTI

Messina 75, Palermo 160, Rome 747 km
Pop. 12,971 ⊠ 98066 ☎ 0941   E2

SW of Catania on the coast, Patti looks out to sea above the beach of **Marina di Patti**. Its 13C cathedral has a *Madonna* by Antonello de Saliba (16C) and the tomb of Adelasia, wife of the Norman Roger I. E of Marina di Patti, excavations have unearthed a grandiose **Roman villa★** *(9 a.m.-sunset);* it has a courtyard with pillars with beautiful coloured mosaics, some in geometrical patterns, others with pictures of domestic and wild animals (4C-5C).   ☐

Practical information ―――――――――

≋
ℹ️ p. Sciacca, ☎ 21327.
⚓ hydrofoil departures twice daily summer (except Wed) for Vulcano, *SNAV,* at Messina, ☎ 364044.

⚠ ★★ *Simenzaru Beach,* at Galice, ☎ 37110.

Recommended
Hang gliding: *Volo Libero Cacciavento,* at Patti Marina, ☎ 361026.

PIAZZA ARMERINA*

Enna 34, Palermo 164, Rome 866 km
Pop. 21,467 ⊠ 94015 ☎ 0935   D4

Piazza Armerina, S of Enna in central Sicily, stands on three hillocks nearly 2,500 ft above sea level. It has a woolen industry and a trade in olive oil and wine.

▶ In the oldest and higghest part of the town are a 13C Norman **castle** and the **Duomo** (17C Baroque). The Duomo houses a marvelous painting of the **Crucifixion★** (1495), possibly by P. Ruzzolone. ▶ Other interesting churches are the Baroque **S. Pietro** with sculptures by the Gagini, the old 13C **S. Giovanni di Rodi** and, just outside the town, the old **Priory of S. Andrea** (11C), which has a series of frescos from the 12C-15C. ▶ The most famous place in the region is the **Roman Villa Casale★★**, 5 km SW of town *(9 a.m.-1 hr before sunset)*. This was built in the 3C-4C and was the country house of a millionaire of the time. The man is thought to have been a rich importer of wild animals for the gladiatorial games, since many of the floor mosaics depict such animal scenes in a manner usually found only in Roman villas in N. Africa. The house is built around a **large Peristyle★** (square columned courtyard), which has mosaics of the proprietor, his family and maidservants; to the N are the many bedrooms: one has a **small hunting scene★**, while the owners' bedroom has erotic floor mosaics. Nearby the **baths**, also with beautiful mosaics, are divided in Roman fashion into *frigidarium* (cold room), *tepidarium* (lukewarm) and *calidaria* (hot). The **large hunting scenes corridor★** is decorated with a whole series of pictures of the hunt. The **Room of the 10 Girls★** is perhaps the most celebrated of all and shows young women in a gymnasium running. ▶ Some of the rooms off the **basilica** have some truly splendid mosaic floors depicting myths. Another courtyard is before a **dining-hall★** with mosaics of **The 12 Labours of Hercules★**, of **Hercules beating the Giants★** and of the **Glorification of Hercules★**. ▶ 15.8 km NE is **Morgantina** where, in an excavated site *(9 a.m.-1 hr before sunset)*, it is possible to see the agora, theatre, council chambers, gymnasium, sanctuary and two residential parts of an **ancient Graeco-Roman city**. Some of the finds from this site can be seen in the antiquarium of **Aidone** on the road from Piazza Armerina.☐

Practical information ―――――――――
ℹ️ p. Garibaldi, ☎ 81201.

Hotel:
★★★ *Park Hotel Paradiso,* at Ramaldo, ☎ 81841, 26 rm
Ⓟ ♨️ 📶 ℘ 45,000.

5. Il Ponente Siculo

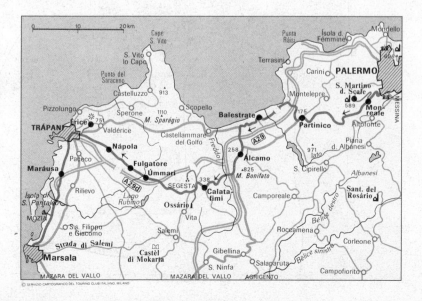

Restaurants:

♦ *Centrale da Totò,* v. Mazzini 29, ☎ 81153, closed Mon and 1-15 Jul. Regional cuisine: cannelloni alla Siciliana, roast meats, 15/25,000.

♦ *Pepito,* v. Roma 140, ☎ 82737, closed Tue and Dec. Regional cuisine: cannelloni alla Siciliana, lamb cutlets, 15/20,000.

Recommended
Events: *Palio* (race) *of the Normans* (13-14 Aug).

Il PONENTE SICULO

From Palermo to Marsala *(138 km, 1 day; map 5)*

According to Thucydides, the Greek historian, the early Sicilian people known as the Sicani came originally from the banks of the River Sicano in Spain 'and the island that was previously called *Trinacria* took the name of Sicania from them and even today they still inhabit the western part of the island'. After the fall of Troy some came from this city 'to Sicily on board their ships and settled alongside the Sicanians

and the two peoples together were known as the Elimi. Eryx (Erice) and Segesta were their cities'. From Italy the Siculi people 'crossed the straits on rafts', and were responsible for 'the change of the name of the island from Sicania to Sicilia'. The Phoenicians also came 'and occupied certain islands and forelands to be near the Siculi, in order to trade with them'. This itinerary leads over much of the W Sicily referred to by Thucydides, with visits to Egesta, Eryx and the Phoenician town of Mozia.

▶ Leaving Palermo, the itinerary goes inland to **Monreale** (→) and climbs to the forests of **San Martino delle Scale.** Here, the Benedictine abbey, founded in the 6C by Gregory the Great, has been changed to a grandiose 17C monastery (Venanzio Marvuglia, 1770-86) with a 15C church containing many excellent paintings, sculptures and a choir with carved woodwork; also by the church is the 17C fountain d'Oreto. ▶ **Partinico** is dominated by the rock of Mt. Cesaro. ▶ **Balestrate** is a seaside resort with a fine beach in the Gulf of Castellamare. ▶ **Alcamo,** on a height at the foot of Mt. Bonifato, is of Arab origin and the birthplace of Ciullo d'Alcamo, the 12C poet who was one of the earliest to use Italian, instead of Latin. In the churches of **S. Francesco, Badia**

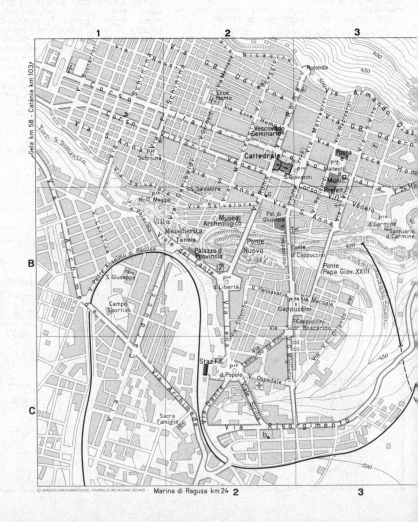

Grande and Matrice, there are some fine sculptures by the Gaginis; the church of **S. Oliva** has a statue of Saint Oliva★ by Antonello Gagini (1511). ► **Calatafimi** lies on a ridge between two hills; it has a few 18C churches and the remains of a medieval castle; it was near this town that Garibaldi defeated the Neapolitans. The monument and cemetery for those who fell in the battle is 4.3 km SW. ► The theatre and the solitary temple at **Segesta** (→) are among the highlights of the itinerary. ► At **Erice** (→), another famous site, the sea once more appears. ► From **Trapani** (→), the route follows the W coast. ► **Mozia** *(8:30 a.m.-1 p.m.; closed Mon; telephone in advance,* ☎ *0923/959598)* is on the island of S. Pantaleo in the Gulf of Stagnone. On the island, the town of **Motya** was a Phoenician settlement in the 8C BC and later became the main Carthaginian base in Sicily. It was destroyed by the Syracusans in 397 BC. Excavation has unearthed a city **wall**, with towers and gates, a Phoenician **temple** with sacrificial altar, the remains of some buildings and a burial ground. A **museum** has on display finds from the surroundings as well as from Lilibeo and from the necropolis of Birgi. ► Once back on the coast of the larger island the route nears the destination of Marsala (→). □

RAGUSA

Palermo 271, Rome 862, Milan 1,437 km
Pop. 65,793 ✉ 97100 ☎ 0932   E5

Ragusa is situated on a long rocky spur on the S slopes of the Iblei Mountains. It consists of upper Ragusa and lower Ragusa Ibla. Upper Ragusa is a modern town, laid out to a regular plan, while Ragusa Ibla is supposed to have been built on the site of the ancient Sicilian town of Hybla Heraia. It is picturesque and Baroque.

► In **upper Ragusa**, the **cathedral** (A2; 1706-60) towers above the central piazza S. Giovanni, flanked by its campanile; behind it stands the **Casa Canonica**, built at the same time. ► The **Ibleo Archaeological Museum** (B2; *9 a.m.-2 p.m.; Sun 9 a.m.-1 p.m.; closed Mon*), with finds from the surrounding sites, is divided into six sections: prehistoric with neolithic material; Greek with vases from the Camerina burial ground; Hellenic finds with ceramics from Scornavacche and a reconstructed model of an ancient pottery shop; rebuilt models of ancient sites including part of the burial ground of Hybla Heraia; late Roman section with floor mosaics from a small church near Santa Croce Camerina and material from the Byzantine port of Caucana, while the last section displays material actually

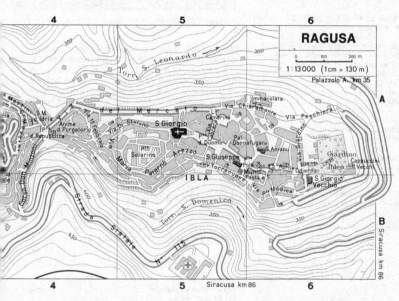

bought by the museum. ► There is a splendid view over the S. Domenico gully from the **bridge of the Capuchins** (B2-3) which crosses it. ► The church of **S. Maria delle Scale** (A-B4) was rebuilt after the terrible earthquake of 1693, but still retains parts of its original 15C-16C structure including its Gothic-Renaissance naves. ► The **Scale** (242 steps) in front of the church go down to Lower Ragusa Ibla; where they end are two Baroque palaces and the church of **S. Maria dell'Idria** (A4).

► In **lower Ragusa Ibla**, the church of **S. Giorgio★** stands imposingly above the p. del Duomo (A5); it is a splendid example of 18C Baroque, built in 1738-75 to a design by Rosario Gagliardi and finished with a Neoclassical dome. ► Other interesting churches are **S. Giuseppe**, attributed to Gagliardi, with an elliptical interior, rich altars and a 15C statue in silver of S. Giuseppe *(not displayed in public, ask nuns)*, and **S. Antonio** (A6), with, on its r.

Practical information

ALCAMO, ✉ 91011, ☎ 0924.

Restaurant:
♦♦ *Funtanazza,* at Monte Bonifato, ☎ 25314, closed Fri. With garden for dining in summer. Italian cuisine: fusilli Gattopardo, grilled meats, 15/25,000.

Recommended
Cycling: *G.S. Alcamese,* v. P. M. Rocca 96, ☎ 25922.

CALATAFIMI, ✉ 91013, ☎ 0924.

Restaurant:
♦ *Mille Pini,* p. Vivona 2, ☎ 51260, closed Tue and Nov-Dec. Regional cuisine: spaghetti all marinara, grilled lobster, 15/25,000.

Recommended
Events: *Festival of the Holy Crucifix* (May).

side, a Gothic portal which was part of the original 13C church. ▶ A fine view of the town is possible from the **Giardino Ibleo** (A6); on the r. of the entrance are the ruins of the church of **S. Gregorio Vecchio** with a Gothic Catalan 15C portal. In the gardens is the **church of the Cappuccini Vecchi** with a tryptych by P. Novelli. ▶ The **asphalt works** are 2 km S with some open-cast mines. ▶ Nearby is an **archaeological park** *(wkdays 9 a.m.-1 p.m.)* close to some quarries and an ancient Christian (4C-5C) burial ground. ▶ From the mines it is 24 km to the coast and the port of **Marina di Ragusa.** ▶ 9 km SW some excavations near **Castiglione** have unearthed the site of an ancient (7C-6C BC) village and the remains of tombs dug from the rock. □

Practical information ———————————————

ℹ v. Natalelli (B2), ☎ 21421.
▨▨ (C2), ☎ 21239.
▨▨ from p. Stazione (C2), ☎ 21249.

Hotel:
★★★ *Montreal*, corso Italia 70 (A3 a), ☎ 21123, 63 rm Ⓟ
ᵫ 52,000; bkf: 4,000.

Restaurants:
♦♦♦ *Jonio*, v. Risorgimento 49 (C2-b), ☎ 24322, closed Fri. Regional cuisine: gnocchi alla Ragusana, risotto all' Iblea, 15/25,000.
♦♦♦ *Villa Fortugno*, 5 km SW toward Marina di Ragusa, ☎ 28656, closed Mon. In old country villa, garden with fountain. Italian cuisine: gnocchi in meat sauce, ravioli with ricotta cheese, 20/30,000.
♦ *Orfeo*, v. S. Anna 117 (B2 c), ☎ 21035, closed Sat and 1-15 Aug. Italian cuisine: lasagne, roast veal with mushrooms, 15/22,000.

Recommended
Craft workshops: *Busacca De Bernardo*, v. Fogazzaro 8, ☎ 47852 (cloth printed by hand).
Events: *Festival of S. Giorgio* (25 Apr at Ragusa Ibla) and *Festival of St. John the Baptist* (27-29 Aug).
Swimming: at Selvaggia, ☎ 28909.
Tennis: at Villa Margherita, ☎ 27378.

Environs

MARINA DI RAGUSA, ⊠ 97010, ☎ 0932, 24 km SW.

Restaurant:
♦♦ *Alberto*, lungomare Doria 48, ☎ 39023, closed Wed and Nov, fine veranda. Seafood: risotto with shellfish sauce, red mullet, 20/28,000.

ᴧ ★★★ *Baia del Sole*, lungomare Doria, ☎ 39844 (all year).

RANDAZZO

Catania 64, Palermo 212, Rome 764 km
Pop. 11,639 ⊠ 95036 ☎ 095   E3

Randazzo is a medieval town on the N slopes of Etna, looking out over the valley of the Alcantara. The Gothic church of **S. Maria★**, built with lava stone, has three powerful apses and two 15C Gothic-Catalan portals. The church of **S. Nicolo**, rebuilt in the 16C-17C, still retains a 14C apse and has sculptures by the Gaginis as well as a tryptych of the Messina school. The splendid **campanile★** of the church of **S. Martino** was built in the 14C; in the interior there are 15C-16C sculptures and a polyptych of the Messina school. The medieval **fort** was a prison during the 15C. □

Practical information ———————————————

Restaurants:
♦ *Arturo*, v. Roma 8, ☎ 921565, closed Sat and Sep. Regional cuisine: tortellini with vegetable sauce, lasagne, 15/25,000.
♦ *La Trottola*, v. Basile 27, ☎ 921187, closed Tue. Regional cuisine: cannelloni, saltombocca alla romana, 15/25,000.

RAVANUSA

Agrigento 49, Palermo 173, Rome 921 km
Pop. 15,556 ⊠ 92029 ☎ 0922   C4

Ravanusa is near the **Mount Saraceno** site, an ancient Greek settlement thought to be that of the city of **Kakyron.** Excavation is going on at present. On the citadel are the remains of a sanctuary with a temple; in the lower part of the excavated city are two villages, one on top of the other. The oldest one, underneath, dates from 7C-6C BC and the other from 6C-4C BC.   □

SAMBUCA DI SICILIA

Agrigento 92, Palermo 125, Rome 1,032 km
Pop. 7,394 ⊠ 92017 ☎ 0925   B3

Sambuca di Sicilia is near an important archaeological site in the Mazara Valley, **Monte Adranone.** These are the ruins of a Hellenized ancient Sicilian town and have been excavated. Its encircling walls are 5 km long and inside it another wall runs around the citadel with a temple, a cistern and a building of two floors (4C-3C BC) which probably had shops or was used as a depot. Outside the citadel, in the larger part of the city where the mass of the population resided, some buildings have been unearthed.   □

SANT'AGATA DI MILITELLO

Messina 119, Palermo 132, Rome 774 km
Pop. 12,678 ⊠ 98076 ☎ 0941   D-E2

Sant'Agata di Militello is on a long beach on the N coast, with a 17C castle which offers a wide view across the sea from Capo d'Orlando to Cefalù.   □

Practical information ———————————————

Hotel:
★★★ *Roma Palace*, at Cannamelata, v. Nazionale, ☎ 703516, 48 rm Ⓟ ⤳ 50,000; bkf: 5,000.

SANT'ALESSIO SICULO

Messina 37, Palermo 266, Rome 712 km
Pop. 1,307 ⊠ 98030 ☎ 0942   F3

Sant'Alessio Siculo is on the coast facing the Ionian Sea, a little N of the craggy Cape of S. Alessio. 4 km away, the village of **Forza d'Agro**, of picturesque and medieval aspect, lies beneath the cliff-top ruins of a 16C **castle.** In the **Triade** church is a 16C, Gothic wooden banner, while the **chiesa Matrice** contains a statue of **S. Catherine of Alessandria**, by M. Montanini (1559), a 14C painted Crucifixion and beautifully carved 17C wooden stalls in the choir. 13.5 km along the road to Messina is **Ali Terme**, surrounded by hills with citrus trees and vineyards.   □

Practical information _____

SANT'ALESSIO SICULO

Hotel:
★★★ *Elihotel,* v. Lungomare, ☎ 751194, 57 rm 👑 closed 26 Oct-14 Mar, 52,000; bkf: 7,000.

Environs

ALI TERME, ✉ 98021, ☎ 0942, 13.5 km N.
♨ (closed Nov-mid May) *Terme Granata Cassibile,* ☎ 715029; *Terme Marino,* ☎ 715031.

SAN VITO LO CAPO

Trapani 39, Palermo 108, Rome 1,015 km
Pop. 3,903 ✉ 91010 ☎ 0923   A2

San Vito Lo Capo is at the extreme end of the W point of the large Bay of Castellammare on the N coast of Sicily. The fishing village of the same name is in a sandy inlet nearby. The **chiesa Madre** on the main street is part of a 15C fortress.   □

Practical information _____

≋
ℹ office on main street (in season).

Hotel:
★★ *Capo San Vito,* v. Principe Tommaso 29, ☎ 972284, 35 rm ৬ ⌘ closed Oct-Mar, 55,000; bkf: 7,000.

⚠ ★ *Soleado,* v. della Secca, 300 pl, ☎ 972688.

Recommended
Events: *Gastronomic Week* (Aug).
Marina: ☎ 972733.

SCIACCA

Agrigento 62, Palermo 134, Rome 1,041 km
Pop. 38,040 ✉ 92019 ☎ 0925   B4

Sciacca, a name of Arab origin, is one of the oldest spas in Europe; it lies on the SW side of the island and is built on a series of steps, on a hill sweeping down to the sea.

▶ **Piazza A. Scandaliato,** the town's centre, has the Mediterranean as a background. ▶ The nearby 17C **Duomo** still retains parts of its original 12C edifice; it contains statues and work on its façade and in its interior by the Gagini. ▶ One of the side **portals**★ of the church of **S. Margherita** is Renaissance Gothic, the work of Francesco Laurana and Pietro de Bonitate (*c.* 1485). ▶ The **Palazzo Steripinto**★ (15C) is notable for its façade, embossed with diamond-shaped projections. ▶ By the **porta S. Calogero** are part of the 15C town **walls** and **Mt. San Calogero** (1,300 ft). ▶ On its summit is the **sanctuary of San Calogero**, built on a plateau and surrounded by pine trees (in its interior is a statue of the saint Calogero by G. Gagini, 1538). From this height there is a splendid view over the surroundings. Also interesting are the **smoky stoves of San Calogero**; these are natural grottos giving off steam. Archaeological finds here prove that they were used for therapeutic purposes from the most ancient times.   □

Practical information _____

≋
♨ (from 15 Apr-15 Nov), ☎ 21620.
ℹ corso Vittorio Emanuelle 94, ☎ 22744.

Hotels:
★★★★ *Torre Macauda,* SS 115, ☎ 26800, 249 rm 🅿 👑 ⬛ ⌦ Pens. 90,000.
★★★ *Grand Hotel delle Terme,* v. Nuove Terme 1, ☎ 23133, 72 rm 🅿 👑 ৬ ⬛ closed Dec-Feb, 59,500.

Restaurant:
♦ *Corsaro,* at Stazzone, v. Esperando 51, ☎ 24120. Seafood: risotto with shellfish sauce, spaghetti with sardine sauce, 20/30,000.

⚠ ★★ *Baia Makauda,* at Tranchina, 200 pl, ☎ 92092.

Recommended
Cycling: *G.S. Amatori Sciacca,* v. degli Aceri 8, ☎ 92330.
Marina: ☎ 22219; ☎ 25710.

SEGESTA*

Trapani 41, Palermo 75, Rome 982 km
✉ 91013 ☎ 0924   A3

Segesta is the name of an ancient city on the slopes of **Mt. Barbaro** whose inhabitants were Elymians, that is, who belonged to the original inhabitants of the island who were there before the Greeks or the Carthaginians arrived. After their arrival, the town had to contend with occupation and massacres; it finally surrendered to Roman authority.

▶ In the now deserted but grandiose landscape are the ruins of the city's famous **Doric temple**★★. The temple had a peristyle of thirty-six columns around it, supporting the entablature and pediments. Worship and sacrifices, on the altar in the open centre, would have been made to the Elymian goddess. Farther up the mountain are the remains of an **ancient city** (a fortified gate, an old wall and a tower) and a **theatre**★, which is Hellenistic and dates from the 3C-2C BC. It has an auditorium that can be reached by climbing about twenty steps carved out of the rock; the stage has as a backdrop a magnificent view over the whole Gulf of Castellammare, as far as the distant Mt. Erice.   □

Practical information _____

Recommended
Events: classical plays at theatre (Jul-Aug).

SELINUNTE*

Trapani 71, Palermo 118, Rome 1,021 km
✉ 91022 (Marinella) ☎ 0924   A4

Selinunte was one of the most important ancient towns in Sicily, situated on a hill on the SW coast. Perhaps this name comes from *Selinon* (Greek for parsley), which grows wild in profusion in this area. The town was founded by Dorians, from Megara Hyblaea on the E coast of Sicily in 628 BC and it soon attained great prosperity. It had many quarrels with the inhabitants of neighbouring Segesta, who were not Greeks, but autochtonous Sicilians, and they finally called in the Carthaginians who destroyed Selinunte in 409 BC and sold those of its people that hadn't been massacred as slaves. It is said that Syracusans returned to the site of the city and eventually it grew and prospered once again, but in the 3C BC, during the First Punic War it was again destroyed (250 BC) by the Carthaginians, and this time for good. Most of its inhabitants managed to escape and went to live in Lilybaeum (Marsala). Religious communities and hermits still continued to live in the surviving parts of the town, but whatever was still standing was finally destroyed during the terrible earthquake during the Byzantine era. It was not until the 16C that a learned Sicilian rediscovered the site, when he saw people from neighbouring villages go there to collect material with which to build their houses. The city, as demonstrated by excavation, stood on a spur (B1-2) between the Modione River and the Gorgo

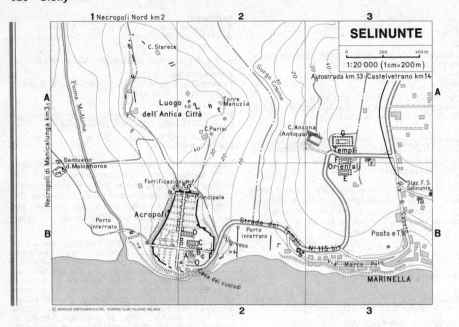

Cotone, which have at their mouths the two buried ports of the ancient city; the citadel and the city itself are behind (A1-2) while to the E (A-B3) lies the sacred area where the temples were built. The Arab traveler and writer, Idrisi, in the 11C, speaks of a village called *Rahl el Asnam*, literally village of the pillars, and he was probably referring to the surviving Doric columns at Selinunte.

▶ The **archaeological** site, covering the ruins of the city that have been excavated, can be visited *(9 a.m.-1 hr before sunset);* an **antiquarium** to house the finds is in preparation at Cascina Ancona. Because the deities to whom the temples were erected are, for the most part, unknown, they have been given letters of the alphabet for identification purposes. The **eastern temples★** (A2-3) number three; of these **temple G** (A3) is one of the greatest known monuments of Greek antiquity; its front has eight pillars and the main part of the building, three naves. It was begun in 550 BC and never finished, perhaps because of the Carthaginian invasion of 409. ▶ **Temple E★★** is majestic and eight of its columns have been set upright. It was built during the first two decades of the 5C BC. ▶ The smallest temple, between the two already mentioned, is **temple F** (560-540 BC). ▶ Passing along the **walls** of huge square blocks, a route ascends to the **acropolis★** (B1-2), which was crossed by two main streets and where it is still possible to see the remains of various temples, such as the base of temple O, the base and some columns of temple A, twelve columns, which have been set upright, of temple C, the oldest one on the acropolis (mid-6C BC). It is also possible to see the ruins of some Carthaginian houses (4C-3C BC) and the base of a small, very early temple. ▶ N of the citadel, the main gate (B2) had **huge fortifications** on the outside. ▶ A large quantity of votive statuettes have been found, some with a pomegranate in their hand, and the nearby sanctuary has been called that of the **Malophoros** (A-B1), after a divinity similar to Demeter. The remains comprise part of a temple and two altars; funer-

al processions stopped at it and then went on to the burial ground at Manicalunga.   ☐

Practical information _____

ℹ office at entrance, near Eastern Temples (A3).

Hotel:
★★ *Alceste,* v. Alceste 21 (B2-3 a), ☎ 46184, 26 rm Ⓟ ♿ closed 16 Nov-28 Feb, 43,000; bkf: 4,500.

Restaurant:
♦♦ *Pierrot,* v. Marco Polo 108 (B2-3 a), ☎ 46025, closed Jan-Feb. Windows and veranda facing sea. Seafood: spaghetti with shellfish sauce, grilled fish, 20/30,000.

Å ★ *Maggiolino,* at Garraffo, ☎ 46044 (all year).

SYRACUSE★★

Palermo 258, Rome 823, Milan 1,398 km
Pop. 118,690 ⊠ 96100 ☎ 0931   F5

In ancient times Syracuse was the richest and most populous city in Sicily. It was founded *c.* 734 BC by settlers from Corinth led by Archias the Corinthian. It was at first an aristocracy, then a democracy until Gelon made himself tyrant in 485 BC; under his rule the city was raised to wealth and power. His successors, however, were rapacious and cruel and were chased from the city which again became a democracy. In a war with the Athenians, the Syracusans, in 413 BC, defeated them, and later in 397 BC, led by Dionysius, they defeated the Carthaginians. Their mistake was to ally themselves later with Carthage, in its struggle against Rome. In 214 BC the city was besieged by the Romans under Marcellus. The Syracusans held out for 13 years, helped considerably by their most famous citizen, the scientist Archimedes, who built war machines capable of throwing boulders at great speed over a considerable distance. This artillery caused panic and demoralization among the Romans who nevertheless, by ruse, managed to take the city. Archimedes was put to death and Syracuse, as a Roman town, declined in importance. It was later occupied by the Saracens (878), the Normans (1085) and later still by the Genoese and the Pisans. Today Syracuse is a Baroque city, having been rebuilt after the earthquake of 1693. The island of Ortygia (D-F4) is where the first Greeks settled, and today it is a picturesque section with many narrow streets and monuments. The city expanded on to the mainland where, around the agora, the district of Acradina evolved (C1). Two other districts were formed later toward the hills, Neapolis and Tiche (A3). Neapolis (B1) is behind Acradina and the hill of Temenite where there is a famous Greek theatre. N of the Neapolis district are the famous quarries where prisoners were put to work and which today are public gardens.

▶ **The island of Ortygia.** On the side of p. Pancali (D3), which faces the **new bridge** connecting the island to the mainland, are the ruins of the **temple of Apollo** (or Artemis), the oldest of the Sicilian Doric temples (end of 7C BC). They comprise two columns, the base of the sanctuary and the walls of the main hall, as well as signs of the transformation of the temple into a Byzantine church, an Arab mosque and a Norman basilica. ▶ In the centre of the island the **piazza Archimedes** (E4) has a modern fountain of Artemide. ▶ The **piazza del Duomo** (E4) is a busy centre with Baroque buildings. ▶ The **Duomo**★★ has a 17C Baroque façade by G. Palma, but it incorporated some parts of the ancient Doric temple of Athena (5C BC). The capitals of the pillars of the temple can clearly be seen in the wall of the church in v. Minerva, while the cella, or centre hall, of the temple has become the central nave of the church. A Hellenistic basin has been given the support of 12C Norman bronze lions and turned into a baptismal font. The painting of *S. Zosimo*★ has been attributed to Antonello da Messina *(recently removed for security reasons)*, the paintings of *Madonna della Neve*★ and *S. Lucia* are by A. Gagini (16C). ▶ From the Duomo, the v. Picherale leads along the seafront to the **Fountain of Arethusa**★ (F4). There is a Greek myth that tells that the nymph Arethusa was pursued, in Greece, by the god Alphaeus in the river in which she was bathing and Artemis changed her into a fountain on the island of Ortygia. The god pursued the nymph under the sea and tried to mix his waters with those of the fountain. There is a spring of fresh water rising in the middle of the port *(occhio della Zillica)*, but the Syracusans prefer to think it is the god Alphaeus pursuing the waters of the Arethusa fountain. ▶ The **Palazzo Bellomo** (E4) is a Swabian edifice, rebuilt in the 15C; it houses the **Galleria Regionale** *(9 a.m.-2 p.m.; Sun 9 a.m.-1 p.m.; closed Mon)*. The beautiful interior of the palace is a suitable site for the gallery's fine collection of sculpture, ranging from the Byzantine period to the Renaissance. Its picture gallery has a splendid *Annunciation*★★ by Antonello da Messina (1474) and a beautiful *Burial of S. Lucia*★ by Caravaggio. It also houses collections of silverware, sacred vestments, furniture, fabrics, goldplate and a large 17C detailed plan of the city. ▶ The church of **S. Martino** (F4) was originally a 6C Christian church, but was rebuilt in the 13C; it has a trypt102 of the 15C Syracusan school. At the end of the island is the **Castello Maniace**★, named after a Byzantine general who for a time reconquered the city from the Saracens, in 1038. The castle, however, was built in 1239 by Frederick II in the form of a square with a tower on each angle; it has a magnificent Gothic portal★ and mullioned windows looking over the sea. ▶ On the W side of the island, the **Arethusa promenade** runs from the Fountain of Arethusa (F4) to the 14C **Porta Marina** (E3), over the Foro Italico; it offers a splendid view of the

larger port and the Iblei Mountains. ▶ At one end of the promenade (E4) is the **Tropical Fish Aquarium** *(9 a.m.-2 p.m.; closed Sun)*; at the other the small church of **S. Maria dei Miracoli** (D-E3-4), built at the end of the 15C. ▶ The medieval part of the island is on the E side; it contains many Baroque churches and palaces. The v. Vittorio Veneto (D-E4) was the **Mastrarua** (main street) of the town when it was ruled by the Spaniards.
▶ **Acradina.** Of the Greek quarters of the city, this is the one of least interest. ▶ All that remains of the agora are parts of a pillar in the vast modern **Foro Siracusano** (C-D2). There are few signs of the colonnaded porch that ran around the **Roman gymnasium** (C2; 1C) or the temple that stood in the middle of the agora. There was a theatre here too, and, although it was once possible to see part of its auditorium and some of its steps, the sea level has risen and they are now submerged.
▶ The highlight of a tour of Syracuse is the **Neapolis Archaeological Park**★★ (A-B1-2; *9 a.m.-1 hr before sunset; closed Mon*), which contains the ruins of Neapolis. Among these are the **altar of Hieron II**, of which the base remains; the altar was used for public sacrifices of animals in the 3C BC. The Romans built a vast piazza with colonnaded porches in front of it and a swimming pool. ▶ The **Roman amphitheatre**★ (B1) is thought to have been built in the 3C and it was almost as large as the one in Verona. ▶ The small church of **S. Nicolo**, at the entrance to the amphitheatre, has an apse and a small side door from the 11C-12C. ▶ The marvelous **Greek theatre**★★ (A-B1), dug almost entirely out of rock, is the one that Hieron II rebuilt in 230 BC, but the original was certainly much older, and the tragedies of Aeschylus and the comedies of Epicharmus were performed in it in the 5C BC. The extant auditorium is very big (it could accommodate 15,000 spectators), and forty-six of its original sixty-one steps are still visible. Little remains of the stage (it is said that Charles V took the stone blocks from it and used them for the fortifications around Ortygia). There is a splendid view★ of the city from the top of the steps. ▶ The **latomia del Paradiso**★★ (A1) is an ancient quarry that has now been partly turned into a public garden; it opens onto two grottos, one, which was called by Caravaggio **the ear of Dionysius** because of the peculiar shape of its entrance, gave rise to the myth that the ancient tyrant could listen in, at the entrance to the grotto, to the conversations of the prisoners he had chained in the quarry. ▶ For centuries, and until quite recently, rope-makers exercised their profession in the **grotta dei Cordari**★ *(closed at present)*. ▶ By means of a gallery in the wall of the latomia del Paradiso, it is possible to pass to the **latomia Intagliatella** (A1), another old quarry that has been transformed into a magnificent citrus orchard. From here there is an arch into another old quarry, the **latomia di S. Venera** (A1), which has been turned into a garden surrounded by tall vertical walls, in which are niches where votive offerings were placed in memory of the dead. From this quarry there is a rocky path up to the **Grotticelli burial ground** (A2) with Greek, Hellenic, Roman and Byzantine tombs dug out of the limestone. A Roman vault for cremation urns from the 1C is called the **tomb of Archimedes**. However, Archimedes' tomb, which is mentioned by Cicero, has never been found. ▶ The beautiful **viale Rizzo** (A-B1) is a scenic route around the parco archeologico.
▶ **The Tiche district.** There are large rectangular pits, not far from the railway station, which once served as dry docks for ships; these are all that remain of the old **Syracuse Arsenal** (C3). ▶ In **piazza della Vittoria** (B2) excavations have unearthed a paved road running E to W; it seems that this artery was used, in Hellenic-Roman times, to plan the layout of the area. ▶ In a large tree-lined square the church of **S. Lucia al Sepolcro** (B3; rebuilt in the 17C) is supposed to be on the site where the Syracusan virgin was martyred in 304. Many of the splendid works of art that were originally in the church, like the *Burial of S. Lucia*★ by Caravaggio, have moved to the Palazzo Bellomo. ▶ Nearby in the octagonal church del **Sepolcro** (17C), it is possible to visit the place where the saint is supposed to have been buried *(accompanied by*

friar); under the church are the **catacombs of S. Lucia** which have only been partly explored and are not open to visitors. ▶ Farther inland is the **Villa Landolina** (A-B3) in which are some pagan burial sites, as well as the city's Protestant cemetery which contains the tomb of August von Platen, the German poet who died in Syracuse in 1835. The Villa Landolina also houses the **Museo Regionale★** *(9 a.m.-2 p.m.; Sun 9 a.m.-1 p.m.),* one of the most important in Italy. It contains prehistoric Sicilian objects, as well as collections of Greek, Roman and early Christian material; among the more recent finds now on display are those from the **secret cache at Adrano★**. There are also sculptures from Megara Hyblaea of a **Kouros★★** and a **Kourotrophos★** (early Greek statuettes of boys), a marble cornice with rain-catching basins in the form of lion's heads, the famous *Winged Victory* from the temple of Athena in Syracuse and a prehistoric head sculpted from the limestone found at the source of the Ciane River. ▶ The small church of **S. Giovanni★** (A2), destroyed by the 1693 earthquake *(9 a.m.-12 noon and 3-5:30 p.m.)* leads to the **crypt of S. Marciano** (first bishop of Syracuse); it is laid out in the form of a Greek cross and has frescos from various periods. The nearby **catacomb of S. Giovanni★** is an underground burial ground of the 4C-5C, with thousands of funeral niches and tombs. ▶ From the **piazza dei Cappuccini** (A4) there is a fine view over the sea. From here it is possible to descend to the **latomia dei Cappuccini★** *(closed temporarily),* another large and picturesque quarry.

Environs

▶ 8 km W is the **Castello Eurialo★★** *(9 a.m.-1 hr before sunset;* from A1), one of the finest and almost complete fortresses from Greek times. It was built by Dionysius to defend the city from the Carthaginians (402-397 BC) and was partly rebuilt by the Byzantines. There are interesting finds in the **Antiquarium** in the caretaker's house. ▶ 7 km SW are the springs of the Ciane River, which can be visited by crossing the plain by road or by going from the Foro Italico by boat up the river. The scenery is very beautiful and the surroundings romantic. □

Archimedes

When Roman forces under the Consul Marcellus besieged Syracuse, they were extremely shocked. Rocks rained down on them from a distance from the city walls, while arrows were showered at them, mowing them down. When the Roman fleet entered the harbour to blockade the city, enormous boulders were hurled into the air as if they were pebbles and crashed down on the Roman galleys and their oarsmen. To the amazement of Marcelus and his generals, long grappling irons emerged from holes in the walls and were operated by men completely concealed behind them; they grabbed the unfortunate ships and, lifting them into the air as if they were toys, hurled them against the harbour walls and rocks, smashing them to pieces. Marcellus knew that this was the work of the great Syracusan Greek scientist Archimedes and withdrew his forces some distance from the city, telling his terrified men, according to Plutarch: 'This man is like the giants of old, some of whom had a hundred arms and hands and could hurl showers of rocks great distances at the same time.'

Practical information

ⓘ v. S. Sebastiano 47 (A2), ☎ 67710 or 67607; archaeological area (B1), ☎ 60510; v. Maestranza 33 (E4), ☎ 66932.

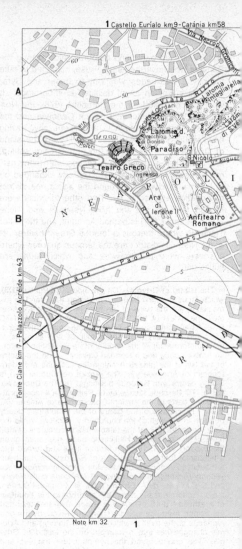

Noto km 32   1

🚋 (C2), ☎ 67964.
🚌 from v. Elorina (D1), ☎ 69555 and v. Trieste (D4), ☎ 66710.
🚢 sailings (E3) for Naples, Reggio di Calabria, Catania and Malta, *Tirrenia*, ☎ 66956.
Car rental: *Avis,* p. della Republica 11, ☎ 65207; *Maggiore,* v. Tevere 14, ☎ 66548.

Hotels:
★★★★ **Jolly,** corso Celone 45 (C2 a), ☎ 64744, 102 rm
Ⓟ 130,000.
★★★ **Grand Hotel Villa Politi,** v. Politi Laudien 2 (A4 b), ☎ 32100, 94 rm Ⓟ 🔧 ⚙ 🛍 ➹ 🖂 70,800; bkf: 7,000.
★★★ **Park Hotel,** v. Filisto 80, ☎ 32644, 102 rm Ⓟ 🖻 🖂 69,000; bkf: 6,000.

Restaurants:
● ◆◆◆ **Jonico-A' Rutta e Ciàuli,** riviera Dionisio il Grande (A4 f), ☎ 66639, closed Tue. In a villa on a rocky spur on seafront. Creative cuisine: risotto alla Siracusana, mackerel alla Dionisio, 28/40,000.

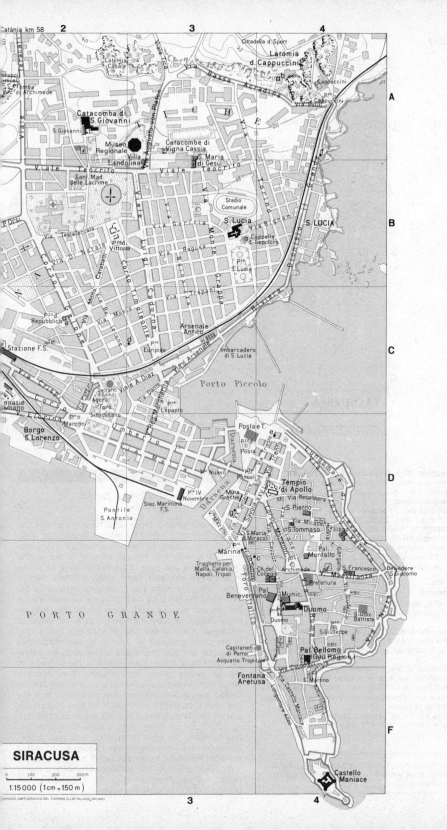

A

B

C

D

F

Citadella d. Sport

Latomia
d. Cappuccini

Cappuccini

Latomia
Casale

Via Tica

Via Bassa Acradina

Via Polti

P.a Cappuccini

Catacomba di
S.Giovanni

S.Giovanni

Museo
Regionale

Villa
Landolina

Catacombe di
Vigna Cassia

S.Maria
di Gesù

S.Maria
delle Lacrime

Viale   Teocrito

Viale   Teocrito

Stadio
Comunale

Via Monte Grappa

Sant. Mad.
delle Lacrime

S.Lucia

S. LUCIA

Cappella
d. Sepolcro

S.Lucia

Via Testaferrata

P.a d.
Vittoria

Arsenale
Antico

Stazione F.S.

Imbarcadero
di S.Lucia

Euripide

Pza d.
Repubblica

Porto   Piccolo

Secc.no
d. Caduti

Agorà e
Foro
Siracusano

Lepanto

Postae T.

Darsena

Borgo
S.Lorenzo

P.a
Posta

Manconi

 Pza
Pancali

Tempio
di Apollo

Via Resalibera

P.a Nuovo

Mura
Greche

S.Pietro

P.a IV
Novembre

Staz. Marittima
F.S.

Via Minerva

Pontile
S. Antonio

S.Tommaso

S.Filippo

S.Maria
d.Miracoli

Pal.
Montalto

Marina

S.Francesco

Belvedere
S.Giacomo

Traghetto per
Malta, Catania,
Napoli, Tripoli

Ch. del
Collegio

Archimede

Maestranza

Prefettura

Pal.
Beneventano

Munic.

Duomo

Duomo

S.Giov.
Battista

S.Giuseppe

Capitaneria
di Porto

Pal. Bellomo
(Gall. Region.)

Acquario Tropicale

Fontana
Aretusa

S.Martino

P O R T O   G R A N D E

Castello
Maniace

SIRACUSA

0   100   200   300m

1:15000 (1cm = 150 m)

SERVIZIO CARTOGRAFICO DEL TOURING CLUB ITALIANO, MILANO

3   4

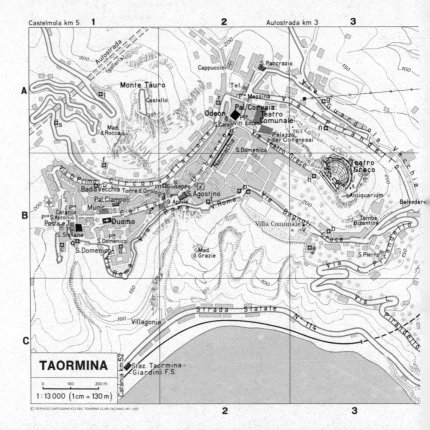

Castelmola km 5 **1** **2** Autostrada km 3 **3**

TAORMINA

0   100   200 m
1 : 13 000 (1cm = 130 m)

© SERVIZIO CARTOGRAFICO DEL TOURING CLUB ITALIANO, MILANO

♦♦♦ *Arlecchino,* largo Empedocle 8 (C2-3 d), ☎ 66386, closed Mon and Aug. Regional cuisine: pennette alla Roberto, grilled meat and fish, 25/40,000.
♦♦♦ *Fratelli Bandiera,* v. G. Perno 6 (D4 e), ☎ 65021, closed Mon and Oct. Regional cuisine: rigatoni Norma, red mullet Sicilian style, 25/35,000.
♦♦ *Archimede,* v. Gemmellaro 8 (E3-4 c), ☎ 69701, closed Sun and 5-20 Jul. Seafood: risotto with shellfish, swordfish with orange sauce, 20/30,000.
♦ *Pippo,* v. XX Settembre 13 (D3 g), ☎ 65945, closed Mon and Oct. Seafood: spaghetti with cuttle-fish, fish soup, 20/30,000.

Recommended
Aquarium: (E4), ☎ 69590.
Canoeing: *Canottieri Siracusa,* v. Testaferrata 22, ☎ 64340.
Clay pigeon shooting: at Armenia, ☎ 741222.
Craft workshops: *L'Altro Egitto,* v. Senofonte 28 (papyrus makers); *G. Samminito,* v. dei Platani, ☎ 52842 (embroidery).
Events: classical opera at *Teatro Greco* in summer, in even yrs, *National Institute of Ancient Drama,* ☎ 65373; *International Festival of Music* and *Open Air Opera* (Jun-Sep); *Festival and Procession of Santa Lucia* (13 Dec); *Festival of San Sebastian* (20 Jan).
Sailing: *Lega Navale,* p. Lepanto 24, ☎ 69147.
Swimming: v. Delfica, ☎ 37412 (also tennis).

If you enjoy sports, consult the pages pertaining to the regions; there you will find addresses for practicing your favorite sport.

TAORMINA**

Messina 49, Palermo 255, Rome 724 km
Pop. 10, 254 ⊠ 98039 ☎ 0942   F3

Goethe was among those who have contributed to making Taormina one of the world's best-known places. In his *Travels in Italy,* he writes: 'If you place yourself among the highest tiers of seats in the Greek theatre, you have to admit that no other public in a theatre has ever been presented with such a vista. On your right you have fortresses and castles filling the hill tops, further away, beneath you is the city with houses which, even though they may be more recent, occupy the same space as those of antiquity. On your left you have the sea and a view of the coast going up to Catania, or even further, to Syracuse, and then the picture is closed by the colossal, smoking volcano, Etna, which, in the softness of the air seems gentle and distant'. Two hundred years later the picture is exactly the same and the city seems suspended between the mountains and the sea, with Etna gazing down on it. It was built on the side of Mt. Taurus and it had much the same history as other towns in Sicily, being Greek, Roman, Arabic and Norman. Its most prosperous time was probably under the Normans in the Middle Ages, and it remains, in spite of its famous Greek ruins, essentially a medieval town. It has glorious weather and lovely subtropical vegetation in which the perfumes of the orange and the almond are foremost.

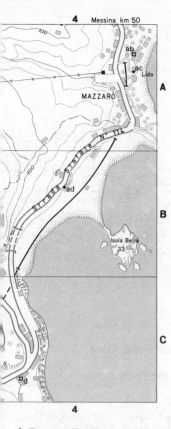

4 Messina km 50

MAZZARÒ

A

B

C

4

▶ The **porta Messina,** an entrance to the town, leads to the **piazza Vittorio Emanuele** (A2), which is on the site of the Roman Forum. The **Palazzo Corvaia★** is located here, a 15C edifice with a crenellated façade, mullioned windows and a Gothic-Catalan portal on its side, near which is the church of S. Caterina. ▶ Behind the church, the **Odeon** (A2) is a building from the days of imperial Rome, when it was used for musical performances. Some of the steps leading to it can still be seen; the front of the stage joined the side of a Hellenistic temple and traces of this can also be detected. ▶ Also in the p. Vittorio Emanuele, recent excavations have unearthed the remains of an imperial Roman bath. The nearby **Greek theatre★★** (B3; *9 a.m.-5:30 p.m.; closed Mon*) is from the later Hellenistic period (3C BC); the Romans (perhaps in the 2C) completely rebuilt it. The stage had niches and pillars and some of these remain; the view★★ from the front of the theatre or on the tiers is exactly as described by Goethe. ▶ An **antiquarium** in the house of the caretaker *(9 a.m.-1 p.m.)* has fragments of marble, reliefs and inscriptions giving accounts of the duties performed by the city's principal magistrates. ▶ The **corso Umberto** (B1-2) is the main street and it cuts across the town from one end to the other, lined with smart shops and sumptuous cafés. The first street, on the r. (v. Naumachia) leads to a long wall with niches which is called **Naumachia** (A-B2). This construction dates from the late Roman Empire and at one time supported a large vaulted cistern. ▶ The corso Umberto crosses the **piazza IX Aprile,** an animated and colourful square with a splendid view out to sea; on one side is the former Gothic church of **St. Augustine** (1448), now the public library. ▶ The gate of the **torre dell'Orologio** (clock tower) leads to the medieval part of town where many of the houses still preserve their ancient portals and Roman-Gothic win-

dows. To the r., the **Palazzo Ciampoli** (now a hotel) is a fine example of Catalan-Gothic architecture (1412). ▶ A little farther is piazza del Duomo with a 17C fountain. The **Duomo★** (B1) is a crenellated building of a rather severe appearance, reminiscent of a Norman cathedral. It was built in the 13C, underwent some alterations in the 15C and the 16C and was renovated in 1636. In its interior are three naves, separated by ogival arches resting on single pillars. The altars are ornamented with tryptychs by the painters of the Messina school (*Visitation* by A. Giuffré; *Madonna and Saints* by Antonello de Saliba). ▶ The corso ends at the **porta Catania** (B1), with, on the l., the **Palazzo Duca di San Stefano★** (B1), a fine 14C-15C building. ▶ A little farther back on the corso, by a fountain, a short street leads to the p. del Carmine, which contains the **Badia Vecchia** (B1), a large crenellated tower pierced by tall ogival windows. It is the remains of a 13C palace. ▶ About halfway along the corso is the **piazzale S. Domenico** (B1); here only the Baroque campanile remains of the old church of S. Domenico which was destroyed by an Allied air raid in 1943. A hotel has taken over the former convent that has a fine 16C cloister. ▶ From the piazzale, the v. Roma leads to the lovely public gardens of the **Villa Comunale;** there are fine views of the city on the way.

Environs

▶ Immediately outside the **porta Messina** is the little church of **S. Pancrazio** with the remains of a small Greek temple dedicated to Serapis. ▶ The **Belvedere** (B3) offers a splendid view over the coast from a point straight above the sea. ▶ The medieval **castle of Taormina** (A1) above the city can be reached by footpaths *(30 mn from Circonvallazione)* or by car along the Castelmola road. It is on the site of an old citadel and offers a magnificent view. ▶ 5 km farther (from A1) is the picturesque village of **Castelmola** on a cliff top; the surroundings are medieval and the terrazzo of the Caffè S. Giorgio affords a famous view★. ▶ Taormina has a marvelous beach at **Mazzaro** (A4; *4 km by road; 15 mn from St. Pancrazio by path and steps; 2.5 mn by cablecar)* and another equally beautiful at **Isola Bella** (B4). It is also possible to go by boat to the marine **caves of Cape St. Andrea,** the cape that divides the two beaches. The coast below Taormina is fascinating. As Goethe said, 'we enjoyed the view of this beautiful shore, under the loveliest of skies, from a small balcony, looking at the roses and listening to the nightingales'. □

Practical information _____

≋ **TAORMINA**
ⓘ p. S. Caterina Palazzo Corvaia (A2), ☎ 23243; corso Umberto (B2), ☎ 23751.
🚂 (C1), ☎ 50177.
Car rental: *Avis,* v. S. Pancrazio 6, ☎ 23041.
Hotels:
★★★★★ *San Domenico Palace,* p. San Domenico 5 (B1a), ☎ 23701, 117 rm 🅿 ≮ ᠔ ▦ ▭ 350,000
★★★★ *Bristol Park,* v. Bagnoli Croci 92 (B3b), ☎ 23006, 58 rm 🅿 ▭ closed Nov-Feb, 137,500; bkf: 18,000.
★★★★ *Excelsior Palace,* v. Toselli 8 (B1c), ☎ 23975, 89 rm 🅿 ≮ ᠔ ▦ ♿ ▭ closed 16 Nov-28 Feb, 100,000; bkf: 15,000.
★★★★ *Grande Albergo Capo Taormina,* at Capo Taormina (C4d), ☎ 24000, 208 rm 🅿 ≮ ▦ ♿ ✻ ▭ closed Nov-14 Apr, 175,000.
★★★★ *Jolly Diodoro* (J), v. Bagnoli Croce 75 (B3e), ☎ 23312, 102 rm 🅿 ≮ ▦ ▭ ᠔ 170,000.
★★★★ *Méditerranée,* v. Circonvallazione 61 (B1f), ☎ 23901, 50 rm 🅿 ≮ ▦ ▭ closed Nov-Mar, 129,500.
★★★★ *Miramare,* v. Guardiola Vecchia 27 (A3g), ☎ 23401, 49 rm 🅿 ▦ ▭ closed 1 Nov-19 Mar and Christmas, 92,000.
★★★ *Continental,* v. Dionisio 1 (B1i), ☎ 23805, 43 rm ▦ 65,000; bkf: 7,000.
★★★ *Lido Méditerranée,* at Lido Spisone, v. Nazionale, ☎ 24422, 72 rm 🅿 ▦ ♿ Pens. Closed Nov-Mar, 125,000.
★★★ *Park Hotel Silemi,* at Letoianni, ☎ 36228, 49 rm 🅿 ᠔ ✻ ♿ closed Nov-Mar, 90,000.

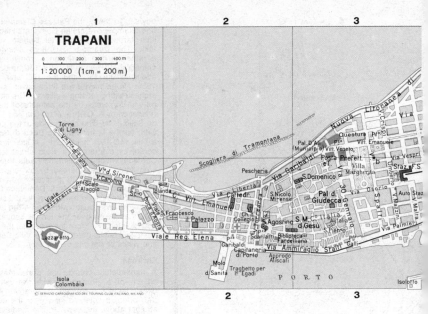

TRAPANI

0 100 200 300 400 m

1 : 20 000 (1 cm = 200 m)

★★★ **Sole Castello,** rotabile Castelmola (A1 l), ☎ 28036,
57 rm P ≮ ैं ❀ ⌂ ↗ 60,000; bkf: 12,000.
★★★ **Vello d'Oro,** v. Fazzello 2 (B2 m), ☎ 23788, 59 rm
≮ closed Nov-Feb, 64,000; bkf: 8,000.
★★★ **Villa Fiorita,** v. Pirandello 39 (A3 n), ☎ 24122, 24 rm
P ≮ ⚜ ⌂ No restaurant, 68,000; bkf: 5,500.
★★★ **Villa Paradiso,** v. Roma 2 (B2 p), ☎ 23922, 33 rm ≮
85,000; bkf: 10,000.
★★★ **Villa Riis,** v. Rizzo 13 (B1 q), ☎ 24874, 30 rm   P
≮ ⚜ ैं ⌂ closed Nov-Mar, 85,000; bkf: 10,000.
★★ **Campanella,** v. Circonvallazione 3 (A2 r), ☎ 23381,
12 rm ⚜ ❀ No restaurant, 60,000.
★★ **Corona,** v. Roma 7 (B2 p), ☎ 23021, 33 rm, closed
1 Nov-14 Feb, 48,000.
★★ **Villa Kristina,** rotabile Castelmola 23 (A1 s), ☎ 28366,
32 rm P ⌂ closed Nov-Jan, 60,000.
★★ **Villa Schuler,** p. Bastione (B2 t), ☎ 23481, 27 rm P
⚜ closed Dec-Feb. No restaurant, 46,000; bkf: 6,000.
★ **Peppe,** at Letoianni, v. Nazionale 345, ☎ 36159, 28 rm
⚜ ैं closed 16 Sep-14 Mar, 30,000; bkf: 3,500.

Restaurants:
● ◆◆◆◆ **Villa le Terrazze,** corso Umberto 172 (B1 z),
☎ 23913, Closed Mon and Nov-Mar. 15C dining room
and terrace facing city. Seafood: papardelle with lobster, risotto caprice, 40/55,000.
◆◆ **Luraleo,** v. Bagnoli Croce 31 (B3 v), ☎ 24279, closed
Tue in winter and 10 Jan-15 Feb. Seafood: trenette with
cuttle-fish, swordfish, 25/35,000.
◆ **Giova Rosy Senior,** corso Umberto 38 (A2 u), ☎ 24411,
closed Mon and 7 Jan-28 Feb. One of best-known and
oldest in town. Seafood: spaghetti del Capitano, swordfish, 25/40,000.

⚑ ★ *San Leo,* at Capo Taormina, ☎ 24658 (all year).

Recommended

Events: *Sicilian Cart and Costume Display* (May); *International Cinema Festival* (Jul); *summer theatre season*
at *Teatro Greco,* ☎ 23220; *summer festival of classical music.*
Excursions: by cablecar from Mazzaro (A3), ☎ 23906.
Farm vacations: at Blandina, ☎ 23712 or 36376.
Tennis: v. Bagnoli Croce, ☎ 23282.

Environs

MAZZARO, ⊠ 98030, ☎ 0942, 4 km E.

Hotel:
★★★★★ **Mazzaro Sea Palace,** v. Nazionale 147 (A4 ab),
☎ 24004, 81 rm P ≮ ⚜ ैं ⌂ closed Nov-Mar, 300,000;
bkf: 20,000.

Restaurants:
● ◆◆ **Pescatore,** v. Nazionale 107 (B4 ad), ☎ 23460,
closed Mon and Nov-Feb. On a rocky spur with excellent service. Seafood: cannelloni Giovanni, sea perch,
20/40,000.
◆ **Delfino,** v. Nazionale 107 (A4 ac), ☎ 23004, closed
16 Oct-14 Mar. Splendid terrace over the sea. Seafood: cannelloni alla domenicana, lobster on spit,
20/30,000.

TERMINI IMERESE

Palermo 38, Rome 869 km
Pop. 25,389 ⊠ 90018 ☎ 091   C3

Termini Imerese is divided into an **upper City** and a
lower City, both of which sit on the slopes of a headland on the N coast. In the **Villa Palmeri** public gardens are the remains of an old **Roman curia** and,
nearby, those of an **amphitheatre.** 15C-16C frescos
inside the church of **S. Catherine** depict the life of the
saint in a popular style with descriptive handwritten
texts in the dialect of the time. In the **Gancia**
church (also called S. Maria del Gesù) is a painting
of *St. George and the Dragon* by Nicola da Voltri. In
the **Duomo** (rebuilt in the 16C; *now being renovated*) are statues and reliefs of the 16C-18C. There is
a magnificent view from the small square behind the
church where the belvedere is located. In the church
of **S. Maria della Misericordia** *(now being renovated)*
on the piazza Mazzini, the main centre of the upper
City, is a large tryptych attributed to Gaspare da
Pesaro (1453). 10 km S is **Càccamo** with a picturesque 12C **castle★** with towers and battlements; it

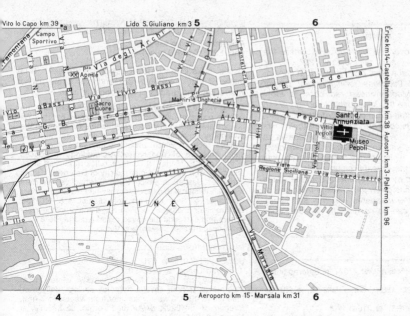

Vito lo Capo km 39   Lido S.Giuliano km 3 **5**   **6**

Érice km 14 - Castellammare km 38 Autostr. km 3 - Palermo km 96

4   **5** Aeroporto km 15 - Marsala km 31   **6**

was partly rebuilt in the 17C and can be visited. It offers some splendid views. ☐

Practical information _____

⚓ ★★ *Torre Battilamano*, at Buonfornello, v. Ugdulena 66, 80 pl, ☎ 8140044 (all year).
Recommended
Marina: ☎ 8141007.

TINDARI

Messina 65, Palermo 177, Rome 734 km
Pop. 73 ⊠ 98060, ☎ 0941   E2

Tindari rests by the sea, on the beautiful site of the ancient Greek city of Tyndaris. It was founded by the Syracusans in 396 BC and destroyed by the Arabs.

▶ The **piazzale Belvedere** has an extraordinary view of the sea, from Cape Calavà to the Milazzo foreland and the Lipari Islands. On the piazzale is the modern sanctuary of the **Madonna Nera** (the Black Madonna), a Byzantine statue that arrived miraculously from the East. ▶ Excavations include *(9 a.m.-1 hr before sunset; Sun 9 a.m.-1:45 p.m.; closed Mon)* a **Greek theatre**★ (2C-3C BC, rebuilt during Roman period) with auditorium and foundations of the stage; a **decuman** (ancient gate) with original pavement and a whole settlement with **taverns** and a **Roman house** (1C BC) with a peristyle with twelve pillars and a mosaic floor. There is also a **basilica**★ from imperial times, which served as an entrance to the agora. ▶ Many interesting finds are kept in the **museum** *(9 a.m.-2 p.m.; Sun 9 a.m.-1 p.m.; closed Mon)* including a rebuilt **front of the stage of the Roman theatre.** ▶ The **walls**, which surrounded the entire hill, are among the most splendid and best preserved anywhere (3C BC), and the S part, with towers and a gate with two arches, is almost intact. ☐

Practical information _____

Restaurant:
♦ **Agora**, v. Teatro Greco 6, ☎ 369013, closed Fri. Close

to Greek theatre. Mixed cuisine: tagliatelle all francescana, cannelloni and meat sauce, 15/20,000.

TRAPANI

Palermo 105, Rome 1,006, Milan 1,581 km
Pop. 71,708 ⊠ 91100 ☎ 0923   A3

Because of its position on the extreme W tip of Sicily, Trapani has always been an important port and it does much trade in salt, wine and tuna. For centuries it was a Carthaginian stronghold, and it was here that in 249 BC the Carthaginian fleet was victorious over the Roman one.

▶ **Corso Vittorio Emmanuele** (B2), with many imposing Baroque buildings, is the principal street in the old part of the city. ▶ The seafront boulevard, **lungomare Regina Elena** (B1-2), goes by the port where there is a fine view of the salt works and the Aegadean Islands. ▶ In the piazzetta Saturno (B2) is the beautiful **fountain of Saturn** (late 15C), as well as the church of **St. Augustine** (14C) with a Gothic portal with a beautiful rosette. ▶ In the church of **S. Maria del Gesù** (B2-3), is a glazed terra-cotta **Madonna degli Angeli**★ by Andrea della Robbia, under a marble canopy by Antonello Gagini (1521). ▶ In the old ghetto, the **Palazzo della Giudecca** (B3) is a 16C building with diamond-shaped bosses and richly decorated windows. ▶ The town's chief monument is the **sanctuary of the Annunziata**★ (A6), a church that still retains its old 13C façade, with a Gothic portal and rosette, while its campanile is Baroque. In the interior, also 17C, there is a single nave and chapels of the Fishermen (15C) and of the Sailors (16C), and the *Madonna di Trapani* in the beautifully decorated chapel of the Madonna behind the high altar. ▶ The former **convent dell'Annunziata** (18C), with a fine cloister, houses the **Museo Regionale Pepoli**★ *(9 a.m.-2 p.m.; Wed and Fri also 3-5 or 5:30 p.m. winter; Sun 9 a.m.-1 p.m.; closed Mon)* with collections of archaeological finds, paintings, sculpture, traditional Trapani coral work and mirror arts. ▶ Among its masterpieces are the *San Giacomo*★ of Antonello Gagini (1522), a *Pietà*★ by Roberto Oderisi and a *San Francesco Receiving the Stigmata*★ by Tiziano. ☐

Coral

Coral is found all over the world in seas where the temperature does not fall below 20° C or 68° Fahr. In tropical waters coral grows to a considerable height and thickness forming great barrier reefs. However, Mediterranean red coral is most highly prized because it is susceptible to a high polish and is much used for ornamental purposes. Extensive fisheries for this coral are operated off the coasts of Sardinia, in the Bay of Naples, on the coasts of N. Africa and in the sea around Sicily. Traditionally, on the island the fishing and working of coral has been carried on in the Trapani region. It is said that this art was learned by the Trapanese from the Arabs centuries ago and has given the Sicilians their love of the Baroque and the mannered carvings and sculptures in coral that can be seen in the Museo Pepoli of Trapani.

Practical information _____

ⓘ via Serba (head office; A4), ☎ 27077; p. Saturno (information; B2), ☎ 29000.
✈ at Birgi, ☎ 841130; *Alitalia*, corso Italia 52, ☎ 23819.
🚂 (B3), ☎ 40416.
🚢 from v. Malta (B3), ☎ 21641.
🚢 sailings to Aegadean Islands and for Pantelleria, for Cagliari and for Tunis; several hydrofoil sailings daily for the Aegadean Islands, *Siremar* and *Tirrenia*, ☎ 40515; *Traghetti delle Isole*, ☎ 22467.

Hotels:
★★★ *Astoria Park*, lungomare Alighieri, ☎ 62400, 93 rm ℗ ▥ ♿ ▤ ⁀ 90,000.
★★ *Cavallino Bianco*, lungomare Alighieri, ☎ 21549, 60 rm 43,000; bkf: 5,000.

Restaurants:
● ◆◆◆ *P & G*, v. Spalti 1 (A-B3 b), ☎ 47701, closed Sun and Aug. In garden full of flowers. Regional cuisine: grilled fish, meat on spit, 25/30,000.
◆◆ *Arco*, v. Bixio 110 (A4 a), ☎ 27796, closed Fri. Seafood: risotto with shellfish, pasta with sardine, 18/25,000.

Recommended
Archery: *Compagnia Arcieri Casasanta*, v. XXX Gennaio 22, ☎ 29832; *Compagnia Arcieri Tirreno*, ☎ 21972.
Events: *Procession of the Mysteries of Good Friday; Trapanese Musical July* (Opera, theatre, ballet at Villa Comunale), ☎ 22934.
Sailing: *Lega Navale*, v. Duca d'Aosta, ☎ 29200.

For help in understanding terms when visiting museums or other sites, see the *Art and Architectural Terms Guide* at the end of the Practical Holiday Guide.

The island of USTICA

Palermo 60, Rome 968 km
Pop. 1,202 ✉ 90010 ☎ 091   B1

Ustica looks like a tortoise asleep on the sea. It is made of black, volcanic rock and has fertile plains where figs and grapes ripen alongside cacti.

▶ The village of **Ustica** is on a tufa plateau, between the landing points of cala Santa Maria and cala Giaconi. Its houses are painted and decorated (some frescoed on the outside by contemporary artists) and lie beneath the **Falconiera** rock, in which ancient tombs were dug. ▶ A small **Museum of Underwater Archaeology** is housed in the Torre S. Maria. It contains relics of ancient ships and material from the submerged city of **Osteodes** (Greek name for Ustica), in which 6,000 Carthaginian soldiers were left to starve to death after they had revolted against Carthage. ▶ Near the Faraglioni district is a 14C-13C BC prehistoric **village**. ▶ Fish are plentiful in the clear waters that surround the **caves** called Azzurra, della Pastizza, delle Barche, Segreta and Verde.   □

Practical information _____

USTICA, ✉ 90010, ☎ 091.
ⓘ p. Vito Longo, ☎ 8449190.
🚢 daily car ferries (several weekly winter) from Palermo (*c.* 2 hrs); several hydrofoil sailings daily from Palermo (*c.* 1 hr), 3 weekly summer from Naples (*c.* 4 hrs), *Siremar*, ☎ 8449002; *SNAV*, at Palermo, ☎ 329990; at Naples, ☎ 081/660444.

Hotel:
★★★ *Grotta Azzura*, ☎ 8449048, 52 rm ♿ ▤ closed 16 Sep-14 Jun, 66,000; bkf: 6,000.

Restaurant:
◆ *Clelia*, v. Magazzino 7, ☎ 8449039. Regional cuisine: pasta and sardine, risotto and shellfish, 18/23,000.

Recommended
Events: international meeting on undersea activities (Jul).

VITTORIA

Ragusa 24, Palermo 243, Rome 876 km
Pop. 52,994 ✉ 97019 ☎ 0932   D5

Vittoria, on a ledge on the S slopes of the Iblei, is a new town laid out like a chessboard. It was founded in 1607 by Vittoria Colonna, daughter of the Viceroy of Sicily, Marcantonio Colonna, and wife of the feudal Count of Modica. The town is named after her. The first inhabitants came from the surrounding villages and towns.

▶ The **chiesa Madre** and **Madonna delle Grazie** are elegant, as is the Neoclassical **Teatro Communale**. ▶ The private collection of the craftsman Giovanni Virgadavola served as a basis for the **Museo del carretto Siciliano** (Sicilian cart) which is presently being created *(inquire at municipio).*   □

Trentino-Alto Adige ●

In Trentino ethnic origins, culture and language vary. The course of the Adige and its tributaries resembles the veins of a leaf. The regional boundaries include the Sarca basin, the upper valley of the Chiese in the W, and the Valsugana, the upper valley of the Brenta in the E. This mountainous region should be enjoyed valley by valley. The valleys have several different levels. At the top are alpine peaks with glittering glaciers. Next, in the shoulders and hollows of high pastures, fir plantations are reflected in lakes. Where rivers have gouged channels in the cliffs and ravines, villages nestle with wooden spires and onion domes on campaniles. Castles are everywhere. Vineyards spread over slopes high and low and orchards are full of peaches, pears and apples. The first snows are on the peaks by harvest time. Central to the region are the Dolomites. They are named after Déodat de Dolomieu, a French geologist, who identified their composition as largely calcium and magnesium carbonate. There are two groups: the lesser, in Trentino, is the Brenta Dolomites; the larger group — the Dolomites — extends over Trentino, Bolzano and Cadorino and is part of Venetia. The rocky masses are alive with animal and plant life: bears in the Brenta Dolomites, deer in the Panaveggio woods, gamebirds of every description, amid rhododendron, gentian and crocus. Between the Italian Trentino and the German-speaking Tyrol there still exists a separate Ladin (neo-Latin-speaking) community. Culture and customs vary with language. In certain valleys the people wear their colourful traditional costumes. This is not folklore for the tourists, but a reflection of their profound sense of identity. □

● Don't miss

Visitors come for mountains, dense forests, picturesque villages and especially the Dolomites. Lake Carezza★ is a well-known Dolomite feature. Famous resorts are Ortisei★, Madonna di Campiglio★, San Martino di Castrozza★, in the mountains, and Riva del Garda★ on Lake Garda. There are excellent views from Sass Pordoi★ (cableway from the Pordoi Pass), Belvedere I★ (cableway from Canazei), Col Rodella★ (chair lift from Campitello di Passa), Cune★ (cableway from Moeno), la Rosetta★ (chair lift and cableway from San Martino di Castrozza), the Rifugio Livrio (cableway and chair lift from the Stelvio Pass) and the Rifugio Presena★ (cableway from the Tonale Pass). The artistic heritage is considerable: Merano★★; Bressanone★ (cathedral cloister★); Trento★ (Duomo★★, Castello del Buonconsiglio★★ and frescos of the months★ in the Torre dell'Aquila). Rare works of art include the Dance of Death★ in the Dominican church at Bolzano, the Carolingian frescos in the church of S. Benedetto in Malles Venosta and the painted doors★ at Vipiteno.

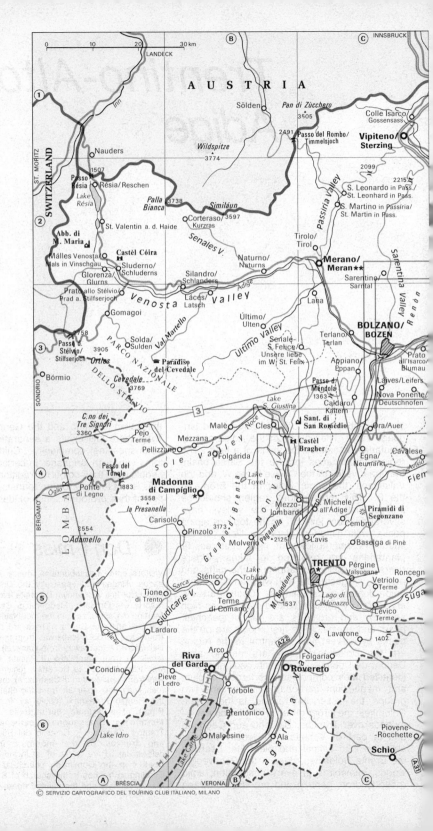

● *Brief regional history*

4C BC-5C AD
The Romans. The region was important for communication (the Brenner Pass was crossed before recorded history), but had only minor cultural links with neighbouring areas. ● The **Rhaetian culture** flourished in the late Iron Age (4C-1C BC). ● The **Romans** were already in Trentino by the end of the 2C BC. ● Under the later (Augustan) emperors the region was divided into *Venetia et Histria* and the provinces of *Betia et Vindelicia* (N of Chiusa) and *Noricum* (la Pusteria). ● Christian evangelization began in the 2C and progressed rapidly under **Bishop Vigilio** (4C), and conversion was complete by the end of the 8C.

6C-11C
The imperial road. After the barbarian invasions and the fall of the Roman Empire, Theodoric the Goth considered the region an outpost of his Italian kingdom. At his death (526), the **Bavarians** seized the Alto Adige; slightly later (569) the Lombards made Trentino into a dukedom. After a long conflict, the Franks designated the Tridentine dukedom as a march (border territory). ● When Charlemagne's empire was dismantled (9C), **Berengarius of Friuli** ceded the Tridentine marches to Arnolfo di Carinzia (888) in exchange for the ephemeral title of King of Italy. ● Then the Holy Roman Emperor Conrad II the Salic reorganized his feudal empire and conferred the title of prince on the bishops of **Trento and Bressanone** (1027). The duty of these feudal lords was to keep open the imperial road **(Brenner-Isarco-Adige)**, through which the emperor tried to control the Italian peninsula. ● Under imperial sovereignty, the power of the two bishops lasted until the 18C.

Duomo in Trento

12C-14C
The prince-bishops and counts of the Tyrol. A family from Venosta, which took the title of count from a castle above Merano **(Castel Tirolo)**, held the title of *advocatus ecclesiae* (representative of the church) from the prince-bishops of Trento (1240) and Bressanone (1248). ● When the male line died out in 1253, the **county of Tyrol** passed by marriage to the **counts of Gorizia** and, when that line was extinguished in 1363, **Margherita**, the last of the Tirolo family, ceded the county to Duke **Rudolph IV of Hapsburg.** ● The castles of Trentino and the Alto Adige are reminders of the region's feudal past, of the balance of power between the prince-bishops and the counts of Tirolo, the other noble families and the **Communes**, which enjoyed varying degrees of autonomy.

Duomo in Bressanone

15C
Venice. In the S part of the region the rule of the Venetian Republic was strengthened when it took **Rovereto** in 1416 and **Riva del Garda** in 1441. ● Venetian rule came to an end in 1509 with the War of the League of Cambrai. The territories controlled by Venice were annexed by the county of Tirolo. The title of count was then held by Maximilian I of Hapsburg, who also occupied the imperial throne.

15C-19C
The Hapsburgs. Transfer of Tirolo to the Hapsburgs meant that a new factor was introduced into the power structure of the region. However, the Hapsburgs' rise to imperial power (which became permanent with **Maximilian I)** was of great significance to the region. ● The culture of **Trento** flourished under the humanist Prince-Bishop **Bernardo Clesio** (1514-39). ● Under his successor, **Christoforo Madruzzo**, Trento was chosen as the seat for the **Council of Trent** (1546-63), held in the hope of finding common ground between Lutherans and Roman Catholics — Trento lay midway between the Latin and Germanic worlds. ● In the 17C, **Claudia de' Medici**, regent of the Tirolo, agreed to the development of **Bolzano** as the commercial and financial centre of the region. ● In 1665, Emperor **Leopold I** began to govern the region directly from Vienna (the governor established himself in **Innsbruck**). ● The Bishop of Trento surrendered his last powers to Emperor **Joseph II** (1780-90).

19C-20C
Italian nationalism. Nationalism arose relatively late in the multilingual Hapsburg Empire. Italian, German and Romansch speakers had lived together for centuries. ● The identity of the Tyrolean people took shape with the rebellion led by **Andreas Hofer** (1809-10), which followed Napoleon's transfer of the Tyrol to Bavarian rule in 1805. The essentially Italian character of Trentino was demonstrated by its active participation in the Risorgimento. ● The end of World War I brought a German-speaking minority within the confines of the Italian state. The problems thus caused were underestimated and aggravated by errors, especially by the events . of World War II. ● The region of Trentino-Alto Adige was formalized in 1948 by the **Gasperi-Gruber Agreement** (5 September 1946). Today the region includes the two **autonomous provinces** of Trento (Trentino, S) and bilingual Bolzano (Alto Adige, N).

Duomo in Bolzano

● *Practical information*

Information: *Assessorato al Turismo,* at Trento, corso 3 Novembre 132, ☎ 0461/980000; *Ufficio provinciale del Turismo,* at Bolzano, p. Parrocchia 11/12, ☎ 0471/993880; *Uffici Turismo Trentino,* at Rome, Galleria Colonna 7, ☎ 06/6794216; at Milan, p. Diaz 5, ☎ 02/874387.

SOS: public emergency assistance, ☎ 113; police emergency, ☎ 112; road breakdown *(ACI),* ☎ 116; snow emergencies, ☎ 0461/33166 or 0471/971694.

Weather: forecast, ☎ 0471/49191; road conditions, ☎ 0471/49000 or 06/4212 *(ACI);* snow reports, ☎ 02/67509, 051/993162 or 992992.

Vacation villages: *Sciliar 2145,* at Siusi Alps (alpine office of *TCI*); *Hotel Village Valtur Marilleva,* at Mezzana; *Hotel Majestic Dolomiti,* at San Martino di Castrozza.

Farm vacations: *Associazione regionale Agriturist,* at Bolzano, v. Brénnero 7/A, ☎ 0471/972145; *Associazione Agriturismo trentino,* at Trento, v. Brénnero 23, ☎ 0461/36211.

Masi chiusi

The word maso *recurs frequently in the place-names and language of Alto Adige. It indicates a landed estate, large farm or temporary building connected with stock-raising. It comes from the medieval Latin* mansum, *with its root in the verb* manere *(to stay). A* mansum *was the area that one family could cultivate with two oxen and one plough. It was the basic unit used in Roman colonization for the organization of agricultural land, military conscription and the collection of taxes. In Alto Adige today, the* maso chiuso *(in German* erbhof*) is a commercial unit in the mountains, in arable farming or in stock-raising that, whether transferred or sold, must remain undivided. A* maso chiuso *must be sufficient to sustain a whole family; its indivisibility had great positive effects, avoiding the excessive fragmentation over generations that damaged upland agriculture elsewhere. It had negative social effects, however, on younger sons, who were excluded from the estate.*

Facts and figures

Location: *Trentino-Alto Adige forms a triangle of mountains and valleys, stretching from the alpine watershed down to Lake Garda. This is the upper basin of the River Adige, the second longest river in Italy. The region is notable for the Dolomites. The region borders on Switzerland and Austria and includes the northernmost point in the republic of Italy, the Vetta d'Italia (9,554 ft). The name combines those of the region's two provinces: Alto Adige or the province of Bolzano in the N; Trentino or the province of Trento in the S.*
Area: *13,613 sq km.*
Climate: *Alpine, but with mild winters compared with other European regions of the same latitude. Abundant sunshine allows wine-grape cultivation; low winter rainfall encourages winter sports.*
Population: *873,415 (third lowest population density in Italy).*
Administration: *The special constitution (1948) provides for the autonomous provinces of Trento and Bolzano.*

Fairs and markets: *international trade fair,* at Bolzano; *agricultural exhibition and market,* at Trento; *mountaineering exhibition,* at Trento.

Events: *May festival,* exhibition with tasting of Alto Adige wines, *Busoni international piano-playing competition,* at Bolzano; *Trentino Autumn,* exhibition of Trentino wines, at Trento; *International mountain and exploration film festival; Marcialonga cross-country ski race* from Moena to Cavalese; *3-Tre slalom* (World Cup), at Madonna di Campiglio; *Topolino skiing trophy* for young contestants, at Trento.

Nature parks: *Stelvio national park,* at Bormio (→ Lombardy), v. Monte Braulio 56, ☎ 0342/901582; regional nature parks of Sciliar, Dolomiti di Sesto, Fanes-Braies, Gruppo di Tessa, Monte Corno and Puez-Odle: office at Bolzano, *Ufficio Parchi Naturali,* v. Battisti 21, ☎ 0471/994300; regional natural parks of Adamello-Brenta and Paneveggio-Pale di S. Martino: office at Trento, *Servizio Parchi e Foreste Demaniali,* p. Dante 15, ☎ 0461/895831.

Conservation: regional delegation of *WWF,* at Trento, v. Malpaga 8, ☎ 0461/915182; Bolzano division, v. Eggerlienz 1, ☎ 0471/47444 (nature tours); *LIPU,* at Trento, v. Mantova 41, ☎ 0461/31170 or 36339 (bird-

Two cuisines

The Salorno Dam, on the Adige, divides the Italian culture of Trentino from the German-speaking culture of Alto Adige. The region has two traditional cuisines, one a mountain version of Venetian cuisine, the other Hapsburg. That doesn't mean dishes have not been exchanged. The German-style dumplings called knödel, for instance, in Trentino are canéderli. Cornmeal and mushrooms are very important in Trentino cooking. In the summer and autumn as many as 250 varieties of mushrooms are to be found in the daily mushroom market in Trento. Specialties of the Alto Adige have spread throughout Italy. One such is speck, the German word for bacon, which in Alto Adige is pork pickled in salt, garlic, bay leaves, juniper and aromatic herbs and then smoked. Trout is also smoked — Passirio trout are famous — and served with horseradish. A popular salad is made of fresh cabbage served with fried speck and sprinkled with vinegar. You can find excellent goulash and soups, in which you dip schuttelbrot, one of the rye and malt breads from the mountains. The hard, flat discs of bread are rather like ship's biscuit. The pastry-makers of Merano prepare exquisite desserts in the Viennese style. The classic regional dessert is strudel with honey, although there are endless local variations.

watching courses, tours); at Bolzano, v. Segantini 18 ☎ 0471/43170 (nature park tours).

Excursions: signposted long-distance routes: Alte Vie of the Dolomites include Bocchette path (crossing Brenta group from Madonna di Campiglio, Jun-Sep) and Alta Via dei Ladini (from Lake Braies to Lake Carezza, Jun-Sep); information, *SAT*, at Trento, ☎ 0461/21522 or 986462; *CAI*, at Bolzano, ☎ 0471/978172 or 971654; at Merano, ☎ 0473/48944; at Bressanone, ☎ 0472/2293.

Horseback riding: centres (associates of *ANTE*) at Bolzano, Cógolo di Pejo and on Renon plateau.

Mountaineering: information at Trento, *SAT (Società alpinistica tridentini)*, v. Manci, ☎ 0461/21522 or 986462; *Comitato trentino Guide alpine*, ☎ 0461/987090; at Bolzano, *CAI*, p. Erbe 46, ☎ 0471/978172 or 971694, alpine information office, ☎ 0471/993809; *Associazio altoatesina Guide alpine*, ☎ 0471/977317.

Young people's facilities: *Comitato italiano Orientamento e Sport nella Natura*, at Trento, v. Cavour 34, ☎ 0461/983900; affiliated organizations at Arco, v. Mantova 16/A; Borgo Valsugana, v. Vicenza 31; Bolzano, v. Vittorio Veneto 5.

Canoeing: *Federazione italiana canoa-kayak*, at Trento, v. Brescia 29, ☎ 0461/21586; affiliated schools at Bressanone, Merano and Trento.

Skindiving: *Club Rane Nere*, at Trento, p. Dante 1, ☎ 0461/23299; *Gruppo Sommozzatori Riva*, at Riva del Garda, v. Trento 140, ☎ 0464/533251 (instruction).

Skiing: There are ski resorts throughout the region; extensive connections between various resorts can be made with a single ski pass. Summer skiing is possible at Stelvio Pass, Tonale Pass, Marmolada and in upper Senales Valley (→ Venosta Valley, Corteraso). Cross-country skiing circuits at Alpe di Siusi, Anterselva, Canazei, Dobbiaco, Braies Valley and elsewhere.

Golf: *Campo Carlo Magno*, at Madonna di Campiglio.

Flying: *Aeroclub Trento, Man di Mattarello Airport*, ☎ 0461/945265 (also gliding); *Aeroclub S. Giacomo*, Bolzano Airport, ☎ 0471/940165 (also gliding, parachuting, free fall, model aircraft flying).

Fishing: *Federazione italiana pesca sportiva*, at Bolzano, v. Goethe 21, ☎ 0471/975332; at Trento, v. A. da Trento 24, ☎ 0461/983083; for information on fishing conditions (controlled waters, bans, etc.) apply to appropriate section of Federation or local anglers' associations.

Ladin speakers

The affinity between the three neo-Latin linguistic groups of the Trentino-Alto Adige and their separation from true Italian dialects can be explained by geographical and political separation from the other dialects of the Alps. The Ladin dialect of the Dolomites, preserved by a community of only a few thousand, is a Latin remnant from the valley of the Isarco, which became a German linguistic area beginning at the time of the Ottoman Empire. Latin must have displaced the earlier languages of the Rhaetian peoples after the last period of the Roman Republic, and the Ladin dialects are the Romance tongues that evolved from that source. They were spread by the people who, after the 11C, colonized the valleys of the Dolomites and moved outwards from the basin of the Isarco.

 # Towns and places

Trento 40, Milan 170 km
Pop. 6,722 ✉ 38061 ☎ 0464   B6

Ala is an isolated town where cobbled alleyways climb toward the church flanked by ancient **palaces.** Some have 16C-17C portals and frescos; the Palazzi Angelini and Taddei have interesting loggias. The Palazzo Pizzini is Baroque. A **museum** displays natural history exhibits, local artifacts and archaeological remains.

Environs

▶ Among vineyards near Sabbionara *(6 km SW)*, the medieval **Castello di Avio** has rare frescos of secular subjects from the late 14C *(Apr-Sep 9 a.m.-1 p.m.*

and 2-6 p.m.; hols p.m. only; winter 1-4 p.m.; closed Mon except Jul and Aug). ☐

The ALPE DI SIUSI

From Bolzano to Corvara in Badia *(99 km, 1 day; map 1)*

The Alpe di Siusi are a series of undulating meadows speckled with woodland that open above the sharp brim of the l. side of the Val Gardena. At its SW end, separating it from the gorge of the Isarco, rises Sciliar. Viewed from the Isarco, this Dolomite massif rises vertical and flat-topped above rockfalls and woods, topped by a steep, regular pyramid. Farmhouses have white-washed walls and churches have fronts like cottages and onion-domed campaniles.

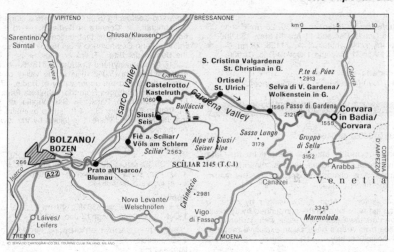

1. The Alpe di Siusi

▶ From **Bolzano** (→) the route enters the valley of the Isarco but soon, at **Prato all'Isarco-Blumau**, it leaves the bottom of the valley and climbs to the first plateau, at the foot of Sciliar and the village of **Fié allo Sciliar-Völs am Schlern** (2,887 ft). The parish church of S. Maria Assunta is late Gothic (16C). ▶ **Siusi-Seis** (3,274 ft) is on the edge of another plateau. ▶ A little farther is a turn which leads up to the **Alpe di Siusi-Seiser Alpe**. The plateau has an average height of 7,000 ft and is bordered by the peaks of Sciliar, Sassolungo and Catinaccio *(it is crossed by several roads, but in summer access for cars is prohibited beyond parking lot by Plaza Hotel; traffic throughout area of the Alpe is banned except for access to hotels for visits of more than 3 days).* ▶ Continuing the route, return by way of the start of the detour to **Castelrotto-Kastelruth** (3,477 ft), again on a plateau. ▶ The scenic descent below the Bullaccia leads to **Ortisei** (→), where the Val Gardena rises through **Santa Christina Valgardena** and **Selva di Val Gardena** (→ Val Gardena). ▶ At the end of the valley, beneath the cliffs of the Sella, the route crosses the **Passo di Gardena** (→), eventually descending into the wide basin of the upper Val Badia at **Corvara in Badia** (→ Val Badia). ☐

Practical information _____

ALPE DI SIUSI-SEISER ALPE, 5,990 ft, ✉ 39040, ☎ 0471.
🎿 Ortisei cableway, cable cars, ski lifts, more than 80 km of cross-country skiing, instruction, ice skating, sled runs at Bullaccia and Spitzbühel.
ⓘ at Castelrotto, ☎ 71333.

Hotels:
★★★★ **Eurotel Sciliar,** ☎ 72928, 84 rm P ⸜ ⸜ 💧 ⌂ closed 6 Apr-19 Jun and 21 Sep-19 Dec, 114,000.
★★★★ **Plaza,** ☎ 72973, 42 rm P ⸜ 💧 ✈ closed Easter-May and Oct-Nov, 136,000.
★★★ **Steger-Dellai,** ☎ 72964, 59 rm P ⸜ ⸜ 💧 ⌂ closed 21 Apr-31 May and 1 Oct-19 Dec, 70,000.

Recommended
Rock climbing: ☎ 71285 (instruction).
Vacation villages: Sciliar 2145 (alpine office of *TCI*, closed May and Oct-Dec), ☎ 02/85261.

CASTELROTTO-KASTELRUTH, ✉ 39040, ☎ 0471.
🎿 cable car, ski lifts, cross-country skiing, instruction, ice skating.
ⓘ in piazza, ☎ 71333.

Hotels:
★★★ **Agnello Posta-Post Hotel Lamm,** p. Kraus 3, ☎ 71375, 43 rm P 💧 ⸜ ⌂ closed 10 Nov-15 Dec, 77,000; bkf: 7,000.
★★★ **Cavallino d'Oro-Goldenes Roessi,** v. Buhl 2, ☎ 71337, 25 rm 💧 1/2 Pens. closed Nov-Dec, 50,000.
★★★ **Madonna,** v. Kleinmichl 35, ☎ 71194, 22 rm P 💧 ⌂ closed May and 20 Oct-20 Dec, 68,000.
★★★ **Razzes-Bad Ratzes,** v. Ratzes 29, ☎ 71131, 49 rm P ⸜ ⸜ 💧 ⸜ ✈ ⌂ closed 16 Apr-19 May and 1 Oct-19 Dec, 76,000.

Recommended
Horseback riding: Maso Oberlanziner Hof, ☎ 71575.
Swimming: at Telfen, ☎ 71535.

FI ALLO SCILIAR-VÖLS AM SCHLERN, ✉ 39050, ☎ 0471.
🌲 (mid-Jul-mid-Sep), ☎ 72020.
🎿 ice skating, sled runs.
ⓘ on the statale, ☎ 72047.

Hotel:
★★★ **Emmy,** at Fié di Sopra 75, ☎ 72006, 33 rm P 💧 ⸜ ⸜ ⌂ closed Nov-Dec, 115,000.

Restaurant:
♦♦♦ **Tschafon,** la Fié di Sopra 57, ☎ 72024, closed Mon noon except hols, Nov and Jan. Elegant, in a mountain guest-house. Regional and French cuisine:filet au poivre dijonnaise, fish buffet, 40/45,000.

🏕 Alpe di Siusi, at San Constantino, 108 pl, ☎ 71459 (all year).

Recommended
Farm vacations: Hanighof, Aica di Fié 22, ☎ 53228.

Horseback riding: Maso Trafunserhof, ☎ 71459.

SIUSI-SEIS AM SCHLERN, ✉ 39040, ☎ 0471.
🎿 cross-country skiing, skating, sled run, curling.
ⓘ ☎ 71124.

Hotels:
★★★★ *Edelweiss,* v. Ibsen, ☎ 71130, 28 rm 🅿 ≼ ░ ▣
꙯ closed 16 Oct-19 Dec and 11 Apr-14 May, 130,000.
★★★ *Dolomiti,* v. Hauenstein 3 ☎ 71128, 28 rm 🅿 ≼ ░
▣ closed 21 Apr-31 May and 1 Oct-19 Dec, 81,000.

Recommended
Tennis: ☎ 70090 (also heated swimming pool).

ARCO

Trento 35, Milan 176 km
Pop. 11,796 ✉ 38062 ☎ 0464   B5

Arco was a popular lakeside resort in the late
19C. Olive trees, magnolias, laurels, oleanders and
palms thrive in a climate moderated by the warm
waters of the nearby lake.

▶ The old sector of Arco is overlooked by cliffs on
which stand the ruins of a **castle** surrounded by cypresses. ▶ The new town has many villas with gardens and
hotels dating from Arco's days as an exclusive resort at
the end of the last century.   □

Practical information

ℹ p. Vicenza 7 (bus station), ☎ 516161.

Hotels:
★★★★ *Palace Hotel Citt,* v. Roma 10, ☎ 531100, 90 rm 🅿
░ ♿ ▣ closed 21 Jan-31 Mar and 1 Nov-19 Dec, 105,000;
bkf: 8,000.
★★★ *Marchi,* v. Ferrera 22, ☎ 517171, 17 rm, 46,000;
bkf: 5,000.
★★★ *Sole,* v. S. Anna 35, ☎ 516676, 16 rm, closed Nov,
40,000; bkf: 3,000.

Restaurant:
♦♦ *Lega,* v. Vergolano 4, ☎ 516205, closed Wed except
Jul-Aug and 20 Oct-20 Dec. 16C with Renaissance frescos and charming courtyard. Regional cuisine: strangolapreti, sguazet di lumache, 16/25,000.

⚔ ★★★ *Arco,* at Prabi, v. Caproni Maini, 192 pl,
☎ 517491 (all year); ★★ *Bellavista,* at Linfano, 114 pl,
☎ 505644.

Recommended
Motocross: *Ciclamino* track, at Pietramurata, man-
agement at *Moto club Arco,* ☎ 507317.
Swimming: at Prabi, ☎ 517000.
Tennis: v. Palme 8, ☎ 516824.
Wines: *festival of Trentino sparkling wine* (Sep).

BADIA VALLEY

D-E3

This is one of the most beautiful valleys in the Dolomites. Leaving the Pusteria (→) and slightly downstream of Brunico in the lower valley, the River Gadera
rushes between steep cliffs and wooded slopes. In
the middle and upper sections and the wide Marebbe
Valley, however, it is broad and bright. The two
roads to the Gardena and Campolongo Passes climb
through the upper basin towards the Sella massif. Another valley (San Cassiano) leads to the Valparola Pass. The local Ladin population speaks a
neo-Latin dialect called *badiotto.* The village architecture has a wealth of detail and local carpenters and
carvers have a high reputation.

▶ It is possible to experience the charms of the Badia Valley at **La Villa-Stern** (4,865 ft) in the upper valley. There
is a wonderful view from Piz la Villa (6,814 ft, cableway). ▶ The route from **Pedràces-Pedratsches** (4,314 ft)
to the Croda di S. Croce (6,036 ft) also offers a fine view★
(chair lift from S. Lorenzo). ▶ Still in the upper valley

Colfosco-Kollfuschg (5,397 ft) clings to a slope below the
Sassongher. ▶ **Corvara in Badia** (5,144 ft) is the junction of the two roads that descend from the Gardena
Pass (→) and Campolongo Pass (6,151 ft), which leads to
the **Bacino del Bite.** There are views★ from Boé Lake
(7,217 ft, cableway) and Col Alto (6,513 ft). ▶ **San Cas-
siano-St.Kassian** (5,042 ft) is in the valley of the same
name adjacent to the upper valley of Badia. There is a
scenic route that goes from the **Valparola Pass** (7,191 ft)
to the Falzárego Pass. ▶ **San Vigilio di Marebbe-
St. Vigil in Enneburg** (3,924 ft) is in a beautiful section of
the Val Marebbe, where it is joined by the lower Badia,
on the r. side.   □

Practical information

COLFOSCO-KOLLFUSCHG, ✉ 39030, ☎ 0471.
⌁ ski lifts, cross-country skiing, instruction.
ℹ at Corvara, ☎ 836145.

Hotel:
★★★★ *Cappella,* ☎ 836183, 40 rm 🅿 ≼ ░ ▣ closed
1 Oct-19 Dec and 1 Apr-19 Jun, 106,000.

CORVARA IN BADIA-CORVARA, ✉ 39033, ☎ 0471.
⌁ Boé cableway, ski lifts, cross-country skiing, instruction, skating.
ℹ municipio, ☎ 836176.

Hotels:
★★★★ *Posta Zirm,* v. Centro 16/19, ☎ 836175, 79 rm 🅿
≼ ▣ closed May and Nov, 96,000.
★★★★ *Sassongher,* at Pescosta, ☎ 836085, 50 rm 🅿 ≼
♿ ▣ Pens. closed 21 Apr-31 May and 1 Oct-30 Nov,
120,000.
★★★ *Villa Eden,* v. Centro 59, ☎ 836041, 34 rm 🅿 ≼
░ closed 16 Apr-19 Jun and 1 Oct-14 Dec, 72,000;
bkf: 10,000.

Recommended
Excursions: by cableway to Boé Lake, ☎ 83266.
Swimming: on road to Colfosco.

LA VILLA-STERN, ✉ 39030, ☎ 0471.
⌁ cableway, ski lifts, cross-country skiing, instruction,
skating.
ℹ on the Statale, ☎ 85037.

Hotels:
★★★★ *Christiania,* ☎ 847016, 31 rm 🅿 ░ ▣ closed
1 May-20 Jun and 1 Oct-15 Dec, 110,000; bkf: 13,000.
★★★ *Ladinia,* v. Nazionale 37, ☎ 847044, 35 rm 🅿 ░ ♿
⚘ closed 16 Apr-31 May and 16 Oct-30 Nov, 60,000;
bkf: 3,000.
★★★ *Savoy,* ☎ 847088, 28 rm 🅿 closed 16 Apr-19 Jun
and 26 Sep-30 Nov, 62,000.
★★★ *Villa,* v. Boscdaplan 48, ☎ 847035, 39 rm 🅿 ≼ ⚘ ░
⚘ closed 21 Apr-19 Jun and 16 Sep-4 Dec, 59,000;
bkf: 10,000.

PEDRACES-PEDRATSCHES, ✉ 39036, ☎ 0471.
⌁ ski lifts, cross-country skiing, instruction, sled run,
ice skating.

Recommended
Hang gliding: *Helmut Striker* school of hang gliding,
☎ 85770.

SAN CASSIANO-SANKT KASSIAN, ✉ 39030, ☎ 0471.
⌁ ski lifts, cross-country skiing at Armentarola, instruction.
ℹ at Badia, ☎ 849422.

Hotels:
★★★ *Rosa Alpina,* ☎ 849500, 45 rm 🅿 ░ ♿ ▣ closed
Easter-14 Jun and 1 Oct-30 Nov, 70,000; bkf: 13,000.
★★★ *Stua,* ☎ 849456, 28 rm 🅿 ≼ ░ ▣ ꙯ Pens. closed
Easter-14 Jun and 1 Oct-Christmas, 75,000.
★★ *Stres,* v. Plang 146, ☎ 849486, 20 rm 🅿 40,000;
bkf: 4,000.

SAN VIGILIO DI MAREBBE-SANKT VIGIL IN ENNEBERG
✉ 39030, ☎ 0474.

⚡ ski lifts, cross-country skiing, instruction, skating, sled run, ski jump.
🛏 ☎ 51037.

Hotels:
★★★ *Condor,* ☎ 51017, 24 rm P ⚡ ⚓ ₪ Pens. closed Easter-May and Oct-Nov, 71,000.
★★★ *Olympia,* ☎ 51028, 22 rm P ⚓ ♿ closed May and Oct-Nov, 60,000; bkf: 4,000.
★★★ *Park Hotel Posta,* ☎ 51010, 55 rm P ⚡ ₪ ▣ ⚐ closed month after Easter, 100,000; bkf: 12,000.

Recommended
Sports centre: ☎ 51138.

BASELGA DI PINE

Trento 18, Milan 260 km
3165 ft pop. 3,994 ⊠ 38042 ☎ 0461   C5

Baselga di Pine is pleasantly situated on a plateau in the Valle di Piné near Lake Serraia and the Piazze reservoir. Near Montagnana is the **santuario della Madonna** (18C-19C) in the woods with numerous votive offerings.   □

Practical information _____

⚡ cross-country skiing, skating (speed rink at Miola), ski lifts.
🛏 at Serraia, v. C. Battisti 9, ☎ 557028.

Hotels:
★★★ *Villa Due Pini,* at Vigo, ☎ 557030, 20 rm P ⚡ ⚓ ₪ ▣ closed 21 Sep-9 Jun, 48,000; bkf: 6,000.
★★ *Nazionale,* at Miola ☎ 557211, 60 rm P ⚡ ₪ ⚘ ▣ ⚐ closed 15 Oct-30 Nov, 48,000; bkf: 4,000.
★★ *Scoiatallo,* at Bedolé *(3 km),* ☎ 557739, 25 rm P ₪ ▣ ⚐ closed Oct-May except Christmas, 42,000; bkf: 6,000.

Restaurant:
● ♦♦♦ *Due Camini,* at Miola, v. Pontara 352, ☎ 557200, closed Mon and Nov. Fireplaces and garden. Italian and international cuisine, 20/30,000.

Recommended
Tennis: at Lake Serraia, ☎ 557676.

BOLZANO - BOZEN

Trento 58, Milan 295, Rome 648 km
Pop. 103,009 ⊠ 39100 ☎ 0471   C3

Historically, Bolzano owed its success to four renowned annual markets and to the city's geographical position, which favoured trade. In 1635, Claudia de' Medici, Countess of the Tyrol, drew up commercial legislation and set up the Trade Council, which continued to function until 1851. Agriculture is a mainstay of Bolzano's economy. Visitors arriving from the S find it particularly striking that Bolzano is both the last Italian city and the first German city, gateway to the Alto Adige and Tyrol.

▶ The **piazza Walther** (B4) is a good place to start a tour of the city, whose centre can conveniently be seen on foot. ▶ The **Duomo★** is 14C-15C Gothic, badly damaged by bombs in the Second World War but faithfully restored. The roof is covered with polychrome tiles and above it rises the campanile with its perforated spire (1519). A Gothic portal in the apse, called the 'wine door', is decorated with vine shoots and figures of vine dressers to commemorate the church's special license to sell wine, granted in 1387. The interior has frescos from the 14C and the Renaissance; a fine sandstone **pulpit** decorated with bas-relief (1514) and in the r. aisle a 15C wooden **cross.** The high altar is Baroque; in the sanctuary are four Gothic altars. ▶ The Gothic **church of the**

Dominicani (B4), traditional place of worship for the Italian community in Bolzano, was rebuilt after bomb damage in the Second World War. It is the most important repository for painting in the city; there are frescos from the Giotto-Paduan school in the **Capella di S. Giovanni★,** among which is a *Triumph of Death* (c. 1340). In the adjacent Gothic cloister *(entrance at 19A)* and in the Cappella di S. Caterina are other frescos of the Giotto school. ▶ Palazzi ring the **piazza delle Erbe** (B4), site of the fruit market; the 18C fountain of Neptune stands where malefactors were once pilloried. ▶ There is a Gothic **church of the Francescani** (B4) with a richly carved altar (1500) in the Cappella della Vergine and a graceful 14C **cloister.** ▶ A Romanesque-Gothic campanile identifies the little church of **S. Giovanni in Villa** (A5). ▶ The commercial importance of the old city is evident in the narrow **via dei Portici★** (B4-5). Stylish shops retain the atmosphere of 15C-18C houses; the shop called Erker (bay window) and the Baroque **Palazzo Mercantile** at no. 39 must not be missed. ▶ In the **Museo Civico★** (B3, *9 a.m.-12 noon and 3-5 p.m.; closed hols*) the works of local 15C and Baroque artists and 13C-16C wood carvings illustrate the artistic spirit of the region; the archaeological material is interesting, especially the ethnographic exhibits, including costumes, domestic objects and reconstructions of interiors. ▶ From the **ponte Talvera** (B3) there is a promenade along the **lungotalvera Bolzano** which, leaving the 13C-16C Castel Mareccio to the r., joins the passeggiata S. Osvaldo which climbs the slopes of the Renon. ▶ Among the suburban gardens and vineyards of **Gries** (A1) stand the Benedictine monastery and the Baroque church of S. Agostino (1771) with frescos in the vault; in the 15C-16C Gothic parish church (A1) is a carved and painted altarpiece dating from 1475.

Environs

▶ The **Passegiate del Gùncina** (from Gries to the Hotel Castel Gùncina) has views over the Bolzano Valley towards the Dolomites. ▶ There is a steep old road or an easier new road to **S. Genesio Atesino.** ▶ 2.5 km along the Sarentina Valley road stands the **Castel Róncolo,** a 13C manor (partly rebuilt 19C) with 14C-15C frescos *(10 a.m.-12 noon and 3-5 p.m.; closed Sun and Mon).* ▶ There are cableways to **Col di Villa** and Soprabolzano.   □

Walther von der Vogelweide

The main square of Bolzano is named p. Walther, because in the last century a monument was erected there to a medieval Tyrolean poet. In the political context of the time, this symbolic act served to affirm the German national identity of the region in the polyglot Hapsburg empire. It is by no means certain that Walther von der Vogelweide was a native of the Tyrol. Poor but of noble birth, he aspired to the court of Vienna and a life of travel (12C-13C). The poet was one of the most illustrious minnesänger, German lyric poets of the 12C-13C, who sang of love (as did the Provençal troubadours) as understood in the medieval code of chivalry and courtly love. When a struggle began between Pope Innocent III and Otto of Brunswick, he glorified the idea of empire, while lambasting papal policy and the decadence of the church. As an old man, he encouraged the anachronistic crusade of Emperor Frederick II of Swabia.

Practical information _____

🛏 p. Parrocchia 11 (B4), ☎ 993808; p. Walther 8 (B4), ☎ 970660.
✈ at San Giacomo, ☎ 941040.
🚂 (C5), ☎ 974292.

1　　　　　　2　　　　　3 S. Genésio A. km 6

© SERVIZIO CARTOGRAFICO DEL TOURING CLUB ITALIANO, MILANO

2　　Trento　Autostrada km 5 - Trento km 57

from bus station, v. Perathoner 4 (C5), ☎ 975117.
Car rental: *Avis,* p. Verdi 18, ☎ 971467; *Hertz,* v. Alto
Adige 30, ☎ 977155; *Maggiore,* railway station,
☎ 971531.

Hotels:
★★★★ *Grifone-Greif,* p. Walther 7 (B4 b), ☎ 977056,
130 rm P ⁂ ⅏ ▣ 135,000; bkf: 12,000. Rest. ●
◆◆◆ closed Sun. Typical Alto Adige building dates from
Renaissance, 29/45,000.
★★★★ *Luna-Mondschein,* v. Piave 15 (B5 c), ☎ 975642,
90 rm P ⁂ 100,000; bkf: 7,000.
★★★★ *Park Hotel Laurin,* v. Laurin 4 (B5 d), ☎ 47500,
110 rm P ⁂ ▣ 160,000; bkf: 10,000.

★★★★ *Scala-Stiegl,* v. Brennero 11 (B4 e), ☎ 976222,
60 rm P ⁂ ▣ 80,000; bkf: 8,000.
★★★ *Asterix,* p. Mazzini 35 (A2 f), ☎ 43301, 24 rm P
Pens. 76,000.
★★★ *Lewald,* at San Giacomo, v. Maso della Pieve 17/19,
☎ 940330, 9 rm P ⁂ ▣ ⟋ 47,000; bkf: 5,000.
★★ *Herzog,* p. del Grano 2 (B4-5 g), ☎ 26267, 31 rm P
closed Jan. No restaurant, 66,000.

Restaurants:
● ◆◆◆ *Abramo,* p. Gries 16 (A1 h), ☎ 30141, closed
Sun. Service outdoors in summer. Regional cuisine:
certosino risotto, pappardelle with stewed hare,
28/40,000.

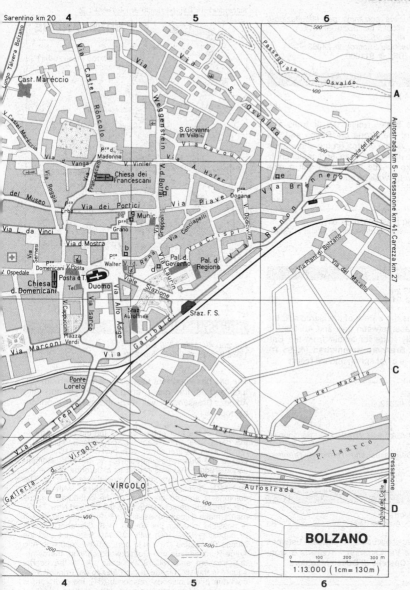

Sarentino km 20

BOLZANO

0   100   200   300 m

1:13.000 (1cm= 130m)

♦♦♦ *Pircher,* v. Merano 52, ☎ 917513, closed Tue and 15-30 Jun. Regional cuisine: spinach canederli with butter, escalopes of veal with mushrooms, 25/35,000.
♦♦ *Moritzingerhof,* v. Merano 113, ☎ 917491, closed Mon. Regional cuisine: prosciutto cured in brine, ristretto in white wine, 20/25,000.

⚐ *Moosbauer,* at San Maurizio, 47 pl, ☎ 918492 (all year).

Recommended

Archery: *Compagnia Arcieri Bolzano Merano,* v. Beato Arrigo 5, ☎ 978678; *Arco Club Laives,* v. Parma 9/A, ☎ 913362.

Clay pigeon shooting: at Castelfirmiano, ☎ 633154.
Craft workshops: *O. Kastowsky,* v. Goethe 34, ☎ 26368 (glass); v. Bottai 8, ☎ 24299 (handmade dolls).
Events: *Alto Adige wine tasting* (Mar-Apr); *flower festival* (Apr); *May festival; Busoni international piano competition* (Aug-Sep), ☎ 973579.
Excursions: to Renon plateau (→), starting from v. Renon (B6), cableway as far as Soprabolzano, then tramway to Collalbo, ☎ 978479; cableway to San Genesio Atesino, ☎ 978436; cableway to Col di Villa from v. Campiglio (C-D5), ☎ 978545.
Fairs and markets: *international trade fair* (Sep); *Fiera di Bolzano* (C2), ☎ 280211.
Flying: at *San Giacomo Airport,* ☎ 940165.

Horseback riding: *Società bolzanina per l'equitazione,*
v. Campofranco 2, ☎ 940025 (associate of *ANTE*).
Ice skating: v. Roma 18, ☎ 282586.
Mountaineering: *Alpinschule Südtirol,* ☎ 24033.
Swimming: v. Trieste (D3), ☎ 911000.

Lake BRAIES

Bolzano 98, Milan 366 km

E2

The waters of Lake Braies reflect the fir trees and
the Dolomite cliffs of the Croda del Becco and the
Sasso del Signore. A little church on the shore adds
a romantic touch to the celebrated and melancholy
landscape. The lake is little more than half a mile
long; it is possible to walk around it through the
woods in an hour.   □

Practical information _____

BRAIES-PRAGS, 3,980 ft, ⊠ 39030, ☎ 0474.
𝄢 ski lifts at Prali Camerali, cross-country skiing in valley,
instruction, sled runs.
ⓘ ☎ 78660.

BRENNERO - BRENNER

Bolzano 75, Milan 343 km
Pop. 2,410 ⊠ 39041 ☎ 0472   D1

The ridge that divides the waters of the Isarco and the
Inn is the busiest pass between Italy and Austria. It
was once the supply route for amber from the Baltic. The **Terme di Brennero-Brennerbad** (4,295 ft),
3 km from the pass, is a hot spring and ski resort.   □

Practical information _____

BRENNERO-BRENNER
ⓘ at Colle Isarco, ☎ 62372.

Environs

TERME DI BRENNERO-BRENNERBAD   ⊠ 39041,
☎ 0472.
⚓ (all year), at *Silbergasses* and *Terme di Brennero*
hotels.
𝄢 ski lifts at Malga Zirago.

BRENTONICO

Trento 40, Milan 223 km
2,270 ft pop. 3,128 ⊠ 38060 ☎ 0464   B6

This scattered village occupies a plateau between
Lake Garda and the Val Lagarina. There is a wonderful view from the **Castello di Dosso Maggiore.**   □

Practical information _____

𝄢 ski lifts and instruction at Polsa *(12 km S)*; ski lifts, instruction, cross-country skiing at San Valentino *(9 km SW)*
and San Giacomo *(6 km SW)*.
ⓘ v. Roma, ☎ 95149.

Hotels:
★★ *Bucaneve,* at San Valentino, ☎ 86557, 66 rm Ⓟ ⌂⌂
⌘ ⊡ ⌂ closed 1 Apr-19 Jun and 6 Sep-19 Dec, 53,000;
bkf: 3,500.
★★ *San Giacomo,* at San Giacomo, ☎ 86560, 32 rm Ⓟ ⌂⌂
♿ ⌘ ⊡ ⌂ closed 1-20 Oct, 45,000; bkf: 5,000.

For the translation of a name of a meat, a fish or a
vegetable, for the composition of a dish or a sauce,
see the *Menu Guide* at the end of the Practical Holiday Guide; it lists the most common culinary terms.

Autostrada km 6 **1** Vipiteno km 30-Brunico km 34 **2**

BRESSANONE

0   100   200   300   400 m

1 : 20.000 (1cm=200m)

Bolzano km 40   Pláncios km 20

BRESSANONE - BRIXEN*

Bolzano 40, Milan 336 km
1,835 ft pop. 16,232 ⊠ 39042 ☎ 0472   D2

The city has important associations with German culture and is the major artistic centre of the Alto
Adige. Bressanone was once the seat of a prince-
bishop.

▶ Three of the four entrances into the old city centre —
the porta Sole, porta Sabiona and porta S. Michele —
remain from the first set of walls built in the 11C. ▶ The
piazza del Duomo is impressive. ▶ The 13C Romanesque **Duomo** (A2) was rebuilt to a Baroque plan in the
latter 18C. Two campaniles frame the façade. ▶ The
13C-14C Romanesque-Gothic **cloister★** with paired
columns is entered on the r. of the cathedral; frescos
(14C-16C) that depict events from the Old and New Testaments make it most interesting. ▶ From the cloisters it
is possible to enter the church of **S. Giovanni Battista**
or baptistery (11C-14C) with 13C-14C **frescos★** and the
Museo Diocesano *(10 a.m.-5 p.m.; closed hols)* with Alto
Adige Romanesque and Gothic wood carving, the cathedral treasure and 18C-19C crèches. ▶ In the nearby
square is the 18C façade of the **Palazzo dei Principi Vescovi** (the prince-bishops' residence; B1); the courtyard is
decorated with twenty-four terra-cotta statues (1599) of
members of the Hapsburg family. ▶ On the l. of the
cathedral, in the p. della Parrocchia, the 15C Gothic parish
church of **S. Michele** (A2) has a spire called the **Torre
Bianca** that adds to the town its memorable skyline. ▶ In
the same square the Renaissance **Casa Pfaundler** combines German and Italian elements with unusual
effect. ▶ The old cemetery is between the parish church
and the cathedral; on its outside walls and on the façades
of the two churches are memorials to nobles and prelates, including one to a Garda troubadour, Oswald von
Wolkenstein. ▶ The p. della Parrocchia leads to the
sombre medieval **via dei Portici Maggiori★**, lined by
16C-17C houses. No. 14, the former **municipio**, has
a painting of the *Judgment of Solomon* in the courtyard. ▶ From the ponte Widmann (B2), there is an
interesting view of the **confluence** of the Rienza and
the Isarco.

Environs

▶ The **abbazia di Novacella** (→) is 3 km N. ▶ In the **Castello di Velturno** *(3 km SW)*, Renaissance summer residence of the bishops, are frescoed rooms with fine ceilings *(guided tours 10-11 a.m. and 2:30-3:30 p.m.; closed Mon; apply next door at casa Stern)*. ▶ Near the **Rio di Pusteria-Mühlbach** is the **Castello di Rodengo-Rodeneck** with a cycle of secular frescos from the early 13C *(guided tours mid-May-mid-Oct 11 a.m.-3 p.m.)*. ▶ It is 27 km by cableway or scenic drive to the **Plose massif.** □

Practical information ———————

⚡ cableways, cable car, ski lifts, cross-country skiing, instruction, skating.
ⓘ v. Stazione 9 (B1), ☎ 22401.

Hotels:
★★★★ *Dominik*, v. Terzo di Sotto 13 (A2 a), ☎ 30144, 29 rm 🅿 ⌁ 🅐 ❄ 🖻 ⌐ closed Nov, 180,000.
★★★★ *Elefante*, Rio Bianco 4 (A1 b), ☎ 22288, 44 rm 🅿 🅐 ⚇ 🖻 closed 16 Nov-28 Feb except Christmas. 14C post house, period furnishings, 140,000. Rest. ●
◆◆◆◆ closed Mon. Regional cuisine: Vipiteno gnocchi, Valle Isarco wine soup, 25/40,000.
★★★ *Albero Verde-Stremitzer*, v. Stufles 11 (A2 e), ☎ 21333, 71 rm 🅿 ⌁ ⚇ 🖻 closed 15 Nov-15 Dec, 78,000; bkf: 8,000.
★★★ *Corona d'Oro-Goldene Krone*, v. Fienili 6 (A1 c), ☎ 24154, 36 rm 🅿 ⌁ 🅗 closed 16 Nov-28 Feb except Christmas, 66,000.
★★★ *Gasser*, v. Giardini 19 (A2 d), ☎ 22105, 30 rm 🅿 🅐 ⚇ ⌐ closed 21 Oct-Easter, 96,000; bkf: 10,000.
★★★ *Temlhof*, v. Elvas 76, ☎ 22658, 52 rm 🅿 ⌁ 🅐 ⚇ 🖻 ⌐ closed 10 Nov-25 Dec, 90,000; bkf: 6,000.

Restaurant:
● ◆◆◆ *Fink*, v. Portici Minori 4 (A1 f), ☎ 23883, closed Wed eve, Thu and 10-30 Jun. Tyrolean decor, long tradition. Regional cuisine: wine soup, spinach gnocchetti, ricotta croquettes, 20/35,000.

Recommended

Canoeing: v. Bastioni Minori 4/A, ☎ 24568.
Swimming: v. Mercato Vecchio, ☎ 22860 (indoor pool).
Technical tourism: visits to *Ostheimer* candle factory, v. Mercato Vecchio 10, ☎ 22203.
Tennis: lungoisarco Sinistro, ☎ 22992 (indoor courts).

BRUNICO - BRUNECK

Bolzano 74, Milan 369 km
2,750 ft pop. 11,758 ⊠ 39031 ☎ 0474   E2

This tightly knit town, entered through an archway, must be explored on foot. The v. Centrale, backbone of the historical town, perfectly illustrates how elegant modern design can blend with an ancient environment.

▶ The houses of the old **centre** on the l. of the Rienza display quaint old signs and have battlemented gables. ▶ The **Castello** (13C-14C, altered in 15C-16C) is on a hill. ▶ The **Museo degli usi e costumi della provincia di Bolzano** *(Mon-Fri 9 a.m.-12 noon and 1-5 p.m.)* stands partly outdoors and partly inside a 16C building. □

Practical information ———————

⚡ cableways, ski lifts at Plan de Cornes, cross-country skiing, instruction, skating, sled runs.
🚋 ☎ 85722.

Hotels:
★★★★ *Royal Hotel Hinterhuber*, at Riscone, Pfaffenthal Ried 1, ☎ 21221, 56 rm 🅿 ⌁ 🅐 ⚇ ⌃ 🖻 ⌐ closed 25 Apr-5 Jun and 3 Oct-20 Dec, 130,000.
★★★ *Andreas Hofer*, v. Campo Tures 1, ☎ 85469, 50 rm 🅿 ⚇ ⌃ Pens. closed 5-20 May and 1-15 Dec, 56,000.

⚲ *Bersaglio*, v. Dobbiaco 4, 50 pl.

Recommended

Excursions: by cableway to Plan de Cornes, ☎ 85925.
Horseback riding: indoor riding school, at Riscone, ☎ 84778.
Ice skating: v. Castel Lamberto 1, ☎ 85599.
Swimming: at Riscone, ☎ 21296 (indoor pool).
Tennis: v. Tennis, ☎ 85768; lungofiume S. Giorgio, ☎ 20444.

CALDARO S. STRADA DEL VINO

Bolzano 15, Milan 292 km
Pop. 5,820 ⊠ 39052 ☎ 0471   C3-4

This name evokes vineyards, which are particularly beautiful here. Equally attractive are the landscape with wooded mountains, glimpses of castles and the charm of the foothills.

▶ The local architecture shows an unusual adaptation of Italian Renaissance design to the local Gothic tradition (**Casa Ruedl**, 16C, in main square). The Gothic church of **S. Caterina** has 15C frescos of the Bolzano school (restored). ▶ There are late 15C frescos (restored) in the 13C-14C Gothic **parish church** of the hamlet of S. Antonio. ▶ In the 14C castle of Montetondo-Ringberg is the **Museo atesino del vino** *(hols Apr-Oct 9:30 a.m.-12 noon and 2-6 p.m.; closed Mon)*. ▶ **Caldaro Lake** is popular for swimming and boating. ▶ The **wine road** passes from Caldaro through vineyards to Termeno-Tramin, Cortaccia-Kurtasch and Magrè all'Adige-Margreid.   □

Practical information ———————

CALDARO SULLA STRADA DEL VINO
ⓘ p. del Mercato, ☎ 963169.

Hotels:
★★★★ *Kartheinerhof*, v. Karthein 20/22, ☎ 963240, 33 rm 🅿 ⌁ ⚇ 🖻 128,000.
★★★ *Europa*, v. Europa 21, ☎ 963370, 22 rm 🅿 ⚇ 55,000; bkf: 3,500.
★★ *Tannof*, at Pianizza di Sopra, ☎ 52377, 18 rm 🅿 ⌁ ⚇ ❄ 🖻 closed Nov-Mar, 52,000.

⚲ *San Giuseppe al Lago*, at San Giuseppe al Lago, 130 pl, ☎ 963170.

Recommended

Events: *Wine festival* (last wk in Aug; procession in costume on the Sun).
Farm vacations: *Haus Edi*, v. Malga 4, ☎ 962343.

Environs

LAKE CALDARO, ⊠ 39052, ☎ 0471, 4 km S.
≋

Hotel:
★★★ *Seehof*, v. Klughammer 3, ☎ 960098, 27 rm 🅿 ⌁ 🅐 ⚇ 1/2 Pens. closed Dec-Mar, 77,000.

Recommended

Wind surfing: *Gretl am See*, ☎ 960273 (instruction).

CANAZEI

Trento 93, Milan 345 km
4,805 ft pop. 1,633 ⊠ 38032 ☎ 0462   D3

The Dolomites offer a variety of pleasures: meadows, forests, walks, excursions, climbing and skiing in winter. Canazei is a base for the Dolomite **Sella, Sassolungo** and **Marmolada** (→) groups.

▶ There is a cableway to **Belvedere I** (A1) for views★ of these and of the Catinaccio; 45 minutes to the Pordoi Pass, 2 hours of easy walking down a path to **Fedaia Lake** (→ Marmolada).   □

Practical information ———————

⚡ cableways, ski lifts, cross-country skiing, instruction, skating.
ⓘ v. Roma 16, ☎ 61113.

Hotels:
★★★ **Croce Bianca,** v. Roma 3, ☎ 61111, 41 rm Ⓟ ⫞
⬚ closed 6 May-19 Jun and 21 Oct-14 Dec, 90,000;
bkf: 8,000.
★★★ **Jan Maria,** v. Dolomiti Est 28, ☎ 62145, 31 rm Ⓟ ✗
closed 25 Apr-19 Jun and 21 Sep-19 Dec, 65,000.
★★★ **Rosa,** v. Dolomiti 142, ☎ 61107, 40 rm Ⓟ ⫞ ⬧
closed Jun and 15 Oct-20 Dec, 60,000; bkf: 8,000.
★★★ **Tyrol,** v. alla Cascata 2, ☎ 61156, 36 rm Ⓟ ⫞ ⬚
✗ closed 16 Apr-19 Jun and 1 Oct-19 Dec, 56,000;
bkf: 7,000.
★★ **Chalet Pineta,** v. Roma 114, ☎ 61162, 20 rm Ⓟ ⫞
⬚ closed Easter-31 May and Oct-Christmas, 58,000;
bkf: 7,000.
⚠ ★★★ **Marmolada,** at Pian de Pareda, 253 pl, ☎ 61660
(all year).

Recommended
Discothèque: *Le streghe,* v. Dolomiti, ☎ 61349.
Ice skating: at Alba, ☎ 62004.
Swimming: v. Pareda, ☎ 61348 (indoor pool).
Tennis: Baita al Parco, ☎ 62035.

CAVALESE

Trento 52, Milan 302 km
3,280 ft pop. 3,489 ✉ 38033 ☎ 0462   C4

Lots used to be drawn to assign the inhabitants of the Val di Fiemme (→) to meadows for hay-making. Mowers and rakers worked their way across the plateau as far as the fir forests, staying there for weeks, sleeping in tents and subsisting on polenta with cheese. Summoned by the bell for Sunday mass, the workers would troop down to the village. Cavalese today is a centre for tourism and winter sports in Trentino, but the 'Magnificent Community of Fiemme', which organized the communal hay-making, is still operating.

▶ The Magnificent Community of Fiemme, which includes eleven communes in the valley and administers a huge area of woods and meadows, operates from a 16C **palazzo** with a frescoed facade, originally a summer residence of the prince-bishops of Trento. It contains a collection of 17C-18C paintings *(3-5 p.m. except Sat and hols).* ▶ In the public park, a stone table and two rows of stone seats recreate the atmosphere of traditional valley life: this was the meeting place of the representatives of the Community, where twice a year the steward administered justice in the presence of the head of the valley and a jury of four men. ▶ The 12C **parish church** has been rebuilt many times. ▶ There is a cableway to the **Alpe Cermis** (6,500-7,000 ft). ☐

Practical information ———————

⚡ cableways, ski lifts to Alpe Cerms, cross-country skiing, instruction.
ⓘ v. Fratelli Bronzetti 4, ☎ 30298.

Hotels:
★★★ **Bellavista,** v. Pizzegoda 5, ☎ 30205, 27 rm Ⓟ ⬚ ✗
closed May and Nov, 55,000; bkf: 7,000.
★★★ **Park Hotel Azalea,** v. Cesure 1, ☎ 30109, 35 rm Ⓟ
⬚ closed May and Nov, 58,000; bkf: 6,000.
★★★ **San Valier,** v. Marconi 2, ☎ 31285, 30 rm Ⓟ ⬚ ⬧
⬚ closed Nov, 88,000; bkf: 5,000.
★★★ **Veronza,** at Carano, p. Dolomiti 15, ☎ 32222, 74 rm
Ⓟ ⬚ ⬧ ✗ ⬚ ⬗ Pens. closed May and 20 Sep-20
Dec, 70,000.
★★ **Panorama,** v. Cavazal 3, ☎ 31724, 31 rm Ⓟ ⫞ ⬚ ⬚
closed 16 Apr-31 May and Oct-Nov, 46,000; bkf: 7,000.

Restaurant:
♦♦♦ **Orso Grigio,** v. Giovanelli 5, ☎ 31481, closed Wed and Nov. Regional cuisine: bocconcini alla ricotta, gnocchi parigina, 17/27,000.

Recommended
Events: *Marcialonga* (long cross-country ski race, last Sun in Jan).
Excursions: by cableway to Alpe Cermis, ☎ 31137.
Ice skating: p. funivia Cermis, ☎ 31935.
Tennis: Parco della Pieve, ☎ 30228.

CEMBRA

Trento 23, Milan 267 km
Pop. 1,443 ✉ 38034 ☎ 0461   C4

Cembra is the principal village and also the name of the lower section of the Avisio Valley, a narrow gorge enclosed between ravines and gullies. 750 ft above the bed of the torrent, the gorge opens onto terraces covered with vineyards, orchards and woods and dotted with attractive houses.

▶ There are Gothic frescos in the portico of the **parish church,** 16C frescos in the church of **S. Pietro** originally built in the 12C. ▶ 5 km away is **Lake Santo** surrounded by woods; trout, tench and carp are caught there. ▶ 6 km away are pyramids of Segonzano (→). ☐

Practical information ———————

ⓘ v. IV Novembre 3, ☎ 683110.

Hotel:
★★ **Caminetto,** v. Battisti 3, ☎ 683007, 32 rm Ⓟ ⬚ ✗
closed Nov,44,000; bkf: 6,000.

CHIUSA - KLAUSEN

Bolzano 28, Milan 329 km
Pop. 4,073 ✉ 39043 ☎ 0472   D2

The road to the Brenner Pass used to go straight through this town in an arrow part of the Isarco Valley. 15C-16C houses with handsome portals and wooden shutters are typical of the area. Chiusa was once a customs post for the Bishop of Bressanone.

▶ The 13C **Torre del Capitano** dominates the town. ▶ The Gothic **parish church** and the **church of the Twelve Apostles** date from the 15C. ▶ The **treasury** of Loreto in the Capuchin church displays objects bestowed by an 18C Queen of Spain on her confessor, a Capuchin friar from Chiusa *(10-11 a.m. and 4-5 p.m. mid-May-Sep, ask at neighbouring convent).* ▶ Private **museum** of local folklore in the hamlet of Gudon (☎ 47401 in advance). ▶ It is possible to climb by path or mule-track to the **Monastery of Sabiona** (2,392 ft, *30 mn).* This is the site of the Roman outpost of Sabiona, on a clifftop overlooking Chiusa. A church founded here in the 6C became the seat of a bishop under the patriarch of Aquileia (the seat of the diocese was moved to Bressanone *c.* 1000). In a vineyard near the 13C walls of the convent traces have been found of an early Christian basilica. The monastery is a complex of Romanesque, Gothic and 17C buildings, surrounded by walls and turrets. ☐

Practical information ———————

ⓘ p. Tinne 40, ☎ 47424.

Hotel:
★★★ **Sylvanerhof,** v. Brennero 52, ☎ 47557, 21 rm ⬚ ▭
closed 6 Jan-15 Feb, 65,000.

> The arrow (→) is a reference to another entry.

⚓ *Gamp*, v. Gries 22, 50 pl, ☎ 47425 (all year).

Recommended
Farm vacations: *Haus Waldruhe*, at Villandro-San Valentino, ☎ 53181.

CLES

Trento 40, Milan 284 km
Pop. 5,789 ⊠ 38023 ☎ 0463   B4

The Noce, a tributary on the r. side of the Adige, has dug deep into the valley (the Val di Non or Anàunia) to form a twisting gorge. Geological conditions combined with a dam created the reservoir, **Lake S. Giustina**, which dominates the orchard-covered plateau and its old centre, Cles. Like other villages in the valley, Cles retains interesting architectural features, including late Gothic elements and local interpretations of the Venetian Renaissance.

▶ In the p. Municipio, the 15C-16C **Palazzo Assessorile** has graceful paired windows on the façade and a balcony. ▶ The 16C Gothic-Renaissance **chiesa archipretale** has a campanile with paired windows. ▶ In the hamlet of Pez is the Romanesque church of **S. Vigilio** with 14C-15C frescos. ▶ 1.5 km away, the turreted **Castel Cles** *(private)* owned by Cardinal Bernardo Clesio, a local humanist prince-bishop (16C); it contains important **frescos**.   □

Practical information _____

ⅈ v. Dante 30, ☎ 21376.

Hotel:
★★★ *Cles*, p. Navarrino 7, ☎ 21300, 40 rm 🅿 ♨ ♿ closed 15-30 Jun, 48,000; bkf: 5,000.

Recommended
Children's facilities: *Casa degli scoiattoli* children's residence, at Sfruz *(12 km E)*, ☎ 36209 or ☎ 055/283877 (children 4-13, open Jun-Sep and Christmas-Easter).

COLLE ISARCO - GOSSENSASS

Bolzano 76, Trento 136, Milan 375 km
3,605 ft pop. 813 ⊠ 39040 ☎ 0472   C1

There is evidence of the town's mining past in the **Miners' House** to the l. of the parish church, the 16C chapel of **S. Barbara**. The mountain landscape is dominated by a viaduct of the motorway to the Brenner Pass.   □

Practical information _____

⚡ ski lifts, cross-country skiing, instruction, skating, curling.
ⅈ in piazza, ☎ 62372.

Hotel:
★★ *Erna*, v. Fléres 2, ☎ 62307, 15 rm 🅿 ♙ ♨ ⌘ ✈ closed 1 Oct-15 Dec, 43,000; bkf: 6,000.

Terme di COMANO

Trento 28, Milan 193 km
⊠ 38077 ☎ 0465   B5

Curative springs arise in the **Grotta della Sibilla** in this spa town.

Environs

▶ 6 km NW in a valley below the spurs of the Brenta range is the pleasant village of **Sténico**. Its **Castle** is one of the most interesting in Trentino (12C-13C with 14C-15C

alterations and additions, recently restored; *guided tours 9 a.m.-12 noon and 2-5 or 5:30 p.m.; closed Mon*). It has mullioned windows and a Renaissance loggia; inside, 15C-16C frescos and decoration. In front of the castle are the Riobianco falls.   □

Practical information _____

⚘ (Apr-Oct), ☎ 71277.
ⅈ at Ponte Arche, v. Marconi 68, ☎ 71465.

Hotels:
★★★ *G. A. Terme*, ☎ 71421, 65 rm 🅿 ♨ closed Nov-Mar, 93,000; bkf: 9,000.
★★★ *Plaza*, v. Battisti 19, ☎ 71442, 68 rm 🅿 ♨ ♿ ✈ 70,000; bkf: 7,000.

La Grande Strada delle DOLOMITI

From Bolzano to Cortina d'Ampezzo *(110 km, 1 day; map 2)*

In Ladin (neo-Latin) *enrosadira* describes the rocks of the Dolomites when they seem to burst into flames of pink and violet at dawn and sunset. From the slopes above Bolzano where the route begins, it is possible to see the *enrosadira* of the peaks of the Catinaccio, which in German is called *Rosengarten* (rose garden).

▶ From **Bolzano** (→) the route enters the **Val d'Ega**. The **Castel Cornedo**, on a rocky crag, guards the entrance to the gorge between lofty cliffs. The **bridge by the falls** with the view of the gorge is most striking. ▶ The damp air of the gorge has been left behind by the time the route reaches **Ponte Nova-Birchabruck**. There are views of the Latemar on the r. and the Catinaccio on the l. as the route climbs to **Nova Levante-Welschnofen** (3,878 ft). ▶ The two Dolomite groups, especially the Latemar, become more clearly visible as the route ascends. The rocks, rising like organ pipes above the forests, are reflected in **Lake Carezza**★. ▶ **Carezza al Lago-Karersee** (5,278 ft, chair lift to Rifugio Paolina on the Catinaccio) is slightly below the **Costalunga Pass-Karerpass** which opens into the Val di Fassa. ▶ The descent into the **Val di Fassa** (→) ends at **Vigo di Fassa**. ▶ The climb out of this valley as far as **Canazei** (→) offers a different view of the Dolomites; the main interest is the Sassolungo and the Sella group. ▶ At Canazei the winding ascent of the **Pordoi Pass** begins. This was a notorious stage of the Tour of Italy cycle race. ▶ The route now leaves Trentino and enters Venetia, descending to **Pieve di Livinalongo**. The mountains are now the Marmolada and the more distant Pelmo and Civetta; the appearance of the villages changes in descending the upper valley of the Cordévole. ▶ At **Cernadoi** begins the climb to the third Dolomite pass of the tour, through a bracing valley partly covered in forest, with at one point a final full view of the Marmolada glacier. The route then reaches the **Falzarego Pass** (6,966 ft). From the valley of the River Cordévole it crosses the pass to the valley of the River Bóite, both of which are tributaries of the Piave. ▶ Descending, there is new Dolomite scenery at the foot of the impressive cliffs of the Tofane with the solitary Cinque Torri to the r. ▶ At the woods of **Pocol** the dramatic basin of **Cortina d'Ampezzo**, final destination of the route, comes into view.   □

Practical information _____

CAREZZA AL LAGO-KARERSEE, ⊠ 39056, ☎ 0471.
⚡ ski lifts.
ⅈ at Nova Levante, ☎ 613126; at Vigo di Fassa, ☎ 0462/64093.

Hotel:
★ *Simhild*, v. Belvedere 1, ☎ 616869, 9 rm 🅿 ✈ closed 16 Apr-14 Jun and 1 Oct-25 Dec, 50,000.

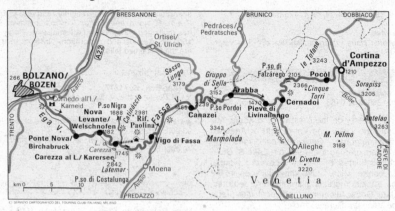

2. La Grande Strada delle Dolomiti

NOVA LEVANTE-WELSCHNOFEN, ⊠ 39056, ☎ 0471. ⚡ cable car, ski lifts, instruction, cross-country skiing, skating.
ⓘ at the crossing point, ☎ 613126.

Hotels:
★★★★ *Posta-Cavallino Bianco*, v. Carezza 30, ☎ 613113, 48 rm 🄿 ⫽ ⛲ 👍 ▣ 🏊 closed 25 Apr-20 May and 1 Nov-20 Dec, 90,000; bkf: 8,000.★★★ *Angelo-Engel*, v. S. Valentino 3, ☎ 613131, 45 rm 🄿 ⫽ ⛲ ▣ closed 21 Apr-4 Jun and 6 Oct-19 Dec, 59,000; bkf: 8,000.
★★ *Panorama*, ☎ 613232, 18 rm 🄿 ⫽ ⛲ 🏊 closed May and 16 Oct-19 Dec, 42,000; bkf: 9,000.
★★ *Pardeller*, v. Roma 18, ☎ 613144, 14 rm 🄿 ⫽ 🏊 closed 1 May-10 Jun, 42,000.

Recommended
Horseback riding: ☎ 613153.
Mountaineering school: ☎ 613365 or 713352.
Sports centre: v. Dolomiti, ☎ 613273.

DOLOMITI DI BRENTA

From San Michele all'Adige to Mezzolombardo *(152 km, 1 day; map 3)*

Bears still frequent the forests of the Brenta Massif. Although in local sanctuaries there are votive offerings in gratitude for the dramatic escape of a villager from a bear, the animal is timid and is always the first to flee. Bears are strictly protected and have withdrawn to the few areas rarely entered by man. In certain areas, such as Spormaggiore on the slopes of the Brenta group, it is possible to find traces: fur on tree trunks, wasp nests destroyed, ant-hills dug up. The Brenta Dolomites are the only group to the r. of the Adige: they are far removed from the other Dolomite groups. Small glaciers full of crevices lie at the head of barren valleys and icy gullies drop steeply from the gaps between the peaks, the two highest of which are Cima Tosa (10,410 ft) and Cima Brenta (10,335 ft). Geographically, the group is clearly bounded by the River Sarca and the torrents Meledrio and Noce; the route takes in the varied landscapes of the upper Val di Non and the Giudicarie, the Val Rendena and the Val di Sole.

▶ Starting in **San Michele all'Adige** (→) the route winds through vineyards to **Mezzolombardo**. ▶ A steep climb leads to the plateau at **Fai della Paganella** (*chair lift for Paganella*, 6,972 ft). ▶ **Andalo** (3,419 ft), in a green hollow also has a cableway ascending Paganella and a chair lift to La Roda (6,890 ft, *panorama*★). ▶ At **Molveno** (2,838 ft) is the first exhilarating view of the Brenta group. Hydroelectric exploitation has somewhat spoiled the beauty of **Lake Molveno**. ▶ Descending to **Ponte Arche** on the Sarca, the route enters Giudicarie. ▶ The centre of the region is **Tione di Trento** at the mouth of the Val Rendena. ▶ At **Pelugo** the church of S. Antonio Abate with cemetery has 15C frescos all around its external walls. The artist belonged to a Bergamo family of painters who left many works in the W Trentino valleys. ▶ The most interesting is at **Pinzolo** (2,526 ft), farther up the Val Rendena: the *Dance of Death*★, a 16C fresco on the church of S. Vigilio, portrays forty figures representing all the social classes and accompanied by skeletons, in a stern warning on the vanity of life with a commentary in dialect verse. There are other frescos in the church of S. Stefano at **Carisolo**. ▶ At Carisolo it is worthwhile to take a detour into the unspoiled **Val Genova**★. ▶ 6.5 km away is the **cascata di Nardis**★, a waterfall of more than 300 ft in two parallel streams with two masses of granite at its base, which legend says are demons turned to stone. The valley climbs through the woods as far as **Pian de Bédole** between the peaks of Adamello and Presanella *(the use of private motor vehicles in Jul or Aug is inadvisable)*. ▶ After climbing through the Valle di Campiglio from Carisolo, the route reaches the NW side of the Brenta group at **Madonna di Campiglio** (→). ▶ Crossing the **Campo Carlo Magno** (5,518 ft), the road descends into the Val Meledrio. ▶ The facilities at the ski resort of **Folgàrida** (4,272 ft) are connected with those of Madonna di Campiglio and Marilleva (→ Mezzana). ▶ The route returns to the Val di Sole at **Dimaro**. The landscape is now very different; open and covered by orchards passing through **Malè** (→) and **Cles** (→) in the Anàunia. ▶ One last detour from **Tuenno** is noteworthy. In the valley that divides the N part of the Brenta group into two parallel ranges is **Lake Tovel**★. The basin beneath the N faces of the Brenta group is beautiful; the lake was famous for the pink colouration of its water that occurred between July and September as a result of a micro-organism on the S side. Pollution was probably responsible for its disappearance some years ago. ▶ Returning through Tuenno,

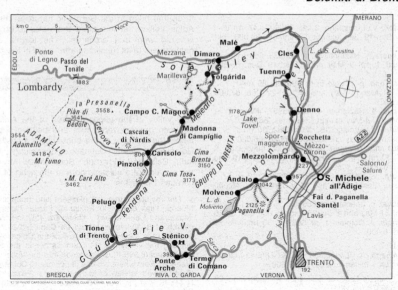

km 0   5   10   Noce

MERANO

EDOLO

Ponte
di Legno Passo del
Tonàle
1883

Lombardy

Mezzana Dimaro Malè
768
Marilleva Folgárida

Sola valley

Cles L. di S. Giustina

Tuenno

Noce valley

BOLZANO

la Presanella
Piàn di 3558
1641
Bèdole
3554 ADAMELLO
Adamello 3418
M. Fumo

Campo C. Magno

Cenova V.

Cascata
di Nàrdis

Carisolo

Pinzolo

M. Caré Alto
3462

Rendena V.

Meledrio v.

Madonna
di Campíglio

Cima
Brenta
3150

Cima Tosa
3173

GRUPPO DI BRENTA

1178
Lake
Tovel

Denno

Spor-
maggiore

Mezzolombardo

Ándalo

Molveno
L. di
Molveno 2125
Paganella

Rocchetta
Mezzo-
corona

A22

227

952

Salorno/
Salurn

S. Michele
all'Ádige

Fai d. Paganella
Santèl

Lavis

Adige

Pelugo

Tione
di Trento

Giud carie V.

Sténico H

393
Ponte Terme
Arche di Comano

Sarca

TRENTO
192

BRESCIA RIVA D. GARDA VERONA

3. Dolomiti di Brenta

the route passes by **Denno** and the Chiusa della Rocchetta and ends in San Michele all'Adige. □

Practical information

ANDALO, ⊠ 38010, ☎ 0461.
⚡ cable cars, ski lifts, cross-country skiing at lake, instruction, skating.
ⓘ p. Centrale, ☎ 585836.

Hotels:
★★★ **Cristallo,** v. Paganella 18, ☎ 585744, 31 rm Ⓟ ↻
closed 11 Apr-14 Jun and 16 Sep-30 Nov, 44,000; bkf:
6,000.
★★★ **Olimpia,** v. Paganella 17, ☎ 585715, 27 rm Ⓟ ↻ ▦
❄ closed 16 Apr-14 Jun and 16 Sep-14 Dec, 50,000;
bkf: 6,000.
★★★ **Piccolo Hotel,** v. Pegorar 2, ☎ 585710, 38 rm Ⓟ ↻
▦ closed 21 Apr-14 Jun and 16 Sep-19 Dec, 39,000;
bkf: 5,000.
★★★ **Splendid,** v. Paganella, ☎ 585777, 57 rm Ⓟ ↻ ▦
❄ closed 16 Apr-14 Jun and 16 Sep-14 Dec, 80,000;
bkf: 4,000.

Recommended

Excursions: to Paganella by cable car and chair lift
(2 stages).
Swimming: v. Trento 17, ☎ 585776 (indoor pool).

CAMPO CARLO MAGNO, ⊠ 38084, ☎ 0465.
⚡ Grosté cableway (two stages), Spinale chair lifts,
ski lifts.

Hotels:
★★★★ **Carlo Magno Zeledria,** v. Cima Tosa 25,
☎ 410101, 100 rm Ⓟ ↻ ▦ ❄ 🖵 closed 26 Apr-22 Jun
and 21 Sep-30 Nov, 160,000.
★★★★ **Golf Hotel,** ☎ 41003, 124 rm Ⓟ ↻ ▦ ⌿ (9 holes)
closed 1 Apr-14 Jul and 26 Aug-22 Dec. Once a summer residence of the Hapsburgs, 160,000; bkf: 12,000.

Recommended

Golf: ☎ 41003 (9 holes).

DIMARO, ⊠ 38025, ☎ 0463.

Hotel:
★★ **Vittoria,** v. Ponte di Ferro 41, ☎ 94113, 25 rm Ⓟ ↻
↻ ▦ closed 16-30 Jun and 21 Sep-30 Nov, 58,000;
bkf: 6,000.
⚡ ★★ **Dolomiti di Brenta,** SS 42 at 173.5-km marker,
200 pl, ☎ 94332.

FAI DELLA PAGANELLA, ⊠ 38010, ☎ 0461.
⚡ ski lifts, cross-country skiing, instruction, ice skating.
ⓘ ☎ 583130.

Hotels:
★★★ **Santellina,** at Santel, ☎ 583120, 40 rm ↻ ▦ ❄ ⌿
closed 16 Apr-31 May and 16 Sep-30 Nov, 45,000;
bkf: 7,000.
★★★ **Sole-Beppin,** ☎ 583127, 13 rm Ⓟ ▦ ❄ 45,000;
bkf: 7,000.

FOLGARIDA, ⊠ 38025, ☎ 0463.
⚡ cable car, ski lifts, instruction.
ⓘ ☎ 96113.

Hotels:
★★★ **Gran Baita Palace Hotel,** v. Nazionale, ☎ 96263,
54 rm Ⓟ ▦ ❄ closed 16 Apr-30 Jun, and 1 Sep-30 Nov,
79,000; bkf: 7,000.
★★ **Derby,** ☎ 96163, 58 rm Ⓟ ❄ closed 6 Apr-30 Jun
and 1 Sep-4 Dec, 58,000; bkf: 5,000.

LAKE TOVEL, ⊠ 38019, ☎ 0463.
ⓘ at Tuenno, ☎ 31149.

MEZZOLOMBARDO, ⊠ 38017, ☎ 0461.

Recommended

♥ wines: Barone de Cles, v. Mazzini 18, ☎ 602673
or 601082.

MOLVENO, ⊠ 38018, ☎ 0461.
⚡ cable car, ski lifts, instruction, skating.
ⓘ p. Marconi 1, ☎ 586924.

Hotels:
★★★ *Ariston*, v. Lungolago 3, ☎ 586907, 47 rm ℗ ∉ closed 21 Sep-19 Jun except Christmas, 80,000; bkf: 5,000.
★★★ *Belvedere*, v. Nazionale 9, ☎ 586933, 65 rm ℗ ∉ ⬥⬥⬥ ⬥ ⊡ closed 1 Apr-9 May and 1 Oct-19 Dec, 65,000; bkf: 6,000.
★★★ *Cima Tosa*, p. Scuole 5, ☎ 586928, 36 rm ℗ ∉ ⬥⬥⬥ ⬥ closed 21 Mar-14 May and 11 Oct-22 Dec, 57,000; bkf: 5,000.
★★★ *Du Lac*, v. Nazionale 4, ☎ 586957, 44 rm ℗ ⬥⬥⬥ Pens. closed Oct-May except Christmas, 60,000.
★★★ *Gloria*, v. Lungolago 15, ☎ 586962, 30 rm ℗ ∉ ⬥⬥⬥ Pens. closed Apr-May and Oct-Christmas, 65,000.
★★★ *Ischia alle Dolomiti di Brenta*, v. Lungolago 8, ☎ 586057, 30 rm ℗ ∉ ⬥⬥⬥ closed May and 1 Oct-19 Dec, 58,000; bkf: 6,000.
★★★ *Londra*, v. Nazionale 26, ☎ 586943, 32 rm ℗ ∉ ⬥⬥⬥ ⬥ closed Easter-May and Nov-Christmas, 46,000; bkf: 6,000.
★★★ *Miralago*, p. Scuole 3, ☎ 586935, 35 rm ℗ ⬥⬥⬥ ⊡ closed 26 Mar-31 May and 1 Oct-25 Dec, 55,000; bkf: 5,000.
★★★ *Olympia*, v. Dolomiti 1, ☎ 586961, 30 rm ∉ ⬥⬥⬥ ⬥ 45,000; bkf: 6,000.

Restaurant:
♦♦♦ *Caminetto*, v. Lungolago 4, ☎ 586949, closed 21 Sep-19 Jun. Italian cuisine, 25/40,000.

⚠ ★★★ *Spiaggia-Lago di Molveno*, v. Lungolago 27, 264 pl, ☎ 586978 (all year).

Recommended
Alpine guides: v. Roma, ☎ 586191.
Swimming: at Spiaggia, ☎ 586015.

PINZOLO, ⊠ 0465.
⚡ cable car, ski lifts, cross-country skiing, instruction.
ⓘ v. del Sole, ☎ 51007.

Hotels:
★★★★ *Valgenova*, at Giustino, v. Dolomiti, ☎ 51542, 50 rm ℗ ⬥⬥⬥ ⬥ ⊡ closed 21 Apr-9 Jun and 21 Sep-4 Dec, 52,000; bkf: 8,000.
★★★ *Corona*, ☎ 51030, 45 rm ℗ ⬥⬥⬥ ⬥ closed May and Nov, 62,000; bkf: 7,000.
★★★ *Pinzolo Dolomiti*, corso Trento 24, ☎ 51024, 44 rm ℗ ∉ ⬥⬥⬥ ⬥ closed May and Oct-Nov, 70,000; bkf: 10,000.
★★ *Beverly*, v. Caré Alto 2, ☎ 51158, 25 rm ℗ ⬥⬥⬥ ⬥ closed May and Oct-Nov, 36,000; bkf: 5,000.

Restaurant:
♦♦♦ *Prima o Poi*, SS for Madonna di Campiglio, ☎ 57175, closed Wed and Jun. Italian cuisine: rabbit terrine, grilled meats, baked radicchio, 25/35,000.

⚠ ★★ *Parco Adamello*, at Magnab, 82 pl, ☎ 51793 (all year).

Recommended
Events: *Pinzolo 24-hour Nordic ski race* (Feb).
Ice skating: v. alla Pineta, ☎ 52470.
Tennis: v. Miliani, ☎ 51015.

TIONE DI TRENTO, ⊠ 38079, ☎ 0465.
ⓘ on circonvallazione, ☎ 21051.

Hotel:
★★ *Milano*, v. Circonvallazione 36, ☎ 21096, 18 rm ℗ ⬥⬥⬥ ⬥ 46,500.

Recommended
Children's facilities: *Dolomiti* children's residence, ☎ 22093; management, ☎ 02/3186691 (children 5-14; open Jun-Sep, Christmas hols, ski vacations until Mar).
Tennis: Parco Paletti, ☎ 21798.

EGNA - NEUMARKT

Bolzano 24, Milan 244 km
Pop. 3,812 ⊠ 39044 ☎ 0471   C4

The Gothic **parish church** has a Romanesque campanile with double- and treble-arched windows — fea-

tures that point to the Germanic nature of the upper Adige Valley. At this point the valley is broad and covered with fruit orchards. The town's German name refers to its rebuilding after a fire in the 14C. □

The FASSA VALLEY

D3-4

This valley of the upper reaches of the Avisio runs between grass-covered hills and belts of woodland below the summits of the best-known massifs in the Dolomites: Latemar, Catinaccio, Sassolungo, Marmolada, Sella and Monzoni. Surprisingly, Monzoni is the remains of a volcanic core at the heart of the calcareous Dolomites.

▶ The major centres, all pleasant and hospitable, are: Moena, Vigo di Fassa, Pozza di Fassa, Campitello di Fassa, and Canazei (→). There are 15C frescos in the church of S. Volfango. From **Le Cune** (7,220 ft; *cableway*) there is a breathtaking view of the Dolomite groups flanking the valley. ▶ 11.5 km farther is the **S. Pellegrino Pass** (6,295 ft), which leads into the Valley of Biòis (Venetia), from where a cable car climbs to **Col Margherita** (8,240 ft) with a view of Marmolada. ▶ **Pozza di Fassa** (4,345 ft) is at the foot of Catinaccio. 9 km farther is the Rifugio Gardeccia (6,390 ft), from which it is one hour to the **Rifugio Vaiolet** (7,360 ft) beneath the Torri del Vaiolet. A cable car ascends to **Buffaure** (6,625 ft) with a view★ of Catinaccio and Sella. ▶ At **Vigo di Fassa** (4,535 ft) the Grande Strada delle Dolomite (→) enters the valley. The 15C church of S. Giuliana (paintings) stands alone above the village; the 15C Gothic church of S. Giovanni, in the hamlet of the same name, has 16C frescos, a campanile with spire, and portals. The cableway climbs to **Ciampede** (6,560 ft). ▶ From **Campitello di Fassa** (4,750 ft) a chair lift climbs to **Col Rodella★** (8,155 ft, *panoramic view★*). From here it is possible to climb on foot *(30 mn)* or by chair lift to the Sella Pass (→) or go along a footpath leading on level ground to the Alpe di Siusi (→). □

Practical information ⸻⸻⸻⸻⸻⸻

CAMPITELLO DI FASSA, ⊠ 38031, ☎ 0462.
⚡ chair lifts to the Sella Pass (→), ski instruction.
ⓘ ☎ 61137

Hotels:
★★★ *Gran Paradis*, v. Dolomiti 4, ☎ 612221, 39 rm ℗ ∉ ⬥⬥⬥ ⬥ ⊡ closed Oct-Dec and Apr-Jun, 58,000; bkf: 6,000.
★★★ *Salvan*, v. Dolomiti 20, ☎ 61427, 26 rm ℗ ⬥⬥⬥ ⬥ ⊡ closed 16 Apr-14 Jun and 1 Oct-4 Dec, 96,000; bkf: 7,000.
★★ *Crepes de Selà*, v. Dolomiti 30, ☎ 61538, 16 rm ℗ ⬥⬥⬥ ⬥ closed May and 1 Oct-14 Dec, 40,000; bkf: 6,000.
★★ *Villa Kofler*, v. Dolomiti, ☎ 61244, 22 rm ℗ ∉ 45,000; bkf: 7,000.

Recommended
Alpine guides: *Casa delle guide*, SS 48, ☎ 61459.

MOENA, ⊠ 38035, ☎ 0462.
⚡ cableway, ski lifts at Moena and Alpe Lusia, instruction, ice skating.
ⓘ p. C. Batisti 18, ☎ 53122.

Hotels:
★★★ *Alpi*, v. Moene 47, ☎ 53194, 38 rm ℗ ∉ ⬥⬥⬥ ⬥ closed 16 Apr-14 Jun and 1 Oct-14 Dec, 54,000; bkf: 6,000.
★★★ *Catinaccio*, v. Domeda 6, ☎ 53235, 41 rm ℗ ⬥⬥⬥ closed 21 Mar-30 Jun and 11 Sep-19 Dec, 90,000; bkf: 6,000.
★★★ *Laurino*, v. Löwy 15, ☎ 53238, 42 rm ℗ ⬥⬥⬥ closed 16 Apr-14 Jun and 16 Sep-19 Dec, 73,000; bkf: 5,000.
★★★ *Leonardo*, v. Ciroch 5, ☎ 53355, 21 rm ℗ ⬥⬥⬥ closed 1 May-14 Jun and 1 Oct-20 Dec, 100,000.

★★ *Campagnola*, v. dei Colli 40, ☎ 53232, 30 rm P ⫣ ⌂
⌇ 58,000; bkf: 6,000.
Recommended
Events: *Marcialonga* (last Sun in Jan, → Cavalese).
Tennis: ☎ 54013.

PASSO DI SAN PELLEGRINO, ⊠ 38035, ☎ 0462.
⚡ cableway, ski lifts, cross-country skiing.
ⓘ at Moena, ☎ 53122.

POZZA DI FASSA, ⊠ 38036, ☎ 0462.
⚡ cable car, ski lifts, cross-country skiing, instruction, skating.
ⓘ p. Municipio, ☎ 64136.

Hotels:
★★★ *Gran Baita*, v. Roma 57, ☎ 64284, 30 rm P ⌂ ▣
closed 16 Apr-14 Jun and 26 Sep-19 Dec, 80,000; bkf: 12,000.
★★★ *Mater Dei*, v. Dassé 7, ☎ 64255, 55 rm P ⫣ ⌂ &
⌇ closed 21 Apr-14 Jun and 21 Sep-14 Dec, 57,000; bkf: 5,000.
★★★ *Trento*, v. Roma, ☎ 64279, 49 rm P ⫣ ⌂ ⌇ ▣
closed 16 Apr-14 Jun and 6 Oct-31 Dec, 110,000; bkf: 5,000.
★★ *Crepei*, at Pera, v. Giumella 2, ☎ 64103, 34 rm ⌂ ⌇
closed 16 Apr-14 Jun and 1 Oct-19 Dec, 80,000.
★★ *Montana*, v. Roma 106, ☎ 64193, 42 rm P ⫣ ⌂ ⌇
closed 16 Apr-24 Jun and 21 Sep-19 Dec, 42,000; bkf: 5,000.

Restaurant:
◆◆◆ *Augusto Salin*, at Pera, v. Dolomiti 19, ☎ 64147, closed Wed, 10 May-10 Jun and 10 Oct-10 Nov. Regional cuisine: orzetto, homemade pasta, 15/25,000.

△ ★★★ *Catinaccio Rosengarten*, v. Avisio 15, 208 pl, ☎ 63305; ★★★ *Soal*, at Pera, v. Dolomiti, 220 pl, ☎ 64519 (all year).

Recommended
Excursions: to the Rifugio Vaiolet, ☎ 63292.

VIGO DI FASSA, ⊠ 38039, ☎ 0462.
⚡ cableway, ski lifts at Vigo and the Costalunga Pass, cross-country skiing, instruction, skating.
ⓘ v. Roma 2, ☎ 64093.

Hotels:
★★★★ *Park Hotel Corona*, v. Roma 8, ☎ 64211, 70 rm P ⌂ ▣ ⁄° closed 16 Apr-4 Jun and 11 Oct-19 Dec, 130,000; bkf: 8,000.
★★★ *Gran Mugon*, at Tamion, ☎ 64208, 17 rm P ⫣ ⌂
closed 16 Apr-24 Jun and 16 Oct-19 Dec, 40,000; bkf: 3,500.
★★★ *Savoy*, at Passo di Costalugna, ☎ 0471/616824, 40 rm P ⫣ ▣ 90,000.
★★ *Catinaccio*, p. Europa 9, ☎ 64209, 26 rm P ⫣ ⌂
closed 16 Apr-19 Jun and 21 Sep-19 Dec, 58,000; bkf: 6,000.

Recommended
Excursions: by cableway to Ciampede, ☎ 63242 (*CAI* rifugio, ☎ 63332).

The FIEMME VALLEY

C-D4

This valley was one of the areas from which the Venetian Republic obtained timber for its ships. The early system of government in Fiemme incorporated certain features of democracy, with the result that the rulers of Venice viewed the Fiemme community almost as a sister to the Venetian Republic. In contrast to other valleys in the region, there are no castles here because, in the 12C, the valley avoided the feudal system by submitting to direct rule by the prince-bishops of Trento.

▶ The historic centre of the valley is **Cavalese** (→). The valley runs along the middle reaches of the River Avisio;

its meadows and woods are dominated by the Latemar group of the Dolomites on one side and by the Lagorai range (seams of porphyry) on the other. ▶ At **Predazzo** (3,340 ft) is the **Museo Civico di Etnologia, Mineralogia e Geologia** (*Casa della Cultura, v. Molini, open summer and Christmas, 5-7 p.m.; other times visits on request,* ☎ *51237*). Local minerals and fossils, along with traditional costumes, are on display. The road branches at Predazzo and leads to the **Rolle Pass** (→). Other charming spots are **Panchi** (3,220 ft) and **Tésero** (3,280 ft). □

Practical information

PREDAZZO, ⊠ 38037, ☎ 0462.
⚡ cable car, ski lifts, more than 30 km of cross-country skiing, ski instruction, skating, ski jumps.
ⓘ p. della Chiesa, ☎ 51237.

Hotels:
★★★★ *Ancora*, v. IX Novembre 1, ☎ 51651, 38 rm P ⌂
closed May and Nov, 65,000; bkf: 10,000.
★★★ *Bellamonte*, at Bellamonte, v. Prai de Mont 52, ☎ 56250, 31 rm P ⫣ ⌂ closed May and Oct-Nov, 90,000; bkf: 5,000.
★★★ *Bellaria*, v. De Gasperi 20, ☎ 51369, 58 rm P ⌂ ⌇ ▣ closed 15-31 May and Oct, 72,000; bkf: 5,000.
★★★ *Sole*, v. de l'Or 8, ☎ 56299, 35 rm P ⌂ & ⌇ 52,000; bkf: 6,000.
★★ *Margherita*, v. Prai de Mont 1, ☎ 56140, 28 rm P ⌂ & ⌇ Pens. closed 21 Apr-19 Jun and 21 Sep-19 Dec, 47,000.

△ ★★★ *Bellamonte*, at Bellamonte, v. Cece 16, 300 pl, ☎ 56119 (all year).

Recommended
Alpine guides: ☎ 51573.
Events: *national horse show* (Jul); *Marcialonga* (Jan, → Cavalese).
Swimming: v. Venezia, ☎ 51365 (indoor pool).

TÉSERO, ⊠ 38038, ☎ 0462.
⚡ ski lifts at the Alpe Pampeago (7.5 km N), cross-country skiing at Lake Tésero, instruction.
ⓘ ☎ 83032.

Hotel:
★★★ *Alma*, v. Roma 4, ☎ 83185, 30 rm P ⫣ ⌂ ⌇
closed May and Nov, 42,000; bkf: 10,000.

Recommended
Swimming: v. Rossini, ☎ 31810 (indoor pool).

FOLGARIA

Trento 27, Milan 236 km
3,830 ft pop. 3,087 ⊠ 38064 ☎ 0464   C5-6

Folgaria is the largest village on the plateau to the l. of the River Adige. It looks onto Lagarina Valley. □

Practical information

⚡ cable cars, ski lifts, cross-country skiing, instruction, skating, rope-drawn sled lift at Costa.
ⓘ v. Roma 15, ☎ 71133.

Hotels:
★★★ *Cristallo*, at Fondo Grande, ☎ 71320, 34 rm P ⌲ & ⌇ closed 11 Apr-19 Jun and 11 Sep-30 Nov, 70,000; bkf: 8,000.
★★★ *Park Hotel Miramonti*, v. Dante 12, ☎ 71461, 45 rm P ⌲ ⌂ closed May and Oct-Nov, 60,000; bkf: 10,000.
★★★ *Sporting*, at Costa, v. Maffei 229, ☎ 71367, 21 rm P ⌂ ⌇ 50,000.
★★★ *Vittoria*, v. Cadorna 4, ☎ 71122, 39 rm P ⌂ ⌇
closed May and Oct-Nov, 60,000; bkf: 8,000.

Recommended
Bowling: *Palameeting*, ☎ 70044.
Events: *Marcia degli Altipiani* (alpine market, Jul).
Tennis: ☎ 71100 (indoor courts).

The GARDENA PASS

Bolzano 54, Milan 353 km
6,960 ft ⊠ 39048 ☎ 0471 D3

This saddle between the N slope of Sella and the Pizzes da Cir is one of four Dolomite passes that permit a circuit of the Sella group. It links the Badia Valley to the Gardena Valley. □

Practical information

chair lift and cable car to Selva di Val Gardena, ski lifts on the Colfosco slope.
ℹ at Selva di Val Gardena, ☎ 75122.

Hotel:
★★ ***Rifugio Cir,*** ☎ 75127, 34 rm Ⓟ closed 1 May-14 Jun and Oct-Nov, 50,000; bkf: 10,000.

The GARDENA VALLEY

D3

Wood carving began in this valley in the mid-17C at Pescosta, a district of Ortisei. There were about 300 wood-carvers working here by the end of the following century and by the early 19C more than that number of valley dwellers were spreading far and wide to sell the products. The tradition is very much alive today. The valley branches off from the River Isarco at Ponte Gardena-Waidbruck, where there is a gorge whose wildest point is at Pontves, the Ladin gate. Upstream, Ladin is spoken. The valley broadens out into meadows, knolls and woodland, above which the Sassolungo, Odle and Sella massifs loom.

▶ The main town is **Ortisei** (→). ▶ **Santa Cristina Valgardena-St. Christina in Gröden** (4,685 ft) has picturesque Ladin-Gardanese houses among its hotels and villas. ▶ **Selva di Val Gardena-Wolkenstein in Gröden** (5,130 ft) has the majestic backdrop of the Sella and Sassolungo groups. **Ciampinoi** (7,340 ft) can be reached by cableway or chair lift. ▶ Near **Plan de Gralba** (5,940 ft; *cableway to* ***Piz Sella,*** 7,345 ft), the valley road branches in two, one fork ascending to the Sella Pass (→), the other to the Gardena Pass (→). □

Practical information

SANTA CRISTINA VALGARDENA-SANKT CHRISTINA IN GRÖDEN, ⊠ 39047, ☎ 0471.
cableway, ski lifts, cross-country skiing, instruction, skating.
ℹ ☎ 76346.

Hotels:
★★★★ ***Diamant,*** at Sacun, ☎ 76780, 34 rm Ⓟ Pens. closed Easter-31 May, and 1 Nov-Christmas, 82,000.
★★★★ ***Sporthotel Monte Pana,*** at Monte Pana, ☎ 76128, 71 rm Ⓟ closed 21 Apr-30 Jun and 16 Sep-19 Dec, 160,000.
★★★ ***Cristallo,*** v. Dursan 33, ☎ 76499, 36 rm Ⓟ closed Easter-19 May and 1 Oct-19 Nov, 96,000.
★★★ ***Dosses,*** v. Dursan 48, ☎ 73326, 48 rm Ⓟ closed 20 Apr-31 May and 4 Nov-20 Dec, 64,000; bkf: 7,000.

Recommended
Rock climbing: ☎ 76302 or 76369 (instruction).

SELVA DI VAL GARDENA-WOLKENSTEIN IN GRÖDEN, ⊠ 39048, ☎ 0471.
cable car, ski lifts, cross-country skiing, instruction, skating.
ℹ on the Statale, ☎ 75122.

Hotels:
★★★★ ***Alpenroyal,*** v. Meisules 43, ☎ 75178, 33 rm Ⓟ 86,000; bkf: 10,000.
★★★★ ***Antares,*** v. Centro, ☎ 75400, 50 rm Ⓟ 1/2 Pens. closed 16 Apr-30 Jun and 21 Sep-30 Nov, 98,000.
★★★★ ***Genziana,*** v. Ciampinei 2, ☎ 75187, 29 rm Ⓟ 1/2 Pens. closed 16 Apr-19 Jun and 1 Oct-19 Dec, 90,000.
★★★★ ***Sporthotel Gran Baita,*** v. Meisules 145, ☎ 75210, 60 rm Ⓟ Pens. closed 21 Apr-14 Jun and 1 Oct-7 Dec, 123,000.
★★★★ ***Tyrol,*** v. Centro 73, ☎ 75270, 40 rm Ⓟ closed Easter-31 May and Nov, 140,000; bkf: 15,000.
★★★ ***Armin,*** v. Centro 301, ☎ 75347, 20 rm Ⓟ closed 16 Apr-4 Jun and 16 Sep-19 Dec, 94,000.
★★★ ***Chalet Portillo,*** v. Meisules 65, ☎ 75205, 25 rm Ⓟ closed 11 Apr-19 Jun and 21 Sep-19 Dec, 90,000.
★★★ ***Condor,*** v. Dantercepies 53, ☎ 75055, 26 rm Ⓟ closed 1 May-14 Jun and Oct-Nov, 80,000.
★★★ ***Malleier,*** v. Cir 58, ☎ 75296, 37 rm Ⓟ 16 Apr-9 Jun and 1 Oct-14 Dec, 76,000.
★★★ ***Olympia,*** v. Centro 138, ☎ 75145, 42 rm Ⓟ closed Easter-31 May and 1 Oct-Christmas, 80,000; bkf: 10,000.
★★★ ***Sporthotel Maciaconi,*** v. Plan da Thiesa 3, ☎ 76229, 40 rm Ⓟ closed Jun and Nov, 90,000.
★★ ***Stella,*** v. Meisules 283, ☎ 75162, 48 rm Ⓟ closed 16 Apr-19 Jun and 21 Sep-19 Dec, 50,000; bkf: 10,000.

Recommended
Alpine guides: ☎ 75568.
Tennis: ☎ 75122.

GLORENZA - GLURNS

Bolzano 83, Milan 260 km
Pop. 734 ⊠ 39020 ☎ 0473 A2

As the Val Venosta road climbs out of the valley bottom, Glorenza presents a picture postcard view amid pastures and mountains.

▶ The wall of the square **village★** dates from 1555, with corner towers and three gates; the 16C layout has hardly changed since the wall was built. ▶ Glorenza was an important market (Tyrolean salt, Lombard grain) by virtue of its position at the point where the Monastero Valley enters the Adige Valley. ▶ The base of the 14C campanile of the **parish church** (1481) stands outside the walls on the other side of the Adige and is decorated with a fresco of the *Last Judgment* (1496).

Environs

▶ 2.8 km away at Sluderno-Schluderns is **Castel Coira★**, a 13C castle rebuilt in the 16C *(guided tours 10 a.m.-12 noon and 2-4:30 p.m.; closed Mon).* Features include courtyard with loggias, a 16C chapel, furnishings and an armory. One of the suits of armour is Milanese and belonged to a knight 6 ft 11 in tall. ▶ There are 13C-14C frescos in the church of S. Giovanni at **Tubre-Taufers in Münstertal.** □

Practical information

ℹ at Sluderno, ☎ 75858.

Hotel:
★★ ***Posta-Zur Post,*** v. Flora 15, ☎ 81208, 25 rm Ⓟ closed 10 Jan-25 Mar, 32,000; bkf: 5,000.

LANA

Bolzano 24, Milan 322 km
Pop. 7,957 ⊠ 39011 ☎ 0473 C3

Lana is a picturesque spot in the Adige Valley near Merano.

► The **church of the Assunta** near the cemetery has a 16C **high altar★** *(guided tours 9:30-11:30 a.m. and 2-6 p.m.).* ► 4 km S is **Foiana** with the ruins of Castel Maggio. ► A trip *(5 mn)* can be made by cableway to M. San Vigilio whose meadows look down on the valley of Merano; then by chair lift to Dosse dei Larici (6,025 ft). ► The **Val d'Ultimo** cuts in as far as the Cevedale group *(passable by road for 34 km to Santa Gertrude-St. Gertraud);* at **San Nicolò-St. Nicolaus** is a museum of ethnography *(open Jun-Sep; Tue, Fri, Sun 11 a.m.-12 noon and 3-5 p.m.).* ☐

Practical information ───────────

ⓘ v. A. Hofer 6, ☎ 51770.

Hotels:
★★★★ *Poeder,* v. Andreas Hofer 11, ☎ 51258, 48 rm ℗ ⊞ ▭ 126,000. Rest. ♦♦♦ closed Mon off season. Central European cuisine, 20/30,000.
★★★★ *Teiss-Cavallino Bianco,* v. Merano 5, ☎ 51101, 38 rm ℗ ▭ ▭ Pens. closed Nov-Mar, 85,000.
★★★★ *Völlanerhof,* at Foiana, ☎ 58033, 38 rm ℗ ⫤ ⚘ ▭ ⫫ Pens. closed 1 Dec-24 Mar, 106,000.
★★★★ *Waldhof,* at Foiana, v. Mayenburg, ☎ 58081, 28 rm ℗ ⫤ ⚘ ⊞ ▭ ⫫ closed Nov-May, 87,000; bkf: 20,000.

Recommended
Swimming: v. Bolzano 33, ☎ 51416.
Tennis: zona sportiva Valsura, ☎ 53535 (also mini-golf).

LAVARONE

Trento 32, Milan 245 km
3,840 ft pop. 1,152 ⊠ 38046 ☎ 0464   C5

Lavarone is scattered over a plateau SE of Trento, separated from the Valsugana by Mt. Cimone. **Lake Lavarone** lies below the hamlet of Chiesa at the bottom of a karst sink-hole surrounded by conifers. The lake is used for fishing and bathing in summer, skating in winter. ► 1.5 km from Cappella is the Austrian **Fort Belvedere** *(open summer),* which once controlled the Astico Valley and the Asiago plateau: it contains a photographic exhibition and a museum of weapons and mementos. ☐

Practical information ───────────

⚡ ski lifts, more than 50 km of cross-country skiing on the plateau, instruction, skating.
ⓘ at Gionghi, municipio, ☎ 73226.

Hotels:
★★★ *Monteverde,* at Gionghi, ☎ 73174, 31 rm ℗ ⫤ ▭ 50,000; bkf: 4,000.
★★★ *Villa Maria,* at Chiesa, v. Dolomiti 5, ☎ 73230, 37 rm ℗ ⫤ ▭ closed 11 Mar-19 Jun and 11 Sep-19 Dec, 56,000; bkf: 8,000.
★★ *Capriolo,* at Bertoldi, ☎ 73187, 28 rm ℗ ⫤ ⚘ ▭ ⫫ closed 1 Apr-19 May except Easter and 1 Oct-14 Dec, 50,000; bkf: 4,000.
⚠ ★★★ *Lago di Lavarone,* at Chiesa, v. Trieste 36, 160 pl, ☎ 73300.

Recommended
Events: *Millegrobbe* (Nordic skiing, Jan).
Swimming: at Chiesa, ☎ 73112; at Cappella, ☎ 73588.

MADONNA DI CAMPIGLIO*

Trento 74, Milan 214 km
4,995 ft pop. 777 ⊠ 38084 ☎ 0465   B4

In the 12C monks built a hospice in this valley. In the late 19C an entrepreneur built a hotel and the road that leads from Pinzolo. Today Madonna di Campiglio is an elegant and popular mountain resort.

► **Malga Nambino** is 3 km away and from there **Lake Nambino** (5,795 ft) can be reached on foot *(20 mn).* ► **Mt. Spinale** (6,905 ft) is accessible by cableway. ► 2.5 km away is **Campo Carlo Magno,** an expanse of pastures forming a pass between the Campiglio Valley and Meledrino Valley, a tributary of the Val di Non. It is said that Charlemagne passed through here in 776 on his way to crush Lombard rebels in Friuli; this incident is commemorated in frescos in the church of S. Stefano at Carisolo, a village in the Rendena Valley. There is a cableway to **Grosté★** (8,205 ft), with a superb view of the Brenta Dolomites. ☐

Practical information ───────────

⚡ cableways (Cinque Laghi, Spinale-Grosté, Pradalago), ski lifts, cross-country skiing, instruction, skating (Olympic speed-skating rink).
ⓘ centro Rainalter, ☎ 42000.

Hotels:
★★★★ *Grifone,* v. Vallesinella 7, ☎ 42002, 40 rm ℗ ⫤ ▭ Pens. closed 21 Apr-30 Jun and 11 Sep-30 Nov, 130,000.
★★★★ *Savoia Palace,* v. Dolomiti di Brenta, ☎ 41004, 57 rm ℗ ▭ closed 16 Apr-4 Dec, 160,000.
★★★ *Bonapace,* v. Spinale 18, ☎ 41019, 50 rm ℗ ⚘ ▭ ⫫ closed 7 Apr-9 Jul except Easter and 26 Aug-4 Dec, 112,000; bkf: 6,000.
★★★ *Chalet dei Pini,* v. Campanile Basso 16, ☎ 41489, 10 rm ℗ ⚘ ▭ ⫫ closed 23 Apr-6 Jul except Easter and 16 Sep-3 Dec. No restaurant, 74,000.
★★★ *Cristiania,* v. Pradalago 24, ☎ 41470, 30 rm ℗ ⫫ closed 21 Apr-19 Jun and 16 Sep-30 Nov, 112,000; bkf: 9,500.
★★★ *Oberosler,* v. Monte Spinale 27, ☎ 41136, 38 rm ℗ ▭ ⫫ closed 16 Apr-30 Nov, 112,000; bkf: 13,000.
★★★ *St. Hubertus,* v. Dolomiti di Brenta 7, ☎ 41144, 32 rm ℗ ⫤ ⊞ closed Easter-30 Jun and 16 Sep-30 Nov, 112,000; bkf: 12,000.
★★★ *Touring,* v. Belvedere 10, ☎ 41051, 27 rm ℗ ⚘ ▭ closed May-Jun and 21 Sep-30 Nov, 112,000; bkf: 10,000.

Recommended
Alpine guides: ☎ 41570 or 41140 (rock-climbing school).
Events: *3-Tre slalom* (world cup in alpine skiing); *Galopera* (30-km Nordic ski race); *international speed-skating competitions.*
Excursions: by cableway to M. Spinale and Grosté, ☎ 41001.
Golf: at Campo Carlo Magno, ☎ 41003 (9 holes).
Horseback riding: ☎ 42660.
Swimming: at centro Rainalter, ☎ 42766 (indoor pool).

MALE

Trento 55, Milan 236 km
2,420 ft pop. 2,026 ⊠ 38027 ☎ 0463   B4

Val di Sole is the upper part of the Valle del Noce and Malé stands at the point where the Rabbi Valley enters on the l. Next to the 15C-16C church of the **Assunta** is the former chapel of **S. Valentino** (15C) with an open arcade in which services are said to have been celebrated in times of plague. The **Museo della Civiltà Solandra** houses local exhibits.

Environs

► 12 km NW is **Bagni di Rabbi** (4,010 ft). ► 3 km towards Trento is **Caldés** and its deserted 13C **castle.** ☐

Practical information ───────────

MALE
⚡ torch-lit cross-country skiing.
ⓘ v. Marconi, ☎ 91280.

Hotel:
★ *Rauzi,* v. Molini 31, ☎ 91228, 33 rm ℗ ⫤ ▭ ⫫ closed 1 Apr-24 Jun and 11 Sep-21 Dec, 51,000; bkf: 5,000.

Restaurant:
♦♦ *Segosta,* v. Trento 59, ☎ 91390; closed Thu and
Jun. A *segosta* is an old-fashioned pot used for cooking in a fireplace. Regional cuisine: canederli, strangolapreti, lucanega, 15/20,000.

Recommended
Alpine guides: ☎ 91151 or 92535.
Swimming: ☎ 91003 (indoor pool, sauna).

Environs

BAGNI DI RABBI, ⊠ 38020, ☎ 0463.
♨ (Jul-Aug), ☎ 95144.

MALLES VENOSTA - MALS

Bolzano 85, Milan 260 km
3,450 ft pop. 4,590 ⊠ 39024 ☎ 0473   A2

Campaniles and sturdy Romanesque towers are features of this Alto Adige village. The exceptional
monuments and works of art that it contains enhance
the charm of its setting.

▶ The Gothic **parish church** has a 16C campanile; the
small church of **S. Michele** has early 16C frescos. ▶ A
little way off, the remains of Frölich Castle include a
Romanesque **tower** (12C-13C) and a Lombard Romanesque **campanile** from a church that has been destroyed. ▶ The fragments of frescos and stucco (9C) that
decorate the church of **S. Benedetto★** *(N of village, keys
in same street at no. 29)* are among the finest works of
art in the region; the atmosphere harks back to Charlemagne. ▶ From the **park,** there is a splendid view of the
valleys of Venosta, Monastro and l'Ortles.

Environs

▶ 5.2 km away, beyond Burgusio-Burgeis and leaving the
castle of Fürstenburg on the l., is the Benedictine **abbey
of Monte Maria.** This imposing group of buildings clinging to the mountainside was founded in the 12C, later
altered and enlarged (mainly 18C-19C). It has a 16C
Gothic **cloister** and 12C **frescos★** *(Redeemer, Angels and
Saints)* in the central apse of the church crypt.   □

Practical information _____

⚡ ski lifts, cross-country skiing, instruction at Watles
(8 km NW).
ⓘ ☎ 81190.

Hotel:
★★★ *Garberhof,* v. Nazionale 25, ☎ 81399, 29 rm Ⓟ ⚒
♿ ☐ closed 20 Nov-20 Dec, 94,000.

⚘ *Zum Lwen,* at Tarces, v. Resia, 45 pl, ☎ 81598
(all year).

La MARMOLADA

10,965 ft   D-E3

La Marmolada is the highest peak in the Dolomites. It takes its name from the **Marmolada glacier**
that covers the N slope and runs down towards the
Pian Fedaia.

▶ 12 km along the road from Canazei (→) are the **Pian
Fedaia** and **Lake Fedaia,** an extensive artificial reservoir. The road next arrives at the **Fedaia Pass** (6,750 ft),
where it descends to **Malga Ciapelo** (4,685 ft; *cableway
to Marmolada*) and passes through the **Serrai di Sotto-
guda★** ravine *(road open only summer)* to reach **Rocca
Piétore** in the Cordévole Valley (Venetia).   □

Practical information _____

⚡ cableway from Malga Ciapela, cable car from the
Fedaia Pass, ski lifts, cross-country skiing, instruction,
summer skiing.

ⓘ at Alleghe (→ Venetia), ☎ 0437/723333; at Rocca Piétore (→ Venetia), ☎ 0437/21319; at Canazei,
☎ 0462/61113.

The MENDOLA PASS

Bolzano 25, Milan 300 km
4,470 ft ⊠ 38011 ☎ 0471   C3

The Mendola Pass cuts through the wall of mountains
that tower above the River Adige on one side, but
slope gently towards the Anàunia on the other. This
pass was highly fashionable in the early years of
this century. From the belvedere on **Mt. Pénegal**
(5,700 ft, *4 km, toll for cars*) there is an extensive
view of the Adige, the Bolzano Valley and the mountains from the Presanella to the Dolomites.   □

Practical information _____

⚡ ski lifts, cross-country skiing, instruction.
ⓘ at Ruffrè, ☎ 0463/82127.

MERANO - MERAN★★

Bolzano 28, Milan 326 km
Pop. 33,502 ⊠ 39012 ☎ 0473   C2

The Hapsburgs took up temporary residence in the
castle at Merano in the 17C to escape from an epidemic raging in the Inn Valley. Some time later Merano
was established as a health resort. In the first half of
the 19C local doctors publicized Merano as a holiday
resort, encouraging tourism by referring to the temperate climate and extolling the grape cure. Both climate and grapes are still excellent, and the town has
a splendid position facing S over the orchards of
the Adige Valley. In spring and autumn, Merano is
enchanting. Relics of the *belle époque* are evident in
the promenades along the River Passirio, in the gardens, in the hotels and in the cafés with their Viennese pastries. This atmosphere of a bygone age is
striking and Merano also has works of art and monuments.

▶ The rectangular old town encloses the Duomo and rows
of medieval houses. Later expansion took place across
the River Passirio in the suburbs of **Maia Alta** (B3) and
Maia Bassa (C2-3). ▶ The town centre is the p. del Teatro (B2). ▶ The **Kursaal** (B2), in the corso Libertà facing the
Passirio, is a meeting place and venue for events. ▶ The
14C-15C Gothic **Duomo★** (A-B2) has an elegant campanile, portals, statues, reliefs and frescos outside. Inside
is an altar with a 15C carved Gothic altarpiece. Behind
the Duomo is the octagonal Gothic church of **S. Barbara.** Nearby is the **Museo Steiner** *(11 a.m.-12:30 p.m.
and 3-5 p.m.; closed Sat p.m. and hols).* ▶ The **via dei
Portici★** (A-B2) is elegant, lively and typical of the Alto
Adige. ▶ The ivy-clad **Castello Principesco** (A2) is partly
hidden among trees and contains noteworthy furnishings
*(9 a.m.-12 noon and 3-6 p.m.; Sat 9 a.m.-12 noon and
2-4 p.m.; closed hols).* Opposite is the chair lift to
Mt. Benedetto (1,560 ft). ▶ In the **Museo Civico** (A2,
10 a.m.-12 noon and 4-6 p.m.; closed Sat p.m. and hols)
are natural history, folklore and archaeology collections;
in the art gallery, wood carvings and Gothic frescos by
the Merano school. ▶ Merano is ideal for strolling. The
Passeggiata Lungo Passirio★ runs along the r. bank of
the river and is shaded by a long row of poplars. After
the ponte della Posta (B2), it continues as the **Passegiata d'inverno** (winter walk), partly covered with luxuriant vegetation beyond the Roman bridge (A3) and
continuing as far as the base of the ruins of Castel
S. Zeno. The **Passeggiata d'estate** (summer walk) follows the l. bank of the River Passirio between the ponte
della Posta, with its 15C Gothic church of S. Spirito, and

Castel Tirolo km 7 — 1 — 2 — 3

MERANO

0 100 200 300 400 m

1:20.000 (1cm = 200m)

Fondo km 40 — 2 — Bolzano km 28 © SERVIZIO CARTOGRAFICO DEL TOURING CLUB ITALIANO, MILANO

the Passirio bridge (B3), from which Maia Alta can be climbed. Finally, the **Passegiata Tappeiner★** (A2) winds among gardens and vineyards on the hill offering views of the Merano Valley.

Environs

▶ **Avelengo-Hafling** (4,235 ft) is reached by cableway then by road *(2 km)* from Maia Alta or else directly by road *(6 km).* The plateau commands superb views. ▶ 4 km away is **Tirolo-Tirol,** the town that gave the region its name, with a Gothic parish church; from here to **Tirolo Castle** it is a 20-mn walk. The interior of this castle of the Counts of Tyrol is being restored. Nearby is the **Museo Agricolo Brunenburg** *(9:30-11:30 a.m. and 2-5 p.m.; closed Tue).* ▶ 5 km NE is **Scena-Schenna** with a **castle** containing extensive collections of arms *(guided tours every 45 mn 10-11:30 a.m. and 2:30-5 p.m.).* There are cableways to Mt. Scena (4,595 ft) and, from the hamlet of Verdins, to Talle di Sopra (4,730 ft) and the area of the Rifugio Punta Cervina (6,505 ft, *this ski area can also be reached by cableway from Saltusio Pass on the Passiria Valley road).* ▶ **Merano 2000,** a ski resort with excellent facilities, adjoins the Avelengo plateau and has a majestic view★, with the Monte Ivigna cableway from Val di Nova *(3 km from Merano).* ☐

Practical information ────────────

MERANO
⚓ (all year), ☎ 37724.
ℹ corso Libertà 47 (B2), ☎ 35223.
🚂 (A1), ☎ 47500.

🚂 from p. della Stazione, ☎ 42002.

Hotels:
★★★★ *Palace,* v. Cavour 2 (B2 a), ☎ 34734, 124 rm 🅿 ♨
♨♨ ♿ ☐ closed 11 Nov-14 Mar except Christmas. Period furniture; in a park with exotic plants, 200,000; bkf: 20,000.
★★★★ *Adria,* v. Gilm 2 (B3 b), ☎ 36610, 55 rm 🅿 ♨ ♨♨
♿ ☐ 1/2 Pens. closed 1 Nov-14 Mar, 77,000.
★★★★ *Augusta,* v. Otto Huber 2 (B1 c), ☎ 49570, 26 rm
🅿 ♨♨ ♿ closed Nov-Mar, 90,000; bkf: 7,000.
★★★★ *Castel Freiberg,* at Castel Verruca, v. Monte Franco, ☎ 44196, 36 rm 🅿 ⚞ ♨♨ ☐ ♪ closed 4 Nov-14 Apr. An isolated castle, 14C in origin, 230,000.
★★★★ *Eurotel Merano,* v. Garibaldi 5 (B2 f), ☎ 34900, 135 rm 🅿 ♨♨ ♿ closed 16 Nov-28 Feb except Christmas. No restaurant, 90,000.
★★★★ *G. H. Bristol,* v. Otto Huber 14 (A-B1 d), ☎ 49500, 146 rm 🅿 ♨♨ ☐ closed 16 Nov-28 Feb, 140,000.
★★★★ *G. H. Emma,* p. Mazzini 1 (A1 e), ☎ 47522, 130 rm 🅿 ♨♨ ♿ ☐ ♪ closed 15 Nov-20 Dec, 140,000.
★★★★ *Irma,* v. Belvedere 17, ☎ 30124, 50 rm 🅿 ♨ ♨♨ ♿
☐ ♪ closed 6 Nov-14 Mar, 124,000; bkf: 5,000.
★★★★ *Juliane,* v. dei Campi 6 (C3 g), ☎ 30195, 39 rm 🅿
♨ ♨♨ ♿ ☐ closed 6 Nov-14 Mar, 120,000.
★★★★ *Kurhotel Castel Rundegg,* v. Scena 2 (B3 h),
☎ 34364, 30 rm 🅿 ♨♨ ☐ closed 10-31 Jan. In a 15C castle, 160,000; bkf: 20,000.
★★★★ *Parc Hotel Mignon,* v. Grabmayr 5 (B3 i), ☎ 30353, 52 rm 🅿 ♨♨ ☐ 1/2 Pens. closed 1 Nov-14 Mar, 89,000.
★★★★ *Villa Mozart,* at Maia Bassa, v. S. Marco 26, ☎ 30630, 10 rm 🅿 ♨ ♨♨ ⚡ ☐ closed 6 Nov-

14 Mar. Early 20C villa with furniture in the Viennese Secession style, 242,000; bkf: 22,000. Rest. ● ◆◆◆◆ closed 10 Jan-15 Mar. Refined and exclusive; outstanding chef; menu reserved for hotel guests and advance reservations (minimum of 6 persons), 80/100,000.
★★★ *Europa Splendid,* corso Libert 178 (B2 1), ☎ 32376, 55 rm Ⓟ closed 1 Nov-20 Dec, 64,000; bkf: 7,000.
★★★ *Fragsburg-Castel Verruca,* at Castel Verruca, v. Fragsburg, ☎ 44071, 18 rm Ⓟ ⫤ ◔ ▥ ▱ closed 4 Nov-Easter, 104,000.
★★★ *Isabell,* v. Piave 58 (B2 m), ☎ 34700, 25 rm Ⓟ ▥ ❺ closed 11 Nov-28 Feb, 70,000.
★★★ *Schloss Labers,* v. Labers 25, ☎ 34484, 32 rm Ⓟ ⫤ ◔ ▥ ▱ ⌕ closed Nov-Mar. Isolated medieval castle with view, 124,000.
★★★ *Windsor,* v. Rezia 2 (B1 n), ☎ 46556, 14 rm Ⓟ ▥ ▱ No restaurant, 50,000; bkf: 5,000.
★★ *Conte di Merano-Graf von Meran,* v. delle Corse 78 (A2 p), ☎ 32181, 26 rm Ⓟ 50,000; bkf: 7,000.

Restaurants:
● ◆◆◆ *Andrea,* v. Galilei 44 (A2 q), ☎ 37400, closed Mon and 5 Jan-15 Mar. Regional cuisine: prosciutto alla meranese, Angus beef, 50/70,000.
◆◆ *Flora,* v. Portici 75 (A2 r), ☎ 31484, closed Sun, Jan-Feb and Jul. Looks onto courtyard garden. Creative cuisine: tasting menu of six dishes, 30/50,000
◆◆ *Terlaner Weinstube,* v. Portici 231 (B2 s), ☎ 35571, closed Wed, Jan-Feb and Jul. Typical Tyrolean establishment. Regional and Italian cuisine: hunter's pappardelle, venison carpaccio, 14/26,000.

⚹ *Merano,* v. Piave 44, 150 pl, ☎ 31249.

Recommended
Canoeing: v. Portici 204, ☎ 32126.
Events: *race meetings* (spring and autumn) and the *Gran Premio di Merano* (Sep) at the Ippodromo di Maia Bassa; *Grape Festival* (second Sun in Oct); *concerts* on the promenades and at the Kursaal; fashion shows.
Ice skating: v. Mainardo, ☎ 47544.
Mountaineering: v. Portici 6, ☎ 33022.
Race course: Maia Bassa, v. Palade (C1), ☎ 36154.
♥ gastronomy: speck, Tyrolean desserts.

Environs

MERANO 2000-MERAN 2000, 7,875 ft, ⊠ 39012, ☎ 0473.
⚑ ski lifts, instruction.
Access: from Merano by cableway, ☎ 34821; from Falzében by chair lift.

MEZZANA

Trento 66, Milan 239 km
3,080 ft pop. 862 ⊠ 38020 ☎ 0463   B4

Mezzana is a lively village in the alpine setting of the Val di Sole.

▶ **Piano** (*3 km*, 2,790 ft), one of the hamlets of Commezzadura, contains the 16C church of **S. Agata** with a free-standing campanile; frescos (1499) in sanctuary. ▶ **Marilleva** (4,600 ft) is 10 km by road then cable car. Its ski lifts are linked to those of Folgrida and Madonna di Campiglio (→). ❏

Practical information _____

MEZZANA
⚑ cableway to Marilleva, cross-country skiing, instruction.
ⓘ ☎ 71934.
Hotels:
★★★ *Ravelli,* v. IV Novembre 18, ☎ 77122, 38 rm Ⓟ ⫤ ◔ ⌔ closed 11 Apr-14 Jun and 26 Sep-4 Dec, 80,000; bkf: 6,000.
★★★ *Val di Sole,* v. Nazionale 75, ☎ 77240, 50 rm Ⓟ ▥ ⌔ ▱ 37,000; bkf: 5,000.
★★ *Eccher,* v. IV Novembre 60, ☎ 77146, 17 rm Ⓟ ⌔ closed May and Nov, 40,000.

Environs

MARILLEVA, 4,600 ft, ⊠ 38020, ☎ 0463.
⚑ ski lifts, instruction.

Recommended
Vacation villages: *Hotel Villaggio Valtur Marilleva* (closed May-Nov), ☎ 02/791733.

MOUNT BONDONE

Trento 19, Milan 263 km
5,415 ft ⊠ 38040 ☎ 0461   B5

The pyramidal peaks of this massif between the Adige and Sarca Rivers dominate the Trento landscape.

▶ The main village is **Vason**; the others are **Sardagna, Candriai** and **Vaneze.** ▶ Some of the grasses are used in baths to treat rheumatism. ▶ In the valley of **Le Viotte,** 2,200 species of alpine plants from all over the world are grown in the **Giardino Botanico Alpino** *(May-Oct 8 a.m.-12 noon and 2-6 p.m.).* ❏

Practical information _____

MOUNT BONDONE
⚑ Vaneze-Vason cable car, ski lifts, instruction, ice skating.
ⓘ at Trento, ☎ 983880; at Vaneze, ☎ 47128.
Hotels:
★★★ *Montana,* at Vason, ☎ 47171, 53 rm Ⓟ ⫤ ◔ ❺ ⌔ closed 16 Apr-14 Jun and 16 Sep-30 Nov, 60,000; bkf: 6,000.
★★★ *Nevada,* at Vason, ☎ 47317, 25 rm Ⓟ ⫤ closed May-Nov, 46,000; bkf: 5,000.

Recommended
Nature park: *Tre Cime del Monte Bondone* Reserve; information, at Trento, *Ufficio Foreste demaniali,* ☎ 982117; at Le Viotte, *stazione forestale,* ☎ 47123.
Tennis: at Candriai.

Environs

LE VIOTTE, 5,045 ft.
⚑ high-altitude ski zone, cross-country skiing, instruction.
Recommended
Botanical garden: ☎ 47540 (open May-Oct).

NOVACELLA ABBEY

Bolzano 43, Milan 339 km
⊠ 39042 (Bressanone) ☎ 0472   D2

The 12C-18C abbey is interesting both for its associations with the region's religious culture and the historical function of the monastic buildings. A hospice for pilgrims once stood here. The circular battlemented chapel of **S. Michele** was built in 1199 in imitation of the Church of the Holy Sepulchre in Jerusalem. The **abbey** was founded in the 15C *(10-11 a.m. and 2:30-3:30 p.m.; closed hols).* In the courtyard is the **Pozzo delle Meraviglie** (a well decorated with frescos depicting the seven wonders *(meraviglie)* of the world, the eighth being the abbey itself). There are also a Gothic **cloister** with 14C-15C frescos, a Baroque **library** with 65,000 volumes and paintings by the 14C-15C Adige school. The Baroque decoration in the **church of the Madonna** is remarkable. ❏

Practical information _____

Recommended
♥ wines: the abbey's wine cellar.

NOVA PONENTE - DEUTSCHNOFEN

Bolzano 25, Milan 323 km
4,450 ft pop. 3,071 ⊠ 39050 ☎ 0471   C3

Once a silver mining village, Nova Ponente stands on a plateau above the Ega Valley, commanding magnificent views of two Dolomite groups, Catinaccio and Latemar.

▶ The church of **S. Elena**, near an abandoned mine, has frescos★ in the early 15C Bolzano style. ▶ The 17C shrine of **Madonna di Pietralba**, 8 km away among fir-woods, is the most popular shrine in the Alto Adige.   □

Practical information _____

⌇ ski lifts, cross-country skiing (45-km run heading SE to the Oclini Pass), ski lifts at San Floriano *(10 km SE)*.
ⓘ on main road, ☎ 616567.

Hotels:
★★★ *Peter,* at Monte San Pietro, ☎ 615143, 35 rm P ∰
ⓔ ⁀° closed 1 Nov-14 Dec, 60,000; bkf: 6,000.
★★★★ *Sporthotel Obereggen,* at San Floriano-Obereggen, ☎ 615797, 55 rm P ⊰ ⌓ ∰ ⅄ ⅋ ⓔ ⁀° closed 26 Apr-31 May and 2 Oct-4 Dec, 128,000.

L'OLTRADIGE

                                                        C3-4
This hilly area extends between the Adige and the Méndola Mountains. Fertile, sunny and with a relatively mild climate, it is covered with vineyards and strewn with medieval castles and palazzi. The Oltradige style, a late adaptation of local architecture to the models of the Italian Renaissance, flourished here in the second half of the 16C. The results still lend grace to the many villages: **Caldaro sulla Strada del Vino** (→) is the main centre of the area.

▶ **Appiano sulla Strada del Vino-Eppan an der Weinstrasse** consists of several hamlets scattered among vineyards and orchards. ▶ Fine small palazzi are to be seen, especially along the colourful main road of **San Michele-St. Michael**, which is the administrative centre. The **lakes of Montcolo**, small lakes left by glaciers, are 5.2 km SE. Only ruins on a cliff still remain of the 12C **Castello di Appiano**, 4 km N, then footpath *(20 mn)*. The 12C chapel of S. Maddalena, beside the castle, has frescos from the first half of the 13C. ▶ At **Termeno sulla Strada del Vino-Tramin an der Weinstrasse** are interesting houses and frescos in the church of S. Valentino, the parish church of SS. Quirico e Giulitta and the small Romanesque church of S. Giacomo on a hill above the village. These last frescos, including one depicting *Battles of Monstrous Animals* (mid-13C), were derived from medieval bestiaries. ▶ The Oltradige villages are linked by an attractive **Strada del Vino** (wine route).   □

Practical information _____

APPIANO SULLA STRADA DEL VINO-EPPAN AN DER WEINSTRASSE, ⊠ 39057, ☎ 0471.
ⓘ at San Michele, ☎ 52206; at San Paolo, ☎ 51557.

Hotels:
★★★★ *Schloss Korb,* at San Paolo, ☎ 633222, 56 rm P ⊰ ⌓ ∰ ⁀° Pens. closed 6 Nov-31 Mar, 100,000.
★★★ *Girlanerhof,* at Cornaiano, v. Belvedere 7, ☎ 52442, 31 rm P ⊰ ⌓ ∰ ⅋ ⓔ Pens. closed 16 Nov-14 Mar, 65,000.

Restaurant:
♦♦♦ *Bellavista-Marklhof,* at Cornaiano, v. Belvedere, ☎ 52407, closed Mon and Jun-Jul. In former convent with summer terrace and garden. Regional cuisine: cros-

tini di milza in brodo, cheese canederli, homemade wines, 25/36,000.

Recommended
Swimming: at Cornaiano.
Youth hostel: *Ostello Castel Masaccio,* Organizzazione Alpetour di Baviera, ☎ 50111.

ORA - AUER

Bolzano 20, Milan 282 km
Pop. 2,521 ⊠ 39040 ☎ 0471   C4

Maximilian of Hapsburg, later Emperor Maximilian II, halted here during his return in 1551 from a journey to Portugal. The Portuguese king had presented Maximilian with the exotic gift of an elephant. This was probably the first elephant to cross the Alps after those of Hannibal. The elephant's passage is recorded in the name and sign of a hotel here and at Bressanone, another stop on the journey. Ora is surrounded by vineyards and orchards.

▶ The Gothic church of **S. Pietro** has a campanile with double- and treble-arched windows. ▶ For those following the Adige up from Trento, Ora marks the start of the Dolomites, with the **San Lugano Pass** leading to Cavalese, and the Fiemme and Fassa valleys, where the route joins the **Grande Strada delle Dolomiti** (→) from Bolzano and the Val d'Ega. The initial climb to the pass offers a superb view of the Adige Valley. ▶ 4.5 km S of Ora at **Villa-Vill** is the Gothic church of **S. Maria**, with an early 15C polygonal apse and 15C-16C frescos.   □

Practical information _____

ⓘ ☎ 80231.

Hotel:
★★★ *Elefant,* p. Principale 45, ☎ 80129, 32 rm P ⅋ closed 10 Nov-25 Dec, 60,000.
⚘ *Cascata,* v. Cascata 32, 60 pl, ☎ 80519.

ORTISEI - SANKT ULRICH*

Bolzano 36, Milan 334 km
4,050 ft pop. 4,154 ⊠ 39046 ☎ 0471   D3

Ortisei, lively and elegant, is the centre of the Val Gardena. The area has a strong tradition of **wood-carving** and the **Palazzo dei Congressi** has a permanent exhibition of the valley's products.

▶ **Museo della Val Gardena** in Cesa di Ladins *(Mon-Fri p.m.; ☎ 76245)* houses prehistoric and natural history collections, as well as paintings and sculptures from this Ladin-speaking valley. ▶ There is a cableway to the **Alpe di Siusi** (→ Alpe di Siusi). ▶ Another cableway leads to **Mt. Seceda** (8,260 ft), then there is a walk *(30 mn)* to the foot of the Odle. ▶ From **San Giacomo** there is a view★ of Sassolungo. There are 15C Gothic frescos in the little church near the village.   □

Practical information _____

⌇ cableways (Seceda and Alpe di Siusi), chair lifts, cross-country skiing, instruction.
ⓘ Palazzo dei Congressi, ☎ 76328.

Hotels:
★★★★ *Aquila-Adler,* v. Rezia 7, ☎ 76203, 85 rm P ⊰ ∰ ⓔ ⁀° closed 16 Apr-31 May and 11 Oct-14 Dec, 174,000.
★★★★ *Hell,* v. Promenade 3, ☎ 76785, 27 rm P ⊰ ∰ ⅋ ⅋ ⓔ closed 11 Apr-5 Jun and 11 Oct-14 Dec, 94,000.
★★★ *Angelo-Engel,* v. Petlin 35, ☎ 76336, 37 rm P ⊰ ∰ closed 1 Nov-20 Dec, 76,000.
★★★ *Gardena-Groednerhof,* v. Vidalong 3, ☎ 76315, 45 rm P ∰ ⅋ closed Easter-31 May and from 1 Oct-14 Dec, 80,000.

★★★ *Perla,* v. Digon 8, ☎ 76421, 36 rm P ◄ ⟨ ⅷ ḋ ⊡
↗ closed 21 Apr-9 Jun and 11 Oct-14 Dec, 80,000;
bkf: 7,000.
★★★ *Rainell,* v. Vidalong 19, ☎ 76145, 28 rm P ◄ ⅷ
closed 1 Apr-15 Jun and 1-20 Oct, 51,000; bkf: 5,000.
★★★ *Villa Emilia,* v. Mureda 61, ☎ 76171, 33 rm P ◄ ⅷ
closed 1-20 May and 15-30 Nov, 80,000; bkf: 8,000.

Restaurant:
◆◆ *Ramoser,* v. Purger 8, ☎ 76460, closed Thu, Jun
and 1 Nov-20 Dec. Regional cuisine: venison ragu, grilled
venison with porcini, 35/55,000.

Recommended
Events: *international ski races and ice-hockey competitions; Garda Folklore Day* (first Sun in Aug, alternating with Santa Cristina and Selva).
Excursions: cableway to Alpe di Siusi, ☎ 76210.
Horseback riding: *Country Club S. Durich,* v. Vidalong
2/1, ☎ 76904.
Ice skating: v. Setil, ☎ 76779.
Swimming: v. Decima, ☎ 77131.
Tennis: at Roncadizza, ☎ 76019.
♥ crafts: permanent exhibition at Palazzo dei Congressi,
☎ 77620; Comune di Ortisei, *Sezione artigianato artistico
gardenese,* ☎ 77552 (information on visits to workshops);
wood carving: *Istituto d'arte,* ☎ 76328 (instruction, Jul-
Sep).

PASSIRIA VALLEY

C1-2

When they don their picturesque costumes with red-
lapeled leather jackets, the men of the valley wear
pointed hats decorated with green rings if they are
married and red rings if they are bachelors. The
River Passirio, which gives its name to the valley, is
known for trout. It rises near the alpine watershed
at the Rombo Pass and flows into the Adige after
passing through Merano. Upstream, the landscape
becomes increasingly wild.

▶ The lower valley is full of vineyards, orchards, cultivated fields, pretty villages and isolated farmhouses. **Sal-
tusio-Saltaus** is the most important of the eleven *Masi
dello Scudo.* These historical curiosities were medieval
fiefs whose holders were obliged to serve their prince as
bodyguards at ceremonies and as horsemen in war. In
return they enjoyed tax privileges along with hunting and
fishing rights. ▶ **San Leonardo in Passiria-St. Leonhard
im Passeier,** the main centre, lies in a green hollow at the
junction with the Vannes Valley. Between San Leonardo
and **San Martino in Passiria-St. Martin im Passeier** is the
birthplace of Andreas Hofer (small museum,
8:30 a.m.-12 noon and 2-6 p.m.). He was the mountain
dweller who aroused the inhabitants of the Tyrol when it
was assigned to Bavaria by Napoleon. He fought tenaciously for the Hapsburgs and was executed by firing
squad in Mantua in 1810. He is still the hero of Tyrolean nationalism. A road climbs up from San Leonardo
in Passiria to the **Monte Giovo Pass** (6,870 ft), linking the
valley to Vipiteno. ▶ Between San Leonardo in Passiria and **Moso in Passiria-Moos im Passeier** (4,100 ft,
at mouth of beautiful Plan Valley), the valley sides slope
steeply; there are terraces and waterfalls. ▶ The upper
valley from Moso to the **Rombo Pass** (8,175 ft), which
leads into Austria, is even more wild; larch and fir woods
cling to steep slopes punctuated by crags and landslips. ☐

Practical information _____

SAN LEONARDO IN PASSIRIA-SANKT LEONHARD
IM PASSEIER, ⊠ 39015, ☎ 0473.
⚡ ski lifts at Vàltina and Malga Giovo.
ⓘ ☎ 86188.

Hotel:
★★★ *Stroblhof,* ☎ 86128, 70 rm P ⅷ ḋ ⊡ ↗ Pens.
closed 1 Nov-19 Feb except Christmas, 45,000.

Recommended
Horseback riding: ☎ 85272.
Swimming: ☎ 86220.

SAN MARTINO IN PASSIRIA-SANKT MARTIN IN PAS-
SEIER, ⊠ 39010, ☎ 0473.

Hotels:
★★★ *Kennenhof,* ☎ 85440, 15 rm P ⟨ ⅷ ⊡ ↗ 90,000.
★★★ *Quellenhof,* ☎ 85474, 50 rm P ⅷ ⊡ ↗ Pens.
45,000.

PEIO TERME

Trento 80, Milan 256 km
4,520 ft pop. 31 ⊠ 38020 ☎ 0463   A4

Peio Terme sits in a hollow surrounded by conifer
woods in the Monte Valley.   ☐

Practical information _____

⚕ (Jun-Sep, mid-Dec-Easter), ☎ 73226.
⚡ cable car, ski lifts, cross-country skiing, instruction, ice
skating at Cógolo.
ⓘ at Mal, ☎ 91280.

Hotels:
★★★ *Cevedale,* at Cógolo, v. Roma 23, ☎ 74067, 33 rm
P ◄ ⅷ closed May, 66,000; bkf: 7,000.
★★★ *Kristiania,* at Cógolo, ☎ 74157, 33 rm P ⅷ ⌀
closed Easter-31 May and Oct-Nov, 60,000.

Å ★ *Val di Sole,* in Dossi di Cavia, 175 pl, ☎ 73177.

Recommended
Horseback riding: *Alpen Ranch,* at Cógolo (associate
of *ANTE*).

PELLIZZANO

Trento 69, Milan 215 km
Pop. 826 ⊠ 38020 ☎ 0463   B4

Pellizzano is in the valley bottom of the Val di
Sole. The r. side of the Gothic-Renaissance **parish
church** has a frescoed porch. Inside are carved and
gilded 16C wooden altars, 15C frescos and a large
fresco dating from 1571. **Lake Caprioli** is reached
by way of the Fazzon Valley. **Ossana** is a little farther up the Val di Sole; it has a campanile with spire
and a ruined castle.   ☐

Practical information _____

ⓘ ☎ 71183.

PIEVE DI LEDRO

Trento 54, Milan 184 km
2,165 ft pop. 449 ⊠ 38060 ☎ 0464   A-B6

Pieve di Ledro stands along with **Mezzolago** and
Molina di Ledro in pleasant countryside by **Lake
Ledro.** The climb to the valley is by a steep, scenic road from Riva del Garda (→) or from Lake Idro
(→ Lombardy) via the Ampola Valley. At periods of
low water, remains of Bronze Age **stilt houses** are
visible on the shores of the lake near Molina. Artifacts, mostly Bronze Age, are in a **museum**
(9 a.m.-12 noon and 1-6 p.m.) near the lake, where a
prehistoric lake-dwellers' hut has been rebuilt.   ☐

Practical information _____

⚡ ski lifts at Bezzecca *(3 km NW).*

Recommended
Swimming: ☎ 591070.

PORDOI PASS

Trento 105, Belluno 85, Milan 356 km
7,345 ft ⊠ 38032, ☎ 0462   D-E3

This is perhaps the most famous of the Dolomite passes. Extremely scenic, it is one of four that ring the **Sella group** and it links the Fassa (Trentino) and the Cordévole (Venetia) valleys. A cableway *(4 mn)* climbs to **Sass Pordoi★** (9,680 ft) with its view★★, among the most extensive in all the Dolomites.   □

Practical information

✂ cableway to Sass Pordoi, ski lifts.
ⓘ at Canazei, v. Roma 16, ☎ 61113; at Arabba (→ Venetia), ☎ 0436/79130.

La PUSTERIA

D-F2

La Pusteria is the major valley of the E Italian Alps, running between the range on the border with Austria to the N and the Dolomites to the S. The main river is the Rienza, but the Drava also runs along it for a short stretch inside Italian territory; the two are separated by the sloping saddle of Dobbiaco.

▶ The major towns are **Brunico** (→) and **San Candido** (→). Everywhere the buildings are graceful and the climate and views invigorating. ▶ At **San Lorenzo di Sebato-St. Lorenzen** the Egerer chapel in the old parish church contains painted wood Baroque statues vividly depicting *Christ's Passion*. ▶ **Valdàora-Olang** (3,520 ft), with hamlets scattered over terraced meadows, is in one of the most beautiful parts of the valley. ▶ **Monguelfo-Welsberg** (3,565 ft) has an 18C parish church with Baroque altars and altarpieces and a 16C Castel Monguelfo. ▶ **Villabassa-Niederdorf** (3,800 ft) has fine old buildings. ▶ **Dobbiaco-Toblach** (4,080 ft) has an old centre, the Paese, around the Baroque parish church of S. Giovanni and a 16C castle. ▶ The side valleys offer varied scenery; those on the r. run into the Aurine Alps and those on the l. are flanked by the Dolomites. ▶ A little downstream from Brunico, the **Val Badia** (→) cuts S. ▶ The **Valley of Tùres** branches off N from Brunico and **Campo Tùres-Sand in Taufers** (2,865 ft) is its main centre, standing between two castles: the late 16C Castello Neumelans *(not open for visits)* and the older Castello di Tùres with 17C furnishings and frescos in the chapel *(10 a.m.-12 noon and 3-5 p.m. summer)*. Upstream, the long **Aurina Valley** and the **Riva Valley** begin. From the latter, at **Riva di Tùres-Rain in Taufers**, in a dip covered by meadows and surrounded by woods, is a splendid view of the Ries cirque near the church of S. Volfango. ▶ The **Anterselva Valley** extends from Valdora to the **Stalle Pass** (6,735 ft) on the border with Austria. The valley's administrative centre is **Rasun di Sotto-Niederrasen** with a nature reserve *(ask at Pro Loco)*. **Lake Anterselva**, surrounded by forests, is reached from Anterselva di Sopra. ▶ The **Bràies Valley**, upstream from Monguelfo, is known for **Lake Bràies** (→). ▶ The Landro Valley leads from Dobbiaco to **Carbonin-Schluderbach**, facing an amphitheatre of Dolomite peaks: Cadini, Cristallo and Croda Rossa. Here the roads to Cortina d'Ampezzo and Misurina (→ Venetia) branch off. ▶ From San Candido, the Sesto Valley runs to delightful **Sesto-Sexten** (4,230 ft) and to the **Monte Croce di Comélico Pass** (5,365 ft), from where it descends to Cadore (→ Venetia).   □

Practical information

CAMPO TURES-SAND IN TAUFERS, ⊠ 39032, ☎ 0474.
✂ ski lifts, cross-country skiing, instruction, ice skating, sled runs.

ⓘ v. Jungmann, ☎ 68076.

Hotels:

★★★ **Feldmüllerhof,** v. Castello 9, ☎ 68127, 30 rm 🅿 ⌨ ⌧ closed 16 Apr-14 May and 21 Oct-14 Dec, 41,000; bkf: 8,000.
★★★ **Panoramic-Speikboden,** at Molini, ☎ 68212, 21 rm 🅿 ⌨ ⌧ ⤴ closed 16 Apr-9 May and 16 Oct-19 Dec, 55,000; bkf: 8,000.

Recommended

Mountain climbing: ☎ 68290 or 68175 or 68514 (instruction).
Swimming: v. Dr. Daimer 145, ☎ 68257; at Lutago, ☎ 61216.

DOBBIACO-TOBLACH, ⊠ 39034, ☎ 0474.
✂ ski lifts, cross-country skiing (more than 70 km; one 35-km run ends at Cortina d'Ampezzo), instruction, ice skating.
ⓘ ☎ 72132.

Hotels:

★★★ **Alpino Monte Rota,** at Monte Rota, ☎ 72213, 25 rm 🅿 ⌨ ⌧ 🅲 ⌧ closed 15 Apr-20 May and 20 Oct-20 Dec. Accessible by chair lift, 40,000; bkf: 6,000.
★★★ **Park Hotel Bellevue,** v. Roma 37, ☎ 72101, 36 rm 🅿 ⌨ ✂ closed 11 Apr-19 May and 1 Oct-19 Dec, 58,000; bkf: 6,000.
★★★ **Toblacherhof,** v. Pusteria, ☎ 72217, 25 rm 🅿 ⌨ ⌨ 64,000.
★★ **Sole-Sonne,** v. Roma 19, ☎ 72225, 45 rm 🅿 ⌨ closed 15-30 Apr and 1 Nov-20 Dec, 40,000; bkf: 7,000.

▲ Olympia, v. Pusteria 49, ☎ 72147 (all year).

Recommended

Swimming: ☎ 72453.

MONGUELFO-WELSBERG, ⊠ 39035, ☎ 0474.
✂ ski lifts, ice skating.
ⓘ at Tésido, ☎ 74010.

Hotel:

★★ **Dolomiti-Dolomiten,** v. Stazione 13, ☎ 74146, 21 rm 🅿 ✂ closed 1 Nov-15 Dec, 36,000; bkf: 7,000.

Restaurant:

♦ **Hell,** p. Centrale 3, ☎ 74126, closed Mon and 1 Oct-15 Nov. Regional cuisine: house speck, tournedos of venison, 20/25,000.

Recommended

Farm vacations: Haslerhof, v. Tésidio 19, ☎ 74040.
Tennis: v. Stazione, ☎ 74167.

PASSO DI MONTE CROCE DI COMELICO-KREUZBERG-PASS, ⊠ 39030, ☎ 0474.

Hotel:

★★★ **Passo Monte Croce-Kreuzbergpass,** ☎ 70328, 55 rm 🅿 ⌨ ⌨ ⌧ ⤴ closed May, Oct-Nov, 50,000.

SESTO-SEXTEN, ⊠ 39030, ☎ 0474.
✂ cableway, ski lifts, cross-country skiing, instruction, ice skating, curling.
ⓘ at San Vito, v. Dolomiti 9, ☎ 70310.

Hotels:

★★★★ **Sporthotel Fischleintal,** at Moso, v. Fiscalina 27, ☎ 70365, 48 rm 🅿 ⌨ ⌧ ❧ ⌧ closed Nov-May, 90,000.
★★★ **Berghotel Tyrol,** at Moso, ☎ 70386, 27 rm 🅿 ⌨ ⌧ ⌨ ✂ closed 21 Apr-19 May and 11 Oct-19 Dec, 57,000; bkf: 8,000.
★★★ **Monika,** v. del Parco 2, ☎ 70384, 27 rm 🅿 ⌧ ⌨ ✂ ⤴ Pens. closed 11 Apr-19 May and 11 Oct-19 Dec, 55,000.
★★★ **Sesto,** v. Dolomiti 13, ☎ 70314, 32 rm 🅿 ⌧ ⌨ closed 1 May-4 Jun and 21 Nov-19 Dec, 60,000; bkf: 6,000.
★★★ **Tre Cime-Drei Zinnen,** at Moso, v. S. Giuseppe 28, ☎ 70321, 41 rm 🅿 ⌨ ⌨ ⌧ Pens. closed 1 Apr-24 Jun and 26 Sep-19 Dec, 75,000.

⚓ *Sesto,* at Moso, 250 pl, ☎ 70444.

Recommended
Alpine guides: ☎ 70375.
Tennis: v. Tennis Waldheim, ☎ 70402.

VALDAORA - OLANG, ⊠ 39030, ☎ 0474.
⚡ ski lifts at Plan de Corónes, cross-country skiing, instruction, ice skating, run for sled races.
① ☎ 46277.

Hotel:
★★★ *Posta-Post,* at Valdaora di Sopra, ☎ 46127, 38 rm ℗ ⋘ ⊟ closed 26 Apr-9 May and 21 Oct-9 Dec, 80,000; bkf: 8,000.

Recommended
Swimming: at Valdàora di Mezzo, ☎ 46344.

VALLE DI ANTERSELVA-ANTHOLZER TAL, ⊠ 39030, ☎ 0474.
⚡ ski lifts at Anterselva di Mezzo and di Sopra, more than 60 km of cross-country skiing.
① at Anterselva di Mezzo, ☎ 42116; at Rasun di Sotto, ☎ 86269.

Hotel:
★★★ *Antholzerhof,* ☎ 42148, 30 rm ℗ ⋘ ⊟ closed 21 Apr-31 May and 16 Oct-19 Dec, 105,000.

⚓ *Anterselva,* at Anterselva di Sopra, 100 pl, ☎ 42204 (all year); *Corónes,* at Rasun di Sotto, 120 pl, ☎ 46490.

Recommended
Nature park: nr Rasun di Sotto, ☎ 86269.

VILLABASSA-NIEDERDORF, ⊠ 39039, ☎ 0474.
⚡ ski lifts, over 40 km of cross-country skiing, instruction, ice skating.
① ☎ 75136.

Hotel:
★★★ *Aquila d'Oro-Goldener Adler,* p. Municipio 108, ☎ 75128, 45 rm ℗ ⋘ ♿ ⊟ closed Nov-Dec, 70,000; bkf: 4,000. Rest. Regional cuisine: canederli with speck, smoked pork or sausage with sauerkraut.

Restaurant:
♦♦ *Friedlerhof,* v. Dante 40, ☎ 75003, closed Tue and Jun-Jul. Regional cuisine: gnocchetti with spinach, schlutzkrapfen, Tyrolean delicacies, 20/45,000.

The RENON PLATEAU

Bolzano 15, Milan 310 km

C3

This plateau extending between the rugged Isarco and Tàlvera Valleys is graced with small villages, a network of roads and footpaths, charming landscapes and distant views of mountains. The main villages, pleasant places to stay, include: **Collalbo-Klobenstein, Costalovara-Wolfsgruben** and **Soprabolzano-Oberbozen. Eroded earth pillars** can be seen near Soprabolzano in the small Rivellone Valley.

Practical information _____

RENON-RITTEN, 3,785 ft ⊠ 39054, ☎ 0471.
⚡ ski lifts, cross-country skiing, instruction, ice skating.
① at Collalbo, ☎ 56100.

Hotels:
★★★ *Bemelmans-Post,* at Collalbo, ☎ 56127, 49 rm ℗ ⋘ ⊟ ⁄º closed 26 Apr-19 May and 6 Nov-19 Dec, 46,000.
★★★ *Maier,* at Costalovara, ☎ 55114, 31 rm ℗ ≼ ⚘ ⋘ ⊟ ⁄º closed Nov-Mar, 52,000; bkf: 6,000.
★★★ *Parkhotel Holzner,* at Soprabolzano, ☎ 55231, 41 rm ℗ ≼ ⚘ ⋘ ⊟ ⁄º closed Dec-Apr, 110,000.
★★★ *Wieserhof,* at Collalbo, v. Monte di Mezzo 87, ☎ 56186, 23 rm ℗ ⋘ ⊟ ⁄º Pens. 52,000.

Recommended
Horseback riding: *Maneggio Tony,* at Collalbo (associate of *ANTE*).
Swimming: at Collalbo, ☎ 56296; at Soprabolzano, ☎ 55169.

RIVA DEL GARDA*

Trento 41, Milan 170 km
Pop. 13,177 ⊠ 38066 ☎ 0464   B5-6

Riva del Garda, at the N tip of Lake Garda's long panhandle, still retains the impression of a brief period of Venetian rule during the 15C.

▶ The centre of Riva is the **piazza 3 Novembre** facing the lake and partly surrounded by 14C arcades. Its dominant feature is the **Torre Apponale** (13C-14C) and on the opposite side the **municipio** (1482) and the 14C **Palazzo Pretoria.** ▶ The four-sided, turreted **Rocca** (12C) is surrounded by water. The Rocca has been enlarged, altered and destroyed several times. It now houses the library and the **Museo Civico** *(closed for restoration).* Finds★ from the lake-village at Ledro Lake stand out among the collections of fossils, natural history, antiques, paintings, prints, weapons, folklore and crafts. ▶ **Spiaggia degli Olivi** is a delightful spot beyond the Rocca. ▶ The Baroque **church of the Inviolata,** with an octagonal ground plan, has an interior rich in stuccos and paintings. It is the work of an anonymous Portuguese architect who began building in 1603. ▶ A chair lift leads to **Bastione,** a cylindrical tower (1508) below the jutting rocks of Mt. Rocchetta. ▶ The **Varone waterfall★** *(4 km toward Tenno)* drops 295 ft into a cleft in the rock, creating interesting light effects.   ▫

Practical information _____

≋
① Spiaggia degli Olivi gardens, ☎ 554444.
🚌 from the bus station, ☎ 552323.
⛴ boats and hydrofoils, ☎ 552625.
Car rental: *Avis,* v. Rovereto 76, ☎ 514030 (Apr-Oct).

Hotels:
★★★★ *Du Lac et Du Parc,* v. Rovereto 44, ☎ 520202, 169 rm ℗ ⋘ ⊟ ⁄º closed 16 Oct-31 Mar. In a park by lake shore, 160,000; bkf: 15,000.
★★★★ *Liberty,* v. Carducci 3/5, ☎ 553581, 69 rm, ℗ ♿ ⊟ 95,000.
★★★ *Astoria,* v. Trento 9, ☎ 552658, 96 rm ℗ ⋘ ⊟ closed 16 Oct-31 Mar, 85,000.
★★★ *Europa,* p. Catena 9, ☎ 521777, 63 rm ⋘ ♿ closed Feb and 15 Nov-20 Dec, 110,000.
★★★ *Gardesana,* v. Brione 1, ☎ 552793, 38 rm ℗ ⋘ ⚞ ⊟ closed 11 Oct-31 Mar, 50,000; bkf: 7,000.
★★★ *Luise,* v. Rovereto 9, ☎ 552796, 58 rm ℗ ⋘ ⊟ ⁄º 65,000; bkf: 6,000.
★★★ *Riviera,* v. Rovereto 95, ☎ 552279, 36 rm ℗ ⋘ ⊟ closed Nov-Dec and Feb, 42,000; bkf: 6,000.
★★★ *Sole,* p. III Novembre 35, ☎ 552686, 50 rm ⋘ closed 16 Oct-31 Mar, 98,000.
★★★ *Venezia,* v. Rovereto 62, ☎ 552216, 24 rm ℗ ⋘ ⊟ closed Dec-Feb, 74,000; bkf: 9,000.

Restaurants:
♦♦♦ *San Marco,* v. Roma 20, ☎ 554477, closed Mon and 15 Jan-15 Feb. Seafood, 25/45,000.
♦♦ *Ponale-Casa della Trota,* at Cascata del Ponale, ☎ 554666, closed Wed and 15 Nov-15 Dec. On lake with terrace. Mixed cuisine: 18/26,000.
♦ *Rocca,* p. Battisti 4, ☎ 552217, closed Wed and 16 Nov-28 Feb. Park on lake shore. Mixed cuisine, 25/40,000.

⚓ ★ *Bavaria,* v. Rovereto 100, 75 pl, ☎ 552524.

Recommended
Cycling: *G. S. Leoni,* v. S. Nazzaro 60, ☎ 513030.
Events: *international sailing regattas* (mid-Mar and Jul); *Expo Riva Surf* (May).

Marina: ☎ 552460.
Sailing: *Nautic club Riva,* v. Dante 70, ☎ 554440.
Swimming: v. Martini 44, ☎ 520078.
Tennis: Cascina delle Magnolie, ☎ 552225; v. Carducci 10, ☎ 521878.
Wind surfing: at Gola, ☎ 551730 (instruction).
Youth hostel: *Ostello Banacus,* p. Cavour 10, ☎ 38066.
♥ olive oil: *Associazione Agraria,* ☎ 512133.

ROLLE PASS

Trento 86, Milan 308 km
6,465 ft pop. 15 ⊠ 38030 ☎ 0439   D-E4

A majestic landscape, with the **Pale di S. Martino,** forms a backdrop to the meadows of this pass that links the Travignolo and Císmon Valleys. 2.5 km away is **Baita Segantini** (7,515 ft) with a view of the Pale. From Baita Segantini, the route descends via the **Val Venegia** to join the road from Paneveggio, then climbs to the **Valles Pass** (6,670 ft). It drops down again into the Falcade Valley with the **San Pellegrino Pass** (6,295 ft). ☐

Practical information ―――――――――――――

↑ ski lifts, cross-country skiing, instruction.
ⓘ at San Martino di Castrozza, ☎ 68101.

Hotel:
★★★ *Venezia,* ☎ 68315, 28 rm Ⓟ ⚞ ⚘ closed May-Jun and 11 Sep-30 Nov, 44,000; bkf: 6,000.

RONCEGNO

Trento 31, Milan 277 km
Pop. 2,318 ⊠ 38050 ☎ 0461   C5

The **Palazzo delle Terme,** a spa surrounded by a park, offers a variety of treatments. There is an important **altarpiece** on the high altar of the 18C parish church. ☐

Practical information ―――――――――――――

♨ Direzione Terme, at Lévico, ☎ 706481.
ⓘ p. De Giovanni 2, ☎ 764028.

Hotel:
★★★★ *Palace Hotel,* ☎ 764012, 85 rm Ⓟ ⚟ ▭ ⚓ closed 11 Sep-9 Jun, 150,000; bkf: 12,000.

ROVERETO

Trento 24, Milan 216 km
Pop. 33,071 ⊠ 33068 ☎ 0464   B-C6

In rare moments of candour the people of Trentino confess that when they descend into the Po Valley they feel like strangers in their own country: too German for other Italians and too Italian in comparison to other Tyroleans in this region. Rovereto dates from the Middle Ages and is therefore recent in comparison to other settlements, which were started in Roman times and earlier. During the 15C, when Rovereto was taking shape as a town, it belonged to Venice and bordered on the lands of the prince-bishops of Trentino. Under Venetian rule, Rovereto's silk industry developed to such an extent that an early 19C French traveler noted similarities between the local silk-weavers and the French silk workers of Lyon.
▸ Every evening at sunset the **Campana dei Caduti**★ (bell of the fallen) tolls to commemorate the victims of all wars waged around the world. The bell is known as **Maria Dolens** (weeping Mary) and is the largest ever cast (11 ft 2

in high). The bell is rung in a piazza decorated with the flags of various nations. From here the whole of Rovereto, the Lagarina Valley and Mt. Baldo can be seen. ▸ The imposing **Castello** was built in the 14C by the feudal lords of the town and enlarged in the following century by the Venetians. The **Museo Storico della Guerra**★ *(9 a.m.-12 noon and 2-5 or 7 p.m.)* has the largest Italian collection relating to World War I, occupying 30 rooms. ▸ The 15C-16C **Palazzo del Municipio** has the remains of frescos on the façade and there is a fine courtyard. To the l. of the entrance is a marble plaque in which the old metal standards of measurement used to be inserted. Opposite the municipio is the memorial to the Fallen of the Legione Trentina. ▸ The **Museo Civico** in v. Calciari *(Apr-Sep 9 a.m.-12 noon and 2:30-5:30 p.m.; other months 9 a.m.-12 noon; closed Mon and 15 Dec-15 Feb)* has collections dealing with archaeology, art, history, numismatics, folklore and natural history. ▸ The **Museo Depero** has works by this futuristic painter *(apply a.m. at municipio, Ufficio Economato).* ▸ 2 km S is the **Sacrario di Castel Dante,** a chapel containing the bodies of Italians, Austrians and Czechs who fell in World War I. There are also the ruins of the medieval castle of Lizzana, where Dante is said to have stayed in 1303.

Environs

▸ A steep road leads to **Lake Cei,** 15 km NW. ▸ 9 km NE, above the village of Calliano, is the **Castel Beseno** (12C-18C), the largest fortress in the region. In the 15C-16C palace are remains of frescos *(under restoration).* There are 15C frescos in the **Castel Pietra,** a little way before Calliano. ☐

Practical information ―――――――――――――

ⓘ v. Dante 63, ☎ 30363.

Hotels:
★★★ *Leon d'Oro,* v. Tacchi 2, ☎ 37333, 52 rm Ⓟ ⚟ No restaurant, 75,000; bkf: 7,000.
★★★ *Rovereto,* corso Rosmini 82/D, ☎ 35222, 49 rm Ⓟ ⚟ 65,000; bkf: 7,000.

Restaurant:
♦♦♦ *Borgo,* v. Garibaldi 13, ☎ 36300, closed Mon, Feb and Jul-Aug. Mixed cuisine: crostone with eggplant, seafood, 30/44,000.

Recommended
Archery: *Compagnia Arcieri Linea Arco,* v. Donizetti 19/A; *Compagnia Arcieri Kappa,* v. Cavour 14, ☎ 21569.
Swimming: v. Lungo Leno Destro, ☎ 35440.
Wines: *Bossi Federigotti,* v. Vimone 43, ☎ 24950.

SAN CANDIDO - INNICHEN

Bolzano 106, Milan 409 km
3,055 ft pop. 2,985 ⊠ 39038 ☎ 0474   F2

The houses of San Candido with thick walls and small windows — protection against the winter cold — are neatly whitewashed on the outside and have cosy wood-paneled rooms *(stuben)* on the inside. The balconies are carved and the window-sills bright with pots of geraniums. This typically Tyrolean town is the watershed between the Pusteria Valley and the Valley of the Drava whose waters flow to the Black Sea.

▸ The **Collegiata**★ is the finest Romanesque monument in Alto Adige; it originated as an 8C Benedictine abbey. The massive campanile is 14C. Behind the high altar is a 13C wooden Crucifix; there are 13C-14C frescos in the crypt. ▸ In the presbytery is the **Museo Comunale** (archaeological finds and folk culture, *weekly guided tours on Wed).* ▸ There have been recent excavations in a building from the Roman period which suggest that the site was the Roman *Littamum*. ☐

Practical information ———————————

⚡ ski lifts, cross-country skiing, instruction, ice skating, curling.
ⓘ v. Canonici, ☎ 73149.

Hotels:
★★★★ *Cavallino Bianco-Weisses Roessl*, v. Duca Tassilo 1, ☎ 73135, 56 rm Ⓟ ⚒ ⓖ ⌂ closed 16 Apr-31 May and 16 Oct-19 Dec, 92,000; bkf: 7,000.
★★★ *Parkhotel Sole Paradiso*, v. Sesto 13, ☎ 73120, 45 rm Ⓟ ≼ ⚒ ⌂ ⌁ closed Apr-May and 6 Oct-18 Dec, 110,000.
★★★ *Posta*, v. Sesto 1, ☎ 73355, 39 rm Ⓟ ⚒ ⓖ closed 11 Apr-19 May and 1 Oct-19 Dec, 76,000; bkf: 6,000.
★★★ *Sporthotel Tyrol*, v. Rainer 12, ☎ 73198, 27 rm Ⓟ ≼ ⚒ ⌁ closed 16 Apr-19 May and 11 Oct-19 Dec, 100,000.

Restaurant:
♦♦ *Schmieder-Teestube 1911*, v. Duca Tassilo 16, ☎ 73144, closed noon, Mon, 10 Apr-31 May and 10 Oct-20 Dec. Regional cuisine: gnocchetti with spinach, canederli with speck, 20/30,000.

Recommended
Swimming: ☎ 73282.

SAN MARTINO DI CASTROZZA*

Trento 96, Milan 349 km
4,740 ft pop. 568 ⊠ 38058 ☎ 0439   D4

A thousand years ago monks founded a monastery (suppressed 1418) in this pine-clad valley at the foot of the **Pale di San Montano.**

▶ By cable car it is possible to ascend to the **Alpe Tognola** (7,095 ft) with a view★ of the Pale. There is also a chair lift to **Punta Ces** (7,315 ft).. ▶ From Malga Ces (5,425 ft, *accessible by car*) it is one hour on foot to the **Colbricon** lakes (6,320 ft), where prehistoric artifacts have been unearthed. ▶ There is a chair lift to **Col Verde** (6,280 ft), then a cableway ride to the Rifugio Pedrotti (8,460 ft) and the **Cima della Rosetta** (9,000 ft) with view★. ☐

Practical information ———————————

⚡ cableway, cable car, ski lifts, cross-country skiing, instruction, ice skating.
ⓘ v. Passo Rolle 15, ☎ 68101.

Hotels:
★★★★ *Des Alpes*, v. Passo Rolle 128, ☎ 68518, 55 rm Ⓟ ⚘ closed 6 Apr-27 Jun and 6 Sep-19 Dec, 90,000; bkf: 8,000.
★★★★ *Savoia*, v. Passo Rolle 233, ☎ 68094, 72 rm Ⓟ ≼ ⓖ closed 11 Apr-30 Jun and 11 Sep-19 Dec, 100,000; bkf: 11,000. Rest. ● ♦♦♦ *Drei Tannen* ☎ 68325, closed Mon, Apr-Jun and Oct-Dec. International cuisine, some regional dishes: gnocchetti with cream, filet of beef with gorgonzola, 30/45,000.
★★★ *Belvedere*, v. Passo Rolle 247, ☎ 68000, 32 rm Ⓟ ≼ ⚒ ⚘ closed 16 Apr-19 Jun and 16 Sep-19 Dec, 90,000.
★★★ *Colfosco*, v. Passo Rolle 20, ☎ 68224, 53 rm Ⓟ ≼ closed 16 Apr-19 Jun and 16 Sep-30 Nov, 74,000; bkf: 9,000.
★★★ *Cristallo*, v. Passo Rolle 51, ☎ 68134, 27 rm Ⓟ ≼ closed 16 Apr-30 Jun and 1 Sep-19 Dec, 70,000; bkf: 8,000.
★★★ *San Martino*, v. Passo Rolle 279, ☎ 68011, 53 rm Ⓟ ≼ ⚒ ⓖ ⌂ ⌁ closed 16 Apr-30 Jun and 16 Sep-19 Dec, 65,000; bkf: 7,000.

Restaurant:
♦♦♦ *Malga Ces*, ☎ 68145, closed 10 Oct-10 Dec and 15 Apr-10 Jun. Regional cuisine, 20/25,000.

△ ★★ *Sass Maor*, v. Laghetto, 184 pl, ☎ 68347 (all year).
Recommended
Alpine guides: ☎ 68795 or 68620.
Excursions: by chair lift to Col Verda, by cableway to Rifugio Pedrotti, ☎ 68308.
Swimming: *Vecchia Fornace centre*, ☎ 68648.
Vacation villages: *Hotel Majestic Dolomiti* (closed Apr-May and Oct-Nov), ☎ 02/85391 (organized by *Vacanze*).

SAN MICHELE ALL'ADIGE

Trento 15, Milan 257 km
Pop. 1,972 ⊠ 38010 ☎ 0461   C4

At the E edge of the Campo Rotaliano, an immense vineyard, San Michele all'Adige is known as a winegrowing centre. The Castello di S. Michele, which towers above the village and was formerly an Augustinian monastery, contains the **Museo Provinciale degli usi e costumi della Gente trentina** (*8:30 a.m.-12 noon and 2:30-6 p.m.; closed Sun and Mon*) with a collection of domestic objects and implements relating to farming and associated crafts. ☐

Practical information ———————————

Hotel:
★★★ *Lord Hotel*, at Masetto, ☎ 650119, 33 rm Ⓟ ⚒ ⓖ ⌁ closed Christmas, 50,000.
Restaurant:
● ♦♦♦ *Silvio*, at Masetto, v. Nazionale 2, ☎ 650324, closed Mon. Regional and creative cuisine: chagall, Altamira dish, 30/40,000.

Recommended
Wines: *Istituto agrario*, ☎ 650111; *Stazione sperimentale di viticoltura ed enologia* (experimental centre for vinegrowing and the wine industry), ☎ 650148.

SAN ROMEDIO AND SANZENO

Trento 45, Milan 254 km
Pop. 882 ⊠ 38010 ☎ 0463   C4

San Romedio was a hermit who lived in the Val di Non in the 4C. His horse was killed by a bear while he was on his way to visit St. Vigilius, his bishop, in Trento, but Romedio supposedly tamed the beast and arrived riding the bear. His shrine is reached from **Sanzeno**, a village on the road through the Val di Non to Mendola. The way is flanked by marble reliefs depicting the Stations of the Cross. The shrine stands on a cliff and consists of four chapels (11C-18C) one above the other and linked by steps. ☐

SEGONZANO PYRAMIDS

Trento 24, Milan 234 km
Pop. 1,405 ⊠ 38047 ☎ 0461   C4

The **ómeni di Segonzano**, pyramids shaped by erosion, are along the River Regnana, on the r. slope of the Valle di Cembra (→). Some are as much as 130 ft high. They consist of pebbles and rocky debris mixed with clay and each pyramid is surmounted by a large boulder. ☐

———————————

In preparing for your trip, consult the pages pertaining to the regions. You will find there the description of the region you wish to visit, as well as a list of sites that must be seen, a brief history and practical information.

The SELLA PASS

Bolzano 53, Trento 104, Milan 352 km
7,260 ft ⊠ 33010 ☎ 0433   D3

The Sella Pass is one of the four that ring the **Sella group**. It links the Gardena and Fassa Valleys. To the E is the bastion of the Sella; to the W are the Dolomite peaks of Sassolungo, Cinque Dita, Sassopiatto — the **Sassolungo group**.   ☐

Practical information ⎯⎯⎯⎯⎯⎯
⌇ cable car at Forcella del Sassolungo, ski lifts.

STELVIO PARK

A3-4/B3

This park covers 334,000 acres and consists of the majestic massif of Ortles-Cevedale and Valfurva, together with the Martello, Ultimo, Solda and Trafoi Valleys. Entrance to the park is free to visitors who are asked to observe the regulations regarding the protection of nature. Deer, roebuck, chamois, ibex, marmot, eagles, capercaillie and willow grouse are among the fauna encountered here. Besides the firs, larches and pines, there is a great variety of rare alpine flowers.   ☐

Practical information ⎯⎯⎯⎯⎯⎯
ⓘ park office, at Bormio (→ Lombardy), v. Monte Braulio 56, ☎ 0342/901582; *Ufficio provinciale parchi*, at Trento, ☎ 0461/895831. Guard posts and information offices, at Cógolo, ☎ 0463/74186; Bagni di Rabbi, ☎ 0463/95190; Malé, ☎ 0463/92155; Silandro, ☎ 0473/70447; Prato allo Stelvio, ☎ 0473/76140.

The STELVIO PASS

Bolzano 109, Sondrio 87, Milan 220 km
9,045 ft ⊠ 23030 ☎ 0342   A3

The Ortles glaciers provide an awe-inspiring view from the second-highest pass in Europe, which links the Venosta Valley (Alto Adige) with the Valtellina (Lombardy). The area is part of Stelvio Park (→). A cable car and cableway *(15 mn)* lead to the **Rifugio Livrio** (10,415 ft) on the glacier. This offers a magnificent view★.   ☐

Practical information ⎯⎯⎯⎯⎯⎯
⌇ cableways, ski lifts, instruction, summer skiing (→ Bormio, Lombardy).
ⓘ at Prato allo Stelvio, ☎ 0473/76034; at Bormio, v. Stelvio, ☎ 0342/903300.

Hotels:
★★★ **Folgore**, ☎ 903141, 37 rm ℗ ⌇ ⚲ closed Nov-May, 55,000; bkf: 6,000.
★★★ **Passo dello Stelvio-Stilfserjoch**, ☎ 903162, 60 rm ℗ ⌇ Pens. closed 6 Nov-31 May, 75,000.
★★★ **Sport Hotel Sertorelli**, ☎ 904565, 42 rm ℗ ⌇ ⚲ ⚹ Pens. closed 6 Nov-24 May, 78,000.

TERLANO - TERLAN

Bolzano 10, Milan 307 km
Pop. 3,050 ⊠ 39018 ☎ 0471   C3

This town stands amid vineyards and orchards on the road from Bolzano to Merano.

▶ The Gothic **parish church** has two campaniles, one of which is 14C, while the other is modern and very tall (it

replaced an older campanile demolished because it was leaning dangerously). Inside the church is a 15C fresco cycle. ▶ Crossing the Adige either here or farther upstream at **Vilpiano-Vilpian** leads to **Nalles-Nals** on the other side of the valley. This, with the other centres along the ridge (**Prissiano-Prissian, Grissiano-Grissian**), constitutes a group of picturesque, isolated towns with frescoed churches and several castles. In particular, the Romanesque church of S. Jacopo is beautifully situated to the S of Grissiano with early 13C frescos★ that are among the best examples of Romanesque painting in this region.   ☐

Practical information ⎯⎯⎯⎯⎯⎯
ⓘ ☎ 57165; at Vilpiano, ☎ 678648.

Hotels:
★★★ **Sparerhof**, at Vilpiano, v. Nazionale 91, ☎ 678671, 21 rm ℗ ⌇ ⚸ ⊡ 40,000; bkf: 5,000.
★★★ **Weingarten**, v. Nazionale 32, ☎ 57174, 18 rm ℗ ⚸ ⊡ closed Nov-Mar, 47,000; bkf: 5,000.

Recommended
Excursions: by cableway from Vilpiano to Méltina.

TIRES - TIERS

Bolzano 17, Milan 316 km
3,375 ft pop. 828 ⊠ 39050 ☎ 0471   D3

Tires is the main town of the beech-covered valley that runs up from the Isarco Valley towards Catinaccio. 2 km away is a view★ of Catinaccio from the chapel of **S. Cipriano**. 3.3 km farther is **Bagni di Lavina Bianca-Weisslahnbad**.   ☐

Practical information ⎯⎯⎯⎯⎯⎯
⌇ ski lifts, cross-country skiing, sled run.
ⓘ ☎ 642127.

Hotel:
★★ **Stefaner**, at San Cipriano, ☎ 642175, 17 rm ℗ ⚲ ⚸ 1/2 Pens. closed 1 Nov-10 Dec, 38,000.

Lake TOBLINO

Trento 17, Milan 226 km
⊠ 38070 ☎ 0461   B5

The turreted and battlemented **Castello** stands on a peninsula. It dates from the 11C but appears today as it did in the Renaissance under the Madruzzo family, whose members included several prince-bishops of Trento. An isthmus separates this stretch of water from **S. Massenza Lake.** Slavonian grapes are grown in the vineyards here.   ☐

Practical information ⎯⎯⎯⎯⎯⎯

Restaurant:
♦♦ **Valentino**, v. Nazionale 118, ☎ 44039, closed Tue in winter and Jan-Feb, 18/22,000.

The TONALE PASS

Trento 86, Brescia 128, Milan 177 km
6,180 ft pop. 145 ⊠ 38020, ☎ 0364   A4

The meadows of this pass lie between the Ortles-Cevedale and Adamello-Presanella groups and the pass links the Val di Sole (Trentino) to the Valcamnica (Lombardy). In the 15C it had a reputation as a place where witches met to perform their rituals.

▶ The area contains an **ossuary** for the dead of World War I. ▶ There is a cableway *(6 mn)* to the **Paradiso Pass** (8,465 ft), then a footpath *(30 mn)* or cable car

(10 mn) to the **Rifugio Presena** (9,025 ft) with a view★ of the Presanella group. The Presena glacier is reached after 2 hours of hard walking and it is possible to descend by way of the Maroccaro Pass (9,760 ft) to the **Rifugio Città di Trento** (8,135 ft), commanding views of the slopes of the Val Genova. □

Practical information

⚡ cableway, cable car, ski lifts, cross-country skiing, instruction, summer skiing at Presena glacier.
ⓘ ☎ 91343; at Ponte di Legno, ☎ 91122.

Hotels:
★★★ **Redivalle,** v. Nazionale 67, ☎ 92266, 45 rm Ⓟ ✆ closed May-Jun and Oct-Nov, 46,000; bkf: 6,000.
★★★ **Savoia,** ☎ 91340, 41 rm Ⓟ closed May and Oct-Nov, 65,000.
★★★ **Sporthotel Vittoria,** v. Nazionale 16, ☎ 91348, 40 rm Ⓟ ✆ 🛆 closed 3 May-24 Jun and 26 Sep-30 Nov, 80,000; bkf: 7,000.

TORBOLE

Trento 41, Milan 174 km
Pop. 2,246 ☒ 38069 ☎ 0464   B6

Torbole is a pleasant little town on Lake Garda. A short walk with lovely views leads to Nago and the road from Nago descends towards Arco and reveals traces of glacial erosion, the **marmitte dei Giganti** ('giants' kettles'). The Sarca glacier once covered the lake up to the moraines on its S shore. □

Practical information

ⓘ lungolago Verona, ☎ 505177.
🚢 boats and hydrofoils.

Hotels:
★★★★ **Piccolo Mondo,** v. Matteotti 7, ☎ 505271, 36 rm Ⓟ 🎱 🛆 🖾 🎮 closed 16 Oct-31 Mar, 94,000.
★★★ **Baia Azzurra,** at Linfano 68, ☎ 505168, 36 rm Ⓟ 🎱 closed Nov-Mar, 75,000; bkf: 7,000.
★★★ **Ifigenia,** lungolago Verona 23, ☎ 505134, 35 rm 🎱 🛆 closed Nov-Mar, 72,000; bkf: 8,000.
★★ **Paradiso,** lungolago Verona 49, ☎ 505126, 28 rm Ⓟ 🎱 ✆ closed 11 Oct-31 Mar, 72,000; bkf: 8,000.
🛆 ★★ **Europa,** v. Al Cor, 78 pl, ☎ 505888.

Recommended
Marina: ☎ 505600 or 505350.
Tennis: v. Strada Granda, ☎ 505460.
Wind surfing: *Windsurf Torbole,* v. Matteotti, ☎ 505899; *Centro Windsurf,* Colonia Pavese, ☎ 505385.

TRENTO*

Trento 58, Milan 240, Rome 592 km
Pop. 99,457 ☒ 38100 ☎ 0461   C5

The Palazzo Galasso in v. Manci, built for a member of the Augsburg family of bankers, the Fuggers, is also known as *Casa del Diavolo* (the Devil's House) and was said to have been built in a single night with stones provided by the evil one. The Council of Trent was held at Trento from 1545 to 1563. Opening and closing sessions took place at the Duomo, but most sessions were held in the Renaissance church of S. Maria Maggiore. The fifty-one prince-bishops who governed the town and county from 1000 to 1803 followed a secular form of rule. The town is beautiful, simple and noble. Geographical features have played a role in the development of Trento including the Adige-Isarco-Brennero axis, a route between the Adriatic and Baltic used in ancient times for the amber trade, the Valsugana cleft, which runs from Trento toward Venice, and the fan of valleys that radiates from the town. Trento was important to the Holy Roman Emperors, who needed an open passage to Italy. With the permanent transfer of the imperial crown to the house of Hapsburg, Trento's fate was sealed until the end of World War I, when the Austrian yoke was finally lifted from N Italy. The architectural style of Trento is distinctive, as is the local dialect.

▶ Archaeological excavation has located the grid-plan of the Roman city of *Tridentum,* which was contained within the perimeter formed by the p. del Duomo, v. Rossini, the railway station, p. Battisti and p. delle Erbe. ▶ The centre of town is the **piazza Duomo★** (C2) with the fountain of Neptune, the **Palazzo Pretorio** whose double- and treble-arched windows reveal its 13C origin and the 16C **Case Rella** with frescos on the façades. ▶ The severity of the 12C-13C Romanesque-Gothic **Duomo★★** (C2) is softened by loggias at the side and rose-windows in the façade and transept. The cathedral has an octagonal dome and a 16C campanile. Inside, stairs are cut into the walls. The decrees of the Council of Trent were pronounced from the Cappella del Crocifisso on the r.; remains of 13C and 15C frescos are in the transepts. Underneath the church are the remains of the **early Christian basilica** and its successive rebuildings *(Mon-Fri 10 a.m.-12 noon and 3-6 p.m.),* a pavement mosaic and bishops' tombs. ▶ The history of the Duomo is illustrated in the **Museo Diocesano** *(mid-Feb-mid-Nov 9 a.m.-12 noon and 2-7 p.m.; closed Wed)* in the Palazzo Pretorio: it houses seven 16C Flemish **tapestries★**, Trentino carved altars and wooden statues (14C-15C), mementos of the Council, a 10C ciborium and other treasures. ▶ **Via Belenzani★** (C2), with Renaissance palazzi (some with frescoed façades), is typical of the town; the **via Manci** is also lined with palazzi and ends at the **Cantone** crossroads (C2), which was the old town centre. ▶ The Renaissance church of **S. Maria Maggiore** (C1-2) has a superb marble balustrade (1534) supporting the organ and a large altarpiece dating from 1541. ▶ The **Castello del Buonconsiglio★★** (B3), residence of the prince-bishops, played an important role in the history of Trentino. It comprises a series of rather diverse units: the 13C battlemented **Castelvecchio,** the 17C **Albertine giunta** and the **Magno Palazzo** of 1536. ▶ The Magno Palazzo and the Castelvecchio have rooms that are worth visiting, with fine wooden ceilings and 16C frescos. The **Museo Provinciale d'Arte★** *(9 a.m.-12 noon and 2-5 p.m. winter or 5.30 p.m. summer; closed Mon)* covers archaeology, art and ethnography and the Aquila tower is decorated with 15C frescos of the *Twelve Months★*. The **Museo del Risorgimento e della Lotta per la Libertà** *(same opening times as the Museo Provinciale)* records Italy's struggle for liberty. ▶ A tower from the 13C town walls, the **Torre verde** with green-and-yellow tiled roof, is in the p. Raffaello Sanzio (B2) and other sections of the walls still stand. ▶ The **Dante monument** in the public garden (B2) was erected in 1896 under the Austrians as a symbol of Italy. ▶ The church of **S. Lorenzo** (B1) is Romanesque (12C). ▶ The **Torre Vanga** (C1) dates from the 13C and guards a bridge over the Adige. ▶ **S. Apollinare** (B1), a 14C Romanesque-Gothic church, has a polygonal apse. ▶ The **Palazzo delle Albere** (D1) is a villa built by the ruling Madruzzo family in the early 16C. It now houses the contemporary section of the **Museo Provinciale d'Arte;** parts of the original fresco cycles can also be seen here. ▶ Palazzo Sardagna, v. Calepina 14 (C2), houses the **Museo tridentino di Scienze naturali** *(9 a.m.-12 noon and 3-5.30 p.m.; closed Sun and Mon).*

Environs

▶ 3 km away is the **Doss Trento★** (B1), a rock that is a distinctive feature of the local landscape with a monument to a local patriot, Cesare Battisti, and a splendid view. Nearby are the remains of an early-Christian basilica from the first half of the 6C, as well as the **Museo**

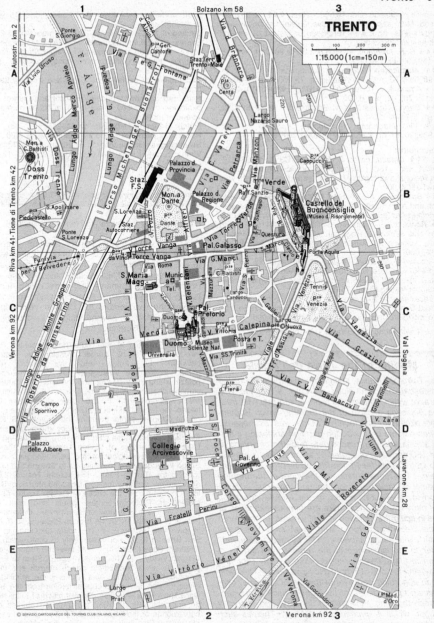

Nazionale degli Alpini *(summer 9:30 a.m.-12 noon and 2-5:30 p.m.; winter 10:30 a.m.-12 noon and 2:30-4 p.m.; closed Mon).* ▶ There is a good view of the town from the **Belvedere** (1,950 ft; *cableway from the S. Lorenzo bridge).* ▶ 16 km W is the **castello di Toblino** (→). ▶ **San Michele all'Adige** (→) is 16 km N. □

Practical information _____

ⓘ corso III Novembre 134 (E2), ☎ 980000; v. Alfieri 4 (B2), ☎ 983880; p. Duomo (C2; in season), ☎ 981289.
🚂 (B1-2), ☎ 34545; Trento-Malé electric railway (A2), ☎ 823671.
🚌 from bus station, v. Pozzo 1 (B1), ☎ 25186.

Hotels:
★★★★ *Accademia,* vicolo Colico 4/6 (C2 a), ☎ 981011,

40 rm ℗ 90,000; bkf: 10,000. Rest. ♦♦♦ ☎ 981580, closed Mon and Aug. Creative cuisine: gnocchi with poppy seeds, trout with Teroldego or pistachio, venison with juniper, 25/35,000.

★★★★ *G. H. Trento*, v. Alfieri 3 (B2 b), ☎ 981010, 94 rm ℗ 150,000; bkf: 10,000.

★★★ *Alessandro Vittoria*, v. Romagnosi 14/16 (B2 c), ☎ 980089, 70 rm ℗ No restaurant, 75,000; bkf: 7,000.

★★★ *America*, v. Torre Verde 50 (B2 d), ☎ 983010, 43 rm ℗ ♿ 70,000; bkf: 6,000.

★★★ *Capitol*, at Gardolo, v. Soprasasso 32, ☎ 993232, 44 rm ℗ 70,000; bkf: 7,000.

★★★ *Villa Madruzzo*, at Cognola, v. Ponte Alto 26, ☎ 986220, 51 rm ℗ ♿ ♪ 74,000; bkf: 8,000.

Restaurants:

● ♦♦♦ *Chiesa*, parco S. Marco (B-C3 f), ☎ 986677, closed Sun. 18C palazzo by a public garden. Excellent regional and creative cuisine: strangolapreti, light veal stew, 35/50,000.

♦♦♦ *Bollicine*, v. dei Ventuno 1 (B3 e), ☎ 983161, closed Mon and Aug. Cellar of sparkling wines. Italian cuisine: pancakes stuffed with cheese, rabbit in pastry, 30/45,000.

♦♦ *Roma*, v. S. Simonino 6 (C2 i), ☎ 984150, closed Sun and summer. Regional cuisine: risotto al Marzemino, spinach roll with melted butter, old-style stufato, 22/27,000.

♦ *Hostaria dell'Erba Voglio*, v. Suffragio 23 (B2 g), ☎ 986619, closed Sat, Sun, Easter, Aug 15 and Christmas. In one of oldest streets in city. Regional cuisine: seasonal tasting menu, 25/30,000.

♦ *Locanda Port'Aquila*, v. Cervara 66 (C3 h), ☎ 30420, closed Sun and 1-15 Sep. Regional cuisine: orzetto, stufato with Teroldego, torta di fregolotti, 25/30,000.

⚠ ★ *Trento*, lungadige Braille 1, 64 pl, ☎ 25162.

Months of the Torre dell'Aquila

The Torre dell'Aquila, standing within the walls of the Castello del Buonconsiglio in Trento, is reached by a parapet walk. The middle room is adorned with frescos depicting a cycle of the months, which is complete except for one month. March was lost because it was painted on a wooden partition enclosing a spiral staircase. The frescos date from the beginning of the 15C and were executed by an anonymous artist in the Gothic style for Prince-Bishop George of Lichtenstein. The representation of the work of the months against a background of changing seasons is common in the figurative arts of the Middle Ages and the early Renaissance; there are famous examples of this in sculpture, painting and miniatures. The Trento cycle, recently restored with great skill, has particularly interesting aspects. The paintings frequently refer to the landscape of the region: the Castello di Stenico (Jan), the hills surrounding the city (Apr and May) and the city of Trento (Nov and Dec). The cycle is an absorbing portrayal of the life of the time, contrasting the pastimes of the nobility (ladies and gentlemen throwing snowballs in January) and everyday labour, which is omitted only in May. Themes such as hay-making, harvesting, scything and falconry are common; especially relevant to the mountain life of Trentino are milking herds in high pastures, harvesting grapes on the slopes, wine making and bear hunting.

Recommended

Alpine guides: *Comitato trentino*, v. Grazioli 5, ☎ 987090; *Giorgio Graffer school of mountaineering*, v. Manci 57, ☎ 21522.

Canoeing: *Canoa club*, v. Druso 7, ☎ 985362.

Craft workshops: *I. Moscati*, at Padergnone *(15 km W)*, ☎ 44058 (copper).

Cycling: *G.S. Cicli Baldo*, v. Tre Novembre 70, ☎ 21486.

Events: *festival internazionale Film della Montagna* (Apr-May); *exhibition of mountaineering* (May); *Trentino Autumn* (typical dishes, excursions, folklore); *Trofeo Topolino* (Feb).

Excursions: by cableway to Belvedere from S. Lorenzo bridge (C1).

Fairs and markets: *Agricultural show and market* (Mar), *exhibition of Trentino wines* (Apr); *antiques market* (last wkend in month).

Flying: at Man di Mattarello, ☎ 945265.

Horseback riding: at Madonna Bianca, ☎ 924480.

Swimming: at Gocciadoro, v. Fogazzaro, ☎ 911006.

Wines: *Lunelli* wine cellar, largo Carducci 12 (C2), ☎ 21646.

La VALSUGANA

From Trento to Predazzo *(146 km, 1 day; map 4)*

This route within the SE part of Trentino reveals the variety of the region's scenery and combines two different atmospheres. The first is the spacious, verdant Valsugana. This is the basin of the upper Brenta; it was a Roman military post called *Ausugum* during the imperial era. After crossing two mountain passes the road enters the Cismon Valley and the Pale di S. Martino, beyond which a third pass leads into the Val di Fiemme.

▶ From **Trento** (→) the route heads toward Pérgine through the Férsina gorge, crossing the watershed between the Adige and the Brenta (Valsugana). ▶ **Pérgine Valsugana** has small Renaissance palazzi along the v. Mayer and the late 15C **Castello** includes a chamber where some bizarre water-torture equipment was installed. ▶ The route skirts **Lake Caldonazzo**, the largest lake in the region (**Calcerànica al Lago**, on the opposite shore, contains the church of S. Ermete, thought to be the oldest in the valley and on the site of a temple of Diana whose altar survives), and passing above **Lake Lévico** arrives at **Lévico Terme** where the Parco delle Terme is redolent of the *belle époque*. ▶ After **Borgo Valsugana** the route climbs to **Strigno** and joins the road to the Brocon Pass. ▶ **Castello Tesino** (2,860 ft) on a plateau contains the 15C frescoed church of S. Ippolito. ▶ Farther on, the **caves of Castel Tesino** (3,150 ft; inquire at *Proloco*) contain pools and rock formations. ▶ There is a view of the Primiero Dolomites, the Pale di S. Martino, from the **Brocon Pass** (5,230 ft, *brocon* in dialect is heather). ▶ The route descends to **Canal San Bovo** in the Vanoi Valley, only to climb again to the **Góbbera Pass** (3,240 ft). ▶ At **Imèr** the route enters the Cismon Valley. ▶ The alpine village of **Fiera di Primiero** (2,340 ft) has a fine Gothic **parish church** and the 16C **Casa del Dazio** which was formerly the administrative office for iron, silver and copper mining from the 14C onward. The village was also the birthplace of Luigi Negrelli, an engineer who, in 1838, commenced studies on the construction of the Suez Canal. ▶ As the road ascends, the curtain-like peaks of the Pale di S. Martino can be seen above the trees: the summits of the Cima di Val Roda, the red wall of the Pale di S. Martino, the Cima della Madonna and the Sass Maor. ▶ **San Martino di Castrozza** (→) lies in a valley. ▶ As the route emerges from the fir woods, the Cimon della Pala appears on the road across the **Rolle Pass** (6,463 ft, →), the highest point of the journey. ▶ The descent by way of the Val Travignolo, which runs into the Avisio Valley, passes across the **Paneveggio-Pale di S. Martino nature park**, which includes the Paneveggio forest (8,600 acres, largest in Italian Alps) with Norway spruce, larch, Swiss pine, silver fir and dwarf pine. Roebuck, marmot, foxes, martens, capercaillie and willow grouse abound. The golden eagle

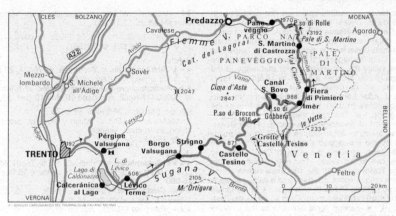

4. La Valsugana

is sometimes seen. ▶ **Predazzo** (4,650 ft) is where the road reaches the Val di Fiemme (→). ☐

Practical information

CASTELLO TESINO, ⊠ 38053, ☎ 0461.
🎿 ski lifts at Brocon Pass, cross-country skiing.
ⓘ ☎ 594136.

FIERA DI PRIMIERO, ⊠ 38054, ☎ 0439.
🎿 ski lifts, 35 km of cross-country skiing, instruction, skating.

Hotels:
★★★ **Aurora,** v. Piave 8, ☎ 62504, 26 rm Ⓟ 🐾 closed 10-31 Oct, 50,000; bkf: 4,000.
★★★ **Mirabello,** v. Montegrappa 2, ☎ 64241, 43 rm Ⓟ 🐾 ⁂ ▣ closed 11 Apr-31 May and 1 Oct-14 Dec, 60,000; bkf: 4,000.
★★★ **Park Hotel Iris,** v. Roma 18, ☎ 62000, 92 rm Ⓟ 🐾 ⦀ 60,000; bkf: 5,000.

Recommended
Swimming: ☎ 62568.

LEVICO TERME, ⊠ 38056, ☎ 0461.
♨ (May-Oct), ☎ 706481.
ⓘ v. Dante Alighieri, ☎ 706101.

Hotels:
★★★ **Bellavista,** v. Vittorio Emanuele 7, ☎ 706474, 78 rm Ⓟ 🐾 ⦀ ⅋ ▣ closed Oct-Apr except Christmas, 60,000; bkf: 5,000.
★★★ **Romanda,** v. Garibaldi 7, ☎ 707122, 40 rm ⁑ closed 20 Oct-20 Dec, 50,000; bkf: 6,000.
★★★ **Sorriso,** lungolago Segantini 14, ☎ 707029, 45 rm Ⓟ ⦀ ⅋ ▣ ✤ closed 1 Nov-Easter except Christmas, 70,000; bkf: 8,000.
★★ **Levico,** v. Vittorio Emanuele 54, ☎ 706335, 39 rm Ⓟ ⦀ ⁑ closed Oct-May, 45,000; bkf: 5,000.
★★ **Parc Hotel du Lac,** at Lago 3, ☎ 706590, 34 rm Ⓟ ⦀ ⁑ closed 16 Oct-4 Apr, 46,000.

Restaurant:
● ◆◆ **Stua,** v. Battisti 62, ☎ 707028, closed Tue and 15-30 Jun. Regional and creative cuisine: pasticcio of aubergines, strudel with cheese, salmon with Riesling, 20/36,000.

> Don't forget to consult the Practical Holiday Guide: it can help in solving many problems.

△ ★★★ *2 Laghi,* at Costa, 360 pl, ☎ 707381.

Recommended
Swimming: v. Lido, ☎ 38056.
Tennis: v. Segantini, ☎ 706896 (also minigolf).

PERGINE VALSUGANA, ⊠ 38057, ☎ 0461.
≈ at Lake Caldonazzo.
ⓘ p. Gavazzi 1, ☎ 531258; at San Cristoforo al Lago, ☎ 51119.

Hotels:
★★★ **Lido-Seehof,** at San Cristoforo al Lago, ☎ 531044, 49 rm Ⓟ ⦀ ⅋ closed 6 Oct-30 Apr, 67,000; bkf: 6,000.
★★★ **Turismo,** v. Venezia 20, ☎ 531073, 33 rm Ⓟ ⦀ ⚆ ▣ closed Nov, 50,000; bkf: 4,000.

Restaurant:
◆◆ **Castello,** ☎ 531158, closed Mon and 15 Oct-30 Apr. Italian cuisine: spiedini reali, escalopes forester's style with polenta, 25/35,000.

Recommended
Horseback riding: at Lochere di Caldonazzo, ☎ 38056.
Sailing: *Associazione velica trentina,* Lake Caldonazzo at Valcanova, ☎ 987028 (instruction in wind surfing and canoeing).
Water skiing: at Lake Caldonazzo.

The VENOSTA VALLEY

A-B2-3

This upper valley of the Adige runs between the alpine watershed on the one side and the Ortles and Cevedale groups on the other. Interesting side valleys branch off it, and the undulating landscape of the main valley is marked by fans of matter washed downhill by the tributaries, forcing the Adige from side to side along the valley bottom. Medieval campaniles stand out amid the typical Alto Adige architecture. They, together with a few remnants from the early Middle Ages, provide clues to the history of the valley. There are numerous castles.

▶ The church of **S. Procolo★** (8C-9C and 13C) at **Naturno-Naturns** has frescos (probably 8C-9C) on the inside walls and a triumphal arch. These exceptional works are of major importance. ▶ A little upstream, the road through the Val Senales drives on toward the alpine watershed. At **Certosa-Karthaus** is a restored group of buildings that once made up a 14C Carthusian monastery. **Madonna-Unserfrau in Schnals** stands below the dam across Lake Vernago; from **Corteraso-Kurzras** at the head of the valley the cableway *(5 mn)* that leads to the Croda Grigia glacier reaches a height of 10,500 ft. From here a chair lift descends to the Rifugio Bellavista (9,380 ft). ▶ After **Làces-Latsch** (2,095 ft) the Val Martello road branches to the l. and leads to the foot of the Cevedale group. ▶ The road that goes up to **Gomagoi** branches off at **Spondigna-Spondinig.** From Gomagoi the road leads to **Solda-Sulden** (6,255 ft) in a valley dominated by the ice-capped peaks of the Ortles, Gran Zebrù and Zebrù groups; the Rifugio Città di Milano (8,470 ft) is two hours away. The road continues from Gomagoi to **Trafoi** (5,060 ft); the 18C Tre Fontane shrine here shelters unique votive offerings and a cable car leads to the Rifugio Forcola (7,185 ft) with a view★ of the Ortles group. The road continues from Trafoi as far as the **Stelvio Pass** (→). ▶ Farther upstream and to the l. is the road to **Glorenza** (→) and the Tubre border post between Italy and Switzerland. ▶ **Màlles Venosta** is the historic centre of the valley. ▶ **San Valentino alla Muta-St. Valentin auf der Haide** (4,825 ft) lies between della Muta and di Resia, adjacent artificial lakes. ▶ **Résia-Reschen** (5,005 ft) lies at the N tip of the lake of the same name (source of the Adige) near the Resia Pass on the border with Austria. ☐

Practical information ————————————

CERTOSA-KARTHAUS, ⊠ 39020, ☎ 0473.
ⓘ ☎ 89148.

CORTERASO-KURZRAS, ⊠ 39020, ☎ 0473.
⌁ cableway, ski lifts, cross-country skiing, instruction, summer skiing on Croda Grigia glacier, ☎ 89669.

LACES-LATSCH, ⊠ 39021, ☎ 0473.
⌁ ski lifts.
ⓘ ☎ 73109.

NATURNO-NATURNS, ⊠ 39025, ☎ 0473.
ⓘ v. della Stazione, ☎ 87287.

Hotels:
★★★★ *Sunnwies,* v. Kleeberg 7, ☎ 87157, 37 rm 🅿 🔍 ⚒ ⌂ ⏐₀ closed 4 Nov-19 Mar, 80,000; bkf: 10,000.
★★★ *Lindenhof,* v. della Chiesa 2, ☎ 87208, 25 rm 🅿 ⚒ ⌂ closed 4 Nov-24 Mar, 70,000; bkf: 10,000.
★★★ *Schnalserhof,* at Stava, v. Venosta 121, ☎ 87219, 23 rm 🅿 ⌂ Pens. closed Jan, 62,000.

Recommended
Horseback riding: *Scuola ippica Plaus,* ☎ 87239.

PRATO ALLO STELVIO-PRAD AM STILFSERJOCH,
⊠ 39026, ☎ 0473.
ⓘ v. Nazionale, ☎ 76034.

Hotel:
★★ *Prato-Prad,* v. Principale 103, ☎ 76006, 28 rm 🅿 ⚒ ⌂ closed Oct-May, 48,000.
⚓ *Sgemühle,* v. Principale 25, 70 pl, ☎ 76078 (all year).

RÉSIA-RESCHEN, ⊠ 39027, ☎ 0473.
⌁ ski lifts, instruction, skating.
ⓘ at Curon Venosta, ☎ 83233; on the SS, ☎ 83101.

Recommended
Swimming: at Curon Venosta, ☎ 83245.

SAN VALENTINO ALLA MUTA-SANKT VALENTIN AUF DER HAIDE, ⊠ 39020, ☎ 0473.
⌁ cable car, ski lifts, cross-country skiing, instruction, skating.
ⓘ at Curon Venesta, ☎ 83233; on the SS, v. ☎ 84603.

Hotel:
★★ *Stocker,* v. Principale 44, ☎ 84632, 21 rm 🅿 ⚒ ⚒ closed 26 Apr-31 May and 6 Oct-14 Dec, 47,000. Rest.

◆◆ Regional cuisine: pappardelle with venison, Val Venosta soup, 12/18,000.

SILANDRO-SCHLANDERS, ⊠ 39028, ☎ 0473.
ⓘ v. Principale 123, ☎ 70155.

Hotels:
★★★ *Schlossgarten,* v. Pretura 8, ☎ 70424, 22 rm 🅿 🔍 ⚒ 🔍 ⌂ closed Nov-Mar, 60,000.
★★ *Montone Nero-Schwarzer Widder,* v. Principale 96, ☎ 70000, 47 rm 🅿 ⚒ closed 10 Nov-10 Dec, 52,000.

SOLDA-SULDEN, ⊠ 39029, ☎ 0473.
⌁ cableway to Città di Milano, ski lifts, cross-country skiing, instruction, skating.
ⓘ ☎ 75415.

Hotels:
★★★★ *Suldenhotel,* v. Principale 50, ☎ 75481, 50 rm 🍴 ⌂ ⏐₀ 1/2 Pens. closed 16 Apr-19 Jun and 16 Sep-19 Dec, 75,000.
★★★ *Cristallo,* ☎ 75436, 35 rm 🅿 ⚒ 🔍 ⌂ closed 1 May-14 Jun and 21 Sep-14 Nov, 70,000.
★★★ *Eller,* ☎ 75421, 50 rm 🍴 ⚒ ⚒ ⏐₀ closed 21 Apr-31 May and 21 Sep-19 Dec, 60,000.
★★★ *Gampen,* ☎ 75423, 26 rm 🅿 🍴 ⚒ 80,000.

Recommended
Excursions: by cableway to Rifugio Città di Milano, ☎ 75409.

TRAFOI, ⊠ 39020, ☎ 0473.
⌁ cable car, ski lifts, cross-country skiing, instruction.
ⓘ at Prato allo Stelvio, ☎ 76034.

Hotel:
★★★ *Madaccio-Madatsch,* ☎ 75767, 42 rm 🅿 🍴 ⚒ ⚒ ⌂ ⏐₀ closed 26 Apr-14 Jun and 3 Nov-19 Dec, 48,000.

VETRIOLO TERME

Trento 32, Milan 242 km
4,921 ft pop. 4 ⊠ 38056 ☎ 0461   C5

Vetriolo Terme rests among woods on the slopes of Panarotta with a great view of the Valsugana. Therapeutic waters, which also flow at Lévico Terme at the bottom of the valley, spring from artificial caves known as Vetriolo and Ocra.   ☐

Practical information ————————————

⚕ (Jul-mid-Sep), ☎ 706481.
⌁ cable car, ski lifts, cross-country skiing, instruction at Panarotta 2002.
ⓘ at Lévico, ☎ 706101.

Hotels:
★★★ *Compet,* at Compet ☎ 706466, 39 rm 🅿 🍴 🔍 ⚒ 🔍 ⚒ closed 10 Oct-30 Nov, 48,000.
★★★ *Italia Grand Chalet,* ☎ 706414, 50 rm 🅿 🍴 🔍 ⚒ ⏐₀ closed 16 Apr-19 Jun and 16 Sep-14 Dec, 46,000; bkf: 6,000.

VIPITENO - STERZING

Bolzano 70, Milan 369 km
3,110 ft pop. 5,338 ⊠ 39049 ☎ 0472   C1

This is the first Italian town on the descent from the Brenner Pass. In character it is thoroughly Tyrolean. It lies in the basin where the Valleys of Ridanna, Racines and Vizze join the upper Isarco Valley. Its origin as a stop on a much-traveled route is revealed by its ribbon-like development along the old road from the Brenner Pass. The newer section of this road, the v. Città Nuova, is elegant and colourful. In the past the town flourished both because of the Brenner traffic and because of the minerals washed down the Ridanna and Fleres Valleys. So prosperous was Vipiteno that a Florentine money-changer had a branch office here as early as the 14C.

▶ The **via Citta Nuova**★ is lined with 15C-17C arcades and palazzi. These are battlemented and adorned with oriels, balconies brimming with flowers and heraldic devices. The Torre di Città stands at the end of the street. ▶ The late-Gothic **Palazzo Comunale** (16C) has a courtyard with a gallery on the first floor and a collection of 15C-16C paintings and sculpture *(office hrs).* ▶ The street through the old town continues beyond the **Torre di Città.** ▶ In the p. Mitra is a Mithraic cult **relief** from the Roman period, showing Mithras slaying a bull, personifications of the sun and moon in two medallions and other Mithraic scenes not yet interpreted. This most important work indicates how widespread this Eastern cult was in the Roman Empire. ▶ The Gothic church of **Spirito Santo** has 15C frescos. ▶ The **Museo Multscher** *(in Casa della Commenda near Ospedale Civile; 10 a.m.-12 noon and 3-5 p.m.; closed Sat p.m. and Sun)* has four 15C **doors**★ formerly at the high altar of the parish church illustrating scenes from the Passion and the life of the Virgin Mary. The Gothic parish church of **S. Maria in Vibitin** (1417-1525), standing alone away from the town centre, has 18C frescos, wooden statues and a 15C wooden group of the *Stations of the Cross.* ▶ In the **Racines gorges** 5 km from Stanga are waterfalls with a natural rock bridge. ▶ 13 km away is **Colle-Bichl** where a chair lift climbs to the ski area of the Mt. Giovo Pass. □

Practical information _____

⚡ cableway, ski lifts, cross-country skiing, instruction, skating.
ⓘ p. Città 3, ☎ 765325.

Hotel:
★★★ *Corona-Krone,* v. Città Vecchia 31, ☎ 765210, 22 rm Ⓟ ← ⚿ ❀ closed Dec-Jan, 72,000.

Recommended
Sports: v. Kofler, ☎ 764406 (swimming pools, bowling, tennis).

Tuscany

▶ Tuscany is a region of curving beaches, headlands, offshore islands, scrub and pine. Farther inland are silvery olive groves covering the hills and mountains and rows of the black cypresses which so attracted the Sienese painters. Throughout all this meanders the Arno valley. In the fields, although less so now than in the past, are the distinctive white cattle with curving horns as painted by Fattori. Villages of stone houses and walled towns sit on the hills— 'mounts on mounts' as Petrarch referred to them. All combine to convey a sense of Tuscany. Tuscans are a collection of smaller groupings: Pisans, Livornese, Luccans, Sienese, Maremmans — each with their local individualities. This individualism, which is prevalent throughout Italy, finds its most extreme form in Tuscany. It is not by accident that it is immediately possible to distinguish a Sienese painter from a Florentine one, a Pisan architect from one from Pistoia. When St. Bernardino of Siena asked, 'where is more delightful to live than Italy' except for 'the curse of divisions', he was thinking, above all, of Tuscany. There is a proud individuality in each Tuscan city and town. In the towns the Middle Ages still predominate, the time of the city-states. They contain the rough yet proud buildings, built by the councils, and magnificent cathedrals, built to glorify God and the towns. The additions, changes and innovations of the Renaissance— the Tuscan revolution— spring forth quite naturally from this background. Everywhere in the region there appears that ingenuity, clear wisdom and native creativity, the genius that Tuscans absorb from their marvelous land. Perhaps Michelangelo was right when he said that what little 'ingenuity' he showed was due to the 'subtlety' of his native air. ☐

● Don't miss

At Arezzo★, S. Francesco★★ with Piero della Francesca's frescos★★, S. Maria★★; at Cortona★, the Madonna del Calcinaio★★, the Museo dell'Accademia Etrusca★ and the Museo Diocesano★; at Verna★, the convent★. At Lucca★★, the Duomo★★ with the tomb of Ilaria del Carretto★★, S. Michele in Foro★★, S. Frediano★★. At Massa Marittima★, the Duomo★★; not far from Montalcino, the abbey of S. Antimo★★; at Montecatini Terme★, the Parco delle Terme★; at Monte Oliveto Maggiore★★, the frescos of the Life of St. Benedict; at Montepulciano★, S. Biagio★★; at Pienza★, the Cathedral★★ and the Palazzo Piccolomini★★; at Pisa★★, the Campo dei Miracoli★★ with the Duomo★★, the Leaning Tower★★, the Baptistery★★ and the Camposanto★★, the Museo Nazionale di S. Matteo★★ and S. Maria della Spina★★. At Pistoia★, the Duomo★★, the Baptistery★★, S. Giovanni Fuorcivitas★★ and S. Andrea★★ with Giovanni Pisano's pulpit★★. At Prato★, the Duomo★★ and S. Maria delle Carceri★★. The abbey of San Galgano★★; San Gimignano★ and its collegiate church★★. At Siena★★, the piazza del Campo★★, the Palazzo Pubblico★★, the Duomo★★ with the Libreria Piccolomini ★★, the Baptistery★★, the Museo dell'Opera Metropolitana★, which houses the Maestà★★ by Duccio da Boninsegna, the Pinacoteca Nazionale★★. The isolated medieval village of Sovana★★. At Volterra★, the piazza dei Priori★, the Duomo★ and the Museo Etrusco Guarnacci★.

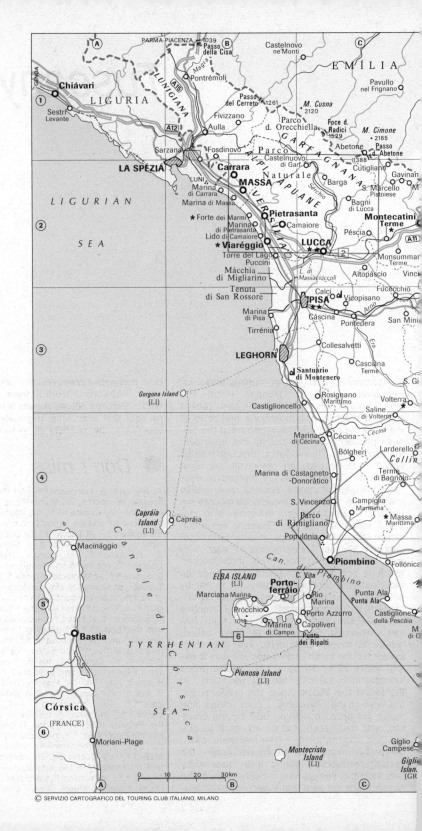

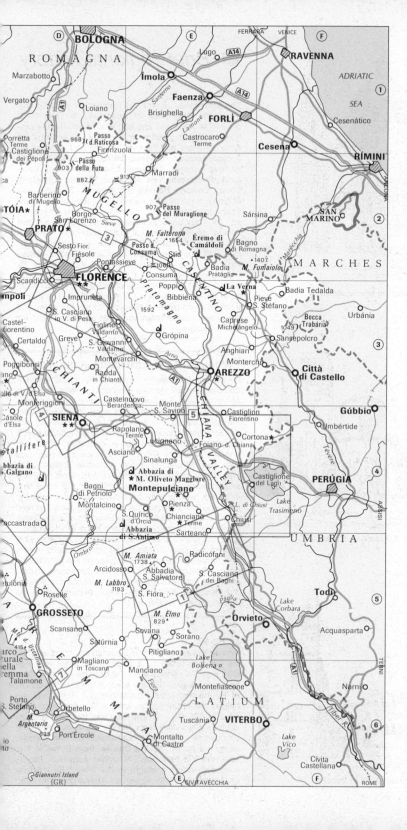

S. Biagio in Montepulciano

● *Brief regional history*

8C-3C BC

The Etruscans. It was the Romans who named this group the **Etruscans** (or *Tuscans*). ● Their great civilization appeared and flourished following the prehistoric Villanova culture in the area bordered by the Arno, the Tiber and the sea. ● The Etruscans set up a **confederation of twelve cities,** which are thought to have included: **Tarquinii, Caere (Cerveteri), Vetulonia, Populonia, Veii, Rusellae, Volsinii (Orvieto?), Chiusi, Cortona, Perugia** and **Arezzo.** Each city was originally ruled by a *lucumone* but in many cases republican, oligarchic or popular regimes developed. ● They became more prosperous through **iron** mining on the island of Elba and other minerals throughout Tuscany. They were also great fishermen. ● They expanded into Campania and across the Apennines into the Po Valley (6C BC). In its early years, Rome went through its own Etruscan period. ● The naval battle of **Cumae** (474 BC) resulted in defeat at the hands of the Greeks. The migrations of Celtic peoples **(Gauls)** into the Po Valley and the progressive **Roman conquest** spelled the end for the Etruscans.

abbey of S. Antimo in Montalcino

Where did the Etruscans come from?

Herodotus, the Greek historian of the 5C BC, claimed that the Tyrrhenians had emigrated to Italy from Asia Minor. These Tyrrhenians are the people we now know as the Etruscans. But another historian from the same period, Hellanicus of Lesbos, believed that the Etruscans' origins went back to a mythical Greek people in Thessaly. Some centuries later, yet another historian, Dionysios of Halicarnassus, said that the Etruscans were a native Italian people. Modern Etruscan scholars find none of these explanations correct. The arrival of the Etruscans into Italy, with a fully developed cultural identity, is now seen as a legend that might have been believed or even developed in certain Etruscan cities. Today the question of the development of the Etruscan civilization is seen within the context of the complex pre- and early history of the Italian peninsula and events in continental Europe and along the Mediterranean. One crucial element in this continuing investigation is the Etruscan language, which incorporates old Mediterranean tongues which existed before the Indo-European invasions.

piazza dei Priori in Volterra

3C BC-5C AD

Roman Etruria. The first Etruscan city conquered by the Romans following a siege of ten years was **Veii** (396 BC). A century later the decisive battle of **Sentino** was fought. By the start of the Punic Wars, all of Etruria had been Romanized and Rome had the help of the entire region when it fought against Hannibal in 205 BC. ● The Romans founded colonies such as *Sena Julia* (now Siena), previously an Etruscan centre. They also built roads: the **Via Aurelia,** along the coast, the **Via Cassia,** from Rome to Fiesole, the **Via Flaminia.** ● Under Augustus, Etruria extended from the Magra to the Tiber. By the time of Diocletian, it was known as **Tuscia** and had been

combined with Umbria. It was ruled by an adminis-
trator in Florence, another Roman colony which had
been an Etruscan centre.

6C-12C

The duchy, the counts and the marquisate. Tuscia was a duchy under the Lombards (568-744) and
its main centre was **Lucca.** ● The region was then
ruled by the counts of Lucca, descendants of a follower of Charlemagne. By the 9C, one of these counts
had declared himself Marquis of Tuscany. ● The
marquisate passed to the Attoni of Canossa in the
middle of the 11C; thus the famous **Matilda** came to
rule over Tuscany.

11C-15C

The city-states. The cities' independence and future
depended on the individual from whom they had
received their 'privileges'. **Lucca, Pistoia** and **Pisa**
obtained them from the Emperor, **Florence** owed
them to Matilda. ● At the same time, **manufacturing**
and trade were developing in the countryside. The
artistic identity of the region was also forged during
these turbulent centuries. ● The city-states fought
among themselves. **Pisa** gained control over **Lucca**
and finally fell to **Genoa** in the naval battle of **Meloria**
(1284). **Florence** controlled **Pistoia** and **Arezzo** and
its leadership in the region grew, although this was
fiercely contested by **Siena.** ● By the start of the
15C, the whole of Tuscany was Florentine, except
for Siena and Lucca. ● As a city-state, Florence
became the bastion of the **Medici.**

S. Maria in Arezzo

Arlotto, the parish priest

*During a violent storm, a parish priest named Arlotto
was crossing the Consuma Pass, an area of beech
woods, pines, firs and meadows, which links the Valdarno and the Casentino. Freezing and soaked to
the bone, the priest took shelter in an inn. The inn
was so crowded with peasants that the priest could
hardly reach the fire. Lamenting loudly to the inn-
keeper that he had lost a purse full of Florentine flo-
rins — gold coins weighing three and a half grams —
on the climb up, he tried to get through the
crowd. Making various excuses, the peasants began
to drift out in search of the mythical purse, leaving
Arlotto alone by the fire. This is just one example
of the good-natured, witty and sharp humour of the
character of Arlotto Mainardi. Florentine by birth, he
lived well into his eighties during the 15C and for
several decades was the parish priest of San
Cresci. There is a portrait of him in the Pitti, painted
long after his death. He owes his fame to a book
of stories, which were collected by a friend and
published. The book was a hit and has been reprint-
ed many times, and translated into French and German. It combines jokes, anecdotes, sayings partly
derived from an old popular tradition and it enjoys a
great reputation in the art of story telling.*

Duomo in Lucca

16C-19C

The grand duchy. After the Italian states fought for
their freedom, and following the struggle between
France and the Hapsburgs, the victorious Charles V
made Alessandro Medici Duke of Florence. He was
assassinated and succeeded by **Cosimo I.** Pius V

Certosa di Pisa in Calci

piazza del Duomo in Pistoia

S. Maria della Spina in Pisa

piazza del Campo in Siena

in 1815 after having been expelled by the **French** in 1799. ● On 27 April 1859, during the Second War of Independence, the Italian tricolour was unfurled over the fortress of Florence and Leopoldo II, the last grand duke, left Tuscany. Baron **Bettino Ricasoli,** the 'dictator', voted for union with Piedmont, a move which was supported by a plebiscite on 15 March 1860. ● The **State of the Presidi,** formed by the Spanish in the second half of the 16C, was not absorbed into the grand duchy until 1814, and the **Principality of Piombino** in 1815, as well as the **island of Elba,** which had been given to Napoleon. **Massa** became part of the Duchy of Modena in 1790 and was incorporated into Italy with the duchy. **Lucca** remained an independent backwater until 1847, when it became part of the grand duchy. ● From 1859, Tuscany's history has been part of Italy's.

The Macchiaioli

This 19C school of painters emphasized landscapes and simple subjects from the countryside of Fiesole, amongst the gardens of Pergentina, along the Arno or in the squares of Florence. The first 'macchia' painting was a study of a black pig against a white wall by Vincenzo Cabianca (1856). The painters had rejected the rules of the Academy and met every day to discuss painting at the Caffè Michelangelo in Florence. The group included Giovanni Fattori, Telemaco Signorini, Silvestro Lega, Giuseppe Abbati, Adriano Cecioni, Rafaello Sernesi, Cristiano Banti, Odoardo Borrani, Vincenzo Cabianca, Vito d'Ancona, Giovanni Boldini, Nino Costa and Serafino de Tivoli, whose return from Paris in 1855 had prompted the new approach. 'Many believe that macchia means sketch', wrote Cecioni. 'But this is a misunderstanding: the macchia is of basic importance, and as such remains in the picture'. The school was successful and in 1862 the painters exhibited at the Società Promotrice in Florence. Their art is an enchanting chapter in the Tuscan tradition, but it is only relatively recently that their role in the rebirth of nineteenth century painting has been recognized.

● *Practical information*

Information: tourist offices in provincial capitals and main towns.

SOS: public emergency services, ☎ 113; police emergency, ☎ 112; *ACI* breakdown, ☎ 116.

Weather: forecast, ☎ 055/2691; road conditions, ☎ 055/2692 or *ACI,* ☎ 06/4212; snow reports, ☎ 055/2694; shipping forecast, ☎ 055/2696 or ☎ 050/996996.

Farm vacations: *Associazione regionale Agriturist,* at Florence, p. S. Firenze 3, ☎ 055/287838.

Vacation villages: *Club Méditerranée,* at Marina di Castagneto-Donoratico (closed Oct-Apr).

Nature parks: *Parco naturale della Maremma* (→ Alberese, La Maremma); *Parco naturale di Migliarino, San Rossore e Massaciùccoli* (→ La Tenuta di San Rossore); *Parco naturale di Rimigliano* (→ Marina di Castagneto-Donoratico); *Parco naturale dell'Orecchiella* (→ La Garfagnana and the Apuan Alps); *Riserva naturale del lago di Burano* (→ Ansedonia, L'Argentario); *Oasi di protezione*

then conferred the title of Grand Duke of Tuscany on Cosimo and, apart from the Napoleonic era, the grand duchy remained virtually unchanged until the unification of Italy in the late 19C. The Medici dynasty died out in 1737 and the European powers gave the grand duchy to Franz Stephan who was married to Maria Theresa of Austria. ● Like the Medici, the **House of Lorraine** were good rulers and they returned to power

della laguna di Ponente di Orbetello (→ Orbetello); *Rifugio faunistico Le Marze* (→ Castiglione della Pescaia, La Maremma itinerary); *Rifugio faunistico di Bólgheri* (→ Marina di Castagneto-Donoratico). Currently being established: *Parco naturale delle Alpi Apuane.*

Nature conservation: regional *WWF* delegation, at Florence, v. S. Gallo 32, ☎ 055/475079 (summer work camps at Uccellina, in collaboration with *Ente Parco* → Alberese, La Maremma), local branches at: Arezzo, v. Tolletta 8, ☎ 0575/27280; Grosseto, v. Unione Sovietica (Quartiere Pace); Livorno, v. Corsica 27 (Circoscrizione 8); Lucca, v. S. Croce 84; Pisa, v. S. Martino 108, ☎ 050/28302; Pistoia, corso Gramsci 150 (Circoscrizione 1); Siena, v. S. Martino 106 (ENPA); Piombino, v. XX Settembre 15. *LIPU* branches: Livorno, Pisa office, ☎ 050/65696 (visits to the *Centro italiano recupero uccelli marini*— the Italian sea bird rescue centre, ☎ 0586/401250; summer camps for study and protection); Capraia, ☎ 0586/905071 (birdwatching and botany courses); Massaciùccoli, ☎ 0584/975186 (guided tours of the *parco naturale lacustre di Massaciùccoli;* Mar-Sep, reserve in advance); Pisa, ☎ 050/25025 (Istituto di Biologia Generale dell'Università; natural history courses); Pistoia, ☎ 0573/33382 (visits to the Fucécchio marshes); Grosseto, ☎ 0564/21628 (summer work camps at the *Parco Naturale della Maremma*).

Events: *Corsa del Palio,* horse race in piazza del Campo, Siena; *Giostra del Saracino* (joust), at Arezzo; *Gioco del Ponte,* an illuminated, historical regatta held on Festa di S. Sisto, at Pisa; the *Palio marinario* and *Coppa Barontini,* at Livorno; the *Balestro del Girifalco* (crossbows), at Massa Marittima; the *Palio della Balestra,* at Sansepolcro; *Giostra dell'Orso* (joust), at Pistoia; the *carnival,* at Viareggio; the *Concorso polifonico internazionale Guido d'Arezzo* (choral festival), at Arezzo; *festival lirico internazionale* (opera festival), at Barga; *Festival Pucciniano,* at Torre del Lago Puccini; *summer music festival* and *international singing competition,* at Lucca; *music weeks* and international courses in the Accademia Musicale Chigiana, at Siena; international culture and study courses, at Cortona; international art workshop, at Montepulciano; literary prize, the *Viareggio,* at Viareggio and the *Bancarella,* at Pontrémoli; prize for political satire, at Forte dei Marmi; *international comic-strip and science fiction convention,* at Prato; *international television film fair,* at Chianciano; biannual flower festival, at Pescia.

Fairs and markets: *international marble and machine show,* at Marina di Carrara; *international goldsmiths' fair,* at Arezzo; *Italian antique furniture and worked copper show-market,* at Cortona; *mineral exchange-market,* at Massa Marittima; *Italian white truffle show-market,* at San Miniato; *honey fair,* at Montalcino; *antiques markets,* at Arezzo, Lucca, Pistoia.

Excursions: long distance, signposted routes: *Grande Escursione Appenninica del Lago Scaffaiolo* (from Pracchia, in stages, along the ridge of the Apennines to the

Cacciucco

There are five *c*'s in *Cacciucco,* and there are five different kinds of fish in this popular soup. The word comes from the Arabic *shakshuklì, or mixture.* Traditionally, the soup includes fat, moray eel, gurnard, goby, mullet and scorpion fish. Cuttlefish, octopus and lobster give it the 'taste of the sea'. The base is an onion sauce with oil and red chilis. Peeled onions, garlic and red wine are added and the fish are cooked in this sauce. The soup is then served in a bowl, with croutons rubbed with garlic. One of the great Mediterranean fish soups, it is typical of Livorno. There are, however, variants in every town along the coast and the Viareggio cacciucco rivals Livorno's, but uses more pepper.

Tuscan trattoria

The region's gastronomic tradition stresses simplicity and respect for natural flavours. The basic elements are the roasting spit, the grill and virgin olive oil. Aromatic herbs, especially rosemary, are used in abundance. One can only begin to give an outline of the dishes themselves. To stimulate the appetite there is crostino, a paste of calf's liver fried with onion, anchovy, capers and pepper. Next, one can choose between ribollita (a bean and black cabbage soup served with just a dash of cold oil) and pappardelle 'sulla' lepre (pasta with sauce made from hare cooked in red wine, oil and tomato). 'Fiorentina' is a sirloin steak grilled over hot charcoal. Arista is pork roasted on a spit or in an oven with herbs. It takes its name from a Greek Orthodox monk who exclaimed 'Aristos' (excellent) when he tasted it at the Council of Florence in 1439. Anatra all'arancia (duck à l'orange) was a Florentine dish which Catherine de Medici's chefs introduced to their Parisian colleagues. Fagioli al fiasco are small, white beans placed in terra-cotta flasks and cooked over charcoal with water, oil, garlic, rosemary and a few sage leaves. Cieche alla pisana: small eels found in the local rivers in February. They are fried in oil, garlic and sage; and parmesan is added before serving.

Chianti

Chianti here refers to the famous wine and not to the area from which it takes its name. Baron Bettino Ricasoli, the great Florentine lord and farmer, was twice Prime Minister of the infant Kingdom of Italy. He owned the castle of Brolio, whose vineyards were to define the style of Chianti (a wine known as far back as the 17C). Dry and full of taste, a brilliant ruby colour becoming garnet as it ages, and a hint of violet in its bouquet: it can be served with any meal (at 18°C). Chianti is made from a mixture of grapes, 75 to 90% Sangiovese, 5 to 10% Canaiolo nero and 5 to 10% Trebbiano toscano and Malvasia dei Chianti. Chianti classico is produced at Barberina Val d'Elsa, San Casciano Val di Pesa, Greve in Chianti, Tavarnelle Val di Pesa in the province of Florence; Castellina in Chianti, Castelnuovo Berardenga, Gaiole in Chianti, Poggibonsi and Radda in Chianti in the province of Siena. In addition there is the Chianti Colli Aretini, the Chianti Colli Fiorentini, the Chianti Colli Pisane, the Chianti Colli Senesi, the Chianti Montalbano and the Chianti Rufina, each term referring to the area of production.

border between Tuscany and Emilia); circuit of La Garfagnana, from Castelnuovo (best in late spring and autumn); *Alta Via delle Alpi Apuane* (in four stages from the Rifugio Carrara, ☎ 0585/317110; best end Apr-end Oct); route heading S from Siena to Monte Argentario (not yet fully signposted; best in spring and autumn). Short excursions in the Maremma nature park and to the Monti dell'Uccellina from Alberese (→ La Maremma itinerary), in the Casentino forests from Badia Prataglia and Stia →; paths in the Valle Graziosa, managed by the Comune di Calci →. Information: *La Roncola,* Florence, v. del Campuccio 98, ☎ 055/2298298; *L'Istrice,* Rosignano Solvay (25 km SE of Livorno), v. Amednola 7, ☎ 0586/760400. *CAI* offices: at Arezzo, v. S. Giovanni

Decollato 37; Carrara, v. Giorgi, ☎ 0585/76782; Grosseto, v. Trieste 9; Lucca, Palazzo Provinciale (cortile Carrara); Massa, p. Mazzini 13, ☎ 0585/488081; Prato, v. Ricasoli 7; Siena, v. di Città 25; San Giovanni Valdarno, v. N. Sauro 20. *Comunità montana Garfagnana*, ☎ 0583/63306; *Comunità montana dell'Amiata*, ☎ 0564/967064; *Comunità montane dell'Appennino:* at Pieve Santo Stefano, ☎ 0575/733611; at La Verna-Badia Prataglia-Camàldoli, ☎ 0575/52571; at Casaglia-Badia di Moscheta, ☎ 055/8456551; at Montepiano-Cascina di Spedaletto, ☎ 0574/957018; at Pràcchia, ☎ 0573/630790; at San Pellegrino in Alpe, ☎ 0583/62033; at the Due Santi Pass, ☎ 0187/830359.

Cycling: assistance and information from various groups affiliated with *UDACE* (58) in all parts of region. *Giro della Toscana*, a bicycle race in nine stages (Florence, Siena, Massa Marittima and La Maremma, Populonia, Volterra and San Gimignano; 31 miles a day), organized by *Ciao e Basta*, at Florence (→), ☎ 055/263985.

Horseback riding: numerous riding centres associated with *ANTE* throughout region.

Instruction: in Italian cooking and entertaining at Lamporecchio (→ Montecatini Terme), ☎ 0572/70151 or 02/874360; nature observation and painting on island of Giglio, ☎ 0564/809034.

Sailing: Lega Navale branches at Follonica, v. Bicocchi 2/C, ☎ 0566/42310; Livorno, v. Spianata Molo Mediceo 12/A, ☎ 0586/23567; Marina di Pisa, v. D'Annunzio 250, ☎ 050/36652; Viareggio, darsena Europa, ☎ 0584/31085. *Casa di Vela dell'Elba*, Livorno, v. Mare, ☎ 0586/505562; Portoferraio, ☎ 0565/966265; *Scuola di vela di Torre del Lago Puccini*, ☎ 0584/342084 (sailing school).

Skiing: best facilities are at Abetone and Cutigliano (→ San Marcello Pistoiese) and at Monte Amiata.

Motocross: tracks at Castellina Marittima (→ Cécina), Montevarchi, Ponte a Égola (→ San Miniato).

Motor racing: *Autodromo internazionale del Mugello*, at Scarperia (→ Borgo San Lorenzo), ☎ 055/84631 (world championship motorcycle races; Formula 2 races).

Golf: at Monsummano-Montecatini Terme, Orbetello, Portoferraio, Punta Ala, Tirrenia.

Tennis: courses with renowned players at the *Ciocco* international tourist centre, Castelvecchio Pascoli (→ La Garfagnana and the Apuan Alps itinerary), ☎ 0583/710021; reservations through the *Alitur* agency, Milan, v. Napo Torriani 29, ☎ 02/6575941 and the *Centro milanese per lo Sport e la Ricreazione*, Milan, p. Lotto 15, ☎ 02/391667-355100.

Flying: at Arezzo, Molin Bianco airport, ☎ 0575/34282-351279 (pilot school); Grosseto, *Ali Maremma* airport, v. Orcagna, ☎ 0564/933096-415136; Livorno, Livorno-Stagno airport, SS 555, at the 2-km marker, ☎ 0586/942675; Lucca, Capànnori-Tassignano airport, ☎ 0583/46677; Marina di Massa, Massa-Cinquale airport, ☎ 0585/309088; Siena, Ampugnano airport,

☎ 0577/349150; Marina di Campo (island of Elba) airport, ☎ 0565/97011.

Parachuting: *Aeroclub centrale Paracadutismo*, Siena, Ampugnano airport, ☎ 0577/349150.

Potholing: sites equipped for potholing at Monsummano Terme, Montecatini Alto, Sarteano.

Fishing: *Federazione italiana pesca sportiva*, at Arezzo, p. Sopra i Ponti 6, ☎ 0575/24201; Grosseto, v. Matteotti 78; Livorno, Scali d'Azeglio 3, ☎ 0586/29398; Lucca, v. Santa Croce 105, ☎ 0583/46597; Pisa, v. R. Fucini 49, ☎ 050/45370; Siena, p. Tolomei 5, ☎ 0577/41111; Massa, office at Aulla (33 km NW), v. Nardi 20, ☎ 0187/408212. For fishing conditions (controlled waters, bans, etc.), apply to the appropriate federal office.

Racecourses: *Casalone*, at Grosseto, ☎ 0564/24214; *Caprilli*, at Ardenza (→ Livorno); Follonica, ☎ 0566/51298; Montecatini Terme, ☎ 0572/78262; *San Rossore*, at Pisa, ☎ 050/531132; *Pian delle Fornaci*, at Siena, ☎ 0577/394347.

Facts and figures

Location: *Tuscany is shaped like a large triangle, with one side running along the coast between the mouth of the Magra and the headland of Argentario, and the other two sides roughly following the great arc of the Apennine mountains. The Tyrrhenian coast is magnificent, and from it one can see Elba and the other islands of the Tuscan archipelago. The Tyrrhenian slopes of the Apennine range dominate the mountainous and hilly landscape. Very little of the countryside is actually flat. It is a varied landscape, wild in certain places and settled in others. Its splendid skylines, its vegetation (scrub-bush, chestnut, cypress) and its hilltop villages and towns are quintessentially Italian. The Arno, the eighth longest river in Italy, is entirely in Tuscany. Only a short stretch of the Tiber runs through the region.*
Area: *22,992 sq km.*
Climate: *Mediterranean on the coast. Away from the sea, the climate progressively becomes Mediterranean-continental, with variations caused by hills and mountains. The Apennine mountains provide shelter, and the result is often a true spring and autumn. Snow is rare in winter on the plains and hills, but heavy snows fall in the mountains.*
Population: *3,581,291 inhabitants, an eighth of whom live in Florence.*
Administration: *Regional capital: Florence; the eight other provincial capitals are: Arezzo, Grosseto, Livorno, Lucca, Massa-Carrara, Pisa, Pistoia and Siena.*

● *Towns and places*

ABBADIA SAN SALVATORE

Siena 73, Florence 143, Rome 181 km
Pop. 7,719 ⊠ 53021 ☎ 0577   E5

Like the other old settlements on Amiata (→), Abbadia San Salvatore was built at a point where rainfall from the mountains emerges as springs amid rocks and groups of chestnut trees. Minerals have played an important part in the town's history. Today, the

modern furniture industry and tourism are also part of the economy.

▶ Little remains of the famous abbey of **S. Salvatore**, which was built in Lombard times as a Benedictine monastery and which rose to become one of the most powerful in Tuscany. The church was rebuilt in the 11C and subsequently altered several times. One fascinating feature does survive from the original building: the **crypt**, which dates from the 8C and includes columns displaying extraordinary Barbarian decorative elements. ▶ The **medieval village★** is virtually intact, with its stone buildings now gray or black with age. In one of its narrow streets stands the small church of **S. Leonardo** with its Gothic façade. ▫

Practical information _____

ⓘ v. Mentana 97, ☎ 778608.

Hotels:
★★★ **Adriana,** v. Serdini 76, ☎ 778116, 39 rm ⑱ 44,000; bkf: 5,000.
★★★ **Italia,** v. Roma 30, ☎ 778007, 24 rm ⑱ closed Sep-Jun except 20 Dec-31 Jan, 35,000; bkf: 3,000.
★★★ **K 2,** v. del Laghetto 15, ☎ 778609, 14 rm ⫽ ⌖ closed 1-20 Oct, 60,000; bkf: 4,000.
★★ **Roma,** v. Matteotti 32, ☎ 778015, 20 rm Ⓟ ⑱ 33,000.

Restaurant:
♦ **Fonte Magria-Il Trotaio,** ☎ 778539, closed Mon. In a fir forest, trout fishing. Regional cuisine: pici, gnocchi, 20/30,000.

Recommended
Swimming: v. Asmara, ☎ 779204.

ABETONE

Pistoia 49, Florence 90, Milan 271 km
4,554 ft   pop. 816 ⊠ 51021 ☎ 0573   C1

Abetone was cut off from the rest of the world until the 1930s, when automobiles and the increasing popularity of winter sports led to a road being built. The town is located in a **pass in the Apennines** (4,554 ft) between Tuscany and Emilia, and is surrounded by **forests** (larch, pine, Turkey oak, beech, birch and fir). It is a favourite resort for weekends, summer holidays and winter sports. ▫

Practical information _____

⚡ cable cars, ski lifts, cross-country skiing, instruction.
ⓘ at pass on piazzale, ☎ 60001.

Hotels:
★★★★ **Palazzaccio,** p. Piramidi, ☎ 60067, 57 rm Ⓟ closed May-Jun and Sep-Nov, 85,000.
★★★ **Bellavista,** v. Brennero 287, ☎ 60028, 18 rm Ⓟ ⑱ closed 16 Apr-14 Jun and 16 Sep-14 Dec, 63,000; bkf: 6,000.
★★ **Regina,** v. Uccelliera 9, ☎ 60007, 26 rm Ⓟ ⅄ closed 16 Apr-24 Jun and 16 Sep-19 Dec, 55,000; bkf: 4,000.

Restaurants:
♦♦ **Capannina,** v. Brennero 256, ☎ 60562, closed Tue eve, Wed, Jun and Oct. Regional cuisine: tortelli alla contadina, roast shank of pork, 25/35,000.
♦♦ **Pierone,** v. Brennero 288, ☎ 60068, closed Thu, Jun and Oct. Regional cuisine: truffle dishes, roast trout, 25/40,000.

⚄ ★★ **Pinguino,** at Pian di Novello, 71 pl, ☎ 673008 (all year).

Recommended
Botanical garden: Abetone forest, at Fontana Vaccaia (information at Florence, ☎ 055/486943).
Sled lift: ☎ 60292.
Swimming: at *Residence Bosco Lungo,* ☎ 60582.
Youth hostel: *Ostello Renzo Bizzarri,* SS dell'Abetone, ☎ 60117.

Il monte AMIATA

From Chiusi *(107 km, 1 day; map 1)*

The main attraction of this route is the scenery. The itinerary heads out of the Valdichiana, circles Amiata and then returns to the valley. Between Chiusi (→) and Radicófani (→), and heading toward Sarteano (→), the landscape is typically Sienese: olive groves

and woods. Further on, across the awesome Orcia, there is an agricultural area with clay soil. Then, suddenly, a magnificent vista opens up onto the rocca of Radicófani perched on a basalt crag against the background of the green peak of Amiata. Farther up, the road climbs toward Abbadia San Salvatore (→), where there is a view over the valley of the Paglia. The return trip between San Casciano dei Bagni and Chiusi also offers fine vistas as the road climbs and dips along a series of hills whose slopes are covered with pines, cypresses and olive trees. However, the major feature is the Amiata peak itself. This beautiful mountain, almost violet in colour, overlooks southern Tuscany like the dome of a cathedral. An extinct volcano, it is now covered with springs and, on its higher slopes, extensive beech and chestnut forests. There are also extensive mineral deposits which were mined by the Etruscans (for the precious dye cinnabar) and in modern times (for mercury).

▶ The **scenic road** which climbs from Abbadia San Salvatore to the foot of Amiata runs through chestnut, pine and fir forests before reaching a refuge *(10 km)* and a group of hotels *(12.5 km)*. ▶ From the **summit of Amiata** (5,702 ft) there is a vast **panorama★** over the whole Tuscan region. ▶ At **Castel del Piano,** there is a 16C quarter and an older **medieval** area. ▶ **Arcidosso** is another town with steep narrow streets lined with tightly built old houses. ▶ **Santa Fiora** is another medieval village which features the remains of a castle and dark stone houses. Its parish church houses some terra-cottas from the school of della Robbia and at the entrance to the village there is an 18C fish pond. ▶ **Piancastagnaio,** now a holiday resort, still has the remains of a gate flanked by a powerful castle *(open to visitors)*. The castle houses a tapestry and furniture museum. The façade of the elegant 17C Palazzo Bourbon Del Monte opens on to the piazza. ▶ **San Casciano dei Bagni** (a popular and ancient spa) and **Cetona** (still surrounded by its 15C Sienese walls) both stand on the slopes of Mt. Cetona and offer fine vistas. Above Cetona, near the former convent of S. Maria a Belverde, there are a number of caves which were inhabited in prehistoric times. ▫

Practical information _____

AIOLE, 4 km toward Santa Fiora.

Hotel:
★★★ **Parco Hotel Faggio Rosso,** ☎ 967274, 70 rm Ⓟ ⑱ ⌖ ☒ ⟋ 55,000; bkf: 8,000.

ARCIDOSSO, ⊠ 58031, ☎ 0564.

Restaurant:
♦ **Tagliola,** at Bagnoli, v. del Centro 2, ☎ 967351, closed Mon, 15-30 Jun and 15 Nov-15 Dec. Regional cuisine: tagliatelle, risotto, 25/30,000.

BAGNOLO, ⊠ 58030, 4 km E.

Restaurant:
♦ **Fungo,** v. Provinciale 32, ☎ 953025, closed Tue and 1 Nov-15 Dec. Beautifully situated with veranda and pergola. Regional and Italian cuisine: tortelloni di ricotta, penne norcina, 18/25,000.

BAGNORE, ⊠ 58032, 2.7 km NW.
⚓ (Jun-Oct), ☎ 977079.

CASTEL DEL PIANO, ⊠ 58033, ☎ 0564.
ⓘ p. Garibaldi, ☎ 955284.

Hotel:
★★★ **Impero,** v. Roma 7, ☎ 955337, 53 rm Ⓟ ⑱ ⟋ closed 20 Sep-15 Dec, 53,000; bkf: 4,500.

⚄ ★★ **Amiata,** at Montoto, v. Roma 15, 161 pl, ☎ 955107 (all year).

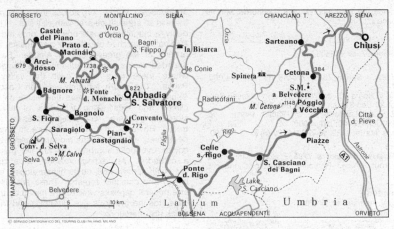

1. Il monte Amiata

MONTE AMIATA, 5,702 ft, ⊠ 53021, ☎ 0577.
丈 ski lifts, cross-country skiing, instruction.
ⓘ at Abbadia San Salvatore, v. Mentana 97, ☎ 778608.

Hotel:
★★★ *Capannina,* ☎ 789751, 30 rm P ⚲ ﷼ ⚸ closed
21 Apr-Jun and 11 Sep-19 Dec, 60,000; bkf: 7,000.

Restaurant:
♦ *Contessa,* at Prato della Contessa, ☎ 955378, closed
Oct-Nov. 4,921 ft up, by ski lifts. Regional cuisine: spinach and ricotta tortelli, roast haunch of pork with
apples, 22/33,000.

PIANCASTAGNAIO, ⊠ 53025, ☎ 0577.

Hotel:
★ *Bosco,* v. Grossetana 31, ☎ 786090, 26 rm P ﷼ ⚸
35,000; breakfast: 4,500.

SAN CASCIANO DEI BAGNI, ⊠ 53040, ☎ 0578.
⚱ (mid-May-mid-Oct), ☎ 58023.
ⓘ p. Matteotti, ☎ 58141.

SANTA FIORA, ⊠ 58037, ☎ 0564.
ⓘ p. Garibaldi, ☎ 977091.

ANGHIARI

Arezzo 27, Florence 105, Rome 242 km
Pop. 6,021 ⊠ 52031 ☎ 0575   E3

In the Middle Ages, Perugia, Arezzo and Florence
fought to control this part of the upper Tiber Valley. The town overlooks an extensive plain and its
hilltop **old centre** has survived largely intact.

▶ In the 14C, Anghiari produced and dyed wool
cloth. Most of the **medieval town** survives: stone houses, narrow lanes, picturesque arched passageways and
worn steps. ▶ The fine Renaissance **Palazzo Taglieschi**
houses a museum *(ring bell)* with artworks and an
extensive and unusual collection of domestic items and
tools. ▶ On the road down to Sansepolcro (→) stands
the 7C or 8C brick church of **S. Stefano,** which has Byzantine features. ◻

Practical information _____

Hotel:
★★ *Meridiana,* p. IV Novembre 8, ☎ 788102, 22 rm P
⚸ 27,000.

Restaurant:
♦♦ *Locanda al Castello di Sorci,* at San Lorenzo,
☎ 789066, closed Mon. In group of houses at centre
of farm. Regional cuisine: special every day, homemade
wines, 15/20,000.

Recommended
Events: *upper Tiber Valley craft fair* (end Apr-early May).

AREZZO*

Florence 77, Rome 219, Milan 376 km
Pop. 91,691 ⊠ 52100 ☎ 0575   E3

The ancient city of Arezzo stands on a hilltop at a
point where the Casentino Valley, the upper Valdarno
and the Valdichiana converge. For centuries it occupied a semicircular area, and the old layout can still
be traced in the long, curving v. Garibaldi, which follows the line of the now vanished walls built around
1200. The Etruscan layout roughly corresponds to
the area where the Duomo, the Passeggio del Prato
and the Medici fortress now stand. To reach the historic heart of the city, one has to climb up the corso
Italia, one of the streets which radiate from the centre. The buildings are mostly Renaissance, and
many of them date back to a time when Arezzo was
under Florence's control. There is, however, much
evidence of the Middle Ages, as seen in the layout
of the roads.

▶ The gardens of the Passegio del Prato extend as far
as the **Fortezza** (B3, 16C) and offer a superb view of the
city from the ramparts. Landmarks include the tower of
the Palazzo dei Priori (14C) and the campanile of the
Duomo. ▶ Streets such as the v. dei Pileati and the
v. di Borgunto still retain much of their old character and
the latter opens on to the dramatic **piazza Grande★** (B2),
the other end of which is marked by Vasari's **Palazzo**

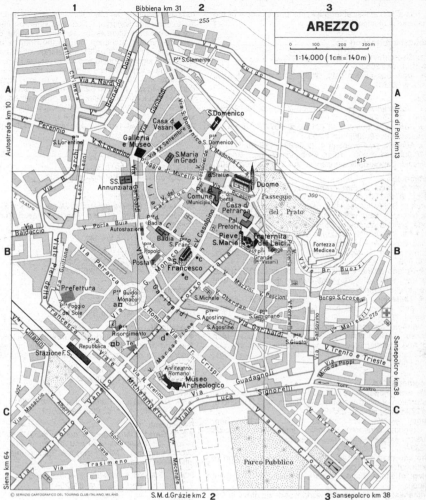

AREZZO

0   100   200   300m
1:14.000 (1cm = 140m)

A   Alpe di Poti km13

Autostrada km 10

Siena km 64

Sansepolcro km38

© SERVIZIO CARTOGRAFICO DEL TOURING CLUB ITALIANO, MILANO

S.M. d.Grázie km 2 **2**

3 Sansepolcro km 38

---

delle Logge. Opposite is a typical Aretine brick house with a tall tower. On the W side is the Romanesque **apse★** of the parish church of S. Maria, the Palazzo del Tribunale, with its 18C staircase, and the **Palazzo della Fraternità dei Laici★** (14C), one of Arezzo's most beautiful buildings displaying an unusual but highly successful blend of Gothic grace and Renaissance harmony. On the first Sunday of every month there is an antiques market in the piazza. ► The parish church of **S. Maria★★** (B2) has a façade with tall loggias, **bas-reliefs★** on its portals and a solemn interior including a crypt and Pietro Lorenzetti's splendid **polyptych★** (1320) on the high altar. Its highly original campanile with its plethora of paired windows has been dubbed 'tower of a hundred openings'. ► There are a number of fine paintings and sculptures in the **Galleria e Museo Medievale e Moderno★** (A1-2; *9 a.m.-2 p.m.; hols 9 a.m.-1 p.m.; closed Mon*). ► Equally interesting is the **Museo Archeologico Mecenate★** (C2; *9 a.m.-2 p.m.; hols 9 a.m.-1 p.m.; closed Mon*), which contains the ruins of the Roman amphitheatre nearby and includes Etruscan mirrors, gold,

coins, amphoras, statuettes, amulets, mosaic fragments, urns, spectacular archaic bronzes and, the pride of the collection, the 1C BC-1C AD **coralline vases** produced in Roman Arezzo with their magnificent colour and relief decoration. ► Not far away is the **house of G. Vasari** (A2; *8 a.m.-2 p.m.; hols 9 a.m.-1 p.m.; closed Mon; ring bell*). ► The Gothic church of **S. Domenico★** (A2), which forms the backdrop to a tree-lined piazza, contains Cimabue's magnificent *Crucifix★*. ► However, most people come to Arezzo to see Piero della Francesca's **fresco cycle★★** of the *Legend of the True Cross*, painted in 1453-64 in the choir of the church of **S. Francesco** (B2) and one of the supreme achievements of the art of painting *(closed for restoration)*. ► The **Duomo★** (B2) contains another della Francesca fresco, *Mary Magdalene★*, and there is also the large **tomb★** of Guido Tarlati, 14C bishop and lord of Arezzo. Another of the Duomo's points of interest is the series of **stained-glass windows** by 16C French master Guillaume de Marsillat. ► **S. Maria delle Grazie,** at the SE edge of the city, has a 15C classical **loggia**★, just one example of the Renaissance element in Arezzo. ◻

Practical information _____

ⓘ p. Risorgimento 116 (B1), ☎ 20839.
🚃 (C1), ☎ 22663.
🚌 from bus station (B2), ☎ 8550322 and p. Monaco (B1-2), ☎ 23687.

Hotels:
★★★ *Continentale,* p. G. Monaco 7 (B1 a), ☎ 20251, 74 rm ℗ ♿ ⌀ 74,000; bkf: 6,000.
★★★ *Europa,* v. Spinello 43 (C1 b), ☎ 357701, 46 rm ⌀ No restaurant, 79,000; bkf: 7,500.
★★★ *Minerva,* v. Fiorentina 4, ☎ 27891, 118 rm ℗ ⅏ ♿ ⌀ 76,000; bkf: 8,000. Rest. ◆◆◆ closed Aug. Regional cuisine: pappardelle alla caccia, spit roasts, 20/35,000.

Restaurants:
● ◆◆◆ *Buca di San Francesco,* v. S. Francesco 1 (B2 c), ☎ 23271, closed Mon eve, Tue and Jul. Near church of S. Francesco, 14C decor with antique furniture and frescos. Regional cuisine: taglioni caserecci with ricotta, pollo in porchetta, 25/34,000.
● ◆◆◆ *Torrino,* at Madonna del Torrino, ☎ 360264, closed Mon. On a hill with towers and veranda. Regional and Italian cuisine: cappelli d'alpino, spit roasts, 18/30,000.
◆◆◆ *Spiedo d'Oro,* v. Crispi 12 (C2 d), ☎ 22873, closed Thu and 1-15 Jul. Regional cuisine: pappardelle with hare stew, spaghetti carbonara, 15/25,000.
◆◆◆ *Tastevin,* v. de' Cenci 9 (B2 e), ☎ 28304, closed Mon and Aug. Piano bar. Regional cuisine: ribollita, carpacci, 20/35,000.
◆◆ *Antica Trattoria al Principe,* at Giovi-Ponte alla Chiassa, v. Giovi d'Arezzo 25, ☎ 362046, closed Mon and Aug. Modernized 18C post house. Regional cuisine: homemade maccheroni with meat sauce, fried frogs, 20/30,000.

Recommended
Craft workshops: *M. Crulli,* v. Fontanella 50, ☎ 27346 (restoration of inlaid furniture); *P. Valenti,* p. S. Martino 8, ☎ 29793 (lacquer and gilding).
Events: *giostra del Saracino* (joust, first Sun Sep, p. Grande); *concorso polifonico internazionale Guido d'Arezzo* (choral festival, last week Aug, Teatro Petrarca, ☎ 23975).
Fairs and markets: *antique fair* in p. Grande first Sun of month; *international goldsmiths' show* (Sep).
Flying: at Molin Bianco, airport, ☎ 34282-351279 (pilot school).
Purchases: gold, lace, metal work, wood and straw items.
Sports stadium: v. della Palestra, ☎ 23791.
Youth hostel: *Ostello Pier della Francesca,* v. Borg'Unto 6 (B2), ☎ 354536.

L'ARGENTARIO

D6

Recent building developments have affected this beautiful and mountainous headland. The same is unfortunately true across the Orbetello lagoon (on the hill side of Ansedonia). The damage has been even further aggravated by a devastating fire that raged a few summers ago, destroying the scrub-brush and forests that made the coastline so attractive. Scattered throughout the area are remains of walls, forts and towers built by the Spaniards at strategic points in the 16C-17C to defend and control the region.

▶ On the flat summit of the headland of **Ansedonia** are the **ruins of Cosa**★, a Roman city and now an important archaeological site. Excavations have uncovered white, cyclopean walls, a well-preserved gate built of massive polygonal blocks, the regular grid of streets, the ruins of the forum and its buildings and, on the acropolis, several

temples, including the *Capitolium* (which was dedicated to Jove, Juno and Minerva). Near the water, on the site of the ancient port, there is the so-called **Tagliata Etrusca,** which is, in fact, a channel dug by the Romans between high rock walls. ▶ **Port'Ércole** stands on a bay sheltered by a small headland and it has retained a number of older features, particularly in the lower town: steep flights of steps are cut into the rock, with low arches and dark passages. ▶ **Porto Santo Stefano** is another charming and colourful old fishing port, now well equipped to receive visitors and bustling with boats which ferry passengers to the island del Giglio (→). The slopes behind the town rise in terraces and are covered with vines and olive trees. ◻

Practical information _____

ANSEDONIA, ✉ 58016, ☎ 0564.
ⓘ at Porto Santo Stefano, ☎ 814208.

Recommended
Nature park: *Riserva del lago di Burano (10 km E),* closed Jun-Jul, Mon-Wed, Fri and Sat; information from *WWF Rome,* ☎ 06/854892.

CALA DEI SANTI, 5 km SW.

Hotel:
★★★★ *Pellicano,* ☎ 833801, 34 rm ℗ ♿ ⅏ ▱ ⌀° closed 16 Oct-14 Apr, 435,000; bkf: 20,000.

Recommended
Marina: ☎ 833923.

CALA MORESCA, 6 km SW.

Restaurant:
◆◆◆ *Moresco,* v. Panoramica 156, ☎ 824158, closed Tue and 10 Jan-Feb. In villa with olive groves. Seafood: risotto di mare, mazzancolle al vino, 30/45,000.

PORT'ERCOLE, ✉ 58018, ☎ 0564.
ⓘ at Porto Santo Stefano, ☎ 814208.

Hotel:
★★★ *Don Pedro,* v. Panoramica 23, ☎ 833914, 44 rm ℗ ⌀ closed Nov-Mar, 62,000; bkf: 6,000.

Restaurant:
◆◆ *Il Gatto e la Volpe,* v. dei Cannoni 3, ☎ 833306, closed Tue except summer and 20 Sep-10 Apr. Terrace overlooking sea. Mixed cuisine: Spezia mussels, fusili alla paesana, 25/40,000.

PORTO SANTO STEFANO, ✉ 58019, ☎ 0564.
ⓘ corso Umberto 55/A, ☎ 814208.

Hotel:
★★★ *Girasole,* at Poggio Calvello, ☎ 812647, 18 rm ℗ ⅏ closed Oct-Easter, 72,500; bkf: 8,000.

Restaurant:
◆◆ *Fontanina di San Pietro,* at San Pietro, ☎ 812029, closed Wed and Jan. Dining under pergola in summer. Regional cuisine: risotto with shrimps and pine nuts, spaghetti alla pirata, 25/45,000.

SANTA LIBERATA, ✉ 58010, 4 km E.

Hotel:
★★★ *Villa Domizia,* ☎ 812735, 24 rm ℗ ⅋ ⅏ ⌀ closed Oct-Mar, 66,000; bkf: 5,000.

Recommended
Marina: ☎ 812529.
Swimming: at Campone, ☎ 813133.
Yacht club: ☎ 814002 (sailing school, Jul-Aug).

ASCIANO

Siena 26, Florence 94, Rome 120 km
Pop. 6,097 ✉ 53041 ☎ 0577   D-E4

Although Sardinian immigrants introduced sheep grazing to this barren area near Siena, it has not been enough to revitalize it economically. Unusual white clay domes, known as *biancane*, are the main feature of the countryside. However, Etruscan and Roman finds prove that the area was settled in antiquity, and buildings dating from the 12C-15C also show that there was considerable activity in the Middle Ages.

▶ Near the Romanesque **collegiate church** is the **Museo d'Arte Sacra★** *(see parish priest)*, which contains a large number of 14C-15C Sienese works, including several major paintings and pieces of sculpture, such as the famous *Nativity of the Virgin★* by the so-called Master of the Osservanza. ▶ The **Museo Etrusco** *(open on request)* also houses an interesting collection in the former church of S. Bernardino: urns, vases — some with inscriptions — bronze objects and necklaces. ▶ V. del Canto 11 is a house with a fine 2C Roman **mosaic pavement★** *(for admission, ask at the pharmacy on corso Matteotti).* ☐

BADIA PRATAGLIA

Arezzo 47, Florence 73, Rome 265 km
Pop. 1,050 ✉ 52010 ☎ 0575   E2

A well-equipped vacation centre in the Casentino, it includes a number of houses scattered through an extensive forest at different altitudes; plenty of streams and small waterfalls.

▶ A scenic road *(9 km)* leads to the hermitage of **Camaldoli** (→). ▶ 3 km away is the **Mandrioli Pass** (3,848 ft) and a little farther, a superb view★ over the Savio Valley.☐

Practical information _____

ⓘ on the Statale, ☎ 509054 (high season).

Recommended
Excursions: guided tours of surrounding forests, Stazione forestale, ☎ 559002.

BARGA

Lucca 37, Florence 111, Milan 277 km
Pop. 10,748 ✉ 55051 ☎ 0583   C2

At the foot of the old town, a network of steep, narrow streets lined with palazzi and fine churches forms the modern 'Giardino' area. Its houses were built by emigrants who returned from the Garfagnana.

▶ The 9C-14C **Duomo★** overlooks the town and has a splendid view. On the façade, there are Romanesque decorative features and inside, a superb 12C marble **pulpit★** and polychrome wooden statue of St. Christopher.

Environs

▶ A path leads from Fornovalasco *(17 km)* up through a chestnut forest to the foot of the Pania della Croce and the **grotta del Vento**, a wonderful series of caves with galleries studded with deep holes and small lakes *(guided tours follow two routes, the first takes one hr and departs every day at 10 a.m., noon, 3 and 6 p.m. in summer; the second takes two hrs and departs at 11 a.m. and 3, 4 and 5 p.m.; in winter the cave is only open on hols, excluding Christmas and New Year; management at Barga, ☎ 763084; reserve for groups).* ☐

Practical information _____

ⓘ p. Angelico, ☎ 73499.

Hotel:
★★★★ *Ciocco,* at Ciocco, ☎ 710021, 234 rm ℗ ⚏ ▣
✍ 130,000.

Restaurant:
♦ *Terrazza,* at Albiano, ☎ 766141, closed Wed except

summer. Maremma cuisine: penne with wild boar, roast kid, 15/25,000.

Recommended
Events: *international opera festival* (Jul-Aug), horse racing at Ciocco.

BORGO SAN LORENZO

Florence 26, Milan 292 km
Pop. 14,815 ✉ 50032 ☎ 055   D2

The Mugello, home of Giotto and Fra Angelico, is the famous valley in which the aristocrats and rich citizens of Renaissance Florence first discovered the delights of a country retreat. Even before seeing the industrial suburbs of Borgo San Lorenzo or the Scarperia race track, the visitor will realize that the area has been changed by contemporary civilization. However, the countryside remains enchanting with its bright colours and variety of flatlands, rolling hills and steeper slopes. Borgo San Lorenzo is the traditional business and social centre of the middle and upper Sieve valley.

▶ The unusual monument to the **dog Fido** graces the p. Dante and proves that man is capable of gratitude toward his best friend. ▶ Also of some interest are the campaniles of the Romanesque church of **S. Lorenzo** *(c. 3 km from centre)* and the parish church of **S. Giovanni Maggiore.** The latter also contains a Romanesque **pulpit★** with marble panels inlaid with symbolic figures. ▶ There is an unusual **Torre dell'Orologio.** After passing beneath it, one enters the **historical centre.** Quite a few of the buildings have been altered and rebuilt over the years, in some cases due to damage caused by the earthquake of 1919.

Environs

▶ The **Mugello,** which from the time of Boccaccio has been regarded as the most beautiful area near Florence, is dotted with **old villas,** half-castle, half-farmhouse. The humbler dwellings in the countryside are normally plastered, as opposed to the bare stone structures generally found in Casentino and Chianti. ▶ At **Scarperia** *(9.7 km),* there is the impressive **Palazzo Pretorio** (1306), whose façade is decorated with stone coats-of-arms. The oratory of the Madonna di Piazza houses a touching 14C *Madonna and Child★* painted by Jacopo di Casentino. In old Tuscany, the **cutlers** of Scarperia were renowned, and their modern successors have not forgotten the old skills. ▶ 1.7 km from Scarperia, at **Fagna,** there is perhaps the finest piece of architecture in the Mugello, the parish church of **S. Maria.** Inside is a Romanesque **pulpit★** with white and green marble panels inlaid with images of animals. ☐

Practical information _____

Environs

SCARPERIA, ✉ 50038, ☎ 055, 10 km NW.

Recommended
Motor racing: *Mugello* international circuit, ☎ 846351 (Formula 2 motor-racing and world championship motorcycling.)
♥ cutlery: visits possible to see traditional production of cutlery.

For help in understanding terms when visiting museums or other sites, see the *Art and Architectural Terms Guide* at the end of the Practical Holiday Guide.

CALCI

Pisa 10, Florence 80, Milan 285 km
Pop. 5,126 ⊠ 56011 ☎ 050   C3

The River Zambra runs down through the olive groves of the gently sloping and broad Valgraziosa, as it comes down the sides of Mt. Pisano toward the plain.

▶ The Verrucano stone façade of the 11C **parish church** makes a great impact, although it is devoid of ornaments and is reduced to a bare minimum. Almost as if to avoid detracting from these simple lines, the campanile has been left unfinished. ▶ 1 km from the village is the **Certosa di Pisa★**, one of the largest monasteries in Italy. Founded in 1366, it was rebuilt in the 17C-18C. The front of the monastery looks on to a large courtyard in the centre of which is the animated 18C white façade of the church *(guided tours: May-Oct 9:30-11:30 a.m. and 3-6 p.m.; Nov-Apr 10 a.m.-12 noon and 2-5 p.m.; closed Sun and Mon).*   □

Practical information _____

⚓ (Jun-Sep), at Uliveto Terme *(5 km S)*, ☎ 788002.

Recommended
Horseback riding: *Cooperativa Agrituristica*, v. Tre Colli 11.

CAMALDOLI

Arezzo 46, Florence 71, Rome 261 km
Pop. 46 ⊠ 52010 ☎ 0575   E2

Falcons and other birds of prey soar high above. A magnificent fir forest scattered with ferns lies below. Nearby facilities have turned this into a vacation area. There is also a **monastery** available for retreats.

▶ The **monastery** has a richly stocked **library,** paintings by Giorgio Vasari in the church and a **pharmacy** which now sells herbal products and spirits. ▶ Higher up *(2.5 km; 3,622 ft)* is a **hermitage** which is attached to the monastery and is in fact the original foundation, dating back to St. Romuald in the 11C. Behind a grille *(women not admitted)* is an enclosure with twenty cells where the monks live in silence and isolation.   □

Practical information _____

ⓘ at Bibbiena, ☎ 593098.

⚐ ★ *Fonte del Menchino*, on road to hermitage, 150 pl, ☎ 556075.

CAMPIGLIA MARITTIMA

Livorno 70, Florence 186, Rome 252 km
Pop. 12,476 ⊠ 57021 ☎ 0565   C4

Perched on the steep slopes of a hill covered by vegetation and crowned by the ruins of an old castle, Campiglia looks as if it belonged to the Middle Ages. The village is made up of old stone houses and narrow lanes. A gate, the **Porta S. Antonio,** bears the coat-of-arms of the Della Gherardesca, the lords of the village from the 11C on. A little farther, there is a **parish church** with a portal decorated with a superb Romanesque bas-relief. In fact, this hill just a few miles from the sea was settled by the Etruscans, who had moved into the area for its copper deposits.

> Send us your comments and suggestions; we will use them in the next edition.

Environs

▶ The **Terme di Caldana** *(5 km)* is a spa with hot water springs offering baths and mud treatments for a variety of ailments.   □

Practical information _____

CAMPIGLIA MARITTIMA

⚐ ★★ *Blucamp*, at Pozzatello, 80 pl, ☎ 838553.

Environs

TERME DI CALDANA, ⊠ 57029, ☎ 0565, 5 km W.
⚓ (May-Oct), ☎ 851066.

The island of CAPRAIA

Livorno 67, Florence 228, Rome 331 km
Pop. 387 ⊠ 57032 ☎ 0586   A-B4

The island is volcanic in origin and has a range of low, rugged hills running N-S. A third of it is now taken up by a prison farm. The island owes its name to the bold Greek sailors who discovered it. There are, however, no more wild goats.

▶ The **harbour** is on the NE coast, and from there one climbs to the white houses of **Capraia** and then the **Fortezza di S. Giorgio** which was built in the 15C by the Genoese. ▶ Lanes and paths climb up the hill sides, offering superb views, and finally reach the S tip of the island, the wild headland of **Punta dello Zenobito,** where there is an old Spanish tower. ▶ It is possible to take a **boat trip** around the island *(half a day)*. The sights include the precipitous cliffs of the **Punta della Manza,** the bay of Peruccia and the famous **Cala Rossa,** where red and gray rocks rise up out of the sea.   □

Practical information _____

≋
ⓘ v. Roma 2, ☎ 905025.
⛴ boat from Livorno (Tue, Wed, Thu and Sat, *c.* 3 hrs) and from Portoferraio on island of Elba (weekly, *c.* 2 hr 20 mn), information: *Toremar*, at Livorno, ☎ 24113; at Capraia, ☎ 905069.

⚐ ★★★ *Sughere*, v. delle Sughere 1, 180 pl, ☎ 905066.

Recommended
Young people's facilities: birdwatching and botany courses, nature rambles, ☎ 905071.

CAPRESE MICHELANGELO

Arezzo 45, Florence 123, Rome 260 km
Pop. 1,803 ⊠ 52033 ☎ 0575   E3

Perched on a rugged height of the E Alpe di Catenaia, this is the birthplace of Michelangelo. His father had been sent by Florence to act as town magistrate for a year.

▶ The modest Casa del Podestà where Michelangelo was actually born has been restored. It houses a **museum** with photographs of his works. The 14C **castello,** which has also recently been restored, contains casts of his sculptures and works by modern artists.   □

Practical information _____

Restaurant:
♦♦♦ *Fonte della Galletta*, at Alpe Faggeta, ☎ 793925, closed Wed from May-Oct. With extensive view over valley. Regional cuisine: tortellini with truffles, prosciutto flambé, 15/25,000.

⚐ *Michelangelo*, 40 pl, ☎ 793886.

CARRARA

Massa 7, Florence 126, Milan 233 km
Pop. 68,621 ⌧ 54033 ☎ 0585   B2

The town deserves its title of 'marble capital'. Quarrying began over two thousand years ago, well before the industry started up in other areas. Today, it is still the largest marble producer, with half a million tons quarried annually. There are quite a few varieties of marble, the very finest of which are used for sculpture. Carrara has had many rulers, but for over three centuries it was governed by the Malaspina and then by the Cybo-Malaspina. Even so, it would be difficult to find people anywhere else in Italy more fiercely attached to their freedom than the Carrarese, and the anarchist movement had strong roots here.

▶ The 11C-14C **Duomo**★ has a fine marble façade surmounted by a graceful Gothic loggia which flanks a splendid rose window. ▶ The 16C **Palazzo Cybo-Malaspina** now houses the Accademia di Belle Arti, with an interesting **gallery of plaster casts.**

Environs

▶ The **Cave di Colonnata** (quarries, *8.5 km*) show just how extensive the marble beds are and the scale of the industry. ▶ Another impressive set of quarries is the **Cave dei Fantiscritti** *(4 km).* ▶ **Campo Cécina** (4,265 ft, *20.5 km*), a vast plateau, offers a splendid **view**★ over the quarries. ☐

The marble of Carrara

In 1505, Pope Julius II sent thirty-year-old Michelangelo to Carrara to purchase marble for the mausoleum he was building in St. Peter's. Michelangelo stayed in Carrara for eight months and travelled through the Apuan Alps. He chose marble from Monte Altissimo and dreamed of carving a colossus which, from afar, would appear to sailors as a block of marble on top of a mountain. When he returned to Rome, the Pope had turned to other projects. The Romans got the marble from Luni and traded with the capital around 70 BC. Trajan's Column and the Apollo Belvedere were both carved from this marble. The village of Colonnata seems to have been founded as a colony of quarry slaves. The Romans quarried the marble beds by first cutting grooves with chisels along the natural cracks, then by forcing in iron wedges. Once the blocks had been cut free, they were moved on iron balls. More recently, explosives have been used. Since 1895, cutting has been done with a helical blade which cuts between two and fifteen cm per hour. Today, there are about three hundred quarries in production in the Apuan Alps, a total of a thousand including those now abandoned.

Practical information

ℹ p. 2 Giugno 14, ☎ 70894.
🚃 at Avenza, ☎ 56124.

Hotel:
★★★ **Michelangelo,** corso Rosselli 3, ☎ 70863, 32 rm 🅿 70,000; bkf: 5,000.

Restaurants:
♦♦♦ **Soldaini,** v. Mazzini 11, ☎ 71459, closed Mon and Aug. Family run, long tradition. Mixed cuisine: Piero crayfish, brodetto, 20/38,000.
♦♦ **Roma-Prioreschi,** p. Battisti 1, ☎ 70632, closed Sat

and 20 Aug-10 Sep. Mixed cuisine: four cheese lasagne, stuffed mussels, 20/30,000.
♦ **Venanzio Vannucci,** at Colonnata, p. Palestro 3, ☎ 73617, closed Sun eve, Thu and Dec-Jan. Lunigiana cuisine: rabbit with rosemary, snails in sauce with parmesan, 25/40,000.

Recommended
Events: *international marble and machinery show,* at Marina di Carrara, ☎ 840561 (May-Jun); *marble crafts show* (Jul-Aug).
♥ purchases: marble, natural minerals and crystals.

CASCIANA TERME

Pisa 35, Florence 77, Rome 330 km
Pop. 3,108 ⌧ 56034 ☎ 0587   C3

The waters of Casciana have long been famous. The Pisans built a spa here in the 14C, following in the footsteps of the Romans. At **Casciana Alta** (656 ft, *2.5 km*) there is a polyptych by Lippo Memmi in the church of S. Niccolò. The medieval structure of the hamlet of **Rivolto** *(6 km S)* is virtually intact. ☐

Practical information ⎯⎯⎯⎯⎯⎯⎯⎯⎯⎯

♨ (Apr-Nov), ☎ 646211.
ℹ v. Galilei 1, ☎ 646257.

Hotel:
★★★ **Villa Margherita,** v. Marconi 20, ☎ 646113, 42 rm 🅿 ⚒ & ⌂ closed Nov-Apr, 60,000; bkf: 5,000.

CASCINA

Pisa 13, Florence 79, Milan 288 km
Pop. 35,649 ⌧ 56021 ☎ 050   C3

Although the surrounding countryside is devoted to agriculture, Càscina has been an important centre for the furniture industry for more than a century. In recent decades, it has expanded and merged with neighbouring towns. However, the most interesting part of Càscina is still the old quarter within the medieval walls.

▶ In the centre, a long, uniform series of **arcades** lines the main street. ▶ A visit to the three **permanent furniture exhibitions,** to the **Scuola d'Arte del legno,** or to one of the many workshops, will convince the visitor that it is possible for an industry to preserve its old crafts. ▶ The 12C parish church of **S. Maria** is built in the restrained and simplified form of Pisan Romanesque. ▶ Inside, the oratory of **S. Giovanni** *(apply to the Istituto di Suore Teresiane, next door, if closed)* are **frescos** (1398) of Old Testament scenes by the Sienese painter Martino di Bartolomeo. ☐

Practical information ⎯⎯⎯⎯⎯⎯⎯⎯⎯⎯

Hotel:
★★★ **Villa Guelfi,** at Sant'Anna, v. Tosco-Romagnola 1301, ☎ 775182, 20 rm 🅿 ⚒ ⌂ 50,000; bkf: 5,000.

Recommended
Cycling: *Pedale Pecciolese,* at Péccioli, ☎ 0587/635043.
Furniture: permanent exhibitions; show of hand-crafted furniture (autumn).

⎯⎯⎯⎯⎯⎯⎯⎯⎯⎯⎯⎯⎯⎯⎯⎯⎯⎯⎯⎯⎯⎯⎯⎯⎯
For help in understanding terms when visiting museums or other sites, see the *Art and Architectural Terms Guide* at the end of the Practical Holiday Guide.

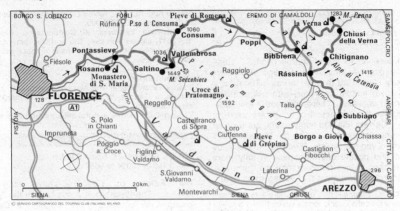

2. The Casentino

The CASENTINO

From Florence to Arezzo *(138 km, 1 day; map 2)*

This is an elliptical basin which covers over 300 square miles and is surrounded by mountains. It is not simply the upper valley of the Arno, but a world of its own within Tuscany. The green stretches of the Vallombrosa, the Verna and Camàldoli (→) saw the likes of saints such as Francis of Assisi. It was the home of the feudal Guidi counts, who still clung to their bleak castles at a time when Florence was entering the Renaissance and modern history. The famous fir forests of the Casentino still stand, largely unscathed.

▶ This itinerary starts on the SS 67 from **Florence** (→) to **Pontassieve**, known for its wines. Across the Arno, the Benedictine monastery of **S. Maria di Rosano** houses numerous works of art. ▶ Further on, a provincial road branches off to the right from the SS 70 to Consuma and climbs to **Vallombrosa**, where the vast monastery complex, which dates mainly from the 15C, contrasts with the humble 11C buildings of the early communities of Benedictine monks. ▶ A short distance from the monastery *(1.5 km W)* are hotels at **Saltino**. The route climbs through an ancient forest of firs and silver firs *(c. 9 km)* to the top of **Mt. Secchieta** (4,754 ft), which offers sweeping vistas★ of a large part of NE Tuscany. In winter the area is popular with skiers. ▶ Having returned to the SS 70 by another provincial road, the route climbs up through beech forests, meadows and firs to the **Consuma Pass** (3,363 ft). This is the traditional gateway to the **upper Casentino** for travelers from Florence and is now a vacation and winter sports centre with a wide range of facilities. After a brief detour to the r. to **Poppi** (→), the route reaches **Bibbiena**, which dates back to the Etruscans and stands on one of the many hilltops that dot the Casentino. It includes a number of Renaissance buildings: the **Palazzo Dovizi**, the church of **S. Lorenzo** and (outside town) the **sanctuary of S. Maria del Sasso**. The church of **SS. Ippolito e Donato** includes elements from the 12C to the Baroque and contains many fine works of art. Bibbiena has expanded down the slopes of the hill and out across the bottom of the Arno Valley. ▶ From here the SS 208 climbs upwards and after a while turns off to **La Verna** which has been described as the 'most

important of the Franciscan sanctuaries'. ▶ Modern villas overlook the steep road at **Chiusi della Verna**, a popular summer vacation centre. The road then goes down through woods, alpine meadows and, finally, fields of crops and a number of sites connected with the life of St. Francis. It reaches **Ràssinia**. The SS 71 then goes down the valley to Arezzo (→).   □

Practical information _____

BIBBIENA, ⊠ 52011, ☎ 0575.
ℹ v. Cappucci, ☎ 593098.

Hotels:
★★ *Amoroso Bei*, at Bibbiena Alta, v. Dovizi 18, ☎ 593046, 20 rm 🛉 37,000; bkf: 3,000. Rest. ● ♦♦ closed Wed. Old building with period furnishings. Regional and Italian cuisine: homemade ravioli, bistecche of venison, 20/25,000.
★★ *Giardino*, at Bibbiena Stazione, p. Palagi, ☎ 593194, 20 rm, Ⓟ ⅋ No restaurant, 34,000.

LA VERNA, ⊠ 52010, ☎ 0575.
ℹ at Bibbiena, ☎ 593098; information office at Doccione (at road junction).

PASSO DELLA CONSUMA, ⊠ 50060, ☎ 055.
ℹ ☎ 8306534.

Hotels:
★★★★ *Parco dei Faggi*, v. la Ripresa 25, ☎ 8306401, 16 rm Ⓟ ⌨ ▭ ⅋ 101,000; bkf: 11,000.
★★★ *Laghetto nel Bosco*, v. la Ripresa 25, ☎ 8306401, 31 rm Ⓟ ⌨ ▭ ⅋ 101,000; bkf: 11,000.

PONTASSIEVE, ⊠ 50065, ☎ 055.

Hotel:
★★★★ *Moderno*, v. Londra 5, ☎ 8315541, 120 rm Ⓟ 🛉 No restaurant, 110,000; bkf: 9,000.

Restaurant:
♦♦ *Girarrosto*, v. Garibaldi 27, ☎ 8302048, closed Mon. Large and lively with spit and grills in Tuscan style. Regional cuisine: pappardelle with wild boar, skewered song bird spit roast, 25/35,000.

Recommended
Wine: *Toscanello d'oro wine show* (May).

VALLOMBROSA, 3,143 ft, ⊠ 50060, ☎ 055.
⚞ ski lifts, cross-country skiing at Mt. Secchieta *(7.5 km N)*.

ⓘ at Reggello, v. Dante Alighieri 55, ☎ 868977; at Saltino, ☎ 862003 (seasonal).

Hotel:
★★★ *Vallombrosa at Saltino,* ☎ 862012, 76 rm ℗ 彡 冬 ▩ ⁄◈ closed Sep-Jun, 93,000.

Recommended
Horseback riding: *Centro equitazione Vallombrosa,* ☎ 862018 (associate of *ANTE;* accommodation available). **Technical tourism:** visits to experimental arboretum at Vallombrosa, Guardia forestale, ☎ 862008 (arrange in advance).

CASOLE D'ELSA

Siena 42, Florence 63, Rome 269 km
Pop. 2,709 ⊠ 53031 ☎ 0577   D4

The walls of the village are now gone, but the **castle** stands as a reminder that Casole was a Sienese fortress in the mid-16C.

▶ Fine examples of 14C-15C Sienese art can be found in the two **funerary monuments** inside the **collegiate church** and in the adjacent presbytery.   ◻

CASTELFIORENTINO

Florence 39, Rome 279 km
Pop. 17,368 ⊠ 50051 ☎ 0571   D3

The Valdelsa is so rich in works of art that one is tempted to refer to it as a museum scattered through the hills. One of the most important stops in this museum is Castelfiorentino. Like many other towns in the area it is made up of an old quarter on a hilltop and newer suburbs down in the valley.

▶ In the finely frescoed 18C church of **S. Verdiana** there is an important **art gallery** *(see parish priest)* with an outstanding 14C Sienese *Madonna★* attributed to Duccio di Boninsegna, a triptych by Taddeo Gaddi and a *Madonna★* by F. Granacci. ▶ Across the Elsa, in the church of **S. Chiara**, is a 15C Gothic *Annunciation* made up of two fine polychrome wooden statues. ▶ The **Cappella della Visitazione** is completely covered with **frescos★** by a 15C painter, Benozzo Gozzoli, who worked mostly in the Valdelsa.   ◻

CASTIGLION FIORENTINO

Arezzo 17, Florence 100, Rome 209 km
Pop. 11,289 ⊠ 52043 ☎ 0575   E4

Like Cortona (→), Castiglion Fiorentino looks down on to the Valdichiana from a hilltop and the slopes are dominated by the massive bulk of an old castle. The medieval origins of the town can be seen in both the layout of its streets and in its architecture.

▶ Grouped around p. del Municipio are the 16C **Logge del Vasari** and the Palazzo Comunale, which houses the **Pinacoteca Civica** *(8 a.m.-2 p.m. wkdays; apply to porter)*. It contains a startling *St. Francis Receiving the Stigmata★* by Bartolomeo della Gatta (15C) and a precious 15C Franco-Rhenish reliquary bust in gilded silver. ▶ To the SE outside the Roman gate, the church of the **Madonna della Consolazione** is a fine example of elegant late Renaissance architecture.

Environs

▶ 3.8 km away on a hilltop is the striking vista of the fortified wall of the 13C **Castello di Montecchio Vesponi.**   ◻

Practical information _____

Recommended
Events: *Palio dei Rioni* (3rd Sun in Jun).

CECINA

Livorno 36, Florence 122, Rome 285 km
Pop. 24,561 ⊠ 57023 ☎ 0586   C4

Cecina is a modern town only founded halfway through the last century when land reclamation made it possible to reoccupy an area that had been marsh since the Middle Ages. It has expanded rapidly and has now merged with the pleasant seaside resort of **Marina del Cecina.** An **antiquarium** houses a collection of Etruscan and Roman finds.   ◻

Practical information _____

CECINA

Hotel:
★★★ *Palazzaccio,* v. Aurelia Sud 300, ☎ 682510, 30 rm ℗ ◈ 63,000; bkf: 6,000.

Restaurant:
◆ *Antico Ponte,* corso Matteotti 21/25, ☎ 680065, closed Sun. Family-run trattoria by bridge over the Cecina. Regional cuisine: bistecca alla fiorentina, wild boar, 20/25,000.

⩜ ★★★ *Bocca di Cecina,* at San Pietro in Palazzi, 476 pl, ☎ 620509 (all year).

Recommended
Horseback riding: *Azienda agricola S. Francesco di Casaglia,* at Casino di Terra, ☎ 0588/37424 (associate of *ANTE*).
Motocross: *Malandrone circuit,* at Castellina Marittima *(23 km NE),* run by *Moto club Livorno,* ☎ 69701.

Environs

MARINA DI CECINA, ⊠ 57023, ☎ 0586, 2.5 km W.
≋
ⓘ largo Cairoli 17, ☎ 620678.

Hotels:
★★★ *Gabbiano,* v. della Vittoria 109, ☎ 620183, 26 rm ℗ 冬 ◈ closed Nov, 63,000; bkf: 6,000.
★★★ *Settebello,* v. della Vittoria 96, ☎ 620039, 33 rm ℗ closed Nov-Jan, 65,000; bkf: 8,000.

Restaurant:
◆◆ *El Faro,* v. della Vittoria 70, ☎ 620164, closed Wed and Nov. On the sea. Regional seafood: red mullet Livornese, squid Giuliano, 30/45,000.

Recommended
Horseback riding: *Società sport equestri,* at Pineta Cavalleggeri, ☎ 620228 (instruction).
Marina: ☎ 642202.
Tennis: sports centre at Mazzanta, ☎ 621069.

CERTALDO

Florence 41, Rome 270 km
Pop. 15,895 ⊠ 50052 ☎ 0571   D3

The home of Boccaccio, Certaldo is made up of an old hilltop centre and newer suburbs down in the valley. These two distinct quarters have existed for quite some time but **Borgo** (in the valley) has evolved with the times, while **Castello** (up the hill) remains virtually untouched.

▶ Medieval **Castello** is beautiful in itself, but also commands a magnificent view. ▶ There are some enchanting streets, such as the **via Boccaccio,** flanked by houses and towers built in red brick. It climbs up to the Palazzo Pretorio★ or the via del Rivellino, which takes the visitor back into the Middle Ages. There is also the via della Rena, which ends in a Gothic archway looking out toward a distant hill. ▶ The Porta del Sole should also be visited. ▶ In the Palazzo Pretorio★ (15C; *9 a.m.-12 noon and 3-6 or 4-7 p.m.; closed Mon)* are frescoed rooms, a tower and jail cells on whose walls unfortunate prisoners have carved messages. ▶ Boccaccio's house was rebuilt after the last war. The visitor may also find his cenotaph in the 13C church of SS. Michele e Jacopo. ▫

Practical information ─────────────

Restaurant:
♦♦ Osteria del Vicario, at Certaldo Alta, v. Rivellino 3, ☎ 668228, closed Wed and 10 Jan-Feb. Within walls of a small 13C monastery, garden for meals in summer. Regional and Italian cuisine: lamb, Maremma wild boar, 25/35,000.

CHIANCIANO TERME*

Siena 73, Florence 132, Rome 167 km
Pop. 7,223 ⊠ 53042 ☎ 0578   E4

At least one of the mineral water springs was known to the Etruscans, but it was during this century that the area was transformed into a large and popular spa. It was carefully planned after the First World War, so that it is laid out with baths, hotels and villas arranged along broad tree-lined avenues, interspersed with parks and quiet streets. What was originally Chianciano has now become Chianciano Vecchia.

▶ There are four springs: Acqua Santa, Sillene, Fucoli and S. Elena, each associated with a different spa. ▶ The p. Italia is the spa's centre and the v. le Roma which leads up to it is lined with luxury shops and cafés. ▶ Chianciano Vecchia, the medieval quarter, has preserved its castello, the Torre dell'Orologio, the Palazzo del Podestà and the buildings that line the v. Solferino. ▶ The Museo d'Arte Sacra in the Palazzo dell'Arcipretura has a number of Sienese and Florentine works from the 14C-15C as well as some archaeological finds. ▫

Practical information ─────────────

⚓ ☎ 63037.
ⓘ p. Italia, ☎ 63167; p. Gramsci, at Chianciano, ☎ 63953; parco Acqua Santa, ☎ 64054 (seasonal).

Hotels:
★★★★ Ambasciatori, v. della Libertà 512, ☎ 64371, 116 rm 🅿 ⅏ ⅋ 🖵 83,000; bkf: 6,000.
★★★★ Continentale, p. Italia 56, ☎ 63272, 45 rm 🅿 🖵 71,000; bkf: 5,000.
★★★★ G. H. Capitol Garibaldi, v. della Libertà 492, ☎ 64681, 63 rm 🅿 ⅏ ⅋ ⅋ 🖵 closed Nov-Mar, 75,000; bkf: 6,000.
★★★★ G. H. Excelsior, v. S. Agnese 6, ☎ 64351, 78 rm 🅿 ⅏ ⅋ 🖵 closed Nov-9 Apr, 120,000; bkf: 10,000.
★★★★ G. H. Fortuna, v. della Valle 76, ☎ 64661, 88 rm 🅿 ⅋ ⅋ 🖵 ⅌ closed Nov-Apr, 85,000; bkf: 10,000.
★★★★ Majestic, v. Buozzi 70, ☎ 63042, 70 rm 🅿 ⅏ ⅋ 🖵 closed Nov-14 Apr, 66,000; bkf: 8,000.
★★★★ Raffaello, v. dei Monti 3, ☎ 64633, 70 rm 🅿 ⅋ ⅋ 🖵 ⅌ closed Nov-14 Apr, 73,000; bkf: 6,000.
★★★ Ardea, v. Piave 12, ☎ 63783, 28 rm 🅿 ⅏ ⅋ closed Nov-Mar, 47,000; bkf: 5,000.
★★★ Bellaria, v. Verdi 57, ☎ 64014, 54 rm 🅿 ⅏ ⅋ closed Nov-14 Apr, 47,000; bkf: 3,000.
★★★ Cosmos, v. delle Piane 42, ☎ 60496, 43 rm 🅿 ⅏ 🖵 closed Nov-14 Apr, 48,000; bkf: 5,000.
★★★ Cristallo, v. Lombardia 35, ☎ 64051, 85 rm 🅿 🖵 closed Nov-14 Apr, 60,000; bkf: 5,000.

★★★ G. H. Terme, p. Italia 8, ☎ 63254, 43 rm 🅿 ⅏ ⅋ 🖵 closed 26 Oct-Apr, 69,000; bkf: 5,000.
★★★ Irma, v. della Libertà 302, ☎ 63941, 70 rm 🅿 ⅏ ⅋ closed 1 Nov-14 Apr, 46,000; bkf: 6,000.
★★★ Macerina, v. Macerina 27, ☎ 64241, 80 rm 🅿 ⅋ ⅏ closed Nov-Apr, 60,000; bkf: 3,000.
★★★ Montecarlo, v. della Libertà 478, ☎ 63903, 25 rm 🅿 ⅏ closed Nov-Apr, 53,000; bkf: 4,000.
★★★ Park Hotel Chianciano, v. Roncacci 30, ☎ 63603, 60 rm 🅿 ⅋ ⅋ closed Nov-Apr, 46,000; bkf: 3,000.
★★★ San Paolo, v. Ingegnoli 22, ☎ 60221, 26 rm 🅿 ⅏ ⅌ closed Nov-Mar, 48,000; bkf: 4,000.

Restaurants:
● ♦♦♦ Casanova, strada della Vittoria 10, ☎ 60449, closed Wed and Jan-Feb. In house in the country, veranda with good views. Regional cuisine: tortelloni with ricotta and nettles, sweet and sour duck, 50/70,000.
♦♦♦ Casale, v. delle Valli Cavine 36, ☎ 30445, closed Tue and 2 Jan-10 Mar. In a farmhouse. Regional cuisine: mixed roasts, truffled filet, 30/50,000.

Recommended
Events: *international television film festival* (May-Jun); concerts and art shows (May-Oct).
Sports centres: *Parco Fùcoli,* ☎ 64577 (tennis, bowls, skating); *Parco Monti di Sopra,* ☎ 64515 (cycle track, skating, fishing).

Il CHIANTI

From Siena *(163 km, 1 day; map 3)*

The most famous of Italy's wines takes its name from a land of hills and mountains. Olive trees, cypresses and, of course, vines add pattern and colour to an otherwise severe landscape. Older buildings in the area (churches, castles and farms) are mostly built of stone. In the 14C, Gaiole, Radda and Castellina were the three centres which formed the League of Chianti under the banner of the black cockerel. Here, as is so often the case in Tuscany, the Middle Ages left the deepest mark.

▶ The first stop on this itinerary, which starts and finishes at Siena (→), is Castelnuovo Berardenza, a bastion of Siena in the 14C and now a wine industry centre. To reach it, turn r. off the SS 408 at Piranella on to a provincial road and then turn l. ▶ Castello di Brolio *(NW, via the SS 484)* developed along similar lines, but started as a Florentine outpost. It stands on an isolated hill and behind its ring of walls are the feudal palace (with a beautiful chapel), the old keep and towers. In the valley below are the buildings of the famous Ricasoli estate. ▶ The SS 408 is found further N and passes the fine Castello di Meleto, a typical old castle with massive towers. Farther along is Gaiole in Chianti, a town in the valley surrounded by vine covered hills. A r. turn leads to Badia a Coltibuono. This old foundation is now a Chianti estate but still retains a fine Romanesque church and a few remains of the Benedictine abbey. ▶ The route then heads for Radda in Chianti *(W via the SS 429)* and Greve *(NW, turn r. on to the SS 222 Chiantigiana)*. Radda is the unofficial capital of Chianti and has a number of 15C (Palazzo Comunale) and 16C palaces amid its predominantly medieval buildings. Greve has a fine piazza, flanked by two arcades, which converge diagonally on the façade of the church of S. Croce. ▶ The SS 222 Chiantigiana heads N toward Florence, but the itinerary turns off to the l. to reach Mercatale, which was in the past a commercial centre. ▶ Next follows San Casciano in Val di Pesa, an old wine centre with a considerable amount of modern industrial development. It was long a commercial and artistic centre, and a visit to the church of the Misericordia is a must (fine works★ by Simone Martini, Giovanni di Balduccio, Taddeo Gaddi and Ugolino di Nerio). ▶ The route then follows the Cassia S through enchanting countryside past the straggling town of Tavernelle Val di Pesa

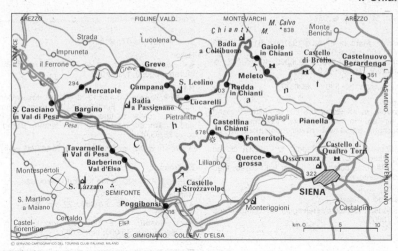

3. Il Chianti

to the fortified walls of **Barberino Val d'Elsa.** It too boasts a number of works of art and the municipio has a good collection of Etruscan finds. ▶ **Poggibonsi** is a lively modern town. It has undergone a fair amount of industrial development and is now an important wine and oil market. ▶ **Castellina in Chianti** stands on a hill to the E *(via the SS 429)* between the Arbia, Elsa and Pesa Valleys. Now a vacation centre, its medieval v. delle Volte offers a splendid view of this historic part of Tuscany. The countryside is breathtaking and remains so for the rest of the route, as it follows the SS 222 into Siena. □

Practical information ─────────────

BADIA A COLTIBUONO, ⊠ 53013, ☎ 0577.

Restaurant:
● ♦♦♦ *Badia a Coltibuono,* ☎ 749424, closed Mon and 4 Nov-15 Dec. In country amid pines and cedars. Regional cuisine: homemade tagliatelle, meat with seven herbs, homemade Chianti Classico, 25/45,000.

Recommended
Wine: visit to *P. Stucchi Prineti,* ☎ 749498 (reserve in advance).

BARBERINO VAL D'ELSA, ⊠ 50021, ☎ 055.

⚐ ★★ *Semifonte,* 95 pl, ☎ 8075454.

Recommended
Youth hostel: *Ostello del Chianti,* at Tavarnelle Val di Pesa, v. Cassia, ☎ 8077009.

CASTELLINA IN CHIANTI, ⊠ 53011, ☎ 0577.

Hotels:
★★★★ *Tenuta di Ricavo,* at Ricavo, ☎ 740221, 25 rm 🅿 ⚐ ⚒ ✵ ▱ 1/2 Pens. closed Nov-Mar, 100,000.
★★★★ *Villa Casalecchi,* ☎ 740240, 16 rm 🅿 ⚐ ⚒ ▱ closed Nov-27 Mar, 118,000; bkf: 10,000.

Restaurant:
♦ *Antica Trattoria La Torre,* p. Umberto I 17, ☎ 740236, closed Fri and 1-15 Sep. Family-run, 100 years old. Regional cuisine: risotto with fungi, game, 20/28,000.

⚐ ★ *Luxor Quies,* at Trasqua, ☎ 743047.

Recommended
Wine: visit to *Villa Cerna,* v. Chiantigiana, ☎ 743023 (Chianti Classico, Galestro); *Casa vinicola Cecchi,* at Casina dei Ponti, ☎ 743024.

CASTELNUOVO BERARDENGA, ⊠ 53019, ☎ 0577.

Recommended
Wine: visit to *Fattoria Pagliarese,* ☎ 359070 (Mon-Sat, also oil and grappa).

GAIOLE IN CHIANTI, ⊠ 53013, ☎ 0577.

Hotel:
★★★ *Castello di Spaltenna,* at Spaltenna, ☎ 749483, 11 rm 🅿 ⚒ closed 20 Jan-Feb. Fortified 13C monastery, 90,000; bkf: 10,000. Rest. ♦♦♦ closed Mon and Tue noon. Regional cuisine: gnocchi with gorgonzola, mixed brochettes with fennel, best local Chianti, 30/40,000.

Recommended
Horseback riding: *Club ippico Cavalieri del Chianti,* at Fattoria S. Giusto, ☎ 363011 (associate of *ANTE*).
Wine: visit to *Cantine Barone Ricasoli,* at Madonna di Brolio *(10 km S),* (reserve in advance, ☎ 055/311961).

GREVE IN CHIANTI, ⊠ 50022, ☎ 055.

Hotel:
★★★ *Villa le Barone,* at Panzano, v. S. Leolino 19, ☎ 852215, 26 rm 🅿 ⚒ ⚐ ▱ closed Nov-Mar, 95,000.

Restaurants:
♦♦ *Trattoria dei Montagliari,* ☎ 852184, closed Mon and Aug. Large fireplaces and a garden. Regional cuisine: farmhouse tripe, spit roast game, 30/40,000.
♦ *Omero Casprini,* at Passo dei Pecorari, ☎ 850716, closed Wed and Aug. Regional cuisine: cannoli with ricotta, tagliatelle with porcini, 20/28,000.

Recommended
Wine: *Enoteca del Consorzio Chianti Classico,* p. S. Croce 8, ☎ 853297.

POGGIBONSI, ✉ 53036, ☎ 0577.

Hotels:
★★★ *Alcide,* v. Marconi 67/A, ☎ 937501, 61 rm Ⓟ ⌀
closed Jul, 53,000; bkf: 6,000.
★★★ *Europa,* v. Senese 293, ☎ 936069, 40 rm Ⓟ ♨ &
⌀ No restaurant, 54,000; bkf: 6,000.

RADDA IN CHIANTI, ✉ 53017, ☎ 0577.

Restaurants:
● ◆◆◆ *Petroio,* v. XX Settembre 23, ☎ 738094, closed
Thu and Dec-Feb. In former oil mill. Regional cuisine:
green gnocchetti, rabbit with olives, homemade wines,
25/35,000.
◆◆ *Villa Miranda,* at Villa a Radda, ☎ 738021, closed
Tue. Long-standing family management, produce from
the estate. Regional cuisine: wild boar with olives, fried
chicken, homemade wines, 25/35,000.

Recommended
Farm vacations: *Fattoria Castelvegghi,* at Santa Maria
Novella, ☎ 738050.

Siena 78, Florence 126, Rome 159 km
Pop. 9,284 ✉ 53043 ☎ 0578   E4

During the late Middle Ages the S part of the Valdichiana was an area of contention between Orvieto,
Perugia, Siena and Florence. However, in the much
more distant past (7C-5C BC) Chiusi was a power in
its own right, with an Etruscan city surrounded by
massive walls on the hilltop. It was so prosperous that its soldiers were able to lay siege to
Rome. Today, the Museo Nazionale contains finds
from this extraordinary period. Virtually nothing survives of the Etruscan civilization except for the layout
of the roads, which was in turn adopted by the
Romans in the 4C.

▶ The Romanesque **Duomo** was poorly restored in the
last century, but it still has a fine interior with a series of
columns taken from Roman buildings. ▶ In the **Museo
della Cattedrale** are a number of superbly illuminated 15C
choir books. ▶ Late medieval and Renaissance palazzi
line the v. Arunte and the v. Porsenna, which follow the
lines of the main streets of the Etruscan
town. ▶ Beneath the campanile *(apply to caretaker of
Museo Etrusco)* are large **cisterns★** from the 1C BC and
also one of the entrances to the extensive network of tunnels dug by the Etruscans under the city. ▶ The **Museo
Nazionale Etrusco** *(8 a.m.-2 p.m.; hols 9 a.m.-1 p.m.;
closed Mon)* houses an extremely interesting collection
which includes a series of **canopic vases** — ossu-
aries with lids shaped like a human head, typical of this
region. Another part of the collection contains a number of **buccheri,** brilliant, decorated black ceramic vases
produced in Chiusi. There are also amphoras, cups, pitch-
ers, funeral pillars, statues, urns and sarcophaguses,
including one large alabaster **sarcophagus★.** ▶ The
Piazza Vittorio Veneto includes a park with **Etruscan and
Roman remains.** ▶ Outside town are a number of large
frescoed **tombs** cut into the rock *(tours with a guide from
the museum)* although the **Tomba della Scimmia★** (of the
ape) at Poggio Renzo is temporarily closed. The **Tomba
Bonci Casuccini** has a beautiful original Etruscan travertine gate. The **frieze★,** which was painted with scenes
of dances and gymnastic competitions, has been partly replaced with copies and the originals are now in
the museum. Other interesting tombs include the **Tomba
della Pellegrina** (pilgrim) and the **Tomba del Granduca** (grand
duke) and the **Tomba della Tassinaia.** ▶ **Lake Chiusi**
and the smaller Lake Montepulciano offer an attractive
array of water plants.   □

Practical information _____
CHIUSI
ⓘ v. Porsenna 67, ☎ 227667.

Hotel:
★★ *Sfinge,* v. Marconi 2, ☎ 20157, 10 rm Ⓟ ⌀ No restaurant, 42,000; bkf: 3,000.

Restaurant:
● ◆◆◆ *Zaira,* v. Arunte 12, ☎ 20260, closed Mon except
summer and Nov. Furnished with Etruscan archaeological finds, cellar of tufa, family management. Regional
and Italian cuisine: rabbit with lemon, baked guinea
fowl, 25/35,000.

⚲ *Pesce d'Oro,* at Sbarchino, ☎ 21403 (all year).

Environs

QUERCE AL PINO, 4 km toward Chianciano.

Hotels:
★★★ *Patriarca,* ☎ 274007, 22 rm Ⓟ ♨ ⚬ 50,000;
bkf: 7,000.
★★★ *Rosati,* ☎ 274008, 27 rm Ⓟ ♨ & closed
20 Dec-15 Jan, 43,000; bkf: 5,000.

Siena 24, Florence 49, Rome 255 km
Pop. 16,300 ✉ 53034 ☎ 0577   D3

This town is divided into a lower part, the **Piano,** and
an upper part, the **Colle Alta.** Recent developments
in the **Piano** have changed its character, but the **Colle
Alta,** a long ribbon of stone that looks down on the
valley, remains untouched.

▶ In the lower town stands the fine church of **S. Agostino,**
with a Gothic façade and a Renaissance interior. ▶ In
the Colle Alta a massive arch stands in the middle of the
magnificent **Palazzo Campana★** (1539), through which
the main street of the Castello quarter runs. The street is
lined with 15C-16C houses and even older **tower houses,** although most of these are beyond the p. del
Duomo. The medieval texture of this area is preserved
in the streets which run parallel and at right angles to the
main street. The **via delle Volte★** is actually covered and
forms a tunnel running for over a hundred yards. ▶ The
borgo di S. Caterina and the **via dell'Amore** include a
number of picturesque features. The **Porta Nuova★** is a
fine example of Renaissance military architecture. ▶ The
Museo d'Arte Sacra and the **Museo Civico** house works
of art from the 12C-16C whereas the **Museo Archeologico** in the Palazzo Pretorio contains Etruscan finds.   □

Practical information _____

ⓘ p. Arnolfo di Cambio 5, ☎ 921692.

Hotels:
★★★ *Arnolfo,* v. Campana 8, ☎ 922020, 32 rm Ⓟ ⌀
closed Dec, 54,000; bkf: 5,500.
★★★ *Vecchia Cartiera,* v. Oberdan 5/9, ☎ 921107, 41 rm
Ⓟ & ⌀ closed Aug, 60,000.

Recommended
Events: craft show (Sep).
Swimming: v. XXV Aprile, ☎ 920883.
♥ purchases: glassware, blown-glass tumblers.

Arezzo 28, Florence 117, Rome 200 km
Pop. 22,819 ✉ 52044 ☎ 0575   E-F4

Cortona stands on a hill overlooking the Valdichiana
and has witnessed the transformation of the valley
below over the years. The Etruscans were the first to
cultivate the great plain through which flows a small
river. The Romans then built the Via Cassia (which

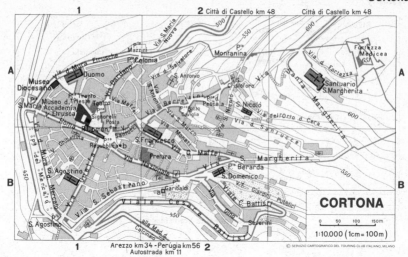

ran past the base of the hill) as the main route between Latium and the middle section of the Arno Valley. In the Middle Ages the entire area was progressively transformed into a marsh, resulting in a decline in trade. In the 16C and at the end of the 18C, large-scale reclamation projects reversed the original course of the river, carrying its waters down a gentle slope N to the Arno and restoring the land to agriculture. Today, the city has been bypassed by major roads and rail routes which follow the valley bottom and which have developed newer centres. Cortona is by no means isolated from the modern world even though it is one of the most important archeological, architectural and artistic sites in Tuscany. Besides its cultural attractions, the town has managed to combine agriculture and work by craftsmen with a brisk antiques trade.

▶ Approaching from Camucia, Cortona appears on a hill rising from a landscape of olive groves. In front of the hill stands its finest piece of architecture, the church of the **Madonna del Calcinaio★★**, a perfect example of Renaissance space and purity of design. ▶ The old, walled town itself is 3 km further up the hill and there is a climb of over 650 ft from the **Porta S. Maria** (A1). Outside and to the r. is a stretch of the old **Etruscan walls**. The **Fortezza Medicea** (A3) is the highest point in Cortona and offers breathtaking views★. ▶ The streets of the city exude history and atmosphere. The v. Maffei is lined with 16C mansions, while the v. Janelli has older 14C stone houses. ▶ The **v. Guelfa** and the **v. Ghibellina** were the main streets of the old town and they are lined with medieval and Renaissance buildings, while the major public buildings are grouped around the p. della Repubblica (E1). These include the **Palazzo Comunale** and, in the nearby p. Signorelli, the **Palazzo Pretorio** which houses the **Museo dell'Accademia Etrusca★** (10 a.m.-1 p.m. and 4-7 p.m.; winter 9 a.m.-1 p.m. and 3-5 p.m.; closed Mon), with its collections of Etruscan, Roman and Egyptian antiquities, as well as medieval and modern paintings, coins★ and costumes. Among its exhibits is an Etruscan bronze **lamp★** dating from the 5C BC. Another fine piece is the Egyptian funerary boat (XII dynasty) with carved wooden figures. There is also an important collection of paintings by the modern painter Gino Severini, who was born in Cortona. ▶ Shrines with a mosaic by Severini line the steep final stretch of the v. S. Mar-

gherita which leads up to the sanctuary of the same name. ▶ The **Duomo** (A1; 15C-16C) faces the former church of of the Gesù, which now houses a magnificent **Museo Diocesano** (A1; 9 a.m.-1 p.m. and 3-5 or 6:30 p.m.; closed Mon). It contains works by Pietro Lorenzetti and Luca Signorelli (also from Cortona) as well as a marvelous *Annunciation★★* by Fra Angelico. ▶ It is a relief from climbing to arrive at the level **Passeggiata in piano**, which starts at the church of S. Domenico (B2).

Environs

▶ A short distance W amid cypress trees is a famous Etruscan tomb known as the **Tanella di Pitagora**. ▶ 11.3 km SE, the **Abbazia di Farneta** (→ Crete Senesi to Valdichiana) stands on a small hill.   □

Practical information _____

ℹ v. Nazionale 72 (B2), ☎ 603056.

Hotels:
★★★ **Portole,** at Pórtole, ☎ 691008, 20 rm ℗ ≼ ⬚ ⤴ closed Nov-Easter, 55,000; bkf: 3,000.
★★★ **San Luca,** p. Garibaldi 2 (B2 a), ☎ 603787, 56 rm ≼ 59,000.

Restaurant:
◆◆◆ **Loggetta,** p. Pescheria 3 (B1 b), ☎ 603777, closed Mon, Sun eve in winter and Jan-Feb. In restored wine cellars, family management. Regional and Italian cuisine: cannelloni, prosciutto in porchetta, 25/30,000.

Recommended
Cycling: G. S. Fratta, at Santa Caterina, ☎ 603009.
Events: worked copper fair (late Apr); national antique furniture fair (late Aug-Sep); festival of Tuscan food and produce (14-15 Aug); international cultural and study courses (Jun-Oct).
Farm vacations: Azienda San Lorenzo, ☎ 692005.
Horseback riding: Centro equitazione Casale, v. Teverina 134, ☎ 616088.
Swimming: at Sodo, ☎ 612638.
Youth hostel: Ostello San Marco, v. Maffei 57 (A1), ☎ 601392.

For the translation of a name of a meat, a fish or a vegetable, for the composition of a dish or a sauce, see the *Menu Guide* at the end of the Practical Holiday Guide; it lists the most common culinary terms.

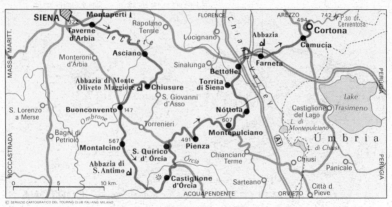

4. Crete Senesi to Valdichiana

CRETE SENESI TO VALDICHIANA

From Siena to Cortona *(161 km, 1 day; map 4)*

The countryside at either end of the route, from Siena to Cortona, is very different, but each is typically Tuscan. The Crete Senesi, at the start of the itinerary, are a succession of long rounded hills almost completely barren. After a brief burst of green in the spring, the hills become bare and the soil is parched and cracked. The Valdichiana, on the other hand, is lush and has extensive flat areas (unusual in an area with so many hills and mountains). Between these two extremes, the route passes hillsides covered with vines and barren slopes. The itinerary also includes many places of historical or artistic interest, many of which date from the Middle Ages. They include such marvels as the abbey of Monte Oliveto Maggiore and the churches of S. Antimo and Farneta, as well as towns like Pienza and Montepulciano. However, these are just the high points of the route that has something to offer at every point, whether it is the unusual landscape of Asciano or the splendid castle at Montalcino.

► The **Taverne di Arbia**, at the junction where the SS 438 turns off the SS 73 from Siena (→), recalls the great battle of Montaperti in 1260. The actual site of the battle is a short distance to the NE and is marked by a small pyramid on a hill surrounded by a double ring of cypresses. ► After the **Crete**, also known as 'Tuscan desert', the route arrives at the abbey of Monte Oliveto Maggiore★, which stands alone on a wooded hill. The gatehouse *(9 a.m.-12:45 p.m. and 3-6:45 p.m. or 5 p.m. in winter)* features a tower and a large glazed terra-cotta over the gate. It opens onto a broad avenue with a botanical garden on one side and cypresses on the other. At the end is the apse of the church with a Gothic façade and an elegant portal. The cloisters of the monastery house an outstanding Renaissance fresco cycle of the *Life of St. Benedict*★★ by Luca Signorelli and Sodoma. Inside the church is a magnificent set of 16C wooden **choir stalls**★ with images of birds and fountains and views of Siena. The abbey has a beautiful **library**, divided into three aisles by colonnades. It displays illuminated choir books. ► The road then winds down to the reddish

medieval walls and to the farmhouses of **Buonconvento**, where the **Museo d'Arte Sacra della Val d'Arbia** *(Tue and Thu 10 a.m.-12 noon; Sat also 4-6 p.m.; Sun 9 a.m.-1 p.m.)* has been open for several years. ► A few km S along the Cassia, turning r. down a provincial road and going through **Montalcino** (→), is the famous 12C Romanesque church of **S. Antimo★★**. It stands in a small valley by a stream, and it makes an immediate impression with its fascinating sculptures and reliefs of animals and imaginary creatures which adorn the portals of the façade. Inside *(caretaker, normally on site, lives at Castelnuovo dell'Abate, v. del Centro 12, ☎ 835676)* the architecture displays French influences. Features include the capitals, some carved of brilliant onyx. ► Continuing SE and turning l. on the SS 323, the route reaches **Castiglione d'Orcia**, with its lovely cobbled and brick piazza. Here is a magnificent view of Mt. Amiata and the Orcia Valley. ► The route rejoins the Cassia further N and then leaves it at **San Quirico d'Orcia** (→). It follows the SS 146, which leads to **Pienza** (→) and **Montepulciano** (→), both of which contain many works of art. At the Nóttola junction the route follows the SS 326 to the l. ► The old churches of **Torrita di Siena** (a farming and industrial centre) feature some fine paintings. ► A few km beyond the **Bettole** junction along the road to Cortona the church of the **abbey of Farneta** stands to the l. on a hill. Its **crypt★** is of particular interest both because of its unusual layout and because its vaults are held by columns removed from classical buildings which once stood in the area. In the sacristy are a number of exhibits including several palaeontological finds. ► From this point, Cortona (→) is a fifteen-minute drive. □

Practical information

CASTIGLIONE D'ORCIA, ⊠ 53023, ☎ 0577.
⚓ (May-Oct), at Bagni di San Filippo, ☎ 872982.
🛈 at Vivi d'Orcia, v. Amiata, ☎ 873820.

MONTE OLIVETO MAGGIORE ABBEY, ⊠ 53020, ☎ 0577.

Restaurant:
♦ *Torre,* ☎ 707022, closed Tue. In tower of abbey gatehouse. Regional cuisine: hunter's hare, escalopes with truffles, 20/25,000.

TORRITA DI SIENA, ⊠ 53049, ☎ 0577.

Restaurant:
● ♦♦♦ *Chiusa,* at Montefollonico, ☎ 669668, closed Tue except summer and 2 Jan-15 Mar. Combined farm

and restaurant, own produce and authentic local cooking. Regional cuisine: herb risotto, guinea fowl in white truffle sauce, homemade wines, 50/80,000.

The island of ELBA

From Portoferraio *(112 km, 1 day; map 5)*

Elba offers a rich and varied landscape which features deep gulfs and long headlands. However, this is the only constant feature. The rest of the coastline is at times made up of high, precipitous cliff, and at others, of gentle bays with pebble beaches or again of broad expanses of sand with pine forests or lush vegetation. To the N, the island has been transformed and is covered by terraced slopes and vineyards. Further inland the land rises and temperatures drop. The scrub-brush at the W end of the island reminds one of its original, untouched state. On the S slopes, cactus plants show that this is a Mediterranean climate. To the E there are vine covered hills beyond the reddish rocks.

▶ This itinerary around Elba leaves from the capital, **Portoferraio** *(→)*, and heads W. It starts with two brief detours, the first to **Capo d'Énfola**, at the tip of a small peninsula with clear waters teeming with fish; and the second to the **Villa Napoleonica di S. Martino** *(summer 9 a.m.-2 p.m.; hols 9 a.m.-1 p.m.; closed Mon)*, one of Napoleon's residences on the island. Next to it, the Neoclassical Villa Demidoff houses the Pinacoteca Foresiana. ▶ The itinerary proper begins at **Procchio**, now a popular tourist resort with a sandy beach. ▶ The houses of **Marciana Marina**, an old fishing village, are reflected in the waters of a harbour guarded by a round tower, built centuries ago by Pisa. Behind the semicircular beach, a valley covered with vineyards climbs into the interior and, higher up, there are chestnut forests. ▶ **Poggio** stands on a granite cliff, covered with oak and alder. ▶ The road reaches **Marciana**, after running along the coast. It features the picturesque ruins of a castle as well as a small **archaeological museum.** It is also a centre of the modern wine industry and has much to offer visitors who can stay overnight or use it as a base for the ascent of **Mt. Capanne** (3,340 ft); Elba's

highest mountain *(cableway).* ▶ Having gone around Mt. Capanne, the route now heads E. The deserted beach of **Fetovaia** contrasts sharply with the now fashionable **Marina di Campo** with its elegant restaurants. The old harbour was once reserved for fishermen, but now welcomes water skiers and luxury yachts. ▶ **Lacona** is the place for a quiet holiday by a sandy beach soaking up the Mediterranean's sun and salty air. ▶ In the SE corner of the island the neat houses which cling to **Capoliveri** hill are a reminder of the past of a village which has now been turned into a holiday resort. ▶ **Porto Azzurro** has changed its name to avoid confusion with Portolongone (the grim Spanish fortress, still used as a prison, which looks down on the town). With the expansion of its harbour basin, now teeming with pleasure boats, it has become a major tourist centre. ▶ The visitor enters a completely different world by taking a short detour to the I. along the Rio nell'Elba road to the **sanctuary of Monserrato.** It was built by the Spaniards in the 17C, possibly out of nostalgia for their famous Catalan monastery of Montserrat. ▶ Another detour leads to **Rio Marina,** in the heart of Elba's mining region. The rocks are a distinctive reddish colour and to the N of the village, long conveyors carry the ore to the sea. In the Palazzo Comunale is the small **Museo Minerario Elbano,** and it is possible to visit the mines during summer *(Sat 8-10 a.m.; reserve with management, ☎ 962001).* ▶ **Cavo,** which involves another detour along a hilly route, is also a seaside resort. ▶ The route then returns to the mining area and the old town of **Rio nell'Elba.** ▶ There are scant remains of the famous **Roman villa** at Le Grotte. □

Practical information

ⓘ at Portoferraio, calata Italia 26 (in harbour), ☎ 92671. ⚓ from Piombino: car ferries for Portoferraio *(→; c.* 1 hr, several sailings per day; advisable to reserve in summer); several boats a day for Porto Azzuro *(c.* 1 hr 20 mn) and Rio Marina *(c.* 45 mn); several hydrofoils a day for Cavo and Portoferraio *(c.* 30 mn); from Livorno: daily boats (direct, *c.* 3 hrs; with stops at islands of Gorgona and Capraia *(→)* and at Marciana Marina, *c.* 5 hrs); information and reservations: at Piombino (harbour), *Toremar,* ☎ 0565/31100, *Novarma,* ☎ 0565/33031; at Livorno, *Toremar,* ☎ 0586/24113; at Elba, *Toremar Portoferraio,* ☎ 0565/918080, Rio Marina, ☎ 0565/962073, Porto Azzurro, ☎ 0565/95004, Cavo, ☎ 0565/949871, *Novarma* Portoferraio, ☎ 0565/918101.

5. The island of Elba

CAPOLIVERI, ⊠ 57031, ☎ 0565.

Hotels:
★★★ *Acacie,* at Naregno, ☎ 968526, 100 rm P ⅏ ⌷ ⌁
closed 11 Oct-14 May, 70,000.
★★★ *Capo Sud,* at Lacona, ☎ 964021, 39 rm P ⌇ ⅏ ⋖
⌁ closed Oct-14 May, 70,000; bkf: 9,000.
★★★ *Elba International Hotel e Residence,* at Naregno,
☎ 968611, 242 rm P ⅏ ⌷ ⌁ closed Oct-Mar, 67,000.

Recommended
Horseback riding: *Costa dei Gabbiani equestrian centre,*
☎ 968402; at Verona, ☎ 045/30140 (4-day riding trips,
except Jul-Aug).
Skindiving: *Corsaro Sub,* at Pareti, ☎ 968679 (instruction).

MARCIANA, ⊠ 57030, ☎ 0565.

Hotels:
★★★ *Bel Tramonto,* at Patresi-II Mortaio, ☎ 908027,
25 rm P ⌇ ⌇ ⅏ closed Nov-14 Mar, 75,000.
★★★ *Cernia,* at Sant'Andrea, ☎ 908194, 20 rm P ⌇ ⅏
⌷ ⌁ Pens. closed Nov-14 Mar, 75,000.
★★★ *Gallo Nero,* at Sant'Andrea, ☎ 908017, 21 rm P ⌇
⅏ ⌷ ⌁ closed 21 Oct-Mar, 70,000; bkf: 8,000.

Restaurant:
♦♦ *Publius,* at Poggio, p. XX Settembre 13, ☎ 99208,
closed Mon except summer and 20 Oct-20 Mar. Mixed
cuisine: spaghetti with lobster, homemade tagliatelle,
25/40,000.

Recommended
Excursions: cable cars up Mt. Capanne, ☎ 901020.

MARCIANA MARINA, ⊠ 57033, ☎ 0565.
≋

Hotels:
★★★ *Conchiglia,* v. XX Settembre 31, ☎ 99016, 41 rm P
⅏ ⌹ ⌷ closed 15 Oct-15 Nov, 70,000.
★★★ *Gabbiano Azzurro,* v. Amedeo 46, ☎ 99226, 43 rm
P ⋖ ⌷ No restaurant, 60,000.

Recommended
Marina: ☎ 99169; *Circolo della vela,* ☎ 99027.

MARINA DI CAMPO, ⊠ 57034, ☎ 0565.
≋

Hotels:
★★★★ *Select,* v. Mascagni 2, ☎ 97100, 77 rm P ⌇ ⅏ ⋖
⌷ closed 6 Oct-14 Apr, 180,000.
★★★ *Bahia,* at Cavoli, ☎ 987055, 40 rm ⌇ ⅏ ⌁ closed
Nov-Mar, 70,000; bkf: 15,000.
★★★ *Barcarola Due,* v. Mascagni 38, ☎ 97255, 28 rm P
⅏ closed Oct-Mar, 68,000; bkf: 10,000.
★★★ *Coralli,* v. degli Etruschi 81, ☎ 97336, 60 rm P ⅏
⌷ ⌁ closed Oct-May. No restaurant, 95,000.
★★★ *Galli,* at Fetovaia, ☎ 987065, 18 rm P ⌇ ⅏ ⋖
closed 21 Oct-9 Apr, 69,000; bkf: 10,000.
★★★ *Riva,* v. degli Eroi 11, ☎ 97316, 40 rm P ⌇ ⋖ ⌁
21 Oct-Mar, 66,000.
★★★ *Santa Caterina,* v. Elba, ☎ 976745, 39 rm P ⅏
closed Oct-Mar,70,000; bkf: 10,000.

Restaurant:
♦ *Triglia,* v. Roma 52, ☎ 97059, closed Thu except
summer and Nov-Feb. Regional seafood: cacciucco, red
mullet livornese, 25/35,000.

⌂ ★★★ *La Foce,* at La Foce, 100 pl, ☎ 97456.

Recommended
Flying: airport, at La Pila, ☎ 97011.
Marina: *Club del mare,* ☎ 976805.
Tennis: at La Serra, ☎ 976771.

PORTO AZZURRO, ⊠ 57036, ☎ 0565.
≋

Hotel:
★★★ *Belmar,* v. IV Novembre, ☎ 95012, 26 rm ⌇ closed
Nov, 55,000; bkf: 6,000.

⌂ ★★ *Roclan's,* at Barbarossa, 124 pl, ☎ 957803.

Recommended
Horseback riding: *Country Place,* at Reale, ☎ 95572
(associate of *ANTE*).
Marina: ☎ 95195.

PROCCHIO, ⊠ 57030, ☎ 0565.
≋

Hotels:
★★★★ *Désirée,* ☎ 907502, 72 rm P ⌇ ⅏ ⌇ ⌷ ⌁
closed 11 Oct-14 Apr, 80,000.
★★★★ *Golfo,* ☎ 907566, 95 rm P ⌇ ⅏ ⌷ ⌁ closed
Oct-14 Apr, 64,000.
★★★ *Valle Verde,* ☎ 907545, 32 rm P ⅏ closed Oct-Mar,
75,000; bkf: 10,000.

Recommended
Windsurfing: *Elba Surf,* v. del Mare, ☎ 907833 (instruction).

RIO MARINA, ⊠ 57038, ☎ 0565.
≋

Hotels:
★★★ *Cristallo,* at Cavo, p. Matteotti, ☎ 949898, 46 rm P
⅏ ⌁ closed Oct-May, 70,000; bkf: 7,000.
★★★ *Marelba,* at Cavo, ☎ 949900, 70 rm P ⌇ ⅏ closed
Oct-14 May, 70,000; bkf: 10,000.
★★★ *Maristella,* at Cavo, v. Kennedy, ☎ 949859, 24 rm
P ⌇ ⅏ ⌇ closed Oct-May, 70,000; bkf: 8,000.
★★★ *Rio,* v. Palestro 31, ☎ 962016, 38 rm, closed Oct-
Mar, 68,000; bkf: 8,000.

Restaurant:
♦ *Canocchia,* v. Palestro 3, ☎ 962432, closed Mon and
Dec-Feb. Mixed cuisine: penne with lobster, bistecca alla
fiorentina, 25/40,000.

⌂ ★★ *Canapai,* at Ortano, 76 pl, ☎ 943271.

Recommended
Marina: ☎ 962109; *Circolo velico Elbano,* ☎ 962005; at
Cavo, ☎ 949910.

EMPOLI

Florence 32, Rome 302 km
Pop. 44,821 ⊠ 50053 ☎ 0571   D3

Since the end of the Second World War, Émpoli and
Pontedera (→) have been central in transforming the
lower Arno Valley from an essentially agricultural area
into a highly industrialized one. This has perhaps
been the single most important development in Tuscany in this century. Émpoli has long had a glass
industry, but to this has been added a garment sector
(specializing in raincoats). In this context, the major
events of past centuries, such as the famous Ghibelline meeting of 1260 during which the question of
razing Florence to the ground was discussed, seem
very distant.

▶ However, as soon as the visitor steps into the p. Farinata degli Uberti, the white and black Romanesque patterns on the façade of the **Collegiata★** make it clear
that there is another side to Émpoli: its art. The city's art
remained influenced by Florence for centuries. ▶ This
becomes even more apparent at the **Museo della Colle-
giata★** *(10 a.m.-12 noon; closed Mon; apply to sacristan
of S. Agostino on Sun)* with its rich collection of 14C-17C
works of art, including paintings by Filippo Lippi, Lorenzo
Monaco and Pontormo, bas-reliefs by Mino da Fiesole
and Tino da Camaino and an outstanding *Pietà★* fresco
by Masolino da Panicale. ▶ Examples of the beauty of
Masolino's painting can also be seen in the 14C Augustinian church of **S. Stefano,** where there is a particularly
fine *Madonna and Child★* (1424).

Environs

▶ There are a number of places to visit nearby, but special emphasis should be placed on **Fucecchio** *(11.7 km)*. Set amid the rolling hills of Cerbaie covered with forests and olive trees, it features a tall brick collegiate church on its piazzale. □

Practical information

🛈 p. Farinata degli Uberti 8/9, ☎ 76115.

Hotel:
★★★ **Commercio**, p. Ristori 16, ☎ 77247, 21 rm P closed Aug. No restaurant, 75,000; bkf: 6,000.

Restaurant:
♦♦ **Bianconi**, at Bianconi, v. Tosco-Romagnola 70, ☎ 90675, closed Wed and Jul. Regional and Italian cuisine: risotto, baked fish, 20/30,000.

Recommended
Events: Busoni piano days (Oct-Nov).

FIGLINE VALDARNO

Florence 32, Rome 241 km
Pop. 15,585 ⊠ 50063 ☎ 055   D3

The **historical centre** still has long sections of its old walls. The dignity and elegant lines of some of the houses and churches show a certain amount of taste and prosperity. The town prospered for centuries through its trading activities, which were so extensive that, by the 13C, its merchants had for decades been well known in France and in Flanders.

▶ There is a magnificent 14C *Madonna and Child with Angels and Two Saints*★ in the collegiate church of **S. Maria** in the p. Marsilio Ficino. ▶ Opposite are the 15C loggias of the former **Spedale Serristori.**

Environs

▶ One of the odder sights in Tuscany is the **Villa Sanmezzano** *(12 km N, then short distance to the r.)*, now a hotel. A *belle époque* villa, its enchanting Byzantine and Peacock Rooms have been decorated in Arab-Moorish style. □

Practical information
FIGLINE VALDARNO

⚐ ★★★ *Figline Agriturismo*, v. Norcenni 7, ☎ 959666 (all year).

Environs
VILLA SANMEZZANO, ⊠ 50066, ☎ 055, 12 km N.

Hotel:
★★★★ **Castello di Sanmezzano**, ☎ 867911, 18 rm P ⚐ 🕮 155,000; bkf: 10,000.

FIVIZZANO

Massa 43, Florence 163, Milan 221 km
Pop. 11,064 ⊠ 54013 ☎ 0585   B1

A number of elegant Renaissance palaces stand inside the ring of walls of Fivizzano.

Environs

▶ 1 km distant, standing on a hilltop at Verrùcola, there is a **Malaspina** castle (partly 14C) with a free-standing watch tower. ▶ Romanesque capitals are the main features of two parish churches; **S. Maria Assunta**, 3 km away in a deserted area with a fine view; and **S. Paolo Vendaso**, 4 km away on the road leading to the Cerreto Pass. ▶ 15 km S is the **Equi Terme** spa and a lit-

tle way outside the village is a **cave** which has yielded palaeontological finds *(9 a.m.-12 noon and 2-5 or 4-7 p.m.).* □

Practical information

FIVIZZANO
🛈 v. Roma 133, ☎ 92017.

Hotel:
★★ **Giardinetto**, v. Roma 151, ☎ 92060, 16 rm P 🕮 ⚐ closed Oct, 31,000; bkf: 3,000. Rest. ♦♦ closed Mon. Regional cuisine: polenta with porcini, charcoal grilled meats, 20/25,000.

⚐ ★ *Alboino*, at Gassano, SS 63 at 10.7-km marker, 80 pl, ☎ 93073.

Recommended
Events: *challenge between archers of Land and Court* (2nd Sun in Jul).

Environs

EQUI TERME, ⊠ 54022, ☎ 0585, 15 km S. ⚐ (Jun-mid-Oct), ☎ 97690.

FOIANO DELLA CHIANA

Arezzo 28, Florence 109, Rome 188 km
Pop. 7,706 ⊠ 52045 ☎ 0575   E4

There are a number of craft and industrial firms in Foiana della Chiana, but the area is primarily devoted to farming.

▶ Foiano contains a number of interesting old buildings including the remains of a **castle**, the **scalinata della torre** and the 18C **Logge del grano**. ▶ The **collegiate church** contains an important group of Renaissance terra-cottas and a painting by Luca Signorelli. ▶ Inside the church of **S. Maria della Fraternità** are fine examples of 17C-18C carved wooden furniture.

Environs

▶ *C.* 5 km NW near the cemetery of Pozzo is the octagonal temple of **S. Vittoria** (16C), commissioned by Cosimo I to celebrate the battle of Scannagallo in 1554. □

Practical information

Recommended
Events: *Carnival* with parade of floats.

FOSDINOVO

Massa 22, Florence 137, Milan 228 km
Pop. 3,629 ⊠ 54035 ☎ 0187   B1

The original town was clustered around the base of the imposing and spectacular **Castello de Malaspina** (13C-14C; *9 a.m.-12 noon and 3-6 p.m.; closed Mon*), which commands splendid vistas from its hilltop position. □

Practical information

Hotel:
★★★ **Don Rodrigo**, v. Cucco, ☎ 68861, 17 rm P ⚐ 🕮 closed Nov, 44,000.

La GARFAGNANA

From Lucca *(125 km, 1 day; map 6)*

Borgo a Mozzano, Bagni di Lucca, Coreglia Antelminelli. These villages fueled a dispersal that has become legendary: that of the statue makers who

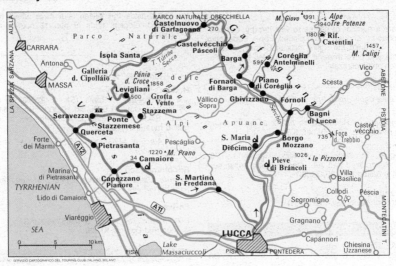

6. La Garfagnana

emigrated, carrying their plaster statuettes as far as America. There was also a great deal of emigration from the Garfagnana, the beautiful but impoverished wooded valley which runs between the Apennine mountains and the Apuan Alps. At the lower levels, the hillsides are terraced for farming, while sheep graze on the high pastures. Over the centuries, the main source of food has been chestnut flour. The Versiliese people, on the other hand, are rooted to their land, to their mountain rich with minerals and beds of marble. Here, historical centres such as Seravezza and Camaiore have developed along the coastal plain, at the foot of the Apuan Alps, with their jagged peaks and immense, overhanging cliffs. It is amid these mountains that the visitor comes across one of the most spectacular sights in Italy: the centuries old, white marble quarries.

▶ From Lucca (→ the route follows the r. bank of the Serchio to **Diécimo,** where there is the 13C parish church of S. Maria set amid vines, fields and olive trees. ▶ At **Borgo a Mozzano** is a humpbacked bridge over the Serchio. ▶ Across the river and on the Abetone SS the route reaches **Bagni di Lucca,** which was popularized as a spa by Elisa Baciocchi (Napoleon's sister) although its warm mineral waters have been consumed and used for baths, mud treatments and to treat arthritis and similar ailments for centuries. ▶ From **Piano di Coreglia,** on the l. of the Serchio, a turn-off from the Garfagnana SS leads to **Coreglia Antelminelli,** once the fief and stronghold of the mighty Castracani family. There is also a very beautiful 16C **processional cross** *(see the parish priest)* and a **museum** *(summer 4-7 p.m.; winter 10 a.m.-12 noon; apply to Comune),* which houses a collection of plaster figurines. ▶ From Fornaci di Barga, still at the bottom of the valley, the route climbs to **Barga** (→) and then descends again to **Castelvecchio Pascoli** where the house in which the poet Giovanni Pascoli lived and wrote for many years is still intact. ▶ At **Castelnuovo di Garfagnana,** back in the Serchio Valley but further upstream, the castle where

The poet governor

Since he had to provide for four brothers and five sisters, Ludovico Ariosto, the greatest Italian poet of the 16C and the author of Orlando Furioso, chose to work for Cardinal Ippolito d'Este. He went with him into battle, he acted as his envoy but also brought him drinks in bed, and he waited at night to help him undress. He left the service when the cardinal became Bishop of Buda in Hungary and transferred his employ to that of Ippolito's brother, Alfonso I d'Este, Duke of Ferrara and Modena. Alfonso made him governor of the Garfagnana, one of the Este dominions, and Ariosto spent 1522-25 in the Rocca di Castelnuovo di Garfagnana (still extant), settling disputes and fighting brigands. He was a shrewd and wise official but was not happy in his post and longed for Ferrara and his beloved. 'This, where I live, is a deep ditch', he bemoaned. Of his task he wrote, 'I confess honestly that I am not the man to govern other men, I have too much pity and I have not the heart to deny what is asked of me'.

Ludovico Ariosto lived is today a picturesque group of towers and turrets, massive, sloping walls and slender columns. This marks the lower boundary of the Alta Garfagnana, a land of extraordinary and sometimes wild vistas, as well as areas such as **Parco dell'Orecchiella** (NW of Pania di Corfino), where nature can be enjoyed in all its glory. ▶ In the valley of the Tùrrite Secca is **Isola Santa,** which was a stopping point and shelter for travelers in the Middle Ages. It is still an oasis with a reservoir which reflects the houses that are half hidden in the greenery. ▶ Further on, there is the tunnel of Cipollaio, then Levigliani to the l. (a good base for excursions to the famous cave of Corchia, 2,625 ft deep). Finally the road descends to **Seravezza,** which stands at the confluence of two torrents, spanned by a series of small bridges. The beautiful 16C **villa** designed by Bartolomeo Ammanati was commissioned by the Medici, who wanted to work the quarries in the Altissimo (Michelangelo helped pull the blocks of marble out in 1517). ▶ Among Seravezza, **Pietrasanta** (→) and **Camaiore**, it is perhaps Camaiore which is the oldest, since its regular layout possibly dates back to the Romans. The parish church, known as the **Collegiata**, the church of **S. Michele** and the **Badia Benedettina** (Benedictine abbey) are all Romanesque. ▶ From here the road back to Lucca follows the Freddana Valley. ☐

Practical information _____

BAGNI DI LUCCA, ☒ 55022, ☎ 0583.
♨ (Feb-Nov), ☎ 87223.
ⓘ at Villa, v. Umberto I 101, ☎ 87245.

Hotel:
★★ *Bridge,* at Ponte a Serraglio, ☎ 87147, 14 rm ℗ ⌘ No restaurant, 36,000; bkf: 5,000.

Restaurant:
♦♦ *Ruota,* at Fornoli, v. Giovanni XXIII 29/A, ☎ 86071, closed Mon eve, Tue and Aug. Regional cuisne: risotto, polenta and mushrooms, 25/30,000.

Recommended
Convention centre: Casino Municipale, ☎ 87123.

CAMAIORE, ☒ 55041, ☎ 0584.
ⓘ at Lido di Camaiore, ☎ 64397.

Restaurant:
♦♦ *Emilio & Bona,* at Lómbrici, ☎ 989289, closed Mon and Jan. Regional cuisine: ravioli ai pinoli, roast shank of pork, 30/45,000.

Recommended
Events: *Giotto d'oro,* international prize for madonnari (pavement artists, late Jun).

CASTELNUOVO DI GARFAGNANA, ☒ 55032, ☎ 0583.
ⓘ at the Rocca, ☎ 62268.

Hotel:
★★ *Carlino,* v. Garibaldi 13, ☎ 62045, 33 rm ℗ ⫿⫿⫿ closed Jan, 48,000; bkf: 4,000.

⚴ ★★ *Parco Agrituristico la Piella,* at La Piella, 500 pl, ☎ 62916 (all year).

Recommended
Swimming: v. Puccini, ☎ 63310.
♥ gastronomy: cheese, walnuts, honey.

PARCO DELL'ORECCHIELLA, 3,707 ft.
ⓘ forestry administration, at Lucca, v. Giusti 23, ☎ 0583/955525; forestry station at Corfino *(13 km N of Castelnuovo di Garfagnana),* ☎ 0583/660096.

The island of GIGLIO

Grosseto 74, Florence 214, Rome 183 km
Pop. 1,644 ☒ 58013 (Giglio Porto), 58012 (Campese)
☎ 0564   C-D6

Even groups of modern tourists are preferable to the repeated conquests and incursions by pirates which the island was subjected to until 1799. Until relatively recently, the only sources of employment for the population were fishing, vine growing and a small pyrite mine. Now hotels, tourist villages and camp sites have multiplied, and a new town (Campese) has sprung up next to Giglio Porto and Giglio Castello.

▶ **Giglio Porto** is located on a bay on the E coast. The soft, pleasant colours of its houses are set off against a background of hills covered with terraces and vineyards. ▶ The fortified village of **Giglio Castello** stands at the top of a steep hill (1,329 ft) overlooking the sea and is completely different in character. It is surrounded by a high ring of medieval walls with rectangu-

lar and cylindrical towers and once inside the walls becomes a maze of lanes and steep staircases up to the castle. ▶ A tower built by the Medici looks out over the bay toward **Campese** and the island's largest beach. ▶ From **Poggio della Pagana,** the highest point on the island (1,634 ft), there is a superb **view★** and, on a clear day, it is possible to see Corsica. ▶ A mule trail then leads S down a slope covered with granite boulders and outcrops to **Punta del Capel Rosso,** where there is a lighthouse. ☐

Practical information _____

≋
ⓘ at Giglio Porto, v. Umberto I, ☎ 809265 (seasonal).
⚓ several sailings a day from Porto Santo Stefano *(c.* 1 hr), cars can be taken (reserve in summer); information: *Toremar,* Porto Santo Stefano, ☎ 0564/814615; island of Giglio, ☎ 809349; *Maregiglio,* Porto Santo Stefano, ☎ 0564/812920, island of Giglio, ☎ 809309.

Hotels:
★★★ *Arenella,* at Giglio Porto, v. Arenella 5, ☎ 809340, 24 rm ⌘ 65000; bkf: 4,000.
★★★ *Campese,* at Giglio Campese, ☎ 804003, 39 rm ℗ ⫿⫿⫿ ⌘ closed Oct-Apr, 58,000.
★★★ *Castello Monticello,* at Giglio Porto, v. Provinciale ☎ 809252, 31 rm ℗ ⫿⫿⫿ ⁓ closed Oct-Mar (except Christmas), 65,000; bkf: 8,000.

Restaurants:
♦ *Beatrice,* at Giglio Campese, v. Provinciale 66, ☎ 804087, closed Tue and 15 Nov-15 Mar. Seafood: cold pasta, sailor's risotto, 20/30,000.
♦ *Maria,* at Castello, v. della Casamatta 12, ☎ 806062, closed Wed and 7 Jan-10 Mar. In medieval building declared a national monument. Seafood: risotto alla crema di gamberi, shellfish, 30/40,000.
⚴ ★ *Baia del Sole,* at Sparvieri, Giglio Campese, ☎ 804036.

Recommended
Marina: at Giglio Porto, ☎ 809036.
Young people's facilities: birdwatching and natural history courses; watercolour courses (flowers and plants); *Hotel Hermitage,* Cala degli Alberi, ☎ 809034 (Apr-Jun).

The church of San Pietro di GROPINA

Arezzo 32, Florence 68, Rome 251 km
☒ 52024 ☎ 055   E3

The **church★** stands on the slope of Pratomagno and is one of the finest in the Valdarno. It dates from the start of the 11C — the massive campanile was built later — and inside it has a nave and two aisles with very pure lines. The historiated capitals have simple, archaic figures and they include two tigers and a pony bearing a knight with a shield. There is an unusual round marble **pulpit★** which is decorated with reliefs.☐

GROSSETO

Florence 142, Rome 181, Milan 440 km
Pop. 69,760 ☒ 58100 ☎ 0564   D5

Like many of the habitations in the countryside around it, Grosseto is virtually entirely new, except for the historical town centre within the hexagonal Medici town walls. However, even this historical heart is very much a part of the modern world, serving the Maremma area (→) as a commercial and administrative centre even more today than in the past.

▶ The 14C **Duomo★** in the p. Dante has been restored several times and features a brick campanile (1402). ▶ In the last century the ramparts and bastions of the old **walls,** which were built after the city passed from Siena to Florence, were transformed into avenues and gardens

1   Marina di Pisa km 17   2   Autostrada km 5 - Pisa km 19

A

Staz.
Marittima

S.Ferdinando

Fortezza
Vecchia

Traghetto
per Corsica,
Elba e Sardegna

Capitaneria
di Porto

Porto
Mediceo

Mon.
4Mori

Molo Mediceo

Faro

Staz.
S.Marco
F.S.

P.za
XI Maggio

S.Giuseppe

Via Garibaldi

Campo
Sportivo

Fosso Reale

Fortezza
Nuova

S.Andrea

Garibaldi

S.Andrea

Cisternone

Giardino
Pubblico

Munic
Larga
Municipio

Prefettura

Via S.Giov.

Via Grande

Duomo
Tel.

Via d. Bastione

Viale   Carducci

Barriera
Garibaldi

P.za Ferrucci

Campo
Sportivo

De Laderel

P.za d.
Repubblica

Guerrazz

Serlembra

Posta e
Tel.

Giardino
Pubblico

B.Chiesa

Fosso Reale

P.za Cavour

Via G. Verdi

Via F. Rossi

Via Maggi

P.za d.
Vittoria

S.Maria d.
Soccorso

Via Deni

Via G. Ferrigni

B

Mazzini

Corso Mazzini

Borgo dei

Via G. Borsi

Villa Maria
(Museo d'Arte
Contemporanea)

P.za
Mazzini

Orlando

Scoglio
d. Regina

Cappuccini

Matteotti

Viale

Viale della Libertà

COTETO

Autostrada km 7

V. Montebello

Museo Civico
(Villa Fabbricotti)

Acquario

Terrazza
Mascagni

Bagni Pancaldi
Acquaviva

Modigliani

Via S.Iacopo in Acquaviva

Via Roma

C

S.Iacopo
in Acquaviva

Accademia
Navale

Viale N.Sauro

Stadio

Rio M.

T Y R R H E N I A N

Ippodromo

Via dei Pensieri

Via Machiavelli

Bagni Fiume

ARDENZA

Staz. Ardenza
F.S.

Via G. Salvestri

Via Ricci

D

S E A

Via del Mare

V. O. Franchini
S.Simone

M.a d. Pastore

Bagni Lido

La
Rotonda

Rio Ardenza

LEGHORN

0   250   500m

1 : 27.000 (1cm=270m)

© SERVIZIO CARTOGRAFICO DEL TOURING CLUB ITALIANO, MILANO

2   Antignano

3   Grosseto km 134

A

by the last grand duke of Tuscany. It is possible to walk around them in half an hour. ▶ The **Museo Archeologico e d'Arte della Maremma** (*9:30 a.m.-12:30 p.m. and 4:30-8 p.m.; closed Wed and hol. p.m.*) contains a collection of Etruscan and Roman finds from the Maremma around Grosseto and provides excellent information about the exhibits (bronze statuettes, tufa carvings, coins, urns, antefixae and other architectural fragments). There is also a collection of religious art and of paintings which provide evidence of the long-lasting influence of Siena. One of the outstanding exhibits is a masterpiece by Sassetta, *Madonna of the Cherries* (15C).

Environs

▶ **Marina di Grosseto,** a growing seaside resort, is 13 km away, sandwiched between a **pine forest** and a fine sand beach. □

Practical information

GROSSETO
ⓘ v. Monterosa 20/B, ☎ 22534.
🚌 ☎ 22366.
🚖 from railway station, ☎ 25380.
Car rental: *Maggiore,* v. Ximenes 38, ☎ 20467.
Hotels:
★★★ *Nalesso,* v. Senese 35, ☎ 412441, 38 rm ℗ ⌇ No restaurant, 55,000; bkf: 6,000.
★★ *Maremma,* v. Fulceri Paolucci 11, ☎ 22293, 30 rm ⌇ closed Christmas. No restaurant, 47,000.
★★ *MotelAgip,* v. Aurelia Sud, at 179-km marker, ☎ 24100, 32 rm ℗ 58,500.
Restaurants:
● ◆◆◆ *Enoteca Ombrone,* v. Matteotti 71, ☎ 22585, closed Sat eve, hols, Jul and Dec-Jan. Converted Maremma villa, terrace in summer, fine cellar. Regional cuisine: Cecchino tagliatelle; prosciutto porchettato, 30/60,000.
◆◆◆ *Maremma,* v. Fulceri Paolucci 5, ☎ 21117, closed Sun eve, Tue and Jul-Aug. Veranda summer and winter. Maremma cuisine: fisherman's risotto, deviled chicken, 20/30,000.
◆◆ *Canapone,* p. Dante 3, ☎ 24546, closed Sun eve and Mon except Jun-Sep and 1-20 Jul. Maremma cuisine: charcoal grilled meats, hunter's wild boar, 21/31,000.

Recommended

Baseball: v. Repubblica, ☎ 492419.
Flying: at Maremma airport, v. Orcagna, ☎ 933096 or 492346; v. Oberdan 24, ☎ 415136.
Nature park: office at Alberese *(14 km S),* ☎ 407098.
Racecourse: *Casalone,* ☎ 24214 (horse racing at night, Wed and Sat, Jun-Aug; Grosseto international horse show, first Sun in Oct).
Tennis: *Circolo tennis Grosseto,* ☎ 493162.

Environs

MARINA DI GROSSETO, ✉ 58046, ☎ 0564, 13 km E.
≋
ⓘ v. Piave 10, ☎ 34449.

Hotels:
★★★ *Mediterraneo,* v. XXIV Maggio 70, ☎ 345000, 62 rm ⌇ closed 5 Nov-28 Dec, 70,000; bkf: 8,000.
★★★ *Rosmarina,* v. delle Colonie 33, ☎ 34408, 16 rm ℗ ⌇ 65,000; bkf: 7,000.

Restaurant:
◆ *Mario,* v. Baracca 2, ☎ 34472, closed Mon and Nov. Seafood: cacciucco, spaghetti alla pirata, 20/30,000.

⚠ ★★★★ *Cieloverde,* strada della Trappola, 900 pl, ☎ 30084; ★★★ *Rosmarina,* v. delle Colonie 37, 70 pl, ☎ 36319.

Recommended
Marina: ☎ 34475.

PRINCIPINA A MARE, 6 km SW.

Hotels:
★★★★ *Principe,* v. dello Squalo 100, ☎ 34598, 65 rm ℗ ⌇ 🖐 ⅙ ⌇ closed 16 Oct-Easter, 120,000.
★★★ *Grifone,* v. Pesce Persico 2, ☎ 34300, 38 rm ⌇ ⌇ closed 11 Oct-Mar, 70,000; bkf: 7,000.

LEGHORN

(Livorno)

Florence 115, Milan 295, Rome 310 km
Pop. 176,298 ✉ 57100 ☎ 0586   B3

Livorno was only a small village before the Medici commissioned Buontalenti to build an 'ideal' city in the second half of the 16C. Buontalenti laid the city out as a pentagon with a large harbour, and by the end of the 18C Leghorn (as it was then known to the English) was the second largest city in Tuscany. It owed its growth to its ideal position along the trade routes between Europe and the East. The tax exemptions that were granted and the fact that foreigners who settled here were allowed freedom to worship also contributed to growth. In the '20s and '30s, a new industrial port was built to the N and the outskirts of the city now include refineries and modern factories. The Italian Naval Academy is located here.

▶ Many parts of Livorno were destroyed during the last World War, but much has been rebuilt. ▶ The feeling of light and space along the **Fosso Reale** (A-B 1-2), lined with 19C palazzi with magnificent façades, is impressive. ▶ The broad **piazza delle Repubblica** (A2), which spans the canals, provides a splendid vantage point to see the red block of the **Fortezza Nuova** (A2, built by Medici architects in 1590). ▶ To see and visit the impressive 16C **Fortezza Vecchia** (A1; *open in summer*), the visitor must go to the **Vecchia Darsena** (Old Basin), not far from Livorno's most famous monument, the **Four Moors★** (A-B 1; 17C). ▶ **Venezia Nuova** (A1-2), the 17C part of the city, criss-crossed by canals between the two fortresses, was the heart of Livorno at the time. ▶ 19C Livorno has left two unusual Neoclassical monuments, the **Cisternone** (A3) and the **Cisternino** (A3), cisterns for the aqueducts which hide behind the impressive forms of ancient temples. ▶ Along the **viale Italia★,** (B-C 1, D2) the *belle époque* reigns as the avenue runs S past rows of vil-

Don't forget to consult the Practical Holiday Guide: it can help in solving many problems.

las.   On the way, one can stop at the **city aquarium** (C1; *summer 10 a.m.-12 noon and 3-6 p.m.*) or at the **Terrazza Mascagni**.   ▶ The **Museo Civico Fattori** houses paintings from the Tuscan Macchiaioli school and by Modigliani (C2; *10 a.m.-1 p.m.; Thu and Sat also 4-7 p.m.; closed Mon*) and the works of contemporary artists are on display in the **Museo Progressivo d'Arte Contemporanea** (B2; *same hours*).   However, no visitor ever really gets to know Livorno without mingling with the locals who crowd its **markets**.   The famous fish market is at the Darsena Vecchia, the daily market in the v. Buontalenti or the weekly market *(Fri)* in the v. Galilei (A2).

Environs

▶ The **Santuario di Montenero** *(9 km)* stands on a hill and houses numerous votive offerings (colourful images of accidents on sea and land which have befallen the local inhabitants, testaments to a naive but passionate faith).   There is a fine view★ from the piazza in front of the chapel.   ▶ 22 km S along the coast, **Castiglioncello** is an elegant seaside resort set amid headlands and bays and against a backdrop of pine trees.   ☐

Practical information _____

LEGHORN
≋

① p. Cavour 6 (B2), ☎ 33111 (main office); Palazzo Dogana, at harbour, ☎ 25320 (B1; information, seasonal).
🚋 (A2), ☎ 401105.
🚂 from p. Grande (A2) and v. Meyer (B2).
⚓ services to Elba and other islands of the Tuscan Archipelago (*Toremar*, ☎ 24113), Sardinia (*Sardinia Ferries*, ☎ 31001); Corsica (*Corsica Ferries*, ☎ 31001, *Novarma*, ☎ 28314) and Sicily (*Tirrenia* ☎ 34732).
Car rental: *Avis*, v. Garibaldi 49, ☎ 24090; *Hertz*, v. Mastacchi 59-63, ☎ 410515; *Maggiore*, v. Fiume 31-33, ☎ 30240.

Hotels:
★★★ **Boston,** p. Mazzini 40 (B1 a), ☎ 37333, 35 rm Ⓟ ✲ No restaurant, 66,000; bkf: 8,000.
★★★ **Giappone Inn,** v. Grande 65 (A2 b), ☎ 880241, 60 rm Ⓟ 64,000; bkf: 5,000.
★★★ **Gran Duca,** p. Micheli 16 (A-B1 c) ☎ 32024, 50 rm Ⓟ ♿ 65,000; bkf: 5,000.
★★★ **MotelAgip,** at Stagno, v. Aurelia 25, ☎ 943067, 50 rm Ⓟ ✲ 61,000.
★★ **Giardino,** p. Mazzini 85 (B1 d), ☎ 806330, 21 rm Ⓟ ▩ ✲ closed Christmas, 48,000.

Restaurants:
● ♦♦♦ **Gennarino,** v. S. Fortunata 11 (A2 i), ☎ 888093, closed Wed and Jan. Lovely veranda with plants. Regional seafood: penne scoglio, spaghetti pozzolana, 25/40,000.
♦♦♦ **Banditella da Cappa,** at Ardenza, v. Angioletti 3, ☎ 501246, closed Sun and Jul-Aug.   Mixed cuisine: white fish risotto, lobster with tomato, 45/60,000.
♦♦♦ **Barcarola,** v. Carducci 63 (A3 g), ☎ 402367, closed Sun and Aug.   Seafood: brochettes with squid and crayfish, cuttlefish alla parigina, 35/40,000.
♦♦♦ **Fanale,** Scali Novi Lena 15 (B1 h), ☎ 25346, closed Tue and 20 Aug-10 Sep.   Mixed cuisine: tagliatelle, crayfish, 30/40,000.
♦♦♦ **Oscar,** v. Franchini 78 (D3 l), ☎ 501258, closed Mon, 1-15 Sep and Christmas.   Seafood: scampi with linguine, brochettes of scampi, 30/45,000.
♦♦♦ **Torre di Calafuria,** at Calafuria, v. del Litorale 248, ☎ 580547, closed Tue and Nov.   In 16C Medici tower standing between the sea and the Aurelia.   Regional mixed cuisine: pappardelle mare, red mullet alla livornese, 28/32,000.
♦♦ **Sottomarino,** v. Terrazzini 48 (A2 m) ☎ 887025, closed Thu and 15 Jun-15 Jul.   Typical trattoria.   Regional fish cuisine— cuttlefish or shellfish risotto, spaghetti panna mare, cacciucco, red mullet alla livornese, fried fish, baked fish, several regions, 23/35,000.
♦ **Antico Moro,** v. Enrico Bartelloni 59 (B1 f), ☎ 884659, closed Wed. and Aug.   Simple, longstanding family tra-

dition, resembles a bistro.   Regional fish cuisine— shellfish spaghetti, penne with crab, risotto with cuttlefish, cacciucco; grilled fish, scampi and crayfish in guazzetto, elvers with sage (winter), regional, 20/25,000.

△ ★★ *Miramare,* at Antignano, SS Aurelia at 307-km marker, 200 pl, ☎ 580402.

Recommended
Aquarium: v. Italia (C1), ☎ 805504.
Events: *palio marinaro,* off Terrazza Mascagni (C1, Jul); *Coppa Barontini,* rowing competition on canals (Jul); *Coppa dei risicatori,* on open sea (Jul).   *Race meetings* at Ippodromo Caprilli.
Fencing: v. dei Pensieri, ☎ 505555.
Flying: *Livorno-Stagno Airport,* SS 555 at 2-km marker, ☎ 942675.
Horseback riding: *Società livornese di equitazione,* v. Condotti Vecchi 53, ☎ 400333.
Marina: *Molo Mediceo,* at yachtclub ☎ 30142; *Nazario Sauro,* ☎ 807354; *Antignano,* ☎ 580295.
Purchases: variety of items (particularly clothing) at *mercatino americano,* p. XX Settembre (A2).
Racecourse: *Caprilli,* at Ardenza.
Sailing: *Lega Navale,* v. Spianata Molo Mediceo 12/A, ☎ 23567; *Casa di vela Elba 74,* v. Mare, ☎ 505562.
Sports arena: v. dei Pensieri, ☎ 505452.

Environs

CASTIGLIONCELLO, ✉ 57012, ☎ 0586, 22 km S.
≋
① v. Aurelia 959, ☎ 752017 (seasonal).
Hotels:
★★★ **Martini,** v. Martelli 3/A, ☎ 752140, 30 rm Ⓟ ♿ ♨ ♿ closed Oct-Mar, 63,000.
★★★ **Miramare,** v. Marconi 8, ☎ 752435, 64 rm ⟨ ♨ ▩ closed Oct-Mar, 60,000; bkf: 10,000.
★★ **Guerrini,** v. Roma 12, ☎ 752047, 22 rm ♨ ▩ ✲ closed Nov, 43,000; bkf: 6,000.

Restaurant:
♦♦ **Poggetto,** v. del Sorriso 8, ☎ 752754, closed Mon and Oct-Jan.   With veranda and views.   Mixed cuisine: spaghetti with rosemary, salt fish, homemade wines, 25/45,000.

Recommended
Marina: ☎ 752310.
Tennis: v. Pineta, ☎ 752102.

LUCCA★★

Florence 71, Milan 275, Rome 349 km
Pop. 90,022 ✉ 55100 ☎ 0583   C2

By the time Napoleon declared Lucca a principality for his sister Elisa Baciocchi, it already had two thousand years of history to look back on as a town.   For several centuries, Lucca had also been the capital of a small independent republic.   It reached its peak between the 11C and the 13C.   Silk from Lucca was found in all the markets of the world; it had trading colonies everywhere and lent money to sovereigns and emperors.   Then, in the 16C, as its dynamic merchants settled down to become a landed aristocracy, the city built its last set of walls.   The construction took more than a century and after its completion Lucca enjoyed a long period of peace, resisting even the Jesuits and the Inquisition.   At the beginning of the 19C the broad ramparts of the walls were turned into a tree-lined ring.

▶ The city displays a wide range of moods, from the somewhat melancholy **via del Rosso** to the lively **via Fillungo★** (B-C 3), the favourite promenade of the people of Lucca.   It offers old goldsmiths' shops; a 13C **Torre delle Ore**, which has been a clock tower since 1471; and 14C **brick houses**.   ▶ At one point, the v. Fillungo runs alongside the **Anfiteatro Romano** (B3; 2C). At the beginning of the 19C, this superb amphitheatre was cleared of all the buildings which had sprung up inside it to form a piazza. ▶ The **Duomo★★** (C3) and the adjacent white and red Opera del Duomo form a striking corner of the p. S. Martino, which is the heart of medieval Lucca. Although the walls and interior of the cathedral are Gothic, the two-coloured marble **façade★** is Romanesque and features an asymmetrical portico crowned by graceful loggias. The portals and entrance wall bear fine Romanesque **reliefs★** but the cathedral's most important treasures are inside: the octagonal **Tempietto of the Volto Santo★**, which houses an ancient wooden crucifix, and the famous **Tomb of Ilaria del Carretto★★**, a masterpiece by Jacopo della Quercia (1408). ▶ There are a number of other churches in Lucca with Romanesque features, although each displays individual features. The oldest, **S. Alessandro** (C2), is compact and simple; **S. Pietro Somaldo** is decorated with Pisan-style horizontal green and white stripes, while **S. Anastasio** combines red brick and white stone. **S. Maria Forisportam** (C4) includes blind arcades, whereas **S. Frediano★★** (B3) has a smooth stone façade crowned by brilliant 13C mosaic. Its interior is richly decorated and contains a tall Romanesque **font★** and **reliefs★★** by Jacopo della Quercia. ▶ **S. Michele★★** (C2) is another splendid Romanesque church which displays very individual features. Its façade is crowned by a gigantic statue of an archangel and below are four tiers of highly ornate marble loggias with inlaid and carved polychrome columns. ▶ Lucca's palazzi are just as beautiful and diverse as the churches. The finest of these houses include the **Palazzo Bernardini**, a model of a 16C residence, and the **Palazzo Controni Pfanner**, which houses a permanent exhibit of silk and Lucchesi costumes. In the medieval quarter of the city, there are the no less fascinating 14C **Case dei Guinigi★** (B3). ▶ **Porta S. Gervasio** (C4) is one of the gates from the 13C walls and the two massive cylindrical towers give an idea of these massive defenses. In graceful contrast, there is the 14C oratory in the v. della Rosa (C3). ▶ The major museums include the **Pinacoteca Nazionale** (B1-2; *9 a.m.-2 p.m.; hols 9 a.m.-1 p.m.; p.m. opening is planned; closed Mon*), which is housed in the 17C **Palazzo Mansi★** with its splendid **Camera degli Sposi★** and paintings from the Renaissance to the 18C; the **Museo Nazionale★** in the 15C Villa Guinigi (B4; *9 a.m.-2 p.m.; hols 9 a.m.-1 p.m.; p.m. opening in summer is planned; closed Mon*), which displays archaeological finds and numerous paintings, sculptures, furniture and fabrics. Even the smaller collections contain a number of delightful surprises, such as the 15C gilded and dyed leather **casket★** (probably Spanish in origin) in the **Tesoro del Duomo**, or the splendid 12C Arab bronze falcon in the **museum** attached to S. Frediano.

Environs

▶ Over the centuries, Lucca's aristocracy built many splendid villas in the surrounding countryside. Outstanding examples include the **Villa Mansi**, 10 km NE, **Villa Torreggiani**, 1.5 km S and at **Marlia** *(1.5 km)* the **Villa Pecci-Blunt★**, a former Royal villa *(park only open to visitors)*. ☐

Practical information _____

LUCCA
ⓘ p. Guidiccioni 2 (B3), ☎ 41205 (main office); v. Vittorio Veneto 40 (C2), ☎ 43639 (information).
🚃 (D3), ☎ 47013.
🚌 from p. Verdi (C1).

Hotels:
★★★★ *Napoleon*, v. Europa 1, ☎ 53141, 63 rm Ⓟ ⅋ No restaurant, 115,500; bkf: 10,000.
★★ *Ilaria*, v. del Fosso 20 (C4 a), ☎ 47558, 17 rm. No restaurant, 53,000; bkf: 4,000.

Restaurants:
● ◆◆◆ *Buca di Sant'Antonio*, v. della Cervia 3 (C2 b), ☎ 55881, closed Sun eve, Mon and Jul. Rebuilt taverna

retaining original character. Regional cuisine: pappardelle with hare sauce, spit roast kid, 25/35,000.
◆ *Giglio*, p. del Giglio 2 (C2-3 c), ☎ 44058, closed Tue eve and Wed. Mixed cuisine: spaghetti with crab meat, giant sailor's scampi, 19/29,000.
◆ *Giulio*, v. S. Tommaso 29 (B1-2 d), ☎ 55948, closed Sun, Mon, Aug and Christmas. Regional cuisine: polenta with mushrooms, eels in sauce, 15/22,000.

Recommended
Botanical garden: (C4), ☎ 46665.
Events: *Sagra Musicale Lucchese* (Apr-Jun); *Estate Musicale; international singing competition* (Nov); *Settembre Lucchese* (philatelic and numismatic show); *opera season* in the Teatro del Giglio, ☎ 46147, *Festa della Santa Croce*); summer festival of music, theatre and cinema, at Màrlia.
Farm vacations: *Villa Casanova*, at Balbano *(10 km SW)*, ☎ 548429.
Flying: airport, at Capànnori, at Tassignano, ☎ 46677.
Sports arena: v. delle Tagliate, ☎ 46677 (fencing).
Youth hostel: *Ostello Il Serchio*, at Salicchi, v. del Brennero, ☎ 953686.
♥ antiques: market in p. S. Martino and p. Antelminelli (C3), 3rd Sun of month; café: *Antico Caffè di Simo*, v. Fillungo 58 (B3), ☎ 41148.

Environs

MASSA PISANA, ✉ 55050, 4 km toward Pisa.

Hotel:
★★★★ *Villa la Principessa*, v. Nuova for Pisa, ☎ 370037, 43 rm Ⓟ ♨ 〰 ☒ closed Nov-9 Apr. 19C villa built on ruins of villa of Castruccio Castracani, Lord of Lucca, 270,000; bkf: 15,000.

PIEVE SANTO STEFANO, 9 km NW.

Restaurant:
◆◆◆ *Vipore*, ☎ 59245, closed Mon and Tue noon. In 18C farmhouse with lovely terrace for dining in summer and splendid view. Regional cuisine: tortelli with ragù, lamb with olives, 30/40,000.

PONTE A MORIANO, ✉ 55029, 9 km toward Abetone.

Restaurant:
● ◆◆◆ *Mora*, v. Sesto 104, ☎ 57109, closed Wed eve, Thu and 1-15 Jul. First tavern, then rural trattoria and now a traditional restaurant with fine pergola for dining in summer. Regional cuisine: Serchio delicacies, trout al peperone dolce, 30/45,000.

SAN MACARIO IN PIANO, ✉ 55056, 6 km W.

Restaurant:
● ◆◆◆ *Solferino*, ☎ 59118, closed Tue eve, Wed, Christmas, Jan and Aug. Covered terrace with garden, long-standing family management. Regional cuisine: island turbot, duck stuffed with truffles, 30/50,000.

LUCIGNANO

Arezzo 28, Florence 109, Rome 194 km
Pop. 3,251 ✉ 52046 ☎ 0575   E4

Lucignano is another of the Valdichiana's hilltop towns, but is unusual in its compact, elliptical layout. The main road entering the town follows a spiral toward the centre, making two complete circuits.

▶ Housed in the 14C **Palazzo Comunale**, the Museo Civico contains the **Tree of St. Francis**, a famous old Sienese gold reliquary. ▶ The paintings in the 13C church of **St. Francis** are also Sienese. Nearby, the **Museo della Campagna** is devoted to old household implements and tools. ▶ 1 km outside the porta S. Giusto stands a 16C **Medici fortress**, and a little farther, the Renaissance sanctuary of the **Madonna delle Querce**, probably designed by Vasari. ☐

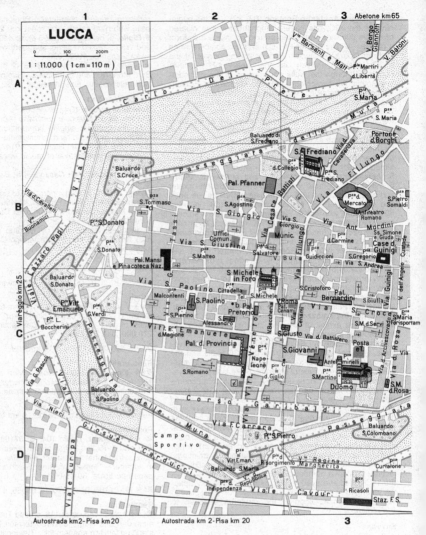

LUCCA

0   100   200m
1 : 11.000 (1 cm = 110 m)

Abetone km 65

Autostrada km 2 - Pisa km 20

Autostrada km 2 - Pisa km 20

Practical information

Hotel:
★★★ *Totò,* p. del Tribunale 6, ☎ 836763, 20 rm P
45,000; bkf: 7,000.

Recommended
Events: *Maggiolata,* festival of folk singing (last two Sun in May).

MAGLIANO IN TOSCANA

Grosseto 28, Florence 170, Rome 171 km
Pop. 4,215 ⊠ 58051 ☎ 0564   D5-6

Although Magliano has its own artworks and monuments, the main reason for the climb is the age-old **Ulivo della Strega** (the Witch's Olive Tree). It stands a little outside town, near the church of the Annunziata, and is one of the most famous olive trees in Tuscany. According to tradition, orgiastic pagan ceremonies were once performed near the tree in honour of woodland divinities.

▶ The Renaissance did not leave much of a mark on the Maremma and it is surprising to find as beautiful a piece of architecture as the elegant façade of the church of **S. Giovanni Battista.** The best buildings in Magliano are examples of Sienese Gothic. They include the beautiful 15C **walls,** which are crowned by arches; the **Palazzo dei Priori,** with a Gothic portal; and the so-called **Palazzo di Checco il Bello,** which has elegant double windows.
▶ 2.5 km SE lie the isolated ruins of the church of **S. Bruzio.** Several **Etruscan tombs** are to be found in the area.   □

Practical information

Restaurant:
♦ *Aurora,* p. Marconi 2, ☎ 592030, closed Wed and Sep-

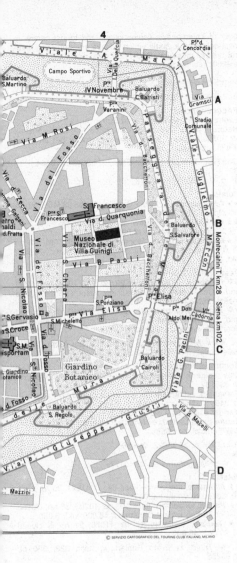

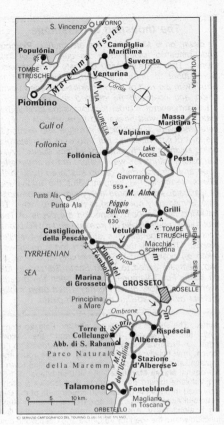

7. La Maremma

Oct. Family trattoria. Regional cuisine: wild asparagus pasticcio, roast guinea fowl or pigeon, 15/25,000.

Recommended
Horseback riding: at *Il Cardo*, ☎ 597126; *Centro Turismo Equestre*, ☎ 592347 (associate of *ANTE*).

La MAREMMA

From Piombino to Talamone *(140 km, 1 day; map 7)*

The legendary herdsmen of the area are no more. They disappeared about a century ago along with the marshes which covered as much as 162,500 acres of the Maremma on the borders of Tuscany and Latium. Gone are the herds of livestock, as well as the seasonal labourers who would arrive to harvest the grain and often die from malaria. Drainage and agrarian reform have changed the face of Grosseto Maremma. The waters have dried out, the dunes have been leveled and now the area stretches as a flat plain, criss-crossed by geometrical patterns of fields, roads and canals. The region is dotted with farmhouses and villages. While several of the towns inland have more to offer in terms of their medieval past, the reverse is true on the coast. These coastal towns are not just mere relics of old Pisan, Sienese, Florentine or Spanish strongholds. Industry and tourism have breathed new life into them.

▶ The itinerary starts by taking a l. turn off the road from **Piombino** (→) to San Vincenzo and heads for **Populonia,** the walled town which overlooks the N tip of the headland jutting out toward Elba. All that remains of the Etruscan city is a small museum and the **necropolis★** *(9 a.m.-12 noon and 4-8 p.m.; winter 2-6 p.m.),* with its burial mounds, chamber and niche tombs. ▶ The route then heads back toward Piombino and turns l. on to the SS 398 where v. Aurelia is joined at **Venturina.** Etruscan furnaces for smelting copper have been discovered nearby. A provincial road curves through a typical landscape of olive groves up to **Campiglia Maríttima** (→) and the SS 398 continues on to **Suvereto.** This old town stands on a hill in the Cornia Valley, but it is no longer surrounded by the cork oak woods from which it derives its

The thousand at Talamone

At dawn, on 6 May 1860, the steamships Piemonte *and* Lombardo *appeared in the quiet port of Talamone. They were carrying Garibaldi's troops which were about to unite the Bourbon kingdom of the South with the rest of Italy. Garibaldi needed ammunition and coal and he donned the uniform of a Savoyard general in order to impress the local authorities. He got what he wanted from officials and officers who were in awe of his prestige and excited by the idea of national unity, but who were also fearful of doing anything which contravened their duties. All of Garibaldi's volunteers went ashore at two in the afternoon and the disorderly group scattered through the village, terrifying the women. But the appearance of Garibaldi, who ordered everybody back on board ship, immediately put a stop to the disturbance. The following day Garibaldi inspected the castle of Talamone and requisitioned an iron gun and a 17C bronze cannon from the castle's store of ancient artillery pieces. That night the ammunition and supplies were taken on board, and on the morning of 8 May, the two steamers sailed to Porto Santo Stefano to take on coal. For Talamone, this had been the greatest event in its history since the day it had been sacked in 1544 by Khair-ad-Din, the Turkish pirate.*

name. The church of S. Giusto and the Palazzo Comunale are, however, remnants from the Middle Ages. ▶ From Venturina, the v. Aurelia heads SE to **Follónica**, now mainly a seaside resort. ▶ The route then zigzags up past Valpiana, to the most beautiful town in Maremma, **Massa Marittima** (→). It then heads SE from the Valpiana toward the v. Aurelia and follows a secondary road through the gentle, lush countryside of the **Laghetto dell'Accesa**. Nearby is an old silver mine. ▶ Heading S along the v. Aurelia, the route reaches the Grilli junction where the road for Vetulonia and Castiglione della Pescaia branches off to the r. ▶ The massive **Tumulo del Diavolino**, a monumental example of Etruscan funerary architecture, is just one of the interesting features of the vast and extraordinary **necropolis of Vetulonia**. Many of the finds from this site are now in the archaeological museum in Florence but some are in the small **antiquarium** *(9:30 a.m.-12:30 p.m. and 3:30-6:30 p.m.; closed Mon)* at the entrance to the village, which was one of the most powerful cities of pre-Roman Etruria. ▶ Yachts now outnumber fishing boats in the picturesque harbour and canal basin of **Castiglione della Pescaia**. Tourism now rules in the fortified town which looks down on the harbour from a crag above the sea. ▶ The road to **Marina di Grosseto** is shaded by the Tómbolo pine forest, which extends for some 15 km along the coast. ▶ The road heading inland (the SS 322 as far as Grosseto (→) and then, heading S toward Uccellina, the SS 1) initially crosses an immense area of reclaimed land in a series of long straight stretches and then reaches **Rispescia**, a typical modern rural village. ▶ Rispescia marks the start of the final section of the itinerary. The road branches r. to Alberese and the Torre di Collelungo on the sea; and then along the v. Aurelia from the resort of Alberese to the Fonteblanda junction; finally, to the r. toward Talamone. ▶ The **mouth of the Ombrone** and the **Monti dell'Uccellina** form the Maremma nature park. The Monti dell'Uccellina is a range of hills which runs *c.* 15 km. They are covered with Mediterranean scrub-brush and dotted with old watch towers and the ivy-clad ruins of the abbey of **S. Rabano**. There are no modern settlements in this untouched paradise. The magic of the coastal lake and the steep sea cliffs, the splendid sandy bays and the pine and oak forests are unspoiled. Here is the only stretch of Italian coastline that remains in its original state. ▶ The colourful har-

bour of **Talamone**, a fishing village and tourist centre, is overlooked by a castle which houses an interesting natural history **museum** *(8:30-11:30 a.m. and 4-7 p.m.)* with exhibits relating to the Uccellina park.　　□

Practical information

ALBERESE, ⊠ 58010, ☎ 0564.
Recommended
Event: *Rodeo dei Butteri* (2nd Sun in Aug).
Natural park: office at Pianacce (Aurelia Antica), ☎ 407098; guided tours in summer (Wed, Sat and hols 9 a.m. and 5 p.m., fee).

CASTIGLIONE DELLA PESCAIA, ⊠ 58043, ☎ 0564.
≋
🏠 p. Garibaldi, ☎ 933678.
Hotels:
★★★★ **Approdo**, v. Ponte Giorgini 29, ☎ 933466, 50 rm 🏊 closed Jan, 93,000; bkf: 5,000.
★★★★ **David**, v. degli Ulivi, ☎ 939030, 26 rm 🅿 🔧 ≼ 🎰 ▭ 🏊 closed Nov-Mar, 140,000.
★★★ **Piccolo Hotel**, v. Montecristo 7, ☎ 937081, 22 rm 🅿 ὃ 🏊 closed 1 Oct-14 May except Easter, 70,000; bkf: 6,000.

Restaurants:
♦♦ **Gambero**, v. Ansedonia 29, ☎ 937110, closed Wed and 1 Oct-15 Nov. Mixed cuisine: sailor's penne, grilled meats, 25/35,000.
♦♦ **Tana del Cinghiale**, at Tirli, ☎ 945810, closed Wed and Jan. Maremma cuisine: tortellini with ricotta, wild boar with apple, 25/35,000.

⚔ ★★★ *Maremma Sans Souci*, at Casa Mora, strada delle Collacchie, 400 pl, ☎ 933765.
Recommended
Clay pigeon shooting: at Fattoria delle Anatre, ☎ 935132.
Horseback riding: *Centro ippico La Briglia*, v. Pegaso 3, ☎ 24581 (associate of *ANTE*).
Marina: sailing club, ☎ 937098.
Nature park: *Le Marze* animal sanctuary; information from WWF official, ☎ 26588.

FOLLONICA, ⊠ 58022, ☎ 0566.
≋
🏠 v. Italia (lungomare), ☎ 40177.
Hotels:
★★ **Miramare**, lungomare Italia 84, ☎ 41521, 25 rm 🅿 🎰 🏊 closed Nov-Feb, 50,000; bkf: 7,000.
★★ **Parrini**, lungomare Italia 103, ☎ 40293, 38 rm, closed 21 Oct-28 Feb except Christmas, 48,000; bkf: 5,000.
★★ **Touring**, v. Bellini 31, ☎ 41578, 21 rm ὃ closed 10-25 Oct, 48,000.

⚔ ★ *Tahiti*, at Prato Ranieri, v. Italia 320, 320 pl, ☎ 60255.
Recommended
Racecourse: ☎ 51155.
Sailing: *Lega Navale*, v. Bicocchi 2/C, ☎ 42310.
Swimming: Capannina, ☎ 51298.

TALAMONE, ⊠ 58010, ☎ 0564.
🏠 at Porto Santo Stefano, ☎ 814208.
Hotel:
★★★ **Capo d'Uomo**, ☎ 887077, 24 rm 🅿 ≼ 🔧 🎰 🏊 closed Oct-Mar. No restaurant, 70,000; bkf: 5,000.
Recommended
Horseback riding: *Le Cannelle*, in Maremma nature park, ☎ 887020.
Marina: ☎ 887079.

In preparing for your trip, consult the pages pertaining to the regions. You will find there the description of the region you wish to visit, as well as a list of sites that must be seen, a brief history and practical information.

MARINA DI CASTAGNETO

Livorno 57, Florence 143, Rome 272 km
Pop. 5,416 ⊠ 57024 ☎ 0565   B-C4

The town stands on the edge of the Tyrrhenian sea, its back against a pine forest and long, straight expanses of soft sand on either side. It is also a good point from which to visit inland. For example, **San Guido** is 7.8 km along the v. Aurelia and is the starting point for a famous **cypress avenue**, which climbs for almost 5 km up to **Bolgheri**. 12 km S along the coast is **San Vincenzo**, which features a long beach. Further S is the **Riva degli Etruschi** and the protected area of the **Parco di Rimigliano** (875 acres). ☐

Practical information _____

MARINA DI CASTAGNETO-DONORATICO

Hotel:
★★★ *Torre,* Torre 42, ☎ 775268, 11 rm ⬕ ▦ ⬥ 60,000.

⚐ ★★ *Etruria,* at Marina di Donoratico, 600 pl, ☎ 744254.

Recommended
Children's facilities: *Centri Rousseau* camp, (6-12 yrs, Jun-Aug), information at Milan, v. Vico 10, ☎ 02/468496.
Nature park: *Rifugio faunistico di Bólgheri* (at 270-km marker on v. Aurelia, between railway and sea); open mid-Oct-mid-Apr, Fri and 1st and 3rd Sat of the month; reserve with the Donorático police, ☎ 777125.
Vacation village: *Club Méditerranée* (closed Oct-Apr), ☎ 02/778663.

Environs

PARCO DI RIMIGLIANO
ⓘ   at San Vicenzo, municipio (cultural office), ☎ 0565/701871; park restoration and assistance centre, ☎ 0565/701970 (summer).

SAN VICENZO, ⊠ 57027, ☎ 0565, 12 km S.
≋
ⓘ p. Umberto I 7, ☎ 701533.

Hotels:
★★★ *Riva degli Etruschi,* v. della Principessa 120, ☎ 702351, 95 rm ℗ ▦ ⬥ ⌗ 63,000; bkf: 5,000.
★★★ *Vela,* v. Vittorio Emanuele 72, ☎ 701529, 14 rm ▦ ⬥ No restaurant, 60,000; bkf: 6,000.
★★★ *Villa Marcella,* v. Serristori 41, ☎ 701646, 33 rm ℗ ⬕ ▦ ♿ closed 20 Oct-10 Nov and 10-20 Jan, 70,000; bkf: 5,000.
★★ *Delfino,* v. Colombo 15, ☎ 701179, 39 rm ℗ ▦ ⬥ 47,000; bkf: 5,000.

Restaurant:
● ♦♦♦ *Gambero Rosso,* p. della Vittoria 13, ☎ 701021, closed Tue and Nov. Within sight of harbour. Creative cuisine: ravioli with clams and broccoli, duck with raspberries, 50/75,000.

⚐ ★★★ *Park Albatros,* Torre Nuova pine forest, strada Provinciale della Principessa, 678 pl, ☎ 702414.

MASSA

Florence 114, Milan 235, Rome 373 km
Pop. 66,157 ⊠ 54100 ☎ 0585   B2

The castle stands on a high ridge, surrounded by a long wall. The old town with narrow medieval streets clusters at the bottom of the hill. On the plain below, the spacious new town built by the Cybo-Malaspina dukes in the 16C spreads out toward the Frigido. In the last sixty years the city has experienced substantial growth due to industrial development and in-

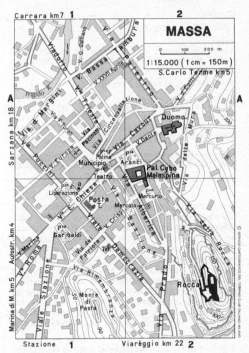

Carrara km 7 **1**   **2**

MASSA

0   100   200 m
1:15.000 (1 cm = 150 m)
S.Carlo Terme km 5

Stazione **1**   Viaréggio km 22 **2**

creased tourism. Massa now spreads down the Apuan Alps toward the coast.

▶ The **Rocca**★ (B2; *9 a.m.-12 noon and 4-7 p.m. summer; 2-5 p.m. winter; closed Mon*) was built by the Obertenghi in the 11C. However, none of the original fortifications survive, and the oldest section still standing dates from the 14C. Substantial additions were made in the 15C-16C. ▶ The p. degli Aranci is at the center of this Renaissance and Baroque city. There stands the **Palazzo Cybo-Malaspina** (A2), once the seat of the ducal and princely court. The exuberant decoration of its 18C windows shows the Ligurian influence. ▶ In the church of **S. Maria degli Ulivi** is a 15C wooden statue of St. Leonard (attributed to Jacopo della Quercia).

Environs

▶ 15 km along the road to Arni there is a small **botanical garden** at **Pian della Fioba** (*c.* 2,950 ft), a *CAI* rifugio *(permanently open)* and a **view**★ over the Apuan Alps and the sea. ☐

Practical information _____

MASSA
⚲ (May-Sep), at San Carlo Terme *(5 km NE),* ☎ 880233.
ⓘ at Marina di Massa *(5 km SW),* lungomare Vespucci 24, ☎ 240063.
▄▄▄ (B1), ☎ 41029.

Restaurant:
♦♦♦ *Manfredi,* p. della Liberazione 21 (B1 a), ☎ 42650, closed Sun. Regional and Italian cuisine: Francis IV kid, rabbit with apple, 15/26,500.

Recommended
Events: concerts, shows and summer entertainment, at the Castello Malaspina, ☎ 44774.
Sports stadium: v. degli Oliveti, ☎ 331084.

Environs

CINQUALE, ⊠ 54030, 6 km S.

Hotel:
★★★ *Giulio Cesare,* v. Giulio Cesare 29, ☎ 309319, 15 rm ℙ ⚉ ⚘ closed Oct-24 May except Easter. No restaurant, 72,000.

MONTIGNOSO, ⊠ 54038, 3 km SE.

Restaurant:
● ◆◆◆◆ *Bottaccio,* v. Bottaccio 1, ☎ 340031, closed Mon except summer. In converted 18C oil mill. Creative cuisine: scampi in verbena sauce, tagliolini with red mullet and seaweed, 45/60,000.

MASSA MARITTIMA*

Grosseto 51, Florence 132, Rome 249 km
Pop. 10,049 ⊠ 58024 ☎ 0566   C4

The decline of the coastal towns of the Maremma in the early Middle Ages was a result of raids by Arab pirates and of the constant expansion of marshland across the flat land. In turn, this led to the settlement of the hills from the 11C onward. Massa Marittima began to develop at that time. Massa established itself as a free commune and resumed mining in the hills, which the Etruscans had worked centuries before. It became a wealthy city, and eventually fell under Sienese domination in the 14C. Massa is not to be missed by anyone wanting to rediscover the fascination and beauty of the late Middle Ages in Tuscany.

▶ In the heart of the older medieval center is the dramatic 14C **piazza Garibaldi★** (B1). The superb Romanesque-Gothic **Duomo★★** is set at an angle to the slightly sloping square. The refined manipulation of perspective in the square means unexpected views and angles from every side. Other buildings ring the piazza; the **Palazzo Pretorio,** which is covered with coats-of-arms, and the 13C-14C **Palazzo Comunale★** and tower. ▶ A fierce **Sienese wolf** stands on a column of granite at the corner of the Palazzo Vescovile. ▶ The Palazzo Pretorio houses the **museo archeologico** *(summer 10 a.m.-12:30 p.m. and 3:30-7*

p.m.; winter 9-11 a.m. and 3-4 p.m.; closed Mon), with its collection of Etruscan tomb furnishings from nearby Lake dell'Accesa. It also houses the **pinacoteca,** with a 14C *Maestà★* by Ambrogio Lorenzetti. In the **Duomo** are a number of fine medieval works, including the 13C **font★,** a splendid Sienese painting of the *Madonna delle Grazie★,* and (in an underground chapel) the **tomb of S. Cerbone★,** signed by Goro di Gregorio. ▶ The v. Moncini (B1) climbs up from the 'Città Vecchia' to the Porta alle Silici of the 'Città Nuova'. Having passed this gate, one can still see the regular layout of streets in this 13C residential quarter. The dominant feature is the **Fortezza dei Senesi★,** built after the city's capture in 1335. A soaring 14C arch links one of the fortress walls to the 13C **Torre del Candeliere.** ▶ The **Biblioteca Comunale** (p. Cavour, A1) houses an original copy of the first **mining code** drawn up in Europe (1310). ▶ Although mining is no longer a major source of employment in Massa, the **Museo della Miniera** (B1) is of great interest and displays minerals such as pyrites and machines and tools used at the time *(guided tours at 11:15 a.m., 12 noon and 4:15 p.m. winter and 10:10, 11, 11:50 a.m. and 3:40, 4:30, 5:20 and 6:20 p.m. summer).*   □

Practical information

♨ (Jun-Sep), at Terme del Bagnolo, ☎ 916633.

Hotel:
★★ *Duca del Mare,* p. Alighieri 1, ☎ 902284, 18 rm ≮ ℙ ⚘ ⚉ 46,000; bkf: 5,000.

Recommended

Events: *Balestro del Girifalco,* a competition between crossbowmen drawn from the various quarters in medieval costume (20 May if hol or following Sun and 2nd Sun in Aug); craft show (Jul-Aug); *mineral exchange and market* (last Sun in Jul).
Youth hostel: *Ostello Apuano,* v. delle Pinete 89, ☎ 20288.

MONSUMMANO TERME

Pistoia 13, Florence 49, Milan 301 km
Pop. 17,365 ⊠ 51015 ☎ 0572   C2

One day, in the middle of the 19C, a farmer moved a boulder on his land, revealing the entrance to a **cavern.** The cavern ran back several hundred yards into the mountain and ended in a small **lake.** Even the Grand Duke of Tuscany hurried to visit the vast chambers filled with steam and covered in stalactites and stalagmites. Monsummano was a farming village built in the 17C around a sanctuary, but this discovery turned it into a spa specializing in steam baths which were used to cure arthritic and rheumatic ailments. In the 1960s, the town was transformed again as the local shoe industry grew and more than one hundred new companies sprang up. Today, the town has a decidedly modern and industrial feel.

▶ The 17C sanctuary of **S. Maria di Fontenuova** is an interesting example of Tuscan Baroque. ▶ On the hill above the spa, 3.8 km away, **Monsummano Alto** (the old settlement) has been abandoned, but its beautiful old Romanesque **parish church** still stands. Amid the cypresses and junipers are also the ruins of the **medieval castle.** Extensive vista★ over the Valdiniévole.   □

Practical information

♨ (Apr-Nov), *Grotto Giusti,* ☎ 51165 or 51008; (May-Oct); *Grotta Parlanti,* ☎ 51029.

Hotel:
★★★ *Grotta Giusti,* v. Grotta Giusti 171, ☎ 51165, 34 rm ℙ ⚒ ⚘ ⚘ craft closed Nov-Mar, 67,000.

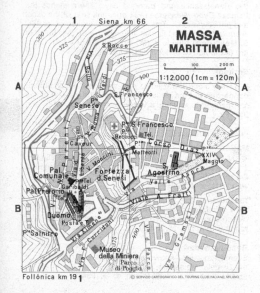

MASSA MARITTIMA

0   100   200 m
1:12.000 (1cm = 120m)

Siena km 66

Follónica km 19

Recommended
Caves: Grotta Giusti (Apr-Nov); information at centro termale, ☎ 51165.
Golf: v. Villa Galeotti, ☎ 628714 (9 holes).

MONTALCINO

Siena 40, Florence 109, Rome 213 km
Pop. 5,470 ⊠ 53024 ☎ 0577   D4

It was in Montalcino that the Italian city-states lost their independence, something they had cherished for centuries. Montalcino was the last bastion of the ancient Sienese republic, and when Siena itself fell to the Hapsburgs and the Medici in 1555, hundreds of its citizens fled here to carry on a final desperate resistance which lasted a few years.

▶ The famous 14C **rocca** *(9 a.m.-1 p.m. and 3-8 p.m.)*, which crowns the hill of Montalcino, now contains wine cellars. Local wines are tasted here (Brunello, Moscadello, Rosso di Montalcino). On the upper floors is a series of beautiful rooms. Splendid views from the bastions and towers. ▶ On the p. del Popolo is the 13C-14C **Palazzo Comunale.** ▶ There is a good collection in the **Museo Civico e Diocesano** *(summer: open every day 10 a.m.-12 noon and 3-7 p.m.; winter: 10 a.m.-12 noon and 3-5 p.m.; closed Mon)*, which includes old paintings and statues, a 12C illuminated Bible, gold objects and objets d'art. Note the *Painted Cross*★, one of the oldest examples of Sienese painting, and the unusual series of painted **jugs** made in Montalcino in the 13C-14C. ▶ The abbey of **Sant'Antimo** (→ from the Crete Senesi to the Valdichiana) is 8 km away.   □

Practical information _____

ⓘ v. Mazzini 41, ☎ 848242.

Restaurants:
● ♦♦♦ *Cucina di Edgardo,* v. Saloni 33, ☎ 848232, closed Wed except summer and Jan-Feb. Tiny, refurbished in local style: Italian and creative cuisine: pasticci di verdure, Lombard veal, 30/35,000.
♦♦ *Taverna dei Barbi,* ☎ 848277, closed Wed and Jul. Authentic rustic setting. Regional cuisine: grilled meat, chicken al Brunello, homemade wines, 25/30,000.

Recommended
Events: Classical concerts in the Fortezza (Jul-Aug); *national honey fair* (early Sep); *Sagra del tordo* (thrush festival, late Oct).
Wine: *Greppo farm,* ☎ 848087 (Sant'Antimo road, arrange in advance); *Cantine dei Barbi,* ☎ 848277 (Sant'Antimo road, turn after 5 km, arrange in advance).

MONTECATINI TERME*

Pistoia 14, Florence 49, Milan 301 km
Pop. 21,256 ⊠ 51016 ☎ 0572   C2

Like other European spas, Montecatini has its great temples of health, built in classical or floral style with sumptuously-decorated rooms, galleries, walks, colonnades and statues. The establishments, including the three most famous (the **Tettuccio**, the **Excelsior** and the **Terme Leopoldine,** built in 1775 but rebuilt in the 1920s), are scattered across the large Parco delle Terme★. There, the waters can be consumed or baths taken. There are cures involving mud treatments or inhalation for digestive problems, metabolic disorders, liver and respiratory problems. However, the atmosphere is not that of a large health centre. Montecatini is also a fashionable resort, with excellent hotels and meeting places, such as the **Kursaal** or the **Circolo dei Forestieri.** There is also the racecourse, and an extensive range of fashionable and cultural events.

5 km away, on the hill above the spa, stands **Montecatini Alto,** with towers and other vestiges from its medieval past (take funicular railway).   □

Practical information _____

MONTECATINI TERME
♨ ☎ 75851.
ⓘ v. Verdi 66, ☎ 70109.
Car rental: *Avis,* v. Manin 8, ☎ 72945.

Hotels:
L★★★★★ *G. H. Bellavista Palace e Golf,* v. Fedeli 2, ☎ 78122, 104 rm 🅿 ⬜ ♿ 🖵 ♫ ⏟ (9) 290,000.
L★★★★★ *Grand Hotel & La Pace,* v. Torretta 1, ☎ 75801, 150 rm 🅿 🔍 ⬜ ♿ 🖵 ♫ ⏟ (9) closed Nov-Mar, 350,000.
★★★★ *Ambasciatori G.H. e Cristallo,* v. IV Novembre 12, ☎ 73301, 66 rm 🅿 ♿ 🖵 closed 11 Nov-Feb, 130,000; bkf: 15,000.
★★★★ *Croce di Malta,* v. IV Novembre 18, ☎ 75781, 115 rm 🅿 ⬜ 🖵 190,000.
★★★★ *G.H. Nizza et Suisse,* v. Verdi 72, ☎ 79691, 108 rm 🅿 ⬜ closed Nov-Mar, 130,000; bkf: 9,000.
★★★★ *G.H. Tamerici & Principe,* v. IV Novembre 2, ☎ 71041, 157 rm 🅿 ⬜ 🖵 ♫ closed Dec-Mar, 220,000; bkf: 10,000.
★★★★ *Panoramic,* v. Bustichini 65, ☎ 78381, 104 rm 🅿 ⬜ ♿ 🖵 closed Nov-Mar, 110,000; bkf: 7,000.
★★★★ *Park Hotel le Sorgenti,* at Pieve a Nievole, corso Matteotti 198, ☎ 83116, 52 rm 🅿 ⬜ 🖵 closed Nov-Dec, 100,000.
★★★ *Astoria,* v. Fedeli 1, ☎ 71191, 65 rm 🅿 ⬜ 🖵 closed Nov-Mar, 75,000; bkf: 8,000.
★★★ *Belvedere,* v. Fedeli 10, ☎ 70251, 103 rm 🅿 ⬜ ♿ ⯒ 🖵 ♫ closed Nov-Mar, 80,000; bkf: 6,000.
★★★ *Biondi,* v. IV Novembre 83, ☎ 71341, 91 rm 🅿 🖵 closed 11 Oct-19 Mar, 70,000; bkf: 4,500.
★★★ *Boston,* v. Bicchierai 20, ☎ 70379, 57 rm 🅿 🖵 closed Nov-Mar, 68,000; bkf: 4,000.
★★★ *Cappelli - Croce di Savoia,* v. Bicchierai 139, ☎ 71151, 73 rm 🅿 ⬜ 🖵 closed 11 Nov-Mar, 78,000; bkf: 8,000.
★★★ *Hermitage,* v. Baragiola 31, ☎ 78241, 35 rm 🅿 ⬜ closed Nov-Mar, 73,000; bkf: 4,000.
★★★ *Michelangelo,* v. Fedeli 9, ☎ 74571, 65 rm 🅿 ⬜ ♿ 🖵 ♫ closed 16 Nov-31 Mar, 70,000; bkf: 4,000.
★★★ *Parma e Oriente,* v. Cavallotti 135, ☎ 78313, 45 rm 🅿 ⬜ 🖵 closed Nov-Easter, 80,000.
★★★ *President,* corso Matteotti 119, ☎ 767201, 37 rm 🅿 ⬜ 78,000; bkf: 6,000.
★★★ *Santabarbara,* v. Marlianese 4, ☎ 67353, 37 rm 🔍 ⬜ 55,000; bkf: 6,000.
★★★ *Settentrionale-Esplanade,* v. Grocco 2, ☎ 70021, 60 rm 🅿 ⬜ 🖵 Pens. closed 7 Nov-31 Mar, 76,000.
★★★ *Terme Pellegrini,* p. del Popolo 34, ☎ 71241, 80 rm 🅿 ♿ 82,000; bkf: 7,000.
★★ *Palo Alto,* v. Bruceto 10, ☎ 78554, 12 rm, closed 7 Jan-15 Mar, 50,000; bkf: 4,000.
★ *Giusti,* v. Salsero 7, ☎ 70006, 30 rm ⤬ Pens. closed 1 Nov-14 Feb, 50,000.

Restaurants:
● ♦♦♦♦ *Gourmet,* v. Amendola 6, ☎ 771012, closed Tue, Jan and Jul. Art Nouveau furnishings, well appointed. International cuisine: risotto with spider crab and champagne, gnocchetti parigina, 35/50,000.
♦♦♦ *Pietre Cavate,* at Pieve a Nievole, v. Pietre Cavate 11, ☎ 73664, closed noon except Sun and Wed. Fine view. Regional mixed cuisine: charcoal grilled fish, lamb chops, 25/40,000.
♦♦♦ *San Francisco,* corso Roma 112, ☎ 79632, closed Thu. Italian and international cuisine: risotto al verde, truffled filet, 30/45,000.
♦♦ *Enoteca Giovanni,* v. Garibaldi 25, ☎ 71695, closed Mon. Regional and creative cuisine: pancakes stuffed with asparagus, strawberry or nettle risotto, 40/50,000.

Recommended
Clay pigeon shooting: v. Ponte Monsummano, ☎ 767585.
Craft workshops: *Arte del gesso,* at Margine Coperta, ☎ 72263 (Mon-Sat).
Golf: at Monsummano Terme, v. Villa Galeotti, ☎ 628714 (9 holes).
Racecourse: v. Leonardo da Vinci, ☎ 78262.
Tennis: v. dei Bari, ☎ 767587.
♥ cooking and entertaining: Villa Bernini Rospigliosi, at Lamporecchio, information at *Hotel Centrale,* p. del Popolo 20, ☎ 70151, or at Milan, *Angolo della Gastronomia,* p. del Carmine, ☎ 02/874360.

Environs

MONTECATINI ALTO, ⊠ 51010, ☎ 0572, 6 km N.

Recommended
Caves: visit to Grotta Maona (Apr-Oct), Ente Grotta, ☎ 74581.

MONTEPULCIANO*

Siena 66, Florence 119, Rome 176 km
Pop. 14,154 ⊠ 53045 ☎ 0578   E4

Montepulciano is known for its fine wines (such as 'Nobile di Montepulciano') and for the **Bruscello,** an ancient form of popular theatre. The town was already well developed in the 14C, but much of its fine architecture dates from the 16C.

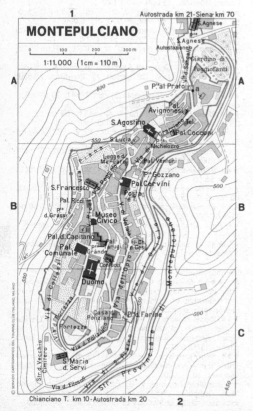

MONTEPULCIANO
0   100   200   300m
1:11.000 (1cm = 110m)

► The church of **S. Biagio★★** by Antonio da Sangallo the Elder (1518-45) stands outside town, at the foot of the hill. ► The original layout of the streets survives in the steep medieval **alleys,** many of which run beneath vaults and arches. ► After going through the **Porta al Prato** (A2), the **via di Gracciano★** displays two monumental products of the 16C: the **Palazzi Avignonesi** and **Bucceli.** The road continues (although it changes name several times) right through the city and it is lined with numerous fine palaces. ► Another major Renaissance architect whose work is found in Montepulciano is Michelozzo. He built Cosimo de' Medici's palace in Florence and was partly responsible for the church of **S. Agostino★** here. ► In the centre of the city is the beautiful **piazza Grande★** (B1). Here stand the **Duomo★ (funerary monument** carved by Michelozzo, and an *Assumption★* on the high altar by Taddeo di Bartolo); the 14C **Palazzo Comunale★;** and such majestic 16C buildings as the **Palazzo Nobili-Tarugi,** and the **Palazzo Contucci.** The **well** in front of the Gothic **Palazzo del Capitano** displays an absolute perfection of line found in the best of Renaissance work. ► The **Logge del mercato** (B1) in the piazzetta delle Erbe and the v. delle Arti both recall Montepulciano's past as a commercial and manufacturing centre. ► An unusual figure made of metal plate strikes the hours on the **Torre di Pulcinella** in the p. Manin. ► The **Museo Civico★** (B1; *9:30 a.m.-12:30 p.m. and 4-7 p.m.; closed Mon*) houses 13C-17C paintings, terra-cottas by the Florentine workshop of the della Robbias and 15C illuminated choir books.   □

Practical information _____

☼ (mid-Apr-Oct), at Terme di Montepulciano, ☎ 798086 or 798153.
ℹ v. Ricci (B1), ☎ 757935.

Hotels:
★★★ *Palio,* at Montepulciano Stazione, ☎ 738236, 27 rm
P ⚏ ఈ No restaurant, 61,000; bkf: 10,000.
★★★ *Panoramic,* v. di Villa Bianca 12, ☎ 798398, 25 rm
P ⟋ 🔲 ⚏ ♨ closed Oct-Mar, 69,000; bkf: 8,000.

Restaurants:
● ♦♦♦ *Fattoria Pulcino,* SS 146 for Chianciano, ☎ 716905, closed Mon in winter. With large fireplace and grill in farmhouse that was once a friary, local produce on display and for sale. Regional and Italian cuisine: penne all'arrabbiata, spit roast suckling pig, homemade wines, 25/30,000.
♦♦♦ *Porta di Bacco,* v. Graciano nel Corso 100 (A2 a), ☎ 716907, closed Fri except summer. Refreshment room of small museum. Regional cuisine: ewe's cheese and Sienese salume, roast suckling pig and beans, homemade Nobile di Montepulciano, 20/25,000.

Recommended
Events: international art workshops (theatre, concerts, figurative arts; Jul-Aug).

MONTERCHI

Arezzo 28, Florence 109, Rome 246 km
Pop. 1,885 ⊠ 52035 ☎ 0575   E-F3

Monterchi began as one of the many feudal castles which were built in the wooded upper Tiber Valley in the early 11C. It is now a typical hill town, still surrounded by greenery but with a strong historical heritage. Features include the old **castle walls** and the curious medieval arcaded passage that runs around the apse of the parish church. Its prized possession, however, is Piero della Francesca's extraordinary fresco, the *Madonna del Parto★,* in a chapel standing amid the cypresses of the cemetery outside town.   □

If you enjoy sports, consult the pages pertaining to the regions; there you will find addresses for practicing your favorite sport.

MONTERIGGIONI

Siena 15, Florence 55, Rome 245 km
Pop. 6,835 ⊠ 53035 ☎ 0577   D3-4

Monteriggioni's formidable 13C **walls★** caught the imagination of Dante, who mentions them in his *Inferno.* The town stands on a hill, and its walls run in a rough circle for a little over 600 yards. They are defended by a series of square towers (originally fourteen in number). When the fortress was built by the Sienese to counter Florentine expansion, they were even higher than they are today. As time passed, the military stronghold inside the walls turned into a country town, but its buildings and streets still bear traces of their original role. The parish church, which dates from the Middle Ages, has a rough late-Romanesque stone façade. Less than 5 km away are the massive fortifications built by the Florentines at **Staggia** in the 14C.   □

Practical information

Restaurant:
● ◆◆◆ *Pozzo,* p. Roma 2, ☎ 304127, closed Sun eve, Mon, Jan and Aug. Inside ring of walls of medieval town, run by experienced couple. Regional cuisine: pappardelle with wild boar, homemade pici, 28/40,000.

Recommended
Clay pigeon shooting: at Santa Colomba, ☎ 57050.

MONTE SAN SAVINO

Arezzo 20, Florence 86, Rome 197 km
Pop. 7,760 ⊠ 52048 ☎ 0575   E3-4

In order to secure the pope's good graces, the Medici gave Monte San Savino, in the mid-14C, to Pope Julius III's family, the Del Monte. Although this transfer to the Del Monte was not permanent, it did result in the transformation of the buildings of the old medieval town and in a marked improvement in their architecture.

▶ The main road runs from the **Porta Fiorentina** to the **Porta Romana** and features a 17C obelisk and the small church of **S. Chiara,** which houses terra-cottas by the Della Robbias and by Sansovino. Further on is the **Loggia dei Mercanti★,** a splendid example of 16C Florentine architecture with classical lines and rich ornamentation. Opposite is the massive façade of the **Palazzo Comunale,** dating from the same period and built by Antonio da Sangallo. It served as model for many of Monte San Savino's palaces. ▶ In contrast, the high tower of the **Palazzo Pretorio,** further along the route, dates from the late Middle Ages, as do the circular towers of the walls. The **cloister of S. Agostino** is typical of the spacious harmony of the Renaissance. ▶ 2.4 km to the E, on a hill covered with cypresses, stands the church of **S. Maria delle Vertighe.** The nearby Franciscan convent has important examples of paintings by Margaritone d'Arezzo (13C) and Lorenzo Monaco (14C).   □

Practical information

ⓘ p. Gamurrini.

Hotel:
★★★ *Domenico,* at Vertighe, ☎ 844040, 27 rm ℗ ≼ ᕼ ⅋ 55,000.

Recommended
Events: *ceramics show* (Sep-Oct); *Sagra della porchetta* (festival of the suckling pig, 2nd Sun in Sep).
Farm vacations: *Azienda Castello di Gargonza,* ☎ 847021.

MONTEVARCHI

Arezzo 31, Florence 52, Rome 235 km
Pop. 22,162 ⊠ 52025 ☎ 055   D-E3

Montevarchi's nickname used to be 'chickens and hats', due largely to its two best-known industries. Today's reality is more complex, but the town is still at the centre of the Valdarno's agricultural trade, as it has been since the 13C.

▶ The church of **S. Lorenzo** (rebuilt in the 18C) stands in the town's old centre. Inside is a reliquary of the 'Holy Milk'. ▶ The museum attached to the church features a fine example of the glazed terra-cotta work of Andrea della Robbia and his school, and a **monumental tempietto★** decorated inside and out with friezes of cherubs. ▶ There is also an important **palaeontological musem** *(9 a.m.-noon and 4-6 p.m.; Sun 10 a.m.-12 noon; closed Mon, hols and Aug)* with a specimen of *Elephas meridionalis,* several million yrs old.   □

Practical information

Hotel:
★★★ *Delta,* v. Diaz 137, ☎ 901213, 40 rm ℗ ᕼ ᕼ ⅋ No restaurant, 64,000; bkf: 8,000.

Recommended
Archery: *Compagnia arcieri Valdarno,* v. Dante 60, ☎ 982939.
Horseback riding: *Rendola Riding* at Réndola, ☎ 987045, (Jul-mid-Sep).
Motocross: *Miravalle,* run by *Moto club Brilli Peri,* at Mercatale, ☎ 987188 or 987222.

ORBETELLO

Grosseto 44, Florence 183, Rome 152 km
Pop. 14,972 ⊠ 58015 ☎ 0564   D6

Orbetello stands at the tip of a strip of land which juts out from the coast toward **Mt. Argentario** (→). On either side of the dyke which connects with the Argentario are lagoons. Currents have moved sandbanks and transformed Mt. Argentario from an island to part of the mainland.

▶ The town owes much of its present appearance to the Spanish, who turned it into the capital of a small state in the 16C-17C. Traces of their military presence can be seen in the **bastions** which jut out into the lagoons, in the town gates and in the **former powder mill.** ▶ The **Duomo** was extended in the 17C, but its façade incorporates the graceful 14C Gothic façade. ▶ The **Antiquarium Civico** *(10:30 a.m.-12:30 p.m. and 5:30-8:30 p.m.; closed Mon a.m.)* contains various Etruscan finds, including sculptures and ceramics, as well as the **pediment★** of a 2C BC temple depicting the myth of Oedipus. ▶ For nature lovers, the more interesting of the two lagoons is the **laguna di Ponente:** its islets and dunes covered in vegetation are home to flocks of herring gulls, mallards, herons and thousands of other birds. ▶ The two sandbanks which enclose the lagoons are known as 'tmboli'. The S one, the **Tómbolo a mezzogiorno★,** has been least disturbed by man and is richest in animal life. Covered with pine, cork oak and oak, it provides a home for fallow deer and pheasants.   □

Practical information

ⓘ at Porto Santo Stefano, ☎ 814208.

Hotel:
★★★ *Presidi,* v. Mura di Levante 34, ☎ 867601, 63 rm ℗ ᕼ No restaurant, 73,000; bkf: 5,000.

Restaurants:
◆◆ *Egisto,* corso Italia 190, ☎ 867469, closed Mon and

Nov. Regional cuisine: sailor's risotto, charcoal grilled fish and meats, 18/28,000.
♦♦ *Pitorsino,* at Orbetello Scalo, v. Aurelia, at 140-km marker, ☎ 881433, closed Wed and Jan-Feb. In old farmstead with terrace and garden. Italian cuisine: potatoes with caviar, charcoal grilled fish and meats, 25/40,000.
♦♦ *Poggio al Pero,* at Albinia, v. Maremmana 181, ☎ 870012, closed Wed and 7 Jan-Feb. Maremma cuisine: acquacotta, grilled meat, 30/40,000.

⚠ ★★★ *Gianella-La Costa,* at Gianella, 240 pl, ☎ 820049; ★ *Haway,* at Albinia, SS Aurelia, at 154.5-km marker, 204 pl, ☎ 870164; ★ *Voltoncino,* at Albinia, SS Aurelia, at 153.6-km marker, 264 pl, ☎ 870158.

Recommended
Golf: *Golf Argentario,* v. Tagliata, ☎ 882062.
Nature park: *Laguna di Ponente di Orbetello reserve* (Sep-Apr; information WWF Rome, ☎ 06/854892).
Tennis: at La Pista, ☎ 867539.

PESCIA

Pistoia 23, Florence 61, Milan 299 km
Pop. 18,411 ⊠ 51017 ☎ 0572   C2

Over the past centuries Pescia has been famous for a number of different activities: mulberry growing, paper making and leather tanning. Today, it is best known for its production of cut flowers, carnations in particular. The town seems to be surrounded by one enormous garden, the scents and colours of which enliven its great Mercato dei Fiori every day. Its horticultural industry is also active in the nursery sector, and grows large numbers of olive trees.

▶ The pure lines of the façade of the oratory of the **Madonna di Piè di Piazza** emphasize its 15C origins. ▶ The powerful **campanile** beside the Duomo dates from the previous century. ▶ Buonaventura Berlinghieri's panel of *Scenes from the Life of St. Francis*★, in the Gothic church of S. Francesco, dates from 1235, only a few years after the saint's death, and is one of the masterpieces of 13C Tuscan painting.

Environs

▶ 12.5 km N is one of the gems of Romanesque art in the Valdiniévole, the **parish church of Castelvecchio**★. ▶ The village of **Collodi** lies on a green ridge 6 km W. It was the birthplace of the mother of Carlo Lorenzini, author of *Pinocchio,* and provided him with his pseudonym. A **park,** with statues, mosaics and sculptures devoted to the famous puppet and other characters from the book, was opened here in 1963 *(8 a.m.-9 p.m.; winter 9 a.m.-6 p.m.).* ▶ The dramatic **Giardino Garzoni**★ occupies a hillside crowned by the Villa Garzoni *(8 a.m.-8 p.m.; winter 9 a.m.-4:30 p.m.),* and is one of the most beautiful gardens in Italy.   ☐

Practical information _____

Ⓘ p. Mazzini 1 (municipio), ☎ 476392.

Hotels:
★★★ *Villa delle Rose,* at Castellare, ☎ 451301, 106 rm Ⓟ △ ▥ ☞ 63,000; bkf: 7,000.
★★ *Fiori,* v. VIII Settembre 10, ☎ 4778671, 48 rm Pens. 52,000.

Restaurants:
♦♦ *Cecco,* v. Forti 84, ☎ 477955, closed Mon, Jul and Nov-Dec. Some walls date from original 19C inn. Regional cuisine: hunter's style penne, chicken baked in a brick, 25/35,000.
♦♦ *Fortuna-da Piero e Franca,* v. Colli per Uzzano 18, ☎ 477121, closed noon except hols, Mon and Aug. Dining in summer outside under olive trees. Regional cuisine: spaghetti with seafood, sea bass with aromatic herbs, 30/40,000.
♦ *Buca,* p. Mazzini 4, ☎ 477339, closed Tue and Jul-Aug.

Opposite Palazzo Comunale. Regional cuisine: pappa al pomodoro, bistecca alla fiorentina, 20/30,000.

Recommended
Events: *Biennale del fiore* (flower show, even-numbered yrs, Sep).

PIENZA*

Siena 52, Florence 120, Rome 188 km
Pop. 2,441 ⊠ 53026 ☎ 0578   E4

'Nobody, upon pain of excommunication, may sully the whiteness of the walls. No one may hang other pictures here. No one may add altars or open new chapels. No one may disturb the beauty of the church, which must remain as it is.' These words are part of an order signed in 1462 by Pope Pius II. They referred to the cathedral at Corsignano which the Pope had just built and decorated with individually chosen works of art. This Sienese village was the Pope's birthplace and he went about transforming it by building palaces, houses and squares. It was meant to be the ideal Renaissance city, but Pius II's death interrupted the project. Bernardo Rossellino worked on the town between 1459 and 1462 and retained part of the old medieval street layout. Nevertheless, Pienza is still a city conceived as a unified whole, a pure expression of beauty.

▶ Half way down the **corso Rossellino,** the visitor comes to the **piazza Pio II**★ (A1), the heart of the Renaissance city. The cathedral forms the backdrop, and on either side of the square are the Palazzo Piccolomini and the Palazzo Vescovile. On the road side, the square is closed off by the **Palazzo Comunale** and the **Palazzo Ammannati.** ▶ The **cathedral**★★ has a classical, tripartite façade with tall arches crowned by a pediment bearing the Piccolomini arms. Although Renaissance on the outside, the interior has touches of German Gothic. There is a magnificent wooden **choir**★ (1462) and several fine paintings, including an *Assumption*★ by the Sienese artist Vecchietta (15C). The **baptismal font**★ by Rossellino is in the crypt. ▶ Also by Rossellino, the **Palazzo Piccolomini**★★ closely resembles the Palazzo Rucellai in Florence. In fact one might see it as Rossellino's tribute to his master, Alberti. The splendid arcaded courtyard gives access to the **garden**★ to the rear, above which is the finest piece of architecture in Pienza: the S front of the palace. The rooms on the first floor *(10 a.m.-12:30 p.m. and 3-6 p.m.)* house mementos, weapons, paintings and objets d'art. ▶ In the Casa dei Canonici is the **Museo della Cattedrale**★ *(10 a.m.-1 p.m. and 3-6 p.m.; 2-4 p.m. winter)* and its prized exhibits include a 14C English embroidered cope★ belong-

PIENZA

1:7,000 (1cm = 70m)

0   50   100 m

Autostrada km 23

ing to Pius II, as well as Etruscan antiquities. ▶ Toward the Porta al Ciglio, in the **via delle Case Nuove** (A2), are twelve houses which Pius II had built for the poor. ▶ The Gothic church of **S. Francesco** (A1) was left untouched by Rossellino and features old frescos and a panel painting by Luca Signorelli. ▶ 10 min walk out into the country is the **pieve di Corsignano** (the original 11C-12C parish church) with the remains of a campanile. □

Practical information ───────────

ⓘ vicolo della Canonica 1 (at side of cathedral).

Hotel:
★★★ *Corsignano,* v. Madonnina 11, ☎ 748501, 36 rm Ⓟ ⑭ ✿ closed 11 Nov-9 Mar except Christmas, 42,000; bkf: 5,000.

Restaurant:
◆ *Falco,* p. Dante 7 (A1 a), ☎ 748551, closed Fri and 10 Nov-10 Dec. Regional cuisine: homemade ravioli, filet with porcini, 18/26,000.

Recommended
Events: *molten cheese competition* (1st Sun Sep); popular theatre, in piazza at Monticchiello (*6 km E,* Jul).

PIETRASANTA

Lucca 30, Florence 104, Milan 246 km
Pop. 25,425 ✉ 55045 ☎ 0584   B2

The regular layout of the town suggests a distant, Roman origin. Due to its position near the Apuan Alps, it is likely that its inhabitants worked the marble from the nearby Valle di Seravezza. Pietrasanta is surrounded by hills, covered with green vines and silver olive trees. It is difficult to imagine that Eugenio Barsanti, one of the inventors of the internal combustion engine, was born here.

▶ The town's historical and cultural importance can be seen from the buildings on the p. del Duomo. The **Duomo★** itself (13C-14C) has a fine marble façade with a frieze of arches and a large rose window. Next to it is a Renaissance brick **campanile.** Other buildings on the square: the church of **S. Agostino,** with an elegant marble front (14C), and the **Palazzo Pretorio.** In the square itself is a 16C fountain with three basins and the Florentine column of the Marzocco (1514). ▶ 3.5 km away is **Valdicastello Carducci.** □

Practical information ───────────

ⓘ at Marina di Pietrasanta, ☎ 20331.

Restaurants:
◆◆ *Gatto Nero,* p. Carducci 10, ☎ 70135, closed Mon, 1-20 Oct and Christmas. Regional mixed cuisine: shellfish soup, bistecca alla fiorentina, 40/50,000.
◆ *Rocchetta,* at Strettoia, v. Montiscendi 29, ☎ 775728, closed Wed and 15 Oct-15 May. Regional cuisine: tagliatelle and risottos with porcini, chicken alla Marchi, 20/30,000.

Recommended
Events: *permanent marble exhibition; Pietrasanta music season* (May-Jun, in the churches).

PIOMBINO

Livorno 82, Florence 161, Rome 264 km
Pop. 38,780 ✉ 57025 ☎ 0565   C5

The industrial area of Piombino is the major centre of the Tuscan metal and steel industries, a landscape of smokestacks and steelworks. Its harbour is busy loading and unloading goods as well as passengers going to and from Elba.

▶ Little of Piombino's architectural past remains. Much of the damage was done in the 30s, due to restoration. ▶ However, the **view★** from the seafront **piazza Bovio,** onto the Piombino canal, is as enchanting as ever. 14.5 km away, **Populonia** (→ The Maremma) features a famous Etruscan necropolis. □

Practical information ───────────

ⓘ at harbour, ☎ 36432 (seasonal).
⚓ ferries and hydrofoils for Elba (→), information at the harbour: *Toremar,* ☎ 31100, *Novarma,* ☎ 33031; for Bastia in Corsica and for Palau in Sardinia.

Hotel:
★★★★ *Centrale,* p. Verdi 2, ☎ 32581, 38 rm Ⓟ ✿ 122,000; bkf: 9,000.

⚠ ★★★ *Torre Mozza,* at Riotorto, Torre Mozza, 300 pl, ☎ 20821.

PISA**

Florence 83, Milan 275, Rome 329 km
Pop. 103,894 ✉ 56100 ☎ 050   C3

No traces remain of the Romans, or of the Lombards and Franks who ruled the area in the early Middle Ages. However, there is plenty of evidence of the Medici presence in the 16C, particularly in the p. dei Cavalieri. It is not the splendour of this square that will remain in the visitor's mind, but rather the great series of buildings on the Campo dei Miracoli: the Duomo, the Baptistery, the Leaning Tower and the Camposanto, which date 11C-13C. Curiously, they stand away from the centre of town, almost on their own. The cool evening air still carries the salt tang of the sea even though the coast has receded further and further over the centuries. These buildings did not suffer from the political decline of the city, nor from its devastating defeats by Genoa and Florence, which culminated in Pisa losing its independence. Instead they remain, immutable, universal and miraculous in their beauty, bearing witness to one of the most important of the Italian republics of the late Middle Ages. The milling crowds of students along the banks of the Arno conjure up the other face of Pisa, that of a city which has for centuries been a centre of study. It received the active support of both the Medici and of Napoleon, and Galileo Galilei taught at its famous university.

▶ **Borgo Stretto** (C4), lined with old arcades, is the most typical and interesting section of the main street and, in the evening, is the gathering spot for local strollers. The street crosses the Arno over the modern **ponte di Mezzo,** which spans the river with a single arch of white stone. Its S section passes the grand 17C **logge di Banchi,** the orignal silk and wool markets. It continues as the corso Italia, flanked by luxury shops. ▶ On the **piazza dei Cavalieri★** (B4) stands the 16C **Palazzo dei Cavalieri★.** Since the last century, it has housed the Scuola Normale Superiore founded by Napoleon. To the r. of the palace, the church of **S. Stefano dei Cavalieri★** was designed by Vasari (1569) and has a 17C marble façade. The **Palazzo dell'Orologio** is believed to stand on the remains of the 'Torre della fame' immortalized in Dante's *Inferno* (the tower in which Ugolino della Gherardesca died of hunger along with his sons and nephews). ▶ 17C-18C buildings line the **via S. Maria,** where there is also the **Domus Galileana** (C3) with mementos of the great scientist) and a 13C **tower-house,** which is perhaps the oldest example of a load-bearing structure with brick and stone dressings. ▶ The extraordinary and innovative architecture of the **Duomo★★** (A3; 11C-12C) shows a mixture of vigorous Romanesque forms, classical echoes and a decorative use of colour which underlines Pisa's contacts with

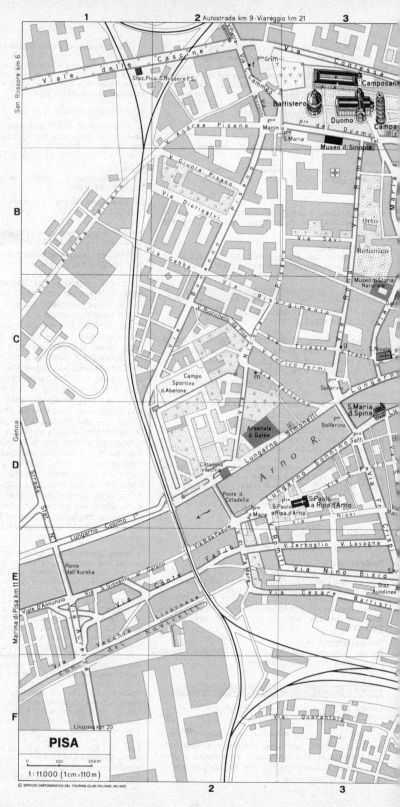

PISA

0   100   200m

1:11.000 (1cm=110m)

© SERVIZIO CARTOGRAFICO DEL TOURING CLUB ITALIANO, MILANO

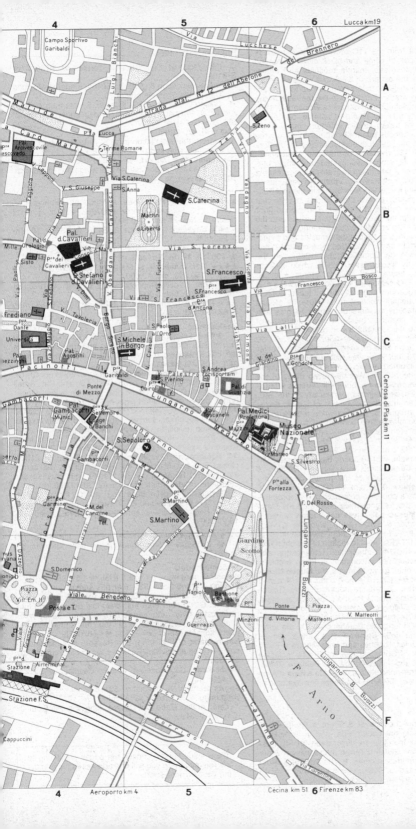

the Muslim Orient from the 11C onward. The exterior is covered with stripes of white and black stone, recessed lozenges and inlaid roses, marble mosaics and enameled glass. Inside, the pattern of black and white stripes is repeated and four majestic colonnades run up to the transept. Outstanding works of art include the **leaves★** of the door of S. Ranieri, with bronze panels by Bonanno (1180); the **tomb of Henry VII★** by Tino da Camaino, one of the finest examples of Italian Gothic sculpture (early 14C); Giovanni Pisano's famous **pulpit★★**, with scenes from the Life of Christ and the Last Judgment; paintings by Andrea del Sarto and the 13C **mosaic★** of the apse's half dome. The lamp whose movements suggested the simple harmonic movement of a pendulum to Galileo hangs almost in front of the pulpit. ▶ It took more than two centuries to build the **Baptistery★★**, which was begun in the mid-12C, and the exterior clearly shows the changes in style that occurred during the course of the work. The ground floor is Romanesque, with the two-colour stone stripes and the restrained ring of blind arcades, while the loggia above is surmounted by a series of trefoils, tabernacles and pinnacles. The wonderful interior is vaulted by a conical dome and contains Guido da Como's **font★** (1246) and the famous **pulpit★★** by Nicola Pisano (1260), which is decorated with reliefs, figures and colossal statues★ by N. and G.Pisano. ▶ The campanile or **Leaning Tower★★** is famous for the precarious angle at which it leans, but it is also a dazzlingly elegant piece of architecture. Its ground floor is surmounted by six tiers of circular loggias and crowned by a bell chamber. Inside, a spiral staircase of 294 steps leads to the top (182 ft 7 in on the S side and 179 ft 9 in on the N side; *9 a.m.-4:30, 5:30, 6 or 7:30 p.m., depending upon time of year*). The Leaning Tower was begun in 1173, but work was halted half way up the third storey and resumed in 1275. It was finally completed in the middle of the 14C. ▶ War destroyed many of the frescos of the **Camposanto★★**, but it still remains a fascinating gallery of Tuscan painting, particularly of the 14C, and also houses an important collection of Greek, Etruscan and Roman antiquities. Its long white façade forms a backdrop to the piazza and consists of four arcaded wings, each large arch enclosing four smaller ones built 1283-1464; *(Oct-Mar 9 a.m.-4:30 or 5:30 p.m.; Apr-Sep 8 a.m.-6 p.m. or 7:30 p.m.)*. On the N side is the large **Salone degli Affreschi**, which houses the major detached frescos from the Camposanto, including the *Triumph of Death★★*. ▶ On the S side of the p. del Duomo, the **Museo delle Sinopie★** *(9:30 a.m.-12:30 p.m. and 3-4:30 or 7 p.m.)* contains a priceless collection of 14C preparatory drawings for the frescos which decorated the Camposanto. ▶ The **Museo dell'Opera del Duomo** *(winter 9 a.m.-5 p.m.; summer 8 a.m.-8 p.m.)* is in the p. Arcivescovado (A4). ▶ A few yards from the tree-lined p. della Libertà, the 12C-13C marble façade of the church of **S. Caterina** (B5; 13C-14C) integrates Romanesque and Gothic, a combination not uncommon in Pisan architecture. ▶ At the end of lungarno Mediceo, the **Museo Nazionale di S. Matteo★★** *(D6; 9 a.m.-7 p.m.; hols 9 a.m.-1 p.m.; closed Mon)* is a treasure house of early Tuscan works of art, including Giunta Pisano's 'painted crosses', the *Madonna and Child with Saints★* by Simone Martini, a *St. Paul★* by Masaccio and the bust of *St. Luxorious★* by Donatello. ▶ On lungarno Gambacorti (D3), the small church of **S. Maria della Spina★★** is a Gothic gem of tabernacles, pinnacles, rosettes and rose windows. There are also a number of Gothic palaces in the city, including the Palazzo Gambacorti (C-D4), now the **Palazzo Comunale**. ▶ Facing a tree-lined square, **S. Paolo a Ripa d'Arno** (D3) on the r. bank of the Arno is another fine example of Pisan Romanesque.

Environs

▶ The Romanesque basilica of **S. Piero a Grado★★** *(6 km)* stands alone in the countryside, and in its solemn interior the walls of the nave are decorated with 14C frescos. ▶ 7.5 km away, **Giuliano Terme** offers mineral water cures, baths and mud treatments. ▶ The **Park of S. Rossore** (→ the Tenutadi S. Rossore) is 6 km away. ▶ At 13 km is the **Certosa di Pisa** (→ Calci). □

Practical information

⌖ (May-Oct), at San Giuliano Terme, ☎ 818047 or 818100.
ℹ p. Arcivescovado 8 (A3), ☎ 560464; lungarno Mediceo 42 (C5), ☎ 20351 (main office).
✈ *Galileo Galilei*, ☎ 28088 (bus no. 5 from train station); *Alitalia*, v. Puccini 21, ☎ 501570, passenger agency, p. Stazione (E-F4), ☎ 48027.
🚃 (F4), ☎ 41385.
🚌 from the bus station in p. S. Antonio (E3), p. Vittorio Emanuele (E4) and p. Stazione (E-F 4).
Car rental: *Avis*, airport, ☎ 42028; *Hertz*, v. Vespucci 106/A, ☎ 44389, airport, ☎ 44426; *Maggiore*, station, ☎ 502429, airport, ☎ 42574.

Hotels:
★★★★ *California Park Hotel*, at Madonna dell'Acqua, v. Aurelia, at 338-km marker, ☎ 890726, 74 rm P 🏨 ⚐ ⊠ closed 16 Nov-31 Mar, 110,000; bkf: 10,000.
★★★★ *Cavalieri*, p. Stazione 2 (E4 a), ☎ 43290, 102 rm ⚐ 223,000; bkf: 16,000.
★★★★ *D'Azeglio*, p. Vittorio Emanuele 18/B (E4 b), ☎ 500310, 29 rm. No restaurant, 160,000; bkf: 10,000.
★★★★ *G.H. Duomo*, v. S. Maria 94 (B3 c), ☎ 27141, 94 rm P ⚐ 150,000; bkf: 12,000.
★★★ *Arno*, p. della Repubblica 6 (C5 d), ☎ 501820, 33 rm 🏨 63,000; bkf: 6,000.
★★★ *Pace*, v. Gramsci-gall. B (E4 e), ☎ 502226, 68 rm P ⚐ 62,000; bkf: 4,000.

Restaurants:
● ◆◆◆◆ *Sergio*, lungarno Pacinotti 1 (C4 l), ☎ 48245, closed Sun, Mon noon and Jan. In ancient fortress from the 11C. Creative and regional cuisine: crayfish with tarragon, tripe alla pisana, 40/70,000.
● ◆◆◆ *Ristoro dei Vecchi Macelli*, v. Volturno 49 (C2 m), ☎ 20424, closed Sun noon, Wed, Aug and Dec. Small and elegant. Creative cuisine: fish ravioli in sweet pepper butter, boned and stuffed pigeon, 35/50,000.
◆◆◆ *Buzzino*, v. Cammeo 44 (A2 f), ☎ 27013, closed Tue. Well-appointed setting. Regional and Italian cuisine: homemade ravioli, fish baked in foil, 30/50,000.
◆◆◆ *Emilio*, v. Roma 28 (C3 g), ☎ 26028, closed Mon. Regional cuisine: elvers alla pisana, grilled fish, 20/30,000.
◆◆ *Schiaccianoci*, v. Vespucci 104/A (E4 i), ☎ 21024, closed Sun eve, Mon and 1-7 Jan. Small inn with family atmosphere. Regional cuisine: risotto with crayfish and courgettes, filets of fish with porcini, 30/40,000.
◆ *Pergoletta*, v. delle Belle Torri 40 (C5 h), ☎ 23631, closed Sun eve, Mon and 20-30 Aug. Pergola for summer dining. Regional cuisine: cuttlefish with herbs, dried cod, 18/24,000.

⚐ ★ *Internazionale*, at Marina di Pisa, v. Litoranea, 410 pl, ☎ 36553; ★ *Torre Pendente*, v. delle Cascine 86, ☎ 561704.

Recommended
Botanical garden: v. L.Ghini 5 (B3), ☎ 561795.
Cycling: v. Nino Bixio (E3), near bus station.
Clay pigeon shooting: v. Campalto, ☎ 532303.
Events: *Gioco del Ponte* and *historical procession* (Jun); historical regatta and *candle-lit festival of San Ranieri* (Jun); festival of San Sisto (6 Aug, folk entertainment); opera season (*Amici della lirica*, ☎ 562007).
Nature park: of Migliarino, San Rossore and Massaciùccoli (→ Tenuta di San Rossore), v. Cesare Battisti 10, ☎ 43512.
Racecourse: *San Rossore*, v. delle Cascine, ☎ 531285 (Jan-Mar).
Sports arena: v. A. Pisano, ☎ 531132.
Swimming: v. A. Pisano, ☎ 532582.
▼ café: *Antico Caffè dell'Ussero*, lungarno Pacinotti 27 (C4), ☎ 25318.

If you enjoy sports, consult the pages pertaining to the regions; there you will find addresses for practicing your favorite sport.

PISTOIA*

Florence 34, Milan 315, Rome 308 km
Pop. 91,619 ⊠ 51100 ☎ 0573   D2
See map on page 718.

For more than five hundred years, until the second half of the 19C, Pistoia stayed within the confines of medieval walls. When it breached them in the immediate post-war years, industrialization accelerated and expansion followed. Nevertheless the heart of the city remains, one of its corners occupied by the large Fortezza di S. Barbara. Pistoia is marked by the gracefulness of its decoration, and its Romanesque churches, with their green and white façades.

► The beautiful **piazza del Duomo**★ (B4) is completely ringed by medieval buildings. The visitor is immediately struck by the contrast between the lively, colourful decoration of the **Baptistery**★★ (14C) and the **Duomo**★ (12C-13C) on the one hand, and the sheer power of the **Palazzo del Podestà** and the **Palazzo del Comune**★ (1294-1385) on the other. The campanile embodies this contrast: its massive lower section is surmounted by a series of graceful loggias faced with bands of green and white marble in the style of the neighbouring Baptistery and church. There is even a touch of whimsy in the **well** which is surmounted by a Florentine puppet, or in the enigmatic black marble head which projects from the façade of the Palazzo del Comune. ► The vault of the central arch of the Duomo's arcade and the **tympanum**★ of the door both bear **glazed terra-cottas** by Andrea della Robbia. Inside, in the Cappella di S. Jacopo *(7 a.m.-12 noon and 4-7 p.m.)*, is one of the finest examples of Tuscan silverwork, the **altar of S. Jacopo**★★. Begun in 1287, it was not completed until the second half of the 15C, by which time it included no fewer than 628 figures, and had involved generations of Sienese, Pistoian and Florentine silversmiths. ► Pistoia took up the green and white marble stripes typical of Pisan Romanesque style with such fervour that they almost became the visual emblem of the city. There are various medieval churches covered this way; two deserve special attention. One is the 12C-14C church of **S. Giovanni Fuorcivitas**★★ (B4), which is a much-photographed feature of the city; the other, **S. Andrea**★★ (A-B3; 12C), contains one of the masterpieces of Italian Gothic sculpture, Giovanni Pisano's **pulpit**★★ (1298-1301), which is famous for its dramatic, touching scenes from the Life of Christ. ► The architecture of the **Madonna dell'Umiltà**★ (B3; 1494-1522) shows how Renaissance Pistoia was under Florence's cultural influence. However, the city still retained its fondness for colourful ornamentation; see the lively **frieze**★ of glazed terra-cottas by G. della Robbia and his workshop above the elegant arcade of the **Ospedale del Ceppo**★ (A-B4). ► The town itself offers a great range of sights to the visitor: from the elegance of the v. Buozzi to the picturesque workshops of the v. di Stracceria; the noble vistas along the v. delle Pappe; and the energy of the v. degli Orafi, which contrasts with the network of alleyways and secluded piazzas where time seems to stand still.   ☐

Practical information

ℹ corso Gramsci 110 (B3), ☎ 34326; p. Duomo (B4), ☎ 21622 (information).
🚋 (C3-4), ☎ 20789.
🚌 from p. S. Francesco (A3) and v. Frosini (C5).

Hotels:
★★★ *Leon Bianco*, v. Panciatichi 2 (B4 a), ☎ 26675, 30 rm ℗ No restaurant, 65,000.

★★★ *Piccolo Ritz*, v. A. Vannucci 67 (C4 b), ☎ 26775, 24 rm ℗ ⏚ ⚙ No restaurant, 61,000; bkf: 7,000.
★★★ *Residence il Convento*, at Pontenuovo, v. S. Quirico 33, ☎ 452651, 24 rm ℗ ≼ ⚙ ⚙ ⣿ ⌂ Former monastery, restored preserving the original fabric, 80,000; bkf: 7,000.
★★ *Appennino*, v. XX Settembre 21 (C3-4 c), ☎ 32243, 26 rm ℗ 44,000; bkf: 3,000.

Restaurants:
♦♦♦ *Cucciolo della Montagna*, v. Panciatichi 4 (B4 a), ☎ 29733, closed 10-30 Jan. Regional cuisine: ribollita, chicken in the brick, 30,000.
♦♦♦ *Rafanelli*, at Sant'Agostino, ☎ 532046, closed Sun eve, Mon and Aug. Small garden and pergola. Regional cuisine: risotto with mushrooms, mixed grills, 20/30,000.

Recommended
Children's facilities: *Città di Pistoia zoo*, v. Pieve a Celle 160/A, ☎ 571280.
Craft workshops: *Bartoletti*, v. Sestini 110, ☎ 452318 (Mon-Sat, wrought-iron); *Picini*, at Quarrata, v. Follonica 79, ☎ 738743 (rustic furniture).
Events: *Giostra dell'Orso* (historical folk pageant, last ten days in Jul).
▼antiques: 2nd Sat and Sun of month (except Jul-Aug), in former Breda hall, v. Pacinotti.

PITIGLIANO

Grosseto 75, Florence 217, Rome 137 km
Pop. 4,381 ⊠ 58017 ☎ 0564   E5

Pitigliano is set on one of a series of steep ridges which rise abruptly above the gentle, undulating countryside. The houses rise out of the cliff and seem to grow from it. Its strategic position made Pitigliano the centre of one of the Orsini fiefs. The family built powerful defenses as well as Renaissance structures.

► The long, narrow **piazza della Repubblica** forms a clear division between the medieval town and the area occupied by the Orsini counts (dominated by the 14C-16C **Palazzo Orsini**. The Palazzo features an elegant Renaissance courtyard. On the S side of the piazza is a superb 18C **fountain** and, through its arches, an extensive view over the valley. ► In the v. Cavour is a dramatic and impressive series of tall arches, which formed part of a 16C **aqueduct**. ► Tortuous, picturesque side alleys, such as the vicolo della Battaglia, branch off the main streets of the **medieval town**. The alleys are sometimes linked by flights of steps. ► There is a particularly fine view down the steps descending to the **Porta Capo di Sotto**, outside which is a stretch of Etruscan **wall**. ► The vicolo Marghera leads into the old **ghetto**, and in the vicolo Manin are the remains of the synagogue built by the Jewish community which settled in Pitigliano in the 15C but which was exterminated during WWII. ► At one end of the p. Gregorio VII is the 18C Baroque façade of the **Duomo**.

Environs
► A path branches off the road to Sorano for the **Parco Orsini** but its ornamental statues and the benches carved in the tufa are now in ruins after several centuries' exposure to the elements. ► **Sovana** (→) is 8 km away. ► At 9 km is **Sorano** (→).   ☐

Practical information

Hotels:
★★ *Corano*, v. Maremmana, ☎ 616112, 29 rm ℗ ⚙ ⌂ 42,000.
★★ *Guastini*, p. Petruccioli, ☎ 616065, closed 20-30 Jun, 25 rm 42,000; bkf: 6,000.

Recommended
Events: *Sagra dell'uva* (12-14 Sep).

PONTEDERA

Pisa 20, Florence 61, Rome 314 km
Pop. 27,884 ⊠ 56025 ☎ 0587　　　　　　　C3

This strategically situated **fortress**, at the confluence of the Era and the Arno rivers, was a key position during the struggle between Pisa and Florence in the late Middle Ages. More recently, in the postwar period, the town's factories produced the *Vespa* scooters which revolutionized Italy's motoring habits. There is a beautiful *Madonna del Rosario del Cigoli* in the church of **SS. Jacopo e Filippo** (17C). The **Duomo** has a fine 19C Neoclassical façade.　□

Practical information _____

Restaurant:
♦♦♦ *Baldini,* v. Tosco-Romagnola, ☎ 52712, closed Sun. Regional cuisine: black risotto, scampi sui carboni, 25/35,000.

PONTREMOLI

Massa 56, Florence 164, Milan 186 km
Pop. 10,017 ⊠ 54027 ☎ 0187　　　　　　　B1

Pontrémoli is located in the Lunigiana, an area which intermingles Tuscan, Emilian and Ligurian influences. The valley has long been a communications route and, although it lies to the S of the Apennine ridge, it does not have quite the full, sunny Mediterranean climate. The terracing of hillsides is a reminder of a longstanding shortage of land which led to much emigration in the past. Due to such a shortage in the last century, many of Pontrémoli's men became strolling booksellers.

▶ The **Torre del Campanone** and the **campanile** of the cathedral are remnants of an unusual wall built in the 14C by Castruccio Castracani to put a stop to the continual clashes between Guelph and Ghibelline factions. ▶ Only the campanile of **S. Francesco** is still Romanesque, but inside the church is a masterpiece of 15C Tuscan sculpture, a polychrome relief of the *Madonna and Child* attributed to Agostino di Duccio. ▶ The 18C **oratory of the Madonna del Ponte** has an elegant elliptical ground plan and is a rare example of rococo architecture.

Environs

▶ 1.6 km S along the state road, the 15C-16C church of **SS. Annunziata** houses an octagonal Renaissance **tempietto** in marble with a bas-relief attributed to Jacopo Sansovino. At the high altar is another 16C work, Luca Cambiaso's fine panel painting of the *Adoration of the Magi.* ▶ In the Castello, which stands on the hill of Piagnaro, is a **museum** *(9 a.m.-12 noon and 2-5 p.m. or 4-7 p.m.; closed Mon)* which houses a collection of curious **stele-statues** carved by the Bronze Age inhabitants of the region. ▶ The **Museo Etnografico** *(9 a.m.-12 noon and 3-6 p.m.; closed Mon)* at **Villafranca in Lunigiana,** 12 km S, is devoted to the old farming, craft and pastoral methods of the region. ▶ 32 km away, above **Aulla** and overlooking the entrance to the Magra Valley is the powerful 16C **Fortezza della Brunella,** which has a square structure with corner bastions *(9 a.m.-12 noon and 2-5 p.m.).*　□

Practical information _____

PONTREMOLI
ℹ municipio, ☎ 831180.

> Send us your comments and suggestions; we will use them in the next edition.

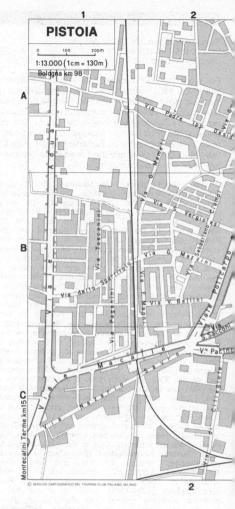

PISTOIA

0　　100　　200m
1:13.000 (1cm = 130m)
Bologna km 98

Montecatini Terme km15

Hotel:
★★★ *Golf,* v. Pineta 6, ☎ 831573, 82 rm Ⓟ ⬚ ⬚ ⬚ 59,000; bkf: 6,000.

Restaurants:
● ♦♦ *Busse,* p. Duomo 9, ☎ 831371, closed Fri and 1-20 Jul. Old trattoria. Lunigiana cuisine: casseroled veal, 20/30,000.
♦ *Bacciottini,* v. Ricci Armani 4, ☎ 830120, closed Thu except summer. Country inn with attached wine shop. Lunigiana cuisine: frittered dried cod, steamed loin of pork, 20/25,000.

Recommended
Events: *Bancarella literary prize* (last Sun Jul); *Bancarella sports prize* (second Sun Sep).

Environs

ZUM ZERI, 4,567 ft, ⊠ 54029, ☎ 0187, 24 km W.
⌇ ski lifts, cross-country skiing.
ℹ at Zeri, ☎ 837127 (municipio).

POPPI

Arezzo 38, Florence 53, Rome 256 km
Pop. 5,619 ⊠ 52014 ☎ 0575　　　　　　　E2-3

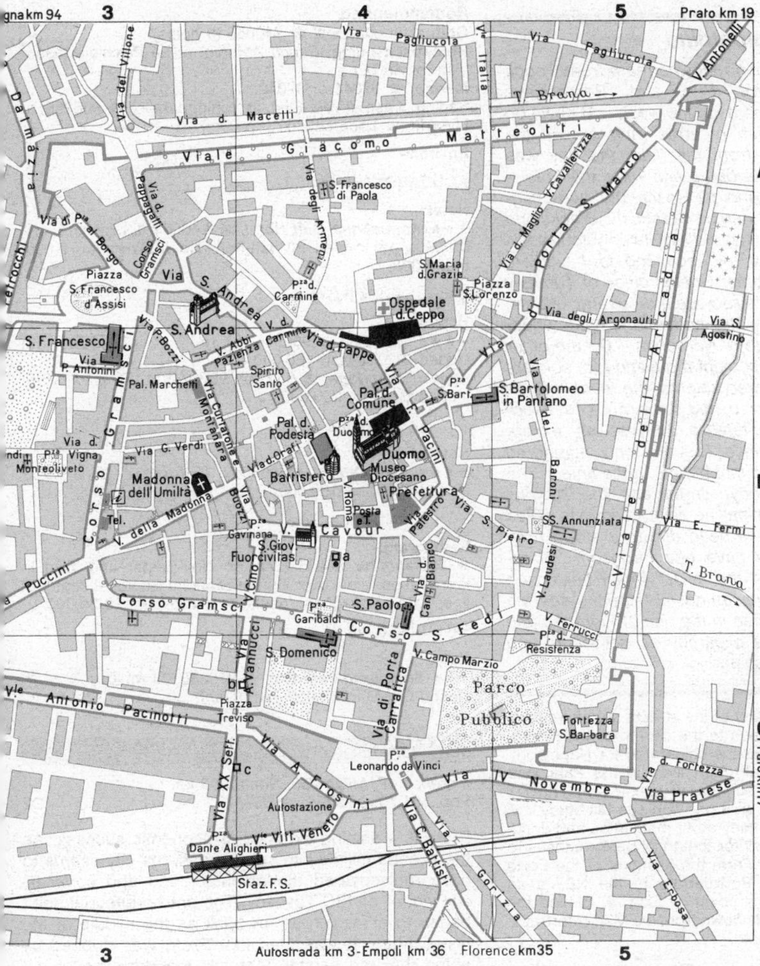
gna km 94
3
4
5
Prato km 19
Via Pagliucola
V. Italia
Via Pagliucola
V. Antonelli
T. Brana
Via d. Macelli
Viale Giacomo Matteotti
Via del Villone
Via Dalmazia
A
Via d. Pappagalli
Via degli Armeni
S. Francesco di Paola
V. Cavallerizza
Porta S. Marco
Via d. Maglio
Via di P.ta al Borgo
Corso Gramsci
S. Maria d. Grazie
Piazza S. Lorenzo
Piazza S. Francesco d'Assisi
Via S. Andrea
P.za d. Carmine
Ospedale d. Ceppo
Via degli Argonauti
Via S. Agostino
S. Francesco
S. Andrea
Via P. Bozzi
V. Abbi Pazienza
V. d. Carmine
Via d. Pappe
Via P. Antonini
Pal. Marchetti
Spirito Santo
Via Curtatone e Montanara
Pal. d. Comune
P.za S. Bart.
S. Bartolomeo in Pantano
Via dei Baroni
Viale dell' Arcadia
Pal. d. Podestà
P.za d. Duomo
Via d. Vigna
P.za Vigna
Via G. Verdi
Monteoliveto
Via d. Orafi
Duomo
Museo Diocesano
Via Pacini
Madonna dell'Umiltà
Battistero
Prefettura
B
Corso
V. della Madonna
Via Buozzi
V. Roma
Via Palestro
Via S. Pietro
SS. Annunziata
Via E. Fermi
Tel.
P.za Gavinana
V. Cavour
Posta e T.
S. Giov. Fuorcivitas
V.d. Canto al Bianco
Via Laudesi
T. Brana
Puccini
Corso Gramsci
V. Cimo
P.za Garibaldi
S. Paolo
Corso S. Fedi
V. Ferrucci
P.za d. Resistenza
Via A. Vannucci
S. Domenico
V. Campo Marzio
Via di Porta Carratica
Parco Pubblico
V.le Antonio Pacinotti
Piazza Treviso
Fortezza S. Barbara
C
Prato km 17
Via XX Sett.
Via A. Frosini
P.za Leonardo da Vinci
Via IV Novembre
Via d. Fortezza
Via Pratese
Autostazione
V.le Vitt. Veneto
P.za Dante Alighieri
Via C. Battisti
Via Gorizia
Via Erbosa
Staz. F.S.
3
Autostrada km 3 - Empoli km 36
Florence km35
5

In the centre of the Casentino (→), Poppi is best known for its formidable castle, the 13C-14C **Castello dei Guidi★**. Behind its moated wall and rather severe façade is a courtyard with a soaring external staircase and walls decorated with coats-of-arms. On the first floor *(apply to the caretaker)* is a hall decorated with 15C Florentine paintings and frescos. The tower commands a panoramic view★ over the Casentino. The 12C church of **S. Fedele** contains a 13C panel painting of the *Madonna and Child★*, a number of other works of art and a crypt. On the plain of **Campaldino,** at the junction of the Stia and Pontassieve roads, a column commemorates the great battle fought in 1289 between the Guelphs and the Ghibellines. A scenic route 17.2 km long leads to **Camáldoli** (→). □

Practical information

ℹ at Bibbiena, ☎ 593098.

Recommended
Children's facilities: *Zoo Fauna Europa,* v. del Parco 16, ☎ 58602.
Farm vacations: *Azienda Corsignano,* ☎ 550279.

PORTOFERRAIO

Livorno 102, Florence 181, Rome 284 km
Pop. 11,490 ✉ 57037 ☎ 0565 B5

Portoferraio was built in the middle of the 16C by Cosimo I de' Medici to be a stronghold and harbour. It is the capital of the island of Elba (→) and it is still ringed by a formidable semicircle of walls. By the end of the 18C, Portoferraio was still strategically important, but it was mainly devoted to mining and fishing. At the beginning of the 19C, Elba's name suddenly became known around Europe. On 3 May 1814, it became the capital of the small state given to Napoleon in his exile and where he remained until 26 February 1815.

▶ The **Porta a Terra** provides access to the **fortifications** on the W side of the city. They rise in a series of steps from the sea, up to the reddish brick bulk of the **Forte del Falcone** (1548). ▶ The **Porta a Mare,** opposite the **Molo Mediceo,** is the other entrance to the town and leads to the **piazza della Repubblica,** the old parade ground, on which the **Palazzo Comunale** stands (inscriptions to Napoleon on the façade). ▶ Near the Duomo is a picturesque

Campaldino

Campaldino is in Casentino, downstream from Poppi, where the roads for Stia and Pontassieve branch. Pratomagno looms to the west. At dawn on 11 June 1289, the clash of arms rang out as the morning mists cleared from the field; the day was hot and stormy. On the battle site were the Magistrate of Florence, Ugolino de'Rossi, the two magnates Corso Donati and Vieri de'Cerchi, the Blacks and the Whites (Corso Donati was killed), twenty-four-year-old Dante Alighieri, and ten thousand foot soldiers from Florence and the other Guelph cities of Tuscany and Romagna. In all, there were a thousand knights, including those sent by the house of Anjou, under the command of Amerigo of Narbonne. On the other side were the Ghibellines: eight thousand foot soldiers from Arezzo, eight hundred knights, the feudal retainers, the Bishop of Arezzo and the army commander, Buonconte da Montefeltro. It was an exceptional show of force since Tuscany only numbered seven hundred thousand inhabitants at the time. The clash was long and bloody. In the end, the Guelphs triumphed since the Ghibelline reinforcements failed to arrive. This may have been due to a storm from Pratomagno, or it may have been treason. Buonconte was 'run through the throat whilst fleeing on foot'; his body was never found. Historians see the battle as an important step in the rise of Florence and the establishment of its oligarchy of merchants and manufacturers over Tuscany.

market and old shops. Many of the streets are staircases, such as the one which leads to the church of the Misericordia (every 5 May, a mass is celebrated for Napoleon). ▶ Napoleon and his small court lived in the **Palazzina Napoleonica dei Mulini** *(summer 9 a.m.-2 p.m.; hols 9 a.m.-1 p.m.; closed Mon)*. In it one can see his study, his bedroom, his library and many other mementos and documents. Do not miss the hall for theatrical performances to the I. of the palazzina. ▶ From the bastions of the **Forte Stella**, which dominates Portoferraio to the NE, an extensive vista over the N coast of Elba. ▶ Behind the city, a fascinating trail leads down from the Medici fortresses to the **spiaggia delle Viste**. □

Practical information _____

PORTOFERRAIO
⚓ (mid-Apr-Oct), at Terme San Giovanni (4 km S), ☎ 92680.
≋
Ⓘ at the harbour, calata Italia 26, ☎ 92671.
⛴ car ferries, boats, hydrofoils from Piombino; daily motor boats from Livorno (→ island of Elba).
Car rental: *Maggiore*, calata Italia 8, ☎ 915368.

Hotels:
★★★ **Nuova Padulella**, v. Einaudi 1, ☎ 915506, 44 rm Ⓟ ⋞ ♿ 66,000.
★★★ **Touring**, v. Roma 13, ☎ 915851, 31 rm ⅋ 70,000.

Restaurants:
♦ **Braciere**, v. Carducci 230, ☎ 915612, closed Wed except summer and Feb. With small covered terrace. Mixed cuisine: penne Giorgio, grilled or baked fish, 25/40,000.
♦ **Ferrigna**, p. della Repubblica 22, ☎ 92129, closed Tue except summer and Dec-Jan. Near harbour. Regional cuisine: mussels gratinéed with aromatic herbs, deviled squid, 23/40,000.

⚠ ★★★ *Rosselba le Palme*, at Ottone, 250 pl, ☎ 966101.

Recommended
Golf: at Acquabona, ☎ 940066 (9 holes).
Horseback riding: *Ranch Antonio*, at Le Picchiaie (associate of *ANTE*).
Marina: ☎ 92041 or 92042.
Sailing: *Casa di vela Elba*, at Schiopparello, ☎ 966265; at Livorno, ☎ 0586/505562 (Apr-Oct).

Environs

ACQUABONA, 9 km SE.

Hotel:
★★★ **Acquabona Golf Hotel**, ☎ 940064, 23 rm Ⓟ ♿ ⅋ ▣ ⅋ (9) closed 20 Jan-Feb. No restaurant, 79,000; bkf: 9,000.

BIODOLA, 9 km SW.

Hotels:
★★★★ **Biodola**, ☎ 969966, 67 rm Ⓟ ⋞ ♿ ▣ ⅌ ∿ (9) closed 21 Oct-Mar, 160,000.
★★★★ **Hermitage**, ☎ 969932, 90 rm Ⓟ ⋞ ♿ ▣ ⅌ ∿ (9) closed Oct-Apr, 200,000.

OTTONE, 10 km E.

Hotel:
★★★★ **Villa Ottone**, ☎ 966042, 68 rm Ⓟ ⋞ ♿ ⅋ ▣ ⅌ closed Oct-Mar, 150,000.

SCAGLIERI, 8 km SW.

Restaurant:
♦ **Luciano**, ☎ 969952, closed Nov-Easter and Wed in low season. View over Gulf of Biodola. Regional seafood: libecciata of spaghetti, penne with octopus, 20/30,000.

VITICCIO, 6 km W.

Hotel:
★★★ **Soggiorno Paradiso**, ☎ 915385, 34 rm Ⓟ ⋞ ♿ ⋞ ⅌ closed Oct-Mar, 68,000; bkf: 8.000.

PRATO*

Florence 19, Milan 293, Rome 293 km
Pop. 161,705 ⊠ 50047 ☎ 0574   D2

Prato is a shining example of economic success. As the second millennium approaches, the city seems to have rediscovered the manufacturing and commercial vigour of 13C Tuscany. The entrepreneurial spirit began to stir again as far back as the middle of the last century. It was then that Prato was dubbed by some the 'rag capital'. Actually the recycling of old dresses to produce low-cost products is just one aspect of an enormous textile industry which has attracted many immigrants since the war. Prato is now the third largest city in Tuscany.

▶ It is not necessary to go to Apulia or to Sicily to see a fine example of 13C Germanic military architecture. Prato's **Castello dell'Imperatore★** (1237-48) was built by Frederick II and is typical of the style. Open to the public *(9 a.m.-12 noon and 4-7 p.m.; closed Wed)*, it has a vast courtyard used for concerts and the walk along the wall offers a splendid view of the city. ▶ The 15C Renaissance basilica of **S. Maria delle Carceri★** is by Giuliano da Sangallo and shows Brunelleschi's influence. ▶ A number of artists active in the Florentine Renaissance worked on the beautiful **Duomo★★** (12C-13C, extended in the 14C). On the exterior is Michelozzo's famous pulpit of the Holy Girdle★. Its panels are copies of ones carved by Donatello and his assistants (the originals are in the **Museo dell'Opera del Duomo**). The glazed white terra-cotta tympanum above the portal is by Andrea della Robbia. Inside is another 15C pulpit, Giovanni Pisano's graceful Gothic *Madonna and Child*★ (14C), frescos such as the *Nativity of the Virgin*★, attributed to Paolo Uccello and, in the sanctuary, the *Lives of St. John the Baptist and St. Stephen*★★, a masterpiece by Filippo Lippi. ▶ The severe Palazzo Pretorio on the p. del Comune houses the **Galle-**

ria Comunale★ *(weekdays 9 a.m.-1 p.m.; hols 9 a.m.-12 noon; closed Mon)*, which has an important collection of 14C-15C Florentine paintings. ▶ The large **piazza del Mercatale** has been a market place for centuries and immediately gives the visitor a feeling for the true Prato. ▶ In keeping with its main industry, Prato has the **Museo del Tessuto** *(wkdays 9 a.m.-12 noon)*, the finest museum of its kind in Italy, with collections of ancient brocades, damasks, velvets and embroideries.   □

Practical information _____

① v. Cairoli 48, ☎ 24112.

Hotels:
★★★★ *Palace*, v. Pier della Francesca 71, ☎ 592841, 85 rm ℗ ⏼ ☐ closed Aug, 130,000; bkf: 15,000.
★★★★ *President*, v. Simintendi 20, ☎ 30251, 78 rm ℗ ⏼ 105,000; bkf: 10,000.
★★★ *Flora*, v. Cairoli 31, ☎ 20021, 31 rm ℗ ⏼ No restaurant, 92,000; bkf: 10,000.
★★★ *Milano*, v. Tiziano 15, ☎ 23371, 70 rm ℗ ⏼ ⏼ 95,000; bkf: 10,000.
★★★ *Villa Santa Cristina*, v. Poggio Secco 58, ☎ 595951, 23 rm ℗ ⏼ ⏼ ☐ closed Aug, 95,000; bkf: 15,000.

Restaurants:
● ♦♦♦ *Piraña*, v. Valentin 110, ☎ 25746, closed Sat, Sun and Aug. Modern and elegant. Creative cuisine: creamed rice with scampi, fettuccine with lobster, 50/55,000.
♦♦ *Tonio*, p. Mercatale 161, ☎ 21266, closed Sun, Mon and Aug. Mixed cuisine: taglioni with salmon, fisherman's risotto, 30/45,000.

Recommended
Events: *international congress of comic strips and science fiction* (Jan-Feb); *stamp show and congress* (Mar). *Display of the Holy Girdle* from the pulpit of the Duomo (Easter, 1 May, 15 Aug, 8 Sep, 26 Dec).
Farm vacations: *Fattoria Bacchereto*, at Carmignano, ☎ 055/8712191.
Wine: trade fair for wines of Carmignano in May-Jun; visit to Capezzana estate, ☎ 8706091.

PUNTA ALA

Grosseto 41, Florence 170, Rome 225 km
Pop. 261 ✉ 58040 ☎ 0564   C5

Until a few decades ago, Punta Ala was simply a rocky headland covered with scrub-brush. Today, it is a luxury tourist and seaside resort with a bustling marina. Fine view★ along the coast from Piombino to Mt. Argentario and the islands of the Tuscan archipelago.   □

Practical information _____

≋
① at Castiglione della Pescaia, ☎ 933678.

Hotels:
★★★★ *Cala del Porto*, v. del Porto, ☎ 922455, 47 rm ℗ ≼ ☾ ⏼ ⏼ ☐ closed 1 Oct-14 May, 170,000; bkf: 25,000.
★★★★ *Gallia Palace Hotel*, v. delle Sughere, ☎ 922022, 98 rm ℗ ☾ ⏼ ⏼ ☐ ⏼ ⏼ (18) closed Oct-24 May, 338,000. Rest. ● ♦♦♦♦ *Pagoda* on private beach of grand hotel. Creative cuisine: mussel soup alla Paul Bocuse, salmon with dill, 40/50,000.
★★★★ *Golf*, v. del Gualdo, ☎ 922026, 180 rm ℗ ☾ ⏼ ⏼ ⏼ ☐ ⏼ closed 16 Oct-9 Apr, 250,000; bkf: 15,000.
★★★★ *Piccolo Hotel Alleluja*, v. del Porto, ☎ 922050, 43 rm ℗ ☾ ⏼ ⏼ ⏼ closed 10 Nov-15 Dec, 300,000.

Restaurant:
♦♦ *Scalino*, v. Porto 12, ☎ 922168, closed Tue and Jan-Feb. View over sea near harbour. Regional cuisine: pappardelle with crab, foil baked fish, 35/70,000.
⋏ ★★★★ *Puntala*, at Torre Civette, 760 pl, ☎ 922294 (all year).

Recommended
Conference centre: at *Golf Hotel*, ☎ 922026.
Golf: ☎ 922121 or 922643 (18 holes).
Horseback riding: ☎ 922013; *Polo club*, ☎ 922013.
Marina: ☎ 922217.
Yacht club: ☎ 921117.

RADICOFANI

Siena 72, Florence 140, Rome 158 km
Pop. 1,393 ✉ 53040 ☎ 0578   E5

As one heads S, down the bleached and bare landscape of the Val d'Orcia, the castle of Radicófani rises above the horizon. The new SS no longer climbs up to the village. In the Middle Ages and under the Medici, the town was a busy stop on the old v. Cassia. In the 17C, it became the customs house of the grand duchy. In the 13C, travelers ran the risk of meeting up with the legendary Ghino di Tacco, a noble turned brigand, who was mentioned by both Dante and Boccaccio.

▶ The village stands on a hill and retains much of its medieval appearance: narrow streets and dark alleys lined by stone houses, picturesque staircases. ▶ A **basalt cliff**, surmounted by the ruins of the fortress, overlooks the village. ▶ Along the v. Cassia, opposite a late Renaissance fountain, the **Palazzo La Posta** was in turn a Medici hunting lodge, a hotel and customs house. Its former guests include the renowned French writers Montaigne and Chateaubriand.   □

RAPOLANO TERME

Siena 27, Florence 96, Rome 202 km
Pop. 5,076 ✉ 53040 ☎ 0577   E4

Still partly enclosed within its medieval walls and towers, Rapolano is set amidst low, oak-covered hills on the W slope of the ridge which divides the Ombrone basin from the Valdichiana. Fertile and sunny, the area is devoted to the cultivation of maize and vines. There are also extensive deposits of travertine, the light, porous stone used in so many Tuscan buildings. Another natural asset is the hot sulphur springs which accommodate the town's two spas (baths, mud treatments, inhalations).

▶ Near the **Terme di S. Giovanni Battista**, 2 km SW of the town, is an impressive natural gas spring, the **Mofeta.** □

Practical information _____

⏀ *Terme Antica Querciolaia* (all year), ☎ 724091; *Terme San Giovanni* (May-Oct), ☎ 724030.

Hotel:
★★ *Motel Due Mari*, SS for Siena, ☎ 724070, 47 rm ℗ ⏼ ⏼ closed Jul, 59,000.

The ruins of ROSELLE

Grosseto 12, Florence 134, Rome 193 km
✉ 58040 ☎ 0564   D5

Devastated first by the barbarians, then by the Saracens, the Roman city of Roselle was never rebuilt. The hilltop site behind Grosseto has been a boon to archaeologists. Beneath the Roman ruins are the remains of an Etruscan city which flourished from the 7C BC-4C BC as the centre of a fertile area which produced grain, millet and barley. Located on an open plateau between two small hills, it is a fascinating site and the dense network of streets and walls, which at first appear like some unfathomable maze, convey a real feeling for its ancient past.

▶ The almost-intact **ring of Etruscan walls**★ consists of large, partly-dressed, polygonal blocks and extends for nearly two miles. Some parts of the wall are 16 ft high. The five gates were opened at such an angle that attackers were forced to expose parts of their bodies not protected by shields. ▶ The most important discovery is the first example of an archaic house dating from the 7C BC. These houses were square on the outside, but oval inside and are made of unfired bricks. ▶ Features of the **Roman city** include the ruins of the forum, which was paved in the 1C AD. On the N hill are the remains of baths and a small amphitheatre. ▶ Finds from Roselle (with an accompanying map) are housed in the Museo Archeologico e d'Arte della Maremma at Grosseto (→). □

The abbey of SAN GALGANO**

Siena 33, Florence 90, Rome 254 km
✉ 53012 ☎ 0577   D4

Few places in Tuscany have the rare atmosphere of the silent, isolated ruins of the abbey of San Galgano. The monks, inspired by their order's churches in France, built this masterpiece of Cistercian architecture in the 13C. The monastery soon became rich and powerful. Its slow decline began in the 15C and its buildings gradually began to crumble.

▶ Today the **monastery** has been restored; but not the famous **church**★★, which is the first example of Cistercian Gothic in Tuscany. From the outside, the ruins of the façade, flanks and apse convey a sense of grand, desolate beauty. The roof has collapsed and, inside, the high Gothic arches of the nave flank a carpet of grass. ▶ The **chiesetta of S. Galgano**★, a short distance away, is a gem of Sienese Romanesque architecture. It features a beautiful dome built in concentric circles of brick and stone. An adjoining chapel houses a 14C **fresco cycle**★ by Ambrogio Lorenzetti. □

SAN GIMIGNANO*

Siena 38, Florence 54, Rome 268 km
Pop. 7,369 ✉ 53037 ☎ 0577   D3

The town occupies a strong position on top of a hill, from where it overlooks the Valdelsa. A compact curtain wall (13C), over 1 mile long, encloses it completely, but the town's unique feature is its series of massive towers. There are fourteen in all, scattered across the town, some of them over 165 ft high. San Gimignano is a virtually untouched medieval city-state. The walls, gates, houses and towers, streets and piazzas have survived the centuries almost unaltered (much of San Gimignano dates from the mid-14C). It was at that time that its fortunes began to collapse, its population to decline and its independence to come to an end.

▶ The town's backbone is a small hilly segment of what was, between the 9C-13C, the great v. Francigena, the main road to the trade fairs of France. The road is known as the **via S. Giovanni** (and, beyond the centre, the **via S. Matteo**). It is lined with churches, inns, houses, towers and medieval palazzi, interspersed with picturesque side alleys. ▶ The centre is divided into the adjacent and intercommunicating piazze della Cisterna and del Duomo (B1-2) where, in the 12C-14C, the major public and religious buildings were built, along with the palazzi and towers of the most powerful families in the city. Several towers, such as the twin 13C **Torri degli Ardinghelli** (E side) and the **Torre del Diavolo** (N side), stand on the sloping **piazza della Cisterna**★, which has a central well dating from 1263. The **Piazza del Duomo**★, the monu-

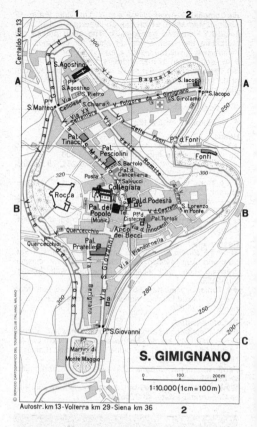

S. GIMIGNANO

0   100   200 m
1:10.000 (1 cm = 100 m)

Autostr. km 13 - Volterra km 29 - Siena km 36

mental heart of San Gimignano, is flanked by a series of tall buildings. To the N are the twin **Torri dei Salvucci**; to the E the 14C **Palazzo del Podestà**★, which has an open loggia on the ground floor and is flanked by the powerful **Torre Rognosa** (165 ft); to the S is the **Palazzo del Popolo** with the **Torre Grossa**★ (175 ft); to the W, is the rough façade of the Duomo or **Collegiata**★★, which rises at the top of a broad flight of steps. ▶ The medieval **via della Romite** (A1-B2) offers an enchanting mix of buildings and open spaces devoted to orchards and gardens. ▶ Of the smaller towns in Tuscany, San Gimignano is certainly one of the richest in works of art, particularly religious works from the 14C-15C. In these pieces, one can follow the town's cultural evolution, in the mid-14C, toward Florence's influence. The **Museo d'Arte Sacra** is known for its sculptures, while the Palazzo del Popolo houses the **Pinacoteca Civica**★ (B1; *Apr-Sep 9:30 a.m.-12:30 p.m. and 3:30-6:30 p.m.; Oct-Mar 10 a.m.-1 p.m. and 2:30-5:30 p.m.; closed Mon in winter; combined ticket for all museums and the Cappella di S. Fina*). There are a number of outstanding works in the highly-decorated Duomo: the Renaissance **Cappella di S. Fina** (*same opening hrs as the Pinacoteca Civica; combined ticket valid for both buildings; also open Mon*) and, in the Romanesque-Gothic church of **S. Agostino** (A1), the **fresco**★ cycle by Benozzo Gozzoli and the stupendous panel painting of the *Coronation of the Virgin Mary*★ by Piero del Pollaiolo. □

Don't forget to consult the Practical Holiday Guide: it can help in solving many problems.

Practical information

🛈 p. del Duomo (B1), ☎ 940008.

Hotels:
★★★ *Bel Soggiorno*, v. S. Giovanni 89 (C1 a), ☎ 940375, 27 rm ℗ ⪅ ✤ 50,000; bkf: 5,000.
★★★ *Cisterna*, p. della Cisterna 24 (B2 b), ☎ 940328, 46 rm ℗ ⪙ closed 11 Nov-9 Mar, 67,000; bkf: 7,000. Rest.
✦✦ *Terrazze*, closed Tue and Wed noon. Original medieval monastery, fine views of the Val d'Elsa. Regional cuisine: hunter's style rabbit, Parma-style tripe, 30/50,000.
★★★ *Leon Bianco*, p. della Cisterna 13 (B2 c), ☎ 941294, 21 rm ℗ ✤ No restaurant, 50,000; bkf: 5,000.
★★★ *Pescille*, at Pescille, ☎ 940186, 33 rm ℗ ⪅ 🕮 ✤ 🖂 ⚲ closed 2 Jan-Feb. No restaurant, 55,000; bkf: 5,000.
★★★ *Renaie*, at Pancole, ☎ 955044, 26 rm ℗ 🕮 🖂 55,000; bkf: 6,000. Rest. ✦✦ *Leonetto* ☎ 955072, closed Tue and 15-30 Nov. In countryside. Regional cuisine: rigatoni montanara, fusilli pancolana, 20/35,000.

🜁 ★★ *Boschetto di Piemma*, at Santa Lucia, 130 pl, ☎ 940352.

Recommended
Events: *Sangimignanese summer* (operas performed in piazzas, concerts, exhibitions of painting).
Purchases: wrought-iron work, straw baskets, handicrafts.

SAN GIOVANNI VALDARNO

Arezzo 37, Florence 44, Rome 255 km
Pop 19,303 🖂 52027 ☎ 055   D-E3

The military needs of the Florentine republic in the 14C led to the construction of this town which today focuses on industry and is the most important centre in the upper Valdarno.

▶ In the old quarter, many of the narrow alleys which lead to the **arcaded piazza** retain their medieval character as does the **Palazzo Pretorio** on the piazza. ▶ Underneath the portico of the **S. Maria delle Grazie** basilica is a lively, glazed, polychrome **terra-cotta** attributed to Giovanni della Robbia. The ornate 17C interior features a *Madonna and Child with Four Saints*, attributed to Masaccio; the 14C fresco of the *Miracle of Monna Tancia* is also of interest; there is a fine *Annunciation* attributed to Jacopo del Sellaio. ▶ About 2 km away, on top of a hill, stands the restored **Franciscan monastery of Montecarlo**, which features some fine Renaissance architecture. ☐

Practical information

Hotel:
★★★ *River*, v. F.lli Cervi 10, ☎ 941345, 40 rm ℗ 55,000.

SAN MARCELLO PISTOIESE

Pistoia 29, Florence 66, Milan 291 km
Pop. 8,305 🖂 51028 ☎ 0573   C2

Although it was a Ghibelline commune in the Middle Ages, San Marcello Pistoiese is today an important vacation resort surrounded by fine scenery. The wax *Ecce Homo* in the parish church bears witness to the impassioned, sorrowful religious spirit of the 17C. 3 km away, near **Mamiano**, is an unusual **footbridge** suspended between the two banks of the River Lima.

Environs

▶ **Cutigliano** *(9 km N)* is a vacation resort with a **cableway** to Doganaccia (5,050 ft). The 14C **Palazzo Pretorio**, rebuilt in the 16C, reminds the visitor that Cutigliano was once an administrative centre for the Pistoiese Apennines. ▶ Until a few decades ago **Gavinana** *(3.5 km E)* was simply a name in history books (the site of the famous battle of 1530 which marked the Medici's return to power).

Today, it is a summer and winter vacation resort. There is a small **museum** *(10 a.m.-12 noon and 5-7 p.m., every day in summer; Thu and Sat in winter)*, with weapons and coins from the period of the famous battle. ▶ The beeches, pines and chestnut trees which dot the valley surrounding **Maresca** *(6.3 km E)* give only a hint of the great state-owned **Teso forest** which climbs over 3,000 ft to the Apennine watershed. A vacation resort in summer, Maresca hosts snow sports enthusiasts in winter: a road *(6 km)* leads to the **rifugio Casetta Pulledrari** and to the nearby ski lifts. ▶ From either Cutigliano or Maresca, one can take a trip to the **Corno delle Scale** (6,380 ft). Further on, at the foot of Mt. Cupolino, is a small lake: the **Scaffaiolo**. ☐

Practical information

SAN MARCELLO PISTOIESE
🛈 v. Marconi 16, ☎ 630145.

Hotels:
★★★ *Cacciatore*, v. Marconi 87, ☎ 630533, 25 rm ⪅ 🕮 ✤ closed Oct, 53,000; bkf: 5,000.
★★ *Villa Ombrosa*, v. D'Azeglio 18, ☎ 630156, 27 rm ℗ 🜁 🕮 ✤ closed 11 Sep-24 Jun, 50,000; bkf: 6,000.

Recommended
Events: traditional launching of hot air balloon for S. Celestina (8 Sep).
Tennis: v. Nazionale, ☎ 65486.

Environs

CUTIGLIANO, 2,224 ft, 🖂 51024, ☎ 0573, 9 km N.
⚡ cableways, ski lifts, cross-country skiing and instruction at Doganaccia and at Pian di Novello.
🛈 v. Tigri, ☎ 68029.

Hotels:
★★★ *Italia*, p. Ferrucci 5, ☎ 68008, 34 rm 🕮 ✤ closed May and 30 Sep-20 Dec, 55,000; bkf: 4,000.
★★★ *Piandinovello*, at Pian di Novello, v. Sestaione 131, ☎ 673076, 68 rm ℗ 🜁 🕮 ✤ 🖂 ⚲ closed 21 Apr-Jun and Sep-19 Dec, 55,000; bkf: 5,000.
★★★ *Villa Patrizia*, v. Europa 9, ☎ 68024, 19 rm ℗ 🕮 ✤ closed 6 Apr-19 Jun and 16 Sep-19 Dec, 55,000; bkf: 5,000.

Restaurant:
✦ *Fagiolino*, v. Carega 1, ☎ 68014, closed Tue and Wed and Oct-Nov. Typical rural trattoria. Regional cuisine: ravioli with ricotta and vegetables, roast kid, 18/28,000.

🜁 ★★ *Neve e Sole*, at Pianosinatico, SS dell'Abetone, 90 pl, ☎ 670079 (all year).

Recommended
Events: exhibition of crafts and *midsummer festival* (Aug).
Purchases: porcini mushrooms (seasonal market at Pian di Novello), chestnuts, woodland fruits.

GAVINANA, 2,685 ft, 🖂 51025, ☎ 0573, 3.5 km E.
⚡ ski lifts, instruction at Pratorsi.
🛈 p. Ferrucci, ☎ 66191.

Hotel:
★★ *Villa Ada*, v. Apiciana 43, ☎ 66034, 41 rm ℗ 🜁 🕮 closed 11 Jan-9 Jun and 21 Sep-19 Dec, 50,000; bkf: 3,000.

MARESCA, 2,625 ft, 🖂 51026, ☎ 0573, 6 km E.
⚡ ski lifts, cross-country skiing, instruction.
🛈 p. L. Appiano, ☎ 64040 (in season).

Hotel:
★★ *Miramonti*, v. Mazzini 20, ☎ 64021, 37 rm ℗ ⪅ 🜁 🕮 ✤ closed Sep-14 Jun, 51,000.

SAN MINIATO

Pisa 41, Florence 43, Rome 296 km
Pop. 25,183 🖂 56027 ☎ 0571   C3

There are superb vistas from the top of the hill, and on clear days the view extends from the hills of Fiesole to the sea, from the Apuan Alps to the cliffs of

Volterra. One can understand why the medieval German emperors established their Tuscan residence here. The palazzi, and the churches rich in works of art, show that even under Florentine rule San Miniato continued to build with elegance and beauty.
▶ San Miniato is to be enjoyed more as a whole than for any individual work. In the 14C church of **S. Domenico** *(cloister open to the public)* are a number of fine pieces displaying the influence of Masolino, Pisanello, Bernardo Rossellino and della Robbia. The **Duomo's** Romanesque brick facing incorporates marble sculptures and has three 16C portals; a series of 13C glazed bowls is also here.
▶ Religious art, paintings and sculpture from the 16C-19C are on display in the **Museo Diocesano** *(not always open,* ☎ 418071; closed Mon). ▶ Napoleon visited one summer day in 1797, since a member of his family lived here. He stayed the night at the **Palazzo Buonaparte.**
▶ One climbs up the hill from the Prato del Duomo. The **tower** at the top is a post-WWII reconstruction of the last remnant of the fort built by the Emperor Frederick II in 1240. □

Practical information ───────────────

Hotel:
★★★ *Miravalle,* p. del Castello, ☎ 418075, 23 rm ╬ ◁ ఈ ⊛ closed Christmas, 68,000; bkf: 8,000.

Recommended
Archery: *Compagnia arcieri Michele Salvini da Montopoli,* at Montópoli Vald'Arno, v. S. Stefano 11.
Events: *drama festival* in the piazza (end of Jul). *Kite-flying festival* (1st Sun after Easter). *White truffle fair* (last Sun in Nov).
Motocross: *S. Barbara* track, at Ponte a Egola *(6 km W),* run by *Moto club Pelli corse,* at La Serra, ☎ 460197.

SAN QUIRICO D'ORCIA

Siena 43, Florence 111, Rome 196 km
Pop. 2,220 ⊠ 53027 ☎ 0577   E4

This old Sienese hilltop town is located between the Orcia and Asso valleys. Its outstanding feature is the old parish church (the Collegiata), rebuilt in the 12C-13C when the bishops and cities of Arezzo and Siena were fighting for control of the village. In the 18C, a pottery factory began producing fine ceramics which are still known today. They are marked by the Chigi coat-of-arms or, simply, S.Q.

▶ The extraordinary portals of the famous **Collegiata★** are its main attraction. On the façade the portal is preceded in the Lombard manner by a small porch with knotted columns held by lionesses; and on the r. flank the first portal shows powerful 13C sculptures★. ▶ 5.5 km S is one of the countless small Tuscan spas: **Bagno Vignoni,** which can boast Lorenzo il Magnifico as one of its former guests. □

Practical information ───────────────

ℹ p. Libertà 2.
♨ (Jun-Sep), at Bagno Vignoni, ☎ 887365.

SANSEPOLCRO

Arezzo 35, Florence 114, Rome 260 km
Pop. 15,641 ⊠ 52037 ☎ 0575   F3

Sansepolcro's prosperity at the end of the Middle Ages can still be seen in its towers, tower-houses, Gothic buildings and large numbers of palaces dating from between the Renaissance and the 18C. Piero della Francesca was born here and there are quite a number of his works in town.

▶ The main road, the v. XX Settembre, runs from the porta Fiorentina and the porta Romana and is flanked by magnificent Gothic, Renaissance and Mannerist buildings. There are also some **medieval workshops.** ▶ Five arches cross the **via del Buon umore.** Next to the church of S. Maria delle Grazie is the elegant small portico of the oratory of the **Compagnia della Visitazione.** The v. di Santa Maria dei Servi is lined with humble medieval houses. ▶ The church of **S. Lorenzo** contains a memorable 16C *Deposition* by Rosso Fiorentino. The **Museo Civico★** *(9:30 a.m.-12 noon and 3-6:30 p.m. or 2:30-6 p.m.)* houses some beautiful works by Piero della Francesca, including his fresco of the *Resurrection★★,* the polyptych of the *Virgin of the Mantle★★,* the fragment of *S. Giuliano★* and the fragment of *S. Ludovico★.* There is also *S. Quintino★,* a canvas by Pontormo. ▶ There is another fresco by della Francesca at Monterchi (→ ; *17 km S).* □

Practical information ───────────────

Hotels:
★★★ *Balestra,* v. dei Montefeltro 29, ☎ 735151, 54 rm ℙ ▧ ఈ 45,000; bkf: 3,000.
★★★ *Fiorentino,* v. Pacioli 60, ☎ 734233, 26 rm ℙ ▧ ⊛ 39,000; bkf: 2,500. Rest. ● ◆◆◆ closed Fri and 20 Jun-10 Jul. Family-run with long tradition. Regional cuisine: roulades with artichokes, pigeon with olives, 15/30,000.

Recommended
Events: *Palio della Balestra* (contest between local crossbowmen and crossbowmen from Gubbio, 2nd Sun in Sep), Comune, ☎ 76461.
Horseback riding: *Club ippico Sansepolcro,* ☎ 72044 (ANTE affiliate).
Purchases: embroidery and pillow lace.

SARTEANO

Siena 84, Florence 135, Rome 168 km
Pop. 4,359 ⊠ 53047 ☎ 0578   E4-5

Sarteano's location on the slopes of Mt. di Cetona makes it a pleasant place for a vacation. The thermal springs of **Bagno Santo** (some 500 yards from town) are mainly used to supply two swimming pools.

▶ There were settlements on Mt.di Cetona by the end of the Neolithic period and a small **antiquarium** (with prehistoric and Etruscan finds) has been opened in the Municipio. ▶ The **castle** which overlooks the town is a well-preserved medieval fortress. ▶ There are some fine buildings in the **old section,** including the palazzo at the top of v. Roma, with the old town **sundial;** the Renaissance **palazzo Piccolomini,** with an elegant arcaded courtyard; the Flamboyant Gothic **cloister** of the former monastery of S. Francesco; and the house in the piazzetta della Chiesina, with a delightful little 15C loggia. ▶ An *Annunciation★* by Beccafumi, the 16C Mannerist painter, is housed in the church of **S. Martino.** □

Practical information ───────────────

♨ (mid-May-Sep), park with heated swimming pool, ☎ 265531.
ℹ p. XXIV Giugno, ☎ 265312.

Restaurant:
◆ *Giara,* v. Europa 2, ☎ 265511, closed Mon except summer. Typical trattoria. Regional cuisine: homemade tagliatelle, charcoal-grilled meats, 20/30,000.

⋏ ★★★★ *Delle Piscine,* v. Campo dei Fiori, 450 pl, ☎ 265531.

Recommended
Horseback riding: *Centro ippico Casa Bocca,* v. di Chianciano, ☎ 265368.
Spelunking: visits to Grotte di Belvedere (Mar-Oct); information at Cetona, ☎ 25531.

SATURNIA

Grosseto 57, Florence 199, Rome 172 km
Pop. 372 ⊠ 58050 ☎ 0564   D-E5

According to ancient writers, Saturnia is the oldest town in Italy, a cradle of Italic civilization, which flourished before the arrival of the Etruscans. The modern village is situated on a plateau in the Albegna Valley. At different periods in its history, Saturnia was controlled by Etruscans, Romans, Saracens, Sienese and Florentines. Each group added or demolished parts of the city in a process which still continues today. Recent aerial photographs have revealed a **network of streets** that pre-dates the regular Roman grid.

▶ Behind the parish church, the remains of the 14C **fortifications** built by the Sienese can still be seen. ▶ The arch of a 2000-year-old **gate** is Roman. But the origin of the **walls**, with their large masses of polygonal and squared stone marvelously well-fitted together, is more enigmatic. Before concluding that they were from the same period as the arch, scholars debated whether the walls might not even be pre-Etruscan. ▶ However, the **tombs** discovered in the area are definitely Etruscan and pre-Etruscan. A small group of finds is on display in a **local collection.** ▶ 7 km away, in a green valley, is the **Terme di Saturnia,** whose warm sulphur waters are used for therapeutic purposes.   ◻

Practical information _____

♨ (all year), at Terme di Saturnia, ☎ 601191.

Hotel:
★★★★ **Terme di Saturnia,** ☎ 601061, 104 rm Ⓟ ⌕ ⅏ ⅊
⊡ ✍ 210,000; bkf: 15,000.

Restaurant:
◆◆◆ **Due Cippi-da Michele,** p. Vittorio Veneto 26/A, ☎ 601074, closed Tue and Jan. Regional cuisine: triangolini with ricotta, roast suckling pig, 20/30,000.

SIENA**

Florence 68, Rome 219, Milan 365 km
Pop. 61,337 ⊠ 53100 ☎ 0577   D4

Siena is the most uniform, homogenous and harmoniously beautiful of the large Tuscan cities. Its streets are spread over three steep hills, which the city has enfolded within its walls. However, the main feature is not this impressive barrier which separates Siena from the outside world, but the magical attraction of the city centre: the piazza del Campo. The whole city converges upon this piazza, in which the Palazzo Pubblico and the tall tower of the Mangia stand tall as if the world revolved around them. Siena's strikingly 14C appearance is the result of a conscious decision to remain faithful to the past and to tradition. Here, the Renaissance's influence was hardly felt. Not even after losing its independence in the mid-16C did the city change its appearance. Siena has not singled out just one of its districts for preservation; instead, it sees itself as an integral whole. Today Siena feels like a unique, slightly labyrinthine household. In the 14C-15C, this household was inhabited by some of the greatest painters and sculptors Italy has seen.

▶ The paving of the **piazza del Campo★★** (D3) is superb: flagstones are arranged in a circle, and an expanse of brick is subdivided into nine sections by stone strips. Among all the magnificent palazzi surrounding the piazza the most outstanding is the **Palazzo Pubblico★★** (1297-1342). Above the ground floor, the massive

The palio of Siena

The first of these horse races was held on the feast of the Madonna of Provenzano, 2 July 1656. They have been held every year since without fail. In 1701, it was decided to hold two races a year, the second on 16 August (the Feast of the Assumption) and so it has been ever since. The word palio comes from the Latin and means mantle or cloak, since the custom of offering a a piece of precious fabric as a prize for a race was commonplace in many towns in the Middle Ages. In the 16C and the 17C races using buffalos and asses were also run. The palio finally took its present form in the piazza del Campo, thought to be the most beautiful racecourse in the world. The riders representing the different areas take part in the splendid parade dressed in historical costume. This is a prelude to the race itself which only lasts a few electrifying moments. The steeds line up on the rope in an order determined by lottery. The rope falls and the horses shoot forward. Mounts which have lost their riders can still win the race and the victorious town holds a great celebration.

palazzo is built of pinkish brick with triple windows; the black-and-white arms of Siena appear on all the tympanums. To one side is the **Torre del Mangia★** (1348), with a white stone top-section surmounting its slender brick shaft. At the base of the palazzo, the square **Cappella di Piazza** is an open loggia with a single arch on each of three sides. At the other end of the palazzo is a column surmounted by a Sienese wolf. The monumental **Gaia fountain★** occupies the top of the piazza and now has 19C copies of original statues by Jacopo della Quercia. The **Palazzo Sansedoni,** with its majestic curving brick façade on the piazza and three rows of triple windows, was originally made up of several buildings until alterations were made in the 18C. It is a brilliant example of Siena's 'anachronistic' fidelity to its medieval and Gothic vision. ▶ Inside the Palazzo Pubblico is the **Museo Civico** *(9 a.m.-6:30 p.m. Apr-Sep; 9 a.m.-1:30 p.m. Oct-Mar; 9 a.m.-1 p.m. hols).* The frescos in its spectacular rooms include some famous works by Simone Martini: the *Virgin Mary in Glory★★* (1315) and *Guidoriccio da Fogliano at the Siege of Montemassi★★* (1328). There are also frescos by Ambrogio Lorenzetti, including the enchanting depiction of the *Effects of Good Government in Town and Country★★,* with quiet scenes of everyday life: masons working on roofs, craftsmen in their workshops and a group of dancing girls. The frescos' scenes show the hilly countryside, ploughing and grape-harvesting. In the loggia of the palazzo are some fragments from the Gaia fountain by Jacopo della Quercia (1419). 503 steps lead to the top of the **Torre del Mangia** *(same opening times as the palazzo),* which offers a splendid **panoramic view★** of the city. ▶ Siena has no finer sight than the **Duomo★★** (D-E2), an outstanding piece of Italian Gothic architecture. It has three broad portals, above which the façade is covered with marble tracery, and the campanile is faced with a pattern of narrow black-and-white stripes. The superb interior contains numerous works of art and an **inlaid pavement★★.** Two of the Duomo's most beautiful features are the famous **pulpit★★** (1266-8) by Nicola Pisano and assistants, and the **Libreria Piccolomini★★** *(open 9 a.m. until the Duomo closes),* whose Renaissance marble front faces the l. aisle; inside are **frescos★★** by Pinturicchio (1502-9). ▶ The Gothic **Baptistery★★** was built beneath the apsidal section of the Duomo, making use of a natural break in the ground. One goes down a flight of steps, which passes through a portal in a high wall — the flank of a new Duomo which was planned but never actually built. Inside is a **font★★** by Jacopo della Quercia

Autostrada

Staz. F.S.
P.za C. Rosselli

Villa Scacciapensieri km 3

3

Viale

Giuseppe

Mazzini

Sardegna

Autostr. Firenze km 65

Antiporto di
Camollia

Viale Vitt. Emanuele

Porta
Camollia

Piazza
G. Amendola

Piscina

B

Via Piave

Via Fiera

Viale di Don Giovanni di Campo

Via N. Bixio

Minzoni

Viale

Memmi

Via N. Sauro

Fontegiusta

Via di Montlupo

Campansi

Barriera
S. Lorenzo

Simone Martini

Beccafumi

Garibaldi

Grosseto km 73

C

Via Cesare Battisti

Viale Vitt. Veneto

Viale A. Diaz

R. Franci

La Lizza

Viale C. Maccari

Campo
Sportivo

Forte
Piazza
d. Libertà
S. Barbara

Stadio

Stadio
Comunale

Viale XXV Aprile

Via F. Tozzi

S. Stefano

P.za
d. Sale

Via S. Sebastiano

S. Andrea

Fonte
Nuova

Via d. Stufasecca

Al Gramsci

Via di Montanini

P.za
d'Ovile

Fonte
d'Ovile

P.za Ovile

300

S. Donato

Via Pian d'Ovile

Via dell'Abbadia

Fonte
d'Ovile

S. Frances

Piazza
S. Frances

Oratorio
S. Bernar

S. Pietro
Ovile

S. Maria di
Provenzano

Via dei Rossi

Via Banchi

Provenzano
Salvani

S. Cristoforo

Via d. Paradiso

Via d. Sapienza

Posta
P.za
Matteotti

P.za
Salimbeni

Pal.
Salimbeni

Banchi

D

Via Vitt. Veneto

Via di Città

Via E. di Fontebranda

Via di Fontebranda

S. Domenico

S. Domenico

Sant'
Cateriniano

Museo
Archeologico

Museo
Tel. G.

Banchi di sotto

Universita

Pal.
Piccolomini

Fonte
Branda

Fontebranda

Pal.
Pellegrini

Loggia
Mercanzia

Il Campo

Logge
d. Papa

Via d. Porrio

Duomo

Pal. d.
Magnifico

Museo
d. Opera

Pal.
Tolomei

S. Caterina

Pal
Pubblico
(Municipio)

R.za d.
Mercato

E

Via Esterna di Fontebranda

Palazzo
Arcivescovile

d. Selva

S. Sebastiano

d. Duomo

Via d. Diacceto

Spedale
d. S. M. d. Scala

Prefettura
Pal.
Piccolomini

Pal. Chigi
Saracini

Pinacoteca
Nazionale

Via S. Ansano

P.za
Postierla

S. Pietro

V. Stalloreggi

V. di Pendola

275

325

Via P. Mascagni

Via d. Tufi

Pal.
Pollini

Pal.
Mantellini

P.za
Laterina

Via d. Laterino

a

Niccolò
al Carmine

Via d. Scuole

Via d. Cerchia

S. Agostino

Erato

S. Agostino

Orto

Botanico

Via Pier Andrea Mattioli

F

P.za S. Marco

Via della Diana

Via della Sapienza

300

P.za Tufi

325

300

Grosseto km 73

3

(1417-30), a masterpiece of Tuscan sculpture decorated with statues and bas-reliefs in gilded bronze by Jacopo della Quercia himself, and also by Donatello (the *Banquet of Herod*★★) and other artists. ▶ For the visitor in search of a thorough exposure to Sienese painting from the late 12C-early 17C, the main sites to visit are: the **Museo dell'Opera Metropolitana★** (D2; *open daily 9 a.m.-7 p.m. summer; 9 a.m.-2 p.m. winter*), where exhibits include the famous *Maestà*★★ by Duccio di Boninsegna, a triptych by Pietro Lorenzetti with the *Nativity of the Virgin Mary*★★, and ten **statues★★** by Giovanni Pisano. The **Pinacoteca Nazionale★★** (E3; *entrance fee; 8 a.m.-1:45 p.m.; 8:30 a.m.-1 p.m. hols; closed Mon*), with masterpieces by artists such as Simone Martini (*Madonna and Child*★★), Ambrogio Lorenzetti (*City by the Sea*★★), Pietro Lorenzetti, Neroccio, Francesco di Giorgio Martini, Beccafumi and many others. ▶ Siena's cultural heyday finds expression in the Gothic and Renaissance architecture of innumerable splendid palazzi. Some of the finest are: the **Palazzo Buonsignori★** (E3; the Pinacoteca Nazionale), **Salimbeni★** (C3; Monte dei Paschi), **Chigi-Saracini★** (E3; the Accademia Musicale Chigiana), **Tolomei★** (D3) and **Piccolomini★** (D3; the State Archive, with the famous **Tavolette di Biccherna★**: a series of illuminated bindings from the public registers dating from 1258-1659). Siena also has churches such as **S. Francesco★** (C3), **S. Domenico★** (D2) and **S. Maria dei Servi★** (E4), which are worth visiting both for their architecture and for the masterpieces of painting and sculpture they house. ▶ The **Casa di S. Caterina** (D2; *9 a.m.-1 p.m. and 3-6:30 p.m.*) is, in fact, a series of buildings that were built around St. Catherine's house.
▶ Siena's fountains are outstanding. The most famous is the **Branda fountain** (D2; 11C-13C), built entirely of brick with three large Gothic arches. The city gates are also noteworthy, and the **porta Camollia** (B1), which is the northernmost, bears a welcome in Latin to those visiting the city. ▶ Every street has something to offer. The three main roads, the **via di Città, Banchi di Sotto**, and **Banchi di Sopra**, radiate out from one of the busiest parts of the city, the **Croce del Travaglio**, where the 11C **Loggia della Mercanzia★** stands. Other picturesque medieval streets include the **v. Bandini** (D3), the **Corte del Castellare degli Ugurgieri★**, and the **v. della Galluzza.** ▶ The visitor should put some time aside for minor details, such as the **wrought iron** which is a feature of Siena. A fine example of this is the 15C flag bearer on the column in the **piazza della Postierla** (E3) which is surmounted by a marble wolf. ▶ The **Lizza** (C2), a promenade and public park, is near the entrance to the 16C Medici **Forte S. Barbara** (C1). ▶ One can walk to the **monastery of the Osservanza★** *(2.5 km)* by leaving Siena through the porta Ovile (C3) and following the v. Simone Martini and the v. Chiantigiana. The 13C monastery founded by S. Bernardino of Siena stands on the Capriola hill, from which there is a wonderful view. ▶ **Monteriggioni** (→) is 14.5 km away, while **San Galgano** (→) is 33.5 km away. □

Practical information _____

ⓘ v. di Città 5 (D3), ☎ 47051; p. del Campo 55 (D3), ☎ 280551.
▰▰▰ (A1), ☎ 280115.
▰▰▰ from p. S. Domenico (D2) and p. della Lizza (C2), ☎ 221221.

Hotels:
★★★★★ **Park Hotel**, v. Marciano 18, ☎ 44803, 69 rm ℗ ⌕ ▥ ☷ ▱ ✍ Elegant hotel in old fortress, 200,000; bkf: 14,000. Rest.● ◆◆◆◆ **Olivo-Terrazza la Magnolia** in 15C building with park, terraces and sports facilities. Regional cuisine: brochette of mazzancolle, casseroled guinea fowl, 55/80,000.
★★★★ **Athena**, v. Mascagni 55 (E-F2 a), ☎ 286313, 110 rm ℗ closed Feb. No restaurant, 150,000; bkf: 10,000.
★★★★ **Certosa di Maggiano**, v. Certosa 82, ☎ 288180, 14 rm ℗ ⌕ ▥ ☷ ☰ ✍ A 13C Carthusian monastery whose old buildings survive, 265,000.
★★★★ **Jolly Excelsior**, p. La Lizza (C2 b), ☎ 288448, 126

rm, 218,000. Rest. ♦♦♦ *Rotonda* Italian cuisine: penne with olives, fusilli with sausage, 30/35,000.
★★★★ *Villa Scacciapensieri,* v. Scacciapensieri 24, ☎ 41441, 29 rm ℙ ◊ ⚭ ⬛ ↗ closed Nov-20 Mar. 18C villa set in park, 225,000.
★★★ *Garden,* v. Custoza 2, ☎ 47056, 67 rm ℙ ◊ ⬛ 66,500.
★★★ *Vico Alto,* v. delle Regioni 26, ☎ 48571, 46 rm ℙ ⚭ ও 59,000; bkf: 5,000.
Restaurants:
● ♦♦♦ *Marsili,* v. del Castoro 3 (E3 e), ☎ 47154, closed Mon. Housed in ground floor and cellars of 15C Palazzo Marsili, impeccable service. Regional cuisine: pancakes with piquant cheeses, escalopes senesi, 25/35,000.
♦♦♦ *Guido,* vicolo P. Pettinaio 7 (D3 c), ☎ 280042, closed Mon. Genuine restaurant in 14C style. Regional cuisine: charcoal-grilled meats, escalopes alla senese, 25/35,000.
♦♦♦ *Nello-La Taverna,* v. del Porrione 28 (D3 f), ☎ 289043, closed Sun eve and Mon. Informal setting, expert management. Regional and Italian cuisine: ossobuco senese, wild boar stew, 25/35,000.
♦♦♦ *Tullio ai Tre Cristi,* vicolo Provenzano 1 (C3 g), ☎ 280608, closed Mon and Jan-Feb. A former 19C trattoria. Italian cuisine: game, tripe alla senese, 30/40,000.
♦♦ *Mariotti-da Mugolone,* v. dei Pellegrini 8/12 (D3 d), ☎ 283235, closed Sun eve, Thu and 10-30 Jul. Regional cuisine: baked cannelloni, ossibuchialla toscana, 20/30,000.

⚿ ★★★ *Colleverde,* strada Scacciapensieri 47, ☎ 280044.

Recommended
Botanical garden: (F3), ☎ 281248 (closed Sat, Sun and hols).
Events: *Palio horserace* in p. del Campo (2 Jul; *Palio dell'Assunta* on 16 Aug). *Siena summer:* musical weeks (Jul-Sep); international music courses, at Accademia Musicale Chigiana, ☎ 46152.
Flying: *Aeroporto di Ampugnano,* ☎ 349150; *Aeroclub centrale Paracadutismo,* ☎ 349150.
Guided tours: ☎ 280435 or 40219.
Horseback riding: *Club ippico Senese,* at Piano del Lago, ☎ 53277.
Racecourse: at Costalpino, ☎ 394347.
Sports arena: v. Sclavo 8; Palasport *Mens Sana* (basketball), v. Sclavo 12, ☎ 47298.
Swimming: v. Amendola (B1), ☎ 47496.
Wine: *Enoteca Italica Permanente,* Fortezza Medicea, ☎ 288497 (open daily 3 p.m.-midnight).
Youth hostel: *Ostello Guidoricci,* at Stellino, v. Fiorentina, ☎ 52212.
♥ gastronomy: panforte spicy cake, ricciarelli almond biscuits, olive oil, cheeses.

SINALUNGA

Siena 47, Florence 103, Rome 188 km
Pop. 11,656 ⊠ 53048 ☎ 0577   E4

Like all the towns of the Valdichiana which developed in the Middle Ages, Sinalugna stands on high ground since the valley bottom was then marshland.

▶ The **piazza Garibaldi** was named as such as an act of contrition. In 1867 the Italian state arrested Garibaldi, hero of the Risorgimento, in Sinalunga. He was on his way to Rome, in order to liberate it from Papal rule by force of arms. **Three churches** stand on the lively 17C-18C piazza.   □

Practical information _____

Hotels:
★★★★ *Locanda dell'Amorosa,* at Amorosa, ☎ 679497, 7 rm ℙ ⚭ ↗ closed 20 Jan-Feb. In beautiful 14C Sienese farmhouse, 160,000; bkf: 10,000. Rest.● ♦♦♦ closed Mon and Tue noon. Romantic setting, attentive

service. Regional and creative cuisine: ravioli with ricotta, butter and sage, Chianti produced on the farm, 50/60,000.
★★★ *Apogeo,* at Bettolle, ☎ 624186, 36 rm ℙ ⚭ ↗ ⬛ 74,000.
Restaurant:
♦ *Cacciatore,* v. Di Vittorio 12, ☎ 624192, closed Thu. Regional cuisine: rabbit alla boscaiola, wild boar with mushrooms, 20/25,000.

Recommended
Cycling: *G.S. Bar Sport,* v. Trento, ☎ 69473.

SORANO*

Grosseto 84, Florence 226, Rome 136 km
Pop. 4,645 ⊠ 58010 ☎ 0564   E5

Sorano, which like other towns in the region stands on a ridge, has been partially undermined by landslides and shows obvious signs of structural collapse. Its inhabitants are abandoning this picturesque town, whose old houses spring from a cliff, and it has been the subject of many works of art.

▶ The **houses** crowded together along **streets** and **alleyways** are beautiful, if modest. They frequently display small ornamental details, as if to show the loving care of their former owners. ▶ Changes in height from street to street are so abrupt that **flights of steps** were built to link them. ▶ Two fortresses stand opposite one another and overlook the town. In the SE, the massive 16C **Fortezza** is entered through a rustic gate. The medieval **castle**, which stands on the far side of the picturesque courtyard, belonged to the Orsini, who were counts of Sorano for centuries. In the NW is the 18C **Sasso Leopoldino** with a steeply sloping wall.   □

SOVANA**

Grosseto 82, Florence 226, Rome 149 km
Pop. 188 ⊠ 58010 ☎ 0564   E5

The first part of the road from Pitigliano (→) to Sovana runs between walls of porous rock. This archaic passageway prepares the visitor for medieval Sovana and the remarkable Etruscan tombs in the countryside nearby. This was the birthplace of Pope Gregory VII, who carried out the first reform of the Church in the 11C. The town holds a strong position on a plateau above two gorges, and still seems to live in the 11C-12C, when it was the centre of an immense fief.

▶ The walls no longer stand, but in the Middle Ages they surrounded the town and linked it with the **Aldobrandescha castle**. Some impressive remains of the castle can still be admired today. ▶ Major restoration work has been done in the **village**, and it has lost the air of melancholy decay it exuded some twenty years ago. The streets paved with bricks in the 16C (in a herringbone pattern) still remain and so do the small, single-storeyed old houses built of warm, golden porous rock. ▶ The enchanting **'strada di mezzo'** leads to the tranquil **piazza del Pretorio** (13C-15C). The **Palazzo Pretorio** and the **Loggetta del Capitano** stand in a corner of this piazza and their façades are decorated with coats-of-arms. The front façade of the late Renaissance **Palazzo Bourbon del Monte** is arcaded on the ground floor. Next to it is the 12C church of *S. Maria,* inside which there are early Romanesque reliefs and an unusual 8C-9C ciborium. The small, plain palazzo, which stands at the back of the piazza and houses the archive, has a clock and a small campanile. ▶ Outside town is the famous **Duomo★** (12C-14C) which stands in proud, religious isolation in an open space surrounded by olive trees. ▶ The apse of the Duomo faces town and one side has a portal decorated with fragments of ancient sculpture, some of them pagan. Perhaps the finest features of the solemn interior *(ring bell)* are the figures on some of the capitals (12C). ▶ 1.5 km away, green hills and high rock walls provide the magical natural setting for the **Etruscan necropolis** *(apply to the Taverna Etrusca, in the p. del Pretorio)*. The tombs are cut into the rock and each contains a burial chamber with a bench along the wall for the body. Many of the tombs have architectural façades. See especially the **Tomba Ildebranda** (2C BC), in the form of a temple and still imposing even though it is in ruins. Equally interesting are the **Grotta Pola**, the opening of which is in the side of the Poggio Prisca; the **Tomba del Tifone**, a niche tomb in the Poggio Stanziale; and the countless other tombs which, although more humble, are still admirable. □

Practical information ─────────────

Restaurant:
◆◆ *Taverna Etrusca,* p. Pretorio 16, ☎ 615539, closed Mon. Maremma cuisine: pappardelle with wild boar sauce, tortelli with ricotta, 15/30,000.

STIA

Arezzo 48, Florence 47, Rome 266 km
Pop. 3,004 ⊠ 52017 ☎ 0575   E2

Stia stands on a ridge at the confluence of the Arno and Staggio rivers, with Mt. Falterona to its rear. The area is typical of the upper Casentino Valley and there are numerous traces of the town's long history. One section is still largely medieval. But today, Stia is best known for its various crafts and industries: wrought iron and wool mills. The latter follows centuries-old traditions: strong thick woolen cloths were woven here in the 14C. They were fairly coarse, in a single bright colour, mostly red. Their fame extended outside Tuscany, and they were known as 'casentinesi' (due to their origins in Casentino Valley).

▶ The 18C façade of the parish church of **S. Maria Assunta** stands on a long arcaded piazza in the **medieval section**. The interior is Romanesque and houses a *Madonna*★ by Andrea della Robbia.

Environs

▶ Remains of Guidi castles are to be found at **Porciano** *(1.7 km)* and Pratovecchio *(3.5 km;* remains of the **Castello di Romena**). ▶ The marvelous Romanesque parish church of **S. Pietro di Romena**★ is nearby and is worth visiting. Inside *(caretaker at the house next door)* are monolithic columns with unusual carved capitals. □

Practical information ─────────────

Recommended
Craft workshops: *L. Detti,* v. Sanarelli 19, ☎ 583250 (Mon-Sat; wrought iron).
Guided tours: to Casentino forests; Stazione forestale di Pratovecchio, ☎ 58763.

La TENUTA DI SAN ROSSORE

                                                            B3

Over the centuries, this estate belonged to the Empire, to the grand duchy, to the Kingdom of Italy and to the Presidency. But the visitor comes here more for the place's natural beauty than for its history. The estate's main features are the majestic colonnades formed by stone pines, oaks, poplars, ash trees and alders.

▶ Hundreds of species of birds are found regularly on the **Tenuta di San Rossore.** Deer, roebuck, wild boars, hares, wild rabbits, martens and foxes also live here. The section of the estate open to the public *(hols only, 9 a.m.-sunset)* is limited to parts of the avenues running from the Cascine Vecchie (the old farmhouses). The estate extends over 7,500 acres along the coastal strip of Tuscany, from the Arno River to the Serchio River. ▶ Between the Serchio and Lake Massaciùccoli (→ Torre del Lago Puccini) is the **Migliarino scrub-brush:** pines and evergreen oaks, a multicoloured abundance of tamarisks, myrtles, junipers and ferns. □

Practical information ─────────────

ⓘ office of the *Consorzio Parco Naturale di Migliarino, San Rossore e Massaciùccoli,* at Pisa, v. C. Battisti 10, ☎ 050/43512 (guided group tours). For permission and advance reservations for individual visits to the Tenuta di San Rossore, apply to the management, ☎ 050/27271; for visits to the Tenuta di Migliarino: duchi Salviati, ☎ 050/8040361.

Restaurant:
◆◆ *Ugo,* at Migliarino, v. Aurelia Nord, 342-km marker, ☎ 804455, closed Mon. Mixed cuisine: scampi in guazzetto, baked bream with potatoes, 30/40,000.

TERME DI PETRIOLO

Siena 32, Florence 100, Rome 228 km
⊠ 58040 ☎ 0564   D4

Once considered out-of-the-way and isolated, Terme di Petriolo had all but been forgotten. Now that a superhighway runs nearby, the old **thermal baths** visited by Pope Pius II Piccolomini during the Renaissance have been restored. A new spa has also sprung up on the hill. □

Practical information ─────────────

♨ (Easter-New Year), ☎ 908871.

Hotel:
★★★★ *Terme di Petriolo,* at Pari, ☎ 908871, 55 rm Ⓟ ∭ ♿ ⊡ ♪ᵒ closed Dec-Apr, 160,000; bkf: 15,000.

TIRRENIA

Pisa 15, Florence 98, Rome 322 km
Pop. 2,000 ⊠ 56018 ☎ 050   B3

Tirrenia lies 6 km S of the mouth of the Arno, on the edge of an old **pine forest.** It is today known for its cinemas, bathing establishments and splendid **beach.** □

Practical information ─────────────

≋
ⓘ largo Belvedere, ☎ 32510 (in season).

Hotels:
★★★★ *G.H. Continental,* largo Belvedere 26, ☎ 37031, 200 rm Ⓟ ∭ ⊡ ♪ᵒ 143,000.
★★★★ *G.H. Golf,* v. dell'Edera, ☎ 37545, 86 rm Ⓟ ∭ ⊡ ♪ᵒ ♩ (9) 140,000; bkf: 15,000.
★★★ *Baleari,* v. del Tirreno 13, ☎ 37497, 22 rm Ⓟ ♿ ∭ ♿ closed Nov-Mar, 65,000; bkf: 5,500.
★★★ *Medusa,* v. degli Oleandri 37, ☎ 37125, 32 rm Ⓟ ∭ closed Oct-Mar, 60,000; bkf: 7,000.

Recommended
Children's facilities: zoo, p. dei Fiori, ☎ 33111.
Golf: v. S. Guido, ☎ 37518 (9 holes).
Sailing: Lega Navale, at Marina di Pisa, v. D'Annunzio 250, ☎ 36652.
Tennis: v. Pisorno, ☎ 37579.
Youth hostel: *Ostello San Francesco,* at Calambrone, ☎ 37442.

TORRE DEL LAGO PUCCINI

Lucca 33, Florence 107, Milan 261 km
Pop. 7,246 ⊠ 55048 ☎ 0584   B2

Giacomo Puccini's sweet melodies seem to ring through this town. An avenue of lime trees leads *(1.5 km)* to the shore of **Lake Massaciùccoli**, where the composer's **villa** *(9 a.m.-12 noon and 3-7 p.m. summer; 2-5 p.m. winter)* and his **tomb** are both located. The placid lake is a remnant of the lagoons which were once a feature of this stretch of the Tuscan coast.   □

Practical information ────────────

Restaurant:
♦♦ *Cecco,* Belvedere Puccini, ☎ 341022, closed Mon and Nov-Dec. Fireplace for grills. Regional cuisine: salumi of wild boar, chicken cacciucco, 20/30,000.

⚔ ★ *Burlamacco,* v. Marconi, 300 pl, ☎ 340797; ★ *Italia,* v. dei Tigli, 410 pl, ☎ 341504.

Recommended
Events: *Festival Pucciniano,* Belvedere Puccini, ☎ 343322 (summer).
Sailing: circolo velico, porticciolo Si-Sa, ☎ 342084.

The VERSILIA RIVIERA

                                                             B2

The Versilia Riviera features sunshine, fine sandy beaches, swimming, excursions into the Apuan Alps (and their famous quarries), boat trips on the Tyrrhenian Sea, and walks in the cool pine forests. The Riviera is a 15-mile stretch of modern vacation resorts: villas, hotels, vacation homes, camp sites. A long coastal boulevard runs from Viareggio (→) to Marina di Carrara, passing through Lido di Camaiore, Marina di Pietrasanta, Forte dei Marmi and Marina di Massa.

▶ **Forte dei Marmi★.** The town takes its name from the fortress built two centuries ago by a grand duke of Tuscany which still stands on the main piazza. The marble blocks from which it was built came from the Apuan Alps. The town has a fine reputation as an elegant resort. ▶ **Lido di Camaiore**, Forte dei Marmi and **Marina di Pietrasanta** make up the Versilia Riviera proper. Lido di Camaiore is a particular favourite with Tuscan vacationers. ▶ The old marble industry exists side by side with tourism at **Marina di Carrara**, where the harbour breaks the sweep of the shore. The **ruins of Luni** (→ Luni, in Liguria) are 3.5 km NW. **Marina di Massa** is a stretch of beach a few miles long, hemmed in between the sea and pine forests. The beautiful **Cinquale** is some 4 km away on the way to Viareggio. ▶ **Marina di Pietrasanta** includes *(from N to S)* **Fiumetto, Tónfano, Motrone** and the **Focette.** The famous **Versiliana,** the last remnant of what was once an extensive coastal forest, starts here: evergreen oaks, umbrella pines, myrtles and juniper trees.   □

Practical information ────────────

FORTE DEI MARMI, ⊠ 55042, ☎ 0584.
≋
ⓘ p. Marconi, ☎ 80091.

Hotels:
★★★★★ *Augustus,* v. Morin 169, ☎ 80202, 68 rm Ⓟ ⚒ ⅏ closed Oct-19 May, 345,000.
★★★★ *Adam's Villa Maria,* v. Lungomare 110, ☎ 80901, 41 rm Ⓟ ⅏ ▤ closed Oct-Apr, 120,000; bkf: 10,000.
★★★★ *Alcione,* v. Morin 137, ☎ 89952, 45 rm Ⓟ ⅏ ⅜ closed Oct-May, 100,000; bkf: 6,000.

★★★★ *Astoria Garden,* v. Leonardo da Vinci 10, ☎ 80754, 40 rm Ⓟ ⚒ ⅏ ⅌ closed Oct-14 May, 90,000; bkf: 10,000.
★★★★ *Hermitage,* v. Battisti, ☎ 80022, 67 rm Ⓟ ⚒ ⅏ ⚒ ▤ closed 16 Sep-May, 212,000.
★★★★ *Pineta al Mare,* v. Mazzini 65, ☎ 81043, 29 rm Ⓟ ⅏ closed Oct-Mar, 115,000; bkf: 8,000.
★★★★ *Raffaelli Park,* v. Mazzini 37, ☎ 81494, 36 rm Ⓟ ⅏ ⚒ ▤ ⅌ 152,000; bkf: 12,000.
★★★★ *St. Mauritius,* v. XX Settembre, ☎ 82131, 36 rm Ⓟ ⅏ ⅜ closed Oct-May, 140,000.
★★★ *Pleiadi,* v. Civitali 51, ☎ 881188, 30 rm Ⓟ ⚒ ⅏ ⅜ closed Oct-9 May, 74,000; bkf: 10,000.
★★★ *Raffaelli-Villa Angela,* v. Mazzini 64, ☎ 80652, 56 rm Ⓟ ⅏ ⚒ ▤ ⅌ closed Oct-Apr, 87,000; bkf: 9,000.

Restaurants:
♦♦ *Barca,* v. Italico 3, ☎ 89323, closed Tue, Mon eve in winter and Nov-Dec. With summer terrace. Mixed cuisine: lobster risotto, sea bream pirata, 35/50,000.
♦♦♦ *Bruno,* v. Arenile 22, ☎ 89972, closed Thu in spring and Sep-20 Apr. Seafood: spaghetti with clams, risotto provenzale, 45/55,000.
♦♦♦ *Cervo Bianco,* v. Risorgimento 9, ☎ 89640, closed Wed, Thu noon in Jan-Jun and 15 Jan-15 Feb. Mixed cuisine: date-shell soup, grilled scamponi, 35/50,000.
♦♦♦ *Lorenzo,* v. Carducci 61, ☎ 84030, closed Mon and 15 Dec-30 Jan. Seafood: zuppetta with small curled octopuses, shellfish alla catalana, 50/60,000.

Recommended
Cycling: *G.S. Guidi,* v. S. Stagi 50, ☎ 80994; *G.S. Cicloturistica,* v. Spinetti 10, ☎ 81261.
Events: *international display of children's art* (Jul-Aug); *prize for political satire* (Aug).
Marina: ☎ 89826.
Tennis: v. dell'Acqua, ☎ 89167 (also swimming pool); v. dell'Acqua 102, ☎ 82482; v. Colombo, ☎ 81153; v. XX Settembre, ☎ 89775.

LIDO DI CAMAIORE, ⊠ 55043, ☎ 0584.
≋
ⓘ p. Umberto 1, ☎ 64397.

Hotels:
★★★★ *Ariston,* v. Colombo 355, ☎ 66333, 35 rm Ⓟ ⅏ ▤ ⅌ closed 16 Oct-14 Apr, 135,000.
★★★ *Bacco,* v. Rosi 20, ☎ 67177, 21 rm ⚒ ⅏ closed Oct-14 May, 53,000; bkf: 6,500.
★★★ *Capri,* v. Pistelli 6, ☎ 60001, 47 rm Ⓟ ⅜ closed Nov-24 Dec, 70,000; bkf: 6,000.
★★★ *Rialto Suisse,* p. Umberto, ☎ 65051, 50 rm, 69,500.
★★ *Sylvia,* v. Manfredi 15, ☎ 64994, 21 rm Ⓟ ⚒ ⅏ ▤ closed Oct-14 May, 52,000; bkf: 5,000.

Restaurants:
● ♦♦♦ *Squalo Charlie,* v. Colombo 760, ☎ 65597, closed Tue and 15-30 Nov. Quiet, elegant restaurant. Regional mixed cuisine: shark soup, sliced beef with herbs, 45/65,000.
♦♦ *Clara,* v. Aurelia 289, ☎ 904520, closed Wed and 10-25 Jan. Regional cuisine: spaghetti alla palombara, baked turbot, 35/50,000.

⚔ ★★★ *Versiliamare,* v. Trieste 175, 141 pl, ☎ 67824.

Recommended
Tennis: v. del Magazzeno, ☎ 67403.

MARINA DI CARRARA, ⊠ 54036, ☎ 0585.
≋
ⓘ p. Marconi 6/B, ☎ 632218.

Hotels:
★★★★ *Maestrale,* v. Colombo, ☎ 635371, 60 rm Ⓟ ⅏ ▤ ⅌ closed Nov-Apr, 110,000; bkf: 8,000.
★★★ *Mediterraneo,* v. Genova 2/H, ☎ 635222, 50 rm Ⓟ ⅏ ⅜ 56,000; bkf:5,000.

⚔ ★ *Carrara,* v. Litoraneo, 210 pl, ☎ 635260.

Recommended
Children's facilities: *Montessori* children's residence, v. Micheli 35, ☎ 58085; management, ☎ 55316-73270 (children 4-14 years, open mid-Jun-Aug).

Events: the Marmo-Macchine exhibition, in the exhibition centre of v. Colombo, ☎ 632044 (May-Jun).
Marina: ☎ 635150.

MARINA DI MASSA, ⊠ 54037, ☎ 0585.

≋
Ⓘ lungomare Vespucci 24, ☎ 240063; at Cinquale di Montignoso, ☎ 29317 (in season).

Hotels:
★★★★ *Excelsior,* lungomare Vespucci 51, ☎ 240141, 73 rm Ⓟ ⨺ ⊟ 112,000; bkf: 10,500.
★★★ *Eco del Mare,* corner of v. Lungomare and v. Verona, ☎ 240459, 20 rm Ⓟ ⨺ ⊟ 80,000; bkf: 10,000.
★★★ *Hermitage,* at Ronchi, v. Verdi 17, ☎ 240856, 24 rm Ⓟ ⨺ ⌁ ⊟ closed 26 Sep-24 May, 75,000; bkf: 7,000.
★★★ *Marina,* at Ronchi, v. Magliano 3, ☎ 245261, 30 rm Ⓟ ⨺ ⌁ closed Oct-May, 72,000; bkf: 10,000.
★★★ *Pergola,* at Poveromo (3 km), v. Verdi 41, ☎ 240118, 26 rm Ⓟ ⨺ closed Oct-Mar, 70,000.
★★★ *Villa Irene,* at Ronchi, v. delle Macchie 125, ☎ 308678, 42 rm Ⓟ ⚲ ⨺ ⅙ ⊟ closed Nov-Mar, 105,000; bkf: 12,000.

Restaurants:
♦♦ *Cenacolo,* v. delle Pinete 2, ☎ 241200, closed Mon. Fine summer garden. Mixed cuisine: crayfish brochettes, charcoal-grilled meats, 25/35,000.
♦♦ *Riccà,* lungomare di Ponente, ☎ 241070, closed Mon and 15 Oct-15 Nov. On the shore. Seafood: penne with lobster, sea bream in salt crust, 30/40,000.
⚖ ★ *Città di Massa,* v. delle Pinete, 400 pl, ☎ 241225.

Recommended
Flying club: *Aeroporto Massa-Cinquale,* at Ronchi, ☎ 309088.
Horseback riding: *Scuola apuana d'equitazione,* v. Mura Frati, ☎ 241202.

MARINA DI PIETRASANTA, ⊠ 55044, ☎ 0584.
≋
Ⓘ at Tónfano, v. Donizetti 14, ☎ 20331.

Hotels:
★★★★★ *Palazzo della Spiaggia,* at Focette, lungomare Roma 303, ☎ 21195, 47 rm Ⓟ ⨺ ⊟ closed Oct-Apr, 195,000; bkf: 10,000.
★★★★ *Ermione,* at Tonfano, v. Roma 183, ☎ 20652, 50 rm Ⓟ ⨺ ⊟ closed 16 Oct-9 May, 150,000; bkf: 10,000.
★★★★ *Verdemare,* at Focette, v. Cipro 27, ☎ 20621, 40 rm Ⓟ ⚲ ⨺ closed 16 Oct-30 Apr, 90,000.
★★★ *Caravaggio,* at Fiumetto, v. Carducci 127, ☎ 20128, 27 rm Ⓟ ⨺ closed 21 Sep-19 May, 53,000; bkf: 4,000.
★★★ *Mistral,* at Motrone, v. Tolmino 5/B, ☎ 21391, 34 rm Ⓟ ⨺ closed Oct-Easter, 70,000; bkf: 7,000.
★★★ *Mondial,* at Tonfano, v. Ricasoli 18, ☎ 21121, 50 rm Ⓟ ⨺ ⌁ closed Nov-Mar, 68,000; bkf: 7,000.
★★★ *Oceano,* at Focette, v. Roma 347, ☎ 20851, 39 rm Ⓟ ⨺ ⊟ closed Nov-Apr, 69,500.
★★★ *Tierra Brasilia,* at Motrone, v. Roma 333, ☎ 21521, 42 rm Ⓟ ⨺ ⌁ closed 16 Sep-Easter. No restaurant, 80,000; bkf: 10,000.
★★★ *Venezia,* at Motrone, v. Firenze 48, ☎ 20731, 34 rm Ⓟ ⨺ ⌁ closed 21 Sep-14 May, 70,000.

Recommended
Discothèque: *La Cannicia,* v. Unità d'Italia 1, ☎ 23225.
Horseback riding: Maneggio *La Versiliana,* v. Morin, ☎ 24280.
Tennis: at Fiumetto, v. Apua, ☎ 20895; at Focette, v. Cavour, ☎ 20720; at Tónfano, v. Unità d'Italia 56, ☎ 21991.

▉ VIAREGGIO* ▉

Lucca 24, Florence 97, Milan 255 km
Pop. 58,454 ⊠ 55049 ☎ 0584   B2

Viareggio became a vacation resort in the middle of last century, when the first seaside hotels were established here. The old **Burlamacca canal** cuts through the town and flows into the sea. Each side of town has a large park: the S is the **Pineta di Levante,** and the N is the **Pineta di Ponente** (which extends into the centre of town). The various darsene (basins), the harbour (protected by breakwaters which are open to the public and which extend hundreds of yards into the sea), the gardens with their palm trees, oleanders and tamarisks, the fine sand on the extensive beach, the elegant buildings and facilities (a number of *belle époque* buildings), cultural and social venues, and events such as the famous carnival — all these elements combine to make Viareggio the largest resort on the Tyrrhenian Sea. The mild, dry climate attracts visitors all year round.

Practical information _____

≋
Ⓘ v. Carducci 10, ☎ 962233.
✈ at Pisa, ☎ 050/28088.
▬▬ ☎ 44350.
Car rental: *Avis,* v. Margherita 48, ☎ 46111; *Maggiore* office, v. Mascagni 8, ☎ 502429.

Hotels:
★★★★ *Astor Hotel & Residence,* v. Carducci 54, ☎ 50301, 68 rm Ⓟ ⚲ ⌁ ⊟ 230,000; bkf: 12,000.
★★★★ *Palace,* v. Gioia 2 ☎ 46134, 68 rm Ⓟ 170,000; bkf: 12,000.
★★★★ *Plaza & De Russie,* v. Manin, ☎ 46546, 52 rm Ⓟ No restaurant, 135,000; bkf: 11,000.
★★★ *Garden,* v. Foscolo 70, ☎ 44025, 41 rm, closed Nov, 70,000; bkf: 8,000.
★★★ *Liberty,* v. Manin 18, ☎ 46247, 49 rm Ⓟ closed Nov-Apr (except Carnival and Easter). No restaurant, 67,000; bkf: 6,000.
★★★ *Mirage,* v. Zanardelli 12, ☎ 32222, 10 rm Ⓟ closed Nov, 69,500.
★★★ *Miramare,* v. Carducci 27, ☎ 48441, 30 rm, closed Nov-Dec 72,000; bkf: 6,000.
★★★ *San Francisco,* v. Carducci 68, ☎ 52666, 31 rm Ⓟ closed Dec-Jan. No restaurant, 69,500.
★★ *Kursaal,* v. Mentana 19, ☎ 49713, 38 rm ⌁ closed Mar and Oct-Jan, 53,000.
★★ *Lupori,* v. Galvani 11, ☎ 962266, 19 rm Ⓟ No restaurant, 53,000; bkf:5,000.

Restaurants:
● ♦♦♦ *Margherita,* v. Regina Margherita 30, ☎ 962553, closed Wed. *'Belle époque'* café on fine avenue. Creative cuisine: conchigliette with sea bass, sea bass with balsam vinegar, 35/45,000.
● ♦♦♦ *Romano,* v. Mazzini 122, ☎ 31382, closed Mon and Jan. Well appointed. Creative regional cuisine: squid soup, stuffed sea bream al cartoccio, homemade Montecarlo, 40/45,000.
♦♦♦ *Angelo,* v. Coppino 409, ☎ 393958, closed Wed in winter. Piano bar, open until late at night. Seafood: pappardelle with conger eel, scampi alla catalana, 35/55,000.
♦♦♦ *Montecatini,* v. Manin 8, ☎ 962129, closed Mon and Jan. Aristocratic villa with surviving fireplace and vaults. Mixed cuisine: spaghetti with mullet sauce, sea bream al cartoccio, 34/45,000.
♦♦♦ *Oca Bianca,* v. Aurelia 312, ☎ 64191. Closed Wed, Thu noon and 6-31 Jan. In well-restored farm building. Mixed cuisine: canoli with lobster, sea bass with celery mousse, 40/60,000.
♦♦♦ *Patriarca,* v. Carducci 79, ☎ 53126, closed Wed. Outdoor service in summer. Mixed cuisine: salt or steamed fish, bistecca alla fiorentina, 45/65,000.
♦♦♦ *Tito del Molo,* lungomolo Corrado del Greco 3, ☎ 962016, closed Wed and Jan. Terrace facing harbour and canal. Regional cuisine: baked fish with vegetables, scampi brochettes, 40/65,000.
♦♦ *Buonamico,* v. S. Andrea 27/29, ☎ 43038, closed Mon and Nov. Old fashioned Tuscan atmosphere. Regional cuisine: risotto alla marinara, sea bass al cartoccio, 30/55,000.

Recommended
Archery: *Compagnia arcieri Matilde di Toscana*, v. Fratti, ☎ 53115.
Cycling: *G.S. Cicloamatori*, v. Leopardi 164, ☎ 391964.
Events: *carnival* with a parade of allegorical floats, ☎ 962568; *Viareggio prize for literature* (Jun); *nautical exhibition*, ☎ 395334 (late Apr); *international children's football competition* (Feb-Mar); *Elica d'oro* motorboat trophy (Jul).
Horseback riding: *Società ippica viareggina*, v. Comparini 8, ☎ 391176 (riding ground for national horse show, v. dei Tigli).
Marina: ☎ 961594.
Sailing: *Lega Navale*, darsena Europa, ☎ 31085.
Sports arena: v. Salvatori, ☎ 394253; children's football centre, ☎ 390747.

VICOPISANO

Pisa 18, Florence 68, Milan 293 km
Pop. 7,428 ⊠ 56010 ☎ 050   C3

Not far from Mt. Pisano, this hill was once surrounded by water (from the Arno River and a lake). It was therefore the ideal site to build a castle to control the plain. The geography of the area has changed completely, but there are still remnants of the Middle Ages, including fortifications, the castle with its central group of towers, the intertwining network of streets and the fine 12C Pisan Romanesque parish church.   □

VINCI

Florence 38, Rome 313 km
Pop. 13,732 ⊠ 50059 ☎ 0571   C2

Leonardo's birthplace stands amid vineyards and olive groves, on the slopes of Mt. Albano. Like so many other Tuscan towns, Vinci was built around a feudal castle.

▶ Today, the **museum** *(9:30 a.m.-12 noon and 2:30-5 p.m. or 3-7 p.m. summer),* **library** and **castle** have been transformed into a centre for the documentation and celebration of the artist's multifaceted genius. ▶ In the church of **S. Croce**, a stone tablet bears a note dating from 1452 recording the baptism of a child 'named Lionardo', born on 15 April 'at 3 o'clock at night'. ▶ Tradition has it that Leonardo was actually born in the hamlet of **Archiago**, 3 km SE of Vinci. The small rustic dwelling was restored a few decades ago *(9:30 a.m.-12 noon and 2:30-5 p.m. or 3-7 p.m. in summer).*   □

Environs

▶ At **Cerreto Guidi** *(5.5 km SW)*, the **Ponti Medicei** are majestic 16C staircases, designed by Bernardo Buontalenti. They lead up to the austere **Villa Medicea** *(2-7 p.m. summer; 9 a.m.-2 p.m. winter; 9 a.m.-1 p.m. hols).*   □

Practical information ⎯⎯⎯⎯⎯⎯⎯⎯⎯⎯⎯

Restaurant:
♦♦ *Torretta,* v. della Torre 19, ☎ 56100, closed Mon. With view over roofs, vines, olive groves. Regional cuisine: pappardelle, bistecca alla fiorentina, 25/35,000.

VOLTERRA*

Pisa 61, Florence 81, Rome 287 km
Pop. 13,937 ⊠ 56048 ☎ 0588   C3

Volterra is located so high in the hills which separate the valleys of the Cécina and Era that it became known as the 'city of the wind'. The visitor will be

struck immediately by the city's monochrome aspect, with little in the way of ornament. The rooms of the Guarnacci museum give the visitor a different feeling entirely. Here are terra-cotta and alabaster reliefs on hundreds of Etruscan funerary urns found in local excavations. They convey a sense of imagination, individual detail and ornament. There is a strange contradiction between what appears on the surface and what was kept hidden beneath the ground for two thousand years. The land itself is dramatic. Volterra stands on eroding clay and sand soils. This slow and ancient process is practically impossible to stop, and, century by century, it has brought the city closer to the edge of the cliff.

⎯⎯⎯⎯⎯⎯⎯⎯⎯⎯⎯⎯⎯⎯⎯⎯⎯⎯⎯⎯⎯⎯⎯⎯⎯⎯⎯

Larderello

The landscape in this part of the metal-bearing hills to the south of Pomarance looks like something out of science fiction: wreaths of steam and network of pipes, drilling rigs and cooling towers. Larderello is the site of a power station which produces electricity from geothermal energy released from boric acid gases. In 1777, the German chemist Franz Höfer discovered boric acid in the muddy waters of the lakes of Montecerboli. The water was kept boiling by steam which bubbled to the surface. The white plumes of the steam fumaroles only appeared at the end of the last century when drilling began. Earlier in the same century, a Frenchman, François de Larderel, had emigrated to Livorno but had been reduced to hawking ribbons and fabric. In 1818, he had a stroke of genius — use the natural steam to heat cauldrons in which the boric acid solution was processed. He made a fortune, using highlanders from Parma and Modena as labourers. He devoted a share of his profits to assisting widows and the sick, and also built a workers' community theatre, school and church. He recovered some of these expenses from the houses he rented to workers and from the sale of goods from his shops. In 1837 Grand Duke Leopoldo II made him Count of Montecerboli, and in 1846 the industrial village became Larderello.

⎯⎯⎯⎯⎯⎯⎯⎯⎯⎯⎯⎯⎯⎯⎯⎯⎯⎯⎯⎯⎯⎯⎯⎯⎯⎯⎯

▶ The old acropolis is partly occupied by the long and formidable **Fortezza** (B2-3; now used as a prison). From the v. dei Ponti one can see that a wall which links the 14C **Rocca Vecchia** (to the E) to the **Rocca Nuova** (to the W; 15C). The latter has a square layout. ▶ The **Museo Etrusco Guarnacci★** (B2-3; *daily 9:30 a.m.-1 p.m. and 3-6:30 p.m.; Oct-Mar 10 a.m.-2 p.m.*) is of great interest. It contains over 600 funerary urns★ made locally (6-1C BC) and occupying several rooms. On the lids, the deceased are depicted stretched out at a banquet, sometimes idealized as heroes, sometimes depicted with a lively realism. The urns are decorated with floral patterns or scenes from Greek myths, connected in some way with the theme of withdrawal from life. In addition to this exceptional collection, there are also: small bronze sculptures, among them the wonderful figurine, the *Ombra della Sera* ('shadow of evening', 2C BC); weapons; lanterns; amulets; gold items. ▶ The art of **alabaster carving** is still very much alive in Volterra today: many alabaster workshops are found in the long **via Porta dell'Arco** (B1), which descends a steep slope to the **Arco Etrusco** (part of the 4C-3C BC wall). ▶ The harmonious **piazza dei Priori★** (B2) is one of Volterra's finest medieval piazzas. ▶ The massive **Palazzo dei Priori★** (1208-54) is the oldest medieval palazzo still standing in Tuscany and its tower offers a fine vista★. ▶ The **'porcellino' ('piglet') tower** in the **Palazzo Pretorio** (13C) on the same piazza

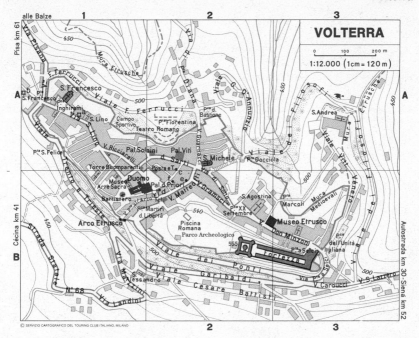

VOLTERRA

0   100   200 m
1:12.000 (1cm = 120 m)

© SERVIZIO CARTOGRAFICO DEL TOURING CLUB ITALIANO, MILANO

takes its name from the curious image which appears on a high stone corbel. ▶ Some fine examples have survived from Volterra's past as a city-state, including the **tower-houses** and the **Quadrivio dei Buomparenti★** viaduct (corner of v. Roma and v. Ricciarelli). In the Romanesque **Duomo★** (B1) is a beautiful **pulpit★** with sculptures, and a wooden group, dating back to the 13C. There are also a number of Renaissance works: the **ciborium★** and the carved angels by Mino da Fiesole, and the *Adoration of the Magi★* fresco by Benozzo Gozzoli. There are other works and objets d'art in the **pinacoteca** and in the **Museo Civico** (A2; *9:30 a.m.-1 p.m. and also 2:30-6:30 p.m. summer; closed Mon*) which are housed in the Palazzo Minucci-Solaini. Another collection is exhibited in the **Museo Diocesano d'Arte Sacra** (B1; *10 a.m.-1 p.m.; closed Mon*). Works by Domenico Ghirlandaio, Luca Signorelli and Rosso Fiorentino are to be found in the pinacoteca and Museo Civico, while the diocesan museum has pieces by Andrea della Robbia, with a fine *S. Linus★*. ▶ Outside the Porta Fiorentina, the archaeological site of the **Roman theatre** (A2) lies to the l. ▶ The road from the Porta S. Francesco (A1) passes a long section of **Etruscan walls** *(on the l.)* which extended here for nearly 7 km. ☐

Looking for a locality? Consult the index at the back of the book.

Practical information

⒤ v. Turazza 2 (B2), ☎ 86150.

Hotels:

★★★★ *San Lino,* v. San Lino 26 (A1 a), ☎ 85250, 44 rm ℗ ⌂ Formerly a monastery, 75,000; bkf: 6,000.

★★★ *Villa Nencini,* borgo S. Stefano 55 (A1 b), ☎ 86386, 14 rm ℗ ⌂ ⌂ ⌂ No restaurant, 57,000.

Restaurants:

◆◆ *Etruria,* p. dei Priori 6/8 (B2 d), ☎ 86064, closed Thu and 15 Nov-15 Dec. In period palazzo. Regional cuisine: pappardelle with hare sauce, rabbit Doccia, 18/30,000.

◆ *Beppino,* v. delle Prigioni 15/19 (A-B2 c), ☎ 86051, closed Wed and Jan. Regional cuisine: ravioli di magro, wild boar alla maremmana, 13/25,000.

◆ *Poggio,* v. Matteotti 39 (B2 e), ☎ 85257, closed Tue and Nov. Regional cuisine: spaghetti Poggio, bistecca alla fiorentina, 18/33,000.

◆ *Porcellino,* v. delle Prigioni 16 (B2 f), ☎ 86392, closed Tue and 10 Oct-20 Mar. Near Duomo. Regional cuisine: rabbit hunter's style, wild boar with olives, 20/30,000.

⚠ ★★ *Le Balze,* borgo San Giusto, 100 pl, ☎ 87880.
Recommended
Events: *Astiludio* (1st Sun in Sep, tournament of crossbowmen and flag wavers from various towns); *international choir festival* (last Sat in Sep).
Tennis: Villaggio Giardini, ☎ 87206.

Umbria

▶ Umbria's landscape is soft, as in the paintings of Perugino and in the early work of Raphael, with hills and mountains rolling into the distance, oak woods in pleasant valleys, vines, olive trees, fields, scattered cottages, poplar trees and small towns silhouetted on the crest of hillocks. The mountains are ever-present in the background. The area seems like a continuation of Tuscany and a prelude to Latium; part of the theme that forms the essence of central Italy. Green and mystical are adjectives often applied to the region. The history of Umbria abounds with religious figures: St. Benedict and St. Scholastica from Norcia, St. Rita from Cascia, St. Clare and St. Francis. The Convent of St. Damian on the slopes of Mt. Subasio is where St. Francis received his call and where St. Clare put Frederick II and the Saracens to flight. Giotto came to paint here, replacing mysticism with his sense of human reality, and Italian art embarked upon its adventurous journey. Many Umbrian towns, such as Perugia, Orvieto, Spello, Gubbio, Todi, Spoleto and Bevagna, still look predominantly medieval, but this is deceptive. Here as in few other places, the sense of the ancient town as a historical and artistic centre has been incorporated into modern life and the spirit of the past lives on, shaping the character of the region.

● Don't miss

In Perugia ★★: the Fontana Maggiore ★★, the Cathedral ★★, the Palazzo dei Priori ★★ with the National Gallery of Umbria ★★, the frescos by Perugino ★★ in the Collegio del Cambio ★★, S. Bernardino ★★ and S. Pietro ★★. In Assisi ★★: S. Francesco ★★ and the frescos by Giotto ★★, S. Chiara ★★, S. Maria degli Angeli ★★ and S. Damiano ★★. In Gubbio: the Palazzo dei Consoli ★★. In Montefalco: S. Francesco ★. In Orvieto ★: the Duomo ★★ and the Palazzo del Popolo ★★. In Spello ★: the Baglioni Chapel ★★ in S. Maria Maggiore ★. In Spoleto ★: the Duomo ★★, S. Salvatore ★★, S. Pietro ★★ and the Marmore falls ★★ just outside the town. In Todi ★: the Piazza del Popolo ★ and its monuments and S. Maria della Consolazione ★.

● Brief regional history

10C-4C BC
Umbrians and Etruscans. In the historical period from the 7C-6C BC, the region became divided between the **Umbrians** (Italic-Indo-European) to the l. of the Tiber and the **Etruscans**, to the r., the two principal towns being **Perugia** and **Orvieto.** ● The two peoples vied for supremacy, and, as a result, **Todi,** which was an Umbrian settlement, came under strong Etruscan influence.

4C BC-5C AD
The Romans. The Roman conquest was easy and swift (310-295 BC) and the region remained loyal even after Hannibal defeated the Romans at **Lake Trasimene** (217 BC). *Narnia* **(Narni)**, *Spoletium* **(Spoleto)** and *Carsulae* **(Spello, Todi)** were all Roman settlements. ● **Perugia**, which was on the losing side in the **battle between Antony and Octavian,** was besieged (40 BC) and burnt down by Octavian (Augustus), who then rebuilt it and named it *Augusta Perusia.*

6C-12C
The Duchy of Spoleto, the Benedictines, the Church. After the Roman Empire and the subsequent reign of the Goths, the vast Lombard Duchy of **Spoleto** was set up by **Faroaldo** in 571, which meant that the **Byzantines** still had a corridor linking the exarchate territory of Ravenna to Rome. ● **Chris-**

tianity had advanced through Flaminia, *c.* 4C. In the 6C, **Benedictine monasteries** were built high up in the safety of the hills and mountains: **Sant'Eutizio, San Benedetto del Subasio, Montelucco, San Pietro in Valle.** ● The famous **donations** of the Frankish emperors Pippin and Charlemagne (8C) gave rise to the rule of the Papal See, which was long opposed, and only became effective at the beginning of the 16C.

12C-14C
The city-states. San Francesco, Perugia, Spoleto, Foligno, Gubbio and **Assisi** were all sizeable city-states. San Francesco featured predominantly in local rivalries and struggles. ● The religious revival associated with **St. Francis of Assisi** (1181-1226) was part of a mood of spiritual urgency later reflected in Raniero Fasani's 'disciplinati' (1260) and in **Jacopone da Todi** (13C-14C). ● The **Franciscan Order** was approved by Innocent III (1209) and also by Honorius III (1223). The building of the basilica began in 1228, and **Assisi** became the centre of the order.

14C-15C
Lords and commanders of mercenaries. In the middle of the 14C, Cardinal **Albornoz** managed to establish direct papal rule for a time, but **Perugia** was unwilling to give up its liberty. ● Peace was brought about by giving the city local government, with limited powers. ● At the time of the bands of mercenaries, Umbria produced some famous captains, **Gattamelata** for example, whose influence was felt in political affairs throughout the peninsula. ● The mercenary leader, **Braccio da Montone** made a bid for overall power, but was eventually defeated and killed at L'Aquila in 1424. After this, papal power was restored in the region.

Palazzo dei Consoli in Gubbio

16C-19C
The Papal State and Italy. Work on the **Rocca Paolina** in Perugia began in 1540, finally establishing papal rule in Umbria and marking the end of the city-states which had long been in existence there and throughout Italy. ● The heyday of Umbrian painting was now over. **Perugino, Pinturicchio** and **Raphael** (who began his career as a painter of the Umbrian school) had all been dead for some time. Umbria remained isolated and stagnant within the **Papal State,** which included the whole of central Italy, apart from Tuscany. ● In the short term, not even the

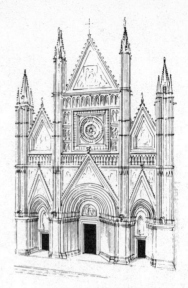

Duomo in Orvieto

events of the Napoleonic era seemed to make much impact. ● Then in 1848, when Rome was under siege by the French, Umbrian patriots sprang to the defense of Mazzini and his **Republic of Rome.** ● During the troubled events of the spring of 1859 (the war against Austria by Victor Emmanuel II and Napoleon III), **Perugia** rebelled, formed a temporary government and offered 'dictatorship' to the king of Sardinia. Swiss papal supporters took the town on 20 June. They sacked it and killed unarmed civilians (the **'Perugia massacre'**). ● Next came the **Piedmontese** on 11 September 1860. Gubbio and several other towns were then united within the **'Province of Umbria'.**

Duomo in Spoleto

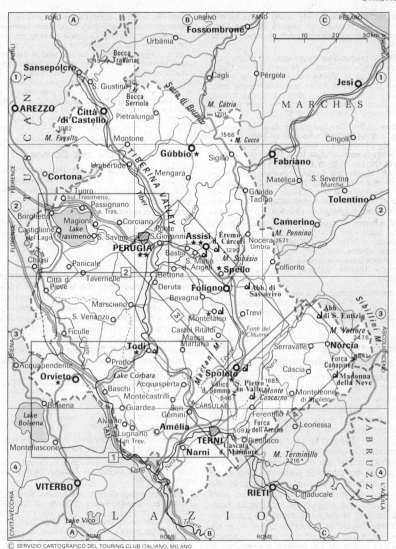

© SERVIZIO CARTOGRAFICO DEL TOURING CLUB ITALIANO, MILANO

Palazzo dei Priori in Perugia

● *Practical information*

Information: tourist offices in provincial capitals and main resorts; regional tourist advisor at Perugia, corso Vannucci 30, ☎ 696448.

Weather: forecast, ☎ 075/991991; roads open and closed, ☎ 075/994994 or *ACI*, 06/4212; snow information, ☎ 075/992992. From Perugia and its dialing code area, 191 (weather), 194 (roads), 162 (snow).

Farm vacations: *Associazione regionale Agriturist*, at Perugia, p. B. Michelotti 1, ☎ 075/30174.

Zoos and theme parks: *Città della Domenica* (→ Lake Trasimeno); *Monte Peglia* zoo (→ Orvieto).

Young peoples' activities: weekly sailing stages for children between the ages of 12 and 15 at Isola Maggiore in Lake Trasimeno; information from *Mastio*, Milan, ☎ 02/6141391.

Nature parks: in preparation: *Nera-Piedilucco* nature park; *Tiber* nature park; (from Todi to Alviano); *Monte Cucco* territorial nature park; *Monte Subasio* territorial nature park; *Monti Coscerno e Aspra* territorial nature park; *Monti Sibillini* territorial nature park. Information from the Ufficio Piano Urbanistico Territoriale della Regione Umbra, at Perugia, p. Giotto 42, ☎ 075/31341.

Conservation: *WWF* Delegazione Umbria, at Perugia, v. Cotogno 1, ☎ 075/65816; branches at: Terni, v. Muratori 2/A, ☎ 0744/49520; Foligno, v. Pignattara 2, ☎ 0742/55181; Orvieto, v. delle Ripe 16, ☎ 0763/28623; Todi, v. delle Caselle 19/C, ☎ 075/882078 (summer work camps at Mt. Malbe, the Sibillini mountains and other places of natural interest). *LIPU*, regional headquarters at Assisi, v. S. Agata, ☎ 075/813456; Terni, v. del Serpente 6, ☎ 0744/427201 (promotion of oases in cooperation with the regional authorities and local communities).

Instruction: summer courses in painting and sculpture, *Accademia Belle Arti Pietro Vannucci*, at Perugia, p. S. Francesco al Prato 5, ☎ 075/29106, summer courses in dance, drama and languages, winter courses in ecology, *Associazione femminile Casa Balena*, at Castel Ritaldi (→ Umbria Valleys), v. Torregrosso 51, ☎ 0743/51679.

Fairs and markets: market and exhibition of black truffles and other products of Valnerina and Norcia; tasting stand for Italian wines, at Torgiano (→ Umbria Valley); craftwork exhibition and market at Todi.

Umbrian delicacies

The small, black pigs used for roast pig can be found all over central Italy. Originally, however, they came from Umbria and are reared in the wild on acorns and chestnuts. The pig is first stuffed with small pieces of its liver, heart and lungs seasoned with pepper, garlic, salt and wild fennel and then roasted on a spit in a wood oven. The spit and the grill are the basic instruments used in Umbrian cooking. Woodcock is also cooked on a spit *alla norcina, i.e.* stuffed with giblets, sausage and aromatic herbs including sweet marjoram, which is a popular seasoning in the region. Assisi is famous for its *palombacci* (wild migratory doves) and, despite the fact that St. Francis used to preach to the birds, these are placed on a spit and then basted with a sauce of red wine, oil, capers and sage. Large carp from Lake Trasimeno are cooked *in porchetta, i.e.* using the same procedure as for roast pig. There are three different types of homemade pasta; *ciriole ternane, tagliatelle* seasoned with garlic lightly fried in oil; *strascinati, rough* macaroni with *sautéed* sausage and beaten eggs mixed with Parmesan cheese, and *umbrici, large,* handmade spaghetti. In Perugia and Norcia, grated truffles are sometimes used to flavour spaghetti. The black truffle of Norcia is highly prized, and the principal truffle market is in Scheggino. Black olives marinated in a mixture of oil, orange rind, garlic and bay leaf are sometimes used as an accompaniment to aperitifs.

Events: *Festival dei Due Mondi*, at Spoleto; *Umbria Jazz*, at Perugia and Terni; *Umbrian Festival of Music, Sagra Musicale Umbra* and *Amici della Musica*, all at Perugia; *Cantamaggio Ternano*, at Terni; *International Chamber* *Music Festival*, at Città di Castello; *drama season*, at the Morlacchi theatre, at Perugia and other Umbrian towns; *Ceri races*, at Gubbio; *Quintana jousting tournament*, at Foligno; strewing of flowers for *Corpus Christi*, at Spello; *Calendimaggio*, (medieval festival held in the first part of May), at Assisi; *Anello Races*, at Narni; historic procession for *Corpus Christi*, at Orvieto; *international folk review*, at Castiglione del Lago; *national antiques fair*, at Todi; *national antiques exhibition*, at Assisi; *international ceramics competition*, at Gualdo Tadino; *national and international boat races*, at Lake Piedilucco.

Facts and figures

Location: *Umbria is the only region in the peninsula without a coast. It is hilly and mountainous. However, the highest peaks, which are in the Apennines, rarely exceed 4,920 ft, and the hilly landscapes around the Tiber, Italy's third largest river, are renowned for their gentleness. The region takes its name from an ancient Italian people known as the Umbri, who in fact inhabited an area larger than modern Umbria.*
Area: *8,456 sq km.*
Climate: *The Mediterranean characteristics of the climate are tempered by the fact that it is inland. The summer is relatively mild, and the serenity of the sky makes spring and autumn very pleasant. The rains, which are brought by the wind from the Tyrrhenian Sea, are hardest in November and December.*
Population: *813,507 inhabitants.*
Local government: *There are two provincial capitals, Perugia and Terni, the former also being the regional capital.*

Motor racing: Magione (→ Lake Trasimeno), *vocabolo Bacanella*, ☎ 075/840303.

Cycling: help and information from groups belonging to *UDACE* (18) throughout the region.

Hang gliding: schools belonging to *Federazione Italiana Volo Libero*, at Sigillo (→ Gualdo Tadino) and Terni, ☎ 015/538703.

Horseback riding: *Federazione Italiana Sport Equestri*, at Rome, v. Flaminia Nuova 213, ☎ 06/3278457; riding schools, at Foligno and Corciano (→ Lake Trasimeno). Centre at Corciano (→ Lake Trasimeno): rides daily, longer treks to Tyrrhenian coast, overnight accommodation available; associated centres in Amelia (→ Tevere and Nera), Corciano (→ Lake Trasimeno) and Orvieto (associate of *ANTE*).

Excursions: numerous areas of interest to hikers (no specially marked long routes); information from *CAI*, at Foligno, v. Piermarini; at Perugia, v. della Gabbiaia 9; at Spoleto, v. Pianciani 4 ☎ 0743/28233 and at Terni, v. Roma 96.

Golf: at Ellera (→ Perugia, Corciano, Lake Trasimeno).

Fishing: *Federazione Italiana Pesca Sportiva*, at Perugia, v. Piaggia Colombata 2, ☎ 075/65072 and at Terni, corso Tacito 84, ☎ 0744/409235. For fishing regulations (permitted and prohibited waters, etc.) apply to relevant federal departments.

Spelunking: *CAI Speleology Group*, at Perugia, ☎ 075/28613. *Monte Cucco National Speleology Centre*, at Costacciaro, ☎ 075/9170236; fully equipped speleology centre, at Mt. Cucco (→ via Gualdo Tadino).

Flying: *Aeroclub Foligno*, at airport, ☎ 0742/670201 (also gliding and hang gliding); *S. Egiaio* airport, at Perugia, ☎ 075/6929445 (also gliding).

● *Towns and places*

ACQUASPARTA

Terni 21, Perugia 61, Rome 111 km
Pop. 4,648 ✉ 05021 ☎ 0744   B3

Perched high on a hill, the ancient Terra Arnolfa, named after its first feudal lord, has always been a renowned thermal watering place and still has ample spa facilities. The **Amerino** (N) and **Furapane** springs (S) rise near the town. Parts of the medieval walls with cylindrical towers have survived. In the town centre is the majestic 16C **Palazzo Cesi,** with arcaded courtyard and a loggia along one side.   ☐

Practical information ─────────────────
⚓ (mid-May-Sep), ☎ 93921.

ALVIANO

Terni 40, Perugia 113, Rome 103 km
Pop. 1,402 ✉ 05020 ☎ 0744   A4

Situated within a circle of hills scarred by erosion, Alviano enjoys a good view of the Tiber Valley. It still retains its characteristic medieval appearance. The 15C castle has angular towers and a fine Renaissance courtyard. The chapel contains a 17C fresco depicting a miracle performed there by St. Francis in 1212.   ☐

ASSISI**

Perugia 23, Rome 177 km
Pop. 24,668 ✉ 06081 ☎ 075   B2

The magic of Assisi lives on. It is a medieval town almost down to the last stone, but its fame and spiritual atmosphere derive mainly from St. Francis, who was born, worked and died here, 'opening his arms to God'. It sits perched high on a spur of Mt. Subasio, overlooking much of the green vale of Umbria, in the broad valley through which the Chiascio and Topino Rivers flow. The medieval town was built over an existing Roman settlement. It is ranged along a slope with the main streets linked by narrow alleyways, and the town walls culminate in a fortress at the top. From a distance, this fortress seems part of the mountain, while the town resembles a cascade of churches, houses and campaniles.

▶ The main entrance to the town is the 14C **Porta S. Francesco** (A1-2), part of the defensive wall, which is almost 5 km long and contains eight gates. ▶ V. Frate Elia leads up to the **piazza inferiore di S. Francesco★** (A1),which is dominated by the basilica and **campanile★** (1239) and surrounded by low 15C arcades, originally built to provide shelter for pilgrims. ▶ The basilica of **St. Francis★★** (A1) is one of the greatest shrines in the Christian world, begun in 1228 according to the wishes of brother Elia (appointed vicar of the order by St. Francis), who may also have designed it. It consists of two churches, one above the other. The lower one, which is the shrine proper, is a low Romanesque-Gothic building, while the upper church is tall, slender and full of light. The interior of the **lower church** has a nave with five dividing bays, a transept, an apse and side chapels. The chapel of St. Catherine leads to an evocative **cloister★**, once a cemetery. The frescos are steeped in medieval piety. In the nave: *Stories of Christ and St. Francis★*, by the master of St. Francis (13C) on the walls between the

entrance arches to the side chapels, and in a niche at the far end, on the l., *Coronation of the Virgin★* by Puccio Campana (14C). In the cross-vault, above the high altar, are the famous **allegorical frescos★** by Giotto and pupils (in the apse, is a **wooden choir★**, 1471). The walls and vaults in the r.-hand transept are decorated with **frescos★** by Giotto and followers; on the r. wall is the *Madonna with Angels and St. Francis★★*, and, on the back wall, the figures of the *5 Saints*, by Simone Martini. On the walls and in the vaulted ceiling of the l.-hand transept are *Episodes of the Life and Passion of Christ★★*, a remarkable work by P. Lorenzetti, who also painted the *Madonna with Saints★★* (l. wall), *St. Francis' Stigmata* (r. wall) and the *Madonna with Saints★* in the chapel at the far end underneath the 14C stained glass window. The r.-hand chapel is decorated with frescos by Simone Martini (1322) including the *Life of St. Martin★★*, and the third one with *Saints and Stories of the Madonna★*, by Giotto and his pupils (*c.* 1314). The crypt contains St. Francis' tomb. The **upper church** has nave,transepts and polygonal apse. The upper part of the walls of the nave contain fine 13C stained glass windows and are decorated with frescos depicting *Stories from the Old and New Testaments★*. Along the lower part is the famous cycle of twenty-eight frescos depicting the *Life of St. Francis★★*. Begun in 1296, they are all the work of Giotto apart from the last few, which he entrusted to his pupils. There are **frescos★** by Cimabue in the transept, the cross-vault and the apse. ▶ The **Tesoro★** (*9.30 a.m.-12.30 p.m. and 2.30-5 p.m. summer only; closed Mon*) houses some interesting works of art: a chalice★ by Guccio di Mannaia (*c.* 1288) which belonged to Nicholas IV, a *Madonna and Child★* (*c.* 1260-70), the Missal of St. Louis★, (1260-70), the antependium★ (a covering in front of the altar) of Sixtus IV designed by Pollaiolo and Botticini, the 15C Flemish tapestry, *The Tree of St. Francis★* and an exceptional collection of Florentine and Sienese school paintings on wood★ (14C-15C). ▶ The **via San Francesco★** (A2) leads uphill to the town centre and is lined with medieval buildings and a few baroque palaces. ▶ The central square, **p. del Comune★** (B3-4) is on the site of the old Roman Forum. Facing it are the **Palazzo dei Priori** (1337) and the 13C **Palazzo del Capitano del Popolo,** together with the Torre del Popolo, and beside it the **Temple of Minerva★**, dating from the Augustan age, with its elegant fluted columns, Corinthian capitals and pediment. ▶ The Palazzo dei Priori houses the **Pinacoteca Comunale** with frescos and fragments from the Romanesque period up to the 16C (*9 a.m.-12:30 p.m. and 3-6 p.m or 4-7 p.m. summer; 9 a.m.-12:30 p.m. wkends, closed Mon.*). ─ The **Museo Civico** (B3, *9:30 a.m.-12:30 p.m.and 3-7 p.m.; 9:30 a.m.-12:30 p.m. wkends, closed Mon.*) is housed in the Romanesque crypt of St. Nicholas, where St. Francis heard the sermon that changed his life. It contains fragments of Roman statues, sarcophagi, inscribed tablets and Etruscan and Roman memorial stones. The crypt leads to the remains of the Roman Forum. ▶ The **Duomo★** (B4) (12C-13C) stands on the site of a former 11C basilica. It has a beautiful sloping façade with statues, three carved portals and three rose windows. The interior has nave and three aisles on pilasters and a domed ceiling. In the apse is a valuable 16C wooden choir. The **Museo del Duomo** (*8:30 a.m.-1 p.m. and 3-6 p.m.; apply to caretaker*) contains detached frescos, paintings and a Gothic reliquary of Wood from the Cross, the Roman cistern and the original crypt. ▶ The church of **S. Chiara★★** (C4) has a fine portal and stained glass window. The tall campanile with a spire stands next to the apse. Among its paintings are a *Crucifixion* on wood in the apse, *St. Clare* in the r.-hand transept and a *Madonna* in the l.-hand transept (all late 13C). Off the nave is the Chapel of the Sacrament containing 14C frescos and panel paintings. On the l. is the 12C Crucifixion, which, according to legend, spoke to St. Francis in the

Convent of St. Damian. ▶ The 12C church of **S. Maria Maggiore** (B3) was once the Cathedral. ▶ The 13C Romanesque-Gothic church of **S. Pietro★** (B2) was built over an earlier church. The façade has an elegant central portal and three beautiful rose windows. Nearby is the **Porta S. Pietro** (14C). ▶ To get to **Rocca Maggiore** on foot (A3-4), follow the quaint v. Maria delle Rose (B4), beginning at the Duomo, and continue along a secluded lane and up a grassy slope. The present fortress was rebuilt by Albornoz in 1367 and consists of a trapezoid surrounding wall and towers, and a square keep with **view★**. Various parts of the interior are of interest *(8 a.m.-sunset)*.

Environs

▶ The basilica of **S. Maria degli Angeli★★** (1569-1679) is in the modern town of the same name, 5 km away. It stands on the spot where the Franciscan order began and where St. Francis died. It incorporates the **Cappella della Porziuncola**, a little oratory in the wood where St. Francis and his companions lived (14C-15C, exterior frescos). In the presbytery on the r. is the **Cappella del Transito**, the cell where the saint died. On the altar is a statue of *St. Francis★* by Andrea della Robbia. To the r. of the church is a garden of the roses of St. Francis, the nearby Cappella del Roseto and the 14C convent which now houses an ethnographical museum and another small **museum** *(8:30 a.m.-12:30 p.m. and 2:30-6:30 p.m.)* which has a portrait of *St. Francis* by Cimabue (13C), a crucifix★ by Giunta Pisano and religious ornaments. ▶ 25 km from the Porta Nuova (C4-5) stands the Convent of **S. Damiano★★** which grew up around the **oratory** where, according to legend, the crucifix spoke to the young St. Francis in 1205 showing him the path he must follow. The convent and the little garden of St. Clare can be visited. Off the cloister is the refectory with its low cross-vaulted ceiling. The original tables and benches (c. 1200) are still there. ▶ **L'Eremo delle Carceri★** *(4 km)* is situated on the slopes of Mt. Subasio. It was St. Francis' first retreat, and St. Bernard built a small convent there in the 15C. In the courtyard facing the small church is St. Francis' well, from which, according to tradition, water flowed miraculously. In the wood are St. Francis' cave and those of his companions. From the hermitage, the road goes on past St. Benedict's abbey (11C crypt) and up to the summit of Mt. Subasio (4,232 ft) with a splendid **view★**.

Practical information _____

♨ (all year), ☎ 816064.
ℹ p. del Comune 12 (B3-4), ☎ 812534.

Hotels:
★★★★ *Fontebella*, v. Fontebella 25 (A-B2 a), ☎ 812883, 37 rm ℙ No restaurant, 120,000; bkf: 9,000.
★★★★ *Subasio*, v. Frate Elia 2 (A1 b), ☎ 812206, 66 rm ℙ ∰ ⚄ Converted from 14C monastery and linked to basilica of St. Francis by ancient porticos, 90,000; bkf: 10,000.
★★★ *Castel San Gregorio*, at San Gregorio *(12 km N)*, ☎ 8038009, 12 rm ℙ ⚄ ∰ ⚄ Converted 13C castle, 58,000.
★★★ *Priori*, corso Mazzini 15, (B4 c) ☎ 812237, 28 rm ℙ closed 16 Nov-14 Mar, 57,000; bkf: 5,000.
★★★ *San Francesco*, v. S. Francesco 48 (A2 d), ☎ 812281, 47 rm ⚄ 57,000;bkf: 10,000.
★★★ *San Pietro*, p. S. Pietro 5 (A B2 e) ☎ 812452, 46 rm closed Nov-Feb, 56,000; bkf: 6,000.
★★★ *Windsor Savoia*, v. Marconi 1 (A1-2 f), ☎ 812210, 33 rm ℙ ∰ 56,000; bkf: 7,000.
★★ *Berti*, p. S. Pietro 24 (A-B2 g), ☎ 813466, 10 rm ⚄ No restaurant, 40,000; bkf: 5,000.
★★ *Roma*, p. S. Chiara (B-C4 h), ☎ 812390, 29 rm ℙ ⚄ 40,600.
★★ *Villa Elda*, at Santa Maria degli Angeli *(5 km SW)*, v. S. Pietro Campagna 137/139, ☎ 8041756, 50 rm ℙ ∰ ⚄ 40,500; bkf: 4,000.

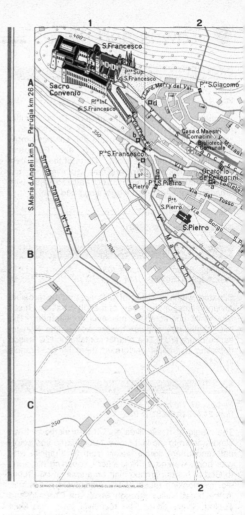

© SERVIZIO CARTOGRAFICO DEL TOURING CLUB ITALIANO, MILANO

Restaurants:
● ♦♦♦ *Buca di San Francesco*, v. Brizi 1 (B3 i), ☎ 812204, closed Mon, Sun eve in winter and Jul. Authentic 14C cellar dug out of volcanic tufa. Regional cuisine: garlic toast soaked in olive oil, wild boar ham, 20/30,000.
♦♦♦ *Umbra*, vicolo degli Archi 6 (B3 m), ☎ 812240, closed Tue, Nov-Feb. Elegant restaurant with seating in attractive garden. Regional cuisine: Umbrian style pancakes, cappelletti delight, 25/38,000.
♦♦ *Frantoio*, vicolo Illuminati (A-B2 a), ☎ 812977, closed Wed (in off season). Converted olive mill; seating outside in summer on large terrace. Regional cuisine: country style strangozzi, small macaroons with ricotta, 25/50,000.
♦ *Pozzo della Mensa*, v. Pozzo della Mensa 11 (B4 1), ☎ 816247, closed Wed and 10 Jan-10 Feb. The 'mensa' of the Franciscan. Regional cuisine: tagliatelle with truffles and sausage, escalopes with black truffles, 18/25,000.

⚐ ★★ *Fontemaggio*, strada Eremo delle Carceri 9, 246 pl, ☎ 813636 (all year).
Recommended
Farm vacations: *Azienda Le Silve*, at Armenzano, ☎ 812659.

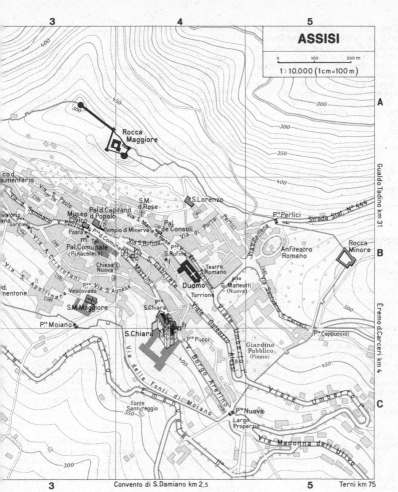

3   **4**   **5**

ASSISI

0   100   200 m

1 : 10,000 (1cm=100 m)

3   Convento di S.Damiano km 2,5   **5**   Terni km 75

Events: *Calendimaggio* (medieval pageant, first ten days of May); *ceremonies for Holy Week; festival of the Ascent of Mt. Subasio; Pardon at the Porziuncola* (1-2 Aug); *festival of St. Francis* (3-4 Oct), *Christmas celebrations; national antiques exhibition* (Apr-May).

Swimming: *Centro turistico sportivo,* at Fossa Caroncia, ☎ 812991 or 813009 (also tennis).

BASTIA

Perugia 18, Rome 176 km
Pop. 15,273 ⊠ 06083 ☎ 075   **B2**

Situated on the beautiful plain below Assisi, this modern-looking town still retains its ancient centre with remains of interesting buildings and fortifications. The 14C church of **S. Croce,** with its pink-and-white Subasio limestone façade, stands in p. Mazzini. The interior contains some interesting works of art. 9 km N, on a hillock, is **Rocca Sant'Angelo** with medieval walls and towers and one of the oldest Franciscan convents in existence. ☐

Practical information _____

Hotels:
★★★ *Olivera Inn,* at Ospedalicchio, SS 75 at 1.8-km marker, ☎ 809182, 72 rm Ⓟ ⚿ ♿ ⌷ 56,000.

★★★ *Spedalicchio,* at Ospedalicchio *(5 km W),* p. Buozzi 3, ☎ 809323, 25 rm Ⓟ ⚿ Renaissance palace with interesting tiled vaults, 53,000; bkf:6,000.

★★ *Santa Lucia,* villaggio XXV Aprile, ☎ 8000303, 53 rm Ⓟ 40,000; bkf: 6,000.

BEVAGNA

Perugia 35, Rome 148 km
Pop. 4,560 ⊠ 06031 ☎ 0742   **B3**

This ancient Umbrian town is situated at the W edge of the plain of Foligno in a loop of the River Timia. At the time of the Roman Empire, when it was known as *Mevania,* it was a flourishing community. The prevailing atmosphere, however, is medieval, especially in the historic town centre which is still intact, as are the walls (1249-1377).

▶ **Piazza Silvestri★**, the central square, is medieval in atmosphere. In it stands the Gothic **Palazzo dei Consoli** (1270). ▶ Two remarkable Romanesque churches are **S. Silvestro★** (1195) and **S. Michele★** (late 12C). ▶ The Palazzo Comunale, in corso Matteotti, houses the **Pinacoteca F. Torti**, with paintings from the 15C-18C and a collection of Roman coins *(8 a.m.-2 p.m.; closed wkends)*. ▶ The town also has Roman remains: a temple (2C BC), a mosaic (v. di Porta Guelfa, *apply to caretaker at no. 2*) and stretches of the surrounding walls (1C BC). □

Practical information _____

ⓘ p. Silvestri (palazzo dei Consoli).

Restaurant:
◆ *G. T. Nina,* p. Garibaldi 6, ☎ 62161, closed Tue and Jul. Classic, simple home cooking. Regional cuisine: pappardelle with pheasant, penne primavera, 20/30,000.

⚊ ★★★ *Pian di Boccio,* at Pian di Boccio, 450 pl, ☎ 62472

CASTIGLIONE DEL LAGO

Perugia 41, Rome 181 km
Pop. 13,434 ⊠ 06061 ☎ 075   A2

Castiglione del Lago sits on a promontory on the shores of Lake Trasimeno, among hills covered with olive trees.

▶ The **Palazzo Comunale** faces **piazza Ducale** with gardens and a view of the lake. The building once belonged to the Della Corgna family (dukes of the town from the 16C-17C) and is an adaptation, by Alessi, of an older building. The rooms contain 16C Roman school frescos. ▶ Along a short road are the remains of the medieval castle. ▶ The **church of la Maddalena** contains a panel painting of the *Madonna and Child★* (1500). □

Practical information _____

≋
ⓘ p. Mazzini 10, ☎ 952184.
⛴ boats to Isola Maggiore, Tuoro and Passignano, ☎ 827157.

Hotel:
★★ *Fazzuoli,* p. Marconi 25, ☎ 951119, 27 rm Ⓟ ♿ closed Jan. No restaurant, 40,500; bkf: 4,000.

⚊ ★★ *Badiaccia,* at Badiaccia, 147 pl, ☎ 954147.

Recommended
Events: *international folk festival* (at the castle, end of Jul-mid-Aug).
Motocross: *Gioiella track,* management *Moto Club Trasimeno,* ☎ 957107.
Sailing school: *Club Velico,* ☎ 953227 (also wind surfing).

CITTA DELLA PIEVE

Perugia 43, Rome 154 km
Pop. 6,438 ⊠ 06062 ☎ 0578   A3

Situated on a ridge above the Chiani Valley, Città della Pieve still has remains of medieval walls and a 14C fortress.

▶ It was the home of the painter, Pietro Vannucchi, known as Perugino. Some of his works are to be found in the **Duomo** (12C, rebuilt) with its tall Romanesque-Gothic **campanile**, which faces the town square. In the same square stands the **Palazzo Mazzuoli**, attributed to Alessi. ▶ Other frescos by Perugino are found in the oratory of **S. Maria dei Bianchi** *(when closed apply to the nearby convent)* and in the church of **S. Pietro** *(outside the town, near the hospital).* □

Practical information _____

ⓘ p. Matteotti 1, ☎ 298031.

Hotel:
★ *Villa Maraska,* at Po Bandino *(7 km toward Chiusi),* SS 71 50, ☎ 20524, 6 rm ▦ 32,000; bkf: 3,000.

Restaurant:
◆◆ *Barzanti,* v. S. Lucia 53, ☎ 298010, closed Tue. Italian cuisine: homemade spaghetti, pappardelle with hare, 20/30,000.

CITTA DI CASTELLO

Perugia 50, Rome 222 km
Pop. 37,918 ⊠ 06012 ☎ 75   A1

Located among the hills of the Tiber Valley, this town still retains some 16C walls. At the centre is p. Matteotti, dominated by the **Palazzo del Podestà** (14C, extended 17C).

▶ The **Palazzo Comunale★** is a Gothic building in ashlar-work (1322-52) with portal and mullioned windows with two lights. In front of it stands the **Torre Comunale**. ▶ The 11C **Duomo** (extended 1356, renovated 1466 and 1529) may have been built on the site of a Roman temple. It has a round campanile (13C). The small annexed **museum** *(apply to the sacristy)* contains a 12C silver altar frontal★, several 5C and 6C communion vessels★ and a *Madonna* by Pinturicchio. ▶ The **Palazzo Vitelli alla Cannoniera** (16C) has a graffito work façade. It houses the **Pinacoteca Comunale★** *(9 a.m.-1 p.m. and 3-6 p.m.; closed Mon),* second only to the Pinacoteca in Perugia for Umbrian paintings. Among the exhibits are paintings by Raphael★, Luca Signorelli, Neri di Bicci and Ghirlandaio. ▶ Other places of interest are: the **Museo Burri** *(10 a.m.-12 noon and 3-5 p.m.; closed Mon)* with works donated by this locally born painter, the church of **S. Francesco** with Vitelli chapel and the Gothic church of **S. Domenico**.

Environs

▶ At **Garavalle** *(2 km along the old SS to Perugia)* is the **Centro di Tradizioni Popolari** with a Museum of Folk Art and Culture and other collections. ▶ The **Terme di Fontecchio** is 3.5 km E. ▶ At **Umbértide** *(20 km S)* is the church of S. Croce, with a *Descent from the Cross* by Signorelli. □

Practical information _____

ⓘ v. De Cesare 2/B, ☎ 8554922.

Hotels:
★★★ *Europa,* v. V. E. Orlando 2, ☎ 8550551, 54 rm ♿ 47,000; bkf: 5,000.
★★★ *Garden,* v. Bologni, ☎ 8550587, 61 rm Ⓟ ▦ ♿ 50,000; bkf: 4,000.
★★★ *Park Hotel Geal,* v. Piero della Francesca 24, ☎ 8559441, 34 rm Ⓟ ▦ closed 1-26 Dec and 5 Jan-1 Feb, 47,000; bkf: 5,000.
★★★ *Tiferno,* p. Raffaello Sanzio 13, ☎ 8550331, 47 rm. One of oldest in Umbria, housed in former patrician palace, 50,000; bkf: 5,000. Rest. ◆◆◆ Closed Mon. Regional cuisine: risotto with green vegetables, costata di midollo, 25/35,000.

⚊ ★★★ *Montesca,* at Montesca, 100 pl, ☎ 8558566.

Recommended
Fairs and markets: sale of bric-à-brac every third Sun of month.
Events: *international chamber music festival* (Aug-Sep), *exhibition of period furniture* (Apr-May), *white truffle show* (Nov).
Swimming: v. Engels, ☎ 8550785.
Tennis: v. Bologni, ☎ 8559825 (also bowling green), ☎ 8550919).

Environs

TERME DI FONTECCHIO, ⊠ 06012, ☎ 075, 3 km E.
♨ (Mar-Nov), ☎ 8559440 or 8558150.

DERUTA

Perugia 19, Rome 153 km
Pop. 7,441 ⊠ 06053 ☎ 075   B3

Deruta is a town with ancient origins, situated in the Tiber Valley. It is interesting not only for its works of art, but also for the famous traditional decorative pottery industry, dating from the 14C and at its height in the first half of the 16C. Today, it is still one of the town's principal resources and is fostered by the Istituto Statale d'Arte per la Ceramica and by the International Ceramics Exhibition.

▶ The 14C church of **S. Francesco** is in the p. dei Consoli. Inside are Umbrian-Sienese school frescos (14C-16C). ▶ In the same square is the medieval **Palazzo Comunale**, which houses a **Pinacoteca** *(apply to secretary or police)* containing 15C-18C works, and a **Museo delle Ceramiche** containing both old and contemporary local pottery. ▶ 2.5 km toward Todi is the church of **Madonna di Bagno** whose interior is decorated with votive majolica work (17C-18C).   □

Practical information _____

ⓘ corso Umberto 1, ☎ 9711559.

Hotel:
★★★ *Melody,* SS 3 bis at 55.8-km marker, ☎ 9711186, 44 rm Ⓟ ᠔ ᠗ 55,000; bkf: 5,000.

Restaurant:
♦ *Asso di Coppe,* SS 3 bis at 73.4-km marker, ☎ 9710279, closed Tue. Italian cuisine: rigatoni montanara, tagliatelle puttanesca, 20/25,000.

FOLIGNO

Perugia 36, Rome 158 km
Pop. 53,179 ⊠ 06034 ☎ 0742   B3

In 1472, 300 copies of the *Divine Comedy,* the first book in Italy to be printed in Italian, were published in Foligno by the local master. The town was also the birthplace of Giuseppe Piermarini, the architect of La Scala in Milan.

▶ The town centre is around the p. della Repubblica and adjoining p. del Duomo. ▶ The **Duomo★**, originally built in 1133, has been altered several times (16C-18C). It has a secondary **façade★** (in p. della Repubblica), dating back to 1201, with portal decorated with classical style reliefs and mosaics. The interior was rebuilt by Piermarini in the 18C, but the 12C crypt and the 16C Cappella del Sacramento, by A. Sangallo, have survived. ▶ The **Pinacoteca★** is housed on the upper floor of the **Palazzo Trinci** (1389-1407), which has been largely disfigured, but still retains traces of old frescos *(9 a.m.-1 p.m. and 3-7 p.m. or 2-4 p.m. winter, 9 a.m.-2 p.m. wkends; if closed apply to library).* ▶ The Romanesque church of **S. Maria Infraportas★** has a portico (11C-12C) and campanile. Inside are 13C-14C frescos.

Environs

▶ 6 km away in the Renaro Valley is the **Abbazia di Sassovivo★**, founded in the 11C by the Benedictines, who turned it into a cultural and study centre. It has a splendid 13C Romanesque **cloister★** on 128 slender columns.   □

─────────────────────────────
Be advised that hotels and restaurants in this Guide have perhaps changed addresses; prices indicated are also subject to modifications.
─────────────────────────────

Practical information _____

ⓘ porta Romana, ☎ 60459.

Hotels:
★★★★ *Nuovo Poledrini,* v. Mezzetti 3, ☎ 60581, 42 rm Ⓟ ᠗ ᠔ 68,000; bkf: 7,000.
★★★ *Italia,* p. Matteotti 12, ☎ 50412, 29 rm Ⓟ 58,000; bkf: 7,000.
★★★ *Umbria,* v. Battisti 3, ☎ 52821, 47 rm Ⓟ 56,000.

Restaurant:
♦♦♦ *Remo,* v. Battisti 49, ☎ 50079, closed Sun eve and Mon. Regional cuisine: strangozzi al profumo di bosco, pigeon alla folignata, 20/30,000.

Recommended
Events: *Quintana joust* (second and third Sun in Sep) and, historic *eating contest* with each district of the town competing; also 17C *theatre performances* in dialect.
Flying club: *Aeroporto turistico,* ☎ 670201 (also gliding and hang gliding).
Horseback riding: *Società ippica,* in San Bartolomeo, ☎ 50461 (riding school).
Sports centre: ☎ 53845.
Youth Hostel: *Ostello Fulginium,* p. S. Giacomo 11, ☎ 52882.

Le FONTI DEL CLITUNNO

Perugia 52, Rome 141 km
⊠ 06042 (Campello) ☎ 0743   B-C3

Poets throughout the ages, from Virgil to Carducci, have sung the praises of this famous spot. The fountains are situated in a wide valley of the plain of Spoleto, where their clear springs form a small **lake** dotted with green islands and surrounded by poplars and weeping willows *(information from the nearby Ufficio Turistico).* 1 km along the v. Flaminia is the **Tempietto del Clitunno★** (church of S. Salvatore; *ring the bell on the gate),* an Early Christian building of uncertain date (4C-5C or 8C-9C) with remains of 8C frescos in the apse.   □

Practical information _____

Restaurant:
♦ *Casaline,* at Casaline *(5 km E),* ☎ 520811, closed Mon. Regional cuisine, 20/30,000.

GUALDO TADINO

Perugia 53, Rome 193 km
Pop. 14,155 ⊠ 06023 ☎ 075   B-C2

Situated at the foot of Mt. Serra Santa, Gualdo Tadino has a long-standing tradition of pottery-making, its speciality being polychrome earthenware with metallic flecks.

▶ The historic centre and the **Rocca Flea** (a fortification rebuilt in part by Frederick II in the 13C and again in the 14C and 16C) give it an old-world appearance. ▶ In the central square are the Palazzo Comunale (late 18C), the Torre Civica and the **Duomo**, built in 1256, which has a fine central portal and a rose window in the façade (the interior is decorated with paintings and has a Renaissance font). The former Gothic church of **S. Francesco** has 15C frescos. It now houses the **Pinacoteca Comunale** *(apply to the chief of police).* ▶ The church of **S. Maria**, in p. XX Settembre, has a triptych by Matteo da Gualdo.   □

Practical information _____

ⓘ p. Calai 39, ☎ 912172.

Hotel:
★★ *Gigiotto,* v. Morone 5, ☎ 912283, 30 rm, closed Nov,

36,000; bkf: 4,000. Rest. ♦♦ closed Wed except Jul-Aug. Regional and Italian cuisine: risotto with salmon, cappelletti with truffles, 20/30,000.

Recommended
Events: *international ceramics competition* (Aug-Sep), *Good Friday Passion Play, Giochi delle Porte* (late Sep); *traditional festival* at San Pellegrino,the night of 1 May.
Hang gliding: *Monte Cucco* gliding school, at Sigillo *(13 km NW),* at Scirca, ☎ 917185.
Spelunking: visit to the Grotta di Mt. Cucco *(c. 25 km NW);* information from *Centro nazionale di speleologia Monte Cucco,* in Costacciaro, ☎ 9170236.
Swimming: v. Valsorda, ☎ 916250.

GUBBIO*

Perugia 40, Rome 217 km
Pop. 32,323 ⊠ 06024 ☎ 075   B2

This town in the Apennines is splendidly sited at various levels on the side of Mt. Ingino, where St. Francis is said to have tamed the 'savage wolf'. Its plan is simple and linear, but highly picturesque, with intact medieval buildings and walls and towers made of limestone from the nearby mountains. Many of the houses have the so-called *porta del morto* (door of the dead) next to the main door. It is narrow and set above street level. According to tradition, it only opened to allow coffins through, but, in reality, it was probably the entrance to the upper

floors. At dawn on the 15th May, the *Corsa dei Ceri* begins. The *ceri* (candles) are three large wooden structures, one belonging to the stone masons, with a statue of S. Ubaldo, the second to the merchants, with a statue of St. George, and the third to the peasants, with a statue of St. Antony of Egypt. The *ceri* are raised at midday, when the bell on the Palazzo dei Consoli tolls, and carried through the streets by chosen bearers, who perform spectacular *birate* (turns). Late in the afternoon, at a sign from the mayor, they are taken, at a great pace, up the side of the mountain to the church of S. Ubaldo. In Italian folklore, this festival is second in fame only to the Sienese Palio.

▶ The **piazza della Signoria**★ (B2) opens like a balcony onto the plain below, offering a breathtaking view. On the piazza is the 14C **Palazzo Pretorio** and the **Palazzo dei Consoli**★★ (A-B2), the latter a magnificent example of 14C architecture and home of the **museum**★ and Art Gallery *(9 a.m-1 p.m. and 3-5 p.m. winter; 9 a.m.-12:30 p.m. and 3:30-6 p.m. spring and autumn; open until 7 p.m. summer).* It contains Roman and medieval marbles, archaeological exhibits, coins, pottery and the *Eugubian tables* — seven bronze tablets bearing religious inscriptions in Umbrian and Latin characters (the most important surviving example of the Umbrian language). The **Pinacoteca**★ has works of the Gubbio and Tuscan schools. ▶ The **via Ducale** (B2), flanked by old buildings, leads to the Duomo★ (A2, 13C, renovated 16C).The façade retains the original Gothic portal and sculptures. The interior has a nave supported by large trans-

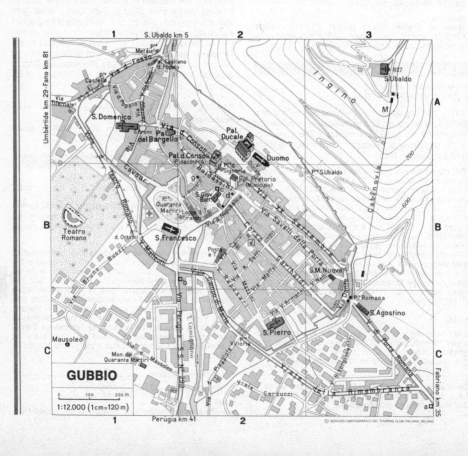

verse arches. The altars and walls are decorated with 16C paintings and frescos of the Umbrian/Marche school. The Duomo's **museum** *(apply to the caretaker)* contains 15C detached frescos and a fine 16C Flemish cope. ▶ Opposite the Duomo is the 15C **Palazzo Ducale★★** (A2, *9 a.m.-1 p.m., closed Mon*). It has an attractive **courtyard★★** with an arcade on brick and stone columns with graceful capitals. In a number of the rooms old floors, elegantly decorated fireplaces, inlaid wooden doors and old furniture remain. ▶ The **via Galeotti★** is a quaint street with narrow, dark alleys leading off it; it leads to **via dei Consoli★** (A1-2) with interesting old houses and towers. ▶ After the 13C Gothic **Palazzo del Bargello** (A1) is the 14C church of **S. Domenico** (A1). Inside are 15C-17C paintings and frescos. ▶ Nearby is the late 13C **Palazzo del Capitano del Popolo** (A1). ▶ Some 12C and 14C houses with the characteristic *porta del morto* may be seen in the **via Baldassini** (A-B2). Overhanging the p. della Signoria are the Palazzo dei Consoli, held up by four colossal arches, and the Palazzo Comunale. ▶ The 13C church of **S. Giovanni Battista** (B2) has a wide Gothic portal in the façade and an attractive interior with transverse arches. ▶ **Piazza Quaranta Martiri** (B1-2), at the foot of the town, is dedicated to war victims. In it stands the medieval Loggiato dei Tiratori dell'Arte della Lana (wool spinners' lodge) with its long rustic portico and the 13C church of **S. Francesco★** (B1). The inside is decorated with 13C-15C frescos. In the former convent are sacred vessels, paintings and pottery from Greece and Apulia. ▶ The **Roman theatre★** (B1) was a majestic building of the Augustan age (1C BC). Some of the pilasters and arcades plus the steps of auditorium have survived. Nearby are the ruins of the **Mausoleo di Pomponio Grecino** (C1), a Roman aristocratic tomb. The burial chamber has a barrel-vaulted ceiling. ▶ Back in the town centre is the v. Savelli della Porta (B2-3). The elegant **Palazzo della Porta** (no.16) has a Renaissance portal; a little further on is the 14C church of **S. Maria Nuova** (B3). The interior *(caretaker at v. Dante 64)* contains frescos, including the *Madonna del Belvedere★*. ▶ Beyond the Porta Romana (C3) the 13C church of **S. Agostino** houses valuable frescos by O. Nelli and his pupils. The church of **S. Pietro** (C2), originally built before 1000 and rebuilt 13C and 16C, has frescos and paintings, a *Crucifixion* in wood (1200) and a splendid carved organ by Maffei (1598). ▶ The church of **S. Ubaldo** stands 2,713 ft up on the side of Mt. Ingino, (B3; *5 km on foot or by car; can also be reached by cable car*). Originally a medieval basilica, it was rebuilt and enlarged in the 16C. It has a Renaissance portal and a fine cloister with the altar containing the body of S. Ubaldo★. There is a wonderful view of the town from the front of the church. ◻

Practical information _____

ℹ p. Oderisi 5 (B2), ☎ 9273693, v. della Repubblica 13 (B2), ☎ 9273341.

Hotels:
★★★ *Pinolo*, v. di Porta Romana (C3 a), ☎ 9272747, 25 rm ℗ No restaurant, 48,000; bkf: 4,000.
★★★ *San Marco*, v. Perugia 5 (B1-2 b), ☎ 9272349, 52 rm ℗ ⚒ ♨ 50,000; bkf: 5,000.
★★ *Gattapone*, v. Beni 11 (B2 c), ☎ 9272489, 15 rm, closed Jan, 36,000; bkf: 4,500.

Restaurants:
♦♦♦ *Balestra*, v. della Repubblica 41 (B2 d), ☎ 9273810, closed Wed and Feb. Service in garden in summer. Regional cuisine: tagliatelle with truffles, friccò with fritters, 16/25,000.
♦♦♦ *Federico da Montefeltro*, v. della Repubblica 35 (B2 e), ☎ 9273949, closed Thu and Feb. Outside service in summer. Regional and Italian cuisine: maccheroncini with shellfish, agnolotti etrusca, 13/30,000.
♦♦♦ *Porta Tessenaca*, v. Piccardi 21 (B2 g), ☎ 9273327, closed Wed. Quaint converted stable building. Regional cuisine: risotto with herbs, cappelletti Mario, 15/30,000.
♦♦♦ *Taverna del Lupo*, v. Ansidei 21 (B2 g), ☎ 9271269, closed 10-31 Jan. 14C vaulted ceilings. Regional cui-

sine: cannelloni francescana, risotto with mushrooms or truffles, 25/35,000.
♦ *Funivia*, on Monte Ingino (A3 f; *3 km by funicular*), ☎ 9273464, closed Wed and Jan. Regional cuisine: risotto Vinicio, gnocchi with cèpes, friccò, 15/25,000.

Recommended
Cycling: *G. S. Albertcar*, in Torre Calzolari *(10 km SE)*, ☎ 9256257.
Events: *Corsa dei Ceri* (15th May); *cross bow tournament* with the Sansepolcro archers (last Sun in May); *Good Friday procession*, classical plays at the Roman theatre (Jul-Aug), *stamp and coin exhibition* (Sep).
Excursions: cablecar to Mt. Ingino, depart v. S. Gerolamo (B3), ☎ 9273881.
Fairs and markets: *antiques fair* (second Sun of the month) v. Baldassini (A-B2).
Farm vacations: *Azienda Castel'Alfiolo*, at Padule, ☎ 9258128, *Residenza Cortevecchio*, at Nogna, ☎ 9255446.

LUGNANO IN TEVERINA

Terni 35, Perugia 118, Rome 98 km
Pop. 1,624 ⊠ 05020 ☎ 0744   A-B4

Lugnano in Teverina is beautifully located on the ridge of hills to the E of the winding River Tiber. The **walls**, largely rebuilt by Pius II in the 15C, still stand. The Romanesque church of **S. Maria Assunta★** (12C) has a façade with a rose window and mullioned windows with two lights framed by sculptures and mosaics. At the front is a portico with wooden beams over the columns (13C). The interior has a *schola cantorum* with partition walls in coloured stone, two pulpits, a rood screen and a crypt below the presbytery. ◻

MONTEFALCO*

Perugia 41, Rome 145 km
Pop. 5,526 ⊠ 06036 ☎ 0742   B3

Situated high above the plains around the Topino and Clitunno Rivers, Montefalco, with its towered walls, is known as the 'balustrade of Umbria', because of the splendid view it affords. An account of the life of St. Francis, painted by B. Gozzoli in 1452, may be seen in the apse of the church of S. Francesco.

▶ The tower of the 13C **Palazzo Comunale** in the p. della Repubblica offers a splendid view of the town. ▶ The 14C church of **S. Francesco★**, rich in frescos, is now a **Pinacoteca** *(8 a.m.-12 noon and 3-6 p.m.; 9 a.m.-12 noon hols; caretaker at v. Severini 16, ☎ 79146, closed for repairs)*. It contains work by Umbrian artists from the 14C-16C *(Nativity★* by Perugino). The cycle of frescos by B. Gozzoli in the centrally positioned apse *(Stories of St. Francis★*) is exceptional. ▶ Nearby is v. Ringhiera Umbra, which goes up to the famous view★ over the valleys of the Topino (l.) and the Clitunno (r.). ▶ Also see the 13C church of **S. Agostino**, the Romanesque church of **S. Bartolomeo** and the nearby **Porta di Federico II** (1244) and the church of **S. Chiara**, with frescos painted in 1333 *(ring the doorbell of adjacent Augustinian monastery)*. ▶ Along the Spoleto road is the 16C church of **S. Illuminata**, containing frescos *(apply to convent of Poor Clares, opposite)*. ▶ 1.5 km SE is the church of **S. Fortunato** (15C), containing **frescos★** by B. Gozzoli in the lunette of the portal and at the r.-hand altar. ◻

Practical information _____

ℹ corso Mameli 68 (Palazzo Comunale), ☎ 79122.

Recommended
Craft workshops: *L. Reali*, v. dei Vasari (ceramics).

Terni 13, Perugia 84, Rome 89 km
Pop. 20,802 ⊠ 05035 ☎ 0744   B4

On a hill covered with olive trees and overlooking the
gorge of the River Nera and the lowlands of Terni,
this ancient fortress with its towered castles can be
seen from far away. Much about the medieval-
looking town is interesting; not only its monuments, but
also the back streets, squares, fountains and façades
of former aristocratic dwellings. Erasmo da Narni,
the famous condottiere known as Gattamelata (Sly-
boots) was born here in 1370.

▶ The Romanesque **Duomo★** (11C-12C) has a 15C portico at the front with Renaissance frieze. The main portal
is decorated with classical motifs. Inside, note the 12C
frescos and the chapel of S. Giovenale and S. Cassio, installed in the 15C-16C, using Romanesque and early Christian elements (high up is a late 11C mosaic depicting
the *Redeemer★*). ▶ Facing the long, narrow medieval
piazza dei Priori are the **Loggia dei Priori** (14C) with
two big arcades, and the **Palazzo del Podestà★**, comprising three 13C houses combined into one (in the Council Chamber are paintings including a large altarpiece by
Ghirlandaio in 1486). ▶ **Via Mazzini** is a street flanked
by medieval towers and 13C houses. At one end is the
Romanesque church of **S. Maria in Pensole** (1175), which
has a portico with longitudinal arches. Nearby is the
12C church of **S. Domenico**, converted into a studio
and museum *(wkdays 8 a.m.-2 p.m., inquire at municipio):*
it houses 13C-14C frescos and other works, including an
Annunciation★ by Gozzoli. ▶ The church of **S. Agostino**
(15C) contains some remarkable frescos, a 16C wooden
Crucifixion and a 15C painting on wood. The **Rocca** was
erected by Cardinal Albornoz in 1370 (view★). At the foot
of the town, by the River Nera, 1.5 km along the road
that leads to the station, are the ruins of the magnificent
Ponte d'Augusto★ which had four rows of arches, 98 ft
high and 525 ft long.   □

Practical information _____

Ⓘ p. dei Priori 18, ☎ 715362.
Car rental: Maggiore, v. Tuderte 10, ☎ 737997.

Hotel:
★★★ *Minareto*, v. Cappuccini Nuovi 32, ☎ 726343, 10 rm
⚏ Charming Arab style building with small lake, 50,000;
bkf: 5,000.

Restaurant:
♦♦♦ *Loggia*, vicolo del Comune 4, ☎ 722744, closed Mon
and 15-31 Jul. Charming internal courtyard. Regional,
Italian and international cuisine: noodles fattoressa style,
fried sandwiches Valnerina style, 18/25,000.

⚐ ★★ *Monti del Sole*, on road to Borgheria, 100 pl,
☎ 746336.

Recommended
Events: Anello races (Apr-May), ☎ 726233.

Perugia 55, Rome 179 km
Pop. 6,184 ⊠ 06025 ☎ 0742   B2

Nocera Umbra, a small town of ancient appearance
noted for its mineral waters, is on a piece of high
ground in the Topino Valley. The waters come from
springs which emerge at **Bagni di Nocera** *(5.6 km SE)*
and **Schiagni** *(4.5 km NE)*. ▶ The former church of
S. Francesco (14C-15C) now houses the **Pinacoteca Comunale** *(8 a.m.-2 p.m. and 3-7 p.m.), apply
to police headquarters),* containing paintings of the
Umbrian and Tuscan schools. Frescos by Matteo di

Gualdo decorate the walls. ▶ At the top of the town,
the **Duomo** (11C, rebuilt 15C) has a Romanesque portal on the l.-hand side and a remarkable majolica floor
in the sacristy.   □

Practical information _____

♨ (May-Oct), ☎ 81255.

Hotel:
★★ *Europa*, largo Bisleri 9, ☎ 81274, 20 rm Ⓟ ⚘ closed
10-25 Sep, 40,000; bkf: 3,000.

Restaurant:
♦♦ *Pennino*, at Bagnara, ☎ 81391, closed Wed, Easter
and Christmas. Regional cuisine: tagliatelle, venison with
cranberries, 15/28,000.

Perugia 96, Rome 157 km
Pop. 4,727 ⊠ 06046 ☎ 0743   C3

Norcia is at the edge of the large, green plain of
S. Scolastica, which is watered by a number of
rivers and surrounded by a cluster of green mountain peaks. It is a beautiful town known for its artistic heritage, but even more famous for the fact that it
was the home of St. Benedict, the founder of Western monasticism.

▶ The town still has its 14C **walls**. The centre is the
piazza S. Benedetto, which contains the most important buildings. ▶ The church of **S. Benedetto★**is a typical example of 13C-14C Gothic architecture. In the crypt
are the remains of a house from the late Roman Empire,
and which, according to tradition, was St. Benedict's
home. ▶ The fortress or **Castellina★**, erected by Vignola
from 1554-63 on the orders of Julius III, is now the home
of the interesting **Museo Civico Diocesano**
*(8 a.m.-12:30 p.m. and 2-4 p.m. winter; closed
Mon).* ▶ The **Duomo**, in the southernmost corner of the
town, was rebuilt in the 18C. It has a massive campanile
and a Gothic portal. ▶ The **Palazzo Comunale** still has
its 13C portico. Its many works of art include the reliquary of St. Benedict, made of gilded and enameled silver
(15C). ▶ Interesting too are the 14C church of **S. Francesco** and the so-called **Edicola**, a building dating from
1345. ▶ 23.3 km away *(about 20 km along the Porca
Canapine road and then turn l.)* is the **Piano Grande★**,
a magnificent natural amphitheatre 6 km long, dominated
by the Sibillini to the E. ▶ The ancient abbey of **S. Eutizio** is reached by going 16 km NW (with a short detour
by Piedivalle) along a road that climbs and descends. □

Practical information _____

⚲ ski lifts and instruction at Forca Canapine *(2 km SE),*
cross-country slopes at Pian Piccolo, Pian Grande and
Pian Perduto.

Hotels:
★★★ *Europa*, v. Europa 7, ☎ 816322, 54 rm Ⓟ ⚏ ⚘
closed Nov, 52,000; bkf: 3,000.
★★★ *Grotta Azzurra-Granaro del Monte*, v. Alfieri 12,
☎ 816513, 40 rm Ⓟ & ⚘ 52,000; bkf: 4,000.
★★★ *Posta*, v. Battisti 10, ☎ 816274, 30 rm ⚏ 55,000.

Restaurant:
♦ *Francese*, v. Riguardati 16, ☎ 816290, closed Fri
except summer. Regional cuisine: tortelloni with crema
di tordi and truffles, chop in vinegar with sugar and truffles, 35/50,000.

Recommended
Fairs and markets: exhibition and market, black truffles
and products of Valnerina (Feb).

ORVIETO**

Terni 72, Perugia 86, Rome 121 km
Pop. 22,761 ⊠ 05018 ☎ 0763   A3

Orvieto stands on a flat-topped, elliptical block of volcanic tufa in the middle of the Paglia Valley. From the town, it is possible to see beyond the plain to hilly countryside with many deep incisions carved by numerous rivers. Olive trees and vines grow in the volcanic soil. The medieval structure of the town remains largely unchanged; the streets are narrow and winding and flanked by low houses made of tufa stone or basalt. There are a few 16C buildings along the main streets. The old town occupied most of the flat surface of the cliff as long ago as the Etruscan era; all modern expansion has taken place below it.

▶ The central square is the **piazza della Repubblica★** (B2), probably on the site of the Etruscan-Roman forum. ▶ Its most prominent feature is the long façade of the **Palazzo Comunale**, erected in the 16C and incorporating an existing medieval building, remains of which can be seen at the back and inside. ▶ Also in the square is the church of S. **Andrea★** (6C, rebuilt several times). Beside it stands a dodecagonal **campanile★**. The interior has traces of 14C-15C frescos. In the underground vaults are remains of the 6C basilica, and, below those, Roman remains. ▶ Leading off the square is **corso Cavour**, the winding main road through the town, flanked by 16C buildings and medieval houses. ▶ Around the small clock tower (at the top is a figure which strikes the hour) and l. into v. Duomo, is the quiet **piazza del Duomo**. ▶ The **Duomo** (C2-3) is one of the great masterpieces of Italian Gothic architecture. Begun in 1290, probably to a design by Arnolfo di Cambio, it was completed by Lorenzo Maitani (façade and apse) from 1310-30. It has a splendid tripartite Gothic **façade★** entirely covered in mosaics (renovated 17C-18C) and sculptures; a portal in the centre and **rose window★** by Orcagna above it (14C); four pilasters decorated with **reliefs★★** by Maitani between each portal and bronze leaves of a central door (by Emilio Greco 1964-70). Among the works of art inside are the fresco by Gentile da Fabriano of the *Madonna★*, at the near end of the l.-hand aisle, the *Crucifixion★* on the high altar, the Cappella Nuova or Cappella della Madonna di San Brizio (at the end of the r.-hand arm of the transept) containing splendid **frescos★★** by L. Signorelli (1499-1504), the Cappella del Corporale (at the end of the l.-hand arm of the transept) with the **Madonna dei Raccomandati★** by Lippo Memmi on the r. wall and, above the altar, within the Gothic tabernacle, the magnificent **reliquary★★**. ▶ In the same square stands the **Palazzo Soliano★** (C3, 1297-1304). This huge tufa building with an outside staircase houses the **Museo dell'Opera del Duomo** *(9 a.m.-1 p.m. and 3-6 or 7 p.m. summer; 9 a.m.-12 noon and 2:30-4:30 p.m. winter; closed Mon)*. Among the major works are *Madonna and Saints★* by Simone Martini, a sculpture of the *Madonna and Child★* by Andrea Pisano, two wooden statues *(Madonna and Child★* and *Christ Blessing)* and the reliquary of S. Savinio★. ▶ The **archaeological section** of the museum (in the building opposite the Duomo) contains remains from ancient Etruscan burial grounds throughout the area. ▶ Other important archaeological remains can be found in the nearby **Palazzo Faina** (C2), housing the foundation of the same name and the **Musei Civici** *(9 a.m.-1 p.m. and 3-6.30 p.m. summer; 2.30-4.30 p.m. winter)*. Exhibits include the three large Etruscan vases of the so-called Vanth★ group, which depict the passage of the deceased into the after life. ▶ The church of S. **Francesco** (C2) still retains the façade, the three Gothic portals and the small rose windows from the original 13C building. ▶ The 13C church of S. **Lorenzo de Arari** (C2) has a curious high altar made from an ancient Etruscan pagan altar. The **Palazzo del Popolo★★** (B2) is a splendid 12C Romanesque-Gothic tufa building with arcades, out-

side staircase, mullioned windows and crenellated battlements. ▶ The church of S. **Domenico** (B2-3) has a **monument to Cardinal de Braye★**, by Arnolfo di Cambio. ▶ In p. Cahen (B3-4) is the **Rocca** built on the orders of Albornoz in 1364. From here, a lane goes past the ruins of an Etruscan temple (5C BC, on the l.) and down to the S. **Patrizio Well★** (A-B4, *9 a.m.-7 p.m.*), designed by Antonio da Sangallo the Younger and built (1527-37) to provide the town with a reservoir in case of siege. It is 203 ft deep and consists of a round chamber 42 ft in diameter and two wide spiral staircases, each with 284 steps. It has 72 large windows.

Environs

▶ Turning l. off the SS leading to the railway station is the Etruscan **Necropoli del Crocifisso del Tufo** *(1.6 km,* B1) at the foot of the tufa cliff upon which the town stands. It dates from the 6C BC and consists of a series of chambers made out of blocks of tufa. ▶ About 2.5 km beyond the Porta Romana (C1-2) is the 12C-13C Romanesque-Gothic abbey of SS. **Severo e Martirio★**, once a Premonstratensian (an order founded at Prémontré, France, in 1119) monastery with abbot's house, church and dodecagonal campanile.   □

Orvieto wine

'... His holiness liked to drink this wine, especially when he was in Orvieto.' His holiness in this case was Pope Paul III (Farnese), and the words were spoken in the 16C by Sante Lancerio, the man who took care of his cellar. The painter Pinturicchio, who came from Perugia, also liked the wines of his own native region. In a contract for certain of his works, it stipulates that, besides money, he was to have *vinum quantum libuerit (as much wine as he wished)* while working. It is doubtful whether he was speaking of Orvieto, and yet, it was this wine, in its squat round flasks, that became the most famous in Umbria, unjustly overshadowing all others. Today, the zone of production laid down by the protecting authority is confined to the province of Terni and five places in the adjoining province of Viterbo, in Lazio. In accordance with the prescribed controls, the grapes used must be 50 to 65 percent Tuscan Trebbiano, 15 to 25 percent Verdello, 20 to 30 percent Drupeggio, Grechetto and Tuscan Malvasia (any one or else a mixture) but never more than 20 percent Malvasia. Orvieto is a straw-coloured white wine and comes in two types, Orvieto Abboccato and Orvieto Secco. Some consider the Abboccato variety suitable for serving with the main meal, while others say it should only be served with dessert. Orvieto Classico, even when it comes within the two stated types, is a geographical specification, and refers to wine coming from the oldest production area, i.e., the hills to the r. and to the l. of the River Paglia.

Practical information

ⓘ p. del Duomo 24 (C2), ☎ 41772.

Hotels:
★★★★ *Aquila Bianca*, v. Garibaldi 13 (C2 a), ☎ 41246, 37 rm ℙ ⊗ No restaurant, 84,000; bkf: 9,000.
★★★★ *G. H. Italia*, v. di Piazza del Popolo 13 (B2 b), ☎ 42065, 37 rm ℙ ⊗ No restaurant, 120,000; bkf: 12,000.
★★★★ *Maitani*, v. Maitani 5 (C2 c), ☎ 42011, 43 rm ℙ ▨ ⊗ No restaurant, 118,000.
★★★ *Virgilio*, p. Duomo 5 (C2 d), ☎ 41882, 18 rm ℙ No restaurant, 56,000; bkf: 10,000.

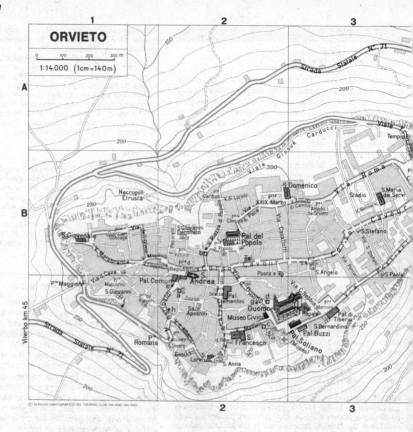

ORVIETO

1:14.000 (1cm=140m)

© SERVIZIO CARTOGRAFICO DEL TOURING CLUB ITALIANO, MILANO

Restaurants:

● ♦♦♦♦ *Morino*, v. Garibaldi 37/45 (C2 h), ☎ 41952, closed Wed and Jan. Elegant, with modern decor. Regional cuisine: agnolotti with fondue and truffles, kid scottadito style, home-produced Orvieto, also wine tasting, 40/60,000.

♦♦♦ *Maurizio al Duomo*, v. Duomo 78 (C2 g), ☎ 41114, closed Tue. In heart of historic centre. Regional cuisine: homemade tortellini with cèpes, spit roast lamb, 20/35,000.

♦♦♦ *Pino - da Checco*, p. del Popolo 15 (B2 i), ☎ 35381, closed Tue and Jan-Feb. 13C building with modern decor. Regional cuisine: cannelloni ducali, gnocchi orvietana, milk-fed lamb scottadito style, 21/33,000.

♦♦ *Grotte del Funaro*, v. Ripa Serancia 41 (C1 f), ☎ 43276, closed Mon and Christmas. Converted from a former rope-making workshop dug out of tufa. Regional cuisine: tagliatelle with fish sauce, grilled wild boar and piglet, 20/30,000.

♦ *Cocco*, v. Garibaldi 4 (C2 e), ☎ 42319, closed Fri and Jan. Next door to Palazzo Comunale. Regional cuisine with some international dishes: tortellini certosina, risotto norcina, 20/30,000.

Recommended

Cycling: *Gruppo Sportivo*, at Torre San Severo, ☎ 28693.
Events: pageant for the festival of *Corpus Christi* (Jun); *Palombella Festival at Pentecost* (Jun); *national horse show*, at Porano (*8 km S*, May).
Horseback riding: *Azienda Agricola Camorena*, ☎ 92625 (associate of *ANTE*).
Zoo: at *Monte Peglia* (*c. 22 km NE*); for information and

guided tours apply to the *Comunità Montana*, ☎ 075/875175.

Environs

BADIA, ✉ 05019, 5 km S.

Hotel:

★★★★ *Badia*, ☎ 90359, 22 rm ℗ ⚲ ♨ ⅋ ⊗ ▣ .✄
closed Jan-Feb. Converted 12C abbey, 148,000.

ORVIETO SCALO, 5 km E, ✉ 05019.

Hotels:

★★★ *Europa*, v. Gramsci 5 (A4 1), ☎ 90771, 52 rm ℗ 55,000; bkf: 6,000.

★★★ *Kristal*, v. Costanzi 69, ☎ 90703, 22 rm ℗ ⅋ 53,000; bkf: 4,000.

★★★ *Villa Ciconia*, at Ciconia, v. dei Tigli 69, ☎ 90677, 4 rm ℗ ♨ closed 5-30 Nov and Christmas. 17C villa with centuries-old park, 56,000; bkf: 8,000.

PASSIGNANO SUL TRASIMENO

Perugia 30, Rome 211 km
Pop. 4,535 ✉ 06065 ☎ 075   A2

On a promontory on the N shore of Lake Trasimeno, Passignano sul Trasimeno is a picturesque village with winding streets, still surrounded by its medieval **walls,** and with the remains of the **castle** above.

▶ It is possible to take a boat to **Isola Maggiore**, the most beautiful island in the lake, upon which stands the church of **S. Michele Arcangelo**, decorated with 14C-16C fres-

cos. ▶ There is a splendid view from the old village of **Castel Rigone** *(10.5 km NE)*, which has remains of a 13C castle as well as the Renaissance church of the **Madonna dei Miracoli**★, containing numerous 16C paintings. ☐

Practical information _____

≋
ℹ in Castiglione del Lago, ☎ 952184.
🚢 boat trips to Isola Maggiore, Castiglione and Tuoro; also to Sant'Arcangelo and San Feliciano, summer weekends only, ☎ 827157 (boats can be hired for outings).

Hotels:
★★★ **Lido**, v. Roma 1, ☎ 827219, 52 rm P ⚌ ⅊ ⅏
closed Nov-Jan, 56,000; bkf: 5,000.
★★★ **Sayonara**, San Donato, ☎ 827442, 25 rm P ⅊ ⅃ ⅊
▭ closed at Christmas and Jan, 56,000; bkf: 4,500.
★ **Florida**, v. ℓ Giugno, ☎ 827228, 15 rm P ⚌ ⅏ closed 1-20 Feb, 32,000; bkf: 4,000.

Restaurant:
♦♦ **Cacciatori - da Luciano**, v. Nazionale 11, ☎ 827210, closed Wed and 10 Nov-10 Dec. Rustic, overlooking lake, also small hotel. Seafood: rice with scampi, barbecued lobster, 30/60,000.

⚱ ★★ **Kursaal**, at San Donato, v. Europa, 140 pl, ☎ 827182.

Recommended
Marina: mooring places for motor boats (private), ☎ 951195, 52115 or 954120 and for sailboats, *Club Velico*, ☎ 827400 (sailing and wind surfing school).

PERUGIA★★

Rome 175, Milan 450 km
Pop. 144,064 ✉ 06100 ☎ 075   A-B2

Perugia, located on an uneven hillside, is one of the most beautiful towns in Italy, with its Etruscan walls, medieval buildings, clear, graceful marbles by Agostino di Duccio in the church of S. Bernardino, frescos by Perugino and other Umbrian artists and the 16C baroque edifices of papal Perugia. The town is an example of the vitality of Italian art throughout its history and of the incredible mastery with which the urban environment was shaped in medieval and Renaissance times. A cosmopolitan atmosphere is added by the Italian University for Foreigners. The layout of Perugia lends itself to certain routes; monuments and sites are thus described in the order in which they will be encountered.

▶ The artistic centre is **p. IV Novembre**★ (C3) with its ancient buildings, the Fontana Maggiore, the Cathedral, the 15C Loggia di Braccio Fortebraccio and the Palazzo dei Priori. ▶ The **Fontana Maggiore**★★ (C3), with sculptures by Nicola and Giovanni Pisano consists of two marble basins with a small bronze basin above them. It is decorated with beautiful **reliefs**★★. ▶ The Gothic **Cathedral**★★ (C3) (1345-1490), has a rough façade with a Baroque portal. Its magnificent l. side is of red-and-white marble. The interior has a polygonal apse and a carved and inlaid wooden **choir**★ (1486-91). Off the sacristy, with its 16C frescos, and at the far end of a cloister is the **Museo Capitolare** *(9-11:30 a.m. and 3:30-5:30 p.m.; closed Mon; apply to the sacristy)* containing detached paintings and frescos by 14C-16C Umbrian and Sienese artists, including a *Pietà*★, an *Enthroned Madonna*★ and a *Madonna with Saints*★. Other exhibits include illuminated manuscripts, jewelry and sacred vessels. ▶ The **Palazzo dei Priori**★★ (C3) one of the most stately medieval palaces in Italy, was built in several stages between 1293 and 1443. On the first floor, in the **Sala dei Notari**★, a magnificent hall supported by eight transverse arches and decorated with frescos, are the coats of arms of various mayors (13C-15C). On the third floor *(elevator)* the **Galleria Nazionale dell'Umbria** *(9 a.m.-2 p.m, 9 a.m.-1 p.m. wkends, closed Mon)* has a striking collection of 13C-18C Umbrian paintings by the great masters. Among these are: *Madonna and Angels*★, by Duccio (1308); sculptures★by Arnolfo di Cambio; *Madonna with Child, Angels and Saints*★★, by Beato Angelico; *Madonna with Child and Saints*, by Piero della Francesca; *Adoration of the Magi*★ and *Pietà*★, by Perugino (1475); a niche of S. Bernardino da Siena★ with small paintings on wood by Perugino and Pinturicchio; as well as *The Body of Christ*★ and the *Madonna of the Consolation*★ by Perugino. The **Sala del Collegio della Mercanzia**★ (Chamber of Commerce; *entrance at no. 15 to the r. of the main door, 9 a.m.-12.30 p.m. and 3-6 p.m.; 9 a.m.-12.30 p.m. wkends; closed Mon*), is in late Gothic style and has walls and vaults entirely covered in carved wood as well as sculptured officials' seats around the walls. ▶ The **Collegio del Cambio**★ (C3, *9 a.m.-12:30 p.m. and 3-5 or 6 p.m.; 9 a.m.-12:30 p.m. wkends; closed Mon*), built between 1452-57, was once the town's exchange. Beyond the entrance hall, with its 17C benches, is the **Sala dell'Udienza del Cambio**★, a major artistic achievement of the Renaissance. The walls have **frescos**★★ by Perugino and his pupils, among them possibly Raphael (1496-1500). ▶ **Via delle Volte**, between p. IV Novembre and p. Cavallotti (C3), is flanked by 13C and 14C houses and palaces. At its end is the Oratory of the **Maestà delle Volte**, with a red-and-white 14C stone arch. ▶ A 4C or 3C BC **Etruscan well** may be seen at no. 18 **piazza Dante** (C3; *wkdays 8 a.m.- 1:30 p.m.*). From the square, v. Rocchi leads to the **Arco Etrusco**★ (B3), the main gate of the Etruscan wall (3C-2C BC, the upper part adapted by the Romans after

PERUGIA

0   100   200 m

1:12.000 (1cm=120m)

Ripido M.

S.Angelo

P.ta S.Angelo

ELCE

Via Annibale Vecchi

Via Franc Innamorati

Università

Via dell'Elce di Sotto

S.Agostino

Bola

Via Antinori

Via Aless. Pascoli

Mosaico Romano

Via S.Isabetta

Pal. Gallenga

Fortebrado

P.za Conca

Via Aless. Pascoli

Viale Z. Ferrarino Faina

Via Garibaldi

S. Fabretti

Via A. Fabretti

Arco d'Etrusco

Accademia di Belle Arti

S.Francesco al Prato

P.za S.Francesco

San Bernardino

Mad d. Luce

Cavallotti

Cattedrale

Piccinino

Volte d.Pa

Via Roggero D'Andreotto

Via S. Galigano

Viale Z. Orazio

Via Sporza

Via Toree d.Sciri

Via Priori

Via Sant'Ercolano

Mod Jacchi

P.za Dante

Fontana Maggior

S.Filippo Neri

S.Agata

Pal d.Priori

(Municipio)

P.za S.Susanna

P.za S.Agata

Collegio d.Cambio

Posta e T.

Pal.Cap d.Popol

Piazza Colombaria

Vannucci

Repubblica

Bagliotti

Corso Vannucci

Via S. Prospero

Pontugo Perugia

Via della Cupa

A Mariotti

Via Caporali

Pal d. Regione

P.za Italia

Via S. Prospero

Arco d. Mandorla

Prefettura

Da

Giardini Carducci

P.za Marzia

S.Ercola

P.ta Eburnea

Tre Archi

Via Indipendenza

Via Cortonese

Via Ferrovia

FONTIVEGGE

Fiorenzo di Lorenzo

Staz. S.Anna

Largo Cacciatori d.Alpi

P.za Partigiani

Autostaz.

P.za Europa

P.za Vitt. Veneto

S. Giuliana

Stadio

Via Cacciatori d.Alpi

Via Fr. Pellas

Staz.F.S.

Via Settembre

Via Sicilia

Via Ferroviari

Via Campo di Marte

Fratelli Pellas

Via della Pescara

Via del Lavoro

Autostrada del Sole km 62

© SERVIZIO CARTOGRAFICO DEL TOURING CLUB ITALIANO, MILANO

Racc. Autostr. Rome-Assisi

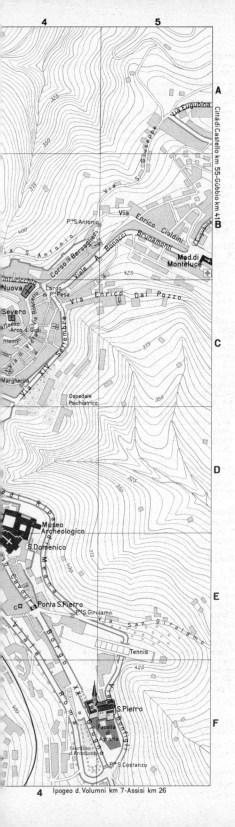

40 BC). ▶ On the other side of the arch is piazzale Fortebraccio (B3) with the Baroque **Palazzo Gallenga Stuart,** now housing the Italian University for Foreigners. ▶ Through corso Garibaldi, is the church of **S. Angelo★** (A2), a 5C-6C Early Christian building on a central plan. The interior has a circular nave on sixteen Roman columns with Gothic elements, added in the late Middle Ages. ▶ The 13C church of **S. Maria Nuova** has a carved wooden **choir★** (1456). ▶ The nearby church of **S. Severo** (C4, *ring the doorbell of no. 11, 10 a.m.-12:30 p.m. and 3 p.m.-sunset*) contains a fresco by Raphael (1505) in the adjacent oratory, depicting the *Holy Trinity and Saints★.* ▶ V. Bonacci Brunamonti nearby (B4-5) leads to the 13C church of **Madonna di Monteluce★** (altered 15C) with 14C frescos behind the apse. ▶ Back in p. IV Novembre, an arch below the Palazzo dei Priori leads to **via dei Priori,** medieval quarter. Along this street are the Gothic church of **S. Agata** (C3) with pointed portal and 14C frescos, the Baroque church of **S. Filippo Neri** and the **Torre degli Sciri** (C2). ▶ Beyond the ancient Etruscan Porta Trasimena (C2) is the picturesque piazzetta della Madonna della Luce with its church (1512-18). ▶ In the nearby **piazza S. Francesco** (C2) is the 13C Gothic church of **S. Francesco al Prato** *(under restoration)* and the church of **S. Bernardino★★,** a Renaissance architectural and sculptural gem by Agostino di Duccio (1457-61). It has a simple Gothic interior and an altar consisting of a carved 4C sarcophagus. ▶ The p. IV Novembre leads to **piazza Matteotti** (C3), on the E side of which are the **Palazzo dell'Università Vecchia** (Old University Building, 1453) with cruciform windows and the **Palazzo del Capitano del Popolo★,** an elegant building (1472) with a fine portal, four mullioned windows with two lights and a balcony supported by richly decorative corbels. Passing on underneath the arch at no. 18, a 14C loggia and a terrace (**view★**) next appear. Behind the square is the picturesque, arcaded 14C **v. Volte della Pace.** ▶ Off p. IV Novembre to the S is the main street, **corso Vannucci** (C-D3), with the **Collegio dei Notari** (medieval council hall, 1446) at the near end and the 18C **Palazzo Donini** at the far end. ▶ In **piazza Italia** (D3), which stands on the site of the 16C Rocca Paolina is the 19C Prefecture. Behind are the Carducci Gardens, with a fine **view★★** toward the Valle Umbra, and **viale Indipendenza,** with remains of the Etruscan walls. ▶ The Etruscan **Porta Marzia** (D3) was incorporated by Sangallo in the Rocca Paolina. It leads to **via Bagliona,** which runs underground through the remains of the medieval houses incorporated in the fortress *(9 a.m.-12:30 p.m. and 3-6 p.m. or 4-7 p.m.).* ▶ **Corso Cavour** leads to the Gothic basilica of **S. Domenico★** (B4, 14C, rebuilt 17C). The parts of the original building that remain are the outside buttresses and a few side chapels. The truncated campanile is 15C. The interior is majestic and austere. The **altar★** of the fourth chapel on the r. has polychrome architectural and sculptural decorations by Agostino di Duccio. In the apse is a wooden Renaissance choir lit by a large 15C window. In the chapel on the r. of the apse is the **monumental tomb of Benedict XI★.** ▶ Part of the old Dominican convent houses the **Museo Archeologico Nazionale dell'Umbria★** (D4, *9 a.m.-1:30 p.m.; wkends 9 a.m.-1 p.m.; closed Mon*) with a prehistoric section containing exhibits from the palaeolithic era to the Stone Age, and an Etruscan-Roman section containing engraved stones, sarcophagi, urns and grave finds. ▶ After the **Porta di S. Pietro★** (or Porta Romana, E4), an elegant Renaissance construction by Agostino di Duccio (1475) with 14C elements on the inside, is the church of **S. Pietro★★** (F4-5), one of the town's most interesting monuments. A late 10C building with a tall campanile built in 1464; it has a 17C arcaded courtyard at the front. The ceiling of the nave is of wood and there are eleven canvases by Aliense (1592). Works by Guercino and Perugino are among the noteworthy paintings on the altars in the two aisles. The sacristy (1451) contains woodcarvings (1472), four paintings by Perugino and one by Caravaggio. In the presbytery see two carved stalls (1556) and a magnificent wooden **choir★** (1526-35). A door at the back of the

choir opens onto a balcony which offers a superb view★ *(apply to the caretaker).* Between the second and first altars of the l.-hand aisle are a *Pietà*★ (late work by Perugino) and a 15C *Crucifixion.*

Environs

▶ After viale Roma (F4), the SS 75 bis goes toward Ponte San Giovanni to the **Ipogeo dei Volumni**★ *(7 km),* an aristocratic Etruscan tomb dating from the late 2C BC *(9 a.m.-5 p.m. or 6.30 p.m.; wkends 9 a.m.-1 p.m., closed Mon).* From the modern entrance hall containing funerary urns from the surrounding necropolis, a steep staircase goes down to an underground chamber consisting of an atrium and numerous recesses, the last one of which contains seven funerary urns. Particularly interesting is the one of the head of the family (Arunte Volumnio), which is adorned with his statue and an angel of death on either side. ▶ Lake Trasimeno is approximately 26 km away (→).

Braccio da Montone

He was buried in the convent church of S. Francesco dei Minori eight years after his death, because he had been excommunicated. He lived in the troubled Italy of the early 15C, before the country was organized into independently governed states under foreign domination, an arrangement which lasted until the Unification. He was one of those men who by 'prowess' and 'fortune' (to quote Machiavelli's theory written not long after) built dominions. In rank, somewhere between a commander of mercenary troops and a Renaissance prince, according to chroniclers of the time, 'nec enim desperabat italicum sibi regnum vindicare' ('he hoped to become king of Italy'). His name was Andrea Fortebracci, and he was born in Montone Castle near Perugia. He learned to be a mercenary soldier under Alberico da Barbiano and had as a companion in arms Muzio Attendolo, known as Sforza, a man who was to become his relentless enemy. Braccio wanted to rule Perugia, from where his father, the nobleman Oddo Fortebracci, had been exiled. He succeeded in taking it, together with Umbria and other territories, and defended it against the new pope, Martin V, and his ally, Sforza. Eventually, he was made a Vicar of the Church of Rome. He went on to capture the principality of Capua and a number of strongholds in Abruzzi, and in breach of his promise to Martin V (hence the excommunication) attacked L'Aquila. The battle fought beneath the walls of L'Aquila on 2 June 1424, the bloodiest of the century according to some historians, decided the fate of much of the peninsula. Braccio was defeated and wounded. He refused food and medicine and died, without a word, after three days. He was 56 years old.

Practical information

ⓘ corso Vannucci 96, Palazzo della Regione (D3), ☎ 23327; v. Mazzini 21, ☎ 25341 (headquarters, C3); *Assessorato al Turismo Regione Umbria* (Tourist Advice), corso Vannucci 30, ☎ 6961 (headquarters, C3).
✈ *S. Egidio airport (12 km E),* ☎ 6929447 (flights to and from Milan).
🚉 (EI), ☎ 70980; *Ferrovia Centrale Umbra,* S. Anna station (E3), ☎ 23947.
🚌 from p. Italia (D3), ☎ 74641; p. Partigiani (E3), ☎ 61807 and from S. Anna station (E3).
Car rental: *Avis,* at S. Egidio airport, ☎ 6929796.

Hotels:

★★★★★ *Brufani,* p. Italia 12 (D3 a), ☎ 62541, 24 rm Ⓟ ← 230,000; bkf: 14,000.
★★★★ *Colle della Trinità,* at Fontana *(9 km toward Lake Trasimeno),* ☎ 79548, 53 rm Ⓟ ← 🏊 🎱 ⛴ 🍽 closed Feb, 115,000.
★★★★ *Grifone,* v. Pellico 1, ☎ 32049, 50 rm Ⓟ ⛴ 80,000. Rest. ◆◆◆ closed Mon and 25 Jul-14 Aug. Elegant, medieval Umbrian décor. Regional and Italian cuisine: taglierini alla francescana, braciola alla spoletina, 22/32,000.
★★★★ *Hit Hotel,* at Ferro di Cavallo *(4 km W),* strada Trasimeno Ovest 159/10, ☎ 799247, 80 rm Ⓟ 🍽 80,000; bkf: 7,000.
★★★★ *Perugia Plaza Hotel,* v. Palermo 88, ☎ 34643, 103 rm Ⓟ ⛴ 100,000; bkf: 9,000.
★★★★ *Rosetta,* p. Italia 19 (D3 b), ☎ 20841, 97 rm Ⓟ ⛴ 80,000; bkf: 6,000.
★★ *Signa,* v. del Grillo 9 (E4 c), ☎ 61080, 23 rm Ⓟ 🏊 ⛴ 🍽 41,000; bkf: 6,000.

Restaurants:

● ◆◆◆ *Mario Ragni,* v. de' Priori 78 (C2 f), ☎ 21889, closed Sun and Aug. In former aristocratic home with 17C vaulted ceilings, service outside in summer. Excellent creative cuisine: menu according to availability, predominance of prized Umbrian wines, 50/65,000.
◆◆◆ *Taverna,* v. delle Streghe 8 (D3 i), ☎ 61028, closed Mon and 15-31 Jul. Housed on two floors of historic building. Regional cuisine: tagliolini with truffles, agnolotti, 25/35,000.
◆◆ *Bocca Mia,* v. Rocca 36 (B-C3 d), ☎ 23873, closed Sun and 1-15 Aug. Regional and Italian cuisine: roast piglet, agnello a scottadito, 20/25,000.
◆◆ *Falchetto,* v. Bartolo 20 (C3 e), ☎ 61875, closed Mon. Period style furnishing. Regional cuisine: risotto Fregoli, pasta with chick peas, torello perugina, 20/30,000.
◆◆ *Ricciotto 1888,* p. Danti 20 (C3 g), ☎ 21956, closed Sun and Jul-Aug. Regional and some international cuisine: maccheroni with cream and mushrooms, risotto verde, 25/35,000.
◆◆ *Sole,* v. della Rupe 1 (D3 h), ☎ 65031, closed Sat and Christmas. Terrace-garden with view. Regional and Italian cuisine: risotto lamolese, country style tagliatelle, penne norcina, 21/30,000.
⚠ ★★ *Il Rocolo,* at L'Olmo, strada Fontana 1/N, 100 pl, ☎ 798550.

Recommended

Archery: *Compagnia Arcieri Braccio Fortebraccio,* v. R. Torelli.
Botanical garden: v. S. Costanzo, ☎ 32643 (telephone in advance).
Events: *concert season* (Amici della Musica, ☎ 25264) and *play season,* at the Teatro Morlacchi, ☎ 61255; Sagra musical umbra (international festival of religious music, Sep); *Umbria Jazz* (Jul, also in Terni); *theatre in the square* (Jul); *Monteluce festival* (15 Aug) and *Festival of the Dead* (Pian di Massiano, 1-5 Nov).
Flying club: *S. Egidio airport (12 km E),* ☎ 6929445.
Golf: at Ellera *(10 km SW),* ☎ 79704 (9 holes).
Guided tours: *Associazione guide umbre,* information offices in corso Vannucci (Palazzo Donini), ☎ 65124.
Sports centre: v. Pellini (C2), ☎ 24654.
Swimming: v. Pellini (C2), ☎ 65160, in Montebello, ☎ 388172.
Wines: v. Rocchi 16, ☎ 24824.
♥ painting instruction: *Accademia delle Belle Arti P. Vannucci,* p. S. Francesco al Prato 5, ☎ 29106 (Jul-Aug).

PIEDILUCO

Terni 13, Perugia 97, Rome 116 km
Pop. 707 ✉ 05038 ☎ 0744   B-C4

Piediluco lies at the foot of a cone-shaped mountain with a straight wall leading up to a 14C **fortress** at the top. It has a lovely lake★, set among green hills. It also contains a late 13C church, **S. Francesco. Mt. Caperno** has a famous perfect echo★. 3 km NW are the **Marmore Falls** (→ Terni). ☐

Practical information _____

Restaurant:
♦♦ **Miralago,** v. Noceta 2, ☎ 68108, closed Wed. Country setting near lake. Mixed cuisine: crepes with ricotta and spinach, pasta alla chitarra with nuts, fresh and saltwater fish, 25/30,000.

Recommended
Events: *national yachting championships* and *international regattas,Federazione Italiana,* at I Quadri, ☎ 69156; *Società Canottieri,* ☎ 68147.

SAN GEMINI

Terni 12, Perugia 72, Rome 99 km
Pop. 3,919 ⊠ 05029 ☎ 0744   B4

The town, a flourishing spa situated in a pleasant, hilly area, is famous for its mineral water, which comes from a spring nearby. It still retains part of its old medieval centre.

▶ The Gothic church of **S. Francesco** (14C) contains a number of Umbrian school frescos. ▶ In p. di Palazzo Vecchio is the **Palazzo del Popolo**, with its truncated tower, to which a clock was added in the 18C. Nearby is the parish church of **S. Giovanni**, with its 12C Romanesque façade on the l.-hand side. ▶ The Romanesque church of S. Nicolò *(9 a.m.-12 noon and 3-7 p.m.; closed Mon; apply to caretaker)* with 13C frescos is on the SS just outside town. ▶ The **ruins of Carsulae**, a prosperous Roman town on the via Flaminia (destroyed 9C), are 4 km N. On the site stands the church of **S. Damiano**, built in the early Middle Ages over a Roman building. ☐

Practical information _____

♨ (May-Oct), ☎ 630426.
ⓘ v. Garibaldi 1, ☎ 630130.

Hotel:
★★★ **Duomo,** p. Duomo, ☎ 630015, 20 rm ♨ ᕼ ⌖ closed Jan, 52,000; bkf: 6,000.

Recommended
Events: *jousting tournament in medieval costumes* (first ten days Oct).

L'abbazia di SANT'EUTIZIO

Perugia 95, Rome 173 km
⊠ 06047 ☎ 0743   C3

This green valley, a retreat for hermits who lived in caves in the area, was the cradle of the Benedictine order, the place where St. Benedict realized his spiritual vocation. The monastery, built before 1000, brought the hermits under his rule. It prospered from the 9C until the 13C. The beautiful Romanesque **church** (1190) has a nave with trussed roof and a raised presbytery above a crypt. Behind the main altar is the burial monument of St. Eutizio; there are interesting objets d'art in the sacristy. ☐

SPELLO*

Perugia 31, Rome 165 km
Pop. 7,649 ⊠ 06038 ☎ 0742   B2-3

Pinturicchio came here in 1500 to paint the Cappella Bella (or Baglioni chapel, from the name of an aris-

tocratic family) in S. Maria Maggiore. The frescos were finished a year later; they are as magnificent and fascinating as the town itself, with its Subasio limestone houses, narrow, winding medieval streets, covered passageways, orchards and unexpected views caused by the uneven terrain.

▶ There are a number of Roman remains: parts of the amphitheatre, walls and gates that have survived since the age of Augustus, including the monumental **Porta Consolare**, which still forms the S entrance to the town. ▶ Once through this gate, the v. Consolare leads to p. Matteotti and the church of **S. Maria Maggiore★** (12C-13C). The façade was rebuilt in 1644 using old materials. Inside, on the l., is the **Cappella Baglioni★★**, decorated with Pinturicchio's splendid frescos; it has a beautiful Deruta majolica floor (1566). Other frescos by Pinturicchio are in the transept chapels and in a room next to the chapel on the l. The presbytery contains frescos by Perugino and an elegant canopy above the high altar (1515). The Cappella del Santo Sepolcro houses a **museum** *(8 a.m.-12 noon and 3-6 p.m.; apply to parish priest)* with 13C-14C wooden statues, church ornaments, vestments and jewelry. ▶ Nearby is the church of **S. Andrea** (13C) with a large panel painting by Pinturicchio *(Madonna and Saints★).* ▶ The **Palazzo Comunale** stands in p. della Repubblica. It has a 13C Gothic portico and mullioned windows with two lights. ▶ A little further on is the church of **S. Lorenzo** which incorporates remains of the 12C building and contains some interesting paintings, sculptures and works in carved wood. ▶ The v. Belvedere leads to the **Belvedere★** on top of the hill on the site of the Roman acropolis, now occupied by the remains of the 14C **Rocca** (the little Roman arch was once the entrance to the acropolis); there is a splendid view of the hills and the Topino Valley. ▶ Going N from the Porta Consolare along v. Roma (where there is a stretch of wall dating back to the Augustan era containing the Porta Urbica) and viale Centrale, past the ruins of the Roman amphitheatre and the Romanesque church of S. Claudio, is the Renaissance **Chiesa Tonda** *(2.5 km),* built in 1517 on the Greek cross plan with an octagonal dome. ▶ 1.5 km away, near the cemetery, is the church of **S. Girolamo** (1474), with Renaissance portico at the front, decorated with 15C-16C frescos. The interior contains noteworthy works of art and a cloister with 16C frescos. ☐

Practical information _____

ⓘ v. Garibaldi 21.

Hotels:
★★ **Bastiglia,** v. Salnitraria 15, ☎ 651277, 15 rm Ⓟ ⋞ ⌖ closed Jan-Feb, 40,600; bkf: 5,000.
★★ **Cacciatore,** v. Giulia 42, ☎ 651141, 17 rm Ⓟ ⌖ closed Jun-Jul and Christmas, 40,600; bkf: 3,000.
★★ **Julia,** v. S. Angelo 22, ☎ 651174, 22 rm, 40,600; bkf: 5,000.

Restaurant:
● ♦♦ **Molino,** p. Matteotti 6/7, ☎ 651305, closed Tue. Converted 18C mill with remarkable vaulted ceilings and large fireplace. Regional cuisine: misto molinara, pancakes Franciscan style, 20/30,000.

Recommended
Events: *festivals of flowers for the Corpus Christi procession* (Jun).
Technical tourism: visit to the agricultural firm of *Cianetti,* v. Bulgarella 10, ☎ 652781 or 652834 to see olive press (working Dec-Jan and Jul-Aug, reserve in advance).

SPOLETO*

Perugia 63, Rome 130 km
Pop. 37,972 ⊠ 06049 ☎ 0743   B3

A neatly paved route leads to Spoleto's secluded Cathedral and from the square inviting glimpses of

SPOLETO

0   100   200 m

1 : 12.000 (1 cm = 120 m)

© SERVIZIO CARTOGRAFICO DEL TOURING CLUB ITALIANO, MILANO

Terni km 28

greenery can be seen.   The façade spans the whole period from the Romanesque era to the Renaissance, incorporating some existing Roman elements.   The *Festival dei Due Mondi* (Festival of the Two Worlds) was established in 1958 by the composer Gian Carlo Menotti (born in Italy but an American resident).   Its fame has not overshadowed the town's image as a repository of artistic treasure.   Spoleto, in fact, is an example of how a city can combine a great cultural heritage with up-to-date aesthetic activities.   Perhaps it was to acknowledge this that Alexander Calder offered the town his sculpture *Teodolapio* (1962) now in front of the station.

▶ In **piazza della Libertà** (C2), in the upper part of the town, is the 17C **Palazzo Ancaiani;** on its r. are the ruins of the **Roman theatre** (built in the early years of the Empire) dominated by the medieval church of S. Agata and the adjacent former monastery. ▶ The **Arch of Drusus★** (C2, 23 BC) is next to the ruins of a **Roman temple** (1C BC) and rests against the Romanesque side of the church of **S. Ansano,** rebuilt in the 18C *(access from inside to the crypt of S. Isacco,* 12C, detailed frescos). ▶ On the side of a mound overlooking p. Campello (C2) is the majestic **Rocca,** begun in 1359 and surrounded by walls, once the seat of the papal governors *(visitors allowed).* ▶ The **Palazzo Comunale** (B-C2, 13C, rebuilt 18C) houses the **Civic Art Gallery** *(9 a.m.-1 p.m. and 3:30-5:30 p.m. winter; 5:30-8 p.m. summer; closed*

Tue). Among the exhibits are frescos by Spagna, paintings on wood, wooden sculptures and jewelry. The remains of a **Roman house** said to have been the home of the mother of the Emperor Vespasian (7-79 AD) are in nearby v. di Visiale *(keys with caretaker).* ▶ The Romanesque church of **S. Eufemia★** (B2, early 12C) with its simple façade, is in the courtyard of the Archbishop's Palace . ▶ In the adjacent **piazza del Duomo** (B2), next to the Duomo, there is the elegant 16C **Palazzo Arroni,** which has graffito work on the façade and a courtyard with a nymphaeum, and the **Teatro Melisso** (1880). Behind the latter *(entrance from the square)* is the 14C building which houses the **Museo Civico** *(10 a.m.-1 p.m. and 4-6 p.m. winter; 10 a.m.-12:30 p.m. and 4-6:30 p.m. summer).* ▶ The **Duomo★★** (B2-3) is the most important monument in the town. Built in the 12C, it has retained its original Romanesque structure in the majestic campanile and the **façade.** The latter is preceded by a Renaissance portico and has a large detailed mosaic at the top (1207). The interior, renovated in the 17C, has traces of the 12C floor in the nave. Among the works of art are the bronze bust of **Urban VIII** by Bernini above the central portal, a fresco by Pinturicchio *(Madonna and Saints★)* in the first chapel on the r. *(apply to the sacristy if closed),* the tomb of Filippo Lippi (d. Spoleto 1469) designed by his son Filippino and the **frescos★★** in the apse by Lippi and his pupils (1467-69). In the Cappella delle Reliquie are some 16C wooden sculptures carved locally and a crucifix (1187). ▶ In p. Mentana stands the Romanesque church of SS. Giovanni e Paolo (B2, *caretaker at no. 6),* containing votive frescos from the late 12C-16C. ▶ The 13C church of **S. Domenico** (B1) is built with bands of red-and-white stone and has an elegant Gothic portal on the r. side. Inside are 14C-15C frescos and a 14C *Crucifixion* painted on wood. ▶ The medieval **Porta Fuga** (in the street of the same name, B2) is named after the defeat suffered by Hannibal when he tried to occupy the town. Next to it is the 12C-14C **Torre dell'Olio.** ▶ Part of nearby **via Cecili** (B2) is flanked by the imposing town **walls,** (6C, 5C and 3C BC). Layers were added by the Romans, and again in the Middle Ages, and houses were built on top. Protruding from these walls are the tall polygonal apse of the 14C church of **S. Nicolò** (B2), now a centre for cultural events. ▶ The **Galleria d'Arte Moderna** *(10 a.m.-1 p.m. and 3-6 p.m., closed Tue),* which contains work by contemporary artists competing in the Premio Spoleto. ▶ In v. Anfiteatro (A-B2) are the remains of the **Roman amphitheatre,** an imposing structure dating from the 2C BC. ▶ A flight of steps leads from p. della Vittoria (A2) to the **Ponte Romano** (or Ponte Sanguinario, A2), a bridge with three arches made out of blocks of travertine. It dates from the times of Augustus *(to visit apply to municipio).* ▶ The 12C church of **S. Gregorio Maggiore★** (A2) has a Renaissance portal at the front and a colossal campanile to one side. The presbytery is raised above the crypt, which has a nave and four aisles supported by very old columns, on the walls are remains of 12C-15C frescos.

Environs

▶ The **giro del Ponte** *(2.5 km)* is a walk that offers both interesting scenery and monuments. From p. della Libertà (C2), follow viale Matteotti, which runs alongside the park (C1), then turn l. at v. Roma. Across the Tessino is the flight of steps leading up to the church of **S. Pietro★★** (D2),which may date from the 5C. The 13C façade is decorated with Romanesque reliefs. Hugging the slopes of Monteluco, with a view of the Rocca (on the l.) is the grandiose **Ponte delle Torri★** (C3, *footbridge),* a majestic 14C construction with ten arches supported by sturdy piers. It is 262 ft high and 754 ft long. ▶ **S. Salvatore★★** (A3), 1.2 km away near the cemetery, is an important Early Christian church (4C-5C), although it has been extensively altered. Elements of the original building can be seen in the beautiful façade, which has three portals and three windows with fine decorations. Inside, the semicircular presbytery has survived *(8 or 9 a.m.-12 noon and 2-5 or 7 p.m.).* Nearby is the Roman-

esque church of **S. Ponziano** (A3), built in the 12C in honour of the town's patron saint. ▶ 8 km away is **Monteluco,** the mountain which was sacred to the Anchorites, who settled there in the 7C and stayed until the 18C. It is a highly evocative spot, with a magnificent ilex wood and the Convent of **S. Francesco,** founded by St. Francis in 1218, perched on the summit. From the **belvedere,** there is a fine view★ of the town and the Umbrian hills. □

Practical information _____

ℹ️ p. Libertà 7 (C2), ☎ 28111 or 49890.

Hotels:
★★★★ **Gattapone,** v. del Ponte 6 (C3 a), ☎ 36147, 11 rm ≪ ▥ ঌ Two extraordinary buildings with a flower garden in between, 89,000.
★★★ **Charleston,** p. Collicola 10 (B1 d), ☎ 38135, 19 rm ⌘ No restaurant, 40,600; bkf: 5,000.
★★★ **Clarici,** p. Vittoria 32 (A2 b), ☎ 46706, 24 rm Ⓟ No restaurant, 55,000; bkf: 8,000.
★★★ **Duchi,** v. Matteotti 4 (C1 c), ☎ 44541, 50 rm Ⓟ ≪ ▥ ঌ 56,000; bkf: 8,000.
★★★ **Europa,** v. Trento e Trieste 201, ☎ 46949, 24 rm Ⓟ No restaurant, 56,000; bkf: 8,000.
★★★ **Motel Agip,** v. Flaminia, at 127-km marker, ☎ 49340, 57 rm Ⓟ ঌ 56,000; bkf: 7,000.

Restaurants:
● ♦♦♦ **Tartufo,** p. Garibaldi 24 (A2 f), ☎ 40236, closed Wed and Jul-Aug. Elegant establishment, also has tavern with 4C floor. Quality regional and Italian cuisine: risotto with parmesan cheese and truffles, fried truffle sandwich, 23/45,000.
♦♦ **Pentagramma,** v. Martani 4 (C2 e), ☎ 47838, closed Mon and 1-20 Jan. In historic town centre. Regional cuisine: homemade strangozzi, sliced mutton browned on the outside and pink inside, 20/35,000.
♦ **Trattoria del Festival,** v. Brignone 8 (C2 g), ☎ 32198, closed Thu and 10 Jan-20 Feb. Regional cuisine: strangozzi with truffles, cappelletti with cream and truffles, 14/30,000.

🅰 ★★ **Girasole,** in Petrognano, 60 pl, ☎ 51335 (all year).

Recommended
Events: *Festival dei Due Mondi* (opera, plays, music, dance, Jun-Jul), ☎ 06/3614009.
Farm vacations: *Azienda Ciri,* at Petrognano, ☎ 51106.
Motocross: *Città di Spoleto* motordrome, at Poreta.
Swimming: p. D'Armi, ☎ 49565.

Environs

MONTELUCO, ⊠ 06049, ☎ 0743, 8 km SE.

Hotel:
★★★ **Paradiso,** ☎ 37182, 24 rm ≪ ▥ ⌘ 56,000.

Recommended
Clay pigeon shooting: 37198.

TERNI

Perugia 84, Rome 105, Milan 530 km
Pop. 111,147 ⊠ 05100 ☎ 0744   B4

Terni is chiefly known for the Marmore Falls, a few km away. A modern town, it is the heart of one of the most industrialized areas in central Italy. Nevertheless, it has a surprising number of fine ancient monuments.

▶ The **Pinacoteca** (C2, *9 a.m.-1 p.m.; closed Mon)* in the 17C Palazzo Manassei. It contains a number of interesting works, such as the *Nuptials of St. Catherine★* by B. Gozzoli and the triptych of the *Madonna of the Annunciation* by Maestro Gardner (1485). ▶ **Palazzo Spada** (C2), an imposing building with a large portal and decorative cornice, is the last work of Antonio da Sangallo the Younger (16C). ▶ The oldest building in the town is the

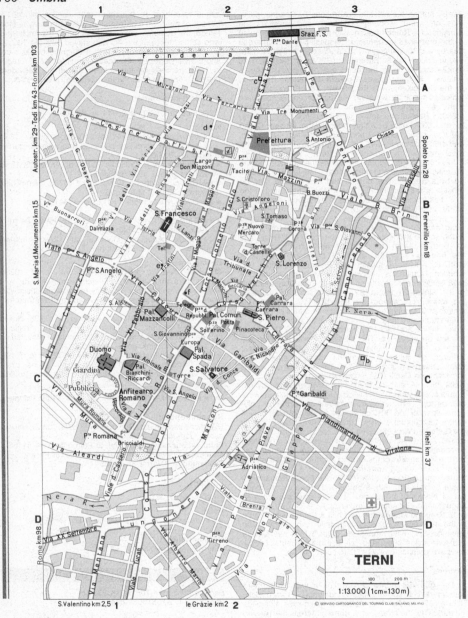

TERNI

1:13.000 (1cm=130m)

© SERVIZIO CARTOGRAFICO DEL TOURING CLUB ITALIANO, MILANO

early Christian church of **S. Salvatore★** (C2, 5C), circular in plan and standing on the site of an earlier Roman building. Inside, the Manassei chapel contains interesting 14C frescos. ▶ The **Duomo** (C1) was rebuilt in the 17C. Beneath the portico at the front are a beautiful Romanesque portal with reliefs (12C) and a Gothic portal. Inside is an interesting *Presentation in the Temple* by L. Agresti (1560). ▶ Opposite the Duomo stands the 16C **Palazzo Bianchini-Riccardi.** ▶ Nearby are the ruins of the **Roman amphitheatre** (C1), built in 32 BC. ▶ The

11C church of **S. Alò** (B1, *ring doorbell of convent of Poor Clares next door*) has a nave and two aisles on pillars and columns with beautiful capitals. It is decorated with 13C-14C frescos. ▶ The Gothic church of **S. Francesco★** (B1-2; 1265, enlarged in1437, altered 17C) has a fine 15C campanile. At the far end of the r.-hand aisle is the 14C Cappella Paradisi. The walls are decorated with frescos by a 15C Umbrian painter, depicting scenes inspired by Dante. ▶ The only surviving parts of the original 14C building of the church of **S. Pietro** (C2) are the l.-hand side and the portal. The interior has a polygon-al apse and contains 14C-15C frescos. There is also an interesting 14C cloister *(apply to school caretaker).* ▶ The church of S. **Lorenzo** (C2) was built in 1200 and altered in the 17C. It has two mullioned windows with three lights and a 15C portal in the façade. The interior contains a painting of the *Martyrdom of S. Biagio* (late 16C).

Environs

▶ 1 km away near the cemetery is the 15C church of S. **Maria del Monumento,** containing the cycle of fres-cos known as *Golden Apples* and other paintings. ▶ The present basilica of S. **Valentino** *(2 km away on road to Poggio Mirteto)* was built in the 12C on the site of a primitive Early Christian church that stood in the ceme-tery where St. Valentine (patron saint of the town and of lovers) is said to be buried. ▶ The **Marmore Falls**★★ can be reached in two ways: the high road *(8 km along the SS 79)* leads to the Observatory, where it is possible to see the falls from above; the low road *(7 km along the SS 209),* which affords a complete view of the three spec-tacular drops *(water is released every Sun and hols at the following times: 3-4 p.m. Nov to mid-Mar; 10 a.m.-12 noon and 3-9 p.m., 6-9 p.m. Sat, spring and autumn; 10 a.m.-1 p.m. and 3-11 p.m., 5-10 p.m. Sat, May-Aug; also wkdays, 5-6.30 p.m. from 15 Jul-31 Aug. The falls are illuminated by night).* □

Marmore Falls

The waters of the River Velino fall steeply in three stages from the plain of Rieti to the Nera Valley 540 ft below, forming the Marmore Falls, the highest in Italy. The basin of the plain of Rieti is enclosed on all sides by the mountains of Sabina and the massif of Terminillo. Water rich in calcium salts flows down from the mountains and into the Velino. The mouth of the Nera and therefore, the waterfall, was created artificially by the Romans in 271 BC in order to drain the Rieti marshes. The calcium salts form deposits which look very similar to marble, hence the name of the falls, marmore being an old Italian word for mar-ble. Normally, a waterfall tends to erode the ground it falls from, wearing it away, sometimes complete-ly. Here, however, strangely enough, chalky depos-its actually build up and, in the past, they have blocked the flow so that the waterfall had to re-form higher up. Today the potential of a waterfall for pro-ducing energy is far too tempting for scientists not to try and use it. Such is the case with the Marmore Falls, which 'function' only on set days and at set times. They provide a spectacular sight.

Practical information _____

ℹ v. Battisti 5/7 (A2), ☎ 43047.

🚌 (A2-3), ☎ 401283; *Ferrovia Centrale Umbra,* ☎ 415297.

🚕 from railway station (A2-3), ☎ 59541.

Hotels:
★★★★ *Valentino,* v. Plinio il Giovane 5 (B2-3 a), ☎ 55246, 60 rm Ⓟ 112,000.
★★★ *Allegretti,* strada Staino 7/B (C3 b), ☎ 57747, 35 rm Ⓟ 🍽 ⛶ No restaurant, 54,000.
★★★ *De Paris,* v. Stazione 52 (A2 c), ☎ 58047, 64 rm Ⓟ ⛶ 🍽 No restaurant, 54,000; bkf: 3,000.
★★★ *Garden,* v. Bramante 2/6, ☎ 43846, 58 rm Ⓟ 🍽 ⛶ 🔲 57,000; bkf: 5,000.

Restaurants:
♦♦♦ *San Marco,* v. San Marco 4 (B1 e), ☎ 44178, closed Mon and Aug. 16C building with modern furnishings;

17C sand pits and ruins of Roman baths have been con-verted to wine cellar. Regional cuisine: tagliatelle with black truffles, thinly sliced raw beef in a spicy sauce with truffles, 25/40,000.
♦♦♦ *Tre Colonne - da Lodovico,* v. Plebiscito 13 (B2 f), ☎ 54511, closed Mon and Aug. Elegant and rus-tic. Regional cuisine: ciriole alla ternana, gramigna with cream, 20/30,000.
♦♦ *Alfio,* v. Galilei 4 (A2 d), ☎ 420120, closed Sat and Aug. Secluded and traditional. Regional cuisine: ciriole ternana, penne, 20/30,000.

Recommended
Clay pigeon shooting: at Campacci Marmore, ☎ 67510.
Cycling: *GS Cicli Roma,* v. Bligny 2, ☎ 86286; *GS Tom-besi,* v. Colleroletta 10, ☎ 58271.
Events: *Cantamaggio Ternano* (medieval festival, Apr-May), *international piano competition* (Jun, even-number-ed years).
Hang gliding: *Umbria Delta,* v. Piemonte 25, ☎ 56768 (in-struction).
Swimming: v. Stadio, ☎ 58000, Borgo Bovio, ☎ 428137; Borgo Rivo, ☎ 242777.

Between TIBER AND NERA

From Orvieto *(137 km, 1 day; map 1)*

The most striking aspect of this route is the scenery: the quiet, gentle beauty of the hills in this southern-most part of Umbria with its ancient little towns, built high up away from the unhealthy marshes that form-ed from time to time when the rivers (especially the Tiber) flooded. Traveling the provincial roads, well-worn tracks are visible leading to farmyards sur-rounded by vineyards and olive groves. There are numerous thickets of cluster pines and oaks in the small valleys. The River Nera has carved a deep bed through limestone massifs, and light green Aleppo pines grow on its steep banks, which are full of holes made by nesting mountain swallows. There are numerous Roman and Etruscan settlements; the *magna arva Etruriae,* which provided grain for Rome, began in the Nera Valley.

▶ On leaving **Orvieto** (→), the route commences on the SS 79 bis to Todi (a winding road, with beautiful scen-ery). This runs along the Tiber. ▶ At **Prodo** there is an interesting 15C **castle** with many towers. ▶ After Cano-nica (view of Todi), the road descends steeply and cross-es the Tiber at **Pontecuti,** a village of medieval appear-ance with remains of the old walls and a gate tower at the end of an imposing bridge. ▶ After leaving **Todi** (→), it is possible to glimpse the harsh slopes of Mt. Martano (3,589 ft) in the distance on the l. as the route goes down through oak woods into the valley of the River Naia. Along the river are the thermal resorts of **Acquas-parta** (→) and **San Gémini** (→), as well as the ruins of *Car-sulae.* ▶ Beyond San Gémini, continuing along the edge of the Terni plain the route leads toward Narni, situated on a hill beyond the River Nera and close to the imposing Roman bridge of Augustus. ▶ From **Narni** (→) the road goes NW along the wooded slopes of Mt. Amerini, where there are breathtaking views★ of the Tiber Valley, the vil-lages and isolated huts along the riverside and, on the far horizon, a panorama from the Cimini to the Amiata moun-tains. ▶ In **Amelia** parts of the **polygonal walls**★ built in the 6C-4C BC have survived. The church of S. **Fran-cesco** with its 13C façade contains six Geraldini family tombs (those of Matteo and Elisabetta are by Agostino di Duccio, 1477). ▶ Going through the centres of **Lugnano in Teverina** (→) and **Alviano** (→) there is a brief detour to the l. that leads along a road with a view over artificial Lake Alviano, formed by damming the River Tiber. ▶ On the r. is a hill with ruins, and the **Guardea Vecchia** tower and **Guardea.** ▶ There is a magnificent view going down

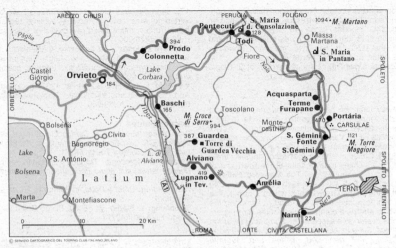

1. Between Tiber and Nera

towards the bottom of the valley. ▶ The route continues N to **Baschi,** high on a projection. It has a 16C parish church with an altarpiece★ by Giovanni di Paolo (c. 1440). ▶ Here the route crosses the Autostrada del Sole and the Tiber, which flows through a narrow gorge at this point, and arrives back at Orvieto. □

Practical information ————————————

AMELIA, ⊠ 05022, ☎ 0744
ⓘ porta Romana, ☎ 982559.

Hotel:
★★★ *Scoglio dell'Aquilone,* v. Orvieto 23, ☎ 982445, 38 rm ℗ ≼ ⋙ ⋘ 53,000; bkf: 8,000.

Recommended
Horseback riding: *Circolo ippico Amerino,* v. Rietta 15 (associate of *ANTE*).

TODI*

Perugia 45, Rome 130 km
Pop. 17,090 ⊠ 06059 ☎ 075   A-B3

Three things come to mind at the mention of the name of Todi: first, the religious poems of Jacopone da Todi (Jacopo dei Benedetti); second, the image of the town itself — typically medieval, but, at the same time, joyously Gothic and full of imaginatively created spaces ideally suited to urban life — and last, the Renaissance church of the Consolazione, standing alone, outside the town walls, on a slope next to a grassy meadow.

▶ In **Piazza del Popolo★** (A2) at the top of the hill are the Duomo, the **Palazzo dei Priori** (B2, 1293-1337) with its battlements and Renaissance windows (1514) and the enormous Gothic **Palazzo del Popolo★** (A2), with a portico on the ground floor, leading by an outside staircase to the **Palazzo del Capitano★** (A2, 1290). The latter is the home of the **Pinacoteca Civica** *(closed for repairs),* which contains archaeological exhibits from Etruscan and Roman times, coins, Umbrian school paintings and medieval pottery. ▶ The **Duomo★** (12C, renovated 13C and 16C) is situated at the top of a long flight of steps. Inside, among other works, are two panel paintings by Spagna and three statues by Andrea Pisano. ▶ The Franciscan poet Jacopone da Todi

(1230-1306) is buried in the crypt of the church of **S. Fortunato★** (B2), built between 1292 and the late 15C. Among the numerous works of art are a chapel of the **Madonna e due Angeli★** by Masolino da Panicale and a wooden choir in the apse (1590). ▶ Of interest are the **large recesses** in p. del Mercato Vecchio (B2), perhaps the remains of a Roman basilica; medieval **walls** and square towers. ▶ On a bank outside the walls stands the church of **S. Maria della Consolazione★** (B1, 1504-1617). It is built on the Greek cross plan with large apses and a dome. An outstanding work of the Renaissance, it is only attributed to Bramante, but bears the stamp of his calm, imposing style. □

Practical information ————————————

♨ *Terme di San Faustino,* (May-Oct, *13 km SE*), ☎ 8856109.
ⓘ p. del Popolo 38 (A2), ☎ 883062; v. Mazzini 19 (B2), ☎ 882406.

Hotels:
★★★★ *Bramante,* v. Orvietana 48 (B1 a), ☎ 8848381, 43 rm ℗ ⋙ � ♪ Tastefully converted 14C convent, 92,000; bkf: 7,000.
★★★ *Villa Luisa,* v. Cortesi 147, ☎ 8848571, 43 rm ℗ ⋙ ᴪ ⋘ 56,000; bkf:6,000.

Restaurant:
♦♦ *Umbria,* v. S. Bonaventura 13 (A2 b), ☎ 882737, closed Tue and Dec-Jan. Service outside in summer. Regional cuisine: spaghetti with truffles, venison with juniper berries, 28/36,000.

Recommended
Clay pigeon shooting: at Massa Martana, ☎ 8855179.
Cycling: *GS Pantalla,* at Pantalla, v. Tiberina, ☎ 888316.
Events: *antiques fair* (Apr), *national exhibition of crafts* (Aug-Sep).

Lake TRASIMENO

From Perugia (124 km, 1 day; map 2)

Lake Trasimeno is the largest stretch of inland water in the Italian peninsula, set among hills, vineyards, olive orchards and crenellated castles. It has flat shores with scythe-like inlets bordered by thick reed beds in parts. There are three islands, Maggiore and

TODI

0   100   200 m
1:12.000 (1cm=120m)

Minore near the N shore and Polvese close to the SE corner. The name of the lake appears in both legend and history: the love of the demigod Trasimeno for the nymph Agille, the famous battle of 217 BC between the Carthaginians and the Romans and St. Francis' retreat on the Isola Maggiore. The fishermen still use simple techniques dating from antiquity; particularly striking are their flat-bottomed boats with raised prows, which do not get caught in the reeds.

▶ This route starts in **Perugia** (→) on the SS 75 bis W. A short detour to the r. leads to Spagnolia or **Città della Domenica**, an unusual amusement park in a scenic position. ▶ There is a junction where it is possible to turn off to the r. for **Corciano**, a village of medieval appearance with numerous towers dominated by a 14C **castle**. ▶ A long, straight route through low, rounded hills goes across the Cáina and Formanuova Rivers to **Magione**. Entering the town, on the r. is the multi-towered castle of the Knights of Malta, known as the **Badia** (15C). 8.5 km N is the village of **Castel Rigone** with a fine view and the remains of a **castle** (rebuilt in 1297) and the elegant church of the **Madonna dei Miracoli**★, begun in 1494 by builders from Lombardy. ▶ From there, it is a short journey to **Lake Trasimeno**; the route goes around the lake in a counterclockwise direction. ▶ After **Passignano sul Trasimeno** with its splendid view of the lake and islands, a short detour to the r. leads to **Tuoro sul Trasimeno**, close to the site of the bloody battle between the Romans and the Carthaginians. ▶ On the NW shore of the lake is the turning for nearby **Borghetto** (15C tower), after which the route proceeds S to **Castiglione del Lago** (→). ▶ From the SE edge of the lake, a wide road goes up to **Panicale** (c. 8 km), a medieval-looking village situated on a spur and offering a view. Note the collegiate church of **S. Michele**★, with its Renaissance portals and the frescos by Perugino in the church of S. Sebastiano. ▶ The route next goes around Montalera Castle

situated on a hillock and continues along back toward the lake. At one turning there is a view★ of the entire lake and its islands. ▶ **San Savino**, dominated by a castle rebuilt in the 14C, is near the point at which the water flows out of the lake. ▶ After **San Feliciano** *(boats to nearby Polvese island)* is **Monte del Lago**, situated on a promontory. ▶ From nearby Magione, the road leads back to Perugia. □

Practical information ———————

CASTEL RIGONE, ✉ 06060, ☎ 075.

Hotel:
★★★ *Fattoria*, v. Rigone 1, ☎ 845197, 30 rm P ▨ ◈ closed Nov, 60,000.

CITTA DELLA DOMENICA, ✉ 06100, ☎ 075.

Recommended
Amusement park: *Città della Domenica*-Spagnolia, ☎ 754941 or 70306 (daily Apr-Sep, wkends only Oct-Feb).

CORCIANO, ✉ 06073, ☎ 075.

Hotel:
★★★ *Conca del Sole*, at Chiugiana *(3 km SE)*, ☎ 79249, 39 rm P ≪ ◁ ▨ & 55,000; bkf: 5,500.

Restaurant:
♦♦♦ *Ottavi*, at Chiugiana, v. A. Garibaldi 20, ☎ 774718, closed Sun and Aug. Italian and international cuisine: seasonal risottos, tripe stew, 30/45,000.

Recommended
Clay pigeon shooting: at Monte Malbe, v. Cappuccini, ☎ 690396.
Discothèque: *Quasar*, at Ellera *(7 km SE)*, ☎ 798800.
Golf: at Ellera, ☎ 79704 (9 holes).
Horseback riding: at *Cape Horse* at Capocavallo, ☎ 605858 or 605705 (associate of *ANTE*); Club ippico Santa Sabina, at Ellera, ☎ 780198 (instruction).
Sports centre: *Santa Sabina*, ☎ 78195.

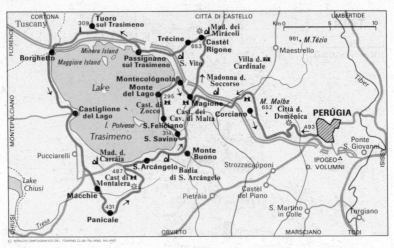

2. Lake Trasimeno

MAGIONE, ⊠ 06063, ☎ 075.

Hotels:
★★ *Cantalodole,* at La Rocca, strada Leopardi 3/A, ☎ 840458, 38 rm Ⓟ ⚏ ⚄ 40,000; bkf: 4,500.
★ *Settimio,* at San Feliciano *(7 km SW),* ☎ 849104, 15 rm Ⓟ ⚄ ⚘ closed 5-30 Nov, 32,000. Rest. ● ◆◆ closed Thu in winter and Nov. Grill and spits in view and terrace. Cuisine of lake fish: fritto misto, queen carp with garlic and wild fennel, 20/25,000.

Recommended
Cycling: *Pedale Magionese,* v. Roma 10, ☎ 840216.
Motor racing: in Bacanella, ☎ 840303.

PANICALE, ⊠ 06064, ☎ 075.

Recommended
Motocross: *Crossodromo Del Poggio,* at Poggio, ☎ 837424.

TUORO SUL TRASIMENO, ⊠ 06069, ☎ 075.
≋
⚓ boats to Castiglione del Lago and Passignano, ☎ 827157.

⚑ ★★ *Punta Navaccia,* at Tuoro Lido, 250 pl, ☎ 826357.

Recommended
Farm vacations: *Agriturismo Azienda La Dogana,* v. Dogana 107, ☎ 846011.

TREVI

Perugia 50, Rome 150 km
Pop.7,232 ⊠ 06039 ☎ 0742　　　　　　　　　B3

Trevi is situated on a hill covered with olive trees overlooking the plain of Spoleto. It is a typical medieval town with winding streets and a pervasive feeling of antiquity.

▶ The church of **S. Emiliano** still contains part of the original Romanesque building (12C). Inside is the altar of the Sacrament★ by Rocco da Vicenza (1522). ▶ The 13C Gothic church of **S. Francesco** contains 14C-15C frescos and a panel painting of the *Crucifixion* (14C). ▶ The 15C Palazzo Comunale houses the *Pinacoteca (8 a.m.-2 p.m., apply to municipio),* which contains a valuable collection of Umbrian paintings. ▶ 1.8 km away, towards the via Flaminia, is the Renaissance church of **Madonna delle**

Lacrime (1487) containing 16C frescos including one by Perugino *(apply to institute next door).* ▶ 3 km S is **Bovara** and the Romanesque church of **S. Pietro:** the frieze on the pediment is believed to be 5C.　　□

Practical information _____

ⓘ voltone Palazzo Comunale.

Hotels:
★★★★ *Torre,* v. Flaminia at 147-km marker, ☎ 670644, 140 rm Ⓟ ⚏ ⚄ ⊠ ⚘ 98,000.
★★ *Cocchetto,* v. Dogali 13, ☎ 78229, 22 rm, 46,000.

Recommended
Farm vacations: *Azienda Casa Bozzi,* at San Lorenzo, ☎ 799162.
Technical tourism: visit to olive oil manufacturers, *Cooperativa agricola Trevi,* v. Flaminia at 141-km marker, ☎ 78448 (Mon-Sat).

The UMBRIA VALLEY

From Perugia *(145 km, 1 day; map 3)*

SE of Perugia in the midst of the winding hills between Assisi, Foligno and Spoleto on one side of the ridge and Bevagna, Montefalco and Castel Ritaldi on the other is a fertile plain with canals and numerous farms and churches. Its southernmost corner is in the harsh countryside around Spoleto, with the Martani Mountains to the W and the wooded hummocks of Valnerina to the E. It has always been a cereal-growing area, but also contains sugar beet and vines supported by mulberry trees. Olive trees grow as high up as 2,300 ft, where they meet with oak coppices. The whole of the area to one side of the Tiber, around the Chiascio, Topino and Clitunno Rivers, is known as the Valle Umbra or Valle Spoletina and can be seen in its entirety from Montefalco, the balustrade of Umbria.

▶ Leaving Perugia (→), the route descends (extensive view of the Tiber Valley) until reaching the plain which unfolds as far as Spoleto. ▶ Going up to **Assisi** (→) there is a fine view of the town and surrounding area. ▶ Enchanting, too, is the entrance to Roman

3. The Umbria Valley

Spello (→), beautifully situated at the far end of the Subasio. ▶ The countryside grows gentler as it heads S from **Foligno** (→), which lies stretched out across the plain. ▶ **Trevi**, on a hill covered with olive trees, can be seen long before actually reaching it. ▶ Going around the romantic **fonti del Clitunno** (springs) the route arrives in **Spoleto** (→), which can be seen against the dark wooded background of Monteluco. ▶ Continuing N along the W edge of the valley the route comes to **Maiano** (14C castle), **San Brizio** (remains of 13C walls) and **Bruna**, dominated by the sanctuary of S. Maria della Bruna (1510). The route then heads NW to **Castel Ritaldi** *(1.8 km)*, an agricultural centre which grew up on the site of a Roman village. Its 13C castle is in good condition. A little further on, a detour to the r. *(c. 4 km)* leads to the sanctuary of the **Madonna delle Stelle** in a green clearing near a cypress and ilex wood. ▶ After **Montefalco** (→) the route descends to the medieval town of **Bevagna** (→) at a bend of the River Timia. ▶ Continuing along the edge of the plain the route reaches **Bettona**, perched in a panoramic position on a hill covered with olive trees. It is of Etruscan origin (stretch of wall dating back to the 4C BC) and the medieval centre and some 14C and 16C houses have survived. There are works by Perugino in the church of **S. Maria Maggiore** (banner depicting *Madonna and Saints*) and in the **Pinacoteca**, which is housed in the 14C Palazzo del Podestà *(open a.m.)*. 1 km N is an **Etruscan underground tomb** dating from the late 3C BC *(caretaker in house nearby)*. ▶ **Torgiano** stands above the Tiber Valley at the point where the Tiber and the Chiascio meet. In the medieval town centre are remains of the walls and an isolated tower. ▶ Finally, the route crosses the Tiber and arrives back at Perugia. ☐

Practical information _____

CASTEL RITALDI, ✉ 06044, ☎ 0743.

Recommended

Young people's activities: summer courses in dance, drama and languages; winter courses in ecology, *Associazione femminile Casa Balena*, v. Torregrosso 51, ☎ 51679.

TORGIANO, ✉ 06089, ☎ 075.

Hotel:
★★★★★ *Tre Vaselle*, v. Garibaldi 48, ☎ 982447, 48 rm Ⓟ ⅏ ✿ ⬙. Elegantly converted 16C house, 190,000; bkf: 15,000. Rest. ● ♦♦♦♦ Outstanding regional cuisine: ghiottoneria with truffles, pike marinated in oil with white wine, home-produced Torgiano, 40/55,000.

Recommended
Wines: *Lungarotti* wine shop, v. M. Angeloni 16, ☎ 982348 (Torgiano wine); wine tasting stall in Nov (Italian wines).

La VALNERINA

From Terni to Norcia *(106 km, 1 day; map 4)*

It has been said that the idyllic part of Umbria ends at Terni and that E of the town is a wilder landscape where there are still wolves in the heart of the ilex woods and wild boar in the glens among the wooded mountain slopes. However, leaving Terni, the landscape becomes beautiful again. Beyond the fork of the Arrone the landscape becomes more vivid, even violent in places, and the region opens out, offering glimpses of turbulent beauty. The towns appear suddenly: Cascia is like a miniature town inhabited by a race of peasant kings; Norcia is severe with its ancient surrounding walls. The characteristic gentleness of Umbria also remains.

▶ Leaving **Terni** (→), the route enters the green, silent Valnerina with its steep sides and travels along the winding, foaming River Nera. ▶ In **Papigno** are the remains of a small round-towered castle and the Villa Graziani, in which Byron stayed in 1817. ▶ Suddenly, at a bend, the white mass of the waters of the Nera appears and, shortly afterwards, the **Marmore Falls** (→ Terni). ▶ Continuing SE the route overshadows the valley bottom and the tranquil River Velino. ▶ After **Piediluco** (→) on the shores of the lake of the same name a winding road goes N to the **fork of the Arrone** and then goes back down into Valnerina. ▶ The route now follows the SS 209 NE to **Ferentillo**, a small town situated in a gorge guarded by two rocks and divided by the River Nera into the two areas of Materella and Precetto. In the latter is the 15C church of S. Stefano, famous for the fact that the bodies placed in the crypt have undergone a process of natural mummification *(apply to house nearby, no. 7)*. ▶ The valley bottom now widens out and the River Nera winds its way peacefully through. On a spur on the r. is the **Castello di Umbriano** with its tall tower. ▶ Just before Sambucheto, a road on the l. *(1.8 km)* with a beautiful view of the valley leads up to the abbey of **S. Pietro in Valle** at the foot of Mt. Solenne. Founded in the 8C and rebuilt in the 12C, it is a venerable monument to the history and art of the early Middle Ages. Of the original church, the apses, the transept and the front part of the altar★ still remain. The nave has a cycle of Roman school frescoes★ which, like the cloister★ and the campanile★, date from the 12C. ▶ On the other side of the Nera is **Sant'Anatolia di**

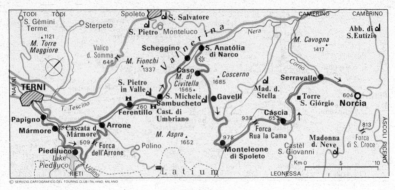

4. La Valnerina

Narco, with its medieval centre which grew up around the castle built in 1198. The surrounding walls are 14C, but the two keeps are 15C. ▶ Traveling SE along a steep uphill road with hairpin turns and a view over the countryside below Mt. Civitella, the route reaches **Caso** and **Gavelli,** which both have parish churches containing 12C-14C frescos. ▶ There is a steep descent and a r. turn to **Monteleone di Spoleto** (3,208 ft), perched high on a hill above the Corno Valley. In the medieval town centre are the remains of a castle and a church containing valuable works of art. ▶ When the route reaches the valley bottom it continues N along the river. ▶ After **Forca Rua la Cama** it goes down to **Cascia** on a spur in a broad hollow within the valley. This was the birthplace of St. Rita, whose body is kept in a modern **shrine.** There are many mementos of the saint in the **monastery** next door *(group visits 9-11:30 a.m. and 2:30-5:30 p.m.; 8 a.m.- 12:30 p.m. wkends),* as well as a 15C cloister, an oratory and rose garden. The church of **S. Francesco** (1424) contains 15C-16C frescos. ▶ **Serravalle** is to the r. of the River Corno, at the point where it meets the Sordo. Not far from the town is the church of S. Claudio (13C). ▶ Norcia stands upon a plateau, from which the pretty and peaceful Sordo Valley opens out suddenly into a delightful landscape of green meadows and tall poplar trees, with an encircling cluster of mountains. ☐

Send us your comments and suggestions; we will use them in the next edition.

Practical information

ARRONE, ⊠ 05031, ☎ 0744.

Restaurants:
♦♦ *Grottino del Nera,* at Casteldilago, ☎ 78104, closed Wed, Jan and Jun. Regional cuisine: risotto with freshwater crayfish, tagliatelle with truffles or a choice of eight other sauces, 14/22,000.
♦♦ *Rossi,* at Casteldilago, vocabolo Isola 6, ☎ 78104, closed Fri and Christmas. Regional cuisine: fettuccine with trout sauce, freshwater crayfish in cold green sauce, 15/30,000.

CASCIA, ⊠ 06043, ☎ 0743.
ⓘ p. Garibaldi 1, ☎ 71147.

Hotels:
★★★ *Cursula,* v. Cavour 3, ☎ 76206, 30 rm Ⓟ 50,000; bkf: 3,500. Rest. ● ♦♦ closed Wed. Regional cuisine: fettuccine nere, pappardelle with truffles, 20/30,000.
★★★ *Monte Meraviglia,* v. Roma 15, ☎ 76142, 90 rm Ⓟ & 50,000; bkf: 4,000.
★★★ *Rose,* v. Fasce 2, ☎ 76241, 160 rm Ⓟ ⑳ & closed Nov-Easter, 47,000; bkf: 5,000.
★★ *Casa del Pellegrino,* at Roccaporena *(5 km W),* ☎ 71205, 82 rm Ⓟ ⑳ ⌇ closed Nov-Mar, 36,000; bkf: 3,000.

SELLANO, ⊠ 06030, ☎ 0743.

Recommended
Craft workshops: *Scaramucci,* at Villamagina, ☎ 96225 (ironwork).

Valle d'Aosta

▶ The Valle d'Aosta is a region of Italy of great beauty through which runs the River Dora Baltea enclosed by a magical ring of peaks, steep and inaccessible to all but a few. Even the pass linking the valley with the Canavese hills and the plains below, through the nearby valley of Pont-Saint-Martin, is little more than a break in the rocks. Down in the valley are fields and vineyards and even small factories and higher up, hilltop villages (whose access roads cannot be seen), alpine meadows, bare rocks, waterfalls that become columns of ice in the winter and, high against the sky, the brilliance of the glaciers. In the space of a few hundred yards there is a change of environment equivalent to almost 45° of latitude. The two ancient routes over the mountains by the Pennine Alps Pass and the Graian Alps Pass (later to be named the Great St. Bernard and the Little St. Bernard Passes) went through the Valle d'Aosta, and where they crossed the Roman praetor Aulus Terentius Varro founded the colony of *Augusta Praetoria* (Aosta). These roads have always been more important internationally (more than ever today with tunnels under the Alps replacing the old passes) than they have been to the people living in the valley. The history of the region, with the intermixing of invading tribes with the indigenous population, can be traced from the prehistoric people who carved mysterious figures on cave walls to the Celts and to the more recent arrivals who occupied various sites in the valley and who came over narrow passes used only by the chamois. Mountaineering was born here among the most beautiful peaks in the world (the Mont Blanc, the Monte Rosa, the Matterhorn and the Gran Paradiso) and it was soon followed by winter sports and mass tourism. ☐

 ## Don't miss

The valley is prized for its superb alpine scenery (Mont Blanc, 15,780 ft from Courmayeur★; the Matterhorn, 14,691 ft from Breuil-Cervinia★; Monte Rosa, 15,200 ft; Gran Paradiso, 13,323 ft from Cogne, the centre of the National Park of Gran Paradiso), but also unforgettable are Aosta with the cloister★★ of the Collegiate Church of S. Orso★ and the castles of Issogne and Fénis. The crossing by cable car of Mont Blanc from Courmayeur★★ is an exhilarating experience.

 ## Brief regional history

3rd millennium-2C BC
Prehistory and the Salassi. Archaeological research, stimulated by regional autonomy, has revealed two points of interest. The first concerns the neolithic culture of Vollein, which it is thought may have spread from the Mediterranean through the Ligurian Gulf during the first half of the 3rd millennium. Secondly, the megalithic site at **Saint-Martin-de-Corléans,** on the edge of Aosta, has yielded large anthropomorphic figures dating from the second half of the 3rd millennium. ● In ancient times, probably before 500 BC, the valley was inhabited by the **Salassi,** a Celtic people who, according to Strabo, exploited the gold mines, washing the precious mineral in the waters of the Dora. The **cromlech** in the Little Saint Bernard Pass is associated with the Salassi.

2C BC-5C AD
The Romans. The Consul Aprius Claudius Pulcrus, who intervened to force the Salassi to make peace with the neighbouring tribes, was heavily defeated in 143 BC and only two years later did he achieve victory. ● Subsequently there were periods of calm but also periods of tension in relations between the Romans and the Salassi. ● It was not until 25 BC that the praetor Aulus Terentius Varro, acting on orders from Augustus, finally crushed a rebellion

among the Salassi, many of whom were sold as slaves in the market at *Eporedia* (Ivrea) to recover the cost of the war. The colony of *Augusta Praetoria* (Aosta, whose remains are among the most interesting of all Roman cities) was founded in the following year to control the road to Gaul, from *Eporedia* through the *Alpis Graia* (the lower pass of Saint Bernard) to *Lugdunum* (Lyons).

6C-11C

Three saints. The incursions of the **Burgundians** began to penetrate into the valley at the end of the 5C. ● From 570 the valley above the Bard pass belonged to the **Varovingians** who then ruled Burgundy. ● Also in the 6C came the founding of the collegiate church of S. Orso. Ploceanus, Bishop of Aosta, was an Arian, while **Orso,** Archdeacon of the cathedral, rejected the Arian heresy. The latter consequently withdrew from the cathedral and founded a chapel which later became the collegiate church bearing his name and which is today the most famous sacred monument in the valley. ● The link with **Burgundy** survived events throughout northern Italy during the Carolingian period and subsequent times of feudal division. ● However, one event of particular importance was the arrival in the 10C of the **Saracens,** who passed through the valleys of the Rhône, the Jura and the Vallese, built fortifications on the Greater Pass of Saint Bernard and various other sites and sacked the region. They were defeated, put to flight or exterminated through the efforts of the Archdeacon of Aosta, **Bernard of Menton,** who then built for the protection of travelers two hostels on the passes that now bear his name. ● A contemporary of Saint Bernard was **Anselm of Aosta** (1033-1109), a man of immense learning and one of the great figures of the Middle Ages. He became Archbishop of Canterbury and courageously carried through the Gregorian reforms despite the opposition of the King of England.

11C-15C

Savoy and the Challants. In a document dating from 1032 there appears as Count of Aosta one **Umberto of the white hand,** founder of the Savoy family, Count of Moriana and councilor to Rudolf III, King of Burgundy; he shared the position of count with the Bishop of Aosta in recognition of the sovereignty of Emperor Conrad the Salic. ● At first, the Savoy family were counts in name only; power was effectively divided between the bishop and the small, troublesome, local landowners. ● At the end of the 12C **Thomas I of Savoy** defeated the landowners after concluding a pact of friendship with **Bishop Gualberto. The Charter of Immunity** (1191), a document of fundamental importance in the history of the valley, gave him jurisdiction over the inhabitants of Aosta 'who had seen and experienced calamities, oppression and injuries'. The nobles then moved out into the countryside, acquiring and reinforcing their estates, of which the many **castles** so characteristic of the valley remain, testifying to a world that remained feudal for so long. ● The Counts of Savoy were represented in the valley by a viscount until the mid-13C. The first of these, in the 11C, was a certain **Bavo,** founder of the family that in the 13C took the name of **Challant.** The Challants reappear frequently in the history of the valley. ● The castles of **Aymaville, Fénis, Verrès, Ussel** and **Issogne** were all built during the 14C-15C by members of this family.

15C-20C

From the kingdom of Savoy to Italy. The valley saw the rise of Savoy (whose capital moved to Turin in 1563) and its relative autonomy, safeguarded by an assembly of representatives of the three states after the fashion of the *Ancien Régime* and lasting until the second half of the 18C. ● The valley also had four brief periods of direct **French** rule: in 1691, 1704-6, 1798-9 and 1800-14. The penultimate period followed the war between revolutionary France and the King of Sardinia and saw fierce resistance on the alpine ridges on the part of Piedmontese soldiers and volunteers from the Valle d'Aosta. One famous event of this period was the **crossing of the Great Saint Bernard Pass** by Napoleon and his army in May 1800. ● In the new State of Italy, Aosta was the capital of a province in Piedmont, which, apart from the Valle d'Aosta, included Ivrea and the Canavese hills. The autonomy of the region dates from 1948.

Castle of Fenis

S. Orso in Aosta

© SERVIZIO CARTOGRAFICO DEL TOURING CLUB ITALIANO, MILANO

Facts and figures

Location: *Surrounded by the highest and most beautiful mountains in the Alps (indeed in Europe), occupies the NW corner of Italy, around the valley of the Dora Baltea (running from W to E), with numerous tributaries which have fascinating upper valleys with almost perpendicular sides. Of all the alpine regions it is one of the most varied and unspoiled. Roman monuments and medieval churches and castles add unexpected interest to the mountain landscapes.*
Area: *3,262 sq km, it occupies approximately one hundredth of the area of Italy and is the smallest of its regions.*
Climate: *Continental but temperate, dry, mild in the lower valleys; harsh at higher altitudes. Clear skies and low rainfall in spring and autumn but abundant snowfalls.*
Population: *113,418 inhabitants; the smallest population and lowest population density in Italy.*
Administration: *An autonomous region, administered by the Regional Council which is located at the capital, Aosta, and officially bilingual (Italian and French).*

● *Practical information*

Information: tourist office at Aosta, p. Narbonne 3, ☎ 0165/303725.

SOS: public emergency service, ☎ 113; police emergency, ☎ 112; *ACI* breakdown services, ☎ 116; mountain rescue service linked to mountain huts, main office at Aosta, ☎ 0165/362543.

Weather: forecast, ☎ 011/57601; road conditions, ☎ 011/5711, ☎ 06/4212 *(ACI)*; snow conditions,

☎ 02/67509 or 011/5731; avalanche information, ☎ 31210.

Farm vacations: *Assessorato Regionale Agricoltura-Ufficio Agriturismo*, at Aosta, p. Deffeyes, ☎ 0165/553392.

Vacation village: at Pila-Aosta, *Hotel Villaggio Valtur* (closed May-Nov).

Events: at Aosta, *Bataille des Reines* (fight between cows) regional finals; international festival of organ music; cultural and social events at Saint-Vincent.

Fairs and markets: *Millenarian fair of S. Orso*, at Aosta.

Nature parks: *Gran Paradiso national park* (partly in Piedmont); guided tours from Cogne, p. E. Chanoux, ☎ 0165/74040; visitors' centres at Rhêmes-Notre-Dame and Dégioz Valsavarenche (open Jul-Aug).

Mountain walk: along Alte Vie 1 and 2 (along the l. and r. sides of the valley respectively); 175 miles of well-laid-

Coffee of the Valle d'Aosta

Perfectly suited to the harsh climate of the alpine winter and the earthy cuisine of the valley, the local manner of drinking coffee is a pleasant way to end the day's exertions in the snow. Served in a squat, wooden cup with four, six, eight or more mouthpieces, the drink is a mixture of generous quantities of lemon-rind and grappa added to boiling coffee. This is then ignited and sugar is thrown into the flames of the evaporating spirit. Drinkers take turns, each from a different mouthpiece. The picturesque receptacle used for the coffee in the Valle d'Aosta is often incorrectly called a grolla, but a grolla is a wooden goblet with a lid. The name is connected by some with that of the Holy Grail, mentioned in the legends and poems of the Knights of the Round Table and believed to be the cup Christ used at the Last Supper and the one in which Joseph of Arimathea collected his blood as it flowed from his side.

out walks, best period from mid-Jul-mid-Sep. Information: branch offices of *CAI*, at Aosta, ☎ 0165/40194 and Verrès, ☎ 0165/92016; nature guides, at Cogne, ☎ 0165/74040; *Unione valdostana guide d'alta montagna*, ☎ 0165/34983.

Natural history course: *LIPU Valle d'Aosta*, at Aosta, v. Montagnayes, ☎ 0165/41047 (courses in bird-watching, organized trips to *Gran Paradiso*).

Mountaineering: ascents of Mont Blanc from Courmayeur; of Matterhorn from Breuil-Cervinia and Valtournenche; of Monte Rosa from Gressoney and Champoluc; of Gran Paradiso from Cogne and Valsavarenche. 38 mountain huts *(rifugi)*, 37 permanent huts. Mountaineering instruction at Courmayeur; schools of rock-climbing at Arnad, Breuil-Cervinia, Cogne, Courmayeur, Pollein, Pontey, Valgrisenche. Alpine skiing routes from Breuil-Cervinia, Champoluc, Cogne, Courmayeur, Gressoney-La-Trinité, La Thuile. Information: *CAI,* branch offices at Aosta, p. Chanoux, ☎ 0165/40194, and Gressoney-La-Trinité; at *Studio Camisasca Rial,* Verrès, v. Martorey, ☎ 0165/92016; *Unione valdostana guide d'alta montagna,* Aosta, v. Vevey 17, ☎ 0165/34983.

Skiing: Breuil-Cervinia (summer skiing at Plateau Rosà); Brusson (cross-country skiing, 70 km); Champoluc; Cogne (cross-country skiing, 50 km); Courmayeur (summer school at Colle del Gigante; cross-country skiing, 35 km); Gressoney-La-Trinité-La Thuile (summer skiing in the Rutor glacier, with helicopter service); Pila; Valtournenche.

Ice skating and hockey: Aosta ice rink, Tzamberlet region, ☎ 0165/361039.

Golf: at Breuil-Cervinia (9 holes); at Plan-Pincieux (9 holes; → Courmayeur).

Archery: *Fitarco* regional committee, at Aosta, v. Voison 8, ☎ 0165/361178.

Bowling: at Aosta, v. Lancieri d'Aosta, ☎ 0165/31271; Châtillon, ☎ 0166/62355; Saint-Vincent, v. Conti Challand 10, ☎ 0166/2443.

Hang gliding: *Alpi delta air sport,* at Nus, v. Stazione 3, ☎ 0165/767015. Information at Saint-Pierre, ☎ 0165/903646.

Parachuting and gliding: *Aosta Saint-Christophe Airport,* strada Nazionale, ☎ 0165/362442.

⬤ *Towns and places*

AOSTA*

Milan 185, Rome 729 km
Pop. 37,355 ⊠ 11100 ☎ 0165   B1

If the alpine climate had been as severe two thousand years ago as it is now, the Roman settlement of *Augusta Praetoria,* founded in 25 BC, would not have benefited from its special position at the bottom of the valley where the consular roads from the Isère and the Rhône regions cross. From that time onward its position as a junction for transalpine traffic has always been uncertain, depending as it does on favourable climatic conditions. No other Italian city shows so clearly the original layout of the Roman

fortifications along with its walls and a complex of Roman monuments all dating from the same period, which have given it the title 'Rome of the Alps'. In other respects there is evidence of an unusual transformation that has reversed the historical relationship between the city and its environs. The mineral and hydroelectric resources and the development of motorways, alpine tunnels and the tourist industry mean that the mountains no longer constitute a threat, but rather a source of riches for the economy of the Valle d'Aosta.

▶ Outside the city, beyond the Buthier torrent, a Roman **bridge** throws its imposing but quite useless stone arch over the dry bed of the river which was diverted in the

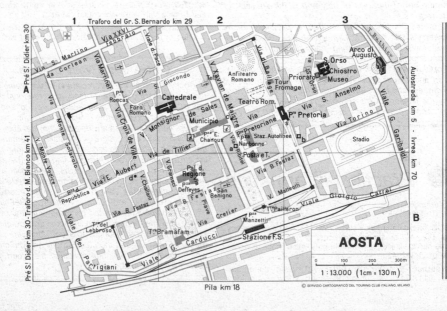

AOSTA

0   100   200   300m
1 : 13.000 (1cm = 130m)

Traforo del Gr. S. Bernardo km 29

Pila km 18   © SERVIZIO CARTOGRAFICO DEL TOURING CLUB ITALIANO, MILANO

13C. ▶ Nearby is the **Arch of Augustus**★★ (A3), erected in 25 BC to celebrate victory over the Salassi. From the square there is a panoramic view, taking in mountains and glaciers along with the city with its ancient architecture. ▶ A few steps away is **S. Orso**★ (A3), the most perfect jewel of medieval and Renaissance architecture in the whole valley. In the small 16C square nearby stands a magnificent and ancient lime tree, its luxuriant foliage softening the lines of the powerful Romanesque **campanile** (1131) and the still older **Collegiate Church**. All that remains of the 11C church is the crypt and traces of frescos in the gallery *(inquire at the sacristy)*. The simple façade, the other frescos and the Gothic groin vaults date from the 15C. The sanctuary has a fine wooden, carved **choir**★ from the 16C. The pride of S. Orso and a masterpiece of Romanesque sculpture is the 12C **cloister**★★, whose columns have forty marble capitals painted in black. Behind the 15C **Priory** (which has fine red terracotta window frames and an octagonal tower with a spire), at v. S. Orso 10, is the **Museo Archeologico Regionale** *(closed for reorganization)*. ▶ V. S. Anselmo (A3) leads quickly to the centre of the city, which, with the old quarter, corresponds with the perimeter of the Roman city, still in part enclosed by the Roman walls; today, as in earlier times, in order to pass through the original gates the city must be entered by the **Porta Pretoria**★ (A2-3), an edifice of unique dimensions with walls made of a double ring of enormous ashlars. ▶ The **Roman Theatre**★ (A2) is not so well preserved. But one glance at the gargantuan ruins of the 72 ft high façade pierced by four tiers of arches and rectangular windows gives some indication of the magnificence of the original building. Behind the façade are the partially restored remains of the **tiers of seats** (which held 3,000 people) and of the stage, which ran parallel to the **gates**. ▶ The adjacent **Roman Amphitheatre**, which, when it was built in the 1C BC, could hold 20,000 spectators, must have been even more impressive. Of the sixty original arches only seven can now be seen and these have been incorporated into the façade of a house in the courtyard of the convent of S. Caterina (13C), slightly to the N of the theatre *(ask for permission to visit)*. ▶ A worthwhile conclusion to a tour of Aosta's civil Roman architecture is a visit to the remains of the **Forum**, in the p. Giovanni XXIII (A1), in the enclosure next to the Cathedral *(curator on site)*. Descend into the cryptoporticus (an underground gallery extending in part under the church; *excavation in progress)*, which has two aisles, the arches of which are supported on massive tufa pillars. ▶ The Neoclassical façade (1848) of the **Cathedral**★ (A2) is flanked by two Romanesque campaniles, which are all that remain of the original edifice (11C-12C; restored and altered on several occasions after the 15C). The vestibule has a fine façade, both carved and painted (1522-6). The Gothic interior (late 15C-early 16C) has groin vaults and 15C stained glass. In the sanctuary, beyond the fine mosaic pavement laid in two sections (the lower one, depicting year, months and four rivers of the earthly paradise, dates from the 12C, whereas the other dates from the 13C or 14C), there is a splendid Gothic wooden **choir** (*c.* 1468) with two rows of stalls carved in the form of saints, prophets, angels and grotesques. The apsidal chapel on the l. has the tomb of Count Thomas II of Savoy, from the 14C or 15C. The newly re-opened arcades house the **Treasury Museum** *(weekdays summer only 10 a.m.-12 noon and 3-5 p.m.; wkends all year 3-5:45 p.m.)*, which have an ivory diptych with the image of Emperor Honorius (406), a wooden altar with twenty carved panels (local school 15C), the 13C crucifix once placed beneath the Arch of Augustus, shrines, sculptures in wood and stone, jewelry, glass and enamels. Through a door in the l. side of the cathedral is the part-Gothic **cloister**★ completed in 1460, in which are gathered the remains of the Challant tombs. ▶ The intersection of v. Croix de Ville with v. de Tillier (B1) was for centuries the centre of the economic and social life of the city. Nearby, a cross over a fountain records the flight of Calvin, who attempted, without success, to spread the reformed church in the valley. ▶ The centre of the city consists of the vast but pleasant piazza

Chanoux (A2). In the arcade of the ancient v. de Maistre there is the **permanent exhibition of local crafts**. ▶ The v. de Sales (A2) is flanked by the seminary and the Bishop's palace (Vescovado). ▶ Start at the **Bramafan Tower** (B2), a massive 13C building which belonged to the Challant family, viscounts of Aosta, to explore the Roman **walls** (from the 1C BC), sections of which are extremely well preserved. Forming a rectangle 2,473 ft by 1,876 ft, they enclose the central areas of the city and the site of the ancient *castrum*. Some of the towers are particularly fine, e. g., the Pailleron (B2) and the Lebbroso (B1), incorporated into the castle of the lords of Friours in the 13C and which held the poor, sick prisoner whose pathetic story inspired Xavier de Maistre's famous tale.

Environs

▶ The ski resort **Pila** (5,875 ft; *18 km)* offers a splendid panorama of the Pennine Alps, across the Gran Combin and Mt. Rosa (ascents of Chamolè and Mt. Emilius). A scenic route passes through **Peroulaz** (4,448 ft) and **Les Fleurs** (4,461 ft). ▶ **Sarre** *(5 km)*, with a castle built in the 12C by the Savoy family and rebuilt in the 17C, has an exhibition of interesting garments, hangings and curious hunting trophies *(Jul-mid-Sep 10-11 a.m. and 2-4:30 p.m. except Tue; group visits in other months by arrangement,* ☎ 57027). **Saint-Pierre** (2,398 ft; *8 km)* contains the **Museo Regionale di Scienze Naturali** *(May-Sep 9:30-11:30 a.m. and 3-5:30 p.m.; closed Mon)* in 4 rooms of a 17C castle. ▶ **Saint-Nicolas** (2,624 ft; *16 km)*, a vacation centre straight above the valley of the Dora, has views of the mountains. ▶ Above Aosta on the r. side of the Dora are the valleys of Cogne (→), Valsavarenche (→), Rhêmes (→ Rhêmes-Notre-Dame) and **Valgrisenche**; the last of these is the wildest. ▶ From **Valgrisenche** (5,459 ft; *30 km)*, a small tourist resort, there are excursions (to the **Rifugio Scavarda**, 9,573 ft, and to the **Rifugio Bezzi**, 7,493 ft) and alpine ascents of the Grande Rousse, the Grande Sassière and the Rutor. A little to the S a dam has created the large artificial lake of Beauregard. □

Practical information _____

AOSTA
ⓘ (A2) regional tourist office at municipio, p. E. Chanoux 8, ☎ 35655.
▦▦ (B2), ☎ 362057.
▭▭▭ p. Narbonne (A2).

Hotels:
★★★★ *Valle d'Aosta*, corso Ivrea 146, ☎ 41845, 104 rm Ⓟ ⬭ ⅙ No restaurant, 125,000; bkf: 6,500.
★★★ *Ambassador*, v. Duca degli Abruzzi 2, ☎ 42230, 44 rm Ⓟ ⬭ ⬿ 73,500; bkf: 7,000.
★★★ *Europe*, p. Narbonne 8 (A2 a), ☎ 40566, 80 rm Ⓟ 75,000; bkf: 7,000.
★★★ *Rayon de Soleil*, v. Gran S. Bernardo, ☎ 362247, 39 rm Ⓟ ⬭ ▣ closed Nov-Feb, 68,000.
★★★ *Roma*, v. Torino 7 (A3 b), ☎ 40821, 33 rm Ⓟ closed Jan-Feb. No restaurant, 70,000; bkf: 6,000.
★★ *Mignon*, v. Gran S. Bernardo 7, ☎ 43227, 22 rm Ⓟ Pens. 46,000.

Restaurants:
● ♦♦♦ *Cavallo Bianco*, v. E. Aubert 15 (B1 d), ☎ 362214. Built on Roman walls. Creative cuisine with seasonal specialties: dégustation menu, 65/80,000.
● ♦♦♦ *Casale*, at Saint-Christophe *(3 km E)*, regione Condemine 1, ☎ 541203, closed Sun eve, Mon and Nov. Managed by brothers, one responsible for kitchen, other for dining room. Regional cuisine: snail soup; salt beef, 35/40,000.
♦♦ *Brasserie Valdôtaine*, v. Xavier De Maistre 8 (A2 c), ☎ 32076, closed Thu, Jun and Nov. In old alehouse. Italian and international cuisine: risottos, scampi all'orientale, dishes cooked on individual stove at table, 30/40,000.
♦♦ *RistorAgip*, corso Ivrea 138, ☎ 44565, closed Mon and Feb. Looking on to garden. Regional and Piedmontese cuisine: pancakes valdostana, risotto with fontina cheese, agnolotti pasta envelopes, 22/26,000.

� ★★ *Milleluci,* Roppoz 15, 300 pl, ☎ 32437 (all year).

Recommended
Cheeses: visits to *Cooperativa caseficio,* at Saint-Marcel *(11 km E),* nr Ru Herbor, ☎ 768897.
Clay pigeon shooting: Cogne region.
Craft workshops: at Saint-Christophe *(c.* 2 km), Grand Chemin, ☎ 45716 (woodworking).
Events: *final of the Bataille des Reines* (mid-Oct); *organ concerts* (Jul-Aug) and *other musical events* held in summer.
Fair: *Millenarian fair of S. Orso* (typical wood carvings, wrought iron and earthenware), held on 31 Jan and, in summer, on the first Sat of Ferragosto.
Flying: at Saint-Christophe, strada Nazionale, ☎ 362442.
Guided tours: fee charged (2 hrs), inquire at information office, ☎ 35655.
Horseback riding: *Società Ippica Valdostana,* v. Grand Eyvia 25, ☎ 551580 (associate of *ANTE).*
Swimming: v. Lancieri Aosta, ☎ 31271; at Tzamberlet, ☎ 40275 (closed Jul).
Tennis: v. Mazzini 1, ☎ 40420.
Vacation village: *Hotel Villaggio Valtur,* at Pila *(18 km S),* closed May-Nov, ☎ 521041.
Wines and distilleries: visits to vineyards and wine cellars of regional agricultural institute (permission required, ☎ 553392); to *Saint-Roch* distilleries, at Quart *(7 km E),* Villair, ☎ 765203 and *La Valdôtaine,* at Saint-Marcel, ☎ 768919.
Young people's activities: kayak courses and trips, ☎ 42476.

Environs

PILA, ⊠ 11020, ☎ 0165, 18 km S.
𝔁 cableway, ski lifts, cross-country skiing, instruction.

SAINT-PIERRE, ⊠ 11010, ☎ 0165, 8 km W.

Recommended
Craft workshops: *La Grolla,* nr Cognein, ☎ 95021 (cups and goblets; telephone a few days before visit).

SARRE, ⊠ 11010, ☎ 0165.

Recommended
Fishing: *Pescatori sportivi Valle d'Aosta,* Villa dei Fiori Chezallet, ☎ 57050.
Liqueurs: visits to *Amaro Aosta* distillery, SS 26, ☎ 551500.

BREUIL-CERVINIA*

Aosta 51, Milan 187 km
6,580 ft pop. 756 ⊠ 11021 ☎ 0166   B-C 1

The Matterhorn (Fr. Mont Cervin; It. Monte Cervino) peak of the Pennine Alps is on the Swiss-Italian border (altitude 14,691 ft). Its appearance is most striking owing to its isolation and unusual steepness. The ascent by the NE or Zermatt ridge was first made in 1865 by Whymper, Lord Douglas, Hudson and others, when several of the party lost their lives. A few days later it was climbed via the Italian ridge, the N face, by Abbot Gorret, and ultimately via all four ridges and faces. All routes are difficult, especially in bad weather, but there are now fixed ropes on the NE and Italian ridges which lessen the climbing expertise required and reduce the risks.

▶ **Breuil-Cervinia** is a part of Valtournenche (→). The two areas were only linked by a passable road in 1934, but Breuil had already been attracting crowds of tourists, alpinists and skiers for at least twenty years. ▶ Today it is a large, modern and attractive resort and climbing centre and one of the most important all-year ski resorts in Europe. The hotels, condominiums and villas have changed the original character of the area. In return, a continuous network of cable cars and ski lifts ascend

to the vast expanses of permanent snow at high altitudes. The landscape is splendid and the slopes are endless.

Environs

▶ By cableway to Plan Maison (8,389 ft) then **Platen Rosà★** (11,417 ft) or the **Cresta del Furggen★★** with a superb view★★ of the **Matterhorn★**; climbers can reach the latter by ascending from the Rifugi J. A. Carvel (12,569 ft) and Luigi Amedeo (12,598 ft).   ☐

Practical information _____

𝔁 cableways at Plan Maison, Plateau Rosà and Furggen, ski lifts, cross-country skiing, bobsleigh runs, skating, summer skiing at Plateau Rosà, ☎ 949076.
ℹ v. Carrel 29, ☎ 949136.

Hotels:
★★★★ *G. H. Cristallo,* v. Piolet 6, ☎ 948121, 85 rm ℗ ≮ ⼁ ☐ ℘ closed May-Jun and Sep-Nov, 280,000.
★★★★ *Hermitage,* strada Cristallo, ☎ 948998, 32 rm ℗ ≮ ⼁ ℘ ☐ closed 11 May-9 Jul and 11 Sep-9 Nov, 120,000; bkf: 15,000.
★★★ *Breuil,* ☎ 949537, 45 rm ℗ ≮ ℘ closed 16 May-30 Jun and 16 Sep-30 Nov, 72,000; bkf: 7,500.
★★★ *Chalet Valdôtain,* ☎ 948776, 35 rm ℗ ≮ closed May-14 Jun and Oct-Nov, 73,500; bkf: 7,500.
★★★ *Europa,* v. Planet, ☎ 948660, 39 rm ℗ ≮ closed 11 May-30 Jun and Oct-Nov, 73,500; bkf: 6,000.
★★★ *Planet,* p. Planet 1, ☎ 949426, 32 rm ≮ closed 1 May-14 Jun and 16 Sep-31 Oct, 70,000; bkf: 6,000.
★★★ *President,* ☎ 949476, 48 rm ℗ ℗ ≮ 1/2 Pens. closed May-Jun and 11 Sep-31 Oct, 98,500.
★★ *Neiges d'Antan,* at Cret Perrères, ☎ 948775, 24 rm ℗ ≮ ⼁ closed 10 Sep-30 Nov and May-Jun, 50,000. Rest. ◆◆◆ closed Mon. Old converted mountain hut, rustic furnishings, quiet location. Regional cuisine: polenta with cheese, chamois (in season), Donnaz red wine, 36/50,000.

Restaurant:
◆◆ *Sole-da Pavia,* Casa del Sole, ☎ 949010, closed Thu and 10 May-15 Jul and 10 Sep-30 Nov. In view of the Grandes Murailles. Regional and Piedmontese cuisine: agnolotti, chamois with polenta, 30/40,000.

Recommended
Alpine guides: *Hostellerie des Guides,* v. Carrel, ☎ 948169.
Golf: ☎ 949131 (9 holes).
Swimming: at *Residence Cielo Alto,* ☎ 948755 and *Hotel Cristallo,* ☎ 948121.
Young people's activities: courses in summer skiing and slalom skate (skiing on roads) near Lago Blu, ☎ 02/744570.

The CASTLES IN THE VALLEY*

From Pont-Saint-Martin to Fénis *(49 km, 1 day; map 1)*

There are in fact 130 castles, but half a dozen of the most important and best preserved are sufficient to give the Dora Baltea the reputation of being an Italian Loire, albeit of a harsher character. It is not by chance that the most famous chateaux are concentrated along the banks of the river, on heights strategically overlooking the only major route of communication across the region. Nor is it a matter of chance that most of them belonged to the Challants, the eminent family of the counts of Savoy who produced famous warriors and religious and political figures, emulated their princes and introduced into the rough and rambling feudal mansions a taste for the arts and fine clothing of court.

▶ The strategic importance of **Pont-Saint-Martin** in the first basin of the Dora Baltea as a natural gateway to the

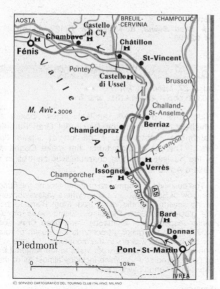

1. Castles in the Valley

Valle d'Aosta is obvious. An elegant 1C **Roman bridge** crosses the river Lys, its one tall and slender arch still perfectly intact. ▶ At **Donnas** it is worth taking the old road to Aosta. After roughly 1.5 km is the most impressive surviving stretch of a **Roman consular road** with an arch and a milestone carved in the rock. ▶ Suddenly at **Bard** appears a narrow passage between menacing cliffs, always thought of as the 'key to the valley'. Its natural strategic position is reinforced by the **Forte di Bard**. On the top of the overhanging cliffs, as early as the 11C Hugo I of Lorraine had erected a castle, which was seized by the Savoy rulers in 1242. A proper fort was built toward the end of the 15C. Napoleon bypassed it during his Second Italian Campaign, but his artillery was forced to pass at night along the narrow local roads and he had it demolished in 1810. The fort as it is today, with its casemates clinging to the cliffs, was reconstructed by Carlo Alberto (1831), who imprisoned Cavour there when he was a young official with liberal ideas. ▶ The **Castle of Verrès**, on a rocky buttress where the Dora joins the Evançon, was built at the turn of the 14C by Ibleto di Challant *(9:30 a.m.-12 noon and 2-4:30 p.m.; winter 9:30-11:30 a.m. and 2-4 p.m.; closed Mon)*. This stern and massive edifice, a cube with 100 ft sides, is the most powerful example of the local type of four-square castle. ▶ By contrast, roughly 1 km beyond the Dora, stands the **Castle of Issogne★**, a classic example of the local type of luxurious princely residence, a mixture of Gothic and Renaissance styles. It is not the external architecture (square with angular towers) which is so important but rather the elegant little courtyard, with an ironwork **pomegranate** over the fountain, the famous frescoed **lunettes** of the arcade and the noble rooms, decorated in fine cosmopolitan style. The building provides a clear reflection of the spirit of its creator, the churchman Giorgio di Challant, a great patron of local crafts in the 15C and 16C, who, *c.* 1480, decided to build a 'dream palace' for his niece Margherita *(9:30 a.m.-12 noon and 2-4:30 p.m.; winter 9:30-11:30 a.m. and 2-4 p.m.; closed Mon)*. ▶ The Challants also left two castles at **Châtillon**. One of them is in the old centre of the village a few hundred yards above the parish church. Particularly worthy of a visit is the nearby **Castle of Ussel** *(5 km N)*, a simple fortress of rectangular design built on a rocky outcrop in 1350 by Ebalo di Challant, an interesting illustra-

tion of the transition from the four-square military castle to the noble residence. ▶ The **Castle of Cly** was built in 1250 and is the third and oldest of the Challant family's castles. The ruins of a square tower and walls stand on a rocky outcrop N of **Chambave**. ▶ On the other hand the **Castle of Fénis★**, roughly 2 km beyond the Dora and the motorway, is the best preserved in the whole Valle d'Aosta *(9:30 a.m.-12 noon and 2-4:30 p.m.; Dec-Feb 9:30-11:30 a.m. and 2-4 p.m.; closed Tue)*. It is the most picturesque of its kind, containing all the features of a medieval castle: double outer walls with redoubts, massive square towers and pointed turrets, spiral staircases, loop holes, portcullises, embrasures and battlements. Inside are wooden furniture, pewter tableware, high-ceilinged kitchens and an armoury with a man trap. Built 1337-40 by Aimone di Challant and subsequently enlarged, it boasts a fine 15C courtyard with unusual semicircular steps which divide to give access to a double loggia with wooden balconies and **frescos** *(c.* 1426), mostly attributed (together with those in the chapel) to the Turin school of Giacomo Jaquerio, a master of the elegant French Gothic style.   □

Practical information ⎯⎯⎯⎯⎯⎯⎯⎯

CHATILLON, ✉ 11024, ☎ 0166.

Hotel:
★★ *Rendez-Vous*, Soleil 3, ☎ 61662, 24 rm Ⓟ ⴟ 44,000; bkf: 4,000.

Restaurants:
◆◆◆ *Parisien*, Panorama 1, ☎ 37053, closed Thu, noon except Sat and hols and Jun. Elegant and French-inspired. International cuisine: risotto allo champagne, chateaubriand with tarragon sauce, 35/60,000.
◆◆ *Terrazza di Pietro e Paola*, Panorama 3, ☎ 2548, closed Jun, Jan and Oct. With fine terrace. Regional and international cuisine: pancakes alla valdostana, agnolotti Savoy-style, 35/40,000.

Recommended
Cheeses: visits to *Cooperativa Latte-Fontina* cheese factory, ☎ 61681 (closed Thu p.m. and Fri a.m., Sun open by request).
Events: at Chambave *(5 km E)*, *Tableau vivant of crèche* on Christmas Eve, grape festival with a parade in traditional costumes in late Sep. Information at Aosta, ☎ 0165/40526.

FENIS, ✉ 11020, ☎ 0165.

⎗ ★★ *Les Chataigniers*, at Pleod, 50 pl, ☎ 764297 (all year).

Recommended
Horseback riding: *Cooperativa Steva*, ☎ 764117.
Sledge runs: at Combasse (5,595 ft), ☎ 768887.

PONT-SAINT-MARTIN, ✉ 11026, ☎ 0125.

Restaurant:
◆◆ *Dora*, v. della Resistenza 120, ☎ 82035, closed Mon and Nov. Regional cuisine: dumplings with gorgonzola or fondue, goat valdostana with polenta, 18/35,000.

VERRES, ✉ 11029, ☎ 0125.
ⓘ v. Caduti per la Libertà 20, ☎ 929550.

Hotel:
★★★ *Evançon*, v. Circonvallazione 9, ☎ 929035, 20 rm Ⓟ ▦ ⴟ closed 10-30 Nov, 56,000; bkf: 5,000.

Restaurant:
● ◆◆◆ *Pierre*, v. Martorey 43, ☎ 920404, closed Tue except Jul-Aug and 1-15 Jun. Privately owned renovated villa and small garden. Regional and Piedmontese cuisine: dumplings alla valdostana, trout with cream, 35/55,000.

Recommended
Events: *historic carnival*.
Swimming: ☎ 920420 (closed mid-Jun-mid-Jul).

CHAMPOLUC

Aosta 63, Milan 175 km
5,145 ft pop. 343 ⊠ 11020 ☎ 0125   C1

Rocks and glaciers abound in the upper valley of the river Evançon, which above Brusson and the Joux Pass is called the Val d'Ayas. The many streams descending from the massif of Mt. Rosa (Breithorn, Gemelli, Lyskamm) sweep down on the valley of Champoluc, a famous and popular ski resort. The Matterhorn, its appearance unmistakable, may be seen from the head of the valley.

▶ The lifts at **Champoluc** are to the E of the town, on the N side of the valley of Cuneaz. ▶ However, lifts can also be found at other nearby centres: **Periasc** (4,931 ft), **Antagnod** (5,574 ft) on the r. side of the valley, which here opens into a particularly wide hollow, and the picturesque village of **Saint-Jacques** (5,541 ft) at the head of the valley. ▶ From here there are various ascents and excursions, for example, to the **Santuario di Barmasc** (5,997 ft) with a fine view of Mt. Rosa. There are also several interesting old houses, including a 16C fortified house from the days of Challant rule. In the parish church there is a fine carved, wooden altar (18C, Valsesia).   ☐

Practical information ─────────────

CHAMPOLUC
⚡ cableway, ski lifts, cross-country skiing, instruction, ice skating.
ⓘ v. Varasco 16, ☎ 307113.

Hotels:
★★★ **Anna Maria,** ☎ 307128, 20 rm Ⓟ ⚲ ⋙ closed 7 Jan-24 Jun and 1 Sep-19 Dec, 73,500; bkf: 5,000.
★★★ **Castor,** v. Ramey 2, ☎ 307133, 32 rm Ⓟ ⋙ ⋙ closed 15 Sep-5 Dec and 27 Apr-28 Jun, 65,000; bkf: 5,000.

Recommended
Alpine guides: ☎ 307194.
Handicrafts: wooden clogs.

Environs
ANTAGNOD, 5 km SW.
⚡ ski lifts, instruction.

CHAMPORCHER

Aosta 60, Milan 156 km
4,675 ft pop. 443 ⊠ 11020 ☎ 0125   B-C2

King Victor Emmanuel II often went hunting in the valley of the Ayasse torrent which is enclosed and wooded in its lower sections. Some parts of Champorcher (Mellier, Rosier, Chardonney, Dondenaz and Château) are still connected by roads that were once the hunting paths of the Savoyard rulers.

▶ The chief town of the region, **Château** (4,681 ft), retains just one tower from the Challant castle destroyed in 1212. ▶ From **Dondenaz** (6,889 ft) there is a climb up to **Miserin** (8,458 ft), one of the most beautiful lakes in the Graian Alps. Every year the people of the valley arrive on its banks in procession from the nearby **Sanctuary of the Madonna** rebuilt on the site of a chapel founded in 1880 by Abbot Chanoux, a famous botanist and a native of Champorcher who was rector of the Little St. Bernard hospice. From the lake the **Finestra di Champorcher** (9,271 ft) can be reached; it is a narrow ravine in the rocks with splendid views.   ☐

Practical information ─────────────

⚡ cableway, ski lifts, cross-country skiing, instruction.
ⓘ at Château, ☎ 37134.

Hotel:
★★ **Beau Séjour,** at Mellier, ☎ 37122, 21 rm Ⓟ ⋙ ⋙ 32,000.

COGNE

Aosta 27, Milan 212 km
5,033 ft pop. 1,490 ⊠ 11012 ☎ 0165   B2

Wide green meadows, ancient mines, ibexes and whistling marmots in the Parco del Gran Paradiso, handmade embroidery, a garden of alpine flowers... The list of attractions that make Cogne one of the busiest and most characteristic centres in the Valle d'Aosta is endless.

▶ The buildings of **Cogne** are grouped around the famous meadow of Saint Orso, in a basin where valleys converge, giving several splendid views from Mont Blanc round to the glaciers of Gran Paradiso. Skiing takes place in winter (especially at **Montzeuc** and **Gran Crot**, above 6,000 ft), but the major attraction is the wealth of routes for climbers and walkers in the mountains. Cogne is the principal point of departure for visits to the **National Park of Gran Paradiso** (→), which includes almost all of the r. side of the Grand'Eyvia Valley.

Environs

▶ The valley of Valnontey is the best known and most spectacular in the Park. At **Valnontey** (5,465 ft) is the **Giardino Alpino Paradisia★** (5,577 ft; *15 Jun-15 Sep 9 a.m.-12 noon and 2-6 p.m.*) with its collection of interesting and rare species of alpine flowers. Easy mule tracks and paths presenting no difficulty lead up to three outstanding viewpoints, which are themselves departure points for various excursions and climbs: the **Rifugio dell'Alpe Money** (7,627 ft), the cabins at **Herbetet** (7,988 ft) and the **Rifugio Vittorio Sella** (8,477 ft) in the vale of Lauson. ▶ Visitors go to **Lillaz** (5,298 ft) to admire the wild mountain scenery of the valleys of Urtier and Valeille, with its glacier and Balma waterfalls. ▶ An unusual excursion is to the ancient **magnetite mines** in the valley of Liconi, near Colonna (7,919 ft), which were exploited for two centuries by the Bishops of Aosta before they were taken over by Cogne in 1672. The iron industry, which was already flourishing here in the 15C, then spread throughout the Valle d'Aosta, which could boast as many as twelve functioning blast-furnaces in the 17C-18C. Even today the local deposits that are being worked provide high-grade ore for the steelworks at Aosta. ▶ At the start of the valley of Cogne, **Aymaville** is dominated by the castle where the last of the Challant family died in 1804. ▶ At Poyaz, a road on the r. climbs up to **Pondel** with a startling 3C **Roman bridge,** which also functioned as an aqueduct.   ☐

Practical information ─────────────

COGNE
⚡ cableway, ski lifts, cross-country skiing, skating.
ⓘ p. E. Chanoux, ☎ 74040.

Hotels:
★★★★ **Bellevue,** v. Grand Paradis 20, ☎ 74825, 45 rm Ⓟ ⋇ ⋙ ⚲ closed 21 Mar-31 Jan except Easter, Jun, Sep and Christmas, 85,000; bkf: 7,000.
★★★ **Grand Paradis,** v. Grappein 26, ☎ 74070, 28 rm ⋙ closed May, Oct and Nov, 64,000; bkf: 6,000.
★★★ **Miramonti,** v. Cavagnet 28, ☎ 74030, 25 rm Ⓟ ⋇ ⋙ ⚲ closed 24 Apr-31 May and 16 Oct-6 Dec, 73,000; bkf: 6,000.
★★★ **Notre Maison,** at Cretaz, ☎ 74104, 12 rm Ⓟ ⋇ ⋙ closed Oct-Nov, 60,000; bkf: 5,000.
★★ **Herbetet,** at Valnontey ☎ 74180, 22 rm Ⓟ ⋇ ⋙ ⋙ closed Oct-Apr, 36,000; bkf: 4,000.

Restaurant:
◆◆ **Lou Ressignon,** v. Bourgeois 91, ☎ 74034, closed

Tue, 15-30 Jun and 15-30 Sep. Regional cuisine: soup Cogne, salt beef and game with polenta, 20/24,000.

ᴧ ★★ *Raggio Verde,* at Epinel, 150 pl, ☎ 74259 (all year).

Recommended
Excursions: by cable car to Montzeuc (6,890 ft, closed May, Oct, Nov), ☎ 74008; to *Giardino Alpino Paradisia,* at Valnontey, ☎ 74147 (admission free); *Gran Paradiso National Park* with guided tours, ☎ 74040 or 74008 *(Società funivie Cogne).*

Environs

LILLAZ, 4 km SE.

Hotel:
★★★ *Arolla,* ☎ 74052, 14 rm ᱻ ぷ closed 8 Jan-4 Feb and 16 Sep-7 Dec, 65,000; bkf: 6,000.

COURMAYEUR*

Aosta 35, Milan 220 km
4,015 ft pop. 2,760 ☒ 11013 ☎ 0165   A1

Four famous natural springs attracted the first vacationers in the second half of the 17C. From that point on the beauty of the mountains began to exert its influence over visitors to the valley and at the beginning of the 19C, when Shelley's letters from Chamonix started a flood of English pilgrims to the alpine regions, the summit of Mont Blanc had already been conquered some thirty years before. Stretched out at the foot of the Alps Courmayeur was fated to become the true home of alpinism. The reputation of its guides equals or even exceeds that of the celebrities who visit, or have visited its inns, in order to climb the cliffs or take cable cars to the refuges and ski-runs. The impressive spectacle of the highest mountain range in Europe, framed by the natural barriers of two mountain ridges at the head of the valley, is quite irresistible.

▶ Courmayeur is modern and constantly growing. In its older section are the **Maluquin tower-house** (12C) and the **parish church** (rebuilt 18C) with Romanesque campanile. In the Casa delle Guide facing the church is the **Museo Alpino Duca degli Abruzzi** *(9:30 a.m.-12:30 p.m. and 3-6:30 p.m.; closed Mon).* It contains exhibits from alpine climbs as well as from expeditions to the Arctic and other parts of the world. ▶ The Courmayeur-Mont Blanc skiing area is the second largest in the Valle d'Aosta.

Environs

▶ **Val Ferret**★ lies at the foot of the Dente del Gigante and the Grandes Jorasses. The road goes around the picturesque village of **Entrèves** (4,284 ft), through **La Palud** (from which there is a cable car to Mont Blanc) and up to **Arnouvaz** (5,803 ft). From here a cart track leads to **Pré de Bar** (6,765 ft), at the head of the valley, from which point a mule track climbs to the **Colle del Gran Ferret** (8,323 ft the Swiss-Italian border) which was once used by travelers crossing into the Valle d'Aosta. ▶ The **Val Veny**★, overlooked by the Aiguille Noire de Peutérey and the imposing face of the Brenva glacier (the lowest on the S side of the Alps), ends only a few hundred yards from the Mont Blanc tunnel. The tiny sanctuary of **Notre Dame de la Guérison** on the site of an ancient cross on the rocks of the moraine is permanently threatened by the movement of the glacier. The scenic route to Mont Blanc climbs to **Purtud** (4,885 ft), **La Visaille** (5,442 ft) and the beautiful natural amphitheatre round **Lake Combal** (6,423 ft; *now being drained).* From here roads dug out of the mountainside and mule tracks lead to L'Alpe Inferiore della Lex Blanche *(18 km)* and then to the Rifugio Elisabetta (7,545 ft) and the Colle della Seigne (8,248 ft), on the French border.   ☐

Practical information

COURMAYEUR
ᴣ Val Veny, Plan Chécrouit and Mont Blanc cableways, cable cars, ski lifts, instruction, cross-country skiing (35 km), skating, summer skiing at the Colle del Gigante, ☎ 842477, skiers carried by helicopter.
ⓘ p. Monte Bianco, ☎ 842060.

Hotels:
★★★★ *Palace Bron,* v. Plan Gorret 42, ☎ 842545, 29 rm Ⓟ ⚿ ᱻ ㎝ closed May-Jun and Oct-Nov, 180,000; bkf: 16,000.
★★★★ *Pavillon,* strada Regionale 60, ☎ 842420, 40 rm Ⓟ ⚿ ☐ closed 1 May-19 Jun and 1 Oct-5 Dec. A few steps from cableway to Plan Chécrouit, 210,000; bkf: 15,000.
★★★★ *Royal,* v. Roma 87, ☎ 843621, 96 rm Ⓟ ㎝ ᱻ ☐ ⟋ (9) closed 16 Apr-27 Jun and 11 Sep-5 Jan, 302,000; bkf: 16,000.
★★★ *Bouton d'Or,* superstrada Traforo Monte Bianco, ☎ 842380, 21 rm Ⓟ ⚿ ㎝ closed May-Jun and Nov-Dec. No restaurant, 70,000; bkf: 7,000.
★★★ *Centrale,* v. Puchoz 7, ☎ 842944, 32 rm Ⓟ ㎝ ᱻ closed Easter-27 Jun and 11 Sep-4 Dec, 73,000; bkf: 8,000.
★★★ *Chetif,* v. Villette 11, ☎ 843503, 20 rm Ⓟ ㎝ ᱻ closed 21 Apr-24 Jun and 1 Oct-30 Nov, 74,000; bkf: 8,000.
★★★ *Crampon,* v. Villette 8, ☎ 842385, 26 rm Ⓟ ⚿ ㎝ ぷ closed May-Jun and 11 Sep-19 Dec. No restaurant, 70,000.
★★★ *Cristallo,* v. Roma 142, ☎ 842015, 27 rm Ⓟ ㎝ closed 21 Apr-24 Jun and 21 Sep-4 Dec, 74,000; bkf: 8,000.
★★★ *Majestic-Parigi,* strada Regionale 38, ☎ 841025, 56 rm Ⓟ ⚿ ㎝ closed Oct-Nov, 74,000; bkf: 8,000.
★★★ *Viale,* v. Monte Bianco 74 ☎ 842227, 23 rm Ⓟ ㎝ 74,000; bkf: 10,000.

Restaurants:
♦♦ *Pierre Alexis 1877,* v. Marconi 54, ☎ 843517, closed Mon and 15 Oct-30 Nov. Regional cuisine: leg of pork with sauerkraut, salt beef with polenta, 25/35,000.
♦♦ *Vieux Pommier,* p. Monte Bianco 25, ☎ 842281, closed Mon and Oct. Regional cuisine: crêpes Mont Blanc, polenta with cheese, 25/35,000.

Recommended
Alpine guides: p. A. Henry, ☎ 842064 (group excursions along paths at foot of Mont Blanc, in summer).
Discothèque: *L'Abajour,* v. Regionale, ☎ 842990.
Events: *torchlight procession and firework displays,* New Year's Eve.
Excursions: to Chamonix, France *(23 km NW)* through the Mont Blanc tunnel (11.6 km, toll).
Golf: at Plan-Piucieux *(6 km N),* ☎ 89103 (9 holes).
Horseback riding: ☎ 89276.
Swimming: at Courba Dzeleuna (6,825 ft) and Plan Chécrouit (5,600 ft).

Environs

ENTRÈVES, 3 km N.

Hotels:
★★★ *Brenva,* ☎ 89285, 14 rm Ⓟ 72,000.
★★★ *Grange,* strada La Brenva, ☎ 89274, 23 rm Ⓟ ⚿ ㎝ closed May-Jun and Oct-Nov. 14C, rebuilt in mountain style, 70,000; bkf: 7,000.
★★★ *Pilier d'Angle,* ☎ 89129, 20 rm Ⓟ ㎝ 73,500; bkf: 9,000.
★★ *Astoria,* at La Palud, ☎ 89910, 35 rm Ⓟ ⚿ closed May-Jun and Oct-Nov, 50,000; bkf: 5,000.

Restaurant:
♦♦ *Maison de Filippo,* ☎ 89968, closed Tue. Typical mountain hut with local antiques. Regional cuisine: polenta pasticciata, mutton in civet, 30/35,000.
ᴧ ★★ *Tronchey,* at Tronchey (Val Ferret), 170 pl, ☎ 89251.

VAL VENY, 12 km NW.

Hotels:
★★ *Purtud,* at Purtud *(6 km from Courmayeur),* ☎ 89960, 32 rm Ⓟ ⚿ ㎝ closed 11 Sep-24 Jun, 50,000; bkf: 6,000.

★★ **Val Veny,** at Plan Ponquet *(4 km from Courmayeur),* ☎ 89904, 20 rm P ⓦ closed Sep-Jun, 55,000; bkf: 6,000.

⚠ ★★ *Monte Bianco-La Sorgente,* at Peuterey, 150 pl, ☎ 89372.

Park of GRAN PARADISO

A-B2

Ibexes, which were threatened with extinction in the last century, owe their survival to Victor Emmanuel II, a king who loved hunting. He set up reserves (given to the nation in 1918) in order to protect alpine fauna and flora and especially the ibex which has become one of the main attractions of the Gran Paradiso National Park. Practically unspoiled by man, the park is home to a whole variety of animals, plants and flowers.

▶ The Gran Paradiso extends over the entire massif within the area bounded by the Dora Baltea and the River Orco in Piedmont, comprising about 180,000 acres on the map (or 500,000 on the ground) with a perimeter of 112 miles. In the Valle d'Aosta it includes the r. side of the Rhêmes valley (→ Rhêmes-Notre-Dame) and the Valsavarenche (→) with the plain of Nivolet and the W side of Gran Paradiso, the l. side of the valley of Cogne (→), with the valleys of Bardoney, Valeille and Valnontey and the E side of the Grivola. ▶ From April to October, at 3,000 to 10,000 ft, it is easy to catch sight of the **ibexes** (numbering around 3,000), the **chamois** (about 5,000) and the **marmots.** There are also alpine hares, wolves, badgers, martens, weasels, ermine, squirrels, bats, moles, shrews and about eighty species of birds (including the golden eagle, the ptarmigan, the quail and the raven). ▶ The **flora** is equally rich with many rare alpine plants, prize specimens of the most interesting of which are cultivated in the **Giardino Alpino Paradisia,** near Cogne (→).   □

Bells and the Gran Paradiso

The chimes of bells can be traced back to man's remotest times and until recently their sound was part of everyday life — telling him when to start work, when to eat in the middle of the day, and when to come home from the fields in the evening. The city church bells rang out in joyful peals for the happy occasions of birth and marriage, as well as sounding the tocsin. Now the bells are silent. Even living beside a campanile, bells are rarely heard because they have been replaced by other noises. Fortunately, this is not true everywhere. On the mountains and in the high valleys around Aosta, there are still plenty of bells, the clinking coming from those around the necks of the animals. The tinkles are not all the same, because the bells are in different sizes, shapes and metals. There are bronze bells for cows and mountain goats, and smaller ones, clochettes, for sheep, but they all blend together to give sweet sounds.

GREAT ST. BERNARD PASS

Aosta 36, Milan 218 km
8,115 ft ⊠ 11010 ☎ 0165   A-B1

The harsh winds of the pass, mist, blizzards, frost and snow twelve months of the year are enough to discourage even the most intrepid traveler. However, in antiquity no alpine pass was more heavily used than this one. Crossing the Monte di Giove, as it was known then, the Roman legions went from Rome to Geneva in as little as eight days. Today the motorway tunnel provides an even better service while, some distance away, the pass (8,113 ft) has retained the same scenery that was honoured by the presence of sovereigns and warriors such as Charlemagne, Henri IV, the Savoyards and Napoleon.

▶ Further along and slightly over the Swiss-Italian border is the **Ospizio,** which, according to tradition, was founded by Bernard, Archdeacon of Aosta, in 1050. The modern building, reconstructed in 1837, also contains a Baroque church (1686), a small museum, a library and a weather observatory. However, the hostel is most famous as the place where the Saint Bernard dogs were originally bred and trained to rescue travelers lost in the storms. ▶ From **Cerisey** (4,396 ft) the motorway climbs into the **tunnel of Gran San Bernardo** *(toll; open all year),* which is 5.8 km long and whose Swiss end is near Bourg-St.-Bernard (6,292 ft).   □

Practical information _____

⚡ ski lifts at Flassin Valley, cross-country skiing (at Saint-Oyen and Saint-Rhémy), instruction at Etroubles.

Hotel:
★★ *Italia,* ☎ 780908, 16 rm P ⚡ ⚠ closed 1 Oct-9 Jun, 49,000.

Recommended
Events: *Comba Freida,* a historic carnival, takes place in the valley.

The valley of GRESSONEY

C1-2

The River Lys, which flows from the glacier of the same name, rushes impetuously between steep banks to the bottom of the valley. The road climbs gently, crossing belts of vegetation ranging from vineyards to chestnut groves, and from conifers to meadows. The landscape changes appreciably, becoming more and more irregular, and when the massif of Mt. Rosa appears in the background, it becomes truly magnificent. The cultural aspects of the area are just as complex, if not more so. As is the case at the heads of all the valleys around Mt. Rosa, there still survives an original ethnic group, which has preserved its ancient language (a German dialect) and customs. In the lower part of the valley, however, they still speak the dialect of the Valle d'Aosta, which explains why 'the most beautiful mountain in the world' is named after its glaciers (from *roise, roese* or *rosa,* glacier) and not its romantic hue at dawn.

▶ From **Pont-Saint-Martin** (→ the Castles in the Valley) the road climbs into the valley of the Lys. ▶ **Issime,** in a depression between the meadows and the woods, has a 16C parish church with a 17C gilded wooden altar. ▶ Another tourist attraction is **Gaby,** in a steep-sided hollow at the mouth of the falls of Niel, whose four-tiered cascades are worth visiting. ▶ The road enters a long straight-sided valley with the Lyskamm glacier in the background. Here are numerous old houses with the ground floor in stone and the upper part in wood in the manner of the Walser immigrants from Germany. They are known as 'rascards'. ▶ At **Valdobbia,** deep in the forest, the castle was built by Queen Margherita in 1894 as a summer residence. ▶ **Gressoney-Saint-Jean** (4,543 ft) was probably founded in the 13C, when Bishop Sion encouraged the immigration of Walser shepherds to guarantee his control of the area against the Challant family. The 18C parish church is of interest, with a portico dating from 1630, but the area is best known as an

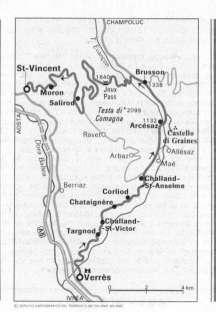

2. Joux Pass

© SERVIZIO CARTOGRAFICO DEL TOURING CLUB ITALIANO, MILANO

Napoleon in the Alps

On 23 May 1800, Napoleon was leading his army over the Great St. Bernard Pass on his way to Italy and the village of Marengo where he was to win a great victory over the Austrians. Accompanied by high-ranking officers with maps, he was on reconnaissance in the Forest of Joux above St. Vincent and some distance away from his escort of guards when he found himself surrounded by a detachment of 40 Austrian soldiers, commanded by Lieutenant Le Breux from Brussels. Staggered by the importance of his prisoner, the lieutenant stood talking to Napoleon, allowing him to question him and gain time until the French forces arrived and silently surrounded the Austrian troops. Seeing this Napoleon remarked: 'Well, Sir, I was your prisoner, now you are mine. But please do not worry. I will take good care of you and your men.' And Napoleon kept his word, for five days later Le Breux was seen in Lausanne, Switzerland, a free man. This gave rise to rumours that the lieutenant had traitorously released the general when he was his prisoner, instead of handing him over to the Austrians.

elegant and attractive centre for tourism both in winter and summer. ▶ Even more important in this respect is **Gressoney-la-Trinité** (5,364 ft), the starting point for climbs and excursions in the Mt. Rosa group. ▶ From **Orsia** (5,688 ft) it is possible go by cable car to the Alpe Gabiet (7,732 ft), and then by chair lift and by foot over the Col d'Olen (9,452 ft) to the **Rifugio Città di Vigevano** (9,396 ft). The view★ on the Valsesia side of Mt. Rosa is spectacular. There are also chair lifts leading to **Punta Jolanda** (7,372 ft) and the **Colle della Bettaforca** (8,766 ft), another magnificent viewpoint★. □

Practical information

GABY, ⊠ 11020, ☎ 0125.

Hotel:
★★ *Mologna,* v. Provinciale 108, ☎ 345939, 47 rm [P] ⌂
⌘ closed 11 Sep-6 Dec, 44,000; bkf: 4,500.

Recommended
Clay pigeon shooting: ☎ 345998.
Events: *Folk festival (with polenta)* on first Sun in Aug.

GRESSONEY-LA-TRINITÉ, ⊠ 11020, ☎ 0125.
ϟ cable cars, ski lifts, cross-country skiing, instruction, skating.
ⓘ p. Tachen, ☎ 366143.

Hotels:
★★★★ *Busca-Thedy,* ☎ 366136, 34 rm [P] ⌂ ⌂ & ⌂
closed 16 Apr-31 May and 16 Sep-30 Nov, 80,000;
bkf: 5,000.
★★★ *Residence,* at Elselboden, ☎ 366148, 35 rm [P] ⌂
closed May-Jun and Oct-Nov, 74,000.

▲ ★ *Stafal,* 187 pl, ☎ 366283 (all year).

Recommended
Alpine guides: ☎ 366143.

GRESSONEY-SAINT-JEAN, ⊠ 11020, ☎ 0125.
ϟ ski lifts, cross-country skiing, instruction, skating.
ⓘ municipio, ☎ 355185.

JOUX PASS

From Verrès to Saint-Vincent *(38 km, 1 day; map 2)*

In its names, its many castles and towers, the lower valley of the Evançon records the rule of the Challants, whose birthplace it was. The triangle bounded by the ancient 'wine road', the road climbing the so-called 'hill of Saint-Vincent' as far as Brusson and the l. bank of the Dora, is rich in ancient evidence of the labour and skill of the valley's inhabitants. For example, the great canal, which took forty years to dig at the beginning of the 15C, is still in operation, carrying the waters of the glaciers of Mt. Rosa to the hillsides.

▶ From **Verrès** (→ the Castles in the Valley) the road climbs through a dark passage to the basin across which the villages of **Challand-St.-Victor** and **Challand-St-Anselme** are scattered. ▶ Above **Arcesaz** a r. fork climbs to the ruins of the **Castello di Graines**, built in the 12C, which for centuries the administrative centre of the estate of the upper valley. ▶ Near the villages there are many mine-shafts, spoil heaps, rough ore-crushers for **gold** dug out of the rock and foundries from different periods, which show the importance of mining activities in the area until the beginning of this century. ▶ At **Brusson** (2,122 ft), a tourist centre, the route descends into the valley across the **Joux Pass** (5,380 ft), an ancient site for offerings to Jove, its broad saddle carpeted with pines, and arrives in **Saint-Vincent** (→). □

Practical information

BRUSSON, ⊠ 11022, ☎ 0125.
ϟ ski lifts, 70-km cross-country skiing, instruction, skating.
ⓘ p. del Municipio 1, ☎ 300240.

Hotels:
★★ *Italia,* at Pasquier, ☎ 300114, 59 rm [P] ⌂ ⌂ closed
Sep-Jun, 58,000; bkf: 6,000.
★★ *Moderno,* v. Tre Villaggi 20, ☎ 300118, 26 rm [P] ⌂
⌘ closed 26 Apr-31 May and 23 Sep-31 Oct, 55,000;
bkf: 4,000.
★ *Laghetto,* at Toule, ☎ 300179, 17 rm [P] ⌘ closed Nov,
40,000; bkf: 5,000.

⚴ ★★ *Monte Rosa*, at Extrepieraz, 250 pl, ☎ 300282 (all year).

CHALLAND-SAINT-ANSELME, ⊠ 11020, ☎ 0125.

Hotel:
★★ *Torretta*, at Maé, ☎ 965218, 24 rm Ⓟ ♨ ও ⌘ closed Oct-Nov, 50,000; bkf: 4,500.

COLLE DI JOUX, ⊠ 11022, ☎ 0125.
ϟ ski lifts, instruction.
ⓘ at Saint-Vincent, ☎ 0166/2239.

Restaurant:
♦♦ *Stella Alpina*, ☎ 3527, closed Wed, 1-23 Dec, Oct-Mar closed Mon, Tue and Thu.   Regional cuisine: polenta pasticciata, game in civet, 25/45,000.

LA THUILE

Aosta 39, Milan 227 km
4,730 ft pop. 731 ⊠ 11016 ☎ 0165   A1

Today La Thuile is a well-known and well-equipped winter tourist centre, but in the past it was notorious for less happy reasons. Strategically placed below the ancient Little Saint Bernard Pass, it often had to serve as a bastion against attempted invasions.

▶ La Thuile is crowded in all seasons.   For skiers there are the most up-to-date facilities and mile after mile of slopes.

Environs

▶ The visitor must not miss the spectacular **Cascate del Rutor★**; also of interest are the plateau of **Les Suches** (7,152 ft), the crossing of the **Colle San Carlo** (6,466 ft) and the **Tête d'Arpy** (6,633 ft) with very good views★. ▶ At the **Little Saint Bernard Pass** (7,178 ft, *13.2 km*) the road cuts across the so-called 'ring of Hannibal', a cromlech consisting of forty-six standing stones, dating from the Bronze Age or earlier, wrongly associated with the passage of the Carthaginian general.   Behind the French customs house, a Roman column dedicated to Jove is topped by a wooden statue of Saint Bernard.   □

Practical information ⎯⎯⎯⎯⎯⎯

ϟ cableway, ski lifts, cross-country skiing, instruction, skating, summer skiing at Rutor glacier with helicopter service.
ⓘ municipio, ☎ 884179.

Hotels:
★★★★ *Planibel*, at Entrèves, ☎ 884541, 294 rm Ⓟ ▣ ⌁ closed Dec-Apr, 150,000.
★★★ *Kristal*, v. Collomb 54, ☎ 884117, 25 rm Ⓟ ♨ ⌘ closed May-Jun and Oct-Nov, 65,000; bkf: 7,000.

⚴ ★★ *Rutor*, at La Sapiniera, v. Villaret 32, 70 pl, ☎ 884165 (all year).

Recommended
Alpine guides: ☎ 884123 or 884193.

MONT BLANC

15,780 ft   A1

De Saussure, the great Swiss naturalist who realized his dream of exploring the highest ice-covered peak and camping on the Colle del Gigante (in the summer of 1787) would never have believed that one day crowds of tourists would contemplate the same place from the comfort of a viewing platform.   Criss-crossed by long steel cables, Mont Blanc is like a giant Gulliver carved out of rock and ice, tolerating with an air of benign resignation the endless comings and goings of the inquisitive Lilliputians.   This does not, however, diminish its stature, for whoever makes the crossing,

albeit insulated inside a cable car, realizes that it is quite impossible to look at this colossus from top to bottom without a feeling of awe.

▶ The **cableway crossing** of Mont Blanc★★ normally lasts 1.5 hr. From **La Palud**, 3.5 km from Courmayeur (→), the cable car rises to the pavilion of **Mt. Fréty** (7,132 ft), then to the old **Rifugio Torino** (10,898 ft) near the Colle del Gigante (11,003 ft), and finally to the viewing platform at the **Punta Helbronner** (11,358 ft; *national frontier, passport control and checkpoint*). This was named after the geologist who explored and surveyed the summits of Mont Blanc and the W Alps at the end of the 19C and the beginning of the 20C. Whether from the shelter or from the terrace, the view★★ is extraordinary. It is possible to see for miles, with a view including the highest peaks in the Alps and in Europe. But the real fascination of the crossing is in the next section. From the Punta Helbronner, the **cableway of the glaciers**, anchored with reinforced pylons to the rock buttresses, touches the **Gros Rognon** (11,312 ft) and after a crossing of more than half a mile above the **Glacier du Géant** and the **Vallée Blanche** it arrives just below the **Aiguille du Midi** (12,604 ft), on the French side. A gallery leads from here to the terminal station of the **Chamonix-Mont-Blanc** cableway. There is an elevator up to the terrace on the Aiguille du Midi, the highest point in the elevator system.   This is another breathtaking view★★.   □

Ascent of Mont Blanc

Mont Blanc at 15,782 ft is the highest mountain in the entire chain of the Alps and in Europe, with the exception of certain peaks in the Caucasus.   Its old name, Les Glacières, had its origin in the distinguishing feature of the mountain, the immense glaciers which are found on all sides of it.   The first ascent of Mont Blanc was made on 8 August 1786 by two Chamonix men, Dr. Michel Paccard and Jacques Balmat, a mountain guide, to win an award offered by the Genevese naturalist H. B. de Saussure.   In the following year J. Balmat and two other local men again made the ascent while Saussure himself climbed the mountain on 3 August 1787.   These ascents were all made from Chamonix although in the course of time ascents have been made from every side.   The view from the summit of the mountain is very extensive, Lyons being visible.   Marie Paradis was the first woman to reach the summit on 14 July 1808.   The first ascent ever effected in winter was made by a woman.   She was Miss Isabella Stratton, an Englishwoman who climbed the mountain in January 1876.

MORGEX

Aosta 26, Milan 210 km
Pop. 1,703 ⊠ 11017 ☎ 0165   A1

Morgex is the centre of the Valdigne, in the upper valley of the Dora Baltea, a resort popular with gourmets for its splendid sausage (called a *boudin*) and above all for its wine 'Blanc de Morgex'. It contains a **parish church** rebuilt in the 17C with Romanesque campanile and restored 14C-15C wall paintings inside.

Environs

▶ There is an attractive route to **La Thuile** *(17.5 km)* via **Tête d'Arpy** (6,633 ft) and the **Colle San Carlo** (6,466 ft). The road continues through magnificent woods and offers an exceptional view★ of Mont

Blanc. At the **Campo del Principe Tommaso** (5,875 ft) are trenches where the Piedmontese resisted the incursions of the French (1792-6). □

Practical information _____

Ⅰ v. Valdigne 82, ☎ 809912.

Hotel:
★★ *Grivola,* v. del Monte Bianco 132, ☎ 809550, 22 rm P ⓦ closed Nov, 46,000; bkf: 5,000.

A ★ *Arc en Ciel,* at Feisoulles, 104 pl, ☎ 809257 (all year).

Recommended
Wines: vintage local wines and *Blanc de Morgex wine festival* in Aug (every two years, alternating with La Salle).

PRE-SAINT-DIDIER

Aosta 30, Milan 217 km
Pop. 890 ⊠ 11010 ☎ 0165   A1

The ancient Romans prized the medicinal powers of the waters from the nearby springs and at one time the baths of this tranquil holiday resort were extremely popular. In the square, with its fine view of the Mont Blanc range, stands the **parish church** which is interesting for its 11C campanile and three carved and gilded wooden **Baroque altars**. Near the **baths,** which were built in 1830 and rebuilt after being damaged in the war *(restoration in progress),* are an impressive gorge and the falls of the Dora di Verney, where the river flows down through its high, vertical banks. □

Practical information _____

Hotels:
★★★ *Etoile des Neiges,* at Verrand, ☎ 842368, 25 rm P ⓦ ⧉ closed 27 Apr-9 Jul and 11 Sep-4 Dec. No restaurant, 73,500.
★★ *Beau Séjour,* at Pallusieux, ☎ 87961, 33 rm P ⧖ ⓦ closed May and Oct-Nov, 50,000; bkf: 5,500.
★★ *Edelweiss,* strada del Monte Bianco 1, ☎ 87841, 38 rm P ⓦ closed 1 Oct-15 Dec, 47,000; bkf: 4,000.

Recommended
Children's facilities: *Le Marmotte* kindergarten, ☎ 87820.
Swimming: ☎ 87827 (closed end May-end Jun).

RHEMES-NOTRE-DAME

Aosta 30, Milan 216 km
5,660 ft pop. 89 ⊠ 11010 ☎ 0165   A2

Rhêmes-Notre-Dame is a romantic hamlet among meadows and woods in the upper valley of Rhêmes, which marks the NW boundary of the Parco del Gran Paradiso. Overhung in its lower sections, the valley opens up above the village, where the forest thins out and gives way to alpine meadows and then to great rock falls, moraines, glaciers and high peaks.

▶ In the region of Breuil (5,659 ft) the **Renzo Videsott Information Centre** *(open in summer or on request)* houses interesting records concerning wildlife in the parks. ▶ Excursions to the Parco del Gran Paradiso are available, especially from the **Rifugio Benevolo** (7,496 ft). □

Practical information _____

ϟ ski lifts, cross-country skiing.
Ⅰ municipio, ☎ 96114.

Hotel:
★★ *Granta Parey,* at Chanavey, ☎ 96104, 26 rm P ⧖ ⓦ closed May and Oct-Nov, 44,000; bkf: 5,000. Rest. ◆◆ Rural setting on edge of Parco del Gran Paradiso. Regional cuisine: salt beef with polenta, chamois in civet, 20/30,000.

A ★★ *Val di Rhêmes,* at Rhêmes-Saint-Georges *(10 km N),* 139 pl, ☎ 95648.

SAINT-VINCENT

Aosta 27, Milan 159 km
Pop. 4,678 ⊠ 11027 ☎ 0166   C1

The two major attractions — the Casino and the Fonti Curative Mineral Springs — lie at opposite ends of the town, in a symbolic separation of pleasure-seekers from those seeking relief from pain. Around the bustling, elegant and fashionable centre, the town is expanding. As early as the 19C it had one of the largest populations in the valley; today it is merging into a single conurbation together with neighbouring Châtillon.

▶ The **Casino de la Vallée** on the W edge of the town is not solely used for gambling. Along with the neighbouring conference centre, this famous building forms a complex in which international exhibitions and other activities are held. ▶ Between May and September people visit the **Nuove Terme,** which is served by a funicular railway at the E end of the town, to drink the waters of the *Fonti,* used since the 18C as a remedy for digestive, liver or metabolic complaints. ▶ Excursions to the **Castello di Issogne★** and **Castello di Fenis★** (→ the Castles in the Valley), the **Joux Pass** (→) and **Breuil-Cervinia★** (→) are available from here. □

Practical information _____

♨ (May-Oct), ☎ 2694.
Ⅰ v. Roma 50, ☎ 2239.

Hotels:
★★★★★ *G. H. Billia,* v. Piemonte 18, ☎ 3446, 250 rm P ⓦ ⧖ ⧉ ⌁ 250,000; bkf: 14,000.
★★★ *Elena,* v. Biavaz 2, ☎ 2140, 48 rm P ⧖ ⌇ closed Nov. No restaurant, 73,500.
★★★ *Posta,* p. XXVIII Aprile 1, ☎ 2250, 39 rm ⓦ ⌇ 62,000; bkf: 6,000.
★ *Du Soleil,* v. Marconi 20, ☎ 2685, 20 rm P ⌇ No restaurant, 40,500.

Restaurants:
● ◆◆◆ *Batezar-da Renato,* v. Marconi 1, ☎ 3164, closed Wed, Thu noon and Jul. Elegant atmosphere, refined cooking. Creative cuisine: filet of trout with lettuce and basil, leg of lamb, 50/70,000.
◆◆◆ *Grenier,* p. Zerbion 1, ☎ 2224, closed Mon noon, Tue, 15-30 Jan and 15-30 Jul. Rural setting. Regional and French cuisine: pancakes valdostane, duck en croûte, 35/70,000.
◆◆ *Tre Porcellini,* v. Roma 30, ☎ 3407, closed Thu and Nov. Regional and international cuisine: salmon pancakes, game, 30/40,000.

A ★★ *Glereyaz,* at Glereyaz, 40 pl, ☎ 3669 (all year).

Recommended
Casino: *de la Vallée,* ☎ 2011.
Events: *S. Vincent Press Award* and *Grolle d'Oro Film Award* take place in the casino at a *Gala Evening* with fashion shows, concerts and ballet performances, ☎ 2011; *exhibition* of local handicrafts (Jul).
Swimming: v. Trento 7, ☎ 3690.

Send us your comments and suggestions; we will use them in the next edition.

VALPELLINE

Aosta 12, Milan 196 km
Pop. 543 ⊠ 11010 ☎ 0165   B1

The village, close to Aosta, lies at the entrance to two quiet and not as yet very frequented valleys. The area is one of woods, torrents and mountain houses against a background of rocky heights.

▶ **Valpelline** is a farming village set amid meadows and orchards whose old houses have long wooden balconies, like the 12C house known as **La Tour** near the centre. ▶ Higher up, the Valpelline Valley divides, one arm becoming the valley of **Ollomont**, a starting point for ascents of Mt. Velan (12,165 ft), Mt. Avril (10,980 ft) and Mt. Gele (11,542 ft). The road ends at **Glacier** (5,082 ft), but a mule track leads to the beautiful pastures of the **Conca di By** (6,719 ft; *fine views*). ▶ From Valpelline via **Oyace** and **Bionaz** is the artificial **lake of Place Moulin**, which is contained by one of the largest dams in Europe (479 ft). Beyond the lake is **Prarayer**, reached only by cart track and mule track, as the waters of the lake flooded the road. The old village (inhabited all year round until the 19C) is an important base for climbers.   □

VALSAVARENCHE

Aosta 27, Milan 214 km
5,056 ft pop. 204 ⊠ 11010 ☎ 0165   B2

Valsavarenche is the centre of the valley of the same name below Grivola and the Gran Paradiso. Today the 186 miles of mule tracks laid out by Victor Emmanuel II are very useful to visitors to the park, providing a gradual climb to the glorious vantage points on the higher summits.

▶ **Valsavarenche** is situated where the ravines and steep slopes of the valley open out into a hollow formed by an ancient landslide, and is near two more villages, **Eau Rousse**, near a cliff speckled with red, and **Pont**, a village of shepherds' huts. All three are starting points for excursions into the Parco del Gran Paradiso (→), which includes the valley. From the **Rifugio Vittorio Emanuele II** (8,963 ft), built in 1932 with a corrugated-iron roof, it is possible to climb the Gran Paradiso. ▶ The **Colle del Nivolet** (8,569 ft) is one of the most interesting high plateaus in the Alps, with plentiful water and herds of ibexes.   □

Practical information _____

VALSAVARENCHE
⚡ ski lifts, cross-country skiing.
ⓘ municipio, ☎ 95703.

Recommended
Alpine guides: ☎ 95774.

Environs
PONT, 8 km S.
Hotel:
★★★ *Genzianella*, ☎ 95709, 27 rm Ⓟ ⚡ ♨ ∰ closed 16 Sep-14 Jun, 55,000; breakfast: 6,000.

⚠ ★★ *Pont Breuil*, 157 pl, ☎ 95728.

VALTOURNENCHE

Aosta 42, Milan 178 km
5,013 ft pop. 2,116 ⊠ 11021 ☎ 0166   B-C1

Valtournenche is the main village of the valley of the same name at the foot of the Matterhorn. It is a popular resort, with a glorious past linked with the history of mountaineering.

▶ Local guides and mountaineers who performed heroic mountaineering feats or died in accidents in the mountains are commemorated on numerous memorial stones in the village's main square.

Environs
▶ **Gouffre des Busserailles** (5,666 ft) is an awesome and spectacular chasm 341 ft long and 115 ft deep, into which the River Marmore pours down in a 33 ft drop. ▶ From **Losanche** (5,380 ft), cable cars run to **Madonna de la Salette** (7,218 ft; *ski slopes*), where a ski lift goes to the lower **Col of the Cime Bianche** (8,966 ft).   □

Practical information _____
⚡ cableway, ski lifts, cross-country skiing, instruction, skating.
ⓘ p. Municipio 1, ☎ 92029.

Hotels:
★★ *Alpi*, at Paquier, ☎ 92230, 26 rm Ⓟ closed 20 Sep-30 Nov, 50,000; bkf: 6,000.
★★ *Caminetto*, at Paquier, ☎ 92150, 15 rm Ⓟ ♨ 45,000.
★★ *Meridiana*, at Paquier, ☎ 92218, 11 rm Ⓟ No restaurant, 50,000; bkf: 5,000.

The VALTOURNENCHE LOWLAND

                                            B-C2

To some extent this whole valley lives in the shadow of the Matterhorn. The small villages in its lower section have preserved an individuality, however, and thus are good bases from which to take advantage of the local tourist attractions.

▶ **Antey-Saint-André** is mainly a summer resort. The lower section of the campanile of the old **parish church** was formerly part of a tower of the **castle** of the lords of Cly. There are skiing facilities at **La Magdaleine** (5,393 ft; *6 km*) and at **Torgnon** (4,885 ft), where interesting wood carvings (16C-18C) can be seen in a small **museum**. Wood carving is still practiced in the winter months. A fine view★ of the Matterhorn is possible from the chapel of **S. Pantaleone** (5,397 ft). ▶ A little above Antey-Saint-André is a muletrack or cableway (from Buisson) up to **Chamois** (5,954 ft), a small rural village with skiing facilities.   □

Practical information _____

ANTEY-SAINT-ANDRÉ, ⊠ 11020, ☎ 0166.
ⓘ Grand Moulin, ☎ 48266.

Hotels:
★★ *Des Roses*, at Poutaz, ☎ 48248, 23 rm Ⓟ ∰ closed 11 May-24 Jun and 21 Sep-30 Nov, 42,000; bkf: 4,500.
★★ *Filey*, at Filey, ☎ 48212, 55 rm Ⓟ ∰ ♨ closed 20 Sep-2 Dec, 57,500; bkf: 4,500.

⚠ ★★ *Cervino*, at Buisson, 500 pl, ☎ 48421 (all year).

CHAMOIS, ⊠ 11020, ☎ 0166.
⚡ cableway, ski lifts, instruction.
ⓘ at Antey-Saint-André, ☎ 48266.

TORGNON, ⊠ 11020, ☎ 0166.
⚡ ski lifts, cross-country skiing, instruction.
ⓘ at Antey-Saint-André, ☎ 48266.

Hotel:
★★ *Panoramique*, at Mongnod, ☎ 40216, 35 rm Ⓟ Ⓟ ⚡ ∰ closed May-Jun and Oct-Nov, 58,000; bkf: 4,500.

Venetia

▶ The first impression in Venetia is of the link with Venice, for the region was ruled by the Venetian Republic from 1420 to 1797 and these centuries have left their mark. Building façades recall those on the Grand Canal. Everywhere the winged lion of St. Mark, symbol of Venice, appears with the book and words of the evangelist. Nevertheless, each city or town has an individual character, and, often, traces of what preceded Venice, whether Rome, the city republics of the Po Valley, feudal Goths, or even hints of a more ancient past, back to the Celts or the Veneti. In the 16C the nobility of Venice and the mainland aristocracy revelled in the life of the landed gentry. Over a period of 300 years they built country houses in a style that owed most to the Neoclassicism of the architect Andrea Palladio. Instead of the stone of classical architecture, the builders of the Venetian villas used brick, plaster and stucco. In a sense, the villa of Venetia was an illusion met with another illusion. The first was set up by the owner-patrons, who wished to dignify their new-found titles and wealth with hints of ancient lineage. The second illusion was the creation of the architects, builders and artisans. The handsome architecture of the finest Venetian villas is embellished with frescoed scenes of peasants frolicking in idealized landscapes (such as those of Giandomenico Tiepolo at the Villa Valmarana) or incredibly lifelike trompe l'oeil figures gazing down from the painted balconies or through doorways (Paolo Veronese at the Villa di Maser). Yet these beautiful country houses, nestled in a gentle countryside that is seen, practically unchanged, in the backgrounds of paintings from the Renaissance to the 18C, were both elegant residences and working farmhouses. In the Palladian plan, the farm outbuildings are very often integrated into the overall design of the main house. Palladio based this eminently practical plan, with only minor modifications, on the villas of the Romans. The mountains that close off the plain of Venetia to the N were, on one hand, obstacles to the free flow of trade from Venice to a Europe eager to buy. On the other, they were also the source of timber for the busy Venetian shipyards. Venice is no longer Europe's main port for trade from the east, and her shipyards no longer can — or need to — build and equip an entire warship in a sin gle day. Still, the landscapes that bask in the eternal sun of Tiepolo and the mountains that Titian painted in the backgrounds of his masterpieces are recognizable today in the golden light that softens the contours of Venetia. ☐

● Don't miss

Padua (Padova)★★ offers the Cappella degli Scrovegni★★ with Giotto's frescos, the Gattamelata monument★★ by Donatello, the basilica of S. Antonio (il Santo)★★ with Donatello's bronzes★★. In Treviso, the piazza dei Signori★ with the Palazzo dei Trecento★, the Duomo★★, S. Nicolò★★ and frescos by Tommaso da Modena★ in the chapterhouse of the Seminario. Verona★★ has the Arena★★, the piazza delle Erbe, the piazza dei Signori★ and the Scaliger tombs★, S. Anastasia★ with Pisanello's fresco of St. George and the Dragon★, the Castelvecchio★★ with the Civico Museo d'Arte★ and the Scaliger bridge★, S. Zeno Maggiore★★. In Vicenza★★, the piazza dei Signori★★ with Palladio's buildings, the Loggia del Capitanio★ and the basilica★★, the Duomo★★, the Palazzo Chiericati★ with the Museo Civico★, the Teatro Olimpico★★, the basilica of Monte Bérico with Veronese's Feast of St. Gregory the Great★★, the Villa Valmarana★ with frescos★★ by the Tiepolos, father and son, Palladio's Rotonda★★. The lesser centres include Arquà Petrarca, with the poet's house★, Asolo, Bassano del Grappa★, with the covered bridge★, Castelfranco Veneto, with Giorgione's pala★, Este★ and the Museo Atestino★, Feltre, Maróstica, Montagnana★, Thiene, Vittorio Veneto★ and the abbey of Praglia★★ and the Visconti bridge★ at Valeggio on the Mincio. The Euganean hills, the shore of Lake Garda, with Peschiera, Garda, the Punta S. Vigilio★ and Malcesine. In the Dolomites are Cortina d'Ampezzo★★ and Lake di Misurina★★. Besides the Villa Rotonda mentioned above there are the splendid Palladian villas, Villa di Maser★, with Veronese's frescos★★, the Villa Godi★ at Lugo di Vicenza, the Villa Emo at Fanzolo di Vedelago and the Villa Badoer at Fratta Polésine.

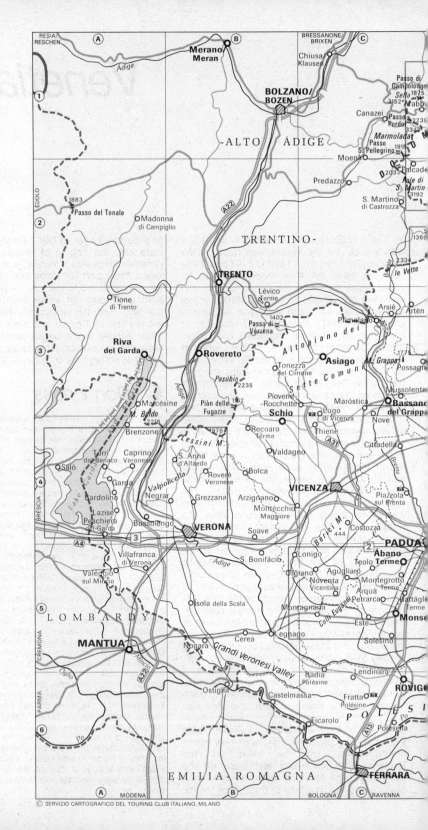

Venezia

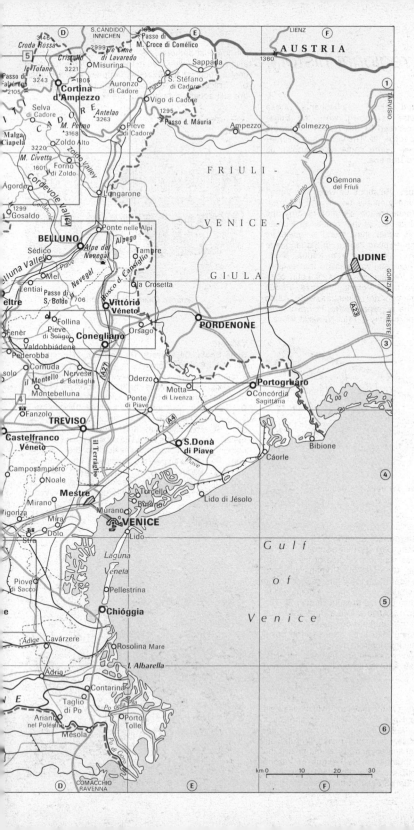

● *Brief regional history*

Before the 3C BC
Euganei and Veneti. The first inhabitants, whose name, but little else, is known, were the **Euganei.** They were absorbed by the occupying **Veneti,** an Indo-European people. ● The Veneti had an interesting culture whose centre came to be known as *Ateste* (Este) by the Romans.

3C BC-5C AD
Veneti and Romans. Relations between the Veneti and the Romans were generally friendly and the gradual process of **Romanization** did not destroy the ethnic and cultural identity of the Veneti, as Roman grammarians noted when they found a *quendam patavinitas,* a certain Paduan flavour, in the language of the historian **Livy,** who came from Padua. ● In 1C BC a law (lex Pompeia) was passed that extended to the cities of Venetia the rights of Latin colonies. ● In Roman times **Verona, Vicenza, Padua** and **Treviso** were important cities, as were **Altino** and **Concordia.** The principal centre, however, was **Aquileia,** a major port today in Friuli-Venezia Giulia.

Palazzo dei Rettori in Belluno

5C-7C
Mainland and lagoons. Environmental factors played an important part in the history of Venetia. The region was vital to the trade of the Roman Empire but, by the 4C, while the Romans still held sway, problems in controlling the rivers had led to the resurgence of marshes, which have continued to plague governments up to the present century. ● The devastation caused by **Attila** and the Huns (5C) was soon repaired, but the **Lombard conquest** (starting in 589) exerted a lasting influence. It led to the political separation of the interior from the Byzantine coastal strip. The interior was held first by the Lombards, then by the Franks and finally by the Holy Roman Empire.

7C-13C
League of Verona. On the mainland, which was held by vassals of the Holy Roman Emperor, the cities were **Communes,** the same that had flourished under the Romans: **Padua, Vicenza, Treviso, Verona,** as well as a number of lesser centres. ● In the 12C the four cities joined together in the **League of Verona** (later absorbed into the larger Lombard League) to resist **Frederick II Barbarossa's** attempts to re-estab-

lish imperial authority. ● The freedom of the cities also had to be defended in the middle of the following century against the **Ezzelini,** deputies of the Emperor. Traces of this intense struggle by the city-states are still apparent throughout the region.

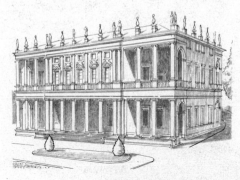

Palazzo Chiericati in Vicenza

13C-14C
Della Scala, Da Carrara, Da Camino. The cities of Venetia, as everywhere else in Italy at this period, saw a change in their form of government to rule by feudal lords. ● In Venetia the most important of these lords were the **Della Scala** or Scaligers of Verona, the **Da Carrara** or Carraresi in Padua, the **Da Camino** at Treviso and the **Este** of Ferrara, who held the Polésine. ● The ambitions and outward expansion of these ruling houses aroused hostility and the formation of coalitions that resulted in their destruction. ● For example, the **Scaligers,** after annexing Vicenza, Padua, Treviso and Belluno, sought to expand further but were checked by the ruling Visconti family of Milan, the Florentines and Venice (mid-14C).

S. Antonio in Padua

piazza Castello in Marostica

Villas of Venetia

At the beginning of the 16C, a Venetian nobleman lamented that his fellow Venetian patricians, neglecting maritime trade, 'wished to attend to giving themselves pleasure and delectation and greenery on terra firma'. Indeed at this time well-to-do Venetians transferred the source of their wealth from the sea to the mainland, from trade to agriculture. In doing so they built beautiful villas throughout the region under the rule of Venice, and a priceless artistic heritage came into being. In many places, unfortunately, these houses are now in decay or have been lost. The mainland gentry, nobles of the subject cities, followed the example of the Venetian patricians. Villas were built from Venice toward Padua along the banks of the Brenta, and toward Treviso along the Terraglio and the River Sile. They were built in the valleys of the Marca Trevigiana, the lower Po Valley, and the region of Verona as far as the Polésine, Friuli, the Euganean and Bérici hills, Montello, Asolo and the pre-Alpine valleys. The architecture of the villas is largely based on the Renaissance designs of Andrea Palladio (1508-1580) and incorporates the classical Roman elements of arches, columns and pediments. 'Two sorts of building are required in the villa', wrote Palladio, who was able to interpret with such imagination the aspirations of his sophisticated and wealthy clientele, 'one for the dwelling of the master and his family, the other to oversee and guard the goods and animals'. His example was followed for the next two centuries. The villa of Venetia is in fact the heart of a farm. The outbuildings (dwellings for the foreman and workers, tool sheds, storehouses, sheds for vehicles, stables, stalls and barns) are generally arranged in two symmetrical wings known as barchesse, linked by arcades. 'One can walk to any place under cover, so that neither the rain nor the rays of the sun may trouble the master in going about his business.'

15C-18C

The rule of Venice. The government of Venice had always considered the shore of the lagoon as the limit of the dogeship; its concerns further inland were for freedom of passage and security on trade routes. The possibility of a strong territorial state developing in Venetia was one of the reasons for Venice adopting a **'mainland policy'.** By 1420, the whole of Venetia was Venetian, and by 1483, so was the Polésine. The long period of **rule by the Venetian republic** went through major crises. It survived the first **(War of the League of Cambrai,** 1509), caused by French and imperial expansion. The second, which grew out of the ferment of the **French Revolution,** saw its fall (in 1797). ● Under Venetian rule, the people of Venetia were able to address problems of regulating the river systems and to begin reclamation schemes in the Polésine and around Verona.

19C-20C

Austrian rule and Italy. Napoleon ceded Venice and its mainland possessions to Austria in the Treaty of **Campoformio** of 1797, although he reneged on the

Veneti and Venedi

The civilization of the Veneti is recorded in the Museo Atestino, and most of the inscriptions in their language (Venetic) were found in the area of Este (Ateste in antiquity). The age of the Veneti, an Indo-European people, lasted from the 6C BC until their slow Latinization, which began in the 3C. On the linguistic map of Indo-European peoples in the second millennium BC, the Veneti and the proto-Latins occupy an area N of the Danube, roughly corresponding to Slovakia. To the E there were the Thracians and the Slavs; to the W, the Celts. To the S there were the Oscan-Umbrians and the Illyrians. All these races subsequently migrated to the territories they held in the historical era. It is claimed that a group of the Veneti moved N to settle in the lands between the Oder, the Vistula and the Baltic. These Baltic Veneti were slowly assimilated by the Slavs. In 1C BC the Germans who bordered them to the E called them Venedi. Cremation, animal figurines and symbols connected with cults of the sun and fertility are among the evidence that points to a link between the two groups.

Ponte Coperto in Bassano del Grappa

agreement some years later. ● The division of Europe at the Congress of Vienna in 1815 united Venetia and Lombardy in the **Kingdom of Lombardy-Venetia** within the Hapsburg Empire. The Austrian rulers became more and more at odds with those patriots who yearned for a united Italy. ● In 1866 a campaign mounted by the army of the Kingdom of Italy failed, but its ally, Prussia, defeated the Austrians at Sadowa, and the subsequent peace finally united Venice and the Venetia, including Friuli, with **Italy.** ● During the final phase of World War I (1917-18), the region from the eastern border up to the Piave was occupied by the Austro-Hungarian army and the guns could be heard in Venice. ● The 20C transformation of an agricultural region with extensive areas of poverty into a prosperous one with thriving industries is a significant development in the social history of the republic.

 Practical information

Information: tourist offices in principal towns and other centres.
SOS: public emergency service, ☎ 113; police emergency, ☎ 112; *ACI* emergency breakdown, ☎ 116.
Weather: forecasts, ☎ 041/993191, for provinces of Verona and Vicenza, ☎ 045/993191 (if calling from Venice, ☎ 191); road conditions, ☎ 041/993194, for province of Belluno, ☎ 0471/49000 (if calling from Venice, ☎ 194) or ☎ 06/4212 for *ACI;* shipping forecasts, ☎ 041/993196 (from Venice, ☎ 196); snow reports, ☎ 041/993162 (from Belluno, Treviso and Venice, ☎ 162).
Farm vacations: regional Agrituristi association, Venice-Marghera, *Federazione Agricoltori,* v. Palladio 26/4, ☎ 041/935801.
Fairs and markets: large trade fairs in the Verona exhibition area *(Fieragricola, Vinitaly, Herbora, Samoter, Fieracavalli); Padua international sample fair; international jewelery, goldsmith and gemology show* at Vicenza; regular antiques' markets at Asolo and at Brugine (→ Piove di Sacco).
Events: *opera and summer theatre season* at Verona; *classic plays* at Teatro Olimpico, Vicenza; *chess game* with pieces played by people at Marostica; *international violin festival, symphonic and drama season* at Teatro Verdi, Padua; *international archery competitions, national mountain walking races* at Belluno; *national balloon meeting,* Treviso.
Nature parks: *Parco naturale dei Colli Euganei* (→ Padua); regional parks planned for the areas of Cansiglio, Càorle and Monte Baldo.
Wildlife and entertainment parks: *Gardaland entertainment park* (→ Peschiera del Garda); *Parco giardino Villa Sigurta,* at Valeggio sul Mincio; *Parco-zoo del Garda* (→ Lazise); *Parco-zoo dei Colli Euganei,* at Torreglia (→ Abano Terme); *Città di Verona* zoological garden, at Verona.
Nature conservation: Venetian *WWF* delegations, at Verona, v. Chiodo 6, ☎ 045/594872; sections at Belluno, v. Corte Caorera 1; Padua, v. A. Cornaro 1/B, ☎ 049/8070465, Treviso, corso del Popolo, Vicenza, Contrà Riale 12, ☎ 0444/31777, Baldo-Garda, at Caprino Veronese (32 km NW of Verona), v. Unità d'Italia 8; excursions and summer work camps in the Baldo area and other areas of natural interest. *LIPU,* at Belluno, v. Feltre 17, ☎ 0437/212423, Padua, *C.L.A.C.,* v. A. Cornaro 1/B, ☎ 049/8070465, Verona, v. Dietro Filippini 6; Vicenza, v. Pozzetto 9, ☎ 0444/237321; birdwatching; *LIPU* Treviso, corso del Popolo 29, ☎ 0422/361094; guided tours of Venice lagoon, the lagoon of Càorle and the Isola di Corvara reserve (7 km SW), open Sat-Sun, (☎ 0422/379068 Comune di Quinto di Treviso). *Italia Nostra,* regional council in Vicenza, contrà Riale 14,

☎ 0444/543636. Po delta group at Porto Tolle, Polesine Camerini, v. Piazza.
Walks: long distance, signposted routes in the foothills of the Alps and in the plain: Valbrenta circuit between Bassano del Grappa and Cismon (Apr-late autumn): in the Alpine zone: Alte Vie Dolomitiche (7): one, from Cortina d'Ampezzo to Belluno (8 stops in a *rifugio:* Jul-mid-Sep); four, from San Candido to Pieve di Cadore (9 stops in a *rifugio:* late Jun-mid-Sep). Alta Via dei Ladini from Cortina d'Ampezzo; Cadore circuit from Pieve di Cadore. Short excursions along signposted *CAI* paths on Monte Baldo and the Lessini, along the Brenta and in the Cadore valleys. Information: *CAI* offices at Agordo, p. Marconi 13; Auronzo, v. Dante 4, ☎ 0435/99454; Bassano del Grappa, v. Schiavonetti 26; Cortina d'Ampezzo, largo Poste 2; Feltre, porta Imperiale 3, ☎ 0439/81140; Pieve di Livinallongo (→ La val Cordévole), v. Zanon 121/B; Padua, Galleria S. Biagio 5/10, ☎ 049/22678; Pieve di Cadore, v. Nazionale 5; San Vito di Cadore (in the tourist offices), v. Nazionale 9, ☎ 0436/9405; Verona, stradone Maffei 8, ☎ 045/30555; Vicenza, Contrà Rieale 12, ☎ 0444/545369; Vittorio Veneto, v. della Vittoria 321; tourist offices at Agordo, Alleghe, Auronzo, Bassano del Grappa, Calalzo di Cadore, Cortina d'Ampezzo, Falcade, Pieve di Cadore, San Vito di Cadore, Sappada, Vittorio Veneto.
Cycling: information and assistance from cycling groups affiliated to *UDACE* (250) throughout the region. *TCI* bicycle touring route maps *Il Veneto e La Laguna,* routes for the Adige and the Lagoon from Cavanella d'Adige (11 km S of Chioggia), for the villas of the Brenta from Stra, from Venice (→) to Chioggia, from Po di Levante (Contarina, 14 km E of Adria) to Po di Maistra, for the Isola della Donzella from Porto Tolle-Ca'Tiepolo, from Po di Gnocca (Mesola, 36 km S of Chioggia) to Po di Goro, for the Bosco della Mésola.
Horseback riding: *Federazione italiana sport equestri,* regional committee (for the Three Venetias), at Vicenza, corso Padova 83, ☎ 0444/507423. Numerous centres associated with ANTE throughout the region. **23 Race courses:** Le Padovanelle, at Ponte di Brenta (→ Padua), strada S. Marco 219, ☎ 049/625107; *Lancenigo* (→ Treviso), S. Artemio district, ☎ 0422/63357.

Venetian cuisine

It has been written that Venetia is 'in gastronomic terms, the most complete and refined of Italian regions'. Polenta, the corn-meal porridge, may be served alone, as an accompaniment to oven dishes or fried. There are at least forty different ways of preparing rice. The Adriatic, the rivers (eels) and the lagoon provide a wealth of fish and shellfish (capesante, clams, mussels), the moleche or baby crabs caught in spring when still tender. Granseola, the white flesh of dried lamb, kid and poultry; hare and venison from Belluno and Trevigiano and songbirds for polenta e osei mark the bounds of la Serenissima's rule no less surely than the stones engraved with the Lion of St. Mark. The regional fare is based on cheeses, prosciutti (hams) from the Euganean and Bérici hills, and charcuterie such as ossocollo (from the neck of a pig) and soppressa (pork and garlic). Typical hors d'œuvres include delicious dried cod in pastry, granseola and fish in saor (soused with herbs); bigoli with duck; vicentini (duck giblets); bellunese casunziei (ravioli), risi e bisi (rice with peas); to follow, guinea fowl in tecia (baked in special earthenware dishes), liver in the Venetian style with onions, torresani (pigeons wrapped in thin slices of fat bacon and grilled). Asparagus alla bassanese and grilled Treviso chicory are vegetable specialities.

River trips: from Padua to Venice down the Riviera del Brenta, 3 times a week, aboard the *Burchiello* (Tue, Fri, Sun, Mar-Oct; stopping at the villas Pisani and Malcontenta); information at Padua, *Siamic*, v. Trieste 42.
Lake trips: public boat services on Lake Garda (also summer cruises), office at Desenzano del Garda, p. Matteotti 2, ☎ 030/9141323-9142419.
Instruction: *Laboratorio di ceramica*, at Schio, v. della Campagna 14, ☎ 0445/27628 (4 hours a day, followed by trips and excursions); bookbinding at Este, *Villa Albrizzi*, ☎ 0429/2063 (Sep); gemology, woodcutting, precious stone and graphic art production, *Scuola di arti e mestieri*, at Vicenza, Contrà Mure S. Rocco, ☎ 044/23926.
Skindiving: courses from *Club sommozzatori Padova*, v. Cornaro 1, ☎ 049/8071941; *Gruppo sub Bassano*, v. Bassanese 3/B, ☎ 0424/34789; *Scuola sub Treviso*, v. S. Nicolò 21, ☎ 0422/53071.

Facts and figures

Location: Like Venice, the region takes its name from its pre-Roman inhabitants, the Veneti, whose Indo-European language, Venetic, has survived in several hundred inscriptions. Since the separation of Friuli in 1947, the region has comprised the NE of Italy between Lake Garda and the Mincio to the W and the Livenza and the Tagliamento to the E; the Po and the Adriatic in the S and part of the Alps to the N. The alluvial plain that forms the S half of the region extends down to the sea and the unique natural phenomenon of the Venetian lagoon. The mountainous part, which is more pre-Alpine than Alpine, includes some of the peaks of the Dolomites.
Area: *18,377 sq km.*
Climate: Continental, with variations due to altitude, which ranges to more than 6,600 ft in the pre-Alps, and relatively mild winters where there is shelter, such as that provided by the Euganean hills.
Population: *4,361,527 inhabitants.*
Administration: The regional capital is Venice; the other six provinces are Belluno, Padua, Rovigo, Treviso, Verona and Vicenza.

Mountain climbing: information: local *CAI* branches at Agordo, p. Marconi 13, Auronzo; v. Dante 4, ☎ 0435/99454; Bassano del Grappa, v. Schiavonetti 26; Belluno, v. Ricci 1, ☎ 0437/26841; Cortina d'Ampezzo, largo Poste 2; Pieve di Cadore, v. Nazionale 5; San Vito di Cadore at the tourist offices; Verona, stradone Maffei 8, ☎ 045/30555; Vicenza, Contrà Riale 12, ☎ 0444/545369; Vittorio Veneto, v. della Vittoria 321; Alpine guides at Alleghe, ☎ 0437/723766; Cortina d'Ampezzo, ☎ 0436/4740.
Skiing and winter sports: main skiing areas are in Cadore, Agordino, Zoldano and the Asiago plateau. Summer skiing at Marmolada (→ Zoldano and La Marmolada).
Golf: courses in all provinces.
Bowls: *Federazione italiana bocci*, Verona, v. SS. Trinità 7, ☎ 045/917725; *Unione bocciofila italiana*, Treviso, v. Giacomelli, ☎ 0422/549908.
Canoeing: *Federazione italiana canoa-kayak*, affiliated schools at Bardolino, Padua, Valstagna (→ Bassano del Grappa), Verona.
Rugby: *Comitato interregionale triveneto rugby*, Silèa (4 km E of Treviso), v. Treviso 17, ☎ 0422/360928.
Air sports: flying club, at Belluno, v. Caduti 14 Settembre 1944, airport, ☎ 0437/30667; Legnago, airport, ☎ 0422/22065; Padua, v. Sorio 89, ☎ 049/665611 (also gliding); Thiene, v. Rozzampia airport, ☎ 0445/362723; Treviso, v. Noalese 63, ☎ 0422/20251; Verona, Boscomantico airport, ☎ 045/563200 (also gliding and parachuting); Vicenza, v. S. Antonino airport, ☎ 0444/23079 (also

Recioto

Verona, the source of Recioto, is the most important of Venetia's wine-producing areas and Venetia is among Italy's foremost wine regions. Recioto is a special type of three different Veronese wines: Gambellara, Soave and Valpolicella. The name is derived from the regional dialect term, recia meaning ear; the recie of a bunch of grapes are its upper stems. Specially ripened grapes are picked from the recie only. In addition the selected grapes are dried for between one and three months, thus the wine is usually made at the turn of the year or even as late as February. Its fermentation therefore takes place at a time when the weather is very different from the autumn, when fermentation usually occurs. It is possible to produce sweeter recioto, with more sugar, or drier wine by bringing forward or delaying the vinification. Recioto di Gambellara is golden yellow, very fruity and is suggested as an accompaniment to uncooked shellfish or desserts. Recioto di Soave is a pale golden yellow with an intense bouquet and should be drunk at the end of a meal, as should Recioto della Valpolicella, a brilliant red with a warm, velvety taste. Finally, Recioto della Valpolicella Amarone, the dry version of the previous wine, accompanies red meats and game.

Grappa

Grappa is a liquor resulting from the fermentation of grapes, pips, stems and skins. There are those who remember how, once wine-making was over, country lanes among the vineyards of northern Italy would be redolent with the scent of distilling grappa from the cottages. The only true Italian spirit, it has held its ground against successive commercial offensives and fashions for French cognac, Spanish brandy, Scotch whisky, American bourbon and Russian or Polish vodka. It can be dull or magnificent and it is made in all the regions of the Alpine arc (Valle d'Aosta, Lombardy, Venetia, Trentino, Friuli). Grappa is usually drunk neat, either sipped or thrown back in a single gulp, according to two opposite schools of thought. New grappa, from the vintage of the same year, is drunk chilled. Older grappa, the colour of topaz, is usually drunk at room temperature.

gliding). *Aeroclub volovelistico* (gliding) at Asiago, *Aeroporto R. Sartori*, v. Cinque.
Hang gliding: *Federazione italiana*, information, ☎ 015/538703; affiliated schools at Pastrengo (→ Lazise), Pieve d'Alpago (→ the Cansiglio itinerary), Rosà (→ Bassano del Grappa) and Schio.
Pot holing: *Gruppi speleologici CAI*, at Verona, ☎ 045/30555; Padua, ☎ 049/22678; Oderzo, ☎ 0422/710640; Vittorio Veneto, casella postale 117, ✉ 31029 ; sites equipped for pot-holing at Oliero (→ Bassano del Grappa).
Fishing: *Federazione italiana pesca sportiva*, at Belluno, v. Cipro 13, ☎ 0437/24854; Padua, v. Lippi 4/1, ☎ 049/606408; Rovigo, v. Puccini 16, ☎ 0425/361165; Treviso, v. Sant'Ambrogio di Fiera 7, ☎ 0422/50695; Verona, v. Albere 43, ☎ 045/578126; Vicenza, v. Mazzini 161, ☎ 0444/23212. For fishing conditions (controlled waters, bans, etc.), apply to the appropriate office of the Federation.

Towns and places ═══════════════

ABANO TERME*

Padua 14, Venice 49, Milan 246 km
Pop. 16,647 ⊠ 35031 ☎ 049   C5

Abano, a spa, has tree-lined roads, large hotels, gardens, modern buildings and efficient facilities. Its **130 springs** make it one of the largest thermal centres in Italy. As long ago as the Roman Empire it was frequented by wealthy Romans taking the cure. The nearby **Euganean hills** (→) offer pleasant walks and excursions.

Environs

▶ 3 km away the **Sanctuary of Monteortone★** (or Madonna della Salute), begun in 1435, has a 15C brick campanile. The interior has frescos and a Renaissance high altar. ▶ 6 km W stands the Benedictine **abbey of Praglia★★**, founded in 1080 and rebuilt in the 15C-16C. It includes the Renaissance church of the **Assunta** (1490-1548) with a Latin cross ground plan. Above the high altar there is a painted wooden crucifix by the school of Giotto. To the r. of the church is the abbey entrance *(p.m.; closed Mon and religious festivals; apply to monks)*. It contains a cloister (1495), refectory, library and chapterhouse. ▶ At **Torreglia** *(5 km SW)* is the Belvedere della Croce and, in the Luvigliano district, the 15C **Villa dei Vescovi** (bishop's residence). Farther on *(10 km from Abano)* and, at 1,365 ft, offering fine views, is the **Eremo di Monte Rua** (hermitage, *no visitors*), founded in the 15C, rebuilt in the 16C.   ☐

Practical information _____

ABANO TERME
⚓ (all year), ☎ 669455.
ⓘ v. P. d'Abano 16, ☎ 669455.
🚌 from v. P. d'Abano.
Car rental: *Hertz,* at Padua, ☎ 657877.

Hotels:
★★★★★ *Sheraton G. H. Orologio,* v. delle Terme 66, ☎ 669111, 165 rm ℙ ⅏ 🛁 🖃 ✧ closed Dec-Feb, 214,000.
★★★★ *Bristol Buja,* v. Monteortone 2, ☎ 669390, 148 rm ℙ ⅏ 🖃 115,000; bkf: 9,000.
★★★★ *G H. Magnolia,* v. Volta 6, ☎ 667233, 145 rm ℙ ⅏ 🖃 closed Jan-Feb and Nov-Dec, 134,000; bkf: 13,000.
★★★★ *G.H. Trieste & Victoria,* v. P. d'Abano 1, ☎ 669101, 101 rm ℙ ⅏ 🖃 ✧ closed Nov-Feb, 130,000.
★★★★ *President Terme,* v. Montirone 31, ☎ 668288, 117 rm ℙ ⅏ 🖃 135,000.
★★★★ *Savoia Todeschini,* v. P. d'Abano 49, ☎ 667111, 180 rm ℙ ⅏ 🛁 🖃 ✧ closed Dec-Feb, 160,000; bkf: 10,000.
★★★★ *Terme Internazionale,* v. Mazzini 5, ☎ 668000, 140 rm ℙ ⅏ 🛁 🖃 ✧ closed Dec-Feb except Christmas 110,000; bkf: 8,000.
★★★ *Centrale,* v. Jappelli 37, ☎ 669860, 135 rm ℙ ⅏ 🛁 🖃 ✧ closed Dec-Feb, 80,000; bkf: 6,000.
★★★ *Columbia,* v. Augure 15, ☎ 669606, 102 rm ℙ ⅏ 🛁 🖃 Pens. closed Dec-Feb except Christmas, 67,500.
★★★ *Europa,* v. Flacco 13, ☎ 669080, 142 rm ℙ ⅏ 🖃 ✧ closed Dec-Feb except Christmas, 80,000; bkf: 10,000.
★★★ *Harry's Terme,* v. Marzia 50, ☎ 668500, 79 rm ℙ ⅏ 🖃 closed Dec-Feb except Christmas, 74,000; bkf: 6,000.
★★★ *Panoramic Hotel Plaza,* p. della Repubblica 23, ☎ 669333, 126 rm ℙ ⅏ 🖃 ✧ closed Jan-Mar, 83,000; bkf: 9,000.
★★★ *Ritz Terme,* v. Monteortone 19, ☎ 669990, 149 rm ℙ ⅏ 🖃 ✧ 76,000; bkf: 9,000.
★★★ *Salus,* v. Marzia 2, ☎ 669056, 76 rm ℙ 🖃 73,000.
★★★ *Smeraldo,* v. Busonera 174, ☎ 669865, 73 rm ℙ ⅏ 🛁 🖃 ✧ Pens. closed Dec-Feb except Christmas, 66,500.

★★★ *Terme Alexander,* v. Martiri d'Ungheria 24, ☎ 668300, 221 rm ℙ ⅏ ✧ 🖃 closed Jan-Feb, 133,000.
★★★ *Terme Italia,* v. Mazzini 7, ☎ 669600, 132 rm ℙ ⅏ 🛁 ✧ 🖃 ✧ closed Dec-Feb, 86,000; bkf: 7,000.
★★ *Alba,* v. Flacco 32, ☎ 669115, 132 rm ℙ ⅏ 🛁 🖃 ✧ 55,000; bkf: 4,000.
★★ *Milano,* v. delle Terme 169, ☎ 669444, 101 rm ℙ ⅏ 🖃 ✧ closed Jan-Mar, 62,000; bkf: 6,500.

Recommended
Conference centre: nr *Alexander Hotel,* ☎ 668300.
Cycling: *Cicli Bassan,* v. Stella 35, ☎ 810862.
Golf: at Valsanzibio (→ Euganean hills), ☎ 9130078 or 9130215 (18 holes).
Tennis: v. U. Foscolo, ☎ 810952; v. Colli Euganei 22, ☎ 812411.

Environs

TORREGLIA, ⊠ 35038, ☎ 049, 6 km SW.

Recommended
Animal park: *Parco-Zoo dei Colli Euganei,* at Tramonte *(5 km W),* ☎ 9900232 (entrance fee; 9 a.m.-12 noon and 2 p.m.-dusk).
Wine: at Luvigliano, cellar devoted to wines of Euganean hills, ☎ 5211896.

ADRIA

Rovigo 22, Venice 64, Milan 290 km
Pop. 21,712 ⊠ 45011 ☎ 0426   D6

Adria was once a part of its namesake sea, the Adriatic. Greeks established themselves here in the 6C BC and named the site *Adrias*. After Etruscan occupation it remained a major trading port and provided entry into the Po Valley for the influence of Greek culture. Adria ceased to be a port early in the Christian era because of silt brought down by the Adige. Today the Canal Bianco links the city with the sea some 15 miles distant. One of its citizens, L. Groto, 'the blindman of Adria' (16C, portrait by Tintoretto in Biblioteca Civica), is an example of courage in the face of adversity. He lost his sight in early infancy, but until his death at the age of 44 was a renowned poet, comic playwright and translator from Greek and Latin. Groto was also a powerful orator. Swayed by of one of his speeches, the Venetian Doge Pietro Loredan built a channel to divert the flood waters of the Po away from the town.

▶ The **Museo Archeologico** *(9 a.m.-2 p.m.; hols 9 a.m.-1 p.m.; closed Mon)* displays local finds, including an iron **chariot★** from the tomb of a Celtic warrior (4C BC), black-and-red figure vases (6C-4C BC), Iron Age ceramics, Etruscan bells, Greek and Etruscan bronzes, gold, Egyptian and Phoenician glass, Roman coins and glass and ceramics. ▶ The 18C church of **S. Maria Assunta** has an 8C font and 15C terra-cottas in the Cappella della Madonna.   ☐

Practical information _____

ⓘ corso Vittorio Emanuele 53, ☎ 21675.

Restaurants:
● ♦♦♦ *Due Leoni,* at Ariano del Polesine, corso del Popolo 21, ☎ 71138, closed Mon and 1-15 Jul. Regional cuisine: la torchiata, baked wild boar, 23/33,000.
♦♦ *Molteni,* v. Ruzzina 2, ☎ 21295, closed Sat and Christmas. Summer service in garden. Mixed cuisine: fish stew, cannelloni, 22/35,000.

Recommended
Boat trip: along Canal Bianco to sea, *Fratelli Vicentini*, ☎ 95426.
Cycling: *Cicloamatori Adriesi*, v. Corte Corazza 8, ☎ 41081.

AGORDO

Belluno 29, Venice 135, Milan 338 km
Pop. 4,269 ⊠ 32021 ☎ 0437   D2

Agordo lies in a hollow along the course of the Cordévole, surrounded by wooded hills backed by the peaks of the Dolomites.

▶ The 17C-18C **Palazzo Crotta** has a fine façade and a small garden with an enclosure decorated with statues. It stands on the p. della Libertà, where an ancient fountain is adorned with the lion of St. Mark. ▶ The 19C **parish church** contains two altarpieces and two paintings in the sacristy. ▶ A **Mineralogical Museum** is attached to the Istituto Minerario.   ☐

Practical information _____

ⓘ p. Libertà, ☎ 62105.
Hotel:
★★ *Milano*, v. Praganda 5, ☎ 62046, 34 rm ℗ ⬚ ⌂ 60,000; bkf: 5,000. Rest. ◆◆◆ closed Mon. Italian cuisine: venison with polenta, stew with Barolo, 25/40,000.

Restaurant:
◆ *Caneva*, v. Carrera 28, ☎ 62037, closed Thu and Nov. Bellunese cuisine: casunziei with pumpkin, filet with juniper berries, 20/35,000.

Recommended
Tennis: v. Paganin, ☎ 63156.

ARQUA PETRARCA

Padua 22, Venice 61, Milan 268 km
Pop. 1,997 ⊠ 35032 ☎ 0429   C5

The poet and humanist Petrarch (1304-74) came to stay here in the autumn of 1369. He spent his final years in the village, living simply in a small house that he had built in an olive grove and vineyard. He was found dead in his study at dawn on 19 July 1374. His favourite cat, stuffed, is still displayed inside his house. The village is medieval in appearance, admirably situated in the Euganean hills.

▶ The **Casa del Petrarca★** (14C-15C) is in the upper village *(summer 9:30 a.m.-12:30 p.m. and 3-7:30 or 7 p.m. hols; winter 9:30 a.m.-12:30 p.m. and 1:30-4:30 or 4 p.m. hols; telephone in advance)*. Inside, the decoration is partly original and partly 17C. Mementos include the chair in which the poet died and signatures of famous visitors. ▶ The **Tomba del Petrarca** (Petrarch's tomb; 1380) is a sarcophagus standing on low pilasters in the piazzetta in the centre of the village. Behind it is the church of **S. Maria**, with 11C, 13C-14C frescos and a 14C polyptych.   ☐

Practical information _____

Restaurants:
◆◆◆ *Aganoor*, v. Aganoor 14, ☎ 718140, closed Tue eve, Wed, Jan-Feb and Jul. International cuisine: guinea fowl alla zingara, pheasant creole, home-produced Colli Euganei wine, 25/30,000.
◆◆◆ *Montanella*, v. Costa 33, ☎ 718200, closed Tue eve, Wed, Jan-Feb and Aug. Fireplace for grilling and outdoor service. Regional and Italian cuisine: quail risotto, tagliatelle with nettles, 28/35,000.
◆◆ *Contarine*, v. Bignago 29, ☎ 718218, closed Mon eve, Tue, Jan and Jul-Aug. Regional and Italian cuisine: dried salt cod alla vicentina, donkey stew, 20/25,000.

ASIAGO

Vicenza 52, Venice 121, Milan 261 km
Pop. 6,867 ⊠ 36012 ☎ 0424   C3

Asiago is the main centre of the plateau of the same name. On a hill to the E of the town is the **Sacrario Militare** *(9 a.m.-12 noon and 2-7 or 5 p.m. in winter)*, a cemetery for Italian and Austro-Hungarian dead from the fighting on the plateau during World War I. Nearby, the University of Padua has two astrophysical **observatories**. The **Sasso** district is connected to Valstagna in the Valsugana by a flight of 4,444 steps. The Asiago plateau is also known as the **Plateau of the Seven Communes**, undulating plains and hollows surrounded by conifer forests between the Brenta and Astico valleys. People of German stock settled here from the millennium onwards. They spoke a dialect called *cimbro*, a mistaken reference to the Cimbri who, according to Roman historians, made incursions into Italy in the closing years of the 2C BC. Villages include: **Gallio, Roana,** comprising the districts of **Canove (Museo della Guerra** in former railway station, *Jun-Sep 9 a.m.-12 noon and 3-5:30 p.m.*)**, Camporóvere, Cesuna, Treschè-Conca, Foza, Enego, Lusiana** and **Conco.**   ☐

Practical information _____

𝕏 ski lifts (more than 60 on the plateau), 150 km of cross-country skiing on the plateau, skating, sledge runs, instruction.
ⓘ p. Carli 1 (municipio), ☎ 62221.
Hotels:
★★★★ *Linta Park*, v. Linta 6, ☎ 62270, 108 rm ℗ ⬚ ⌂ 🔄 closed Sep-Christmas and Mar-Jun, 91,000; bkf: 13,000.
★★★ *Bellevue*, at Kaberlaba *(5 km S)*, ☎ 63367, 28 rm ℗ ⬚ ⌂ ⌯ closed 16 Oct-20 Nov and 1-31 May, 83,000.
★★★ *Croce Bianca*, corso IV Novembre 30, ☎ 62858, 36 rm ℗ ⬚ closed Oct-Nov, 60,000; bkf: 7,000.
★★ *Erica*, v. Garibaldi 55, ☎ 62113, 27 rm ℗ ⬚ ⬚ closed 11 Sep-14 Dec and 1 Apr-14 Jun, 48,000.
★★ *Europa*, corso IV Novembre 65, ☎ 64259, 27 rm ⬚ closed 15 Apr-31 May and Oct, 46,000; bkf: 6,000.

Restaurant:
◆ *Casa Rossa*, ☎ 62017, closed Thu and Oct. Former peasant's house at edge of a wood. Regional cuisine: homemade spaghetti in duck broth, gnocchetti with Asiago cheese, 25/30,000.

⚑ ★★★ *Asiago Ekar*, at Ekar, strada della Fratellanza, ☎ 63752 (all year).

Recommended
Children's facilities: *Maria Paola* children's residence, at Canove di Roana, v. Bettinadi 22, ☎ 540759 (from 3-12 yr); open Christmas hol, Feb and summer.
Clay pigeon shooting: at Kaberlaba *(5 km S)*, *Casa Rossa Restaurant*, ☎ 62017.
Flying: *Carlo Deslex*, gliding club at *R. Sartori Airport*, v. Cinque.
Gastronomic specialties: cheese, butter, spirits.
Golf: strada Colombaretta, ☎ 56310 (9 holes).
Horseback riding: *Hotel Orthal*, ☎ 62119, at Gallio *(4 km NE)*, ☎ 658280 (instruction).
Skating: ☎ 64144; *Hockey club*, v. Stazione, ☎ 64580.
Swimming: at Camena, ☎ 65224.
Youth hostel: *Ostello Ekar*, v. Costalunga, ☎ 62777.
♥ Observatory: astrophysical observatories of University of Padua (Jul-Aug p.m.; permission from information office, ☎ 62221).

Don't forget to consult the Practical Holiday Guide: it can help in solving many problems.

ASOLO

Treviso 34, Venice 65, Milan 255 km
Pop. 6,359 ⊠ 31011 ☎ 0423   D3

Asolo's fame rests on two women. The first was Caterina Cornaro, the Venetian who was made Queen of Cyprus. She ceded the kingdom to Venice in exchange for the town of Asolo and 8,000 ducats a year. Here she held court, surrounded by men of letters for more than thirty years. In 1509 she fled to Venice and died there soon after. The second was the actress Eleonora Duse (1850-1924) who was born in Asolo. The poet Robert Browning was also captivated by Asolo, staying here on three occasions and coining the unlikely gerund *Asolando,* as the title for one of his poems.

▶ The 18C **Duomo** has a portico on the side facing the piazza and contains Renaissance paintings. ▶ The porticoed 15C **Loggia del Capitano**, former seat of the town authorities, has a frescoed façade and houses the **Museo Civico** *(Tue-Fri 9:30 a.m.-12 noon and 4-7 p.m.; closed Mon).* It contains Venetian paintings, sculptures (Canova), fossils and archaeological finds and mementos of Caterina Cornaro, Duse and Gabriele D'Annunzio (→ Lake Garda). ▶ A medieval tower survives from Caterina Covanovo's **Castello della Regina.** ▶ The porta del Colmarion leads to the **Rocca**, with its massive walls (abandoned, view). ▶ There are frescos in the churches of **S. Gottardo** (14C) and **S. Caterina.** Fine fabrics are hand-woven in the **Tessoria** and there is a school of embroidery. ▶ At **Onè di Ponte** *(5 km toward Bassano)* there is a **Museum of Ancient Trades** *(9 a.m.-12 noon and 4-6 p.m.; closed Mon and Tue).*   ▢

Practical information _____

ℹ v. Regina Cornaro 209, ☎ 55045.

Hotel:
★★★★ *Villa Cipriani,* v. Canova 298, ☎ 55444, 32 rm ℗ ⚜ ≼ ₩ ⅛ 16C Venetian villa with Italian-style garden, 264,000; bkf: 18,000. Rest. ● ♦♦♦♦ Service on veranda facing garden. Excellent regional and international cuisine: fagotti della nonna, curried scampi with pilau rice, 50/80,000.

Recommended
Antiques market: in historic centre, 2nd Sun of every month except Aug, ☎ 55841.
Craft workshops: *Tessoria,* ☎ 52062; *Scuola del ricamo antico e dell'arazzo,* v. Sottocastello, ☎ 52187 (9 a.m.-5 p.m.; Sat and Sun, reserve in advance; embroidery and lace).
Tennis: v. Dante 19, ☎ 52351.

BADIA POLESINE

Rovigo 24, Venice 97, Milan 216 km
Pop. 10,183 ⊠ 45021 ☎ 0425   C5-6

Polésine is on the r. bank of the Adige, on the edge of the Valli Grandi Veronesi (→ Legnano), in countryside criss-crossed by canals and embankments designed to manage the water system.

▶ The **Palazzo degli Estensi,** in the street of the same name, is a 15C Venetian Gothic building. ▶ The **Museo Civico Baruffaldi** in the p. Vittorio Emanuele *(apply Biblioteca Civica)* displays weapons and other military artifacts, agricultural tools and 14C-15C ceramics. ▶ The remains of the **abbey of Vangadizza** *(apply to caretaker)* give the town its name (badia is derived from abbazia which means abbey). It has a 10C foundation and was extended in the 15C. Two sarcophagi stand in the piazza in front of it and there is a leaning campanile from the late 12C. The Cappella della Madonna (1490) has a marble entrance archway.   ▢

Practical information _____

Restaurant:
♦♦ *Fontana,* v. Monte Pegni 41, ☎ 51412, closed Sat. Regional cuisine: bigoli with sauce, hare in wine sauce with polenta, 15/25,000.

Mount BALDO

A3-4

Mount Baldo rises between the Adige Valley and the E shore of Lake Garda. Rocky cliffs slope down to the lake, but on the Adige side they are gentler and rise to form a parallel range. The long, almost straight ridge reaches its highest points at Cima Valdritta (7,277 ft) and Punta del Telegrafo (7,218 ft). There is little woodland but the meadows contain a number of rare plants and the area was of interest to botanists as long ago as the 16C.

▶ **San Zeno di Montagna** (1,765 ft) dominates Lake Garda, a little N of Torri del Benaco. A chair lift runs from **Prada** (3,445 ft) to **Ortigaretta** (5,085 ft). ▶ A cableway *(15 mn)* connects **Malcesine** (→) on the shore of the lake with **Tratto Spino** (5,840 ft). ▶ **Ferrara di Monte Baldo** (2,808 ft) is on the E slope. The trip to Pra' Alpesina *(13 km by difficult road; impassable in winter)* has interesting views. ▶ From **Spiazzi** it is possible to descend to the sanctuary of the **Madonna della Corona,** built in the 16C on a crag overhanging the Adige Valley.   ▢

Practical information _____

FERRARA DI MONTE BALDO, ⊠ 37020, ☎ 045.
⚡ ski lifts, cross country skiing.
ℹ v. Quattro Novembre, ☎ 7220058.

Hotel:
★★ *Stella Alpina,* at Spiazzi, v. Peretti, ☎ 7220004, 41 rm ℗ ≼ ₩ closed 3 Nov-10 Dec, 45,000.

SAN ZENO DI MONTAGNO, ⊠ 37010, ☎ 045.
⚡ cableway, ski lifts and instruction at Prada *(10 km NE).*
ℹ municipio, ☎ 7285076.

Hotels:
★★★ *Diana,* at Ca' Montagna, ☎ 7285211, 44 rm ℗ ≼ ₩ ⚘ closed spring and autumn, 60,000; bkf: 6,000.
★★ *San Zeno,* at Castello, ☎ 7285031, 55 rm ℗ ≼ ⅙ ⚘ closed Nov, 43,000; bkf: 4,000.

BARDOLINO

Verona 28, Venice 145, Milan 147 km
Pop. 5,835 ⊠ 37011 ☎ 045   A4

The name of the wine from the Verona shore of Lake Garda is better known than the town itself, which is a popular resort. The 12C Romanesque church of **S. Severo** has a campanile above its apse; inside are 12C-13C frescos. The small church of **S. Zeno,** which retains its 9C form, is one of the few surviving Carolingian structures. The church of **S. Maria** at **Cisano** *(2.5 km S)* retains the 11C-12C porch, campanile and apse from its Romanesque foundation.   ▢

Practical information _____

ℹ p. Matteotti 53, ☎ 7210078 or 7210872.
🚤 boats, hydrofoils (Mar-Oct).
Car rental: Avis, v. Mirabello 9, ☎ 7210390 (Apr-Oct).

Hotels:
★★★ *San Pietro,* v. Madonnina 15, ☎ 7210139, 44 rm ℗ ₩ ⚘ ☐ closed Nov-Feb, 60,000; bkf: 8,000.
★★ *Kriss Hotel Internazionale,* lungolago Cipriani, ☎ 7210242, 33 rm ℗ ₩ closed Dec-Feb, 45,000; bkf: 9,000.
★★ *Speranza,* v. Garibaldi 49, ☎ 7210355, 22 rm, 60,000.

Restaurant:
♦♦♦ **Aurora,** p. S. Severo, ☎ 7210038, closed Mon and Nov-Dec. Outside service in square. Regional and international cuisine: pennette with vodka, trout filets with grapes, 28/35,000.

⚎ *Cisano,* at Cisano, v. Peschiera, 800 pl, ☎ 7210107; *Continental,* at Reboin, v. Gardesana Orientale, 280 pl, ☎ 7210192; *Serenella,* at Serenella, ☎ 7211333.

Recommended
Canoeing: *Centro Nautico,* lungolago, ☎ 7211109.
Cycling: *Polisportiva Bardolino,* v. Valsorda 1.
Marina: *Nautica La Serenissima,* ☎ 7210353.
Tennis: v. S. Colombano, ☎ 7211320.

BASSANO DEL GRAPPA*

Vicenza 34, Venice 76, Milan 234 km
Pop. 38,619 ⊠ 36061 ☎ 0424   C3

In the past six centuries Bassano has been destroyed eight times — by war or by the Brenta in flood. Each time it has been rebuilt in wood, except in 1524 when stone was tried, but the bridge stood for only two years. The present town dates from 1945, but is a copy of the original. Three generations of 16C painters belonging to a Bassano family took their surname of Da Ponte from the bridge. The city itself is pleasant to wander through. Shop windows display rustic and sometimes amusing ceramics that carry on a tradition of craftsmanship and manufacture dating from the 17C. Bassano also produces — as its name proclaims — one of the best *grappe* (brandies) of the region.

► In the p. Garibaldi, dominated by the 13C **Torre di Ezzelino,** stands the Romanesque-Gothic church of **S. Francesco** (A2) with a fine porch (1306). Inside are 15C frescos and a 15C wooden crucifix. ► The former convent of S. Francesco houses the **Museo Civico★** (A2; *10 a.m.-12.30 p.m. and 2.30-6.30 p.m.; Sun 10 a.m.-12.30 p.m.),* where the picture gallery displays a number of paintings by Jacopo Bassano (1516-92); *(Flight into Egypt★; Charity of St. Martin★; St. Valentine Baptizing St. Lucilla★★).* Other collections include the

BASSANO
DEL GRAPPA

0   100   200   300 m
1 : 18.000 (1cm=180m)

© SERVIZIO CARTOGRAFICO DEL TOURING CLUB ITALIANO, MILANO

1   2 Primolano km 29
Marostica km 7
                           Montebelluna km 25
A
B   B
                           2   Padua km 42

bequest *(access upon request)* of the Remondini family, who had a printing house at Bassano from the late 17C until 1861 and a flourishing business producing colour prints. The collection includes more than 10,000 engravings from the 15C-19C. ► The 16C **Municipio** (A1) has a 15C loggia on the ground floor. ► Piazza Monte Vecchio is surrounded by handsome houses decorated with frescos. ► The **Palazzo Sturm** (A1) is an 18C nobleman's house. ► There are several paintings by members of the Bassano family in the **Duomo** (A1), which stands within the walls of the upper castle (Castello degli Ezzelini); the campanile was once one of the castle's towers. ► The **viale dei Martiri** (A2) follows the line of the city fortifications and offers a view of the Brenta Valley, the plateau of the Sette Comuni (seven communes) and Mt. Grappa. ► Across the **Ponte Coperto★** (covered bridge) is the 17C Palazzo Bonauguro (A1). ► At Nove *(7.75 km),* the **Museo delle Ceramiche** *(apply to Istituto Statale d'Arte per la Ceramica,* ☎ 82022) has a collection of local majolica, porcelain and earthenware (17C).   ▢

Practical information _____

⒤ v. delle Fosse 9 [A2], ☎ 24351.

Hotels:
★★★★ **Belvedere,** p. Gen. Giardino 14 (A2a), ☎ 29845, 96 rm P ⓹ ⚘ 92,000; bkf: 10,000. Rest. ♦♦♦ v. Fosse 1, ☎ 26602, closed Sun. Mixed cuisine: ravioli of trout and asparagus, house style gnocchetti, 30/45,000.
★★★ **Camin,** at Cassola *(3 km),* v. Valsugana 64, ☎ 25164, 50 rm ⚐ ⚘ closed 1-15 Aug, 80,000.

Restaurants:
● ♦♦♦ **Villa Ca' 7,** v. Cunizza da Romano 4, ☎ 25005, closed Sun eve, Mon and Nov. 18C Venetian villa with period furnishings. Mixed regional cuisine: raw scampi, seasonal dishes with asparagus, mushrooms, radicchio or artichokes, 30/50,000.
♦♦ **Ponte-da Renzo,** v. Volbato 60 (A1 b), ☎ 25269, closed Tues and Jan. Pergola for summer service and room with veranda, both overlooking bridge and old town. Seafood: spaghetti with lobster sauce, mixed fried fish from the Adriatic, 25/35,000.
♦♦ **Sole,** v. Vittorelli 41/43 (A2 c), ☎ 23206, closed Mon and Jul. Vicenza cuisine: homemade pastas with locally grown mushrooms or asparagus, polenta and dried salt cod, 25/30,000.

Recommended
Archery: *Compagnia arcieri Romano d'Ezzelino,* v. Tito Speri 12, ☎ 29327.
Canoeing: *Canoa Club Valstagna,* ☎ 99813.
Caves: *Grotta Parolini,* at Oliero *(11 km N),* tour by boat, fee; information, ☎ 98463 or 98285.
Craft workshops: *Ceramiche Bonato,* v. Augurano 5, ☎ 22812 (Mon-Fri a.m.; ceramics); at Borso del Grappa *(9 km NE;* pipe manufacture).
Cycling: *Cicli Cavalera,* v. Monte Grappa 70, ☎ 37353.
Events: *asparagus show* (May); *ceramic, antique furniture and wrought-iron fair* in the Palazzo Bonauguro (A1; mid-Jul-Sep).
Hang gliding: *Monte Grappa school,* at Rosa *(5 km S),* v. Ca' Diedo, ☎ 848210.
Swimming: v. Gobbi, ☎ 29995.
Tennis: v. Col Fagheron 24, ☎ 31853; v. Ognissanti, ☎ 26670.
Wine: *Bottega del Vino Italiano,* v. Pio X 47, ☎ 30669.
Young peoples' activities: *Polisportiva Bassano,* v. Scalabrini 76 (outdoor activities).
♥ historic inns: *Grapperia Nardini,* ponte degli Alpini, ☎ 27741.

BELLUNO*

Venice 108, Milan 321, Rome 617 km
Pop. 36,450 ⊠ 32100 ☎ 0437   D2

Belluno stands on a spur above the confluence of the Ardo torrent and the Piave. Many of the streets are

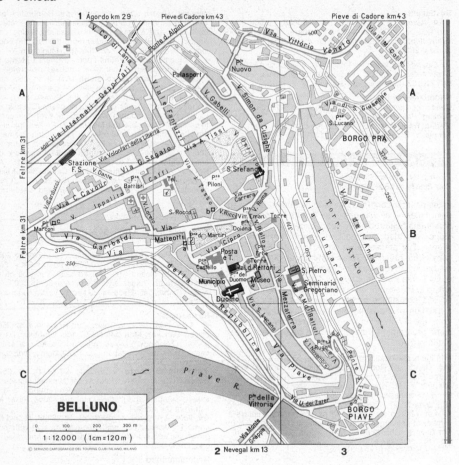

1 Ágordo km 29 Pieve di Cadore km 43 Pieve di Cadore km 43

BELLUNO

0 100 200 300 m
1:12.000 (1cm=120 m)

© SERVIZIO CARTOGRAFICO DEL TOURING CLUB ITALIANO, MILANO

2 Nevegal km 13 3

arcaded and there are Gothic houses, ancient fountains and numerous Renaissance palazzi in the Venetian style. Venice gained control of Belluno in 1404 and extensive rebuilding forged links with the architecture of the republic, although with a rustic, alpine flavour.

▶ A garden, the **piazza dei Martiri** (B2), with the Neoclassical Palazzo Cappellari della Colomba, is both the heart of the city and the entrance to the old quarter. ▶ The **piazza del Duomo★** (B2) is the most beautiful of the city's squares. The **Duomo★** was rebuilt at the beginning of the 16C. Inside are altarpieces by Venetian artists and, in the crypt, a 15C Rimini school polyptych on the altar. ▶ The **Palazzo dei Rettori★** (begun 1491) is the best known of the city's monuments. This Venetian Renaissance building has a porticoed façade surmounted by a loggia. To the r. is the 11C-12C city tower, a remnant of the castle of the count-bishops. ▶ The **Museo Civico** (B2; *Apr-Oct 10 a.m.-12 noon and 3-6 p.m.; hols 10 a.m.-12 noon; winter 10 a.m.-12 noon, closed hols; ☎ 24836; closed Mon)* displays prehistoric material and Roman antiquities; the picture gallery has works by Venetian artists and Renaissance bronzes, medals and tablets. ▶ Surrounded by arcaded Renaissance buildings, the **piazza delle Erbe** (B2) has a beautiful fountain at its centre and forms one end of the **via Mezzaterra** (B-C 2-3), which follows the major thoroughfare of the Roman town

and is lined by palaces in regional style. ▶ In the church of **S. Pietro** (B3) are interesting paintings and two 17C carved wooden altarpieces by the local carver Andrea Brustolon. There are two cloisters (14C-15C) in the adjacent **Seminario Gregoriano.** ▶ Built in 1486, the Gothic church of **S. Stefano★** (B2) has a 16C gilded wooden altarpiece, frescos and wood carvings. ▶ There are two gates, the **porta Doiona** (B2), built 1286, enlarged in the 16C and decorated with sculptures; and the **porta Rugo** (C3), 12C restored in the 18C. □

Practical information _____

☲ at Nevegal (→ Cansiglio).
ⓘ v. Pesaro 21 (B2), ☎ 22043; v. Matteotti 3, ☎ 28746.
▦ (A1), ☎ 25438.
▦ from p. Stazione (A-B 1), ☎ 25112.

Hotels:
★★★ **Astor,** p. dei Martiri 26/E (B2 a), ☎ 24921, 32 rm ₺ No restaurant, 64,000.
★★★ **Dolomiti,** v. Carrera 46 (B2 b), ☎ 27077, 32 rm Ⓟ ₺ No restaurant, 54,000; bkf: 4,000.
★★★ **Villa Carpenada,** v. Mier 158, ☎ 28343, 28 rm Ⓟ ⏅ 78,500; bkf: 9,000.
★★ **Sole,** p. Marconi 11 (B1 c), ☎ 25146, 24 rm Ⓟ 55,000; bkf: 6,000.

Restaurants:
♦♦♦ **Borgo,** v. Anconetta 8, ☎ 926755, closed Mon eve,

Tue and 30 Jun-15 Jul. 18C Venetian villa in attractive garden. Regional cuisine: pumpkin gnocchi, rabbit bellunese style, 20/30,000.
♦♦♦ *Daj Dam*, p. Resistenza 6, ☎ 26513, closed Mon. Regional and Italian cuisine: sliced raw beef in spicy sauce, schiz with polenta, 20/25,000.

Recommended
Cycling: *G. S. Eaton*, v. F. del Vesco 2, ☎ 30650.
Events: *international archery tournaments* (Jul-Aug); *national mountain walking races.*
Flying: *Aeroclub dell'Oro*, at San Pietro in Campo, v. Caduti 14 Settembre 1944, ☎ 30667.
Skating: at Lambioi, ☎ 20576 or 20560 (also swimming pool).
Specialties: antiques, rustic furniture.
Sports stadium: v. Gabelli, ☎ 28300.
Tennis: at Fisterre, ☎ 20482; v. Lante, ☎ 28983 (also bowling).

BIBIONE

Venice 92, Milan 352 km
Pop. 2,480 ⊠ 30020 ☎ 0431   F4

Bibione is a new development on the shore of the Adriatic to the r. of the mouth of the Tagliamento. The adjacent resort is known as **Bibione Pineda** because of the pine plantations.   □

Practical information _____

BIBIONE
≋
ⅈ v. Aurora 20, ☎ 43362.

Hotels:
★★★★ *Principe*, v. Ariete 41, ☎ 43256, 80 rm 🅿 ⚌ ⁄∘ closed Oct-Apr, 120,000.
★★★ *Leonardo da Vinci*, corso Europa 92, ☎ 43416, 54 rm 🅿 ⚌ closed 16 Sep-14 May, 76,000; bkf: 6,000.
★★★ *Nevada*, at Lido del Sole, v. Veneto 1, ☎ 43346, 40 rm 🅿 ⚌ ⚅ closed 16 Sep-14 May, 60,000.
★★★ *Palace*, v. del Leone 44, ☎ 43135, 80 rm 🅿 ⚌ ☐ closed 16 Sep-19 May, 80,000; bkf: 8,000.
★★ *Garni Renania*, v. Acquario 41, ☎ 43391, 40 rm 🅿 ⚌ closed Oct-Apr. No restaurant, 54,000.

Restaurant:
♦♦ *Piccolo Mondo-da Ori*, v. Adromeda 118, ☎ 430249, closed Mon and 15 Oct-30 Nov. Regional seafood: oyster risotto, gnocchetti with spider crab, 35/40,000.
⅄ ★★★★ *Internazionale*, v. delle Colonie 2, 390 pl, ☎ 43232.

Recommended
Horseback riding: school at entrance to village.
Tennis: v. Europa, ☎ 43604; v. Natisone, ☎ 430801.

Environs

BIBIONE PINEDA, ⊠ 30020, ☎ 0431, 4 km W.

Hotels:
★★★ *Esplanada*, v. delle Dune 6, ☎ 43260, 80 rm 🅿 ⚖ ⚌ ⚘ ☐ ⁄∘ closed 21 Sep-14 May, 75,000; bkf: 10,000.
★★★ *San Marco*, v. delle Ortensie 2, ☎ 43301, 57 rm 🅿 ⚖ ⚌ ⚘ ☐ closed 16 Sep-14 May, 75,000; bkf: 7,000.

⅄ ★★★ *Capalonga*, v. della Laguna, ☎ 43341.

BOLCA

Verona 51, Venice 102, Milan 204 km
Pop. 222 ⊠ 37030 ☎ 045   B4

Bolca is the centre of the Lessinia at the head of the Alpone Valley. It is famous for the fossils in its basalt formations.

▶ At Villa di Bolca, the **Museo dei Fossili** *(10 a.m.-12 noon and 3-6 p.m.; winter 2-5 p.m.; closed Mon)* has a collection of rare, well-preserved fossils found in the area. Exhibits cover fish, reptiles, crustacea, palms and other plants and shells. ▶ A **palaeontological walk** *(3 km)* leads to the Pesciara, Mt. Postale (2,220 ft), Mt. Vegroni (2,460 ft) and Mt. Purga (3,060 ft), all with quarries where fossils from the Eocene Epoch have been found.   □

La Riviera del BRENTA
C4

The Venetian Republic diverted the rivers that flowed into the lagoon to prevent it from silting up. The drainage scheme completed in 1896 which divided the River Brenta into two channels near Stra, E of Padua, was a continuation of the policy. The main branch (Brenta or La Cunetta) was canalized into long, straight stretches and runs around the S end of the lagoon, entering the sea a little S of Chioggia. The **Naviglio di Brenta** (older branch), which was also canalized and has locks, flows into the lagoon at Fusina.

▶ The Riviera del Brenta consists of the banks of the Naviglio di Brenta and from the 16C to the end of the 18C it became the area where the patricians of Venice chose to build their water-side villas surrounded by parks. ▶ The villas and villages along the banks suggest a 'fondamenta' (quay) in Venice. Indeed, many of the features represented by Antonio Canaletto (1697-1767) in a series of etchings entitled *Le delizie del fiume Brenta* (The Delights of the River Brenta) are still to be seen. Venetians used to travel to the villas on a regular boat service known as the *Burchiello* which ran between Venice and Padua. A service for tourists along the route now uses the same name (→ Venice). ▶ It is possible to follow the l. bank of the Naviglio di Brenta along the SS 11 from **Stra** to Mira and as far as a junction after Oriago. From there, to reach Mestre, take the road to **Fusina** *(parking lot and boats to Venice).* ▶ The numerous villas include the **Villa Pisani★** (→ Stra); the 18C Villa Lazara Pisani known as **La Barbariga** *(on opposite bank of canal, between Stra and Mira)* and the 16C **Villa Soranza-Favaro** on the l. bank. The 18C **Villa Widmann-Foscari** at Mira Porte has a park with statues and frescoed rooms *(9 a.m.-1 p.m. and 3-6 p.m.).* The beautiful villa **Malcontenta★** (→ Venice) is the work of Andrea Palladio.   □

Practical information _____

Restaurant:
♦♦♦ *Burchiello*, at Oriago, ☎ 472244, closed Mon, Thu eve and Jan. Terrace-garden on banks of Brenta. Seafood: oyster risotto, soused sardines, 35/52,000.

Recommended
River trips: along Brenta between Padua (→) and Venice (→) on the *Burchiello*, stops at Villa Pisani and Villa Malcontenta.

Il CADORE
D-E1

The shipwrights of the Venice Arsenal made extensive use of timber from the Cadore region. In 1420, the local inhabitants voluntarily accepted the rule of Venice. For centuries wood was floated down the Piave to the plain on its way to the Venetian shipyards. There are still old men who can remember lashing the logs together in their youth to form rafts and guiding them in the stream. The barrier at Perarolo, where logs felled in the upper valleys were halted, was demolished a few years ago. However, the area is still important for timber (the province of Belluno, which includes the Cadore, is 40 percent woods). The Cadore region covers the upper Piave basin from its source on the flanks of Peralba, upstream of Sappada, to Longarone. The main valley has three tributaries branching off to the r., the Pàdola (the Comélico basin), the Ansiei and the Bóite, the upper reaches of which are known as the Ampezzano. Downstream from the Bóite, the Piave is joined by the Maé; its valley, the Val Zoldo between Cadore and Agordino, is described in this itinerary although it is not strictly part of the Cadore (→ Zoldano and Marmolada). At the head of the Zoldo Valley the Forcella Staulanza, between Mt. Pelmo and Mt. Civetta, leads into the Val Fiorentina, which is part of the Cadore, even though it is a tributary of the Cordévole. Ringed by the Dolomites (Antelao, the highest peak at 10,705 ft, Tofane, Lavaredo, Sorapis, Cristallo and Pelmo), the area has some fine alpine scenery. Here and there the alpine style of building has survived intact in houses or barns but its features can also be seen in modern buildings. These include the extensive use of wood on house fronts and balconies, projecting eaves and in some cases wooden shingles instead of tiles.

▶ The main centre is **Pieve di Cadore** (→), birthplace of the painter Titian (1488-1576), who painted the mountains of his home in the backgrounds of several works. ▶ Following the Pieve upstream are **Calalzo di Cadore** (2,644 ft), **Lorenzo di Cadore** (2,897 ft), Vigo di Cadore, Santo Stefano di Cadore and Sappada. ▶ At **Vigo di Cadore** (3,120 ft), the 14C church of S. Orsola has frescos from the late 14C-early 15C. The church of S. Margherita, which stands on its own amid meadows 1 km from **Laggio di Cadore**, is frescoed with scenes from the life of St. Margaret. 3 km away on the other side of the valley is **Lozzo di Cadore** where the road for the **Rifugio Marmarole** (5,860 ft) and the Pian dei Buoi (5,988 ft) begins. The **Razzo plateau** (5,725 ft) lies 14 km along the road for Sauris. ▶ **Santo Stefano di Cadore** (6,260 ft), in a hollow at the confluence of the Piave and the Valle del Pàdola, is the main centre of the Comélico. A drive of about an hour leads to the **Val Visdende** with its extensive forest. ▶ **Sappada** (3,993 ft) was probably founded by Germans, who fled here at the beginning of the 11C from the upper Drava Valley to escape the oppression of feudal lords. The **Museo Civico** *(mid-Jul-mid-Sep 2:30-7 p.m.; closed Mon)* is devoted to the houses, environment and activities of this isolated community. **Cima Sappada** (4,219 ft), 4 km distant, stands on the ridge that forms the watershed with the Tagliamento basin. ▶ The hamlets of the Comélico include **San Nicolò di Comélico** with a parish church with frescos from 1492 in the apse; **Candide** with old houses, an 18C parish church which has paintings and a fine organ and the Gothic church of S. Antonio Abate. On the piazza of **San Pietro di Cadore** stands the Villa Poli-Del Pol★ (17C), which has frescos in two rooms. ▶ **Auronzo di Cadore** (2,835 ft), in the Ansiei Valley, is situated near the reservoir of Lago di S. Caterina ringed by Dolomite peaks. Villagrande has an 18C parish church, S. Giustina. It is possible to climb the valley to **Misurina** (→) and its lake★. ▶ The beautiful Bóite or Ampezzo Valley, which is flanked by the Dolomite massifs of Pelmo and Antelao, has **Borca di Cadore** (3,091 ft), **San Vito di Cadore** (3,317 ft; Lago di S. Vito, 3,209 ft; *10 mn by chair lift or 2 km by road* to Rifugio Senes, 4,003 ft, view★), and finally the splendid basin of **Cortina d'Ampezzo** (→). ▶ In the Zoldo Valley, which is flanked by forests of firs and dominated by the peaks of Pelmo and Civetta, lies the scattered community of **Zoldo Alto**. The principal centre is **Fusine**. In the **Mareson** district is a church with two altars and a crucifix by Andrea Brustolon, as well as an 18C altarpiece on the high altar. ▶ The two cen-

tres of the Val Fiorentina, in front of Marmolada, are Colle Santa Lucia and Selva di Cadore. ▶ Toward Andraz from **Colle Santa Lucia** is a splendid view from the **belvedere★**. At 12 km the **Giau Pass** (7,326 ft) is reached. ▶ In **Selva di Cadore** ⁴is the Gothic church of S. Lorenzo (15C); the Landria district has 17C rustic houses and a **Museo di Storia e Tradizioni Locali** *(Jul and Aug p.m.; other times by request).* ☐

Practical information

AURONZO DI CADORE, ⊠ 32040, ☎ 0435.
𝄪 cableway at Mt. Agudo, ski lifts, cross-country skiing, instruction, skating, bobsled run and sledding.
ℹ v. Roma, ☎ 9359 or 9426.
Hotels:
★★ *Juventus*, v. Padova 26, ☎ 9221, 50 rm ℗ ⬅ ♨ ✧ closed 1 Oct-9 Dec and 11 Apr-19 May, 60,000.
★ *Panoramic*, v. Padova 17, ☎ 9398, 32 rm ℗ ⬅ ♨ ✧ closed 21 Sep-19 Jun, 45,000; bkf: 4,000.
Restaurant:
♦♦ *Cavalier*, at Cima Gogna, ☎ 9834, closed Wed, Mon and Tue eve in low season. Bellunese cuisine: tagliatelle with bilberries, armonie with mushrooms, 25/35,000.
△ ★★ *Auronzo*, at Pause, ☎ 9553.

Recommended
Events: *canoe championships* (Jul), *motorboat races on lake* (Aug).
Horseback riding: at S. Marco (*12 km W; instruction*).
Skating: ☎ 723749; *Hockey Auronzo,* ☎ 99532.
Tennis: v. Roma, ☎ 99269.

BORCA DI CADORE, ⊠ 32040, ☎ 0426.
𝄪 ski lifts, cross-country skiing, instruction, skating.
ℹ v. Roma, ☎ 82015.
Hotels:
★★★ *Boite*, at Corte, ☎ 82051, 84 rm ℗ ⬿ ♨ ✧ ⤴ closed 21 Mar-19 Jun and 21 Sep-19 Dec, 77,000.
★★★ *Bories*, v. Roma 4, ☎ 82521, 33 rm ℗ ✧ No restaurant, 48,000; bkf: 6,000.

CALALZO DI CADORE, ⊠ 32042, ☎ 0435.
𝄪 cross-country skiing, skating.
ℹ ☎ 32348 or 32357.
Hotels:
★★ *Calalzo*, v. Stazione 19, ☎ 32248, 38 rm ℗ ♨ closed 20 Sep-15 Oct, 60,000; bkf: 5,000.
★★ *Ferrovia*, v. Stazione 4, ☎ 31115, 18 rm ℗ ♨ ✧ closed 20 Aug-30 Sep, 60,000; bkf: 4,000.

LORENZAGO DI CADORE, ⊠ 32040, ☎ 0435.
𝄪 cross-country skiing, skating, sled run.
ℹ ☎ 75042 (seasonal).

SANTO STEFANO DI CADORE, ⊠ 32045, ☎ 0435.
𝄪 ski lifts, cross-country skiing, instruction.
ℹ v. Venezia, ☎ 62230.
Hotel:
★★ *Monaco*, v. Lungopiave, ☎ 62430, 21 rm ℗ ♨ closed 16 Apr-30 Jun and 1 Oct-19 Dec, 52,000; bkf: 4,000.
△ ★★★ *Comelico*, at Campolongo, v. Tarigole, 200 pl, ☎ 62466.

SAN VITO DI CADORE, ⊠ 32046, ☎ 0436.
𝄪 ski lifts, cross-country skiing, instruction, skating.
ℹ v. Nazionale 9, ☎ 9119.
Hotels:
★★★★ *Marcora*, v. Roma 28, ☎ 9102, 46 rm ℗ ⬅ ♨ ᙚ ▤ ⤴ closed 1 Apr-14 Jun and 16 Sep-19 Dec, 150,000; bkf: 10,000.
★★★ *Ladinia*, v. Ladinia 16, ☎ 99211, 29 rm ℗ ⬅ ▨ ♨ ✧ ⤴ closed Easter-14 Jun and 16 Sep-30 Nov, 78,000; bkf: 10,000.
★★ *Pelmo*, corso Italia 61, ☎ 9125, 46 rm ℗ ♨ closed 16 Mar-19 Jun and 16 Sep-19 Dec, 54,000; bkf: 4,000.

SAPPADA, ⊠ 32047, ☎ 0435.
𝄪 ski lifts, cross-country skiing, instruction, skating.

ⓘ at Bach, ☎ 69131.

Hotels:
★★ **Alpi**, at Cima Sappada, ☎ 69102, 16 rm Ⓟ ⚌ ✎
closed Oct and May, 45,000; bkf: 5,000.
★★ **Corona Ferrea**, at Kratten, ☎ 69103, 25 rm Ⓟ ⚌
closed 16 Apr-14 Jun and 16 Sep-19 Dec, 60,000; bkf:
6,000.

⚠ ★★ *Primo Ponte sul Piave*, at Cretta, ☎ 69293.

VIGO DI CADORE, ✉ 32040, ☎ 0435.
⚡ ski lifts, cross-country skiing.
ⓘ p. S. Orsola, ☎ 77058.

Hotel:
★★ **Sporting**, at Pelos di Cadore, v. Fabbro 32, ☎ 77103,
25 rm Ⓟ ⚌ ⚌ ⚑ ▣ closed 21 Aug-14 Jun except Christmas, 70,000; bkf: 8,000.

ZOLDO ALTO, ✉ 32010, ☎ 0437.
⚡ ski lifts, cross-country skiing, instruction.
ⓘ at Mareson, ☎ 789145 (seasonal).

Hotels:
★★ **Bosco Verde**, at Pecol, ☎ 789151, 24 rm Ⓟ ⚌ ⚌ ⚑
closed Easter-Jun and Oct-Nov, 54,000; bkf: 4500.
★★ **Valgranda**, at Pecol, ☎ 789142, 29 rm Ⓟ ⚌ ⚑ ▣
closed Easter-30 Jun and 16 Sep-Christmas, 66,000.

CANSIGLIO

From Conegliano *(164 km, 1 day; map 1)*

This route makes two crossings of the Venetian pre-
Alps, which lie between the Piave Valley and the plain
around Treviso. It includes Cansiglio, an almost
untouched limestone karst plateau partly covered by
forest; Alpago, a green valley formed by the basin of
the Tesa torrent and its tributaries as they flow down
to Lake S. Croce; and Val Belluna, the name given to
the Piave valley between Ponte in the Alps and Feltre.

The route combines splendid landscape with the
artistic heritage and history of Vittorio Veneto, Belluno
and Feltre.

▶ **Vittorio Veneto** (→) is not far from **Conegliano** (→),
and from there the ascent to the **Cansiglio plateau**
begins. ▶ A short detour *(2.3 km)* at Mezzavilla leads to
the **Calieron Caves★** in a ravine. Bridges carry the steep
path down from cave to cave to the bottom. ▶ At
La Crosetta the **Cansiglio forest★** (beech, fir, larch)
begins. To the Venetians this was the *'oar wood'*,
because its timber was used to make oars for their galleys. ▶ The **Plain of Cansiglio** is an expanse of level
meadows. ▶ At **Spert** the route goes toward **Tambre**
(3,025 ft), then crosses **Alpago**, with views of the Lake
S. Croce, to **Pieve d'Alpago**, the most important village in
the valley. ▶ At **Ponte nelle Alpi** the Piave Valley begins,
which leads to **Belluno** (→). ▶ An interesting detour can
be made from Belluno by taking the scenic road to **Alpe-
del Nevegal** (3,379 ft; chair lift to Mt. Faveghera, 5,282 ft,
and to the **Giardino Botanico delle Alpi Orientali** at
4,921 ft). ▶ From Belluno a road on the r. of the Piave
goes to **Sédico** and **Feltre** (→). ▶ Going in the other
direction the road along the l. bank of the Piave leads to
Lentiai and Mel as far as Trichiana. ▶ The parish church
of **S. Maria Assunta** at **Lentiai** has Renaissance paintings
and a fine coffered ceiling. ▶ At **Mel** are several late
Renaissance and Baroque houses, particularly around the
piazza where the 18C parish church also stands. ▶ At
Trichiana the route leaves the Piave Valley and climbs
to the **S. Boldo Pass** (2,316 ft), then descends a narrow
ravine★ to the valley of the River Soligo. ▶ It then runs
along the shores of the Lago di Lago, through **Tarzo** and
returns to Conegliano. ▢

Practical information ⎯⎯⎯⎯⎯⎯⎯⎯⎯

MEL, ✉ 32026, ☎ 0437.

Restaurant:
● ♦♦♦ **Antica Locanda al Cappello**, p. Papa Luciani
20, ☎ 753651, closed Wed, Feb and Jun-Jul. In a 17C

1. Cansiglio

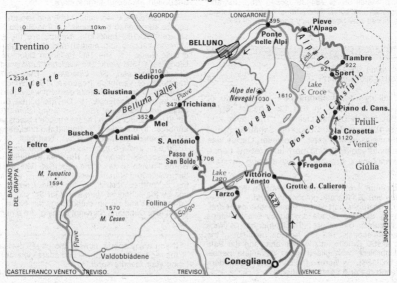

house. Excellent regional and Italian cuisine: tortelloni with radicchio, snail risotto, 23/28,000.

NEVEGAL, ⊠ 32024, ☎ 0437.
⚡ ski lifts (night skiing), cross-country skiing, instruction, skating, sled run.
ℹ️ *Centro servizi sportivi e turistici del Nevegal,* ☎ 298321.

⚊ ★★★★ *Nevegal,* ☎ 298143.

PIANO DEL CANSIGLIO, ⊠ 32010, ☎ 0438.
⚡ ski lifts, 60 km of cross-country skiing, instruction.
ℹ️ at Vittorio Veneto, p. del Popolo, ☎ 57243.

Hotel:
★★★ *Olivier,* v. Col. di Gou 341, ☎ 298165, 32 rm ℗ ⌂
⚲ closed 16 Apr-9 Jun and 16 Sep-30 Nov, 66,000; bkf: 5,000.

Recommended
Golf: at *Hotel S. Marco,* ☎ 585425 (9 holes).
Horseback riding: *Malga Lissandri school,* ☎ 581890.

PIEVE D'ALPAGO, ⊠ 32010, ☎ 0437.

Recommended
Hang gliding: *Monte Dolada school,* v. Catisana 6, ☎ 479040 or 479041.

PONTE NELLE ALPI, ⊠ 32014, ☎ 0437.

Hotels:
★★★ *Boito,* v. Roma 78, ☎ 999514, 16 rm ℗ ⚲ No restaurant, 66,000; bkf: 5,000.
★★ *Benito,* at Pian di Vedoia, ☎ 998157, 26 rm ℗ ≤ ♨
⚲ closed 15 Jul-8 Aug, 69,000; bkf: 5,000. Rest. ♦♦♦
closed Sun eve and Mon. Mixed cuisine: radicchio soup, game with polenta, 21/32,500.

TAMBRE, ⊠ 32010, ☎ 0437.
⚡ ski lifts, instruction.
ℹ️ p. dei Martiri 1, ☎ 49193.

TARZO, ⊠ 31020, ☎ 0438.

⚊ ★★ *Mara,* at Fratta, ☎ 586489.

Recommended
Horseback riding: *Azienda Agricola R. Tessari* (associate of *ANTE*).

TRICHIANA, ⊠ 32028, ☎ 0437.

Restaurant:
♦♦ *Thea,* p. Merlin 36, ☎ 754439, closed Wed, Jun and Sep. Regional and some international cuisine: seasonal pancakes, sliced raw beef in spicy sauce, 15/20,000.

CAORLE

Venice 66, Milan 326 km
Pop. 11,500 ⊠ 30021 ☎ 0421   F4

Caorle's tall cylindrical **campanile**★ in the style of Ravenna is a landmark in this flat coastal region around the mouth of the Livenza. The town was founded by refugees from Concordia Sagittaria (→) at the same time as Venice itself. However, Caorle was merely a picturesque fishing port until recent tumultuous development brought on by a flood of summer visitors.

▶ The old centre, protected from the sea by a high coastal dyke, remains a separate, untouched world. The free-standing campanile is part of the Romanesque **cathedral,** which has a tripartite façade divided by pilaster strips with 12C Byzantine bas-reliefs. The interior has columns with Byzantine capitals, 14C-15C frescos, paintings of the Apostles, a 15C Crucifix at the high altar and the **Pala d'Oro**★ (altarpiece with gilded silver Byzantine panels from the 12C-13C). ▶ Across the Livenza is the modern seaside resort of **Porto Santa Margherita.**   □

Practical information _____

≋
ℹ️ p. Europa 3, ☎ 81085 or 81860.

Hotels:
★★★★ *Airone,* v. Pola 1, ☎ 81570, 68 rm ℗ ♨ ⚲ ⊠ ⤴
closed Oct-Apr, 76,000; bkf: 9,000.
★★★ *Garden,* p. Belvedere 2, ☎ 82836, 50 rm ℗ ♨ ⤴
closed Nov-Mar, 65,000; bkf: 5,000.
★★★ *Metropol,* v. Emilia 1, ☎ 81492, 44 rm ℗ ♨ ⚲ ⊠
⤴ closed Sep-19 May, 70,000; bkf: 8,000.
★★★ *Panoramic,* lungomare Trieste 66, ☎ 81101, 64 rm
℗ ♨ closed Oct-Apr, 62,000; bkf: 8,500.
★★★ *Savoy,* v. Marconi, ☎ 81879, 44 rm ℗ ♨ ♿ closed
Oct-Apr, 80,000; bkf: 7,000.
★★★ *Stellamare,* v. del Mare 8, ☎ 81203, 30 rm ℗ closed
Oct-Easter, 60,000; bkf: 7,000.
★★ *Serena,* lungomare Trieste 39, ☎ 81133, 36 rm ℗ ⚲
closed Oct-Apr. No restaurant, 60,000.

Restaurant:
● ♦♦♦ *Duilio,* v. Strada Nuova 19, ☎ 81087, closed
Mon except hols and 15 Sep-15 May. Spacious and elegant with marine furnishings including hull of sailing boat. Mixed regional cuisine: cuttlefish risotto, roast meats, 20/30,000.

⚊ ★★★★ *San Francesco,* at Porto Santa Margherita, v. Selva Rosata, 1,200 pl, ☎ 89333; *Falconera,* at Falconera, v. dei Casoni, 198 pl, ☎ 84282.

Recommended
Marina: at Santa Margherita (5 km SW), ☎ 860230 (seasonal; opens in May).
Sailing: *Club vela d'altura,* at Santa Margherita, v. Pigafetta 7, ☎ 83346 (school, 6-12-day cruises in the Mediterranean, Jun-Sep).
Swimming: v. Lepanto, ☎ 860437.
Tennis: v. dei Greci, ☎ 860485.

CASTELFRANCO VENETO

Treviso 26, Venice 45, Milan 239 km
Pop. 28,697 ⊠ 31033 ☎ 0423   D4

Castelfranco Veneto was the birthplace of the painter Giorgione (Giorgio Barbarelli, 1477-1510) who breathed new life into Venetian painting although he lived for only a short time. Square walls have governed the shape of the town centre and help guard its unspoiled, peaceful atmosphere.

▶ The **castello's**★ red walls (1199) and five towers form a square surrounded by a moat. ▶ The **Bastia Nuova** has several 16C-18C buildings. Nearby are the piazza del Mercato Vecchio (old market) and the Loggia dei Grani e delle Biade. ▶ The 18C Palladian **Duomo**★ contains Giorgione's 1504 work, *The Madonna Enthroned Between St. Francis and St. Liberale*★. The sacristy has fragments of Veronese **frescos**★ (1551) which were removed from the Villa Soranza before it was pulled down, as well as other paintings. ▶ On the p. del Duomo, the **Casa del Giorgione** *(Sat 3-6 p.m.; Sun 10:30 a.m.-12:30 p.m. and 3-6 p.m.)* has a frescoed **fascia**★ generally attributed to the artist. ▶ Behind the brick façade of the 18C **Teatro Accademico** (v. Garibaldi; *9:30 a.m.-12:30 p.m. and 2-6 p.m.; closed Sat and hols*) is an unusual stuccoed interior. ▶ The **Villa Revedin-Bolasco** at Borgo Treviso 46 has a fine park *(Sat, first Sun of month, summer 3:30-6:30 p.m., winter 2-5 p.m.).* ▶ 4 km SW, in the S. Andrea district, is the **Villa Corner** with frescos by the school of Veronese *(Sat 3-6 p.m.; reserve on other days)* and, in an outbuilding, the **Museo Agricolo e dell'Arte Conciaria** (farming, tanning; *3-6 p.m.*).   □

If you enjoy sports, consult the pages pertaining to the regions; there you will find addresses for practicing your favorite sport.

Practical information

ⓘ v. Garibaldi, ☎ 495000.

Hotels:
★★★ *Roma,* v. Filzi 39, ☎ 495041, 68 rm Ⓟ ৬ 68,000; bkf: 7,000.
★★ *Cà delle Rose,* at Salvarosa, circonvallazione Est 33/A, ☎ 490232, 20 rm Ⓟ ∰ ৬ ⚘ closed Aug, 54,000; bkf: 7,000. Rest. ● ♦♦♦ *Barbesin* ☎ 490446, closed Wed eve, Thu, Jan and Aug. Regional cuisine: guinea fowl in peppery sauce, fricandeau with herbs, 25/35,000.

CITTADELLA

Padua 28, Venice 61, Milan 227 km
Pop. 17,563 ⊠ 35013 ☎ 049   C4

Cittadella exemplifies the medieval town, with an elliptical ring of walls, a moat, thirty-two towers and four gates.

▶ The town stands at the point where the line of foothills gently slopes down to the broad plain. Cittadella was Padua's response to the building of Castelfranco (→) by Treviso and was founded twenty years later. ▶ The grid of streets, formed by the crossing of the Padua-Bassano and the Vicenza-Treviso roads contrasts with the irregular, elliptical ring of the 13C-14C walls★, glacis and moat. ▶ In the Neoclassical **parish church** (late 18C) are 16C-18C Venetian paintings.   ▢

Practical information

ⓘ v. Garibaldi, ☎ 5970986.

Hotel:
★★★★ *Motel Palace,* borgo Vicenza 64, ☎ 5971922, 51 rm Ⓟ ∰ ⚘ 75,000; bkf: 7,000.

CONCORDIA SAGITTARIA

Venice 66, Milan 325 km
Pop. 10,442 ⊠ 30023 ☎ 0421   E-F3

On the banks of the Lémene, Concordia looks like a town in the Venetian lagoon. It is in fact Roman in origin and the name is Latin. During the Barbarian invasions, Concordia was transformed into a stronghold and centre for weapons manufacturing.

▶ The **cathedral,** at the end of a short road lined with sarcophagi and columns, is Gothic-Renaissance (rebuilt 1466). To the side of the church and in front of the 11C-12C Romanesque **baptistery** (Greek cross plan, three apses with 11C-14C frescos) are excavations where discoveries include a group of **early Christian buildings** (4C-5C); **sarcophagus of Faustiniana** (arcaded burial enclosures); martyrium for the veneration of relics; funerary basilica and part of the outer walls of the r. aisle, with a mosaic pavement, of the **basilica of the Apostles** (the remainder lies beneath the present cathedral). ▶ Beyond the cemetery, along the road to San Giusto, are the remains of a 2C **Roman bridge.**   ▢

CONEGLIANO

Treviso 28, Venice 60, Milan 310 km
Pop. 36,051 ⊠ 31015 ☎ 0438   D3

Two wine roads lead out of the town. The red wine route *(68 km, road signs)* heads for Oderzo and twists across the plain along the l. bank of the Piave through a region known for red or rosé wines made with Cabernet, Merlot and Raboso grapes. The white wine route *(42 km, road signs)* passes through gentle hills whose vineyards produce Prosecco, Cartizze and Bianco dei colli, on its way to Valdobbiadene. At intervals along the routes are inns and wine

merchants where it is possible to stop and sample the produce.

▶ Features of Conegliano are arcaded streets, frescoed houses, Venetian-style palaces (15C-18C) and the p. G. B. Cima (named for the painter Giovanni Battista Cima da Conegliano, 1459-1518). ▶ The **Duomo** has a Gothic portico (14C-15C) and a campanile of 1497. The high altar has a splendid altarpiece, *Madonna Enthroned with Saints★* (1493). The late 14C *Sala dei Battuti (apply to sacristan)* is decorated with early 16C frescos. ▶ The **Casa di Cima da Conegliano** (v. Cima 24; *Sat and Sun 4-6 p.m. summer; 3-5 p.m. winter)* is devoted to the painter and displays archaeological finds as well. ▶ The esplanade of the Castello (above the town, view★) has the remains of walls and towers from the medieval **Castelvecchio.** The bell tower houses the **Museum** *(9 a.m.-12 noon and 3:30-7 p.m. summer; 2-5:30 p.m. winter; closed Mon)* exhibiting stones, coins, frescos, paintings, sculpture and historical material.   ▢

Practical information

ⓘ v. Carducci 32, ☎ 21230.

Hotels:
★★★ *Canon d'Oro,* v. XX Settembre 129, ☎ 22171, 26 rm Ⓟ ∰ ৬ 60,000; bkf: 6,000.
★★★ *Sporting Hotel Ragno d'Oro,* v. Diaz 37, ☎ 24955, 17 rm Ⓟ ∰ ⚘ ☐ ⁓ No restaurant, 85,000; bkf: 6,000.
★★ *Cima,* v. XXIV Maggio 61, ☎ 22648, 20 rm Ⓟ ∰ ⚘ closed Jul-Aug, 60,000; bkf: 4,000. Rest. ♦♦♦ closed Tue. Regional cuisine: risottos, venison in rich wine sauce, 17/22,000.

Restaurants:
● ♦♦♦ *Tre Panoce,* v. Vecchia Trevigiana 50, ☎ 60071, closed Mon and Aug. Late 17C former convent with spacious garden. Excellent regional and Italian cuisine: duck in Prosecco grape sauce, game, 25/35,000.
♦♦ *Salisà,* v. XX Settembre 2, ☎ 24288, closed Tue eve, Wed and Aug. Service on terrace in summer. Italian and some international cuisine: duck with brandy, saddle of venison in rich wine sauce, 30/40,000.

Recommended
Bowling: v. Lourdes 274, ☎ 32087.
Clay pigeon shooting: at Santa Lucia di Piave *(5 km S),* v. dell'Argine, ☎ 27388.
Motocross: at San Pietro di Feletto *(9 km NW),* management, *Moto Club Cimetta.*
Water skiing: *Sci Club Orsago,* at Cava Biasuzzi *(12 km NE),* ☎ 90454.
Wine: *Istituto Sperimentale per la Viticoltura,* v. 28 Aprile 1, ☎ 61615 (first Tue of month); *Carpene Malvolti,* ☎ 23531 (reserve, allowing several weeks' notice).

CORDEVOLE VALLEY

D1-2

The Cordévole River rises near the Pordoi Pass and flows down the Belluna Valley to join the Piave. The lower part of the valley, known as the Canale di Agordo, runs between close-set crags. The alpine upper basin is surrounded by the Dolomites (Marmolada, Averau, Nuvolau, Pelmo and Civetta) and has extensive meadows and woods. Numerous villages provide accommodation for vacationers, skiers and climbers.

▶ The main centre of the valley is **Agordo** (→). A side valley to the r. leads to the **Frassenè** basin and then to the meadows and conifers of the **Forcella Aurine.** ▶ Upstream from Agordo, along the valley of the Biois torrent, is **Falcade** (3,757 ft), which offers views of the peaks of the Dolomites and from where a road leads to the **Valles Pass** (6,667 ft) and down to Predazo in the Val di Fiemme (→ in Trentino-Alto Adige) while another leads to the **San Pellegrino Pass** (6,293 ft) and then down to Moena in the Val di Fassa (→ in Trentino-Alto Adige). ▶ **Alleghe** (5,167 ft) lies beneath the immense wall of Civetta (10,558 ft), beside the picturesque Lago di Alleghe, which dates from 1771 when the valley was blocked up by a landslide. ▶ **Rocca Piétore** (3,750 ft) is in a further valley, the Val Pettorina, beneath Marmolada (→ in Trentino-Alto Adige), and both Pelmo and Civetta are within view. ▶ The upper basin of the Val Cordévole is known as the Livinallongo. **Pieve di Livinallongo** lies on the slopes of the Col di Lana, whose outline changed markedly when six tons of explosive were detonated on 17 April 1916. The **Grande Strada delle Dolomiti** (→ in Trentino-Alto Adige) passes through the valley to **Arabba** (5,256 ft), at the foot of the Sella group, where the roads from the **Pordoi Pass** (→ in Trentino-Alto Adige) and the **Campolongo Pass** meet. □

Practical information ─────────────

ALLEGHE, ⊠ 32022, ☎ 0437.
⌇ ski lifts, cross-country skiing, instruction, summer skiing on Marmolada, ☎ 723716.
ⓘ ☎ 723333.

Hotels:
★★★ *Posta,* at Caprile, p. Dogliani 19, ☎ 721171, 46 rm ♿ ⚘ closed 3 May-15 Jun and 25 Sep-30 Nov, 78,000; bkf: 6,000.
★★★ *Sporthotel Europa,* v. Europa 10, ☎ 723362, 33 rm Ⓟ ♦ ⚘ closed May and Oct-Christmas, 80,000; bkf: 7,000.
★★ *Alleghe,* corso Italia 21, ☎ 723527, 16 rm ⚄ ♿ ⚘ closed May and 15 Oct-30 Nov, 70,000; bkf: 7,000.
★★ *Coldai,* v. Coldai 15, ☎ 723305, 29 rm Ⓟ ⚄ ⚘ closed May and Oct, 54,000; bkf: 5,000.

Recommended
Alpine guides: corso Italia Zunaia 8, ☎ 723766.
Skating: ☎ 723749; **Hockey club,** v. Lungolago 18, ☎ 723791.
Tennis: at Masaré *(2 km S)* and Caprile *(4 km N).*

ARABBA, ⊠ 32020, ☎ 0436.
⌇ cableway, ski lifts, cross-country skiing, instruction.

Hotels:
★★★★ *Sporthotel Arabba,* v. Pordoi 80, ☎ 79158, 45 rm Ⓟ ⚄ ⚘ ⚘ ♿ ⚘ closed May and Oct-Nov, 120,000; bkf: 10,000.
★★★ *Boé,* at passo Campolongo, ☎ 79144, 35 rm Ⓟ ⚄ ♿ ⚘ closed May-Jun and Oct-Nov, 71,000; bkf: 10,000.
★★★ *Monte Cherz,* at passo Campolongo, ☎ 79133, 23 rm Ⓟ ⚄ ⚘ closed 16 Apr-Jun and Oct-Nov, 60,000; bkf: 5,000.

Restaurant:
♦ *Grill al Forte,* v. Pezzei 66, ☎ 79150, closed Tue, Jun-Jul and Nov-Dec. Italian cuisine: grilled meats, mushrooms prepared in various ways, 20/27,000.

FALCADE, ⊠ 32020, ☎ 0437.
⌇ ski lifts, cross-country skiing, instruction, skating.
ⓘ municipio, ☎ 59241; at Caviola, ☎ 50116.

Hotels:
★★★ *Scoiattolo,* at Caviola, v. Pineta 3, ☎ 50346, 28 rm Ⓟ ⚄ ⚘ ⚘ ▭ ⚘ closed 16 Apr-14 Jun and 1 Oct-30 Nov, 78,000; bkf: 5,000.
★★ *Serena,* corso Italia 14, ☎ 50134, 26 rm Ⓟ ⚄ ⚒ ⚘ ⚘ closed Easter-May and Oct-Nov, 58,000; bkf: 7,000.

Recommended
Events: *Pizolada delle Dolomiti, international skiing and climbing race,* pairs competition, Sun after Easter.

PIEVE DI LIVINALLONGO, ⊠ 32020, ☎ 0436.
ⓘ ☎ 7157.

ROCCA PIETORE, ⊠ 32020, ☎ 0437.
⌇ ski lifts at Sottoguda.
ⓘ ☎ 721319.

Hotels:
★★ *Digonera,* at Digonera, ☎ 721193, 30 rm Ⓟ ⚄ closed May and Nov, 69,000.

★★ *Rosalpina,* v. Bosca Verde 21, ☎ 722004, 32 rm Ⓟ ⚘ closed May and Oct-Nov, 50,000.

CORTINA D'AMPEZZO**

Belluno 71, Venice 161, Milan 411 km
Pop. 8,005 ⊠ 32043 ☎ 0436   D1

The campanile against the background of the Tofane Dolomites is perhaps the best known symbol of this famous winter resort. The attractions include bracing walks through superb scenery, rock climbing of every degree of difficulty and all kinds of winter sports. Cortina is the main centre of the Venetian **Dolomites**. It lies in an undulating basin of the Bóite Valley, ringed by the mountains of the Tofane group, Pomagagnon, Cristallo, Sorapis, the Cinque Torri, Croda da Lago and the Becco di Mezzodi. Cortina first began to attract tourists in the mid-19C; in 1902 the town staged the first ski race in Italy. The buildings along the corso d'Italia are modern with some interesting and lively architecture.

▶ The 18C **parish church** has a wooden tabernacle (1724) and an altarpiece dating from 1679; there is a view from the top of the campanile. ▶ In the **Ciasa de ra Regoles** are the **Museum,** devoted to geology, minerals and local traditions *(4-7:30 or 7 p.m. in winter; closed Sun)* and the **Rimoldi Collection** of modern Italian art, with works by important painters. ▶ A cableway and chair lift lead to **Tondi di Faloria** (7,677 ft), from where there is a splendid view★. The **Tofana di Mezzo** (10,643 ft) is reached by a cableway known as the *'Freccia del Cielo'*★ (arrow of the skies) and offers a view★ from Adamello to Grossglockner and to the lagoon of Venice. ▶ In the **Tofane** group a chair lift runs from Piemerlo (5,505 ft; *4 km*) to the Duca d'Aosta refuge at 6,883 ft, then to the Forcella Pomedes (7,487 ft) with a view★. ▶ From Rio Geres (5,511 ft; *6 km along road to Tre Croci Pass*) a chair lift and cableway runs to Forcella Staunies beside **Cristallo;** view★ to the Grossglockner; descent by path and steps to the small Cresta Bianca glacier (8,990 ft). ▶ At dusk the **Belvedere di Pocol** (5,049 ft; *bus*) offers a superb view of the Cortina basin; a little farther on is the **Sacrario Pocol** (war cemetery; *summer 7 a.m.-12 noon and 4-7 p.m.; winter 9 a.m.-12 noon and 2-5 p.m.).* ▶ The **Giro del Lago Ghedina** (11 km) is a trout lake surrounded by fir forests. ▶ **Misurina** (→) is reached by crossing the Tre Croci Pass (5,935 ft). ▶ 16 km away is the **Falzàrego Pass** (→) on the Grande Strada delle Dolomiti (→ in Trentino-Alto Adige); there is a cableway to **Lagazuoi Piccolo** (view★). □

Practical information ─────────────

CORTINA D'AMPEZZO
⌇ cableways at Falzarego, Druscè and Faloria; ski lifts, more than 50 km cross-country skiing, instruction, Olympic ice-skating stadium, bob sled run at Ronco, ☎ 867395, sled run, *Italia* Olympic ski jump at Zuel, ☎ 3484.
ⓘ p. Roma, ☎ 2711; p. S. Francesco, ☎ 3231.
▭ from bus station, v. Marconi, ☎ 2741.

Hotels:
★★★★★ *Cristallo,* v. Menardi 42, ☎ 4281, 98 rm Ⓟ ⚄ ⚒ ▭ ⚒ Pens. closed 11 Apr-9 Jul and 11 Sep-Christmas, 278,500.
★★★★★ *Miramonte Majestic G. H.,* v. Pezié 103, ☎ 4201, 134 rm Ⓟ ⚄ ⚒ ⚘ ▭ ⚒ ⚒ (9 holes) Pens. closed Apr-Jun and Sep-Christmas, 240,000.
★★★★ *Cortina,* corso Italia 92, ☎ 4221, 48 rm Ⓟ ⚄ closed 16 Apr-19 Jun and 16 Sep-Christmas, 260,000; bkf: 15,000.
★★★★ *De la Poste,* p. Roma 14, ☎ 4271, 83 rm Ⓟ ⚄ ⚒ Pens. closed 20 Oct-20 Dec, 240,000.
★★★★ *Europa,* corso Italia 207, ☎ 3221, 52 rm Ⓟ ⚄ closed Nov, 280,000; bkf: 15,000.
★★★★ *Savoia G. H.,* v. Roma 62, ☎ 3201, 142 rm Ⓟ ⚄ ⚒

⊠ ✍ closed 11 Apr-4 Jul and 16 Sep-Christmas, 297,000; bkf: 20,000.
★★★★ *Splendid Hotel Venezia,* corso Italia 209, ☎ 3291, 92 rm ℗ ⪡ ᕃ closed 11 Apr-31 May and 21 Sep-19 Dec, 300,000.
★★★ *Capannina,* v. dello Stadio 11, ☎ 2950, 20 rm ℗ ⫘ ⅋ closed Easter-4 Jul and 11 Sep-3 Dec, 190,000. Rest. ◆◆◆ closed Wed. International cuisine: filet with speck, chicken allo cherry, 35/55,000.
★★★ *Columbia,* v. Ronco 75, ☎ 3607, 22 rm ℗ ⪡ ⫘ ⅋ closed May and Oct-Nov. No restaurant, 72,000; bkf: 6,000.
★★★ *Concordia Park Hotel,* corso Italia 28, ☎ 4251, 58 rm ℗ ⫘ closed 21 Mar-30 Jun and 1 Sep-21 Dec, 190,000; bkf: 7,000.
★★★ *Fanes,* v. Roma 136, ☎ 3427, 21 rm ℗ ⪡ ⫘ closed 6 Apr-14 Jun and 6 Nov-18 Dec, 120,000; bkf: 8,000.
★★★ *Franceschi Park Hotel,* v. Battisti 86, ☎ 867041, 44 rm ℗ ⪡ ⫘ ⅋ ✍ closed 1 Apr-24 Jun and 1 Oct-18 Dec, 190,000; bkf: 8,000.
★★★ *Majoni,* v. Roma, ☎ 866945, 50 rm ℗ ⪡ ⫘ ᕃ Pens. closed 21 Apr-19 Jun and 22 Sep-14 Dec, 170,000.
★★★ *MotelAgip,* v. Roma 118, ☎ 61400, 42 rm ℗ ⅋ 140,000.
★★★ *Parc Hotel Victoria,* corso Italia 1, ☎ 3246, 45 rm ℗ ⫘ closed 1 Apr-30 Jun and 21 Sep-19 Dec, 180,000; bkf: 12,000.
★★ *Menardi,* v. Majon 110, ☎ 2400, 43 rm ℗ ⪡ ⫘ closed 11 Apr-19 Jun and 16 Sep-19 Dec, 98,000; bkf: 10,000.

Restaurants:
● ◆◆◆ *El Toulà,* v. Ronco 123, ☎ 3339, closed Mon in low season and 16 Apr-24 Jul and 11 Sep-22 Dec. Regional cuisine, luxurious and full of atmosphere, 45/65,000.
◆◆◆ *Beppe Sello,* v. Ronco 68, ☎ 3236, closed Tue in low season and 16 Apr-14 May and 26 Sep-31 Oct. Bellunese cuisine: tagliatelle with cèpes, pappardelle with venison, 23/38,000.
● ◆◆ *Bellavista-il Meloncino,* at Gillardon, ☎ 61043, closed Tue, Jun and Nov. Bellunese cuisine: canederli, casunziei, 30/40,000.

⚐ ★★ *Olympia,* at Fiames, 283 pl, ☎ 5057 (all year).

Recommended
Alpine guides: p. S. Francesco, ☎ 4740 (trips for adults and children, routes with handrails, rock-climbing school).
Bowling: largo delle Poste, ☎ 2333.
Discothèque: *Vip,* at Hotel Europa, corso Italia 207, ☎ 3221 (closed Easter-Christmas except Aug); *Area,* at Ronco, ☎ 867393.
Excursions: cableway (from railway station) to Tondi di Faloria, ☎ 2517 or 3356; to Tofana de Mezzo, ☎ 5052; to Cristallo (cableway from Rio Geres on climb to Tre Croci Pass), ☎ 861035; cableway to Laguzuoi Piccolo from Falzarego Pass, ☎ 867301.
Golf: at *Miramonti Hotel* (9 holes).
Horseback riding: v. Fraina 6, ☎ 60641.
Mountain guides: *Le settimane di S. Peretti,* v. dello Stadio 23, ☎ 861594 (instruction).
Swimming: at Guargnè, ☎ 60781.
Tennis: v. Sopiazes, ☎ 2937.

Environs
POCOL, 6 km SW.

Hotels:
★★★ *Argentina,* ☎ 5641, 110 rm ℗ ⪡ ⫘ closed 8 Apr-30 Jun and 8 Sep-19 Dec, 110,000; bkf: 8,000.
★★ *Pocol,* ☎ 2602, 22 rm ℗ ⪡ ⫘ closed Apr-19 Jun and 1 Oct-Christmas, 85,000; bkf: 7,000.

ESTE*

Padua 31, Venice 69, Milan 220 km
Pop. 18,032 ⊠ 35042 ☎ 0429   C5

The Este family, who were renowned as rulers of Ferrara and patrons of the arts, took their name from this

little town at the point where the S edge of the Euganean hills gives way to the plain. The Este lived for power, took the title of marquesses of Este in the mid-12C and held the town for at least 100 years before being expelled by Padua and moving on to greater success. The name Este is derived from an older Roman one, *Ateste,* which perhaps comes from *Athesis,* i.e., the river Adige, which used to flow past Este until earthquakes and floods in 589 altered its course.
▶ The **Castello★** (A1-2) was built by the Carrara of Padua (1339). The walls form a vast trapezoid, now a public garden, and continue up the hill on which the keep stands. ▶ A 16C palace to the l. of the garden entrance houses the **Museo Nazionale Atestino★** (A2), with one of N Italy's most important archaeological collections *(Apr-Sep 9 a.m.-1 p.m. and 3-7 p.m.; Oct-Mar 9 a.m.-1 p.m. and 3-6 p.m.; hols 9 a.m.-12 p.m.; closed Mon).* The pre-Roman section has Aeneolithic and Bronze Age finds and funerary artifacts from the early Iron Age. The Roman section has inscriptions, mosaics, architectural fragments, glass and medals. ▶ The historical part of the city occupies the elongated rectangle between the Castello and the Canale d'Este. ▶ The **Duomo** (A1), rebuilt 1708, has an oval interior and contains numerous paintings and sculptures, including Tiepolo's *St. Thecla Liberates Este from the Plague of 1630★* (1759). ▶ The Romanesque-Gothic church of **St. Martin** (A2) has a leaning campanile (1293). ▶ Other interesting buildings include the 16C church of **S. Maria delle Consolazioni** (A1) and the 18C basilica of **S. Maria delle Grazie** (B2), which has a 15C Byzantine-style *Madonna and Child.* ▶ The town has several arcaded streets and old villas.   □

Practical information ———————————

ℹ p. Maggiore (A1-2), ☎ 3635.

Hotels:
★★ *Beatrice d'Este,* v. Rimembranze 1 (A2 a), ☎ 3681, 30 rm ℗ ⫘ 42,000; bkf: 3,000.
★★ *Centrale,* p. Beatrice d'Este 16 (A1-2 b), ☎ 3930, 21 rm ℗ 36,000; bkf: 5,000.

Restaurant:
♦♦ *Tavernetta-da Piero Ceschi,* p. Trento 16 (A1 c), ☎ 2855, closed Thu and Jul, 30/40,000.
Recommended
Craft workshops: *Ceramiche estensi,* v. Volta 26, ☎ 4848 (ceramics).

The EUGANEAN HILLS

From Padua *(119 km, 1 day; map 2)*

The Euganean hills are a compact and isolated group of volcanic hills that takes its name from the most ancient and mysterious inhabitants of Venetia. The varied countryside has extensive woodlands of locust trees, chestnuts, oaks, arbutus, elms and laurels. This route makes a circuit of the hills and has been chosen both for the scenery and the cultural or environmental importance of the places it passes through.

▶ From **Padua** (→) the route leads SW past the **abbey of Praglia**★ (→ Abano Terme) to **Teolo,** which lies in a pleasant basin (the sanctuary of the Madonna del Monte stands on a height at a distance of *2.5 km;* view). ▶ The route then goes to **Noventa Vicentina,** with an arcaded piazza with the 17C Villa Barbarigo and the Duomo, and **Poiana Maggiore,** with the 15C Villa Poiana and another by Palladio, before reaching **Montagnana**★ (→); **Sant'Elena** (Villa Castello, park with lake; interior, *open to visitors,* 16C-18C Venetian paintings); **Monsélice** (→) and **Arqua Petrarca** (→). ▶ At **Battaglia Terme** are the 16C-18C Villa Emo Capodilista and the **Villa del Cataio**★, built 1572 but with later Baroque decorations, set in a large park. ▶ Finally it passes through **Valsanzibo** (**Villa Barbarigo,** beautiful Italian garden★, *open to visitors*), then climbing to the **Eremo di Monte Rua** (→ Abano Terme). ▶ The tour follows the E slopes of the hills through **Torreglia, Monteortone** and **Abano Terme** and returns to Padua.　□

Practical information _____

BATTAGLIA TERME, ⊠ 35041, ☎ 049.
♨ (Mar-Nov), ☎ 525269; at Galzignano, ☎ 525186.
ℹ v. Traversa Terme 23A, ☎ 525269.

Hotels:
★★★ *Green Park Terme,* ☎ 525511, 92 rm ℗ ▥ ▭ ⌇ Pens. closed Dec-Feb, 74,000.
★★★ *Majestic Hotel Terme,* ☎ 525444, 125 rm ℗ ▥ ♿ ▭ ⌇ ⌿ (18 holes) Pens. closed Dec-Feb, 77,500.
★★★ *Splendid Terme,* ☎ 525333, 108 rm ℗ ▥ ▭ ⌇ ⌿ (18 holes) Pens. closed Dec-Feb, 77,500.
★★★ *Sporting Terme,* ☎ 5255000, 106 rm ℗ ▥ ▭ ⌇ ⌿ (18 holes) Pens. closed Dec-Feb, 99,000.

MONTEORTONE, ⊠ 35030, ☎ 049.

Hotels:
★★★★ *Leonardo da Vinci Terme,* Tramonte 70, ☎ 9935057, 105 rm ℗ ♦ ▥ ♿ ▭ ⌇ closed Dec-Feb, 110,000; bkf: 12,000.
★★★★ *Terme Michelangelo,* v. S. Daniele 36, ☎ 9935026, 120 rm ℗ ♦ ▥ ▭ ⌇ closed 16 Nov-28 Feb, 90,000; bkf: 12,000.

NOVENTA VICENTINA, ⊠ 36025, ☎ 0444.

Recommended
Horseback riding: *Gruppo ippico Basso Vicentino,* v. Europa 13 (associate of *ANTE*).

VALSANZIBIO, ⊠ 35030, ☎ 049.

Recommended
Golf: ☎ 528078 (18 holes).

Villa Emo at FANZOLO

Treviso 22, Venice 51, Milan 245 km
Pop. 874 ⊠ 31050 ☎ 0423　　　　　　　　　D3-4

This villa, built *c.* 1550 by Andrea Palladio for the Venetian noble Leonardo Emo, is a fine example of the Palladian farmstead and country house.　The porticoed main building, approached by a flight of steps, is flanked by two long, arcaded wings.　The interior decoration includes frescos *(winter Sat and hols, 2-5 p.m.; summer 2 or 3-6 p.m.; groups on other days, reserve,*☎ 487040).　□

The arrow (→) is a reference to another entry.

2. The Euganean Hills

FELTRE

Belluno 31, Venice 88, Milan 288 km
Pop. 20,691 ⊠ 32032 ☎ 0439   D3

Feltre is decidedly Venetian in atmosphere with its projecting eaves that suggest arcades, façades covered with the remains of frescos and portals adorned with the lions of St. Mark. Feltre was twice sacked by troops of the Holy Roman Emperor (1509 and 1510) because of its allegiance to Venice.

▶ The **via Mezzaterra**★ (A1-2) climbs through the old town to the 16C **Porta Imperiale** (B1). It is lined with picturesque 16C houses with façades covered with worn frescos depicting classical subjects. ▶ Monuments to famous sons of the town (the 15C printer Panfilo Castaldi, the teacher Vittorino da Feltre) adorn the lively **piazza Maggiore**★ (A2) on which the church of **S. Rocco** (1599) faces a Renaissance fountain (1520). Also on the Piazza are the **Palazzo del Comune** by Palladio and the 19C neo-Gothic **Palazzo Guarnieri**. The square keep of the medieval Castello dominates the scene. ▶ The **Galleria Rizzarda** (A1; *9 a.m.-12 noon and 2-6 p.m.*) displays wrought iron and 19C and modern sculpture and paintings. ▶ The **via Luzzo** (A2) is almost entirely lined by Renaissance houses. The **Museo Civico**★ is at no. 23 *(Sat 10 a.m.-1 p.m. and 4-6 p.m.; Sun 11 a.m.-1 p.m. and 4-6 p.m.; closed Mon).* ▶ The **Cathedral** (B2) was rebuilt in the 16C but retains the polygonal Gothic apse and 1392 campanile (15C funerary relief at the base). Inside are a 9C crypt and a Renaissance tomb in the sanctuary. Behind the church, the **baptistery** has a font of 1399; the original early-Christian baptistery is under excavation. ▶ The sacristy of the church of **Ognissanti** (A2) displays a fresco of the *Apparition of Christ*★ *(apply to neighbouring Istituto Neuropsichiatrico).* ▶ 3.8 km SE is the Romanesque church of **SS. Vittore e Corona** (11C-12C), with an interesting loggia in the apse and 13C-14C frescos. □

Practical information _____

⛷ ski lifts, cross-country skiing at Croce d'Aune Pass *(11 km NW).*
ⓘ largo Castaldi 7 (B1), ☎ 2540.

Belluno 1   2

FELTRE

0   100   200   300m
1:16.000 (1cm=160m)

© SERVIZIO CARTOGRAFICO DEL TOURING CLUB ITALIANO, MILANO   2

Hotel:
★★★ Nuovo, v. Fornere Pazze (A1 a), ☎ 81345, 23 rm Ⓟ ⏚ No restaurant, 55,000.

Recommended
Brewery: *Dreher,* at Pedavena *(3 km NW),* v. Vittorio Veneto 78, ☎ 301755 (guided tour; Mon-Fri 9 a.m.-4 p.m.).
Events: *festival of the palio (horse race) in historical costume* (Aug).
Horseback riding: *Associazione turistica Equitazione Feltrino,* at tourist office, ☎ 2540 (associate of *ANTE*).
Skating: at Bosco Drio le Rive, ☎ 89993.
Swimming: at Pedavena, v. U. Foscolo, ☎ 302061.
Youth hostel: *Ostello Feltre,* p. Maggiore, Castello di Alboino (A2), ☎ 81188.

Villa Badoer at FRATTA POLESINE

Rovigo 16, Venice 94, Milan 279 km
Pop. 3,010 ⊠ 45025 ☎ 0425   C6

The Villa Badoer is one of the most chaming of Palladio's designs. The free-standing central section on a gentle rise is approached by a broad flight of steps and preceded by a loggia with six columns. The central building is flanked by two semicircular wings with an arcade of Tuscan columns. In the bare interior the remains of **frescos** have recently been discovered *(2-5 p.m. or 3-7 p.m. Thu and Sun; also summer 9 a.m.-12 noon).* □

FUGAZZE PLAIN

Vicenza 45, Venice 115, Milan 247 km
⊠ 36030 ☎ 0445   B3

The pass between the Vallarsa and the Valle del Léogra in the Venetian-Trentina pre-Alps is the starting point for a visit to the Pasubio, which was the scene of ferocious battles in World War I.

▶ The **Pasubio war cemetery** (4,006 ft; *2 km SE;* warden) has a small historical museum and a good view★. ▶ Two tricky roads lead up to the Pasubio: the **Strada degli Eroi** *(easier access to memorial area)* leaves the pass and through a series of tunnels reaches, after 10.5 km, the **Porte di Pasubio** (6,345 ft). This is also the destination of the **Strada degli Scarubbi**, which turns off the national road at Ponte Verde *(4 km from pass, on Vicenza slope)* and crosses the **Xomo Pass** (3,465 ft) and the **Bocchetta di Campiglia** (3,970 ft). A short stretch to the N ends at the **Selletta Sette Croci** (9,190 ft). The **memorial area**★ comprises the Dente Italiano and the Cima Palon: its boundary is marked by thirty stones commemorating the detachments that distinguished themselves in the fighting of 1916-18. At Bocchetta di Campiglia, the **Strada della l Armata** turns off. □

GARDA

Verona 31, Venice 151, Milan 151 km
Pop. 3,470 ⊠ 37016 ☎ 045   A4

Situated on a bay on Lake Garda, at the base of the foothills of Mt. Baldo (→), this pleasant town has a typical **old quarter.** Trees line the shore of the lake. The 18C **parish church** has a 15C campanile and the remains of a cloister from the same period. □

Practical information _____

ⓘ lungolago Regina Adelaide 25, ☎ 7255194.
🚢 boats and hydrofoils.

Hotels:
★★★★ *Eurotel Garda,* v. Marconi 18, ☎ 7255107, 145 rm Ⓟ ⏝ ⌀ closed Nov-Mar, 136,000; bkf: 8,000.

★★★ **Flora**, v. Madrina 4, ☎ 7255348, 58 rm P 🔒 🏛 ᴃ ⚭ 🖃 ⚡ closed 16 Oct-31 Mar, 70,000; bkf: 12,000.
★★★ **Gabbiano**, v. dei Cipressi 4, ☎ 7255363, 30 rm P 🏛 ⚭ 🖃 closed Nov-Easter, 60,000; bkf: 8,000.
★★★ **Regina Adelaide**, v. XX Settembre, ☎ 7255013, 54 rm P 🏛 88,000.
★★ **Conca d'Oro**, v. Lungolago 28, ☎ 7255275, 19 rm P 🏛 ⚭ closed 6 Nov-28 Feb, 60,000.
★★ **Continental**, v. Giorgione 6, ☎ 7255398, 56 rm P 🏛 🖃 closed Nov-Mar, 45,000; bkf: 6,000.
★★ **Giardinetto**, v. Lungolago 28, ☎ 7255051, 24 rm ⚭ 45,000; bkf: 8,000.
★★ **Tre Corone**, lungolago Regina Adelaide 52, ☎ 7255033, 25 rm P 🏛 ⚭ closed Nov-Feb, 44,000; bkf: 8,000.

Restaurant:
♦ **Beati**, v. Beati Bassi, ☎ 7255780, closed Mon and Jan. View of lake and mountains. Italian and some international cuisine: gnocchi with radicchio, fillet in cider, 25/30,000.

Recommended
Horseback riding: *Centro ippico Rossar,* at Rossar Marciaga di Costermano *(4 km E),* ☎ 7255943 (trekking on the hills around lake; courses for beginners).
Sailing: *Lega Navale,* lungolago Pincherli, ☎ 7256377.
Tennis: v. Don Gnocchi.

GARDA AND THE LESSINI MOUNTAINS

From Verona *(167 km, 1 day; map 3)*

The shores of Lake Garda are known for their mild climate, evident from the olives, palms, cypresses, lemons and cedars that grow there. However, the lake is known to have frozen over completely at least once, in 1709. This suggested route runs along the great E gulf (for the Brescia shore → Lombardy) and returns to Verona by climbing Mt. Baldo (→) and gently descending through the Lessini Mountains, the series of ranges that fan out from N to S to the l. of the Adige and gradually subside into cultivated hills on the plain of Verona. Between 3,600 and 4,900 ft in

the Lessini is the plateau of the 13 Communes. The main interest of the town lies in the variety of its scenery.

▶ From **Verona** (→) the route joins **Lake Garda at Peschiera del Garda** (→). The E shore leads to **Lasize** (→), **Bardolino** (→) and **Garda** (→). ▶ The headland that marks the end of the gulf is the **Punta di San Vigilio★★** and is one of the most romantic spots on the lake, with cypresses and the ancient church of S. Vigilio (dedicated to a 4C bishop of Trento who preached to the people of this shore) and the beautiful 16C Villa Guarienti. ▶ At **Torri del Benaco** (→) the route leaves the lake, crosses Mt. Baldo and descends to **Caprino Veronese** and then, after crossing a basin with numerous vineyards, comes to **Affi**. ▶ Having crossed the Adige downstream of the Rivoli dam, the route follows the **Valpolicella** (known for its wine), into which open the valleys of several rivers descending from the Lessini plateau. ▶ Passing through **Sant'Ambrogio di Valpolicella, San Pietro in Cariano, Negrar, Prun,** over the ridge between the Valle del Progno di Fumane and the Vaio Marchiora, the route finally arrives at **Sant'Anna di Alfaedo,** an alpine village notable for its characteristic roofing material of stone tiles. There is a **museum** in the municipio. ▶ Continuing from valley to valley, with excellent views, and passing through the isolated village of **Erbezzo,** the route next comes to **Bosco Chiesanuova,** the main centre of the Lessini, situated on the edge of the plateau and offering views from Lake Garda to the plain. ▶ The route now descends through **Cerro Veronese** to enter the **Val Pantena** at **Grezzana** with the church of S. Maria. Originally Romanesque, it was rebuilt several times, but retains a campanile with Romanesque lines. ▶ The route ends with a short drive back to Verona. □

Practical information ─────────────────

BOSCO CHIESANUOVA, 3,629 ft, ✉ 37021, ☎ 045.
✠ ski lifts, cross-country skiing, instruction at Branchetto-Monte Tomba *(9 km N)* and at Malga S. Giorgio *(11 km N).*
🖈 p. della Chiesa, ☎ 7050088.

Restaurant:
♦ **Tracchi,** at Tracchi, v. Monti Lessini, ☎ 7050153, closed Mon and 1 May-30 Jun and 16 Sep-9 Dec. Emilian cuisine: lasagne al forno, passatelli, 20/25,000.

3. Garda and the Lessini Mountains

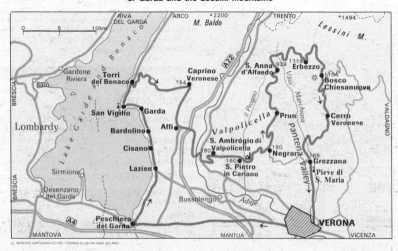

△ ★★★★ *Branchetto,* at Branchetto-Monte Tomba, ☎ 7050392.

Recommended
Skating: ☎ 7050130.
Young people's activities: *Orienteering Boscochiesa-nuova* (at information office, ☎ 7050088).

SANT'AMBROGIO DI VALPOLICELLA, ⊠ 37010, ☎ 045.

Hotel:
★★★★ *Villa Quaranta Park,* at Ospedaletto di Pescan-tina, ☎ 7156211, 43 rm ℗ ⚿ ♿ ☜ ⌧ ➳ 140,000; bkf: 15,000.

GRAPPA AND MONTELLO

From Bassano del Grappa *(162 km, 1 day; map 4)*

No more than 40 km separate the two ends of this itin-erary, which runs between the Brenta and the Piave through the foothills of the Venetian pre-Alps to the N of the Treviso plain. However, the variety of scenery that it offers will demonstrate the diversity of Vene-tia. In terms of art, Possagno has much to offer, and the outstanding Villa Barbaro is at Maser. Mt. Grappa dominates a ring of mountains and the plain as far as the Adriatic. From Bassano the sight of the moun-tain to the r. of the Brenta canal explains its strate-gic importance in 1917-18, when, after the Italian lines were broken at Caporetto, the Austrians flooded into Friuli on this side of the Isonzo and defenses had to be prepared on the r. bank of the Piave. Grappa formed the W bulwark of the line. The entire area has been declared a national monument in memory of those who fought and died here. To the r. of the Piave, the Montello is a most unusual geological structure, elongated, rounded and covered in vegeta-tion. During the last Austrian offensive, which suc-ceeded in crossing the Piave here (June 1918), the mound was an inferno. SE of Grappa and W of the Piave lie the Asolo hills, rounded peaks made yet more gentle by their crops, woods and pictur-esque villas.

▶ From **Bassano del Grappa** (→) the route follows the SS 141 (Strada Cadorna) up **Mt. Grappa**★ (5,823 ft); from the piazzale Milano it climbs to the watershed, where there is the **Italian War Cemetery.** Higher still is the **Sanctuary** with the *Madonna of Grappa* and the Via Eroica, which leads to the **Museum;** it offers a splendid view★. Access to the Galleria Vittorio Emanuele, a mili-tary engineering work nearly 1 mile long, is from the piazzale Milano. ▶ The descent down the E slopes of the Grappa massif leads to the village of **Possagno,** where the **house** in which the Neoclassical sculptor Anto-nio Canova (1757-1822) was born is preserved as it was during the last years of the artist's life. The house dis-plays mementos of the artist *(9 a.m.-12 noon and 3-6 p.m. or 2-5 p.m. winter; closed Mon).* The **Tempio di Canova**★ *(8 a.m.-12 noon and 2-7 p.m. or 1:30-5 p.m. win-ter),* now the parish church, was built 1819-30 to Canova's design. Inside is a bronze *Deposition from the Cross,* the sculptor's last work. His body lies in the urn of the tomb which he carved for the Marchese Berio. There is a fine view from the dome *(access on request).* ▶ At **Pederobba** the road reaches the broad valley floor of the Piave and the river is crossed further upstream at the Fener bridge. ▶ **Valdobbiàdene** (827 ft) on the l. bank of the Piave and at the foot of the pre-Alps of Belluno is the last stop on the **White Wine Road** (→ Conegliano). Its fine 17C-18C church has a Neoclassical façade and paint-ings by Venetian artists. 13 km NE is the **abbey of Fol-lina.** ▶ **Farra di Soligo** has the early 16C Villa Savoini with frescoed façade and the church of **S. Stefano** with noteworthy works of art. ▶ **Pieve di Soligo** has several 17C-18C buildings; the parish church contains a Renais-sance *Assumption.* ▶ The Piave is recrossed at **Ponte della Priula** and soon afterward **Nervesa della Battaglia** is reached on the bank of the river and beneath the Mon-tello. ▶ **Cornuda** can be reached by following the road at the foot of the Montello along the banks of the Piave or by crossing it. Both routes are scenic, although in differ-ent ways. ▶ From **Cornuda** a road climbs to the **Memo-rial-Ossuary** to the Romagnese volunteers who died here on 8 May 1848 in the first clash during the Italian wars of independence. Farther on is the 19C sanctuary of **S. Maria della Rocca** (view★ over the Piave valley, the Montello and the plain stretching to the sea). ▶ The route then enters the **Asolo hills.** At **Maser** is the **Villa Barbaro**★ (now called Villa Maser, *Tue, Sat, Sun and hols, Apr-Sep 3-6 p.m.; Oct-Mar 3-5 p.m.; closed Eas-ter, August hol, 1 Nov-8 Dec and Christmas-Epiphany).* It was built by Palladio *c.* 1560 for Daniele Barbaro and his brother Marc'Antonio Barbaro. It is one of Palladio's masterpieces and the only one of his works that had the

4. Grappa and Montello

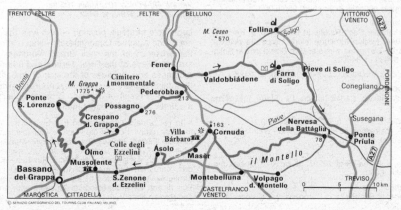

good fortune to be decorated by an artist of equal stature — Paolo Veronese (1528-1588). Veronese's **frescos**★ (1566-8) include several remarkable scenes, such as figures looking down from a *trompe-l'oeil* balustrade or the self-portrait of the painter. The stucco ornament of the vestibule and the rooms is by Alessandro Vittoria, as are the statues in the garden behind the villa. On the nearby hill there is a park with conifers and a **Carriage Museum** *(same opening times as villa).* On the road outside the villa grounds is a circular **temple,** also by Palladio, with a statue in stone on the dome by Orazio Marinali and stuccoes inside by Vittoria. ▶ The beautiful town of **Asolo** (→) is situated a little way farther on. ▶ From **San Zenone degli Ezzelini** it is possible to walk *(2.3 km N)* to the **Colle degli Ezzelini,** where the castle of the Ezzelini stood. The Ezzelini were vassals of the Emperor who extended their dominions to include Treviso, Padua, Vicenza, Verona, Trento and Brescia in the 12C-13C. A stone records the fate of Alberico, brother of the detested Ezzelino III da Romano. Besieged in the castle, he fell into the hands of his enemies in 1260 and was forced to watch his seven sons being beheaded and his wife and daughters burnt alive before he was dragged to death behind a horse. ▶ After passing the **Mussolente** junction, with the large **Villa Negri-Piovene** (1769), the route leads back into Bassano del Grappa.   ◻

Practical information _____

CORNUDA, ⊠ 31041, ☎ 0423.

Restaurants:
◆◆◆ *Cavallino,* v. 8-9 Maggio 23, ☎ 83301, closed Sun eve, Mon and Aug. Seafood: fish stew, spaghetti with clams, 30/35,000.
◆◆ *Armando,* v. 8-9 Maggio 66, ☎ 83390, closed Tue and Sep. Seafood: risottos, salmon al cartoccio, 30/35,000.

NERVESA DELLA BATTAGLIA, ⊠ 31040, ☎ 0422.

Restaurants:
◆◆◆ *Panoramica,* v. VIII Armata 30, ☎ 879068, closed Mon, Tue, Jan and Jul. On hill with view; surrounding slopes covered with vineyards belonging to agricultural firm of same name. Regional cuisine, 20/30,000.
◆◆◆ *Roberto Miron,* p. S.Andrea 26, ☎ 879357, closed Sun eve, Mon, Jan and Aug. Regional cuisine: pancakes with mushrooms, roast or grilled meat, 20/30,000.

PIEVE DI SOLIGO, ⊠ 31053, ☎ 0438.

Hotel:
★★ *Lino,* at Solighetto, v. Brandolini 31 ☎ 82150, 12 rm ℗ ▦ closed Jul and Christmas, 40,000. Rest. ● ◆◆◆ closed Mon. Green setting and large fireplaces. Excellent regional cuisine: duck and mushroom mould, guinea fowl in peppery sauce with polenta, 22/35,000.

Restaurant:
● ◆◆ *Gigetto,* at Miane, v. De Gasperi 4, ☎ 893126, closed Mon eve, Tue, Jan and Aug. Large stone fireplace and summer service under portico. Regional cuisine: pumpkin gnocchi, snail soup, 25/40,000.

Recommended
Craft workshops: *Sech Rattan,* at Barbisano, v. Kennedy 16, ☎ 840446 (wicker furniture; telephone before visiting). **Wine:** Marca Trevigiana wines at *Villa Brandolini,* at Solighetto, ☎ 82630 or 840092.

SAN ZENONE DEGLI EZZELINI, ⊠ 31020, ☎ 0423.

Recommended
Horseback riding: *Centro ippico La Staffa* (associate of *ANTE*).

VALDOBBIADENE, 827 ft, ⊠ 31049, ☎ 0423.
⚞ ski lifts, instruction at Pianezze *(11 km N).*
ⓘ p. Marconi, ☎ 72125.

Hotel:
★★ *Diana,* v. Roma 49 ☎ 72237, 35 rm ℗ ▦ closed Jan, 42,000; bkf: 4,000.

Restaurant:
◆ *Marianna,* at San Pietro di Barbozza, v. Cal Vecchia del

Col, ☎ 72616, closed Wed eve, Thu, Feb and Jun. Summer service under pergola. Regional cuisine: risottos with seasonal green vegetables, grilled and spit roasted meat, locally produced Prosecco wine, 20/30,000.

Recommended
Events: *national sparkling wine show* (Sep).

LAZISE

Verona 22, Venice 146, Milan 141 km
Pop. 5,506 ⊠ 37017 ☎ 045   A4

An almost complete ring of medieval **walls** links the **Castello** (five towers and a keep, rebuilt in 14C), the **porticciolo** and the church of S. Nicolò (12C; 14C frescos) to the 16C building of the **Dogana Veneta.** Lazise was held by Venice from 1405 until the end of the Republic and still bears the stamp of Venetian rule. Now it is a popular lakeside resort with a mild climate and splendid view over a broad section of Lake Garda.   ◻

Practical information _____

ⓘ v. Fontana, ☎ 7580114.
⛴ boats and hydrofoils.

Hotels:
★★★ *Casa Mia,* at Risare, ☎ 7580058, 39 rm ℗ ▦ ⬤ ▭ ♨ closed 1 Dec-4 Mar, 67,000; bkf: 7,000.
★★★ *Lazise,* v. Esperia 38/A, ☎ 7580292, 47 rm ℗ ▦ ♿ ⬤ ▭ ♨ closed Nov-Dec, 80,000.
★★ *Benacus,* v. Roma, ☎ 7580124, 26 rm ℗ ▦ ⬤ closed Nov-Dec, 62,000.

Restaurant:
◆◆ *Forgia,* v. Calle I 26, ☎ 7580287, closed Mon and Nov. Cuisine of lake fish: risotto tench, Lake Garda carp (on request), 14/30,000.
⚑ *Quercia,* at Bottona, 890 pl, ☎ 7580051.

Recommended
Animal parks: Garda zoo-park, between Pastrengo and Bussolengo *(10 km W; fee; 9 a.m.-6 p.m.);* Autosafari, ☎ 7170080; Dinosaur park, tropical greenhouses, vivarium, ☎ 7170052.
Hang gliding: *Il Gabbiano,* at Pastrengo, ☎ 7170448.
Horseback riding: *Centro equestre del Garda,* v. Gardesana 65/A, ☎ 7170202.
Youth facilities: *Caneva* water sports centre, Fossalta, ☎ 7590229.

LEGNAGO

Verona 42, Venice 101, Milan 195 km
Pop. 27,146 ⊠ 37045 ☎ 0442   B5

Legnago's strategic position — this was the SE corner of the Austrian Quadrilateral — was reinforced by the presence of the Valli Grandi Veronesi. These are the valleys of the River Tartaro and its numerous tributaries and, because of the lack of embankments, the region is marshy. The present productivity of the area is the result of drainage projects undertaken in the latter half of the last century.

▶ In the p. della Libertà stand the ruins of the **Torrione,** the only remnant of the old Rocca's four towers. ▶ The Palazzo Fioroni houses the Fondazione Museo Fioroni *(Sun 4:30-7:30 p.m. summer; 3-5:30 p.m. winter; closed Aug),* which comprises a **Historical Museum** with weapons, barbarian and medieval tools, 15C-16C ceramics, furniture and mementos of the Risorgimento and World War II, and an **Archaeological Museum** with prehistoric and Roman finds from the region.   ◻.

Practical information

Recommended
Events: *symphony and drama season,* at Teatro Salieri, ☎ 20116.
Flying: *Basso Veronese,* ☎ 22065.
♥ market: second-hand furniture and antique market at Cerea (first Sun of month).

LENDINARA

Rovigo 16, Venice 94, Milan 269 km
Pop. 13,205 ☒ 45026 ☎ 0425   C6

Lendinara has a number of fine Renaissance and Baroque palaces, gardens and Venetian style houses. The area produces sugar beet and hemp.

▶ In the p. Risorgimento the **Palazzo Comunale** has a portico with 14C columns, a large tower and a clock tower. Both towers are remnants of an Este castle. ▶ The sacristy of the 18C **Duomo** contains a Renaissance *Madonna and Child with Angels* (1511). ▶ The sanctuary of the **Madonna del Pilastrello** (16C-18C) contains an *Ascension* by Veronese. ▶ The most charming quarter of the town lies along the Adigetto; the tree-lined **Riviera S. Biagio** offers a view of the loop of the river flanked by palaces and gardens.   □

LIDO DI JESOLO

Venice 44, Milan 303 km
Pop. 9,742 ☒ 30017 ☎ 0421   E4

One of the principal Adriatic resorts, Lido di Jésolo stretches along the shore between the Porto di Piave Vecchia and the Porto di Cortellazzo (the present mouth of the Piave).   □

Practical information

LIDO DI JESOLO
≋
⚓ (Jun-Sep), ☎ 90071.
ⓘ p. Brescia 13, ☎ 90076.
Car rental: *Avis,* p. Drago 14, ☎ 92461 (Apr-Oct).

Hotels:
★★★★ *Atlantico,* v. Bafile-III accesso, ☎ 91273, 69 rm Ⓟ closed 21 Sep-14 May, 68,000; bkf: 9,000.
★★★★ *Aurore,* p. Aurore 8, ☎ 972027, 77 rm ⅏ ♿ 🄴 closed 21 Sep-19 May, 130,000; bkf: 12,000.
★★★★ *G.H. Las Vegas,* v. Mascagni 2, ☎ 971515, 104 rm Ⓟ ⅏ 🄴 closed Nov-Mar, 130,000; bkf: 10,000.
★★★★ *Majestic Toscanelli:* v. Canova 2, ☎ 971331, 55 rm Ⓟ ⅏ ⅋ 🄴 closed 16 Sep-14 May, 120,000; bkf: 15,000.
★★★★ *Palace Cavalieri,* v. Mascagni 1, ☎ 971969, 56 rm Ⓟ 🄴 closed Oct-Apr, 123,000; bkf: 9,000.
★★★ *Beny,* v. Levantina-IV accesso, ☎ 961792, 44 rm Ⓟ ⅋ 🄴 closed Oct-Apr, 83,000.
★★★ *Bussola,* v. Levantina 4, ☎ 93273, 56 rm Ⓟ 🄴 closed Oct-Apr, 80,000; bkf: 5,000.
★★★ *Christian,* v. Olanda 150, ☎ 961715, 60 rm Ⓟ ⅋ 🄴 closed Oct-Apr, 80,000.
★★★ *Galassia,* v. Treviso 7, ☎ 972271, 64 rm Ⓟ ⅏ 🄴 closed 21 Sep-9 May, 110,000; bkf: 10,000.
★★★ *Heron,* v. Padova 3, ☎ 971242, 90 rm Ⓟ ⅋ 🄴 closed 21 Sep-14 May, 74,000; bkf: 6,000.
★★★ *Imperial Palace,* v. Zara 29, ☎ 972266, 62 rm Ⓟ 🄴 closed Oct-Apr, 90,000.
★★★ *Regina,* v. Bafile 115, ☎ 90383, 47 rm Ⓟ ⅏ ⅋ closed Oct-Apr, 70,000; breakfast: 6,000.
★★★ *Rivamare,* v. Bafile-XVII access, ☎ 90432, 55 rm Ⓟ ⅏ closed 21 Sep-14 May, 69,000; bkf: 7,000.
★★★ *Termini,* v. Altinate 32, ☎ 962312, 45 rm Ⓟ ⅏ 🄴 closed 5 Oct-Easter, 100,000; bkf: 75,000.
★★ *Promenade,* v. delle Nereide 1, ☎ 92205, 52 rm Ⓟ closed Oct-Mar. No restaurant, 66,000.

★★ *Ruhl,* v. Altinate 4, ☎ 962370, 45 rm Ⓟ ⅏ closed 5 Oct-Easter, 80,000; bkf: 7,500.
★ *Colombo,* v. Aquileia 127, ☎ 92279, 52 rm Ⓟ ⅋ closed Oct-Mar, 48,000; bkf: 7,000.

Restaurant:
♦♦♦ *Alfredo,* largo Tempini 113, ☎ 91227, closed 21 Sep-9 May. Mixed regional cuisine: fish risotto, pennette Tempini, 35/45,000.

Recommended
Bowling: at Jésolo Paese.
Excursions: to Venice by road *(21 km)* along Cavallino coast road as far as Punta Sabbioni, embarkation point for the Lido and Venice.
Go-Karts: *Pista azzurra,* v. Roma Destra 90, ☎ 972471.
Sailing: at Cortellazzo *(7 km E),* ☎ 961356.
Tennis: v. Aleardi 205, ☎ 972323; v. Olanda 221, ☎ 961053.
Youth hostel: *Ostello Adriatico Nord,* v. Mameli 103, ☎ 90350.

Environs

COSTELLAZZO, 7 km E.

Restaurant:
♦♦♦ *Darsena,* v. Oriente 166, ☎ 961081, closed Thu except summer and Nov-Dec. At mouth of Piave. Regional seafood: eel and cuttlefish stew, fried blue-fish, 30/45,000.

JESOLO PAESE, 3.5 km N.

Hotel:
★★ *Udinese,* v. Battisti 25, ☎ 951409, 13 rm Ⓟ ⅏ closed Sep-Jun, 55,000; bkf: 3,500. Rest. ♦♦♦ ☎ 951407, closed Wed except Jul-Aug and Jan, 25/37,000.

JESOLO PINETA, 6 km E.

Hotels:
★★★★ *Bellevue,* v. Oriente 100, ☎ 961233, 64 rm Ⓟ ⅏ 🄴 ⅌ closed 16 Sep-9 May, 125,000; bkf: 15,000.
★★★★ *Elite,* v. Oriente 64, ☎ 961133, 45 rm Ⓟ ⅏ ♿ 🄴 closed 16 Sep-14 May, 125,000; bkf: 15,000.
★★★★ *Gallia,* v. del Cigno Bianco, ☎ 961018, 58 rm Ⓟ ⅏ ♿ 🄴 closed 21 Sep-19 May, 110,000; bkf: 15,000.
★★★★ *Negresco,* v. Bucintoro 8, ☎ 961137, 44 rm Ⓟ ⅏ 🄴 ⅌ closed Oct-Apr, 95,000; bkf: 12,000.

⚠ ★★★★ *Malibù Beach,* at Jésolo Pineta, v. Oriente 78, 126 pl, ☎ 962212.

LONIGO

Vicenza 24, Venice 93, Milan 186 km
Pop. 12,535 ☒ 36045 ☎ 0444   B-C5

The road to Lonigo from Vicenza is lined by the typical plane trees of the region.

▶ In the p. IV Novembre near the late 19C neo-Romanesque **Duomo** are two **towers**, ruins of a castle. ▶ Compact and Venetian in style, the p. Garibaldi contains the **Palazzo Comunale**, with an external staircase (two flights, 1557). ▶ Outside the built-up area stands the **Rocca Pisani**. This is in fact a Pisani villa, but there was previously a castle on the site and the name rocca persisted. The villa was built in 1578 by Vincenzo Scamozzi, one of Palladio's followers. ▶ Another Villa Pisani, designed by Palladio himself but incomplete *(Wed and Fri 10 a.m.-12 noon and 3-5 p.m.),* stands at **Bagnolo,** 3.5 km S. ▶ 2.5 km away on the road to San Bonifacio is the sanctuary of the **Madonna dei Miracoli** (1488-1501), which has a fine Lombard façade. Inside around an image of the Virgin and beneath a Turkish flag is a noteworthy collection of votive offerings.   □

Practical information

ⓘ p. Garibaldi 1, ☎ 830948.

Villa Godi at LUGO DI VICENZA

Vicenza 27, Venice 96, Milan 231 km
Pop. 3,573 ☒ 36030 ☎ 0445　　　　　　　　C3

This villa (1542) was Andrea Palladio's first
work. The building's simplicity makes Palladio's skill
all the more apparent. The beautiful loggia and ten
rooms were decorated with frescos. These rooms
house the **Museo dei Fossili** and the **Collezione
Malinverni** of 19C Italian painting *(mid-Mar to end
Oct, Tue, Sat and hols 2-6 p.m. or 3-7 p.m.; groups
every day, reserve,* ☎ 860571). The **Villa Piovene-
Porto Godi** *(2:30-7 p.m.; winter 2-5 p.m.),* another of
Palladio's early works, stands on a nearby hill. In
1587 the Ionic portico was built and in the 18C the
portal and steps were added. In the park are natural caves and the church of S. Girolamo (1496).　□

MALCESINE

Verona 60, Venice 174, Milan 179 km
Pop. 3,488 ☒ 37018 ☎ 045　　　　　　　　A3

Amid olive groves and gardens at the foot of
Mt. Baldo (→), Malcesine is one of the most beautiful
places in the N section of Lake Garda.

▶ The old centre, with the Renaissance **Palazzo dei Capitani del Lago** (now the municipio), is dominated by the
13C-14C **Castello Scaligero** with its tall keep. It houses
a small **museum** *(summer 9 a.m.-8 p.m.; winter Sat and
hols, 9 a.m.-5 p.m.)* with archaeological finds, weapons
and exhibits relating to the Risorgimento and local history. In the Venetian palace is a natural history collection and, in the old powder magazine, a room dedicated
to the German poet Goethe. In 1786, at the beginning of
his Italian journey, Goethe was seen sketching in a lane of
the village (memorial). He was arrested as a German spy
and was briefly detained before clearing himself.　□

Practical information _____

🟄 cableway, ski lifts, instruction at Tratto Spino.
ⓘ v. Capitanato, ☎ 7400044 or 7400555.
🚤 boats and hydrofoils.

Hotels:
★★★ **Du Lac,** v. Lungolago, ☎ 7400156, 47 rm 🅿 ♨ ✿
closed 6 Oct-Easter, 63,000; bkf: 10,000.
★★★ **Maximilian,** at Val di Sogno, ☎ 7400317, 33 rm 🅿
♨ ✿ ▱ ✓ 1/2 Pens. Closed Nov-Mar, 71,000.
★★★ **Vega,** v. Roma 10, ☎ 7400151, 19 rm 🅿 ♨ ✿
closed Nov-Mar, 60,000; bkf: 8,000.
★★ **Piccolo Hotel,** at Campagnola, ☎ 7400264, 21 rm 🅿
▣ closed 1 Oct-19 Mar, 42,000; bkf: 8,000.

⚓ *Claudia,* at Campagnola, ☎ 7400786; *Martora,* at Campagnola, ☎ 7400345.

Recommended
Excursions: cableway up Mt. Baldo (Tratto Spino),
☎ 7400206.
Marina: ☎ 7400274.
Surfing: ☎ 740988 (instruction).
Tennis: at Cassone *(4 km),* ☎ 7400044.
Sailing: *Fraglia della vela,* at Cor de lo Re, ☎ 7400274
(instruction).

MAROSTICA

Vicenza 27, Venice 82, Milan 243 km
Pop. 12,395 ☒ 36063 ☎ 0424　　　　　　　C3

The two castles of Marostica — one at the foot, the
other at the summit of the Colle Pausolino — are
linked by battlemented walls and towers that climb the
slope of the green hillside. This picturesque fortress

was begun in the 14C. The old town lies behind the
Lower Castle.

▶ The **Lower Castle** has a massive, ivy-clad tower and a
courtyard with portico and loggia.　▶ A chess game with
figures in 15C dress is played in the **piazza del Castello**
which, with its arcaded houses, column of St. Mark and
well-head, forms a delightful Romanesque setting. Legend has it that the lord of the castle, Taddeo
Parisio, had two noble suitors for his daughter Leonora's
hand. He forbade them to settle the matter in a duel, as
was normal, and decreed that they should play a game
of chess, with the loser receiving the hand of his younger
daughter. It is this event that the modern game and the
recitals in Venetian dialect evoke.　▶ The 18C church of
S. Antonio has a 12C-13C bell tower and spire. On the
entrance wall is an altarpiece (1574).　▶ The keep and
gates of the **Upper Castle** still stand.　□

Practical information _____

ⓘ p. Castello 7, ☎ 72127.

Restaurant:
◆◆◆ **Scacchiera,** p. Castello 49, ☎ 72346, closed Sun
eve, Mon, Jul-Aug and Dec-Jan. In historic town
square. Vicenza cuisine: homemade spaghetti with duck
broth, guinea fowl scacchiera, 20/30,000.

Recommended
Events: *chess game with people acting as pieces* (second
Sat and second Sun of Sep in even-numbered years);
Umoristi a Marostica (Jun); *cherry festival* (first ten days
of Jun).

MISURINA

Belluno 86, Venice 176, Milan 426 km
5,761 ft pop. 111 ☒ 32040 ☎ 0436　　　　　D1

The **lake★★** for which Misurina is known is in the
foreground of a superb view of the Dolomites. It is
little more than half a mile by 300 yards, but around
the conifer-fringed basin rise the Tre Cime di Lavaredo, the Cadini, the Marmarole and Sorapis. A road
runs around this romantic expanse of water.

▶ A chair lift climbs to **Col de Varda** *(c.* 7,870 ft)
with a view of the Cristallo group.　▶ **Angelo Bosi**
refuge (6,578 ft; *6 km by difficult road)* has a wonderful
view★.　▶ The **Auronzo** refuge★ (7,612 ft; *7.5 km, final
section on foot)* is situated beneath the S walls of the Tre
Cime di Lavaredo with a superb view★.　□

Practical information _____

🟄 chair lift for Col de Varda, ski lifts, cross-country skiing,
instruction, skating.
ⓘ p. Misurina, ☎ 39016 (seasonal).

Hotels:
★★★ **Lavaredo,** v. Monte Piana, ☎ 39127, 39 rm 🅿 ◣ ✿
✓ closed Apr and Nov-Dec, 70,000; bkf: 5,000.
★★ **Miralago,** v. Col S. Angelo 3, ☎ 39123, 23 rm 🅿 ◣ ⬠
♨ ✿ closed 21 Apr-31 May and 16 Oct-14 Dec, 52,000;
bkf: 5,500.

⚓ ★★ *Baia,* ☎ 39039.

Recommended
Excursions: to *Auronzo rifugio,* ☎ 39002.

MONSELICE

Padua 22, Venice 59, Milan 256 km
Pop. 17,639 ☒ 35043 ☎ 0429　　　　　　　C5

Monselice is situated on an isolated cone of rock
rising from the plain to the SE of the Euganean
hills. The rock has been quarried in places for trachyte (*masegna* in local dialect); this is the stone

that has twice been used to pave the p. S. Marco in Venice. The town and its monuments are arranged on three levels.

▶ At the bottom level is the p. Mazzini, dominated by the 13C **Torre Civica** with the 16C **Monte di Pietà** (loggia) and a Gothic palace. ▶ The attractive **via al Santuario★** leads from here and, as it climbs the hill, passes a series of monuments and offers views over the town and the plain. ▶ The **Castello★** dates in part from the 13C and in part from the 15C. Inside are medieval and Renaissance works *(guided tours Apr-Nov 9, 10:30 a.m., 3:30 and 5 p.m.; Sun 9 and 10:30 a.m.).* ▶ The 16C-18C **Villa Nani-Mocenigo** has a curious series of 18C statues of dwarfs in its grounds and a dramatic flight of steps. ▶ The **Duomo Vecchio★** is a Romanesque-Gothic building (1256) with frescos and altarpieces by the 15C Venetian school inside. ▶ The **Santuario delle Sette Chiese** consists of a series of chapels arranged among cypresses along an avenue ending in the **Villa Duodo** (Scamozzi, 1593-1611; extended in 18C). ▶ The ruins of the **Rocca**, built by Frederick II and rebuilt by the Carrara family, occupy the summit of the hill. □

Practical information _____

Hotel:
★★★ *Ceffri*, v. Orti, ☎ 75995, 52 rm Ⓟ ⌂ ✵ ☒ 70,000; bkf: 6,000.

Restaurant:
◆◆ *Torre*, p. Mazzini 14, ☎ 73752, closed Mon, Fri eve and Jul-Aug. Regional and Italian cuisine: seasonal pancakes with mushrooms or asparagus, fresh pasta with truffles, 30/45,000.

Recommended
Bowling: v. S. Giacomo 21, ☎ 72260.

MONTAGNANA*

Padua 47, Venice 85, Milan 211 km
Pop. 9,913 ☒ 35044 ☎ 0429   B-C5

Ubertino da Carrara, Lord of Padua (1338-45) built Montagna's powerful defenses because he was surrounded by covetous neighbours. Two earlier sets of walls (one built by the Ezzelini) were incorporated into the new ring. Half a century later when the Venetian oligarchy decided to conquer the mainland, Montagnana and all the Carrara lands ended up in Venetian hands. Fortunately, the walls remained and the town preserved the unique character of its buildings, with the beams of the arcades, the ancient fittings of some of the shops and the old-fashioned paving of its side streets.

▶ The 13C-14C **walls★** are built of trachyte blocks (the *masegna* of Monsélice), limestone layers and red brick. They form an irregular rectangle, are strengthened by twenty-four towers and run for a little over a mile. Of the four gates, most impressive are the **Rocca degli Alberi★** or Porta Legnano (A1) and the **Porta Padova** (B2) with the **Torre Ezzelina**. The walls and towers may also be viewed for almost their entire length from the road that runs inside them (v. della Mura). ▶ The **Museo Civico di Storia Locale** in the Venetian wing of the Castello di S. Zeno (B2; *apply to Ufficio Turistico or municipio*) has Bronze- and Iron-Age finds (11C-8C BC) from a local site, 1C Roman funerary artefacts and 16C-17C ceramics. Roman inscriptions from the 1C-2C are temporarily in the church of S. Giovanni. ▶ A Gothic-Renaissance (1431-1502) **Duomo★** (A2) stands on the arcaded central piazza. It has a classical portal and inside are three early Renaissance altarpieces (early 16C), frescos (including *Assumption of the Virgin* in the apse) and Veronese's *Transfiguration★* at the high altar. ▶ The **Palazzo del Municipio** (B2) is a severe building. ▶ Also interesting is the 14C-15C church of **S. Francesco** (B1). Outside the Porta Padova is the **Villa Pisani★** (B2), built *c.* 1560 to a design by Andrea Palladio; it contains statues of the *Seasons* by A. Vittoria (1577). □

Practical information _____

ⓘ (A2), ☎ 81320.

Hotel:
★★ *Aldo Moro*, v. Marconi 27 (B2 a), ☎ 81351, 18 rm Ⓟ ⌂ closed Jan, Jul-Aug and Christmas, 45,000; bkf: 7,000. Rest. ◆◆◆ closed Mon. Regional and international cuisine: risotto with asparagus, penne alla vodka, 25/35,000.

Recommended
Cycling: *Cicloamatori*, v. dei Montagnani 13, ☎ 82353.
Gastronomic specialties: salami from donkey meat, ham.
Horseback riding: *Turismo equestre Villa Fava*, at Megliadino San Fidenzio *(5 km E)*, v. Longo Pasquale 8, ☎ 89309 (associate of *ANTE*).
Market: at Casale di Scodósia, first and last Fri of month (furniture).
Youth hostel: *Costello degli Alberi*, Porta Legnano (A1), ☎ 81076.

MONTEBELLUNA

Treviso 21, Venice 51, Milan 257 km
Pop. 24,744 ☒ 31044 ☎ 0423   D3

Montebelluna is a typically Venetian town at the foot of an isolated peak that is linked to the Montello (→ Mount Grappa) on the edge of the plain of Treviso. In the Villa Biagi (corso Mazzini 70; *9 a.m.-12 noon and 3-6 p.m.; 3:30-6:30 p.m. summer; hols 9 a.m.-12 noon)* is the **Museo Civico di Storia e Scienze Naturali**, displaying archaeological finds and natural history collections. □

Practical information _____

ⓘ p. Marconi, ☎ 23827.

Hotels:
★★★ *Bellavista*, v. Zuccareda 21, ☎ 301031, 42 rm Ⓟ ⌂ ✵ closed Aug, 75,000.
★★ *Pineta*, at Biadene, v. Brigata Campania 42/A, ☎ 302831, 32 rm Ⓟ ◁ ⌂ ✵ No restaurant, 40,000.

Colona V. km 13 **1**   **2** Vicenza km 43

Mantua km 60

A

B

MONTAGNANA

Badia P. km 19

Monsélice km 25

0   100   200   300 m
1:14.000 (1cm=140m)

© SERVIZIO CARTOGRAFICO DEL TOURING CLUB ITALIANO, MILANO   **2**

Restaurant:
♦♦♦ *Falconera-da Celeste*, at Volpago del Montello, v. Diaz 11, ☎ 820445, closed Mon eve, Tue, Jan and Aug. Fine regional cuisine: tagliatelle with game sauce, guinea fowl alla montelliana, 25/30,000.

Recommended
Motocross: *Angeli*, at Giàvera del Montello *(11 km NE)*; *Motoclub*, v. Stazione,☎ 876271.

MONTECCHIO MAGGIORE

Vicenza 12, Venice 77, Milan 196 km
Pop. 19,762 ⊠ 36075 ☎ 0444   B4

The beautiful countryside of this area initially conceals the fact that it is one of the most heavily industrialized in Venetia. Montecchio Maggiore contains the church of **S. Pietro** with 16C statues and paintings. A road climbs the hill overlooking the town and leads to two 14C Scaliger castles, Villa and Bellaguardia, which have taken their place in romantic legend as the **Castello di Romeo** and the **Castello di Giulietta**; with view★. On the road to Sovizzo is the 18C Palladian **Villa Cordellina-Lombardi**. The central hall was frescoed by Tiepolo in 1743 *(13-18 Apr, 4 May-18 Jul, 17 Aug-15 Oct: Wed, Sat and Sun 9 a.m.-12 noon and 3-6 p.m.).*   ☐

Juliet

Castles said to be those of the Cappelletti and Montecchi (Capulet and Montague in Shakespeare's Romeo and Juliet) are at Montecchio Maggiore, not far from Vicenza. They are known as the Castello di Bellaguardia and the Castello della Villa. Romeo's house, battlemented and with an arcaded courtyard, is in Verona and so, not far away in the v. Cappella, is Juliet's house, complete with balcony. An old, lidless sarcophagus in the cloisters of the church of S. Francesco al Corso is visited as the tomb of Juliet. The church is the scene of the pair's hasty wedding and the cloisters serve as the setting for the tragic denouement of the love story, in which the girl, recovering from Friar Laurence's potion, but seeing her lover dead, takes her own life. All this is legend: the star-crossed lovers of Verona are pure invention. In Shakespeare's Romeo and Juliet, as in his other 'Italian' plays (Two Gentlemen of Verona and The Merchant of Venice), however, references to local geography are so precise as to suggest that the English dramatist could actually have spent time in Italy during the period when the London stage was dark because of the plague (1592-94). Shakespeare's source for Romeo and Juliet was a novel, Giulietta e Romeo, written by Luigi da Porto of Vicenza and published in Venice at the beginning of the 16C.

Practical information —————————————

Hotels:
★★★ *Castelli*, at Alte Ceccato, v. Trieste, ☎ 697366, 64 rm P ₩ ⊁ closed Christmas, 78,000; bkf: 6,500.
★★ *Plaza*, p. Marconi 39, ☎ 696421, 13 rm P closed Aug and Christmas, 47,000; bkf: 5,000.

> For the translation of a name of a meat, a fish or a vegetable, for the composition of a dish or a sauce, see the *Menu Guide* at the end of the Practical Holiday Guide; it lists the most common culinary terms.

MONTEGROTTO TERME

Padua 12, Venice 49, Milan 246 km
Pop. 9,194 ⊠ 35036 ☎ 049   C5

At the foot of the Euganean hills, Montegrotto Terme offers the same range of treatments as nearby Abano Terme (→), with which it now forms a single spa. It takes its name from *Mons Aegrotorum* (mountain of the sick). The remains of 1C baths and a small theatre (v. della Stazione) prove that the waters and muds have been sought after since ancient times.   ☐

Practical information ——————————————

♨ (all year), ☎ 793384.
ⅰ v. della Stazione 37, ☎ 793384.

Hotels:
★★★★ *Caesar*, v. Aureliana, ☎ 793655, 135 rm P ₩ ⊟ ⊁ closed Dec-Feb except Christmas, 104,000; bkf: 11,000.
★★★★ *Esplanade Tergesteo*, v. Roma 54, ☎ 793444, 136 rm P ⚲ ₩ & ⊟ ⊁ closed 16 Nov-9 Mar, 125,000; bkf: 12,000.
★★★★ *Garden*, corso Terme 7, ☎ 794033, 112 rm P ₩ & ⊟ ⊁ ⌁ (18) closed Dec-Feb, 90,000; bkf: 8,000.
★★★★ *G.H. Terme*, v. Stazione 23, ☎ 793111, 125 rm P ₩ & ⊟ ⊁ 90,000; bkf: 15,000.
★★★★ *International Bertha*, largo Traiano 1, ☎ 793100, 126 rm P ₩ & ⊟ ⊁ closed Jan-Feb, 135,000; bkf: 12,000.
★★★ *Continental*, v. Neroniana 8, ☎ 793522, 108 rm P ⚲ ₩ & ⊟ ⊁ closed Dec-Feb except Christmas, 80,000.
★★★ *Montecarlo*, v. Stazione 109, ☎ 793301, 106 rm P ₩ & ⊟ ⊁ closed 4 Nov-17 Mar, 88,000.
★★★ *Petrarca Touring*, p. Roma 23, ☎ 793422, 129 rm P ₩ & ⊟ ⊁ closed 1 Dec-14 Feb except Christmas, 68,000; bkf: 8,000.
★★★ *Terme Cristallo*, v. Roma 69, ☎ 793377, 119 rm P ₩ ⊟ ⊁ closed Dec-Feb, 66,000; bkf: 7,000.
★★★ *Terme delle Nazioni*, v. Mezzavia 20, ☎ 793228, 100 rm P ₩ & ⊟ ⊁ closed Dec-Jan, 68,000; bkf: 8,000.
★★★ *Terme Neroniane*, v. Neroniana 21, ☎ 793466, 91 rm P ₩ ⊟ ⊁ closed Jan-Feb, 85,000.
★★ *Marconi Terme*, v. Catajo 6, ☎ 793144, 115 rm P & ⊟ ⊁ 39,000.

MOTTA DI LIVENZA

Treviso 36, Venice 59, Milan 309 km
Pop. 7,923 ⊠ 31045 ☎ 0422   E3

The name 'Motta' (heap, pile) may refer to the rise on which the Strazzolini della Motta family built a castle in the 11C on the r. of the Livenza, where Venetia meets Friuli. Today the area is covered with vineyards. In the 16C-17C **Duomo** are noteworthy paintings, a stone altar and a Venetian altarpiece (1590). On the road to Oderzo is the sanctuary of the **Madonna dei Miracoli** (1510-13). The façade has a curved pediment and inside are several Venetian paintings and a marble bas-relief on the high altar. The attached convent has two 16C **cloisters** with frescos from 1674.   ☐

Practical information ——————————————

Restaurant:
♦ *Bertacco*, v. Argine Destro 4, ☎ 766129, closed Thu and Aug-Sep. Mixed regional cuisine: soup coada, fried and grilled fish, 16/30,000.

Recommended
Bowling: v. Risorgimento, ☎ 766245.

ODERZO

Treviso 27, Venice 57, Milan 291 km
Pop. 16,406 ⊠ 31046 ☎ 0422   E3

This farming and commercial centre is situated on the plain of Treviso, between the rivers Piave and Livenza. As the Roman *Opitergium*, in the 7C it was the seat of the governor of the Byzantine province of *Venetia*, which was gradually absorbed by the Lombards. When it fell in 639 the governor withdrew to the lagoon and Cittanova and Oderzo became the first seat of the dogeship of Venice. Several churches in Venice date their foundation to a bishop of *Opitergium*, who also took shelter on the islands in the lagoon. However, it is post-medieval Venice that has left its stamp on the town, as seen in its arcaded streets and palace façades.

▶ The central piazza is dominated by buildings with frescoed façades and the **Duomo**, rebuilt in Gothic-Renaissance style in the 14C-15C. The slender campanile and spire are built on the remains of a tower from the 13C medieval walls. The Duomo has 14C-16C frescos and 16C paintings. ▶ In the **Museo Civico** (at v. Garibaldi 18; *8 a.m.-1 p.m. and 3-6 p.m.; Sat 10 a.m.-12 noon; closed Mon*) are Roman finds, medieval exhibits and a collection of medals. The **Pinacoteca A. Martini**, v. Garibaldi 80, *(2:30-6:30 p.m. or 3-7 p.m.; closed wkends)* is devoted mainly to modern local artists. ▶ 9 km towards Pordenone, at **Portobuffolé**, are the remains of a medieval river port on the Livenza.   □

Practical information _____

Hotel:
★★ *Postumia*, v. Battisti 6, ☎ 717562, 25 rm P 35,000; bkf: 5,000.

Restaurant:
● ♦♦♦ *Gambrinus*, at San Polo di Piave, v. Gambrinus 22, ☎ 742043, closed Mon except hols and Jan. Elegant rustic-style rooms with antiques, garden for dining outside in summer. Excellent creative and regional cuisine: prawns alla Gambrinus, eels, homemade wines, 25/40,000.

Recommended
Archery: *Compagnia arcieri franchi*, v. S. Pio X 49, ☎ 716416.

PADUA**

(Padova)

Venice 38, Milan 234, Rome 493 km
Pop. 230,744 ⊠ 35100 ☎ 049   C4-5

Padua exudes an extraordinary dynamism and has been in the forefront of the post-World War II industrialization of Venetia. The university is the second oldest in Italy and one of the oldest in Europe, having been founded in 1222. Padua was a burgeoning city-state at that time. The university buildings (16C) are in the heart of the city. During the first century of Padua's rule by Venice (15C), the city was the major artistic centre in Venetia and it was through Padua that the Renaissance reached Venice. The monuments, which are among the most important in Italy, and the streets in the old quarter do not dominate the visitor's initial impression, which is one of modernity and activity.

▶ The River Bacchiglione winds around the edge of the old city in an L-shape, which governs the form of the historical centre. Long sections of the city **walls** still stand. ▶ The Neoclassical **Caffé Pedrocchi** (1831;

named for original proprietor, Antonio Pedrocchi) stands on a piazzetta leading off the p. Cavour (C3). ▶ Farther on are the **municipio** (13C and 16C sections) and the 16C **university** (C3) which is Mannerist in style and has an arcaded courtyard with loggias. Inside *(wkdays, guided tour every hr, 9 a.m.-1 p.m.)* is the **Anatomy Theatre** of 1594, the first in Europe — Padua, along with Bologna, was a cradle of medicine. Noteworthy, too, is the wooden lectern where Galileo taught from 1592-1610. ▶ A short distance away is the Romanesque-Gothic church of **S. Maria dei Servi** (D 2-3), with Renaissance frescos and sculpture. ▶ Behind the municipio, between the p. delle Erbe (vegetable market) and the p. della Frutta stands the **Palazzo della Ragione★** (lawcourts; 1218-19, rebuilt 1306), with loggias on all sides and a keel-shaped roof (C2-3). Inside is a large hall *(9:30 a.m.-12:30 p.m. and 2:30-5:30 p.m.; hols 9:30-12:30; closed Mon)* with religious and astrological frescos and a large wooden horse used for jousting (1466). ▶ On the p. dei Signori (C2) are the **Loggia della Gran Guardia** (1496-1523) and the Palazzo del Capitanio with the **Arco dell'Orologio** (1532), the oldest clock in Italy (1344, rebuilt 1437) which marks not only the hours but also the phases of the planets. ▶ The **Liviano** (C2) is the seat of the Faculty of Letters; in the atrium are frescos by Campigli and a statue of **Livy**, the Roman historian (59 BC-17 BC), who was born near Padua. ▶ Beside the **Duomo** (C2; 1522), with a rough façade and spare interior, is the 13C Romanesque Baptistery★ with an important cycle of frescos★ (1374-6; *closed for restoration*). ▶ The **Scuola di S. Rocco** (C2-3) was built in the 15C-16C and has 16C frescos. ▶ The **Eremitani★** (B3) is a 13C Romanesque-Gothic church, which was faithfully restored after bomb damage in 1944 *(8:15 or 9 a.m.-12 noon and 3:30-5:30 or 6:30 p.m.)*. Few of the original frescos in the **Cappella Ovetari★** survived the bombing. ▶ The adjacent Augustinian monastery *(under restoration)* houses archaeological collections and the Renaissance bronzes of the Museo Civico *(9 a.m.-1:30 p.m.; hols 9 a.m.-1 p.m.; closed Mon)*. ▶ The public gardens of the Arena (remains of 1C Roman amphitheatre) contain the **Cappella degli Scrovegni★★** (B3) which was built by Enrico Scrovegni to expiate his notorious father's sins of usury. The interior is covered by Giotto's frescos★★ (1303-1309). The thirty-eight panels relate the lives of Christ and the Virgin Mary. Above the altar there is an important sculpture of the *Madonna with Two Angels★*. ▶ The **Carmini** (B2-3) or S. Maria del Carmine (16C Gothic apse) displays splendid architectural decoration and has a Renaissance sacristy★. For entrance to the **Scuola del Carmine** (16C frescos) apply to the sacristan. ▶ In the **Santuario dell'Arcella** (from v. Guariento, A3, via v. Tiziano Aspetti and the v. dell'Arcella) the modern church encloses the cell of the monastery in which St. Antony of Padua (born Lisbon 1195) died in June 1231.

▶ In the city centre, on the p. Antenore (C3) is an urn within a 13C tabernacle, which is by tradition the **tomb of the Trojan Antenor**, the legendary founder of the city. ▶ The 15C Gothic church of **S. Francesco** (C-D3) has important works of art, including bronzes dating from 1498. ▶ In the p. del Santo (D3) is Donatello's **Gattamelata monument★★** (1453). This equestrian statue of Erasmo da Narni, the soldier of fortune who served Venice, is a masterpiece of classical heroism and restraint. ▶ **Il Santo★★** (S. Antonio) is a Romanesque-Gothic basilica that displays Byzantine, Venetian and French Romanesque (Perigord) influence. It was built between 1232 and the mid-14C to enclose the tomb of the Franciscan preacher, St. Antony of Padua. It has eight domes and two slender campaniles. The most important works of art are the 15C **bronzes★★** by Donatello and assistants on the high altar *(apply to sacristan)*. In the r. transept, the Cappella di S. Felice has 14C **frescos★**. The fifth chapel houses the **Treasury★**, and in the 16C **Cappella di S. Antonio★** (l. transept) are nine reliefs depicting the *Life of Saint Antony*. Entry to the 13C-15C cloisters is from the r. aisle. ▶ To the r. of the basilica is the **Oratorio di San Giorgio** *(7 a.m.-12 noon and 2:30-6 p.m.)*, with frescos★ dating from 1377, and the

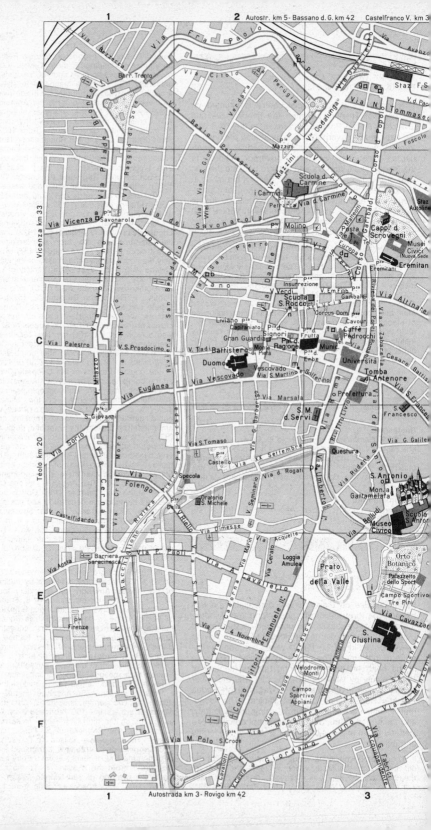

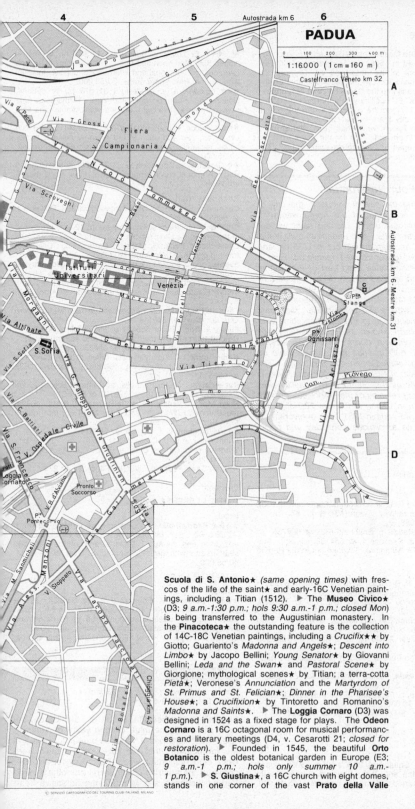

Map labels and text:

4   5   Autostrada km 6   6

PADUA

807

0   100   200   300   400 m

1:16.000 (1 cm = 160 m)

Castelfranco Veneto km 32

A

Autostrada km 6: Mestre km 31

B

C

D

Scuola di S. Antonio★ *(same opening times)* with frescos of the life of the saint★ and early-16C Venetian paintings, including a Titian (1512). ▶ The **Museo Civico**★ (D3; *9 a.m.-1:30 p.m.; hols 9:30 a.m.-1 p.m.; closed Mon*) is being transferred to the Augustinian monastery. In the **Pinacoteca**★ the outstanding feature is the collection of 14C-18C Venetian paintings, including a *Crucifix*★★ by Giotto; Guariento's *Madonna and Angels*★; *Descent into Limbo*★ by Jacopo Bellini; *Young Senator*★ by Giovanni Bellini; *Leda and the Swan*★ and *Pastoral Scene*★ by Giorgione; mythological scenes★ by Titian; a terra-cotta *Pietà*★; Veronese's *Annunciation* and the *Martyrdom of St. Primus and St. Felician*★; *Dinner in the Pharisee's House*★; a *Crucifixion*★ by Tintoretto and Romanino's *Madonna and Saints*★. ▶ The **Loggia Cornaro** (D3) was designed in 1524 as a fixed stage for plays. The **Odeon Cornaro** is a 16C octagonal room for musical performances and literary meetings (D4, v. Cesarotti 21; *closed for restoration*). ▶ Founded in 1545, the beautiful **Orto Botanico** is the oldest botanical garden in Europe (E3; *9 a.m.-1 p.m.; hols only summer 10 a.m.-1 p.m.*). ▶ **S. Giustina**★, a 16C church with eight domes, stands in one corner of the vast **Prato della Valle**

(E3).   Behind a bare façade, the Renaissance interior has choir stalls★ carved in 1566, the *Martyrdom of St. Justina*★ by Veronese in the apse and *St. Gregory the Great*★ by Sebastiano Ricci in the second chapel on the l.   The transept leads into the **Cappella della Madonna**★, the remains of a 5C-6C basilica with a marble iconostasis and inlaid stalls (1477) in the old choir★ of 1462.   ▶ In the E part of the city there is the church of **S. Sofia**★ (C4), the oldest in Padua, which has been altered many times from the 11C onward.   The façade dates from the 11C-14C and the apse has Byzantine-style niches.   The interior is Romanesque-Gothic.   □

Four No Trumps

In a popular song the city of Padua is the city of a meadow with no grass, of the horse without a rider, the café without doors and the saint without a name.   The first is the Prato (meadow) della Valle, the great piazza and garden laid out in 1775 on land that the Venetian governor had reclaimed from a marsh.   The site had once been part of the Roman city.   The second, in the Palazzo della Ragione (law courts) is a large wooden horse which was made for a tournament in 1446.   The design has been attributed to Donatello, who, a few years earlier, fashioned the equestrian monument to the Venetian commander Erasmo da Narni, known as Gattamelata (Tabby Cat).   The café without doors is the neoclassical Caffè Pedrocchi, built in 1831 and said to have no doors because it stayed open day and night.   The last is the basilica of St. Anthony of Padua, who is referred to locally as the 'Santo'.   The basilica was built to enclose the remains of the Franciscan preacher who was born in Lisbon in the late 12C and died on the outskirts of Padua in 1231.   His anniversary is commemorated as a religious feast day and popular holiday.

Practical information ─────────────

PADUA

ⓘ riviera Mugnai 8 (B3), ☎ 651856; p. Pedrocchi 18 (C3), ☎ 44711; office in railway station (A3), ☎ 27767.
▦ (A3), ☎ 657688.
☞ from bus station, p. Boschetti (B3), ☎ 664755.
Car rental: *Avis*, p. Stazione 1, ☎ 664198; *Hertz*, p. Stazione 5, ☎ 657877; *Maggiore*, Stazione corso del Popolo 61, ☎ 30031.

Hotels:
★★★★ *Milano*, v. P. Bronzetti 62 (B1 a), ☎ 663788, 58 rm ℙ ♿ No restaurant, 95,000; bkf: 7,500.
★★★★ *Plaza*, corso Milano 40 (B-C2 b), ☎ 656822, 142 rm ℙ ♿ 130,000.
★★★★ *Villa Altichiero*, v. Altichiero 2, ☎ 615111, 71 rm ℙ ▦ ♿ ▱ 79,500; bkf: 8,000.
★★★ *Biri*, v. Grassi 2 (C6 c), ☎ 776566, 87 rm ℙ ♿ 74,000; bkf: 9,000.
★★★ *Europa*, largo Europa 9 (B3 d), ☎ 621200, 59 rm ℙ 85,000; bkf: 8,000.
★★★ *Grande Italia*, corso del Popolo 81 (A3 e), ☎ 650877, 64 rm ℙ ♿ 89,000.
★★★ *Leon Bianco*, p. Pedrocchi 12 (C3 f), ☎ 22514, 22 rm ℙ No restaurant, 76,000; bkf: 10,000.
★★★ *Monaco:* p. Stazione 3 (A3 g), ☎ 664344, 57 rm ℙ 70,000.
★★ *Cason*, v. P. Sarpi 40 (A2 h), ☎ 662636, 48 rm ℙ ⚐ 31,000; bkf: 5,000.

Restaurants:
● ♦♦♦ *Dotto*, v. Squarcione 23 (C2 m), ☎ 25055, closed Sun eve, Mon, Jan and Aug.   Regional cuisine: risotto alla campagnola, dried salt cod alla padovana, 35/45,000.

● ♦♦♦ *El Toulà*, v. Belle Parti 11 (C2 n), ☎ 26649, closed Sun, Mon noon and Aug.   In 16C palace in historic town centre.   Regional and international cuisine: tortellini with pigeon, fried shore crabs, 30/50,000.
♦♦♦ *Falconiere*, v. Umberto I 31 (D3 p), ☎ 656544, closed Thu, noon on hols and Aug.   Romagnese cuisine: garganelli casalinghi, tagliata with Atlantic sea salt, 35/50,000.
♦♦♦ *Cavalca*, v. Manin 8/10 (C2 l), ☎ 39244, closed Tue eve, Wed, Jan and Jul.   Mixed regional cuisine: homemade tagliatelle and tortellini, cuttlefish alla veneziana, 30/35,000.
♦♦ *Giovanni*, v. Moroncelli 22, ☎ 772620, closed Sun and Aug.   Regional cuisine: homemade pastas, roast meats, 25/35,000.

Recommended
Canoeing: *Società canottieri* school, strada Polveriera, ☎ 680857.
Children's facilities: sailing courses (8-12 yrs) organized in the spring by *Lega Navale*, v. Trieste 38/A, ☎ 45750.
Cycle-racing track: *G. Monti*, v. Carducci 3; *CONI* cycle training centre, v. Venturina, ☎ 38575.
Events: *opera season* (Oct), *theatre season* (Nov-May) at *Teatro Verde* (C2), ☎ 20431; *concerts* at the *Liviano* (autumn-spring); *international violin festival* (May-Jun); *Teatro Estate (summer theatre)* in the *Roman Arena* (Jul-Aug).
Fairs and markets: *international sample fair* (May); *leisure time fair* (Nov), ☎ 840111.
Flying: v. Sorio 89, ☎ 665611 or 25699 (also gliding).
Guided tours: to old town in spring and autumn (daily).
Horseback riding: v. Libia 30, ☎ 654635 (instruction).
Nature park: of Euganean hills, office at p. Antenore 3, ☎ 30369; *Orto Botanico* (Botanical Garden; E3), ☎ 656614.
Race course: *Le Padovanelle*, at Ponte di Brenta *(5 km E)*, strada S. Marco 219, ☎ 625107 or 625531.
River trips: to Venice along the Riviera del Brenta (→) on the *Burchiello* (Wed, Fri and Sun, Mar-Oct); information from *Siamio*, v. Trieste 42.
Sports stadium: v. T. Aspetti, ☎ 600811.
Wine: cellar at p. S. Croce 31, ☎ 23767.
Youth hostel: *Ostello Città di Padova*, v. A. Aleardi 30 (D2), ☎ 28369.
♥ café: *Caffè Pedrocchi*, v. Otto Febbraio, ☎ 27397.

Environs

PONTE DI BRENTA, 5 km E.

Hotel:
★★★★ *Padovanelle*, v. Ippodromo, ☎ 625622, 40 rm ℙ ♿ ▥ ⚐ ▱ 150,000.   Rest.   ● ♦♦♦ closed Sun eve, Mon and Jul-Aug.   Regional and international cuisine: risotto with green peppercorns, liver alla veneta, 40/65,000.

RUBANO, 8 km W.

Hotels:
★★★★ *Bulesca*, v. Fogazzaro 2, ☎ 630288, 59 rm ℙ ♿ ▥ ⚐ 100,000; bkf: 4,000.   Rest.   ♦♦♦ closed Sun.   Regional cuisine: strangolapreti in partridge and orange sauce, pancakes with mushrooms, 30/45,000.
★★★★ *Rustego*, v. Rossi 16, ☎ 631466, 41 rm ℙ ▥ ♿ 83,000; bkf: 7,000.

PESCHIERA DEL GARDA

Verona 24, Venice 138, Milan 133 km
Pop. 8,811 ⊠ 37019 ☎ 045   A4

Situated on the beautiful E gulf of Lake Garda, the town still bears the mark of long years of Venetian rule.   Peschiera was a Venetian border fortress and the **fortifications** that still surround the town were even more important when Peschiera formed one corner of the Austrian Quadrilateral (the others being Verona, Legnano and Mantua), the defensive heart of Lombardy-Venetia. One room in the palace of the Comando del Presidio displays exhibits connected with the meeting of the Allied leaders, held here on 8 Nov 1917 to organize the defense of Piave after the Austrian breakthrough at Caporetto *(9-11 a.m. and 3-5 p.m.).* 2.5 km SW is the 16C sanctuary of the **Madonna del Frassino** (15C altarpiece and 16C-18C paintings). □

Practical information

ℹ p. Betteloni 15, ☎ 7550381.
⚓ boats and hydrofoils.

Hotels:
★★ *Papa,* at San Benedetto, v. Bella Italia 40, ☎ 7550476, 19 rm 🅿 ⬛ ⟲ ⅋ ⬛ closed Nov, 40,000; bkf: 3,500.
★★ *Peschiera,* at San Benedetto, v. Parini 4, ☎ 7550526, 30 rm 🅿 ⬛ ⬛ ⅋ ⬛ 40,000; bkf: 3,500.
⚘ *Bella Italia,* at Bella Italia, 700 pl, ☎ 7550138; *Garda,* v. Marzan, 1,053 pl, ☎ 7550540.

Recommended
Entertainment park: *Gardaland,* 9 a.m.-dusk, ☎ 7551397.
Wines: at Castelnuovo del Garda, v. Montini 16, ☎ 644121; *Zenato* farm company, ☎ 7550300.

PIAZZOLA SUL BRENTA

Padua 17, Venice 54, Milan 226 km
Pop. 10,768 ⊠ 35016 ☎ 049   C4

This villa, set in an extensive park with a lake and fish pool, is dramatic in appearance. The central section (1546), possibly by Palladio, is flanked by 17C-19C wings completed by a semicircular arcade with rusticated columns. Inside *(9 a.m.-12 noon and 3-8 p.m.; 1-5 p.m. winter)* are several rooms with paintings and frescos. The most interesting feature is the Music Room, known as **La Chitarra** (guitar) because of its shape. The musicians stand on four balconies and the sound is reflected off special angled boards through a hole in the middle of the floor into the Sala delle Audizioni below, where the audience sits. □

Practical information

Recommended
Horseback riding: *Centro ippico Brenta,* at Villa Simes-Contarini, ☎ 5590595.
Speedway: *Vaccarino,* at Curtarolo *(7 km SE),* v. Papa Giovanni XXIII 57, ☎ 551125 or 557041.

PIEVE DI CADORE

Belluno 43, Venice 133, Milan 386 km
2,881 ft pop. 4,146 ⊠ 32044 ☎ 0435   D-E1

Pieve is the main centre of Cadore (→) and the birthplace of Titian. His home can be visited *(summer 9 a.m.-12 noon and 3-6 p.m.; winter apply to warden).* It contains a small museum of mementos (autographs, prints, reproductions). To the l. there is a house with a façade said to have been frescoed by Titian as a boy. On the central p. Tiziano stands the **Palazzo della Magnifica Comunità Cadorina** *(summer 9 a.m.-12:30 p.m. and 4-7:30 p.m.; closed Mon)* with numerous exhibits and a museum with finds from excavations at Làgole. The 19C **parish church** has several paintings, including Titian's *Madonna and Saints★*. □

Send us your comments and suggestions; we will use them in the next edition.

Practical information

⚡ ski lifts, cross-country skiing, instruction, skating.
ℹ v. XX Settembre 18, ☎ 31644.

Hotels:
★★ *Canada:* at Tai di Cadore, v. Manzago 15, ☎ 31741, 35 rm 🅿 ⬛ ⬛ closed Sep-Oct, 60,000. Rest.◆◆◆ closed Sat and Sep-Oct. Regional cuisine: potato gnocchi alla cadorina, cannelloni ai formaggi, 25/30,000.
★★ *Giardino,* v. Carducci 20, ☎ 33141, 24 rm 🅿 ⬛ ⅋ 50,000; bkf: 5,000.
★★ *Tabià,* at Pozzale, ☎ 31693, 8 rm 🅿 ⬛ ⅋ closed 1 Apr-19 Jun and 21 Sep-19 Dec, 40,000; bkf: 4,000.

Recommended
Children's facilities: *Casetta di Babbo Natale* (Father Christmas's House in woods, 10 mn from village, open to visitors).
Swimming: at Valcalda, ☎ 31189.

PORTOGRUARO

Venice 66, Milan 323 km
Pop. 24,862 ⊠ 30026 ☎ 0421   E-F3

Medieval and Renaissance buildings line the arcaded streets of Portogruaro and the River Lémene flows through the town. The origin of its name is the subject of dispute; some scholars trace it to a low Latin word *groa,* meaning marsh (the area was a marsh until being drained), others to *gruarius,* a Celtic word meaning guardian of the wood. In the town itself the question has been resolved with scant respect for linguistics by placing two cranes (gru) with curving necks on the town arms. The town was long a port on the Lémene, which is still navigable down to the sea.

▶ The picturesque 14C-15C Gothic **Palazzo Comunale★** has battlemented roofs, Gothic windows and an external staircase. ▶ Next to the 19C **Duomo,** which contains 16C Venetian altarpieces, is a leaning campanile. ▶ The **Museo Nazionale Concordiese** (v. del Seminario 22; *9 a.m.-2 p.m.; hols 9 a.m.-1 p.m.; closed Mon*) contains stones with inscriptions, sculptures and various finds from excavations at Concordia Sagittaria including a bronze of Diana★ (3C), a collection of stone weights and a piece of early-Christian glass portraying Daniel in the lions' den. □

Practical information

Restaurant:
◆ *Botte,* v. Pordenone 46, ☎ 74026, closed Fri. Regional cuisine: rabbit alla campagnola, charcoal grilled meat, 19/35,000.

Recommended
Bowling: v. Cadorna, ☎ 73033.
Horseback riding: *Circoli ippici* at Fossalta di Portogruaro *(6 km E),* v. King, ☎ 700059; v. Matteotti, ☎ 700093 (instruction).
Wine: Venetian wines (national wine show, Apr-May, at Pramaggiore, *12 km NW),* v. Vittorio Veneto 13, ☎ 799025.

PORTO TOLLE AND THE PO DELTA

Rovigo 51, Venice 90, Milan 336 km
Pop. 11,034 ⊠ 45018 ☎ 0426   D-E6

The **Po Delta** thrusts out from the Adriatic coast and extends nearly 40 miles between the mouths of the Adige and the Volano. In Roman times the shoreline was straighter and set farther back, but the Delta has moved seaward, particularly over the last three centuries, as a result of silt carried by the river and deposited in the coastal shallows. The landscape includes islands surrounded by irregular expanses of water or by reclaimed lands that are now farmed. Canals wind through it, flanked by high embankments on which roads have been laid. The Po divides for the first time near Santa Maria in Punta, S of Adria, into the Po di Venezia and the Po di Goro. A series of channels, the Po di Levante, the Po della Donzella or della Gnocca and the Po di Maistra branch off the Po di Venezia or Po Grande until finally it forks into the Po delle Tolle and the Po della Pila. The mouth of the Po della Pila is the easternmost of the outlets, while the Po di Levante is the northernmost and the Po di Goro the southernmost. The Po di Goro also marks the boundary between Venetia and Emilia-Romagna. The Delta landscape is best viewed in the **Isola della Donzella** (between the Po di Venezia and delle Tolle and the Po della Gnocca; starting point, Ca' Tiepolo); in the **Polésine dello Schiavone** or Isola di Polésine (between the Po della Pila and the Podelle Tolle, entered from Ca' Dolfin); in the **Isola di Ca' Venier** (between the Po di Maistra and the Po di Venezia, starting point Contarina) and along the lower stretch of the **Po di Levante** (starting point Contarina).

▶ **Porto Tolle** is a community with several centres scattered over the islands of the delta. The main centre is **Ca' Venier**. In front of the municipio is a monument to Ciceruacchio — Angelo Brunetti of Trastevere, an ardent supporter of the Roman Republic (1849) who, like Garibaldi, fled towards the Romagna, from where he hoped to reach Venice, which was still holding out. He was captured and executed here by an Austrian firing squad together with his two young sons and six companions on 10 August 1849. □

Practical information _____

ⓘ v. Matteotti 417, ☎ 81150.

Restaurant:
♦ **Brodon**, at Cà Dolfin *(10 km E)*, ☎ 84021, closed Mon and Jul. Mixed cuisine: fish risotto, grilled meat, 18/36,000.

Recommended
Boat trips: in Po Delta (summer, 3-5 hrs) from Ca' Tiepolo, from Scardovari *(15 km SE)*, from Pila *(15 km E* of Ca' Venier, accessible by car from Contarina), from Taglio di Po *(14 km NW)* and from other places; information from *Consorzio Pro Loco Delta Padano*, ☎ 660531.
Canoeing: *Gruppo Canoa Delta Po*, ☎ 82501 (guided tours of delta).
Cycling: *C.S. Taglio di Po (14 km NW)*, v. Kennedy.

RECOARO TERME

Vicenza 42, Venice 108, Milan 227 km
Pop. 7,717 ⊠ 36076 ☎ 0445   B4

Here in the lush upper valley of the Agno, against the background of the Piccole Dolomiti, life has all the attractions of the old-fashioned spas.

▶ There are nine springs, of which five are incorporated in the **Fonti Centrali**, which stands in a beautiful park. The first was discovered in 1689 by Count Lelio Piovene; years later he began to exploit them. ▶ **Recoaro Mille** is a ski area (3,300-5,600 ft) reached by chair lift or by road *(11 km)* from San Quirico *(7.5 km downstream)*. □

Practical information _____

♨ (May-Sep), ☎ 75016.
🎿 ski lifts, cross-country skiing, instruction at Recoaro Mille.
ⓘ v. Roma 25, ☎ 75070.

Hotels:
★★★★ **Dolomiti**, v. Mattinale, ☎ 75025, 40 rm 🅿 🔍 ⌗ ⌀ closed Oct-May, 80,000; bkf: 6,000.
★★ **Pittore**, v. Roma, ☎ 75039, 25 rm ♿ ⌀ closed Oct-Apr, 45,000; bkf: 4,000.
★★ **Seggiovia**, p. Duca d'Aosta, ☎ 75050, 37 rm ⌀ closed 10 Oct-20 Dec, 45,000; bkf: 4,000.
★★ **Verona**, v. Roma 60, ☎ 75065, 40 rm ⌀ closed Oct-Apr, 45,000; bkf: 3,000.

Recommended
Conference centre: at Fonti Termali.
Cycling: *Cicli Cornale*, v. Giara 27, ☎ 75395.
Excursions: to *Alpe di Campogrosso refuge*, ☎ 75030 and to *C. Battisti CAI refuge*, ☎ 75235 (alpine guides).

ROSOLINA MARE

Rovigo 49, Venice 74, Milan 334 km
Pop. 185 ⊠ 45010 ☎ 0426   D-E5

Rosolina Mare is a recently developed resort along the coast to the r. of the mouth of the Adige. The road that leads to Rosolina along the embankments of the river conveys an inescapable sense of the delta landscape. Immediately to the S, on the **Isola di Albarella** (private) is a holiday centre in natural surroundings with hotels and sports facilities. It is 22 km by road from Rosolina Mare and the interesting route runs through the lagoons. □

Practical information _____

ROSOLINA MARE
≋
ⓘ p. Albertini 16, ☎ 664541; at Rosolina Mare, v. dei Pini 60, ☎ 68012 (seasonal).

Hotel:
★★★ **Alexander**, v. dei Pini 60, ☎ 68047, 66 rm 🅿 ⌗ ☐ closed Oct-Apr, 49,000; bkf: 6,000.
⛺ ★★★ *Rosapineta*, strada Nord 24, ☎ 68033.

Recommended
Children's facilities: *Villa Serena* children's residence, v. Trieste 15, ☎ 68094, information, ☎ 0444/544788 (2-12 yrs, open 15 Jun-30 Aug).
Tennis: v. S. Antonio, ☎ 68103; p. Europa, ☎ 68040.
Water skiing: *Sci nautico Albarella*, v. Approdo, ☎ 0421/67310.

Environs

ISOLA DI ALBARELLA, ⊠ 45010, ☎ 0426, 6 km S.

Hotels:
★★★★ **Golf**, ☎ 67078, 22 rm 🅿 🔍 ⌗ ♿ ☐ ⌀ ⌁ (18) closed Nov-Feb, 126,000; bkf: 15,000.
★★★ **Capo Nord**, ☎ 67139, 43 rm 🅿 🔍 ⌗ ☐ ⌀ closed Oct-Apr, 80,000; bkf: 10,000.

Recommended
Golf: ☎ 67124 (18 holes).

ROVIGO

Venice 80, Milan 285, Rome 457 km
Pop. 52,373 ⊠ 45100 ☎ 0425   C6

Rovigo is the main centre of the Polésine. At its centre, in the p. Vittorio Emanuele, stands a column with a Lion of St. Mark (the city passed to Venice in 1482). Noteworthy buildings include the **Loggia dei Notai** (16C, now the municipio); the 18C **Torre dell'Orologio**; the **Palazzo Roverella** (the columns and pilasters of the portico and part of the courtyard are from the original 15C building) and the **Palazzo dell'Accademia dei Concordi**.

▶ The **Pinacoteca dei Concordi**★, housed in the Palazzo dell' Accademia dei Concordi *(10 a.m.-12 noon and 4-6:30 p.m.; Sat and Sun 10 a.m.-12 noon; closed hols)*, has an interesting collection of 15C-18C Venetian paintings *(Madonna and Child*★ by Giovanni Bellini and *Venus in the Mirror*★ by Mabuse). Attached to this gallery are the **Pinacoteca del Seminario** (*St. John the Baptist*★ by Piazzetta, *Peasant*★ by P. Longhi) and an archaeological department with Egyptian artefacts as well as prehistoric and Roman finds from the Polésine. ▶ Rebuilt in the 19C and incorporating the remains of the Romanesque-Gothic church along the r. flank, the church of **S. Francesco** (v. Silvestri) contains several 16C Ferrarese paintings. ▶ The **Rotonda** or Beata Vergine del Soccorso (p. XX Settembre) is a late 16C building; inside are several 17C Venetian paintings (1655). ▶ The **Duomo** was rebuilt in the 17C and has an 18C dome. The interior has several sculptures and paintings. ▶ Two leaning **towers** in the public garden are all that remain of the medieval castle, which, according to tradition, was begun in the 10C by the bishop of Adria *(summer 8 a.m.-1 p.m. and 4-8:30 p.m.; winter 9:30 a.m.-12:30 p.m. and 2-5 p.m.).* ▶ In the abbey of S. Bartolomeo (v. A. Oroboni), the **Museo Civico della Civiltà in Polésine** *(Mon-Fri 8:30 a.m.-12:30 p.m.; Wed also 3-6 p.m.)* records the development of the cultures of the middle and upper Polésine from early historical times, with finds from the proto-Villanova culture, Roman antiquities and incised 16C-18C ceramics from Rovigo and Badia Polésine. ☐

Practical information _____

ⓘ corso del Popolo 78, ☎ 361481.
🚂 ☎ 33396.
🚌 from bus station, v. Petrarca 12.

Hotels:
★★★★ *Europa Palace,* v. Porta Po 92, ☎ 29504, 56 rm Ⓟ ⬜ 💸 84,000.
★★★ *Corona Ferrea,* v. Umberto I 21, ☎ 26201, 30 rm. No restaurant, 74,000; bkf: 5,500.
★★★ *Cristallo,* v. Porta Adige 1, ☎ 30701, 50 rm Ⓟ 57,000; bkf: 5,000.
★★ *Bologna,* v. Regina Margherita 6, ☎ 361410, 16 rm Ⓟ ⬜ 💸 39,000; bkf: 6,000.

Restaurant:
● ◆◆◆ *Tre Pini,* v. Porta Po 68, ☎ 27111, closed Sun and Aug. In small villa among pines. Creative cuisine: gratinéed lobster tails, calf liver with grapes, 25/40,000.

Recommended
Cycling: *Pedale Rodigino,* v. Puccini 26, ☎ 30613; *G.S. Fausto Coppi,* at Guarda Veneta *(11 km S),* v. Roma 11, ☎ 98130.
Horseback riding: *Circolo ippico Rodigino,* at Guarda Veneta, v. Kennedy 20/A, ☎ 98276 (associate of *ANTE*).
Sports stadium: v. Gramsci.
Swimming: v. Porta Adige, ☎ 30120.

SCHIO

Vicenza 24, Venice 94, Milan 225 km
Pop. 36,320 ✉ 36015 ☎ 0445   B3-4

The industrialized zones of Italy are centred around the foot of the Alps. There are two reasons: labour could easily be attracted from farming that was only marginally profitable and there is abundant water that can be used as a source of power. Schio lies at the foot of the pre-Alps, at the opening of the Val Léogra. The wool industry dates back to the 12C, when weaving was carried out by the Umiliati, a brotherhood of Milanese origin, which combined religious penitence with labour. The modern development of the industry began under Nicolò Tron, a Venetian nobleman, who opened a factory in 1738, importing both machines and experts. This enterprise suffered as a result of political changes during

the Napoleonic era but recovered in the 19C under the Rossi family.

▶ The Neoclassical 18C **Duomo** is approached by a double flight of steps (view) and in front of it is a **Monument to the Weaver.** ▶ The Gothic church of **S. Francesco,** near the park known as *Grumi dei Frati,* has an elegant portico and campanile. Inside are an altarpiece, frescos and wooden choir stalls carved in the early 16C. ▶ In the v. Pasubio are the **Stabilimenti Lanerossi,** old woollen mills. ☐

Practical information _____

Hotel:
★★★ *Nuovo Miramonti,* v. Marconi 3, ☎ 29900, 70 rm, 64,000. Rest. ◆◆◆ *Bruno* ☎ 20119, closed Sun and Aug. Vicenza cuisine: dried salt cod alla vicentina, seasonal dishes with radicchio, mushrooms or asparagus, 25/35,000.

Recommended
Events: *organ concerts* in Duomo (every Sun in Sep).
Hang gliding: *Delta Club Schio,* v. Fleming 11, ☎ 640002.

SOAVE

Verona 21, Venice 95, Milan 178 km
Pop. 5,536 ✉ 37038 ☎ 045   B4

The castle standing amid the vineyards on the spurs of the Lessini is named not from the Italian adjective meaning sweet, but from Swabia (Svevia). The wine, which takes its name from the castle, is not sweet but dry in taste with a hint of bitterness.

▶ The historical centre is ringed by 14C **walls** strengthened by twenty-four towers which climb the hill to the castle. ▶ In the p. dell'Antenna, the **Palazzo di Giustizia** (1375) has a portico with Gothic arches and an external staircase and the **Palazzo Cavalli** is Venetian Gothic (1411). ▶ The old **castle** *(summer 9 a.m.-12 noon and 3-7 p.m.; winter 9 a.m.-12 noon and 2-4 p.m.; closed Mon)* was enlarged in the 14C and again in the 15C. It is possible to enter some of the rooms of the residence from the second courtyard ; view★. ▶ 2 km on the SS for Vicenza, at **Villanova di San Bonifacio,** is the Romanesque abbey of S. Pietro with 14C frescos. ▶ There are 15C votive frescos in the Romanesque church of S. Abbondio at **San Bonifacio** (4.5 km SE of Soave). ☐

Practical information _____

ⓘ municipio, ☎ 7680648.

Restaurant:
◆◆ *Grio,* at Costeggiola *(4 km NW),* p. Salvo D'Acquisto 3, ☎ 7675184, closed Mon eve, Tue and Aug-Sep. Within view of Scaliger castle. Italian cuisine: pappardelle and cannoli Can Grande, risotto al Soave, 22/30,000.

Recommended
Wine: *Cantine sociali di Soave* and *Cantia del Castello,* ☎ 7680093.

STRA

Venice 30, Milan 246 km
Pop. 6,347 ✉ 30039 ☎ 049   D4-5

The **Villa Pisani**★ *(9 a.m.-1.30 p.m.; park 9 a.m.-6 p.m.; closed Mon)* is the largest and most monumental of the villas on the Brenta. It was built between 1736 and 1756 in celebration of the election of Alvise Pisani as Doge of Venice. Since the time of Napoleon it has been the property of the Italian ruling family or, latterly, of the State. It was decorated by the foremost artists of the 18C. The fresco *Apotheosis of the Pisani*★ is by Tiepolo (1762) and decorates the ceiling of the ballroom. In a corner of the magnificent **park**★ is a **maze**. ☐

Practical information ───────────

Hotel:
★★★ *Venezia*, v. Venezia 31, ☎ 503182, 59 rm P ⚏ ᵭ closed 20 Dec-31 Jan. No restaurant, 48,000; bkf: 5,000.

Recommended
Horseback riding: *Centro ippico*, at Vigonovo *(4 km S)*, v. Fratelli Bandiera 1, ☎ 5090154 (associate of *ANTE*).

THIENE

Vicenza 20, Venice 91, Milan 241 km
Pop. 19,099 ⊠ 36016 ☎ 0445   C4

Thiene lies on the edge of the plain of Vicenza, at the foot of the Asiago plateau. At its heart is the 15C Venetian Gothic **Palazzo Thiene**★ or Porto Colleoni, whose façade has a portico, loggia and battlemented side towers. Inside *(guided tours Sat and hols 9, 10, 11 a.m. and 3, 4, 5 p.m.; other days only p.m.; for groups reserve, ☎ 362121)* are frescos. The park has a 15C oratory and 17C stables. ▶ A 15C Gothic church of the **Natività** (brick with stone ornament) stands in the piazza before the villa. ▶ The 17C **Duomo** has a coffered ceiling (1796) and 17C-18C Venetian paintings. ☐

Practical information ───────────

Hotels:
★★★ *Torre*, v. del Lavoro 2, ☎ 364386, 41 rm P ⚏ ᵭ 60,000; bkf: 6,000.
★★ *Belvedere*, v. Val Posina 65, ☎ 361605, 19 rm P ⚏ closed Aug, 47,000; bkf: 3,500.

Restaurants:
♦ *Milanesi-da Elio e Angelo*, v. del Costo 57, ☎ 362486, closed Sun. Vicenza and Lombard cuisine: ravioli di magro, fusilli all'arrabbiata, 20/30,000.
♦ *Roma*, v. Fogazzaro, ☎ 361084, closed Thu and Aug. Vicenza cuisine: risottos with herbs, dried salt cod alla vicentina, 17/25,000.

Recommended
Flying: *Aeroporto A. Ferrarin*, v. Rozzampia, ☎ 362723 (also gliding and parachuting).
Motocross: *Prà Fontana*, at Fara *(7 km NW)*.

TORRI DEL BENACO

Verona 38, Venice 159, Milan 159 km
Pop. 2,432 ⊠ 37010 ☎ 045   A4

Benaco, the original name for Lake Garda, is now little used. Torri, set amid olive groves, is one of the most pleasant spots on the Verona shore. Typical lakeside houses and the small church of SS. Trinità surround the **porticciolo**, overlooked by the **Scaliger Castle** (1383) with its battlemented towers. ☐

Practical information ───────────

ⓘ p. Portici, ☎ 7225120.
⛴ boats, hydrofoils, car ferry for Maderno.

Hotels:
★★★ *Gardesana*, p. Calderini 20, ☎ 7225005, 34 rm ⚏ ᵭ closed Feb and Nov, 70,000.
★★ *Caval*, v. Gardesana 160, ☎ 7225666, 22 rm P ⚏ closed 15 Oct-15 Dec, 47,000; bkf: 8,000.
★★ *Europa*, v. D'Annunzio 20, ☎ 7225086, 18 rm P ⚏ ⚏ ⬚ closed 6 Oct-Easter, 46,000; bkf: 10,000.

⚓ *Oliveti*, at San Faustino, ☎ 7225522.

Recommended
Windsurfing: school on beach and at *Hotel Baia dei Pini*, ☎ 7225215.
Yacht club: *Yachting Club Torri*, v. G. Marconi, ☎ 7225124.

TREVISO*

Venice 30, Milan 285, Rome 544 km
Pop. 86,527 ⊠ 31100 ☎ 0422   D4

Treviso bestrides the Rivers Sile and Botteniga. It has a profusion of houses and palaces in a handsome blend of late Gothic, early Renaissance, Mannerist and other styles. Although the walls and the course of the Sile form a fairly regular rectangle, the network of streets is medievally intricate and invites detours that offer pleasant surprises and subtle pleasures.

▶ At the centre is the **Piazza dei Signori**★ (A2), a medieval square surrounded by the Palazzo dei Podestà, the Torre del Comune, the former Palazzo Pretorio and the **Palazzo dei Trecento**★ (1217). ▶ In the p. del Monte di Pietà is the **Cappella dei Rettori**★ decorated with paintings and gilded leather *(Mon-Fri 8:30 a.m.-12 noon; apply at no. 12)*. ▶ There are two churches in the p. San Vito (A2); **S. Lucia** (14C frescos) and **S. Vito** (12C, rebuilt 16C). ▶ **Calmaggiore** (A2) is the lively main street of the old city with 15C-16C arcades and houses. ▶ The medieval **Duomo**★★ has Romanesque fragments on the l. flank and column bases in the form of lions on either side. It was rebuilt in the 15C-16C (apse) and again in the 18C-19C. Inside are several works of art (*Adoration of the Shepherds*★ by Paris Bordone, second altar on the r., *Annunciation*★ by Titian at the 16C altar of the Cappella dell'Annunziata, Renaissance sculptures in the sanctuary). To the l. of the cathedral is a Romanesque **baptistery**. ▶ The **Museo della Casa Trevigiana** is in a 15C Gothic house (A2; *closed for restoration*). ▶ The **Museo Civico**★ (A1; *9 a.m.-12 noon and 2-5 p.m.; hols 9 a.m.-12 noon; closed Mon*) has an interesting series of prehistoric weapons★ in the archaeological department and paintings in the gallery, mostly Venetian but some by local artists (*Madonna* by Giovanni Bellini; *Madonna* by Cima da Conegliano; *Portrait of a Dominican*★ by Lorenzo Lotto; *Portrait of Sperone Speroni*★ by Titian, *Crucifixion*★ by Jacopo Bassano). There is also an important collection of modern sculpture by the local Treviso artist, Arturo Martini. ▶ The Gothic church of **S. Nicolò**★★ (B1; 13C-14C) is perhaps the most important building in the city. There are frescos on the cylindrical pillars in the interior. In the sanctuary the 16C Onigo tomb★ is noteworthy. The attached monastery, now a seminary, has a chapterhouse with a fresco of *Figures of the Dominican Order*★ *(apply to porter's lodge)*. ▶ The 13C church of **San Francesco**★ (A2) has several 13C-15C frescos. It is the burial place of Francesca, daughter of the poet Petrarch, and of Pietro, son of Dante. ▶ Tommaso da Modena, an artist from Emilia and a follower of Giotto, left a considerable body of work in Treviso. Several of his frescos, including the *Life of St. Ursula*★, are displayed in the deconsecrated church of **S. Caterina dei Servi di Maria** (A3; *8:45-11:45 a.m.; Apr-Oct also 2-7 p.m.; closed hols*). ▶ The 12C-13C **Loggia dei Cavalieri** (A2) is an arcaded Romanesque building. ▶ On an islet in the Botteniga is the **Peschiera** (A2), or fish market. ▶ The 18C **Villa Manfrin** is in a park that is open to the public on the road out to Conegliano. ▶ The **Porta S. Tommaso** of 1518 (A3) bears a Lion of St. Mark on its outer face (the town was Venetian from 1389). ▶ The **Villa Lattes** at Istrana *(9.7 km on the SS for Castelfranco Veneto)* houses several collections, some of oriental art and one of bells *(Tue and Fri 9 a.m.-12 noon; Sat and Sun 9 a.m.-12 noon and 3-6 p.m.)*. ☐

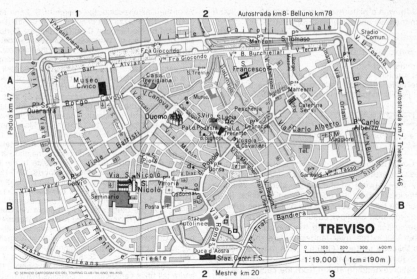

1 **2** Autostrada km8- Belluno km78

TREVISO

0   100   200   300   400 m

1:19.000 (1cm=190m)

2 Mestre km 20   **3**

Practical information

TREVISO

ⓘ v. Toniolo 41 (B2), ☎ 547632.

✈ S. Giuseppe, v. Noalese, ☎ 20393.

🚂 (B2), ☎ 541352.

🚌 from bus station, lungosile Mattei, ☎ 546268 or 541281.

Hotels:

★★★★ *Continental,* v. Roma 16 (B2 a), ☎ 543774, 82 rm Ⓟ No restaurant, 115,000; bkf: 7,000.

★★★ *Cà del Galletto,* v. S. Bona Vecchia 30, ☎ 23831, 47 rm Ⓟ ⚒ 🍴 96,000; bkf: 7,000.

★★★ *Carletto,* v. Bibano 42, ☎ 60371, 89 rm Ⓟ ⚒ 🍴 100,000; bkf: 8,000. Rest. ● ◆◆◆ v. Bibano 46, ☎ 62955, closed Mon and Aug. 19C Venetian style building. Regional cuisine: pumpkin tortelloni, stuffed pigeons, 30/40,000.

★★★ *Carlton,* largo Porta Altinia 15 (B2 b), ☎ 55221, 93 rm Ⓟ 🍴 No restaurant, 91,000; bkf: 6,000.

★★★ *Fogher,* v. della Repubblica 10, ☎ 20686, 48 rm Ⓟ 🍴 83,000; bkf: 6,000.

★★ *Campeol,* p. Ancilotto 4 (A2 c), ☎ 56601, 16 rm 🍴 56,000; bkf: 5,000. Rest. ◆◆◆ *Beccherie* p. Ancillotto, ☎ 540871, closed Thu eve, Fri and Jul, 25/35,000.

Restaurants:

◆◆◆ *Alfredo,* v. Collalto 26 (B2 d), ☎ 540275, closed Mon and Aug. Regional and international cusine: blinis al brie, cuttlefish alla veneziana, 30/45,000.

◆◆◆ *Bersagliere,* v. Barberia 21 (A2 f), ☎ 541988, closed Sun and Aug. 14C building with period furnishings. Regional and some international cuisine: spring risotto, curried scampi, 30/40,000.

◆◆ *Antica Torre,* v. Inferiore 55 (A2 e), ☎ 53694, closed Sun and Aug. On ground floor of old palace. Mixed cuisine: pasticcio of fish, sea bass al Prosecco, 20/40,000.

Recommended

Craft workshops: *Laboratorio Benetton,* v. Caselle 3, ☎ 63352 (wrought iron; telephone before visiting).

Events: *national balloon meeting* (Mar); *radicchio show* (Tue before Christmas).

Flying: v. Noalese 63, ☎ 20251.

Golf: at Zerman di Mogliano Veneto *(12 km S),* Golf Club *Villa Condulmer,* v. Zermanese 1, ☎ 041/457062.

Horseback riding: at Lancenigo *(6 km NW),* ☎ 63357;

at Mogliano Veneto *(12 km S),* ☎ 041/942253; at Grave di Papadopoli *(19 km NE), Equitazione di campagna,* ☎ 743710.

Motocross: race-track at Spresiano *(14 km N),* ☎ 880975.

Race course: S. Artemio, ☎ 63357.

Skating: v. Cairoli (A2), ☎ 263250.

Environs

PADERNO DI PONZANO VENETO, 7 km NW.

Hotel:

★★★★★ *Relais el Toulà,* v. Postumia 63, ☎ 969191, 10 rm Ⓟ ⚒ 🍴 ☐ 270,000; bkf: 18,000. Rest. ◆◆◆ closed Tue. Venetian villa among vineyards. Good regional and some international cuisine: blinis with salmon, rocchio with citrus fruits, 60/80,000.

PREGANZIOL, 7 km S.

Hotel:

★★ *Magnolia,* v. Terraglio 98, ☎ 93375, 30 rm Ⓟ ⚒ 49,000; bkf: 4,000. Rest. ◆ ☎ 93131, closed Sun eve, Mon and Aug. Mixed cuisine: date-shell stew, cuttlefish alla veneziana, 20/35,000.

Restaurants:

◆◆◆ *Bolognese,* at San Trovaso, v. Terraglio 175, ☎ 380888, closed Mon. In park with fountains. Seafood: pasticcio of shrimps, scampi alla busara, 17/33,000.

◆◆◆ *Grazie,* v. Terraglio 114, ☎ 381615, closed Thu eve, Fri, Jan and Aug. Veranda facing garden. Regional cuisine: goose ham, pappardelle, 20/35,000.

VALDAGNO

Vicenza 32, Venice 103, Milan 219 km
Pop. 28,323 ☒ 36078 ☎ 0445   B4

Valdagno is an important wool centre in the Agno Valley. The **old town** has several 18C buildings: the Villa Valle (now Marzotto) attributed to Frigimelica; the Neoclassical Villa Gajanigo; the Palazzo Festari; the Palazzo Nanti and the Palazzo Pedoni. The church of **S. Clemente** dates from 1748. 10 minutes NW by car, in the Torrazzo Valley, is **Montagna Spaccata**

(1,542 ft), with a picturesque gorge formed by a 300 ft cleft in the rock and a waterfall *(open Apr-Oct)*. ☐

Practical information ─────────────

ⓘ v. Trento, ☎ 401190.

Recommended
Sports stadium: v. A. Volta 6, ☎ 404435.
Textile mills: *Marzotto Stabilimenti Tessili e d'Abbigliamento* (textile andgarment factories), ☎ 402000 (reserve).

VALEGGIO SUL MINCIO

Verona 25, Venice 147, Milan 143 km
Pop. 9,233 ⊠ 37067 ☎ 045   A5

Lake Garda is enclosed in the S by a ring of vine- and cypress-covered hills which are the moraine deposited by the thawing of the Sarca glacier. Valeggio sul Mincio stands at the point where the Mincio flows through the hills. It contains the picturesque **ruins** of a many-towered Scaliger castle (13C-14C) on the hill that separates the town from the Mincio. 2 km distant but still in the river landscape are the remains of the **Visconti bridge★** (1393). This may be the last section (before **Borghetto**) of the **Serraglio**, a massive fortification extending 16 km from the castle of Nogarole to Villafranca di Verona, Valeggio and then Borghetto. It was built by the feudal lords Mastino II and Cangrande II della Scala to prevent Mantuan incursions. The road to Verona passes the **Sigurtà garden-park** *(drive through; Thu, Sat and hols)*. ☐

Practical information ─────────────

ⓘ p. C. Alberto, ☎ 7951880.

Restaurants:
♦♦♦ *Antica Locanda Mincio,* at Borghetto, v. Michelangelo 12, ☎ 7950059, closed Wed eve, Thu, Feb and Nov. Summer service in garden on banks of Mincio. Mixed cuisine: tortellini with butter, pumpkin tortelli, 28/38,000.
♦♦♦ *Lepre,* v. Marsala 5, ☎ 7950011, closed Wed, Thu noon, Jan and Jul. Italian cuisine: pappardelle with hare sauce, trout in sour-sweet sauce, 26/32,000.

Recommended
Horseback riding: *Centro ippico del Mincio* (associate of *ANTE*).
Nature park: *Parco-giardino Sigurtà,* ☎ 7950203.

VERONA★★

Venice 114, Milan 160, Rome 506 km
Pop. 261,947 ⊠ 37100 ☎ 045   B4

The medieval battlements of the Scaliger bridge resemble a stage set. The picturesque piazza delle Erbe and the passageways linking a series of squares as far as the Scaliger tombs are extremely beautiful. The promenade of the piazza Bra and the Roman arches of the Arena come to vivid life during the opera season in June. The terraces of the Giardini Giusti rise up the side of the hill. Verona is the largest and most modern city in Venetia. The city's monuments attest to every stage in Verona's history from the Renaissance through the medieval, Lombard-Romanesque and Scaliger-Gothic periods, back to its Roman foundation.

▶ The Adige flows from N to S through the city, describing two loops like the letter S. The old centre (B-C-D4-5) occupies a tongue of land within the second loop. Verona's regular grid of streets is a relic of the Romans. The most important monuments are to be found in this quarter, along with those of the l. bank and,

W of the Castelvecchio, the church of S. Zeno Maggiore (C2). ▶ The **Piazza Bra** is now the city centre (D4). It is bounded by the Baroque **Gran Guardia**; the **Portoni della Bra** of 1389 (r. of entrance to **Museo Lapidario Maffeiano,** *9 a.m.-7 p.m.; closed Mon);* the houses and palaces along the **Liston** — the lively public promenade and the vast **Arena★★** *(9 a.m.-7 p.m.; during opera season 8 a.m.-2 p.m.; closed Mon),* which is one of the largest surviving Roman amphitheatres (1C). ▶ Now for pedestrians only, the elegant v. Mazzini (C4-5) leads to the **piazza delle Erbe,** where the daily market adds life to the 14C houses and Renaissance palaces. In the piazza are the market column, the 16C stocks, the Madonna Verona fountain (1368) and the Column of St. Mark (the city became Venetian in 1404). ▶ After the **Arco della Costa** (the name refers to a whale rib hung beneath it) is the fine **piazza dei Signori★** (C5). On one side is the **Palazzo del Comune** or della Ragione (lawcourts; 12C-16C), with an arcaded Romanesque courtyard and a Gothic external staircase, and the **Torre dei Lamberti** (12C-15C, *winter 8 a.m.-2 p.m.; summer 9 a.m.-7 p.m.; closed Mon; elevator).* On the other side is the **Loggia del Consiglio★** (late 15C). ▶ The monumental **Arche Scaligere★** (B-C 5) are tombs in the form of Gothic tabernacles with statues by the Campionese school. They stand in a small square redolent of the medieval atmosphere of Verona under the rule of the Scaligers. ▶ **S. Anastasia★** (B5) is a Dominican Gothic church (1290-1481) with a double 14C portal and a tall brick campanile. It contains many great works of art: Altichiero's **fresco★** (1395; second apsidal chapel on the r.); *St. George Riding to Free the Maiden,* a detached fresco in Pisanello's elegant, courtly style (in the Cappella Giusti, *apply to sacristan);* sculpted hunchbacks support the holy water stoups. ▶ The 12C **Duomo★** (B5) is Romanesque with 15C Gothic alterations and Renaissance additions. Outside, features to note are the porch★ with reliefs by Maestro Nicolò (12C) and the apse (12C). Inside is a Titian *Assumption★* (first altar on l.). ▶ East of the p. Bra, at the end of the Stradone Maffei and the Stradone S. Fermo with their Renaissance houses and palaces, is the church of **S. Fermo Maggiore★** (D5). One of the city's most interesting churches, it is 13C-14C Gothic with a keel roof. It contains a *Madonna and Saints★* (1528) and the **Benzoni Monument** (1439), framed by Pisanello's fresco of the *Annunciation★.* The sacristy *(apply to sacristan)* gives access to the Romanesque cloister and the 11C-12C lower church. ▶ **Juliet's tomb★** (E5, *9 a.m.-7 p.m.; closed Mon)* is full of atmosphere. ▶ From the p. delle Erbe, the **Corso di Porta Borsari** runs to the **Porta dei Borsari★** (C4), which takes its name from the *bursarii* (tax collectors). This was one of the gates of Verona during Roman times and it was much studied and copied by the architects of the Renaissance. ▶ After the gate the road continues as the **corso Cavour,** which is flanked by noble palaces (19, the **Palazzo Bevilacqua★,** is a masterpiece by the Veronese architect, Michele Sammicheli, 1530) until it reaches the **Castelvecchio★★** (C-D3), Verona's most important medieval building. It dates back to the mid-14C, when it served as both fortress and residence for the Scaliger lords. It now houses the **Civico Museo d'Arte★** *(9 a.m.-7 p.m.; closed Mon)* with a collection of Venetian art from 14C-18C. The school of Verona is well represented: *Madonna del Roseto★* by Stefano da Verona; *Madonna della Quaglia★* by Pisanello; *Boy with Drawing★* by Caroto; two Giovanni Bellini *Madonnas★;* the *Madonna of the Passion★* by Carlo Crivelli; Tintoretto's *Concert in the Open★* and *Heliodorus and the Talents of the Temple★* by Tiepolo. The important **Tesoro★** (Treasury) is in the v. Trezza (13C-14C enamels, gold and bindings). The outstanding **equestrian statue★** of Cangrande I with his enigmatic smile (13C) was taken from the Arche Scaligere. Behind the Castelvecchio the battlemented **Ponte Scaligero★** spans the Adige. ▶ In the W part of the city, still within the walls, are several notable monuments, including S. Zeno Maggiore, S. Bernadino and the Porta Palio. ▶ **San Zeno Maggiore★★** (C1-2) is, together with the Duomo at Modena, perhaps the masterpiece of Italian Romanesque architecture

(12C-13C, apse 1398). Outside, features to admire are the ivory-coloured façade, the **portal★**, the porch (reliefs dating from 1138; **door★**, bronze panels illustrating the life of St. Zeno and the Old and New Testament, 12C) and the free-standing campanile (11C-12C). Over the nave is a keel roof. The decoration includes 13C **statues of Christ and the Apostles★** and, on the high altar, a triptych of the *Madonna and Saints★★*, a key work by Andrea Mantegna (1459). The Romanesque cloister has paired columns (12C-14C; enter from l. aisle). ▶ The 15C church of **S. Bernardino★** (D2) is transitional in style between the Gothic and the Renaissance (frescos and paintings of the Verona school inside and in the attached monastery). ▶ The **Porta Palio★** is the finest of the gates built in 1542-57 for the new ring of walls.

▶ Across the ponte Garibaldi, on the l. bank of the Adige, is **S. Giorgio in Braida★** (A4-5), a Renaissance church with a dome by Sammicheli and a 17C façade. Its paintings include a *Martyrdom of St. George★* by Veronese. ▶ The **Teatro Romano★** (B5-6; *summer 9 a.m.-7 p.m.; winter 8 a.m.-2 p.m.; closed Mon)* is cut out of the slope of the hill. From the top tier of seats there is an elevator to the **Museo Archeologico** in the former convent of S. Girolamo. It contains Etruscan, Greek and Roman bronzes, Roman mosaics, glass, funerary artifacts, terra-cottas and vases; there is a view★ from the terrace. ▶ **Santa Maria in Organo★** (B6) dates from 1481. The Renaissance interior is richly decorated with superb inlay in the choir and sacristy (15C-16C). ▶ The **Palazzo Giusti** (C6) has a beautiful 18C Italian garden with an avenue of cypresses and a belvedere on a terrace. ▶ The **Palazzo Pompei★** (1530, D6) houses the **Museo di Storia Naturale★** *(9 a.m.-12:30 p.m. and 3-6 p.m.; Jun-Aug 3:30-6:30 p.m.; closed Fri),* one of Italy's most interesting natural history museums with a collection of fossils★ from the Bolca layers. □

Practical information

VERONA

⚕ at Caldiero *(15 km E),* ☎ 7650933.
ⓘ v. Valverde 34 (E3), ☎ 30086; v. Dietro Anfiteatro 6/B (C4), ☎ 592828; p. Europa (Casello Verona Sud), ☎ 584019.
✈ at Villafranca, ☎ 513700; *Alitalia,* corso Porta Nuova 61, ☎ 594222; Villafranca airport stop, ☎ 513617.
🚆 (F2), ☎ 590688.
🚌 from Porta Nuova station, ☎ 34125.
Car rental: *Avis,* at railway station, ☎ 26636; *Hertz,* at railway station,☎ 8000832; *Maggiore,* at railway station, ☎ 34808.

Hotels :
★★★★★ ***Due Torri,*** p. S. Anastasia 4 (B5 a), ☎ 595044, 100 rm Ⓟ ♿ 17C palazzo furnished with antiques, 280,000; bkf: 18,000.
★★★★ ***Accademia,*** v. Scala 12 (C4-5 b), ☎ 596222, 116 rm Ⓟ ❄ 120,000; bkf: 12,000.
★★★★ ***Firenze,*** corso di Porta Nuova 88 (E3 c), ☎ 590299, 60 rm Ⓟ ♿ closed Christmas. No restaurant, 102,000; bkf: 12,000.
★★★★ ***Grand Hotel,*** corso Porta Nuova 105 (E3 d), ☎ 595600, 48 rm Ⓟ ♨ ♿ 115,000; bkf: 12,000.
★★★★ ***Nuovo Hotel San Pietro,*** v. S. Teresa 1, ☎ 582600, 58 rm Ⓟ ♿ closed Christmas. No restaurant, 110,000; bkf: 10,000.
★★★★ ***Victoria,*** v. Adua 8 (C4 e), ☎ 590566, 44 rm Ⓟ 🐚 ♿ ❄ 123,000; bkf: 15,000.
★★★ ***Bologna,*** p. Scalette Rubiani 3 (C-D4 f), ☎ 26830, 33 rm Ⓟ ♿ ❄ 69,000; bkf: 8,000.
★★★ ***De' Capuleti,*** v. del Pontiere 26 (E4-5 g), ☎ 32970, 36 rm Ⓟ ❄ closed Christmas, 80,000; bkf: 8,000.
★★★ ***Italia,*** v. Mameli 58/64 (A4 h), ☎ 918088, 53 rm Ⓟ ❄ closed Christmas, 69,000; bkf: 7,500.
★★★ ***Rossi,*** v. Coste (F1 i), ☎ 569022, 40 rm Ⓟ ♨ No restaurant, 77,000; bkf: 8,000.
★★ ***Torcolo,*** vicolo Listone 3 (D4 l), ☎ 21512, 19 rm Ⓟ ♿ No restaurant, 63,000; bkf: 7,500.

Restaurants:
● ♦♦♦ ***Arche,*** v. Arche Scaligere 6 (C5 m), ☎ 21415, closed Sun, Mon noon and Jun-Jul. Managed by same family for a century. Outstanding seafood: sea bass ravioli with crustacean sauce, warm lobster salad with basil, 48/58,000.
● ♦♦♦ ***Dodici Apostoli,*** vicolo Corticella S. Marco 3 (C4 q), ☎ 596999, closed Sun eve, Mon, Jun-Jul and Christmas. Historic inn with frescos and arches. Outstanding regional cuisine: truffle pie, salmon cooked in bread, 50/65,000.
● ♦♦♦ ***Nuovo Marconi,*** v. Fogge 4 (B5 r), ☎ 595295, closed Tue eve and Sun. Regional and Italian cuisine: meat rolls with green vegetables, escalopes of salmon with green vegetables, 35/50,000.
♦♦♦ ***Desco,*** v. Dietro S. Sebastiano (C5 p), ☎ 595358, closed Sun. In old palace. Creative cuisine: cream of cèpes en croûte, breast of duck allo champagne, 45/60,000.
♦♦♦ ***Re Teodorico,*** p. Castel S. Pietro 1 (A6 s), ☎ 49990, closed Wed and Nov. Mixed cuisine: Florentine pancakes, grilled swordfish, 35/55,000.
♦♦♦ ***Serra di Mamma Sinico,*** v. Leoncino 1 (D5 t), ☎ 26150, closed Tue eve and Wed. Regional cuisine: risotto with radicchio, veal chops with cream of olives, 16/35,000.
♦♦♦ ***Tre Corone,*** p. Bra 16 (D4 v), ☎ 22462, closed Thu and Jan. Regional and Italian cuisine: gnocchetti verdi with Gorgonzola, riblets with polenta, 35/65,000.
♦♦ ***Bragozzo,*** v. del Pontiere 13 (E5 n), ☎ 30035, closed Mon and Jan. Mixed cuisine: fish stew, seafood brochette, 35/40,000.
♦♦ ***Torcoloti,*** v. Zambelli 24 (C5 u), ☎ 26777, closed Sun, Mon eve, Jun-Jul and Christmas. In comfortably refitted 19C inn. Regional and Italian cuisine: fili d'erba with onions, homemade spaghetti with olives, 30/40,000.
♦♦ ***Veronantica,*** v. Sottoriva 10 (C5 z), ☎ 34124, closed Sun, Mon noon and Jul-Aug. Mixed international cuisine: champagne risotto, cheese pancakes, 32/44,000.

⛺ ★★★ *Romeo e Giuletta,* at San Massimo all'Adige, v. Bresciana 54, ☎ 989243.

Recommended
Archery: *Compagnia arcieri scaligeri,* at Isola della Scala, v. Matteotti 1,☎ 7300177.
Canoeing: *Canoa Club,* corte Dogana 6 (D5), ☎ 37186.
Children's entertainments: toy fair in p. Bra for S. Lucia (10-13 Dec); zoo in v. Oriani, ☎ 528656.
Clay-pigeon shooting: v. Torricelle 5.
Events: opera, ballet and concert festival in the *Arena* (Jul-Sep), ☎ 590966; *Estate Teatrale* (Shakespeare festival) in *Teatro Romano, international Film Week,* ☎ 594363; symphonic and opera season in the *Teatro Filarmonico,* ☎ 22880; *display of crèches* (Dec-Jan); *Due Valli National Rally* (Oct).
Fairs and markets: *Fieragricola* (Mar), *Vinitaly* (Apr), *Herbora* (May), *Fieracavalli* (Nov), ☎ 588111.
Flying: *Boscomantico airport,* ☎ 563200 (flying, gliding and parachuting).
Gastronomic specialities: *Bauli establishment* (Veronese cake, pandoro), v. del Perlar, ☎ 512388 (open 40 days before Easter).
Golf: at Sommacampagna, Cà del Sale 15, ☎ 510060.
Guided tour: *Agenzia Cangrande,* v. G. della Casa 5, ☎ 38018 (Jul-Sep, reservations up to day before).
Horseback riding: at Boschetto, lungadige Galtarossa, ☎ 31854; *Equitazione di campagna,* at Mizzole, v. Villa Piatti 1, ☎ 558570 (associates of *ANTE*).
Purchases: antiques, tapestries, paintings, prints in v. S. Anastasia, v. Massalongo and v. Sottoriva (B5); elegant shops in v. Mazzini and v. Cappello (C4-5).
Squash: *Squash e bowling center di Verona,* at Bussolengo, strada Padana Superiore, ☎ 7153273.
Swimming: v. Col. Galliano (C-D 1), ☎ 567622.
Technical tourism: *Mondadori* printing works, v. Zeviani 2, ☎ 934391 (apply several days in advance); *Borsa Merci,* corso Porta Nuova 96, ☎ 591011 (agricultural produce, Mon 9:30 a.m.-4 p.m.).
Tennis: v. Col. Galliano, ☎ 566372; v. Gioia 9, ☎ 508908.

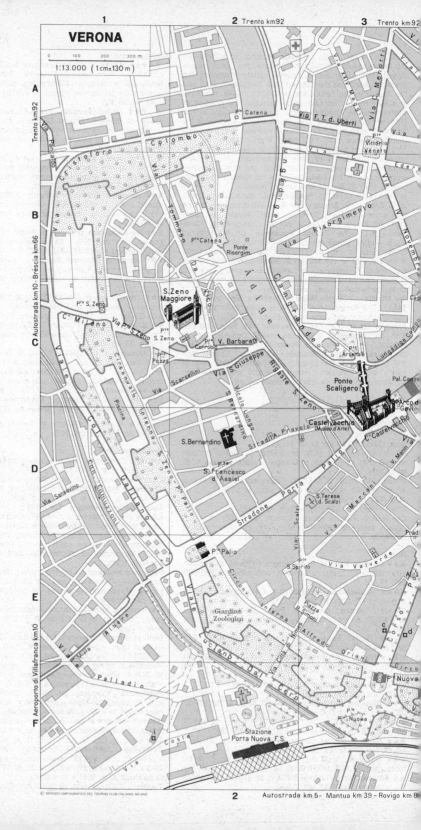

VERONA

0   100   200   300 m

1:13.000 (1cm=130 m)

Autostrada km 5- Mantua km 39 - Rovigo km 8

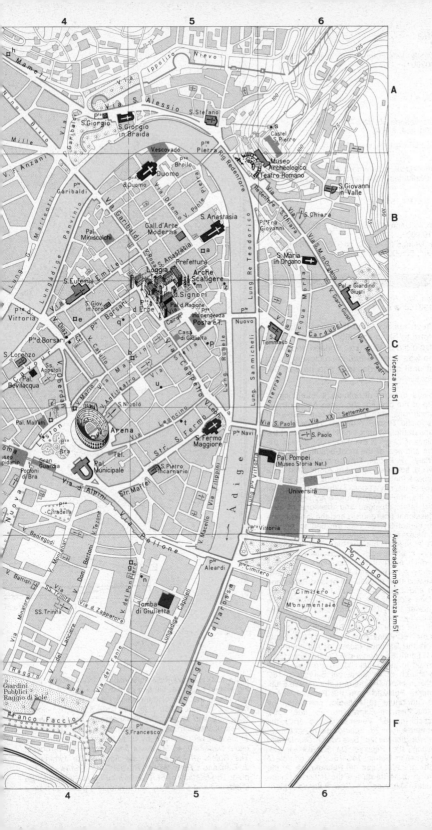

Youth hostel: *Ostello Villa Francescatti,* salita Fontana del Ferro 15, ☎ 590360.

Environs

CROCE BIANCA, 4 km W.

Hotel:
★★ *Garda,* v. Gardesane 35, ☎ 572877, 13 rm P ♨ No restaurant, 52,000; bkf: 5,000.

PERONA DI VALPOLICELLA, 6 km NW.

Hotel:
★★ *Brennero Mini Hotel,* v. Brennero 3, ☎ 941100, 20 rm P ⌖ closed Christmas. No restaurant, 52,000; bkf: 5,500.

SAN MICHELE EXTRA, 5 km E.

Hotels:
★★★ *MotelAgip,* v. Unità d'Italia 346, ☎ 972033, 116 rm P 97,000; bkf: 10,000.
★★ *Gardenia,* v. Unità d'Italia 350, ☎ 972122, 28 rm P ♨ ⌖ closed Jun-Jul, 52,000; bkf: 6,000.

VICENZA**

Vicenza 68, Milan 205, Rome 525 km
Pop. 112,771 ⊠ 36100 ☎ 0444   C4

No other architect has ever had the good fortune to give concrete form to his imagination and innovations as Andrea Palladio did at Vicenza. Indeed, the name of Palladio (who was from Padua) is so closely linked to Vicenza that until a few decades ago he was believed to be a native of the city.

▶ The key buildings, in terms of both architectural importance and the life of the city, line the corso Andrea Palladio (D2-C2-3) which runs from the piazza of a castle that no longer exists to the Teatro Olimpico. There are also two further groups of monuments, one N and one S of the corso, but the place to begin is the piazza dei Signori, the heart of the town and one of the most beautiful architectural groups in Italy. ▶ Padua, Treviso and a number of other cities have a so-called 'drawing room', that is, a large enclosed space that served the needs of the townspeople at the time of the city-states. When the people of Vicenza decided that their political future lay with Venice (1404), the social fabric changed and the sons of merchants, the professional bourgeoisie and the landed gentry could aspire to nobility. It was decided to provide the 15C Gothic Palazzo della Ragione, the city's 'drawing room', with a magnificent marble exterior. Palladio produced his masterpiece, the **Basilica**★★ (C-D3, 1549-1617), in which each of the four sides of the old building is faced by a portico and loggia in perfect proportion. The basilica now houses the **Museo Palladiano** *(9 a.m.-12 noon and 2:30-5 p.m.; Sun 10 a.m.-12 noon; closed Mon).* One side of the Basilica, flanked by the slender piazza tower (12C-15C), faces onto the **piazza dei Signori**★, which has two Venetian columns: one with a Lion of St. Mark, the other with the Redeemer. On the opposite side is the 16C Palazzodel Monte di Pietà, in the centre of which is the Baroque façade of the church of S. Vincenzo (1617) and the **Loggia del Capitanio**★ (1571, Palladio). ▶ Linked to the p. dei Signori are the p. delle Biade, with the church of S. Maria dei Servi (C3; 18C façade, 15C Gothic interior) and the graceful p. delle Erbe. ▶ On corso Andrea Palladio★ are the Palazzo Bonin-Thiene (no. 13, attributed to Palladio, completed by V. Scamozzi); the Palazzo Capra (no. 45, late 15C); the Palazzo Braschi (no. 67, Venetian Gothic, 15C); the **Palazzo del Comune**★ (no. 98, Scamozzi's masterpiece; apply to porter for access to Sala della Giunta and Sala degli Stucchi); the **Palazzo Da Schio**★ or Ca' d'Oro (no. 147, Venetian Gothic, 14C-15C); the church of S. Corona and the graceful **Casa del Palladio.** ▶ At the end of the corso in p. Matteotti are the Palazzo Chiericati and the Teatro Olimpico. ▶ The **Palazzo Chieri-**

cati★ (C3) displays Palladio's inspired innovation in placing a solid expanse, flanked by the two wings of the loggia, above the void of the portico. It houses the **Museo Civico**★ *(9 a.m.-12:30 p.m. and 2:30-5:30 p.m.; closed Sun p.m. and Mon).* The **Pinacoteca**★ has a splendid series of Venetian paintings from the 14C-18C (*Madonna Enthroned with Saints*★ by B. Montagna; G. Buonconsiglio's *Deposition*★; *Madonna and Saints*★ by Veronese; *The Rulers of Vicenza at the Feet of the Virgin*★ by J. Bassano; *Time Which Reveals the Truth*★ by Tiepolo; *The Ecstasy of St. Francis*★ by Piazzetta), sculpture (*Madonna and Child*★ by Sansovino) and paintings from a

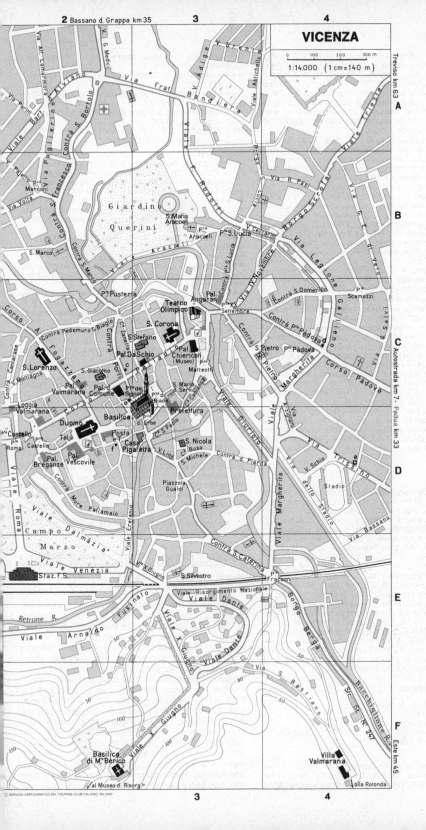

VICENZA

0   100   200   300 m

1:14.000 (1 cm=140 m)

Treviso km 63

Autostrada km 7 - Padua km 33

Este km 45

Giardino
Querini

S.Maria
Aracoeli

S.Marco

P.ta Pusteria
Teatro
Olimpico
S.Corona
S.Stefano
Pal.Da Schio
S.Lorenzo
S.Giacomo
Pal.d.
Valmarana   Pal.d.
Comune
Loggia
Valmarana
Duomo
Castello   Posta
e T.
Casa
Pigafetta
Pal.
Breganze   Pal.
Vescovile

Pal.
Angaran

S.Pietro
S.Maria
d. Servi
Prefettura
S.Nicola
da Busa
S.Michele
Piazzola
Gualdi

Pal.
Chiericati
(Museo)
Matteotti

Contrà S.Domenico
Contrà P.ta Pádova
P.ta Pádova
Corso Pádova

Stadio

Via Bassano

Campo
Marzo
Viale Dalmazia
Viale Venézia
Staz.F.S.

Contrà S.Caterina
S.Silvestro
P.ta Fracon

Retrone R.
Viale   Arnaldo

Viale Risorgimento Nazionale
Viale Dante

Basilica
di M.Bérico

Villa
Valmarana

al Museo d. Risorg.to   alla Rotonda

number of other schools (*Crucifixion*★ by Hans Memling; *The Three Ages of Man*★ by van Dyck). ▶ The **Teatro Olimpico**★★ (C3; *summer, 9:30 a.m.-12:20 p.m. and 3-5:20 p.m.; hols 9:30 a.m.-12:15 p.m.; winter 9:30 a.m.-12:20 p.m. and 2-4 p.m.; closed Sun p.m.*), Palladio's last work (1580, completed by Scamozzi 1584), is a wood and stucco reworking of the theatre of antiquity. The fixed stage is cunningly built and painted to offer false perspectives. ▶ **S of corso Andrea Palladio.** ▶ **Palazzo Porto Breganza** (D2, p. Castello 18) built by Scamozzi. Its present narrow façade, articulated by three columns, reveals only a part, although an important one, of Palladio's grand design. ▶ The **Duomo**★ (D2; 14C-16C) has a Gothic façade (1467) and a Renaissance apse (1482-1508). The Gothic interior contains several paintings. On the piazza, the **Palazzo Vescovile** (D2) has a splendid Renaissance loggia★ facing the courtyard. Below the Palazzo Proti is a **Roman crypt** (*Wed, Fri and Sat 9:30-11:30 a.m.; apply to C.T.G., p. Duomo 2).* ▶ **Casa Pigafetta** (D3; v. Pigafetta 9) is in Venetian Gothic style. It is the birthplace of the nobleman from Vicenza who accompanied Magellan on the first circumnavigation of the world and chronicled the voyage. ▶ The interior of the Oratory of **S. Nicola da Tolentino** (D3; 16C-18C; *bell on l. side*) is decorated with paintings framed by 17C stucco. ▶ **N. of corso Andrea Palladio.** ▶ In the corso Fogazzaro (C2) are the **Palazzo Valmarana** (no. 16, Palladio) and the 13C Franciscan Gothic brick church of **S. Lorenzo**★. ▶ Several superb palaces line the **Contrà Porti**★ (C2); Palladio was responsible for the **Palazzo Porto-Barbaran** (no. 11), the courtyard and rear façade (in Contrà Zanella) of the **Palazzo Thiene** (no. 12) and the **Palazzo Iseppo da Porto** (no. 21). ▶ The Contrà Zanella (C2) also has a number of fine buildings. Palma Vecchio's *Madonna and Saints*★ is in the transept of the Baroque church of **S. Stefano**. ▶ The Dominican church of **S. Corona**★ (C3; *9:30 a.m.-12:15 p.m. and 3-6 p.m.; closed Mon a.m.*) has various works of art, including Veronese's *Adoration of the Magi*★ and the *Baptism of Christ*★★ by Giovanni Bellini. ▶ Some distance from the centre, the church of **SS. Felice e Fortunato**★ (D1) has played a prominent role in the city's religious history (10C-12C).

Environs

▶ The **Basilica di Monte Bérico**★ (F2) stands on the site of an apparition of the Virgin in 1426, although the present building is late 17C. It contains two masterpieces: the *Pietà*★ by B. Montagna (altar to r. of sanctuary) and the *Supper of St. Gregory the Great*★★ by Veronese (monastery refectory); there is an extensive view★ from the piazzale. ▶ The **Villa Valmarana**★ (*c. 3 km by car on SS 247 for Rovigo; Thu and Sat 10 a.m.-12 noon and 3-6 p.m., other days 3-6 p.m.; hols 10 a.m.-12 noon*) is famous for the frescos★★ by Giambattista Tiepolo and his son Giandomenico (1757) that decorate both the Palazzina and the Foresteria. The chinoiserie fantasy of some and the idealization of country life in others put them among the most cheerful and poetic of 18C Venetian decorative cycles. ▶ A short distance away the **Rotonda**★★ or Villa Capra, begun in 1550 and completed by Scamozzi in 1606, is the most famous of Palladio's villas (*entrance to park 9 a.m.-12 noon and 3-7 p.m.; access to the villa not always allowed,* ☎ 21793). Standing on a small hill, it is a Mannerist masterpiece. ☐

Practical information _____

ℹ️ p. Matteotti (C3), ☎ 228944.
🚃 (E2), ☎ 239427.
🚐 from bus station, v. Milano, ☎ 232950.
Car rental: *Avis,* v. Milano 88, ☎ 221622; *Maggiore,* at railway station, ☎ 545962.

Hotels:
★★★★ *Alfa Hotel,* v. dell'Oreficeria 52, ☎ 565455, 87 rm ℗ closed Christmas, 92,500; bkf: 10,000. Rest. ◆◆◆
Incontro ☎ 571577, closed Sun. Vicenza cuisine: dried

salt cod alla vicentina, turkey with pomegranate, 25/40,000.
★★★★ *MotelAgip,* v. Scaligeri 64, ☎ 564711, 132 rm ℗ 🅿️ ⚅ 110,000.
★★★ *Continental,* v. Trissino 89 (D4 a), ☎ 505476, 52 rm ℗ ⚘ 73,000; bkf: 6,000.
★★★ *Cristina,* corso S. Felice 32 (D1 b), ☎ 543656, 30 rm ℗ No restaurant, 76,000.
★★★ *Europa,* v. S. Lazzaro, ☎ 564111, 72 rm ℗ ⚘ No restaurant, 88,000; bkf: 8,000.

Restaurants:
● ◆◆◆ *Antica Trattoria Tre Visi,* opposite Porti 6 (C2 c), ☎ 238677, closed Sun eve, Mon, Jul and Aug. In 15C palace with fireplace. Vicenza cuisine: loin with mushrooms, guinea fowl in sauce, 25/36,000.
● ◆◆◆ *Remo,* v. Caimpenta 14, ☎ 500018, closed Sun eve, Mon, Dec-Jan and Jul-Aug. Country style with summer service outside. Vicenza cuisine: seasonal risottos, fillet alla bassanese, 30/40,000.
◆◆◆ *Cinzia e Valerio,* v. Porta Padova 65/67 (C4 d), ☎ 505213, closed Mon. Seafood: black risotto of cuttlefish, monkfish tail casserole, 30/50,000.
◆◆◆ *Dinosauro,* v. Edolo 50, ☎ 564463, closed Tue and Aug. Mixed cuisine: homemade pastas, grilled meat and fish, 20/25,000.
◆◆◆ *Gran Caffè Garibaldi,* p. dei Signori (C2-3 e), ☎ 544147, closed Tue eve, Wed and Nov. In view of basilica Palladiana. Vicenza and Italian cuisine: fillet with green peppercorns, 20/35,000.
◆◆◆ *Pozzo-da Sergio e Ciacio,* v. S. Antonio 1 (D2 f), ☎ 21411, closed Sun, Tue and Jul-Aug. Regional and Italian cuisine: fresh salmon with cognac, leg of pork en croûte, 25/35,000.

Recommended
Events: at *Teatro Olimpico,* ☎ 234381: *Mozart festival* (May-Jun) and *classical drama* (Sep).
Fairs and markets: *international goldsmiths show* (Jan and Jun); *Orogemma* (Sep), ☎ 969111.
Horseback riding: *Scuola vicentina,* at Monteviale, v. Mioli 12, ☎ 552355.
Swimming: v. Forlanini, ☎ 546745; v. Giuriato 71, ☎ 513783; v. Ferrarin 71 (B1), ☎ 232754.
Tennis: v. Monte Zebio 42 (B1), ☎ 565547.
Wines: v. Mazzini 227 (C1), ☎ 45544; DOC wine and food show (Mar).
Young people's facilities: outdoor activities, *Comitato vicentino,* v. Machiavelli 18, affiliated societies at Barbarano (*22 km S); CSI,* v. Zanella 17; at Castelgomberto (*22 km NW), GEC lux,* v. Rigallo 6.
♥ cafe and pastry shop: *Antica Ofelleria della Meneghina,* v. Cavour 18, ☎ 43687.

VILLAFRANCA DI VERONA

Verona 16, Venice 131, Milan 150 km
Pop. 25,118 ☒ 37069 ☎ 045   A5

A meeting of two emperors, Napoleon III of France and Franz Josef of Austria, took place on 8 July 1859 in the Villa Gandini Morelli-Bugna (v. della Pace 38/B). The armies (the French were fighting alongside the Piedmontese) had fought a fortnight earlier in the moraine landscape of Garda at Solferino and at San Martino. The Austrian Emperor had personally commanded his troops and been defeated, but the sunny June day was a massacre for both sides, with some 17,000 Franco-Piedmontese and 22,000 Hapsburg subjects left dead on the field. 'Better to lose a province than to spill so much blood', wrote the Austrian Emperor to his wife Elisabeth after the battle. Lombardy was ceded to Napoleon III, then handed over to the French ally Savoy. It was too little for Cavour, who temporarily resigned, and for the Italian patriots. In the space of less than two years the political map of the peninsula was totally transformed, with a king, a grand-duke, two dukes, and several Papal legates all forced out and the Kingdom of Italy proclaimed. The rectangular layout of Villafranca, which is traversed by the Mantua-Verona road, stems from its foundation at the end of the 12C as a fortified 'free town' *(Villafranca)*.

▶ The battlemented walls and towers of the 12C-14C **Scaliger Castle**★ cut across the main street of the town. It formed the E end of the Serraglio, a large-scale fortification that extended for 16 km to Valeggio sul Mincio (→). □

Practical information _____

✈ Verona-Villafranca, ☎ 513700.

Hotel:
★★★ *Roveda,* v. Postumia 88, ☎ 7901377, 48 rm P 🏨 ♿ ♨ 76,000; bkf: 8,000.

Recommended
Events: *national antiques fair,* at *Palazzo Gandini Bugna* (Jun).
Horseback riding: *Circolo ippico Moira,* at Alpo di Villafranca, ☎ 513003; *Amici del cavallo,* at Mozzecane, v. Brensani 20 (associates of *ANTE*).

VITTORIO VENETO*

Treviso 40, Venice 70, Milan 320 km
Pop. 30,040 ✉ 31029, ☎ 0438   D3

In 1866, after the union of Venetia with the Kingdom of Italy, Serravalle to the N and Céneda to the S were joined into a single town and named Vittorio Veneto in honour of Victor Emmanuel II, King of Italy. With time, these two original centres have grown together, along the path of the railway, river and road as they leave the mountains. The road is the road to Germany and was built in the mid-19C by the Austrian government. However, the two old centres — Serravalle in particular — provide most of the attractions and features of artistic interest. The city gave its name to the battle of Vittorio Veneto, the last battle on the Italian front in World War I.

▶ **Céneda** has an 18C **cathedral** with a 13C campanile. Inside are two 15C altarpieces and paintings in the sacristy. ▶ The piazza in front of the cathedral has a Renaissance fountain and the **Loggia Cenedese** (1538), which houses the **Museo della Battaglia** *(10 a.m.-12 noon and 2-5 p.m. or 4-6:30 p.m. summer; closed Mon).* ▶ The **Museo Diocesano,** with Venetian paintings, silver, vestments and church furnishings, is being established in the Seminario Vescovile. ▶ An *Annunciation*★ stands at the high altar of the church of **S. Maria del Meschio.** ▶ **Serravalle,** which lies between steep mountain slopes covered with the remains of fortifications, still looks like a 15C-16C town. ▶ At the entrance to the town is the **Ospedale Civile,** whose façade has a Gothic portico and the chapel of S. Lorenzo decorated with 15C frescos *(3-4 p.m. summer; 2-3 p.m. winter; closed Tue).* ▶ The arcaded **via Martiri della Libertà**★ is lined with arcaded Gothic and Renaissance palazzi, including the **Palazzo Troyer** (no. 4-12) and the Renaissance **Palazzo Minucci** (no. 35; *Mon-Fri 9 a.m.-12 noon),* which has a collection of pictures, sculpture, ceramics and *objets d'art.* ▶ In the p. Marc'Antonio Flaminio, the **Loggia Serravallese**★ (1462) houses the **Museo del Territorio Cenedese** *(winter 10 a.m.-12 noon and 3-5 p.m.; summer 4-6 p.m.; closed Tue),* with archaeology (prehistoric and Roman), medieval sculpture (including a Sansovino relief), paintings and detached frescos. ▶ The high altar of the 18C **Duomo** has a Titian *Madonna and Saints*★. ▶ S. Andrea or **Pieve di Bigonzo** (14C) is an unusual church with four Renaissance shrines in each corner of the interior. ▶ The 14C church of **S. Giovanni Battista** has a Renaissance portal, a Gothic interior with paintings and

15C-16C frescos. ▶ There is a view of the city from the **Santuario di S. Augusta** (from p. Flaminio, *25 mn).* □

_____

Mozart's Librettist

Emanuele Conegliano was born in the 18C in the ghetto of Céneda, one of two towns which merged to form modern-day Vittorio Veneto. Since his father had abandoned his Jewish faith to marry a Catholic, Emanuele was baptized together with his father and brothers and, as was usual in such cases, the bishop gave him his own name, Lorenzo da Ponte. He was ordained priest, but later abandoned clerical life to persue adventure and fortune. He had a gift for verse improvisation and at various stages in his career was poet to the emperor in Vienna, librarian and theatrical agent in London and Italian master in the United States, where he died in 1838. During his Viennese period, he wrote the librettos for Mozart's Marriage of Figaro, Don Giovanni and Così fan Tutte. He left lively and entertaining memoirs.

_____

Practical information _____

ℹ p. del Popolo, ☎ 57243.

Hotels:
★★★ *Terme,* v. della Vittoria, ☎ 554345, 39 rm P 🏨 ♿ ♨ 90,000.
★★ *Sanson,* at S. Giacomo di Veglia, p. Fiume 38/39, ☎ 500161, 28 rm P ♨ No restaurant, 46,000; bkf: 5,000.

Restaurant:
♦♦♦ *Postiglione,* v. Cavour 39, ☎ 556924, closed Tue and Jun-Jul. Regional cuisine: pasticcios, spit roasted meat, 20/30,000.

Recommended
Craft workshops: foundry, v. Rizzera 97, ☎ 53304 (bells; telephone before visiting).
Swimming: v. Toniolo, ☎ 59398.
Tennis: v. della Cava 11, ☎ 550540; v. Sabotino 53, ☎ 500008.
♥ gastronomy: salami, head cheese, mushrooms, bilberries.

ZOLDANO AND MARMOLADA

From Agordo to Cortina d'Ampezzo *(80 km, 1 day; map 5)*

This itinerary runs through the Dolomites of Venetia, crossing four passes and ending in the magnificent basin of Cortina d'Ampezzo. The detour to climb the Marmolada group is the high point of a memorable outing.

▶ From **Agordo** (→) the route over the range that separates the Cordévole (Agordino) and Zoldo Valleys climbs through the village of **La Valle Agordino** and along a green plateau to the grass-covered saddle of the **Duran Pass** (5,252 ft). ▶ There is a magnificent view here of Pelmo and Antelao; the road then descends to **Dont** in the Zoldo Valley. In the past, iron ore was mined here and the place names recall this. For example, Dont is a district of Forno (furnace) di Zoldo (furnace) and the village of **Fusine** (forge) is on the other side of the valley at the foot of Pelmo as the road climbs to the **Forcella Staulanza** (5,817 ft), the second pass along the route. ▶ The descent into the Fiorentina Valley passes through the villages of **Selva di Cadore** and **Colle Santa Lucia,** then rejoins the Cordévole Valley at **Caprile.** ▶ At this point the route detours to the Marmolada group, climbing the Pettorina Valley to **Rocca Piétore** (3,750 ft) and the awesome ravine of the **Serrai di Sottoguda**★ to the **Malga**

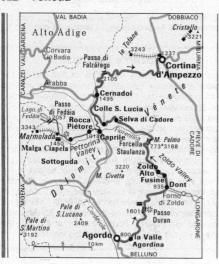

5. Zoldano and Marmolada

Ciapela basin (4,757 ft; cableway for **Marmolada**) and the

Fedaia Pass (6,749 ft).　From here it is possible to reach the nearby **lake** of the same name at the foot of the glacier of the Marmolada.　▶ After the detour, the route continues up the Cordévole Valley, reaching the small cluster of houses at **Cernadoi**.　▶ Following the final section of the **Grande Strada delle Dolomiti** (→ in Trentino-Alto Adige), via the **Falzàrego Pass** (→), the last pass on the route, the route arrives at **Cortina d'Ampezzo** (→), set in its magnificent Dolomite valley.　　　　□

Practical information ――――――――――――――

COLLE SANTA LUCIA, ⊠ 32020, ☎ 0437.

Hotel:
★★ *Posta,* at Villagrande, ☎ 720000, 28 rm Ⓟ ⋙ ⅁ closed 1 Oct-30 Jun except Christmas, 38,000.

FORNO DI ZOLDO, 2,782 ft, ⊠ 32012, ☎ 0437.
☧ ski lifts, cross-country skiing.
ⓘ municipio, ☎ 78341.

Hotels:
★★ *Corinna,* v. al Pez 3, ☎ 78564, 33 rm Ⓟ ⋙ ⅋ closed May and Sep, 63,500: bkf: 5,000.
★★ *De Feo,* v. Roma 5, ☎ 78191, 27 rm Ⓟ ⋙ ⅋ closed 15 Mar-15 Jun, 46,000; bkf: 4,000.

MALGA CIAPELA, ⊠ 32020, ☎ 0437.
☧ Marmolada cableway, Fedaia Pass cableway, ski lifts, cross-country skiing, instruction (summer, ☎ 722027); summer skiing on Marmolada.

Hotel:
★★★ *Tyrolia,* ☎ 722054, 23 rm Ⓟ ⅋ ⅁ ⅋ ⊟ closed 3 May-19 Jun and 1 Oct-21 Dec, 57,000.

Recommended
Excursions: by cableway to Marmolada, ☎ 722144.

Venice ●

▶ There is only one Venice and its uniqueness is not just a matter of water and canals. It is due to the way it receives the sun, mirrors the moonlight on its canals, shimmers in the lagoon while the warm sirocco wind blows through its streets, and to the way its monuments and buildings reflect light and shadow, chiaroscuro and colour. When its decline set in, after a long period as a world power, Venice became a city of indolence and pleasure, attracting with its picturesque carnival, colourful pageants, musical festivals, theatres and gambling houses visitors from all over Europe. This new role for the old mercantile republic began in January 1782 when the city arrayed itself in gonfalons and banners and organized an unprecedented series of festivities in honour of some visiting Russian nobles. The episode was recorded in many paintings of the time, the most famous being Francesco Guardi's splendid *Fêtes for the Archduke Paul of Russia and Maria Teodorovna,* now in Munich's Alte Pinakothek. The image of Venice as an escapist's paradise is interwoven with the romantic one of moonlight trysts and barcarole-singing gondoliers, and is further enhanced by the memory of the famous people who in the past have lived in this or that palace, now slowly crumbling into the canals. Writers and artists are also prominent among the visitors to the city. They come to study its political institutions, art and history and, looking a little more closely than the ordinary visitor, they have uncovered a less pleasant side to Venice's past, bringing to light the cynicism of its ruling cliques and the grasping behaviour of its merchant class. They have also shown that Venice must be considered a Mediterranean and European power, rather than an Italian one, influenced by Byzantine, Lombard, Islamic, Florentine, Flemish, Balkan and Graeco-Roman culture, and, philosophically, by Neoplatonism and Cartesianism. But all these cultural influences were absorbed by the city and transformed by it so that the resultant creativity has always been clearly stamped with Venice's own mark. Braudel, the French historian, has written 'In the strangeness of this city, full of myth and magic, we find ourselves in a world half real and half dream, a world each of us comes to love in his own special way'. When Paolo Sarpi, patriot and ecclesiastic, lay dying in 1623, he used, when referring to his native Venice, the Latin quotation 'Esto perpetua' (May she last forever), and that is surely a wish that all visitors to this enchanting city will want to echo.

● Don't miss

The Piazza S. Marco★★ and the Piazzetta★★ with visits to the Basilica of S. Marco★★ and its mosaics★★ and the Pala d'Oro★★, the Doge's Palace★★ and the view from the campanile★★. A gondola ride down the Grand Canal★★. The Accademia Gallery★★. S. Maria Gloriosa dei Frari★★, the Scuola Grande di S. Rocco★★. The Equestrian Statue of Colleoni★★. The islands of Murano, Burano and Torcello★ in the lagoon.

● *Brief regional history*

Venice and Byzantium. Fugitives had started to move to the **lagoon** as early as the first Barbarian Invasions, but they only began to organize themselves with the arrival of a fresh influx after the Lom-

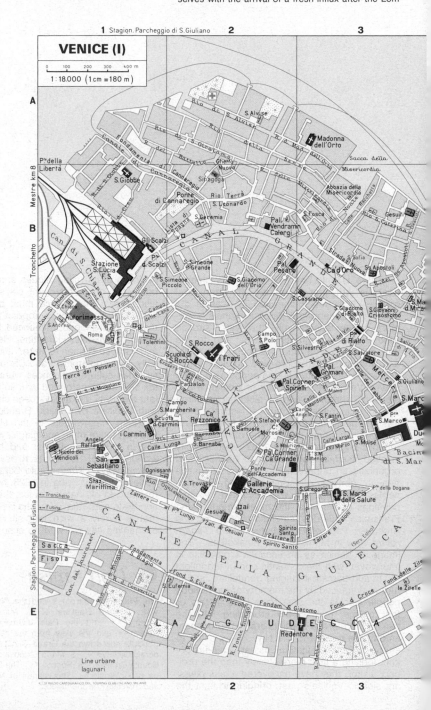

VENICE (I)

0   100   200   300   400 m

1:18.000 (1cm = 180 m)

bard conquest (6C). ● According to tradition, the first doge was **Paoluccio Anafesto** (697), but he was in fact the Byzantine Exarch of Ravenna. ● The seat of this march of the Byzantine Empire was first established at **Cittanova** (Heraclea), then **Malomocco** and finally on the **islands of the Rialto.** ● In 828, in an action that symbolized Venice's independence, the body of Mark the Evangelist was brought from Alexandria in Egypt and placed in the doge's palace chapel. At the same time work began on a new doge's

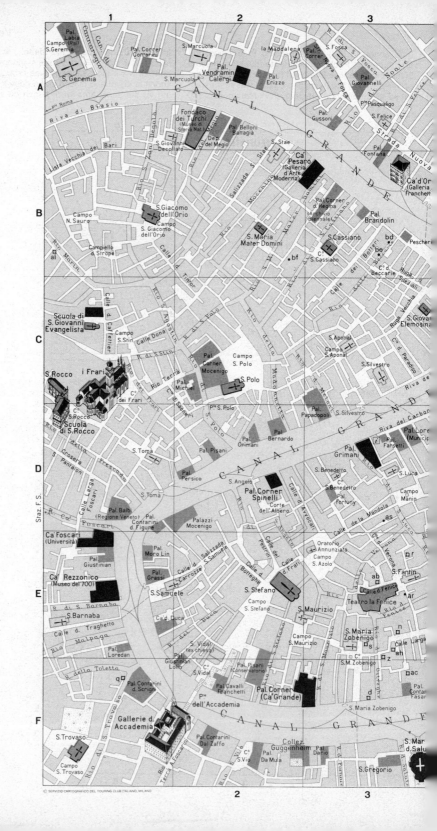

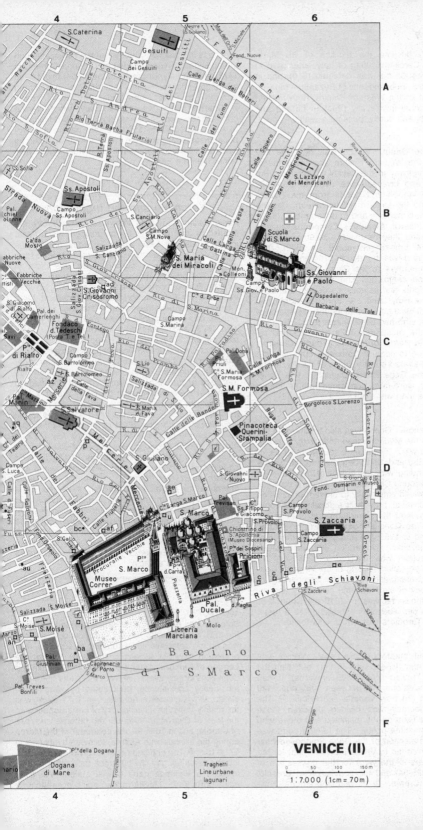

VENICE (II)

Traghetti
Line urbane
lagunari

0   50   100   150m

1:7.000 (1cm = 70m)

chapel, which became the basilica of **St. Mark.**
● **Pepin,** the Carolingian king of Italy, attempted to
conquer the lagoon but was defeated (810), and in
840 **Doge Pietro,** independently of Byzantium but with
the agreement of the Western Empire, renewed the
treaty of territorial inviolability **(Pactum Latarii)** and
Venice, the city and duchy, became a reality.

10C-13C
Trade and the Orient. Venice was now the key
link between the Western Empire and the Adriatic,
the maritime highway to the Levant. The rivers Po,
Adige, Piave and Livenza were used to transport
salt from the lagoon and goods from the Byzantine Empire and the eastern Mediterranean. ● The
Venetians were a maritime and trading people. They
helped the Emperor **Alexius I Comnenus** against
the Normans and they received in return privileges
throughout the Empire (**chrysobul** of 1082). The
Arsenale shipyard was founded in 1104 and its ships
carried the **Crusaders** to the East. Venice's fleets
fought in these campaigns and in return the city
was granted rights and established depots and trading posts in the **Holy Land.** ● **Enrico Dandolo,** the
ninety-year-old, blind doge, obtained the assistance of
the Crusaders, who had been unable to pay for their
transport, in the recapture of Zara, which had rebelled. ● The same Crusaders (Fourth Crusade,
1201-4) went on to capture **Constantinople** with the
Venetians and shared out the spoils of the Byzantine
Empire with the Doge Enrico Dandolo. The Venetians, however, were more concerned with setting up
trading centres than with booty.

13C-14C
Venice and Genoa. Genoa was also trading with the
eastern half of the Mediterranean and rivalry between
the two led to war. There were four wars in all, in
1257, 1294, 1350 and 1378, beginning in the waters
of Acre and ending with the defeat of the Genoese
in the lagoon around Chioggia. ● Venice's complex
institutions, devised empirically to prevent domination
by any one individual, brought it a stability and continuity which aroused the admiration and envy of the
rest of Italy. The **Consiglio dei Pregadi,** or Senate,
was established c. 1255; the procedure for the **election of the doge,** which involved ten alternating stages
of lot and election, was finalized in 1268; in 1297
took place the so-called 'locking of the **Maggior Consiglio',** as a consequence of which membership of
the highest body of state became hereditary and restricted to patrician families; in 1310 the **Council of
Ten** (Consiglio dei Dieci) was established as a result
of **Bajamonte Tiepolo's plot,** which was foiled.

15C
Terra firma and 'mastery of the seas'. Venice was
the strongest and richest state in Italy but, with the
exception of Treviso (from 1339 onwards), it had
no Italian possessions. ● Between 1389 and 1420
it gained what are now **Venetia** and **Friuli.** ● The
Venetian aristocracy was divided between those
favouring expansion on the mainland and those who
supported a maritime policy. The turning point was
marked by the election of the Doge **Francesco Foscari** (1423), which led to Venice's involvement for the
next thirty years in the wars for the possession of
Lombardy (1425-54) and the acquisition of **Brescia,
Bergamo** and **Crema.** ● Its maritime empire, how-

ever, was threatened by the rise of the **Turks,** although
the addition of Cyprus (ceded by Caterina Cornaro in
1473) and, in Italy, of the **Polésine** (1484) might have
given grounds for feeling that the city was strong
enough to fight and win on two fronts.
● **Charles VIII's** descent into Italy, which Venice
opposed, opened up the struggle for the domination
of the peninsula. In 1503 Venice, paying a heavy
price, made peace with the Turks and, in what can be
seen as the crucial moment in its history, chose Italy
rather than the East.

Veronese and the Inquisition

*Paolo Caliari, known as Veronese, came before the
Inquisition as a result of his magnificent work,* Feast
in the House of Levi, *which is today one of the
jewels of the Accademia. The Dominican monastery
of San Zanipólo was burned down one night in
1571. The building was quickly restored and Father
Andrea Buono commissioned a Last Supper from
Veronese for the refectory as a replacement for a
Titian that had been destroyed in the fire. The work
was shown to the public on the Feast of the Ascension 1573, and it was then that the painter's troubles began. The Council of Trent had only ended
ten years previously and Daniele da Volterra had been
entrusted with covering up the nudity in Michelangelo's Last Judgment in̄ the Sistine Chapel. Such was
the spirit of the times. Veronese's painting had no
nudes but there were certain details — a dog, a jest-
er, a servant whose nose was bleeding and two German halberdiers — which appeared unsuitable to the
inquisitors. According to the report of the interroga-
tion which the painter underwent on 18 July 1573, in
the chapel of S. Teodoro, he was asked 'Did it appear
fitting to him that at the last Supper of Our Lord he
should portray clowns, drunks, Germans, dwarfs and
similar scurrilous items?.' Veronese nervously
attempted to explain: 'We painters take the same
license as poets and madmen...', adding humbly that
he had not dreamed of committing irregularities. In
the end a compromise was reached by changing the
title of the painting from* The Last Supper *to its present one of the* Feast in the House of Levi, *a banquet
at which, as the Evangelist said, 'many tax collectors
and sinners were at table'.*

16C-18C
Splendour in decline. Both artistically and culturally
the 16C was Venice's heyday, but politically the city
was on the defensive and struggling to survive. ● It
overcame its most serious crisis in the **War of the
League of Cambrai** (1505) and preserved its mainland
dominions largely intact. ● With the **Turks** there was
an uneasy coexistence, punctuated by wars which
ended with successive retreats. In 1571 there was
the mainly Venetian naval victory of **Lepanto,** but also
the loss of Cyprus; in 1645-69, the defense and loss
of **Candia;** and in 1684-99, the **conquest of the Morea**
during the alliance with Austria, followed by its loss in
1714-18. ● The rich and powerful grew used to visiting the beautiful, gay city but trade took other routes.
In 1733 a Venetian trade official stated, 'We have
many ports in the Mediterranean doing no trade'.

18C-20C

Austria and Italy, 'They have made a man from Friuli doge, the Republic is dead', said a patrician when **Lodovico Manin** was elected the one hundred and twentieth doge in 1789. ● Not many years later, in 1797, Napoleon handed the Serenissima to **Austria.** ● Apart from two interludes Venice was to remain subject to Austria until 1866, when, along with Venetia, it became part of Italy. The first of the breaks in Austrian rule was in 1805-14, when the Emperor Napoleon made it part of his Kingdom of Italy, and the second was when the city rose under **Daniele Manin** and established itself as a republic in 1848-9, withstanding an Austrian siege.

Facts and figures

Location: *Capital of Venetia, situated on the Adriatic coast in the middle of the lagoon of the same name. 270 km from Milan; 531 km from Rome.*
Area and Population: *The commune of Venice is one of the most extensive in Venetia, covering 457.47 sq km and including Mestre and the mainland, the area of Marghera and the islands of the lagoon. Venice proper, however, only occupies a small part of this area and has a population of about 92,000 (as against 340,873 for the whole commune).*
Postal Code: *30100.*
Dialing Code: *041.*

La Tempesta

In 1530 the Venetian gentleman, Marcantonio Michiel, the author of A Treatise on Drawing, *saw a painting in the house of Gabriele Vendramin, the Venetian noble who had probably commissioned it some twenty years earlier. He describes it as 'a landscape on canvas with a storm, gypsy and soldier by Zorzi of Castelfranco'. It was, of course, by Giorgione. Since 1932 it has been the pride of the Accademia, although prior to then it had always been in private hands. It is one of the most famous paintings in the world and also one of the most mysterious. Giorgione probably painted it 1505-8 although there is disagreement as to its exact date. He made no preliminary drawing but reworked the painting on the canvas with his brush, as x-ray studies have shown. For example, the 'soldier' or shepherd in the left foreground was originally a second female nude. The critics will not allow that the painting is simply as it appears — a landscape with a stormy sky which makes its impression by what it suggests rather than what it depicts. More than ten critical interpretations have been advanced, each seeing it as the depiction of a different myth. The best known of these is perhaps the finding of Paris by the shepherd. Other interpretations see it as an allegory for the composition of the world from the four elements or the union of Heaven and Earth. Another sees it as the contrast between Sin and Salvation while others explain the painting in the context of the* Dream of Polyphilus, *a highly original allegorical work attributed to the Dominican Francesco Colonna and published in Venice by Aldus Manutius in 1499, with illustrations which led to its being regarded as the most beautiful book of the Renaissance.*

▶ ACCADEMIA**

II F1-2

Galleries whose origins go back to the foundation in 1750 of the Academy of Painters and Sculptors under the direction first of Piazzetta and then of Tiepolo occupy the former complex of S. Maria della Carità. This comprises a church, school and convent, the last of which was rebuilt by Palladio. The rebuilding was not completed but a fine wing with loggias can be seen from the windows of the picture galleries. It is the world's greatest collection of the unique art of Venice. It is an art in which, as the seventeenth century Venetian Marco Boschini wrote, 'the painter creates without form,' 'rather with form he deforms the true formality in appearance', and so, with Baroque images he touched on the essential point of Venetian art, the dominance of colour.

▶ The Accademia *(9 a.m.-2 p.m.; wkends 9 a.m.-1 p.m.; closed Mon)* covers the history of Venetian painting from the 14C to the 18C and its exhibits include masterpieces by Venice's finest artists. Examples include Paolo Veneziano's *Coronation of the Virgin★*, Mantegna's *St. George★★*, the *Miracles of the Cross* (G. Mansueti and Gentile Bellini) and the *Legend of St. Ursula★★* by Carpaccio, which are also the most poetic descriptions of the city and life in it. There are the marvelous works of Giovanni Bellini, Giorgione's *Tempesta★★* and *Old Woman★*; Titian's *The Presentation of the Virgin in the Temple★*; *Portrait of a Gentleman★★* by Lorenzo Lotto; Veronese's *Feast in the House of Levi★★*; the *Miracles of St. Mark★★* by Tintoretto; the *Fortune-teller* by Piazzetta and Rosalba Carriera's delicate pastels★. Outside the field of Venetian art there is, among others, one of Piero della Francesca's masterpieces, *St. Jerome and Follower★★*. □

▶ L'ARSENALE*

I C5

The Signoria took important visitors to see the Arsenal, believing that the impression of power and efficient production that they would receive and report outweighed the risks of espionage. So, Dante, who visited it as ambassador of the Da Polenta, used it to describe the horrors of Hell, 'boils in winter the viscous pitch'. To understand the impression it would have made in today's terms one must imagine the pouring of molten iron in a steel works. It was, in actual fact, the state's shipyard for the building of both warships and merchantmen, a base from which the fleet was armed, and both a factory and warehouse for military equipment. In short, it was everything a modern naval base is and more. It was an outstanding early example of industrial organization both technically and in social terms. The 'arsenalotti' (the workers at the arsenal) were a privileged group for their time and position. Tradition has it that it was founded at the start of the 12C by Doge Ordelaffo Falier.

▶ Now the basins, which were gradually extended from their original core, are deserted and quiet and the vast complex awaits a role that will revitalize it. The Italian armed forces now own it, with its huge **Gaggiandre** (covered quays for shipbuilding designed by Sansovino), the **Corderie** (some 300 yds long, for the twisting of ropes) and the shed for the Bucintoro. It can be visited upon request, and the vaporetti of Line 5 pass through it down the Rio delle Galeazze and the Darsena Arsenale Vecchio. ▶ Outside its walls, the names of the calli (del Piombo, lead; della Pegola, pitch; delle Vele, sails; delle

Ancore, anchors) evoke the memory of the great centre of industry. ▶ In 1692-4, the Serenissima, ever ready for self-congratulation, built an impressive terrace with allegorical statues in front of the monumental 15C **portal**. The four lions are spoils of war and were carried off from Piraeus and Delos. □

▶ CA' CORNER DELLA REGINA
II B3

18C, Neoclassical, with a façade on the Grand Canal, it houses the **Archivio Storico delle Arti Contemporanee** (archive of contemporary art) of the Venice Biennale *(wkdays 9 a.m.-1 p.m.)*, a comprehensive and well-regarded institution devoted to recording the contemporary international art scene. □

▶ CA' D'ORO*
II B3

It is known as the Ca' d'Oro (gold) because most of the decorative features — the window dressings, the cornices and the battlemented roof — of the Grand Canal façade were gilded. It was built by Giovanni and Bartolomeo Bon and Matteo Roverti between 1422 and 1440 for Marino Contarini, a merchant who was rich enough to be able to employ the craftsmen and stonemasons who had just finished work on the doge's palace.

▶ It is the city's most famous late Gothic or Flamboyant palace, despite the alterations carried out in the last century. There are two significant departures from the normal arrangement and these are one of the reasons for its enduring fascination. The **façade** is asymmetric. On one side is the portico, above which there are two light, elegant loggias with interlaced arches, and on the other side, not on both, there is the single wing. Behind this there is the second unusual feature, a picturesque **courtyard** with an outside staircase in the corner. ▶ The courtyard, which has a well-head★ by B. Bon (1427), and Greek, Roman and medieval marbles, is visible when entering the **Galleria Giorgio Franchetti★**, which has recently been rearranged here and in the adjacent Palazzo Giusti *(9 a.m.-2 p.m.; wkends 9 a.m.-1 p.m.; closed Mon)*. Originally this was the collection of the Baron Giorgio Franchetti, who tried to recreate the environment of the house at the time of Contarini by means of works of art, furniture and other items from the 15C. ▶ Outstanding pieces include A. Vivarini's polyptych of *the Passion★*, Mantegna's *St. Sebastian★★*, paintings by Carpaccio, Giovanni da Rimini, B. Diana, M. Giambono, L. Signorelli, Titian, Tintoretto, H. van Eyck and other Flemish and Dutch painters, a German Christ★, frescos by Pordenone, fragments of frescos by Titian and Giorgione and two *Views of Venice* by F. Guardi. Sculptures include an *Apollo* by dell'Antico (1498) and Tullio Lombardo's *Pair of Youths*. There are also Renaissance medals, 16C Flemish tapestries, Bernini sketches and Venetian ceramics from the 12C onward. □

▶ CA' FOSCARI
II B1

Ca' Foscari is the home of the university. It stands on the Grand Canal at the mouth of the Rio di Ca' Foscari and is a fine example of the features of a 15C palace. The tripartite **façade** has loggias flanked by wings with relatively few windows. This distribution reflects the internal arrangement, in which there is a large central salon flanked by private rooms. On the

ground floor, the central area forms an atrium; this served as a warehouse for goods in Venetian-Byzantine palaces, which were both house and place of business. These elements recur in virtually all Venetian palaces even when overlaid by Renaissance, Baroque or 18C styles, which impose a classical language of columns, round arches, trabeations and stricter rules of proportion. In the Ca' Foscari, the style is late Gothic or Flamboyant. In 1858-9 Richard Wagner composed the second act of *Tristan and Isolde* in the adjacent **Palazzo Giustinian** (15C). □

▶ IL CAMPANILE*
II E5

On the morning of 14 July 1902, the Campanile collapsed as a result of the decay of its walls without causing serious damage or harming anyone. At the top of the pile of masonry lay the Archangel Gabriel, the weather vane that had stood at the point of the spire. The Venetians promptly rebuilt the Campanile 'as it was and where it was'. It is 317 ft 8 in high and the bell chamber *(lift, 10 a.m.-4 p.m.)* offers a splendid view★ of the buildings and the unique arrangement of the city and its position in the lagoon. The only surviving old bell is the 'marangona' which called the carpenters of the Arsenal to work. The **Loggetta★**, an exquisite work built by Jacopo Sansovino and decorated with marbles and bronzes (1537-49), stands at the foot of the Campanile and also had to be rebuilt. It was originally a meeting place for the nobles, but it soon became a post for the Arsenalotti who formed the guard for sessions of the Maggior Consiglio. The architect's plans to continue the loggetta around the other sides of the Campanile never came to fruition and until the last century it was backed by shops. □

▶ CANAL GRANDE**

I from D3 to B1; opening into the Bacino di S. Marco, II F4

'The finest street that I believe there is in all the world.' So said Philippe de Commynes, the representative of Charles VIII of France in negotiations with the Signoria. He is only one of many who have used this singular image. In fact, when he saw it at the end of the 15C, the Grand Canal was very different from its present form. The Rialto bridge was still made of wood, there were none of the beautiful 16C palaces or the 18C Baroque ones. Many of those begun in the 15C were still unfinished and there were probably more gardens along the canal. The ships of merchants would also have been travelling up it to unload at the warehouses. The great S which divides the islands of the Rialto, on which the modern city stands, into two groups was the course of a river which exhausted itself among the sandbanks of the lagoon. Today there is nothing else like it in the world.

▶ There are various ways of traveling down the Grand Canal, but the cheapest is a seat in the bow of a vaporetto of Line 1. Setting off from the landing stage at the railway station (Ferrovia), there is the green-domed Neoclassical church of **S. Simeon Piccolo** to the r. and one then passes under the bridge of the Scalzi, with, to the l., the Baroque façade of the **Scalzi** (→). ▶ After the 18C church of **S. Geremia** (l.) comes the mouth of the **Canale** di **Cannaregio** and then the 17C Palazzo Correr Contarini (l.). ▶ After S. Marcuola there is the **Fondaco dei Turchi** (r. →) and the **Palazzo Vendramin Calergi★** (l. →). ▶ Beyond the S. Stae landing stage are the Baroque façade of the church of **S. Stae**, the **Ca' Pesaro★** (→) and the Ca' Corner della Regina (→ r.) and the Palazzo Fontana-Rezzonico (l.) in Sansovino's late style. Back on the r. is the Gothic Palazzo Brandolin-Morosini, with two elegant loggias and, finally, on the l. the famous **Ca'd'Oro★★** (→). ▶ On leaving the Ca' d'Oro landing stage there are the Rialto markets (r.), with the Pescheria (fish market) followed by Sansovino's Fabbriche Nuove di Rialto (1556) and the Fabbriche Vecchie (1522). On the l. there is the **Fondaco dei Tedeschi** (now the post office), which no longer has the frescos by Titian and Giorgione on its outside walls, and to the r. is the delicate Renaissance **Palazzo dei Camerlenghi** (1528). ▶ The Rialto landing stage is the only section of the Grand Canal bordered by a fondamenta on both sides: the Riva del Vin (r.) with the Palazzo dei Dieci Savi (1521) and, opposite, the Riva del Ferro, with the Palazzo Manin. There then follows the Riva del Carbon with the **Palazzi Farsetti and Loredan** (now the city hall), typical Venetian-Byzantine houses and warehouses of the 12C-13C with unbroken loggias. ▶ After S. Silvestro comes the **Palazzo Grimani★** (→ l.) and, to the r., the Palazzi Papadopoli, Bernardo★, Grimani-Marcello, Pisani-Moretta and Persico, which display a variety of the Canal's architectural styles. Finally, on the l., comes the **Palazzo Corner-Spinelli★** (→). ▶ Beyond S. Angelo on the l. are the four **Palazzi Mocenigo** (16C-18C), in which Giordano Bruno and Byron stayed, and the Renaissance **Palazzo Contarini delle Figure.** ▶ After S. Tomà, the Canal curves round and on the r. there is the **Ca' Foscari★** (→) and the **Ca' Rezzonico★** (→), while on the l. are the **Palazzo Grassi★** and the church of S. Samuele, with a picturesque Romanesque campanile. ▶ Following the Ca' Rezzonico landing stage, the **Ca' del Duca** (l.) houses a collection of 18C Venetian porcelain and Oriental art *(Mon, Wed, Fri 9:30 a.m.-12:30 p.m.; Sat 3-6 p.m.)* and the Baroque Palazzo Giustinian-Lolin; on the r. are the Palazzo Loredan dell'Ambasciatore, with two pages bearing shields in niches on the façade, the Palazzo Contarini degli Scrigni and the **Gallerie dell'Accademia** (→). ▶ The Accademia landing stage is immediately before the wooden Accademia bridge and after it, to the l., is the **Palazzo Corner della Ca' Grande★**, a magnificent example of Sansovino's work. On the r. there is the unfinished Palazzo Venier dei Leoni, which houses the **Peggy Guggenheim Collection** (→), and the unique, elegant **Palazzo Dario,** possibly by Pietro Lombardo (1487). ▶ The Salute landing stage, at the foot of the great church of **S. Maria della Salute★** (→), is the last stop on the Canal. Beyond the Salute the only buildings on the r. are the Dogana da Mare (rebuilt in the 19C), which ends in the **Punta della Dogana** (1637), with the figure of Fortune, which turns on a sphere. On the l. are the Palazzo Ducale, the Libreria Marciana, the domes of S. Marco, the campanile: the heart of the city. □

▶ CA' PESARO*

II B2-3

The palace which Baldassarre Longhena designed for the Pesaro family (1628, completed in 1710 by Antonio Gaspari) is one of the masterpieces of Venetian Baroque. The Grand Canal **façade** has two dramatically handled piani nobili with large, arched windows opening on to continuous balconies above a powerful ground floor of diamond rustication, and the play of light and shadow created by the architectural elements produces an impressive chiaroscuro effect.

▶ The **Galleria d'Arte Moderna** (first and second floors; *closed for restoration*) contains paintings, sculptures and drawings by modern and contemporary artists of all nationalities donated or bought at the Venice Biennale. There

is also a section devoted to 19C works. ▶ The **Museo di Arte Orientale★** (third floor) houses mainly Japanese works of the 17C-19C (Edo period) including a rare and outstanding group of **suits of armour.** There are sections devoted to other parts of Asia, such as China (porcelain and jade) and Indonesia (weapons, fabrics, shadow puppets). Since the collection's origins go back to the objects collected by Enrico di Borbone during his travels in the closing decades of the last century, it also displays a hint of *fin-de-siècle* exotic. □

Water stories

In February 1986, the water began to rise and finally almost covered the whole city. The alarm was sounded once more. Saving Venice from the water is almost a superhuman task. There are about 200 palaces in danger on the Grand Canal, and other structures on 77 smaller canals. The work is both extremely delicate and gigantic. For example, to save the Palazzo Grassi, its foundations and walls were practically sawed through to slide a layer of lead and plastic between them in order to stop the water from seeping into the palace. In 1984, a law was passed to subsidize up to 80 percent of all the restorations. A first project cost 4 billion lire ($3.5 million, £2 million) and involved about 40 different sites. Efforts to save the lagoon began in October 1986. Secondary canals are being dammed up to spread the tides out over a wider area. At the same time, the waterline foundations are being consolidated in order to stop erosion by the water. Saving the city requires work throughout the Venice lagoon, which is 50 km long. A group of 26 different public work companies is involved on the different restoration sites and administers the 3,000 billion lire budget ($2.5 million, £1.5 million) voted in by the government.

▶ CA' REZZONICO*

II E1

Baldassarre Longhena began work on the palace for the Bon family in 1649 and like the Ca' Pesaro (→), it is one of the masterpieces of Venetian Baroque, although he was not able to complete it. Halfway through the following century, the Rezzonico family, who had acquired it, engaged Giorgio Massari to finish it. He was responsible for, among other items, the splendid **ballroom,** with frescos by G.B. Crosato. The Rezzonico family were originally from Como but they entered the Maggior Consiglio in 1687, and they numbered two Procurators of St. Mark and two cardinals, one of whom became Pope Clement XIII (1758-69), among their members. Tiepolo frescoed the ceilings of a number of the rooms on the upper floors for the Rezzonico family.

▶ The historical background and the interior of this restored palace form a fitting setting for the **Museo del Settecento Veneziano★** *(10 a.m.-4 p.m.; wkends 9:30 a.m.-12:30 p.m.; closed Fri),* which, with objects and furniture, brings back to life the precious atmosphere of 18C Venice in glorious decline. Tapestries, furniture, lacquer work, costumes, fittings, a puppet theatre, an 18C pharmacy are interspersed with paintings by G.B. Piazzetta, F. Maffei, G.B. Tiepolo and Canaletto. ▶ Two of Guardi's works deserve a special mention both on account of their artistic value and for the information they give on 18C dress: *Il Ridotto★* and *Il Parlatorio delle Monache★* (The Nun's Parlatory). The museum houses the most important collection of Pietro Longhi's **paintings★**, with their domestic and rustic scenes, masquerades and figures. The frescos of Giandomenico Tiepolo (no less a painter than his more famous father, Giambattista) have been installed in rooms that have been rebuilt from the **Villa di Zianigo**. ☐

▶ I CARMINI*

I D1

The Scuola Grande dei Carmini (→) and the Renaissance façade and curved pediment of the church of S. Maria del Carmelo, attached to the former Carmelite monastery, both look onto a small campo that in turn opens onto the rio S. Margherita. On its l. side there is a fine portal with a 14C porch. Originally 13C, the basilican interior is now Renaissance and has a nave and two aisles. It contains a number of important works of art: Cima da Conegliano's *Adoration of the Shepherds★* (c. 1509) at the second altar (r.); a bronze bas-relief of the *Deposition★* by Francesco di Giorgio Martini (c. 1474) in the chapel to the r. of the sanctuary; a *St. Nicholas between St. John the Baptist, St. Lucy and Angels★* by Lotto (1529). The former monastery has a fine 16C **cloister**. ☐

Venetian lace

A Venetian sailor once offered his beloved an aquatic plant commonly known as mermaid lace. When the sailor had once again left for distant shores, the young woman tried to copy the plant's strange pattern with her needle — and so was born, as legend has it, Venice's famous lace industry. Lacemaking started here in the 16C and developed to such a point that its reputation spread through the world. Originally reserved for religious garments, lace soon adorned blouses, dresses, men's clothes, linen, curtains, even shoes! Today Venice's lace industry is in a slump. Despite this, tradition and quality are still the hallmark of the few lacemaking houses that survive, such as Jesurum (ponte Canonica 4310, ☎ 52706177, behind the basilica) where the visitor can find superb Venetian lace for sale.

▶ COLLEONI STATUE**

(Monumento al Colleoni)

II B6

Bartolomeo Colleoni of Bergamo was a condottiere leader who served the Serenissima from 1448 onward, at a time when it had recently conquered and had to defend its mainland possessions in Venetia and Lombardy. He left the state a part of his wealth on condition that an equestrian statue be erected to him in front of the Basilica of S. Marco. Its site on the campo in front of the Scuola Grande di San Marco (→) was a piece of disingenuous sleight of hand which the Senate resorted to in order to remain true to the principle that the Republic would not grant so important a site to any one individual, even for a monument. The commission for the statue (1481-8), which is one of the great masterpieces of the Renaissance and remarkable for its restrained, virile energy,

was given to the famous Florentine sculptor Andrea Verrocchio. The bronze was cast and the fine pedestal executed in 1490 after Verrocchio's death by the Venetian Alessandro Leopardi. ☐

▶ La FENICE

II E3

Venice's most important theatre was almost completely rebuilt after the fire of 1836, although it retains the Neoclassical grace of Antonio Selva's original design of 1790, which, by means of a number of technical developments, overcomes the problem of fitting so vast a building into the crowded urban environment. It was opened on 17 May 1792 with a work by Paisiello. ☐

▶ FONDACO DEI TURCHI

II A2

Extensive restoration in the 19C removed all its original atmosphere but it does, however, survive as an interesting example of the Venetian-Byzantine palace cum warehouse of the 12C-13C. It opens through a portico on to the Canal, above which there is a loggia, and on either side there is a tower. It was originally built for the Pesaro family, but in the 17C it was granted to Turkish merchants for use as a warehouse and they continued to use it until 1838. In the courtyard there are well-heads, fragments of buildings and sculptures. It houses the **Museo di Storia Naturale** *(9:30 a.m.-1:30 p.m.; wkends 9 a.m.-12 noon; closed Mon).* ☐

▶ I GESUITI

II A5

The 18C church of S. Maria Assunta dei Gesuiti has an imposing Baroque façade and its founders specified a design that was closer to Roman than to Venetian models. Even the **decoration of the interior★** — white-and-green marble intarsia in imitation of tapestries and white and gold stucco (pulpit and the steps of the sanctuary) — is unique in Venice.

▶ It contains a masterpiece by Titian, the *Martyrdom of St. Lawrence★* (1558) at the first altar (l.). ▶ In the nearby **Oratorio dei Crociferi** there is a cycle of paintings by Palma Giovane depicting the history of the order and of the Zen and Cicogna doges *(Jul-Sep 4:30-6:30 p.m.; Apr-Jun and Oct 10 a.m.-12 noon).* ☐

▶ Il GHETTO

I A-B2

Between 1516 and 1797, the Jews of Venice were obliged to live in an area between the Cannaregio canal and the rio di S. Girolamo, and five synagogues ministering to different nations still survive.

▶ The campo of the **Ghetto Nuovo** is surrounded by very tall houses, which are the result of the need to build the maximum number of dwellings in a restricted space. ▶ The **Museo di Arte Ebraica** *(10:30 a.m.-12:30 p.m. and 3-5 p.m.; closed Sat)* displays interesting relics and objects relating to the Jewish community of Venice. ▶ Two synagogues, the **Scuola Spagnola** and the **Scuola Levantina,** face onto the campiello delle Scuole in the **Ghetto Vecchio.** These were rebuilt in the 17C, probably by Longhena, and they have sumptuous interiors. At the opening onto the fondamenta di Cannareggio, in the jambs of the sottoportico of the Ghetto Vecchio, one can still see the marks of the hinges for the doors which were closed at dusk. ▶ It is thought that the word 'ghetto', pronounced with a hard *g* by German Jews, is in fact 'getto', meaning to cast, and was derived from the fact that the area was a foundry. There are, however, other theories for the origin of the term, which came to be used throughout Europe. ☐

▶ The island of the GIUDECCA

(L'isola della Giudecca)
I E1-2-3

This forms the southern suburb of Venice and separates the canal of the Giudecca from the lagoon. The most important of the buildings on the fondamenta that follows the canal is the **Redentore** (→). At the W end of the island stands the red mass of the **Mulino Stucky** (mill), an important if somewhat odd element in the cityscape of Venice. It is doubtful whether the island's present name (originally Spinalonga) is derived from the presence in the 14C of a Jewish community. This, in any case, is not documented. ☐

▶ GUGGENHEIM COLLECTION*

(Collezione Guggenheim)
II F2-3

Only the ground floor of the 18C **Palazzo Venier dei Leoni** facing the Grand Canal was ever built. It was bought by Peggy Guggenheim in 1949 and houses her collection *(12 noon-6 p.m.; Sat 6-9 p.m.; closed Mon)* of modern art — one of the most important in the world. She herself is buried in the garden, which lies behind the palace, near the tombs of her dogs. The works are arranged by the various styles of the avant-garde from 1910 onward (Dadaism, Cubism, abstract, Surrealism, etc.) and they are all of the first order. ☐

▶ LIBRERIA MARCIANA**
II E5

The Tuscan architect Jacopo Sansovino left Rome when it was sacked in 1527 and was welcomed to Venice by Aretino, the writer and art critic, who played an important role in the cultural life of the city. Sansovino's architectural ideas proved a splendid vehicle for the ambitions of Venice's aristocracy, who regarded their city as the true heir of the mythical wisdom and power of the ancients. The Libreria was built between 1537 and 1588 to house the great collection of ancient manuscripts which Cardinal Bessarione, the Greek humanist, bequeathed to the Republic. In the aristocratic architecture of 16C Classicism the building gives a feeling of the culture of the time and influenced the subsequent development of architectural style. Sansovino succeeded in combining classical plasticity with the sense of drama, colour and play of light and shade which were a feature of the Venetian style, and in so doing he became one of the most important, if not the most important, creators of the work of art that is Venice.

Libreria Marciana

▶ From no. 13 in the portico of the piazzetta, A. Vittoria's monumental **staircase** leads up to public rooms. These were once part of the library but are now used for temporary exhibitions. The walls and ceilings have **paintings★** by Titian, Veronese, Tintoretto and A. Schiavone. ▶ One of the outstanding items in this splendid library is the **Grimani Breviary★**, a codex from the end of the 15C illuminated by Flemish artists. ▶ Turning from the piazzetta along the canal bank, by the Libreria Marciana, is the **Zecca** or Mint (J. Sansovino, 1536). Since 1905 it has housed the Public Library (entrance, piazzetta n° 7). ☐

▶ MADONNA DELL'ORTO*
I A3

This is one of Venice's most interesting churches, since it displays elements of transition from the Romanesque to the Gothic and the Renaissance. Its fine brick façade stands on a campo which opens on to a quiet canal at the edge of the city. Inside it has a nave and two aisles, with wooden tie beams, and a series of splendid Tintorettos (he was buried here in 1594): *Presentation of the Virgin in the Temple★*, *St. Agnes Raising Licinius★*, *Last Judgment★* and the *Adoration of the Golden Calf★*. In contrast to the dramatic passion of Tintoretto's canvases is the luminous serenity of Cima da Conegliano's *St. John the Baptist and Saints★* (c. 1493). ☐

▶ Le MERCERIE
II D4-5

These are the main shopping streets of Venice. They offer an unbroken succession of shops with a wide variety of goods, and they are always crowded with both locals and visitors.

▶ Starting from the archway of the **Torre dell'Orologio** (→) as the merceria dell'Orologio, they continue as the mercerie di S. Zulian, del Capitello, di S. Salvador and 2 Aprile, crossing just one bridge before reaching the **campo S. Bartolomeo,** one of the centres of Venetian life, with the lively Carlo Goldoni monument, and a few yards from the Grand Canal and the Rialto bridge (→). The mercantile origins of the streets are revealed by their names and historically they linked the political and religious centre of the city (S. Marco and the Palazzo Ducale) with the commercial and financial heart at the Rialto. ▶ At the start of the merceria dell'Orologio (no. 149, l.) there is a historical curiosity, a relief commemorating the old woman with a mortar who dropped it on the head of the man leading the conspirators against the Palazzo Ducale at the time of Bajamonte Tiepolo's uprising against Doge Pietro Gradenigo (15 June 1310). This led to the failure of the rebellion and the establishment of the *Consiglio dei Dieci* (Council of Ten) to prevent further ones. □

▶ MUSEO ARCHEOLOGICO
II E5

A collection of classical sculpture is somewhat surprising in Venice, since it is the only major Italian city to have been founded after the fall of the Roman Empire.

▶ The Venetian archaeological collection (no 17, portico of the Libreria Marciana; *9 a.m.-1 p.m.; wkends 9 a.m.-12:30 p.m.; closed Mon*) is another result of the classical taste of the 16C Venetian aristocracy, which had conferred on Sansovino, the architect of the Library itself, a sort of superintendency of building in the city. ▶ The initial core of the museum was the bequest by Cardinal Domenico Grimani (1523) of marbles and bronzes found in Rome. This was then combined (1587) with another collection of sculptures, including Greek ones, donated by his nephew, Giovanni, Patriarch of Aquileia. The museum's outstanding items are the **statues★** of goddesses, Greek 5C-6C BC, the Hellenistic **Grimani altar★** and the **Zulian cameo★**, again Hellenistic. □

▶ MUSEO CORRER*
II E4

In 1830 the Venetian patrician Teodoro Correr, who as an adult had witnessed the sad end of the thousand-year Serenissima, left his collections to the city.

▶ This gift, supplemented by further bequests, donations and purchases, forms the basis of the splendid **museum** *(10 a.m.-4 p.m.; wkends 9:30 a.m.-12:30 p.m.; closed Tue).* The exhibits fall into two main groups. In one are curiosities, mementos, documents, weapons and instruments which evoke the history of the Republic and its trade, the operation of its institutions and the life of the city. This section also contains the decorative art collections, with fabrics, lace, ivories, Islamic bronzes and 16C Italian ceramics. The second part comprises the **Quadreria★**, an important picture gallery that complements the Accademia (→) in providing a view of Venetian art. It contains a number of key masterpieces, such as Jacopo Bellini's *Crucifixion★*; the *Portrait of Doge Mocenigo★* by Gentile Bellini; Giovanni Bellini's *Transfiguration★*, *Crucifixion★* and *Pietà★*; Carpaccio's *Venetian Ladies★* (also known as *The Courtesans*); the *Pietà* by Cosmè Tura; a *Pietà* by Antonello da Messina and a *Portrait★* by Lorenzo Lotto. ▶ The Museo Correr gives access to the **Museo del Risorgimento★** *(same opening hrs).* □

▶ MUSEO DIOCESANO
II D5

At no. 4312 on the short fondamenta S. Apollonia stands the small Romanesque **cloister** of S. Apollonia which, with its mainland architectural forms, is rather out of place on the lagoon. Once part of a Benedictine monastery, it now houses the **museum** in which silver, books, liturgical vestments and other objects

are placed, sometimes on a temporary basis, when the churches they come from are no longer able to guarantee their display or their security. □

▶ MUSEO FORTUNY
II D3

The Palazzo Pesaro degli Orfei, a picturesque 15C Gothic building by S. Beneto, was bought at the beginning of the century by Mariano Fortuny y Madrazo, the Spanish painter, stage designer and collector. The **museum** on the first floor *(8:30 a.m.-7 p.m.; closed Mon and wkends)* displays in rooms left as the artist furnished them paintings, carpets, tapestries and his fabric designs, as well as models of the 'Fortuny cupola', an advance in set design. The agreeable atmosphere evokes the way of life of an artist in the early part of this century in an ancient Venetian palace. The building also houses exhibitions and the Virgilio Guidi bequest. □

▶ MUSEO STORICO NAVALE*
I D5

This museum is housed in a 15C building that was once the granary of the Republic, and it is one of the most important museums of its kind in Italy *(9 a.m.-1 p.m.; Sat 9 a.m.-12 noon; closed Sun).* It has a famous **model of the Bucintoro** (the ceremonial galley in which, each Ascension Day, the doge would celebrate the 'wedding with the sea' by throwing a ring into the water at the mouth of the Lido), models of Venetian ships, decorative fragments from lost galleys and the abate Maffioletti's views of the Arsenal at the fall of the Republic. Other diverse exhibits provide information on many aspects of Venice's past maritime life. There is also an important section dealing with the history of the Italian Navy. □

▶ PALAZZO CONTARINI
from Campo Manin, II D3

From the calle, the courtyard façade appears as one of the most unusual creations in the varied and charming secular architecture of Venice. The loggias are flanked by a cylindrical tower with an arcaded external spiral (*bóvolo* in Venetian) **staircase**, the spiral making two turns per storey. This elegant Renaissance work (1499) is by Giovanni Candi. The well-head and arches in the courtyard are from the demolished church of S. Paternian. □

▶ PALAZZO DUCALE**
II E5

The site was the centre of political power in the Venetian state from the 9C, when the doge and the government moved from the Rivo Alto (Rialto), until the fall of the Republic (1797). However, the two wings of the marvelous palace which face on to the piazzetta and the molo (the bank on the Bacino di S. Marco) are essentially Gothic and the wing between the courtyard and the rio di Palazzo is late Renaissance. The main object of the work which began in 1340 was to build a room suitable for sessions of the Maggior Consiglio, a body on which it was not just the right but the duty of every Venetian patrician to sit. The wing on the molo was built for this purpose and in its arcades the crews of the galleys were enlisted. Then, starting in 1424 and in the same architectural style, the façade was extended along the piazzetta as far as the **Porta della Carta★** (G. and B. Bon, 1438), in the corner by the side of the Basilica (note the individual carvings of the capitals of the arcade and the three corners). The interior had to be almost entirely rebuilt after two disastrous fires in 1574 and 1577, which explains its sumptuous, late Renaissance character.

▶ The beautiful **courtyard★★** has 16C bronze **wellheads★**, a Baroque **clock façade** (1515); the **Arco Foscari** (1470), transitional between the Gothic and the Renaissance, and the **Scala dei Giganti★** (designed by A. Rizzo, late 15C, statues of Mars and Neptune by Sansovino, 1556). At the top of this staircase the newly elected doge would receive his ducal beret, or cornu. ▶ A tour of the interior *(summer 8:30 a.m.-6 p.m.; winter 8 a.m.-2 p.m.)* is both an occasion to admire the rich and refined rooms and the paintings of the great masters which decorate them and a chance to gain an idea of the complex mechanisms of the political institutions which for so long and with such success guided the Serenissima. ▶ The normal route proceeds up the **Scala d'Oro★** (1558) through the rooms of the **Doge's Apartments,** with their richly decorated ceilings and fine Renaissance chimneypieces (the paintings include a *Pietà★* by Giovanni Bellini and the *Lion of St. Mark* by Carpaccio); then to the **Sala delle Quattro Porte** (*Doge Grimani Adores the Faith★*, Titian; *Venice Receives the Homage of Neptune★*, Tiepolo); the **Sala dell'Anticollegio** (four panels★ by Tintoretto; the *Rape of Europa★★* by Veronese); the **Sala del Collegio,** again with canvases by Tintoretto and Veronese, as have the **Sale del Senato** and **del Consiglio dei Dieci;** the **Sale della Bussola** (with the 'bocca del leone' for secret denunciations) and **dei Tre Capi dei Consiglio dei Dieci;** the **Sala del Guariento** (remains of Guariento's fresco, *Paradise,* 1367, destroyed in the fire of 1577), the loggia with *Adam★* and *Eve★* by A. Rizzo (1464) previously on the Arco Foscari; the magnificent **Sala del Maggior Consiglio,** with portraits of 76 doges (that of Marin Falier, who was beheaded in 1355, is occupied by a black space) and Tintoretto's famous *Paradise★*. On the ceiling there is Veronese's *Apotheosis of Venice*. Finally there are the **Sale della Quarantia Civil Nuova, dello Scrutino, della Quarantia Criminal, del Magistrato al Criminal** and **del Magistrato alle Leggi.** The **Pozzi,** the former prisons, are entered from the loggia. ☐

▶ **PALAZZO GRASSI**
II E1

Unusually for Venice, this great Neoclassical building (begun by G. Massari in 1749) was arranged around a square courtyard, now covered. The decoration of the staircase with frescos of figures by M. Morlaiter looking out from *trompe l'oeil* balconies is a typical touch of 18C Venice. It is used for major art exhibitions and it has recently been restored by Gae Aulenti on behalf of *FIAT*. ☐

▶ **PALAZZO LABIA★**
II A1

Originally from Catalonia, the Labia family commissioned the palace as soon as they were enrolled as

Venetian patricians (1646). There is a story that in a boastful display, one of the house, saying the words 'I may or may not have it but I will always be a Labia', threw a gold plate from the window into the canal (the Italian used being a play on the word Labia, 'L'abia o non l'abia sarò sempre Labia'). The family did, however, have the good taste to engage Giambattista Tiepolo to decorate the ballroom with **frescos★**. These include *The Embarkation of Cleopatra* and the *Banquet of Antony and Cleopatra*, and the cycle is one of his most splendid masterpieces, *(3-6 p.m. Wed, Thu and Fri, book in advance with RAI, which operates from the palace)*. The nearby **ponte delle Guglie** offers a good view along the Cannaregio canal. ☐

▶ **PALAZZO PISANI**
II F2

There is an imposing 16C-18C front on the campiello Pisani (off the campo S. Stefano) and it extends down to a narrow façade on the Grand Canal. It now houses the **Conservatorio Benedetto Marcello.** The 18C former church of **S. Vidal,** also on the campo S. Stefano, contains a fine altarpiece by Carpaccio *(St. Vitale on Horseback and Eight Saints★,* 1514). ☐

▶ **PALAZZO VENDRAMIN CALERGI★**
II A2

Commissioned by the Loredan family in 1481 and completed in the early years of the following century, the palace is Mauro Coducci's masterpiece of secular architecture. His use of large paired windows within a semicircular arch, and other classical elements, rewrote the Gothic model of the palace with loggias still current at that time. In his subtle play of light and shadow he beautifully interpreted the essentially colouristic nature of Venetian architecture. Carved into the stone under the windows of the mezzanine are the words *Non nobis Domine* ('Not unto us O Lord'). The palace is the winter home of the **Casino.** Richard Wagner stayed in it, and died here in 1883. ☐

▶ **PIAZZA SAN MARCO★★**
II E4-5

What other square in the world exerts the same fascination? It is difficult to think of one. There are certainly squares that are grander or more rigorous architecturally, and some may even be more picturesque. However, in terms of charm — and by that is meant the pleasure of aesthetic appreciation combined with the delight of being there — it has no equal. The same could be said for the whole of Venice. It is a magnificent 'drawing room', 'for which', as Napoleon observed, 'only the sky is worthy to serve as a vault'. It is an interesting point that the final touch, which brought the square to the form we see today, is linked to Napoleon. It is the Ala Napoleonica, the arcaded wing which forms the E side, facing the Basilica. It was built in 1810, on the site of Sansovino's church of S. Geminiano, which was demolished. This, however, was just the last step in the creation of this marvel, a process which had been going on for a millennium, indeed for almost as long as the city itself has existed.

▶ The site was chosen when the church of S. Teodoro (Theodore was the first patron saint of Venice) was founded in 560 on the present piazzetta dei Leoni. Its importance then greatly increased in the 9C with the transfer of the centre of political power from the Rivo Alto (Rialto) and the building of the Palazzo Ducale (→) and the ducal chapel of S. Marco (→). The palace and the chapel were to be rebuilt many times, and they both created the piazza and defined its role in the life of the city. ▶ Apart from the backdrop formed by the **façade of S. Marco,** the architectural fabric of the square only began to take its present form in the 16C. The long building on the N side (l. when facing the church) is the **Procuratie Vecchie** (office of the Procurators of St. Mark's), built in 1514 to a design attributed to the Tuscan architect Giovanni Celestro in the immature Renaissance style of those years, although still displaying late Gothic rhythms. The portico conceals the entrances to the alleys and streets, and the only one that is in fact visible is the beginning of the Mercerie (→), which is emphasized by the Torre dell'Orologio (→). When Sansovino, who had completed the Procuratie Vecchie without breaking from the already existing forms, built the Libreria Marciana (→) on the piazzetta S. Marco (→) he decided to make a fundamental stylistic advance, introducing into the architecture of Venice his version, marked by chiaroscuro and a pictorial approach, of the aristocratic, classical language of architecture, while remaining true to the *genius loci.* Sansovino also unfettered the **Campanile,** which had been backed on to by a hospice, and made it the focal point of the piazza and the piazzetta. The **Procuratie Nuove** (the buildings along the S side of the piazza) were begun by Vincente Scamozzi (1582) and completed by Longhena (1640). Although there are some differences, the Procuratie Nuove essentially take up and continue Sansovino's approach with the Libreria and so, moreover, does the Ala Napoleonica. Thus the stage was set for the whirling masses of pigeons and the customers sitting in the neo-Gothic rooms of Florians, or at the tables of the various cafés. ▶ The flag poles, which have bronze bases by A. Leopardi, are a highly symbolic feature of the square, having been erected in the early years of the 16C when the Venetian oligarchy, equally strong on both land and sea, felt itself at its peak. □

▶ **PIAZZETTA SAN MARCO****

II E5

The image of Venice rests on nothing. No hills or mountains, no rivers, no valleys or rocky coasts, no forests; nothing. In the beginning there was only marsh, but even that has disappeared; everything is made by man. As has been said, Venice is a shimmer at the meeting point between two pure expanses, the sea and the sky. Everything is colour. The point where this view of the city is most clearly vindicated is the piazzetta. This architectural space is firmly joined to the piazza S. Marco (→), but while the emphasis of the latter is on the façade of the Basilica and its domes, the focus of the piazzetta, which is at right angles to the piazza, with the Campanile forming the point around which it turns, is on the sky and the sea, as represented by the Basin, the salt in the air, the slap of the waves on the gondolas. This sense of the sea must have been even more acute when, as in the views of Guardi or Canaletto, a galley was moored alongside the molo in front of the Palazzo Ducale and sailing ships of every nation lay at anchor between the Dogana and the island of S. Giorgio.

▶ Two sides of the piazzetta are formed by buildings that are the quintessence of the 'miracle' of Venice: on one side is the **Palazzo Ducale** (→), on the other the **Libreria Marciana** (→). The palace is radiant, with its great polychrome walls rising above the Gothic loggia and the arcades of the portico — a shadowy void framed by Istrian stone. This reversal of the norm — mass above the void — is a highly successful device as both mass and void take on light and colour. In the Libreria the reflections of the sea play across the Istrian stone, and the monumental classical language of columns, capitals, arches and cornices is transformed into touches of light gradually emerging from the shade. ▶ The side opening onto the riva has two **columns** (12C; pedestals 16C; capitals Venetian-Byzantine, with the Lion of St. Mark and St. Theodore at the top), which form a kind of proscenium in the air. The fact that executions used to take place between the columns sharply reminds one that the 'actors' were a part of the harsh realities of history. The aesthetic side is but one aspect of Venice. □

Street names of Venice

Venice is unique in its layout. There is only one piazza, S. Marco; and the splendid piazzetta, which opens on to the lagoon, is also one of a kind. All the other open spaces are known as campo, campiello *or* campazzo. *The alleys are referred to as* calle *(from the Latin* callis*),* calletta *or* callesella. *Sometimes the term* ruga *is used (analogous to the French* rue*) or* rughetta. *Salizzada is a term used for the first alleys paved with stone;* fondamenta *means the path along the side of a canal or rio and derives from the fact that it serves as the base for the buildings.* Piscina *indicates that in the past there was an expanse of water.* Ramo *is used for the branch of a* calle, rio terra *signifies a canal or rio that has been filled in. The names of the calli and campi are often taken from crafts or trades;* bareteri *are hatters and make caps;* calegheri *and* zavater *are cobblers,* cuoridoro *are gilded leather workers,* marangon *refers to carpenters and joiners;* murer *means masons;* pistor *the people who knead dough, which is then baked by the* forner. *The* pestrin *sells milk;* pizieta *refers to tinsmiths,* varotari *tan hides. The* gatte *of the campo of the same name were the 'legates' or papal nuncios who once resided there. The* barbaria delle tolle *was possibly the calle where* tole *(planks) were planed and the* barbe *or roughness removed.* Carampane *were the whores who established themselves in the former palace of the Rampani family, the Ca' (casa) Rampani, from which they took their name.*

▶ **PINACOTECA MANFREDINIANA**

II F4

Left to the Seminario Patriarcale by the Florentine Federico Manfredini, it contains sculptures and fine paintings by Cima da Conegliano, Filippino Lippi, Beccafumi and an *Apollo and Daphne*★ by Giorgione *(telephone to arrange a visit).* □

▶ **PINACOTECA QUERINI STAMPALIA***

II D5-6

Housed in twenty rooms in the 16C palace of the same name, with 18C furniture, the gallery has a fine collection of Venetian paintings, as well as ones from other Italian and foreign schools *(10 a.m.-2:45 or 3:45 p.m.; closed Mon)*. Among the Venetian paintings (14C-18C), the outstanding works are those by Donato and Catarino Veneziano *(Coronation of the Virgin★)*, Palma Vecchio, Vincenzo Catena *(Judith★)* and Giambattista Tiepolo. There is a fine series of paintings by Pietro Longhi, the chronicler of 18C Venice: the *Seven Sacraments★*, the *Hunt in the Valley* and the *Duck Shoot on the Lagoon★*. Gabriele Bella's *Venetian Festivals* (18C) records, in popular style, this aspect of Venetian life. □

▶ **PONTE DEI SOSPIRI***

II E5

The Ponte dei Sospiri or Bridge of Sighs is one of Venice's best known landmarks, dear to the Romantics, who probably invented its name. Baroque in form and pierced by stone grilles, it links the Palazzo Ducale with the Prigioni Nuove (New Prisons). It was commissioned in 1602 by Doge Marino Grimani in order to bring prisoners awaiting trial from the prisons to the courts. It is always beautiful, although its appearance varies with the position of the sun, whether seen from ponte della Paglia on the Riva degli Schiavoni or from ponte della Canonica. □

▶ **PONTE DI RIALTO***

II C4

Until the last century, this was the only bridge across the Grand Canal (there are now three, the other two being the Accademia, II F2, and Scalzi, I B1, bridges). The present bridge was built between 1588 and 1591. It is an impressive single-arched structure, with three pedestrian walkways and two rows of **shops**. All Venetian buildings stand on unstable sands, and these are consolidated by driving in dense clusters of piles which support slabs and the foundations of Istrian stone. In the case of the Rialto bridge, each end rests on 6,000 piles. The previous bridge was a wooden one and, since the Grand Canal was a true port, its central section could be raised to allow the passage of ships on their way to the places of business of the merchants. Carpaccio's *Miracle of the Cross* (in the Accademia) provides a good impression of the old bridge. When the Republic decided to build a stone bridge a competition was launched. Some leading architects of the time — Sansovino, Palladio, Michelangelo, Vignola — submitted designs, but the winner was Antonio da Ponte, curator of the Magistratura del Sale, a choice which has aroused a number of regrets for what might have been. □

▶ **IL REDENTORE***

I E3

Andrea Palladio, who came from Padua and was the greatest of Venetia's architects, already had a solid reputation when he came to work in Venice. However, he did not find the favour of private clients and all his commissions were public ones. He left the city two undisputed master-pieces. One of these is S. Giorgio Maggiore (→) and the other is the Redentore (1577-1692), which was completed, strictly according to his plans, after his death. The church was built by the Senate of the Republic in thanks for the end of a plague (1576). It consists of three sections, one behind the other, which form an interior that Palladio himself incorrectly referred to as a Latin cross. He would have welcomed the luminosity of the interior, the solemnity of the articulation and the brightness of the surfaces. There are a number of altarpieces by Venetian artists (F. Bassano, Palma Giovane) and in the sacristy there are works by A. Vivarini, Veronese and L. Bastiani. □

▶ **La RIVA DEGLI SCHIAVONI***

I D4, II E6

A broad thoroughfare (the end section of which has recently changed name) which runs from the Canal Grande (→) to the eastern tip of Venice. It derives its name from the Dalmatian *(Schiavoni means Slavs)* sailors who traded there. The riva was predominantly commercial until the time of Napoleon when, with the opening of the Giardini Pubblici, it became the city's principal promenade and, with the change in architecture, its magnificent 'façade'. There is a fine view from the Punta della Dogana to the r. past the island of Giudecca (→), the island of S. Giorgio Maggiore (→), to the distant Lido (→) which forms the coastal barrier. The façade of the 18C church of the **Pietà** is on the riva degli Schiavoni and inside there are paintings by Tiepolo (ceiling of the church and sanctuary) and Moretto da Brescia (in the choir above the entrance). Antonio Vivaldi taught music to the orphans at the attached hospital. □

▶ **SAN CASSIANO**

II B3

Rebuilt several times, its interior is 17C. There are three Tintorettos in the presbytery, including a *Crucifixion★* (1568); paintings by Leandro Bassano in the chapel to the r. of the high altar. Note the **Cappellina del Medico** (1746), decorated with marbles and paintings by G.B. Pittoni. □

▶ **SAN FRANCESCO DELLA VIGNA***

II C4

It owes its name to the bequest of a vineyard to the Franciscans in 1253 by Marco Ziani, son of Doge Pietro. The present 16C church was designed by Jacopo Sansovino (the **façade** is by Andrea Palladio), but the plans were altered during the building in an effort to achieve harmonic proportions that corresponded to the Pythagorean ideas held by Francesco Zorzi, the friar who oversaw the work. The single-aisled **interior** is rich in works of art: *Madonna★* by Antonio da Negroponte (1450; altar in the r. transept); tombstone of A. Bragadin (c. 1487, pavement of the sanctuary); sculptures by P. Lombardo and pupils (15C; chapel to the l. of the sanctuary); *Sacra Conversazione* by Veronese (1551; 5th chapel, l.); *Madonna and Saints★* by Giovanni Bellini (in the **Cappella Santa;** entered from the l. transept). □

▶ SAN GIACOMO DELL'ORIO

II B1

An ancient foundation, the church was rebuilt in 1225 and still retains the apses and campanile from this period. Additions and alterations were made to it between the 14C and the 17C and its timber-ridged roof is 14C. It contains numerous works of art, including Lotto's *Madonna and Saints*★ (1546; in the sanctuary). The **New Sacristy** has paintings by Veronese (1577; ceiling) and Francesco Bassano (walls). The **Old Sacristy** is decorated throughout with paintings by Palma Giovane (1575). □

Saints in Venice

The saints to whom the churches of Venice are dedicated and after whom many of the streets are named are those of the church calendar, but they appear in their Venetian dialect form. Sometimes this is similar to their form in standard Italian, sometimes it is very different. Basegio, Boldo and Lio are Basilio (Basil), Ubaldo (Hubald) and Leone (Leo), Marcilian is Marziale (Martial), Pantalon is Pantaleone (Pantaleon), Polo is Paolo (Paul), Stin is Stefanino (Stephen), Stae is Eustachio (Eustace), Marcuola combines the names of Saints Ermacora and Fortunato (Hermagoras and Fortunatus), Trovaso is Gervasio and Protasio (Gervase and Protase), Zaniplo is Giovanni and Paolo (John and Paul). Aponal is Apollinare (Apollinaris), Tomà is Tommaso (Thomas), Zuliar is Giuliano (Julian), San Zan Degolà is S. Giovanni Decollato (St. John Decollate), Santa Ternita is the santissima Trinità (Holy Trinity). Other names connected with churches include San Giorgio in Bragora, which is perhaps derived from bragolà, market place, or bragolare, to fish. The Carmini is the church Santa Maria del Carmelo; Santa Maria Formosa because a beautiful (formosa in Latin) vision of the Madonna appeared to St. Magnus, Bishop of Oderzo in the 7C. The Frari is the church of Santa Maria Gloriosa dei Frari, named after the Franciscan Friars who founded it; the Gesuati is the church of Santa Maria del Rosario on the Zattere, built on the site of a former monastery of the same order; San Giacomo dell'Orio is perhaps derived from alloro, laurel, as a laurel tree once stood on the site; Santa Maria del Giglio and also Santa Maria Zobenigo because they were founded by the Lubanico family. The Zitelle (the 'old maids') is the nickname of the church of Santa Maria della Presentazione because it was near a sixteenth-century conservatorio or hospice for single women.

▶ SAN GIACOMO DI RIALTO

II C4

Popularly known as S. Giacometto, tradition has it that this is the oldest church in Venice (actually it is 11C-12C, rebuilt at the beginning of the 17C). It is at the heart of the interesting Rialto area, which was re-laid out in the 16C on rational lines and is still the site of the public markets. In the campo, in front of the church, is the **Gobbo di Rialto**, which supports the steps up which the 'comandador' ascended to the Colonna del Bando, from where he proclaimed laws and judgments. The sottoportico del Banco Giro

used to contain the tables of the bankers, where the merchants would make payments and transfers of money by simple entries in the books — on the basis of their 'credit'. □

▶ SAN GIOBBE*

I B1

Tullio and Pietro Lombardo completed the church in Renaissance style in the second half of the 15C, although it was originally Gothic. The portal★ and the interior, the **sanctuary**★ (tombstone of Doge Moro★) with two altars in niches flanking it are by P. Lombardo. The second chapel on the l. was built by Tuscan artists for the Martini family from Lucca and has terra-cottas by the della Robbias and marble pala by Rossellino. The famous altarpieces painted by Marco Basaiti, Giovanni Bellini and Carpaccio for this church are now in the Accademia; but a number of important works by artists such as G. Savoldo and A. Vivarini remain. □

▶ SAN GIORGIO DEI GRECI

II D6

This is the Renaissance church of the Greek Orthodox community, once the most important group of foreigners in the city. Its interior is in the traditional Orthodox form and therefore has a marble iconostasis covered with late Byzantine icons in front of the altar. To the l., in the Istituto Ellenico, the **museum** *(9 a.m.-12:30 p.m. and 3:30-6 p.m.; wkends 9 a.m.-12 noon; closed Tue)* has some eighty Byzantine pictures and Venetian-Cretan icons which are of considerable interest, not only to specialists, for the light they shed on the unfamiliar aspects of Orthodox iconography. □

▶ SAN GIORGIO MAGGIORE*

I D4

The church occupies a small island facing the Molo of S. Marco, and from its forecourt the monumental front of Venice appears in all its beauty. For an even more extensive view it is possible to go up the campanile in an elevator. It has a fine façade and is one of Andrea Palladio's most beautiful works (built 1565-83). The complex arrangement of the interior combines a Latin cross ground plan with some of the dimensions and features of a centrally planned church. Two of Tintoretto's masterpieces are hung on the walls of the sanctuary *(Last Supper*★ and the *Shower of Manna*★); carved wooden **choir stalls**★ (1598).

▶ In the adjacent monastery *(apply in sacristy)* there is the Sala del Conclave, where the election of Pope Pius VII was held in 1800, with Carpaccio's *St. George and the Dragon*★; and the Chapel of the Dead with a *Deposition*★ by Tintoretto. ▶ The monastery also houses the **Fondazione Cini**, an important cultural institution which organizes and plays host to major exhibitions. There are also two pleasant cloisters★ *(open on request)*, the refectory, also by Palladio, and a magnificent monumental staircase by Longhena. The various rooms contain numerous works of art. □

▶ SAN GIOVANNI CRISOSTOMO
II B-C4

Fine Renaissance church with a Greek cross ground plan, designed by Mauro Coducci (1497-1504). It contains one of the masterpieces from Giovanni Bellini's old age, his *Three Saints*★ (1513) and a pala by Sebastiano del Piombo (*c.* 1509). □

▶ SAN GIOVANNI IN BRAGORA*
I C4

A late Gothic church, rebuilt in 1475. Inside it has a number of fine works of art, including Alvise Vivarini's *Risen Christ*★ (1498) and the *Baptism of Christ*★ by Cima da Conegliano (1494). □

▶ SAN GIULIANO
II D5

Tommaso Rangone, the Venetian doctor, scientist and philosopher, paid for the 16C rebuilding of this church, which was founded in the 9C, and the work was carried out by Jacopo Sansovino, with Alessandro Vittoria assisting him with the sculptures. The donor is commemorated with a bronze statue (Sansovino or Vittoria) over the portal. It contains some fine works of art. □

▶ SAN MARCO**
II E5

San Marco and Palazzo Ducale

In 828 two Venetian sailors stole the remains of Mark the Evangelist from Alexandria in Egypt. On the fragile and perhaps incorrect basis of a legend that the Evangelist had preached in the lagoon, Venice chose him as its patron, adopting his symbol, the winged lion, for the State and founding a church dedicated to him. It was a political act, a statement of independence from the Patriarch of Aquileia, from the Bishop of Grado (Byzantine rite) and from the Metropolitan of the lagoon itself, whose seat was on the island of Olivolo (Castello). San Marco was in fact simply

the doge's chapel and it only became the seat of the Patriarch in 1807.

▶ Laid out on a Greek cross ground plan with five domes, it is believed to have been modelled on the *Holy Apostles* in Constantinople. The present church — Byzantine, Romanesque, Gothic — is the result of several phases of rebuilding and expansion undertaken between the 11C and the 17C. The result is a monument of immense importance which generates intense and complex aesthetic sensations. ▶ The central arch (13C) of the **façade** is decorated with **reliefs** *(Months, Virtues, Prophets)*. The N side has four 15C **water bearers**★; the S side has the *Tetrarchs*★, possibly a 4C Syrian work, and, standing in front of it, two pillars from Acre, which may be 6C Syrian. The domes of the **narthex** are covered by magnificent 12C-13C Venetian-Byzantine **mosaics**★ depicting Biblical stories. ▶ In the Byzantine **interior**★★ each arm of the cross has three aisles divided by piers which support galleries (matroneum). **Mosaics**★★ cover the whole upper portion of the basilica. They are the work of Venetian and Byzantine artists (12C-14C), although in the 16C and 17C they were partly replaced by mosaics based on cartoons by Titian, Tintoretto and Veronese. The contrast between the hieratic Byzantine approach and the style of the Renaissance, defining two distinct periods in the building of the church, can clearly be seen in the **sanctuary** *(9:30 a.m.-4:30 or 5:30 p.m.; wkends 2-5 p.m.)*. Four 13C **columns**★ with historiated capitals support the baldacchino over the high altar, and behind it is the famous *pala d'oro*★★, a magnificent Venetian and Byzantine work in gold and enamel (10C-14C). ▶ The **Treasury** *(same hours as the sanctuary)* is entered from the transept, while the **Baptistery** and the **Cappella Zen** (13C mosaics) are entered from the r. aisle. ▶ The **Museo S. Marco** (entrance in the narthex, *10 a.m.-5 p.m.*) has the **four horses**★ (4C Roman or 4C-3C BC Greek, taken from Constantinople) which used to be on the façade. From the museum there is access to the galleries inside the church or to the terrace on the façade (view★ over piazza and piazzetta). □

▶ SAN MOISE
II E4

It is in the nature of Venetian architecture to transpose the formal architectural elements into colour, light and shade. It is this feature which unites all the variations of Venetian style. The Baroque **façade** of San Moisè, built in 1668 by Alessandro Tremignon with an overabundance of plastic elements and sculptures (by Heinrich Meyring, in honour of the donors, the Fini), is one of the most cogent examples of this. Inside the church is single-aisled and contains sculptures and paintings, including a late Tintoretto, *Washing of the Feet*.

▶ SAN NICOLO DEI MENDICOLI
I D1

The old inhabitants of this out-of-the-way quarter were referred to as *mendicoli*, or beggars, and were poor fishermen or involved in uncertain trades. The community of the 'nicolotti' was tolerated by the Signoria for the sake of good government and was granted a certain formal independence, electing a representative or 'doge of the nicolotti'. The tree-lined campo conserves the base of their standard. The church itself has a Romanesque campanile and is one of the oldest in Venice (17C), although it has been rebuilt numerous times and is now in the form of a 13C Venetian-Byzantine church. □

▶ SAN PIETRO DI CASTELLO

I C6

It stands on the out-of-the-way island of San Pietro, on a deserted campo, and it still appears as it did when work finished on it at the end of the 16C and the beginning of the 17C. It was the bishop's church from 775 onward and the patriarch's from 1451 to 1807. The **campanile★** is by Mauro Coducci. ☐

▶ SAN POLO

II C2

The apse of this ancient and much rebuilt church stands on the campo di S. Polo, which is the largest in Venice. It has a free-standing campanile (1362) and a large 15C Gothic side **portal**. Inside there are a nave and two aisles, with paintings by Tintoretto, Veronese and G.B. Tiepolo. All the works in the attached Oratorio del Cristo are by Giandomenico Tiepolo, and they include *Stations of the Cross★*. ☐

▶ SAN ROCCO**

II C1

Adjacent to the famous Scuola Grande di San Rocco (→), the church, which was rebuilt in the 18C, contains eight Tintorettos, including *S. Rocco Cures the Plague Victims★*. ☐

▶ SAN SALVADOR*

II D4

A 16C church with a Baroque façade. Inside it has a severely elegant nave and two aisles and it houses a number of important works of art: the monument to Doge Francesco Venier★ by J. Sansovino (1561, r. aisle); an *Annunciation★* (r. aisle) and a *Transfiguration★* (1560, high altar) by Titian; the beautiful *Supper at Emmaus★* by Giovanni Bellini (chapel to the l. of the sanctuary). The silver pala (14C-15C) on the high altar is rarely shown. ☐

▶ SAN SEBASTIANO*

I D1

It is Paolo Veronese's splendid frescos and canvases, painted in several phases between 1555 and 1565, which form the point of interest of this 16C church *(9-11 a.m. and 4-6 p.m., wkends 12 noon-1 p.m.; custodian)*. Veronese is buried in front of the chapel to the l. of the sanctuary. The church contains his greatest series of religious paintings, outstanding among which are three panels of the ceiling depicting scenes from the *Story of Esther★★*; the doors of the organ; the canvases in the sanctuary, including the *Martyrdom of St. Sebastian★* and *St. Mark and St. Marcellian being encouraged to Martyrdom by St. Sebastian★*; the panels of the ceiling in the sacristy, which are among the painter's first works in Venice. Climb up from the sacristy to the nuns' **choir** *('barco')*, where there is a view of the frescos of *St. Sebastian before Diocletian* and *Martyrdom of the Saint*, and a closer view of the paintings of the vault. ☐

▶ SANTA MARIA DEI MIRACOLI**

II B5

The church, Pietro and Tullio Lombardo's masterpiece, provides an example of the 15C classical architectural forms of Tuscany clothed with the Venetian feeling for colour, with polychrome marble inlay and the distinctive curved pediment. The **interior★** continues the spirit of the exterior and offers an undivided space, vaulted by a dome and clad with marble. There are 50 wooden panels bearing busts of prophets and saints. ☐

▶ SANTA MARIA DELLA SALUTE*

II F3

A regular octagon with its entrance formed by a triumphal arch and a high drum linked to the lower section by Baroque volutes and crowned by a great hemispherical **dome,** Baldassarre Longhena's church represents a brillant advance in form, even for the Baroque, a period of tremendous experiment in the use of space.

Santa Maria della Salute

▶ Its position at the mouth of the Grand Canal makes it one of the landmarks of Venice, and its key place in the cityscape sometimes means that the church itself, as a building, does not get the attention it merits. Note, for example, the clear lines of the apses, with the second dome and the two campaniles, which are in contrast to the splendour of the canal front, with its marbles and statues. ▶ The **interior** is solemn and light. At the third altar l. there is a late Titian, the *Descent of the Holy Spirit*, and the high altar, designed by Longhena, has a Byzantine Greek Madonna and sculptures by Juste Le Court. ▶ The **Great Sacristy** has *St. Mark Enthroned with Saints★* (1512, altar) and three further Titians★ (1543, ceiling), as well as Tintoretto's *Marriage at Cana★*. Work on the church lasted from 1631 to 1687, in fulfilment of a vow made for the end of a plague. ☐

The Plague and Santa Maria della Salute

The plague was rife in Italy as a result of the war over the succession in Mantua and it was probably brought to Venice by the Marchese di Strigis, the ambassador of the Duke of Mantua to the Emperor, on 8 June 1630. The effects were devastating. Trade broke down; those who could fled to the towns on the mainland, 'the entire city turned beggar' and people lowered baskets from their windows to ask for charity. Records show that 46,490 people died in the city itself and 93,661 in the whole dogate, including Murano, Malamocco and Chioggia, and that these deaths represented over 30 percent of the population. At the height of the plague, on 20 October 1630, the Senate invoked the protection of the Virgin which was 'preserved with a special reverence since the early days of the Republic'. It pledged to build a church 'which would be splendid and magnificent', to be known as the Madonna della Salute. A similar pledge had been made 54 years before during another plague and it had been fulfilled by the building of Palladio's church of the Redentore. Eleven architects took part in the competition for the Salute and the winner was a Venetian, Baldassarre Longhena, whose design was for a centrally planned church 'in the form of a crown to be dedicated to the Virgin'. Work began in 1631 and the church was consecrated in 1687, five years after the architect's death. At the top of the lantern, the statue of the Virgin is clothed as 'captain of the sea', with a baton of command, and St. Mark stands beside as helmsman. Thus, allegorically, the church links the Virgin and the Republic and jointly glorifies them.

▶ SANTA MARIA FORMOSA*

II C-D5

'Formosa', that is, most beautiful, is how the Madonna appeared to St. Magno, Bishop of Oderzo, in the 7C, and this suggests that the church is one of the oldest in Venice. However, the present building, on the busy campo of the same name, is essentially early Renaissance (Mauro Coducci, 1492), with two 16C Neoclassical façades and an 18C Baroque campanile. The **interior★** has a nave and two aisles, with deep side chapels; a triptych by Bartolomeo Vivarini (1473, 1st chapel r.), and a polyptych by Palma Vecchio (*St. Barbara and Four Saints★*, r. transept) and a *Last Supper* by L. Bassano.

▶ SANTA MARIA GLORIOSA**

II C1

Just as in many of Italy's other historical centres, the two orders of friars (Franciscans and Dominicans) made an impression on the Venice of the Middle Ages, building their great churches across the city from each other. The Franciscan church is S. Maria Gloriosa dei Frari, usually known simply as the Frari, and the Dominican one is Santi Giovanni e Paolo (→). The original structure of both is typical of the monastery church: transepts arranged to form a T

with the enormous nave and two aisles, and transept chapels on either side of the apse, all in the restrained forms of 14C Italian Gothic. However, in Venice one structural element, the wooden tie beams between the piers of the Gothic arches, attained a decorative importance not seen elsewhere.

▶ The Frari was built between 1340 and 1443. Note, outside, the apse and the portals, both of the façade and at the sides. The **interior★** *(9 or 9:30 a.m.-12 noon and 2:30 or 3-5:30 p.m.; wkends 3-5:30 or 6 p.m.)* contains so many exceptional works of art and monuments to doges and famous Venetians that it is almost a museum. ▶ The monks' **choir★** stands in the middle of the nave. Its outer walls are marble (1475) and its wooden stalls are carved and inlaid (1468). ▶ In the r. aisle there is the Titian monument (1852, 2nd bay) and A. Vittoria's statue of *St. Jerome★* (3rd altar). ▶ In the l. aisle there is the Neoclassical monument to Canova (1827), to his own design; Longhena's Baroque mausoleum for Doge G. Pesaro (1669) and (2nd altar) the *Madonna di Ca' Pesaro★★* by Titian (1526), one of the jewels of the church and of Italian painting. ▶ On the r. in the sanctuary is the Gothic-Renaissance monument to Doge F. Foscari★ (A. and P. Bregno, *c.* 1457); on the l. is the monument to Doge N. Tron★, a masterpiece of Venetian Renaissance sculpture (A. Rizzo, *c.* 1476). Behind the high altar there is Titian's **Assumption★★** (1518), a daringly innovative composition with warm, vibrant colouring. ▶ The chapels of the transept contain a painted wooden statue of *St. John the Baptist★* by Donatello (1450, 1st r.); and *St. Ambrose and Saints★* by A. Vivarini and M. Basaiti (1503, 3rd l.). ▶ In the sacristy there is a triptych of the *Madonna and Child Enthroned with Saints★★*, one of Giovanni Bellini's masterpieces (1488). □

▶ SANTA MARIA ZOBENIGO

II E3

Its exuberant façade, an example of Venetian Baroque, celebrates the Barbaro family — and Antonio, the *'Capitano da Mar'*, in particular — who paid for its building (1678-83) by G. Sardi. Inside there are Tintoretto's *Four Evangelists★* (behind the altar) and *Christ with Saints.* □

▶ SANTI GIOVANNI E PAOLO**

II B-C6

Standing on a beautiful campo, beside the Scuola Grande di S. Marco (→) and the Colleoni Monument (→), this great Gothic church — known to Venetians as S. Zanipólo — was built by the Dominicans between 1246 and 1430. ▶ The portal is by B. Bon (1461) and there are five polygonal **apses★** (mid-15C).

▶ The vast **interior** displays the typical arrangement of a monastery church, with a nave and two aisles, and it contains monuments to doges, captains and famous figures from the history of the Republic, together with numerous works of art. ▶ On the entrance wall there are three Mocenigo monuments, including one to Doge Pietro★ by P. Lombardo (1481). ▶ The r. aisle has a *Madonna and Child Enthroned with Saints★* attributed to F. Bissolo and Giovanni Bellini's polyptych, *St. Vincent Ferrer★* (*c.* 1465). ▶ At the end of the r. aisle, the ceiling of the **Chapel of St. Dominic** (1716) has Piazzetta's *St. Dominic in Glory★* (1727). ▶ The l. aisle has a statue of *St. Jerome★* by A. Vittoria. ▶ In the **sanctuary** there are tombs of doges on the walls and, between them, the monument to Doge A. Vendramin★, a masterpiece of Venetian funerary art of the 15C by P. Lombardo or A. Vittoria, with bas-reliefs and statues by A. and T. Lombardo. There is also the Gothic monument to Doge M. Corner, with the *Madonna and Child and Four Saints*★ by Nino Pisano. ▶ In the r. transept there is *St. Anthony and Supplicants*★, an altarpiece by Lorenzo Lotto (1542). At the end of the l. transept is the **Chapel of the Rosary**★ with four works by Veronese on its ceiling. ◻

▶ SANTO STEFANO*

II E2

A 14C-15C Gothic church with its r. side running along the campo S. Stefano or Morosini, which is ringed by fine palaces. Superb Gothic-Flamboyant portal. Inside the church is divided into a nave and two aisles by columns and has a ridged ceiling. Polygonal apse containing the sanctuary with a Gothic choir (1488). Its paintings include three Tintorettos★ in the sacristy. ◻

Living in Venice

The name 'Venice' immediately conjures up images of canals, lagoons and gondolas, but it is also a vital industrial and business centre. The city includes three areas: the historical city centre, where visitors spend most of their time; the port of Marghera, which continues to expand; and Mestre, a bedroom community on the mainland. While the administrative commune totals some 350,000 inhabitants, there are only about 90,000 permanent residents of the old city centre, and their exodus toward 'solid ground' continues. Venice is experiencing a severe housing shortage, partly because many of its old houses are no longer habitable. Often hundreds of years old, these houses are particularly difficult to restore because of the artistic and architectural considerations which take precedence over more efficient and less aesthetic repairs. Saving Venice means restoring the stone which time has eaten away. It will also mean bringing new life into the city and re-establishing a human balance in its various districts. Venice must live, but it mustn't simply become a gigantic museum without human resources.

▶ SAN ZACCARIA*

II D-E6

Entered from the quiet campo S. Zaccaria through a Gothic portal, the church has a 13C brick campanile to the r. and to the l. shops occupy the 15C arcades bordering the cemetery of the former monastery. The scene is dominated by the **façade** which Mauro Coducci completed in 1485-90.

▶ The church itself has an ancient foundation but was rebuilt in Gothic style in the 15C and the curved pediments, arcades and elongated windows crowned by semicircular arches provide clear evidence for what had reached Venice, then firmly late Gothic, of the new architectural style of 15C humanism. ▶ The **interior** is divided into a nave and two aisles by columns and has a Gothic apse with ambulatory and radial apsidal chapels. It is covered with 17C and 18C paintings, but on the second altar on the l. there is Giovanni Bellini's splendid *Madonna and Child with Angel and Saints*★ (1505). ▶ The crypt has three aisles and two chapels (entrance r. aisle) and is a remnant of the first, Gothic church. In the **Chapel of St. Athanasius** *(admission charge)* there are inlaid 15C

choir stalls and paintings by Tintoretto. The apse of the **Chapel of St. Tarasius**★ has important frescos *(Holy Father and Saints*★) by Andrea del Castagno and Francesco da Faenza (1442) and also three Gothic polyptychs by A. Vivarini and Giovanni d'Alemagna (1443). ◻

▶ Gli SCALZI*

I B1

A Baroque church built by Longhena (1654) for the Discalced Carmelites, the façade is by G. Sardi. The splendid decoration of the **interior**, with its polychrome marbles, sculptures and gilding, was carried out under the supervision of the Carmelite artist Giuseppe Pozzo and displays the influence of the Roman Baroque. Tiepolo frescoed the vaults in the second chapel on the r. and the first one on the l. but his most important work in the church, *The Transport of the Holy House of Loreto*, which used to decorate the ceiling of the nave, was destroyed in an air raid in 1915. ◻

▶ SCUOLA GIOVANNI EVANGELISTA*

II C1

An elegant Renaissance courtyard by Pietro Lombardo leads into a small courtyard in front of the Gothic church and the school itself *(9:30 a.m.-12:30 p.m.; closed Sat and Sun)*. An imposing double **staircase**★ ascends from the ground floor to the first floor salone, which has late 16C and 18C paintings. The altar of the Oratorio della Croce has a crystal and silver Gothic reliquary. ◻

▶ SCUOLA GRANDE DEI CARMINI

II C-D1

In Venice the 'schools' were charitable and religious organizations which were loosely associated with the guilds. The main ones took their names from their patron saints, or from their nationalities of origin, and the monumental buildings in which they were based often housed works by major artists. By extension, the synagogues were also known as 'schools'.

▶ The **Scuola Grande dei Carmini**, a confraternity devoted to the Virgin of Carmelo, held almost half the population of the city in 1675. ▶ The façade of the 17C building *(9 a.m.-12 noon and 3-6 p.m.; closed Sun)* is attributed to Longhena and inside it is richly decorated with 17C paintings and stucco. ▶ On the ceiling of the upper hall there are nine **paintings**★ by Tiepolo (1739-44) which are among his finest works. ◻

▶ SCUOLA GRANDE DI SAN MARCO*

II B6

The **façade** of the school, at right angles to that of Santi Giovanni e Paolo (→), on the campo beside the rio dei Mendicanti, is one of the most beautiful of Venetian 'scenes' and was painted several times by Canaletto and Guardi. The building, which is today part of the civic hospital, is the work of Pietro Lombardo, Mauro Coducci and Jacopo Sansovino, the three architects who together sum up the development of the Venetian Renaissance from the tenuous linearity of the 15C to the sumptuous Mannerist chiaroscuro of mature Classicism. The overall tone of the delightful asymmetric façade is in keeping with the 15C humanist models, with its curved pediments and delicate polychrome marble panels. There are surprising *trompe l'oeil* with bas-reliefs of the Lion of St. Mark and two scenes from the life of the saint by Tullio Lombardo. □

▶ **SCUOLA GRANDE S. ROCCO****

II D1

'A flash, a clap, indeed even a thunderbolt which has struck all the loftiest heights of painting.' This was said of Tintoretto by Marco Boschini (*Carta del Navegar Pitoresco*, 1660). The school *(summer 9 a.m.- 1 p.m. and 3:30-6:30 p.m.; winter 10 a.m.-1 p.m.; wkends 3-6 p.m.)* is an outstanding gallery devoted to this great visionary painter.

▶ It was built between 1516 and 1560 and the façade is by B. Bon and Scarpagnino. ▶ A competition was held (1564) for the decoration of the central section of the Sala dell'Albergo. Tintoretto, one of whose rivals was Veronese, submitted a completed painting rather than a sketch and offered it as a gift. He was chosen, not without opposition, and he then painted at the school until 1587. ▶ His splendid **works★★**, which display invention and a daring use of light, include: the *Annunciation★*, the *Flight into Egypt★*, *Mary Magdalene★*, *St. Mary of Egypt★*; stories from the Old and New Testaments occupy the compartments of the ceiling and walls of the chapterhouse, which has severe wooden carvings all round. The Sala dell'Albergo contains the *Crucifixion★* and the dramatic scenes of the *Passion★*. ▶ *Christ Carrying the Cross★*, attributed to Giorgione or Titian, is displayed on an easel, and there is also an *Ecce Homo* by Titian. □

▶ **SCUOLA S. GIORGIO SCHIAVONI***

I C4

Schiavonia or Slavonia was the Venetian term for Dalmatia, over which Venice held sway until the end of the Republic and which supplied loyal regiments of soldiers.

▶ The school of the Confraternity of the Dalmatians or of St. George and St. Tryphone *(summer 9:30 a.m.- 12:30 p.m. and 3-6:30 p.m.; winter 10 a.m.-12:30 p.m. and 3-6:30 p.m.; wkends 10 or 10:30 a.m.-12:30 p.m.; closed Mon)* offers one of the most fascinating series of **paintings★★** in Venice. These were painted by Vittore Carpaccio in 1502-11, and by the middle of the 16C they had been moved from the upper hall of the brotherhood to the lower one, where they are now on display. They show scenes from the lives of St. George, St. Tryphone (patron of Cattaro) and St. Jerome (patron of the Dalmatians). They are pervaded with poetic feeling, and they have an immediate attraction because of the imagination they display and the accuracy of their depiction. □

▶ **La TORRE DELL'OROLOGIO**

II D-E5

It is possible to climb up it to get a closer view of the **'Mori'**, two bronze statues cast in 1497 which strike the hours (entrance n° 147, Mercerie, *9 a.m.-12 noon and 3-5 p.m.; wkends 9 a.m.-12 noon).* The tower was built in 1496-9, possibly by Mauro Coducci,

and the archway at its base leads from the piazza S. Marco into the Mercerie and to the Rialto. The face of the clock indicates the hours, the phases of the moon and the movement of the sun through the Zodiac. During Ascension week, the **Magi,** preceded by an angel, emerge from the l. doorway and bow before the gilded Madonna on the terrace above the clock, before disappearing through the r. doorway. Above there is a gilded **Lion of St. Mark** in full relief against a blue ground scattered with gold stars. □

▶ **Le ZATTERE**

I D1-2-3

The fondamenta along the Giudecca canal makes a very pleasant walk. To the r. of the Zattere landing stage, when disembarking, is the 18C church of the **Gesuati** (I D2), which contains works by Piazzetta, Tiepolo (ceiling frescos) and sculptures by G.M. Morlaiter. To the l. of the landing stage, a short walk along the fondamenta of the rio di S. Trovaso brings one opposite the **Squero di S. Trovaso,** a picturesque relic, although still active, of the many small shipyards of Venice. □

● *Practical information*

Information: S. Marco 71/C (II E4), ☎ 5226356; Castello, calle del Remedio 4421, ☎ 5222373; p. Roma ☎ 27402; Rialto 4089, Palazzo Martinengo (II C5), ☎ 5226110; S. Lucia railway station (I B1), ☎ 715016. Municipal tourist office, Ca' Giustinian, S. Marco 1364/A (II E-F4), ☎ 5209955.

✈ Marco Polo international airport, ☎ 661111; *Alitalia,* S. Marco 1463, S. Moisé (II E4), ☎ 700355; *Terminal* p. Roma 597/l (I C1), ☎ 705593.

🚄 (I B1), ☎ 715555.

Visiting Venice

The best way to move through Venice is on foot. The steamers which sail through the lagoon are limited to a top speed of 8 km/h. If they went any faster they might damage the foundations of houses and palaces. Various public transport projects have been drawn up and abandoned such as a subway and elevated rail link from the mainland to the Lido. However, Venetians already have a variety of public transport systems available to them: the vaporetti or water buses; the motoscafi, the famous speedboats; the water taxis; the traghetti; and, of course, the gondolas. The gondola's design evolved from the first flat-bottomed boats used in the lagoon. The hull is asymmetrical because the skiff is propelled forward by a single back rudder on the starboard side. All gondolas were painted in bright colours until 1562 when an outbreak of the plague led to a Senate decree that all the skiffs be painted black. The metal piece at the bow which looks like a six-toothed comb represents Venice's six districts; the top tooth section represents the Dorsoduro district and Giudecca island.

▓▓▓ from bus station in p. Roma (I C1); taxi ranks in p. Roma, ☎ 5237774.

⌒ **public transport within Venice:** tourist routes: *line 1* (accelerata) from p. Roma to Ferrovia, to Rialto, to S. Marco and to the Lido with numerous stops on both sides of the Canal Grande; *line 2* (direct), same route but fewer stops; *line 4* (summer only) from p. Roma to the Lido via the Canal Grande; *line 5, right-hand circuit,* from S. Zaccaria to Giudecca, to Zattere, to S. Basilio, to p. Roma, to Fondamenta Nuove and to Murano; *left-hand circuit,* from S. Zaccaria to Fondamenta Nuove and to Murano, then to S. Basilio, Zattere and Giudecca; *line 6,* direct from the riva degli Schiavoni to the Lido; *line 11,* riva degli Schiavoni - Lido - Pellestrina - Chioggia (steamer and bus); *line 12,* Fondamenta Nuove - Murano - Burano - Torcello; *line 14,* Venice - Punta Sabbioni. For *Murano: line 5* (departures every 15 minutes from S. Zaccaria, riva degli Schiavoni, p. Roma, Ferrovia and Fondamenta Nuove); for *Burano* and *Torcello: line 12* (terminus at Fondamenta Nuove; departures every hour, more frequently in the afternoons). Transport company: information, ☎ 5287886. Public-transport motoscafi (fixed fares for the most common trips), departure points in piazzetta S. Marco (II E5), ☎ 5229750; Ponte della Paglia, ☎ 5228538; Rialto Riva Carbon, ☎ 5230575; S. Marco (Giardinetti), ☎ 5222303; Tronchetto, Isola Nuova, ☎ 5237836. At various points gondola ferries (traghetti) cross the Canal Grande; rates vary with time of day and number of passengers. Boats and ferries, mostly to Greece and the Eastern Mediterranean countries: *Adriatic shipping company,* Zattere 1411, ☎ 781611; car ferries to the Lido and to Punta Sabbioni.

S.O.S: emergency calls, and calls to the public utilities: Croce Azzurra, ☎ 5230000; urgent medical assistance, ☎ 5205622; medical staff working at night and during festivals, ☎ 113; chemist's shops open out of hours, ☎ 192. Carabinieri, ☎ 5204777; civil police, ☎ 981400; municipal police, ☎ 5224063; fire brigade, ☎ 5222222. Offices for trunk and international telephone calls: Palazzo delle Poste, campo S. Bartolomeo (II C4), open 24 hours; Stazione S. Lucia (I B1), open 8 a.m.-8 p.m.; Tessera airport, open 8 a.m.-8 p.m.; SIP, p. Roma (I C1), open 8 a.m.-9.30 p.m. Dictated telegrams, ☎ 186.

Weather: ☎ 993191; road conditions, ☎ 194 from Venice; tides, *Da un giorno all'altro* column of *Gazzettino,* local newspaper, and in the glass cases at the vaporetto landing stages (during the high-water period: end of Oct-beginning of Apr).

Festivals: *contest between the four maritime republics (Jun); Festival of the Redeemer* (3rd Sat in Jul), with processions of decorated and illuminated boats; *historical regatta* (first Sun in Sep); *parade of historical boats,* and *race between gondolas; Festival of Madonna della Salute* (21 Nov); procession to the church of Santa Maria della Salute on a bridge of boats extending across the Canal Grande; *Vogalonga* (May), a non-competitive rowing course of 30 km in the lagoon; during the *Carnival of Venice,* there is an almost uninterrupted succession of events.

Events: *Venice Biennale,* one section of which is devoted to the visual arts (*International Exhibition of Modern Art* (summer, even-numbered years), various pavilions in the Giardini Pubblici II D-E 5-6) and in the cinema (*International Cinema Exhibition,* (Aug-Sep), Palazzo del Cinema al Lido, ☎ 5260188); secretary's office, ☎ 700311. *International Festival of Contemporary Music* (Sep-Oct) and of *Prose* (May-Jul); *Il Campiello* Prize for Literature (Sep); exhibitions devoted to ancient and modern art and to aspects of Venetian culture are organized annually in the Palazzo Ducale, the Palazzo Grassi, at the Accademia, and in the Correr and Fortuny museums; at the Teatro La Fenice operas are given in the winter season, while orchestral music is performed from spring to autumn, ☎ 5203544; drama is performed at the Teatro del Ridotto, ☎ 5222939 and the Teatro Goldoni, ☎ 5205422.

Environmental protection: supervision of the environment and architecture of Venice, palazzo Ducale, ☎ 5204077; *WWF* at Mestre, calle Sale 15, ☎ 950800; *Italia Nostra,* S. Marco 1260, ☎ 5204822; *LIPU* at Marghera, p. Parmesan 12, ☎ 920444.

Nature reserve: protected area in the Averto valley (at the edge of the lagoon, along the Romea road between Chioggia and Mestre, entrance, Lugo hill); guided tours on Tue and Fri, reservations and information from the Venice *WWF,* ☎ 950800.

Guided tours: by gondola or on foot with guides recognized by the Comune: inquire at travel agencies. Tourist boats to Murano, Burano and Torcello, leaving from the riva degli Schiavoni, with visits to the glassworks of Murano and to the lacemaking school at Burano.

Entertainment: information on films, ☎ 198; information on films, plays, concerts, exhibitions, conferences, festivals is published in the local news pages of the two dailies, *Il Gazzettino di Venezia* and *La Nuova Venezia,* and in the *Carnet del turismo* booklet edited by *Chiavi d'oro,* the international association of hotel porters (published weekly in summer, every three weeks in winter; distributed free of charge at three- and four-star hotels).

Boat trips: along the Riviera del Brenta (→) on the *Burchiello* which departs three times a week (Tue, Thu and Sat; Mar-Oct); information from travel agencies.

Motorboat trips: to Chioggia (→) departing from the Riva degli Schiavone (the trips lasts about 2 hrs).

Sailing instruction: *Glénans Italia (Glénans nautical club),* at Isola di S. Clemente, ⊠ 403, ☎ 5200320 (1- and 2-week courses from Jun to Sep: introduction to sailing, courses for non-beginners, instruction in seafaring and introduction to cruising, cruising instruction with nights spent aboard); *Italian nautical league,* Castello, fondamenta dell'Arsenale (near the Comando Marina), ☎ 5289294 (courses in sailing and navigation); *high-seas sailing club,* at Chioggia (→); *high-seas sailing club,* at Porto S. Margherita di Càorle (→ Veneto).

Children's facilities: Drawing and painting courses at the *Planetarium delle arti,* calle della Testa 6125 (II B5), ☎ 5287272.

Young people's facilities: Drama and dancing classes at the *Centro teatrale di ricerca,* Castello - S. Lorenzo 5068 (II D6), ☎ 5231039.

Motorboating: *Venice motorboating club,* S. Marco 1364, ☎ 5222692; *Italian Federation,* S. Marco 3927, ☎ 5208325.

Rowing: Castello (I D5), ☎ 5207899.

Swimming: *Gandini swimming pool,* at Isola di S. Giorgio (I D4), ☎ 5231932.

Yacht club: *Olivolo Yachting Club,* Castello 40/B, ☎ 5224970.

Canoeing: lessons given by the *Venice canoeing group,* Calle Favret 47, ☎ 716122; *Italian federation,* S. Marco 3927, ☎ 5238952.

Archery: *Venetian archery club,* Lista di Spagna 228 (I B1), ☎ 715189.

Bowling: Dorsoduro 2531, ☎ 5231407; Cannaregio 3253, ☎ 715736.

Fencing: *Fencing club,* Cannaregio 47, ☎ 717960 (annual trial for the World Cup).

Horseback riding: *Marco Polo horse-riding centre,* Campalto (I E3), at v. Irlanda 190, ☎ 900065.

Golf: at the Lido (→), ☎ 731015; at Martellago (→ Mestre), ☎ 540021.

Flying club: *Ancillotto flying club,* at the Lido (→), ☎ 5260808.

Rugby: *Venice rugby club,* v. Malamocco 74, ☎ 765263.

● Hotels

★★★★★ **Bauer Grunwald & Grand Hotel,** campo S. Moisè 1459 (II E-F4 A), ☎ 5231520, 214 rm Ⓟ ≼ 357,000.

★★★★★ **Cipriani,** Giudecca 10 (I E4 B), ☎ 5207744, 98 rm Ⓟ ◿ ⚌ ⚐ ◢ ⚲ closed Nov-Mar. Rooms in 18C Venetian style and Art Deco, swimming pool surrounded by romantic garden, 660,000; bkf: 40,000.

★★★★★ **Danieli,** riva degli Schiavoni 4196 (II E6 C), ☎ 5226480, 236 rm Ⓟ ≼ ⚌ 520,000. Rest. ● ◆◆◆◆ **Terrazza Danieli** Neoclassical style with terrace overlooking lagoon and S. Giorgio. Mixed regional cuisine: sea bass alla Caleghera, cuttlefish al nero, 80/120,000.

★★★★★ **Gritti Palace,** campo S. Maria del Giglio 2467 (II F3 D), ☎ 5226044, 96 rm Ⓟ ≼ ⚌ 589,000. Rest. ● ◆◆◆◆ **Club del Doge** ☎ 794611. Refined with antiques and terrace. Mixed cuisine: spring risotto, scampi in erbaria, 80/100,000.

★★★★★ **Londra Palace,** riva degli Schiavoni 4171 (II E6 E), ☎ 5200533, 69 rm Ⓟ ≼ 23,600. Rest. ● ◆◆◆◆ **Do Leoni** closed noon, Tue and 15 Nov-15 Dec. With elegant service by canal in summer. Regional cuisine: taglionini with crabs, fish alla piastra, 75/115,000.

★★★★★ **Monaco & Grand Canal,** calle Vallaresso 1325 (II E-F4 M), ☎ 5200211, 80 rm Ⓟ ≼ 380,000.

★★★★ **Cavalletto & Doge Orseolo,** calle del Cavelletto 1107 (II E4 F), ☎ 5200955, 81 rm Ⓟ ⚘ 265,000.

★★★★ **Etap-Park,** giardini Papadopoli (I C1 G), ☎ 5285394, 100 rm, 280,000.

★★★★ **Gabrielli-Sandwirth,** riva degli Schiavoni 4110 (I D4-5 H), ☎ 5231580, 91 rm ⚌ closed Nov-Mar, 320,000.

★★★★ **Luna,** calle dell'Ascensione 1243 (II E4 I), ☎ 5289840, 125 rm ≼ 320,000.

★★★★ **Metropole,** riva degli Schiavoni 4149 (I C4 L), ☎ 5205044, 64 rm ≼ 293,000.

★★★★ **Saturnia & International,** calle larga XXII Marzo 2399 (II E3 N), ☎ 5208377, 99 rm, 250,000. Rest. ● ◆◆◆ **Caravella** closed Wed in winter. Prestigious and fashionable. Regional and international cuisine: bigoli al sugo, dumplings al Gorgonzola, 50/70,000.

★★★★ **Splendid Suisse,** ponte dei Baretteri 760 (II D4 P), ☎ 5200755, 157 rm ⚘ 310,000.

★★★ **Accademia,** Dorsoduro 1058 (II F1 Q), ☎ 5237846, 26 rm ⚌ ⚘ No restaurant, 129,000.

★★★ **Ateneo,** calle Minelli 1876 (II E3 R), ☎ 5200588, 20 rm. No restaurant, 158,000.

★★★ **Bel Sito,** campo S. Maria del Giglio 2517 (II E3 S), ☎ 5223365, 40 rm. No restaurant, 146,000.

★★★ **Bisanzio,** calle della Pietà 3651 (I C4 T), ☎ 5203100, 39 rm, closed Jan. No restaurant, 160,000.

★★★ **Concordia,** calle larga San Marco 367 (II D5 U), ☎ 5206866, 60 rm ≼ No restaurant, 183,000.

★★★ **Continental,** lista di Spagna 166 (I B2 V), ☎ 715122, 104 rm ⚌ 130,000; bkf: 16,000.

★★★ **Do Pozzi,** calle larga XXII Marzo 2373 (II E-F3 Z), ☎ 5207855, 35 rm ⚌ closed Jan-Feb, 155,000.

★★★ **Fenice et Des Artistes,** campiello Fenice 1936 (II E3 AB), ☎ 5232333, 68 rm ⚘ No restaurant, 130,000.

★★★ **Flora,** calle larga XXII Marzo 2283/a (II F3 AC), ☎ 5205844, 44 rm ⚌ ⚌ closed Dec-Jan. No restaurant, 158,000.

★★★ **Malibran,** S. Giovanni Grisostomo 5864 (II C4 AD), ☎ 5228028, 29 rm ⚌ closed Nov-Dec, 140,000; bkf: 13,000.

★★★ **Montecarlo,** calle degli Specchieri 463 (II D5 AE), ☎ 5207144, 48 rm Ⓟ No restaurant, 160,000.

★★★ **San Marco,** calle dei Fabbri 877 (II D-E4 AF), ☎ 5204277, 60 rm Ⓟ 172,000.

★★★ **Santa Chiara,** S. Croce 548 (1 C1 AG), ☎ 5206955, 28 rm Ⓟ ⚘ No restaurant, 149,500.

★★★ **Torino,** calle larga XXII Marzo 2356 (II E3 AH), ☎ 5205222, 20 rm Ⓟ No restaurant, 163,000.

★★ **Alboretti,** Accademia 884 (I D2 AI), ☎ 5230058, 19 rm ⚌ closed Nov-Dec. No restaurant, 66,000; bkf: 9,000.

★★ **Basilea,** at Santa Croce, rio Marin 817 (II B1 AL), ☎ 718477, 30 rm ⚌ No restaurant, 69,000; bkf: 11,000.

★★ **Calcina,** Zattere 780 (I D2 AM), ☎ 5227045, 36 rm, 89,000.

★★ **Lisbona,** Corte Barozzi 2153 (II E4 AN), ☎ 5286774, 15 rm. No restaurant, 91,500.

★★ **Residenza,** campo Bandiera e Moro 3608 (I C4 AP), ☎ 5285315, 17 rm ⚘ closed Jan-Feb and Nov-Dec. No restaurant, 87,500.

● Restaurants

● ◆◆◆◆ **Antico Martini,** campo S. Fantin 1983 (II E3 AR), ☎ 5224121, closed Tue, Wed noon and 10 Dec-Carnival. Meeting place for art and music world of Venice. Mixed cuisine: cannelloni alla dogaressa, grilled scampi, 60/100,000.

● ◆◆◆◆ **Harry's Bar,** calle Vallaresso 1323 (II E4 BA), ☎ 5236797, closed Mon, Sun eve and Jan-Feb. Prestigious and renowned. Regional and international cuisine: risotto with cuttlefish, sliced filets of raw beef, 65/110,000.

Venetian cooking

Venetian cooking is based largely on products from the sea. Of the different fish and shellfish dishes, the most original is granscole, small sea spiders served cold after cooking in olive oil and lemon juice; moleche are tiny grilled crabs which are eaten whole, including the pincers. Also worthy of interest are cuttlefish with polenta (seppie in tecia) and cod with cinnamon and anchovies (baccala mantecato). Venetian risotto generally consists of fish or other seafood cooked in a chicken broth with rice; risi e bisi is a variant including small green peas. Green or black pasta (bigoli in salsa) is served with an anchovy sauce. However, Venice's best-known dish is still fegato alla veneziana: thin slices of calf's liver cooked with onions. The local beer is light and pleasant. The area's fine wines include reds, such as Bardolino, Merlot, Valpolicella; white wines include Soave, Poesecco, Gambellara.

● ◆◆◆ **Poste Vece,** Pescherie 1608 (II B3 BC), ☎ 721822, closed Tue. Paneled ceilings, stone fireplace and charming access bridge. Mixed regional cuisine: bigoli al sugo, soused sardines, 35/55,000.

◆◆◆ **Campiello,** calle Fuseri 4346 (II D4 AT), ☎ 5206396, closed Mon and Aug. Quiet atmosphere, with a sophisticated American bar. Mixed cuisine: tagliatelle Saint-Jacques, scampi alla busara, 35/60,000.

◆◆◆ **Colomba,** piscina di Frezzeria 1665 (II E4 AU), ☎ 5221175, closed Wed. Trattoria dating from 18C. Regional seafood: fish risotto, cuttlefish alla veneziana with polenta, 39/75,000.

◆◆◆ **Colombo,** corte del Teatro (II D3-4 AV), ☎ 5237493, closed Mon and Jan-Feb. Paintings by well-known artists and open-air service in small square. Mixed cuisine: pappardelle with seafood, Sardinian dumplings with salmon, 30/50,000.

◆◆◆ **Graspo de Ua,** calle Bombaseri 5094 (II C4 AZ), ☎ 5223647, closed Mon, Mar and Christmas. In operation for over a century. Mixed regional cuisine: vermicelli fisherman's style, cuttlefish alla veneziana, 40/65,000.

◆◆◆ **Noemi,** calle dei Fabbri 909 (II D4 BC), ☎ 5225238, closed Sun eve, Mon noon and Jan-Feb. Regional seafood: shrimp pâté, taglioni with crayfish, 45/65,000.

● ◆◆◆ *Regina,* Santa Croce 2330 (II B2 BF), ☎ 5241402, closed Mon. Fireplace, summer terrace with gondolas skimming by. Regional cuisine: bigoli in anchovy sauce, turbot alla Raffaele, 70/80,000.
◆◆◆ *Taverna la Fenice,* campiello Fenice (II E3 AB), ☎ 5223856, closed Sun and Jan. Near famous La Fenice theatre. Mixed regional cuisine: black spaghetti, bigoli al sugo, 45/75,000.

● Recommended

Auction rooms: public auctions for antiques, *Semenzato and C.S.A.S.,* Cannaregio 2292 (II A3), ☎ 721811.
Casino: at Lido (→), ☎ 767054, in winter, at the Palazzo Vendramin Calergi (II A2), ☎ 720444.
Cinema: at Lido (→), ☎ 5260188.
Discothèque: Club *El Souk,* Accademia 1056/A, ☎ 5200371 (80 places, always open).
Gondolas: visits to small shipyards: the *San Trovaso boatyard,* at Dorsoduro, fondamenta Bollani (II F1); *squero* (boatyard) *of Maestro Giuponi* by the Giudecca; the *sheds of the Fratelli Serafin* by the Redentore church (I E-D3).
Racecourse: *Zelarino Racecourse,* at Trevignano (14 km NW), v. Ca' Lin 75, ☎ 909488.
Youth hostel: *Ostello Venezia,* Giudecca fondamenta Zitelle 86, ☎ 5238211.
♥ glassware: artistic glassworking, *Brudo Amadi glassworks,* at So Polo, Calle dei Saoneri (II C-D 1-2); historical restaurants: *Caffè Florian,* San Marco 56/9, ☎ 5285338; *Caffè Quadri,* p. San Marco 120, ☎ 5222105; items worth purchasing: Murano glass, lace, carpets, furniture covers, ceramics, mosaics, lacquered period furniture, and antiques. Deluxe shops are found along the Mercerie running from p. San Marco to the Rialto (II D4-5) and in many other city centre streets; masks: *mask-makers' workshop,* at Barbaria de le Tole, Castello 6657 (II C6), ☎ 5223110; *Tragicomica,* at S. Polo, calle dei Botteri 1566 (II B-C3), ☎ 5230102; *Mondonovo* workshop, at Dorsoduro, Rio Terrà Canal (II E1); *Mangiafuoco* (puppets), at S. Polo 2718, calle dei Saoneri (II C-D1); paper and prints: sheets of marbled paper at *Ebrù* workshop, calle della Fenice (II E3); workshop, salizzada San Samuele (II E2); photographs, lithographs, historical prints obtainable from *Bohm,* the photographers and publishers, at San Moisè, S. Marco 1349/50, ☎ 5222255; textiles: precious fabrics worked by hand, *M* workshop, at piscina di Frezzeria 1651 (II E4); furnishing fabrics, *Rubelli* laboratory, at Campo S. Gallo, San Marco 1089 (II D-E4), ☎ 5236110.

● Environs

ALTINO

Mestre 16, Venice 20 km
Pop. 54 ⊠ 30020 ☎ 0422

This ancient Roman town was at the intersection of three important roads: the *Emilia Annia* leading to Aquileia and the E, the *Popilia* leading to Rome, and the *Claudia Altinatis Augusta* leading northwards. After the town was sacked by Attila and the Lombards, its inhabitants took refuge on the islands in the lagoon, especially Torcello, and were involved in the creation of Venice.

▶ The **Archaeological Museum** *(9 a.m.-2 p.m.; closed Mon)* has mosaics, architectural fragments, stones, stele, small sculptures, statues and burial objects taken from excavations in the ancient town and burial grounds. ☐

BURANO

Venice 9 km
Pop. 4,729 ⊠ 30012 ☎ 041

This fishing village stands on four small islands in the lagoon. Its colours are enchanting, and it is a popular subject for painters. The art of lacemaking flourished here from the 14C. The Gothic palazzo in the p. Galuppi houses the school of lacemaking. The **lacemaking museum** *(9 a.m.-6 p.m.; closed Tue)* is also in the palazzo. ☐

Practical information _____

 Burano is served by *Line 11,* which has its terminus at the fondamenta Nuove and departs every hour (more frequently in the afternoon). The Venezia-Murano-Burano-Torcello boat service for tourists departs from the riva degli Schiavoni (visits to the school of lacemaking).

Restaurant:
● ◆◆ *Romano,* p. Galuppi 221, ☎ 730030, closed Tue and 15 Dec-15 Feb. Meeting place for artists and intellectuals. Seafood: risotto with cuttlefish, roast eel, 30/55,000.

Recommended
♥ lacemaking: p. Galuppi 184, ☎ 730034 (9 a.m.-6 p.m.).

Coast of CAVALLINO

Lido di Jésolo 10, Venice 51 km
Pop 10,065 ⊠ 30013 ☎ 041

This is the low-lying sandy strip which separates the E part of the Venetian lagoon from the sea between the porto di Lido and the porto di Piave Vecchia. The countryside around **Tre Porti** and **Cavallino,** two districts of the Venice municipality, is distinctive. ☐

Practical information _____

 Cavallino is reached from the riva Schiavoni in Venice by *Line 14* as far as Sabbioni, and then by bus.

Hotels:
★★★ *Fenix,* at Cavallino, v. Baracca 45, ☎ 968040, 64 rm Ⓟ ☖ ⌂ ♨ closed 1 Oct-14 May, 92,000; bkf: 8,000.
★★★ *Lio Grando,* at Punta Sabbioni, p. Lio Grando 17, ☎ 966136, 62 rm Ⓟ ⌂ 〇 closed Nov-Jan, 75,000; bkf: 8,000.

Restaurant:
◆ *Laguna,* at Cavallino, v. Pordelio 444, ☎ 968058, closed Thu and Nov-Dec. Seaside trattoria with a fine terrace looking out on lagoon. Seafood: dumplings and bigoli with cuttlefish in its ink, agnolotti with oysters and ricotta, crêpes with cheese and smoked salmon, 25/45,000.

▲ ★★★★ *Fiori,* at Ca' Vio, v. delle Batterie 52, 453 pl, ☎ 966448; ★★★★ *Mediterraneo,* at Ca' Vio, v. delle Batterie 38, 812 pl, ☎ 966721; ★★★★ *Union Lido,* at Ca' di Valle, ☎ 968080; ★★★ *Europa,* at Ca' di Valle, 556 pl, ☎ 968068.

CHIOGGIA*

Venice 52, Milan 279 km
Pop. 53,886 ⊠ 30015 ☎ 041

A factor contributing to the atmosphere of this humble little Venice in miniature is the memory of the world of common fishermen and their gossipy ladies so wittily described by Goldoni in his play *Baruffe chiozzotte* (Quarrels of Chioggia). There is also the picturesque ambience of its canals and colourful alleyways (the town is the result of the intelligent town planning which guided the rebuilding after the 'War of Chioggia') and the ever-present reminders of seafaring and fishing. Separated from the mainland at the southern tip of the lagoon, Chioggia was an important bulwark in the defence of Venice. The Genoese captured it in 1379, but were themselves besieged by the Venetian galleys of Vettor Pisani, to whom they finally surrendered in June 1380. This was known as the 'War of Chioggia', and was the final crucial episode in the war between the two maritime republics.

▶ The **corso del Popolo★** is the main thoroughfare, which crosses the town from N to S; picturesque alleys branch off from it, extending down to the Lombardo Interno canal on one side, and to the canal of S. Domenico on the other. The **canal della Vena** (fishing) runs close to the corso del Popolo and parallel with it. ▶ The Gothic oratory of **S. Martino** *(inquire at the cathedral)* contains a polyptych attributed to Paolo Veneziano. ▶ The 11C **cathedral** was rebuilt in Baroque style by Longhena (1674); it has marble inlay on the high altar and two chapels beside the sanctuary (the right-hand chapel has canvases of the 18C Venetian school, with an early work by Tiepolo among them). ▶ The **piazza Vescovile★**, with a balustrade decorated by 18C statues including the venerated *Virgin Mary of Refugium peccatorum,* is a charming spot. ▶ The isolated 18C church of **S. Domenico,** with a 14C campanile, contains some excellent works of art. ▶ A long bridge over the Lusenzo lagoon leads to Sottomarina and its beach. □

Practical information

CHIOGGIA

ℹ at Sottomarina, lungomare Centro, ☎ 401068.

Restaurants:
♦♦♦ ***Bragosso,*** at Sant'Anna, strada Romea, ☎ 4950395, closed Wed and Nov. Seafood: fish pie, risotto alla marinara, 25/40,000.
♦ ***Bella Venezia,*** calle Corona 51, ☎ 400500, closed Thu and Jan. Regional cuisine, 15/30,000.

⛺ ★★★★ *Isamar,* at Isola Verde, 450 pl, ☎ 498100.

Recommended
Events: *Summer festival* (2nd week in Jul); *festival of fishing and parade of boats (2nd week in Aug).*
Excursions: by motorship to Venice (→).
Sailing: *High-seas sailing club,* v. Canal Lombardo 1423, ☎ 403506 (summer courses in Mediterranean cruising, lasting 6-20 days); Milan office, ☎ 02/745578.
Technical tourism: visits to a fish-preserving factory at Saloni, v. della Marittima, ☎ 403130.

SOTTOMARINA, ⊠ 30019, ☎ 041, 1 km.
≋
ℹ lungomare Centro, ☎ 401068.

Hotels:
★★★★★ ***Ritz,*** lungomare Adriatico 48, ☎ 491700, 90 rm Ⓟ ♨ ✂ ⊡ closed Oct-Apr, 95,000.
★★★ ***Anzoletti,*** lungomare Adriatico 30, ☎ 5540660, 45 rm Ⓟ ♨ ✂ closed Oct-Easter, 65,000.
★★★ ***Florence,*** v. Pegaso 36, ☎ 490010, 24 rm Ⓟ closed Jan, 50,000; bkf: 4,000.
★★★ ***Florida,*** v. Mediterraneo 9, ☎ 491505, 55 rm Ⓟ ♿ closed Nov-Feb, 60,000; bkf: 6,000.
★★★ ***Mosella,*** v. S. Felice 3, ☎ 405488, 51 rm Ⓟ ♨ ♿ ⊡ closed Nov-Mar, 60,000; bkf: 6,000.
★★★ ***Park,*** lungomare Adriatico, ☎ 490740, 41 rm Ⓟ ♨ closed Oct-Mar, 65,000.

⛺ ★★ *Adriatico,* v. Vespucci, 180 pl, ☎ 492907; ★★ *Atlanta,* v. Barbarigo, 249 pl, ☎ 491311; ★★ *Miramare,* v. Barbarigo, 270 pl, ☎ 490610.

Recommended
Children's facilities: *Bagni Clodia,* ☎ 401910 (water chute).
Swimming: *Villaggio marino comunale,* ☎ 400300; *Centro Astoria,* front, ☎ 404844; *Bagni Clodia,* ☎ 401910 or 400520 (also tennis courts at these pools).

LIDO DI VENEZIA

Venice 4 km
Pop. 20,954 ⊠ 30126 ☎ 041

The long, thin island between the porto di Lido and the porto di Malamocco separates the central part of the lagoon from the sea. The **Lido** is a famous seaside resort and Venetian patricians bathed here collectively in the nude as long ago as the 18C, provoking denunciations to the Inquisitors. **Malamocco,** at the S tip of the island, was the political centre of the lagoon in the 8C, before its transfer to the Rivo Alto (Rialto). □

Practical information

≋
ℹ in Venice.
✈ *G. Nicelli* civil airport, at S. Nicolò, ☎ 765427.
🚌 from S. Nicolò, Ca' Bianca, S.M. Elisabetta.
⛴ Boats from p. Roma; motoscafi direct from the railway station and from p. Roma; boats direct from the degli Schiavoni; the lagoon coach service follows the route Schiavoni-Lido-Alberoni-San Pietro in Volta-Pellestrina-Chioggia; ships and ferries from the riva degli Schiavoni to Punta Sabbioni (Lido di Jésolo) which stop at the Lido. Car ferry from Venice-Tronchetto; motorboats depart from p. S.M. Elisabetta, ☎ 5260059.

Hotels:
★★★★★ ***Excelsior,*** lungomare Marconi 41, ☎ 5260201, 220 rm Ⓟ ♨ ♿ ⊡ closed Nov-Mar. Popular with jet set, this is the hotel that made the Lido famous, 500,000.
★★★★ ***Des Bains,*** lungomare Marconi 17, ☎ 765921, 266 rm Ⓟ ♨ ⊡ ✂ closed Nov-Mar. Art Nouveau building facing beaches in a splendid park, 285,000; bkf: 17,000.
★★★★ ***Villa Mabapa,*** riviera S. Nicolò 16, ☎ 5260590, 63 rm Ⓟ ♨ ♿ closed 16 Nov-9 Feb and Christmas, 200,000.
★★★ ***Biasutti,*** v. Dandolo 24/29, ☎ 5260120, 100 rm Ⓟ closed Nov-Mar, 160,000.
★★★ ***Helvetia,*** Gran Viale 4/6, ☎ 5260105, 50 rm Ⓟ ♨ ✂ closed Nov-Mar. No restaurant, 125,000; bkf: 15,000.
★★★ ***Petit Palais,*** lungomare Marconi 54, ☎ 5261707, 25 rm Ⓟ ♨ closed Nov-Feb. No restaurant, 153,000.
★★★ ***Villa Otello,*** v. Lepanto 12, ☎ 5260048, 34 rm Ⓟ ♨ ⊡ closed Nov-Mar. No restaurant, 146,000.

Restaurant:
♦♦ ***Valentino,*** v. Gallo 81, ☎ 5260128, closed Mon and 15 Oct-15 Nov. Mixed cuisine: risotto with seafood, game according to season, 35/50,000.

Recommended
Aeroclub: *Ancillotto Aeroporto,* at S. Nicolò, ☎ 5260808.
Archery: *Del Leon archery club,* lungomare Marconi 85, ☎ 766359.
Bowling: *Lido bowling club,* v. Quattro Fontane, ☎ 765298.
Casino: lungomare Marconi 4, ☎ 767054.
Cinema: lungomare Marconi, ☎ 5260188.
Clay pigeon shooting: at Ca' Bianca, ☎ 765980.
Discothèque: *Club 22,* lungomare Marconi 22, ☎ 5260466.
Golf: at Alberoni *(9 km S.),* v. del Forte, ☎ 731015.
Horseback riding: at Ca' Bianca, ☎ 765162 (associate of *ANTE,* instruction).
Skating: v. Quattro Fontane, ☎ 5260382.
Tennis: lungomare Marconi, ☎ 765689; v. S. Gallo 163, ☎ 5260954; v. Fausta, ☎ 968134.

Villa MALCONTENTA*

Venice 14, Mestre 6 km
Pop. 2,435 ⊠ 30030 ☎ 041

A fresco in the stanza dell'Aurora depicts a lady entering through a door; this is the 'malcontenta' from which the villa takes its name (Elisabetta Dolfin or Elisabetta Loredon, the wives of Nicolo and Alvise Foscari respectively), who was banished for being unfaithful. Set amid greenery on the banks of the Brenta, the site is romantic in a languid way and the villa is among the most successful designs by Andrea Palladio *(May-Sep, Tue, Sat and first Sun in month, 9 a.m.-12 noon).* Built by Nicola and Alvise Foscari *c.* 1555; interior decoration by B. Franco and G.B. Zelotti. This villa still belongs to the founders' descendants. Of the many villas along the Brenta (→ Venetia), Malcontenta is the nearest to the lagoon. ☐

Practical information ─────────

Hotel:
★★ *Gallimberti*, v. Malcanton 3, ☎ 698099, 22 rm P ⅋ 68,000; bkf: 5,000. Rest. ♦ *Bepi el Ciosoto* ☎ 969137, closed Mon. Seafood: risotto, fish in foil, 20/40,000.

MESTRE

Venice 9, Milan 261 km
Pop. 197,952 ⊠ 30170 ☎ 041

Along with nearby **Marghera** (they are both industrial centres), Mestre, which stands on the margin of the lagoon, now has a much larger population than Venice itself. It is this simple fact which certainly complicates, if it does not totally cause, the very serious problems associated with the preservation of Venice. ☐

Practical information ─────────

ⓘ Marghera, on the bypass toward Padua, ☎ 921638.

Hotels:
★★★★ *Ambasciatori*, corso del Popolo 221, ☎ 5310699, 104 rm P ⅋ 127,000; bkf: 12,000.
★★★★ *Michelangelo*, v. Forte Marghera 69, ☎ 986600, 51 rm P & ⅋ No restaurant, 190,000; bkf: 18,000.
★★★ *Bologna & Stazione*, v. Piave 214, ☎ 931000, 130 rm P ⅋ 94,000; bkf: 8,000.
★★★ *Plaza*, p. Stazione 36, ☎ 929388, 226 rm P & 95,000; bkf: 8,000.
★★★ *President*, v. Forte Marghera 99/A, ☎ 985655, 51 rm P ⅋ No restaurant, 92,000; bkf: 9,000.
★★ *San Giuliano*, v. Forte Marghera 193/A, ☎ 957604, 58 rm P & ⅋ closed Dec, 62,000; bkf: 7,000.
★★ *Venezia*, p. XXVII Ottobre, ☎ 985533, 100 rm P ⅋ 62,000; bkf: 7,000.
★★ *Vivit*, p. Ferretto 73, ☎ 951385, 19 rm P ⅋ 62,000.

Restaurants:
♦♦♦ *Amelia*, v. Miranese 113, ☎ 913951, closed Wed except summer. Regional seafood: fish pies with chicory and nettles, risotto with goby and hop shoots, 35/56,000.
♦♦♦ *Hostaria Dante*, v. Dante 53, ☎ 959421, closed Sun, Aug and Christmas. Mixed cuisine: snails in purgatorio sauce, spinach in pastry, 30/40,000.
♦♦♦ *Molini*, at Mirano, v. Belvedere 8, ☎ 430063, closed Mon and Wed noon. Conversion of 18C mill. Mixed regional cuisine: seafood spaghetti, liver alla veneziana, 30/50,000.
♦♦♦ *Tinelo dei Molini*, at Mirano, v. Belvedere 10, ☎ 430063, closed Mon and Tue noon. 18C building with simple furnishings contrasting with elegant ser-

vice. Mixed regional cuisine: capesante en croûte, liver alla veneziana, 30/50,000.
♦♦♦ *Valeriano*, v. Col di Lana 18, ☎ 926474, closed Sun eve, Mon and Aug. Regional seafood: pasta al tovagliolo, scampi alla busara, 35/50,000.
♦♦ *Tonin Geremia*, calle Legrenzi 20, ☎ 972574, closed Sat eve, Sun and 1-15 Aug. Service on piazza outside in summer. Mixed cuisine: fish in foil, various meats, 25/35,000.
♣ ★★ *Fusina*, at Fusina, v. Moranzini, 285 pl, ☎ 969055 (all year).

Recommended
Archery: *Compagnia arcieri mestrini Conte di Carmagnola*, at Spinea *(7 km W)*, v. Desenzano 2/3, ☎ 994750.
Canoeing: *Mestre canoeing club*, Punta S. Giuliano, ☎ 958389 (instruction).
Cycling: *G.S. Mestre*, v. San Marco 94/3, ☎ 983862.
Fishing: *Italian angling association*, corso del Popolo 32, ☎ 984871.
Golf: *Golf club Villa Morosini*, at Martellago (18 holes); *Ca' della Nave*, p. Vittoria 14, ☎ 5400521 or 5400543 (also swimming pools and tennis).
Horse riding: *Circolo ippico Dolo*, at Arino *(13 km SW)*, v. Covinello 1, ☎ 708691; *Club ippico dell'Elfo*, at Martellago *(10 km NW)*, v. Frassinelli Maerne, ☎ 909009; *Miranese horse-riding centre*, at Mira *(11 km SW)*, v. Matteotti 82, ☎ 432289.
Motorboating: *Manta motorboating club*, at Marghera, v. Macchine 19, ☎ 987766.
Sports centre: v. Porto di Cavergnago, ☎ 5311583.
Swimming pool: *CONI*, ☎ 961936; *Olimpia*, v. Bixio 30, ☎ 982973; *Jolly*, at Marghera, v. delle Querce 52, ☎ 923783.
Tennis: v. Olimpia 12, ☎ 989611; v. Scaramuzza 42, ☎ 907425; Ca' Alverà 6, ☎ 630544.

MURANO

Venice 2 km
Pop. 6,247 ⊠ 30121 ☎ 041

In the late 13C, the glassworks were moved here for what would today be termed environmental reasons: they were a fire risk. From that time on, the fame of Murano glass has never been eclipsed. This picturesque town on the lagoon stands on five little islands immediately to the N of Venice.

▶ The **Museum of Glassmaking** in the Palazzo Giustinian (I A6; *10 a.m.-4 p.m.; wkends 9 a.m.-12:30 p.m.; closed Wed)* displays ancient glass and, in particular, the marvellous history of Venetian glassmaking in the 15C-18C. The **Barovier wedding cup** (*c.* 1470-80) is the celebrated pride of the collection; one section is devoted to modern works produced by local glassworks. ▶ A fine feature of the 12C basilica of **SS. Maria e Donato**★ (I A6) is its beautiful apse★; the interior decoration includes mosaic pavement (1140), 13C Byzantine mosaics in the apse, early-15C frescos and some paintings. ▶ The 15C Gothic **Palazzo Da Mula** (I B5-6) is also of interest. ▶ The mid-15C church of **S. Pietro Martire** (I B5-6), altered in the early 16C, has good paintings by Giovanni Bellini, Tintoretto and Veronese. ☐

Practical information ─────────

🚢 *Line 5* departs every 15 minutes from San Zaccaria (riva degli Schiavoni), from p. Roma, from the railway station and from the Fondamente Nuove; *line 12*, a terminus at Fondamente Nuove with departures every hour, more frequently in the afternoons (continues via Burano and Torcello). Tourist service on the route Venice-Murano-Burano-Torcello, departure from the riva degli Schiavoni, visits to the glassworks and to the Scuola dei Merletti.

Restaurants:
♦ *Busa alla Torre,* campo S. Stefano 3, ☎ 739662, closed Sun and Dec-Jan. In 13C house. Seafood, 25/40,000.
♦ *Frati,* fondamenta Venier 4, ☎ 736694, closed Thu and Feb. Regional seafood: eel baked with bay leaves, cuttlefish with polenta, 25/45,000.

PELLESTRINA

Chioggia 6, Venice 20 km
Pop. 5,289 ⊠ 30010 ☎ 041

A colourful and picturesque village on the lagoon side of the coast, between the port of Malamocco and the port of Chioggia. On the sea coast, there are 7 miles of **murazzi** (1744-82), powerful embankments protecting the lagoon from the sea. The last great public work of the Serenissima, they stretch for about 12 miles from Porto di Lido up to Chioggia. □

Practical information

⚓ From Venice (riva Schiavoni), *Line 11,* boat and bus.

Restaurant:
♦♦ *Nane,* at San Pietro in Volta, ☎ 688100, closed Mon, Jan and Feb. Veranda facing lagoon. Regional cuisine: fish pie, spaghetti with spider crab, 30/40,000.

SAN LAZZARO DEGLI ARMENI

Venice 4 km

Situated only half a kilometre from the tumultuous Lido, the island offers an opportunity for serene and cultivated withdrawal. It houses a community of Armenian monks, who have been here since the early 18C, thanks to the work of Father Mechitar, and are actively engaged in preserving Armenian culture. Buildings worth visiting are a small **museum,** with a collection of some 2,000 Armenian manuscripts (some illuminated), and the **picture gallery.** The printing house of the Mechitarist monks, opened in 1796, is today still able to print in 36 languages. The island can be reached from Venice (riva degli Schiavoni) via *Line 10,* departing every hour. □

TORCELLO*

Venice 10 km
Pop. 52 ⊠ 30012 ☎ 041

The bishop of Altino (→) took refuge on the island of Torcello, which was then the main town of the lagoon from the 7C to the 9C. There are two important monuments from this period, and they vie with the relaxed enchantment of this place on the lagoon. The 7C **cathedral**★★ *(8 a.m.-12 noon),* rebuilt in the 11C, has a nave and two aisles with classical and Byzantine capitals, and a marble and mosaic

pavement (11C). A large mosaic of the *Last Judgment* (12C-13C) occupies the entrance wall. The nave has two ambos and iconostases with 11C transennae, and 15C paintings in the architrave; in the vault of the central apse is a 13C mosaic, on a gold ground, depicting the *Madonna and Child*★★; 12C-13C mosaics in the right-hand apse. The sturdy 11C **campanile** is behind the church. **Santa Fosca**★ is a centrally planned 11C Romanesque building, surrounded by a portico and having Greek marble columns in its cruciform interior. The Palazzi dell'Archivio and del Consiglio (14C) house the **Museum of Torcello** *(10:30 a.m.-12:30 p.m. and 2-6 or 4:30 p.m. in winter; closed Mon),* which displays archaeological finds from Altino and the lagoon, and various objects from the 11C-16C, including some remains of the 13C silver pala from the cathedral. □

cathedral in Torcello

Practical information

⚓ *Line 12,* terminus at the Fondamento Nuovo with departures every hour, more frequently in the afternoons. A tourist service following the route Venice-Murano-Burano-Torcello, departing from the riva degli Schiavoni.

Hotel:
★★★ *Locanda Cipriani,* p. S. Fosca 29, ☎ 730757, 4 rm ⌂ ⌘ closed 11 Nov-14 Mar. Sought-after place to stay. Rest. ● ♦♦♦ closed Tue. Romantic setting, open-air service. Regional seafood: green tagliolini au gratin, fritto misto del mare, 65/90,000.

Index

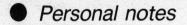

Personal notes

● *Personal notes*